KU-542-659

HUTCHINSON

The Encyclopedia of BRITAIN

HUTCHINSON

The Encyclopedia of BRITAIN

Helicon

Helicon Publishing Ltd
42 Hythe Bridge Street
Oxford
OX1 2EP
email: admin@helicon.co.uk
Web site: http://www.helicon.co.uk

Printed and bound in Slovenia by
DELO-Tiskarna, d.d.,
by arrangement with Korotan-Ljubljana

ISBN 1-85986-275-6

Contributors
Anne Baker
Ian Chilvers
Nick Coleman
Ian Derbyshire
Clarissa Hyman
Antony Kamm
Richard Martin
David Milsted
Anna Papadoupolos
Ben Ramos
Adrian Room
Julian Rowe
Joseph Spooner
Jill Turton

Project manager
Barbara Fraser

Text editors and proofreaders
Eileen Auden
Clare Collinson
Malgorzata Colquhoun
Caroline Cowan
Christine Cowley
Jane Crone
Christine Delaney
Denise Dresner
Keith Hopper
Stephen Pavlovich
Sue Purkis
Joseph Spooner
Alison Smith
Edith Summerhayes
Catherine Thompson

Picture research
Elizabeth Loving

Cartography
Olive Pearson

Production
Tony Ballsdon

Design manager
Terence Caven

Page design
Paul Saunders

Contents

The United Kingdom of Great Britain and Northern Ireland
Shetland Islands
ATLANTIC OCEAN
Orkney Islands
Kirkwall
Thurso
Wick
North Sea
Outer Hebrides
Inner Hebrides
Inverness
Aberdeen
Dee
Mallaig
SCOTLAND
Tay
Dundee
Oban
Glasgow
Edinburgh
Clyde
Tweed
UNITED KINGDOM
Londonderry
NORTHERN IRELAND
Belfast
Dumfries
Carlisle
Newcastle upon Tyne
Middlesbrough
Isle of Man
Leeds
Aire
Kingston upon Hull
Irish Sea
Manchester
Liverpool
Holyhead
Dublin
Sheffield
REPUBLIC OF IRELAND
Caernarfon
Derby
Nottingham
Trent
Leicester
Norwich
Gt Ouse
Severn
Birmingham
Nene
Aberystwyth
Cambridge
WALES
Fishguard
Cork
ENGLAND
Oxford
Swansea
London
Thames
Cardiff
Bristol
Dover
Celtic Sea
Southampton
Brighton
Exeter
Plymouth
English Channel
Isles of Scilly
Channel Islands (UK)
0
50 mi
0
100 km
FRANCE

Preface

THIS IS A GOOD TIME to be considering what the UK has achieved and what it means to be British. Against the backdrop of the Millennium there are some fundamental changes afoot in Britain. The policies promised by the Labour government elected in 1997 are being put to the test. Devolution of power in Scotland, Wales and Northern Ireland mean that some nine million people from a population of 55 million will be looking to their elected national assembly for a more direct response to their needs. There is a will for lasting peace in Northern Ireland. Meanwhile, what may seem just one more technological development, the advent of new digital television channels, may have a greater cultural impact than we guess: the time when everyone talked about the same programme they saw the previous night, may be over. And alongside all these, there is the developing role of the UK within Europe, and especially the 'will-we won't-we' sidestep of whether the UK will join the European Single Currency and introduce the Euro alongside the pound.

This encyclopedia focuses on Britain's cultural, historical, and geographical heritage. It uses the term Britain in its colloquial sense, meaning the United Kingdom, or Great Britain and Northern Ireland. Matters relating to Ireland before the country divided in 1921 into Northern Ireland, as part of the UK, and the Republic of Ireland as a separate nation-state, are included, but details of geography are restricted to Northern Ireland.

In its coverage of people, the book's aim has been to include people who have made a significant contribution to the UK in particular, and UK-born citizens who have made a contribution on the world stage. The first category is made up mostly, though not entirely, of UK nationals. For non-nationals, where a person chooses to live, and the nature of their work, has had a bearing on inclusion. Thus Shaw and Wilde, two Irishmen who lived in Britain and wrote very specifically about Britain and for a British audience, are included as main entries, while two other giants of Irish and world literature, Joyce (who never lived in England) and Beckett (who lived mostly in Ireland and France), are not. Prominent historical figures in Anglo-Irish affairs, such as Parnell and O'Connell, are included. Influential non-nationals who mostly live elsewhere, for instance Rupert Murdoch, may be referred to in entries relating to their work, rather than given their own entry. In sport, British citizens from Commonwealth countries who have played as, and are known as, representatives of their own country, have not been included.

One aspect of compiling an encyclopedia of Britain is that every British reader can legitimately see themself as an expert in the subject and will expect to find certain entries. We cannot hope to satisfy every reader, most especially in the field of popular culture where television, newspapers, and magazines have made so many people not just into household names but familiar as personalities, too. The aim here has been to be representative. At the back of the book there are brief details for a range of television personalities past and present, and contemporary figures in acting and films, writing and sport, to supplement the main entries.

In named works, coverage is particularly, and unashamedly, selective. Books have been included by title where it seems they have a known identity quite distinct from their author – perhaps the real definition of a classic. In films there is a bias to recent releases that have done unusually well, where the film title may yet be more widely known than the names of individuals within the team. There are none the less entries for genres of film, for example Carry On films and Bond films, and a feature on the history of the British film industry. A tribute to the British sense of humour, and the array of comic writing and performing talent in this country, is the number of television comedies that have entered the national psyche, and some of these are recognized with main entries, as well as in the entry for comedy.

For animals, coverage has been restricted to noted British breeds of livestock, and does not extend to domestic or wild animals.

To make finding an entry as easy as possible, the encyclopedia attempts to list entries under their most common name, whether an abbreviation or a full name: the BBC, AA, and ACAS, for example, are listed as such, while entries that are known broadly by their full, explanatory title, such as the Royal Opera House, and London Contemporary Dance Theatre, are under the name in full.

December 1998

List of features

AA

Abbreviation for the British **Automobile Association**, motoring organization founded in 1905. Originally designed to alert members to the presence on the road of police, it gradually broadened its services to include signposting, technical and legal services, as well as roadside help for members. In 1914 membership stood at 83,000 and in the 1990s exceeded 8 million.

Abbots Langley

Town in Hertfordshire, England, 8 km/5 mi north of Watford; population (1991) 4,300. It is said to be the birthplace of Nicholas Breakspear (later Pope Adrian IV). The parish church in Abbots Langley dates from 1154.

abdication crisis

The constitutional upheaval of the period 16 November 1936 to 10 December 1936, brought about by the British king ◊Edward VIII's decision to marry Wallis Simpson, a US divorcee. The marriage of the 'Supreme Governor' of the Church of England to a divorced person was considered unsuitable and the king abdicated on 10 December and left for voluntary exile in France. He was created Duke of Windsor and married Mrs Simpson on 3 June 1937.

Abel, Frederick Augustus (1827–1902)

English scientist and inventor who developed explosives. As a chemist to the War Department, he improved gun-cotton manufacture by showing that it is essential to remove all traces of the acids used in the process. He was joint inventor with James ◊Dewar of the explosive cordite and also invented the Abel close-test instrument for determining the flash point (ignition temperature) of petroleum. Baronet 1893.

Aberaeron

Coastal resort and administrative headquarters of ◊Ceredigion (Cardiganshire), central Wales, 20 km/13 mi south of Aberystwyth. It has a harbour surrounded by brightly painted Georgian houses, and facilities for sailing and sea angling.

Abercrombie, (Leslie) Patrick (1879–1957)

English architect. A pioneer of British town planning, he was involved in replanning British cities, including London, after damage in World War II. He initiated the ◊new town policy, which drew on the idea of the ◊garden city.

In 1913 Abercrombie won a competition for replanning Dublin. With J H Forshaw (1895–1973), he prepared the County of London Plan (1943) and Greater London Plan (1944); detailed, comprehensive schemes which were illustrated on an unprecedented scale. The term ◊green belt, an

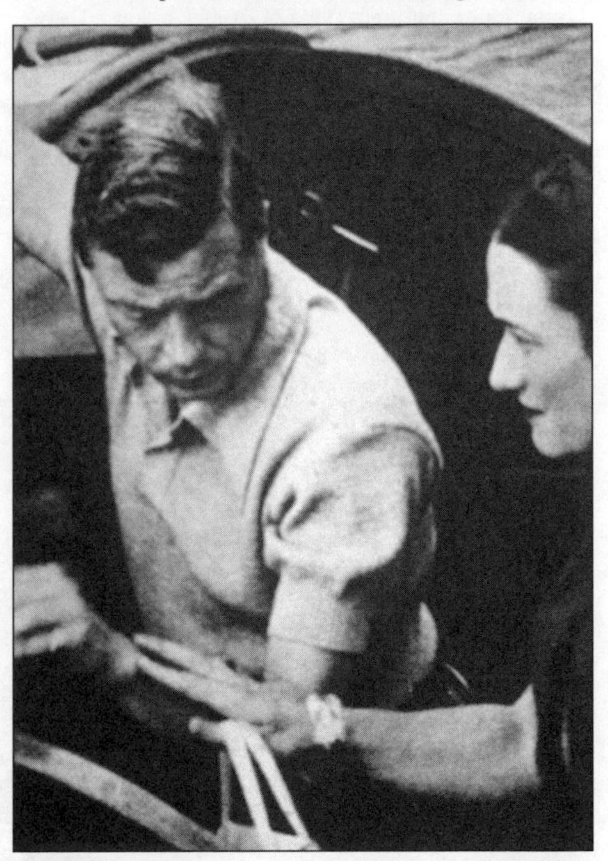

ABDICATION CRISIS *King Edward VIII and Wallis Simpson holidaying on board the* Nahlin *during the summer of 1936. Edward reigned for just 11 months before giving up the throne to marry the twice-divorced American. Image Select*

area designated not to be built on, generally refers to the 'outer ring' he proposed around London to prevent urban sprawl; new towns were envisaged beyond this boundary. He also created plans for Edinburgh, Plymouth, Hull, the West Midlands, Clydeside, Bath, Bristol, Sheffield, and Bournemouth.

His schemes aimed to improve means of transport, distribution of population and industry, conditions of housing, and provision of open spaces, with regard for the welfare of the people and the preservation or creation of amenities. He was knighted in 1945.

Aberdare, Welsh Aberdâr

Town in Rhondda Cynon Taff, south Wales, 32 km/20 mi north of Cardiff at the confluence of the Rivers Dare and Cynon; population (1982 est) 38,000.

Once an important coalmining and iron-working town, its industries now include the manufacture of electrical cables and light engineering.

Aberdeen

City and port on the east coast of Scotland, administrative headquarters of ◊Aberdeen City and ◊Aberdeenshire unitary authorities; population (1995) 219,100. It is situated between the mouths of the rivers Dee and Don and has 3 km/2 mi of sandy beaches. Aberdeen has the most prosperous local economy in Scotland. Industries include oil and gas service industries, fish processing, and papermaking. It is the main centre in Scotland and Europe for offshore oil exploration and there are shore-based maintenance and service depots for the North Sea oil rigs. Aberdeen is Scotland's third largest city and has the third largest economic output.

The city has many fine buildings, including the Municipal Buildings (1867); St Andrew's Episcopal Cathedral (consecrated in 1816); King's College (from 1500) and Marischal College (founded in 1593, and housed in one of the world's largest granite buildings constructed in 1836), which together form Aberdeen University; St Machar Cathedral (from 1370); and the Brig O'Balgownie (1314–18). Aberdeen's granite buildings have given it the name of 'Silver City', although the last granite quarry, in Rubislaw, closed in 1971. Oil discoveries in the North Sea in the 1960s–70s transformed Aberdeen into the European 'offshore capital'. An airport and heliport at Dyce, 9.6 km/6 mi northwest of the city, link the mainland to the rigs.

Among the more imposing of the city's buildings are the art gallery (1884), the grammar school (1861–63), Robert Gordon's Institute of Technology (1731), and St Nicholas Kirk (restored 1835–37, but dating from the 12th century). King's College was founded by Bishop Elphinstone in Old Aberdeen, and Marischal College, in New Aberdeen, was founded by Earl Marischal of Scotland as a Protestant

ABERDEEN *The construction of a ship in Aberdeen. From the mid-1970s, the city's service and manufacturing industries have benefited greatly from oil exploration in the North Sea, with vessels being built locally to service the many offshore drilling and accommodation platforms. Brian Shuel/Collections*

alternative to King's College. Aberdeen has a large fish market.

Its oil-related services include supplying precision tools, spare parts, catering equipment, food, and domestic supplies for the 90 operational oil fields in the North Sea.

History

In 1178 ◊William the Lion granted Aberdeen a charter and it became a royal burgh, but it was burned down in 1337 by ◊Edward III. Rebuilt as New Aberdeen, it became a flourishing town.

Aberdeen, George Hamilton Gordon, 4th Earl of Aberdeen (1784–1860)

British Tory politician, prime minister from 1852 until 1855, when he resigned because of criticism provoked by the miseries and mismanagement of the ◊Crimean War.

Aberdeen began his career as a diplomat; he was ambassador in Vienna in 1813 and signed the Treaty of Teplitz. He was foreign secretary under Wellington (1828–30), and again under Robert Peel (1841–46). In 1852 he became prime minister in a government of Peelites and Whigs (Liberals). Although a Tory, he supported Catholic emancipation and followed Peel in his conversion to free trade.

He succeeded as a Scottish earl in 1801, and was created an English viscount in 1814.

Aberdeen Angus

Former name of the ◊Angus breed of dairy cattle.

Aberdeen City

Unitary authority in northeast Scotland, created in 1996 from the district of the same name which was part of Grampian region

Area 185 sq km/71 sq mi

Towns ◊Aberdeen (administrative headquarters)

Physical low-lying coastal area on the banks of the rivers Dee and Don

Features St Andrew's Cathedral, King's and Marischal Colleges, Brig O'Balgownie

Industries North Sea oil, paper manufacturing, textiles, engineering, food processing, chemicals

Agriculture white and salmon fishing

Population (1995) 219,100.

Administrative history

Aberdeen City was part of Aberdeenshire prior to 1974.

Aberdeenshire

Unitary authority in northeast Scotland, created in 1996 from three districts within the former Grampian region; its administrative headquarters, Aberdeen, lies outside the authority

Area 6,308 sq km/2,436 sq mi

Towns Banff, Fraserburgh, Huntly, Peterhead, Stonehaven, Inverurie

Physical area of contrast with mountainous western interior, intensively farmed core, and coastal plain; Cairngorm Mountains; rivers Deveron, Ythan, Don, and Dee

Features Balmoral Castle; Braemar Games

Industries oil and gas, papermaking, whisky distilling, seafood, tourism

Agriculture beef cattle, fishing, cereal crops

Population (1995) 226,500.

Economy

This prosperous part of Scotland has both traditional and modern economic enterprise. Agriculturally rich, the area is well known for cereal production, livestock, such as pedigree Angus and Beef Shorthorn cattle, and fishing, at Peterhead, Fraserburgh, and MacDuff, in particular.

The eastern seaboard also serves the oil and gas industry of the North Sea and the western area has an important tourist industry because of its association with royalty and its mountain environment.

Environment

There are 80 Sites of Special Scientific Interest, eight National Nature Reserves, three Ramsars (wetland sites), five Special Protection Areas, two Biogenetic Reserves, two National Scenic Areas, and four country parks.

Architecture

The area has many examples of historic buildings and is particularly rich in castles, including that at Huntly (16th century); in the Dee valley, Crathes (16th century), Drum, Aboyne, and Braemar (all 17th century), and Dunnottar Castle (about 1392). Balmoral Castle, the Queen's Highland residence, is situated 15 km/9 mi west of Ballater in the Dee valley.

Administrative history

Aberdeenshire is the only Scottish unitary authority with its administrative headquarters outside its administrative area. It was created from the districts of Banff and Buchan, Gordon, and Kincardine and Deeside. Aberdeenshire includes the pre-1974 county of the same name, Kincardinshire, and parts of Banffshire.

Aberfan

Former coalmining village in Merthyr Tydfil unitary authority, south Wales. Coal waste from a slag heap overwhelmed a school and houses in 1966; of the 144 dead, 116 were children.

Aberfeldy

Town and former burgh in Perth and Kinross unitary authority, Scotland, on the right bank of the River Tay, 35 km/22 mi northwest of Perth; population (1991) 1,700. Tourism and distilling are the principal industries. The town is the home of the Dewars family distillery.

A watermill, restored in the 19th century, and the silver birch trees which line the banks of Urlar Burn as it flows into the River Tay at Aberfeldy, are among the principal tourist attractions. The river is spanned at Aberfeldy by a bridge erected by the military roadbuilder George Wade in 1733. Designed by the architect William Adam, the bridge is of a hump-backed construction with five arches.

Abergavenny, Welsh Y-Fenni

Town in Monmouthshire, south Wales, at the confluence of the Usk and Gavenny rivers; population (1991) 13,900. It is overlooked by Mynydd Pen-y-fal (596 m/1,955 ft), the 'Sugar Loaf' mountain. Abergavenny is a market town and a shopping centre for a large agricultural area. Tourism is a growing industry.

The town was a Roman settlement (**Gobannium**), and there are the remains of a Norman castle and of a Benedictine priory.

Abertillery

Town in Blaenau Gwent, south Wales; population (1991) 11,700. The town has a steelworks, working in Ebbw Vale steel. Coal mining used to take place here, but the collieries are no longer in operation.

Aberystwyth

Commercial, tourist, and educational centre in Ceredigion, mid-Wales, situated at the mouths of the rivers Ystwyth and Rheidol in Cardigan Bay; population (1991) 11,150. It is the site of the University College of Wales (1872), the National Library of Wales (1911), the College of Librarianship (Wales), the Welsh Plant Breeding Station, and the office of the Royal Commission on Ancient Monuments in Wales. It is the unofficial capital of the Welsh-speaking area of Wales. The Welsh Language Society was founded here in 1963.

The town is overlooked by Pen Dinas, an Iron Age hillfort. The remains of Edward I's castle dominate the sea front. Built by his brother, Edmund of Lancaster, it was finally completed in 1307 but was destroyed by Cromwellian forces during the Civil War. A mint was opened here by Charles I; it used silver from a local mine. Some of the coins produced can be seen in the university museum.

Abingdon

Market town in Oxfordshire, south-central England, at the confluence of the River Ock with the Thames, 10 km/6 mi south of Oxford; population (1991) 35,200. Light industries include brewing and the manufacture of electronics and scientific instruments. The remains of a Benedictine abbey, founded in 675, include the 14th-century Checker Hall, now restored as an Elizabethan-type theatre, the 16th-century Long Gallery, and the 15th-century gateway. The abbey was largely destroyed in 1538 at the Dissolution of the Monasteries.

The County Hall (1677–82) houses a local museum. Other historic buildings include the Long Alley almshouses (1446). Abingdon was the county town of Berkshire until 1870. Late 20th-century excavations suggest Abingdon may be the oldest continually inhabited town in England.

abolitionism

A movement culminating in the late 18th and early 19th centuries that aimed first to end the slave trade, and then to abolish the institution of slavery and emancipate slaves.

In the UK, the leading abolitionist was William ◊Wilberforce, who secured passage of a bill abolishing the slave trade in 1807.

Aboukir Bay, Battle of

Also known as the **Battle of the Nile**; naval battle during the Napoleonic Wars between Great Britain and France, in which Admiral Horatio Nelson defeated Napoleon Bonaparte's fleet at the Egyptian seaport of Aboukir on 1 August 1798. The defeat put an end to French designs in the Middle East.

Abraham, Edward Penley (1913–)

English biochemist who isolated the antibiotic cephalosporin, capable of destroying penicillin-resistant bacteria. He also had a major role in early studies of penicillins. Knighted 1980.

Abse, Dannie (1923–)

Welsh poet, novelist, and dramatist. His first volume of verse was *After Every Green Thing* (1949), and among subsequent volumes are *White Coat, Purple Coat: Collected Poems 1948–1988* (1989), and *Remembrance of Crimes Past* (1990). *Ash on a Young Man's Sleeve* (1954) and *There Was a Young Man from Cardiff* (1991) are semi-autobiographical novels about his Jewish upbringing.

Absolutely Fabulous

British sitcom (1992–96) satirizing the fashion industry and middle-aged baby boomers. The alcohol and drugs intake, interest in fads, disposable income, sex drives, and shopping sprees of Edina Monsoon (Jennifer ◊Saunders, who also wrote the scripts) and her comatose, boozy sidekick Patsy Stone (Joanna ◊Lumley) are counterpointed by the 'normalcy' of Eddie's studious daughter Saffron (Julia Sawalha) and mother (June Whitfield). Directed by Bob Spiers and created by Saunders and her comedy and business partner Dawn ◊French, the series is popularly known as *Ab Fab*. A US version of the show, *High Society*, was broadcast in 1995.

ACAS, Advisory, Conciliation, and Arbitration Service

Government-funded independent body set up under the Employment Protection Act 1975 to improve industrial relations through its advisory, conciliation, and arbitration services. Specifically, ACAS aims to encourage the extension of collective bargaining and, wherever possible, the reform of collective-bargaining machinery.

It provides advice about employment law and encourages employers and unions to adopt best practice in this field. Most of its work is advisory but occasionally it becomes involved as a conciliator or arbitrator in an important national dispute.

Its chair is appointed by the secretary of state for employment and a third of its nine-member council is nominated by the TUC, a third by the CBI, and a third are independents. In 1998 it had more than 600 staff.

Accrington

Industrial town in Lancashire, northwest England, at the northern end of the ◊Rossendale upland, 35 km/22 mi north of Manchester; population (1991) 36,500. A former cotton-weaving town, its industries include the manufacture of textiles, engineering, and brickmaking.

The Haworth Art Gallery in the town houses the largest collection of Tiffany glass in Europe.

Ackroyd, Peter (1949–)

English novelist, biographer, reviewer, and poet. His novel *Hawksmoor* (1985) won the Whitbread award, and *T S Eliot* (1984) won the Whitbread prize for biography. Ackroyd's other books include the novels *Chatterton* (1987), *The House of Doctor Dee* (1993), and *Milton in America* (1996), and biographies of Dickens (1990), William Blake (1995), and Thomas More (1998). He has been chief book reviewer of *The Times* since 1986.

acre

Traditional English land measure equal to 4,840 square yards (4,047 sq m/0.405 ha). Originally meaning a field, it was the size that a yoke of oxen could plough in a day.

As early as Edward I's reign, the acre was standardized by statute for official use, although local variations in Ireland, Scotland, and some English counties continued. It may be subdivided into 160 square rods (one square rod equalling 25.29 sq m/30.25 sq yd).

ActionAid

UK charity founded in 1972 to help people in the Third World to secure lasting improvements in the quality of their lives. It has sister organizations in other industrialized countries and by 1990 had projects in 18 countries in Africa, Asia, and Latin America, concentrating on long-term integrated rural development in the areas of water, health, agriculture, education, and income generation and reaching 3 million of the world's poorest people. It has over 110,000 active individual supporters and an annual income in excess of £35 million.

Sinn Féin believe the violence we have seen must be for all of us now a thing of the past – over, done with and gone.

GERRY ADAMS President of Sinn Féin and member of the Northern Ireland Assembly.
A statement – approved by the British, Irish, and US governments – issued on the eve of President Clinton's visit to Ireland, September 1998

---

act of Parliament

A change in the law, originating in Parliament and called a statute. Before an act receives the royal assent and becomes law it is a **bill**. An act of Parliament may be either public (of general effect), local, or private. The body of English statute law comprises all the acts passed by Parliament: the existing list opens with the Statute of Merton, passed in 1235. See House of ◊Commons for how a bill becomes law.

Acton, Eliza (1799–1859)

English cookery writer and poet, whose *Modern Cookery for Private Families* 1845 influenced ◊Mrs Beeton.

Modern Cookery was an immediate success and there were five editions in two years. It continued in print until 1914. Acton also wrote *The English Bread Book*. Some of her poetry was published in the 1820s and 1830s.

Adam

Family of Scottish architects and designers. **William Adam** (1689–1748) was the leading Scottish architect of his day, and his son **Robert Adam** (1728–1792) is considered one of the greatest British architects of the late 18th century, responsible for transforming the prevailing Palladian fashion in architecture to a Neo-Classical style.

William Adam trained his three sons Robert, John, and James in his Edinburgh office. Robert travelled in Italy and Dalmatia, and was appointed architect to King George III in 1762. His commissions included the remodelling of Kenwood House (1764) and Osterley Park, London (1760s); Culzean Castle, South Ayrshire (1775); and Nostell Priory, West Yorkshire. At Kedleston Hall (1759–70) he exquisitely balanced Antiquarian and Neo-Classical influences. In his interiors, such as those at Saltram, Harewood House, Luton Hoo, and Syon House, he employed delicate stucco decoration with Neo-Classical motifs. He also earned a considerable reputation as a furniture designer.

Robert, John, and James designed and speculatively developed the district of London between Charing Cross and the Thames, which was named the ◊Adelphi after them (Greek for 'brothers'). The area was largely rebuilt in 1936.

Adams, Douglas (Noël) (1952–)

English novelist and script-writer, author of a series of bestselling space-fiction books which began with ◊*The Hitch-Hiker's Guide to the Galaxy* (originally a radio serial in 1978 and published in 1979). He has also written the absurdist detective books *Dirk Gently's Holistic Detective Agency* (1987) and *The Long Dark Tea-Time* (1988), and the nonfiction *Last Chance to See* about endangered species.

Adams, Gerry (Gerard) (1948–)

Northern Ireland politician, president of ◊Sinn Féin (the political wing of the Irish Republican Army, IRA) from 1978. He was elected member of Parliament for Belfast West in 1983 but declined to take up his Westminster seat, as he refused to take an oath of allegiance to the Queen; he lost his seat in 1992 but regained it in 1997, still refusing to sit in the Westminster parliament. Since June 1998 he has represented Sinn Féin in the Northern Ireland Assembly.

Despite doubts about his ability to influence the IRA, he has been a key figure in Irish peace negotiations. He was the main architect of the IRA cease-fire in 1994 and in 1997 he entered into multi-party talks with the British government. This culminated in the 1998 Good Friday Agreement for a political settlement, which was subsequently ratified in Irish referenda. Later in 1998 he met the Unionist leader, David Trimble, at Stormont, Belfast, in a historic meeting, the first of its kind for several generations.

Adams was interned 1972–77 on suspicion of involvement in terrorist activity. In 1993 it was revealed that he had held talks about a possible political solution with the leader of the

ADAMS, GERRY *The leading Northern Ireland Republican politician Gerry Adams has been central to the negotiations aimed at bringing peace to the province, and has taken a seat in the Northern Ireland National Assembly. Adams has repudiated political violence, but concerns remain over whether the IRA, the paramilitary wing of his party Sinn Féin, will decommission its stockpile of weapons. Erik Pendzich/Rex*

Social Democratic Labour Party, John ◊Hume, and with representatives of the British government. In August 1994, when Adams announced the IRA cease-fire, the British government removed all restrictions on his public appearances and freedom to travel to mainland Britain (in force since 1988).

Adams, John Couch (1819–1892)

English astronomer. He mathematically deduced the existence of the planet Neptune in 1845 from the effects of its gravitational pull on the motion of Uranus, although it was not found until 1846 by J G Galle. Adams also studied the Moon's motion, the Leonid meteors, and terrestrial magnetism.

Adams was born in Landeast, Cornwall, and educated at Cambridge, where he spent virtually his entire career. He became professor of mathematics at the University of St Andrews, Fife 1858, Lowndean professor of astronomy and geometry at Cambridge 1859–92, and director of Cambridge observatory 1861–92.

Adams, Neil (1958–)

English judo champion. He won two junior and five senior European titles 1974–85, eight senior national titles, and two Olympic silver medals (1980 and 1984). In 1981 he was world champion in the 78 kg class.

Adams, Richard George (1920–)

English novelist. He wrote *Watership Down* (1972), a story of rabbits who escape from a doomed warren and work together to establish a new one. *Tales from Watership Down* (1996) continues the mythology. His other novels using animals as main characters are *Shardik* (1974), *The Plague Dogs* (1977), and *Traveller* (1988), while *The Girl on the Swing* (1980) and *Maia* (1984) have human protagonists. He has also written *The Days Gone By: An Autobiography* (1990).

Addington, Henry, 1st Viscount Sidmouth (1757–1844)

British Tory politician, prime minister 1801–04. As home secretary 1812–1822, he was responsible for much reprieve legislation, including the notorious ◊Six Acts. He was created viscount in 1805.

Addison, Joseph (1672–1719)

English poet and dramatist, and one of the most celebrated of English essayists. His essays set a new standard of easy elegance in English prose and his work foreshadows modern journalism. In 1704 he commemorated ◊Marlborough's victory at Blenheim in a poem commissioned by the government, 'The Campaign'. He subsequently held political appointments and was MP for Malmesbury from 1708 until his death. From 1709 to 1711 he contributed to the *Tatler* magazine, begun by Richard ◊Steele, with whom he was cofounder in 1711–12 of the *Spectator*.

In 1715 he launched a periodical published in support of the government entitled *The Freeholder*.

Addison, Thomas (1793–1860)

English physician who first recognized the condition known as Addison's disease in 1855. He was the first to correlate a collection of symptoms with pathological changes in an endocrine gland. He is also known for his discovery of what is now called pernicious (or Addison's) anaemia.

Addled Parliament

The English Parliament that met for two months in 1614 but failed to pass a single bill before being dissolved by James I.

Adelaide (1792–1849)

Queen consort of ◊William IV of Great Britain and Ireland. Daughter of the Duke of Saxe-Meiningen, she married William, then Duke of Clarence, in 1818. No children of the marriage survived infancy.

Adelphi (Greek **adelphoi**, 'brothers')

District in central London, south of the Strand. It was developed in the late 18th century by the architect Robert

◊Adam and his brothers James and William. Thanks to its architecture and location, the Adelphi soon became a high-class residential district. Adelphi Terrace was demolished in 1936 and few Adam buildings now remain.

In 1768 the Adam brothers obtained a 99-year lease for the area from the Duke of St Albans. Until the late 17th century it had been the site and grounds of Durham House, built in the early 13th century for the Bishop of Durham. For the Adams' development, land was reclaimed from the River Thames, and great arched vaults served as foundations for the houses nearer the river. Despite the appeal of the development, the Adam brothers lost much money in the speculation.

Admiral's Cup

Sailing series first held in 1957 and held biennially. National teams consisting of three boats compete over three inshore courses (in the Solent, off the English coast) and three offshore courses culminating at the Fastnet race (established 1925), which is 973 km/605 mi long.

Admiralty, Board of the

The controlling department of state for the Royal Navy from the reign of Henry VIII until 1964, when most of its functions – apart from that of management – passed to the Ministry of Defence. The 600-year-old office of Lord High Admiral reverted to the sovereign.

Admiralty Court

English court that tries and gives judgement in maritime cases. The court is now incorporated within the Queen's Bench Division of the High Court and deals with such matters as salvage and damages arising from collisions between ships.

Prize court

The Admiralty Court also sits as a prize court, in which capacity it has jurisdiction in matters of capture in port or on land if the capture has been effected by a naval force or a mixed naval and military force. The court can also try any questions referred to it by the Privy Council concerning booty of war; that is, property captured by land forces.

Scotland

The Scottish Court of Admiralty lost its prize jurisdiction to the English Court of Admiralty in 1825, and in 1830 its civil and criminal jurisdiction was transferred respectively to the Court of Session and the High Court of Justiciary. The maritime law of Scotland is the same as that of England.

Adrian IV, Nicholas Breakspear (*c.* 1100–1159)

Pope 1154–59, the only English pope. He secured the execution of Arnold of Brescia (1100–55), who attacked the holding of property by the Catholic Church, and crowned Frederick I Barbarossa (*c.* 1123–90) as German emperor. When he died, Adrian IV was at the height of a quarrel with Barbarossa over papal supremacy. He allegedly issued the controversial bull giving Ireland to Henry II of England in 1154. He was attacked for false representation, and the bull was subsequently refuted.

Adrian, Edgar Douglas (1889–1977), 1st Baron Adrian

English physiologist. He received the Nobel Price for Physiology or Medicine in 1932 for his work with Charles Sherrington in the field of nerve impulses and the function of the nerve cell. Adrian was also one of the first to study the electrical activity of the brain. Created baron 1955.

adult education

Voluntary classes and courses for adults provided mainly in further-education colleges, adult-education institutes, and school premises. Adult education covers a range of subjects from electronics to flower arranging. Courses are either vocational, designed to fill the gaps in earlier education and leading to examinations and qualifications, or nonvocational, to aid the adult's cultural development and contribute to his or her general education. The ◊Open College, ◊Open University, and Workers' Educational Association are adult-education bodies.

Most adult education is provided by local education authorities (LEAs) and fees for classes are subsidized. In 1992 the government restricted subsidy to work-related courses, a proposal which met with strong opposition from bodies as diverse as the LEAs and the Women's Institute. Adult students are also provided for by extramural departments of universities and by a small number of residential colleges, such as Ruskin College, Oxford, and Fircroft, Birmingham.

Advertising Standards Authority, ASA

Organization founded by the UK advertising industry 1962 to promote higher standards of advertising in the media (excluding television and radio, which have their own authority). It is financed by the advertisers, who pay a 0.1% supplement on the cost of advertisements. It recommends to the media that advertisements which might breach the British Code of Advertising Practice are not published, but has no statutory power.

advisory committee

Nonelected body whose members are answerable only to the minister who appointed them. Their deliberations are secret and members have no obligation to reveal their financial interests. They are chiefly made up of outside experts, working part-time and meeting infrequently.

There were 807 advisory committees in 1995, including the Committee on the Safety of Medicines (CSM), which approves new drugs; the Medicines Commission, which acts as a court of appeal to the CSM; the Committee on Toxicity, which advises on food additives; the Citizen's Charter Panel; the Spongiform Encephalopathy Advisory Committee, which advises on BSE; and Royal Comissions.

Advocates, Faculty of

Professional organization for Scottish advocates, the equivalent of English ◊barristers. It was incorporated in 1532 under James V.

Advocates' Library

Legal and general library founded in 1680 in Edinburgh by the Faculty of Advocates. From the early 18th century it was a copyright library entitled to claim a copy of every book published in Britain from the publishers. Until 1925 it was the principal library in Scotland, and in that year the nonlegal books were presented by the Faculty of Advocates to the nation to form the National Library of Scotland.

Aelfric (*c.* 955–1020)

English writer and abbot. Between 990 and 998 he wrote in vernacular ◊Old English prose two sets of sermons known as *Catholic Homilies*, and a further set known as *Lives of the Saints*, all of them largely translated from Latin.

Aesthetic Movement

English artistic movement of the late 19th century, dedicated to the doctrine of 'art for art's sake' – that is, art as a self-sufficient entity concerned solely with beauty and not with any moral or social purpose. Associated with the movement were the artists Aubrey Beardsley and James McNeill Whistler and writers Walter Pater and Oscar Wilde, while John Ruskin and William Morris were staunch critics of the movement.

AESTHETIC MOVEMENT *A drawing of* St John the Baptist and Salome *by the English artist Aubrey Beardsley. His bold and original use of line and pattern, combined with his fascination with the erotic and the grotesque, made him a leading and controversial member of the Aesthetic Movement at the end of the 19th century. Linda Proud*

Afghan Wars

Three wars waged between Britain and Afghanistan to counter the threat to British India from expanding Russian influence in Afghanistan.

First Afghan War 1838–42, when the British garrison at Kabul was wiped out.

Second Afghan War 1878–80, when General Roberts captured Kabul and relieved Kandahar.

Third Afghan War 1919, when peace followed the dispatch by the UK of the first aeroplane ever seen in Kabul.

Africa, the scramble for

Drive by European nations to establish colonies in Africa. It began in the 1880s, and by 1914 only Ethiopia and Liberia remained completely independent. The rest of Africa was under the control of seven European powers, including Britain. Britain and France had the most colonies.

The British, moving from their already established base in Cape Colony, seized territory in East Africa. Britain had already gained control over Egypt, which had been under Ottoman Turkish rule, and ruled Sudan jointly with Egypt. Despite the speed at which colonization by the Europeans took place, all these colonies were short-lived, and the majority attained their independence in the 1960s and 1970s.

Afro-Caribbean

West Indian person of African descent. Afro-Caribbeans are the descendants of West Africans captured or obtained in trade from African procurers and shipped by European slave traders to colonies in the West Indies from the 16th century. Since World War II many Afro-Caribbeans have migrated to Europe, including the UK. According to the 1991 census, there are some 500,000 Afro-Caribbeans, or black Caribbeans, living in the UK.

> *My voice as a writer has its source very much in the Caribbean region, which means that psychically you're at once connected to the Americas, Africa, Asia, and Europe.*
>
> GRACE NICHOLS British writer. *A Virago Keepsake* (1993)

Agate, James (Evershed) (1877–1947)

English essayist and theatre critic. His reviews, many of which were published, were noted for their wit, clarity, and seriousness. He wrote *Ego*, a diary in nine volumes published 1935–49.

Born in Manchester, he worked on the staff of the *Manchester Guardian* 1907–14, and was a drama critic for the *Saturday Review* 1921–23 and the *Sunday Times* 1923–47. His published novels include *Responsibility* (1919) and *Blessed Are the Rich* (1924).

The English instinctively admire any man who has no talent and is modest about it.

JAMES AGATE English essayist and theatre critic.
Attributed remark

Age Concern

UK charity that cares for the elderly. Founded in 1940, it now has nearly 1,000 groups. Its services include the provision of day centres and lunch clubs and home visits to elderly people. As well as offices in London, Age Concern has regional centres in Wales, Scotland, and Northern Ireland.

Agincourt, Battle of

Battle of the ◊Hundred Years' War in which Henry V of England defeated the French on 25 October 1415, mainly through the overwhelming superiority of the English longbow. The French lost more than 6,000 troops compared with about 1,600 English casualties.

As a result of the battle, Henry gained France and the French princess Catherine of Valois as his wife. The village of Agincourt (modern **Azincourt**) is south of Calais, in northern France.

Agricola, Gnaeus Julius (AD 40–93)

Roman general and politician. Born at Forum Julii (Fréjus) in Provence, he became consul in AD 77, and then governor of Britain 78–85. Having won in the battle of Mons Graupius (an identified location in Scotland) in AD 84, he was able to extend Roman rule to the Firth of Forth in Scotland. His fleet sailed round the north of Scotland and proved Britain was an island.

agricultural revolution

Sweeping changes that took place in British agriculture over the period 1750–1850. The changes were a response to the increased demand for food from a rapidly expanding population. Major events included the ◊enclosure of open fields; the development of improved breeds of livestock; the introduction of four-course crop rotation; and the use of new crops such as turnips as animal fodder.

Recent research has shown that these changes were only part of a much larger, ongoing process of development: many were in fact underway before 1750, and other breakthroughs, such as farm mechanization, did not occur until after 1859.

The introduction of new crops – such as potatoes, red clover, and turnips – into Britain in the 17th century led to a considerable advance in farming practices, since farmers could use them to feed their livestock throughout the winter. Their use did away with the practice of slaughtering animals in the autumn and salting the meat for storage through the winter, which had been particularly detrimental to the health of the community. In the latter part of the 18th century, moreover, Jethro ◊Tull demonstrated the advantage of thorough soil cultivation, and, with the invention of the first practical mechanized seed drill in about 1701, initiated the practice of drilling rather than broadcasting seed.

Four-course rotation

Tull's invention allowed crops to be planted in regular rows, while the intervals between rows could be stirred and cleaned by horse-hoeing. It also afforded a place for turnips and other root crops, and eventually led to the replacement of the 'three-field' system of the village community by the four-course rotation system, which was designed to ensure that no land would need to lie fallow between periods of cultivation and, to this end, rotated crops which absorb different kinds and quantities of nutrients from the soil. The four-course rotation system was subsequently developed by enlightened landowners such as Viscount 'Turnip' ◊Townshend and Thomas ◊Coke (1752–1842), who used it to produce greatly increased crop yields on his farmland in Norfolk, and encouraged other farmers and landowners to use the same method. Because both Coke and Townshend lived in Norfolk the system also became known as the 'Norfolk System'.

Livestock farming

Other pioneers of the new farming methods developed in Britain in the latter part of the 18th century included Arthur ◊Young, the first secretary of the British Board of Agriculture and the author of numerous works on agriculture; and the livestock farmer Robert Bakewell, who improved the quality of horned stock and sheep, largely by means of inbreeding. His work resulted in a great reduction in the age at which bullocks and sheep were ready for the butcher.

agriculture

In 1996 74% of land in Britain was in use for agriculture, of which the majority is grassland used for grazing animals, with just under 30% used for crops. There were approximately 230,000 farm holdings (excluding very small operations) in the same year. Overall, British agriculture employs some 2% of the country's workforce. Britain's main agricultural exports are livestock (reduced since 1995 because of the BSE crisis, see ◊bovine spongiform encephalopathy), food products, agrochemicals, and agricultural machinery. See chronology on pages 10 and 11 for some key dates in the history of British agriculture.

Agriculture, Fisheries, and Food, Ministry of, MAFF

UK government department established in 1955, through the combination of existing agriculture, fisheries, and food ministries. It is responsible for agriculture, horticulture, fisheries, and food policies. In 1998, including agencies such

Agriculture: Some Key Dates

***c.* 4400 BC** As knowledge spreads from continental Europe, communities in the British Isles begin to develop agricultural practices to replace the hunter-gatherer lifestyle.

80 BC The second wave of Celtic Belgae arrives in Britain from Gaul during this period. They settle mostly in the southeast and tackle the less well drained and still forested land, farming with a plough that can turn the sod.

1128 Norman monks of the Cistercian order arrive in England and begin to farm. The order lives entirely off the land and is to introduce many improvements in agricultural practice.

1236 The Statute of Merton (followed in 1285 by the Statute of Westminster) attempts to ensure that sufficient common land is left for the tenants of a lord who is appropriating open fields for private use, often for grazing sheep. The process is known as enclosure, and becomes widespread in the 15th and 16th centuries. It causes poverty, homelessness, and rural depopulation, leading to revolts.

June 1381 Riots known as the Peasants' Revolt start in southeast England in reaction to a new poll tax.

February 1607–May 1607 Resistance by English peasants to enclosures and the consequent deprivation of common land, rights, and subsistence, leads to the Midlands Rising (large-scale fence-breaking and rioting throughout the heavily enclosed counties), culminating in a peasant assembly and insurrection in Northamptonshire.

1663 The Royal Society calls for the widespread cultivation of potatoes as a precaution against famine in Britain.

1700–1800 The weight of cattle reaching market in England doubles over the century, thanks to the introduction of selective breeding, pedigrees, and new animal husbandry techniques.

***c.* 1701** English farmer Jethro Tull invents the first practical mechanized seed drill.

1714 English farmer and inventor Jethro Tull introduces the horse-hoe to England from France, advocating its use for releasing nutrients from the soil.

1788 Scottish millwright Andrew Meikle patents a threshing machine for separating the grain from the straw.

1801, 1836, and 1845 General Enclosure Acts complete the enclosure of open fields for private use.

1817 Irish farmer James Murray invents superphosphate, a fertilizer made from bones and sulphuric acid.

1843 English agronomist John Bennet Lawes and English chemist Joseph Henry Gilbert establish the Rothamsted Experimental Station, Hertfordshire, England, the world's first agricultural research station.

1845 The potato blight fungus *Phytophthora infestans* causes potato crops to fail throughout Europe. In Ireland, where the potato is a staple, over half the crop is lost causing devastating famine. Over 1 million die and 1.5 million emigrate over the next two years.

26 June 1846 The British prime minister, Robert Peel, repeals the Corn Laws to allow the unhindered importation of grain into Ireland in an effort to alleviate the famine caused there by the failure of the potato crop.

1873 In the first example of biological pest control, British-born US entomologist Charles Riley exports the acarid *Rhizoglyphus phylloxerae* to France to destroy aphids.

23 July 1889 The British Board of Agriculture is founded.

1917 The Women's Land Army is set up in Britain.

1953 Infectious myxomatosis is introduced from continental Europe to Britain, killing millions of rabbits.

25 October 1967 An epidemic of the cattle disease foot-and-mouth begins in Shropshire, England, ending in March 1968.

14 October 1979 France imposes a prohibitive tariff on British lamb exports in defiance of the European Court.

1984 The pesticide DDT is banned in Britain.

1985 An epidemic of bovine spongiform encephalopathy (BSE), or 'mad cow disease', is reported in beef cattle in Britain; it is later traced to cattle feed containing sheep carcasses infected with scrapie; in following years the consumption of infected beef is linked to CJD (Creutzfeld Jakob disease) in humans.

16 December 1988 The junior British health minister Edwina Currie resigns after her claim that most British eggs are infected with salmonella leads to a slump in egg sales.

January 1996 The first genetically engineered salmon are hatched, at Loch Fyne in Scotland. The salmon contain genes from white fish as well as a salmon growth hormone gene that causes them to grow five times as fast as other salmon.

25 March 1996 The European Union bans the export of British beef abroad following anxiety over the potential for transmission of the BSE infection to humans as CJD (Creuzfeld Jakob disease).

27 February 1997 Scottish researcher Ian Wilmut of the Roslin Institute in Edinburgh, Scotland, announces that British geneticists have cloned an adult sheep. A cell was taken from the udder of the mother sheep and its DNA (deoxyribonucleic acid) combined with an unfertilized egg that had had its DNA removed. The fused cells were grown in the laboratory and then implanted into the uterus of a surrogate mother sheep. The resulting lamb, Dolly, came from an animal that was six years old. This is the first time cloning has been achieved using cells other than reproductive cells. The news is met with international calls to prevent the cloning of humans.

4 March 1998 The Countryside March, a demonstration in London of around 250,000 people, aims to promote understanding of the issues facing rural Britain. Issues that had caused controversy and led to the march included the 1997 bill to ban hunting with dogs, and government policies on farming.

November 1998 The government announces a £120 million emergency aid package for Britain's farmers, especially hill farmers, partly funded by the European Union. In the same month, the EU lifts the ban on the export of British beef.

as the Meat Hygiene Service, it had more than 9,000 staff. The minister of agriculture from 1998 was Nick Brown.

Ahmed, Nazir, Baron Ahmed (1955–)

Pakistani-born British Labour working peer, created in 1998, one of three Muslim members of the House of Lords. Elected to Rotherham Council in 1990, he was the founder of the British Muslim Councillors Forum. A Yorkshire businessman, Lord Ahmed is chairman of the South Yorkshire Labour Party and vice-chairman of the South Yorkshire Euro-constituency; he also campaigns on Kashmiri issues.

Aidan, St (*c.* 600–651)

Irish monk who converted Northumbria to Christianity and founded Lindisfarne monastery on Holy Island off the northeast coast of England. His feast day is 31 August.

AIDS

Between 1982 and October 1997 just under 15,000 people in the UK were reported as suffering from AIDS, of whom 10,663 died in that time. See also ◊National AIDS Trust and ◊Terrence Higgins Trust.

Ailsa Craig, Gaelic Fairy Rock

Rocky islet in the Firth of Clyde, Scotland, about 16 km/10 mi off the coast of South Ayrshire, opposite Girvan. It forms a cone rising abruptly from the sea to a height of 338 m/1,114 ft, with a circumference of about 3 km/2 mi. Ailsa Craig's fine grained granite rock, 'Ailsite', was used in the manufacture of ◊curling stones. The islet is a breeding ground for sea birds and home to one of the largest colonies of gannets in Britain. There is a lighthouse at the southern tip which has been operating since 1886.

Aintree

Racecourse situated on the outskirts of Liverpool, northwest England. The ◊Grand National steeplechase (established 1839) is held at Aintree every spring.

There is also a car-racing circuit, used only for club racing. The British Grand Prix was held here in 1955, 1957, 1959, and 1961–62.

Airdrie

Industrial town in North Lanarkshire unitary authority, Scotland, approximately 8 km/5 mi north of the River Clyde, and 18 km/11 mi east of Glasgow; population (1991) 37,000. Originally a centre for cotton weaving, its industries are now diverse, ranging from paper manufacture to the production of pharmaceuticals.

Aire

River in northern England; length 110 km/68 mi. It rises in the Pennine Hills near Malham, North Yorkshire, and flows through West and East Yorkshire to join the River Ouse near Goole. It also flows through **Airedale**, a valley lying between Malham Cove and Leeds.

Early in its course, the Aire flows east through the Aire Gap. The **Aire and Calder Navigation** is a system of rivers and canals; its chief branches are from Goole to Leeds, and from Castleford to Wakefield.

air raid

Aerial attack, usually on a civilian target such as a factory, railway line, or communications centre. Air raids began during World War I with the advent of military aviation, but it was the development of long-range bomber aircraft during World War II that made regular attacks on a large scale possible.

The first air raids in World War I were carried out by airships, since only they had the necessary range, but later in the war aeroplanes were also used as their performance improved. Bombing was generally indiscriminate due to the difficulty of accurately aiming the primitive bombs in use at the time. Despite the relatively limited nature of these early raids, there were 4,830 British and 2,589 German casualties in air raids 1914–18.

Many thousands died in attacks by both sides in World War II, notably the ◊Blitz on London and other British cities 1940–41, and the firebombing of Dresden in February 1945, and air raids by both bombers and rockets have been a standard military tactic ever since.

Airy, George Biddell (1801–1892)

English astronomer. He installed a transit telescope at the Royal Observatory at Greenwich, England, and accurately measured ◊Greenwich Mean Time by the stars as they crossed the meridian.

Airy became the seventh Astronomer Royal in 1835. He began the distribution of Greenwich time signals by telegraph, and Greenwich Mean Time as measured by Airy's telescope was adopted as legal time in Britain in 1880. Knighted 1872.

Alamein, El, Battles of

Two decisive battles of World War II in the western desert of northern Egypt. In the first (1–27 July 1942), the British 8th Army under Auchinleck held off the German and Italian forces under Rommel; in the second (23 October–4 November 1942), ◊Montgomery defeated Rommel.

Montgomery began the second battle with a diversionary attack in the south so that the main attack in the north could create a gap for the British armoured divisions to pass through German minefields. He changed tactics constantly, switching the main emphasis of his attack to wear down Rommel's front line. By 3 November Rommel had only 30 serviceable tanks in action and on the following day began organizing his withdrawal.

Alba

Gaelic name for Scotland.

Alban, St (lived 3rd century)

First Christian martyr in England. In 793 King Offa founded a monastery on the site of Alban's martyrdom, around which the city of St Albans grew up. His feast day is 20 June.

According to tradition, he was born at Verulamium, served in the Roman army, became a convert to Christianity after giving shelter to a priest, and, on openly professing his belief, was beheaded.

Albany, Alexander Stewart, 3rd Duke of (*c.* 1454–1485)

Son of James II of Scotland. He usurped the throne of Scotland with English help. He was arrested by his brother, King James III of Scotland, in 1479, but escaped to England and was recognized as king of Scotland in June 1482 by Edward IV. Edward invaded Scotland in support of his claim; in return Albany acknowledged English suzerainty over Scotland, an acknowledgement he made again when he held the throne in 1484. He was subsequently forced to flee to France, where he died.

Albany, John Stewart, 4th Duke of (1484–1536)

Son of Alexander, 3rd Duke of Albany, he was made regent for the infant king James V in 1514, acting as an agent for the French king Francis I. He fled to France in 1517 where he was detained for a time under an agreement with the English, but was allowed to return to Scotland when the English declared war on France and Scotland in 1521. He led two invasions of England, in 1522 and 1523, but was finally forced to leave Scotland for France in May 1524.

Albany, Robert Stewart, 1st Duke of (*c.* 1340–1420)

Scottish noble and governor of Scotland 1402–20. His brother, Robert III of Scotland, was an invalid and so deemed unable to rule. Albany vied with Robert's elder son, David, Duke of Rothesay, for dominance and became de facto ruler after Rothesay's disgrace and death in 1402. He increased his power after the capture of Robert's second son (the future James I) by the English, and Robert's subsequent death in 1406, ruling as governor of Scotland until his own death in 1420, when he was succeeded by his son, Murdoch.

Albert, Prince Consort (1819–1861)

Husband of Queen ◊Victoria from 1840. A patron of the arts, science, and industry, Albert was the second son of the Duke of Saxe Coburg-Gotha and first cousin to Queen Victoria, whose chief adviser he became. He planned the Great Exhibition of 1851, the profits from which were used to buy the sites in London of all the South Kensington museums and colleges and the Royal Albert Hall, built in 1871. Albert also popularized the Christmas

ALBERT, PRINCE CONSORT *Albert photographed with Queen Victoria in 1854; he received the title 'Prince Consort' in 1857. Victoria adored him, but government ministers resented his involvement in politics, and the British public mistrusted him because of his German origins. After his death the Queen was inconsolable and spent the next 40 years as a virtual recluse. Corbis*

tree in England. He was regarded by the British people with groundless suspicion because of his German connections. He died of typhoid. The Queen never fully recovered from his premature death, and remained in mourning for him for the rest of her life.

Albert Memorial, the

Imposing Gothic Revival monument in Kensington Gardens, London. It was erected 1863–72 in memory of ◊Albert, the Prince Consort, husband of Queen Victoria. The monument was designed by George Gilbert ◊Scott, who earned a knighthood from Queen Victoria for his work on it.

Resoration work on the Albert Memorial was completed in 1998.

Albion

Name for Britain used by the ancient Greeks and Romans. It was mentioned by Pytheas of Massilia (4th century BC), and is probably of Celtic origin, but the Romans, having in mind the white cliffs of Dover, assumed it to be derived from the word *albus* (white).

Alcock, John William (1892–1919)

English aviator. On 14 June 1919, he and Arthur Whitten Brown (1886–1948) made the first non-stop transatlantic flight, from Newfoundland to Ireland. KBE 1919.

Alcuin, Flaccus Albinus Alcuinus (735–804)

English scholar. Born in York, he went to Rome in 780, and in 782 took up residence at Charlemagne's court in Aachen. From 796 he was abbot at St Martin's in Tours. He disseminated Anglo-Saxon scholarship. Alcuin organized education and learning in the Frankish empire and was a prominent member of Charlemagne's academy, providing a strong impulse to the Carolingian Renaissance.

Aldeburgh

Small town and coastal resort in Suffolk, eastern England, 33 km/20 mi from Ipswich; population (1991) 2,700. It maintains a small fishing fleet, serving the local market. The **Aldeburgh Festival**, founded in 1948 by the English composer Benjamin Britten, is held annually at the Snape Maltings, 8 km/5 mi west of the town. It is the home of the Britten–Pears School for Advanced Musical Studies.

Features

An important and prosperous port in the 16th century, Aldeburgh retains some Tudor buildings, including the timber-framed Moot Hall, built in about 1520–40, which is now a museum. Once near the centre of the town, the hall presently stands only a short distance from the sea because the shoreline has gradually been eroded.

Alde House was home to Elizabeth Garrett Anderson, the first English woman to qualify in medicine. She was elected mayor of Aldeburgh in 1908, becoming the first woman mayor in Britain.

The Church of St Peter and St Paul contains a statue of the poet George Crabbe who was born in Aldeburgh. His collection of tales about the life of the fishermen of Aldeburgh, *The Borough* (1810), was the inspiration for *Peter Grimes*, the opera by Benjamin Britten.

alderman (Old English **ealdor mann** 'older man')

Anglo-Saxon term for the noble governor of a shire; after the Norman Conquest the office was replaced with that of ◊sheriff. From the 19th century aldermen were the senior members of the borough or county councils in England and Wales, elected by the other councillors, until the abolition of the office in 1972.

In Britain in more recent times aldermen were members of county, town, and city corporations, and held certain powers in local affairs. The Local Government Act 1933 provided that one-half of the total numbers of the aldermen of a council had to retire in every third year, being the year in which councillors are elected. Although the office of alderman was abolished by the Local Government Act 1972, it was retained in the City of London and on the Greater London Council until 1977 and in the London boroughs until 1978. The title of **honorary alderman** can be conferred on former councillors, but does not entitle the holder to sit on the council.

Aldermaston

Village in West Berkshire, England, and site of an atomic and biological weapons research establishment, which employs some 5,000 people working on the production of nuclear warheads. During 1958–63 the Campaign for Nuclear Disarmament (CND) made it the focus of an annual Easter protest march.

Alderney

Third largest of the ◊Channel Islands, with its capital at St Anne's; area 8 sq km/3 sq mi; population (1991) 2,300. It exports early potatoes. Alderney is the former name for all breeds of dairy cattle of the Channel Islands, including the ◊Jersey and ◊Guernsey breeds.

Aldershot

Town in Hampshire, southern England, 56 km/35 mi southwest of London; population (1991) 51,400. Industrial products include electronics and vehicle components for cars and tankers. It contains the largest permanent military and training camp in the UK.

A small village until the mid-19th century, Aldershot grew in importance when permanent barracks and a military training centre were established in 1854. Very large numbers of troops were stationed in Aldershot during both world wars. Cambridge Hospital (1854–1996), founded along with the camp, became the birthplace of plastic surgery in the British Empire. The only two surviving 19th-century barrack blocks now house the Military Museum, one of nine museums in the town.

Aldgate
Area and street in the City of London, connecting Fenchurch Street with Whitechapel. The old gate, which was called Eastgate in the Saxon period and, later, Alegate, was the most easterly gate of the City. Excavations have established that it was formerly the site of a Roman gate; it was rebuilt in 1608 and finally demolished in 1761. The remains of the Aldgate Pump, a water pump, can still be seen. Geoffrey Chaucer lived in the old gatehouse.

Aldington, Richard pen name of Edward Godfree Aldington (1892–1962)
English poet, novelist, and critic. A leading Imagist (see ◊Imagism), he published the collection *Images* (1915). He wrote biographies of the English writers D H Lawrence and T E Lawrence and his novels include *Death of a Hero* (1929) and *All Men are Enemies* (1933).

Aldiss, Brian Wilson (1925–)
English novelist, science-fiction writer, anthologist, and critic. His futuristic novels include *Non-Stop* (1958), *Barefoot in the Head* (1969), the 'Helliconia' trilogy (1982–85), and *Somewhere East of Life* (1994). He has also published several volumes of short stories, including *Seasons in Flight* (1984). *Trillion Year Spree* (1986) is a revised edition of his history of science fiction, *Billion Year Spree* (1973). *Bury My Heart at W H Smith's*, a volume of autobiography, was published in 1990.

Aldwych
Thoroughfare in London. It was constructed between 1900 and 1905, and forms a loop on the northern side of the Strand. The name Aldwych was revived to commemorate an ancient Danish settlement in the area.

A level, or **Advanced level**
In England, Wales, and Northern Ireland, examinations taken by students usually at the age of 18, after two years' study, in no more than four subjects at one time. Two A-level passes are normally required for entry to a university degree course. Scottish students sit Highers.

Alexander, Conel Hugh O'Donel (1909–1974)
Irish-born British chess player and intelligence officer. He was an international master and British champion 1938 and 1956. In 1946 in a radio chess match he beat the future world champion, Mikhail Botvinnik.

Born in Cork, he moved to England as a child. He was a mathematics teacher at Winchester College 1932–38 before joining the Foreign Office. Recruited by British Intelligence, during World War II he was a member of the team that cracked the German Enigma code. CBE 1955.

Alexander, Harold Rupert Leofric George, 1st Earl Alexander of Tunis (1891–1969)
British field marshal, a commander in World War II in France, Burma (now Myanmar), North Africa, and the Mediterranean. He was governor general of Canada 1946–52 and UK minister of defence 1952–54.

In World War II he was the last person to leave in the evacuation of Dunkirk in 1940. In Burma he fought a delaying action for five months against superior Japanese forces. In Aug 1942 he went to North Africa, and in 1943 became deputy to Eisenhower in charge of the Allied forces in Tunisia. After the Axis forces in North Africa surrendered, Alexander became supreme Allied commander in the Mediterranean, and field marshal in 1944. He was appointed KCB in 1942, Viscount in 1946, and Earl Alexander of Tunis in 1952, and was awarded the OM in 1959.

Alexander
Three kings of Scotland:

Alexander I (*c.* 1078–1124)
King of Scotland from 1107, known as **the Fierce**. He ruled over the area to the north of the rivers Forth and Clyde, while his brother and successor David ruled over the area to the south. He assisted Henry I of England in his campaign against Wales in 1114, but defended the independence of the church in Scotland. Several monasteries, including the abbeys of Inchcolm and Scone, were established by him.

Alexander II (1198–1249)
King of Scotland from 1214, when he succeeded his father, William the Lion. Alexander supported the English barons in their struggle with King John after ◊Magna Carta. The accession of Henry III of England allowed a rapprochement between the two countries, and the boundaries between England and Scotland were agreed by the Treaty of York in 1237. By the treaty of Newcastle in 1244 he pledged allegiance to Henry III. Alexander consolidated royal authority in Scotland and was a generous patron of the church.

In 1221 he married Joanna, the sister of Henry III. In 1239, after her death he married Marie de Coucy, with whom he had a son, Alexander III.

Alexander III (1241–1286)
King of Scotland from 1249, son of Alexander II. After defeating the Norwegian forces in 1263, he was able to extend his authority over the Western Isles, which had been dependent on Norway. The later period of his reign was devoted to administrative reforms, which limited the power of the barons and brought a period of peace and prosperity to Scotland.

He died as the result of a fall from his horse, leaving his granddaughter Margaret, the Maid of Norway, to become queen of Scotland.

Alexandra (1936–)
Princess of the UK. Daughter of the Duke of Kent and Princess Marina, she married Angus Ogilvy (1928–), younger son of the earl of Airlie. They have two children, James (1964–) and Marina (1966–).

Alexandra (1844–1925)
Queen consort of ◊Edward VII of England, whom she married in 1863. She was the eldest daughter of Christian IX

of Denmark. She bore five children, two boys and three girls. The elder son, Albert Victor, Duke of Clarence, died in 1892, and his brother reigned as George V.

Alexandra was extremely popular in Britain; she had great charm, and showed a genuine interest in charitable work of all kinds. An annual Alexandra Rose Day in aid of hospitals commemorates her charitable work.

Alfred, the Great (*c.* 849–*c.* 901)

King of Wessex from 871. He defended England against Danish invasion and founded the first English navy. A new legal code came into force during his reign. He encouraged the translation of scholarly works from Latin (some he translated himself), and promoted the development of the ◊Anglo-Saxon Chronicle.

Alfred was born at Wantage, Oxfordshire, the youngest son of Ethelwulf (died in 858), King of the West Saxons. In 870 Alfred and his brother Ethelred fought many battles against the Danes. Alfred gained a victory over the Danes at Ashdown in 871, and succeeded Ethelred as king in April 871 after a series of battles in which the Danes had been defeated. Five years of uneasy peace followed while the Danes were occupied in other parts of England. In 876 the Danes attacked again, and in 878 Alfred was forced to retire to the stronghold of ◊Athelney, from where he finally emerged to win the victory of Edington, Wiltshire. By the Peace of Wedmore in 878 the Danish leader Guthrum (died in 890) agreed to withdraw from Wessex and from Mercia west of Watling Street. A new landing in Kent encouraged a revolt of the East Anglian Danes, which was suppressed 884–86, and after the final foreign invasion was defeated 892–96, Alfred strengthened the navy to prevent fresh incursions.

> *In England, then, being Canadian was like being cross-eyed, only less interesting: most people would gamely pretend not to notice, or throw you a look of pity and then swiftly escape to talk to someone else.*
>
> MARGARET ATWOOD Canadian writer. Writing in *A Virago Keepsake* (1993) about being a Canadian in London in the 1970s

Alice's Adventures in Wonderland

Children's story, published in 1865, by Lewis ◊Carroll (originally published as *Alice's Adventures Under Ground*). Alice dreams she follows the White Rabbit down a rabbit hole and meets fantastic characters such as the Cheshire Cat, the Mad Hatter, and the King and Queen of Hearts. With its companion volume *Through the Looking-Glass, and What Alice Found There* (1872), it is one of the most quoted works in the English language. Both volumes were illustrated by John ◊Tenniel.

Aliens Act

Act of Parliament passed by the Conservative government in 1905 to restrict the immigration of 'undesirable persons' into Britain.

Undesirable persons were defined as people who might be a charge on the poor rates because they were without means or infirm. Since the act appeared to be stimulated by the arrival of large numbers of impoverished Europeans, many of them Jews from the Russian Empire, Prime Minister Balfour was accused of anti-Semitism.

Allenby, Edmund Henry Hynman, 1st Viscount Allenby (1861–1936)

British field marshal. In World War I he served in France before taking command 1917–19 of the British forces in the Middle East. After preparations in Egypt, he captured Gaza, Beersheba and, in 1917, Jerusalem. His defeat of the Turkish forces at Megiddo in Palestine in September 1918 was followed almost at once by the capitulation of Turkey. He was high commissioner in Egypt 1919–35. KCB 1915, Viscount 1919.

Alleyn, Edward (1566–1626)

English actor. The only actor of his time to rival Richard Burbage, he appeared in Marlowe's plays. With his father-in-law, theatre manager Philip Henslowe, he built the Fortune Theatre in 1600 and was also part owner of the Rose Theatre. He founded Dulwich College in 1619.

Alliance, the

In UK politics, a loose union (1981–87) formed by the ◊Liberal Party and ◊Social Democratic Party (SDP) for electoral purposes.

The Alliance was set up soon after the formation of the SDP, and involved a joint manifesto at national elections and the apportionment of constituencies in equal numbers to Liberal and SDP candidates. The difficulties of presenting two separate parties to the electorate as if they were one proved insurmountable, and after the Alliance's poor showing in the 1987 general election the majority of the SDP voted to merge with the Liberals to form the Social and Liberal Democrats.

Allies, the

In World War I the 23 countries allied against the Central Powers (Germany, Austro-Hungary, Turkey, and Bulgaria), including France, Italy, Russia, the UK, Australia and other Commonwealth nations, and, in the latter part of the war, the USA. In World War II they were the 49 countries allied against the Axis Powers (Germany, Italy, and Japan), including France, the UK, Australia and other Commonwealth nations, the USA, and the former Soviet Union.

In the 1991 Gulf War, there were 28 countries in the Allied coalition.

Allingham, Margery Louise (1904–1966)

English detective novelist. She created detective Albert Campion in *The Crime at Black Dudley* (1929). Her detective fiction displays wit and ingenuity and includes *More Work for the Undertaker* (1949). Her mystery thrillers include *Tiger in the Smoke* (1952) and *The Beckoning Lady* (1955). *The Oaken Heart* (1941) is an account of village life during World War II.

Alloa
Town and former burgh in Clackmannanshire, Scotland, on the River Forth, 10 km/6 mi east of Stirling; population (1991) 18,800. Originally a port and coalmining centre, its principal industries are now brewing and distilling, and the manufacture of bottles and knitwear.

allotment
Small plot of rented land used for growing vegetables and flowers. Allotments originated in the UK during the 18th and 19th centuries, when much of the common land was enclosed (see ◊enclosure) and efforts were made to provide plots for poor people to cultivate.

Later, acts of Parliament made this provision obligatory for local councils. In 1996 there were 296,923 allotments in England, with 15 plots for every 1,000 households (1 plot for every 65 households). Half of the allotments are 10 rod in size, as the average; one-quarter are 5 rod in size. Some 87% of allotments are owned by local councils, the remainder being private or unlisted. Under the 1922 Enclosure Act, councils are entitled to charge a rate to maintain and buy allotments. During both world wars, growing vegetables on allotments to supplement food supplies was encouraged.

Alloway
Village in South Ayrshire unitary authority, Scotland, on the River Doon, now a suburb of Ayr, lying 6 km/4 mi south of its centre. Alloway is the birthplace of Robert Burns, and is the site of several tourist attractions associated with the Scottish poet, including Burns Cottage, a museum converted from his family home; the kirk, scene of the witches' dance in *Tam o' Shanter*; the Auld Brig o' Doon over which Tam o' Shanter escaped; and the Burns Monument and gardens.

All Saints
Vocal pop group formed in London in 1993, whose music combines pop, rhythm and blues, and hip hop. Its members are Melanie 'Mello-Deeeee' Blatt (1975–), Shaznay 'Bart' T Lewis (1975–), and the Canadian sisters Nicole 'The Fonz' Appleton (1974–) and Natalie 'Nona' Appleton (1973–). Following their hit single 'I Know Where It's At' (1997) they secured their popularity with 'Never Ever' and the hit album *All Saints* (1997).

Alma-Tadema, Lawrence (1836–1912)
Dutch artist who worked in England from 1870. He painted romantic, idealized scenes from ancient Greek, Roman, and Egyptian life, such as *Phidias at Work on the Parthenon* (1869; Tate Gallery) and the *Pyrrhic Dance* (1869; Guildhall, London), which combined Victorian sentiment with detailed historical accuracy. He was knighted in 1899.

almshouse, also known as *poor house*
House built and endowed for the support of those disabled from work by age or poverty.

Almshouses were founded by private charities and privately funded. Formerly (in the Middle Ages), an almshouse was the house belonging to a monastery or a section of a monastery, where alms and hospitality were dispensed. The most ancient example in England is the hospital of St Cross, Winchester (1136). The name 'hospital' is also used for almshouses in Scotland.

Alnwick
Town in Northumberland, England; population (1991) 7,200. It is situated 53 km/33 mi north of Newcastle, on the River Aln. **Alnwick Castle**, originally dating from the 12th century, was the home of the ◊Percy family. It was the site of battles in 1092 and 1174 following Scottish invasions of Northumberland. The castle was much restored in the 19th century. The 15th-century Hotspur Tower was the original gateway to the town.

Alston, Richard (1948–)
English choreographer. A modernist, or post-modernist, his style remains lyrical, characterized by lightness and speed. He was a founder member of the London Contemporary Dance Theatre and artistic director of the Rambert Dance Company 1986–92. The Richard Alston Dance Company was launched in 1994.

Among his principal works are *Rainbow Bandit* (1974, revived 1992 and 1994), *Doublework* (1978), *The Rite of Spring* (1981), *Soda Lake* and *Dutiful Ducks* (solos for Michael ◊Clark, 1981 and 1982), *Wildlife* (1984), *Strong Language* (1987), *Roughcut* (1990), *Le Marteau sans Maître* (1992), *Stardust* (1995), and *Rumours, Visions* (1996).

Althorp
Village in Northamptonshire, England, 11km/7m north of Northampton, site of the **Althorp Park** estate owned by the Spencer family since 1508. Diana, Princess of Wales, whose family home this was, is buried on an island in the park.

Earl Spencer, Diana's brother, opened a museum to her memory at Althorp in 1998.

Alton
Town in northeast Hampshire, England, 20 km/12 mi southeast of Basingstoke; population (1991) 15,600. The church of St Laurence was built in the early Norman period; a second nave and chancel were added in the 15th century. The south door of the church still bears the bullet holes where a Royalist, Captain Boles, was shot in 1643 while holding out against the Parliamentarians. The poet Edmund Spenser lived in Alton for a time; his cottage can still be seen.

Alton Towers
Theme park in Alton, Staffordshire, England, 24 km/15 mi east of Stoke-on-Trent; it opened in 1979. It was once the home of the earls of Shrewsbury. The gardens of Alton Towers lie above the gorge of the River Churnet, and are decorated with statues, grottoes, ornamental fountains, and temples. They were landscaped in the early 19th century by Charles, 15th Earl of Shrewsbury. The house – originally called Alveton Lodge – was enlarged in Gothic style in the 1830s by John, the 16th Earl, who renamed it Alton Towers. It contains a picture gallery and armoury. In 1924 the estate was sold to a private company who opened it to the public.

ALMSHOUSE *A 16th-century half-timbered almshouse in Thame, Oxfordshire. Almshouses, charitable foundations to house old and needy people, are found in many ancient towns in England. This one was built by Lord Williams of Thame in the 1550s. Corbis*

Alwyn, William (1905–1985)

English composer. He was professor of composition at the Royal Academy of Music 1926–55; he wrote film music (*Desert Victory*, *The Way Ahead*), and composed symphonies and chamber music. He also published *The Technique of Film Music* (1957).

Ambleside

Town in the Cumbrian Lake District, England; population (1981) 3,200. It is situated 20 km/12 mi northwest of Kendal, and extends to the head of Lake Windermere in the Vale of Rothay. Ambleside is a busy tourist centre for much of the year, with many hotels and guest houses.

Ambleside's literary associations include William and Dorothy Wordsworth, who lived at nearby Grasmere and later at Rydal Mount. Harriet Martineau, who died at Ambleside in 1876, lived at The Knoll, just outside the town.

A sports festival is held here every summer which includes traditional events, such as Cumberland and Westmorland wrestling, and fell running.

American Independence, War of

Alternative name of the ◊American Revolution.

American Revolution

Revolt 1775–83 of the British North American colonies, resulting in the establishment of the United States of America. It was caused by colonial opposition to British economic exploitation and by the unwillingness of the colonists to pay for a standing army. It was also fuelled by the colonists' antimonarchist sentiment and their desire to participate in the policies affecting them.

Resentment had been growing in the American colonies from 1763 onward as a result of high-handed British legislation, like the ◊Stamp Act of 1765, and the Townshend Acts of 1767, which imposed taxes on various goods, including tea. The first casualties of the revolution occurred in the Boston Massacre of 1770, when British troops opened fire on protesters. In the Boston Tea Party of 1773, protesters disguised as Indians emptied 342 chests of cheap imported tea into the harbour. In 1775 fighting broke out at Lexington and Concord, and in the same year the Americans invaded Canada and George Washington was appointed commander in chief of the America forces. The Declaration of Independence was issued in 1776, but Washington's troops suffered a series of defeats at the hands of General Howe.

The turning point in the war came with the decisive American victory at the Battle of Saratoga Springs in 1777, which prompted the French to enter the war on the American side. American military success culminated in British defeat

THE COLLAPSE OF THE COLONIAL SYSTEM: GEORGE III AND THE LOSS OF AMERICA

THE THIRTEEN Colonies of North America were central to the British imperial system; nowhere outside Britain itself did so many people of European descent live under British rule. A major British achievement of the mid-18th century had been the ending of the French threat to the colonies and the conquest of Canada in the Seven Years' War (1756–63).

Reasons for rebellion

Yet this empire was to collapse rapidly and George III (1760–1820) was the last king of the Thirteen Colonies. There were a number of reasons why relations between Britain and the colonies, hitherto fairly amicable, broke down so rapidly. British determination to make colonies, not represented in Parliament, pay a portion of their defence burden was crucial, although many other factors came into play, such as the increasing democratization in American society, a rejection of British authority, concern about British policy in Canada, anxiety that the British were trying to limit American expansion in order to please the native peoples, and the borrowing of British conspiracy theories about the supposed autocratic intentions of George III: in fact, he was not so much autocratic as stubborn and his lack of flexibility was partly responsible for the ultimate loss of the colonies. The Seven Years' War had left the British government with an unprecedentedly high level of national debt and it looked to America to meet a portion of the burden. The Americans, however, no longer felt threatened by French bases in Canada and were, therefore, no longer willing to see British troops as saviours. The Stamp Act of 1765 led to a crisis as Americans rejected Parliament's financial demands; thereafter, relations were riven by a fundamental division over constitutional issues.

Nonetheless, the fact that Britain's most important colonies in the western hemisphere, those in the West Indies, did not rebel, despite the sensitivity of their elites on questions of constitutional principle, suggests that there was no inevitable crisis in the British imperial system, but rather that factors particular to the American colonies were crucial.

The war

Fighting broke out near Boston in 1775 because of the determination of the government of Lord North to employ force, and the willingness of sufficient Americans to do likewise. An ill-advised government attempt to seize illegal arms dumps led to clashes at Lexington and Concord on 19 April, and the British were soon blockaded by land in Boston. Their attempt to drive off the Americans led to very heavy losses at the Battle of Bunker Hill on 17 June. The Americans hardened their position and declared independence in 1776. British forces were largely driven out of the Thirteen Colonies, though they held Canada, and then counterattacked to win the Battle of Long Island on 27 August 1776 and regain New York. The British seizure of Philadelphia was matched by defeat at Saratoga (19 September and 6 October 1777), and, after the French entered the war on the revolutionary side in 1778, the British were pushed on to the defensive in a world war for which they lacked the necessary resources. Spain joined France in 1779, and at the end of 1780 so did the Dutch, in what was becoming a truly global conflict. Though the Franco-Spanish attempt to invade England in 1779 failed, and the British held on to Gibraltar, India, and Jamaica, surrender of a besieged British army at Yorktown on 19 October 1781 was followed by the collapse of British will to fight on and by the acceptance of American independence.

The war can be seen as both revolutionary and traditional: revolutionary in that it was one of the first important instances of a people's war, of the nation-in-arms; and traditional in that it was essentially fought on terms that would have been familiar to those who had been engaged in recent conflicts in Europe and North America. The American response to battle was to adopt the lines of musketeers of European warfare. British troops fought well, but Britain's failure to destroy George Washington's army was, in the end, crucial. The British needed a decisive victory and the Americans displayed skill and determination in avoiding such a defeat, despite casualty rates higher than in either of the World Wars.

Consequences

American independence split the English-speaking world. America was to be the most dynamic of the independent states in the western hemisphere, the first of the decolonized countries. Its people were best placed to take advantage of the potent combination of a European legacy, independence, and the opportunities for expansion and growth that were to play an increasingly important role in the new world after 1776. Paradoxically, American independence also ensured that aspects of British culture, society, and ideology, albeit in altered forms, were to enjoy great influence outside and after the span of British empire, down to the present day.

BY JEREMY BLACK

and surrender at Yorktown in 1781. The defeat forced the resignation of the prime minister Lord ◊North, one of the war's main advocates. Under the Peace of Versailles, on 3 September 1783 Britain recognized the independence of the USA, and in return was allowed to retain Canada and recovered its West Indian territories.

Amersham

Market town in Buckinghamshire, England, 12 km/7 mi northeast of High Wycombe; population (1981) 21,490. It is situated on the edge of the Chiltern Hills. Its main industries include the manufacture of cosmetics, textile printing, food production, timber haulage, and chemical and pharmaceutical research and development.

Amesbury

Town in Wiltshire, England; population (1991) 6,400. It is situated 13 km/8 mi north of Salisbury, by the River Avon, on Salisbury Plain; Stonehenge, Woodhenge, and a Roman rampart are all nearby.

Amesbury Abbey, the former residence of the dukes of ◊Queensberry, was built by Inigo Jones; John Gay wrote *The Beggar's Opera* while staying as a guest here in 1727. The nunnery of Elfreda, wife of King Edgar, was erected in Amesbury in 980. St Mary's Church, an example of Early English architecture, was later built on this site.

Amies, (Edwin) Hardy (1909–)

English couturier. He is noted for his tailored clothes for women and menswear designs. He was formerly one of Queen Elizabeth II's dressmakers.

In 1950 he opened a ready-to-wear boutique and was awarded a royal warrant in 1955. In 1961 he became linked with Hepworths and known mainly as a designer of menswear. KCVO 1989.

Amis, Kingsley (William) (1922–1995)

English novelist and poet. He was associated early on with the ◊Angry Young Men group of writers. His sharply ironic works include the bestselling *Lucky Jim* (1954; his first novel), a comic portrayal of life at a provincial university. His later novels include the satiric comedy *The Old Devils* (1986), for which he won the Booker Prize.

His other novels, written in a variety of genres, include the spy story *The Anti-Death League* (1966), the ghost story *The Green Man* (1969), *The Riverside Villas Murder* (1973), which imitates a classic detective story, and *The Alteration* (1976), which imagines a 20th-century society dominated by the Catholic Church. His last novel *The Biographer's Moustache* was published in 1995. He was the father of writer Martin Amis. Knighted 1990.

Amis, Martin Louis (1949–)

English novelist and journalist, the son of novelist and poet Kingsley Amis. His works are characterized by their acerbic black humour and include *The Rachel Papers* (1973), a memoir of adolescence told through flashbacks, *Dead Babies* (1975), which addresses decadence and sadism, *Money* (1984), *London Fields* (1989), and *Time's Arrow* (1991). Later works include *Night Train* (1997), a novella-length thriller, and *Heavy Water and Other Stories* (1998).

Ammanford, Welsh Rhydaman

Town in Carmarthenshire, southwest Wales, 20 km/12 mi from Swansea; population (1991) 12,100. It has one of very few coal mines still operating in Wales, and also has some light industry.

Amnesty International

Human-rights organization established in the UK in 1961 to campaign for the release of prisoners of conscience worldwide; fair trials for all political prisoners; an end to the death penalty, torture, and other inhuman treatment of all prisoners; and the cessation of extrajudicial executions and 'disappearances'. It is politically and economically unaligned. Amnesty International has over a million members in more than 100 countries, and section offices in 54 countries. The organization was awarded the Nobel Prize for Peace in 1978. It is based in London.

Amstrad

Electronics company founded in 1968 by Alan ◊Sugar. In 1985 Amstrad introduced a complete word-processing system at the low price of £399. Subsequent models consolidated the company's success internationally. The business expanded rapidly during the 1980s, but encountered problems at the end of the decade, and Sugar took the company back into private ownership. Amstrad is a contraction of Alan M Sugar Trading.

> *Bad behaviour, sleaze, decadence certainly go on appearing. They must be my subject. But I didn't choose them.*
>
> Martin Amis English writer.
> On recurring themes in his novels; interviewed in *New Writing* (1992)

Ancient Britain

Period in Britain extending through prehistory to the Roman occupation (1st century AD).

Settled agricultural life evolved in Britain during the 3rd millennium BC. A peak was reached in Neolithic society in southern England early in the 2nd millennium BC, with the construction of the great stone circles of Avebury and ◊Stonehenge. It was succeeded in central southern Britain by the Early Bronze Age Wessex culture, an aristocratic society which had strong trade links across Europe. The Iron Age culture of the Celts, a warrior aristocracy that introduced horse-drawn chariots and their own distinctive art forms (see ◊Celtic art), was predominant in the last few centuries BC.

The Belgae (of mixed Germanic and Celtic stock) were responsible for the earliest British sites large and complex enough to be called towns. They settled in southern Britain, and resisted the Romans from centres such as Maiden Castle, Dorset. However, they were partially Romanized in the century between the first Roman expedition to Britain under Julius Caesar (54 BC) and the Roman conquest (AD 43). For later history, see ◊Roman Britain; ◊United Kingdom.

'Ancient Mariner, The Rime of the'

Poem by Samuel Taylor ◊Coleridge, published in 1798, describing the curse that falls upon a mariner and his ship when he shoots an albatross.

Anderson, Elizabeth Garrett (1836–1917)

English physician, the first English woman to qualify in medicine. Unable to attend medical school, Anderson studied privately and was licensed by the Society of Apothecaries in

London in 1865. She was physician to the Marylebone Dispensary for Women and Children (later renamed the Elizabeth Garrett Anderson Hospital). She became the first woman member of the British Medical Association in 1873 and in 1908 was elected mayor of Aldeburgh, becoming the first woman mayor in Britain.

Anderson, Lindsay (1932–1994)

British film director. As critic and then filmmaker, he championed the cause of commitment to moral and social beliefs; his best-known film *If...* (1968) enunciated a message of social protest using surrealist humour and distancing effects.

His first feature film was *This Sporting Life* (1963); his later work includes *O Lucky Man* (1973). Anderson also pursued a parallel career in the theatre, directing a variety of productions, which ranged from work by ambitious modern writers, such as David ◊Storey, to popular plays and occasional classic revivals.

In 1988 he directed his only American film, *The Whales of August*, a portrait of two elderly sisters, played by Bette Davis and Lillian Gish.

Anderson shelter

A simple air raid shelter used during World War II which could be erected in a garden to provide protection for a family. Tens of thousands were produced and they undoubtedly saved thousands of lives during the air raids on the UK. It was named after Sir John Anderson, Home Secretary 1939–40.

Andover

Market town in Hampshire, England, 22 km/14 mi northwest of Winchester; population (1981) 30,900. It is situated on the River Anton, a tributary of the River Test, and is the trading and commercial centre of an extensive agricultural district, with paper milling, printing, and iron industries.

There are a number of prehistoric earthworks and tumuli in the area. Bury Hill, an early Iron Age camp lies 1.5 km/1 mi southwest of the town. The Anglo-Saxon national council, the Witan, met in Andover.

Andrew (Andrew Albert Christian Edward) (1960–)

Prince of the UK, Duke of York, second son of Queen Elizabeth II. He married Sarah Ferguson in 1986; see Duchess of York. Their first daughter, Princess Beatrice, was born in 1988, and their second daughter, Princess Eugenie, was born in 1990. The couple separated in 1992 and were officially divorced in May 1996. Prince Andrew was a naval helicopter pilot, and in 1998 accepted a naval post in international relations.

Andrew, Rob (Christopher Robert) (1963–)

English rugby union player. He is England's record points scorer with 396 points in 71 internationals between 1985 and 1997. He also played five times for the British Lions, and is the most capped fly-half in international rugby. Renowned for his all-round kicking skills, his 23 drop goals are an international record.

Andrew, St (lived 1st century AD)

New Testament apostle and patron saint of Scotland and Greece. According to tradition, he went with John to Ephesus, preached in Scythia, and was martyred at Patrai in Greece on an X-shaped cross (**St Andrew's cross**).

Some time before the 8th century bones claimed to be his were brought to St Andrews in Scotland. The X-shaped cross represents Scotland in the Union Jack. Feast day 30 November.

Andrews, Julie stage name of Julia Elizabeth Wells (1935–)

English-born US actress and singer. She was the original Eliza Doolittle in the Broadway production of Lerner and Loewe's musical *My Fair Lady* (1956), and also appeared in their *Camelot* (1960). She is particularly associated with the hit film *The Sound of Music* (1965).

A child performer with her mother and stepfather in British music halls, she first appeared in the USA in the Broadway production of the musical *The Boy Friend* (1954). Her other films include *Mary Poppins* (1964), *Torn Curtain* (1966), *'10'* (1979), *Victor/Victoria* (1982), and *A Fine Romance* (1992).

She is married to the film director Blake Edwards, who directed *Victor/Victoria*.

ANDREWS, JULIE *The singer and actress Julie Andrews in the film* Victor/Victoria *(1982). She first came to prominence in the 1960s, starring in a number of hit musicals, notably* The Sound of Music. *In 1998 a throat operation placed Andrews' future singing career in some doubt. The Ronald Grant Archive*

Aneirin
Welsh poet. He wrote the core of the epic poem *Y Gododdin* (*c.* 600), one of the earliest known poems in Welsh. It describes a battle at Catraeth (Catterick) where the tribe from Dun Edin (Edinburgh) were heavily defeated by the Northumbrians.

Angevin
Term used to describe the English kings Henry II and Richard I (also known, with the later English kings up to Richard III, as the **Plantagenets**). Angevin derives from Anjou, a region in northwestern France. The **Angevin Empire** comprised the territories (including England) that belonged to the Anjou dynasty.

King John is sometimes known as the last of the Angevin dynasty because he was the last English king to reign over Anjou, which he lost in 1204.

Angle
Member of the Germanic tribe that occupied the Schleswig-Holstein district of North Germany known as Angeln. The Angles, or Angli, invaded Britain after the Roman withdrawal in the 5th century and settled in East Anglia, Mercia, and Northumbria. The name 'England' (Angleland) is derived from this tribe. See ◊Anglo-Saxon.

Anglesey, Welsh Ynys Môn (island), Sir Ynys Môn (authority)
Island and unitary authority off the northwest coast of Wales
Area 720 sq km/278 sq mi (34 km/21 mi long and 31 km/19 mi broad)
Towns ◊Llangefni (administrative headquarters), Holyhead, ◊Beaumaris, Amlwch
Features separated from the mainland by the Menai Strait, which is crossed by the Britannia tubular railway bridge and Telford's suspension bridge, originally built between 1819 and 1826 but rebuilt since; rich fauna, notably bird life, and flora; many buildings and relics of historic interest
Industries manufacture of toys and electrical goods; bromine extraction from the sea
Agriculture sheep farming, varied agriculture
Population (1996) 71,100.

The port of Holyhead, on the adjoining ◊Holy Island, has an aluminium smelting plant and a ferry service to Ireland. The Wylfa nuclear power station is located 10 km/6 mi west of Amlwch. Lead, copper, and zinc were once mined here. Anglesey was the ancient granary of Wales.

Anglesey Abbey
House in Cambridgeshire, England, 10 km/6 mi northeast of Cambridge, dating from 1600 and built on the site of an Augustinian abbey.

The landscaped garden and arboretum here were created by Lord Fairhaven who left the house and 202 ha/499 acre estate to the National Trust in 1966, along with his vast collection of furnishings and European works of art. The house has a 13th-century crypt.

Anglo-Irish agreement
See ◊Northern Ireland.

Anglo-Saxon
One of several groups of Germanic invaders (including Angles, Saxons, and Jutes) that conquered much of Britain between the 5th and 7th centuries. Initially they established conquest kingdoms, commonly referred to as the **Heptarchy**; these were united in the early 9th century under the overlordship of Wessex. The Norman invasion in 1066 brought Anglo-Saxon rule to an end. See next page for a map of Kingdoms in Britain and Ireland in c. AD 600.

The Jutes probably came from the Rhineland and not, as was formerly believed, from Jutland. The Angles and Saxons came from Schleswig-Holstein, and may have united before invading. The Angles settled largely in East Anglia, Mercia, and Northumbria; the Saxons in Essex, Sussex, and Wessex; and the Jutes in Kent and southern Hampshire.

There was probably considerable intermarriage with the Romanized Celts of Ancient Britain, although the latter's language and civilization almost disappeared. The English-speaking peoples of Britain, the Commonwealth, and the USA are often referred to today as Anglo-Saxons, but the term is inaccurate, as the Welsh, Scots, and Irish are mainly of Celtic or Norse descent, and by the 1980s fewer than 15% of US citizens were of British descent.

Anglo-Saxon architecture
The architecture of the Anglo-Saxon period of English history, from the 5th century to the early 11th century. For architecture in Britain after the Anglo-Saxon period, see ◊Norman architecture and ◊architecture.

Little evidence remains of the timber buildings which the first Anglo-Saxon settlers must have erected during the period 410–597. However, St Augustine's landing in Kent in 597, and his speedy conversion of the Kentish king Ethelbert resulted in the erection of Christian churches in Canterbury (St Peter and St Paul, 597); St Pancras (about 600); St Mary (around 620); and in Kent (St Andrew, Rochester, 604; St Mary, Lyminge, about 633; and St Mary, Reculver, 669). St Peter, Bradwell (Essex), was built about 660; and at Brixworth (Northamptonshire) a large church was erected around 670, which still survives. It has a long aisled nave with semicircular brick arches, a small apsidal chancel and a timber roof.

Only a few years later, a second group of Christian churches was erected in the former 'Kingdom of Northumbria', as a result of missionary activity by Benedict Biscop, who had studied in Rome. His three churches, all very small and roughly built, are at Monkwearmouth (674), Jarrow (chancel only, 682), and Escomb (about the same date). In Hexham Abbey and Ripon Cathedral are crypts of this period, built about 675 by St Wilfrid, who was the Archbishop of York.

Danish invasions from the 8th century resulted in a lull in church-building, but it recommenced early in the 10th century and a number of Pre-Conquest Romanesque churches were erected before 1066. Examples include the 10th-century St Benet's, Cambridge, and churches at Bradford-on-Avon, Wiltshire; Wing, Buckinghamshire; and Barton-on-Humber, Leicestershire. The foundations of Elmham

Cathedral, Norfolk, and St Augustine's Abbey, Canterbury, are 11th century. The first abbey church at Westminster, London, was begun around 1050 and dedicated in 1065

Anglo-Saxon art

The art of the Anglo-Saxon period of English history, from the 5th to the 11th century. Sculpted crosses and ivories, manuscript painting, and gold and enamel jewellery demonstrate a love of intricate, interwoven designs in the Anglo-Saxon period. Influences include the late Celtic arts of the native Britons, Roman styles deriving from the introduction of Christianity, and Norse art following the Viking invasions of the 8th century.

Much metalwork has survived, including simple bronze brooches, remarkable circular silver brooches with tracery and niello decoration, and gold and silver jewels with cloisonné inlays of garnet and lapis lazuli, and decoration of interlaced gold filigree. The relics of the ◊Sutton Hoo ship burial (7th century; British Museum, London) have typical Celtic ornamental patterns and include the finest examples of the Saxon goldsmiths' art yet known.

Church books of a high standard were produced by the early illuminators. In Northumbria the ◊*Lindisfarne Gospels* were embellished in the early 8th century with illuminated capital letters and elaborate paintings of the evangelists deriving unmistakably from the Celtic applied arts. In the manuscripts of southern England, in particular those produced at Winchester and Canterbury, a different style emerged in the 9th century, with delicate, lively pen-and-ink figures and heavily decorative foliage borders.

Saxon sculpture incorporated Roman, Norse, Scottish, and Irish elements, as seen in the inscriptions carved on standing stones and crosses. Great development occurred in Northumbria in the 7th century, marked in particular by Acca's cross, Hexham; and standing crosses at Ruthwell, Dumfriesshire and Bewcastle, Cumbria. In 9th-century Mercia sculpture was used to decorate churches, notably at Breedon-on-the-Hill, Derbyshire.

Anglo-Saxon Chronicle

A history of England from the Roman invasion to the 11th century, consisting of a series of chronicles written in Old English by monks, begun in the 9th century (during the reign of King Alfred), and continuing until 1154.

The Chronicle, comprising seven different manuscripts, forms a unique record of early English history and also of the development of Old English prose up to its final stages. By 1154 Old English had been superseded by Middle English.

Anglo-Saxon language

Group of dialects, also known as Old English, spoken between the 5th and 12th centuries by peoples of Saxon origin who invaded and settled in central and southern England in the 5th–7th centuries; thus the term properly does not include the language of the Angles who settled in the areas to the north. See ◊Old English; ◊Old English literature.

Anglo-Saxon literature

Another name for ◊Old English literature.

Angry Young Men

Journalistic term applied to a loose group of British writers who emerged in the 1950s after the creative hiatus that followed World War II. They revolted against the prevailing social mores, class distinction, and 'good taste'. Their dissatisfaction was expressed in works such as Kingsley Amis's *Lucky Jim* (1954), John ◊Osborne's *Look Back in Anger* (1956), Colin Wilson's *The Outsider* (1956), John Braine's *Room at the Top* (1957), and John Wain's *Hurry on Down* (1953).

Anguilla

Island in the eastern Caribbean; a British dependency
Area 160 sq km/62 sq mi
Population (1992) 8,960.

A British colony from 1650, Anguilla was long associated with St Christopher–Nevis but revolted against alleged domination by the larger island and seceded in 1967. A small British force restored order in 1969, and Anguilla retained a special position at its own request; since 1980 it has been a separate dependency of the UK.

Angus

Unitary authority on the east coast of Scotland. A former county, it was part of Tayside region 1975–96

Area 2,187 sq km/844 sq mi

Towns Arbroath, Brechin, Carnoustie, ◊Forfar (administrative headquarters), Kirriemuir, and Montrose

Physical the ◊Grampian Mountains in the north are dissected by the fertile valleys of the rivers Isla, Clova, Prosen, Water of Saughs, and North Esk; the wide Vale of Strathmore separates the Grampian Mountains from the low-lying Sidlaw Hills in the south

Features Pictish and Iron Age remains

Industries textiles, light engineering (declining), fish processing

Agriculture some fishing (mainly in Arbroath), cereal production

Population (1995) 111,800.

Economy

It is essentially a rich and important agricultural area, although the towns have a manufacturing tradition and, increasingly, a service sector base.

Environment

There are 34 Sites of Special Scientific Interest, two National Nature Reserves, three Ramsars (wetland sites), three Special Protection Areas, one National Scenic Area, and three country parks.

Archaeology

There are several large Iron Age hill forts in the area, such as the two Caterthuns, and impressive souterrains (earth houses) at Ardestie and Carlungie. Other remains include brochs, sculptured stones, and hut circles. Many of these remains are situated on the fringes of the Vale of Strathmore.

Angus

Breed of black polled beef cattle, formerly known as **Aberdeen Angus**. They originated in northeast Scotland and are a beef breed of the highest rank, winning regular places of honour at leading fatstock shows in Britain and the USA. Within the breed, the strain of **Red Angus** was gaining in popularity in the late 20th century.

Animal Farm

Novel by George ◊Orwell published in 1945. In this political fable based on the Russian revolution, farm animals, led by the pigs Snowball and Napoleon, eject their human exploiters and try to turn their farm into a Utopia. The enterprise fails because of corruption and weakness from within, the leaders end up masquerading as humans, and their society becomes a totalitarian police state. Written in stark, simple prose, it is perhaps the most read of Orwell's novels.

Animals, The

English rock and rhythm-and-blues group 1960–1966, reformed in 1976 and 1983. In 1964 their 'House of the Rising Sun' reached number one in the UK and USA. Other hits include 'I'm Crying' (1964) and 'Don't Let Me Be Misunderstood' (1965).

The group's members were Eric Burdon (1941–) (vocals and harmonica), Alan Price (1942–) (vocals and keyboards), Bryan Chandler (1938–1996), Hilton Valentine (1943–) (guitar), and John Steel (1941–) (drums).

Annan

Town and former royal burgh in Dumfries and Galloway unitary authority, Scotland, on the mouth of the River Annan as it enters the Solway Firth, 26 km/16 mi southeast of Dumfries; population (1991) 8,900. Salmon fishing forms an important part of the local economy, and the town is a market centre for cattle and sheep trading. Engineering and clothing industries have also been developed.

> *As I know my heart to be entirely English, I can very sincerely assure you that there is not one thing you can expect or desire of me which I shall not be ready to do for the happiness or prosperity of England.*
>
> ANNE Queen of Great Britain and Ireland. First speech to Parliament, March 1702

Anne (1665–1714)

Queen of Great Britain and Ireland 1702–14. She was the second daughter of James, Duke of York, who became James II, and his first wife, Anne Hyde, daughter of Edward Hyde, Earl of Clarendon. She succeeded William III in 1702. Events of her reign include the War of the Spanish Succession, Marlborough's victories at Blenheim, Ramillies, Oudenarde, and Malplaquet, and the union of the English and Scottish parliaments in 1707.

Anne received a Protestant upbringing, and in 1683 married Prince George of Denmark (1653–1708). Of their many children only one survived infancy: William, Duke of Gloucester (1689–1700). For the greater part of her life Anne was a close friend of Sarah Churchill (1650–1744), the wife of John Churchill (1650–1722), afterwards created 1st Duke of ◊Marlborough in 1702. The Churchills' influence was partly responsible for her desertion of her father for William of Orange, her brother-in-law, later William III, during the ◊Glorious Revolution of 1688. The Churchills' influence later also led her to engage in Jacobite intrigues. Although her sympathies were Tory, she accepted a predominantly Whig government 1704–10. The influence of the Churchills began to decline from 1707. After a violent quarrel in 1710, Sarah Churchill was dismissed from court, and Abigail Masham succeeded the duchess as Anne's favourite, using her influence to further the Tories.

Anne (Anne Elizabeth Alice Louise) (1950–)

Princess of the UK, second child of Queen Elizabeth II, declared Princess Royal in 1987. She is actively involved in global charity work, especially for children. An excellent horsewoman, she won silver medals in both individual and team events in the 1975 European Championships, and competed in the 1976 Olympics.

In 1973 she married Capt Mark Phillips (1949–); they separated in 1989 and were divorced in 1992. In December 1992 she married Commander Timothy Laurence. Her son Peter (1977–) was the first direct descendant of the Queen not to bear a title. She also has a daughter, Zara (1981–).

Anne of Cleves (1515–1557)

Fourth wife of ◊Henry VIII of England, whom she married in 1540. She was the daughter of the Duke of Cleves, and was recommended to Henry as a wife by Thomas Cromwell, who wanted an alliance with German Protestantism against the Holy Roman Empire. Henry did not like her looks, had the marriage declared void after six months, pensioned her, and had Cromwell beheaded.

Anne of Denmark (1574–1619)

Queen consort of James VI of Scotland (from 1603 ◊James I of Great Britain). She was the daughter of Frederick II of Denmark and Norway, and married James in 1589. She bore him five children, two of whom survived: Charles I and Elizabeth of Bohemia. Anne was suspected of Catholic leanings and was notably extravagant but seems to have had little influence on state affairs.

Antarctic Territory, British

British dependent territory created in 1961 and comprising all British territories south of latitude 60° south and between 20° and 80° west longitude, including the South Orkney Islands, the South Shetland Islands, the Antarctic Peninsula and all adjacent lands, and Coats Land, extending to the South Pole; total land area 1,810,000 sq km/700,000 sq mi; population (exclusively scientific personnel) *c.* 300.

Anti-Corn Law League

An extra-parliamentary pressure group formed in September 1838 by Manchester industrialists, and led by Liberals Richard ◊Cobden and John ◊Bright. It argued for free trade and campaigned successfully against duties on the import of foreign corn to Britain imposed by the ◊Corn Laws.

Campaigning on a single issue, the league initiated strategies for popular mobilization and agitation including mass meetings, lecture tours, pamphleteering, opinion polls, and parliamentary lobbying. Reaction by the conservative landed interests was organized with the establishment of the Central Agricultural Protection Society, nicknamed the Anti-League. In June 1846 political pressure, the state of the economy, and the Irish situation prompted Prime Minister ◊Peel to repeal the Corn Laws.

Antonine Wall

Roman line of fortification built in AD 142 in the reign of Antoninus Pius. It was the Roman empire's furthest northwest frontier, between the Clyde and Forth rivers in Scotland. It was defended until about 200, after which the frontier returned to ◊Hadrian's Wall.

Antony and Cleopatra

Tragedy by William Shakespeare, written and first performed in 1607–08. Mark Antony falls in love with the Egyptian queen Cleopatra in Alexandria, but returns to Rome when his wife, Fulvia, dies. He then marries Octavia to heal the rift between her brother Augustus Caesar and himself. Antony returns to Egypt and Cleopatra, but is finally defeated by Augustus. Believing Cleopatra dead, Antony kills himself, and Cleopatra takes her own life rather than surrender to Augustus.

Antrim

Town in County Antrim, Northern Ireland; population (1991) 23,500. It is situated on the Six Mile Water where it enters the northeast corner of Lough Neagh, 28 km/17 mi northwest of Belfast. Antrim is a manufacturing and market town with engineering, electronics, and construction industries as well as computer-software development. The Round Tower (28 m/92 ft high) is all that remains of the 10th-century Aentrebh monastery after which the town is named.

Antrim was burnt by Scottish Covenanters in 1643; in 1798 it was the site of the **Battle of Antrim**, at which the ◊United Irishmen were defeated by English troops.

On the outskirts of the town, in Antrim Castle Demesne, are the remains of formal gardens laid out by André Le Nôtre (also responsible for the gardens at Versailles, France). Clotworthy House, an arts centre and theatre, is located here, as is a golf course.

Castle Upton, designed in the late 18th century by Robert ◊Adam, is 9 km/5.5 mi east of Antrim at Templepatrick. Shane's Castle Park and deer park are 8 km/5 mi west of Antrim, and Randalstown Forest wildlife reserve is nearby.

A number of archaeological sites are located near Antrim: 3 km/2 mi east are the ring forts of Rathmore and Rathbeg (the possible seat of the kings of Dál nAraide during the 6th and 7th centuries); 5 km/3 mi east on Donegore Hill is a Neolithic enclosed settlement; and at nearby Ballywee ring fort excavations show evidence of house foundations and souterrains (underground dwellings).

Antrim

County of Northern Ireland

Area 2,830 sq km/1,092 sq mi

Towns and cities ◊Belfast (county town), Larne (port), Antrim, Ballymena, Lisburn, Carrickfergus

Physical peat bogs; Antrim borders Lough Neagh, and is separated from Scotland by the North Channel, which is only 21 km/13 mi wide at Torr Head, the narrowest point; the main rivers are the Bann and the Lagan

Features ◊Giant's Causeway, a World Heritage Site, consisting of natural hexagonal and pentagonal basalt columns on

the coast; Antrim Mountains (highest point Trostan 554 m/1,817 ft) and the Glen of Antrim; Kebble National Nature Reserve, on Rathlin Island, off the coast near Ballycastle; Bushmills Distillery, in the village of Bushmills, has the oldest known licence for distilling whiskey; there are a number of early fortifications, castles, and medieval ecclesiastical remains in the county; the village of Cushendun was built by Clough Williams-Ellis; Gobbins Cliff Path (19th century), to be restored as a millennium project
Industries shipbuilding; traditional linen production largely replaced by the manufacture of man-made fibres, whiskey, agriculture (the Bann Valley is particularly fertile)
Agriculture potatoes, oats, flax
Population (1981) 642,000.

The most dangerous thing in the world is to make a friend of an Englishman, because he'll come sleep in your closet rather than spend ten shillings on a hotel.

Truman Capote US writer.
Sayings of the Week, the *Observer*, March 1968

Apostles

Discussion group founded 1820 at Cambridge University, England; members have included the poet Tennyson, the philosophers G E Moore and Bertrand Russell, the writers Lytton Strachey and Leonard Woolf, the economist J M Keynes, and the spies Guy Burgess and Anthony Blunt.

Appleby, or Appleby-in-Westmorland

Market town in Cumbria, England, formerly the county town of Westmorland; population (1991) 1,300. It is situated on the River Eden, 21 km/13 mi southeast of Penrith. The castle, built on the site of a Norman keep, was restored by Lady Anne Clifford in the 17th century.

The church of St Lawrence has a monument to Lady Anne, and a church organ – one of the oldest in England – which was brought here from Carlisle Cathedral in 1684. Appleby holds an annual horse fair in June.

Appleton, Edward Victor (1892–1965)

English physicist. He worked at Cambridge under Ernest ◊Rutherford from 1920. He proved the existence of the Kennelly–Heaviside layer (now called the E layer) in the atmosphere, and the Appleton layer beyond it, and was involved in the initial work on the atom bomb.

Appleton became interested in radio as signals officer during World War I, and his research into the atmosphere was of fundamental importance to the development of radio communications.

By periodically varying the frequency of the BBC transmitter at Bournemouth and measuring the intensity of the received transmission 100 km/62 mi away, Appleton found that there was a regular fading in and fading out of the signals at night but that this effect diminished considerably at dawn as the Kennelly–Heaviside layer broke up. Radio waves continued to be reflected by the atmosphere during the day but by a higher-level ionized layer. By 1926 this layer, which Appleton measured at about 230 km/145 mi above the Earth's surface (the first distance measurement made by means of radio), became generally known as the Appleton layer (it is now also known as the F layer). Nobel prize 1947. KCB 1941, GBE 1946.

April Fools' Day

The first day of April, when it is customary in western Europe and the USA to expose people to ridicule by a practical joke, causing them to believe some falsehood or to go on a fruitless errand.

The victim is known in England as an April Fool and in Scotland as a gowk (cuckoo or fool).

Apsley House

Mansion at the southeast corner of ◊Hyde Park, London. Home of the dukes of Wellington from 1820; now the Wellington Museum. It was originally built in 1771–8 for Baron Apsley, 2nd Earl Bathurst (1774–94), from designs by Robert ◊Adam.

The house was bought in 1820 by the Duke of ◊Wellington from his brother the Marquess Wellesley. The house was enlarged in 1828 by Benjamin Dean Wyatt (1775–1850), and has a palatial interior. The house and its contents were presented to the nation by the 7th Duke of Wellington in 1947. Now the Wellington Museum, it contains many Wellington relics and a famous collection of pictures captured during the Peninsular War, including Velázquez's *Water Carrier*.

It used to be known as 'No. 1, London' (being the first house that travellers reached on entering London). The Duke of Wellington held the commemorative Waterloo dinner there annually until his death.

Arbroath

Fishing town in Angus, on the east coast of Scotland, 26 km/16 mi northeast of Dundee, at the mouth of Brothock Water; population (1991) 23,500. In 1320 the **Declaration of Arbroath** was signed by the Scottish Parliament in **Arbroath Abbey**, proclaiming Scotland's independence to the pope. The town has a number of oil-related firms, a fishing industry and produces smoked haddock (Arbroath smokies).

There are the remains of a Benedictine abbey, built in 1178 by ◊William the Lion. The town was celebrated by Walter Scott as 'Fairport' in *The Antiquary* (1816).

Arbroath, Declaration of

Declaration made on 26 April 1320 by Scottish nobles of their loyalty to King Robert I ('The Bruce') and of Scotland's identity as a kingdom independent of England. A response to papal demands that the Scots should yield to English claims, the document was probably composed by Robert the Bruce's chancellor, Bernard de Linton. In the 20th century, it has become a manifesto for Scottish nationalism.

Arbuthnot, John (1667–1735)

Scottish writer and physician. He attended Prince George and then Queen Anne from 1705 to 1714. He was a friend of Alexander Pope, Thomas Gray, and Jonathan Swift and was the chief author of the satiric *Memoirs of Martinus Scriblerus* (1741). He created the English national character of ◊John Bull, a prosperous farmer, in his 'History of John Bull' (1712) pamphlets advocating peace with France.

Born at Arbuthnott, Kincardineshire, he studied at Aberdeen, Oxford, and St Andrews universities, where he obtained the first recorded MD degree in 1696.

Archer, Frederick (1857–1886)

English jockey. He rode 2,748 winners in 8,084 races between 1870 and 1886, including 21 classic winners. He won the Derby five times, the Oaks four times, the St Leger six times, the Two Thousand Guineas four times, and the One Thousand Guineas twice. He rode 246 winners in the 1885 season, a record that stood until 1933 (see Gordon ◊Richards).

Archer, Jeffrey Howard, Baron Archer of Weston-super-Mare (1940–)

English writer and politician. He was a Conservative member of Parliament 1969–1974, and lost a fortune in a disastrous investment, but recouped it as a bestselling novelist and dramatist. His books, which often concern the rise of insignificant characters to high political office or great business success, include *Not a Penny More, Not a Penny Less* (1975), *Kane and Abel* (1979) (which was dramatized for television), *First Among Equals* (1984) (also televised), and *The Fourth Estate* (1997). Collected short stories are in *To Cut a Long Story Short* (1997).

In 1985 he became deputy chair of the Conservative Party, but resigned in November 1986 after a scandal; he subsequently cleared his name in a successful libel action against the *Daily Star*. Baron 1992.

Archer, William (1856–1924)

Scottish drama critic. He did much to popularize the work of Ibsen in England and advocated a more serious and realistic drama. His works include *English Dramatists of To-day* (1882), *Masks or Faces* (1888), and *The Old Drama and the New* (1923). His plays include *War is War* (1919) and *The Green Goddess* (1923).

He translated (either alone or in collaboration with his brother, Charles Archer) a number of Ibsen's plays, as well as editing Ibsen's prose dramas in five volumes (1890–91).

Archers, the

Longest-running drama serial in the world. It began on BBC radio in 1951 and continues to be broadcast in six episodes per week, with an omnibus edition on Sundays. Originally designed as a means of disseminating farming news and information, it still retains a farming advisor and refers to contemporary farming issues. The serial is set in the fictional village of Ambridge.

The programme prompted acute controversy when, in 1955, on the opening night of commercial television, it killed off a leading character in a fire. Programme-makers later admitted that this was deliberate sabotage. At its peak, also in 1955, the serial attracted 20 million listeners.

In my own case I 'find' G major by singing the signature tune of 'The Archers'.

ANTONY HOPKINS English educator, conductor, writer on music, and composer.
On pitch, in *Downbeat Music Guide* (1977)

Archigram

London-based group of English architects (1960–75) whose designs were experimental and polemical. Central to their philosophy was the belief that architecture should be technological, flexible, and disposable.

The group included Peter Cook (1936–), Dennis Crompton (1935–), David Greene (1937–), Ron ◊Herron, and Mike Webb (1937–). Cook's concept of 'plug-in, clip-on' architecture was exemplified in Instant City, an idea for an airship that descended from the sky and rejuvenated a sleeping town. Herron designed a mobile 'walking city', 3 km/2 mi long.

architecture

For architecture before the 11th century, see ◊Anglo-Saxon architecture.

Norman

(11th–12th century) William the Conqueror inaugurated an enormous building programme. He introduced the **Romanesque style** of round arches, massive cylindrical columns, and thick walls. At Durham Cathedral (1093–*c.* 1130), the rib vaults were an invention of European importance in the development of the Gothic style.

Gothic

The three main styles, Early English, Decorated, and Perpendicular, are distinguishable by the design of their windows, and in particular by the development of vaulting and buttressing, whereby the thick walls and heavy barrel-vaults, the flat buttresses and the narrow windows of the 12th century came to be replaced by bolder buttresses with thinner walls between them, thinner vaults supported on stone ribs, and much larger windows filled with tracery.

Ghastly Good Taste, or a depressing story of the rise and fall of English architecture.

JOHN BETJEMAN English poet and essayist.
Book title

◊Early English (late 12th–late 13th century), a simple elegant style of lancet windows, deeply carved mouldings, and slender, contrasting shafts of Purbeck marble, began with the east end of Canterbury Cathedral in 1175, and reached its peak in the cathedrals of Wells, Lincoln, and Salisbury. ◊Decorated (late 13th–14th century), as found at Exeter Cathedral, introduced features such as the ogee arch, elaborate window tracery, and vault ribs woven into star patterns. Dramatic gridded and panelled cages of light characterize the ◊Perpendicular (late 14th–mid-16th century) period; the chancel of Gloucester Cathedral is early Perpendicular; Kings College Chapel, Cambridge, is late Perpendicular.

Tudor and Elizabethan

(1485–1603) This period saw the Perpendicular style interwoven with growing Renaissance influence. Buildings developed a conscious symmetry elaborated with continental Patternbrook details. Hybrid and exotic works result such as Burghley House, Cambridgeshire (1552–87), and Hardwick Hall, Derbyshire (1590–97).

Jacobean

(1603–25) A transition period, with the Renaissance influence becoming more pronounced, as in Hatfield House, Hertfordshire (1607–12), and Blicking Hall, Norfolk (completed 1628).

English Renaissance

(17th–early 18th century) The Jacobean scene of half-timbered and turreted buildings was revolutionized by Inigo Jones, who introduced Palladianism with his Queen's House, Greenwich (1616–35) and Banqueting House, Whitehall (1619–22). With Christopher Wren a restrained Baroque evolved showing French Renaissance influence, for example St Paul's Cathedral (1675–1710). Nicholas Hawksmoor and John Vanbrugh developed a theatrical Baroque style in their design for Blenheim Palace, Oxfordshire (1705–20).

Georgian

(18th–early 19th century) Richard Boyle Burlington, reacting against the Baroque, inspired a revival of the pure Palladian style of Inigo Jones, as in his Chiswick House, London (1725–29). William Kent, also a Palladian, invented the picturesque garden, as at Rousham, Oxfordshire. Alongside the great country houses, an urban architecture evolved of plain, well-proportioned houses, defining elegant streets and squares; John Wood the Younger's Royal Crescent, Bath, was built from 1767 to 1775. The second half of the century mingled Antiquarian and Neo-Classical influences, exquisitely balanced in the work of Robert Adam at Kedleston Hall (1759–70). John Nash carried Neo-Classicism into the new century, his designs including Regent Street, London (begun 1811), and the Royal Pavilion, Brighton (1815–21).

19th century

Throughout the Victorian period Classic and Gothic engaged in the 'Battle of the Styles': Gothic for the Houses of Parliament (1840–60) (designed by Barra and Pugin), Renaissance for the Foreign Office (1860–75). Meanwhile advances in engineering and the needs of new types of buildings, such as railway stations, transformed the debate. Joseph Paxton's prefabricated Crystal Palace (1850–51) was the most remarkable building of the era. The Arts and Crafts architects Philip Webb and Norman Shaw brought renewal and simplicity inspired by William Morris.

20th century

The early work of Edwin Landseer Lutyens and the white rendered houses of Charles Voysey maintained the Arts and Crafts spirit of natural materials and simplicity. Norman Shaw, however, developed an Imperial Baroque style. After World War I Classicism again dominated, grandly in Lutyens' New Delhi government buildings (1912–31). There was often a clean Scandinavian influence, as in the RIBA building, London (1932–34), which shows growing Modernist tendencies. The Modern Movement arrived fully with continental refugees such as Bertholdt Lubetkin, the founder of the Tecton architectural team that designed London Zoo (1934–38).

The strong social dimension of British 20th-century architecture is best seen in the garden city and new town movement. Welwyn Garden City was begun in 1919 and

ARCHITECTURE *Uppark, an imposing country house high on the South Downs near Chichester in West Sussex, is a good example of English Renaissance architecture. This square, red-brick building of around 1690 shows a fine sense of proportion. It was severely damaged by fire in 1989, but was painstakingly restored by its owners, the National Trust. Matthew Antrobus/National Trust Photographic Library*

developed after World War II. The latest of the new towns, Milton Keynes, was designated in 1967. British architects have also achieved international recognition, for example, Norman Foster and Richard Rogers for their High-Tech innovative Lloyds Building, London (1979–84). Post-Modernist architecture includes the Sainsbury Wing of the National Gallery, London, designed by Robert Venturi in 1991.

archives

Collections of historically valuable records, ranging from papers and documents to photographs, films, videotapes, and sound recordings. The **National Register of Archives**, founded 1945, is in London; the **Public Record Office** (London and Kew) has documents of law and government departments from the Norman Conquest, including the ◊Domesday Book and ◊Magna Carta. Some government documents remain closed, normally for 30 years, but some for up to 100 years. The **National Portrait Gallery** has photographs, paintings, and sculptures; the **British Broadcasting Corporation Archives** have sound recordings, 500,000 cans of films, 1.5 million videotapes (1990), and a contemporary Archive Unit to make films about the background to current events. In 1989 the British Film Institute launched a campaign for a national television archive to be funded from ITV advertising revenues.

Private archives have been increasingly made available to users by their transfer to public custody in the manuscript departments of, for example, the British Library, university and larger public libraries, and to record offices of local authorities. The **Historical Manuscripts Commission**, through its National Register of Archives, acts as a central clearing house of information as to the whereabouts and accessibility of private (and other) archives. The National Register of Archives is the central collecting point for information about manuscripts relating to British history.

Arden, John (1930–)

English dramatist. His early plays *Serjeant Musgrave's Dance* (1959) and *The Workhouse Donkey* (1963) contain trenchant social criticism and show the influence of Brecht. Subsequent works, often written in collaboration with his wife, Margaretta D'Arcy, express increasing concern with the political situation in Northern Ireland and dissatisfaction with the professional and subsidized theatre world.

Arden first came to attention with a prize-winning radio play, *The Life of Man* (1956). This was followed by *The Waters of Babylon* (1957) and *Live Like Pigs* (1958). *Serjeant Musgrave's Dance* is generally regarded as his finest work; it deals with the realities of war and the tragically unsuccessful attempt by a group of deserters to act effectively against those guilty of encouraging war.

Later plays include *The Happy Haven* (1960) (written with Margaretta d'Arcy), *Armstrong's Last Goodnight* (1964), and *Left-handed Liberty* (1965). *The Island of the Mighty* provoked considerable controversy when performed by the Royal Shakespeare Company in 1973.

Arden, Forest of

Former woodland region of north Warwickshire, central England, the setting for William Shakespeare's play *As You Like It*.

The Forest of Arden lay north of Stratford-upon-Avon, and was originally part of an ancient forest which covered much of the Midlands. Most of the trees in the region were cut down during the Industrial Revolution for use as fuel for iron works in the area. Since 1993 a local government reafforestion project has been established, encouraging landowners and farmers to replace lost woodland and trees.

Ardglass

Village and port in County Down, Northern Ireland, 11 km/7 mi southeast of Downpatrick; population (1991) 1,300. Ardglass is built on a natural harbour, and was the most important fishing port in the north of Ireland during the 19th century; it still has a thriving herring and prawn industry. Jordan's Castle, a tower house in the centre of the town, dates from the early 15th century.

Ardress House

17th-century manor house in County Armagh, Northern Ireland, 14 km/9 mi north of Armagh. It has two 18th-century wings added by the Dublin architect George Ensor, who married the heiress to Ardress in 1760. The Ulster Land Fund gave Ardress to the National Trust in 1960.

The decorative plasterwork in the main rooms is by Michael Stapleton, a talented stuccoist.

Ardrossan

Seaport and industrial town in North Ayrshire unitary authority, Scotland, on the Firth of Clyde, 19 km/12 mi south of Largs; population (1991) 10,800. Its harbour, first constructed in 1806, plays a central role in the town's economy: there is a ferrypoint for the island of Arran, a shipbuilding industry, and an oil refinery. With two local sandy bays, the town is also a minor holiday resort.

Ardrossan's ruined castle contains a dungeon known as Wallace's Larder.

Argyll

Line of Scottish peers who trace their descent to the Campbells of Lochow. The earldom dates from 1457, and was created by James I, who conferred the title on Lord Campbell (died 1493). The 4th Earl was the first of the great Scottish nobility to become Protestant.

Argyll, Archibald Campbell, 5th Earl of Argyll (1530–1573)

Adherent of the Scottish presbyterian John ◊Knox. A supporter of Mary Queen of Scots from 1561, he commanded her forces after her escape from Lochleven Castle in 1568. Following her defeat at Langside, he revised his position, made peace with the regent, James Stuart, Earl of Murray, and became Lord High Chancellor of Scotland in 1572. Succeeded to earldom 1558.

Argyll and Bute

Unitary authority in western Scotland, created in 1996 from the district of the same name and part of Dumbarton district, which were both parts of Strathclyde region; it includes the

islands of Gigha, Bute, Mull, Islay, Jura, Tiree, Coll, Colonsay, Iona, and Staffa
Area 7,016 sq km/2,709 sq mi
Towns Campbeltown, Dunoon, Helensburgh, Inveraray, ◊Lochgilphead (administrative headquarters), Oban, Rothesay
Physical rural area consisting of mainland and islands; the coast is heavily indented. Inland the area is mountainous; highest peak, Ben Cruachan (1,126 m/3,693 ft). Lochs Fyne and Long are the largest sea lochs; freshwater lochs include Loch Awe and Loch Lomond; Fingal's Cave (Staffa); Corryvrekan Whirlpool (Jura-Scarba); Ben Arthur (The Cobbler), 884 m/2,900 ft
Features Bronze, Stone, and Iron Age remains
Industries limited manufacture, seaweed processing, fish, timber harvesting
Agriculture sheep, forestry
Population (1995) 91,300.

Economy
With land of marginal agricultural capability and located far from the urban core, the area has a typical rural economy. Tourism, fishing, forestry, and less intensive agriculture are each important components of the area's economy.

Archaeology
There are standing stones, stone circles, vitrified forts, inscribed stones, and Neolithic chambered cairns. The capital of Dalriada, the ancient Scottish kingdom founded in about 503, was at Dunadd, near Crinan until shortly after the union of the Picts and Scots, whereafter it moved to Forteviut in Strathearn.

Environment
There are 112 Sites of Special Scientific Interest, seven Special Protection Areas, eight Ramsars (wetland sites), nine Special Protection Areas, one Biosphere Reserve, eight National Scenic Areas, and one regional park.

Administrative history
Argyll and Bute was part of the two counties of Argyllshire and Bute prior to 1974.

Arkwright, Richard (1732–1792)

English inventor and manufacturing pioneer who in 1768 developed a machine for spinning cotton (he called it a 'water frame'). In 1771 he set up a water-powered spinning factory and in 1790 he installed steam power in a Nottingham factory.

Arkwright was born in Preston, Lancashire, and experimented in machine designing with a watchmaker, John ◊Kay, until, with Kay and John Smalley (died 1782), he set up the water frame, the first machine capable of producing sufficiently strong cotton thread to be used as warp. In 1771 he went into partnership with Jebediah Strutt (1726–1797), a Derby man who had improved the stocking frame, and Samuel Need (died 1781), and built a water-powered cotton mill at Cromford in Derbyshire, where he also built the first mill village for his workers.

In 1773 Arkwright produced the yarn ('water twist') for the first cloth made entirely from cotton; previously, the warp had been of linen and only the weft was cotton. A special act of Parliament was passed in 1774 to exempt Arkwright's fabric from the double duty imposed on cottons by an act of 1736. By 1782 Arkwright employed 5,000 workers, mainly women and children. Knighted 1786.

Arlington Court

19th-century neo-Grecian house in Devon, England, 11 km/7 mi northeast of Barnstaple. It was built for John Chichester, whose family owned the estate from the 14th century. The house was bequeathed to the National Trust in 1949 by Rosalie Chichester, together with over 1200 ha/2964 acres of land, including three hamlets, thirteen farms, an animal sanctuary and a nature reserve.

The bequest also included interesting collections of costumes, pewter, 19th-century furniture, horse-drawn carriages (now displayed in the stables), model ships, and shells.

Armada

Fleet sent by Philip II of Spain against England in 1588. See ◊Spanish Armada.

Armagh

City and county town of County ◊Armagh, Northern Ireland; population (1991)14,300. Industries include textiles (Armagh's chief product), engineering, the manufacture of linen, whisky, shoes, optical instruments, and chemicals, and food processing. The city became the religious centre of Ireland in the 5th century when St Patrick was made archbishop. Armagh was also a noted seat of learning; St Patrick founded a monastic school here, and in 1169 Ruari O'Connor, the last Irish king, founded a 'professorship'. The city was the seat of the kings of Ulster for 700 years, and is now the seat of both the Roman Catholic and Protestant archbishops of Ireland, each of whom bears the title 'Archbishop of Armagh and Primate of All Ireland'.

The Church of Ireland cathedral occupies the traditional site of the church built by St Patrick. The Protestant cathedral houses several fine monuments, including pre-Christian stone statues (one of which is reputed to be of Queen Mhacha), and a statue of Thomas Molyneaux by Roubiliac; in the library is an annotated handwritten copy of Jonathan Swift's *Gulliver's Travels*.

Eamhain Macha, 3 km/2 mi to the west of Armagh, is a large earthwork and tumulus reputed to be the burial site of Queen Mhacha; it was also the seat of the Ulster kings until AD 332. At Beal an Atha Buidhe, 3 km/2 mi to the north of Armagh, is the site of a battle where English troops under Henry Bagenal were defeated by Hugh O'Neill's army in 1598.

There are a number of fine Georgian houses lining The Mall, and the 18th-century Protestant Archbishop's Palace now contains the council offices. Ardress House, a 17th-century mansion, is 14 km/9 mi north of the city, and is now owned by the National Trust. The ruins of a 13th-century Franciscan friary have been restored to form an equestrian heritage centre. There is an observatory, founded in 1791, a planetarium, and a number of museums.

ARMAGH *The Argory, near Armagh, is a country house from the early 19th century in the Neo-Classical style of architecture. Along with other local buildings from the Georgian period, it points to the prosperity once enjoyed by the gentry of this important linen-manufacturing town. Matthew Antrobus/National Trust Photographic Library*

Armagh (Irish *Ard Mhacha* 'the height of Mhacha' (a legendary queen))

County of Northern Ireland
Area 1,250 sq km/483 sq mi
Towns and cities ◊Armagh (county town), Lurgan and Portadown (merged to form ◊Craigavon), Keady
Physical smallest county of Northern Ireland; flat in the north, with many bogs and mounds formed from glacial deposits; low hills in the south, the highest of which is Slieve Gullion (577 m/1,893 ft); principal rivers are the Bann, the Blackwater and its tributary, the Callan
Agriculture good farmland (apart from the marshy areas by Lough Neagh) with apple orchards; potatoes; flax; emphasis on livestock rearing in the south; fruit-growing and market gardening in the north
Industries linen manufacture (Portadown and Lurgan were the principal centres of the linen industry); milling; light engineering; concrete; potato crisps
Population (1981) 119,000.

Borders

The River Blackwater, which flows into Lough Neagh, forms the western boundary with County Tyrone; County Down lies to the east. The hills of igneous rock encircling Slieve Gullion form part of the border with County Louth in the Republic of Ireland.

History

The county of Armagh has been significant in many conflicts over territory, including battles over Ulster between the British and Irish during the 17th–19th centuries.

Armatrading, Joan (1950–)

West-Indies-born folk singer and songwriter. She grew up in England and following the album *Joan Armatrading* (1976) established a wide international following. She maintained her reputation with other albums including *Show Some Emotion* (1977), *The Key* (1983), and *What's Inside* (1995).

armed forces

The armed forces of the UK are made up of the Army, the Royal Navy, and the Royal Air Force. The Queen is the commander-in-chief for all branches of the armed forces. The Ministry of Defence (MoD) is concerned with the control, administration, equipment, and support of the armed forces of the Crown. The research, development, production, and purchase of weapons is the concern of the Procurement Executive of the MoD. All three armed services are professionals, with no conscript element.

The Chief of Staff of the Defence Staff is the professional head of the armed forces and under him each Service's Chief of Staff is responsible for the fighting effectiveness, efficiency, and morale of his Service. They and other senior officers and officials at the head of the department's main functions form the MoD's corporate board, chaired by the Permanent Under-Secretary. The Secretary of State chairs the Defence Council (established in 1964) and is responsible to Parliament for the formulation and conduct of defence policy, and the provision of the means to implement it.

Defence and security

The defence and security of the UK are pursued through membership of the European Union (EU), the Western European Union (WEU), the Organization for Security and Cooperation in Europe (OSCE), and the United Nations (UN). The majority of the armed forces are committed to NATO. The UK contributes significantly to the peacekeeping work of the UN both financially and in terms of the deployment of personnel.

Army

Control of the British Army is vested in the Defence Council and is exercised through the Army Board. The Secretary of State is Chairman of the Army Board. The military members of the Army Board are the Chief of the General Staff, the Adjutant General, the Quartermaster General, the Master General of the Ordnance, the Commander-in-Chief Land Command, and the Assistant Chief of the General Staff. Women serve throughout the Army in the same regiments and corps as men. There are only a few roles in which they are not employed, such as the Infantry and Royal Armoured Corps.

Royal Air Force

The Royal Air Force (RAF) was formed in 1918 by the merger of the Royal Naval Air Service and the Royal Flying Corps. The RAF is administered by the Air Force Board, which is chaired by the Secretary of State for Defence. Other members of the Board include the Chief of the Air Staff, Air Member for Personnel, Air Member for Logistics, and Air Officer Commander-in-Chief Strike Command. The RAF is organized into three commands: Strike Command, Personnel and Training Command, and Logistics Command.

Royal Navy

Control of the Royal Navy is vested in the Defence Council and is exercised through the Admiralty Board, chaired by the Secretary of State for Defence. Naval members of the Defence Council are the Chief of Naval Staff (First Sea Lord), responsible for management, planning, fighting efficiency, and operational advice; the combined Second Sea Lord and Commander-in-Chief Naval Home Command, responsible for procurement of ships, their weapons, and equipment; the Chief of Fleet Support, responsible for logistic support, fuels and transport, naval dockyards, and auxiliary services; the Commander-in-Chief Fleet and the Assistant Chief of Staff, responsible for coordinating advice on certain policy and operational matters.

The principal roles of the Royal Navy are to deploy the national strategic nuclear deterrent, to provide maritime defence of the UK and its dependent territories, to contribute to the maritime elements of NATO forces, and to meet national maritime objectives outside the NATO area. The Commander-in-Chief Fleet, with headquarters at Northwood, is responsible for the command of the fleet, while command of naval establishments in the UK is exercised by the Commander-in-Chief Home Command from Portsmouth.

Royal Marines

The British Corps of Royal Marines was founded in 1664. It is primarily a military force also trained for fighting at sea, and providing commando units, landing craft crews, and frogmen. The Royal Marines corps provides a commando brigade comprising three commando groups. Each commando group is approximately 1,000 strong, with artillery, engineering and logistic support, air defence, and three helicopter squadrons. The Royal Marine corps' strength is completed by the Special Boat Squadron and specialist defence units.

Royal Naval Reserve/Royal Marines Reserve

The Royal Naval Reserve (RNR) and the Royal Marines Reserve (RMR) are volunteer forces that provide trained personnel in war to supplement regular forces. The RMR principally provides reinforcement and other specialist tasks with the UK–Netherlands Amphibious Force. Personnel who have completed service in the Royal Navy and the Royal Marines have a commitment to serve in the Royal Fleet Reserve.

Territorial Army

The Territorial Army (TA) is a force of volunteer soldiers, created from volunteer regiments (incorporated in 1872) as the Territorial Force in 1908. It was raised and administered by county associations, and intended primarily for home defence. It was renamed Territorial Army in 1922. Merged with the Regular Army in World War II, it was revived in 1947, and replaced by a smaller, more highly trained Territorial and Army Volunteer Reserve, again renamed Territorial Army in 1979. The Army Chief of the General Staff is responsible for the TA.

The role of the TA is to act as a general reserve for the Army, reinforcing it, as required, with individuals, sub-units, and other units, both overseas and in the UK. It also provides the framework and basis for regeneration and reconstruction in the event of unforeseen needs in times of national emergency.

Arminianism

High church school of Christian theology opposed to Calvin's doctrine of predestination which flourished under James I and Charles I, and later formed the basis of Wesleyan Methodism. Named after a Dutch Protestant theologian, Jacob Arminius (1560–1609), it was associated in England with William Laud, bishop of London and later archbishop of Canterbury. It was first promoted by Charles, as Prince of Wales, and the Duke of Buckingham, to the annoyance of James I. Arminianism was denounced when Parliaments were called again in 1640, after the 11-year period of Charles's personal rule.

Armistice Day

Anniversary of the armistice signed 11 November 1918, ending World War I. In the UK it is commemorated on the same day as ◊Remembrance Sunday.

Armitage, Kenneth (1916–)

English sculptor. His works are mostly executed in bronze, and based on the human figure, characteristically depicted with large, flat, squarish bodies, small heads, and spindly limbs. His figures are often fused into a single form, as in *People in the Wind* (1950; Tate Gallery, London) and *Sentinels* (1955–56; Brooklyn Museum, New York).

Army

See ◊armed forces.

Arnaud, Yvonne Germaine (1892–1958)

French actress. She trained as a pianist and toured Europe as a child prodigy. At 18 she appeared in London in *The Quaker Girl* and had a long and distinguished career on the English stage. In 1963 a repertory theatre named after her opened in Guildford, where she lived for many years with her husband, Hugh McLellan.

Arne, Thomas Augustine (1710–1778)

English composer. He wrote incidental music for the theatre and introduced opera in the Italian manner to the London stage with works such as *Artaxerxes* (1762; revised 1777). He is remembered for the songs 'Where the bee sucks' from *The Tempest* (1746), 'Blow, blow thou winter wind' from *As You Like It* (1740), and 'Rule Britannia!' from the masque *Alfred* (1740).

Arnold, Malcolm Henry (1921–)

English composer. His work is tonal and includes a large amount of orchestral, chamber, ballet, and vocal music. His overtures *Beckus the Dandipratt* (1948), *A Sussex Overture* (1951), and *Tam O'Shanter* (1955) are well known. His operas include *The Dancing Master* (1951), and he has written music for more than 80 films, including *The Bridge on the River Kwai* (1957), for which he won an Academy Award.

Arnold, Matthew (1822–1888)

English poet and critic. His poem 'Dover Beach' (1867) was widely regarded as one of the most eloquent expressions of the spiritual anxieties of Victorian England. In his highly influential critical essays collected in *Culture and Anarchy* (1869), he attacked the smugness and philistinism of the Victorian middle classes, and argued for a new culture based on the pursuit of artistic and intellectual values. He was he son of Thomas Arnold, headmaster of Rugby school.

Arnold's poems, characterized by their elegiac mood and pastoral themes, also include 'The Forsaken Merman' (1849), 'Sohrab and Rustum' (1853), 'Thyrsis' (1867), and 'The Scholar-Gipsy' (1853). His *Essays in Criticism* were published in 1865 and 1888, and *Literature and Dogma*, on biblical interpretation, in 1872. Arnold served as an inspector of schools from 1851 to 1886 and many of his advocated reforms were carried out in schools and universities.

Arnold, Samuel (1740–1802)

English composer. In 1765 he became composer to Covent Garden theatre and produced the pasticcio *The Maid of the Mill*. He was appointed organist of the Chapel Royal in 1783 and Westminster Abbey in 1793. He composed or arranged many works for the stage, including the pasticcio *The Maid of the Mill* (1765), *The Spanish Barber* (1777), *Gretna Green* (1783), and *Turk and No Turk* (1784). He also wrote oratorios and church music.

Arnold, Thomas (1795–1842)

English schoolmaster, father of the poet and critic Matthew ◊Arnold. He was headmaster of Rugby School 1828–42. His regime has been graphically described in Thomas Hughes's *Tom Brown's Schooldays* (1857). He emphasized training of character, and had a profound influence on public school education.

> *My object will be, if possible, to form Christian men, for Christian boys I can scarcely hope to make.*
>
> Thomas Arnold English schoolmaster.
> Letter, on appointment to headmastership of Rugby 1828

Arran

Large island in the Firth of Clyde, lying between the Kintyre peninsula and the mainland of North Ayrshire, Scotland; area 427 sq km/165 sq mi; population (1991) 4,500. The economy is largely service based, with tourism and craft industries, such as knitwear. Other industries include whisky distilling and food processing. The island, which is mountainous to the north and undulating to the south, is a popular holiday resort. The chief town is Brodick.

Arran is the largest island in the Firth of Clyde, and is 32.5 km/20 mi long and 17 km/11 mi broad at its widest part. The highest point is Goat Fell (874 m/2,868 ft). Machrie Moor dates from the Bronze Age (3000–4000 years ago) and has stone circles, single stones, hut circles, and burial cists. Drumadoon Point is the site of an Iron Age fort.

The shoreline that encircles the coast of Arran forms a low platform, which rises abruptly to the high peaks in the north and northeast. Much of the southern half of the island is forested. There are red deer in the wilder hilly district, and grouse, wild geese, and duck. The geology of Arran is of particular interest, as within its comparatively confined limits the distinct sections of several geological formations can be observed. The oldest part of Brodick Castle dates from the 13th century. Arran villages include Lamlash, which possesses a fine natural harbour, and Whiting Bay. Car ferries link Brodick and Ardrossan on the mainland and Lochranza and Claonaig (Kintyre); in summer there is also a ferry link between Brodick and Rothesay (Bute).

array, commission of

In England, system of universal military conscription dating from the 13th century, when the obligation to serve the king was extended to serfs. Able-bodied men between the ages of 15 and 60 in each shire were selected by local commissioners to serve in a force paid for by the county. Although hired soldiers predominated in royal armies by the following century, in the 16th century the power of array was accorded to lords-lieutenant. During the Civil War, Charles I issued commissions to raise troops for the royalist armies.

art

For British art before the 10th century, see ◊Celtic art and ◊Anglo-Saxon art.

Medieval: 10th–15th centuries

The strong traditions of Celtic art and Anglo-Saxon art continued in manuscript illumination. One of the few named figures of the period was the 13th-century illuminator and chronicler Matthew Paris. Few examples of medieval British painting survived the Reformation. The late 14th-century *Wilton Diptych* (National Gallery, London), showing Richard II presented to the Virgin and Child, is a rare example of medieval panel painting.

Tudor and Elizabethan: 15th–16th centuries

The reign of Henry VIII virtually put an end to church art. Painting survived largely through the influence and example of the German Hans Holbein, who painted portraits of Henry's court. In Elizabeth's reign miniature portrait painting developed, most notably by Nicholas Hilliard and his pupil Isaac Oliver.

ARRAN *The Machrie standing stones on the island of Arran, in Strathclyde region, Scotland, date from around 2000 BC. The variety of landscapes on Arran, from rocky fells in the north to gentler hills in the south, has led to it being dubbed 'Scotland in miniature'. Corel*

17th century

British art was once again revitalized by foreign artists, in particular the Flemish painter Anthony van Dyck, who settled in England to become court painter to Charles I. His Baroque elegance dominated 17th-century portraiture. Among his successors were William Dobson (1610–1646), the cavalier court painter to Charles I. During the Commonwealth and after the Restoration, the influence of foreign artists working in Britain continued, in particular Peter Lely, Godfrey Kneller, and the sculptors, John Michael Rysbrack and Grinling Gibbons.

18th century

British art at last became robustly independent, with great achievements in portraiture and landscape.

Portraiture was transformed by two outstanding figures, Gainsborough and Reynolds, who brought a new subtlety and refinement to portraits, their images expressing the wealth and confidence of British society. The Royal Academy was founded in 1768, and as its first president Reynolds was able to promote a Classicism based on Italian High Renaissance art. Other important portraitists were Thomas Lawrence, George Romney, and John Hoppner. The fashionable portraiture of the 18th century was challenged by William Hogarth, who painted contemporary life with a vigorous and unapologetic frankness. He was the first English artist to gain an international reputation. Other leading caricaturists, earthy and bitingly satirical, were James Gillray and Thomas Rowlandson. Their favourite targets were the Georgian court, the follies and evils of society, and, during the Napoleonic Wars, Napoleon.

Landscape painting was established in England by the work of foreign artists such as Canaletto. The first British artist to excel at landscape was Richard Wilson, who painted landscape in the 'Italian manner', based on the works of Claude Lorrain. Gainsborough brought to his landscapes a more personal and romantic feeling, his influences being Dutch 17th-century landscapists.

The poet and etcher William Blake was a unique figure, fashioning his own highly individual style to express a complex personal mythology. His visionary creations, among the first powerful expressions of Romanticism, briefly inspired Samuel Palmer, who brought a strong note of mysticism to landscape painting.

At the very end of the century John Flaxman became the leading exponent of Neo-Classical sculpture.

19th century

Constable and Turner gave a depth and range to landscape painting which made it not only one of the most popular expressions of British art, but also one of its most important. Their achievements were complemented by a host of other landscape painters, including Richard Bonington, John Crome, John Sell Cotman, Robert Cozens, Thomas Girtin, and David Cox.

The Pre-Raphaelite movement, which was established in the 1840s, dominated British art for the rest of the century. Its members – such as Holman Hunt, Dante Gabriel Rossetti, and John Everett Millais – concentrated on religious, literary, and genre subjects, their style colourful and minutely detailed.

In the late 19th century the Arts and Crafts movement, led by William Morris, promoted a revival of crafts and good design. Book illustration flourished under the inspiration of both the Pre-Raphaelites and the Arts and Crafts movement, its leading practitioners being Walter Crane, Kate Greenaway, Arthur Rackham, and Aubrey Beardsley.

Among the most popular artists of the day were Edward Landseer, who specialized in animal pictures; and Lord Leighton and Lawrence Alma-Tadema, both of whom made their reputations with lavish recreations of ancient Greek and Roman life.

By the end of the century British art was being influenced by French artists, in particular Edgar Degas and the Impressionists. The US-born artist James McNeill Whistler was typical, rejecting the story pictures that characterized so much Victorian art in favour of the aesthetics of form, colour, and tone. English Impressionists founded the New English Arts Club in 1886, and French influence, which continued well into the 20th century, can be seen in the work of Wilson Steer, John Singer Sargent (another American working in England), Walter Sickert, and Augustus John.

20th century

In 1910 an exhibition arranged by the critic Roger Fry introduced British artists to Post-Impressionism and Fauvism. The Camden Town Group was formed in 1911 to encourage artists who were bringing a new sense of form and colour to the depiction of scenes of everyday London life. Walter Sickert, Charles Ginner, and Harold Gilman (1876–1919) were its leading figures. Artists of the Bloomsbury Group, such as Duncan Grant, Dora Carrington, and Vanessa Bell, were more adventurous in their development of the same influences.

Just before World War I Vorticism, the one specifically English art movement, was created by Wyndham Lewis, one of the few artists to be directly influenced by Cubism and Futurism. Paintings by David Bomberg and sculptures by Henri Gaudier-Brzeska and Jacob Epstein are among the movement's main achievements.

Between the world wars, artists soon began to reflect a wide range of styles and intentions. Matthew Smith worked in a Fauvist style and L S Lowry developed a childlike naivety. Using a finely detailed realism, Stanley Spencer sought to express a visionary apprehension of everyday life. Ben Nicholson evolved an entirely abstract art; Paul Nash, Ceri Richards (1903–1979), and Graham Sutherland responded to Surrealism. Surrealism was also an influence on the sculptor Henry Moore. Other important sculptors to emerge at this time were Barbara Hepworth and Ben Nicholson (both abstract), and Jacob Epstein (who soon outgrew Vorticism), Eric Gill, and Frank Dobson (all figurative).

After World War II British art became increasingly pluralistic. A strong figurative tradition was continued, in very different styles, by Francis Bacon, Lucian Freud, and others. Associated with the introduction of Pop art in the 1950s were Richard Hamilton, Peter Blake, David Hockney, and R B Kitaj. Abstract painting, which has never had a strong following in Britain, was practised by Victor Pasmore, Patrick Heron, William Turnbull, Terry Frost, and Bridget Riley, the leading figure in Op art. Outstanding among sculptors – who also have explored a range of creative possibilities – are Reg Butler, Lynn Chadwick, Kenneth Armitage, Anthony Caro, Elizabeth Frink, Eduardo Paolozzi, Richard Long, and Antony Gormley. In the late 20th century mixed and sometimes unusual media have been utilized, such as dead sheep (Damien Hirst) and chocolate (Helen Chadwick, 1953–1996). Performance artists include Gilbert and George (who styled themselves 'living sculptures') and Bruce McLean (1944–).

> ***Do not imagine that Art is something which is designed to give gentle uplift and self-confidence. Art is not a brassière. At least, not in the English sense. But do not forget that brassière is the French for life-jacket.***
>
> Julian Barnes English novelist. *Flaubert's Parrot* (1984) ch 10

Art Deco

Originally called 'Jazz Modern', Art Deco emerged in Europe in the 1920s and continued to influence art, architecture, and product design through the 1930s. A self-consciously modern style, it was characterized by angular, geometrical patterns and bright colours, and by the use of materials such as enamel, chrome, glass, and plastic. Art Deco style in Britain was epitomized by the innovative work of pottery designers Clarice Cliff and Susie Cooper. Other exponents included Betty Joel, creator of curved, easy-care, functional furniture; the cabinetmaker Ambrose Heal; the sculptor Eric Gill; industrial designer Douglas Scott; and Giles Gilbert Scott, who designed Battersea Power Station (1932–34) with an Art Deco interior.

Long-established pottery and glass manufacturers such as Doulton, Coulton, Crown Devon, Pilkington, and Wedgwood created Art Deco ranges, and the Carter, Stabler & Adams company, established at Poole in 1921, produced painted earthenware in the style.

Arthur (lived 6th century AD)

Legendary British king and hero in stories of ◊Camelot and the quest for the ◊Holy Grail. Arthur is said to have been born in Tintagel, Cornwall, and been buried in Glastonbury (see ◊Avalon), Somerset. He may have been a Romano-Celtic leader against pagan Saxon invaders.

The legends of Arthur and the knights of the Round Table were developed in the 12th century by Geoffrey of Monmouth, Chrétien de Troyes, and the Norman writer Wace. Later writers on the theme include the anonymous author of *Sir Gawayne and the Greene Knight* (1346), Thomas Malory, Tennyson, T H White, and Mark Twain.

Arthur's Seat

Hill of volcanic origin to the east of the centre of Edinburgh,

Scotland; height 251 m/823 ft. It forms the core of Holyrood Park and is a dominant landmark.

The easiest ascent is from Dunsappie Loch to the south.

articles of association

The rules governing the relationship between a registered company, its members (the shareholders), and its directors. The articles of association are deposited with the Registrar of Companies along with the memorandum of association.

Art Nouveau

Decorative style of the visual arts, interior design, and architecture flourishing from 1890 to 1910. Characterized by organic, sinuous patterns and ornamentations based on plant forms, its style was notable in the sophisticated decadence of Aubrey Beardsley's illustrations, and in the fluent interior and exterior designs of Charles Rennie Mackintosh.

Art Nouveau may, in part, be traced back to late Pre-Raphaelite floral patterns, as in the designs of William Morris, founder of the Arts and Crafts movement. The influence of Morris and Beardsley was strongly felt in Austria, Belgium, and Germany, propagated by early numbers of the *Studio* (1893), the first issue of which contained Beardsley's work. In Italy Art Nouveau was known as *stile Liberty* after the London department store, which was celebrated for its Arts and Crafts and Art Nouveau houseware.

Arts and Crafts movement

English social and aesthetic movement of the late 19th century which stressed the importance of manual skills and the dignity of labour. It expressed a rejection of Victorian industrialization and mass production, and a nostalgic desire to return to a medieval way of life. The movement influenced Art Nouveau and, less directly, the Bauhaus school of design.

Its roots lay in the ideas of the architect A W N Pugin and the art critic John Ruskin, both of whom believed that a country's art reflected its spiritual state and was damaged by the loss of traditional skills. The most important practitioner of their ideals was William Morris, who in 1861 founded the firm of Morris, Faulkner and Co, producing a wide range of high-quality goods, including fabrics, furniture, stained glass, and wallpaper. Artists who worked for the firm included Edward Burne-Jones, Dante Gabriel Rossetti, and Philip Webb.

In 1884 the **Art Workers Guild** was formed to bridge the gap between the 'craftsman' and the 'artist', and in 1886 several of its members founded the **Arts and Crafts Exhibition Society**, from which the movement derived its name. Both organizations sought to produce 'art made by the people for the people', encompassing pottery, book illustration and production, metalware, and architectural design. The Guild came to be inspired by socialism, and was led by William Morris (a member of the Socialist League) until his death in 1896. His ideas on the social importance of good design were influential, but he failed to reach the masses as such high-quality products were necessarily expensive.

Other important members included the designer and architect Charles Ashbee (1863–1942), the architect Norman Shaw, and the illustrator Walter Crane.

Arts Councils

UK organizations that aid music, drama, opera, and visual arts with government funds. They came into being in April 1994 when the Arts Council of Great Britain was divided into the separate and independent Arts Councils of England, Scotland, Wales, and Northern Ireland.

Arun

River in southeast England; length 60 km/37 mi. It rises in the inner Weald and is joined by the River Rother in West Sussex; it then flows southwards past ⇨Arundel towards Littlehampton on the coast. The Arun is navigable for approximately 33 km/20 mi inland.

Arundel

Market town in West Sussex, southern England, on the River Arun; population (1991) 3,300. Tourism is an important summer industry. Its Norman castle, much restored, is the seat of the Duke of Norfolk and Earl of Arundel, Earl Marshal of England.

Arundel Castle, the seat of the Fitzalan-Howard family, Dukes of Norfolk, was built in 1067 by the cousin of William (I) the Conqueror, Roger Montgomery, to defend the Arun valley; its large stone keep dates from the 12th century. During the English Civil War the castle was besieged from 1643 to 1644 and almost ruined by Oliver Cromwell's Parliamentary troops. It was rebuilt in the 18th century and much restoration work was carried out in 1890.

The church of St Nicholas, dating from 1380, has a pre-Reformation pulpit and 14th-century wall paintings. The 14th-century Fitzalan Chapel stands behind the altar, separated from the rest of the church by an iron grille and glass screen. Catholic services are held in the chapel, which belongs to the estate of the Duke of Norfolk and can be entered from the castle. It was restored by the 15th Duke of Norfolk in 1886. The Roman Catholic church of St Philip Neri, built by the 15th Duke in 1873, became a cathedral in 1965. Its name was changed to Our Lady and St Philip Howard following the saint's canonization in 1970, and the transfer of his remains to a new shrine in the cathedral in 1971.

A reedbed on the Arun, part of a Wildfowl and Wetlands Trust reserve at Arundel, is a Site of Special Scientific Interest, supporting a population of warblers.

Arup, Ove (1895–1988)

Danish civil engineer. He founded the British-based architectural practice, Arup Associates, a firm noted for the considered and elegant manner in which modern materials, especially concrete, are employed in its designs. Set up in 1963, the practice represented Arup's ideal of interdisciplinary cooperation. Examples of its work are at Somerville College, Oxford (1958–62); and Corpus Christi, Cambridge (1961–64).

During the 1930s Arup worked with Berthold ⇨Lubetkin and the Tecton group on a number of projects, including the Penguin Pool, London Zoo (1934–35), which used reinforced concrete in a sculptural fashion (later developed in Arup's own designs). He later prepared the structural designs for Coventry Cathedral (1951), designed by Basil Spence; and the Sydney Opera House (1956–73), by Jørn Utzon.

Arup was born in Newcastle-upon-Tyne of Danish parents, and studied in Denmark before moving to London in 1923.

Ascham, Roger (*c.* 1515–1568)

English scholar and royal tutor. He wrote *Toxophilus* (1545), a treatise on archery (King Henry VIII's favourite sport). Written in dialogue form, it provided the model for later treatises, including *The Compleat Angler* by Izaak ◊Walton. His chief work is *The Scholemaster*, published by his widow in 1570, a humane and attractively written treatise on education.

In 1548 Ascham was appointed tutor to Princess Elizabeth. He retained favour under Edward VI and Queen Mary (despite his Protestant views), and returned to Elizabeth's service as her secretary after she became queen.

Ascot

Small town in Windsor and Maidenhead unitary authority, southern England, about 10 km/6 mi southwest of Windsor; population (1991) 6,200. The Royal Ascot race meeting, established by Queen Anne in 1711, is held annually in June. It is a social as well as a sporting event.

The June meeting is a showcase for fashion and extravagant hats, particularly on Ladies Day. Principal races include the Gold Cup, Ascot Stakes, Coventry Stakes, and the King George VI and Queen Elizabeth Stakes.

Ascott

Half-timbered house in Wing, Buckinghamshire, England. The house and its estate of over 100 ha/247 acres were given to the National Trust in 1950 by Mr and Mrs Anthony de Rothschild, together with their collections of French and English furniture, paintings by Gainsborough, Rubens, Hogarth and Hobbema, and an outstanding collection of oriental porcelain.

Ashbee, Charles Robert (1863–1942)

English designer, architect, and writer. He was one of the major figures of the ◊Arts and Crafts movement. He founded a Guild and School of Handicraft in the East End of London in 1888, but ultimately modified his views, accepting the importance of machinery and design for industry. The guild and school employed over 100 craftworkers at its peak.

Ashbourne

Market town in Derbyshire, England; population (1991) 6,100. It is situated 21 km/13 mi northwest of Derby, on the River Dove. The cruciform church, dating from the 13th century, has a spire over 60 m/197 ft high, known as the 'Cathedral of the Peaks'. Ashbourne forms the gateway to Dovedale.

Ashburner, Michael (1942–)

English geneticist and one of the world's leading authorities on the genetics of the fruit fly *Drosophila melanogaster*. His work has advanced the study of genes involved in the development of living organisms, including the human body, since many of the *Drosophila* genes are also present and play a similar part in human cells.

He is known for his detailed studies of the structure and function of genes. In his studies he chose to use 'heat shock genes' (genes that are activated by increased temperature) in *Drosophila*, as a model for gene regulation. He also cloned many genes involved in the inheritance of interesting characteristics of *Drosophila* flies.

Ashby-de-la-Zouch

Market town and former spa in Leicestershire, central England, 26 km/16 mi northwest of Leicester; population (1991) 11,000. It is the service centre of an agricultural area and manufactures biscuits. Mary Queen of Scots was imprisoned in its castle (now ruined) in 1569, and fields nearby were the scene of the tournament in Walter Scott's novel *Ivanhoe* (1819).

The town derives its name from its first Norman overlord, Alain de Parrhoet la Zouch, and the Saxon *ashby*, meaning 'homestead where ash trees grow'.

Ashby-de-la-Zouch has Georgian architecture and a Classical-style terrace of houses built in the 19th century when it developed as a spa town. The late Perpendicular church of St Helen contains the only known example of a 'finger pillory', a device used until the 19th century to punish those who misbehaved in a place of worship. Originally a Norman manor house, Ashby Castle was acquired in 1461 by William, Lord Hastings, chancellor of Edward IV, who fortified the house and added the Hastings Tower. The fortification was destroyed by Oliver Cromwell's Parliamentary troops during the English Civil War; little remains of the external walls but the Hastings Tower has survived.

Ashcroft, Peggy (1907–1991)

English actress. She worked with the English Stage Company, the Royal Shakespeare Company and the National Theatre. Her Shakespearean roles included Desdemona in *Othello* (with Paul Robeson) and Juliet in *Romeo and Juliet* (1935) (with Laurence Olivier and John Gielgud), and she appeared in the British TV play *Caught on a Train* (1980) (BAFTA award), the series *The Jewel in the Crown* (1984), and the film *A Passage to India* (1984).

She was born in Croydon, Surrey, where a theatre is named after her. She was made a DBE in 1956.

Ashdown, Paddy (Jeremy John Durham) (1941–)

British politician, leader of the merged Social and Liberal Democrats 1988–99. He became a Liberal member of Parliament in 1983. His constituency is Yeovil, Somerset. His party significantly increased its seat holding in the 1997 general election and cooperated in areas such as constitutional reform with the new Labour government of Tony Blair. Ashdown now sits on a cabinet committee with prime minister Blair.

Ashdown served in the Royal Marines as a commando, leading a Special Boat Section in Borneo, and was a member of the Diplomatic Service 1971–76.

Ashdown Forest

Area of heathland in West and East Sussex, England. It is

situated between East Grinstead and Uckfield, and is part common and part private land. It is a popular recreation area with a golf course, Royal Ashdown.

Ashdown House

17th-century house in Oxfordshire, England, 12 km/7 mi east of Swindon. It was given to the National Trust in 1956 by Cornelia, Countess of Craven, whose ancestor, the 1st Lord Craven, built the house for Elizabeth of Bohemia in 1665.

The house is of unusual design, and is constructed of chalk blocks with stone quoins (dressed corner-stones). It is four storeys high, and crowned by a cupola (dome) with a golden ball.

Ashes, the

Cricket trophy theoretically held by the winning team in the England–Australia Test series.

The trophy is permanently held at ◊Lord's cricket ground no matter who wins the series. It is an urn containing the ashes of stumps and bails used in a match when England toured Australia 1882–83. The urn was given to the England captain Ivo Bligh by a group of Melbourne women. The action followed the appearance of an obituary notice in the *Sporting Times* the previous summer announcing the 'death' of English cricket after defeat by the Australians in the Oval test match.

ASHCROFT, PEGGY *English actress Peggy Ashcroft. In addition to her accomplishments in Shakespearean roles on stage, she appeared in films, notably* The Thirty-Nine Steps *(1935) and* A Passage to India *(1984) (for which she won an Academy Award). Corbis*

Ashford

Market town in Kent, southeast England, on the Great Stour River, 22 km/14 mi southwest of Canterbury; population (1991) 52,000. It expanded in the 1980s as a new commercial and industrial centre for the southeast. Industries include a railway works, light engineering, brewing, and the manufacture of agricultural goods. A terminus of the ◊Channel Tunnel is sited here.

Regular livestock auctions, traditionally known for the sale of ◊Romney Marsh sheep, are held in the town.

Ashford, Daisy (Margaret Mary Julia) (1881–1972)

English writer. *The Young Visiters* (1919), a novel of unconscious humour, was written when she was nine. Sponsored by the novelist and playwright J M Barrie, the book won instant success by its artless charm. It retained its popularity and became a juvenile classic. She also wrote *Where Love Lies Deepest* (1920) and *Love and Marriage* (1965). All her published work was written by the time she was 15.

Ashmole, Elias (1617–1692)

English antiquary. His collection forms the basis of the ◊Ashmolean Museum, Oxford, England. He wrote books on alchemy, astrology, and on antiquarian subjects, and amassed a fine library and a collection of curiosities, both of which he presented to Oxford University in 1682.

Ashmolean Museum

Museum of art and antiquities in Oxford, England, founded in 1683 to house the collections given to Oxford University by the historian and antiquary Elias ◊Ashmole. Its collections include European, Near Eastern, and Oriental art and archaeology; paintings and drawings by Raphael, Michelangelo, and other Renaissance artists; watercolours by J M W Turner; and works by Pre-Raphaelite and major British and European artists of the 18th, 19th, and 20th centuries. It was the first museum in Britain to open to the public.

The original collection included natural and artificial curiosities left to Ashmole by John Tradescant in 1659. For two centuries it was housed in the old Ashmolean building in Broad Street, Oxford. About 1860 the natural history exhibits went to the University Museum and the manuscripts, books, and coins to the Bodleian Library; in 1886 the ethnographic specimens went to the Pitt Rivers Museum. In 1894 the archaeological material, greatly expanded by the English archaeologist Arthur Evans, was moved to an extension of the galleries in Beaumont Street; in 1908 this joint institution was renamed the Ashmolean Museum of Art and Archaeology.

Ashton, Frederick William Mallandaine (1904–1988)

English choreographer and dancer. He was director of the Royal Ballet, London, 1963–70. He studied with Marie

Rambert before joining the Sadler's Wells (now Royal) Ballet in 1935 as chief choreographer. His choreography is marked by a soft, pliant, classical lyricism. His many works and long association with Margot Fonteyn, for whom he created her most famous roles, contributed to the worldwide reputation of British ballet and to the popularity of ballet in the mid-20th century.

His major works include *Façade* (1931) and *Les Rendezvous* (1933) for Rambert; *Symphonic Variations* (1946), *Cinderella* (1948), *Ondine* (1958), *La Fille mal gardée* (1960), *Marguerite and Armand* – for Margot Fonteyn and Rudolf Nureyev – (1963), and *A Month in the Country* (1976). He was knighted in 1962.

Ashton-under-Lyne

Town and administrative headquarters of Tameside metropolitan borough, Greater Manchester, northwest England, on the River Tame; population (1994 est) 177,000. Industries include light engineering and cotton-milling, and the manufacture of rubber, textiles, tobacco, plastics, leather goods, and footwear.

St Michael's church has stained glass dating from about 1500.

Asian Times, The

Weekly newspaper for the Asian community in Britain, covering UK and international news, business, cultural, and other general subject areas. It was established in 1983 and in 1998 had a circulation of just over 30,000.

AS level, General Certificate of Education

Or **Advanced Supplementary level**; examinations introduced in the UK in 1988 as the equivalent to 'half an ◊A level' as a means of broadening the sixth-form (age 16–18) curriculum and including more students in the examination system.

Asquith, Herbert Henry, 1st Earl of Oxford and Asquith (1852–1928)

British Liberal politician, prime minister 1908–16. As chancellor of the Exchequer, he introduced old-age pensions in 1908. He limited the powers of the House of Lords and attempted to give Ireland ◊Home Rule.

Asquith was born in Yorkshire, and on completing his education became a barrister, achieving prominence in 1889 as junior counsel for the Irish Nationalist members in a case involving Charles ◊Parnell. Asquith was first elected Liberal member of Parliament for East Fife in 1886 and held the seat until 1918. He was home secretary in William Gladstone's 1892–95 government. When Henry Campbell-Bannerman formed his government in 1905, Asquith was made chancellor of the Exchequer, becoming prime minister on Campbell-Bannerman's resignation in 1908.

Forcing through the radical budget of his chancellor David ◊Lloyd George led Asquith into two elections in 1910; this resulted in the Parliament Act of 1911, which limited the right of the Lords to veto legislation. His endeavours to pass the Home Rule for Ireland Bill led to the ◊Curragh 'Mutiny' and incipient civil war. Unity was re-established by the outbreak of World War I in 1914, and a coalition government was formed in May 1915. However, Asquith's attitude of 'wait and see' was not suitable to all-out war. In December 1916 he was driven to resign and was replaced by Lloyd George. This event caused a disastrous split in the Liberal Party, which went into eclipse after 1918, though Asquith remained its official leader until 1926.

assize

In medieval Europe, the passing of laws, such as the Constitutions of Clarendon passed by Henry II of England in 1164. The term remained in use in the UK for the courts held by judges of the High Court in each county (see also ◊Bloody Assizes). Assize courts were abolished under the Courts Act in 1971, their civil jurisdiction taken over by the High Court, and their criminal jurisdiction by the Crown Court.

Aston, Francis William (1877–1945)

English physicist who developed the mass spectrometer, which separates isotopes by projecting their ions (charged atoms) through a magnetic field. For his contribution to analytic chemistry and the study of atomic theory he was awarded the 1922 Nobel Prize for Chemistry.

Astor

Prominent US and British family. **Waldorf Astor**, 2nd Viscount Astor (1879–1952), was a British politician, and served as Conservative member of Parliament for Plymouth from 1910 to 1919, when he succeeded to the peerage. His US-born wife Nancy Witcher Langhorne (1879–1964), **Lady Astor**, was the first woman member of Parliament to take a seat in the House of Commons, when she succeeded her husband in the constituency of Plymouth in November 1919. She remained in parliament until 1945, as an active champion of women's rights, educational issues, and temperance.

Astronomer Royal

Honorary post in British astronomy. Originally it was held by the director of the Royal Greenwich Observatory; since 1972 the title of Astronomer Royal has been awarded separately as an honorary title to an outstanding British astronomer. The Astronomer Royal from 1995 is Martin Rees. There is a separate post of Astronomer Royal for Scotland.

Athelney, Isle of

Area of firm ground in marshland near Taunton in Somerset, England, the headquarters of King ◊Alfred the Great in 878, when he was in hiding from the Danes. The legend of his burning the cakes is set here.

Athelstan (*c.* 895–939)

King of Mercia and Wessex, son of Edward the Elder and grandson of Alfred the Great. He was crowned king in 925 at Kingston-upon-Thames. He subdued parts of Cornwall and Wales, and defeated the Welsh, Scots, and Danes at Brunanburh in 937.

Atherton, Michael Andrew (1968–)

English cricketer. A right-handed opening batsman from Lancashire who captained England in a record 52 Tests 1993–98. Atherton first played for Lancashire when a Cambridge University student in 1987. He captained Cambridge University in 1988–89, made his Test debut in 1989, and took over as England captain in 1993. In his 68th Test in 1997 he became the 12th England cricketer to score 5,000 test runs. At the Second Test against Australia at Lord's in 1997 he led England for the 43rd time in Tests, breaking the record for captaining England set by Peter May in the 1950s.

Atkinson, Rowan (1955–)

English comedian, screen actor, and writer. Atkinson's awkward screen presence, based as much on physical clownishness as verbal wit, first gained widespread attention on the 1979 comedy show *Not the Nine O'Clock News*. His position as one of the UK's leading small-screen comic actors was cemented with the series *Blackadder* (1983), which he co-wrote with frequent collaborator screenwriter Richard Curtis. Together they created a new hit series for the 1990s, *Mr Bean*, a throwback to the physical comedy of silent cinema, which has sold to television stations throughout the world, and which spawned a feature film, *Bean* (1997), in which Atkinson starred.

Atlantic triangle

18th-century trade route. Goods were exported from Britain to Africa where they were traded for slaves, who were then shipped to either Spanish colonies in South America, or British colonies in North America; in return, staple goods such as cotton were sent to Europe. See next page for a map showing trade routes and cargoes.

attainder, bill of

Legislative device that allowed the English Parliament to declare guilt and impose a punishment on an individual without bringing the matter before the courts. Such bills were used intermittently from the Wars of the Roses until 1798. The guilty party was deemed to be 'tainted' and so could neither inherit property nor bequeath it to an heir.

Bills of attainder were used under Henry VIII and revived by James I and Charles I, whose best-known bill of attainder involved the Earl of ◊Strafford in 1641. The last bill of attainder was passed against Lord Edward Fitzgerald (1763–1798) for leading a rebellion in Ireland. The use of the device has generally been deplored as it does not require the accusers to prove their case and was usually employed to punish 'new' crimes of treason that were detrimental to those in power.

Attenborough, David Frederick (1926–)

English traveller and zoologist who has made numerous

ATKINSON, ROWAN *Following a career path trodden by many postwar British comics, Rowan Atkinson had an Oxbridge education and appeared in student revues before taking up comedy professionally. One of his most successful creations is the hapless, and silent, Mr Bean, who has become one of British television's greatest exports. A Mr Bean film won Atkinson recognition in the United States in 1997. Edward Hirst/Rex*

wildlife films for television. He was the writer and presenter of the television series *Life on Earth* (1979), *The Living Planet* (1983), *The Trials of Life* (1990), *The Private Life of Plants* (1995), and *The Life of Birds* (1998).

After studying natural sciences at Cambridge, Attenborough joined the BBC as a television producer in 1952. Between 1954 and 1964 he made annual trips to film and study wildlife and human cultures in remote parts of the world; these expeditions were recorded in the *Zoo Quest* series of TV programmes and books. He was director of programmes for BBC Television 1969–72 and a member of its board of management. He is the brother of the actor and director Richard Attenborough. He was knighted in 1985.

Attenborough, Richard (Samuel), Baron Attenborough (1923–)

English director, actor, and producer. He appeared in such films as *Brighton Rock* (1947) and *10 Rillington Place* (1971), and directed *Oh! What a Lovely War* (1969), and such biopics as *Gandhi* (which won eight Academy Awards) (1982) and *Cry Freedom* (1987).

He made his screen acting debut in *In Which We Serve* (1942), and co-produced the socially conscious *The Angry Silence* (1960). He subsequently concentrated on directing – other films include *Chaplin* (1992) and *Shadowlands* (1993) – but returned to the other side of the camera in Steven Spielberg's *Jurassic Park* (1993) and in the 1994 remake of *Miracle on 34th Street*. He features in *Elizabeth I* (1998) and is scheduled to film *Grey Owl* for release in 1999.

His films as a director are infused with a degree of human liberalism. Grandiose in scale, they often focus on the personal dramas of historical figures whose lives have helped shape 20th-century culture and history. He is the brother of naturalist David Attenborough.

Attingham Park

Late 18th-century house near Shrewsbury, Shropshire, England. It stands in a 1620 ha/4000 acre estate acquired in 1953 by the National Trust under the will of the 8th Lord Berwick. The house has a John ◊Nash picture gallery and staircase, and the park was landscaped by Humphry ◊Repton.

Attlee, Clement (Richard), 1st Earl Attlee (1883–1967)

British Labour politician. In the coalition government during World War II he was Lord Privy Seal 1940–42, dominions secretary 1942–43, and Lord President of the Council 1943–45, as well as deputy prime minister from 1942. As prime minister 1945–51 he introduced a sweeping programme of nationalization and a whole new system of social services.

ATLANTIC TRIANGLE *The trade routes and the cargoes carried, including slaves, between Britain, the North American colonies and the Caribbean in the 18th century.*

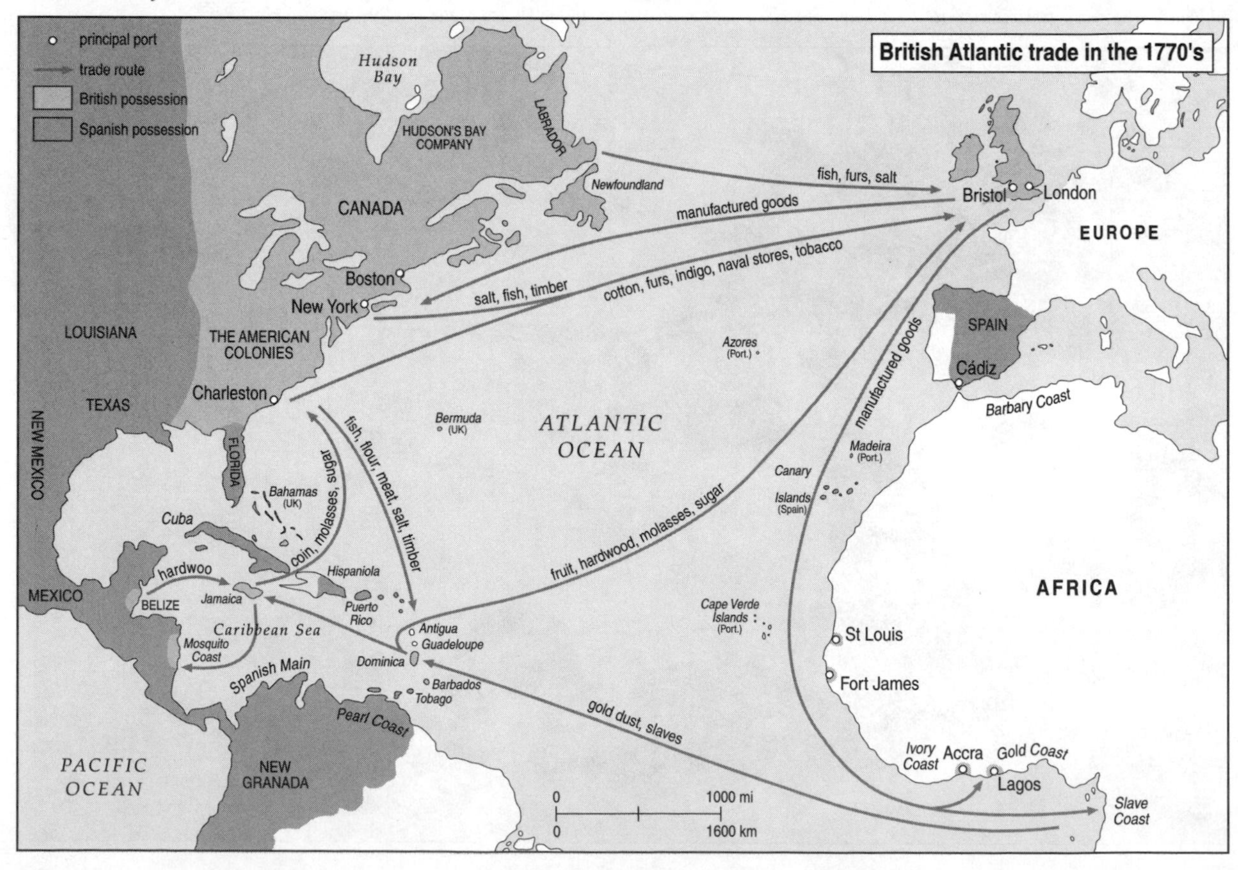

Attlee was educated at Oxford and practised as a barrister 1906–09. Social work in London's East End and cooperation in poor-law reform led him to become a socialist; he joined the Fabian Society and the Independent Labour Party in 1908. He became a lecturer in social science at the London School of Economics in 1913. After service in World War I he was mayor of Stepney in east London 1919–20, and Labour member of Parliament for Limehouse (1922–50) and for West Walthamstow (1950–55). In the first Labour government he was undersecretary for war (1924) and in the second chancellor of the Duchy of Lancaster and postmaster general (1929–31). In 1935 he became leader of the opposition. In July 1945 he became prime minister after a Labour landslide in the general election. The government was returned to power with a much reduced majority in 1950 and was defeated in 1951. He was created 1st Earl in 1955 on his retirement as leader of the opposition.

I think the British have the distinction above all other nations of being able to put new wine into old bottles without bursting them.

CLEMENT ATTLEE British Labour politician. *Hansard* 24 Oct 1950

Attorney General
Principal law officer of the crown and head of the English Bar; the post is one of great political importance.

In England, Wales, and Northern Ireland, the consent of the Attorney General is required for bringing certain criminal proceedings where offences against the state or public order are at issue (for example, the ◊*Spycatcher* litigation). Under the Criminal Justice Act 1988, cases can be referred to the Court of Appeal by the Attorney General if it appears to him or her that the sentencing of a person convicted of a serious offence has been unduly lenient.

Attwell, Mabel Lucie (1879–1964)
English artist. She illustrated many books for children, including her own stories and verse, with cherubic-styled figures in comic and poignant settings. Her name was also used by her daughter, who continued to work in the same idiom.

Aubrey, John (1626–1697)
English biographer and antiquary. He was the first to claim Stonehenge as a Druid temple. His *Lives*, begun in 1667, contains gossip, anecdotes, and valuable insights into the celebrities of his time. It was published as *Brief Lives* in 1898. *Miscellanies* (1696), a work on folklore and ghost stories, was the only work to be published during his lifetime.

Auchinleck
Coalmining town in East Ayrshire unitary authority, Scotland, 22 km/14 mi east of Ayr; population (1991) 4,100. **Auchinleck House**, situated within the town, is the former family seat of James Boswell, the Scottish biographer and diarist.

Auden, W(ystan) H(ugh) (1907–1973)
English-born US poet. He wrote some of his most original poetry, such as *Look, Stranger!* (1936), in the 1930s when he led the influential left-wing literary group that included Louis MacNeice, Stephen Spender, and C Day-Lewis. He moved to the USA in 1939, became a US citizen in 1946, and adopted a more conservative and Christian viewpoint, for example in *The Age of Anxiety* (1947).

He also wrote verse dramas with Christopher ◊Isherwood, such as *The Dog Beneath the Skin* (1935) and *The Ascent of F6* (1936), and opera librettos, notably for Igor Stravinsky's *The*

ATTLEE, CLEMENT *British Labour politician Clement Attlee, photographed in about 1950. Attlee was prime minister 1945–51, and reforms under his leadership included the introduction of the National Health Service, mass nationalization, and the independence of India and Burma. Corbis*

Rake's Progress (1951). Auden was professor of poetry at Oxford from 1956 to 1961. His last works, including *Academic Graffiti* (1971) and *Thank You, Fog* (1973), are light and mocking in style and tone, but are dazzling virtuoso performances by a poet who recognized his position as the leading writer in verse of his time. He returned to live in England a year before his death.

Audit Commission

Independent body established by the Local Government Finance Act 1982. It administers the District Audit Service (established in 1844) and appoints auditors for the accounts of all UK local authorities. The Audit Commission consists of 15 members: its aims include finding ways of saving costs, and controlling illegal local-authority spending. In 1992 it was given the duty to direct local authorities to publish comparative indicators of performance annually.

Auerbach, Frank Helmuth (1931–)

German-born British painter. He is best known for his portraits and views of Primrose Hill and Camden Town, London; his style, formatively influenced by David ◊Bomberg, is characterized by the heavy reworking of charcoal or thickly applied paint. In 1986 he was Britain's representative at the Venice Biennale.

Augustine, St (died 605)

First archbishop of Canterbury, England. Originally prior of the Benedictine monastery of St Andrew, Rome, he was sent from Rome to convert England to Christianity by Pope Gregory I. He landed at Ebbsfleet in Kent in 597 and soon after baptized Ethelbert, King of Kent, along with many of his subjects. He was consecrated bishop of the English at Arles in the same year, and appointed archbishop in 601, establishing his see at Canterbury.

In 603 he attempted unsuccessfully to unite the Roman and native Celtic churches at a conference on the Severn. He founded Christ Church, Canterbury, in 603, and the abbey of Saints Peter and Paul, now the site of Saint Augustine's Missionary College. Feast day 26 May.

Auld Alliance

Intermittent alliance between Scotland and France that lasted from the end of the 13th century until 1560, when Protestantism displaced Catholicism as the dominant faith in Scotland.

'Auld Lang Syne'

Song written by the Scottish poet Robert Burns about 1789, which is often sung at New Year's Eve gatherings. The title means 'old long since' or 'long ago'.

Austen, Jane (1775–1817)

English novelist. She described her raw material as 'three or four families in a Country Village'. *Sense and Sensibility* was published in 1811, *Pride and Prejudice* in 1813, *Mansfield Park* in 1814, *Emma* in 1816, and *Northanger Abbey* and *Persuasion* together in 1818, all anonymously. Many of her works have been successfully adapted for film and television.

Austen was born in Steventon, Hampshire, where her father was rector. She was sent to school in Reading with her elder sister Cassandra, who was her lifelong friend and confidante, but she was mostly taught by her father. In 1801 the family moved to Bath and after the death of her father in 1805, to Southampton, settling in 1809 with her mother and sisters in a house in Chawton, Hampshire, provided by her brother Edward (1768–1852). She died in Winchester, and is buried in the cathedral.

Jane Austen's novels deal mainly with middle-class families, set usually in rural communities, though occasionally in a town, such as Bath. Her plots hinge mostly on the development of a love affair leading to the heroine's marriage.

Her novels reveal Jane Austen as a scrupulous and conscious artist; absolute accuracy of information is allied to absolute precision of language. Describing individuals coping with ordinary life and social pressures, she probes the centres of human experience, using a sharp, satiric wit to expose the follies, hypocrisies, and false truths of the world. She observed speech and manners with wit and precision, and her penetrating observation of human behaviour results in insights that transcend period. Her genius and place among the great English novelists was at once recognized by such critics as S T Coleridge, Robert Southey, Thomas Macaulay, and Walter Scott.

AUSTEN, JANE *English novelist Jane Austen, whose uneventful life belied her ability to produce insightful novels concerning relationships and the nuances of social interaction amongst the landed gentry. Although she had several suitors, Austen never married. She died in 1817 of Addison's disease. Corbis*

Austin, Herbert, 1st Baron Austin (1866–1941)

English industrialist who began manufacturing cars in 1905 in Northfield, Birmingham, notably the Austin Seven (1921). KBE 1917, Baron 1936.

Avalon

In Celtic mythology, the island of the blessed, or paradise; in the legend of King ◊Arthur, the land of heroes, ruled over by Morgan le Fay, to which King Arthur is conveyed after his final battle with Mordred. It has been identified since the Middle Ages with Glastonbury in Somerset, southwest England.

Avebury

Europe's largest stone circle (diameter 412 m/1,350 ft), in Wiltshire, England. This megalithic henge monument is thought to be part of a ritual complex, and contains 650 massive blocks of stone arranged in circles and avenues. It was probably constructed around 3,500 years ago, and is linked with nearby ◊Silbury Hill.

The henge, an earthen bank and interior ditch with entrances on opposite sides, originally rose 15 m/49 ft above the bottom of the ditch. This earthwork and an outer ring of stones surround the inner circles. The stones vary in size from 1.5 m/5 ft to 5.5 m/18 ft high and 1 m/3 ft to 3.65 m/12 ft broad. They were erected by a late Neolithic or early Bronze Age culture. The remains that can be seen today may cover an earlier site – as may be the case at a number of prehistoric sites.

When the village of Avebury developed within the circle, many of the blocks were used for building material. In the Middle Ages many of the stones were buried.

Alexander Keiller, former owner of the site, did much to restore and preserve the monument. He founded the Avebury Museum, where finds from this site and the nearby Neolithic defensive earthwork of Windmill Hill are preserved. The site was acquired by the National Trust in 1943, and the area now protected includes the majority of the stone circles, Windmill Hill, and the manor farm.

> *For what do we live, but to make sport for our neighbours, and laugh at them in our turn?*
>
> JANE AUSTEN English novelist. *Pride and Prejudice* (1813) ch 57

AVIATION *The Anglo-French* Concorde *supersonic airliner, which made its maiden flight in 1969 and is still operating regular services, is a technological triumph. However, it has not enjoyed great commercial success; its noise levels brought early landing restrictions by US airport authorities, while its high operating costs deterred other airlines from buying it. Corel*

Avengers, the

British television series (1961–69), combining espionage, mystery, and, occasionally, science fiction. The series followed the fortunes of cultured British intelligence officer John Steed (Patrick Macnee) and his female partner as they did battle with underworld figures, using their wits and physical prowess to extricate themselves from dangerous situations. Steed's sidekicks included Cathy Gale (Honor Blackman, 1961–64), Emma Peel (Diana Rigg, 1966–68), and Tara King (Linda Thorson, 1968–69).

A sequel, *The New Avengers*, featuring Steed and his new accomplices Purdey (Joanna Lumley) and Mike Gambit (Gareth Hunt), ran from 1976 to 1977. The original series, which continued to be broadcast on British television in the 1990s, acquired a cult following, and a feature film adaptation starring Ralph Fiennes and Uma Thurman was released in 1998.

aviation

See chronology on the next page for some key dates in British aviation; see also ◊civil aviation.

Aviemore

All-year sports and tourist centre, in the Highland unitary authority, Scotland, 45 km/28 mi southeast of Inverness and adjacent to the Cairngorm Mountains. The centre specializes in winter sporting activities. It was extensively developed in the 1960s as Britain's first complete holiday and sports centre.

Avison, Charles (1709–1770)

English organist and composer. A pupil of Geminiani and organist at St Nicholas' Church, Newcastle (1736–70). He is chiefly remembered for his treatise *An Essay on Musical Expression* (1752), but also wrote a quantity of instrumental music, including 48 concertos for chamber orchestra. He edited (with fellow composer John Garth, 1722–1810) 50 of Benedetto Marcello's Psalms in 1757. He is recognized as the foremost English concerto composer of his time.

Avon

Former county of southwest England, formed in 1974 from the city and county of Bristol and parts of northeast Somerset and southwest Gloucestershire. It was abolished in 1996 when the unitary authorities of Bristol, Bath and North East Somerset, North Somerset, and South Gloucestershire were created.

Avon, Upper Avon or Warwickshire Avon (Celtic *afon* 'river')

River in southern England; length 154 km/96 mi. It rises in the Northamptonshire uplands near Naseby and flows southwest through Warwick, Stratford-upon-Avon, and Evesham, before joining the River Severn near Tewkesbury, Gloucestershire.

Aviation: Some Key Dates

1 December 1804 English aviation pioneer George Cayley develops an instrument to measure wind resistance. About this time he also begins to construct models of gliders with fixed wings, fuselage, elevators, and a rudder – the basic configuration of the modern aeroplane.

1896 British aeronautical engineer Percy Sinclair Pilcher builds a successful monoplane glider called the *Hawk*, which is controlled by moving the body from side to side under the wings.

11 November 1902 English balloonist J M Bacon crosses the Irish Channel in a balloon.

25 July 1909 French aviator Louis Blériot crosses the English Channel by monoplane in 37 minutes from Le Boraques, France, to Dover, England.

18 December 1915 The British firm Hadley-Page test-flies the HP 0/100, the first purpose-built bomber.

14 June 1919–15 June 1919 The British aviators John Alcock and Arthur Whitten Brown fly, in a Vickers-Vimy twin-engined biplane, from Newfoundland to Ireland in 16 hr 12 min, winning the £10,000 prize offered by the *Daily Mail* for the first nonstop transatlantic flight.

1928 British aviators Charles Kingsford-Smith and Charles Ulm are the first to fly across the mid-Pacific by air – from Oakland California, to Brisbane, Australia, via Honolulu and Fiji.

May 1930–July 1930 The British aviator Charles Kingsford-Smith, piloting the *Southern Cross*, makes the first solo around-the-world flight.

4 May 1936–7 May 1936 English aviator Amy Johnson flies from England to Cape Town, South Africa, in 3 days 6 hr 25 min.

1936 Gatwick Airport, in the Surrey countryside south of London, England, opens.

August 1938 The Spitfire fighter plane goes into service with the RAF. It is the only British combat aircraft to remain in production throughout World War II.

15 May 1941 The Gloster E 28/39, using a Whittle jet engine, is the first British jet to fly.

June 1941 The Lancaster bomber, which carries bouncing bombs, is launched.

21 May 1946 Heathrow Airport opens in Hounslow, London, England.

1946 The British Overseas Airways Corporation (BOAC) starts a transatlantic passenger service, using Lockheed Constellation airliners to operate between London, England, and New York, New York.

1954 The first vertical take off and landing (VTOL) aircraft, known as the 'flying bedstead', is developed in the UK.

1967 British pilot Sheila Scott sets a world record for flying between London and Cape Town. In all, she breaks over 100 records for light-aircraft flying, and is the first British pilot to fly solo round the world.

21 January 1976 The British–French supersonic airliner *Concorde* begins a regular passenger service across the Atlantic; it is the world's first scheduled supersonic passenger service.

10 September 1976 The world's worst mid-air collision occurs when a British Airways Trident and a Yugoslav DC-9 collide in the air near Zagreb; 176 people are killed.

15 March 1977 The government nationalizes the aircraft industry.

29 April 1977 British Aerospace is formed to run Britain's nationalized aviation industry.

26 September 1977 The first Laker 'Skytrain' flies from London to New York for $102 a ticket, launching Laker Airways' no-frill low-cost service. The company collapses in 1982.

22 June 1984 Virgin Atlantic Airlines makes its first flight from London to New York.

21 December 1988 A terrorist bomb explodes on a Pan Am Boeing 747 airliner flying over Lockerbie in Scotland, killing all 259 passengers on board and 11 people on the ground.

1991 The Terminal at Stansted Airport in Essex designed by the English architect Norman Foster, is completed.

22 December 1997 After three years of delays, the defence ministers of Britain, Germany, Italy, and Spain sign an agreement to begin producing a new military aeroplane, the 'Eurofighter'.

8 June 1998 British deputy prime minister John Prescott announces plans for the privatization of Britain's air-traffic control.

Avonmouth

Suburb of the city of Bristol, England. Situated at the mouth of the River Avon (Bristol Avon), it has extensive docks. A new deep-water harbour was opened here in 1977.

Awe, Loch

Loch in Argyll and Bute unitary authority, Scotland. The loch, lying 36 m/118 ft above sea level, is 37 km/23 mi long (the longest in Scotland) and reaches a depth of 100 m/328 ft. Fed in the northeast by the rivers Orchy and Strae, it empties to the northwest into the River Awe. Hydroelectricity is generated above the loch at the Cruachan Dam.

Kilchurn Castle, a stronghold of the Campbell clan with a keep dating from 1440, stands on a peninsula which is transformed into an island by high tide.

axe factories

Neolithic and later (*c.* 3500–1400 BC) sites of volcanic rock where axe-heads were shaped. Some 550 axe factories have been identified in the Lake District of Cumbria, and it is thought that scree at Pike O'Stickle in the Langdales represents the debris from as many as 75,000 stone axe-heads. Elsewhere, axe factories have been identified in the Lleyn Peninsula in Wales and in Cornwall. They are rare in southern and eastern England, where axe-heads were made chiefly from flint.

Axholme, Isle of

Low-lying area of 2,000 ha/5,000 acres in North Lincolnshire, eastern England, bounded by the Trent, Don, Idle, and Torne rivers, where a form of 'medieval' open-field strip farming is still practised. The largest village, Epworth, was the birthplace of the Methodists John and Charles Wesley.

It is thought that the area was originally covered with forest. Later the isle became a swamp which was settled in the early 17th century by Dutch and Flemish immigrants, and drained by the Dutch water engineer Charles Vermuyden (*c.* 1596–1683) between 1625 and 1630.

Axminster

Town in Devon, England, on the River Axe, 38 km/24 mi east of Exeter; population (1991) 3,400. Its original carpet industry, which was established in 1755, came to an end 80 years later. A new carpet factory was opened in 1937, and still produces ⇨Axminster carpets.

The town grew up at the intersection of two Roman roads, Portway and the ⇨Fosse Way. It derives its name from the River Axe and the old abbey church, or minster, which combines Norman, early Decorated, and Perpendicular Gothic architectural styles.

Axminster carpet

Type of cut-pile, patterned carpet originally made in Axminster, Devon, England. It is produced by a method which permits up to 240 colours.

Ayckbourn, Alan (1939–)

English playwright and artistic director of the Stephen Joseph Theatre, Scarborough, North Yorkshire, from 1970. His prolific output, characterized by comic dialogue and teasing experiments in dramatic structure, includes *Relatively Speaking* (1967), *Absurd Person Singular* (1972), a trilogy *The Norman Conquests* (1974), *Intimate Exchanges* (1982), *A Woman in Mind* (1986), *Haunting Julia* (1994), and *Things We Do For Love*. He has also written a number of plays for children, including *Invisible Friends* (1989) and *This Is Where We Came In* (1990).

> *Few women care to be laughed at and men not at all, except for large sums of money.*
>
> ALAN AYCKBOURN English dramatist. *The Norman Conquests* (1974)

Ayer, A(lfred) J(ules) (1910–1989)

English philosopher. He wrote *Language, Truth and Logic* (1936), an exposition of the theory of 'logical positivism', presenting a criterion by which meaningful statements (essentially truths of logic, as well as statements derived from experience) could be distinguished from meaningless metaphysical utterances (for example, claims that there is a God or that the world external to our own minds is illusory). Knighted 1970.

Aylesbury

Market town and administrative headquarters of Buckinghamshire, England, 60 km/37 mi northwest of London; population (1991) 50,000. It is the centre of the fertile Vale of Aylesbury and lies to the north of the Chiltern Hills. Industries include printing, publishing, food production, and light engineering. Aylesbury gives its name to a breed of large white domestic duck.

Ayot St Lawrence

Village in Hertfordshire, southern England, 13 km/8 mi north of St Albans. The playwright George Bernard Shaw lived in the village from 1906 until his death in 1950, and his former home, Shaw's Corner, is preserved as it was in his lifetime.

Ayr

Administrative headquarters of ⇨South Ayrshire, southwest Scotland, at the mouth of the River Ayr; population (1991) 48,000. Ayr has strong associations with the poet Robert ⇨Burns. Industries include fishing, electronics, shipbuilding in Troon, and aircraft parts.

Ayr is a popular holiday resort, with a long sandy beach. It has a racecourse, which hosts the Scottish Grand National, Scotland's only professional ice-hockey team, and several golf courses. Glasgow Prestwick International Airport is 6 km/4 mi to the north of the town centre. Robert Burns was born at Alloway, 4 km/2.5 mi south of the town centre. The first bridge was built in the 13th century and was replaced by a stone built one in 1491. This was reconstructed in 1588 and is known as the Auld Brig.

Ayrshire

Former county of southwest Scotland, on the Firth of Clyde, which was merged to form the greater part of four districts in Strathclyde region in 1975.

Ayrshire was merged into the districts of Kyle and Carrick, Kilmarnock and Loudoun, and Cumnock and Doon Valley, and forming the greater part of the district of Cunninghame in 1975. It is now divided into three unitary authorities, which bear its name – East, North, and South.

Ayrshire

Breed of hardy dairy cattle originating in the former county of Ayrshire, Scotland, in the latter part of the 18th century and considered to be the only special dairy breed to have originated in the British Isles. Their body colour ranges from almost pure white to almost all cherry red or brown. They are found worldwide. Their beef quality is of secondary importance.

Babbage, Charles
(1792–1871)

English mathematician who devised a precursor of the computer. He designed an analytical engine, a general-purpose mechanical computing device for performing different calculations according to a program input on punched cards (an idea borrowed from the Jacquard loom). This device was never built, but it embodied many of the principles on which digital computers are based.

In 1991, the British Science Museum completed Babbage's second difference engine (to demonstrate that it would have been possible with the materials then available). It evaluates polynomials up to the seventh power, with 30-figure accuracy.

Babington, Anthony (1561–1586)

English traitor. He was the son of Henry Babington and Mary, daughter of Lord Darcy, and was a fanatical Catholic. As page to the Earl of Shrewsbury, who was jailer to ◊Mary Queen of Scots, he became strongly attached to her and her cause. He was the chief promoter of a plot to assassinate Elizabeth I and replace her with Mary. The plot was discovered by the intelligence chief Francis Walsingham, and Babington was arrested, tried, and executed. The discovery of the plot also led to Mary's own execution.

Backley, Steve (1969–)

English javelin thrower who in 1990 became the first Briton to break the men's world javelin record. Three times European champion, 1990–98, and two times Commonwealth champion, 1990–94.

Back to Basics

Phrase used by British prime minister John Major during his keynote address to the Conservative Party conference in October 1993, in which he argued for a return to 'traditional British values'; it was subsequently adopted as a slogan by the Conservative Party, some members of which emphasized the morality aspect. In the following months, media revelations of sexual indiscretions by Conservative politicians and corrupt practices by Conservative-run councils and government departments caused deep embarrassment to the party.

Bacon, Francis
(1909–1992)

Irish painter. Self-taught, he practised abstract art, then developed a stark Expressionist style characterized by distorted, blurred figures enclosed in loosely defined space. His aimed to 'bring the figurative thing up onto the nervous system more violently and more poignantly'. One of his best-known works is *Study after Velázquez's Portrait of Pope Innocent X* (1953; Museum of Modern Art, New York).

Bacon moved to London in 1925, began to paint about 1930, and held his first show in London in 1949. He destroyed much of his early work. *Three Studies for Figures at the Base of a Crucifixion* (about 1944; Tate Gallery, London) is an early example of his mature style, which is often seen as a powerful expression of the existential anxiety and nihilism of 20th-century life.

Bacon, Francis, 1st Baron Verulam and Viscount St Albans (1561–1626)

English philosopher, politician, and writer, a founder of modern scientific research. His works include *Essays* (1597; revised and augmented 1612 and 1625), characterized by pith and brevity; *The Advancement of Learning* (1605), a seminal work discussing scientific method; *Novum organum* (The New Instrument) (1620), in which he redefined the task of natural science, seeing it as a means of empirical discovery and a method of increasing human power over nature; and *The New Atlantis* (1627), describing a utopian state in which scientific knowledge is systematically sought and exploited. He was briefly Lord Chancellor in 1618 but lost his post through corruption.

Satirist Alexander Pope called Bacon 'the wisest, brightest, and meanest of mankind'. The **Baconian theory**, originated by James Willmot in 1785, suggesting that the works of Shakespeare were written by Bacon, is not taken seriously by scholars.

Bacon, Roger (*c.* 1214–1294)

English philosopher and scientist. He was interested in alchemy, the biological and physical sciences, and magic. Many discoveries have been credited to him, including the magnifying lens. He foresaw the extensive use of gunpowder and mechanical cars, boats, and planes. Bacon was known as *Doctor Mirabilis* (Wonderful Teacher).

In 1266, at the invitation of his friend Pope Clement IV, he began his *Opus majus/Great Work*, a compendium of all branches of knowledge. In 1268 he sent this with his *Opus minus/Lesser Work* and other writings to the pope. In 1277 Bacon was condemned and imprisoned by the Christian church for 'certain novelties' (heresy) and not released until 1292.

Bacon wrote in Latin and his works include *On Mirrors*, *Metaphysical*, and *On the Multiplication of Species*. He followed the maxim 'Cease to be ruled by dogmas and authorities; look at the world!'

Baden-Powell, Robert Stephenson Smyth, 1st Baron Baden-Powell (1857–1941)

British general, founder of the Scout Association. He was commander of the garrison during the 217-day siege of Mafeking (now Mafikeng) in the Second South African War (1899–1900). After 1907 he devoted his time to developing the Scout movement, which rapidly spread throughout the world.

Baden-Powell began the Scout movement in 1907 with a camp for 20 boys on Brownsea Island, Poole Harbour, Dorset. He published *Scouting for Boys* (1908) and about 30 other books. He was World Chief Scout from 1920. With his sister Agnes (1858–1945) he founded the Girl Guides in 1910. Knighted 1909, Baron 1929.

Bader, Douglas Robert Steuart (1910–1982)

British fighter pilot. He lost both legs in a flying accident in 1931, but had a distinguished flying career in World War II. He was credited with 22 ½ planes shot down (20 on his own and some jointly) before himself being shot down and captured in August 1941. The film *Reach for the Sky* (1956) was based on his experiences; he was played by Kenneth More.

He was twice decorated for his war service and was knighted in 1976 for his work with disabled people.

badminton

Racket game similar to lawn tennis but played on a smaller court and with a shuttlecock (a half sphere of cork or plastic with a feather or nylon skirt) instead of a ball. The object of the game is to prevent the opponent from being able to return the shuttlecock. In Britain there are estimated 4 million badminton players.

The sport is named after Badminton House, the seat of the duke of Beaufort, where the game was played in the 19th century.

Badminton

Village in Gloucestershire, England. **Badminton House**, the seat of the Duke of Beaufort, is a mansion in the Palladian style; it has given its name to the game of badminton, and to the Badminton Library. An annual three-day equestrian event is held at Badminton, which is often attended by members of the British Royal Family.

Baffin, William (1584–1622)

English explorer and navigator. In 1616 he and Robert Bylot explored Baffin Bay, northeast Canada, and reached latitude 77° 45' N, which for 236 years remained the 'furthest north'.

In 1612, Baffin was chief pilot of an expedition in search of the Northwest Passage, and in 1613–14 commanded a whaling fleet near Spitsbergen, Norway. He piloted the *Discovery* on an expedition to Hudson Bay led by Bylot in 1615. After 1617, Baffin worked for the ◊East India Company and made surveys of the Red Sea and Persian Gulf. In 1622 he was killed in an Anglo-Persian attack on Hormuz.

BAFTA

Acronym for **British Academy of Film and Television Arts**, formed in 1959 as a result of the amalgamation of the British Film Academy (founded in 1948) and the Guild of Television Producers (founded in 1954). It gives annual awards to the film and television industries for craft, production, and performance.

Bagehot, Walter (1826–1877)

British writer and economist. His *English Constitution* published in 1867, a classic analysis of the British political system, is still a standard work.

bagpipes

Any of an ancient family of double-reed folk woodwind instruments employing a bladder, filled by the player through

BAGPIPES *Although played in a number of regions in Britain, bagpipes are most commonly associated with Scotland. Characteristic types of tunes for the pipes are stirring military marches performed by massed regimental pipers (for example at the annual Edinburgh Tattoo) or* pibrochs, *haunting laments for the dead played by a lone piper. Corel*

a mouthpiece, or bellows as an air reservoir to a 'chanter' or fingered melody pipe, and two or three optional drone pipes providing a continuous accompanying harmony.

The Highland bagpipes are the national instrument of Scotland.

Bailey, David (1938–)

English fashion photographer. His work for *Vogue* magazine in the 1960s and his black-and-white portraits of fashionable celebrities did much to define the image of 'swinging London'. He has also directed documentaries and commercials for television. His books include *Box of Pin-ups* (1965) and *Goodbye Baby and Amen* (1969).

Bailey, Donald Coleman (1901–1985)

English engineer, inventor in World War II of the portable **Bailey bridge**, made of interlocking, interchangeable, adjustable, and easily transportable units. Knighted 1946.

bailiff

Officer of the court whose job, usually in the county courts, is to serve notices and enforce the court's orders involving seizure of the goods of a debtor.

Bainbridge, Beryl (1934–)

English novelist. Her writing has dramatic economy and pace, it is acutely observed, peppered with ironic black humour, and often deals with the tragedy and comedy of human self-delusion. She achieved critical acclaim with *The Dressmaker* (1973), set in wartime England. *Birthday Boys* (1991), *Every Man for Himself* (1996), and *Master Georgie* (1998) are novels of historical realism centring respectively on R F Scott's expedition to the South Pole, the sinking of the Titanic, and the Crimean War.

Her other works include *The Bottle Factory Outing* (1974), *Injury Time* (1977), and *An Awfully Big Adventure* (1989).

Bainbridge, Simon (1952–)

English composer and conductor. As a conductor he has worked with the BBC Symphony Orchestra and the Scottish Sinfonia. In April 1997 he was awarded the Grawemeyer Award for musical composition. His works include: *Heterophony* for orchestra (1970); viola concerto (1977); *Landscape and Magic Words* for soprano and chamber ensemble (1981); *A cappella* for six voices (1985); *Metamorphosis* for ensemble (1988); *Cantus contra cantum* (1989); Double Concerto for oboe and clarinet (1990); Clarinet quintet (1993).

Baird, John Logie (1888–1946)

Scottish electrical engineer who pioneered television. In 1925 he gave the first public demonstration of television, transmitting an image of a recognizable human face. The following year, he gave the world's first demonstration of true television before an audience of about 50 scientists at the Royal Institution, London. By 1928 Baird had succeeded in demonstrating colour television.

Baker, Benjamin (1840–1907)

English engineer who designed, with English engineer John Fowler (1817–1898), London's first underground railway (the Metropolitan and District) in 1869; the Forth Rail Bridge, Scotland in 1880; and the original Aswan Dam on the River Nile, Egypt.

In the construction of the Central Line of the London Underground, Baker incorporated an ingenious energy-conservation measure: he dipped the line between stations to reduce the need both for braking to a halt and for the increase in power required to accelerate away. Knighted 1890.

Baker, Kenneth Wilfrid (1934–)

British Conservative politician, home secretary 1990–92. He was environment secretary 1985–86, education secretary 1986–89, and chairman of the Conservative Party 1989–90, retaining his cabinet seat, before becoming home secretary in John Major's government. After his dismissal in 1992, he became a frequent government critic. He retired from parliament in 1997.

Bakewell

Town in Derbyshire, England, on the River Wye, 40 km/25 mi from Derby; population (1991) 3,600. Bakewell is in the scenic surroundings of the ◊Peak District; nearby are the historic stately homes Haddon Hall and Chatsworth House.

There are Saxon remains on Castle Hill near Bakewell; the church of All Saints is mentioned in the ◊Domesday Book; on its southern side stands an 8th-century carved stone cross. Bakewell Bridge is one of the oldest bridges in England. Lead mining was practised from early times, and chert limestone is still worked.

Balaclava, Battle of

A Russian attack on 25 October 1854, during the Crimean War, on British positions, near a town in Ukraine, 10 km/6 mi southeast of Sevastopol. The Russian army had broken through Turkish lines on 25 October and entered the valley of Balaklava, intending to attack the British supply base and relieve Sevastopol by attacking British positions from the rear. Balaklava was the scene of the ill-timed ◊Charge of the Light Brigade of British cavalry against the entrenched Russian artillery, following which the 93rd Highland Regiment broke up a Russian cavalry attack. The battle ended with the Russians retaining their guns and their position. **Balaclava helmets** were knitted hoods worn here by soldiers in the bitter weather.

Bala Lake, Welsh Llyn Tegid

Lake in Gwynedd, north Wales, about 6.4 km/4 mi long and 1.6 km/1 mi wide. It has a unique primitive species of fish, the gwyniad (a form of whitefish), a protected species from 1988. It has facilities for water sports.

Balcon, Michael Elias (1896–1977)

English film producer. He entered film production in the early 1920s and was instrumental in developing the career of the young Alfred ◊Hitchcock. Subsequently, he was responsible for the influential Ealing comedies of the 1940s and early

1950s (see ◊Ealing Studios), such as *Kind Hearts and Coronets* (1949), *Whisky Galore!* (1949), and *The Lavender Hill Mob* (1951).

Baldwin, Stanley, 1st Earl Baldwin of Bewdley (1867–1947)

British Conservative politician, prime minister 1923–24, 1924–29, and 1935–37. He weathered the general strike of 1926, secured complete adult suffrage in 1928, and handled the ◊abdication crisis of Edward VIII in 1936, but failed to prepare Britain for World War II.

Baldwin was born in Bewdley, Worcestershire, the son of an iron and steel magnate. In 1908 he became Unionist member of Parliament for Bewdley, and in 1916 he was made parliamentary private secretary to Andrew Bonar ◊Law. Baldwin was financial secretary to the Treasury 1917–21, and then appointed to the presidency of the Board of Trade. In 1919 he anonymously gave the Treasury £50,000 of War Loan for cancellation, representing about 20% of his fortune. He was a leader in the disruption of the David ◊Lloyd George coalition in 1922, and, as chancellor under Bonar Law, achieved a settlement of war debts with the USA.

As prime minister 1923–24 and again 1924–29, Baldwin passed the Trades Disputes Act of 1927 after the general strike, granted widows' and orphans' pensions, and equal voting rights for women in 1928. He joined the national government of Ramsay ◊MacDonald in 1931 as Lord President of the Council. He handled the abdication crisis during his third premiership 1935–37, after the resignation of MacDonald, but was later much criticized for his failures to resist popular desire for an accommodation with the dictators Hitler and Mussolini, and to rearm more effectively.

Balfour, Arthur James, 1st Earl of Balfour (1848–1930)

British Conservative politician, prime minister 1902–05, and foreign secretary 1916–19. He issued the ◊Balfour Declaration in 1917 and was involved in peace negotiations after World War I, signing the Treaty of Versailles.

Son of a Scottish landowner, Balfour was elected a Conservative member of Parliament in 1874. In Lord Salisbury's ministry he was secretary for Ireland in 1887, and for his ruthless vigour was called 'Bloody Balfour' by Irish nationalists. In 1891 and again in 1895 he became First Lord of the Treasury and leader of the Commons, and in 1902 he succeeded Salisbury as prime minister. His cabinet was divided over Joseph Chamberlain's tariff-reform proposals, and in the 1905 elections suffered a crushing defeat.

Balfour retired from the party leadership in 1911. In 1915 he joined the Asquith coalition as First Lord of the Admiralty. As foreign secretary 1916–19 he issued the ◊Balfour Declaration in favour of a national home in Palestine for the Jews. He was Lord President of the Council 1919–22 and 1925–29. He also wrote books on philosophy.

Balfour, Eve (1898–1990)

English agriculturalist and pioneer of modern organic farming. She established the Haughley Experiment, a farm research project at New Bells Farm near Haughley, Suffolk, to demonstrate that a more sustainable agricultural alternative existed. The experiment ran for almost 30 years, comparing organic and chemical farming systems. The wide-ranging support it attracted led to the formation of the ◊Soil Association in 1946.

Balfour Declaration

Letter, dated 2 November 1917, from British foreign secretary A J Balfour to Lord Rothschild (chair, British Zionist Federation) stating: 'HM government view with favour the establishment in Palestine of a national home for the Jewish people.' It helped form the basis for the foundation of Israel in 1948.

> *I look forward to a time when Irish patriotism will as easily combine with British patriotism as Scottish patriotism combines now.*
>
> Arthur Balfour British politician and prime minister. Speech 1889

Baliol, John de, or Balliol (*c.* 1249–1315)

King of Scotland 1292–96. As an heir to the Scottish throne on the death of ◊Margaret, the Maid of Norway, he had the support of the English king, Edward I, against 12 other claimants. Baliol was proclaimed king, having paid homage to Edward. When English forces attacked Scotland, Baliol rebelled against England and gave up the kingdom.

Baliol was unpopular with the Scots, who dubbed him Toom Tabbard ('empty garment'). After Edward's invasion, Baliol and his three sons were sent to London and confined to the Tower for three years. Released at the request of Pope Boniface, Baliol died in France at his patrimonial estate of Ballieul. His son Edward invaded Scotland in 1332 and became king for various short periods between 1332 and 1346.

Ball, John (died *c.* 1381)

English priest. He was one of the leaders of the ◊Peasants' Revolt of 1381, known as 'the mad priest of Kent'. A follower of John ◊Wycliffe and a believer in social equality, he was imprisoned for disagreeing with the archbishop of Canterbury. During the revolt he was released from prison, and when in Blackheath, London, incited people against the ruling classes by preaching from the text 'When Adam delved and Eve span, who was then the gentleman?' When the revolt collapsed he escaped but was captured near Coventry and executed.

ballad (Latin *ballare* 'to dance')

Form of traditional narrative poetry, usually metrically simple and in short stanzas. Concerned with some strongly emotional event or popular story, the ballad is halfway between the lyric and the epic. Most English ballads date from the 15th century but may describe earlier events.

Historically, the ballad was primarily intended for singing at the communal ring-dance, the refrains representing the chorus. Opinion is divided as to whether the authorship of the ballads may be attributed to individual poets or to the community. Later ballads tend to centre on a popular folk hero, such as Robin Hood (as in *A Lytell Geste of Robyn Hode*, *c.* 1495). The ballad form was adapted in 'broadsheets', with a satirical or political motive, and in the 'hanging' ballads purporting to come from condemned criminals.

In the UK collections of ballads were made in the 17th and 18th centuries, for example Bishop Percy's *Reliques of Ancient Poetry* (1765), including the early Scottish ballad *Sir Patrick Spens*, Scott's *Minstrelsy of the Scottish Border* (1802–03), a collection of traditional ballads as well as adaptations, and F J Child's *English and Scottish Popular Ballads*, (1857–59).

Poets of the Romantic movement in Britain were greatly influenced by the ballad revival, as seen in, for example, the *Lyrical Ballads* (1798) of Wordsworth and Coleridge. During the 19th and 20th centuries the ballad form has influenced the work of poets such as Keats (as in *La Belle Dame Sans Merci*), A E Housman, John Masefield, and Charles Causley.

ballad opera

An English light operatic entertainment, the fashion for which was set by John Gay's *The Beggar's Opera* in 1728 and continuing its vogue until the 1760s. The most distinctive feature of its music is that it consists mainly of short songs interspersed with dialogue and that they are not specially composed for the piece, but chosen from popular songs of the day.

Ballantyne, R(obert) M(ichael) (1825–1894)

Scottish writer of children's books. Six years with the Hudson's Bay Company provided material for *The Young Fur Traders* (1856), after which he produced numerous moral adventure tales set in various parts of the world, such as *The Coral Island* (1857), *Martin Rattler* (1858), and *The Dog Crusoe* (1861).

Ballard, J(ames) G(raham) (1930–)

English novelist. He became prominent in the 1960s for his science fiction works on the theme of catastrophe and collapse of the urban landscape. His first novel was *The Drowned World* (1962), and later works include *Crash!* (1973), *High-Rise* (1975), the partly autobiographical *Empire of the Sun* (1984), dealing with his internment in China during World War II, and the autobiographical novel *The Kindness of Women* (1991).

ballet (Italian *balletto* 'a little dance')

Western ballet as we know it today first appeared in Renaissance Italy, where it was a court entertainment. From there it was brought by Catherine de' Medici to France in the form of a spectacle combining singing, dancing, and declamation. This reached its height in the mid-17th century, in the reign of Louis XIV, who founded the Académie Royale de Danse, to which all subsequent ballet history can be traced.

Top Ten Most Popular Ballet Productions in the UK 1996–7

April 1996–March 1997

Rank	Repertoire	Company	Tickets sold
1	*Nutcracker*	English National Ballet	80,430
2	*Nutcracker*	Kirov Ballet	47,690
3	*Alice in Wonderland*	English National Ballet	41,100
4	*Sleeping Beauty*	Birmingham Royal Ballet	39,217
5	*Dracula*	Northern Ballet Theatre	36,651
6	*Coppelia*	English National Ballet	35,579
7	*Nutcracker*	Birmingham Royal Ballet	32,869
8	*A Christmas Carol*	Northern Ballet Theatre	32,723
9	*Swan Lake*	Birmingham Royal Ballet	27,657
10	*Sleeping Beauty*	Royal Ballet	21,255

Source: Arts Councils of England, Scotland, Wales, and Northern Ireland

16th–17th centuries

In England, the masque, a composite art form similar to the court ballet, originated in the late 16th century but was given its definitive form by the architect Inigo Jones and playwright Ben Jonson. Masques used visual images to express moral and philosophical truths, and represented a belief in human ability to control nature; in the reign of Charles I, the 'antimasques' evolved as a mimed or danced episode preceding the main spectacle, often portraying 'grotesque' characters (a relationship may be drawn with the Italian commedia dell'arte tradition, which in turn influenced the pantomimes of English fairgrounds). The masque entertainment came to an abrupt end with the monarchy in 1649.

18th–19th centuries

The English choreographer John Weaver emerged in the 1700s, with his theories and 'dramatick entertainments' going back to ancient Greek traditions. In 1734 the French dramatic ballerina Marie Salle, a student with the French dancer Marie-Anne Camargo, came to London to premiere her most famous ballet, *Pygmalian*. The choreographer Jules Perrot presented his work in London in the 19th century. He was ballet master for Her Majesty's Theatre 1842–48,during which time he presented some 20 ballets, including *Ondine* (which later influenced Frederick ◊Ashton) and *Giselle* (which formed the basis of the interpretation performed today). His work in London contributed to the international expansion of Romantic ballet, which first appeared about 1830 but survives only in the ballets *Giselle* (1841) and *La*

Sylphide (1832). Perrot specialized in dramatic ballets, using dance to advance the action.

20th century

The next major development was initiated by the Russian entrepreneur Sergei Diaghilev with his Ballets Russes, founded in 1909, which first visited London in 1911 and mounted several triumphant seasons there until the company folded with the death of Diaghilev in 1929; there were also visits to Manchester in 1919 and regional tours of England in 1927 and 1929.

In 1926 Marie ◊Rambert founded the company that developed into the Ballet Rambert, and launched the careers of choreographers such as Frederick Ashton and Anthony Tudor (1908–1987). The national company, the ◊Royal Ballet (so named in 1956), grew from foundations laid by Ninette de Valois and Frederick Ashton in 1928. The London Festival Ballet, formed in 1950, was renamed the English National Ballet in 1989. The Northern Ballet Theatre was founded in 1987. Leading British dancers include Alicia ◊Markova, Anton ◊Dolin, Margot ◊Fonteyn, Antoinette ◊Sibley, Beryl Grey (1927–), Anthony ◊Dowell, Merle ◊Park, and Lesley Collier (1947–); choreographers include Kenneth ◊MacMillan, Derek Deane, artistic director of the English National Ballet, and Christopher Gable (1940–1998), director of the Northern Ballet Theatre from 1987.

See table for the most popular ballets in the UK 1996–97; see also ◊modern dance and ◊contemporary dance.

ballot act

Legislation introduced by Gladstone's Liberal administration in 1872, providing for secret ballots in elections. The measure was opposed by landowners who would no longer be able to monitor, and hence control, the voting of their tenants. They defeated the measure when it was first presented in the Lords in 1871 but William Forster eventually secured its passage in July 1872.

ballroom dancing

The origins of ballroom dancing in Britain go back to the 16th century, when country dancing became very popular. In England both Henry VIII and Elizabeth I were enthusiastic dancers, the latter specifically encouraging the activity as an assertion of Englishness. Other dances were European imports, such as the pavane (originally from Padua, Italy, a favourite of Elizabeth I) and the gavotte (or la volta). The farandole can be traced back to the ancient Greeks (it is described in Homer's *Iliad*). In Scotland, Mary Queen of Scots imported the French courtly dances which gained popularity alongside Scottish reels and country dancing.

Contredanses (also known as square dances) became established in Britain where sets of couples danced in opposition to each other, instead of all facing the front (towards the monarch). Such ball dances became a proper accomplishment for 'gentlefolk'. Later in the 18th century, popular dances such as the waltz (originally from Germany), the polka (originally from Bohemia and made fashionable by the French), and the mazurka and the polonaise (from Poland) became popular in Britain.

The dance band years, starting from the Rag Time era of the late 19th century, brought more new dances to Britain, most of which originated in America. Some were a fusion of dances from the Afro-Caribbean (Latin American) dances, for example the mambo, cha cha cha, tango, samba, rumba, and habanera; others include the cakewalk, fox trot (1914), and the Lindy or Jitterbug.

In the early to mid-20th century ballroom dancing came to be specifically associated with a standardization of steps drawn from several of the above forms by dance teachers, most of them English, and eventually represented in competitive ballroom dancing. The first official Ballroom Dancing World Championships were held in London in 1960, organized by the International Council of Ballroom Dancing. The championships are held in Britain every other year; they have also been staged in West Germany, Australia, Japan, and the USA. These and the national and regional versions of both amateur and professional competitions held all over Britain are the subject of the televised *Come Dancing* series.

Ballroom dancing was also enjoyed at social and tea dances held from the 1930s onwards in venues all over Britain, ranging from village halls to the Palais de Danses dance halls (such as the Hammersmith Palais, London).

Ballycastle

Market town and seaside resort in the north of County Antrim, Northern Ireland; population (1991) 3,300. It is the port from which Rathlin Island is reached. Ballycastle's large Lammas Fair has been held on the last Tuesday in August since 1606.

There are a number of medieval ruins around Ballycastle, including Bonamargy friary (1 km east), an 11-m/35-ft round tower (8 km/5 mi south near Armoy), and Dunaneanie Castle (1 km west). Knocklayd Mountain (517 m/1,695 ft) is to the south, as is Ballycastle Forest; the sheer columnar basalt cliffs of Fairhead (190 m/626 ft) are 10 km/6 mi to the east, and impressive basaltic columns are also found at Grace Staples Cave to the west of Ballycastle.

The Italian inventor Guglielmo Marconi made the first successful wireless transmissions over water from Ballycastle to Rathlin Island in 1898.

Ballymena

Town in County Antrim, Northern Ireland, on the River Braid, 45 km/28 mi northwest of Belfast; population (1991) 28,300. The town has a range of textile, food-processing, and light engineering industries, and there are fish farms nearby. It was created as a Lowland Scots plantation in the 17th century.

Harryville Motte and Bailey, a 12th-century earthwork, is located on the southern outskirts of the town. Some 2 km/1 mi to the southwest is Galgorm Castle, built at the time of the plantation (1618–19), and Gracehill, a settlement established in 1746 by the Moravian Brethren sect of Protestants. Linen manufacture was introduced in Ballymena in 1733.

Balmoral Castle

Residence of the British royal family in Scotland on the River Dee, 10 km/6 mi northeast of Braemar, Aberdeenshire. The castle, built of granite in the Scottish baronial style, is dominated by a square tower and circular turret rising 30 m/100 ft. It was rebuilt between 1853 and 1855 by Prince Albert, who bought the estate in 1852 from Robert Gordon, and gave it to Queen Victoria.

Baltic, Battle of the

Naval battle fought off Copenhagen on 2 April 1801, in which a British fleet under Sir Hyde Parker, with ◊Nelson as second-in-command, annihilated the Danish navy.

Baltic Exchange, in full the Baltic Mercantile and Shipping Exchange

Market in London mainly for the chartering of freight. Most of the world's chartering of freight is carried out here, where cargo space on ships and aeroplanes is bought and sold. It originated in the 17th century when merchants and ships' captains met in coffee houses to organize cargoes, and was concentrated in the Baltic coffee house in 1810. It was destroyed by an IRA bomb in 1992.

When people say England, they sometimes mean Great Britain, sometimes the United Kingdom, sometimes the British Isles – but never England.

GEORGE MIKES Hungarian-born English writer.
How To Be An Alien (1946)

Bamburgh Castle

Castle in the village of Bamburgh on the coast of Northumberland, England. An imposing structure of red sandstone, it is situated 26 km/16 mi southeast of Berwick, and is built on a rock rising 46 m/151 ft above the North Sea. Founded in 547 by Ida, the first king of Northumbria, it was rebuilt in Norman times, and underwent extensive restoration in the 18th and 19th centuries. It was the scene of many battles in the Border wars of the 14th century, and changed hands several times during the Wars of the Roses. Henry VI ruled briefly from Bamburgh, but after the Battle of Hexham in 1464 it became the first English castle to fall to artillery. The castle is now open to the public.

Banbridge

Town in County Down, Northern Ireland, on the River Lower Bann, 35 km/22 mi southwest of Belfast; population (1991) 9,700. It is a shopping and service centre with a small textile industry and shoe manufacturing. In the past, the main industry in Banbridge was the manufacture of linen.

Lisnagade ring fort 5 km/3 mi southwest of Banbridge is the largest of the forts that marked the boundary of the ancient kingdoms of Ulaidh and Oriel. Scarva, 6 km/4 mi southwest of Banbridge, was the site where William III's armies gathered before marching to the Battle of the Boyne in 1690, and is therefore an important focus in the annual celebrations of Protestant Orangemen.

Banbury

Market town in Oxfordshire, central England, on the River Cherwell, 40 km/25 mi north of Oxford; population (1991) 39,900. Industries include food-processing (Kraft-Jacobs), traditional brewing (Hook Norton, Merivales), printing, and the manufacture of car components, electrical goods, and aluminium. The **Banbury Cross** of the nursery rhyme 'Ride a Cock Horse to Banbury Cross' was destroyed by the Puritans in 1602, but replaced in 1859. **Banbury cakes** are made from flaky or puff pastry with a filling of dried, spiced fruit.

Features

Nothing remains of the town's castle, built in 1125 and demolished by Banbury's inhabitants during the English Civil War. The townspeople also destroyed Banbury's medieval church with gunpowder in 1792, but it was replaced by a Neo-Classical church designed by Samuel Cockerell (1754–1827). The 19th-century Banbury Cross was erected to celebrate the marriage of the Princess Royal to the Prince of Prussia, although it was completed 18 months after the wedding. Broughton Castle, a moated 14th-century fortified manor house, lies 5 km/3 mi to the southwest. Banbury Museum illustrates the history of clothmaking in the town.

History

During the 13th century the town was an important wool-trading centre. New industries appeared after the opening of the Oxford Canal in 1790, which connected Banbury to the Midlands.

In 1469, during the Wars of the Roses, the Yorkists suffered a defeat nearby at the Battle of Banbury. During the English Civil War, Banbury surrendered to Charles I in 1642, and was besieged by the Parliamentarians led by John Fiennes in 1643 and 1644, and in 1646 when the garrison finally surrendered.

Banff

Town, holiday resort, and former royal burgh in Aberdeenshire unitary authority, Scotland, at the mouth of the River Deveron on the Moray Firth, 80 km/50 mi northwest of Aberdeen; population (1991) 4,100. Sea and river fishing, and a golf course, attract tourists.

The town received its first charter from Malcolm IV in 1163, and has many old buildings, including fine examples of 18th- and 19th-century Scottish architecture. Duff House, designed by the architect William ◊Adam, is now the main outpost of the National Galleries of Scotland.

Bangor

Resort and Belfast commuter town in County Down, Northern Ireland, on the shore of Belfast Lough, 20 km/12 mi northeast of Belfast; population (1991) 52,400. It is the site of a famous missionary abbey of the Celtic church, founded by St Comgall in 555 and sacked by the Danes in the 9th century. The abbey was the home of St Columbanus and St Gall. A Protestant church, the Abbey Church, was built on the site in 1617 by Thomas Hamilton (later Viscount Clandeboye). **Bangor Castle**, built by Robert Ward in 1852, is now the town hall and a heritage centre. Bangor has the largest marina in Ireland, and the Royal Ulster Yacht Club is based here.

A 7th-century prayer book, **The Antiphonary of Bangor**, one of the oldest ecclesiastical manuscripts in the world, was created in Bangor; the original manuscript is now housed in Milan, but a facsimile is housed in the museum of the Bangor Heritage Centre. The lands of Bangor were granted by James I to Thomas Hamilton in the 17th century, and planted with Scottish settlers. The lands were inherited by the Wards in the 18th century, the descendants of whom were responsible for promoting the textile industry in the area during the early 19th century.

Bangor

Cathedral, university and market town in Gwynedd, north Wales, on the Menai Strait 15 km/9 mi northeast of Caernarfon; population (1981) 12,300. Industries include chemicals, electrical goods, and engineering. Slate from Penrhyn quarries is exported.

Construction of the present cathedral, cruciform in shape, began in 1495. It was restored by Gilbert Scott between 1868 and 1880 and contains tombs of Welsh princes. A constituent college of the University of Wales is situated here, founded in 1884. Prehistoric and Roman remains are housed in the museum. Nearby Penrhyn Castle was built between 1820 and 1837 in mock-Norman style.

bank holiday

A public holiday, when banks are closed by law. Bank holidays were instituted by the Bank Holiday Acts 1871 and 1875.

In addition to Good Friday and Christmas Day, bank holidays in England and Wales are: New Year's Day, Easter Monday, 1 May, the last Monday in May, the last Monday in August, and the first weekday after Christmas (Boxing Day). In Scotland, although there is some local variation, there are bank holidays on: New Year's Day, 2 January (and 3 January if either 1 or 2 January falls on a Sunday), the first Monday in May, the first Monday in August, and Christmas Day. Northern Ireland has all the English holidays, with the addition of St Patrick's Day (17 March) and 12 July. The Channel Islands have all the English holidays, plus Liberation Day (9 May).

banking

Services of a financial institution, primarily a bank or ◊building society, offered to and used by the public and small businesses (retail banking) and large, often multinational or international organizations (wholesale banking). Other financial institutions include ◊friendly societies. The UK's central bank is the ◊Bank of England.

Changes in the banking sector

Banking in the UK changed dramatically in the last quarter of the 20th century. The traditional types of specialist financial institution have largely disappeared, with many companies originally in other sectors (especially retailing) now offering a wide range of services. This change, prompted by intense competition for clients, has been accompanied by the introduction of credit and debit cards, cash dispensing machines, telephone and computer banking, and a range of financial products such as ◊TESSAs and PEPs. Retail banking now offers not only the basic deposit and withdrawal facilities, money lending, money transmission, and foreign exchange, but also a selection of account and credit card types, insurance policies, mortgages, pension schemes, investment facilities and advice, accounting services, and so on.

Conversion of building societies to banks

In 1997, in a great wave of change in the banking world, five of the largest UK building societies became banks – the Halifax, Woolwich, Alliance and Leicester, Bristol and West, and Northern Rock plc – in order to diversify into a wider range of financial services. Following the flotation of the societies on the stock market, there were windfall gains for the former members to compensate for ceding their position of joint ownership to the new banking shareholders.

Other companies enter banking

Supermarkets, notably Tesco, Sainsbury, and Safeway, and insurance companies, including Prudential, Standard Life, and Legal and General, also introduced banking services in the 1990s, offering a convenient service to their customers. The greater ease of banking provided to the public, with increased flexibility and facilities at the site of spending, have contributed to the closure of many small local bank branches, which have also been edged out by greater centralization and the increase in use of telephone and computer banking.

International banking

The City of London is one of the world's major financial centres, together with New York and Tokyo, and a huge

Top Ten Largest Banks in the UK

Source: *FT500, FT Surveys, Financial Times*
This table is ranked by market capitalization. Market capitalization is the market value of a company's issued share capital, that is the quoted price of its shares multiplied by the number of shares issued.
(As of 22 January 1998)

Rank	Bank	1997 Market capitalization (£ millions)
1	HSBC Holdings	56,986.6
2	Lloyds TSB Group	44,980.0
3	Barclays	25,352.8
4	Halifax	18,323.0
5	National Westminster Bank	16,044.6
6	Abbey National	13,475.8
7	Standard Chartered	8,400.6
8	Bank of Scotland	6,147.1
9	Royal Bank of Scotland Group	5,972.8
10	Woolwich	4,976.0

BANKING: SOME KEY DATES

1672 Britannia makes her first appearance on British coins when a copper halfpenny and farthing are introduced.

27 July 1694 The Bank of England is founded by Parliament with capital of £1.2 million to fund the siege of Namur in the Spanish Netherlands. William Pateson is appointed the first governor.

1695 The Bank of England introduces banknotes for the first time.

1 January 1772 British banker Robert Herries issues the first traveller's cheques, in London, England. Sold as 'Circular Notes', they can be exchanged in 90 European cities.

1861 The Post Office Savings Bank opens in Britain.

1881 Postal Orders are introduced in Britain.

1916 The National Savings movement is launched in Britain to raise money for the war effort.

1 March 1946 The British government nationalizes the Bank of England.

1959 The first drive-in bank in Britain is opened in Liverpool.

7 March 1966 The Midland Bank in Britain is the first to introduce cheque guarantee cards.

29 June 1966 The first British credit card, the Barclaycard, is launched.

15 February 1971 Decimal currency is introduced in Britain: the pound is now worth 100 pence rather than 240 pennies.

2 June 1975 The British government introduces index-linked National Savings Certificates, which become known as 'Granny bonds'.

1 November 1983 The Nottingham Building Society and the Bank of Scotland jointly launch Homelink, the first telephone banking system in Britain. Operating through the television, using Prestel technology, it also offers teleshopping.

1986 The Building Societies Act allows building societies to offer many of the same services as banks.

1987 The Conservative government in Britain introduces Personal Equity Plans (PEPs), a scheme for tax-free share investment.

1987 The building society Nationwide Anglia in Britain introduces its Flex Account, the first cheque account giving interest.

3 June 1987 Barclay's Bank launches its Connect Card, the first debit card in Britain.

February 1989 Midland Bank introduces the first smartcard (which uses programmable microchips to store information rather than 'read-only' magnetic chips) in Britain, for students and staff at Loughborough University in England.

October 1990 Britain joins the European Community's Exchange Rate Mechanism (ERM), aimed at stabilizing currencies of member states.

September 1992 Britain abruptly pulls out of ERM, on what became known as Black Wednesday.

1995 The Royal Bank of Scotland becomes the first bank in the UK to offer its customers computer access to their accounts through a modem.

amount of international banking business is conducted here each year. See table for the largest UK banks.

Bank of England

UK central bank founded by act of Parliament in 1694. It was entrusted with issuing bank notes in 1844 and nationalized in 1946. It is banker to the clearing banks and the UK government.

As the government's bank, it manages and arranges the financing of the public sector borrowing requirement and the national debt, implements monetary policy and exchange-rate policy by intervening in foreign-exchange markets, sets interest rates (from 1997), and supervises the UK banking system. It is known by its London site as the *Old Lady of Threadneedle Street*.

Banks, Gordon (1937–)

English footballer. Banks kept goal for England's 1966 World Cup-winning side. Widely recognized as one of the world's greatest goalkeepers, his brilliant reflexes were most memorably displayed by his famous save from Pelé in the 1970 World Cup finals, which has been called the 'save of the century'. He won 73 full England caps between 1963 and 1972 before an eye injury sustained in a car accident prematurely ended his international career.

Banks, Iain (Menzies) (1954–)

Scottish novelist and writer of science fiction. His controversial first novel *The Wasp Factory* (1984) was criticized for its violence but critically acclaimed for its original style. His subsequent novels include *The Crow Road* (1992) (subsequently adapted for television) and *A Song of Stone* (1997). As Iain M Banks he produces works of science fiction, including *Against A Dark Background* (1993) and *Inversions* (1998).

Banks, Jeff (1943–)

English textile, fashion, and interior designer. He helped establish the Warehouse Utility chain in 1974 and combines imaginative designs with inexpensive materials to provide stylish and affordable garments for the younger market. He has presented the TV programme *The Clothes Show*, which encouraged broader interest in fashion among the British public.

Banks, Thomas (1735–1805)

English sculptor, one of the leading Neo-Classicists of the 18th century. He worked in Italy between 1772 and 1779, where he studied Greek and Roman art. In 1781 he went to St Petersburg, Russia, where he won the patronage of Catherine II, though he soon returned to London. There are monuments by Banks in Westminster Abbey and St Paul's Cathedral, London.

Bann

Name of two rivers in Northern Ireland: the Upper and Lower Bann. The **Upper Bann** rises in the Mourne Mountains and flows 65 km/40 mi northwest into Lough ◊Neagh on its southern side. The **Lower Bann** runs northwards from the northwest corner of Lough Neagh, flowing through Lough Beg and entering the Atlantic 8 km/5 mi south of Coleraine. For most of its 64 km/40 mi length it forms the boundary between counties Antrim and Londonderry.

There is much fishing in the Bann, particularly for roach, bream, pike, and sea trout, with salmon and eel fisheries on the Lower Bann. It is also a habitat for a variety of wildlife, with nature reserves and bird sanctuaries at Lough Neagh and Coleraine.

Bannister, Roger Gilbert (1929–)

English track and field athlete. He was the first person to run a mile in under four minutes. He achieved this feat at Oxford, England, on 6 May 1954, in a time of 3 min 59.4 sec.

Bannister broke the four-minute barrier on one more occasion: at the 1954 Commonwealth Games in Vancouver, Canada, when he was involved with John Landy (1930–) from Australia, in the 'Mile of the Century', so called because it was a clash between the only two people to have broken the four-minute barrier for the mile at that time. An eminent neurologist, he was knighted 1975.

Bannockburn, Battle of

Battle on 23–24 June 1314 in which ◊Robert (I) the Bruce of Scotland defeated the English under Edward II, who had come to relieve the besieged Stirling Castle. The battle is named after the town of Bannockburn, south of Stirling, central Scotland.

On 23 June the English vanguard attempted to force the road to Stirling, but their mounted attack was broken up by the Scots. The English knights then attempted to bypass the Scottish position via some low, boggy ground known as the Carse, but were again driven back again. The main army then camped below the Scottish position. The next morning, Bruce launched his pikemen in an attack downhill on the cramped English position. The battle hung in the balance until Scottish reserves came up, and the English position collapsed. English losses are reckoned at about 10,000 troops against about 4,000 Scots.

> *I felt like an exploded flashlight ... There is a certain oblivion at that point.*
>
> Roger Bannister English athlete. On crossing the finishing line at Oxford after running the mile in under four minutes, 6 May 1954

Bantock, Granville Ransome (1868–1946)

English composer and conductor; professor of music at the University of Birmingham 1908–34. He is chiefly known today for his colourful *Pierrot of the Minute* overture (1908). Also notable amongst his vast output in all genres, much of it inspired by the East, are the *Hebridean Symphony* (1915), the oratorio *Omar Khayyám* (1906–09), for chorus and orchestra, *Atalanta in Calydon* (1911), symphony for unaccompanied chorus and *Sappho*, an orchestral song cycle.

Bar, the

In law, the profession of ◊barristers collectively. To be **called**

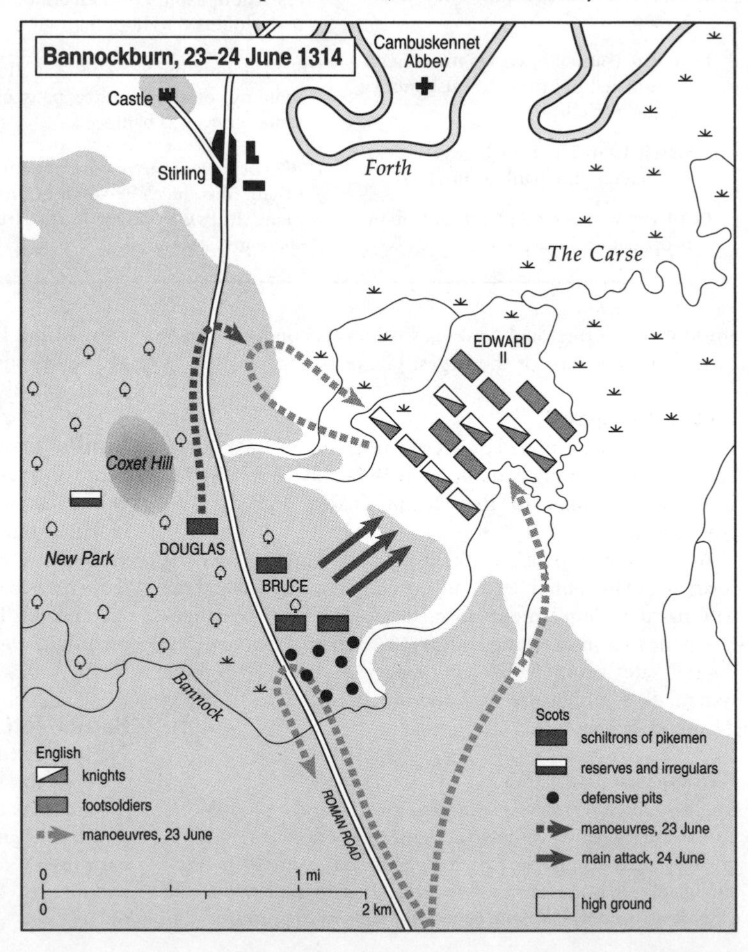

to the Bar is to become a barrister. Prospective barristers in the UK must not only complete a course of study in law but also be admitted to one of the four Inns of Court before they can be 'called'. The General Council of the Bar and of the Inns of Court (known as the Bar Council) is the professional governing body of the Bar.

barbarian conspiracy

Joint attack in AD 367 on Roman Britain from the north by Picts, Scots and Attacotti, and from Continental Europe by Franks and Saxons. Nectaridus, probably *comes* (count) of the Roman coastal defences known as the Saxon Shore, was killed in the raids. The Roman commanders in Britain, Jovinus and Severus, were unable to repel the raiders and the Emperor Valentinian sent Theodosius to restore order. He landed at Richborough in 368, marched on London, and reorganized Britain's defences. Despite his capable efforts, the attack was a great shock to Britain's defence system.

Barbican, the

Arts and residential complex in the City of London. The Barbican Arts Centre (1982) contains theatres, cinemas, and exhibition and concert halls. The architects were Powell, Chamberlin, and Bon.

Barbirolli, John (Giovanni Battista) (1899–1970)

English conductor. Barbirolli excelled in the Romantic repertory, especially the symphonies of Elgar, Sibelius, Mahler, and Vaughan Williams. Trained as a cellist, he succeeded Toscanini as conductor of the New York Philharmonic Orchestra 1937–43 and was conductor of the Hallé Orchestra, Manchester, 1943–70.

Barbour, John (*c.* 1320–1395)

Scottish poet. His epic 13,000-line poem *The Brus* (written 1374–75, printed 1571) chronicles the war of Scottish independence and includes a vivid account of Robert Bruce's victory over the English at Bannockburn in 1314. It is among the earliest known works of Scottish poetry.

Barbour was ordained a priest and was promoted by King David II to the archdeaconry of Aberdeen in about 1356. In 1357 he gained permission from Edward III of England to study in Oxford for a time. Under Robert II he became one of the auditors of the Exchequer.

Bardsey Island, Welsh Ynys Enlli (Welsh 'island of the currents')

Island in Gwynedd, off the coast of northwest Wales. It is a former pilgrimage centre, and has a 6th-century ruined abbey. It is sometimes called the island of 20,000 graves, as that number of saints are reputed to be buried here. It is a Site of Special Scientific Interest and has a bird and field observatory.

Barebones Parliament

English assembly called by Oliver ◊Cromwell to replace the 'Rump Parliament' in July 1653. Although its members attempted to pass sensible legislation (civil marriage; registration of births, deaths, and marriages; custody of lunatics), their attempts to abolish tithes, patronage, and the court of chancery, and to codify the law, led to the resignation of the moderates and its dissolution in December 1653.

The assembly consisted of 140 members selected by the army and derived its name from one of its members, Praise-God Barbon.

Baring Brothers

UK merchant bank, founded in 1763 by John (1730–1816) and Francis Baring (1740–1810). The bank went into administration in February 1995 after its leading trader in Singapore, Nicholas Leeson, lost around £250 million of its assets in unauthorized transactions, mainly high-risk derivative contracts. The bank was able to resume trading in March 1995 after being purchased by a Dutch company, Internationale Nederlanden Groep NV.

Leeson was sentenced by a Singapore court in December 1995 to six and a half years in prison for his actions in the affair. In May 1995 21 executives, who had also been found to be partially responsible for the bank's crash, resigned.

History

The oldest merchant bank in London, Baring Brothers adopted its name in 1807. By the 1830s it was one of the world's most important banking houses, underwriting the purchase of Louisiana from the French, for example, and financing much of the railway development in North America.

The bank collapsed in 1890 following a default on debt repayments by the Argentine government, leading to the first ever intervention in the British banking system by the Bank of England, which injected some £17 million to prevent the bank suspending payments and consequent financial catastrophe. The business was later refounded and control subsequently passed back to descendants of the original founders.

Barker, George Granville (1913–1991)

English poet. He is known for his vivid imagery, as in *Calamiterror* (1937), *The True Confessions of George Barker* (1950), *Collected Poems* (1930–50), and the posthumously published *Street Ballads* (1992).

Barker, Howard (1946–)

English playwright whose plays examine the human spirit when it is subjected to dictatorship, whether mental or physical. Among his works are *Victory* (1982), *The Castle* (1985), *The Last Supper*, *The Possibilities*, and *The Bite of the Night* (all 1988), *Seven Lears* (1989), *Hated Nightfall* (1993), and *Wounds to the Face* (1994). In 1988 he formed The Wrestling School, a theatre company dedicated to the performance of his own work. He directed *Hated Nightfall* in 1994 and *Judith* in 1995.

Barker, Pat (Patricia Margaret) (1943–)

English author. She received critical acclaim for her 'Regeneration' trilogy, an evocative exploration of World War I blending fact and fiction, and comprising *Regeneration* (1991), *The Eye in the Door* (1993) which won the Guardian Fiction Prize, and *The Ghost Road* (1995) which won the Booker Prize. *Another World* was published in 1997.

Barker, Ronnie, stage name of Ronald William George Barker (1929–)

English comedian, actor, and radio performer. For much of his performing career he was associated with comic sketch series, from the television series *The Frost Report* in the 1960s, to (from 1971) the long-running *The Two Ronnies* in which he performed alongside Scottish comedian Ronnie Corbett.

During the 1970s he also created the popular character of recidivist Norman Stanley Fletcher in the comedy series *Porridge* and *Going Straight*, and the curmudgeonly cornershop owner Arkwright in *Open All Hours*. Following the television series *Clarence* (1988), he retired from acting to run an antiques business.

> *The marvellous thing about a joke with a double meaning is that it can only mean one thing.*
>
> Ronnie Barker English comic actor and writer.
> *Sauce*, 'Daddie's Sauce'

Barking and Dagenham

Outer London borough of east Greater London

Features 15th–16th-century St Margaret's Church; Barking Abbey, with its 15th-century tower; Cross Keys Inn at Dagenham (about 1500); Quaker burial ground where Elizabeth Fry is buried

Industries paint; telephone cables; pharmaceuticals

Population (1991) 143,700.

Barnardos

UK's largest child-care charity, founded by Thomas Barnardo (1845–1905), who opened the first of a series of homes for destitute children in 1867 in Stepney, east London. Barnardo was known as Dr Barnardo although he was not medically qualified, and the homes came to be known as Dr Barnardo's Homes. Eventually there were more than 90 of them. The charity, now known as Barnardos, no longer runs homes, but instead directs its funds towards supporting disadvantaged children in the community.

Barnes, Julian (Patrick) (1946–)

English novelist. His first novel, *Metroland*, was published in 1981, followed by *Before She Met Me* in 1982. It was his third novel, *Flaubert's Parrot* (1984) – skilfully combining fiction, biography, and essay – that brought him an international reputation, winning the French *Prix Medicis Etrangère* (the first British book to do so). Later works include *The Porcupine* (1992), a political parable, *Cross Channel* (1996), a collection of stories about the British in France, and *England, England* (1998), a futuristic comedy with a moral for the present.

He has also published detective novels under the name Dan Kavanagh.

Barnet

Outer London borough of northwest Greater London. It includes the district of Hendon

Features

site of the Battle of Barnet (1471) in one of the Wars of the ◊Roses; Lawrence Campe almshouses (1612); Hadley Woods; department for newspapers and periodicals of the British Library at Colindale; Metropolitan Police Training Centre and Royal Air Force Battle of Britain and Bomber Command museums in Hendon; Hampstead Garden Suburb

Population

(1991) 293,600.

Barnet, Battle of

In the Wars of the ◊Roses, the defeat of Lancaster by York on 14 April 1471 in Barnet (now in northwest London).

Barnsley

Town and administrative headquarters of Barnsley metropolitan borough, South Yorkshire, England, on the River Dearne, 26 km/16 north of Sheffield; population (1991) Barnsley 75,100; Dearne Valley urban area 211,500. It lies on one of Britain's richest coal fields, although the industry is in decline. Manufactured products include steel, glass, paper, carpets, cakes (Lyons), sports equipment (Dunlop-Slazenger), and clothing. The headquarters of the National Union of Mineworkers are sited here.

Barnsley was mentioned in the Domesday Book of 1086. The town received the right to hold a market in 1249, and open-air and covered markets are still held. The Classical-style town hall was built in 1933. Cannon Hall, built in about 1765, is now a country-house museum. The Cooper Art Gallery includes a collection of English drawings and 19th- and 20th-century watercolours.

> *It [the Isle of Wight] was one of the first places in Great Britain to be perverted by becoming a tourist destination. It was a rather undeveloped, old-fashioned, quite primitive offshore island until sunbathing became fashionable. Queen Victoria and Tennyson went there and that did for it. Sea-bathing became all the rage. The traditional industries of smuggling and boat-building lost out to tourism.*
>
> Julian Barnes English author.
> Interviewed in the *Daily Telegraph* about *England, England* (1998).

Barnsley, Michael

British computer graphics researcher who in the mid-1980s developed fractal image compression. In *Fractals Everywhere* (1988) he sets out the use of fractal geometry as a language that allows the precise description of any object, thereby making it possible to program computers to produce even the most complex images.

Barnstaple

Town and port in Devon, England, 96 km/60 mi northwest of Exeter; population (1981) 24,900. It is situated 10 km/6 mi from the mouth of the River Taw, and has a tidal harbour; the Taw is crossed by a 12th-century bridge with 16 arches. Barnstaple is the centre for agriculture, commerce, administration, and tourism in north Devon. Lace, gloves, furniture, and pottery are also manufactured here.

Barnstaple has a 14th-century parish church, a castle mound, and a grammar school, endowed in 1649, which occupies part of a ruined monastery. The poet John Gay was educated at the school.

baron

Rank in the ◊peerage of the UK, above a baronet and below a viscount. Historically, any member of the higher nobility, a direct vassal (feudal servant) of the king, not bearing other titles such as duke or count. The term originally meant the vassal of a lord, but acquired its present meaning in the 12th century.

The first English barony to be created by 'patent' was created in 1387, but barons created by 'writ' existed earlier. Life peers, created under the Act of 1958, are always of this rank. The wife of a baron, or a woman holding a title in her own right, is a **baroness**.

baronage

Collective title for all the landed nobility of medieval England, including earls and other important tenants-in-chief, as well as the barons.

baronet

Order of chivalry below the rank of baron, but above that of knight, created in 1611 by James I to finance the settlement of Ulster. It is a hereditary honour, although women cannot succeed to a baronetcy. A baronet does not have a seat in the House of Lords but is entitled to the style *Sir* before his name. The sale of baronetcies was made illegal in 1937.

Barons' Wars

Civil wars in England:

1215–17 between King ◊John and his barons, over his failure to honour ◊Magna Carta; **1264–67** between ◊Henry III (and the future ◊Edward I) and his barons (led by Simon de ◊Montfort); **1264** 14 May Battle of Lewes at which Henry III was defeated and captured; **1265** 4 August Simon de Montfort was defeated by Edward at Evesham and killed.

Baroque

Expressive, flamboyant, and dynamic, Baroque style flourished mainly in the Catholic countries of Europe from 1600 to 1750, and had a comparatively small impact in the predominantly Protestant north of Europe, including Britain. Rubens and Van Dyck, two of the greatest Baroque painters, both worked in England for Charles I, but there were no native British painters of comparable quality at this time to sustain their influence.

The most important British contribution to Baroque art came in a brief period at the end of the 17th century and beginning of the 18th century, when Christopher ◊Wren (in his late work), Nicholas ◊Hawksmoor, and John ◊Vanbrugh created a number of superb buildings that have all the vigour of Continental Baroque art combined with a distinctive British robustness. At the same time there was a short-lived fashion for wall and ceiling painting in a flamboyant Baroque style. Several foreign painters, including Laguerre and Verrior, worked in Britain in this vein; the leading native-born exponent was James ◊Thornhill. By about 1720 taste was turning away from Baroque in favour of the more sober Palladianism.

The term Baroque has also been used to describe the music and literature of the period but is more a convenient label than a stylistic description. George Frideric ◊Handel and Henry ◊Purcell were Britain's foremost Baroque composers.

Barra

Southern island of the larger Outer ◊Hebrides, Scotland, part of the Western Isles unitary council area; area 90 sq km/35 sq mi; population (1991) 1,300. It is separated from South Uist by the Sound of Barra. The principal town is Castlebay. The main industries are fishing and tourism.

Scheduled air services land at low tide on the beach at Traigh Mhor in the north. Car ferries sail from Castlebay to and from Oban, Lochboisdale on South Uist, and Mallaig on the mainland. The medieval Kisimul Castle, once home of the piratical clan McNeil, is situated on a rock off Castlebay. The novelist Compton ◊Mackenzie is buried at St Barr's church.

Barrett Browning, Elizabeth

English poet; see ◊Browning, Elizabeth Barrett.

Barrie, J(ames) M(atthew) (1860–1937)

Scottish dramatist and novelist. His work includes *The Admirable Crichton* (1902) and the children's fantasy *Peter Pan* (1904).

After early studies of Scottish rural life in plays such as *A Window in Thrums* (1889), his reputation as a dramatist was established with *The Professor's Love Story* (1894) and *The Little Minister* (1897). Later plays include *Quality Street* (1901) and *What Every Woman Knows* (1908).

> *You've forgotten the grandest moral attribute of a Scotsman, Maggie, that he'll do nothing which might damage his career.*
>
> JAMES MATTHEW BARRIE Scottish dramatist and novelist. *What Every Woman Knows* II

Barrington Court

Tudor mansion in Somerset, England, 5 km/3 mi northeast of Ilminster. Although purchased by the National Trust in 1907, the derelict mansion and adjoining 17th-century stable block were not restored and refurnished until after World War I. The mansion has a garden designed by Gertrude ◊Jekyll.

barrister

A lawyer qualified by study at the ◊Inns of Court to plead for a client in court. In Scotland such lawyers are called advocates. Barristers also undertake the writing of opinions on the prospects of a case before trial. They act for clients through the intermediary of ◊solicitors.

Traditionally, in the highest courts, only barristers could represent litigants, but this distinction between barristers and solicitors was abolished in the 1990s. When pupil barristers complete their training they are 'called to the Bar': this being the name of the ceremony in which they are admitted as members of the profession. Barristers remain outside the bar until they become ◊Queen's Counsel, appointed on the recommendation of the Lord Chancellor, when they 'take silk' (wear a silk instead of a stuff gown) and are called 'within the Bar'.

In Britain, a barrister is obliged to accept instructions from any client who wants their services, provided the case is within the lawyer's expertise and the client can pay the fee – the 'cab rank rule'. The barrister is not, therefore, personally vouching for a client's case, and cannot turn down a case because of their perception of a client's guilt or innocence.

barrow

Burial mound, usually composed of earth but sometimes also of stones. The two main types are **long**, dating from the Neolithic period (New Stone Age), and **round**, dating from the Mesolithic period (early Bronze Age). Barrows made entirely of stones are known as cairns.

Some **long** barrows may be mere mounds, typically higher and wider at one end. The body or bodies of the deceased were usually placed in a turf-lined cavity, or a chamber of wood or stone slabs with a single entrance. This type is common in southern England from Sussex to Dorset. The remains of these stone chambers, once their earth covering has disappeared, are known as **dolmens**, and in Wales as **cromlechs**.

Round barrows belong mainly to the Bronze Age. In Britain they are commonly associated with the Wessex culture (2000–1500 BC). There are also some barrows from the Roman era; these have a distinctive steep and conical outline, and often contain the graves of wealthy merchant traders; similar mounds are also found in Belgic Gaul, where the traders had commercial links. The Saxons buried the remains of important chieftains in large barrows (see ◊Sutton Hoo), but clusters of small burial mounds are more commonly found.

Barrow, Isaac (1630–1677)

English mathematician, theologian, and classicist. His *Lectiones geometricae* (1670) contains the essence of the theory of calculus, which was later expanded by Isaac ◊Newton and Gottfried Leibniz.

Barrow was born in London and studied at Cambridge, where he was professor of mathematics 1663–69. Isaac Newton attended his lectures and was inspired by Barrow's work in the field of optics. To Barrow is due the credit for two original contributions: the method of finding the point of refraction at a plane interface, and his point construction of the diacaustic of a spherical interface.

Barrow-in-Furness

Industrial port in Cumbria, northwest England, at the south end of the ◊Furness peninsula; population (1991) 48,900. Industries include shipbuilding, engineering, the manufacture of chemicals and nuclear submarines, and those industries associated with offshore gasfields; the British Gas pipeline from Morecambe Field in the Irish Sea comes ashore here. Nearby to the northeast are the ruins of Furness Abbey (1127). ◊Walney Island is linked to Barrow by a bridge over Walney Channel.

Barrow developed with the growth of the iron, steel, and shipbuilding industries in the 19th century. The steel works closed in 1983. Contraction within the shipbuilding industry was alleviated in the mid-1990s by UK government orders; two Royal Navy amphibious warfare ships (Landing Platform Docks), requested in 1996, were the first surface vessels to be built in Barrow since 1980. The Dock Museum traces the history of shipbuilding in the town.

BARRY, CHARLES *Charles Barry, one of the leading British architects of the 19th century. Much of his work is in a rich classical style recalling the palaces of the Italian Renaissance, but his most famous building, the Houses of Parliament in London, is Gothic Revival. However, the detailing was not by Barry himself, but by the Gothic specialist A W N Pugin. Corbis*

Barry, Welsh Y Barri

Port and administrative centre of the ◊Vale of Glamorgan, south Wales, 12 km/7 mi southwest of Cardiff; population (1991) 49,900. With **Barry Island**, it is a holiday resort. Its large docks (0.46 sq km/0.29 sq mi), opened in 1889 to export coal, led to its emergence as an important port for trade with the Windward Islands in the West Indies. Since the decline of the docks they have become the site of tourist-related development, including pleasure steamers. The chemical industry is a major source of local employment. There is a tidal basin of 360,000 sq m/3,875,000 sq ft between the mainland and Barry Island in the Bristol Channel.

Barry, Charles (1795–1860)

English architect. He designed the Neo-Gothic new Palace of Westminster, London (the Houses of Parliament; 1840–60), in collaboration with A W N ◊Pugin. His early designs for the Travellers Club (1829–23) and for the Reform Club (1837), both in London, were in Renaissance style.

His winning design for the new Houses of Parliament was picked from a field of 97 submissions in 1836. Later works included Dulwich College schools (1841), Halifax town hall (1859–62), and several very large mansions, notably Eynsham Hall, Oxfordshire (1843); and ◊Cliveden House, Buckinghamshire (1851).

He was knighted in 1852.

Barstow, Stan (1928–)

English novelist. His realist novels describe northern working-class life and include *A Kind of Loving* (1960) (filmed in 1962), a first-person, present-tense narrative of a young man trapped into marriage. He ranks with John Braine, Alan Sillitoe, David Storey, and Keith Waterhouse as a contributor to the modern regional novel.

Bart, Lionel (1930–)

English composer. He wrote both the words and music for many musicals including *Fings Ain't Wot They Us'd T'Be* (1959) and *Oliver!* (1960).

Barton, Derek Harold Richard (1918–)

English organic chemist. Barton investigated the stereochemistry of natural compounds. He showed that their biological activity often depends on the shapes of their molecules and the positions and orientations of key functional groups. He created the branch of organic chemistry known as conformational analysis. He shared the 1969 Nobel Prize for Chemistry.

Barton, John (1928–)

English theatre director. He became associate director of the Royal Shakespeare Company in 1960 and directed and devised numerous productions for the company, including *The Hollow Crown* (1961), *The Wars of the Roses* (1963), Shakespeare's history plays (1964), *The Greeks* (1980), and *Life's a Dream* (1984). Television work includes the series of workshops *Playing Shakespeare* (1982).

Barton-upon-Humber

Ancient market town in North Lincolnshire, England; population (1991) 9,100. It is situated on the south bank of the River Humber, close to the southern end of the Humber Bridge. Barton is a centre for chemical manufacturing, oil refining, and engineering.

Barton-upon-Humber was one of the main ports on the Humber during the Norman Conquest.

Bart's

Shortened form of St Bartholomew's Hospital in Smithfield, London, one of the great teaching hospitals of England. It was founded by Henry VIII at the Reformation.

Basic English

Simplified form of English devised and promoted by the writer and scholar C K ◊Ogden and the literary critic I A ◊Richards in the 1920s and 1930s as an international auxiliary language; as a route into ◊Standard English for foreign learners (little used now); and as a reminder to the English-speaking world of the virtues of plain language. Its name derives from the initial letters of *B*ritish, *A*merican, *s*cientific, *i*nternational, and *c*ommercial.

Basic has a vocabulary of 850 words (plus names, technical terms, and so on), only 18 of which are verbs or 'operators'. *Get* therefore replaces 'receive', 'obtain', and 'become', while *buy* is replaced by the phrase 'give money for'.

Basildon

Industrial town in Essex, eastern England, 19 km/12 mi southwest of Chelmsford; population (1994 est) 101,000. It was designated a ◊new town in 1949 to accommodate overspill population from London. Industries include printing, engineering, and the manufacture of chemicals and clothing.

Basingstoke

Town in Hampshire, England, 72 km/45 mi west-southwest of London; population (1991) 77,800. It is a financial and insurance service centre, containing the headquarters of the Automobile Association and Sun Life Insurance. Industries include light engineering, food-processing, printing, publishing, and the manufacture of cosmetics (Wella, Alberto-Culver), scientific instruments, medical equipment, agricultural machinery, and electronics.

The Milestones museum, a major cultural project to mark the millennium, will explore developments in transport and technology, and their effects on people's lives.

The population of Basingstoke grew rapidly when it began to take overspill population from London in the 1960s, and developed as a business and industrial centre.

Features

Many traces of Roman occupation have been discovered in the area. The Willis Museum and Art Gallery, in the Old Town Hall, includes local archaeological exhibits, as well as a collection of clocks, watches, costumes, and textiles.

In the nearby village of **Basing** are the ruins of Basing House, a Tudor mansion built on the site of a Norman castle, and the scene of a two-year siege during the English Civil War. In 1645 Parliamentary forces, led by Oliver Cromwell, overwhelmed the Marquess of Winchester and his Royalist followers here; the architect Inigo Jones was among those taken prisoner.

Bassey, Shirley (1937–)

Welsh cabaret singer with a huge voice and large following. Early hits such as 'Kiss Me Honey Honey Kiss Me' (1958), and 'As I Love You' (1959), were followed by a number of others, including 'What Now My Love?' (1962) and 'Hey Big Spender' (1967). She sang the theme tune for the James Bond film *Diamonds Are Forever* (1971), but record hits declined in the mid-1970s and she devoted herself mainly to concert and cabaret performing. However in 1998 she featured on the single 'History Repeating', with the Propellerheads.

Bass Rock

Volcanic islet in the Firth of Forth, Scotland, 5 km/3 mi from North Berwick. It is about 107 m/350 ft high, and has a ruined castle, a chapel, and a lighthouse. It is a seabird sanctuary, home to the third largest gannetry in the world and the largest in Britain.

Bass Rock's castle, which dates from the 16th century, was converted by the English government after 1671 into a state prison in which several eminent Covenanters were confined. The rock was captured in 1691 and held until 1694 for James II by 16 Jacobites against a small army of William III.

Bateman's

Jacobean farmhouse, 1 km/0.6 mi south of Burwash, East Sussex, England. It is built in local stone and was Rudyard ◊Kipling's home from 1902 to 1936. The house and 120 ha/296 acres, including the gardens, were left to the National Trust in 1939 by Mrs Kipling.

The stories 'Rewards and Fairies' and 'Puck of Pook's Hill' were written here; Pook's Hill can be seen from the lawn.

BATES, ALAN *English film actor Alan Bates. Bates, pictured in 1970, first came to prominence in the early 1960s, and went on to produce a series of commanding screen performances in such films as* Whistle Down the Wind *(1961),* Far From the Madding Crowd *(1967),* Women in Love *(1969),* The Go-Between *(1971), and* An Unmarried Woman *(1978). Corbis*

Bates, Alan (Arthur) (1934–)

English actor. He has proved himself a versatile male lead in over 60 plays and films. His films include *Zorba the Greek* (1965), *Far from the Madding Crowd* (1967), *Women in Love* (1970), *The Go-Between* (1971), *The Shout* (1978), *Duet for One* (1986), and *We Think the World of You* (1988). Recent film work includes *Varya* (1998), a Greek adaptation of Chekhov's *The Cherry Orchard*.

Throughout his lengthy career on stage and screen Bates has studiously avoided being stereotyped, serving up fresh, rounded characters in every performance, whether as Shakespeare's Anthony in the National Theatre's production of *Anthony and Cleopatra* (1998), the romantic lead of *The Go-Between* and *An Unmarried Woman* (1978), or Marcel Proust in the television movie *102 Boulevard Haussmann* (1991). He was made a CBE in 1996.

Bates, H(enry) W(alter) (1825–1892)

English naturalist and explorer. He spent 11 years collecting animals and plants in South America and identified 8,000 new species of insects. He made a special study of camouflage in animals, and his observation of insect imitation of species that are unpleasant to predators is known as 'Batesian mimicry'.

Bates was born in Leicester and left school at 13, but studied natural history in his spare time. In 1844 he met English naturalist Alfred Russel ◊Wallace, and together they travelled to the Amazon region of South America in 1848 to study and collect its flora and fauna. Wallace returned to England in 1852 but Bates remained until 1859. He returned with a vast number of specimens, including more than 14,000 species of insects.

Bates, H(erbert) E(rnest) (1905–1974)

English writer. He was most successful in capturing the feeling of life in the changing English countryside, and his stories are written in a simple, direct, and deeply compassionate manner. Of his many novels and short stories, *The Jacaranda Tree* (1949) and *The Darling Buds of May* (1958) particularly demonstrate the fineness of his natural observation and compassionate portrayal of character. *Fair Stood the Wind for France* (1944) was based on his experience as a squadron leader in World War II, during which he also wrote stories under the pseudonym Flying Officer X.

The five chronicles of the Larkin family began with *The Darling Buds of May*, and also included *A Breath of French Air* (1959), *When the Green Woods Laugh* (1960), *Oh! To be in England* (1963), and *A Little of What You Fancy* (1970). The novels were filmed as a television series in the 1990s.

Bateson, William (1861–1926)

English geneticist. Bateson was one of the founders of the science of genetics (a term he introduced), and a leading proponent of Austrian biologist Gregor Mendel's work on heredity. Bateson also made contributions to embryology and to the theory of evolution.

Bath

Historic city and administrative headquarters of ◊Bath and North East Somerset unitary authority, southwest England, 171 km/106 mi west of London; population (1991) 78,700. Industries include printing, plastics, engineering, and tourism. Bath was the site of the Roman town of **Aquae Sulis**, and in the 18th century flourished as a fashionable spa, with the only naturally occurring hot mineral springs in Britain. Although the baths were closed to the public in 1977, a Millennium Spa Project is intended to bring back public bathing to Bath's hot springs. The city of Bath is a World Heritage Site.

History

The Roman town of Aquae Sulis ('waters of Sul' – the British goddess of wisdom) was established in the first 20 years after the Roman invasion of AD 43. In medieval times the springs were crown property, administered by the church, but the city was transformed in the 18th century to a fashionable spa, presided over by 'Beau' ◊Nash.

Features

The remains of the Roman baths and adjacent temple are among the finest Roman remains in Britain. The Gothic Bath Abbey has an unusually decorated west front and fine fan-vaulting. The city has much 18th-century architecture, including Queen Square and the Circus, designed by John Wood the Elder, the Assembly Rooms (1771) and Royal Crescent, designed by the younger John Wood (1728–1782). The Bath Festival Orchestra is based here and the University of Bath was established in 1966.

Roman baths and temple

The remains of the Roman baths and the temple dedicated to Sulis Minerva, established around the hot springs after AD 60 and built over during the medieval period, were not excavated until the late 19th century. Now about 6 m/20 ft below street level, the open-air Great Bath was originally covered and occupied a hall measuring about 34 m/110 ft by 21 m/68 ft; the pillars date from the 19th century, but the bath itself has its original lead floor, and the surrounding pavement is well preserved. The baths complex also includes a tepid bath, a small semicircular bath, a cold circular bath, remains of the hypocaust (floor raised on tile piers, heated by hot air circulating beneath it), and the Norman King's Bath. Excavations in 1979 revealed thousands of coins and 'curses', offered at a place which was thought to be the link between the upper and lower worlds. The museum adjoining the baths complex displays examples of these offerings; other exhibits include a bronze head of Sulis Minerva and the reconstructed pediment of the temple, with a gorgon's head at its centre.

Hot springs

Rich in radium emanation, the hot spring water (46.5°C/116°F) which surfaces at Bath is thought to have medicinal and therapeutic properties, beneficial in the treatment of gout, rheumatism, and skin diseases. The waters may still be taken in the Pump Room.

Architectural features

The 18th-century buildings of Bath are mostly built of Bath Stone, a white freestone. The shop-lined Italianate Pulteney Bridge (1769–74) was designed by Robert Adam. The Pump Room dates from 1792–96. The Assembly Rooms were destroyed in an air raid in 1942 and re-opened in 1963; they now house the Museum of Costume. The Royal Crescent (1767–74), to the northwest of the city centre, comprises an arc of 30 houses overlooking a sloping lawn. The Guildhall (1768–75) includes the Victoria Art Gallery. The astronomer William Herschel discovered Uranus while working here in 1781; his house is now a museum.

The city suffered heavy aerial attacks during World War II, particularly in the 'Baedeker raids' (April 1942). Over 200 buildings of architectural or historic value were either destroyed or seriously damaged.

Bath Abbey

The present Abbey church, a fine example of Perpendicular Gothic architecture, was begun in 1499. It was built on the site of a Saxon abbey (founded in 775), in which Edgar, the first King of All England, was crowned in 973. The carved decoration on the west front of the present Abbey depicts angels ascending and descending ladders on the turrets on each side of the window.

Bath and North East Somerset

Unitary authority in southwest England created in 1996 from part of the former county of Avon

Area 351 sq km/136 sq mi

Towns and cities ◊Bath (administrative headquarters), Keynsham, Chew Magna, Paulton, Radstock, Peasedown St John, Midsomer Norton

Features River Avon and tributaries; Chew Valley Lake; Beckford's Tower (Bath) built in 1827 for William Beckford; Roman baths with hot springs and Regency architecture (Bath); Stanton Drew bronze age stone circles including second largest in Great Britain.

Industries tourism, central government administration, clothing manufacture

Population (1996) 158,700.

Bathgate

Town in West Lothian unitary authority, Scotland, 10 km/6 mi south of Linlithgow; population (1991) 13,800. Originally a coalmining centre, with the Easton colliery nearby, Bathgate's economy subsequently diversified, with the motor industry becoming a principal employer.

James Young Simpson, pioneer of the use of chloroform in

surgery in 1847, was born in Bathgate in 1811. The experiments of his namesake James Young (1811–83) around 1850 led to the first commercial refinement of oil from coal set up locally at the village of Pumpherston.

Bath, Order of the

British order of knighthood (see ◊knighthood, orders of), believed to have been founded in 1399 by Henry IV. The order now consists of three classes: Knights of the Grand Cross (GCB), Knights Commanders (KCB), and Knights Companions (CB).

Batley

Town in West Yorkshire, England, 14 km/9 mi southwest of Leeds; population (1991) 34,600. Batley originated the heavy reprocessed cloth known as 'shoddy', and is still a centre for the heavy woollen trade. It has a 13th-century church and a Victorian Gothic mansion which is now a museum of ethnography. Oakwell Hall, in nearby Birstall, is a 15th-century manor house, and was the inspiration for 'Fieldhead' in Charlotte Brontë's novel *Shirley*.

Battenberg

Title conferred in 1851 on a German noble family. Members of the family included Louis ◊Mountbatten, who anglicized his name to Mountbatten in 1917 due to anti-German feeling in Britain during World War I.

Battersea

District of the Inner London borough of Wandsworth on the south bank of the Thames. It has a park (including a funfair 1951–74), Battersea Dogs' Home (opened in 1860) for strays, and Battersea Power Station (1937, designed by Giles Gilbert Scott, with an Art Deco interior), closed in 1983. A listed building from 1980, a scheme to convert the power station to an Edwardian theme park and leisure centre collapsed in 1989 after removal of the roof and gutting of the interior led to escalating costs. Failure to refinance the project led to the sale of the power station in 1993 to the Hwang family, Hong Kong property developers. Plans were approved in 1996 for its conversion into a leisure complex. Work was scheduled for completion in 2000.

Battle

Town in East Sussex, southeast England, named after the Battle of ◊Hastings, which took place here in 1066. The remains of the Benedictine abbey of St Martin's, founded by William (I) the Conqueror to commemorate his victory over Harold II, lie nearby.

The abbey was built on the ridge above the hamlet of Senlac. It is said that the high altar was erected on the spot where Harold was killed, and the site is now marked by a memorial stone. The foundation was dissolved in 1537, but remnants of the turreted abbey gatehouse (1338) and the refectory survive.

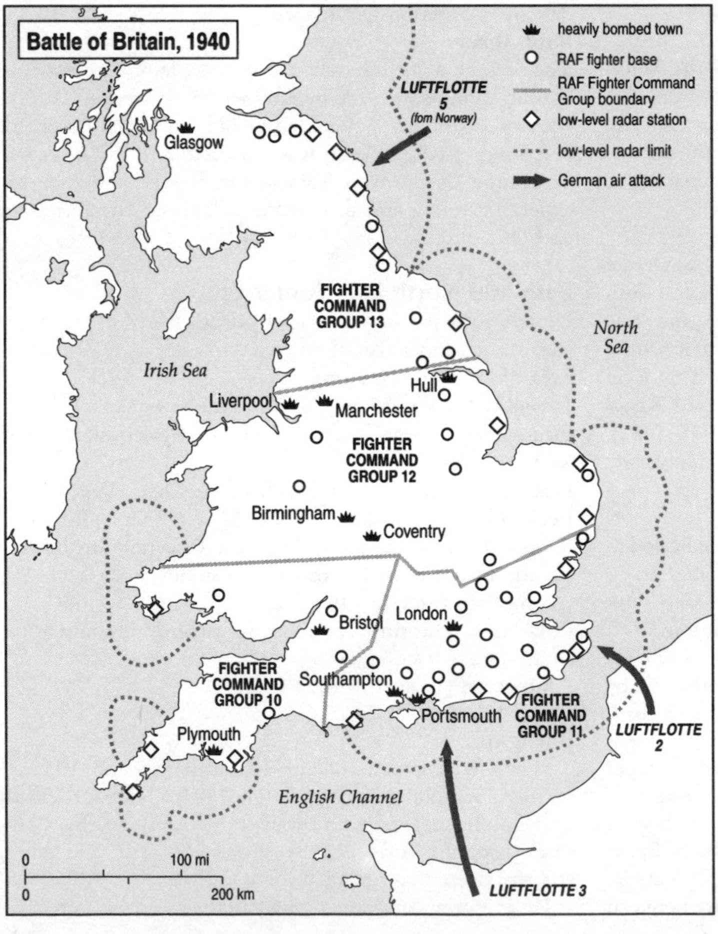

Battle of Britain

World War II air battle between German and British air forces over Britain 10 July–31 October 1940.

At the outset the Germans had the advantage because they had seized airfields in the Netherlands, Belgium, and France, which were basically safe from attack and from which southeast England was within easy range. The Battle of Britain had been intended as a preliminary to the German invasion plan, which Hitler postponed indefinitely on 17 September and abandoned on 10 October, choosing instead to invade the USSR. The battle has been divided into five phases: a preliminary phase; an attack on coastal targets; an attack on Fighter Command airfields; and two daylight attacks on London. See table opposite for aircraft losses on both sides.

Bawden, Nina Mary (1925–)

English novelist and writer of books for children. Her novels for adults, which focus on the lives of the middle classes, include *Who Calls the Tune* (1953), *Circles of Deceit* (1987) (short-listed

Battle of Britain: Aircraft Losses

aircraft losses 10 July–31 Oct 1940

period	RAF		Luftwaffe		
	fighter	other	bomber[1]	fighter[2]	other
10–30 July	75 (27)	8 (1)	116 (31)	49	9 (6)
31 July–27 Aug	284 (30)	30 (7)	306 (53)	268 (35)	21 (9)
28 Aug–1 Oct	471 (32)	12 (5)	345 (78)	400 (41)	28 (18)
2–31 Oct	174 (57)	11 (7)	194 (68)	162 (36)	19 (9)
total	1,004 (146)	61 (20)	961 (230)	879 (112)	77 (42)

figures in brackets indicate aircraft lost in accidents (included in total figures)

[1]Luftwaffe bombers include Ju 87 divebombers [2]Luftwaffe fighters include Me110 twin-engine fighters

for the Booker Prize), and *Family Money* (1991). Among her novels for children are *The Witch's Daughter* (1966), the acclaimed *Carrie's War* (1973) (the story of a child being evacuated to Wales during World War II), *Keeping Henry* (1988), and *The Real Plato Jones* (1994).

Bayes, Thomas (1702–1761)
English mathematician whose investigations into probability led to what is now known as Bayes' theorem.

Bayeux Tapestry
Linen hanging made about 1067–70 which gives a vivid pictorial record of the invasion of England by William I (the Conqueror) in 1066. It is an embroidery rather than a true tapestry, sewn with woollen threads in blue, green, red, and yellow, 70 m/231 ft long and 50 cm/20 in wide, and containing 72 separate scenes with descriptive wording in Latin. It is exhibited at the museum of Bayeux in Normandy, France.

All writers are liars. They twist events to suit themselves. They make use of their own tragedies to make a better story. They batten on their relations. They 'put people in books' – although by the time the book is underway they are honestly convinced that the character they are writing about has sprung entirely from their imagination.

NINA BAWDEN English writer.
A Virago Keepsake (1993)

Baylis, Lilian Mary (1874–1937)
English theatre manager. She was responsible for re-opening Sadler's Wells Theatre, London, in 1931. From 1934 Sadler's Wells specialized in productions of opera and ballet: the resultant companies eventually became the Royal Ballet and the English National Opera.

She managed the Old Vic Theatre from 1912, starting a complete series of productions of Shakespeare's plays. The National Theatre Company performed at the Old Vic 1961–76.

Bayliss, William Maddock (1860–1924)
English physiologist who discovered the digestive hormone secretin, the first hormone to be found, with Ernest ◊Starling in 1902. During World War I, Bayliss introduced the use of saline (salt water) injections to help the injured recover from shock. Knighted 1922.

BBC, British Broadcasting Corporation
The state-owned broadcasting network. It operates television and national and local radio stations, and is financed by the sale of television (originally radio) licences. It is not permitted to carry advertisements but has an additional source of income through its publishing interests and the sales of its programmes. The BBC is controlled by a board of governors, each appointed by the government for five years. The BBC was converted from a private company (established in 1922) to a public corporation under royal charter in 1927. Under the charter, news programmes were required to be politically impartial. A new charter in 1996 safeguarded the BBC's role and status as a public corporation until 2006, with the licence fee guaranteed as the chief source of revenue until 2002. The first director general was John Reith (1922–38). John ◊Birt was appointed director general in 1993.

Television

Television services began in 1936, although they were suspended 1939–46 during World War II. A second channel, BBC2, was launched on 20 April 1964, aimed at minority interests, and in 1991 BBC World Service Television began broadcasting English-language transmissions round the world. Under the terms of the 1989 Broadcasting Act, 25% of programmes must be supplied by external contractors. Producers are entitled to buy services for their productions inside the BBC or elsewhere. The BBC's key production centre is in London, with regional centres in Glasgow, Cardiff, Belfast, Birmingham, Manchester, and Bristol. In 1998 the BBC launched a digital channel, BBC Choice.

Radio

The BBC has five national radio channels, as well as a number of local regional stations. Overseas radio broadcasts (World Service) have a government subsidy. The World Service broadcasts in 47 languages, including English (1998). Listeners have increased from 130 million a week in 1990 to over 140 million in 1998. Countries that have attempted to ban the World Service include the USSR, which jammed the airwaves for 24 years during the Cold War, and finally allowed the BBC to creep through in January 1988. Libya, Iran, and China have all attempted to stifle BBC transmissions.

Programme library

In March 1997, the BBC signed a 30-year agreement to open its television-programme library for commercial use in the UK for the first time. The 50–50 venture with Flextech plc will lead to new pay-TV channels that use the library.

See also ◊television, ◊broadcasting, and ◊comedy.

BBFC

Abbreviation for the ◊British Board of Film Classification.

Beachy Head (French *beau chef*, 'beautiful head')

Chalk headland on the south coast of England, between Seaford and Eastbourne in East Sussex. Rising to 163 m/535 ft, it is the eastern end of the South Downs. The lighthouse at the foot of the cliff is 38 m/125 ft high.

France and the Isle of Wight can be seen across the English Channel from the headland. Belle Tout lighthouse, erected in 1828, was replaced in 1902 by the present cliff-base lighthouse.

In June 1690 allied English and Dutch fleets were defeated by the French at the Battle of Beachy Head.

Beaconsfield

Town in Buckinghamshire, southern England, 37 km/23 mi northwest of London; population (1991) 12,300. Its economy includes light engineering, the manufacture of scientific instruments, and the importing and wholesaling of wine. The National Film and Television School is located here.

In the 18th century the town was an important coaching stop on the routes from London to Oxford and from Windsor

BAYEUX TAPESTRY *Harold II of England and William of Normandy meet in this scene from the Bayeux Tapestry. Harold had been sent to Normandy by Edward the Confessor to offer the throne of England to William. The tapestry shows Harold taken prisoner by a French count and rescued by William who subsequently knighted Harold before his return to England. The tapestry shows Harold's death at the subsequent Battle of Hastings in 1066. Corbis*

to Aylesbury, making the surrounding countryside notorious for its highwaymen. Several old coaching inns remain, including the half-timbered Royal Saracen's Head, and the Royal White Hart where Elizabeth I is said to have stayed. Other features of the town include Bekonscot Model Village, a miniature landscape and railway network.

Distinguished figures associated with the town include the political theorist Edmund Burke and the poet Edmund Waller, former inhabitants who are buried at the 15th-century church; and G K Chesterton, who wrote many of his *Father Brown* stories while living in Beaconsfield between 1909 and 1935. Former British prime minister Benjamin Disraeli was created Earl of Beaconsfield in 1876.

Beaker people

Prehistoric people thought to have been of Iberian origin, who spread out over Europe from the 3rd millennium BC. They were skilled in metalworking, and are associated with distinctive earthenware drinking vessels with various designs, in particular, a type of beaker with a bell-shaped profile, widely distributed throughout Europe.

In Britain, the Beaker people built circular earthwork enclosures with ditches and entrances on opposite sides known as henges, sometimes containing stone circles. They have been associated with later stages of the construction of ◊Stonehenge and with ◊Avebury in Wiltshire.

Beale, Dorothea (1831–1906)

English pioneer of higher education for women, whose work helped to raise the standard of women's education and the status of women teachers.

Beale was headmistress of the Ladies' College in Cheltenham from 1858, and she helped to found St Hilda's Hall, Oxford (1892), for former pupils of Cheltenham Ladies' College desiring to study at Oxford. She was also active in founding the first residential training college for teachers at St Hilda's, Cheltenham.

Beamish, Sally (1956–)

English composer and viola player. She studied at the Royal Northern College of Music and with Lennox Berkeley. She played viola in various London ensembles. In 1989 she became resident in Scotland, cofounding the Chamber Group of Scotland, after which she received a steady stream of commissions; she often writes for non-professional forces. Recent works include a cello concerto (1997) and *The Flight of the Eagle*, a children's introduction to the woodwind instruments of the orchestra, Symphony No.2 (1998), and *The Caledonian Road* for chamber orchestra (1998).

Beardsley, Aubrey Vincent (1872–1898)

English illustrator and leading member of the ◊Aesthetic Movement. His meticulously executed black-and-white

BBC *John Reith, centre, who was to become the first director general of the BBC, pictured c.1924 with other founding figures of British broadcasting outside 2, Savoy Hill, in London, one of the early centres of television research. Reith's belief that television should educate, inform, and entertain shaped the development of public service broadcasting in the UK. Hulton Getty*

drawings show the influence of Japanese prints and French Rococo, and also display the sinuous line, asymmetry, and decorative mannerisms of Art Nouveau. His work was often charged with being grotesque and decadent.

He became known through *The Yellow Book* magazine, for which he was the art editor, and through his drawings for Oscar Wilde's *Salome* (1893).

Beatles, the

English pop group 1960–70. The members, all born in Liverpool, were John ◊Lennon (1940–1980, rhythm guitar, vocals), Paul ◊McCartney (1942– , bass, vocals), George Harrison (1943– , lead guitar, vocals), and Ringo Starr (formerly Richard Starkey, 1940– , drums). Using songs written largely by Lennon and McCartney, the Beatles dominated rock music and pop culture in the 1960s.

The Beatles gained early experience in Liverpool and Hamburg, West Germany. They had a top-30 hit with their first record, 'Love Me Do' (1962).

At the peak of Beatlemania they starred in two films, *A Hard Day's Night* (1964) and *Help!* (1965), and provided songs for the animated film *Yellow Submarine* (1968). Their ballad 'Yesterday' (1965) was covered by 1,186 different performers in the first ten years. The album *Sgt Pepper's Lonely Hearts Club Band* (1967), recorded on two four-track machines, anticipated subsequent technological developments.

The Beatles were the first British group to challenge the US dominance of rock and roll, and continued to influence popular music beyond their break-up in 1970.

beat music

Pop music that evolved in the UK in the early 1960s, known in its purest form as ◊Mersey beat, and as British Invasion in the USA. The beat groups characteristically had a simple, guitar-dominated line-up, vocal harmonies, and catchy tunes. They included the Beatles (1960–70), the Hollies (1962–), and the Zombies (1962–67).

Beatles *From left to right Paul McCartney, George Harrison, Ringo Starr, and John Lennon, the Beatles remain the most successful British pop group ever. They topped the charts with a succession of hits, and were the first British band to gain widespread recognition in America. Their appearances often unleashed 'Beatlemania', mass adulation by hysterical teenage girls. Rex*

Beaton, Cecil Walter Hardy (1904–1980)

English photographer. His elegant and sophisticated fashion pictures and society portraits often employed exotic props and settings. He adopted a more simple style for his wartime photographs of bomb-damaged London. He also worked as a stage and film designer, notably for the musicals *Gigi* (1959) and *My Fair Lady* (1965). He was knighted in 1972.

Beatty, David, 1st Earl Beatty (1871–1936)

British admiral in World War I. He commanded the cruiser squadron 1912–16 and bore the brunt of the Battle of Jutland in 1916. In 1916 he became commander of the fleet, and in 1918 received the surrender of the German fleet. He was created an earl in 1919.

Beaufort, Francis (1774–1857)

British admiral, hydrographer to the Royal Navy from 1829; the Beaufort scale and the Beaufort Sea in the Arctic Ocean are named after him.

Drawing up the scale named after him, Beaufort specified the amount of sail that a full-rigged ship should carry under the various wind conditions. It was officially adopted by the Admiralty in 1838. Modifications were made to the scale when sail gave way to steam. KCB 1848.

Beaufort, Henry (1375–1447)

English politician and cleric. As chancellor of England, he supported his half-brother ◊Henry IV and made enormous personal loans to Henry V to finance war against France. As a guardian of Henry VI during his minority, from 1421 he was in effective control of the country until 1426. In the same year he was created a cardinal.

He had a long-running personal feud with Humphrey, Duke of Gloucester, which led to his fall from power in 1426. In 1427 he was sent by the pope to Germany to lead a crusade against Hussites. He crowned Henry VI king of France in Paris in 1431.

Beaufort, Margaret, Countess of Richmond and Derby (1443–1509)

English noble. She was the granddaughter of ◊John of Gaunt, Duke of Lancaster. In 1455 she married Edmund Tudor, Earl of Richmond, and their son became ◊Henry VII of England.

Her father was John Beaufort, Duke of Somerset. After the death of Edmund she married Henry Stafford, son of the Duke of Buckingham. Her third husband, Thomas Stanley, Earl of Derby, defected from the Yorkists to the Lancastrians, aiding Henry's victory over Richard III at the battle of ◊Bosworth 1485, which ended the Wars of the ◊Roses.

Beaulieu

Village in Hampshire, southern England, on the estuary of the River Beaulieu and the edge of the New Forest, 9 km/6 mi southwest of Southampton. The National Motor Museum (1952) and the remains of a Cistercian abbey, established by King John in about 1204, are in the grounds of the home of Lord Montagu of Beaulieu; parts of Palace House, the family residence, were opened to the public in 1952.

Another part of the Montagu estate, the 18th-century shipyard of Buckler's Hard, is situated 3 km/2mi southwest of Beaulieu on the river estuary. Admiral Nelson's HMS *Agamemnon* was built and launched here. The yard and cottages are under restoration, and the site contains a Maritime Museum.

Beauly Firth

Arm of the North Sea north and west of Inverness, Scotland. It is separated from the North Sea by the Moray Firth and is spanned by the Kessock Bridge (1982).

Beaumaris

Town and tourist resort on the Isle of Anglesey, northwest Wales; population (1991) 1,600. It is situated on Beaumaris Bay, to the north of the Menai Strait, and has a large harbour. There is an annual regatta, and a music festival is held in early summer. **Beaumaris Castle**, one of the finest European examples of the concentric type, was founded by Edward I in 1295, and is classified by the United Nations as a World Heritage site.

Beaumont, Francis (1584–1616)

English dramatist and poet. He collaborated with John ◊Fletcher from about 1606 to 1613. Their joint plays include the tragicomedies *Philaster* (1610), *A King and No King* (about 1611), and *The Maid's Tragedy* (about 1611). *The Woman Hater* (about 1606) and *The Knight of the Burning Pestle* (about 1607), which is a satire on the audience, are ascribed to Beaumont alone.

Beaumont was a close friend of Michael Drayton and Ben ◊Jonson, for some of whose plays he wrote commendatory verses.

BEAUMARIS CASTLE *One of ten massive castles built in the then-hostile region of North Wales by the English king Edward I. It is of the concentric type, being protected by two rings of defensive walls. When construction began, in 1295, 400 stonemasons and 2,000 labourers were engaged on the project. Corel*

Beautiful South, The

English pop group formed in 1989. Following their hit debut album *Welcome to the Beautiful South* (1989), they continued their success with a string of UK chart-topping albums and singles including the single 'A Little Time', and the albums *Carry On Up The Charts – The Best Of The Beautiful South* (1995) and *Blue Is The Colour* (1996).

Members are Paul Heaton (1962–) (vocals), Dave Hemingway (1960–) (vocals), Jacqueline Abbott (1973–) (vocals), Dave Rotheray (1963–) (guitar), Sean Welch (1965–) (bass), and Dave Stead (1966–) (drums).

Beaverbrook, (William) Max(well) Aitken, 1st Baron Beaverbrook (1879–1964)

British financier, newspaper proprietor, and politician, born in Canada. He bought a majority interest in the *Daily Express* in 1919, founded the *Sunday Express* in 1921, and bought the London *Evening Standard* in 1923. He served in Lloyd George's World War I cabinet and Churchill's World War II cabinet.

Between the wars he used his newspapers, in particular the *Daily Express*, to campaign for empire and free trade and against Prime Minister Baldwin.

Bebington

Town in Wirral, Merseyside, England, on the ◊Wirral peninsula south of Birkenhead; population (1991) 60,100. Industries include engineering, and the manufacture of soap and chemicals. Oil-refining is conducted at neighbouring Eastham. Nearby is ◊Port Sunlight, originally built in 1888 as a model housing estate for workers at the Lever Brothers (now Unilever) soap and margarine factory.

Beccles

Market town in Suffolk, England; population (1991) 6,600. It is situated on the River Waveney, 15 km/9 mi southwest of Lowestoft, in the Norfolk Broads area. Beccles is a favoured holiday yachting resort; an annual regatta is held in August. Its main industry is printing.

Becker, Lydia Ernestine (1827–1890)
English botanist and campaigner for women's rights. She established the Manchester Ladies' Literary Society in 1865 as a forum for women to study scientific subjects. In 1867 she co-founded and became secretary of the National Society for Women's Suffrage. In 1870 she founded a monthly newsletter, the *Women's Suffrage Journal*.

Becket, St Thomas à (1118–1170)
English priest and politician. He was chancellor to ◊Henry II 1155–62, when he was appointed archbishop of Canterbury. The interests of the church soon conflicted with those of the crown and Becket was assassinated; he was canonized in 1172.

A friend of Henry II, Becket was a loyal chancellor, but on becoming archbishop of Canterbury transferred his allegiance to the church. In 1164 he opposed Henry's attempt to regulate the relations between church and state, and had to flee the country; he returned in 1170, but the reconciliation soon broke down. Encouraged by a hasty outburst from the king, four knights murdered Becket before the altar of Canterbury cathedral. He was declared a saint, and his shrine became the busiest centre of pilgrimage in England until the Reformation.

Beckett, Margaret born Jackson (1943–)
British Labour politician, president of the board of trade 1997–98, President of the Council and leader of the Commons, 1998–. On John ◊Smith's death in 1994, Beckett took over as acting party leader, but was defeated by Tony Blair in the 1994 leadership election. She also lost in the concurrent deputy leadership contest to John ◊Prescott. Beckett became president of the board of trade when the new Labour government was formed in 1997, but in the July 1998 cabinet re-shuffle was moved sideways to become Leader of the Commons.

Drawn from the party's Bennite left-wing, Beckett was first elected to parliament in 1974 and served as a party whip, until being defeated at the 1979 general election. She returned to parliament in 1983, representing Derby South, and, having moderated her policy approach yet still attracting strong trade union support, she was elected deputy leader in 1992 and worked loyally alongside John Smith.

... they fell upon him and killed him (I say it with sorrow). I fear the anger I had recently shown against him may have been the cause of this misdeed. I call God to witness that I am extremely disturbed, but more with anxiety about my reputation than qualms of conscience.

Henry II King of England.
Referring to the killing of Thomas à Becket, in a letter to Pope Alexander III, 1171

Beckham, David Robert Joseph (1975–)
English footballer, born in Leytonstone, London. A midfielder with great passing ability, he was a member of the

BECKET, ST THOMAS À *The murder of Thomas à Becket, Archbishop of Canterbury, depicted by the artist and chronicler Matthew Paris. After his death, Becket's tomb in Canterbury became one of the most important English pilgrimage sites of the Middle Ages. Philip Sauvain Picture Collection*

Manchester United sides that won the FA Premier League in the 1995–96 and 1996–97 seasons, and also won an FA Cup-winner's medal with Manchester United in 1996. Beckham was the Professional Footballers' Association Young Player of the Year in 1996–97. By August 1998 he had played 18 times for England. In the 1998 World Cup, Beckham was notoriously sent off early in the second half of the team's second round match defeat against Argentina for kicking an opponent who had fouled him.

Beddgelert

Village in Gwynedd, northwest Wales, 20 km/12 mi southeast of Caernarfon. Lying at the foot of Snowdon (1,085 m/3,560 ft), the village is close to the pass of Aberglaslyn. Its name means 'grave of Gelert'. Gelert was the hound of Llewelyn (Prince of Wales in the 13th century) and his grave is marked by a stone recalling the legend that he saved his master's child from a wolf and was then killed by Llewelyn in error.

The nearby Sygun copper mine is open to tourists. The pass of Aberglaslyn contains the rock known as the 'chair of Rhys Goch' (the 15th-century bard).

Bede (*c.* 673–735)

English theologian and historian, known as **the Venerable Bede**. Active in Durham and Northumbria, he wrote many scientific, theological, and historical works. His *Historia Ecclesiastica Gentis Anglorum* (*Ecclesiastical History of the English People*) of 731 is a primary source for early English history, and was translated into the vernacular by King Alfred.

Born at Monkwearmouth, Durham, Bede entered the local monastery at the age of seven, later transferring to Jarrow, where he became a priest about 703. He devoted his life to writing and teaching; among his pupils was Egbert, archbishop of York. He was canonized in 1899. Much of our knowledge of England in the Dark Ages prior to the 8th century depends on Bede's historical works and his painstaking efforts to research and validate original sources, both documentary and oral testimony. He popularized the system of dating events from the birth of Christ.

Bedford

Town and administrative headquarters of ◊Bedfordshire, southern England, on the River Ouse, about 80 km/50 mi north of London; population (1991) 73,900. Industries include light engineering and food-processing, activities associated with aircraft services, and the manufacture of agricultural machinery, diesel engines, pumps, bricks, communications systems, and electronic equipment and components. The writer John ◊Bunyan is said to have written part of *The Pilgrim's Progress* (1678) while imprisoned in the town. A large Italian community has settled here.

Museums and galleries

The Cecil Higgins Art Gallery includes a collection of English watercolours, 20th-century prints, porcelain, glass, and Bedfordshire lace. A museum adjoining the Bunyan Meeting House, built on the site of the chapel in which John Bunyan preached, displays relics of the author and copies of *The Pilgrim's Progress* in many languages. The Moot Hall at the nearby village of Elstow, where Bunyan was born in 1628, contains exhibits illustrating life in the time of the writer.

Features

St Paul's Church dates from the 14th and 15th centuries. The interior was restored in the 19th century. It contains monuments to the important local benefactor William Harpur (1496–1573) and his wife, Alice Harpur. Outside the church is a statue of John Howard, the prison reformer, who was appointed high sheriff of Bedfordshire in 1773.

William Harpur, who was born in Bedford and became Lord Mayor of London in 1561, founded a grammar school in the town. The Harpur Trust was established to administer the school and later founded others in the town; it still supports Bedford School, a private boys' school, and other educational institutions.

Bedfordshire

County of south central England (since April 1997 Luton has been a separate unitary authority)

Area 1,192 sq km/460 sq mi

Towns ◊Bedford (administrative headquarters), Dunstable

Physical the Great Ouse River and its tributary, the Ivel; the county is low lying with the Chiltern Hills in the southwest

Features Whipsnade Wild Animal Park, near Dunstable (200 ha/494 acres), belonging to the London Zoological Society; Woburn Abbey, seat of the duke of Bedford; Cranfield Institute of Technology

Agriculture cereals (especially wheat and barley); vegetables

Industries agricultural machinery; cement manufacture (using local chalk); clay; electrical goods; gravel; motor vehicles and parts; packaging; sand; brickworks at Stewartby

Population (1995 est) 373,000.

Topography

Bedfordshire is bounded on the northeast by Cambridgeshire; on the northwest by Northamptonshire and Milton Keynes; on the west by Buckinghamshire; and on the southeast by Luton and Hertfordshire. The Great Ouse, flowing through the centre of the county to the east, is navigable to Little Barford.

Bedlam, abbreviation of Bethlehem

The earliest mental hospital in Europe. It was opened in the 14th century in London and is now sited in Surrey. It is now used as a slang word meaning chaos.

Bedruthan Steps

Rock formation on the north coast of Cornwall, England, 8 km/5 mi north of Newquay. Bedruthan Steps are natural granite stacks, 61 m/200 ft high.

Bedser, Alec Victor (1918–)

English cricketer. A right-arm seam bowler renowned for his accuracy, he took 236 Test wickets at an average of 24.89, 1946–55. During the 1953 Ashes series, in which he took 39 Australian wickets, he passed Clarrie Grimmett as the most prolific wicket-taker in Test cricket. He played for Surrey 1939–60 and was a crucial member of the side which won seven consecutive county championships, 1952–58.

Bedyngham, John (died *c.* 1460)

English composer. He wrote Masses, motets, and chansons, possibly including *O rosa bella*, often ascribed to John Dunstable. His music was widely known in Continental Europe; one of his two Mass cycles is derived from a ballade by Binchois.

Beecham, Thomas (1879–1961)

English conductor and impresario. He established the Royal Philharmonic Orchestra in 1946 and fostered the works of composers such as Delius, Sibelius, and Richard Strauss. He was knighted and suceeded to the baronetcy in 1916.

Beeching Report

1963 official report on the railway network of Britain, which recommended the closure of loss-making lines and the improvement of money-making routes. Hundreds of lines and several thousand stations were closed as a result.

These closures were not evenly spread throughout the country. Networks in East Anglia, south Wales, and the West Country fared worst, whereas the densely populated southeast retained more of its routes. Richard Beeching was chair of the British Railways Board 1963–65.

beer

Alcoholic drink made from water and malt (fermented barley or other grain), flavoured with hops. Beer contains between 1% and 6% alcohol and is one of the oldest alcoholic drinks. See ◊public house for a feature on the development of brewing and pubs.

The medieval distinction between beer (containing hops) and ale (without hops) has now fallen into disuse and beer has come to be used strictly as a generic term including ale, stout, and lager. Stout is top fermented, but is sweet and strongly flavoured with roasted grain; lager is a light beer, bottom fermented and matured over a longer period (German *Lager* 'store').

Beerbohm, (Henry) Max(imilian) (1872–1956)

English caricaturist and author. A perfectionist in style, he contributed to *The Yellow Book* (1894); wrote a novel of Oxford undergraduate life, *Zuleika Dobson* (1911); and published volumes of caricature, including *Rossetti and His Circle* (1922). He succeeded George Bernard Shaw as critic to the *Saturday Review* in 1898.

Beeston and Stapleford

Town in Nottinghamshire, England, 5 km/3 mi southwest of Nottingham; population (1991) 35,900. The area comprises Beeston, Stapleford, Chilwell, Bramcote, and Toton. The main industries include telecommunications, manufacturing chemists, lace and hosiery manufacture, light engineering, and iron founding.

Good ale, the true and proper drink of Englishmen.

George Henry Borrow English author and traveller.
Lavengro ch 48

Beeton, Mrs, Isabella Mary Mayson (1836–1865)

British writer on cookery and domestic management. She produced *Mrs Beeton's Book of Household Management* (1861), the first comprehensive work on domestic science.

Mrs Beeton's Book of Household Management appeared originally in monthly instalments of *The Englishwoman's Domestic Magazine* (1859–60), and was published in book form in 1861, becoming an immediate bestseller. Mrs Beeton was assistant editor of the magazine, which was published by her husband, Samuel Beeton.

BEF

Abbreviation for ◊**British Expeditionary Force**.

Beggar's Opera, The

Ballad opera, produced London, Theatre in Lincoln's Inn Fields, 29 January 1728, consisting of a play by John Gay interspersed with songs. The music, popular tunes of the day but for the most part not folksongs, was arranged by John Christopher Pepusch, who also composed the overture. There have been several modern realizations, including one by Britten (1948).

Behn, Aphra (1640–1689)

English novelist and dramatist. She was the first

BEECHAM, THOMAS *British conductor Thomas Beecham. One of the most important figures in British musical life in the 20th century, he was not only a superb conductor but also an impresario who founded several orchestras and promoted opera. He lived stylishly and was celebrated for his wit and flamboyant manner. Corbis*

woman in England to earn her living as a writer. Her works were criticized for their explicitness; they frequently present events from a woman's point of view. Her novel *Oroonoko* (1688), based on her visit to Surinam, is an attack on slavery.

Between 1670 and 1687 fifteen of her plays were produced, including *The Forced Marriage* (1670) and *The Rover* (1677). As in *The Lucky Chance* (1686), condemnation of forced and mercenary marriages was a recurring theme in her work. She was employed as a government spy in Holland in 1666.

All I ask is the privilege for my masculine part, the poet in me ... if I must not, because of my sex, have this freedom, I lay down quill and you shall hear of me no more.

APHRA BEHN English writer.
Preface to *The Lucky Chance* (1686)

Belfast (Gaelic Beal Feirste 'the mouth of the Farset')

City and industrial port in County Antrim and County Down, Northern Ireland, at the mouth of the River Lagan on Belfast Lough; county town of County ⇨Antrim, and capital of Northern Ireland since 1920.

Population

(1994 est) 290,000 (Protestants form the majority in east Belfast, Catholics in the west)

Industries

aircraft and aircraft components, engineering, electronics, fertilizers, food processing, rope, textiles, tobacco; linen and shipbuilding have declined in importance since the 19th century, although some attempt is being made to revive these industries. The city is currently undergoing major redevelopment, both in terms of physical infrastracture (particularly along the River Lagan) and industrial investment, which is partly funded by the EU

Features

City hall (1906); ⇨Stormont (the former parliament buildings and from 1998 the seat of the Northern Ireland Assembly); Waterfront Hall, opened in 1997; the Linen Hall Library (1788); Belfast Castle (built 1870; former home of the Donegall family); Queen's University (1909)

History

Belfast grew up around a castle built in 1177 by John de Courcy. With the settlement of English and Scots, Belfast became a centre of Irish Protestantism in the 17th century. An influx of Huguenots after 1685 extended the linen industry, and the 1800 Act of Union with England resulted in the promotion of Belfast as an industrial centre. It was created a city in 1888, with a lord mayor from 1892. From 1968 onwards the city was heavily damaged by civil disturbances and terrorist activity.

Location and public buildings

On the landward side Belfast is dominated by the basalt hills of County Antrim. The city centre is built on reclaimed land, the larger buildings being supported on piles sunk deep into alluvial deposits.

Most of its major public buildings have been built since the late 19th century: the royal courts of justice (1933), the museum and art gallery (1929), the public library (1888), the harbour office (1896), St Anne's Cathedral (1904), and the parliament buildings, Stormont (1932). The Customs House dates from 1857.

Queen's University was founded as Queen's College in 1849. It was associated with the other Queen's Colleges at Cork and Galway until it received its royal charter as an independent university in 1909. In addition to the public and university libraries, the Linen Hall Library, founded in 1788, still flourishes as a subscription library. It has an important collection of publications on the linen trade and concerning the political life of Northern Ireland since 1966. The grounds of the 19th-century Belfast Castle, presented to the city by Lord Shaftesbury in 1934, lie on the slopes of Cave Hill, as do the public parks of Hazelwood and Bellevue, where there is a public zoo.

Transport

Belfast is 180 km/112 mi north of Dublin, and is the centre of the Northern Ireland's road and rail network. It is a terminus for ferries from Liverpool and the Isle of Man, and has an international airport at Aldergrove, 31 km/19 mi to the west. The port of Larne 32 km/20 mi to the north is a terminus for ferries to Scotland.

Belfast harbour

The harbour of Belfast is under the management of the Belfast Harbour Commissioners, established by the Belfast Harbour Act in 1847. Extensive land reclamation has been carried out; Belfast City airport was opened on reclaimed land in 1937. The harbour area covers 668 ha/1650 acres and includes a shipyard, an oil refinery, and an aircraft factory as well as 102 ha/252 acres of commercial docks.

Regeneration in the 1990s

The city underwent extensive redevelopment in the 1990s, especially along the River Lagan, including the building of the Waterfront Hall and Conference Centre, which includes a major theatre opened in 1997. Industrial development and regeneration also took place during the 1990s, particularly in the service and tertiary industries.

Early history

Belfast grew up around a castle built in 1177 by John de Courcy. After the invasion of Ulster in 1177 de Courcy built his castle on the site of an earlier fort at the ford over the River Lagan as a stronghold to command the crossing-point. This was destroyed by the troops of Edward Bruce in 1316, but later rebuilt. Throughout medieval times Belfast was a small settlement, much less important than the neighbouring port of Carrickfergus, which was the main Anglo-Norman stronghold in the north of Ireland. For about 300 years the Lagan valley was controlled by the O'Neill family. The castle and surrounding settlement were subject to frequent dispute between the O'Neills and English forces, changing hands several times until 1574 when the lands were captured by the Earl of Essex.

BELFAST *The Parliament building at Stormont was built in 1932 to house Northern Ireland's government, and became a byword for the Unionist (Protestant) domination of political life in the province. In 1972, Stormont became redundant after the British government imposed direct rule from Westminster but in 1998 it became the seat of the Northern Ireland National Assembly. Alain Le Garsmeur/ Image Ireland/Collections*

17th-century history
In 1604 the settlement at Belfast came under the control of Arthur Chichester, as part of the ◊Plantation of Ireland. Under Chichester Belfast received a charter in 1613, and it grew to be the market town for the Lagan valley. Belfast was settled by Protestant families from Devon and Scotland and became a centre of Irish Protestantism. Real growth came with the establishment of linen manufacture after an influx of Huguenots in 1685. Belfast also became an important trading port with Scotland.

18th-century history
The shipbuilding industry was established in Belfast by William Hugh Ritchie in 1791. Also in 1791 the Society of the United Irishmen was founded in Belfast to fight the repression of the Penal Laws. This united both Catholic and Presbyterian inhabitants of the city in a bid for independence. Henry Joy McCracken (1767–1798), a member of the United Irishmen who led the Irish troops at the Battle of Antrim in 1798 was later executed in the city.

19th-century history
The 1800 Act of Union with England resulted in the promotion of Belfast as an industrial centre, and the shipbuilding industry developed throughout the 19th century. Between 1831 and 1901 Belfast's population grew from 30,000 to 350,000. Belfast was incorporated into a borough in 1842, created a city in 1888, with a lord mayor from 1892.

20th-century history
Belfast has been at the centre of the Northern Ireland 'Troubles' since 1968. See ◊Northern Ireland.

The parliament of Northern Ireland
The first ◊Northern Ireland parliament sat in the city hall in Belfast, the state opening being performed in 1921 by King George V. The parliament buildings at Stormont were opened by the Prince of Wales in 1932, and were used until the parliament's suspension in 1972. The multi-party peace talks of 1997–98, leading up to the agreement of 10 April 1998, were held at Stormont, which since summer 1998 has been the seat of the Northern Ireland Assembly.

Belfast Lough

Inlet on the east coast of Northern Ireland, between the counties of Antrim and Down. It is an estuary of the River Lagan, and is 11 km/7 mi wide at its mouth. Belfast Lough extends 24 km/15 mi inland, and has the towns of Belfast, Carrickfergus, Holywood, and Bangor on its shores. The area adjacent to Port Belfast is heavily industrialized.

Belgravia

Residential district of west central London, laid out in squares by Thomas Cubitt (1788–1855) between 1825 and 1830, and bounded to the north by Knightsbridge.

Bell, Alexander Graham (1847–1922)

Scottish-born US scientist and inventor. He was the first

person ever to transmit speech from one point to another by electrical means. This invention – the telephone – was made in 1876. Later Bell experimented with a type of phonograph and, in aeronautics, invented the tricycle undercarriage.

Bell also invented a photophone, which used selenium crystals to apply the telephone principle to transmitting words in a beam of light. He thus achieved the first wireless transmission of speech.

Bell was born in Edinburgh, where his grandfather was a speech tutor. As a boy he constructed an automaton simulating the human organs of speech, using rubber, cotton, and a bellows. He was educated at the universities of Edinburgh and London, and in 1870 went first to Canada and then to the USA, where he opened a school for teachers of the deaf in Boston and in 1873 became professor of vocal physiology at the university. With the money he had made from his telephone system, Bell set up a laboratory in Nova Scotia, Canada; in 1880 he established, in addition, the Volta Laboratory in Washington DC.

Bell, Charles (1774–1842)

Scottish anatomist and surgeon who carried out pioneering research on the human nervous system. He gave his name to Bell's palsy, an extracranial paralysis of the facial nerve, and to the long thoracic **nerve of Bell**, which supplies a muscle in the chest wall. Knighted 1829.

Bell, John (1928–1990)

Northern Irish physicist who in 1964 devised a test to verify a point in quantum theory: whether two particles that were once connected are always afterwards interconnected even if they become widely separated. As well as investigating fundamental problems in theoretical physics, Bell contributed to the design of particle accelerators.

In the early 1980s, a French team tested Bell's criteria, and a connection between widely separated particles was detected.

Bell, Vanessa (1879–1961)

English painter and designer. She was one of the first English artists to paint abstracts, but most of her work was in a Post-Impressionist style. She was the sister of Virginia ◊Woolf and wife of the art critic Clive Bell, and like them she was a leading figure of the ◊Bloomsbury Group.

From 1916 she lived with Scottish painter Duncan ◊Grant, and their home at Charleston, Sussex practically became a Bloomsbury memorial.

Bellany, John (1942–)

Scottish painter and printmaker. He is best known for large Expressionistic figure compositions, brightly coloured and vigorously handled. Often they have imagery taken from the sea, reflecting his upbringing in a Scottish fishing village. He has also painted numerous portraits, and in the 1990s he began making coloured etchings.

Bell Burnell, (Susan) Jocelyn (1943–)

English astronomer. In 1967 she discovered the first pulsar (rapidly flashing star) with Antony ◊Hewish and colleagues at Cambridge University, England.

Bell spent her first two years in Cambridge building a radio telescope that was specially designed to track quasars. The telescope had the ability to record rapid variations in signals. In 1967 she noticed an unusual signal, which turned out to be composed of a rapid set of pulses that occurred precisely every 1.337 sec. One attempted explanation of this curious phenomenon was that it emanated from an interstellar beacon, so initially it was nicknamed LGM, for Little Green Men. Within a few months, however, Bell located three other similar sources. They too pulsed at an extremely regular rate but their periods varied over a few fractions of a second and they all originated from widely spaced locations in our Galaxy. Thus it seemed that a more likely explanation of the signals was that they were being emitted by a special kind of star – a pulsar.

The English think incompetence is the same thing as sincerity.

Quentin Crisp British writer and model.
The Naked Civil Servant (1968)

Belleek

Village in County Fermanagh, Northern Ireland. Belleek is situated on the border with County Donegal, 39 km/24 mi from Enniskillen. It gives its name to a type of china with a mother-of-pearl lustre, which has been made here since 1857.

Belloc, (Joseph) Hilaire (René Pierre) (1870–1953)

French-born British writer. He is remembered primarily for his nonsense verse for children *The Bad Child's Book of Beasts* (1896) and *Cautionary Tales for Children* (1907). Belloc also wrote historical, biographical, travel, and religious books (he was a devout Catholic). With G K ◊Chesterton, he advocated a return to the late medieval guild system of commercial association in place of capitalism or socialism. He wrote some 16 novels, nearly all of which were illustrated by G K Chesterton.

Belloc was born in St-Cloud on the outskirts of Paris, and educated at Oxford University. He became a British subject in 1902.

bell ringing, or campanology

The art of ringing church bells individually or in sequence by rhythmically drawing on a rope fastened to a wheel rotating the bell, so that it falls back and strikes in time. **Change ringing** is an English art, dating from the 17th century, of ringing a patterned sequence of permutations of 5–12 church bells, using one player to each bell.

Bell Rock, or Inchcape Rock

Reef off the east coast of Scotland, over 600 m/1,968 ft long, in the opening of the bay at the mouth of the River Tay, 19 km/12 mi southeast of Arbroath. A lighthouse, 37 m/121 ft high, was erected on the reef between 1807 and 1811,

BELLOC, HILAIRE *English author Hilaire Belloc, photographed in about 1940. Although remembered chiefly for his children's verse, he also wrote serious poetry, novels, travel books, political and religious essays, and biographies of, among others, Marie Antoinette, Cromwell, and Charles II. Corbis*

designed by Robert Stevenson and John Rennie; a new lightroom was built in 1902.

Bellshill and Mossend

Town in North Lanarkshire unitary authority, Scotland, 6 km/4 mi northeast of Hamilton; combined population (1991) 21,600. Its diverse industries are situated mainly in Mossend, which has extensive iron and steel works.

Belper

Market town in Derbyshire, England; population (1991) 16,500. It is situated on the River Derwent, 11 km/7 mi north of Derby. Belper's main industries are its cotton mills and hosiery factories. The first cotton mill in Belper was opened by Richard Arkwright and Jedediah Strutt in 1776.

Belvoir Castle

Neo-Gothic castle near Bottesford, Leicestershire, England; the seat of the Duke of Rutland. The original fortress of 11th to 13th centuries was rebuilt in 1528, and again in 1654–58 as a mansion. Around 1800 the 5th duke employed James Wyatt to reconvert it to a castle, altering the apartments at the same time. Further rebuilding and redecoration after a fire in 1816 included the construction of a Romanesque-style mausoleum (1820–30). The castle has an important art collection which includes works by Holbein, Poussin, Reynolds, and Gainsborough.

Benbecula, or Beinn na Faoghla

Island of the Outer ◊Hebrides in Western Isles unitary authority, Scotland, about 25 km/16 mi west of Skye; population (1991) 1,700. It lies between North and South Uist, with causeway links, and covers an area of about 9,200 sq km/3,552 sq mi. An airport is located at Balivanich (or Baile a Mhanaich).

The highest point is Rueval, barely 124 m/406 ft above sea level. Numerous lochan (inland waters) provide freshwater fishing. Crofting (a form of subsistence farming) is the main occupation of the islanders, and a large military base administers a rocket range on South Uist.

Ben Cruachan

Mountain in Argyll and Bute unitary authority, Scotland, between Loch Awe and Loch Etive, about 19 km/12 mi east of Oban. It has eight peaks, the highest of which rises to 1,126 m/3,694 ft.

One of the largest hydroelectric pumped storage schemes in Europe is situated on its south flank at the Cruachan Dam near the Falls of Cruachan. Water is raised to the reservoir from Loch Awe during off-peak hours.

Benedictine order

Religious order of monks and nuns in the Roman Catholic Church, founded by St Benedict at Subiaco, Italy, in the 6th century. It was brought to England by St Augustine in 597. A number of Oxford and Cambridge colleges have a Benedictine origin.

At the Reformation there were nearly 300 Benedictine monasteries and nunneries in England, all of which were suppressed. The English novice house survived in France, and in the 19th century monks expelled from France moved to England and built abbeys at Downside, Ampleforth, and Woolhampton. The monks from Pierre-qui-vive, who went to England in 1882, rebuilt Buckfast Abbey in Devon on the ruins of a Cistercian monastery.

Benjamin, George William John (1960–)

English composer, conductor, and pianist. He was a pupil of the French composer Messiaen (1908–92), and his colourful and sonorous works include *Ringed by the Flat Horizon* (1980), *At First Light* (1982), *Antara* (1987), and *Cascade* (1990).

Ben Macdhui, or Beinn MacDuibh

Second highest mountain in Britain, rising to 1,309 m/4,294 ft in the ◊Cairngorm Mountains, Aberdeenshire unitary authority, Scotland, 16 km/10 mi southeast of Aviemore. The summit is flat and bare.

Benn, Tony (Anthony Neil Wedgwood) (1925–)

British Labour politician, formerly the leading figure on the party's left wing. He was minister of technology 1966–70 and secretary of state for industry 1974–75, but his campaign against entry to the European Community (EC; now the European Union) led to his transfer to the Department of Energy 1975–79. A skilled parliamentary orator, he twice unsuccessfully contested the Labour Party leadership.

Born the son of the 1st Viscount Stansgate, a Labour peer, Benn was educated at Oxford. He was member of Parliament for Bristol Southeast 1950–60, when he succeeded to his father's title. Despite refusing to accept the title and being re-elected in Bristol in 1961, he was debarred from sitting in the House of Commons by a judgement of the Electoral Court. His subsequent campaign to enable those inheriting titles to disclaim them led to the passing of the Peerage Act in 1963; Benn was the first person to disclaim a title under this act.

Bennett, (Enoch) Arnold (1867–1931)

English novelist, playwright, and journalist. His major works are set in the industrial 'five towns' of the Potteries in Staffordshire (now Stoke-on-Trent) and are concerned with the manner in which the environment dictates the pattern of his characters' lives. They include *Anna of the Five Towns* (1902), *The Old Wives' Tale* (1908), and the trilogy *Clayhanger, Hilda Lessways*, and *These Twain* (1910–15).

Bennett, Alan (1934–)

English dramatist and screenwriter. His works (often set in his native north of England) treat such subjects as class, senility, illness, and death with macabre comedy. They include the series of monologues for television, *Talking Heads* (1988) and *Talking Heads 2* (1998), and the play *The Madness of George III* (1991), made into the critically acclaimed film *The Madness of King George* (1995) (Academy Award for best adapted screenplay).

He began writing professionally when he appeared in *Beyond the Fringe*, a stage revue (1959–64), with Peter Cook, Dudley Moore, and Jonathan Miller. His other screenwriting credits include *A Private Function* (1985) and *Prick Up Your Ears* (1987), based on the relationship between the dramatist Joe Orton and his lover Kenneth Halliwell. Other works include the TV films *An Englishman Abroad* (1982) and *A Question of Attribution*, and plays such as *Forty Years On* (1968), *Getting On* (1971), and *Kafka's Dick* (1986).

And it was for one of these smoking-concerts that I wrote a cod Anglican sermon, something I found no problem doing as I'd sat through so many in my youth. It took me half an hour to put together, and, since it later figured in (indeed earned me my place in) Beyond the Fringe, *it was undoubtedly the most profitable half-hour I've ever spent.*

Alan Bennett English dramatist and screenwriter. In *Writing Home* (1994), describing how he began writing comedy while studying at Exeter College, Oxford, in the 1950s

---

Bennett, Richard Rodney (1936–)

English composer of jazz, film music, symphonies, and operas. His film scores for *Far from the Madding Crowd* (1967), *Nicholas and Alexandra* (1971), and *Murder on the Orient Express* (1974) all received Oscar nominations. His operas include *The Mines of Sulphur* (1963) and *Victory* (1970).

Ben Nevis

Highest mountain in the British Isles (1,344 m/4,409 ft), 7 km/4 mi southeast of Fort William, Scotland.

The northeast side of Ben Nevis has a precipice of 450 m/1,480 ft. From the summit, which consists of a large plateau, there is an extensive view of the Scottish Highlands and islands, as far as the Hebrides. There is a well-marked and easily negotiated path to the summit, but also more difficult rock-climbing routes.

An observatory was built in 1823 to study sun spots. It was closed in 1904, having also been used for the collection of meteorological data. The base of the mountain, which measures about 48 km/30 mi, is composed mainly of granite and gneiss, while the upper part (the visible cliff) if formed chiefly of andesite, lavas, and agglomerate.

All punishment is mischief: all punishment in itself is evil.

Jeremy Bentham English philosopher, and legal and social reformer. *Principles of Morals and Legislation* (1789)

Benson, Frank (Francis) Robert (1858–1939)

English actor and theatre manager. He played in Henry ◊Irving's production of *Romeo and Juliet* at the Lyceum in London in 1882, and in 1883 acquired a Shakespeare repertory company, which he managed until his death. He played about 100 parts, the majority from Shakespeare. He was also responsible for many of the Shakespeare festivals at Stratford-upon-Avon, Warwickshire. He was knighted in 1916.

Bentham, Jeremy (1748–1832)

English philosopher, legal and social reformer, and founder of utilitarianism. The essence of his moral philosophy is found in the pronouncement of his *Principles of Morals and Legislation* (written in 1780, published in 1789): that the object of all legislation should be 'the greatest happiness for the greatest number'.

Bentham declared that the 'utility' of any law is to be measured by the extent to which it promotes the pleasure, good, and happiness of the people concerned. In 1776 he published *Fragments on Government*. He made suggestions for the reform of the poor law in 1798, which formed the basis of the reforms enacted in 1834, and in his *Catechism of Parliamentary Reform*, published in 1817, he proposed annual elections, the secret ballot, and universal male suffrage. He was also a pioneer of prison reform.

Bentham left his body for dissection. His clothed skeleton, with a wax head, is on view at University College, London.

Bentley, Edmund Clerihew (1875–1956)

English writer. He invented the four-line humorous verse form known as the ◊clerihew, first collected in *Biography for Beginners* (1905) and then in *More Biography* (1929). He was also the author of the classic detective story *Trent's Last Case* (1913), introducing a new naturalistic style that replaced Sherlock Holmesian romanticism. It was followed by *Trent's Own Case* (1936), in which he collaborated with H Warner Allen, and *Trent Intervenes* (1938), a volume of short stories.

Beowulf

Old English poem of 3,182 lines, thought to have been composed in the first half of the 8th century. It is the only complete surviving example of Germanic folk epic and exists in a single manuscript copied in England about 1000 and now housed in the Cottonian collection of the British Museum, London.

Berger, John Peter (1926–)

English left-wing art critic and writer. In his best-known book, *Ways of Seeing* (1972), he valued art for social rather than aesthetic reasons. He also attacked museums for preserving what is by nature ephemeral. His novels include *A Painter of Our Time* (1958) and *G* (1972) (Booker Prize).

Berkeley

Town in southern Gloucestershire, England, between Bristol and Gloucester; population (1991) 2,200. It is situated in the Vale of Berkeley, rich dairy and pasture country once celebrated for its 'Double Gloucester' cheese. Berkeley has a nuclear power station, which began production in 1962. **Berkeley Castle**, in which Edward II was murdered in 1327, is regarded as one of the finest castles in England. The castle was completed in 1153 by Lord Maurice Berkeley. The Norman keep can still be seen within the great courtyard of the castle. It is still occupied, after 800 years, by the Berkeley family. Dr Edward Jenner, who discovered vaccination, was born and buried in Berkeley.

Berkeley, Lennox Randal Francis (1903–1989)

English composer. His works for the voice include *The Hill of the Graces* (1975), verses from Spenser's *Faerie Queene* set for eight-part unaccompanied chorus; and his operas *Nelson* (1954) and *Ruth* (1956).

Berkhamsted

Town in the Chiltern Hills in Hertfordshire, England; population (1991) 14,800. It is situated 45 km/28 mi northwest of London, on the banks of the River Bulborne and the Grand Union Canal. The main industry in Berkhamsted is chemical manufacturing.

The grammar school in the town dates from 1541. The church of St Peter, dating from the 13th century but heavily restored in the 19th century, consists of many styles from different periods, especially Perpendicular. There are also the remains of an 11th-century castle where John II of France was imprisoned in 1356. The half-timbered Incent's House dates from the 16th century.

Berkoff, Steven (1937–)

English dramatist and actor. His abrasive and satirical plays include *East* (1975), *Greek* (1979), and *West* (1983). Berkoff's production of Oscar Wilde's *Salome* was staged in 1991. His *Collected Plays* (2 vols) were published in 1994.

He formed the London Theatre Group in 1968 as a vehicle for his own productions, which have included his adaptations of Kafka's *Metamorphosis* (1969) and *The Trial* (1970), and Edgar Allan Poe's *The Fall of the House of Usher* (1974). Recent theatre credits include *Coriolanus* (1995–97), *One Man* (1997), and *Massage* (1997). In his acting career, he has often been cast as a villainous 'heavy' as in the films *Beverly Hills Cop* (1984) and *The Krays* (1990). His autobiography *Free Association* was published in 1996.

Berkshire, or Royal Berkshire

Former county of south-central England; from April 1998 split into six unitary authorities: ◊West Berkshire, ◊Reading, ◊Slough, ◊Windsor and Maidenhead, ◊Wokingham and ◊Bracknell Forest.

Berkshire

Breed of domestic pig named for Berkshire, England, where it evolved from strains of differing origin and type. Berkshires are of medium size and mainly black in colour, with white on the face, legs, and tail-tip. They are used for pork production in many countries.

Berkoff, Steven *English actor, playwright, and stage director Steven Berkoff. Frequently cast as a villain in the films in which he appears, Berkoff is perhaps best known for his stage work, as in this 1980 contemporary production of* Hamlet. *Corbis*

Berlin, Isaiah (1909–1997)

Latvian-born British philosopher and historian of ideas. In *The Hedgehog and the Fox*, he wrote about Leo Tolstoy's theory of irresistible historical forces; and in *Historical Inevitability* (1954) and *Four Essays on Liberty* (1969), he attacked all forms of historical determinism. His other works include *Karl Marx* (1939) and *Vico and Herder* (1976).

Berlin emigrated to England with his family in 1920, and was professor of social and political theory at Oxford 1957–67. Knighted 1957.

Bermuda

British colony in the Northwest Atlantic Ocean, consisting of about 150 small islands, of which 20 are inhabited, linked by bridges and causeways
area 54 sq km/21 sq mi;
Population (1994) 60,500.

Under the constitution of 1968, Bermuda is fully self-governing. It is Britain's oldest colony, officially taken by the crown in 1684. Racial violence in 1977 led to intervention, at the request of the government, by British troops. A 1995 referendum rejected independence.

Berners-Lee, Tim(othy) (1955–)

English inventor of the World Wide Web in 1990. He developed the Web whilst working as a consultant at CERN. He currently serves as director of the W3 Consortium, a neutral body that manages the Web. In 1996, the British Computing Society (BCS) gave him a Distinguished Fellow award.

Bernstein, Sidney Lewis (1899–1993)

English entrepreneur and film and television producer. As founder of Granada Television, chair of the Granada group (1934–79), and president of the group until his death, he was a dominant influence on commercial television in the UK.

Cinema

Bernstein left school at 15 and soon became responsible for the entertainment side of his father's property business, managing the picture palaces and music halls the company acquired near the housing estates it built. In 1922 Bernstein founded a chain of Granada cinemas, first acquiring derelict theatres and converting them. His first purpose-built cinema was opened in Dover, Kent, in 1927. Also active in the theatre, Bernstein built the Phoenix in Charing Cross Road, London, which opened in September 1930 with the premiere of Noël Coward's *Private Lives*. Although this production was successful, others were not, and Bernstein sold the theatre two years later. During World War II, Bernstein was films adviser to the Ministry of Information, while his chain of 30 cinemas flourished. After the war, he spent five years in Hollywood, where he produced three films directed by Alfred Hitchcock: *Rope* (1948), *Under Capricorn* (1949), and *I Confess* (1953).

Television

In 1954, when the passage of the Television Act opened the way for commercial broadcasting, Bernstein applied for a licence, despite being a long-time believer in public-service broadcasting. After struggles in the early years, the television company became hugely successful, and Granada diversified into TV-set rentals, motorway service centres, and publishing. Bernstein remained active on the board of the company until he was 80.

Berwickshire

Former border county of southeast Scotland, which largely became the district of the same name within Borders region in 1975. It is now part of the Scottish Borders unitary authority.

Berwick, treaties of

Three treaties between the English and the Scots signed at Berwick, on the border of the two countries.

In the first treaty, made in January 1560, Queen Elizabeth I of England and the Calvinist Lords of the Congregation in Scotland agreed to an alliance, and the expulsion from Scotland of French troops who were supporting the Catholic regent, Mary of Guise, mother of Mary Queen of Scots.

In the second treaty, made in July 1586, James VI of Scotland signed a treaty with Elizabeth by which, in return for an English pension of £4,000, both sides agreed to maintain their established religions, and cooperate in case of an invasion of Britain by Catholic forces.

The third treaty, made in June 1639 ended the first Bishops' War. King Charles I of England agreed with the Scottish rebels that a General Assembly of the Scottish Church, the Kirk, would determine religious matters and that a parliament would be summoned in Edinburgh, and in return they stood down their forces.

Berwick-upon-Tweed

Town and port in Northumberland, northeast England, at the mouth of the River Tweed; population (1991) 13,500. Lying 5 km/3 mi southeast of the Scottish border, it is England's most northerly town. Salmon-netting and sea fishing are important, salmon and grain being the port's principal exports. Other industries include agricultural engineering, and the manufacture of foodstuffs and fertilizers.

History

Berwick was held alternately by England and Scotland for centuries, changing hands at least 13 times before being surrendered to the English in 1482. It was attached to Northumberland in 1885.

Features

Three bridges cross the Tweed: the Old Bridge with 15 arches (1611–34); the 28-arched Royal Border Railway Bridge, constructed by Robert Stephenson and opened by Queen Victoria in 1850; and the Royal Tweed Bridge (1928).

A thick defensive Elizabethan wall, 6 m/20 ft high and over 4 m/12 ft wide, surrounds the town centre. Begun in the 1550s by Elizabeth I to protect the town from possible attack by allied Scottish and French forces, it is an early example of new military architecture designed for gunpowder warfare. The remnants of a bell tower, used to alarm the neighbourhood during border raids, still survive.

Besant, Walter (1836–1901)

English writer. He wrote novels in partnership with James Rice (1843–1882), and produced an attack on the social evils of the East End of London, *All Sorts and Conditions of Men* (1882), and an unfinished *Survey of London* (1902–12). He was the brother-in-law of the feminist activist Annie Besant. In 1884 he founded the Society of Authors to protect the rights of new writers; he was its chair until 1892. Knighted 1895.

Bessemer, Henry (1813–1898)

English engineer and inventor who developed a method of converting molten pig iron into steel (the **Bessemer process**) in 1856.

During the Crimean War of the early 1850s Bessemer turned to the problem of high gas pressures causing guns to explode. The British military commanders showed no interest in Bessemer's work which was as yet unsuccessful owing to the use of phosphoric iron, but Napoleon III of France encouraged Bessemer in his experiments. By modifying the standard process, he found a way to produce steel without an intermediate wrought-iron stage, reducing its cost dramatically. However, to obtain high-quality steel, phosphorus-free ore was required. In 1860 Bessemer erected his own steel works in Sheffield, importing phosphorus-free iron ore from Sweden. Knighted 1879.

Best, George (1946–)

Northern Irish footballer. One of football's greatest talents, he was a vital member of the great Manchester United side which won the league championship in 1965 and 1967, and the European Cup in 1968, when he was voted both English and European footballer of the year. A goal provider as much as a goal scorer, he scored 134 goals in his 349 appearances for the club 1963–73.

Born in Belfast, he joined Manchester United as a youth and made his full debut at 17. Seven months later he won the first of 37 international caps for Northern Ireland. Although he subsequently made a series of short-lived comebacks, trouble with managers, fellow players, and the media, his career as a player was in decline by the time he left Manchester United in 1973.

Betjeman, John (1906–1984)

English poet and essayist, poet laureate from 1972. He was the originator of a peculiarly English light verse, nostalgic, and delighting in Victorian and Edwardian architecture. He also wrote prose works on architecture and social history which reflect his interest in the ◊Gothic Revival. His *Collected Poems* appeared in 1958 and a verse autobiography, *Summoned by Bells*, in 1960.

Betjeman's verse, seen by some as facile, has been much enjoyed for its compassion and wit, and its evocation of places and situations. His verse is traditional in form – favouring iambic lines and a conversational clarity – and subject matter. He recalls with great precision and affection details of his childhood in north London and holidays in Cornwall. His letters, edited by his daughter, Candida Lycett Green, were published in two volumes (1994 and 1995). He was knighted in 1969.

Betws-y-coed

Village in Conwy, north Wales, situated 25 km/15 mi south of Llandudno. It is a tourist centre for ◊Snowdonia and there are waterfalls nearby. The best known are Swallow Falls, Conwy Falls, and Fairy Glen.

The Conwy Valley Railway Museum is here, as is a Motor Museum. Artists are also attracted to the area, and trout and salmon are fished.

Bevan, Aneurin (Nye) (1897–1960)

British Labour politician. Son of a Welsh miner, and himself a miner at 13, he was member of Parliament for Ebbw Vale 1929–60. As minister of health 1945–51, he inaugurated the National Health Service (NHS); he was minister of labour January–April 1951, when he resigned (with Harold Wilson) on the introduction of NHS charges and led a Bevanite faction against the government. In 1956 he became chief Labour spokesperson on foreign affairs, and deputy leader of the Labour party in 1959. He was an outstanding speaker.

Bevan, Brian (1924–1991)

Australian-born rugby league winger who spent almost his entire playing career in England. Bevan's total of 796 tries for Warrington, Blackpool Borough, and representative sides 1945–64 is an unequalled record. Lean and almost scrawny in appearance, he was known for speed, swerve, and a characteristic sidestep which enabled him to score many of his tries untouched.

BETJEMAN, JOHN *English poet John Betjeman, photographed in 1955. He was poet laureate from 1972. As well as several volumes of poetry, Betjeman wrote a blank-verse autobiography,* Summoned by Bells *(1960), and various works on architecture. Corbis*

Beveridge, William Henry, 1st Baron Beveridge (1879–1963)

British economist. A civil servant, he acted as Lloyd George's lieutenant in the social legislation of the Liberal government before World War I. The ◊Beveridge Report of 1942 formed the basis of the welfare state in Britain.

Beveridge Report, the

Popular name of *Social Insurance and Allied Services*, a report written by William Beveridge in 1942 that formed the basis for the social-reform legislation of the Labour government of 1945–50.

Also known as the *Report on Social Security*, it identified five 'giants': illness, ignorance, disease, squalor, and want. It proposed a scheme of social insurance from 'the cradle to the grave', and recommended a national health service, social insurance and assistance, family allowances, and full-employment policies.

Beverley

Town in, and administrative headquarters of, the East Riding of Yorkshire, England, 13 km/8 mi northwest of Hull, and connected with the River Hull by canal; population (1991) 12,300. Beverley Minster (13th century) is an outstanding example of Gothic church architecture. The town is an agricultural centre with a flourishing cattle market and bakery, and the Beverley race course. Leather tanning, shipbuilding, manufacture of car accessories, aircraft assembly, industrial plastics, and metal plating are the chief industries.

Bevin, Ernest (1881–1951)

British Labour politician. Chief creator of the Transport and General Workers' Union, he was its general secretary 1921–40. He served as minister of labour and national service 1940–45 in Winston Churchill's wartime coalition government, and organized the 'Bevin boys', chosen by ballot to work in the coalmines as war service. As foreign secretary in the Labour government 1945–51, he played a leading part in the creation of NATO.

Bewick, Thomas (1753–1828)

English wood engraver. He excelled in animal subjects, some of his finest works appearing in his illustrated *A General History of Quadrupeds* (1790) and *A History of British Birds* (1797–1804). His birthplace, Cherryburn, Mickley, Northamptonshire, is a museum of wood engraving, with many of his original blocks. Bewick's swan (*Cygnus bewicki*) is named after him.

Bexhill-on-Sea

Seaside resort in East Sussex, England, 10 km/6 mi southwest of Hastings; population (1991) 38,900. Manufactured products include industrial machinery and scientific instruments. The centre of the seafront development is the de la Warr pavilion (1935–36), designed by the German architects Erich Mendelsohn and Serge Chermayeff (1900–1996).

Bexley

Outer borough of southeast Greater London. It includes the suburbs of Crayford, Erith, Sidcup

Features 16th-century Hall Place; Red House (1859), home of William Morris 1860–65; 18th-century Danson Park, with grounds landscaped by 'Capability' ◊Brown

Industries armaments manufacture (important since the 19th century at Crayford, site of Vickers Factory)

Population (1991) 215,600.

BG plc, formerly British Gas plc

Company formed in 1986 when the state-owned British Gas Corporation was privatized. This reversed the nationalization of the gas industry of 1949, when more than 1,000 separate private or municipally owned companies were taken into state ownership. In February 1997 British Gas was separated into Centrica plc, for the supply of gas, and British Gas plc, renamed BG plc, for the production and storage of gas; Transco, which owns the national gas pipeline network, is part of BG plc. BG also supplies electricity.

Following the opening up of the domestic gas market by the Gas Act 1995, new competitors have emerged to create a much more competitive market. By the late 1990s independent supply companies were providing around 60% of the energy used in British homes.

bhangra

Pop music evolved in the UK in the late 1970s from traditional Punjabi music, combining electronic instruments and ethnic drums. Bhangra bands include Holle Holle, Alaap, and Heera. A 1990s development is **bhangramuffin**, a reggae-rap-bhangra fusion popularized by Apache Indian (stage name of Steve Kapur, 1967–).

Bible (Greek *ta biblia* 'the books')

The first English translation of the entire Bible was by a priest, Miles Coverdale, in 1535; the **Authorized Version**, or **King James Bible** 1611, was long influential for the clarity and beauty of its language. A revision of the Authorized Version carried out in 1959 by the British and Foreign Bible Society produced the widely used American translation, the Revised Standard Version. A conference of British churches in 1946 recommended a completely new translation into English from the original Hebrew and Greek texts; work on this was carried out over the following two decades, resulting in the publication of the New English Bible (New Testament 1961, Old Testament and Apocrypha 1970). Another recent translation is the Jerusalem Bible, completed by Catholic scholars 1966.

The King James Bible has probably sold more copies than any other book in history, and is still popular, especially among fundamentalists. The **Good News Bible** has been the most popular translation into modern colloquial English.

Bibury

Village in Gloucestershire, England. It is situated in the Cotswold Hills, 11 km/7 mi north of Cirencester, on the River Coln. Bibury's riverside setting and honey-coloured old stone houses make it one of the Cotswold's most popular tourist destinations.

Arlington Row, a group of early 17th-century cottages in the village, is now the property of the National Trust; Arlington Mill, which was built in the 17th century, is now a museum.

Bicester

Market town in Oxfordshire, England, 21 km/13 mi northeast of Oxford; population (1991) 19,400. A retail park of factory outlet stores attracts many thousands of shoppers to the town each week. One of the British Army's largest ordnance depots is 3 km/2 mi away. A weekly street market and an annual fair are held in Bicester.

There are the remains of an Augustinian priory here, and the town has a number of gabled 16th-century houses. The ruins of the Roman settlement of Alchester lie 2 km/1.2 mi southwest of Bicester, on the line of the Roman road known as Akeman Street.

Biddulph

Town in Staffordshire, England, 11 km/7 mi north of Stoke-on-Trent; population (1991) 18,700. The main industries are mining, engineering, and textiles. The source of the River Trent is on nearby **Biddulph Moor**. Also on the moor is the Bridestones, a Neolithic burial-chamber.

Bideford

Town and port in north Devon, England; population (1991) 12,600. It is situated 13 km/8 mi southwest of Barnstaple, on both banks of the River Torridge, 6 km/4 mi above its confluence with the estuary of the River Taw. An old 24-arched bridge unites the two parts of the town. Industries include the making of fabric gloves and toys, boat building, and light engineering. There are regular sailings from Bideford to ◊Lundy Island, 18 km/11 mi offshore.

The port handled considerable trade up to the late 18th century, including cloth, salted fish, and tobacco. It was the starting-place of the last voyage of the 16th-century adventurer Sir Richard Grenville. The town also figures prominently in Charles Kingsley's *Westward Ho!*.

Big Bang

In economics, popular term for the changes instituted in late 1986 to the organization and practices of the City of London as Britain's financial centre, including the liberalization of the London stock exchange. This involved merging the functions of jobber (dealer in stocks and shares) and broker (who mediates between the jobber and the public), introducing negotiated commission rates, and allowing foreign banks and financial companies to own British brokers/jobbers, or themselves to join the London Stock Exchange.

The aim of the Big Bang was to ensure that London retained its place as one of the leading world financial centres. In the year before and after the Big Bang the City of London was marked by hyperactivity. This level of activity could not be sustained, and in October 1987 the frenzied trading halted abruptly and share prices fell sharply around the world on what became known as ◊Black Monday.

Big Ben

Popular name for the bell in the clock tower of the Houses of Parliament in London, cast at the Whitechapel Bell Foundry 1858, and known as 'Big Ben' after Benjamin Hall, First Commissioner of Works at the time. It weighs 13.7 tonnes. The name is often used to mean the tower as well.

Biggin Hill

Airport in the southeast London borough of Bromley. It was the most famous of the Royal Air Force stations in the Battle of Britain in World War II.

Biggles, Captain James Bigglesworth

Fictional World War I flying hero created by the English author W E ◊Johns. Biggles was first introduced in short stories published in *Popular Flying*, a magazine founded by Johns in 1932; the character, together with his companions Algy and Ginger, later featured in over 70 novels.

Big Issue, The

Magazine, published weekly, founded in 1991 to give homeless people the chance to earn income as vendors. It also campaigns on behalf of the homeless, but covers a range of social issues. The **Big Issue Foundation** is a separate charity supported financially by the magazine.

The Big Issue vendors buy the magazine at a fixed price and sell it on the streets for a fixed cover price, making a profit. They must have proved themselves homeless or 'vulnerably accommodated'. The magazine is published in five regional editions, including editions for Scotland and Wales.

bill

The name of a piece of proposed legislation, before it is enacted. See ◊Parliament for a glossary of parliamentary terms.

Billericay

Town in Essex, England, 8 km/5 mi east of Brentwood; population (1991) 22,800. In 1381 Billericay was the scene of the ◊Peasants' Revolt. The Pilgrims (Pilgrim Fathers) assembled here in Chantry Hall before leaving for America in 1620.

The church of St Mary Magdalen has a 16th-century tower which is considered to be one of the finest examples of brick architecture in the country.

Billingham

Industrial town in Stockton-on-Tees unitary authority, England, on the north bank of the River Tees. Billingham has a major electronics industry (Samsung), as well as chemical, metal and engineering works.

Billingham became an industrial town after World War I, when Imperial Chemical Industries developed an extensive chemicals works here. The tower of the church of St Cuthbert is Anglo-Saxon, dating from the 10th century.

Billingsgate

Chief London wholesale fish market, formerly (from the 9th

century) near London Bridge. It re-opened in 1982 at the new Billingsgate market, West India Dock, Isle of Dogs.

Bill of Rights

An act of Parliament of 1689 which established Parliament as the primary governing body of the country. It made provisions limiting ◊royal prerogative with respect to legislation, executive power, money levies, courts, and the army, and stipulated Parliament's consent to many government functions.

The Bill of Rights embodied the Declaration of Rights which contained the conditions on which William and Mary were offered the throne in the ◊Glorious Revolution. The act made illegal the suspension of laws by royal authority without Parliament's consent; the power to dispense with laws; the establishment of special courts of law; levying money by royal prerogative without Parliament's consent; and the maintenance of a standing army in peacetime without Parliament's consent. It also asserted a right to petition the sovereign, freedom of parliamentary elections, freedom of speech in parliamentary debates, and the necessity of frequent parliaments.

The Bill of Rights is the nearest approach to a written constitution that the United Kingdom possesses. Its provisions, where applicable, were incorporated in the US constitution ratified in 1788.

Billy Bunter

Fat, bespectacled schoolboy who featured in stories by Frank Richards (Charles Hamilton, 1876–1961), set at Greyfriars School. His adventures, in which he attempts to raise enough money to fund his passion for eating, appeared in the children's paper *Magnet* between 1908 and 1940, and subsequently in books in the 1940s and on television from 1952–62.

Bilston

Town in West Midlands, England, 6 km/4 mi southeast of Wolverhampton; population (1991) 25,100. At one time Bilston was one of the UK's most important centres for iron smelting and a focal point of industrial expansion; it is now engaged in a variety of industrial activities ranging from atomic power station development to sheet metal work.

The poet Sir Henry Newbolt was born in Bilston.

Bird, Isabella Lucy, Mrs Bishop (1831–1904)

British traveller and writer who wrote extensively of her journeys in the USA, Persia, Tibet, Kurdistan, China, Japan, and Korea. A fearless horsewoman, she generally travelled alone and in later life undertook medical missionary work.

Her published works include *The Englishwoman in America* (1856), *A Lady's Life in the Rocky Mountains* (1874), *Unbeaten Tracks in Japan* (1880), *Among the Tibetans* (1894), and *Pictures from China* (1900). She made her last great journey in 1901, when she travelled over 1,600 km/1,000 mi in Morocco.

Birdcage Walk

Area in St James's Park, London, connecting Buckingham Gate with Storey's Gate. It is named after the aviary established here during the reign of James I.

Birkbeck, George (1776–1841)

English doctor and pioneer of workers' education. Born in Settle, Yorkshire, he studied medicine and philosophy in Edinburgh. As professor of natural philosophy at Anderson's College, Glasgow, he started giving free lectures to workers in 1799 and these classes later became the Glasgow Mechanics' Institution. He moved to London as a doctor in 1804 and established a similar scheme of free classes for workers there. This scheme became the London Mechanics' Institute in 1824 and then evolved to become Birkbeck College, a college offering part-time degrees in the new University of London, which he also helped found.

> *Living in England, provincial England, must be like being married to a stupid but exquisitely beautiful wife.*
>
> MARGARET HALSEY US writer.
> *With Malice Toward Some* (1938)

Birkenhead

Seaport and industrial town in Wirral, Merseyside, England, opposite Liverpool on the Wirral peninsula, on the west bank of the Mersey estuary; population (1994 est) 93,100; Birkenhead urban area 270,200. It developed as a shipbuilding town with important dock facilities, but other principal industries now include engineering and flour-milling. The Mersey rail tunnel (1886), the Queensway road tunnel (1934), and a passenger ferry service link Birkenhead with Liverpool. After the decline of the shipbuilding industry and the closure of the last Cammell Laird shipyard in 1993, the former warehouses and industrial buildings on the Birkenhead waterfront were redeveloped as a heritage centre.

Features

The Williamson Art Gallery and Museum includes a collection of English watercolours and Liverpool porcelain, and a separate gallery has exhibits illustrating the history of the town's shipbuilding industry. The warships HMS *Plymouth* and HMS *Onyx* are preserved as museums.

History

The first settlement on the site of Birkenhead developed around a Benedictine priory founded in 1150. Birkenhead was still a small village when William Laird established a boilermaking and shipbuilding yard in the town in 1824, the forerunner of the immense Cammell Laird yards, and in 1829 the first iron vessel in the UK was built here. The first ferries across the Mersey from Birkenhead were operated by Benedictine monks in the 12th century. When steamboats were introduced in 1817, Birkenhead became a centre for pleasure trips, and inhabitants on the north side of the estuary were encouraged to settle in Birkenhead and other parts of the Wirral peninsula. Birkenhead was designed largely on a Scottish model, with streets and squares laid out between 1835 and 1846. Birkenhead Park, opened in 1847, was the first public park in the country. Much of the 19th-century housing has been demolished and large areas have been redeveloped. The Scout Movement was inaugurated in Birkenhead by Robert Baden-Powell in 1908.

Birkenhead, F(rederick) E(dwin) Smith, 1st Earl of Birkenhead (1872–1930)

British lawyer and Conservative politician. He was a flamboyant and ambitious character, and played a major role in securing the Anglo-Irish Treaty in 1921 which created the Irish Free State (now the Republic of Ireland). As a lawyer, his greatest achievement was the Law of Property Act of 1922, which forms the basis of current English land law.

Although characterized by the press and politicians as a swashbuckling orator, Smith proved himself a tireless, responsible, and far-sighted statesman. He also wrote a number of popularist literary works.

Birmingham

Industrial city and administrative headquarters of ◊West Midlands metropolitan county, central England, second-largest city in the UK, 177 km/110 mi northwest of London; population (1994 est) 1,220,000, metropolitan area 2,632,000. It is a major manufacturing, engineering, commercial, and service centre. The city's concert halls, theatres, and three universities also make it an important cultural and educational centre. Its chief products are motor vehicles, vehicle components and accessories, machine tools, aerospace control systems, electrical equipment, plastics, chemicals, food, chocolate (Cadbury), jewellery, tyres, glass, cars, and guns.

Features

National Exhibition Centre and National Indoor Arena; International Convention Centre; Birmingham International Airport; the Bull Ring shopping and office complex; restored canal walks ('Britain's Canal City'); Millennium Point science, technology, and entertainment complex, a Millennium Commission Landmark Project, due for completion in 2001.

Music and theatre

Symphony Hall (opened 1991), within the International Convention Centre, home to the City of Birmingham Symphony Orchestra, with a capacity of over 4,000; ◊Birmingham Royal Ballet; Birmingham Conservatoire, now part of the University of Central England; the repertory theatre founded in 1913 by Barry Jackson (1879–1961); D'Oyly Carte Opera Company.

Museums and galleries

Barber Institute of Fine Arts (Birmingham University, Edgbaston); the City Museum and Art Gallery (1864–81), containing a fine Pre-Raphaelite collection; the Museum of Science and Industry; Gas Hall, displaying temporary art exhibitions.

Educational institutions

University of Birmingham (1900); Aston University (1966), and University of Central England (formerly Birmingham Polytechnic), established in 1992.

Industry

Birmingham supplied large quantities of weapons to the Parliamentary forces of Oliver Cromwell during the English Civil War. Its location on the edge of the south Staffordshire coalfields, its skilled workforce, and its reputation for producing small arms allowed it to develop rapidly during the 18th and 19th centuries – much of the city was rebuilt between 1875 and 1882. It was a centre for munitions manufacture during both world wars. High-tech and service industries have gradually overtaken the city's traditional but declining large-scale metal industry.

History

After the Norman Conquest Birmingham passed into the possession of the Bermingham family, and it was mentioned in the Domesday Book of 1086, valued at 20 shillings. By the end of the 13th century a market town had grown up around the Bull Ring, the meeting point of several roads. It remained in the hands of the Bermingham family until 1527, when John Dudley, Duke of Northumberland, gained control of the town. In the English Civil War Birmingham supported the Parliamentarians, and it was sacked by the Royalist general Prince Rupert in 1643. The plague of 1665 caused many deaths in the city.

During the 19th century Birmingham was a centre of religious Nonconformity, supporting the movements of Unitarianism, Wesleyan Methodism, and Baptism. The chemist and Unitarian minister Joseph Priestley preached at the chapel known as the New Meeting from 1780. Riots occurred in 1791, and in 1832 the city played an important part in the agitation leading to the ◊Reform Acts. Further disturbances took place in 1839 in support of Chartism, a radical democratic movement.

Birmingham was not represented in parliament until 1832. It became a borough, electing its first town council in 1838, and it was made a city in 1889. In 1911 the boundaries were extended to include the borough of Aston Manor and other districts.

Industrial heritage

Birmingham was known from early times as a centre for the manufacture of swords, firearms, and jewellery. In the 14th century it was notable for its ironwork, and the metal trade was the basis of the city's rapid expansion during the Industrial Revolution.

Matthew Boulton and James Watt established the Soho Manufactory in Birmingham to produce steam engines. Other pioneers of industry and science in the city included the printer John Baskerville, the chemist Joseph Priestley, and William Murdock, the first person to develop gas lighting on a commercial scale. Birmingham's industrial heritage is illustrated at the Museum of Science and Industry, with exhibits including working steam, gas, and hot-air engines, and the oldest working steam engine in the world, made by Boulton and Watt in about 1779.

From the 1750s Birmingham became notable for the manufacture of jewellery, its silversmiths and goldsmiths being concentrated into one area of the city. The Jewellery Quarter Discovery Centre illustrates the growth and decline of this trade.

Redevelopment

In the 1870s and 1880s a major slum improvement scheme

and extensive rebuilding was initiated by Joseph ◊Chamberlain, mayor of the city between 1873 and 1875. Since the end of World War II, a programme of rebuilding and modernization has altered the city's landscape.

The Inner Ring Road, constructed in the 1940s, later enclosed the cylindrical Rotunda office block, and the Bull Ring shopping and office complex designed by Sydney Greenwood. Built between 1961 and 1964 on the site of the old town centre, the Bull Ring was one of the first inner-city shopping precincts with multi-level shops, offices, and car parks. New schemes for the redevelopment and modernization of the area include the demolition of the Rotunda. 'Spaghetti Junction', a complex multi-level motorway intersection, was constructed at Gravelly Hill, 3 km/2 mi northeast of the city centre, the first sections being opened from 1968. Much of the cramped industrial housing has been demolished, and areas of the city have been redeveloped with high-rise blocks and local shopping centres.

Suburbs

To the southwest of the city centre is Bournville, a worker's model village with some 8,000 houses, constructed in the 1890s by George Cadbury (1839–1922) and Richard Cadbury (1835–1899). The Cadbury World Museum, an exhibition centre, is sited here. ◊Edgbaston was first developed in the 1790s as a residential estate, and includes Cannon Hill Park, Midland Arts Centre, Edgbaston Cricket Ground, and Birmingham University with the Barber Institute of Fine Arts. It is also the site of the botanical gardens, and King Edward VI's school, which was originally founded in 1552 and moved here in 1936.

Birmingham Royal Ballet

Formerly the **Sadler's Wells Royal Ballet**. The company relocated to new purpose-built facilities at the Birmingham Hippodrome in 1990, when it was renamed the Birmingham Royal Ballet. David Bintley became artistic director in 1995.

The company was originally founded in 1946 as a touring company for the ◊Royal Ballet, when it was known as the Sadler's Wells Opera Ballet (later Theatre Ballet). It was renamed the Sadler's Wells Royal Ballet in 1976, and under the direction of Sir Peter Wright from 1977 continued to

BIRMINGHAM *Once known chiefly for its manufacturing industry, Britain's second city has a growing reputation for its cultural life. Created in the early 1990s, the Birmingham Royal Ballet company is seen here in its production of* Nutcracker Sweeties, *a jazz adaptation of Tchaikovsky's ballet by Duke Ellington and Billy Strayhorn. Bill Cooper/Birmingham Royal Ballet*

operate under the wing of the Royal Opera House, also performing at Sadler's Wells and on tour. Wright produced a much acclaimed version of the *Nutcracker* in 1991.

Birmingham Six

Irish victims of a miscarriage of justice who spent nearly 17 years in British prisons convicted of an IRA terrorist bombing in Birmingham in 1974. They were released in 1991 when the Court of Appeal quashed their convictions. The methods of the police and prosecution were called into question.

Birt, John (1944–)

English television executive, since 1993 director general (chief executive) of the BBC. His initial television work was in current affairs, especially *World In Action*, and with Peter Jay (1937–) he proposed an approach to reporting that placed emphasis on giving greater context to news and opinion. At the commercial station London Weekend Television 1974–87 he moved from head of current affairs to controller of programmes, then left to become the BBC's deputy director general in the same year.

His time at the BBC has been controversial, characterized by a drive to streamline production processes, at the same time separating production from the commissioning of programming, and by the bringing together of radio and television news and current affairs operations. Knighted 1998.

> *... the country is at a turning point like that of the 1630s, 1680s, 1830s, 1900s, and 1940s. In each of these periods there was a conflation of economic, social, and political crises which forced the decaying network of institutions to admit new demands for inclusion and participation.*
>
> Will Hutton English journalist. *The State We're In* (1995)

Birthday Odes

Works for solo, chorus, and orchestra written by English composers from the Restoration onwards to commemorate royal birthdays. Purcell wrote six for Queen Mary, consort of William III, as follows: 1. *Now does the glorious day appear* (1689), 2. *Arise my Muse* (1690), 3. *Welcome, welcome, glorious morn* (1691), 4. *Love's goddess sure was blind* (1692), 5. *Celebrate this festival* (1693), 6. *Come ye sons of art away* (1694).

Birtwistle, Harrison (1934–)

English avant-garde composer. He has specialized in chamber music, for example, his chamber opera *Punch and Judy* (1967) and *Down by the Greenwood Side* (1969). Birtwistle's early music was influenced by US composer Igor Stravinsky and by the medieval and Renaissance masters, and for many years he worked alongside Peter Maxwell ◊Davies.

His operas include *The Mask of Orpheus* (1986) (with electronic music by Barry Anderson (1935–1987)) and *Gawain* (1991), a reworking of the medieval English poem 'Sir Gawain and the Green Knight', described as 'Birtwistle's *Parsifal*'. It was followed by *The Second Mrs Kong*, in which the composer returned to Orphic myth.

Bishop, Ronald Eric (1903–1989)

British aircraft designer. He joined the de Havilland Aircraft Company in 1931 as an apprentice, and designed the Mosquito bomber, the Vampire fighter, and the Comet jet airliner.

Bishop Auckland

Town in Durham, England, 14 km/9 mi southwest of Durham City; population (1991) 3,900. Bishop Auckland has engineering, electrical, and other light industries.

In the northeast of the town is the bishop's palace, **Auckland Castle**, originally built by Anthony Bec during the reign of Edward I. The palace has been the country residence of the Bishops of Durham since the 12th century and is now the official residence. It lies in Bishop's Park, a park of 324 ha/800 acres.

Bishop's Stortford

Town in Hertfordshire, England, 47 km/29 mi northeast of London on the River Stort; population (1991) 26,700. Its main industries are brewing and malting. Stansted Airport lies to the northeast of the town. Cecil Rhodes was born here in 1853. His birthplace, The Old Vicarage, is now a museum.

In the late Saxon and early Norman period the town was the property of the Bishop of London; the ruins of the so-called Bishop's Prison can still be seen.

Bishops' Wars

Struggles between King Charles I of England and Scottish Protestants 1638–40 over Charles' attempt to re-impose royal authority over the church in Scotland. The name derives from the Arminian bishops in England who were seen as the driving force behind Charles' attempt.

Black, James Whyte (1924–)

Scottish physiologist, director of therapeutic research at Wellcome Laboratories (near London) from 1978. He was active in the development of beta-blockers (which reduce the rate of heartbeat) and anti-ulcer drugs. He shared the Nobel Prize for Physiology or Medicine in 1988 with US scientists George Hitchings (1905–) and Gertrude Elion (1918–). Knighted 1981.

Black, Joseph (1728–1799)

Scottish physicist and chemist. In 1754 he discovered carbon dioxide (which he called 'fixed air'). By his investigations in 1761 of latent heat and specific heat, he laid the foundation for the work of his pupil James Watt.

In 1756 Black described how carbonates become more alkaline when they lose carbon dioxide, whereas the taking-up of carbon dioxide reconverts them. He discovered that carbon dioxide behaves like an acid, is produced by fermentation, respiration, and the combustion of carbon, and guessed that it is present in the atmosphere. He also discovered the bicarbonates (hydrogen carbonates).

Blackadder, Elizabeth (1931–)

Scottish painter. Most of her paintings are landscapes and still lifes (although she has also done some commissioned portraits), and she is particularly well known for her sensitive studies of flowers, which often take her months to complete. She works with equal facility in oils and watercolour.

Black and Tans

Nickname of a special auxiliary force of the Royal Irish Constabulary employed by the British from 1920 to 1921 to combat the Sinn Féiners (Irish nationalists) in Ireland; the name derives from the colours of the uniforms, khaki with black hats and belts.

Black Beauty

Novel by Anna ◊Sewell, published in 1877. It describes the experiences of the horse, Black Beauty, under many different owners, and revived the genre of 'animal autobiography' popular in the late 18th and early 19th centuries. Although now considered to be a children's book, it was written to encourage sympathetic treatment of horses by adults.

Blackburn

British aircraft manufacturer; their aircraft were employed in both world wars, mainly by the Royal Navy.

The Kangaroo, a twin-engined biplane, was used by the Royal Naval Air Service in World War I for antisubmarine operations in the North Sea.

The Skua was a two-seat fighter and dive bomber used by the Fleet Air Arm in World War II. A Skua shot down the first German aircraft claimed by the Fleet Air Arm, and another sank the German cruiser *Königsberg* in Bergen harbour, but the model was withdrawn from combat duty 1941 to become a trainer.

Blackburn

Industrial city and administrative headquarters of ◊Blackburn and Darwen unitary authority, northwest England, on the Leeds–Liverpool canal, 32 km/20 mi northwest of Manchester; population (1991) 106,000. Until April 1998 it was part of the county of Lancashire. Industries include engineering, brewing, and high-tech industries. Textiles, electronics, radio and television components, leather, chemicals, paper, tufted carpets, and compact discs (Polygram) are produced.

Blackburn lies in the Calder valley, between the ◊Rossendale upland to the south and hilly country to the north. Flemish weavers settled here in the 14th century, and the town grew rapidly after the completion of the Leeds and Liverpool Canal in 1816. The town prospered as the centre of Lancashire's cotton-weaving industry until the industry's decline in the 1930s and 1940s.

Features

A working model of the ◊spinning jenny, invented in 1764 by James Hargreaves (born near Blackburn in about 1720), can be seen at the Lewis Textile Museum. Some of Blackburn's spinning-mills, weaving sheds, and chimneys survive, and the town's Victorian prosperity is reflected in large public buildings, including the town hall and the exchange building. The cathedral was originally a parish church, rebuilt in 1826 and enlarged in 1937–1950 as the cathedral of an Anglican diocese founded in 1926. The museum and art gallery contains a collection of Japanese prints and English watercolours.

Blackburn, with its public buildings and domestic housing blackened by smoke from factories and chimneys, benefited from anti-pollution laws and the development of smokeless zones. Much redevelopment has taken place and the Victorian town centre has been replaced by a modern shopping precinct.

Blackburn and Darwen

Unitary authority (borough status) in northwest England created in 1998, formerly part of Lancashire

Area 136 sq km2/53 sq mi

Towns and cities ◊Blackburn (administrative headquarters), Darwen

Features Leeds–Liverpool canal; River Darwen; Darwen Hill and Tower (372 m/1,220 ft); western foothills of Rossendale uplands; Lewis Textile Museum (Blackburn); Blackburn Museum and Art Gallery has largest display of European icons in Britain

Industries engineering, brewing, high technology industries, and the manufacture of chemicals, textiles, leather, electronics, paint, paper, carpets, and compact discs

Population (1995) 140,300.

Black Country

Central area of England, to the west and north of Birmingham, incorporating the towns of ◊Dudley, ◊Walsall, ◊Wolverhampton, and Sandwell. Heavily industrialized, it gained its name in the 19th century from its belching chimneys and mining spoil. Anti-pollution laws and the decline of heavy industry have changed the region's landscape. Coalmining in the area ceased in 1968.

The Black Country Museum was opened in 1975 at Dudley to preserve the region's industrial heritage. The area evolved with a dialect and culture distinct from that of nearby Birmingham.

There is still some quarrying in the region, and engineering, metal-processing, and the manufacture of motor accessories are important.

Black Death

Great epidemic of bubonic plague that ravaged Europe in the mid-14th century, killing between one-third and half of the population (about 75 million people). The cause of the plague was the bacterium *Yersinia pestis*, transmitted by fleas borne by migrating Asian black rats. The name Black Death was first used in England in the early 19th century.

It was recognized at Weymouth in August 1348, and before waning in the winter of 1349 had reduced the population of England by a third. The dramatic impact on localities is perpetuated in accounts which have entered folklore, such as the Reverend Mompesson's handling of the outbreak in the village of Eyam, Derbyshire, where he persuaded the people of the village not to flee, and so prevented the disease from spreading further.

Blackett, Patrick Maynard Stuart, Baron Blackett (1897–1974)

English physicist. He was awarded a Nobel prize in 1948 for work in cosmic radiation and his perfection of the cloud chamber, an apparatus for tracking ionized particles, with which he confirmed the existence of positrons.

Blackfriars Bridge

Bridge over the River Thames in London. It crosses the river at the approximate point where the River Fleet once entered the Thames. The first Blackfriars Bridge was begun in 1760, completed in 1770, and removed in 1860. The present bridge, which was begun in 1865 and opened in 1869, was designed by J Cubitt.

Blackfriars Bridge was widened by the London County Council for an electric tramway along the Embankment to Westminster Bridge in 1907–09. The name commemorates the Dominican monastery of Blackfriars, which is situated on the northern side of the river.

Blackheath

Suburb of London, lying south of Greenwich Park on the London–Dover road. It falls within the Greater London boroughs of ◊Greenwich and ◊Lewisham and takes its name from the common, where Wat Tyler encamped during the 1381 Peasants' Revolt. It developed as a residential suburb from the late 18th century.

For centuries the common was used as a place of assembly: Henry V was welcomed here after the Battle of Agincourt 1415; Henry VIII met Anne of Cleves at a Blackheath pageant; Charles II was welcomed here 1660; and the Methodist John Wesley held religious meetings on the heath in the 18th century. The common is crossed by Shooters Hill, a former haunt of highwaymen.

Black Hole of Calcutta

Incident in Anglo-Indian history: according to tradition, the nawab (ruler) of Bengal confined 146 British prisoners on the night of 20 June 1756 in one small room, of whom only 23 allegedly survived. Later research reduced the death count to 43, assigning negligence rather than intention.

Black Monday

Worldwide stockmarket crash that began on 19 October 1987, as fears of a US recession were voiced by the major industrialized countries. Between 19 and 23 October, the London Stock Exchange Financial Times 100 Index fell by 25%. The total paper loss on the London Stock Exchange and other City of London institutions during Black Monday was £94 billion.

Blackmore, R(ichard) D(oddridge) (1825–1900)

English novelist. His romance *Lorna Doone* (1869), set on Exmoor, southwest England, in the late 17th century, won him lasting popularity.

He published 13 other novels, including *Cradock Nowell* (1866), *The Maid of Sker* (1872), *Alice Lorraine* (1875), and *Springhaven* (1887).

Black Mountain, Welsh Mynydd Du

Ridge of hills in the ◊Brecon Beacons National Park in Carmarthenshire and Powys, south Wales, stretching 19 km/12 mi north from Swansea. The hills are composed of limestone and red sandstone. They are estimated to be 280–295 million years old and contain a coal seam. The highest peak is Carmarthen Van (Fan Foel) (802 m/2,630 ft).

Black Mountains

Upland massif with cliffs and steep-sided valleys in ◊Powys and ◊Monmouthshire, southeast Wales, lying to the west of ◊Offa's Dyke largely within the ◊Brecon Beacons National Park. The highest peak is Waun Fach (811 m/2,660 ft).

Blackpool

Seaside resort and unitary authority in northwest England, 45 km/28 mi north of Liverpool; area 35 sq km/14 sq mi; population (1995 est) 153,600; Blackpool urban area (1991) 261,400. It was part of the county of Lancashire until April 1998. Blackpool is the largest holiday resort in northern England, and provides important conference business facilities. Other industries include light engineering and the production of confectionery and biscuits.

Features include 11 km/7 mi of promenades, known for their autumn 'illuminations' of coloured lights; **Blackpool Tower**, 157 m/518 ft high; and the Pleasure Beach, an amusement park which includes Europe's largest and fastest roller-coaster, 75 m/235 ft high and 1.5 km/1 mi long (opened in 1994).

With its neighbours Lytham St Annes to the south and Fleetwood to the north, Blackpool is part of an urban ribbon between the Ribble estuary and Morecambe Bay.

Features

Blackpool Tower, built in 1894 and modelled on the Eiffel Tower in Paris, includes an aquarium, an indoor circus, and a ballroom. There are three 19th-century piers and other features include the Wintergardens, Grand Theatre, and Sealife Centre. A tram, which first operated in 1885, transports visitors along the promenade. Recreational facilities include swimming pools, tennis courts, golf courses, and bowling greens.

History

Blackpool developed as a resort in the 18th century and, following the opening of the railway in 1846, workers travelled to the town from all over industrial Lancashire and Yorkshire for 'Wakes Weeks', when factories and mills closed for the annual holiday. The promenade opened in 1856, the North Pier in 1863, and the outdoor Pleasure Gardens in 1872. Growth was more rapid after 1879, when the borough was the first in England permitted to spend money on advertising; large hotels, boarding houses, and lodgings, many of them in closely-packed terraces, were built to cater for the visitors. Holiday habits in the late 20th century have been changed by the increase in car ownership, making coastal resorts without railway termini more accessible, and the availability of cheap holidays abroad. However, the resort still attracts over 8 million people a year, a large percentage from the north of England, many of whom visit on more than one occasion.

Black Prince

Nickname of ◊Edward, Prince of Wales, eldest son of Edward III of England.

Black Rod, full title Gentleman Usher of the Black Rod

Official of the House of Lords whose duties include maintaining order and who has the power to arrest a peer for breach of privilege of the House or other offences noticed by the House. Black Rod is also the official messenger from the House of Lords to the House of Commons, most notably during the state opening of Parliament. These duties correspond to those of the ◊Serjeant at Arms in the House of Commons and may also be performed by a deputy, the **Yeoman Usher of the Black Rod**.

The name 'Black Rod' is derived from the staff, the insignia of the office, an ebony rod topped with a golden lion. The office dates from the reign of Henry VIII. Appointed by letters patent, Black Rod is also the first usher of the court and the kingdom, and as such takes part in all court and other ceremonials. Furthermore, Black Rod is the principal usher of the Order of the Garter, with duties including the guarding of the door at a chapter of the knights.

> *Our England is a garden, and such gardens are not made / By singing:– 'Oh, how beautiful!' and sitting in the shade.*
>
> Rudyard Kipling English writer. *The Glory of the Garden* (1911)

Blackshirts

Term widely used to describe fascist paramilitary organizations and applied to the followers of Oswald Mosley's British Union of Fascists.

Blackwall Tunnel

Road tunnel under the River Thames, London, linking the Bugsby Marshes (south) with the top end of the Isle of Dogs (north). The northbound tunnel, 7,056 km/4,410 ft long with an internal diameter of 7.2 m/24 ft, was built in 1891–97 to a design by Alexander Binnie; the southbound tunnel, 4,592 km/2,870 ft long with an internal diameter of 8.25 m/27.5 ft, was built in 1960–67 to a design by Mott, Hay, and Anderson.

Blackwater

River in Northern Ireland, rising in the southeast of County Tyrone, and flowing into Lough Neagh at its southwestern corner. It forms the boundary between counties Tyrone and Armagh.

Blackwell, Elizabeth (1821–1910)

English-born US physician, the first woman to qualify in medicine in the USA in 1849, and the first woman to be recognized as a qualified physician in the UK in 1869. Her example inspired Elizabeth Garrett ◊Anderson and many other aspiring female doctors.

Blaenau Ffestiniog

Town in Gwynedd, northwest Wales, 15 km/9 mi northeast of Porthmadog; population with Ffestiniog (1991) 4,500. The slate quarries are no longer operating but are open to tourists. A pumped storage scheme is also open to visitors. The Ffestiniog Railway, the oldest independent railway company in the world, runs steam trains on a narrow-gauge track from Blaenau to Porthmadog.

Blaenau Gwent

Unitary authority in south Wales, created in 1996 from part of the former county of Gwent

Area 109 sq km/42 sq mi

Towns ◊Ebbw Vale (administrative headquarters), ◊Tredegar, ◊Abertillery

Features Mynydd Carn-y-Cefn (550 m/1,800 ft); rivers Sirhowy and Ebbw; part of the ◊Brecon Beacons National Park is here

Population (1996) 73,000.

The area no longer depends on coal, iron, and steel industries, and former industrial land is being redeveloped.

Blair, Tony (Anthony Charles Lynton) (1953–)

British politician, leader of the Labour Party from 1994, prime minister from 1997. A centrist in the manner of his predecessor John ◊Smith, he became Labour's youngest leader by a large majority in the first fully democratic elections to the post in July 1994. In 1995 he won approval of a new Labour Party charter, intended to distance the party from its traditional socialist base and promote 'social market' values. He and his party secured a landslide victory in the 1997 general election with a 179-seat majority. He retained a high public approval rating of 60% in February 1998.

Blair retained a remarkably high level of public approval throughout his first year as prime minister, which included the key initiatives of Scottish and Welsh devolution and a peace agreement in Northern Ireland. Along with the creation of an elected mayor for London, they were approved in 1997-98 referenda. The economic strategy of the Blair government differed little from that of the preceding Conservative administrations, involving tight control over public expenditure and the promotion, the Private Finance Initiative, of 'public-private partnerships'.

He has governed in presidential style, delegating much to individual ministers, but intervening in key areas, such as welfare reform, in an effort to build up public support. He has been supported by a large 'Number 10' team of political advisers and media 'spin doctors'.

BLAIR, TONY *Labour politician Tony Blair, pictured with his wife Cherie, ended 18 years of Conservative government in Britain when he led his party to an overwhelming general election victory in 1997. His centrist approach, combining policies of the right (such as strict public spending controls) and left (social and constitutional reform) has been called the 'third way'. J. Sutton Hibbert/Rex*

Blair practised as a lawyer before entering the House of Commons in 1983 as member for the Durham constituency of Sedgfield. He was elected to Labour's shadow cabinet in 1988 and given the energy portfolio; he shadowed employment from 1991 and home affairs from 1992. Like John Smith, he did not ally himself with any particular faction and, in drawing a distinction between 'academic and ethical socialism', succeeded in winning over most sections of his party, apart from the extreme left.

Blake, George (1922–1994)

British double agent who worked for MI6 and also for the USSR. Blake was unmasked by a Polish defector in 1960 and imprisoned, but escaped to the Eastern bloc in 1966. He is said to have betrayed at least 42 British agents to the Soviet side.

Blake, Peter (1932–)

English painter, sculptor, and designer. He was one of the leading exponents of Pop art and his work evokes the spirit of the 'Swinging Sixties'. In particular he is remembered as the designer of the cover of the Beatles' album *Sergeant Pepper's Lonely Hearts Club Band* (1967).

Blake's main training was at the Royal College of Art, 1953–56. At this time he was influenced by folk and popular art, but by the end of the decade he was more concerned with mainstream Pop-art subjects such as film stars and singing idols. From 1975 to 1983 he was a member of the Brotherhood of Ruralists, a group of seven painters who aimed to evoke 'the spirit of the countryside'. From 1994 to 1996 he was Associate Artist at the National Gallery.

Blake, QuentinSaxby (1932–)

English book illustrator and author of books for children. His animated pen-and-ink drawings are instantly recognizable. A prolific illustrator of children's books written by others, including Roald Dahl, Stella Gibbons, George Orwell, and Evelyn Waugh, he has also written and illustrated his own books, including *Mr Magnolia* (1980) (Kate Greenaway Medal) and *Mrs Armitage and the Big Wave* (1997).

Blake, Robert (1599–1657)

British admiral of the Parliamentary forces during the English ◊Civil War. Appointed 'general-at-sea' in 1649, the following year he destroyed Prince Rupert's privateering Royalist fleet off Cartagena, Spain. In 1652 he won several engagements against the Dutch navy. In 1654 he bombarded Tunis, the stronghold of the Barbary corsairs, and in 1657 captured the Spanish treasure fleet in Santa Cruz.

Blake represented his native Bridgwater, Somerset, in the Short Parliament of 1640, and distinguished himself in defending Bristol in 1643 and Taunton in 1644–45 in the Civil War. In the naval war with the Netherlands (1652–54) he was eventually defeated by Maarten Tromp off Dungeness, but had his revenge in 1653 when he defeated the Dutch admiral off Portsmouth and the northern Foreland. Blake was elected lord warden of the ◊Cinque Ports in 1654, and constable of Dover Castle.

Blake, William(1757–1827)

English poet, artist, engraver, and visionary, and one of the most important figures of English ◊Romanticism. His lyrics, often written with a childlike simplicity, as in *Songs of Innocence* (1789) and *Songs of Experience* (1794), express a unique spiritual vision. In his 'prophetic books', including *The Marriage of Heaven and Hell* (1790), he created a vast personal mythology. He illustrated his own works with hand-coloured engravings.

Songs of Innocence was the first of his own poetic works that he illustrated and engraved, his highly individual style ultimately based on Michelangelo and Raphael. The complementary volume, *Songs of Experience*, which contains the poems 'Tyger! Tyger! burning bright' and 'London', expresses Blake's keen awareness of cruelty and injustice. Blake's poem 'Jerusalem' (1820) was set to music by Charles Parry.

Central themes in his work are the importance of passion and imagination, his visionary spirituality – he often claimed that he saw angels – and a political radicalism that made him a keen supporter of the French Revolution and of Mary Wollstonecraft's views on the rights of women.

Blakeney

Village on the north coast of Norfolk, England, 10 km/6 mi east of Wells-next-the-Sea; population (1991) 1,500. A lagoon-like stretch of sea is used for sailing, and at **Blakeney Point** there is a bird sanctuary covering an area of over 4 sq km/1.5 sq mi. There is also a colony of seals.

Blanchflower, Danny (Robert Dennis) (1926–1993)
Northern Irish football player, captain of Tottenham Hotspur from 1959 to 1964, during which time it became the first club since Victorian times to win both the Championship and FA Cup in one season (1960–61). He also captained Northern Ireland in the 1958 World Cup finals, when the team reached the quarterfinals, and was Footballer of the Year in 1958 and 1961. His play was characterized by its inventiveness and subtlety.

blanketeers
Manchester hand-loom weavers who began a march on London in March 1817, in protest against the suspension of the ◊Habeas Corpus Act and the economic slump after the end of the Napoleonic Wars. They were so named because they carried their blankets on the march. The march was broken up in Stockport, Cheshire, the day after it began. See also ◊Peterloo massacre.

Blantyre, or **High Blantyre**
Town in South Lanarkshire unitary authority, Scotland, near the River Clyde, adjoining northwest Hamilton, 12 km/8 mi southeast of Glasgow; population (1991) 18,500. The district was once a major coal producer, but engineering is now the principal industry, conducted on a large industrial estate. Blantyre was the birthplace of the 19th-century missionary explorer David Livingstone, and his home is now a national memorial. The ruins of Blantyre priory, founded in the late 13th century, are sited upriver on the banks of the Clyde.

Blashford-Snell, John (1936–)
English explorer and soldier. His expeditions have included the first descent and exploration of the Blue Nile (in 1968); the journey north to south from Alaska to Cape Horn, crossing the Darien Gap between Panama and Colombia for the first time (1971–72); and the first complete navigation of the Congo-Zaïre River, Africa (1974–75).

From 1963 he organized adventure training at Sandhurst military academy. He was director of Operation Drake (1977–81) and Operation Raleigh (1978–82). His books include *A Taste for Adventure* (1978).

Bleasdale, Alan (1946–)
English dramatist. He gained a national reputation with the series of television dramas *The Boys From the Blackstuff* (1982), which portrayed the pressures and tensions of unemployment on a group of men. It was followed by *GBH* (1991), a psychological study of the leader of a city council in northern England. His stage plays include *Having a Ball* (1981) and *On the Ledge* (1993).

He wrote several early plays including *Down the Dock Road* (1976) for the Everyman Theatre in Liverpool, where he was artistic director from 1977. His early *Scully* stories about an adolescent boy were adapted for television in 1984.

Blech, Harry (1910–)
English conductor and violinist. He played with the BBC Symphony Orchestra before World War II and was a founder member of the Blech quartet 1933–50. He founded the London Mozart Players in 1949 and was their music director until 1984.

Blenheim Palace
House near Woodstock, Oxfordshire, England. Blenheim is the seat of the Duke of ◊Marlborough. Conceived as a national monument and virtually as a royal palace, it was the gift of Queen Anne and Parliament to the 1st Duke in gratitude for his victory over the army of Louis XIV at the Battle of Blenheim in 1704. It was built from 1705 to 1725, and designed by John ◊Vanbrugh, assisted by Nicholas ◊Hawksmoor. Grinling ◊Gibbons supervised the carving. Blenheim Palace exemplifies Vanbrugh's style of 'heroic architecture'. Blenheim Palace was designated a World Heritage Site in 1987.

Vanbrugh's formal gardens disappeared between 1764 and 1774 when the whole park was landscaped by Capability ◊Brown, who made a lake and planted trees, reputedly arranged according to the battle plan at Blenheim.

Bletchley
Town in Buckinghamshire, England, 72 km/45 mi northwest of London, situated just south of Milton Keynes. It was originally a railway town and has developed through the expansion of Milton Keynes.

Bletchley Park was the home of Britain's World War II code-breaking activities. German codes generated by the Enigma enciphering machine were cracked here. It is now used as a training post for GCHQ (Britain's electronic surveillance centre). It is open to the public at certain times for tours, exhibitions, and lectures.

Blethyn, Brenda (1946–)
English stage and screen actress. A versatile performer, her roles include that of a downtrodden working-class heroine in Mike ◊Leigh's *Secrets and Lies* (1996), which earned her universal acclaim, Cordelia in the 1982 BBC production of *King Lear*, and a matriarch in the US feature film *A River Runs Through It* (1992). Her British television credits include *Chance in A Million* (1986) and *The Buddha of Suburbia* (1993). She also featured in the films *Night Train* and *Girl's Night* (both 1998).

Blickling Hall
Large Jacobean house near Aylsham, Norfolk, England. It was built in rose-red brick by Henry Hobart, Lord Chief Justice of England, who pulled down the 14th-century manor house in which Anne Boleyn spent much of her childhood. Blickling Hall, its contents, and 1933 ha/4774 acres, including the village of Blickling, were left to the National Trust by the 11th Marquess of Lothian in 1940.

A family of Norwich architects called Ivory made alterations to the interior of the Hall and also built the Orangery and Temple. The 19th-century formal garden was redesigned in 1930; the park is in the style of Capability Brown and contains a lake.

Bligh, William (1754–1817)

English sailor. He accompanied Captain James ◊Cook on his second voyage around the world (1772–74), and in 1787 commanded HMS *Bounty* on an expedition to the Pacific. On the return voyage, in protest against harsh treatment, the crew mutinied. Bligh was sent to Australia as governor of New South Wales in 1805, where his discipline again provoked a mutiny in 1808 (the Rum Rebellion).

Bligh went to Tahiti with the *Bounty* to collect breadfruit-tree specimens, and gained the nickname 'Breadfruit Bligh'. In the mutiny, he and those of the crew who supported him were cast adrift in a boat with no map and few provisions. They survived, after many weeks reaching Timor, near Java, having drifted 5,822 km/3,618 mi. Many of the crew settled in the ◊Pitcairn Islands. On his return to England in 1790, Bligh was exonerated for his conduct.

Blighty (Hindi *bilati*, 'foreign')

Popular name for England among British troops in World War I. The term was also used to describe serious but non-fatal wounds requiring hospitalization in Britain; for example, 'He caught a Blighty one'.

blimp

Airship: any self-propelled, lighter-than-air craft that can be steered. A blimp with a soft frame is also called a **dirigible**; a **zeppelin** is rigid-framed.

During World War I British lighter-than-air aircraft were divided into A-rigid and B-limp (that is, without rigid internal framework), a barrage balloon therefore becoming known as a blimp. The cartoonist David Low adopted the name for his stuffy character **Colonel Blimp**.

Blind Harry

Another name for ◊Harry the Minstrel, Scottish poet.

Bliss, Arthur Edward Drummond (1891–1975)

English composer and conductor. He became Master of the Queen's Musick in 1953. Among his works are *A Colour Symphony* (1922); music for the ballets *Checkmate* (1937), *Miracle in the Gorbals* (1944), and *Adam Zero* (1946); an opera *The Olympians* (1949); and dramatic film music, including *Things to Come* (1935). He conducted the first performance of US composer Igor Stravinsky's *Ragtime* for 11 instruments in 1918.

Blitz, the

Abbreviation for Blitzkrieg (German for lightning war), applied to the attempted saturation bombing of London by the German air force between September 1940 and May 1941. It has been estimated that about 40,000 civilians were killed, 46,000 injured, and more than a million homes destroyed and damaged in the Blitz, together with an immense amount of damage caused to industrial installations.

The first raid was against London on 7–8 September 1940, and raids continued on all but 10 nights until 12 November. The raids then targeted industrial cities such as Coventry (14 November), Southampton, Birmingham, Bristol, Cardiff, Portsmouth, and Liverpool, with occasional raids on London. In spring 1941 the air defences began to take a larger toll of the attackers, due to improvements in radar for night fighters and for artillery control. The raids fell away during the early summer as Luftwaffe forces were withdrawn from the west in preparation for the invasion of the USSR.

Blood, Thomas (1618–1680)

Irish adventurer, known as Colonel Blood. In 1663 he tried to seize the Lord Lieutenant of Ireland at Dublin Castle, and in 1670 he attempted to assassinate the Duke of Ormonde in 1670, possibly on instructions from the Duke of ◊Buckingham. In 1671 he and three accomplices succeeded in stealing the crown and orb from the Tower of London, but were captured soon afterwards.

Blood received estates in Ireland in return for military services rendered to the Parliamentary party during the English Civil War. These were forfeited at the Restoration of the monarchy but were later returned by Charles II. In 1671 Charles II visited him in prison, and through his favour Blood obtained his release.

Bloody Assizes

Courts held by judges of the High Court in the west of England under the Lord Chief Justice, Judge ◊Jeffreys, after ◊Monmouth' s rebellion in 1685. Over 300 rebels were executed and many more flogged or imprisoned.

Bloody Sunday

Shooting dead of 13 unarmed demonstrators in Londonderry, Northern Ireland, on 30 January 1972, by soldiers from the British Army's 1st Parachute Regiment. One wounded man later died from an illness attributed to the shooting. The demonstrators were taking part in a march to protest against the British government's introduction of internment without trial in Northern Ireland on 9 August 1971. The British government-appointed Widgery Tribunal found that the paratroopers were not guilty of shooting dead the 13 civilians in cold blood. In January 1998, however, British prime minister Tony Blair announced a new inquiry into the events of Bloody Sunday.

Bloomsbury

Area in the borough of Camden, London, a series of squares between Gower Street and High Holborn. It contains London University, the British Museum (1759), and the Royal Academy of Dramatic Arts. Between the world wars it was the home of the ◊Bloomsbury Group of writers and artists.

Bloomsbury Group

Intellectual circle of writers and artists based in Bloomsbury, London, which flourished in the 1920s. It centred on the house of publisher Leonard Woolf (1880–1969) and his wife, novelist Virginia ◊Woolf. Typically Modernist, their innovative artistic contributions represented an important section of the English avant-garde.

The circle included the artists Duncan ◊Grant and Vanessa Bell (1879–1961), the biographer Lytton ◊Strachey, and the

HOLBORN CIRCUS IN THE BLITZ *Holborn Circus in London burns at the height of the Blitz. London was bombed on 76 consecutive nights as part of the Battle of Britain campaign by the German airforce during 1940. Corbis*

economist John Maynard ◊Keynes. From their emphasis on close interpersonal relationships and their fastidious attitude towards contemporary culture arose many accusations of elitism.

Blount, Charles, Earl of Devonshire, 8th Baron Mountjoy (1563–1606)

English soldier, a friend of the 2nd Earl of Essex. Blount accompanied him and ◊Raleigh on their unsuccessful expedition to the Azores in 1597. He became Lord Deputy of Ireland 1601 and quelled the revolt led by the Irish chief Hugh O'Neill, 2nd Earl of Tyrone, when the Irish failed in their attempt to reach a Spanish force that had arrived at Kinsale 1601. He subdued most of Ireland and was created earl 1603. Knighted 1586.

blue books

Former official reports published by the government and Parliament on domestic and foreign affairs in the 19th and early 20th centuries, so named for their blue paper covers. They were usually the reports of a royal commission or a committee, but short acts of Parliament were also sometimes known as blue books, even when they had no cover.

Blue John Cavern

Cave in Derbyshire, England. It is situated in Treak Cliff in the north of the county, 3 km/2 mi from Castleton. Blue John is the name of a distinctive local variety of fluorspar. Blue John Cavern and Treak Cliff Cavern are both open to the public.

Blue Peter

Long-running British children's television program (1958–). Usually hosted by three young adults, and following a magazine-style segmented structure, it has been a source of information on such topics as popular culture, pet care, gardening, and creative use of everyday household objects for several generations of children.

The show has been responsible for raising thousands of pounds for charity by organizing campaigns and urging its young viewers to get involved. Presenters have included Valerie Singleton, Peter Purves, John Noakes, Simon Groom, Sarah Greene, Anthea Turner, and Konnie Huq.

Blueprint for Survival

Environmental manifesto published in 1972 in the UK by the editors of the *Ecologist* magazine. The statement of support it attracted from a wide range of scientists helped draw attention to the magnitude of environmental problems.

Blunden, Edmund (Charles) (1896–1974)
English poet and critic. He served in World War I and published the prose work *Undertones of War* (1928). His poetry is mainly about rural life.

His poems were published as early as 1914, but his first notable volume was *The Waggoner and other Poems* (1920), followed by *The Shepherd and other Poems of Peace and War* (1922). Among his scholarly contributions was the discovery and publication of some poems by the 19th-century poet John ◊Clare.

Blunkett, David (1947–)
British Labour politician, secretary of state for education and employment from 1997. He was leader of Sheffield city council from 1980 before becoming MP for Sheffield Brightside in 1987. He was shadow spokesperson on local government 1988–92, shadow health secretary 1992–94, and shadow education and employment secretary 1994–97. Blunkett overcame the disability of blindness to rise through the ranks of the trade union movement and local government to the forefront of national politics.

Blunt, Anthony Frederick (1907–1983)
English art historian and double agent. As a Cambridge lecturer, he recruited for the Soviet secret service and, as a member of the British Secret Service 1940–45, passed information to the USSR. In 1951 he assisted the defection to the USSR of the British agents Guy ◊Burgess and Donald Maclean (1913–1983). He was the author of many respected works on French and Italian art. Unmasked in 1964, he was given immunity after his confession.

He was director of the Courtauld Institute of Art 1947–74 and Surveyor of the Queen's Pictures 1945–1972. He was stripped of his knighthood in 1979 when the affair became public.

Blur
English pop group. Their album *Parklife* (1994) won wide admiration for its catchy melodies and quirky 'Cockney' attitude. Members are singer Damon Albarn (1968–), guitarist Graham Coxon (1969–), bassist Alex James (1968–), and drummer Dave Rowntree (1963–).

The release of the single 'Girls and Boys' (1994) and the third album *Parklife* saw a recreation of Blur as the quintessentially English pop group, combining a feel for 'classic' English pop with a 1990s sensibility. Blur's subsequent mainstream success led to a renewed interest in modern English pop (termed 'Britpop').

Blyth
Town in Northumberland, England; population (1991) (Blyth Valley district) 77,200. It is situated at the mouth of the River Blyth (32 km/20 mi long), where it enters the North Sea, and is 11 km/7 mi north of the River Tyne. Blyth has two power stations.

In the 19th century Blyth was a coal-shipping and shipbuilding port.

Blyth, Chay (Charles) (1940–)
British sailing adventurer who rowed across the Atlantic with Capt John Ridgeway in 1966 and sailed solo around the world in a westerly direction during 1970–71. He sailed around the world with a crew in the opposite direction 1973–74, and in 1977 he made a record-breaking transatlantic crossing from Cape Verde to Antigua.

Blyton, Enid Mary (1897–1968)
English writer of children's books. She used her abilities as a trained teacher of young children and a journalist, coupled with her ability to think like a child, to produce books at all levels which, though criticized for their predictability and lack of characterization, and more recently for social, racial, and sexual stereotyping, satisfy the reader's need for security. Her bestselling series were, the ◊*Famous Five* series, the 'Secret Seven', and 'Noddy'.

In 1951 she had 31 different titles published, and ten years after her death she was the fourth most translated author in the world. In 1996 Trocadero plc, a British property and leisure company, paid £14.25m for the residual copyrights in over 700 of her books.

BMA
Abbreviation for ◊British Medical Association.

BNFL
See ◊British Nuclear Fuels.

Boadicea
Alternative (Latin) spelling of British queen ◊Boudicca.

Boardman, Chris (1968–)
English cyclist who first came to prominence in 1992 when he won the individual pursuit gold medal at the Barcelona Olympics.

In July 1993 he set a new world one-hour record of 52.270 km, beating the previous record by 0.674 km. In 1994 he made his debut in the Tour de France and led the race for the first three days. Then at the World Cycling Championships he won both the individual pursuit and road time-trial titles. In 1996, just days after winning back the world pursuit title and twice breaking the world record, he regained the world one-hour record, extending the distance to 56.38 km.

Boateng, Paul Yaw (1951–)
British Labour politician and broadcaster. Elected member of Parliament for Brent South in 1987, he was appointed to Labour's Treasury team in 1989, the first black appointee to a front-bench post. He served on numerous committees on crime and race relations. In May 1997 he was appointed

parliamentary under-secretary in the health department in the new Labour government.

Boat Race, the

Annual rowing race between the crews of Oxford and Cambridge universities. It is held during the Easter vacation over a 6.8 km/4.25 mi course on the River Thames between Putney and Mortlake, southwest London.

The Boat Race was first held in 1829 from Hambledon Lock to Henley Bridge. Up to and including the 1998 race it had been staged 142 times; Cambridge had 76 wins, Oxford 68 and there had been one dead heat in 1877. The reserve crews also have their own races. The Cambridge reserve crew is called Goldie, Oxford's is called Isis.

Bocking

Town in Essex, England; population (1991) 10,900. It is situated on the River Blackwater, 1 km/0.6 mi northeast of Braintree. The firm of Courtauld's, specializing in the production of artificial silk, was founded here in 1816 by Samuel Courtauld.

Bodiam

Village in East Sussex, England. It is situated 16 km/10 mi north of Hastings, on the River Rother. **Bodiam Castle** was built by Sir Edward Dalyngruge in 1385, and was one of the last castles to be constructed in England. The towers, walls, gateway, portcullis, and moat of this large rectangular castle remain intact, although the interior is less well-preserved. The castle, attractively set in a large moat, now belongs to the National Trust.

Bodley, Thomas (1545–1613)

English scholar and diplomat, after whom the Bodleian Library in Oxford is named. After retiring from Queen Elizabeth I's service 1597, he restored the university's library, which was opened as the Bodleian Library 1602.

The library had originally been founded in the 15th century by Humphrey, Duke of Gloucester (1391–1447). Knighted 1604.

Bodmin

Market town in Cornwall, southwest England, 48 km/30 mi

BODIAM CASTLE *This fortress in Sussex was constructed in 1385–88 in response to French raids on the south coast of England. Its sheer walls rise from a wide moat, which can only be crossed by a narrow causeway. It has been in ruins since the English Civil War. Corel*

northwest of Plymouth; population (1991) 12,500. It is the commercial centre of a farming area. Other activites include some light industry and the provision of tourist services. **Bodmin Moor**, to the northeast, is a granite upland culminating in Brown Willy, the highest point in Cornwall at 419 m/1,375 ft.

History

Situated midway between the north and south coasts of Cornwall, Bodmin became an important trading town in medieval times. It was the capital of Cornwall from 1835 until 1989 when it was replaced by Truro. The scholar and writer Arthur Quiller-Couch was born here in 1863.

Features

St Petroc's Church is the largest medieval church in Cornwall. Dating mostly from the late 15th century, it contains a 12th-century font. There is a 44 m/144-ft obelisk on the hill to the southwest of the town, erected in 1856 in memory of Walter Raleigh Gilbert (1785–1853), a descendant of the adventurer Walter Raleigh. Lanhydrock House, 4 km/2.5 mi southeast of Bodmin, is a 17th-century house now owned by the National Trust, which was largely rebuilt after a fire in 1881.

Body Shop

UK cosmetics company, founded by Anita Roddick. The first shop opened in Brighton in 1976. The company has a 'green' image, selling only natural toiletries, not tested on animals, and in refillable plastic containers. Its emphasis on natural ingredients has been influential in the field of cosmetics retailing.

In 1998 Body Shop had 1,594 outlets in 47 countries (263 in the UK, 527 in the rest of Europe, 290 in the USA, 130 in the rest of the Americas, 308 in Asia, 76 in Australia and New Zealand). Of these, 308 were company owned and the rest (approx 81%) franchised.

Boer War

The second of the ◊South African Wars 1899–1902, waged between Dutch settlers in South Africa and the British.

There's something wrong with actors. We've always been a suspect breed. Socially, I find myself more admissible now in England because I've written books.

Dirk Bogarde English actor.
Ritz April 1983

Bogarde, Dirk stage name of Derek Niven van den Bogaerde (1921–)

English actor. He appeared in comedies and adventure films such as *Doctor in the House* (1954) and *Campbell's Kingdom* (1957), before acquiring international recognition for complex roles in Joseph Losey's *The Servant* (1963) and *Accident* (1967), and Luchino Visconti's *Death in Venice* (1971).

His other films include *The Night Porter* (1974), *A Bridge Too Far* (1977), and Bertrand Tavernier's *Daddy nostalgie/These Foolish Things* (1990). He has also written autobiographical books and novels, including *A Postillion Struck by Lightning* (1977), *Backcloth* (1986), *A Particular Friendship* (1989), and *A Short Walk from Harrods* (1993). He was knighted in 1992.

Bogdanov, Michael, born Michael Bogdin (1938–)

English theatre director. He became Artistic Director of the English Shakespeare Company in 1986. He produced the opening production at the Theatre Upstairs at the Royal Court Theatre in 1969, *A Comedy of the Changing Years*. He has directed plays at the Royal National Theatre and at the Royal Shakespeare Company, including the seven-play history cycle *The Wars of the Roses*, which won the Laurence Olivier Award for Director of the Year in 1989.

Anne Boleyn was not a catalyst in the English Reformation; she was an element in the equation.

E W Ives
Anne Boleyn (1986)

Bognor Regis

Seaside resort in West Sussex, southern England, 105 km/66 mi southwest of London; population (1991) 56,700. High-tech industries such as refrigeration and light engineering are being developed alongside Bognor's traditional tourist economy. It developed as a resort in the late 18th century and 19th century and was popular with Queen Victoria. The word 'Regis' was added to its name after George V visited nearby Aldwick to convalesce in 1929.

Boksenberg, Alexander (1936–)

English astronomer and physicist. Boksenberg devised a light-detecting system that can be attached to telescopes, vastly improving their optical powers. His image photon-counting system (IPCS) revolutionized observational astronomy, enabling Boksenberg and others to study distant quasars.

Boleyn, Anne (*c.* 1507–1536)

Queen of England 1533–36 as second wife of Henry VIII. She gave birth to the future Queen Elizabeth I in September 1533. Although she subsequently produced a still-born son in January 1536, she produced no living male heir to the throne, and was executed on a false charge.

Having no male heir by his first wife, Catherine of Aragón, Henry broke from Rome and the pope (starting the Reformation) in order to divorce Catherine and marry Anne. Three years after Anne had married Henry she was accused of adultery and incest with her half-brother (a charge invented by Thomas Cromwell), and sent to the Tower of London. She was declared guilty, and was beheaded on 19 May 1536 at Tower Green.

Bolingbroke

Title of Henry of Bolingbroke, ◊Henry IV of England.

Bolingbroke, Henry St John, 1st Viscount Bolingbroke (1678–1751)

British Tory politician and political philosopher. He was foreign secretary 1710–14 and a Jacobite conspirator. His books, such as *Idea of a Patriot King* (1738) and *The Dissertation upon Parties* (1735), laid the foundations for 19th-century Toryism.

Secretary of war 1704–08, he became foreign secretary in Robert Harley's ministry in 1710, and in 1713 negotiated the Treaty of Utrecht. His plans to restore the 'Old Pretender' James Francis Edward Stuart were ruined by Queen Anne's death only five days after he had secured the dismissal of Harley in 1714. He fled abroad, returning in 1723, when he worked to overthrow Robert Walpole.

Bolsover

Town in Derbyshire, England; population (1991) 11,000. It is situated on a ridge of the Pennines, 10 km/6 mi east of Chesterfield. Coalmining used to be the principal local industry. **Bolsover Castle** was originally built by William Peveril in the 11th century; what remains, however, is a mixture of Gothic and Renaissance styles dating from the 17th century. The castle is now owned by English Heritage.

Bolt, Robert (Oxton) (1924–1995)

English dramatist and screenwriter. He wrote historical plays, such as *A Man for All Seasons* (1960; filmed 1966); his screenplays include *Lawrence of Arabia* (1962), *Dr Zhivago* (1965) (both Academy Awards), *Ryan's Daughter* (1970), *Lady Caroline Lamb*, which he also directed, *The Bounty* (1984), and *The Mission* (1986).

Widely considered his most important play, *A Man for All Seasons* deals with the tragic relationship between Henry VIII and Sir Thomas More, and illustrates Bolt's ability to dramatize political and moral issues using a clear dramatic structure, strong characterization, and expressive dialogue. Later plays were less successful, though *Vivat! Vivat Regina!* (1970) again illustrates his ability to bring history vividly to life, and *Revolution* (1977), a critical but not popular success, shows Bolt's continued willingness to tackle intellectually ambitious works.

Bolton

Town and administrative headquarters of Bolton metropolitan borough, Greater Manchester, northwest England, on the River Croal, 18 km/11 mi northwest of Manchester; population (1994 est) 210,000. Industries include engineering and the manufacture of chemicals, paper, and textiles. Bolton developed rapidly in the 18th century as a cotton-spinning town. Samuel Crompton, inventor of the spinning mule in 1779, was born nearby.

History

Bolton was a centre for the wool trade in medieval times. During the Industrial Revolution its prominent cotton-spinning industry specialized in fine counts; engineering developed as a complementary activity to textile production. Growth was encouraged by the opening of the canal to Manchester in 1791 and the railway in 1838. Bolton's cotton-textile industry suffered a slower decline than that of many other towns, but the demand for fine counts eventually diminished and the town's economy diversified.

Features

Dating from 1251, the Old Man and Scythe is the oldest inn in Bolton; following a Royalist massacre in the town in 1651 during the English Civil War, James Stanley, Earl of Derby, reputedly spent his last night at the inn before being executed by Oliver Cromwell. Nearby Smithill's Hall, dating from the 14th century, is one of Greater Manchester's oldest manor houses. The Textile Museum, to the north of the town, illustrates the early machinery used in the industry. Exhibits include examples of Samuel ◊Crompton's spinning mule, and the spinning frame invented in 1768 by Richard ◊Arkwright, who lived and worked in Bolton.

Bolton was the birthplace of William Lever (1851–1925), the first Viscount Leverhulme and founder of Lever Brothers (which later became Unilever). An important local benefactor, he bought and restored Hall i'th' Wood, a 15th-century manor house and the former home of Samuel Crompton, presenting it to the town in 1902. Lying north of the town centre, the house now contains a folk museum with relics of Crompton.

Bolton Priory

Priory situated on the banks of the River Wharfe, in the village of Bolton Abbey near Ilkley, North Yorkshire, England. Its Augustinian community was founded in 1120 by William de Meschines and his wife Cicely de Romily, and moved to Bolton around 1154. The nave survives as the parish church.

The chancel, transepts and unfinished tower are picturesque ruins with notable features from the 13th to 16th centuries. The 14th-century gatehouse is now part of the the mainly 19th-century Bolton hall.

Bomberg, David (Garshen) (1890–1957)

English painter and founder member of the London Group. He applied forms inspired by Cubism and Vorticism to figurative subjects, treating them as patterns of brightly coloured interlocking planes in such early works as *The Mud Bath* (1914; Tate Gallery, London). After World War I he turned to landscape painting. Moving away from semi-abstraction in the mid-1920s, his work became more representational but remained outstanding for its freedom of handling and brilliant colour. He gained recognition only towards the end of his life.

Bonar Law

British Conservative politician; see ◊Law, Andrew Bonar.

Bond, Edward (1934–)

English dramatist. His early work aroused controversy because of the savagery of some of his imagery, for example, the brutal stoning of a baby by bored youths in *Saved* (1965). Other works include *Early Morning* (1968); *Lear* (1972), a reworking of Shakespeare's play; *Bingo* (1973), an account of Shakespeare's last days; *The War Plays* (1985); and *Jackets*

2/Sugawara and *In the Company of Men* (both 1990). For television he wrote *Olly's Prison* (1991) and *Tuesday* (1993).

Early Morning was the last play to be banned in the UK by the Lord Chamberlain.

Bondfield, Margaret Grace (1873–1953)

British socialist who became a trade-union organizer to improve working conditions for women. She was a Labour member of Parliament 1923–24 and 1926–31, and was the first woman to enter the cabinet – as minister of labour 1929–31.

Originally a shop assistant, Bondfield began her political career in the National Union of Shop Assistants, of which she was assistant secretary 1898–1908. She was the only woman delegate to the Trades Union Congress (TUC) in 1899, and in 1923 she was its first woman chair.

Bond films

Series of films featuring novelist Ian ◊Fleming's creation, the urbane British spy and womanizer James Bond (also known as 007). Blending comedy and drama, gunplay and sex scenes, and deploying every conceivable mode of transport, the series has exerted an enduring appeal for mainstream cinemagoers since *Dr No*, the first instalment, premiered in 1962. The series has produced such classics of the British cinema as *Goldfinger* (1964) and *On Her Majesty's Secret Service* (1969), and has added a memorable array of evil masterminds to the pantheon of screen villains. Five actors have played the charismatic leading man: Sean ◊Connery, George Lazenby, Roger ◊Moore, Timothy Dalton, and Pierce ◊Brosnan.

BOND FILMS *The Scottish actor Sean Connery was the first to portray the suave secret agent James Bond on screen, in a series of films that helped raise the international profile of the British film industry in the 1960s. So popular are the Bond films that they continue to be made, despite no longer being based on scripts from the original novels of Bond's creator, Ian Fleming. Rex*

The series was produced until the late-1980s by Albert R 'Cubby' Broccoli (1909–96) and, 1962–74, by his business partner Harry Saltzman (1915–94). *Casino Royale* (1967), based on Fleming's novel of the same title and starring David Niven as the intrepid adventurer, is the only Bond feature film to be made outside the series.

The series was much influenced by Alfred Hitchcock's espionage thriller *North by Northwest* (1959). Other Bond films include *From Russia with Love* (1964), *Diamonds Are Forever* (1971), *The Man with the Golden Gun* (1974), *The Spy who Loved Me* (1977), *Octopussy* (1983), *Licence to Kill* (1989), and *Tomorrow Never Dies* (1997).

Bondi, Hermann (1919–)

Austrian-born British cosmologist. In 1948 he joined with Fred ◊Hoyle and Thomas Gold in developing the steady-state theory of cosmology, which suggested that matter is continuously created in the universe.

The steady-state model stimulated much debate for, while its ideas were revolutionary, it was fully compatible with existing knowledge. However, evidence that the universe had once been denser and hotter emerged in the 1950s and 1960s, and the theory was abandoned by most scientists. KCB 1973.

Bond Street

Street and shopping centre in London, running between Piccadilly and Oxford Street. The southern section, known as Old Bond Street, was built in 1686 by Thomas Bond, a member of Queen Henrietta Maria's household, and after whom the street was named. The northern section, New Bond Street, was built around 1721.

The composer Georg Friedrich Handel lived at 25 Brook Street, close to the junction of Brook Street and New Bond Street, from 1723 until his death.

Bone, Muirhead (1876–1953)

Scottish graphic artist. As official war artist from 1916 to 1918, during World War I, he made drawings of the Western Front and battleships (Imperial War Museum and Tate Gallery, London). He also produced many views of London, recording the effects of the Blitz in World War II.

Bonham-Carter, (Helen) Violet, Baroness Asquith of Yarnbury (1887–1969)

President of the Liberal party in Britain 1945–47. DBE 1953, Baroness 1964.

Bonham Carter, Helena (1966–)

English actress. Her early career saw her typecast as an aristocratic or upper-middle-class heroine in such films as

Room with a View (1985) and *Howard's End* (1992), and her work continues to be dominated by period costume dramas, including *The Wings of the Dove* (1997). She has become a key company member in the film productions of both Kenneth ◊Branagh and Ismail Merchant and James Ivory.

Bonington, Chris(tian John Storey) (1934–)

British mountaineer. He took part in the first ascent of Annapurna II in 1960, Nuptse in 1961, and the first British ascent of the north face of the Eiger in 1962, climbed the central Tower of Paine in Patagonia in 1963, and was the leader of an Everest expedition in 1975 and again in 1985, reaching the summit.

Bonnie Prince Charlie

Scottish name for ◊Charles Edward Stuart, pretender to the throne.

Booker Prize for Fiction

British literary prize of £20,000 awarded annually (from 1969) to a Commonwealth writer by the Booker company (formerly Booker McConnell) for a novel published in the UK during the previous year.

The first recipient of the prize in 1969 was P H Newby for *Something to Answer For*. Other notable winners have included V S Naipaul (1971), Iris Murdoch (1978), William Golding (1980), Anita Brookner (1984), and Kingsley Amis (1986). In 1997 the winner was Arundhati Roy for *The God of Small Things* and in 1998 the prize was awarded to Ian McEwan for *Amsterdam*.

Boole, George (1815–1864)

English mathematician. His work *The Mathematical Analysis of Logic* (1847) established the basis of modern mathematical logic, and his **Boolean algebra** can be used in designing computers.

Boole's system is essentially two-valued. By subdividing objects into separate classes, each with a given property, his algebra makes it possible to treat different classes according to the presence or absence of the same property. Hence it involves just two numbers, 0 and 1 – the binary system used in the computer.

Boorman, John (1933–)

English film director, screenwriter, and producer. He started out in television, and has directed a number of visually stylish films in both Hollywood and Britain. They include *Deliverance* (1972), *Excalibur* (1981), *The Emerald Forest* (1985), *Hope and Glory* (1987), and *Beyond Rangoon* (1995).

Boorman's narratives frequently betray his interest in mythology and the work of the Swiss psychologist C G Jung, an interest shared by his early collaborator Lee Marvin, who starred in his *Point Blank* (1967) and *Hell in the Pacific* (1968). Among Boorman's recent works are the feature film *The General* and the documentary *Lee Marvin: A Personal Portrait* (both 1998).

Booker Prize

This UK literary prize of £20,000 is awarded annually in October.

Year	Winner	Awarded for
1969	P H Newby	*Something to Answer For*
1970	Bernice Rubens	*The Elected Member*
1971	V S Naipaul	*In a Free State*
1972	John Berger	*G*
1973	J G Farrell	*The Siege of Krishnapur*
1974	Nadine Gordimer	*The Conservationist*
	Stanley Middleton	*Holiday*
1975	Ruth Prawer Jhabvala	*Heat and Dust*
1976	David Storey	*Saville*
1977	Paul Scott	*Staying On*
1978	Iris Murdoch	*The Sea, The Sea*
1979	Penelope Fitzgerald	*Offshore*
1980	William Golding	*Rites of Passage*
1981	Salman Rushdie	*Midnight's Children*
1982	Thomas Keneally	*Schindler's Ark*
1983	J M Coetzee	*The Life and Times of Michael K*
1984	Anita Brookner	*Hotel du Lac*
1985	Keri Hulme	*The Bone People*
1986	Kingsley Amis	*The Old Devils*
1987	Penelope Lively	*Moon Tiger*
1988	Peter Carey	*Oscar and Lucinda*
1989	Kazuo Ishiguro	*The Remains of the Day*
1990	A S Byatt	*Possession*
1991	Ben Okri	*The Famished Road*
1992	Barry Unsworth	*Sacred Hunger*
	Michael Ondaatje	*The English Patient*
1993	Roddy Doyle	*Paddy Clarke Ha Ha Ha*
1994	James Kelman	*How Late It Was, How Late*
1995	Pat Barker	*The Ghost Road*
1996	Graham Swift	*Last Orders*
1997	Arundhati Roy	*The God of Small Things*
1998	Ian McEwan	*Amsterdam*

He is the author of a telling book on film finance, *Money into Light* (1985), and since 1992 has been co-editor of Faber & Faber's annual film journal *Projections*. He was made a CBE in 1994.

Booth, Hubert Cecil (1871–1955)

English inventor of the vacuum cleaner. A mechanic and engineer by trade, he patented an electric machine in 1901 that went into production the following year.

Booth conceived the principle of his vacuum cleaner after witnessing the cleaning of a railway carriage by means of compressed air which simply blew a great cloud of dust around. In his machine, one end of a tube was connected to an air pump, while the other, with nozzle attached, was pushed over the surface being cleaned. The cleaner incorporated an air filter.

Because of the large size and high price of early vacuum cleaners and the fact that few houses had mains electricity, Booth initially offered cleaning services rather than machine sales. The large vacuum cleaner, powered by petrol or electric engine and mounted on a four-wheeled horse carriage, was parked in the street outside a house while large cleaning tubes were passed in through the windows. The machine was such a novelty that society hostesses held special parties at which guests watched operatives cleaning carpets or furniture. Transparent tubes were provided so that the dust could be seen departing down them. Booth's machines received a great popular boost when they were used to clean the blue pile carpets laid in Westminster Abbey for the coronation of King Edward VII in 1902.

Smaller, more compact indoors vacuum cleaners followed, but until the first electrically powered model appeared, two people were required to operate them – one to work the pump by bellows or a plunger, the other to handle the cleaning tube.

Booth, William (1829–1912)

British founder of the ◊Salvation Army (1878), and its first 'general'.

Booth experienced religious conversion at the age of 15. In 1865 he founded the Christian Mission in Whitechapel, east London, which became the Salvation Army in 1878. 'In Darkest England, and the Way Out' (1890) contained proposals for the physical and spiritual redemption of the many down-and-outs. His wife Catherine (1829–1890, born Mumford), whom he married in 1855, became a public preacher in about 1860, initiating the ministry of women. Their eldest son, **William Bramwell Booth** (1856–1929), became chief of staff of the Salvation Army in 1880 and was general from 1912 until his deposition in 1929.

Boothby, Robert John Graham, Baron Boothby (1900–1986)

Scottish politician. He became a Unionist member of Parliament in 1924 and was parliamentary private secretary to Churchill 1926–29. He advocated Britain's entry into the European Community (now the European Union), and was a powerful speaker. KBE 1958, Baron 1958.

Boothroyd, Betty (1929–)

British Labour politician, Speaker of the House of Commons from 1992. A Yorkshire-born daughter of a textile worker and weaver, and a former West End dancer, she was elected MP for West Bromwich in the West Midlands in 1973 and was a member of the European Parliament 1975–77. The first woman to hold the office of Speaker, she has controlled Parliamentary proceedings with a mixture of firmness and good humour.

Bootle

Town and seaport in Merseyside, northwest England, at the mouth of the River Mersey, adjoining Liverpool; population (1991) 65,500. It exports timber, and industries include engineering and tanning. The headquarters of the National Girobank are here.

Features

Bootle includes the northern section of the docks of the Mersey estuary, with their associated warehouses and factories. It also has a large number of industrial buildings beside the Leeds and Liverpool Canal.

History

A proposal to unite Bootle with Liverpool was

Boothroyd, Betty *In 1992, Betty Boothroyd became the first woman to be elected as Speaker of the House of Commons. This is part of a trend in British politics that has seen the first female premier (Margaret Thatcher 1979–90) and a great increase in the number of women MPs elected at the 1997 general election. Nevertheless, women still remain proportionally under-represented in Parliament. Geoff Wilkinson/Rex*

defeated by the House of Lords in 1903. Extensive areas were rebuilt after damage caused during World War II bombing raids.

Boots

UK's largest pharmacy chain, founded by **Jesse Boot** (1850–1931). In 1863 Boot took over his father's small Nottingham shop trading in medicinal herbs. Recognizing that the future lay with patent medicines, he concentrated on selling cheaply, advertising widely, and offering a wide range of medicines. In 1892 Boots also began to manufacture drugs. The chain grew rapidly. By 1900 there were 126 shops and more than 1,000 when Jesse Boot died in 1931. In 1968 Boots took over another chain of chemists, Timothy White's. The shops now sell photographic and audio equipment, small household wares, and children's clothing, as well as cosmetics and pharmaceuticals.

Borders

Former region of Scotland (1975–96) which consisted of four districts and was replaced in 1996 by the Scottish Borders unitary authority.

The districts of Tweeddale, Ettrick and Lauderdale, Berwickshire, and Roxburgh made up the Borders region. The region was created in 1975 with lands from the five counties of Midlothian, Peeblesshire, Selkirkshire, Roxburghshire, and Berwickshire.

borough, Old English **burg** 'a walled or fortified place'

Urban-based unit of local government which existed from the 8th century until 1974, when it continued as an honorary status granted by royal charter to a district council, entitling its leader to the title of mayor. In England in 1998 there were 32 London borough councils and 36 metropolitan borough councils.

County and non-county boroughs disappeared in the reorganization which took place in 1974. Existing boroughs lost their status, but the newly created district councils were allowed to petition for a charter conferring the status of borough and many did so. Prior to the reorganization of local government in 1974 there were 83 county boroughs and, excluding the 32 London boroughs, 259 non-county boroughs.

See also ◊local government.

Borrowers, The

Story for children by the British writer Mary Norton (1903–), published in 1952. It describes a family of tiny people who live secretly under the floor in a large country house and subsist by 'borrowing' things from the 'human beans' who live above. Their survival and way of life come under threat in several sequels. The book has been adapted for television and cinema.

Boston

Port and market town in Lincolnshire, eastern England, on the River Witham, 50 km/31 mi southeast of Lincoln; population (1991) 34,600. Industries include food-processing and shell-fishing, and the manufacture of labels and tags. Trade is conducted particularly with Scandinavia and the Baltic countries, agricultural products forming the bulk of the traffic.

St Botolph's Church, dating from the 14th century, is said to be England's largest parish church. Its 83-m/272-ft high tower, known as **Boston stump**, is the highest parish church tower in England and a landmark for sailors. The town is situated in the flat, fertile agricultural district of the Lincolnshire Fens.

History

Boston was the second-largest port in Britain during the 13th and 14th centuries, and its prosperity was based on the wool trade with Flanders. Its importance declined as ports on the west coast of Britain were favoured for trade with the New World, and as the River Witham silted up.

The town became a centre of Nonconformism in the early 17th century, and a group of pilgrims, later known as the Pilgrim Fathers, were imprisoned in the town in 1607 following their failed attempt to find religious freedom by sailing to Holland. The cells in which the pilgrims were confined can be seen in Boston's Guildhall. In 1630 John Winthrop emigrated to North America on the *Arbella*, and founded a settlement on Massachusetts Bay named after his hometown, Boston. The colony was joined by a party of Puritans led by John Cotton, who sailed for Massachusetts Bay in 1633 to escape religious persecution.

Boswell, James (1740–1795)

Scottish biographer and diarist. He was a member of Samuel ◊Johnson's Literary Club and the two men travelled to Scotland together in 1773, as recorded in Boswell's *Journal of a Tour to the Hebrides* (1785). His *Life of Samuel Johnson* was published in 1791. Boswell's ability to record Johnson's pithy conversation verbatim makes this a classic of English biography.

Boswell was born in Edinburgh. He qualified as a lawyer in 1766 but centred his ambitions on literature and politics. He first met Johnson in 1763, and following a European tour, established a place in his intimate circle, becoming a member of the Literary Club in 1773.

Bosworth, Battle of

Last battle of the Wars of the ◊Roses, fought on 22 August 1485. Richard III, the Yorkist king, was defeated and slain by Henry of Richmond, who became Henry VII. The battlefield is near the village of Market Bosworth, 19 km/12 mi W of Leicester, England.

Richard's oppressive reign ensured that Henry, landing in Wales, gathered an army of supporters as he marched into England to meet Richard's army which was drawn up on a hill at Bosworth. A third, smaller, army led by Lord Stanley stood off from both sides, undecided upon which to join. Henry opened the battle by advancing up the hill and charging into the opposition. Lord Stanley now made his decision and fell on the rear of King Richard's position, causing the King's force to break and flee. Richard was unhorsed in the rush and beaten to death as he lay. As the battle ended, Lord Stanley

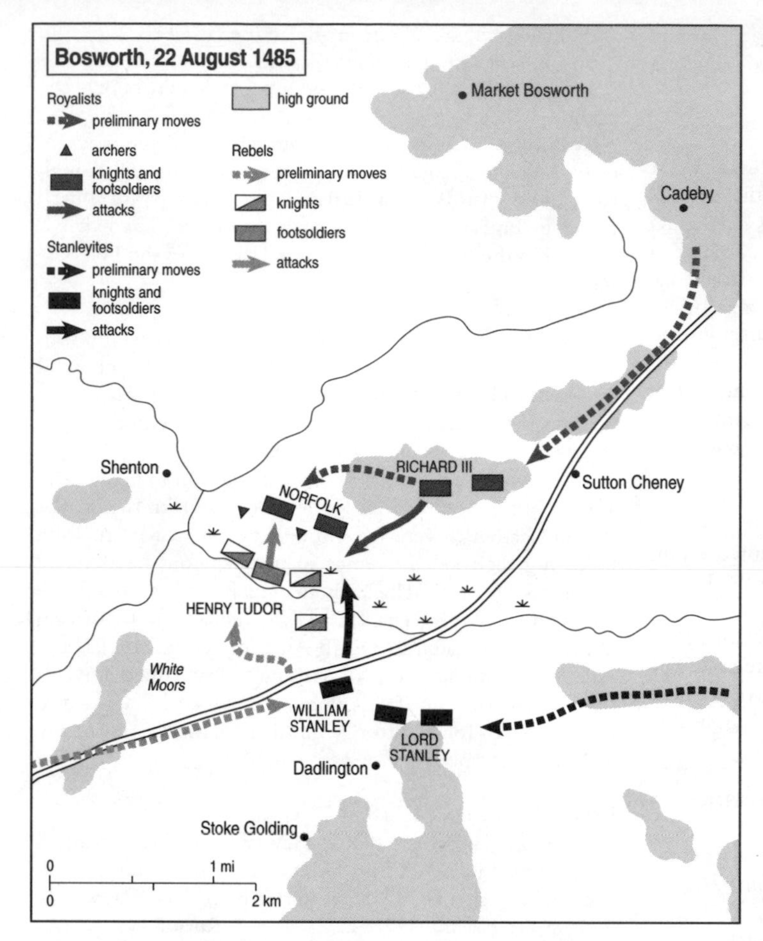

crowned Henry as king; Henry later married Edward IV's daughter Elizabeth, uniting the houses of York and Lancaster to bring the Wars to an end.

Botham, Ian Terence (1955–)

English cricketer. One of the world's greatest all-rounders, in 102 Tests for England between 1977 and 1992 he scored 5,200 runs and took 383 wickets to become the first player in Test cricket to score over 5,000 runs as well as take over 300 wickets. He played county cricket for Somerset, Worcestershire, and Durham, and briefly represented Queensland in the Sheffield Shield.

Botham made his Somerset debut in 1974 and first played for England against Australia at Trent Bridge in 1977; he took five wickets for 74 runs in Australia's first innings. In 1987 he moved from Somerset to Worcestershire and helped them to win the Refuge Assurance League in his first season.

Botham also played Football League soccer for Scunthorpe United 1979–84. He raised money for leukaemia research with much-publicized walks from John o'Groats to Land's End, and Hannibal-style across the Alps.

Bothwell, James Hepburn, 4th Earl of Bothwell (*c.* 1536–1578)

Scottish nobleman. The third husband of ◊Mary Queen of Scots, 1567–70, he was alleged to have arranged the explosion that killed Darnley, Mary's previous husband, in 1567.

Tried and acquitted a few weeks after the assassination, he abducted Mary and married her on 15 May. A revolt ensued, and Bothwell was forced to flee. In 1570 Mary obtained a divorce, and Bothwell was confined in a castle in the Netherlands where he died insane. Succeeded as Earl 1556, Duke 1567.

Boudicca (died AD 61)

Queen of the Iceni (native Britons), often referred to by the Latin form of her name, **Boadicea**. Her husband, King Prasutagus, had been a tributary of the Romans, but on his death AD 60 the territory of the Iceni was violently annexed. Boudicca was scourged and her daughters raped. Boudicca raised the whole of southeast England in revolt, and before the main Roman armies could return from campaigning in Wales she burned Londinium (London), Verulamium (St Albans), and Camulodunum (Colchester). Later the Romans under governor Suetonius Paulinus defeated the British between London and Chester; they were virtually annihilated and Boudicca poisoned herself.

Boughton, Rutland (1878–1960)

English composer. He idolized Wagner, and determined to found an English centre of opera on the same lines as Bayreuth. He began in a very modest way at Glastonbury with a series of music dramas on the Arthurian legends, producing *The Immortal Hour* (1914). A special theatre was to be built at Glastonbury, but the project had to be abandoned.

Boult, Adrian Cedric (1889–1983)

English conductor. He conducted the BBC Symphony Orchestra 1930–50 and the London Philharmonic 1950–57. He promoted the work of Holst and Vaughan Williams, and was a celebrated interpreter of Elgar.

Boulting, John Edward (1913–1985) and Roy (1913–)

English director–producer team that was successful in the years after World War II. Their films include *Brighton Rock* (1947), *Lucky Jim* (1957), and *I'm All Right Jack* (1959). They were twins.

Bounty, Mutiny on the

Naval mutiny in the Pacific in 1789 against British captain William ◊Bligh.

Bournemouth

Seaside resort and unitary authority in southern England; population (1995 est) 160,900; area 46 sq km/18 sq mi. The town lies on Poole Bay, 40 km/25 mi southwest of

Southampton, and was part of the county of Dorset until 1997. Industries include tourism, the provision of insurance, banking, and financial services, and the manufacture of communications systems (Siemens). An International Conference Centre is situated here.

History

The area was undeveloped until the early 19th century when a local squire, Louis Tregonwell, built a house on the coastal moorland. Pine trees were planted in the Bourne valley and Bournemouth, with its sheltered position, mild climate, and long sandy beach, developed as a popular summer and winter resort.

Features

Bournemouth has a 10 km/6 mi stretch of sands, as well as parks, winter gardens, and two piers, one of which is 305 m/1,000 ft long. Undercliff promenades extend for 7 km/4 mi. The Russell-Cotes Museum and Art Gallery houses a collection of Japanese art and 17th–20th century paintings. The Pavilion, opened in 1929, includes a theatre and dance hall. Bournemouth University was founded in 1992 (formerly Bournemouth Polytechnic). Bournemouth Airport is at Hurn to the north of the town.

Bovey Tracey

Town in Devon, England; population (1991) 5,200. It is situated 14 km/9 mi northwest of Teignmouth, on the edge of Dartmoor. The **Bovey Beds** are a deposit of sands, clays, and lignite, 60–90 m/197–295 ft thick, which extends from Bovey Tracey to Newton Abbot. The extracted clay is valuable, and is used for pipe- and pottery-making.

bovine spongiform encephalopathy, BSE or mad cow disease

Disease of cattle, related to ◊scrapie in sheep, which attacks the nervous system, causing aggression, lack of coordination, and collapse. First identified in 1985, it is almost entirely confined to the UK. By 1996 it had claimed 158,000 British cattle.

The source of the disease has been traced to manufactured protein feed incorporating the rendered brains of scrapie-infected sheep. Following the ban on the use of offal in feed in 1988, the epidemic continued, indicating that the disease could be transmitted from cows to their calves. It was not until 1996 that government scientists admitted that this was so.

In 1996, when links between BSE and Creutzfeldt-Jakob disease (CJD) in humans were demonstrated, export of British beef was prohibited. Support for the beef industry amounting to £1,370 million came from the government and the EU. In 1996, consumption of beef in Britain fell 15–20% compared with 1995, and the price fell 14% in the same period.

It was revealed in 1997 that the British government had allowed more than 6,000 carcasses suspected of having BSE to be buried in landfill sites across Britain – in direct contravention of its own regulations. Because of fears that BSE could get into drinking water, or the food chain, both the British government and the EU have insisted the carcasses should be incinerated.

In November 1998 the government announced a £120 million emergency aid package for Britain's farmers, partly to compensate for the effects of the BSE crisis.

See feature on next page.

Bow Bells

The bells of St Mary-le-Bow church, Cheapside, London; a person born within the sound of Bow Bells is traditionally considered a true Cockney. The bells also feature in the legend of Dick ◊Whittington. The church was nearly destroyed by bombs in 1941. The bells, recast from the old metal, were restored in 1961.

Bowdler, Thomas (1754–1825)

English editor. His expurgated versions of Shakespeare and other authors gave rise to the verb **bowdlerize**.

BSE: Some Key Dates

1985 An epidemic of bovine spongiform encephalopathy (BSE or 'mad cow disease') is reported in beef cattle in Britain; it is later traced to cattle feed containing sheep carcasses infected with scrapie.

15 May 1990 Home-produced beef is banned in UK schools and hospitals as a result of concern about bovine spongiform encephalopathy.

25 March 1996 The European Union bans the export of British beef abroad following anxiety over the potential for transmission of the BSE infection to humans as CJD (Creutzfeldt-Jakob disease).

1 April 1996 The agriculture minister Douglas Hogg proposes a scheme to eradicate BSE in Britain and get the export ban on British beef lifted; 4.6 million cattle over 6 years old would be culled.

1 August 1996 The UK Central Veterinary Laboratory publishes a report indicating that BSE can be transmitted from cow to calf.

2 October 1997 UK scientists Moira Bruce and, independently, John Collinge and their colleagues show that the new variant form of the brain-wasting CJD is the same disease as bovine spongiform encephalopathy in cows.

3 December 1997 Agriculture Secretary Jack Cunningham announces that the government will ban the sale of beef on the bone to help prevent the transmission of BSE to humans.

March 1998 Public inquiry into BSE opens; it is scheduled to report mid-1999.

November 1998 The government announces a £120 million emergency aid package for Britain's farmers, partly to compensate for the BSE crisis. Later that month, the European Union lifts the ban on the export of British beef.

BSE: THE DEBATE GOES ON

BSE (BOVINE spongiform encephalopathy) is the cattle version of a group of diseases known as TSEs (transmissible spongiform encephalopathies), which degenerate the nerve cells in mammals. The human version is known as Creutzfeldt-Jakob Disease or CJD, and causes brain degeneration and death.

BSE was first identified in 1985. In 1988, UK government epidemiologists announced that the source was probably scrapie, the form of TSE in sheep. They linked the emergence of the cattle disease to changes in industrial plants where protein was recovered from animal carcasses to produce cattle feed. Feeds containing animal products were developed in the 1970s, when scientists found that they could bypass the ruminant process in cows and get protein – from fishmeal or animal remains – into the animals' first 'true' stomach, thus maximizing production. As the price of soya and fishmeal rose, feed-makers turned to sheep remains.

Government action to deal with the initial crisis involved a ban on animal remains (except fishmeal) being included in sheep and cattle feed, the slaughter of animals suspected of having the disease, and the removal from the human food chain of offal believed to carry the disease such as the spinal cord and brain. However, beef itself is not the only product affected. Food which contains beef, beef bone stock, mechanically recovered meat, suet, gelatine or animal fats includes such products as chicken gravy granules, Christmas pudding, frankfurters, baby food, cakes, and jellies.

The government was initially confident that these steps would contain the problem. By April 1995, however, there had been approximately 147,000 cases of BSE recorded in UK cows – 18,000 of which had been born since the feed ban – with about 220 new cases being reported each week. It was obvious that things were not as simple as had been hoped. One problem was the UK government's failure to carry out research to assess the scrapie/BSE link. The government's reported view was that a single, highly resilient strain of scrapie must have escaped inactivation in the rendering plants, and was thus passed onto cattle. However, a variety of other hypotheses are now emerging. Robert Rohwer, who studies spongiform encephalopathies in the US, suggests that BSE is a new disease that first arose in a few British cows and then built over several years as the carcasses were repeatedly recycled in animal feed. Another theory is that the routine use of organophosphate insecticides to eradicate warble fly has affected the nervous system of treated cattle and made them more susceptible to disease.

The human link

A new crisis was triggered by the government announcement in March 1996 that 10 young people had died from a variant of CJD probably caused by eating infected meat. Stephen Dorrell, the Health Secretary, stated that although there was no actual 'scientific proof' that BSE can be transmitted to humans, the scientists concluded that 'the most likely explanation' for the 10 cases was exposure to BSE before the offal ban in 1989. Although the government tried to persuade processors, retailers, and consumers that eating beef had become progressively safer since the controls introduced in 1989, the statements that the risk from eating beef was only 'extremely small' did little to reduce people's fears. Nor did it allay fears in the European Union, which imposed a bitterly contested ban on beef from the UK.

By November 1997 a further 12 cases of new variant CJD had come to light and the Spongiform Encephalopathy Advisory Committee in the UK recommended that white blood cells be removed from donor blood, by a process known as leucodepletion. This advice follows research published by Professor Adriano Aguzzi of Zurich University, Switzerland – who had been working on the problem of how the disease could transmit itself from the gut to the brain – which suggests that white blood cells, lymphocytes, could play an important role in transmitting the infection. The UK government announced in July 1998 that all blood transfusions would be filtered to remove white blood cells to reduce the risk of vCJD being transmitted in this way.

Other scientists, notably Dr Bruno Oesch of the company Prionics in Zurich, Switzerland, have been busy developing tests that could screen for the disease agent – abnormal prion proteins – in milk and blood, but a lot of work still needs to be done.

The situation remains unclear. There have been over 400 times as many reported cases of BSE in the UK compared to the rest of the world put together, but there is no evidence that CJD-related deaths are more prevalent in the UK. This, however, could be because of the long lead time for development of CJD. Researchers are still not precisely sure how BSE developed in the British cattle herd. The number of cases are rising elsewhere and some observers believe that countries have been under-reporting the level of incidence to prevent a public panic.

Undoubtedly, earlier British complacency about the risks to humans in government assurances that the situation was under control, in conjunction with poor implementation of controls, has not helped further our knowledge of the disease. The Spongiform Encephalopathy Research Campaign has argued that by the year 2000 the British could have eaten as many as 1.8 million infected beasts.

The reaction

Fears over safety of beef has brought the £500 million per annum UK beef industry to its knees, and had repercussions throughout the world. Schools have take beef off dinner menus and burger chains are sourcing beef products from outside the UK. A worldwide ban on UK beef products was put in place by the EU. Much discussion has also ensued about wide-scale slaughter policies and who will provide the farmers with financial compensation. Perhaps more importantly, in the long term, the issue has focused attention on the the safety aspects of modern, intensive agricultural practice.

BY NIGEL DUDLEY AND SUE STOLTON

In 1818 he published the *Family Shakespeare*, in ten volumes, in which 'those words and expressions are omitted which cannot with propriety be read aloud in a family'. In 1826 he edited Edward Gibbon's *History of the Decline and Fall of the Roman Empire*, 'with the careful omissions of all passages of an irreligious or immoral tendency'. His prudery was much ridiculed.

Bowen, Elizabeth (Dorothea Cole) (1899–1973)
Novelist and short-story writer, born in Dublin of Anglo-Irish descent, and taken to England as a child. She published her first volume of short stories, *Encounters* in 1923. Her novels include *The Death of the Heart* (1938), *The Heat of the Day* (1949), and *The Little Girls* (1964).

Bowie, David, Stage name of David Robert Jones (1947–)
English pop singer, songwriter, and actor. His career has been a series of image changes. His hits include 'Jean Genie' (1973), 'Rebel, Rebel' (1974), 'Golden Years' (1975), and 'Underground' (1986). He has acted in plays and films, including Nicolas Roeg's *The Man Who Fell to Earth* (1976).

Bowie's albums include *Aladdin Sane* (1973), *Station to Station* (1976), *Low* (1977), *Heroes* (1977), *Lodger* (1979), *Let's Dance* (1983), and *Black Tie/White Noise* (1993). In 1989 he formed the hard-rock band Tin Machine. In 1997 Bowie released the album *Earthling* and received his best reviews for 20 years.

Bowlby, (Edward) John (Mostyn) (1907–1990)
English psychologist and author of *Child Care and the Growth of Love* (1953), in which he argued that a home environment for children is preferable to an institution, and stressed the bond between mother and child. He was consultant in mental health for the World Health Organization 1972–90.

bowls
Outdoor and indoor game popular in Commonwealth countries. It has been played in Britain since the 13th century and was popularized by Francis Drake, who is reputed to have played bowls on Plymouth Hoe as the Spanish Armada approached in 1588.

The sport's major international events include the World Outdoor Championship first held in 1966 for men and in 1969 for women, the World Indoor Championship first held in 1979 for men and in 1988 for women

Two popular forms of the game are played in Britain: **lawn bowls**, played on a flat surface, and **crown green bowls**, played on a rink with undulations and a crown at the centre of the green. This latter version is more popular in the Midlands and northern England. The Waterloo Handicap, crown green bowling's principal tournament, was first held in 1907 at the Waterloo Hotel, Blackpool.

Bowness, or **Bowness-on-Windermere**
Residential and holiday town in Cumbria, England. It is situated on the eastern shore of Lake Windermere, 13 km/8 mi northwest of Kendal. Bowness is a centre for pleasure trips and water sports on the lake. The Windermere Steamboat Museum is nearby, and there is a regular car ferry service from Bowness to Belle Isle on the lake.

Bow Street
Street in London, between Long Acre and Russell Street, the location of a famous police court. The work of the Bow Street magistrates formerly embraced executive functions which are now performed by the commissioner of the Metropolitan Police; the ◊Bow Street Runners served writs and acted as detectives until 1829.

The first Bow Street magistrate was Sir Thomas de Veil, who, when an acting justice in 1735, lived in Bow Street, and the court owes its subsequent establishment to him.

Bow Street Runners
Informal police force organized in 1749 by Henry ◊Fielding, chief magistrate at Bow Street in London. The scheme was initially established as a force of detectives to aid the Bow Street Magistrates' court but from 1757 it was funded by the government to cover the rest of London. It formed the basis for the Metropolitan police force established by Robert Peel's government in 1829.

Box Hill
Wooded hill overlooking the valley of the River Mole near Dorking in Surrey, England; height 170 m/558 ft. The National Trust owns 400 ha/988 acres of woods and chalk downland here. Box Hill is one of the best-known beauty spots in southeast England. Box trees give the area its name.

Boyce, William (1710–1779)
English composer and organist. He wrote church music, symphonies, and chamber music, but is best known for his song 'Heart of Oak' (1759). He was one of the most respected English composers of his time. Much of his music exhibits a fresh liveliness, particularly his many dance movements.

Boycott, Charles Cunningham (1832–1897)
English land agent in County Mayo, Ireland, who strongly opposed the demands for agrarian reform by the Irish Land League 1879–81, with the result that the peasants refused to work for him; hence the word **boycott**, meaning to isolate an individual, organization or country, socially or comercially.

Boycott, Geoffrey (1940–)
English cricketer. A prolific right-handed opening batsman for Yorkshire and England, he made 8,114 Test runs in 108 matches 1964–82 at an average of 47.72. In all first class cricket career he made 48,426 runs at an average of 56.83, 1962–86. He is one of only five players to have hit over 150 first-class centuries.

In 1981 he overtook Gary Sobers' world record total of Test runs. Twice, in 1971 and 1979, his average was over 100 runs in an English season. He was released by Yorkshire after a dispute in 1986.

Boyd Orr, John Boyd, 1st Baron Boyd Orr (1880–1971)

British nutritionist and health campaigner. He was awarded the Nobel Prize for Peace in 1949 in recognition of his work towards alleviating world hunger. Knighted 1939, Baron 1945.

Boyne, Battle of the

Battle fought on 1 July 1690 in eastern Ireland, in which the exiled king James II was defeated by William III and fled to France. It was the decisive battle of the War of English Succession, confirming a Protestant monarch. It took its name from the River Boyne which rises in County Kildare and flows 110 km/69 mi northeast to the Irish Sea.

James's forces had taken up a position on the south side of the river, and William launched the attack by sending a force to cross the river some miles upstream. While the French soldiers in James's army were countering this attack, William sent his cavalry across the river in a frontal assault on James's position. After fierce fighting the Irish foot soldiers broke and James's cavalry was routed. James fled to Dublin.

BP

Abbreviation for ◊British Petroleum.

BR

Abbreviation for **British Rail**, the nationalized railway system from 1948 (as British Railways) until provatization began in 1992 (completed 1997). See ◊railways and ◊Railtrack.

Brackley

Market town in Northamptonshire, England, 14 km/9 mi east of Banbury; population (1991) 8,700. It is situated 10 km/6 mi southwest of Silverstone motor-racing circuit, and is the administrative and shopping centre for the surrounding rural district.

Magdalen College School was founded in 1548; the college chapel is derived from the 12th-century Hospital of St James and St John.

Bracknell

Town and, since April 1998, administrative headquarters of ◊Bracknell Forest unitary authority in southern England, 16 km/10 mi southeast of Reading; population (1991 est) 93,800. It was designated a ◊new town in 1949; before 1998 it was part of the county of Berkshire. The headquarters of the Meteorological Office are here. Bracknell is one of the world's two global area forecasting centres which monitor upper-level winds and temperatures for all air traffic; the other is in Washington DC, USA. Industries include engineering, electronics, and the manufacture of biscuits (Burtons).

Bracknell Forest

Unitary authority (borough status) in central south England created in 1998 from part of the former county of Berkshire
Area 109 sq km/42 sq mi
Towns ◊Bracknell (administrative headquarters), Sandhurst, Crowthorne
Features Royal Military Academy at Sandhurst (established in 1799 for officer training); the Meteorological Office at Bracknell (one of two global forecasting centres for the world's airlines); Transport Research Laboratory
Industries high technology industries, engineering, electronics, manufacture of clothing and furniture, bakery products
Population (1995) 107,700.

Bradbury, Malcolm (Stanley) (1932–)

English novelist and critic. His fiction includes comic and satiric portrayals of provincial British and US campus life: *Eating People is Wrong* (1959) (his first novel), *Stepping Westward* (1965), and *The History Man* (1975). *Dr Criminale* (1992) is an academic satire with a 1990s setting. His critical works include *The Modern American Novel* (1983, 2nd edition 1992) and *The Modern British Novel* (1993).

Bradbury was professor of American studies at the University of East Anglia 1970–94, where, with Angus Wilson, he established a MA course in creative writing to complement the programmes which had long been taught in the USA; among its most notable graduates are Kazuo Ishiguro and Ian McEwan.

> *I like the English. They have the most rigid code of immorality in the world.*
>
> MALCOLM BRADBURY English novelist and critic. *Eating People is Wrong* (1959)

Bradford

Industrial city and metropolitan borough in West Yorkshire, England, 14 km/9 mi west of Leeds; population (1994 est) 357,000. The manufacture of wool textiles, traditionally the base of Bradford's prosperity, declined in the 1970s but remains important. Other principal industries now include printing, precision and construction engineering, and the manufacture of chemicals and electronics. Stone-quarrying, brewing, photo-engraving, and publishing make a notable contribution to the city's economy. Bradford is also a major centre for financial services.

Features

The National Museum of Photography, Film, and Television (opened 1983), with Britain's largest IMAX cinema screen, 14×20 m/46×66 ft, and the Pictureville Cinerama Screen (opened in 1992), which features the only 1950s-style three-projector format in the world. The museum was closed for renovation and expansion in September 1997, relocating temporarily to a mill in Bradford's Little Germany district. The Colour Museum and the Bradford Industrial Museum illustrate the history of the textile industry; the Alhambra Theatre, an Edwardian music hall restored as a major venue for ballet, opera, plays, and pantomime; a 14th–15th-century cathedral, where a National Faith Centre is planned as part of a millennium project; Bradford University, opened in 1966. The charter of the Bradford Grammar School was granted by Charles II in 1662.

Museums and galleries
Cartwright Memorial Hall, built in 1904 in Lister Park, houses the City Art Gallery and Museum and includes a collection of 19th-and 20th-century British sculpture and painting. Saltaire, an industrial model village north of the city centre, includes Salt's Mill which houses the Gallery (1853) with a large collection of works by the 20th-century artist David Hockney, a native of Bradford.

Architecture and public buildings
Bradford's parish church, built in the 14th and 15th centuries, became a cathedral when the city was created a bishopric in 1919. The chancel, lady chapel, and chapter house were rebuilt by the architect Edward Maufe between 1951 and 1963. Little Germany, the city's historic quarter, includes many 19th-century warehouses. The Gothic-style town hall, completed in 1873 and enlarged from 1902 to 1909, has a tower which contains a clock with carillon chimes. Other notable public buildings include Commerce House, a seven-storey building; St George's Hall (1853), once Bradford's public assembly rooms, which opened in 1953 for orchestral and other concerts, public meetings, and exhibitions; and the Wool Exchange, which includes a statue of the politician and economist Richard Cobden.

Industrial products
Bradford is a major centre for the sorting of fleeces, and produces wool 'tops' (long fibres), 'noils' (short fibres), and wastes of various kinds. Finished cloths include heavy worsted coatings and lighter weaves such as linings. Mercerized cotton fabrics and goods are manufactured in large quantities. Other materials include velvet, plush, alpaca, mohair, silk, and synthetic fibres.

Bradford's wide range of engineered products encompasses machine tools, marine and lift machinery, industrial and domestic motors, traction motors for electric and diesel electric trains, turbines, boilers, pumps, and condensing plants.

Early history
From the 13th century woollen-textiles manufacturing was the city's staple industry, but in the 17th century the worsted trade began to move to Bradford from East Anglia, and the city grew steadily during the early part of the Industrial Revolution. The introduction of steam power and the factory system led to rapid development in the early 19th century, and Bradford became the world's largest producer of worsted cloth.

20th-century history
Following the textile industry's decline in the 1970s owing to overseas competition, an Economic Development Unit was established in Bradford to attract new industries and develop the city's potential as a tourist destination. Bradford City Football Club was the scene of a disaster in 1985, when the stand caught fire killing 56 people. Areas of the city experienced severe rioting by local vigilante groups in June 1995 after a confrontation with the police.

Population
Bradford contains a great diversity of immigrant communities, making it a highly multi-cultural society. Newcomers have included Irish in the 1840s, German merchants in the mid-19th century, Poles and Ukrainians, and more recently West Indians and Asians. Ethnic minorities presently account for 18% of Bradford's population, of which 86% are Asian and 7% are Afro-Caribbean in origin.

Bradlaugh, Charles (1833–1891)
British freethinker and radical politician. In 1880 he was elected Liberal member of Parliament for Northampton, but was not allowed to take his seat until 1886 because, as an atheist, he claimed the right (unsuccessfully) to affirm instead of taking the oath. He was associated with the feminist Annie Besant.

He served in the army, was a lawyer's clerk, became well known as a speaker and journalist under the name of Iconoclast, and from 1860 ran the *National Reformer*. He advocated the freedom of the press, contraception, and other social reforms.

Bradley, James (1693–1762)
English astronomer. In 1728 he discovered the aberration of starlight. From the amount of aberration in star positions, he was able to calculate the speed of light. In 1748, he announced the discovery of nutation (variation in the Earth's axial tilt).

Braemar
Village in Grampian, Scotland, where the most celebrated of the ◊Highland Games, the **Braemar Gathering**, takes place on the first Saturday in September.

Bragg, Melvyn (1939–)
English television presenter and executive, also author, who began presenting and editing the subsequently long-running ITV arts documentary series *The South Bank Show* in 1978. He was head of arts at London Weekend Television from 1982 until 1990, when he was appointed LWT's controller of arts and also chairman of Border Television. His novel *A Time to Dance* was adapted for television in 1992. He has also presented *Start the Week* for BBC Radio. In 1997 he conducted a revealing Channel 4 studio interview with Dennis Potter, shortly before Potter died. Melvyn Bragg was created a life peer in 1998.

Bragg, William Henry (1862–1942)
English physicist. In 1915 he shared with his son Lawrence Bragg the Nobel Prize for Physics for their research work on X-rays and crystals.

Crystallography had not previously been concerned with the internal arrangement of atoms but only with the shape and number of crystal surfaces. The Braggs' work gave a method of determining the positions of atoms in the lattices making up the crystals, and for accurate determination of X-ray wavelengths. This led to an understanding of the ways in which atoms combine with each other and revolutionized mineralogy and later molecular biology, in which X-ray diffraction was crucial to the elucidation of the structure of DNA. Knighted 1920.

Braine, John (Gerard) (1922–1986)
English novelist. His novel *Room at the Top* (1957) cast Braine

BRAGG, MELVYN *Television and radio presenter and cultural commentator Melvyn Bragg. His LWT arts programme,* The South Bank Show, *has brought many cultural topics to wider public attention, while his stint on the BBC Radio 4 show* Start the Week *encouraged informative discussions among diverse guests. Tim Rooke/Rex*

as one of the leading ◊Angry Young Men of the period. It created the character of Joe Lampton, one of the first of the northern working-class antiheroes, who reappears in *Life at the Top* (1962).

Braintree

Market town on the River Blackwater in Essex, England, 18 km/11 mi north of Chelmsford; population (1991) 19,400. The town has engineering and printing works and textile factories. Braintree merges with the nearby town of Bocking. In medieval times Braintree was a centre for the woollen industry. The church of St Michael the Archangel dates from the 13th century.

Nicholas Udall, the author of the first known English comedy, was vicar here 1537–44.

Braithwaite, Lilian (1873–1948)

English actress. She had a long career on the London stage and was outstanding in modern comedy. Among her parts were Margaret Fairfield in Clemence Dane's *Bill of Divorcement* (1921), Florence Lancaster in Noël Coward's *The Vortex* (1924), and the eccentric Abbey Brewster in Joseph Kesselring's *Arsenic and Old Lace* (1942). She was made a DBE in 1943.

Bramah, Joseph adopted name of Joe Brammer (1748–1814)

English inventor of a flushing water closet (1778), an 'unpickable' lock (1784), and the hydraulic press (1795). The press made use of Blaise Pascal's regulation (that pressure in fluid contained in a vessel is evenly distributed) and employed water as the hydraulic fluid; it was used in cotton baling and in forging.

Bramah took out patents for 18 inventions, but his training of a whole generation of engineers in the craft of precision engineering and the manufacture of machine tools at the dawn of the Industrial Revolution was probably an even greater legacy.

Branagh, Kenneth (Charles) (1960–)

Northern Irish stage and film actor, director, and producer. He co-founded the Renaissance Theatre Company in 1987. His first film as both actor and director was *Henry V* (1989); he returned to Shakespeare with lavish film versions of *Much Ado About Nothing* (1993) and *Hamlet* (1996).

His first Hollywood film was *Dead Again* (1992), a stylish *film noir* in which he played two roles. He also demonstrated a deft comic touch with *Peter's Friends* (1992) and *In the Bleak Midwinter* (1995), although his extravagant interpretation of *Mary Shelley's Frankenstein* (1994) was coolly received.

Branagh was born in Belfast. He trained at the Royal Academy of Dramatic Art and began his career with the Royal Shakespeare Company. After starting the Renaissance Theatre Company with David Parfitt, he earned comparisons with Laurence Olivier for his performances, notably in *Hamlet* (1988) and (1992) and *Much Ado About Nothing* (1988). He has also appeared in *High Season* (1987), *A Month in the Country* (1987), *Swing Kids* (1993), Oliver Parker's reworking of *Othello* (1995), Robert Altman's adaptation of the John Grisham thriller *The Gingerbread Man*, and Woody Allen's *Celebrity* (both 1998). In 1989 he married his regular co-star Emma ◊Thompson; they separated in 1995.

Brancaster

Village in Norfolk, England, 29 km/18 mi northeast of King's Lynn. It stands on the ancient site of the Roman fort of **Branodunum**. The parish of Brancaster includes Brancaster Staithe and Deepdale, a fishing village with a harbour from which boats depart for Scolt Head Island, now a nature reserve belonging to the National Trust.

Brandt, Bill (Hermann Wilhelm) (1904–1983)

English photographer. During the 1930s he made a series of social records contrasting the lives of the rich and the poor, some of which were presented in his book *The English at Home* (1936). During World War II he documented conditions in London in the Blitz. The strong contrasts in his black-and-white prints often produced a gloomy and threatening atmosphere. His outstanding creative work was his treatment of the nude, published in *Perspective of Nudes* and *Shadows of Light* (both 1966).

Branson, Richard (1950–)

English entrepreneur, founder of the ◊Virgin company. The 1968 launch of *Student* magazine was the first of his many successful business ventures, and in 1969 he started the Virgin mail-order business. He is a keen sailor and balloonist. In 1986 he made the fastest sea-crossing of the Atlantic, winning the Blue Riband title. He was the first to cross the Atlantic in a hot-air balloon in 1987, and in 1991, with Per Lindstrand, he made the first balloon crossing of the Pacific. His 1997 and 1998 attempts to circumnavigate the world by balloon were unsuccessful.

In 1995 he claimed that the chairman of GTech, a company owning part of the National Lottery organizer, Camelot, tried to bribe him before the concession was awarded to prevent him making a rival bid. He has also successfully sued British Airways for conducting a 'dirty tricks campaign' aimed at putting his airline (Virgin Atlantic Airlines) out of business.

Bratby, John (1928–1992)

English painter. He was one of the leading exponents of the 'kitchen sink' school of the 1950s whose work concentrated on working-class domestic life. He also wrote and illustrated his own novels, for example *Breakdown* (1960), which had a similar bold energy of style.

Brave New World

Novel by Aldous ◊Huxley published in 1932. It is set in the future when Humanity is totally controlled on scientific principles by eugenics and drugs. A Savage from outside the boundaries is brought inside and is ultimately maddened by the emotional triviality and meaninglessness of this society's life. The ironic title is taken from Shakespeare's *The Tempest* when Miranda delightedly exclaims 'Oh brave new world that has such people in it'.

Brazil, Angela (1868–1947)

English writer. She founded the genre of girls' school stories, writing over 50; among them are *A Pair of Schoolgirls* (1912), *Captain Peggie* (1924), and *The New School at Scarsdale* (1940).

bread and baking

Afternoon tea remains a showcase for traditional tea breads and buns, scones, cakes and biscuits. Many traditional cakes have retained their popularity, such as sponge, plain or Victoria, cherry or lemon, as well as parkin and gingerbread, fruit cake, and chocolate cake. Imported newcomers, such as carrot cake and banoffee pie have, however, taken the place of former favourites such as seed and Madeira cake, jam tarts, and rock cakes.

Foreign loaves, such as ciabatta, sourdough and baguettes, have changed the face of bakery shelves, but there has been a new enthusiasm for home breadmaking which has arisen as a result of the blandness of the sliced white loaf. For crumpets and muffins, buns, barms and baps or teacakes, however, you need the skills of a master-baker.

Regional specialities remain popular, for instance Scottish shortbread and drop scones, Cornish fairings, Devonshire splits, Welsh cakes, bara brith, Yorkshire curd tarts, lardy cake, saffron cake, and Richmond Maids of Honour. Chelsea, Bath, and hot-cross buns are also part of British social history.

breakfast

British culinary institution, nowadays more frequently enjoyed in its traditional form on a weekly, rather than a daily basis. W Somerset Maugham said that 'To eat well in England, you should have breakfast three times a day'. Changing lifestyles mean orange juice, cereals and toast, plus the occasional croissant, have largely replaced eggs and bacon as the morning meal, but a 'full cooked breakfast' is still often found in hotels and guest houses.

Breakfast literally means the meal that 'breaks the fast of the night'. Saxons started the day's work with ale, cold pork, and coarse dark bread; in the Middle Ages the rich ate boiled beef, mutton and salt herring and wine, while the poor subsisted on bread, salt pork, and fish on Fridays. This was much the pattern for the next 500 years. In Scotland, oatmeal boiled with water became the staple morning food; along with marmalade and kippers, Scotch porridge is now an integral part of the British breakfast repertoire.

In the 17th and 18th centuries, tea and coffee began to replace the 'morning draught'; by the end of the 19th century, the Edwardians had turned breakfast into an art form. In its heyday, the classic breakfast line-up, served on silver dishes on a hotplate, included eggs boiled, scrambled or fried, bacon, ham, devilled kidneys, sausages, mushrooms, smoked fish, kedgeree, cold meats and game, rolls, and conserves. Such breakfasts were only served in affluent households with plenty of servants – the poor had to make do with stale bread and watery gruel.

Breakspear, Nicholas

Original name of ◊Adrian IV, the only English pope.

Breathalyzer

Trademark for an instrument for on-the-spot checking by police of the amount of alcohol consumed by a suspect driver. The driver breathes into a plastic bag connected to a tube containing a chemical (such as a diluted solution of potassium dichromate in 50% sulphuric acid) that changes colour in the presence of alcohol. Another method is to use a gas chromatograph, again from a breath sample.

Breath testing was introduced in the UK in 1967. The approved device is now the Lion Intoximeter 3000, which is used by police to indicate the proportion of alcohol in the blood.

Breckland

Area of heathland in Norfolk and Suffolk, England, near Thetford. The soil in the area is poor, but much of the area has been planted with conifers by the Forestry Commission. Breckland is also used for military training.

Brecon Beacons

Group of mountains in the south of Powys, central Wales. Pen y Fan (885 m/2,904 ft) and Corn Du (873 m/2,864 ft) are the major peaks. It is the highest mountain mass of Old Red Sandstone in the British Isles. The area is designated as a National Park. There is a mountain centre near Defynog.

Brent

Outer borough of northwest Greater London. It includes the suburbs of Wembley and Willesden

Features

Wembley Stadium (1923); a new National Sports Stadium to be built at Wembley, designed by Norman Foster; former State Cinema in Willesden (1937), the largest cinema in Europe when built; Brent Cross shopping centre (1976), first regional shopping centre in Europe

Population (1991) 243,000.

Brenton, Howard (1942–)

English dramatist. His political theatre, deliberately provocative, includes *The Churchill Play* (1974) and *The Romans in Britain* (1980).

Bloody Poetry (1984) is an examination of the poet Shelley, and he co-wrote *Pravda* (1985) with David Hare and *Moscow Gold* (1990) with activist/writer Tariq Ali.

Brentwood

Market town in Essex, England, about 17 km/11 mi southwest of Chelmsford; population (1991) 67,400. Brentwood is situated in wooded countryside, and has a school founded in 1557 and dedicated to the English martyr St Thomas à Becket.

Brett, John (1831–1902)

English landscape and marine painter. His early, minutely detailed pictures were inspired by Pre-Raphaelite principles. An example is *The Stonebreaker* (1857–58; Walker Gallery, Liverpool), which was highly praised by the critic John Ruskin. Later he specialized in Cornish coastal and geological scenes. He became ARA in 1881.

Bretwalda (from Old English *Bretenanwealda*, 'ruler of Britain')

9th-century Anglo-Saxon title for a powerful king who exercised authority over England south of the Humber. The term was initially used in Bede's list of hegemonic rulers, but also extended to include more recent kings, such as Egbert of Wessex. Other powerful kings holding much the same sway, such as Offa of Mercia, were not included. The existence of the title provides important evidence for the early concept of an English 'nation'.

brewing

Making of beer, ale, or other alcoholic beverage, from malt and barley by steeping (mashing), boiling, and fermenting.

See ◊public house for a feature on the development of the British pub and with it, brewing.

Brideshead Revisited

Novel (1945) by Evelyn ◊Waugh. The plot revolves around the deep fascination Charles Ryder feels for the Roman Catholic Flyte family who own the great house, Brideshead. The conclusion contains a melancholy affirmation of spiritual values in spite of human unhappiness. It marked a development beyond Waugh's previous career as a satirist. The book was successfully dramatized for television in the 1980s.

Bridge, Frank (1879–1941)

English composer. His works include the orchestral suite *The Sea* (1912), and *Oration* (1930) for cello and orchestra. He taught English composer Benjamin Britten.

As a composer he possessed a formidably polished technique, and in his inter-war compositions developed a radical cosmopolitan idiom, influenced by the atonality of Schoenberg. He is now recognized as one of the finest composers of his generation, particularly in the field of chamber music.

Bridgend

Unitary authority in south Wales created in 1996 from part of the former county of Mid Glamorgan

Area 40 sq km/15 sq mi

Towns ◊Bridgend (administrative headquarters), Porthcawl (resort and residential area), ◊Maesteg

Physical most of the authority consists of the western end of a lowland plateau, Bro Morgannwg, a rich agricultural area of mixed farming and large villages; in the north is the Cymer Forest and Mynydd Caerau (556 m/1,824 ft)

Industries civil engineering; chocolate manufacture

Population (1996) 128,300.

Bridgend

Industrial and market town in ◊Bridgend unitary authority, south Wales, situated on the

BREWING *Lauter tuns used in making beer. Here the malt and barley are steeped in water before being sent to the copper. Courage Ltd*

River Ogmore 31 km/19 mi west of Cardiff; population (1981) 31,600. A Royal Ordnance factory, established here in 1936, was turned into an industrial estate for a wide variety of light industries in 1945.

Bridgewater, Francis Egerton, 3rd Duke of Bridgewater (1736–1803)

Pioneer of British inland navigation. With James ◊Brindley as his engineer, he constructed the ◊Bridgewater Canal. Succeeded as Duke 1748.

Bridgewater Canal

Canal in northwest England, initially built to carry coal from the Duke of Bridgewater's mines at Worsley (where underground waterways were constructed), to Manchester and on to the Mersey, a distance of 67.5 km/42 mi. The canal crosses the Irwell Valley on an aqueduct.

The Duke of Bridgewater began its construction, under the direction of James Brindley, in 1759. By 1761 it had opened as far as Stretford, and was extended to the Cornbrook wharf in Manchester by 1763.

An extension to the River Mersey was opened in 1776; another extension, from Worsley to Leigh, was built from 1795. In 1796 passenger services were first tried, and by 1781 there were packet boats from Manchester to Runcorn, and from Manchester to Worsley. By 1824 there were services to Wigan, using the connection with the Leeds and Liverpool Canal at Leigh. These services were later discontinued.

The canal, which was sold to the Manchester Ship Canal Company in 1887, continued to be used for goods traffic until the mid-1970s. It is now used mainly by pleasure craft.

Bridgnorth

Town in Shropshire, England, 22 km/14 mi southeast of Wellington; population (1991) 11,100. Bridgnorth is a market centre in a rich agricultural area; industries include carpet-making, light engineering, and electronics. The Town Hall was built between 1650 and 1652. The 18th-century North Gate is now a museum.

Bridgnorth is situated in the Severn Valley, which divides the town into High Town on the west bank and Low Town on the east bank; both sides are linked by steps and the Castle Hill Railway.

Bridgwater

Market town and port in Somerset, southwest England, on the River Parrett northeast of Taunton; population (1991) 34,600. Industries include engineering and the manufacture of furniture, wickerwork, industrial chemicals, fibre fabrics, cellophane, footwear, plastics, electrical goods, and preserves. A nuclear power-station stands to the northwest at Hinkley Point on **Bridgwater Bay**. The site of the Battle of ◊Sedgemoor is 5 km/3 mi to the east.

The annual **Bridgwater Carnival** is held on the nearest Thursday to 5th November, in commemoration of the Gunpowder Plot in 1605; its two-hour procession, containing over 130 floats and carts, culminates in a huge fireworks display. The Blake Museum includes relics of Admiral Blake and the Battle of Sedgemoor.

Bridgwater Three

Three victims of a miscarriage of justice who spent 18 years in prison for the murder of Carl Bridgwater. The convictions were declared unsafe in February 1997.

Following the discovery of the body of the 13-year-old paperboy at an isolated farmhouse near Stourbridge, Worcestershire, and a subsequent investigation by the West Midlands police, four men were charged. In February 1979, three of them, Michael Hickey, Vincent Hickey, and Jim Robinson, were convicted of murder, and the fourth, Patrick Molloy, of manslaughter. All were committed to prison. The case against them rested mainly on confessions by Vincent Hickey and Molly. The accused have always proclaimed their innocence and 18 years after they were convicted, it was accepted by the UK government that the confessions had been forged by the police and that the convictions were unsafe. The two Hickeys and Robinson were released on bail, pending a full judicial hearing. Molloy had died in prison 1981.

Bridie, James pen name of Osborne Henry Mavor (1888–1951)

Scottish dramatist and professor of medicine. He was a founder of the Glasgow Citizens' Theatre. His plays include the comedies *Tobias and the Angel* and *The Anatomist* (both 1930).

His work shows a richness of imagination and outstanding theatrical technique, though the problems set out in the first acts are not always satisfactorily resolved.

Bridlington

Seaside resort in the East Riding of Yorkshire, England; population (1991) 31,000. It is situated on Bridlington Bay, 10 km/6 mi southwest of Flamborough Head. The town is the headquarters of the Royal Yorkshire Yacht Club; its harbour accommodates numerous small vessels. Its main industry lies in the entertainment sector.

The lodgings in Bridlington of Queen Henrietta Maria, wife of Charles I, were bombarded by the Parliamentary ships of Admiral Batten in February 1643.

Bridlington agreement

In industrial relations, a set of principles agreed in 1939 at a Trades Union Congress conference in Bridlington, Humberside, to prevent the poaching of members of one trade union by another, and to discourage breakaway unions.

Brief Encounter

Classic 1945 British film directed by David ◊Lean, starring Celia Johnson as a housewife who falls in love with Trevor ◊Howard and struggles to stay faithful to her husband. Scripted by Noel ◊Coward from a one-act play, its themes of parting and thwarted love struck an immediate chord with audiences as World War II came to an end, and it has since gained a cultish following. The film uses the music of Russian composer Sergei Rachmaninov to haunting effect.

Briers, Richard (1934–)

English stage and screen actor. Along with Felicity Kendall, he became a household name following his role in the television sitcom *The Good Life* (1975–77). He continued to work in television in such series as *Ever Decreasing Circles* (1987) and *If You See God, Tell Him* (1993), and has appeared in several films. He has supplemented his stage, film, and television acting work with providing voice-overs for numerous advertisements and narrating the *Survival* nature programs of the mid-1980s.

Briggs, Henry (1561–1630)

English mathematician, with John Napier one of the founders of calculation by logarithms. Briggs's tables remain the basis of those used to this day.

In 1614 Scottish mathematician John Napier had published his discovery of logarithms, and Briggs went to Edinburgh to meet him in 1616. On this and subsequent visits the two men worked together to simplify Napier's original logarithms. It seems most probable that the idea of having a table of logarithms with 10 for their base was originally conceived by Briggs; the first such tables were published by him in 1617.

Bright, John (1811–1889)

British Liberal politician. He was a campaigner for free trade, peace, and social reform. A Quaker millowner, he was among the founders of the ◊Anti-Corn Law League in 1838, and was largely instrumental in securing the passage of the Reform Bill of 1867.

He sat in Gladstone's cabinets as president of the Board of Trade 1868–70 and chancellor of the Duchy of Lancaster 1873–74 and 1880–82, but broke with him over the Irish Home Rule Bill.

Brighton

Seaside resort in ◊Brighton and Hove unitary authority, on the south coast of England; population (1994 est) 155,000. The town was part of the county of East Sussex until 1997. It is an education and service centre with two universities, language schools, and tourist and conference business facilities.

The town developed in the 18th century as a fashionable health resort patronized, from 1783, by the Prince of Wales (later George IV). The ◊Royal Pavilion, extensively remodelled by John Nash between 1815 and 1822 in a mixture of Classical and Oriental styles, reopened in 1990 after nine years of restoration. Other features include the Palace Pier and an aquarium.

Originally a fishing village mentioned in the Domesday Book of 1086 as Brighthelmstone or Brithelmeston, the town became known as Brighton at the beginning of the 19th century.

Features

Brighton has 6 km/4 mi of promenade. Palace Pier was built in 1899 to replace the Chain Pier which had been destroyed by a storm in 1896. The Lanes area of the town contains 18th-century buildings on the medieval street plan of the original village. French raids in the 16th century destroyed much of the town's early architecture, the oldest surviving building being the church of St Nicholas, founded in the 14th century.

Other features include the Dome Theatre, originally the royal stables; the Museum and Art Gallery, which includes Art Deco, English pottery, and British paintings from the 19th and early 20th centuries; Booth's Museum of Natural History housing a large collection of stuffed birds; and a racecourse near the regal Kemptown estate. Devil's Dyke, a large cleft in the 200 m/700 ft-high downs to the north of the town, offers long views across the Weald.

Educational institutions

The University of Sussex was founded in 1961. Built on the Stanmer estate, to the northeast of the town, it contains buildings designed by Basil Spence. The University of Brighton (formerly Brighton Polytechnic) was established in 1992. Roedean Girls' School was founded in 1885.

Brighton and Hove

Unitary authority in southern England created in 1997

Area 84 sq km/32 sq mi

Towns Brighton, ◊Hove (administrative headquarters), Woodingdean, Rottingdean, Portslade-by-Sea

Features English Channel; South Downs; Royal Pavilion (Brighton); Palace Pier (Brighton); Hollingbury Castle fort; Booth Museum of Natural History (Brighton); British Engineerium (Hove)

Industries financial services (including American Express), tourism, conference facilities, language schools

Population (1995 est) 248,000.

Brighton Rock

Novel published in 1938 by Graham ◊Greene. Seventeen-year-old Pinkie, seeking distinction through crime, commits a squalid murder. He marries Rose, a fellow Roman Catholic, to prevent her giving evidence against him, but he is finally brought to justice through the efforts of Ida, an acquaintance of the murdered man. Although there are detective story elements, the main interest of the novel lies in its early expression of Greene's lifelong struggle with moral and spiritual questions.

Brindley, James (1716–1772)

English canal builder. He was the first to employ tunnels and aqueducts extensively, in order to reduce the number of locks on a direct-route canal. His 580 km/360 mi of canals included the Bridgewater (Manchester–Liverpool) and Grand Union (Manchester–Potteries) canals.

In 1759 Brindley was engaged by the Duke of Bridgewater to construct a canal to transport coal to Manchester from the duke's mines at Worsley. Brindley's revolutionary scheme for this included a subterranean channel and an aqueduct over the River Irwell. He constructed impervious banks by puddling clay, and the canal simultaneously acted as a mine drain. The success of this project established him as the leading canal builder in the UK.

Bristol

Industrial port and unitary authority in southwest England, at the junction of the rivers Avon and Frome; unitary authority area 109 sq km/42 sq mi; population (1996) 374,300, urban area (1991) 516,500. It was part of the former county of Avon to 1996. Industries include engineering, microelectronics, tobacco, printing, metal refining, banking, insurance, sugar refining, and the manufacture of aircraft engines, chemicals, paper, soap, Bristol 'blue' glass, and chocolate. The old docks have been redeveloped for housing, industry, yachting facilities, and the National Lifeboat Museum. Further developments include a new city centre, with British engineer and inventor Isambard Kingdom ♢Brunel's Temple Meads railway station as its focus.

Features

The Clifton Suspension Bridge (completed in 1864), was designed by Brunel. His ship *SS Great Britain*, the first propeller-driven ocean-going iron ship, was launched from Bristol in 1843 and brought back from the Falklands in 1970; it is now in dry dock at the Great Western dock, where it is being restored, although it can still be visited and hired out by the public. There is an aerospace complex at the suburb of Filton. The city is home to the University of Bristol (founded 1909) and the University of the West of England (established in 1992), formerly the Bristol Polytechnic. Ashton Court mansion is to the west of the city on an 850 acre estate, which hosts the annual International Balloon Fiesta and North Somerset show. Bristol 2000, a Millennium Commission Landmark Project in the city's harbour area, includes Wildscreen World, the world's first electronic zoo.

History

An important commercial centre and port in medieval times, Bristol was the second-most important town in England between the 15th and 18th centuries. The town developed in the 17th–18th centuries as the principal British port for trade with the American colonies and the West Indies. The port was especially important for the slave trade, and was part of a triangular trading system between West Africa and the West Indian and American plantations. Jamaican sugar and molasses and West African cocoa were brought into Britain along this trade route, leading to the development of sugar and chocolate industries in Bristol. The city was important for shipbuilding from the 18th century; the *Great Western*, Isambard Kingdom Brunel's first steam ship and the first steamer intended for transatlantic trade, was built in Bristol in 1838. The importance of the port declined in the 19th century when it was unable to berth increasingly large vessels. Bristol underwent heavy aerial attacks during World War II. Approximately 1,299 persons were killed and over 3,300 injured. More than 3,000 houses were totally destroyed.

BRISTOL *Clifton Suspension Bridge is one of Bristol's most notable landmarks. Spanning the Avon Gorge, it is a wrought-iron construction designed by the engineer Isambard Kingdom Brunel and completed after his death, in 1864. In the late 19th century, a woman fell from the bridge but was saved when her crinoline and ample skirts acted as a parachute, breaking her fall. Robert Hallmann/Collections*

Cathedral and churches
The cathedral, originally the abbey church of St Augustine (founded in about 1140), is the only 'hall-church' in England (with aisles, nave, and choir all of the same height). It retains its Norman chapter house and its Norman gate house, and the choir dates from 1298–1300. It became a cathedral in 1542 at the time of the Dissolution of the Monasteries when the see of Bristol was created. St Mary Redcliffe church was described by Queen Elizabeth I as 'the fairest church in England'. It has a large 13th-century tower with an 87 m/285 ft-high spire. The Roman Catholic cathedral of St Peter and St Paul in Clifton was dedicated in 1973, and is of an open circular design. John Wesley's chapel, dating from 1739, is England's earliest Methodist building.

Clifton
Northwest of the city centre, the Georgian residential district of Clifton includes England's longest Georgian crescent, the Royal York Crescent. The Clifton Suspension Bridge, spanning the Avon Gorge, is 214 m/702 ft long and 75 m/246 ft high. It was completed after Brunel's death. Clifton is also the site of Bristol Zoo and Clifton College, a private school founded in 1862.

Galleries, museums, and architectural features
The City Museum and Art Gallery includes collections of local archaeology, natural history, Chinese glass, Assyrian reliefs dating from the 8th century BC, European paintings, and a large display of English delftware (a type of porcelain). The redeveloped city docks include the Bristol Industrial Museum (home to the *Mayflower*, Britain's oldest working tug) and the Maritime Heritage Centre. The Merchants' Almshouses date from 1699. The Theatre Royal, home to the Bristol Old Vic since 1946, was a Georgian playhouse which opened in 1766.

Bristol Channel

Inlet in the southwest of England; coastline length 352 km/219 mi. Situated on the Atlantic Ocean, it is an extension of the ◊Severn estuary, and is surrounded by South Wales to the north, and by Devon, Somerset and North Somerset to the south. The Bristol Channel is Britain's largest inlet, with a length of about 128 km/79 mi, a breadth which varies from 8 km/5 mi to 69 km/43 mi, and a depth from 9 m/30 ft to 73 m/240 ft.

Features
A feature of the channel is its extraordinary tides, which sometimes rise to a height of 10 m/33 ft at King Road on the mouth of the River Avon, and even to 15 m/49 ft or more at Chepstow. This marked rise causes the Severn bore, a rush of the tide in the form of a wall of water, located further upstream where the Severn estuary narrows.

The rivers Towy, Taff, Usk, Wye, Severn, Avon, Axe, Ely, Parret, Taw, and Torridge all flow into the Bristol Channel. There are several islands, including Steep Holm, Flat Holm, and Lundy Island.

Bristow, Eric (1957–)

English darts player, nicknamed 'the Crafty Cockney'. He has won all the game's major titles, including the world professional title a record five times between 1980 and 1986.

Britain

Island comprising England, Scotland, and Wales (together officially known as ◊Great Britain), part of the ◊United Kingdom. The word is often used colloquially to cover the whole of the United Kingdom including Northern Ireland.

Britannia

The Roman name for Britain, later a national symbol of Great Britain in the form of a seated woman with a trident. Also the name of the royal yacht, decommissioned in 1997.

British Academy

Academy founded in 1901, whose primary purpose is to promote research and scholarship in the humanities and social sciences. It receives the bulk of its income from the government.

British Academy of Film and Television Arts

See ◊BAFTA.

British Aerospace plc, BAe

British civil and military aviation company. It is one of the world's largest aerospace concerns, producing aircraft, missiles, spacecraft, and parts for various jointly produced commercial and military aircraft. Formerly state-owned, it was privatized in 1979–81.

The company was incorporated in 1978 when the Aircraft and Shipping Industries Bill merged the Aircraft and Dynamics divisions of Hawker-Siddeley with the British Aircraft Corporation and Scottish Aviation. It continued to be operated by the British government as a state-owned corporation until privatization. The government held 48% of the company's share capital until 1985 when it offered to sell its shares (worth £550 million) to institutional investors.

British Airways, BA

Largest British airline, formed in 1974 by the merger of British European Airways (BEA) and British Overseas Airways Corporation (BOAC). Originally state-owned, British Airways was privatized in 1987.

British Board of Film Classification, BBFC

Independent UK body established in 1912; until 1985 it was known as the British Board of Film Censors. The BBFC ensures that a proper national standard is maintained in films offered for cinema exhibition and in videos supplied to the public primarily for viewing at home. It is financed by fees charged for the examination of cinema films.

Films and videos intended for public viewing are submitted by the industry for examination. The board grants certificates in the following categories: **U** (Universal) suitable for all; **Uc** (Universal) particularly suitable for children (video only); **PG** (Parental Guidance) general viewing, but some scenes may be unsuitable for young children; **12** suitable only for persons of 12 years and over (film only); **15** suitable only for persons of

15 years and over; **18** suitable only for persons of 18 years and over; **R18** (Restricted) to be exhibited only in licensed sex shops (video) to persons of not less than 18 years of age.

British Commonwealth of Nations

Former official name of the ◊Commonwealth.

British Council

Semi-official organization set up in 1934 (royal charter 1940) to promote a wider knowledge of the UK, excluding politics and commerce, and to develop cultural relations with other countries. It employs more than 6,000 people and is represented in 109 countries, running libraries, English-teaching operations, and resource centres.

British Empire

Empire covering, at its height in the 1920s, about a sixth of the landmass of the Earth, all of its lands recognizing the United Kingdom as their leader. See feature on next page and table of member countries.

British Empire, Order of the

British order of knighthood (see ◊knighthood, orders of) instituted in 1917 by George V. There are military and civil divisions, and the ranks are GBE, Knight Grand Cross or Dame Grand Cross; KBE, Knight Commander; DBE, Dame Commander; CBE, Commander; OBE, Officer; MBE, Member.

In 1974 awards for civilian gallantry previously made within the order were replaced by the Queen's Gallantry Medal (QGM), which ranks after the George Cross and George Medal.

Membership of the order is awarded to both men and women for services rendered to the British Empire. Its motto is 'For God and Empire'. The order uses the crypt of St Paul's Cathedral, London, as its chapel.

British Expeditionary Force, BEF

During World War I (1914–18) the term commonly referred to the British army serving in France and Flanders, although strictly speaking it referred only to the forces sent to France in 1914; during World War II it was also the army in Europe, which was evacuated from Dunkirk, France in 1940.

British Film Institute, BFI

Organization founded in 1933 to promote the cinema as a 'means of entertainment and instruction'. It includes the National Film Archive (founded in 1935) and the National Film Theatre (founded in 1951), and is involved in publishing books and periodicals such as the monthly *Sight and Sound*.

The BFI provides funding for film distribution and exhibition in Britain, and also releases films on its video label Connoisseur Video. It is responsible for programming and

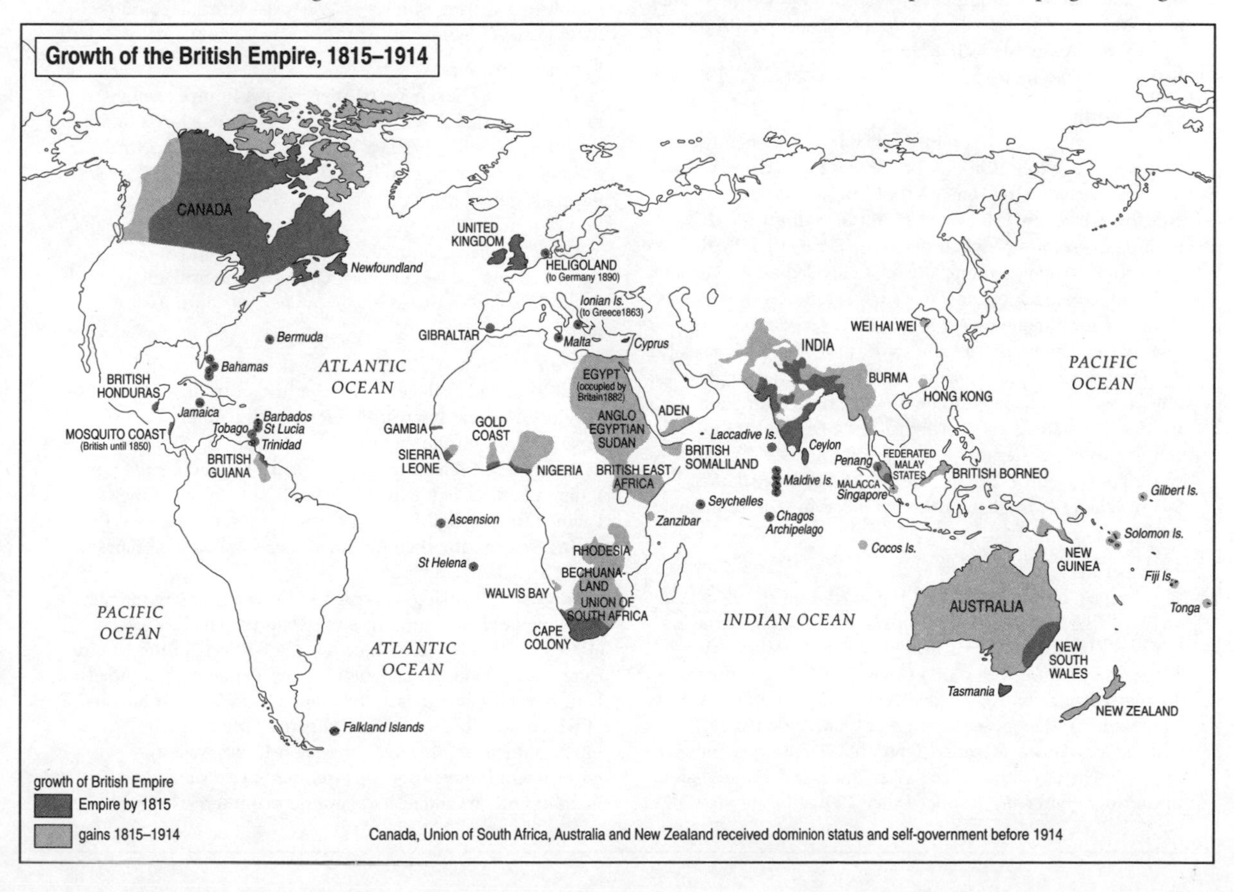

Growth of the British Empire, 1815–1914

Canada, Union of South Africa, Australia and New Zealand received dominion status and self-government before 1914

THE GROWTH AND DECLINE OF THE BRITISH EMPIRE

At its height in the 1920s, the British Empire consisted of the Empire of India, four self-governing countries known as dominions, and dozens of colonies and territories, all recognizing the UK as their leader. After World War II it began to dissolve as colony after colony became independent, and today the UK has only 13 small dependent territories. With 52 other independent countries, it forms the Commonwealth. Although Britain's monarch is accepted as head of the Commonwealth, most of its member states are republics.

The present Commonwealth is a voluntary association of independent states. Only one of its members, Mozambique, which joined in 1995, was never a British colony (it was Portuguese). The Commonwealth's links are mainly cultural and economic, depending upon the fact that the English language is the lingua franca of all educated people in the territories that formed the British Empire, on the continuing ties of trade, and on the financial and technical aid provided by the economically developed members to the developing members.

A major factor in the break-up of the British Empire was that while in its earlier days it brought wealth to the mother country, later it became a liability which Britain could no longer afford. In addition, people's attitudes toward colonies had changed. In the 19th century many Britons believed that they had a mission to improve the lot of other peoples. The poet Rudyard Kipling summed up this philosophy in the phrase 'the White Man's burden'; this idea is now regarded with distaste by many people.

Early empire

The story of the British Empire began in 1497 when the Italian seafarer John Cabot sailed across the Atlantic Ocean in the service of King Henry VII of England and reached Newfoundland. In 1583 the explorer Sir Humphrey Gilbert took possession of Newfoundland for Elizabeth I. By this time the Portuguese and Spanish had divided between them a considerable part of the Earth's land surface. England was already a formidable power at sea, but its seafarers were mainly freebooters engaged in trade, piracy, and slavery. The defeat of the Spanish Armada in 1588 reinforced English sea power, which continued to be mostly privately organized. Unlike the Spanish and Portuguese, the English in the 16th century were neither missionaries nor colonists. England was a poor country, lacking the wealth of Portugal and Spain; when the English put to sea it was to seek immediate profits.

17th century

This pattern began to change in the 17th century. Between 1623 and 1632 English settlers occupied St Kitts, Barbados, St Croix (later lost), Nevis, Antigua, and Montserrat. In 1655, Oliver Cromwell's forces took Jamaica from the Spaniards, who officially ceded it in 1760. British Honduras (now Belize) was governed as part of Jamaica until 1884, and the tiny South Atlantic island of St Helena was annexed in 1673. The attraction of the West Indies for the English lay in the sugar and rum produced there. Virginia, the first permanent English colony in mainland America, was established in 1607 by the Virginia Company, which also took over Bermuda in about 1610. Shortly after this, in 1620, the Pilgrim Fathers landed from the ship *Mayflower* to found the colony of Massachusetts. By 1733, the English had established 13 colonies along the Atlantic seaboard between French Canada and Spanish Florida. The colonists began to plant cotton in the 17th century, and this plantation crop was being grown on a very large scale by the late 18th century.

18th century

In 1707 England had united with Scotland to form, as Great Britain, the largest free-trade area then existing, and by the late 18th century Britain had become the leading industrial nation. Its main pattern of trade was based on the 'triangular route'; British ships took manufactured goods and spirits to West Africa to exchange them for slaves, whom they landed in the West Indies and the southernmost of the 13 colonies. The ships then returned to Britain with cargoes of cotton, rum, sugar, and tobacco, produced mainly by the labour of the black slaves. Britain's prosperity was bound up with the slave trade until this became illegal in 1807. By that time the importance of the slave trade had diminished and other forms of commerce had become more profitable. With other western European nations, the British had already established a string of forts in West Africa to safeguard the trade in slaves, gold, and ivory.

Seven Years' War

In 1756–63 the Seven Years' War against France brought Britain lands in Canada and India, plus more islands in the West Indies, and Gibraltar. The 13 colonies on the North Atlantic seaboard won independence as the USA 1776–83. Britain acquired the Bahamas in 1783, and the defeat of France in the Napoleonic Wars enabled Britain to add Malta, St Lucia, Grenada, Dominica, St Vincent, Trinidad, Tobago, part of Guiana (now Guyana), Ceylon (now Sri Lanka), the Seychelles, and Cape Colony (now part of South Africa) to its empire.

Spread of science

In the 17th and 18th centuries the British ruling class developed a great interest in science, which had repercussions on the growth of the British Empire. Between 1768 and 1780 scientific naval expeditions commanded by Captain James Cook explored islands and coasts of the Pacific Ocean, from the entrance to the Arctic Ocean at the Bering Strait to the then unknown coasts of New Zealand and Australia.

Successive British governments showed no more interest in annexing these southern lands than they had in places elsewhere. In most cases they left the building of the empire to private individuals such as William Penn (who founded Pennsylvania) or to chartered companies, the most famous of which was the East India Company (1660–1858). An important exception was in the West Indies, where government intervention was frequent because many members of Parliament had commercial interests there.

Members of the British Empire

current name	colonial names and history	colonized	independent
India	British East India Company	18th century–1858	1947
Pakistan	British East India Company	18th century–1858	1947
Myanmar	Burma	1866	1948
Sri Lanka	Portuguese, Dutch 1602–1796; Ceylon 1802–1972	16th century	1948
Ghana	Gold Coast; British Togoland integrated 1956	18th–19th centuries	1957
Nigeria		1861	1960
Cyprus	Turkish to 1878, then British rule	1878	1960
Sierra Leone	British protectorate	1788	1961
Tanzania	German East Africa to 1921; British mandate from League of Nations/UN as Tanganyika	19th century	1961
Jamaica	Spanish to 1655	16th century	1962
Trinidad & Tobago	Spanish 1532–1797; British 1797–1962	1532	1962
Uganda	British protectorate	1894	1962
Kenya	British colony from 1920	1895	1963
Malaysia	British interests from 1786; Federation of Malaya 1957–63	1874	1963
Malawi	British protectorate of Nyasaland 1907–53; Federation of Rhodesia & Nyasaland 1953–64	1891	1964
Malta	French 1798–1814	1798	1964
Zambia	Northern Rhodesia – British protectorate; Federation of Rhodesia & Nyasaland 1953–64	1924	1964
The Gambia		1888	1965
Singapore	Federation of Malaya 1963–65	1858	1965
Guyana	Dutch to 1796; British Guiana 1796–1966	1620	1966
Botswana	Bechuanaland – British protectorate	1885	1966
Lesotho	Basutoland	1868	1966
Bangladesh	British East India Company 18th century–1858; British India 1858–1947; eastern Pakistan 1947–71	18th century	1971
Zimbabwe	Southern Rhodesia from 1923; UDI under Ian Smith 1965–79	1895	1980
Belize	British Honduras	17th century	1981
Hong Kong	Hong Kong	1841	1997 (returned to China)

Convict settlements

One reason for the British government's interest in the 13 American colonies was as a dumping ground for convicts, debtors, and political prisoners, many of whom were sentenced to transportation rather than to gaol or the gallows (at that time the law provided the death sentence for stealing a sheep). American independence posed the problem for Britain of where to send its surplus prison population, so in 1788 a new convict settlement was established in Australia at Botany Bay in New South Wales, near where Sydney is now located. This territory had been recently discovered by the voyages of James Cook.

19th century
Britain annexed New Zealand in 1840, Tristan da Cunha in 1816, the Falkland Islands in 1833, and Papua in 1884. In 1878 Turkey handed over Cyprus to a British administration.

India
At the heart of the British Empire was India, which was controlled not by the government but by the East India Company, whose power extended from Aden (annexed in 1839) in Arabia to Penang (leased in 1786) in Malaya. Both places were vital ports of call for company vessels travelling between Britain, India, and China. Politically, the East India Company was the most powerful private company in history. It controlled India partly by direct rule and partly by a system of alliances with Indian princes, whose powers and security were backed by the company's powerful army. Finally, in 1857, a mutiny by its Indian troops terminated the company's affairs, and in 1858 the British government took over its functions. In 1877, Benjamin Disraeli, then prime minister, made Queen Victoria Empress of India. Her new empire included present-day India, Pakistan, Sri Lanka, Bangladesh, and most of Myanmar (Burma). In 1879 the nearby Maldive Islands were annexed.

Imperialism
By this time British policy was becoming imperialistic. In the last quarter of the 19th century Britain tended to annex countries not just for commercial gain but for reasons of national prestige. The commercial operations of the East India Company extended into the East Indies, a vast area that had come under Dutch control. When the Netherlands were occupied by the French under Napoleon (1793–1815), parts of the Dutch East Indies were occupied by the East India Company and held until 1824. When the British government took over from the East India Company it also acquired the Straits Settlements. These comprised Penang, Malacca (not returned to the Dutch), and Singapore, founded by Stamford Raffles in 1819. Increasingly the British became involved in the affairs of the Malay Sultanates, several of which sought British protection from the domination of Siam (now Thailand). By 1914 all of Malaya was under British control. Eastward, in Borneo, Sarawak had become the personal possession of James Brooke, a freebooting, British ex-soldier of the East India Company. The British North Borneo Company acquired present-day Sabah in 1888. In the same year the once powerful adjoining sultanate of Brunei, which had formerly possessed Sarawak and Sabah, itself came under British protection.

This vast empire had been assembled without any coordinated plan, and it was held together and administered by whatever means seemed most expedient for a particular place. Pirates, traders, soldiers, explorers, financial speculators, missionaries, convicts, and refugees all played a part in creating the British Empire, but increasingly British governments were drawn in to maintain it. To protect India's northwest frontier, the British army fought two wars with Afghanistan (1839–41 and 1878–80) and in 1904 invaded Tibet.

Hong Kong
The acquisition of Hong Kong was typical of the way in which western countries seized colonies between about 1840 and 1890. In 1839 China stopped the importation by the East India Company of opium, which China complained was having a debilitating effect upon its people. When British and American ships defied the ban, Chinese officials publicly destroyed 20,000 cases of the drug. Faced with the collapse of its Far Eastern operations (for without the opium trade it was not financially viable) the company persuaded the British government, then led by Lord Palmerston, to declare war on China. As a result of the Opium War, Britain gained Hong Kong island. Kowloon was added to the colony after a second Opium War (1856–58) and more mainland territory was taken in 1898.

Colonizing Africa
Before the 1880s the British showed little interest in Africa apart from Cape Colony. The first large group of British settlers landed in the Cape in 1820. They were bitterly resented by the Boers (Dutch farmers), descendants of Dutch Protestants who had settled in the Cape nearly 200 years earlier. When slavery was ended throughout the British Empire in 1833, the Boers were forced to free their African slaves. Although the British government gave them generous financial compensation, the Boers regarded this further interference by the British as too much to accept. In 1836 they began the 'Great Trek' northward to found the Orange Free State and the South African Republic. By 1856 the British had recognized the independence of these states but had themselves founded a new colony in Natal. After heavy fighting, beginning in 1879, the British conquered the African military state of Zululand and added it to Natal in 1897.

The discovery of diamonds and gold in southern Africa led to disputes between the Boers and the British. Britain annexed the South African Republic, but the Boers struck back. They won the first Boer War (1880–81) and regained the lost territory, which the Boers renamed the Transvaal Republic.

Britain had maintained a few forts in West Africa, where gold and ivory kept their importance after the slave trade ended. An exception was Sierra Leone, where Granville Sharp, an Englishman opposed to slavery, established a settlement of freed American slaves in 1787. This coastal strip of Sierra Leone was made a British colony in 1808. In 1821 the British established a coastal colony around the tiny town of Bathurst on the River Gambia. Only later were colonies established on the coasts of present-day Ghana and Nigeria.

From the 1880s onward Belgium, Britain, France, Germany, Italy, Portugal, and Spain vied with each other to establish colonies in Africa. British protectorates were established to cover roughly the area of present-day Gambia, Sierra Leone, Ghana, and Nigeria. Because of the climate, which gave West Africa its reputation as 'the white man's grave', these colonies attracted very few British settlers.

In East Africa the situation was different, for on high ground the land proved suitable for settlement by white colonists. Private companies under charter from the British government established control over Kenya in 1888 and Uganda in 1890. In 1890 Germany, which had already relinquished its interests in Uganda, ceded Zanzibar (now part of Tanzania) to Britain in exchange for Heligoland, an island off the German coast. By 1900 all Kenya and Uganda was under the control of the British government. Northern Somalia had come under direct control of the British in 1884. By the time the European scramble for Africa ended, Britain held the second-largest share of the continent.

British missionaries of all denominations spread the Christian religion throughout the empire. They made proportionately little impression in places where the religions of Buddhism, Hinduism, or Islam dominated, but even in those areas their converts numbered several millions. Their success was greater in the West Indies, and in Africa south of the Sahara.

David Livingstone, a Scottish missionary, explored much of the area that is now Botswana, Zambia, and Zimbabwe. Like several other intrepid explorers, who included Richard Burton, John Hanning Speke, and Sir Samuel Baker, Livingstone explored the River Nile. His journeys also took him to the Zambezi River and to lakes Tanganyika and Nyasa. Following Livingstone's journeys, the Free Church of Scotland set up a mission in Nyasaland (now Malawi) in 1875, and the country became a British protectorate in 1891, a year after Bechuanaland (now Botswana). Basutoland (now Lesotho) became a British colony in 1884.

In the late 1880s the British South Africa Company, which was largely controlled by Cecil Rhodes, negotiated land mineral rights from African chiefs in Matabeleland and Mashonaland. By 1889 the company had conquered these two territories and united them as Rhodesia, named after Rhodes. The company intervened further northwards, stamping out the slave trade and bringing that area under their control too. They named it Northern Rhodesia (which later became Zambia).

In 1890 Rhodes became prime minister of Cape Colony, at a time when tension was again mounting between the Boers and the British. The Boers resisted encroachments in their territories by British speculators interested in the diamonds and gold known to exist there. After three years of the second Boer War (1899–1902), the two Boer republics, plus Swaziland, were annexed by Britain.

Dominions and independence

Britain took care not to lose any more colonies through wars of independence. Canada, Australia, and New Zealand had special problems. Their great distance from Britain made it desirable that they should have a great measure of control over their own affairs. The concept of self-government was first formulated in the 'Report on the Affairs of British North America' in 1839 by Lord John Durham, Canada's governor-general. This report recommended that responsible government (the acceptance by governors of the advice of local ministers) should be granted to Upper Canada (Ontario) and Lower Canada (Quebec), which should be merged into one. The merge took place immediately, but responsible government did not come into being until 1847 under the governorship of Lord Elgin, the son-in-law of Lord Durham.

This pattern was subsequently applied to the other Canadian provinces and to the Australian colonies. The Australian colonies had attained responsible government by 1859, except for Western Australia, which attained it in 1890. New Zealand obtained responsible government in all but native affairs in 1856, and this reservation disappeared by 1870. Cape Colony achieved responsible government in 1872, followed by Natal in 1893.

The British devised a further intermediate stage between colonial status and independence, which came to be called dominion status. Canada became a dominion in 1867, Australia in 1901, New Zealand in 1907, and the Union of South Africa (Cape Colony, Natal, Orange Free State, and Transvaal) by 1910. These constitutional changes were effected without rancour. Eire (southern Ireland), which had been part of the UK, also became a dominion as the Irish Free State in 1922. It did not acknowledge this status, and declared itself independent in 1938. Eire's breakaway was accomplished only with much violence and bitterness.

To improve communications with India, Disraeli purchased for Britain shares in the Suez Canal in 1875. This led to British involvement in Egypt, a country supposedly under Turkish suzerainty, but in fact largely independent. In 1882 Egypt came under British occupation, and shortly after this British and Egyptian troops were jointly involved in Sudan, to the south. By 1899, a protectorate had been established, setting up a condominium called Anglo-Egyptian Sudan. The great dream of Rhodes had been that one day the British Empire in Africa would stretch from the Cape to Cairo. By 1899 this dream was almost a reality; only German East Africa (Tanganyika) stood in the way. The defeat of Germany and Turkey in World War I not only gave Britain a mandate over Tanganyika, but also over Palestine, Transjordan, Iraq, and part of Cameroon. German Southwest Africa (now Namibia) went to South Africa, German New Guinea to Australia, German Samoa to New Zealand, and the Pacific island of Nauru to Britain, Australia, and New Zealand jointly.

20th century

By the 1920s the British Empire had reached its zenith. As well as the places already mentioned, it included part of Antarctica and many small territories, mainly Pacific islands. Its continuance depended upon British superiority at sea, upon the ability of Britain to maintain its industrial and financial supremacy, and also upon the psychological acceptance of British (and Western) superiority. However, all three were waning. In the 1920s there had been stirrings in India, where Mahatma Gandhi led unarmed protests, called 'civil disobedience', to British rule. By 1939 the end of all empires was near, and World War II speeded their end. After the war ended the rest of the empire began to break up. India was the first to acquire independence, dividing as it did so into two countries, India and Pakistan. The rest of the colonies then became independent, most of them before 1980. With the return of Hong Kong to China in 1997 Britain was left with only 13 small dependencies.

running the annual London Film Festival. A library of film books and journals, a stills and posters department, and research facilities are housed at the BFI's headquarters in London. The BFI, in conjunction with Birkbeck College, also operates a master's degree course in film and television studies.

British Isles

Group of islands off the northwest coast of Europe, consisting of Great Britain (England, Wales, and Scotland), Ireland, the Channel Islands, the Orkney and Shetland islands, the Isle of Man, and many other islands that are included in various counties, such as the Isle of Wight, Scilly Isles, Lundy Island, and the Inner and Outer Hebrides. The islands are divided from Europe by the North Sea, Strait of Dover, and the English Channel, and face the Atlantic to the west.

British Legion

Organization to promote the welfare of British veterans of war service and their dependants. Established under the leadership of Douglas Haig in 1921 (royal charter 1925) it became the **Royal British Legion** in 1971; it is nonpolitical. The sale on Remembrance Sunday of Flanders poppies raises much of its funds.

British Library

National library of the UK. Created in 1973, it comprises the **reference division** (the former library departments of the British Museum, rehoused in Euston Road, St Pancras, London); **lending division** at Boston Spa, Yorkshire, from which full text documents and graphics can be sent by satellite link to other countries; **bibliographic services division** (incorporating the British National Bibliography); and the **National Sound Archive** in South Kensington, London.

The Humanities Reading Room of the new library at St Pancras was opened in November 1997, with smaller reading rooms opening 1998–99. The new library holds 12 million volumes, can accommodate 1,200 readers, and includes a conference centre and exhibition facilities.

Construction work on the site began in 1982. Its escalating costs (£511million in total), delays in completion, and ultra-modern design caused controversy.

Great Britain has lost an empire and has not yet found a role.

Dean Acheson US Democratic politician.
Speech at the Military Academy, West Point
5 December 1962

British Lions

Rugby union side selected from the best players in the British Isles for tours of Australia, New Zealand or South Africa. The first tour by a British side representing two or more countries took place in 1888, however the first one composed of players from all four Home Unions (England, Ireland, Scotland, and Wales) occurred in 1910. To wear the red shirt of the British Lions is considered one of the highest honours in the game.

British Medical Association, BMA

Association founded in 1832 to promote the medical and allied sciences, and to maintain the honour and interests of the medical profession, exercising disciplinary powers when necessary. It is recognized by the government and others as the representative body of the profession in the UK. It was founded as the Provincial Medical and Surgical Association and took its present name in 1856. Its official organ is the *British Medical Journal*.

British Museum

Largest museum of the UK. Founded in 1753, it opened in London in 1759. Rapid additions led to the construction of the present buildings (1823–47). In 1881 the Natural History Museum was transferred to South Kensington.

The museum began with the purchase of Hans Sloane's library and art collection, and the subsequent acquisition of the Cottonian, Harleian, and other libraries. It was first housed at Montagu House in Bloomsbury. Its present buildings were designed by Robert Smirke; later extensions were the circular reading room built of 1857, and the north wing or Edward VII galleries of 1914.

British Nuclear Fuels, BNFL

State-owned company manufacturing nuclear fuel and recycling used nuclear fuel, also handling the associated waste management.

British Petroleum, BP

One of the world's largest oil concerns, with more than 58,150 employees in Britain (1997). It was formed as the Anglo-Persian Oil Company in 1909 and acquired the chemical interests of the Distillers Company in 1967.

In 1917 British Petroleum was established as a marketing subsidiary of the Anglo-Persian Oil Company (from 1935 the Anglo-Iranian Oil Company), and the latter was renamed the British Petroleum Company in 1954.

British Rail

The nationalized railway system, 1948–97. See ◊Railways and ◊Railtrack.

British Standards Institution, BSI

UK national standards body. Although government funded, the institution is independent. The BSI interprets international technical standards for the UK, and also sets its own.

For consumer goods, it sets standards which products should reach (the BS standard), as well as testing products to see that they conform to that standard (as a result of which the product may be given the BSI 'kite' mark).

British Steel

Company manufacturing iron and steel. Originally state-owned, British Steel was privatized in 1988.

British Technology Group, BTG

UK corporation exploiting inventions derived from public or private sources, usually jointly with industrial firms. It was set

Top Ten Exhibitions at the British Museum, London, by Total Attendance

Figures are for temporary exhibitions as at March 1998.

Rank	Name	Date	Total attendance number
1	Treasures of Tutankhamun	1972	1,694,117
2	Turner Watercolours	1975–76	585,046
3	The Vikings	1980	465,000
4	Thracian Treasures from Bulgaria	1976	424,465
5	From Manet to Toulouse-Lautrec: French Lithographs 1860–1900	1978	355,354
6	The Ancient Olympic Games	1980–81	334,354
7	Treasures for the Nation – Conserving our Heritage	1988–89	297,837
8	Excavating in Egypt: The Egypt Exploration Fund 1882–1992	1982–83	285,736
9	Heraldry: British Heraldry from its Origins to 1800	1978	262,183
10	Drawings by Michelangelo	1975	250,000

Source: The British Museum

up in 1967 under the Development of Inventions Acts 1948–65 and known as the National Research Development Council until 1981. BTG holds more than 8,000 patents and was responsible for marketing the hovercraft, magnetic resonance imaging, and cephalosporin antibiotics. In 1990 it returned royalties worth £13 million to British research bodies.

British Virgin Islands

UK dependency, part of the Virgin Islands group in the West Indies.

The British Virgin Islands consist of Tortola (with the capital, Road Town), Virgin Gorda, Anegada, and Jost van Dykes, and about 40 islets (11 islands are inhabited); area 150 sq km/58 sq mi; population (1991) 16,100. They were taken over from the Dutch by British settlers in 1666, and have partial internal self-government.

Brittain, Vera (Mary) (1893–1970)

English socialist writer. She was a nurse to the troops overseas from 1915 to 1919, as told in her *Testament of Youth* (1933); *Testament of Friendship* (1940) commemorates English novelist Winifred ◊Holtby.

She married political scientist George Catlin (1896–1979); their daughter is the politician Shirley ◊Williams, aspects of whose childhood are recorded in her mother's *Testament of Experience* (1957).

Brittan, Leon (1939–)

British Conservative politician and lawyer. Chief secretary to the Treasury 1981–83, home secretary 1983–85, secretary for trade and industry 1985–86 (resigned over his part in the ◊Westland affair), and senior European commissioner from 1988. Appointed commissioner for external trade from 1993, he was at the forefront of the negotiating team that concluded the Uruguay round of GATT trade talks, leading to greater trade liberalization. He later became vice president of the European Commission. Knighted 1989.

Britten, (Edward) Benjamin, Baron Britten (1913–1976)

English composer. He often wrote for the individual voice; for example, the role in the opera *Peter Grimes* (1945), based on verses by George Crabbe, was written for his life companion, the tenor Peter Pears. Among his many works are the *Young Person's Guide to the Orchestra* (1946); the chamber opera *The Rape of Lucretia* (1946); *Billy Budd* (1951); *A Midsummer Night's Dream* (Shakespeare) (1960); and *Death in Venice* (after Thomas Mann) (1973).

By intellectual conviction and personal disposition Britten was an outsider; the themes of lost innocence, persecution, and isolation are constantly repeated in his music, especially the operas. Once treated with caution by both conservatives and the avant garde, he has now reached a wider acceptance.

BRM

Abbreviation for **British Racing Motors**, a racing-car manufacturer founded in 1949 by Raymond Mays (1899–1980). Their first Grand Prix win was in 1959, and in the next 18 years they won 17 Grands Prix. Their only world champion was Graham Hill.

broadcasting

The transmission of sound and vision programmes by ◊radio and ◊television. Broadcasting is operated in Britain under a compromise system, where a television and radio service controlled by the state-regulated British Broadcasting Corporation (◊BBC) operates alongside commercial channels operating under franchises granted by the ◊Independent Television Commission (known as the Independent Broadcasting Authority before 1991) and the Radio Authority.

Television broadcasting entered a new era with the introduction of high-powered communications satellites in the 1980s. The signals broadcast by these satellites are sufficiently strong to be picked up by a small dish aerial located, for example, on the roof of a house. Direct broadcast by satellite thus became a feasible alternative to land-based television services. A similar revolution is taking place as digital ◊television becomes widely available.

A royal charter and agreement govern the constitution, finances, and obligations of the BBC, which has a regional structure and provides 20,000 hours of regional and national broadcasting a year. In 1996, the BBC was substantially reorganized to strengthen its existing services and develop digital services. The franchizing of cable television systems is carried out by the Programme and Cable Division of ITC.

Digital technologies being introduced will support 500 television channels, video-on-demand, home shopping and banking, security and alarm services, electronic mail, and high-speed internet access.

History

Although television transmissions began shortly after the end of World War II, radio continued for several years to be the dominant medium. On the more serious side of broadcasting, the BBC's Third Programme (now Radio 3) began to present speech and music on a pattern which was speedily copied in other European countries and which aimed at the consistent treatment of the arts, philosophy, literature, and music. However, television soon began to expand its audience and to challenge radio. Radio reacted slowly to the competition, but it was soon exploiting its immediacy and flexibility as a medium for reporting and for making a new type of documentary made possible by light, portable tape-recorders. Music, discussions, talks, quizzes, and magazine programmes were the staple of radio, which now left to television those large areas of entertainment, drama, and documentary which were better suited to visual presentation.

Technological developments

The development of television programmes was greatly advanced by the adoption of light, portable equipment using 16-mm film; this gave news and current-affairs reporting a flexibility unknown with cumbersome 35-mm gear. This technical advance enabled news documentary programmes to develop a new kind of television journalism, recording events with sometimes horrifying immediacy. The development of portable video cameras and recorders brought the advent of electronic news gathering, while the introduction of ◊satellite television made it possible to convey pictures from one side of the Earth to the other and, in due course, to the Earth from the Moon.

The consumer

Two other areas of debate have been concerned with the concepts of accountability: the extent to which broadcasting organizations should be answerable to the public they serve, and the desire by members of the community to air their views without the intervention of television or radio producers in the role of censors and editors.

Broadcasting Complaints Commission

Former UK body responsible for dealing with complaints of invasion of privacy or unjust treatment on television or radio. It was replaced by the ◊Broadcasting Standards Commisssion in 1997.

Broadcasting Standards Council

Former UK body concerned with handling complaints on treatment of sex and violence. It was replaced by the ◊Broadcasting Standards Commisssion in 1997.

Broadcasting Standards Commission, BSC

UK body created in April 1997 to take over and combine the roles of the former Broadcasting Standards Council and Broadcasting Complaints Commission. It monitors the portrayal of violence, sex, and other morally sensitive areas on television and radio, endeavours to ensure fair representation of situations and individuals, and deals with complaints of invasion of privacy or unjust treatment.

Broads, Norfolk

Area of navigable lakes and rivers in England; see ◊Norfolk Broads.

Broadstairs

Seaside resort in east Kent, England, 5 km/3 mi southeast of Margate; population (1991) 24,000. The North Foreland lighthouse is nearby. Broadstairs is closely associated with the novelist Charles Dickens, who wrote *David Copperfield* here. Many places in Broadstairs are mentioned in Dickens's works and the town is now the site of an annual Dickens festival.

A house where the novelist Charles Dickens spent much time in the 1850s and 1860s stands on the cliff above the harbour. The house was renamed Bleak House after Dickens's novel of the same name, and is now the Dickens and Maritime Museum.

Broadwood, John (1732–1812)

English piano manufacturer and music editor. He married Barbara, daughter of the Swiss-born harpsichord maker Burkat Shudi, in 1769, and was sole proprietor of Shudi & Broadwood from 1782. By 1781 he had built the first Broadwood grand piano, developed from Johannes Zumpe's (fl. 1735–83) square pianos.

Bromley

Outer borough of southeast Greater London

Features ◊Crystal Palace, re-erected at Sydenham in 1854 and burned down in 1936, site now partly occupied by the National Sports Centre; 13th-century parish church of SS Peter and Paul; 17th-century Bromley College; chalk caves and tunnels at Chislehurst; Keston Common has a Roman cemetery and traces of a Roman villa; Holwood Park contains 'Caesar's Camp', the site of a British encampment with earthworks dating from about 200 BC. It is the best surviving field monument in Greater London.

Bromsgrove

Market town in Worcestershire, 20 km/12 mi southwest of Birmingham; population (1991) 88,500. The Lickey Incline (274 m/900 ft) is the steepest gradient on the main lines of the British rail network; a headstone in the churchyard commemorates two engine drivers whose train engine exploded while trying to climb it in November 1840. The church of St John the Baptist has a 61 m/200 ft tower and spire, both dating from the 14th century.

Bronowski, Jacob (1908–1974)

Polish-born British scientist, broadcaster, and writer, who enthusiastically popularized scientific knowledge in several books and in the 13-part television documentary *The Ascent of Man*, issued as a book 1973.

Bronowski fled with his family to Germany when, in World War I, Russia occupied his native Poland. Moving to the UK in 1920, he studied mathematics at Cambridge. He lectured at University College, Hull, 1934–42, and then did military research during World War II, remaining a government official until 1963. His last appointment was at the Salk Institute for Biological Studies in California, from 1964.

His book *The Common Sense of Science* (1951) displayed the history and workings of science around three central notions: cause, chance, and order. *Science and Human Values* (1958) collected newspaper articles written for the *New York Times* about nuclear science and the morality of nuclear weapons. *The Western Intellectual Tradition* (1960) is an illuminating survey of the growth of political, philosophical, and scientific knowledge from the Renaissance to the 19th century, written with Bruce Mazlish. Bronowski also wrote about literature; for example, *William Blake and the Age of Revolution* (1965).

Brontë

Three English novelists, daughters of a Yorkshire parson. **Charlotte** (1816–1855), notably with ◊*Jane Eyre* (1847) and *Villette* (1853), reshaped autobiographical material into vivid narrative. **Emily** (1818–1848) in ◊*Wuthering Heights* (1847) expressed the intensity and nature mysticism which also pervades her poetry (*Poems*, 1846). The more modest talent of **Anne** (1820–1849) produced *Agnes Grey* (1847) and *The Tenant of Wildfell Hall* (1848).

The Brontës were brought up by an aunt in their father's rectory (now a museum) at ◊Haworth in Yorkshire. During 1848–49 Emily, Anne, and their brother Patrick Branwell (1817–1848) all died of tuberculosis, aided in Branwell's case by alcohol and opium addiction; his portrait of the sisters survives. Charlotte married her father's curate, A B Nicholls, in 1854, and died during pregnancy. The sisters share a memorial in Westminster Abbey, London.

Charlotte

Charlotte attended a school for clergymen's daughters at Cowan Bridge with her older sisters, Maria and Elizabeth, and Emily. She suffered intensely, watching her older sisters rapidly fail in health; after their deaths from consumption the two younger girls were brought home. Throughout her early years, Charlotte was writing and, with Patrick, she created an elaborate imaginary world, described and illustrated in many volumes of verse and prose.

From 1835 to 1838 she worked as a teacher for her former headmistress, but this ended in a quarrel and estrangement. Various posts as governess in private families proved equally uncongenial. Charlotte, however, was ambitious for herself and her sisters, and her aunt agreed to support them in the venture of a small private school. With this scheme in mind, Charlotte lived in Brussels from 1842 to 1844 to improve her French. After her return, Charlotte's letters to her teacher, M Héger, show that she was deeply and unhappily in love with him. Her last novel, *Villette*, embodies her experiences in Brussels.

Emily

Emily was passionately attached to the wild countryside around her home. In her only novel, the extraordinary *Wuthering Heights*, she portrays the influence of the elements and elemental passions on human souls; the strangeness of the characters contrasts with the realistic description of the bleak moorland setting, yet the two are inseparable. Charlotte was astonished by her poetry and regarded her work as unparalleled. Much of Emily's poetry supposedly describes events in the history of her imaginary country, Gondal. She endured her last illness with the stoic fortitude expressed in the 'Last Lines', written some months before her death from tuberculosis.

Anne

Anne successfully held posts as a governess in England. She was particularly close to Emily, and shared with her the imaginary world which gave rise to the bulk of Emily's Gondal poetry. Although her reputation has been overshadowed by that of her sisters her two novels, completed when she was already seriously ill, represent a considerable achievement. More than Charlotte's works, they need to be considered as period pieces, but they are notable for their realism and the then advanced and unconventional ideas on such themes as the position of women in society.

Brook, Peter Stephen Paul (1925–)

English theatre director with a particularly innovative style. His work with the Royal Shakespeare Company (which he

BRONTË, CHARLOTTE *English novelist Charlotte Brontë, who is best known for her novel* Jane Eyre, *which achieved great success when she published it under the pseudonym Currer Bell in 1847. She lived in Haworth, Yorkshire with her sisters Emily and Anne; all the sisters worked for brief periods as governesses and teachers. Corbis*

joined in 1962) included a production of Shakespeare's *A Midsummer Night's Dream* (1970), set in a white gymnasium and combining elements of circus and commedia dell'arte. In the same year he founded an independent initiative, Le Centre International de Créations Théâtrales/The International Centre for Theatre Research in Paris. Brook's later productions aim to combine elements from different cultures and include *The Conference of the Birds* (1973), based on a Persian story, and *The Mahabarata* (1985–88), a cycle of three plays based on the Hindu epic.

His films include *Lord of the Flies* (1962), *Meetings with Remarkable Men* (1979), and *The Mahabarata* (1989). He is the author of the influential study of contemporary theatre *The Empty Space* (1968), and of the essays and observations published in *The Shifting Point* (1988).

Brooke, Rupert (Chawner) (1887–1915)

English poet. He stands as a symbol of the World War I 'lost generation'. His five war sonnets, including 'The Soldier', were published posthumously. Other notable poems are 'Grantchester' (1912) and 'The Great Lover', written in 1914.

Brooke's war sonnets were published in *1914 and Other Poems* (1915); they caught the prevailing early wartime spirit of selfless patriotism.

Brooke was awarded a fellowship at King's, his own college at Cambridge University, in 1913, but having had a nervous breakdown he travelled abroad. He toured America (*Letters from America*, 1916), New Zealand, and the South Seas, and in 1914 became an officer in the Royal Naval Volunteer Reserve. After fighting at Antwerp, Belgium, he sailed for the Dardanelles, but died of blood poisoning on the Greek island of Skyros, where he is buried.

Brookeborough, Basil Stanlake Brooke, Viscount Brookeborough (1888–1973)

Unionist politician of Northern Ireland. He entered Parliament in 1929, held ministerial posts 1933–45, and was prime minister of Northern Ireland 1943–63. He was a staunch advocate of strong links with Britain.

Brooklands

Former motor racing track near Weybridge, Surrey. One of the world's first purpose-built circuits, it was opened 1907 as a testing ground for early motorcars. It was the venue for the first British Grand Prix (then known as the RAC Grand Prix) in 1926. It was sold to aircraft-builders Vickers 1946. The circuit has been rejuvenated, and now houses the Brooklands Museum.

Brookner, Anita (1928–)

English novelist. Her books include *Hotel du Lac* (1984) (Booker Prize), *A Misalliance* (1986), *Latecomers* (1988), *A Closed Eye* (1991), *Family Romance* (1993), *A Private View* (1994), *Incidents in the rue Laugier* (1995), *Altered States* (1996), and *Falling Slowly* (1998). Her skill is in the subtle portrayal of hopelessness and lack of vitality in her female characters. *Soundings* (1997) is a collection of lectures and reviews. She was Reader at the Courtauld Institute 1977–88, and Slade Professor of Fine Art at Cambridge 1967–68, the first woman to hold the post.

Brookside

Channel 4 drama serial created by Phil Redmond (creator also of the BBC's children's soap opera *Grange Hill*), shown since 1982. See ◊soap operas.

Broome, David (1940–)

Welsh show jumper. He won the 1970 world title on Beethoven and helped Britain to the team title in 1978. He was European champion in 1961, 1967, and 1968, and he won the King George V Gold Cup a record six times, 1960–91. His sister Liz Edgar was also a top-class show jumper.

Brophy, Brigid (Antonia) (1929–1995)

English writer. Opera is a frequent element in her work, for example in the novel *The Snow Ball* (1964). The narrator of *In Transit* (1969) is in the predicament of having forgotten his or her sex as well as identity.

Her lives of the artist Aubrey Beardsley (*Black and White*, 1968) and the writer Ronald Firbank (*Prancing Novelist*, 1973) were written as much in defence of her own views as the lives of her subjects. She also campaigned successfully for the introduction in the UK of ◊public lending right.

Brosnan, Pierce (1953–)

Irish actor. In *Goldeneye* (1995), he became the fifth actor to play the role of secret agent James Bond; his second Bond film was *Tomorrow Never Dies* (1997). He first found success in a string of elegantly mounted television roles, especially in the thriller series *Remington Steele*.

Brosnan is known for his suave and sophisticated screen presence, a persona cultivated in *Remington Steele*. Other films include *The Lawnmower Man* (1992) and *Dante's Peak* (1997). He is scheduled to star in the next instalment in the James Bond series in 1999.

Brown, Capability (Lancelot) (1716–1783)

English landscape gardener and architect. He acquired his nickname because of his continual enthusiasm for the 'capabilities' of natural landscapes. He worked on or improved the gardens of many great houses and estates, including Hampton Court; Kew; Blenheim, Oxfordshire; Stowe, Buckinghamshire; and Petworth, West Sussex.

From about 1740 to about 1749 he collaborated with the architect William ◊Kent, but from 1751 he had his own very large architectural practice.

Brown, Ford Madox (1821–1893)

English painter, associated with the ◊Pre-Raphaelite Brotherhood through his pupil Dante Gabriel Rossetti. His pictures, which include *The Last of England* (1855; City Art Gallery, Birmingham) and *Work* (1852–65; City Art Gallery, Manchester), are characterized by elaborate symbolism and abundance of realistic detail. His later subject pictures, romantic treatments of scenes from history and literature such as *Christ Washing St Peter's Feet* (Tate Gallery, London), are not always harmonious in design and colour, but as a colourist he excels in some small landscapes.

Brown, George Alfred, Baron George-Brown (1914–1985)
British Labour politician. He entered Parliament in 1945, was briefly minister of works in 1951, and contested the leadership of the party on the death of Gaitskell, but was defeated by Harold Wilson.

He was secretary for economic affairs 1964–66 and foreign secretary 1966–68. He was created a life peer in 1970.

Brown, (James) Gordon (1951–)
British Labour politician, chancellor of the Exchequer from 1997. He entered Parliament in 1983, rising quickly to the opposition front bench, with a reputation as an outstanding debater. He took over from John Smith as shadow chancellor in 1992. After Smith's death in May 1994, he generously declined to challenge his close ally, Tony Blair, for the leadership, retaining his post as shadow chancellor, and assuming the chancellorship after the 1997 general election.

On becoming chancellor in 1997, Brown ceded to the Bank of England full control of interest rates. He has used his position as chancellor to promote key initiatives, notably the 'welfare to work' programme directed against unemployment and funded by a windfall tax imposed on privatized utilities. He has gained the reputation of being an 'iron chancellor', maintaining firm control over public expenditure. This has led to criticisms within his party from those seeking more funds for welfare reform and the National Health Service.

Brown, Robert (1773–1858)
Scottish botanist who in 1827 discovered Brownian motion. As a botanist, his more lasting work was in the field of plant morphology. He was the first to establish the real basis for the distinction between gymnosperms (pines) and angiosperms (flowering plants).

The concept of Brownian motion arose from his observation that very fine pollen grains suspended in water move about in a continuously agitated manner. He was able to establish that inorganic materials such as carbon and various metals are equally subject to it, but he could not find the cause of the movement (now explained by kinetic theory).

Brown also described the organs and mode of reproduction in orchids. In 1831, he discovered that a small body that is fundamental in the creation of plant tissues occurs regularly in plant cells – he called it a 'nucleus', a name that is still used.

Browning, Elizabeth (Moulton) Barrett (1806–1861)
English poet. In 1844 she published *Poems* (including 'The Cry of the Children'), which led to her friendship with and secret marriage to Robert ⇨Browning in 1846. She wrote *Sonnets from the Portuguese* (1850), a collection of love lyrics, during their courtship. She wrote strong verse about social injustice and oppression in Victorian England, and she was a learned, fiery, and metrically experimental poet.

BROWNING, ELIZABETH BARRETT *An English poet of the Romantic movement, Elizabeth Barrett Browning was highly regarded as a poet in her own right and was considered for the post of poet laureate in 1850. A passionate interest in Italian and French politics and spiritualism fired her vivacious life. She secretly married Robert Browning in 1846. Corbis*

She suffered illness as a child, led a sheltered and restricted life, and was from the age of 13 regarded by her father as an invalid.

A brief stay in Torquay, Devon, with her brother Edward ended with his death by drowning in 1840. Her *The Battle of Marathon* was privately printed in 1820. Her translation of Aeschylus' drama *Prometheus Bound* was published in 1833 and *The Seraphim* in 1838; she also contributed to the *Athenaeum* and other periodicals. With the appearance of *Poems*, her reputation was established.

Correspondence from Robert Browning, also a rising poet, led to their meeting and secret marriage. The story of their love, vividly reflected in their own letters, has been retold in many novels and plays.

She was freed from her father's oppressive influence by her marriage and move to Italy, where her health improved and she produced her mature works.

She died in Florence, and a volume of *Last Poems* was issued in 1862.

Browning, Robert (1812–1889)
English poet. His work is characterized by the accomplished use of dramatic monologue (in which a single imaginary

speaker reveals his or her character, thoughts, and situation) and an interest in obscure literary and historical figures. It includes *Pippa Passes* (1841) (written in dramatic form) and the poems 'The Pied Piper of Hamelin' (1842), 'My Last Duchess' (1842), 'Home Thoughts from Abroad' (1845), and 'Rabbi Ben Ezra' (1864). He was married to Elizabeth Barrett ◊Browning.

From 1837 Browning achieved moderate success with his play *Strafford* and several other works, though the narrative poem *Sordello* (1840) was initially criticized.

In 1845 he met Elizabeth Barrett; they eloped the following year and went to Italy. There he wrote *Christmas Eve and Easter Day* (1850) and much of *Men and Women* (1855), the latter containing some of his finest love poems and dramatic monologues. He published no further collection of verse until *Dramatis Personae* (1864), which was followed by *The Ring and the Book* (1868–69), based on an Italian murder story.

After his wife's death in 1861 Browning settled in England and enjoyed an established reputation, although his later works, such as *Red-Cotton Night-Cap Country* (1873), *Dramatic Idylls* (1879–80), and *Asolando* (1889), prompted opposition by their rugged obscurity of style.

Brownsea Island, or **Branksea Island**

Island in Dorset, England. It is situated at the entrance of Poole harbour and is 1.6 km/1 mi long by 1.1 km/0.7 mi broad. Brownsea Island is owned by the National Trust. It can be reached via passenger ferry from Poole Quay. Part of the island is a nature reserve. Baden-Powell held the first Boy Scout camp here in 1907.

Bruce

One of the chief Scottish noble houses. ◊Robert (I) the Bruce and his son, David II, were both kings of Scotland descended from Robert de Bruis (died 1094), a Norman knight who arrived in England with William the Conqueror in 1066. See genealogy opposite.

Bruce, Christopher (1945–)

English choreographer and dancer. He became artistic director of the Rambert Dance Company in 1994. His work integrates modern and classical idioms and often chooses political or socially conscious themes, as in *Ghost Dances* (1981), which treats the theme of political oppression. Other works include *Cruel Garden* (1977), *Sergeant Early's Dream* (1984), *The Dream is Over* (1987) – a tribute to John Lennon, *Swansong* (1987), *Rooster* (1991), *Moonshine* (1993), *Quicksilver* (1996) – a tribute to Marie Rambert, and *Four Scenes* (1998), created for the opening of the new Sadler's Wells theatre in October 1998.

As a dancer, Bruce took key roles in Glen Tetley's *Pierrot lunaire* (1967), the recreation of Nijinsky's *L'Après-midi d'un faune* (late 1960s), his own *Cruel Garden* (1977), and Foukine's *Petrushka* (1988).

Bruce, James (1730–1794)

Scottish explorer who, in 1770, was the first European to reach the source of the Blue Nile and, in 1773, to follow the river downstream to Cairo.

Bruce, Robert

King of Scotland; see ◊Robert (I) the Bruce, and genealogy opposite.

Bruce, Robert de, 5th Lord of Annandale (1210–1295)

Scottish noble, one of the unsuccessful claimants to the throne at the death of Alexander II in 1290. His grandson was ◊Robert (I) the Bruce. See genealogy.

Brummell, Beau (George Bryan) (1778–1840)

English dandy and leader of fashion. He introduced long trousers as conventional day and evening wear for men. A friend of the Prince of Wales, the future George IV, he later quarrelled with him. Gambling losses drove him in 1816 to exile in France, where he died in an asylum.

Brunel, Isambard Kingdom (1806–1859)

English engineer and inventor. In 1833 he became engineer to the Great Western Railway, which adopted the 2.1-m/7-ft gauge on his advice. He built the Clifton Suspension Bridge over the River Avon at Bristol and the Saltash Bridge over the River Tamar near Plymouth. His shipbuilding designs include the *Great Western* (1837), the first steamship to cross the Atlantic regularly; the *Great Britain* (1843), the first large iron ship to have a screw propeller; and the *Great Eastern* (1858), which laid the first transatlantic telegraph cable.

In 1833 he was appointed to carry out improvements on the Bristol docks, and while working on this project his interest in the potential of railways was fired. In all, Brunel was responsible for building more than 2,600 km/1,600 mi of the permanent railway of the west of England, the Midlands, and South Wales. He also constructed two railway lines in Italy, and acted as adviser on the construction of the Victoria line in Australia and on the East Bengal railway in India.

Brunel's last ship, the *Great Eastern*, was to remain the largest ship in service until the end of the 19th century.

With over ten times the tonnage of his first ship, it was the first ship to be built with a double iron hull. It was driven by both paddles and a screw propeller. A report of an explosion on board brought on his death.

Brunel, Marc Isambard (1769–1849)

French-born British engineer and inventor, father of Isambard Kingdom Brunel. He constructed the tunnel under the River Thames in London from Wapping to Rotherhithe 1825–43.

Brunel fled to the USA in 1793 to escape the French Revolution. He became Chief Engineer of New York advising on defence. In 1799 he moved to England to mass-produce marine blocks, which were needed by the navy. Brunel demonstrated that with specially designed machine tools 10 men could do the work of 100, more quickly, more cheaply, and yield a better product. He made a large profit and invested it in sawmills in Battersea, London. Cheating partners and fire damage to the sawmills caused the business to fail and Brunel was imprisoned for debt in 1821. He spent the latter part of his life working on the Rotherhithe tunnel. Knighted 1841.

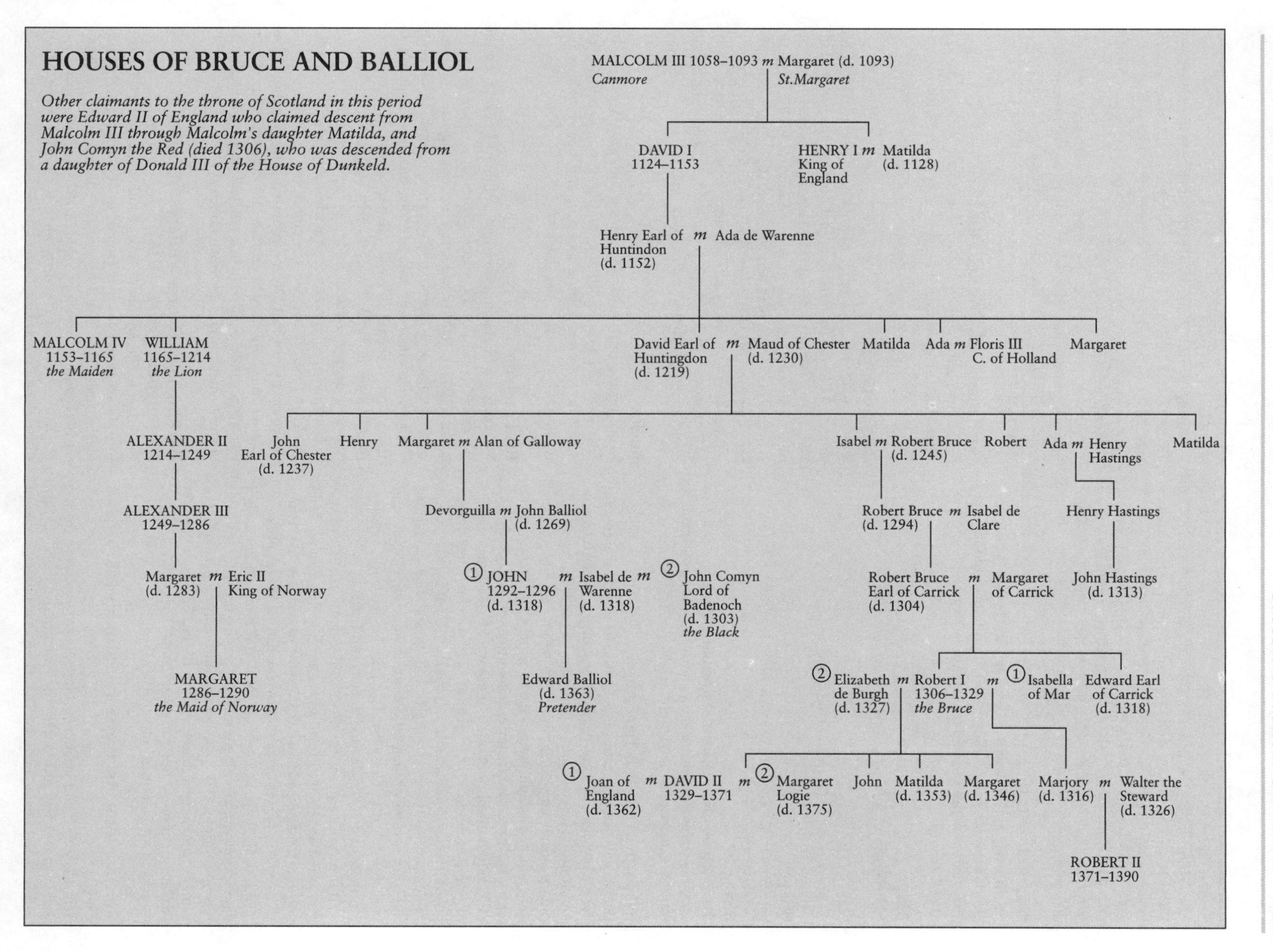
HOUSES OF BRUCE AND BALLIOL
Other claimants to the throne of Scotland in this period were Edward II of England who claimed descent from Malcolm III through Malcolm's daughter Matilda, and John Comyn the Red (died 1306), who was descended from a daughter of Donald III of the House of Dunkeld.
MALCOLM III 1058–1093 m Margaret (d. 1093)
Canmore
St.Margaret
DAVID I
1124–1153
HENRY I m Matilda
King of England
(d. 1128)
Henry Earl of Huntindon (d. 1152)
m Ada de Warenne
MALCOLM IV
1153–1165
the Maiden
WILLIAM
1165–1214
the Lion
David Earl of Huntingdon (d. 1219)
m Maud of Chester (d. 1230)
Matilda
Ada m Floris III C. of Holland
Margaret
ALEXANDER II
1214–1249
John Earl of Chester (d. 1237)
Henry
Margaret m Alan of Galloway
Isabel m Robert Bruce (d. 1245)
Robert
Ada m Henry Hastings
Matilda
ALEXANDER III
1249–1286
Devorguilla m John Balliol (d. 1269)
Robert Bruce (d. 1294)
m Isabel de Clare
Henry Hastings
Margaret (d. 1283)
m Eric II King of Norway
① JOHN 1292–1296 (d. 1318)
m Isabel de Warenne (d. 1318)
m ② John Comyn Lord of Badenoch (d. 1303) the Black
Robert Bruce Earl of Carrick (d. 1304)
m Margaret of Carrick
John Hastings (d. 1313)
MARGARET
1286–1290
the Maid of Norway
Edward Balliol
(d. 1363)
Pretender
② Elizabeth de Burgh (d. 1327)
m Robert I 1306–1329 the Bruce
m ① Isabella of Mar
Edward Earl of Carrick (d. 1318)
① Joan of England (d. 1362)
m DAVID II 1329–1371
m ② Margaret Logie (d. 1375)
John
Matilda (d. 1353)
Margaret (d. 1346)
Marjory (d. 1316)
m Walter the Steward (d. 1326)
ROBERT II
1371–1390

Bruno, Frank (1961–)
English heavyweight boxer. He won the World Boxing Association (WBA) world title after defeating Oliver McCall 1995. Bruno had made three previous unsuccessful attempts to win a world title, against Tim Witherspoon 1986 (WBA title), Mike Tyson 1989 (undisputed world title), and Lennox Lewis 1993 (World Boxing Council (WBC) title). He lost his WBA title to Mike Tyson in 1996. An eye injury forced him to retire from boxing in August 1996.

Bryant, David John (1931–)
English flat-green (lawn) bowls player. He has won every honour the game has offered, including four outdoor world titles (three singles and one triples) 1966–88 and three indoor titles 1979–81.

BSE
Abbreviation for ◊bovine spongiform encephalopathy.

BSI
Abbreviation for ◊British Standards Institution.

BSkyB
Satellite service started as Sky in 1989; see ◊television.

BST
Abbreviation for **British Summer Time**, March to October, when clocks are set an hour ahead of standard UK time to gain benefit of daylight hours.

BT, formerly British Telecom
British telecommunications company. Its principal activity is the supply of local, long-distance, and international telecommunications services and equipment in the UK, serving 27 million exchange lines. BT also offers an international direct-dialled telephone service to more than 200 countries and other overseas territories – covering 99% of the world's 800 million telephones. One of the world's leading providers of telecommunications services and one of the largest private-sector companies in Europe, in 1997 BT had a market capitalization in excess of £28 billion and had established operations in more than 30 countries worldwide, with joint ventures in Spain, Germany, Italy, the Netherlands, Sweden, South Africa, New Zealand, Japan, and India.

BT formed part of the Post Office until 1980, and was privatized in 1984. Previously a monopoly, it now faces commercial competition for some of its services. BT is not allowed to offer other cable services apart from telephones.

BT deals with 103 million local and international calls a day. It is now a prominent internet service provider, and also provides Campus, the educational and training network. BT is the second largest shareholder in INTELSAT and operates satellite stations at London Docklands, Goonhilly Downs, Cornwall, in Hereford, and at Aberdeen.

Buchan, John, 1st Baron Tweedsmuir (1875–1940)
Scottish writer and politician. His popular adventure stories, today sometimes criticized for their alleged snobbery, sexism, and anti-Semitism, include *The Thirty-Nine Steps*, a tale of espionage published in 1915, *Greenmantle* (1916), and *The Three Hostages* (1924).

During World War I he served on the Headquarters staff 1916–17 and in 1917 became director of information. He travelled extensively, in 1937 making a journey of some 16,000 km/10,000 mi into the Arctic Circle and British Columbia.

He was Conservative member of Parliament for the Scottish universities 1927–35, and governor general of Canada 1935–40. He also wrote historical and biographical works, literary criticism, and poetry. Created baron in 1935.

Buchanan, Jack (Walter John) (1890–1957)
Scottish musical-comedy actor. His songs such as 'Good-Night Vienna' epitomized the period between World Wars I and II.

Buckfastleigh
Town in Devon, England; population (1991) 3,400. It is situated 11 km/7 mi northwest of Totnes, in the valley of the River Dart. Nearby is **Buckfast Abbey**, which lies on the site of a medieval Cistercian monastery and was built by French Benedictine monks between 1907 and 1938. The town is the terminus for the Dart Valley Railway.

Fossilized remains of prehistoric animals have been found in local caves. Buckfastleigh is the headquarters of the Devon Speleological Society (for the study of caves).

Buckie
Major fishing port in Moray unitary authority, Scotland, on Spey Bay, 20 km/13 mi east of Elgin; population (1991) 8,500. It possesses a large harbour, and boat-building and repair yards to service the trawlers.

Buckingham
Market town in Buckinghamshire, southern England, on the River Ouse, 27 km/17 mi northwest of Aylesbury; population (1991) 10,200. Industries include agriculture, light engineering, and the manufacture of paints. University College, Britain's only independent university, opened in 1976, and received a royal charter as the University of Buckingham in 1983. It was the first UK university to offer two-year degree courses.

Buckingham was mentioned as a borough in the Domesday Book of 1086. It became the county town, but was partly destroyed by fire in 1725 and superseded by Aylesbury. The 18th-century Old Gaol houses a local history museum. Other features include a Georgian town hall and a 15th-century chantry chapel with a Norman doorway.

Buckingham, George Villiers, 1st Duke of Buckingham (1592–1628)
English courtier, adviser to James I and later Charles I. He was introduced to the court of James I in 1614 and soon became his favourite. He failed to cement the marriage of Prince Charles and the Infanta of Spain in 1623, but on returning to England negotiated Charles's alliance with Henrietta Maria, sister of the French king. After Charles's accession, Bucking-

ham attempted to form a Protestant coalition in Europe, which led to war with France; however, he failed to relieve the Protestants (Huguenots) besieged in La Rochelle in 1627. His policy on the French Protestants was attacked in Parliament, and when about to sail for La Rochelle for a second time, he was assassinated in Portsmouth. Earl 1617, Duke 1623.

Buckingham, George Villiers, 2nd Duke of Buckingham (1628–1687)

English politician, a member of the ♦Cabal under Charles II. A dissolute son of the first duke, he was brought up with the royal children. His play *The Rehearsal* satirized the style of the poet Dryden, who portrayed him as Zimri in *Absalom and Achitophel*. He succeeded to the dukedom in 1628.

Buckingham Palace

London home of the British sovereign, it stands at the west end of St James's Park. The original Buckingham House, begun in 1703 for the 1st Duke of Buckingham, was sold to George III in 1761. George IV obtained a parliamentary grant from for its repair and enlargement, but instead he and the architect, John ♦Nash, began a new building (1821–26). The palace was incomplete at George IV's death in 1830, when Nash was displaced by Edward Blore, who reputedly covered most of Nash's work.

Nash's gateway was removed in 1851 and became Marble Arch. William IV did not like the palace, and it did not become a regular royal residence until the accession of Queen Victoria. In 1914 a new façade by Aston Webb replaced Blore's. The palace retains a park of 17 ha/42 acres.

The Queen's Gallery presents exhibitions of portions of the royal collections, and the state rooms and Royal Mews are also open to visitors.

Buckinghamshire

County of southeast central England

Area 1,565 sq km/604 sq mi

Towns ♦Aylesbury (administrative headquarters), Beaconsfield, Buckingham, High Wycombe, Olney

Physical Chiltern Hills; Vale of Aylesbury

Features ♦Chequers (country seat of the prime minister); Burnham Beeches; the church of the poet Gray's 'Elegy' at Stoke Poges; Cliveden, a country house designed by Charles Barry (now a hotel; it was once the home of Nancy, Lady Astor); Bletchley Park, home of World War II code-breaking activities, now used as a training post for GCHQ (Britain's electronic surveillance centre); homes of the poets William Cowper at Olney and John Milton at Chalfont St Giles, and of the Tory prime minister Disraeli at Hughenden; grave of William Penn, Quaker founder of Pennsylvania, at Jordans, near Chalfont St Giles; Stowe landscape gardens

Industry engineering; furniture (chiefly beech); paper; printing; railway workshops; motor cars

Agriculture about 75 % of the land under cultivation, fertile soil; cereals (barley, wheat, oats); cattle, pigs, poultry, sheep

Population (1997 est) 468,700.

History The refusal of the politician John ♦Hampden to pay ship-money in 1636 was partly instrumental in precipitating the English Civil War; an early skirmish was fought on the outskirts of Aylesbury in 1642.

Topography

Buckinghamshire is one of the Home Counties, and is bounded by Northamptonshire and Milton Keynes to the north; Oxfordshire to the west; Wokingham, and Windsor and Maidenhea to the south, where the River Thames forms part of the county boundary; and by Greater London, Hertfordshire, and Bedfordshire to the east. The county is partly commuter belt for London. Buckinghamshire is divided into eight 'hundreds': Ashendon, Aylesbury, Buckingham, Burnham Cottesloe, Desborough, Newport, and Stoke; Burnham, Desborough and Stoke form the ♦Chiltern Hundreds.

Buckland, William (1784–1856)

English geologist and palaeontologist, a pioneer of British geology. He contributed to the descriptive and historical stratigraphy of the British Isles, inferring from the vertical succession of the strata a stage-by-stage temporal development of the Earth's crust.

Budget

Annual statement delivered to the House of Commons by the Chancellor of the Exchequer. It sets out taxation levels for the coming years and is accompanied by a financial statement budget report, which includes the treasury's short-term economic forecast and medium-term financial strategy. The budget has traditionally been delivered on a Tuesday in March, although between 1993–97 it was moved to November–December so that it could be combined with the announcement of departments' public spending levels for the year ahead.

The budget's taxation changes are legislated in an annual Finance Bill. These changes are debated for a week on the floor of the House and are then considered in detail in standing committee before being passed as the Finance Act, typically in July. The word 'budget' is derived from the leather wallet from which early Chancellors withdrew their papers when delivering this annual address.

building society

A financial institution that attracts investment in order to lend money, repayable at interest, for the purchase or building of a house on security of a mortgage. The largest building societies in the UK in 1996, in order, were the Halifax, Nationwide, Woolwich, Alliance and Leicester, Bradford and Bingley, Britannia, Bristol and West, and Northern Rock. In 1997 five of these became banks or were taken over by banks in order to extend their range of financial services: the Halifax, Woolwich, Alliance and Leicester, Bristol and West, and Northern Rock.

History

Building societies originated in 1781 from the ♦friendly societies in England. The Building Societies Act 1986 enabled societies to raise up to 20% of their funds on the international capital market. Among other changes, the act provided that building societies could grant unsecured loans of up to £5,000; they were also able to offer interest-bearing cheque accounts, a challenge to the clearing banks' traditional role in this area. From 1988 societies were able to operate in other EC countries.

Bulge, Battle of the, or **Ardennes offensive**

In World War II, Hitler's plan for a breakthrough by his field marshal Gerd von Rundstedt, aimed at the US line in the Ardennes, 16 December 1944–28 January 1945. Hitler aimed to isolate the Allied forces and create a German salient (the prominent part of a line of attack, also known as a 'bulge'). Although US troops were encircled for some weeks at Bastogne, the German counteroffensive failed.

Bull, John

Imaginary figure personifying England; see ◊John Bull.

Bull, John (*c.* 1562–1628)

English composer, organist, and virginalist. Most of his output is for keyboard, and includes ◊'God Save the King'. He also wrote sacred vocal music.

Bullard, Edward Crisp (1907–1980)

English geophysicist who, with US geologist Maurice Ewing, founded the discipline of marine geophysics. He pioneered the application of the seismic method to study the sea floor. He also studied continental drift before the theory became generally accepted. Knighted 1953.

Buller, John (1927–)

English composer. From 1959 he studied with Anthony Milner and in the 1970s produced a series of works based on James Joyce's *Finnegan's Wake*. The opera *Bakxai* (after Euripides) was premiered by English National Opera in 1992.

Bunhill Fields

Public gardens and cemetery in Finsbury in the London borough of Islington, England. It was originally part of an estate belonging to St Paul's Cathedral. In the 17th century it became a burial-ground for dissenters; the writers John Bunyan and Daniel Defoe are buried here. The Fields were opened as a public garden in 1869.

Bunyan, John (1628–1688)

English writer, author of *The ◊Pilgrim's Progress* (first part 1678, second part 1684), one of the best-known religious allegories in English. A Baptist, he was imprisoned in Bedford 1660–72 for unlicensed preaching and wrote *Grace Abounding* in 1666, which describes his early spiritual life. He started to write *The Pilgrim's Progress* during a second jail sentence 1676–77. Written in straightforward language with fervour and imagination, it achieved immediate popularity and was highly influential.

Bunyan was born in Elstow, near Bedford. At 16, he was drafted into the Parliamentary army to fight in the Civil War. His military career, probably his first experience of stern and impassioned Puritanism, was brief, and in 1647 he returned to Elstow. In 1649 he married Margaret Bentley who introduced him to the religious work *The Plaine Man's Path-way to Heaven* which exerted a powerful influence on Bunyan.

Following a period of religious doubts and struggles, he underwent a conversion experience and joined the Baptists in 1653. He began preaching in neighbouring villages and publishing religious pamphlets. In 1660 he was committed to Bedford county jail, where he remained for 12 years, refusing all offers of release conditional on his not preaching again. Set free in 1672, he was elected pastor of the Bedford congregation, but in 1676 he was again arrested and imprisoned for six months in the jail on Bedford Bridge.

Burbage, Richard (*c.* 1567–1619)

English actor. He is thought to have been Shakespeare's original Hamlet, Othello, and Lear. He also appeared in first productions of works by Ben Jonson, Thomas Kyd, and John Webster. His father **James Burbage** (*c.* 1530–1597) built the first English playhouse, known as 'the Theatre'; his brother **Cuthbert Burbage** (*c.* 1566–1636) built the original ◊Globe Theatre in 1599 in London.

Burbidge, (Eleanor) Margaret, born Peachey (1919–)

British astrophysicist who, with her husband Geoffrey Burbidge, discovered processes by which elements are formed in the nuclei of stars. Together they published *Quasi-Stellar Objects* (1967), based on her research. Later, they suggested that quasars and galaxies are linked in some way.

In addition to the work done jointly with her husband, Margaret Burbidge measured the red shifts of several objects suspected of being quasars, and in the process she found that some quasars do not give off any radio radiation.

Bure

River in Norfolk, England; length 80 km/50 mi. It flows southeast through the Norfolk Broads, where it joins the River Yare at Yarmouth.

Burgess, Anthony pen name of John Anthony Burgess Wilson (1917–1993)

English novelist, critic, and composer. A prolific and versatile writer, Burgess wrote about 60 books as well as screenplays, television scripts, and reviews. His work includes *A Clockwork Orange* (1962) (made into a film by Stanley Kubrick in 1971), a despairing depiction of high technology and violence set in a future London terrorized by teenage gangs, and the panoramic *Earthly Powers* (1980), a vast survey of the 20th century narrated by a fictional world-famous novelist, which was short-listed for the Booker Prize. Equally ambitious was *The Kingdom of the Wicked* (1985), a spectacular retelling of the biblical Acts of the Apostles.

Burgess's works often show an experimental approach to language – *A Clockwork Orange* is written in 'nadsat', the imaginary argot of the teenage narrator, and his fictional biography of Shakespeare, *Nothing Like the Sun* (1964), is written in a mock-Elizabethan dialect. His vision has been described as bleak and pessimistic, but his work is also comic and satiric, as in his novels featuring the poet Enderby.

BURGESS, ANTHONY *English writer Anthony Burgess, photographed in 1980. As well as novels including* A Clockwork Orange *(1962) (which was made into an Academy Award-nominated film by Stanley Kubrick in 1971) and* Earthly Powers *(1980), he produced criticism, biography, screenplays, and orchestral works. Corbis*

Burgess wrote many works of literary criticism, particularly on James Joyce, as well as several on language and on music and composing. His memoirs, *Little Wilson and Big God* (1987) and *You've Had Your Time* (1990), are as exciting as his fiction and in many respects an extension of it.

> *Without class differences, England would cease to be the living theatre that it is.*
>
> ANTHONY BURGESS English novelist and literary critic. Sayings of the Week, the *Observer*, May 1985

Burgess, Guy Francis de Moncy (1911–1963)

British spy, a diplomat recruited by the USSR as an agent. He was linked with Kim ◊Philby, Donald Maclean (1913–1983), and Anthony ◊Blunt.

Burgess Hill

Town in West Sussex, England, 14 km/9 mi north of Brighton; population (1991) 24,400. Burgess Hill is a commuter town on the London to Brighton railway.

burgh

Former unit of Scottish local government, referring to a town enjoying a degree of self-government. Burghs were abolished in 1975; the terms **burgh** and **royal burgh** once gave mercantile privilege but are now only an honorary distinction.

History

Burghs had their origin as early as the 12th century as local communities granted a royal monopoly of trade in the surrounding district. In addition to these royal **regality burghs** there developed **barony burghs** established by the Scottish barons and enjoying similar trading privileges.

The burghs provided the framework for municipal reform in Scotland after 1832 and remained the basic urban unit of local government until the reorganization of local government in Scotland in 1975.

Burgh, Hubert de (died 1243)

English justiciar and regent of England. He began his career in the administration of Richard I, and was promoted to the justiciarship by King John; he remained in that position under Henry III from 1216 until his dismissal in 1232. He was a supporter of King John against the barons, and ended French intervention in England by his defeat of the French fleet in the Strait of Dover in 1217. He became the most powerful figure in Henry III's minority following the death of the regent, William Marshall, in 1219. He reorganized royal administration and the Common Law.

Burghley, William Cecil, 1st Baron Burghley (1520–1598)

English politician, chief adviser to Elizabeth I as secretary of state from 1558 and Lord High Treasurer from 1572. He was largely responsible for the religious settlement of 1559, and took a leading role in the events preceding the execution of Mary Queen of Scots in 1587.

One of Edward VI's secretaries, he lost office under Queen Mary, but on Queen Elizabeth's succession became one of her most trusted ministers. He carefully avoided a premature breach with Spain in the difficult period leading up to the attack by the Spanish Armada in 1588, and did a great deal towards abolishing monopolies and opening up trade. Baron, 1571.

Burghley House

House in Cambridgeshire, England, near Stamford, Lincolnshire. Built between 1556 and 1587 by William Cecil, first Lord ◊Burghley, it is now the seat of his descendants, the Marquesses of Exeter. Capability ◊Brown laid out the surrounding park from 1756.

Burgon, Geoffrey (1941–)

English composer. He studied with Peter Wishart and Lennox Berkeley at the Guildhall School of Music. His music shows a range of influences, including jazz and medieval French music. He is best known for his themes for successful TV series, including *Brideshead Revisited*.

Burke, Edmund (1729–1797)

British Whig politician and political theorist, born in Dublin, Ireland. In Parliament from 1765, he opposed the government's attempts to coerce the American colonists, for example in *Thoughts on the Present Discontents* (1770), and supported the emancipation of Ireland. However, he denounced the French Revolution, for example in *Reflections on the Revolution in France* (1790), and attacked the suggestion of peace with France in *Letters on a Regicide Peace* (1795–97).

Burke also wrote *A Philosophical Inquiry into the Origin of our Ideas on the Sublime and Beautiful* (1756), on aesthetics. He was a skilled orator and is regarded by British Conservatives as the greatest of their political theorists.

Burke, William (1792–1829)

Irish murderer. He and his partner William Hare, living in Edinburgh, sold the body of an old man, who had died from natural causes in their lodging house, to an anatomist as a subject for dissection. After that, they increased their supplies by murdering at least 15 people. Burke was hanged on the evidence of Hare. Hare is said to have died a beggar in London in the 1860s.

Burke's Peerage

Popular name of the *Genealogical and Heraldic History of the Peerage, Baronetage, and Knightage of the United Kingdom*, first issued by John Burke 1826. The most recent edition was 1970.

Burkitt, Denis Parsons (1911–1993)

Northern Irish surgeon who first described the childhood tumour named after him, **Burkitt's lymphoma**, a malignant tumour of the lymph nodes. He also pioneered the trend towards high-fibre diets.

Burlington, Richard Boyle, 3rd Earl of Burlington (1695–1753)

Anglo-Irish architectural patron and architect. He was one of the premier exponents of the Palladian style in Britain. His buildings are characterized by absolute adherence to the Classical rules. William ◊Kent was his major protégé.

Burlington based Chiswick House, London (1725–29), on Palladio's Villa Rotonda, Italy. He succeeded to the earldom in 1704, and was made lord high treasurer of Ireland in 1715.

Burne-Jones, Edward Coley (1833–1898)

English painter. In 1856 he was apprenticed to the Pre-Raphaelite painter and poet Dante Gabriel ◊Rossetti, who remained a dominant influence. His paintings, inspired by legend and myth, were characterized by elongated forms and subdued tones, as in *King Cophetua and the Beggar Maid* (1880–84; Tate Gallery, London). He also collaborated with William ◊Morris in designing stained-glass windows, tapestries, and book decorations for the Kelmscott Press. His work influenced both Symbolism and ◊Art Nouveau. He was created a baronet in 1894.

Burnell, Jocelyn Bell

English astronomer. See ◊Bell Burnell.

Burnett, Frances Eliza Hodgson (1849–1924)

English writer. Her novels for children include the rags-to-riches tale *Little Lord Fauntleroy* (1886) and *The ◊Secret Garden* (1911), which has its values anchored in nature mysticism. She emigrated with her family to the USA in 1865.

Burney, Fanny (Frances) (1752–1840)

English novelist and diarist. She achieved success with *Evelina*, an epistolary novel published in 1778, became a member of Samuel ◊Johnson's circle, and received a post at court from Queen Charlotte. She published three further novels, *Cecilia* (1782), *Camilla* (1796), and *The Wanderer* (1814).

Burnham Beeches

Forest northwest of Slough, near the village of Burnham, Buckinghamshire, England; area 324 ha/600 acres. It is the remains of an ancient forest, and consists of a number of large beech trees. In 1879 the City of London Corporation acquired the trees for public use. Dorneywood, owned by the National Trust, lies 1 km/1.5 mi north of the village of Burnham.

Thomas ◊Gray, in a letter to Horace Walpole dated September 1737, remarked on the picturesque beauty of the woods.

Burnley

Town in Lancashire, northwest England, on the Leeds and Liverpool Canal, at the confluence of the Calder and Brun rivers, 19 km/12 mi northeast of Blackburn; population (1991) 74,700; Burnley–Nelson urban area 149,900. Formerly a cotton-manufacturing town, its industries include aerospace and light engineering, and the manufacture of textiles, plastics, vehicle components, and footwear.

Mainly built of the local stone, the town is situated in the Calder valley while its suburbs lie on the northern side of the ◊Rossendale upland. Burnley prospered during the Industrial Revolution with the growth of cotton-weaving. Numerous mills were established beside the Calder and the Leeds and Liverpool Canal, and by the end of the 19th century the town was a centre of Lancashire's cotton-textiles industry. Since the decline of coalmining and cotton manufacture, Burnley's industries have diversified, and redevelopment of the town centre and areas of poor industrial housing have modernized the town's landscape.

Weaving sheds, weavers' cottages, foundries, and mills, are preserved in the Weavers' Triangle, and the town's industrial history is illustrated at the Canal Toll House Heritage Centre.

Burns, Robert (1759–1796)

Scottish poet. He used a form of Scots dialect at a time when it was not considered suitably 'elevated' for literature. Burns's first volume, *Poems, Chiefly in the Scottish Dialect*, appeared in 1786. In addition to his poetry (such as 'To a Mouse'), Burns wrote or adapted many songs, including 'Auld Lang Syne'. **Burns Night** is celebrated on 25 January, his birthday.

Burns is recognized as the culminating figure in two centuries' tradition of folk song and genre poetry and one of the greatest of all writers of love songs. Although not a Romantic himself, the example of his work was one of the vital influences in the coming Romantic movement. He contributed some 300 songs to James Johnson's *Scots Musical*

Museum (1787–1803) and Thomson's *Select Collection of Original Scottish Airs* (1793–1841). Whether composing original pieces or, as in the case of 'Auld Lang Syne', revitalizing a song which had already passed through more than one version, he had the touch of lyric genius. To this he added a power of vitriolic satire, shown in such poems as 'Holy Willie's Prayer', and a command of vivid description that appears at its best in 'Tam o' Shanter' and 'The Jolly Beggars'.

Born in Alloway, near Ayr, he became joint tenant with his brother Gilbert of his late father's farm at Mossgiel in 1784, but it was unsuccessful. Burns intended to emigrate to Jamaica with Mary Campbell as his wife, but she died. In 1786, to earn money for his passage, he published *Poems, Chiefly in the Scottish Dialect*. It was an immediate success and contained much of his best work especially in social criticism. Burns was thereafter welcomed among intellectuals and aristocrats and was dissuaded from going abroad.

In 1788 he used his capital to try a new farm, Ellisland, on the banks of the Nith near Dumfries. This farm also proved unsatisfactory and in 1791 he moved to Dumfries and became a full-time excise officer.

My heart's in the Highlands, my heart is not here; / My heart's in the Highlands a-chasing the deer; / Chasing the wild deer, and following the roe, / My heart's in the Highlands, wherever I go.

Robert Burns Scottish poet.
'My Heart's in the Highlands'

Burra, Edward John (1905–1976)

English painter. He was devoted to themes of city life, its bustle, humour, and grimy squalor. Characteristic are *The Snack Bar* (1930; Tate Gallery, London) and his watercolour scenes of Harlem, New York created 1933–34. Postwar works include religious paintings and landscapes influenced by El Greco and Goya.

Burrell, Diana (1948–)

English composer. She studied at Cambridge and has played the viola in various orchestras. Her music is skilfully crafted. Her works include: *Albatross* (1987), *Creator of the Stars of Night* (1989), *You Spotted Snakes* (1991), and *Gulls and Angels* for string quartet (1994).

Burslem

Town in Staffordshire, England. Since 1910 the town has been included in the city of ◊Stoke-on-Trent. For many years Burslem was the chief English centre for the manufacture of earthenware, and is still called 'the mother of the Potteries'. Josiah Wedgwood was born here in 1730, and a Wedgwood Memorial Institute was opened in 1869. As well as earthenware manufacture, there is some light engineering and tile-making.

The Burslem Tunstall and Hayward War Memorial Hospital were opened in 1930.

Burt, Cyril Lodowic (1883–1971)

English psychologist. A specialist in child and mental development, he argued in *The Young Delinquent* (1925) the importance of social and environmental factors in delinquency. After his death it was claimed that he had falsified experimental results in an attempt to prove his theory that intelligence is largely inherited. Knighted 1946.

Burton, Decimus (1800–1881)

English architect. Befriended by John ◊Nash, he later became a leading figure in the Classical Revival before he had studied in Italy or Greece. Buildings by his enormous London practice included the Athenaeum Club (1829–30), his masterpiece; and the Palm House at Kew (1844–48).

Outside London he laid out the Calverley Estate, Tunbridge Wells (1828 onwards); Adelaide Crescent, Brighton (1830–34); and many country mansions.

Burton, Richard stage name of Richard Walter Jenkins (1925–1984)

Welsh stage and screen actor. He had a rich, dramatic voice but his career was dogged by personal problems and an often poor choice of roles. Films in which he appeared with his wife Elizabeth ◊Taylor include *Cleopatra* (1963) and *Who's Afraid of Virginia Woolf?* (1966). Among his later films are *Equus* (1977) and *Nineteen Eighty-Four* (1984).

Other films include *Beckett* (1964) and *The Spy Who Came in from the Cold* (1966). His rendition of Dylan Thomas's *Under Milk Wood* for radio was another of his career highlights. He also won acclaim for his stage performances in both Shakespearean and contemporary dramas throughout his film career.

Burton, Richard Francis (1821–1890)

English explorer and translator (he knew 35 oriental languages). He travelled mainly in the Middle East and northeast Africa, often disguised as a Muslim. He made two attempts to find the source of the White Nile, 1855 and 1857–58 (on the second, with John ◊Speke, he reached Lake Tanganyika), and wrote many travel books. He translated oriental erotica and the *Arabian Nights* (1885–88).

Burton upon Trent

Town in Staffordshire, central England, on the River Trent, northeast of Birmingham; population (1991) 60,500. It is a former cotton-spinning town. Brewing is the principal industry, with five major breweries in operation; Marmite savoury spread is produced from the yeast by-products. Engineering, food-processing, and the manufacture of tyres and rubber goods are also important. The Benedictine monks of Burton Abbey (founded in 1002) began the town's tradition of brewing in the 11th century.

Gypsum deposits in the area make the local well water high in calcium sulphate, which is particularly good for the production of beer. The earliest-known reference to Burton ale was in 1295, it was noted in London in 1630, and commercial production began in the mid-18th century. The history of brewing in Burton is illustrated at the Bass Museum. Marmite was first produced here in 1902.

Bury

City and administrative headquarters of Bury metropolitan borough, Greater Manchester, northwest England, on the River Irwell, 16 km/10 mi north of central Manchester; population (1991) 62,600. The principal industries are textiles, paper-making, and engineering. Other activities include printing and the manufacture of chemicals, textile machinery, felt, and paint.

Features

The town is known for its black pudding. Bury Art Gallery includes a collection of paintings by Turner, Constable, and other 19th-century artists.

Industrial history

Bury prospered during the Industrial Revolution when the cotton, wool, paper-making, and engineering industries flourished, using water from the Irwell as a source of power. A canal linking Bury to Bolton and Manchester was built in 1791, and from 1846 the East Lancashire Railway Company provided a rail link with Manchester. Although cotton production has declined, textile industries such as calico-printing, bleaching, dyeing, and the manufacture of clothing are still important.

Famous people

Bury was the birthplace of the politician Robert Peel, founder of the modern police force, in 1788; and John Kay, inventor of the flying shuttle (used to speed up the work of hand-loom weaving) was born nearby in 1704.

Bury St Edmunds

Market town in Suffolk, eastern England, on the River Lark, 43 km/27 mi east of Cambridge; population (1991) 31,200. Industries include engineering, brewing, sugar beet-refining, printing, and the manufacture of agricultural machinery, electronic equipment, cameras, lamps, and confectionery. It was named after St Edmund, last Saxon king of East Anglia, and there are remains of a large Benedictine abbey.

History

Bury St Edmunds was the first planned town in Norman Britain, laid out on a grid pattern by Abbot Baldwin (1065–97). On 14 November 1214 (St Edmund's Day) Cardinal Langton, archbishop of Canterbury, and the barons swore at the high altar of the abbey church to force King John to sign the Magna Carta.

Features

A large collection of watches and clocks are housed at the Manor House Museum. The Angel Hotel features in the *Pickwick Papers* of Charles Dickens. William Wilkins, architect of the National Gallery in London, built the Regency Theatre Royal in 1819. Moyse's Hall, a 12th-century dwelling now a museum, was possibly a Jewish merchant's house, and may be the oldest domestic building in East Anglia.

Religious foundations

Sigebert, king of the East Angles, founded a monastery at Beodericsworth in about 537, and the remains of St Edmund, killed by the Danes in 869 and canonized as a martyr in 870, were interred there. An abbey established on the site in 945 was renamed St Edmundsbury in the early 11th century, and given abbey status in 1020. It was rebuilt by the Normans in the 11th and 12th centuries, and became an important site of pilgrimage. Before its dissolution in 1539, the abbey was one of the richest in England. Remains include part of the west front of the abbey church, into which a number of Georgian houses have been incorporated, the chapter-house, two gateways, and a 13th-century abbot's bridge.

Other foundations include the large 15th-century church of St Mary, which has a hammerbeam roof and contains the tomb of Mary Tudor, sister of Henry VIII.

Busby, Matt(hew) (1909–1994)

Scottish football player and manager, synonymous with the success of Manchester United both on and off the field. He was best known as manager of Manchester United 1945–1969. His 'Busby Babes' won the championship in 1952, 1956, and 1957, before eight members were tragically killed in an air crash in Munich in 1958. Busby's reassembled team reached the 1958 FA Cup final, and won the FA Cup in 1963. Championship wins in 1965 and 1967 ensured a further onslaught on European Cup competition, and the team went on to win the European Cup in 1968, the first English side to do so.

Busby, Thomas (1755–1838)

English organist and composer. He sang at Vauxhall as a boy with great success, and later became a pupil of Battishill. He worked at a music dictionary with Samuel Arnold, and was appointed church organist at St Mary's, Newington, Surrey, around 1780. He gained a doctorate of music at Cambridge in 1801. He wrote several books on music, including a history (1825).

Bush, Alan Dudley (1900–1995)

English composer. He adopted a didactic simplicity in his compositions in line with his Marxist beliefs. He wrote a large number of works for orchestra, voice, and chamber groups. His operas include *Wat Tyler* (1948–51) and *Men of Blackmoor* (1955), both of which had their first performances in East Germany.

Bush, Kate (1958–)

English pop singer, songwriter, and pianist. Her first single 'Wuthering Heights', released in 1978, was number one in the UK for a month and was followed by the hit album *The Kick Inside* (1978). Her other albums include *Never For Ever* (1980) and *Hounds Of Love* (1985) which both entered the UK chart at number one.

Buss, Frances Mary (1827–1894)

British pioneer in education for women. She first taught in a school run by her mother, and at 18 she founded her own school for girls in London. It became the North London Collegiate School in 1850. She founded the Camden School for Girls in 1871. Her work helped to raise the status of women teachers and the academic standard of women's education in the UK. She is often associated with Dorothea ◊Beale, a fellow pioneer.

Bussell, Darcey (Andrea) (1969–)
English ballerina who joined the Royal Ballet in 1988 and is particularly noted for her roles in George Balanchine's ballets. She joined the Sadler's Wells Royal Ballet in 1987, progressing to the Royal Ballet as soloist, first soloist, and then principal ballerina.

Butcher, Rosemary (1947–)
English choreographer and dancer. She is a leading exponent of contemporary dance. Her minimalist pieces, often created in collaboration with her dancers and performed in unusual spaces such as on beaches and in art galleries, display a quiet assurance and fluidity. *Touch the Earth* (1986), created for the Whitechapel Gallery, London, with a soundscape of chamber music and eight dancers, is one of her best-known works.

US choreographers such as Lucinda Childs and Trisha Brown were formative influences on Butcher, who founded her own dance company in 1975. Among her other works are *Space Between* (1977), *Flying Lines* (1986), *d1, d2 & d3* (1989–90), *Body as Site* (1993), *Unbroken View* (1996), and *Fractured Landscapes, Fragmented Narratives* (1997).

Bute
Island in the Firth of Clyde, Scotland; area 120 sq km/46 sq mi. The chief town and resort is Rothesay. Farming and tourism are the principal industries. It is separated from the mainland in the north by a winding channel, the **Kyles of Bute**. With Arran and the Cumbraes it comprised the former county of Bute. In 1975 Bute merged into the district of Argyll and Bute in Strathclyde region, and is now part of the Argyll and Bute unitary authority.

Bute lies 8 km/5 mi from the north Ayrshire coast and 10 km/6 mi from Arran. The coast is rocky, and in the interior are several small lochs, including Fad, Ascog, and Quien. The soil is light and gravelly, but produces good crops, especially oats. Cattle and sheep are reared, and dairying is important. Soft red sandstone, slate, whinstone, and grey granite are found. Rothesay was the most popular of the traditional holiday venues for the people of Glasgow, prior to the popularization of international travel in the 1970s. At Rothesay are the ruins of a 13th-century castle and award-winning Victorian toilets at the Winter Gardens by the sea front. Mount Stuart, 6 km/4 mi south of Rothesay, dating from the late 19th century, is a seat of the Marquis of Bute. Prince Charles is the current title holder of the Duke of Rothesay.

Daily ferry services for vehicles and passengers operate between Rothesay and Wemyss Bay, and across the Kyles of Bute between Rhubodach and Colintraive. Seasonal car ferry services connect Rothesay and the Isle of Arran.

Bute, John Stuart, 3rd Earl of Bute (1713–1792)
British Tory politician, prime minister 1762–63. On the accession of George III in 1760, he became the chief instrument in the king's policy for breaking the power of the Whigs and establishing the personal rule of the monarch through Parliament.

Bute succeeded his father as Earl in 1723, and in 1737 was elected a representative peer for Scotland. His position as the king's favourite and supplanter of the popular prime minister Pitt the Elder made him hated in the country. He resigned in 1763 after the Seven Years' War.

Butler, Josephine Elizabeth born Gray (1828–1906)
English social reformer. She promoted women's education and the Married Women's Property Act, and campaigned against the Contagious Diseases Acts of 1862–70, which made women in garrison towns suspected of prostitution liable to compulsory examination for venereal disease. Refusal to undergo examination meant imprisonment. As a result of her campaigns, the acts were repealed in 1883.

Butler, Reg(inald Cotterell) (1913–1981)
English sculptor. He taught architecture from 1937 to 1939 and was then a blacksmith for many years before becoming known for cast and forged iron works, both abstract and

BUSSELL, DARCEY *The dancer Darcey Bussell enjoyed early success with the Royal Ballet, becoming a prima ballerina by the age of 20. Her talent, youth, and glamour have helped broaden the appeal of ballet among a younger audience. Tim Rooke/Rex*

figurative. In 1953 he won an international competition for a monument to *The Unknown Political Prisoner* (a model is in the Tate Gallery, London).

Butler, Richard Austen ('Rab'), Baron Butler of Saffron Walden (1902–1982)
British Conservative politician. As minister of education 1941–45, he was responsible for the 1944 Education Act; he was chancellor of the Exchequer 1951–55, Lord Privy Seal 1955–59, and foreign minister 1963–64. As a candidate for the prime ministership, he was defeated by Harold Macmillan in 1957 (under whom he was home secretary 1957–62), and by Alec Douglas Home in 1963.

Politics is the art of the possible.

Richard Austen ('Rab') Butler British Conservative politician.
Attributed remark

Butler, Samuel (1612–1680)
English satirist. His best-known poem *Hudibras*, published in three parts in 1663, 1664, and 1678, became immediately popular for its biting satire against the Puritans and on other contemporary issues.

Butler also wrote minor poetic satires, and prose 'characters' not published until 1759. He was a strong influence on the poetry of Jonathan ◊Swift.

Butler, Samuel (1835–1902)
English writer. He made his name in 1872 with a satiric attack on contemporary utopianism, *Erewhon* (an anagram of *nowhere*). He is now remembered for his unfinished, semi-autobiographical discursive novel, *The Way of All Flesh*, a study of Victorian conventions, the causes and effects of the clash between generations, and religious hypocrisy (written and frequently revised 1873–84 and posthumously published in 1903).

Erewhon shows remarkable foresight into the development of some phases of 20th-century society, and has invention, wit, and grace, as well as originality.

The Fair Haven (1873) examined the miraculous element in Christianity. *Life and Habit* (1877) and other works were devoted to a criticism of the theory of natural selection.

Butlin, Billy (William Heygate Edmund Colborne) (1899–1980)
British holiday-camp entrepreneur, born in South Africa. He went in early life to Canada, but later entered the fairground business in the UK and originated a chain of camps (the first at Skegness in 1936) that provided accommodation, meals, and amusements at an inclusive price. Knighted 1964.

Butterworth, George (Sainton Kaye) (1885–1916)
English composer. He collected folk songs, and cultivated folk dancing and composition, but enlisted on the outbreak of World War I and was killed in action. He suggested the idea for Vaughan Williams's *London Symphony* (1911–13), and the work is dedicated to his memory.

Buxton
Town and former spa in Derbyshire, central England, 54 km/34 northwest of Derby, on the River Wye, surrounded by the Peak District National Park; population (1991) 19,900. Known from Roman times for its hot springs, it is now a tourist centre and a source for bottled mineral water.

At about 300 m/984 ft above sea level, Buxton is the highest town of its size in England. It has a restored Edwardian opera house, and the **Buxton Festival** is held annually.

History
The Roman settlement of **Aquae Arnemetiae** was founded here in about AD 79, the Romans being attracted by the natural spring water supplied at a constant temperature of 28°C/82°F. In the Middle Ages the town became a centre of pilgrimage, and Mary Queen of Scots was treated for rheumatism at the spa. In the 1780s, under the guidance of the 5th Duke of Devonshire, the Crescent and other buildings were built, modelled on the architecture of the fashionable spa town of Bath.

Features
The Devonshire Royal Hospital, opened in 1859, was originally an 18th-century stables; its wide dome is 48 m/156 ft in diameter. **Buxton Country Park**, to the southwest of the town, includes Poole's Cavern, a limestone cave near the source of the Wye, which has large chambers with complex stalactite and stalagmite formations. Other features are St Ann's Hotel in the Crescent; St Ann's Well; and the Micrarium, which displays exhibits as seen through a microscope, situated in the old Pump Room.

Byatt, A(ntonia) S(usan) (1936–)
English novelist and critic. Her fifth novel, *Possession*, won the 1990 Booker Prize. *The Virgin in the Garden* (1978) is a confident, zestfully handled account of a varied group of characters putting on a school play during the coronation year of 1953. It has a sequel, *Still Life* (1985). The third part of this projected quartet is *Babel Tower* (1996), set in the 1960s. *Angels and Insects* (1992) has twin themes of entomology and spiritualism.

by-election
See ◊elections.

Byland Abbey
Large ruined Cistercian abbey, 32 km/20 mi north of York, England. It was built from around 1170, and its west end and monastery foundations still survive.

Byng, George, 1st Viscount Torrington (1663–1733)
British admiral. He captured Gibraltar in 1704; commanded the fleet that prevented an invasion of England by the 'Old Pretender' James Francis Edward Stuart in 1708; and destroyed the Spanish fleet at Messina in 1718. John Byng was his fourth son.

At the Battle of Beachy Head in 1690 he advised protecting the Thames and awaiting the return of the rest of the fleet, but Queen Mary ordered him to give battle. He was subsequently court-martialled and acquitted. Knighted 1704, Viscount 1721.

Except for his genius, he was an ordinary nineteenth-century English gentleman, with little culture and no ideas.

MATTHEW ARNOLD English writer and critic.
On Lord Byron, in *Essays in Criticism*

Byrd, William (1543–1623)
English composer. His sacred and secular choral music, including over 200 motets and Masses for three, four, and five voices, exemplifies the English polyphonic style.

Byrd studied under Thomas Tallis as one of the children of the Chapel Royal in London. He became organist at Lincoln Cathedral in 1563. He married Juliana Birley there in 1568, and was elected a Gentleman of the Chapel Royal in 1569, but continued his duties at Lincoln until 1572, when he became organist of Queen Elizabeth's Chapel Royal jointly with Tallis. In 1575 Queen Elizabeth granted Byrd and Tallis an exclusive licence for printing and selling music and they dedicated to her their *Cantiones sacrae* published that year.

Byrd's popular reputation rests with his three great Masses, in three, four, and five parts, in which his contrapuntal mastery is most fully displayed. Other aspects of his genius are found in the ornate *Cantiones sacrae* and the large body of consort songs and instrumental music.

Byron, (Augusta) Ada, Countess of Lovelace (1815–1852)
English mathematician, a pioneer in writing programs for Charles ◊Babbage's analytical engine. In 1983 a new, high-level computer language, Ada, was named after her.

She was the daughter of the poet Lord Byron.

Byron, George Gordon, 6th Baron Byron (1788–1824)
English poet. He became the symbol of ◊Romanticism and political liberalism throughout Europe in the 19th century. His poetic strength can be clearly seen in his romantic and self-dramatizing poems which, together with the events of his life, have given rise to the concept of the Byronic hero. His reputation was established with the first two cantos of *Childe Harold* (1812). Later works include *The Prisoner of Chillon* (1816), *Beppo* (1818), *Mazeppa* (1819), and, most notably, the satirical *Don Juan* (1819–24). He left England in 1816 and spent most of his later life in Italy.

Byron published his first volume *Hours of Idleness* in 1807 and attacked its harsh critics in *English Bards and Scotch Reviewers* (1809). Overnight fame came with the first two cantos of *Childe Harold*, which romantically describes his tours in Portugal, Spain, and the Balkans. In 1815 he married mathematician Ann Milbanke (1792–1860), with whom he had a daughter, Augusta Ada Byron. The couple separated shortly after the birth amid much scandal. He then went to Europe and became friendly with Percy and Mary Shelley. He engaged in Italian revolutionary politics and sailed to Greece in 1823 to further the Greek struggle for independence, but died of fever at Missolonghi. He succeeded to the title of baron in 1798.

CAB
Abbreviation for ◊Citizen's Advice Bureau.

Cabal, the (from *kabbala*)
Group of politicians, the English king Charles II's counsellors 1667–73, whose initials made up the word by coincidence – Clifford (Thomas Clifford 1630–1673), Ashley (Anthony Ashley Cooper, 1st Earl of ◊Shaftesbury), ◊Buckingham (George Villiers, 2nd Duke of Buckingham), Arlington (Henry Bennett, 1st Earl of Arlington 1618–1685), and ◊Lauderdale (John Maitland, Duke of Lauderdale). The word cabal, meaning 'association of intriguers', is now applied to any faction that works in secret for private or political ends.

caber, tossing the (Gaelic *cabar* 'pole')
Scottish athletic sport, a ◊Highland Games event. The caber (a tapered tree trunk about 6 m/20 ft long, weighing about 100 kg/220 lb) is held in the palms of the cupped hands and rests on the shoulder. The thrower runs forward and tosses the caber, rotating it through 180 degrees so that it lands on its opposite end and falls forward. The best competitors toss the caber about 12 m/40 ft.

Cabot, Sebastian (1474–1557)
Italian navigator and cartographer, the second son of Giovanni ◊Caboto. He explored the Brazilian coast and the Rio de la Plata for the Holy Roman Emperor Charles V, 1526–30.

Cabot was also employed by Henry VIII, Edward VI, and Ferdinand of Spain. He planned a voyage to China by way of the North-East Passage, the sea route along the north Eurasian coast, encouraged the formation of the Company of Merchant Adventurers of London in 1551, and in 1553 and 1556 directed the company's expeditions to Russia, where he opened British trade.

Caboto, Giovanni, or **John Cabot** (*c.* 1450–*c.* 1498)
Italian navigator. Commissioned, with his three sons, by Henry VII of England to discover unknown lands, he arrived at Cape Breton Island on 24 June 1497, thus becoming the first European to reach the North American mainland (he thought he was in northeast Asia). In 1498 he sailed again, touching Greenland, and probably died on the voyage.

Cadair Idris, or **Cader Idris**, 'Chair of Idris'
Mountain in Gwynedd, northwest Wales; height 892 m/2,926 ft. It is composed of basalt and porphyry, with beds of slag and pumice. It can be ascended from Minffordd on the Tal-y-Llyn side, or from Dolgellau. The area, which is of special interest to botanists and geologists, lies within the boundaries of the Snowdonia National Park. 390 ha/960 acres of the mountain belong to the National Trust.

CABER, TOSSING THE *This feat of strength is associated with the Highland Games at Braemar, Scotland, revived in the 19th century when Queen Victoria's residence at Balmoral made all things Scottish popular. The caber thrower does not just aim for distance, but straightness as well. Brian Shuel/Collections*

Cade, Jack (died 1450)

English rebel. He was a prosperous landowner, but led a revolt in 1450 in Kent against the high taxes and court corruption of Henry VI and demanded the recall from Ireland of Richard, Duke of York. The rebels defeated the royal forces at Sevenoaks and occupied London. After being promised reforms and pardon they dispersed, but Cade was hunted down and killed near Heathfield in Sussex.

Cadwalader (died *c.* 664)

Semi-mythical British king, the son of ◊Cadwallon, king of Gwynedd, North Wales, described by Geoffrey of Monmouth in his book *Historia Regum Britanniae* (*History of the Kings of Britain*).

Cadwallon (lived 6th century), also Caedwalla

King of Gwynedd (*c.* 625–34), in North Wales. He allied with Penda of Mercia and in 632 defeated and killed Edwin of Northumbria at Hatfield Chase. The following year he was himself defeated and killed near Hexham by Edwin's nephew, Oswald.

> *The only British king of historic times who overthrew an English dynasty, and the British peoples never found an equal leader.*
>
> F M Stenton
> Referring to Cadwallon, *Anglo-Saxon England* 2nd ed (1947)

Caedmon (lived *c.* 660–670)

Earliest known English Christian poet. According to the Northumbrian historian Bede, when Caedmon was a cowherd at the monastery of Whitby, he was commanded to sing by a stranger in a dream, and on waking produced a hymn on the Creation. The poem is preserved in some manuscripts. Caedmon became a monk and may have composed other religious poems.

Caerleon, Welsh Caerllion

Small town in Newport unitary authority, south Wales, situated on the River ◊Usk 5 km/3 mi northeast of Newport. Formerly a separate settlement, it is now a suburb of ◊Newport. It stands on the site of the Roman fortress of Isca Silurum. There is a legionary museum and remains of an amphitheatre.

History

Isca Silurum, planned by governor of Britain Sextus Julius Frontinus from 74 to 78, was the headquarters of the Second Legion, which arrived here in about 75 and remained until late in the 3rd century. The place was a focal point from which a network of roads spread west and north into Wales, and was therefore one of the most important points in Roman Britain. The military quarters and amphitheatre had already been excavated when, in 1954 on an adjacent site, there was discovered a large town distinct from, but once dependent on, the fortress. It was occupied, as were similar towns at York and Chester, by the wives and families of the legionaries.

Caernarfon, or Caernarvon

Administrative centre of ◊Gwynedd, north Wales, situated on the southwest shore of the ◊Menai Strait; population (1991) 9,700. Formerly the Roman station of **Segontium** (Caer Seint), it is now a market town, port, and tourist centre. Industries include the manufacture of plastics and metal-working.

Caernarfon castle, one of the finest examples of medieval fortifications in the British Isles, lies to the west of the town. It was built by Edward I in 1284, and is in an excellent state of preservation. It is an irregularly shaped building with 13 polygonal towers; the famous Eagle Tower was built by Edward II. The castle was besieged by Owain Glyndwr in 1402.

The first Prince of Wales (later ◊Edward II) was born in Caernarfon Castle; Edward VIII was invested here in 1911 and Prince Charles in 1969. The Earl of Snowdon became constable of the castle in 1963.

Caerphilly

Unitary authority in south Wales, created in 1996 from parts of the former counties of Mid Glamorgan and Gwent
Area 270 sq km/104 sq mi
Towns Hengoed (administrative headquarters), ◊Caerphilly, Bargoed, Newbridge, Rhymney
Physical rivers Rhymney and Sirhowy
Industries iron and steel production and coal mining have been replaced by a wide range of light industries
Population (1996) 172,000.

Caerphilly, Welsh Caerffili

Market town in the unitary authority of Caerphilly, south Wales, 11 km/7 mi north of Cardiff; population (1991) 35,900. The 13th-century castle, built by Edward I, is the second-largest in Britain. The town gives its name to a mild, white cheese. There is some light industry.

When the Welsh rebellions ended, the castle started to fall into decay; during Elizabethan times the stone was taken for other building work. Restoration work began in the 19th century and has continued in the 20th century.

Caesar, (Gaius) Julius (100–44 BC)

Roman statesman and general. He formed with Pompey and Crassus the First Triumvirate in 60 BC. He conquered Gaul 58–50 and came to Britain in 55 and 54. He was assassinated by conspirators on the Ides of March 44 BC.

Caine, Michael stage name of Maurice Joseph Micklewhite (1933–)

English screen actor. He is a prolific and versatile performer with an enduring Cockney streak. He has played historical roles as in *Zulu* (1964) and *The Man Who Would Be King* (1975), hardboiled psychopaths as in *Get Carter* (1971) and *Mona Lisa* (1986), and comic buffoons as in *Educating Rita* (1983) and *Sweet Liberty* (1986). He won an Academy Award for his supporting role in *Hannah and Her Sisters* (1986).

Caine first rose to international prominence as the philandering leading man of the swinging London set in *Alfie*

CAERNARFON *An aerial view of Caernarfon Castle shows the imposing walls and battlements of this medieval fortification, built on a strategic site between the River Seiont and the Menai Strait. Caernarfon was one of several castles constructed by King Edward I in the late 13th century to protect his newly conquered lands in Wales. Michael St Maur Sheil/Collections*

(1966), for which he won the first of four Academy Award nominations. He was made a CBE in 1993.

Cairngorm Mountains

Granite mountain group in Scotland, northern part of the ⇨Grampian Mountains, between the River Dee and the upper Spey. The central range includes four out of five of Britain's highest mountains: Ben Macdhui (1,309 m/4,296 ft), Braeriach (1,296 m/4,251 ft), Cairn Toul (1,291 m/4,235 ft), and Cairn Gorm (1,245 m/4,084 ft). Cairn Gorm can be accessed by chair-lift.

The winter snowfall is heavy, and winds are higher than normally encountered in mountain ranges on the exposed and extensive plateau. Mountaineering, rock- and snow-climbing, skiing, deer hunting, grouse shooting, and angling are popular. Large herds of red deer are found in the hills, as are Britain's only herd of reindeer. The Ptarmigan restaurant near the summit of Cairn Gorm is Britain's highest restaurant.

The range also includes Ben Avon (1,171 m/3,843 ft), and Beinn a'Bhuird (1,196 m/3,925 ft).

Caldecott, Randolph (1846–1886)

English artist and illustrator. He illustrated books for children, including *John Gilpin*, and became an illustrator for the magazine *Punch* during the 1870s.

Calder

River in West Yorkshire, England; length 72 km/45 mi. It rises in the Pennine moors northwest of Todmorden, and joins the River Aire at Castleford. Several large reservoirs supplying water to West Yorkshire towns lie within its catchment area.

The Aire and Calder Navigation forms a link in the system of rivers and canals that provides a waterway from the River Mersey to the River Humber.

The Calder valley (see Calderdale), via Hebden Bridge, Sowerby Bridge, Mirfield, to Wakefield, is one of the main road and rail routes through the Pennines.

Caldey Island, or Caldy Island, Welsh Ynys Bŷr

Island in ⇨Carmarthen Bay off the coast of Pembrokeshire, southwest Wales, 4 km/2.5 mi south of Tenby; area 1.82 sq km/0.7 sq mi. It is separated from the mainland by **Caldey Sound**. It was inhabited by Celtic monks as early as the 6th century. A monastery, built by Anglican Benedictines in 1906, is now occupied by Trappist monks from a sect which came here from Belgium in 1929. There is a small village, and a lighthouse on the southern cliffs.

Caledonia

Roman term for the Scottish Highlands, inhabited by the Caledoni. The tribes of the area remained outside Roman control – they were defeated but not conquered by Agricola in AD 83–84 and again by Septimius Severus who reached beyond modern Aberdeen in 208. Since the 18th century, the name has been revived as a romantic alternative for the whole of Scotland.

Caledonian Canal

Waterway in northwest Scotland, 98 km/61 mi long, linking the Atlantic and the North Sea. Situated between the Moray Firth and Loch Linnhe, the canal was constructed as a transport route to save the long sail around Scotland. It is one of Scotland's largest marina facilities. Of its total length, only a 37 km/22 mi stretch is artificial, the rest being composed of lochs Lochy, Oich, and Ness.

Thomas ◊Telford began construction of the canal in 1803 and it was completed by 1822.

Callaghan, (Leonard) James, Baron Callaghan of Cardiff(1912–)

British Labour politician. He was home secretary 1967–70 and prime minister 1976–79 in a period of increasing economic stress. As chancellor of the Exchequer 1964–67, he introduced corporation tax, capital-gains tax, and selective employment tax, and resigned following devaluation.

As foreign secretary in 1974, Callaghan renegotiated Britain's membership of the European Community (now the European Union). In 1976 he succeeded Harold Wilson as prime minister and in 1977 entered into a pact with the Liberals to maintain his government in office. Strikes in the so-called 'winter of discontent' 1978–79 led to the government's losing a vote of no confidence in the Commons, forcing him to call an election in May 1979, when his party was defeated by the Conservatives.

Britain has lived too long on borrowed time, borrowed money, and even borrowed ideas.

JAMES CALLAGHAN British Labour politician. Sayings of the Week, the *Observer*, October 1976; as Prime Minister, he had applied to the International Monetary Fund for a $3.9 billion loan the week before

---

Callanish, or Calanais, or Challernish

Village on the Isle of ◊Lewis, in the Outer Hebrides group, Western Isles unitary authority, Scotland, situated on the east shore of East Loch Roag, 25 km/16 mi west of Stornoway. The megalithic standing stones of Callanish are regarded as one of the most impressive prehistoric monuments in Britain.

The monument features an alignment of parallel stones culminating at one end in a circle, which contains a large stone cairn and is intersected by a cross.

Callcott, John Wall (1766–1821)

English organist and composer. Having obtained a deputy organist's post, he found time to compose and in 1785 gained three of the four prizes offered by the Catch Club. Two years later he took part in founding the Glee Club. He obtained a doctorate from Oxford University in 1800. In 1809 he went insane, and died having reached letter P of a music dictionary, feeling unable to proceed further.

Callow, Simon (1949–)

English character actor, stage and screen director, and author. A commanding screen presence, he is equally adept at both dramatic and comic roles. He first won acclaim as Mozart in the theatre production of *Amadeus* (1979). He has worked in both US and British cinema, appearing in films as diverse as *A Room with a View* (1985), *Street Fighter* (1994), and *Four Weddings and a Funeral* (1994). In 1991 he directed the film *The Ballad of the Sad Café* and in 1998 featured in *The Scarlet Tunic*.

He has published several books, including studies of actor Charles Laughton and actor-director Orson Welles.

Calman, Mel (1931–1994)

English cartoonist, designer, and writer. He produced cartoons for a wide variety of magazines and newspapers, and also designed book jackets and advertising campaigns. In 1970 he founded the Workshop Gallery, London, later known as the Cartoon Gallery, which became a leading showcase for humorous art. His books include *Calman and Women* (1967).

Calne, Roy Yorke (1930–)

British surgeon who developed the technique of organ transplants in human patients and pioneered kidney-transplant surgery in the UK. Knighted 1986.

Cam

River in southeast England. It rises in Ashwell, Hertfordshire, and flows 65 km/40 mi northwest and northeast through Cambridgeshire, and then into the River Ouse, 6 km/4 mi south of Ely. The Cam is joined at Hauxton by the River Granta, which rises in Essex, and is known thereafter as either the Cam or the Granta. It is navigable as far as the city of Cambridge.

Camberley

Town in Surrey, England, north of Aldershot; population (1981) 45,700. The Royal Military Academy Sandhurst, was built in 1810, and the Staff College in 1862. Broadmoor prison, for the criminally insane, is nearby.

Camborne-Redruth

Town in Cornwall, southwest England, 16 km/10 mi southwest of Truro; population (1991) 35,900. Industries include engineering and milk production. The town lies in a former copper- and tin-mining area; the last working tin mine, South Crofty, near Camborne, closed in 1998. There is a School of Metalliferous Mining.

In the 1850s the Camborne-Redruth area was the most

productive copper-mining area in the world, but overseas competition caused the industry's decline in the late 19th century. In Redruth the former home of the Scottish inventor William Murdock, who was the first to develop gas lighting commercially, has been restored as a museum. Camborne was the birthplace of Arthur Woolf (*c.* 1766–1837), inventor of the compound steam engine. Richard Trevithick, the engineer and pioneer of steam locomotives, was born in 1771 at Illogan, Redruth.

Nearby to the southwest of Redruth is Carn Brea, a 225 m/738 ft-high hill with Druid remains and castle ruins. To the southeast of the town is Gwennap Pit where John Wesley, the founder of Methodism, preached to the miners.

Cambrian Mountains

Region of hills, plateaux, and deep valleys in Wales, 175 km/ 110 mi long, linking Snowdonia in the northwest and the Brecon Beacons and Black Mountains in the south.

The Cambrian Mountains are in the heart of Wales, the source of the Severn, Towy, and Wye rivers. The highest peak is Aran Fawddwy (905m/ 2,950 ft) in the Berwyn Mountains in the centre. The area is sparsely populated, with livestock farming the chief occupation.

Cambridge

City and administrative headquarters of ◊Cambridgeshire, eastern England, on the River Cam, 80 km/50 mi north of London; population (1994 est) 117,000. It is the seat of ◊Cambridge University (founded in the 13th century). Industries include the manufacture of computers and electronic products, scientific instruments, and paper, printing, publishing, financial services, and insurance. Between the 1960s and 1980s many Cambridge University graduates stayed in the area and founded a range of high-technology companies (mostly computer-related). This attracted others and led to the area being dubbed 'Silicon Fen'.

Features

Apart from those of Cambridge University, fine buildings include St Benet's church, with a Saxon tower (about 1000), the oldest building in Cambridge; the Holy Sepulchre or Round Church (about 1130, restored in 1841), the oldest of four round churches in England; and the Guildhall (1939). The Backs is an ancient strip of land between the backs of the colleges and the Cam. Cambridge lies in the low-lying plain on the southern edge of the Fens, commanding a ford over the River Cam (sometimes known by its former name Granta). Excavations have uncovered remains of Belgic (1st century BC), Roman (1st–4th century AD), and late-Saxon settlements. A castle was built here by the Normans.

Museums

The Fitzwilliam Museum was built in the mid-19th century. Its varied collections include Egyptian sarcophagi and

CAMBRIDGE UNIVERSITY *Members of Queens' College, Cambridge in traditional summer garb. The observance of tradition in the colleges of Cambridge and Oxford, Britain's two oldest universities, has fuelled a widespread belief that they are bastions of outmoded privilege; both have recently made substantial efforts to attract more state-school applicants. Alain Le Garsmeur/Impact*

mummies, 5th-century black- and red-figure Greek vases, Chinese vases, and sculpture; its collection of paintings includes works by Titian, Hogarth, and Picasso. Other museums include the Folk Museum, the Museum of Archaeology and Anthropology, the Sedgwick museum which includes the oldest geological collection in the world, the Scott Polar Research Institute, with displays illustrating the expeditions of Captain Scott and other polar adventurers.

Cambridgeshire

County of eastern England, which has contained the unitary authority Peterborough since April 1998

Area 3,410 sq km/1,316 sq mi

Towns and cities ◊Cambridge (administrative headquarters), Ely, Huntingdon, March, Wisbech, St Neots, Whittlesey

Physical county is flat with fens, whose soil is very fertile; Bedford Level (a peaty area of the fens); rivers: Nene, Ouse (with tributaries Cam, Lark, and Little Ouse), Welland

Features Cambridge University; Britain's second cruise missile base at RAF Molesworth, near Huntingdon, was deactivated in January 1989

Agriculture the county is one of the chief cereal and sugar-beet producing districts of England; fruit and vegetables are grown; there is also dairy farming and sheep-rearing

Industry brewing, paper, electronics, food processing, mechanical engineering; there are scientific and pharmaceutical research establishments

Population (1994) 686,900.

History The inhabitants of the district resisted the Norman invasion, and it was at Ely that ◊Hereward the Wake held out against the Normans for some years.

The county's boundaries

Cambridgeshire is bounded to the north by Lincolnshire and Peterborough; to the east by Norfolk and Suffolk; to the south by Essex and Hertfordshire; and to the west by Bedfordshire and Northamptonshire. The boundaries of the county were altered in 1965 when the two then counties of Cambridgeshire and the Isle of Ely united to form one county. In 1974 the county was extended to include Huntingdon and Peterborough district.

Topography

Although the county is generally very flat, there are hills in the south (the Gog Magog Hills), in the southeast (near Weston Colville, West Wickham, and Castle Camps), and in the west. The hills are mainly boulder clay on top of chalk, although geologically, the county is mainly oolite covered with boulder clay. The south is more wooded than the rest of the county. The river channels are chiefly man-made, and the rivers flow extremely slowly.

Early history

In Celtic times, the northern part of Cambridgeshire was in the territory of the Iceni, while the remainder was controlled by the Catuvellauni. There are remains of pre-Roman earthworks, while relics of the Roman occupation, such as roads, amphorae, and coins, are common. The county was later prominent in the bitter struggles under kings Stephen, John, Henry III, and Charles I.

Cambridge University

English university, one of the earliest in Europe, founded in the 12th century. The university was a centre of Renaissance learning and Reformation theology, and more recently has excelled in scientific research.

According to tradition the university was founded by scholars who had left Oxford because of conflict with the people of the town. Friction between the townspeople of Cambridge and the scholars of the university led to a riot during the Peasants' Revolt of 1381, and five people from the town were hanged. The university was a centre of church Reformism in the sixteenth century, and the church reformers Thomas Cranmer, Hugh Latimer and Nicholas Ridley were educated there. Oliver Cromwell (leader of the Parliamentarian side in the English Civil War), was a graduate of Sidney Sussex college and the local member of Parliament, but the university was largely Royalist. In the 18th century the university had a reputation for noise and drunkenness, but in the 19th century its reputation was restored when the curriculum was broadened to include natural science and history and the number of students increased greatly. The first two women's colleges, Girton and Newnham, were founded in the 1870s but women did not have full academic status and were not awarded degrees until 1948.

Other colleges include Peterhouse, founded in 1284, the oldest college; King's College (1441); Queen's College (1448); Jesus College (1496); St John's College (1511); and Trinity College (1546), the largest college. Emmanuel College chapel was built by Christopher Wren in 1666. The newest college, Robinson, was founded in 1977. The collection of books in the university library (built 1931–34) includes the first book ever printed in English.

Famous students of the university include Rupert Brooke, Samuel Taylor Coleridge, Thomas Gray, Christopher Marlowe, John Milton, Samuel Pepys, and William Wordsworth. In 1996–97, there were 11,223 undergraduates in residence. All colleges are now coeducational except for three women's only colleges: Lucy Cavendish, New Hall, and Newnham.

Among the departments held in high repute is the Cavendish Laboratory for experimental physics, established in 1873. The Cambridge Science Park was set up by Trinity College in 1973. The Royal Greenwich Observatory moved there in 1990.

Some of the colleges of the university back onto the gardens and lawns through which the River Cam flows (known as 'the Backs'). King's College Chapel, dating from 1446, has a richly decorated interior with extravagant fan-vaulting and a carved organ screen which is one of the earliest examples of Italianate Renaissance woodcarving in England. The altarpiece, the *Adoration of the Magi* by Rubens, was donated to King's in 1961. Bridges spanning the Cam include the Bridge of Sighs – a covered bridge built in 1831 – at St John's College; the Mathematical Bridge at Queens' College, which was originally built in the 18th century without nuts or bolts; Clare Bridge; and St John's Bridge.

Cambuskenneth

Ruined abbey on the River Forth near Stirling, Scotland,

Cambridge University Colleges

year founded	college
1284	Peterhouse
1326	Clare
1347	Pembroke
1348	Gonville and Caius
1350	Trinity Hall
1352	Corpus Christi
1441	King's
1448	Queen's
1448	Christ's
1473	St Catharine's
1496	Jesus
1511	St John's
1542	Magdalene
1546	Trinity
1584	Emmanuel
1596	Sidney Sussex
1695	Homerton
1800	Downing
1869	Girton
1871	Newnham[1]
1882	Selwyn
1885	Hughes Hall[2]
1896	St Edmund's
1954	New Hall[1]
1960	Churchill
1964	Lucy Cavendish[1,2]
1964	Darwin
1965	Wolfson[2]
1966	Clare Hall
1966	Fitzwilliam
1977	Robinson

[1] women's colleges [2] colleges for mature students

founded in 1147 by ◊David I. The first Scots parliament met here in 1326. The remains of ◊James III and his queen, Margaret of Denmark, were discovered here in 1864 and reinterred with an altar memorial by command of Queen Victoria in 1865.

Camden

Inner borough of northwest Greater London. It includes the districts of ◊Bloomsbury, Fitzrovia, ◊Hampstead, Highgate, Holborn, and Somers Town

Population

(1991) 170,400.

Features

St Pancras station (1868), chosen 1994 as the international terminal for the high-speed rail link between the Channel Tunnel and London; Highgate Cemetery (1839), burial place of George Eliot, Michael Faraday, Karl Marx, and Herbert Spencer; new British Library (opened 1997); Inns of Court; Hatton Garden, centre of the diamond trade; the London Silver Vaults; Camden lock street market; Hampstead Heath; the Roundhouse, Chalk Farm (1846), a former engine shed, to be converted into the British Architectural Library; Kenwood; British Museum.

Camden Town Group

School of British painters (1911–13), based in Camden, London, led by Walter ◊Sickert. The work of Spencer Gore (1878–1914) and Harold Gilman (1876–1919) is typical of the group, rendering everyday town scenes in Post-Impressionist style. In 1913 they merged with another group to form the London Group.

Camelot

Legendary seat of King ◊Arthur and name of the company that operates the National Lottery.

A possible site of Authur's Camelot is the Iron Age hillfort of South Cadbury Castle in Somerset, England, where excavations from 1967 have revealed remains dating from 3000 BC to AD 1100, including those of a large 6th-century settlement, the time ascribed to Arthur.

> *Whilst all that we love best in classic art / is stamped forever on the immortal face.*
>
> JULIA MARGARET CAMERON English photographer. Poem 'On a Portrait' September 1875

Cameron, Julia Margaret born Pattle (1815–1879)

British photographer. She made lively and dramatic portraits of the Victorian intelligentsia, often posed as historical or literary figures. Her sitters included her friends the English astronomer Sir John Herschel, the poet Alfred Lord Tennyson, whose *Idylls of the King* she illustrated in 1872, and Charles Darwin. She used a large camera, five-minute exposures, and wet plates.

CAMPBELL, MRS PATRICK *English actress Mrs Patrick Campbell as Militza in* For the Crown *(1896). Corbis*

Campaign for Nuclear Disarmament, CND

Nonparty-political British organization advocating the abolition of nuclear weapons worldwide. Since its foundation in 1958, CND has sought unilateral British initiatives to help start, and subsequently to accelerate, the multilateral process and end the arms race.

The movement was launched by the philosopher Bertrand Russell and Canon John Collins and grew out of the demonstration held outside the government's Atomic Weapons Research Establishment at Aldermaston, Berkshire, at Easter 1956. CND held annual marches from Aldermaston to London 1959–63, after the initial march in 1958 which was routed from London to Aldermaston. From 1970 CND has also opposed nuclear power.

Its membership peaked in the early 1980s, during the campaign against the presence of US Pershing and cruise nuclear missiles on British soil, which left in 1991. It is part of Abolition 2000, a global network, founded in 1995 and with organized support in 76 countries, to press for the elimination of nuclear weapons.

Campbell

Family name of the dukes of Argyll, seated at Inveraray Castle, Argyll, Scotland.

Campbell, Colen (1676–1729)

Scottish architect. He was one of the principal figures in British Palladian architecture. His widely influential book *Vitruvius Britannicus* was published in 1712. Among his best-known works are Burlington House, London (1718–19); Mereworth Castle, Kent (1722–25); and Houghton Hall, Norfolk (1722–26). His revision of Palladio's *First Book of Architecture* was published in 1728.

Campbell, Donald Malcolm (1921–1967)

British car and speedboat enthusiast, son of Malcolm Campbell, who simultaneously held the land-speed and water-speed records. In 1964 he set the world water-speed record of 444.57 kph/276.3 mph on Lake Dumbleyung, Australia, with the turbojet hydroplane *Bluebird*, and achieved the land-speed record of 648.7 kph/403.1 mph at Lake Eyre salt flats, Australia. He was killed in an attempt to raise his water-speed record on Coniston Water, England.

Campbell, Malcolm (1885–1948)

British racing driver who once held both land- and water-speed records. He set the land-speed record nine times, pushing it up to 484.8 kph/301.1 mph at Bonneville Flats, Utah, USA, 1935, and broke the water-speed record three times, the best being 228.2 kph/141.74 mph on Coniston Water, England, 1939. His car and boat were both called *Bluebird*. His son Donald ◊Campbell emulated his feats.

Campbell, Mrs Patrick born Beatrice Stella Tanner (1865–1940)

English actress. Her roles included Paula in Pinero's *The Second Mrs Tanqueray* (1893) and Eliza in *Pygmalion*, written for her by George Bernard Shaw, with whom she had an amusing correspondence.

Campbell, Steven (1953–)

Scottish painter. He specializes in large, offbeat figure paintings and helped to inspire a flourishing group of figurative painters in Glasgow, among them Stephen Conroy. He studied at Glasgow School of Art and by his early 30s was recognized as a leading figure in Scottish art.

Campbell-Bannerman, Henry (1836–1908)

British Liberal politician, prime minister 1905–08, leader of the Liberal party 1898–1908. The 'Entente Cordiale' was broadened to embrace Russia during his premiership, which also saw the granting of 'responsible government' to the Boer republics in southern Africa. He was succeeded as prime minister and Liberal leader by H H ◊Asquith, who had effectively led the House during Campbell-Bannermann's premiership, as the latter was dogged by ill health.

Campion, Edmund (1540–1581)

English Jesuit and Roman Catholic martyr. He became a Jesuit in Rome in 1573 and in 1580 was sent to England as a missionary. He was betrayed as a spy in 1581, imprisoned in the Tower of London, and hanged, drawn, and quartered as a traitor. Feast day 1 December.

Campion, Thomas (1567–1620)

English poet and musician. He was the author of the critical *Art of English Poesie* (1602) and four books of *Ayres* (1601–17), for which he composed both words and music.

The *Art of English Poesie* is an attack on the use of rhyme and a plea for the adoption of unrhymed metres formed on classical models.

He composed masques that are among the best of their kind, including *The Mask of Flowers*, and produced many fine lyrics notable for their metrical finish. The best known of his songs are 'There is a Garden in her Face' and 'My Sweetest Lesbia, Let Us Live and Love', a translation from Catullus.

canals

The first major British canal was the Bridgewater Canal 1759–61, constructed for the 3rd Duke of Bridgewater to carry coal from his collieries to Manchester. The engineer, James ◊Brindley, overcame great difficulties in the route. Today, many of Britain's canals form part of an interconnecting system of waterways some 4,000 km/2,500 mi long. Many that have become disused commercially have been restored for recreation and the use of pleasure craft. In 1998 167 km of canals in the UK were classed as Sites of Special Scientific Interest.

Canary Wharf

420 thousand-sq m/4.5 million-sq ft office development on the Isle of Dogs in London's ◊Docklands, the first phase of which was completed in 1992, along with the foundations for a further 740 thousand sq m/8 million sq ft. The complex of offices, surrounding landscaped squares, is best known for its central skyscraper, the second tallest in Europe at 244 m/800 ft. Designed by US architect Cesar Pelli (1926–), it sports a pyramid-shaped crown in stainless steel. After the collapse of the developer Olympia York in 1992, the site gained notoriety as a symbol of the economic recession in the UK, with much of its office space remaining unlet. By the end of 1995, following a rescue package, 75% had been let, but the cost to the taxpayer, in development grants and tax breaks, was estimated at £3 billion.

Canning, Charles John, 1st Earl Canning (1812–1862)

British administrator, son of George ◊Canning and first viceroy of India from 1858. As governor general of India from 1856, he suppressed the Indian Mutiny with a fair but firm hand which earned him the nickname 'Clemency Canning'. Viscount 1837, Earl 1859.

Canning, George (1770–1827)

British Tory politician, foreign secretary 1807–10 and 1822–27, and prime minister in 1827 in coalition with the Whigs. He was largely responsible, during the ◊Napoleonic Wars, for the seizure of the Danish fleet and British intervention in the Spanish peninsula.

Canning entered Parliament in 1793. His verse, satires, and parodies for the *Anti-Jacobin* (1797–98) led to his advancement by Pitt the Younger. His disapproval of the Walcheren expedition in 1809 involved him in a duel with the war minister, ◊Castlereagh, and led to Canning's resignation as foreign secretary. He was president of the Board of Control 1816–20. On Castlereagh's death in 1822, he again became foreign secretary, supported the national movements in Greece and South America, and was made prime minister in 1827. When Wellington, Peel, and other Tories refused to serve under him, he formed a coalition with the Whigs. He died in office.

Canterbury

Historic cathedral city in Kent, southeast England, on the River Stour, 100 km/62 mi southeast of London; population (1991) 36,500. The city is the metropolis of the Anglican Communion and seat of the archbishop of Canterbury. It is a popular tourist destination. Paper, paper products, and electrical goods are manufactured.

Canterbury was the site of an important Roman town and military station situated on the Roman road between Dover and London. It is believed that a settlement was maintained from Roman times until the Saxon period, and in the 6th century the town, now known as **Cantwarabyrig**, was the capital of Ethelbert, king of Kent. ◊Augustine, sent from Rome to convert England to Christianity, was welcomed here in 597 by Ethelbert, and became the first archbishop of England in 601.

Canterbury Cathedral

Established on the site of previous churches possibly dating back to Roman times, the present cathedral represents the

CANTERBURY CATHEDRAL *A view of Canterbury Cathedral from the north-west. Historically and artistically, it is one of the most important buildings in England. The oldest part of the building is the crypt, dating from the late 11th century. Externally, the dominant feature is the majestic central tower (known as 'Bell Harry'), built in the 15th century. Corbis*

finest work of four centuries, initiated by Archbishop Lanfranc, the first Norman archbishop (1070–89), following a great fire in 1067. It is in the form of a double cross, with a central and two west towers. The total length is 160 m/525 ft, the east transept measuring 47 m/154 ft. Canterbury's Norman crypt remains in its entirety, with exceptionally fine carvings. Its 12th-century choir is the most important specimen of Transitional-Norman work in England in the nascent Gothic style, using both the pointed and the rounded arch, carved capitals, and a ribbed vault. The late 14th-century nave is a masterpiece of Perpendicular style, with lierne vaults and strikingly lofty aisles. The cathedral's stained glass is among the finest and oldest surviving in quantity, many specimens dating from around 1200, or earlier.

Until the Reformation (1538) the Trinity Chapel was the site of Thomas à ◊Becket's shrine, indicated by the marks worn in the stones by many generations of pilgrims. The framework for Chaucer's ◊*Canterbury Tales* is a group of pilgrims on their way to visit the shrine of Thomas à Becket. Nearby is the tomb of Edward the Black Prince (1376), and facing it the tomb of Henry IV and his consort, Joan of Navarre.

Canterbury, archbishop of

Archbishop of the Church of England (Anglican), the primate (archbishop) of all England, and first peer of the realm, ranking next to royalty. He crowns the sovereign, has a seat in the House of Lords, and is a member of the Privy Council. He is appointed by the prime minister.

Formerly selected by political consultation, since 1980 the new archbishops have been selected by a church group, the Crown Appointments Commission (formed in 1977). The first holder of the office was St Augustine (601–04). George Carey was appointed in 1991.

The archbishop's official residence is at Lambeth Palace, London, and second residence at the Old Palace, Canterbury. See full list of Archbishops of Canterbury, opposite.

Canterbury Tales, The

Unfinished collection of stories in prose and verse (*c.* 1387) by Geoffrey ◊Chaucer, told in Middle English by a group of pilgrims on their way to Thomas à ◊Becket's tomb at Canterbury. The tales and preludes are remarkable for their vivid character portrayal and colloquial language, and they were a major influence on the development of English literature.

Each of the thirty or so pilgrims was meant to tell two stories on the way, and two on the return journey. Though it comprises 17,000 lines of prose and verse, including prologues and epilogues, the 24 stories only constitute less than a fifth of the projected work, which was never put into any proper order. They range from the sublimity of the 'Knight's Tale', to the mock heroism of the 'Nun's Priest's Tale', the humour of the 'Merchant's Tale', and the sheer bawdiness of the 'Miller's Tale'.

Canute (*c.* 995–1035)

King of England from 1016, Denmark from 1018, and Norway from 1028. Having invaded England in 1013 with his father, Sweyn, king of Denmark, he was acclaimed king on his father's death in 1014 by his ◊Viking army. Canute defeated ◊Edmund (II) Ironside at Assandun, Essex, in 1016, and became king of all England on Edmund's death. He succeeded his brother Harold as king of Denmark in 1018, compelled King Malcolm to pay homage by invading Scotland in about 1027, and conquered Norway in 1028. He was succeeded by his illegitimate son Harold I.

Under Canute's rule English trade improved, and he gained favour with his English subjects by sending soldiers back to Denmark. The legend of Canute disenchanting his flattering courtiers by showing that the sea would not retreat at his command was first told by Henry of Huntingdon in 1130.

Canvey Island

Island in the Thames estuary, England, 48 km/30 mi east of London; area 18 sq km/7 sq mi; population (1991) 35,700. It is situated off the Essex coast to the west of Southend-on-Sea, and was reclaimed from the sea in the 17th century. Canvey Island is reached from Benfleet station, with which it is connected by a bridge. A major oil storage terminal is located here.

In 1953 the island was damaged by storms which killed 58 people.

Cape Wrath (Norse **huaf** 'point of turning')

Headland at the northwest extremity of Scotland, extending 159 m/523 ft into the Atlantic Ocean. It is one of a series of rugged cliffs formed of gneiss. Its lighthouse dates from 1827.

Caractacus (died *c.* 54)

British chieftain who headed resistance to the Romans in southeast England AD 43–51, but was defeated on the Welsh border. Shown in Claudius's triumphal procession, he was released in tribute to his courage and died in Rome.

Cardew, Cornelius (1936–1981)

English composer and pianist. He belonged at one time to the avant-garde school, whose ideas are much influenced by John Cage, but he later espoused Marxist principles and published a book, *Stockhausen Serves Imperialism* (1974). In 1969 he founded the Scratch Orchestra for non-performers, who are free to produce any sounds or no sounds on conventional or improvised instruments. His works have been widely performed in Europe.

Cardiff

Unitary authority in south Wales, created in 1996 from part of the former county of South Glamorgan; population 306,500 (1996); area 139 sq km/54 sq mi. The administrative headquarters is ◊Cardiff.

Cardiff, Welsh **Caerdydd**

Seaport, capital of Wales (from 1955), and administrative centre of ◊Cardiff unitary authority, situated at the mouth of the ◊Taff, Rhymney, and Ely rivers; population (1994 est) 290,000. Industries include car components, flour milling, ship repairs, electrical goods, paper, and cigars; there are also high-tech industries.

Succession List of the Archbishops of Canterbury

Date elected	Name	Date elected	Name	Date elected	Name
597	Augustine	1093	Anselm	1556	Reginald Pole
604	Laurentius	1114	Ralph d'Escures	1559	Matthew Parker
619	Mellitus	1123	William de Corbeil	1576	Edmund Grindal
624	Justus	1139	Theobald	1583	John Whitgift
627	Honorius	1162	Thomas à Becket	1604	Richard Bancroft
655	Deusdedit	1174	Richard (of Dover)	1611	George Abbot
668	Theodore	1184	Baldwin	1633	William Laud
693	Berthwald	1193	Hubert Walter	1660	William Juxon
731	Tatwine	1207	Stephen Langton	1663	Gilbert Sheldon
735	Nothelm	1229	Richard le Grant	1678	William Sancroft
740	Cuthbert	1234	Edmund of Abingdon	1691	John Tillotson
761	Bregowine	1245	Boniface of Savoy	1695	Thomas Tenison
765	Jaenbert	1273	Robert Kilwardby	1716	William Wake
793	Ethelhard	1279	John Peckham	1737	John Potter
805	Wulfred	1294	Robert Winchelsey	1747	Thomas Herring
832	Feologeld	1313	Walter Reynolds	1757	Matthew Hutton
833	Ceolnoth	1328	Simon Meopham	1758	Thomas Secker
870	Ethelred	1333	John de Stratford	1768	Frederick Cornwallis
890	Plegmund	1349	Thomas Bradwardine	1783	John Moore
914	Athelm	1349	Simon Islip	1805	Charles Manners-Sutton
923	Wulfhelm	1366	Simon Langham	1828	William Howley
942	Oda	1368	William Whittlesey	1848	John Bird Sumner
959	Aelfsige	1375	Simon Sudbury	1862	Charles Thomas Longley
959	Brithelm	1381	William Courtenay	1868	Archibald Campbell Tait
960	Dunstan	1396	Thomas Arundel	1883	Edward White Benson
c. 988	Ethelgar	1398	Roger Walden	1896	Frederick Temple
990	Sigeric	1399	Thomas Arundel[1]	1903	Randall Thomas Davidson
995	Aelfric	1414	Henry Chichele	1928	William Cosmo Gordon Lang
1005	Alphege	1443	John Stafford	1942	William Temple
1013	Lyfing	1452	John Kempe	1945	Geoffrey Francis Fisher
1020	Ethelnoth	1454	Thomas Bourchier	1961	Arthur Michael Ramsey
1038	Eadsige	1486	John Morton	1974	Frederick Donald Coggan
1051	Robert of Jumieges	1501	Henry Deane	1980	Robert Alexander Kennedy Runcie
1052	Stigand	1503	William Warham	1991	George Leonard Carey
1070	Lanfranc	1533	Thomas Cranmer		

[1] Restored.

The city dates from Roman times, the later town being built around a Norman castle. The castle was the residence of the earls and marquises of Bute from the 18th century and was given to the city in 1947 by the fifth marquis. Coal was exported until the 1920s. As the coal industry declined, iron and steel exports continued to grow, and an import trade in timber, grain and flour, tobacco, meat, and citrus fruit developed. Cardiff Airport is at Roose, 19 km/12 mi to the southwest.

The docks

Cardiff grew into a major city when the docks on the Bristol Channel were opened in 1839. They were greatly extended by the second Marquis of Bute (1793–1848), and have now been redeveloped for industry. Cardiff became the largest Welsh town in 1881, and has remained thus.

Office development

The city's main function is as an administrative centre, and office employment has consequently expanded greatly. In Cathays Park is a group of public buildings including the Law Courts, City Hall, the National Museum of Wales, the Welsh Office (established 1964), and the Temple of Peace and Health.

Features

Llandaff, on the right bank of the River Taff 3 km/1.9 mi to the northwest, was included in Cardiff in 1922; its cathedral, virtually rebuilt in the 19th century and restored between 1948 and 1957 after air-raid damage in World War II, contains Jacob Epstein's sculpture *Christ in Majesty*. At St Fagan's 5 km/3 mi to the west is the Welsh National Folk Museum, containing small, rebuilt historical buildings from rural Wales in which crafts are demonstrated. The city is the headquarters of the Welsh National Opera. A 75,000-seat Millennium Stadium at Cardiff Arms Park, to be completed in time for the 1999 Rugby World Cup, is a Millennium Commission Landmark Project. **Cardiff Bay** is the site of the new National Assembly for Wales building (see ◊Welsh Assembly).

Cardiff Arms Park, Welsh Parc yr Arfau

Welsh rugby ground, officially known as the National Stadium, situated in Cardiff. The stadium became the permanent home of the Welsh national team 1964 and has a capacity of 64,000. The existing stadium is to be demolished and replaced by the 73,000-seater Millennium Stadium in time for the 1999 Rugby World Cup.

Cardigan Bay

Wide inlet of St George's Channel, west Wales, stretching from Braich-y-Pwll in the north to Strumble Head in the south. It is bounded to the north by the Lleyn Peninsula and to the south by St David's Peninsula, and borders the counties of Gwynedd, Ceredigion (Cardiganshire), and Pembrokeshire. Dolphins have often been sighted here.

CARDIFF *The Inner Harbour and the Pierhead Building in Cardiff Bay. In common with many other such sites around Britain, changing patterns of manufacture and overseas trade left this former bustling dockland area derelict by the 1980s. Urban regeneration in the 1990s has seen it become the site of a marina and other leisure facilities; it will be the site of the Welsh National Assembly. Gena Davies/Collections*

Carew, Thomas (*c.* 1595–*c.* 1640)

English poet. Often associated with the ◊'Cavalier poets', he was a courtier and gentleman of the privy chamber to Charles I, for whom he wrote the spectacular masque *Coelum Britannicum* (1634). *Poems* (1640) revealed his ability to weave metaphysical wit, eroticism, and a jewelled lyricism in his work.

His first important work was an elegy written on the death of the metaphysical poet John Donne, which was published in 1633 in the first edition of Donne's poetry.

Carewe, John (1933–)

English conductor. After studying with Boulez and Messiaen he founded the New Music Ensemble in 1957 and gave the first performances of works by Peter Maxwell Davies and Harrison Birtwistle with works by Stockhausen and Boulez. He conducted the Fires of London 1980–84, and the first performance of Elliott Carter's oboe concerto, in Zurich, 1988. He was appointed chief conductor of Chemnitz Opera and the Robert Schumann Philharmonic Orchestra in 1993.

Carey, George Leonard (1935–)

103rd archbishop of Canterbury from 1991. A product of a liberal evangelical background, he was appointed bishop of Bath and Wells 1987.

His support of the ordination of women priests brought disagreement during his first meeting with Pope John Paul II 1992.

Caribbean Times, The, incorporating *The African Times*

Weekly newspaper of the Afro-Caribbean and black community in Britain, established in 1981. In 1998 it had a circulation of 24,500.

caricature

Exaggerated portrayals aiming to ridicule or expose an individual or type, or satirizing British society and politics, have appeared in the arts and literature since medieval times. Notable caricaturists were James Gillray, William Hogarth, and Thomas Rowlandson in the 18th century; George Cruikshank, Edward Lear, Richard Doyle, and George Du Maurier in the 19th century; and Max Beerbohm, David Low, 'Vicky', 'Giles', Ronald Searle, Osbert Lancaster, Mel Calman, Gerald Scarfe, and Ralph Steadman in the 20th century. Illustrators associated with the satirical magazine *Punch* (founded 1841) included John Tenniel, Richard Doyle, John Leech, Leonard Raven-Hill, Edward Reed, and Phil May.

Within television Peter Fluck and Roger Law created three-dimensional puppets for their satirical television series *Spitting Image* (from 1984).

Carisbrooke

Village southwest of Newport, Isle of Wight, England. It was once the capital of the Isle of Wight, and remains traditionally the island's principal town. Charles I was imprisoned in its Norman castle from 1647 to 1648. The castle houses the Isle of Wight County Museum.

Carling, Will (William David Charles) (1965–)

English rugby union player. A centre, he won 72 caps for England between 1988 and 1997 including a record 59 as captain. He made his full England debut in January 1988, and was appointed England captain when only 22 years old. He captained England to Grand Slam Championships in 1991, 1992, and 1995, the World Cup final in 1991, and the World Cup semi-final in 1995. He was sacked as captain in 1995 after remarks made in a television interview, but was quickly reinstated by popular demand. He holds the world record for international appearances as captain, having captained England 59 times 1988–96. In 1997 Carling announced his retirement from international rugby, having played for England 72 times; he also terminated his contract with Harlequins and announced his retirement from competitive rugby.

Carlingford Lough

Inlet of the Irish Sea at the mouth of the River Newry, between County Louth in the Republic of Ireland and County Down in Northern Ireland. It is 16 km/10 mi long and 3 km/2 mi wide, with a shingle shore, and is a popular centre for sea angling and sailing, with rich wildlife.

Carlisle

City and administrative headquarters of ◊Cumbria, northwest England, on the River Eden at the western end of Hadrian's Wall, 14 km/9 mi south of the Scottish border; population (1991) 72,400. It is a leading railway and service centre. Industries include engineering and brewing (Scottish and Newcastle), and the manufacture of textiles, agricultural machinery, metal goods, confectionery, and processed foods. Carlisle was the Roman settlement of **Luguvalium**. There is a Norman cathedral and a restored castle dating from 1092.

Features

The cathedral, completed in 1123, was originally the church of an Augustinian priory; the diocese was founded in 1133 by Henry I. Rebuilt and embellished at various stages, it has a fine Early English choir and an east window with 14th-century stained glass. Traces of the town's Roman street plan have survived, and part of the medieval walls remain around the inner town. The Guildhall dates from the 14th century. The Tullie House Museum, originally a Jacobean mansion, includes a collection of Roman remains.

History

Surrounded by wide and fertile lowland, the town developed on a low sandstone hill with the River Eden to the north, the Petteril tributary to the west, and the Caldew tributary to the east. During the Roman occupation the settlement was raided by the Picts and other Scottish tribes, and the Saxon town was sacked by the Danes in the 9th century. William Rufus built the castle as a stronghold against the Scots and frequent border raids followed. The Scots gained control of the town from 1136 to 1157 and, in the English Civil War, the town surrendered to the Scots after suffering considerable damage during a siege from 1644 to 1645. Carlisle was captured again by the Scots in 1745, during the Jacobite rising led by Charles Edward Stuart, but the Duke of recaptured it some weeks later.

Throughout its history, Carlisle has been a thriving market centre, and it developed rapidly in the 19th century as a railway hub. It remains an important focus of trade and commerce, and a major railway centre, with extensive marshalling yards, on the main line from London to Glasgow and Edinburgh.

Carlyle, Jane (Baillie) born Welsh (1801–1866)

Scottish letter-writer, wife of the historian Thomas ◊Carlyle from 1826. She resented her husband's preoccupation with his books, and their relationship became increasingly strained. However, her affection for her husband is apparent in her voluminous correspondence, which also illustrates her natural vivacity and wit.

Carlyle, Robert (1961–)

Scottish actor. He made his film debut in Ken ◊Loach's *Riff-Raff* (1990), a building-site-set examination of class struggle, and went on to enjoy a string of successes in British film and television, notably in the films ◊*Trainspotting* (1996) and ◊*The Full Monty* (1997). He has emerged as one of the leading British actors of his generation, often playing working-class men either down on their luck or embroiled in the criminal underworld. He has a talent for both comedy and drama, and great skill in reproducing regional accents.

His versatility as an actor has also been demonstrated in his television work, since 1995 starring as the eponymous police constable in *Hamish Macbeth* and as a violent drug dealer in *Looking After Jo Jo* (1998). His other films include *Priest* (1993), *Carla's Song* (1996), and *Face* (1997).

Carlyle, Thomas (1795–1881)

Scottish essayist and social historian. His works include the partly autobiographical *Sartor Resartus/The Tailor Retailored* (1833–34), reflecting his loss of Christian belief; *The French Revolution* (1837); and the long essay 'Chartism' (1839), attacking the doctrine of *laissez faire*. His prose style was idiosyncratic, encompassing grand, thunderous rhetoric and deliberate obscurity.

Carlyle was born in Ecclefechan, Dumfriesshire. Leaving Edinburgh University without taking a degree, he supported himself by teaching while he devoted several years to intensive study of German literature. In 1826 he married Jane Baillie Welsh and they moved to her farm at Craigenputtock, where *Sartor Resartus* and many of his most influential essays were written. His reputation was established with *The French Revolution* and in 1834 they moved to London.

In 1853 Carlyle began his *History of Frederick the Great* (1858–65). After the death of his wife in 1866 he edited her letters (1883) and prepared his *Reminiscences* (1881), which shed an unfavourable light on his character and his neglect of her, for which he could not forgive himself. The house in Cheyne Row, Chelsea, London, where Carlyle and his wife lived from 1834, is a museum.

Carmarthen, Welsh Caerfyrddin

Town and administrative centre of ◊Carmarthenshire, south-west Wales, situated on the River Towy, 15 km/9 mi north of Kidwelly; population (1991) 13,200. It is the agricultural centre for the productive dairy region of the Vale of Tywi. It was formerly the Roman settlement of **Maridunum**. There is a museum in the Bishop's palace, and the Gwili steam railway is nearby.

Carmarthen Bay

Large bay on the south coast of Wales, in the county of Carmarthenshire. Commercial cockle-fishing takes place here. The principal towns on its coast are Tenby and Llanelli.

Carmarthenshire, Welsh Sir Gaerfyrddin

Unitary authority in south Wales; a former county, it was part of Dyfed between 1975 and 1996
Area 2,390 sq km/923 sq mi
Towns ◊Carmarthen (administrative headquarters), ◊Llanelli
Physical rivers ◊Tywi, Taf, ◊Teifi; ◊Black Mountain range in the east, southern spur of the Cambrian Mountains in the north, including Mynydd Mallaen (459 m/1,1,506 ft); along the coast are extensive sands and marshes. Carmarthenshire is dominated by the Vale of Tywi, but there are numerous grassy

CARLYLE, THOMAS *Scottish essayist and historian Thomas Carlyle, who was acclaimed as one of the most brilliant and unconventional historians of his day. He became a fierce critic of Victorian values, arguing passionately for a moral, political, and intellectual renewal of society.* Corbis

hills, mostly under 300 m/1,000 ft; the valleys are fertile and the hillsides afford good pasturage
Features ◊Brecon Beacons National Park on the eastern border; Museum of the Woollen Industry at DreFach-Felindre; home of Dylan ◊Thomas in the village of ◊Laugharne, 6 km/3.7 mi southeast of St Clears; the National Botanic Garden of Wales, to be established in the Regency park of Middleton Hall, is a Millennium project
Agriculture dairy farming, stock-raising
Population (1996) 68,900.

Carnarvon

Alternative spelling of ◊Caernarfon, a town in Wales.

Carnegie Medal, full name Library Association Carnegie Medal

Annual award for an outstanding book for children written in English and published in the UK. The medal was first awarded in 1937 to Arthur Ransome's *Pigeon Post* (in the ◊*Swallows and Amazons* series). It is named after US industrialist and philanthropist Andrew Carnegie (1835–1919).

The 1998 Carnegie Medal was awarded to Tim Bowler for *River Boy*.

Caro, Anthony (Alfred) (1924–)

English sculptor. His most typical work is large, brightly coloured abstract sculpture, horizontal in aspect, and made from prefabricated metal parts, such as I-beams, angles, and mesh visibly bolted together. An example is *Early One Morning* (1962; Tate Gallery, London). From the 1980s Caro turned to more traditional sculptural techniques and subjects; in the 1990s, for example, he made a series of bronze figures inspired by the story of the Trojan War. He was knighted in 1987.

Caroline of Brunswick (1768–1821)

Queen consort of George IV of Great Britain. King George attempted to divorce her, unsuccessfully, on his accession to the throne in 1820.

Second daughter of Karl Wilhelm, Duke of Brunswick, and Augusta, sister of George III, she married her first cousin, the Prince of Wales, in 1795, but after the birth of Princess Charlotte Augusta a separation was arranged. When her husband ascended the throne in 1820 she was offered an annuity of £50,000 provided she agreed to renounce the title of queen and to continue to live abroad. She returned forthwith to London, where she assumed royal state. In July 1820 the government brought in a bill to dissolve the marriage, but Lord Brougham's brilliant defence led to the bill's abandonment. On 19 July 1821 Caroline was prevented by royal order from entering Westminster Abbey for the coronation. Her funeral a few weeks later was the occasion of popular riots.

Carrickfergus

Seaport on Belfast Lough, County Antrim, Northern Ireland; population (1991) 32,800. There is some light industry, and the town is a major centre for the man-made fibre industry. The well-preserved **Carrickfergus Castle** was begun in 1180, and now houses a museum. The church of St Nicholas dates partly from the 12th century. The port has a large marina and a sailing school. Carrickfergus was the main port of medieval Ulster but declined from the 17th century onwards, with the development of Belfast.

Carrickfergus is reputedly named after Fergus McErc, ruler of the former kingdom of Dalriada, and a king of Scotland during the 6th century. The town was the site of a number of conflicts between English and Irish troops from the 14th–17th centuries, and was briefly held by the French army under Thurot in 1760.

Some remains of the town walls, dating from the 17th century, can still be seen, and there is a statue at the harbour commemorating the landing of William III (William of Orange) here in 1690. There is an historical theme park in the centre of the town. 3 km/2 mi north of Carrickfergus is the Andrew Jackson Centre, a restored 17th-century cottage housing a museum commemorating the life of Andrew Jackson (1767–1845), 7th president of the USA, whose father emigrated from Carrickfergus in 1765. The ruins of Kilroot church, where Jonathan Swift was minister between 1694 and 1696, are 3 km/2 mi northeast of the town.

Carrington, Dora (1893–1932)

English painter, a member of the ◊Bloomsbury Group. She developed a style which, in its emphasis on design and bold colours, is typical of English Post-Impressionism of the period from World War I to the 1930s. Among her best known works are an elegant portrait of her close friend, the writer Lytton ◊Strachey (1918), and the landscape *The Mill House at Tidmarsh* (1918).

Her style, broadly similar to that of her Bloomsbury friends Duncan Grant and Vanessa Bell, was well suited to the decorative arts, and her work includes sign boards, painted tiles and furniture, and designs for book covers; for several years she worked for Roger Fry's ◊Omega Workshop.

A film of her life, *Carrington*, appeared in 1995.

Carrington, Peter Alexander Rupert, 6th Baron Carrington (1919–)

British Conservative politician. He was defence secretary 1970–74, and led the opposition in the House of Lords 1964–70 and 1974–79. While foreign secretary 1979–82, he negotiated independence for Zimbabwe, but resigned after failing to anticipate the Falklands crisis. He was secretary general of NATO 1984–88 and chaired the European Community-sponsored peace talks on Yugoslavia in 1991. Knighted 1958; succeeded as Baron 1938.

Carroll, Lewis Pen name of Charles Lutwidge Dodgson (1832–1898)

English author of the children's classics ◊*Alice's Adventures in Wonderland* (1865) and its sequel *Through the Looking-Glass, and What Alice Found There* (1872). Among later works was the mock-heroic narrative poem *The Hunting of the Snark* (1876). He was a lecturer in mathematics at Oxford University from 1855–81 and also published mathematical works.

Dodgson first told his fantasy stories to Alice Liddell and her sisters, daughters of the dean of Christ Church, Oxford University. His two Alice books brought 'nonsense' literature to a peak of excellence, and continue to be enjoyed by children and adults alike. The reasons for their success include the illustrations of John ◊Tenniel, the eminently quotable verse, and the combination of exciting adventures, imaginative punning, and humorous characters, with a more sophisticated level of ingenious imagination which parodies everything from mathematical to literary theories. Dodgson was a prolific letter writer and one of the pioneers of portrait photography (his sitters included John Ruskin, Alfred Tennyson, and D G Rossetti, as well as children). He is said to be, after Shakespeare, the most quoted writer in the English language.

'O frabjous day! Callooh! Callay!'/He chortled in his joy.

LEWIS CARROLL English author.
Alice Through the Looking-Glass (1872) ch 1

Carry On films

Series of low-budget, highly profitable British comedies with an emphasis on the unsubtle double entendre. The first was *Carry On Sergeant* (1958) and the series continued for 20 years with such titles as *Carry On Nurse*, *Carry On Spying*, *Carry On Screaming*, and *Carry On Doctor*. *Carry On Columbus* (1992), starring a combination of *Carry On* regulars and contemporary comic talent, was a late and anachronistic addition to the series.

All were produced by Peter Rogers and directed by Gerald Thomas. Regular stars included Kenneth Williams, Charles Hawtrey, Sid James, Joan Sims, Barbara Windsor, and Hattie Jacques.

Carse of Gowrie

Fertile lowland plain bordering the north bank of the Firth of Tay, Scotland. It is 24 km/15 mi long, and is one of the country's most productive agricultural areas, including soft fruit. William III landed here before the Battle of the Boyne in 1690.

Carson, Willie (William Fisher Hunter) (1942–)

Scottish jockey who rode 17 English classic winners including four Epsom Derby winners, and was the champion flat-racing jockey in 1972, 1973, 1978, 1980 and 1983. He retired in 1997 with a career total of 3,828 winners.

Carter, Angela (1940–1992)

English writer of the magic realist school. Her works are marked by elements of Gothic fantasy, a fascination with the erotic and the violent, tempered by a complex lyricism and a comic touch. Her novels include *The Magic Toyshop* (1967) (filmed in 1987) and *Nights at the Circus* (1984). She co-wrote the script for the film *The Company of Wolves* (1984), based on one of her stories. Her last novel was *Wise Children* (1991).

Shaking a Leg: Collected Writings and Journalism, edited by Jenny Uglow, was published posthumously in 1997.

Carter, Howard (1873–1939)

English Egyptologist. He discovered the virtually intact tomb of Tutankhamen, an Egyptian king of the 18th dynasty. This important archaeological find was made in 1922 in the Valley of the Kings at Luxor with the British archaeologist Lord Carnarvon, although the sealed door was not opened until February 1923.

Carter worked on numerous Egyptian sites, including the ancient city of Tell el Amarna in Upper Egypt with the archaeological survey led

CARTER, HOWARD *British archaeologist Howard Carter (right) at the opening of Tutankhamen's tomb at Luxor, Egypt, in 1922. Carter spent ten years making a detailed record of the tomb; his work here is regarded as the most important single piece of excavation in the history of Egyptology. Corbis*

by Flinders ◊Petrie (1891–99), and conducted excavations as an inspector in the antiquities department of the Egyptian government.

The contents of Tutankhamen's tomb included many works of art and his solid-gold coffin, which are now displayed in a Cairo museum. An exhibition in the British Museum in 1972 celebrated the 50th anniversary of the discovery of the royal tomb and attracted a record 1.6 million visitors.

He described his discoveries in a number of publications, including *The Tomb of Thoutmosis IV* with P E Newberry (1904), *Description and Excavation of the Tomb of Hatshopsitu* (1906), and *The Tomb of Tutankhamen* with A C Mace (1923–33).

Cartland, (Mary) Barbara (Hamilton) (1904–)

English romantic novelist. She published her first book, *Jigsaw* in 1921 and since then has produced a prolific stream of stories of chastely romantic love, usually in idealized or exotic settings, for a mainly female audience. Her novels include *Love Climbs In* (1978) and *Moments of Love* (1981).

She claims to have written 23 books a year for the last 18 years. They include several volumes of autobiography, including *Reach for the Stars* (1994). DBE 1991.

Cartwright, Edmund (1743–1823)

English inventor. He patented the power loom (1785), built a weaving mill (1787), and patented a wool-combing machine (1789).

Visiting the spinning mills of manufacturing pioneer Richard Arkwright inspired Cartwright to try to invent a weaving mill. He patented his first, water-driven power loom in 1785, and gradually improved it. It was followed by the wool-combing machine, which did the work of 20 hand-combers. The wool-combers – some 50,000 in number – organized a protest, but nothing came of it.

Cartwright's Doncaster factory was enlarged when a steam engine was erected to power it, and in 1799 a Manchester firm contracted with Cartwright for the use of 400 of his power looms and built a mill where some of these were powered by steam. The Manchester mill was burned to the ground, probably by workers who feared to lose their jobs, and this prevented other manufacturers from repeating the experiment.

Cary, (Arthur) Joyce (Lunel) (1888–1957)

British writer. He used his experiences gained in the Nigerian political service (which he entered in 1913) as a backdrop to such novels as *Mister Johnson* (1939), and he used the trilogy form to look at a subject from different viewpoints. The first and best known of his trilogies was about the life of an artist, Gulley Jimson, and comprised the novels *Herself Surprised* (1941), *To Be a Pilgrim* (1942), and *The Horse's Mouth* (1944).

Casement, Roger David (1864–1916)

Irish nationalist. While in the British consular service, he exposed the ruthless exploitation of the people of the Belgian Congo and Peru, for which he was knighted in 1911 (degraded 1916). He was hanged for treason by the British for his involvement in the Irish nationalist cause.

In 1914 Casement went to Germany and attempted to induce Irish prisoners of war to form an Irish brigade to take part in a republican insurrection. He returned to Ireland in a submarine in 1916 (actually to postpone, not start, the Easter Rising), was arrested, tried for treason, and hanged.

Cassivelaunus

Chieftain of the British tribe, the Catuvellauni, who led the British resistance to the Romans under Caesar in 54 BC.

Casson, Hugh Maxwell (1910–)

English architect. He was professor at the Royal College of Art from 1953 to 1975, and president of the Royal Academy from 1976 to 1984. He was director of architecture for the Festival of Britain on the South Bank in London (1948–51), in which pavilions designed by young architects helped to popularize the Modern Movement. His books include *Victorian Architecture* (1948). He was knighted in 1952.

> *The British love permanence more than they love beauty.*
>
> HUGH CASSON English architect.
> *Observer* 1964

castles

Fortified buildings or group of buildings, characteristic of medieval Britain. Outstanding examples are the 13th-century Caernarfon castle, with its unique polygonal towers; and the 14th-century Warwick castle.

The **motte and bailey** castle was introduced to England after the Norman Conquest in 1066. The motte was a mound of earth, topped by a wooden tower, while the bailey was a courtyard below, containing the main dwellings. The first **rectangular stone keep** was the White Tower in the ◊Tower of London, begun in 1078. Entrance was usually at first floor level.

During the 12th century more substantial defensive systems were developed, based in part on the Crusaders' experiences of sieges during the First Crusade of 1096. The first **curtain walls** with projecting towers were built at this time, as at Framlingham, Suffolk. In the 13th century **round towers** were introduced, both for curtain walls, as at Pembroke, Wales, and for keeps, as seen at Conisbrough, Yorkshire. **Concentric planning**, with two rings of walls protecting the inner buildings, may be found in the castles built by Edward I in Wales, such as Caernarfon, ◊Beaumaris, and Harlech. **Fortified town walls** became increasingly common during this period.

With the first use of gunpowder in the 14th century, gunports were included in curtain walls, such as those at Bodiam, Sussex, but in the face of this new weapon castles became less defensible, and increases in civil order led to their replacement in the 15th century by unfortified manor houses. Fortified coastal defences, however, continued to be built in the 16th century, as at Falmouth, Cornwall.

In the late 19th and early 20th centuries castlelike buildings were built as residences for the wealthy as part of the Romantic revival in Britain, ◊Castle Drogo, Devon, being a notable example.

Castle, Barbara Anne, Baroness Castle born Betts (1911–)

British Labour politician; a cabinet minister in the Labour governments of the 1960s and 1970s. She led the Labour group in the European Parliament 1979–89 and became a life peer in 1990.

Castle was minister of overseas development 1964–65, transport 1965–68, employment 1968–70 (when her White Paper *In Place of Strife*, on trade-union reform, was abandoned because it suggested state intervention in industrial relations), and social services 1974–76, when she was dropped from the cabinet by Prime Minister James Callaghan. She criticized him in her *Diaries* (1980).

She campaigned vigorously against Britain's entry into the European Economic Community between 1970 and the referendum of 1975.

Castle, Roy (1932–1994)

English entertainer. Noted for his versatility, he combined the talents of comic, singer, dancer, and musician; he was a particularly enthusiastic trumpeter. He presented the long-running TV series, *Record Breakers*, based on entries in *The Guinness Book of Records*, and held two records himself; for tap dancing and wing walking. In his last years he was an active campaigner for cancer research.

Castle Coole

Classical house southeast of Enniskillen, County Fermanagh, Northern Ireland. It was built 1790–96 by James Wyatt, and contains plasterwork by Joseph Rose (1745–99) and furniture lent by the Earl of Belmore. The 32 ha/79 acre estate was given to the National Trust by the Ulster Land Fund in 1951.

Castle Donington

Town in Leicestershire, England, at the confluence of the rivers Trent and Soar, 11 km/7 mi northeast of Ashby de la Zouch; population (1991) 6,100. It lies at the centre of a largely agricultural district. Castle Donington has a large power station, a hosiery factory, and industries manufacturing springs, trimmings and lace.

Extensive gravel working takes place in the Trent Valley near Castle Donington. To the south is the East Midlands airport. A rock festival is held here annually. There is a motor-racing circuit and a museum of veteran cars at Donington Park.

Castle Drogo

20th-century granite castle near Drewsteignton, Devon, built by Edwin ◊Lutyens between 1910 and 1930 on a 274 m/899 ft rocky outcrop above the River Teign. The castle was given to the National Trust in 1974, together with the Elizabethan Whiddon Deer Park.

Castleford

Town in Wakefield, West Yorkshire, northern England, at the confluence of the rivers Aire and Calder, 15 km/10 mi southeast of Leeds; population (1991) 36,000. A former coalmining town, Castleford now manufactures chemicals, glass, clothing, flour, confectionary, and bakery products. Under the Romans it was **Lagentium** on the Roman road Watling Street.

Castlereagh, Robert Stewart, Viscount Castlereagh (1769–1822)

British Tory politician. As chief secretary for Ireland 1797–1801, he suppressed the rebellion of 1798 and helped the younger Pitt secure the union of England, Scotland, and Ireland in 1801. As foreign secretary 1812–22, he coordinated European opposition to Napoleon and represented Britain at the Congress of Vienna 1814–15.

Castlereagh sat in the Irish House of Commons from 1790. When his father, an Ulster landowner, was made an earl in 1796, he took the courtesy title of Viscount Castlereagh. In Parliament he was secretary for war and the colonies 1805–06 and 1807–09, when he had to resign after a duel with foreign secretary George ◊Canning. During his time as foreign secretary, he devoted himself to the overthrow of Napoleon and subsequently to the congress system. His policy abroad favoured the development of material liberalism, but at home he repressed the Reform movement, and popular opinion held him responsible for the Peterloo massacre of peaceful demonstrators in 1819.

In 1821 he succeeded his father as Marquess of Londonderry, but committed suicide the following year.

Castle Rising

Village in Norfolk, England, 6 km/4 mi northeast of King's Lynn. There are the ruins of a large Norman castle here, built around 1150 by William de Albini, Earl of Sussex, and now managed by English Heritage. The keep is one of the largest in England. Isabella of France was exiled to Castle Rising following the murder of Edward II.

Castle Rising is also the site of the 12th-century church of St Lawrence, and of Bede House, founded by Henry Howard in 1614 for poor women. Today Bede House is an almshouse for elderly women, who wear Jacobean costume to attend church on Sundays.

Castleton

Village in Derbyshire, England, 25 km/16 mi west of Sheffield. It is situated at the foot of a hill, on the summit of which stands Peak Castle, originally built by William Peveril on land granted to him by William the Conqueror in 1068. The keep was built by Henry II in 1176. Today the castle is managed by English Heritage. The castle features in Walter Scott's novel *Peveril of the Peak*. The area around the village contains the Peak, Speedwell, and Treak Cliff Caverns, as well as the Blue John Cavern, which is known for its coloured fluorspar.

Castle Ward

Imposing 18th-century mansion in County Down, Northern

Ireland, 11 km/7 mi northeast of Downpatrick. Castle Ward was reputedly one of the first houses in Ireland to exemplify 'the modern Gothic'. Standing on the southern shore of Strangford Lough, the house boasts an unusual compromise of west and east fronts in both Classical and neo-Gothic styles. The estate includes a Victorian laundry and a wildfowl collection (the Strangford Lough Wildlife Centre), and was given to the National Trust by the Northern Ireland Government in 1953.

catch

A part-song, in vogue in England from the early 17th to the 19th centuries, in which the voices follow each other in the manner of a canon or round, with the difference in the most characteristic examples that the words, thus mixed up, acquire new and ludicrous meanings, often of an indecent nature in the 17th century.

cathedrals

In Britain cathedrals, the principal church of a bishop or archbishop, were formerly distinguished as either monastic or secular, the clergy of the latter not being members of a regular monastic order. Some are referred to as 'minsters', such as Southwell and York, the term originating in the name given to the bishop and cathedral clergy who were often referred to as a *monasterium*. After the ◊Dissolution of the Monasteries by Henry VIII, most of the monastic churches were refounded and called Cathedrals of the New Foundation. Cathedrals of dioceses founded since 1836 include St Albans, Southwark, Truro, Birmingham, and Liverpool.

Most cathedrals were built during the Middle Ages and reflect the many styles of Norman architecture, as at Durham Cathedral, and Gothic architecture as at Ely Cathedral, Exeter Cathedral, Winchester Cathedral, and York Minster. Canterbury Cathedral spans the Norman to Perpendicular periods. Among the few built since medieval times are the 17th-century St Paul's Cathedral and 19th-century Westminster Cathedral, London. The 20th-century saw the construction of the Liverpool (Catholic) and Guildford cathedrals, and the rebuilding of Coventry Cathedral after World War II.

In British ecclesiastical architecture, the enclosed space forming the precinct of a cathedral or monastery is known as the close, as found at Salisbury Cathedral.

Catherine of Aragón (1485–1536)

First queen of Henry VIII of England, 1509–33, and mother of Mary I. Catherine had married Henry's elder brother Prince Arthur in 1501 and on his death in 1502 was betrothed to Henry, marrying him on his accession. She failed to produce a surviving male heir and Henry divorced her without papal approval, thus creating the basis for the English Reformation.

Born at Alcala de Henares, she was the youngest daughter of Ferdinand and Isabella of Spain. After Prince Arthur's death, Catherine remained in England, virtually penniless, until her marriage to Henry in 1509. Of their six children, only Mary survived infancy. Wanting a male heir, Henry sought an annulment in 1526 when Catherine was too old to bear children. When the pope demanded that the case be referred to him, Henry married Anne Boleyn, afterward receiving the desired decree of nullity from Thomas Cranmer, the archbishop of Canterbury, in 1533. The Reformation in England followed, and Catherine went into retirement until her death.

Catherine of Braganza (1638–1705)

Queen of Charles II of England, 1662–85. Her childlessness and Catholic faith were unpopular, but Charles resisted pressure for divorce. She was instrumental in Charles II's return to Catholicism on his deathbed. After his death in 1692, she returned to Lisbon.

The daughter of John IV of Portugal (1604–1656), she brought the Portuguese possessions of Bombay and Tangier as her dowry and introduced tea drinking and citrus fruits to England.

Catherine of Valois (1401–1437)

Queen of Henry V of England, whom she married 1420; the mother of Henry VI. After the death of Henry V, she secretly married Owen Tudor (*c.* 1400–1461) in about 1425, and their son Edmund Tudor was the father of Henry VII. See genealogy on page 906.

Catholic Emancipation

In British history, acts of Parliament passed 1780–1829 to relieve Roman Catholics of civil and political restrictions imposed from the time of Henry VIII and the Reformation.

Cato Street Conspiracy

Unsuccessful plot hatched in Cato Street, London, to murder the Tory foreign secretary Robert Castlereagh and all his ministers on 20 February 1820. The leader, the Radical Arthur Thistlewood (1770–1820), who intended to set up a provisional government, was hanged with four others.

cat's eyes

Reflective studs used to mark the limits of traffic lanes, invented by Percy Shaw (1890–1976) as a road safety device in 1934.

A cat's eye stud has two pairs of reflective prisms (the eyes) set in a rubber pad, which reflect the light of a vehicle's headlamps back to the driver. When a vehicle goes over a stud, it moves down inside an outer rubber case; the surfaces of the prisms brush against the rubber and are thereby cleaned.

Catterick

Village in North Yorkshire, northern England, 6 km/4 mi southeast of Richmond, 56 km/35 mi northwest of York. It is the site of a large military camp and there is a racecourse nearby at Catterick Bridge. Also nearby there are traces of the Roman military camp **Cataractonium**.

Catuvellauni

Leading southern British tribe of the time of the Roman invasions under Caesar and Claudius, with a fortified stronghold at what is now Wheathampstead, Hertfordshire. ◊Cassivelaunus, ◊Cymbeline, and his son ◊Caractacus were kings of the Catuvellauni.

Caulfield, Patrick (1936–)
English painter and printmaker. He works in a style related to Pop art, with strong flat colours enclosed within thick black outlines, but his subjects are traditional – typically, landscapes and still lifes – rather than the contemporary ones usually favoured by Pop artists.

Causley, Charles Stanley (1917–)
English poet. His first volume of verse, *Farewell Aggie Weston* (1951), reflected his service in the Royal Navy during World War II. Recent collections of his verse include *Collected Poems 1951–1997* (1997) and *Collected Poems for Children* (1996). His work is rooted in the life and folklore of his native Cornwall and makes use of ballad material and religious themes. He was awarded the Queen's Gold Medal for Poetry in 1986.

cavalier
Horseman of noble birth, but mainly used as a derogatory nickname to describe a male supporter of Charles I in the English Civil War (Cavalier), typically with courtly dress and long hair (as distinct from a Roundhead); also a supporter of Charles II after the Restoration.

Cavalier poets
Poets of Charles I's court, including Thomas ◊Carew, Robert ◊Herrick, Richard ◊Lovelace, and John ◊Suckling. They wrote witty, lighthearted lyrics about love and loyalty to the monarch.

Cavell, Edith (Louisa) (1865–1915)
English nurse. As matron of a Red Cross hospital in Brussels, Belgium, in World War I, she helped Allied soldiers escape to the Dutch frontier. She was court-martialled by the Germans and condemned to death. The British government made much propaganda from her heroism and execution, which was cited as an example of German atrocities.

I realize that patriotism is not enough. I must have no hatred or bitterness towards any one.

EDITH CAVELL English hospital matron in World War I.
Last words 12 October 1915, quoted in *The Times* 23 October 1915

Cavendish
Family name of dukes of Devonshire; the family seat is at Chatsworth, Derbyshire, England.

Cavendish, Henry (1731–1810)
English physicist and chemist. He discovered hydrogen (which he called 'inflammable air') in 1766, and determined the compositions of water and of nitric acid. The Cavendish experiment (1798) enabled him to discover the mass and density of the Earth.

Cavendish demonstrated in 1784 that water is produced when hydrogen burns in air, thus proving that water is a compound and not an element. He also worked on the production of heat and determined the freezing points for many materials, including mercury.

Cavendish, Lord Frederick Charles (1836–1882)
British administrator, second son of the 7th Duke of Devonshire. He was appointed chief secretary to the lord lieutenant of Ireland in 1882. On the evening of his arrival in Dublin he was murdered in Phoenix Park with Thomas Burke, the permanent Irish undersecretary, by members of the Irish Invincibles, a group of Irish Fenian extremists founded 1881.

Cavendish, Spencer
See ◊Hartington, Spencer Compton Cavendish, British politician.

Cavendish, William, 4th Duke of Devonshire (1720–1764)
British Whig politician, prime minister and First Lord of the Treasury 1756–57. His appointment was chiefly a convenience to secure the services of William ◊Pitt the Elder as secretary of war, and when by mismanagement he lost the support of Pitt, he was forced to resign.

Career
Cavendish's career was a classic example of the importance of patronage and family connections in the way British politics was conducted at this time. He entered the House of Lords in 1754, becoming a privy councillor and Master of the Horse, and being appointed to the key position of Lord Lieutenant to Ireland. In that post he made important friends and appeased hostile factions. He ended his political career as Lord Chamberlain of the royal household 1757–62.

Caxton, William (*c.* 1422–1491)
First English printer. He learned the art of printing in Cologne, Germany, in 1471 and set up a press in Belgium where he produced the first book printed in English, his own version of a French romance, *Recuyell of the Historyes of Troye* (1474). Returning to England in 1476, he established himself in London, where he produced the first book printed in England, *Dictes or Sayengis of the Philosophres* (1477).

The books from Caxton's press in Westminster included editions of the poets Chaucer, John Gower, and John Lydgate (*c.* 1370–1449). He translated many texts from French and Latin and revised some English ones, such as Malory's *Morte d'Arthur.* Altogether he printed about 100 books.

And certaynly our langage now used varyeth ferre from that which was used and spoken when I was borne.

WILLIAM CAXTON The first English printer.
1490

Cayman Islands
British island group in the West Indies
Area 260 sq km/100 sq mi;

CAXTON, WILLIAM *William Caxton produced both the first printed book in English,* Recuyell of the Historyes of Troy *(1475), and also the first book to be printed in England,* Dictes or Sayengis of the Philosophers *(1477). Philip Sauvain Picture Collection*

Population (1993 est) 31,150.

Acquired by Britain following the Treaty of Madrid in 1670 the Cayman Islands became a dependency of Jamaica in 1863. In 1959 the islands became a separate crown colony, although the inhabitants chose to remain British.

CBI

Abbreviation for ◊**Confederation of British Industry**.

Cecil, Henry Richard Amherst (1943–)

Scottish-born racehorse trainer with stables at Warren Place, Newmarket. The leading trainer ten times between 1976 and 1993, in 1985 he became the first trainer to win over £1 million in a season (1985). He trained Slip Anchor and Reference Point to win the Epsom Derby.

Cecil, Robert, 1st Earl of Salisbury (1563–1612)

Secretary of state to Elizabeth I of England, succeeding his father, Lord Burghley; he was afterwards chief minister to James I (James VI of Scotland) whose accession to the English throne he secured. He discovered the ◊Gunpowder Plot, the conspiracy to blow up the King and Parliament 1605. James I created him Earl of Salisbury 1605. Knighted 1591, Baron 1603, Viscount 1604.

Ceefax ('see facts')

One of Britain's two teletext systems (the other is Teletext), or 'magazines of the air', developed by the BBC and first broadcast on television in 1973.

In 1995 the BBC began testing a scheme to allow Ceefax (repackaged in HTML, hypertext markup language, to enable it to behave like Web pages) to be viewed on a PC by connecting a DAB (digital audio broadcasting) radio to the PC like a modem.

Celt

Member of an Indo-European tribal people that originated in Alpine Europe about 1200 BC and spread throughout Europe and beyond, settling in the British Isles from about the 5th century BC (see ◊Ancient Britain). The Celts had a distinctive religion, led by Druids, and were renowned for their horsemanship, ferocity in battle, and their ritual savagery. They were subjugated by the invading Romans after AD 43, leaving only Ireland unscathed.

There was a resurgence of ◊Celtic art and culture after the end of the Roman era, and a thriving Celtic church. After the 11th century the Celts were gradually absorbed, conquered, and mostly assimilated into English-based culture. The most important legacy of the Celtic presence is in language, both in place names, especially those of rivers, and in Scottish Gaelic, Irish Gaelic, Welsh, Manx, and Cornish. The island of Iona is regarded as the cradle of the Celtic kingdom of Scotland.

Celtic art

Art of the Celtic peoples of western Europe, emerging about 500 BC, probably on the Rhine, and flourishing only in Britain and Ireland from the 1st century BC to the 10th century AD. In Britain, Celtic art may be divided into two broad periods: the pre-Christian (from 250 BC) and the Christian (from AD 597); the influence of Anglo-Saxon culture may be found from AD 400.

Pre-Christian metalwork was commonly in bronze or possibly gold (for example, the Ipswich torques, about 50 BC), and weapons, bracelets, and horse harness and trappings were frequently decorated. Repoussé work has been found throughout the British Isles, and the designs are sometimes enriched by yellow, blue, green, and red enamel, millefiori glass, or patches of coloured vitreous pastes. A unique oval bronze shield, recovered from the River Thames, has 27 settings of red enamel. Typical designs were based on animal and plant motifs and formed semi-abstract patterns of divergent spirals of whorls and elliptical curves. Engraved lines or dots filled the pattern, highlighting the plain groundwork.

With the arrival of Christianity and the introduction of new artefacts, many fresh elements of ornament appeared, such as fretwork (geometrical carving), interlaced work, and shaped designs. Sculpture in the form of large stone crosses is also a distinctive feature of this period. The Lindisfarne Gospels (690; British Museum, London), with their intricately illuminated pages, clearly show the flowing designs previously associated with Celtic applied arts. The main collections of Celtic art are in the British Museum.

CELTIC ART *The Celtic cross, a distinctive feature of Celtic Christianity. The Celtic religion spread to Britain and Ireland from the 1st century* BC, *and prevailed until the 10th century* AD. *The design of this symbol, a cross in a circle, is said to derive ultimately from the ancient Egyptian symbol of life, known as the* ankh. *Corbis*

Celtic languages

Branch of the Indo-European family, divided into two groups: the **Brythonic** or **P-Celtic** (◊Welsh language, Cornish, Breton, and Gaulish) and the **Goidelic** or **Q-Celtic** (Irish, Scottish, and Manx ◊Gaelic languages). Celtic languages once stretched from the Black Sea to Britain, but all Celtic languages are generally in decline despite the efforts of broadcasters, 'revitalist' organizations, and pressure groups. The most notable efforts have been in Welsh.

Celtic Sea

Sea area bounded by Wales, Ireland, and southwest England. The Celtic Sea is separated from the Irish Sea by St George's Channel.

Cenotaph (Greek 'empty tomb')

Monument in the Whitehall, London, designed by Edwin Lutyens to commemorate the dead of both world wars.

Central

Former region of Scotland (1975–96); replaced in 1996 by Clackmannanshire, Falkirk, and Stirling unitary authorities.

The new unitary authorities were formerly the four districts of Central region. Central region was formed from lands within the counties of Perthshire, Stirlingshire, and Clackmannanshire.

Central Criminal Court

Crown court in the City of London, able to try all treasons and serious offences committed in the City or Greater London. First established 1834, it is popularly known as the **Old Bailey** after part of the medieval defences of London; the present building is on the site of Newgate Prison.

Central Lowlands

One of the three geographical divisions of Scotland, being the fertile and densely populated plain that lies between two geological fault lines, which run nearly parallel northeast–southwest across Scotland from Stonehaven to Dumbarton and from Dunbar to Girvan.

Cerdic

Saxon king of Wessex. He is said to have come to Britain about AD 495, landing near Southampton. He defeated the British in Hampshire and founded Wessex about AD 500, conquering the Isle of Wight about AD 530.

Ceredigion

Unitary authority in southwest Wales, created in 1996 from part of the former county of Dyfed, of which it was a district
Area 1,793 sq km/ 692 sq mi
Towns ◊Aberaeron (administrative headquarters), ◊Aberystwyth, Cardigan, ◊Lampeter, Llandyssul, Tregaron
Physical part of the Cambrian Mountains, including ◊Plynlimon Fawr (752 m/2,468 ft); rivers ◊Teifi, Rheidol, Ystwyth, Aeron, and ◊Tywi
Features remains of Roman roads and military stations, and inscribed stones; ruins of 12th-century Strata Florida Abbey southeast of Aberystwyth; ◊Devil's Bridge) (spanning the Rheidol Falls)
Industries tourism, woollens production
Agriculture sheep-rearing, dairy production
Population (1996) 68,900.

Topography

Washed on the west by Cardigan Bay, Ceredigion extends from the mouth of the Dovey to the mouth of the Teifi, and has an extensive eastern boundary with Powys. The surface of the district is comprised of Cambrian and Silurian rocks, and the interior is mountainous.

Commerce
The main occupation is agriculture. In the north and northeast there are large sheep farms, while in the lower parts of the district, milk production plays the main part in farming activity. There are a number of small woollen mills, and a considerable amount of tourist traffic at the coastal resorts of Borth, Aberystwyth, Aberaeron, New Quay, Tresaith, Llangranog, and Aberporth. The rivers and lakes are noted for freshwater fishing, while coracle fishing still survives on the River Teifi. Formerly, mineral deposits of lead, copper, and zinc were mined here.

Chadderton
Town in Greater Manchester, England; population (1991) 31,200. Some of the surviving cotton mills are now used for manufacturing industries, including electrical and aircraft engineering.

Chadwick, James (1891–1974)
English physicist. In 1932 he discovered the particle in the nucleus of an atom that became known as the **neutron** because it has no electric charge. He received the Nobel Prize for Physics in 1935.

Chadwick established the equivalence of atomic number and atomic charge. During World War II, he was closely involved with the atomic bomb, and from 1943 he led the British team working on the Manhattan Project in the USA. Knighted 1945.

Chadwick, Lynn (1914–)
English sculptor. He is known for his 1940s mobiles (influenced by Alexander Calder) and for welded ironwork from the 1950s, typically spiky, pyramidal 'creatures' suggesting the human figure. In the 1960s his work became chunkier, influenced by Minimal art, but subsequently he returned to more figurative work. He has worked in various materials, including sheet steel, which he began using in the 1980s.

Chain, Ernst Boris (1906–1979)
German-born British biochemist. After the discovery of penicillin by Alexander ◊Fleming, Chain worked to isolate and purify it. For this work, he shared the 1945 Nobel Prize for Medicine with Fleming and Howard Florey. Chain also discovered penicillinase, an enzyme that destroys penicillin. Knighted 1969.

Chalfont St Giles
Town in Buckinghamshire, England, 7 km/4 mi northeast of Beaconsfield; population (1991) 5,800. The poet John Milton lived in Chalfont St Giles during the Great Plague of 1665–66. He finished *Paradise Lost* and began *Paradise Regained* here; his cottage is now open to the public.

Chalmers, Thomas (1780–1847)
Scottish theologian. At the Disruption of the ◊Church of Scotland in 1843, Chalmers withdrew from the church along with a large number of other priests, and became principal of the Free Church college, thus founding the ◊Free Church of Scotland.

Chamberlain, (Arthur) Neville (1869–1940)
British Conservative politician, son of Joseph Chamberlain. He was prime minister 1937–40; his policy of appeasement toward the Italian fascist dictator Benito Mussolini and German Nazi Adolf Hitler (with whom he concluded the ◊Munich Agreement in 1938) failed to prevent the outbreak of World War II. He resigned in 1940 following the defeat of the British forces in Norway.

Younger son of Joseph Chamberlain and half-brother of Austen Chamberlain, he was born in Birmingham, of which he was lord mayor in 1915. He was minister of health in 1923 and 1924–29, and his policies centred on slum clearance. In 1931 he was chancellor of the Exchequer in the national government, and in 1937 succeeded Stanley Baldwin as prime minister. Trying to close the old Anglo-Irish feud, he agreed to return to Eire those ports that had been occupied by the navy.

He also attempted to appease the demands of the European dictators, particularly Mussolini. In 1938 he went to Munich and negotiated with Hitler the settlement of the Czechoslovak question. He was ecstatically received on his return, and claimed that the Munich Agreement brought 'peace in our time'. Within a year, however, Britain was at war with Germany.

CHAMBERLAIN, NEVILLE *British prime minister Neville Chamberlain (left) and the British ambassador to Germany, Neville Henderson. Both were proponents of the policy of appeasement towards Germany and Italy in the 1930s, hoping to avoid war by making concessions. This policy had the support of much of the British population, who dreaded the thought of another war, and resented money spent on rearmament. Corbis*

Chamberlain, (Joseph) Austen (1863–1937)

British Conservative politician, elder son of Joseph Chamberlain; as foreign secretary 1924–29 he negotiated and signed the Pact of Locarno, which fixed the boundaries of Germany; for this he won the Nobel Peace Prize in 1925. In 1928 he also signed the Kellogg–Briand pact to outlaw war and provide for peaceful settlement of disputes.

He was elected to Parliament in 1892 as a Liberal-Unionist, and after holding several minor posts was chancellor of the Exchequer 1903–06. During World War I he was secretary of state for India 1915–17 and member of the war cabinet in 1918. He was chancellor of the Exchequer 1919–21 and Lord Privy Seal 1921–22, but failed to secure the leadership of the party in 1922, as many Conservatives resented the part he had taken in the Irish settlement of 1921.

Chamberlain, Joseph (1836–1914)

British politician, reformist mayor of and member of Parliament for Birmingham. In 1886, he resigned from the cabinet over William Gladstone's policy of home rule for Ireland, and led the revolt of the Liberal-Unionists.

By 1874 Chamberlain had made a sufficient fortune in the Birmingham screw-manufacturing business to devote himself entirely to politics. He adopted radical views, and took an active part in local affairs. Three times mayor of Birmingham, he carried through many schemes of municipal development. In 1876 he was elected to Parliament and joined the republican group led by Charles Dilke, the extreme left wing of the Liberal Party. In 1880 he entered Gladstone's cabinet as president of the Board of Trade. The climax of his radical period was reached with the unauthorized programme, advocating, among other things, free education, graduated taxation, and smallholdings of 'three acres and a cow'.

As colonial secretary in Salisbury's Conservative government, Chamberlain was responsible for relations with the Boer republics up to the outbreak of war in 1899. In 1903 he resigned to campaign for imperial preference or tariff reform as a means of consolidating the empire. From 1906 he was incapacitated by a stroke. Chamberlain was one of the most colourful figures of British politics, and his monocle and orchid made him a favourite subject for political cartoonists.

Chamberlain, Lord

The only officer of state whose position survives from Norman times; responsibilities include the arrangements for the opening of Parliament, assisting with the regalia at coronations, and organizing the ceremony when bishops and peers are created. The post is part-time and the symbols of the office are a white staff and key, which are carried on ceremonial occasions. In the middle ages, the King's Chamberlain often acted as the monarch's spokesman in council and parliament. It remained a political appointment until 1924.

The Lord Great Chamberlain was originally the financial officer of the royal household but he now performs only a small number of ceremonial duties. At coronations he helps to invest the sovereign with the regalia; when the sovereign opens Parliament in person the Lord Great Chamberlain is responsible for the arrangements, including the appointment of a peer to carry the sword of state, and walks in the procession from the robing room. Until April 1965 he also controlled the Palace of Westminster and its precincts, but that authority now extends only to the robing room, with the staircase and ante-room adjoining, and to the royal gallery.

chamber music

Music intended for performance in a small room or chamber, rather than in the concert hall, and usually written for instrumental combinations, played with one instrument to a part, as in the string quartet.

Chamber music developed as an instrumental alternative to music for voices such as the madrigal; madrigals published in England in the 16th and 17th centuries were often designed to be playable on instruments. A peculiarly English form was the 'fantasy' or 'fancy' for stringed instruments or keyboard, a free composition not restricted by the structures of dance or variation form. The idea of 'fantasy' chamber music was revived in Britain in the early 20th century, with the establishment of a composition prize for such pieces. Byrd also wrote works specifically for instruments, to which texts were set subsequently.

Chamber music continued to develop during the 17th and 18th centuries, through musical clubs (such as those that existed in London and Oxford) and the partronage of royalty – Charles II had a private band of musicians. The expertise of English viol players was much in demand in the courts of Europe at this time. In the mid-18th century, London was an important centre for the publication of 'accompanied keyboard sonatas', works for keyboard with violin or cello accompaniment, that are the direct precursors of intrumental sonatas and piano trios.

In the 19th century few British composers wrote for chamber forces, although works from the Classical repertoire were heard in concert series. In the 20th century the human voice began to be used in chamber music; in Britain chamber works with voice were written by Vaughan Williams, Maxwell Davies, and Holst, among others. Chamber operas and symphonies have also been written, the size of their forces partly dictated by commercial considerations. Many British festivals now present concerts of chamber music, and a number of universities have resident chamber ensembles.

chambers

Rented offices used by a group of barristers. Chambers in London are usually within the precincts of one of the four law courts.

Chancellor, Lord, (Latin cancellarius)

State official, originally the royal secretary, today a member of the cabinet, whose office ends with a change of government. The Lord Chancellor acts as Speaker of the House of Lords, may preside over the Court of Appeal, and is head of the judiciary; the office is now always held by a lawyer. Lord Irvine of Lairg was appointed Lord Chancellor in 1997.

The chancellor is properly known as the Lord High Chancellor of Great Britain, but is commonly referred to as the Lord Chancellor. He or she is also Keeper of the Great Seal, although historically the two offices have sometimes been separated. In rank the lord chancellor takes precedence immediately after the royal family and the Archbishop of Canterbury. The holder of the office is now normally a peer or is elevated to the peerage on appointment. The Lord Chancellor is appointed by the prime minister and leaves office when the government resigns.

The office of Lord Chancellor illustrates the fusion of the three branches of government, in that the Lord Chancellor fulfils executive, legislative, and judicial functions. In an executive capacity the Lord Chancellor is a member of the cabinet and is the government's principal legal and constitutional adviser. In the absence of the sovereign he also reads the Queen's speech at the opening of Parliament; he also reads all other messages from the sovereign to Parliament, and announces in the House of Lords the royal assent to bills. In a legislative capacity he is Speaker of the House of Lords and, unlike the Speaker of the House of Commons, participates in debates and votes in divisions, but has no casting vote. When speaking in debates he leaves the seat, known as the ◊woolsack, and speaks from the government benches.

In a judicial capacity the Lord Chancellor is head of the judiciary, may preside over the House of Lords when it is sitting as a final court of appeal, and over the Judicial Committee of the Privy Council (see ◊Privy Council). He is also president of the Court of Appeal, the High Court, and the Chancery Division, although he does not normally preside over them.

Chancellor of Scotland

The Chancellor of Scotland, like his English counterpart, was always a high officer of the Crown and developed considerable legal and political authority. The office expired, however, in 1707, following the Treaty of Union with England.

chancellor of the Duchy of Lancaster

Honorary post held by a cabinet minister who has other nondepartmental responsibilities. The chancellor of the Duchy of Lancaster was originally the monarch's representative controlling the royal lands and courts within the duchy. Jack Cunningham was appointed to the post in 1998, being also minister for the cabinet office, with responsibility for overseeing government policy and sorting out disputes between ministers.

chancellor of the Exchequer

Senior cabinet minister responsible for the national economy. The office, established under Henry III, originally entailed keeping the Exchequer seal. The current chancellor of the Exchequer from 1997 is Gordon Brown. See table below for post holders since 1945.

The chancellor is responsible for national finance, the coordination of economic policy, and presents the annual ◊Budget to Parliament in which he or she reviews the state of the economy and reveals proposals for its regulation. These proposals are subsequently given parliamentary approval through the annual Finance Act. Since 1997 the chancellor had ceded control over setting United Kingdom interest to the Bank of England.

In the past the office of chancellor of the Exchequer was sometimes held by the prime minister, but the last to do so was W E Gladstone in 1873–74 and 1880–82. The chancellor also originally had important judicial functions, but these lapsed and were finally abolished in the 19th century.

The chancellor of the Exchequer has an official residence at 11 Downing Street, although the current chancellor, Gordon Brown, a bachelor, lives in the residential quarters of 10 Downing Street, allowing the prime minister and his family to live in 11 Downing Street, where the residential quarters are more spacious.

Chancery

A division of the High Court that deals with such matters as the administration of the estates of deceased persons, the execution of trusts, the enforcement of sales of land, and foreclosure of mortgages. Before reorganization of the court

Chancellors of the Exchequer since 1945

Date appointed	Name	Date appointed	Name
July 1945	Hugh Dalton	November 1967	Roy Jenkins
November 1947	Sir Stafford Cripps	June 1970	Iain Macleod
October 1950	Hugh Gaitskell	July 1970	Anthony Barber
October 1951	'Rab' Butler	March 1974	Denis Healey
December 1955	Harold Macmillan	May 1979	Sir Geoffrey Howe
January 1957	Peter Thorneycroft	June 1983	Nigel Lawson
January 1958	Derick Heathcoat Amory	October 1989	John Major
July 1960	Selwyn Lloyd	November 1990	Norman Lamont
July 1962	Reginald Maudling	May 1993	Kenneth Clarke
October 1964	James Callaghan	May 1997	Gordon Brown

system 1875, it administered the rules of ◊equity as distinct from common law.

Chanctonbury Ring

Iron Age hillfort on the West Sussex Downs, England; situated 3 km/2 mi west of Steyning; height 250 m/820 ft. There are also the remains of two Roman buildings here.

Channel ferry

Ferry service carrying cars, passengers, and goods lorries across the English Channel between England and France and Holland. Several operators run roll-on/roll-off (ro-ro) ships, now in competition with the Channel Tunnel. The service began in World War I as a train ferry, constructed early in 1918 for the rapid movement of vehicles, tanks, guns, and trainloads of stores across the English Channel.

The key English ports from which ferries operate are Dover, Folkestone, Southampton, Portsmouth, Newhaven, and Harwich.

Channel 4

Britain's fourth national television channel, launched on 2 November 1982 as a wholly-owned subsidiary of the IBA (Independent Broadcasting Authority; now known as the ITC or ◊Independent Television Commission). Its brief was to serve minority interests, encourage innovation through the use of independent producers, and develop a character distinct from the other channels.

The company's financial involvement in film production, both at home and abroad, played a significant part in a revival of the fortunes of filmmaking in the UK. Films it has commissioned include *My Beautiful Laundrette* (1985), *Four Weddings and a Funeral* (1994), and *Trainspotting* (1996). It became a public broadcasting service in 1993. Channel 4 makes very few programmes, typically buying from external production companies. A separate company, S4C, serves Wales.

The first director of Channel 4 was Jeremy Isaacs, succeeded in 1989 by Michael Grade, who in turn was succeeded by Michael Jackson as chief executive in 1997.

Channel tunnel: chronology

1751 French farmer Nicolas Desmaret suggested a fixed link across the English Channel.

1802 French mining engineer Albert Mathieu-Favier proposed to Napoleon I a Channel tunnel through which horse-drawn carriages might travel. Discussions with British politicians ceased 1803 when war broke out between the two countries.

1842 De la Haye of Liverpool designed an underwater tube, the sections of which would be bolted together underwater by workers without diving apparatus.

1851 Hector Horeau proposed a tunnel that would slope down towards the middle of the Channel and up thereafter, so that the carriages would be propelled downhill by their own weight and for a short distance uphill, after which compressed air would take over as the motive power.

1857 A joint committee of British and French scientists approved the aim of constructing a Channel tunnel.

1875 Channel-tunnel bills were passed by the British and French parliaments.

1878 Borings began from the French and British sides of the Channel.

1882 British government forced abandonment of the project after public opinion, fearing invasion by the French, turned against the tunnel.

1904 Signing of the Entente Cordiale between France and the UK enabled plans to be reconsidered. Albert Sartiaux and Francis Fox proposed a twin-tunnel scheme.

1930–40 British prime minister Winston Churchill and the French government supported the digging of a tunnel.

1955 Defence objections to a tunnel were lifted in the UK by prime minister Harold Macmillan.

1961 Study Group plans for a double-bore tunnel presented to British government.

1967 British government invited tunnel-building proposals from private interests.

1975 British government cancelled project because of escalating costs.

1984 Construction of tunnel agreed in principle at Anglo-French summit.

1986 Anglo-French treaty signed; design submitted by a consortium called the Channel Tunnel Group accepted.

1987 Legislation completed, Anglo-French treaty ratified; construction started in Nov.

1990 First breakthrough of service tunnel took place in December.

1991 Breakthrough of first rail tunnel in May; the second rail tunnel was completed in June.

1994 6 May: The Queen and President Mitterrand officially inaugurated the Channel Tunnel. November: Limited commercial Eurostar services (for foot passengers) commenced. December: Limited commercial shuttle services (for cars) commenced.

1995 April: Eurotunnel chairman Alistair Morton warned of the risk of financial collapse. Cost of project reported at £8 billion. Complete service for cars started. September: Eurotunnel suspended interest payments on its £8 billion debt. November: The millionth car was carried through the tunnel.

1996 18 November: A fire broke out in a freight train injuring 34 people, and resulting in the tunnel being closed for repair.

1997 Passengers and freight services resumed fully.

Channel 5

Britain's fifth television channel. Launched on 30 March 1997, it was set up by the 1990 Broadcasting Act, under which the ◊Independent Television Commission (ITC) was required to create a fifth national channel. It was awarded by competitive tender in 1995 to Channel 5 Broadcasting Ltd, a consortium of companies including Pearson, owners of the *Financial Times*, and United News and Media, owners of the *Daily Express* and Anglia Television.

The ITC's aim in launching Channel 5 was to introduce more competition to the advertising market. Early indications were that the channel was to pitch at a downmarket audience. Its stated aim was to include seven hours of live broadcasting, and a feature film, each day, both of which targets were compatible with its low commissioning budget. Channel 5 is the first UK TV channel to display a continuously broadcast on-screen logo.

Channel Islands

Group of islands in the English Channel, off the northwest coast of France; they are a possession of the British crown. They comprise the islands of Jersey, Guernsey, Alderney, Great and Little Sark, with the lesser Herm, Brechou, Jethou, and Lihou.

Area 194 sq km/75 sq mi

Features very mild climate, productive soil; financially the islands are a tax haven

Industries farming, fishing, and tourism; flowers, early potatoes, tomatoes, butterflies, and dairy cattle are exported

Currency English pound, also local coinage

Population (1991) 145,600

Language official language French (◊Norman French) but English more widely used

Religion chiefly Christian

Government the main islands have their own parliaments and laws. Unless specially signified, the Channel Islands are not bound by British acts of Parliament, though the British government is responsible for defence and external relations

History originally under the duchy of Normandy, they are the only part still held by Britain. The islands came under the same rule as England 1066, and are dependent territories of the British crown. Germany occupied the islands June 1940–May 1945, the only British soil to be occupied by the Germans during World War II.

Channel swimming

Test of endurance first undertaken by Captain Matthew Webb (1848–1883) who swam across the English Channel from Dover to Calais 1875. His time was 21 hr 45 min for the 34 km/21 mi journey.

The current record is 7 hr 17 min by Chad Hundeby of the USA 1978. The first to swim nonstop in both directions was the Argentine Antonio Abertondo 1961. The Channel Swimming Association was formed 1927, and records exist for various feats; double crossing, most crossings, and youngest and oldest to complete a crossing.

Channel Tunnel

Tunnel built beneath the ◊English Channel, linking Britain (from just west of Dover) with mainland Europe. It comprises twin rail tunnels, 50 km/31 mi long and 7.3 m/24 ft in diameter, located 40 m/130 ft beneath the seabed. Construction began in 1987, and the French and English sections were linked in December 1990. It was officially opened on 6 May 1994. The shuttle train service, Le Shuttle, opened to lorries in May 1994 and to cars in December 1994. The tunnel's high-speed train service, Eurostar, linking London to Paris and Brussels, opened in November 1994. See chronology opposite.

The estimated cost of the tunnel has continually been revised upwards to a figure of £8 billion (1995). In 1995 Eurotunnel plc, the Anglo-French company that built the tunnel, made a loss of £925 million.

High-speed link

The contract to build the London–Dover high-speed rail link was awarded to the London and Continental Railways Consortium in February 1996. The link, due to be completed in 2003, would allow Eurostar trains to maintain their high speeds within Britain; under existing legislation, Eurostar trains that travel at up to 300 kph/186 mph in France are

CHANNEL TUNNEL *One of the two main rail tunnels that carry shuttle and Eurostar trains operated by British, French, and Belgian national railways beneath the English Channel. Channel Tunnel Group Ltd*

forced to slow to 80 kph/50 mph once in Britain. Transit time between London and Paris is 3 hours, and 2 hours 40 minutes between London and Brussels.

A fire broke out in a freight train in the tunnel on 18 November 1996, involving 34 people who were removed to safety.

Chantrey, Francis Legatt (1781–1841)

English sculptor. His portrait busts and monuments include celebrities of his time such as the Duke of Wellington, William Wordsworth, Walter Scott, Horatio Nelson, and George Washington. His unaffected studies of children were much loved in his day, notably *Sleeping Children* (1817; Lichfield Cathedral).

The **Chantrey Bequest** provides for the ◊Royal Academy of Arts to buy works of art for the nation, which are housed in the Tate Gallery, London. He was knighted in 1835.

Chapel Royal

A group of musicians and clergy serving the English monarch. Dating back at least to 1135, the Chapel Royal fostered some of England's greatest composers, especially prior to the 18th century, when many great musical works were religious in nature. Members of the Chapel Royal have included Tallis, Byrd, and Purcell.

There are chapels royal, in the sense of chapel buildings, at the former royal palaces of St James's, Hampton Court, the Tower of London (St John the Evangelist, and St Peter ad Vincula), and Windsor Castle (with a royal chapel also in Windsor Great Park), and a royal church at Sandringham, Norfolk.

Chaplin, Charlie (Charles Spencer) (1889–1977)

English film actor and director. One of cinema's most popular stars, he made his reputation as a tramp with a smudge moustache, bowler hat, and twirling cane in silent comedies, including *The Rink* (1916), *The Kid* (1921), and *The Gold Rush* (1925). His work combines buffoonery with pathos, as in *The Great Dictator* (1940) and *Limelight* (1952).

Chaplin was born in London and first appeared on the music-hall stage at the age of five. He joined Mack Sennett's Keystone Company in Los Angeles in 1913. Along with Mary Pickford, Douglas Fairbanks, and D W Griffith, Chaplin formed United Artists in 1919 as an independent company to distribute their films. His other films include *City Lights* (1931), *Modern Times* (1936), and *Monsieur Verdoux* (1947). *Limelight* (1952) was awarded an Academy Award for Chaplin's musical theme. When accused of communist sympathies during the Joe McCarthy witchhunt, he left the USA in 1952 and moved to Switzerland. He received special Academy Awards in 1928 and 1972, and was knighted in 1975.

Chapman, George (*c.* 1559–1634)

English poet and dramatist. His translations of the Greek epics of Homer (completed 1616) were the earliest in England; his plays include the comedy *Eastward Hoe* (with Ben ◊Jonson and John Marston) (1605) and the tragedy *Bussy d'Ambois* (1607).

Chard

Market town in Somerset, England, 19 km/12 mi southeast of Taunton; population (1991) 12,700. It is situated near the Devon border, on high ground between the Bristol and English Channels. Chard was the scene of a victory by the Parliamentary forces during the Civil War; Judge Jeffreys, the 'hanging judge', held one of his Bloody Assizes here in 1681.

Chard was the birthplace of John Stringfellow, inventor of a heavier-than-air flying machine, and of Margaret Bondfield, the first woman cabinet minister.

Charge of the Light Brigade

Disastrous attack by the British Light Brigade of cavalry against the Russian entrenched artillery on 25 October 1854 during the Crimean War at the Battle of Balaclava. Of the 673 soldiers who took part, there were 272 casualties. The Brigade was only saved from total destruction by French cavalry.

Charing Cross

District in Westminster, London, around Charing Cross railway station. It derives its name from the site of the last of 12 stone crosses erected by Edward I in 1290 at the resting-places of the coffin of his queen, Eleanor. The present cross was designed by A S Barry in 1865.

Charing Cross is regarded as the centre of London for the purposes of calculating distances from other towns.

Charity Commission

UK government body, established in 1993, that keeps a public register of all charities in the UK, gives information and advice to charity trustees and checks abuse. The Charity Commission does not itself have any funds to grant to charitable organizations. At the end of 1996 the number of registered charities was 181,824 with a combined income of around £18,000 million.

Charles, John (William John) (1931–)

Welsh footballer. The first British player to achieve fame in club football abroad, he scored 93 goals in 155 appearances for Juventus 1957–62, and gained three Italian championship and two Italian cup winner's medals. A tall broadly-built striker, renowned for his heading ability, his sense of sportsmanship earned him the nickname, the 'Gentle Giant'. He had made his Football League debut for Leeds United 1949 at the age of 17. Switching from centre-half to centre-forward 1951 he became a prolific goalscorer, and his 42 goals for Leeds in Division 2 in 1953–54 is still a club record. He won 38 Welsh caps, 1950–65, scoring 15 goals.

Charles

Two kings of Great Britain and Ireland:

Charles I (1600–1649)

King of Great Britain and Ireland from 1625, son of James I of England (James VI of Scotland). He accepted the petition of right in 1628 but then dissolved Parliament and ruled without a parliament 1629–40. His advisers were ◊Strafford and Laud, who persecuted the Puritans and provoked the Scots to revolt.

The ◊Short Parliament, summoned in April 1640, refused funds, and the ◊Long Parliament of later that year rebelled. Charles declared war on Parliament in 1642 but surrendered in 1646 and was beheaded in 1649. He was the father of Charles II.

Charles was born in Dunfermline, Scotland, and became heir to the throne on the death of his brother Henry in 1612. He married Henrietta Maria, daughter of Henry IV of France. Friction with Parliament began shortly after Charles succeeded his father. Charles dissolved the parliaments of 1625, 1626, and 1629. During his period of rule without parliament, Charles raised money by unpopular expedients, such as ◊ship money, while the ◊Star Chamber suppressed opposition. He caused unrest in 1637 by attempting to force a prayer book on the English model on Presbyterian Scotland. After the Short Parliament, the Scots advanced into England and forced their own terms on Charles. The Long Parliament declared extraparliamentary taxation illegal, abolished the Star Chamber, and voted that Parliament could not be dissolved without its own consent.

Confident that he had support among those who felt that Parliament was becoming too radical, Charles declared war on Parliament on 22 August by raising his standard at Nottingham (see ◊Civil War, English). Charles was defeated at the ◊Battle of Naseby, in June 1645. In May 1646 he surrendered to the Scots, who handed him over to Parliament in January 1647.

In November 1647 Charles escaped from Hampton Court Palace, where he had been confined by the army, but was recaptured and held at Carisbrooke Castle on the Isle of Wight. He was tried by a high court of justice set up by the House of Commons in January 1649, and was executed on the 30 January in front of the Banqueting House in Whitehall, London.

Charles II (1630–1685)

King of Great Britain and Ireland from 1660, when Parliament accepted the restoration of the monarchy after the collapse of Oliver Cromwell's Commonwealth; son of Charles I. His chief minister Edward ◊Clarendon, who arranged Charles's marriage in 1662 with Catherine of Braganza, was replaced in 1667 with the ◊Cabal of advisers. His plans to restore Catholicism in Britain led to war with the Netherlands 1672–74 in support of Louis XIV of France and a break with Parliament, which he dissolved in 1681. He was succeeded by James II.

During the Civil War, Charles lived with his father in Oxford 1642–45, and after the victory of Cromwell's Parliamentary forces he withdrew to France. Accepting the Covenanters' offer to make him king, he landed in Scotland in 1650, and was crowned at Scone on 1 January 1651. An attempt to invade England was ended 3 September by Cromwell's victory at Worcester. Charles escaped, and for nine years he wandered through Europe. In April Charles issued the Declaration of Breda, promising a general amnesty and freedom of conscience. Parliament accepted the Declaration and he was proclaimed king on 8 May 1660.

In 1673, Parliament forced Charles to withdraw the Declaration of Indulgence (which had suspended all penal laws against Catholics and Dissenters) and accept a Test Act excluding all Catholics from office. The following year Parliament forced the end of the Dutch War started in 1672. The Test Act was responsible for the end of the Cabal. In 1681 Charles summoned Parliament to Oxford, but dissolved it when compromises failed. He now ruled without a parliament, financed by Louis XIV. Charles was a patron of the arts and science, and had several mistresses.

Charles (Charles Philip Arthur George) (1948–)

Prince of the UK, heir to the British throne, and Prince of Wales since 1958 (invested 1969). He is the first-born child of Queen Elizabeth II and the Duke of Edinburgh. He studied at Trinity College, Cambridge, 1967–70, before serving in the Royal Air Force and Royal Navy. The first royal heir since 1660 to have an English wife, he married Diana, Princess of Wales (then Lady Diana Spencer), daughter of the 8th Earl Spencer, in 1981. There are two sons and heirs, William (1982–) and Henry (1984–). Amid much publicity,

PRINCE CHARLES *The heir to the British throne faces pressures unknown to previous generations of the Royal Family. Intense media interest has caused friction between Buckingham Palace and sections of the press. Charles supports a number of contemporary causes, such as organic farming, but will become king in a Britain where many question the role of monarchy in a modern democracy. Jiri Jiru/Rex*

Charles and Diana separated in 1992 and were divorced in 1996. Following the death of Diana, Princess of Wales in 1997 his popularity with the British public seemed in some doubt; however opinion polls in 1998 indicated that public feeling had warmed towards him and to his long-standing relationship with Camilla Parker Bowles(1946–).

His concern with social issues and environmental issues has led to many projects for the young and underprivileged, of which the Prince's Trust is the best known, and he has been outspoken on the subject of the unsympathetic features of contemporary architecture.

Charles Edward Stuart, the **Young Pretender** or **Bonnie Prince Charlie** (1720–1788)

British prince, grandson of James II and son of James, the Old Pretender. In the Jacobite rebellion of 1745 Charles won the support of the Scottish Highlanders; his army invaded England to claim the throne but was beaten back by the duke of ⇨Cumberland and routed at ⇨Culloden on 16 April 1746. Charles fled; for five months he wandered through the Highlands with a price of £30,000 on his head before escaping to France. He visited England secretly in 1750, and may have made other visits. In later life he degenerated into a friendless drunkard. He settled in Italy in 1766.

Charlton, Bobby (Robert) (1937–)

English footballer who between 1958 and 1970 scored a record 49 goals for England in 106 appearances. An elegant attacking midfield player who specialized in fierce long-range shots, he spent most of his playing career with Manchester United and played in the England team that won the World Cup 1966. He is the younger brother of Jack ⇨Charlton and the nephew of the Newcastle and England forward Jackie Milburn.

Charlton, Jack (John) (1935–)

English footballer. A tall commanding centre-half he spent all his playing career with Leeds United and played more than 750 games for them. He appeared in the England team that won the World Cup 1966. He is the older brother of Robert (Bobby) ⇨Charlton and the nephew of the Newcastle and England forward Jackie Milburn.

Charnwood Forest

Area of northwestern Leicestershire, England. It is no longer thickly wooded. An area of rocky outcrops, it lies over 120 m/400 ft above sea level, with its highest point at Bardon Hill (278 m/912 ft). The Leicestershire coalfields lie on the western and northwestern fringes, and the area is traversed from north to south by the M1 motorway.

In the forest are the remains of Ulverscroft Priory, founded about 1153. Also in the forest is the Cistercian Abbey of Mount St Bernard.

charter

Open letter recording that a grant of land or privileges had been made on a specific date, as in the ⇨Magna Carta. Witnesses either signed, made their mark, or affixed their seal. Based on the Roman **diploma**, the charter was reintroduced into Britain after the departure of the Romans to record donations of land to the Christian Church. These early charters were written in Latin, but from the 9th century charters were written in the vernacular; Latin again came into use after the Norman Conquest.

Charter 88

British political campaign begun in 1988, calling for a written constitution to prevent what it termed the development of 'an elective dictatorship', and for freedom of information and reform of the electoral register. Those who signed the charter, including many figures from the arts, objected to what they saw as the autocratic premiership of Margaret ⇨Thatcher.

They were consciously influenced by Charter 77, the human rights manifesto signed in communist Czechoslovakia by intelligentsia dissidents (including Václav Havel) in response to the 1975 Helsinki Agreements. Charter 88 was launched in a letter to *New Statesman* by 348, mostly Labour and Liberal Democrat party-leaning intellectuals. In 1998 it had 75,000 members and many of its ideas on modernizing the UK constitution were implemented by the 'New Labour' government.

Chartism

Radical British democratic movement, mainly of the working classes, which flourished around 1838–48. It derived its name from the People's Charter, a six-point programme comprising universal male suffrage, equal electoral districts, secret ballot, annual parliaments, and abolition of the property qualification for, and payment of, members of Parliament.

Two petitions were presented to Parliament (in 1839 and 1842), and were rejected. Under the leadership of Fergus O'Connor, Chartism became a powerful expression of working class frustration, and a third petition was presented in 1848. The long-term demise of the movement was probably due to greater prosperity among the populace as a whole, lack of organization, and rivalry among the leadership of the movement.

Chartwell

House near Westerham, Kent, England, bought by Winston ⇨Churchill in 1922, and where he lived, with the exception of the war years, until his death in 1965. He decided to sell the house after losing the 1945 General Election, but a group of close friends bought Chartwell and gave it to the National Trust on the understanding that he continued living there undisturbed during his lifetime.

Chatham

Town in Medway Towns unitary authority, southeast England, on the River Medway, between Rochester to the west and Gillingham to the east; population (1991) 71,700. Until 1998 the town was part of Kent. From 1985, as a focus of revival for the whole Medway area, the Royal Dockyard (1588–1984) was converted to an industrial area, marina, and museum, with part of the docks being preserved as the Chatham Historic Dockyard. The University of Greenwich has had a campus here since 1996. Industries include tourism, and the manufacture of electronics and cement.

Features
Chatham Historic Dockyard, covering a 34 ha/85-acre site, includes displays illustrating nautical crafts and the history of the yard. The Ropery, the dockyard's rope-making centre, is the longest brick building in the UK, extending for approximately 402 m/1,320 ft. The campus of the University of Greenwich was formerly HMS Pembroke, a Royal Navy training base for officers and ratings.
History
First established by Henry VIII, the dockyard was developed by Elizabeth I and, by the reign of Charles II, Chatham had become the largest naval base in England. Following an attack on the docks by Dutch ships in 1667, the defences were strengthened, firstly by guardships and booms and later by lines of fortification. The *Victory*, later the flagship of Admiral Nelson at the Battle of Trafalgar, was launched here in 1765. Fort Pitt was built in 1779 and the dockyards were further expanded during the Napoleonic Wars (1803–15). Chatham remained the principal naval dockyard in England in the 19th century. Charles Dickens lived at Chatham between 1817 and 1821 when his father worked in the naval offices, and the area is featured in many of his novels.

Chatsworth
House and seat of the dukes of Devonshire, 7 km/4 mi west of Chesterfield, Derbyshire, England. It was commenced by William Cavendish (1505–57). Chatsworth was gradually rebuilt in classical style from 1688 to 1707 by William, 1st Duke of Devonshire (1640–1707) with a curved north front. The courtyard plan of the Elizabethan house was retained, but a long wing was added by the 6th duke from 1820.

The house contains one of the world's finest collection of drawings, as well as outstanding picture and book collections. Joseph Paxton was gardener here, and some of his work remains.

It was here that Mary Queen of Scots was imprisoned under the care of the Earl of Shrewsbury.

Chatterton, Thomas (1752–1770)
English poet. His medieval-style poems and brief life were to inspire English Romanticism. Having studied ancient documents, he composed poems he ascribed to a 15th-century monk, 'Thomas Rowley', and these were at first accepted as genuine. Seeking a patron, he sent examples to the writer Horace ◊Walpole, who, after originally being taken in, was advised that they were forgeries. He committed suicide after becoming destitute. His death gripped the imagination of the Romantic poets and tributes were paid to his memory by Coleridge, Shelley, Keats, and Wordsworth. Chatterton's importance in English literature lies not in his use of terms from old glossaries, but in his command of rhythm and his breaking away from 18th-century conventions.

Chatwin, (Charles) Bruce (1940–1989)
English writer. His works include *The Songlines* (1987), written after living with Australian Aborigines; the novel *Utz* (1988), about a manic porcelain collector in Prague; and travel pieces and journalism collected in *What Am I Doing Here* (1989).

Chaucer, Geoffrey (*c.* 1340–1400)
English poet, the most influential English poet of the Middle Ages. *The ◊Canterbury Tales*, a collection of stories told by a group of pilgrims on their way to Canterbury, reveals his genius for metre and characterization, his knowledge of human nature, and his stylistic variety, from urbane and ironic to simple and bawdy. His *Troilus and Criseyde*, is a substantial narrative poem about the tragic betrayal of an idealized courtly love.

Chaucer presented English society as had never been done before, and he wrote in English rather than in French, the language of the court and of many of his originals. Thus he developed English as a literary medium, and in doing so ensured that the Southeast Midland dialect used in London was the one ultimately to become standard English.

His early work shows formal French influence, as in the dream-poem *The Book of the Duchess* and his adaptation of the French allegorical poem on courtly love, *The Romaunt of the Rose*. More mature works reflect the influence of Italian realism, as in *Troilus and Criseyde*, adapted from Boccaccio.

Chaucer was born in London, the son of a vintner. Taken prisoner in the French wars, he had to be ransomed by Edward III in 1360. In 1366 he married Philippa Roet, becoming in later life the brother-in-law of ◊John of Gaunt, Duke of Lancaster. He became justice of the peace for Kent in 1385 and knight of the shire in 1386. In 1389 he was made clerk of the king's works, and superintended undertakings at Woolwich and Smithfield. In 1391 he gave up the clerkship and accepted the position of deputy forester of North Petherton, Somerset in 1391. Late in 1399 he moved to Westminster and died the following year; he was buried in the Poets' Corner of Westminster Abbey.

Chaudhuri, Nirad Chandra (1897–)
Indian writer and broadcaster. He attracted attention with his *Autobiography of an Unknown Indian* (1950) which illuminates the clash of British and Indian civilizations. A first visit to England, previously known to him only through its literature, produced the quirky *A Passage to England* (1959). Later works include *The Continent of Circe* (1965), an erudite critique of Indian culture, and *Thy Hand Great Anarch* (1987), critical of the impact of British culture on India.

Cheapside (Old English *ceap*, 'barter')
Street running from St Paul's Cathedral to Poultry, in the City of London. Now a business district, it was the scene of the 13th-century 'Cheap', a permanent fair and chief general market in the city. The church of St Mary-le-Bow in Cheapside, designed by Christopher Wren, has the ◊Bow Bells.

Various side lanes were named after their services in the market, including Milk Street, Bread Street, and Wood Street, while Cheapside itself was a centre of the goldsmiths and silversmiths trade. In the Middle Ages Cheapside was the scene of ceremonies and pageants and a place of penance and punishment. Royal tournaments were held in the open ground on the northern side, the king and nobility watching from a balcony on Bow Church. An Eleanor Cross, erected by Edward I in memory of his wife, Eleanor of Castile, stood at the junction with Wood Street until its destruction by Parliament in 1643. Cheapside extends to the east as far as Poultry, formerly the poultry-selling area of the market, which was noted for its numerous inns before the Great Fire of London in 1666.

Cheapside suffered severely from bombing in World War II. The Mercers' and Saddlers' halls were destroyed, but have since been restored.

Cheddar

Village in Somerset, southwest England, in the Mendip Hills, 32 km/20 mi southwest of Bristol. It gives its name to Cheddar cheese, a hard variety first produced here around the beginning of the 12th century. Nearby are the limestone **Cheddar Gorge** and caves, owned by the National Trust. Tourism is important and the village is part of an agricultural, market-gardening, and strawberry-growing district.

Features

Cheddar Reservoir, about 3 km/2 mi in circumference, lies to the west of the village. Archaeological excavations have uncovered evidence of prehistoric, Stone Age, Saxon, and Roman occupation in the area. Roman lead-mines have been found on the Mendip Hills near Cheddar, and in 1962 the site of a Saxon palace was discovered nearby. The 10,000 year-old skeleton of Cheddar Man, who lived in the gorge at the end of the last Ice Age, is on display in the museum.

Cheddar Gorge and caves

Limestone cliffs rise to nearly 150 m/490 ft on either side of Cheddar Gorge; 274 steps known as Jacob's Ladder lead to the cliff-top. The caves beneath the gorge, including Gough's Cave and Cox's Cave, have complex and richly coloured stalactites and stalagmites. Stone Age communities are believed to have lived in Gough's Cave.

cheesemaking

Cheesemaking in Britain can be traced back to 2000 BC and the perforated curd strainers discovered on Bronze Age sites. The monks of the Middle Ages developed cheesemaking as an important way of preserving milk. Cheese became a largely uninterrupted staple of British dairy farms until 1933 when the creation of the Milk Marketing Board provided a dependable market for milk and this, together with wartime rationing, led to a decline in farmhouse cheesemaking.

The decline was nearly fatal as some cheeses came close to extinction. In their place came mass produced block and vacuum-packed cheese. The modern revival in British cheese dates to the imposition of EEC milk quotas which led dairy farmers to diversify again.

At the end of the 20th century there were some 1,000 British cheeses on the market, with new artisan cheesemakers producing some of the best and most distinctive cheese. They include Beenleigh Blue from Devon; Mary Holbrook's award-winning ewe and goat's milk cheeses; Keen, Quicke and Montgomery Cheddars; Appleby's Cheshire; Kirkham's Lancashire and Yorkshire's Richard III Wensleydale and Cotherstone.

The resurgence is also strong in the Celtic fringes from Cornish Yarg and Welsh Llangloffan to Scotland's Lanark Blue and Ireland's Cooleeney and Gubbeen. The best of modern British include Blue Stilton and Irish Cashel Blue; and soft cheeses such as Gedi Moillion goat's milk cheese. Rind washed cheeses such as Stinking Bishop and Tornegus are repeatedly washed in brine, wine or cider to give a soft texture and pungent flavour. The mould-ripened cheeses such as Bonchester and Milleens which are allowed to form a soft, bloomy rind like Camembert.

The best-selling British cheeses are those commercially produced in large-scale creameries. The most famous are still Cheddar, Cheshire, Lancashire, Wensleydale, Stilton, Double Gloucester, Derby, Red Leicester and Caerphilly. Geographic names can be deceptive, as most cheeses are also produced outside their region of origin. Uniquely, Stilton is protected by its own trade mark which prescribes the method of production and limits its manufacture to the counties of Leicestershire, Derbyshire, and Nottinghamshire.

CHEESEMAKING *Testing Wensleydale for maturity in a Yorkshire creamery. The 1980s and 1990s saw a revival in the art of farmhouse cheesemaking, and a wide variety of cheeses are now made from cow's, ewe's and goat's milk. Traditional British hard cheeses such as Cheddar, Lancashire, or Wensleydale have been supplemented by a range of soft-rind products. Roger Scruton/Collections*

Chelmsford

Market town and administrative headquarters of ◊Essex, southeast England, at the confluence of the Chelmer and Can rivers, 48 km/30 mi northeast of London; population (1991) 97,500. Corn and cattle are traded. Industries include agricultural services, radio communications, engineering, flour-milling, brewing, and the manufacture of electrical equipment, plastics, and soft drinks (Britvic).

It was the Roman **Caesaromagus**. In 1920 the first wireless-telegraph broadcasting service in the world was transmitted from Chelmsford by Marconi.

The Anglia Polytechnic University was established here in 1992; other campuses of the university are sited in Cambridge and Brentwood. The 15th-century Perpendicular church of St Mary the Virgin became a cathedral in 1914.

Chelsea

Historic area of the Royal Borough of Kensington and Chelsea, London, immediately north of the Thames where it is crossed by the Albert and Chelsea bridges.

The Royal Hospital was founded 1682 by Charles II for old and disabled soldiers, 'Chelsea Pensioners', and the National Army Museum, founded 1960, covers the history of the British and Commonwealth armies. The Physic Garden for botanical research was established in the 17th century; the home of the essayist Thomas Carlyle in Cheyne Row is a museum. The **Chelsea Flower Show** is held annually by the ⟡Royal Horticultural Society in the grounds of the Royal Hospital. Ranelagh Gardens (1742–1804) and Cremorne Gardens (1845–77) were popular places of entertainment.

Chelsea porcelain factory

Porcelain factory thought to be the first in England. Based in southwest London, it dated from the 1740s, when it was known as the Chelsea Porcelain Works. It produced softpaste porcelain in imitation of Chinese high-fired porcelain. Later items are distinguished by the anchor mark on the base. Chelsea porcelain includes plates and other items decorated with botanical, bird, and insect paintings.

The factory was taken over by William Duesbury of Derby in 1769 (after which the so-called 'Chelsea-Derby' was produced), and pulled down in 1784.

Cheltenham

Spa town at the foot of the Cotswold Hills, Gloucestershire, England, 12 km/7 mi northeast of Gloucester; population (1991) 91,300. The town has light industries including aerospace electronics and food-processing (Kraft). Tourism and the conference business are also important. Annual events include the Cheltenham Festival of Literature in October, the International Festival of Music, the National Hunt Festival in March, and the Cheltenham Cricket Festival (see ⟡Cheltenham Festival). The headquarters of Gulf Oil and the centre of the British government's electronic surveillance operations (⟡GCHQ) are here.

History

Cheltenham was a small village until the early 18th century. After the discovery of mineral spring water here in 1716, the only alkaline spring in the UK, the town gradually developed as a spa and fashionable health resort. A pump room was built in 1738 and the town was visited by George III in 1788. During the 19th century the town's education services were its main source of income.

Architecture

The town has much Georgian and Regency architecture, with avenues, squares, crescents, and terraces, reflecting the town's development as a fashionable spa.

Galleries and museums

Spa waters can still be taken at the domed Pittville Pump Room, which houses a museum displaying costumes and local history exhibits. The Art Gallery and Museum includes a collection of furniture, silver, and arts and crafts, and there are special exhibits for the blind. The former home of the composer Gustav Holst, who was born in Cheltenham in 1874, is now a museum. Prinknash Abbey, to the southwest, is a Benedictine house which produces pottery.

Educational institutions

A grammar school was founded here in 1576, Cheltenham College in 1841, and Cheltenham Ladies' College in 1853. The Universities and College Admission Service (UCAS) is based here.

Cheltenham Festival

The premier National Hunt fixture in British horse racing, known formally as the National Hunt Meeting. It has been held at Cheltenham Racecourse in Gloucestershire since 1910. The highlights of the three-day festival are the Cheltenham Gold Cup (first run 1924) and the Champion Hurdle (first run 1927).

Chemical Brothers

English pop group formed in 1989. Their 'big-beat' debut *Exit Planet Dust* (1995) combined elements of dub, techno, funk, and rock, and they reached number one in the UK with the single 'Setting Sun' and the album *Dig Your Own Hole* (1997).

Its members are Tom Rowlands (1971–) (keyboards) and Ed Simons (1970–) (keyboards).

Chepstow, Welsh Cas-Gerent

Market town in Monmouthshire, south Wales, on the River ⟡Wye near its junction with the Severn. The high tides, sometimes 15 m/50 ft above low level, are the highest in Britain. The Norman castle was possibly the first stone castle in Britain. The ruins of Tintern Abbey lie 6.5 km/4 mi to the north of the town. There are light industries, farming, and tourism.

The town lies on a slope between steep cliffs and is surrounded by beautiful scenery; it is a holiday centre for the Wye Valley and the Forest of Dean. The castle was built by William the Conqueror's friend, William FitzOsbern, starting in 1067; it sustained several sieges during the Civil War and is now in ruins. The remains of the town wall lead from the castle through the town. Brunel's 19th-century tubular suspension bridge across the Wye has been replaced by a modern structure.

Chequers, popular name for Chequers Court

Country home of the prime minister. It is an Elizabethan mansion in the Chiltern hills near Princes Risborough, Buckinghamshire, and was given to the nation by Lord Lee of

CHEPSTOW CASTLE *The site of Chepstow Castle, on an outcrop of rock overlooking the River Wye in Gwent, east Wales, was long considered of strategic importance and was fortified from prehistoric times. This great Norman castle has stood there since the 12th century. Corel*

Fareham under the Chequers Estate Act 1917, which came into effect in 1921.

The mansion dates from 1565 or earlier, but was extensively altered by Lord Lee. It contains a collection of Cromwell portraits and relics.

Cherwell

River in southern England. A tributary of the River Thames, it rises 19 km/12 mi northeast of Banbury, and flows south for 48 km/30 mi through Northamptonshire and Oxfordshire to join the main stream near Oxford.

Cheshire

County of northwest England, which has contained the unitary authorities Halton and Warrington since April 1998
Area 2,320 sq km/896 sq mi
Towns and cities ◊Chester (administrative headquarters), Crewe, Congleton, Macclesfield
Physical chiefly a fertile plain, with the Pennines in the east; rivers: Mersey, Dee, Weaver; a sandstone ridge extending south through central Cheshire together with Delamere Forest constitute a woodland and heath landscape
Features salt mines and geologically rich former copper workings at Alderley Edge (in use from Roman times until the 1920s); Little Moreton Hall; discovery of Lindow Man, the first 'bogman' to be found in mainland Britain, dating from around 500 BC; Museum of the Chemical Industry on Spike Island; Quarry Bank Mill at Styal is a cotton-industry museum
Agriculture arable farming in the north; cheese (at one time produced entirely in farmhouses) and dairy products in the centre and south of the county
Industries aerospace industry, chemicals, pharmaceuticals, salt, silk and textiles (at Congleton and Macclesfield), vehicles
Famous people the novelist Elizabeth Gaskell lived at Knutsford (the locale of *Cranford*); Charles Dodgson (Lewis Carroll)
Population (1995) 978,100.

Boundaries

Cheshire is bounded on the north by Warrington, Halton, Merseyside, and Greater Manchester; on the east by Derbyshire and Staffordshire; on the south by Shropshire; and on the west by Wrexham and Flintshire. The new unitary authority of Halton consists principally of the former Cheshire towns Widnes and Runcorn.

History

Chester was a Roman fortress. Many Cheshire towns were market centres serving large rural areas in which there were comparatively few villages. In Nantwich there is a splendid 14th-century church, and also many houses from the Tudor and Georgian periods. Sandbach has two Saxon crosses and many villages have handsome churches, almost all built in the local red sandstone. From the Norman Conquest to the Tudor period Cheshire was a county palatine (an area under an overlord that did not send representatives to Parliament).

Cheshire, (Geoffrey) Leonard (1917–1992)

English pilot and philanthropist. Commissioned into the Royal Air Force on the outbreak of World War II, he was decorated several times. A devout Roman Catholic, he founded the first **Cheshire Foundation Home** for the Incurably Sick in 1948.

He won the Victoria Cross, Distinguished Service Order (with 2 bars), and Distinguished Flying Cross. In 1945 he was an official observer at the dropping of the atom bomb on Nagasaki. Baron 1991.

In 1998 there were over 200 Cheshire Homes in about 45 countries and the Ryder-Cheshire foundation supported projects in several countries.

Chesil Beach (Anglo-Saxon *ceosil*, 'pebble-bank')

Shingle bank extending 18 mi/29 km along the coast of Dorset, England, from Bridport in the west to the Isle of Portland in the east.

Chesil Beach connects Portland with the mainland and encloses a tidal lagoon known as the Fleet. At the Portland end the bank is about 13 m/43 ft above high water mark, and 183 m/600 ft broad. The pebbles gradually decrease in size from east to west; they are 2.5– 7.5 cm/1–3 in in diameter at Portland and reach the size of peas at Bridport. At the western end of the Fleet is the Abbotsbury swannery, a wetland reserve for a breeding herd of mute swans.

The bank was formed 10,000 years ago at the end of the last glacial period, when the rise in sea level and large waves from the southwest pushed vast quantities of rock debris and sediments inshore.

The whole area of Chesil Beach and the Fleet is proposed for designation as a protected site under the European Union's habitats directive.

Chester

City and administrative headquarters of ◊Cheshire, England, on the River Dee 26 km/16 mi south of Liverpool; population (1991) 80,100; Chester urban area 89,629. There are engineering, aerospace (airbus), metallurgical, and clothing industries, and car components are manufactured. It is a centre of trade and commerce, and tourism is also important.

Chester was the site of **Deva**, a Roman legionary fortress, and remains include the largest stone-built military Roman amphitheatre to have been discovered in Britain. The town has a medieval centre and the most complete city walls in England, extending for 3 km/2 mi. Other features include the cathedral, dating from the 11th century, and the 'Rows', half-timbered shops with continuous galleried footwalks at first-floor level, dating from the medieval period.

The city hosts one of the four surviving mystery play cycles performed in the UK, the others taking place at Coventry, Wakefield (or Townley), and York. Chester Zoo is the largest in area in the country, spreading over 324 ha/80 acres; a National Pondlife Centre is planned there, to mark the millennium.

History

The Roman fortress was constructed some time between AD 70 and 79 on a sandstone bluff beside an easy crossing place of the Dee; it commanded the route to North Wales. The fort was abandoned in the late 4th century. Chester became an important town in Saxon times. It did not submit to the Normans until William (I) the Conqueror gave it to his nephew Hugh Lupus in 1070. From this time, until it reverted to the crown in 1237, Chester was ruled by a succession of earls as a ◊county palatine (a county whose lord exercised some of the roles usually reserved for the monarch).

In the medieval period it was a major centre and port for trade with Ireland, although its importance declined when the Dee estuary began to silt up and traffic transferred to Liverpool. During the English Civil War Chester suffered a two-year siege by the Parliamentarians. The city prospered during the 19th century when the development of the railway network made it an important trading centre once more.

Roman remains

The rectangular town grid planned by the Romans still survives with little modification. Parts of the Roman walls remain and many Roman relics are displayed in the Grosvenor Museum. The Deva Roman Experience museum also includes archaeological finds. It is thought that the excavated Roman amphitheatre, built in about AD 100, would have seated about 8,000 people.

Chesterfield

Market town in Derbyshire, central England, on the River Rother, to the east of the Peak District National Park, 40 km/25 mi north of Derby; population (1991) 71,900. Industries include iron-founding, engineering, and the manufacture of chemicals, pottery, and glass. Extensive coalfields are mined to the southeast.

The locomotive engineer George Stephenson is buried in Trinity Church. All Saints' Church, dating from the 14th century, is renowned for its twisted 69 m/228 ft tall spire which leans nearly 3 m/9.5 ft from the true centre.

Chesters

Park containing the site of the Roman station of **Cilurnum**, on the banks of the North Tyne near Chollerford in Northumberland, England. Cilurnum is one of the most important forts of ◊Hadrian's Wall, since 1987 a World Heritage Site. It was a garrison for 500 troops. The fort site is managed by English Heritage.

Remains of its gateway and streets can still be seen, and its military bathhouse, between the fort and the river, is well preserved. Much excavation work has been carried out. A collection of Roman artefacts is housed in a museum in the park of Chesters.

In 1832 the estate of Chesters was inherited by the classical scholar John Clayton, who carried out important archaeological investigations at the site.

Chesterton, G(ilbert) K(eith) (1874–1936)

English novelist, essayist, and poet. He wrote numerous short stories featuring a Catholic priest, Father Brown, who solves crimes by drawing on his knowledge of human nature. Other novels include the fantasy *The Napoleon of Notting Hill* (1904) and *The Man Who Was Thursday* (1908), a deeply emotional allegory about the problem of evil.

He was also active as a political essayist, and with the writer Hilaire ◊Belloc advocated a revolt against capitalism in the direction opposite to socialism by discouraging big business.

Cheviot

Breed of hardy, medium-wool, white-faced, hornless sheep developed in the Cheviot Hills in the border region of Scotland and England. The wool of their fleece is straight, moderately long, close set, and free of black fibre. The breed is frequently used in crossbreeding.

Before the Roman came to Rye or out to Severn strode, / The rolling English drunkard made the rolling English road.

G K CHESTERTON English novelist, essayist, and poet.
The Rolling English Road (1914)

Cheviot Hills

Range of hills, 56 km/35 mi long, mainly in Northumberland but also extending into the Scottish Borders; they form the border between England and Scotland for some 48 km/30 mi. The Cheviots lie between the Pennines and the Southern Uplands ranges. The highest point is the **Cheviot** at 816 m/2,676 ft. For centuries the region was a battleground between the English and the Scots. The area gives its name to a breed of white-faced sheep.

The range lies in the northern part of the Northumberland National Park. In the 1920s and 1930s a major afforestation scheme was carried out, mainly over areas to the northwest, and this became a national forest park in 1955.

The Cheviots are thinly populated, largely grassy, and used for sheep grazing. Other peaks include Cairn Hill reaching 776 m/2,546 ft; Hedgehope Hill, 716 m/2,349 ft; Windy Gyle, 621 m/2,037 ft; Peel Fell, 602 m/1,975 ft; and Carter Fell, 553 m/1,814 ft. Rivers rising in the range include the North Tyne, feeding the Kielder reservoir, and the River Rede.

The centre of the Cheviot is formed of granite surrounded by andesitic lavas of Old Red Sandstone age.

Chichester

City and market town and administrative headquarters of ◊West Sussex, southern England, 111 km/69 mi southwest of London; population (1991) 27,100. It lies in an agricultural area, and has a harbour. It was a Roman town, **Noviomagus Regnensium**, and the nearby remains of ◊Fishbourne Palace (about AD 80) is one of the finest Roman archeological sites outside Italy.

It has a cathedral which is mainly Norman, and the Chichester Festival Theatre (1962). Chichester has become a cultural centre, with an annual arts festival in July. Goodwood Park racecourse is nearby to the north.

Chichester, Francis Charles (1901–1972)

English sailor and navigator. In 1931 he made the first east–west crossing of the Tasman Sea in *Gipsy Moth*, and in 1966–67 circumnavigated the world in his yacht *Gipsy Moth IV*. KBE 1967.

child abuse

A local authority can take abused children away from their parents by obtaining a care order from a juvenile court under the Children's and Young Persons Act 1969 (replaced by the Children's Act 1989). Controversial methods of diagnosing sexual abuse led to a public inquiry in Cleveland, England 1988, which severely criticized the handling of such cases. The standard of proof required for criminal proceedings is greater than that required for a local authority to take children into care. This has led to highly publicized cases where children have been taken into care but prosecutions have eventually not been brought, as in Rochdale, Lancashire, and the Orkneys, Scotland in 1990.

In 1996 there were an estimated 8,000 children in residential care in England and Wales, costing approximately £1,500 per week for each child. Some are in council-run homes, others are in private homes; abuses have been revealed in both sectors.

Childers, (Robert) Erskine (1870–1922)

British civil servant and, from 1921, Irish Sinn Féin politician, author of the spy novel *The Riddle of the Sands* (1903).

Before turning to Irish politics, Childers was a clerk in the House of Commons in London. In 1921 he was elected to the Irish Parliament as a supporter of the Sinn Féin leader de Valera, and took up arms against the Irish Free State in 1922. Shortly afterwards he was captured, court-martialled, and shot by the Irish Free State government of William T Cosgrave. His son, Erskine Hamilton Childers (1905–74) was Irish president from 1973.

Childline

Charity set up in 1986 providing a special telephone number which children who are being physically or sexually abused can ring for confidential help or advice.

children's literature

Works of prose or verse specifically written for children. The earliest known illustrated children's book in English is *Goody Two Shoes* (1765), possibly written by Oliver Goldsmith. Early children's stories were written with a moral purpose; this was particularly true in the 19th century, apart from the unique case of Lewis Carroll's ◊*Alice* books. The late 19th century was the great era of children's literature in the UK, with Lewis ◊Carroll, Beatrix ◊Potter, Charles ◊Kingsley, and J M ◊Barrie. It was also a golden age of illustrated children's books, with such artists as Kate ◊Greenaway and Randolph Caldecott.

Adventure stories have often appealed to children even when these were written for adults; examples include *Robinson Crusoe* by Daniel Defoe and the satirical *Gulliver's Travels* by Jonathan Swift.

Among the most popular children's writers in the early 20th century were Kenneth Grahame (*The Wind in the Willows*, 1908) and A A Milne (*Winnie the Pooh* 1926). Richmal ◊Crompton introduced the character of ◊William in 1922, and in 1942 Enid ◊Blyton introduced her 'Famous Five' series and produced many more bestselling works of escapist fiction.

Since the end of World War II, paperback sales have increased and many children's libraries have been established, encouraging writers to explore new areas. Many children's writers have been influenced by J R R ◊Tolkien, whose *The Hobbit* (1937) and its sequel, the three-volume *Lord of the Rings* (1954–55), are set in the comprehensively imagined world of Middle Earth. C S ◊Lewis produced the allegorical chronicles of ◊*Narnia*, including *The Lion, the Witch and the Wardrobe* (1950). Rosemary Sutcliff's *The Eagle of the Ninth* (1954), Philippa Pearce's *Tom's Midnight Garden* (1958), and Penelope Lively's *The Wild Hunt of Hagworthy* (1971) are other outstanding books by children's authors who have exploited a perennial fascination with time travel. Recently, more realistic stories for teenagers have included *Junk* (1996) by Melvin Burgess.

Writers for younger children combining stories and illustrations of equally high quality include Janet and Allan Ahlberg (including *The Jolly Postman*, 1986), Quentin Blake (including *Mr Magnolia* 1980), Shirley Hughes (including *Dogger*, 1977), and Raymond Briggs (*The Snowman*, 1979).

In recent years sales of books for young children such as the 'Thomas the Tank Engine' series, which began with *The Three Railway Engines* (1945), by Rev W V Awdry, the 'Postman Pat' series by John Cunliffe, and 'Spot' by Eric Hill, have increased with the popularity of associated television series, videos, and products.

Chiltern Hills

Range of chalk hills extending for some 72 km/45 mi in a curve from a point north of Reading to the Suffolk border. Coombe Hill, near Wendover, 260 m/852 ft high, is the highest point.

Chiltern Hundreds, stewardship of

A nominal office of profit under the crown. British members of Parliament may not resign; therefore, if they wish to leave office during a Parliament, they may apply for this office, a formality that disqualifies them from being an MP. There were originally two further offices, the stewardship of the manors of East Hundred and Hempholme, but these have not been used since the middle of the 19th century.

chintz

Printed fabric, usually glazed, popular for furnishings. In England in the late 16th and 17th centuries the term was used for Indian painted and printed cotton fabrics (calicos) and later for European printed fabrics.

Chintz had become so popular by the early 18th century that in 1722 Parliament legislated against its importation and manufacture, to protect the British silk and wool industries. The legislation against manufacture was repealed in 1744. In the mid-19th century chintz was superseded by a stronger fabric, cretonne, but it has become popular again for soft furnishings.

Chippendale, Thomas (1718–1779)

English furniture designer. He set up his workshop in St Martin's Lane, London, in 1753. His trade catalogue *The Gentleman and Cabinet Maker's Director* (1754), was a significant contribution to furniture design, and the first of its type to be published. Although many of his most characteristic designs are Rococo, he also employed Louis XVI, Chinese, Gothic, and Neo-Classical styles. He worked mainly in mahogany, newly introduced from South America.

Chippendale's work is characterized by solidity without heaviness; his ribbon-backed chairs are perhaps his most notable work, followed by his settees of two or three conjoined chairs. His business was carried on by his eldest son, Thomas (1749–1822), until 1813.

Chippenham

Town in north Wiltshire, England; population (1991) 21,500. It is situated 20 km/12 mi northeast of Bath and 35 km/22 mi east of Bristol. A bridge with 21 arches crosses the River Avon here. The main industries are meat- and milk-processing, engineering, and electronics. Chippenham was once a centre for the making of broadcloth.

There is a Georgian church designed by John Wood the Younger and dating from 1779 at nearby Hardenhuish. Chippenham was formerly occupied by the Saxon kings of Wessex, and King Alfred was forced to flee the town when surprised by the Danes.

Lodowicke Muggleton, founder of the Muggletonians, a group of 17th-century radical religious dissidents, is said to have been born in Chippenham.

Chislehurst

Part of the Greater London borough of Bromley, England; population (1991) 14,900. A extensive system of subterranean caves is found here. The origin of the caves is uncertain, but they are believed to be ancient storehouses and hiding-places. The caves were used for shelter from air-raids during World War II.

Cholmondeleys

British all-female dance company founded 1984 by Lea Anderson, its chief choreographer and dancer. The group specializes in short, dry-humoured pieces characterized by a sharp and quirky movement style. *Baby, Baby, Baby* (1985), a pastiche of 1960s pop girl groups, illustrates their deadpan approach. Other more serious pieces include *No Joy*, an exploration of human behaviour that uses sign language.

The all-male counterpart, also founded by Lea Anderson (1988), is called the Featherstonehaughs (pronounced 'fan-shaws').

Chorley

Industrial town in south Lancashire, England; population (1991) 33,500. It is situated 32 km/20 mi northwest of

Manchester on the road to Preston. The former cotton mills are now used for a variety of industries, including paper, medical supplies, plastics, furniture, and carpets.

Astley Hall, a 16th-century house with many later additions, is set in an attractive park 1.6 km/1 mi west of the town centre.

Christchurch

Resort town in Dorset, southern England, at the junction of the Stour and Avon rivers, 8 km/5 mi east of Bournemouth; population (1991) 36,400. Industries include seasonal tourism, and the manufacture of plastics and electronics. The Norman and Early English Holy Trinity church is the longest parish church in England, extending for 95 m/312 ft. The church contains a monument to the poet Percy Bysshe Shelley. North of Holy Trinity are the ruins of a Norman castle, built in Henry I's reign. Christchurch is noted for salmon fishing and sailing. Nearby to the south is Hengistbury Head, a nature reserve.

Christian, Fletcher (*c.* 1764–*c.* 1794)

English seaman who led the mutiny on HMS *Bounty* in 1789.

Christian Aid

Charity, founded in 1945, that raises funds for practical aid and relief operations in developing countries.

Christie, Agatha (Mary Clarissa) born Miller (1890–1976)

English detective novelist. She is best known for her ingenious plots and for the creation of the characters Hercule Poirot and Miss Jane Marple. She wrote more than 70 novels, including *The Murder of Roger Ackroyd* (1926) and *The Body in the Library* (1942). Her play *The Mousetrap*, which opened in London in 1952, is the longest continuously running show in the world.

Her first crime novel, *The Mysterious Affair at Styles* (1920), introduced the Belgian detective Hercule Poirot. She often broke purist rules, as in *The Murder of Roger Ackroyd* in which the narrator is the murderer. She was at her best writing about domestic murders in the respectable middle-class world. A number of her books have been filmed, for example *Murder on the Orient Express* (1934) (filmed in 1975).

Under the name Mary Westmacott she wrote several successful romantic novels. DBE 1971.

Christie, Julie (Frances) (1940–)

British film actress, born in Chukua, Assam, India. She made her name in John Schlesinger's *Billy Liar* (1963), reuniting with the same director for *Darling* (1965), in which she gave an Academy Award-winning performance, and *Far from the Madding Crowd* (1967). She confirmed her status as an international star as Lara in David Lean's adaptation of *Dr Zhivago* (1965).

In Nicolas Roeg's cult thriller *Don't Look Now* (1973), she starred opposite Donald Sutherland. She made a trio of films with Warren Beatty: *McCabe and Mrs Miller* (1971) (for which she received her second Academy Award nomination), *Shampoo* (1975), and *Heaven Can Wait* (1978). Recent films include *Hamlet* (1996) and *Afterglow* (1997), for which she earned a further Academy Award nomination.

Christie, Linford (1960–)

Jamaican-born British sprinter who, with his win in the 1993 world championships, became the first track athlete ever to hold World, Olympic, European, and Commonwealth 100-metres titles simultaneously.

He has won more medals in major events than any other athlete in British athletics history. His time of 9.87 seconds was, in 1993, the second-fastest time ever recorded for a 100-metre sprinting event.

Christie's

English fine-art saleroom, the oldest in the world, founded in 1766 by Australian-born auctioneer James Christie. The sales of paintings that the firm held during the 18th and 19th centuries were the basis for the present collections in museums worldwide, including those in Berlin, Boston, Leningrad, and London. Christie's has overseas branches internationally, and, in addition to the daily sales in London, sales are held several times a year in its branches in Geneva, Rome, Amsterdam, Sydney, and Montreal.

Another facet of Christie's work were the 'Studio' sales of famous artists such as Joshua Reynolds, Edwin Henry Landseer, Henry Raeburn, Dante Gabriel Rossetti, Edward Burne-Jones, and John Singer Sargent, and Augustus John.

James Christie was born in Perth in 1730; he became a midshipman in the Royal Navy, but resigned his commission before he was 20 and became an auctioneer in Covent Garden, London. At the age of 33 he set up on his own in modest rooms in Pall Mall, moving in 1779 to 125 Pall Mall, next door to the painter Thomas Gainsborough.

Christmas

Anniversary of the birth of Christ, celebrated on 25 December, though it is unlikely that this was the actual date of Jesus' birth. The day is traditionally spent with family and friends, and marked by present-giving, a practice that can be traced back to the Romans; eating a special **Christmas dinner**, usually roast turkey followed by **Christmas pudding**; and, often, watching television and playing family games. Children are particularly indulged. The day after Christmas is Boxing Day, which may be named after the practice of opening charity boxes hung in churches, to distribute the contents to the poor. This ceased in the early 19th century.

The custom of decorating houses and churches is probably pagan in origin, though the idea of bringing into the house and decorating a **Christmas tree** came from Germany in the reign of Queen Victoria. **Christmas cards**, exchanged in the weeks before Christmas, were introduced in 1846. **Father Christmas**, who supposedly comes down the chimney and places gifts in the children's stockings hanging by the fireplace or at the end of the bed, has a parallel in every European country. **Christmas carols** and the image of the **manger** (attributed to Francis of Assisi) date from the Middle Ages. The beginning of the celebration of Christmas cannot be dated.

Christmas truce

In World War I, unofficial cessation of hostilities between British and German troops in the front lines on Christmas Day 1914.

Soldiers of both sides emerged from their trenches and fraternized in 'No Man's Land', exchanging food and drinks, playing football and singing carols. They then returned to their trenches but no shots were exchanged for the rest of the day.

Church Army

Religious organization within the Church of England founded in 1882 by Wilson Carlile (1847–1942), an industrialist converted after the failure of his textile firm, who became a cleric in 1880. Originally intended for evangelical and social work in the London slums, it developed along Salvation Army lines, and has done much work among ex-prisoners and for the soldiers of both world wars.

Churchill, Caryl (1938–)

English dramatist. Her plays include the innovative and feminist *Cloud Nine* (1979) and *Top Girls* (1982), a study of the hazards encountered by 'career' women throughout history; *Serious Money* (1987), which satirized the world of London's brash young financial brokers; and *Mad Forest* (1990), set in Romania during the overthrow of the Ceauşescu regime. Recent works include a translation of Seneca's *Thyestes*, and *The Skriker* (both 1994).

Churchill, Lord Randolph Henry Spencer (1849–1895)

British Conservative politician, chancellor of the Exchequer and leader of the House of Commons in 1886; father of Winston Churchill.

Born at Blenheim Palace, son of the 7th duke of Marlborough, he entered Parliament in 1874. In 1880 he formed a Conservative group known as the Fourth Party with Drummond Wolff (1830–1908), J E Gorst, and Arthur Balfour, and in 1885 his policy of Tory democracy was widely accepted by the party. In 1886 he became chancellor of the Exchequer, but resigned within six months because he did not agree with the demands made on the Treasury by the War Office and the Admiralty. In 1874 he married Jennie Jerome (1854–1921), daughter of a wealthy New Yorker.

Churchill, Winston (Leonard Spencer) (1874–1965)

British Conservative politician, prime minister 1940–45 and 1951–55. In Parliament from 1900, as a Liberal until 1923, he held a number of ministerial offices, including First Lord of

CHURCHILL, WINSTON *The British politician Winston Churchill had an eventful early career as a war correspondent before entering Parliament. It is as premier of a coalition government during World War II that he is best remembered; his pugnacious attitude and defiant, rousing radio broadcasts typified the nation's 'bulldog spirit' when Britain stood alone in Europe against Nazi Germany. Rex*

the Admiralty 1911–15 and chancellor of the Exchequer 1924–29. Absent from the cabinet in the 1930s, he returned in September 1939 to lead a coalition government 1940–45, negotiating with Allied leaders in World War II to achieve the unconditional surrender of Germany in 1945; he led a Conservative government 1951–55. He received the Nobel Prize for Literature in 1953.

He was born at Blenheim Palace, Woodstock, Oxfordshire, the elder son of Lord Randolph Churchill. Educated at Harrow and Sandhurst, he joined the army 1895. In the dual role of soldier and military correspondent he served in the Spanish-American War in Cuba, and then in India, Egypt, and South Africa, where he made a dramatic escape from imprisonment in Pretoria.

In 1900 he was elected Conservative member of Parliament for Oldham, but he disagreed with Joseph Chamberlain's tariff-reform policy and joined the Liberals. In 1906 he won Northwest Manchester for the Liberals. He had in the meantime been appointed undersecretary of state for the colonies in the Henry Campbell-Bannerman administration. Herbert Asquith made Churchill president of the Board of Trade 1908, where he introduced legislation for the establishment of labour exchanges. As home secretary 1910, he lost much of his previously won reputation as a radical by his action in sending in the military to aid police against rioting miners in Tonypandy, south Wales.

> *The British are unique in this respect: they are the only people who like to be told how bad things are, who like to be told the worst.*
>
> WINSTON CHURCHILL British Conservative prime minister.
> Speech, Guildhall, 1921

In 1911 Asquith appointed Churchill First Lord of the Admiralty, a position he still held on the outbreak of World War I. He devised an ill-fated plan to attack the Dardanelles 1915 in order to relieve pressure on the Russians fighting Turkish troops in the Caucasus. The disaster of the Dardanelles expedition brought political attacks on Churchill that led to his demotion to the Duchy of Lancaster and to his resignation later that year. In 1915–16 he served in the trenches in France, but then resumed his parliamentary duties and was minister of munitions under David Lloyd George 1917, when he was concerned with the development of the tank. After the armistice he was secretary for war 1918–21 and then as colonial secretary played a leading part in the establishment of the Irish Free State. During the postwar years he was active in support of the Whites (anti-Bolsheviks) in Russia.

During the period 1922–24 Churchill was out of Parliament. He left the Liberals 1923, and was returned for Epping as a Conservative 1924. Baldwin made him chancellor of the Exchequer, and he brought about Britain's return to the gold standard. During the General Strike of May 1926, Churchill edited the government newspaper the *British Gazette* and was prominent in the defeat of the strike. He was out of office 1929–39, and as a back-bench MP he disagreed with the Conservatives on India (he was opposed to any abdication of British power), rearmament (he repeatedly warned of the rate of German rearmament and Britain's unpreparedness), and Neville Chamberlain's policy of appeasement.

On the first day of World War II he went back to his old post at the Admiralty. In May 1940 he was called to the premiership as both prime minister and defence minister at the head of an all-party administration, and made a much-quoted 'blood, tears, toil, and sweat' speech to the House of Commons. He had a close relationship with US president Roosevelt, and in August 1941 concluded the Atlantic Charter with him. He travelled to Washington, DC; the Casablanca Conference, Morocco; Cairo, Egypt; Moscow, USSR; and the Tehran Conference, Iran, meeting the other leaders of the Allied war effort. He met Stalin and Roosevelt in the Crimea at the Yalta Conference February 1945 to draw up plans for the final defeat of Germany and for its occupation and control after its unconditional surrender.

The coalition government was dissolved 23 May 1945, and Churchill formed a caretaker government drawn mainly from the Conservatives. In June he went to the Potsdam Conference in Germany to discuss the final stages of the war. He was already worried by Soviet intentions in Eastern Europe, the 'iron curtain descending' as he later described it. But he could have no part in the eventual decisions of the conference, because in July his government was defeated in a general election and he had to return to Britain. He became leader of the opposition until the election October 1951, in which he again became prime minister until his resignation April 1955.

His peacetime government saw an apparent abatement of the Cold War, and a revival in the country's economy. There was, however, little progress towards the united Europe of which Churchill had proclaimed himself an advocate. He remained in Parliament as MP for Woodford until the dissolution 1964.

His home from 1922, Chartwell in Kent, is a museum. His books include a six-volume history of World War II (1948–54) and a four-volume *History of the English-Speaking Peoples* (1956–58).

The British government agreed in 1995 to pay Winston Churchill's family £13.25 million for his pre-1945 writings, the Chartwell papers. The offer followed a long-running legal battle to prevent the possible sale of the papers to a US university. Knight of the Garter 1953.

Churchill tank

British heavy tank of World War II. First designed in 1940 for trench-crossing and infantry support, it was later modified, and the resulting model, though officially called the A22, was known as the 'Churchill' as a morale-raising measure. As well as proving to be an effective battle tank, it also provided the basis for conversion into specialist vehicles.

Church in Wales

The Welsh Anglican church; see ⇨Wales, Church in.

Church of England

Established form of Christianity in England, a member of the Anglican Communion. It was dissociated from the Roman Catholic Church in 1534 under Henry VIII; the British monarch is still the supreme head of the Church of England today. The service book is the Book of ◊Common Prayer.

The Church of England suffered its largest annual decline in Sunday service attendance for 20 years in 1995, according to the annual Church Statistics report. The average attendance was 1,045,000 – a drop of 36,000 from 1994.

In November 1992 the General Synod of the Church of England voted in favour of the ordination of women, and the first women priests were ordained in England in 1994. By 1998 there were some 860 stipendiary women clergy (see feature on the Ordination of Women Priests on page 180).

Organization

Two archbishops head the provinces of Canterbury and York, which are subdivided into bishoprics (see Archbishop of ◊Canterbury for a full list of appointees since Augustine). The Church Assembly (established in 1919) was replaced in 1970 by a **General Synod** with three houses (bishops, other clergy, and laity) to regulate church matters, subject to Parliament and the royal assent. A **Lambeth Conference** (first held in 1867), attended by bishops from all parts of the Anglican Communion, is held every ten years and presided over in London by the archbishop of Canterbury. It is not legislative but its decisions are often put into practice. The **Church Commissioners** for England (dating from 1948) manage the assets of the church and endowment of livings.

Main groups

The main parties, all products of the 19th century, are: the **Evangelical** or **Low Church**, which maintains the church's Protestant character; the **Anglo-Catholic** or **High Church**, which stresses continuity with the pre-Reformation church and is marked by ritualistic practices, the use of confession, and maintenance of religious communities of both sexes; and the **Liberal** or **Modernist** movement, concerned with the reconciliation of the church with modern thought. There is also the **Pentecostal Charismatic** movement, emphasizing spontaneity and speaking in tongues.

> *As for the British churchman, he goes to church as he goes to the bathroom, with the minimum of fuss and with no explanation if he can help it.*
>
> RONALD BLYTHE English writer.
> *Age of Illusion* (1963)

Church of Scotland

Established form of Christianity in Scotland, first recognized by the state in 1560. It is based on the Protestant doctrines of the reformer Calvin and governed on Presbyterian lines.

History

The church went through several periods of episcopacy (government by bishops) in the 17th century, and those who adhered to episcopacy after 1690 formed the Episcopal Church of Scotland, an autonomous church in communion with the Church of England. In 1843 there was a split in the Church of Scotland (the Disruption), in which almost a third of its ministers and members left and formed the ◊Free Church of Scotland. By an Act of Union of 3 October 1929 the Church of Scotland was united with the United Free Church of Scotland to form the United Church of Scotland. There are over 680,000 members of the Church of Scotland (1998).

Government

The government of the Church of Scotland is by kirk sessions, presbyteries, synods, and the General Assembly, the supreme court. The kirk session consists of the parish minister and ruling elders, elected by the congregation. The presbyteries consist of all parish ministers in a specified district, with one ruling elder from every congregation. The provincial synods, of which there are 12, comprise three or more presbyteries. The presbyteries elect the two commissioners who sit in the General Assembly.

Cibber, Colley (1671–1757)

English actor, dramatist, and poet. He wrote numerous plays, such as *Love's Last Shift, or The Fool in Fashion* (1696) and *The Careless Husband* (1705), and acted in many parts. In 1709 he became a joint proprietor of the Drury Lane Theatre, London, and was the first manager to run a theatre on strictly business lines. He was poet laureate from 1730.

His first play, *Love's Last Shift* (written to provide a bigger part for himself), was so successful that John Vanbrugh wrote a sequel to it, *The Relapse* (1696), in which Cibber played Lord Foppington.

CID

Abbreviation for ◊**Criminal Investigation Department**.

cider

A fermented drink made from the juice of the apple. Cider has been made for more than 2,000 years, and for many centuries has been a popular drink in France and England, which are now its main centres of production.

The French output is by far the greater, mainly from Normandy and Brittany. In Britain in a good year about 500 million litres/111 million gallons are produced, mainly in western England from Hereford to Devon, and in Kent and Norfolk.

Cinque Ports

Group of ports in southern England, originally five, Sandwich, Dover, Hythe, Romney, and Hastings, later including Rye, Winchelsea, and others. Probably founded in Roman times, they rose to importance after the Norman conquest and until the end of the 15th century were bound to supply the ships and men necessary against invasion. Their importance declined in the 16th and 17th centuries with the development of a standing navy.

The office of Lord Warden of the Cinque Ports survives as an honorary distinction (Winston Churchill 1941–65, Robert Menzies 1965–78, the Queen Mother from 1979). The official residence is Walmer Castle.

THE ORDINATION OF WOMEN PRIESTS

The first women ordained in the Church of England

From 12th March to August 1994 some 1,200 women were ordained priests in the Church of England. This followed the vote by the General Synod of the Church of England on 11 November 1992, an event that was a cause of rejoicing for those who had campaigned for many years to allow women to become priests in the Church of England.

Other parts of the Anglican Communion had already voted in favour, notably the USA, Canada, and New Zealand. More recently, enabling legislation has been passed by the Church of Scotland, but rejected by the Church in Wales.

Opposition at Anglican bishops' conference

Within the Church of England many are still opposed to the ordination of women. The plans that were drawn up by the Anglican bishops' conference in Manchester in early 1993 allowed for certain areas to be havens of male priesthood. There were fears that some dioceses would be no-go areas for women, since parish priests are appointed by the bishop. However, women may be ordained by those bishops who agree with women's ordination and then given special license to function in a diocese where the acting bishop is opposed.

Effect of the ordination of women

John Austin Baker, the bishop of Salisbury, suggested that no-one should be ordained who did not accept women's ordination. His statements are likely to continue to fuel the debate. However, the forecast split in the Anglican church has never materialized. Out of more than 10,000 priests, some 140 have left the Church of England for the Roman Catholic Church and 80 more have indicated their intention to do, depending on the specific terms for settlement.

Provision made for opponents of women's ordination

Many of those who oppose women's ordination have decided to remain within the Church of England, which reflects the somewhat complex provision made for them within the structures of the church. An Act of Synod, for example, states clearly that no-one should be discriminated against in terms of responsibility in the Church of England on the grounds of their views on the ordination of women.

Bishops who oppose women's ordination are given the pastoral care of those priests who hold similar views, which may mean caring for those in a neighbouring diocese, after permission has been given by the local diocesan bishop. Where this is not possible, so-called 'flying bishops', or more correctly Provincial Episcopal Visitors, take pastoral care of those opposed to women's ordination. Each Parochial Church Council has the power to vote against having women priests in its parish, and may request alternative episcopal oversight.

The Church of Scotland's acceptance of women's ordination is controversial because of the lack of legislation to protect those who are opposed to women priests.

Reaction from the Roman Catholic Church

As might be expected, the Roman Catholic Church was cautious in allowing Anglicans entry into the Catholic church simply because they rejected women's ordination. The Conference of Roman Catholic Bishops which met at the end of April 1993 decided that each and every person and priest who sought to become Roman Catholic should go through the usual period of testing.

The authority of the Roman Catholic Church could not recognize the official validity of the Anglican priesthood, which rules out an automatic transfer from Anglican to Catholic priesthood. Thus many priests find it as painful to go as to stay.

The issue of authority

One of the arguments of those opposed to women's ordination has been that the real issue is one of authority: What right had the General Synod to go back on hundreds of years of history and the tradition of the wider church, that is the Catholic church? The anti-ordination lobby is predominantly Anglo-Catholic; that is, those who stress the historical rootedness of the Anglican church in the Catholic faith.

The irony is that the church to which the rebels are seeking union is still open as far as the ordination of women is concerned. The Catholic Commission on Women set up by the present pope as far back as 1976 concluded that the New Testament was ambiguous over the possible accession of women to the priesthood. The pope has made clear statements expressing his own personal resistance to the idea of women's ordination, but these statements were not made *ex cathedra*, which would have made them part of the infallible dogma of the Roman Catholic Church.

Can a woman represent Christ?

Other arguments against the ordination of women have been used such as: How can a female represent Christ at the altar? Those who are in favour of women's ordination argue that if Christ cannot be represented by women at the altar, how can he represent women at the cross? In other words, arguments such as these imply Christ came to save one half of humanity.

The issue has helped to create an atmosphere of debate on the role of women and the whole question of women's ministry. At its best this could be an opportunity to discuss the model of priesthood accepted by the Anglican church as well as the role of women generally.

'A moment of liberation'

The feminist theologian, Sara Maitland, who chose to be received into the Roman Catholic Church remarked that the vote to ordain women was 'a moment of liberation', believing that 'much of the best feminist theology in Britain is coming from Roman Catholicism'. Like all churches the Roman church is seeking to expand and develop its ministerial tasks for women. To do otherwise would be a failure to keep in touch with contemporary society.

by Celia Deane-Drummond

Cirencester

Market town in Gloucestershire, England, on the River Churn, in the Cotswold Hills, 25 km/16 mi southeast of Gloucester; population (1991) 15,200. Industries include agriculture, precision engineering, and the manufacture of electrical goods. The Royal Agricultural College is situated here. Cirencester was the important Roman settlement of **Corinium Dobunnorum**, and flourished in the Middle Ages as the centre of the Cotswold wool trade.

Features

Cirencester's medieval prosperity is reflected in the 15th-century Perpendicular church of St John the Baptist, one of the largest in England. The church contains a wineglass pulpit dating from about 1450, one of the few surviving pre-Reformation pulpits in England. There are remains of the Hospital of St John, founded by Henry II, and the 15th-century Weavers' Hall. The remains of a Roman amphitheatre seating 8,000 spectators have been excavated, and the Corinium Museum displays a collection of Roman exhibits, including sections of mosaic pavement.

Cissbury Hill

Hill in West Sussex 5 km/3 mi north of Worthing, England; height 184 m/604 ft. On the summit of the hill lies **Cissbury Ring**, the largest hillfort on the South Downs, which dates from around 300 BC. The fort has more than 200 pits containing prehistoric flint works.

Citizens' Advice Bureau, CAB

organization established in 1939 to provide information and advice to the public on any subject, such as personal problems, financial, house purchase, or consumer rights. If required, the bureau will act on behalf of citizens, drawing on its own sources of legal and other experts. There are more than 900 bureaux located all over the UK.

Citizen's Charter

Series of proposals aimed at improving public services in the UK, unveiled by prime minister John Major in 1991. Major's 'programme for a decade' covered the activities of a range of public-sector bodies, including the police, the health service, schools, local authorities, and public and private utility companies. It promised better quality for consumers through the publication of service standards, the right of redress, performance monitoring, penalties for public services, tighter regulation of privatized utilities, and the increased pressures resulting from competition and privatization.

The Labour government of Tony Blair has sought to build on the charter programme, aiming to make it more 'locally owned' and improve public access to performance information. New charters are planned for those in long-term care and for 'prison users'.

City, the

Financial centre of ◊London, England. It is situated on the north bank of the River Thames, between Tower Bridge and London Bridge, in the oldest part of the capital. The ◊Bank of England, Lloyd's, the Royal Exchange, and the head offices of the 'big four' banks (Barclays, Lloyds, Midland, National Westminster) are in the City.

The City also contains the law courts of the Old Bailey (Central Criminal Court) and Royal Courts of Justice.

city technology college (CTC)

One of a network of some 20 proposed schools, financed jointly by government and industry, designed to teach the national curriculum with special emphasis on technological subjects in inner-city areas to students aged 11 to 18. The first school was opened in 1988. By 1994 only 15 schools had opened in England and Wales (still 15 in mid-1998), industry having proved reluctant to fund the scheme, which was abandoned in its original form.

CTCs caused controversy (a) because of the former Conservative government's plans to operate the schools independently of local education authorities; (b) because of selection procedures; and (c) because of the generous funds they receive compared with other schools. The Conservative government encouraged local authority and also grant-maintained schools to opt for CTC status at reduced expense, and began to make grants available to selected maintained and grant-maintained schools to enable them to update their technology facilities.

civil aviation

Operation of passenger and freight transport by air.

In the UK there are about 140 civil airports. Heathrow, Gatwick, and Stansted (all serving London), Southampton, Glasgow, Edinburgh, and Aberdeen are managed by the British Airports Authority (founded 1965). Close cooperation is maintained with authorities in other countries, including the Federal Aviation Agency, which is responsible for regulating development of aircraft, air navigation, traffic control, and communications in the USA. See ◊aviation for some key dates in British aviation.

civil list

Annual sum provided from public funds to meet the official expenses of the sovereign and immediate dependents; private expenses are met by the ◊privy purse.

The amount is granted by Parliament on the recommendation of a Select Committee. It has to be renegotiated within the first six months of a new reign. In 1991 a fixed 10-year annual sum of £7.9 million was agreed for all of the royal family but this was changed in 1992 to provide only for the Queen, the Queen Mother, and the Duke of Edinburgh. Outside the Civil List Parliament makes payments for the upkeep of the royal palaces and the Queen's Flight, through the respective government departments. Other payments, such as those to members of the Queen's extended family come from her private income.

Since 1995 the Queen has paid income tax on her private income, the amount of which is not publicly disclosed. Additional royal income has been generated since 1993 by the opening of Buckingham Palace, between August and October each year, to paying public visitors. The income generated has been used to fund the restoration of Windsor

Castle. In 1998 the Royal Yacht *Britannia* was decomissioned and the prime minister floated plans for joint use of the royal aircraft.

History

Before 1689 all expenses of government in peacetime and of the royal household were supposed to be met from the hereditary revenues of the Crown and from taxes voted for life to the sovereign on accession. In 1689 Parliament attempted to secure some control over the monarch by voting an annual sum of £600,000. This was raised to £700,000 and given statutory effect by the Civil List Act 1697.

On the accession of George III in 1760 an important change occurred when the hereditary revenues and such tax yields as Parliament decided were no longer paid to the monarch, but to the exchequer account (known as the consolidated fund) and the civil list was paid out of the consolidated fund. Finally, on the accession of William IV in 1830 all government expenses were removed from the civil list and it was restricted to the expenses of the royal household.

civil-list pension

Pension paid to people in need who have just claims on the royal beneficence, who have rendered personal service to the crown, or who have rendered service to the public by their discoveries in science and attainments in literature, art, or the like. The recipients are nominated by the prime minister, and the list is approved by Parliament. The pensions were originally paid out of the sovereign's civil list, but have been granted separately since the accession of Queen Victoria.

civil service

Body of administrative staff appointed to carry out the policy of a government. Members of the UK civil service may not take an active part in politics, and do not change with the government.

History

Civil servants were originally in the personal service of the sovereign. They were recruited by patronage, and many of them had only nominal duties. The great increase in public expenditure during the Napoleonic Wars led to a move in Parliament for reform of the civil service, but it was not until 1854 that two civil servants, Charles Trevelyan and Stafford Northcote, issued a report as a result of which recruitment by competitive examination, carried out under the Civil Service Commission 1855, came into force. Its recommendations only began to be effective when nomination to the competitive examination was abolished 1870.

Structure

The two main divisions of the British civil service are the **home** and **diplomatic** services, the latter created in 1965 by amalgamation of the Foreign, Commonwealth, and Trade Commission services. All employees are paid out of funds voted annually for the purpose by Parliament. Since 1968 the Civil Service Department has been controlled by the prime minister (as minister for the civil service), but everyday supervision is exercised by the Lord Privy Seal. In 1981 the secretary to the cabinet was also made head of the Home Civil Service. The present emphasis is on the professional specialist, and the **Civil Service College** (Sunningdale Park, Ascot, Berkshire) was established in 1970 to develop training.

Size and scope of the civil service

A basic distinction is usually drawn between non- industrial and industrial staff in the civil service. There are about 476,000 civil servants, a decrease of 37% from a peak of 751,000 in 1976.

About half of all civil servants are engaged in the provision of public services, a further quarter are employed in the Ministry of Defence, and the rest are divided between central administrative and policy duties, support services, and largely self-supporting services, such as National Savings and the Royal Mint. Four-fifths of the total work outside London. About 3,000 comprise the senior civil service: the most senior managers and policy advisers.

In 1988 the Next Steps Programme was launched with the aim of delivering services more efficiently and effectively. This involved the setting up of separate units or agencies, within or attached to departments, to perform executive functions. Agencies remain part of the civil service but enjoy greater freedom in pay, personnel, and financial matters than normal departments. An agency cannot be created until 'prior options' have been considered and ruled out. These include complete abolition of the operation, or its privatization, or its contracting out. In September 1997 there were 137 Executive Agencies, together with 24 executive units of Customs and Excise and 24 Executive Offices of the Inland Revenue. Some 80% of all civil servants now work in organizations run on Next Steps lines.

The ◊Diplomatic Service is a separate service, employing some 5,800 people for the Foreign and Commonwealth Office and diplomatic missions abroad. It has its own grade structure.

Civil War, English

Conflict between King Charles I and the Royalists (also called Cavaliers) on one side and the Parliamentarians (also called Roundheads) under Oliver ◊Cromwell on the other. Their differences centred initially on the king's unconstitutional acts, but later became a struggle over the relative powers of crown and Parliament. Hostilities began in 1642 and a series of Royalist defeats (at Marston Moor in 1644, and then at Naseby in 1645) culminated in Charles's capture in 1647, and execution in 1649. The war continued until the final defeat of Royalist forces at Worcester in 1651. Cromwell then became Protector (ruler) from 1653 until his death in 1658. See feature and chronology on pages 183 and 184.

Clackmannanshire

Unitary authority in central Scotland, bordering the north side of the Firth of Forth. A former county (until 1974), it was a district of Central region (1975–96)

Area 161 sq km/62 sq mi

Towns ◊Alloa (administrative headquarters), Tillicoultry

Physical compact geographical area comprising the extensive flat flood plain of the River Devon, which rises dramatically at the Ochil Hills to Ben Cleuch (721 m/2,365 ft)

THE WORLD TURNED UPSIDE DOWN: CIVIL WAR AND REVOLUTION

From 1640 to 1660 the British Isles witnessed some of the most dramatic events of their history. In this period, the English, Scottish, and Irish states all experienced major, and interconnected, internal convulsions.

Scotland

In the late 1630s the Scots rose in armed insurrection to defend their Calvinist, or presbyterian, church against a new 'popish' prayer book which Charles I was attempting to impose. In 1640 the Scots Covenanters defeated Charles's army at Newburn, precipitating the deep political crisis in England which led to civil war in 1642. In 1643 they entered into a military alliance with the English Parliamentarians, and Scottish forces contributed much to the defeat of the Royalists. The Scots had assumed that Charles's defeat would be followed by the introduction of a Scottish-style church in England, but by 1649 the presbyterian English Parliament had lost power to the soldiers of the New Model Army, most of whom firmly rejected the concept of any national church.

The Scots then transferred their allegiance, backing the attempts of Charles I and then his son to win back the English crown. They were, however, defeated at Preston (1648), Dunbar (1650), and Worcester (1651) by Cromwell, who then brought all of Lowland Scotland under direct English rule for the first time in its history. In 1654 he forced Scotland into a union with England. While this union was overturned at the Restoration in 1660, the English hegemony it had established ensured that England entered the union of 1707 as much the dominant partner.

Ireland

In Ireland the mid-century crisis erupted with the Ulster Rising of 1641, during which several thousand native Catholics rose up against Protestant colonists planted on their lands earlier in the century. The rebellion quickly spread. A provisional Catholic government was set up at Kilkenny, and in 1643 Charles I recognized its authority in exchange for Irish military assistance in England. The recovery of Ireland was entrusted to Cromwell in 1649. Within nine months he broke the back of the rebellion with an efficiency and ruthlessness for which he has never been forgiven by the Irish people. This military reconquest was swiftly followed by the Cromwellian Land Settlement, which ejected most of the Catholic population from their lands and gave them the famous choice of going to 'Hell or Connaught'. These events laid the foundations for the English Protestant Ascendancy.

England

It was in England, however, that the revolutionary nature of the 1640s and 1650s was most apparent. Here a full-scale civil conflict resulted in the public trial and execution of a king who many still regarded as divinely appointed, the establishment of a republic, and the emergence of a military junta. In the religious sphere, the established national church was dismembered in favour of a large number of unorthodox radical sects, including the Ranters, who encouraged indulgence in alcohol, tobacco, and casual sex, and the Quakers, whose refusal to defer to social superiors made them especially subversive.

These 20 years were marked by an extraordinary intellectual ferment. Many English men and women began to espouse very radical solutions to a wide range of social and political problems. The Levellers advocated universal male suffrage. Gerrard Winstanley established a short-lived commune on St George's Hill near Weybridge, and argued in print for a communist solution to social inequalities. The poet John Milton sought liberal divorce laws, and other writers debated women's rights, polygamy, and vegetarianism.

England had fallen into civil war in 1642 for want of a peaceful solution to the serious differences between Charles I and some of his most influential subjects. Some of these differences had been political, but more important was a religious struggle manifested in the opposition of many English Calvinists to a clique of anti-Calvinists, or Arminians, who (under Charles's patronage) had gained control of the established church in the 1630s. Parliament's victory in the Civil War owed much to the organizational ability of its early leader John Pym, its access to the financial and demographic resources of London, and the creation of the New Model Army in 1645. After his defeat, Charles's own obstinate refusal to settle with his opponents finally drove the leaders of the army to the desperate expedient of regicide.

From 1649 to 1660, England remained a military state. Cromwell struggled to reconcile the country to his rule, but failed because of his association with the army in a nation now thoroughly fed up with the military. Moreover, Cromwell and his puritan colleagues considered it their duty to impose their own godly culture on the nation. Initiatives such as the introduction of the death penalty for adultery were met with widespread hostility. In restoring the Stuarts in 1660, the English were decisively rejecting this puritan culture in favour of a world once more turned right way up.

BY CHRISTOPHER DURSTON

Industries brewing, distilling, manufacture of bottles and knitwear
Agriculture intensive on flood plain of Forth; less intensive on Ochil Hills
Population (1995) 48,800.

Economy
This is based largely on small enterprises in a mixed economy.
Environment
There are ten Sites of Special Scientific Interest and one country park.

CHRONOLOGY OF THE ENGLISH CIVIL WAR

1625 James I died, succeeded by Charles I, whose first Parliament was dissolved after refusing to grant him tonnage and poundage (taxation revenues) for life.

1627 'Five Knights' case in which men who refused to pay a forced loan were imprisoned.

1628 Coke, Wentworth, and Eliot presented the Petition of Right, requesting the king not to tax without Parliamentary consent, not to billet soldiers in private homes, and not to impose martial law on civilians. Charles accepted this as the price of Parliamentary taxation to pay for war with Spain and France. Duke of Buckingham assassinated.

1629 Parliament dissolved following disagreement over religious policy, tonnage and poundage, beginning Charles' 'Eleven Years' Tyranny'. War with France ended.

1630 End of war with Spain.

1632 Strafford made lord deputy in Ireland.

1633 Laud became archbishop of Canterbury. Savage punishment of puritan William Prynne for his satirical pamphlet 'Histriomastix'.

1634 Ship money first collected in London.

1634–37 Laud attempted to enforce ecclesiastical discipline by metropolitan visits.

1637 Conviction of John Hampden for refusal to pay ship money infringed Petition of Right.

1638 Covenanters in Scotland protested at introduction of Laudian Prayer Book into the Kirk.

1639 First Bishops' War. Charles sent army to Scotland after its renunciation of episcopacy. Agreement reached without fighting.

1640 Short Parliament April–May voted taxes for the suppression of the Scots, but dissolved to forestall petition against Scottish war. Second Bishops' War ended in defeat for English at Newburn-on-Tyne. Scots received pension and held Northumberland and Durham in Treaty of Ripon. Long Parliament called, passing the Triennial Act and abolishing the Star Chamber. High Commission and Councils of the North and of Wales set up.

1641 Strafford executed. English and Scots massacred at Ulster. Grand Remonstrance passed appealing to mass opinion against episcopacy and the royal prerogative. Irish Catholic nobility massacred.

1642 January Charles left Westminster after an unsuccessful attempt to arrest five members of the Commons united both Houses of Parliament and the City against him.

February Bishop's Exclusion Bill passed, barring clergy from secular office and the Lords.

May–June Irish rebels established supreme council. Militia Ordinance passed, assuming sovereign powers for parliament. Nineteen Propositions rejected by Charles.

August Charles raised his standard at Nottingham. Outbreak of first Civil War.

October General Assembly of the Confederate Catholics met at Kilkenny. Battle of Edgehill inconclusive.

1643 Irish truce left rebels in control of more of Ireland. Solemn League and Covenant, alliance between English Parliamentarians and Scots, pledged to establish Presbyterianism in England and Ireland, and to provide a Scottish army. Scots intervened in Civil War.

1643–49 Westminster Assembly attempted to draw up Calvinist religious settlement.

1644 Committee of Both Kingdoms to coordinate Scottish and Parliamentarians' military activities established. Royalists decisively beaten at Marston Moor.

1645 Laud executed. New Model Army created. Charles pulled out of Uxbridge negotiations on a new constitutional position. Cromwell and the New Model Army destroyed Royalist forces at Naseby.

1646 Charles fled to Scotland. Oxford surrendered to Parliament. End of first Civil War.

1647 May Charles agreed with Parliament to accept Presbyterianism and to surrender control of the militia.

June–August Army seized Charles and resolved not to disband without satisfactory terms. Army presented Heads of Proposals to Charles.

October–December Army debated Levellers' Agreement of the People at Putney. Charles escaped to the Isle of Wight, and reached agreement with the Scots by Treaty of Newport.

1648 January Vote of No Addresses passed by Long Parliament declaring an end to negotiations with Charles.

August Cromwell defeated Scots at Preston. Second Civil War began.

November–December Army demanded trial of Charles I. Pride's Purge of Parliament transferred power to the Rump of independent MPs.

1649 January–Februrary Charles tried and executed. Rump elected Council of State as its executive.

May Rump declared England a Commonwealth. Cromwell landed in Dublin.

September–October Massacres of garrisons at Drogheda and Wexford by Cromwell. Large numbers of native Irish were transplanted.

1650 September Cromwell defeated Scots under Leslie at Dunbar

1651 Scots under Charles II invaded England, but were decisively defeated at Worcester (3 September) by Cromwell. Charles fled to the Continent and lived in exile for 9 years.

Clacton-on-Sea

Seaside resort in Essex, eastern England, 19 km/12 mi southeast of Colchester; population (1991) 45,100. It possesses nearly 11 km/7 mi of sandy beaches, a pier, and a promenade and marine parade over 6 km/4 mi long. The Essex county cricket ground is here.

To the west of the town is St Osyth's priory, dating largely from the 12th century.

With the ascension of Charles I to the throne, we come at last to the Central Period of English History (not to be confused with the Middle Ages, of course), consisting in the utterly memorable Struggle between the Cavaliers (Wrong but Wromantic) and the Roundheads (Right and Repulsive).

W C SELLAR AND R J YEATMAN English writers.
1066 and All That, A Memorable History of England (1930)

claim of right

Declaration by the Scottish estates in 1689 accompanying
their recognition of the new regime of William and Mary following the 'Glorious Revolution' of 1688. The declaration asserted the right to depose any monarch who violated the law, listing grievances against James VII and II, as well as denouncing the Lords of the Articles and episcopacy in Scotland.

clan (Gaelic *clann* 'children')

Social grouping based on kinship. Some traditional societies are organized by clans, which are either matrilineal or patrilineal, and whose members must marry into another clan in order to avoid in-breeding.

Familiar examples are the Highland clans of Scotland. Theoretically each clan is descended from a single ancestor from whom the name is derived – for example, clan MacGregor ('son of Gregor').

Clans played a large role in the Jacobite revolts of 1715 and 1745, after which their individual tartan Highland dress was banned 1746–82. Rivalry between them was often bitter.

Clandon Park

House near Guildford, Surrey, England, which was built around 1735 by Giacomo Leoni (1686–1746) for the 2nd Lord Onslow. It was given to the National Trust by the Countess of Iveagh in 1956.

The house contains the Onslow family pictures and furniture, the Gubbay collection of furniture, porcelian and needlework, and the Ivo Forde collection of Meissen Italian comedy figures.

Clapham sect

Early 19th-century evangelical group within the Church of England which advocated paternalist reforms for the underprivileged. Based on Rev. John Venn's church in Clapham between 1792 and 1830, the group consisted largely of liberal-minded wealthy families and had a profound influence on many of the most prominent social reformers of the time, including William Wilberforce and the Earl of Shaftesbury.

Clapton, Eric (1945–   )

English blues and rock guitarist, singer, and songwriter. Originally a blues purist, then one of the pioneers of heavy rock with Cream 1966–68, he returned to the blues after making the landmark album *Layla and Other Assorted Love Songs* (1970) by Derek and the Dominos. Solo albums include *Journeyman* (1989) and the acoustic *Unplugged* (1992), for which he received six Grammy awards (1993). He won a Grammy award for Record of the Year with 'Change the World' in 1997.

CLAPTON, ERIC *British guitarist and singer Eric Clapton. He won acclaim as a virtuoso guitarist in various rock bands before making his first solo album in 1970. After being sidelined with a drugs problem in the early 1970s, he returned with great success in live performance and on record, and is now probably as much admired for his easygoing vocal style as for his guitar playing. Corbis*

Clare, John (1793–1864)

English poet. His work includes *Poems Descriptive of Rural Life and Scenery* (1820), *The Village Minstrel* (1821), *The Shepherd's Calendar* (1827), and *The Rural Muse* (1835). The dignified simplicity and truth of his descriptions of both landscape and emotions were rediscovered and appreciated in the 20th century.

Clare spent most of his life in poverty. He was given an annuity by the duke of Exeter and other patrons, but had to turn to work on the land. He spent his last 20 years in Northampton asylum. His early life is described in his autobiographical writings, first published in 1931.

Clare, Richard de, Earl of Pembroke and Striguil (known as 'Strongbow') (died 1176)

English soldier. At the request of Dermot MacMurrough he invaded Ireland in 1170 and captured Waterford and Dublin, beginning English intervention in Ireland. He was forced to hand over his conquests to Henry II but after helping him in Normandy was granted Wexford, Waterford, and Dublin, the first Anglo-Norman lordship. He is buried in Dublin Cathedral.

Claremont Park

Palladian mansion in Esher, Surrey, England, built for Robert ◊Clive, and now a girls' school. Clive bought the original house, designed by ◊Vanbrugh, in 1768, and in 1770 began the rebuilding to designs by Capability ◊Brown.

Other distinguished residents were Princess Charlotte of Wales (died 1817) and Louis Philippe of France. The property was later owned by Queen Victoria.

Clarence

English ducal title, which has been conferred on a number of princes. The last was Albert Victor (1864–92), eldest son of Edward VII.

Clarence House

House in London, residence of HM Queen ◊Elizabeth the Queen Mother. It stands immediately opposite Friary Court, St James's Palace, and was built by John ◊Nash in 1825–29 for William IV when he was Duke of Clarence. It was enlarged by one storey in 1873.

Clarendon, Edward Hyde, 1st Earl of Clarendon (1609–1674)

English politician and historian, chief adviser to Charles II 1651–67. A member of Parliament 1640, he joined the Royalist side 1641. The **Clarendon Code** 1661–65, a series of acts passed by the government, was directed at Nonconformists (or Dissenters) and was designed to secure the supremacy of the Church of England.

In the ◊Short and ◊Long Parliaments Clarendon attacked Charles I's unconstitutional actions and supported the impeachment of Charles's minister Strafford. In 1641 he broke with the revolutionary party and became one of the royal advisers. When civil war began he followed Charles to Oxford, and was knighted and made chancellor of the Exchequer. On the king's defeat in 1646 he followed Prince Charles to Jersey, where he began his *History of the Rebellion*, published 1702–04, which provides memorable portraits of his contemporaries. In 1651 he became chief adviser to the exiled Charles II. At the Restoration he was created Earl of Clarendon, while his influence was further increased by the marriage of his daughter Anne to James, Duke of York. His moderation earned the hatred of the extremists, however, and he lost Charles's support by openly expressing disapproval of the king's private life. After the disasters of the Dutch war 1667, he went into exile.

Clarendon, George William Frederick Villiers, 4th Earl of Clarendon (1800–1870)

British Liberal diplomat, lord lieutenant of Ireland 1847–52, foreign secretary 1853–58, 1865–66, and 1868–70.

He was posted to Ireland at the time of the potato famine. His diplomatic skill was shown at the Congress of Paris in 1856 and in the settlement of the dispute between Britain and the USA over the *Alabama* cruiser.

Claridge's Hotel

Hotel in Brook Street, London, opened in 1855 by William Claridge, a butler from a noble household. It was bought by the Savoy Company in 1895 and rebuilt. It is known as the best-equipped hotel in London to accommodate royalty and the rich.

Clarissa

Novel (1747–48) by Samuel ◊Richardson in the form of letters between the characters. The heroine is pursued by the attractive but unprincipled Lovelace. He rapes her and the consequent loss of autonomy and identity leads to her tragic decline and eventual death. The book's length (originally eight volumes) helps to explain its current lack of popularity, but Richardson's psychological subtlety and inexhaustible sympathy for his women characters ensure a place for the book in the development of the novel form.

Clark, Jim (James) (1936–1968)

Scottish-born motor-racing driver who was twice world champion 1963 and 1965. He spent all his Formula One career with Lotus. He won 25 Formula One Grand Prix races, a record at the time, before losing his life at Hockenheim, West Germany during a Formula Two race 1968.

Clark, Kenneth (Mackenzie), Baron Clark (1903–1983)

English art historian, director of the National Gallery, London, from 1934 to 1945. Clark was chair of the Arts Council between 1953 and 1960. His books include *Leonardo da Vinci* (1939), *Landscape into Art* (1949), and *The Nude* (1956).

He popularized the history of art through his television series *Civilization* (1969), published as a book in the same year. He was made KCB in 1938, and baron in 1969.

Clark, Michael (1962–)

Scottish avant-garde dancer. His provocative and outlandish costumes and stage props have earned him as much celebrity as his innovative dance technique. A graduate of the Royal Ballet school, he danced with the Ballet Rambert 1979–81, where Richard ◊Alston created works for him, and formed his own company, the Michael Clark Dance Company, in 1984.

His works include *Swamp* (1986), *Because We Must* (1987), *I Am Curious Orange* (1988), *Mmm... Modern Masterpiece* (1992), incorporating elements of *The Rite of Spring*, and *O* (1994), featuring the birth of Apollo in a perspex cube. In 1991 he played Caliban in Peter Greenaway's film *Prospero's Books*. Injury and personal loss took him out of dance for three years in the late 1990s.

Clarke, Arthur C(harles) (1917–)

English science-fiction and nonfiction writer. He originated the plan for a system of communications satellites in geostationary orbit in 1945. His works include the short story 'The Sentinel' (1951) (filmed in 1968 by Stanley Kubrick as *2001: A Space Odyssey*), and the novels *Childhood's End* (1953), *2010: Odyssey Two* (1982), *3001: The Final Odyssey* (1997), *Rendezvous with Rama* (1997), and *A Fall of Moondust* (1998).

Clarke served in the Royal Air Force during World War II as a radar instructor, and then studied physics at King's College, London. He became chair of the British Interplanetary Society 1946, the year his first story was published. In 1956 he moved to Sri Lanka. His popular-science books generally concern space exploration; his fiction is marked by an optimistic belief in the potential of science and technology. He was knighted in 1998.

Clarke, Gillian (1937–)

Welsh poet and editor. Typically her poems begin with an everyday incident that leads to a reflection on the history, landscape, or changing social life of Wales – and in particular on the role of women in Welsh life. Her first collection of poems, *The Sundial*, was published in 1978 in Wales; and it was a third collection, *Letter from a Far Country* (1982), that won her critical acclaim and a wider readership. Other volumes include *Letting in the Rumour* (1989).

Gillian Clarke's critical success is based on her ability to merge these specific, local subjects – closely observed and sensitively portrayed – with universal themes.

Clarke, Kenneth Harry (1940–)

British Conservative politician. A cabinet minister 1985–97, he held the posts of education secretary 1990–92 and home secretary 1992–93. He succeeded Norman Lamont as chancellor of the Exchequer in May 1993, bringing to the office a more open and combative approach. Along with his colleagues Malcolm Rifkind, Tony Newton, and Patrick Mayhew, in 1996 he became the longest continuously serving minister since Palmerston in the early 19th century.

He was a contestant for the leadership of the Conservative Party after its defeat in the 1997 general election. At odds over the new leader's anti-European policy, he declined to accept a position in the shadow cabinet of William Hague.

Clash, the

English rock band 1976–85, a driving force in the British ◊punk movement. Reggae and rockabilly were important elements in their sound. Their albums include *The Clash* (1977), *London Calling* (1979), and *Combat Rock* (1982).

classical music

Term used to distinguish 'serious music' from pop music, rock music, folk music, and jazz.

Middle Ages to the Reformation

One of the earliest English composers of note was John Dunstable (died 1453), a master of vocal polyphony known in Europe whose influence was especially felt in Flanders. Eminent composers of church music in this period were Robert Fayrfax (1464–1521), organist at St Alban's cathedral; William Cornyshe (*c.* 1468–1523), master of the choristers at Westminster Abbey, who also organized court pageants and masques for Henry VII; and John Taverner, who produced masses in a florid style.

A Golden Age

With the introduction of a new liturgy after the Reformation, church music became relatively restrained and was dominated by Thomas Tallis, William ◊Byrd and Orlando ◊Gibbons. Various secular forms of music also developed: lute music and songs with lute were composed by Thomas ◊Campion and John ◊Dowland; keyboard music by Byrd and John ◊Bull; and vocal music of all kinds, especially madrigals, by composers such as Thomas ◊Morley, Thomas Weelkes and John Wilbye. These last three composers all contributed to *The Triumphs of Oriana* (1601), a madrigal collection in honour of Elizabeth I.

There were many continental musicians working in England at this period, but English musicians in their turn made careers for themselves abroad: Dowland in Denmark, for instance, and Bull in the Netherlands. Notable composers in the mid-17th century were Henry Lawes (1596–1662), who wrote mainly vocal music; his brother William (1602–45), who wrote consort-music; and Matthew ◊Locke, who composed instrumental music, and collaborated with Henry Lawes and others on a setting of Davenant's *The Siege of Rhodes* (1656), creating what could be regarded as an early English opera.

Restoration

With the Restoration, Locke became court composer to Charles II. Many of the other musicians who found favour with the King were French. A new generation of native composers came to the fore: Pelham Humfrey (1647–74), John Blow (1649–1708), and Jeremiah Clarke (1673–1707) among them, but it was Henry ◊Purcell, a pupil of Blow and Humfrey, who was the greatest force in late 17th-century English music, writing in and enriching a variety of forms.

Influence of Handel

The gap left by Purcell's early death was filled by the German-born ◊Handel, who lived most of his life in England. His musical roots were German and Italian, and at a time when there was a taste for Italian opera, he wrote several which were well received in London, where the Royal Italian Opera House was opened at Covent Garden in 1732 (a precursor of the ◊Royal Opera House). A native tradition of ballad opera, exemplified by John ◊Gay's *Beggar's Opera* is found throughout the century.

Foreign musicians and composers continued to come to England in large numbers, among them J C Bach (1735–82), who settled in London in 1762. Public concerts became fashionable. Against this background English composers tended to adopt a style influenced by Handel, although Thomas ◊Arne, William ◊Boyce, and (later) Charles ◊Dibdin, among others, strove to create individual styles of their own. The two Thomas Linleys, father (1733–95) and son, were theatre composers and contributed to the development of English opera. The 18th centuryalso saw the beginnings of musical scholarship at university level.

1780–1880

There are few British figures of note in the field of music from the late 18th and 19th centuries. Cipriani Potter's (1792–1871) symphonies show him to be a composer of individuality and sure orchestral command – even Beethoven acknowledged that Potter was gifted; and Irishman John Field (1782–1837) was a great pianist, and is known principally for the nocturnes he composed for piano. Victorian audiences lionised Mendelssohn and (later) Gounod, but their tastes seem to have been for bland oratorios and sensational operas. Only English operetta flourished, Arthur ◊Sullivan being its principal exponent.

Late-19th century renaissance

The late 1870s and early 1880s witnessed the start of a renaissance in English musical life. Two eminent figures were Hubert ◊Parry – at once composer, teacher, theorist, and administrator – and Charles ◊Stanford, who founded the Royal College of Music in 1882. The College proved an excellent training-ground for young composers. Two great figures of this renaissance were Edward ◊Elgar and Frederick ◊Delius, both of whom were largely self-taught. Each formulated personal musical languages that were recognisable English, yet exhibited the influence of music being composed on the European continent. The honours gradually paid to Elgar were a measure of the increase in status of music in England.

At the start of the 20th century, research into folk-music was being undertaken by several musicians in Europe, notably by Bartók in Romania and Hungary. The research undertaken in England, notably by Cecil ◊Sharp and later by Ralph ◊Vaughan Williams, provided a nationalist impetus to composition in England. Impetus was also provided by the republication of much early English music, which initiated a tradition of exploring musical resources from the past. By 1914, musical life in Britain was flourishing. Rising talent included Arnold Bax (1883–1953), Frank ◊Bridge, George ◊Butterworth, Ivor ◊Gurney, and Herbert ◊Howells. There was an active musical press and the popularity of orchestral concerts increased, largely on account of the extrovert conductors Thomas ◊Beecham and Henry ◊Wood.

Post-World War I

World War I dealt musical life in Britain a severe blow. The post-war generation was suspicious of grand designs, real structural complexity, and unabashed expressiveness, the dominant mood being satirical. Stravinsky and French composers were much admired. To the new generation of composers belonged Arthur ◊Bliss, Lennox ◊Berkeley, Constant Lambert (1905–51), Alan Rawsthorne, William ◊Walton, Havergal Brian (1876–1972), Frank ◊Bridge, and Gustav ◊Holst. The British song tradition was cultivated by Gerald Finzi and Peter ◊Warlock.

Two composers who came to prominence just before World War II, Benjamin ◊Britten and Michael ◊Tippett went on to dominate the British music scene, though Tippett had to wait many years for official recognition. Britten made several exceptional contributions to the English opera repertoire. The influence of music composed on the European continent continued – the serial procedures of the Viennese School were used by Elisabeth Lutyens.

Late 20th century

Since the late 1950s, the development of music in England has been closely linked with developments in western classical music around the world. The range of individual compositional styles has increased enormously, as has the number of influences on classical music – for example, the works of John ◊Tavener show the influence of Greek Orthodox church music. Purely electronic music has been written by several composers (including Jonathan Harvey), and electronic instruments have featured often in new works.

Prominent British composers at the end of the 20th century

included Peter Maxwell ◊Davies, Alexander ◊Goehr and Harrison ◊Birtwistle, whose works have provoked much fertile discussion in the media as to the nature and accessibility of contemporary classical music.

Claudius I, Tiberius Claudius Drusus Nero Germanicus (10 BC–AD 54)

Nephew of Tiberius, and son of Drusus Nero, made Roman emperor by the Praetorian Guard AD 41, after the murder of his nephew Caligula. Claudius was a scholar and historian. During his reign the Roman empire was considerably extended, and in 43 he took part in the invasion of Britain.

Claverhouse, John Graham, Viscount Dundee (*c.* 1649–1689)

Scottish soldier. Appointed by Charles II to suppress the Covenanters from 1677, he was routed at Drumclog in 1679, but three weeks later won the battle of Bothwell Bridge, by which the rebellion was crushed. Until 1688 he was engaged in continued persecution and became known as 'Bloody Clavers', regarded by the Scottish people as a figure of evil. His army then joined the first Jacobite rebellion and defeated the loyalist forces in the pass of Killiecrankie, where he was mortally wounded.

Claydon House

House in Buckinghamshire, England, 21 km/13 mi northwest of Aylesbury. Claydon was the home of the Verney family from 1463. The present house was built 1752–68, but all that now remains is the west wing, containing magnificent rococo state rooms, including Florence ◊Nightingale's bedroom and museum. She was the sister of Parthenope Verney, and a constant visitor to Claydon. The Verney family gave Claydon to the National Trust in 1956, but continue to live in the house.

Clean Air Act

Legislation designed to improve the quality of air by enforcing pollution controls on industry and households. The first Clean Air Act in the UK was passed in 1956 after the London Smog killed 4,000 people.

Clee Hills

Range of hills in southern Shropshire, England. The principal summits are Brown Clee Hill (546 m/1791 ft) and Titterstone Clee Hill (533 m/1749 ft). Some coal reserves remain here, although they are no longer mined. A noted hard rock called Dhu stone, which is used mainly for road metal, is quarried here.

Cleese, John (Marwood) (1939–)

English actor and comedian. He has written for and appeared in both television programmes and films, and has worked in television advertising. On British television, he is particularly associated with the comedy series ◊*Monty Python's Flying Circus* and *Fawlty Towers*. His films include *Monty Python and the Holy Grail* (1974), *The Life of Brian* (1979), and *A Fish Called Wanda* (1988).

In the 1990s he appeared in the films *Mary Shelley's Frankenstein* (1994), *Fierce Creatures* (1997), which he also wrote and produced, and Michael Winner's black comedy *Parting Shots* (1998).

Cleethorpes

Seaside resort in North East Lincolnshire, northeast England, on the Humber estuary, adjacent to Grimsby; population (1987 est) 35,500. Fishing is important to the local economy.

Features include a sea wall, nearly 2 km/1 mi long, about 5 km/3 mi of sandy beaches, a zoo, and a pier. Until 1994 when the line was standardized, Cleethorpes Coast light railway was unique as the country's only 36 cm/14.25 in-gauge track because of a mistake made during construction.

> *This parrot is no more. It's ceased to be. It has expired. The parrot has gone to meet its maker. This is a late parrot ... If you hadn't nailed it to the perch, it would be pushin' up the daisies.*
>
> JOHN CLEESE English actor and comedian. 'Monty Python's Flying Circus' (1969)

Clements, John Selby (1910–1988)

English actor and director. His productions included revivals of Restoration comedies and the plays of George Bernard Shaw. He was knighted in 1968.

Cleopatra's Needle

Name given to two ancient Egyptian granite obelisks erected at Heliopolis in the 15th century BC by Thutmose III, and removed to Alexandria by the Roman emperor Augustus about 14 BC; they have no connection with Cleopatra's reign. One of the pair was taken to England in 1878 and erected on the Victoria Embankment in London. It is 21 m/68.5 ft high.

clerihew

Humorous verse form invented by Edmund Clerihew ◊Bentley, characterized by a first line consisting of a person's name.

The four lines rhyme AABB, but the metre is often distorted for comic effect. An example, from Bentley's *Biography for Beginners* (1905), is: 'Sir Christopher Wren/Said, I am going to dine with some men./If anybody calls/ Say I am designing St Paul's.'

Clevedon

Resort in North Somerset, England; population (1991) 20,800. It is situated on the Severn estuary at the foot of Dial Hill, 17 km/11 mi southwest of Bristol. **Clevedon Court** was built by John de Clevedon in the 14th century, and added to in practically every century since then. It was in the possession of the Elton family from 1709 to 1961, when it was transferred to the National Trust through the Treasury. It has extensive collections of pottery and glass.

Samuel Coleridge lived at nearby Myrtle Cottage in 1795.

Henry Hallam, the historian, and his poet son, Arthur Hallam – in whose memory Tennyson's 'In Memoriam' was written – are buried in the parish church here.

Cleveland

Former county of northeast England, formed in 1974 from parts of Durham and northeast Yorkshire. It was abolished in 1996 when the unitary authorities of Hartlepool, Middlesborough, Redcar and Cleveland, and Stockton-on-Tees were created.

Cliff, Clarice (1899–1972)

English pottery designer. Her Bizarre ware, characterized by brightly coloured floral and geometric decoration on often geometrically shaped china, became increasingly popular in the 1930s and increasingly collectable in the 1970s and 1980s. Contemporary artists such as Laura Knight and Vanessa Bell also designed for her Bizarre range.

Born in the ◊Potteries, she started as a factory apprentice at the age of 13, trained at evening classes and worked for many years at Wilkinson's Newport factory. By 1929 production was given over exclusively to her work. In 1963 she became art director of the factory, which was part of the Royal Staffordshire Pottery in Burslem.

Clitheroe

Market town in Lancashire, England, 16 km/10 mi northeast of Blackburn. It is situated in the Ribble Valley between Pendle Hill and the Forest of Bowland, and is a stone-built town centred around a Norman castle, the grounds of which are now used as a War Memorial park. Clitheroe serves as a market centre for a wide rural area, and has a variety of industries, including light engineering, printing, lime, and cement works.

Clive, Robert, 1st Baron Clive (1725–1774)

British soldier and administrator who established British rule in India by victories over French troops at Arcot and over the nawab of Bengal at Plassey in 1757. This victory secured Bengal for the East india Company, and Clive was appointed governor of the province from 1757. He returned to Britain on account of ill health in 1760, but was governor for a further year in 1765–6. On his return to Britain in 1766, his wealth led to allegations that he had abused his power. Although acquitted by a Parliamentary enquiry, he committed suicide.

Clive became a clerk in the East India Company's service in Madras in 1743, then joined the army. During a dispute in 1751 over the succession to the Carnatic, an important trading region, Clive marched from Madras with 500 troops, seized Arcot, capital of the Carnatic, and defended it for seven weeks against 10,000 French and Italian troops. He then sallied out and relieved the British forces besieged in Trichinopoli. He returned to Britain a national hero, and was hailed as 'Clive of India'. He returned to India in 1755 as governor of Fort St David, and after the incident of the ◊Black Hole of Calcutta, when the city was besieged by the nawab of Bengal, Clive defeated the nawab's 34,000 strong army, with a force of only 1,900 troops outside Calcutta in February 1757.

Cliveden

Large Victorian house near Maidenhead, England, on the Buckinghamshire–Berkshire border. The 2nd Viscount ◊Astor gave Cliveden to the National Trust in 1942, together with its gardens and woods which dominate the Cliveden reach of the Thames. The house is now a privately owned hotel, but the grounds are open to the public.

closure, or clôture

Method of bringing a question under discussion to an immediate decision in parliamentary procedure. It was introduced in 1881 by William Gladstone to combat the obstructive tactics of the Irish Nationalist party, and was embodied in a permanent standing order in 1887.

Clôture was the name applied to it in the French assembly and by which it was sometimes called when first introduced in the UK.

Clwyd

Former county of north Wales, created in 1974 and, in 1996, divided between ◊Conwy, ◊Denbighshire, ◊Flintshire, ◊Powys, and ◊Wrexham unitary authorities.

Clwyd

River in northeast Wales, rising in the Denbigh Moors and Clwydian Hills, and flowing past St Asaph and Rhuddlan into the Irish Sea at Rhyl; length 64km/40 mi. The Elwy is the main tributary. The Clwyd valley has fine scenery.

Clyde

Third longest river and firth in Scotland, and longest in southern Scotland; 171 km/106 mi long. Formerly one of the world's great industrial waterways, and famed for its shipbuilding, its industrial base has declined in recent years and the capacity of the ports on the Clyde has reduced.

Daer Water and Portrail Water, which unite near Elvanfoot, are the river's chief headstreams. The headwaters of the Daer were dammed (1948–54) as part of a scheme to serve the growing needs of industry and new housing in central Scotland.

Near Lanark the Clyde rapidly falls 70 m/230 ft within 6 km/4 mi, forming the four Falls of Clyde.

The chief towns on the Clyde's banks from Elvanfoot to Glasgow are Lanark, Hamilton, Bothwell, and Blantyre. The junction with the Forth and the Clyde Canal is at Bowling. Ports on the river are Glasgow, Port Glasgow, and Greenock, and on the Firth of Clyde, are Ardrossan, Troon, and Ayr. The Firth, which reaches from Dumbarton to Ailsa Craig, is over 100 km/62 mi long. The chief islands in the Firth are Arran, Bute, Great Cumbrae, and Little Cumbrae, and among the sea lochs are Gare Loch, Loch Long, Holy Loch, and Loch Fyne.

Clydebank

Town on the River Clyde, part of West Dunbartonshire unitary authority, Scotland, 10 km/6 mi northwest of Glasgow; population (1991) 29,200. At the John Brown yard, liners such as the *Queen Elizabeth II* were built and launched. Shipbuilding is now in decline.

Some of the largest passenger and other ships were launched from here. The town was badly damaged by bombing in World War II.

CND

Abbreviation for ◊**Campaign for Nuclear Disarmament**.

coaching

Conveyance by coach – a horse-drawn passenger carriage on four wheels, sprung and roofed in. Public **stagecoaches** made their appearance in the middle of the 17th century; the first British mail coach began in 1784, and they continued until 1840 when railways began to take over the traffic.

The main roads were kept in good repair by turnpike trusts, and large numbers of inns – many of which still exist – catered for stagecoach passengers and horses. In the UK, coaches still in use on ceremonial occasions include those of the Lord Mayor of London (1757) and the state coach built in 1761 for George III.

Coalbrookdale

Village in the Telford and Wrekin unitary authority, England, effectively a suburb of Telford, situated in the Severn Gorge; population (1991) 1,000. Sometimes known as the 'cradle of the Industrial Revolution', Coalbrookdale became the world's most important iron-producing area following Abraham Darby I's successful attempt in 1709 to use coke – rather than coal or charcoal – to smelt iron in a blast-furnace, thereby allowing for a massive increase in production. It is now the site of the Coalbrookdale Museum of Iron which forms part of the ◊Ironbridge Gorge World Heritage Site.

coalmining

Traditionally one of Britain's key industries. Coal was mined on a small scale from Roman times, but production expanded rapidly between 1550 and 1700. Coal became the main source of energy for the Industrial Revolution; by 1700 over 50% of the country's energy needs was supplied by coal, and Britain became the world's largest coal producer. Under the Coal Industry Nationalization Act (1946) Britain's mines were administered by the National Coal Board, but the industry was privatized in 1994. The York, Derby, and Notts coalfield, which extends north of Selby in Yorkshire, is Britain's chief reserve.

Competition from oil as a fuel, cheaper coal from overseas (USA, Australia), the decline of traditional users (town gas, railways), and the exhaustion of many underground workings resulted in the closure of mines: 850 mines in 1955; 54 in

COALMINING *A* Punch *cartoon of 1844, entitled* Capital and Labour, *contrasts the luxurious life of a mineowner with the harsh working conditions in the pits. Although the Industrial Revolution brought Britain as a whole greater material prosperity, it also caused massive social upheavals. Philip Sauvain Picture Collection*

1992. However, rises in the price of oil, greater productivity, and the discovery of new, deep coal seams suitable for mechanized extraction improved the position of the British coal industry from 1973–90. Britain remains very dependent on the use of coal in electricity generation (although the percentage of electricity generated from coal dropped from 74% in 1992 to just over 50% in 1995).

Pit closures

In October 1992, Trade and Industry Secretary Michael Heseltine announced that 31 of the country's coal mines would be closed, putting some 30,000 miners out of work. After widespread protest, the government announced that 10 pits would close and the remaining 21 would be put under review. In March 1993 a revised closure programme reprieved 12 of the 21 collieries while they were assessed for economic viability. By August 1993, 18 collieries had closed. In 1995, 30 major deep mines and 35 opencast mines formerly owned by British Coal, were still being worked. However, in 1997 doubts were expressed about the future of even these pits.

More that 100,000 miners died in mining accidents in the 20th century – over 1,000 times more deaths than in the nuclear industry.

Coastal Command

Combined British naval and Royal Air Force system of defence organized during World War II (1939–45).

coastal erosion

The erosion of the land by the constant battering of the sea's waves, primarily by the processes of hydraulic action, corrasion, attrition, and corrosion. Hydraulic action occurs when the force of the waves compresses air pockets in coastal rocks and cliffs. The air expands explosively, breaking the rocks apart. Rocks and pebbles flung by waves against the cliff face wear it away by the process of corrasion. Chalk and limestone coasts are often broken down by solution (also called corrosion). Attrition is the process by which the eroded rock particles themselves are worn down, becoming smaller and more rounded.

In Britain, the southern half of the coastline is slowly sinking (on the east coast, at the rate of half a centimetre a year) whilst the northern half is rising, as a result of rebounding of the land mass (responding to the removal of ice from the last Ice Age). Some areas may be eroding at a rate of 6 m/20 ft per year. Current opinion is to surrender the land to the sea, rather than build costly sea defences in rural areas. In 1996, it was reported that 29 villages had disappeared from the Yorkshire coast since 1926 as a result of tidal battering.

Coatbridge

Town in North Lanarkshire unitary authority, Scotland, 13 km/8 mi east of Glasgow; population (1991) 43,600. Coatbridge lies in the centre of a mineral district with a mining and manufacturing tradition.

There is a technical college (Coatbridge College) and a country park (Drumpellier). The town is almost joined to Airdrie to the east, with which there is great rivalry based on religious traditions (Coatbridge is predominantly Catholic, Airdrie is predominantly Protestant).

Coates, Eric (1886–1957)

English composer. He is remembered for the orchestral suites *London* (1933), including the 'Knightsbridge' march; 'By the Sleepy Lagoon' (1939); 'The Dam Busters March' (1942); and the songs 'Bird Songs at Eventide' and 'The Green Hills of Somerset'. He is best known as the composer of the signature tune for BBC Radio's 'Desert Island Discs' (the *By the Sleepy Lagoon*).

Coates, Nigel (1949–)

English architect. While teaching at the Architectural Association in London in the early 1980s, Coates and a group of students founded NATO (Narrative Architecture Today) and produced an influential series of manifestos and drawings on the theme of the imaginative regeneration of derelict areas of London.

Drawing parallels with the ideas of the Situationists in the 1960s and of punk in the 1970s, Coates promoted an eclectic and narrative form of architecture that went against the contemporary grain.

coat of arms

See ◊heraldry.

cob

Traditional building material made from a sun-dried mixture of clay and straw, mostly found in Devon and Dorset. Chalk and gravel were also introduced to the composition. **Cob-walls** were gradually built up in thick 30 cm/12 in layers, and finished with plaster or lime. Cob was also sometimes compressed into moulds and used with flint as walling in areas where stone was scarce.

Walls constructed from a mixture of wet chalk and straw, known as wichert, are also found, mainly in Buckinghamshire.

Cobbett, William (1763–1835)

English Radical politician and journalist, who published the weekly *Political Register* (1802–35). He spent much of his life in North America. His crusading essays on the conditions of the rural poor were collected as 'Rural Rides' (1830).

Born in Surrey, the self-taught son of a farmer, Cobbett enlisted in the army in 1784. After a period of service in Canada, he lived in the USA as a teacher of English, and became a vigorous pamphleteer, at this time supporting the Tories. In 1800 he returned to England. With increasing knowledge of the sufferings of the farm labourers, he became a Radical and leader of the working-class movement. He was imprisoned 1809–11 for criticizing the flogging of British troops by German mercenaries. He became a strong advocate of parliamentary reform, and represented Oldham in the Reformed Parliament after 1832.

Cobden, Richard (1804–1865)

British Liberal politician and economist, cofounder with John Bright of the Anti-Corn Law League in 1838. A member of Parliament from 1841, he opposed class and religious privileges and believed in disarmament and free trade.

Born in Sussex, the son of a farmer, Cobden was a typical early Victorian radical; he believed in the abolition of privileges, a minimum of government interference, and the securing of international peace through free trade and by disarmament and arbitration. He opposed trade unionism and most of the factory legislation of his time, because he regarded them as opposed to liberty of contract. His opposition to the Crimean War made him unpopular. He was largely responsible for the commercial treaty with France in 1860.

Cochran, C(harles) B(lake) (1872–1951)

English impresario. He promoted entertainment ranging from wrestling and roller-skating to Diaghilev's Ballets Russes. He was knighted in 1948.

Cockcroft, John Douglas (1897–1967)

British physicist. In 1932 he and Irish physicist Ernest Walton succeeded in splitting the nucleus of an atom for the first time. For this they were jointly awarded a Nobel prize in 1951.

The voltage multiplier built by Cockcroft and Walton to accelerate protons was the first particle accelerator. They used it to bombard lithium, artificially transforming it into helium. The production of the helium nuclei was confirmed by observing their tracks in a cloud chamber. They then worked on the artificial disintegration of other elements, such as boron. Knighted 1948, awarded the Order of Merit 1957.

Cockerell, Charles Robert (1788–1863)

English architect. He built mainly in a Neo-Classical style derived from antiquity and from the work of Christopher ◊Wren. His buildings include the Cambridge University Library (now the Cambridge Law Library; 1837–42) and the Ashmolean Museum and Taylorian Institute in Oxford (1841–45).

Cockerell, Christopher Sydney (1910–)

English engineer who invented the ◊hovercraft in the 1950s.

Cockerell tested various ways of maintaining the air cushion. In 1957 he came up with the idea of a flexible skirt, an idea derided by sceptics who could not believe that a piece of fabric could be made to support a large vessel.

Employed by the Marconi Company 1935–50, Cockerell made a major contribution to aircraft radio navigation and communications. During this period he filed 36 patents.

Trained as a development engineer, he set himself the task of trying to make a boat go faster. First he experimented with air lubrication of the hull, but concluded that a major reduction in drag could be obtained only if the hull could be supported over the water by a really thick air cushion. In 1953 he began work on the hovercraft, carrying out his early experiments on Oulton Broad, Norfolk, and filing his first hovercraft patent in 1955. Finally in 1958 he found commercial backing; the first full-size hovercraft was built and crossed the English Channel with the inventor on deck. Knighted 1969.

Cockerill, William (1759–1832)

English engineer. Born in Lancashire, he is generally regarded as the founder of the European textile-machinery industry. His working career began with the building of spinning jennies and flying shuttles. In 1794 he went to St Petersburg, Russia, and enjoyed the patronage of Catherine II. Her successor, however, imprisoned Cockerill for failing to complete a contract within the given time. Eventually he escaped via Sweden to Belgium in 1799, where he established himself as a manufacturer of textile machinery, first in Verviers and from 1807 in nearby Liège. There, together with his three sons William, Charles, and John, he made rotary carding machines, spinning frames, and looms for the French woollen industry.

cockney

Native of the City of London. According to tradition cockneys must be born within sound of ◊Bow Bells in Cheapside. The term cockney is also applied to the dialect of the Londoner, of which a striking feature is rhyming slang.

Coe, Sebastian Newbold (1956–)

English middle-distance runner, Olympic 1,500-metres champion in 1980 and 1984. He became UK's most prolific world-record breaker with eight outdoor world records and three indoor world records (1979–81).

Coe's world record for the 800 metres, set in 1981, stood for 16 years until it was broken by Wilson Kipketer of Denmark in 1997. After his retirement from running in 1990, Coe pursued a political career with the Conservative party, and in 1992 was elected member of Parliament for Falmouth and Camborne in Cornwall. He lost his seat in the 1997 general election.

It is folly of too many to mistake the echo of a London coffee house for the voice of the kingdom.

JONATHAN SWIFT Irish satirist and Anglican cleric.
The Conduct of the Allies (1711)

---

coffee house

Alternative to ale-houses as social meeting place, largely for the professional classes, popular in the 17th and 18th centuries. Christopher Bowman opened the first Coffee House in London (later known as the 'Pasqua Rosee') in St. Michael's Alley, Cornhill, in 1652 and others soon followed in both London and Oxford so that by 1708 London alone boasted 3,000 coffee houses. Their popularity stemmed from their reputations as centres for the dissemination of news and ideas, making them good places to meet others of a like mind and also to conduct business. For this reason, coffee houses were often associated with radical readings and an attempt was made to suppress them by royal proclamation in 1675 but the

COFFEE HOUSE *A contemporary picture of a coffee house from c. 1700. Coffee, chocolate, and tea were all introduced to England in the mid-17th century, and coffee houses rapidly became popular meeting places for the discussion of business affairs and literature. Philip Sauvain Picture Collection*

coffee houses were too popular and the attempt was abandoned within a matter of days. The coffee houses declined in popularity toward the end of the 18th century as coffee itself was largely superseded by the new fashion for tea.

Coggeshall

Town in Essex, England; population (1991) 5,000. It is situated on the River Blackwater, 10 km/6 mi southeast of Braintree. Coggeshall is an important seed-growing area. Clothing is also manufactured here.

Paycocke's House, built around 1500, is a half-timbered building that now belongs to the National Trust. The Grange Barn at Coggeshall, also owned by the National Trust, is the oldest surviving timber-framed barn in Europe. It dates from the 12th century and was originally part of a Cistercian abbey.

Coke, Edward (1552–1634)

Lord Chief Justice of England 1613–17. He was a defender of common law against royal prerogative; against Charles I he drew up the petition of right 1628, which defines and protects Parliament's liberties.

Coke became a barrister in 1578, and in 1592 speaker of the House of Commons and solicitor-general. As attorney-general from 1594, he conducted the prosecution of Elizabeth I's former favourites Essex and Raleigh, and of the Gunpowder Plot conspirators. In 1606 he became Chief Justice of the Common Pleas, and began his struggle, as champion of the common law, against James I's attempts to exalt the royal prerogative. An attempt to silence him by promoting him to the dignity of Lord Chief Justice proved unsuccessful, and from 1620 he led the parliamentary opposition and the attack on Charles I's adviser Buckingham. Coke's *Institutes* are a legal classic, and he ranks as the supreme common lawyer.

Coke, Thomas William, 1st Earl of Leicester (1754–1842)

English pioneer and promoter of the improvements associated with the Agricultural Revolution. His innovations included regular manuring of the soil, the cultivation of fodder crops in association with corn, and the drilling of wheat and turnips.

He also developed a fine flock of Southdown sheep at Holkham, Norfolk, which were superior to the native Norfolks, and encouraged his farm tenants to do likewise. These ideas attracted attention at the annual sheep shearings, an early form of agricultural show, which Coke held on his home farm from 1776. By the end of the century these had become major events, with many visitors coming to see and discuss new stock, crops, and equipment.

Colchester

City and river port in Essex, eastern England, on the River Colne, 80 km/50 mi northeast of London; population (1991)

96,100. It is the market centre of an agricultural and shell-fishing area, roses and oysters being notable products. Industries include engineering, printing, and the manufacture of clothing. The oldest recorded town in England, Colchester was the capital of the kingdom of ◊Cymbeline, until his death in about AD 40. As **Camulodunum**, it was the first capital of Roman Britain, and it was burned by ◊Boudicca in AD 60.

Features

Remains of the Roman walls and gateway; ruins of a castle dating from 1070, with the largest Norman keep in the country; the gateway of the 11th-century monastery of St John; and the ruins of the 12th-century St Botolph's priory church. There is an army base in the town, and the University of Essex opened in 1965 at nearby Wivenhoe Park.

History

Following the Roman invasion in AD 43, Camulodunum became the headquarters of the Romans in Britain. A temple dedicated to the Divine Claudius was erected here, and it became a colony for Roman ex-soldiers in AD 50, and one of the most prosperous towns in Roman Britain. Boudicca devastated the town in AD 60 when she led a rising of the Trinobantes and Iceni against the Romans. After her defeat a new town was established on the site of modern Colchester. The Roman occupation of Colchester lasted until about the end of the 4th century.

The settlement later became the Saxon stronghold of **Colneceaster**, and William (I) the Conqueror built a castle on the site of the Roman temple. The town flourished as a centre of the weaving and cloth trade from the 14th to 17th centuries. During the English Civil War, the town surrendered to the Parliamentarians in 1648 after an 11-week siege. In 1884 the town was badly shaken by the Essex earthquake and several buildings were damaged.

Museums

Holly Tree Mansion (1718) houses a museum of 18th- and 19th-century social life. A museum in the castle contains a large collection of Romano-British antiquities. All Saints' Church houses a natural history museum.

Cole, Henry (1808–1882)

English public official, art critic, and editor. He organized the ◊Great Exhibition of 1851 and played a major part in founding the Victoria and Albert Museum, the Science Museum, the Royal Albert Hall, and the Royal College of Music, all in London. Employed at the Treasury on the postal project (1839–42), he introduced the penny postage system in 1840, and the adhesive stamp.

The Henry Cole Wing of the Victoria and Albert Museum is named after him.

Coleman, Edward (died 1669)

English singer, lutenist, and composer. He composed incidental music to Shirley's play *Contention of Ajax and Achilles* in 1653, contributed songs to *Select Musicall Ayres and Dialogues* the same year, and pieces of his appeared in Playford's *Musical Companion* in 1672.

Coleraine

Town in County Londonderry, Northern Ireland, on the River Bann, 6 km/4 mi from the sea; population (1991) 16,100. It is a market town with textile and food-processing industries and salmon fisheries. Coleraine is the site of the New University of Ulster, which opened in 1968.

Coleraine was originally the site of a monastery dedicated to St Patrick, of which nothing remains. The present town owes its origins to the granting of lands to the London companies as part of the Londonderry plantation in the early 17th century.

The mesolithic site at Mount Sandel, 2 km/1 mi to the south, has yielded much archaeological information. It was also the site of the stronghold of Fintan, who ruled Derry in the 1st century AD.

Coleridge, Samuel Taylor (1772–1834)

English poet, critic, and philosopher. A friend of the poets Robert ◊Southey and William ◊Wordsworth, he collaborated with the latter on the highly influential collection *Lyrical Ballads* (1798), which was the spearhead of the English Romantic Movement. His poems include 'The Rime of the Ancient Mariner', 'Christabel', and 'Kubla Khan' (all written 1797–98); his critical works include *Biographia Literaria* (1817).

Coleridge was educated at Cambridge University where he became friends with Southey. In 1797 he moved to Nether Stowey, Somerset, and worked closely with Wordsworth on *Lyrical Ballads*, producing much of his finest poetry during this period. In 1798 he went to Germany where he studied philosophy and literary criticism. In 1800 he settled in the Lake District with Wordsworth and from 1808 to 1819 gave a series of lectures on prose and drama. Suffering from rheumatic pain, Coleridge became addicted to opium and from 1816 lived in Highgate, London, under medical care. Here he produced his major prose work *Biographia Literaria* (1817), a collection of autobiographical pieces in which he develops his philosophical and critical ideas. Much of it based on German ideas, and it is full of insight but its formlessness represents a partial failure of promise.

Coleridge-Taylor, Samuel (1875–1912)

English composer. He wrote the cantata *Hiawatha's Wedding Feast* (1898), a setting in three parts of Longfellow's poem. The son of a West African doctor and an English mother, he was a student and champion of traditional black music.

He sang at a church at Croydon as a boy, and entered the Royal College of Music as a violin student in 1890, but also studied composition under Charles Stanford. He had works performed while still at college and in 1899 he was represented at the North Staffordshire Festival at Hanley. He was appointed conductor of the Handel Society in 1904, and visited the USA that year, as well as in 1906 and 1910; but otherwise devoted all his time to composition and private teaching. In the last years of his life he did some teaching at the Guildhall School of Music, London.

His works include the opera *Thelma* (1907–09); settings for solo voices, chorus, and orchestra of portions from Longfellow's 'Hiawatha' (three parts, 1898), Coleridge's 'Kubla Khan' (1905), Noyes's 'A Tale of Old Japan'; 'Five Choral Ballads' (Longfellow), 'Sea Drift' (Whitman) for chorus; oratorio *The Atonement*; and incidental music for Shakespeare's *Othello*.

College of Arms, or Heralds' College

English heraldic body formed in 1484. There are three kings-of-arms, six heralds, and four pursuivants, who specialize in genealogical and heraldic work. The college establishes the right to a coat of arms, and the kings-of-arms grant arms by letters patent. The office of king-of-arms for Ulster was transferred to the College of Arms in London in 1943.

The College of Arms is presided over by the Earl Marshal (whose office is hereditary in the family of the duke of Norfolk), and consists of the Garter King-of-Arms; the Clarenceux King-of-Arms (with jurisdiction south of the River Trent); the Norroy King-of-Arms, who now also holds the office of Ulster King of Arms (with jurisdiction north of the Trent as well as in Northern Ireland); the heralds (named Chester, Windsor, Lancaster, Richmond, York, and Somerset); and four pursuivants (named Bluemantle, Portcullis, Rouge Dragon, and Rouge Croix). The College has no jurisdiction in Scotland, whose heraldry is under control of the Lyon King-of-Arms. See also ◊heraldry.

college of higher education

A college in which a large proportion of the work undertaken is at degree level or above. Colleges of higher education are centrally funded by the Universities and Colleges Funding Council, and some of the largest became universities in 1992 at the same time as the former polytechnics.

Collier, Constance (1878–1955)

English actress. She worked with the theatre manager Herbert Beerbohm ◊Tree 1901–08. Later she divided her time between England and the USA, playing Gertrude to John Barrymore's Hamlet in 1925, and appearing in such parts as Mrs Cheveley in Oscar Wilde's *An Ideal Husband* in London and Anastasia in G B Stern's *The Matriarch* in New York.

Collingwood, Cuthbert, 1st Baron Collingwood (1750–1810)

British admiral who served with Horatio Nelson in the West Indies against France and blockaded French ports 1803–05; after Nelson's death he took command at the Battle of Trafalgar. Baron 1805.

Collins, Joan (Henrietta) (1933–)

English film and television actress. From the late 1960s she gained a glamorous reputation on and off screen, especially after *The Stud* (1979). Her role as Alexis Carrington in the TV series *Dynasty* (1981–89) brought her international fame. Screen appearances in the 1990s include Kenneth Branagh's *In the Bleak Midwinter* (1995) and the US television series *Pacific Palisades* (1997).

She has written some 'sex and shopping' novels, and is the sister of the novelist Jackie Collins.

Collins, Michael (1890–1922)

Irish nationalist. He was a ◊Sinn Féin leader, a founder and director of intelligence of the Irish Republican Army (see ◊IRA) in 1919, minister for finance in the provisional government of the Irish Free State in 1922, commander of the Free State forces in the civil war, and for ten days head of state before being killed by Irishmen opposed to the partition treaty with Britain.

Born in County Cork, Collins became an active member of the Irish Republican Brotherhood, and in 1916 fought in the Easter Rising. In 1918 he was elected a Sinn Féin member to the Dáil (lower chamber of parliament), and became a minister in the Republican Provisional government. In 1921 he and Arthur Griffith (1872–1922) were mainly responsible for the treaty that established the Irish Free State. During the ensuing civil war, Collins took command and crushed the opposition in Dublin and the large towns within a few weeks. When Griffith died on 12 August Collins became head of the state and the army, but he was ambushed near Cork by fellow Irishmen on 22 August and killed.

Collins, Pauline (1940–)

English stage and screen actress. She rose to international prominence in 1989 as the middle-aged heroine on the road to self-discovery in the comedy *Shirley Valentine*. Known for her stage work in the play of the same name and *Come As You Are*, she had previously appeared on British television in the

COLLINS, JOAN *English actress Joan Collins, with US actors Bing Crosby (left) and British-born Bob Hope (right), in a 1961 publicity still from* Road to Hong Kong *(1962). Shot at Shepperton Studios in England, this was the last of the* Road *films, a series which had begun with* Road to Singapore *in 1940. Corbis*

comedy *The Liver Birds* (1969), in *Upstairs, Downstairs* (1971–76) and various comedy series with her husband, John Alderton. She also starred in the Calcutta-set film drama *City of Joy* (1992) and featured as the protagonist of the television miniseries *The Ambassador* (1998).

Collins, Phil(lip David Charles) (1951–)

English pop singer, drummer, and actor. A member of the group Genesis from 1970, he has also pursued a successful middle-of-the-road solo career since 1981, with hits (often new versions of old songs) including 'In the Air Tonight' (1981), 'Groovy Kind of Love' (1988), 'Another Day in Paradise' (1989), 'I Wish it Would Rain' (1990), and 'Both Sides of the Story' (1993). He starred as the train robber Buster Edwards in the film *Buster* (1988).

Collins, (William) Wilkie (1824–1889)

English author of mystery and suspense novels. He wrote *The Woman in White* (1860) (with its fat villain Count Fosco), often called the first English detective novel, and *The Moonstone* (1868) (with Sergeant Cuff, one of the first detectives in English literature).

Collins was born in London and qualified as a barrister. In 1848 he wrote a life of his father, the painter William Collins, and in 1850 published his first novel, *Antonina*. In 1851 he formed a friendship with the novelist Charles ◊Dickens, with whom he collaborated on a number of works, including the play *A Message from the Sea* (1861).

Collins, William (1721–1759)

English poet. His *Persian Eclogues* four short effusions in heroic couplets published anonymously in 1742, were followed in 1746 by his *Odes on Several Descriptive and Allegorical Subjects*, 12 lyric poems which include 'Ode To Evening' and 'The Passions'. The 'Ode on the Superstitions of the Highlands', written in 1749, is an important poem in the early Romantic movement.

Colman, George, the Elder (1732–1794)

English dramatist and theatre manager. He wrote a great number of plays, including *The Jealous Wife* (1761) and (in collaboration with David ◊Garrick) *The Clandestine Marriage* (1766). He was one of the lessees of the Covent Garden Theatre 1766–74 and manager of the Haymarket Theatre 1776–94, both in London.

His son **George Colman the Younger** (1762–1836) followed him in this position and also wrote for the stage. His output was vast, his most notable piece being *John Bull* (1803).

Colman, Ronald (Charles) (1891–1958)

English film actor. In Hollywood from 1920, he played suave and dashing roles in *Beau Geste* (1924), *The Prisoner of Zenda* (1937), and *Lost Horizon* (1937). He received an Academy Award for his role as a murderous schizophrenic in George Cukor's *A Double Life* (1947).

Coltrane, Robbie stage name of Anthony McMillan (1950–)

Scottish comedian, actor, and television presenter. He first gained widespread recognition in the early 1980s as part of the team behind the British television series *The Comic Strip Presents*, which was later followed by a leading role in the comedy series *Tutti Frutti* (1987). In the 1990s he won acclaim for his performances in the television crime drama *Cracker*.

He has also appeared in a number of films, including *Mona Lisa* (1986), *Nuns on the Run* (1990), and 1990s James Bond films. Coltrane diversified in the 1990s, presenting television series on pet subjects, such as *Coltrane in a Cadillac* (1993) and *Coltrane's Planes and Automobiles* (1997).

Columba, St (Latin form of Colum-cille, 'Colum of the cell') (521–597)

Irish Christian abbot, missionary to Scotland. He was born in County Donegal of royal descent, and founded monasteries and churches in Ireland. In 563 he sailed with 12 companions to Iona, and built a monastery there that was to play a leading part in the conversion of Britain. Feast day 9 June.

Colwyn Bay, Welsh Bae Colwyn

Seaside town in Conwy, north Wales, situated 7 km/4 mi east of Conwy; population (1991) 29,900. Known as the 'garden resort of Wales', it has a good sandy beach.

Combination Acts

Laws passed in Britain in 1799 and 1800 making trade unionism illegal. They were introduced after the French Revolution for fear that the unions would become centres of political agitation. The unions continued to exist, but claimed to be friendly societies or went underground, until the acts were repealed in 1824, largely owing to the radical Francis Place.

comedy

Drama of a humorous nature, usually with a happy or amusing ending. British comedy has a strong tradition in the genres of pantomime, satire, and farce and, more recently, in black comedy. Great British comic theatrical dramatists include ◊Shakespeare, Ben ◊Jonson, George Bernard ◊Shaw, and Oscar ◊Wilde. In the second half of the 20th century, comedy in a traditional half-hour format has been a key part of television programming, attracting large audiences and, in the case of a few outstanding classics, bearing many repeats.

Theatrical comedy

The first known English comedy, *Ralph Roister Doister* by Nicholas Udall (*c.* 1505–1556), was written in the middle of the 16th century. It had its origins in the plays of the Roman comic dramatists Plautus and Terence. The stock comic characters of the Renaissance **comedy of humours**, however, had their origins in medieval morality plays. One such is the villain Mosca in Ben Jonson's *Volpone* (1606).

The main development in comedy after Shakespeare was the witty **comedy of manners** of Restoration writers such as George Etherege, William Wycherley, and William Congreve. The often coarse nature of these comedies was toned down in the later Restoration dramas of Richard Sheridan and Oliver Goldsmith. Sentimental comedy dominated most of the 19th century, though these plays were not often

COMEDY *The zany humour of the radio comedy* The Goon Show *(from left to right, at the microphones: Spike Milligan, Peter Sellers, and Harry Secombe) in the 1950s and 1960s was characterized by surreal situations and wildly improbable accents. Offbeat experimentation has been an enduring feature of British comedy, also apparent in* Monty Python's Flying Circus *of the 1960s and 1970s and* The Fast Show *of the 1990s. Rex*

performed in the late 20th century, the realistic tradition of Shaw and the elegant social comedies of Wilde proving more popular.

The polished comedies of Noël ◊Coward and Terence ◊Rattigan from the 1920s to 1940s were eclipsed during the late 1950s and the 1960s by a trend towards satire and cynicism as seen in the works of Joe ◊Orton and Peter ◊Nichols, alongside the absurdist comedies of Tom ◊Stoppard. From the 1970s the black comedies of Alan ◊Ayckbourn have dominated the English stage. As with television comedy, the work of a few extremely skilled dramatists continues reliably to draw audiences.

Satirical revue, a traditional part of the musical cabaret performed in European cafés and bars in the early 20th century, was revived by the Cambridge Footlights theatre group in *Beyond the Fringe* (1961). Cabaret and alternative comedy later combined to provide a new generation of stand-up entertainers during the 1980s, notably from the Comedy Store and Comic Strip clubs in London. In the 1990s Eddie Izzard (1962–) has been a leading live solo performer. The Edinburgh Fringe Festival gives a Perrier award for stand-up comedy.

Radio comedy

Radio brought to national audiences established variety performers such as Arthur Askey (1900–1982), Ted Ray, and Tommy ◊Handley, whose sketch programme *ITMA* attracted huge audiences hungry for humour during World War II. *The Navy Lark* (1959–1977) became one of the longest-running comedy shows, while Tony ◊Hancock's classic *Hancock's Half Hour* was one of the first formats to switch successfully to television. Like Hancock, the anarchic humour of Spike ◊Milligan, Michael Bentine (1921–96), Peter ◊Sellers, and Harry Secombe (1921–) as *The Goons* was to have a formative influence on a new generation of comedians such as John ◊Cleese, who led *I'm Sorry I'll Read That Again* (1967), in turn a direct precursor of television's *Monty Python's Flying Circus* and *The Goodies*. A stalwart of radio comedy, Kenneth Williams continued the sketch show tradition, with others, in the long-running *Round The Horne*, and then found he was in demand for quizzes based on quick wit, notably *Just a Minute*. Radio continued to be a valuable training ground for comedians and comic writers in the 1980s and 1990s, among them Armando Iannucci (1963–), one of the creators of the mock news shows *On the Hour* and *The Day Today*, and, for television, *Knowing Me, Knowing You... with Alan Partridge* (Steve Coogan).

Television sketch shows

Divided broadly into sketch shows and sitcoms, television

comedy has produced some of the nation's favourite entertainers, most remembered sketches, and most enduring characters. ◊Morecambe and ◊Wise took the variety format into the new medium in 1961and developed it to dominate television comedy for almost two decades. *The Two Ronnies* kept to their own hugely successful sketch format for the 1970s and 1980s, while Dick Emery (1917–83), Stanley Baxter (1926–), Benny ◊Hill, Marty Feldman (1933–82), and Les Dawson (1934–93) all had their own sketch shows in the 1970s that revolved entirely around their individual comic and mimetic talent. Ned Sherrin and David ◊Frost's topical show *That Was The Week That Was* (1963) broke new ground with its up-to-the-minute references and biting satire, but lasted only a couple of series before the BBC used the forthcoming 1964 general election as an excuse to take it off. Peter ◊Cook and Dudley Moore's *Not Only But Also* (1966) often parodied television itself, and scored in creating characters who reappeared week after week. Sadly not all the programmes survived the then common practice of wiping tapes for re-use.

In 1969 *Monty Python's Flying Circus* unleashed its unique brand of off-beat mania; *The Goodies* remained a quieter, safer, but still popular sketch collection. Often sketch shows would launch further careers: *Not the Nine O'Clock News* set Griff Rhys Jones (1953–) and Mel Smith on their way as a duo, while Rowan ◊Atkinson went on to make the silent knockabout *Mr Bean*, a huge overseas seller, and the novel historical sitcom *Blackadder.* In the 1990s *The Fast Show* featured Paul Whitehouse (1958–)who was to join up with Harry ◊Enfield for *Harry Enfield and Chums* from 1994.

Television sitcoms

A peculiarly fertile area of British programming, sitcoms have the benefit of building up characters over time and have often taken some years to be truly popular. From early successes with strong themes, such as *The Army Game* (1957–62) and *The Rag Trade* (1962), the genre developed a variety of approaches, one being the ups and downs of a flat- or house-share, as in *The Liver Birds* (1969) (girls sharing) and *Man About the House* (1975) (two girls and a boy sharing), a format that reached a zenith with *Rising Damp* (1974) (an eclectic houseful, drawn together by irksome landlord) and, in the 1980s, *The Young Ones* (boys sharing). This in turn paved the way for comedies that dealt with life as a man in the 1990s, again sharing housespace, in *Bottom* and *Men Behaving Badly. Till Death Us Do Part* (from 1966) set the argumentative Alf Garnett in the bosom of his exasperated family, and confronted an uncomfortable bigotry. In something of the same domestic vein, but reaching far beyond the confines of four walls to give a view of life near the edge in Peckham, *Only Fools and Horses* (from 1981) by John Sullivan won continuing popularity for its blend of warmth, feeling, and situation humour, as the Trotter brothers move through life.

Nostalgia for World War II proved a winner for one of comedy's most productive writing duos, Jimmy Perry and David Croft, creators of both ◊*Dad's Army* (from 1968, and still a favourite 30 years on) and *It Ain't Half Hot Mum* (from 1974). Another duo, Ray Galton and Alan Simpson, who had written for Tony Hancock, created the enduring classic of aspirations set against the reality of social limitations, ◊*Steptoe and Son* (from 1963), while Dick Clement and Ian La Frenais brought alive the divergent but loyal friends *The Likely Lads* (from 1966, with a sequel from 1973). Responsible for another classic, *Porridge*, in what seemed at first an unlikely setting of a prison, they went on to develop the comedy drama *Auf Wiedersehen, Pet* based on a real trend for builders to go abroad looking for work. Another pair of writers, Anthony Jay and Jonathan Lynn, created the hugely successful *Yes, Minister* (1984) and *Yes, Prime Minister* (1986) from their observations of life in the corridors of power.

Some of the best sitcoms rely almost completely on just one or two stars to carry a good script, for instance Michael ◊Crawford in *Some Mothers Do 'Ave 'Em* (from 1973), Ronnie Barker and David Jason in *Open All Hours* (from 1976), and Richard Wilson supported by Annette Crosbie in *One Foot in the Grave* (from 1990), this being one of several latterday comedies that have looked at life from the pensioner's point of view. Foremost in that genre has been the quirky *Last of the Summer Wine* (from 1973), based on the meanderings of three old fogeys and their neighbours.

In a class of its own, the phenomenal and enduring success of the brief *Fawlty Towers*, written by and starring John ◊Cleese and Connie Booth, with Andrew Sachs and Prunella Scales, hit a nerve of understanding about the British character.

A key development in the 1990s was the increase in funny women demonstrating extreme comic versatility and taking lead roles. *Birds of a Feather*, with Pauline Quirke, Linda Robson, and Leslie Joseph, broke new ground as a predominantly female sitcom. Dawn ◊French and Jennifer ◊Saunders graduated from the parody series *The Comic Strip Presents* (1982) to their own sketch show, *French and Saunders*, then on to sitcom. For Jennifer Saunders, this was *Absolutely Fabulous* (from 1992), and for Dawn French the timely *Vicar of Dibley*. Victoria Wood has shown a similar range of talent, moving from her own sketch shows such as *Victoria Wood on TV* to her scripted *Dinnerladies* (1998).

Commission for Racial Equality

Executive body established in 1976 to promote racial equality in England, Scotland and Wales. In 1996 it registered 1750 applications for assistance in cases of racial discrimination and handled 142 litigation cases. A Commission for Racial Equality for Northern Ireland was established in 1997 with similar powers.

The commission gives advice to employers and others on arrangements for implementing equal opportunity policies. It also has the power to investigate unlawful discrimination practice and to issue notices requiring such practice to cease. It can undertake or fund research, give grants to suitable groups or projects as well as supporting the work of 84 racial equality councils.

Committee on Safety of Medicines, CSM

UK authority processing licence applications for new drugs. The members are appointed by the secretary of state for health. Drugs are licensed on the basis of safety alone,

HOW THE HOUSE OF COMMONS OPERATES

The House of Commons is the lower chamber of Parliament. It consists of 659 elected members of Parliament, each of whom represents a constituency. Its functions are to debate, legislate, and to scrutinize the activities of government. Constituencies are kept under continuous review by the Parliamentary Boundary Commissions 1944. The House of Commons is presided over by the Speaker. Proceedings in the House of Commons began to be televised from November 1989. After the 1997 election, the Commons included a record 120 women members, including 101 female Labour MPs.

The members of the House of Commons are directly elected by universal adult suffrage. The maximum period between general elections is five years, but the prime minister may advise a dissolution at any time. In order to remain in office the prime minister and his or her government must retain the confidence of a majority of the members of the House of Commons, whereas it does not need the confidence of a majority of the House of Lords. The majority of ministers are drawn from the House of Commons and it is there that the government must defend its actions and policies.

Members of Parliament

Members of Parliament must be British subjects and at least 21 years of age. The following are ineligible to become MPs: aliens; people medically certified as suffering from mental illness; peers; holders of offices of profit under the Crown; many clergymen; convicted prisoners; undischarged bankrupts; members of any police force. Under the Peerages Act 1963 a person who succeeds to a peerage may disclaim the peerage and thus become, or remain, eligible to sit in the House of Commons.

Although the rise of the Labour Party in the 20th century dramatically increased the proportion of working-class candidates elected to the House of Commons, the proportion has been declining since 1945 and Parliament has become increasingly middle class.

Salaries and facilities

Members of Parliament receive a salary (1998) of £43,860 and an office cost allowance of up to £47,568. The salaries of ministers in the House of Commons range from £23,623 for junior ministers to £60,000 for those in the cabinet. The prime minister is entitled to a salary of £100,000. These amounts are additional to their parliamentary pay.

Officers

The principal officers of the House of Commons are the Speaker, the Chairman of Ways and Means, the Clerk to the House of Commons and the Serjeant at Arms.

The leader of the House of Commons, who usually holds the office of Lord President of the Privy Council, is in charge of the government's business in the House of Commons. He or she is assisted by the government chief whip, who holds the office of parliamentary secretary to the Treasury, and about a dozen junior whips.

Constituencies

The practice of periodic reviews of constituencies was established by the House of Commons (Redistribution of Seats) Act 1949. The boundary commissioners apply an electoral quota of approximately 65,000 per constituency and adhere as far as possible to local government boundaries.

Government and opposition

The UK Parliament operates on the adversarial principle in which the government of the day presents its proposals to and defends its policies in Parliament and these are in turn criticized by the Opposition.

The members of the government and its supporters occupy the benches to the right of the Speaker and the Opposition and its supporters the benches to his or her left. MPs holding ministerial office and members of the shadow cabinet are commonly known as **frontbenchers**, since they occupy the benches nearest to the Speaker; all other MPs are known as **backbenchers** or private members.

Parliamentary sessions

The House of Commons meets for approximately 160 days a year. The parliamentary session normally begins in October or November. On Mondays to Thursdays the House meets from 2.30 to 10.30 p.m. On Fridays, most of which are devoted to private members' business, the sitting is from 11 a.m. to 4.30 p.m. It is possible, however, for the House to extend any sitting and late-night sittings add the equivalent of more than 30 days to the session.

Questions to the prime minister may be put for 30 minutes on Wednesday.

Divisions

Every matter is determined upon a question put from the chair, and resolved in the affirmative or negative. If, having collected the voices on either side, the Speaker's opinion as to which side has the majority is challenged, he or she puts the question again two minutes later. If challenged a second time, he or she directs the **ayes** into the lobby on the right and the **noes** into that on the left. Members' names are recorded in the lobby by the clerks, and they are counted by the tellers (usually whips) as they leave the lobby. The tellers announce the result, which the Speaker then declares to the House.

Parliamentary debate

The rules for the conduct of debate are as far as possible adapted to the maintenance of certain standards of behaviour and to the curtailment of unnecessary argument. Except in committee of the whole House or in standing committee, no member may speak twice to the same question. No member is supposed to read his or her speech (though ministers often do), but the use of copious notes is customary.

Supply

Twenty-nine days are allotted each session for the discussion of the annual estimates of expenditure presented by the civil and defence departments. The Opposition has the right to choose the estimates set down for discussion, and they generally use this right not to discuss expenditure but to raise questions of policy and administration.

Parliamentary time
Only about half the time available is directly at the government's disposal for dealing with its business. Approximately a fifth is at the disposal of the Opposition (mainly its 29 supply days) and another fifth is devoted to private members' business. This leaves a small amount which the government makes available for such contingencies as emergency and censure debates, which cannot be anticipated.

Legislation
Bills may be public or private, the latter being required primarily for local authorities wanting additional powers. Private bills should not be confused with private members' bills, which are so named simply because they are not introduced by the government, but by a private member.

Public bills are considered and debated in stages as follows:

(1) First Reading. This is simply the introduction of the bill when it is normally carried without discussion.

(2) Second Reading. The main principles of the bill are fully debated and difficulties of detail are noted.

(3) Committee Stage. The bill is discussed in detail either by a standing or select committee, or by a committee of the whole House.

(4) Report Stage. The committee reports to the House and any changes in it are accepted or rejected.

(5) Third Reading. The concluding general debate at which only small verbal changes are normally agreed. The bill is then sent to the House of Lords where the legislative procedure is repeated.

Where the bill originates in the upper House the procedure is similar but reversed.

Although private members normally introduce more bills than the government, government legislation is far more likely to be passed. In a normal session approximately 60 to 80 public bills are passed, of which 15 to 20 are private members' or private peers' bills.

Parliamentary committees
Parliament has long made use of committees to cope with an increasing volume of work. Standing committees are used to deal with the committee stage of all bills, unless the House orders otherwise. Bills of constitutional importance are usually taken in 'committee of the whole House' so that as many members as possible have the opportunity to participate in the debate.

Other committees include: select committees, committees on private bills, Scottish and Welsh Grand Committees and specialized committees.

How well the House of Commons performs its functions is a matter of dispute. There are some observers who regard Parliament in general and the House of Commons in particular as a talking-shop reduced to impotence by the rigours of party discipline. Conversely, there are others who argue that this view ignores many of the subtleties of politics and that governments ignore Parliament at their peril.

according to the manufacturers' own data; usefulness is not considered.

The CSM operates a 'yellow card' reporting system: once a drug has entered clinical use doctors are expected to report any side effects. If these prove unacceptable the CSM can withdraw the drug's licence.

Common Prayer, Book of

The service book of the Church of England and the Episcopal Church, based largely on the Roman breviary.

The first service book in English was known as the *First Prayer Book of Edward VI*, published in 1549, and is the basis of the *Book of Common Prayer* still, although not exclusively, in use. The *Second Prayer Book of Edward VI* appeared in 1552, but was withdrawn in 1553 on Mary's accession. In 1559 the *Revised Prayer Book* was issued, closely resembling that of 1549. This was suppressed by Parliament in 1645, but its use was restored in 1660 and a number of revisions were made. This is the officially authorized *Book of Common Prayer* but an act of 1968 legalized alternative services, and the Worship and Doctrine Measure (1974) gave the church control of its worship and teaching. The church's *Alternative Service Book* (1980), in contemporary language, is also in use.

Commons, House of

Lower chamber of ◊Parliament, in Westminster, London; see feature opposite for how it operates. See also House of ◊Lords.

> *The British, being brought up on team games, enter the House of Commons in the spirit of those who would rather be doing something else.*
>
> C NORTHCOTE PARKINSON English writer and historian.
> *Parkinson's Law* (1958)

Commonwealth Games

Multisport gathering of competitors from British Commonwealth countries, held every four years. The first meeting (known as the British Empire Games) was in Hamilton, Canada, August 1930. It has been held in Britain on four occasions: London 1934; Cardiff 1958; Edinburgh 1970 and 1986. Manchester will host the 2002 games.

Commonwealth Immigration Acts

Successive acts to regulate the entry into the UK of British subjects from the Commonwealth. The Commonwealth Immigration Act, passed by the Conservative government in 1962, ruled that Commonwealth immigrants entering Britain must have employment or be able to offer required skills. Further restrictions have been added since.

Commonwealth, the

Republican rule by Parliament during the Interregnum of 1649–60, more precisely the periods 1649–53 and 1659–60 – in the intervening years Oliver Cromwell ruled by direct personal government under the protectorate. After the abolition of the monarchy in 1649, the ◊Rump Parliament declared England to be a 'Commonwealth or Free State'. The House of Commons held supreme authority, with the former executive powers of the monarchy being vested in a 40-member Council of State. However, Parliament was not sufficiently radical for the army, and was dissolved in May 1653 by Cromwell.

In December, the ◊Barebones Parliament passed the 'Instrument of Government', placing supreme authority in the hands of Cromwell personally. Cromwell ruled under the terms of the Protectorate until his death in 1659, when he was succeeded briefly by his son Richard. Richard was unable to provide the strong leadership of his father, and in May the army restored the Rump Parliament. Parliament and the army were unable to cooperate any better than in the first phase of the Commonwealth, and the House of Commons began negotiations for the ◊Restoration of Charles II.

Commonwealth, the (British)

Voluntary association of 54 countries and their dependencies, the majority of which once formed part of the ◊British Empire and are now independent sovereign states. They are all regarded as 'full members of the Commonwealth'; the newest member being Mozambique, which was admitted in November 1995. Additionally, there are some 20 territories that are not completely sovereign and remain dependencies of the UK or one of the other fully sovereign members, and are regarded as 'Commonwealth countries'. Heads of government meet every two years, apart from those of Nauru and Tuvalu; however, Nauru and Tuvalu have the right to participate in all functional activities. The Commonwealth, which was founded in 1931, has no charter or constitution, and is founded more on tradition and sentiment than on political or economic factors. However, it can make political statements by withdrawing membership; a recent example was Nigeria's suspension in November 1995 because of human-rights abuses. Fiji was readmitted in October 1997, ten years after its membership had been suspended as a result of discrimination against its ethnic Indian community.

In 1995 Queen Elizabeth II was the formal head but not the ruler of 17 member states; 5 member states had their own monarchs; and 31 were republics. The Commonwealth secretariat, headed from October 1989 by Nigerian Emeka Anyaoko (1933–) as secretary general, is based in London. The secretariat's staff come from a number of member countries, which also pay its operating costs.

Communist Party of Great Britain, CPGB

British Marxist party founded in 1920, largely inspired by the Russian Revolution of 1917. Its affiliation with the Labour Party (it has originally been intended as a branch of the Labour Party) ended in the late 1920s, when the organization was proscribed. The party enjoyed its greatest popularity in the 1930s and 1940s, particularly after Britain allied with the

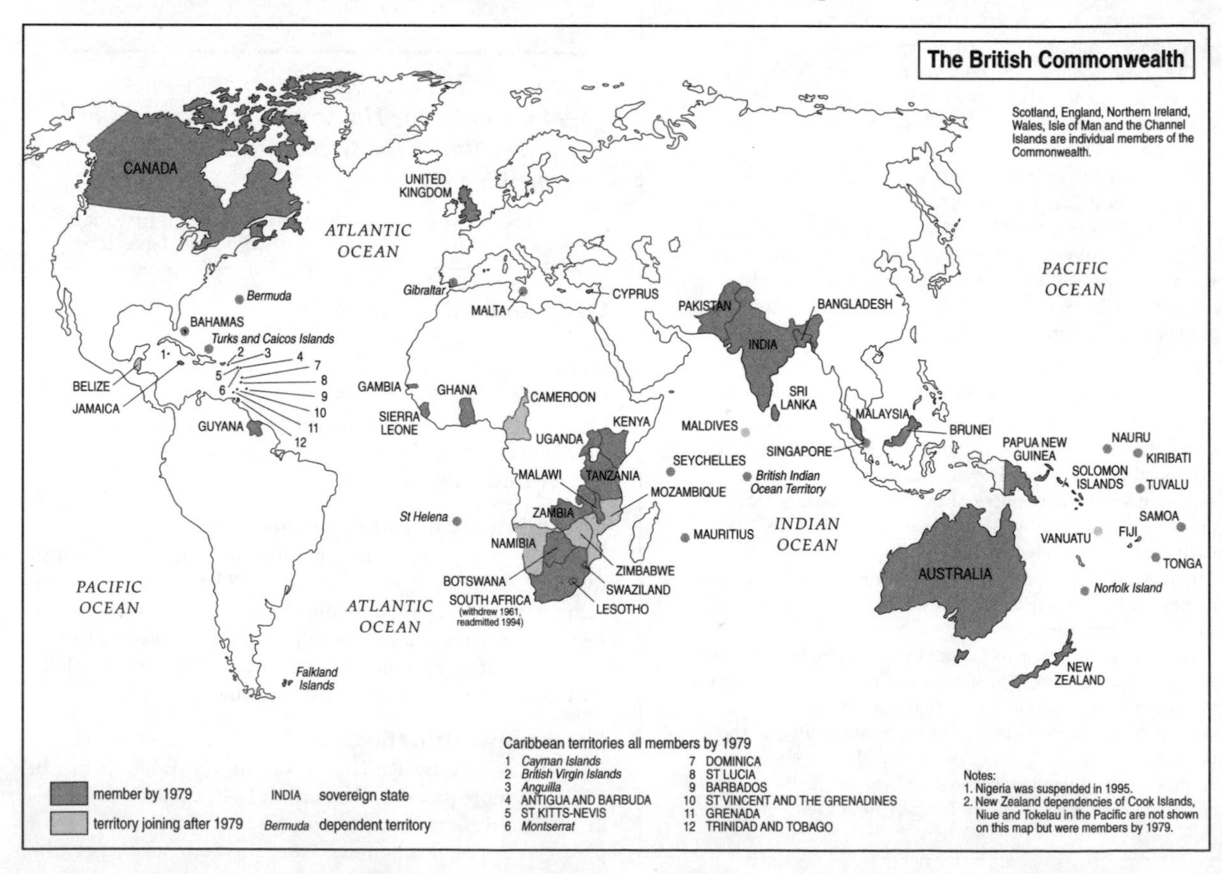

Countries of the British Commonwealth

country	date joined	constitutional status
	in Africa	
Botswana	1966	sovereign republic
British Indian Ocean Territory	1965	British dependent territory
Cameroon	1995	emergent democratic republic
Fiji	1970, 1997	sovereign republic
Gambia	1965	sovereign republic
Ghana	1957	sovereign republic
Kenya	1963	sovereign republic
Lesotho	1966	sovereign constitutional monarchy
Malawi	1964	sovereign republic
Mauritius	1968	sovereign republic
Mozambique	1995	emergent democratic republic
Namibia	1990	sovereign republic
Nigeria[4]	1960	sovereign republic
St Helena	1931	British dependent territory
Seychelles	1976	sovereign republic
Sierra Leone	1961	sovereign republic
South Africa	1910[2]	sovereign republic
Swaziland	1968	sovereign republic
Tanzania	1961	sovereign republic
Uganda	1962	sovereign republic
Zambia	1964	sovereign republic
Zimbabwe	1980	sovereign republic
	in the Americas	
Anguilla	1931	British dependent territory
Antigua and Barbuda	1981	sovereign constitutional monarchy[1]
Bahamas	1973	sovereign constitutional monarchy[1]
Barbados	1966	sovereign constitutional monarchy[1]
Belize	1982	sovereign constitutional monarchy[1]
Bermuda	1931	British dependent territory
British Virgin Islands	1931	British dependent territory
Canada	1931	sovereign constitutional monarchy[1]
Cayman Islands	1931	British dependent territory
Dominica	1978	sovereign republic
Falkland Islands	1931	British dependent territory
Grenada	1974	sovereign constitutional monarchy[1]
Guyana	1966	sovereign republic
Jamaica	1962	sovereign constitutional monarchy[1]
Montserrat	1931	British dependent territory
St Christopher–Nevis	1983	sovereign constitutional monarchy[1]
St Lucia	1979	sovereign constitutional monarchy[1]
St Vincent and the Grenadines	1979	sovereign constitutional monarchy[1]
Trinidad and Tobago	1962	sovereign republic
Turks and Caicos Islands	1931	British dependent territory
	in the Antarctic	
Australian Antarctic Territory	1936	Australian external territory
British Antarctic Territory	1931	British dependent territory
Falkland Islands Dependencies	1931	British dependent territories
Ross Dependency	1931	New Zealand associated territory
	in Asia	
Bangladesh	1972	sovereign republic
Brunei	1984	sovereign monarchy
Hong Kong	1931	

continued on page 204

Countries of the British Commonwealth

country	date joined	constitutional status
India	1947	sovereign republic
Malaysia	1957	sovereign constitutional monarchy
Maldives	1982	sovereign republic
Pakistan	1947[3]	sovereign republic
Singapore	1965	sovereign republic
Sri Lanka	1948	sovereign republic
in Australasia and the Pacific		
Australia	1931	sovereign constitutional monarchy[1]
Cook Islands	1931	New Zealand associated territory
Norfolk Island	1931	Australian external territory
Kiribati	1979	sovereign republic
Nauru	1968	sovereign republic
New Zealand	1931	sovereign constitutional monarchy[1]
Niue	1931	New Zealand associated territory
Papua New Guinea	1975	sovereign constitutional monarchy[1]
Pitcairn Islands	1931	British dependent territory
Solomon Islands	1978	sovereign constitutional monarchy[1]
Tokelau	1931	New Zealand associated territory
Tonga	1970	sovereign monarchy
Tuvalu	1978	sovereign constitutional monarchy[1]
Vanuatu	1980	sovereign republic
Western Samoa	1970	sovereign republic
in Europe		
Channel Islands	1931	UK crown dependencies
Guernsey		
Jersey		
Cyprus	1961	sovereign republic
Gibraltar	1931	British dependent territory
Malta	1964	sovereign republic
Isle of Man	1931	UK crown dependency
United Kingdom	1931	sovereign constitutional monarchy[1]
England		
Northern Ireland		
Scotland		
Wales		

[1] Queen Elizabeth II constitutional monarch and head of state [2] withdrew from membership 1961 and readmitted 1994 [3] left 1972 and rejoined 1989 [4] suspended 1995

USSR during World War II. It had 18,000 members in 1939 and had two MPs elected in 1945, representing West Fife in Scotland and Mile End in London. The party was riven internally by the Soviet invasion of Hungary in 1956 and moved away from the USSR during the 1960s, particularly after the invasion of Czechoslovakia of 1968. Disbanded in 1991, the party was relaunched as 'Democratic Left', although some splinter factions still lay claim to the old name.

community charge

A charge (commonly known as the ◊poll tax) levied by local authorities from 1989 in Scotland and 1990 in England and Wales; it was replaced in 1993 by a council tax.

community council

In Wales, name for a ◊parish council.

Community law

Law of the member states of the ◊European Union, as adopted by the Council of Ministers. The European Court of Justice interprets and applies EU law. Community law forms part of the law of states and prevails over national law. In the UK, community law became effective after enactment of the European Communities Act 1972.

community service

Unpaid work in the service of the community (aiding children, the elderly, or the disabled), performed by a convicted person by order of the court as an alternative to prison.

The scheme was introduced in Britain by the Criminal Justice Act 1972. In English law, the person must be over 16 years, have been convicted of a nonviolent offence punishable with imprisonment, and consent to the making of the order. Breach of a community service order may result in a fine or the court revoking the order so that an alternative sentence may be given. If the convicted person lives in Scotland or Northern Ireland, no order may be made unless arrangements can be made under equivalent Scottish or Northern Ireland provisions.

Companion of Honour

British order of knighthood (see ◊knighthood, orders of) founded in 1917 by George V. It is of one class only, and carries no title, but Companions append CH to their names, next to and after the initials GBE (Knight or Dame Grand Cross). The number is limited to 65 and the award is made to both men and women for conspicuous national service.

comprehensive school

Secondary school that admits pupils of all abilities, and therefore without any academic selection procedure. In England 86.8% of all pupils attend a comprehensive school. Other state secondary schools are middle, deemed secondary (5.2%), secondary modern (2.6%), secondary grammar (4.2%), and technical (0.1%). There were 4,462 state secondary schools in 1995–96, with 3,675,600 pupils.

In England, the 1960s and 1970s saw a slow but major reform of secondary education, in which most state-funded local authorities replaced selective grammar schools (taking only the most academic 20% of children) and secondary modern schools (for the remainder), with comprehensive schools capable of providing suitable courses for children of all abilities. By 1987, only 3% of secondary pupils were still in grammar schools. Scotland and Wales have switched completely to comprehensive education, while Northern Ireland retains a largely selective system.

Compton, Denis Charles Scott (1918–1997)

English cricketer and football player. He played for Middlesex and England, and was a right-handed batsman of prodigious talent and great style, who in 78 tests between 1937 and 1957 scored 5,807 runs at an average of 50.06. In the 1947 English season he scored 3,816 runs (at an average of 90.85) and 18 hundreds, records which are unlikely ever to be surpassed. As a footballer he won Football League and FA Cup winners' medals with Arsenal and played in 12 wartime internationals for England.

Compton-Burnett, Ivy (1884–1969)

English novelist. She used dialogue to show reactions of small groups of characters dominated by the tyranny of family relationships. Her novels, set at the turn of the century, include *Pastors and Masters* (1925), *More Women than Men* (1933), and *Mother and Son* (1955).

Her plots deal exclusively with middle- and upper-class characters and often involve mystery and violence. DBE 1967.

Compton Wynyates

Tudor mansion, once moated, 20 km/12 mi southeast of Stratford-upon-Avon, Warwickshire, England. Begun in 1480, it is built round a courtyard, with the arms of Henry VIII and Catherine of Aragon over the porch.

The house has a number of secret staircases and hiding-places. The Great Hall is panelled, with two minstrels' galleries, carved screens and a timber roof.

In the grounds is a church, rebuilt in 1665, with many memorials of the Compton family. Compton Wynyates is the seat of the Marquess of Northampton.

Compulink Information eXchange, CIX

London-based electronic conferencing system founded in 1987. Owned by Frank and Sylvia Thornley, CIX is the oldest and largest native British conferencing system. In 1996 it had approximately 16,000 users, including most of the country's technology journalists.

Computer Misuse Act

British law passed in 1990 which makes it illegal to hack into computers. The first prosecution under the Act was that of British hacker Paul Bedworth, who in 1993 was acquitted on the grounds that he was addicted to computing.

The law was inspired by the Law Lords' acquittal on appeal of Robert Schifreen and Steve Gold, two journalists who had hacked into Prince Philip's mailbox in 1984 on the British Telecom service Prestel. The Lords ruled that the Forgery Act did not cover deceiving a computer.

Concorde

The only supersonic airliner, which cruises at Mach 2, or twice the speed of sound, about 2,170 kph/1,350 mph. Concorde, the result of Anglo-French cooperation, made its first flight in 1969 and entered commercial service seven years later. It is 62 m/202 ft long and has a wing span of nearly 26 m/84 ft. Developing Concorde cost French and British taxpayers £2 billion.

Confederation of British Industry, CBI

UK organization of employers, established in 1965, combining the former Federation of British Industries (founded in 1916), British Employers' Confederation, and National Association of British Manufacturers. It acts as a pressure group for businesses, promoting their interests to government, overseas, and to workers.

Congleton

Market town in west Cheshire, England; population (1991) 20,800. It is situated on the River Dane, 13 km/8 mi southwest of Macclesfield. Congleton has a wide range of minor textile and engineering industries. In the 19th century it was a silk- and cotton-weaving town; it has since become a residential area for the ◊Potteries.

Congreve, William (1670–1729)

English dramatist and poet. His first success was the comedy *The Old Bachelor* (1693), followed by *The Double Dealer* (1694), *Love for Love* (1695), the tragedy *The Mourning Bride*

CONGREVE, WILLIAM *A portrait of the English dramatist and poet William Congreve. One of the principal writers of Restoration comedy, which flourished on the reopening of the theatres after the restoration of Charles II to the throne, Congreve wrote witty and satirical plays about affectation and manners. Corbis*

(1697), and *The Way of the World* (1700). His plays, which satirize the social affectations of the time, are characterized by elegant wit and wordplay, and complex plots.

Conisbrough

Town in South Yorkshire, England, 8 km/5 mi southwest of Doncaster; population (1991) 14,500. **Conisbrough Castle**, with a fine circular keep, is a Norman castle built by Hamelin, a half-brother of Henry II, in around 1180.

Coniston Water

Lake in the Cumbrian Lake District, England. It has a length of 8 km/5 mi and a width of 1 km/0.6 mi, which makes it one of the smaller lakes in the area. The village of Coniston (population (1991) 1,200) lies 14 km/9 mi west of Bowness, between the lake and Coniston Old Man, which is 802 m/2631 ft high.

Donald Campbell died while attempting to improve his world water-speed record on Coniston Water in 1967.

Peel Island, one of three small islands on the lake, is the 'Wild Cat Island' of Arthur Ransome's novel *Swallows and Amazons* (1931). Brantwood, once the home of John Ruskin, stands above the eastern shore of Coniston Water; Ruskin is buried in Coniston churchyard.

Connery, Sean (Thomas) (1930–)

Scottish film actor. He was the first interpreter of James Bond in several films based on the spy thrillers of Ian Fleming. He has since enjoyed success as a mature actor in such films as *The Name of the Rose* (1986), *Highlander* (1986), and *Indiana Jones and the Last Crusade* (1989). He won an Academy Award for his supporting performance in the crime thriller *The Untouchables* (1987).

Other films include the Bond movies *Dr No* (1962) and *Goldfinger* (1964), *Marnie* (1964), *The Man Who Would Be King* (1975), *Robin and Marian* (1976), *The Hunt for Red October* (1990), *Rising Sun* (1993), *Dragonheart* and *The Rock* (both 1996), and *The Avengers* (1998).

Connery endows his film roles with grace and wit and, since his resurgence as a mature performer, a degree of worldly wisdom. From Bond to more recent roles, he has conveyed himself on screen as a charismatic masculine adventurer. In 1998 he won the ▷BAFTA life achievement award. He has frequently portrayed mythical patriarchs such as an ageing Robin Hood alongside Audrey Hepburn in *Robin and Marian* and King Arthur in *First Knight* (1995).

Connolly, Billy (1942–)

Scottish comedian, actor, and musician. He is best-known in the UK for his stand-up comedy routines, his accomplished performance as Queen Victoria's aide John Brown in *Mrs Brown* (1997), and his television series *Billy Connolly's World Tour of Australia* (1996).

A former welder in the Glasgow shipyards, he has also enjoyed a successful career in the USA, playing Billy MacGregor in his own sitcom *Billy* (1992), a spin-off from *Head of the Class* in which he also featured 1990–91. He is an accomplished banjo player and released several albums.

I nauseate walking; 'tis a country diversion, I loathe the country.

WILLIAM CONGREVE English dramatist and poet.
The Way of the World (1700) IV. iv

Conrad, Joseph pen name of Teodor Józef Konrad Na eøcz Korzeniowski (1857–1924)

British novelist, born in Ukraine of Polish parents. His greatest works include the novels *Lord Jim* (1900), *Nostromo* (1904), *The Secret Agent* (1907), and *Under Western Eyes* (1911); the short story *Heart of Darkness* (1902); and the short novel 'The Shadow Line' (1917). These combine a vivid and sensuous evocation of various lands and seas with a rigorous, humane scrutiny of moral dilemmas, pitfalls, and desperation.

The novel *Chance* (1912) was Conrad's first triumphant success. Thereafter he was regarded as one of the greatest modern authors, although his subsequent output was small. His critical reputation and influence have grown steadily since his death.

He was brought up in Russia and Poland. He landed at

Lowestoft, Suffolk, in 1878 with no knowledge of English, but in 1886 he gained his master mariner's certificate and became a naturalized British subject. He retired from the sea 1894 to write, living in Kent from 1896.

Conran, Jasper Alexander Thirlby (1959–)

English fashion designer. He is known for using quality fabrics to create comfortable garments. He launched his first collection in 1978 and has rarely altered the simple, successful style he then adopted. He has also designed costumes for the stage. He is the son of Terence ◊Conran.

Conran, Terence Orby (1931–)

English designer and retailer of furnishings, fashion, and household goods. He was founder of the Storehouse group of companies, including Habitat and Conran Design, with retail outlets in the UK, the USA, and elsewhere. He has been influential in popularizing French country style in the UK.

In 1964 he started the Habitat company, then developed Mothercare. The Storehouse group gained control of British Home Stores in 1986. He was knighted in 1983.

Conroy, Stephen (1964–)

Scottish painter. His enigmatic figure compositions owe something to those of Steven ◊Campbell, but they are more studied and inward-looking. He achieved recognition while still a student at Glasgow School of Art and has become a leading figure in Scottish art.

CONRAD, JOSEPH *English writer Joseph Conrad, photographed in about 1905. Conrad, who first learned English at the age of 21, is now regarded as one of the greatest of modern English novelists. His works include the novels* Lord Jim *(1900) and* Nostromo *(1904), and the short story 'Heart of Darkness' (1902). Corbis*

conscription

Legislation for all able-bodied male citizens (and female in some countries) to serve with the armed forces. It originated in France in 1792, and in the 19th and 20th centuries became the established practice in almost all European states.

In Britain conscription was introduced for single men between 18 and 41 in March 1916 and for married men two months later, but was abolished after World War I. It was introduced for the first time in peace in April 1939, when all men aged 20 became liable to six months' military training. The National Service Act, passed in September 1939, made all men between 18 and 41 liable to military service, and in 1941 women also became liable to be called up for the women's services as an alternative to industrial service. Men reaching the age of 18 continued to be called up until 1960.

consent, age of

Age at which consent may legally be given to sexual intercourse by a girl or boy.

In the UK it is 16 (18 for male homosexual intercourse). The Criminal Law Amendment Act 1885 raised the age of consent from 13 to 16, and that of abduction from 16 to 18, after a campaign by William Thomas Stead (1849–1912), editor of the *Pall Mall Gazette*, exposed the white slave trade from England to Paris and Brussels. Stead's purchase of a girl to demonstrate the existence of the trade led to his prosecution, conviction, and imprisonment for three months.

UK MPs in late June 1998 voted overwhelmingly to lower the age of consent for homosexuals to 16. The leaders of all three main parties supported the vote for equality along with most of the Cabinet. However, the House of Lords in late July decisively threw out the amendment by 290 votes to 122.

conservation

In the life sciences, action taken to protect and preserve the natural world, usually from pollution, overexploitation, and other harmful features of human activity.

Conservation groups in Britain originated in the 1860s; they include the Commons Preservation Society (1865), which fought successfully against the enclosure of Hampstead Heath (1865) and Epping Forest (1866) in London; the National Footpaths Preservation Society (1844); and the ◊National Trust (1895). More recently ◊English Heritage (1983), ◊English Nature (1991) (formerly the Nature Conservancy Council), and the ◊Countryside Commission (1968) have become heavily involved.

See list starting on page 208 of Areas of Outstanding Natural beauty, designated by the Countryside Commission. See also ◊World Heritage Sites.

Natura 2000

Twelve coastal sites in Great Britain, including five Special Areas of Conservation, have been designated by the European

Areas of Outstanding Natural Beauty and National Scenic Areas

The Countryside Commission designates Areas of Outstanding Natural Beauty in England, and in Wales similar areas are the responsibility of the Countryside Council for Wales. No Areas of Outstanding Natural Beauty are designated in Scotland. The Scottish Natural Heritage recognizes equivalent sites called National Scenic Areas.
(N/A = not available.)

Name	**Region**	**Established (year)**	**Area**	
			sq km	**sq mi**
	England			
Arnside and Silverdale	Cumbria, Lancashire	1972	75	29
Blackdown Hills	Devon, Somerset	1991	370	143
Cannock Castle	Staffordshire	1958	68	26
Chichester Harbour	Hampshire, West Sussex	1964	74	29
Chilterns	Bedfordshire, Buckinghamshire, Hertfordshire, Oxfordshire	1965; extended 1990	833	322
Cornwall	Cornwall	1959; Camel estuary 1983	958	370
Cotswolds	South Gloucestershire, Bath and Northeast Somerset, Gloucestershire, Herefordshire, Worcestershire, Oxfordshire, Wiltshire, Warwickshire	1966	2,038	787
Cranborne Chase and West Wiltshire Downs	Dorset, Hampshire, Somerset, Wiltshire	1983	983	379
Dedham Vale	Essex, Suffolk	1970; extended 1978, 1991	90	35
Dorset	Dorset, Somerset	1959	1,129	436
East Devon	Devon	1963	268	103
East Hampshire	Hampshire	1962	383	148
Forest of Bowland	Lancashire, North Yorkshire	1964	802	310
High Weald	Sussex, Kent, Surrey	1983	1,460	564
Howardian Hills	North Yorkshire	1987	204	79
Isle of Wight	Isle of Wight	1963	189	73
Isles of Scilly	Isles of Scilly	1976	16	6
Kent Downs	Bromley, Kent	1968	878	339
Lincolnshire Wolds	Northeast Lincolnshire	1973	558	215
Malvern Hills	Gloucestershire, Herefordshire and Worcestershire	1959	105	40
Mendip Hills	Northwest Somerset, Bath and Northeast Somerset	1972	198	76
Nidderdale	North Yorkshire	1994	603	233
Norfolk Coast	Norfolk	1968	451	174
North Devon	Devon	1960	171	66
North Pennines	Cumbria, Durham, Northumberland	1988	1,983	766
Northumberland Coast	Northumberland	1958	135	52
North Wessex Downs	Berkshire, Hampshire, Oxfordshire, Wiltshire	1972	1,730	668

Name	Region	Established (year)	Area	
			sq km	sq mi
Quantock Hills	Somerset	1957	99	38
Shropshire Hills	Shropshire	1959	804	310
Solway Coast	Cumbria	1964	115	44
South Devon	Devon	1960	337	130
South Hampshire Coast	Hampshire	1967	77	30
Suffolk Coast and Heaths	Suffolk	1970	403	156
Surrey Hills	Surrey	1958	419	162
Sussex Downs	Sussex	1966	983	379
Tamar Valley	Devon, Cornwall	1995	195	115
Wye Valley (England)	Gloucestershire, Herefordshire and Worcestershire	1971	209	126
Northern Ireland				
Antrim Coast and Glens	Co. Antrim	1988	706	273
Causeway Coast	Co. Antrim	1989	42	16
Lagan Valley	Co. Down	1965	21	8
Lecale Coast	Co. Down	1967	31	12
Mourne	Co. Down	1986	570	220
North Derry	Co. Londonderry	1966	130	50
Ring of Gullion	Co. Armagh	1991	154	59
Sperrin	Co. Tyrone, Co. Londonderry	1968	1,010	390
Strangford Lough	Co. Down	1972	186	72
Wales				
Anglesey	Anglesey	1967	221	85
Clwydian Range	Denbighshire, Flintshire	1985	157	60
Gower	Swansea	1956	189	73
Llyn	Gwynedd	1957	161	62
Scotland				
Assynt-Coigach	Highland	N/A	902	348
Ben Nevis and Glen Coe	Highland, Argyll and Bute, Perth and Kinross	N/A	1,016	392
Cairngorm Mountains	Highland, Aberdeenshire, Moray	N/A	672	259
Cuillin Hills	Highland	N/A	219	85
Deeside and Lochnagar	Aberdeenshire, Angus	N/A	400	154
Dornoch Firth	Highland	N/A	75	29
East Stewartry Coast	Dumfries and Galloway	N/A	45	17
Eildon and Leaderfoot	Scottish Borders	N/A	36	14
Fleet Valley	Dumfries and Galloway	N/A	53	20
Glen Affric	Highland	N/A	193	75

Areas of Outstanding Natural Beauty and National Scenic Areas continued

Name	Region	Established (year)	Area	
			sq km	sq mi
Glen Strathfarrar	Highland	N/A	38	15
Hoy and West Mainland	Orkney Islands	N/A	148	57
Jura	Argyll and Bute	N/A	218	84
Kintail	Highland	N/A	155	60
Knapdale	Argyll and Bute	N/A	198	76
Knoydart	Highland	N/A	395	153
Kyle of Tongue	Highland	N/A	185	71
Kyles of Bute	Argyll and Bute	N/A	44	17
Lochna Keal, Mull	Argyll and Bute	N/A	127	49
Loch Lomond	Argyll and Bute, Stirling, West Dunbartonshire	N/A	274	106
Loch Rannoch and Glen Lyon	Perth and Kinross, Stirling	N/A	484	187
Loch Shiel	Highland	N/A	134	52
Loch Tummel	Perth and Kinross	N/A	92	36
Lynn of Lorn	Argyll and Bute	N/A	48	19
Morar, Moidart, and Ardnamurchan	Highland	N/A	135	52
Ninth estuary	Dumfries and Galloway	N/A	93	36
North Arran	North Ayrshire	N/A	238	92
North-West Sutherland	Highland	N/A	205	79
River Earn	Perth and Kinross	N/A	30	12
River Tay	Perth and Kinross	N/A	56	22
St Kilda	Western Isles	N/A	9	3
Scarra, Lunga, and the Garvellachs	Argyll and Bute	N/A	19	7
Shetland	Shetland Islands	N/A	116	45
Small Isles	Highland	N/A	155	60
South Lewis, Harris, and North Uist	Western Isles	N/A	1,096	423
South Uist Machair	Western Isles	N/A	61	24
The Trossachs	Stirling	N/A	46	18
Trotternish	Highland	N/A	50	19
Upper Tweeddale	Scottish Borders	N/A	105	41
Wester Ross	Highland	N/A	1,453	561

Commission to be part of a network of Natura 2000 sites. The EC will provide funds to help preserve these sites from development, overfishing, and pollution, and to monitor rare plants. They include the north Northumberland coast, with its sea caves, its breeding population of grey seals in the Farne Islands, and Arctic species such as the wolf fish; the Wash and north Norfolk coast, with its population of common seals, waders, and wildfowl, and its extensive salt marshes; and

Plymouth Sound and estuaries, with their submerged sandbanks.

'Turning the Tide'

A £10 million project, launched in 1997 by the Millennium Commission, to protect and restore Britain's only magnesium limestone cliffs, between Hartlepool and Sunderland. The area is rich in wild flowers, with grassland and denes (steep, wooded valleys). Intensive farming and the use of fertilizers have damaged the flora and fauna of the area. The beaches are polluted as a result of over two centuries of coal mining along the Durham coast. Waste from the mines was dumped into the sea and on to the beaches, leaving heaps of spoil 3.7–4.6 m/12–15 ft high. The restoration project aims to remove spoil from the beaches and return the cliffs to their natural grassland.

conservation, architectural

Attempts to maintain the character of buildings and historical areas in Britain are subject to a growing body of legislation which has designated around a million listed buildings, the largest number in Western Europe. There are now over 6,000 conservation areas and 500,000 listed buildings throughout England alone. See also ◊English Heritage.

Conservative Party

One of the two historic British political parties; the name replaced **Tory** in general use from 1830 onwards. Traditionally the party of landed interests, it broadened its political base under Benjamin Disraeli's leadership in the 19th century. The present Conservative Party's free-market capitalism is supported by the world of finance and the management of industry. In recent history, the Conservative Party was in power under Margaret Thatcher (1979–90) and John Major (1990–97). After the party's defeat in the 1997 general election, John Major resigned and was succeeded by William Hague. The party's Central Office is located in Smith Square, London and the current party chairman is Cecil Parkinson.

In the 1980s the party's economic policies increased the spending power of the majority, but also the gap between rich and poor; nationalized industries were sold off (see ◊privatization); military spending and close alliance with the USA were favoured; and the funding of local government was overhauled with the introduction of the ◊poll tax. The Conservative government of John Major 1990–97 repudiated some of the extreme policies of Thatcherism, notably the poll tax, introduced the new ◊Citizen's Charter, and promoted further privatization or market testing.

Opposed to the *laissez-faire* of the Liberal manufacturers, the Conservative Party supported, to some extent, the struggle of the working class against the harsh conditions arising from the Industrial Revolution. The split of 1846 over Robert Peel's Corn Law policy led to 20 years out of office, or in office without power, until Disraeli 'educated' his party into accepting parliamentary and social change, extended the franchise to the artisan (winning considerable working-class support), launched imperial expansion, and established an alliance with industry and finance. The Irish Home Rule issue of 1886 drove Radical Imperialists and old-fashioned Whigs into alliance with the Conservatives, so that the party had nearly 20 years of office, but fear that Joseph Chamberlain's protectionism would mean higher prices led to a Liberal landslide in 1906. The Conservative Party fought a rearguard action against the sweeping reforms that followed and only the outbreak of World War I averted a major crisis. During 1915–45, except briefly in 1924 and 1929–31, the Conservatives were continually in office, whether alone or as part of a coalition, largely thanks to the break-up of the traditional two-party system by the rise of Labour.

Labour swept to power after World War II, but the Conservative Party formulated a new policy in their Industrial Charter of 1947, visualizing an economic and social system in which employers and employed, private enterprise and the state, work to mutual advantage. Antagonism to further nationalization and postwar austerity returned the Conservatives to power in 1951 with a small majority, and prosperity kept them in office throughout the 1950s and early 1960s. Narrowly defeated in 1964 under Alec Douglas-Home, the Conservative Party from 1965 elected its leaders, beginning with Edward Heath, who became prime minister in 1970. The imposition of wage controls led to confrontation with the unions; when Heath sought a mandate in February 1974, this resulted in a narrow defeat, repeated in a further election in October 1974.

Margaret Thatcher replaced Heath, and under her leadership the Conservative Party returned to power in May 1979. She was re-elected in 1983 and 1987, but was ousted in November 1990 following an intra-party challenge by Michael ◊Heseltine. The Conservative government continued in office under John Major who went on to be re-elected in 1992. By 1995 a clear division had emerged in the party's approach to Europe, with pro-Europeans, including Kenneth ◊Clarke, the ◊chancellor of the Exchequer, mainly to the left and 'Eurosceptics', including Michael ◊Portillo, the defence secretary, and John Redwood, the former Welsh secretary who later challenged John Major's leadership (1995), mainly to the right. The Macleod Group was formed in 1995 by party left-wingers, but several on the left defected to the Labour and Liberal Democrat parties.

In the 1997 general election, Conservative support fell to 31%, its lowest level since 1832, and the party fell to a landslide defeat, winning no seats in Scotland or Wales. It held the smallest number of seats (165) since 1906.

The new leader, William Hague, sought to draw a ' line in the sand' over the party's European policy, by ruling out United Kingdom membership of the European Monetary Union for at least 10 years. He also reformed the party's organization, giving the rank-and-file a say in the election of future leaders. In September 1998 a £1 million recruitment drive was launched, with the aim of doubling membership from 325,000 within two years.

Conspicuous Gallantry Cross

British military award, second only to the ◊Victoria Cross in honour, instituted in October 1993. It is awarded regardless of rank. It replaced the Conspicuous Gallantry Medal, the Distinguished Conduct Medal, and the Distinguished Service

BRITAIN'S UNWRITTEN CONSTITUTION

Parliamentary sovereignty

Unlike most modern democracies that have written constitutions and bills of rights, Britain has never written down a set of rules that governs its democracy. Instead, the British constitution was settled in 1688 through a division of power between Parliament and the King, embodied in the English Bill of Rights. At the core of this arrangement is the doctrine of parliamentary sovereignty, established by the 1688 settlement. This itself was the product of decades of struggle between Parliament and monarchs.

According to this doctrine, Parliament is the only source of political authority; it is sovereign and can make and unmake laws at will. Unlike countries with a written constitution, there are no fundamental laws that can bind Parliament. Although certain practices, such as universal suffrage, are deeply ingrained in British culture, there is nothing to stop Parliament – perfectly lawfully – abolishing voting and extending its own life indefinitely. Nor does our society possess fundamental rights. Instead, broadly speaking, our laws tell us what we cannot do and our freedom exists, to use Thomas Hobbes' phrase, 'in the silence of the law'.

The problems with parliamentary sovereignty

In practice, this doctrine often ends up being the sovereignty of government – the will of the largest political party – rather than Parliament. Away from Westminster, as we live in a unitary state (as opposed to a federal state), all other tiers of government – local government, development boards, health authorities, regional assemblies – are creatures of Parliament. They can be made and unmade at will. At Westminster itself, the House of Commons is dominated by the government. About one-third of MPs of the majority party hold a government post – they are known as the 'payroll vote'. There is a generally effective system of party discipline through the whips. Prime Ministerial favour deals out political honours, decides who goes on foreign trips, who is preferred for office and so on, creating a considerable concentration of patronage. So, without formal checks and balances, Parliament is often dominated by the government.

Crown in Parliament

The government in Britain is known as the Crown in Parliament. This means that the government functions with the power of a monarch. Governments can make or amend treaties and declare war without reference to Parliament, as was shown by the legal advice given the government relating to the Maastricht Treaty. It can govern through statutory instrument or orders in council, which in other countries would be known as government by decree. Indeed, the UK is best understood not as a democracy in the real sense of the word, but as a limited monarchy.

Composition of Parliament

Members of Parliament are elected by a first-past-the-post system. As a result, no government in the last 30 years has commanded a majority of votes cast, let alone a majority vote among the population as a whole. It is generally accepted that there have been three great electoral victories this century that have changed the face of the country – the Liberals in 1906, Labour in 1945, and the Conservatives in 1979. All were won on a minority of the popular vote: a minority of the population has elected governments that have then been able to wield vast concentrations of power.

It is little wonder that Lord Hailsham, when in Opposition, called this situation 'elective dictatorship'. It is scarcely surprising that, in the past few years, judges have become increasingly active in challenging the actions of ministers, arguing from the belief that Parliament is failing to hold government to account. People feel that a determined government can and does ignore widely held views. And there is an increasing sense that our political institutions are not capable of responding to the challenges of the modern world.

Changes: a Bill of Rights

Public concern at the state of British democracy has led to strong public support for constitutional reform. Many people believe that a Bill of Rights would enshrine those basic civil and political freedoms that are necessary to a democratic society. The basis for such a Bill already exists in the European Convention of Human Rights, which Britain has pledged to uphold. If this were appropriately updated, it could be made law – or incorporated – in the UK. This would provide a means for redress for breaches of our rights in British courts that is currently only available after lengthy and expensive legislation in Strasbourg.

Freedom of information

A Freedom of Information Act would establish our right to know. This legislation would be based on the presumption

Order for particular acts of heroism. The first CGC was awarded in May 1995.

Constable, John (1776–1837)

English artist; one of the greatest landscape painters of the 19th century. He painted scenes of his native Suffolk, including *The Haywain* (1821; National Gallery, London), as well as castles, cathedrals, landscapes, and coastal scenes in other parts of Britain. Constable inherited the Dutch tradition of sombre Realism, in particular the style of Jacob Ruisdael. He aimed to capture the momentary changes of the weather as well as to create monumental images of British scenery, as in *The White Horse* (1819; Frick Collection, New York) and *Salisbury Cathedral from the Bishop's Grounds* (1827; Victoria and Albert Museum, London).

Constable's paintings are remarkable for their atmospheric effects and were admired by many French painters, including Eugène Delacroix. Notable are *The Leaping Horse* (1825; Royal Academy, London); *The Cornfield* (1826; National Gallery, London); and *Dedham Vale* (1828; National Gallery of Scotland, Edinburgh). His many oil sketches are often considered among his best work.

that all information in the hands of the government should be made available to its citizens. Any exceptions to this rule should be limited and specific. They must be necessary to protect life, or to guarantee the security of the nation. This would mean an end to blanket terms such as 'national security', which have often been abused by governments in their own narrow party political interest. A Freedom of Information Act should also set up a new framework of public law to regulate the way in which policy is made, ensuring that policy bodies cannot be lobbied in secret, or make decisions based on inadequate, or biased, research.

Parliament brought up to date

Parliament itself needs to be more independent of government, returning to the spirit of 1688, but updated to suit a modern setting. Backbench MPs, who arrive in Parliament at the moment with no clear task to perform, must be provided with a proper job. This could be achieved by expanding the existing Select Committees (bodies that monitor Parliament's work in particular areas) into departmental committees with a space for every MP. The new committees should have tough powers to scrutinize the work of government with the resources of the National Audit Office at their disposal to make sure they have the information they need. They should also have the power to undertake pre-legislative scrutiny of Bills, including the right to take evidence in public, so that the process of policy-making can be broadened. Looking at Bills before they become law could help to stop poor-quality legislation such as the Dangerous Dogs Act. Moreover, fixed-term Parliaments would help to prevent the flagrant manipulation of politics in the government's interests.

Decentralize power

But even a reformed Parliament could not cope with the volume of business of a modern state. It cannot possibly provide adequate scrutiny for everything, or know all there is to know about legislation affecting a particular region of the country. The volume of business of primary and secondary legislation is beyond any minister or MP. The forthcoming Parliament in Scotland and Assembly in Wales, should mean that decisions affecting local people are taken closer to the communities they affect. An equivalent regional government in England might be a logical addition. Some people argue that these changes could destroy the UK, but we need not be afraid of flexibility in our political arrangements – other countries, such as Germany, survive with it.

Electoral reform

Some consideration is also being given to electoral reform. We need a system where seats in Parliament are held in proportion to the number of votes cast by the people. A first step could be a referendum giving voters in this country a choice of options for their voting system for the first time in our history.

Europe

In parallel, it is also necessary to tackle the accountable nature of European Community institutions. Any country that wishes to join the European Community has to fulfil certain democratic criteria. It is one of the ironies of history that the European Community would fail its own admissions requirements. Its only democratic body, the Parliament, has virtually no power, and the powerful European Commission is in many ways accountable to nobody. As discussions of economic and political union grow more intense and heated, and as Britain approaches the convergence criteria for Monetary Union, it is vitally important that questions about the democratic nature of European institutions are raised now. As a minimum, this would mean applying a European Bill of Rights throughout the European Community to create minimum accountability of the European Commission to the citizens of Europe, which it lacks at present.

Prerogative powers

The role of the monarch as the head of state also needs to be considered. It is vital that the royal powers of the 'prerogative' that are used by government ministers are taken away from the monarch and placed under Parliamentary control. Whether the monarchy would continue to be the ceremonial head of state, or whether people would prefer an elected head of state, could then be the subject of a referendum.

Culture of liberty

None of this is a comprehensive 'answer' to the question of improving democracy. The defence of democracy requires vigilance in the population as a whole. As a US Supreme Court judge said, 'When liberty dies in the hearts of men and women, no law can revive it'. The culture of liberty in this country is very real but it needs nurturing, strengthening, and modernizing – like any other aspect of life.

BY ANDREW PUDDEPHATT

The flat lands, streams, water meadows and cornfields of his native East Anglia, and especially the part of the Stour valley near his home are now known as the 'Constable country'.

In England his immediate influence was practically nil; in France, on the other hand, his influence was felt by the Barbizon School, and later by the Impressionists.

constitution

The UK is one of the few countries not to adopt a written constitution; instead it has an accumulation of customs and precedents, together with a body of laws defining certain of its aspects. See feature above on some implications of Britain's unwritten constitution. See also ◊Parliament for a glossary of Parliamentary terms, and House of ◊Commons for how a bill becomes law.

contemporary dance

New and experimental dance forms that have evolved away from (and often in opposition to) conventions of classical ballet.

In the UK, leading exponents of ◊new dance or avant-garde techniques include Michael ◊Clark from the

CONTI, TOM *Scottish stage and television actor Tom Conti. He received an Academy Award nomination for his role in* Reuben, Reuben *(1983). Corbis*

mid-1980s, Rosemary ◊Butcher, and Lloyd ◊Newson. There is a wide diversity of style within new dance in Britain, with individual choreographers developing their own response to the idiom, drawing on influences from other movement and theatre methods, installation and site-specific work, and new technology.

Conti, Tom (1942–)

Scottish stage and film actor. Specializing in character roles, he has appeared in *The Duellists* (1977), *Merry Christmas Mr Lawrence* (1982), *Reuben, Reuben* (1983), *Beyond Therapy* (1987), *Shirley Valentine* (1989), *Something to Believe In* (1997), and *Out of Control* (1998), among others. On stage he has appeared in *Jeffrey Bernard is Unwell* (1990); he both acted in and directed *Present Laughter* (1993), and *Chapter 2* (1996).

> *It fills the page so I don't have to do a background.*
>
> Beryl Cook British artist.
> On 'why she likes painting fat people'; *Independent on Sunday*, 8 February 1998

Continuity IRA

An extremist Irish Republican terrorist group which split away from the ◊IRA in 1995. It was responsible for blowing up Killyhevlin Hotel, near Enniskillen, in July 1996 and car bombings during 1997 and 1998. It is based in the Irish Republic, just south of the border with Northern Ireland, and is aligned with Republican Sinn Fein, which broke away from Sinn Fein proper in 1986 when the latter decided to take a seat in the Irish Parliament. Although its membership was estimated to be below 50, from September 1998 it was the only Republican terrorist body which remained officially active.

Conwy

Unitary authority in north Wales, created in 1996 from parts of the former counties of Clwyd and Gwynedd
Area 1,107 sq km/427 sq mi
Towns ◊Conwy (administrative headquarters), Abergele, ◊Llandudno, Llanrwst
Physical rivers Conwy and Elwy
Features ◊Snowdonia National Park; coastline of sandy beaches, including the seaside resort of ◊Colwyn Bay
Industries tourism
Population (1996) 113,000.

Conwy

Port, market town and administrative centre of the ◊Conwy unitary authority, north Wales, situated on a steep slope at the estuary of the River Conwy; population (1991) 3,600. It was known until 1972 by the anglicized form **Conway**. Still surrounded by walls, it has the ruins of a castle rebuilt by Edward I in 1284 to subjugate the Welsh. Bodnant Gardens are situated on the east bank of the river.

Castle Conwy, one of the finest feudal fortresses of Britain, has very thick walls and eight vast towers. It was held for Charles I in the Civil War. The Cistercian monks who inhabited the abbey, built in 1185 in the same area, were removed by Edward I to Maenan, near Llanwrst; the abbey ruins can still be seen. The ancient church at Conwy, which contains part of the old abbey building, has a magnificent 15th-century rood screen. Plas Mawr, an old Elizabethan mansion, is now the home of the Royal Cambrian Academy of Art. The remains of the Roman fort of Conovium (Caerhun) are 8 km/5 mi from Conwy. The site was excavated in 1926–27, showing that it was probably built in about 80 and evacuated about 140. A road bridge built in 1958 now stands beside Telford's suspension bridge built in 1826.

Cook, Beryl (1926–)

English naive painter. She depicts plump, jovial figures in everyday situations, often with a sense of saucy humour. She started painting when she was in her 40s and had her first exhibition in 1975, at Plymouth Arts Centre.

After this she became nationally known, and a collection of her paintings was published as *The Works* (1978), the first of several books to her credit. Her work has also been widely reproduced on greetings cards.

Cook, James (1728–1779)

English naval explorer. After surveying the St Lawrence River in North America in 1759, he made three voyages: 1768–71 to Tahiti, New Zealand, and Australia; 1772–75 to the South Pacific; and 1776–79 to the South and North Pacific, attempting to find the Northwest Passage and charting the Siberian coast. He was largely responsible for Britain's initial interest in acquiring colonies in Australasia. He was killed in Hawaii early in 1779 in a scuffle with islanders.

I suppose I've had a few. But I can't seem to remember what they are.

Peter Cook English satirist and entertainer. On being asked towards the end of his life whether he had any regrets

Cook, Peter (Edward) (1937–1995)
English satirist and entertainer. With Dudley ◊Moore, Alan Bennett, and Jonathan Miller, he appeared in the revue *Beyond the Fringe* (1959–64). He opened London's first satirical nightclub, the Establishment, in 1960, and backed the satirical magazine *Private Eye*. He appeared with Dudley Moore in the television series *Not Only But Also* (1965–73), which they also wrote. Cook's distinctive humour was at times as little restrained by any concern for people's feelings as by good taste, and frequently tended towards a kind of verbal surrealism.

Cook, Robin (Robert Finlayson) (1946–)
British Labour politician, foreign secretary from 1997. A member of the moderate-left Tribune Group, he entered Parliament in 1974 and became a leading member of Labour's shadow cabinet, specializing in health matters. When John Smith assumed the party leadership in July 1992, Cook remained in the shadow cabinet as spokesman for trade and industry. He became shadow foreign secretary under Smith's successor, Tony ◊Blair, in October 1994. As foreign secretary, he placed a new emphasis on human rights as part of an ethical foreign policy.

It's better to send middle-aged men abroad to bore each other than send young men abroad to kill each other.

Robin Cook British Labour MP, foreign secretary from 1997.
On UN negotiations with Saddam Hussein; *Independent*, 14 February 1998

Cook, Thomas (1808–1892)
Pioneer British travel agent and founder of Thomas Cook & Son. He organized his first tour, to Switzerland, in 1863. He introduced traveller's cheques (then called 'circular notes') in the early 1870s.

Cooke, (Alfred) Alistair (1908–)
British-born US journalist. He was *Guardian* correspondent in the USA 1948–72, and broadcasts a weekly *Letter from America* on BBC radio.

Cooke, Deryck (1919–1976)
English musicologist. His best-known works include the book *The Language of Music* (1959) and his performing version of Mahler's unfinished tenth symphony, heard in London on 13 August 1964 (revised 1972).

Cookham-on-Thames
Village in Windsor and Maidenhead unitary authority, southern England, on the River Thames, 43 km/27 mi west of London. A memorial gallery of the work of the artist Stanley ◊Spencer, who lived in Cookham for many years, was opened here in 1962. The Keeper of Royal Swans is based in the village.

The British especially shudder at the latest American vulgarity, and then they embrace it with enthusiasm two years later.

Alistair Cooke British-born US journalist.
American Way (magazine of American Airlines), March 1975.

Cookson, Catherine (Ann) (1906–1998)
English popular novelist. From 1950 she was a prolific author of bestselling fiction set in her native Tyneside, northeast England. Her books, characterized by romance and tragedy, are set in various periods from the 19th century onwards. They include the Mallen trilogy (1973–74) and the Tilly Trotter series (1980–82). More recent novels include *The House of Women* (1992), *A Ruthless Need* (1995), *The Branded Man* (1996), and *The Bonny Dawn* (1996).

Cool Britannia
Popular phrase associated with Tony Blair and New Labour, commonly attributed to the magazine *Newsweek*, which in July 1998 denied it had coined the phrase. While it had described London in 1996 as 'the coolest city on the planet' it did not 'extend the adjective to the whole nation, because we know it would have been crazy to do so'.

Cooney, Ray(mond George Alfred) (1932–)
English actor, director, and dramatist. He is known for his farces *Two into One* (1981) and *Run for Your Wife* (1983). More recent work includes *Out of Order* (1990), *Funny Thing* (1994), and *Wife Begins at Forty* (1996).

Cooper, Henry (1934–)
English heavyweight boxer, the only man to win three Lonsdale Belts outright (1961, 1965, and 1970). He held the British heavyweight title 1959–71 and lost it to Joe Bugner. He fought for the world heavyweight title but lost in the sixth round to Muhammad Ali in 1966.

Cooper, Samuel (1609–1672)
English portrait miniaturist. His subjects included Milton, members of Charles II's court, the diarist Samuel Pepys' wife, and Oliver Cromwell.

Cooper, Susie married name Susan Vera Barker (1902–1995)
English pottery designer. Her designs varied from colourful Art Deco to softer, pastel decoration on more classical shapes, with simply-styled patterns of bands, spots, flowers, and animals. She started her own company in 1929 for painting ready-made pottery, and this later became part of the Wedgwood factory, where she was senior designer from 1966.

Cooper, William pen name of Harry Summerfield Hoff (1910–)
English novelist. After *Trina* (1934), set in Yugoslavia, and three further novels under his own name, he published *Scenes from Provincial Life* (1950) under his pen name, to protect identities. Subsequent novels in a similar vein of amused observation include *Scenes from Married Life* (1961) and *Scenes from Later Life* (1983).

Cooperative Party
Former political party founded in Britain in 1917 by the cooperative movement to maintain its principles in parliamentary and local government. A written constitution was adopted in 1938. The party had strong links with the Labour Party; from 1946 Cooperative Party candidates stood in elections as Cooperative and Labour Candidates and, after the 1959 general election, agreement was reached to limit the party's candidates to 30.

Copenhagen, Battle of
Naval victory on 2 April 1801 by a British fleet under Sir Hyde Parker (1739–1807) and ◊Nelson over the Danish fleet. Nelson put his telescope to his blind eye and refused to see Parker's signal for withdrawal.

Corbett, Ronnie, stage name of Ronald Balfour Corbett (1930–)
Diminutive Scottish comedian and actor. He delievered easy-chair, rambling monologues in the long-running television sketch show *The Two Ronnies*, in which he co-starred with Ronnie ◊Barker from 1971; he revived the format later, in *The Ben Elton Show* (1998). In the early 1980s he featured in the television sitcom *Sorry!* as a middle-aged mummy's boy. He also appeared in the television series *Timbuctoo* (1998).

Corby
Town in Northamptonshire, England, 32 km/19 mi north of Northampton; population (1991) 49,100. A small village until the 1930s, Corby expanded rapidly as a centre of the steel-making industry. The steelworks closed in 1979 and the town is now an enterprise zone producing plastics. Other industries include engineering, electronics, and the manufacture of steel tubing, crisps, and cosmetics (Avon).

Corby was designated a ◊new town in 1950.

Corelli, Marie, pseudonym of Minnie Mackay (1855–1924)
English romantic novelist. Trained for a musical career, she turned instead to writing (she was said to be Queen Victoria's favourite novelist) and published *A Romance of Two Worlds* in 1886. This was the first of a string of bestsellers. Her works were later ridiculed for their pretentious style.

Corfe Castle
Village in the Isle of Purbeck, Dorset, southern England, 8 km/5 mi southwest of Poole; population (1981) 1,300. It was built around the ruins of a Norman castle, destroyed during the English Civil War. Industries include electronics and oil, and tourism is important.

The castle is situated on a high ridge, separated from the village by a ravine over which a bridge has been built. It was built in the 11th century on the site of a Saxon stronghold where King ◊Edward the Martyr was murdered in 978. It was captured by the Earl of Devonshire in the reign of Stephen, and during the English Civil War the castle was a Royalist stronghold and the home of John Bankes, chief justice to Charles I. In 1643 his wife defended it for six weeks against 600 Parliamentary troops, but the castle was finally captured and largely destroyed in 1646.

Cornhill
Street in the City of London, running from the Royal Exchange to Leadenhall Street. It contains the churches of St Michael and St Peter, both built by Christopher Wren, as well as many banks and insurance offices.

The Royal Exchange, situated between Cornhill and Threadneedle Street, was originally built by Sir Thomas Gresham between 1566 and 1571 as a centre for the meetings of merchants and bankers. It was destroyed in the Fire of London in 1666 and rebuilt between 1667 and 1669; it was again destroyed by fire in 1838, and rebuilt between 1842 and 1844.

A Roman basilica used to stand at the eastern end of Cornhill, partly on the site now occupied by Leadenhall Market. A general market appears to have existed here in the 14th century.

Cornish language
Extinct member of the ◊Celtic languages, a branch of the Indo-European language family, spoken in Cornwall, England, until 1777. In recent years the language has been revived in a somewhat reconstructed form by people interested in their Cornish heritage.

Cornish literature
The earliest surviving written Cornish is found in some 10th-century glosses. The late Middle Ages produced some religious writing. Other literature is scanty, consisting mainly of folk tales and verses.

The first connected text is a fragment of 41 lines of verse dating from about 1400. The principal literary texts of the 15th century are a poem *Pascon agan Arluth/The Passion of Our Lord* of 1,036 lines and *Ordinalia*, three plays (8,744 lines in all) telling the biblical story from the Creation to the Ascension.

Corn Laws
In Britain until 1846, laws used to regulate the export or import of cereals in order to maintain an adequate supply for

consumers and a secure price for producers. For centuries the Corn Laws formed an integral part of the mercantile system in England; they were repealed because they became an unwarranted tax on food and a hindrance to British exports.

Although mentioned as early as the 12th century, the Corn Laws only became significant in the late 18th century. After the Napoleonic wars, with mounting pressure from a growing urban population, the laws aroused strong opposition because of their tendency to drive up prices. They were modified in 1828 and 1842. The Corn Laws became a hotly contested political issue, as they were regarded by radicals as benefiting wealthy landowners at the expense of the ordinary consumer. The Anti-Corn Law League was formed to campaign for the repeal of the laws in 1838. Partly as a result of the league, and also partly on account of the Irish potato famine, the laws were repealed by prime minister Robert ◊Peel in 1846.

Cornwall

County in southwest England including the Isles of ◊Scilly (Scillies)

Area (excluding Scillies) 3,550 sq km/1,370 sq mi

Towns and cities ◊Truro (administrative headquarters), Camborne, Launceston; Bude, Falmouth, Newquay, Penzance, St Ives (resorts)

Physical Bodmin Moor (including Brown Willy 419 m/1,375 ft); Land's End peninsula; rivers Camel, Fal, Fowey, Tamar

Features St Michael's Mount; Poldhu, site of first transatlantic radio signal 1901; the Stannary or Tinners' Parliament; Tate Gallery, St Ives; the Mineral Tramways Project, which aims to preserve the mining landscape, once the centre of the world's hard-rock mining industry; Eden Project, two 'biomes' (tropical rainforest and Mediterranean) being built in disused china-clay pit near St Austell, scheduled to open in 2000 as a Millennium Commission Landmark Project; the 'Lost' Gardens of Heligan

Industries tourism; electronics; kaolin (a white clay used in the manufacture of porcelain; St Austell is the main centre for production)

Agriculture crops are early in some places: fruit, oats, and vegetables, including swedes, turnips, and mangolds (a root vegetable used as cattle fodder); spring flowers; cattle and sheep rearing; dairy farming; fishing (Mevagissey, Newlyn, and St Ives are the principal fishing ports)

Population (1994) 479,600

History tin was mined from the Bronze Age until 1998, when the last mine, at South Crofty, near Camborne, was closed; The Stannary, or Tinners' Parliament, has six members from each of the four Stannary towns: Losthwithiel, Launceston, Helston, and Truro. It was established in the 11th century, ceased to meet in 1752 but its powers were never rescinded at Westminster, and it was revived in 1974 as a separatist movement. The flag of St Piran, a white St George's cross on a black ground, is used by separatists.

Topography

Cornwall is bounded on the north and northwest by the Atlantic Ocean, on the east by Devonshire, and to the south and southwest by the English Channel. The Scilly Isles are 38 km/24 mi west of ◊Land's End.

CORNWALL *Cotehele House, which stands above the River Tamar valley in Cornwall, was built by a prosperous family 1485–1627, largely from the local materials of granite and slatestone. It is one of numerous attractions in the richly varied duchy of Cornwall. Andrew Besley/National Trust Photographic Library*

The northern coastline is formed of rugged cliffs, and is famous for its wild scenery. Although it has only two harbours of any importance – one formed by the estuary of the River Camel (where Padstow is situated), the other at ◊St Ives bay – there are numerous small creeks, formerly used by smugglers.

The southern coast is also rocky, but to a lesser degree, and has headlands covered with luxuriant vegetation; the most important harbour is at Falmouth.

The surface of Cornwall is extremely irregular; from the River ◊Tamar (on the eastern border) to Land's End it is a series of rugged hills, alternating with wide stretches of moorland. The Tamar is the county's chief river; it is tidal, and navigable for 30 km/19 mi.

Plant life

The climate is mild, particularly in the south, and vegetation there grows prolifically; fuchsias, geraniums, camellias, myrtles, and hydrangeas flourish around Penzance and Falmouth during the winter. Exotic plants that would normally have to be grown under glass in Britain grow in the open in the Scilly Isles.

Mining

Cornwall's mines were formerly a great source of wealth, yielding the elements arsenic, bismuth, copper, iron, lead, tin, and zinc. At one time Cornwall supplied half of the world's copper, and all of Britain's tin. The tin industry declined in the first half of the 20th century, because sources in Malaysia were found to be easier to work. However, following renewed interest in Cornish tin in the 1960s, production increased greatly in the 1970s; Cornish mines supplied Britain with nearly a quarter of its tin ore requirement in 1974, but the collapse in world tin prices in the 1980s led to rapid decline, and the last mine closed in 1998. Serpentine rock is also quarried, mainly in the Lizard district; ornaments are produced from it.

Prehistoric remains

There are several types of prehistoric remains in Cornwall: cromlechs, such as Lanyon, Mulfra, and Zennor (all in the Land's End district; the Lanyon cromlech is high enough for a person to ride under); rough monoliths, found in all parts of Cornwall; stone circles, of which the principal one is the Hurlers, near Liskeard; stone avenues, an example being the Nine Maidens near St Colomb Major; and the remains of hut dwellings.

Cornwall's historic remains include many ruined cliff-top and hill-top castles; famous examples are the castles at ◊Tintagel and Launceston, parts of which date from Norman times.

Cornwallis, Charles, 1st Marquis and 2nd Earl (1738–1805)

British general in the ◊American Revolution until 1781, when his defeat at Yorktown led to final surrender and ended the war. He then served twice as governor general of India and once as viceroy of Ireland. Succeeded to Earldom 1762, Marquis 1792.

Coronation Street

Drama serial produced for ITV by Granada since 1961. See ◊soap operas.

Corporation Act

In England, statute of 1661 which effectively excluded religious dissenters from public office. All magistrates in England and Wales were obliged to take sacrament according to the Church of England, to swear an oath of allegiance, to renounce the Covenant, and to declare it treason to carry arms against the King. The measure reflected the wishes of parliament rather than Charles II, though it was later circumvented prior to its repeal in 1828.

corresponding society

In British history, one of the first independent organizations for the working classes, advocating annual parliaments and universal male suffrage. The London Corresponding Society was founded in 1792 by politicians Thomas Hardy (1752–1832) and John Horne Tooke (1736–1812). It later established branches in Scotland and the provinces. Many of its activities had to be held in secret and government fears about the spread of revolutionary doctrines led to its being banned in 1799.

Cort, Henry (1740–1800)

English iron manufacturer. For the manufacture of ◊wrought iron, he invented the puddling process and developed the rolling mill (shaping the iron into bars), both of which were significant in the Industrial Revolution.

Cort's work meant that Britain no longer had to rely on imported iron and could become self-sufficient. His method of manufacture combined previously separate actions into one process, removing the impurities of pig iron and producing high-class metal relatively cheaply and quickly.

Cosgrave, William Thomas (1880–1965)

Irish politician. He took part in the ◊Easter Rising of 1916 and sat in the Sinn Féin cabinet of 1919–21. Head of the Free State government 1922–33, he founded and led the Fine Gael opposition 1933–44.

From January 1922 Cosgrave was minister for local government in the Irish Free State, and acted as deputy for President Griffith during the latter's absence in London. After Griffith's death in August 1922 and the assassination of his successor, Michael ◊Collins, the same month, Cosgrave was chosen as president.

> *I don't want to go cruising in Hollywood or hang out at all the star parties. I'm not interested in any of that ... I'm just interested in playing.*
>
> ELVIS COSTELLO English rock musician.
> Irwin Stambler *The Encyclopedia of Pop, Rock and Soul* 1989

Costello, Elvis stage name of Declan Patrick McManus (1954–)

English rock singer, songwriter, and guitarist. He emerged in the late 1970s as part of the New Wave. His intricate yet impassioned lyrics have made him one of Britain's foremost songwriters, and he dominated the UK rock scene into the early 1980s. His hits range from the political rocker 'Oliver's Army' (1979) to the country weepy 'Good Year for the Roses' (1981) and the punning pop of 'Everyday I Write the Book' (1983).

Cosway, Richard (1742–1821)

English artist. He led an 18th-century revival of the miniature, painting portraits of the Prince Regent's court. His works show an exceptional lightness of touch.

He became very successful through the favour of the Prince of Wales, who greatly admired his *Portrait of Mrs Fitzherbert* (about 1784; Wallace Collection, London), and appointed him painter-in-ordinary.

Cotehele

Medieval house near Calstock, Cornwall, England, on the west bank of the River Tamar. The house, which is virtually unaltered, was acquired by the National Trust, together with 520 ha/1284 acres, through the Treasury in 1947.

The original furniture, fabrics and armour remain in the house. The estate includes a valley shrub garden with many subtropical plants; **Cotehele Quay** on a bend of the river, 1 km/0.5 mi below the house; and Morden Mill, the manorial water-mill, are now restored to working order.

Cotman, John Sell (1782–1842)

English landscape painter. With John Crome, he was a founder of the ◊Norwich School. His early watercolours were bold designs in simple flat washes of colour; *Greta Bridge, Yorkshire* (about 1805; British Museum, London) was a classic in the art.

In the simplification of design to broad, expressively silhouetted areas, he was highly original and unlike any of his contemporaries. Time spent on drawing antiquities for his patron in Norfolk, Dawson Turner (1775–1858), was largely wasted, and his later work is unequal, but it included oil paintings in his own distinct manner as well as some drawings.

Of his two painter sons, **Joseph John Cotman** (1814–1878) and **Miles Edmund Cotman** (1810–1858), the latter is the more distinguished for his river and sea views.

Cotswold Hills, or Cotswolds

Range of limestone hills in Gloucestershire, South Gloucestershire, and Bath and North East Somerset, England, 80 km/50 mi long, between Bath and Chipping Camden. They rise to 333 m/1,086 ft at Cleeve Cloud, near Cheltenham, but average about 200 m/600 ft. The area is known for its picturesque villages, built with the local honey-coloured stone. Tourism is important.

History

Old tracks and evidence of early British forts and Roman camps indicate that the area was important in ancient times. It prospered in the 14th and 16th centuries when the woollen industry of Flemish weavers flourished. The decline of the area's wool industry was primarily triggered by the industrialization of the 1830s, which led to labour disputes, fluctuating markets, strikes, failing machinery, and mill closures.

The artist William Morris, founder of the Arts and Crafts movement, spent his holidays in Broadway and lived at Kelmscott Manor, Lechlade, from 1871 until his death in 1876; he is buried in the churchyard with his wife Jane. Following his patronization of the town, Broadway quickly became a favourite venue for visiting artists; at one stage Broadway Green was so busy that easel space had to be rented.

Features

The oolitic limestone ridge forming the Cotswolds is about 48 km/30 mi wide in some parts, and the range is roughly divided into two portions by the valley of the River Churn. The hills provide good grazing, and large flocks of sheep are bred in the district.

Great parish churches, imposing houses, and solidly built inns are evidence of the wealth of the area in the Middle Ages. Chipping Campden, Northleach, and Cirencester contain fine examples of wool churches, built on the prosperity of the medieval wool trade and heavily adorned with gargoyles and story pictures.

The River Thames rises on the eastern slopes the hills, 5 km/3 mi southwest of Cirencester. The **Cotswold Way** is a long-distance path which runs along the top of the ridge, stretching about 160 km/100 mi from Chipping Campden to Bath.

Near Winchcombe is Belas Knap, a burial chamber dating from about 3000 BC, and there are traces of a Roman camp at Battledown Knoll. Oak trees in the grounds of Ashley Manor, near Charlton Kings, are reputed to be the biggest in the country.

Principal towns and villages

Among the chief towns in the region are ◊Stroud, ◊Cirencester, Chipping Norton, Chipping Campden, Stow-on-the-Wold, ◊Malmesbury, Bourton-on-the-Water, Northleach, Lechlade, Burford, and Tetbury. Gloucester, Cheltenham, Tewkesbury, and Evesham are on the periphery of the Cotswolds area. The main villages are Winchcombe, Cleeve-Hill, Upper and Lower Slaughter, Sherborne, Painswick, Bibury, Sapperton, Fairford, and Broadway, which is known as the 'gateway' to the Cotswolds.

cottar, or cotter

In feudal time, a free smallholder and tenant of a cottage, mainly in southern England.

Cotton, (Thomas) Henry (1907–1987)

English golfer. He won the British Open three times, in 1934, 1937 and 1948, an achievement which, with the exception of Nick ◊Faldo no other British golfer has matched since World War I. He turned professional 1924 at the age of 17. In 1932 he won the first of three PGA Match Play championships. He played in three Ryder Cups in 1929, 1937 and 1947, the last as captain. He was also a non-playing captain 1953.

Cotton, William (1786–1866)

English inventor, financier, and philanthropist. In 1864 he invented a knitting machine for the production of hosiery. This machine had a straight-bar frame which automatically made fully fashioned stockings knitted flat and sewn up the back.

In 1821 Cotton was elected a director of the Bank of

England, and was its governor 1843–46. He invented an automatic weighing machine for sovereigns.

council

In local government in England and Wales, a popularly elected local assembly charged with the government of the area within its boundaries. Under the Local Government Act 1972, they comprise three types: ◊county councils, ◊district councils, and ◊parish councils.

Council for the Protection of Rural England

Countryside conservation group founded in 1926 by Patrick ◊Abercrombie with interests ranging from planning controls to energy policy. A central organization campaigns on national issues and 42 local groups lobby on regional matters.

The **Campaign for the Preservation of Rural Wales** is the Welsh equivalent.

Council in the Marches

Royal court with jurisdiction over Wales and the English border counties; established as part of the process of imposing the King's rule over the semi-independent Marcher Lords of the Welsh border regions. The Council in the Marches was formally established in January 1543 in the reign of Henry VIII and was abolished in 1641. Though primarily a judicial court, it acted as a spearhead of Protestantism at the time of the Reformation.

Council of Estates

Executive committee, composed of members of parliament and others, convened in the 17th century to govern Scotland during conflicts with the Crown, notably during the Civil War (1640–51), at the time of the Restoration (1660–61), and during the Glorious Revolution (1688–89).

Council of the North

In England, royal council which supervised Yorkshire, Cumberland, Durham, Northumberland, and Westmoreland. Though its origins lay in the 15th century, it was reconstituted in 1537 after the Pilgrimage of Grace and was like the Council in the Marches, imposed royal policies on the North, overseeing the introduction of Protestantism. It was abolished along with other regional councils in 1641.

council tax

Method of raising revenue for local government in Britain. It replaced the community charge, or ◊poll tax, from April 1993. The tax is based on property values at April 1991, but takes some account of the number of people occupying each property.

It is levied by local authorities on the value of dwellings in their area. Each dwelling is valued and then placed into one of eight bands. The owners of properties worth more than £320,000 in the highest band pay three times as much in council tax as those in the lowest band of properties worth less than £40,000.

Country Diary of An Edwardian Lady, The

Journal by the English artist and naturalist Edith Holden (1871–1920), published in 1977, and illustrated with Holden's own watercolours. One of the longest-running bestsellers in the UK, it was one of the first books in Britain to achieve continuing sales through the development and promotion of a wide range of associated products.

Country Landowners' Association

British organization open to anyone owning land in the countryside. Its principal aims are to protect the interests of landowners and to promote private enterprise in farming and other land use.

Originally formed as the Central Land Association in 1907, its activities were for many years directed towards agricultural prosperity. In 1949 the present name was adopted, and the Association has widened its membership and interests to cover all aspects of rural life.

country park

Pleasure ground or park, often located near an urban area, providing facilities for the public enjoyment of the countryside. Country parks were introduced in the UK following the 1968 Countryside Act and are the responsibility of local authorities with assistance from the Countryside Commission. They cater for a range of recreational activities such as walking, boating, and horse-riding.

Countryside Commission

Official conservation body created for England and Wales under the Countryside Act 1968. It replaced the National Parks Commission, had by 1980 created over 160 country parks, and designates Areas of Outstanding Natural Beauty (see conservation for a full list of these areas).

Countryside Council for Wales

Welsh nature conservation body formed in 1991 by the fusion of the former Nature Conservancy Council and the Welsh Countryside Commission. It is government-funded and administers conservation and land-use policies within Wales.

Countryside March

Demonstration in London on 4 March 1998 to promote understanding of the issues facing rural Britain. Issues that had caused controversy and led to the march included the 1997 bill to ban hunting with dogs, and government policies on farming. Around 250,000 people joined the march through central London.

county (Latin **comitatus** through French **comté**)

The name given by the Normans to Anglo-Saxon 'shires'; the boundaries of many present-day English counties date back to Saxon times. There are currently 34 English administrative non-metropolitan counties and 6 metropolitan counties, in addition to 34 unitary authorities. Welsh and Scottish counties were abolished in 1996 in a reorganization of local government throughout the UK, and replaced by 22 and 33 unitary authorities respectively. Northern Ireland has 6

COUNTRYSIDE MARCH *The Countryside March was organized in 1998 by the Countryside Alliance, a loose coalition of rural interest groups. The immediate cause of the demonstration was a parliamentary bill to ban hunting with dogs, but it also raised long-standing concerns of country dwellers that their lifestyle might be changed in an increasingly urban Britain. Simon Shepheard/Impact.*

geographical counties, although administration is through 26 district councils.

In England, a major review overseen by the Local Government Commission in 1996 put emphasis on the creation of unitary 'all purpose' authorities in 10 counties and in others retaining the existing structure or producing a blend of two-tier and unitary bodies.

Under the Local Government Act 1972, which came into effect in 1974, the 13 Welsh counties were reduced by amalgamation to eight. Under the Local Government (Scotland) Act 1973 the 33 counties of Scotland were amalgamated in 1975 in nine regions and three island areas.

county council

In England, a unit of local government whose responsibilities include broad planning policy, highways, education, personal social services, and libraries; police, fire, and traffic control; and refuse disposal. The tier below the county council has traditionally been the district council, but with local government reorganization from 1996, there has been a shift towards unitary authorities (based on a unit smaller than the county) replacing both. By 1998 there were 34 two-tier non-metropolitan county councils under which there were 274 district councils. (See also ◊local government.)

County councils were originated as a level of local government in 1889. Since the Local Government Act 1972, the county councils in England and Wales consist of a chair and councillors (the distinction between councillors and aldermen has been abolished). Councillors are elected for four years, the franchise being the same as for parliamentary elections, and elect the chair from among their own number. Metropolitan county councils, including the Greater London Council, were abolished 1986.

county court

English court of law created by the County Courts Act 1846 and now governed by the Act of 1984. It exists to try civil cases, such as actions on contract and tort where the claim does not exceed £5,000, and disputes about land, such as between landlord and tenant. County courts are presided over by one or more circuit judges.

County Hall

Building in central London, on the River Thames opposite the Palace of Westminster. Opened in 1922, it was the headquarters of the governing body for London until the abolition of the ◊Greater London Council (GLC) by the Conservative government in 1986. Part of the building now houses the London Aquarium. The main building was designed by Ralph Knott.

County Hall was built in the borough of Lambeth, on a site partly reclaimed from the Thames foreshore, running northwards along the southern bank of the river from Westminster Bridge. The main building was begun in 1911 and the southern part of the river frontage completed in 1922. The building comprised nine floors, 8.4 km/5.2 mi of corridors, and nearly 1,000 rooms. County Hall continued to expand throughout the 1930s; building work finally came to an end in 1963, with completion of the southern block extension. Later buildings, between Belvedere Road and York Road, were the work of the London County Council architects E P Wheeler and F R Hiorns, with Giles Gilbert ◊Scott acting as consultant.

On the abolition of the GLC by the government of Margaret Thatcher, County Hall was sold to private investors.

county palatine

In medieval England, a county whose lord held particular rights, in lieu of the king, such as pardoning treasons and murders. Under William I there were four counties palatine: Chester, Durham, Kent, and Shropshire.

Courtauld, Samuel (1793–1881)

English industrialist who developed the production of viscose rayon and other synthetic fibres from 1804. He founded the firm of Courtauld's in 1816 in Bocking, Essex, and at first specialized in silk and crepe manufacture.

His great-nephew **Samuel Courtauld** (1876–1947) was chair of the firm from 1921, and in 1931 gave his house and art collection to the University of London as the Courtauld Institute.

courtesy title

Any title allowed by custom to the progeny of members of the peerage, though the holder has no legal right to it. For example, the eldest son of a duke, marquess, or earl may bear one of his father's lesser titles; thus the duke of Marlborough's son is the marquess of Blandford. Since they are commoners, not peers, they do not sit in the House of Lords but remain eligible for the House of Commons.

court martial

Court convened for the trial of persons subject to military discipline who are accused of violations of military laws.

British courts martial are governed by the code of the service concerned – Naval Discipline, Army, or Air Force acts – and in 1951 an appeal court was established for all three services by the Courts Martial (Appeals) Act. The procedure prescribed for the US services is similar, being based on British practice.

The European Court of Human Rights ruled in February 1997 that Britain's courts martial system violates the right to a fair trial. The Strasbourg judges unanimously ruled in favour of a Falklands veteran who was court martialled for actions undertaken while suffering post-traumatic stress disorder.

Courtneidge, Cicely Esmeralda (1893–1980)

English comic actress and singer. She appeared both on stage and in films. She married comedian Jack Hulbert (1892–1978), with whom she formed a successful variety partnership. She was made a DBE in 1972.

Court of Appeal

UK law court comprising a Civil Division and a Criminal Division, set up under the Criminal Appeals Act 1968. The Criminal Division of the Court of Appeal has the power to revise sentences or quash a conviction on the grounds that in all the circumstances of the case the verdict is unsafe or unsatisfactory, or that the judgement of the original trial judge was wrong in law, or that there was a material irregularity during the course of the trial.

The Court of Appeal consists of 16 Lord Justices of Appeal and a number of ex-officio judges, for example, the Lord Chancellor, the Master of the Rolls, and the President of the Family Division. Usually, three judges sit, but where a case raises new or important issues, up to seven judges may form the court.

Court of Protection

In English law, a department of the High Court that deals with the estates of people who are incapable, by reason of mental disorder, of managing their own property and affairs.

Court of Session

Supreme civil court in Scotland, established 1532. Cases come in the first place before one of the judges of the Outer House (corresponding to the High Court in England and Wales), and from that decision an appeal lies to the Inner House (corresponding to the Court of Appeal) which sits in two divisions called the First and the Second Division. From the decisions of the Inner House an appeal lies to the House of Lords. The court sits in Edinburgh.

Court of the Lord Lyon

Scottish heraldic authority composed of one king-of-arms (the Lord Lyon, or Lyon King-of-Arms, three heralds, and three pursuivants who specialize in genealogical work. The court sits in Edinburgh, and has jurisdiction over questions of the right to Scottish titles, clan chieftainships, and coats of arms.

Coutts, Thomas (1735–1822)

British banker. He established with his brother the firm of Coutts & Co (one of London's oldest banking houses, founded in 1692 in the Strand), becoming sole head on the latter's death in 1778. Since the reign of George III an account has been maintained there by every succeeding sovereign.

Covent Garden

Popular name of the Royal Opera House at Covent Garden, London. The present building was completed 1858 after two previous ones burnt down. The Royal Ballet is also in residence here. Financial uncertainty has put the building's future in some doubt.

Covent Garden

London square (named from the convent garden once on the site) laid out by Inigo Jones 1631. The buildings that formerly housed London's fruit and vegetable market (moved to Nine Elms, Wandsworth 1973) have been adapted for shops and restaurants. The Royal Opera House, also housing the Royal Ballet, is here; also the London Transport Museum.

The Theatre Museum, opened 1987, is in the Old Flower Market.

Coventry

Industrial city in the West Midlands, England, on the River Sherbourne, 29 km/18 mi southeast of Birmingham; population (1994 est) 303,000. Principal industries are engineering and the manufacture of electronic equipment, machine tools, agricultural machinery, manmade fibres, aerospace components, telecommunications equipment, and vehicles, including London taxis and Massey Ferguson tractors.

Features

Coventry cathedral, incorporating the ruins of the old cathedral destroyed in an air raid in 1940, was designed by Basil Spence and consecrated in 1962; Belgrade Theatre (1958); the Herbert Art Gallery and Museum; Museum of British Road Transport; the University of Warwick (1965); Coventry University (1992), formerly Coventry or Lanchester Polytechnic. Every three years the city hosts one of the four surviving mystery play cycles performed in England. Under the Phoenix Initiative, a project to mark the millennium, parts of the city centre will be rebuilt to provide public open spaces.

History

Leofric, Earl of Mercia and husband of Lady Godiva, founded a Benedictine priory here in 1043. A centre of armaments manufacture during World War II, the city was the target of a massive German air raid on 14–15 November 1940 in which 550 people were killed, and over 60,000 buildings were destroyed. Comprehensive redevelopment of the city's commercial, cultural, and civic facilities has since taken place.

Industrial history

The city has long maintained a reputation as a manufacturing centre. Before the 15th century Coventry had established itself as the focus for the wool trade and cloth industry in the Midlands. In the late 15th and the 16th centuries the city was known for its caps and bonnets, and for a particular blue dye (hence the saying 'true as Coventry blue'). From the 17th to the 19th centuries the manufacture of clocks, watches, and silk ribbons was important. Bicycle manufacture began in 1870; the last two major manufacturers, including Raleigh, left in the 1950s, but an adult BMX-type bike is still produced. The first British production car was built here in 1896.

Coventry Cathedral

On the east side of the porch is Jacob Epstein's statue *St Michael overcoming the Devil*. The west wall of the cathedral is made of glass; designed by John Hutton, it depicts angels and Christian figures.

The nave is inset with a series of long windows, each strikingly different, while the massive baptistry window, by John ◊Piper, is intended to represent the Love of God flowing into the world. Behind the altar hangs Graham ◊Sutherland's tapestry *Christ in Majesty* made at Felletin, in France, and measuring 23×11 m/75×36 ft. The font consists of a boulder taken from a Bethlehem hillside. Among the side chapels is one dedicated to Christ the Servant, and intended to serve industry. Also connected to the cathedral, and administered jointly by Anglican and Free Churchmen, is the Chapel of Unity.

The cathedral's fabric and furnishings were contributed by churches and individuals from all over the world. In 1964 the cathedral sponsored a fund for the rebuilding of a church hospital in Dresden, destroyed by Allied bombing in 1945, while German students have played a major part in the International Centre established in the ruins of the old cathedral vestries. Benjamin Britten composed his *War Requiem* for the consecration ceremony.

Coverdale, Miles (1488–1568)

English Protestant priest whose translation of the Bible, *Coverdale's Bible*, (1535) was the first to be printed in English. In 1539 he edited the *Great Bible* which was ordered to be placed in churches. His translation of the psalms is that retained in the Book of Common Prayer.

Mad dogs and Englishmen / Go out in the midday sun.

NOËL COWARD English dramatist and composer. 'Mad Dogs and Englishmen'

Coward, Noël Peirce (1899–1973)

English dramatist, actor, revue-writer, director, and composer. He epitomized the witty and sophisticated man of the theatre. From his first success with *The Young Idea* (1923), he wrote and appeared in plays and comedies on both sides of the Atlantic such as *Hay Fever* (1925), *Private Lives* (1930) with Gertrude Lawrence, *Design for Living* (1933), *Blithe Spirit* (1941), and *A Song at Twilight* (1966). His revues and musicals included *On With the Dance* (1925) and *Bitter Sweet* (1929).

Coward also wrote for and acted in films, including the patriotic *In Which We Serve* (1942) and the sentimental *Brief Encounter* (1945). After World War II he became a nightclub and cabaret entertainer, performing songs like 'Mad Dogs and Englishmen'. He was knighted in 1970.

Cowdrey, (Michael) Colin (1932–)

English cricketer. An orthodox but elegant right-handed batsman and a brilliant slip fielder, who when his international career ended in 1975 held the record for both the most runs (7,624) and the most catches (120) in Test match cricket. He scored 42,719 first class runs, 1950–76, a career total which only 12 players have exceeded.

He captained England in 27 Tests between 1959 and 1969, providing the team with solid if not inspirational leadership. He also captained Kent from 1957 to 1971, and in 1970 he led the team to its first County Championship title for 57 years.

Cowes

Seaport and resort on the north coast of the Isle of Wight, England, on the Medina estuary, opposite Southampton Water, 14 km/9 mi southwest of Portsmouth; population (1981) 19,600. A major yachting centre, Cowes is the starting point for the Around the World Yacht Race, finishing at Cape Town; and **Cowes Castle** is the headquarters of the Royal Yacht Squadron, which holds the annual **Cowes Week** regatta. Maritime-related industries include boatbuilding, marine engineering, sail-making, hovercraft construction, and the manufacture of radar equipment. Tourism is important; facilities include the island's ferry connection with Southampton.

Features

East and West Cowes, divided by the Medina estuary, are connected by a floating bridge. East Cowes is the location of ◊Osborne House, built by Albert, the Prince Consort, and Thomas Cubitt. The house was a seaside residence of Queen Victoria, who died there in 1901. To the south of Osborne House is Whippingham Church (1854–62), reputedly designed by Prince Albert. East Cowes Castle, now in ruins, was the former home of the architect John Nash. Yachting and sailing clubs include the Royal Corinthian Yacht Club, the Royal London Yacht Club, and the Island Sailing Club.

Cowley, Abraham (1618–1667)

English poet. He introduced the Pindaric ode (based on the work of the Greek poet Pindar) to English poetry, and published metaphysical verse with elaborate imagery, as well as essays. His best-known collection is *Poems* (1656).

Cowling, Thomas George (1906–1990)

English applied mathematician and physicist. He contributed significantly to modern research into stellar energy, with special reference to the Sun.

Cowling was responsible for demonstrating the existence of a convective core in stars, suggesting that the Sun may behave like a giant dynamo whose rotation, internal circulation, and convection produce the immensely powerful electric currents and magnetic fields associated with sunspots. With Swedish physicist Hannes Alfvén, Cowling showed that such currents and fields are likely to have existed since the Sun was first formed.

Cowper, William (1731–1800)

English poet. His verse anticipates ◊Romanticism and includes the six books of *The Task* (1785). He also wrote hymns (including 'God Moves in a Mysterious Way').

Cowper's work is important for its directness and descriptive accuracy, and it deals with natural themes later developed in Wordsworth's poetry. Cowper was also among the finest of English letter writers. His letters contain humorous accounts of the trivia of rural life and sensitive descriptions of nature, disrupted from time to time by the expression of irrational fear.

Cox, David (1783–1859)

English artist. He studied under John ◊Varley and made a living as a drawing master. His watercolour landscapes, many of scenes in North Wales, show attractive cloud effects, and are characterized by broad colour washes on rough, tinted paper.

In later years he painted much in North Wales, including a celebrated inn sign for the Royal Oak, Bettws-y-Coed. He is noted for watercolours in which broken touches and atmospheric effect give a distant anticipation of Impressionism. He took to oils late in life, adapting his watercolour technique. *A Windy Day* (Tate Gallery) well shows his special gift.

Cozens, John Robert (1752–1797)

English landscape painter, a watercolourist. His romantic views of Europe, mostly Alpine and Italian views, painted on tours in the 1770s and 1780s, were very popular and greatly influenced the development of English landscape painting.

He was taught painting by his father, the painter Alexander Cozens (*c.* 1717–1786). He became mentally ill in 1794 and was cared for by Dr Thomas Monro (1759–1833), a patron of art. Cozens's drawings in his collection influenced the young Thomas Girtin and J M W Turner, employed by Monro in copying them. John Constable claimed that Cozens was 'the greatest genius who ever touched landscape' and 'all poetry'.

CPVE

Abbreviation for **Certificate of Pre-Vocational Education**, an educational qualification introduced in 1986 for students over 16 in schools and colleges who want a one-year course of preparation for work or further vocational study.

Crabbe, George (1754–1832)

English poet. He wrote grimly realistic verse about the poor: *The Village* (1783), *The Parish Register* (1807), *The Borough* (1810) (which includes the story used in Benjamin Britten's opera *Peter Grimes*), and *Tales of the Hall* (1819).

Cragg, Tony (1949–)

English sculptor, based in Germany since 1977. His early work consisted of almost flat arrangements of junk material, sometimes displayed like a picture on a wall, sometimes on the floor. From the mid 1980s, he made freestanding abstract sculptures, often of heavy and bulky materials. He won the Turner Prize in 1988.

Craig, (Edward Henry) Gordon (1872–1966)

English director and stage designer. His innovations and theories on stage design and lighting effects, expounded in *On the Art of the Theatre* (1911), had a profound influence on stage production in Europe and the USA. He was the son of actress Ellen Terry.

Craig, James, 1st Viscount Craigavon (1871–1940)

Ulster Unionist politician, the first prime minister of Northern Ireland 1921–40. Craig became a member of Parliament in 1906, and was a highly effective organizer of Unionist resistance to Home Rule. As prime minister he carried out systematic discrimination against the Catholic minority, abolishing proportional representation in 1929 and redrawing constituency boundaries to ensure Protestant majorities. Viscount 1927.

Craigavon

City in Armagh county, Northern Ireland; population (1990 est) 62,000. It was created by integrating Lurgan and Portadown, with a new town centre and new residential and industrial areas, and was designated a 'new town' in 1965. It was named after ◊James Craig (Viscount Craigavon), the first prime minister of Northern Ireland (1921–40).

Craigievar Castle

Stately 17th-century castle built on a hillside 5 km/3 mi north of Lumphanan, Aberdeenshire, Scotland, by William Forbes. The castle is little altered, and contains magnificent plasterwork in the Elizabethan style. Craigievar was acquired by the National Trust for Scotland in 1963.

Cram, Steve (Stephen) (1960–)

English middle distance runner who won the 1500 metres at the inaugural world championships in 1983, and between 1982 and 1990 also won two European and two Commonwealth gold medals and an Olympic silver medal at the same distance. In 1985, within the space of 19 days he broke world records in the mile, 1,500, and 2,000 metres, with times of 3:46.32, 3:29.67, and 4:51.39 respectively.

CRAM, STEVE *One of three British athletes who dominated the world of middle-distance running in the 1980s (along with Sebastian Coe and Steve Ovett). His succession of medal-winning performances at international events was crowned by three different world records in 1985. Nils Jorgensen/Rex*

Cranborne

Village in Dorset, England, 41 km/25 mi northeast of Dorchester; population (1991) 1,600. Cranborne lies in a area of natural beauty known as **Cranborne Chase**, covering some 260 sq km/100 sq mi. Heavily wooded in the Middle Ages, it used to be a royal hunting ground.

Crane, Walter (1845–1915)

English artist, designer, and book illustrator. While apprenticed to William J Linton (1812–1898), a wood engraver, he came under the influence of the Pre-Raphaelites. In the 1880s he was closely associated with William Morris in both the ◊Arts and Crafts movement and the Socialist League. His book illustrations, both for children's and for adult books, included an edition of Edmund Spenser's *Faerie Queene* (1894–96).

Cranmer, Thomas (1489–1556)

English clergyman, archbishop of Canterbury from 1533. A Protestant convert, he helped to shape the doctrines of the Church of England under Edward VI. He was responsible for the issue of the Prayer Books of 1549 and 1552, and supported the succession of Lady Jane Grey in 1553.

Condemned for heresy under the Catholic Mary I, he at first recanted, but when his life was not spared, resumed his position and was burned at the stake, first holding to the fire the hand which had signed his recantation.

Cranmer suggested in 1529 that the question of Henry VIII's marriage to Catherine of Aragón should be referred to the universities of Europe rather than to the pope, and in 1533 he declared it null and void. Three years later he annulled the marriage with Anne Boleyn in the same fashion. In 1540 he divorced Henry from Anne of Cleves.

Crashaw, Richard (*c.* 1613–1649)

English religious poet of the metaphysical school. He published a book of Latin sacred epigrams, *Epigrammatum Sacrorum Liber* (1634). His principal sacred poems were published in *Steps to the Temple* (1646). Some secular poems were added to this work under the title *Delights of the Muses*.

Crathes Castle

Castle near Crathes, Aberdeenshire, Scotland, built 1546–96 on the north side of the River Dee by the Burnett family. It contains original tempera painted ceilings, and the problem of preserving these has prompted the establishment of a centre for the restoration of tempera in Edinburgh. Crathes was given to the National Trust for Scotland in 1951.

Crawford, Michael stage name of Michael Patrick Dumble-Smith (1942–)

English actor and singer. He played the title role in Andrew Lloyd Webber's musical *The Phantom of the Opera*, which opened in London in 1986 and New York in 1988.

His early television, film, and stage appearances were mainly in comedy, including the TV series *Not so Much a Programme, More a Way of Life* (1964) and *Some Mothers Do 'ave 'em* (1973–78), the film *A Funny Thing Happened on the Way to the Forum* (1966), and the play *No Sex, Please – We're British* (1971). His musical theatre performances included *Barnum* (1981), in which he played the part of the circus impresario P T Barnum. He toured the USA, UK, and Australia 1990–91 in *The Music of Andrew Lloyd Webber*, a revue.

Crawley

Town in West Sussex, England, northeast of Horsham, 45 km/28 mi south of London; population (1991) 88,200; Crawley urban area 114,600. It was chartered by King John in 1202 and developed as a ◊new town from 1947. Industries include light engineering, electronics, printing, and the manufacture of plastics, pharmaceuticals, and furniture. London's ◊Gatwick Airport is to the north.

Crécy, Battle of

First major battle of the Hundred Years' War, on 26 August 1346, in which Philip VI of France was defeated by Edward III of England at the village of Crécy-en-Ponthieu, now in Somme *département*, France, 18 km/11 mi northeast of Abbeville.

Edward's forces were arranged in three divisions on foot, with Welsh archers and spearmen in the front ranks. The Genoese crossbowmen in the French army opened the battle, but rain had affected their bowstrings and they were rapidly annihilated by the Welsh bowmen, who had managed to keep their strings dry. The French knights then rode forward but were soon picked off by bowmen and spearmen on the confined battlefield. The battle then resolved itself into a series of charges by the French knights, but the French were eventually beaten off.

Creutzfeldt–Jakob disease, CJD

Rare brain disease that causes progressive physical and mental deterioration, leading to death usually within a year of onset. It claims one person in every million and is universally fatal. It has been linked with ◊bovine spongiform encephalopathy (BSE), and there have also been occurrences in people treated with pituitary hormones derived from cows for growth or fertility problems.

Research published by British pathologists in 1997 proved that the new variant of CJD (vCJD) is caused by the same agent that causes BSE, indicating that the disease has jumped species, from cattle to humans.

There were 55 deaths from CJD in Britain in 1994. In March 1996 the UK government announced that 10 young people had died from a variant of CJD probably caused by eating beef infected with BSE. The average age of victims is normally 63; the average age for this group was 27. The UK government launched a study to assess the risk of transmission of vCJD through blood transfusions, in November 1997.

Crewe

Town in Cheshire, England; population (1991) 63,400. It grew as a major railway junction, containing the chief construction workshops of British Rail. Crewe is also the centre of the dairy industry, providing cattle breeding, management, and animal health services. Other industries include food-processing and the manufacture of chemicals, vehicles, and clothing.

History

Between 1837 and 1858 Crewe became the hub of a six-point star of railway lines, leading to London (through Birmingham), Manchester, Liverpool, Chester, Shrewsbury, and Stoke. Locomotive works were established in 1840. The population of Crewe in 1841 was 300, and houses for workers were initially built by the railway company. A local board was established in 1860 and the town became a municipal borough in 1877. Britain's last steam engine was constructed here.

Crichton, James (1560–1582)

Scottish scholar. He was known as 'the Admirable Crichton' because of his extraordinary gifts as a poet, scholar, and linguist; he was also an athlete and fencer. According to one account he was killed in Mantua, Italy, in a street brawl by his pupil, a son of the Duke of Mantua, who resented Crichton's popularity.

Crick, Francis Harry Compton (1916–)

English molecular biologist. From 1949 he researched the molecular structure of DNA, and the means whereby characteristics are transmitted from one generation to another. For this work he was awarded a Nobel prize (with Maurice ◊Wilkins and James Watson) in 1962.

Using Wilkins's and others' discoveries, Crick and Watson postulated that DNA consists of a double helix consisting of two parallel chains of alternate sugar and phosphate groups linked by pairs of organic bases. They built molecular models which also explained how genetic information could be coded – in the sequence of organic bases. Crick and Watson published their work on the proposed structure of DNA in 1953. Their model is now generally accepted as correct. See DNA for a feature of the discovery.

Later, this time working with South African Sidney Brenner, Crick demonstrated that each group of three adjacent bases (he called a set of three bases a codon) on a single DNA strand codes for one specific amino acid. He also helped to determine codons that code for each of the 20 main amino acids. Furthermore, he formulated the adaptor hypothesis, according to which adaptor molecules mediate between messenger RNA and amino acids. These adaptor molecules are now known as transfer RNAs.

cricket

The exact origins of cricket are unknown, but it certainly dates back to the 16th century. The name is thought to have originated from the Anglo-Saxon word *cricc*, meaning a shepherd's staff. The first players were the shepherds of south-east England, who used their crooks as bats and the wicket gate and movable bail of the sheep pens as a target for

BRITISH CRICKET: SOME KEY DATES

c. **1550** An English court case of 1598 refers to 'crickett' being played at the 'Free School' at Guildford, Surrey, at this time. It is the first certain reference to cricket.

1646 The first recorded cricket match in England is played at Coxheath, Kent.

1709 Kent play Surrey in the first 'county' cricket match, at Dartford Brent, England.

1744 The first known Laws of Cricket, probably a revision of an existing code, are issued by the cricketers of the London Star and Garter Club.

18 June 1744 Kent defeat All England at the Artillery ground, London, in the first major cricket match of which a full record of the score survives.

c. **1767** The Hambledon Club, the first great cricket club, is formed near the village of Hambledon in Hampshire.

1787 The Marylebone Cricket Club (MCC) is founded by Thomas Lord and members of the White Conduit Club, at Thomas Lord's new private ground at Dorset Square, Marylebone, London.

1814 The Marylebone Cricket Club (MCC) moves Lord's cricket ground to its present site at St John's Wood, London.

1839 Sussex County Cricket Club, the oldest first-class English county cricket club, is established as the Royal Sussex Cricket Club.

1871 The English cricketer W(illiam) G(ilbert) Grace and his brothers found the Gloucestershire Cricket Club.

1890 Surrey wins the first official English County Cricket Championship.

24 June 1938–27 June 1938 Test Cricket from Lord's is broadcast on British television for the first time.

1947 In the course of the English first-class cricket season, the English batsman Denis Compton of Middlesex scores a record 3,816 runs, including an unprecedented and unsurpassed 18 centuries.

27–31 July 1956 In the fourth Cricket Test between England and Australia at Old Trafford, Manchester, the England offspinner Jim Laker becomes the first bowler to take all ten wickets in a Test match innings. His match analysis of 19–90 beats the previous Test record of 17–159 set by S F Barnes in 1913–14.

16–20 July 1962 The Gentlemen v. Players cricket match, established in 1806, is played for the last time at Lord's, London, as the Marylebone Cricket Club (MCC) votes to abolish the distinction between amateurs ('gentlemen') and professionals ('players').

7 September 1963 Cricket's first limited-overs competition, sponsored by Gillette, is held in England. In the final at the Lord's ground, Sussex beat Worcestershire by 14 runs.

21 July 1981 In the third Test at Leeds against Australia, England becomes only the second side in 104 years of Test cricket to win a match after being forced to follow on. Ian Botham saves England from defeat with an innings of 149 not out, then Bob Willis takes 8 for 43 in Australia's second innings to give England victory.

19 March 1982 Fifteen England cricketers led by Graham Gooch are banned from Test cricket for three years for participating in a cricket tour of South Africa, breaking an international ban on sporting links with that country because of its policy on apartheid.

September 1998 The Marylebone Cricket Club votes in favour of admitting women members for the first time in its 211 year history.

the bowlers. In the 18th century, runs were recorded by notches cut on a stick. The wicket consisted of two stumps and a crosspiece (the third stump was added in the late 1770s). Until about 1773 bats retained the curve akin to a hockey stick, suited to deal with the prevalent under-arm bowling of the time. By about 1780 the straight bat was in almost universal use to counter the advance in bowling technique whereby the ball rose from the pitch on a 'length'. The first major alteration in the laws for which the Marylebone Cricket Club (MCC) was responsible was the licence given to the bowler in 1835 to raise his arm as high as the shoulder and bowl round-arm. Formerly he was compelled to deliver the ball underarm and the new method had for years been the subject of heated argument. This concession was the prelude to the legalization of overarm bowling in 1864. Modern bat blades are made of willow (*salix coerulea*) with handles of compressed cane and rubber; early bats were in one piece. The early Victorian period saw the introduction of protective clothing.

It is hard to tell where the MCC ends and the Church of England begins.

J B Priestley English novelist and playwright. *New Statesman* 20 July 1962

Test cricket and the International Cricket Council

The first Test match held in England was in 1880. In 1882 Australia's victory over England at the Oval inspired a journalist to write a mock obituary notice of English cricket, in which he coined the term the ◊Ashes. The introduction of the six-ball over in England in 1900 aided higher scoring; bowlers countered the batting dominance by the practice of swing bowling (by fast bowlers), and the introduction in the early 1900s of the 'googly', a style quickly adopted around the world. In 1909 the Imperial Cricket Conference (renamed the International Cricket Conference in 1965 and the

International Cricket Council in 1989) was set up with England, Australia, and South Africa as founder members; they were later joined by the West Indies, New Zealand, India, Pakistan, Sri Lanka, and Zimbabwe.

Great English cricketers have included W G Grace, Jack Hobbs, and Len Hutton. Major grounds in England include Lord's (London), Kennington Oval (London), Old Trafford (Manchester), Edgbaston (Birmingham), Trent Bridge (Nottingham), and Headingley (Leeds). The UK is to host the World Cup in 1999.

crime

In English law a crime is defined as an act prohibited by law which is punishable by some sanction applied by the courts of criminal jurisdiction, known as the Crown Court and magistrates' courts. Some criminal acts may also be the subject of civil proceedings; for instance, a motorist found guilty of dangerous driving may subsequently be sued for damages for negligence in a civil court. No act, however antisocial, may be punished as a crime unless it is prohibited by law ('nulla poena sine lege'). Despite the widely differing punishments which they attract, murder, theft, dangerous or careless driving, adulteration of milk, and riding a bicycle without lights are all considered crimes in English law.

Juvenile crime

Since the beginning of the 20th century English law has made a number of provisions for the punishment of specifically juvenile crimes (crimes committed by persons between the ages of ten and seventeen). Juvenile courts were first legislated for in England in 1908. Juvenile courts cannot deal with cases of murder, but do have the power to commit young adults to special detention centres, formerly known as 'borstals'. The juvenile courts may also enforce care orders, where juvenile offenders are removed from their normal surroundings and relocated in an institution or 'community home' for their own protection; and supervision orders, where the juvenile offender is placed under the supervision of a social worker and may also be required to abide by a curfew or take part in reformative activities.

Crimean War

War 1853–56 between Russia and the allied powers of England, France, Turkey, and Sardinia. The war arose from British and French mistrust of Russia's ambitions in the Balkans. It began with an allied Anglo-French expedition to the Crimea to attack the Russian Black Sea city of Sevastopol. The battles of the River Alma, ◊Balaclava (including the charge of the Light Brigade), and Inkerman 1854 led to a siege which, owing to military mismanagement, lasted for a year until September 1855. The war was ended by the Treaty of Paris in 1856. The scandal surrounding French and British losses through disease led to the organization of proper military nursing services by Florence Nightingale.

Criminal Injuries Compensation Board

UK board established 1964 to administer financial compensation by the state for victims of crimes of violence. Victims can claim compensation for their injuries, but not for damage to property. The compensation awarded is similar to the amount that would be obtained for a court in damages for personal injury.

Criminal Investigation Department, CID

Detective branch of the London Metropolitan Police, established in 1878, comprising in 1998 a force of 3,834 (3,458 men and 376 women) recruited entirely from the uniformed police and controlled by an assistant commissioner. Such branches are now also found in the regional police forces. In London, a number of the detectives are stationed at New Scotland Yard.

In 1979 new administrative arrangements were introduced so that all police officers, including CID, came under the uniformed chief superintentendent of the regional division. Regional crime squads are composed of detectives drawn from local forces to deal with major crime, and are kept in touch by a London-based national coordinator.

The CID at New Scotland Yard has the following departments: **1** Central Office: deals with international crime and serious crime throughout the country. It controls the Flying Squad (a rapid deployment force for investigating serious crimes). **2** Criminal Intelligence Department: studies criminals and their methods. **3** Fingerprint Department: holds some 2 million prints of convicted criminals. **4** Criminal Record Office: holds information on known criminals and publishes the *Police Gazette*. **5** The Scientific Laboratory. **6** The Stolen Car Squad. **7** Special Branch: deals with crimes against the state. **8** National coordinator for the Regional crime squads (detectives drawn from local forces to deal with major crime).

Criminal Justice and Public Order Act, also known as the Criminal Justice Act

Act of Parliament of November 1994, which created a broad range of new offences and made substantial changes to existing laws in an attempt to tackle those areas where the law was felt to be failing. The act caused considerable controversy, with civil liberties and legal reform groups protesting against the act's restrictions on a suspect's 'right to silence'. Many young people also viewed the restrictions on protests and unlicensed 'rave' parties as an attack on their freedom.

The act was proposed by Conservative Home Secretary Michael ◊Howard as a way of 'getting tough' with criminals, but was controversial from the start because of its perceived attacks on civil liberties. The act also attracted criticism for being too diverse: it contains over 100 separate sections, dealing with a huge scope of matters from lowering the age of homosexual consent (lowered to 18 in 1994), to powers enabling the establishment of a DNA database of offenders.

Some of the main provisions are:

Right to silence

The law previously allowed a suspect to remain silent when interviewed by the police and not give evidence at trial. The act retained this right but allowed a jury or magistrates to draw adverse inferences from a suspect's refusal to provide an explanation for prosecution evidence.

Trespass
The act created a new offence of aggravated trespass, when a trespasser interferes with a lawful activity taking place on private land, primarily aimed at protests against foxhunts and road schemes. Trespassory assemblies, large gatherings on private land without the owner's consent, were also prohibited and the police given new powers to prevent people from going to such assemblies. This power, together with new powers to seize sound equipment belonging to the organizers of unlicensed parties in the open air, were aimed at 'rave' parties. The police and local councils were also given new powers to deal with travellers moving vehicles onto land and living there.
Young offenders
A new type of 'youth detention', a combination of a custody order and a probation order was created. The measure was designed to deal with persistent offenders between the ages of 12 and 15 after public outrage at a series of highly publicized cases in which the courts were unable to act against juvenile criminals who had committed dozens of offences.
Sexual offences
Male rape was recognized by the act for the first time in British law. The increasing use of new technology in creating and distributing pornography was also recognized with the creation of a new offence of making or owning computer-generated child pornography. Existing legislation had only covered books, photographs, and videos, allowing child pornographers a loophole which was widely exploited.

criminal law

Body of law that defines the public wrongs (crimes) that are punishable by the state and establishes methods of prosecution and punishment. It is distinct from civil law, which deals with legal relationships between individuals (including organizations), such as contract law.

In England and Wales crimes are either: **indictable offences** (serious offences triable by judge and jury in a crown court); **summary offences** dealt with in magistrates' courts; or **hybrid offences** tried in either kind of court according to the seriousness of the case and the wishes of the defendant. Crown courts have power to punish more severely those found guilty than a magistrates' court. Punishments include imprisonment, fines, suspended terms of imprisonment (which only come into operation if the offender is guilty of further offences during a specified period), probation, and ◊community service. Overcrowding in prisons and the cost of imprisonment have led to recent experiments with noncustodial sentences such as electronic tags fixed to the body to reinforce curfew orders on convicted criminals in the community. The total cost of criminal justice services for England and Wales was £7 billion in 1990, an increase of 77% in real terms from 1980.

Crippen, Hawley Harvey (1861–1910)

US murderer who killed his wife, variety artist Belle Elmore, in 1910. He buried her remains in the cellar of his London home and tried to escape to the USA with his mistress Ethel le Neve (dressed as a boy). He was arrested on board ship following a radio message, the first criminal captured 'by radio', and was hanged.

Croft, William (1678–1727)

English organist and composer. His most famous work is his setting of the Burial Service, which is still in use. Much other church music survives, including two volumes of anthems published under the title *Musica Sacra* in 1724. Other works include theatrical pieces and keyboard music.

Cromarty Firth

Inlet in Highland unitary authority, Scotland, north of the ◊Moray Firth, extending for 29 km/18 mi, with a width of up to 8 km/5 mi, and depth of 9–60 m/20–196 ft. Almost landlocked, it is entered by a narrow strait between two promontories, the North and South Sutors. During World War II, it was used as a safe harbour by the British navy. It has since been used as a servicing area for oil rigs.

In the 19th century, the Scottish writer and geologist Hugh Miller discovered fossilized fish in the local red sandstone, including *Pterichthys* and *Osteolepis*.

Crome, John (1768–1821)

English landscape painter. He was a founder of the ◊Norwich School with John Sell Cotman in 1803. His works, which show the influence of Dutch landscape painting, include *Boy Keeping Sheep* (1812; Victoria and Albert Museum);*Mousehold Heath* (about 1814–16), 'painted for air and space', and *The Poringland Oak* (1818; National Gallery); and *The Slate Quarries* (about 1802–05) and *Moonrise on the Yare* (about 1811–16), both in the Tate Gallery, London.

Crome was largely self-taught, studying Dutch and other paintings in a local collection: he seems to have learned mainly from Meindert Hobbema, Thomas Gainsborough, George Morland, and, as regards luminous effect, from Richard Wilson. Cotman inspired him to produce some watercolours and he also made a number of etchings, but his main work is in oil paintings, broadly treated and with true grandeur of design.

As 'Old Crome' he is distinguished from his son **John Bernay Crome** (1794–1842), who also worked in Norwich as painter and art teacher and specialized in effects of moonlight.

Cromer

Seaside resort on the northeast coast of Norfolk, England, 37 km/23 mi north of Norwich; population (1991) 4,800. Apart from tourism, fishing (especially for crabs) is the main activity.

Cromer became popular as a holiday destination because of its favourable location, sheltered on the land side by hills and woods. There are golf links to the west of the town. The sea has greatly encroached on parts of the coast; the cliffs are protected by sea walls at Cromer, but subject to rapid erosion between Cromer and Overstrand. There is a lifeboat station and a lighthouse, whose light is visible for 37 km/23 mi.

Crompton, Richmal pen name of Richmal Crompton Lamburn (1890–1969)

English writer. A writer of marginally feminist novels, such as her third, the semi-autobiographical *Ann Morrison* (1925), she is remembered for her stories about the mischievous schoolboy ◊William, the first of which was *Just William* (1922).

Crompton, Rookes Evelyn Bell (1845–1940)

English engineer. He pioneered the use of the dynamo, electric lighting, and road transport. On his return from military service in India he began importing dynamos from France and set up his own company to develop and manufacture generating systems for lighting town halls, railway stations, and small residential areas. Direct-current electricity of about 400 volts was generated and used with large storage batteries (accumulators). This competed, in the end unsuccessfully, with the alternating-current system of Sebastian ◊Ferranti.

During the Boer War, Crompton served in South Africa as commandant of the Electrical Engineers' Royal Engineers Volunteer Corps. He then returned to road transport, and contributed both to the principles of automobile engineering and the maintenance and design of roads. During World War I he was an adviser on the design and production of military tanks. He also contributed to the development of industry standards, both electrical and mechanical, and was involved in the founding of the ◊National Physical Laboratory and what is now the British Standards Institution.

Crompton, Samuel (1753–1827)

English inventor at the time of the Industrial Revolution. He developed the 'spinning mule' in 1779 in Bolton, combining the ideas of Richard ◊Arkwright and James ◊Hargreaves. This span a fine, continuous yarn and revolutionized the production of high-quality cotton textiles.

Crompton's invention was called the mule because it was a hybrid. It used the best from the spinning jenny and from Richard Arkwright's water frame of 1768. The strong, even yarn it produced was so fine that it could be used to weave delicate fabrics such as muslin, which became fashionable among the middle and upper classes, creating a new market for the British cotton trade. Spinning was taken out of the home and into the factories.

Cromwell, Oliver (1599–1658)

English general and politician, Puritan leader of the Parliamentary side in the ◊Civil War. He raised cavalry forces (later called **Ironsides**) which aided the victories at Edgehill in 1642 and ◊Marston Moor in 1644, and organized the New Model Army, which he led (with General Fairfax) to victory at Naseby in 1645. He declared Britain a republic ('the Commonwealth') in 1649, following the execution of Charles I. As Lord Protector (ruler) from 1653, Cromwell established religious toleration and raised Britain's prestige in Europe on the basis of an alliance with France against Spain.

Cromwell was born at Huntingdon, northwest of Cambridge, son of a small landowner. He entered Parliament in 1629 and became active in the events leading to the Civil War. Failing to secure a constitutional settlement with Charles I 1646–48, he defeated the 1648 Scottish invasion at Preston. A special commission, of which Cromwell was a member, tried the king and condemned him to death, and a republic, known as 'the Commonwealth', was set up.

The ◊Levellers demanded radical reforms, but he executed their leaders in 1649. He used terror to crush Irish clan resistance 1649–50, and defeated the Scots (who had acknowledged Charles II) at Dunbar 1650 and Worcester 1651. In 1653, having forcibly expelled the corrupt 'Rump Parliament', he summoned a convention ('◊Barebones Parliament'),

CROMWELL, OLIVER *Oliver Cromwell, in a painting attributed to Van Dyck. Lord Protector and virtual dictator of England after the execution of Charles I, Cromwell inherited a divided and war-weary nation, to which he forcibly united Scotland and Ireland for the first time in their histories. His rule became associated with an unpopular type of Puritan zeal, and the Stuart Charles II was welcomed back by most of Britain after Cromwell's death. Philip Sauvain Picture Collection*

soon dissolved as too radical, and under a constitution (the 'Instrument of Government') drawn up by the army leaders, became Protector (king in all but name). The Parliament of 1654–55 was dissolved as uncooperative, and after a period of military dictatorship, his last Parliament offered him the crown; he refused because he feared the army's republicanism.

Take away these baubles.

Oliver Cromwell English general and politician. Referring to the symbols of Parliamentary power when he dismissed Parliament 1653

Cromwell, Thomas, Earl of Essex (*c.* 1485–1540)
English politician who drafted the legislation that made the Church of England independent of Rome. Originally in Lord Chancellor Wolsey's service, he became secretary to ◊Henry VIII 1534 and the real director of government policy; he was executed for treason.

Cromwell had Henry divorced from Catherine of Aragón by a series of acts that proclaimed him head of the church. From 1536 to 1540 Cromwell suppressed the monasteries, ruthlessly crushed all opposition, and favoured Protestantism, which denied the divine right of the pope. His mistake in arranging Henry's marriage to Anne of Cleves (to cement an alliance with the German Protestant princes against France and the Holy Roman Empire) led to his being accused of treason and beheaded.

Cromwell tank
British cruiser tank produced 1943–44. One of the fastest tanks of World War II, it could reach 65 kph/40 mph though later production had the engine governed so as to keep the speed down to 55 kph/35 mph.

Cronin, A(rchibald) J(oseph) (1896–1981)
Scottish novelist. The success of his novel *Hatter's Castle* (1931) enabled him to leave his practice as a physician and take up writing full time. His medical stories gave rise in the 1960s to the popular television series *Dr Finlay's Casebook* for which Cronin contributed a number of scripts.

Other novels include *The Citadel* (1937) and *The Judas Tree* (1961). *Jupiter Laughs* (1940) is a play.

Crookes, William (1832–1919)
English scientist whose many chemical and physical discoveries include the metallic element thallium (1861), the radiometer (1875), and the Crookes high-vacuum tube used in X-ray techniques.

The radiometer consists of a four-bladed paddle wheel mounted horizontally on a pinpoint bearing inside an evacuated glass globe. Each vane of the wheel is black on one side (making it a good absorber of heat) and silvered on the other side (making it a good reflector). When the radiometer is put in strong sunlight, the paddle wheel spins round.

During the 1870s Crookes's studies concerned the passage of an electric current through glass 'vacuum' tubes containing rarified gases; such discharge tubes became known as Crookes tubes. The ionized gas in a Crookes tube gives out light – as in a neon sign – and Crookes observed near the cathode a light-free gap in the discharge, now called the **Crookes dark space**. He named the ion stream 'molecular rays' and demonstrated how they are deflected in a magnetic field and how they can cast shadows, proving that they travel in straight lines. Knighted 1897.

Crossley, Paul Christopher Richard (1944–)
English pianist. He was artistic director of the London Sinfonietta 1988–94. A specialist in the works of such composers as Ravel, Messiaen, and Tippett, he studied with Messiaen and French pianist Yvonne Loriod (1924–). He was appointed CBE in 1993.

Crossman, Richard Howard Stafford (1907–1974)
British Labour politician. He was minister of housing and local government 1964–66 and of health and social security 1968–70. His posthumous 'Crossman Papers' (1975) revealed confidential cabinet discussions.

Crotch, William (1775–1847)
English composer. He was a child prodigy who played the organ at the age of four, went to Cambridge at the age of 11 to assist Randall at the organs of Trinity and King's Colleges, and produced an oratorio *The Captivity of Judah* there in 1789. In 1788 he moved to Oxford to study theology. In 1790 he began to study music and was appointed organist at Christ Church, Oxford; he succeeded Philip Hayes as professor in 1798. On the establishment of the Royal Academy of Music in London in 1822 he became its first principal.

By yesterday morning British troops were patrolling the streets of Belfast. I fear that once Catholics and Protestants get used to our presence they will hate us more than they hate each other.

Richard Crossman British Labour politician. *Diaries* 17 August 1969

Crown colony
Any British colony that is under the direct legislative control of the Crown and does not possess its own system of representative government. Crown colonies are administered by a crown-appointed governor or by elected or nominated legislative and executive councils with an official majority. Usually the Crown retains rights of veto and of direct legislation by orders in council.

crown court
In England and Wales, any of several courts that hear serious criminal cases referred from ◊magistrates' courts after committal proceedings. They replaced ◊quarter sessions and assizes, which were abolished 1971. Appeals against convic-

tion or sentence at magistrates' courts may be heard in crown courts. Appeal from a crown court is to the Court of Appeal.

Crown Derby

See ◊Derby.

Crown Estate

Title (from 1956) of land in UK owned by the monarch. The income from it was handed to Parliament by George III in 1760 in exchange for an annual payment (the ◊civil list).

The Crown Estate is one of the largest landed estates in the UK, and owns all Mines Royal (mines of gold and silver) and valuable sites in central London, which, along with 268,400 acres in England and Scotland, are valued in excess of £1.2 billion.

Crown jewels, or regalia

Symbols of royal authority, used by royalty on state occasions. The British set (except for the Ampulla and the Anointing Spoon) were broken up at the time of Oliver Cromwell, and the current set dates from the Restoration. In 1671 Colonel ◊Blood attempted to steal them, but was captured, then pardoned and pensioned by Charles II. The Crown Jewels are kept in the Tower of London in the Crown Jewel House.

Crown Prosecution Service

Body established by the Prosecution of Offences Act 1985, responsible for prosecuting all criminal offences in England and Wales. It is headed by the Director of Public Prosecutions (DPP), and brought England and Wales in line with Scotland (which has a procurator fiscal) in having a prosecution service independent of the police.

Croydon

Outer borough of south Greater London; it is a residential area and commercial centre, and includes the suburbs of Purley and Coulsdon.

Features an 11th-century Palace, former residence of archbishops of Canterbury, now a school; Whitgift School, originally founded in 1599 for 20 poor boys and girls by John Whitgift, a resident of the borough; Whitgift's 16th-century almshouses; Surrey Street market (dating from the 13th century); Fairfield Halls (1962), including Ashcroft Theatre, Fairfield concert hall, and Arnhem Gallery; it is the largest office centre in the south of England (outside central London)

Industries financial and insurance services, pharmaceuticals, electronics, engineering, foodstuffs

Population (1991) 298,500.

History

Settlement in the area dates back to the Stone Age; traces of prehistoric man have been found at Sanderstead, Coulsdon, and Purley.

Croydon had a market from 1276, becoming the trading centre of the surrounding agricultural area. Industries in the medieval period included tanning and brewing. From the late 17th century the town became a popular residential area for London commuters, and its growth accelerated with the opening of the London to West Croydon railway in 1839. Other small villages in the area rapidly became commuter suburbs, among them Upper and South Norwood, Thornton Heath, Addiscombe, and Purley. By 1900 Croydon was the largest town in Surrey. In 1965 it amalgamated with Purley and Coulsdon to become a borough of Greater London.

Archbishops' Palace

The manor of Croydon was given by William (I) the Conqueror to Archbishop Lanfranc of Canterbury, and he and subsequent archbishops had their palace here until 1758. Remains of the medieval palace include the 12th-century undercroft, the great hall and Arundel's Hall, the library and chapel dating from the 15th century, and the 14th-century entrance porch. From 1808 to 1896 the archbishops lived at Addington Palace, built between 1773 and 1779.

Churches

Medieval foundations include All Saints, Sanderstead; St John the Evangelist, Old Coulsdon; and St Mary, Addington. Croydon parish church was rebuilt in 1867 by George Gilbert Scott on the original 15th-century plan.

Town planning

Croydon suffered severe bomb damage during World War II, and was subsequently redeveloped with many new houses, a large town centre, and a greatly extended shopping area. Recreational facilities include over 1,200 ha/2,965 acres of parks and woodland, including Farthing Down, Coulsdon Common, Selsdon Woods, and Happy Valley Park.

Crufts

UK's largest dog show. The first show was organized in 1886 by the dog expert **Charles Cruft** (1852–1938), and from that year annual shows bearing his name were held in Islington, London. In 1948 the show's venue moved to Olympia and in 1979 to Earl's Court. Since 1991 it has been held at the NEC in Birmingham.

Cruikshank, George (1792–1878)

English painter and illustrator. He is remembered for his political cartoons and illustrations for Charles Dickens' *Oliver Twist* and Daniel Defoe's *Robinson Crusoe*. From 1835 he published the *Comic Almanack*, a forerunner of *Punch*.

Following his father, he began with political and social caricatures in the Gillray and Rowlandson style for *The Scourge* (1811–16) and *The Meteor* (1813–14), but evolved a grotesque and humorous manner of his own in sketches of Victorian London life and in book illustration. Notable productions are his etchings, made from 1823 to 1826, for Grimms' fairy-tales and the spirited melodrama of those for Dickens's *Oliver Twist* and Harrison Ainsworth's *Old St Paul's*. His brother Robert (1789–1856) was also a caricaturist and a miniature painter. They collaborated in 1821 in illustrating the late-Georgian humours of Pierce Egan's *Life in London*.

Crusades, the (French *croisade*)

Series of wars undertaken 1096–1291 by European rulers intended, among other things, to recover Palestine from the Muslims. Motivated by religious zeal, the desire for land, and the trading ambitions of the major Italian cities, the Crusades had varying degrees of success in their aims and effects.

CRUFTS *Run by the Kennel Club, the annual Crufts dog show dates from 1886; since 1991 it has been held at the National Exhibition Centre, Birmingham. Dogs compete to win their particular category, and then go on to contest the title of supreme champion. These quintessentially British bulldogs await their moment in the limelight in suitably patriotic quarters. Nigel Hawkins/Collections*

Several expeditions were mounted towards the end of the 1100s in response to the conquests of Saladin, Sultan of Egypt, who had captured Damascus in 1174, Aleppo in 1183, and Jerusalem in October 1187. The most important of these expeditions was the Third Crusade led by Philip II of France, Frederick I Barbarossa of Germany, and Richard I of England in 1189. Richard distinguished himself in the capture of Acre, but quarrelled with his allies, who left him to carry on the war alone. After a year of brilliant but useless exploits, he made a truce with Saladin, and returned to Europe.

Almost a century later, in 1270 Prince Edward of England (later ◊Edward I), led his own followers to Acre, but achieved no results.

Crystal Palace

Glass and iron building designed by Joseph Paxton (1801–65), housing the Great Exhibition of 1851 in Hyde Park, London. It was later rebuilt in modified form at Sydenham Hill in 1854 but burned down in 1936.

CSE

Abbreviation for **Certificate of Secondary Education**, in the UK, the examinations taken by the majority of secondary school pupils who were not regarded as academically capable of GCE ◊O level, until the introduction of the common secondary examination system, ◊GCSE, in 1988.

Cudlipp, Hugh, Baron of Aldingbourne (1913–1998)

British publishing and newspaper magnate, a dynamic pioneer of British tabloid journalism. He was chairman of Odhams Press, Daily Mirror Newspapers, and the International Publishing Corporation.

Cudlipp was managing editor of the *Sunday Express* 1950–52, and editorial director of the *Daily Mirror* and *Sunday Pictorial* 1959–63. His books include *Publish and Be Damned* (1955), *At Your Peril* (1965), and his autobiography, *Walking on the Water* (1976). He was made a life peer in 1974.

Cuillin Hills

Range of mountains in southern ◊Skye, the largest island of the Inner Hebrides, in Highland unitary authority, Scotland, running southwestwards from Sligachan to Loch Coriusk. The Cuillin Hills have an average height of 895 m/2,936 ft to 965 m/3,166 ft, and their precipitous ridges attract numerous climbers. The highest point is Sgurr Alasdair, which rises to 993 m/3,257 ft.

Culloden, Battle of

Defeat in 1746 of the ◊Jacobite rebel army of the British prince ◊Charles Edward Stuart (the 'Young Pretender') by the Duke of Cumberland on a stretch of moorland near Inverness, Scotland. This battle effectively ended the military challenge of the Jacobite rebellion.

Although both sides were numerically equal, the English were a disciplined force, while the Jacobites forces were virtually untrained. Although the Jacobites broke through the first English line, they were caught by the musket fire of the second line. They retired in confusion, pursued by the English cavalry which broke the Jacobite lines completely. See map on page 234.

Culshaw, John Royds (1924–1980)

British record producer who developed recording techniques. Managing classical recordings for the Decca record company in the 1950s and 1960s, he introduced echo chambers and the speeding and slowing of tapes to achieve effects not possible in live performance. He produced the first complete recordings of Wagner's *Ring* cycle.

Culture, Media, and Sport Department, DCMS

Government department formed in 1997 to succeed the Department for National Heritage. It is responsible for broadcasting and the media, the arts, libraries, museums, and galleries, architectural and archaeological heritage, tourism, sport, and recreation, and the National Lottery. Including agencies, such the Historic Royal Palaces and Royal Parks agencies, the department had more than 1,000 staff in 1998.

Culzean Castle

Castle 6 km/4 mi west of Maybole, South Ayrshire, Scotland. In 1775 Robert ◊Adam was employed to reconstruct the old castle, and to build a brew-house which was replaced a century later by the present west wing. The castle and over 200 ha/494 acres were given to the National Trust for

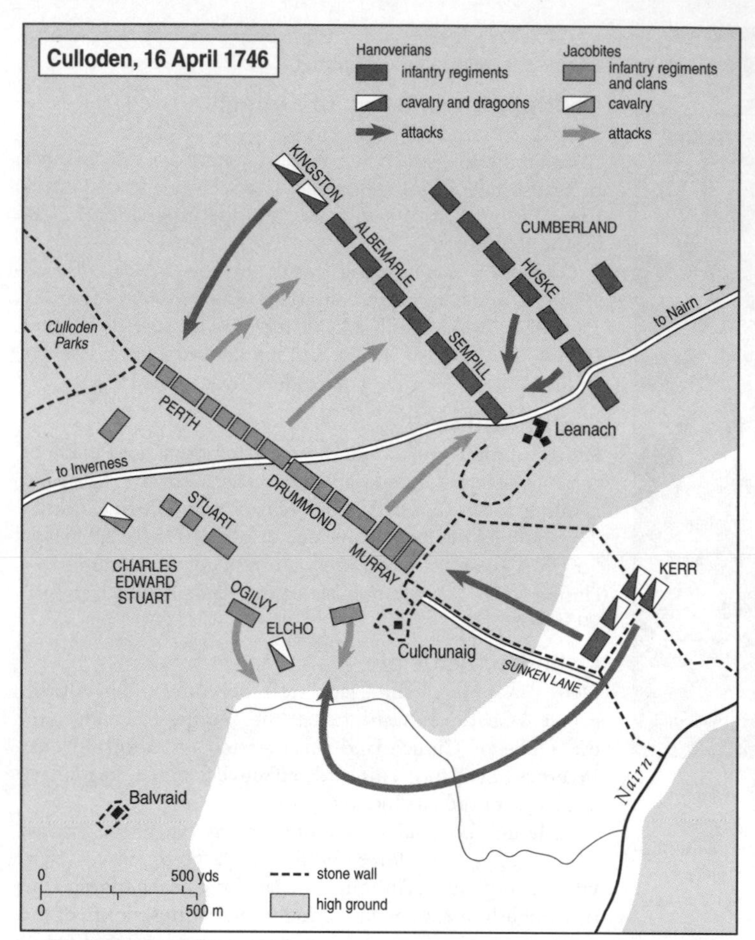

Scotland in 1945, and in 1971 Scotland's first Country Park was established on the estate.

Cumberland

Former county in northwest England, becoming part of Cumbria in 1974.

After the Roman withdrawal from Britain, Cumberland became part of Strathclyde, a British kingdom. In 945 it passed to Scotland, but in 1157 it went to England, and the region became the scene of frequent battles between the two countries until the union of the English and Scottish crowns in 1603.

Cumberland, William Augustus, Duke of Cumberland (1721–1765)

British general who ended the Jacobite rising in Scotland with the Battle of ◊Culloden in 1746; his brutal repression of the Highlanders earned him the nickname of 'Butcher'. KCB 1725, Duke 1726.

Cumbernauld

Town in North Lanarkshire, Scotland, 18 km/11 mi from Glasgow; population (1991) 48,800. It was founded as a ◊new town in 1956 to take in Glasgow city overspill. Industries include electronics.

Cumbria

County of northwest England, created in 1974 from Cumberland, Westmorland, the Furness district of northwest Lancashire, and the Sedbergh district of northwest Yorkshire

Area 6,810 sq km/2,629 sq mi

Towns and cities ◊Carlisle (administrative headquarters), Barrow, Kendal, Penrith, Whitehaven, Workington

Physical Scafell Pike (978 m/3,210 ft), the highest mountain in England, Helvellyn (950 m/3,118 ft); Lake Windermere, the largest lake in England (17 km/10.5 mi long, 1.6 km/1 mi wide), and other lakes (Derwentwater, Grasmere, Haweswater, Ullswater); the rivers Eden and Derwent; the M6 motorway runs north to south through the centre of the county

Features Lake District National Park; Grizedale Forest sculpture project; Furness peninsula; western part of Hadrian's Wall

Power permission granted in 1992 to build fifteen 24 m/80 ft-high wind generators; nuclear power stations at Calder Hall (1956) and Sellafield (formerly Windscale, the first to produce plutonium in the United Kingdom); British Nuclear Fuels' THORP nuclear reprocessing plant began operating 1994

Industries the traditional coal, iron, and steel industries of the coast towns have been replaced by newer industries including chemicals, plastics, marine engineering, electronics, and shipbuilding (at Barrow-in-Furness, nuclear submarines and warships); tourism; salmon fishing

Agriculture in the north and east there is dairy farming; sheep are also reared; the West Cumberland Farmers is England's largest agricultural cooperative

Population (1994) 490,200.

Famous people Thomas de Quincey; Beatrix Potter; John Ruskin's home, Brantwood, on Coniston Water; homes of Robert Southey and Samuel Taylor Coleridge at Keswick; birthplace of William Wordsworth at Cockermouth, and home at Grasmere; Stan Laurel born at Ulverston

History Cumbria's varied history is reflected in its historic remains, which include barrows, stone circles, the western section of Hadrian's Wall, and a number of castles. In the 7th century it was part of Northumbria. In the 10th and 11th centuries it alternated between Scottish and English rule, until taken by the English in 1157.

A Health and Safety Executive report in 1993 showed that children of men working at Sellafield risked fourteen times the national average of developing leukaemia.

Cumbrian Mountains

The mountains of the ◊Lake District, in the county of Cumbria, England; of these, ◊Scafell Pike (978 m/3,210 ft) is the highest peak in England.

CUMBRIA *Castlerigg stone circle near Keswick in Cumbria. Human settlement of this area, with its plentiful fresh water and natural defensive sites, began in Neolithic times. Cumbria is characterized by its lakes and mountain scenery; behind the stone circle is the peak Blencathra, also called Saddleback. Corel*

Cunedda, Wledig (lived 5th century)

British chieftain. He came with his sons and followers from Scotland to northwest Wales to defend Britain against barbarian invaders from Ireland. He laid the foundations of the kingdom of Gwynedd, which was named after him.

Cunningham, John A ('Jack') (1939–)

British Labour politician, secretary of state for Agriculture 1997–98, minister for the cabinet office and chancellor of the Duchy of Lancaster 1998–. He was arguably the most experienced member of Tony Blair's first cabinet, having served as parliamentary private secretary to James Callaghan 1974–76 and parliamentary under-secretary for Energy 1976–79. He was elected to the Labour shadow Cabinet in 1983 and afterwards shadowed Environment 1983–89, Leader of the House of Commons 1989–92, Foreign and Commonwealth Affairs 1992–94, Trade and Industry 1994–95, and National Heritage 1995–97.

He represented Whitehaven 1970–83 and Copeland 1983– in the House of Commons. He was promoted in the July 1998 cabinet re-shuffle to minister of state for the cabinet office and chancellor of the Duchy of Lancaster, with the task of 'ensuring that the prime minister's objectives are delivered'.

Cure, the

English rock band formed in 1976, part of the ◊goth pop scene and enduringly popular with fans. Albums include *Three Imaginary Boys* (1979), *The Head on the Door* (1985), and *Wish* (1992). Their singer, songwriter, and guitarist is Robert Smith (1957–).

curling

Game played on ice with stones; sometimes described as 'bowls on ice'. One of the national games of Scotland, it has spread to many countries. It can also be played on artificial (cement or tarmacadam) ponds.

Curragh 'Mutiny'

Demand in March 1914 by the British general Hubert Gough and his officers, stationed at Curragh, Ireland, that they should not be asked to take part in forcing Protestant Ulster to participate in Home Rule. They were subsequently allowed to return to duty, and after World War I the solution of partition was adopted.

currency

See table overleaf for currency in the UK.

Curry, John (1949–1994)

English ice skater, British champion 1970 and 1972–75, and European, Olympic, and world champion 1976. He excelled

Currency in the UK

The monetary unit in use in the UK is **Pound Sterling** (£). The unit is divided into 100 **Pence** (p).

Notes

UK notes are issued by the Bank of England in the following denominations: £5, £10, £20, and £50. Series D £10 note was withdrawn on 20 May 1994. Series E £50 note came into circulation on 20 April 1994.

Coins

Coins in general circulation are: nickel brass £2, nickel brass £1, cupro-nickel 5p, 10p, 20p and 50p, and bronze 1p and 2p. 1p and 2p coins are, since September 1992, issued in copper-plated steel.

Coins that remain a legal tender and can sometimes be found in circulation are silver or cupro-nickel crowns dating from 1816 onwards. These had been equivalent to 25p; in 1990 the face value of the crown changed from 25p to £5.

Gold coins dating from 1838 onwards in denominations of £1, £2, £5, and 10s (=50p) are legal tender but only at face value. Gold coins introduced in October 1987 as Britannia Gold Bullion Coins, in denominations of £100, £50, £20, and £10, are not found in general circulation.

---

in the free interpretation of music on ice, and moved the emphasis of the sport from the athletic to the artistic.

Curwen, John (1816–1880)

English cleric and educator. In about 1840 he established the **tonic sol-fa** system of music notation (originated in the 11th century by Guido d'Arezzo) in which the notes of the diatonic major scale are named by syllables (doh, ray, me, fah, soh, lah, te) to simplify singing by sight.

Curzon, George Nathaniel, 1st Marquess Curzon of Kedleston (1859–1925)

British Conservative politician, viceroy of India 1899–1905. During World War I, he was a member of the cabinet 1916–19. As foreign secretary 1919–24, he negotiated the Treaty of Lausanne with Turkey.

As viceroy of India, Curzon introduced various reforms, including the creation of the North-West Frontier Province, reorganization of Indian finance, and the establishment of the imperial cadet corps. He resigned this post in 1905, after a dispute with Horatio Kitchener, commander of the British forces in India. Baron (Irish peerage) 1898, Earl 1911, Marquess 1921.

Cushing, Peter (1913–1994)

English actor. Elegant and often sinister, he specialized in horror roles in films made at Hammer studios 1957–73, including *Dracula* (1958), *The Mummy* (1959), and *Frankenstein Must Be Destroyed* (1969). Other films include *Doctor Who and the Daleks* (1966), *Star Wars* (1977), and *Top Secret* (1984).

Cushing first played the role of Baron Frankenstein in 1957 and Count Dracula in 1958, bestowing on each a touch of class and quality. Although his success in the Hammer films led to his being typecast within that genre, he was able to venture into other fields, and played Sherlock Holmes in the film *Hound of the Baskervilles* (1959).

Customs and Excise

Government department responsible for taxes levied on imports (customs duty). Excise duties are levied on goods produced domestically or on licences to carry on certain trades (such as sale of wines and spirits) or other activities (theatrical entertainments, betting, and so on) within a country.

In the UK, both come under the Board of Customs and Excise, which also administers VAT generally, although there are independent tax tribunals for appeal against the decisions of the commissioners.

Cuthbert, St (died 687)

English Christian saint. A shepherd in Northumbria, England, he entered the monastery of Melrose, Scotland, after receiving a vision. He travelled widely as a missionary and because of his alleged miracles was known as the 'wonderworker of Britain'.

He became prior of Lindisfarne in 664, and retired in 676 to Farne Island. In 684 he became bishop of Hexham and later of Lindisfarne. Feast day 20 March.

Cutty Sark

British sailing ship, built in 1869, one of the tea clippers that used to compete in the 19th century to see which clippers could bring its cargo most quickly from China to Britain.

The biennial Cutty Sark International Tall Ships Race is named after it. The ship is preserved in dry dock at Greenwich, London.

Cwmbran (Welsh 'Vale of the Crow')

Town and administrative centre of ⇨Monmouthshire, south-east Wales, situated on the Afon Lywel, a tributary of the River Usk; population (1991) 46,000. It was established in 1949 to provide a focus for new industrial growth in a depressed area, and produces scientific instruments, car components, nylon, and biscuits. There are also engineering and electrical industries.

Cymbeline (lived 1st century AD), or Cunobelin

King of the Catuvellauni AD 5–40, who fought unsuccessfully against the Roman invasion of Britain. His capital was at Colchester.

Cymru

Welsh name for ⇨Wales.

Cynewulf (lived 8th century or 9th century)

Anglo-Saxon poet. He is thought to have been a Northumbrian monk and is the undoubted author of 'Juliana' and part of the 'Christ' in the Exeter Book (a collection of poems now in Exeter Cathedral, England).

Dad's Army
Television comedy series (1968–77). It follows the trials and tribulations of a group of Home Guard volunteers in the fictitious town of Walmington-on-Sea during World War II. Too old, or considered unfit for full military service, the group is led by the pompous Captain Mainwaring (Arthur Lowe), supported by the urbane Sergeant Wilson (John Le Mesurier) and the hysterical Lance-Corporal Jones (Clive Dunn). An institution of BBC television, the series has been rerun many times, becoming popular with successive generations.

A feature-length spin-off was filmed in 1971. Other cast members include John Laurie, James Beck, Arnold Ridley, Ian Lavender, and Bill Pertwee.

daffodil
A national symbol of Wales, worn on St David's Day (1 March), which is traditionally the first day it blooms. In the Scilly Isles Prince Charles is paid one daffodil annually as rent. **National Daffodil Day** has been promoted by Marie Curie Cancer Care since 1990 and the daffodil has also been adopted as a symbol by the Irish Cancer Society.

Dafydd ap Gwilym (*c.* 1340–*c.* 1400)
Welsh poet. His work exhibits a complex but graceful style, concern with nature and love rather than with heroic martial deeds, and has references to Classical and Italian poetry.

Some of his themes recall those of the troubadours and perhaps derive indirectly from them.

Daglish, Eric Fitch (1892–1966)
English artist and author. He wrote a number of natural history books, and illustrated both these and classics by Izaak Walton, Henry Thoreau, Gilbert White, and W H Hudson with exquisite wood engravings.

Dahl, Roald (1916–1990)
British writer, of Norwegian ancestry. He is celebrated for short stories with a twist, such as *Tales of the Unexpected* (1979), and for his children's books, including *James and the Giant Peach* (1961), *Charlie and the Chocolate Factory* (1964), *The BFG* (1982), and *Matilda* (1988). Many of his works have been successfully adapted for television or film. He also wrote the screenplay for the James Bond film *You Only Live Twice* (1967), and the script for *Chitty Chitty Bang Bang* (1968).

The enormous popularity of his children's books can be attributed to his weird imagination, the success of his child characters in outwitting their elders, and his repulsive detail. *The Collected Short Stories* was published in 1991. His autobiography *Going Solo* (1986) recounted his experiences as a fighter pilot in the RAF. After surviving a crash landing he was posted to Washington, where he worked with British security.

Daily Mail
Tabloid newspaper, founded by Lord ◊Northcliffe in 1896. Politically, the paper is conservative but often takes an independent line. It is the flagship newspaper of the Daily Mail and General Trust media company, which also owns the *Mail on Sunday* and the *Evening Standard*. In 1998 it had sales in excess of two million.

The *Mail* was the first exponent of modern journalism in Britain, and from the start Northcliffe's policy was to present the day's news in such a way that it could be absorbed at a glance. Northcliffe had gained control of the *London Evening News* in 1894 and started the *Daily Mail* with an initial capital of less than £15,000. Under his direction, the newspaper's circulation grew until it was far larger than that of any other paper of the day, and several major scoops during the Boer War consolidated its position. Associated Newspapers Limited was formed by Northcliffe to run the *Daily Mail*, *Evening News*, and *Sunday Dispatch*. In 1960 the *Daily Mail* took over the *News Chronicle*, and in 1971 it became a tabloid.

Daily Record
Daily morning newspaper covering Scotland, published in Glasgow. A sister paper of the *Mirror*, it was established in 1895. It had a circulation of around 700,000 in 1998, reaching nearly 50% of all Scottish adults.

Daily Telegraph, The
British newspaper, the first penny paper to be published in London, founded in 1855. In 1937 the *Daily Telegraph*, itself politically conservative, amalgamated with the *Morning Post*,

the former conservative daily. Owned by the Telegraph Group, it had a circulation of over 1,100,000 in 1998.

The *Daily Telegraph* has always specialized in foreign news, and had famous correspondents in many parts of the world. The paper helped to send US explorer Henry Morton Stanley on his expedition to the Congo and helped pay the cost of his search for Scottish explorer David Livingstone.

Dales, or Yorkshire Dales

Series of river valleys in northern England, running east from the Pennines in West Yorkshire; a National Park was established in 1954. The principal valleys are Airedale (see ◊Aire), Nidderdale, ◊Swaledale, ◊Wensleydale, and ◊Wharfedale. The three main peaks are Ingleborough, ◊Whernside, and Pen-y-Ghent.

Dairy farming is the main agricultural activity, Wensleydale cheese being the most notable product. Tourism is also important; the Dales offer magnificent scenery, and walking and potholing are popular activities. Dry stone walls and barns are regular features of the landscape.

Dalglish, Kenny (Kenneth Mathieson) (1951–)

Scottish footballer and football manager. A prolific goalscorer for Glasgow Celtic and then Liverpool, he was the first player to score 100 goals in both the English and Scottish first divisions. He won nine trophies as a player with Celtic and 12 with Liverpool including three European Cups. As a manager he won the league championship with Liverpool 1986, 1988 and 1990, and with Blackburn Rovers 1995. He managed Newcastle United 1996–98 but without success. He made a record 102 international appearances for Scotland and equalled Denis Law's record of 30 goals.

He played for Celtic 1967–77, who won four Scottish League Championships, four Scottish Cups and one Scottish League Cup. He moved to Liverpool and won 12 major medals in the next eight years; five League Championships, four League Cups, and three European Cups. He was Footballer of the Year 1979 and 1983, and Players' Player of the Year 1983. He was player-manager of Liverpool when they won the Cup and League double 1985–86; as manager he added two more League titles 1987–88 1989–90 and another FA Cup win 1989. He became manager of Blackburn Rovers 1991, taking them into the Premier League and on to the Championship 1994–95. He is one of only three managers to win the English Championship with two clubs. He replaced Kevin Keegan as manager of Newcastle United January 1997 but was sacked in August 1998.

Dalkeith

Market town and administrative headquarters of Midlothian unitary authority, Scotland, 10 km/6 mi southeast of Edinburgh; population (1991) 11,600. Grain is the principal trading commodity. The town originally lay between the North Esk and South Esk rivers, but has since been developed to the east of River South Esk. Extensive coalfields lie in the vicinity, and ironmoulding, carpet weaving, brushmaking, brewing, and electronics industries have been established in the town.

Dalkeith Palace, rebuilt in 1700, is located in the town. The 15th-century Rosslyn (Roslin) Chapel stands nearby, decorated with stone carvings of which the 'Prentice Pillar' is considered the finest example.

Dallaglio, Lawrence Bruno Nero (1972–)

English rugby union player. A powerful and highly mobile flank forward, he was appointed England captain in 1997, just two years after making his full international debut. He captained Wasps to their first ever English club championship in 1996–97, and made a major contribution to the British Lions victorious tour of South Africa in 1997.

Dalton, John (1766–1844)

English chemist who proposed the theory of atoms, which he considered to be the smallest parts of matter. He produced the first list of relative atomic masses in 'Absorption of Gases' 1805 and put forward the law of partial pressures of gases (**Dalton's law**).

From experiments with gases, Dalton noted that the proportions of two components combining to form another gas were always constant. He suggested that if substances combine in simple numerical ratios, then the macroscopic weight proportions represent the relative atomic masses of those substances. He also propounded the law of partial pressures, stating that for a mixture of gases the total pressure is the sum of the pressures that would be developed by each individual gas if it were the only one present.

Dalton-in-Furness

Market town in the county of Cumbria, England, 7 km/4 mi northeast of Barrow-in-Furness; population (1991) 11,300. It has increasingly become a commuter settlement for workers in Barrow. At one time Dalton had haematite mining.

Dame

In the UK honours system, the title of a woman who has been awarded the Order of the Bath, Order of St Michael and St George, Royal Victorian Order, or Order of the British Empire. It is also the legal title of the wife or widow of a knight or baronet, placed before her name.

Dampier, William (1651–1715)

English explorer and hydrographic surveyor who circumnavigated the world three times.

On his final voyage 1708–11 he rescued Alexander ◊Selkirk (on whose life Daniel Defoe's *Robinson Crusoe* is based) from Juan Fernandez in the South Pacific.

Dance, Charles (1946–)

English film and television actor. He became known when he played the sympathetic Guy Perron in *The Jewel in the Crown* (1984). He has also appeared in *Plenty* (1986), *Good Morning Babylon*, *The Golden Child* (both 1987), *White Mischief* (1988), *China Moon* (1994), and *Michael Collins* (1996).

He played the title role in the Royal Shakespeare Company's 1989 production of *Coriolanus*, and has appeared in the London-based comedy *What Rats Don't Do* (1998).

Dancer, John Benjamin (1812–1887)

British optician and instrumentmaker. He pioneered microphotography and by 1840 he had developed a method of taking photographs of microscopic objects using silver plates. The photographic image was capable of magnification up to 20 times before clarity was lost. By 1859 he was showing microscope slides which carried portraits or whole pages of books.

Dancer improved many of the standard laboratory practices of the period. He introduced unglazed porous jars in voltaic cells to separate the electrodes. Dancer improved on the ⟩Daniell cell by crimping or corrugating its copper plates to increase the electrode surface area. He also constructed the apparatus with which James ⟩Joule determined the mechanical equivalent of heat.

Dance Umbrella

Annual British dance festival, held in London, established 1978. Its aim is to develop contemporary dance in Britain at all levels. Its artistic director and founder is Val Bourne (1938–).

danegeld

Tax imposed from 991 by Anglo-Saxon kings to pay tribute to the Vikings. After the Norman Conquest the tax continued to be levied until 1162, and the Normans used it to finance military operations.

Danelaw

11th-century name for the area of north and east England settled by the Vikings in the 9th century. It occupied about half of England, from the River Tees to the River Thames. Within its bounds, Danish law, customs, and language prevailed. Its linguistic influence is still apparent.

Daniell, John Frederic (1790–1845)

English chemist and meteorologist who invented a primary electrical cell in 1836. The **Daniell cell** consists of a central zinc cathode dipping into a porous pot containing zinc sulphate solution. The porous pot is, in turn, immersed in a solution of copper sulphate contained in a copper can, which acts as the cell's anode. The use of a porous barrier prevents polarization (the covering of the anode with small bubbles of hydrogen gas) and allows the cell to generate a continuous current of electricity.

The Daniell cell was the first reliable source of direct-current electricity.

Danielli, James Frederic (1911–1984)

British cell biologist who hypothesized that the molecular structure of the cell membrane was a sandwich of two layers of proteins. In 1943, Danielli and Hugh Davson published their seminal theory on transport of substances across cell membranes in *The Permeability of Natural Membranes*. Their work provided a framework for future physiologists and cell biologists working on the role of the membrane in different cellular activities.

Daniels, Sarah (1957–)

British dramatist. Her plays explore contemporary feminist issues, and include *Ripen Our Darkness* (1981), *Masterpieces* (1983), *Byrthrite* (1987), *Neaptide* (1984), *Beside Herself* (1990), and *Head-Rot Holiday* (1992), concerning women condemned to mental institutions.

Dankworth, John Philip William (1927–)

English jazz musician, composer, and bandleader. He was a leading figure in the development of British jazz from about 1950. His film scores include *Saturday Night and Sunday Morning* (1960) and *The Servant* (1963).

He also composed television music, for example, for the series *The Avengers* (1964).

Darling, Alistair Maclean (1953–)

British Labour politician and lawyer, chief secretary to the

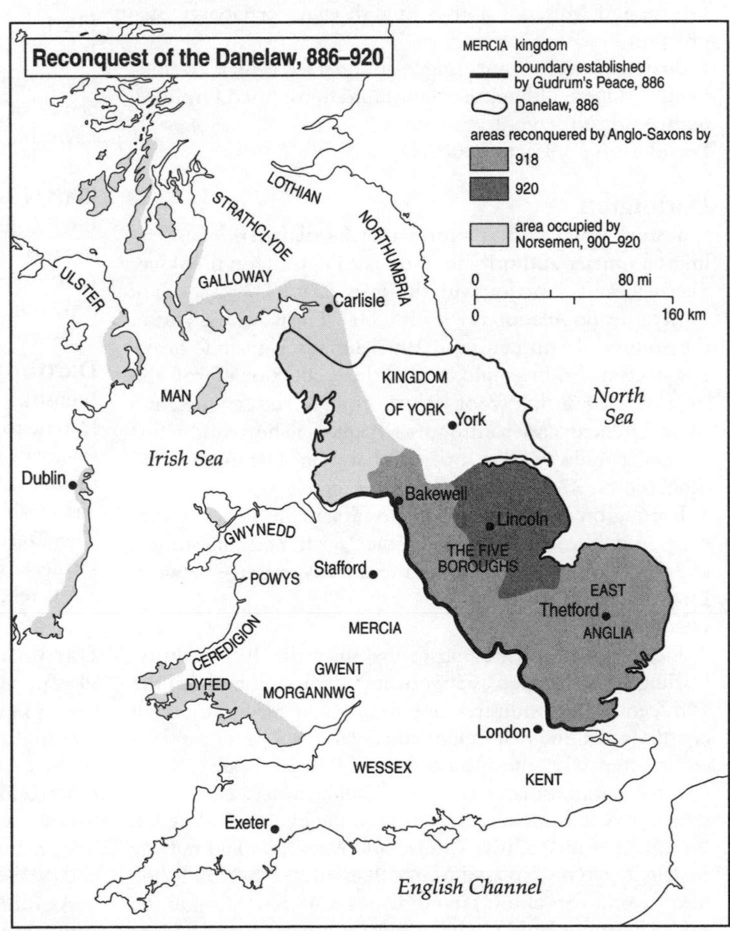

Treasury 1997–98, secretary of state for Social Security 1998–. He was Chairman of the Lothian Regional Transport Committee 1986–87 before being elected to the House of Commons in 1987, representing Edinburgh Central. He served as Opposition spokesman on Home Affairs 1988–92, on Treasury, Economic Affairs and the City 1992–96, and as shadow chief secretary to the Treasury 1996–97.

Darling, Grace Horsley (1815–1842)

British heroine. She was the daughter of a lighthouse keeper on the Farne Islands, off Northumberland. On 7 September 1838 the *Forfarshire* was wrecked, and Grace Darling and her father rowed through a storm to the wreck, saving nine lives. She was awarded a medal for her bravery.

Darlington

Unitary authority (borough status) in northeast England, created in 1997

Area 199 sq km/77 sq mi

Towns and cities ⇨Darlington (administrative headquarters); villages of Hurworth on Tees, Middleton St George, Heighington, Hurworth Place

Features River Skerne flows through Darlington, River Tees forms southern boundary of authority; Darlington Railway Centre and Museum houses English engineer George Stephenson's locomotion engine

Industries heavy engineering, iron and steel, vehicle components, bridge building, telecommunications, fitted furniture, textiles, knitting wool, agriculture

Population (1995) 100,600.

Darlington

Industrial town and administrative headquarters of ⇨Darlington unitary authority in northeast England, on the River Skerne near its junction with the Tees, 53 km/33 mi south of Newcastle; population (1996) 100,600. The town was part of the county of Durham until 1997. Industries include heavy engineering, bridge-building, and the production of iron and steel goods, knitting wool, vehicle components, textiles, and fitted kitchens and bathrooms (Magnet). The world's first passenger railway was opened between Darlington and Stockton on 27 September 1825.

Darlington occupies a central position in the Tees lowland, lying in the broad gap between the North Yorkshire moors and the Pennines, which forms the east coast passage between England and Scotland.

History

A local service and trading centre since the 10th century, Darlington developed as a wool and textiles centre until the 19th century. Its industrial importance increased in the 19th century when the first freight railway to carry passengers was constructed with the sponsorship of Edward Pease, a local Quaker businessman. George ⇨Stephenson's *Locomotion*, which pulled the first train to run on the line, is displayed at the Darlington Railway Centre and Museum. The railway was built to transport coal from collieries, 13 km/8 mi to the northwest, to Stockton's riverside quays, 18 km/11 mi to the east. The route later extended eastwards into Cleveland and westwards into Cumbria, and the London–Newcastle–Edinburgh line opened in 1841. Rapid expansion followed and Darlington became a centre for railway engineering and the manufacture of locomotives, tracks, and wagons. The railway engineering workshops were closed in 1966.

Darnley, Henry Stewart or Stuart, Lord Darnley (1545–1567)

Scottish aristocrat, second husband of Mary Queen of Scots from 1565, and father of James I of England (James VI of Scotland).

On the advice of her secretary, David ⇨Rizzio, Mary refused Darnley the crown matrimonial; in revenge, Darnley led a band of nobles who murdered Rizzio in Mary's presence. Darnley was assassinated in 1567.

He was born in England, the son of the 4th Earl of Lennox (1516–1571) and Lady Margaret Douglas (1515–1578), through whom he inherited a claim to the English throne. Mary was his first cousin. Mary and Darnley were reconciled after the murder of Rizzio 1566, but soon Darnley alienated all parties and a plot to kill him was formed by ⇨Bothwell. Mary's part in it remains a subject of controversy. Knighted and became Earl of Ross and Duke of Albany 1565.

Dart

River in Devon, southwest England; length 57 km/35 mi, 16 km/10 mi of which is tidal. It rises near Cranmere Pool in the centre of ⇨Dartmoor, widens into a broad estuary, and is navigable to Totnes.

Dart, (Robert) Thurston (1921–1971)

English harpsichordist and musicologist. His pioneer reinterpretations of Baroque classics such as Bach's *Brandenburg Concertos* helped to launch the trend towards authenticity in early music.

Dartford

Industrial town in Kent, southeast England, on the River Darent to the south of the Thames estuary, 27 km/17 mi southeast of London; population (1991) 59,400. Industries include milling, engineering, and the manufacture of cement, chemicals, paper, and pharmaceuticals (Glaxo-Wellcome). The **Dartford Tunnel** (1963) runs under the Thames to Purfleet, Essex. The Queen Elizabeth II bridge opened in 1991, relieving congestion in the tunnel.

Dartmoor

Plateau of southwest Devon, England; mostly a national park, 956 sq km/369 sq mi in area. Over half the region is around 300 m/1,000 ft above sea level, making it the highest and largest of the moorland areas in southwest England. The moor is noted for its wild aspect and the tors, rugged blocks of bare granite, which crown its loftier points. The highest are Yes Tor, rising to 619 m/2,030 ft; and High Willhays, which climbs to 621 m/2,039 ft.

At Princetown, 11 km/7 mi east of Tavistock, is **Dartmoor Prison**, a high-security long-term institution, opened in 1809 during the Napoleonic Wars, initially for the confinement of French prisoners-of-war. The region provides grazing for sheep, cattle, and **Dartmoor ponies**, a semi-wild breed probably descended from animals turned out on the moor in the Dark Ages. Dartmoor was the setting for Arthur Conan Doyle's *The Hound of the Baskervilles.*

Physical features

The slopes beneath the granite tors are covered by gorse and heather, and the low-lying areas are characterized by broad tracts of dark peat and bog with bright green grass. The region has no natural lakes, but Devon's chief rivers, including the ◊Dart, the Tavy, the Plym, the Avon, and the Erme, have their sources on the moor. Eight reservoirs have been constructed, covering a total 209 ha/516 acres.

The main areas of broad-leaved woodland, mainly oak, lie in deep valleys at the southern edge of the moorland, such as the Dart and the Teign valleys. Originally oak and birch forest covered all but the very highest reaches of the moor, but only three ancient upland copses of oak trees survive at Black Tor Beare, Piles Copse, and Wistman's Wood. The valley woodlands were managed as coppice until the 20th century, being used for building, fuel, and other local purposes, but these woods are no longer generating naturally because of grazing pressure and lack of management. Tree preservation orders now cover over 1,100 ha/2,500 acres, and the Forestry Commission manages 1,740 ha/4,300 acres of conifer plantations. In 1990 severe storms destroyed 3% of Dartmoor's woodland, about 107,000 trees.

Rainfall is particularly heavy on the moor. Princetown has an average annual precipitation of 2150 mm/85 in, compared with 889 mm/35 in at Exeter.

Historic remains and architectural features

Extensive evidence of the region's prehistoric occupation includes stone rows, cairns, and the remains of hillfort settlements of the Bronze and Iron ages. Several simple clapper bridges, slabs supported on stones, are preserved. Buckfast Abbey, completed in 1938, occupies the site of an 11th-century abbey near ◊Buckfastleigh, in the southeast region of Dartmoor. A Ministry of Defence artillery range lies in the northern part of the moor to the south of Okehampton.

Mining

Tin, copper, lead, and manganese were mined in the Middle Ages. The tin industry was ruled through the ◊stannaries courts at Ashburton, Tavistock, Chagford, and Plympton. Offenders breaking the laws of the stannaries were imprisoned in ◊Lydford Castle. The last working tin mine on Dartmoor closed in 1930. Hemerdon, just outside the national park boundary, contains reserves of tungsten, and the southwestern area of the moor has china clay deposits.

Chief towns

Okehampton lies on the northern boundary of the moor, Ashburton and Buckfastleigh in the east, Widecombe-in-the-Moor in the southeast, Ivybridge in the south, ◊Tavistock and Lydford in the west, and ◊Princetown and Postbridge in the centre of the moor. Ashburton, with about 3,500 inhabitants, is the largest settlement within the national park boundary.

Dartmouth

English seaport at the mouth of the River Dart; 43 km/27 mi east of Plymouth, on the Devon coast; population (1996 est) 6,000. It is a centre for yachting and has an excellent harbour. The Britannia Royal Naval College dates from 1905. Dartmouth Castle (15th century), 1.6 km/1 mi southeast of the town, guards the narrow entrance of the Dart estuary.

Darwin, Charles Robert (1809–1882)

English naturalist who developed the modern theory of evolution and proposed, with Alfred Russel ◊Wallace, the principle of natural selection.

After research in South America and the Galápagos Islands as naturalist on HMS *Beagle* 1831–36, Darwin published *On the Origin of Species by Means of Natural Selection or the Preservation of Favoured Races in the Struggle for Life* (1859). This book explained the evolutionary process through the principles of natural selection and aroused bitter controversy because it disagreed with the literal interpretation of the Book of Genesis in the Bible.

Darwin's work marked a turning point in many of the

DARWIN, CHARLES *English naturalist Charles Darwin, author of one of the most influential scientific books ever published,* On the Origin of Species by Means of Natural Selection *(1859). At a time when most people still believed in the literal truth of the Bible's account of creation, Darwin's idea that species had evolved gradually caused a storm of controversy. The first edition of the book sold out on the day of publication. Corbis*

sciences, including physical anthropology and palaeontology. But, before the voyage of the *Beagle*, Darwin, like everyone else at that time, did not believe in the mutability of species. In South America, he saw fossil remains of giant sloths and other animals now extinct, and on the Galápagos Islands he found a colony of finches that he could divide into at least 14 similar species, none of which existed on the mainland. It was obvious to him that one type must have evolved into many others, but how they did so eluded him. Two years after his return he read Malthus's 'An Essay on the Principle of Population' (1798), which proposed that the human population was growing too fast for it to be adequately fed, and that something would have to reduce it, such as war or natural disaster. This work inspired Darwin to see that the same principle could be applied to animal populations.

Darwin's theory of natural selection concerned the variation existing between members of a sexually reproducing population. Those members with variations better fitted to the environment would be more likely to survive and breed, subsequently passing on these favourable characteristics to their offspring. He avoided the issue of human evolution, however, remarking at the end of *The Origin of Species* that 'much light will be thrown on the origin of man and his history'. It was not until his publication of *The Descent of Man and Selection in Relation to Sex* (1871), that Darwin argued that people evolved just like other organisms. He did not seek the controversy he caused but his ideas soon caught the public imagination. The popular press soon published articles about the 'missing link' between humans and apes.

Darwin never understood what caused newly formed advantageous characteristics to appear in animals and plants because he had no knowledge of heredity and mutations. The irony is that the key work on heredity by the Austrian scientist Gregor Mendel was carried out during Darwin's own lifetime and published in 1865, but was neglected until 1900. Neo-Darwinism, the current theory of evolution, is a synthesis of Darwin's theories and genetics based on Mendel's work.

Darwin, Erasmus (1731–1802)

English poet, physician, and naturalist; he was the grandfather of Charles Darwin. He wrote *The Botanic Garden* (1792), which included a versification of the Linnaean system entitled *The Loves of the Plants*, and *Zoonomia* (1794–96), which anticipated aspects of evolutionary theory, but tended to French naturalist J B de Lamarck's interpretation.

Darwin Initiative

Government conservation initiative announced at the Earth Summit in 1992, pledging an annual budget of £10 million in grants to British researchers. This was reduced to £3 million in 1993.

Dave Clark Five, The

English pop group formed in 1958 and disbanded in 1973. They reached number one in the UK with their single 'Glad All Over' (1964), and they continued their success, in the UK and USA, with a string of hits including 'Bits and Pieces'.

Members of the group were Dave Clark (1942–) (drums), Mike Smith (1943–) (vocals and keyboards), Rick Huxley (1942–), Lenny Davidson (1944–), and Denis Payton (1943–) (guitar and saxophone).

Daventry

Town in Northamptonshire, central England, 19 km/12 mi west of Northampton; population (1991) 18,000. Because of its central position, the BBC's high-power radio transmitter was erected on Borough Hill, to the east of the town, in 1925. Originally specializing in footwear manufacture, the town received London and Birmingham overspill from the 1950s, and developed diverse light industries such as the manufacture of metal products, motor accessories, and vehicle components (Ford).

David, Elizabeth, born Gwynne (1914–1992)

British cookery writer. Her *A Book of Mediterranean Food* (1950) and *French Country Cooking* (1951) helped to spark an interest in foreign cuisine in Britain, and also inspired a growing school of informed, highly literate writing on food and wine.

Her other books include *Italian Food* (1954), *French Provincial Cooking* (1960), and *English Bread and Yeast Cookery* (1977).

David

Two kings of Scotland.

David I (1084–1153)

King of Scotland from 1124. The youngest son of Malcolm III Canmore and St ◊Margaret, he was brought up in the English court of Henry I, and in 1113 married ◊Matilda, widow of the 1st earl of Northampton.

He invaded England in 1138 in support of Queen Matilda, but was defeated at Northallerton in the Battle of the Standard, and again in 1141.

David II (1324–1371)

King of Scotland from 1329, son of ◊Robert (I) the Bruce. David was married at the age of four to Joanna, daughter of Edward II of England. In 1346 David invaded England, was captured at the battle of Neville's Cross, and imprisoned for 11 years.

After the defeat of the Scots by Edward III at Halidon Hill in 1333, the young David and Joanna were sent to France for safety. They returned in 1341. On Joanna's death in 1362 David married Margaret Logie, but divorced her in 1370.

David Copperfield

Novel by Charles ◊Dickens, published in 1849–50. The story follows the orphan David Copperfield from his school days and early poverty to eventual fame as an author. Among the characters he encounters are Mr Micawber, Mr Peggotty, and Uriah Heep. It is perhaps the most popular of Dickens' novels and it was his own favourite.

David, St (lived 5th–6th century), or **Dewi**

Patron saint of Wales, Christian abbot and bishop. According to legend he was the son of a prince of Dyfed and uncle of King Arthur. He was responsible for the adoption of the leek as the national emblem of Wales, but his own emblem is a dove. Feast day 1 March.

Davie, Donald Alfred (1922–)
English poet and literary critic. His verse has a highly wrought style and grace, wedded to interests in history and politics, as exemplified in *The Forests of Lithuania* (1959). His later work is as carefully constructed, but explores freer syntactic and metrical forms. Among Davie's critical writings are *Purity of Diction in English Verse* (1952), *Thomas Hardy and British Poetry* (1972), and a book on the poet Ezra Pound (1976).

Davies, (Henry) Walford (1869–1941)
English composer and broadcaster. His compositions include the cantata *Everyman* (1904), the 'Solemn Melody' (1908) for organ and strings, chamber music, and part songs. He also wrote sacred music and pieces for children. He was a popular radio broadcaster, particularly in his British Broadcasting Corporation (BBC) series, *Music and the ordinary listener* (1926–30).

Davies, Gerald (Thomas Gerald Reames) (1945–)
Welsh rugby union player. A fast, elusive wing-threequarter renowned for his sidestep, his 20 tries in 46 internationals 1966–78 was a Welsh record (shared with Gareth ◊Edwards). He scored three more tries in five appearances for the British Lions 1968–71.

Davies, Jonathan (1962–)
Welsh rugby union and rugby league player. He was capped 27 times between 1985 and 1988 for the Wales rugby union team. In 1988 he changed codes, joining Widnes for a fee of £225,000, and became a member of the Great Britain XIII. He was rugby league Player of the Year 1991 and 1994. He returned to rugby union 1995, when he joined Cardiff.

Davies, Laura (1963–)
English golfer. One of the longest hitters in the history of women's golf who in 1987 became the first British player to win the US Women's Open. She won the British Women's Open in 1986, the McDonalds LPGA Championship in 1993 and 1996, when she also won the Du Maurier Classic. In 1994 she became the first European to top the US LPGA Money List, and she was a member of the 1998 Solheim Cup team.

A member of the British Curtis Cup team in 1984, she turned professional in 1985, and finished her first professional season as top of the European order of merit. She was a member of Europe's Solheim Cup team in 1990, 1992, 1994, and 1996.

Davies, Peter Maxwell (1934–)
English composer and conductor. His music combines medieval and serial codes of practice with a heightened Expressionism as in his opera *Taverner* (1972), based on the life and works of the 16th-century composer John Taverner. Other works include the opera *The Lighthouse* (1980), the music- theatre piece *Miss Donnithorne's Maggot*, and the orchestral piece *Mavis in Las Vegas*. He is the Associate Conductor/Composer of the Royal Philharmonic Orchestra, and the BBC Philharmonic, and the Composer Laureate of the Scottish Chamber Orchestra.

Davies, Ron (1946–)
British Labour politician, secretary of state for Wales 1997–98. After serving as a local government councillor 1969–84 he was elected to the House of Commons in 1983, representing Caerphilly. He was placed in the Whips Office 1985–87 and then made steady progress within the party. He was Opposition spokesman on Agriculture and Rural Affairs 1987–92, to which was added Food 1989, and then, after a short period as shadow minister of Agriculture, he served as shadow secretary of state for Wales 1992–97. In 1997 he oversaw the successful introduction of legislation to create an elected assembly with devolved powers in Wales. In October 1998 he resigned as Secretary of State for Wales and withdrew as the Labour Party's candidate for the leadership of the National Assembly for Wales.

Davies, Siobhan (Susan) (1950–)
English choreographer and dancer. She was a founding member of the London Contemporary Dance Theatre (LCDT) in 1967 and became its resident choreographer

DAVIES, LAURA *The golfer Laura Davies has had an extremely successful career, winning both the British and US Women's Open tournaments. However, like many other sports, women's golf lives in the shadow of the men's game, and Davies does not enjoy the instant recognition commanded by some of her contemporaries on the men's circuit. Tony White/Times/Rex*

1983–87, continuing as associate choreographer 1988–93. She is the founder and director of Siobhan Davies and Dancers (1981), and her Siobhan Davies Dance Company was launched at the 1998 Dance Umbrella festival. Her style is modernist or postmodern, sometimes cool and intense as in *Bridge the Distance* (1985), sometimes fleet and rhythmic, exploring relationships in space and dynamics.

Davis, Colin Rex (1927–)

English conductor. He was musical director at Sadler's Wells 1961–65, chief conductor of the BBC Symphony Orchestra 1967–71, musical director of the Royal Opera, Covent Garden, 1971–86, chief conductor of the Bavarian Radio Symphony Orchestra 1986–92, and principal conductor of the London Symphony Orchestra from 1995. He is particularly associated with the music of Berlioz, Mozart, and Tippett.

Davis, Joe (Joseph) (1901–1978)

British billiards and snooker player. He was world snooker champion a record 15 times 1927–46 and responsible for much of the popularity of the game. His brother Fred (1913–98) was also a billiards and snooker world champion.

> *England is a country infested with people who love to tell us what to do, but who very rarely seem to know what's going on.*
>
> Colin MacInnes English novelist. *England, Half English* (1960)

Davis, Steve (1957–)

English snooker player who has won every major honour in the game since turning professional in 1978. He has been world champion six times.

Davison, Emily Wilding (1872–1913)

English militant ◊suffragette who died after throwing herself under the king's horse at the Derby at Epsom (she was trampled by the horse). She joined the Women's Social and Political Union in 1906 and served several prison sentences for militant action such as stone throwing, setting fire to pillar boxes, and bombing Lloyd George's country house.

Davitt, Michael (1846–1906)

Irish nationalist. He joined the Fenians (forerunners of the Irish Republican Army) in 1865, and was imprisoned for treason 1870–77. After his release, he and the politician Charles Parnell founded the ◊Land League in 1879. Davitt was jailed several times for land-reform agitation. He was a member of Parliament 1895–99, advocating the reconciliation of extreme and constitutional nationalism.

Davy, Humphry (1778–1829)

English chemist. He discovered, by electrolysis, the metallic elements sodium and potassium in 1807, and calcium, boron, magnesium, strontium, and barium in 1808. In addition, he established that chlorine is an element and proposed that hydrogen is present in all acids. He invented the safety lamp for use in mines where methane was present, enabling miners to work in previously unsafe conditions. Knighted 1812, baronet 1818.

Dawkins, (Clinton) Richard (1941–)

British zoologist whose book *The Selfish Gene* (1976) popularized the theories of sociobiology (social behaviour in humans and animals in the context of evolution). In *The Blind Watchmaker* (1986) he explained the modern theory of evolution.

In *The Selfish Gene* he argued that genes – not individuals, populations, or species – are the driving force of evolution. He suggested an analogous system of cultural transmission in human societies, and proposed the term 'mimeme', abbreviated to 'meme', as the unit of such a scheme. He considered the idea of God to be a meme with a high survival value. His contentions were further developed in *The Extended Phenotype* (1982), primarily an academic work.

Dawkins was born in Nairobi, Kenya, and educated at Oxford, where from 1975 he held academic posts.

Dawlish

Town in Devon, England, 18 km/11 mi south of Exeter; population (1991) 11,400. The town, together with **Dawlish Warren** – a sand spit extending into the mouth of the River Exe – is a holiday resort. A stream called Dawlish Water runs through the town centre.

Dawson, Les (1934–1993)

English comedian, born in Manchester. After a long apprenticeship in working men's clubs and similar venues, he gained popularity on television, first in his own long-running series *Sez Les* and especially as host of the quiz show *Blankety Blank*. In mining a vein of determinedly glum humour, full of derogatory references to wives and mothers-in-law, Dawson was a natural successor to bygone exponents of northern working-class comedy. However, his best routines possessed qualities of verbal elaboration and near-surreal fantasy.

Day, Robin (1923–)

English broadcasting journalist. A barrister, he pioneered the probing political interview, notably when he questioned Harold Macmillan on the composition of his cabinet in 1958.

After studying law at Oxford, Day was called to the Bar in 1952. He worked for Independent Televison News (ITN) 1955–59, then joined the BBC, where he presented *Panorama* 1967–72 and hosted *Question Time* 1979–89. Knighted 1981.

Day-Lewis, Cecil (1904–1972)

Irish poet brought up in England who wrote under the name **C Day Lewis**. With W H Auden and Stephen Spender, he was one of the influential left-wing poets of the 1930s. His later poetry moved from political concerns to a more traditional personal lyricism. He also wrote detective novels under the pseudonym **Nicholas Blake**. He was British poet laureate 1968–1972.

His poetry, which includes *From Feathers to Iron* (1931) and *Overtures to Death* (1938), is marked by accomplished lyrics and sustained narrative power. *The Complete Poems* was published in 1992.

Day-Lewis, Daniel (1958–)

English actor. He first came to prominence in *My Beautiful Laundrette* and *A Room With a View* (both 1985). He won an Academy Award for his performance as a painter suffering from cerebral palsy in *My Left Foot* (1989).

An actor of great versatility, he has also appeared in *The Unbearable Lightness of Being* (1987), *The Last of the Mohicans* (1992), *The Age of Innocence* (1993), *In the Name of the Father* (1993), *The Crucible* (1996), and *The Boxer* (1997).

DBE

Abbreviation for Dame Commander of the Order of the British Empire.

D-day

6 June 1944, the day of the Allied invasion of Normandy under the command of General Eisenhower to commence Operation Overlord, the liberation of Western Europe from German occupation. The Anglo-US invasion fleet landed on the Normandy beaches on the stretch of coast between the Orne River and St Marcouf. Artificial harbours known as 'Mulberries' were constructed and towed across the Channel so that equipment and armaments could be unloaded on to the beaches. After overcoming fierce resistance the allies broke through the German defences; Paris was liberated on 25 August, and Brussels on 2 September.

Deal

Port and resort on the east coast of Kent, southeast England; population (1991) 28,500. Industries include fishing, boatbuilding, and tourism. Julius Caesar is said to have landed at nearby ◊Walmer in 55 BC, and Deal became one of the ◊Cinque Ports. The castle, built by Henry VIII, houses the town museum.

Deal Castle was one of many fortifications built along the south coast in about 1540, resulting from Henry's fear of invasion by Catholic France after the English Reformation. Together with the castles of Walmer to the south and Sandown to the north (now in ruins), Deal protected the ◊Downs roadstead, an area of safe anchorage between the coast and the hazardous sandbanks known as the ◊Goodwin Sands. The castle has a unique circular form, with a central keep surrounded by two rings of six semi-circular bastions.

In the 18th century, Deal gained notoriety as a centre of smuggling.

de Bono, Edward Francis Charles Publius (1933–)

Maltese-born British medical doctor and psychologist whose concept of lateral thinking, first expounded in *The Use of Lateral Thinking* (1967), involves thinking round a problem rather than tackling it head on.

From 1976 to 1983 de Bono was lecturer in Medicine at the Department of Investigative Medicine, Cambridge University. He was appointed director of the Cognitive Research Trust, Cambridge in 1991 and secretary-general of the Supranational International Thinking Organization in 1983. He has written many books on lateral thinking, including *Teaching Thinking* (1976), *de Bono's Thinking Course* (1982), *I am Right, You are Wrong* (1990), and *Teach Your Child to Think* (1992).

Debrett's Peerage

Directory of the British peerage, first published in 1802 by John Debrett (1753–1822) under the title *Peerage of England, Scotland and Ireland*, but based on earlier compilations. Debrett aimed to avoid spurious genealogies and confine himself to authenticated facts.

Declaration of Rights

The statement issued by the Convention Parliament in February 1689, laying down the conditions under which the crown was to be offered to William III and Mary. Its clauses were later incorporated in the ◊Bill of Rights.

Decline and Fall of the Roman Empire

Historical work by Edward Gibbon, published in the UK in 1776–88. One of the best-known historical works in English literature, it spans 13 centuries and is arranged in three parts. It covers the history of the empire from Trajan and the Antonines through to the Turkish seizure of Constantinople in 1453.

Decorated

In architecture, the second period of English Gothic, covering the latter part of the 13th century and the 14th century. Chief characteristics include ornate window tracery, the window being divided into several lights by vertical bars called mullions; sharp spires ornamented with crockets and pinnacles; complex church vaulting; and slender arcade piers.

The reconstruction of ◊Exeter Cathedral (begun about 1270) was in the Decorated style. Other examples include the naves of Lichfield Cathedral, Beverley Minster, and the parish church of Heckington, Lincolnshire; the choirs of Bristol, Lincoln and St Albans cathedrals; the choir, west front and chapter-house of York; and the chapter-houses of Salisbury, Southwell, and Wells cathedrals.

Dee

River which flows through Aberdeenshire, Scotland and the city of Aberdeen; length 137 km/85 mi. From its source in the Cairngorm Mountains, it flows east into the North Sea at Aberdeen (by an artificial channel in this latter stage). Near Braemar the river passes through a rock gorge, the **Linn of Dee**. ◊Balmoral Castle is on its banks. It is noted for salmon fishing and is the fifth longest river in Scotland.

Defence, Ministry of

British government department created in 1964 from a temporary Ministry of Defence established after World War II together with the Admiralty, Air Ministry, and War Office. It is headed by the secretary of state for defence, with ministers of state for the armed forces and defence procurement.

The Ministry of Defence's annual expenditure totalled £22.5 billion, or 3.3% of gross domestic product (1994–95). With more than 100,000 staff in 1998, it is the largest central government department.

It was announced in the government's 1998 strategic defence review that the defence budget will fall in real terms by more than £900 million over the next three years. The strategic emphasis has been shifted from preparing to fight a land war in Europe to intervening further afield, with an expanded rapid reaction force.

defence policy

As an imperial power – still retaining control over 13 overseas dependent territories – a nuclear power and a permanent member of the UN Security Council, the UK has far wider defence interests than might be anticipated from its population size and economic weight. In the early 1990s, at more than 4% of GDP, UK defence spending was more than double the EU norm. With the ending of the Cold War, defence spending has subsequently fallen sharply and, in 1997, at 2.7% of GDP, was at its lowest proportionate level since the 1930s.

In 1998, there were British forces deployments in 28 locations overseas, including 5,000 troops in Bosnia, part of the international peacekeeping mission. In the 1991 Gulf War, 42,000 UK troops participated in the US-led international coalition against Iraq.

At the cornerstone of UK defence policy since 1949 has been membership of NATO, an organization formed to provide collective defence for Western Europe against the threat of invasion by Communist Russia. As part of its NATO commitment, large British army garrisons were based in Germany, while the British Navy defended the sea-lanes of northwest Europe from Russian submarines. Britain has also been a member of the Western European Union, since its inception in 1955, a consultative forum for military issues among western European governments.

With decolonization from the late 1940s, Britain has progressively reduced the number of its overseas military bases and commitments. Yet still, in 1997, it maintained a substantial naval fleet, including 12 nuclear submarines, three Trident strategic submarines, two aircraft carriers, 12 destroyers and 23 frigates. This fleet was used to support the ground forces in the 1991 Gulf Conflict and was crucial in the British success in the 1982 Falklands War. Since 1969, political instability and terrorism in Northern Ireland, has also meant that large troop deployments have been necessary in the Province.

The collapse of communism in eastern Europe and the disbanding, in 1991, of NATO's adversary, the Warsaw Pact, has led to successive fundamental reviews of British defence policy and a reduction in troop numbers, bringing what has been termed a 'peace dividend'. The most recent review, the Strategic Defence Review, was undertaken between 1997 and 1998 by the new Labour government. It concluded that British defence policy should remain based around maintaining Trident as an effective nuclear deterrent and making a strong contribution to an enlarged NATO, to help oversee security across Europe. However, the review recognized that Britain no longer needed to prepare expensively for a large land war in Europe. In a world made unstable by the new threats posed by international terrorism, the drugs trade, the proliferation of weapons of mass destruction, ethnic rivalries (as in the Balkans), and Islamic fundamentalism, the future defence capability needed to be more flexible. At its core will be a larger and better integrated, air and sea-based Rapid Reaction Force.

Defence Research Agency

Military organization set up 1991 to make the Ministry of Defence's non-nuclear research and development institutions more profitable. It incorporates the Admiralty Research Establishment, the Royal Aerospace Establishment, the Royal Armament Research and Development Establishment, and the Royal Signals and Radar Establishment.

Defender of the Faith

One of the titles of the English sovereign, conferred on Henry VIII in 1521 by Pope Leo X in recognition of the king's treatise against the Protestant Martin Luther. It appears on coins in the abbreviated form **F.D.** (Latin *Fidei Defensor*).

Your Roman-Saxon-Danish-Norman English.

Daniel Defoe English writer. *The True-Born Englishman*

Defoe, Daniel (1660–1731)

English writer. His ◊*Robinson Crusoe* (1719), though purporting to be a factual account of shipwreck and solitary survival, was influential in the development of the novel. The fictional *Moll Flanders* (1722) and the partly factual *A Journal of the Plague Year* (1722) are still read for their concrete realism. A prolific journalist and pamphleteer, he was imprisoned in 1703 for the ironic *The Shortest Way with Dissenters* (1702).

Defoe was educated for the Nonconformist ministry but became a hosier. He took part in ◊Monmouth's rebellion in 1685, and joined William of Orange in 1688. He was bankrupted three times as a result of various business ventures. After his business had failed, he held a civil-service post from 1695 to 1699.

He wrote numerous pamphlets and first achieved fame with the satirical poem *The True-Born Englishman* (1701). His version of the contemporary short story 'True Relation of the Apparition of One Mrs Veal' (1706) revealed a gift for realistic narrative. Since Defoe's death, an increasing number of works have been attributed to him, bringing the total to more than 600.

De Havilland, Geoffrey (1882–1965)

English aircraft designer who designed and whose company produced the Moth biplane, the Mosquito fighter-bomber of

World War II, and in 1949 the Comet, the world's first jet-driven airliner to enter commercial service.

After designing a fighter and a bomber for use in World War I, he founded the De Havilland Aircraft Company in 1920. This was eventually absorbed into the Hawker Siddeley conglomerate.

In the 1920s and 1930s the De Havilland Company produced a series of light transport aircraft and the Moth series of private planes, starting with the Cirrus Moth in 1925. The all-wood Mosquito was at first rejected by the Air Ministry, but went into squadron service in September 1941. Faster than the Spitfire, it could out-fly virtually anything in the air.

After World War II the De Havilland Company put a range of jet-powered aircraft into production, many of which used the company's own engines. Knighted 1944.

Deheubarth

Southern Welsh kingdom which resisted English domination until the reign of Edward I. Its name derives from the Latin *dextralis pars* (i.e. 'the right-hand side') of Wales and it comprised most of southern Wales, apart from Monmouthshire and Glamorgan. The kingdom was consolidated during the 9th and 10th centuries by a series of strong and capable rulers such as Seisyll and Hywel Dda. It succeeded in holding off the Normans, although with some setbacks, until Henry II of England recognized the kingdom's independence under the leadership of Rhys ap Gruffydd (1155–97). Squabbling among his descendants left the kingdom open to subjugation and it was absorbed by 1277 when Edward I of England was accepted as overlord of Wales.

DEFOE, DANIEL *English writer Daniel Defoe, sometimes described as the first true novelist. A prolific journalist and pamphleteer, he travelled throughout Europe before settling as a hosiery merchant in London. His life was colourful; he was pilloried and imprisoned for his pamphlet 'The Shortest Way with Dissenters' (1702), bankrupted three times, and spent 11 years as a secret agent for Tory politicians. His* Tour through the Whole Island of Great Britain *(1724–6) is a guide book and an account of the state of the country gained on his many travels. Corbis*

Deighton, Len (Leonard Cyril) (1929–)

English author of spy fiction. His novels include *The Ipcress File* (1963) and the trilogy *Berlin Game*, *Mexico Set*, and *London Match* (1983–85), featuring the spy Bernard Samson. Samson was also the main character in Deighton's trilogy *Spy Hook* (1988), *Spy Line* (1989), and *Spy Sinker* (1990). A further spy trilogy is *Faith* (1994), *Hope* (1995), and *Charity* (1996).

Dekker, Thomas (*c.* 1572–*c.* 1632)

English dramatist and pamphleteer. He wrote mainly in collaboration with others. His play *The Shoemaker's Holiday* (1600) was followed by collaborations with Thomas Middleton, John Webster, Philip Massinger, and others. His pamphlets include *The Gull's Hornbook* (1609), a lively satire on the fashions of the day.

Dekker's plays include *The Honest Whore* (1604–05) and *The Roaring Girl* (1611; both with Middleton), *Famous History of Sir Thomas Wyat* (1607, with Webster), *Virgin Martyr* (1622, with Massinger), and *The Witch of Edmonton* (1621, with John Ford and William Rowley).

De la Beche, Henry Thomas born Beach (1796–1855)

English geologist. He secured the founding of the Geological Survey in 1835, a government-sponsored geological study of Britain, region by region.

De la Beche wrote books of descriptive stratigraphy, above all on the Jurassic and Cretaceous rocks of the Devon and Dorset area. He also conducted important fieldwork on the Pembrokeshire coast and in Jamaica. He prided himself upon being a scrupulous fieldworker and a meticulous artist. Such works as *Sections and Views Illustrative of Geological Phenomena* (1830) and *How to Observe* (1835) insisted upon the primacy of facts and sowed distrust of theories. His main work is *The Geological Observer* (1851).

Delafield, E M, pen name of Edmée Elizabeth Monica Dashwood, born de la Pasture (1890–1943)

English writer. Her amusing *Diary of a Provincial Lady* (1931) skilfully exploits the foibles of middle-class life. This was so successful that she followed it with three sequels, the last being *The Provincial Lady in War Time* (1940).

A voluntary ambulance driver in Exeter during World War I, she wrote of her experiences in *The War Workers* (1918). In 1919 she settled in Devon, where she was a justice of the peace. Her novels include *Consequences* (1919) and *The Way Things Are* (1927). *Messalina of the Suburbs* (1924) and *Women Are Like That* (1929) are collections of short stories.

de la Mare, Walter John (1873–1956)

English poet and writer. His works include verse for children, such as *Peacock Pie* (1913), and the novels *The Three Royal Monkeys* (1910) (for children) and *The Memoirs of a Midget* (1921) (for adults). He excelled at creating a sense of eeriness and supernatural mystery.

The Listeners (1912) established his reputation as a writer of delicately imaginative verse in the twin domains of childhood and dreamland.

de la Rue, Warren (1815–1889)

British astronomer and instrument maker. He was a pioneer in the field of celestial photography; besides inventing the first photoheliographic telescope, he took the first photograph of a solar eclipse in 1860 and used it to prove that the prominences observed during an eclipse are of solar rather than lunar origin.

delftware

Term used in England for a once-fired pottery object dipped in a slurry made up of a glossy lead glaze made opaque by the addition of tin oxide. A design is painted on in blue, yellow, and other colours, and then fired. This ware was produced throughout Europe from about the 12th century onwards, but it was not until 1584 that it was made at the Dutch town of Delft. Its manufacture was introduced into England by Dutch potters about 1575 and it was made at three main centres: Lambeth (London), Bristol, and Liverpool. The Old English name for this ware was 'gallyware'.

Delius, Frederick Theodore Albert (1862–1934)

English composer. His haunting, richly harmonious works include the opera *A Village Romeo and Juliet* (1901); the choral pieces *Appalachia* (1903), *Sea Drift* (1904), *A Mass of Life* (1905); orchestral works such as *In a Summer Garden* (1908) and *A Song of the High Hills* (1911); chamber music; and songs.

Del Mar, Norman Rene (1919–1994)

English conductor, composer, and horn player. He founded the Chelsea Symphony Orchestra 1944, and was a guest conductor with leading orchestras. He conducted an enormously wide range of music, but was especially known for his Mahler, Elgar, and other late Romantics, above all Strauss, and was noted for his clear interpretations of complex scores. He also composed two symphonies, a string quartet, and a number of horn pieces. He wrote three volumes on Richard Strauss (1960–72), as well as *Orchestral Variations* (1981) and *Companion to the Orchestra* (1987).

Democratic Unionist Party, DUP

Northern Ireland political party, which is orientated towards the Protestant Unionist community and opposes union with the Republic of Ireland. The DUP originated in 1971 as a breakaway from the Official Ulster Unionist Party. It was co-founded by the Reverend Ian Paisley, a Presbyterian minister and militant Unionist MP for North Antrim, who continues to lead it. At the May 1997 general election the DUP won two of Ulster's 18 seats. The party gained 18.1% of votes in the June 1998 elections to the new 108-seat Belfast assembly.

The party has a populist, blue-collar appeal and, with its motto 'Service ever, Surrender never', has taken an unyielding stance on sectarian issues and efforts by successive British governments to settle the 'Troubles'. The DUP fiercely opposed the 1985 Anglo-Irish Agreement, which gave the Irish Republic some say in Ulster's affairs. It has also rejected the 1998 Good Friday Peace Agreement: Paisley's North Antrim seat was the only Ulster constituency in which there was a majority against the Agreement in the referendum held in May 1998.

Demon Internet

In computing, Britain's first and largest mass-market Internet Service Provider. Founded in 1992 by English hardware salesman Cliff Stanford with 200 founding subscribers who each paid £120 in advance for a year's service, Demon set the price (£10 a month plus VAT) for Internet access in the UK.

demonstrations

Official response to demonstrations in Britain was first codified by the Public Order Act 1936. This was provoked by the Cable Street riot of that year, when an anti-Jewish march through east London by Oswald Mosley and 2,500 of his Blackshirts gave rise to violent clashes. Later demonstrations include the nonstop anti-apartheid presence in front of South Africa House in London April 1986–February 1990; the women's peace camp at ◊Greenham Common; the picketing of the News International complex in Wapping, east London, by print workers in 1986; and the anti-poll-tax demonstrations in Trafalgar Square, London, March 1990. In March 1998 an estimated 280,000 attended the Countryside March in London in protest against the new Labour government's policies affecting rural areas. Unusually, the majority of these demonstrators was drawn from the conservative middle class.

During the 1990s resort to 'direct action', through demonstrations, has spread to include environmentalists, for example protesting against housing developments, rubbish dumps, new road building, notably the Newbury bypass, and extension of Manchester airport, and animal welfare groups, protesting against fox-hunting and grouse-shooting.

Current legislation

The Public Order Act 1986 gave police extensive new powers to restrict demonstrations and pickets. It requires those organizing a demonstration to give seven days' notice to the police and gives the police the power to say where demonstrators should stand, how long they can stay, and in what numbers, if they believe the protest could cause 'serious disruption to the life of the community' (traffic and shoppers) even though no disorder is anticipated.

History

In England, the Peasants' Revolt of 1381 began as a demonstration against the poll tax. A later instance of violent suppression of demonstrators was the ◊Peterloo massacre 1819. The ◊hunger marches organized in the 1920s and 1930s, notably the ◊Jarrow Crusade, were demonstrations in reaction to the Depression.

de Morgan, William (Frend) (1839–1917)

English pottery designer and novelist. He set up his own factory 1888 in London, producing tiles and pottery painted with flora and fauna in a style typical of the ◊Arts and Crafts movement. When he retired from the pottery industry, he began writing novels in the style of Charles Dickens. *Joseph Vance* (1906) was a great success; it was followed by six other novels.

De Morgan studied art at the Royal Academy School, where he formed friendships with William Morris, Dante Gabriel Rossetti, Edward Burne-Jones, and others of the ◊Pre-Raphaelite Brotherhood. For 40 years he devoted himself to designing artistic pottery and stained glass, starting out with designs for Morris's Merton Abbey factory. In 1871 he established a pottery industry in Chelsea, London, and rediscovered the process of making coloured lustres (covering pottery with an iridescent metallic surface), before building his factory in Fulham. His work was influenced by Persian and Italian styles – he spent many months in Italy in later years.

Denbigh, Welsh Dinbych

Town in Denbighshire, northeast Wales; population (1991) 8,400. It stands on a steep limestone hill, which is crowned by an ancient castle on the site of a fortress erected by William the Conqueror. The gatehouse is one of the finest in Britain. The newer part of the town was built at the bottom of the hill, after the destruction of much of the old town in about 1468.

There are fine views of the valley and hills from the castle gatehouse. In 1645 Charles I took refuge in the castle after the Battle of Rowton Heath.

Denbighshire, Welsh Sir Ddinbych

Unitary authority in north Wales. A former county, between 1974 and 1996 it was largely merged, together with Flint and part of Merioneth, into Clwyd; a small area along the western border was included in Gwynedd

Area 844 sq km/326 sq mi

Towns Ruthin (administrative headquarters), ◊Denbigh, ◊Llangollen

Physical Clwydian range of mountains rises to a height of 555 m/1,820 ft, with ◊Offa's Dyke along the main ridge; rivers ◊Clwyd, Dee, Elwy

Features Denbigh and Rhuddlan castles; seaside resorts of ◊Rhyl and Prestatyn

Industries agriculture (chiefly dairy), tourism

Population (1996) 91,000.

Topography the area is rugged and mountainous except for the fertile Vales of Llangollen and Clwyd. The rocks are chiefly Silurian clay and graywacke slates, with some granite and trap, and bands of Devonian, Carboniferous, and Permian strata. Coal and limestone are found with minor quantities of mineral ores.

Dench, Chris (1953–)

English composer. He is self-taught and a leading member of the avant garde; his music has been performed by the London Sinfonietta, Ensemble InterContemporain, and the Arditti Quartet. He has appeared at Darmstadt, the Venice Biennale, and the International Society for Contemporary Music's World Music Days.

Dench, Judi (Judith Olivia) (1934–)

English actress. She made her professional debut as Ophelia in *Hamlet* (1957) with the Old Vic Company. Her Shakespearean roles include Viola in *Twelfth Night* (1969), Lady Macbeth (1976), and Cleopatra (1987). Her films include *Wetherby* (1985), *A Room with a View* (1986), *A Handful of Dust* (1988), and *Mrs Brown* (1997).

Since 1995 she has played M in the Bond films *Goldeneye* (1995) and *Tomorrow Never Dies* (1997). She worked with Kenneth Branagh on *Henry V* (1989) and the long version of *Hamlet* (1996). She won international plaudits, a ◊BAFTA award, and an Academy Award-nomination for best actress for her powerful performance as Queen Victoria in *Mrs Brown*. Recently she played Elizabeth I in *Shakespeare in Love* (1998). She was created a DBE in 1988.

Denning, Alfred Thompson, Baron Denning of Whitchurch (1899–)

British judge, Master of the Rolls 1962–82. In 1963 he conducted the inquiry into the ◊Profumo scandal. A vigorous and highly innovative civil lawyer, he was controversial in his defence of the rights of the individual against the state, the unions, and big business. Knighted 1944, Baron 1957.

> *There are many things in life more worthwhile than money. One is to be brought up in this our England which is still the envy of less happy lands.*
>
> Lord Denning British judge.
> Sayings of the Week, the *Observer* August 1968.

Dent, Edward J(oseph) (1876–1957)

English musicologist and composer. His books include works on Alessandro Scarlatti, Mozart's operas, English opera, Handel, and Busoni, and his compositions include polyphonic motets and a version of *The Beggar's Opera*. He was president of the International Society for Contemporary Music from its foundation in 1922 until 1938.

Denton

Town southeast of Manchester, England, now within the Tameside borough of Greater Manchester Metropolitan county (see ◊Manchester, Greater); population (1991) 34,700. Light engineering is the main local industry. Denton was formerly a centre of hat manufacture.

Depeche Mode

English synth-rock group formed in 1980. Among their 32 singles to have reached the UK Top Thirty chart are 'New Life', 'Just Can't Get Enough', and 'The Meaning Of Love'; their albums include *Songs Of Faith And Devotion* (1993), which entered the chart at number one in both the UK and USA, and the UK chart-topping *Ultra* (1997).

Its members are Dave Gahan (1962–) (vocals), Martin Gore (1961–) (keyboards and guitar), Andy Fletcher (1961–) (keyboards), and Alan Wilder (1959–) (keyboards).

dependent territories

Term used as a means of referring collectively to colonies, protectorates, protected states, and trust territories for which Britain remains responsible. The term 'dependencies' is normally used to refer to territories placed under the authority of another; for example Ascension Island and Tristan da Cunha are dependencies of St Helena.

In 1998 there were 11 inhabited British dependent territories: Anguilla; Bermuda; British Virgin Islands; Cayman Islands; Falkland Islands; Gibraltar; Montserrat; Pitcairn Islands; St Helena; South Georgia and the South Sandwich Islands; and the Turks and Caicos Islands. There were also two offshore Crown dependencies: the Channel Islands and the Isle of Man.

Depression, the

The world economic crisis precipitated by the Wall Street crash of 29 October 1929 when millions of dollars were wiped off US share values in a matter of hours. Britain was already weakened by the 1926 General Strike and unemployment rose to over 2 million. International loss of confidence in sterling in 1931 led to a crisis that caused a coalition government to be in power until World War II. The economy was slow to recover, as witnessed by a series of hunger marches, notably the ◊Jarrow Crusade.

Although most European countries experienced a slow recovery during the mid-1930s, the main impetus for renewed economic growth was provided by rearmament programmes later in the decade. See map opposite.

DEPRESSION *A photograph illustrating poverty in Wigan, England (1939) by Kurt Hutton. He moved to England in 1934 to escape the Nazi regime in Germany and did a good deal of work for the magazine* Picture Post. *He specialized in human interest stories and summed up his attitude in the words: 'A photograph should suggest that behind the face, whatever sort of face it may be:young or old, pretty, plain or ugly, lively or quiet, there is a thinking and feeling human being.' Corbis*

Deptford

District in southeast London, in the Greater London borough of ◊Lewisham, on the River Thames west of Greenwich. It was a major royal naval dockyard (1513–1869), established by Henry VIII to build the flagship *Great Harry*. Now mainly residential, its industries include engineering and chemicals.

Francis Drake was knighted at Deptford, and Peter the Great, tsar of Russia, studied shipbuilding here 1698. John ◊Evelyn lived at Sayes Court near the dockyard and helped Grinling ◊Gibbons establish himself as a woodcarver. Deptford was the last stopping place for coaches on the Dover road.

De Quincey, Thomas (1785–1859)

English writer. His works include *Confessions of an English Opium-Eater* (1821) and the essays 'On the Knocking at the Gate in Macbeth' (1825) and 'On Murder Considered as One of the Fine Arts' (in three parts, 1827, 1839, and 1854). He was a friend of the poets William ◊Wordsworth and Samuel Taylor ◊Coleridge, and his work had a powerful influence on Charles Baudelaire and Edgar Allan Poe, among others.

De Quincey's literary career began with the anonymous publication of *The Confessions of an English Opium-Eater* in the *London Magazine*. Reprinted in book form in 1822, it brought him fame. Thereafter he produced a long series of articles, some of them almost on the scale of books, in *Blackwood's* and *Tait's* magazines, the *Edinburgh Literary Gazette*, and *Hogg's Instructor*.

In the essays 'Suspiria de Profundis' (1845) and 'The English Mail Coach' (1849), he began a psychological study of dreaming, examining how childhood experiences can through symbols in dreams affect the dreamer's personality. In this way he gave lasting expression to the fleeting pictures of his usually macabre dreams, and it could be said that he explored the subconscious before it was formally discovered.

Derby

Industrial city and, as **Derby City**, a unitary authority in north central England; unitary authority area 87 sq km/30 sq mi; population (1996) 218,800. The city lies on the River Derwent, 200 km/124 mi north of London, and was part of the county of Derbyshire until 1997. Products include cars

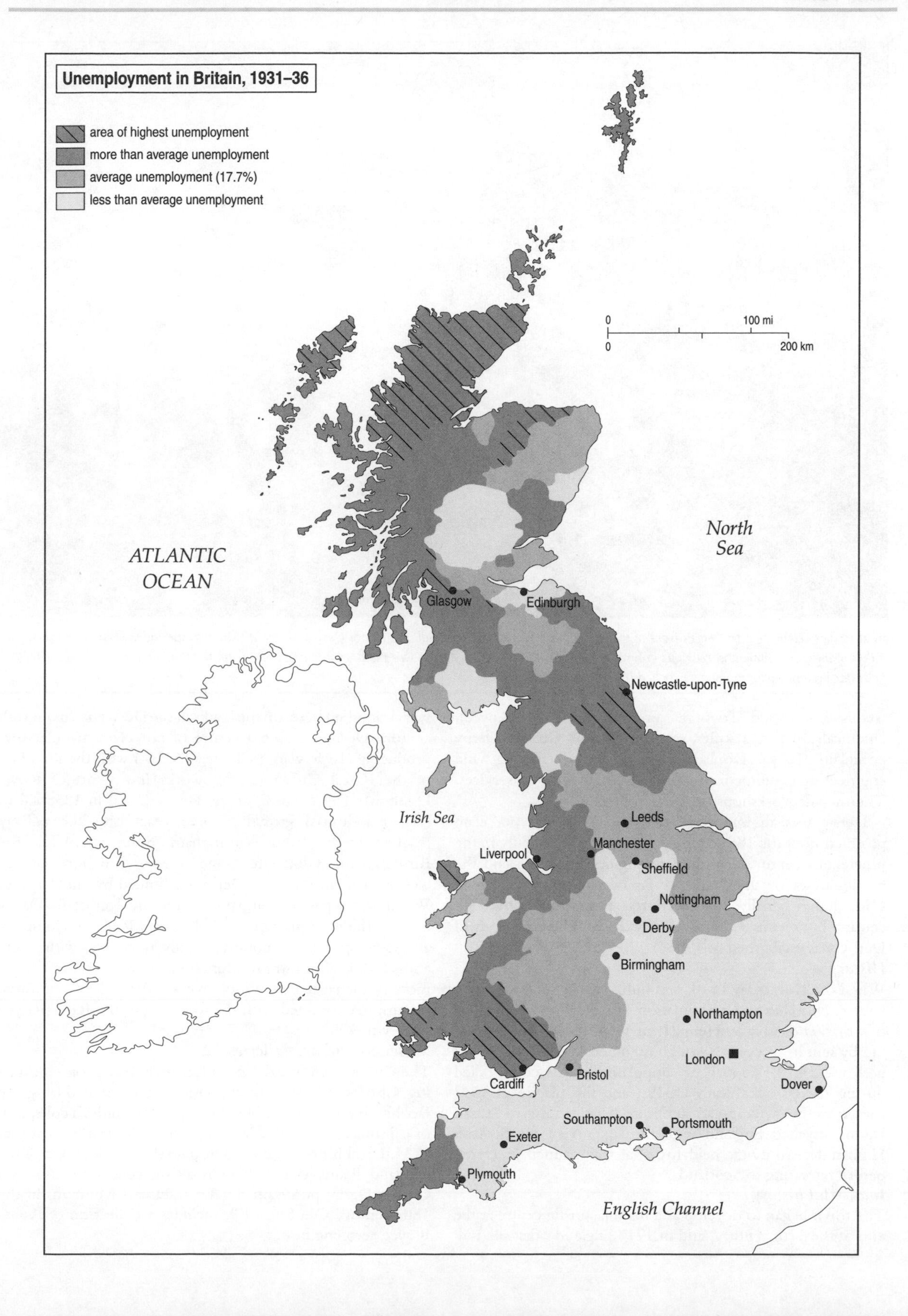
Unemployment in Britain, 1931–36
area of highest unemployment
more than average unemployment
average unemployment (17.7%)
less than average unemployment
0
100 mi
0
200 km
ATLANTIC OCEAN
North Sea
Irish Sea
English Channel
Glasgow
Edinburgh
Newcastle-upon-Tyne
Leeds
Manchester
Liverpool
Sheffield
Nottingham
Derby
Birmingham
Northampton
London
Cardiff
Bristol
Dover
Southampton
Portsmouth
Exeter
Plymouth

DERBY *Sikhs celebrate a festival in front of their gurdwara (temple) in the Midlands city of Derby. Many of Britain's cities have been enriched by an influx of different ethnic and religious groups in the 20th century. While Derby was the destination of Sikhs from the Punjab in India, in the 1970s Leicester became home to Asians expelled from Uganda. Robin Weaver/Collections*

(Rolls-Royce and Toyota), aero engines (Rolls-Royce), chemicals, paper, textiles, plastics, Royal Crown Derby porcelain (Royal Doulton), and electrical, mining, and engineering equipment. It is also a base for financial services. Train repair workshops are located here.

Derby was an important centre for silk and porcelain production in the 18th century, and expanded rapidly in the nineteenth century as a railway engineering town and the headquarters of the Midland Railway Company. Derby Cathedral, originally a parish church, was rebuilt in the 18th century but retains its 16th-century tower. The University of Derby was established in 1993.

History

When the Domesday Book was published in 1086 the town had six churches and a population of 2,000. It was given its first market charter by Henry II in 1154. Records show that Derby sent its first two borough members to Edward I's 23rd parliament in 1295. Half the population of the county died during the ◊Black Death (1349), and the plague of 1592 caused further widespread suffering. Charles Edward Stuart, having invaded England with the support of the Scottish Highlanders in 1745, held his final war council in Derby before retreating to Scotland.

Industrial history

The town began to develop as a manufacturing centre at the end of the 17th century, and in 1717 England's first silk mill was established here, on the banks of the Derwent. In the 18th century Derby became a centre of porcelain manufacture, producing classic ware ('Chelsea–Derby') with the founding of the Royal Crown Derby works (now part of Royal Doulton). The opening of the Derby Canal in 1836 led to further industrial growth. Three years later the railway reached Derby from Nottingham. Soon afterwards the Birmingham, Gloucester, and Derby Junction railway was opened, and in 1841 Derby was linked by rail to Leeds. When the separate companies were amalgamated, Derby became the headquarters of the Midland Railway Company and developed as an important railway centre, with operational and administrative functions as well as large locomotive, carriage, and wagon works. After 1900 industrial expansion continued with the founding of the Rolls-Royce factory in 1908.

Museums and art galleries

The City Museum and Art Gallery includes a room illustrating Charles Edward Stuart's visit to the town during the Jacobite Rebellion of 1745. The gallery includes a collection of paintings by Joseph ◊Wright, who was born in Derby in 1734. Local history exhibits illustrate the development of the Midland Railway and there is also a collection of Royal Crown Derby porcelain. Derby Industrial Museum, in the 18th-century Old Silk Mill, includes a collection of Rolls-Royce aero engines.

Cathedral and churches
Derby Cathedral was originally built as All Saints' parish church, and its 16th-century tower, 64 m/178 ft high, was the second highest parish church tower in England (second only to ⇨Boston Stump). Only the tower of the 16th-century foundation survived demolition in the early 18th century, being incorporated into a new church built by Scottish architect James Gibbs. It has an unusual wrought-iron screen designed by the local smith Robert Bakewell (died 1752). The church became a cathedral in 1927.

Other religious foundations include St Mary's Roman Catholic church (1838), designed by Augustus ⇨Pugin. St Mary's on the Bridge, dating from the 13th century, is one of the few remaining bridge chapels in England.

Derby

Blue riband of the English horseracing season, run over 2.4 km/1.5 mi at Epsom Downs, Surrey, every June. It was established 1780 and named after the 12th Earl of Derby.

Derby City

Unitary authority in north central England since April 1997; see ⇨Derby.

Derbyshire

County of north central England (since April 1997 Derby City has been a separate unitary authority)
Area 2,550 sq km/984 sq mi
Towns ⇨Matlock (administrative headquarters), Buxton, Chesterfield, Glossop, Ilkeston, Long Eaton
Physical Peak District National Park (including Kinder Scout 636 m/2,088 ft); rivers Dane, Derwent, Dove, Goyt, Rother, Trent, Wye; Dove Dale
Features Chatsworth House, Bakewell (seat of the Duke of Devonshire); Haddon Hall; Hardwick Hall; Kedleston Hall (designed by Robert Adam); well-dressing at Tissington, Wirksworth, ⇨Eyam and other villages; Castleton Caverns
Industries heavy engineering; manufacturing (cotton, hosiery, lace, porcelain, textiles); mineral and metal working (barytes, gypsum, lead, zinc); quarrying (marble, sandstone, pipeclay); motor cars; limestone quarrying
Agriculture cereals, root crops, and dairy farming (in the south); sheep farming (in the northern hills)
Population (1995 est) 726,000.

Topography
Derbyshire is bounded on the northwest by Greater Manchester, West Yorkshire and South Yorkshire; on the east by Nottinghamshire; on the southeast by Leicestershire; on the south by Warwickshire; and on the west by Cheshire and Staffordshire. The southern part of the county is very fertile, the north very rugged and mountainous. The county's many rivers, including tributaries of the rivers Don, Mersey, and Trent, have their source in the Peak District, at the southern end of the Pennine chain. There are springs near Buxton and Matlock, both of which were fashionable spa towns.

History
Arkwright opened the world's first water-powered cotton spinning mill on the banks of the River Derwent at Cromford, near Matlock, in 1771. Cresswell Crags (in the northeast of the county) is one of the earliest known human settlements in the British Isles. Buxton was a Roman spa town. In 1665–66 the bubonic plague killed 80% of the inhabitants of Eyam.

Historic sites and houses
Derbyshire contains numerous antiquities, including the prehistoric stone circle of Arbor Low, the most important in England after Stonehenge and Avebury. There are several ceremonial Bronze Age sites east of the River Derwent. Other places of interest include the ruined abbey of Dale, and the Saxon crypt at Repton.

Derry

One of four districts in the county of Londonderry, Northern Ireland; population (1991) 99,000. The name is also commonly used in the Republic of Ireland for the city and county of Londonderry.

Derwent

River in North Yorkshire, northeast England; length 92 km/57 mi. Rising in the North Yorkshire moors, it flows south through Malton and joins the River Ouse southeast of Selby.

Derwent Water

Lake in Cumbria, England, part of the ⇨Lake District. Derwent Water stretches for 5 km/3 mi south of Keswick into Borrowdale. The lake was part of the area forming the core of the ⇨National Trust when it was founded.

De Savary, Peter John (1944–)

British entrepreneur. He acquired Land's End, Cornwall, England, in 1987 and built a theme park there. He revived Falmouth dock and the port of Hayle in north Cornwall.

A yachting enthusiast, he sponsored the Blue Arrow America's Cup challenge team.

deselection

Removal or withholding of a sitting member of Parliament's official status as a candidate for a forthcoming election. The term came into use in the 1980s with the efforts of many local Labour parties to revoke the candidature of MPs viewed as too right-wing.

Desert Orchid

One of the most popular steeplechase horses in Britain. A grey gelding, he won more than 30 National Hunt races, including the King George VI Chase 1986, 1988–89, Cheltenham Gold Cup 1989, and the 1990 Irish Grand National. He was ridden to most of his wins by Colin Brown, Simon Sherwood, and Richard ⇨Dunwoody.

Desert Rats

Nickname of the British 8th Army in North Africa during World War II. Their uniforms had a shoulder insignia bearing a jerboa (a North African rodent, capable of great leaps). The Desert Rats' most famous victories include the expulsion of the Italian army from Egypt in December 1940 when they captured 130,000 prisoners, and the Battle of El ◊Alamein. Their successors, the 7th Armoured Brigade, fought as part of the British 1st Armoured Division in the 1991 Gulf War.

Design Council

Organization that promotes the improvement of design. Set up as a government-sponsored body in 1944, focussing on British industry, the Council was restructured in 1994 and works as a think-tank with government, industry, and education. In 1996 it launched Design in Business Week. The Design Council is also involved in assessing innovative Millennium products for display in 2000.

Design Museum

Museum in London's Docklands dedicated to mass-produced goods with an emphasis on design. Opened in 1989 and supported by the designer-entrepreneur Terence Conran, it sets out to promote 'awareness of the importance of design in education, industry, commerce and culture'.

The museum is unique in exhibiting design outside the traditional contexts of fine art or technology. It houses a permanent study collection, a 'review' section for contemporary products, and temporary exhibits.

DETR

Abbreviation for ◊Environment, Transport, and the Regions, Department of.

de Valera, Éamon (1882–1975)

Irish nationalist politician, prime minister of the Irish Free State/Eire/Republic of Ireland 1932–48, 1951–54, and 1957–59, and president 1959–73. Repeatedly imprisoned, he participated in the ◊Easter Rising in 1916 and was leader of the nationalist ◊Sinn Féin party 1917–26, when he formed the republican Fianna Fáil party; he directed negotiations with Britain in 1921 but refused to accept the partition of Ireland until 1937.

De Valera was born in New York, the son of a Spanish father and an Irish mother, and sent to Ireland as a child, where he became a teacher of mathematics. He was sentenced to death for his part in the Easter Rising, but the sentence was commuted, and he was released under an amnesty in 1917. In the same year he was elected member of Parliament for East Clare, and president of Sinn Féin. He was rearrested in May 1918, but escaped to the USA in 1919. He returned to Ireland in 1920 and directed the struggle against the British government from a hiding place in Dublin. He authorized the negotiations of 1921, but refused to accept the ensuing treaty which divided Ireland into the Free State and the North.

Civil war followed. De Valera was arrested by the Free State government in 1923, and spent a year in prison. In 1926 he formed a new party, Fianna Fáil, which secured a majority in 1932. De Valera became prime minister and foreign minister of the Free State, and at once abolished the oath of allegiance and suspended payment of the annuities due under the Land Purchase Acts. In 1938 he negotiated an agreement with Britain, under which all outstanding points were settled.

DE VALOIS, NINETTE *Irish dancer, choreographer, and teacher Ninette de Valois, who was also an excellent administrator. She founded the Vic-Wells Ballet in 1931 and her drive and enthusiasm enabled the company to achieve standards of excellence through which it was transformed into the Royal Ballet in 1956. Corbis*

de Valois, Ninette stage name of Edris Stannus (1898–)

Irish choreographer, dancer, and teacher. In setting up the Vic-Wells Ballet in 1931 (later the Royal Ballet and Royal Ballet School) she was, along with choreographer Frederick ◊Ashton, one of the architects of British ballet. Among her works are *Job* (1931), *The Rake's Progress* (1935), *Checkmate* (1937), and *The Prospect Before Us* (1940), revived by the Birmingham Royal Ballet in honour of her 100th birthday in June 1998. She is reverentially and affectionately known as 'Madam' in the ballet world.

She worked with Sergei Diaghilev in Paris (1923–25) before opening a dance academy in London in 1926. She was created a DBE in 1951.

Devil's Bridge, Welsh Pontarfynach

Village in Ceredigion (Cardiganshire), central Wales, 17 km/11 mi east of Aberystwyth, situated on the River Mynach where it joins the River Rheidol. There are three bridges over a deep gorge (35 m/115 ft) here. The site of Devil's Bridge provides important evidence for Ice-Age landscape evolution and river capture.

The lowest and oldest bridge (12th century) is believed to have been built by the monks of Strata Florida Abbey (see Pontrhydfendigaid); the middle one dates from 1753; and an iron road-bridge was constructed in 1901.

Devizes

Historic market town in Wiltshire, England; population (1991) 13,200. It was formerly known for its trade in cloth, but is now a centre for brewing, engineering, agricultural products, and food-processing. Features include ancient earthworks and fragments of a Norman castle destroyed by Oliver Cromwell in 1645.

Devizes lies at the mouth of the Vale of Pewsey. Nearby to the west of the town, the course of the Kennet and Avon Canal is interrupted with a series of 29 locks.

devolution

Delegation of authority and duties; in the later 20th century, the movement to decentralize governmental power. The Labour government which took office in May 1997 introduced legislation to establish Scottish and Welsh assemblies and their membership . The ⟩Scottish Parliament is located in Edinburgh and the National Assembly for Wales (see ⟩Welsh Assembly) in Cardiff. The ⟩Northern Ireland Assembly, which was proposed in 1998 as part of the ⟩Good Friday Agreement, came into being later that year and sits at Stormont. See also ⟩Scotland and ⟩Wales for features on devolution.

Devon, or Devonshire

County of southwest England; Plymouth and Torbay unitary authorities have been separate since April 1998

Area 6,720 sq km/2,594 sq mi

Towns and cities ⟩Exeter (administrative headquarters); resorts: Barnstaple, Bideford, Exmouth, Ilfracombe, Sidmouth, Teignmouth, and Tiverton

Physical rivers: Dart, Exe (86 km/53 mi), Plym, Tamar (94 km/58 mi), Taw, Teign, Torridge; National Parks: Dartmoor, Exmoor

Features Lundy bird sanctuary and marine nature reserve in the Bristol Channel

Agriculture sheep and dairy farming, beef cattle; cider and clotted cream; fishing

Industries kaolin in the south; lace (at Honiton); Dartington glass; carpets (Axminster); quarrying (granite, limestone, sandstone); minerals (copper, iron, lead, manganese); tourism

Population (1995) 1,058,800

Boundaries

Devon is bounded by the Bristol Channel on the north; by Cornwall on the west; by the English Channel on the south; and by Dorset and Somerset on the east.

Topography

The surface of Devon is hilly, with the rolling uplands of Dartmoor, and its numerous rugged tors, in the southwest. On the lower slopes of hills the soil is fertile, especially in the lower Exe valley, which has orchards and market gardens. The northern coast is very rugged, with cliffs 122–152 m/400–500 ft high; there are also rocky inlets, the largest of which is Bideford Bay. On the southern coast are the headlands Bolt Tail and Start Point, and the harbours Tor Bay and Plymouth Sound, one of the best harbours in Britain.

History

Parts of Devon, particularly Dartmoor, are rich in prehistoric remains. It was one of the last counties to be conquered by the Saxons, and became one of the wealthiest parts of England, with an economy based on farming, fishing, mining, and the tin and woollen trades. There was also a large overseas trade; however, this began to decline during the 17th century.

Devonshire, 8th Duke of

See ⟩Hartington, Spencer Compton Cavendish, British politician.

Dewar, Donald Campbell (1937–)

British Labour politician, secretary of state for Scotland 1997–. He joined the Labour Party while at university and contested the Aberdeen South parliamentary seat at the age of 27, later winning it 1966–70. Following a period out of Parliament, he has represented Glasgow Garscadden since 1978. He was Opposition spokesman on Scottish Affairs 1981–92, on Social Security 1992–95, and then Opposition chief whip 1995–97. He successfully oversaw the passage of legislation in 1997 to create a devolved parliament for Scotland.

Dewar, James (1842–1923)

Scottish chemist and physicist who invented the vacuum flask (Thermos) in 1872 during his research into the properties of matter at extremely low temperatures.

Working on the liquefaction of gases, Dewar discovered, in 1891, that both liquid oxygen and ozone are magnetic. In 1895 he became the first to produce liquid hydrogen, and then in 1899 succeeded in solidifying hydrogen at a temperature of −259°C/−434°F. He also invented, jointly with Frederick ⟩Abel, the explosive cordite in 1889. Knighted 1904.

de Wint, Peter (1784–1849)

English landscape painter of Dutch-American descent, born in Staffordshire, USA. He was apprenticed to the painter and engraver John Raphael Smith (1752–1812), but was directed towards watercolour by the advice of the painter John Varley and the example of Thomas Girtin, whose work he greatly admired in the art collection of Dr Thomas Monro (1759–1833). From 1806 watercolour was his chief means of expression, his best work being executed with broad washes summarizing natural forms. The city of Lincoln and the lush countryside round it, home of his wife, were his main subjects.

Dewsbury

Town in West Yorkshire, England, on the River Calder; population (1991) 30,400. Dewsbury is a textile-manufacturing town; industries include blanket-making, carpet-making, engineering, and dyeing.

Among the public buildings are the parish church of All Saints, with some remains of Early English Gothic architecture (rebuilt in the 18th century), the town hall (1888), the Wheelwright grammar schools, a covered market and an extensive open market.

The Roman missionary Paulinus is believed to have preached Christianity to the Saxons on the site of the parish church in 627.

DHSS

Abbreviation for **Department of Health and Social Security**, UK government department until divided in 1988; see ⟩social security.

dialect

Dialect has long been a prominent feature of English in Britain. In England it developed from the Northern, West Midland, East Midland, Southern and Kentish dialects in Middle English. Standard English evolved from the East Midland dialect, with an increasing Scandinavian overlay. Today, while vocabulary is becoming increasingly standardized, differences of pronunciation are still marked in certain regions.

Among them are the 'flat' vowels of 'Brummie' spoken in the Birmingham area, the substitution of 'f' or 'v' for 'th' and the dropping of initial 'h' in 'Cockney', the long 'a' in words such as 'talk' and 'walk' and the rising tone in statements, making them sound like questions, in 'Geordie', spoken in northeast England, the short 'a' in both 'gas' and 'grass' in Lancashire and Yorkshire, the 'flat' intonation and adenoidal voice quality in 'Scouse', in the Liverpool area, and the distinctive burr in West Country speech, sometimes known as 'Zummerzet', with 'z' for initial 's' ('zum' for 'some') and 'v' for 'f' ('varm' for 'farm').

Many such dialects and their individual turns of speech become generally familiar through television drama, with 'Brummie' heard in *Crossroads*, 'Cockney' in *EastEnders*, 'Geordie' in *Auf Wiedersehen, Pet* and 'Scouse' in *Bread* and *Brookside*.

Dialects in Scotland fall into four main groups: the Northern Isles (Orkney and Shetland) with 'f' for 'wh' in such words as 'who' and a rounded front vowel 'ui' in such words as 'good' ('guid') and 'school' ('scuil'), Northern Scots with 'ee' for 'oo' in such words as 'moon', 'shoe', Central Scots with 'ai' or 'i' for 'oo' in those words, and Southern Scots with 'twae' for 'two', 'whae' for 'who' and 'waiter' for 'water'. Speech in Wales often has a distinctive 'sing-song' quality, reflecting that in Welsh itself. Dialects in Northern Ireland are much as south of the border, with a distinctive 'burring' 'r' in such words as 'worse' and 'hard' and phonological features similar to those of American English.

DIANA, PRINCESS OF WALES *Diana, Princess of Wales, talking with children at the Khanum Memorial Cancer Hospital in Lahore, Pakistan in February 1996. Diana was well-known for her work supporting charitable organisations. Corbis*

Diamond Jubilee

Celebration in 1897 of the 60th year of Queen Victoria's rule. The jubilee was a celebration of both Crown and Empire at the peak of British colonial power. The scions of other royal houses, many related to Victoria, joined the celebrations and paid their respects to Victoria's rule, heightening Britain's sense of superiority over the continental powers. Ironically, even while the jubilee was being celebrated there was renewed tension between the Crown and the Boers in South Africa, which was to lead to the Boer War, a significant blow to British imperial prestige and morale. In retrospect, the jubilee celebrations neatly encapsulated both the splendour and the superficiality of Britain's achievements in the 19th century.

Diana, Princess of Wales born Diana Frances Spencer (1961–1997)

Daughter of the 8th Earl Spencer, Diana married Prince Charles in St Paul's Cathedral, London, in 1981. She had two sons, William and Harry, before her separation from Charles in 1992. In February 1996 she agreed to a divorce, after which she became known as Diana, Princess of Wales. Her worldwide prominence for charity work contributed to a massive outpouring of public grief after her death in a car crash in Paris, France, on 31 August 1997. Her funeral proved to be the biggest British televised event in history.

In 1995 in a BBC *Panorama* interview with Martin Bashir, she said that she would like to be a 'queen of people's hearts, in people's hearts'. Her divorce was settled shortly after.

Following a suggestion made by her son William, an auction of some of Diana's dresses was held in New York in June 1997, raising $5 million for cancer and AIDS research.

Diana Memorial Fund

This fund set up and granted charitable status within four days of Diana's death, raised over £40 million in its first seven months. It is run by a board of trustees, among them Lady Sarah McCorquodale, one of Diana's two sisters, and Christopher Spence, founder of the London Lighthouse AIDS care centre. On March 10 1998 six organizations of which Diana was patron at the time of her death were awarded £21 million each from the fund: Centrepoint, English National Ballet, Great Ormond Street Hospital, the National AIDS Trust, the Royal Marsden NHS Trust, and the Leprosy Mission. Smaller amounts went to a range of arts, health and sports charities.

Her brother, Earl Spencer, has opened a museum in her memory at Althorp, the Spencer family home, where she is buried.

Dibdin, Charles (1745–1814)

English singer, author, and composer. He began his career as a singing actor at Covent Garden, where his pastoral *The Shepherd's Artifice* was produced in 1764. Over 100 dramatic works followed. In 1789 he began his series of 'Table Entertainments', in which he was author, composer, narrator, singer, and accompanist. One of the most successful, *The Oddities*, contained the song 'Tom Bowling'. Many other sea-songs achieved great popularity.

Dickens, Charles (John Huffam) (1812–1870)

English novelist. He is enduringly popular for his memorable characters and his portrayal of the social evils of Victorian England. Dickens was born in Portsea, Hampshire, and received little formal education. In 1827 he became a lawyer's clerk, and then a reporter for the *Morning Chronicle*, to which he contributed the *Sketches by Boz*. In 1836 he published the first number of the *Pickwick Papers*. They were originally intended merely as an accompaniment to a series of sporting illustrations, but the adventures of Pickwick outgrew their setting and established Dickens's reputation.

In 1842 he visited the USA, where he was welcomed as a celebrity. After his visit, American feeling was deeply offended by *American Notes* (1842), attacking the pirating of English books by American publishers. On his return home, he satirized US democracy in *Martin Chuzzlewit* (1844). *Dombey and Son* (1848) was largely written abroad. *David Copperfield*, his most popular novel and his own favourite, contains many autobiographical incidents and characters; Mr Micawber is usually recognized as a sketch of his father. Dickens inaugurated the weekly magazine *Household Words* in 1850, reorganizing it in 1859 as *All the Year*

DICKENS, CHARLES *English novelist Charles Dickens, whose immense creative energy made him the most popular novelist of his age. Born into a family on the fringes of gentility, he was always acutely conscious of the social and economic abysses of Victorian society. Corbis*

Dickens: Major Works

title	date	well-knowcharacters
The Pickwick Papers	1836	Mr Pickwick, Sam Weller, Mr Snodgrass, Mr Jingle, Mr and Mrs Bardell
Oliver Twist	1837	Oliver Twist, Fagin, Mr Bumble, The Artful Dodger
Nicholas Nickleby	1838	Nicholas Nickleby, Wackford Squeers, Madame Mantalini, Smike, Vincent Crummles
The Old Curiosity Shop	1840	Little Nell, Dick Swiveller, Daniel Quilp
Barnaby Rudge	1841	Simon Tappertit (Sim), Miss Miggs, Gashford
A Christmas Carol	1843	Ebenezer Scrooge, Bob Cratchit, Marley's Ghost, Tiny Tim
Martin Chuzzlewit	1844	Martin Chuzzlewit (Junior), Mr Pecksniff, Mrs Gamp, Tom Pinch
Dombey and Son	1848	Dombey, Paul and Florence Dombey, Edith Granger, James Carker, Major Bagstock
David Copperfield	1850	David Copperfield, Mr Micawber, Mr Dick, Uriah Heep, Little Em'ly, Betsey Trotwood
Bleak House	1853	John Jarndyce, Esther Summerson, Harold Skimpole, Lady Dedlock, Mrs Jellyby
Hard Times	1854	Tom and Louisa Gradgrind, Josiah Bounderby Gradgrind, Cissy Jupe Bitzer
Little Dorrit	1857	Amy Dorrit, Flora Finching, Mr Merille
A Tale of Two Cities	1859	Dr Manette, Charles Darnay, Sydney Carton, Jerry Cruncher, Madame Defarge
Great Expectations	1861	Pip, Estella, Miss Havisham, Joe Gargery, Wemmick, Magwitch
Our Mutual Friend	1865	Noddy Boffin, Silas Wegg, Mr Podsnap, Betty Higden, Bradley Headstone, Reginald Wilfer
The Mystery of Edwin Drood (unfinished)	1870	Rosa Bud, John Jasper

Round; many of his later stories were published serially in these periodicals. In 1858 he began giving public readings from his novels, which proved such a success that he was invited to make a second US tour in 1867–68. *Edwin Drood*, a mystery story influenced by the style of his friend Wilkie ◊Collins, was left incomplete on his death.

Dickens's novels are characterized by strong satire, inclining to caricature; the protest against injustice, indignant but too humorous to be shrill; pathos, tending to sentimentality; well-observed characters, and the melodrama. See table for dates of major works and their characters.

Dickens, Monica (Enid) (1915–1992)

English writer. Her first books were humorous accounts of her experiences in various jobs, beginning as a cook (*One Pair of Hands*, 1939). Her first novel, *Mariana*, was published in 1940.

In the early years of World War II she worked as a hospital nurse and then later as a fitter in a factory producing aircraft spare parts. Her experiences again provided material for her next books, *One Pair of Feet* (1942), *The Fancy* (1943), and *Thursday Afternoons* (1945), the latter two attracting much praise. A close friend of the Samaritans' founder, Chad Varah, she founded the Samaritans in the USA. She was a great-granddaughter of Charles Dickens.

Dick-Read, Grantly (1890–1959)

English gynaecologist. In private practice in London 1923–48, he developed the concept of natural childbirth: that by the elimination of fear and tension, labour pain could be minimized and anaesthetics, which can be hazardous to both mother and child, rendered unnecessary.

Dicksee, Cedric Bernard (1888–1981)

British engineer. He was a pioneer in developing the compression-ignition diesel engine into a suitable unit for road transport. This became standard in commercial vehicles.

Dicksee built his first engine in 1930 and kept improving on it. The 1933 model became the standard; a further development of this engine used combustion chambers of a toroidal shape and was subsequently adopted for larger engines in the company's range. Dicksee's engines ran at speeds ranging from 1,800 to 2,400 (governed) rpm, higher than comparable engines of the day. With this performance, the way was opened for the adoption of compression-ignition engines instead of petrol engines for road transport.

dictionaries

The first dictionaries of English (*glossa collectae*), in the 17th century, served to explain difficult words, generally of Latin or Greek origin, in everyday English. Samuel ◊Johnson's *A Dictionary of the English Language* (1755) was one of the first dictionaries of standard English, and the first to give extensive coverage to phrasal verbs. The many-volume *Oxford English Dictionary*, begun in 1884 and subject to continuous revision (and now computerization), provides a detailed historical record of each word and, therefore, of the English language. See chronology below.

Didcot

Town in Oxfordshire, England, 11 km/7 mi south of Abingdon; population (1991) 15,400. Didcot is the site of an important railway junction, where the main line from London to the West Country joins that to Oxford and Birmingham. A large coal-fired power station serving central England and known as Didcot A, is situated near the town. A smaller power station, using natural gas to produce electricity, and known as Didcot B, opened on the same site in July 1997.

Didcot expanded rapidly during the 1980s, as large housing developments were constructed on the outskirts to cater for commuters to London, Swindon, and the high-tech industries of the Thames Valley. Harwell atomic-energy research station is 6 km/4 mi east of the town.

Dieu et mon droit

(French 'God and my right') motto of the royal arms of Great Britain.

ENGLISH DICTIONARIES: SOME KEY DATES

1225 John Garland used the term *dictionarius*.

1530 The first English–English dictionary appeared (appendix to William Temple's *Pentateuch*).

1538 Thomas Elyot's *Shorte Dictionarie for Yonge Begynners* (English–Latin) was published.

16th century The first vernacular–vernacular dictionaries were prepared by William Salesbury, Welsh–English 1547, and Giovanni Florio, Italian–English 1599.

1604 Robert Cawdrey's *Table Alphabeticall of hard usuall English wordes* aimed at converting Latin to Latinate English.

1730 Nathan Bailey published his *Dictionarium Britannicum*.

1755 Samuel Johnson's dictionary of standard English, *A Dictionary of the English Language*, appeared.

1773 William Kenrick published the first dictionary to indicate pronunciations.

1828 Noah Webster published *An American Dictionary of the English Language*.

1852 Peter Mark Roget's *Thesaurus of English Words* was published.

1884–1928 The *Oxford English Dictionary* was compiled.

1992 The *Oxford English Dictionary* was published on CD-ROM.

Digger, or True Leveller

Member of an English 17th-century radical sect that attempted to seize and share out common land. The Diggers became prominent in April 1649 when, headed by Gerrard Winstanley (*c.* 1609–1660), they set up communal colonies near Cobham, Surrey, and elsewhere. These colonies were attacked by mobs and, being pacifists, the Diggers made no resistance. The support they attracted alarmed the government and they were dispersed in 1650. Their ideas influenced the early ◊Quakers.

digital television

See ◊television.

Dillon, James (1950–)

Scottish composer. His music has had Renaissance and non-Western influences and is densely composed. Works by him have ben featured at Bath, Darmstadt, Warsaw, and Paris festivals.

Dimbleby, David (1938–)

English broadcaster, presenter of *Question Time* and *Panorama* for BBC television. He joined the BBC in 1960 and has presented the BBC Election and Results programmes for all the general elections since 1979. He won an Emmy Award in 1991 for his television documentary 'The Struggle for South Africa', and has provided live commentary on many public occasions, including the funeral of Diana, Princess of Wales in 1998. Richard Dimbleby was his father.

Dimbleby, Jonathan (1944–)

English broadcaster and writer. He has been chairman of BBC Radio's *Any Questions* since 1987. He wrote and presented *Charles: The Private Man, The Public Role* (1994), a documentary about Prince Charles in which the Prince of Wales admitted he had been unfaithful to Diana, Princess of Wales after their marriage had broken down.

He has made many television documentaries, including *The Last Governor*, a series about Chris Patten and the handover of Hong Kong, in 1997. His books include biographies of his father, Richard Dimbleby (1975) and Prince Charles (1994). ITV coverage of the 1997 General Election was presented by him, rivalling his brother, David Dimbleby's, coverage for the BBC. He was President of the Council for the Protection of Rural England (CPRE) for five years from 1992.

Dimbleby, Richard Frederick (1913–1965)

English broadcaster. He was the leading commentator on royal and state occasions on radio and television. He began as a journalist, working on the family newspaper, the *Richmond and Twickenham Times*, before joining the BBC in 1936 as its first news observer. He was the first BBC war correspondent, with the British Expeditionary Force in France in World War II in 1939, and went on to cover campaigns in 15 countries.

He was subsequently the first war correspondent to fly with Bomber Command, in 1943; he directed the BBC War Reporting Unit from D-Day onwards; and he entered Berlin with the British army in 1945. After the war, while continuing as a radio broadcaster, presenting such programmes as *Twenty Questions* and *Down Your Way*, he began commentating for television, and covered the Queen's coronation in 1953. He commentated on the Royal Tour of the Commonwealth in 1954, and other occasions covered by him included the first televised state opening of Parliament in 1958, the wedding of Princess Margaret in 1960, the funeral of President Kennedy in 1963, and the funeral of Sir Winston Churchill in 1965. He presented *Panorama* for many years. He is commemorated in the annual Dimbleby Lecture.

It is part of the Constitution that all major events have to be presented by a Dimbleby.

JEREMY PAXMAN British television presenter and author.
Independent, 5 April 1997

Dinorwig

Location of Europe's largest pumped-storage hydroelectric scheme, completed in 1984, in Gwynedd, North Wales. It is used as a backup to meet heavy demands for electricity. Six turbogenerators are installed, with a maximum output of some 1,880 megawatts. The working head of water for the station is 530 m/1,740 ft.

The main machine hall is twice as long as a football field and as high as a 16-storey building.

Diplock court

In Northern Ireland, a type of court established in 1972 by the British government under Lord Diplock (1907–1985) to try offences linked with guerrilla violence. The right to jury trial was suspended and the court consisted of a single judge, because potential jurors were allegedly being intimidated and were unwilling to serve. Despite widespread criticism, the Diplock courts continued to operate into the 1990s.

Diplomatic Service, British

Body that represents Britain abroad in regard to its international interests, comprising diplomatic agents and occasionally consuls, although the latter are in general concerned exclusively with the interests of British subjects resident abroad. Diplomatic agents include ambassadors, or envoys, who are officials permanently accredited to a foreign state, and *chargés d'affaires* who either act as deputy for an ambassador or are accredited as the British representative to a foreign country of minor importance.

The Diplomatic Service employs some 5,500 (1998) people for the Foreign and Commonwealth Office and diplomatic missions abroad.

Dirac, Paul Adrien Maurice (1902–1984)

English physicist who worked out a version of quantum mechanics consistent with special relativity. The existence of antiparticles, such as the positron (positive electron), was one of its predictions. He shared the Nobel Prize for Physics in 1933 with Austrian physicist Erwin Schrödinger.

In 1928 Dirac formulated the relativistic theory of the electron. The model was able to describe many quantitative aspects of the electron, including such properties as the half-quantum spin and magnetic moment, and introduced the first antiparticle.

Dirac noticed that those particles with half-integral spins obeyed statistical rules different from the other particles. For these particles, Dirac worked out the statistics, now called **Fermi–Dirac statistics** because Italian physicist Enrico Fermi had done very similar work. These are used, for example, to determine the distribution of electrons at different energy levels.

Director of Public Prosecutions, DPP

The head of the Crown Prosecution Service (established 1985), responsible for the conduct of all criminal prosecutions in England and Wales. The DPP was formerly responsible only for the prosecution of certain serious crimes, such as murder.

Dire Straits

Rock group formed in 1977 by guitarist, singer, and songwriter Mark Knopfler (1949–). Their tasteful musicianship, influenced by American country rock, was tailor-made for the new compact-disc audience, and their 1985 LP *Brothers in Arms* went on to sell 20 million copies. Other albums include *On Every Street* (1991). Knopfler is also much in demand as a producer.

disclaimed peerage

The Peerage Act (1963) allows a peerage to be disclaimed for life provided that it is renounced within one year of the succession, and that the peer has not applied for a writ of summons to attend the House of Lords.

Members of Parliament and Parliamentary candidates who succeed to peerages must disclaim their titles within one month of succeeding; until that period expires they are not disqualified from membership of the House of Commons, provided that they do not sit or vote in the House of Lords within that time.

Discovery

The ship in which Captain ◊Scott, commanding the National Antarctic Expedition in 1900–04, sailed to the Antarctic and back. In 1980, it became a Maritime Trust museum of exploration at St Katharine's Dock, London.

disestablishment

The formal separation of a church from the State by ceasing to recognize it as the official church of a country or province. The special status of the Church of Ireland, created by Henry VIII in 1541, was a major source of grievance to Irish Catholics in the 19th century and it was disestablished by Gladstone in 1869, with its endowments converted to charitable ends. In 1920, after a bitter struggle lasting over 50 years, the Welsh Anglican Church was disestablished as the Church in Wales; it gained its own archbishop and was detached from the province of Canterbury. There have been several attempts to disestablish the Church of England which would involve the abolition of the Royal Supremacy over the Church and the concomitant right of the Prime Minister to advise the Crown on episcopal appointments.

Disraeli, Benjamin, 1st Earl of Beaconsfield (1804–1881)

British Conservative politician and novelist. Elected to Parliament in 1837, he was chancellor of the Exchequer under Lord Derby 1852, 1858–59, and 1866–68, and prime minister 1868 and 1874–80. His imperialist policies brought India directly under the crown, and he was personally responsible for purchasing control of the Suez Canal. His trilogy of popular, political novels (*Coningsby*, 1844, *Sybil*, 1845, and *Tancred*, 1847) reflect an interest in social reform.

Disraeli entered Parliament in 1837 after four unsuccessful attempts. Initially laughed at as a dandy, he was excluded from ◊Peel's government of 1841–46. When the government fell, Disraeli came to be recognized as the leader of the Conservative Party in the Commons. Disraeli became prime minister in 1868, but was defeated by Gladstone, the Liberal leader with whom he had many political duels, in the general election shortly afterwards. During the six years of opposition that

Disraeli, Benjamin *Twice prime minister, Benjamin Disraeli in 1876 introduced a bill in Parliament which gave Queen Victoria the additional title of 'Empress of India'. Victoria afterwards referred to Disraeli as 'her kind, good and considerate friend'. Private collection*

followed, he established Conservative Central Office, the prototype of modern party organizations.

Disraeli took office again in 1874. Some useful reform measures were carried, but the outstanding feature of the government's policy was its imperialism. Following the Bulgarian revolt of 1876 and the subsequent Russo-Turkish War of 1877–78 Disraeli was the principal British delegate at the Congress of Berlin in 1878. He brought home 'peace with honour' and Cyprus. The government was defeated in 1880, and a year later Disraeli died. He was created an earl in 1876.

The Continent will not suffer England to be the workshop of the world.

BENJAMIN DISRAELI British Conservative prime minister and novelist.
Speech in House of Commons 15 March 1838

dissenting academies

Schools founded in late 17th and 18th centuries for children of religious nonconformists who were otherwise banned from local schools and universities. They became a model of advanced education, with their emphasis on the sciences and modern languages.

Dissolution of the Monasteries

Closure of the monasteries of England and Wales from 1536 to 1540 and confiscation of their property by ◊Henry VIII. The operation was organized by Thomas Cromwell and affected about 800 monastic houses with the aim of boosting royal income. Most of the property was later sold off to the gentry.

district council

Lower unit of local government in England. In 1998 there were 274 district councils under 34 (two-tier) non-metropolitan county councils, and 36 single-tier metropolitan district councils. Their responsibilities cover housing, local planning and development, roads (excluding trunk and classified), bus services, environmental health (refuse collection, clean air, food safety and hygiene, and enforcement of the Offices, Shops and Railway Premises Act), council tax, museums and art galleries, parks and playing fields, swimming baths, cemeteries, and so on.

Under the Local Government Act 1972, 300 district councils were created to replace the former county borough, borough, and urban and rural district councils. The district councils are headed by an annually elected chair or, in an honorary borough or city, mayor or lord mayor. Councillors are elected for four years, and one-third retire at a time, so that district elections are held in three out of four years, county-council elections taking place in the fourth. The Local Government Commission for England 1992–95 identified the district council as the major unitary authority of the future. Since 1997, many district councils have either disappeared or become 'single tier' unitary authorities.

Ditchling Beacon

The second highest point on the ◊South Downs, 9 km/6 mi north of Brighton, East Sussex, England. Ditchling Beacon is 248 m/814 ft high and is surmounted by an ancient earthwork. From here, sightseers can see far across the Weald. It lies on the South Downs long-distance footpath.

On top of Ditchling Beacon, one of a great chain of fires was lit in 1588 to warn of the approach of the Spanish Armada.

divine right of kings

Christian political doctrine that hereditary monarchy is the system approved by God, hereditary right cannot be forfeited, monarchs are accountable to God alone for their actions, and rebellion against the lawful sovereign is therefore blasphemous.

The 17th and 18th centuries

James I of England, in his *Trew Law of Free Monarchies*, insisted on divine right as a principle. This was carried to extremes by the supporters of his son. Charles I's claim to divine right was a direct cause of the Royalist and Parliamentary struggles of the 17th century.

The doctrine was again invoked in the Exclusion Crisis and in the ◊Glorious Revolution of 1688 when James II was replaced in an aristocratic coup by William of Orange. The most influential exposition of divine right in English is to be found in Sir Robert Filmer's *Patriarcha* (1680), which argues by analogy that the powers of God over the universe, of father over family, and sovereign over people, are all divinely ordained and absolute. The success of John Locke's *Two Treatises on Government* (1690), signalled the decline of the theory of divine right in England, although versions are found, especially in France until 1789, where it was opposed by Rousseau.

divorce

Legal dissolution of a lawful marriage. It is distinct from an annulment, which is a legal declaration that the marriage was invalid. In England and Wales, divorce could only be secured by the passing of a private act of Parliament until 1857, when the Matrimonial Causes Act set up the Divorce Court and provided limited grounds for divorce. The grounds for divorce were gradually liberalized by further acts of Parliament, culminating in the Divorce Reform Act 1969, under which the sole ground for divorce is the irretrievable breakdown of the marriage. The court places great emphasis on provision for the custody and maintenance of any children. It may also order other financial arrangements, including the transfer of property. Although not worded exactly the same, the grounds for divorce in Scotland are the same as in England and Wales.

DNA

See feature on page 262 on the discovery of DNA.

D-notice

A censorship notice issued by the Department of Defence to the media to prohibit the publication of information on

THE DISCOVERY OF THE STRUCTURE OF DNA

The first announcement

'We wish to suggest a structure for the salt of deoxyribose nucleic acid (DNA). This structure has novel features which are of considerable biological interest.'

So began a 900-word article that was published in the journal *Nature* in April 1953. Its authors were British molecular biologist Francis Crick and US biochemist James Watson (1928–). The article described the correct structure of DNA, a discovery that many scientists have called the most important since Austrian botanist and monk Gregor Mendel (1822–1884) laid the foundations of the science of genetics. DNA is the molecule of heredity, and by knowing its structure, scientists can see exactly how forms of life are transmitted from one generation to the next.

The problem of inheritance

The story of DNA really begins with British naturalist Charles Darwin. When, in November 1859, he published 'On the Origin of Species by Means of Natural Selection' outlining his theory of evolution, he was unable to explain exactly how inheritance came about. For at that time it was believed that offspring inherited an average of the features of their parents. If this were so, as Darwin's critics pointed out, any remarkable features produced in a living organism by evolutionary processes would, in the natural course of events, soon disappear.

The work of Gregor Mendel, only rediscovered 18 years after Darwin's death, provided a clear demonstration that inheritance was not a 'blending' process at all. His description of the mathematical basis to genetics followed years of careful plant-breeding experiments. He concluded that each of the features he studied, such as colour or stem length, was determined by two 'factors' of inheritance, one coming from each parent. Each egg or sperm cell contained only one factor of each pair. In this way a particular factor, say for the colour red, would be preserved through subsequent generations.

Genes

Today, we call Mendel's factors **genes**. Through the work of many scientists, it came to be realized that genes are part of the chromosomes located in the nucleus of living cells and that DNA, rather than protein as was first thought, was a hereditary material.

The double helix

In the early 1950s, scientists realized that X-ray crystallography, a method of using X-rays to obtain an exact picture of the atoms in a molecule, could be successfully applied to the large and complex molecules found in living cells.

It had been known since 1946 that genes consist of DNA. At King's College, London, New Zealand–British biophysicist Maurice Wilkins had been using X-ray crystallography to examine the structure of DNA, together with his colleague, British X-ray crystallographer Rosalind Franklin, and had made considerable progress.

While in Copenhagen, US scientist James Watson had realized that one of the major unresolved problems of biology was the precise structure of DNA. In 1952, he came as a young postdoctoral student to join the Medical Research Council Unit at the Cavendish Laboratory, Cambridge, where Francis Crick was already working. Convinced that a gene must be some kind of molecule, the two scientists set to work on DNA.

Helped by the work of Wilkins, they were able to build an accurate model of DNA. They showed that DNA had a double helical structure, rather like a spiral staircase. Because the molecule of DNA was made from two strands, they envisaged that as a cell divides, the strands unravel, and each could serve as a template as new DNA was formed in the resulting daughter cells. Their model also explained how genetic information might be coded in the sequence of the simpler molecules of which DNA is comprised. Here for the first time was a complete insight into the basis of heredity. James Watson commented that this result was 'too pretty not to be true!'

Cracking the code

Later, working with South African–British molecular biologist Sidney Brenner (1927–), Crick went on to work out the genetic code, and so ascribe a precise function to each specific region of the molecule of DNA. These triumphant results created a tremendous flurry of scientific activity around the world. The pioneering work of Crick, Wilkins, and Watson was recognized in the award of the Nobel Prize for Physiology or Medicine in 1962.

The unravelling of the structure of DNA led to a new scientific discipline, molecular biology, and laid the foundation stones for genetic engineering – a powerful new technique that is revolutionizing biology, medicine, and food production through the purposeful adaptation of living organisms.

BY JULIAN ROWE

matters alleged to be of national security. The system dates from 1922.

Dobson, Frank (1940–)

British Labour politician, secretary of state for Health 1997–. Sponsored by the National Union of Railwaymen (NUR), he has represented the London constituency of Holborn and St Pancras since 1979. He was Opposition spokesman on Education 1982–83, shadow Health minister 1983–87, shadow Leader of the Commons 1987–89, and Opposition spokesman on Energy 1989–92. After John Smith became Labour Leader, Frank Dobson served as Opposition spokesman on Employment 1992–93, Transport and London 1993–94, and Environment and London 1994–97, under the new Labour Leader, Tony Blair.

Dobson, Frank (1889–1963)

English sculptor and painter. Beginning as a painter working in the Post-Impressionist idiom, Dobson soon turned to sculpture, his early works showing the strong influence of Vorticism. He later developed a sleekly contoured Classicism inspired by the French sculptor Aristide Maillol. Dobson's works are usually heavy-limbed nudes and portrait busts, such as *Sir Osbert Sitwell* (1923; Tate Gallery, London).

Docklands

Urban development area east of St Katherine's Dock, London, occupying the site of the former Wapping and Limehouse docks, the Isle of Dogs, and Royal Docks. It comprises 2,226 hectares/5,550 acres of former wharves, warehouses, and wasteland. Plans for its redevelopment were set in motion in 1981 and by 1993 over 13,000 private housing units had been built, including terraced houses at Maconochies Wharf, Isle of Dogs. Distinguished buildings include the Tidal Basin Pumping Station in Royal Docks, designed by Richard Rogers, and the printing plant for the *Financial Times*, designed by Nicholas Grimshaw. The Limehouse Link motorway and tunnel, linking Tower Hill and Canary Wharf, opened in 1993. The tallest building is the ◊Canary Wharf tower. Docklands is served by the London City airport (Stolport) and the Docklands Light Railway (DLR). The London Underground Jubilee Line was extended to Canary Wharf in 1998.

During World War II, one-third of the warehouses and half of the storage areas belonging to the Port of London Authority were destroyed, together with large residential areas, and by 1981 all the docks had closed. The London Docklands Development Corporation (LDDC) was formed in 1981, at a time of economic boom, to develop the Docklands area as an international business centre.

Doctor Who

Hero of a British science-fiction television series of the same name, created in 1963 by Sidney Newman and Donald Wilson; his space vehicle is the *Tardis* and his most famous enemies are the Daleks, robotlike aliens. The actors who have played Doctor Who include William Hartnell (1908–1975), Patrick Troughton (1920–1987), Jon Pertwee (1919–), Tom Baker (1936–), Peter Davison (1951–), Colin Baker (1943–), Sylvester McCoy (1943–), and Peter Cushing (1913–).

Dogger Bank

Submerged sandbank in the North Sea, about 115 km/70 mi off the coast of Yorkshire, England. It is about 270 km/168 mi long by 110 km/68 mi wide. In places the water is only 11 m/36 ft deep, but the general depth is 18–36 m/60–120 ft; it is a well-known fishing ground.

In World War I, it was the site of the Battle of Dogger Bank, a substantial naval engagement on 24 January 1915 between British and German forces under the commands of Admiral Sir David (later Earl) Beatty and Admiral Franz von Hipper, respectively.

Doggett, Thomas (*c.* 1670–1721)

Irish actor. He was associated with Colley ◊Cibber and others in the management of the Drury Lane and Haymarket theatres. He founded the rowing prize **Doggett's Coat and Badge** in 1715, in honour of George I's accession the year before.

The prize, consisting of a red coat with a large silver badge on the arm, was competed for by Thames watermen who had completed their apprenticeship within the previous 12 months. The race took place on 1 August, and the course was from London Bridge to Chelsea. Under modified conditions, the race is still held annually.

Dogs, Isle of

District of east London, part of the Greater London borough of ◊Tower Hamlets. It is bounded on three sides by the River Thames, and is part of the Docklands urban development area.

The Isle of Dogs is home to the ◊Billingsgate fish market (based since 1982 in the West India Dock) and the ◊Canary Wharf development. The ◊Blackwall Tunnel provides a road link with the south side of the Thames.

Dolgellau, formerly **Dolgelly**

Market town at the foot of the ◊Cadair Idris mountain range in north Wales, situated on the River Wnion, 38 km/24 mi northeast of Aberystwyth; population (1991) 2,400. The town lies within the Snowdonia National Park and is a tourist

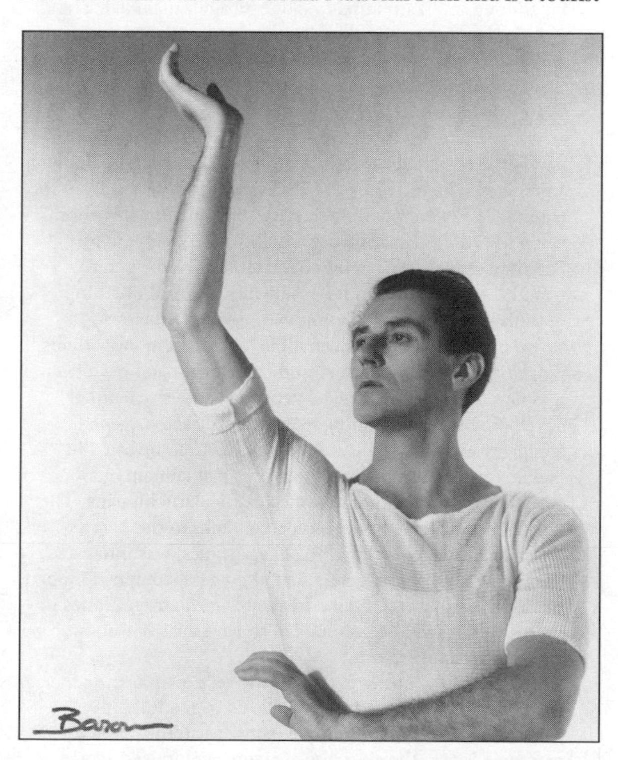

DOLIN, ANTON *British dancer and choreographer Anton Dolin, who formed the Markova-Dolin Ballet with Alicia Markova in 1935. Dolin was important as a role model for later British male dancers. Technically brilliant, he was criticized by some for theatricality and mannerist movements. Corbis*

DOLLY: THE CLONING DEBATE

Dolly, the most famous sheep in the world, has been the subject of debate ever since her existence was announced in February 1997. For Dolly is a clone, produced without sex from a single cell scraped from the udder of an adult sheep. The experiments that produced Dolly were done at the Roslin Institute, a research establishment just outside Edinburgh, but there has been interest in cloning animals for several decades. The intense publicity that surrounded Dolly arose because, as a mammal, she is closely related to humans. And if genetically identical individuals, or clones, can be produced from adult sheep cells, then it seems likely that the same process could be applied to humans. Very soon after Dolly met the world's photographers, a House of Commons committee summoned Ian Wilmut, the team leader of Roslin's Dolly project, to explain the meaning of his work. Wilmut confirmed that his technology could be applied to humans, and given the resources, might lead to cloned humans 'within a couple of years'.

Advantages of cloning

It is important in assessing the significance of Dolly, to understand the background to cloning, and to appreciate why Wilmut's small agricultural research institute persisted for so long in its attempts to clone an adult mammal. The motive is simple, and relates to the commercial breeding of animals. If a farmer has a successful animal, for example a cow that produces a great quantity of excellent milk, similar cows would also be welcome. Normally, breeders obtain the animals they want by mating one favoured individual with another. Yet sexual reproduction produces variation among animals, so the offspring are always a little different from the parents. If it were possible to reproduce an animal without using sex, then the offspring would be identical to its single parent: a clone. Any useful characteristics in the parent would then be found in its genetically identical offspring.

With plants the application was obvious: tomatoes, strawberries, and carrots can all be cloned from individuals judged successful by farmer and consumer – and have been. It is harder to clone animals, yet soon another scientific development made cloning even more attractive: genetic engineering. Much time and money has been invested in making transgenic animals: creatures that contain one or more genes from another species, particularly humans. The Roslin Institute, with its commercial links to the pharmaceutical company PPL Therapeutics, was interested in making sheep with genes that altered the composition of the milk, so that it contained valuable medicines. Clones of such sheep would be guaranteed to have the same ability, and the investment would be secure.

The basis of cloning is that all the cells of an organism, with the exception of the sex cells, contain a full set of genes. A liver cell, for example, contains all the genes for making a brain, the skin, the skeleton, and indeed every other part of the body, yet when a liver cell reproduces it only ever makes other liver cells. It is as if all the other genes it contains were permanently switched off. Therefore, in order to grow an animal from a single cell, a way had to be found to switch back on every gene.

Early cloning attempts

Early cloning experiments, unsurprisingly, used cells taken from an embryo. The method followed was always this: take the nucleus (where the genes are found) out of a cell and then inject it into a fertilized egg – one that has been prepared by having its own nucleus removed. Success came in 1952 in Philadelphia, Pennsylvania, when Robert Briggs and Tom King took a frog embryo, separated out all the cells, and inserted each nucleus into a prepared egg. Twenty-seven tadpoles developed, each genetically identical. It was a world first: an animal had been experimentally cloned.

While US researchers followed this with work developing cloned beef cattle, researchers at the Roslin Institute were developing their interest in transgenic sheep. Sheep embryos were being injected with human genes, and some of these genes were finding their way into the sheep genetic apparatus. One such gene caused the sheep to produce in their milk the drug alpha-1 antitrypsin, used in treating some lung diseases. However, the technique is hit-and-miss: the sheep embryos only incorporate the human genes occasionally. Yet if it were possible to clone transgenic sheep, especially from those individuals with a proven drug-producing history, then the offspring would be guaranteed to contain the gene, and there would be no need for those gene injections with their low success rates. Ian Wilmut had already had success with cloning from embryonic cells, but believed that it should be possible to use adult cells instead. He argued that all the genes contained within an adult nucleus could be reactivated; it was just a matter of finding the right method. Oddly enough, a period of starvation was found to produce the desired effect. Cells taken from a sheep's udder were starved for a short period and this produced in the nucleus a change: the genes became active again. Egg cells were prepared by having their own nuclei removed and replaced by the udder nuclei. Out of 277 eggs that received the nuclei, just 29 developed into embryos, all of which were implanted in surrogate mothers. Fourteen pregnancies began, but most miscarried; only one pregnancy went through to term – this was Dolly.

Ethical issues

It is no exaggeration to say that the scientific world was astonished by the achievement. Scientists' widespread feeling had been that cloning from adult mammals was impossible; indeed, throughout the long-running but sporadic debate about the ethics of cloning, running since the 1970s, scientific commentators tended to downplay the possibility of cloning from adults. In any event, with the attention of the media focused on the concept of human cloning, scientists have had little opportunity to explain that Dolly is not simply an example of scientists in white coats 'playing God' but might constitute instead a serious medical advance.

Following the birth of Dolly, the public debate focused entirely on this question: will humans be cloned? The prospect of dictators cloning themselves and of women giving birth to their father were all discussed as serious possibilities. One reader, writing to *The Times*, suggested that if his son, who had died in a car accident, were cloned 'he would be able to resume his relationship with my wife and myself and our younger son in a meaningful way and our family would be complete again'. Yet a clone of a person would have their own personality, wrought by the environment. They would have their own identity. In reality no-one could clone themselves and predict the outcome, any more than one can predict the future. Controlling the outcome of human cloning, in any civilized society, would most likely be illegal, as human clones would have the same rights as any other human. The scientific reasons commonly given for cloning humans all fail when considered alonside the social and ethical problems. However, if research into human cloning gets under way, there are useful applications that involve the cloning of tissues, not individuals. Cloned bone marrow, genetically identical to the patient in need, would save lives. More lives would be saved if whole organs could be grown, genetically matched to someone with heart or kidney disease. For the moment research in such areas is banned in the UK. In the USA federal funds cannot be used for human embryo research, but private laboratories have greater freedom. Research into mammal cloning, if not human cloning, is bound to continue. The debate too will continue, and will raise the most profound of questions about human and animal rights, about the question of personal identity, and about the purposes and methods of science. Meanwhile, Dolly the sheep thrives in her pen in Scotland, the centre of attention, but a reminder that the end of the century has seen the arrival of another troubling scientific development.

Recent developments

Dolly returned to the headlines in April 1998 when she gave birth to a lamb, Bonnie, conceived in the normal way. This was good news for the Roslin scientists because it showed that a cloned sheep can be fully healthy and able to pass on her genetic characteristics in the simplest and easiest way – by sexual reproduction. However, there was less welcome publicity, too. The simple fact is that Dolly remains unique. Neither Roslin nor any other laboratory has managed to repeat the original feat of cloning a mammal from an adult cell. In science, repeatability is an important part of the process by which a scientific result becomes not a fluke but a useful advance. Dolly was the single success from 277 attempts and this has raised the question that perhaps the original udder cell was unusual in some respect. Among the possibilities are that the cell was undifferentiated or, if the original sheep was pregnant, fetal in origin. The research carries on therefore, and several laboratories, both in Europe and the USA, are striving to produce adult clones of sheep and cows. Given the doubts about Dolly, and the strength of the debate over cloning, it is certain that the next cloned adult animal will generate another rash of headlines.

BY STEPHEN WEBSTER

centre. Nearby are the Gwynfynydd ('White Mountain') and Clogau gold mines; a nugget from the latter has supplied gold for the wedding rings of royal brides since 1923.

Dolgellau beds are a series of rocks of the Upper Cambrian system exposed near Dolgellau and Blaenau Ffestiniog, and consist of slates and shales containing characteristic trilobites.

Dolin, Anton stage name of (Sydney Francis) Patrick (Chippendall Healey) Kay (1904–1983)

English dancer and choreographer. He was the first British male dancer to win an international reputation. As a dancer, his reputation rested on his commanding presence, theatricality, and gymnastic ability. His most famous partnership was with Alicia Markova. After studying under Nijinsky, he was a leading member of Diaghilev's company 1924–29. He formed the Markova–Dolin Ballet Company with Markova 1935–38, and was a guest soloist with the American Ballet Theater 1940–46.

Doll, (William) Richard Shaboe (1912–)

British physician who, working with Bradford Hill (born 1897), provided the first statistical proof of the link between smoking and lung cancer in 1950. In a later study of the smoking habits of doctors, they were able to show that stopping smoking immediately reduces the risk of cancer. Knighted 1971.

Dolly

Sheep cloned at the Roslin laboratory in Scotland in 1996. See feature opposite.

Dolmetsch, (Eugène) Arnold (1858–1940)

English musician and instrument maker, born into a Swiss family settled in France. Together with his family, including his son Carl (1911–), he revived interest in the practical performance of solo and consort music for lute, recorders, and viols, and established the Baroque soprano (descant) recorder as an inexpensive musical instrument for schools.

Domesday Book

Record of the survey of England carried out in 1086 by officials of William the Conqueror in order to assess land tax and other dues, ascertain the value of the crown lands, and enable the king to estimate the power of his vassal barons. The name is derived from the belief that its judgement was as final as that of Doomsday.

Northumberland and Durham were omitted, and also London, Winchester, and certain other towns. The Domesday Book is preserved in two volumes at the Public Record Office, London.

Dominions

Term formerly used to describe those countries of the ◊British Empire and Commonwealth enjoying complete autonomy in internal and external affairs. In this context the term was first applied to Canada, the formal title of which is the **Dominion of Canada**. It was subsequently applied as a generic term, though not as a formal title (except in the case of New

Zealand, which has since ceased to use it), to describe Australia, South Africa, and, in 1922, the Irish Free State.

Don

River in northeast England, a tributary of the ◊Ouse; length 115 km/71 mi. It rises in the Pennines and flows through Sheffield and Doncaster to join the Ouse at Goole, East Yorkshire.

Don

River in Aberdeenshire unitary authority, Scotland, rising in the Ladder Hills and flowing 133 km/83 mi east to the North Sea near Aberdeen.

Donald, Ian (1910–1987)

English obstetrician who introduced ultrasound (very high-frequency sound wave) scanning. He pioneered its use in obstetrics as a means of scanning the growing fetus without exposure to the danger of X-rays. Donald's experience of using radar in World War II suggested to him the use of ultrasound for medical purposes.

Donald III, Bane ('fair') (*c.* 1039–*c.* 1100)

King of Scotland. He came to the throne in 1093 after seizing it on the death of his brother ◊Malcolm III. He was dethroned in 1094 by his nephew, Malcolm's son, ◊Duncan II. He regained power in 1094 but was defeated and captured in 1097 by Edgar, fourth son of Malcolm III, who had him blinded and imprisoned until his death.

Donat, (Friederich) Robert (1905–1958)

English actor. He started out in the theatre and made one film in Hollywood (*The Count of Monte Cristo* (1934)). His other films include *The Private Life of Henry VIII* (1933), Alfred Hitchcock's *The Thirty-Nine Steps* (1935), *Goodbye, Mr Chips* (1939) (for which he won an Academy Award), *The Winslow Boy* (1948), and *The Inn of the Sixth Happiness* (1958).

Doncaster

Industrial town and administrative headquarters of Doncaster metropolitan borough, South Yorkshire, England, on the River Don, 56 km/35 mi southwest of York; population (1991) 71,600. It has been an important centre for railway engineering (locomotives and rolling stock) since the 19th century. Traditional iron, steel, and coal production has declined, although active collieries remain, including the Rossington deep mine. Synthetic textiles, confectionery (butterscotch), agricultural equipment, wallpaper, electrical equipment, fencing, brass fittings, nylon yarn, and wire rope are produced.

The St Leger (1776), the world's oldest classic race, is held annually at Doncaster racecourse in September, and the Lincolnshire Handicap is held in March. The Earth Centre, Europe's largest centre for ecological research and display, is being built here as a Millennium Commission Landmark Project.

Features

The Mansion House (built 1744–1748) contains a fine banqueting hall and is one of only three civic mansion houses in England (the others being in London and York). The town's museum and art gallery includes a local history collection, including Roman artefacts, horse-racing exhibits, and a collection of Yorkshire pottery. Nearby is Cusworth Hall, built in the mid-18th century, which houses a museum of social and industrial history. At Conisbrough to the southwest of the town, there is a ruined Norman castle with a well-preserved circular keep. The castle features in Walter Scott's novel *Ivanhoe* as Athelstan's stronghold.

History

The Romans established the military station of **Danum** here, which occupied an important position on the Great North Road. It was later the site of a Saxon settlement and in the Domesday Book of 1086 the town repeatedly occurs as **Donecastre**. In 1194 Richard I gave Doncaster its first known charter, and in 1467 Edward IV authorized the election of a mayor.

Although Doncaster has street names such as French Gate, Baxter Gate, and St Sepulchre Gate, suggesting that the town was fortified in the Middle Ages, the 16th-century antiquary John Leland recorded that it was never a walled town, gate in this context simply meaning 'street'. Names such as Priory Place and Greyfriars Road indicate the former presence of religious orders.

The town was an important focus for trading in the Middle Ages. In the mid-17th century the English diarist and author John Evelyn described Doncaster as a large, fair town, famous for great wax lights and good stockings. For its loyalty in the English Civil War, Charles II granted the town the privilege of being a free borough. In the 18th century the town was a busy coaching stop and agricultural centre, and figured in Robert Southey's *The Doctor, etc* (published in seven volumes 1834–47), fictional memoirs of Dr Daniel Dove. Following the opening of the railway in 1849 and the establishment of the Great Northern Railway works in 1853, it developed rapidly as a railway engineering town. The development of the South Yorkshire coalfield encouraged growth.

Donellan, Declan (1953–)

British theatre director. He was cofounder of the Cheek by Jowl theatre company in 1981, and associate director of the National Theatre from 1989. His irreverent and audacious productions include many classics, such as Racine's *Andromaque* (1985), Corneille's *Le Cid* (1987), and Ibsen's *Peer Gynt* (1990).

Donington, Robert (1907–1990)

English instrumentalist and musicologist. He edited music, wrote learned articles, performed with various teams on early instruments, and produced books on instruments and ornaments, including *The Interpretation of Early Music* (1963).

Donne, John (1572–1631)

English metaphysical poet. His work consists of love poems, religious poems, verse satires, and sermons. His sermons rank him with the century's greatest orators, and his fervent poems of love and hate, violent, tender, or abusive, give him a unique position among English poets.

His poems are characterized by the imaginative power of their imagery and the use of irregular meter and colloquial diction. His religious poems show the same passion and ingenuity as his love poetry, and his sermons, written in an elegant prose style, reflect his preoccupation with humanity's place in the universe and its approaching end. His verse was not published in collected form until after his death, and was long out of favour, but he is now recognized as one of the greatest English poets.

Born into a Catholic family, Donne matriculated early at Oxford University to avoid taking the compulsory oath of supremacy at the age of 16. In 1596 he joined a naval expedition against Spain with the Earl of Essex and Walter Raleigh, and on his return became private secretary to Sir Thomas Egerton (about 1540–1617), Keeper of the Seal. This appointment was ended by his secret marriage in 1601 to Ann More (died 1617), niece of Egerton's wife. They endured many years of poverty and had 12 children (of whom seven survived childhood).

In 1610 he made a bid for the patronage of James I with the prose work *Pseudo-Martyr* and in 1615 he was ordained in the Church of England, urged on by the King. From 1621 to his death he was dean of St Paul's.

Donoghue, Steve (Stephen) (1884–1945)

English jockey who between 1915 and 1925 won the Epsom Derby six times, equalling the record of Jem Robinson (since beaten by Lester Piggott). Donoghue is the only jockey to have won the race in three successive years (1921–23).

Donovan (1946–)

Scottish pop-folk singer and songwriter whose hit songs include 'Mellow Yellow' (1966). *A Gift From a Flower to a Garden* (1968) was a novel double-album. He wrote the score of the film *Brother Sun, Sister Moon* (1972) for Franco Zeffirelli.

Dorchester

Market town and administrative headquarters of ◊Dorset, southern England, on the River Frome, north of Weymouth, 192 km/119 mi southwest of London; population (1991) 15,000. It is the service centre of an agricultural region and has light engineering industries. Tourism plays an important role in the town's economy. The hillfort ◊Maiden Castle to the southwest was occupied from about 4000 BC, although the first identifiable settlement dates from 2000 BC. The novelist Thomas ◊Hardy was born nearby.

In 1685 Judge ◊Jeffreys held his 'Bloody Assizes' here after the Monmouth Rebellion and the ◊Tolpuddle Martyrs were sentenced in the local court house in 1834.

Roman remains

Dorchester occupies the site of the Roman town of **Durnovaria**, established in about 70 AD. The line of the town's Roman walls is marked by avenues known as 'The Walks'. The foundations of a Roman villa with a mosaic floor, discovered in 1937 in the grounds of the county hall, are preserved. Maumbury Rings, a prehistoric earthwork dating back to 2000 BC, was converted into an amphitheatre for the Roman town, seating an audience of about 10,000; later the site was used for public hangings until 1705.

History

In the 17th century the Puritans gained control of the town, using money gained from the town brewhouse monopoly to pay for poor relief from 1622. In 1642 Dorchester was a centre of Parliamentary revolt, but was captured by the Royalists in 1643.

Features

The Dorset County Museum contains collections illustrating the archaeology, natural history, and geology of Dorset. Judge Jeffreys is said to have held his Bloody Assizes in the Oak Room of the Antelope Hotel. In the Shire Hall of 1797, the room where the Tolpuddle Martyrs were tried is preserved. St Peter's church dates from the 15th century; and Napper's Mite was formerly a 17th-century almshouse. The Keep Military Museum includes displays on the Dorset and Devon regiments. Dorchester contains the only museum in Britain totally devoted to dinosaurs, and the only permanent exhibition on the ancient Egyptian king Tutankhamun outside Egypt.

Literary associations

The poet William Barnes, who published poems in the Dorset dialect, lived in the town. Thomas Hardy was born 5 km/3 mi from Dorchester at Higher Bockhampton in 1840, and lived for the last 50 years of his life at Max Gate, which he built on the outskirts of the town. Dorchester featured as 'Casterbridge' in his novel *The Mayor of Casterbridge*.

Dorchester-on-Thames

Town in Oxfordshire, England, 14 km/9 mi southeast of Oxford; population (1991) 2,100. Traces of Neolithic, Iron, and Bronze Age settlements have been found on the Sinodun hills southwest of the town. Dorchester was the seat of a bishop in the early Middle Ages, and has an abbey church dating from the 12th century.

The Dyke Hills just south of Dorchester are an ancient British earthwork. The town was also the site of a Roman station and a Romano-British town.

Dorking

Town in the county of Surrey, England, in the North ◊Downs near Box Hill; population (1991) 10,000. Dorking is now mainly a dormitory town for commuters working in London.

The recreational areas of Leith Hill, Ranmore Common, and Mickleham Down are easily accessible from Dorking.

dormancy

State of a peerage or baronetcy when it is believed that heirs to the title exist, but their whereabouts are unknown. This sometimes occurs when a senior line dies out and a cadet line has long since gone abroad.

Dorneywood

Country house near Burnham Beeches, Buckinghamshire, England. Presented to the nation by Lord Courtauld-Thomson (1865–1954) as an official residence for a minister of the crown, it is used by the foreign secretary.

Dorset

County of southwest England (since April 1997 Bournemouth and Poole have been separate unitary authorities)

Area 2,541 sq km/981 sq mi

Towns and cities ◊Dorchester (administrative headquarters), Shaftesbury, Sherborne; Lyme Regis, Weymouth, Poole (resorts)

Physical Chesil Beach, a shingle bank along the coast 19 km/11 mi long, connecting Isle of Portland to the mainland; Dorset Downs (chalk); River Stour, and rivers Frome and Piddle (which flow into Poole Harbour); clay beds in the north and west; Canford Heath, the home of some of Britain's rarest breeding birds and reptiles (including the nightjar, Dartford warbler, sand lizard, and smooth snake)

Features Isle of Purbeck, a peninsula where china clay and Purbeck 'marble' are quarried, and which includes Corfe Castle and the holiday resort of Swanage; Cranborne Chase; Maiden Castle (prehistoric earthwork); Tank Museum at Royal Armoured Corps Centre, Bovington, where the cottage of the soldier and writer T E ◊Lawrence is a museum; Wimborne Minster; abbey church of Sherborne

Industries Wytch Farm is the largest onshore oilfield in the UK; production at Wareham onshore oilfield started 1991; quarrying (marble from the Isle of Purbeck, and Portland stone, which has been used for buildings all over the world); manufacturing (rope, twine, and net at Bridport); sand and gravel extraction; tourism

Agriculture dairy farming

Population (1994 est) 374,800.

Topography

Dorset is bounded on the west by Devon; on the northwest by Somerset; on the northeast by Wiltshire; on the east by Hampshire; and on the south by Poole, Bournemouth, and the English Channel. Bridport, Poole, and Weymouth are the chief seaports. Chesil Bank has been augmented with additional breakwaters at Portland Roads to form Portland Harbour. The coast around Lyme Regis has yielded significant dinosaur remains.

Doughty, Charles Montagu (1843–1926)

English travel writer, author of *Travels in Arabia Deserta* (1888), an account of an astonishing and dangerous journey in

DORSET *The coast of Dorset in southern England is characterized by soft limestone cliffs eroded by the action of the waves. One of the most striking formations is the archway pierced through a prominent headland at Durdle Door, just west of the small harbour of Lulworth Cove. Corel*

an unusual literary style, written after two years in the Middle East searching for Biblical relics. He was a role model for English soldier T E ◊Lawrence ('Lawrence of Arabia'). Latterly he wrote epic poems of an experimental linguistic and metrical nature.

Douglas

Capital of the Isle of Man in the Irish Sea; population (1991) 22,200. It is situated in the southeast of the island, and is a holiday resort and terminus of shipping routes to and from Fleetwood and Liverpool. Banking and financial services are important, and the Manx Parliament, Tynwald meets here.

Douglas, Alfred (Bruce), Lord Douglas (1870–1945)

English poet. He became closely associated in London with the writer Oscar ◊Wilde. Their relationship led to Wilde's conviction for homosexual activity, imprisonment, and early death, through the enmity of Douglas's father, the 8th Marquess of ◊Queensberry. Douglas wrote the self-justificatory *Oscar Wilde and Myself* (1914) and the somewhat contradictory *Oscar Wilde, A Summing-Up* (1940).

Douglas, Bill (1937–)

Scottish film director and screenwriter. Although his output has been minimal, he has made a significant contribution to British realist cinema of the 1970s. He established his reputation with a trilogy of films – *My Childhood* (1972), *My Ain Folk* (1973), and *My Way Home* (1977) – a documentary-like account of a poverty-stricken boy growing up in a Scottish mining town.

Comrades (1987) is an equally unsentimental filmic account of the Tolpuddle Martyrs and their exile to an Australian penal colony in the 19th century. Douglas's work draws on his own working-class experiences and the influence of such filmmakers as the Indian Satyajit Ray.

Douglas, Gavin, or Gawin (*c.* 1475–1522)

Scottish poet. His translation into Scots of the Roman poet Virgil's *Aeneid* (1513) was the first translation from the classics into a vernacular of the British Isles. He wrote the allegorical *The Palace of Honour* in about 1501.

> *There are two problems in my life. The political ones are insoluble and the economic ones are incomprehensible.*
>
> ALEC DOUGLAS-HOME British prime minister. Speech Jan 1964

Douglas-Hamilton

Family name of dukes of Hamilton, seated at Lennoxlove, East Lothian, Scotland.

Douglas-Home, Alec, Alexander Frederick) Baron Home of the Hirsel (1903–1995)

British Conservative politician. He was foreign secretary 1960–63, and succeeded Harold Macmillan as prime minister 1963. He renounced his peerage (as 14th Earl of Home) and re-entered the Commons after successfully contesting a by-election, but failed to win the 1964 general election, and resigned as party leader in 1965. He was again foreign secretary 1970–74, when he received a life peerage. Knighted 1962.

Douglas-Home, William (1912–1992)

Scottish dramatist. He is noted for his comedies, which include *The Chiltern Hundreds* (1947), *The Secretary Bird* (1968), *Lloyd George Knew My Father* (1972), and *The Kingfisher* (1977). He was the younger brother of the politician Alec Douglas-Home.

As a captain in the Royal Armoured Corps during World War II, he disobeyed orders by refusing to take part in the bombardment of Le Havre because the citizens had not been evacuated. This led to a court martial and a year in prison, an experience upon which his first real success, *Now Barabbas* (1945), was based.

> *Every morning I read the obits in* The Times. *If I'm not there, I carry on.*
>
> WILLIAM DOUGLAS-HOME Scottish playwright. Quoted in the *Observer* 16 August 1987

Doulton, Henry (1820–1897)

English ceramicist. He developed special wares for the chemical, electrical, and building industries, and established the world's first stoneware-drainpipe factory in 1846. From 1870 he created art pottery and domestic tablewares in Lambeth, South London, and Burslem, near Stoke-on-Trent. He was knighted in 1887.

Dounreay

Site of the world's first fast-breeder nuclear reactor (1962) on the north coast of Scotland, in the Highland unitary authority, 12 km/7 mi west of Thurso. It is now a nuclear reprocessing plant.

The first nuclear reactor was active until 1977, when an explosion contaminated beaches. It has since been linked to the high incidence of childhood leukaemia in the area. A second reactor opened in 1974 and continued until the site was decommissioned in 1994 and replaced with a nuclear reprocessing plant. A 1996 survey by the UK Atomic Energy Authority found 1,500 patches of radioactive contamination. There was a plutonium leak in September 1996 into the sea. One of its reprocessing plants had to be temporarily shut down. Fishing was banned within 2 km/1.5 mi of Dounreay in October 1997.

Dove

River in Derbyshire, England, a tributary of the ◊Trent; length 65 km/40 mi. The Dove rises on Axe Edge, 6 km/4 mi from Buxton, and forms the southwestern border between

Derbyshire and Staffordshire as it flows south to join the Trent near Burton. Izaak ◊Walton, author of *The Compleat Angler* (1653), fished the Dove.

The valley of **Dovedale**, below Hartington, where the river runs through a rocky, wooded gorge some 3 km/2 mi long, is popular with walkers.

Dove Cottage

Small house at Grasmere in the English Lake District where the poet William ◊Wordsworth settled with his sister Dorothy in 1799, and later with his wife Mary Hutchinson in 1802. Wordsworth wrote much of his best work here, including 'Ode: Intimations of Immortality', 'Michael', and 'Resolution and Independence', before reluctantly moving to a larger house in 1808. It is now a museum.

Dover

Market town and seaport in Kent, southeast England, on the coast of the English Channel; population (1991) 34,200. It is Britain's nearest point to mainland Europe, 34 km/21 mi from Calais, France. Dover is the world's busiest passenger port and England's principal cross-channel port, with ferry, hovercraft, and cross-channel train services. Industries include electronics, paper manufacturing, and light engineering

As Roman **Dubris**, the port was an important naval base and the starting point of ◊Watling Street. The Roman beacon or 'lighthouse', dating from about 50 AD, in the grounds of the Norman castle, is one of the oldest Roman buildings in the country. Dover was the largest of the original ◊Cinque Ports.

Features

Dover is known for its white cliffs, and views from the castle keep, 116 m/380 ft above sea level, can include the French coast from Boulogne to Gravelines, the shoreline from Folkestone to Ramsgate, and many of the fortifications honeycombing the Dover cliffs. The White Cliffs Experience Museum illustrates the history of Dover from Roman times to World War II. The Roman Painted House describes the Roman occupation and includes Roman wall paintings and the remains of an underground Roman heating system. The Duke of York's Royal Military School is located in the town.

Dover Castle

Dover Castle was built on the cliffs overlooking the town, on the site of earlier fortifications. An important military headquarters and defensive garrison for centuries, it has a massive keep built by Henry II in the 1180s, with walls 5–7 m/17–22 ft thick. The castle was seized by Oliver Cromwell during the English Civil War, and it was strengthened during the Napoleonic Wars. Within the grounds of the castle is the Saxon church of St Mary in Castro.

20th-century history

The town was the centre of the Dover Patrol during World War I. Dover suffered considerable damage from bombing and shelling during World War II, and much of the town and the seafront have since been redeveloped. A network of tunnels underneath the castle known as Hellfire Corner, built originally during the Napoleonic Wars, was used during World War II as the control base for the Dunkirk evacuation. The Channel Tunnel, to the west of Dover, opened in 1994.

Dover, Strait of, French Pas-de-Calais

Stretch of water separating England from France, and connecting the English Channel with the North Sea. It is about 35 km/22 mi long and 34 km/21 mi wide at its narrowest part (from Dover pier to Cap Griz-Nez); its greatest depth is 55 m/180 ft. It is one of the world's busiest sea lanes. The main ports are Dover and Folkestone (England), and Calais and Boulogne (France).

By 1972 increasing traffic, collisions, and shipwrecks had become so frequent that traffic-routeing schemes were enforced.

The geological formation of the channel bed points to the fact that at one time England was joined to continental Europe.

dowager

The style given to the widow of a British peer or baronet.

Dowell, Anthony James (1943–)

English classical ballet dancer. He is known for his elegant poise, accurate finish, and exemplary classical style. He was principal dancer with the Royal Ballet 1966–86, and became artistic director in 1986.

Dowell joined the Royal Ballet in 1961. The choreographer Frederick Ashton chose him to create the role of Oberon in *The Dream* (1964)

DOVER *Ferry traffic at Britain's busiest passenger port, Dover in Kent. Ferry operators here have faced stiff competition since the Channel Tunnel undersea rail link to France opened in 1994. Among the incentives to travellers to take the slower sea crossing has been the 'booze cruise', a one-day excursion to stock up on cheap liquor and cigarettes. David Bowie/Collections*

opposite Antoinette Sibley, the start of an outstanding partnership. His other noted performances include those in Anthony Tudor's *Shadowplay* (1967), Ashton's *Monotones* (1965), and van Manen's *Four Schumann Pieces* (1975).

During his tenure as artistic director of the Royal Ballet, he has staged new productions of *Swan Lake* (1987) and *The Sleeping Beauty* (1994). He continues to perform character roles with the company, such as Carabosse in *Sleeping Beauty*.

Dowland, John (*c.* 1563–*c.* 1626)

English composer of lute songs. He introduced daring expressive refinements of harmony and ornamentation to English Renaissance style in the service of an elevated aesthetic of melancholy, as in the masterly *Lachrymae* (1605).

Down

County of southeastern Northern Ireland

Area 2,470 sq km/953 sq mi

Towns and cities Downpatrick (county town), Bangor (seaside resort), Newtownards, Newry, and Banbridge; the northern part lies within the commuter belt for Belfast, and includes part of the city of Belfast, east of the River Lagan.

Physical Mourne Mountains; Strangford sea lough

Industries light manufacturing, plastics, linen, high technology and computer companies, fishing, quarrying

Agriculture County Down has very fertile land. The principal crops are barley, potatoes, and oats; there is livestock rearing and dairying

Population (1981) 339,200.

Government the county returns two members to the UK Parliament.

Physical

Down is a largely lowland county. The Silurian bedrock, and the low hills that are scattered all over the north were formed from the debris deposited and moulded by glacial action. In contrast, the south is dominated by the Mourne Mountains, a granitic intrusion the highest point of which is Slieve Donard (852 m/2,796 ft). The coast at Dundrum Bay, where the mountains rise abruptly, is sandy, but elsewhere the coastline is mainly low and rocky. In the east it is penetrated by the long sea inlet Strangford Lough, a noted habitat for birds and grey seals.

Features

There are a number of fortifications and early ecclesiastical remains in the county, including: the prehistoric Giant's Ring earthwork; Legananny Dolmen, a Stone Age monument; the well-preserved tower house, Audley's Castle; 5th-century Nendrum Monastery on Mahee Island in Strangford Lough; Grey Abbey, a Cistercian foundation dating from 1193; Mount Stewart House and Gardens, the 18th-century former home of the Marquess of Londonderry, noted for its statues and carvings dating from the early 20th century; the Strangford Stone, 10 m/33 ft high, to be erected on the shores of Strangford Lough on Midsummer's Day, June 1999, to mark the millennium.

Downing Street

Street in Westminster, London, leading from Whitehall to St James's Park, named after Sir George Downing (died 1684), a diplomat under Cromwell and Charles II. **Number 10** is the official residence of the prime minister and **number 11** is the residence of the chancellor of the Exchequer. **Number 12** is the office of the government whips. After his appointment as prime minister May 1997, Tony Blair chose to use Number 11 to accommodate his family, using Number 10 as his office and for Cabinet meetings. The chancellor of the Exchequer, Gordon Brown, retained his office in Number 11 but used the flat above Number 10 as his residence.

Downing Street Declaration

Statement, issued jointly by UK prime minister John ◊Major and Irish premier Albert Reynolds on 15 December 1993, setting out general principles for holding all-party talks on securing peace in ◊Northern Ireland. The Declaration was warmly welcomed by mainstream politicians in both the UK and the Republic of Ireland, but the reception by Northern Ireland parties was more guarded. However, after initial hesitation, Republican and ◊Loyalist cease-fires were declared in 1994 and an Ulster framework document, intended to guide the peace negotiations, was issued by the UK and Irish governments in February 1995.

Downpatrick

County town of County ◊Down, Northern Ireland, 45 km/28 mi southeast of Belfast; population (1991) 8,300. Local employment is mainly in service industries, but residents also commute to Belfast. Downpatrick has been an important settlement since prehistoric times, and its first church may have been founded by St Patrick in the 5th century.

Downpatrick has been the cathedral town of the (now Protestant) diocese of Down since the Middle Ages. A major borough in Anglo-Norman times, it became the market centre for the rich farming area of Lecale, but declined in importance during the 19th century. The Ulster Harp National horserace is held annually at the racecourse.

Downs, the

Roadstead (partly sheltered anchorage) in the English Channel, off ◊Deal on the coast of east Kent, southeast England. Lying between the coastline and the treacherous sandbanks of the ◊Goodwin Sands, the waters extend over an area 13 km/8 mi long and 10 km/6 mi broad. Henry VIII built the castles of Deal, Walmer, and Sandown to defend the Downs, each fortress being about 2 km/1 mi apart. Several 17th-century naval battles took place here, including a defeat of Spain by the Dutch in 1639.

Downs, North and South

Two lines of chalk hills in southeast England; see ◊North Downs and ◊South Downs.

Doyle, Arthur Conan (1859–1930)

Scottish writer. He created the detective Sherlock ◊Holmes and his assistant Dr Watson, who first appeared in *A Study in Scarlet* (1887) and featured in a number of subsequent stories, including *The Hound of the Baskervilles* (1902). Among Doyle's other works is the fantasy adventure *The Lost World* (1912). In his later years he became a spiritualist and wrote a *History of Spiritualism* (1926).

The Sherlock Holmes character featured in several books, including *The Sign of Four* (1890) and *The Valley of Fear* (1915), as well as in volumes of short stories, first published in the *Strand Magazine*. Knighted 1902.

Doyle, Richard (1824–1883)

English caricaturist and book illustrator. In 1849 he designed the original cover for the humorous magazine *Punch*. He illustrated many books, among them William Thackeray's *The Newcomes* (1853–55) and *In Fairy Land* (1869) by the Irish writer William Allingham (1824–1889). He also painted landscapes, usually fantastic fairyland scenes.

D'Oyly Carte, Richard (1844–1901)

English producer of the Gilbert and Sullivan operas. They were performed at the Savoy Theatre, London, which he built. The D'Oyly Carte Opera Company, founded 1876, was disbanded 1982 following the ending of its monopoly on the Gilbert and Sullivan operas. The present company, founded 1988, moved to the Alexandra Theatre, Birmingham, 1991.

Drabble, Margaret (1939–)

English writer. Her novels include *The Millstone* (1965), *The Middle Ground* (1980), the trilogy *The Radiant Way* (1987), *A Natural Curiosity* (1989), and *The Gates of Ivory* (1991), and *The Witch of Exmoor* (1996). She portrays contemporary life with toughness and sensitivity, often through the eyes of intelligent modern women.

After a brief period as an actress, she began her career as a novelist with *A Summer Bird-Cage* (1963). She has been a lecturer and critic, and her works also include biographies of Virginia Woolf (1973) and Arnold Bennett (1974).

She edited the 1985 and 1995 editions of the *Oxford Companion to English Literature*.

Drake, Francis (*c.* 1540–1596)

English buccaneer and explorer. Having enriched himself as a pirate against Spanish interests in the Caribbean 1567–72, he was sponsored by Elizabeth I for an expedition to the Pacific, sailing round the world 1577–80 in the *Golden Hind*, robbing Spanish ships as he went. This was the second circumnavigation of the globe (the first had been by the Portuguese explorer Ferdinand Magellan). Drake also helped to defeat the ◊Spanish Armada in 1588 as a vice-admiral in the *Revenge*.

When the Spanish ambassador demanded that Drake be punished for robbing Spanish ships on his round the world trip, the Queen knighted him on the deck of the *Golden Hind* at Deptford, London. In a raid on Cádiz in 1587 he burned 10,000 tons of shipping ('singed the King of Spain's beard'), and delayed the invasion of England by the Spanish Armada for a year. He was stationed off the French island of Ushant 1588 to intercept the Armada, but was driven back to England by unfavourable winds.

On his last expedition to the West Indies, Drake captured Nombre de Dios on the north coast of Panama but failed to seize Panama City. In January 1596 he died off the coast of Panama.

Dreadnought

Class of battleships built for the British navy after 1905 and far superior in speed and armaments to anything then afloat. The first modern battleship to be built, it was the basis of battleship design for more than 50 years. The first Dreadnought was launched in 1906, with armaments consisting entirely of big guns.

Drinkwater, John (1882–1937)

English poet and dramatist. He was a prolific writer of lyrical and reflective verse, and also wrote many historical plays, including *Abraham Lincoln* (1918) and *Mary Stuart* (1921). His work had an important influence on the revival of serious drama.

The advantage of time and place in all practical actions is half the victory; which being lost is irrecoverable.

Francis Drake English buccaneer and explorer.
Letter to Queen Elizabeth I, 1588

Droitwich

Town in Worcestershire, England, 9 km/6 mi northeast of Worcester; population (1991) 20,300. Housing and light industry have developed as a result of overspill from Birmingham.

The saline springs, or 'wyches', of Droitwich have been used since Roman times and are mentioned in the Domesday Book. Their medicinal properties were realized in 1830, during a cholera epidemic.

drove roads

Trackways for cattle, maintained by constant usage. They were probably established in prehistoric times, when communities moved their livestock from one grazing area to another. They were in continual use until the first half of the 19th century, when enclosures and the advent of the railway made long-distance drove roads obsolete.

Druidism

Religion of the Celtic peoples of the pre-Christian British Isles and Gaul. The word is derived from the Greek *drus* ('oak'), a tree regarded by the Druids as sacred. One of the Druids' chief rites was the cutting of mistletoe from the oak with a golden sickle. They taught the immortality of the soul and a reincarnation doctrine, and were expert in astronomy. The Druids are thought to have offered human sacrifices.

In Britain the Druids had their stronghold was Anglesey, Wales, until they were driven out by the Roman governor Agricola. They existed in Scotland and Ireland until the coming of the Christian missionaries. What are often termed Druidic monuments – cromlechs and stone circles – are of

New Stone Age (Neolithic) origin, though they may later have been used for religious purposes by the Druids. A possible example of a human sacrifice by Druids is Lindow Man, whose body was found in a bog in Cheshire in 1984.

drum 'n' bass

The most original formal development of the mid-1990s in UK pop music, being a hybrid form of assorted US and Anglo-Caribbean popular musical styles, focusing on the relationship between the two chief components of the rhythm section. Drum 'n' bass departs from reggae and hip-hop convention by making drum patterns the subject of the music (usually realized in double or quadruple time against deep, slow bass lines), then overlaid with vocal and instrumental edits.

Goldie has been the doyen of the style, essentially an underground phenomenon, championed by such artists as Roni Size, 4Hero, and LJK Bukem, though the group Everything But The Girl have helped popularize it in the pop mainstream.

Drury Lane

London street connecting Aldwych with High Holborn. It has been a part of the theatre district since the 17th century. Charles II's mistress Nell Gwyn was born here and is traditionally supposed to have sold oranges in the Drury Lane Theatre. The same theatre was leased by the dramatist Richard Brinsley Sheridan from 1776.

Drury Lane takes its name from Drury Place, a 15th-century house owned by the Drury family. It was here that Robert Devereux, 2nd Earl of Essex, planned his rebellion of 1601, which led to his execution.

Drury Lane Theatre

Theatre in the London, first opened in 1663 on the site of earlier playhouses. It was twice burned; the present building dates from 1812.

Dryburgh Abbey (Gaelic *Darach-bruach* 'bank of oaks')

Monastic ruin in the Scottish Borders region of Scotland, on the River Tweed, near Melrose. It was founded about 1150 for Premonstratensian canons by Hugo de Morville, constable of Scotland. The style is mainly Decorated.

Dryburgh was burned by Edward II (1322), and was partly restored by Robert Bruce. Under Richard II it again suffered (1385), and was reduced to ruins by Bowes and Latoun (1544), and by the Earl of Hertford's expedition (1545).

DRY STONE WALLING *Building a dry stone wall in North Yorkshire. Making walls without the aid of mortar is a highly skilled task requiring careful selection of the right size and shape of block for maximum stability. Square openings, known as 'sheep-creeps' are often left in the base of the wall to let livestock pass through. Roger Scruton/Collections*

St Mary's aisle in the north transept has the tombs of the novelist Walter Scott, his biographer, John Gibson Lockhart, and Field Marshal Earl Haig.

Dryden, John (1631–1700)

English poet and dramatist, one of the leading writers of the Restoration period. He is noted for his satirical verse and for his use of the heroic couplet. His poetry includes the verse satire *Absalom and Achitophel* (1681), *Annus Mirabilis* (1667), and 'A Song for St Cecilia's Day' (1687). Plays include the heroic drama *The Conquest of Granada* (first performed in 1670, printed in 1672), the comedy *Marriage à la Mode* (first performed in 1672, printed in 1673), and *All for Love* (first performed in 1677, printed in 1678). Critical works include the essay 'Of Dramatic Poesy' (1668).

Dryden was born in Northamptonshire, and educated at Cambridge University. In 1657 he moved to London, where he worked for the republican government of Oliver Cromwell. His stanzas commemorating the death of Cromwell appeared in 1659 and *Astraea Redux*, in honour of the Restoration, was published in 1660. He followed this with a panegyric in honour of Charles II's coronation in 1661. Dryden was much involved in the intellectual spirit of the 'new age', and was one of the first to liken the reign of Charles II to that of the Roman emperor Augustus. In 1668 he became the first poet officially to hold the title of poet laureate. He converted to Roman Catholicism following the accession of James II, but lost the post of poet laureate after the Revolution of 1688.

dry stone walling

The practice of building walls by bonding the stones without mortar. In upland farming areas dry stone walls often replace hedges and fences as field boundaries. Typically dry stone walls consist of an outer layer of large stones concealing a core of smaller stones.

Early examples include prehistoric walls and tombs (for example at Skara Brae, in the Orkneys), and in British agriculture it has been used since the early Middle Ages for buildings and animal pens. Most existing walls are the result of the extensive ◊enclosure of farmland in the 18th and 19th centuries, when the first professional wallers appeared.

DSO

Abbreviation for Distinguished Service Order, British military medal.

Dudley

Industrial town and metropolitan borough in the West Midlands, 14 km/9 mi northwest of Birmingham, England; population (1994 est) 141,000. Formerly an important centre for coalmining and iron-smelting at the heart of the industrial ◊Black Country, Dudley now manufactures clothing, glass, and light engineering products.

Features

The Black Country Museum illustrates the area's industrial heritage and includes reconstructed period buildings. There are ruins of a Norman castle, with a zoo in the grounds.

Industrial history

Dudley was an important industrial centre from medieval times, with abundant coal, ironstone, limestone, and refractory clay. Coalmining existed in the late 13th century, and the coalmining and iron-smelting industries expanded in the 17th century. The hand-wrought rail trade flourished in the early 16th century, and the manufacture of glass and bricks began in the early 17th century. Heavy engineering was established later. Dudley's limestone quarries were closed in the 1920s.

Dudley, Lord Guildford (died 1554)

English nobleman, fourth son of the Duke of Northumberland. He was married by his father to Lady Jane Grey in 1553, against her wishes, in an attempt to prevent the succession of ◊Mary I to the throne. The plot failed, and he and his wife were executed.

duke

Highest title in the English peerage. It originated in England in 1337, when Edward III created his son Edward, Duke of Cornwall.

The premier Scottish duke is the Duke of Hamilton (created in 1643).

Dukeries

Area of estates in northwest Nottinghamshire, central England, formerly with magnificent stately homes. Few of these now survive, however. The area includes the northern part of ◊Sherwood Forest. Thoresby Hall, said to be the largest house in England (about 365 rooms), was sold as a hotel in 1989 and the contents were dispersed.

The estates in the area originally belonged to four ducal families. They comprise the parks of Welbeck, Clumber (now National Trust property), Thoresby, and Rufford.

Dukes, Ashley (1885–1959)

English dramatist and theatre manager. Among his plays are *The Man with a Load of Mischief* (1924), a Regency conversation piece, and two adaptations from German, *Such Men are Dangerous* (1928), from *Der Patriot* by Alfred Neumann (1895–1952), and *Jew Süss* (1929), from the novel by Lion Feuchtwanger. In 1933 he opened the Mercury Theatre, Notting Hill Gate, London, for the production of new and foreign plays.

Dulwich

District of the Greater London borough of Southwark. It includes Dulwich College (1619); the Horniman Museum (1901), with a fine ethnological collection; Dulwich Picture Gallery (1814), the first public art gallery to be opened in London; Dulwich Park; and Dulwich Village.

Dulwich Village lies at the heart of the area, with a street of fine Georgian buildings. Dulwich College was founded in 1619 by the actor Edward Alleyn; the authors P G Wodehouse and Raymond Chandler were pupils. The college was originally established in the manor house of Dulwich, but the present building, designed by Charles Barry, was erected between 1866 and 1870. Dulwich Park was opened to the public in 1890.

Dulwich Picture Gallery, designed by John Soane in 1814, houses an important collection including paintings of the Dutch school.

Du Maurier, Daphne (1907–1989)

English novelist. Her romantic fiction includes *Jamaica Inn* (1936), *Rebecca* (1938), *Frenchman's Creek* (1942), and *My Cousin Rachel* (1951), and is set in Cornwall. Her work is made compelling by her storytelling gift.

Jamaica Inn, *Rebecca*, and her short story *The Birds* were made into films by the English director Alfred Hitchcock. DBE 1969.

Dumbarton

Administrative headquarters of ⇨West Dunbartonshire, Scotland, on the River Leven near its confluence with the Clyde, 23 km/14 mi northwest of Glasgow; population (1991) 22,000. Traditional heavy industries have been contracting, other industries include whisky distilling and electronics.

Dumbarton Castle, built on a basalt rock, dates from the 6th century; Dumbarton was then capital of the kingdom of Strathclyde until 1034 when it was absorbed into the kingdom of Scotland. William ⇨Wallace was confined within the castle's walls in 1305, and in 1571 it was captured for James VI.

Dumfries

Administrative headquarters of ⇨Dumfries and Galloway unitary authority, Scotland; population (1991) 32,100. It is situated on the River Nith, 53 km/33 mi northwest of Carlisle. Industries include plastics, light engineering, and textiles. Robert Burns is buried in the graveyard of St Michael's church.

The site of a Franciscan friary where ⇨Robert (I) the Bruce killed the Red Comyn is now built on; a stone marks the site of the old castle of Dumfries which Robert captured after Comyn's death. This death started the long war of independence.

Sweetheart Abbey, southwest of Dumfries, was founded in 1273 by Devorgilla Balliol in memory of her husband. Devorgilla Balliol, with her husband, also founded Balliol College, Oxford. Caerlaverock Castle (1290) is situated nearby.

Robert Burns worked at Ellisland Farm, 10 km/6 mi north of the town, from 1788 until 1791, when he moved to

DU MAURIER, DAPHNE *English novelist Daphne Du Maurier, photographed in about 1930. Her popular period novels include* Jamaica Inn *(1936),* Rebecca *(1938), and* My Cousin Rachel *(1951). Her grandfather, George Du Maurier, was also a writer. Corbis*

Dumfries, where he worked as an exciseman until he died in 1796. The playwright JM Barrie was educated at the town's academy and is understood to have conceived *Peter Pan* at this time.

Two foot bridges and four traffic bridges span the river. Devorgilla's Bridge (1426) is the oldest and is now reserved for pedestrians.

Dumfries and Galloway

Unitary authority in southern Scotland, formed in 1996 from the regional council of the same name (1975–96)
Area 6,421 sq km/2,479 sq mi
Towns Annan, ◊Dumfries (administrative headquarters), Kirkcudbright, Stranraer, Castle Douglas, Newton Stewart
Physical area characterized by an indented coastline, including Luce Bay and Wigtown Bay, backed by a low-lying coastal strip of varying width; intensively forested in the Galloways. Much of the inland area is upland: east to west this includes Eskdalemuir (Hart Fell 808 m/2,651 ft), the Lowther Hills (Green Lowther 732 m/2,402 ft) and the Galloway Hills (the Merrick 843 m/2,766 ft)
Features Wanlockhead (the highest village in Scotland); the oldest working post office in the world at Sanquhar; Glen Trool National Park; Ruthwell Cross, Whithorn archaeological dig
Industries timber, chemicals, food processing
Agriculture beef and dairy cattle, sheep, forestry
Population (1995) 147,900.

Economy

Agriculture is the most important economic enterprise in the area, with poorer lands being intensively forested and better quality lands being intensively cropped or grazed. Tourism is also important, with many camping and caravan sites along the southern coast. The shortest ferry route to Ireland is via Stranraer.

Archaeology

There are Neolithic tombs and a wide range of later prehistoric sites at Burnswark; also at Burnswark and Birrens are Roman artefacts. Early Christian monuments include those at Whithorn and Ruthwell.

Architecture

There are many earthen mounds (mottes) for timber castles which testify to the Norman penetration of Scotland. Caerlaverock Castle is one of the foremost examples of medieval secular architecture in Scotland.

Environment

There are 93 Sites of Special Scientific Interest, five National Nature Reserves, four Ramsars (wetland sites), three Special Protection Areas, three Biosphere Reserves, and three National Scenic Areas.

Other features

The Galloway Hills provided the setting of John Buchan's *The Thirty-Nine Steps*. The region had a number of early innovators during the agricultural revolution, and has associations with Robert the Bruce, the poet Robert Burns, and the writer Thomas Carlyle.

Administrative history

Prior to 1975, the area was part of the counties of Wigtownshire, Kirkcudbrightshire and Dumfriesshire.

Dumfriesshire

Former county of southern Scotland, which was merged into two districts of Dumfries and Galloway region in 1975.

Dumfriesshire merged into the districts of Nithsdale, and Annandale and Eskdale in 1975. Dumfriesshire is now part of Dumfries and Galloway unitary authority.

Dunbar

Scene of Oliver ◊Cromwell's defeat of the Scots in 1650, now a port and resort in Lothian, Scotland. Torness nuclear power station is nearby.

Dunbar, William (*c.* 1460–*c.* 1520)

Scottish poet at the court of James IV. His poems include a political allegory, *The Thrissil and the Rois* written in 1503, celebrating James IV's marriage with Margaret Tudor, and the lament with the refrain 'Timor mortis conturbat me' printed in 1508.

Dunbar, Battles of

Two English victories over the Scots at Dunbar, now a port and resort in Lothian.

27 April 1296 defeat by John de Warenne, Earl of Surrey, of Scottish king John Balliol. The defeat all but ended Scottish resistance to Edward I. Edinburgh fell shortly after and in July John surrendered his throne to Edward and fled the country.

3 Sept 1650 crushing defeat by Oliver Cromwell of a Scottish army under David Leslie supporting Charles II. Combined with Charles's defeat at Worcester the following year, it effectively ended Scotland's independence of action.

Dunbartonshire

Former county of west central Scotland, bordering the north bank of the Clyde estuary, which merged into five districts of Strathclyde region in 1975.

Dunbartonshire merged into the districts of Dumbarton, Clydebank, Bearsden and Milngavie, Cumbernauld and Kilsyth, and Strathkelvin in 1975. It is now part of the unitary authority of Argyll and Bute and of two others which bear its name – East and West.

Dunblane

Town and former burgh in Stirling unitary authority, Scotland, 23 km/14 mi southwest of Crieff; population (1991) 7,400. Its long-established textiles industry specializes in the manufacture of knitwear. In March 1996 a lone gunman entered the local primary school, killing 16 infants and their teacher, and wounding 17 other children and a member of staff.

The massacre led to the banning of all privately held handguns in the United Kingdom and further tightening of the gun laws.

Duncan

Two Kings of Scotland.

Duncan I

He succeeded his grandfather, Malcolm II, as king in 1034,

but was defeated and killed by ◊Macbeth. He is the Duncan in Shakespeare's play *Macbeth* (1605).

Duncan II

Son of ◊Malcolm III and grandson of ◊Duncan I. He gained English and Norman help to drive out his uncle ◊Donald III in 1094. He ruled for a few months before being killed by agents of Donald, who then regained power. See genealogy on pages 278–279.

Dundas, Henry, 1st Viscount Melville (1742–1811)

Scottish Conservative politician. In 1791 he became home secretary and, with revolution raging in France, carried through the prosecution of the English and Scottish radicals. After holding other high cabinet posts, he was impeached in 1806 for corruption and, although acquitted on the main charge, held no further office.

Dundee

City in eastern Scotland, on the north side of the Firth of Tay, administrative headquarters of Dundee City unitary authority; authority area 62 sq km/24 sq mi; population (1996) 155,000. Industries include engineering, textiles, electronics, printing, and food processing. The city, which developed around the jute industry in the 19th century, is Scotland's fourth largest city.

Dundee rests on a gentle slope, rising from the Firth of Tay to a hill known as The Law (174 m/570 ft). The Tay estuary is 3 km/2 mi wide at this point and is easily navigable for large vessels.

There is a university (1967), developed from Queen's College (founded in 1881). Other notable buildings include the Albert Institute (1867) and Caird Hall. *Discovery*, the ship used by Robert Falcon Scott on his expedition to the Antarctic (1901–04) is moored on the Tay, to the west of the Tay road bridge. At Broughty Ferry, 5 km/3 mi to the east, is a 15th-century castle, with a museum documenting Dundee's 18th-century whaling industry.

Dunfermline

Industrial town north of the Firth of Forth in Fife, Scotland; population (1991) 55,100. Industries include engineering, electronics, and textiles. It was the ancient capital of Scotland, with many sites of royal historical significance. Many Scottish kings, including Robert the Bruce and Malcolm Canmore, are buried in **Dunfermline Abbey**.

Dunfermline was the birthplace of the industrialist and philanthropist Andrew Carnegie (1835–1919), who presented the city with Pittencrieff Park and Glen, a free library, and an annual income of £25,000. A royal 'square mile' includes a royal palace, a 12th-century abbey, and a royal burial site.

Dunfermline has had to overcome the economic downturn associated with the closure of the naval base at nearby Rosyth.

Dungannon

Market town in County Tyrone, Northern Ireland, 64 km/40 mi southwest of Belfast; population (1991) 8,300. It was the main seat of the O'Neill family, former kings of Ulster. Dungannon is now a retail centre with some fine Georgian terraces. Its industries include Tyrone crystal, mechanical engineering, meat processing, and food packaging.

Dungannon was a significant scene of conflict with the English crown during the 16th and 17th centuries.

Dungeness

Shingle headland on the south coast of Kent, southeast England, on the edge of ◊Romney Marsh. It has two nuclear power stations and two lighthouses, one operational and the other, now inland, turned into a museum. Other inland features include Denge Marsh, a bird sanctuary; and Derek Jarman's Garden, near the old lighthouse.

Dunkeld, House of

Royal house of the kingdom of Scotland 1030–1290. Despite its origins in the struggle between Duncan I and his cousin Macbeth and almost constant pressure from Anglo-Norman and Plantagenet England, the house of Dunkeld provided a series of strong and competent monarchs of Scotland. Among the more successful rulers were Malcolm III Canmore (1058–1093), William I the Lion (1165–1214), and Alexander II and his brother Alexander III (1249–1286), under whom medieval Scotland enjoyed something of a golden age.

See genealogy on pages 278–279.

Dunkery Beacon

Hill in Somerset, England, 519 m/1,705 ft high, the highest point on ◊Exmoor, with views across the Bristol Channel. Dunkery Beacon is owned by the National Trust.

Dunlop, John Boyd (1840–1921)

Scottish inventor who founded the rubber company that bears his name. In 1888, to help his child win a tricycle race, he bound an inflated rubber hose to the wheels. The same year he developed commercially practical pneumatic tyres, first patented by Robert William Thomson (1822–1873) in 1845 for bicycles and cars.

Dunlop was born in Dreghorn, Ayrshire, and studied veterinary medicine at Edinburgh University before setting up a practice in Ireland near Belfast, in 1867. He founded his own company for the mass production of tyres, and in 1896, after trading for only about five years, Dunlop sold both his patent and his business for £3 million.

Dunlop's first simple design consisted of a rubber inner tube, covered by a jacket of linen tape with an outer tread also of rubber. The inner tube was inflated using a football pump and the tyre was attached by flaps in the jacket which were rubber-cemented to the wheel. Later, he incorporated a wire through the edge of the tyre which secured it to the rim of the wheel.

Dunmow, Little

Village in Essex, eastern England, 4 km/2 mi southeast of Great Dunmow. It was the original scene of the **Dunmow Flitch** trial (dating from 1111), in which a side of bacon is presented to any couple who 'will swear that they have not quarrelled nor repented of their marriage within a year and a day after its celebration'. Couples are judged by a jury whose

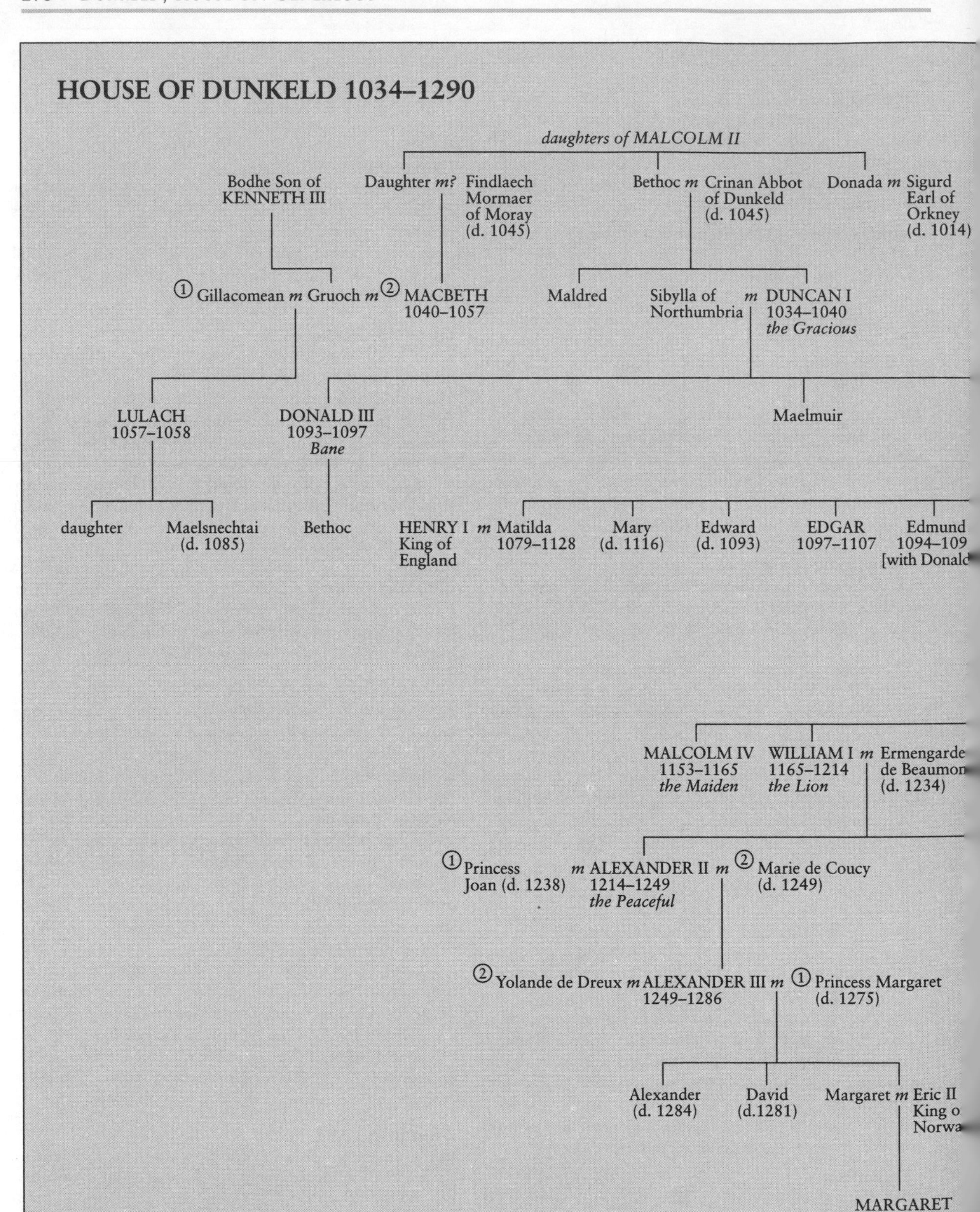
HOUSE OF DUNKELD 1034–1290
daughters of MALCOLM II
Bodhe Son of KENNETH III
Daughter m? Findlaech Mormaer of Moray (d. 1045)
Bethoc m Crinan Abbot of Dunkeld (d. 1045)
Donada m Sigurd Earl of Orkney (d. 1014)
① Gillacomean m Gruoch m ② MACBETH 1040–1057
Maldred
Sibylla of Northumbria m DUNCAN I 1034–1040 the Gracious
LULACH 1057–1058
DONALD III 1093–1097 Bane
Maelmuir
daughter
Maelsnechtai (d. 1085)
Bethoc
HENRY I King of England m Matilda 1079–1128
Mary (d. 1116)
Edward (d. 1093)
EDGAR 1097–1107
Edmund 1094–109
[with Donald
MALCOLM IV 1153–1165 the Maiden
WILLIAM I 1165–1214 the Lion m Ermengarde de Beaumon (d. 1234)
① Princess Joan (d. 1238) m ALEXANDER II 1214–1249 the Peaceful m ② Marie de Coucy (d. 1249)
② Yolande de Dreux m ALEXANDER III 1249–1286 m ① Princess Margaret (d. 1275)
Alexander (d. 1284)
David (d.1281)
Margaret m Eric II King o Norwa
MARGARET 1286–1290 the Maid of Norw

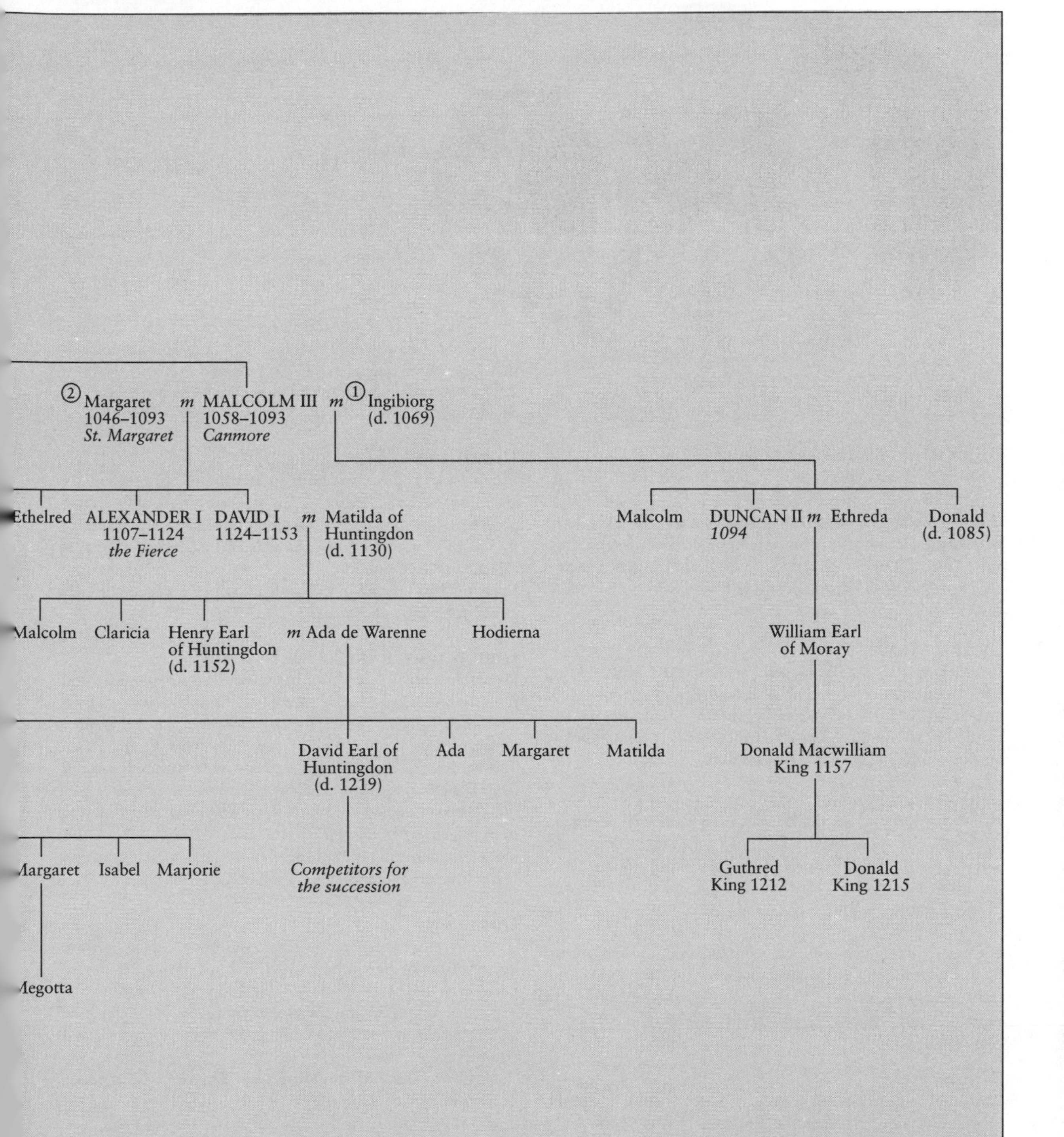

From 1058 the House of Dunkeld was also known as the House of Canmore (after Malcolm III). The descendants of David Earl of Huntingdon included both the House of Balliol and the House of Bruce.

Dunlop, John Boyd *An 1887 photograph of John Boyd Dunlop demonstrating an early pneumatic tyre. Though he had not invented the pneumatic tyre, he was the first to successfully develop the concept. Linda Proud*

members are all unmarried. The trial, which is carried out every four years, now takes place at Great Dunmow.

Dunn, Douglas (Eaglesham) (1942–)

Scottish poet and short-story writer. His first book of verse, *Terry Street* (1969), mainly reflected working-class life. *Elegies* (1985), recalling his wife's death from cancer in 1981, won the Whitbread Book of the Year award. A recent more substantial collection is *Dante's Drum Kit* (1993). Short stories with a variety of Scottish situations and settings are in *Secret Villages* (1985) and *Boyfriends and Girlfriends* (1995).

Dunnet Head

Rocky peninsula in Highland unitary authority, Scotland, and the northernmost point on mainland Britain. It rises to a height of 127 m/417 ft; a lighthouse stands below this viewpoint to the west. The small village of Dunnet lies below on the southeast shore of **Dunnet Bay**.

Dunoon

Holiday resort and former burgh in Argyll and Bute unitary authority, Scotland, on the Firth of Clyde, at the southwest end of the Cowal peninsula, 45 km/28 mi northwest of Glasgow; population (1991) 9,000. On its north side lies ⇨Holy Loch, which until 1992 was the site of a US nuclear submarine base.

Over 1,000 pipers converge on Dunoon for the annual Cowal Gathering. Local antiquities include the ruins of a castle, and a monument to Mary Campbell, the heroine of Robert Burns' poem 'Highland Mary', who was born in Dunoon.

Dunrossness

Southernmost peninsula and parish of Mainland, in the Shetland Islands, Scotland; population (1991) 2,000. The parish incorporates Fair Isle. On the tip of the peninsula lies Jarlshof, an impressive archaeological site displaying layers of settlement from Bronze Age to medieval times.

St Ninian's Isle, joined to the western shore by a spit of sand, was the hiding-place of an ancient treasure trove unearthed in 1958. The area is referred to as the Ness by Shetlanders.

Duns

Town and former burgh in Scottish Borders unitary authority, Scotland, 24 km/15 mi west of Berwick-on-Tweed; population (1991) 2,400. Destroyed in 1545, the town was rebuilt on its present site from 1588, and later became the county capital of former Berwickshire.

In 1639 the Covenanters camped on the hilltop of Duns Law. John Duns Scotus, a Franciscan monk and theologian who taught in Paris, is believed to have been born in Duns about 1265. Criticism of his teachings brought about the derogatory term 'dunce'.

Dunsinane

Elevation of the Sidlaw Hills in Perth and Kinross unitary authority, Scotland, rising 15 km/9 mi northeast of Perth to a height of 308 m/1,010 ft. On its summit lie the remains of 'Macbeth's Castle', where Siward, Earl of Northumbria, is reputed to have defeated Macbeth in 1054. The playwright William Shakespeare produced a dramatic version of the event in his tragedy *Macbeth*.

Duns Scotus, John (*c.* 1265–*c.* 1308)

Scottish monk, a leading figure in the theological and philosophical system of medieval scholasticism, which attempted to show that Christian doctrine was compatible with the ideas of the Greek philosophers Aristotle and Plato. The church rejected his ideas, and the word **dunce** is derived from Dunses, a term of ridicule applied to his followers.

In the medieval controversy over universals he advocated nominalism, maintaining that classes of things have no independent reality. He belonged to the Franciscan order, and was known as *Doctor Subtilis* (the Subtle Teacher).

Dunstable

Town in southwest Bedfordshire, southern England, at the northern end of the Chiltern Hills; 48 km/30 mi northwest of London; population (1991) 49,700. Industries include printing, engineering, communication technology, and the manufacture of paper, cement, plastic and rubber mouldings, and commercial vehicles.

Nearby to the south, on **Dunstable Downs**, is Whipsnade Wild Animal Park.

In 1533 Archbishop Thomas Cranmer annulled the marriage of Henry VIII and Catherine of Aragon in the church of Dunstable's Augustinian priory. Founded by Henry I in the early 12th century, the priory is reputedly the scene of the first mystery play, or miracle play, performed in England in the Middle Ages. The church of St Peter still contains much of the original priory church including the original Norman nave. Until 1643 Dunstable possessed an Eleanor Cross, a memorial to ◊Eleanor of Castile. During the 18th century Dunstable was a coaching town, and noted for the manufacture of straw hats.

The headquarters of the London Gliding Club were established on the nearby Dunstable Downs in 1930.

Dunstable, John (*c.* 1385–1453)

English composer of songs and anthems. He is considered one of the founders of Renaissance harmony.

Dunstaffnage

Ruined castle in Argyll and Bute unitary authority, Scotland, on Loch Etive, 4 km/2.5 mi northeast of Oban. It is traditionally believed to be the royal seat of the ancient Dalriadan kings of Scotland, and held the Stone of Destiny (the Scottish throne) before its removal to ◊Scone. Dunstaffnage was captured by Robert (I) the Bruce in 1308, and became the stronghold of the Campbells and Macdougals.

During the Jacobite risings of 1715 and 1745 it formed an English military station. Flora Macdonald, the Scottish heroine who rescued Prince Charles Edward Stuart, was imprisoned in the fortress in 1746.

The Duke of Argyll is the hereditary keeper of the castle; Campbell of Dunstaffnage is the hereditary captain.

Dunstanburgh Castle

Ruined castle on the Northumberland coast, England, 11 km/7 mi northeast of Alnwick. It is the largest castle in Northumbria, and served as an outpost of the Lancastrian side during the Wars of the Roses.

Dunstanburgh Castle was built in 1316 by Thomas, Earl of Lancaster, and later enlarged by John of Gaunt. The site is geologically interesting, as the point where the Whin Sill (the rock system on which Hadrian's Wall is built) reaches the coast in basalt cliffs. The quartz crystals found in the area are called 'Dunstanburgh diamonds'.

Dunstan, St (924–988)

English priest and politician, archbishop of Canterbury from 960. He was abbot of Glastonbury from 945, and made it a centre of learning. He became bishop of Worcester in 957 and of London in 959. Feast day 19 May.

Dunwich

Fishing village on the eastern coast of Suffolk, England, 7 km/4 mi southwest of Southwold; population (1991) 130. In the early Middle Ages Dunwich was the capital of the kingdom of ◊Mercia and a thriving seaport with a bishop's seat and a king's palace, but the site of the former town is now underwater, and the sea continues to encroach on the land. Immediately to the south of Dunwich lies the Minsmere bird reserve.

Dunwoody, (Thomas) Richard (1964–)

Northern Irish jockey who has ridden more winners in British National Hunt than any other jockey except for Peter ◊Scudamore. The champion jockey three seasons in a row, 1992/93–94/95, he won all the leading races including the Grand National in 1986 and 1994, the Cheltenham Gold Cup in 1988, and the Champion Hurdle in 1990.

DUP

Acronym for the ◊Democratic Unionist Party.

Duran Duran

English synth-pop band, led by singer Simon Le Bon (1958–), whose hit singles included 'Rio' (1982) and 'Is There Something I Should Know?' (1983).

Durham

City and administrative headquarters of the county of Durham, northeast England, on the River Wear, 19 km/12 mi south of Newcastle-upon-Tyne; population (1991) 36,900. Formerly a centre for the coalmining industry (the last pit closed in 1993), the city now has light engineering industries and manufactures textiles, carpets, and clothing.

Features

Durham has a fine Norman cathedral and the remains of a castle built in 1072 by William I. The cathedral and castle are together a World Heritage Site. Other features include the university's Gulbenkian Museum of Oriental Art and Archaeology (1960), the UK's only museum wholly devoted to the subject, and the annual Miners' Gala. The university was founded in 1832.

Cathedral and castle

Durham Cathedral and castle are situated on a 30 m/98 ft-high sandstone hill which forms a peninsula surrounded on three sides by the River Wear. According to tradition, Bishop Aldhun and his community of monks from Lindisfarne brought the uncorrupted body of St Cuthbert (died 687) here from Chester-Le-Street in 995, guided by a girl looking for her lost dun cow. They established a church to serve as St Cuthbert's shrine, which became a place of pilgrimage for Saxons and Normans. The site was then called **Dunholme**, or 'hill island'. Little remains of the original Saxon cathedral.

The present Cathedral was begun in 1093 by Bishop William of St Carileph and remains largely as he conceived it. It was one of the earliest vaulted cathedrals in Europe and the first to employ rib vaults. These, combined with massive cylindrical piers, strikingly ornamented, create one of the most impressive of all English cathedrals.

The interior is as originally built except for the choir. The nave, built from 1104 to 1128 and vaulted by 1135, contains some of the earliest pointed arches used in vaulting. From 1242 to 1280 the Norman east end was replaced with the unusual Chapel of Nine Altars, and the chancel, except for its aisles, was revaulted at the same time. The culmination of building at Durham also produced the visual climax, the tall Perpendicular crossing tower, built from 1465 to 1490.

The cathedral housed a Benedictine monastery in its precincts until 1540. Its former dormitory, now used as a library and museum, contains the Cuthbert relics, including the oldest needlework in England, a stole and maniple presented to St Cuthbert's shrine by King Athelstan in 934. In the Galilee Chapel is the tomb of the Venerable Bede, historian and monk of Jarrow.

The castle, situated on Palace Green opposite the cathedral, was the palace of the bishops of Durham until it was transferred to the new Durham University in 1836, when the bishops moved their home to the palace at Bishop Auckland. The university now occupies most of the castle buildings, and the keep is a student hall of residence. Other features include the kitchen, built in 1499; the Black Staircase, added by Bishop Cosin in the 1665; and the Norman chapel dating from about 1080. The Great Hall was originally built in Norman times but the present structure was built by Bishop Hatfield in the early 14th century.

The building nearest the castle gate, now part of the university library, was once the exchequer built by Bishop Neville in 1450. Nearby is the library built by Bishop Cosin in 1669. On the opposite side are the 17th-century almshouses, now lecture rooms, also built by Bishop Cosin.

Durham

County of northeast England (since April 1997 Darlington has been a separate unitary authority)

Area 2,232 sq km/862 sq mi

Towns and cities Durham (administrative headquarters), Newton Aycliffe, Peterlee, Chester-le-Street

Physical Pennine Hills; rivers Wear and Tees

Features Beamish open-air industrial museum; site of one of Britain's richest coalfields (pits no longer functioning); Bowes Museum; Barnard Castle; Durham Cathedral; University of Durham, (1832) housed in Durham Castle; dales in the west of the county

Industries clothing; chemicals; iron and steel processing; light engineering industries; quarrying; cement; pharmaceuticals

Agriculture sheep; dairy produce; hill farming

Population (1995 est) 492,900.

History Between 1071 and 1836, Durham was a Palatinate county, that is the Bishop of Durham exercised such jurisdiction over the territory as in other counties belonged to the sovereign.

Topography

County Durham extends from the North Sea west to the Pennines between the rivers Tyne and Tees. It is bounded on the north by Northumberland, and Tyne and Wear; on the west by Cumbria; and on the south North Yorkshire, Stockton-on-Tees, and Hartlepool. East of the River Wear, Durham occupies a low plateau (100–120 m/328–394 ft above sea-level) with a coast lined by cliffs. The rock here is magnesian limestone, which is covered by glacial deposits. Seams of coal, which are underneath the limestone in the east, form the surface rock in the centre of the county, covered only by deposits from post-glacial lakes. Coal seams are also found in the west of the county.

The county Palatinate

County Durham was made a county Palatinate in 1071 because of its strategic position on the then main route to Scotland and its distance from the English government in London. The bishops fortified an outcrop on a loop of the River Wear at Durham, and built an imposing cathedral there. From here they repelled, generally successfully, a series of Scottish incursions during the 12–14th centuries. Hartlepool was the bishops' port, Bishop Auckland their country residence, and the 'forest' of Weardale their hunting ground.

Industrial past

Until the 18th century, lead and coal were worked on a very small scale. Long wagonways were built from the north of the county to the River Tyne in the late 18th century, facilitating exports. From 1825 coal was transported by railway from southwest Durham to the Tees. Both the coal from the west of the county, used to produce coke, and that from the north and centre of the county, used for steam engines, were in great demand. The number of mines grew, until even the coal concealed beneath the limestone in the east of the county was being mined by the late 19th century. From 1801 to 1921 the population rose tenfold as mining villages of 500–10,000 people spread across the county.

The largest firms were the Consett steelworks (closed in 1980) and the engineering and railway workshops at Darlington. By the 1920s the demand for coal was falling and the older pits in the west and centre of the county were becoming more expensive to work. In these areas postwar rationalization led to a rundown of coal production. Government

DURHAM *The nave of Durham Cathedral, England. Dating from the 12th century, Durham Cathedral is one of the finest examples of Norman architecture. This picture clearly shows two typical features of the Norman style, massive piers, and round arches. Corbis*

regional policies encouraged light engineering, electrical, and clothing factories on industrial estates across the coalfield, especially in the centre and east of the county. Housing was improved, and new towns built at Peterlee (designated in 1948) and Newton Aycliffe (1947). Many people now work outside the county in the industrial areas on Tyneside and ◊Teesside.

Durrell, Gerald (Malcolm) (1925–1995)

English naturalist, writer, and zoo curator. He became director of Jersey Zoological Park in 1958, and wrote 37 books, including the humorous memoir *My Family and Other Animals* (1956). He was the brother of the writer Lawrence Durrell.

Critical of the conditions in which most zoos kept animals, the lack of interest in breeding programmes, and the concentration on large species Durrell founded the Jersey Zoological Park. Through his work in conservation – within his zoo and as chair of the Flora and Fauna Preservation Society – and perhaps more particularly his many books and television programmes, Durrell encouraged and inspired a whole generation of naturalists, zoologists, and zoo keepers.

Durrell also set up an international training centre near the zoo, which is now the world's foremost centre for training animal keepers.

Durrell, Lawrence (George) (1912–1990)

British novelist and poet. He lived mainly in the eastern Mediterranean, the setting of his novels, including the Alexandria Quartet: *Justine*, *Balthazar*, *Mountolive*, and *Clea* (1957–60). He also wrote travel books, including *Bitter Lemons* (1957) about Cyprus.

He began writing prolifically in the late 1930s, and published several novels, and many volumes of verse, including *Collected Poems* (1968) but commercial and critical success came in the late 1950s with the publication of the Alexandria Quartet.

His heady prose and bizarre characters reflect his exotic sources of inspiration. He was the brother of the naturalist Gerald Durrell.

Dyck, Anthony van (1599–1641)

Flemish painter. He was an assistant to Rubens from 1618 to 1620, then worked briefly in England at the court of James I before moving to Italy in 1622. In 1627 he returned to his native Antwerp, where he continued to paint religious works and portraits.

Living in England from 1632, by invitation of Charles I, he produced numerous portraits of the royal family and English aristocracy, such as *Charles I on Horseback* (about 1638; National Gallery, London). His refinement of style and colour, and dignity of composition, left a profound impression on subsequent portraiture in England. The portrait of Charles I, now in the Louvre, and the many memorable works still in the Royal Collection, are distinct creations and, despite the large extent to which van Dyck employed studio assistants, never fall into superficiality. His landscape studies (British Museum) anticipate John Constable in conveying the atmosphere of the English countryside.

He was knighted by Charles I in 1632.

Dyfed

Former county of southwest Wales, created in 1974 and, in 1996, divided between the unitary authorities of ◊Carmarthenshire, ◊Ceredigion, and ◊Pembrokeshire.

Ealing

Outer borough of west Greater London

Features 18th-century Pitshanger Manor; Gunnersbury House and Gunnersbury Park, both Regency-style houses; ◊Ealing Studios(1931), the first British sound-film studios; Hoover factory (1932), now a supermarket

Industries engineering, chemicals

Population (1991) 283,600.

Ealing Studios

British film-producing company headed by Michael ◊Balcon (1937–58). The studio made a distinctive series of comedies, which had an understated, self-deprecating humour, such as *Passport to Pimlico*, *Kind Hearts and Coronets*, *Whisky Galore!* (all 1949), *The Man in the White Suit* (1951), and *The Ladykillers* (1955).

The studios also made movies in other genres, such as the crime thriller *The Blue Lamp* (1950) and the war story *The Cruel Sea* (1952). In 1994 film production began again at Ealing after an interval of nearly 40 years.

earl

In the British ◊peerage, the third title in order of rank, coming between marquess and viscount; it is the oldest of British titles, deriving from the Anglo-Saxon post of ealdorman. For some time earls were called counts, and their wives are still called countesses.

Earl Marshal (Anglo-Saxon mearh 'horse', sceale 'groom')

In England, one of the great officers of state. The king's marshal early became one of the chief officers of state, and, under the Norman and Plantagenet kings, a judge in the Courts of Chivalry. The Earl Marshal is now head of the ◊College of Arms, through which he regulates all matters connected with armorial bearings and standards, and controls the arrangements for state functions. The office has been hereditary since 1672 in the family of Howard, the dukes of Norfolk. In Scotland a similar dignity was hereditary in the family of Keith from the 14th century until 1716.

Early English

In architecture, the first of the three periods of the English Gothic style, late 12th century to late 13th century. It is characterized by tall, elongated windows (lancets) without mullions (horizontal bars), often grouped in threes, fives, or sevens; the pointed arch; pillars of stone centres surrounded by shafts of black Purbeck marble; and dog-tooth (zig-zag) ornament. Salisbury Cathedral (begun in 1220) is almost entirely Early English.

Most of Wells Cathedral, including the west front, and Lincoln Cathedral, except for the choir and west front, were built in the Early English style. Other examples include the west fronts of Peterborough and Ripon cathedrals; the choirs of Lichfield, Southwark, Southwell and Worcester cathedrals; the nave of York Minster; and the 'Chapel of the Nine Altars' at Durham Cathedral.

The choirs of Westminster Abbey and of the Temple Church in London, and the choir and transepts of Beverley Minster are also Early English.

Easington

Town in County Durham, England, 14 km/9 mi south of Sunderland; population (1991) 95,700. Easington was a centre of extensive coal mining in the region, but the colliery here was closed in the 1980s.

Because the coal seams at Easington and the surrounding area lie beneath thick strata of limestone, mining did not begin here until the 1820s; it reached its peak in the early 20th century. The mine galleries of Easington pit extended far out under the North Sea.

East Anglia

Region of eastern England, formerly a Saxon kingdom, including Norfolk, Suffolk, and parts of Essex and Cambridgeshire. Norwich is the principal city of East Anglia. The Sainsbury Centre for Visual Arts, opened in 1978 at the University of East Anglia, has a collection of ethnographic art and sculpture. East Anglian ports such as Harwich and Felixstowe have greatly developed as trade with the rest of Europe has increased.

East Ayrshire

Unitary authority in southwest Scotland, created in 1996 from two districts of Strathclyde region
Area 1,269 sq km/490 sq mi
Towns ◊Kilmarnock (administrative headquarters), Cumnock, Stewarton, Galston, Crosshouse
Physical predominantly low lying and undulating in the north, mountainous toward the south; Loch Doon; rivers Ayr, Irvine; Blackcraig Hill (700 m/2,298 ft); Loudoun Hill
Features Burns' House Museum, Mauchline; Loudoun Castle Theme Park; Dunaskin Heritage Museum
Industries textiles, light engineering, food and drink, printing
Agriculture dairy farming, sheep, beef cattle
Population (1995) 123,100.
History at Loudoun Hill, Robert the Bruce defeated 6,000 of the Earl of Pembroke's men with a force of 600 in 1306.

Economy

Agriculture is an important industry in a predominantly rural area. However, the area is most notable for its economic problems which is particularly evident in the many rural towns which have lost their traditional industrial base of mining or textile production.

Environment

There are 15 Sites of Special Scientific Interest and one country park.

Administrative history

The districts of Cumnock and Doon Valley, and Kilmarnock and Loudoun were merged to form East Ayrshire in 1996. Prior to 1975, this area was part of the county of Ayrshire.

Eastbourne

Seaside resort in East Sussex, southeast England, 103 km/64 mi southeast of London; population (1991) 94,800. Originally a small village, Eastbourne developed in the mid-19th century as a resort and model of town planning under the direction of the 7th Duke of Devonshire. The modern town, which extends along the coast for 5 km/3 mi, has become a popular place for retirement.

To the east the South Downs terminate in ◊Beachy Head.

Eastbourne was originally the four hamlets of East Bourne, Southbourne, Sea Houses, and Meads. The Transitional Norman St Mary's Church, built in the 12th century in the old village of Eastbourne, lies about 2 km/1 mi inland. The resort has terraced promenades, tree-lined streets, theatres, winter gardens, and golfing facilities. The Carpet Gardens have been established for more than a century. Tennis tournaments are held at Devonshire Park, and other features include the pier, opened in 1872; and a bandstand, built to seat over 3,000 spectators. The Lifeboat Museum illustrates the work of Eastbourne's sea-rescue service.

East Dunbartonshire

Unitary authority in central Scotland, created in 1996 from two districts of Strathclyde region
Area 175 sq km/67 sq mi
Towns Kirkintilloch (administrative headquarters), Bearsden, Milngavie
Physical low-lying lands to the south give way dramatically to the Campsie Fells in the north; Earl's Seat (578 m/1,896 ft); River Kelvin
Features Forth and Clyde Canal; Antonine Wall
Population (1995) 111,100.

Economy

The area is an affluent commuter belt for the city of Glasgow. Smaller industrialized villages, such as Croy, are also evident.

Environment

There are four Sites of Special Scientific Interest and one country park.

Administrative history

The districts of Bearsden and Milngavie, and Strathkelvin were merged into East Dunbartonshire in 1996. Prior to 1975 the area was part of the county of Dunbartonshire.

EastEnders

Drama serial produced by the BBC. See ◊soap operas.

Easter Rising, or Easter Rebellion

In Irish history, a republican insurrection that began on Easter Monday, April 1916, in Dublin. It was inspired by the Irish Republican Brotherhood (IRB) in an unsuccessful attempt to overthrow British rule in Ireland. It was led by Patrick Pearce of the IRB and James Connolly of Sinn Féin.

Arms from Germany intended for the IRB were intercepted but the rising proceeded regardless with the seizure of the Post Office and other buildings in Dublin by 1,500 volunteers. The rebellion was crushed by the British Army within five days, both sides suffering major losses: 220 civilians, 64 rebels, and 134 members of the Crown Forces were killed during the uprising. Pearce, Connolly, and about a dozen rebel leaders were subsequently executed in Kilmainham Jail. Others, including Éamon de Valera, were spared due to US public opinion, to be given amnesty in June 1917.

> *... establish such a politie of civil and military power and create and secure a large revenue ... as may be the foundation of a large, well-grounded sure English dominion in India for all time to come.*
>
> East India Company
> Letter from the East India Company, London, to its agent in Surat 1687

East India Company (British)

Commercial company (1600–1858) chartered by Queen Elizabeth I and given a monopoly of trade between England and the Far East. In the 18th century, the company became, in effect, the ruler of a large part of India, and a form of dual control by the company and a committee responsible to Parliament in London was introduced by Pitt's India Act 1784. The end of the monopoly of China trade came in 1834, and after the ◊Indian Mutiny of 1857 the crown took complete control of the government of British India. The India Act 1858 abolished the company.

By 1652 there were some 23 English factories in India. Bombay came to the British crown in 1662, and was granted to the East India Company for £10 a year. The British victory in the Battle of Plassey in 1757 gave the company control of Bengal. See also ◊British Empire.

East Kilbride

Town in South Lanarkshire, Scotland; population (1991) 70,400. It was designated a ◊new town in 1947 to take overspill from Glasgow, 11 km/7 mi to the northeast. It is the site of the National Engineering Laboratory and headquarters of British Energy. There are various light industries, including electrical equipment and electronics, and some engineering, including jet engines (Rolls Royce).

Eastleigh

Town in Hampshire, England, 8 km/5 mi north of Southampton; population (1991) 26,500. The Ford Motor Company has a large commercial-vehicle plant on the Eastleigh–Southampton boundary. Other industries include cable manufacture, light engineering, and the production of pharmaceuticals and confectionery. On the outskirts of the town lies Southampton (Eastleigh) Airport, which has regular services to the Channel Islands.

Eastleigh developed around the London–Southampton railway line in the 19th century, growing into the principal carriage and locomotive works of the Southern Railway. With the shrinkage of the rail network in the late 20th century, railway-related work decreased.

The first flight of the World War II fighter plane Supermarine Spitfire took place at Eastleigh aerodrome in 1936.

East Lothian

Unitary authority in southeast Scotland which was previously a district within Lothian region (1975–96) and a county until 1974

Area 677 sq km/261 sq mi

Towns ◊Haddington (administrative headquarters), North Berwick, Dunbar

Physical area of contrasts, with coastal plains of cliffs, beaches and estuarine marines, broad river valley of the Tyne, volcanic outcrops (Bass Rock, Traprain Law) and gentle slopes of the Lammermuir Hills

Features Tantallon Castle; Muirfield golf course; Traprain Law fort

Industries whisky distilling, agricultural-based

Agriculture arable farming on plains

Population (1995) 87,600.

History

Traprain Law (221 m/725 ft), a hill of volcanic origin near East Linton, had the most important native stronghold site of the Iron Age in Scotland. A hoard of 4th-century Roman silver coins was found here in 1919 (now in Edinburgh's Museum of Antiquities).

Economy

It is an affluent area with a mixed economy. The western towns are within the Edinburgh commuter belt, with agricultural economies to the south, and tourist-based and service sector enterprise by the coast.

Environment

There are 21 Sites of Special Scientific Interest, one Special Protection Area, and one country park.

Administrative history

The county of East Lothian was more extensive than the present unitary authority to the east, but less extensive to the west.

East Renfrewshire

Unitary authority in central Scotland, created in 1996 from part of Renfrew district in Strathclyde region

Area 174 sq km/67 sq mi

Towns Barrhead, Giffnock (administrative headquarters), Newton Mearns, Clarkston

Physical low-lying plateau rising from the plain of the River Clyde

Industries engineering, cotton textiles

Agriculture sheep, rough grazing, some dairy farming

Population (1995) 88,200.

Economy

There is a sharp contrast between the eastern affluent commuter zone, which is bound into Glasgow's economy, and the de-industrializing Barrhead area. The agricultural lands in the south are of marginal capability.

Environment

There are four Sites of Special Scientific Interest.

Administrative history

Prior to 1975, the area was part of the county of Renfrewshire.

East Riding of Yorkshire

Unitary authority in northern England created in 1996 from part of the former county of Humberside

Area 2,416 sq km/933 sq mi

Towns ◊Beverley (administrative headquarters), Driffield, Goole, Hornsea, Bridlington

Features Humber Estuary to south of authority; North Sea to east; Flamborough Head chalk cliffs; Spurn Head – dynamic spit at mouth of estuary; River Hull; River Ouse; Holderness Peninsula; The Wolds; Hornsea Mere; Beverley Minster (13th century); All Saints Tower (34 m/110 ft) at Driffield; Sledmere House – 18th century mansion with grounds laid out by Capability Brown; Rudstone has Britain's tallest standing stone (8 m/25 ft); Sewerby Hall (Bridlington) – Georgian mansion including museum dedicated to the aviator Amy Johnson (1903–1941); Hornsea Pottery; Withernsea Lighthouse (39 m/127 ft) including museum.

Industries chemicals, pottery, agriculture, agricultural machinery and services, passenger vehicle components, bakery products

Population (1996) 310,000.

Administrative history

Prior to 1974 the area was one of four divisions of Yorkshire.

East Sussex

County of southeast England, created in 1974, formerly part of Sussex (since April 1997 Brighton and Hove has been a separate unitary authority)

Area 1,725 sq mi sq km/666 sq mi

Towns ◊Lewes (administrative headquarters), Newhaven (cross-channel port), Eastbourne, Rye, Winchelsea; Bexhill-on-Sea, Hastings, St Leonards, Seaford (all coastal resorts)

Physical Beachy Head, highest headland on the south coast (180 m/590 ft), the eastern end of the ◊South Downs; the Weald (including Ashdown Forest); Friston Forest; rivers Cuckmere, Ouse, and East Rother (which flows into the sea near Rye); Romney Marsh

Features the 'Long Man' chalk hill figure at Wilmington, near Eastbourne; prehistoric earthworks; Iron Age hillfort at Mount Caburn, near Lewes; Roman villas; Herstmonceux, with a 15th-century castle (conference and exhibition centre) and adjacent modern buildings, site of the Greenwich Royal Observatory (1958–90); other castles at Hastings, Lewes, Pevensey, and Bodiam; Bayham Abbey; Battle Abbey and the site of the Battle of Hastings; Michelham Priory; Sheffield Park garden; University of Sussex at Falmer, near Brighton, founded in 1961

Industries electronics; gypsum; light engineering; timber

Agriculture cereals; hops; fruit and vegetables; fishing (at Hastings)

Population (1995) 482,800

History Two important events that took place in the county are the Battle of ◊Hastings in 1066, and the Battle of ◊Lewes in 1264.

Topography

East Sussex is bounded on the south by the English Channel; on the west by Brighton and Hove and West Sussex; and on the north by Surrey and Kent. It is still one of the most wooded counties in England. Along the South Downs, which lie generally within 15 km/9 mi of the sea, runs the South Downs Way, from Beachy Head through East and West Sussex to the Hampshire border; high points along its path include ◊Ditchling Beacon (248 m/814 ft). The Weald is now a dairy farming area; until the 17th century its iron industry was nationally important. The Ashdown Forest was originally a Norman hunting forest; attempts to cultivate the land have failed because of the forest's sterile soil.

Eastwood

Town in Nottinghamshire, England, 14 km/9 mi northwest of Nottingham; population (1991) 12,400. Formerly a coal-mining town, Eastwood was the birthplace of the novelist and poet ◊D H Lawrence; a museum dedicated to the writer was opened here in 1976.

Ebbw Vale, Welsh Glyn Ebwy

Town and administrative centre of ◊Blaenau Gwent unitary authority, southeast Wales; population (1991) 19,500. It was formerly a coalmining town with iron and steel industries, which ended in the 1970s; tin-plate manufacture and engineering have continued. To the east is Blaenavon, where the Big Pit, although no longer working, is a tourist attraction.

Ecclefechan

Village in Dumfries and Galloway unitary authority, Scotland, 8 km/5 mi north of Annan; population (1991) 800. The essayist and social historian Thomas Carlyle was born and buried in the town.

Eccles

Town in Greater Manchester, northwest England, on the River Irwell and the Manchester Ship and Bridgewater canals, 8 km/5 mi west of Manchester; population (1991) 36,000. Industries include the manufacture of cotton textiles, machinery, and chemicals. **Eccles cakes**, rounded pastries with a dried fruit filling, originated here.

ecclesiastical law

Church law. In England, the Church of England has special ecclesiastical courts to administer church law. Each diocese has a consistory court with a right of appeal to the Court of Arches (in the archbishop of Canterbury's jurisdiction) or the Chancery Court of York (in the archbishop of York's jurisdiction). They deal with the constitution of the Church of England, church property, the clergy, services, doctrine, and practice. These courts have no influence on churches of other denominations, which are governed by the usual laws of contract and trust.

economic activity

The production and distribution of goods and services to satisfy the wants and needs of consumers and other businesses.

EAST SUSSEX *The Seven Sisters are a dramatic succession of chalk headlands that lie on the English Channel east of the East Sussex resort of Eastbourne. The strenuous walk along these exposed clifftops involves a series of sharp descents and climbs. Corel*

In the UK, economic activity is primarily based on private enterprise, which accounts for about 75% of total output in the whole economy, and over two-thirds of total employment.

Economic activity rate

The economic activity rate of a country is the proportion of the population who are in work or looking for work (that is, in the labour force). In recent years, the economic activity rate in the UK has been increasing, and although there was a slight fall in the early 1990s, the economic activity rate in the UK is much higher than the average in the European Community. Figures from 1997 show that of those aged 16 and over, 75% of men and 53% of women are economically active. Women now comprise 44% of all those in employment in Britain. As in other industrialized countries, there has been a marked shift in jobs from manufacturing to service industries. In the last 40 years the numbers employed in the service industries have more than doubled, with significant increases in areas such as business activities, distribution, hotels and restaurants, education, medical services, and social work (although employment numbers have fallen in some areas such as the civil service, defence, and banking).

Manufacturing base and unemployment

In most other sectors of economic activity, that is, in the primary and secondary industries, such as manufacturing, construction, agriculture, mining, and energy and water supply industries, levels of employment have fallen dramatically. This is especially the case in the traditional manufacturing industries such as steel and shipbuilding, which have suffered significant falls, while employment in the mining industries has been reduced by 38% in the 1990s. By 1997, the nation's manufacturing base accounted for only 18% of its workforce, compared with 42% in 1955.

Britain's basic problem in the latter part of the 20th century has been the structural weakness of its industrial sector resulting from low productivity, lack of growth, and the decay of many of its primary and secondary industries – such as coal, steel, shipbuilding, textiles, engineering, and car manufacture. Since these industries were all labour-intensive, their decline has led to a long-term unemployment problem.

ecstasy, or MDMA

Illegal drug in increasing use from the 1980s; according to 1996 government figures, 800,000 young people in the UK have tried the drug. The Home Office estimated that 10% of 14–19 year olds have experimented with it, and nearly half have been offered it. It is estimated that around 1 million ecstasy tablets were consumed weekly by January 1997, and users numbered 0.5 million. The annual death rate through ecstasy is six per year. Most of these deaths have been at clubs or raves where dehydration and over-heating has been a major factor.

Ecstasy is a modified amphetamine with mild psychedelic effects, and works by depleting serotonin (a neurotransmitter) in the brain. Its long-term effects are unknown, but animal experiments have shown brain damage.

Eddington, Arthur Stanley (1882–1944)

English astrophysicist. He studied the motions, equilibrium, luminosity, and atomic structure of the stars. In 1919 his observation of stars during a solar eclipse confirmed Albert Einstein's prediction that light is bent when passing near the Sun, in accordance with the general theory of relativity. In *The Expanding Universe* (1933) Eddington expressed the theory that in the spherical universe the outer galaxies or spiral nebulae are receding from one another.

Eddington discovered the fundamental role of radiation pressure in the maintenance of stellar equilibrium, explained the method by which the energy of a star moves from its interior to its exterior, and in 1924 showed that the luminosity of a star depends almost exclusively on its mass – a discovery that caused a complete revision of contemporary ideas on stellar evolution.

Eddington, Paul born Paul Clark-Eddington (1927–1995)

English actor. He joined the Bristol Old Vic Company in 1962 and played many roles there and in the West End before he starred in the BBC television situation comedy *The Good Life* (1975–78). Perhaps his most memorable role was as Jim

EDDYSTONE LIGHTHOUSE *in the English Channel 22 km/14 mi south of Plymouth warns ships away from Eddystone Rocks. The first lighthouse ever to be built on rocks in the open sea was constructed here in 1698 and was lit by candles. The current structure was built in 1882, and was converted to unstaffed automatic operation in 1982. The light flashes twice every 10 seconds and an audible signal sounds three times a minute in foggy weather. Chris McTernan*

Hacker MP in the television situation comedies *Yes Minister* (1980–82) and *Yes Prime Minister* (1986–88).

He trained at the Royal Academy of Dramatic Art. He was awarded the CBE in 1987.

Eddystone Rocks

Rocks in the English Channel, 23 km/14 mi south of Plymouth. The lighthouse, built in 1882, is the fourth on this exposed site.

Eden

River in Cumbria, northwest England; length 104 km/65 mi. From its source in the Pennines, it flows northwest through Kirkby Stephen, Appleby, and Carlisle before forming a wide estuary and entering the Solway Firth at Rockcliffe, northwest of Carlisle.

Eden, (Robert) Anthony, 1st Earl of Avon (1897–1977)

British Conservative politician, foreign secretary 1935–38, 1940–45, and 1951–55; prime minister 1955–57, when he resigned after the failure of the Anglo-French military intervention in the ◊Suez Crisis.

Upset by his prime minister's rejection of a peace plan secretly proposed by Roosevelt in January 1938, Eden resigned as foreign secretary in February 1938 in protest against Chamberlain's decision to open conversations with the Fascist dictator Mussolini. He was foreign secretary again in the wartime coalition, formed in December 1940, and in the Conservative government, elected in 1951. With the Soviets, he negotiated an interim peace in Vietnam 1954. In April 1955 he succeeded Churchill as prime minister. When Egypt nationalized the Suez Canal in 1956, precipitating the ◊Suez Crisis, he authorized the use of force, and a joint Anglo-French force was sent to Egypt. The force was compelled to withdraw after pressure from the USA and the USSR, and this led to Eden's resignation in January 1957. He continued to maintain that his action had been justified.

Edgar, known as the Atheling ('of royal blood') (*c.* 1050–*c.* 1130)

English prince, born in Hungary. Grandson of Edmund Ironside, he was supplanted as heir to Edward the Confessor by William the Conqueror. He led two rebellions against William, in 1068 and 1069, but made peace in 1074.

Edgar, David (1940–)

English dramatist. After early work as a journalist, Edgar turned to documentary and political theatre. *Destiny*, about the extreme right wing in Britain, was produced by the Royal Shakespeare Company in 1976. Other plays include *The Jail Diary of Albie Sachs* (1978); his adaptation from Dickens for the RSC, *The Life and Adventures of Nicholas Nickleby* (1980); *The Shape of the Table* (1990), on the collapse of the Eastern bloc in Europe; and *Pentecost* (1994).

Edgar the Peaceful (944–975)

King of all England from 959. He was the younger son of Edmund I, and strove successfully to unite English and Danes as fellow subjects.

Edgbaston

Suburb of ◊Birmingham, England, to the southwest of the city centre; population (1991) 18,300. Edgbaston is a residential district, and has the Warwickshire county cricket ground, where international test matches are regularly played. It was opened June 1886 and first hosted a Test May 1902. The ground capacity in 1998 was 20,000. Birmingham University is also located in the suburb.

Edgehill, Battle of

First battle of the English Civil War. It took place in 1642, on a ridge in south Warwickshire, between Royalists under Charles I and Parliamentarians under the Earl of Essex. Both sides claimed victory.

Edinburgh

Capital of Scotland and a unitary authority, located near the southern shores of the Firth of Forth

Area 263 sq km/122 sq mi

Physical Water of Leith, Salisbury Crags, Arthur's Seat

Industries printing, publishing, banking, insurance, chemical manufacture, electronics, distilling, brewing

Population (1995) 447,600.

Features

Edinburgh Castle contains St Margaret's chapel, the oldest building in Edinburgh, dating from the 12th century. The palace of Holyrood House was built in the 15th and 16th centuries on the site of a 12th-century abbey; it is the British sovereign's official Scottish residence.

Edinburgh is to be the site of the Scottish Parliament, a nation–region tier of government in the UK, with tax-varying powers; a new building is planned on the Royal Mile, adjacent to Holyrood House, to house the Parliament. The Parliament House, begun in 1632, is now the seat of the supreme courts. Edinburgh is a cultural centre and hosts the **Edinburgh Festival**, an international arts festival, with the **Edinburgh Fringe Festival** taking place alongside, in August–September each year. The Royal Scottish Academy and the National Gallery of Scotland (renovated in 1989) in Classical style are by William Henry Playfair (1789–1857). A museum of Scotland was opened in 1998. Edinburgh's principal church, St Giles, was consecrated in 1243 and became a cathedral in 1633. The episcopal cathedral of St Mary, opened in 1879, in the New Town area. The Royal Observatory has been at Blackford Hill since 1896. The principal thoroughfares are Princes Street and the Royal Mile.

The city has three universities: the University of Edinburgh (1583), Heriot-Watt University (established in 1885; received university status in 1966), and Napier University. The Conference Centre, designed by Terry Farrell, opened in 1995; Edinburgh Festival Theatre also opened in 1995. A geological visitor centre, the William Younger Centre, to be created in a disused brewery in the Old Town, is due to open in 1999 to mark the millennium. The Old Town and New Town were designated a World Heritage Site in 1995.

EDINBURGH *A courtyard in Edinburgh Castle. The castle stands on top of a granite outcrop that dominates the old part of Scotland's capital city. From its gates the 'Royal Mile', the old town's main thoroughfare, descends the hill to the palace of Holyrood. Edinburgh Castle is the scene of a spectacular annual military tattoo. Joe Cornish*

History

There is evidence of Bronze and Iron Age occupation of Castle Rock, and in Roman times the site was occupied by Celtic peoples; in about 617 the site was captured by Edwin of the Angles of Northumbria; the city took its name from the fortress of Din Eidin which he built. The early settlement grew up around a castle on Castle Rock, while about a mile to the east another burgh, Canongate, developed around the abbey of Holyrood, founded in 1128 by David I. It remained separate from Edinburgh until 1856. Robert the Bruce, having made Edinburgh the capital in 1325, made Edinburgh a burgh in 1329, and established its port at Leith. In 1544 and 1547 the town was destroyed by the English. After the union with England in 1707, Edinburgh lost its political importance but remained culturally pre-eminent. During the 18th century, Edinburgh was known as the 'Athens of the North' because of its concentration of intellectual talent, for example, Adam Smith, David Hume, and Joseph Black. Development of the area known as New Town started in 1767. Parts of the Old and New Towns were designated a World Heritage Site in 1995.

Location

Three eminences which run from east to west form the site of the city, which is surrounded on all sides, except the north, by hills. The steep ridge descending from the castle rock to the Netherbow Port (an old city gateway) constituted the ancient city, and on it the High Street is built. To the north of this ridge was formerly the North Loch. The new town lies on the ground which rises beyond the valley of the North Loch, and its wide streets and stately houses stretch down towards the Firth of Forth. The serried masses of houses forming the old town stretch from Calton Hill as far as the castle; further streets extend south towards the Braid Hills, and east to Arthur's Seat. The valley which formerly was the North Loch, now occupied by Princes Street gardens and railway lines, separates the new town from the old town. The slopes on both sides of the hollow are laid out as public gardens.

Calton Hill is the eastern extremity of Princes Street. It is a rocky eminence studded with monuments, including the unfinished National Monument. The view northwards from Calton Hill includes Leith, the Firth of Forth and the hills of Fife. Salisbury Crags, a huge belt of precipitous rock nearly 177 m/581 ft high, rises beyond the eastern edge of the city centre; behind this is Arthur's Seat, a conical hill 251 m/823.5 ft high, with a narrow rocky summit.

New Town

The streets and squares of the new town were planned by James Craig in the 18th century, and most of the buildings are built of calciferous sandstone quarried locally. There are extensive public open spaces in this part of the city. The principal commercial streets in the new town are Princes Street (1.5 km/1 mi long), George Street, and Queen Street, which all run parallel to each other, east to west.

At the western end of Princes Street are the Caledonian Hotel and St John's Church; at the eastern end are Waverley railway station, Waverley Market, the General Post Office, the Register House (1774), and the St James Centre. On the slopes of Calton Hill are the buildings of the former Royal High School; the Burns Monument; and St Andrew's House, headquarters of the Scottish Office. George Street is the city's chief financial thoroughfare and is bounded by St Andrew Square and Charlotte Square. Queen Street contains the National Portrait Gallery of Scotland and Museum of Antiquities.

The Water of Leith at Canonmills and Stockbridge forms the boundary of the new town; buildings situated in this neighbourhood include the Edinburgh Academy (founded 1824) and Fettes College (founded in 1870.) There are a large number of Georgian buildings in the new town; work by Robert Adam includes a large part of the Old College of Edinburgh University, the north side of Charlotte Square, the tomb of David Hume, and the Register House.

Old Town

The principal street of the old town is that built on the steep ridge which extends from the castle rock to Holyrood. This street is more than 1.5 km/1 mi long and is called at different points, Abbey Strand, Canongate, High Street, Lawnmarket, and Castle Hill, the whole being termed the 'Royal Mile'. The houses in the street are particularly tall.

The High Street opens into Parliament Close or Square, 450 m/500 yds downhill from Edinburgh Castle. The Square contains the old Parliament House (1632–40) and St Giles' Cathedral, built in the later Gothic style, and renovated between 1772 and 1883. The anicent Market Cross of Edinburgh was removed in 1756, and in 1885 Gladstone presented the city with a replacement cross which now stands near the eastern end of the church. John Knox's grave is believed to be in Parliament Square, to the rear of St Giles; a house in which he lived lies further down the Royal Mile.

There are many other historic sites along the Royal Mile including the Old Canongate Tolbooth, and Canongate Kirk Church. Many of the nobility of Edinburgh once lived in Canongate, and the Moray House, the Huntly House, and Queensbury House still remain.

Many of the properties in the Royal Mile have been or are being restored or reconstructed. The closes are narrow lanes which descend laterally in regular rows from the main street; in most cases they are no more than 2 m/7 ft wide at the entrance, and those which admitted the passage of a carriage are called 'wynds'.

The Cowgate runs to the south of and parallel with the High Street, and opens at the western end into the Grassmarket; at one time many aristocratic mansions stood there. The George IV and South bridges, which cross the Cowgate, are several storeys high. The Old College of the university is on South Bridge, and the National Library of Scotland and the Edinburgh Public Library stand on the George IV Bridge.

The oldest part of Edinburgh Castle is St Margaret's Chapel, which stands on the highest point of the castle rock; nearby is a cannon called 'Mons Meg', forged in Belgium in 1448. The Great Hall, built at the beginning of the 16th century, was restored in 1892; the room in which Queen Mary gave birth to James VI in 1566 is situated at the eastern end of the castle.

The Palace of Holyrood House, standing at the lower end of the Royal Mile, was begun by James IV, whilst the greater portion of it was built in the time of Charles II. The apartments occupied by Mary Queen of Scots are in the northwest angle of the building. The ruins of the chapel belonging to the Abbey of Holyrood, founded by David I in 1128, adjoin the chapel of Holyrood Palace on the north side.

Other buildings and monuments

Among other noteworthy public buildings in Edinburgh are the Royal Scottish Academy (1823–6), the National Gallery of Scotland, the Surgeon's Hall, the Royal Scottish Museum, and the Bank of Scotland. The monument to Walter Scott, situated on the south side of Princes Street, and designed by G M Kemp, is the most ornate in the city. It is in the form of an elaborate Gothic spire 60 m/197 ft high. Other monuments in the city are to Robert Burns, David Hume, Allan Ramsay, James Watt, David Livingstone, William Pitt, Dugald Stewart, and John Playfair. The Scottish National War Memorial, opened by the then Prince of Wales on 14 July 1927, is situated on the apex of the castle rock on the site of the old barracks; it contains the names of over 100,000 Scots who died in World Wars I and II.

20th-century development

The postwar years saw substantial changes in Edinburgh. New housing estates were established on the fringes of the city, rehousing the occupants of unsatisfactory housing areas in the central area which were demolished, and industrial estates established. A central bus station beside St Andrew Square has been linked with office and shopping accommodation in the St James Centre. Renovation of parts of the old town has been substantially completed, and new department stores and shops constructed in Princes Street. Much of the new town has been designated a conservation area, and property there has been improved and restored.

Education and culture

Edinburgh University has a famous medical school and the Koestler chair of parapsychology (instituted in 1985), the only such professorship in the UK. The Heriot-Watt University has premises both within the city, and on a campus at Riccarton, within the city district; Moray House College of Education is in the High Street. Schools include the Royal High School, now a comprehensive school in the suburb of Barnton, Edinburgh Academy, Fettes College, Stewart's-Melville College, George Watson's College, and Merchiston Castle School.

A notable annual event in the cultural life of the United Kingdom is the Edinburgh International Festival, which includes music, drama, opera, and art exhibitions. It was founded in 1947 by Rudolph Bing and has been held annually ever since, in August–September. The Edinburgh Fringe

Festival provides a showcase for amateur groups and new talent. The Military Tattoo is held a few days before the Festival on the Esplanade in front of the castle.

Economy

The most important industries of Edinburgh are brewing, whisky distilling (for which it has been noted for more than 200 years), electronics, and printing and publishing, with the connected industries of paper-making, bookbinding, and map-making. The city is also the centre of considerable banking, finance, and insurance expertise. The Edinburgh airport is at Turnhouse.

Malcolm III to James I

Very little is known of the history of Edinburgh until the reign of Malcolm Canmore (the son of Duncan I), when Donald Bane besieged Edinburgh Castle after Malcolm's death. David I lived more at Edinburgh than his predecessors had done, and this custom was followed by his descendants. Robert the Bruce held a parliament at Holyrood in 1327, and his last parliament was held in Edinburgh in the following year, but the chief importance of the town was from a military point of view. Edinburgh was held by the English for several years, but with the outbreak of war between England and France in 1338, the Scots regained their lost ground. A new era began for Edinburgh with the accession of James I.

15th and 16th centuries

Edinburgh may be called the capital of the Stuarts; it shared the vicissitudes of that dynasty, and for a time sank into comparative unimportance when they deserted it. It was not a walled town until 1437. The first printing press was erected in 1507; in the century that followed Edinburgh was recognized as the undisputed capital of the country. At an early period of the Reformation, Edinburgh was converted to the Protestant faith; later the great majority of its inhabitants adopted the Calvinistic creed, led by John Knox the minister of St Giles. ◊Rizzio, the Italian favourite of Mary Queen of Scots, was murdered in 1566 in her apartments in the palace of Holyrood House.

18th and 19th centuries

The Union of England and Scotland (1707) aroused great excitement in Edinburgh, and attempts were made to intimidate the members of the Scottish Parliament who were favourable to the Act of Union, but the Act was eventually passed without bloodshed. An unsuccessful attempt was made by the Jacobites to surprise the castle in the rebellion of 1715. In 1745 the Jacobites were more successful and were masters of the town from 15 September to 31 October, but could not take the castle.

In the Porteous affair of 1736 the populace lynched the captain of the guard, named Porteous, who had fired on the crowd and killed six people. The city was ordered to pay £2,000 to Porteous' widow; the ringleaders were never discovered. The societies which were formed in Edinburgh about the time of the French Revolution in sympathy with the principles prevailing in France, were put down with great severity. In 1822, George IV visited Edinburgh and won popularity by wearing a kilt, at the suggestion of Walter Scott. He was the first sovereign to visit the city since 1650. Holyrood was granted as a residence to the exiled French king, Charles X, in 1830.

Edinburgh, Duke of

Title of Prince ◊Philip of the UK.

Edmonton

A locality, once a town, part of the London borough of Enfield. John Keats lived at Edmonton, and Charles Lamb lived and died here. The Bell Inn is referred to in William Cowper's poem 'John Gilpin'.

Edmund I (921–946)

King of England 939–46. The son of Edward the Elder, he succeeded his half-brother, Athelstan, as king in 939. He succeeded in regaining control of Mercia, which on his accession had fallen to the Norse inhabitants of Northumbria, and of the Five Boroughs, an independent confederation within the Danelaw. He then moved on to subdue the Norsemen in Cumbria and finally extended his rule as far as southern Scotland. As well as uniting England, he bolstered his authority by allowing St Dunstan to reform the Benedictine order. He was killed in 946 at Pucklechurch, Gloucestershire, by an outlawed robber.

Edmund (II) Ironside (*c.* 989–1016)

King of England 1016, the son of Ethelred II the Unready. He led the resistance to ◊Canute's invasion in 1015, and on Ethelred's death in 1016 was chosen king by the citizens of London, whereas the Witan (the king's council) elected Canute. In the struggle for the throne, Edmund was defeated by Canute at Assandun (Ashington), Essex, and they divided the kingdom between them. After Edmund died the same year, Canute ruled the whole kingdom.

education

See pages 294 and 295 for a feature on the education system today and some key dates in education since 1944; see also ◊National Curriculum.

Historic role of Church and state

In England and Wales, prior to the Reformation, the undivided Church was responsible for education. Thereafter, the question of the control of education became a source of bitter sectarian conflict, and it was not until the 19th century that attempts were made to spread literacy throughout society. In Scotland, as early as 1494, freeholders were required by royal statute to send their heirs to school to acquire 'perfect Latin', and from the late 16th century, under the influence of John ◊Knox, churches in every major town had Latin schools attached. The Factory Act of 1802, which applied throughout the UK, required that during the first four years of their apprenticeship children employed by the owners of the newly arising factories were taught reading, writing, and arithmetic. The requirement was not always observed, but it embodied a new principle.

The British and Foreign Schools Society (1808) and the National Society for Promoting the Education of the Poor in the Principles of the Established Church (1811) set up schools in which basic literacy and numeracy as well as religious

HOW THE EDUCATION SYSTEM WORKS

THE ORGANIZATION of the modern school system has been a subject of heated debate in the United Kingdom for more than 30 years. Although political interest has now shifted somewhat to the curriculum and assessment, school organization can still arouse fierce passions.

The situation is further confused because although the Department for Education and Employment in London (and its equivalents in Wales, Scotland, and Northern Ireland) has taken an increasingly centralizing role in what goes on in school, actual control still rests with more than one hundred local education authorities (LEAs) based in town and county halls. As a result, the organization of schools may vary from one part of England to another, although the other three constituent parts of the UK have had more uniform – but different – structures.

Compulsory from age five

Compulsory schooling does not begin for children in the United Kingdom until the age of five, although in practice many children start before that age. Part-time nursery education is widely, although not evenly available, but is not compulsory. The Labour Government elected in 1997 is making places available for all four-year-olds whose parents want it, and intends to extend provision for three year olds.

At five children move from the nursery school or class to primary school, where the emphasis during the early years is very much on the skills of reading, writing, and mathematics. Children generally stay in their primary school until they are eleven (twelve in Scotland) although some local areas provide separate infants and junior schools with a break at seven, or first and middle schools with a break at eight or nine and again at twelve or thirteen, rather than eleven.

Secondary education in the UK is generally 'comprehensive': schools accept children of all abilities without any selective procedure on entry. Only Northern Ireland retains a completely selective system in which children are allocated to grammar (academic) or secondary modern schools on the basis of tests of attainment at the age of eleven. Scotland runs a completely comprehensive secondary system, starting at the age of twelve. In England a few local education authorities have retained some grammar schools, in some cases running them alongside 'comprehensives', which are of course unlikely to be able to recruit the full ability range. Under new legislation, parents will be able to seek a ballot on the retention of grammar schools or a change to a completely comprehensive system in their area.

Specialist schools

Within the comprehensive system, the Labour government is encouraging some schools to specialize by providing grants for subjects such as technology, languages, and the performing arts. These schools will be able to admit a small proportion of children on the basis of their 'aptitude' for the specialist subject.

Another complicating factor is the role of the religious denominations in the provision of education in the UK. Historically the Church of England was responsible for the establishment of many schools, particularly in rural areas. The Roman Catholic Church also established its own schools. In England, Wales, and Scotland most schools are non-denominational 'county' schools, but about a third are run jointly by the local council and a religious denomination. These are known as voluntary schools. In practice, particularly in Northern Ireland, Roman Catholic children attend schools of that denomination, while other schools, both county and voluntary, accept children of all faiths or none.

The former Conservative government allowed parents to vote to transform their existing LEA schools into a new type of school, directly funded by the government and responsible for running their own affairs. The establishment of these grant-maintained schools proved highly controversial in many areas, and they are being brought back into cooperative arrangements with their local authorities under Labour.

There is also a flourishing system of fee-paying private schools which caters for just under 8% of British children. These range from prestigious, academic, and very expensive, boarding schools like Eton and Harrow to small day schools, some of the specializing in the education of children with special needs.

Compulsory education ends at the age of 16, but in practice the majority of young people continue their full-time education at least until the age of 18. At 16 there are four educational options: to remain at school for another one or two years to gain further qualifications such as A Level and GNVQs in a 'sixth form'; to move on to a sixth form college, which will provide mainly the same sort of academic courses offered in a sixth form; to go to a further education college which will provide a range of vocational and prevocational courses; or, in some areas, to go to a tertiary college which will offer academic and vocational courses in one post-16 institution.

After school those who wish to continue their education – and more than one third of the age group now do so – have a choice of higher education courses in almost 200 degree-awarding institutions ranging from international universities of the stature of Oxford and Cambridge, London and Manchester, to new universities which specialize in vocational degree and diploma programmes, and small institutes and colleges which offer a more restricted range of higher education courses.

BY MAUREEN O'CONNOR

knowledge were taught. In 1862, government grants became available for the first time for schools attended by children up to 12. The Elementary Education Act 1870 (Forster's Act) established district school boards all over the country whose duty was to provide facilities for the elementary education of all children not otherwise receiving it. The school boards were abolished by the Education Act 1902 and their responsibilities transferred to county and borough councils,

BRITISH EDUCATION IN THE 20TH CENTURY: SOME KEY DATES

1944 The 1944 Education Act in England and Wales introduces primary, secondary, and further education, sanctions the Eleven Plus examination, provides for a raised school-leaving age of 15 (16 as soon as possible), and makes religious education compulsory.

1945 Fees are abolished in state-maintained secondary schools in England and Wales.

1947 The school-leaving age in the UK is raised to 15.

1971 Britain's Open University (founded in 1969) is launched, using television and radio broadcasts among its teaching media.

25 June 1971 The education secretary, Margaret Thatcher, announces the end of free milk for primary school children.

25 June 1971 The Department of Education allocates £132 million to get rid of 6,000 slum primary schools.

1973 The school-leaving age is raised to 16.

26 October 1977 The Department of Education announces plans for the national testing of children in mathematics, reading, and writing.

1980 An education act, passed in stages, introduces the 'assisted places scheme', subsidizing independent school places for able children from disadvantaged backgrounds. The scheme is set to begin in September 1981.

1981 An Education Act obliges local education authorities to integrate children with special educational needs into mainstream schools.

1986 An Education Act defines the duties and responsibilities of school governors.

1986 The British government announces a new type of secondary school, the city technology college, to be jointly financed by industry and the state.

1986 A National Council for Vocational Qualifications is established to coordinate standards.

22 July 1986 The House of Commons votes to abolish corporal punishment in state schools.

1988 The Baker Education Reform Act introduces a ten-subject national curriculum that will test at four key stages. It envisages further city technology colleges, and permits schools to opt out of local education authority control.

1988 The GCSE (General Certificate of Secondary Education) examination replaces the GCE (General Certificate of Education) 'O' level and the CSE (Certificate of Secondary Education) in England and Wales.

23 July 1997 The government announces a plan to start charging university students a tuition fee of £1,000 and to scrap grants in favour of student loans.

30 September 1997 In his keynote speech at the Labour Party conference, Prime Minister Tony Blair says that Parliament will appropriate £2 billion for school equipment and repairs, £700 million more than was originally promised. He also announces a new initiative in which the government and private business would cooperate to provide all schools with computers and Internet access by 2002.

January 1998 The Department of Education publishes its annual league tables of tests in literacy and numeracy of 11-year-olds in state schools. The results show an overall improvement throughout England.

January 1998 The education and employment secretary David Blunkett announces a relaxation of the National Curriculum in order to focus on mathematics and English. Primary schools will now be free to choose what to teach in history, geography, music, art, design and technology, and physical education.

10 June 1998 The government announces the first national educational scheme using laptops, the Anytime Anywhere Learning pilot project to be introduced in September at 27 schools. The use of laptops is expected to spread to all schools in the 21st century.

16 June 1998 Junior education minister Estelle Morris announces the launch of 10 pilot schemes in September in which gifted children would be offered extra-curricular 'master classes' in languages, maths, sport, and the arts.

23 June 1998 Education and employment secretary David Blunkett announces plans for a joint business and government £75 million initiative for 25 education action zones, some of which began operating in September. The initiative will experiment with information technology and increased school hours. Each action zone will contain about 20 schools in areas of low educational performance.

which became the local education authorities for both higher and elementary education. A further act in 1918 raised the school-leaving age to 14.

Secondary education, funding and legislation

Once the principle of elementary education for all was established, the idea of widely available higher education began to be accepted. The Education Act 1944 introduced a system of secondary education for all, and formed the foundation of much education policy today. This has been revised by two further acts in 1980, which repealed 1976 legislation enforcing ◊comprehensive reorganization, and gave new rights to parents; by the 1981 Education Act which made new provisions for the education of children with special needs; and by legislation in 1986 giving further powers to school governors as part of a move towards increased parental involvement in schools, and in 1987 on the remuneration of teachers. In 1988 a major act introduced a compulsory ◊national curriculum in state schools, compulsory testing of

EDUCATION *Primary school children in Britain. Successive governments stress the importance of education, yet teaching in the state sector remains chronically underfunded and buildings are often in a poor state of repair. Increasingly, standardized national tests are being applied to children from an early age to assess their competence in a range of basic skills. Peter Arkell/Impact*

children, financial delegation of budgets to schools, and the possibility of direct funding by government for schools that voted to opt out of local council control.

Responsibility for education

The Department for Education and Employment, established in 1944 as the Ministry of Education and headed by a cabinet minister, is responsible for nonmilitary scientific research, for universities throughout Great Britain, and for school education in England. From 1999 the ◊Scottish Parliament and ◊Northern Ireland Assembly take responsibility for education in these areas; in Wales, primary and secondary education remains the responsibility of the Welsh Education Office.

Local education authorities (LEAs) are education committees of county and borough councils, responsible for providing educational services locally under the general oversight of the DES, but certain of their powers have been curtailed by the 1988 act. The Inner London Education Authority (ILEA) was abolished by the 1988 act and responsibility for education in London passed to the borough councils.

Education and Employment, Department for

Government department, established in 1944 as the Ministry of Education. It merged in 1995 with the Department of Employment. It is responsible for education, scientific research policies, employment, and training policies. Including the Employment Service Agency, which had 28,000 staff in 1998, the department employs 33,000 people. The secretary of state for Education and Employment, currently David Blunkett (from 1997), has a seat in the Cabinet.

Edward (Edward Antony Richard Louis) (1964–)

Prince of the UK, third son of Queen Elizabeth II. He is seventh in line to the throne after Charles, Charles's two sons, Andrew, and Andrew's two daughters. In January 1999 his engagement to Sophie Rhys-Jones was announced.

Edward, called the Black Prince (1330–1376)

Prince of Wales, eldest son of Edward III of England. The epithet (probably posthumous) may refer to his black armour. During the Hundred Years' War he fought at the Battle of Crécy in 1346 and captured the French king at Poitiers in 1356. He ruled Aquitaine 1360–71. During the revolt that eventually ousted him, he caused the massacre of Limoges in 1370.

Edward

Eight kings of England or Great Britain:

Edward I (1239–1307)

King of England from 1272, son of Henry III. Edward led the royal forces against Simon de Montfort in the ◊Barons' War 1264–67, and was on a crusade when he succeeded to the throne. He established English rule over all Wales, and secured recognition of his overlordship from the Scottish king, although the Scots (under Wallace and Bruce) fiercely resisted actual conquest. In his reign Parliament took its approximate modern form with the ◊Model Parliament of 1295. He married Eleanor of Castile in 1254; she died in 1290 and in 1299 he married Margaret, daughter of Philip III of France. He was succeeded by his son Edward II.

Edward II (1284–1327)

King of England from 1307, son of Edward I. Born at Caernarfon Castle, he was created the first Prince of Wales in 1301. Incompetent and frivolous, and unduly influenced by his favourite, Piers Gaveston, Edward struggled throughout his reign with discontented barons, who attempted to restrict his power through the Ordinances of 1311. His invasion of Scotland in 1314 to suppress revolt resulted in defeat at ◊Bannockburn. When he fell under the influence of a new favourite, Hugh le Depenser, he was deposed in 1327 by his wife Isabella (1292–1358), daughter of Philip IV of France, and her lover Roger de ◊Mortimer, and murdered in Berkeley Castle, Gloucestershire. He was succeeded by his son, Edward III.

Edward III (1312–1377)

King of England from 1327, son of Edward II. He assumed the government in 1330 from his mother, through whom in 1337 he laid claim to the French throne and thus began the ◊Hundred Years' War. He was succeeded by his grandson Richard II.

Edward improved the status of the monarchy after his father's chaotic reign. He began by attempting to force his rule

THE HAMMER OF THE CELTS: EDWARD I AND WALES

Edward I's conquest of Wales was achieved by the use of force on a scale that the Welsh could not hope to match, and by taking advantage of the divisions within the country. In the early and mid-13th century, the princes of Gwynedd, Llewelyn the Great and his grandson Llewelyn ap Gruffydd, had been remarkably successful in capitalizing on the political difficulties faced in England by King John and then by Henry III. Before he came to the throne, Edward himself had failed to maintain proper control of the lands in Wales granted to him in 1254. Llewelyn ap Gruffydd supported the Crown's opponent Simon de Montfort in the civil war of 1264–65. It was hardly surprising that, when he came to the throne, Edward should wish to take his revenge.

At the same time, Llewelyn's own position in Wales was not secure. His push to achieve dominance over members of his own family, notably his brother Dafydd and the other Welsh princes, had been successful, but left him with dangerous enemies. He overestimated the strength of his position, and his refusal to accept Edward's demands that he acknowledge English overlordship by performing homage left him fatally exposed.

The campaign of 1277

The conquest was achieved in three major campaigns. The first, in 1277, clearly demonstrated that the Welsh could not resist a substantial English army marching along the north Welsh coast; Llewelyn's support was limited, and he had to sue for peace on humiliating terms. Edward I, however, failed to reward those Welshmen, who even included Llewelyn's own brother Dafydd, who had supported him in 1277. Attempts to introduce English law in Welsh affairs were provocative, and there was widespread rebellion 1282–83. The English campaign to put down the rising was lengthy, and Edward's forces suffered a disaster when knights who had crossed to the mainland from Anglesey were ambushed and slaughtered. However, Llewelyn was slain at the battle of Irfon Bridge in December 1282, and Dafydd's attempts to carry on the fight ended in failure in the next year. He was handed over to Edward by men of his own nation. The Welsh ruling dynasties were ruined and Wales virtually became an English colony.

The 1294 rebellion

There was a minor rebellion in the south of the country in 1287, followed by a much more serious rising in 1294. The introduction of English methods of taxation, and general oppression by English officials led to the rebellion, which was timed to coincide with the English involvement in war with France. Edward was able to divert the troops intended for France to Wales and an expensive campaign ended in complete success for the English. Edward was capable of putting as many as 30,000 troops in the field against the Welsh. He had heavily armed cavalry in numbers which his opponents could never hope to match, and while he used the traditional feudal obligation as one means of recruitment, the majority of his troops were either paid, or were serving at their own expense. In 1282 he had hoped that the whole army would serve for wages, but this aroused hostility from the baronage, whose independence was threatened by such a move. Infantry were recruited in large numbers, many of them from south Wales, and the majority were armed with the longbow, a devastating weapon. In addition, during the second war he recruited a force of crossbowmen from his overseas dominion of Gascony. Every effort was made to ensure that food supplies for the armies were sufficient, while ships were brought from the south coast of England and Ireland to provide the naval support which was essential if the armies were to be properly provided for. Edward was able to keep his armies in being over the winter months of 1282–83 and 1294–95. The Welsh could not hold out for long against such unremitting pressure.

The great castles

Edward's campaigns were each marked by a programme of castle-building. New castles on a grand scale were designed to hold down the Welsh. Flint, Rhuddlan, Builth, and Aberystwyth were built after the first Welsh war; after the second Snowdonia was hemmed in much more closely by Conwy, Caernarfon, and Harlech, while after the rebellion of 1294 Beaumaris was founded to establish a secure hold on Anglesey. The castles were largely the work of a single man of genius, Master James of St George, a master mason recruited from Savoy. It was Savoyard, not English, masons who were responsible for much of the design and detail of the castles. Caernarfon was the exception. It was based on the walls of Constantinople, and was built as a grand imperial gesture by a king who wanted to express in stone not only his might, but also legendary connections with the Imperial past of ancient Rome.

BY MICHAEL PRESTWICH

on Scotland, winning a victory at Halidon Hill in 1333. During the first stage of the Hundred Years' War, English victories included the Battle of Crécy in 1346 and the capture of Calais in 1347. In 1360 Edward surrendered his claim to the French throne, but the war resumed in 1369. During his last years his son John of Gaunt acted as head of government.

Edward IV (1442–1483)

King of England 1461–70 and from 1471. He was the son of Richard, Duke of York, and succeeded Henry VI in the Wars of the ◊Roses, temporarily losing the throne to Henry when Edward fell out with his adviser Warwick, but regaining it at the Battle of Barnet 1471. He was succeeded by his son Edward V.

Edward was known as Earl of March until his accession. After his father's death he occupied London 1461, and was proclaimed king in place of Henry VI by a council of peers. His position was secured by the defeat of the Lancastrians at

Towton 1461 and by the capture of Henry. He quarrelled, however, with Warwick, his strongest supporter, who in 1470–71 temporarily restored Henry, until Edward recovered the throne by his victories at Barnet and Tewkesbury.

Edward V (1470–1483)

King of England 1483. Son of Edward IV, he was deposed three months after his accession in favour of his uncle (◊Richard III), and is traditionally believed to have been murdered (with his brother) in the Tower of London on Richard's orders.

Edward VI (1537–1553)

King of England from 1547, only son of Henry VIII and his third wife, Jane Seymour. The government was entrusted to his uncle the Duke of Somerset (who fell from power 1549), and then to the Earl of Warwick, later created Duke of Northumberland. He was succeeded by his sister Mary I.

Edward became a staunch Protestant, and during his reign the Reformation progressed. He died of tuberculosis, and his will, probably prepared by Northumberland, set aside that of his father so as to exclude his half-sisters, Mary and Elizabeth, from the succession. He nominated Lady Jane Grey, a granddaughter of Henry VII, who had recently married Northumberland's son. Technically Jane reigned for nine days, and was deposed by Mary I.

EDWARD I *A 16th-century manuscript depicting Edward I in Parliament. The king is flanked by Alexander II of Scotland on his right and Llewellyn ap Gruffyd of Wales on his left. In front of him the justices and law officers are sitting on woolsacks. Philip Sauvain Picture Collection*

Edward VII (1841–1910)

King of Great Britain and Ireland from 1901. As Prince of Wales he was a prominent social figure, but his mother Queen Victoria considered him too frivolous to take part in political life. In 1860 he made the first tour of Canada and the USA ever undertaken by a British prince.

Edward was born at Buckingham Palace, the eldest son of Queen Victoria and Prince Albert. After his father's death in 1861 he undertook many public duties, took a close interest in politics, and was on friendly terms with the party leaders. In 1863 he married Princess ◊Alexandra of Denmark, and they had six children. He toured India 1875–76. He succeeded to the throne in 1901 and was crowned in 1902.

Although he overrated his political influence, he contributed to the Entente Cordiale of 1904 with France and the Anglo-Russian agreement of 1907.

Edward VIII (1894–1972)

King of Great Britain and Northern Ireland from January to December 1936, when he renounced the throne to marry Wallis Warfield Simpson (see ◊abdication crisis). He was created Duke of Windsor and was governor of the Bahamas 1940–45.

Eldest son of George V, he received the title of Prince of Wales in 1910 and succeeded to the throne 20 January 1936. In November that year a constitutional crisis arose when Edward wished to marry Mrs Simpson; it was felt that, as a divorcee, she would be unacceptable as queen. On 11 December Edward abdicated and left for France, where the couple were married in 1937. He was succeeded by his brother, George VI.

> *I have found it impossible to discharge my duties as King as I would wish to do without the help and support of the woman I love.*
>
> EDWARD VIII
> Abdication speech, broadcast on radio 11 December 1936

Edwards, Gareth Owen (1947–)

Welsh rugby union player. A fast, elusive scrum-half he scored 20 tries in 53 international for Wales between 1967 and 1978. He toured with the British Lions three times winning a

EDWARD VI *King Edward VI's coronation medal. The boy–king was a brilliant scholar, deeply interested in theological speculation, and during his short reign the Protestant Reformation in England advanced significantly. Philip Sauvain Picture Collection*

further 10 international caps. Appointed captain of Wales in 1968 at at the age of only 20 he appeared in seven Five Nations championship winning teams, five Triple Crown winning teams, and three Grand Slam winning teams.

Edwards, Jonathan David (1966–)

English athlete who won the triple jump title at the 1995 World Championships in Gothenburg with a world record leap of 18.29 metres. He won silver medals at the 1996 Olympic Games and the 1997 World Championships, and a gold at the 1998 European Championships.

Edwards, Robert Geoffrey (1925–)

British physiologist. With Patrick ◊Steptoe he devised a technique for fertilizing a human egg outside the body and transferring the fertilized embryo to the uterus of a woman. A child born following the use of this technique is popularly known as a 'test-tube baby'. Edwards's research has added to knowledge of the development of the human egg and embryo.

Edwards, Shaun (1966–)

English rugby league half-back who between 1984 and 1997 won 32 winner's medals with Wigan, his home town club, in major competitions including a record nine in the Challenge Cup. A precocious talent, he signed as a professional for Wigan on his 17th birthday, and at the age of 18 won the first of 36 Great Britain caps.

Edward the Confessor (*c.* 1003–1066)

King of England from 1042, the son of Ethelred II. He lived in Normandy until shortly before his accession. During his reign power was held by Earl Godwin and his son ◊Harold, while the king devoted himself to religion, including the rebuilding of Westminster Abbey (consecrated in 1065), where he is buried. His childlessness led ultimately to the Norman Conquest in 1066. He was canonized in 1161.

Edward the Elder (*c.* 870–924)

King of the West Saxons. He succeeded his father ◊Alfred the Great in 899. He reconquered southeast England and the Midlands from the Danes, uniting Wessex and ◊Mercia with the help of his sister, Athelflad.

By the time Edward died, his kingdom was the most powerful in the British Isles. He was succeeded by his son ◊Athelstan. See genealogy under House of ◊Wessex.

Edward the Martyr (*c.* 963–978)

King of England from 975. Son of King Edgar, he was murdered at Corfe Castle, Dorset, probably at his stepmother Aelfthryth's instigation (she wished to secure the crown for her son, Ethelred). He was canonized in 1001.

Edwy

King of England, son of Edmund I. He succeeded his uncle Edred as king in 955 and drove Edred's chief adviser St ◊Dunstan, then virtually ruler, into exile the same year.

On the revolt in 957 of the Mercians and Northumbrians, who had chosen his brother ◊Edgar as king, he was left to rule Wessex and Kent 957–959.

Egbert (died 839)

King of the West Saxons from 802, the son of Ealhmund, an under-king of Kent. By 829 he had united England for the first time under one king.

Egerton

Family name of dukes of Sutherland, seated at Mertoun, Roxburghshire, Scotland.

Egham

Town in Surrey, England, on the River Thames 12 km/7 mi outside Greater London; population (1991) 6,000. Royal Holloway College, part of the University of London, is located here. Nearby is ◊Runnymede, where King John sealed the Magna Carta in 1215.

Remains of the earliest known river harbour in Britain, dating from the 8th century BC, have been found at Egham.

Eigg

Island of the Inner ◊Hebrides, in Highland unitary authority, Scotland; 20 km/12 mi southwest of Mallaig on the mainland; population (1991) 76. Extending over an area of 40 sq km/15 sq mi, it is one of a group collectively known as the Small Isles. Crofting (a form of subsistence farming) is the main occupation. The residents of Eigg bought their island in April 1997 after an eight-month ownership battle.

The islanders' victory marked the end of private ownership which had dominated the island since 1308. In December 1996, an initial bid by the islanders of £1.2 million had been rejected by the then owner, a German artist, and a month later the trustees of the Heritage Lottery Fund turned down their appeal for financial help. Finally, an English millionairess, who has remained anonymous, was believed to have given them around £900,000 – the bulk of the £1.5 million purchase price.

eisteddfod, Welsh 'sitting'

Traditional Welsh gathering lasting up to a week and dedicated to the encouragement of the bardic arts of music, poetry, and literature. The custom dates from pre-Christian times.

Towns and rural communities often hold their own annual eisteddfod. The national eisteddfod was discontinued from the late 17th century until the beginning of the 19th century. Since then the Royal National Eisteddfod has been held annually, at the beginning of August, at a different site each year. During the meetings bardic degrees are awarded and the traditional eisteddfod culminates with the ceremony of 'chairing' the bard (composer of the best verse in strict metre).

EISTEDDFOD *Members of the Gorsedd gather at the annual National Eisteddfod, the principal celebration of Welsh traditional culture. The Gorsedd is a society of bards, led by the archdruid of Wales, that administers and conducts the pageantry of the festival. Most importantly, it is responsible for crowning and chairing the winners of the poetry contests, the centrepiece of the Eisteddfod. Collier's/ Collections*

Elan

River rising in Powys, central Wales, and joining the Wye south of Rhayader. Four dams have been built on this river to form reservoirs for the city of Birmingham. On the River Claerwen, a tributary of the Elan, one of the highest gravity dams in Great Britain (height 56 m/183 ft, length 355 m/1,165 ft) has been constructed to create another reservoir.

Eleanor of Aquitaine (*c.* 1122–1204)

Queen of France 1137–51 as wife of Louis VII, and of England from 1154 as wife of Henry II. Henry imprisoned her 1174–89 for supporting their sons, the future Richard I and King John, in revolt against him.

Eleanor of Castile (*c.* 1245–1290)

Queen of Edward I of England, the daughter of Ferdinand III of Castile. She married Prince Edward in 1254, and accompanied him on his crusade in 1270. She died at Harby, Nottinghamshire, and Edward erected stone crosses in towns where her body rested on the funeral journey to London. Several **Eleanor Crosses** are still standing, for example, at Northampton.

elections

See feature opposite on how elections are conducted; some key election results since 1945 are on page 302.

electricity supply

In 1990 responsibility for electricity generation and supply in England and Wales, hitherto the responsibility of state, was split between four companies in preparation for privatization. The nuclear power stations remain in the hands of the state through Nuclear Electric (accounting for 20% of electricity generated), while National Power (50%) and PowerGen (30%) generate electricity from fossil-fuel and renewable sources. Transmission lines and substations are owned by the National Grid, which was privatized in 1996.

In 1989, 12 regional electricity companies were created from the former area electricity boards in England and Wales. From 1998, these companies no longer had a monopoly on sales to all consumers as competition was introduced into the domestic electricity market.

In Scotland, three new companies were created in 1989: Scottish Power and Scottish Hydro-Electric which generate, transmit, distribute and supply electricity, and Scottish Nuclear. Northern Ireland Electricity was set up in 1993 and three private companies are responsible for generating electricity from four power stations.

Eleven Plus examination

Test designed to select children for grammar school education in the UK, at the time when local authorities provided separate grammar, secondary modern, and occasionally technical schools for children over the age of 11. The examination became defunct on the introduction of ◊comprehensive schools in Scotland, Wales, and most of England during the 1960s and 1970s, although certain education authorities retain the selective system and the Eleven Plus.

HOW ELECTIONS ARE CONDUCTED

In England, elections have been used as a parliamentary process since the 13th century. The secret ballot was adopted in 1872 and full equal voting rights won for women in 1928. All registered members of the public aged 18 and over may vote in parliamentary elections. The House of Commons is elected for a maximum of five years; the prime minister can call a general election at any time.

The calling of an election

The decision to dissolve Parliament is made by the sovereign on the advice of the prime minister. A general election normally takes place within 21 days of a dissolution. Vacancies in the House of Commons between general elections are filled by means of by-elections.

Parliament may extend its own life by act of Parliament, but such an act must have the consent of the House of Lords. In this way the life of Parliament was extended in both World Wars. In practice, general elections are normally held at less than five-year intervals, much depending on political circumstances. In 1910 and 1974 two elections were held in one year.

By-elections

A writ for a by-election is issued by the clerk of the Crown on receipt of the Speaker's warrant. A by-election must be held not less than 11 or more than 21 days after the issue of the writ. In practice, the time between a seat becoming vacant and the by-election being held is often prolonged whilst the party which held the seat awaits an opportune moment to hold the election.

Nomination of candidates

The House of Commons consists of 659 members, each representing a single-member constituency. Each candidate must be nominated by a proposer, a seconder, and eight other electors. In practice, the overwhelming majority of candidates are nominated by political parties. Each candidate must place a deposit with the returning officer for the constituency and this sum is forfeited if the candidate fails to poll a certain proportion of the total number of votes cast.

Election campaigns and expenses

The election expenses of each candidate are strictly controlled and all must be declared and published.

These provisions apply to the election campaigns of individual candidates; they do not apply to the nationwide campaigns conducted by the parties. There are, however, restrictions on the number and duration of election broadcasts on radio and television. Parties may not purchase broadcasting time at all. There is no restriction, however, on the purchase of advertising space in newspapers and journals, nor on advertising hoardings.

The parliamentary franchise

To qualify as an elector in a particular constituency a person must be resident in that constituency on the annual qualifying date (10 October), be a UK citizen, of at least 18 years of age, and not be subject to any legal disqualification. The latter includes peers, convicted prisoners, people found guilty of corrupt or illegal practices and people detained in a mental hospital.

Electors who are unable to vote in person because of their occupation, physical incapacity, or change of address, may apply for a postal or proxy vote. These are not available to electors absent from the constituency on holiday.

The poll

The conduct of the election in each constituency is the responsibility of the returning officer, usually a local government official. Voting takes place in all constituencies on the same day. Since 1935 polling day has always been a Thursday. This allows for the maximum number of days in the last week of the campaign, without encroaching on the following weekend.

The polling stations are open from 7 a.m. to 10 p.m. In a private polling booth, the voter places an X against the name of the candidate of their choice. The candidates are listed in alphabetical order on the ballot paper and a short description of each candidate is included. The voter then places the ballot paper in a ballot box and, after the close of the polls, all ballot boxes are sealed and taken to a central location in the constituency to be counted. The candidate with the most votes in each constituency wins the election in that constituency.

In many constituencies the counting begins as soon as the polls have closed and the first results of a general election are usually known little more than an hour later. With the aid of computers, forecasts of the final outcome are made as soon as the first results are declared. Television commentators were able to predict Labour's landslide victory in the May 1997 general election within minutes of the polls closing.

In the event of a close result a candidate may demand a recount, and in some cases several recounts may occur. As soon as the result is known the returning officer publicly announces it and in due course is required to return the election writ, endorsed with the name of the successful candidate, to the clerk of the Crown.

Effects of the first-past-the-post system

The simple first-past-the-post system of voting has an important effect on elections since it is possible for a candidate to be elected with only a relative majority of votes. Proposals for the introduction of a system of proportional representation (PR) have been resisted by both the Conservative and Labour parties and favoured by the minor parties, especially the Liberal Democrats.

Electoral behaviour in Britain

Electoral behaviour in Britain is characterized by a considerable degree of homogeneity and the movement of support (or swing) from one party to another at a general election is usually maintained fairly uniformly over the whole country. The rise of the Welsh and Scottish Nationalists has, however, modified this situation to some extent.

In England, both of the major parties command the solid allegiance of about 30% of the electorate, whilst the Liberals command perhaps 8–10%, leaving 30% of the electorate as 'floating voters'. It is the votes of this 30% which generally determines the outcome of elections.

Some Key General Election Results Since 1945

party	seats
1945 – Labour	
Labour	392
Conservative	183
National Liberal	13
Independent	11
Liberal	10
Ulster Unionist	10
Irish Nationalist	2
Nationalist	2
Communist	2
Independent Labour Party	2
Independent Liberal	2
Common Wealth	1
Independent Unionist	1
Independent Labour	1
1964 – Labour	
Labour	317
Conservative	285
National Liberal	6
Liberal	9
Ulster Unionist	12
Independent	1
1974 (March) – Labour	
Labour	284
Labour and Co-op	16
Conservative	296
Liberal	14
United Ulster Unionist	10
Democratic Unionist	1
Republican Labour	1
Scottish Nationalist	7
Plaid Cymru	2
Social Democrat	1
Independent Labour	1
1974 (Oct) – Labour	
Labour	304
Labour and Co-op	15
Conservative	276
Liberal	13
Ulster Unionist	10
Independent	1
Scottish Nationalist	11
Plaid Cymru	3
Social Democrat Labour	1
non-party	1
1979 – Conservative	
Conservative	339
Labour	251
Labour and Co-op	17
Liberal	11
Scottish Nationalist	2
Plaid Cymru	2
Independent	1
Official Unionist	5
United Ulster Unionist	1
Democratic Unionist	3
Ulster Unionist	1
Social Democratic and Labour	1
Speaker	1
1992 – Conservative	
Conservative	336
Labour	270
Liberal Democrats	20
Ulster Unionist Party	9
Plaid Cymru	4
Social Democratic and Labour	4
Scottish National Party	3
Democratic Unionist party	3
Ulster Popular Unionist	1
Speaker	1
1997 – Labour	
Labour	419
Conservative	165
Liberal Democrats	46
Ulster Unionist Party	9
Scottish National Party	6
Plaid Cymru	4
Social Democratic and Labour	3
Democratic Unionist party	2
Sinn Féin	2
Ulster Popular Unionist	1
United Kingdom Unionist	1
Independent	1
Speaker	1

Elgar, Edward (William) (1857–1934)

English composer. Although his celebrated oratorio *The Dream of Gerontius* (1900) (based on the written work by theologian John Henry Newman) was initially unpopular in Britain, its good reception in Düsseldorf (1902) led to a surge of interest in his earlier works, including the *Pomp and Circumstance Marches* (1901). His *Enigma Variations* (1899) brought him lasting fame.

Among his later works, which tend to be more introspective than the earlier ones, are oratorios, two symphonies, a violin concerto, chamber music, songs, and the symphonic poem *Falstaff* (1913), culminating in the poignant cello concerto of 1919. After this piece, Elgar published no further music of significance. He concentrated on transcriptions and made some early gramophone recordings of his own work.

Elgin

Administrative headquarters of ◊Moray unitary authority, northeast Scotland, on the River Lossie, 8 km/5 mi south of its port of Lossiemouth on the southern shore of the Moray

Firth; population (1991) 19,000. There are sawmills and whisky distilleries.

◊Gordonstoun private school is situated to the north. The remains of Elgin Cathedral ('Lantern of the North'), founded in 1224, are evident. The 13th-century Spynie Palace, 3 km/2 mi to the north, was restored in 1994.

Elgin marbles

Collection of ancient Greek sculptures, including the famous frieze and other sculptures from the Parthenon at Athens, assembled by the 7th Earl of Elgin. Sent to England 1803–1812, and bought for the nation in 1816 for £35,000, they are now in the British Museum. Greece has repeatedly asked for them to be returned to Athens.

Eliot, George pen name of Mary Ann (later Marian) Evans (1819–1880)

English novelist. Her works include the pastoral *Adam Bede* (1859); *The Mill on the Floss* (1860), with its autobiographical elements; *Silas Marner* (1861), containing elements of the folk tale; and *Daniel Deronda* (1876). *Middlemarch*, published serially (1871–72), is considered her greatest novel for its confident handling of numerous characters and central social and moral issues. She developed a subtle psychological presentation of character, and her work is pervaded by a penetrating and compassionate intelligence.

George Eliot had a strict evangelical upbringing. In 1841 she was converted to free thought. As assistant editor of the *Westminster Review* under John Chapman 1851–53, she made the acquaintance of Thomas Carlyle, Harriet Martineau, Herbert Spencer, and the philosopher and critic George Henry Lewes (1817–1878). Lewes was married but separated from his wife, and from 1854 he and Eliot lived together in a relationship that she regarded as a true marriage and that continued until his death. Lewes strongly believed in her talent and as a result of his encouragement the story 'Amos Barton' was accepted by *Blackwoods Magazine* in 1857. This was followed by a number of other short stories, and their success persuaded Eliot to embark on writing her full-length novels.

Eliot, T(homas) S(tearns) (1888–1965)

US-born poet, playwright, and critic, who lived in England from 1915. His first volume of poetry, *Prufrock and Other Observations* (1917), introduced new verse forms and rhythms; subsequent major poems were *The ◊Waste Land* (1922), a long symbolic poem of disillusionment, and 'The Hollow Men' (1925). Eliot's plays include *Murder in the Cathedral* (1935) and *The Cocktail Party* (1950). His critical works include *The Sacred Wood* (1920), setting out his views on poetic tradition.

His collection *Old Possum's Book of Practical Cats* (1939) was used for the popular English composer Andrew Lloyd Webber's musical *Cats* (1981).

Eliot was born in St Louis, Missouri, and was educated at Harvard, the Sorbonne, and Oxford University. He married and settled in London in 1917 and became a British subject in 1927. He was for a time a bank clerk, later lecturing and entering publishing at Faber & Faber, where he became a director. As editor of the highly influential literary magazine *Criterion* 1922–39, he was responsible for a critical re-evaluation of metaphysical poetry and Jacobean drama.

Although he makes considerable demands on his readers, he is regarded as the founder of Modernism in poetry: as a critic he profoundly influenced the ways in which literature was appreciated. He won the Nobel Prize for Literature in 1948.

Elizabeth, the Queen Mother (1900–)

Wife of King George VI of England. She was born Lady Elizabeth Angela Marguerite Bowes-Lyon, and on 26 April 1923 she married Albert, Duke of York, who became King George VI in 1936. Their children are Queen Elizabeth II and Princess Margaret.

She is the youngest daughter of the 14th Earl of Strathmore and Kinghorne (died 1944), through whom she is descended

ELIZABETH, THE QUEEN MOTHER *The widow of the former King George VI, the Queen Mother is held in great public affection. During the wartime Blitz, she and her husband remained in London and visited victims of the intensive bombing of the poor industrial eastern districts of the city. On her birthday, crowds gather outside her London residence of Clarence House to sing 'Happy Birthday'. Corel*

from Robert Bruce, king of Scotland. When her husband became King George VI she became Queen Consort, and was crowned with him in 1937. She adopted the title Queen Elizabeth, the Queen Mother after his death.

Elizabeth

Two queens of England or the UK:

> *Though God hath raised me high, yet this I count the glory of my crown: that I have reigned with your loves.*
>
> Elizabeth I Queen of England. The Golden Speech 1601, quoted in D'Ewes' *Journal*

Elizabeth I (1533–1603)

Queen of England 1558–1603, the daughter of Henry VIII and Anne Boleyn. Through her Religious Settlement of 1559 she enforced the Protestant religion by law. She had ◊Mary Queen of Scots executed in 1587. Her conflict with Roman Catholic Spain led to the defeat of the ◊Spanish Armada in 1588. The Elizabethan age was expansionist in commerce and geographical exploration, and arts and literature flourished. The rulers of many European states made unsuccessful bids to marry Elizabeth, and she used these bids to strengthen her power. She was succeeded by James I.

Elizabeth was born at Greenwich, London, 7 September 1533. She was well educated in several languages. During her Roman Catholic half-sister Mary's (◊Mary I) reign, Elizabeth's Protestant sympathies brought her under suspicion, and she lived in seclusion at Hatfield, Hertfordshire, until on Mary's death she became queen. Her first task was to bring about a broad religious settlement.

Many unsuccessful attempts were made by Parliament to persuade Elizabeth to marry or settle the succession. She found courtship a useful political weapon, and she maintained friendships with, among others, the courtiers Leicester, Sir Walter ◊Raleigh, and Essex. She was known as the Virgin Queen.

The arrival in England in 1568 of Mary Queen of Scots and her imprisonment by Elizabeth caused a political crisis, and a rebellion of the feudal nobility of the north followed in 1569. Friction between English and Spanish sailors hastened the breach with Spain. When the Dutch rebelled against Spanish tyranny Elizabeth secretly encouraged them; Philip II retaliated by aiding Catholic conspiracies against her. This undeclared war continued for many years, until the landing of an English army in the Netherlands in 1585 and Mary's execution in 1587, brought it into the open. Philip's Armada (the fleet sent to invade England in 1588) met with total disaster.

The war with Spain continued with varying fortunes to the end of the reign, while events at home foreshadowed the conflicts of the 17th century. Among the Puritans discontent was developing with Elizabeth's religious settlement, and several were imprisoned or executed. Parliament showed a new independence, and in 1601 forced Elizabeth to retreat on the question of the crown granting manufacturing and trading monopolies. Yet her prestige remained unabated, as shown by the failure of Essex's rebellion in 1601.

Elizabeth II, Elizabeth Alexandra Mary (1926–)

Queen of Great Britain and Northern Ireland from 1952, the elder daughter of George VI. She married her third cousin, Philip, the Duke of Edinburgh, in 1947. They have four children: Charles, Anne, Andrew, and Edward.

Princess Elizabeth Alexandra Mary was born in London on 21 April 1926; she was educated privately, and assumed official duties at 16.

During World War II she served in the Auxiliary Territorial Service, and by an amendment to the Regency Act she became a state counsellor on her 18th birthday. On the death of George VI in 1952 she succeeded to the throne while in Kenya with her husband and was crowned on 2 June 1953.

With an estimated wealth of £5 billion (1994), the Queen is the richest woman in Britain, and probably the world. In April 1993 she voluntarily began paying full rates of income tax and capital gains on her private income, which chiefly

Elizabeth II *Queen of Great Britain and Northern Ireland. As a constitutional monarch, representing the supreme legal and political authority, the Queen summons and dissolves Parliament, gives her official approval to acts of Parliament, sanctions government judicial appointments, and confers honours and awards. She is the head of the Commonwealth, and is queen of Canada, New Zealand, Australia, and several other countries. Topham Picture Source*

consists of the proceeds of a share portfolio and is estimated to be worth around £45 million. See ◊monarchy for the line of succession and for a list of members of the Royal Family.

I'm glad we've been bombed. It makes me feel I can look the East End in the face.

Elizabeth, the Queen Mother Wife of King George VI of England.
Remark to a policeman 13 September 1940 following German bombing of Buckingham Palace

Elizabethan literature

Literature produced during the reign of Elizabeth I of England (1558–1603). This period saw a remarkable florescence of the arts in England, and the literature of the time is characterized by a new energy, richness, and confidence. Renaissance humanism, Protestant zeal, and geographical discovery all contributed to this upsurge of creative power. Drama was the dominant form of the age, and ◊Shakespeare and ◊Marlowe were popular with all levels of society; see also ◊theatre. Other writers of the period include Edmund Spenser, Sir Philip Sidney, Francis Bacon, Thomas Lodge, Robert Greene, and John Lyly. See also ◊English literature.

Elizabethan playhouse

Open-air theatre in use in England in the late 16th and early 17th centuries. The first playhouse was the Theatre, Shoreditch, London (1576); the ◊Globe Theatre (built in 1599 by the company to which Shakespeare was attached), the Rose (1587), and the Hope (1613) soon followed in Southwark, where the City's strict regulations on entertainment were waived. Elizabethan or Jacobean playhouses could be circular, octagonal, or square in shape, and accommodated a large number of spectators – the Swan Playhouse could reputedly hold 3,000 people. After the discovery of its original site, the Globe Theatre was reconstructed and reopened in 1996.

Ellesmere Port

Oil port and industrial town in Cheshire, northwest England, on the River Mersey and the Manchester Ship Canal, 11 km/7 mi north of Chester; population (1991) 64,500. Industries include enngineering and the manufacture of petroleum products (Shell), cars (Vauxhall), chemicals, car engines, and paper.

Formerly the biggest transhipment canal port in northwest England, it now contains the Ellesmere Port Boat Museum (opened 1976) which traces the history of canals, with many old narrow boats and a blacksmith's forge.

History

The Shropshire Union Canal, developed to transport iron-ore from the Furness peninsula to the West Midlands, and china clay to the Potteries, reached Ellesmere Port in 1795. A variety of industries were later established, including metal processing, dyestuffs, flour-milling, and paper. From 1894 the opening of the Manchester Ship Canal led to further growth.

The Gowy river marshes, now the site of a large oil refinery at Stanlow, were drained by prisoners during World War I.

Elliott, Denholm (Mitchell) (1922–1992)

English film, stage, and television actor. In his early career he often played stiff-upper-lip Englishmen, and later portrayed somewhat degenerate upper-class characters. In his first film for Hollywood, *King Rat* (1965), he was a cynical prisoner. He followed this a year later with the part of the villainous back-street abortionist in *Alfie* (1966). Later film roles include the conceited butler in *Trading Places* (1983), the Fleet Street hack in *Defence of the Realm* (1985), and Mr Emerson in *A Room with a View* (1986). He also appeared in many TV plays and series, including *Bleak House* (1987).

He received the British Academy of Film and Television Arts award for best TV actor in 1981 and for best supporting film actor in 1984, 1985, and 1986.

Ellis, (Henry) Havelock (1859–1939)

English psychologist and writer of many works on the psychology of sex. His major work, *Studies in the Psychology of Sex* (seven volumes, 1898–1928), was for many years published only in the US after a UK bookseller was prosecuted in 1898 for stocking it.

Elstree

Village in Hertfordshire, England, 8 km/5 mi west of Barnet; population (1991) 5,300. Elstree is the residential area of Borehamwood, and is the site of extensive film and TV studios.

The first film studio in Elstree opened in 1914. The BBC's Elstree Centre now stands on the site of the original studio. Films made at Elstree include *2001: A Space Odyssey* and *Star Wars*.

Elton, Ben(jamin) Charles (1959–)

English stand-up comedian, who is also a prolific playwright, scriptwriter, and novelist. He wrote for the *Blackadder* series in the late 1980s, and wrote the police comedy, *The Thin Blue Line* (1995 and 1997), as well as having his own TV show in 1998. He has written three plays and five novels, including *Blast From the Past* (1998).

Elton, Charles Sutherland (1900–1991)

British ecologist, a pioneer of the study of animal and plant forms in their natural environments, and of animal behaviour as part of the complex pattern of life. He defined the concept of food chains and was an early conservationist. Elton was instrumental in establishing the Nature Conservancy Council (1949), and was much concerned with the impact of introduced species on natural systems.

Ely

City in the Cambridgeshire ◊Fens, eastern England, on the Great Ouse River, 24km/15 mi northeast of Cambridge; population (1991) 10,300. Economic activities include agriculture (sugar beet), engineering, and the manufacture of agricultural machinery, pottery, chemicals, and plastics. The cathedral, dating from 1083, is one of the largest in England.

Ely was the chief town of the former administrative district of the **Isle of Ely**, so called because the town originally lay on a low hill, isolated by the surrounding marshland of the Fens before they were drained in the 17th and 18th centuries. The Anglo-Saxon rebel Hereward the Wake had his stronghold against William (I) the Conqueror here, until it was captured in 1071. At the annual feast of St Etheldreda (Audrey), cheap, low-quality souvenirs were sold; the word 'tawdry', a corruption of St Audrey, derives from this practice.

Ely Cathedral

The Cathedral's long nave, high west tower, adjoining transept tower, octagon, and Lady Chapel, make it a completely original composition that stands out from the flat fenland in every direction. The present cathedral was begun by Abbot Simeon, a kinsman of William the Conqueror, in 1083, though it was not the see of a bishop until 1109.

The site was first colonized by St Etheldreda, who founded a monastery in 673. This was burnt down by the Danes in 870 and replaced with a powerful Benedictine Abbey by Ethelwold, Bishop of Winchester, in 970.

The architecture of the present cathedral is chiefly Norman, of a variety which strikingly foreshadows English Perpendicular, the style of three centuries later. The crossing tower was completely redesigned as an octagon in 1322–28, becoming one of the most celebrated creations of Gothic architecture. Its remarkable lantern, resting apparently on slender wooden rib vaults, was completed in 1342.

Empire Windrush

Ship that brought some 500 West Indian immigrants to Britain, docking at Tilbury in June 1948. This was the first of many waves of Caribbean immigrants to arrive in post-war Britain. To celebrate the 50th anniversary of the arrival of *Empire Windrush*, the BBC in summer 1998 ran a series of programmes under the umbrella title *Windrush*.

> *The first shock in England when I came in was that all the bomb sites were still there. The second shock was that it was unusual for people to respond if you said hello.... It was unlike anything I've ever come across before.*
>
> Ben Bosquet London councillor and anti-apartheid activist (arrived in Britain from St Lucia in 1957). Quoted in *Windrush*, 1998

Employment, Department of, DE

Former UK government department which merged in 1995 with the Department for Education to form the ◊Department for Education and Employment.

Empson, William (1906–1984)

English poet and critic. His critical work examined the potential variety of meaning in poetry, as in *Seven Types of Ambiguity* (1930) (introducing the concept of 'ambiguity' to critical thinking) and *The Structure of Complex Words* (1951). His *Collected Poems* were published in 1955. Knighted 1979.

EMS

Abbreviation for ◊**European Monetary System**.

enclosure

Appropriation of common land as private property, or the changing of open-field systems to enclosed fields (often used for sheep). This process began in the 14th century and became widespread in the 15th and 16th centuries. It caused poverty, homelessness, and rural depopulation, and resulted in revolts in 1536, 1569, and 1607. A further wave of enclosures occurred between about 1760 and 1820.

Government action

Numerous government measures to prevent depopulation were introduced between 1489 and 1640, including the first Enclosure Act (1603), but were sabotaged by landowning magistrates at local level. A new wave of enclosures by Acts of Parliament from 1760 to 1820 reduced the yeoman class of small landowning farmers to agricultural labourers, or forced them to leave the land. The Enclosure Acts applied to 4.5 million acres or a quarter of England. Some 17 million acres were enclosed without any parliamentary act. From 1876 the enclosure of common land in Britain was limited by statutes. See also ◊field.

Enfield

Outer borough of northeast Greater London. It includes the districts of ◊Edmonton and Southgate

Features the royal hunting ground of Enfield Chase partly survives in the 'green belt'; early 17th-century Forty Hall; Lea Valley Regional Park, opened 1967

Industries engineering (the Royal Small Arms factory, which closed 1989, produced the Enfield rifle), textiles, furniture, cement, electronics, metal, and plastic products

Population (1991) 257,400.

Enfield, Harry (1961–)

English comedian and writer. He began his career providing the voices for puppets on the 1980s satirical television show *Spitting Image*. This was followed by slots on the weekend entertainment shows *Saturday Live* and *Friday Night Live*, and then his own television shows, in which he teamed up with fellow comics Kathie Burke and Paul Whitehouse. In 1992 Enfield co-starred in the first season of the sitcom ◊*Men Behaving Badly*, and in 1994 his show *Harry Enfield and Chums* began broadcasting.

Among the early characters he created were the endearing Greek-Briton Stavros and the objectionable product of Thatcherite Britain, plasterer Loadsamoney. In his own shows he added to his repertoire such popular favourites as has-been radio disc-jockey Dave Nice, simpleton Tim Nice But Dim, rebellious teenager Kevin, and working-class layabout Wayne Slob. He has also deployed his various characters extensively in television advertising.

England

Largest division of the ◊United Kingdom

Area 130,357 sq km/50,318 sq mi

Capital London

Towns and cities Birmingham, Cambridge, Coventry, Leeds, Leicester, Manchester, Newcastle upon Tyne, Nottingham, Oxford, Sheffield, York; ports Bristol, Dover, Felixstowe, Harwich, Liverpool, Portsmouth, Southampton

England: Local Government

Beginning in 1995, far-reaching local government changes took effect in England, based on recommendations of a government commission that was set up under the Local Government Act of 1992. The changes were implemented in stages, and resulted in a combination of the existing two-tier structure with new single-tier (unitary) authorities. In 1995 and 1996, unitary authorities were introduced for the Isle of Wight, Avon, Cleveland, and Humberside (with the latter three being abolished as counties); the city of York, formerly in North Yorkshire, also became a unitary authority, with the rest of the county retaining the two-tier system. More counties underwent changes in 1997, with their main urban centres becoming unitary authorities and the rest of the county keeping the existing two-tier system.

Local authority	Administrative headquarters
Bath and North East Somerset	Bath
Bedfordshire	Bedford
Bournemouth	Bournemouth
Blackburn with Darwen	Blackburn
Blackpool	Blackpool
Bournemouth	Bournemouth
Bracknell Forest	Bracknell
Brighton and Hove	Hove
Bristol	Bristol
Buckinghamshire	Aylesbury
Cambridgeshire	Cambridge
Cheshire	Chester
Cornwall	Truro
Cumbria	Carlisle
Darlington	Darlington
Derby City	Derby
Derbyshire	Matlock
Devon	Exeter
Dorset	Dorchester
Durham	Durham
East Riding of Yorkshire	Beverley
East Sussex	Lewes
Essex	Chelmsford
Gloucestershire	Gloucester
Halton	Widnes
Hampshire	Winchester
Hartlepool	Hartlepool
Herefordshire	Hereford
Hertfordshire	Hertford
Isle of Wight	Newport
Kent	Maidstone
Kingston upon Hull	Kingston upon Hull
Lancashire	Preston
Leicester City	Leicester
Leicestershire	Glenfield
Lincolnshire	Lincoln
London, Greater	London
Luton	Luton
Medway Towns	Strood
Middlesbrough	Middlesbrough
Milton Keynes	Milton Keynes
Norfolk	Norwich
Northamptonshire	Northampton
North East Lincolnshire	Grimsby
North Lincolnshire	Scunthorpe
North Somerset	Weston-super-Mare
Northumberland	Morpeth
North Yorkshire	Northallerton
Nottingham City	Nottingham
Nottinghamshire	West Bridgford
Oxfordshire	Oxford
Peterborough	Peterborough
Plymouth	Plymouth
Poole	Poole
Portsmouth	Portsmouth
Reading	Reading
Redcar and Cleveland	Redcar
Rutland	Oakham
Shropshire	Shrewsbury
Slough	Slough

continued on page 308

continued from page 307

Local authority	Administrative headquarters
Somerset	Taunton
Southampton	Southampton
Southend	Southend
South Gloucestershire	Thornbury
Staffordshire	Stafford
Stockton-on-Tees	Stockton-on-Tees
Stoke-on-Trent	Stoke-on-Trent
Suffolk	Ipswich
Surrey	Kingston upon Thames
Swindon	Swindon
Telford and Wrekin	Telford
Thurrock	Grays
Torbay	Torbay
Tyne and Wear	Newcastle upon Tyne
Warrington	Warrington
Warwickshire	Warwick
West Berkshire	Newbury
West Sussex	Chichester
Wiltshire	Trowbridge
Windsor and Maidenhead	Maidenhead
Wokingham	Wokingham
Worcestershire	Worcester
York	York
Nonadministrative Metropolitan Counties	
Manchester, Greater	
Merseyside	
South Yorkshire	
West Midlands	
West Yorkshire	

England: Historic Counties

Bedfordshire
Berkshire
Buckinghamshire
Cambridgeshire and Isle of Ely
Cheshire
Cornwall
Cumberland
Derbyshire
Devonshire
Dorset
Durham
Essex
Gloucestershire
Hampshire
Herefordshire
Hertfordshire
Huntingdonshire and Peterborough
Kent
Lancashire
Leicestershire
Lincolnshire
- Holland
- Kesteven
- Lindsey

Greater London
Norfolk
Northamptonshire
Northumberland
Nottinghamshire
Oxfordshire
Rutland
Shropshire
Somerset
Staffordshire
Suffolk
- East Suffolk
- West Suffolk

Surrey
Sussex
- East Sussex
- West Sussex

Warwickshire
Westmorland
Wight, Isle of
Wiltshire
Worcestershire
Yorkshire
- East Riding
- North Riding
- West Riding

England – local government divisions
BA BATH AND NE SOMERSET
BE BEDFORDSHIRE
BR BRACKNELL FOREST
BT BRISTOL
BU BUCKINGHAMSHIRE
DA DARLINGTON
DC DERBY CITY
GR GREATER MANCHESTER
HA HALTON
HE HERTFORDSHIRE
LC LEICESTER CITY
LE LEICESTERSHIRE
LU LUTON
MK MILTON KEYNES
NH NORTHAMPTONSHIRE
NL NORTH LINCOLNSHIRE
NS NORTH SOMERSET
NT NOTTINGHAMSHIRE
PB PETERBOROUGH
PT PORTSMOUTH
R READING
RU RUTLAND
SG SOUTH GLOUCESTERSHIRE
SO SOUTHAMPTON
SS STOCKTON-ON-TEES
ST STOKE-ON-TRENT
TW TELFORD AND WREKIN
WA WARRINGTON
WK WEST BERKSHIRE
WM WEST MIDLANDS
WN WINDSOR AND MAIDENHEAD
WO WOKINGHAM
WR WORCESTERSHIRE
SCOTLAND
NORTHERN IRELAND
REPUBLIC OF IRELAND
WALES
ENGLAND
FRANCE
Isle of Man
Irish Sea
North Sea
English Channel
Isles of Scilly
NORTHUMBERLAND
TYNE AND WEAR
DURHAM
HARTLEPOOL
REDCAR AND CLEVELAND
MIDDLESBROUGH
CUMBRIA
NORTH YORKSHIRE
YORK
THE EAST RIDING OF YORKSHIRE
KINGSTON UPON HULL
LANCASHIRE
BLACKPOOL
BLACKBURN AND DARWEN
WEST YORKSHIRE
NORTH EAST LINCOLNSHIRE
MERSEYSIDE
SOUTH YORKSHIRE
LINCOLNSHIRE
CHESHIRE
DERBYSHIRE
NOTTINGHAM CITY
STAFFORDSHIRE
NORFOLK
SHROPSHIRE
CAMBRIDGESHIRE
SUFFOLK
WARWICKSHIRE
HEREFORDSHIRE
GLOUCESTERSHIRE
ESSEX
OXFORDSHIRE
SOUTHEND
THURROCK
SLOUGH
GREATER LONDON
SWINDON
WILTSHIRE
MEDWAY TOWNS
SURREY
KENT
HAMPSHIRE
SOMERSET
WEST SUSSEX
EAST SUSSEX
POOLE
BRIGHTON AND HOVE
DEVON
DORSET
ISLE OF WIGHT
BOURNEMOUTH
PLYMOUTH
CORNWALL
TORBAY
unitary authority within another local government area
0 50 mi
0 100 km

English Sovereigns

Henry II became additionally King of Ireland in 1172; Wales united with England in 1536–43; Scotland and England united in 1603. For genealogies of the various houses, see their main entries.

Reign	Name	Relationship
	West Saxon Kings	
899–924	Edward the Elder	son of Alfred the Great
924–39	Athelstan	son of Edward the Elder
939–46	Edmund	half-brother of Athelstan
946–55	Edred	brother of Edmund
955–59	Edwy	son of Edmund
959–75	Edgar	brother of Edwy
975–78	Edward the Martyr	son of Edgar
978–1016	Ethelred (II) the Unready	son of Edgar
1016	Edmund Ironside	son of Ethelred (II) the Unready
	Danish Kings	
1016–35	Canute	son of Sweyn I of Denmark who conquered England in 1013
1035–40	Harold I	son of Canute
1040–42	Hardicanute	son of Canute
	West Saxon Kings (restored)	
1042–66	Edward the Confessor	son of Ethelred II
1066	Harold II	son of Godwin
	Norman Kings	
1066–87	William I	illegitimate son of Duke Robert the Devil
1087–1100	William II	son of William I
1100–35	Henry I	son of William I
1135–54	Stephen	grandson of William II
	House of Plantagenet	
1154–89	Henry II	son of Matilda (daughter of Henry I)
1189–99	Richard I	son of Henry II
1199–1216	John	son of Henry II
1216–72	Henry III	son of John
1272–1307	Edward I	son of Henry III
1307–27	Edward II	son of Edward I
1327–77	Edward III	son of Edward II
1377–99	Richard II	son of the Black Prince
	House of Lancaster	
1399–1413	Henry IV	son of John of Gaunt
1413–22	Henry V	son of Henry IV
1422–61, 1470–71	Henry VI	son of Henry V

Reign	Name	Relationship
	House of York	
1461–70, 1471–83	Edward IV	son of Richard, Duke of York
1483	Edward V	son of Edward IV
1483–85	Richard III	brother of Edward IV
	House of Tudor	
1485–1509	Henry VII	son of Edmund Tudor, Earl of Richmond
1509–47	Henry VIII	son of Henry VII
1547–53	Edward VI	son of Henry VIII
1553–58	Mary I	daughter of Henry VIII
1558–1603	Elizabeth I	daughter of Henry VIII
	House of Stuart	
1603–25	James I	great-grandson of Margaret (daughter of Henry VII)
1625–49	Charles I	son of James I
1649–60	the Commonwealth	
	House of Stuart (restored)	
1660–85	Charles II	son of Charles I
1685–88	James II	son of Charles I
1689–1702	William III and Mary	son of Mary (daughter of Charles I); daughter of James II
1702–14	Anne	daughter of James II
	House of Hanover	
1714–27	George I	son of Sophia (granddaughter of James I)
1727–60	George II	son of George I
1760–1820	George III	son of Frederick (son of George II)
1820–30	George IV (regent 1811–20)	son of George III
1830–37	William IV	son of George III
1837–1901	Victoria	daughter of Edward (son of George III)
	House of Saxe-Coburg	
1901–10	Edward VII	son of Victoria
	House of Windsor	
1910–36	George V	son of Edward VII
1936	Edward VIII	son of George V
1936–52	George VI	son of George V
1952–	Elizabeth II	daughter of George VI

ENGLAND: CHRONOLOGY

For earlier history, see Ancient Britain.

AD **43** Roman invasion.

5th–7th centuries Anglo-Saxons overran all England except Cornwall and Cumberland, forming independent kingdoms including Northumbria, Mercia, Kent, and Wessex.

c. 597 England converted to Christianity by St Augustine.

829 Egbert of Wessex accepted as overlord of all England.

878 Alfred ceded northern and eastern England to the Danish invaders but kept them out of Wessex.

1066 Norman Conquest; England passed into French hands under William the Conqueror.

1172 Henry II became king of Ireland and established a colony there.

1215 King John forced to sign Magna Carta.

1284 Conquest of Wales, begun by the Normans, completed by Edward I.

1295 Model Parliament set up.

1338–1453 Hundred Years' War with France enabled Parliament to secure control of taxation and, by impeachment, of the king's choice of ministers.

1348–49 Black Death killed about 30% of the population.

1381 Social upheaval led to the Peasants' Revolt, which was brutally repressed.

1399 Richard II deposed by Parliament for absolutism.

1414 Lollard revolt repressed.

1455–85 Wars of the Roses.

1497 Henry VII ended the power of the feudal nobility with the suppression of the Yorkist revolts.

1529 Henry VIII became head of the Church of England after breaking with Rome.

1536–43 Acts of Union united England and Wales after conquest.

1547 Edward VI adopted Protestant doctrines.

1553 Reversion to Roman Catholicism under Mary I.

1558 Elizabeth I adopted a religious compromise.

1588 Attempted invasion of England by the Spanish Armada.

1603 James I united the English and Scottish crowns; parliamentary dissidence increased.

1642–52 Civil War between royalists and parliamentarians, resulting in victory for Parliament.

1649 Charles I executed and the Commonwealth set up.

1653 Oliver Cromwell appointed Lord Protector.

1660 Restoration of Charles II.

1685 Monmouth's rebellion.

1688 William of Orange invited to take the throne; flight of James II.

1707 Act of Union between England and Scotland under Queen Anne, after which the countries became known as Great Britain.

For history after 1707, see the chronology at the end of the book.

Features variability of climate and diversity of scenery; among European countries, only the Netherlands is more densely populated
Exports agricultural (cereals, rape, sugar beet, potatoes); meat and meat products; electronic (software) and telecommunications equipment; scientific instruments; textiles and fashion goods; North Sea oil and gas, petrochemicals, pharmaceuticals, fertilizers; beer; china clay, pottery, porcelain, and glass; film and television programmes, and sound recordings. Tourism is important. There are worldwide banking and insurance interests
Currency pound sterling
Population (1993 est) 48,500,000
Language English, with more than 100 minority languages
Religion Christian, with the Church of England as the established church, 31,500,000; and various Protestant groups, of which the largest is the Methodist 1,400,000; Roman Catholic about 5,000,000; Muslim 900,000; Jewish 410,000; Sikh 175,000; Hindu 140,000
Government returns 529 members to Parliament; a mixture of 2-tier and unitary local authorities, with 34 non-metropolitan counties, 46 unitary authorities, 6 metropolitan counties (with 36 metropolitan boroughs), 32 London boroughs, and the Corporation of London. See map for local government divisions from 1997, and list for administrative headquarters; see page 308 for the list of **historic counties** that still retain a ceremonial and sporting role.
History see chronology of English history, above, and also list of sovereigns. For England's union with Wales, Scotland, and Ireland, see Act of ◊Union, and ◊United Kingdom. See also chronology of British history 1707–1998 at the end of the book.

It will be said of this generation that it found England a land of beauty and left it a land of beauty spots.

CYRIL JOAD British philosopher and broadcaster.
Sayings of the Week, the *Observer*, May 1953

English Channel

Stretch of water between England and France, leading in the west to the Atlantic Ocean, and in the east via the Strait of Dover to the North Sea; it is also known as **La Manche** (French 'the sleeve') from its shape. The ◊Channel Tunnel, opened in 1994, runs between Folkestone, Kent, and Sangatte, west of Calais.

The English Channel is 560 km/348 mi long west–east; 27

km/17 mi wide at its narrowest (Cap Gris Nez–Dover) and 177 km/110 mi wide at its widest (Ushant–Land's End). The average depth is 40–60 m/131–197 ft, reaching 120 m/394 ft at the entrance to the Strait of Dover and as much as 180 m/590 ft at Hurds Deep, 30 km/19 mi northwest of Guernsey.

The tides are generally higher on the French coast than the English, with a double tide in areas of the English coast. Westerly winds are the most prevalent, with winter gales and year-round fogs occurring. Regular shipping services are run between Southampton and St Malo, Cherbourg, and Le Havre; between Newhaven and Dieppe; and also across the narrower Strait of Dover. The main islands are the Channel Islands and the Isle of Wight.

English Heritage

The UK's leading conservation organization, responsible for the conservation of historic remains in England. Under the National Heritage Act 1983, its duties are to secure the preservation of ancient monuments and historic buildings; to promote the preservation and enhancement of conservation areas; and to promote the public's enjoyment and understanding of ancient monuments and historic buildings.

Listed buildings

With the advice of English Heritage, the government compiles lists of buildings of special architectural or historical interest. It is against the law to demolish, extend, or alter the character of any listed building without prior consent from the local planning authority or the appropriate secretary of state. At the end of 1994 there were 444,508 entries on the lists of historic buildings.

Work

English Heritage has embarked upon a programme to evaluate all known archaeological remains in England. This is expected to result in a significant increase in the number of scheduled monuments.

English Heritage manages about 400 properties on behalf of the secretary of state for national heritage, advises him or her on applications for consent to alter or demolish scheduled monuments and listed buildings, and gives grants for the repair of ancient monuments, historic buildings, and buildings in conservation areas in England. Most of the monuments are open to the public. All the properties in the care of English Heritage either belong to the nation or are in its guardianship.

Finance

Government funding for English Heritage was £104 million in 1994–95. Membership in 1993–94 was 310,000, and provided an income of £2.9 million; income from visitors was £10.7 million. Grants to help owners preserve and restore listed buildings in 1993–94 totalled £34.4 million. In the same year, £6.2 million was spent on commissions to record and survey archaeological sites and landscapes and on publishing the results of this work.

English language

Language spoken by more than 300 million native speakers, and between 400 and 800 million foreign users. See feature on page 313 on the development of the English language.

English is the official language of air transport and shipping; the leading language of science, technology, computers, and commerce; and a major medium of education, publishing, and international negotiation. For this reason scholars frequently refer to its latest phase as World English.

English law

One of the major European legal systems, Roman law being the other. English law has spread to many other countries, including former English colonies such as the USA, Canada, Australia, and New Zealand.

English law has a continuous history dating from the local customs of the Anglo-Saxons, traces of which survived until 1925. After the Norman Conquest there grew up, side by side with the Saxon shire courts, the feudal courts of the barons and the ecclesiastical courts. From the king's council developed the royal courts, presided over by professional judges, which gradually absorbed the jurisdictions of the baronial and ecclesiastical courts. By 1250 the royal judges had amalgamated the various local customs into the system of common law – that is, law common to the whole country. A second system known as ◊equity developed in the Court of Chancery, in which the Lord Chancellor considered petitions.

In the 17th and 18th centuries common law absorbed the Law Merchant, the international code of mercantile customs. During the 19th century virtually the whole of English law was reformed by legislation; for example, the number of capital offences was greatly reduced.

A unique feature of English law is the doctrine of judicial precedents, whereby the reported decisions of the courts form a binding source of law for future decisions. A judge is bound by decisions of courts of superior jurisdiction but not necessarily by those of inferior courts.

The Judicature Acts 1873–75 abolished a multiplicity of courts, and in their place established the Supreme Court of Judicature, organized in the Court of Appeal and the High Court of Justice; the latter has three divisions – the Queen's Bench, Chancery, and Family Divisions. All High Court judges may apply both common law and equity in deciding cases.

From the Court of Appeal there may be a further appeal to the House of Lords. See also ◊legal system.

'It is my duty to warn you that it will be used against you', cried the Inspector, with the magnificent fair play of the British criminal law.

Arthur Conan Doyle English writer.
The Memoirs of Sherlock Holmes, 'Dancing Men'

English literature

Term commonly applied to all literature in the English language; however what follows is an account of literature in Britain (see also ◊Scottish Gaelic literature, ◊Welsh literature, and ◊Old English literature).

THE DEVELOPMENT OF THE ENGLISH LANGUAGE

Origins of English

English is a member of the West Germanic branch of the Indo-European family of languages. As Old English, it was first spoken by the Angles, Saxons and Jutes from Jutland, Schleswig and Holstein respectively who settled in Britain in the 5th and 6th centuries AD. The Jutes went to what is now Kent, southern Hampshire and the Isle of Wight; the Saxons spread out in the rest of England south of the Thames, as well as modern Middlesex and Essex; and the Angles penetrated the remainder of England as far north as the Firth of Forth. The Anglian-speaking region developed two speech groups, Northumbrian, to the north of the River Humber, and Southumbrian, or Mercian, to the south of it. The dialect of the Jutes became known as Kentish, and that of the Saxons as West Saxon in what emerged as the kingdom of Wessex.

In the 8th century Northumbrian led in literature and culture, but its predominance was broken by the Vikings, who sacked Lindisfarne, off the Northumbrian coast, in 793. They landed in strength in 865. The first raiders were Danes, but they were later joined by Norwegians from Ireland and the Western Isles who settled in northwestern England. In the 9th century, thanks to the economic and political influence of the kingdom of Wessex in the reign of Alfred the Great (871–899), the cultural leadership passed from Northumbria to Wessex. Following the arrival of St Augustine in 597 and the subsequent conversion of England to Latin Christianity, the Roman alphabet superseded the original Germanic runes.

The language of the Celts who inhabited Britain at the time of the arrival of the Angles, Saxons and Jutes is chiefly evident today in river names such as Avon, Exe, Esk, Ouse and Wye, which all mean 'river' or 'water'. The first parts of many city names such as Winchester, Salisbury and Lichfield are also of Celtic origin. The Scandinavians gave such common nouns as band, birth, dirt, egg, knife, race, root, seat, skill, sky, and window.

The effect of the Norman conquest on the English language

The Norman Conquest of 1066 had two chief linguistic consequences. First, it placed all four Old English dialects more or less on a level. Second, it introduced a number of French words to the language. West Saxon lost its supremacy and the centre of culture and learning shifted from Winchester to London. The Northumbrian dialect divided into Lowland Scottish and Northern and the Mercian dialect was split into East and West Midland. West Saxon slightly decreased in area and became known as South Western, while the Kentish dialect extended considerably and became South Eastern.

England was now essentially bilingual. The ordinary people spoke and wrote the Germanic language that was now known as Middle English. The followers of William the Conqueror, who took over most of the important offices of church and state, spoke Norman French, which thus became the language of the court, parliament, law and education. The result was that the language contained many doublets. The cows, sheep and pigs that the English peasant tended became beef, mutton and pork on his Norman master's table. Doublets also evolved in English from Norman French and Central French, such as the pairs canal and channel, catch and chase, real and royal, wage and gage, warden and guardian. Words for basic concepts and things that have remained from their Old English originals include pairs of opposites such as heaven and earth, love and hate, life and death, beginning and end, day and night, month and year, heat and cold. Cardinal numbers also come from Old English as do all ordinal numbers except second, which comes, through French seconde, from Latin secundus.

The transition from middle English to modern English

The death of Chaucer at the close of the 14th century marked the beginning of the transition from Middle English to early Modern English. This period saw three major developments: the rise of London English as the dominant form, Caxton's invention of printing in 1476, which reinforced this dominance, and the spread of the new learning, which introduced Latin and Greek words through French or direct from Latin and Greek respectively. Words that had already entered through French were now borrowed again, giving doublets such as benison and benediction, blame and blaspheme, count and compute, dainty and dignity. There were even triplets, such as Anglo-Norman real, Norman French royal, and Latin regal. Borrowings from Latin and Greek produced further doublets, such as the pairs malnutrition and dystrophy, transfer and metaphor, circumambulatory and peripatetic, and luminiferous and phosphorescent. Printed English, for its part, retained features of written English that no longer reflected the actual pronunciation, and was thus largely responsible for crystallizing the disparity between spelling and pronunciation that is a key characteristic of English today.

The development of modern English

Modern English proper is usually dated from the restoration of the monarchy in 1660. Words from languages other than Latin and Greek were now becoming established, including nautical words from Dutch such as buy, deck, dock, skipper and yacht, musical terms from Italian such as allegro, cantabile, legato and staccato, and many indigenous names for animals and plants. Words from Arabic such as alcohol, algebra, assassin and sugar, or from Hebrew such as cherub, messiah, sabbath and seraph were by now no longer regarded as foreign. Global borrowings have since completed the jigsaw of English in its current form.

BY ADRIAN ROOM

12th–15th century: Middle English period

With the arrival of a Norman ruling class at the end of the 11th century, the ascendancy of Norman-French in cultural life began, and it was not until the 13th century that the native literature regained its strength. Prose was concerned chiefly with popular devotional use, but verse emerged typically in the metrical chronicles, such as Layamon's *Brut*, and the numerous romances based on the stories of Charlemagne, the Arthurian legends, and the classical episodes of Troy. First of the great English poets was Geoffrey Chaucer, whose early work reflected the predominant French influence, but later that of Renaissance Italy. Of purely native inspiration was *The Vision of William Concerning Piers the Plowman* of Langland in the old alliterative verse, and the anonymous *Pearl*, *Patience*, and *Gawayne and the Grene Knight*. Chaucer's mastery of versification was not shared by his successors, the most original of whom was John Skelton. More successful were the anonymous authors of songs and carols, and of the ballads, which (for example, those concerned with Robin Hood) often formed a complete cycle. Drama flowered in the form of miracle and morality plays; and prose, although still awkwardly handled by John Wycliffe in his translation of the Bible, rose to a great height with Thomas Malory in the 15th century.

16th century: Elizabethan

The Renaissance, which had first touched the English language through Chaucer, came to delayed fruition in the 16th century. Thomas Wyatt and Henry Surrey used the sonnet and blank verse in typically Elizabethan forms and prepared the way for Edmund Spenser, Philip Sidney, Samuel Daniel, Thomas Campion, and others. With Thomas Kyd and Christopher Marlowe, drama emerged into theatrical form; it reached the highest level in the works of Shakespeare and Ben Jonson. Elizabethan prose is represented by Richard Hooker, Thomas North, Roger Ascham, Raphael Holinshed, John Lyly, and others.

17th century

English prose achieved full richness in the 17th century, with the Authorized Version of the Bible (1611), Francis Bacon, John Milton, John Bunyan, Jeremy Taylor, Thomas Browne, Izaak Walton, and Samuel Pepys. Most renowned of the 17th-century poets were Milton and John Donne; others include the religious writers George Herbert, Richard Crashaw, Henry Vaughan, and Thomas Traherne, and the Cavalier poets Robert Herrick, Thomas Carew, John Suckling, and Richard Lovelace. In the Restoration period (from 1660) Samuel Butler and John Dryden stand out as poets. Dramatists include Thomas Otway and Nathaniel Lee in tragedy. Comedy flourished with William Congreve, John Vanbrugh, and George Farquhar.

18th century: the Augustan Age

Alexander Pope developed the poetic technique of Dryden; in prose Richard Steele and Joseph Addison evolved the polite essay, Jonathan Swift used satire, and Daniel Defoe exploited his journalistic ability. This century saw the development of the novel, through the epistolary style of Samuel Richardson to the robust narrative of Henry Fielding and Tobias Smollett, the comic genius of Laurence Sterne, and the Gothic 'horror' of Horace Walpole. The Neo-Classical standards established by the Augustans were maintained by Samuel Johnson and his circle – Oliver Goldsmith, Edmund Burke, Joshua Reynolds, Richard Sheridan, and others – but the romantic element present in the poetry of James Thomson, Thomas Gray, Edward Young, and William Collins was soon to overturn them.

19th century

The *Lyrical Ballads* 1798 of William Wordsworth and Samuel Taylor Coleridge were the manifesto of the new Romantic age. Lord Byron, Percy Bysshe Shelley, and John Keats form a second generation of Romantic poets. In fiction Walter Scott took over the Gothic tradition from Mrs Radcliffe, to create the historical novel, and Jane Austen established the novel of the comedy of manners. Criticism gained new prominence with Coleridge, Charles Lamb, William Hazlitt, and Thomas De Quincey. During the 19th century the novel was further developed by Charles Dickens, William Makepeace Thackeray, the Brontës, George Eliot, Anthony Trollope, and others. The principal poets of the reign of Victoria were Alfred Tennyson, Robert and Elizabeth Browning, Matthew Arnold, the Rossettis, William Morris, and Algernon Swinburne. Among the prose writers of the era were Thomas Macaulay, John Newman, John Stuart Mill, Thomas Carlyle, John Ruskin, and Walter Pater. The transition period at the end of the century saw the poetry and novels of George Meredith and Thomas Hardy; the work of Samuel Butler and George Gissing; and the plays of Arthur Pinero and Oscar Wilde. Although a Victorian, Gerald Manley Hopkins anticipated the 20th century with the experimentation of his verse forms.

20th century

Poets of World War I include Siegfried Sassoon, Rupert Brooke, Wilfred Owen, and Robert Graves. A middle-class realism developed in the novels of H G Wells, Arnold Bennett, E M Forster, and John Galsworthy while the novel's break with traditional narrative and exposition came through the Modernists D H Lawrence, Virginia Woolf, Somerset Maugham, Aldous Huxley, Christopher Isherwood, Evelyn Waugh, and Graham Greene. Writers for the stage include George Bernard Shaw, Galsworthy, J B Priestley, Noël Coward, and Terence Rattigan, and the writers of poetic drama, such as T S Eliot, Christopher Fry, W H Auden, Christopher Isherwood, and Dylan Thomas. The 1950s and 1960s produced the 'kitchen sink' dramatists, including John Osborne and Arnold Wesker.

Other notable playwrights who emerged in the 1960s and 1970s included John Arden and Robert Bolt, both much concerned with interpreting the present in terms of the past, Alan Ayckbourn, ingeniously exploring situations often from several viewpoints, enfant terrible Joe Orton, Peter Shaffer, extracting drama from concerns of modern psychology and vengeance, and Harold Pinter and Tom Stoppard, both manipulators of language and characterization.

Post-war novelists of middle class manners include Kingsley Amis, A S Byatt, Margaret Drabble, Elizabeth Jane Howard, Iris Murdoch, Anthony Powell, and Angus Wilson. Malcolm Bradbury and David Lodge have depicted, with considerable wit, academic life in universities. A new

English literature: chronology to 1945

871–99 The Anglo-Saxon king Alfred the Great initiated translations from Latin into English, such as the *Venerable Bede's Ecclesiastical History of the English People*.

10th century The epic poem *Beowulf* was written down. The earliest surviving poem in Old English, it was composed orally about 200 years before and is based on Germanic legend.

*c.*1375 The anonymous *Sir Gawayne and the Greene Knight* was written in Middle English. This epic poem still used the alliterative style of Old English verse rather than the rhyming technique of later poetry.

*c.*1382 The first complete English translation of the Bible appeared, the *'Wyclif' Bible*.

c. 1387 Geoffrey Chaucer's *Canterbury Tales* was the first major work written in modern English.

1476 William Caxton set up his printing press in London, which encouraged the development of English prose writing.

1485 Caxton printed the first great English prose work, Sir Thomas Malory's *Morte D'Arthur*, the main source for the Arthurian legends.

1557 Thomas Wyatt's *Songes and Sonnettes* were published (posthumously), introducing the sonnet form to England. They include translations and imitations of the Italian poet Petrarch's work.

1603 John Florio's translations from French of Montaigne's 'Essais'. Montaigne was the originator of the modern essay.

1611 The Authorized Version (King James Version) of the *Bible* published.

1623 The first collected edition of William Shakespeare's plays, known as the *First Folio*, published seven years after his death.

1633 Posthumous publication of the collected poems of John Donne, the most prominent of the Metaphysical poets.

1667 John Milton's epic poem *Paradise Lost* used elaborate Latinate language and employed many classical and biblical references to create a grand style.

1668 John Dryden's essay *Of Dramatick Poesie* and others made him the first English literary critic (often in defence of his own poetry and plays). He advocated using classical Greek and Roman poetry and drama as models.

1712–14 Alexander Pope's epic poem *The Rape of the Lock* used rhyming couplets in a classical, elevated style to describe the theft of a lock of hair. The wit and satire that it employed flourished in the Age of Reason.

1719 *The Life and Strange and Surprising Adventures of Robinson Crusoe* by Daniel Defoe, sometimes considered the first English novel, was published. Other 18th-century novelists include Samuel Richardson (*Pamela* 1740), Henry Fielding (*Tom Jones* 1749) and Laurence Sterne (*Tristram Shandy* 1759–67).

1726 Jonathan Swift's satire *Gulliver's Travels* was published.

1755 Samuel Johnson published his *Dictionary of the English Language*, which remained the standard dictionary for over a century.

1798 *The Lyrical Ballads*, a selection of poems by William Wordsworth and Samuel Taylor Coleridge, introduced Romanticism in England. The Romantics reacted against the restrictions of rational classicism by emphasizing passion, intuition and the imagination.

1811 With *Sense and Sensibility* Jane Austen became the first major woman novelist.

1824 Lord Byron died while fighting for Greek independence. Having left Britain as the result of a scandal, he was seen throughout Europe as the Romantic poet-hero par excellence.

1837–8 Charles Dickens' novel *Oliver Twist* showed his social concern, seen also in the work of other 19th-century novelists such as the Russian Fyodor Dostoevsky and the Frenchman Émile Zola, about poverty and other social evils.

1865 *Alice's Adventures in Wonderland* by Lewis Carroll (Charles Dodgson) was one of several late 19th-century children's works which are now classics. Other writers included Beatrix Potter and J M Barrie.

1871–2 George Eliot (Mary Ann Evans) published her novel *Middlemarch*; she was already considered the greatest English novelist of her day.

1881 Henry James' novel *The Portrait of a Lady* explores with a new psychological subtlety the theme of young American culture meeting European cultural tradition.

1891 Thomas Hardy shocked the reading public with *Tess of the d'Urbevilles*, his novel about a girl who has had an illegitimate baby.

1893 The poet William Butler Yeats published his collection of stories *The Celtic Twilight*. Based on Irish mysticism and fairy tales, they show his commitment to reviving Irish national culture.

1895 H G Wells' novel *The Time Machine* was published, a seminal work in the genre of science fiction.

1898 George Bernard Shaw's *Plays Pleasant and Unpleasant* demonstrated his socialist vision.

20th century The novel became the dominant literary form, developing in a wide variety of directions and genres.

1913 D H Lawrence expressed in *Sons and Lovers* his idea of the vital and creative force of sexuality; *Lady Chatterley's Lover* (1928) was banned in Britain as obscene until 1960.

1922 James Joyce's novel *Ulysses* broke with traditional narrative and exposition, employing a stream-of-consciousness technique. T S Eliot's bleak view of modern life in his collection of poetry *The Waste Land* was greeted by many as outrageous.

1945 George Orwell's (Eric Blair's) political satire *Animal Farm* was published.

generation of anti-heroes features in the regional novels of Stan Barstow, John Braine, Alan Sillitoe, and David Storey. Chaim Bermant, Dan Jacobson, and Bernice Rubens have extended the scope of the Jewish novel.

Bizarre or futuristic imagination informs much of the fiction of Martin Amis, J G Ballard, Julian Barnes, Anthony Burgess, Angela Carter, Doris Lessing, Ian McEwan, Muriel Spark, Fay Weldon, and A N Wilson. Lawrence Durrell, John Fowles, and William Golding have written distinguished philosophical novels of action. The detective novel has been enriched by Colin Dexter, Nicolas Freeling, Reginald Hill, P D James, Ian Rankin, and Ruth Rendell.

John Betjeman, T S Eliot, C Day-Lewis, and Stephen Spender were among the notable poets of the 1930s who continued to write after the war, if not so intensively. That poetry can still sell has been demonstrated by Douglas Dunn and Ted Hughes, who have laid bare personal tragedies, and Seamus Heaney, who has written of the political tragedy in Northern Ireland. Other poets of the postwar period who have, each in his or her own way, spoken plainly enough to be appreciated by the general public as well as by critics include George Mackay Brown, Charles Causley, Gavin Ewart, W S Graham, Philip Larkin, Elizabeth Jennings, Norman MacCaig, Roger McGough, Ruth Pitter, Kathleen Raine, John Silkin, and Iain Crichton Smith.

English National Ballet

Ballet company based in London. Formerly the London Festival Ballet (founded in 1950), it was renamed in 1989. Derek Deane was appointed artistic director in 1993.

English National Opera

Opera company based at the London Coliseum. The company was founded in 1931 as the Vic-Wells Opera, becoming the English National Opera in 1974. It always performs in English.

English Nature

Agency created in 1991 from the division of the Nature Conservancy Council into English, Scottish, and Welsh sections.

It is one of the five bodies responsible for countryside policy and nature conservancy. It is also involved through the Joint Nature Conservation Committee (JNCC) with international nature conservation matters and those that affect Great Britain.

In 1996–97 English Nature provided £2.2 million to assist local activities to sustain biodiversity and geodiversity, such as recovery programmes for 49 threatened species, including bittern, dormouse, lady's slipper orchid, sand lizard, and fen raft spider.

English Pale

Territory in Ireland where English rule operated after the English settlement of Ireland in 1171. The area of the Pale varied, but in the mid-14th century it was comprised of the counties of Dublin, Louth, Meath, Trim, Kilkenny and Kildare. It then gradually shrank until the ◊Plantation of Ireland 1556–1660.

English Stage Company

British theatre company formed in 1956 for the presentation of contemporary drama. It opened at the ◊Royal Court Theatre in London, its permanent home, under the direction of George Devine. Among dramatists whose plays have been performed are John Arden, Samuel Beckett, Bertolt Brecht, Jean Genet, Eugène Ionesco, John Osborne, and Arnold Wesker. Recent productions include Martin McDonagh's *The Beauty Queen of Leenane* (1996), Mark Ravenhill's *Shopping and Fucking* (1996), and Conor McPherson's *The Weir* (1997). Ian Rickson became the company's artistic director in 1998.

Enlightenment

18th-century intellectual and political movement. See feature opposite.

Enniskillen

County town of ◊Fermanagh, Northern Ireland, between Upper and Lower Lough Erne, 184 km/114 mi from Dublin and 141 km/88 mi from Belfast; population (1991) 11,400. It is a market town and shopping centre with some light industry (engineering, food processing); it has been designated for further industrial growth. An IRA bomb exploded here at a Remembrance Day service in November 1987, causing many casualties.

The lands of Enniskillen were held by the Maguires; under James I the lands were granted to William Cole and settled by the English. It was one of the principal strongholds of the plantation during the late 17th century, and was an important strategic centre in the time of William III. **Enniskillen Castle** houses both the county museum and a military museum.

Enright, D(enis) J(oseph) (1920–)

English poet, novelist, and editor. His style is characterized by a clarity of language and form; by a witty, ironic, and almost conversational tone; and by a concern with moral and social issues, notably social inequality and political oppression. His collections include *Bread Rather Than Blossoms* (1956), *Foreign Devils* (1972), and *Old Men and Comets* (1993). His novel *Academic Year* appeared in 1955.

ENSA, Entertainments National Service Association

Organization formed in 1938–39 to provide entertainment for British and Allied forces during World War II. Directed by Basil Dean from headquarters in the Drury Lane Theatre, it provided a variety of entertainment throughout the UK and also in all war zones.

Entente Cordiale (French 'friendly understanding')

Agreement reached by Britain and France in 1904 recognizing British interests in Egypt and French interests in Morocco. It formed the basis for Anglo-French cooperation before the outbreak of World War I in 1914.

enterprise zone

Former special zone introduced in 1980 and designated by

THE LIGHT OF REASON: BRITAIN AND THE ENLIGHTENMENT

BRITISH PARTICIPATION in the 18th-century intellectual and political movement known as the Enlightenment is often ignored by historians. This is partly because of the difficulty of defining the term 'Enlightenment' itself. For many writers, the ideas encompassed are so diverse that the term can only be defined by reference to the key works of such French thinkers as Diderot, Montesquieu, Voltaire, and Rousseau.

But the Enlightenment was a Europe-wide phenomenon, and British intellectuals played a major role, from early Enlightenment heroes such as John Locke (1632–1704) and Isaac Newton (1642–1727) to later thinkers like Erasmus Darwin (1731–1802) and Thomas Paine (1737–1809). Moreover, the importance of Enlightenment thought in shaping early 19th-century politics and society in Britain was not much less than in France. In Britain, as in France, the Enlightenment saw the failure of the last attempt of an aristocratic intelligentsia to shape the wider society in which they lived. Quite apart from its intellectual legacy, this social dimension makes the Enlightenment in Britain well worthy of the historian's attention.

Enlightenment ideas

The Enlightenment can best be described as an age of critical, reasoned enquiry into all aspects of human experience. The novelty of such an approach can best be appreciated by reference to European history in the 17th century – which had not only seen Galileo forced by the Inquisition to recant his assertion that the Earth revolved around the Sun 1632, but also the continent-wide horrors of religious wars led by kings, popes, and popular religious leaders, all equally fervent in their belief in divine sanction for their actions. In Britain, the excesses of the Stuart kings on the one hand and their Puritan opponents on the other had convinced many thoughtful observers that the ordering of human society was as much in need of rational examination as was the wider, natural world: reason was thus a goal as well as a method of Enlightenment thinkers.

In France, the characteristic preoccupations of the Enlightenment were despotism, feudalism, and the Roman Catholic church: a reasoned critique led some commentators not only to social radicalism, but also to outright atheism. British thinkers tended to pursue an objective in which utilitarianism, religious faith, and the search for human happiness could combine. As early as 1695, Locke's *The Reasonableness of Christianity* had put the case for a faith stripped of its supernatural aspects, but not abandoned altogether. Most intellectuals and clegy alike shared Locke's view that a rational appreciation of the human situation would lead people to be Christians.

Experience and discovery

Experience, not received wisdom, was seen as the key to knowledge. A meticulous examination of human thought by the Scottish philosopher David Hume (1711–1776) resulted in his *A Treatise of Human Nature* (1739–40). The clearest statement to date of the empiricist view that all knowledge was ultimately derived from sense experience, Hume's *Treatise* exemplified the new, scientific approach. A firm belief that the sum total of empirical knowledge could be increased came to characterize the Enlightenment. Activities as diverse as James Cook's exploration of the Pacific and the historian Edward Gibbon's massively researched *Decline and Fall of the Roman Empire* (1776–88) were rooted in this belief. Some sense of the confidence of the age can be seen in Joseph Priestley's *History of the Present State of Electricity* 1767, in which he claimed that recent discoveries would 'extend the bounds of natural science ... New worlds may open to our view'. Evidence that interest in such discoveries reached far beyond the tiny minority actively involved can be seen in the 18th-century proliferation of scientific clubs and societies and scholarly journals, and even in that most obvious indicator of Britain's highly developed culture of print, the newspaper.

The perfection of society

Such confidence extended to the perfectibility of human society. Disciplines such as economics, jurisprudence, and public administration made great strides during the 18th century. In Britain, this was particularly evident in the so-called Scottish Enlightenment, where a distinctive legal system gave focus to the reconstruction of that country after the Jacobite revolt – but it also threw up politicians such as Edmund Burke (1729–1797) and Thomas Paine, and educationalists like Jeremy Bentham (1748–1832).

The turning point was the French Revolution, in which the opportunity to put into practice the theories of the Enlightenment in a major European society was presented. The ultimate failure of the Revolution, the excesses committed in its name, and the violent opposition it aroused in Britain all served to discredit the Enlightenment social theorists. Some, like Paine, were driven abroad, while others withdrew into literary or artistic activities largely ignored by the middle classes their ideas had once galvanized. At the popular level, the 19th century was to see a revival of evangelistic piety and the rise of social movements rooted in other social classes.

BY JEREMY BLACK

government to encourage industrial and commercial activity, usually in economically depressed areas. Investment was attracted by means of tax reduction and other financial incentives. Enterprise zones no longer exist, but assisted area and intermediate areas survive. The Labour government plans to set up regional development agencies in 1999.

Environment Agency

Government agency that from April 1996 took over the responsibilities of the ◊National Rivers Authority, Her Majesty's Inspectorate of Pollution, and local waste regulation authorities for England and Wales. Scotland has its own Scottish Environmental Protection Agency.

Environmentally Sensitive Area, ESA
Scheme introduced by the UK Ministry of Agriculture in 1984, as a result of EC legislation, to protect some of the most beautiful areas of the British countryside from the loss and damage caused by agricultural change. The first areas to be designated ESAs were in the Pennine Dales, the North Peak District, the Norfolk Broads, the Breckland, the Suffolk River Valleys, the Test Valley, the South Downs, the Somerset Levels and Moors, West Penwith, Cornwall, the Shropshire Borders, the Cambrian Mountains, and the Lleyn Peninsula.

The total area designated as ESAs was estimated in 1997 at 3,239,000 hectares. The scheme is voluntary, with farmers being encouraged to adapt their practices so as to enhance or maintain the natural features of the landscape and conserve wildlife habitat. A farmer who joins the scheme agrees to manage the land in this way for at least five years. In return for this agreement, the Ministry of Agriculture pays the farmer a sum that reflects the financial losses incurred as a result of reconciling conservation with commercial farming.

Environment, Transport, and the Regions Department of, DETR
UK government department established in June 1997, amalgamating the Department of the Environment and the ◊Department of Transport. Including its agencies, which include the Driving and Vehicle Licensing Agency and the Highways Agency, the department had 15,000 staff in 1998. Since May 1997 responsibility for the environment portfolio has been held by the deputy prime minister, John Prescott.

The Department of Environment (DOB) was established in 1970, bringing together the ministries of Housing and Local Government, Transport, and Building and Works (although Transport returned to an independent status in 1975). DETR is responsible for housing, construction, local government, sport and recreation policies, and the preservation of the environment.

Epping
Town in Essex, southeast England, about 26 km/16 mi northeast of London; population (1991) 9,000. Industries include electronics, manufacture of generators, power tools and machinery (washing equipment), and light engineering
Epping Forest
To the south of Epping, Epping Forest covers an area of approximately 2,000 ha/5,000 acres. Once part of the ancient forest of Waltham, it originally covered the whole of Essex. It is one of Europe's oldest forests.

Epsom
Residential town in Surrey, southeast England, 30 km/19 mi southwest of London; population (1991) 64,400 (with Ewell). In the 17th century it was a spa town producing ◊Epsom salts. The Derby and the Oaks horse races are held annually at **Epsom Downs** racecourse.

Epsom was a small village until it developed as a spa following the discovery of springs containing sulphate of magnesia in 1618. The Royal Medical College on the downs was founded in 1851 as a school for the sons of doctors. Sculptures by John Flaxman and Francis Chantrey decorate the Gothic church (rebuilt in 1824). The UK's first automatic telephone exchange was installed in Epsom by the Post Office in 1912. The site of Henry VIII's Nonsuch Palace, built mainly between 1538 and 1546, was excavated in 1959.

Epsom salts
Hydrated magnesium sulphate, used as a relaxant and laxative and added to baths to soothe the skin. The name is derived from a bitter saline spring at Epsom, Surrey, England, which contains the salt in solution.

Epstein, (Michael) Anthony (1921–)
English microbiologist who, in collaboration with his assistant Barr, discovered in 1964 the Epstein–Barr virus (EBV) that causes glandular fever in humans and has been linked to some forms of human cancer.

This was the first time a virus had been linked to the development of cancer, and it prompted many subsequent studies by other scientists into the role of viruses in the onset and progression of human tumours.

Epstein, Jacob (1880–1959)
US-born British sculptor. Initially influenced by Rodin, he turned to primitive forms after Brancusi and is chiefly known for his controversial muscular nude figures, such as *Genesis* (1931; Whitworth Art Gallery, Manchester). He was better appreciated as a portraitist; his bust of Albert Einstein (1933) demonstrating a characteristic vigorous modelling in clay. In later years he executed several monumental figures, notably the bronze *St Michael and the Devil* (1959; Coventry Cathedral).

In 1904 he moved to England, where most of his major work was done. An early example showing the strong influence of ancient sculptural styles is the angel of the tomb of Oscar Wilde (1912; Père Lachaise cemetery, Paris), condemned as barbaric for its Assyrian idiom. His sculpture from 1912 to 1913 was harsh and mechanistic, having affinities with ◊Vorticism and the work of Modigliani and Brancusi. The Modernist and semi-abstract *Rock Drill* (1913; Tate Gallery, London) originally incorporated a real drill.

Epworth
Village in North Lincolnshire, England, 16 km/10 mi northwest of Gainsborough. It was the birthplace, in 1703, of John ◊Wesley, the founder of Methodism.

Equal Opportunities Commission
Commission established by the UK government in 1975 (1976 in Northern Ireland) to implement the Sex Discrimination Act 1975. Its aim is to prevent discrimination, particularly on sexual or marital grounds.

equity
System of law supplementing the ordinary rules of law where the application of these would operate harshly in a particular case; sometimes it is regarded as an attempt to achieve 'natural justice'. So understood, equity appears as an element in most

legal systems, and in a number of legal codes judges are instructed to apply both the rules of strict law and the principles of equity in reaching their decisions.

In England equity originated in decisions of the Court of Chancery, on matters that were referred to it because there was no adequate remedy available in the Common Law courts. It developed into a distinct system of law, and until the 19th century, the two systems of common law and equity existed side by side, and were applied in separate law courts. The Judicature Acts 1873–75 established a single High Court of Justice, in which judges could apply both common law and equity to all their decisions. Equitable principles still exist side by side with principles of common law in many branches of the law.

Equity

Common name for the **British Actors' Equity Association**, the trade union for professional actors in theatre, film, and television, founded in 1929.

Erasmus, Desiderius (*c.* 1466–1536)

Dutch scholar and leading humanist of the Renaissance era, who taught and studied all over Europe and was a prolific writer. Through his friendship and correspondence with scholars such as the politician Thomas More, the bible interpreter John Colet, and the physician Thomas Linacre, he directly influenced the development of humanism in England.

He paid the first of a number of visits to England in 1499 and for a time was professor of divinity and Greek at Cambridge University.

Ermine Street

Ancient road of Roman origin, or possibly earlier, running from London to York, and by extension to southern Scotland. The name is also applied to the Silchester to Gloucester route. Ermine Street, along with Watling Street, and the Icknield and Foss Ways, were specially protected by the King's Peace at least from Norman times and probably earlier.

ERNIE

Acronym for **electronic random number indicator**, machine designed and produced by the UK Post Office Research Station to select a series of random 9-figure numbers to indicate prizewinners among ◊Premium Bond holders.

Escherichia coli

Rod-shaped Gram-negative bacterium that lives, usually harmlessly, in the colon of most warm-blooded animals. It is the commonest cause of urinary tract infections in humans. It is sometimes found in water or meat where faecal contamination has occurred and can cause severe gastric problems.

Two outbreaks of food poisoning involving a lethal strain of *E coli* in Scotland in December 1996 and January 1997, resulted in 20 deaths. A resulting report from the Meat and Livestock Commission (MLC) in March 1997 revealed that all stages of food handling in Britain, from the abbatoir to the plate, were suspect to some degree. All stages were identified as needing higher standards. It was revealed that the European Commission had warned the government to clean up Britain's abbatoirs in 1989. Another EC inspection in 1996 still found 'serious weaknesses' in Britain's slaughterhouses, including meat being contaminated by excrement.

Esher

Residential district in Surrey, England, 5 km/3 mi outside Greater London and near the River Mole; population (1991) 5,300. Esher has a Friends' (Quaker) Meeting House dating from 1797. Near the station in Esher is Sandown Park, the first enclosed racecourse in Britain (1875).

To the east of Esher lies Claremont, built by Robert Clive, governor of India, where the exiled French king Louis Philippe lived after his overthrow in 1848. The landscape gardens adjoining Claremont, containing a lake, a grotto, and a huge amphitheatre, are National Trust property.

Esk

River in Dumfries and Galloway unitary authority, southwest Scotland, formed by the confluence of the Black and the White Esk in Eskdalemuir, and flowing 56 km/93 mi to the Solway Firth at Sarkfoot Point near Gretna Green.

Eskdale

The valley of the River **Esk**, which rises between Scafell Pike and Bowfell in the ◊Lake District, Cumbria, England, turns west near Hardknott Castle (a Roman fort), and ultimately flows into the Irish Sea at Ravenglass. A narrow-gauge railway from Ravenglass to Dalegarth has become a tourist attraction of the area.

Essex (Old English East-Seaxe)

County of southeast England, which has contained the unitary authorities Southend and Thurrock since April 1998
Area 3,670 sq km/1,417 sq mi
Towns ◊Chelmsford (administrative headquarters), Basildon, Colchester, Harlow, Harwich (port), Clacton-on-Sea (resort)
Physical flat and marshy near the coast; richly wooded in the southwest; rivers: the Blackwater, Crouch, Colne, Lee, Stour, and Thames
Features former royal hunting ground of Epping Forest (2300 ha/5680 acres, controlled from 1882 by the City of London); since 1111 at Little Dunmow (and later at Great Dunmow) the Dunmow flitch (side of cured pork) can be claimed every four years by any couple proving to a jury they have not regretted their marriage within the year (winners are few); Stansted, London's third airport; new Roman Catholic cathedral at Brentwood (designed by Quinlan Terry) dedicated in 1991
Agriculture cereals (wheat), fruit, sugar beet; livestock rearing, dairy products; oysters
Industries brewing, cars, cement, engineering (at Dagenham, Chelmsford, and Colchester), food processing, oil products (there are large oil refineries at Shellhaven and Canvey)
Population (1995) 1,577,500.

ESSEX *The Flemish Cottages, Southfields, Dedham, Essex, southeast England. Throughout the Middle Ages wool was the most important English export. East Anglia was one of the centres of the woollen industry and Dedham was a thriving weaving community. Linda Proud*

Topography
Essex is bounded by Cambridgeshire and Suffolk to the north; by the North Sea in the east; by the River Thames, Thurrock and Southend in the south, and by Greater London and Hertfordshire to the west. The Tilbury and Victoria and Albert Docks of the Port of London are on the Thames in the south of the county. Harwich is the port for continental traffic. Much of the southern half of the county is now a dormitory area for London commuters.
Historic buildings
The abbey at Waltham is reputedly the oldest Norman building in England. Founded in 1030, it was enlarged by King Harold in 1060.

Essex, Robert Devereux, 3rd Earl of Essex (1591–1646)
English soldier. Eldest son of the 2nd earl, he commanded the Parliamentary army at the inconclusive English Civil War battle of Edgehill in 1642. Following a disastrous campaign in Cornwall, he resigned his command in 1645. He succeeded to earldom in 1604.

Ethelbert (*c.* 552–616)
King of Kent 560–616. He was defeated by the West Saxons in 568 but later became ruler of England south of the River Humber. Ethelbert received the Christian missionary Augustine in 597 and later converted to become the first Christian ruler of Anglo-Saxon England. He issued the first written code of laws known in England.

Ethelred (II) the Unready (968–1016)
King of England from 978, following the murder of his half-brother, Edward the Martyr. He was son of King Edgar. Ethered tried to buy off the Danish raiders by paying Danegeld. In 1002, he ordered the massacre of the Danish settlers, provoking an invasion by Sweyn I of Denmark. War with Sweyn and Sweyn's son, Canute, occupied the rest of Ethelred's reign. His nickname is a corruption of the Old English 'unreed', meaning badly counselled or poorly advised.

Etherege, George (*c.* 1635–1691)
English Restoration dramatist. His play *Love in a Tub* (1664) was the first attempt at the comedy of manners (a genre further developed by Congreve and Sheridan). Later plays include *She Would If She Could* (1668) and *The Man of Mode, or Sir Fopling Flutter* (1676). He was knighted by 1680.

Eton
Town in Windsor and Maidenhead unitary authority,

southern England, on the north bank of the River Thames, opposite Windsor; population (1991) 2,000.

Eton College

One of the UK's oldest, largest, and most prestigious public (private and fee-paying) schools. It was founded in 1440 by Henry VI as a grammar school and, after a stormy history which included a rebellion by pupils in 1783, became dominated by the sons of the aristocracy and the wealthy middle classes. Of the pupils in 1991, 40% were the sons of Old Etonians (former pupils). It has provided the UK with 19 prime ministers and more than 20% of all government ministers between 1900 and 1998. Prince William became a student at Eton in 1995; Prince Harry followed in 1998.

Etruria

Part of the suburb of Hanley in the city of ◊Stoke-on-Trent, Staffordshire, England. Etruria is historically associated with pottery; in 1769, Josiah ◊Wedgwood and Thomas Bentley opened their Etruria Works in the district.

Wedgwood's original factory is now used for other purposes, but the fabric is preserved as an historic building. There is a memorial to Thomas Wedgwood, photography pioneer and patron of Coleridge, in Etruria Park. Etruria has given its name to certain beds of marls and clays found in the west Midlands, which are useful for pottery manufacture and are also used to make Staffordshire 'blue' bricks, a very high-grade, water-resistant type of brick, ideal for engineering work.

European Democratic Group

The group of British Conservative Party members of the European Parliament.

European Monetary System, EMS

Attempt by the European Community (now the European Union) to bring financial cooperation and monetary stability to Europe, established in 1979. The EMS has three components: the European currency unit (ECU), the exchange rate mechanism (ERM), and the credit mechanisms.

Britain left the ERM in October 1992 when doubts about the prospects for movement towards a single European currency caused speculators to sell the weaker ERM currencies, particularly sterling, so forcing the pound out of its ERM band. The Conservative government then adopted a 'wait and see' policy. The Labour government has also effectively adopted the same policy, saying it would not be in Britain's interests to join the single currency (euro) that other countries are joining in 1999 under the terms of the 1992 Maastricht Agreement.

European Union, EU; formerly (to 1993) European Community

European political and economic alliance that the UK joined in 1973, following a referendum. The other members are: Belgium, France, Germany, Italy, Luxembourg, the Netherlands, Denmark, the Republic of Ireland, Greece, Spain, Portugal, Austria, Finland, and Sweden.

The aims of the EU include the expansion of trade, reduction of competition, the abolition of restrictive trading practices, the encouragement of free movement of capital and labour within the alliance, and the establishment of a closer union among European people. A single market with free movement of goods and capital was established in January 1993. In September 1995 the EU's member nations stated their commitment to the attainment of monetary union by 1999, and in December of the same year they agreed to call the new currency the euro. In the course of formalizing the creation of the euro monetary zone in May 1998, the heads of EU governments confirmed that 11 countries – all but Britain, Denmark, Sweden, and Greece – were ready to enter it from 1 January 1999.

See also ◊European Monetary System.

Eurythmics, The

English synth–pop duo formed in 1981, comprising Annie Lennox (1954–) and Dave Stewart (1952–). Their songs included 'Sweet Dreams (Are Made of This)' (1982), a hit in the UK and USA, 'Here Comes the Rain Again' (1983), and 'Sisters Are Doin' It For Themselves' (1985).

Euston Road School

Group of English painters associated with the 'School of Drawing and Painting' founded in 1937 in Euston Road, London by William Coldstream (b. 1908), Victor Pasmore (1908–98), Claude Rogers (b. 1907), and Graham Bell (1910–43). Despite its brief existence, the school influenced many British painters with its emphasis on careful, subdued naturalism.

The painters worked alongside their students in the school and encouraged them to 'keep their eyes on what they saw', without being preoccupied by theory or the dominant influence of the School of Paris. The enterprise flourished until the outbreak of war in 1939.

Evans, Arthur John (1851–1941)

English archaeologist. His excavations at Knossos on Crete uncovered a vast palace complex, and resulted in the discovery of various Minoan scripts. He proved the existence of a Bronze Age civilization that predated the Mycenean, and named it Minoan after Minos, the legendary king of Knossos.

Evans, Chris (1966–)

English radio disc jockey and TV entertainer who made his reputation on TV as a presenter of Channel 4's *The Big Breakfast* (1992–94) before moving on to *Don't Forget Your Toothbrush* (1994) and *TFI Friday* (1997–8), both for Channel 4. He has his own production company and in 1998 was also presenting a breakfast show for Virgin Radio.

Evans, Edith (Mary) (1888–1976)

English character actress. She performed on the London stage and on Broadway. Her many imposing performances include the Nurse in *Romeo and Juliet* (first performed in 1926); her film roles include Lady Bracknell in Oscar Wilde's comedy *The Importance of Being Earnest* (1952). Among her other films are *Tom Jones* (1963) and *Crooks and Coronets* (1969). She was made a DBE in 1946.

Evans, Geraint Llewellyn (1922–1992)

Welsh operatic baritone. In a career spanning 36 years, he sang more than 70 roles. He is best remembered for his singing of the title role in Verdi's *Falstaff*, which he sang and acted at Glyndebourne, Covent Garden, and elsewhere. The warmth of his voice, the clarity of his diction and his engaging stage presence endeared him to opera house audiences, television viewers, and music enthusiasts all over the world.

Evelyn, John (1620–1706)

English diarist and author. He was a friend of the diarist Samuel Pepys, and like him remained in London during the Plague and the Great Fire of London. His fascinating diary, covering the years 1641–1706, and first published in 1818, is an important source of information about 17th-century England. He also wrote some 30 books on a wide variety of subjects, including horticulture and the cultivation of trees, history, religion, and the arts. He was one of the founders of the ◊Royal Society.

Everett, Kenny professional name of Maurice Cole (1944–1995)

English television and radio broadcaster. He developed a zany and surreal style as a disc jockey and comic.

Everett's career began on the pirate radio station Radio London. He moved to the BBC's Radio One, then worked on Capital Radio from 1973 to 1980. He hosted his own shows on ITV and BBC.

Evershed, John (1864–1956)

English astronomer who made solar observations. In 1909, he discovered the radial movements of gases in sunspots (the **Evershed effect**). He also gave his name to a spectroheliograph, the Evershed spectroscope.

Everyman

Popular English morality play of the early 16th century, probably derived from an earlier Dutch play, *Elckerlijc*. Summoned by Death, Everyman is forsaken by his former friends – allegorical abstractions such as Fellowship and Kindred – and is saved only by Good Deeds, who accompanies him to the grave.

Evesham

Market town in Worcestershire, England, on the River Avon, on the fringe of the Cotswolds, 24 km/15 mi southeast of Worcester; population (1990 est) 18,000. Fruit and vegetables are grown in the fertile **Vale of Evesham**.

At the Battle of Evesham (4 August 1265), during the ◊Barons' Wars, Prince Edward (the future Edward I) defeated Simon de Montfort, who was killed.

A Benedictine abbey was founded here in 701. Its detached Perpendicular bell tower, built in the 16th century, is 33 m/108 ft high and contains a clock with chimes and 12 bells. Other remains of the foundation include the 12th-century gateway, a fine arch, and the abbot's stables.

Excalibur

The mystic sword of King ◊Arthur, which, according to the promise of Merlin, he received from the Lady of the Lake. At his death it was thrown back into the lake by the knight Bedivere, and was received by a hand which rose from the waters.

exchequer (Norman-French *eschequier*)

Name of the king's court of revenue which is taken from the fact that in early times the accounts were reckoned up on a chequered cloth, resembling a large chessboard, round which the officers sat. It appears that the sums of money received by the treasurer were scored on the squares of this cloth with counters, the process being suggestive of a game of chess.

See also ◊chancellor of the Exchequer.

Exe

River in England that rises in ◊Exmoor; length 86 km/53 mi. It flows in a southerly direction through the counties of Somerset and Devon, much of its course being through densely wooded countryside.

The chief tributaries of the Exe are the Barle, Loman, Batham, Culm, Creedy, and Clyst. Among the towns on its course are Dulverton, Tiverton, Exeter, and Exmouth. Its wide, shallow estuary is navigable to smaller boats for 12 km/7 mi; larger vessels travel to Exeter via the Exeter ship canal, 13 km/8 mi long.

Executive Agency

Any one of a number of UK government agencies set up from the later 1980s by the Conservative administrations of Margaret Thatcher and John Major as part of a ◊'Next Steps' initiative designed to improve efficiency and quality in the delivery of government services.

By September 1997 there were more than 136 Executive Agencies, along with 51 Executive Offices within the Inland Revenue and Customs & Excise, in which around 360,000 civil servants, over three-quarters of the total, are employed. ◊Next Steps agencies include the Meteorological Office, the Prisons Service, the Benefits Agency, the Employment Service, and the Child Support Agency.

Exeter

City and administrative headquarters of ◊Devon, England, on the River Exe; population (1994 est) 107,000. Principal industries are brewing, iron and brass founding, light engineering, printing, financial services, and tourism. Other industries include the manufacture of agricultural machinery, textiles, and leather goods. Exeter was founded by the Romans as **Isca Dumnoniorum** and has medieval, Georgian, and Regency architecture. Exeter Cathedral was built largely between 1280 and 1369. Exeter University was established in 1955.

Features

A cathedral was first established at Exeter in 1050, and the Normans rebuilt it between 1107 and 1137. The present cathedral is mainly in the Decorated style. From the outside the cathedral is most remarkable for its massive Norman transeptal towers (1112–33), which leave unbroken the great roof, 90 m/295 ft long. The magnificent Gothic interior is built to one plan, unlike any other English cathedral except Salisbury. Notable furnishings include a high wooden bishop's throne, begun in 1313, possibly the finest piece of woodwork of its period in Europe. It has a 14th-century west front with many sculptured figures, and its fine ceiling is the longest stretch of Gothic vaulting in the world. The Cathedral Library contains the *Exeter Book*, a collection of Anglo-Saxon poetry. It also includes the Exeter Domesday Book, the episcopal and chapter archives, and many city archives.

Cathedral Close has buildings dating from medieval to Georgian times, including the Elizabethan Mol's Coffee House. The Guildhall (1330) is one of the oldest surviving civic buildings in England; it has a portico dating from about 1595, and its hall has a fine 15th-century roof. Sections of the Roman and medieval walls survive, and there are some remains of Rougemont Castle. Other features include part of the Benedictine Priory of St Nicholas, the Custom House (1681), and the Maritime Museum at the Quay. The Royal Albert Memorial Museum includes collections illustrating zoology and local archaeology.

History

Evidence suggests that a town may have existed here in the 3rd century BC. The Roman settlement of 'Isca of the Dumnoniorum' was well established by AD 55. It later became the Anglo-Saxon settlement Escancestre. The city was attacked by the Danes in 876. In 928 Athelstan, King of the Mercians and West Saxons, met the Witan (council of the Anglo-Saxon kings) here. In 1003 Exeter was sacked by Sweyn, King of Denmark. In 1067 the town initially resisted William the Conqueror, but submitted after an 18-day siege. William the Conqueror built the strong motte-and-bailey castle of Rougemont – so named from its red masonry and earth – in 1068. The town was a centre for the wool trade in the Tudor period. Royalist forces had their western headquarters here during the English Civil War, until in 1646 the town surrendered to Thomas Fairfax, commander in chief of the Parliamentary forces. The city suffered severe damage during World War II air raids.

Exmoor

Moorland district in north Devon and west Somerset, southwest England, forming (with the coast from Minehead to Combe Martin) a national park since 1954. The park covers an area of around 7,700 ha/19,000 acres, and includes Dunkery Beacon, its highest point at 519 m/1,705 ft; and the Doone Valley.

Exmoor is thinly populated and remains isolated by relatively poor road connections. The principal settlements are the twin coastal resort towns of ◊Lynton and Lynmouth in the north and Dulverton in the southeast; the resort town of Minehead lies just outside the national park to the northeast. Tourism and craft industries are important to the local economy. The moor provides grazing for Exmoor ponies, horned Exmoor sheep, and about 1,000 wild red deer. It is also the habitat of grouse, hawks, and falcons. Stag-hunting in the region attracts widespread controversy. Prehistoric remains, including early stone circles and barrows (burial mounds), are mainly located around the edge of the moor, settlement of the moor occurring around 1800 to 1500 BC. Iron Age hillforts include Shoulsbarrow Castle. Tarr Steps, an ancient packhorse bridge over the River Barle, is a simple, stone-slab clapper construction with 17 spans; it may date from the Bronze Age, although other estimates set it in the medieval period around 1400. Exmoor is the setting for R D Blackmore's romance *Lorna Doone* (1869).

Physical features

A plateau of red sandstone and slate, Exmoor has a varied landscape, with grassy and marshy moorland as well as heathland, and substantial woodland covering about 10% of the area. The coastal region is characterized by a series of headlands with cliffs and wooded valleys. There are gentle contours in the Brendon Hills to the east, and inland is **Exmoor Forest**, at the heart of the moor, an area reserved for royal hunting until 1819. The River Exe rises in the uplands of the moor.

The area is subject to heavy rainfall. In August 1952 exceptionally intense rains caused the East and West Lyn rivers to flood Lynmouth, resulting in great destruction and several deaths. Its twin town Lynton, located 180 m/ 600 ft higher on the clifftop, escaped the torrent. The disaster influenced government policy for designing flood relief channels in the UK.

Wimbleball Reservoir, near Dulverton, is a large, pumped-storage facility built to save surplus flow from the Exe, excess water passing through an 805-m/2,640-ft tunnel under the national park. Water flow on the Exe has been regulated by this scheme since 1997. Fishing and sailing take place on the reservoir.

Exmouth

Resort town and former port in Devon, southwest England, at the mouth of the River Exe, 14 km/9 mi southeast of Exeter; population (1996 est) 31,920. Small industries include engineering and a pottery specializing in novelty teapots. The port was permanently closed to commercial vessels in 1989, but the town remains a yachting and boating centre.

Other tourist facilities include pleasure boat cruises up the Exe to Topsham, just below Exeter, and local angling for salmon and trout. The Exe estuary nature reserve is notable for its bird life.

Express, formerly *Daily Express*

Daily mid-market newspaper owned by United News & Media. It was established in 1900 by Arthur Pearson and bought by Lord Beaverbrook in 1916. In 1998 its circulation was over 1,200,000. Its sister paper the *Express on Sunday* was established in 1918 and in 1998 had a circulation over 1,100,000. Both papers are politically broadly conservative.

In 1936 the Express had the largest circulation in the world (2.25 million), at which time the magnificent Daily Express building in Fleet Street was commissioned. The paper moved from this office to Blackfriars Road in 1989.

Expressionism

Style of painting, sculpture, and literature which expresses inner emotions; in particular, a movement in early 20th-century art in northern and central Europe. In painting natural appearance is often distorted or exaggerated in order to create a reflection of an inner world. Expressionism has always been a marginal influence in British painting and sculpture, featuring mainly in the work of highly individual artists such as Francis Bacon, John Bellany, and Jack Yeats.

Expressionism also influenced the stylization of sets, acting, and lighting in cinema, as seen in the work of British filmmakers Alfred Hitchcock, Michael Powell, and Carol Reed. Sets were distorted and largely abstract, and played as important a role as the actors. Lighting was used to emphasize deep shadows and the camera was oddly angled to highlight the grotesque and fantastic.

Eyam

Village in western Derbyshire, England, 16 km/10 mi northeast of Buxton; population (1991) 1,600. Industries include the manufacture of shoes and the mining of fluorspar and lead.

Eyam lies in a district where many British and Saxon antiquities are found; its churchyard contains a 9th- or 10th-century runic cross, restored in 1788.

In 1665–66, most of the population of Eyam died of plague; this tragedy is commemorated in the annual local ceremony of 'well-dressing': decorating the well with a picture made of moss and flowers in supplication for a clean water supply (also practised in Tissington and Wirksworth).

Eyre, Richard (Charles Hastings) (1943–)

English stage and film director. He succeeded Peter Hall as artistic director of the National Theatre, London, 1988–97. His stage productions include *Guys and Dolls* (1982), *Bartholomew Fair* (1988), *Richard III* (1990), which he set in 1930s Britain; *Night of the Iguana* (1992), *Macbeth* (1993), *Skylight* (1995), and *Amy's View* and *King Lear* (both 1997). His films include *The Ploughman's Lunch* (1983), *Laughterhouse* (1984), *Tumbledown* (1988, for television), *Suddenly Last Summer* (1992), and *The Absence of War* (1995). He also directed the opera *La Traviata* at Covent Garden, London, in 1994. He was knighted in 1997.

Eysenck, Hans Jürgen (1916–1997)

British psychologist. His work concentrated on personality theory and testing by developing behaviour therapy (treating certain clinical conditions by regarding their symptoms as learned patterns of behaviour that therapy can enable the patient to unlearn). He was an outspoken critic of psychoanalysis as a therapeutic method. His theory that intelligence is almost entirely inherited and can be only slightly modified by education aroused controversy.

Eysenck was born in Berlin and became professor of psychology at London University in 1955.

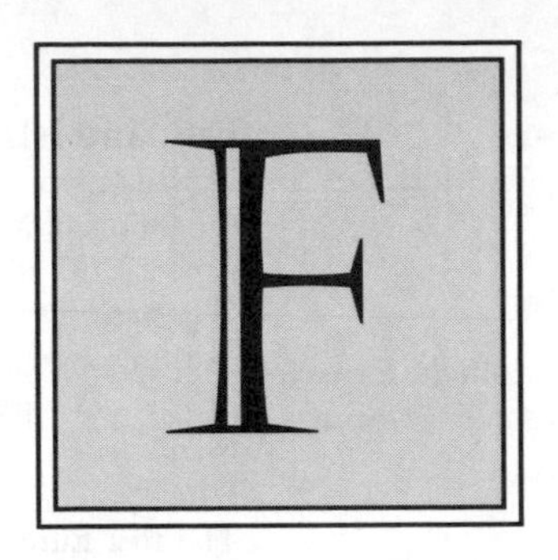

Fabian Society

Socialist organization for research, discussion, and publication, founded in London in 1884. Its name is derived from the Roman commander Fabius Maximus, and refers to the evolutionary methods by which it hopes to attain socialism by a succession of gradual reforms. Early members included the playwright George Bernard Shaw and Beatrice and Sidney Webb. The society helped to found the Labour Representation Committee in 1900, which became the Labour Party in 1906.

factory act

An act of Parliament such as the Health and Safety at Work Act 1974, which governs conditions of work, hours of labour, safety, and sanitary provision in factories and workshops.

In the 19th century legislation was progressively introduced to regulate conditions of work, hours of labour, safety, and sanitary provisions in factories and workshops. The first legislation was the Health and Morals of Apprentices Act 1802.

In 1833 the first factory inspectors were appointed. Legislation was extended to offices, shops, and railway premises 1963. All employees are now covered by the 1974 Act, which is enforced by the Health and Safety Executive.

> *Britain is not a country that is easily rocked by revolution.... In Britain our institutions evolve. We are a Fabian Society writ large.*
>
> WILLIAM HAMILTON Scottish Labour politician. *My Queen and I* (1975)

FA Cup

Abbreviation for **Football Association Challenge Cup**, the major annual soccer knockout competition in England and Wales, open to all member clubs of the English Football Association. First held 1871–72, it is the oldest football knockout competition.

Fairfax, Thomas, 3rd Baron Fairfax (1612–1671)

English general, commander in chief of the Parliamentary army in the English ◊Civil War. With Oliver ◊Cromwell he formed the ◊New Model Army and defeated Charles I at Naseby. He opposed the king's execution, resigned in protest against the invasion of Scotland in 1650, and participated in the restoration of Charles II after Cromwell's death. Knighted 1640, succeeded to barony 1648.

Fair Isle (Old Norse **faar**, 'sheep')

Small island, one of the ◊Shetland Islands group, isolated midway between the Shetlands and the Orkney Islands, Scotland, 38 km/24 mi southwest of Sumburgh Head; population (1991) 87. Covering an area of 15 sq km/6 sq mi, it has a spectacular rocky coastline of high cliff crags. The principal activities are fishing and the production of multicoloured knitted goods with characteristic intricate patterns.

A birdwatching station is based on Fair Isle for research into the origins, routes, wintering areas, and feeding habits of spring and autumn migratory birds. The island passed into the care of the National Trust for Scotland in 1954.

Fairport Convention

English folk rock group formed in 1966. Members are Richard Thompson (1949–) (vocals and guitar), Simon Nicol (1950–) (guitar), Ashley Hutchings (1945–) (guitar), Sandy Denny (Alexandra Denny, 1948–) (vocals), Dave Pegg (1947–) (bass), Dave Swarbrick (1941–) (violin), and Dave Mattacks (1948–) (drums). The album *Unhalfbricking* (1969) contained the hit single 'Si Tu Dois Partir'. The group's van crashed in 1969, killing the original drummer Martin Lamble.

Fairy Queen, The

Semi-opera by Purcell (libretto adapted from Shakespeare's *A Midsummer Night's Dream* by Elkanah Settle), produced in London, Dorset Gardens Theatre, April 1692. The plot broadly follows that of Shakespeare's play, without setting any of the words. It was revived by the English National Opera for the Purcell tercentenary in 1995.

Faldo, Nick (Nicholas Alexander) (1957–)

English golfer who was the first Briton in 54 years to win three British Open titles, and the only person after Jack Nicklaus to win two successive US Masters titles (1989 and 1990). He is one of only seven golfers to win the Masters and British Open in the same year.

Falkirk

Unitary authority in central Scotland, created from the former district of the same name in 1996 from part of the former Central region
Area 297 sq km/115 sq mi
Towns ◊Falkirk (administrative headquarters), Grangemouth
Physical centrally located between Edinburgh and Glasgow, this lowlying area borders the southern side of the Firth of Forth; River Avon flows through
Features Forth and Clyde and Union canals; Rough Castle; Antonine Wall
Industries chemicals and petrochemicals, bus building, soft drinks, toffees
Agriculture some dairy and arable farming
Population (1995) 142,800.

Economy

The area has a broad economic base, but is particularly renowned for chemical industries.

Other features

The remains of the Antonine Wall (about AD 140) and a Roman road, can be seen at Rough Castle, west of Falkirk town. The Scottish Railway Preservation Society is at Bo'ness.

Environment

There are nine Sites of Special Scientific Interest and one country park.

Administrative history

Prior to 1975, the area was part of the county of Stirlingshire.

Falkirk

Administrative headquarters of ◊Falkirk unitary authority, Scotland, 37 km/23 mi west of Edinburgh; population (1991) 35,600. A former iron-founding centre, Falkirk has brewing, distilling, and bus-building industries. Edward I defeated William Wallace here on 22 July 1298, and Charles Edward Stuart defeated the English army here on 17 January 1746.

Two canals pass the town: the Forth and Clyde to the north, and the Union Canal to the south (now closed to navigation). A Millennium Link project to reopen navigation on both canals includes a Millennium Wheel to allow boats to transfer from one to the other. The port of Grangemouth is 4 km/2.5 mi to the east.

Falkland

Town and former royal burgh in Fife unitary authority, Scotland, 4 km/2.5 mi north of Glenrothes; population (1991) 1,200. Its chief industries are the manufacture of linen textiles and linoleum. The burgh was founded in 1458 by James II.

Falkland's ancient palace was the chief hunting lodge of the royal Stuarts from 1400 to 1603. The Renaissance-style south wing remains intact, completed by James V, who died at the lodge in 1542.

Falkland Islands, Argentine Islas Malvinas

British crown colony in the South Atlantic, 300 miles east of the Straits of Magellan
Area 12,173 sq km/4,700 sq mi
Population (1991) 2,120.
Administered with the Falklands, but separate dependencies of the UK, are South Georgia and the ◊South Sandwich Islands; see also British ◊Antarctic Territory.

History

The first European to visit the islands was Englishman John Davis in 1592, and at the end of the 17th century they were named after Lord Falkland, treasurer of the British navy. West Falkland was settled by the French in 1764. The first British settlers arrived in 1765; Spain bought out a French settlement in 1766, and the British were ejected (1770–71), but British sovereignty was never ceded, and from 1833, when a few Argentines were expelled, British settlement was continuous.

Argentina asserts its succession to the Spanish claim to the 'Islas Malvinas', but the inhabitants oppose cession. Occupied by Argentina in April 1982, the islands were recaptured by British military forces in May–June of the same year (see ◊Falklands War). In April 1990 Argentina's congress declared the Falkland Islands and other British-held South Atlantic islands part of the new Argentine province of Tierra del Fuego. In September 1995, the UK and Argentina signed an agreement on oil rights in waters surrounding the Falkland Islands.

Falkland Islands, Battle of the

In World War I, British naval victory (under Admiral Sir Frederick Sturdee) over German forces under Admiral Maximilian von Spee on 8 December 1914.

Von Spee intended to bombard the Falklands in passing before proceeding around the Cape of Good Hope to arouse the disaffected Boers of South Africa. However, there was already a British force stationed off the Falklands and when von Spee realised he had run into a trap he fled the area. The British gave chase and in the ensuing battle von Spee's squadron was entirely destroyed with a loss of 2,100 crew.

Falklands War

War between Argentina and Britain over disputed sovereignty of the ◊Falkland Islands initiated when Argentina invaded and occupied the islands on 2 April 1982. On the following day, the United Nations Security Council passed a resolution calling for Argentina to withdraw. A British task force was immediately dispatched and, after a fierce conflict in which more than 1,000 Argentine and British lives were lost, 12,000 Argentine troops surrendered and the islands were returned to British rule on 14–15 June 1982.

Falmouth

Port and resort on the south coast of Cornwall, southwest England, on the estuary of the River Fal, 11 km/7 mi southwest of Truro; population (1981) 18,500. It is a major yachting centre and the marine rescue and coastguard centre for the southwest region. Principal industries include tourism, ship-repair at Pendennis shipyard, and the construction of aluminium buildings and naval architecture.

Aluminium fabrications constructed here include the NatWest Media Centre at Lord's cricket ground, London. Trade through the port is less significant now, with some fish wholesaling and a specialist traffic in exotic plants for public gardens.

Features

Falmouth has a temperate climate in which sub-tropical plants flourish. The castles of Pendennis and St Mawes, on opposite sides of the estuary, were built in 1543 to guard the entrance to the natural, deepwater harbour. The town contains the headquarters of the Royal Cornwall Yacht Club and hosts a number of local regattas. From 1998 Falmouth will once again be the starting point for the biennial Cutty Sark International Tall Ships Race. Cultural facilities include the Cornwall Maritime Museum and an art gallery.

History

Pendennis Castle was captured during the Civil War by the Parliamentarians after a five-month siege. In 1688 Falmouth became a Mail Packet Station, handling mail destined for North America and the West Indies, and it was an important trading port in the 18th century. The Riot Act (1714) was read for the last time to mutinous crews of packet ships docked at Falmouth. The town developed as a resort after the railway opened in 1863.

Until 1938 Falmouth was the anchorage of the *Cutty Sark*, the last surviving tea clipper, now preserved in dry dock at Greenwich, London.

Tuesday 15 June Stanley woke up to find it was back under British rule. The British soldiers didn't look like men who had just walked across the island but they had, every step of the way on their own two feet. Fifty miles they'd come over mountains and bogs in weather that chilled the bone and soaked the skin, and at the end of it they'd fought bravely and well.

BRIAN HANRAHAN English TV and radio correspondent. BBC TV news report of 25 June 1982, recorded in *I Counted Them All Out and I Counted Them All Back* (1982)

Famous Five

Series of 21 stories for children by Enid ◊Blyton, published in the UK 1942–63, which describe the adventures of the 'Five' (four children and a dog) who spend their holidays together. The same author's *Secret Seven* series (1949–63) has a similar theme.

Faraday, Michael (1791–1867)

English chemist and physicist. In 1821, he began experimenting with electromagnetism, and discovered the induction of electric currents and made the first dynamo, the first electric motor, and the first transformer. Faraday isolated benzene from gas oils and produced the basic laws of electrolysis in 1834. He also pointed out that the energy of a magnet is in the field around it and not in the magnet itself, extending this basic conception of field theory to electrical and gravitational systems.

Chemistry and the discovery of benzene

Faraday was mainly interested in chemistry during his early years at the Royal Institution. He investigated the effects of including precious metals in steel in 1818, producing high-quality alloys that later stimulated the production of special high-grade steels. In 1823, Faraday produced liquid chlorine by heating crystals of chlorine hydrate in an inverted U-tube, one limb of which was heated and the other placed in a freezing mixture. After the production of liquid carbon dioxide in 1835, he used this coolant to liquefy other gases. In the same year, Faraday isolated benzene from gas oils and demonstrated the use of platinum as a catalyst. He also demonstrated the importance in chemical reactions of surfaces and inhibitors, foreshadowing a huge area of the modern chemical industry.

Laws of electrolysis

Faraday's laws of electrolysis established the link between electricity and chemical affinity, one of the most fundamental concepts in science. Electrolysis is the production of chemical changes by passing an electric current through a solution. It was Faraday who coined the terms anode, cathode, cation, anion, electrode, and electrolyte.

Faraday was born in Newington, Surrey, and was apprenticed to a bookbinder; he was largely self-educated. In 1812, he began researches into electricity, and made his first electrical cell. He became a laboratory assistant to Humphry ◊Davy at the Royal Institution in 1813, and in 1833 succeeded him as professor of chemistry. Faraday delivered highly popular lectures at the Royal Institution 1825–62. He refused to take part in the preparation of poison gas for use in the Crimean War.

farce

Broad popular comedy involving stereotyped characters in complex, often improbable situations frequently revolving around extramarital relationships (hence the term 'bedroom farce').

Originating in the physical knockabout comedy of Greek satyr plays and the broad humour of medieval religious drama, the farce was developed and perfected during the 19th century by Arthur Pinero in England. Two successful English series in the 20th century were Ben ◊Travers' Aldwych farces in the 1920s and 1930s and the Whitehall farces produced by Brian Rix during the 1950s and 1960s.

Fareham

Market town in Hampshire, southern England, 10 km/6 mi northwest of Portsmouth; population (1996 est) 102,500. Nearly 80% of employment is in the service sector, mainly retailing, and health and social work. Brickmaking, horticulture (notably strawberries), and leisure sailing industries have recently been supplemented by a fast-growing high-tech industrial sector, which includes the manufacture of scientific instruments (GEC Marconi, IBM).

Fareham was formerly a riverport above Portsmouth Harbour. The ironmaker Henry ◊Cort lived here at the end of the 18th century. His pioneer work on the manufacture of wrought iron and iron bars was central to the development of the Industrial Revolution.

Farjeon, Herbert (1887–1945)

English dramatist and critic. His light plays include *Friends* (1917) and *Many Happy Returns* (1928); he also wrote (in collaboration with his sister Eleanor Farjeon) the musical plays *The Two Bouquets* (1936) and *The Glass Slipper* (1944). He wrote and directed sketches for revues and was drama critic for several papers.

Farnaby, Giles (*c.* 1563–1640)

English composer. He wrote madrigals, psalms for the *Whole Booke of Psalms* (1621), edited by Thomas Ravencroft (1582–1633), and music for virginals (an early keyboard instrument), over 50 pieces being represented in the 17th-century manuscript collection the ◊*Fitzwilliam Virginal Book*.

Farnborough

Town in Hampshire, southern England, 4 km/2.5 mi north of Aldershot; population (1996 est) 53,000. It is the headquarters of the UK Defence Evaluation and Research Agency (until 1995 RAE Farnborough), which carries out research and experimental development in aeronautics and related instrumentation to support the Ministry of Defence. Partnerships with civilian clients are significant. Aeronautical displays are given at the biennial air show.

The mansion of **Farnborough Hill**, now a convent, was occupied by Napoleon III and the Empress Eugénie of France, and she is buried with her husband and son in a mausoleum at St Michael's Catholic Church, built by the empress in 1887.

St Michael's Abbey, adjoining the church, is occupied by a Benedictine community.

Farnham's former Institution of Aviation Medicine became part of the Defence Evaluation and Research Agency (DERA) Centre for Human Sciences in 1996.

Farne Islands

Group of about 28 rocky islands in the North Sea, close to the mainland of northeast England, 2–8 km/1–5 mi from Bamburgh, Northumberland. The islands are a sanctuary for birds and grey seals.

On Inner Farne, the largest of the group, there is a 14th-century chapel on the site of the hermitage at which St Cuthbert stayed from 676 to 684; he returned to die here in 687. The Longstone lighthouse, on one of the most remote of the islands, was the scene of the rescue of shipwrecked sailors by Grace ◊Darling in 1838.

The group has been owned by the National Trust since 1925. The islands are a nature reserve and sanctuary for many species of seabirds, particularly guillemots, puffins, terns, and kittiwakes. To protect the birds only two of the islands are open to visitors. It is the only breeding station of Atlantic seals on the east coast of Britain.

Farnham

Town in Surrey, southeast England, on the River Wey; population (1996 est) 36,200. It is a retailing and business centre, and has an institute of art and design. Industries include biochemical research, software manufacture, and television and video production. Waverley Abbey (1128), the first Cistercian house in England, lies nearby to the southeast; Walter Scott is said to have named his first novel after the foundation.

Farnham Castle, dating from the 12th century, was the palace of the bishops of Winchester until 1925, and then the seat of the bishop of Guildford until 1956. Farnham was formerly the centre of a large hop-growing district and it has many fine Georgian buildings, reflecting its importance as a market centre in the 18th century. The area remains extremely prosperous. Willmer House Museum includes a local history collection and many relics of the radical politician and essayist William Cobbett, who was born here in 1763.

Farrell, J(ames) G(ordon) (1935–1979)

English historical novelist. His work includes *Troubles* (1970), set in Ireland just after World War I, the *The Siege of Krishnapur* (1973) (Booker Prize), describing the Indian Mutiny, and *The Singapore Grip* (1978) which describes the fall of Singapore to the Japanese. His novel *The Hill Station* (1981) was unfinished when Farrell died.

Farrell, Terry (Terence) (1938–)

English architect. He works in a Post-Modern idiom, largely for corporate clients seeking an alternative to the rigours of Modernist or High Tech office blocks. His Embankment Place scheme (1991) sits theatrically on top of Charing Cross station in Westminster, London, and has been likened to a giant jukebox. Alban Gate (1992) in the City of London is a continuation of the language but is more towerlike in form.

Farrell's style is robust and eclectic, and he is not afraid to make jokes in architecture, such as the gaily painted giant egg cups that adorn the parapet of his TV AM building (1981–82) in Camden, London. Other works include studios for Limehouse Productions, Henley Royal Regatta HQ, and the Craft Council Galleries.

farthing

Formerly the smallest English coin, a quarter of a penny. It was introduced as a silver coin in Edward I's reign. The copper farthing became widespread in Charles II's reign, succeeded by the bronze farthing in 1860. It was dropped from use in 1961.

fashion

See chronology opposite for some fashion highlights.

Faulkner, (Arthur) Brian (Deane), Baron Faulkner of Downpatrick (1921–1977)

Northern Ireland Unionist politician. He was the last prime

One of the most rugged terrains in the British Isles is Snowdonia National Park in Gwynedd, North Wales. Such relatively untouched regions must have appeared much the same to the hunter-gatherers who inhabited Britain in prehistoric times.
National Trust Photographic Library/Joe Cornish

The wild coastline at Bedruthan Steps on the North Cornwall coast. Britain became separated from continental Europe some 7,000–8,000 years ago; since then, its position as an island has played a major role in shaping British history and attitudes.
Joe Cornish

The Celts settled in the British Isles during the Iron Age, which began in around 700 BC. As other peoples arrived (the Romans in the 1st century AD, and the Anglo-Saxons in the 5th–7th centuries), Celtic kingdoms remained only on the western fringes. This Celtic monument is the Janus Stone in County Fermanagh, Northern Ireland. *Alain Le Garsmeur/Image Ireland/Collections*

Hadrian's Wall was built to protect the northern frontier of the Roman province of Britannia. After the invasion of AD 43, Celtic Britain was extensively Romanized. Even after the Romans withdrew in AD 410, the British continued to run the country on Roman lines. *Joe Cornish.*

Characteristic Norman chevron decoration on a pillar in Durham Cathedral. When the Normans of northern France conquered Britain after 1066 – the last successful invasion of the country – they seized Anglo-Saxon land and property, imposed their own legal and administrative systems, and exerted an enormous cultural influence.
Joe Cornish

The typical English lowland village arose as settled arable farming developed; farmers gathered together and cooperated to clear woodlands and to till the fields they laid out. The church, like this example at Blyth in Norfolk, often formed the focal point of the village. *Robert Hallmann/Collections*

Sheep farming was widespread in the Middle Ages, and for many centuries wool was Britain's principal product. The Cotswold Hills in southern central England were a major centre of wool production, and the great wealth it generated gave rise to prosperous villages with fine churches, such as here, at Naunton in Gloucestershire.
Michael StMaur Sheil/Collections

Some villages, such as Ditchling, in East Sussex, have remained of moderate size. Although many town dwellers regard rural life as idyllic and aspire to live in the country, only one-quarter of Britain's population now lives in villages. Most of the new inhabitants nowadays are 'incomers', who do not earn their living on the land.
Tony Souter/The Hutchison Library

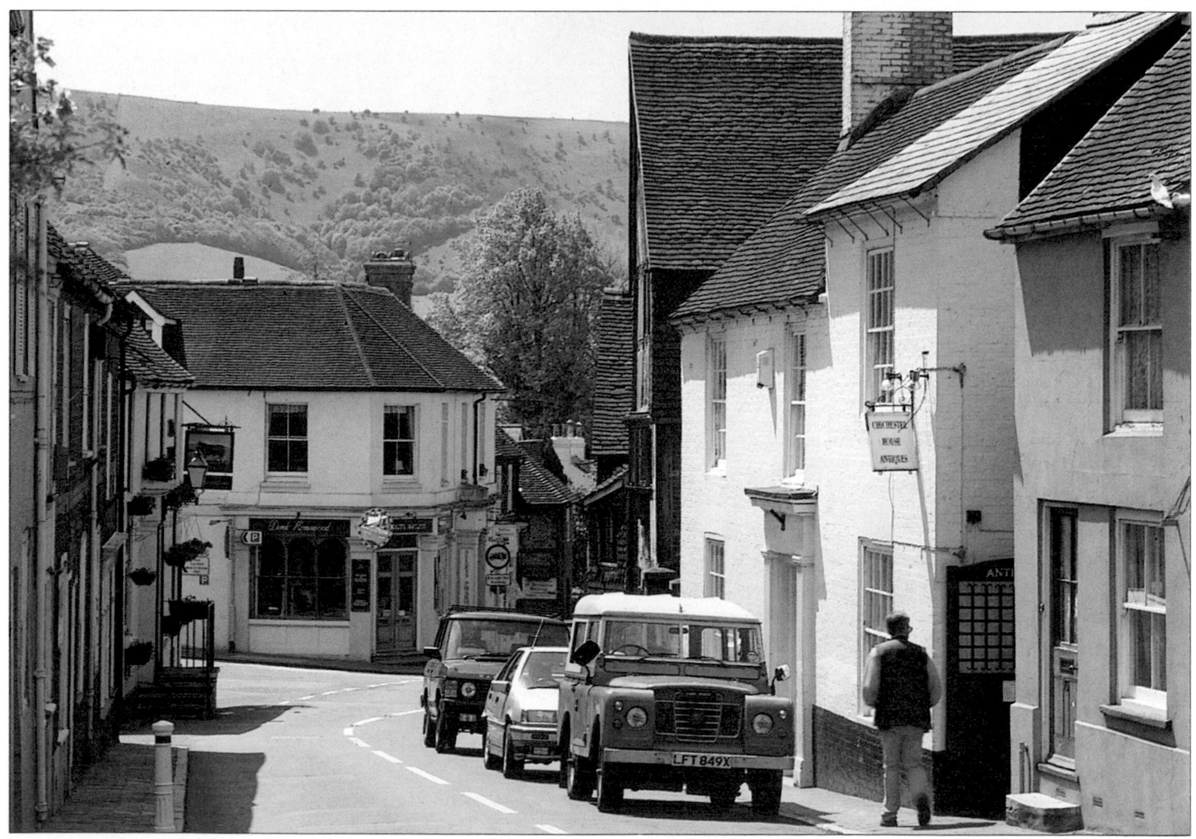

One of the spurs to the growth of urban populations was coal mining, which increased in scale from the 1850s; this mining town is in Wales. Development was particularly intensive in the south of Wales, where, at the height of the coal boom just before World War I, some 150,000 people earned their living from mining. *The Hutchison Library*

A modern view of Manchester, which, like many other UK cities, grew rapidly during the Industrial Revolution of the early 19th century. Then, urban conditions were squalid, with the labour force (many of whom were women and children) working 12-hour days in cotton mills and factories. Today, Manchester's commerce continues to thrive, and it is also a vibrant shopping and cultural centre. *Robin Weaver/Collections*

Sea fishing was formerly an important occupation all around the coast of Britain. Grimsby, on the Humber estuary in the northeast of England, was once the biggest fishing port in the world. Much fishing is still undertaken, but dwindling stocks of cod and herring and the imposition of quotas have brought the decline of the great deep-sea trawler fleets; this small fishing boat sails from Folkestone.
Michael StMaur Sheil/ Collections

Harvesting maize for cattle fodder, in Hampshire. Settled farming began in Britain in around 4400 BC. From the mid-18th century, British farming introduced advances in animal husbandry and crop management (the 'agricultural revolution'), and later pioneered farm mechanization. Modern agribusiness has changed the face of the countryside through factory farming and the replacement of small fields by 'prairie'-style cultivation.
Tony Page

One of the foremost manufacturing industries in Britain has been car manufacture. Production, as at this Rover plant, is now highly automated and efficient, and the industry has been sustained by foreign investment, particularly from Japan and Germany. *John Wender/Collections*

A blast furnace for making steel at Redcar, in northeast England. Plentiful coal and iron-ore deposits stimulated the growth of Britain's heavy industry in the 19th century. Iron and steel production supported the Industrial Revolution, supplying the materials for railways, shipbuilding, and the manufacture of factory machinery. *Mike Kipling/Collections*

Services now form a significant part of the UK economy. Here, the London Water Control Centre regulates distribution of water to industries and homes via the London Ring Main, a huge pipe that encircles the capital and is supplied by 18 reservoirs. Along with other public service utilities, water was privatized in the 1980s.
Tony Page/Impact

Illuminations at the seaside town of Blackpool, which attracts some 8 million visitors annually. The resort developed as a holiday destination for workers from the cotton-manufacturing towns of Lancashire, and is now part of a multi-billion pound leisure and tourism industry that continues to boom throughout the country as changing work practices leave people with more free time. *Sam Walsh/Collections*

FASHION: SOME KEY DATES

1102 Anselm, the archbishop of Canterbury, criticizes the fashions of the court. Men are wearing beards and long curled hair, and are adopting an 'effeminate' style in their dress. Women's dresses have voluminous wide sleeves. Shoes are pointed, often curling up at the toes.

c. **1155** Women's dress is influenced by fashions in France and Italy; trailing gowns with tight bodices become popular.

c. **1460** Dresses with high, full bodices are in fashion.

c. **1480** In the English court, it is the fashion for men to wear fur-lined garments, short doublets and pointed shoes, and their hair long; women wear tight bodices with low-cut necklines and elaborate head-dresses, often in the shape of butterflies or horns.

c. **1520** It is the fashion in the English court for women to wear flowing dresses with elaborately decorated cuffs.

c. **1750** As the grand tour of Europe grows in popularity, the influence of European fashions in clothes and furnishings is seen in Britain. Men increasingly wear gold buttons and buckles; ruffles and embroidered waistcoats are also popular.

1758 English inventor Jedediah Strutt designs a ribbing-machine for the manufacture of hosiery with ribbed or ridged weave.

1797 Haberdasher John Hetherington creates the first top hat, in London, England.

c. **1812** The women's fashion in Britain is for dresses with very high waists, just under the bust.

1823 Charles Macintosh, using a technique developed by James Syme, patents and begins manufacturing the cloth that will help to make 'Macintosh' a synonym for raincoat, in Glasgow, Scotland.

1849 The hatters Thomas and William Bowler create the bowler hat in London, designed to protect the head from branches when shooting. This will become emblematic of the British middle-class professional man.

1858 The English dressmaker Charles Worth launches the first fashion house on the rue de la Paix in Paris, France.

c. **1890** Bloomers, invented in the USA around 1850 by women's rights advocate Amelia Bloomer, become fashionable in Britain as more women take up cycling.

1892 Margaret Tait, a student at the Hampstead Physical Training College, England, designs the gym slip, a short dress which gives girls the freedom to play in team games.

1919 The British company Kynoch of Birmingham introduces the zip fastener, under the name the Ready Fastener.

c. **1930** It becomes socially acceptable for women to wear trousers when playing golf or riding a horse.

December 1946 Nylon stockings, the first commercial nylon goods to be manufactured in Britain, go on sale in London, England.

1 April 1960 R Griggs & Co. begin to produce Doc Martens boots under licence in Britain.

1960s Carnaby Street and the King's Road in London become acknowledged fashion centres.

1966 Women's dresses with mini skirts are being sold as children's clothes in Britain to avoid tax; new tax laws are brought in to close the loophole. Twiggy is named the Face of 1966.

1973 Flared trousers, and platform shoes are in fashion in Britain.

1979 US sports-equipment distributor Paul Fireman obtains the US licence to manufacture British Reebok training shoes. Reebok will go on to challenge Nike's market lead.

1981 Diana Spencer marries Prince Charles in a dress by British designers, the Emmanuels. Her interest in fashion gives British designers new impetus.

1983 London Fashion Week is launched by the British Fashion Council, and is held twice a year.

1996 English designer John Galliano becomes design head of Christian Dior.

minister of Northern Ireland 1971–72 before the Stormont Parliament was suspended. Baron 1977.

Faversham

Town in Kent, England, 15 km/9 mi northwest of Canterbury. Faversham has prehistoric, Roman, and Anglo-Saxon associations, and was an important medieval river port, situated on Faversham Creek. The port now trades in timber, fertilizers, and petroleum spirit. Agricultural produce includes hops, apples, and cherries, and there are fruit-canning, grading, and packing stations. Brewing and brickmaking and several light industries are also present in the town. Faversham is one of England's best-preserved historic towns.

Abbey Street in Faversham has been restored as a complete period piece from before the 19th century, and there are many ancient buildings in the town, including those in Market Place, the Norman church of St Mary of Charity, and the old grammar school.

The former village of Ospringe, now within the town, has the Maison Dieu museum, containing Roman finds. A large abbey – erected by King Stephen in the 12th century, originally for the Cluniac order and later for the Benedictines – was excavated at Faversham in 1965.

Fawcett, Millicent born Garrett (1847–1929)

English ◊suffragette and social reformer, younger sister of Elizabeth Garrett ◊Anderson. A non-militant, she rejected the violent acts of some of her contemporaries in the suffrage movement. She joined the first Women's Suffrage Committee in 1867 and became president of the Women's

Unionist Association in 1889. She was president of the National Union of Women's Suffrage Societies 1897–1919.

She was also active in property reform and campaigned for the right of married women to own their own property, and the higher education and employment of women. DBE 1925.

Fawkes, Guy (Guido) (1570–1606)

English conspirator in the ◊Gunpowder Plot to blow up King James I and the members of both Houses of Parliament. Fawkes, a Roman Catholic convert, was arrested in the cellar underneath the House on 4 November 1605, tortured, and subsequently executed. The event is still commemorated in Britain and elsewhere every 5 November with bonfires, fireworks, and the burning of the 'guy', an effigy.

> *Guido's composure was astonishing. Yes, he had intended to blow up the King and the Lords. No, he had no regrets – except the fact that he had not succeeded. 'The devil and not God', he said firmly, was responsible for the discovery of the Plot. No, he had not sought to warn the Catholic peers, he would have contented himself with praying for them.*
>
> ANTONIA FRASER English writer.
> Describing the questioning of Guido (Guy) Fawkes in *The Gunpowder Plot: Terror and Faith in 1605* (1996)

Feinstein, Elaine born Coolin (1930–)

English poet, novelist, and translator. Her verse, first published in *In a Green Eye* (1966), has an international flavour as well as reflecting a wide variety of forms. Her *Selected Poems* was published in 1994. Her novels, such as her first, *The Circle* (1970), explore family relationships; several, such as *The Border* (1984), have Jewish themes.

Felbrigg Hall

House in Norfolk, England, 3 km/2 mi southwest of Cromer, the home of the Windham family from the mid-15th century. The present house was built in the 17th century and remains outwardly unaltered; the rooms also retain their original furniture and pictures. The house, contents and estate were left to the National Trust in 1969 by Robert Wyndham Ketton-Cremer, the last squire of Felbrigg.

Felixstowe

Port and resort opposite Harwich in Suffolk, eastern England, fronting the estuary of the Orwell at its confluence with the Deben, 20 km/12 mi southeast of Ipswich; population (1996 est) 23,800. It is Britain's busiest container port, handling around 2 million containers a year, 35% of the UK's total traffic. Oil and other bulk liquids are also imported. Ferry services operate from ◊Harwich.

Felixstowe is thought to have derived its name from the Benedictine priory founded here in the late 11th century, which was dedicated to St Felix, bishop of Dunwich. The town developed as a resort at the end of the 19th century, with a promenade, cliff gardens, and boating facilities.

Landguard Point, at the mouth of the Orwell and Deben estuaries, is a nature reserve. Landguard Fort was first built in the mid 16th century by Henry VIII to guard the entrance to the harbour at Harwich. In 1667 the fortress repelled a full-scale naval invasion by the Dutch.

Fenian movement

Irish-American republican secret society, founded in 1858 and named after the ancient Irish legendary warrior band of the Fianna. The collapse of the movement began when an attempt to establish an independent Irish republic by an uprising in Ireland in 1867 failed, as did raids into Canada in 1866 and 1870, and England in 1867.

Fens, the

Level, low-lying tracts of reclaimed marsh in eastern England, west and south of the Wash, covering an area of around 40,000 sq km/15,500 sq mi, about 115 km/70 mi north–south and 55 km/34 mi east–west. They fall within the counties of Lincolnshire, Cambridgeshire, and Norfolk. Formerly a bay of the North Sea, they are now crossed by numerous drainage canals and form some of the most fertile and productive agricultural land in Britain. The southern peat portion of the Fens is known as the Bedford Level.

Features

The main rivers flowing through the area are the Great Ouse, Witham, Welland, and Nene, and many small watercourses also intersect the area. Before the present system of drainage was developed, the whole district was waterlogged and consisted of marshy swamps, wide pools, and lagoons. Woad continues to be grown in some areas for its blue dye. There are a number of windmills, now mostly disused, on the flats. The area is noted for its bulb fields, especially around Spalding.

Ecology

Northeast of Cambridge, attempts have been made to preserve the raised bogs of **Burwell Fen** and Wicken Fen undrained as nature reserves, but agriculture in the surrounding area has affected water levels, partially destroying their ecology. Areas such as **Lopham Fen** and **Redgrave Fen** are also recognized as having important ecological value for specific animal and plant life, including otters, great raft spiders, rare birds, and the marsh hellibore orchid, although their existence is considerably threatened by land drainage and groundwater draw-down for public supplies. Wildfowl and fish remain abundant in the rivers and marshlands, but ecological problems have been caused by the introduction of fish species such as the zander, a voracious predator.

History

The region was once the home of the ancient Iceni, who were led in revolt against the Romans by Queen Boudicca. The Romans dug drainage channels, the Caer or Car Dykes from Lincoln to Ramsey, and constructed earthen embankments along the Welland and the seashore, some stretches of which can still be seen. Following an unsuccessful attempt to drain

Deeping Fen during the reign of William (I) the Conqueror, the district was abandoned, although the forest portions were preserved between the 12th and 14th centuries as royal hunting areas.

Small communities, known as **fen slodgers**, enclosed and embanked portions of the land to create islands with fields and pasture, gathering reed for thatching, and living on wildfowl and fish. The drainage of the land in the 15th and 16th centuries threatened their way of life, and local opposition was expressed by attempts to break down the newly created banks and dams. In 1634 the 4th Earl of Bedford commissioned the Dutch water-engineer Cornelius Vermuyden to drain the Bedford Level, introducing Dutch drainage methods to the Fens. Vast areas were systematically drained in the 17th century by the great landowners, using the Dutch methods, and by the 18th century the way of life of the fen slodgers had almost disappeared. Drainage of the Fens continued during the 18th century and many pumping windmills were installed. In the 19th century steam pumps were introduced, and these were replaced by diesel and electric pumps.

Fenton

Part of the city of ◊Stoke-on-Trent, Staffordshire, England. Earthenware and china are manufactured, and there is light engineering. Formerly a separate town, Fenton merged with other ◊Potteries towns as Stoke-on-Trent in 1910.

Ferguson, Alex(ander) (1941–)

Scottish football manager. One of British football's most successful managers, he has won nine trophies with Manchester United including four league championship titles. In 1996, under his charge, Manchester United became the first club to achieve the league championship and FA Cup double twice. Earlier, as manager of Aberdeen from 1978 to 1986, he won ten trophies including three Scottish championships and the European Cup Winners' Cup. He was also manager of the Scottish national side 1985–86.

Ferguson, Harry George (1884–1960)

Northern Irish engineer who pioneered the development of the tractor, joining forces with Henry Ford in 1938 to manufacture it in the USA. He also experimented in automobile and aircraft development.

Ferguson was born near Belfast. In 1902 he joined his brother in a car- and cycle-repair business. He built his own aeroplane and flew it in 1909, becoming one of the first Britons to do so. He started to import tractors, then, from 1936, designed his own. In 1946, with British government backing, the Ferguson tractor, made by the Standard Motor Company in Coventry, was launched. In the USA Ferguson and Ford fought a massive antitrust suit, largely over a similar machine produced by Ford. Ferguson set up his own US plant in 1948, but sold it to Massey-Harris in 1953.

For the first Ferguson tractor, he designed a plough that would not rear up and crush the driver when encountering an obstacle. But it was his system of draught control, patented in 1925, that revolutionized farming methods by improving the effective traction so that expensive, heavy machines were no longer necessary.

Fermanagh

County of Northern Ireland
Area 1,680 sq km/648 sq mi
Towns ◊Enniskillen (county town), Lisnaskea, Irvinestown
Physical in the centre is a broad trough of low-lying land, in which lie Upper and Lower Lough Erne
Industries clothing, tweeds, cotton thread, food processing, light engineering, china, tourism, electronics
Agriculture small farms, livestock, potatoes
Population (1991) 50,000.

Physical

Upper and Lower Lough Erne bisect the county, the southwest portion of which consists of a series of scenic limestone hills that rise to 663 m/2,175 ft in Mount Cuilcagh, and contain several remarkable cave systems, notably at Marble Arch. Eastwards, the hills are lower and largely composed of sandstone. Lough Erne has many wooded islands and is used for fishing and sailing. Upper Lough Erne is particularly noted for its game fishing.

Features

There are a number of fine castles and tower houses dating from the plantation period, most notably the well-preserved remains of Monea Castle. On Devenish Island, Lower Lough Erne, are the extensive ruins of a monastery, originally founded in the 6th century by St Molaise. Florence Court, a Georgian mansion and forest park, was the home of the Earl of Enniskillen. Castle Coole is a neo-classical, late 18th-century house, and was the home of the Earls of Belmore. Crom Castle Estate, on the shores of Upper Lough Erne, is an important wetland conservation area and has 770 ha/1,903 acres of woodland and parkland, and the ruins of a castle built in 1611 stand in the grounds. (Florence Court, Castle Coole, and Crom Castle are now in the curatorship of the National Trust.)

Ferneyhough, Brian John Peter (1943–)

English composer. His uncompromising, detailed compositions include *Carceri d'invenzione*, a cycle of seven works inspired by the engravings of Piranesi (1981–86), *Time and Motion Studies* (1974–77), and string quartets.

Ferranti, Sebastian Ziani de (1864–1930)

British electrical engineer who established the principle of a national grid and an electricity-generating system based on alternating current (AC) (successfully arguing against Thomas Edison's proposal). He brought electricity to much of central London. In 1881 he made and sold his first alternator.

Ferranti also designed, constructed, and experimented with many other electrical and mechanical devices, including high-tension cables, circuit breakers, transformers, turbines, and spinning machines.

Ferrier, Kathleen Mary (1912–1953)

English contralto. She brought warmth and depth of conviction to English oratorio roles during wartime and subsequently to opera and lieder (songs), including Gluck's *Orfeo ed Euridice*, Mahler's *Das Lied von der Erde/The Song of the Earth*, and the role of Lucretia in Benjamin Britten's *The Rape of Lucretia* (1946).

Ferry, Bryan (1945–)

English pop singer. He was the lead singer of Roxy Music, whose songs include 'Virginia Plain', and his solo albums include *Boys and Girls* (1985) which contained the hit single 'Slave to Love'.

Festival of Britain

Artistic and cultural festival held in London May–September 1951 both to commemorate the 100th anniversary of the Great Exhibition and to boost morale after years of post-war austerity. The South Bank of the Thames formed the focal point of the event and the Royal Festival Hall built specially for the festival is a reminder of the modernist style of architecture promoted at the time.

feudalism (Latin *feudem* 'fief', coined 1839)

The main form of social organization in medieval Europe. A system based primarily on land, it involved a hierarchy of authority, rights, and power that extended from the monarch downwards. An intricate network of duties and obligations linked royalty, nobility, lesser gentry, free tenants, villeins, and serfs. Feudalism was reinforced by a complex legal system and supported by the Christian church. With the growth of commerce and industry from the 13th century, feudalism gradually gave way to the class system as the dominant form of social ranking.

field

Enclosed area of land used for farming.

In Britain, regular field systems were functioning before the Romans' arrival. The open-field system was in use at the time of the Norman Conquest. Enclosure began in the 13th century and continued into the 19th century.

In the Middle Ages, the farmland of an English rural community was often divided into three large fields (the **open-field system**). These were worked on a simple rotation basis of one year wheat, one year barley, and one year fallow. The fields were divided into individually owned strips of the width that one plough team with oxen could plough (about 20 m/66 ft). At the end of each strip would be a turning space, either a road or a **headland**. Through repeated ploughing a **ridge-and-furrow** pattern became evident. A farmer worked a number of strips, not necessarily adjacent to each other, in one field.

The open-field communities were subsequently reorganized, the land enclosed, and the farmers' holdings redistributed into individual blocks which were then divided into separate fields. This ◊enclosure process reached its peak during the 18th century. Twentieth-century developments in agricultural science and technology have encouraged farmers to amalgamate and enlarge their fields, often to as much as 40 hectares/100 acres.

Fielding, Henry (1707–1754)

English novelist. His greatest work, *The History of Tom Jones, a Foundling* (1749) (see ◊*Tom Jones*), which he described as 'a comic epic poem in prose', was an early landmark in the development of the English novel, realizing for the first time in English the form's potential for memorable characterization, coherent plotting, and perceptive analysis. The vigour of its comic impetus, descriptions of high and low life in town and country, and its variety of characters made it immediately popular.

In youth a prolific dramatist, Fielding began writing novels with *An Apology for the Life of Mrs Shamela Andrews* (1741), a merciless parody of Samuel ◊Richardson's *Pamela*.

Fielding gave a new prominence to dialogue in his work, which was to have a marked influence on the development of the English novel. He attempted to portray life realistically, with humour, though his penetrating analysis of human weakness is also compassionate.

He was appointed Justice of the Peace for Middlesex and Westminster in 1748. His *Inquiry into the Increase of Robbers* (1751), with suggested remedies, led to beneficial results and he was instrumental in developing a police force by helping to form the Bow Street Runners.

Fields, Gracie stage name of Grace Stansfield (1898–1979)

English comedian and singer. Much loved by the public, her humorously sentimental films include *Sally in Our Alley* (1931), *Sing as We Go* (1934), *We're Going to be Rich* (1938), and *Holy Matrimony* (1943).

Fiennes, Ralph Nathaniel (1962–)

British film and stage actor. Films include *Emily Brontë's Wuthering Heights* (1992), *Schindler's List* (1993), *Quiz Show*

FIELDING, HENRY *A 1754 portrait of the 18th-century English novelist, Henry Fielding. He broke away from the prevailing epistolary and moralizing tradition of novels to a comic and satiric realism, and frequently wrote parodies of the literary successes of the day. Concern for social justice, seen in his best-known novel* Tom Jones *(1749), was also a feature of his term as a magistrate. Corbis*

(1994), and *Strange Days* (1995). He was nominated for an Academy Award for his leading role in *The English Patient* (1996).

Fiennes established himself as a stage actor with the National Theatre Company (which he joined in 1987) and the Royal Shakespeare Company (1989), and made his screen debut in 1990. He won the 1995 Best Actor Tony Award for his performance in *Hamlet*.

His other films include *The Baby of Maçon* (1993), *Oscar and Lucinda* (1997), and *The Avengers* (1998). He is a cousin of the British explorer Ranulph Fiennes.

Fiennes, Ranulph Twisleton-Wykeham (1944–)

British explorer who made the first surface journey around the world's polar circumference between 1979 and 1982. In 1992 he attempted, with Dr Michael Stroud, the first unsupported crossing of the Antarctic. Though the two men had to airlifted out before they completed the trip, it was none the less the longest unsupported Polar journey ever, recorded in his book *Mind Over Matter* (1993).

His earlier expeditions included explorations of the White Nile in 1969, Jostedalsbre Glacier, Norway, in 1970, and the Headless Valley, Canada, in 1971. Accounts of his adventures include *A Talent for Trouble* (1970), *Hell on Ice* (1979), and the autobiographical *Living Dangerously* (1987). Succeeded to baronetcy 1944.

Fife

Unitary authority in eastern Scotland, which was formerly a region of three districts (1975–96) and a county until 1974

Area 1,321 sq km/510 sq mi

Towns Cupar, Dunfermline, ◊Glenrothes (administrative headquarters), Kirkcaldy, St Andrews

Physical coastal area, predominantly low lying, undulating interior with dramatic escarpment at Lomond Hills; rivers Eden and Leven flow through

Features Rosyth naval base; Old Course, St Andrews

Industries electronics, petrochemicals, light engineering, oil servicing, paper

Agriculture potatoes, cereals, sugar beet, fishing (Pittenweem)

Population (1995) 351,600.

History Tentsmuir, a coastal sand-dune area in the north, is possibly the earliest settled site in Scotland; the ancient palace of the Stuarts (16th century) was at Falkland; eight Scottish kings buried at Dunfermline.

Economy

At one time Fife's economy was dominated by the coal-mining industry, but coalmining is not so important now, although some of the most modern and mechanized pits in Scotland are located in the area. It has a mixed economy, although the economic profiles differ dramatically within the area. St Andrews has a thriving service sector and tourist base, Glenrothes (New Town) has contemporary electronics industries, much of the northeast is predominantly agricultural.

Environment

There are 53 Sites of Special Scientific Interest, three National Nature Reserves, one Ramsar (wetland site), two Special Protection Areas, one regional park, and three country parks.

Administrative history

The districts of Dunfermline, Kirkcaldy and North East Fife made up Fife region, which is now known as Fife unitary authority.

Fifteen, the

◊Jacobite rebellion of 1715, led by the 'Old Pretender' ◊James Edward Stuart and the Earl of Mar, in order to place the former on the English throne. Mar was checked at Sheriffmuir, Scotland, and the revolt collapsed.

film industry

See feature on the British film industry.

Finance Act

The annual act of Parliament which implements the proposals made by the chancellor of the Exchequer in the Budget. Preliminary approval is given to certain changes in taxation, mainly those in which there is a change in the rate at which a tax is levied, by means of resolutions passed immediately after the chancellor's Budget statement.

These resolutions have statutory effect under the Provisional Collection of Taxes Act 1968 (which superseded a similar act of 1913). The Finance Bill must be given a second reading within 20 days of the completion of the debates on the budget statement and, since 1968, some clauses of the bill have been taken in a standing committee, the rest being dealt with in the committee of the whole House.

Financial Times

London newspaper, a morning daily which first appeared in 1888. Incorporated with the *Financial News* (founded in 1884), it contains detailed news of business and finance, including markets, stocks and shares, and industrial developments of interest to the business community. Owned by the Pearson company, it had a circulation of over 300,000 in 1998.

Financial Times Index, FT Index

Indicator measuring the daily movement of 30 major industrial share prices on the London Stock Exchange, issued by the UK *Financial Times* newspaper. Other FT indices cover government securities, fixed-interest securities, gold mine shares, and Stock Exchange activity.

Finch, Peter (William Mitchell) (1916–1977)

Australian-born English film actor. He began his career in Australia before moving to London in 1949 to start on an international career in films such as *A Town Like Alice* (1956), *The Trials of Oscar Wilde* (1960), *Sunday, Bloody Sunday* (1971), and *Network* (1976), for which he won an Academy Award.

Fingal's Cave

Cave on the island of Staffa, Inner Hebrides, Argyll and Bute, Scotland. It is lined with volcanic basalt columns, and is

Still Reliant on Occasional Hits – A Brief History of the British Film Industry

Most historical accounts of the British film industry tend to be tinged with a sense of disappointment and unfulfilled promise. Despite the much vaunted 'renaissance' of British cinema in the 1980s and 90s and the global marketability of British actors and directors, this remains a fairly accurate picture, with the industry still failing to command a significant share of either the domestic or international market. Britain's longterm failure to develop a fully integrated production, distribution, and exhibition network (unlike the US) coupled with the absence of the generous levels of state support and funding enjoyed by some of its European competitors (notably France) has left the industry weak and vunerable, dependent on the occasional box office hit to fuel further investment and production.

The roots of this problem go back as far as the emergence of popular cinema itself in the early 1900s. While primitive film-making had been underway in the UK since the late 1800s, Britain did not have anything resembling a home industry until the early 1930s. By this time, Hollywood had a well-established infrastructure, production network and was already pursuing an aggressive foreign export strategy centred on the British market. As Hollywood films became increasingly popular with British audiences, US distributors introduced the practice of 'blind and block' booking whereby eagerly sought productions could only be rented along with a further series of unknown American films. By the mid 1920s, the percentage of home-produced films exhibited in Britain had dropped from 10% to 5%, a situation which led to first piece of protective cinema legislation: the Cinematagraph Films Act of 1927. This forced British cinemas to exhibit a certain number of British films per year, beginning with a modest 7.5% and rising to 20% in the 1930s. Although this led to the production of many cheap, low quality British productions – dispairingly known as 'quota quickies' – it undoubtedly assisted the growth of the domestic market and the development of the large production studios in and around London: Pinewood, Ealing, Elstree, Denham, and Shepperton.

Countering Hollywood

The difficulty facing British production companies was that generic expectations had, by this point, already been established by Hollywood; Britain's largely working-class audience responded with marked enthusiasm to the vibrancy and breadth of human experience represented in Hollywood genres such as the musical or gangster film, as compared with some of the rather stuffy, class-bound attitudes resonant in British productions. The discovery and promotion of homegrown popular entertainers such as George Formby and Gracie Fields went some way towards luring back the domestic audiences in the 1930s. In addition to this, companies such as the Gaumount-British Picture Corporation – with Michael Balcon at the helm – began producing films of international repute such as Hitchcock's *The Thirty Nine Steps* (1935) and *The Lady Vanishes* (1938). One of the key points in the industry's upturn was the unexpected box office success, in both the UK and US, of London Film Productions' *The Private Life of Henry VIII* (1933).

The moderate successes of the 1930s paved the way for the expansion of the 1940s, the decade generally regarded as the golden age of British cinema. Many of the best-loved, most familiar British film cycles derive from this period: quirky Ealing comedies such as *Kind Hearts and Coronets* (1949) or *Passport to Pimlico* (1949), Gainsborough costume dramas like *The Wicked Lady* or spiv gangster films like *Brighton Rock* (1947) and *The Third Man* (1949). The decade also witnessed the more innovative, groundbreaking work of directors Michael Powell and Emeric Pressburger: *The Life and Death of Colonel Blimp* (1943), *A Matter of Life and Death* (1946), *Black Narcissus* (1947), and *The Red Shoes* (1949). For the first time in the century, British films captured a sizeable

A still from the comedy The Full Monty *(1997), which attracted the largest audiences in Britain of any home-produced film, and also played well abroad. Michele Mattei Productions/Rex*

70 m/230 ft long and 20 m/65 ft high. Visited by the German Romantic composer Felix Mendelssohn in 1829, the cave was the inspiration of his *Hebridean* overture, otherwise known as *Fingal's Cave.*

Finney, Albert (1936–)
English stage and film actor. He created the title roles in Keith Waterhouse's stage play *Billy Liar* (1960) and John Osborne's *Luther* (1961), and was associate artistic director of the Royal Court Theatre 1972–75. Later roles for the National Theatre include Tamburlaine in Marlowe's tragedy (1976) and Macbeth (1978). His films include *Saturday Night and Sunday Morning* (1960), *Tom Jones* (1963), *Murder on the Orient Express* (1974), *The Dresser* (1984), *Miller's Crossing* (1990), and *The Browning Version* (1994).

Finney, Tom (Thomas) (1922–)
English footballer, known as the 'Preston Plumber'. Playing

chunk of the domestic market, the highpoint coming in 1946, when British box office returns actually outstripped that of American imports. Unfortunately, the boom was to be short lived, as post-war competition from other forms of entertainment (chiefly television) resulted in an international slump in cinema audiences. While Hollywood was solid enough to weather the storm, the newly developed, fragile British industry went into longterm decline. Although the 1950s and 60s saw the success of British cycles such as Hammer Horror films, the *Carry On* series, or the largely US-backed Bond films, audiences continued to dwindle, reaching an all-time low in the 1970s.

Fortunes revive

The reinvention and limited recovery of the industry dates from the early 1980s, when, facing imminent collapse, British cinema entered its current phase of quality production. Since attempting to compete with Hollywood was clearly a doomed strategy, Britain has increasingly specialised in either 'heritage' or avant-garde film making, largely financed either by Channel 4 (Film on Four), or as joint Euro–British co-productions (more recently, National Lottery money has been ringfenced for further productions). The film usually credited with almost single-handedly reviving the British film industry, *Chariots of Fire* (1981), is a prime example of the former, as are Merchant–Ivory productions such as *A Room With A View* (1986) or *Howard's End* (1992), while the work of British arthouse directors such as Derek Jarman, Sally Potter, and Peter Greenaway are representative of the latter.

Although this strategy has brought the industry back from the brink (while also securing a clutch of British Oscars) it has perhaps done so at the expense of a popular national cinema or one which captures the nation's cultural diversity. With a few notable exceptions, such as *My Beautiful Laundrette* (1985), *Bhaji on The Beach* (1993) and *The Crying Game*, (1992) British cinema in the last decades of the twentieth century has tended to privilege representations of the sort of upperclass, white Englishness deemed popular with the American market. It remains to be seen whether the recent international success of Scottish productions such as *Shallow Grave* (1994) and *Trainspotting* (1995) or the Sheffield-based comedy *The Full Monty* (1997) will result in a wider, more inclusive conception of British cinema.

BY ROBERTA GARRETT

in every forward position, he socred 30 goals in 76 internationals for England, 1946–58. He was celebrated for his ball control and goal-scoring skills, and was the first person to win the Footballer of the Year award twice.

Fire of London

Fire 2–5 September 1666 that destroyed four fifths of the City of London. It broke out in a bakery in Pudding Lane and spread as far west as the Temple. It destroyed 87 churches, including St Paul's Cathedral, and 13,200 houses, although fewer than 20 people lost their lives.

'Fireworks Music'

Handel's *Music for the Royal Fireworks*, a suite of pieces originally for wind band, was composed for the celebrations of the Peace of Aix-la-Chapelle, first performed London, Green Park, 27 April 1749.

> *This fatal night about ten, began that deplorable fire near Fish Street in London ... all the sky were of a fiery aspect, like the top of a burning oven, and the light seen above 40 miles round about for many nights.*
>
> JOHN EVELYN English diarist and author. *Diary* 23 Sept 1666

Firth, Colin (1960–)

English stage and screen actor. A handsome leading and support performer, he made his film debut in *Another Country* (1984) and has specialized in period pieces such as *Valmont* (1989), *Circle of Friends* (1995), and BBC costume drama *Pride and Prejudice* (1995), often playing the upper-middle-class cad.

FINNEY, ALBERT *A stalwart of both stage and screen, Albert Finney first came to prominence in 1960 in the stage production of* Billy Liar *and film* Saturday Night and Sunday Morning. *He is pictured in 1973 and the following year appeared in* Murder on the Orient Express, *one of four film performances for which he has been Oscar-nominated. Corbis*

He featured in the film *Fever Pitch* (1997) and the television program *Nostromo* (1997).

Fishbourne Palace

Romano-British villa, near Chichester in West Sussex, dating from the 1st century AD; several magnificent mosaics remain. It may have been built for the Roman client king, Tiberius Claudius Cogidubnus who ruled in that area. It was destroyed by fire in the 3rd century.

Fisher, John, St (*c.* 1469–1535)

English cleric, created bishop of Rochester in 1504. He was an enthusiastic supporter of the revival in the study of Greek, and a friend of the humanists Thomas More and Desiderius Erasmus. In 1535 he was tried on a charge of denying the royal supremacy of Henry VIII and beheaded. Canonized 1935. Feast day 22 June.

Fisher, Ronald Aylmer (1890–1962)

English statistician and geneticist. He modernized Charles Darwin's theory of evolution, thus securing the key biological concept of genetic change by natural selection. Fisher developed several new statistical techniques and, applying his methods to genetics, published *The Genetical Theory of Natural Selection* (1930).

This classic work established that the discoveries of the geneticist Gregor Mendel could be shown to support Darwin's theory of evolution.

In statistics, Fisher evolved the rules for decision making that are now used almost automatically, and many other methods that have since been extended to virtually every academic field in which statistical analysis can be applied.

Fishguard, Welsh Abergwaun

Seaport and holiday centre at the mouth of the River Gwaun on the south side of Fishguard Bay, Pembrokeshire, southwest Wales, 30 km/19 mi southwest of Cardigan; population about 5,000. There is a ferry service to Rosslare in the Republic of Ireland.

The town comprises: the original fishing village of Lower Fishguard; modern Fishguard on the cliff above; Goodwick, on the western side; and the harbour village. On the cliff top, the town centres on the market-place; below, the old fishing village retains its quay and pier as reminders of its former industries of herring fishing and pilchard curing. Fishguard Bay has sufficient depth of water to take the largest ocean liners. The crossing to Rosslare, at 87 km/54 mi, is the shortest sea crossing to Ireland.

fishing and fisheries

In terms of food production, British fisheries are almost entirely marine, and two of the main species that are caught in freshwater (salmon and eel) are ones that spend part of their lives in the sea. Increasing numbers of species are being caught and marketed. In addition to fish there are crustaceans (crabs, lobsters, prawns, and shrimps) and molluscs (whelks, winkles, scallops, oysters, mussels, cockles, and squid). The British fishing industry relies heavily on fleets operating from Grimsby in northeastern England and Fleetwood in Lancashire, which fish the distant water grounds off Newfoundland, Greenland, Iceland, and in the Barents Sea, but the North Sea is overall the most important fishing area, and is the source of most of the haddock and plaice landed at UK ports, as well as cod and many other species.

Fishing in general has a long history, as evidenced by fish remains in early cave middens. By the 15th century, decked vessels from England were already line-fishing as far away as Iceland. The introduction of steam power gave great impetus to development in sea fisheries, particularly on the east coast in the latter half of the 19th century. The railway system opened up a greatly increased market for fresh fish and powerful steam-powered trawlers began to replace the sailing smacks. These and other developments, such as the artificial manufacture of ice, the introduction of the otter trawl, and the use of steam-driven winches, helped to open up the trawling grounds in the Arctic.

There have been many changes within the industry since World War II. For example, the Cornish pilchard and East Anglian herring fisheries have declined, but the Cornish mackerel and south-coast lobster fisheries have increased. New fisheries, such as those for sand eels and queen scallops, have been developed and new technology, particularly in the field of acoustic fish detection sonar equipment, is now widely used. Echo sounding has made fishing for many species more efficient and has enabled trawling and purse seining to replace drift netting as the main method for catching pelagic fish. The impact of technology on the industry is reflected in the fact that in 1974 only 18,571 fishers were in regular employment compared with 39,380 in 1938.

In January 1995 the British government increased by £28 million an existing £25 million compensation fund for decommissioned British boats. Under the EU's common fisheries policy, Britain was obliged to open its fishing waters to Spanish trawlers and to reduce its fishing fleet to make room for them.

Regulation and inspection of fisheries

This is the concern of the Ministry of Agriculture, Fisheries and Food (MAFF) and the Department of Agriculture and Fisheries for Scotland (DAFS). Both organizations have research establishments and research vessels for investigating scientific aspects of the fisheries. Their research aims are: (1) the exploitation and conservation of stocks of fish and shellfish; (2) the promotion of the efficiency of the fishing industry by technological development; and (3) the protection of the marine environment. The link between the government and the catching industry is effected by ministry inspectors who provide coverage for the whole coastline.

Britain, through MAFF and DAFS, is a member of the International Council for the Exploration of the Sea (ICES) founded 1902. One of its main functions is to consolidate scientific information from member countries, so that it is in a position to advise the international regulatory body, the North East Atlantic Fisheries Commission (NEAFC), on the scientific aspects of the conservation of fish stocks. Since British vessels fish in the northwestern Atlantic, the UK is also a member of the International Commission for Northwest Atlantic Fisheries (ICNAF). There are similar bodies covering most of the world's oceans and major fish stocks. Until recently the main regulations in the North Atlantic took the form of size limits and net mesh-size limitations, but quotas have now been imposed on the landings of most major fish species.

Fitzalan-Howard

Family name of dukes of Norfolk; seated at Arundel Castle, Sussex, England.

Fitzgerald, Edward (1809–1883)

English poet and translator. His poetic version of the *Rubaiyat of Omar Khayyám* (1859) (and often revised), with its resonant and melancholy tone, is generally considered more an original creation than a true translation. It is known throughout all the English-speaking countries and has passed through innumerable editions.

FitzGerald, Garret Michael (1926–)

Irish politician, leader of the Fine Gael party 1977–87. As Taoiseach (prime minister) 1981–82 and 1982–87, he attempted to solve the Northern Ireland dispute, ultimately by participating in the Anglo-Irish Agreement in 1985. He tried to remove some of the overtly Catholic features of the constitution to make the Republic more attractive to Northern Protestants.

In 1985 he signed the Anglo-Irish Agreement with the British prime minister Margaret Thatcher.

Fitzgerald, Penelope (Mary) born Knox (1916–)

English novelist. She published her first novel, *The Golden Child* (1977), when she was 61. Since then she has applied distinctive, economic style, understanding of human nature, and sense of humour to a variety of situations and settings. Particularly notable novels are *Offshore* (1979), which won the Booker Prize for fiction, *The Gate of Angels* (1990), and *The Blue Flower* (1995).

Fitzherbert, Maria Anne born Smythe (1756–1837)

Wife of the Prince of Wales, later George IV. She became Mrs Fitzherbert by her second marriage in 1778 and, after her husband's death in 1781, entered London society. She secretly married the Prince of Wales in 1785 and finally parted from him in 1803.

Fitzroy

Family name of dukes of Grafton; descended from King Charles II by his mistress Barbara Villiers. The family seat is at Euston Hall, Norfolk, England.

Fitzroy, Robert (1805–1865)

British vice admiral and meteorologist. In 1828 he succeeded to the command of HMS *Beagle*, then engaged on a survey of the Patagonian coast of South America, and in 1831 was accompanied by naturalist Charles ◊Darwin on a five-year survey. Fitzroy was governor of New Zealand 1843–45. In 1855 the Admiralty founded the Meteorological Office, which issued weather forecasts and charts, under his charge.

Fitzsimmons, Robert Prometheus (1863–1917)

English-born boxer who was world champion at three different weight. Born in Cornwall, but raised in New Zealand, he won the world middleweight title in New Orleans in 1891. Although he weighed only 75 kg/165 lb, he also competed as a heavyweight and in 1897 won the title from James J ('Gentleman Jim') Corbett in Carson City, Nevada to become the first British-born world heavyweight champion. He lost that title to James J Jeffries in New York 1899.

Fitzwilliam Virginal Book

Manuscript collection of 297 mainly English 17th-century compositions for keyboard instruments copied by Francis Tregian and acquired by Richard Fitzwilliam (1745–1816) who bequeathed it to Cambridge University. Among composers represented are William Byrd, John Bull, and Giles Farnaby.

five articles of Perth

Reforms imposed on the Kirk (Scottish church) in 1618 by James VI in an attempt to bring it into line with the English church. The articles were ratified by the Scots Parliament in 1621, despite vehement opposition from some Protestant elements who regarded them as an attempt to make the Scottish church more Catholic; they were rejected by the General Assembly of the Kirk in 1638.

Fives

Game of handball, where two or four players hit a hard ball against a wall or walls with padded gloves. In England there are three forms of the game, distinguished from one another by the names of the schools in which they were variously played: Eton, Rugby, and Winchester Fives. Under the name of handball a similar game is played in the USA and Ireland.

Flamborough Head (from 'Flein's burg')

Prominent headland on the coast of the East Riding of Yorkshire, England, 3 km/2 mi east of the village of Flamborough. Flamborough Head is composed of chalk cliffs, which rise in places to a height of 120 m/394 ft. Formerly, beacons were lit on the clifftop; now a lighthouse, whose beam is visible at a distance of 34 km/21 mi, stands 65 m/213 ft above the high-water mark.

An ancient British earthwork, misleadingly called Danes' Dyke, runs across Flamborough peninsula, culminating at the Head.

Flamsteed, John (1646–1719)

English astronomer. He began systematic observations of the positions of the stars, Moon, and planets at the Royal Observatory he founded at Greenwich, London in 1676. His observations were published in *Historia Coelestis Britannica* (1725).

As the first Astronomer Royal of England, Flamsteed determined the latitude of Greenwich, the slant of the ecliptic, and the position of the equinox. He also worked out a method of observing the absolute right ascension (a coordinate of the position of a heavenly body) that removed all

FLAMSTEED, JOHN *After petitioning Charles II for a national observatory, the English astronomer was made the first Astronomer Royal in 1675 and founded the Royal Observatory at Greenwich, London. Private collection*

errors of parallax, refraction, and latitude. Having obtained the positions of 40 reference stars, he then computed positions for the rest of the 3,000 stars in his catalogue.

Flamsteed was born at Denby, near Derby and studied at Cambridge. He began his astronomical studies at home by observing a solar eclipse in 1662. In 1672 he determined the solar parallax from observations of Mars. He early acquired a reputation as an accomplished astronomer, and was appointed astronomer to Charles II in 1675.

Flamsteed's achievements were the construction of a catalogue of the stars more extensive and more precise than any other existing, and the systematic observation of the Sun, Moon, and planets with a view to revising the theories of their apparent motions and constructing tables from which their positions could be accurately computed. He introduced new methods into practical astronomy, many of them still in use today.

Flanagan, Bud stage name of Chaim Reeven Weintrop (Robert Winthrop) (1896–1968)

English comedian. He was the leader of the 'Crazy Gang' from 1931 to 1962. He played in variety theatre all over the world and, with his partner Chesney Allen, popularized such songs as 'Underneath the Arches'.

Flatford

Location on the River Stour, in Suffolk, England. Flatford Mill and Dedham Mill (on the Essex bank of the Stour) formed the sites for paintings by John ◊Constable. Flatford Mill now belongs to the ◊National Trust, which administers the property as a field study centre.

Flavell, Richard Anthony (1945–)

English molecular biologist who is best known for his work on the nature of the genes for human globin chains (the protein components of the blood's oxygen-carrying substance haemoglobin). He showed that thalassaemia, a group of inherited anaemias, were the result of genetic defects. His work led to the development of gene therapies to correct the faulty genes and treat the condition.

Flaxman, John (1755–1826)

English Neo-Classical sculptor and illustrator. From 1775 he worked for the ◊Wedgwood pottery as a designer, and later became one of Europe's leading exponents of the Neo-Classical style. His public works include the monuments to Nelson and Joshua Reynolds in St Paul's Cathedral, London; and to Robert Burns in Westminster Abbey.

From 1787 to 1794 he directed the Wedgwood studio in Rome, where he was able to study Greek, Roman, and medieval Italian art. Apart from designs for Wedgwood ware, he modelled friezes on classical subjects and produced relief portraits. In 1810 he became the first professor of sculpture at the Royal Academy.

Flecker, (Herman) James Elroy (1884–1915)

English poet. During a career in the consular service, he wrote several volumes of lyrical romantic verse, including *The Bridge of Fire* (1907), *Forty-two Poems* (1911), *The Golden Journey to Samarkand* (1913), and *The Old Ships* (1915).

Fleet prison

Royal prison in the City of London dating from the 12th century. It originally received prisoners committed by the Star Chamber, an offshoot of the king's council, and was later used to house debtors until it was closed in 1842. It was pulled down two years later.

Fleet Street

Street in London (named after the subterranean River Fleet). It runs from Temple Bar eastwards to Ludgate Circus. Traditionally the centre of British journalism, it contained (with adjoining streets) the offices and printing works of many leading British newspapers until the mid-1980s, when most moved to sites farther from the centre of London. The earliest extant reference to the street is in about 1188.

Up to the mid-15th century it was, apart from Thames Street, the only paved street in the city and its immediate vicinity. It became celebrated for its taverns, and later became the centre of London's newspaper industry. The *Daily Courant*, Britain's first daily paper, started here in 1702, as did *Punch* magazine, devised in 1841.

Fleetwood

Port and seaside resort in Lancashire, England, at the mouth of the River Wyre, 13 km/8 mi from Blackpool; population (1991) 27,200. Industries include icemaking, fishing, fresh fish wholesaling, and the manufacture of chemicals, plastics, leather goods, and confectionery. The port handles chemicals and miscellaneous containerized goods, mainly trading with Ireland.

The Fleetwood Harbour Village retail park has been developed in the docks area. Tourism and the service sector also provide significant employment.

Fleetwood was formerly one of the chief fishing ports in Britain and, although the industry has declined, it remains England's major west coast fishing centre.

Fleetwood Mac

English blues-influenced rock group formed in 1967, who won a wide following in the UK and USA. Members include Mick Fleetwood (1942–), Stevie Nicks (1948–), and Lindsey Buckingham (1949–), and their songs include 'Albatross' (1968). Their biggest-selling album *Rumours* (1977) spent 31 weeks at number one in the US chart.

Fleming, (John) Ambrose (1849–1945)

English electrical physicist and engineer who invented the thermionic valve in 1904 and devised Fleming's rules. In 1904 he produced experimental proof that the known rectifying property of a thermionic valve was still operative at radio frequencies, and this discovery led to the invention and production of what was first known as the 'Fleming valve'. It revolutionized the early science of radio. Knighted 1929.

Fleming, Alexander (1881–1955)

Scottish bacteriologist who discovered the first antibiotic drug, penicillin, in 1928. In 1922 he had discovered lysozyme, an antibacterial enzyme present in saliva, nasal secretions, and tears. While studying this, he found an unusual mould growing on a culture dish, which he isolated and grew into a pure culture; this led to his discovery of penicillin. It came into use in 1941. In 1945 he won the Nobel Prize for Physiology or Medicine with Howard Florey and Ernst ♢Chain, whose research had brought widespread realization of the value of penicillin. See feature on page 340.

Fleming discovered the antibacterial properties of penicillin, but its purification and concentration was left to Florey and Chain, in Oxford. He identified organisms that cause wound infections and showed how cross-infection by streptococci can occur among patients in hospital wards. He also studied the effects of different antiseptics on various kinds of bacteria and on living cells. His interest in chemotherapy led him to introduce Paul Ehrlich's Salvarsan into British medical practice. Knighted 1944.

Fleming, Ian Lancaster (1908–1964)

English author. His suspense novels feature the ruthless, laconic James Bond, British Secret Service agent 007. The first novel in the series was *Casino Royale* (1953); others include *From Russia with Love* (1957), *Goldfinger* (1959), and *The Man with the Golden Gun* (1965). Most of the novels were made into a successful series of ♢Bond films.

During World War II he worked for British Intelligence where he had the opportunity to give full rein to his vivid imagination in disseminating false information and rumours.

Fletcher, Andrew of Saltoun (1655–1716)

Scottish patriot, the most outspoken critic of the Union of Scotland with England of 1707. He advocated an independent Scotland, and a republic or limited monarchy, and proposed 'limitations' to the treaty, such as annual Parliaments. After the Treaty of Union he retired to private life.

Fletcher, John (1579–1625)

English dramatist. He is remarkable for his range, which included tragicomedy and pastoral dramas, in addition to comedy and tragedy. He collaborated with Francis ♢Beaumont in some 12 plays, producing, most notably, the tragicomedy *Philaster* (1610) and *The Maid's Tragedy* (about 1611). He is alleged to have collaborated with ♢Shakespeare on *The Two Noble Kinsmen* and *Henry VIII* (1613).

Among some 16 plays credited to Fletcher alone are the pastoral drama *The Faithful Shepherdess* (1610), the tragedy *Bonduca* (about 1613–14), *The Chances* (1617), the tragedy *Valentinian* (1618), the comedy *The Humorous Lieutenant* (1619), and the comedies *The Pilgrim* and *The Wild-Goose Chase* (both 1621).

Fletcher was born in Rye, Sussex, and was educated at Benet College, Cambridge, but little is known of his life. Other plays resulting from the collaboration with Beaumont include *The Scornful Lady* (1610), *A King and No King* (about 1611), and *Thierry and Theodoret* (1616), but the pair were credited with a great many more as publishers found that their names on the title page made a good selling line. Of the two, Fletcher is generally reckoned the more fluent and creative, and had a keener sense of 'theatre'.

He also collaborated with Philip Massinger in several plays, and probably with William Rowley and Thomas Middleton in others. He died of the plague.

Flint, Welsh Fflint

Town in Flintshire, northeast Wales, situated on the Dee estuary, 20 km/12 mi from Chester; population (1991) 11,600. Major artificial-fibre factories were formerly located here, but light industry now predominates. Flint Castle was built between 1277 and 1284. It was here that Richard II was betrayed to Henry of Bolingbroke (Henry IV) in 1399.

Flint, William Russell (1880–1969)

Scottish artist. He is known for his watercolours of mildly erotic nudes, and for his book illustrations. He was president of the Royal Society of Painters in Water-Colour from 1936 to 1956, and was knighted in 1947.

Born in Edinburgh, he lived in London from 1930.

Flintshire, Welsh Sir y Fflint

Unitary authority in north Wales. A former county, it was part of Clwyd between 1974 and 1996

Area 437 sq km/167 sq mi

Towns ♢Mold (administrative headquarters), ♢Flint, Holywell, Buckley, Connah's Quay

Physical bounded by the Irish Sea in the north, the Dee estuary in the east, and the Clwydian Range, which rises to 555 m/1,820 ft, in the southwest; rivers Dee, Alyn

THE DISCOVERY OF PENICILLIN

Chance favours the prepared mind

'I think the discovery and development of penicillin may be looked on as quite one of the luckiest accidents that have occurred in medicine.' With these words, Professor Howard Florey (1898–1968), an Australian pathologist, concluded a lecture he gave in 1943 at the Royal Institution. The topic was penicillin: the first, and still perhaps overall the best of a range of natural chemotherapeutic agents called antibiotics.

Together with Ernst Chain (1906–1979), Howard Florey had made the practical exploitation of penicillin possible on a worldwide scale.

A chance discovery

The story of the discovery of penicillin started with a chance observation made by Scottish bacteriologist Alexander Fleming (1881–1955), while he was working in 1928 in his laboratory at St Mary's Hospital in London.

Fleming was doing research on staphylococcus, a species of bacterium that can cause disease in humans and animals. In the laboratory such bacteria are grown in dishes containing a culture medium – a jelly-like substance which contains their food. Fleming noticed that one of his dishes had been accidentally contaminated with a mould. The mould could have entered the laboratory through an open window. All around where the mould was growing, the staphylococci had disappeared.

Fleming investigates the mould

Intrigued, because he had correctly concluded that the mould must contain a substance that killed the bacterium, Fleming isolated the mould and grew more of it in a culture broth. He found that the broth acquired a high antibacterial activity. He tested the action of the broth with a wide variety of pathogenic bacteria, and found that many of them were quickly destroyed.

Fleming was also able to demonstrate that the white corpuscles in human blood were not sensitive to the broth. This suggested to him that other human cells in the body would not be affected by it.

Penicillin is discovered

The mould that Fleming's acute powers of observation had noted in a single culture dish, was found to be *Penicillium notatum*. Fleming named the drug penicillin after this mould.

There the matter rested for 15 years. At the time that penicillin was discovered, it would have been extremely difficult to isolate and purify the drug using the chemical techniques then available. It would also have been quite easily destroyed by them. Without any of the pure substance, Fleming had no way of knowing its extraordinarily high antibacterial activity and its almost negligible toxicity. In fact, penicillin diluted 80,000,000 times will still inhibit the growth of staphylococcus. To translate this number of noughts into something tangible: if one drop of water is diluted 80,000,000 times it would fill over 6,000 whisky bottles.

The first practical application

Then in 1935, German-born British biochemist Ernst Chain joined Professor Florey at Oxford. There in 1939 he began a survey of antimicrobial substances. One of the first he looked at was Fleming's mould. It was chosen because it was already known to be active against staphylococcus, and because, since it was difficult to purify, it represented a biochemical challenge.

A method of purification using primitive apparatus was discovered, and an experiment using penicillin to treat infected mice was carried out with remarkable success. Eventually, enough penicillin was made to treat the first human patient in the terminal stage of a generalized infection. The patient showed an astonishing, although temporary, recovery. Five more seriously ill patients were successfully treated.

Because these patients had already failed to respond to sulphonamide drugs, the value of penicillin was now clearly apparent. For although suphonamides are much more toxic to bacteria than to leucocytes (white blood cells), they do have some poisonous action on the whole human organism.

The new lifesaver

England, then in the midst of World War II, had insufficient resources to manufacture the new wonder drug on a sufficiently large scale. Florey went to the USA to try to interest the large pharmaceutical companies in penicillin. As a result of an outstanding effort, enough penicillin was produced in time to treat all the battle casualties of the Normandy landings in 1944. The use of penicillin in wartime saved countless lives, as it has continued to do ever since.

BY JULIAN ROWE

Industries artificial silk, chemicals, optical glass
Agriculture dairy farming, stock-raising
Population (1996) 144,000

Greenfield Valley was in the forefront of the Industrial Revolution before the advent of steam, and now has a museum of industrial archaeology. There is an airport at ◊Hawarden.

Flodden, Battle of

Defeat of the Scots by the English under the Earl of Surrey on 9 September 1513 on a site, 5 km/3 mi southeast of Coldstream, in Northumberland, England. ◊James IV of Scotland, declaring himself the active ally of France, crossed the border to England with an invading army of 30,000. The Scots were defeated, suffering heavy losses, and James himself was killed.

Florence Court

Mid-18th-century house in County ◊Fermanagh, Northern Ireland, standing 11 km/7 m south of Enniskillen, near the Cuilcagh Mountains which form the Northern Ireland–Eire border. One of the most important historic houses in

Northern Ireland, it contains some outstanding Rococo plasterwork and 18th-century furniture. The house was given to the National Trust in 1954. It was designed by John Cole, father of the 18th Earl of Enniskillen.

Flow Country

Wilderness and wildlife habitat in the northernmost parts of the Highland unitary authority, northern Scotland. Under threat from commercial afforestation, it consists of a treeless peat bog and various lochs, which are home to many rare plants and wading birds.

Vast tracts were sold off at low prices in the 1980s to encourage commercial forestation. However, the land has proven unsuitable for growing trees.

folk dancing

Type of dancing characteristic of a particular people or region. Folk dancing once formed an important part of many ancient rituals, but it has tended to die out since industrialization. The English ◊morris dance and the dance round the fertility 'totem' ◊maypole (linked with regeneration rituals) on the village green are derived from ceremonies of the pre-Christian era. In the early 20th century, the folk historian Cecil ◊Sharp made extensive researches to record English country music and dances, which helped to reactivate interest and encourage revivals where some traditions had been lost. Other English folk dances include the hornpipe, jig, clog dancing, and the sword dance.

The **jig**, mainly associated with Scotland and Ireland (but also found in Wales) and generally identifiable from the 16th century onwards, was usually a solo dance, a forerunner of the galliard. The Frenchified version, the **gigue**, was toned down and assimilated into courtly entertainment and also staged dance (for example, 'Kemps's Jigge', named after the Shakespearean comic actor William Kemp (died 1603) who was celebrated for his jigs at the close of a performance).

Scottish folk dancing, including the Highland fling and the sword dance (to be differentiated from the English version), is generally categorized as the faster reels (almost certainly of northern origin) or the slower strathspey, and often accompanied by the bagpipes.

Irish folk dancing includes the jig (often accompanied by bagpipes, the harp, or the fiddle); céilidhs (social dance gatherings) usually feature jigs, reels, and hornpipes. Irish clog dances are often performed in wooden clogs and are among the most complex versions known of clog dancing (made popular in the mid-1990s by the hit show *Riverdance*).

Welsh folk dancing includes reels with three or four

FOLK DANCING *Sword dancers from the Hampshire town of Farnborough perform outside a pub. Folk dances with swords are of ancient origin, and are thought to have been originally performed to ward off evil spirits or to mime human and animal sacrifice. They are related to the more widespread practice of Morris dancing. Brian Shuel/Collections*

dancers, jigs, and clog dances to a harp or hornpipe, but the dancing tradition was subdued by Welsh presbyterianism or Chapel from the 16th century.

Folkestone

Port and resort on the southeast coast of Kent, England, 10 km/6 mi southwest of Dover; population (1991) 46,200. There are passenger ferry and hovercraft connections with Boulogne, and to the northwest of the town is the British terminal of Eurotunnel, which offers a high-speed train link through the ◊Channel Tunnel to Paris and Brussels for private and haulage traffic.

The physician William Harvey, who discovered the circulation of blood, was born here in 1578; his statue stands on the cliff top.

Features

The Eurotunnel Exhibition Centre illustrates the building of the Channel Tunnel. To the east of the town is the East Cliff and the Warren, a chalk landslip basin between high cliffs, rich in fossil remains. Many of the town's buildings date from the 19th century, reflecting its development as a resort following the arrival of the railway in the mid 19th century. The Leas is a long promenade above the beach along the cliff top. The original fishing quarter and harbour has some of the town's oldest buildings, and is now a popular yachting and cruising venue. There is a racecourse, and the Leas Cliff Hall (1927) is used for concerts and conferences. The town suffered considerable damage during World War II.

The first nunnery in England was established here in 630 by St Eanswythe, grand-daughter of Ethelbert, the first Christian king of Kent. The Early English and Perpendicular church of St Mary and St Eanswythe was built just west of the site of the nunnery.

folk music

Traditional music, especially from rural areas, which is passed on by listening and repeating, and is usually performed by amateurs. The term is used to distinguish it from the ◊classical music of a country, and from urban popular or commercial music. Most folk music exists in the form of songs, or instrumental music to accompany folk dancing, and is usually melodic and rhythmic rather than harmonic in style.

Interest in ballad poetry in the late 18th century led to the discovery of a rich body of folk song in Europe, but it was not until the late 19th century that there was any systematic collection of folk music. In England, this was seen in the transcription and preservation of folk tunes by such people as the Rev Sabine Baring-Gould and Cecil ◊Sharp. The Folk Song Society was founded in 1898 and became the English Folk Dance and Song Society in 1911. In true Victorian fashion, they bowdlerized much of the material they collected, and edited out much of the sophisticated ornamentation and rhythmic complexity, which they felt to be 'primitive', or simply poor performance. The collection of folk music continued through the first half of the 20th century, with important contributions made by Ralph ◊Vaughan Williams (whose collections not only influenced his own music but have been a significant source to the present day), A L Lloyd, and Ewan MacColl; and a unique and invaluable collection gathered by several generations of the Copper family of Sussex.

Different national styles

Recognizably different styles of folk music can be seen within the countries of the British Isles: English, Scottish, Irish, and Welsh folk music all have distinctive characteristics.

In England, folk song is generally in the ballad tradition, either unaccompanied or with a simple concertina or melodeon accompaniment, and, typically for a maritime nation, there is also a large number of shanties. The two folk-dance traditions, Morris dancing and country dance and their many regional variations, each have their own associated tunes, usually played on a pipe and drum, fiddle, or concertina.

Scottish folk music can be divided roughly into two styles: Highland (associated with the Gaelic language), and Lowland (associated with the Scots language). Unusually for a true oral folk tradition, most Scottish folk songs are by known composers and poets whose names have been passed down with their songs, which are mainly in the form of unaccompanied ballads. Instrumental music includes dance music for fiddle and concertina, and a uniquely Scottish genre, the pibroch, a form of theme and variations specifically for the bagpipes.

Irish folk song can similarly be divided according to language, with distinct musical traditions for both Irish and English lyrics. Dances such as the jig and the reel are typical in Irish instrumental music, and are played on the fiddle and pipe, and Irish versions of the harp and bagpipes, almost invariably with the rhythmic accompaniment of the bodhrán, a kind of drum. Much of the traditional repertoire has been preserved and played by groups such as the Chieftains.

Although there is a long tradition of musical culture in Wales, very little true folk music has survived. Welsh traditional music, like Scottish folk music, is mostly by known poets and composers, but because of its association with the Bardic culture, this is perhaps more accurately regarded as a classical rather than a folk culture.

Folk revival in the 20th century

The post-World War II folk revival in the USA had a counterpart in the UK, with both a renewed interest in traditional folk music and a new generation of songwriters and performers in a folk style. The 1960s saw the appearance of performers in many different folk styles: the Watersons, who popularized traditional unaccompanied folk singing; groups such as Pentangle and the Incredible String Band, and the singer Donovan produced new music in a folk style; and folk-rock bands such as Fairport Convention and Steeleye Span brought some of the folk repertoire to a new audience by performing using the instruments of the rock band, as well as introducing new songs in a folk idiom. This folk revival continued through the 1980s, and was furthered by rock guitarist Richard ◊Thompson and such groups as the Pogues (formed 1983), while the singer/songwriter Billy Bragg continued in the tradition of the political protest song. In recent years, there has been a growing interest in roots, or world, music, encompassing traditional as well as modern music from many cultures.

Fonteyn, Margot stage name of Peggy (Margaret) Hookham (1919–1991)
English ballet dancer. She made her debut with the Vic-Wells Ballet in *Nutcracker* (1934) and first appeared as Giselle in 1937, eventually becoming prima ballerina of the Royal Ballet, London. Renowned for her perfect physique, clear line, musicality, and interpretive powers, she created many roles in Frederick ◊Ashton's ballets and formed a legendary partnership with Rudolf Nureyev. She retired from dancing in 1979.

Fonteyn's first major role was in Ashton's *Le Baiser de la fée* (1935); other Ashton ballets include *Symphonic Variations* (1946), *Ondine* (1958, filmed 1959), and *Marguerite and Armand* (1963, filmed 1972). She also appeared in Macmillan's *Romeo and Juliet* (1965, filmed 1966) with Nureyev. She was made a DBE in 1956.

food and drink
See feature on food on page 344 and chronology of some food and drink highlights on page 346.

food poisoning
Any acute illness characterized by vomiting and diarrhoea and caused by eating food contaminated with harmful bacteria (for example, listeriosis), poisonous food (for example, certain mushrooms), or poisoned food (such as lead or arsenic introduced accidentally during processing).

The number of notified cases of food poisoning in Britain for 1997 was 99,976. The actual incidence is as much as ten times higher, as most cases do not get reported.

Two outbreaks of food poisoning involving a lethal strain of *Escherichia coli* in Scotland in December 1996 and January 1997, resulted in 20 deaths.

Foot, Michael Mackintosh (1913–)
British Labour politician and writer. A leader of the left-wing Tribune Group, he was secretary of state for employment 1974–76, Lord President of the Council and leader of the House 1976–79, and succeeded James Callaghan as Labour Party leader 1980–83.

For most of his career Foot was a leading member of the left wing of the Labour Party and a prominent member of the Tribune Group. Not only did he succeed Aneurin Bevan as MP for Ebbw Vale, but was widely regarded as the latter's successor as leader of the Left. He is said to have refused office in the 1964–70 Labour government, but became an Opposition spokesman between 1970 and 1974. Michael Foot was runner-up to Jim Callaghan in the Labour Party leadership contest of 1976.

If this sale goes through, Murdoch can close his fist round the very heart of British culture and shout triumphantly, 'Gotcha!'

SUE MOTT British sports journalist. On the proposed sale of Manchester United plc to BSkyB for £623 million; the *Daily Telegraph*, September 1998

football, association, or **soccer**
Form of football originating in the UK, popular throughout the world. The modern game is played in the UK according to the rules laid down by the home countries' football associations. Slight amendments to the rules take effect in certain competitions and international matches as laid down by the sport's world governing body, Fédération Internationale de Football Association (FIFA, 1904). FIFA organizes the competitions for the World Cup, held every four years since 1930.

Scottish Premier league clubs announced in 1997 that they were breaking away from the Scottish Football Association to form their own league on the model of the English Premiership.

FOOD AND DRINK *Most groceries in Britain are supplied by a few large supermarket chains. Supermarkets are extremely convenient, offering huge choice under one roof. Yet their frequent out-of-town location increases car use and draws trade away from city centres, while their buying power gives them a stranglehold over the food retailing sector. David Davis/Collections*

BRITISH FOOD: TWO DIVERGING PATHS

Within a generation the British have rediscovered their pleasure in food and their talent for cooking. Restaurants are vibrant and diverse. The world's ingredients are flown in around the year while domestic regional produce is championed too. The poor quality of British food used to be an international joke; now London has been touted as the culinary capital of the world.

From *Ready Steady Cook* to *TV Dinners*, food programmes are essential to television schedules. There are even dedicated food channels. Chefs become celebrities and vice versa. Colour supplements, specialist magazines, and coffee-table books feature food of the highest gloss and style. There seems to be no upper limit to Britain's voracious consumer appetite for better food.

And yet there has never been a greater reliance on supermarket ready meals, instant sauces, and take-away food. American fast-food chains serve junk food to an uncritical mass, often on the very High Street sites once occupied by butchers, bakers, and greengrocers. Cookery has all but disappeared from the curriculum, while school meals themselves are losing out to crisps and cola. Fewer and fewer families even sit down and eat a meal together. To understand why Britain has taken such sharply divergent roads one must look to the past.

Traditional culinary strengths

Indigenous ingredients naturally form the basis of the British cuisine, starting with meat. Our earliest ancestors hunted red deer, wild pig and ox and spit-roasted them. The Romans developed farming and animal husbandry, drying and salting their meat to preserve it for winter. They created orchards and cultivated vegetables, herbs, and salads; and imported their own almonds, figs, and raisins from Italy. Early Christianity saw a fishing industry providing white fish, herring, mackerel, and bountiful shellfish. Eel and salmon fisheries were recorded at the time of the Norman Conquest.

Thus a great traditional strength of the national cuisine emerged – the ability to adopt and adapt. As colony and colonizer, Britain has always grafted foreign ingredients and techniques to its own produce. The oriental trade in pepper, ginger, and cinnamon dates to the first century AD. There is no more quintessential British dish than salmon in pastry with ginger and currants, a recipe unimproved since the Middle Ages. Wensleydale cheese was invented by French monks. Macaroni and soy sauce arrived in the 17th century. Grilled anchovies, Parmesan cheese, and curry powder were all as fashionable in the 18th century as today.

Then as now, London became a centre of fine food. The wealthy showed off exotic delicacies: cloves, nutmeg, allspice, sugar, tea, and the drinking chocolate that evolved into the chocolate craze that England exported to the world. Entertaining became ever more outrageous, with banquet dishes laid out by the dozen, sweetmeats piled into pyramids, gross pies filled ever more improbably with live blackbirds, frogs, and small (uneaten) boys.

Home cooking, however, remained relatively plain. Although it was fashionable to employ a French chef many, including England's first influential cookery writer Hannah Glasse, scorned their elaborate dishes. A yawning gap developed between the diet of the rich with their imported truffles and the poor living off bread, lard, porridge, and potatoes. As high bread prices, poor harvests, potato blight, and famine in Ireland and parts of Scotland and England brought 19th-century Britain to the brink of revolution, Alexis Soyer, chef of London's Reform Club, launched soup kitchens and created recipes (of questionable nutritional value – mostly made up of vegetable peelings) for feeding the masses.

The impact of faster distribution and war

Better distribution created by Victorian roads and railways brought fresh milk, meat, and vegetables to the urban middle classes. New industrial processes created self-raising flour, custard powder, blancmange, packet jellies, and sweetened condensed milk. The poor were bequeathed a diet of white bread (thanks to commercial roller mills that destroyed the valuable wheatgerm), margarine, and sweet tea.

Two world wars took the average family's food ever further away from honest farm produce. From the royal household downwards, families who had deserted the kitchen found themselves back at the stove trying to make the best of dried egg and Woolton pie, a parsnip and potato pie created by the Home Front Minister. Rationing cut food imports by two-thirds, and meat, fat, and sugar consumption were reduced. Yet for all its monotony, the wartime diet was nutritionally sound. Fish and chips became institutionalized, although for an island race the British are curiously reticent about cooking fish.

After World War II the British did not easily revert back to either homespun or exotic food. With rationing into the 1950s, post-war governments were understandably determined to make the nation self-sufficient in food. Plentiful cheap food came, but at a price still to be finally reckoned. Farmers were encouraged to abandon mixed farming and rush headlong into prairie and factory farming. Crops were doused with pesticide and fungicide; chickens left the farmyard for battery houses; pigs disappeared into vast indoor units; cattle met the artificial inseminator's syringe and were fed unnatural concoctions from the feed merchants.

Convenience and canned food suppressed true taste and flavour. Restaurants stagnated as dully as the ubiquitous Brown Windsor soup. In 1950, Raymond Postgate was so appalled that he launched a campaign to raise standards. His first *Good Food Guide* found only 22 restaurants worth listing. It remains today a barometer for good restaurant food. Another cry in the dark of 1950 was *A Book of Mediterranean Food* by the unknown Elizabeth David. Although it cited ingredients that were largely unobtainable – mozzarella, olive oil, garlic, and fresh herbs – it was hugely popular. This book and the eight that followed, still in print today, whetted the appetite of a generation whose only experience of a banana was a mashed turnip flavoured with banana essence.

The rise of supermarket culture

As our continental holiday horizons opened up through the 1960s so Anglicized versions of Italian, Chinese, and Indian food took root in British towns and cities. Grocers like John Sainsbury tentatively expanded their shops offering a wider range and an American self-service system: supermarkets. Now overwhelmingly the place where our food is bought, supermarkets dominated supply, and revolutionized purchasing, cooking, and eating habits. Today they offer pre-cooked meals for the microwave; pristine fresh produce, ready washed, peeled, and chopped; and a global market-stall of Thai sauces, Kenyan greens, and Greek farmed fish.

Little by little Britons learned how to cook and respect food again, helped by Jane Grigson, Robert Carrier, Jocelyn Dimbleby, Derek Cooper and, perhaps above all, the TV programmes and books of Delia Smith. People began to differentiate between a sliced white and a home-raised wholemeal loaf. The principles behind vegetarianism and organics played – and still play – a vital role in the drive towards real food. Regional specialities have been clawed back from the edge of extinction. A long inferiority complex about cheese was swept away by a burst of new and revived cheeses made throughout the British Isles.

British cooking today

The best of British produce is peerless: Aberdeen Angus beef, Scottish wild salmon, grouse and venison, finnan haddock, Arbroath smokies, kippers, Welsh saltmarsh lamb, asparagus from the Vale of Evesham, East Anglian mussels, cockles, herring, seakale and samphire, Kent cobnuts and filberts, Whitstable oysters, Wiltshire bacon, Cornish clotted cream, Irish soda bread, a wonderful native range of apples, pears, and berries, and potatoes: Jersey Royal for new and the King Edward for roasting. The best modern British chefs put fresh, seasonal, regional ingredients at the heart of their cooking, reviving historic dishes and traditional cuts, from stews and flummery to tongue and oxtail. And, like their forebears, they draw from the Mediterranean, the Middle and Far East, and the Pacific Rim. Perhaps the strongest unifying characteristic is a desire for clean, clear flavour but attempts to define British cuisine usually prove elusive. It has never stood still for long, always shaped by class, wealth, war and trade routes. It was always reinventing itself and still is.

Not that Britain can feel complacent in mid-renaissance. The poor still eat badly. Obesity grows as government attempts to improve the balance of the national diet fall on deaf ears. British markets are still light years behind French. Salmonella and *E. coli* infection remains disturbingly high, quite apart from the 27 deaths attributed to new variant CJD. Indeed, there is perhaps no greater irony than that at the height of a golden age of British food, the twin engines of science and agribusiness succeeded in making the very symbol of our food, the roast beef of old England, unexportable.

BY JILL TURTON

footpad

Thief or mugger, operating on foot, who robbed travellers on the highway in the 18th and 19th centuries in Britain. Thieves on horseback were termed highwaymen.

Forbes, Bryan (John Clarke) adopted name of John Theobald Clarke (1926–)

English film producer, director, and screenwriter. After acting in such films as *An Inspector Calls* (1954), he made his directorial debut with *Whistle Down the Wind* (1961). Among his other films are *The L-Shaped Room* (1963), *The Wrong Box* (1966), *The Raging Moon* (1971), *The Stepford Wives* (1975), and *The Naked Face* (1985). He directed the TV film *The Endless Game* (1990), and was one of several screenwriters to work on Richard Attenborough's *Chaplin* (1992).

He is married to the actress Nanette Newman and father of the television personality Emma Forbes.

Forbes was a long-serving actor before turning to direction and screenwriting. In the late 1960s and early 1970s he was head of production at Elstree Studios. His early films as a director, including *Whistle Down the Wind*, about a fugitive murderer hiding out in the country, and *The L-Shaped Room*, about a pregnant French woman living in a down-at-heel London Boarding house, were sensitive dramas. *The Stepford Wives* was a chilling thriller about suburban housewives who have been turned into robots by their husbands. His screenplay for *The Angry Silence* was nominated for an Academy Award in 1960.

But the English – what passion.

DANIEL PASSARELLA Argentina's national football coach. After his team's torrid World Cup quarter-final victory over England in 1998

Ford, Ford Madox adopted name of Ford Hermann Hueffer (1873–1939)

English author. He wrote more than 80 books, the best known of which are the novels *The Good Soldier* (1915) and *Tietjen's Saga* (1924–28). As the first editor of the *English Review* from 1908 to 1910, he published works by established writers such as Thomas Hardy and Joseph Conrad, as well as the works of D H Lawrence, Wyndham Lewis, and Ezra Pound.

He was also founder-editor of *The Transatlantic Review* in Paris in 1924, which published work by James Joyce and Ernest Hemingway. He was a grandson of the painter Ford Madox Brown.

Ford, John (*c.* 1586–*c.* 1640)

English poet and dramatist. His play *'Tis Pity She's a Whore* (performed in about 1626, printed in 1633) is a study of

Food and Drink: Some Key Dates

c. **1400** The use of spices and sauces becomes widespread in cooking in England in an effort to counter the repetitive diet of dried and salted foods.

1609 Tea is returned to Europe from China by the Dutch East India Company. It reaches Britain by 1615.

1657 Coffee is sold for the first time in London, England. It is promoted as a patent medicine, capable of curing a variety of ailments.

1741 English doctor William Brownrigg creates the first artificially carbonated mineral water at Whitehaven, Cumberland.

1762 John Montagu, Earl of Sandwich, invents the sandwich (meat between two slices of bread) to stave off hunger while he is at the gaming table in London.

1797 James Keiller starts to manufacture the first orange marmalade, in Dundee, Scotland.

1824 George Smith opens Glenlivet, in Scotland, the first licensed whisky distillery.

1824 English Quaker John Cadbury opens a tea and coffee shop in Birmingham, England, the beginnings of the Cadbury confectionery company.

1831 Edward Adcock of Melton Mowbray, Leicestershire, England, begins to sell the now world-famous pork pies.

1837 Using a recipe from Sir Marcus Sandys, British chemists John Lee and William Perrins produce Worcester Sauce.

1839 Tea from India reaches the British market and quickly becomes more popular than the unfermented green Chinese tea.

1840 James Pimm, of Pimm's Oyster Bar in London, develops Pimms No.1, a mixture of gin, liqueurs, herbs, and spices made to an undisclosed recipe. From 1859 it is available in bottled form.

1862 British food manufacturers Crosse and Blackwell begin producing tinned soups.

c. **1870** Fish and chip shops start to become popular in the north of England.

1875 The British confectionery company Fry's introduces chocolate Easter eggs.

1876 The British confectionery company Slater & Bullock creates lettered rock; they will soon use the names of towns, the first being Blackpool.

1894 The Midland Vinegar Co. in England launches Garton's HP Sauce, using a recipe by Frederick Garton. It will later be renamed simply HP Sauce.

1913 The London company Carter's Crisps launches potato crisps in Britain.

1919 The first Indian cuisine restaurant in London, England, opens.

23 October 1933 Lyons opens its 'Corner House' fast-food restaurant with seats for 2,000 in London.

21 January 1937 Marcel Boulestin shows how to cook an omelette in *Cook's Night Out*, and becomes the first television chef in the UK.

12 January 1948 The London Co-operative Society opens the first supermarket in Britain, at Manor Park in London.

31 December 1971 The Campaign for Real Ale (CAMRA) is founded in Britain.

1974 McDonalds opens its first UK outlet in London.

25 March 1996 The European Union bans the export of British beef abroad following anxiety over the potential for transmission of the BSE (bovine spongiform encephalopathy) infection to humans as CJD (Creuzfeld Jakob disease).

November 1998 The European Union lifts its ban on the export of British beef.

incestuous passion between brother and sister. His other plays include *The Lover's Melancholy* (1629), *The Broken Heart* (1633), *Love's Sacrifice* (1633), in which Bianca is one of Ford's finest psychological studies of women, and *The Chronicle History of Perkin Warbeck* (1634). Dwelling on themes of pathos and frustration, they reflect the transition from a general to an aristocratic audience for drama.

Foreign and Commonwealth Office, or FCO

Government department established in 1782 as the Foreign Office. It is responsible for the conduct of foreign policy, representation of British interests abroad, relations with other members of the ⇨Commonwealth, and overseas aid policy and administration. Robin Cook was appointed foreign secretary in 1997.

Foreland, North and South

Chalk headlands projecting from the east coast of Kent, southeast England. **North Foreland**, with one lighthouse, lies 4 km/2.5 mi east of Margate; **South Foreland**, with two, lies 5 km/3 mi northeast of Dover. The headlands mark the eastern limit of the North Downs.

Forester, C(ecil) S(cott) (1899–1966)

English novelist. He is best known for a series of historical novels set in the Napoleonic era that, beginning with *The Happy Return* (1937), cover the career – from midshipman to admiral – of Horatio Hornblower. One of the series, *A Ship of the Line* (1939), won the James Tait Black Memorial Prize.

His first novel, *Payment Deferred* (1926), was a subtle crime novel, and he also wrote *The African Queen* (1935), filmed in 1952 with Humphrey Bogart and Katharine Hepburn.

FOOTBALL: SOME KEY DATES

1349 Football and other games are banned in England by King Edward III because they interfere with archery practice. The ban is repeated in 1389 and 1401, but with limited effect.

1848 The first football rules are drawn up by students at Cambridge University, most of whom are Old Etonians who object to the Rugby form of the game with its emphasis on handling, mauling, and hacking. Along with the rules of Harrow football they will form the basis of the Football Association's first code of rules in 1863.

1862 Notts County, the oldest club in the English Football League, is founded.

26 October 1863 The Football Association is founded in London, by the representatives of 11 clubs. Their purpose is to establish 'a definite code of rules for the regulation of the game'. All clubs are from the London area.

16 March 1872 A crowd of 2,000 at the Oval cricket ground in London watch Wanderers, a team of ex-public school players, defeat the Royal Engineers 1–0 to win the inaugural Football Association (FA) Cup final.

30 November 1872 At the West of Scotland cricket ground at Patrick, near Glasgow, England and Scotland draw 0–0 in the first ever official international association football match.

13 March 1873 The decision to form the Scottish Football Association is made at a meeting of eight Scottish clubs called by Queen's Park Football Club to organize a cup competition similar to the English Football Association Cup.

20 July 1885 The Football Association in England legalizes professionalism.

1888 The English Football League is founded on the initiative of William MacGregor, a member of Aston Villa Football Club. Twelve teams, all from the Midlands and the north of England, contest the first championship.

28 April 1923 The English Football Association (FA) Cup final is held at Wembley Stadium, London, for the first time. An estimated 200,000 spectators see Bolton Wanderers beat West Ham United 2–0.

1931 Arsenal is the first London team to win the English Football League championship.

25 November 1953 England's footballers lose at Wembley in London, for the first time to an overseas team, beaten 6–3 by Hungary. Six months later, Hungary confirms its overwhelming superiority over England with a 7–1 victory in Budapest, Hungary.

6 February 1958 Eight members of the Manchester United football side from England are killed in an air crash in Munich, West Germany, while returning from a European Cup tie in Belgrade, Yugoslavia.

1961 The maximum wage of £20 a week for English Football League players is abolished; Johnny Haynes of Fulham becomes the first English player to earn £100 a week.

1961 Tottenham Hotspur becomes the first side to win the English League and the Football Association (FA) Cup 'double' since Aston Villa in 1897.

30 July 1966 England wins football's World Cup, beating West Germany in the final at Wembley, 4–2 after extra time. The England forward Geoff Hurst scores the first ever hat trick in a World Cup final.

25 May 1967 Glasgow Celtic becomes the first British football team to win the European Cup, beating the Italian team Inter Milan 2–1 in Lisbon, Portugal.

27 November 1972 The English Football Association decides to abolish amateur status. It announces that from the start of the 1974–75 season (later deferred to the 1975–76 season) all footballers will be known simply as 'players'.

29 November 1978 Viv Anderson of Nottingham Forest becomes the first black footballer to play for England.

26 May 1982 Aston Villa football club defeats Bayern Munich of West Germany 1–0 in the European Cup final in Rotterdam, in the Netherlands; it is the sixth successive year that an English club has won the competition.

11 May 1985 Fifty-five people die when fire destroys the main stand at Bradford City's Valley Parade ground, in Bradford, during a Football League match.

29 May 1985 Thirty-nine people are killed at the Heysel stadium in Brussels, Belgium, following a riot by Liverpool fans before the European Cup Final between Liverpool and Juventus of Italy; as a consequence, English football clubs are banned from all European competitions for five years.

15 April 1989 Ninety-six Liverpool fans die in a crush during the Football Association (FA) Cup semifinal against Nottingham Forest at Hillsborough, Sheffield.

1991 Twenty-two soccer clubs break away from the English Football League, under the auspices of the Football Association (FA), to form the FA Premier League. Play commences in August 1992.

11 May 1996 Manchester United defeats Liverpool 1–0 in the English Football Association (FA) Cup final to complete an unprecedented second league championship and FA Cup double, having first achieved the feat two years earlier.

forest laws

In England, draconian legislation, enacted mainly during the century following the Norman Conquest, which prohibited common or agricultural use of land deemed to be royal hunting grounds and placed all game in such land under royal protection. Infringement of an order protecting royal forests was severely punished, with harsh penalties including mutilation and even death.

The laws were not finally abolished until 1817.

Forestry Commission

Government department responsible for forestry in Britain. Established in 1919, it is responsible for over 1 million hectares/2.7 million acres of land, and is funded partly by government and partly by sales of timber. In Northern Ireland responsibility for forestry lies with the Department of Agriculture's forestry service.

Between 1945 and 1980 the Forestry Commission doubled the forest area in the UK, planting, for example, Kielder Forest, Cumbria. In 1991 woodland cover was estimated at 2.3 million hectares, around 10% of total land area. This huge increase has been achieved mainly by planting conifers for commercial use on uplands or on land difficult to farm. In spite of such massive afforestation, around 90% of the UK's timber needs are imported at an annual cost of some £4 billion.

Forfar

Administrative centre and former royal burgh in Angus unitary authority, Scotland, at the eastern end of Forfar Loch in the fertile valley of Strathmore, 23 km/14 mi northeast of Dundee; population (1991) 13,000. Its principal industries are agricultural engineering and the manufacture of jute and other textiles, ladders, and soft drinks. Two major cattle and sheep markets are held, and it is the trading centre for local soft fruit and seed potato production.

Forfar was the royal residence of Malcolm III, king of Scotland from 1058. Robert (I) the Bruce destroyed Forfar's castle after capturing it from the English in the early 14th century. Its tollbooth was destroyed by British Lord Protector Oliver Cromwell's forces in the mid 17th century, and the town's ancient charters burned. Charles II granted a confirming charter in 1665 to reward the loyalty of Forfar's provost to his father, Charles I.

forfeiture

In England, confiscation of an outlaw's property, usually divided between the crown and the criminal's lord. In cases of treason all property went to the crown, but in most cases the criminal's land would go to his lord and his chattels to the crown. In the case of great lords, however, a portion of the confiscated lands would usually be restored to the heirs to avoid creating a potentially dangerous resentful family. Forfeiture was much used by parliament during the Civil War, and a special Commission for Forfeited Estates was set up after the Scottish rebellions of 1715 and 1745.

Formby, George (1904–1961)

English comedian. He established a stage and screen reputation as an apparently simple Lancashire working lad, and sang such songs as 'Mr Wu' and 'Cleaning Windows', accompanying himself on the ukulele. His father was a music-hall star of the same name.

Forres

Town and former royal burgh in Moray unitary authority, Scotland, on the River Findhorn, 19 km/12 mi southwest of Elgin; population (1991) 8,500. A tower built in honour of Admiral Nelson in 1807 tops Cluny Hill. The nearby monolith of Sueno's Stone, carved in the 11th century, is the largest single stone monument in Scotland.

Forster, E(dward) M(organ) (1879–1970)

English novelist, short-story writer, and critic. He was concerned with the interplay of personality and the conflict between convention and instinct. His novels include *A Room with a View* (1908), *Howards End* (1910), and *A Passage to India* (1924). Collections of stories include *The Celestial Omnibus* (1911) and *Collected Short Stories* (1948), and of essays and reviews 'Abinger Harvest' (1936). His most lasting critical work is *Aspects of the Novel* (1927).

Forster published his first novel, *Where Angels Fear to Tread*, in 1905. He enhances the superficial situations of his plots with unexpected insights in *The Longest Journey* (1907), *A Room with a View*, and *Howards End*. These three novels explore Forster's preoccupation with the need to find intellectual and spiritual harmony in a world dominated by narrow social conventions. His many years spent in India and as secretary to the Maharajah of Dewas provided him with the material for his best-known work *A Passage to India*, which explores the relationship between the English and the Indians with insight and wisdom. It is considered to be one of the most influential of modern English novels. *Maurice*, written in 1914 and published 1971, has a homosexual theme. Many of his works have been successfully adapted for film.

Forster, John (1812–1876)

English biographer and historian. His biography of Charles Dickens (1872–74) was a standard work. He also wrote lives of the leading figures of Oliver Cromwell's Commonwealth (1836–39), a fine biography of Oliver Goldsmith (1848), and the first volume of a life of Jonathan Swift (1875).

Forsyth, Andrew Russell (1858–1942)

Scottish mathematician. His *Theory of Functions* (1893) introduced the main strands of European mathematical study to British mathematicians. Bringing together the work of all the various schools in a single volume, the book completely changed the nature of mathematical thinking.

Forsyth, Bill (1947–)

Scottish film director and screenwriter. Forsyth established a reputation with a series of comedies set in Scotland, including *Gregory's Girl* (1980) and *Local Hero* (1983), which combined whimsy and dry humour.

His first feature film was *That Sinking Feeling* (1979). Other films include *Comfort and Joy* (1984), *Housekeeping* (1987), and *Being Human* (1994). He has recently written and directed a sequel to his most popular success, *Gregory's Two Girls* (1998).

Forsyth, Bruce Bruce Forsyth Johnson (1928–)

English comedian and entertainer who had had many years of live showbusiness experience when in 1958 he became host of TV's variety show, *Sunday Night at the London Palladium*,

FORSTER, E(DWARD) M(ORGAN) *The English writer photographed in 1949. As well as novels, Forster wrote essays, short stories, and biography, and co-wrote the libretto for Britten's opera* Billy Budd. *He was also involved in anticensorship campaigns with PEN and the National Council for Civil Liberties, and appeared as a witness for the defence in the 1960 trial of D H Lawrence's novel* Lady Chatterley's Lover. *Corbis*

which he compered for four years. He went on to present *The Generation Game* (1971–77), *Play Your Cards Right* (from 1980), and *Bruce Forsyth's Generation Game* (1992–94).

Forsyth, Frederick (1938–)

English thriller writer. His books include *The Day of the Jackal* (1970), *The Dogs of War* (1974), *The Fourth Protocol* (1984), and *The Negotiator* (1990). *The Fist of God* (1994) covers the activities of the SAS during the Gulf War; *Icon* (1996) is about intrigue in Russia.

He was a Reuters correspondent and BBC radio and television reporter before making his name with *The Day of the Jackal*, dealing with an attempted assassination of President de Gaulle of France. Later novels were *The Odessa File* (1972) and *The Devil's Alternative* (1979).

Forth

River in central Scotland, with its headstreams, Duchray Water and Avondhu, rising on the northeast slopes of Ben Lomond. It flows east approximately 105 km/65 mi to Kincardine where the **Firth of Forth** begins. The Firth is approximately 80 km/50 mi long, and is 26 km/16 mi wide where it joins the North Sea.

The Forth is the seventh longest river in Scotland. At South Queensferry near Edinburgh are the Forth rail (1890) and road (1964) bridges. The **Forth and Clyde Canal** crosses the lowlands of Scotland and links the east coast and the Firth of Forth to the west coast and the River Clyde, from Grangemouth to Bowling. It was built between 1768 and 1790 and stretches for some 61 km/38 mi. A new coalfield was located beneath the Firth of Forth in 1976. There are salmon and white fisheries in the Forth's basin.

The winding section of the river between Stirling and Alloa is known as the 'Links of Forth'. Its chief tributaries are the Teith (draining Lochs Katrine, Achray, Venachar, and Lubnaig), the Allan Water, and the Devon. The chief rivers flowing into the Firth are the Carron, Almond, Water of Leith, Esk, and Leven. Its principal port is Grangemouth.

Places of historical interest on the river's banks include Stirling (once a royal residence), Cambuskenneth, Alloa, Kincardine, and Aberfoyle.

Fortnum and Mason

High-class store in Piccadilly, London, famous for its exotic range of foods. It was founded in 1707 by William Fortnum, a footman toQueen Anne, and Hugh Mason, a local shopkeeper.

Fort William

Town in Highland unitary authority, Scotland, near the head of Loch Linnhe, at the southern end of the ◊Caledonian Canal, 90 km/56 mi southeast of Inverness; population (1991) 10,400. Straddling a natural route to the Highlands and Great Glen, the provision of tourist services has become a major industry. Distilleries, an aluminium smelter, and a pulp and paper mill offer further employment.

Its military base, built in 1665, was demolished in 1890 to make room for a railway station. The English general George Monk (1608–70) founded the fort, which was named after William, Prince of Orange. It was redesigned in 1690 and besieged by the Jacobites in 1746.

Fort William was formerly an administrative centre for the old district of Lochaber.

Forty-Five, the

◊Jacobite rebellion of 1745, led by Prince ◊Charles Edward Stuart. With his army of Highlanders 'Bonnie Prince Charlie' occupied Edinburgh and advanced into England as far as Derby, but then turned back. The rising was crushed by the Duke of Cumberland at Culloden in 1746.

Fosse Way, or Fosseway

Roman military road in England, from Lincoln in the north to Exeter, Devon, on the south coast. It intersected the Roman ◊Watling Street at a point known as the 'centre of England', and effectively divided the 'barbarian' north and west from the southeast.

The road probably functioned as a frontier in the early years of the Roman conquest and may have been intended as the final limit of the province until fighting spread to Wales. Its route ran through the Celtic territories of the Durotiges, Dobunni, and Corieltauvi, passing through Newark, Leicester, High Cross, Cirencester, Bath, and the hills near Chard, Axminster, and Honiton.

The Fosse Way continued in use until modern times and was one of the four 'royal roads' of 11th-century Britain. It was named after the foss, or ditch, constructed on either side to keep the road well drained.

Foster, Michael (1836–1907)

English physiologist and founder of the School of Physiology at Cambridge University. Foster published a series of textbooks on physiology (the first was published in 1876), in which he hypothesized widely about the mechanism of nerve impulse transmission and subsequent muscle contraction. He proposed that both electrical and chemical processes could be involved in transmission.

He was particularly interested in the control of the heart beat. Since a frog's heart continued to beat for some time after it was extracted from the animal, Albrecht von Haller had proposed that the cardiac muscle possesses an inherent rhythmical power that acts automatically (the myogenic theory). Foster demonstrated this theory by applying a constant current to the apex of a frog's heart devoid of nerve tissue, producing rhythmical activity.

Foster, Norman Robert (1935–)

English architect of the High Tech school. His buildings include the Willis Faber & Dumas insurance offices, Ipswich (1975); the Sainsbury Centre for the Visual Arts, Norwich (1977); the headquarters of the Hong Kong and Shanghai Bank, Hong Kong (1986); and Stansted Airport, Essex (1991).

Foster has won numerous international awards for his industrial architecture and design, including RIBA awards for the Stansted project and the Sackler Galleries extension at the Royal Academy of Art, London (1992), which is a sensitive, yet overtly modern, addition to an existing historic building. He was knighted in 1990.

Fountains Abbey

Cistercian abbey in North Yorkshire, England, situated 13 km/8 mi north of Harrogate. Celebrated as the greatest monument to English monasticism and its architecture, it was founded about 1132, and closed in 1539 at the Dissolution of the Monasteries. The ruins were incorporated into a Romantic landscaped garden (1720–40) with a lake, formal water garden, temples, and a deer park.

fourth estate

Term for the press, coined in the 18th century by the British politician Edmund Burke. It derived from a medieval theory that there were usually three estates – the **nobility**, the **clergy**, and the **commons** – whose functions were, respectively, defending society from foreign aggression and internal disorder, attending to its spiritual needs, and working to produce the base with which to support the other two orders.

Four Weddings and a Funeral

British romantic comedy film set among the upper middle class, released in 1994. The film was scripted by Richard Curtis and directed by Mike Newell. It tells the story of Charles (Hugh ◊Grant) who, apparently unable to sustain a relationship himself while all his friends are getting married, falls for the mysterious American Carrie (Andie MacDowell). The plot follows the conventional highs and lows of classic romantic comedy, and features fine ensemble playing from a predominantly British cast including John ◊Hannah, Simon ◊Callow, Kristin ◊Scott Thomas, and Rowan ◊Atkinson.

Fowey

Port and resort on the south coast of Cornwall, southwest England, on the west bank of the Fowey estuary, 45 km/28 mi southwest of Devonport; population (1995 est) 2,100. It is administered with ◊St Austell. Fowey is the principal outlet for the Cornish china clay mining industry based at St Austell, and is also a centre for recreational sailing.

The port has a deep, sheltered harbour and a lifeboat station. Ferries operate to Brodinnick and Polruan across the Fowey river.

History

Fowey was once an important seaport which fitted out ships for the Crusades. During the reign of Edward III the town equipped a fleet of 47 vessels and supplied about 800 men for the siege of Calais in 1347, and Fowey's seafarers continued to raid the coast of France throughout the Hundred Years' War. The inhabitants were later convicted of piracy by Edward IV, and deprived of their vessels.

The writer and scholar Arthur Quiller-Couch settled here in 1891, and referred to the place as 'Troy Town' in many of his books. Daphne Du Maurier's locally based work, including *Rebecca*, is celebrated at an annual arts and literature festival based in Fowey. Her first novel, *The Loving Spirit* (1931), was written while she lived at Brodinnick.

Fowler, (Peter) Norman (1938–)

British Conservative politician, chairman of the party 1992–94. He was a junior minister in the Heath government, transport secretary in the first Thatcher administration in 1979, social services secretary in 1981, and employment secretary 1987–89.

In 1997 he became the environment secretary in William Hague's shadow cabinet.

Fowler, Henry Watson (1858–1933) and Francis George (1870–1918)

English brothers who were scholars and authors of a number of English dictionaries. *Modern English Usage* (1926), the work of Henry Fowler, has become a classic reference work for matters of style and disputed usage.

Fowler, Jennifer (1939–)

Australian composer, resident in London from 1969. She studied in Perth and at the electronic music studio in Utrecht. Recent works include *Veni Sancte Spiritus* for chamber choir, and *Blow Flute: Answer Echoes in Antique Lands Dying* for solo flute.

Works include:

Look on this Oedipus (1973); *The Arrows of St Sebastian I and II* for ensemble (1981); *Line Spun with Stars* for piano trio (1983); *Between Science and the World* for wind quintet (1987); *Reeds, Reflections* for oboe and string trio (1990).

Fowles, John Robert (1926–)

English writer. His novels, often concerned with illusion and reality and with the creative process, include *The Collector* (1963), *The Magus* (1965), *The French Lieutenant's Woman* (1969) (filmed in 1981), *Daniel Martin* (1977), *Mantissa* (1982), and *A Maggot* (1985).

The Magus attempted to develop a new programme for modern fiction, and created an elaborate and tangled web of bizarre incidents involving a young Englishman teaching on a Greek island; a revised version was published in 1977. *The French Lieutenant's Woman* is a clever semi-historical narrative mystery set largely in Lyme Regis, a 'modern' Victorian novel which uses the story of a passionate young woman to question both modern and 19th-century morals and ideas about fiction.

Fox, Charles James (1749–1806)

English Whig politician, son of the 1st Baron Holland. He entered Parliament in 1769 as a supporter of the court, but went over to the opposition in 1774. As secretary of state in 1782, leader of the opposition to William Pitt the Younger, and foreign secretary in 1806, he welcomed the French Revolution and brought about the abolition of the slave trade.

The 'Old Whigs' deserted to the government headed by Pitt in 1792 over the French Revolution, leaving Fox and a small group of 'New Whigs' to oppose Pitt's war of intervention and his persecution of the reformers. On Pitt's death in 1806 a ministry was formed with Fox as foreign secretary, which at Fox's insistence abolished the slave trade. He opened peace negotiations with France, but died before their completion.

Is peace a rash system? Is it dangerous for nations to live in amity ...? Must the bowels of Great Britain be torn out – her best blood be spilt – her treasure wasted – that you may make an experiment?

CHARLES JAMES FOX English Whig politician.
Speech in the House of Commons February 1800, arguing against war with France

Fox, George (1624–1691)

English founder of the Society of ◊Friends. After developing his belief in a mystical 'inner light', he became a travelling preacher in 1647, and in 1650 was imprisoned for blasphemy at Derby, where the name Quakers was first applied derogatorily to him and his followers, supposedly because he enjoined Judge Bennet to 'quake at the word of the Lord'.

Fox, James (1939–)

English film actor. He is usually cast in roles in which he subtly captures the aloof, condescending qualities of the English aristocracy, as in Joseph Losey's *The Servant* (1963), but he portrayed a psychotic gangster in Nicolas Roeg's *Performance* (1970).

Fox also appeared in *Isadora* (1968). After *Performance* (1970), he took a break from acting until *No Longer Alone* (1978); later films include *Runners* (1984), *A Passage to India* (1984), *The Remains of the Day* (1993), *Anna Karenina*, and *Shadow Run* (both 1998).

In the 1990s he worked extensively in television, appearing in such programmes as *Fall from Grace* (1994) and as Dr Baks in *Gulliver's Travels* (1996).

fox-hunting

The pursuit of a fox across country on horseback, aided by a pack of foxhounds specially trained to track the fox's scent. The aim is to catch and kill the fox. In drag-hunting, hounds pursue a prepared trail rather than a fox.

Described by the playwright Oscar Wilde as 'the unspeakable in pursuit of the uneatable', fox-hunting has met with increasing opposition. Animal-rights activists condemn it as involving excessive cruelty, and in Britain groups of hunt saboteurs disrupt it. Fox-hunting dates from the late 17th century, when it arose as a practical method of limiting the fox population which endangered poultry farming, but by the early 19th century it was indulged in as a sport by the British aristocracy and gentry who ceremonialized it.

English 'hunts' (organized groups of hunters) include the Quorn, Pytchley, Belvoir, and Cottesmore. The recognized fox-hunting season runs from the first Monday in November until the following April. An estimated 12,500 foxes are killed in the UK by hunting each year, and another 100,000 killed by other means. In 1997 there were approximately 200 packs of foxhounds in the UK.

In 1998 the Labour government postponed debate on an anti-fox-hunting bill due to lack of parliamentary time, despite widespread support for the bill.

Foyle, Lough

Sea lough on the north coast of Ireland, traversed by the frontier of Northern Ireland and the Irish Republic. It is noted amongst ornithologists as a site for migratory seabirds.

Frampton, Peter (1950–)

English rock singer, songwriter, and guitarist. He was a member of Humble Pie and went on to succeed in his solo career, with albums including *Frampton Comes Alive!* (1976) and *I'm In You* (1977).

franchise

In politics, the eligibility, right, or privilege to vote at public elections, especially for the members of a legislative body, or parliament. In the UK adult citizens are eligible to vote from the age of 18, with the exclusion of peers, the insane, and criminals.

It was 1918 before all men in the UK had the right to vote, and 1928 before women were enfranchised.

Franciscan order

Catholic order of friars, **Friars Minor** or **Grey Friars**, founded in 1209 by the Italian monk Francis of Assisi. The first Franciscans to establish themselves in England arrived in 1224 and settled at Canterbury, London, and Oxford. By the

FOXHUNTING *Riders and hounds assemble for a hunt in Northumberland. The hunting with dogs of wild animals such as foxes and stags excites great passions. While its supporters defend it as a legitimate country pursuit that helps control overpopulation of wild animals and protects livestock, its opponents regard it as a cruel, unnecessary sport practised by a privileged few. Corel*

middle of the 13th century they had established around 50 friaries with over 1,200 friars. Many friaries subsequently closed, but since the mid-19th century many Franciscan houses have reopened.

An Anglican Franciscan community was established near Batcombe (Cerne Abbas), Dorset, England, in 1921 and is active in evangelistic work. A small Anglican community for women has also been started with headquarters at Freeland, Oxford.

The British scholars Duns Scotus, Roger Bacon, and William of Ockham were members of the Franciscan order.

Francome, John (1952–)

English National Hunt jockey who between 1970 and 1985 rode 1,138 winners from 5,072 mounts. The second person (after Stan Mellor) to ride 1,000 winners, only Peter ◊Scudamore and Richard ◊Dunwoody have ridden more winners in Britain under National Hunt rules. He took up training after retiring from riding and also became a popular TV broadcaster on racing.

Frankenstein, or The Modern Prometheus

Gothic horror story by Mary ◊Shelley, published in England in 1818. It is considered to be the origin of modern ◊science fiction, and there have been many film versions. Frankenstein, a scientist, discovers how to bring inanimate matter to life, and creates a man-monster. When Frankenstein fails to provide a mate to satisfy the creature's human emotions, it seeks revenge by killing Frankenstein's brother and bride. Frankenstein dies in an attempt to destroy his creation.

Franklin, Rosalind Elsie (1920–1958)

English biophysicist whose research on X-ray diffraction of DNA crystals helped Francis ◊Crick and James D Watson to deduce the chemical structure of DNA.

Fraser, Angus Robert Charles (1965–)

English cricketer. A tall right-arm opening bowler renowned for his accuracy, he made his Test debut in 1989 and at the end of the 1998 English season had taken 172 Test wickets in 44 matches at an average of 26.77. His early promise was hampered by a serious hip injury, sustained in 1991, but eventually he recaptured his best form, and in 1998 took 24 wickets and 27 wickets in successive series against the West Indies and South Africa. He made his first-class debut for Middlesex in 1984.

Fraser, Antonia (1932–)
English author. She has published authoritative biographies, including *Mary Queen of Scots* (1969) and *The Six Wives of Henry VIII* (1992), and an investigation of *The Gunpowder Plot* (1996). She has also written historical works, such as *The Weaker Vessel* (1984); and a series of detective novels featuring investigator Jemima Shore.

She is married to the dramatist Harold ◊Pinter, and is the daughter of Lord Longford.

Fraserburgh
Seaport in Aberdeenshire unitary authority, Scotland, on the south side of Kinnaird's Head, west of Fraserburgh Bay, 60 km/37 mi north of Aberdeen; population (1991) 12,800. It is a major fishing centre. Originally called **Faithlie**, the town's name was later changed in honour of its founder, Fraser of Philorth.

Frayn, Michael (1933–)
English writer. A writer of comedy and farce, blended with seriousness, Frayn began as a columnist for the *Guardian* and the *Observer*. His plays include *Donkeys Years* (1976, SWET Best Comedy Award), *Noises Off* (1982, SWET Best Comedy Award), and *Benefactors* (1984, Laurence Olivier Award for Play of the Year). He has written filmscripts, including *Clockwise* (1986); novels, including *The Russian Interpreter* (1966, Hawthornden Prize); and has translated plays by Anton Chekhov.

Frazer, James (George) (1854–1941)
Scottish anthropologist. Frazer's book *The Golden Bough* (12 volumes, 1890–1915), a pioneer study of the origins of religion and sociology on a comparative basis, exerted considerable influence on subsequent anthropologists and writers such as T S Eliot and D H Lawrence. By the standards of modern anthropology, many of its methods and findings are unsound.

He became a fellow of Trinity College, Cambridge in 1876. He was knighted in 1914, and awarded the Order of Merit in 1925.

Frears, Stephen (Arthur) (1931–)
English film director. He received international acclaim for *My Beautiful Laundrette* (1985), a low-budget study of racial, social, and gay prejudice, written by Hanif ◊Kureishi. Frears has also twice teamed with the Irish novelist Roddy Doyle, directing the final two parts of his Barrytown trilogy, *The Snapper* (1993) and *The Van* (1996).

Frears's second collaboration with Kureishi, *Sammy and Rosie Get Laid* (1987), was less well received. After *Prick Up Your Ears* (1987), a life of the playwright Joe Orton, Frears went to Hollywood to make the polished, prize-winning adaptation of the 18th-century novel *Dangerous Liaisons* (1988).

Free Church of Scotland
Body of Scottish Presbyterians who seceded from the Established Church of Scotland in the Disruption of 1843. In 1900 all but a small section that retains the old name (known as the **Wee Frees**) combined with the United Presbyterian Church to form the United Free Church of Scotland. Most of this reunited with the Church of Scotland in 1929, although there remains a continuing United Free Church of Scotland. It has 6,000 members, 110 ministers, and 140 churches.

freehold
In England and Wales, ownership of land for an indefinite period. It is contrasted with a leasehold, which is always for a fixed period. In practical effect, a freehold is absolute ownership.

freeman
One who enjoys the freedom of a borough. Since the early Middle Ages, a freeman has been allowed to carry out his or her craft or trade within the jurisdiction of the borough and to participate in municipal government, but since the development of modern local government, such privileges have become largely honorary.

freemasonry
Beliefs and practices of a group of linked national organizations open to men over the age of 21, united by a common code of morals and certain traditional 'secrets'. Modern freemasonry began in 18th-century Europe. Freemasons do much charitable work, but have been criticized in recent years for their secrecy, their male exclusivity, and their alleged use of influence within and between organizations (for example, the police or local government) to further each other's interests.

History
Freemasonry is descended from a medieval guild of itinerant masons, which existed in the 14th century and by the 16th was admitting men unconnected with the building trade. The term 'freemason' may have meant a full member of the guild or one working in freestone, that is, a mason of the highest class. There were some 25 lodges in 17th-century Scotland, of which 16 were in centres of masonic skills such as stonemasonry.

The present order of **Free and Accepted Masons** originated with the formation in London of the first Grand Lodge, or governing body, in 1717, and during the 18th century spread from Britain to the USA, continental Europe, and elsewhere.

In 1994 there were 359,000 masons registered in England and Wales; there were also an estimated 100,000 in Scotland and 60,000 in Ireland. There are approximately 6 million members worldwide.

French, Dawn (Roma) (1958–)
Welsh comedienne and actress. She rose to fame in partnership with Jennifer ◊Saunders with whom she appeared on the British stand-up comedy circuit, the television series *The Comic Strip Presents* (1982), and subsequently in their own long-running television show, *French and Saunders*. One of the creators of the widely acclaimed sitcom ◊*Absolutely Fabulous*,

she has herself featured in the television series *Girls on Top* (1985), *Murder Most Horrid* (1991), and *The Vicar of Dibley* (1994). She starred in the television film *Sex & Chocolate* in 1997. She is married to Lenny ◊Henry.

Freud, Anna (1895–1982)

Austrian-born founder of child psychoanalysis in the UK. Her work was influenced by the theories of her father, Sigmund Freud. She held that understanding of the stages of psychological development was essential to the treatment of children, and that this knowledge could only be obtained through observation of the child.

Anna Freud and her father left Nazi-controlled Vienna in 1938 and settled in London. There she began working in a Hampstead nursery. In 1947 she founded the Hampstead Child Therapy Course and Clinic, which specialized in the treatment of children and the training of child therapists.

Freud, Lucian (1922–)

German-born British painter. One of the greatest contemporary figurative artists, he combines meticulous accuracy with a disquieting intensity, painting from unusual angles and emphasizing the physicality of his subjects, whether nudes, still lifes, or interiors. His *Portrait of Francis Bacon* (1952; Tate Gallery, London) is one of his best-known works. He is a grandson of Sigmund Freud.

Born in Berlin, he moved to Britain in 1933. Largely self-taught, he was one of the Neo-Romantic group of English painters in his early years, but developed a figurative style from the 1950s. He was awarded an OM in 1993.

Friel, Brian (1929–)

Northern Irish dramatist. His work often deals with the social and historical pressures that contribute to the Irish political situation. His first success was with *Philadelphia, Here I Come!* (1964), which dealt with the theme of exile. Later plays include the critically acclaimed *Dancing at Lughnasa* (1990).

In 1980 he founded the Field Day Theatre Company, which produced *Translations* (1981), a study of British cultural colonialism in 19th-century Ireland. Other plays include *The Freedom of the City* (1973), about victims of the Ulster conflict, *Faith Healer* (1980), *Making History* (1988), and *Molly Sweeney* (1994).

friendly society

Association that makes provisions for the needs of sickness and old age by money payments. In 1995 there were 1,013 orders and branches (17 orders, 996 branches), 18 collecting societies, 294 other centralized societies, 72 benevolent societies, 2,271 working men's clubs, and 131 specially authorized societies in the UK. Among the largest are the National Deposit, Odd Fellows, Foresters, and Hearts of Oak. In the USA similar 'fraternal insurance' bodies are known as **benefit societies**; they include the Modern Woodmen of America (1883) and the Fraternal Order of Eagles (1898).

In the UK the movement was the successor to the great medieval guilds, but the period of its greatest expansion was in the late 18th and early 19th centuries, after the passing in 1797 of the first legislation providing for the registration of friendly societies. In the 20th century the Friendly Societies Act 1992 allowed friendly societies to become companies and offer a wider range of financial services.

Friends of the Earth, FoE, or FOE

Largest international network of environmental pressure groups, established in the UK in 1971, that aims to protect the environment and to promote rational and sustainable use of the Earth's resources. It campaigns on such issues as acid rain; air, sea, river, and land pollution; recycling; disposal of toxic wastes; nuclear power and renewable energy; the destruction of rainforests; pesticides; and agriculture. FoE is represented in 52 countries.

FoE is one of the leading environmental pressure groups in the UK. It has a unique network of campaigning local groups, working in 250 communities in England, Wales, and Northern Ireland. Over 80% of its income comes from individual donations, the rest from special fundraising events, grants, and trading. Friends of the Earth Trust is a charity which commissions detailed research. It provides extensive information and educational materials. Over the years FoE has achieved bans on ozone-destroying chlorofluorocarbons (CFCs), reduced trade in rainforest timber and increased support for cleaner energy technologies. FoE was the first environmental pressure group in the UK to start campaigns for whales, endangered species, and tropical rainforests, and against acid rain, ozone depletion, and climate change.

Friends, Society of, or Quakers

Christian Protestant sect founded by George ◊Fox in England in the 17th century. They were persecuted for their nonviolent activism, and many emigrated to form communities elsewhere; for example, in Pennsylvania and New England. The worldwide movement had about 219,800 members in 1997. Their worship stresses meditation and the freedom of all to take an active part in the service (called a meeting, held in a meeting house). They have no priests or ministers.

The name 'Quakers' may originate in Fox's injunction to 'quake at the word of the Lord'. Originally marked out by their sober dress and use of 'thee' and 'thou' to all as a sign of equality, they incurred penalties by their pacifism and refusal to take oaths or pay tithes. In the 19th century many Friends were prominent in social reform, for example, Elizabeth ◊Fry. Quakers have exerted a profound influence on American life through their pacifism and belief in social equality, education, and prison reform. In 1997 there were about 19,000 members in Great Britain and Ireland.

Frink, Elisabeth (1930–1993)

English sculptor. She created rugged, naturalistic bronzes, mainly based on human and animal forms; for example, the *Alcock Brown Memorial* (1962) for Manchester airport, *In Memoriam* (heads), and *Running Man* (1980).

From 1967 to 1973 she lived in France and expressed her horror of the Algerian War and other troubles in North Africa in a series of 'goggle heads' resembling torturers in sunglasses or the messengers of death in motorcycle goggles in Jean Cocteau's film *Orphée*. In her later years, influenced by the *Riace* bronzes, the Classical Greek figures found off the coast of southern Italy, her male figures became more aggressive. Her use of startling colour effects was inspired by the Aboriginal art she had seen on a visit to Australia.

Frink's other public commissions include the *Dorset Martyrs* in Dorchester and the *Shepherd with Three Lambs* in Paternoster Square, London. She also undertook a few commissions for churches, the last being a bronze *Christ* for Liverpool Cathedral, unveiled only weeks before her death. She was made DBE in 1982 and CH in 1992.

Frith, William Powell (1819–1909)

English painter. His canvases depict large contemporary scenes featuring numerous figures and incidental detail. *Ramsgate Sands* (1854; Royal Collection, London), bought by Queen Victoria, is a fine example, as are *Derby Day* (1856–58; Tate Gallery, London) and *The Railway Station* (1862; Holloway College).

From 1853, possibly influenced by the Pre-Raphaelites, he turned to contemporary society life with great popular success, becoming the wealthiest artist of his day.

Frogmore

Royal residence in the Home Park, Windsor, England, about 2 km/1 mi southeast of the castle. The estate has long been the property of the Crown. The central block of the house dates from the early 18th century, but there have been many later alterations and additions.

Frogmore has two mausolea adjacent, that of the duchess of Kent, mother of Queen Victoria, who lived here for 21 years, and the Royal Mausoleum. The bodies of Queen Victoria and the Prince Consort lie here. Other members of the royal family are buried in the small cemetery adjoining the mausolea.

Fröhlich, Herbert (1905–1991)

German-born British physicist who helped lay the foundations for modern theoretical physics in the UK. He revolutionized solid-state theory by importing into it the methods of quantum field theory – the application of quantum theory to particle interactions.

In particular, he proposed a theory to explain superconductivity using the methods of quantum field theory. He made important advances in the understanding of low-temperature superconductivity. His work also led him to the idea that quantum methods might elucidate some aspects of biological systems, such as the electrical properties of cell membranes.

Frome

Market town in Somerset, England, 40 km/25 mi southeast of Bristol; population (1991) 22,400. Industries in the town include foundries, printing works, and factories producing plastics.

A medieval shopping street (Cheap Street) survives in Frome. The town was once the centre of a prosperous wool trade. It has a 14th-century church.

Frost, David (Paradine) (1939–)

English broadcaster who fronted the radical BBC satirical show, *That Was The Week That Was* (1962–1964). He went on to present *The Frost Report* (1966), *Frost Over England*, and *The Frost Programme* (both 1967). An interview in the latter with Emil Savundra confirmed his ability as a tough interrogator, and he has worked on both British and US TV as a political interviewer, chat show host, and presenter.

frost fairs

Medieval fairs held on rivers that had frozen over. Before bridges with many arches speeded up the flow of water, many English rivers, especially the Thames, were prone to freezing solid for days at a time in the winter and townspeople would take advantage by erecting stalls and holding entertainments on the water.

Froude, William (1810–1879)

English engineer and hydrodynamicist. He first formulated reliable laws for the resistance that water offers to ships and for predicting their stability. He also invented the hydraulic dynameter (1877) for measuring the output of high-power

FRINK, ELISABETH *The bronze statue* War Horse *by Dame Elisabeth Frink stands in the grounds of Chatsworth House, Derbyshire. Frink was one of the leading British sculptors of her time, and specialized in monumental pieces depicting menacing birds, horses, or warrior figures. Robin Weaver/Collections*

engines. These achievements were fundamental to marine development.

In 1838 Froude assisted Isambard Kingdom ◊Brunel on the building of the Bristol and Exeter Railway. Brunel later consulted him on the behaviour of the *Great Eastern* at sea and, on his recommendation, the ship was fitted with bilge keels.

Froude also carried out model experiments and theoretical work on the rolling stability of ships. His general deductions are still the standard exposition of the rolling and oscillation of ships.

Fry, Christopher Harris (1907–)

English dramatist. He was a leader of the revival of verse drama after World War II with *The Lady's Not for Burning* (1948), *Venus Observed* (1950), and *A Sleep of Prisoners* (1951).

Fry, Elizabeth born Gurney (1780–1845)

English Quaker philanthropist. From 1813 she began to visit and teach the women in Newgate Prison who lived with their children in terrible conditions. She formed an association for the improvement of conditions for female prisoners in 1817, and worked with her brother, **Joseph Gurney** (1788–1847), on an 1819 report on prison reform. She was a pioneer for higher nursing standards and the education of working women.

Fry, Roger (Eliot) (1866–1934)

English artist and art critic. An admirer of the French painter Paul Cézanne, he championed Post-Impressionism in Britain, expounding the theory of 'significant form' and colour as the criteria for true art. He was a member of the Bloomsbury Group and founded the ◊Omega Workshops to improve design and to encourage young artists. His critical essays, which were very influential in the 1920s and 1930s, are contained in *Vision and Design* (1920).

Fry, Stephen (1957–)

English comedian, actor, and novelist. A frequent performer, in partnership with Hugh Laurie on the British television show *Friday Night Live*, and as a cast member in the *Blackadder* series, Fry has become a cultured presence on the British comedy scene. He won critical acclaim for his performance of Oscar Wilde in the 1997 film *Wilde*.

FT Index

Abbreviation for ◊**Financial Times Index**, a list of leading share prices.

Fuller, Roy (Broadbent) (1912–1991)

English poet and novelist. His early verse, including the collections *Poems* (1940) and *The Middle of a War* (1944), was concerned with social problems. With *Counterparts* (1954), his work became more personal and allusive. His novels are particularly concerned with mental turmoil and difficult relationships: they include *Image of a Society* (1956), *My Child, My Sister* (1965), and *The Carnal Island* (1970). *The Strange and the Good: Collected Memoirs* was published in 1989.

Full Monty, The

Critically-acclaimed and commercially successful low-budget British comedy film about a group of unemployed Sheffield men who find communal values and renewed self-confidence in their efforts to put together a male strip show. Released in 1997, it was written by Simon Beaufoy and directed by Peter Cattaneo; its cast includes Robert ◊Carlyle, Tom Wilkinson, and Mark Addy.

furlong

Unit of measurement, originating in Anglo-Saxon England, equivalent to 220 yd (201.168 m).

A furlong consists of 40 rods, poles, or perches; 8 furlongs equal one statute mile. Its literal meaning is 'furrow-long', and refers to the length of a furrow in the common field characteristic of medieval farming.

Furness

Peninsula in northwest England, between the Irish Sea and Morecambe Bay, formerly a detached northern portion of Lancashire, separated from the main part by Morecambe Bay. In 1974 it was included in the new county of ◊Cumbria. ◊Barrow-in-Furness is its ship-building and industrial centre. The Michaelson Dock is the principal mooring.

The peninsula is associated with the Cistercian monks of **Furness Abbey**, who planted trees to provide charcoal for the iron industry, and began the reclamation of the nearby marshes. Various coast protection works now exist to prevent sea flooding of the Isle of Walney off the western shore, which is now a nature reserve. Parts of the docks have been drained, including the Graving Dock, and are home to the strikingly-designed Dock Museum.

Furness Abbey

The abbey lies to the northeast of Barrow-in-Furness. It was originally founded in 1123 by Savignac monks and was absorbed by the Cistercian order in 1147. The foundation acquired extensive property in Cumbria, the Isle of Man, and Ireland, and became the second most wealthy Cistercian monastery in Britain after Fountains Abbey. In 1537 the abbey was the first large foundation to be closed in the Dissolution of the Monasteries and it fell into disrepair. Remains include one end of the church, late Norman arches of the cloisters, and the adjoining Early English chapter house.

further education college

Centre of education for students over school-leaving age that provides courses for skills towards an occupation or trade, and general education at a level below that of a degree course. Further education colleges were removed from local authority control in 1993.

fusion

Musical style established in the UK in the 1970s and 1980s as a highly technical, smooth, and relatively commercial alternative to mainstream jazz. Exponents included Morrissey-Mullen and Shakatak. In the late 1980s such diversifications as Acid Jazz connected fusion to jazz culture. Groups of the 1990s such as ⇨Jamiroquai are the pop realization of the fusion ideal.

Fyffe, Will (1885–1947)

Scottish music-hall comedian. He is remembered for his vivid character sketches and for his song 'I Belong to Glasgow'.

Fyne, Loch

Sea-inlet in Argyll and Bute unitary authority, Scotland, extending about 65 km/40 mi north and northeast from the Sound of Bute between the Kintyre peninsula and Argyll on the west and the Cowal peninsula on the east. It reaches a maximum depth of 200 m/656 ft. Inverary stands on its western shore, about 14 km/9 mi from the head of the loch.

Further south, the fishing port of Tarbert is renowned for its herring catches.

Gabor, Dennis (1900–1979)

Hungarian-born British physicist. He worked in Germany until he fled to Britain in 1933 to escape the Nazis. In 1947 he invented the holographic method of three-dimensional photography. Other work included research on high-speed oscilloscopes, communication theory, and physical optics. In 1958 he invented a type of colour TV tube of greatly reduced depth. From 1958 to 1967 he was professor of applied electron physics at the Imperial College of Science and Technology, London.

Gabriel, Peter (1950–)

English rock and pop singer and songwriter who was a member of the group Genesis 1966–75. His first solo album *Peter Gabriel* was released in 1977. He became a champion of 'World Music' with songs such as the anti-apartheid anthem 'Biko'. He rose to international stardom in 1986 with the hit single 'Sledgehammer', which was promoted by a ground-breaking video.

Gaelic language

Member of the Celtic branch of the Indo-European language family, spoken in Ireland, Scotland, and (until 1974) the Isle of Man. Gaelic has been in decline for several centuries, though efforts are being made to keep it alive, for example by means of the government's Gaelic Broadcasting Fund, established in 1993, which subsidises television and radio programmes in Gaelic for transmission in Scotland.

In Scotland in 1991 there were about 70,000 speakers of Gaelic (1.4% of the population), concentrated in the Western Isles and in parts of the northwest coast. See also ◊Scottish Gaelic literature.

Gainsborough

River port and town in Lincolnshire, eastern England, on the River Trent, about 24 km/15 mi northwest of Lincoln; population (1995 est) 17,500. It is an agricultural trading centre with diverse manufactures, including packaging machinery, sheet metal and plastic products, strawboard, animal feed, exhaust systems, instruments and electric motors, golf clubs, and processed foods. Its port handles mainly barge traffic. During spring tides a tidal wave, the 'eagre', sweeps up the river.

The 15th-century Old Hall is a large timber-framed manor house, containing a great hall with a hoop-shaped roof, and a medieval kitchen. A fine three-arched bridge spans the river. Gainsborough is associated with the *Mill on the Floss* by George Eliot, in which it appears as St Ogg's.

Gainsborough, Thomas (1727–1788)

English landscape and portrait painter. In 1760 he settled in Bath, where his elegant and subtly characterized society portraits brought great success. In 1774 he went to London, becoming one of the original members of the Royal Academy

Irish Gaelic Words Borrowed into English

currach	15th century	('boat') a coracle
leprechaun	17th century	('small body') a small and often mischievous supernatural creature
banshee	18th century	('fairy woman') a supernatural female being who wails under the windows of a house where death is imminent
blarney	18th century	flattering or cajoling talk; to talk in such a way, named after a village near Cork
céilidh	19th century	('companion'; also in Scotland) an informal social gathering, with conversation, music, dancing and story-telling
poteen	19th century	('little pot') an alcoholic spirit, illegally brewed (usually from potatoes)
smithereens	19th century	(unknown origin) small fragments
Taoiseach	20th century	('chieftain') the title of the prime minister of the Republic of Ireland

and the principal rival of Joshua Reynolds. He was one of the first British artists to follow the Dutch example in painting realistic landscapes rather than imaginative Italianate scenery, as in *Mr and Mrs Andrews* (about 1750; National Gallery, London).

Although he learned painting and etching in London, Gainsborough was largely self-taught. His method of painting – what Reynolds called 'those odd scratches and marks ... this chaos which by a kind of magic at a certain distance assumes form' – is full of temperament and life. The portrait of his wife (Courtauld Institute, London) and *The Morning Walk* (National Gallery) show his sense of character and the elegance of his mature work. His *Blue Boy* (San Marino, California) is a homage to van Dyck. The landscapes he painted for his own pleasure took on an imaginary look; rhythmic in movement, the *Harvest Wagon* (Birmingham) already has this Utopian character. A foundation member of the Royal Academy and elected to its Council in 1774, Gainsborough moved that year to Schomberg House in London. Influenced in landscape by Rubens now, rather than by Ruisdael as in his youth, he produced the massing and play of light seen in *The Market Cart* (1786; National Gallery).

A constant tendency to experiment produced the remarkable 'fancy pictures' or imaginative compositions of his late years, the *Diana and Actaeon* (Royal Collection), unfinished when he died, being an example. Hundreds of drawings, often in a mixture of media, show his continued pursuit of landscape for its own sake.

Gaitskell, Hugh (Todd Naylor) (1906–1963)

British Labour Party leader from 1955. In 1950 he became minister of economic affairs, and then chancellor of the Exchequer until October 1951. As party leader, he tried to reconcile internal differences on nationalization and disarmament.

In 1955 he defeated Aneurin Bevan for the succession to Clement Attlee as Labour leader, and he was re-elected party leader in 1960. He died suddenly in office in 1963.

Galashiels

Mill town and former burgh in Scottish Borders unitary authority, Scotland, on the Gala Water, 52 km/33 mi southeast of Edinburgh; population (1991) 13,800. A major producer of Scottish tweeds, its Scottish College of Textiles is the headquarters of Scotland's tweed manufacturing industry.

Abbotsford, the residence of the novelist and poet Walter Scott, lies to the southeast.

Galliano, John (1960–)

English fashion designer. His elegant and innovative designs are often inspired by historical motifs (for example, 'Dickensian' clothing), the elements of which he redesigns to create progressive collections. He became known before graduating from St Martin's School of Art in 1984 for his technical expertise and imaginative flair. In 1990 he designed the costumes for a production of Ashley Page's ballet *Corrulao*, performed by the Ballet Rambert. In the same year he began showing his collections in Paris. In 1996 he succeeded Gianfranco Ferré as head of Christian Dior, after only three seasons at Givenchy.

Galsworthy, John (1867–1933)

English novelist and dramatist. His work examines the social issues of the Victorian period. He wrote *The Forsyte Saga* (1906–22) and its sequel, the novels collectively entitled *A Modern Comedy* (1929). His plays include *The Silver Box* (1906). He won the Nobel Prize for Literature in 1932.

Galsworthy first achieved recognition with *The Silver Box* and *The Man of Property* (1906), the first instalment of the *Forsyte Saga* series, which also includes *In Chancery* (1920) and *To Let* (1921). Soames Forsyte, the central character, is the embodiment of Victorian values and feeling for property, and the wife whom he also 'owns' – Irene – was based on Galsworthy's wife.

Galt, John (1779–1839)

Scottish novelist. He was the author of *Annals of the Parish* (1821), in which he portrays the life of a Lowlands village, using the local dialect. An effective interpreter of Scottish rural and small-town life, in which capacity he contributed to the development of the Scottish novel, he was also an instigator of the political novel.

Born in Irvine, Ayrshire, he moved to London in 1804,

GALSWORTHY, JOHN *In his many novels, stories, and plays, the English novelist John Galsworthy created a detailed portrait of English society during its transition from the Victorian era to the Edwardian. Corbis*

then travelled extensively in Europe, and went to Canada as secretary of a land company in 1826. He founded the Canadian town of Guelph, and Galt, on the Grand River, Ontario, was named after him. In 1829 he returned to Scotland.

Galton, Francis (1822–1911)

English scientist, inventor, and explorer who studied the inheritance of physical and mental attributes with the aim of improving the human species. He was the first to use twins to try to assess the influence of environment on development, and is considered the founder of eugenics (a term he coined).

Galton believed that genius was inherited, and was principally to be found in the British; he also attempted to compile a map of human physical beauty in Britain. He invented the 'silent' dog whistle, the weather map, a teletype printer, and forensic fingerprinting, and discovered the existence of anticyclones.

Galton designed several instruments to plot meteorological data, and made the first serious attempt to chart the weather over large areas – described in his book *Meteorographica* (1863). He also helped to establish the Meteorological Office and the National Physical Laboratory.

In *Hereditary Genius* (1869), based on a study of mental abilities in eminent families, Galton formulated the regression law, which states that parents who deviate from the average in a positive or negative direction have children who, on average, also deviate in the same direction but to a lesser extent.

Galton invented instruments to measure mental abilities in some 9,000 subjects. In order to interpret his data, Galton devised new statistical methods of analysis, including correlational calculus, which has since become an invaluable tool in many disciplines. The results were summarized in *Inquiries into Human Faculty and its Development* (1883). Knighted 1909.

Galway, James (1939–)

Irish flautist. He played with the London Symphony Orchestra in 1966, the Royal Philharmonic Orchestra 1967–69, and was principal flautist with the Berlin Philharmonic Orchestra 1969–75 before taking up a solo career.

Gambon, Michael (1940–)

Irish-born actor who won widespread recognition for his performance in Dennis Potter's *The Singing Detective* (1986). An imposing and versatile screen and stage performer, he played the gluttonous gangster in *The Cook, the Thief, his Wife, and Her Lover* (1989) and the subtle eponymous detective in the television series *Maigret* (1992). His other credits include the television series *The Borderers* (1968–69), and the films *The Browning Version* (1994) and *The Wings of the Dove* (1997).

game laws

Legislation from 1671 to 1831 restricting the taking of game to those of high social status. 'Game' itself was defined by the Games Act 1831 as hares, pheasants, partridges, grouse, heath or moor game, black game (the grouse *Lyrurus tetrix*) and bustards, though these last were deleted by the Protection of Birds Act 1954. It is necessary to have a game licence to take or pursue game.

Gang of Four

Four members of the Labour Party who in 1981 resigned to form the ⇨Social Democratic Party: Roy Jenkins, David Owen, Shirley Williams, and William Rodgers.

garden city

Town built in a rural area and designed to combine town and country advantages, with its own industries, controlled developments, private and public gardens, and cultural centre. The idea was proposed by Ebenezer ⇨Howard, who in 1899 founded the Garden City Association, which established the first garden city: Letchworth in Hertfordshire.

A second, Welwyn, 35 km/22 mi from London, was started in 1919. The New Towns Act 1946 provided the machinery for developing ⇨new towns on some of the principles advocated by Howard (for example Stevenage, begun in 1947).

gardening

A national obsession, pride in one's garden being perhaps linked to the ethos 'an Englishman's home is his castle'. See ⇨leisure, for a feature on The British at Play, giving statistics on gardening, and the chronology of some gardening highlights, on the next page.

Gardiner, John Eliot (1943–)

English conductor. He first made his mark establishing the Monteverdi Choir in 1966, which he continues to conduct. He is an authority on 17th- and 18th-century music, and an exponent of the authenticity movement. He has also recorded modern music.

Gare Loch

Northern inlet of the River ⇨Clyde, in Argyll and Bute unitary authority, Scotland, extending about 12 km/8 mi in length, with a width of 1 km/0.6 m. It has a shipbreaking yard, and is mainly used by the Royal Navy, which has a nuclear submarine base at Faslane Bay in the upper reaches of the loch.

Garelochead, a small holiday resort, sits at its northernmost point. The yachting centre of Rhu lies on its east shore, near the opening to the Clyde.

Garforth

Town in West Yorkshire, England, 11 km/7 mi east of Leeds; population (1991) 22,800. Its location on the Leeds–York railway line has contributed to Garforth's development as a dormitory town for Leeds. As a result, it is largely residential, with a large shopping centre.

Garrick, David (1717–1779)

English actor and theatre manager. From 1747 he became joint licensee of the Drury Lane Theatre, London, with his own company, and instituted a number of significant theatrical conventions including concealed stage lighting and banishing spectators from the stage. He played Shakespearean

Gardens and Gardening: Some Key Dates to 1979

1621 The Oxford Physic Garden is opened. The first botanical garden in Britain, it also contains the first rudimentary greenhouse in Britain, a stone greenhouse for the preservation of delicate plants.

1662 Greenwich Park in London, designed by the French garden designer André Le Nôtre, is completed.

c. **1700** Dutch garden designs are fashionable in England.

1724 Horticulturalist Stephen Switzer constructs the first all-glass hothouse in Britain, for the growing of grapes on the Duke of Rutland's estate.

1733 The Serpentine, a curving lake in Hyde Park, London, is laid out for Queen Caroline.

1734 The gardens and garden buildings of Rousham in Oxfordshire, designed by the English architect William Kent, are completed.

1750 The English artist Francis Hayman completes his decoration of the pavilions at Vauxhall Gardens, a fashionable pleasure park in London.

c. **1750** The English landscape gardener Lancelot 'Capability' Brown lays out Warwick Castle Gardens in Warwickshire.

1759 The Botanical Gardens are founded at Kew, near London.

1787 William Curtis sets up the first gardening magazine, the monthly *Botanical Magazine*, in London.

1838 Regent's Park opens in London.

1841 Kew Gardens, London, are opened to the public.

1843 Sir Charles Isham starts the British affection for garden gnomes when he imports them from Nuremberg, Germany.

1845 The tax on glass is dropped in Britain, enabling conservatories to become a feature of suburban houses.

1895 The National Trust is founded in Britain to preserve country houses, parks, gardens, and areas of natural beauty.

20–22 May 1913 The Royal Horticultural Society holds the first Chelsea Flower Show, in London.

21 November 1936 *In Your Garden*, broadcast by the BBC, is the first regular gardening programme.

1942 The 'Dig for Victory' campaign is started in the UK, encouraging the cultivation of gardens and public space to increase food production.

1955–1967 *Gardening Club*, a practical guide for gardeners presented by Percy Thrower, is shown on British television.

March 1979 *Gardening with Michael Barrett* is the first general interest programme to be made for sale on video in the UK.

1992 The 'lost' gardens of Heligan, southern Cornwall are opened to the public, following restoration.

characters such as Richard III, King Lear, Hamlet, and Benedick, and collaborated with George Colman (1732–1794) in writing the play *The Clandestine Marriage* (1766). He retired from the stage in 1766, but continued as a manager.

Garter, Order of the

Senior British order of knighthood (see ◊knighthood, order of), founded by Edward III in about 1347. Its distinctive badge is a garter of dark-blue velvet, with the motto of the order – *Honi soit qui mal y pense* ('Shame be to him who thinks evil of it') – in gold letters. Knights of the Garter write KG after their names.

Gascoigne, Paul, 'Gazza' (1967–)

English footballer who played for Newcastle United 1985–87, Tottenham Hotspur 1988–91, Lazio, Italy 1992–95, Glasgow Rangers 1995–97 and then joined Middlesborough in March 1998. He made his full England debut in September 1988 and in August 1998 had won 57 caps.

He became a national hero after the 1990 World Cup finals in Italy, as much for his tearful response to receiving a booking in the semi-final against West Germany (which would have ruled him out of the final had England won the match), as for his brilliant performances in England's midfield. Lionized by the British media at the time, his subsequent career has been beset by controversy both on and off the field.

The Scottish football writers' Player of the Year in 1996, he helped England to reach the semi-finals of the European Championships. Three months after his move to Middlesborough he was excluded by England manager Glen ◊Hoddle from England's final squad of 22 players for the 1998 World Cup finals in France. The subsequent publication of Hoddle's World Cup diary revealed that it was Gascoigne's mental state as much as his physical condition that was decisive in his exclusion.

Gaskell, Elizabeth Elizabeth Cleghorn, born Stevenson (1810–1865)

English novelist. Her most popular book, *Cranford* (1853), is the study of a small, close-knit circle in a small town, modelled on Knutsford, Cheshire, where she was brought up. Her other books, which often deal with social concerns, include *Mary Barton* (1848), *North and South* (1855), *Sylvia's Lovers* (1863–64), and the unfinished *Wives and Daughters* (1866). She wrote a frank and sympathetic biography of her friend Charlotte ◊Brontë (1857).

The success of *Mary Barton* established her as a novelist; in this work she describes with insight and sympathy the life and feelings of working-class people.

gas lighting

First used in Britain in 1792 to light the office of the Scottish steam engineer William Murdock. Gas lighting was used in

GASKELL, ELIZABETH *English novelist Elizabeth Gaskell lived in Manchester. Set in the slums of the industrial towns of the region, her novels were among the first to portray the moral and social evils of industrialization. Corbis*

1805 in a Manchester factory, and in 1807 Pall Mall, London, was the first public thoroughfare to be lit by gas. The Chartered Gas Light and Coke Company, founded in 1812, was the first of several private companies to produce and supply gas. By 1820 there were seven gasworks in London and the number of gaslights in London streets increased from 4,000 to 51,000 in only five years. By the 1840s gas lights were found in the streets, shops and homes of even small towns. By the end of the 19th century gas-producing companies were beginning to compete with electricity.

gas supply

The UK gas industry was privatized in 1986 with creation of British Gas. In 1997 British Gas demerged into two separate companies: Centrica, owning the supply business, whilst pipelines, storage, exploration, production, research and development were retained by British Gas, subsequently abbreviated to ◊BG. Competition was introduced into the gas market from 1986 and into the domestic gas market from 1996.

History

The gas industry, operating as the Gas Council, was nationalized in 1949. The Gas Council was replaced by the British Gas Corporation in 1972 and privatized as British Gas in 1986. Gas supply to the domestic market was opened to companies other than British Gas in 1996, initially in Cornwall, Devon and part of Wales. This was extended to Scotland and other parts of southern England in 1997 and the rest of England and Wales in 1998. A number of new companies started supplying gas, including several regional electricity companies.

Sources

In 1997 there were 67 offshore gasfields producing natural gas and methane. This gas is transported around Britain by some 267,300 km/166,000 mi of pipelines, which are owned by Transco. BG's competitors are allowed access to these pipelines under a network code.

Gateshead

Port in Tyne and Wear, northeast England; population (1994 est) 127,000. It is situated on the south bank of the River Tyne, opposite Newcastle upon Tyne. Formerly a port for the Tyne coalfields and a railway workshop centre, it now manufactures chemicals, plastics, and glass; other industries include engineering, printing, and tourism.

Features

Metroland, in the Metro Centre shopping complex, is a major tourist attraction. As part of the Tyneside South Bank development (partly funded by the National Lottery), the Baltic Flour Mills are undergoing conversion into an international centre for the visual arts, the New International Art Gallery, scheduled to open in 2000. The *Angel of the North*, a steel sculpture (20 m/65 ft high) overlooking Gateshead, by Anthony Gormley, was erected in 1998. It is sited 5 km/3 mi from the town, and is Britain's largest sculpture.

History

The town received its first charter in 1164. Coal deposits were discovered in the vicinity in the 14th century. It developed as a thriving port and centre of heavy industry during the 19th century. In 1849 a high-level bridge, 34 m/112 ft above river level, was built to carry road and rail traffic between the high ground on either bank of the Tyne. The town was severely damaged by fire in 1854.

Gatting, Michael William (1957–)

Middlesex and England cricketer. He joined Middlesex in 1975 and captained the county from 1983. He was a member of seven championship-winning teams 1976, 1977, 1980, 1982, 1985, 1990, and 1993, and captain of the Sunday League champions 1992. He first played for England 1977 and captained England 1986–88. He led an unofficial England tour to South Africa 1989–90, for which he received a three year ban from test cricket. He played again for England on the 1994–95 tour of Australia, at the end of which he announced his retirement from test cricket. In September 1998 he announced his retirement from first-class cricket. Altogether, he scored 36,347 runs (including 94 centuries) at an average of 49.25 in a first-class career stretching back to 1975. Only 30 players in the history of the game have scored more first class runs.

Gatwick

Site of Gatwick Airport, West Sussex, England, situated 42 km/26 mi south of central London. Designated as London's second airport in 1954, it is now one of the city's three international airport facilities. Nearly 30 million passengers a year pass through its two terminals. A rail connection links Gatwick to Victoria Station, London.

Gatwick 'Airports Ltd' began operating in May 1936 with a scheduled service to Paris. Its official launch followed in June 1936 with the opening of the world's first circular air terminal. During World War II Gatwick was under military control, but it reopened as a civilian airport in 1946. After being designated as London's second airport, new building work began in 1956, and services recommenced in 1958. In 1959 about 368,000 passengers used the facility, mainly in the summer months. Passenger numbers grew rapidly and a second terminal (North Terminal) opened in 1988.

Gaudier-Brzeska, Henri born Henri Gaudier (1891–1915)

French sculptor, active in London from 1911. He is regarded as one of the outstanding sculptors of his generation. He studied art in Bristol, Nuremberg, and Munich, and became a member of the English Vorticist movement, which sought to reflect the energy of the industrial age through an angular, semi-abstract style. His works include the portrait *Horace Brodsky* (1913; Tate Gallery, London); and *Birds Erect* (1914; Museum of Modern Art, New York).

From 1913 his sculptures showed the influence of Constantin Brancusi, Jacob Epstein, and primitive art. He was killed in action during World War I.

Gay, John (1685–1732)

English poet and dramatist. He wrote *Trivia* (1716), a verse picture of 18th-century London. His *The Beggar's Opera* (1728), a 'Newgate pastoral' using traditional songs and telling of the love of Polly for highwayman Captain Macheath, was an extraordinarily popular success. Its satiric political touches led to the banning of *Polly*, a sequel. Bertolt Brecht (1898–1956) based his *Threepenny Opera* (1928) on the story of *The Beggar's Opera*.

> *Life is a jest; and all things show it.*
> *I thought so once; but now I know it.*
>
> John Gay English poet and dramatist.
> 'My Own Epitaph'

GCE

Abbreviation for **General Certificate of Education**, the public examination formerly taken at the age of 16 at Ordinary level (O level) and still taken at 18 at Advanced level (A level). The GCE O-level examination, aimed at the top 20% of the ability range, was superseded in 1988 by the General Certificate of Secondary Education (◊GCSE).

GCHQ

Abbreviation for **Government Communications Headquarters**, the centre of the British government's electronic surveillance operations, in Cheltenham, Gloucestershire. It monitors broadcasts of various kinds from all over the world. It was established in World War I, and was successful in breaking the German Enigma code in 1940.

In addition there are six listening stations: Bude, Cornwall; Culm Head, Somerset; Brora and Hawklaw, Scotland; Irton Moor, North Yorkshire; and Cheadle, Greater Manchester. There is an outpost in Cyprus. In 1982 Geoffrey Prime (1939–), a linguist at GCHQ, was convicted of handing the secrets of US spy satellites to the USSR. The right of GCHQ employees to have trade-union representation, which had been denied by successive Conservative governments, was restored by the Blair government in 1997.

GCSE

Abbreviation for **General Certificate of Secondary Education**, from 1988 the examination for 16-year-old pupils, superseding both GCE O level and CSE, and offering qualifications for up to 60% of school leavers in any particular subject.

The GCSE includes more practical and course work than O level, although course work was reduced in syllabuses from 1993. GCSE subjects are organized as part of the ◊national curriculum.

Geldof, Bob (1954–)

Irish rock singer. He was the leader of the group the Boomtown Rats 1975–86. In the mid-1980s he instigated the charity Band Aid, which raised about £60 million for famine relief, primarily for Ethiopia.

In partnership with musician Midge Ure (1953–), Geldof gathered together many pop celebrities of the day to record Geldof's song 'Do They Know It's Christmas?' (1984), donating all proceeds to charity (it sold 7 million copies). He followed it up with two simultaneous celebrity concerts in 1985 under the name Live Aid, one in London and one in Philadelphia, which were broadcast live worldwide. He was knighted in 1986.

Genée, Adeline stage name of Anina Margarete Kirstina Petra Jensen (1878–1970)

Danish-born British dancer, who settled in England in 1897. She was president of the Royal Academy of Dancing 1920–54. Her most famous role was Swanilda in *Coppélia*, which she danced with infectious vivacity and charm. She was made a DBE in 1950. Her work was commemorated by the Adeline Genée Theatre (1967–89), East Grinstead, Sussex.

general election

See ◊elections.

General Medical Council

Statutory UK body set up under the Medical Act of 1858 to maintain a register of qualified medical practitioners in the UK and to supervise and regulate the standards of medical education and qualifying examinations.

The Council may remove from the Medical Register any medical practitioner it finds guilty of serious professional misconduct, and may restore a name which it has erased. It is composed of representatives appointed by the Crown, by the universities that have medical faculties, by the medical corporations (such as the Royal College of Physicians), and directly by members of the profession as a whole.

The Medical Act of 1950 provided for a new body, the Medical Disciplinary Committee, to be set up within the Council to take over its disciplinary powers. Another provision of this Act is that practitioners found guilty of professional misconduct and ordered to be struck off the Register may within 28 days appeal to the Privy Council; such an appeal was not previously allowed. The law governing registration is set out in the Medical Act 1969.

I don't think that the possible death of 120 million people is a matter for charity. It is a matter of moral imperative.

Bob Geldof Irish rock singer. To Prime Minister Thatcher on the threatened famine in Africa 1985

General Strike

Nationwide strike called by the Trade Union Congress (TUC) on 3 May 1926 in support of striking miners.

The immediate cause of the 1926 general strike was the report of a royal commission on the coalmining industry (*Samuel Report* 1926) which, among other things, recommended a cut in wages. The mine-owners wanted longer hours as well as lower wages. The miners' union, under the leadership of A J Cook, resisted with the slogan 'Not a penny off the pay, not a minute on the day'. A coal strike started in early May 1926 and the miners asked the TUC to bring all major industries out on strike in support of the action; eventually it included more than 2 million workers. The Conservative government under Stanley Baldwin used troops, volunteers, and special constables to maintain food supplies and essential services, and had a monopoly on the information services, including BBC radio. After nine days the TUC ended the general strike, leaving the miners, who felt betrayed by the TUC, to remain on strike, unsuccessfully, until November 1926. The Trades Disputes Act of 1927 made general strikes illegal.

Genesis

English rock/pop group formed in 1967. Its members are Ray Wilson (1968–) vocalist; Mike Rutherford (1950–) on bass and guitar; and Tony Banks (1950–) on keyboards. Peter ◊Gabriel was the lead vocalist 1966–75 and Phil ◊Collins was drummer and lead vocalist until he left the group in 1996. By the end of the 1970s Genesis had established their position as one of the world's leading progressive rock bands and they continued their commercial success during the 1980s and 1990s.

They first had success with the albums *Foxtrot* (1972) and *Genesis Live* (1973). Known for their acclaimed live shows, they broke box office records in North America during their world tour of 1981–82. The hit album *Invisible Touch* (1986) was followed by a string of hit singles in the UK and USA. The album *We Can't Dance* was released in 1991 and *Calling All Stations*, their first album since Ray Wilson became their lead singer, was released in 1997.

genetic fingerprinting, or genetic profiling

Technique developed in the UK by Professor Alec Jeffreys (1950–), and now allowed as a means of legal identification. It determines the pattern of certain parts of the genetic material DNA that is unique to each individual. Like conventional fingerprinting, it can accurately distinguish humans from one another, with the exception of identical siblings from multiple births. It can be applied to as little material as a single cell.

The world's first national DNA database began operating in the UK in April 1995 in accordance with the 1994 Criminal Justice and Public Order Act, which states that those convicted or suspected of sex offences, serious assaults, or burglaries in England and Wales must provide a sample of saliva or hair for DNA analysis. By August 1995 the database held 45,000 genetic samples. In the UK, DNA testing was used nationally for the first time in 1996, involving the testing of 1,200 persons, in a police hunt for a murderer.

gentry

The lesser nobility, particularly in England and Wales, not entitled to sit in the House of Lords. By the later Middle Ages, it included knights, esquires, and gentlemen, and after the 17th century, baronets.

Geoffrey of Monmouth (*c.* 1100–1154)

Welsh writer and chronicler. While a canon at Oxford, he wrote *Historia Regum Britanniae/History of the Kings of Britain* in about 1139, which included accounts of the semi-legendary kings Lear, Cymbeline, and Arthur. He is also thought by some to be the author of *Vita Merlini*, a life of the legendary wizard. He was bishop-elect of St Asaph, North Wales, in 1151 and ordained a priest in 1152.

George

Six kings of Great Britain:

George I (1660–1727)

King of Great Britain and Ireland from 1714. He was the son of the first elector of Hannover, Ernest Augustus (1629–1698), and his wife Sophia, and a great-grandson of James I. He succeeded to the electorate in 1698, and became king on the death of Queen Anne. He attached himself to the Whigs, and spent most of his reign in Hannover, never having learned English.

Parliament, seeking to ensure a Protestant line of succession to oppose the claim of the Catholic ◊James Edward Stuart, made George third in line after Queen Anne and his mother. He was supported upon his succession by the Whigs, especially Stanhope, Charles Townshend, and Robert Walpole. The king grew more and more dependent upon his advisers as scandal surrounded him; his supporters turned against him, demanding freedom of action as the price of reconciliation.

George II (1683–1760)

King of Great Britain and Ireland from 1727, when he succeeded his father, George I. His victory at Dettingen in 1743, in the War of the Austrian Succession, was the last battle to be commanded by a British king. He married Caroline of Anspach in 1705, and was succeeded by his grandson, George III.

Under Queen Caroline's influence, Robert Walpole retained his ministry, begun during the reign of George I, and until his resignation in 1742, managed to keep Britain at peace. The Jacobite rebellion of 1745 was successfully put down by George's favourite son, William Augustus, Duke of Cumberland.

George III (1738–1820)

King of Great Britain and Ireland from 1760, when he succeeded his grandfather George II. His rule was marked by intransigence resulting in the loss of the American colonies, for which he shared the blame with his chief minister Lord North, and the emancipation of Catholics in England. Possibly suffering from ◊porphyria, he had repeated attacks of insanity, permanent from 1811. He was succeeded by his son George IV.

He married Princess Charlotte Sophia of Mecklenburg-Strelitz in 1761.

George IV (1762–1830)

King of Great Britain and Ireland from 1820, when he succeeded his father George III, for whom he had been regent during the king's period of insanity 1811–20. In 1785 he secretly married a Catholic widow, Maria ◊Fitzherbert, but in 1795 also married Princess ◊Caroline of Brunswick, in return for payment of his debts. He was a patron of the arts. His prestige was undermined by his treatment of Caroline (they separated in 1796), his dissipation, and his extravagance. He was succeeded by his brother, the duke of Clarence, who became William IV.

The King's party and mine are like two rival inns on the road, the George and the Angel.

Caroline of Brunswick Queen of George IV of Great Britain.
Remark made during her final attempt to be accepted as Queen, 1821

George V (1865–1936)

King of Great Britain from 1910, when he succeeded his father Edward VII. He was the second son, and became heir in 1892 on the death of his elder brother Albert, Duke of Clarence. In 1893, he married Princess Victoria Mary of Teck (Queen Mary), formerly engaged to his brother. During World War I he made several visits to the front. In 1917 he abandoned all German titles for himself and his family. The name of the royal house was changed from Saxe-Coburg-Gotha (popularly known as Brunswick or Hannover) to Windsor.

George VI (1895–1952)

King of Great Britain from 1936, when he succeeded after the abdication of his brother Edward VIII, who had succeeded their father George V. Created Duke of York in 1920, he married in 1923 Lady Elizabeth Bowes-Lyon (1900–), and their children are Elizabeth II and Princess Margaret. During World War II he visited the Normandy and Italian battlefields.

George Cross/Medal

The highest civilian award in Britain for acts of courage in circumstances of extreme danger. It was instituted in 1940 and was conferred on the island of Malta in 1942. The **George Medal**, also instituted in 1940, is a civilian award for acts of great courage.

George, St (died *c.* 303)

Patron saint of England. The story of St George rescuing a woman by slaying a dragon, evidently derived from the Greek Perseus legend, first appears in the 6th century. The cult of St George was introduced into western Europe by the Crusaders. Feast day 23 April.

He is said to have been martyred at Lydda in Palestine in 303, probably under the Roman emperor Diocletian, but the other elements of his legend are of doubtful historical accuracy.

Georgian

Period of English architecture, furnituremaking, and decorative art between 1714 and 1830. The architecture is mainly Classical in style, although external details and interiors were often rich in Rococo carving. Furniture was frequently made of mahogany and satinwood, and mass production became increasingly common; designers included Thomas Chippendale, George Hepplewhite, and Thomas Sheraton. The silver of this period is particularly fine, and ranges from the earlier, simple forms to the ornate, and from the Neo-Classical style of Robert Adam to the later, more decorated pre-Victorian taste.

Buildings of the period include many vast aristocratic mansions such as Holkham, Kedleston, Harewood, ◊Kenwood, and ◊Chatsworth; many Georgian houses; many churches of the new 'Protestant' type and Nonconformist meeting-houses; and important public buildings such as Chelsea Hospital and Somerset House.

There was keen rivalry during the second half of the 18th century between William Chambers, the upholder of Palladianism, and Robert ◊Adam, the practitioner of a more original style inspired by Greek and Roman archaeology.

John ◊Nash introduced **Regency** style, so-called because of its patronization by the Prince of Wales (later George IV) during his years as Prince Regent (1811–20). Decorous and refined, it is associated with an extensive use of stucco, and may be seen at Hove, Brighton, Weymouth, Cheltenham, Clifton and Tunbridge Wells, as well as in the terraces and mansions around 'the Regent's Park' in London. Examples of **Greek Revival**, which lasted for several decades abreast of the **Regency** style, include the Athenaeum Club, London

(1827–30) by Decimus Burton; and several buildings in Edinburgh by William Henry Playfair.

Gerald of Wales

English name of ◊Giraldus Cambrensis, medieval Welsh bishop and historian.

Gerhard, Roberto (1896–1970)

Spanish-born British composer. He studied with Enrique Granados and Arnold Schoenberg and settled in England in 1939, where he composed twelve-tone works in Spanish style. He composed the *Symphony No 1* (1952–55), followed by three more symphonies and chamber music incorporating advanced techniques.

Gertler, Mark (1891–1939)

English painter. He was a pacifist and a noncombatant during World War I, and his best-known work, *Merry-Go-Round* (1916; Tate Gallery, London), is often seen as an expressive symbol of anti-militarism. He suffered from depression and committed suicide.

Giant's Causeway

Stretch of basalt columns forming a headland on the north coast of Antrim, Northern Ireland. It was formed by an outflow of lava in Tertiary times which has solidified in polygonal columns. The Giant's Causeway and Causeway Coast became a World Heritage Site in 1986.

According to legend, the causeway was built to enable the giants to cross between Ireland and Scotland

Gibberd, Frederick Ernest (1908–1984)

English architect and town planner. He was a pioneer of the Modern Movement in England. His works include the new towns of Harlow, England, and Santa Teresa, Venezuela; the Catholic Cathedral, Liverpool (1962–67); the Central London Mosque, Regent's Park (1970–77), and buildings for London's Heathrow Airport (from 1950). He was knighted in 1967.

Gibbon, Edward (1737–1794)

English historian. He wrote one major work, arranged in three parts, *The History of the Decline and Fall of the Roman Empire* (1776–88), a continuous narrative from the 2nd century AD to the fall of Constantinople in 1453.

He began work on it while in Rome in 1764. Although immediately successful, he was compelled to reply to attacks on his account of the early development of Christianity by a 'Vindication' in 1779.

Gibbon, Lewis Grassic pen name of James Leslie Mitchell (1901–1935)

Scottish novelist. He was the author of the trilogy *A Scots Quair*, comprising *Sunset Song*, *Cloud Howe*, and *Grey Granite* (1932–34), set in the Mearns, south of Aberdeen, where he was born and brought up. Under his real name he wrote anthropological works and novels, which included *Stained Radiance* (1930) and *Spartacus* (1933). It was under his pseudonym, however, that he made his major contribution to Scottish literature in *A Scots Quair*. Ostensibly a story of a Scots peasant's education, series of marriages, and her son's involvement in the working-class struggle, it is also an analysis of the transition from a rural to an industrial economy, with its social consequences, and, at a third level, an allegory of Scottish history with the heroine personifying Scotland.

Gibbons, Grinling (1648–1720)

Dutch woodcarver who settled in England around 1667. He produced delicately carved wooden panels (largely of birds, flowers, and fruit) for St Paul's Cathedral, London, and for many large English country houses including Petworth House, Sussex, and Hampton Court, Surrey. He was carpenter to English monarchs from Charles II to George I.

Features of his style include acanthus whorls in oak, and trophies of musical instruments in oak and limewood. Works in marble and bronze include a statue of James I (Whitehall).

Gibbons, Orlando (1583–1625)

English composer. He wrote many sacred works for the Anglican church; *Cries of London* for voices and strings; instrumental fantasias and other works; and madrigals including *The Silver Swan* for five voices (1612). From a family of musicians, he became organist at Westminster Abbey, London, in 1623.

GIANT'S CAUSEWAY *The strikingly unusual rock formations to be seen at the promontory of Giant's Causeway, in County Antrim, Northern Ireland, are the result of molten basalt cooling rapidly some 60 million years ago. Their name derives from the legend that they are stepping stones used by a giant to cross the Irish Sea. Corel*

Gibbons, Stella (Dorothea) (1902–1989)
English journalist and novelist. Her *Cold Comfort Farm* (1932) is a classic parody of the regional novel, in particular the works of Mary ◊Webb. She followed this with a series of other successful novels.

Gibraltar (Arabic **Jebel Tariq** 'Mountain of Tariq')
British dependency, situated on a narrow rocky promontory at the southern tip of Spain
Area 6.5 sq km/2.5 sq mi
Population (1993) 29,000.

The fortress was taken by the Moors in 711 who finally ceded it to Spain in 1462. Captured from Spain in 1704 by English admiral George Rooke (1650–1709), it was ceded to Britain under the Treaty of Utrecht (1713). A referendum in 1967 confirmed the wish of the people to remain in association with the UK, but Spain continues to claim sovereignty and closed the border from 1969 to 1985. In 1989, the UK government announced it would reduce the military garrison by half. Ground troops were withdrawn in 1991, but navy and airforce units remained.

Gibson, Alexander (1926–1995)
Scottish conductor. He co-founded Scottish Opera in 1962: *Les Troyens* (1969) and *Der Ring des Nibelungen* (1971) were notable achievements.

Gibson, Guy Penrose (1918–1944)
English bomber pilot of World War II. He became famous as leader of the 'dambuster raids' 16–17 May 1943; he formed 617 squadron specifically to bomb the Ruhr Dams, and as wing commander led the raid personally, dropping the first bomb on the Mohne Dam. He was awarded the Victoria Cross for his leadership in this action.

Following the dambuster raid, he was relieved of operational duties and accompanied Churchill to Canada and the USA late in 1944. On returning to Britain he obtained permission for 'one more operation', flying a De Havilland Mosquito on a raid on relatively unimportant targets in Bavaria. On the return flight his plane crashed in Holland and he was killed.

Gielgud, (Arthur) John (1904–)
English actor and director. One of the greatest Shakespearean actors of his time, he made his debut at the Old Vic in 1921 and played Hamlet in 1929. His stage appearances range from roles in works by Anton Chekhov and Richard Sheridan to those of Alan Bennett, Harold Pinter, and David Storey. He won an Academy Award for his role as a butler in the film *Arthur* (1981).

GIELGUD, JOHN *As well as being distinguished as a Shakespearean stage actor, Gielgud has appeared in many popular films, ranging in style from* Murder on the Orient Express *(1974) to* Prospero's Books *(1991). Corbis*

Gielgud's other films include *Secret Agent* (1936), *Richard III* (1955), *Becket* (1964), *Oh! What a Lovely War* (1969), *Murder on the Orient Express* (1974), *Providence* (1977), *Chariots of Fire* (1980), *Prospero's Books* (1991), *Shining Through* and *The Power of One* (both 1992), *First Knight* (1995), and *Portrait of a Lady* (1996).

Television appearances include *The Best of Friends* (1992) and *Scarlett* (1994).

Gilbert, William (1540–1603)
English scientist who studied magnetism and static electricity, deducing that the Earth's magnetic field behaves as if a bar magnet joined the North and South poles. His book on magnets, published in 1600, is the first printed scientific book based wholly on experimentation and observation.

Gilbert was the first English scientist to accept Nicolas Copernicus' idea that the Earth rotates on its axis and revolves around the Sun. He also believed that the stars are at different distances from the Earth and might be orbited by habitable planets, but erroneously thought that the planets were held in their orbits by magnetic forces.

Gilbert discovered many important facts about magnetism, such as the laws of attraction and repulsion and magnetic dip. He also investigated static electricity and differentiated between magnetic attraction and electric attraction (as he called the ability of an electrostatically charged body to attract light objects).

Gilbert, W(illiam) S(chwenck) (1836–1911)
English humorist and dramatist. He collaborated with composer Arthur ◊Sullivan, providing the libretti for their series of light comic operas from 1871 performed by the ◊D'Oyly Carte Opera Company; they include *HMS Pinafore* (1878), *The Pirates of Penzance* (1879), and *The Mikado* (1885). Knighted 1907.

Gilbert and George, Gilbert Proesch (1943–) and George Passmore (1942–)
English painters and performance artists. They became known in the 1960s for their presentations of themselves as

works of art, or 'living sculptures', holding poses for many hours. They also produce large emblematic photoworks. Their use of both erotic and ambiguous political material has made them controversial. They received the Turner Award in 1986. Their work has been very widely exhibited, notably in China in 1993.

Gilchrist, Percy Carlyle (1851–1935)

English metallurgist. He devised a method of producing low-phosphorus steel from high-phosphorus ores, such as those commonly occurring in the UK. This meant that steel became cheaply available to British industry.

Giles, Carl Ronald (1916–1995)

English cartoonist for the *Daily Express* and *Sunday Express* from 1943, noted for his creation of a family with a formidable 'Grandma'.

Self-taught, he became an animator on advertising films after working as an office boy for a film company, and in 1938 joined *Reynolds News* as a cartoonist.

gill

Imperial unit of volume for liquid measure, equal to one-quarter of a pint or 5 fluid ounces (0.142 litre), traditionally used in selling alcoholic drinks.

In southern England it is also called a noggin, but in northern England the large noggin is used, which is two gills.

Gill, (Arthur) Eric (Rowton) (1882–1940)

English sculptor, graphic designer, engraver, and writer. He designed the typefaces Perpetua in 1925 and Gill Sans (without serifs) in 1927, and created monumental stone sculptures with clean, simplified outlines, such as *Prospero and Ariel* (1929–31) on Broadcasting House, London.

He studied lettering at the Central School of Art in London, and began his career carving inscriptions on tombstones. Gill was a leader in the revival of interest in lettering and book design. He engraved for his own press, St Dominic, ánd for the Golden Cockerell Press. His views on art combined Catholicism, socialism, and the Arts and Crafts tradition.

Gill, David (1843–1914)

Scottish astronomer. He pioneered the use of photography to catalogue stars and also made much use of a heliometer, determining the solar parallax and measuring the distances of 20 of the brighter and nearer southern stars. KCB 1900.

Gillingham

Largest of the ◊Medway towns, in Kent, England; population (1991) 92,100. The town, which includes the former village of Rainham within its boundaries, merges with ◊Chatham. Gillingham was closely associated with the Royal Navy until the closure of the dockyard at Chatham in 1994.

The old centre of Rainham village has two old churches, one of them Norman. The Corps of Royal Engineers, with its military museum, founded in 1912, is attached to the town.

Gillray, James (1757–1815)

English caricaturist. Creator of over 1,500 cartoons, his fierce, sometimes gross caricatures satirized George III, the Prince of Wales, politicians, and the social follies of his day, and later targeted the French and Napoleon.

Initially a letter engraver and actor, he was encouraged to become a caricaturist by the works of William Hogarth, and he was celebrated for his coloured etchings, directed against the French and the English court. Gillray's works form a brilliant if unconventional history of the late Georgian and Napoleonic period. He became insane in later life.

Ginner, (Isaac) Charles (1878–1952)

English painter. His street scenes and landscapes were strongly influenced by Post-Impressionism. He settled in London in 1910, and was one of the London Group (an art society formed in 1915 which still exists).

Giraldus Cambrensis, Welsh Gerallt Gymro (*c.* 1146–*c.* 1220)

Welsh historian, born in Pembrokeshire. He studied in Paris, took holy orders in about 1172, and soon afterwards became archdeacon of Brecknock. In 1184 he accompanied Prince John to Ireland. He was elected bishop of St Davids in 1198, but failed to gain possession of his see. He wrote a history of the conquest of Ireland by Henry II.

GILLRAY, JAMES *A satire on King George III and Queen Charlotte by the English caricaturist James Gillray. Gillray was one of the most brilliant of all caricaturists and he was one of the first artists to devote virtually his whole career to this field. His prints made a fortune for their publisher, but Gillray had an unhappy personal life and died insane. Corbis*

Girl Guides

Female equivalent of the ◊Scout organization, founded in 1910 in the UK by Robert Baden-Powell and his sister Agnes. There are three branches: Brownie Guides (age 7–11); Guides (10–16); Ranger Guides (14–20); they are led by Guiders (adult leaders). The World Association of Girl Guides and Girl Scouts (as they are known in the USA) has some 9 million members (1998).

In the UK there are some 660,000 members of the Guide Association (1998).

Girtin, Thomas (1775–1802)

English landscape painter, one of the most important watercolourists of the 18th century. His work is characterized by broad washes of strong colour and bold compositions, for example *The White House at Chelsea* (1800; Tate Gallery, London). He was a friend of J M W Turner.

In addition to scenes of the English countryside, such as *View on the Wharfe*, he created some excellent views of Paris (1801–02) which were subsequently made into soft-ground etchings, and on his return from France worked on a vast panorama of London (the *Eidometropolis*). Six sketches for this work are preserved in the British Museum. Though he died of tuberculosis at the age of 27, he made an important contribution of the development of English watercolour painting.

Gissing, George Robert (1857–1903)

English writer. His work deals with social issues and has a tone of gloomy pessimism. Among his books are *New Grub Street* (1891), about a writer whose marriage breaks up, and the semi-autobiographical *Private Papers of Henry Ryecroft* (1903).

His first novel, *Workers in the Dawn*, appeared in 1880. Between 1885 and 1895 he wrote 14 novels, including *Demos* (1886), his first real success; *The Odd Woman* (1893), which is about early feminists; and *The Nether World* (1889) about the London poor.

Gladstone, William Ewart (1809–1898)

British Liberal politician, four times prime minister. He entered Parliament as a Tory in 1833 and held ministerial office, but left the party in 1846 and after 1859 identified himself with the Liberals. He was chancellor of the Exchequer 1852–55 and 1859–66, and prime minister 1868–74, 1880–85, 1886, and 1892–94. He introduced elementary education in 1870 and vote by secret ballot in 1872 and many reforms in Ireland, although he failed in his efforts to get a Home Rule Bill passed.

In his first term as prime minister he carried through a series of reforms, including the disestablishment of the Church of Ireland, the Irish Land Act, and the abolition of the purchase of army commissions and of religious tests in the universities.

Gladstone strongly resisted Benjamin Disraeli's imperialist and pro-Turkish policy during the latter's government of 1874–80, not least because of Turkish pogroms against subject Christians, and by his Midlothian campaign of 1879 helped to overthrow Disraeli. Gladstone's second government carried the second Irish Land Act and the Reform Act of 1884 but was confronted with problems in Ireland, Egypt, and South Africa, and lost prestige through its failure to relieve General ◊Gordon in Sudan. Returning to office in 1886, Gladstone introduced his first Home Rule Bill, which was defeated by the secession of the Liberal Unionists, and he thereupon resigned. After six years' opposition he formed his last government; his second Home Rule Bill was rejected by the Lords, and in 1894 he resigned. He led a final crusade against the massacre of Armenian Christians in 1896.

Glamis Castle

Fortress near Glamis village, Angus, Scotland, 20 km/12 mi north of Dundee. It has been the seat of the Lyon family, later earls of Strathmore, since 1372. Its central tower dates from the 15th century, but the castle was greatly enlarged from 1650 to 1696. Glamis is the legendary setting of Shakespeare's *Macbeth*.

The castle is also famed for the legend of a secret chamber, supposedly known only to each heir.

Glamorgan, Welsh Morgannwg

Three counties of south Wales – ◊Mid Glamorgan, ◊South Glamorgan, and ◊West Glamorgan – created in 1974 from the former county of Glamorganshire. All are on the Bristol Channel. In 1996 Mid Glamorgan was divided amongst Rhondda Cynon Taff, Merthyr Tydfil, Bridgend, and Vale of Glamorgan; South Glamorgan was divided amongst Cardiff and Vale of Glamorgan; and West Glamorgan was divided into Neath Port Talbot and Swansea.

glam rock, or glitter rock

Pop music in a conventional rock style performed by elaborately made-up and overdressed musicians. English singers Marc Bolan (1947–1977) and David ◊Bowie and the band Roxy Music (1970–83) pioneered glam rock in the early 1970s.

Glasgow

City and unitary authority in west-central Scotland; the unitary authority formed in 1995 from the majority of land from Glasgow District Council of Strathclyde Region
Area 176 sq km/68 sq mi
Industries engineering, chemicals, printing, whisky blending, brewing, electronics, textiles, light manufacturing
Population (1995) 618,400.
Features
Buildings include the Cathedral of St Mungo, which dates mainly from the 13th century; Provand's Lordship (1475; the oldest dwelling-house in the city); the Cross Steeple (part of the historic Tolbooth); the universities of Glasgow, established in 1451 (present buildings constructed in 1868–70 to designs by George Gilbert ◊Scott). Other buildings of note include the Kelvingrove Art Gallery; the Glasgow School of Art, designed by C R ◊Mackintosh; the Burrell Collection at Pollock Park, bequeathed by shipping magnate William Burrell (1861–1958); the Gallery of Modern Art; the Mitchell Library; and 19th-century Greek Revival buildings designed

GLASGOW *The skyline of Glasgow, Scotland's largest and most populous city. Glasgow was once famous as a centre of heavy industry, shipbuilding, and engineering, and infamous as the site of some of Britain's worst slum tenement housing. With the decline of manufacturing and the clearance of the slums, the city has successfully marketed itself since the 1980s as a tourist centre, with attractions such as the eclectic Burrell Collection of art treasures. Hamish Williamson/Collections*

by Alexander Thomson. Glasgow's Hampden Park Stadium is a Millennium Commission Landmark Project.

History

There was a settlement on the Clyde when St Mungo arrived in the 6th century to convert the Strathclyde Britons. Willliam the Lion made Glasgow a burgh of barony in about 1178, and it became a royal burgh under James VI in 1636. The Union of Scotland and England in 1707, though at first resented, brought increasing prosperity; in the 18th century trade with the Americas for tobacco, sugar, and cotton was very important. In the 19th century the Industrial Revolution had a great influence on the city, and its shipbuilding industry developed.

Topography

Glasgow lies on both sides of the River Clyde and is surrounded by hills; the city is partly built on the river terrace and partly on glacially deposited hills (drumlins).

Architecture

Glasgow possesses some of the most impressive buildings in Scotland, situated chiefly in the commercial centre of the city. The main square is George Square (sometimes called the 'Valhalla of Glasgow' because of its many statues) in which a cenotaph occupies a prominent place. The municipal buildings, formally opened by Queen Victoria in 1888, stand on the east side of George Square; the General Post Office occupies the south side; and on the west is the Italianate Merchants' House. Two of the main streets are Sauchiehall Street, in which are the McLellan Galleries, former home of the city art collection; and Argyll Street, the busiest commercial thoroughfare, leading to Trongate, the oldest part of the city. The Trongate steeple is at the eastern end of Trongate, and a little further on lies the cross. St Mungo's Cathedral is situated northeast of the city on the side of the valley of the Molindinar Burn.

Built in the Early English style, the cathedral is in the form of a Latin cross with imperfect transepts. It was used after the Reformation as three separate churches: the Inner High, occupying the choir; the Outer High, occupying the nave; and the Laigh (Low) or Barony, occupying the crypt with its pillars and pointed arches. The stained glass windows in the crypt and chapter house were executed by various British and foreign artists. St Mungo formed a bishopric here in about 543. The see was restored by David, prince of Cumbria, in 1115, and his preceptor John Achaius, bishop of Glasgow, laid the foundations of a cathedral in 1133 (consecrated in 1136). This was probably destroyed by fire in about 1176. Carved bosses in the vaulting of the lower church commemorate those who carried out further building work on the cathedral, including Bishop Jocelyn (1175–99), Bishop Bondington, and Comyn, Lord of Kilbride (13th century). The rood screen and the unfinished south transept were added in the 15th century by Archbishop Blacadder. St Mungo is buried under the central vaulting of the lower church, and a well named after him is nearby.

Education and culture

Glasgow has three universities, the oldest of which is Glasgow University at Gilmorehill in the West End. Strathclyde University is east of George Square, while Glasgow Caledonian University is to the north of George Square. Other important colleges and institutions include the Glasgow School of Art, and the Royal Scottish Academy of Music and Drama.

Glasgow has several excellent art galleries and museums. The outstanding Burrell Collection, gathered by William Burrell, was presented to the city in 1944, but was not unveiled to the public until 1983. The gallery was built especially for the collection. Kelvingrove Art Gallery and Museum was first opened as part of the 1901 International Exhibition and officially opened as an art gallery and museum in 1902. The art gallery is noted for its collection of European painting from the 15th century onwards. The museum has a section on shipbuilding, which includes the Spencer collection of early ship models, and houses the Scott collection of arms and armour. The Kelvin Hall (1927) is the annual venue of the city's exhibitions, fairs, and carnivals. Glasgow's Libraries Department has its headquarters at the Mitchell Library. Stirling's library and the commercial library are housed in the Royal Exchange.

The Scottish Orchestra in Glasgow, where John Barbirolli first won recognition, was established early in the 20th century. The Citizen's Theatre is one of the chief Scottish creative dramatic centres. Parks and open spaces include Glasgow Green in the east; in the southwest are Queen's Park, Bellahouston Park, Roukenglen, and Linn Park; to the north is Springburn Park; to the northeast are Alexandra Park and Hogganfield; and to the northwest is Kelvingrove Park. In Victoria Park is the 'fossil grove', consisting of petrified trees of the Carboniferous period. The botanic gardens contain the Kibble Crystal Palace, a large glass structure and winter garden, at one time used for concerts and meetings. Hampden Park, the ground of Queen's Park Football Club, can accommodate 140,000 spectators. Glasgow is the venue for the 1999 European City of Architecture and Design Festival.

The Clyde

The upper river, originally a fordable salmon river, has been successfully straightened and deepened in such a manner that the scour of the tides keeps the channel clear and comparatively little dredging is required. The rise and fall of the tide at Glasgow bridge varies between 3 m/10 ft and 4 m/13 ft. The River Clyde is spanned by many bridges. The Dalmarnock Bridge was erected in 1891; the Rutherglen Bridge was reconstructed in 1896. St Andrew's suspension bridge spans the river from the Green to Hutcheson Town, a district also approached by the Albert Bridge. The Victoria Bridge, built of granite, replaced the old bridge constructed by Bishop Rae in the middle of the 14th century. The most important of all the bridges, the Glasgow or Broomielaw Bridge, composed of granite, is a continuation of Jamaica Street; reconstructed in 1899, it proved inadequate for the constantly increasing traffic, and the George V Bridge was opened a short distance downstream in 1927. Twin road tunnels have been constructed under the Clyde at Whiteinch in order to relieve traffic congestion in the city.

Glasgow and Clydeside sustained severe bomb damage during World War II, notably in March 1941, when 1,235 people were killed and 40,000 houses damaged. In Clydebank only eight houses were left undamaged.

Communications

Direct transatlantic flights from Glasgow International Airport were introduced in 1990. The city has an urban motorway running through and over the city (including the high Kingston bridge); its construction involved major demolition and reconstruction of the greater part of the inner city. Glasgow has two major railway stations and a small underground system. Glasgow's water supply is taken from Loch Katrine, in Stirling unitary authority. The Loch Katrine waterworks were opened by Queen Victoria in 1859. The supply is augmented with water from Loch Arklet (1914) and Glen Finglass (1958).

Economy

Glasgow maintained the reputation of the Clyde as one of the greatest shipbuilding rivers in the world; many ships of all classes were built there, including the world's largest liners: *Queen Mary*, *Queen Elizabeth*, and *Queen Elizabeth II*, and the battleship *HMS Vanguard*. Most shipbuilding is on the south bank of the Clyde and Glasgow's importance as a world ranking centre has declined considerably. Glasgow engineers built the first airship to cross the Atlantic, and also the Forth Bridge and London's Tower Bridge.

While the heavier industries of shipbuilding and engineering have been predominant, the Clyde area also developed lighter industries, producing textiles, carpets, threads, sewing machines and foods. Industries established include the manufacture of motor trailers, optical equipment, scientific apparatus, jet engines, and motor vehicle components; electric lamps, batteries, and electric household appliances; silk and artificial silk garments; seamless containers; razor blades; and motor service equipment. Established firms have diversified into the manufacture of mechanical loaders and excavators, synthetic resin glues and insulated cloths, machines for bottle-making and labelling, gravel and sand-washing, and the mechanical packing of foodstuffs, and glass silk for heat and sound insulation. The city also has a long tradition of warehousing, commerce, insurance, banking, and general marketing.

Population

Even before local government reorganization in 1975, the population of Glasgow was declining. This was partly a planned dispersal to new towns such as Cumbernauld, but the clearance of 29 specified comprehensive redevelopment areas, including some slum and tenement zones, also caused some displacement of population. The city is the administrative, social, and service centre for the Glasgow conurbation, which extends from Gourock on the west to Carluke on the east; it is thus one of the largest continuously built-up areas in Britain. The majority of the housing stock is owned by the city corporation.

Glasgow School

Either of two distinct groups of Scottish artists. The earlier of the two groups, also known as the **Glasgow Boys**, was a loose association of late-19th-century artists influenced by the Barbizon School and Impressionism. Leading members were James Guthrie and John ◊Lavery. The later, more important group was part of the Art Nouveau movement, and included Charles Rennie ◊Mackintosh.

Glasse, Hannah (1708–1770)

British cookery writer whose *The Art of Cookery made Plain and Easy*, first published in 1747 and in print until 1824, is regarded as the first classic recipe book in Britain.

She was the most influential British cookery writer before ◊Mrs Beeton.

Glastonbury

Market town in Somerset, southwest England, on the River Brue, 8 km/5 mi southwest of Wells; population (1996 est) 8,100. Light industries include injection moulding, and the production of footwear and leather goods. Tourism and warehousing are also important. **Glastonbury Tor**, a hill crowned by a ruined 14th-century church tower, rises to 159 m/522 ft. ◊Glastonbury lake village, occupied from around 150 BC to AD50, lies 5 km/3 mi to the northwest.

Glastonbury Abbey, originally established in the 4th or 5th century, is thought to be on the site of the earliest Christian foundation in England, traditionally established by St Joseph of Arimathaea in about AD 63. Glastonbury has been associated with ◊Avalon, said in Celtic mythology to have been the burial place of the legendary King Arthur and Queen Guinevere. The **Glastonbury Festival** is a pop music festival held outside the town most Junes.

Glastonbury lake village

English Iron Age settlement near Godney, 5 km/3 mi northwest of Glastonbury, Somerset, in the Somerset Levels. Occupied from around 150 BC to AD 50, the lake dwelling was sited in the former marshy seas around **Glastonbury Tor**, and constructed on an artificial island of wooden piles. At its greatest extent the village contained 18 round houses, supporting about 200 people.

Peaty wetland soils have preserved numerous artefacts indicating a prosperous Celtic society; finds include jewellery, pottery, cooking utensils, and farming, hunting, fishing, and weaving implements, many exhibiting the influences of La Tène culture. The Glastonbury Lake Village Museum is housed in the 15th-century Tribunal, Glastonbury.

The settlement was discovered in 1892 by Arthur Bulleid, and a couple of smaller satellite sites have also been identified.

Development

The Somerset Levels have been inhabited during the summer months (the dry season) since Neolithic times. Numerous hunting trails, travelling, and trading routes across the marshes have been detected. The Sweet Track, an ancient raised trackway from Shapwick to Westhay, passing 6 km/4 mi to the west of Glastonbury, has been dated to 3806–7 BC by dendrochronology (tree-ring dating), making it the world's oldest known road. The Glastonbury lake village developed from a very small summer settlement, established in about 150 BC, expanding to accommodate a maximum of 18 dwellings. Remains of round houses found on the site indicate numerous phases of rebuilding, the huts having a life expectancy of around 35 years. Rising water levels in about AD 50 caused the site to be abandoned. The marshes have since been artificially drained.

Culture

Two major trade routes influenced the village, evidenced in the unusually high standard of decoration on pottery found at the site. Links with the Atlantic sea route from Spain and Brittany to Cornwall, Wales, Scotland, and Ireland are indicated by Breton fleur-de-lis designs; while the central trade route of the Southern Belgae, across southern England from Gaul, brought La Tène styles. The community was wealthy, producing a surplus which enabled the acquisition of traded goods. Activities included sheep rearing, weaving, fishing, hunting, and interaction with other local settlements. Its kitchen middens (refuse heaps) indicate the consumption of a large amount of pelican, now extinct in Britain.

An Englishman, even if he is alone, forms an orderly queue of one.

GEORGE MIKES Hungarian-born British writer.
How To Be An Alien (1946). Queueing had become second-nature in Britain during World War II

---

glebe

Landed endowment of a parish church, designed to support the priest. It later became necessary to supplement this with taxation.

glee

Part song, usually for male voices, in not less than three parts, much cultivated by English composers in the 18th and early 19th centuries. The word is derived from the Anglo-Saxon *gliw* ('entertainment'), particularly musical entertainment. Webbe, Stevens, Callcott, Horsley, Attwood, Battishill, Cooke, and others cultivated the glee.

Glencoe

Valley in the Highland unitary authority, Scotland, extending 16 km/10 mi east from Rannoch Moor to Loch Leven. The mountains rise steeply on either side to over 1,000 m/3,300 ft, and the River Coe flows through the valley. Thirty-eight members of the Macdonald clan were massacred in Glencoe on 13 February 1692 by government troops led by Robert Campbell of Glenlyon; 300 escaped.

The area is popular for winter sports and rock-climbing. The Glencoe chair-lift and ski area lies just beyond the glen on the western side of Rannoch Moor.

Glendower, Owen Welsh **Owain Glyndwr (*c.* 1359–*c.* 1416)**

Welsh nationalist leader of a successful revolt against the English in North Wales, who defeated Henry IV in three campaigns 1400–02, although Wales was reconquered 1405–13. Glendower disappeared in 1416 after some years of guerrilla warfare.

Glendower, Sons of, Welsh Meibion Glyndwr

Welsh guerrilla group, active from 1979 against what they perceive to be England's treatment of Wales as a colonial possession. Houses owned by English people in the principality, and offices of estate agents dealing in them, are targets for arson or bombing. It is named after Owen Glendower, the medieval leader of Welsh rebellions against English rule.

Gleneagles

Glen in Perth and Kinross, Scotland, 2 km/1 mi south of Auchterarder, famous for its golf courses, hotel, and for the **Gleneagles Agreement**, formulated in 1977 at the Gleneagles Hotel by Commonwealth heads of government, that 'every practical step (should be taken) to discourage contact or competition by their nationals' with South Africa, in opposition to apartheid.

Glenrothes

Town and administrative headquarters of ◊Fife, Scotland, 10 km/6 mi north of Kirkcaldy, designated a new town from 1948; population (1991) 38,650. Industries include the manufacture of electronics and plastics, and food processing.

Glen Roy

Narrow valley of the River Roy, in Highland unitary authority, west Scotland, about 21 km/13 mi northeast of Fort William. It is 22 km/14 mi in length. Ice Age glaciation has left regular and distinctly formed terraces on each side of the glen, known as the Parallel Roads of Glen Roy, which represent the three levels of a former loch.

Glitter, Gary stage name of Paul Gadd (1944–)

English rock singer and songwriter, known as the 'King of Glam Rock', whose songs include the 1970s hits 'Do You Wanna Touch? (Oh Yeah)', 'I'm The Leader of The Gang (I Am)', and 'I Love You Love Me Love'.

GLOBE THEATRE *In 1989, excavations on the south bank of the River Thames at Bankside in London unearthed the foundations of the Globe Theatre, where most of William Shakespeare's plays were performed during his lifetime. This replica theatre was built on a site close to the original, with the help of funds from the National Lottery. It was completed in 1997, and plays are now regularly staged there. Richard Kalina/Shakespeare's Globe*

Globe Theatre

17th-century London theatre, octagonal and open to the sky, near Bankside, Southwark, where many of Shakespeare's plays were performed by Richard Burbage and his company. It was burned down in 1613, rebuilt in 1614, and pulled down in 1644. The reconstructed Globe Theatre was opened to the public in August 1996, largely due to the campaigning efforts of actor Sam Wanamaker. Mark ◊Rylance was appointed the first artistic director of the Globe in 1995.

The original theatre was built in 1599 by Cuthbert Burbage. It was burned down after a cannon, fired during a performance of *Henry VIII*, set light to the thatch. The site was rediscovered in October 1989 near the remains of the contemporaneous Rose Theatre. The new Globe Theatre opened to the public with a performance of Shakespeare's *The Two Gentlemen of Verona*, the first stage production to be held on the site of the Elizabethan theatre in more than 380 years.

Glorious Revolution

Events surrounding the removal of James II from the throne in 1689; see ◊Revolution, the Glorious, for a feature on the impact of William III's accession to the throne.

Glossop

Town in Derbyshire, England, on the northern fringe of the Peak District National Park and 19 km/12 mi east of the city centre of Manchester. Industries include paper milling and the manufacture of textiles, clothing, and rubber.

Gloster Gladiator

British aircraft; the last biplane fighter to be used by the RAF.

It was introduced in 1936 and saw a good deal of action in the first months of World War II. **Sea Gladiators** (the Fleet Air Arm version) took part in the defence of Malta in 1940. It had a top speed of 400 kph/250 mph and was armed with four machine guns.

Gloster Meteor

First British jet fighter; the only Allied jet aircraft to see combat service during World War II. Its speed made it capable of pursuing the V-1 flying bombs and it was sent to airstrips on the continent to deal with the Messerschmitt Me262, its German equivalent, though the two never actually met in combat.

The Meteor began development in 1941 and entered service in 1944. It was a twin-engine low-wing monoplane, with a top speed of 660 kph/410 mph and four 20 mm cannon.

Gloucester, Roman Glevum

City, port, and administrative headquarters of ◊Gloucestershire, southwest England, on the River Severn, 67 km/42 mi northeast of Bristol; population (1996 est) 106,800. It is a finance and insurance centre, and manufactures aerospace equipment, ice cream and frozen foods, machinery (lifting, fuel vending, compressors), optical equipment, information technology, and camping goods. Salmon fisheries in the Severn are a valuable resource.

Gloucester was the Roman colony of **Glevum**, established in the late 1st century AD. The city's 11th–14th-century cathedral has a Norman nave and includes early examples of Perpendicular-style architecture. The Three Choirs Music Festival is held here every three years (in turn with Hereford and Worcester).

History

Situated to the west of the Cotswold Hills, at the lowest crossing point of the Severn, the Roman settlement of Glevum became one of the four *coloniae* of Roman Britain. It was fortified with walls, and its town plan was based around a central cross at the meeting point of four roads. Henry III was crowned in the cathedral in 1216. Supporting the Parliamentarians in the Civil War, Gloucester withstood a siege in 1643. The city became an important inland port after the opening of the Gloucester and Sharpness Canal in 1827, which linked the city to the Bristol Channel.

Features

The docks have been redeveloped and include the Robert Opie Museum of Advertising and Packaging (opened in 1984) and the National Waterways Museum. The regional offices of the British Waterways Board are located in Gloucester, with responsibility for navigable waterways. The church of St Mary-de-Crypt, dating from the 12th century, includes the tomb of Robert Raikes, who founded the Sunday School movement in Gloucester in 1780. The City Museum and Art Gallery includes Roman relics found in the city, and the Folk Museum illustrates the social history of the area. Redevelopment of the Cheltenham and Gloucester College of Higher Education began in 1993.

Some 9 km/6 mi from Gloucester lies Prinknash Abbey, on the site of a former residence of the abbots of Gloucester, occupied since 1928 by Benedictine monks.

Gloucester Cathedral

This great abbey church did not become a cathedral until 1541, four decades after its completion. The first abbey was founded in 681, and assumed Benedictine rule in 1022. Its post-Conquest rebuilding began in 1089 (completed around 1120), and of this period the nave, crypt and much of the structure survive. The nave has an Early English stone vault, completed in 1242. Edward II, killed at Berkely Castle, was buried here in 1327 and his shrine became an important centre of pilgrimage. The wealth gained from the pilgrims funded the reconstruction of the abbey and church. From 1337 much of the church was remodelled in the Perpendicular style, although the Norman core was preserved. The cathedral's south transept is an early example of the Perpendicular style, and the cloisters (about 1370–1410) include the earliest example of fan vaulting in England. The cathedral's east window is the largest medieval stained-glass window in England, and the first extant Perpendicular window (1331–37). The church received cathedral status from Henry VIII.

Gloucester, Richard Alexander Walter George, Duke of Gloucester (1944–)

Prince of the UK. Grandson of ◊George V, he succeeded his father to the dukedom when his elder brother Prince William (1941–72) was killed in an air crash. In 1972 he married Birgitte van Deurs (1946–), daughter of a Danish lawyer. His heir is his son Alexander, Earl of Ulster (1974–).

Gloucestershire

County of southwest England
Area 2,640 sq km/1,019 sq mi
Towns and cities ◊Gloucester (administrative headquarters), Cheltenham, Cirencester, Stroud, Tewkesbury
Physical Cotswold Hills; River Severn and tributaries
Features Berkeley Castle, where Edward II was murdered; Prinknash Abbey, where pottery is made; Cotswold Farm Park, near Stow-on-the-Wold, which has rare and ancient breeds of farm animals; pre-Norman churches at Cheltenham and Cleeve; Gloucester Cathedral; Tewkesbury Abbey, with early 12th-century nave
Industries aerospace industry; light engineering; manufacturing (bricks, carpets, furniture, glass, pins, pottery, tiles, watches); plastics; timber
Agriculture cereals (in the Cotswolds); fruit (apples and pears); cider; dairy products ('double Gloucester' cheese was formerly made here); sheep farming
Population (1994) 549,500
Famous people Edward Jenner, John Keble, Gustav Holst
History There are Roman and early British remains, mainly in the Cotswolds. The county is mentioned in the Anglo-Saxon Chronicle of 1016. Woollen cloth, previously an important product, is now manufactured only in the Stroud Valley and at Dursley. Silk-weaving was introduced into the Stroud Valley in the 17th century, but has since died out. In the 17th and 18th centuries numerous other minor industries sprang up, including flax-growing and the manufacture of lace, rope, sail-cloth, and stockings.

Topography

Gloucestershire is bounded by Herefordshire, Worcestershire, and Warwickshire on the north; by Oxfordshire on the east; by Swindon and South Gloucestershire on the south; and by Monmouthshire on the west. The county falls into three distinct parts: the uplands of the Cotswold Hills in the east; the Severn valley with its rich pastures, known as the Vale; and to the west the historic Forest of Dean, which lies between the Severn and the River Wye on the border with Monmouthshire. The River Severn runs in a southwesterly direction through the western part of the county and is navigable as far as Sharpness, and between Gloucester and Stourport. The climate is moist, and suitable for root vegetables.

Geology

Gloucestershire's geology is varied, and includes gneissic rocks at the southern end of the Malvern Hills; greenstone at Damory, Charfield, and Woodford; sandy shales and sandstone at Dymock; and iron deposits in the Forest of Dean. Celestine, clay, limestone, and sandstone are all quarried. Rocks dating from the Quaternary period are found in the county.

The Roman period

Gloucestershire was important in Roman times. Camps were established at Gloucester, and also at Cirencester, a station on the Fosse Way known as **Corinium**, which became the second city of Roman Britain.

Preserving the past

In 1933 land was bought through funds provided by the Pilgrim Trust to preserve the surroundings of the church of Chipping Campden and Old Campden House. Dover's Hill, a spur of the Cotswolds not far from Chipping Campden, commanding an extensive view over the Vale of Evesham, was bought by public subscription (1928–9).

Glover, Brian (1934–1997)

English character actor and television presenter. A distinctive screen presence with his bald head and Yorkshire accent, Glover was a long-serving support cast member. He appeared in such films as *Kes* (1969) and *Leon the Pig Farmer* (1992), and in the television series *Campion* (1988–90) and *Rumble* (1995).

His career also embraced a variety of television voice-over and advertising work. One of his last films was the rugby comedy *Up 'n' Under* (1997).

Glyndebourne

Site of an opera house in East Sussex, England, established in 1934 by John Christie (1882–1962). Operas are staged at an annual summer festival and a touring company is also based there. It underwent extensive rebuilding work in the early 1990s.

Godalming

Town in Surrey, southeast England, on the River Wey; population (1996 est) 21,200. A former centre of the Surrey wool trade, the town manufactured textiles until the 1970s. Principal industries are now light engineering, and the manufacture of pharmaceuticals and high-tech products, including remote-sensing image interpretation. The service sector is a major employer, and the UK headquarters of the World Wide Fund for Nature are located here. Charterhouse School, a private school for boys to the north of the town, moved here from London in 1872.

Features

The church of St Peter and Paul is partly Norman, and the town hall, dating from 1814, houses a museum of local history. Nearby to the southeast is Winkworth Arboretum, a 38-ha/95-acre area planted with rare trees and shrubs, owned by the National Trust since 1952.

Famous people

The writer Aldous Huxley was born here in 1894.

Godden, Rumer (1907–)

English novelist, poet, and writer of children's books. Her first popular success was the romantic novel *Black Narcissus* (1939; filmed in 1946). Like several of her finest books it is set in India, where she lived for many years. Among her works of children's fiction is *The Story of Holly and Ivy* (1958).

God Save the King/Queen

British ◊national anthem. The melody resembles a composition by John Bull and similar words are found from the 16th century. It has also been attributed to Henry Carey. In its present form it dates from the Jacobite Rebellion of 1745, when it was used as an anti-Jacobite Party song.

Godwin, William (1756–1836)

English philosopher, novelist, and father of the writer Mary Shelley. His *Enquiry Concerning Political Justice* (1793) advocated an anarchic society based on a faith in people's essential rationality. At first a Nonconformist minister, he later became an atheist. His first wife was Mary ◊Wollstonecraft.

He became an active campaigner for civil liberties and eventually a publisher of children's books. His novel *The Adventures of Caleb Williams* (1794) promoted his views.

Goehr, (Peter) Alexander (1932–)

German-born English composer. He was professor of music at Cambridge from 1976. A lyrical but often hard-edged serialist, he nevertheless usually remained within the forms of the symphony and traditional chamber works, and more recently turned to tonal and even Neo-Baroque models. His output includes four string quartets, the opera *Arianna*, (1995), and *The Mouse Metamorphosed into a Maid* (1991) for solo soprano.

Gog Magog Hills

Chalk hills 6 km/4 mi southeast of Cambridge, England. At some 72 m/236 ft high, they are the most elevated point in the flat landscape of Cambridgeshire. They are named after two biblical figures. There are remains of an Iron Age fort at Wandlebury, on the crest of the hills, and traces of a Roman road.

Golden Jubilee

Celebrations held throughout Britain and the Empire in 1887 to mark the 50th year of Queen Victoria's rule. Colonial leaders gathered in London to attend the celebrations and this made possible the first Imperial Conference. A similar celebration, the Diamond Jubilee, was held on the 60th anniversary.

Golding, William (Gerald) (1911–1993)

English novelist. His work is often principally concerned with the fundamental corruption and evil inherent in human nature. His first book, *Lord of the Flies* (1954; filmed in 1962), concerns the degeneration into savagery of a group of English schoolboys marooned on a Pacific island after their plane crashes; it is a chilling allegory about the savagery lurking beneath the thin veneer of modern 'civilized' life. *Pincher Martin* (1956) is a study of greed and self-delusion. Later novels include *The Spire* (1964). He was awarded the Nobel Prize for Literature in 1983. Knighted 1988.

Golding's novels deal with universal themes and anxieties: evil, greed, guilt, primal instincts, and unknown forces. *Darkness Visible* (1979) is a disturbing book full of symbolism. The Sea Trilogy – *Rites of Passage* (1980) (Booker Prize), *Close Quarters* (1987), and *Fire Down Below* (1989) – tells the story of a voyage to Australia in Napoleonic times through the eyes of a callow young aristocrat.

Conceived as a parody of R M Ballantyne's idealistic classic *Coral Island* (1858), *Lord of the Flies* was initially turned down by 15 publishers; it sold over 2 million copies in the first ten years. It became a cult book and remains a prescribed text for many English-literature courses. The film version by Peter Brook (1962) was also highly successful.

Goldsmith, James Michael (1933–1997)

Franco-British entrepreneur, one of the UK's wealthiest people. Early in his career he built up a grocery empire, Cavenham Foods, then went on to become the owner of several industrial, commercial (he was cofounder of Mothercare), and financial enterprises. He was a member of the European Parliament for France 1994–97. Knighted 1976.

Goldsmith, Oliver (1728–1774)

Irish playwright, novelist, poet, and essayist. His works include the novel *The Vicar of Wakefield* (1766), an outwardly artless and gentle story which is also social and political satire, and in which rural honesty, kindness, and patience triumph over urban values; it became one of the most popular works of English fiction. Other works include the poem 'The Deserted Village' (1770) and the play *She Stoops to Conquer* (1773). In 1761 Goldsmith met Samuel ◊Johnson and became a member of his circle.

Johnson found a publisher for *The Vicar of Wakefield* to save Goldsmith from imprisonment for debt at the instigation of his landlady. With that book Goldsmith's reputation was secured. In 1768 his comedy *The Good Natur'd Man* had considerable success.

In 1773 he produced *She Stoops to Conquer*, also with great success. His last works were *Retaliation, The History of Greece*, and *An History of the Earth and Animated Nature*, all published in 1774.

golf

Outdoor game in which a small rubber-cored ball is hit with a wooden- or iron-faced club into a series of holes using the least number of shots. On the first shot for each hole, the ball is hit from a tee, which elevates the ball slightly off the ground; subsequent strokes are played off the ground. Most courses have 18 holes and are approximately 5,500 m/6,000 yd in length. Golf developed in Scotland in the 15th century.

The ruling body of golf is the Royal and Ancient Golf Club (1754), at ◊St Andrews; the town has six golf courses. The British Golf Open competition began in 1860.

Gollancz, Victor (1893–1967)

English left-wing writer and publisher, founder in 1936 of the Left Book Club. His own firm published plays by R C Sherriff and novels by Daphne Du Maurier, Elizabeth Bowen, and Dorothy L Sayers, among others. Knighted 1965.

Gombrich, Ernst (Hans Joseph) (1909–)

Austrian-born British art historian. One of his abiding concerns is the problems of content and symbolism in painting. His studies are deeply analytical and make connections with other fields, such as the psychology of perception. Among his works are *The Story of Art* (1950; revised 1995), written for a popular audience, and *Art and Illusion* (1959).

Born in Vienna, he came to Britain in 1936 to work at the University of London Warburg Institute, where he was director 1959–76. His books include *Meditations on a Hobby-Horse* (1963), *Norm and Form* (1966), and *Symbolic Images* (1972). Knighted 1972.

Gondoliers, The, or *The King of Barataria*

Operetta by Sullivan (libretto by W S Gilbert), produced at the Savoy Theatre, London, on 7 December 1889. The baby Prince of Barataria is brought up by gondoliers. Not knowing the heir's true identity, the Inquisitor later appoints Marco and Giuseppe as rulers, but it is eventually revealed that servant Luiz is the true king.

Gooch, Graham Alan (1953–)

English cricketer. An attacking right-handed opening batsman he is England's leading run-scorer in Test cricket with 8,900 runs in 118 matches at an average of 42.58 (1975–95). He hit 20 test hundreds with a highest score of 333. He is also England's top scorer in limited overs cricket with 4,295 runs in 125 one-day internationals.

Born in Leytonstone, London he made his first-class debut for Essex in 1973 and his England debut in 1975. Banned for three years for captaining an unofficial England side to South Africa in 1982, he was made England captain during the 1988 Test series against West Indies. Though the choice of Gooch led to the cancellation of the 1988–89 tour of India, he went on to captain England on 34 occasions. In 1990 he scored a world record match total of 456 runs against India and became only the fourth batsman to finish an English season with an average above 100 runs per innings. In 1993 he joined the select band of cricketers to reach the milestone of 100 centuries. He retired from Test cricket in 1995 having played in 118 test matches. He became an England Test Selector in 1996, and in 1997 retired as a player from first-class cricket.

Goodall, Jane, Baroness van Lawick-Goodall (1934–)

English primatologist and conservationist who has studied the chimpanzee community on Lake Tanganyika since 1960, and is a world authority on wild chimpanzees.

Goodall was born in London. She left school at 18 and worked as a secretary and a film production assistant, until she had an opportunity to work for anthropologist Louis Leakey in Africa. She began to study the chimpanzees at the Gombe Stream Game Reserve, on Lake Tanganyika. Goodall observed the lifestyles of chimpanzees in their natural habitats, discovering that they are omnivores, not herbivores as originally thought, and that they have highly developed and elaborate forms of social behaviour. In the 1990s most of Goodall's time was devoted to establishing sanctuaries for illegally captured chimpanzees, fundraising, and speaking out against the unnecessary use of animals in research.

Good Friday agreement

See ◊Northern Ireland.

Good Life, The

Television sitcom (1975–78). The show followed the fortunes of Tom and Barbara Good (Richard ◊Briers and Felicity Kendall), who opt out of the rat race of urban life and become self-sufficient, farming their own back garden, much to the consternation of snooty suburban neighbours Margot and Jerry Ledbetter (Penelope Keith and Paul Eddington). The series was created by John Esmonde and Bob Larbey.

Good Parliament

In English history, the Parliament of April–July 1376 which attacked Edward III's government for excessive expenditure and the lack of success in the Hundred Years' War. The king was forced to change his ministers and to dismiss his mistress, Alice Perrers. The Commons denounced the corruption of many of the government's officials, and created the office of

GOODALL, JANE *English biologist Jane Goodall has studied the behaviour of the chimpanzees of Gombe National Park, Tanzania since 1960. Pictured here with one of her subjects in 1972, her field observations are described in her best-selling books,* In the Shadow of Man *and* The Chimpanzees of Gombe: Patterns of Behaviour. *Corbis*

Speaker to put the case of the Commons to Parliament as whole. Most of its acts were repealed or annulled the following year.

Goodwin Sands

Sandbanks off the coast of Kent, England, about 10 km/6 mi east of Deal, exposed at low tide, and famous for wrecks. According to legend, they are the remains of the island of Lomea, owned by Earl Godwin in the 11th century.

They are divided into the North and South Goodwins, between which is the deep inlet of Trinity Bay. There are three lightships off the Goodwin Sands, and numerous lighted and unlighted buoys.

Goodwood

Racecourse northeast of Chichester, West Sussex, England founded in 1802 by the third Duke of Richmond. Its races include the Goodwood Cup and Sussex Stakes, held in July/August. A motor-racing track used between 1948 and 1966 was reopened in 1998 for historic car and motor cycle racing, and since 1993 Goodwood has hosted the Festival of Speed, an annual celebration of classic motor-racing. Among the drivers and riders taking part at the reopening was Stirling ◊Moss, who had made his circuit racing debut at Goodwood in 1948.

Goole

Port on the River Ouse, in the East Riding of Yorkshire, England, 35 km/22 mi west of Hull; population (1991) 17,700. Principal imports are cereals, wood, iron, steel, and paper; major exports are chemicals, iron, and steel. Maritime industries include shipbuilding, marine engineering, and specialized boat-building. Goole is also a market town serving a wide agricultural area.

The most westerly port on the Humber estuary, Goole is 47 mi/76 km from the open sea and can only accommodate small vessels. There are three dry docks for ship repairs.

Goonhilly

BT satellite-tracking station in Cornwall, England. It is equipped with a communications-satellite transmitter–receiver in permanent contact with most parts of the world.

Goose Green

In the Falklands War, British victory over Argentina at Goose Green, south of San Carlos, on 28 May 1982 during the advance on Port Stanley.

British troops landed at and around Port San Carlos on the western side of the West Falkland island on 21 May and prepared to advance to Port Stanley, some 80 km/50 mi to the east. An Argentine force was known to be at Goose Green, to the south of San Carlos, and this posed a threat to the flank of the British advance. Troops of the Parachute Regiment made an attack with limited support, and a brisk firefight resulted. The Argentine garrison was overrun, and the survivors taken prisoner.

Gorbals

Part of City of Glasgow unitary authority, Scotland, lying south of the River Clyde. Until 1846 it was a separate municipality. Originally an impoverished and crowded area, the Gorbals underwent extensive redevelopment in the period 1958–73, with the first flats being opened in 1962. Many of the tower blocks were designed by the Scottish architect Basil ◊Spence. Built between 1960 and 1966, they were demolished in 1993 in a state of poor repair. A new development programme was initiated in 1992.

Gordon, Charles George (1833–1885)

English general sent to Khartoum in the Sudan in 1884 to rescue English garrisons that were under attack by the Mahdi, Muhammad Ahmed; he was himself besieged for ten months by the Mahdi's army. A relief expedition arrived on 28 January 1885 to find that Khartoum had been captured and Gordon killed two days before.

I would sooner live like a Dervish with the Mahdi, than go out to dinner every night in London.

CHARLES GORDON British general. *Khartoum journal* 1883

Gordon, Douglas (1967–)

Scottish artist. He came to prominence in 1993 with *24 Hour Psycho*, in which Alfred Hitchcock's film *Psycho* was shown in slow motion over a 24-hour period. In 1996 he became the first video artist to win the Turner Prize.

Gordonstoun

◊Public school near Elgin, Scotland, founded by Kurt Hahn in 1935, which emphasizes a spartan outdoor life. It went coeducational in 1972. Prince Philip and Prince Charles attended Gordonstoun School.

Gore, Spencer (1878–1914)

English painter. He was a friend of English artist Walter ◊Sickert and one of his most talented followers in introducing Impressionism and Post-Impressionism to English art. Like Sickert, he enjoyed painting music-hall scenes, and he also produced landscapes, interiors, and still lifes. His later work was very bold in colour.

His early death from pneumonia cut short a career of outstanding promise.

Goring, Marius (1912–1998)

Cosmopolitan English stage and screen actor. Primarily a stage actor, Goring performed in English, French, and German, and was as equally adept at playing dramatic leads as he was in comic supporting roles. He made his screen debut in 1936 in Alexander Korda's *Rembrandt*. He went on to work with director Michael Powell and screenwriter Emeric Pressburger on a series of collaborations, notably the British screen classic *A Matter of Life and Death* (1946) and *The Red Shoes* (1948).

Gormley, Antony (1950–)

English sculptor. In his most characteristic works, he has cast his own body in plaster, lead, and fibreglass to create faceless, featureless nudes, often with outstretched arms. His best-known sculptures are *Derry Sculpture* (1987), two figures, back to back, standing on the ramparts above the city of Derry, Northern Ireland; and *Angel of the North*, the largest sculpture in Britain, erected near Gateshead in 1998.

Gosport

Town and naval base opposite Portsmouth, Hampshire, southern England; borough population (1996 est) 76,000. Industries include mechanical, electrical, and instrument engineering focused on defence research for the maritime industries; and the provision of high-tech services.

As the Ministry of Defence cut back its operations in the late 1990s some associated industries have closed, but high-tech computing companies have taken over in significance, and the waterfront areas are being redeveloped.

A ferry service connects Gosport with Portsmouth, 400 m/1,300 ft across the mouth of Portsmouth Harbour. The construction of a light rapid-transport system link to Fareham and Portsmouth is being funded by a successful bid to the Millennium Commission.

Features

The town centre is surrounded by fortifications developed in the 19th century, and its historic buildings incude the 19th-century sea-defences of Fort Brockhurst. The Royal Navy's Submarine World Museum reflects Gosport's historic association with naval operations.

Naval base

Gosport was an important naval supply base, with ships' anchors, cables, powder magazines, chains, and sails, as well as food supplies, being produced in the town. Priddy's Hard, established in 1770 as a powder magazine, became the Royal Navy's principal armaments depot; it continued to supply the navy until the 1990s, but is now scheduled to become a museum and leisure centre. Gosport naval base was one of the main D-Day embarkation points for troops in 1944. Several active operation centres are located in the town.

Gosse, Edmund William (1849–1928)

English writer and critic. His strict Victorian upbringing is reflected in his masterly autobiographical work *Father and Son* (published anonymously in 1907). As a literary critic and biographer, he was responsible for introducing the works of the Norwegian dramatist Henrik Ibsen to England. He was knighted in 1925.

Gosset, William Sealy (1876–1937)

British industrial research scientist. His work on statistical analysis of the normal distribution opened the door to developments in the analysis of variance.

Gosset spent his career with the Guinness brewery firm, first in Dublin, Ireland, and from 1935 in London. When he arrived in Dublin he found that there was a mass of data concerning brewing which called for sophisticated mathematical analysis. Gosset's main problem was to estimate the mean value of a characteristic on the basis of very small samples, for use by industry when large sampling was too expensive or impracticable.

goth

Member of a youth movement characterized in fashion by black, dramatic clothing and black-and-white make-up, and in music by portentous, swirling synthesizer riffs and angst-ridden lyrics. Goth began in the north of England in the late 1970s. Goth bands include the Sisters of Mercy, Siouxsie and the Banshees, and The Cure.

Gothic architecture

English architecture of the period beginning around 1200 to the mid-16th century. It is usually divided into the following styles: ◊Early English, or Early Pointed (about 1220–about 1300); ◊Decorated, or Middle Pointed (about 1300–about 1370); and ◊Perpendicular, or Late Pointed (about 1370–about 1540).

There was no abrupt line of change between these various periods, each merging into the next as new structural or decorative features were introduced. They demonstrate a gradual development of window design and vaulting and buttressing, whereby the thick walls and heavy barrel-vaults, the flat buttresses, and the narrow windows of the 12th century came to be replaced by bolder buttresses with thinner walls between them, thinner vaults supported on stone ribs, and much larger windows filled with tracery.

Gothic architecture died out very slowly, especially in Oxford, but from about 1640 onwards up to about 1830 all architecture was based on that of Rome, save for a few exceptions that led to the ◊Gothic Revival towards the end of that period.

Gothic novel

Literary genre established by Horace ◊Walpole's *The Castle of Otranto* (1764) and marked by mystery, violence, and horror; other exponents were the English writers Anne ◊Radcliffe, Matthew 'Monk' Lewis, Mary ◊Shelley, and Bram ◊Stoker. In the 20th century elements of the genre are found in popular horror fiction and in the 'Neo-Gothic' works of Emma Tennant (1938–) and Angela ◊Carter.

Gothic Revival

The resurgence of interest in Gothic architecture, as displayed in the late 18th and 19th centuries. Gothic Revival buildings include Charles Barry and Augustus Pugin's Houses of Parliament (1836–65) and Gilbert Scott's St Pancras Station Hotel (1868–74) in London.

The growth of Romanticism led some writers, artists, and antiquaries to embrace a fascination with Gothic forms that emphasized the supposedly bizarre and grotesque aspects of the Middle Ages. During the Victorian period, however, a far better understanding of Gothic forms was achieved, and this resulted in some impressive Neo-Gothic architecture, as well as some desecration of genuine Gothic churches in the name of 'restoration'.

Proponents of ecclesiastical Gothic were usually associated with the ◊Oxford, or Tractarian, Movement. The 19th-century interest in the Middle Ages was reflected in in the writings of Walter Scott, William Morris, and John Ruskin.

Gough, Darren (1970–)

English cricketer. A right-arm fast bowler and hard-hitting late order batsman, he made his England Test debut in 1994, and by the end of the 1998 English season, had taken 104 wickets in 27 matches at an average of 27.79. He made his first-class debut for Yorkshire in 1989.

government

For an overview of how Britain is governed, see feature on Britain's unwritten constitution at ◊constitution. See table of UK government departments, below, and feature on page 382 on how the Cabinet works. See also ◊Parliament (for a Parliamentary glossary); House of ◊Commons; House of ◊Lords; and ◊elections.

UK Government Departments

UK Government Departments
Agriculture, Fisheries, and Food (Ministry of)
Cabinet Office (Office of Public Service)
Culture, Media, and Sport
Defence
Education and Employment
Environment
Foreign and Commonwealth Affairs
Health
Home Office
International Development (formerly the Overseas Development Agency – ODA)
Northern Ireland Office
Scottish Office
Social Security
Trade and Industry
Transport
HM Treasury
Welsh Office

Government Communications Headquarters

Centre of the British government's electronic surveillance operations, popularly known as ◊**GCHQ**.

governor-general

Representative of the British government in a Commonwealth country that regards the British sovereign as head of state. The first Commonwealth country to receive such a representative was Canada in 1929. In almost all Commonwealth countries the governor-general is now a citizen of that country.

Gower, David Ivon (1957–)

English cricketer. An elegant left-handed batsman who in 117 Tests between 1978 and 1992 scored 8,231 runs at an average of 44.25. He was England's record run scorer in Test cricket from 1992, when he surpassed Geoffrey Boycott's record, until 1993, when his total was overtaken by Graham ◊Gooch. He played county cricket for Leicestershire 1975–89 and for Hampshire 1990–93. He retired in 1993.

Gower, John (*c.* 1330–1408)

English poet. He is remembered for his *Confessio Amantis/Lover's Confession*, written in English between 1386 and 1390 and consisting of tales and discussions about love taken from the Roman poet Ovid, the *Gesta Romanorum*, and other sources.

Gower Peninsula, Welsh Penrhyn Gwyr

Peninsula in ◊Swansea unitary authority, south Wales, situated between Swansea Bay and the Burry Inlet and extending into the Bristol Channel. Much of the coastline is the property of the National Trust, and there is tourism on the south coast; the north is marshy.

In the 11th century the area was overrun by the Normans, who built castles and churches; it was thoroughly anglicized in the west and south. It has notable scenery and contains picturesque ruins. As the coastline is principally composed of limestone, there are numerous caves, including Paviland Cave, the site of the important discovery of a skeleton of an old Stone Age man. The old Welsh kingdom of **Gwyr** was much more extensive and included land to the north.

> *All my shows are great. Some of them are bad. But they are all great.*
>
> LEW GRADE English media tycoon. Quoted in the *Observer*, September 1975

Grace, W(illiam) G(ilbert) (1848–1915)

English cricketer. By profession a doctor, he became the most famous sportsman in Victorian England. A right-handed batsman, he began playing first-class cricket at the age of 16, scored 152 runs in his first Test match, and scored the first triple century in 1876. Throughout his career, which lasted nearly 45 years, he scored 54,896 runs and took 2,876 wickets.

Grade, Lew (1906–1998)

English theatrical impresario and television manager. Originally from Russia, Lew Grade emigrated to Britain with his family as a child and was a theatrical agent before founding

CABINET GOVERNMENT: HOW THE CABINET WORKS

THE CABINET is a group of ministers holding the highest executive offices who decide government policy. Cabinet members are chosen by the prime minister; policy is collective and the meetings are secret, minutes being taken by the secretary of the cabinet, a high civil servant. Apart from periodic 'reshuffles', a major change of government, and therefore of the cabinet, normally occurs as a result of a general election at which the government of the day loses its majority in the House of Commons.

The cabinet is collectively responsible to Parliament for the policy it pursues and members of the cabinet are obliged to stand or fall together. If one of them dissents from the rest on a question too important to admit of compromise, it is his or her duty to resign. When the cabinet no longer commands the support of the majority of the House of Commons, the ministers are duty bound to resign en bloc. All members of the cabinet are created privy councillors and are addressed by the prefix 'Right Honourable'.

The size and composition of the cabinet has tended to vary over time. The prime minister normally includes his or her 20 or so most senior colleagues, most of whom head the major departments of state. The cabinet has tended to increase in size in the 20th century as the number of departments has increased.

It is also usual to include in the cabinet the holders of a number of sinecure offices which have no departmental responsibilities, such as the Lord President of the Privy Council, the chancellor of the Duchy of Lancaster, and the Lord ◊Privy Seal. The Lord President is now normally the manager of the government's business in Parliament and is designated leader of the House of Commons.

The cabinet will also include at least two members of the House of Lords: the Lord Chancellor and the leader of the House of Lords, who is usually given a sinecure post, such as Lord Privy Seal.

It has become increasingly rare for heads of departments to be peers on the grounds that they should be directly answerable to the House of Commons. The number of peers in the cabinet is usually no more than four.

The prime minister is also responsible for appointing ministers outside the cabinet, which, including the cabinet, may amount to more than a 100 posts. Of these up to 91 may be members of the House of Commons, the rest normally being drawn from the House of Lords. Thus all ministers are normally expected to be a member of one of the two Houses of Parliament. The only exception to this rule, are the posts of the Lord Advocate and Solicitor General for Scotland, for which offices it is not always possible to find suitably qualified people in Parliament since they must be members of the Scottish Bar.

The 100 or so ministers appointed by the prime minister constitute the 'government', 'administration', or 'ministry' and, in addition to the cabinet, consist of senior non-cabinet ministers, the law officers (the Attorney General and the Solicitor General and the two Scottish law officers mentioned above), ministers of state, parliamentary secretaries (or under-secretaries where the head of department has the title of secretary of state), and whips. Parliamentary private secretaries (PPSs) are not ministers, but MPs who act as personal aides to ministers.

Cabinet secrecy

The cabinet's proceedings are secret and cabinet minutes and papers are not made publicly available at the Public Record Office until 30 years has elapsed. Cabinet decisions are made public at the discretion of the prime minister and members of the cabinet are not supposed to reveal the details of cabinet discussions.

Cabinet committees

The cabinet meets under the chairmanship of the prime minister, who also has the initiative in calling meetings and determining the agenda. A significant part of the cabinet's work, however, is carried out through its committee system. Since 1945 there has been extensive use of cabinet committees. They are usually chaired by a cabinet minister.

The cabinet office

The work of the cabinet is facilitated by the **cabinet secretariat** or **cabinet office**. The cabinet office is headed by the secretary of the cabinet, a civil servant who is also head of the civil service.

Collective responsibility

Constitutionally the cabinet is bound to offer, through the prime minister, unanimous advice to the sovereign, who is

one of Britain's first commercial television stations, ATV (Associated Television), in 1956. His interests extended to films, and he was executive producer of the notoriously expensive *Raise the Titanic*, later joking that it would have been cheaper to lower the Atlantic. A love of fat cigars was his hallmark.

He was created a life peer in 1976. Michael ◊Grade is Lew Grade's nephew.

Grade, Michael (1943–)

English television executive, the second chief executive of Channel 4, 1988–97. He started in journalism and worked for the family theatrical agency before moving to be deputy controller of the commercial station, London Weekend Television, in 1973, where his entertainment background and sports knowledge stood him in good stead. In 1984 he was appointed channel controller of BBC1, and two years later became the Corporation's director of programmes.

Michael Grade is the nephew of Lew Grade.

Graham, Thomas (1805–1869)

Scottish chemist who laid the foundations of physical chemistry (the branch of chemistry concerned with changes in energy during a chemical transformation) by his work on the diffusion of gases and liquids. **Graham's law** (1829) states

constitutionally bound to accept that advice. Ministers are collectively responsible to Parliament for the conduct of the government and for its policies.

History of the cabinet

The cabinet has its origins in the practice of monarchs seeking the advice of a group of confidential advisers. By the end of the 14th century the monarch's advisers constituted a formal body known as the ◊Privy Council and during the minority of Henry VI the Privy Council ruled the country.

The term 'cabinet' became common during the reign of Charles II, when the Privy Council had become a large and unwieldy body, and Charles resorted to the practice of consulting a 'cabal' or clique of confidants. This group of confidential advisers was eventually recognized as a committee of the Privy Council known as the **cabinet council**, and the modern cabinet remains an informal committee of the Privy Council.

Many early cabinets, in the reigns of William III and Anne, included representatives of both the Whig and Tory parties. However, the dependence of George I on the Whigs and his inability to understand English and English affairs led to the formation of ministries normally drawn from one party and, more significantly, ministries which represented the will of a majority in the House of Commons. Furthermore, the withdrawal of the King from attendance at cabinet meetings after 1717 also brought about the development of the office of prime minister.

During the 18th and early 19th centuries the cabinet gradually emerged as the chief executive organ, a process which was facilitated by the mental illness of George III in 1788 and after 1810. The position of the prime minister was also enhanced during this period.

Queen Victoria expressed strong views on cabinet appointments on a number of occasions, but by the end of her reign the constitutional position of the monarch 'to advise, encourage and to warn' (Walter Bagehot), and of the cabinet as ultimately dependent upon and responsible to Parliament, were both firmly established.

The chief development in the 20th century has been the increased power of the prime minister. This had led some commentators to argue that cabinet government has been superseded by prime ministerial government.

that the diffusion rate of a gas is inversely proportional to the square root of its density.

His work on colloids (which have larger particles than true solutions) was equally fundamental; he discovered the principle of dialysis, that colloids can be separated from solutions containing smaller molecules by the differing rates at which they pass through a semipermeable membrane. The human kidney uses the same principle to extract nitrogenous waste.

Graham, W(illiam) S(ydney) (1918–1986)

Scottish poet. His early poetry, published in *Cage Without Grievance* (1942), was compared with that of G M Hopkins, James Joyce, and Dylan Thomas. Subsequently he worked on the development of his verse as a medium of communication, to reflect subjects such as the sea, childhood, language, and love. *Collected Poems 1942–1977* was published in 1977, *Uncollected Poems* (1990), and *Selected Poems* (1996).

Grahame, Kenneth (1859–1932)

Scottish-born writer. The early volumes of sketches of childhood, *The Golden Age* (1895) and *Dream Days* (1898), were followed by his masterpiece *The Wind in the Willows* (1908) which became a children's classic. Begun as a bedtime story for his son, it is a charming tale of life on the river bank, with its blend of naturalistic style and fantasy, and its memorable animal characters, the practical Rat, Mole, Badger, and conceited, bombastic Toad. It was dramatized by A A Milne as *Toad of Toad Hall* (1929) and by Alan Bennett (1990).

Grahame was secretary of the Bank of England from 1898 to 1908.

grammar school

Secondary school catering for children of high academic ability, about 20% of the total, usually measured by the Eleven Plus examination. Most grammar schools have now been replaced by ◊comprehensive schools.

Grampian

Former region of Scotland (1975–96), which consisted of five districts and was replaced by Moray, Aberdeen City, and Aberdeenshire unitary authorities.

The districts of Moray, Banff and Buchan, Gordon, Kincardine and Deeside, and the City of Aberdeen made up Grampian region. The region was created in 1975 with lands from the counties of Morayshire, Banffshire, Aberdeenshire, and Kincardineshire.

Grampian Mountains

Range that includes Ben Nevis, the highest mountain in the British Isles at 1,343 m/4,406 ft, and the Cairngorm Mountains, which include the second highest mountain, Ben Macdhui 1,309 m/4,295 ft. The region includes Aviemore, a winter holiday and sports centre.

The mountains are composed of granite, gneiss, quartzite, marble, and schists. The chief river flowing from the watershed north is the Spey; those flowing east are the Don and the Dee; those flowing south are the Esk and the Tay.

Grand National

Horse-race held in March or April at ◊Aintree, Liverpool, England. The most famous steeplechase race in the world, it was inaugurated in 1839 as the Grand Liverpool Steeple Chase, adopting its present name in 1847. The current course is 7,242 m/4.5 mi long, with 30 formidable jumps. The highest jump is the Chair at 156 cm/5 ft 2in. Grand National steeplechases based on the Aintree race are held in Scotland, Wales, and Ireland at Ayr, Chepstow, and Fairyhouse respectively.

Grand Remonstrance

Petition passed by the English Parliament in November 1641 that listed all the alleged misdeeds of Charles I and demanded parliamentary approval for the king's ministers and the reform of the church. Charles refused to accept the Grand Remonstrance and countered by trying to arrest five leading members of the House of Commons. The worsening of relations between king and Parliament led to the outbreak of the English Civil War in 1642.

Grand Union Canal

Part of the eastern portion of the canal system of Great Britain, connecting London, via Northampton and Leicester, to Nottingham and the River ⇨Trent.

Grangemouth

Seaport and former burgh in Falkirk unitary authority, Scotland, about 4 km/2.5 mi northeast of Falkirk; population (1991) 18,700. Its main industries are oil-related. The refineries are fed by overland pipelines from Loch Finnart and the North Sea fields. Scandinavian timber is a major import.

The town's initial growth was due to the construction of the Forth and Clyde Canal, completed in 1791 but now closed to navigation. Dock improvements in 1843 allowed the settlement to expand. Its industries were mainly maritime-related, but with some brickmaking and coal mining. In 1897 the development of a soap factory initiated a connection with the chemical sector. The first oil refinery was established here in 1924.

Granger, (James Lablache) Stewart (1913–1993)

English film actor. After several leading roles in British romantic melodramas during World War II, such as *The Man in Grey* (1940), he moved to Hollywood in 1950 and appeared in such films as *Scaramouche* (1952), *The Prisoner of Zenda* (1952), *Beau Brummel* (1954), and *Moonfleet* (1955).

Grant, Cary stage name of Archibald Alexander Leach (1904–1986)

English-born actor, a US citizen from 1942. His witty, debonair personality made him a screen favourite for more than three decades. Among his many films are *She Done Him Wrong* (1933), *Bringing Up Baby* (1938), *The Philadelphia Story* (1940), *Notorious* (1946), *To Catch a Thief* (1955), *North by Northwest* (1959), and *Charade* (1963).

Grant was a frequent collaborator with the directors Alfred Hitchcock, Howard Hawks, and George Cukor. Further films include *The Awful Truth* (1937), *Topper* (1937), *His Girl Friday* (1940), *Arsenic and Old Lace* (1944), *Monkey Business*

GRANGEMOUTH *The port of Grangemouth on the east coast of Scotland is a major centre of the petrochemical industry; a refinery was established here in the 1920s. Refining began in Grangemouth with imported crude oil piped from the west coast, and was later supplemented by North Sea oil. David Paterson/ Impact*

(1952), and *An Affair to Remember* (1957). He received an honorary Academy Award in 1969.

Grant, Duncan (James Corrowr) (1885–1978)

Scottish painter and designer. A pioneer of Post-Impressionism in the UK, he was influenced by Paul Cezanne and the Fauves, and became a member of the ◊Bloomsbury Group. He lived with the painter Vanessa Bell from about 1914 and worked with her on decorative projects, such as those at the ◊Omega Workshops. This aspect of his work is represented by interior design, theatrical decor, painted furniture, and designs for pottery and textiles. Later works, such as *Snow Scene* (1921), show great fluency and a subtle use of colour.

One of his finest portraits is *Vanessa Bell* (1942; Tate Gallery, London).

Grant, Hugh (1962–)

English actor. He broke through to widespread popular success with his embodiment of languid romantic charm in the film *Four Weddings and a Funeral* (1994).

Other film roles include *Maurice* (1987), *Impromptu* (1990), *An Awfully Big Adventure* (1994), *The Englishman Who Went Up a Hill But Came Down a Mountain, Nine Months, Sense and Sensibility* (all 1995), and *Extreme Measures* (1996).

Grantham

Market town in southeast Lincolnshire, eastern England, on the River Witham, between Stamford and Lincoln; population (1995 est) 33,300. It is an agricultural centre, with mechanical and electrical engineering, food-processing, and packaging industries. The former UK prime minister Margaret Thatcher was born here in 1925.

History

A farming centre since Saxon times, Grantham was mentioned in the Domesday Book of 1086. The town was sacked in 1461 during the Wars of the Roses, and in 1483 Richard III signed the death warrant of the Duke of Buckingham in the Angel Inn. In 1643 Oliver Cromwell, leader of the Parliamentarians in the Civil War, made Grantham his headquarters. It became an important staging point on the Great North Road from London to Lincoln, and later developed as a railway junction.

Features

The church of St Wulfram has an 86-m/282-ft central spire dating from the 14th century, and a chained library dating from 1598. **Grantham House**, a National Trust property dating from 1380, was formerly known as Hall Place after its owners, the Hall family, who were wealthy wool merchants in medieval times. Its architecture is mainly post-Tudor, and the building was extensively altered in the 18th century. Princess Margaret, daughter of Henry VII, is said to have stayed here in 1503, on her way north to marry James IV of Scotland. The medieval Angel and Royal Hotel has a late 15th-century facade, and is said to be the oldest inn in England, reputedly founded by the Knights Templar in the 12th century. The physicist and mathematician Isaac Newton was born nearby at Woolsthorpe Manor, a 17th-century house built of limestone. He was a pupil at the King's School, a grammar school founded in Grantham in 1528 (now a private school).

grant-maintained school

State school that has voluntarily withdrawn itself from local authority support (an action called **opting out**), and instead is maintained directly by central government. The schools are managed by their own boards of governors. In 1996 there were 1,090 grant-maintained schools, of which 60% were secondary schools.

The first school to opt out was Skegness Grammar School in 1989. The policy was initially quite popular in some local authority areas, particularly some London boroughs and southern counties such as Kent and Essex. By 1995 1,040 schools had opted out, well below government targets, and the rate of opt-out had slowed almost to a standstill.

Granville-Barker, Harley Granville (1877–1946)

English theatre director and author. He was director and manager with J E Vedrenne at the Royal Court Theatre, London, 1904–18, producing plays by Shaw, Yeats, Ibsen, Galsworthy, and Masefield. His works include the plays *Waste* (1907), *The Voysey Inheritance* (1905), and *The Madras House* (1910). His series of *Prefaces to Shakespeare* (1927–47) influenced the staging of Shakespeare for many years.

Grasmere

English lake and village in the Lake District, Cumbria, associated with many writers. William Wordsworth and his sister Dorothy lived at Dove Cottage (now a museum) from 1799 to 1808, Thomas de Quincey later made his home in the same house, and both Samuel Coleridge and Wordsworth are buried in the churchyard of St Oswald's.

Grassholm

Island 25 km/15 mi northwest of St Ann's Head, Pembrokeshire, southwest Wales. Owned and managed by the Royal Society for the Protection of Birds, it is the home of several rare species of birds. The island is of particular interest as a breeding-ground of the gannet (solan goose). Seals abound in the surrounding waters.

Grattan, Henry (1746–1820)

Irish politician. He entered the Irish parliament in 1775, led the patriot opposition, and obtained free trade and legislative independence for Ireland in 1782. He failed to prevent the Act of Union of Ireland and England in 1800, but sat in the British Parliament and pressed for Catholic emancipation.

Graves, Robert (Ranke) (1895–1985)

English poet and writer. He was severely wounded on the Somme in World War I, and his frank autobiography *Goodbye to All That* (1929) contains outstanding descriptions of the war. *Collected Poems* (1975) contained those verses he wanted preserved. His fiction includes two historical novels of imperial Rome, *I Claudius* and *Claudius the God* (both 1934). His most significant critical work is *The White Goddess: A Historical Grammar of Poetic Myth* (1948, revised 1966).

GRAVES, ROBERT *As well as writing a great deal of poetry, Robert Graves wrote historical novels, an autobiography, and works of nonfiction on literature and mythology. He was professor of poetry at Oxford University 1961–66. Corbis*

Graves first achieved notice for his war poetry, but he largely rejected his early poetry and developed much further in his later verse. The poems of his maturity (1926–39), are technically confident, rhetorically simple, and are among the finest of modern love poems. After World War II, he became increasingly interested in Sufist and Eastern religious philosophy and mythology, the subject of many of his later poems. His works include *Collected Poems* (1965), *Poems 1965–68* (1968), *Poems 1968–1970* (1970), and *Poems 1970–72* (1972).

During World War I he served with the Royal Welsh Fusiliers, in the same regiment as the writer and poet Siegfried ◊Sassoon.

Gravesend

Town in Kent, southeast England, 35 km/22 mi east of London, on the River Thames opposite Tilbury, with which it is linked by ferry; borough population (1991) 95,000. Industries include engineering, printing, and the manufacture of electrical goods and a range of paper goods.

Gravesend is the site of the Thames pilot station, at the point where the Thames Estuary narrows and river pilots take control of ships using the Port of London.

History

The town is mentioned in the Domesday Book of 1086 as **Gravesham**. The Native American Matoaka Pocahontas died here in 1617 and was buried in St George's Church. A substantial Sikh community has developed since the 1950s.

Gray, Alasdair (James) (1934–)

Scottish novelist and short-story writer. *Lanark* (1981), begun when he was 18, is an inventive expression of nationalist and anti-nationalist feeling, brimful of literary jokes. *1982, Janine* (1984) and *Something Leather* (1990) are in much the same vein. *Poor Things* (1992), illustrated by himself, presents aspects of Glasgow social history, while *A History Maker* (1994) looks forward to a bizarre future.

Gray, Cecil (1895–1951)

Scottish writer on music and composer. In 1920 he became joint editor of the *Sackbut* with Philip Heseltine, with whom he also wrote a book on the composer Gesualdo (1926), and whose biography as a composer (Peter Warlock) he published. Other books are a *History of Music* (1928), essays 'Predicaments' (1936) and 'Contingencies' (1947) and two works on Sibelius (1931, 1935).

Gray, Henry (*c.* 1827–1861)

British anatomist. He compiled a book on his subject, published in 1858 with illustrations by his colleague H Vandyke Carter. What is now known as *Gray's Anatomy* was based on his own dissections. Through its various editions and revisions, it has remained the definitive work on anatomy.

Unlike other contemporary works on the subject, his book was organized in terms of systems, rather than areas of the body. Such sections as neuroanatomy have been greatly enlarged in later editions but the section that deals with, for example, the skeletal system is almost identical to Gray's original work. It remains a standard text for students and surgeons alike.

Gray, Thomas (1716–1771)

English poet. His *Elegy Written in a Country Churchyard* (1751), a dignified contemplation of death, was instantly acclaimed and is one of the most quoted poems in the English language. Other poems include *Ode on a Distant Prospect of Eton College* (1747), *The Progress of Poesy*, and *The Bard* (both 1757). He is now seen as a forerunner of ◊Romanticism.

A close friend of Horace ◊Walpole at Eton, Gray made a continental tour with him from 1739 to 1741, an account of which is given in his vivid letters. His first poem, *Ode on a Distant Prospect of Eton College*, was published anonymously in 1747 and again in 1748 with *Ode on the Spring* and *Ode on the Death of a Favourite Cat* in *A Collection of Poems By Several Hands*, edited by Robert Dodsley (1703–1764). *Poems by Mr Gray* was published in 1768.

The *Elegy Written in a Country Churchyard*, begun in 1741, was immediately appreciated for its exquisite expression and natural pathos. Gray's works are few in number, yet he was a pioneer, a key figure in a transitional period, and the forerunner of Oliver Goldsmith and William Cowper in developing a style markedly different from that of the poetically dominant Alexander Pope; he was one of the first to celebrate the glories of mountain scenery and in this he was a precursor of the Romantics.

Great Britain

Official name for ◊England, ◊Scotland, and ◊Wales, and the adjacent islands (except the Channel Islands and the Isle of Man) from 1603, when the English and Scottish crowns were united under James I of England (James VI of Scotland). With ◊Northern Ireland it forms the ◊United Kingdom.

Greater London Council, GLC

Local authority that governed London 1965–86. When the GLC was abolished (see ◊local government), its powers either devolved back to the borough councils or were transferred to certain nonelected bodies.

Great Exhibition

World fair held in Hyde Park, London, in 1851, proclaimed by its originator Prince Albert as 'the Great Exhibition of the Industries of All Nations'. In practice, it glorified British manufacture: over half the 100,000 exhibits were from Britain or the British Empire. Over 6 million people attended the exhibition. The exhibition hall, popularly known as the ◊**Crystal Palace**, was constructed of glass with a cast-iron frame, and designed by Joseph Paxton.

Great Expectations

Novel by Charles ◊Dickens, published in 1861. Philip Pirrip ('Pip'), brought up by his sister and her husband, the blacksmith Joe Gargery, rejects his humble background and pursues wealth, which he believes comes from the elderly, eccentric Miss Havisham. Ultimately, through adversity, he recognizes the value of his origins.

Great Glen, or Glenmore

Valley in Scotland following a coast-to-coast geological fault line, which stretches over 100 km/62 mi southwest from Inverness on the North Sea to Fort William on the Atlantic Ocean. The ◊Caledonian Canal, constructed by connecting Loch Ness and the lochs Oich and Lochy, runs the length of the glen.

The Great Glen is a rift valley formed approximately 400 million years ago by volcanic activity and deepened by glacial activity around 10,000 years ago. Movement along the fault has made the rocks particularly susceptible to erosion, and the line is marked by a number of deep lochs.

Although the Great Glen fault was formed in relatively early geological times, it continues to remain slightly unstable, and the neighbouring region is subject to slight earthquake tremors.

great seal

Royal seal used to authenticate the monarch's assent to official documents, required for all the most important acts of state, such as dissolving parliaments and signing treaties.

Great Yarmouth

Holiday resort and port in Norfolk, eastern England, at the mouth of the River Yare, 32 km/20 mi east of Norwich; population (1991) 56,200. It is Norfolk's largest port. Formerly a herring-fishing port, it is now a container port and a base for North Sea oil and gas. Other industries include shipbuilding, tourism and leisure, food processing, engineering, the manufacture of electronic components, shipwreck salvage, and some fishing.

Features

The Rows in the old part of Great Yarmouth are narrow parallel alleys arranged on a grid pattern established in medieval times. The area includes the 17th-century Old Merchant's House, and the 13th-century Tolhouse, once the town's court house and jail, and now housing a museum. The Fishermen's Hospital almshouses date from the early 18th century. The parish church of St Nicholas, founded in 1101, is one of the largest parish churches in England; it was gutted by fire in an air raid in 1942, but has since been restored. There are remains of the 13th-century Greyfriars cloisters and some parts of the medieval town walls survive including some of the town-wall towers. Other features include the Elizabethan House Museum, Maritime Museum, and the Nelson Monument (1819), a column 40 m/131 ft high. There are Roman remains at Burgh Castle nearby to the west. Great Yarmouth includes Gorleston on the other side of the River Yare.

History

Great Yarmouth was an important port in medieval times, and prospered in the 19th century from the herring-fishing industry and from its development in the Victorian era as a holiday resort. The town was attacked by German warships during World War I, and it suffered heavy damage from air raids during World War II. Much reconstruction has since taken place.

Greek Revival

Architectural style that arose in the late 18th-century with the opening up of Greece and its ancient architectural heritage to the West; until then Roman architecture had been considered the only true Classical style. British architects associated with Greek Revival include John Soane, John Nash, Charles Cockerell, Robert Smirke, and William Henry Playfair.

The publication of *Antiquities of Athens* (1762 and 1789) by Nicholas Revett (1725–1804) and James Stuart, and the arrival in London of the Parthenon sculptures (the ◊Elgin marbles) were major catalysts of the movement.

Green, George (1793–1841)

English mathematician. He coined the term 'potential', now a central concept in electricity, and introduced **Green's theorem**, which is still applied in the solution of partial differential equations; for instance, in the study of relativity.

Green, Lucinda Jane born Prior-Palmer (1953–)

British three-day eventer. She won the Badminton Horse Trials a record six times between 1973 and 1984 and was world individual champion in 1982.

Greenaway, Kate (Catherine) (1846–1901)

English illustrator. She specialized in drawings of children. In 1877 she first exhibited at the Royal Academy, London, and began her collaboration with the colour printer Edmund Evans (1826–1905), with whom she produced a number of children's books, including *Mother Goose*.

Since 1955 the **Library Association Greenaway Medal** has been awarded annually to an outstanding illustrated book for children published in the UK. Subsequent winners include Brian Wildsmith (1962), Charles Keeping (1968), Shirley Hughes (1978), and P J Lynch (1996 and 1998).

Greenaway, Peter (1942–)

Welsh film director. His films are highly stylized and cerebral, richly visual, and often controversial. His feeling for perspective and lighting reveal his early training as a painter. *The Draughtsman's Contract* (1983), a tale of 18th-century country-house intrigue, is dazzling in its visual and narrative complexity. *Prospero's Books* (1991), his reworking of Shakespeare's *The Tempest*, has ingenious animated book sequences.

The Falls (1980) established Greenaway's reputation for carefully composed images, a fascination with numbers and lists, and mischievous intellectualism. For all their formal beauty and technical polish, *A Zed and Two Noughts* (1985), *The Belly of an Architect* (1987), and *Drowning by Numbers* (1988) had a mixed critical reception. Other films are *The Cook, the Thief, His Wife and Her Lover* (1989) and *The Baby of Macon* (1992), both of which were erotically controversial, and *The Pillow Book* (1996).

green belt

Area surrounding a large city, officially designated not to be built on but preserved where possible as open space for agricultural and recreational use. The first green belts were established from 1938 around conurbations such as London in order to prevent urban sprawl. New towns were set up to take the overspill population.

The term generally refers to the 'outer ring' proposed in the Greater London Plan by Patrick ◊Abercrombie; Abercrombie envisaged a static population in this ring, with new towns beyond it.

Greene, (Henry) Graham (1904–1991)

English writer. His novels of guilt, despair, and penitence are set in a world of urban seediness or political corruption in many parts of the world. They include ◊*Brighton Rock* (1938), *The Power and the Glory* (1940), *The Heart of the Matter* (1948), *The Third Man* (1949), *The Honorary Consul* (1973), and *Monsignor Quixote* (1982).

Greene worked as a journalist on *The Times*, and in 1927 was converted to Roman Catholicism. When his first novel, *The Man Within*, was published in 1929, he gave up journalism to write full time, but attained success only with his fourth novel, the thriller *Stamboul Train* (1932) which proved the success of a format used by Greene with equal skill in other works. They include *A Gun for Sale* (1936), *The Confidential Agent* (1939), and *The Ministry of Fear* (1943). *Brighton Rock*, about the criminal underworld, is in fact a religious novel, while *The Power and the Glory* explores the inner struggles of a weak, alcoholic priest in Mexico. A World War II period of service for the Foreign Office in Sierra Leone is reflected in the setting of *The Heart of the Matter*. Greene also wrote lighter, comic novels, including *Our Man in Havana* (1958) and *Travels with My Aunt* (1969).

He was one of the first English novelists both to be influenced by, and to recognize, the literary potential of the cinema. His work is marked by an almost cinematic technique and great visual power. Many of his novels have been filmed, and he wrote several screenplays.

God ... created a number of possibilities in case some of his prototypes failed – that is the meaning of evolution.

GRAHAM GREENE English novelist.
Travels With My Aunt pt 2, ch 7

Greenham Common

Site of a continuous peace demonstration (1981–90) on public land near Newbury (then in Berkshire), outside a US airbase. The women-only camp was established in September 1981 in protest against the siting of US cruise missiles in the UK. The demonstrations ended with the closure of the base. Greenham Common reverted to standby status, and the last US cruise missiles were withdrawn in March 1991.

Green Man, or Jack-in-the-Green

In English folklore, a figure dressed and covered in foliage, associated with festivities celebrating the arrival of spring.

His face is represented in a variety of English church carvings, in wood or stone, often with a protruding tongue. Similar figures also occur in French and German folklore, the earliest related carvings being in Trier, France, on the River Mosel (about AD 200).

Greenock

Port and administrative headquarters of ◊Inverclyde, western Scotland, on the southern shore of the part of the Firth of Clyde which runs northwest to southeast to meet the River Clyde; population (1991) 50,000. Traditionally associated with industries such as shipbuilding, engineering, chemicals, and sugar refining, the area now has computer and electronics enterprises. It was the birthplace of the engineer and inventor James Watt, who gave his name to the measurement of power.

The town's public buildings include the custom house (1818). The McLean Museum and Art Gallery houses items relating to the career of James Watt and to the shipping history of the town. The resited (in 1920) Old West Kirk, dating from 1591, contains windows by William Morris, Edward Burne-Jones, and Dante Gabriel Rossetti, and was the first church built after the Reformation.

The Free French naval base was at Greenock (1940–45);

there is a memorial at Lyle Hill to the men of the Free French forces who died in the Battle of the Atlantic.

The town stretches along the river front for nearly 6 km/4 mi. The deep-water facilities of Greenock stimulated the movement of the centre of shipping activity downstream from Glasgow. The Clydeport authority plan to convert the former Scott Lithgow shipyard at nearby Port Glasgow into a retail and residential complex. Shipbuilding capacity is still retained via Clydeport container terminal.

Green Paper

Publication issued by a British government department setting out various aspects of a matter on which legislation is contemplated, and inviting public discussion and suggestions. In due course it may be followed by a ◊White Paper, giving details of proposed legislation. The first Green Paper was published in 1967.

Green Party

Environmentalist party, founded in 1973 as the Ecology Party, and led, initially, by Jonathon ◊Porrit. It adopted its current name in 1985 and campaigns for protection of the environment and the promotion of social justice. The party attracted little electoral support until the 1989 European Parliament elections, when, it won 2.3 million votes, 15% of the total, but received no seats, because Britain was the only country in Europe not to have some form of proportional representation. Internal disagreements from 1990 have reduced its effectiveness and its membership has contracted greatly.

The party's standing was particularly damaged in 1991, when one of its collective leaders, David Icke, a charismatic sports broadcaster, declared himself 'an aspect of the godhead'. The 'greening' of the larger political parties since 1989 has also been a factor in the Greens' failure to make an electoral breakthrough. In the 1992 general election the party lost almost 200 deposits and attracted only 1% of the national vote. In 1997 it contested fewer than 80 seats.

Greenstreet, Sydney (1879–1954)

English character actor. He made an impressive film debut in *The Maltese Falcon* (1941) and became one of cinema's best-known villains. His other films include *Casablanca* (1942) and *The Mask of Dimitrios* (1944).

Greenwich

Outer London borough of southeast Greater London, to the south of the River Thames. It includes the districts of ◊Woolwich and Eltham.

Features Queen's House (1637, designed by Inigo Jones),

GREENWICH *The Queen's House at Greenwich, London, designed by Inigo Jones for Anne of Denmark, the wife of King James I. It was begun in 1616, but work on it temporarily stopped after Anne's death in 1619. The unfinished building was given to her son, Prince Charles, and after he became king as Charles I, it was completed in 1628–35 for his wife, Henrietta Maria. It was one of the first buildings in England in a pure classical style. Corbis*

the first Palladian-style building in England; the **Royal Naval College**, designed by Christopher Wren in 1694 as a naval hospital, and used from 1873 as a college – the Naval College has now closed and the building is occupied by the National Maritime Museum and the University of Greenwich; the **Old Royal Observatory** (see ◊Royal Greenwich Observatory) in Greenwich Park, founded in 1675 by Charles II. The source of ◊Greenwich Mean Time was moved to Herstmonceux, East Sussex, in 1958, and then to Cambridge in 1990, but the Greenwich meridian (0°) remains unchanged. The *Cutty Sark*, built in 1869 and one of the great tea clippers, is preserved as a museum of sail and the *Gipsy Moth IV*, in which Francis Chichester circumnavigated the world in 1966–67, is also here. Greenwich is the site of the Millennium Exhibition, Greenwich 2000, which has as its centrepiece the ◊Millennium Dome. In 1997 Greenwich was designated a World Heritage Site.
Industries tourism
Population (1991) 205,000.

Greenwich became a London borough in April 1965, comprising the former metropolitan boroughs of Greenwich and Woolwich. It is connected by two tunnels with London north of the Thames; one for pedestrians, and the Blackwall Tunnel for vehicles.

The Royal Naval College was built on the site of a former palace (the birthplace of Henry VIII, Mary, and Elizabeth I). Queen's House was designed for Anne of Denmark, the wife of James I, and it was completed in 1637 for Queen Henrietta Maria, wife of Charles I. Part of the buildings of the Old Royal Observatory have been named Flamsteed House after the first ◊Astronomer Royal; other buildings of the observatory are the Meridian Building and the Great Equatorial Building. Greenwich Park, originally a part of Blackheath, was enclosed by Humphrey, Duke of Gloucester for his palace and later laid out for Charles II by André Le Nôtre, the French landscape gardener who planned the gardens at Versailles. Eltham Palace was built in about 1300; it was a royal residence from the time of Edward II until the reign of Henry VIII. The Great Hall, built during the reign of Edward IV, has a fine 15th-century hammerbeam roof. Well Hall in Eltham, once the home of novelist E Nesbitt, has a fine Tudor barn, dating from 1568.

Greenwich Mean Time, or GMT

Local time on the zero line of longitude (the **Greenwich meridian**), which passes through the Old Royal Observatory at Greenwich, London. It was replaced in 1986 by coordinated universal time (UTC), but continued to be used to measure longitudes and the world's standard time zones.

Greet, Ben or Philip (1857–1936)

English actor and theatre manager. He founded the Woodland Players in 1886 and started a long tradition of open-air performances of Shakespeare. He also produced 24 Shakespeare plays at the Old Vic in London (1915–18), including the full text of *Hamlet*. He was knighted in 1929.

Grenville, George (1712–1770)

British Whig politician, prime minister, and chancellor of the Exchequer, whose introduction of the ◊Stamp Act of 1765 to raise revenue from the colonies was one of the causes of the American Revolution. His government was also responsible for prosecuting the radical John ◊Wilkes.

Grenville took other measures to reduce the military and civil costs in North America, including the Sugar Act and the Quartering Act. His inept management of the Regency Act of 1765 damaged his relationship with George III.

Grenville, Richard (*c.* 1541–1591)

English naval commander and adventurer who died heroically aboard his ship the *Revenge* when attacked by Spanish warships. Grenville fought in Hungary and Ireland (1566–69), and was knighted in about 1577. In 1585 he commanded the expedition that founded Virginia, USA, for his cousin Walter ◊Raleigh. From 1586 to 1588 he organized the defence of England against the Spanish Armada.

He became a symbol of English nationalism and was commemorated in the poem 'The Revenge' (1880) by Alfred Tennyson.

Grenville, William Wyndham, 1st Baron Grenville (1759–1834)

British Whig politician, home secretary from 1791, foreign secretary from 1794; he resigned along with Prime Minister Pitt the Younger in 1801 over George III's refusal to assent to Catholic emancipation. He headed the 'All the Talents' coalition of 1806–07 that abolished the slave trade. He was created a baron in 1790.

Gretna Green

Village in Dumfries and Galloway region, Scotland, where runaway marriages were legal after they were banned in England in 1754; all that was necessary was the couple's declaration, before witnesses, of their willingness to marry. From 1856 Scottish law required at least one of the parties to be resident in Scotland for a minimum of 21 days before the marriage, and marriage by declaration was abolished in 1940.

grievous bodily harm, or GBH

In English law, very serious physical damage suffered by the victim of a crime. The courts have said that judges should not try to define grievous bodily harm but leave it to the jury to decide.

Grew, Nehemiah (1641–1712)

English botanist and physician who made some of the early microscopical observations of plants. He studied the structure of various plants' anatomy and introduced the term 'parenchyma' to refer to the ground tissue, or unspecialized cells, of a plant. His observations were included in his book *The Anatomy of Plants* (1682).

Grew and his contemporary Marcello Malpighi were responsible for significant advances in the understanding of botanical anatomy due to their widespread use of the light microscope.

Grey, Charles, 2nd Earl Grey (1764–1845)

British Whig politician. He entered Parliament in 1786, and in 1806 became First Lord of the Admiralty, and foreign secretary soon afterwards. As prime minister 1830–34, he carried the Great Reform Bill of 1832 that reshaped the parliamentary representative system and the act abolishing slavery throughout the British Empire in 1833. He succeeded to earldom in 1807.

Grey, Edward, 1st Viscount Grey of Fallodon (1862–1933)

British Liberal politician, nephew of Charles Grey. As foreign secretary 1905–16 he negotiated an entente with Russia in 1907, and backed France against Germany in the Agadir Incident of 1911. In 1914 he said: 'The lamps are going out all over Europe; we shall not see them lit again in our lifetime.' Baronet 1882, Viscount 1916.

Grey, Lady Jane (1537–1554)

Queen of England for nine days, 10–19 July 1553, the great-granddaughter of Henry VII. She was married in 1553 to Lord Guildford Dudley (died 1554), son of the Duke of Northumberland. Edward VI was persuaded by Northumberland to set aside the claims to the throne of his sisters Mary and Elizabeth. When Edward died on 6 July 1553, Jane reluctantly accepted the crown and was proclaimed queen four days later. Mary, although a Roman Catholic, had the support of the populace, and the Lord Mayor of London announced that she was queen on 19 July. Grey was executed on Tower Green.

Grey, Tanni (1969–)

British athlete. She won gold medals in the 100, 200, 400, and 800 metres wheelchair races at both the 1992 Paralympic Games at Barcelona and the 1994 world championships at Berlin. She won the women's wheelchair event at the London Marathon in 1992, 1994, 1996, and 1998. Also in 1998, she won gold in the 800 metres wheelchair event at the European Championships in Budapest, Hungary.

Grierson, John (1898–1972)

Scottish film producer, director, and theoretician. He pioneered the documentary film in Britain in the 1930s when he produced a series of information and publicity shorts for the General Post Office (GPO). The best known is *Night Mail* (1936), an account of the journey of the London–Glasgow mail train, directed by Basil Wright (1907–1987) and Harry Watt (1906–1987), with a score by Benjamin Britten and a commentary written by poet W H Auden.

Grierson's only film as a director was *Drifters* (1929), a documentary about the North Sea fishing fleet. Among the many impressive films he produced were *Industrial Britain* (1933) by the US documentarist Robert Flaherty, Basil Wright's *Song of Ceylon* (1934), made for the Ceylon Tea Board, and *Coal Face* (1935) by the Brazilian Alberto Cavalcanti (1897–1982).

Griffiths, Richard (1947–)

English character actor. His sharp wit and, in later roles, self-mocking love of food lie at the centre of many of the the roles he plays. A long-serving support player on film and in television, Griffiths appeared in British feature films such as *Chariots of Fire* (1982), *A Private Function* (1985), and *Withnail and I* (1987). In the 1990s he won a wider audience as the policeman-cum-chef in the television programme *Pie in the Sky*, and as the incompetent gourmet-loving politician in the miniseries *In the Red* (1998).

Griffiths, Trevor (1935–)

English playwright and television dramatist. His plays explore revolutionary activity, and include *Occupations* (1970), *The Party* (1973), and *Comedians* (1975).

Born in Manchester, he was a teacher and further-education lecturer, and then Further Education Officer for BBC television in Leeds until 1972.

Grimaldi, Joseph (1779–1837)

English clown. Born in London, he was the son of an Italian actor. He appeared on the stage at two years old. He gave his name 'Joey' to all later clowns, and excelled as 'Mother Goose', performed at Covent Garden in 1806.

Grimond, Jo(seph), Baron Grimond (1913–1993)

British Liberal politician. As leader of the Liberal Party 1956–67, he aimed at making it 'a new radical party to take the place of the Socialist Party as an alternative to Conservatism'. An old-style Whig and a man of culture and personal charm, he had a considerable influence on postwar British politics, although he never held a major public position. During his term of office, the number of Liberal seats in Parliament doubled.

Grimsby

Fishing port and administrative headquarters of ◊North East Lincolnshire, England, on the River Humber, 24 km/15 mi southeast of Hull; population (1995) 89,400. It declined in the 1970s when Icelandic waters were closed to British fishing fleets. Chemicals and processed foods are manufactured, and marine-related industries and tourism are important. The ports of Grimsby and ◊Immingham, 10 km/6 mi up river, are managed jointly from Grimsby, and together deal with 46 million tonnes of freight a year.

The commercial dock at Immingham handles crude oil, iron ore, processed steel, coal, cars, fish, and container traffic. There is also traffic in timber, fertilizers, sugar, grain, and paper.

Industry

Chemical manufacturing is based on the South Humber, and oil refineries are located just outside Immingham. Food- and fish- processing are important, and include icemaking and the provision of cold storage facilities; the principal products are salted and smoked fish, pizzas, and frozen vegetables. Transport and distribution industries and services include an offshore supply base at Immingham; ship engineering and repairing; net, rope, and twinemaking; and box manufacture. Other industries include the preparation of fishmeal and

GRIMALDI, JOSEPH *English clown Joseph Grimaldi in the pantomime* Harlequin and the Red Dwarf. *Grimaldi's first stage appearance was as a dancer at Sadler's Wells when he was only two years old, and he continued to perform there for many years. Corbis*

fertilizers, and animal foods; and the production of medicines and bituminous paints. Neighbouring Cleethorpes is the main tourist centre, attracting around one million visitors a year.

Fishing

In 1860 the total number of fishing vessels using the port was 60 (sailing) and the quantity of fish sent by rail was 4,919 tonnes; in 1880, following dock improvements, the figures were 587 sailing vessels and 47,682 tonnes; and by 1909 the total number of vessels was 608 (29 sailing and 579 steam) and the fish dispatched amounted to 178,780 tonnes. The tonnage of fish landed at Grimsby in 1974 was 170,000 tonnes (about 17% of all fish landed at British ports).

The fishing fleet started to decline in number as a result of overfishing in many of the traditional grounds, the increasing size of vessels, and the extension of territorial waters to 320 km/200 nautical miles by Iceland during 1975–76 with the collapse of cod stocks in the North Atlantic. Numbers have been further reduced largely as a result of the imposition of international quota systems, initially on catches of cod from the North Sea, but latterly incorporating eight other species under pressure from overfishing. Grimsby trawlers now fish as far afield as the Faroes, Iceland, Bear Island, and the White Sea. In 1996 volumes had reduced to 65,000 tonnes of frozen fish landed at Grimsby, but a further 40,000 tonnes of fish arrived overland to be sold in the market. Some containerized fish was imported through Immingham.

In 1992 Grimsby's fish dock was redeveloped to provide the most advanced facility in the UK; it comprises three dock facilities, covering 25 ha/62 acres of water. Grimsby fish market is the newest in Europe. Opened in 1996, the market hall for auctioning fish covers an area of 8,000 sq m/86,000 sq ft. About 27,000 workers depend directly or indirectly on the fishing industry.

Features

The National Fishing Heritage Centre is housed in the redeveloped Alexandra Dock area. The site of the church of St Mary is marked by the three St Mary's Gates (west, south, and east). The church of St James was rebuilt in the Early English style, probably between 1190 and 1225. It was substantially altered in 1718 and restoration work began in 1858 and continued until 1928. The original town hall, built by the burgesses in 1394, was replaced in 1780 by a brick building demolished in 1863; the present town hall was erected on a new site. Various ship and offshore training establishments exist.

History

There is evidence of Roman occupation in the area. It is thought that by the late 12th century it was the main port on the Humber, and Richard I held a meeting here in 1194. King John granted its first charter for 55 marks of gold. In 1319 Edward II granted a charter allowing the burgesses to hold two fairs and to have their own jail and assizes. During the Middle Ages and in Tudor and Stuart times, the prosperity of the town declined owing to silting up of the harbour. However, in 1800 the new dock was opened, in 1848 the Sheffield and Lincolnshire Railway Company extended the line to Grimsby, and in 1852 the Royal Dock opened. In the second half of the 19th century Grimsby's prosperity grew rapidly and it became one of the foremost fishing ports in the world. In 1912 a new commercial dock was opened at Immingham to relieve the congestion in the docks at Grimsby. A new fish dock was opened in 1934. During World War II Grimsby was a naval base.

Origin of the name Grimsby

According to the anonymous 13th-century poem 'Havelock the Dane' (*c.* 1272), Grimsby's name has Danish origins. The poem tells how a Danish fisherman named **Grim** (or Gryem) had been ordered to murder Havelock (or Hablock), the baby heir to the throne. He fled instead to England with the boy, who eventually married an English princess. As king of both England and Denmark, he rewarded Grim for his faithfulness and, according to the poem, the fishing settlement of Grimsby became an important town. Another variation made Grim a Lincolnshire fisherman who rescued the baby from a drifting boat; the child was later recognized as the son of the king of Denmark. His grateful father loaded Grim with riches, and he returned to Lincolnshire to found Grimsby.

The town seal of Grimsby, dating probably from Edward I, shows a large figure of Grim with Havelock and his queen. Grim is also commemorated in a statue in the grounds of Grimsby College.

Grimshaw, Nicholas Thomas (1939–)

English architect. His work has developed along distinctly High Tech lines, diverging sharply from that of his former partner, Terry ◊Farrell. His *Financial Times* printing works, London (1988), is an uncompromising industrial building, exposing machinery to view through a glass outer wall. The British Pavilion for Expo '92 in Seville, created in similar vein, addressed problems of climatic control, incorporating a huge wall of water in its façade and sail-like mechanisms on the roof.

groat ('great penny')

English coin worth four pennies. Although first minted in 1279, the groat only became popular in the following century, when silver groats were produced. Half groats were introduced in 1351.

Grossmith, George (1847–1912)

English actor and singer. Turning from journalism to the stage, in 1877 he began a long association with the Gilbert and Sullivan operas, in which he created a number of parts. He collaborated with his brother **Weedon Grossmith** (1854–1919) on the comic novel *Diary of a Nobody* (1894).

Grosvenor

Family name of the dukes of Westminster. The family's seat is at Eaton Hall, Cheshire, England.

Grove, George (1820–1900)

English scholar. He edited the original *Dictionary of Music and Musicians* (1889), which in its expanded and revised form is still one of the standard music reference sources. He was also the first director of the ◊Royal College of Music. He was knighted in 1882.

Groves, Charles Barnard (1915–)

English conductor. Known both as a choral and symphonic conductor, he is an outstanding interpreter of British music, especially the works of Delius. He was knighted in 1973.

groyne

Wooden or concrete barrier built at right angles to a beach in order to block the movement of material along the beach by longshore drift. Groynes are usually successful in protecting individual beaches, but because they prevent beach material from passing along the coast they can mean that other beaches, starved of sand and shingle, are in danger of being eroded away by the waves. This happened, for example, at Barton-on-Sea in Hampshire, England, in the 1970s, following the construction of a large groyne at Bournemouth.

Grub Street

Road on the north side of the city of London. It became the squalid resort of hack writers in the 17th century, and the term was applied by metaphorical extension to all literary work thought to be scurrilous, pornographic, seditious, or ephemeral and transient.

The street itself was renamed Milton Street in 1830 and was obliterated by the Barbican development in the 1980s, but the metaphoric sense remains.

The actual associations of the place (disease, refuse, poverty, venality) become powerful symbolic associations in satirical literature of the 18th century, for example in Alexander Pope's *The Dunciad* (1728–43).

Gruffydd ap Cynan (*c.* 1054–1137)

King of Gwynedd 1081–1137. He was raised in Ireland, but came to claim the throne of Gwynedd in 1075 and helped halt Norman penetration of Wales. Although defeated and exiled by the Normans in 1098, he returned and was allowed to establish his kingdom after paying homage to Henry I. He led a rising against English dominance in 1135 until his death two years later. He is traditionally regarded as a patron of music and the arts and helped codify much of the previously chaotic bardic tradition.

Gruffydd ap Llewellyn (died 1063)

King of Gwynedd. He had gained control of Gwynedd and Powys by 1039, Deheubarth by 1044, and extended his influence to Gwent by 1055. By the middle of the 11th century, most of Wales was either under his direct control or subject to his wishes, but his successors were unable to retain this dominance after his death. He conducted a series of raids across the English border and formed alliances with dissatisfied elements in Mercia and other English border areas. The English moved against him and defeated him at Rhuddlan in 1063, and he was killed by his own supporters.

Guardian, The

Newspaper, established as a weekly in 1821 and which started appearing daily in 1855. Formerly the *Manchester Guardian*, it was founded to 'advocate the cause of reform' and 'fight scurrility and slander'. The paper is the UK's second oldest national daily newspaper and its leading liberal daily. It is owned by the Guardian Media Group, and, along with its Sunday sibling *The Observer*, has its editorial independence safeguarded by a non-profit trust which owns the Group. Its circulation in 1998 was over 400,000.

The paper changed its name to *The Guardian* in 1959, as two thirds of its circulation lay outside the Manchester area. After 1961 it was printed in London as well as in Manchester and in 1964 the editorial offices were transferred to London.

Guernsey

Second largest of the ◊Channel Islands; area 63 sq km/24.3 sq mi; population (1991) 58,900. The capital is St Peter Port. Products include electronics, tomatoes, flowers, and butterflies; and since 1975 it has been a major financial centre. Guernsey cattle, which are a distinctive pale fawn colour and give rich, creamy milk, originated here.

Guernsey has belonged to the English crown since 1066, but was occupied by German forces 1940–45.

The island has no jury system; instead, it has a Royal Court with 12 jurats (full-time unpaid jurors appointed by an electoral college) with no legal training. This system dates from Norman times. Jurats cannot be challenged or replaced.

Guernsey

Breed of dairy cattle originating in Guernsey, Channel Islands. Like the ◊Jersey, they are of French descent. They are fawn-coloured, marked with white, and are noted for their yellow-coloured milk. Like Jerseys, they are not desirable beef producers.

Guildford

Cathedral city and county town (since 1257) of Surrey, southeast England, on the River Wey, 48 km/30 mi southwest of London; urban population (1991) 60,000; borough population (1996 est) 124,600. Industries include telecommunications, engineering, and the manufacture of plastics and pharmaceuticals. Features include a ruined Norman castle, a cathedral (founded in 1936 and consecrated in 1961), the main campus of the University of Surrey (1966), and the Yvonne Arnaud Theatre (opened in 1965).

Features

Only the ruined 12th-century Norman keep remains of the castle, once a royal residence. Guildford's museum includes relics of the author Charles Dodgson (Lewis Carroll) who died in Guildford in 1898. The Guildhall has a 17th-century facade and a gilded clock dating from 1683 projecting over the street. An inscription over the gate of the Royal Grammar School attributes its foundation to Edward VI in 1552, but it is thought to have been originally founded by Robert Beckingham (d. 1528) and the present building was begun about 1557. The Abbot's Hospital was founded in 1619 by George Abbot, archbishop of Canterbury (d.1633). Battersea College of Advanced Technology was granted a charter as the University of Surrey in 1966. The Yvonne Arnaud Theatre, built on the banks of the Wey, was named after the French actress who lived in Guildford for many years and died here in 1958.

The Tudor mansion Sutton Place, 3 km/2 mi to the northeast of the city, was the 17th-century home of Richard Weston, a noted agricultural innovator and instigator of the 25 km/15.5 mi-long Wey Navigation (1651–53), built to transport grain, timber, gunpowder, and chalk. Sutton Place later became the home of J Paul Getty, the 20th-century US oil millionaire. Loseley House, an Elizabethan manor house, lies 2 km/1 mi to the southwest.

Cathedral and churches

The brick-built cathedral is situated on Stag Hill, to the northwest of the city centre. Designed by Edward Maufe, it was the third entirely new Anglican cathedral to have been built in England since the Reformation. The partly-Saxon St Mary's Church contains medieval wall paintings; the original stone tower of the church, rebuilt in 1050, still survives. Holy Trinity was built in 1740 and the church of St Nicholas in 1875. St Martha's is an ancient cruciform church, restored in the 19th century.

History

In about 880 Alfred the Great bequeathed the town to his nephew Ethelwold, and it began to develop as a defensive and commercial centre. Guildford was a royal mint town until 1100, and the earliest known charters of Guildford are dated 1257. In medieval times Guildford prospered as an important centre of the wool trade, introduced by the Cistercians, and it was an important staging post in the 17th century. The railway replaced this service in 1845.

Guildford Four

Four Irish victims of miscarriage of justice who spent 14 years in prison convicted of terrorist bombings of pubs in Guildford and Woolwich in 1974. They were released in 1989 when an investigation concluded that the arresting Surrey police had given misleading evidence and, in consequence, their convictions were subsequently quashed.

Three former Surrey police officers were subsequently accused of conspiring to pervert the course of justice.

Guildhall

Council hall of the Corporation (governing body) of the City of London. The Great Hall of the present building dates from 1954, designed by Giles Gilbert ◊Scott, and is the venue for ceremonial banquets held by the lord mayor of London. A reference library of books, manuscripts, maps, and prints relating to London is housed in a separate building.

Guildhall School of Music and Drama , or GSMD

Conservatoire established in 1880 as the first municipal music college in Great Britain. It now offers courses in music, acting and technical theatre, and is owned, funded, and managed by the Corporation of London. Since 1977 it has been housed in the Barbican, London.

guillotine

In politics, a device used by governments in which the time allowed for debating a bill in the House of Commons is restricted so as to ensure its speedy passage to receiving the royal assent (that is, to becoming law). The tactic of guillotining was introduced during the 1880s to overcome attempts by Irish members of Parliament to obstruct the passing of legislation.

guinea

English gold coin, notionally worth 21 shillings (£1.05). It has not been minted since 1817, when it was superseded by the gold sovereign, but was used until 1971 in billing professional fees. Expensive items in shops were often priced in guineas.

Guinevere, Welsh Gwenhwyfar

In British legend, the wife of King ◊Arthur. Her adulterous love affair with the knight ◊Lancelot of the Lake led ultimately to Arthur's death.

Guinness

Irish brewing family who produced the dark, creamy stout of the same name. In 1752 Arthur Guinness (1725–1803) inherited £100 and used it to set up a brewery in Leixlip, County Kildare, which was moved to Dublin in 1759. The business grew under his son Arthur (1767–1855) and under Arthur's son Benjamin (1798–1868), who developed an export market in the USA and Europe.

In the 1980s the family interest in the business declined to no more than 5% as the company expanded by taking over large and established firms such as Bells in 1985 and Distillers in 1986 (the takeover of the latter led to a trial in 1990; see ◊Guinness affair).

In 1995 Guinness had 23,297 UK employees; turnover was £4,690,000,000 and pretax profits were £915,000,000.

Guinness, Alec (1914–)

English actor of stage and screen. A versatile performer, he played eight parts in *Kind Hearts and Coronets* (1949); other films include *The Lavender Hill Mob* (1952), *The Ladykillers* (1955), *The Bridge on the River Kwai* (1957) (Academy Award), and *Star Wars* (1977).

Guinness joined the Old Vic in 1936. His film career ranges from *Great Expectations* (1946) to *A Passage to India* (1984) and *Kafka* (1991). A subtle character actor, he played the enigmatic spymaster in TV adaptations of John Le Carré's *Tinker, Tailor, Soldier, Spy* (1979) and *Smiley's People* (1981). He was awarded an honorary Academy Award in 1979. He was made a CBE in 1994.

Guinness affair

In British law, a case of financial fraud during the takeover of Distillers by the brewing company Guinness in 1986. Those accused of acting illegally to sustain Guinness share prices included Ernest Saunders (1935–), the former chief executive. The trial, which lasted February–August 1990, was widely seen as the first major test of the government's legislation aimed at increasing control of financial dealings on London's Stock Exchange.

Ernest Saunders, Gerald Ronson (1939–), and Sir Jack Lyons were found guilty on a variety of theft and false-accounting charges. The trial lasted 107 days at an estimated cost of £20 million. In November 1995 they lost an appeal against their convictions; the appeal had been called for after it emerged that evidence in their favour had been withheld during the original trial.

Gulf War

War between Iraq and a coalition led by the USA, of 28 nations, including the UK, 16 January–28 February 1991. Iraq had invaded and annexed Kuwait on 2 August 1990 on account of a dispute over a shared oilfield, and the price of oil, provoking a build-up of US troops in Saudi Arabia, eventually totalling over 500,000.

An air offensive lasting six weeks destroyed about one-third of Iraqi equipment and inflicted massive casualties. A 100-hour ground war followed, which effectively destroyed the remnants of the 500,000-strong Iraqi army in or near Kuwait. The UK deployed 42,000 troops during the war.

Gulf War Syndrome

Mystery illness suffered by soldiers who fought in the 1991 Gulf War. Symptoms include headaches, memory loss, listlessness, depression, respiratory problems, lethargy, muscle weakness, nausea, and pain. It may be a form of shell shock, or the symptoms could have been caused by a combination of vaccinations (to tropical diseases and diseases likely to be used in biological weapons), nerve gas, anti-nerve gas drugs, and organophosphate (OP) insecticides. In addition, troops were also exposed to Iraqi chemical weapons and smoke from burning oil wells.

The British government admitted in October 1996 that poisoning by OP pesticides may have caused the syndrome that has affected about 1,040 British soldiers and 150,000 Americans, but refused to recognize the existence of one single illness that could be described as Gulf War Syndrome. It was revealed that soldiers had to spray the chemicals without being issued with protective clothing. Ministry of Defence officials, who ordered the use of the pesticides as antimosquito protection, failed to heed a warning by the government's Health and Safety Executive (HSE) about OPs. The Ministry of Defence launched two studies (at a cost of £1.3 million) into Gulf War Syndrome in 1996.

Gulliver's Travels

Satirical novel by Jonathan ◊Swift published in 1726. The four countries visited by the narrator Gulliver ridicule different aspects of human nature, customs, and politics.

Gulliver's travels take him to Lilliput, whose inhabitants are only 15 cm/6 in tall; Brobdignag, where they are gigantic; Laputa, run by mad scientists; and the land of the

GULF WAR *Two British soldiers prepare their Challenger tank during the Gulf War, in preparation for a movement to retake Kuwait from the Iraqis. The war on land was swift and barely opposed, following weeks of US-led UN bombing of Iraqi positions. Many servicemen and women serving during the war later fell ill to an illness known as Gulf War syndrome. Corbis*

Houyhnhnms, horses who embody reason and virtue, while the human Yahoos have only the worst human qualities.

Gummer, John Selwyn (1939–)

British Conservative politician, secretary of state for the environment 1993–97. He was minister of state for employment 1983–84, paymaster-general 1984–85, minister for agriculture 1985–89, secretary of state for agriculture 1989–93, and chairman of the party 1983–85.

A prominent lay member of the Church of England, he left in 1994, after its decision to permit the ordination of women priests, and became a Roman Catholic.

gun laws

The British government announced in October 1996 that 80% of all handguns would be made illegal. The Gun Control Bill resulted from the recommendations of the Cullen report into the March 1996 Dunblane massacre, in which 16 children and their teacher were murdered. The ban covered ownership of handguns over .22 calibre and all handguns unless kept securely at gun clubs. Other key points of the legislation included stringent new security standards for gun clubs, tougher powers to check on firearms holders and dealers, a new national computer for all firearms licences, and stricter rules on holding a licence. The new gun laws are among the most draconian in the world and far tougher than those of other European countries. Under the new legislation, anyone caught in possession of the outlawed higher-calibre handguns can be imprisoned for up to ten years, with a similar penalty applying to people who keep the permitted small-calibre guns outside club premises.

The Labour Party, the Liberal Democrats, and the families and supporters of the Dunblane victims called for a total ban on handguns. The Snowdrop Petition from Dunblane parents and supporters provided much of the impetus for the changes to the laws.

Gunn, Neil Miller (1891–1974)

Scottish novelist. His first novel, *Grey Coast* (1926), at once brought him recognition and was followed by a series of others including *The Lost Glen* (1932), *Butcher's Broom* (1934), *Wild Geese Overhead* (1939), *Highland River* (1937) (Tait Black Memorial Prize), and *The Silver Darlings* (1941).

Gunn excelled in depicting the ordinary life and social and economic history of the Scottish Highlands, and in interpreting the folk wisdom and psychology of the Celts.

Gunnell, Sally (1966–)

English athlete. She won the 1986 Commonwealth 100-metre hurdles gold medal before moving on to 400-metre hurdles. Her career highlights include gold medals over 400-metre hurdles at the 1992 Olympics, 1993 world championships (breaking the world record), 1990 and 1994 Commonwealth Games, and 1994 European Championships. She announced her retirement from competition in 1997.

Gunpowder Plot

Catholic conspiracy to blow up James I and his parliament on 5 November 1605. It was discovered through an anonymous letter. Guy ◊Fawkes was found in the cellar beneath the Palace of Westminster, ready to fire a store of explosives. Several of the conspirators were killed as they fled, and Fawkes and seven others were captured and executed.

In 1604 the conspirators, led by Robert Catesby, took possession of a vault below the House of Lords where they stored barrels of gunpowder. Lord Monteagle, a Catholic peer, received the anonymous letter warning him not to attend Parliament on 5 November. A search was made, and Guy Fawkes was discovered in the vault and arrested.

The event is commemorated annually in England on 5 November by fireworks and burning 'guys' (effigies) on bonfires.

Gunter, Edmund (1581–1626)

English mathematician who became professor of astronomy at Gresham College, London in 1619. He is reputed to have invented a number of surveying instruments as well as the trigonometrical terms 'cosine' and 'cotangent'.

Gurkha

Member of any of several peoples living in the mountains of Nepal, whose young men have been recruited since 1815 for the British and Indian armies. The ten regiments of Gurkhas served in both world wars. When India and Pakistan became independent in 1947, four of the Gurkha regiments were assigned to the British army, and six to the Indian.

Gurney, Ivor (Bertie) (1890–1937)

English poet and composer. He was a poet both of the Gloucestershire countryside and of the war at the front. *Severn and Somme* was published in 1917 and *War's Embers* in 1919. Though his third volume of verse was rejected, he published song-cycles of poems by A E Housman in 1923 and 1926, and settings of poems of Edward Thomas in 1926.

Guscott, Jeremey (1965–)

English rugby union player for Bath, England, and the British Lions. A fast, elusive centre of prodigious talent, he was a key member of the England side which won three Grand Slams in the Five Nations Championship between 1991 and 1995. He has played on three consecutive British Lions tours since 1989, most memorably in the second Test on the 1997 tour of South Africa when he sealed the series for the Lions with a drop goal.

Guthrie, (William) Tyrone (1900–1971)

English theatre director. He was notable for his innovative approach. Administrator of the ◊Old Vic and Sadler's Wells theatres 1939–45, he helped found the Ontario (Stratford) Shakespeare Festival in 1953 and the Minneapolis theatre now named after him. He pioneered the modern concept of open-stage productions for medieval and Renaissance plays. He was knighted in 1961.

Gwent

Former county of south Wales, 1974–1996, now divided between ◊Blaenau Gwent, ◊Caerphilly, ◊Monmouthshire, ◊Newport, and ◊Torfaen unitary authorities.

Gwyn or Gwynn, Nell (Eleanor) (1650–1687)

English comedy actress from 1665. She was formerly an orange-seller at Drury Lane Theatre, London. The poet Dryden wrote parts for her, and from 1669 she was the mistress of Charles II.

Gwynedd

Unitary authority in northwest Wales, created in 1996 from part of the former county of Gwynedd
Area 2,546 sq km/983 sq mi
Towns ◊Caernarfon (administrative headquarters)
Physical area includes the highest mountain in Wales, ◊Snowdon (1,085 m/3,560 ft), and the largest Welsh lake, Llyn Tegid (◊Bala Lake)
Features ◊Snowdonia National Park, seaside resorts, ◊Bardsey Island
Industries gold mining at ◊Dolgellau, textiles, electronics, slate, tourism
Agriculture cattle and sheep-farming
Population (1996) 116,000

Most of Gwynedd lies within ◊Snowdonia National Park. The ◊Lleyn Peninsula, which juts out into the Irish Sea and forms the northern limit of Cardigan Bay, is a rural area with many seaside resorts. Off the tip of the peninsula is the former pilgrimage centre of ◊Bardsey Island, with its 6th-century ruined abbey. In Tremadog Bay is the fantasy resort of ◊Portmeirion, built by Clough ◊Williams-Ellis.

Topography

Other mountains include Carnedd Llywelyn (1,062 m/3,484 ft), Carnedd Dafydd (1,044 m/3,425 ft), Glyder Fawr (999 m/3,278 ft), Aran Mawddwy (926 m/3,038 ft) and Cadair Idris (892 m/2,928 ft). There are several attractive river valleys, including the Dyfi (Dovey), Mawddach, and Maentwrog. There are over 50 lakes among the mountains and several waterfalls. The River Dee drains Bala Lake before passing out of the authority.

Other features

A rack railway to the top of Snowdon can be taken from the village of ◊Llanberis, which also houses the Welsh Slate Museum. Other tourist centres and seaside resorts in the area include Aberdaron, Abersoch, Barmouth, Criccieth, ◊Dolgellau, ◊Harlech, and ◊Pwllheli. Features of Pen y Bryn manor house at Aber, near Bangor, have been identified as surviving from the royal palace of Llewellyn I and Llewellyn II. The castles and town walls of Edward I in the unitary authority are a World Heritage Site. The area includes Caernarfon, Criccieth, and Harlech castles. Caernarfon also

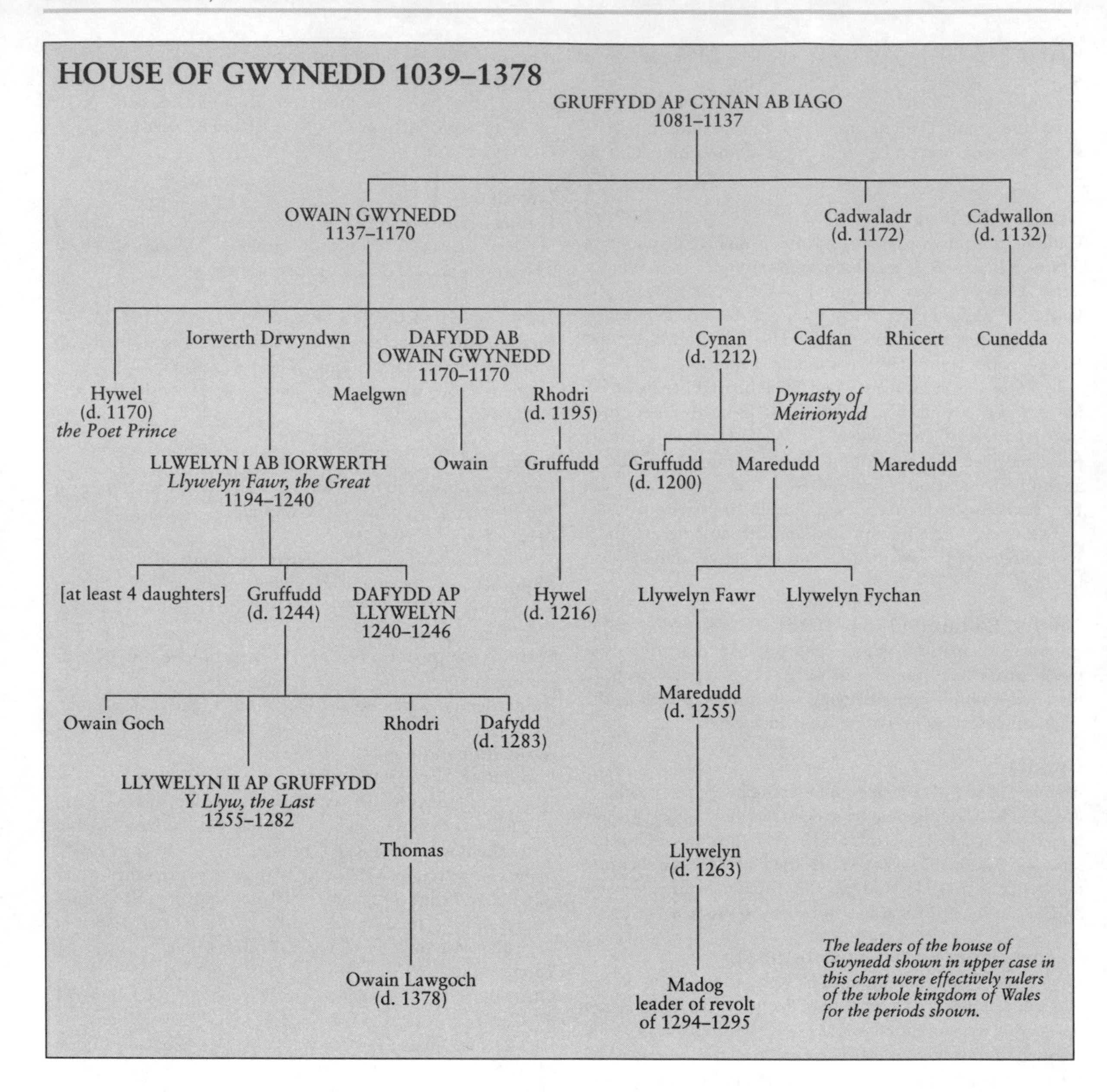

includes the **Sergontium** Roman Fort Museum. Edward II and T E Lawrence were born in the area.

Industry and agriculture

It is generally a region of mixed farming with sheep rearing on the hills and dairy and beef cattle on the lowland fringes. The district is noted for its hardy mountain sheep, rams, and Welsh black cattle. Quarrying for slate and granite were major occupations but have now declined, and light industries are found in the small towns. The Clogau mine at Bontddu supplies the gold for royal wedding rings. Lead, copper, and manganese have been worked near Dolgellau in the past.

Gwynedd, kingdom of

Medieval Welsh kingdom comprising north Wales and Anglesey. It was the most powerful kingdom in Wales during the 10th and 11th centuries: its king ◊Gruffydd ap Llewellyn dominated Wales in the mid-11th century and nearly succeeding in uniting the Welsh. When the Normans invaded England, Gwynedd led Welsh resistance against Norman efforts to extend their writ over the border, with mixed success. Llewellyn ap Gruffydd styled himself Prince of Wales in 1258, and the English king Henry III was forced to acknowledge him as such in 1267. Edward I rightly recognized Gwynedd as the key to subduing the Welsh and he launched a major offensive against Llewellyn in 1277, ultimately destroying the kingdom. Gwynedd was broken up and the lands of the ruling dynasty passed to the English Prince of Wales. See genealogy above.

habeas corpus (Latin 'you may have the body')

In law, a writ directed to someone who has custody of a person, ordering him or her to bring the person before the court issuing the writ and to justify why the person is detained in custody.

Traditional rights to habeas corpus were embodied in the English Habeas Corpus Act 1679. The main principles were adopted in the US Constitution. The Scottish equivalent is the Wrongous Imprisonment Act 1701.

Habitat

Furnishing company, specializing in modern design, founded in 1964 by Terence ◊Conran. Habitat has had a large influence on British interior decoration. In particular, the company's designs have popularized Scandinavian and French country style in the UK.

Conran left Habitat in 1990, and in 1992 it was sold to the Swedish furnishing company Ikea. In 1994–5 Habitat turnover was in excess of £100 million, and operating profits £10 million. There were 39 stores in the UK in 1995 (and one in Ireland), 37 in France, 10 in Italy and 14 elsewhere in Europe.

Hackney, formerly St John at Hackney

Inner borough of north-central Greater London. It includes the districts of Shoreditch and Stoke Newington.

Features Hackney Downs and **Hackney Marsh**, formerly the haunt of highwaymen, now a leisure area; the Theatre, Shoreditch, site of England's first theatre (1576); the Geffrye Museum, housed in early 18th-century almshouses and opened as a museum in 1914; early 16th-century Sutton House, housing the Early Music Centre; early Georgian Christ Church, designed by Nicholas Hawksmoor; Spitalfields market, moved here in 1991. The **hackney carriage**, originally a horse-drawn carriage for hire, is so named because harness horses were bred here in the 14th century

Industries transport, communications, financial services are the largest employers; clothing manufacture remains locally significant in Stoke Newington

Population (1994) 192,500

History

Proximity to the City of London and the railway brought rapid development from the mid 19th century and for a time it was a fashionable residential area. Industries subsequently became established, particularly along the River Lee.

In the 16th century Shoreditch was already a suburb of London, and by the mid 18th century its population was about 10,000. Industrialization in the 19th century led to rapid development, and before World War II it was one of the most overcrowded areas in London. Since World War II there has been a large increase in the ethnic minority population, especially of Afro-Caribbean origin; ethnic minorities now form one third of the total population.

In the 19th and early 20th century Hackney was noted for its poor housing and high crime level. The area has undergone much redevelopment since World War II, including housing estates, not all of which have proved durable. The Kray twins ran a crime syndicate in the area in the 1960s. Unemployment remains the highest in London, standing at 25.5% of the economically active population in 1993, and there are high levels of social deprivation.

Originally a village, Stoke Newington developed rapidly from the mid-19th century onwards. The principal industry in the district is the manufacture of clothing. It was at one time a centre of Nonconformity. Isaac Watts, the Nonconformist hymn writer, lived here for most of his life, and the poet Anna Laetitia Barbauld lived here for many years. The church has a late-medieval nave and a tower built in about 1560.

Haddington

Market town and administrative headquarters of ◊East Lothian, Scotland, on the River Tyne, 16 km/10 mi southwest of Dunbar; population (1991) 8,800. The Protestant reformer John Knox was born here (1505).

The medieval street pattern is a characteristic feature. Buildings in the town include St Mary's church (15th century); St Martin's church (12th century); the Classical town hall (18th century), a creation of William Adam, at least in part; and Haddington House (17th century). Stevenson House (16th century) is 3 km/2 mi east of the town centre, and 1.6 km/1 mi to the south lies Lennoxlove House (17th century), named after Frances Stewart, Duchess of Lennox, and now home of the Duke of Hamilton.

Haddingtonshire

Name until 1921 of the Scottish county of East Lothian, from 1975 part of the region of ◊Lothian.

Haddon Hall

Castellated house, standing on the River Wye, England, 3 km/2 mi southeast of Bakewell, Derbyshire. The first house was fortified around 1195, but little of the Norman structure remains.

The main building periods were the years around 1370 (the hall and parlour), early 15th century to early 16th century (the chapel and lower courtyard), and 1600 (the long gallery). Between 1700 and the careful restoration of the 20th century, the building remained untouched.

Before the Norman Conquest, Haddon was the property of the Crown, but William I granted it to William Peveril. It has been successively in the families of Avenell, Vernon, and Manners. The house is now seasonally open to the public.

Hadfield, Robert Abbott (1858–1940)

English industrial chemist and metallurgist. He invented stainless steel and developed various other ferrous alloys. In making ordinary mild steel, pig iron is oxidized, to lower the carbon content. Hadfield carried out many experiments in which he added other metals to the steel. He found, for example, that a small amount of manganese gave a tough, wear-resistant steel suitable for such applications as railway track and grinding machinery. By adding nickel and chromium he produced corrosion-resistant stainless steels. Knighted 1908, baronet 1917.

Hadid, Zahia (1950–)

British architect, born in Baghdad. An exponent of Deconstructionism, she has been influential through her drawings rather than buildings. Her unbuilt competition-winning entry for Hong Kong's Peak Club in 1983 established her reputation, and in 1993 she completed her first major building, a fire station for the Vitra Furniture Factory at Weil-am-Rhein, Germany.

Hadley, Patrick (Arthur Sheldon) (1899–1973)

English composer. His musical output is small but distinguished, and includes incidental music for Greek plays, choral works *The Trees so High* (1931) and *The Hills* (1944), a rhapsody *One Morning in Spring* for small orchestra, vocal works, church music, and a string quartet.

Hadrian's Wall

Roman frontier system built AD 122–26 to mark England's northern boundary and abandoned in about 383; its ruins run 185 km/115 mi from Wallsend on the River Tyne to Maryport, West Cumbria. It has been referred to colloquially

HADRIAN'S WALL *Marking the northernmost limit of the Roman colonization of Britain, Hadrian's Wall was constructed to prevent tribes such as the Scots and Picts from launching raids into northern England. Skilfully built to take advantage of the lie of the land, and guarded by troops stationed in small forts, the wall was an effective defence, though it was breached in* AD *197, 296, and 367–68. Linda Proud*

as the **Picts' Wall**. In some parts, the wall was covered with a glistening, white coat of mortar. It was defended by 16 forts and smaller intermediate fortifications. It was breached by the Picts on several occasions and finally abandoned in about 383.

In 1985 Roman letters (on paper-thin sheets of wood), the earliest and largest collection of Latin writing, were discovered at Vindolanda Fort. Hadrian's Wall was declared a World Heritage Site in 1987.

Haggard, H(enry) Rider (1856–1925)

English novelist. He used his experience in the South African colonial service in his romantic adventure tales, including *King Solomon's Mines* (1885) and *She* (1887), the best of which also illuminate African traditions and mythology.

His first book, *Cetewayo and his White Neighbours*, appeared in 1882. In 1884 he published *Dawn*, the first of his novels, and followed it with others, most of which were very successful.

Haggard was deeply interested in agricultural and rural questions; *Rural England* (1902) was a valuable study. He was knighted in 1912.

haggis

Scottish dish made from a sheep's or calf's heart, liver, and lungs, minced with onion, oatmeal, suet, spices, and salt, mixed with stock, and traditionally boiled in the animal's stomach for several hours.

Haggis is traditionally served at Hogmanay (New Year's Eve) and on Burns' Night (25 January).

It was inevitable that the Titanic *would set sail, but that does not mean it was a good idea to be on it.*

WILLIAM HAGUE British Conservative party leader.
On the advent of the single European currency;
Daily Telegraph, 7 January 1998

Hague, William Jefferson (1961–)

British Conservative politician, leader of the Conservative party from 1997. He entered the House of Commons in 1989, representing the constituency of Richmond, Yorkshire, and was private secretary to the chancellor of the Exchequer 1990–93, parliamentary under-secretary of state in the Department of Social Security 1993–94, minister for Social Security and disabled people 1994–95, and secretary of state for Wales 1995–97. After the Conservative Party defeat in the May 1997 general election, the then party leader John Major resigned and Hague was elected his successor. He committed the party to oppose joining the European single currency for at least a decade in 1998 and launched major reforms of the party's organization.

He had come to public attention in 1977 when, at the age of 16, he addressed the party's annual conference. The new leader, the youngest for more than 200 years, promised to unite the party and included in his shadow cabinet three of his rivals, Michael Howard, Peter Lilley, and John Redwood, Kenneth Clarke having earlier declined an invitation to join him.

Haig, Douglas, 1st Earl Haig (1861–1928)

Scottish army officer, commander in chief in World War I. His Somme offensive in France in the summer of 1916 made considerable advances only at enormous cost to human life, and his Passchendaele offensive in Belgium from July to November 1917 achieved little at a similar loss. He was created field marshal in 1917 and, after retiring, became first president of the ◊British Legion in 1921.

A national hero at the time of his funeral, Haig's reputation began to fall after Lloyd George's memoirs depicted him as treating soldiers' lives with disdain, while remaining far from battle himself.

Hailsham, Quintin McGarel Hogg, Baron Hailsham of St Marylebone (1907–)

British Conservative politician and lawyer. Having succeeded as 2nd Viscount Hailsham in 1950, he renounced the title in 1963 to re-enter the House of Commons, and was then able to contest the Conservative Party leadership elections. He took a life peerage in 1970 on his appointment as Lord Chancellor 1970–74 and was Lord Chancellor again 1979–87.

Hailwood, Mike (Stanley Michael Bailey) (1940–1981)

English motorcyclist. Between 1961 and 1967 he won nine world titles and a record 14 titles at the Isle of Man TT races between 1961 and 1979.

Haitink, Bernard (1929–)

Dutch conductor. He was associated with the London Philharmonic Orchestra from 1967; musical director at Glyndebourne 1977–87 and at the Royal Opera House, Covent Garden, London, 1987–98. A noted interpreter of Mahler and Shostakovitch, he also conducted Mozart's music for the film *Amadeus* (1984).

Haitink handed in his resignation to the Royal Opera on September 16th 1998, after it was announced that the company, in financial crisis, would close for a year.

Hakluyt, Richard (*c.* 1552–1616)

English geographer whose chief work is *The Principal Navigations, Voyages and Discoveries of the English Nation* (1598–1600). He was assisted by Sir Walter Raleigh.

He lectured on cartography at Oxford, became geographical adviser to the East India Company, and was an original member of the Virginia Company.

The **Hakluyt Society**, established in 1846, published later accounts of exploration.

Haldane, J(ohn) B(urdon) S(anderson) (1892–1964)

Anglo-Indian physiologist, geneticist, and author of popular science books. In 1936 he showed the genetic link between haemophilia and colour blindness. In 1924 Haldane produced the first proof that enzymes obey the laws of thermodynamics.

Haldane carried our research into how the regulation of breathing in man is affected by the level of carbon dioxide in the bloodstream. During World War II, in 1942, Haldane, who often used his own body in biochemical experiments, spent two days in a submarine to test an air-purifying system.

Haldane was convinced that natural selection and not mutation is the driving force behind evolution. In 1932, he estimated for the first time the rate of mutation of the human gene and worked out the effect of recurrent harmful mutations on a population. He is supposed to have remarked: 'I'd lay down my life for two brothers or eight cousins.'

Haldane, John Scott (1860–1936)

Scottish physiologist. His studies of the exchange of gases during respiration led to an interest in the health hazards of coal mining and deep-sea diving. His aim was to bridge the gap between theoretical and applied science.

Haldane devised methods for studying respiration and the blood – the **Haldane gas analyser** and an apparatus for determining the blood gas content. Having investigated the danger to miners of suffocation, he turned to the toxicity of carbon monoxide, which is usually present in mines after an explosion, and showed that haemoglobin in the red blood cells binds this gas in preference to oxygen.

In 1905 Haldane proposed that breathing is controlled by the concentration of carbon dioxide in arterial blood acting on the respiratory centre of the brain. In 1907 he announced the technique of decompression by stages which is still used today to allow deep-sea divers to surface safely. He also researched the reaction of the kidneys to the water content of the blood, and the physiology of sweating.

Hales, Stephen (1677–1761)

English scientist who studied the role of water and air in the maintenance of life. He gave accurate accounts of water movement in plants. He demonstrated that plants absorb air, and that some part of that air is involved in their nutrition. His work laid emphasis on measurement and experimentation.

Hales's work on air revealed to him the dangers of breathing 'spent' air in enclosed places, and he invented a ventilator which improved survival rates when introduced on naval, merchant, and slave ships, in hospitals, and in prisons.

He measured the pressure of sap in growing vines, calculated its velocity, and found that the rate of flow varies in different plants. He measured plant growth and water loss, relating this to the upward movement of water from plants to leaves (transpiration). He also measured blood pressure and the rate of blood flow in animals.

Hales examined stones taken from the bladder and kidney, and suggested possible chemical solvents for their nonsurgical treatment. He also invented the surgical forceps.

Halesowen

Town in the West Midlands metropolitan county, England, 11 km/7 mi west of Birmingham; population (1991) 24,000. Halesowen lies on the fringe of the former industrial area known as the ◊Black Country, but is close to the Clent Hills and other beauty spots. There are extensive iron, steel, and welded-tube works, together with factories producing chains, buttons, prams, and agricultural implements.

The church at Halesowen dates from the 12th century. The town was the birthplace of the 18th-century poet and essayist William Shenstone. To the southwest are the ruins of a 13th-century abbey.

halfpenny, or ha'penny

Originally round silver coins, first minted in the reign of Alfred the Great, and from 1672 the first English copper coin. From the 10th to the 13th centuries, the halfpenny was literally a full penny cut in half but it gradually became a coin in its own right. It was withdrawn with the advent of decimalization in 1969, although it remained legal tender until the 1980s.

Halifax

Town in West Yorkshire, northern England, on the River Calder, 13 km/8 mi northwest of Huddersfield; population (1991) 91,100. Important in the woollen cloth trade since medieval times, the town produces textiles, carpets, and clothing; other industries include engineering and the manufacture of confectionery (Nestlé). It is the headquarters of the Halifax plc (formerly Halifax Building Society).

Features

The restored Piece Hall, built in 1779 as a cloth market; the Calderdale Industrial Museum; the Perpendicular Gothic St John's Church; All Souls' (1857–59), designed by Gilbert Scott; the town hall (1859–62), designed by Charles Barry, architect of the Houses of Parliament; part of the original Halifax gibbet (a predecessor of the guillotine), used to behead cloth stealers (1541–1650), is preserved.

History

There is evidence that the cloth trade was established here in the late 13th century; local records for that period refer to 'websters' (weavers), 'walkers' (fullers), and 'litsters' (dyers). In the 15th century the parish of Halifax produced more cloth than any other place in Yorkshire. The street named Woolshops was once the site of the woolstaplers' (dealers) warehouses. The local weavers began making worsteds in the mid 18th century, the area expanded, and associated industries developed. The rapid increase in the town's population from 12,000 to 34,000 between 1801 and 1851 resulted in overcrowding and poor living conditions. With the arrival of the railways, Bradford became the chief textile-marketing centre for the area.

Architectural features

Piece Hall has 315 rooms and a colonnaded courtyard, and is now used for shops and a market. St John's Church is the third to have been built on the site; of the first church, built by the Cluniac monks of Lewes in about 1120, some Norman fragments survive; three of the windows of the second church (dating from about 1290) remain; the foundations of the present building were probably laid in about 1450. Borough Market is an attractive Victorian building.

Museums and galleries
Shibden Hall, in Shibden Park, is a timbered mansion dating partly from the 15th century; it houses a museum containing 17th-century furniture, a collection of manuscripts relating to the district, early printed books, and court rolls. The Bankfield Museum (opened in 1887) contains art, textiles, archaeology, and natural history collections. Eureka is a museum of technology designed for children.
Parks
Open spaces include Shroggs Park, overlooking Wheatley Valley; Saville Park (formerly Skircoat Moor), with Albert Promenade overlooking Copley Valley; the People's Park; West Vale Park (with Clare House); Shibden Hall and Park; Akroyd Park; Belle Vue Park; and Manor Heath.

Halifax, Edward Frederick Lindley Wood, 1st Earl of Halifax (2nd creation) (1881–1959)
British Conservative politician, viceroy of India 1926–31. As foreign secretary 1938–40 he was associated with Chamberlain's 'appeasement' policy. He received an earldom 1944 for services to the Allied cause while ambassador to the USA 1941–46. Baron 1925, succeeded as Viscount 1934, created Earl 1944.

Hall, James (1761–1832)
Scottish geologist. He was one of the founders of experimental geology and provided evidence in support of the theories of Scottish naturalist James ◊Hutton regarding the formation of the Earth's crust.

By means of furnace experiments, he showed with fair success that Hutton had been correct to maintain that igneous rocks would generate crystalline structures if cooled very slowly. Hall also demonstrated that there was a degree of interconvertibility between basalt and granite rocks; and that, even though subjected to immense heat, limestone would not decompose if sustained under suitable pressure. Baronet 1776.

Hall, Marshall (1790–1857)
English physician and physiologist who distinguished between voluntary and involuntary reflex muscle contractions, proving that the spinal cord is more than a passive nerve trunk transmitting voluntary signals from the brain and sensory signals to the brain.

Hall is best known for his work on the nervous system of frogs. He showed that if the spinal cord of a frog was severed between the front and back limbs, then the front limbs could still be moved voluntarily but the back limbs were useless. He further showed that the back legs could be stimulated to move artificially, but only once for each stimulus. These were reflex (involuntary) muscle contractions. Pain stimuli applied to the back legs were not felt by the animals. From these experiments Hall deduced that the nervous system is made up of a series of reflex arcs. In the intact spinal cord these reflex arcs are coordinated by the ascending and descending pathways in the cord to form movement patterns.

Hall, Peter (Reginald Frederick) (1930–)
English theatre, opera, and film director. He was director of the Royal Shakespeare Theatre in Stratford-upon-Avon 1960–68 and developed the Royal Shakespeare Company 1968–73 until appointed director of the National Theatre 1973–88, succeeding Laurence Olivier. He founded the Peter Hall Company in 1988.

Hall's stage productions include Samuel Beckett's *Waiting for Godot* (1955), *The Wars of the Roses* (1963), Harold Pinter's *The Homecoming* (stage 1967 and film 1973), *The Oresteia* (1981), and Tennessee Williams's *Orpheus Descending* (1988). He has directed operas at Covent Garden, London; Bayreuth, Germany; and New York, and in 1984 was appointed artistic director of opera at Glyndebourne, East Sussex, with productions of *Carmen* (1985) and *Albert Herring* (1985–86).

He established a new repertory company based at the Old Vic Theatre, London, in 1996. In the same year, he directed *Carmen* in New York and *The Oedipus Plays* in London. He was knighted in 1977.

Hall, Radclyffe pen name of **Marguerite Radclyffe-Hall** (1880–1943)
English novelist. *The Well of Loneliness* (1928) brought her notoriety because of its lesbian theme. It was successfully prosecuted for obscenity and banned in the UK, but republished in 1949. Her other works include the novel *Adam's Breed* (1926; Femina Vie Heureuse and Tait Black Memorial prizes) and five early volumes of poetry.

Hallé, Charles (Carl) (1819–1895)
German conductor and pianist. Settling in England in 1848,

HALL, PETER *English director Peter Hall in front of the National Theatre, London. The theatre was designed by Denys Lasdun and built 1965–76; Hall was its director 1973–88.* Corbis

he established and led Manchester's Hallé Orchestra from 1858 until his death. As a pianist, he was the first to play all 32 Beethoven piano sonatas in London (also in Manchester and Paris).

Halley, Edmond (1656–1742)

English astronomer. He not only identified the comet that was later to be known by his name, but also compiled a star catalogue, detected the proper motion of stars using historical records, and began a line of research that, after his death, resulted in a reasonably accurate calculation of the astronomical unit.

Halley calculated that the comet sightings reported in 1456, 1531, 1607, and 1682 all represented reappearances of the same comet. He reasoned that the comet would follow a parabolic path and announced in 1705 in his *Synopsis Astronomia Cometicae* that it would reappear in 1758. When it did, public acclaim for the astronomer was such that his name was irrevocably attached to it.

He made many other notable contributions to astronomy, including the discovery of the proper motions of Aldebaran, Arcturus, and Sirius, and working out a method of obtaining the solar parallax by observations made during a transit of Venus. He was Astronomer Royal from 1720.

hallmark

Official mark stamped on British gold, silver, and (from 1913) platinum, instituted in 1327 (royal charter of London Goldsmiths) in order to prevent fraud. After 1363 personal marks of identification were added. Now tests of metal content are carried out at authorized assay offices in London, Birmingham, Sheffield, and Edinburgh; each assay office has its distinguishing mark, to which is added a maker's mark, date letter, and mark guaranteeing standard.

Hallowe'en

Evening of 31 October, immediately preceding the Christian feast of Hallowmas or All Saints' Day. Customs associated with Hallowe'en include children wearing masks or costumes, and 'trick or treating' – going from house to house collecting sweets, fruit, or money.

Hallowe'en is associated with the ancient Celtic festival of **Samhain**, which marked the end of the year and the beginning of winter. It was believed that on the evening of Samhain supernatural creatures were abroad and the souls of the dead were allowed to revisit their former homes.

Halton

Unitary authority in northwest England, created in 1998 from part of Cheshire

Area 74 sq km/29 sq mi

Towns and cities Runcorn, ◊Widnes (administrative headquarters), Ditton

Features River Mersey divides Runcorn from Widnes and Ditton; Manchester Ship Canal and Bridgewater Canal reach Mersey at Runcorn; St Helen's Canal reaches Mersey via a series of locks at Widnes; Catalyst: the Museum of the Chemical Industry is at Widnes; Norton Priory Museum (Runcorn) is on the site of a 12th-century priory

Industries industrial chemicals, pharmaceuticals, plastics manufacturing and coatings, light engineering, scientific instruments

Population (1995) 123,200.

Hambledon

Village in southeast Hampshire, southern England, 16 km/10 mi north of Portsmouth; population (1996) 836. The first cricket club was founded here in 1750.

A manor of Hambledon had been established and granted by the king to the bishop of Winchester by 1199, and there was a defined settlement at Hambledon by the 13th century.

Hamburger, Michael (Peter Leopold) (1924–)

German-born British poet, translator, and critic. He emigrated with his family to London in 1933, and began to write poetry in English while still at school. His verse was first published in *Later Hogarth* (1945), and he turned in the 1960s from traditional forms to a freer and deeper expression of feeling, in which images of nature and of the Holocaust are frequent. Collected *Poems 1941–1994* was published in 1995.

Hamed, Naseem ('Prince') (1974–)

English boxer. Born in Sheffield of Yemeni extraction and known as 'Prince' Naseem for his showmanship qualities. An exceptionally strong puncher for a featherweight, he is widely regarded as one of British boxing's greatest talents. He made his professional debut in 1992 and by August 1998 he was still unbeaten after 30 fights, He won the European bantamweight title and the WBC International super-bantamweight championship in 1994, before capturing the WBO world featherweight title in September 1995. He won the IBF version of the world featherweight title in February 1997, but relinquished it after a few months.

Ham House

Jacobean-style house near Petersham, Greater London, situated on the south bank of the Thames and owned by the National Trust. It was built in 1660 to an H-shaped Jacobean plan, and is notable for its historic contents, which are under the care of the Victoria and Albert Museum. These include much Elizabethan walnut, lacquered, gilded, and silver furniture, and some portraits by Peter ◊Lely in the Long Gallery.

Hamilton

Family name of the dukes of Abercorn. The family's seat is at Barons Court, County Tyrone. The 3rd duke was the great-grandfather of Diana, Princess of Wales.

Hamilton

Administrative headquarters of South Lanarkshire, Scotland, on the Clyde, 17 km/10.5 mi southeast of Glasgow; population (1991) 50,000. A declining industrial town, its industries include textiles, electronics, and engineering.

There is a racecourse, and between Hamilton and Motherwell is Strathclyde Country Park which is an extensive recreational area, with a theme park, recreational and sporting facilities. The artificial loch in the park was the site of **Hamilton Palace**, one of the largest palaces ever built in Scotland, which was finally demolished in 1927.

The ruins of Cadzow Castle (1744) lie 1.6 km/1 mi south of Hamilton in Chatelherault Country Park and are home to a breed of wild white cattle.

Hamilton, Emma, Lady born Amy Lyon (*c.* 1761–1815)

English courtesan who in 1782 became the mistress of Charles Greville and in 1786 of his uncle Sir William Hamilton (1730–1803), the British envoy to the court of Naples, who married her in 1791. After Admiral ◊Nelson's return from the Nile in 1798 during the Napoleonic Wars, she became his mistress and their daughter, Horatia, was born in 1801.

Hamilton, Iain Ellis (1922–)

Scottish composer. His intensely emotional and harmonically rich works include the ballet *Clerk Saunders* (1951); the operas *Pharsalia* (1968) and *The Royal Hunt of the Sun* (1967–69), which renounced melody for inventive chordal formations; and symphonies. He was one of the first British composers to exploit the serial method.

Hamilton, James, 3rd Marquis and 1st Duke of Hamilton (1606–1649)

Scottish adviser to Charles I. He led an army against the Covenanters (supporters of the National Covenant of 1638 to establish Presbyterianism) in 1639 and subsequently took part in the negotiations between Charles and the Scots. In the second English Civil War he led the Scottish invasion of England, but was captured at Preston and executed. He succeeded as marquis in 1625, and was made a duke in 1643.

Hamilton, Richard (1922–)

English artist, a pioneer of Pop art. His collage *Just What Is It That Makes Today's Homes So Different, So Appealing?* (1956; Kunsthalle, Tübingen, Germany) is often cited as the first Pop art work: its 1950s interior, inhabited by the bodybuilder Charles Atlas and a pin-up, is typically humorous, concerned with popular culture and contemporary kitsch.

He was particularly concerned with the photographic image, which he skilfully combined with oil paint in his *Portrait of Gaitskell as a Monster of Filmland* (1963; Arts Council of Great Britain). For his *Cosmetic Studies* (1969) fragments of fashion photographs were collaged to make a single face. His series *Swingeing London 67* (1967) comments on the prosecution for drugs of his art dealer Robert Fraser and the singer Mick Jagger.

Collected Works, an anthology of his writings, was published in 1982.

Hamlet

Tragedy by William ◊Shakespeare, first performed in 1601–02. Hamlet, after much hesitation, avenges the murder of his father, the king of Denmark, by the king's brother Claudius, who has married Hamlet's mother. The play ends with the death of all three.

Hamlet is haunted by his father's ghost demanding revenge, is torn between love and loathing for his mother, and becomes responsible for the deaths of his lover Ophelia, her father and brother, and his student companions Rosencrantz and Guildenstern. In the monologue beginning 'To be, or not to be' he contemplates suicide.

Hammersmith and Fulham

Inner borough of west central Greater London, north of the Thames

Features Hammersmith Terrace, 18th-century houses on riverside; Parish Church of St Paul (1631); Lyric Theatre (1890); Fulham Palace, residence of the bishops of London from the 12th century until 1973, it is one of the best medieval domestic sites in London, with buildings dating from the 15th century; Riverside studios; Olympia exhibition centre (1884); 18th-century Hurlingham Club; Wormwood Scrubbs prison

Population (1991) 136,500

Famous people Leigh Hunt; Ouida and Henri Gaudier-Brzeska were residents.

Hammond, Wally (Walter Reginald) (1903–1965)

English cricketer. One of the game's greatest players, between 1927 and 1947 he scored 7,249 test runs at an average of 58.45, including 22 centuries. The first test cricketer to reach both 6,000 and 7,000 test runs, he led the English first class averages for eight consecutive seasons, 1933–39, and in 1946. He was also a good medium-fast bowler and a brilliant slip fielder.

He was born in Dover, and made his first class debut for Gloucestershire in 1920 at the age of 17. From 1927, the year he made his first test appearance, to 1939 he was the dominant batsman in English cricket. In Australia, 1928–29, he made the record English test aggregate, 905 runs (at an average of 113.12) including two successive double centuries and a century in each innings of the fourth test. His 336 not out against New Zealand at Auckland in 1933, was then the record individual test score.

Hamnett, Katharine (1948–)

English fashion designer. She is particularly popular in the UK and Italy. Her oversized T-shirts promoting peace and environmental campaigns attracted attention in 1983 and 1984. She produces well-cut, inexpensive designs for men and women, predominantly in natural fabrics. In 1989 she began showing her collections in Paris, and in 1993 launched hand-knitwear and leather collections.

Hampden, John (1594–1643)

English politician. His refusal in 1636 to pay ◊ship money, a compulsory tax levied to support the navy, made him a national figure. In the Short and Long Parliaments he proved himself a skilful debater and parliamentary strategist.

King Charles I's attempt to arrest him and four other

leading MPs made the Civil War inevitable. He raised his own regiment on the outbreak of hostilities, and on 18 June 1643 was mortally wounded at the skirmish of Chalgrove Field in Oxfordshire.

Hampden Park

Scottish football ground, opened 1903, home of the Queen's Park club and the national Scottish team. It plays host to the Scottish FA Cup and League Cup final each year, as well as semifinals and other matches.

Extensive rebuilding work began at the stadium in the early 1990s for completion in 1999 when it will have a capacity of approximately 52,000. It recorded a crowd of 149,547 for the Scotland versus England game in 1937, the largest official attendance for a football match in Britain.

Hampshire

County of south England (since April 1997 Portsmouth and Southampton have been separate unitary authorities)
Area 3,679 sq km/1,420 sq mi
Towns and cities ◊Winchester (administrative headquarters), Aldershot, Andover, Basingstoke, Eastleigh, Gosport, Romsey, and Lymington
Physical New Forest (area 373 sq km/144 sq mi), in the southeast of the county, a Saxon royal hunting ground; rivers Avon, Ichen, and Test (which has trout fishing)
Features Hampshire Basin, where Britain has onshore and offshore oil; Danebury, 2,500-year-old Celtic hillfort; Beaulieu (including National Motor Museum); Broadlands (home of Lord Mountbatten); Highclere Castle (home of the Earl of Carnarvon, with gardens by Capability Brown); Hambledon, where the first cricket club was founded in 1750; site of the Roman town of Silchester; Jane Austen's cottage at Chawton (1809–17), now a museum; Twyford Down section of the M3 motorway was completed in 1994 despite protests
Industries aeronautics; brewing; chemicals; electronics; light engineering (at Basingstoke); oil from refineries at Fawley; perfume; pharmaceuticals
Agriculture market gardening (watercress)
Population (1995) 1,213,600
Famous people Gilbert White, Jane Austen, Charles Dickens
Topography
Hampshire is bounded on the south by the Solent and the Spithead, Southampton, and Portsmouth; on the west by Dorset and Wiltshire; on the north by West Berkshire and Wokingham; and on the east by Surrey and West Sussex. The county is divided by Southampton Water. The South Downs terminate south of Petersfield at Butser Hill (271 m/889 ft). There are also hills in the northern part of the county along the boundary, which are some of the highest chalk downs in England; the highest point of these hills is Sidown Hill (286 m/938 ft). There are the remains of the minor forests at Bere, Woolmer, Alice Holt, and Waltham Chase. About 377 ha/931 acres of common and manorial land on the northern edge of the New Forest were acquired in 1928 for the National Trust.
Historic remains
In addition to Danebury, there are early fortified hilltop refuges at Old Winchester Hill; St Catherine's Hill, Winchester; Ladle Hill, Sydmonton; Beacon Hill, Burghclere; and Quarley Hill. There are convent ruins at Netley, Beaulieu, and Titchfield; notable monastic churches still in use are Winchester Cathedral and Romsey Abbey.
The armed services
The Royal Navy has an establishment at Gosport, and the army has important military depots and training areas at Aldershot and Bordon in the northeast, and at Tidworth in the northwest. At Hamble there is aircraft construction.

HAMPSHIRE *Protesters occupy construction equipment for a new road at Twyford Down, Hampshire. The improvement of the M3 motorway from Southampton to London by excavating a cutting through chalk downland near Winchester provoked clashes between security guards and ecological activists concerned about the road's impact on the environment. Giles Askham/ Impact*

Hampshire

Breed of medium-wool, dark-faced, hornless sheep originating in Hampshire, England. The sheep are large and stocky, yield strong, fine fleece, and are a superior mutton breed.

Hampstead

District in the Greater London borough of ◊Camden. It is the site of Primrose Hill, Hampstead Heath, and Parliament Hill (on which Boudicca is said to have been buried in a barrow); Hampstead Garden suburb was begun in 1907. Notable buildings include Kenwood (about 1616, remodelled by Robert Adam in 1764), containing the Iveagh Bequest of paintings; Fenton House (1693), with a large collection of early keyboard instruments; and Keats House (1815–16), home of the poet John Keats, now a museum. John Constable is buried in the churchyard. Many famous people lived here, including Martin Frobisher, John Galsworthy, Edward Elgar, Ramsay Macdonald, and Anna Pavlova.

Hampton, Christopher (1946–)

English playwright. His plays include *The Philanthropist* (1970; Evening Standard Best Comedy Award). He has translated and adapted many plays for the stage, including the award-winning *Les Liasons Dangereuses* (1985) for the Royal Shakespeare Company, and Malcolm Bradbury's *The History Man* (1981) for BBC television.

Born in the Azores, he was resident dramatist at the Royal Court Theatre from 1968.

Hampton Court Conference

Meeting of the Anglican Church held at Hampton Court Palace near London in 1604. Presided over by King James I, its aim was to consider the objections Puritans had raised to certain Anglican rites, ceremonies, and prayers. Few concessions were made to Puritan demands for change, but the Conference did lead to a major new translation of the Bible, the Authorized Version of 1611.

The Puritan demands were embodied in the Millenary Petition of 1603 (so called because it had a thousand supporters in clergy). John Rainolds was the leading spokesman for the Puritans, and the archbishop of Canterbury, Richard Bancroft (1544–1610), led the bishops' side.

The bishops rejected the Puritans' demands on theological grounds, and King James decided in favour of the bishops, arguing that the logic of the Puritan position meant 'no bishop, no king'. He did however accept Rainolds's suggestion that a new English translation of the Bible should be made, and a strong panel of theologians and scholars was set up to undertake the work.

Hampton Court Palace

Former royal residence near Richmond, England, 24 km/15 mi west of central London. Hampton Court is one of the greatest historical monuments in the UK, and contains some of the finest examples of Tudor architecture and of Christopher ◊Wren's work. It was built in 1515 by Cardinal Wolsey and presented by him to Henry VIII who subsequently enlarged and improved it. In the 17th century William (III) and Mary (II) made it their main residence outside London, and the palace was further enlarged by Wren. Part of the building was extensively damaged by fire in 1986.

The last monarch to live at Hampton Court was George II, who died in 1760. During his life many of the Tudor apartments were pulled down and replaced. The palace was opened to the public, free of charge, by Queen Victoria in 1838 (though visitors now pay an admission fee). Hampton Court has a remarkable collection of pictures housed in the Hampton Court Gallery.

Hanbury-Brown, Robert (1916–)

Indian-born British radio astronomer who participated in the early development of radio-astronomy techniques and later in designing a radio interferometer that permits considerably greater resolution in the results provided by radio telescopes.

Hanbury-Brown became one of the first astronomers to construct a radio map of the sky. In 1949 he detected radio waves emanating from the Andromeda nebula at a distance of 2.2 million light years. To improve resolution, Hanbury-Brown and his colleagues devised the radio interferometer, and as a result Cygnus A became the first radio source traced to a definite optical identification, even though it had a magnitude (brightness) of only 17.9.

Hancock, Tony (Anthony John) (1924–1968)

English lugubrious radio and television comedian. His radio show *Hancock's Half Hour* (1951–53) showed him famously at odds with everyday life; it was followed by a television show of the same name in 1956. He also appeared in films, including *The Rebel* (1961) and *The Wrong Box* (1966).

On radio he teamed up with other British comics including Hattie Jacques, Kenneth Williams, Bill Kerr, and Sid James. The latter would co-star with him in his television show, offering a more upbeat worldview than Hancock's pessimistic vision. Other film credits are *Orders are Orders* (1954), *The Punch and Judy Man* (1963), and *Those Magnificent Men in Their Flying Machines* (1965). He committed suicide.

What the English like is something they can beat time to, something that hits them straight on the drum of the ear.

GEORGE FRIDERIC HANDEL German-born British composer.
Quoted in Schmid *C W von Gluck* 1854

Handel, George Frideric originally Georg Friedrich Händel (1685–1759)

German composer, a British subject from 1726. His first opera, *Almira*, was performed in Hamburg in 1705. In 1710 he was appointed Kapellmeister to the elector of Hanover (the future George I of England). In 1712 he settled in England, where he established his popularity with such works as the *Water Music* (1717), written for George I. His great choral works include the *Messiah* (1742) and the later oratorios *Samson* (1743), *Belshazzar* (1745), *Judas Maccabaeus* (1747), and *Jephtha* (1752).

Visits to Italy 1706–10 inspired a number of operas and oratorios, and in 1711 his opera *Rinaldo* was performed in London. *Saul* and *Israel in Egypt* (both 1739) were unsuccessful, but his masterpiece, the oratorio *Messiah*, was acclaimed on its first performance in Dublin in 1742. Other works include the pastoral *Acis and Galatea* (1718) and a set of variations for harpsichord that were later nicknamed 'The Harmonious Blacksmith'.

Handel's last opera was produced in 1741, after which he devoted his time chiefly to oratorio. *Messiah* was the summation of his life's work, composed in a single burst of inspiration but including some elements from earlier music. Its success encouraged him to write 12 more oratorios, some on Old Testament texts (*Samson*, *Solomon*) others on Classical mythology (*Semele*).

Handley, Tommy (Thomas Reginald) (1892–1949)

English radio comedian. His popular programme *ITMA (It's That Man Again)* ran from 1939 until his death; it had catch phrases such as 'After you, Claud', and characters including 'Mrs Mop' and 'Mona Lot'.

Handley Page, Frederick (1885–1962)

English aeronautical engineer who designed the first large bomber in 1915. His company produced a series of military aircraft, including the Halifax bomber in World War II. He was knighted in 1942.

Hands, Terry (Terence David) (1941–)

English theatre and opera director. He founded the Liverpool Everyman Theatre in 1964, and was Artistic Director of the Royal Shakespeare Company 1986–91 (he joined the company in 1966). He won the SWET Director of the Year Award for his production of *Henry VI* parts I, II, and III in 1978. He directed *Parsifal* for the Royal Opera Company in 1979. He has also directed Shakespearean plays for the Comédie Française.

Hanley

Former ◊Potteries town in Staffordshire, central England, now part of ◊Stoke-on-Trent. It was the birthplace of the novelist Arnold Bennett and the footballer Stanley Matthews.

Features

The City Museum and Art Gallery includes a fine collection of Staffordshire pottery and porcelain. The house where Arnold Bennett lived is now the Bennett Museum.

History

Hanley was made a municipal borough in 1857, a parliamentary borough returning one member to Parliament in 1885, and a county borough in 1888. In 1910 it amalgamated with neighbouring towns Tunstall, Burslem, Fenton, and Longton, to form the city of Stoke-on-Trent.

Hanley, Ellery (1965–)

English rugby league player. A strong, highly versatile player equally adept as a forward or a back he scored 20 tries in 35 internationals for Great Britain, 1984–93. With Wigan between 1985 and 1991 he won 16 trophies including the Challenge Cup five times and the Division One Championship three times. In 1994 six years after becoming the first black player to captain Great Britain, he became Great Britain's first black coach.

Hanley started his career in 1981 with Bradford Northern before his transfer to Wigan in 1985 for a then world record £150,000. He joined Leeds as player-coach in 1991

Hannah, John (1962–)

Scottish screen actor, who, with adept performances in hit British films *Four Weddings and a Funeral* (1994) and *Sliding Doors* (1998) has won international acclaim. A versatile player, Hannah originally made his name on television in *Brond* (1987). He has also featured in the programme *Out of the Blue* (1995), the forensics show *McCallum* (1995–98), and the cinematic adaptation of *The Mummy* (1998).

Hanover, House of

German royal dynasty that ruled Great Britain and Ireland from 1714 to 1901. Under the Act of ◊Settlement of 1701, the succession passed to the ruling family of Hannover, Germany, on the death of Queen Anne. On the death of Queen Victoria, the crown passed to Edward VII of the house of Saxe-Coburg. See genealogy opposite.

Hansard

Official report of the proceedings of the British Houses of Parliament, named after Luke Hansard (1752–1828), printer of the House of Commons *Journal* from 1774. It is published by Her Majesty's Stationery Office. The name *Hansard* was officially adopted in 1943. Hansard can now be consulted on the Internet.

The first official reports were published from 1803 by the political journalist William ◊Cobbett who, during his imprisonment 1810–12, sold the business to his printer Thomas Curson Hansard, son of Luke Hansard. The publication of the debates remained in the hands of the family until 1889.

The first printer of this name, Luke Hansard, was born in Norwich. He went to London and entered the office of John Hughes, printer to the House of Commons, as compositor. In 1774 he became a partner and acting-manager, and began to print the journals of the House of Commons. Subsequently his two sons entered the business, and after their father's death they and their sons continued as printers to the House of Commons.

Thomas Curson Hansard, who had opened his own printing office in 1803, printed Cobbett's *Parliamentary Debates* (founded 1804) and became its owner in 1811, renaming it *Hansard's Parliamentary Debates*. He died in 1833, and was succeeded by his son, Thomas Curson Hansard the second. The name 'Hansard' disappeared from the *Parliamentary Debates* in 1889, when Thomas Curson Hansard sold his interest to the Hansard Publishing Union (Bottomley).

The *Official Report of Parliamentary Debates* reverted to its old name of *Hansard* in 1943. This was a result of the recommendation of the House of Commons' Select Committee on Publications and Debates Reports.

hansom cab

Two-wheeled horse-drawn carriage in which the driver's seat is outside behind the body, the reins passing over the hooded top. Originally called the 'patent safety cab', it was designed in 1834 by Joseph Hansom (1803–1882), who received £300 for his invention.

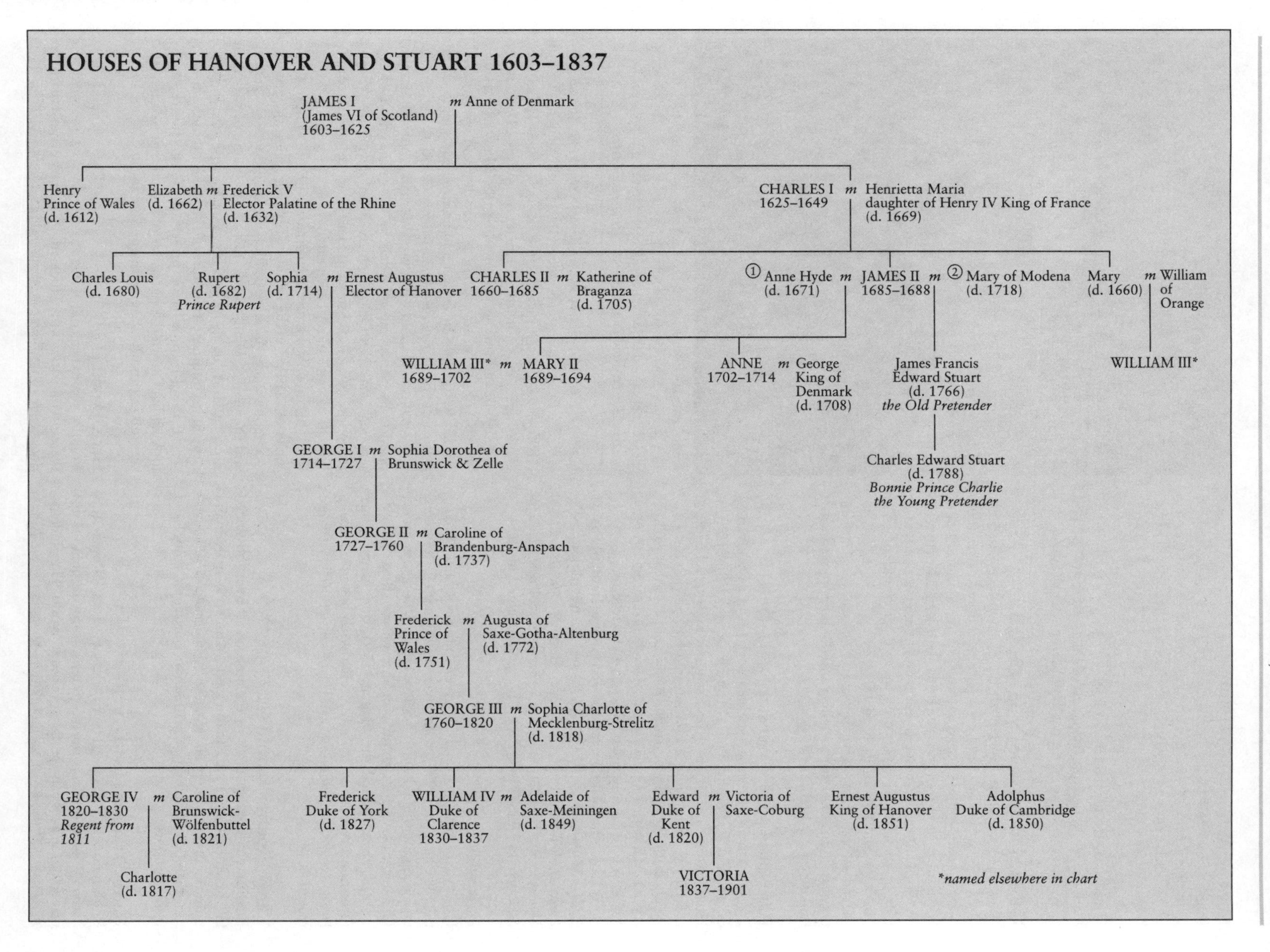
HOUSES OF HANOVER AND STUART 1603–1837
JAMES I (James VI of Scotland) 1603–1625 m Anne of Denmark
Henry Prince of Wales (d. 1612)
Elizabeth (d. 1662) m Frederick V Elector Palatine of the Rhine (d. 1632)
CHARLES I 1625–1649 m Henrietta Maria daughter of Henry IV King of France (d. 1669)
Charles Louis (d. 1680)
Rupert (d. 1682) *Prince Rupert*
Sophia (d. 1714) m Ernest Augustus Elector of Hanover
CHARLES II 1660–1685 m Katherine of Braganza (d. 1705)
① Anne Hyde (d. 1671) m JAMES II 1685–1688 m ② Mary of Modena (d. 1718)
Mary (d. 1660) m William of Orange
WILLIAM III* 1689–1702 m MARY II 1689–1694
ANNE 1702–1714 m George King of Denmark (d. 1708)
James Francis Edward Stuart (d. 1766) *the Old Pretender*
WILLIAM III*
GEORGE I 1714–1727 m Sophia Dorothea of Brunswick & Zelle
Charles Edward Stuart (d. 1788) *Bonnie Prince Charlie the Young Pretender*
GEORGE II 1727–1760 m Caroline of Brandenburg-Anspach (d. 1737)
Frederick Prince of Wales (d. 1751) m Augusta of Saxe-Gotha-Altenburg (d. 1772)
GEORGE III 1760–1820 m Sophia Charlotte of Mecklenburg-Strelitz (d. 1818)
GEORGE IV 1820–1830 *Regent from 1811* m Caroline of Brunswick-Wölfenbuttel (d. 1821)
Frederick Duke of York (d. 1827)
WILLIAM IV Duke of Clarence 1830–1837 m Adelaide of Saxe-Meiningen (d. 1849)
Edward Duke of Kent (d. 1820) m Victoria of Saxe-Coburg
Ernest Augustus King of Hanover (d. 1851)
Adolphus Duke of Cambridge (d. 1850)
Charlotte (d. 1817)
VICTORIA 1837–1901
*named elsewhere in chart

Harden, Arthur (1865–1940)
English biochemist who investigated the mechanism of sugar fermentation and the role of enzymes in this process. For this work he shared the 1929 Nobel Prize for Chemistry. He was knighted in 1936.

Hardicanute (*c.* 1019–1042)
King of Denmark from 1028, and of England from 1040; son of Canute. In England he was considered a harsh ruler.

Hardie, (James) Keir (1856–1915)
Scottish socialist, the first British Labour politician, member of Parliament 1892–95 and 1900–15. He worked in the mines as a boy and in 1886 became secretary of the Scottish Miners' Federation. In 1888 he was the first Labour candidate to stand for Parliament; he entered Parliament independently as a Labour member in 1892 and was a chief founder of the ◊Independent Labour Party in 1893.

A pacifist, he strongly opposed the Boer War, and his idealism in his work for socialism and the unemployed made him a popular hero.

Hardwicke, Cedric Webster (1893–1964)
English actor. He excelled at character parts in a wide variety of plays. After World War II, much of which he spent in Hollywood making films to boost morale in Britain, he joined the Old Vic company in London in 1948, playing Sir Toby Belch in Shakespeare's *Twelfth Night* and Faustus in Christopher Marlowe's *Doctor Faustus*. He then returned to New York, where he continued to act and also to direct.

Among other plays, he appeared in George Bernard Shaw's *Back to Methuselah* in 1924 (London) and Eden Phillpotts's *The Farmer's Wife* in 1924, Rudolph Besier's *The Barratts of Wimpole Street* in 1930, and Paul Vincent Carroll's *Shadow and Substance* in 1938 (New York). He was knighted in 1934.

Hardwick Hall
House in Derbyshire, England, given to the National Trust by the Treasury in 1959, with over 7,200 ha/17,783 acres, including the 6,500 ha/16,055 acre Hope Woodlands Estate. Elizabeth, Dowager Countess of Shrewsbury (Bess of Hardwick), commissioned the Hall in 1591, and many of her furnishings remain in the house. Hardwick has an unusually large expanse of window, and is built entirely of local materials.

Hardy, Godfrey Harold (1877–1947)
English mathematician whose research was at a very advanced level in the fields of pure mathematics known as analysis and number theory. His *Course in Pure Mathematics* 1908 revolutionized the teaching of mathematics at senior school and university levels.

Hardy, Thomas (1840–1928)
English novelist and poet. His novels, set in rural 'Wessex' (his native West Country), portray intense human relationships played out in a harshly indifferent natural world. They include *Far From the Madding Crowd* (1874), *The Return of the Native* (1878), *The Mayor of Casterbridge* (1886), *The Woodlanders* (1887), *Tess of the d'Urbervilles* (1891), and *Jude the Obscure* (1895). His poetry includes the *Wessex Poems* (1898), the blank-verse epic of the Napoleonic Wars *The Dynasts* (1903–08), and several volumes of lyrics. Many of his books have been successfully dramatized for film and television.

HARDY, THOMAS *English writer Thomas Hardy, photographed in the late 19th century. Now remembered chiefly for his novels, including* Tess of the d'Urbervilles *and* Jude the Obscure, *Hardy also wrote eight volumes of poetry and more than 40 short stories. Corbis*

Hardy was born in Dorset and trained as an architect. His first success was *Far From the Madding Crowd* and *Tess of the d'Urbervilles*, subtitled 'A Pure Woman', outraged public opinion by portraying as its heroine a woman who had been seduced. *Jude the Obscure* received an even more hostile reception, which reinforced Hardy's decision to confine himself to verse in his later years.

In his novels Hardy dramatizes with uncompromising directness a belief in the futility of fighting against the cruelties of circumstance, the inevitability of each individual's destiny, and the passing of all beauty. His poems, many of which are now rated as highly as the best of his prose fiction, often contain a compressed version of the same theme, either by seeing ahead from a happy present to a grim future or else looking back from the bitterness of the present to a past that was full of promise. See table opposite for major works.

Hare, David (1947–)
English dramatist and screenwriter. He co-founded the theatre company Joint Stock in 1974. His plays satirize the decadence of post-war Britain, and include *Slag* (1970), *Teeth*

Hardy: Major Works

title	date	well-known characters
Under the Greenwood Tree	1872	Joseph Bowman, Fancy Day, Dick Dewy, Reuben Dewy, William Dewy, Arthur Maybold, Farmer Fred Shiner
Far From the Madding Crowd	1874	William Boldwood, Bathsheba Everdene, Gabriel Oak, Joseph Poorgrass, Fanny Robin, Lyddy Smallbury, Sergeant Francis Troy
The Return of the Native	1878	Christian Cantle, Grandfer Cantle, Diggory Venn, Eustacia Vye, Clym Yeobright, Mrs Yeobright, Thomasin Yeobright, Damon Wildeve
The Trumpet Major	1880	Festus Derriman, Anne Garland, Mrs Garland, Bob Loveday, John Loveday
The Mayor of Casterbridge	1886	Suke Damson, Donald Farfrae, Elizabeth Jane Henchard, Mrs Henchard, Michael Henchard, Richard Newson, Lucetta Templeman/Le Sueur
The Woodlanders	1887	Felice Charmond, Robert Creedle, Edred Fitzpiers, Grace Melbury, Marty South, Giles Winterbourne
Tess of the d'Urbervilles	1891	Mercy Chant, Angel Clare, Rev James Clare, Dairyman Crick, Car Darch, Izz Huett, Marian, Retty Priddle, Alec d'Urberville, Tess Durbeyfield, John and Joan Durbeyfield
Jude the Obscure	1895	Sue Bridehead, Arabella Donn, Jude Fawley, Little Father Time, Richard Phillotson

'n' Smiles (1975), *Fanshen* (1975) on revolutionary Chinese communism, *Plenty* (1978), and *Pravda* (1985) (with Howard ◊Brenton) on Fleet Street journalism.

In a trilogy of plays he looks critically at three aspects of the establishment in Britain: *Racing Demon* (1990) at the Church of England, *Murmuring Judges* (1991) at the legal system, and *The Absence of War* (1994). His screenplays include *Wetherby* and *Plenty* (both 1985), *Paris by Night* (1988), *Damage* (1992), and *The Absence of War* (1994). He wrote the play and screenplay for *The Secret Rapture* (1993) and directed *The Designated Mourner* (1997).

Hare, John (1844–1921)

English actor and theatre manager. He played at the Prince of Wales's Theatre, London, for about nine years before becoming manager of the Court Theatre 1875–79, and was in partnership with William Hunter Kendal (1843–1917) at St James's Theatre 1879–88. The Garrick was built for Hare by the librettist W S Gilbert and opened in 1889. He was knighted in 1903.

Hargreaves, James (*c.* 1720–1778)

English inventor who co-invented a carding machine for combing wool in 1760. About 1764 he invented his 'spinning jenny' (patented in 1770), which enabled a number of threads to be spun simultaneously by one person.

The spinning jenny multiplied eightfold the output of the spinner and could be worked easily by children. It did not entirely supersede the spinning wheel in cotton manufacturing (and was itself overtaken by Samuel ◊Crompton's mule). But for woollen textiles the jenny could be used to make both the warp and the weft.

Haringey

Inner borough of north Greater London. It includes the suburbs of Wood Green, Tottenham, Hornsey, and Harringey

Features Bruce Castle, Tottenham, an Elizabethan manor house (said to stand on the site of an earlier castle built by Robert the Bruce's father); Alexandra Palace (1873), with park; Finsbury Park (1869), one of the earliest municipal parks

Population (1991) 202,200

Industry light industry

Famous people Rowland Hill.

Harlech

Coastal town in Gwynedd, north Wales, 16 km/10 mi from Barmouth; population (1991) 1,230. The castle, now in ruins, was built by the English king Edward I between 1283 and 1289. It was taken by the Welsh chieftain Owen ◊Glendower from 1404 to 1408, and by the Yorkists, in the Wars of the ◊Roses, in 1468. Harlech is now a centre for visitors to ◊Snowdonia National Park.

There is a championship golf course here. The Welsh war song 'March of the Men of Harlech' originated in the Yorkist siege.

During the Civil War the castle held out for Charles I, but eventually became the last one to fall to Parliament. Its ruins overlook the sea and offer impressive views of ◊Lleyn Peninsula, Tremadog Bay and Snowdonia.

harlequinade

Entertainment popular in Britain in the 18th and 19th centuries, in which the principal characters were derived from the Italian commedia dell'arte. The story followed a pattern with the frantic pursuit of the eloping lovers Harlequin and Columbine by the father or guardian Pantaloon and his servant Pierrot. The form was a combination of music and mime, and machinery was used to create striking stage effects.

In the 19th century, Joseph ◊Grimaldi made Clown, a new character, into the central figure, and a tradition grew up by which the opening scene was based on a well-known fairy story. This grew in importance and developed into the British

HARLECH *In Harlech in Gwynedd Edward I sited a forbidding castle on top of a high bluff. From its commanding position, the castle looks out over flat fields and dunes. However, when it was built, in 1283–89, the sea reached the foot of the castle rock. Edward's Welsh castles are now World Heritage sites. Corel*

pantomime, while the harlequinade dwindled into an appendage and, in the 20th century, disappeared altogether.

Harley Street

Road in central London, famed for having many private doctors and other medical specialists. Originally Harley Street was a smart residential area until the doctors moved in, around 1845. It was named after Edward Harley, 2nd Earl of Oxford, the ground landlord.

Harlow

Town on the River Lea in Essex, England, 40 km/25 mi northeast of the centre of London; population (1991) 72,300. Harlow was established as a new town from 1947 onwards, to accommodate the overspill of population and industry from London.

Harman, Harriett (1950–)

British Labour politician and lawyer, secretary of state for Social Security 1997–98. After graduating with a law degree, she was Legal Officer with the National Council for Civil Liberties 1978–82 before entering the House of Commons in 1982, representing Peckham. Within two years of her Commons arrival she joined the Opposition front bench as shadow minister for Social Services 1984–87, later becoming shadow spokesperson on Health 1987–92, shadow chief secretary to the Treasury 1992–94, shadow secretary of state for Employment 1994–95, shadow health secretary 1995–96, and shadow Social Security secretary 1996–97. She faced criticism in 1997 for announcing cuts in benefits for lone parents.

Harold

Two kings of England:

Harold I (1016–1040)

King of England from 1035. The illegitimate son of Canute, known as **Harefoot**, he claimed the throne in 1035 when the legitimate heir Hardicanute was in Denmark. He was elected king in 1037.

Harold II (*c.* 1020–1066)

King of England from January 1066. He succeeded his father Earl Godwin in 1053 as earl of Wessex. In 1063 William of Normandy (◊William the Conqueror) tricked him into swearing to support his claim to the English throne, and when the Witan (a council of high-ranking religious and secular men) elected Harold to succeed Edward the Confessor, William prepared to invade. Meanwhile, Harold's treacherous brother Tostig (died 1066) joined the king of Norway, Harald Hardrada (1015–1066), in invading Northumbria. Harold routed and killed them at Stamford Bridge on 25 September. Three days later William landed at Pevensey, Sussex, and Harold was killed at the Battle of Hastings on 14 October 1066.

Harpenden

Town in Hertfordshire, England, 40 km/25 mi northwest of central London; population (1991) 25,800. It is mainly residential.

At nearby Rothamsted Park in 1843, John Bennet Lawes began systematic experiments in agriculture, providing an endowment of £100,000 for their continuance in 1889. Rothamsted is still an important soil and crop research centre of the Agricultural Research Council.

Harrier

The only truly successful vertical takeoff and landing fixed-wing aircraft, often called the **jump jet**. It was built in Britain and made its first flight in 1966. It has a single jet engine and a set of swivelling nozzles. These deflect the jet exhaust vertically downwards for takeoff and landing, and to the rear for normal flight. Designed to fly from confined spaces with minimal ground support, it refuels in midair.

Harris

Part of the Outer ◊Hebrides, Western Isles, Scotland; area 500 sq km/193 sq mi; population (1971) 2,900. It is joined to Lewis by a narrow isthmus. **Harris tweed** cloths are produced here.

Harris is mountainous in the north. The east coast of Harris is rocky, unlike the western coast with its fine shell sand beaches. Tarbert is the main settlement and terminal for car ferries from Skye and North Uist.

An t'Ob on the south coast was renamed Leverburgh on the death of Lord Leverhulme in 1925. He had a grand economic plan to develop the town into a major fishing port. On his death, the scheme foundered.

Harris, Arthur Travers (1892–1984)
British marshal of the Royal Air Force in World War II. Known as 'Bomber Harris', he was commander in chief of Bomber Command 1942–45.

He was an autocratic and single-minded leader, and was criticized for his policy of civilian-bombing of selected cities in Germany; he authorized the fire-bombing raids on Dresden, in which more than 100,000 died. KCB 1942.

Harrison, John (1693–1776)
English horologist and instrumentmaker. He made the first chronometers that were accurate enough to allow the precise determination of longitude at sea, and so permit reliable (and safe) navigation over long distances. In 1996 Dava Sobel's book about Harrison, *Longitude*, became a bestseller.

Harrison, Rex (Reginald Carey) (1908–1990)
English film and theatre actor. He appeared in over 40 films and numerous plays, often portraying sophisticated and somewhat eccentric characters, such as the waspish Professor Higgins in *My Fair Lady* (1964; Academy Award), the musical version of *Pygmalion*. His other films include *Blithe Spirit* (1945), *The Ghost and Mrs Muir* (1947), and *Dr Doolittle* (1967).

He was also given important and challenging roles on the New York stage, such as that of Sir Henry Harcourt-Reilly in T S Eliot's *The Cocktail Party*. He was knighted in 1989.

Harrison, Tony (1937–)
English poet, translator, and dramatist. He caused controversy with his poem *V* (1987), dealing with the desecration of his parents' grave by Liverpool football supporters, and the play *The Blasphemers' Banquet* (1989), which attacked the death sentence on Salman ⌽Rushdie. He has also translated and adapted Molière.

Recent poetry includes *Black Daisies for the Bride* (1993) and *The Shadow of Hiroshima: and Other Film Poems* (1995). *Plays 3* was published in 1996.

Harrods
Department store in Brompton Road, London, the largest store in the UK and one of the biggest in the world, with about 5,000 staff.

In 1849 Henry Charles Harrod (1800–1885), a wholesale tea merchant, bought a grocer's shop in Knightsbridge. From 1861 his son Charles Digby Harrod gradually expanded the store to cater for his increasingly fashionable clientele. After the premises were destroyed by fire in 1883, C D Harrod designed an even bigger shop, the nucleus of the present store, whose main frontage was built 1901–05. In 1959 it was bought by the House of Fraser, and in the 1980s by the Egyptian Al-Fayed brothers.

Harrogate
Resort and spa town in North Yorkshire, northern England, about 24 km/15 mi north of Leeds; population (1996 est) 69,800. Employment is mainly in the service sector, particularly related to conference business, tourism, and finance. A US communications station is located at Menwith Hill.

History
The town developed as a spa after the discovery of Tewit Well in 1571. It became a fashionable resort and the leading spa in the north of England in Victorian and Edwardian times. The town formerly had over 80 springs (sulphurous, saline, and chalybeate) used for drinking and bathing, and in the treatment of rheumatic, skin, heart, and allied complaints.

Features
Victorian spa facilities include the Royal Baths (1897) and Assembly Rooms; and the Royal Pump Room (1841–42), designed by Isaac Thomas Shutt, and now housing a museum of local history. Turkish baths, sauna, and massage treatments are still available at the Royal Baths. Parks and open spaces include the Stray, a 81-ha/200-acre common to the south of the town centre; and the Harlow Carr Gardens of the Royal Horticultural Society to the west of the town. The resort contains many hotels, a large exhibition hall (a centre for trade fairs), and the new Victoria Shopping Centre.

Annual events
These include the Great Yorkshire Agricultural Show held in July and an International Festival of Music and Arts in July/August. The North of England Horticultural Society organizes annual flower shows.

HARRODS *Britain's most famous department store occupies a large Edwardian building in the fashionable London district of Knightsbridge. Its most notable features are the imposing terracotta facade on the Brompton Road illuminated by thousands of lightbulbs, and a lavish food hall with decorative tilework. Since 1985, the store has been owned by the flamboyant Egyptian businessman Mohammed Al-Fayed. Corel*

Harrow

Outer London borough of northwest Greater London
Features Harrow School (1571)
Population (1991) 200,100
Famous people R B Sheridan, Charles Kingsley, Robert Ballantyne, Matthew Arnold, Anthony Trollope.

Harrow school

Fee-paying independent school in North London, founded in 1571 and opened in 1611; it became a leading public school for boys during the 18th century, and among its former pupils are the writers Byron and Sheridan and the politicians Peel, Palmerston, and Churchill.

harrying of the north

Ruthless Norman repression of Anglo-Saxon rebellion in the north of England (1069–70). After his victory at the Battle of Hastings, William the Conqueror faced a series of revolts against Norman rule across England which he suppressed effectively but ruthlessly. The 'harrying' was effective in deterring potential rebels but the Domesday Book records that large areas of the north were devastated.

Harry the Minstrel, or Henry the Minstrel or Blind Harry

Scottish poet of the later 15th century. He collected popular traditions about the Scottish national hero William ◊Wallace in *Wallace*, a poem of about 12,000 lines in heroic couplets. Written as nationalist propaganda, it is unusually modern in its psychology.

Hartington, Spencer Compton Cavendish, Marquess of Hartington and 8th Duke of Devonshire (1833–1908)

British politician, first leader of the Liberal Unionists 1886–1903. As war minister he opposed devolution for Ireland in cabinet and later led the revolt of the Liberal Unionists that defeated Gladstone's Irish Home Rule bill of 1886. Hartington refused the premiership three times, in 1880, 1886, and 1887, and led the opposition to the Irish Home Rule bill in the House of Lords in 1893.

Hartlepool

Town, port, and, since 1996, a unitary authority in northeast England, formed from part of the county of Cleveland; unitary authority area 94 sq km/36 sq mi; population (1996) 90,400. The local economy depends on metal industries, engineering, support services for the oil industry, fishing, and brewing. A nuclear power station is located 5 km/3 mi southeast of the town at Seaton Carew. The author Compton Mackenzie was born here in 1883.

Features

The docks area has been redeveloped to include the Museum of Hartlepool (opened in 1995). The Gray Art Gallery and Museum includes local history collections. There are remains of the medieval town walls. The Early English church of St Hilda has a Norman doorway and a heavy tower supported by large flying buttresses. The nave consists of six unequal arches on each side, supported by columns, and a clerestory (a window-lined wall) runs the length of both chancel and nave.

History

A settlement was established here in the 7th century when a monastery was founded on the headland north of the harbour. It became a local market centre in the 11th century, and in the 12th century the harbour was improved and Hartlepool became the official port for the Palatinate bishopric of Durham. Town walls were built in medieval times.

The industrialization of Hartlepool began with the building of a railway linking it with the South Durham coalfield in 1835. In 1847 a rival railway reached the coast just south of Hartlepool, and docks were built at its terminus. A new town, West Hartlepool, was established to the south and east of the docks, and the two settlements remained administratively separate until 1969. West Hartlepool grew very rapidly during the mid-19th century, and had a population of 64,000 in 1891. An ironworks was established south of West Hartlepool in 1838 and shipyards in the dock area during the 1870s. With its economy based on heavy industry, the area suffered from severe depression and high unemployment during the 1930s. In 1958 the steelworks south of the town were replaced by a large plant at Greatham, 5 km/3 mi to the southwest.

Shipbuilding

In 1913 there were 42 ship-owning companies in the town, responsible for 235 ships. Due to its importance, the first hostile action by Germany against Britain in World War I was the bombardment of Hartlepool from the sea in 1914. Shipbuilding and steel manufacture were the town's main industries until after World War II, when heavy industry declined in the town. The last ship was built here in 1960–61.The paddle steamer *Wingfield Castle* was built in Hartlepool in 1934 and was used as a ferry on the Humber estuary. HMS *Trincomalee*, the oldest British warship still afloat, was also built here in 1817. Both boats were being restored in Jackson Dock in the late 1990s.

Hartley, L(eslie) P(oles) (1895–1972)

English novelist and short-story writer. His early works explored the sinister. His chief works are the trilogy *The Shrimp and the Anemone* (1944), *The Sixth Heaven* (1946), and *Eustace and Hilda* (1947; Tait Black Memorial Prize), on the intertwined lives of a brother and sister. Later works include *The Go-Between* (1953; filmed 1971) and *The Hireling* (1957), which explore sexual relationships between the classes.

Hartnell, Norman Bishop (1901–1979)

English fashion designer. He was known for his ornate evening gowns and tailored suits and coats. He worked for the designer Lucille from 1923 before founding his own studio. Appointed dressmaker to the British royal family in 1938, he created Queen Elizabeth II's wedding dress, when she was Princess Elizabeth, in 1947, and her coronation gown in 1953. The Hartnell fashion house closed in 1992. Knighted 1977.

Harvey, Jonathan Dean (1939–)

English composer. His use of avant-garde and computer synthesis techniques is allied to a tradition of visionary Romanticism in works such as *Inner Light II* (1977) for voices, instruments, and tape music and *Mortuos plango, vivos voco/I Mourn the Dead, I Call the Living* (1980) for computer-manipulated concrete sounds, realized at IRCAM. Recent works include the opera *Inquest of Love* (1993).

Harvey, Laurence, adopted name of Lauruska Mischa Skikne (1929–1973)

Lithuanian-born British film actor. He worked both in the UK and in Hollywood. Among his films are *Room at the Top* (1958), *The Alamo* (1960), and *The Manchurian Candidate* (1962).

Harvey, William (1578–1657)

English physician who discovered the circulation of blood. In 1628 he published his book *De motu cordis/On the Motion of the Heart and the Blood in Animals.* He also explored the development of chick and deer embryos.

Harvey's discovery marked the beginning of the end of medicine as taught by Greek physician Galen, which had been accepted for 1,400 years.

Harwich

Seaport in Essex, southeast England, on the estuary of the rivers Stour and Orwell, 113 km/70 mi northeast of London; population (1997 est) 15,800. It has an important freight terminal and ferry connections with the Hook of Holland, Germany, Denmark, Sweden, and Norway. Bathside Bay will be developed to add to Harwich's existing port facilities.

The resort of Dovercourt lies to the south.

History

An important trading centre since the 14th century, Harwich has been a fortified port since the time of James I, and was the scene of a naval engagement between the Dutch and English in 1666.

Haslemere

Town in Surrey, England, 20 km/12 mi southwest of Guildford; population (1991) 6,800. ◊Dolmetsch musical instruments are made here, and a festival of early music is held each July.

Nearby is Hindhead heathland area. Haslemere has a museum of the environment and history of the local area.

Hastings

Resort in East Sussex, southeast England, on the English Channel; population (1996) 85,000. Fishing is an important activity; the town has Britain's largest fleet of beach-launched fishing boats and a new wholesale fish market. Other industries include engineering and the manufacture of scientific and aerospace-related instruments, plastics, electronics, and domestic appliances. William the Conqueror landed at Pevensey to the west and defeated Harold at the Battle of ◊Hastings in 1066.

Hastings flourished in the 12th and 13th centuries as the chief of the ◊Cinque Ports. It has the ruins of a Norman castle. The annual **Hastings Premier**, England's leading international chess tournament, is held here in December/January.

Features

The old town in the east part of Hastings is surrounded by high cliffs, and includes the 13th-century St Clement's Church; the old town hall, now housing a museum of local history; and the Perpendicular All Saints' Church. The castle ruins include a museum which gives an account of the invasion of 1066 and the history of the castle. The Fisherman's Museum, housed in a building which was once the fishing community's church, and the Shipwreck Heritage Centre depict the town's fishing and maritime history. The St Clement's Caves, a labyrinth of sandstone caves below the West Hill and East Hill cliff railways, include a museum which illustrates the importance of smuggling to the economy of the town in the 18th century. The West Hill line runs up to the castle. White Rock Pavilion houses the Hastings Embroidery, made by the Royal School of Needlework for the 900th anniversary of the Battle of Hastings. The western part of the town, which developed as a resort in the early 19th century, adjoins St Leonard's to the west, and includes a promenade and a pier. Battle Abbey, built on the site of William the Conqueror's victory, lies 10 km/6 mi to the northwest. The wreck of the Dutch East Indiaman *Amsterdam* (1748) lies buried in mud on the beach near Hastings.

History

The settlement became prominent after the Saxon period and by the 12th century Hastings was the leading member of the Cinque Ports confederation, with William I's castle dominating the town. With the silting-up of the harbour and use of larger ships, the importance of the town declined, and it was known in the early 18th century as a smugglers' haunt. It became a fashionable resort in the early 19th century, but its popularity declined in the late 19th century, and it suffered extensive bomb damage during World War II.

Hastings, Andrew Gavin (1962–)

Scottish rugby union player who scored 755 points in 68 internationals for Scotland and the British Lions. A full-back, he first played for Scotland in 1986, and was a member of Scotland's Grand Slam team in 1990, British Lions in Australia in 1989, and New Zealand in 1993. He scored a record 44 points in a World Cup game against Côte d'Ivoire in 1995. He retired as a player in 1995.

Hastings, Warren (1732–1818)

English colonial administrator. A protégé of Lord Clive, who established British rule in India, Hastings carried out major reforms, and became governor general of Bengal in 1774. Impeached for corruption on his return to England in 1785, he was acquitted in 1795.

Hastings, Battle of

Battle on 14 October 1066 at which William, Duke of Normandy ('the Conqueror') defeated King Harold II of England, and himself took the throne. The site is 10 km/6 mi

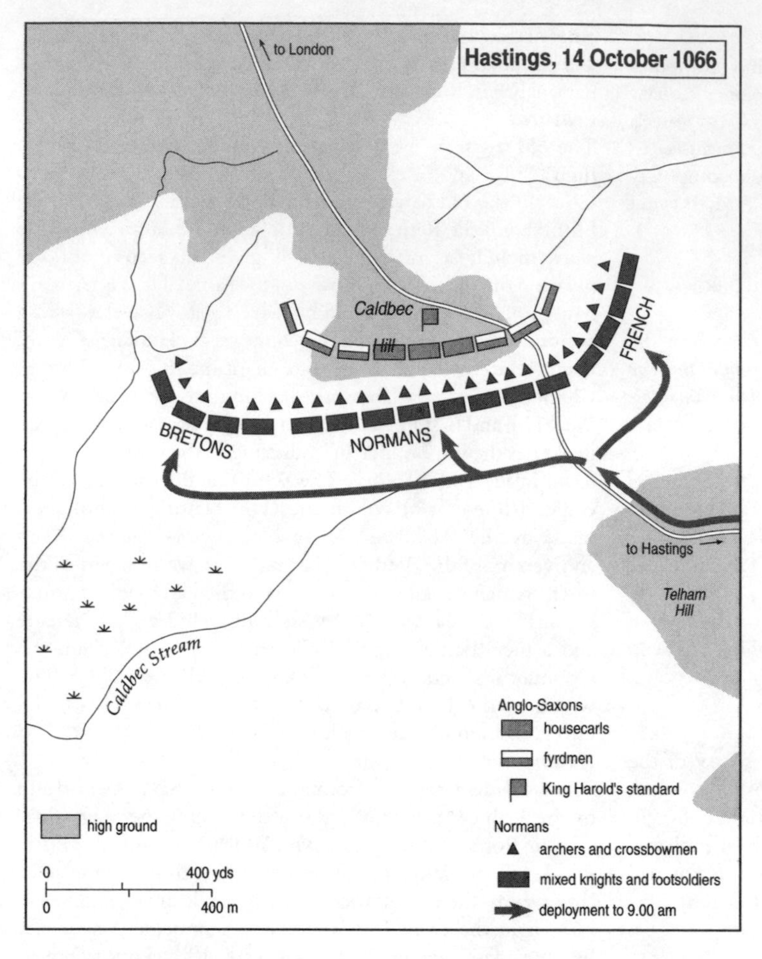

inland from Hastings, at Senlac, Sussex; it is marked by Battle Abbey.

Both sides suffered heavy losses but the decimation of the English army and Harold's death left England open to Norman rule.

The English were attacked by Norman archers, foot soldiers, and finally cavalry with no result. Then some of Harold's personal guard left their places to pursue some stragglers, and William ordered part of his force to simulate panic and flight. The strategy worked – many of the English troops broke ranks to run down the hill after the Normans, who then turned and cut them down. William then resumed his attack on the hill, with his archers shooting into the air. With arrows falling about them, the English opened up, allowing the Norman foot soldiers to get among them. Harold and his two brothers were killed and his army totally destroyed.

Hatfield

Town in Hertfordshire, southeast England, on the River Lea, 8 km/5 mi east of St Albans; population (1991) 31,100. Designated a ◊new town in 1948, it has light engineering industries. It was the site of the 12th-century palace of the bishops of Ely, replaced by the Jacobean mansion, ◊Hatfield House (1607–11). The University of Hertfordshire (previously Hatfield Polytechnic) was established here in 1992.

Hatfield grew as a modern new town around the aircraft industry, close to its historic original town. British Aerospace was the district's largest employer until it closed in 1993; the site is now undergoing redevelopment.

Hatfield House

Jacobean house in Hertfordshire, England, standing in a park 16 km/10 mi in circumference. It is the residence of the Marquess of Salisbury and is one of the best examples of Jacobean architecture in Britain. A surviving wing of the Old Palace of the bishops of Ely, built about 1496 by Cardinal Morton, Henry VII's principal minister, stands in the grounds.

The palace was seized by Henry VIII and inhabited by Edward VI and Elizabeth I before their accession. In James I's reign it was given to Robert ◊Cecil, 1st Earl of Salisbury, in exchange for Theobalds. Three wings of the palace were then pulled down and the materials used for the foundations of Hatfield, which was built between 1607 and 1611, Robert Lyminge being the master carpenter.

Hathaway, Anne (1556–1623)

Englishwoman, daughter of a yeoman farmer, who married William ◊Shakespeare in 1582. She was born at Shottery, near Stratford, where her cottage can still be seen.

Hattersley, Roy Sydney George (1932–)

British Labour politician and author. On the right wing of the Labour Party, he was prices secretary 1976–79, and deputy leader of the party 1983–1992. In 1994 he announced his retirement from active politics, and later expressed disagreement with some policies of the new party leadership which he considered had swung too far to the right in its views on promoting income distribution through the taxation and welfare system.

During Labour's long period in opposition, he was shadow home secretary and shadow chancellor. He also developed a secondary career as a successful author and newspaper columnist.

Hatton, Derek (1948–)

British left-wing politician, former deputy leader of Liverpool Council. A leading member of the ◊Militant Tendency, Hatton was removed from office and expelled from the Labour Party in 1987.

He revealed in his autobiography (1988) how Militant acted as a subversive party-within-a-party. Subsequently he embarked on a career in advertising and public relations.

Havant

Town in Hampshire, England, at the head of Langstone Harbour, 8 km/5 mi northeast of Portsmouth; population (1991) 115,400. The town is largely residential, with some light industry. Hayling Island in Langstone Harbour is a popular holiday centre.

Haverfordwest, Welsh Hwlffordd

Town and administrative headquarters of Pembrokeshire, southwest Wales, on the West Cleddau River, 10 km/6 mi northeast of Milford Haven; population (1991) 13,300. It is the centre of a busy agricultural marketing area. It was a flourishing port from Tudor times to the early part of the 20th century. The castle dates from about 1120.

> *New Labour's most irritating characteristic is the belief that its spokesmen can ignore the facts of history and deny the rules of logic without anybody noticing.*
>
> ROY HATTERSLEY Former British Labour minister. *Independent*, 31 January 1998

Haverhill

Market town in Suffolk, England, on the borders of Essex and Cambridgeshire, 30 km/19 mi southeast of Cambridge. It grew up on the Roman road known as the Via Devana. Most of the town was destroyed by fire in 1665, and extensive housing estates and factories were built in the 1950s to take population overspill from London.

Haverhill's parish church, built in the 14th and 15th centuries, was restored after the 1665 fire. The manor house, latterly the vicarage, was built in the 17th century and contains some impressive wood panelling. To the southeast are indistinct remains of an ancient earthwork known as **Haverhill Castle**. Kedington, 3 km/2 mi to the south, has a church with many tombs and fittings dating from the 13th to the 19th centuries.

Havering

Outer London borough of northeast Greater London. It includes the districts of Hornchurch, Romford, Rainham, and Upminster

Features 15th-century Church House, Romford; St Andrew's, Hornchurch, the only church in England to have a bull's head and horns instead of a cross at the east end (hence Hornchurch); site of The Bower, at Havering-atte-Bower, a small medieval palace used by the wives of Henry VIII, and the official residence of queens of England until 1620, after which time it fell into decay and was sold during the Commonwealth (1649–60); the present Bower House (1729), a small country residence, incorporates the old royal palace's coat of arms; some of the grounds of the medieval palace survive as Havering Country Park and remains of the building are located on the hillside ridge; the church of St John, built in 1876 on the site of a palace chapel

Industries diverse and rapidly changing activities; engineering

Population (1996 est) 230,900

The borough of Havering was created on 1 April 1965, comprising the former municipal borough of Romford and the former urban district of Hornchurch. The name was chosen because most of the newly established borough lay within the bounds of the Royal Liberty of Havering-atte-Bower, granted by charter in 1465. Largely agricultural until the 19th century, the area includes the commuter suburbs of Gidea Park, Mawneys, Redden Court, Nelmes, Bedfords Park, Cranham, and Upminster, all of which were once small villages.

The Bower, built by Edward the Confessor, was used by later monarchs as a hunting-lodge for the neighbouring forest. The church of St Helen and St Giles at Rainham dates from 1160 and has a Saxon font. Parts of St Mary Magdalene, North Ockerdon, and St Lawrence, Upminster, are also medieval. Rainham Hall, now a National Trust property, was built in 1729. Parkland areas include Bedfords and Raphael parks; and the botanical Langton Gardens, Hornchurch, now a registry office.

The rose grower J H Pemberton, propagator of the Alexandra rose, lived in the Round House in the early 20th century; the building, built around 1792, was reputedly constructed in the shape of a tea caddy.

Havers, Robert Michael Oldfield, Baron Havers (1923–1992)

British Conservative politician and lawyer, Lord Chancellor 1987–88. After a successful legal career he became Conservative member of Parliament for Wimbledon in 1970 and was solicitor general under Edward Heath and attorney general under Margaret Thatcher. He was made a life peer in 1987 and served briefly, and unhappily, as Lord Chancellor before retiring in 1988. He was knighted in 1972 and made baron in 1987.

Hawarden, Welsh Penarlâg

Town in Flintshire, northeast Wales, 11 km/7 mi west of Chester. The Liberal politician William ◊Gladstone lived for many years at Hawarden Castle, built in 1752, and founded St Deiniol's theological library and hostel for its students in the town in 1895. There is an airport; its industries include aircraft manufacture.

Hawarden appears in the Domesday Book as Haordine. St Deiniol's church, probably dating from 1275, was restored in 1857 after a fire.

Hawick

Town and former burgh in Scottish Borders unitary authority, Scotland, bounded by the rivers Teviot and Slitrig, 84 km/52 mi southeast of Edinburgh; population (1991) 15,800. The manufacture of woollens is long established; hosiery was being produced in 1771 and tweed in about 1820. The Common Riding, a traditional fair and festival, is held annually in the town.

Hawick's 12th-century castle was demolished by the English in 1570. Its motte, an artificial earthen mound, is the only remaining structure.

SCIENCE IN BRITAIN IN THE 20TH CENTURY

As the 20th century began, Britain was slowly awakening to the realization that the world's first industrial power had not only lost its pre-eminence, but was sliding down the international technological rankings. In part this could be traced to the industrial revolution, which owed very little to university research or scientists. Indeed, the Scottish engineer John Rennie recorded that his father dissuaded him from going to Oxford or Cambridge on the grounds that it would make him unfit for practical work. The industrial world was, however, changing. The new, huge chemical industry was dominated by Germany, a country with some 4000 graduate chemists – Britain could scarcely muster half that number for the entire range of sciences. The universities were still dominated by the public schools, and science was very much a poor relation. In 1913 the USA had four science students per 10,000 of population, Britain only 1.6. It was clear that if Britain was to be internationally competitive, industry must employ more scientists, and more young people would need to turn to science. To attract the best minds, science had to be seen to be both relevant and intellectually exciting. Fortunately, in the 20th century, physicists in Britain were to be seen as among those tackling some of the greatest challenges the world has known.

Achievements in physics

Einstein's theory of relativity, with its fundamental challenge to Newtonian physics and its revolutionary reappraisal of the relationship of space and time, excited the world in a way no scientific theory had done since Darwin. But, for a time, it remained just that – a theory which still required experimental proof. That proof was supplied in 1919 by Arthur Eddington, Professor of Astronomy at Cambridge. The theory predicted that light passing a massive object such as the sun, would be bent by a calculable amount. Eddington's measurements made during a solar eclipse triumphantly confirmed Einstein's theoretical figures: 'Some of the most beautiful results that science has produced,' as Einstein himself proclaimed. Relativity established, speculation turned to such fundamental questions as the origins of the universe itself. One of the earliest theorists was Fred Hoyle, who supported a steady state model, in which matter was continuously created. Even if now discredited, the theory opened up debate, in which the Big Bang came out as the winner. Cosmologists have also had to take into account one of the century's other great ideas – quantum theory – and among those who have wrestled with the problems of uniting this theory with relativity, Stephen Hawking has been pre-eminent.

The theories of the universe continue to give scientists some of their greatest challenges. Yet it is in work on a very different scale, in molecular and particle physics, that advances have impinged most directly on everyday life, and in these areas the work of British scientists has been crucial.

Splitting the atom

By the end of the 19th century, J J Thomson had succeeded in identifying the electron, the first subatomic particle to be isolated. At the start of the new century, he was joined at the Cavendish Laboratory, Cambridge, by a young New Zealander, Ernest Rutherford, who advanced the work, demonstrating that the electron had a definite mass. Further investigation with the positively-charged alpha particles produced in radioactive decay, enabled him to produce a new model for the atom, consisting of a nucleus of heavy, positively charged particles, protons, around which the tiny electrons whirled. In 1932, when James Chadwick established the existence of neutrons in the nucleus, the atomic model seemed complete. We now know that the atom is a good deal more complex than that, but by splitting the atom in 1919, Rutherford had opened the way to a vast array of new subjects.

Paving the way for genetic engineering

Even before the nature of the electron was known, the science of electronics had found practical uses. John Alexander Fleming's diode valve marked a start. In pre-transistor days they were essential components in radio equipment and in the first cumbersome electronic computers. Other developments may not have had such immediately obvious appeal, but scientists were acquiring essential tools for investigating the structures of atoms and molecules. Thomson's assistant, Francis Willliam Aston, devised the mass spectrograph, soon an indispensable tool in organic chemistry analysis. William and Lawrence Bragg – the only father and son to receive a joint Nobel prize – developed X-ray crystallography for solving complex molecular structures. This process culminated in the unravelling of the basic genetic material DNA by Francis Crick and James D. Watson in 1953. The results of this work can be seen in genetic engineering and phenomena that were

Hawking, Stephen (William) (1942–)
English physicist whose work in general relativity – particularly gravitational field theory – led to a search for a quantum theory of gravity to explain black holes and the Big Bang, singularities that classical relativity theory does not adequately explain. His book *A Brief History of Time* (1988) gives a popular account of cosmology and became an international bestseller. His latest book is *The Nature of Space and Time* (1996), written with Roger ◊Penrose.

Hawking's objective of producing an overall synthesis of quantum mechanics and relativity theory began around the time of the publication in 1973 of his seminal book *The Large Scale Structure of Space-Time*, written with G F R Ellis. His most remarkable result, published in 1974, was that black holes could in fact emit particles in the form of thermal radiation – the so-called **Hawking radiation**. See feature on Science in Britain in the 20th century.

Hawkins, Jack (1910–1973)
English film actor. He was often cast in military roles. His

once present only in the realms of science fiction, such as the cloned sheep Dolly.

Co-operation and training

British physicists have been, and are, major players on the world stage, but there have been other equally notable achievements in other sciences. To select just one name from among many, can there have been a more valuable contribution to human health this century than Alexander Fleming's discovery of penicillin? It has, however, become increasingly difficult to talk of any science in terms of national contributions. Particle physics research has become so hugely expensive that projects such as JET in England, investigating nuclear fusion, and CERN on the Swiss–French border, housing a vast particle accelerator, are the results of European co-operation.

If at the beginning of the century, the pattern of education showed the sciences as being the poor relation, the position had been transformed at the end. One notable trend is the increased numbers of women studying science at university level. In medicine, dentistry and allied subjects, female students outnumbered men for the first time in 1995, and even in such traditionally male oriented subjects as engineering and technology, women now represent around 20 per cent of all students. In the most recent statistics, science and technology students now make up nearly half the student body, but the changes have not been uniform. Whereas in the past, universities seemed slow to respond to change, they now reflect the outside world more accurately. In 1985 there were no courses in computer science; ten years later there were over 50,000 students. Even the less obviously commercial subjects, such as the physical sciences, have seen dramatic increases in the last decade of the century.

Has the role of the scientist in Britain changed over the century? Clearly it has, even if British companies regularly spend less on research than their competitors. Paradoxically, as the scientific method has shown itself to be one of the most powerful inventions of the human brain, science itself has become more and more distrusted. Atomic and chemical weapons, nuclear power and genetic engineering are seen as products of a mad, Frankensteinian world, and for every one who contemplates the nature of a black hole, there are hundreds who consult horoscopes. The challenge now seems to be to provide science with a moral framework, and to make scientific ideas comprehensible to a larger public.

BY ANTHONY BURTON

films include *The Cruel Sea* (1953), *Bridge on the River Kwai* (1957), *The League of Gentlemen* (1959), *Zulu* (1963), and *Waterloo* (1970).

Hawkins, John (1719–1789)

English music historian and antiquary. Devoted at first to architecture and then to law, he gradually became interested in literature and music. Having married a wealthy woman in 1753, he was able to retire and to undertake, in addition to minor works, his *General History of the Science and Practice of Music*, published in five volumes in 1776, the same year as the first volume of Charles Burney's similar work.

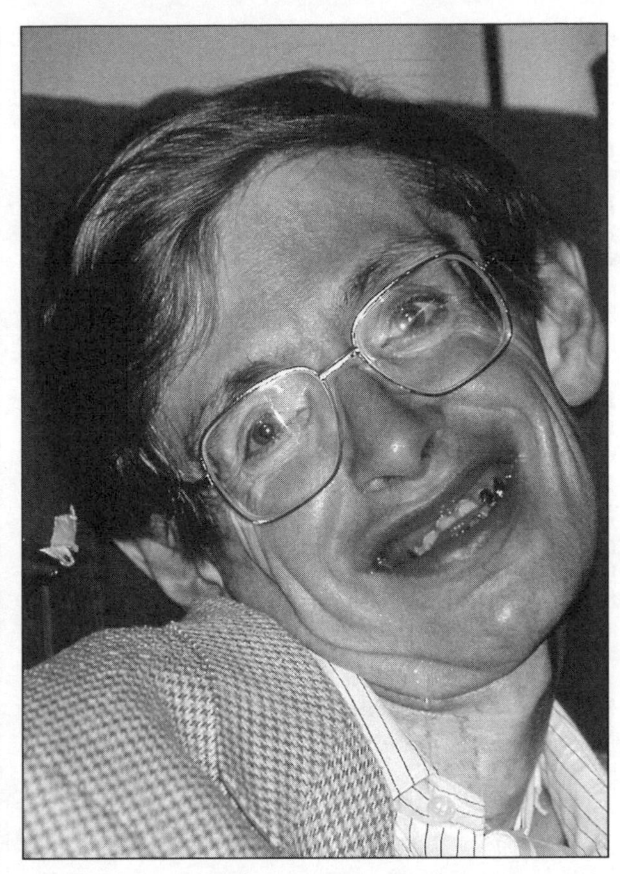

HAWKING, STEPHEN *Widely acknowledged as one of Britain's most brilliant and original scientists, the theoretical physicist Stephen Hawking has made major contributions to the understanding of the origins of the universe. His affliction by motor neuron disease makes it necessary for him to communicate through a voice synthesizer. Rex*

Hawksmoor, Nicholas (1661–1736)

English architect. He was assistant to Christopher ◊Wren in designing various London churches and St Paul's Cathedral, and joint architect of Castle Howard and Blenheim Palace with John ◊Vanbrugh. His genius is displayed in a quirky and uncompromising style incorporating elements from both Gothic and Classical sources.

After 1712 Hawksmoor completed six of the 50 new churches planned for London under the provisions made by the Fifty New Churches Act of 1711: St Alphege, Greenwich (1712–14); St Anne, Limehouse (1712–24); St George-in-the-East (1714–34); St Mary Woolnoth (1716–27); St George, Bloomsbury (1720–30); and Christ Church, Spitalfields (1714–29).

Haworth

Moorland village in West Yorkshire, England, 5 km/3 mi south of Keighley. The writers Charlotte, Emily, and Anne ◊Brontë lived at the parsonage here from their earliest years. The old church of Haworth has been restored, and contains the graves of Charlotte and Emily Brontë. The parsonage is now the Brontë museum.

Vivid descriptions of the local moorland scenery are to be found in their novels, notably *Wuthering Heights* (1847) by Emily Brontë.

Haworth, (Walter) Norman (1883–1950)

English organic chemist who was the first to synthesize a vitamin (ascorbic acid, vitamin C) in 1933, for which he shared a Nobel prize in 1937. He made significant advances in determining the structures of many carbohydrates, particularly sugars. Knighted 1947.

Hawthorne, Nigel (1929–)

English character actor. He gained popular recognition as the machiavellian civil servant Sir Humphrey Appleby in the 1980s television comedies *Yes, Minister* and *Yes, Prime Minister*. A supporting player for many years in such British productions as *Gandhi* (1982), his leading performance as the troubled monarch in *The Madness of King George* (1994) further extended his career and earned him international acclaim. He also featured in Steven Spielberg's *Amistad* (1997) and the family comedy *Madeline* (1998).

Hawtrey, Charles Henry (1858–1923)

British actor, theatre manager, and dramatist. He produced a number of light comedies, playing in them himself in what became known as 'Hawtrey parts'. His greatest success was *The Private Secretary* (1884), which he adapted from a German play, *Der Bibliothekar* by Gustav von Moses. He was knighted in 1922.

Hay, Will(iam Thomson) (1888–1949)

English comedy actor. Originally a music-hall comedian, he made many films in the 1930s, in which he was usually cast as an incompetent in a position of authority, including *Good Morning Boys* (1937), *Oh Mr Porter* (1938), *Ask a Policeman* (1939), and *My Learned Friend* (1944).

Haye, Helen (1874–1957)

British actress, born in India. She was on the stage for 60 years and had some of her greatest successes in later life, particularly as the Dowager Lady Monchensey in T S Eliot's verse drama *The Family Reunion* (1939) and the dowager empress of Russia in *Anastasia* (1953).

Hayes, William (1708–1777)

English organist and composer. He was organist at Worcester Cathedral from 1731 and organist and master of the choristers at Magdalen College, Oxford from 1734; he was appointed professor in 1742. He introduced many of Handel's works to Oxford, Bath, and Winchester; his own works were indebted to Handel.

Hay-on-Wye, Welsh Y Gelli

Market town in Powys, Wales, situated 24 km/15 m northeast of Brecon on the south bank of the River ⇨Wye. It is an angling and walking centre. It is known as the 'town of books' because of the huge second-hand book shop started here in 1961 by Richard Booth; it was followed by others.

Hayter, Stanley William (1901–1988)

English painter and graphic artist. He became influenced by the Surrealists after moving to Paris in 1926. In 1927 he set up Atelier 17, an experimental workshop for printmakers that had an enormous impact on the development of graphic art, attracting such figures as Picasso, Ernst, Miró, and Dalí.

Originally a chemist, Hayter became a master innovator of printmaking techniques, his work combining traditional media (like engraving) with other processes. He played a large part in the revival of printmaking. He was made a CBE in 1967.

Haywards Heath

Market town in West Sussex, England, 20 km/12 mi north of Brighton; population (1991) 25,400. Its growth as a dormitory town was due to the development of the Southern Region railway line from Brighton to London.

Hazlitt, William (1778–1830)

English essayist and critic. His work is characterized by invective, scathing irony, an intuitive critical sense, and a gift for epigram. His essays include 'Characters of Shakespeare's Plays' (1817), 'Lectures on the English Poets' (1818–19), 'English Comic Writers' (1819), and 'Dramatic Literature of the Age of Elizabeth' (1820).

HAZLITT, WILLIAM *The early 19th-century English essayist and critic William Hazlitt. He embarked on training as a minister before deciding to become a painter, and eventually a writer. He wrote political journalism, criticism, travel notes, and biography. Corbis*

Headingley
Leeds sports centre, home of the Yorkshire County Cricket Club and Leeds Rugby League Club. The two venues are separated by a large stand. The cricket ground has been a centre for Test matches since 1899.

The crowd of 158,000 for the five day England Australia Test match at Headingley in 1948 is an English record. Britain's first official Rugby League Test match against New Zealand was at Headingley in 1908. The rugby ground is one of the best in the country and has excellent turf. It was the first club to install undersoil heating. The main stand is one of the biggest in Rugby League.

Heal, Ambrose (1872–1959)
English cabinetmaker. He took over the Heal's shop from his father and developed it into a large London store. He initially designed furniture in the Arts and Crafts style, often in oak, but in the 1930s he started using materials such as tubular steel.

Heal was a founder member of the Design and Industries Association, which aimed to improve the quality of mass-produced items. He was knighted in 1933. Heals is now part of the Conran group of companies called Storehouse.

Healey, Denis Winston, Baron Healey (1917–)
British Labour politician. While secretary of state for defence 1964–70 he was in charge of the reduction of British forces east of Suez. He was chancellor of the Exchequer 1974–79. In 1976 he contested the party leadership, losing to James Callaghan, and again in 1980, losing to Michael Foot, to whom he was deputy leader 1980–83. In 1987 he resigned from the shadow cabinet.

Health and Safety Commission
Government organization responsible for securing the health, safety, and welfare of people at work, and for protecting the public against dangers to health and safety arising from work activities. It was established by the Health and Safety at Work Act 1974 and is responsible to the secretary of state for employment.

The Health and Safety Executive is responsible for carrying out the Commission's decisions, bringing together a number of different inspectorates, including those for factories and mines and quarries.

health care
See ◊NHS, Department of ◊Health, ◊Health Education Authority, and chronology of medicine and health care.

Health, Department of, or DH
Government department established in 1988, following the division of the Department of Health and Social Security into two separate departments. It is responsible for the operation of the National Health Service and overall policies on health. The current health secretary (from 1997) is Frank Dobson.

Health Education Authority, or HEA
Authority established in 1987 to provide information and advice about health directly to the public; promote the development of health education in England and AIDS health education in the UK; and support and advise government departments, health authorities, local authorities, voluntary organizations, and other bodies or individuals concerned with health education. The HEA is also responsible for carrying out national campaigns and promoting research.

Following a review of the HEA's role and functions, a radical change in how it is to be funded was announced in December 1994.

Since 1 April 1996, after a year of shadow operation 1995–96, the HEA has essentially been funded on a contract basis, seeking contracts from the Department of Health and other organizations to deliver health promotion programmes and projects for the supply of health promotion material, research, and expertise.

Heaney, Seamus (Justin) (1939–)
Irish poet and critic. He has written powerful verse about the political situation in Northern Ireland and reflections on Ireland's cultural heritage. Collections include *Death of a Naturalist* (1966), *Field Work* (1979), *The Haw Lantern* (1987), and *The Spirit Level* (1996; Whitbread Book of the Year), *Opened Ground: Poems 1966–1996* (1998). Critical works include *The Redress of Poetry* (1995). He was professor of poetry at Oxford 1989–94 and was awarded the Nobel Prize for Literature in 1995.

Heanor
Town in Derbyshire, England, 16 km/10 mi northwest of Nottingham; population (1991) 16,100. It produces hosiery, structural and mechanical engineering goods, prefabricated timber buildings, and pottery. Large coal mines once operated in the area, but have long been closed.

Heart of Midlothian, The
Novel (1818) by Walter ◊Scott. It centres around Effie Deans, imprisoned for alleged infanticide, and her half-sister, Jeanie Deans, who travels to London and obtains for her a pardon from Queen Caroline. The supposedly murdered child is revealed to have been kidnapped and brutalized; in ignorance, he kills the father who is searching for him. With its convincing and compassionate character studies and substantial social background it is probably the most accessible and lasting of all Scott's novels.

Heath, Edward (Richard George) (1916–)
British Conservative politician, party leader 1965–75. As prime minister 1970–74 he took the UK into the European Community but was brought down by economic and industrial relations crises at home. He was replaced as party leader by Margaret Thatcher in 1975, and became increasingly critical of her policies and her opposition to the UK's full participation in the EC. During John Major's administration, he continued his attacks on 'Eurosceptics' within the party.

In 1990 he undertook a mission to Iraq in an attempt to secure the release of British hostages. He returned in 1993 to negotiate the release of three Britons held prisoner by Iraq.

MEDICINE AND HEALTH CARE: SOME KEY DATES

1518 King Henry VIII founds the Royal College of Physicians at the instigation of his personal physician, Thomas Linacre. It is the first body with the power to license and examine those practising medicine.

1628 English physician William Harvey first describes the circulation of the blood.

1659 Typhoid fever is given a detailed description for the first time by English physician Thomas Willis.

1695 English physician and naturalist Nehemiah Grew isolates magnesium sulphate from Epsom spring water. 'Epsom salts' will become widely used for their purgative properties.

1747 The world's first sexually-transmitted disease clinic is opened at the London Lock Hospital in England.

1761 English naturalist John Hill writes that excessive use of snuff may lead to cancer; this is the first association of tobacco and cancer.

1775 The first evidence that environmental and occupational factors can cause cancer is provided by English surgeon Percivall Pott, who suggests that chimney sweeps' exposure to soot causes cancer of the scrotum and nasal cavity.

1783 English physician Thomas Cawley correctly diagnoses diabetes mellitus by demonstrating the presence of sugar in a patient's urine.

1796 English physician Edward Jenner performs the first vaccination against smallpox.

1819 British surgeon James Blundell makes the first human-to-human blood transfusion. The patient survives for 56 hours.

5 October 1823 English surgeon Thomas Wakley establishes the British medical journal the *Lancet*.

1853 English surgeon John Snow administers chloroform to Queen Victoria during the birth of Prince Leopold. It subsequently becomes a generally accepted anaesthetic.

1858 The Odontological Society of London establishes the first dental school in Great Britain. The College of Dentists of England establishes another school the following year.

1860 English nurse Florence Nightingale founds the Nightingale School for Nurses. The first nursing school in England, it establishes nursing as a profession for women.

1867 English surgeon Joseph Lister, founder of antiseptic surgery, announces his successful use of carbolic acid to keep his wards clear of sepsis.

1877 English physician Sophia Jex-Blake becomes the first women medical doctor to practise in Britain.

25 November 1884 The English surgeon Rickman John Godlee performs the first operation to remove a brain tumour.

1899 Scottish physician Patrick Manson founds the School of Tropical Medicine in London.

1911 The Medical Research Council is founded in Britain.

1915 New Zealand-born British surgeon Harold Delf Gillies develops plastic surgery when he treats war casualties at Sidcup, Kent.

1928 Scottish bacteriologist Alexander Fleming discovers penicillin, the first known antibiotic, when he notices that the mould *Penicillium notatum*, which has invaded a culture of staphylococci, inhibits the bacteria's growth.

1948 The NHS (National Health Service) is founded.

1960 English surgeon John Charnley performs a hip replacement operation, using a two-part joint replacement constructed of plastic and cobalt-chrome.

1962 English orthopaedic surgeon John Charnley discovers a low-friction, high-density polythene suitable for artificial hip joints.

28 March 1974 The National Health Service's family planning service is inaugurated in Britain.

1977 In-vitro fertilization (IVF) is developed by the English gynaecologist and obstetrician Patrick Steptoe.

25 July 1978 Louise Brown is born at Oldham Hospital, London; she is the first 'test tube' baby. Having been unable to remove a blockage from her mother's Fallopian tube, gynaecologist Patrick Steptoe and physiologist Robert Edwards removed an egg from her ovary, fertilized it with her husband's sperm, and re-implanted it in her uterus.

17 December 1986 British surgeons John Wallwork and Roy Calne perform the first triple transplant – heart, lung, and liver – at Papworth Hospital, Cambridge.

1997 The British Medical Association updates the Hippocratic Oath. Changes concern issues of modern medical ethics, such as abortion and treating the terminally ill.

November 1997 The NHS Confederation in the UK reports a growing increase in the number of treatments involving physical manipulation, especially aromatherapy (massage with essential oils), and reflexology (massage of hands and feet). Physiotherapy treatments on the NHS have increased by 26% since 1995.

After Douglas-Home's defeat in the 1964 general election, and the institution of a more democratic system of election for Conservative Party leaders, Heath became leader of the Conservative Party in 1965, when Douglas-Home resigned. Heath, defeated by Harold Wilson in the snap election of March 1966 (which consolidated the Labour government's majority), won the June 1970 general election against all poll indications.

Heath came to power pledged to reduce the increases in prices, put labour relations on a firmer legal basis, and negotiate favourable terms for Britain's entry to the EEC. His government's initial industrial measures brought resentment and discord into industrial relations, and resulted in long confrontations between government and unions.

Heath achieved his ambition of British entry to the Common Market on 1 January 1973, after earlier negotiations and a close vote in Parliament. The entry issue was not put to a referendum until after the fall of the Heath administration, and it remained a political controversy throughout his period of office.

On the domestic front, Heath initiated a policy of expansion, and after a bleak period during which unemployment reached levels of over one million, there was a period of unprecedented prosperity for some sectors of society, before, in the autumn of 1972, inflation reached such a level that the government introduced the Counter Inflation Acts, legislating against rises in office rents, some commodity prices, and basic earnings, but leaving fresh food prices to market elements. His anti-inflation measures were rendered largely inoperative partly by unprecedented rises in world prices of imported foods and raw materials.

In 1972 and the winter of 1973–74 Heath's industrial and economic policies were directly challenged by miners' strikes. In February 1974 Heath took up the miners' challenge by calling a general election. This resulted in a Conservative defeat and the appointment of a minority Labour government. Heath remained leader of the Conservative Party for the election of October 1974, but his leadership and policies came under increasing criticism and in February 1975 he was successfully challenged for the leadership by Margaret Thatcher.

Heathrow

Major international airport to the west of London in the Greater London borough of Hounslow, approximately 24 km/14 mi from the city centre. Opened in 1946, it is one of the world's busiest airports, with four terminals. It was linked with the London underground system in 1977. It was the target of three mortar attacks by the Irish Republican Army (IRA) in March 1994, all of which failed to detonate. In 1998 an inquiry into the proposal to build a fifth terminal was in its third year.

Heaviside, Oliver (1850–1925)

English physicist. In 1902 he predicted the existence of an ionized layer of air in the upper atmosphere, which was known as the **Kennelly–Heaviside layer** but is now called the E layer of the ionosphere. Deflection from it makes possible the transmission of radio signals around the world, which would otherwise be lost in outer space.

His theoretical work had implications for radio transmission. His studies of electricity published in *Electrical Papers* (1892) had considerable impact on long-distance telephony, and he added the concepts of inductance, capacitance, and impedance to electrical science.

heavy horse

Powerful horse specially bred for hauling wagons and heavy agricultural implements. After a decline following the introduction of the tractor, they are again being bred in increasing numbers and used for specialized work.

The four main British breeds all have European ancestry. The Suffolk Punch, the Clydesdale, and the Shire (the heaviest, with an average weight of nearly a ton) have been established in Britain for centuries, but the Percheron was imported from France as recently as 1916.

Their advantages are being rediscovered: they have a working life of 10–14 years and they can be maintained from self-sufficient resources. They are invaluable in forestry work, and some city breweries have found them more economical than lorries for short-range deliveries.

Hebrides

Group of more than 500 islands (fewer than 100 inhabited) off the west coast of mainland Scotland; total area 2,900 sq km/1,120 sq mi. The Hebrides were settled by Scandinavians during the 6th–9th centuries and passed under Norwegian rule from about 890 to 1266.

The **Inner Hebrides** are divided between Highland and Argyll and Bute authorities, and include Raasay, ◊Rum, Muck, Eigg, Scalpay, ◊Skye (Highland) and ◊Mull, ◊Jura, ◊Islay, ◊Iona, Coll, Tiree, Colonsay, and uninhabited Staffa (Argyll and Bute). The **Outer Hebrides** form the islands area of the ◊Western Isles authority, separated from the **Inner Hebrides** by the Little Minch. They include Harris/Lewis, North Uist, South Uist, Benbecula, ◊Barra, and ◊St Kilda.

The island of Eigg, which has been in private ownership since 1308, was bought by its residents in April 1997 after an eight-month ownership battle. In December 1996, an initial bid by the islanders of £1.2 million was rejected by the then owner, a German artist; a month later the Trustees of the Heritage Lottery Fund turned down their appeal for financial help. Finally, an English millionairess, who has remained anonymous, was believed to have given them around £900,000 – the bulk of the £1.5 million purchase price.

hedgerows

A feature of the landscape since Roman times. There is an estimated total of 450,600 km/280,000 miles of hedgerows in Britain, sheltering more than 600 plant species, 1,500 types of insect, 65 birds, and 20 different mammals. Among this diverse flora and fauna are 13 species which are either in very rapid decline or endangered globally. Ancient and species-rich hedgerows were among 14 key wildlife habitats on which the government and leading wildlife charities agreed rescue plans as a follow-up to the 1992 Rio Earth Summit. In 1996 the government estimated that more than 16,000 km/10,000 mi of hedgerows were disappearing each year because of neglect, 'grubbing out', and the spray drift of pesticides. New laws were introduced in 1997 to help combat this decline.

Hedgerows are frequently mentioned in Anglo-Saxon charters, the earliest reference in England to planting a hedge being in Wiltshire in 940. During the period of ◊enclosures, an estimated 321,800 km/200,000 mi of hedges were planted. However, between 1984 and 1990, nearly 25% of Britain's hedgerows were destroyed.

Helensburgh
Holiday resort and residential town in Argyll and Bute unitary authority, Scotland, situated on the Firth of Clyde at the mouth of Gare Loch, 40 km/25 mi northwest of Glasgow; population (1991) 22,600. With neighbouring Rhu, it is a centre for dinghy sailing.

Founded in the 18th century, the town contains many fine villas built by wealthy Glaswegians. The most outstanding example is Hill House, designed by Charles Rennie ◊Mackintosh and built in 1902–3.

Helensburgh was reputedly the birthplace of steam navigation in Europe. Henry Bell (1767–1830), hotelier and builder of the steamship *Comet*, ran the first European commercial steamline in 1812; it went to Glasgow.

Hell-Fire Club
18th-century club devoted to hedonism and debauchery established by Sir Francis Dashwood (1708–1781) in the village of Medmenham, Buckinghamshire, England. The club reputedly engaged in wild orgies, including devil worship, in caves under the village church. Most of these rumours were later proved to be untrue, but the club revelled in the notoriety they caused and it spawned a series of imitators.

Helpmann, Robert Murray (1909–1986)
Australian dancer, choreographer, and actor. The leading male dancer with the Sadler's Wells Ballet, London 1933–50, he partnered Margot ◊Fonteyn in the 1940s.

His forte was characterization rather than virtuosity, best displayed in his memorable role as the comic Ugly Sister in Frederick Ashton's *Cinderella*, for which he used his gift for mime and other theatrical effects. His other comic roles include Doctor Coppelius in *Coppélia* and the bridegroom in Ashton's *A Wedding Bouquet*, but he was equally at home in dramatic roles, such as the Red King in de Valois' *Checkmate*. His film appearances include *The Red Shoes* (1948), *The Tales of Hoffman* (1951), *Chitty Chitty Bang Bang* (1968), and the title role in Nureyev's *Don Quixote* (1973). Knighted 1968.

Help the Aged
Charity providing financial and material aid for poor and disadvantaged elderly people, both in the UK and overseas.

Helston
Market town in Cornwall, England, 16 km/10 mi southwest of Falmouth. Helston was made a borough by King John in 1201; from the reign of Edward I to 1832 it returned two members to Parliament.

The traditional **Helston Furry** or 'Floral' Dance is performed in processional formation through the streets and houses. The steps are in the ◊morris dance tradition, and the dance usually takes place in May in order to welcome spring and drive away evil spirits from the area.

'Furry' is derived from an ancient word 'fer', a fair or festivity. There are many theories regarding the dance's origin, one being that it honours the goddess Flora. Local legend tells of a dragon threatening the town, and the borough seal shows a dragon being slain by St Michael, Helston's patron saint.

Helvellyn
Peak of the ◊Lake District in Cumbria, northwest England; height 950 m/3,118 ft.

The summit is the highest point of the ridge which separates the the valleys containing Thirlemere and Ullswater lakes. The peak may be climbed from Wythburn at the head of Thirlemere on the western side, and from Patterdale or Glenridding on Ullswater to the east. Two sharp ridges, Striding Edge and Swirrell Edge, on the east side, provide more challenging routes. Helvellyn forms part of an annual Three Peaks charity event held in the Lake District; the other peaks are Skiddaw (930 m/3,052 ft) and Scafell Pike (978 m/3,210 ft).

Hemel Hempstead
Town in Hertfordshire, southeast England, 37 km/23 mi northwest of London, on the River Gade; population (1997 est) 80,790. It was designated a ◊new town in 1946. Paper, electrical goods, information systems, software and computers, electronics components, and brushes are manufactured. It has a large administrative and service sector, including telephone call centres for financial concerns.

The town was formerly a centre of the straw-plaiting industry. The mainly Norman church of St Mary's dates from the 12th century. Remains of a Roman villa have been discovered at nearby Boxmoor.

Hendon
Residential district in the Greater London borough of ◊Barnet. The Metropolitan Police Detective Training and Motor Driving schools are here, and the RAF Museum (1972) includes the Battle of Britain Museum (1980).

Hendry, Stephen (1970–)
Scottish snooker player who in 1990 became the youngest ever world champion at the age of 21 years 106 days. He won the title five years in succession (1991–96), an unprecedented achievement in modern snooker. The world number one from 1990 to 1998, he has won more ranking event tournaments than any other player.

Hendry was the youngest winner of a professional tournament when he claimed the 1986 Scottish professional title. He won his first ranking event in the 1987 Rothmans Grand Prix.

Hengist (died *c.* 488)
Legendary leader, with his brother **Horsa**, of the Jutes, who originated in Jutland and settled in Kent about 450, the first Anglo-Saxon settlers in Britain.

Henley-on-Thames
Town in Oxfordshire, south-central England, 56 km/35 mi west of London; population (1996 est) 10,000. It provides financial and other services, and has malting and brewing, and light engineering industries. The Royal Regatta, held here annually since 1839, is in June/July. Henley Management Colllege, established in 1946, was the first in Europe. A River and Rowing museum opened in 1998.

A fine five-arched bridge, built in 1786, spans the River Thames.

Henley Royal Regatta

Rowing festival on the River Thames at Henley, Oxfordshire, inaugurated in 1839. It is as much a social as a sporting occasion. The principal events are the solo *Diamond Challenge Sculls* and the *Grand Challenge Cup*, the leading event for eight-oared shells. The regatta is held in June–July. From 1998 professional rowers were allowed to compete at Henley after the Regatta's stewards had dropped the amateur definition from their rules.

Henman, Tim(othy) (1974–)

English tennis player. In 1998 became the first Briton for 25 years to reach the semi-finals of the men's singles at Wimbledon. In 1996 he won a silver medal in the men's doubles at the Atlanta Olympic Games. In January 1997 he achieved his first win on the ATP Tour and with good performances in other tournaments, including the Australian Open, he made it into the top 15 of the world rankings for the first time. During 1996 he leapt 70 places in the world rankings, an achievement which earned him the ATP Tour most improved player of the year award. In September 1998 he became the first British player to defend a title on the ATP Tour when he retained the President's Cup in Tashkent, Uzbekistan.

Henri, Adrian Maurice (1932–)

English poet and painter. In the 1960s he became known as one of the 'Liverpool Poets' with Roger ◊McGough and Brian ◊Patten. A compilation of his work was published in the bestselling *The Mersey Sound* (1967). His collections include *Tonight at Noon* (1968), *City* (1968), and *From the Loveless Motel* (1980).

Henrietta Maria (1609–1669)

Queen of England 1625–49. The daughter of Henry IV of France, she married Charles I of England in 1625. By encouraging him to aid Roman Catholics and make himself an absolute ruler, she became highly unpopular and was exiled 1644–60. She returned to England at the Restoration but retired to France in 1665.

Henry, (Charles Albert David) known as Harry (1984–)

Prince of the UK; second child of the Prince and Princess of Wales.

Henry, Lenny, Lenworth Henry (1958–)

English comedian and comic actor who first appeared on TV on the talent show *New Faces* when he was 16. He went on to

HENLEY ROYAL REGATTA *Held every summer on a long, straight stretch of the River Thames at Henley-on-Thames in Oxfordshire, the Royal Regatta is both a major international rowing festival and a principal event in the British upper-class social calendar. The Regatta was inaugurated in 1839. Gerry Gavigan/Collections*

HENRY, LENNY *The comedian Lenny Henry was born in Dudley in the West Midlands and makes affectionate mockery in his act of the region's distinctive, lugubrious-sounding accent. His quick-fire comedy has attracted a large following, and includes such outrageous characters as the lascivious American soul singer 'Theophilus P. Wildebeest'. Rex Features*

work on the children's programmes *Tiswas* and *OTT* before starring in *The Lenny Henry Show* (1984). A stalwart of the *Comic Relief* fund-raising programmes, he also took the lead role in the sitcom *Chef!* in the 1990s and in 1998 presented *Lenny Goes to Town* in which he toured Britain. He is married to Dawn ◊French.

Henry, William (1774–1836)

English chemist and physician. In 1803 he formulated **Henry's law**, which states that when a gas is dissolved in a liquid at a given temperature, the mass that dissolves is in direct proportion to the pressure of the gas.

He established that firedamp – the cause of many mining disasters – is methane, and confirmed the composition of methane and ethane. Like English chemist John ◊Dalton, Henry showed that hydrogen and carbon combine in definite proportions to form a limited number of compounds.

In medicine, Henry studied contagious diseases. He believed that these were spread by chemicals which could be rendered harmless by heating; he used heat to disinfect clothing during an outbreak of cholera in 1831.

Henry

Eight kings of England:

Henry I (1068–1135)

King of England from 1100. Youngest son of William the Conqueror, he succeeded his brother William II. He won the support of the Saxons by granting them a charter and marrying a Saxon princess, Matilda, daughter of Malcolm III of Scotland. An able administrator, he established a professional bureaucracy and a system of travelling judges.

His only legitimate son, William, was drowned in 1120, and Henry tried to settle the succession on his daughter ◊Matilda's son Henry (later Henry II). However, Matilda was unpopular and the throne was taken by Henry's nephew Stephen, who, towards the end of his reign, agreed to adopt Matilda's son as his heir.

Henry II (1133–1189)

King of England from 1154. The son of ◊Matilda and Geoffrey of Anjou (1113–1151), and the first of the Angevin kings, he succeeded ◊Stephen. He brought order of England after the chaos of Stephen's reign, curbing the power of the barons and reforming the legal system. His attempt to bring the church courts under control had to be abandoned after the murder of Thomas à ◊Becket. During his reign the English conquest of Ireland began. He was succeeded by his son Richard I.

Henry III (1207–1272)

King of England from 1216, when he succeeded John, but the royal powers were exercised by a regency until 1232, and by two French nobles, Peter des Roches and Peter des Rivaux, until the barons forced their expulsion in 1234, marking the start of Henry's personal rule. His financial commitments to the papacy and his foreign favourites antagonized the barons who issued the Provisions of Oxford in 1258, limiting the king's power. Henry's refusal to accept the provisions led to the second Barons' War in 1264, a revolt of nobles led by his brother-in-law Simon de ◊Montfort. Henry was defeated at Lewes, Sussex, and imprisoned, but restored to the throne after the royalist victory at Evesham in 1265. He was succeeded by his son Edward I.

Henry IV, (Bolingbroke) (1367–1413)

King of England from 1399, the son of ◊John of Gaunt. In 1398 he was banished by ◊Richard II for political activity but returned in 1399 to head a revolt and be accepted as king by Parliament. He was succeeded by his son Henry V.

He had difficulty in keeping the support of Parliament and the clergy, and had to deal with baronial unrest and Owen ◊Glendower's rising in Wales. In order to win support he had to conciliate the church by a law for the burning of heretics, and to make many concessions to Parliament.

Henry V (1387–1422)

King of England from 1413, son of Henry IV. Invading Normandy in 1415 (during the Hundred Years' War), he captured Harfleur and defeated the French at ◊Agincourt. He invaded again 1417–19, capturing Rouen. His military victory forced the French into the Treaty of Troyes (1420), which gave Henry control of the French government. He married ◊Catherine of Valois in 1420 and gained recognition as heir to the French throne by his father-in-law Charles VI, but died before him. He was succeeded by his son Henry VI.

Henry VI (1421–1471)

King of England from 1422, son of Henry V. He assumed royal power in 1442 and sided with the party opposed to the continuation of the Hundred Years' War with France. After his marriage in 1445, he was dominated by his wife, ◊Margaret of Anjou. He was deposed in 1461 in the Wars of the ◊Roses; was captured in 1465, temporarily restored in 1470, but again imprisoned in 1471 and then murdered.

Henry was eight months old when he succeeded to the English throne, and shortly afterwards, by the death in 1422 of his maternal grandfather, Charles VI, he became titular king of France. Unlike his father, Henry was disinclined to warfare, and when Joan of Arc revived French patriotism the English gradually began to lose their French possessions. By 1453 only Calais remained of his father's conquests.

The unpopularity of the government, especially after the loss of the English conquests in France, encouraged Richard, Duke of ◊York, to claim the throne, and though York was killed in 1460, his son Edward IV proclaimed himself king in 1461.

Henry VII (1457–1509)

King of England from 1485, when he overthrew Richard III at the Battle of ◊Bosworth. A descendant of ◊John of Gaunt, Henry, by his marriage to Elizabeth of York in 1486, united the houses of York and Lancaster. Yorkist revolts continued until 1497, but Henry restored order after the Wars of the Roses by the ◊Star Chamber and achieved independence from Parliament by amassing a private fortune through confiscations. He was succeeded by his son Henry VIII.

Born in Pembroke, Wales, the son of Edmund Tudor, Earl of Richmond (*c.* 1430–1456), Henry lived in Brittany, France, from 1471 to 1485, when he landed in Britain to lead the rebellion against Richard III. Henry succeeded in crushing the independence of the nobility by means of a policy of forced loans and fines. His chancellor, Cardinal Morton, was made responsible for the collection of these fines, and they were enforced by the privy councillors Empson and Dudley. This form of taxation became known as **Morton's Fork**, the dilemma being that, if a subject liable for taxation lived an extravagant lifestyle, obviously they could afford to pay the fine; if they lived austerely they should have sufficient funds saved with which to pay. To further curb the pretensions of the nobility, there were no unions of his children with the baronage. He married his son Henry to Catherine of Aragón, daughter of the joint sovereigns of Spain, his daughter Margaret to James IV of Scotland, and his youngest daughter Mary to Louis XII of France.

Henry VIII (1491–1547)

King of England from 1509, when he succeeded his father Henry VII and married Catherine of Aragón, the widow of his brother.

During the period 1513–29 Henry pursued an active foreign policy, largely under the guidance of his Lord Chancellor, Cardinal Wolsey, who shared Henry's desire to make England stronger. Wolsey was replaced by Thomas More in 1529 for failing to persuade the pope to grant Henry a divorce. After 1532 Henry broke with papal authority, proclaimed himself head of the church in England, dissolved the monasteries, and divorced Catherine. His subsequent wives were Anne Boleyn, Jane Seymour, Anne of Cleves, Catherine Howard, and Catherine Parr.

Henry divorced Catherine of Aragón in 1533 because she was too old to give him an heir, and married Anne Boleyn, who was beheaded in 1536, ostensibly for adultery. Henry's third wife, Jane Seymour, died in 1537. He married Anne of Cleves in 1540 in pursuance of Thomas Cromwell's policy of allying with the German Protestants, but rapidly abandoned this policy, divorced Anne, and beheaded Cromwell. His fifth wife, Catherine Howard, was beheaded in 1542, and the following year he married Catherine Parr, who survived him. Henry never completely lost his popularity, but wars with France and Scotland towards the end of his reign sapped the economy, and in religion he not only executed Roman Catholics, including Thomas More, for refusing to acknowledge his supremacy in the church, but also Protestants who maintained his changes had not gone far enough.

Foreign policy

Henry's reign falls naturally into two parts, separated by the year 1529, which can be regarded as the critical year of the divorce. The early period is notable for his skilful foreign policy, guided by Wolsey, although Henry's will was always paramount. Henry and Wolsey exploited the rivalry between Francis I of France and the Holy Roman emperor Charles V by making England the arbiter between them, enhancing the prestige and influence of England. Both kings sought Henry's favour, Francis at the Field of the Cloth of Gold, and Charles, less ostentatiously, in Kent. The policy collapsed disastrously after Henry began supporting Charles in 1522. Charles comprehensively defeated Francis at Pavia in 1525 and no longer needed English support.

Split from Rome

By this time Henry's policy had become dominated by his desire to divorce Catherine as he was becoming desperate for a male heir and was determined to marry Anne Boleyn. At first there seemed a possibility that the divorce might be granted. The papal legate journeyed to England to hear the case, but Catherine appealed direct to the pope and the court was adjourned. The position was complicated by the fact that Charles V, Catherine's nephew, controlled Rome. Unable to obtain the annulment for his monarch, Wolsey was dismissed in 1529. Henry then proceeded to act through Parliament, and had the entire body of the clergy in England declared guilty of treason in 1531. The clergy were suitably cowed and agreed to repudiate papal supremacy and recognize Henry as supreme head of the church in England. The English ecclesiastical courts then pronounced his marriage to Catherine null and void and he married Anne Boleyn in 1533.

Henry continued his attack on the church with the suppression of the monasteries 1536–39; their lands were confiscated and granted to his supporters. However, although he laid the ground for the English Reformation by the separation from Rome, he had little sympathy with Protestant dogmas. As early as 1521 a pamphlet which he had written against Lutheranism had won him the title of *Fidei Defensor* from the pope, and Henry's own religious views are quite clearly expressed in the Statute of ◊Six Articles (1539) which instituted the orthodox Catholic tenets as necessary conditions for Christian belief. As a result Protestants were being burnt for heresy even while Catholics were being executed for refusing to take the oath of supremacy.

Henry's legacy

Henry ended his reign with the reputation of a tyrant, despite the promise of his earlier years – in 1536 the rebellion known as the ◊Pilgrimage of Grace was viciously suppressed, and advisers of the calibre of More and Bishop John Fisher had died rather than sacrifice their own principles to Henry's will. But the power of the crown had been considerably strengthened by Henry's ecclesiastical policy, and the monastic confiscations gave impetus to the rise of a new nobility which was to become influential in succeeding reigns.

He was succeeded by his son Edward VI.

You have sent me a Flanders mare.

HENRY VIII King of England.
Attributed remark on seeing Anne of Cleves for the first time

---

Henry Doubleday Research Association

British gardening group founded in 1954 by Lawrence Hills (1911–1990) to investigate organic growing techniques. It runs the **National Centre for Organic Gardening**, a 10-hectare/22-acre demonstration site, at Ryton-on-Dunsmore near Coventry, England. The association is named after the person who first imported Russian comfrey, a popular green-manuring crop.

Henryson, Robert (*c.* 1430–*c.* 1505)

Scottish poet. His works include versions of Aesop's fables (*The Moral Fables of Esope the Phrygian*) and *The Testament of Cresseid*, a work once attributed to Geoffrey Chaucer, which continues Chaucer's story of *Troilus and Criseyde* by depicting the betrayal and wretched afterlife of Troilus. His *Robene and Makyne* was the first pastoral to be written in Britain.

Hepburn, Audrey born Hepburn-Ruston (1929–1993)

English actress, of Anglo-Dutch descent. She often played innocent, childlike characters. Slender and doe-eyed, she set a different style from the more ample women stars of the 1950s. After playing minor parts in British films in the early 1950s, she became a Hollywood star in *Roman Holiday* (1951), for which she won an Academy Award, and later starred in such films as *Funny Face* (1957) and *My Fair Lady* (1964).

Her break came when the French novelist Colette insisted Hepburn play in the Broadway version of her novel *Gigi*. This led to her casting in *Roman Holiday* and to a succession of films during the 1950s and 1960s: mainly comedies, such as *Sabrina* (1954) and *Charade* (1963), and the anarchic Holly Golightly in the bittersweet *Breakfast at Tiffany's* (1961), but she also played Natasha in *War and Peace* (1956) and the doubting novice in *The Nun's Story* (1959).

Hepplewhite, George (died 1786)

English furnituremaker associated with Neo-Classicism. His reputation rests upon his book of designs *The Cabinetmaker and Upholsterer's Guide*, published posthumously in 1788, which contains over 300 designs, characterized by simple elegance and utility. No piece of furniture has been identified as being made by him.

Hepplewhite's designs were mainly in mahogany or satinwood, delicately inlaid or painted with decorations of feathers, shells, or ears of wheat. He favoured heart- and shield-backs for chairs, and used 'Marlboro' (square-tapered) legs on tables and sideboards. His workshop was in St Giles, Cripplegate, London.

heptarchy

The seven Saxon kingdoms thought to have existed in England before AD 800: Northumbria, Mercia, East Anglia, Essex, Kent, Sussex, and Wessex. The term was coined by 16th-century historians.

Hepworth, (Jocelyn) Barbara (1903–1975)

English sculptor. She developed a distinctive abstract style, creating slender upright forms reminiscent of standing stones or totems; and round, hollowed forms with spaces bridged by wires or strings, as in *Pelagos* (1946; Tate Gallery, London). Her preferred medium was stone, but she also worked in concrete, wood, and aluminum, and many of her later works were in bronze.

Hepworth was an admirer of Henry ◊Moore, Constantin Brancusi, and Hans Arp. She married first the sculptor John Skeaping and in 1933 the painter Ben ◊Nicholson, whose influence encouraged her interest in abstract forms. In 1939 she moved to St Ives, Cornwall (where her studio is now a museum). She was made DBE in 1965.

Her public commissions included *Winged Figure* (1962) for the John Lewis Building, London and *Single Form* (1962–63; United Nations, New York).

heraldry

The science of armorial bearings. In England it developed rapidly during the 13th and 14th centuries, reaching a climax in the reigns of Edward III and Richard II. There was a revival in the 19th century. The English ◊College of Arms, founded in 1484, is the world's oldest heraldic court, and it continues to exercise its function; in Scotland the equivalent body is the ◊Court of the Lord Lyon. In 1672 all older registers in Scotland were superseded by the 'Public Register of All Arms and Bearings in Scotland'.

Heralds' College

Another name for the ◊College of Arms, the English heraldic body.

Herald, The

Daily morning newspaper covering Scotland, published in Glasgow. Established in 1783, it had a circulation of over 100,000 in 1998.

Herbert, George (1593–1633)

English poet. His volume of religious poems, *The Temple*, appeared in 1633, shortly before his death. His intense though quiet poems embody his religious struggles ('The Temper', 'The Collar') or poignantly contrast mortality and eternal truth ('Vertue', 'Life') in a deceptively simple language.

The high regard in which he was held in the 17th century waned early in the 18th, and for a century or more his poetry was considered uncouth. The Romantic poet Coleridge did much to restore it to favour. It is noted for its colloquial phraseology, pliable verse forms, and quiet music; its apparent simplicity is its greatest strength.

Herbert was born at Montgomery Castle in Wales, and educated at Cambridge University, where he was made a fellow in 1615. In 1619 he drew the notice of James I, and for a time he followed the court. He joined the church in 1626, was ordained priest in 1630, and became vicar of Bemerton, Wiltshire, where he wrote his religious poems.

Hereford

City in the county of Herefordshire, west-central England, on the River Wye, 34 km/21 mi southwest of Worcester; population (1996 est) 48,900. It is an agricultural centre, with a livestock market noted for its white-faced Hereford cattle. The city has the UK's largest cider industry. Other activities include brewing, food-processing (chicken), tourism, and the manufacture of non-ferrous alloys and components. The cathedral, dating from 1079, has the largest chained library in the world and a medieval *Mappa Mundi* (map of the world). The Three Choirs Festival is held in the cathedral every third year (in turn with Gloucester and Worcester).

Hereford Cathedral

Founded not later than 680 by its first bishop, Putta, the cathedral was destroyed in 1055 by the Welsh, and rebuilt late in the 11th century, the nave and other Norman parts of the building being completed in about 1140. Since medieval times the structure has been much rebuilt and restored. The finest parts surviving intact are the Lady Chapel (1220–40), the north transept (1250–87), and the early 14th-century crossing tower.

The cathedral's two most treasured possessions are its remarkable chained library, containing almost 1,500 books, including some very rare manuscripts and early printed volumes; and the ⇨Mappa Mundi (map of the world), dated about 1275, and probably the earliest map of its kind in existence. It was made in England around 1285 by Richard of Haldingham, with the Welsh castles added during 1289. Following an appeal in 1988, money was raised to restore and preserve the map.

Features

The Old House is a 17th-century black-and-white timbered residence, now housing a museum. The river is spanned by the Wye Bridge, dating from 1490, and Greyfriars Bridge, opened in 1966. Other features include Castle Green on the site of the old castle; the Coningsby Hospital (1614) almshouses; the Cathedral School, which had its first known headmaster in 1384; St Ethelbert's Hospital; All Saints' Church, with 14th-century carved stalls and a chained library; and the 12th–14th-century church of St Peter's. The Wye is an excellent salmon river.

History

The site of Hereford was seized from the Welsh by the Mercians in about AD 600, and it became the capital of West Mercia and a garrison against the Welsh. King Offa of Mercia later established the Wye as border between Wales and England, and built Offa's Dyke in about 785 to mark the border. Hereford's first castle, built by Ralph, the nephew of Edward the Confessor, was destroyed (along with the original Saxon cathedral) following a defeat by the Welsh in 1055. In Norman times the city was an important garrison, and it received its first charter from Richard I in 1189. It prospered in the Middle Ages as a centre of the wool trade, but it continued to be the scene of warfare until after the English Civil War. Hereford was held by the king for most of the Civil War, suffering several Parliamentary raids from Gloucester, and changing hands more than once. The Earl of Stamford took it for Parliament in September 1642, but evacuated it in early December, after which the Royalists returned. In April 1643 it was garrisoned again by a Parliamentary force for about six weeks. In July and August 1645 a Scottish force unsuccessfully besieged the town, but in November 1645 a large Parliamentary force led by Col John Birch took the town and held it until after the war. The castle was finally demolished in 1660.

Famous people

The actor and theatre manager David Garrick was born here in 1717. It is said that Hereford was the birthplace of the 17th-century actress Nell Gwyn.

Hereford

Breed of beef cattle originating in Herefordshire, England, an area noted for its luxuriant pastures. They are characteristically red with white faces and white markings and thrive well in adverse conditions. They are found in many countries of the world and are the predominant breed in Canada.

Herefordshire

County in west England, created in 1998 from part of the former county, Hereford and Worcester

Area 2,288 sq km/884 sq mi

Towns and cities ⇨Hereford (administrative headquarters), Leominster, Ross-on-Wye, Ledbury

Features River Wye; Herefordshire Beacon (340 m/1,115 ft) Iron Age fort; Hereford Cathedral (11th century) houses the late 13th- early 14th-century Mappa Mundi, and the Chained Library, with almost 1,500 chained books and 200 manuscripts dating from the 8th to 12th centuries; Waterworks Museum (Hereford) in restored Victorian pump house; Croft Castle (Leominster); St Mary's Church (Kempley) with medieval wall paintings; The Prospect, a walled clifftop garden in Ross-on-Wye designed by John Kyrle in the 17th century; Norman Church (Kilpeck) with notable carvings

Industries agriculture, orchards and cider industry, agricultural services and machinery, precision engineering, light engineering, plastics manufacture

Population (1995) 191,250.

HEREFORDSHIRE *Symond's Yat on the border between Gloucestershire and Herefordshire is a well-known site of outstanding natural beauty. Here, the River Wye loops through a narrow gorge surmounted by a steep rocky outcrop that commands panoramic views of the surrounding countryside.*
Joe Cornish

Hereward the Wake (lived 11th century)

English leader of a revolt against the Normans in 1070. His stronghold in the Isle of Ely was captured by William the Conqueror in 1071. Hereward escaped, but his fate is unknown.

Herne Bay

Resort on the north coat of Kent, southeast England, 11 km/7 mi north of Canterbury; population (1991) 32,800.

Herne Bay's pier, formerly the second-longest in England, is storm-severed; its inshore portion remains with an associated sports centre, but the offshore section is inaccessible. A large breakwater contains a viewing gallery.

The coastal area developed in the 19th century. The old village of **Herne** inland has a 13th-century church.

Heron, Patrick (1920–)

English painter, designer, and writer on art. Most of his work is abstract and vibrantly coloured. He has been art critic for several journals, including the *New Statesman*, and has written several books on art.

Heron was born in Leeds, the son of a textiles manufacturer, for whom he made designs in the 1930s and 1940s. In 1956 he settled in Cornwall and he is considered a leading figure of the ◊St Ives School of painters.

Herrick, Robert (1591–1674)

English poet and cleric. He published *Hesperides: or the Works both Humane and Divine of Robert Herrick* (1648), a collection of verse admired for its lyric quality, including the well-known poems 'Gather ye rosebuds' and 'Cherry ripe'.

The 'divine' poems are, on the whole, unremarkable, but the 'humane' works are rich and varied, owing much to Roman models such as Catullus and Martial and to native influences such as Ben ◊Jonson and popular ballads. They range in scale from couplets to Horatian odes and verse epistles, and cover such subjects as religion, politics, love, erotic fantasy, the value of poetry, and the changing cycles of life in the countryside.

Herriot, James pen name of James Alfred Wight (1916–1995)

English writer. A practising veterinary surgeon in Yorkshire from 1939, he wrote of his experiences in a series of humorous books which described the life of a young vet working in a Yorkshire village in the late 1930s. His first three books were published as a compilation under the title *All Creatures Great and Small* (1972).

He wrote his first book, *If Only They Could Talk*, when he was in his 50s. This was quickly followed by *It Shouldn't Happen To A Vet*, and *Let Sleeping Vets Lie*.

The success of Herriot's novels was based on their warm humour, their colourful, larger-than-life characters, and an implicit nostalgia for the pre-war way of life in which there was a strong and enduring sense of community. In 1974 a film version of *All Creatures Great and Small* was made, and by the 1980s his books had been translated into every major language, including Japanese, and a long-running television series was being sold world-wide.

Herron, Ron(ald James) (1930–1994)

English architect and founder member of Archigram, a radical architectural group of the 1960s. He designed Walking City, a proposed city on wheels with full environmental controls, inspired by space exploration. Walking City became a seminal icon of technology and mobility. The Pompidou Centre in Paris was inspired by Herron's drawing *Oasis* (1968).

Archigram was derided by the profession for never building anything, but its aim was to explore the idea of almost possible architecture. Herron continued to collaborate with the group while working for mainstream architectural practices. His buildings include the award-winning headquarters for the design firm Imagination and fabric structures in Japan.

Herschel, Caroline (Lucretia) (1750–1848)

German-born English astronomer, sister of William ◊Herschel, and from 1772 his assistant in Bath, England. She discovered eight comets and worked on her brother's catalogue of star clusters and nebulae.

Herschel, John Frederick William (1792–1871)

English scientist, astronomer, and photographer who discovered thousands of close double stars, clusters, and nebulae. He coined the terms 'photography', 'negative', and 'positive', discovered sodium thiosulphite as a fixer of silver halides, and invented the cyanotype process; his inventions also include astronomical instruments. Knighted 1831.

Herschel, (Frederick) William (1738–1822)

German-born English astronomer. He was a skilled telescopemaker, and pioneered the study of binary stars and nebulae. He discovered the planet Uranus in 1781 and infrared solar rays in 1801. He catalogued over 800 double stars, and found over 2,500 nebulae, catalogued by his sister Caroline Herschel; this work was continued by his son John Herschel. By studying the distribution of stars, William established the basic form of our Galaxy, the Milky Way.

Herschel discovered the motion of binary stars around one another, and recorded it in his *Motion of the Solar System in Space* (1783). In 1789 he built, in Slough, Berkshire, a 1.2-m/4-ft telescope of 12 m/40 ft focal length (the largest in the world at the time), but he made most use of a more satisfactory 46-cm/18-in instrument. He discovered two satellites of Uranus and two of Saturn. Knighted 1816.

Herstmonceux

Village in East Sussex, southeast England, 11 km/7 mi north of Eastbourne; population (1996 est) 2,300. The Royal Greenwich Observatory was sited alongside the 15th-century castle from 1958 until 1990, when it relocated to Cambridge. The Isaac Newton telescope was moved to the Canary Islands in 1979.

The name derives from the 11th-century Norman lord of the manor. **Herstmonceux Castle**, a fortified manor house, is one of the earliest brick buildings in England; fortification was added in 1441. The castle was restored in the 20th century, and is now used as an international study centre for Queen's University, Canada. All Saints' Church dates from the late 12th century and **Herstmonceux Place** was built in the early 18th century with bricks from the castle. Some of the Royal Greenwich Observatory's fine antique telescopes remain in an exhibition centre, open only to school parties.

The village was a centre of trug-making for over 160 years.

Hertford

Market town and administrative headquarters of ◊Hertfordshire, southeast England, on the River Lea, about 40 km/25 mi north of London; population (1997 est) 24,000. Industries include brewing, printing, telecommunications, and plastics manufacturing. Service activities include finance, and research and development for the rubber industry.

Hertford was the site of a Saxon stronghold, and there are remains of a Norman castle, including the Norman mound, parts of the curtain wall of Henry II, and the 15th-century gatehouse. Haileybury College, a co-educational private school, is nearby.

Hertfordshire

County of southeast England
Area 1,630 sq km/629 sq mi
Towns and cities ◊Hertford (administrative headquarters), Bishop's Stortford, Hatfield, Hemel Hempstead, Letchworth (the first ◊garden city; followed by Welwyn in 1919), Stevenage (the first ◊new town, designated in 1946), St Albans, Watford, Hitchin
Physical rivers Lea, Stort, Colne; part of the Chiltern Hills
Features Hatfield House; Knebworth House (home of Lord Lytton); Brocket Hall (home of Palmerston and Melbourne); home of George Bernard ◊Shaw at Ayot St Lawrence; Berkhamsted Castle (Norman); Rothamsted agricultural experimental station
Industries aircraft; computer electronics; electrical goods; engineering; paper and printing; plastics; pharmaceuticals; plastics; tanning; sand and gravel are worked in the south
Agriculture barley for brewing industry; dairy farming; market gardening; horticulture
Population (1991) 975,800
Famous people Henry Bessemer, Cecil Rhodes, Graham Greene
History In 896 a battle took place in Hertfordshire between Alfred and the Danes. During the Wars of the Roses the battles of St Albans and Barnet were fought here. Elizabeth I was at Hatfield palace when she heard of her accession.

Topography

Hertfordshire is bounded to the north by Cambridgeshire, Bedfordshire, and Luton; to the east by Essex; to the south by Greater London; and to the west by Buckinghamshire. The landscape is hilly, with parks and woodlands. The rocks, principally chalk, date mainly from the Upper Cretaceous period. The Grand Union Canal passes through part of the county.

Heseltine, Michael (Ray Dibdin) (1933–)

British Conservative politician, deputy prime minister 1995–97. A member of Parliament from 1966 (for Henley from 1974), he was secretary of state for the environment 1990–92 and for trade and industry 1992–95.

Heseltine was minister of the environment 1979–83, when he succeeded John Nott. As minister of defence from 1983, he resigned in January 1986 over the ◊Westland affair and was then seen as a major rival to Margaret Thatcher. In November 1990, Heseltine's challenge to Thatcher's leadership of the Conservative Party brought about her resignation. After the Conservatives' defeat in 1997, he announced that he would not contest the party's vacant leadership because of heart problems but has continued to make known his views on European issues.

Heseltine, Philip (Arnold)

Real name of the English composer Peter ◊Warlock.

Hever Castle

Castle in Kent, England, 3 km/2 mi east of Edenbridge. It was the Boleyn family home in Tudor times but sank into obscurity with the family's decline after the dissolution of Anne ◊Boleyn's marriage to Henry VIII. In the early 20th century it was modernized by William Waldorf ◊Astor and includes an entire Tudor-style village built to augment the castle's accommodation, and magnificent gardens.

Hewish, Antony (1924–)

English radio astronomer who was awarded, with Martin ◊Ryle, the Nobel Prize for Physics in 1974 for his work on pulsars, rapidly rotating neutron stars that emit pulses of energy.

The discovery by Jocelyn ◊Bell Burnell of a regularly fluctuating signal, which turned out to be the first pulsar, began a period of intensive research. Hewish discovered another three straight away, and more than 170 pulsars have been found since 1967.

Hexham

Market town in Northumberland, northeast England, 34 km/21 mi west of Newcastle upon Tyne; population (1991) 11,342. Woodchip board is the principal manufacture. The town is a tourist centre for ◊Hadrian's Wall, a Roman frontier system and World Heritage Site lying 13 km/8 mi to the north. **Hexham Abbey** dates from the 12th century.

Features

An ancient abbey church was founded on the site of the present Priory Church by Wilfrid, archbishop of York, in 674. It was sacked by the Danes in 876, and an Augustinian priory was founded on the site in 1114. The present Priory Church, a good example of Early English architecture, was built over the Saxon crypt. It contains a fine Perpendicular rood screen of oak and a carved Roman slab. Other features include the 15th-century Moot Hall and the 14th-century Manor Office, built originally as a prison and now housing a museum.

Close to the south of the town is the site of the **Battle of Hexham**, where the Lancastrians suffered a defeat in 1464. Nearby are the remains of Dilston Castle, seat of the last Earl of Derwentwater, who was beheaded in 1716. Hadrian's Wall includes the Roman forts of Chesters and Housesteads; and Vindolanda, site of the remains of eight forts and settlements. A National Trail follows the course of the wall from Bowness-on-Solway to Wallsend. The substantial Kielder Reservoir, about 48 km/30 mi to the northwest, is surrounded by the largest planned forest in Europe, and offers recreational and sailing facilities.

Heyer, Georgette (1902–1974)

English novelist. She wrote her first historical novel, *The Black Moth* in 1921, to amuse a sick brother. Her best, such as *These Old Shades* (1926) and *Regency Buck* (1935), are Regency romances based on considerable research, a fictional form she can be said to have invented.

Heywood

Town in Greater Manchester Metropolitan County, England, 5 km/3 mi southwest of Rochdale; population (1991) 29,100. Heywood has a range of industries, including the manufacture of machinery, carpets, wallpaper, and chemicals, as well as engineering works.

Heywood, Thomas (*c.* 1570–*c.* 1650)

English actor and dramatist. He wrote or adapted over 220 plays, including the domestic tragedy *A Woman Kilde with Kindnesse* (1602–03). He also wrote an *Apology for Actors* (1612), in answer to attacks on the morality of the theatre.

Hick, Graeme Ashley (1966–)

Rhodesian-born cricketer who became Zimbabwe's youngest professional cricketer at the age of 17. A prolific right-handed batsman, he joined Worcestershire, England, in 1984. He achieved the highest score in England in the 20th century in 1988 against Somerset with 405 not out. He made his test debut for England in 1991 after a seven-year qualification period. He has not been able to reproduce his county from at Test level, and in particular has struggled against the top fast bowlers. Many of his best performances for England have come in one-day cricket.

Hicks, (Edward) Seymour (1871–1949)

English actor and theatre manager. He was chief light comedian at the Gaiety Theatre 1894–97. He wrote numerous plays, including *Bluebell in Fairyland* (1901), *The Catch of the Season* (1904), and *The Man in Dress Clothes* (1922). He was knighted in 1935.

Hickstead

English equestrian centre built 1960 at the Sussex home of Douglas Bunn (1928–), a leading figure and administrator in the horse world. The British Show Jumping Derby has been held there since 1961, as well as many other national and international events.

Higgins, Jack

Pseudonym of English novelist Harry ◊Patterson.

high commissioner

Representative of one independent Commonwealth country in the capital of another, ranking with ambassador. Also a high administrative officer in a dependency or protectorate.

The member countries of the Commonwealth exchange high commissioners and not ambassadors. They act as confidential channels of communication between the UK and Commonwealth governments.

Higher

In Scottish education, a public examination taken at the age of 17, one year after the Scottish O grade. Highers are usually taken in four or five subjects and qualify students for entry to higher education. About 90% of Scottish undergraduates choose to study in Scotland.

High Force

Waterfall 21 m/69 ft high, where the River ◊Tees crosses the Whin Sill (the rock system on which Hadrian's Wall is built), near Middleton-in-Teesdale, Durham, England.

Highland

Unitary authority in northern Scotland, created from the region bearing the same name in 1996

Area 26,157 sq km/10,100 sq mi (one-third of Scotland)

Towns ◊Inverness (administrative headquarters), Thurso, Wick, Fort William, Aviemore

Physical mainland Highland consists of a series of glaciated ancient plateau masses dissected by narrow glens and straths (valleys); in the northeast (Caithness), old red sandstone rocks give a softer, lower topography; Ben Nevis (1,343 m/4,406 ft), Cairngorm Mountains; Loch Ness; Cuillin Hills, Skye; includes many of the Inner Hebridean islands

Features Caledonian Canal; John O'Groats; Skye Road Bridge

Industries winter sports, timber, aluminium smelting, pulp and paper production, whisky distilling, cottage and croft industries

Agriculture salmon fishing, sheep farming, grouse and deer hunting

Population (1995) 208,300

History location of many key historical moments in Scottish history, including the 'massacre' of Glencoe, the Battle of Culloden and the Highland Clearances.

Language

Gaelic is spoken by 7.5% of the population.

Economy

Highland is a predominantly rural area comprising of land that is agriculturally marginal, much of which is not amenable to crops or forestry. Subsistence economies in the form of crofting still characterize the least accessible parts of the area. More accessible parts are exploiting their tourist potential and the opportunities afforded by mountain sports, for example, Aviemore and Fort William. Traditional industries, such as whisky distilling and crafts, are sustained by the tourist industry.

Environment

There are 356 Sites of Special Scientific Interest, 27 National Nature Reserves, eight Ramsars (wetland sites), 16 Special Protection Areas, three Biosphere Reserves, and 16 National Scenic Areas.

Administrative history

Prior to 1975, this area was part of the five counties of Caithness-shire, Sutherlandshire, Ross and Cromarty, Inverness-shire, and Nairnshire.

Highland Clearances

Forced removal of tenants from large estates in Scotland during the early 19th century, as landowners 'improved' their estates by switching from arable to sheep farming. It led ultimately to widespread emigration to North America.

Highland fling

Scottish dance-step, rather than a dance itself, although that is often so called. The music is that of the strathspey and the step is a kick of the leg backwards and forwards.

Highland Games

Traditional Scottish outdoor gathering that includes tossing the caber, putting the shot, running, dancing, and bagpipe playing.

The most celebrated is the Braemar Gathering, held annually in August.

Highland Host

Force of highlanders brought into southwest Scotland in 1678 to suppress Scottish Covenanters by the Earl of Lauderdale. For two months the host engaged in pillage and confiscation of lands until their brutality and their local unpopularity led to their being withdrawn.

Highlands

One of the three geographical divisions of Scotland, lying to the north of a geological fault line that stretches from Stonehaven in the North Sea to Dumbarton on the Clyde. It is a mountainous region of hard rocks, shallow infertile soils, and high rainfall.

high sheriff

County or city officer in England and Wales, with wide judicial and executive authority. The sheriff's duties are defined by the Sheriffs' Act of 1887, and include attendance on judges during assizes, the functions of returning officers during parliamentary elections, and the preparation of lists of jurors.

City sheriffs are appointed annually on 9 November.

high steward

In England, one of the great officers of state. The Court of the High Steward formerly decided upon claims to do services at

HIGHLAND GAMES *Contestants in the sword dancing competition at a Highland Games meeting in Scotland. Highland Games are celebrations of clan membership and Scottish identity, and include a number of different athletic events, such as tossing the caber and sword (or Highland) dancing, in which the contestants must perform a sequence of complicated steps and leaps over a pair of crossed swords. Brian Shuel/Collections*

the coronation of the sovereign; this duty is now performed by the Court of Claims, newly appointed on each accession. A high steward was also created to preside over the House of Lords on the trial of a peer.

The original duty of the high steward seems to have been to place the dishes on the lord's table at solemn feasts. On the accession of Henry IV the office was merged in the Crown.

High Tech

In architecture, abbreviation for **high technology**, an approach to design, originating in the UK in the 1970s, which concentrates on technical innovation, often using exposed structure and services as a means of creating exciting forms and spaces.

Outstanding examples are the Lloyds Building (1986) in the City of London, by Richard ◊Rogers, which dramatically exhibits the service requirements of a large building; and Nicholas ◊Grimshaw's *Financial Times* printing works, London (1988).

highwayman

In English history, a thief on horseback who robbed travellers on the highway (those who did so on foot were known as **footpads**). Highwaymen continued to flourish well into the 19th century.

With the development of regular coach services in the 17th and 18th centuries, the highwaymen's activities became notorious, and the ◊Bow Street Runners were organized to suppress them.

High Wycombe

Market town in Buckinghamshire, southern England, on the River Wye, between London and Oxford; population (1991) 62,500. Industries include light engineering and the printing of postage stamps, waste management and corporate services, and the manufacture of furniture, cigarette machines, precision instruments, pharmaceuticals, and software. RAF Strike Command has multi-storey underground headquarters (1984) beneath the Chiltern Hills nearby; they were used as Joint Headquarters in the Gulf War (1991).

Features

The church of All Saints dates from about 1275, but it was considerably altered and enlarged in the 15th and 16th centuries. The tower has a peal of 12 bells. The Local History and Chair Museum illustrates the tradition of furnituremaking in the town and includes a collection of domestic chairs. The Little Market House was built in 1761, and the Guildhall dates from 1757. The ruined hospital of St John dates from about 1180; it was converted into a grammar school in 1550. Wycombe Abbey, built in 1795, is now a girls' school.

Hughenden Manor, home of Benjamin Disraeli from 1847 until his death in 1881, is nearby to the north.

Hill, Archibald Vivian (1886–1977)

English physiologist who studied muscle action and especially the amount of heat produced during muscle activity. For this work he shared the 1922 Nobel Prize for Physiology or Medicine.

Hill, Austin Bradford (1897–1991)

English epidemiologist and statistician. He pioneered rigorous statistical study of patterns of disease and, together with Richard ◊Doll, was the first to demonstrate the connection between cigarette smoking and lung cancer.

His work on smoking and lung cancer, which involved collecting data on the smoking habits and health of over 30,000 British doctors for several years, in the precomputer age, is considered to be among the great medical achievements of the century. He was knighted in 1961.

Hill, Benny born Alfred Hawthorne (1925–1992)

English comedian. His television shows, which first appeared in 1952, combined the bawdy humour of the seaside postcard with the manic slapstick of the silent cinema, a format which he perfected but never really changed.

Regarded as too risqué early in his career, he was later condemned for being sexist, but many critics nevertheless saw him as the last of the great visual comics. His TV shows were sold to 109 countries.

Hill, Damon (1960–)

English racing driver. He won the 1996 Formula One World Drivers' Championship.

The son of ◊Graham Hill, he began his Formula One racing career with Brabham in 1992 before replacing Nigel Mansell at Williams, who had used him as a test driver. He won his first Grand Prix in Hungary in 1993. In both 1994 and 1995 he finished as runner-up to Michael Schumacher in the Drivers' Championship. In 1996 he led the championship from start to finish, winning 8 races and finishing 19 points ahead of his nearest rival, though only clinching the championship at the last Grand Prix of the season. He joined the TWR Arrows team for the 1997 season after Williams did not renew his contract, but moved to Jordan in 1998. In 1998 he won the Belgian Grand Prix at Spa, the first Grand Prix win of his career since leaving Williams.

Hill, (Norman) Graham (1929–1975)

English motor-racing driver. He won the Dutch Grand Prix in 1962, progressing to the world driver's title 1962 and 1968. In 1972 he became the first Formula One World Champion to win the Le Mans Grand Prix d'Endurance (Le Mans 24-Hour Race). He was also the only driver to win the Formula One world championship, Le Mans 24-Hour Race, and the Indianapolis 500 Race in his career as a driver. Hill started his Formula One career with Lotus in 1958, went to BRM 1960–66, returned to Lotus 1967–69, moved to Brabham 1970–72, and formed his own team, Embassy Shadow, 1973–75. He was killed in an air crash. His son Damon won his first Grand Prix in 1993, making them the first father and son to both win a Grand Prix.

Hill, Joseph (1715–1784)

English violin maker. He worked in London. The house of his descendants W E Hill and Sons is now in Great Missenden.

Hill, Octavia (1838–1912)

English campaigner for housing reform and public open spaces. She cofounded the ◊National Trust in 1894.

With encouragement and financial help from John ◊Ruskin she pioneered a successful experiment in social housing. In 1864 she bought slum property in Marylebone, London which she rented to poor families. She served with Beatrice ◊Webb on the Poor Law Commission (1889).

Hill, Robert (1899–1991)

British biochemist who showed that during photosynthesis, oxygen is produced, and that this derived oxygen comes from water. This process is now known as the **Hill reaction**. He also demonstrated the evolution of oxygen in human blood cells by the conversion of haemoglobin to oxyhaemoglobin.

Hill, Rowland (1795–1879)

English Post Office official who invented adhesive stamps. His pamphlet *Post Office Reform* (1837) prompted the introduction of the penny prepaid post in 1840 (previously the addressee paid, according to distance, on receipt).

He was secretary to the Post Office 1854–64, and made a KCB in 1860.

Hill, Susan (Elizabeth) (1942–)

English novelist, short-story writer, and radio dramatist. Her works, which explore the nature of loss, isolation, and grief, include *The Enclosure* (1961) (her first novel), *A Change for the Better* (1969), *I'm the King of the Castle* (1970), and *The Bird of Night* (1972) which won the Whitbread award. The pseudo-Victorian ghost story *The Woman in Black* (1983) was successfully adapted for stage and television. Later works include *Air and Angels* (1991), and *Mrs de Winter* (1993), a sequel to *Rebecca* by Daphne du Maurier.

She has also written books for children, including *Can It Be True* (1988), *The Glass Angels* (1991), and *King of Kings* (1993).

Hiller, Wendy (1912–)

English actress. Her many roles include Catherine Sloper in *The Heiress* (1947) and Eliza in the film version of Shaw's *Pygmalion* (1938). Her other films include *The Elephant Man* (1980). She was made a DBE in 1975.

hill figure

Any of a number of figures, usually of animals, cut from the turf to reveal the underlying chalk. Their origins are variously attributed to Celts, Romans, Saxons, Druids, or Benedictine monks, although most are of modern rather than ancient construction. Examples include 17 ◊White Horses, and giants such as the Cerne Abbas Giant, near Dorchester, Dorset, associated with a prehistoric fertility cult.

Nearly 50 hill figures are known in Britain, of which all but four are on the southern chalk downs of England. Some are landmarks or memorials; others have a religious or ritual purpose. It is possible that the current figures are on the site of, or reinforce, previous ones. There may have been large numbers of figures dotted on the landscape in the Iron Age, which were not maintained. The White Horse at Uffington, on the Berkshire Downs, used to be annually 'scoured' in a folk ceremony.

Other hill-figure designs include the Long Man of Wilmington on Windover Hill, East Sussex; crosses, such as the Bledlow and Whiteleaf crosses on the Chiltern Hills; a collection of military badges made at Fovant Down, Wiltshire (1916); an aeroplane, and a crown. A stag at Mormond Hill, Aberdeenshire, Scotland, is cut into white quartz.

Cerne Abbas Giant

This male figure, 55 m/180 ft in height, is ithyphallic (with an erect penis) and holds a great club in his right hand, his left hand being outstretched as though in the act of grasping. He is represented in outline, marked by a 60 cm/2 ft trench. The figure lies in an area rich in prehistoric remains. Just beyond his head is a small four-sided earthwork, probably of the early Iron Age. The foundations of the Benedictine abbey of Cerne lie nearby.

A number of theories have been postulated concerning the origins of the giant. A traditional annual maypole celebration (involving an intricate weaving dance around a pole, possibly linked to ancient fertility rites) took place in the early Iron Age earthwork until quite recent years, adding weight to the suggestion that the site may be identified with a fertility cult. One theory identifies the giant with Hercules, who is associated with a fertility cult, or Priapus worship, revived by the Roman emperor Commodus in the later 2nd century AD.

Long Man of Wilmington

The Long Man is 70.4 m/231 ft in height and holds a staff in each hand. The figure is outlined by trenches defined by white-painted bricks. Nothing is known of the giant's early history, but there has been a mass of mostly fanciful conjecture associating it with Celts, Romans, Saxons, and Druids as well as various mythological characters, astronomers, and the Benedictine monks of the priory of Wilmington, dissolved in 1414. One recent theory is that the figure may have served as a giant advertisement for the priory, where travellers would receive rest and refreshment.

hillfort

Type of site with massive banks and ditches for defence, used as both a military camp and a permanent settlement, dating from the European Iron Age. Hillforts are found across Europe, and examples in Britain include ⇨Maiden Castle, Dorset, England; Danebury in Hampshire; and Navan Fort near Armagh, Northern Ireland. There are several others in the hill country of Wales and the north. Many of these hillforts were occupied well into the Roman era and can sometimes be linked with the establishment of a Roman town nearby.

Hilliard, Nicholas (*c.* 1547–1619)

English miniaturist and goldsmith. Court artist to Elizabeth I and James I, his sitters included Francis Drake, Walter Raleigh, and Mary Queen of Scots. A fine collection of his brilliant, highly detailed portraits, set in gold cases, including *An Unknown Young Man Amid Roses* (about 1590), is in the Victoria and Albert Museum, London.

He wrote a treatise on miniature painting, *The Arte of Limninge*, in 1593. After 1600 he was gradually superseded by his pupil Isaac ⇨Oliver, and in 1617 was imprisoned for debt. His son **Lawrence Hilliard** (1582–after 1640) was also a miniaturist.

Hillingdon

Outer borough of west Greater London. It includes the district of Uxbridge

Features Cedar House (about 1850); Hillingdon parish workhouse (1747); Swakeleys, Jacobean mansion at Ickenham; Grand Union Canal; Heathrow airport (1946), built on the site of a Neolithic settlement

Industries pharmaceuticals (Glaxo Wellcome at Uxbridge)

Population (1991) 231,600.

Hillsborough

Market town in County Down, Northern Ireland, 20 km/12 mi southwest of Belfast; population (1991) 1,200. It mainly functions as a commuter settlement for Belfast. Hillsborough was developed by a family named Hill in the 17th century, and still retains much of its original character, with a number of fine Georgian buildings. The mansion, built in 1760 for the Hills, became the official residence of the governors of Northern Ireland, and is now the local base for the UK secretary of state for Northern Ireland.

Near Hillsborough is a 17th-century star-shaped fort built for Col Arthur Hill.

Kilwalin Moravian church near Hillsborough has a model of the ancient Greek battlefield of Thermopylae in its grounds. At Moira village, 11 km/7 mi to the west of Hillsborough, a conflict took place in 637 between the high king of Ireland and the king of Ulster, as recounted in a poem by Samuel Ferguson.

Hillsborough Agreement

Another name for the Anglo-Irish Agreement (1985). See ⇨Northern Ireland.

Hillsborough litigation

Test case brought before the court in Liverpool in July 1990, which established that individuals who witness major disasters may be able to recover damages for psychiatric illness including post-traumatic stress disorder. Eight of the claimants had watched the 1989 Hillsborough football-ground disaster (see ⇨Sheffield) on television, knowing their relatives were present at the stadium; another watched in a coach outside as his son died, and a third was sitting in the stand above the terrace where his two brothers died. It was the first case where recovery for nervous shock was extended to siblings.

Police officers who suffered psychological illness as a result of helping dying football fans at the disaster won the legal right to compensation in 1996. The Court of Appeal ruled in favour of compensation claims that were likely to reach £2 million. The decision, overturning a 1995 High Court ruling, could have significant implications for future compensation claims by those whose jobs involve the trauma of confronting disaster.

Hilton, Roger (1911–1975)

English painter. His uncompromising abstract works of the 1950s were heavily influenced by Mondrian. Later associated with the ◊St Ives School, Cornwall, he developed a spontaneous figurative style; his paintings of the 1960s, often landscapes and nudes, being distinguished by an earthy eroticism and great variety in the handling of the oils. The exuberant *Oi yoi yoi* (1963; Tate Gallery, London) is typical.

Hilton Hotel, or London Hilton Hotel

Hotel in Park Lane, London, built in 1963. It is 30 storeys high and belongs to the chain founded in 1919 by US hotelier Conrad Hilton (1887–1949). The **Hilton International**, Kensington also belongs to the group.

Hinckley

Market town in Leicestershire, central England, 20 km/12 mi southwest of Leicester; population (1995 est) 44,900. Industries include transport and distribution services, engineering, and the manufacture of hosiery and motorcycles.

Hinckley was the site of a Roman settlement on the junction of the Fosse Way and Watling Street Roman roads. The site of the Battle of Bosworth (1495), in which Richard III was killed, is 8 km/5 mi north of the town. Hosiery production was advanced with the installation of the first stocking frame in 1640.

Hinshelwood, Cyril Norman (1897–1967)

English chemist who shared the 1956 Nobel prize for his work on chemical chain reactions. He also studied the chemistry of bacterial growth. Knighted 1948.

Hirst, Damien (1965–)

English sculptor, painter, and designer. He won the Turner Prize in 1995 with *Mother and Child Divided*, a bisected cow and calf presented in a glass case. His installation works include *Away from the Flock* (1994), a sheep pickled in formaldehyde and displayed in glass.

The main focus of his work has been an exploration of mortality, notably in his Natural History series in which dead animals are presented as reminders of death, evoking the fragility of life. Some of these works have provoked demonstrations by animal lovers. His other work has included abstract paintings and the design of restaurants. In 1997 he published a large book on his life and work, *I Want to Spend the Rest of My Life Everywhere, with Everyone, One to One, Always, Forever.*

Hirst studied at Goldsmiths' College, London, from 1986 to 1989, and first attracted attention for organizing an exhibition of student work called Freeze in 1988. The talent for publicity shown on this occasion has helped his swift rise as the best-known British avant-garde artist of his generation.

historical novel

Prose narrative set in the past, often concerning fictional as well as historical characters and events. Walter ◊Scott established the modern tradition by setting imaginative romances of love, impersonation, and betrayal in a past based on known fact; his use of historical detail, and subsequent imitations of this technique by European writers, gave rise to the genre.

Some historical novels of the 19th century were overtly nationalistic, but most were merely novels set in the past to heighten melodrama while providing an informative framework. Chief exponents of the genre in Britain included Charles ◊Dickens, William ◊Thackeray, George ◊Eliot, and Thomas ◊Hardy. In the 20th century the historical novel became concerned with exploring psychological states and the question of differences in outlook and mentality in past periods. Examples of this are Robert ◊Graves's novels *I, Claudius* and *Claudius the God*.

The less serious possibilities of the historical novel were exploited by writers in the early 20th century in the form of the **historical romance**, which was revived with some success in the late 1960s. The historical novel acquired subgenres – the stylized **Regency novel** of Georgette Heyer (1902–1974) and her imitators, and the Napoleonic War sea story of C S ◊Forester. Other recent exponents of the genre include Mary ◊Renault and Rosemary ◊Sutcliff.

Hitchcock, Alfred (Joseph) (1899–1980)

English film director, a US citizen from 1955. A master of the suspense thriller, he was noted for his meticulously drawn storyboards that determined his camera angles and for his cameo walk-ons in his own films. His *Blackmail* (1929) was the first successful British talking film. *The Thirty-Nine Steps* (1935) and *The Lady Vanishes* (1938) are British suspense classics. He went to Hollywood in 1940, and his work there included *Rebecca* (1940), *Notorious* (1946), *Strangers on a Train* (1951), *Rear Window* (1954), *Vertigo* (1958), *North by Northwest* (1959), *Psycho* (1960), and *The Birds* (1963).

Hitchens, Ivon (1893–1979)

English painter. His semi-abstract landscapes, influenced by Cubism, were painted initially in natural tones, later in more vibrant colours. He also painted murals, for example *Day's Rest, Day's Work* (1963; Sussex University).

From the 1940s Hitchens lived in a forest near Midhurst in Sussex, which provided the setting for many of his paintings.

Hitch-Hiker's Guide to the Galaxy, The

Bestselling space-fiction novel by Douglas ◊Adams published in 1979. It began as a radio serial in 1978 and was later successfully adapted for television. The first of a series of international bestsellers which achieved cult status, the novel was followed by others which developed the theme including *The Restaurant at the End of the Universe* (1980), *Life, the Universe and Everything* (1982), *So Long, and Thanks for All the Fish* (1984), and *Mostly Harmless* (1992).

Hitchin

Market town in Hertfordshire, southeast England, on the River Hiz, 48 km/30 mi northwest London; population

(1991) 29,300. Industries include engineering, flour milling, electronics, pharmaceutical distilling, computer and software manufacturing, and the provision of financial services. Horticulture is important, notably the cultivation and distillation of lavender, introduced from Naples in the 16th century, and rose-growing.

There are many small businesses specializing in steel tubing, road haulage, transport, and retailing.

Features

The Perpendicular-style St Mary's Church stands on a Norman foundation and has a large buttressed tower and a 13th-century doorway. In the Baptist church is a chair presented by the writer John Bunyan.

Famous people

George Chapman, the dramatist, poet, and translator of Homer, was born here in about 1559. Henry Bessemer, inventor of a method of converting molten pig iron into steel (the Bessemer process), was born in 1813 at Charlton nearby. Eugene Aram, a murderer hanged in 1759, was a self-educated teacher at Church House, a small school at Ramsgill, Hitchin; he left valuable philological writings. The judge Henry Hawkins (later Lord Brampton), nicknamed 'Hanging Hawkins', was born at the Grange in 1817.

HMSO

Abbreviation for ◊Stationery Office, His/Her Majesty's.

Hobbes, Thomas (1588–1679)

English political philosopher and the first thinker since Aristotle to attempt to develop a comprehensive theory of nature, including human behaviour. In *Leviathan* (1651), he advocates absolutist government as the only means of ensuring order and security; he saw this as deriving from the ◊social contract.

Hobbit, The, or *There and Back Again*

Fantasy for children by J R R ◊Tolkien, published in the UK in 1937. It describes the adventures of Bilbo Baggins, a 'hobbit' (small humanoid) in an ancient world, Middle-Earth, populated by dragons, dwarves, elves, and other mythical creatures, including the wizard Gandalf. *The Hobbit*, together with Tolkien's later trilogy *The Lord of the Rings* (1954–55), achieved cult status in the 1960s.

By 1991 35 million copies had been sold worldwide, more than any other work of fiction.

Hobbs, Jack (John Berry) (1882–1963)

English cricketer who has scored more first-class runs and more centuries than any other player. An orthodox right-handed opening batsman, between 1905 and 1934 he scored 61,237 runs including 197 hundreds. He made his Test debut in 1907 and in 61 matches scored 5,410 runs at an average of 56.94. He was knighted in 1953.

hockey

Game played with hooked sticks and a small, solid ball, the object being to hit the ball into the goal. It is played between two teams, each of not more than 11 players. Hockey has been an Olympic sport since 1908 for men and since 1980 for women.

Modern hockey in Britain dates from 1886 when the Men's Hockey Association rules were drafted. Since 1895 international matches have been played and there are now 71 countries in membership of the International Hockey Federation. Apart from the Olympic Games, where entry is restricted to 12 men's teams, world and continental championships exist. The rules of the game are established by the International Hockey Rules Board, a committee set up by the International Hockey Federation. They are common to both the men's and women's games. The women's game is governed by the All England Women's Hockey Association, founded in 1895. Indoor hockey is becoming increasingly popular in the UK.

Hockney, David (1937–)

English painter, printmaker, and designer, resident in California. One of the best-known figures in British Pop art, he developed a distinctive figurative style, as in his portrait *Mr and Mrs Clark and Percy* (1971; Tate Gallery, London). He has experimented prolifically with technique, and produced drawings; etchings, including *Six Fairy Tales from the Brothers Grimm* (1970); photo collages; and opera sets for Glyndebourne, East Sussex, La Scala, Milan, and the Metropolitan, New York.

Born in Yorkshire, he studied at Bradford School of Art and

HOCKNEY, DAVID *English artist David Hockney in 1975 with his sets for Stravinsky's opera* The Rake's Progress. *One of the leading figures of Pop art, Hockney developed a colourful, graphic style that lent itself to bold and innovative stage designs. Corbis*

then at the Royal College of Art, London, from 1959 to 1962. He exhibited at the Young Contemporaries Show in 1961 and held his first solo exhibition in 1963, showing paintings that exploited pictorial ambiguities in a witty, self-consciously naive manner.

In 1964 he went to California and many of his later paintings are concerned with Los Angeles life, his views of swimming pools reflecting a preoccupation with surface pattern and effects of light.

He was the subject of Jack Hazan's semidocumentary film *A Bigger Splash* (1974).

Hoddinott, Alun (1929–)

Welsh composer. In addition to major works in standard genres (including nine symphonies, several concertos, and ten piano sonatas) Hoddinott has composed works in a lighter vein, including carols and *Quodlibet on Welsh Nursery Tunes* for brass quintet.

Hoddle, Glen (1957–)

English football player and coach. In 1996, at the age of 38, Hoddle became the manager of the England team.

An elegant midfield player with brilliant passing skills, he played 484 games for Tottenham Hotspur (1975–87), scoring 106 goals. In 1979 he won the first of 53 full England caps, but despite his abundant talent was never guaranteed a regular place in the side. He enjoyed a season with Monaco in the French League (1987–88) before a knee injury appeared to have ended his career. In 1991 he became player-manager of Swindon Town, moving to Chelsea in 1993. In 1996, just one year after retiring as a player, he was appointed England manager in succession to Terry Venables.

Hodgkin, Alan Lloyd (1914–)

English physiologist engaged in research with Andrew ◊Huxley on the mechanism of conduction in peripheral nerves 1945–60. He devised techniques for measuring electric currents flowing across a cell membrane. In 1963 they shared the Nobel prize. KBE 1972.

Hodgkin, Dorothy Mary Crowfoot (1910–1994)

English biochemist who analysed the structure of penicillin, insulin, and vitamin B_{12}. Hodgkin was the first to use a computer to analyse the molecular structure of complex chemicals, and this enabled her to produce three-dimensional models. She was awarded the 1964 Nobel Prize for Chemistry.

Hodgkin studied the structures of calciferol (vitamin D_2), lumisterol, and cholesterol iodide, the first complex organic molecule to be determined completely by the pioneering technique of X-ray crystallography, a physical analysis technique devised by Lawrence Bragg (1890–1971), and at the time used only to confirm formulas predicted by organic chemical techniques. She also used this technique to determine the structure of penicillin, insulin, and vitamin B_{12}.

In 1964 Hodgkin became the second woman to have ever received the Order of Merit (the first was Florence Nightingale) and – a committed socialist all her life – in 1987 she was awarded the Lenin Peace Prize.

Hodgkin, Howard (1932–)

English painter. Influenced by Indian miniatures, his small pictures are full of movement and colour, the paint frequently spreading over the frame. Though they have a specific subject – often an encounter between friends – they are abstract in appearance, the artist slowly reducing an incident or scene to a highly personal language of a few broad brush strokes and patterned dabs. An example is *Dinner at Smith Square* (1975–79; Tate Gallery, London). He won the Turner Prize in 1985 and was knighted in 1992.

> *Howard's pictures have always been, more or less, erotic – and the more erotic for being inexplicit. He seems incapable of starting a picture without an emotionally charged subject, though his next step is to make it obscure...*
>
> BRUCE CHATWIN English writer.
> On Howard Hodgkin, in *What Am I Doing Here*, published after Chatwin's death in 1989

Hodgkin, Thomas (1798–1866)

English physician who first recognized **Hodgkin's disease**, a rare form of cancer mainly affecting the lymph nodes and spleen. He pioneered the use of the stethoscope in the UK. He was also the first person to stress the importance of postmortem examinations.

Hogarth, William (1697–1764)

English painter and engraver. He produced portraits and moralizing genre scenes, such as the story series of prints *A Rake's Progress* (1735; Soane Museum, London). His portraits are remarkably direct and full of character, for example *Heads of Six of Hogarth's Servants* (about 1750–55; Tate Gallery) and his oil sketch masterpiece *The Shrimp Girl* (National Gallery).

Hogarth was born in London and apprenticed to an engraver. He published *A Harlot's Progress*, a series of six engravings, in 1732. Other story series followed, including *Marriage à la Mode* (1745), *Industry and Idleness* (1749), and *The Four Stages of Cruelty* (1751). A stern critic of 'phizmongering' (traditional portrait painting), his book *The Analysis of Beauty* (1753) also attacked the uncritical appreciation of the arts, advocating the double curved line and serpentine spiral as a key to visual beauty (both traceable in the composition of his own work).

His house in Hogarth Lane, Chiswick, is now a museum.

Hogg, Quintin

British politician; see Lord ◊Hailsham.

Hogmanay

Scottish name for New Year's Eve. A traditional feature is first-footing, visiting the homes of friends and neighbours after midnight to welcome in the new year with salt, bread, whisky, and other gifts. Children may also go from house to house singing carols and receiving oatmeal cakes.

Hog's Back

Narrow part of the North ◊Downs between Guildford and Farnham in Surrey, England. At its highest point, the Hog's Back has an elevation of over 150 m/492 ft, and from it there are panoramic views to both north and south.

The ancient royal hunting ground of Windsor Forest used to extend as far as the Hog's Back.

Holbein, Hans, the Younger (1497–1543)

German painter and woodcut artist, who from 1536 was court painter to Henry VIII. He created a remarkable and unparalleled evocation of the English court in a series of graphic, perceptive portraits. He also travelled in Europe to paint some of Henry's prospective wives, including the Duchess of Milan in Brussels and Anne of Cleves (Louvre). One of his best known works is *The (French) Ambassadors* (1533; National Gallery), remarkable in technical skill and curious detail.

A dynastic group for the Privy Chamber at Whitehall was destroyed by fire in 1698, but one of his numerous portrayals of Henry VIII survives in the Thyssen Collection, Madrid. Other works in England included ornamental designs, such as the drawing for the *Jane Seymour Cup* (Bodleian Library), and the miniatures which inspired Nicholas ◊Hilliard, examples of which are in the Victoria and Albert Museum. He was also one of the finest graphic artists of his age; he designed the title page of Thomas More's *Utopia*.

Holinshed or Hollingshead, Raphael (*c.* 1520–*c.* 1580)

English historian. He published two volumes of the *Chronicles of England, Scotland, and Ireland* (1578), which are a mixture of fact and legend. The *Chronicles* were used as a principal source by Elizabethan dramatists for their plots. Nearly all Shakespeare's historical plays (other than the Roman histories), as well as *Macbeth*, *King Lear*, and *Cymbeline*, are based on Holinshed's work.

Holinshed was probably born in Cheshire. He went to London early in Elizabeth I's reign, and was employed as a translator in Reginald Wolfe's printing office, helping him in the compilation of his *Universal History*. Wolfe died before the work was completed, and it was left to Holinshed to finish in an abridged form. It appeared as the *Chronicles of England, Scotland, and Ireland*. A second enlarged edition was published in 1587. The *Chronicles* basically subscribe to the 'Tudor myth of history', advancing the view that Henry VII was a national saviour, restoring peace and order after the anarchy of the Wars of the Roses.

Holkham Hall

House in Norfolk, England, 13 km/8 mi north of Fakenham. One of the masterpieces of the Palladian style, it was designed by William ◊Kent, advised by Richard ◊Burlington, and built between 1734 and 1759. Capability ◊Brown laid out the grounds in 1762.

Its grey brick exterior contrasts with a palatial interior, the chief feature of which is its pillared, apsidal entrance hall and staircase.

Hollies, The

English pop and rock group, formed in 1962, whose songs include the UK number one hit 'I'm Alive' (1965), 'He Ain't Heavy, He's My Brother' (1969), and 'The Air That I Breathe' (1974).

Holm, Ian stage name of Ian Holm Cuthbert (1931–)

Prolific English stage and screen actor, and one of Britain's foremost character performers. A diminutive, but commanding presence, he started his career as a Shakespearean actor in the 1950s, breaking into film in the late 1960s. A hugely versatile performer, he has played a robot in *Alien* (1979), a demanding athletics trainer in *Chariots of Fire* (1981), Ruth Ellis's doting admirer in *Dance with a Stranger* (1985), and a manic Italian restaurateur in *Big Night* (1996).

In the 1990s he has alternated support and lead roles in a series of British and independent North American productions, effortlessly moving from the comic to the menacing. Later films include *The Madness of King George* (1994), *The Sweet Hereafter* (1997), *A Life Less Ordinary* (1997), and David Cronenberg's *eXistenZ* (1998). He was knighted in 1998.

Holmes, Arthur (1890–1965)

English geologist who helped develop interest in the theory of continental drift. He also pioneered the use of radioactive decay methods for rock dating, giving the first reliable estimate of the age of the Earth.

Holmes, Sherlock

Fictitious private detective, created by the English writer Arthur Conan ◊Doyle in *A Study in Scarlet* (1887) and recurring in novels and stories until 1927. Holmes' ability to make inferences from slight clues always astonishes the narrator, Dr Watson.

The criminal mastermind against whom Holmes repeatedly pits his wits is Professor James Moriarty. Holmes is regularly portrayed at his home, 221b Baker Street, London, where he plays the violin and has bouts of determined action interspersed by lethargy and drug-taking. His characteristic pipe and deerstalker hat were the addition of an illustrator.

Holmfirth

Town in West Yorkshire, England, 10 km/6 mi south of Huddersfield. There are still cloth and wool mills here, as well as stone quarries.

Holnicote Estate

Estate in Somerset, England, west of Minehead. The National Trust owns 4950 ha/12,226 acres of land here, which includes 2400 ha/5999 acres of Exmoor, together with Dunkery and Selworthy Beacons and the greater part of five villages, including Selworthy, famous for its thatch, and five hamlets.

HOLMES, SHERLOCK *Fictional detective Sherlock Holmes with his assistant Dr Watson on a train to Devon to investigate a murder in* The Adventure of Silver Blaze. *The illustration, from the original serialization of Conan Doyle's* The Adventures of Sherlock Holmes *in* The Strand Magazine *(1892), is by Sidney Paget, the first artist to draw Holmes. Image Select*

Holyhead, Welsh Caergybi

Seaport on the north coast of ◊Holy Island, off Anglesey, northwest Wales; population (1988 est) 13,000. The Island is linked by road and railway bridges with Anglesey, and there are regular sailings from Holyhead to Dun Laoghaire in Dublin, Republic of Ireland.

The harbour has an area of 1.08 sq km/0.42 sq mi and a breakwater 32 km/20 mi long; this refuge is extended by 1.62 sq km/0.63 sq mi of roadstead. Construction of the harbour began in 1846 and was completed in 1873; major works to expand both its size and its facilities for Irish traffic were finished in 1977. St Cybi is a notable, old embattled church.

Holy Island, or Lindisfarne

Island in the North Sea, 3 km/2 mi off the coast of Northumberland, northeast England, with which it is connected by a causeway at low tide; area 10 sq km/4 sq mi; population (1991) 179. It is the site of a monastery founded by St ◊Aidan in 635. Tourism and a mead factory provide local employment.

Features

The northern part of the island is mostly sandy, but the rest is fertile. To the southwest of the island is a small village with a harbour. Nothing has survived of the original monastery but there are remains of the 11th-century Benedictine priory. In the 16th century stones from the priory were used to construct **Lindisfarne Castle**, which was converted into a private house by Edwin Lutyens in 1903, and is now the property of the National Trust.

History

The Celtic manuscript known as the ◊Lindisfarne Gospels, dating from about 698, was written here as a memorial to St Cuthbert (prior of Lindisfarne from 664 to 676). The manuscript is now in the British Museum. Following his death on Farne Island in 687, St Cuthbert's body was returned to Lindisfarne, and the monastery became a place of pilgrimage until the monks were driven from the island by the Danes in 875. According to tradition, the monks took with them the remains of St Cuthbert and finally settled in Durham in 995. Benedictine monks from Durham returned to the island in 1082, renamed it Holy Island, and established a Benedictine priory here.

Holy Island, or Holyhead Island, Welsh Ynys Gybi

Rocky and barren island west of the Isle of Anglesey, northwest Wales; length 13 km/8 mi, width 6 km/4 mi. It is

Holst, Gustav(us Theodore von) (1874–1934)

English composer of distant Swedish descent. He wrote operas, including *Sávitri* (1908) and *At the Boar's Head* (1924); ballets; choral works, including *Hymns from the Rig Veda* (1908–12) and *The Hymn of Jesus* (1917); orchestral suites, including *The Planets* (1914–16); and songs. He was a lifelong friend of Ralph ◊Vaughan Williams, with whom he shared an enthusiasm for English folk music. His musical style, although tonal and drawing on folk song, tends to be severe. He was the father of Imogen Holst (1907–), musicologist and his biographer.

Holtby, Winifred (1898–1935)

English novelist and journalist. She was an ardent advocate of women's freedom and of racial equality. Her novel *South Riding* (1936), set in her native Yorkshire, was awarded the Tait Black Memorial Prize and was subsequently filmed and televised. Her other works include an analysis of women's position in contemporary society, *Women in a Changing Civilization* (1934).

Holy Grail

In medieval Christian legend, the dish or cup used by Jesus at the Last Supper, supposed to have supernatural powers. Together with the spear with which he was wounded at the Crucifixion, it was an object of quest by King Arthur's knights in certain stories incorporated in the Arthurian legend.

According to one story, the blood of Jesus was collected in the Holy Grail by Joseph of Arimathaea at the Crucifixion, and he brought it to Britain where he allegedly built the first church, at Glastonbury. At least three churches in Europe possess vessels claimed to be the Holy Grail.

connected to Anglesey by a sandy causeway. The island is a centre for surfing and sea angling, and Trearddur on Penrhos Bay is a seaside resort. Holy Island is designated as an Environmentally Sensitive Area with some Areas of Outstanding Natural Beauty.

The island is one of the oldest sites of human settlement in Wales, and has numerous prehistoric and Roman remains. Ancient remains on the island include an Iron-Age hillfort and a Roman watchtower on Holyhead Mountain (Welsh *Mynydd Twr*), 200 m/656 ft.

Holy Loch

Western inlet of the Firth of Clyde, Argyll and Bute, west Scotland. Formerly a US nuclear submarine base (1961–92), it is one of the most polluted stretches of water in the world, and is being cleaned up by the Ministry of Defence.

It is feared that disturbing the contaminated sediment may cause the toxic chemicals to dissolve and be consumed by fish such as salmon and sea trout.

Holyrood House

Royal residence in Edinburgh, Scotland. The palace was built from 1498 to 1503 on the site of a 12th-century abbey by James IV. It has associations with Mary Queen of Scots, and Charles Edward, the Young Pretender. Holyrood was the royal palace of the Scottish kings until the Union, and is now a palace of the British monarchy, used during state visits but otherwise open to the public.

One wing remains from the original building begun by James IV, but everything else was burnt in 1544. The main part of the palace was built between 1671 and 1679 for Charles II, to the designs of William Bruce (*c.* 1630–1710).

Adjoining the palace are the ruins of Holyrood Abbey, founded in 1128 by David I.

Home, Alec Douglas- (1903–1995)

British Conservative politician. See ◊Douglas-Home.

Home Counties

Counties in close proximity to London: Hertfordshire, Essex, Kent, Surrey, Buckinghamshire, and formerly Berkshire and Middlesex.

home front

Organized sectors of domestic activity in wartime, mainly associated with world wars I and II. Features of the UK home front in World War II included the organization of the black-out, evacuation, air-raid shelters, the Home Guard, rationing, and distribution of gas masks. With many men on active military service, women were called upon to carry out jobs previously undertaken only by men.

Home Guard

Unpaid force formed in Britain in May 1940 to repel the expected German invasion, and known until July 1940 as the Local Defence Volunteers. It consisted of men aged 17–65 who had not been called up, formed part of the armed forces of the Crown, and was subject to military law. Over 2 million strong in 1944, it was disbanded on 31 December 1945, but revived in 1951, then placed on a reserve basis in 1955. It ceased activity in 1957.

Home Office

Government department established in 1782 to deal with all the internal affairs of England except those specifically assigned to other departments. Responsibilities include the police, the prison service, immigration, race relations, and broadcasting. Including the HM Prisons Service, which had 38,000 staff in 1998, it employs more than 50,000 people. The home secretary, the head of the department, currently Jack Straw from 1997, holds cabinet rank.

There is a separate secretary of state for Scotland and another for Wales. The home secretary has certain duties in respect of the Channel Islands and the Isle of Man.

Home Rule, Irish

Movement to repeal the Act of ◊Union of 1801 that joined Ireland to Britain, and to establish an Irish Parliament responsible for internal affairs. In 1870 Isaac Butt (1813–1879) formed the Home Rule Association and the movement was led in Parliament from 1880 by Charles ◊Parnell. After 1918 the demand for an independent Irish republic replaced that for home rule.

Gladstone's Home Rule bills of 1886 and 1893 were both defeated. A third bill was introduced by the Liberals in 1912, which aroused opposition in Ireland where the Protestant minority in Ulster feared domination by the Catholic majority. Ireland appeared on the brink of civil war but the outbreak of World War I rendered further consideration of Home Rule inopportune.

In 1920 the Government of Ireland Act introduced separate Parliaments in the North and South and led to the treaty of 1921 that established the Irish Free State. See ◊Ireland for a feature on the struggle for Home Rule.

honi soit qui mal y pense (French 'shame on him or her who thinks evil of it')

Motto of England's Order of the Garter. See Orders of Chivalry List on page 444.

Honiton

Market town in Devon, southwest England, on the River Otter, 27 km/17 mi northeast of Exeter; population (1996 est) 9,700. It has an important cattle market, although employment is mainly in the service sector. Honiton's handmade pillow-lace industry, introduced by Flemish settlers during the reign of Elizabeth I, is undergoing a revival of interest.

Tourism is significant locally, although the town has only one hotel. The River Otter is renowned for its trout fishing.

honours list

Military and civil awards approved by the sovereign of the UK and published on New Year's Day and on her official birthday in June. Many Commonwealth countries, for example, Australia and Canada, also have their own honours list.

The Political Honours Scrutiny Committee is a group of

privy councillors established after Lloyd George's extravagant abuse of the honours system to reward party benefactors. Names are considered for honours in four ways: (1) from senior government officials; (2) nominated personally by the Queen; (3) directly from the major political parties, through the chief whip; and (4) through the prime minister who can add to or subtract from all the above lists. It became a criminal offence to misuse the honours system in the UK in 1925. John Major, prime minister 1990–97, promised to 'democratize' the honours system, but there was little evidence of change.

See tables for Military Orders, Decorations and Medals, and Orders of Chivalry. See ◊Knighthood, Orders of, for historical background to the Orders of Chivalry.

Hood, Robin

Hero of English legend; see ◊Robin Hood.

Hood, Samuel, 1st Viscount Hood (1724–1816)

English admiral. A masterly tactician, he defeated the French at Dominica in the West Indies in 1783, and in the ◊Revolutionary Wars captured Toulon and Corsica. Baronet 1779, Viscount 1796.

Hooke, Robert (1635–1703)

English scientist and inventor, originator of **Hooke's law**, and considered the foremost mechanic of his time. His inventions included a telegraph system, the spirit level, marine barometer, and sea gauge. He coined the term 'cell' in biology.

He studied elasticity, furthered the sciences of mechanics and microscopy, invented the hairspring regulator in timepieces, perfected the air pump, and helped improve such scientific instruments as microscopes, telescopes, and barometers. His work on gravitation and in optics contributed to the achievements of his contemporary Isaac ◊Newton.

Hooke was born in Freshwater on the Isle of Wight and educated at Oxford, where he became assistant to Irish physicist Robert Boyle. Moving to London in 1663, he became curator of the newly established Royal Society, which entailed demonstrating new experiments at weekly meetings. He was also professor of geometry at Gresham College, London, from 1665.

In geology, Hooke insisted, against the prevailing, Bible-bound view, that fossils are the remains of plants and animals that existed long ago.

Hooke also designed several buildings, including the College of Physicians, London.

Hooker, Joseph Dalton (1817–1911)

English botanist who travelled to the Antarctic and India, and made many botanical discoveries. His works include *Flora Antarctica* (1844–47), *Genera plantarum* (1862–83), and *Flora of British India* (1875–97).

In 1865 he succeeded his father, William Jackson Hooker

UK Military Orders, Decorations, and Medals

VC Victoria Cross
CGC Conspicuous Gallantry Cross
GC George Cross
KG Knight of the Garter
KT Knight of the Thistle
KP Knight of St Patrick
GCB Knight Grand Cross or Dame Grand Cross of the Order of the Bath
OM Member of the Order of Merit
GCSI Knight Grand Commander of the Star of India
CI Order of the Crown of India
GCMG Knight Grand Cross or Dame Grand Cross of the Order of St Michael and St George
GCIE Knight Grand Commander of the Order of the Indian Empire
GCVO Knight Grand Cross or Dame Grand Cross of the Royal Victorian Order
GBE Knight Grand Cross or Dame Grand Cross of the Order of the British Empire
CH Member of the Order of the Companion of Honour
KCB Knight Commander of the Order of the Bath
DCB Dame Commander of the Order of the Bath
KCSI Knight Commander of the Order of the Star of India
KCMG Knight Commander of the Order of St Michael and St George
DCMG Dame Commander of the Order of St Michael and St George
KCIE Knight Commander of the Order of the Indian Empire
KCVO Knight Commander of the Royal Victorian Order
DCVO Dame Commander of the Royal Victorian Order
KBE Knight Commander of the Order of the British Empire
DBE Dame Commander of the Order of the British Empire
CB Companion of the Order of the Bath
CSI Companion of the Order of the Star of India
CMG Companion of the Order of St Michael and St George
CIE Companion of the Order of the British Empire
CVO Commander of the Royal Victorian Order
CBE Commander of the Order of the British Empire
DSO Companion of the Distinguished Service Order
LVO Lieutenant of the Royal Victorian Order
OBE Officer of the Order of the British Empire
ISO Companion of the Imperial Service Order (obsolete)
MVO Member of the Royal Victorian Order
MBE Member of the Order of the British Empire
RRC Member of the Royal Red Cross
DSC Distinguished Service Cross
MC Military Cross
AFC Air Force Cross
ARRC Associate of the Royal Red Cross
DCM Distinguished Conduct Medal (obsolete)
CGM Conspicuous Gallantry Medal (obsolete)
GM George Medal
DSM Distinguished Service Medal (obsolete)
MM Military Medal (obsolete)
DFM Distinguished Flying Medal
QGM Queen's Gallantry Medal
BEM British Empire Medal (obsolete)
RVM Royal Victorian Medal
ERD Army Emergency Reserve Medal
TD Territorial Decoration or Efficiency Decoration
RD Royal Naval Reserve Officer's Decoration
AE Air Efficiency Award

Source: Ministry of Defence

Orders of Chivalry and the Honours List

Modern orders of chivalry are awarded as a mark of royal favour or as a reward for public services. Members of orders are normally created Knights or Dames, titled Sir or Dame; some orders are graded, with the lower grades not being knighted. Honours are awarded by the sovereign and published on New Year's Day, and on the official royal birthday in June.

Order	Created	Ribbon	Motto	Initials	Other
Order of the Garter[1]	1348	blue	*honi soit qui mal y pense* (shame on him who thinks evil of it)	KG	founded by Edward III
Order of the Thistle[2]	1687[3]	green	*nemo me impune lacessit* (no one provokes me with impunity)	KT	ancient Scottish order
Order of the Bath	1725	crimson	*tria juncta in ino* (three joined in one)	GCB, KCB, DCB, CB[4]	founded by Henry IV; divided into civil and military divisions; women became eligible in 1971
Order of Merit[1 5]	1902	blue and crimson	none	OM	founded by Edward VII
Order of the Star of India	1861	light blue with white edges	Heaven's light our guide	GCSI, KCSI, CSI[6]	no new members created since 1947
Order of St Michael and St George	1818	blue with scarlet centre	*auspicium melioris aevi* (token of a better age)	GCMG, KCMG, DCMG, CMG[7]	
Order of the Indian Empire	1868	purple	*imperatricis auspiciis* (under the auspices of the Empress)	GCIE, KCIE, CIE[8]	no new members created since 1947
Imperial Order of the Crown of India[9]	1877	light blue with white edge	none	CI	no new members created since 1947
Royal Victorian Order	1896	blue with red and white edges	Victoria	GCVO, KCVO, DCVO, CVO, LVO, MVO[10]	
Order of the British Empire	1917	pink edged with grey; vertical grey stripe in centre for the military division	for God and the Empire	GBE, KBE, DBE, CBE, OBE, MBE[11]	divided into civil and military divisions in 1918
Companions of Honour[5 12]	1917	carmine with gold edges	none	CH	
Distinguished Service Order	1886	red with blue edges	none	DSO	awarded to members of the armed forces for services in action; a bar may be added for any additional act of service
Imperial Service Order[13]	1902	crimson with blue centre	none	ISO	awarded to members of the Civil Service; no new members created since 1993

[1] Only 24 people may hold this order at any one time. [2] Only 16 people may hold this order at any one time. [3] Revived in this year. [4] GCB (Knight/Dame of the Grand Cross); KCB, DCB (Knight/Dame Commander); CB (Companion). [5] Members are not given a knighthood. [6] GCSI (Knight Grand Commander); KCSI (Knight Commander); CSI (Companion). [7] GCMG (Knight/Dame Grand Commander); KCMG, DCMG (Knight/Dame Commander); CMG (Companion). [8] GCIE (Knight/Dame Grand Commander); KCIE (Knight/Dame Commander); CIE (Companion). [9] For women only. [10] GCVO (Knight/Dame of The Grand Cross); KCVO, DCVO (Knight/Dame Commander); LVO (Lieutenant); MVO (Member). [11] GBE/KBE (Knight/Dame Grand Cross); DBE (Knight/Dame Commander); CBE (Commander); OBE (Officer); MBE (Member). [12] Only 65 people may hold this order at any one time. [13] Membership is limited to 1,900 people.

(1785–1865), as director of the Royal Botanic Gardens, Kew, London. Knighted 1877.

Hooker, Stanley George (1907–1984)

English engineer responsible for the development of aircraft engines such as the Proteus turboprop (1957), Orpheus turbojet (1958), Pegasus vectored-thrust turbofan, Olympus turbojet, and RB-211 turbofan. Knighted 1974.

Hooker, William Jackson (1785–1865)

English botanist and director of Kew Gardens. When he took over Kew Gardens they were only 11 acres, but he increased them to 300 acres, made them a national garden and opened them to the public for the first time. In 1804 he discovered a new moss and also illustrated botanist Dawson Turner's book *Historica fucorum*. Knighted 1836.

Hope, Anthony pen name of Anthony Hope Hawkins (1863–1933)

English novelist. His romance *The Prisoner of Zenda* (1894), and its sequel *Rupert of Hentzau* (1898), introduced the imaginary Balkan state of Ruritania. Other works include *The King's Mirror* (1899), *Second String* (1910), *Captain Dieppe* (1918), and *Little Tiger* (1925). Knighted 1918.

Hope, Bob (Leslie Townes) (1903–)

British-born US comedian. Employing a wise-cracking, cowardly persona, he has starred in a number of films since the 1930s, most notably in the seven *Road* movies (1940–62), with Bing Crosby and Dorothy Lamour, and the two *Paleface* films (1948–52), with Jane Russell. Hope received an honorary British knighthood on 17 May 1998 at the British Embassy in Washington, DC.

His other films include *The Cat and the Canary* (1939), *My Favorite Brunette* (1947), *Fancy Pants* (1950), *Casanova's Big Night* (1954), and *The Facts of Life* (1960). He has received five honorary Academy Awards.

Hopkins, Anthony (Philip) (1937–)

Welsh actor. A successful stage actor both in London and on Broadway, Hopkins won acclaim for his performance as Richard the Lion-Heart in his second film, *The Lion in Winter* (1968). His performance as a cannibalistic serial killer in *The Silence of the Lambs* (1991) gained him an Academy Award.

Throughout the 1970s and 1980s Hopkins continued to work in the theatre (an award-winning performance in *Equus* (1975), for example) as well as alternating a series of restrained (*84 Charing Cross Road*, filmed in 1986) and near-psychotic (*Magic*, filmed in 1978) film roles. He has been lauded for his performances in *Howards End* (1992), *The Remains of the Day* (1993), *Shadowlands* (1993), *Legends of the Fall* (1995), and *Nixon* (1995). In 1996, having staged a production of Anton Chekov's *Uncle Vanya* in Wales, he then made his directorial debut with *August*, adapted from the same text. He played the title role in *Surviving Picasso* (1996); other recent films are *Amistad* (1997) and *The Mask of Zorro* (1998). He was knighted in 1993.

Hopkins, Frederick Gowland (1861–1947)

English biochemist whose research into diets revealed the necessity of certain trace substances, now known as vitamins, for the maintenance of health. Hopkins shared the 1929 Nobel Prize for Physiology or Medicine with Christiaan Eijkman, who had arrived at similar conclusions. Knighted 1925.

Hopkins, Gerard Manley (1844–1889)

English poet and Jesuit priest. His works are marked by originality of diction and rhythm and include 'The Wreck of the Deutschland' (1876), and 'The Windhover' and 'Pied Beauty' (both 1877). His collected works was published posthumously in 1918 by his friend the poet Robert Bridges. His employment of 'sprung rhythm' (the combination of traditional regularity of stresses with varying numbers of syllables in each line) greatly influenced later 20th-century poetry.

His poetry is profoundly religious and records his struggle to gain faith and peace, but also shows freshness of feeling and delight in nature.

Hoppner, John (1758–1810)

English portrait painter. He painted many society figures of the day, including the royal princesses, William Pitt, and Admiral Nelson, and became portrait painter to the Prince of Wales (later George IV) in 1789. A follower of Joshua Reynolds, he rivalled Thomas Lawrence in popularity. His style, especially in his portraits of women and children, was noted for its grace and charm, as in *Mrs Williams* (Tate Gallery, London).

Other notable works include *The Countess of Oxford* (National Gallery), and *William Pitt* and *Lord Grenville* (National Portrait Gallery, London).

Hordern, Michael (Murray) (1911–1995)

English character actor. He appeared in stage roles such as Shakespeare's King Lear and Prospero (in *The Tempest*), and in plays by Tom Stoppard and Harold Pinter. His films include *The Man Who Never Was* (1956), *The Spy Who Came in From the Cold* (1965), *The Bed-Sitting Room* (1969), and *Joseph Andrews* (1976).

In modern drama, notable Hordern roles include the failed barrister in John Mortimer's *The Dock Brief* (1958), the husband in Alan Ayckbourn's *Relatively Speaking* (1967), and the comically anguished philosopher of Tom Stoppard's *Jumpers* (1972). Hordern often played conventional roles in costume epics such as *Cleopatra* (1963), but the offbeat film comedies *A Funny Thing Happened on the Way to the Forum* (1966) and *The Bed-Sitting Room* (1969) afforded full rein to his capacity for the eccentric. He also often acted on television, his final role being in the serial *Middlemarch* (1994). On children's TV he supplied the voice of Paddington Bear. He was knighted in 1983.

Hore-Belisha, (Isaac) Leslie, 1st Baron Hore-Belisha (1893–1957)

British politician. A National Liberal, he was minister of transport 1934–37, introducing **Belisha beacons** to mark pedestrian crossings. He was war minister from 1937, until removed by Chamberlain in 1940 on grounds of temperament, and introduced peacetime conscription in 1939.

Horley

Town in Surrey, England, 6 km/4 mi north of Crawley; population (1991) 18,100. Much industrial and residential development here is linked with Gatwick Airport, which lies immediately to the southwest. The town also has a station on the London–Brighton railway line, which has contributed to Horley's growth as a commuter town.

St Bartholomew's church in Horley is built in the Early English Gothic style.

Horniman, Annie Elizabeth Fredericka (1860–1937)

English pioneer of repertory theatre. She subsidized the Abbey Theatre, Dublin (built 1904), and founded the Manchester company at the Gaiety Theatre 1908.

hornpipe

English dance popular between the 16th and 19th centuries, associated especially with sailors. During the 18th century it changed from triple time (3/4) to common time (4/4). Examples include those by Purcell and Handel.

Horse Guards

The Household Cavalry, or **Royal Horse Guards**, formed in 1661; also their headquarters in Whitehall, London. The building was erected in 1753 by John Vardy (1718–65) to a design by William ◊Kent, on the site of the Tilt Yard of Whitehall Palace. To the rear lies Horse Guards Parade, a large exercise ground where the ceremony of Trooping the Colour takes place annually in early June to mark the sovereign's official birthday.

Horseguards is the centre for two United Kingdom army commands: the London District, responsible for military administration in the City of London, and the Household Division, which has guard, escort, and ceremonial duties.

Horse, Master of the

Head of the department of the British royal household, responsible for the royal stables. The Earl of Westmorland became Master of the Horse in 1978.

horse racing

Sport of racing mounted or driven horses. Two forms in Britain are **flat racing**, for Thoroughbred horses over a flat course, and **National Hunt racing**, in which the horses have to clear obstacles.

History

Racing took place in Stuart times and with its royal connections became known as the 'sport of kings'. Early racecourses include Chester, Ascot, and Newmarket. The English classics were introduced in 1776 with the St Leger (run at Doncaster), followed by the Oaks in 1779 and Derby in 1780 (both run at Epsom), and 2,000 Guineas in 1809 and 1,000 Guineas in 1814 (both run at Newmarket). The first governing body for the sport was the Jockey Club, founded about 1750; it still has a regulatory role, but the British Horseracing Board became the governing body in 1993. The National Hunt Committee was established 1866.

Types of race

Steeplechasing is a development of foxhunting, of which **point-to-point** is the amateur version, and **hurdling** a version with less severe, and movable, fences. Outstanding steeplechases are the Grand National (1839; at Aintree, Liverpool), and Cheltenham Gold Cup (1924; at Cheltenham). The leading hurdling race is the Champion Hurdle (1927; at Cheltenham).

Race horses, UK and Ireland

There are approximately 8,000 Thoroughbred racehorses born each year in Britain and Ireland. The births occur mostly between February and May, but all Thoroughbred foals are registered as being 1 year old on 1 January of the following year. The next autumn, aged 18–20 months, they begin training for racing in the coming spring. Horses are raced between two and eight years old.

Horsham

Town and market centre in West Sussex, southeast England, on the River Arun, 26 km/16 mi southeast of Guildford; population (1996 est) 43,300. Employment is mainly in the service sector and retailing. High-tech industries and pharmaceutical production take place in the district. The private school Christ's Hospital is about 3 km/2 mi to the southwest.

Features include Carfax, the town square; Pump Alley; and the Causeway, with Causeway House (now Horsham Museum). St Mary's is a restored Norman church.

Hosking, Eric (John) (1909–1990)

English wildlife photographer. He is known for his documentation of British birds, especially owls. Beginning at the age of eight and still photographing in Africa at 80, he covered all aspects of birdlife and illustrated a large number of books, published between 1940 and 1990.

Hoskins, Bob (Robert William) (1942–)

English character actor. He progressed to fame from a series of supporting roles, and has played a range of both comic and dramatic roles, effortlessly shifting from humorous sidekick or love interest to menacing sociopath. Films include *The Long Good Friday* (1980), *The Cotton Club* (1984), *Mona Lisa* (1986), *A Prayer for the Dying* (1987), *Who Framed Roger Rabbit?* (1988), *Mermaids* (1990), *Shattered* (1991), *Nixon* (1995), in which he played the FBI chief J Edgar Hoover. He played the lead role of the sheet music salesman in Dennis Potter's TV serial *Pennies From Heaven* (1978).

He recently starred in British filmmaker Shane Meadow's feature film debut *twentyfourseven* (1997) and appeared in Michael Winner's black comedy *Parting Shots* (1998).

Other work includes the film *The Raggedy Rawney* (1988), which he both wrote and directed, and a series of lucrative television commercials for British Telecom (BT) in the mid-1990s.

HOSKINS, BOB *The actor Bob Hoskins rose to screen stardom playing roguish Cockney characters, such as a gangland boss in the violent action film* The Long Good Friday *(1980) and a bodyguard in the thriller* Mona Lisa *(1986). His career broadened to Hollywood films, in which he has convincingly adopted gravelly American working-class accents. Castle Rock-Turner/Rank/Ronald Grant*

hospice

Residential facility specializing in palliative care for terminally ill patients and their relatives.

The first research and teaching hospice in the UK was St Christopher's Hospice in London, founded in 1967 by Cicely ◊Saunders.

Hounsfield, Godfrey Newbold (1919–)

English engineer, a pioneer of tomography, the application of computer techniques to X-raying the human body. He shared the Nobel Prize for Physiology or Medicine in 1979. Knighted 1981.

Hounslow

Outer borough of west Greater London. It includes the districts of Heston, Brentford, and Isleworth

Features reputed site of Caesar's crossing of the Thames in 54 BC at Brentford; Hounslow Heath, formerly the haunt of highwaymen; 16th-century Osterley Park, reconstructed by Robert Adam in the 1760s; 16th-century Syon House, seat of duke of Northumberland, where Lady Jane Grey was offered the crown in 1553; the artist William Hogarth's House, Chiswick; Boston Manor House (1662); Chiswick House, Palladian villa designed by Richard ◊Burlington (1725–29); site of London's first civil airport (1919)

Population (1991) 204,400

Famous people Thomas Gresham.

Housman, A(lfred) E(dward) (1859–1936)

English poet and classical scholar. His *A Shropshire Lad* (1896), a series of deceptively simple, nostalgic, ballad-like poems, has been popular since World War I. This was followed by *Last Poems* (1922), *More Poems* (1936), and *Collected Poems* (1939).

As a scholar his great work was his edition of the Roman poet Manilius, which is a model of textual criticism and marks him as one of the greatest English Latinists.

Hove

Residential town and seaside resort, and from 1998 the administrative headquarters of ◊Brighton and Hove unitary authority, on the south coast of England, adjoining Brighton to the west; population (1996 est) 93,400. One of the world's pioneering filmmaking centres at the beginning of the 20th century, it was home to a group of British filmmakers known as the Brighton School.

Hove developed as a resort in the 19th century and includes Regency-style squares and terraces, as well as many parks and public gardens. The Sussex county cricket ground is here. It was the home of English novelist Ivy Compton-Burnett from 1892 to 1916.

hovercraft

Vehicle that rides on a cushion of high-pressure air, free from all contact with the surface beneath, invented by English engineer Christopher Cockerell in 1959. Hovercraft need a smooth terrain when operating overland and are best adapted to use on waterways. They are useful in places where harbours have not been established.

Large hovercraft (SR-N4) operate a swift car-ferry service across the English Channel, taking only about 35 minutes between Dover and Calais. They are fitted with a flexible 'skirt' that helps maintain the air cushion.

Howard, Alan Mackenzie (1937–)

English actor. His appearances with the Royal Shakespeare Company include the title roles in *Henry V*, *Henry VI*, *Coriolanus*, and *Richard III*.

Howard, Catherine (*c.* 1520–1542)

Queen consort of ◊Henry VIII of England from 1540. In 1541 the archbishop of Canterbury, Thomas Cranmer, accused her of being unchaste before marriage to Henry and she was beheaded in 1542 after Cranmer made further charges of adultery.

Howard, Charles, 2nd Baron Howard of Effingham and 1st Earl of Nottingham (1536–1624)

English admiral, a cousin of Queen Elizabeth I. He commanded the fleet against the Spanish Armada while Lord High Admiral 1585–1618.

He cooperated with the Earl of Essex in the attack on Cádiz in 1596.

Howard, Constance (1919–)

English embroiderer. She helped to revive creative craftwork after World War II. Her work included framed pictures with fabrics outlined in bold black threads, wall hangings, and geometric studies in strong colour.

Howard, Ebenezer (1850–1928)

English town planner. Aiming to halt the unregulated growth of industrial cities, he pioneered the ideal of the ◊garden city through his book *Tomorrow* (1898; republished as *Garden Cities of Tomorrow* in 1902). He also inspired and took an active part in building the garden cities of ◊Letchworth and Welwyn.

His ideas were influenced by the US writers Walt Whitman, Ralph Waldo Emerson, and in particular by the Utopian novel *Looking Backward* (1888) by Edward Bellamy (1850–1898). Every house was to have its own plot of land; land usage was to be arranged zonally with civic amenities at the centre and factories on the edge of the city; and the whole city was to be surrounded by a 'green belt'.

He was knighted in 1927, and died at Welwyn Garden City.

Howard, Elizabeth Jane (1923–)

English novelist and short-story writer. Her novels are carefully written, closely observed stories of contemporary society, about individuals who seek moral and emotional security. *The Beautiful Visit* (1950) was her first novel.

Howard, John (1726–1790)

English philanthropist whose work to improve prison conditions is continued today by the **Howard League for Penal Reform** (a charity formed in 1921 by the amalgamation of the Prison Reform League and the Howard Association).

On his appointment as high sheriff for Bedfordshire in 1773, he undertook a tour of English prisons which led to two acts of Parliament in 1774, making jailers salaried officers and setting standards of cleanliness. After touring Europe in 1775, he published *State of the Prisons in England and Wales, with an account of some Foreign Prisons* (1777). He died of typhus fever while visiting Russian military hospitals at Kherson in the Crimea.

Howard, Leslie stage name of Leslie Howard Stainer (1893–1943)

English actor. His films include *The Scarlet Pimpernel* (1935), *The Petrified Forest* (1936), *Pygmalion* (1938), and *Gone With the Wind* (1939).

HOWARD, LESLIE *English actor, whose qualities of restraint and reserve won him the role of Ashley Wilkes in* Gone With the Wind *(1939). He accepted this part reluctantly and returned to England to make patriotic films such as* Pimpernel Smith *(1941). He was shot down by the Germans in World War II on a mission between Lisbon and London. Private collection*

Howard, Michael (1941–)

British Conservative politician, home secretary 1993–97. On the right of the Conservative Party, he championed the restoration of law and order as a key electoral issue, but encountered stiff opposition to his proposals for changes to the criminal-justice system and for increased police powers, as embodied in the 1994 Criminal Justice and Public Order Bill. A new crime bill, focusing on tougher sentencing, was announced by Howard at the 1995 Conservative Party conference, and immediately condemned by the Lord Chief Justice.

His position as home secretary was seriously threatened in October 1995 following allegations that he had unduly interfered in the operations of the prison service. After the Conservative Party's election defeat in May 1997, he unsuccessfully contested for the party's vacant leadership, but allegations by former colleague Ann Widdecombe about his conduct as home secretary undermined his challenge.

You have less to do, but then you have fewer people to help you do it.

Michael Howard British Conservative MP and former home secretary.
On life in Opposition; *Independent*, 10 January 1998

Howard, Trevor (Wallace) (1913–1988)

English actor. His films include *Brief Encounter* (1945), *Sons and Lovers* (1960), *Mutiny on the Bounty* (1962), *Ryan's Daughter* (1970), and *Conduct Unbecoming* (1975).

Howe, (Richard Edward) Geoffrey, Baron Howe of Aberavon (1926–)

British Conservative politician, member of Parliament for Surrey East. As chancellor of the Exchequer 1979–83 under Margaret Thatcher, he put into practice the monetarist policy which reduced inflation at the cost of a rise in unemployment. In 1983 he became foreign secretary, and in 1989 deputy prime minister and leader of the House of Commons. On 1 November 1990 he resigned in protest at Thatcher's continued opposition to Britain's greater integration in Europe.

Many of the ideas proposed by Howe in the early 1960s were subsequently taken up by the Thatcher government. Under Edward Heath he was Solicitor General 1970–72 and minister for trade 1972–74.

> *The thing I value about Wales and Welsh background is that it has always been a genuinely more classless society than many people present England as being.*
>
> GEOFFREY HOWE British Conservative politician. Remark in 1986

Howe, Richard, 1st Earl Howe (1726–1799)

British admiral. He cooperated with his brother William against the colonists during the American Revolution, and in the French Revolutionary Wars commanded the Channel fleets 1792–96.

Howe, William, 5th Viscount Howe (1729–1814)

British general. During the American Revolution he won the Battle of Bunker Hill in 1775, and as commander in chief in America (1776–78) captured New York and defeated Washington at Brandywine and Germantown. He resigned in protest at lack of home government support.

Howells, Herbert Norman (1892–1983)

English composer, organist, and teacher. His works are filled with an 'English' quality, as with those of Elgar and Vaughan Williams. Often elegiac in expression, as in some of the *Six Pieces for Organ* (1940), much of his music after the mid-1930s reflects his mourning over the death of his son. He wrote choral and chamber music, as well as solo works, both sacred and secular.

Howerd, Frankie (Francis Alex Howard) (1922–1992)

English comedian and actor. He was best known for his role as the Roman slave Lurcio in the television series *Up Pompeii*. The trademark of his rambling monologues was suggestive innuendo followed by aggrieved disapproval when audiences laughed.

Hoy (Scandinavian Hoey, 'high island')

Second largest of the ⟡Orkney Islands, Scotland, 7 km/4 mi south of Stromness, from which it is separated by the Sound of Hoy; population (1991) 500. Rising abruptly from the sea, it is 21 km/13 mi long, and up to 10 km/6 mi wide. Its highest crags are St John's Head (347 m/1,138 ft), Ward Hill (477 m/1,565 ft), and Cuilags Hill (433 m/1,421 ft). The spectacular sandstone stack of the **Old Man of Hoy**, rising to 137 m/449 ft, lies 2 km/1 mi west of Rora Head.

During World Wars I and II, Lyness contained a major Royal Navy base, now deserted. To the south, the bay of Longhope forms an excellent natural harbour.

Hoyland, Vic(tor) (1945–)

English composer. Hoyland's music has been featured at the Bath, Aldeburgh, and California Contemporary Music Festivals. He is a senior lecturer at the Barber Institute of Fine Arts, and reader at the University of Birmingham. His output includes the music theatre piece *Crazy Rosa – La Madre* (1988), and a chamber concerto with piano (1993).

Hoyle, Fred(erick) (1915–)

English astronomer, cosmologist, and writer. His astronomical research has dealt mainly with the internal structure and evolution of the stars. In 1948 he developed with Hermann ⟡Bondi and Thomas Gold the steady-state theory of the universe. In 1957, with William Fowler, he showed that chemical elements heavier than hydrogen and helium may be built up by nuclear reactions inside stars. He was knighted in 1972.

Hucknall, formerly Hucknall Torkard

Town in Nottinghamshire, England, 13 km/9 mi northwest of Nottingham; population (1991) 28,400. It was once dominated by extensive coal mines.

The Romantic poet Lord Byron, whose family home, Newstead Abbey, is nearby, was buried in Hucknall parish church after his body had been brought back from Greece.

Huddersfield, Anglo-Saxon Oderesfelt

Industrial town in West Yorkshire, on the River Colne, between Leeds and Manchester; population (1991) 119,000. A thriving centre of woollen manufacture by the end of the 18th century, it now produces textiles and related products, and has electrical and mechanical engineering, food-processing (biscuits), publishing, and building industries. The service sector is the principal employer.

Features

These include the railway station (completed 1848), with a neo-Classical facade; the restored Brook Street Market (1887–89); the town hall (1978–84), containing a concert hall; and the University of Huddersfield (formerly Huddersfield Polytechnic), established in 1992.

Economy

Industries related to Huddersfield's traditional woollen manufactures include the production of dyestuffs, wool textiles, carpets, and auxiliary textile equipment. Engineering includes sheet-metal working, coach and motor-body building, and the manufacture of machine and hand tools. Publishing activities incorporate printing and bookbinding. Furniture-making and the manufacture of prams, chemicals, paint, and building materials are also important. Principal service sector activities are distribution, hotel business, and catering.

Museums, galleries, and other features

Ravensknowle Park and Hall (1860), includes the Tolson Memorial Museum, illustrating the development of the cloth industry, and some re-erected parts of the original Cloth Hall (built in 1776 and demolished in 1930). The Library and Art Gallery includes a collection of 20th-century art. To the west of the town is Slack, where excavations have revealed evidence of the Roman camp of **Cambodunum**. Nearby at Kirklees Park is the reputed grave of Robin Hood. The Huddersfield Contemporary Music Festival is held annually in November.

Location

Huddersfield lies in the Colne Valley on the edge of the Pennines to the west. To the east and southeast there are farming villages, while on the west and south is thinly populated moorland rising to a height of 600 m/1,968 ft. Rochdale Canal links Huddersfield to Manchester, although the route is no longer used commercially and its tunnel has been closed; proposals have been made to reopen the waterway for recreational purposes.

History

A village in Anglo-Saxon times, Huddersfield was mentioned in the Domesday Book of 1086 as **Oderesfelt**, and in Subsidy Rolls, dated 1297, as Huddersfield. Nearby Almondbury (now a suburb to the south of the town) had a weekly market from 1272 and Huddersfield market was established in 1672. It was an important centre by the end of the 18th century, and developed rapidly in the 19th century as mills grew up along the river. Huddersfield Technical College, now part of the university, began in 1841 as the Young Men's Mutual Improvement Society.

Almondbury

Castle Hill, at the medieval settlement of Almondbury, was the site of an Iron Age camp and is crowned by the Victoria Tower (1897), built to commemorate the diamond jubilee of Queen Victoria. The village contains All Hallows Church, constructed largely in the Perpendicular style but with an Early English chancel. Wormall's Hall, dating from 1631, is a black-and-white half-timbered building.

Famous people

The former UK prime minister Harold Wilson was born here in 1916.

Hudson, Henry (*c.* 1565–1611)

English explorer. Under the auspices of the Muscovy Company 1607–08, he made two unsuccessful attempts to find the Northeast Passage to China. In September 1609, commissioned by the Dutch East India Company, he reached New York Bay and sailed 240 km/150 mi up the river that now bears his name, establishing Dutch claims to the area. In 1610 he sailed from London in the *Discovery* and entered what is now the **Hudson Strait**. After an icebound winter, he was turned adrift by a mutinous crew in what is now **Hudson Bay**.

Huggins, William (1824–1910)

English astronomer and pioneer of astrophysics. He revolutionized astronomy by using spectroscopy to determine the chemical make-up of stars and by using photography in stellar spectroscopy. Knighted 1897.

Hughes, Arthur (1832–1915)

English Pre-Raphaelite painter and illustrator. His depictions of contemporary life are closely observed, their mood often wistful or melancholy. They include *April Love* (1856; Tate Gallery, London) and *The Long Engagement* (1859; Birmingham City Art Gallery).

In 1857 Hughes worked with Dante Gabriel Rossetti, Edward Burne-Jones, and William Morris on the frescoes for the Oxford Union. He also produced many book illustrations, including those for Christina Rossetti's children's verses.

Hughes, Richard (Arthur Warren) (1900–1976)

English writer. His study of childhood, *A High Wind in Jamaica*, was published in 1929; his story of a ship's adventures in a hurricane, *In Hazard* in 1938; and the historical novel *The Fox in the Attic* in 1961.

Hughes was the first English dramatist to write specially for broadcasting and he was also associated with the Welsh National Theatre.

Hughes, Shirley (1927–)

English author and illustrator of books for children. Following her first picture book, *Lucy and Tom's Day* (1960), she has written and illustrated many books, including *Dogger* (1977) which won the Kate Greenaway Medal, a series of books about Alfie including *Alfie's Feet* (1982), *The Big Alfie Out of Doors Story Book* (1992), and *Alfie's Birthday Surprise* (1997). Her works of poetry for children include *Out and About* (1988), and *Rhymes for Annie Rose* (1995).

Hughes, Ted (Edward James) (1930–1998)

English poet, poet laureate from 1984. His work is characterized by its harsh portrayal of the crueller aspects of nature, by its reflection of the agonies of personal experience, and by the employment of myths of creation and being, as in *Crow* (1970) and *Gaudete* (1977). His free-verse renderings, *Tales from Ovid* won the 1997 Whitbread Book of the Year prize.

Collections include *The Hawk in the Rain* (1957), *Lupercal* (1960), *Wodwo* (1967), *Wolfwatching* (1989), and *Winter Pollen: Occasional Prose* (1994). His novels for children include *The Iron Man* (1968).

Hughes worked in various jobs as a gardener, security guard, film reader, and teacher. *Birthday Letters* (1998) is a collection of poems written at various times, following the course of his seven-year marriage to the US poet Sylvia Plath, who committed suicide in 1963. He was awarded the OM in 1998.

Hughes, Thomas (1822–1896)

English writer. He is best known as the author of ◊*Tom Brown's School Days* (1857), a story of Rugby School under Thomas ◊Arnold, with an underlying religious sense, which was the forerunner of the modern school story. It had a sequel, *Tom Brown at Oxford* (1861).

Hugh Town

Capital of the ◊Scilly Isles, off the coast of Cornwall, England. Agriculture and tourism are the principal industries. The town is situated on the largest island, St Mary's.

Huguenot

French Protestant, particularly a Calvinist, persecuted in the 16th and 17th centuries under Francis I and Henry II. In 1598, under Henry IV, the Huguenots were granted toleration by the Edict of Nantes. This edict was revoked by Louis XIV in 1685, prompting large-scale emigration. Some 40,000 Huguenots settled in Britain, bringing their industrial skills with them.

Some were expert craftsmen in silver, an area in which they set new standards. In the next generation Paul de Lamerie (1688–1751) became the best known of English silversmiths. Other craftsmen secured the success of Spitalfields silk. Well-known descendants of the Huguenot immigrants include the actor David Garrick and the textile manufacturer Samuel Courtauld.

Hull

Shortened name of ◊**Kingston upon Hull**, a city and unitary authority on the north bank of the Humber estuary, northeast England.

Hulme, T(homas) E(rnest) (1883–1917)

English poet, philosopher, and critic. He was killed on active service in World War I. As a poet he condemned the vagueness of the romantic Georgian school, demanding instead hardness and precision. His *Speculations* (1924) influenced T S ◊Eliot and his few poems inspired the ◊Imagist movement.

Human Fertilization and Embryology Act

Act of Parliament in 1990 which determined the status of a child born as the result of artificial insemination by donor (AID), of the scientific mixing of sperm and eggs in a woman's fallopian tubes (GIFT), and embryo transfer. A licensing authority was established, and is responsible for the licensing of persons involved in activities covered by the Bill, supervising research carried out on human embryos, and reviewing the resulting information.

Humber

Estuary in northeast England formed by the Ouse and Trent rivers, which meet east of Goole and flow east for 60 km/38 mi to enter the North Sea below Spurn Head. It is an important commercial waterway, and the main ports are ◊Kingston upon Hull on the north side, and ◊Grimsby on the south side. The ◊Humber Bridge (1981) joins the two banks.

The estuary widens from 2 km/1 mi at its head to 13 km/8 mi at the bay below Spurn Head. The area drained by the Humber is 24,000 sq km/9,264 sq mi.

Humber Bridge

Suspension bridge with twin towers 163 m/535 ft high, which spans the estuary of the River Humber in northeast England. When completed in 1981, it was the world's longest bridge with a span of 1,410 m/4,628 ft.

Built at a cost of £150 million, toll revenues over the following 15 years proved inadequate to pay even the interest on the debt.

Humberside

Former county of northeast England, created in 1974 out of north Lincolnshire and parts of the East and West Ridings of Yorkshire. It was abolished in 1996 when the unitary authorities of East Riding of Yorkshire, Kingston upon Hull, North East Lincolnshire, and North Lincolnshire were created.

Hume, (George) Basil (1923–)

English Roman Catholic cardinal from 1976. A Benedictine monk, he was abbot of Ampleforth in Yorkshire 1963–76, and in 1976 became archbishop of Westminster, the first monk to hold the office.

He was ordained in 1950.

Hume, David (1711–1776)

Scottish philosopher whose *Treatise of Human Nature* (1739–40) is a central text of British empiricism (the theory that experience is the only source of knowledge). Examining meticulously our modes of thinking, he concluded that they are more habitual than rational. Consequently, he not only rejected the possibility of knowlege that goes beyond the

HUMBER BRIDGE *When completed in 1981, the Humber Bridge in northeast England was the world's longest suspension bridge, with a centre span of 1,410 m/4,628 ft. British Steel*

bounds of experience (speculative metaphysics), but also arrived at generally sceptical positions about reason, causation, necessity, identity, and the self.

Hume's law in moral philosophy states that it is never possible to deduce evaluative conclusions from factual premises; this has come to be known as the 'is/ought problem'.

Hume, John (1937–)

Northern Ireland politician, leader of the Social Democratic and Labour Party (SDLP) from 1979. Hume was a founder member of the Credit Union Party, which later became the SDLP. An MP since 1969 and a member of the European Parliament, he has been one of the chief architects of the peace process in Northern Ireland.

In 1993 he held talks with Sinn Féin leader, Gerry Adams, on the possibility of securing peace in Northern Ireland. This prompted a joint Anglo-Irish peace initiative, which in turn led to a general cease-fire 1994–96. Despite the collapse of the cease-fire, Hume continued in his efforts to broker a settlement. This was achieved in the 1998 Good Friday Agreement and the SDLP polled strongly in the subsequent June 1998 elections to the new Northern Ireland assembly. In October 1998 he was, jointly with the Ulster Unionist David Trimble, awarded the Nobel Peace Prize for his part in the Northern Ireland peace process.

Hume-Rothery, William (1899–1968)

English metallurgist who studied the constitution of alloys. He established that the microstructure of an alloy depends on the different sizes of the component atoms, the valency electron concentration, and electrochemical differences.

With atoms of widely different sizes, at least two types of crystal lattice may form, one rich in one metal and one rich in the other. The presence of two types of structure can increase the strength of an alloy. This is why some brasses are much stronger than their component metals zinc and copper.

If the two elements differ considerably in electronegativity, a definite chemical compound is formed. Thus steel, an 'alloy' of iron and carbon, contains various iron carbides. Hume-Rothery and his team constructed the equilibrium diagrams for a great number of alloy systems.

Humperdinck, Engelbert (1936–)

English pop singer and cabaret entertainer whose hit songs included 'Release Me' and 'The Last Waltz' (both 1967).

hundred

Subdivision of a shire in England, Ireland, and parts of the USA. The term was originally used by Germanic peoples to denote a group of 100 warriors, also the area occupied by 100 families or equalling 100 hides (one hide being the amount of land necessary to support a peasant family). When the Germanic peoples settled in England, the hundred remained the basic military and administrative division of England until its abolition in 1867.

Hundred Years' War

Series of conflicts between England and France 1337–1453. Its origins lay with the English kings' possession of Gascony (southwest France), which the French kings claimed as their fief, and with trade rivalries over Flanders. The two kingdoms had a long history of strife before 1337, and the Hundred Years' War has sometimes been interpreted as merely an intensification of these struggles. It was caused by fears of French intervention in Scotland, which the English were trying to subdue, and by the claim of England's ◊Edward III (through his mother Isabella, daughter of Philip IV of France) to the crown of France. See feature and chronology.

Hungerford

Town in West Berkshire, England, on the border with Wiltshire and 14 km/9 mi northwest of Newbury; population

Chronology of the Hundred Years' War

1340 The English were victorious at the naval Battle of Sluis.

1346 Battle of Crécy, a victory for the English.

1347 The English took Calais.

1356 Battle of Poitiers, where Edward the Black Prince defeated the French. King John of France was captured.

late 1350s–early 1360s France had civil wars, brigandage, and the popular uprising of the Jacquerie.

1360 Treaty of Brétigny. France accepted English possession of Calais and of a greatly enlarged duchy of Gascony. John was ransomed for £500,000.

1369–1414 The tide turned in favour of the French, and when there was another truce in 1388, only Calais, Bordeaux, and Bayonne were in English hands. A state of half-war continued for many years.

1415 Henry V invaded France and won a victory at Agincourt, followed by conquest of Normandy.

1420 In the Treaty of Troyes, Charles VI of France was forced to disinherit his son, the Dauphin, in favour of Henry V, who was to marry Catherine, Charles's daughter. Most of northern France was in English hands.

1422–28 After the death of Henry V his brother, the duke of Bedford, was generally successful.

1429 Joan of Arc raised the siege of Orléans, and the Dauphin was crowned Charles VII at Rheims.

1430–53 Even after Joan's capture and death the French continued their successful counteroffensive, and in 1453 only Calais was left in English hands.

THE CENTURY OF STRIFE: ENGLAND AND THE HUNDRED YEARS' WAR

THE Hundred Years' War is a 19th-century term for a series of wars fought between 1337 and 1453. Complicated by the legal position of the English kings as vassals of the French for territories held in France, and by English counter-claims to the French throne, these wars saw the culmination of the long quest of the kings of France for territorial dominance in Western Europe.

Edward III's war

The end of the struggle between the Angevins and the French crown in 1259 had left the English monarchs only a narrow strip of territory in Aquitaine (Gascony). In the 1290s Edward I came into conflict with France over French support for Scotland; but it was not until the 1330s that war broke out. As a minor, Edward III (1327–77) had been unable to press his claim to the throne of France and had done homage to Philip VI (1328–50) for Gascony. When Philip used appeals to his law court as a pretext for reclaiming Gascony, Edward decided to fight.

His first campaigns were directed from Flanders, where the cloth towns of Ypres, Bruges, and Ghent were bound to England by the wool trade. In 1338–39 Edward could not draw the French into battle, and 1340 saw a crushing English naval victory off Sluis; but no progress on land.

Edward's ambitions had bankrupted his government, and he now turned to cheaper expedients. First he intervened in the Breton succession dispute, which resulted in a war lasting from 1341 to 1364. Then he tried a *chevauchée* (a plundering raid) across Normandy, sacking Caen and challenging Philip VI to battle outside Paris. His archers delivered him the brilliant victory of Crécy in 1346. Calais fell in 1347, to be held by England until 1558.

In 1356, another *chevauchée* by Edward, the Black Prince, led to the Battle of Poitiers. This time King John of France (1350–64) was captured and held for an enormous ransom. In the Treaty of Bretigny (1360), John ceded a third of his kingdom in return for Edward's renunciation of his claim to the French throne. Prince Edward was made Duke of Aquitaine, but his harsh rule led the Gascon nobles to appeal to Charles V (1364–80). War resumed, and in 1369 Edward III revived his claim.

A change of strategy

The French now adopted a successful strategy of avoiding battle while harassing English *chevauchées*, as on John of Gaunt's expedition of 1373. France was weakened by Charles VI's (1380–1422) attacks of insanity after 1392, but Richard II (1377–99) was eager for peace, and a 28-year truce was agreed in 1396.

Henry V (1413–22) came to the English throne determined to reassert his claim. Charles VI's illness had left France split between Armagnac and Burgundian factions. Their failure to combine in the face of Henry's invasion in 1415 led to his crushing victory at Agincourt. Philip the Good, Duke of Burgundy, threw in his lot with the English after the murder of his father in 1419, substantially shifting the balance of power in Henry's favour. Henry was able to force the Treaty of Troyes in 1420, which declared him heir to the French throne. But he died before Charles, leaving only his baby son Henry VI (1422–71) to inherit.

The Dauphin, later Charles VII (1422–61), still ruled south of the Loire, in what was scornfully called the 'Kingdom of Bourges'. The Burgundian alliance seemed to give the English all the trump cards. They recorded victories at Cravant in 1423 and Verneuil in 1424, and in 1429 besieged Orléans. Here the death of the Earl of Salisbury and the arrival of Joan of Arc turned the tables. Although she was soon captured and executed by the English, Joan helped to inspire a French revival and saw Charles VII crowned at Rheims. When Philip of Burgundy reverted to the French allegiance in 1435, the balance swung firmly against the English.

The triumph of Charles VII

Determined efforts to turn Normandy into an English colony proved unsustainable, and Henry VI was no war leader; a truce was agreed in 1444. In 1449 Charles VII renewed the war and Normandy fell swiftly. Despite the vigorous leadership of John Talbot, Earl of Shrewsbury, Gascony too was threatened, and finally conquered in 1453 when Talbot was killed in battle at Castillon.

The loss of France led to a series of civil wars in England, known as the Wars of the Roses (1455–85, intermittently). Although Edward IV (1461–83) did invade France in 1474, he was bought off. When Charles the Bold of Burgundy (1465–77) was killed fighting the Swiss, the French king was left without a rival in his kingdom. Although there would be many later wars between France and England, the French crown was no longer at issue.

BY MATTHEW BENNETT

(1991) 5,900. Hungerford is a centre for the breeding and stabling of racehorses and offers angling on the River Kennet.

The ancient name for Hungerford was Ingleford, meaning 'Ford of the Angles'.

In 1986 a local man, Michael Ryan, ran amok in Hungerford, shooting dead 13 people before killing himself.

hunger march

Procession of the unemployed, a feature of social protest in interwar Britain.

The first took place in 1922 from Glasgow to London and another in 1929. In 1932 the National Unemployed Workers' Movement organized the largest demonstration, with groups converging on London from all parts of the country, but the most emotive was probably the Jarrow Crusade of 1936, when 200 unemployed shipyard workers marched to the capital.

Hunt, Henry ('Orator') (1773–1835)

British Radical politician who agitated for a wider franchise and the repeal of the Corn Laws. Born into an affluent farming family, he emerged as one of the best-known radical leaders in the agitation for parliamentary reform following the passage of the Corn Laws in 1815, largely due to his inflammatory rhetoric. His speech at St Peter's Field in Manchester on November 1819 caused the militia to intervene, charging the crowd in what became known as the Peterloo Massacre, and Hunt was imprisoned for three years 1820–23. He was elected member of parliament for Preston 1831–33.

Hunt, (James Henry) Leigh (1784–1859)

English essayist and poet. He influenced and encouraged the Romantics. His verse, though easy and agreeable, is little appreciated today, and he is best remembered as an essayist. He recycled parts of his *Lord Byron and some of his Friends* (1828), in which he criticized Byron's character, as *Autobiography* (1850). The character of Harold Skimpole in Charles Dickens's *Bleak House* was allegedly based on him.

The appearance in his Liberal newspaper the *Examiner* of an unfavourable article that he had written about the Prince Regent caused him to be convicted for libel and imprisoned in 1813.

Hunt, James Simon Wallis (1947–1993)

English motor-racing driver who won his first Formula One race at the 1975 Dutch Grand Prix. He went on to win the 1976 world driver's title. Hunt started his Formula One career with Hesketh in 1973 and moved to Maclaren 1976–79, finishing in 1979 with Wolf. He later took up commentating for the BBC's Grand Prix coverage until his sudden death of a heart attack in June 1993.

A stockbroker's son, Hunt was educated at Wellington College. He struggled as a Formula Three driver before joining Hesketh; he had been involved in crashes so often that he was known as 'Hunt the Shunt'. Others claim the epithet derived from a punch that he threw at fellow competitor David Morgan after a collision at Crystal Palace in 1970. Hunt was deeply affected by the death of his friend and fellow racing driver Ronnie Peterson in 1978, whom he had pulled from the blazing wreckage of his car at Monza.

Hunt, (William) Holman (1827–1910)

English painter, one of the founders of the ◊Pre-Raphaelite Brotherhood in 1848. His paintings, characterized both by a meticulous attention to detail and a clear moral and religious symbolism, include *The Awakening Conscience* (1853; Tate Gallery, London) and *The Light of the World* (1854; Keble College, Oxford).

Obsessed with exact historical and archaeological detail, particularly for his religious works, Hunt visited Palestine and Syria in 1854, producing *The Scapegoat* (1856), with a meticulous study of the scenery around the Dead Sea.

He also painted scenes of contemporary life, including *A Hireling Shepherd* (1852) and *Strayed Sheep* (1852). Throughout his career he remained the most fervent adherent to the Pre-Raphaelite conception of 'truth to nature'.

His book *Pre-Raphaelitism and the Pre-Raphaelite Brotherhood* (1907) gives a clear account of his ideals and the history of the movement.

Hunter, John (1728–1793)

Scottish surgeon, pathologist, and comparative anatomist who insisted on rigorous scientific method. He was the first to understand the nature of digestion.

hunting

See ◊fox-hunting.

Huntingdon

Market town in Cambridgeshire, eastern England, on the River Ouse, 26 km/16 mi northwest of Cambridge; population (1996 est) 18,300 (excluding Godmanchester). It is an agricultural centre with diverse industries, including telecommunications, printing, food-processing (frozen foods, meat products), and the manufacture of electrical equipment, fibre optics, computerware, furniture, rubber mouldings, plastics, and chemicals. Oliver Cromwell was born here in 1599.

Huntingdon was formerly the county town of Huntingdonshire (amalgamated with Cambridgeshire in 1974), and in 1961 it was united with Godmanchester, on the south bank of the river. The grammar school (founded in 1565), attended by Oliver Cromwell and the diarist Samuel Pepys, was opened in 1962 as a Cromwell museum. The Environmental Information Centre was opened in 1989.

History

Huntingdon developed at the point where Ermine Street, the Roman road running from London to York, crosses the Ouse. In the 10th century the Danes constructed a defensive earthwork or 'burh' here, remains of which are visible. Edward the Elder, king of the West Saxons, captured the town in 921, but it was destroyed by the Danes in 1010. A castle was built here in the 11th century and the town received its first charter in 1204. Many of Huntingdon's inhabitants died during the ◊Black Death in 1348 and the town's prosperity declined. During the Civil War the town was used as a headquarters first by Oliver Cromwell and then by Charles I. It prospered as a staging post on the Great North Road in the 18th century.

Features

The town is connected with Godmanchester by a fine six-arched bridge (1332). The grammar school was founded in a 12th-century building, formerly part of a medieval hospital. Huntingdon had 16 churches in medieval times, only two of which survive: All Saints', dating from the 13th–16th centuries, and St Mary's, 12th–17th centuries. The town hall dates from 1745. Hinchingbrooke, the former seat of the Cromwell family, west of the town, was built on the site of a nunnery said to have been founded by William the Conqueror. It dates mainly from the 16th century, but incorporates remains of Norman work. The property is now the location of a business park. The site of the Norman castle is now a public open space. Remains of the earthworks consist of a motte, with a bailey partly surrounded by a rampart and a deep ditch. The George Hotel has a 17th-century galleried courtyard. The town has many 17th- and 18th-century houses including Walden House, Ferrar House, Cowper House, and Castle Hill House. Cromwell House occupies the site of a former residence of Cromwell, where he lived from 1617 to 1631 as a young married man, prior to moving to St Ives; the original building was demolished in 1810 and a new house erected.

Hurd, Douglas (Richard) (1930–)

British Conservative politician, home secretary 1985–89 and foreign secretary 1989–95. In November 1990 he was an unsuccessful candidate in the Tory leadership contest following Margaret Thatcher's unexpected resignation.

Hurd entered the House of Commons in 1974, representing Witney in Oxfordshire from 1983. He was made a junior minister by Margaret Thatcher, and the sudden resignation of Leon Brittan projected him into the home secretary's post. He was appointed foreign secretary in 1989 in the reshuffle that followed Nigel Lawson's resignation as chancellor of the Exchequer, and retained his post in prime minister John Major's new cabinet formed after the 1992 general election. He was replaced as foreign secretary in the reshuffle that followed Major's re-election as party leader in July 1995, having earlier announced his intention to retire from parliament at the 1997 election.

Hurst, Geoff(rey Charles) (1941–)

English footballer who scored three goals in England's 4–2 victory in the 1966 World Cup final at Wembley, the only time a hatrick has been scored in a World Cup final. A virtual unknown internationally before the tournament began, having only made his full England debut two months earlier, he was surprisingly preferred to the prolific scoring Jimmy Greaves in the competition's final stages. He went on to make a total of 49 appearances for England, scoring 24 goals. Knighted in 1998.

Hurst Castle

Coastal fortification in Hampshire, England, about 6 km/4 mi southwest of the port of Lymington, at the mouth of the western arm of the ◊Solent. The castle lies at the end of a long shingle spit, and was originally erected by Henry VIII for the purpose of defending the Solent.

Charles I was imprisoned at Hurst Castle in 1648, during the English Civil War, and further fortifications were added when England was threatened with invasion by Napoleon I early in the 19th century. Two lighthouses are also located on Hurst Point. The castle is now administered by English Heritage, and may be reached on foot along the spit, or by a seasonal ferry service across the salt marshes from Keyhaven.

Hurstmonceux

Alternative spelling of ◊**Herstmonceux**, a village in East ◊Sussex.

Hurt, John (1940–)

Leading English stage and screen actor who has enjoyed film success on both sides of the Atlantic. A rugged, sad-eyed screen presence, he has worked with some of the major filmmakers of his generation, turning in a string of accomplished dramatic performances in such films as *The Elephant Man* (1980), as the disfigured Victorian John Merrick; and *Champions* (1983), as the cancer-suffering jockey Bob Champion. Other films include *Midnight Express* (1978), *1984* (1984), *Bandyta* (1997), and *Desert Blue* (1998).

Hutton, James (1726–1797)

Scottish geologist, known as the 'founder of geology', who formulated the concept of uniformitarianism. In 1785 he developed a theory of the igneous origin of many rocks.

His *Theory of the Earth* (1788) proposed that the Earth was incalculably old. Uniformitarianism suggests that past events could be explained in terms of processes that work today. For example, the kind of river current that produces a certain settling pattern in a bed of sand today must have been operating many millions of years ago, if that same pattern is visible in ancient sandstones.

Hutton, Len (Leonard) (1916–1990)

English cricketer, born in Pudsey, West Yorkshire. A right-handed opening batsman he captained England in 23 test matches 1952–56 and was England's first professional captain. In 1938 at the Oval he scored 364 against Australia, a world record test score until beaten by Gary Sobers 1958. He was knighted for services to the game in 1956.

Huxley, Aldous (Leonard) (1894–1963)

English writer of novels, essays, and verse. From the disillusionment and satirical eloquence of *Crome Yellow* (1921), *Antic Hay* (1923), and *Point Counter Point* (1928), Huxley developed towards the Utopianism exemplified by *Island* (1962). His most popular work, the science fiction novel ◊*Brave New World* (1932) shows human beings mass-produced in laboratories and rendered incapable of freedom by indoctrination and drugs.

Huxley's later devotion to mysticism led to his experiments with the hallucinogenic drug mescalin, recorded in *The Doors of Perception* (1954). His other works include the philosophical novel *Eyeless in Gaza* (1936), and *After Many a Summer* (1939; Tait Black Memorial Prize).

Huxley intended to become a doctor, but was hindered by problems with his sight, being blind for a time. Later his eyesight partly recovered. Huxley joined the staff of the *Athenaeum* in 1919 and did miscellaneous literary work. He was in Italy from 1923–30 and associated with D H Lawrence there; in 1934 he visited Central America and in 1938 settled permanently in California.

Huxley, Andrew Fielding (1917–)

English physiologist, awarded the Nobel prize in 1963 with Alan ◊Hodgkin for work on nerve impulses, discovering how ionic mechanisms are used in nerves to transmit impulses. Knighted 1974.

Huxley, Julian Sorell (1887–1975)

English biologist, first director general of UNESCO, and a founder of the World Wildlife Fund (now the World Wide

Fund for Nature). He wrote popular science books, including *Essays of a Biologist* (1923). Knighted 1958.

Huxley, Thomas Henry (1825–1895)

English scientist and humanist. Following the publication of Charles Darwin's *On the Origin of Species* (1859), he became known as 'Darwin's bulldog', and for many years was a prominent champion of evolution. In 1869 he coined the word 'agnostic' to express his own religious attitude, and is considered the founder of scientific humanism.

From 1846 to 1850 Huxley was the assistant ship's surgeon on HMS *Rattlesnake* on its voyage around the South Seas. The observations he made on the voyage, especially of invertebrates, were published and made his name in the UK.

Hyde

Town in Greater Manchester Metropolitan County, England, 7 km/4 mi northeast of Stockport; population (1991) 33,300. Industries include the manufacture of textiles, printing, light engineering, and the production of foodstuffs and rubber goods. The town is a residential area for commuters to Manchester.

Hyde Park

One of the largest open spaces in London, occupying over 138 ha/340 acres in Westminster, and adjoining Gardens to the west. It includes the Serpentine, a boating lake; and Rotten Row, a riding track. Open-air meetings are held at Speakers' Corner, in the northeast corner near Marble Arch. In 1851 the Great Exhibition was held here.

The southeast corner of the park is known as **Hyde Park Corner**.

History

The park was originally part of the **Manor of Hyde**, owned by Westminster Abbey, until it was taken by Henry VIII in 1536 at the time of the Dissolution of the Monasteries. It then became a royal deer park until it was opened to the public by Charles I. It was sold by Parliament in 1652, but reverted to the Crown at the Restoration. It became a fashionable coach- and horse-racing track, a rendezvous for duellists, and from its northwest corner crowds used to watch executions at Tyburn. The Serpentine (1730–33) was formed on the course of the old Westbourne River. The Great Exhibition of 1851 was housed in the ◊Crystal Palace, a glass and iron construction moved to Sydenham Hill in 1854, where it burned down in 1936. In 1855 a large number of people gathered illegally in the northeast corner of the park to demonstrate against the Sunday Trading Bill. There were further demonstrations, and the right of assembly in the park was recognized in 1872, the site becoming Speakers' Corner.

HYDE PARK *Cyclists in Hyde Park, central London, England, in 1898. Hyde Park was traditionally a meeting place for fashionable people, and it was not until 1895 that cyclists were allowed in the park. At that time cycling was becoming a socially acceptable activity for women, and contributed to changes towards less restrictive styles of dress for women. Private collection*

Hyde-White, Wilfrid (1903–1991)
English actor. He played character roles in British and occasionally US films; for example, the role of Colonel Pickering in the screen version of *My Fair Lady* (1964). He tended to be cast as an eccentric or a pillar of the establishment, and sometimes as a mixture of the two.

Hythe
Seaside resort (one of the original ◊Cinque Ports) in the Romney Marsh area of Kent, southeast England; population (1996 est) 15,800. Industries include horticulture and the manufacture of plastics.

Features
St Leonard's Church is partly late-Norman with a large chancel and a crypt containing a large number of human skulls and bones. The Royal Military Canal (constructed 1804–06) was built as a defence against the threatened Napoleonic invasion, and is now a recreation area and scene of an annual water festival. The terminus of the Romney, Hythe, and Dymchurch narrow-gauge railway is here. Said to be the smallest public railway in the world, it runs for 23 km/14 mi from Hythe to Dungeness. Saltwood Castle, dating mainly from the 14th century, lies nearby to the north.

Hytner, Nicholas (1957–)
English theatre and film director. He first made his name in theatre directing the Royal Shakespeare Company's *Measure for Measure* (1988) and the stage production of *Miss Saigon* (1989). In 1994 he broke into feature films, helming the British production of *The Madness of King George*, noteworthy both for its understated visual style and quality of performance. This led to work in the USA, including directing an adaptation of Arthur Miller's play *The Crucible* (1996) and the romance *The Object of My Affection* (1998).

He won a Tony award for directing the revival of *Miss Saigon* in 1994

Hywel Dda Hywel the Good
Welsh king. He succeeded his father Cadell as ruler of Seisyllwg (roughly former Cardiganshire and present Towy Valley), at first jointly with his brother Clydog *c.* 910–920 then alone 920–950. He had extended his realm to Dyfed, Gwynedd, and Powys by 942, creating a larger Welsh kingdom than any before. His reign was peaceful, mainly because he was subservient to the English kings. He is said to have codified Welsh laws, but there is no contemporary record of this.

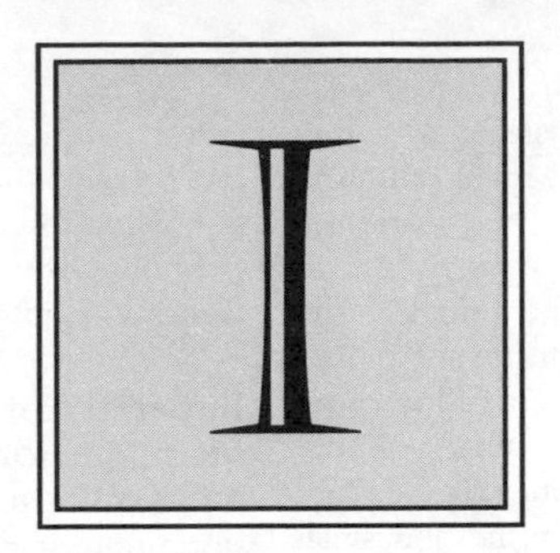

Iceni

Ancient people of eastern England, who revolted against Roman occupation under the chieftainship of ◊Boudicca.

Icknield Way

Major pre-Roman trackway traversing southeast England. It runs from Wells-next-the-Sea on the Norfolk coast in a generally southwesterly direction, passing first through Cambridgeshire and Hertfordshire. The Icknield Way then runs through Luton in Bedfordshire, skirts the Chiltern Hills, crosses the River Thames at Goring and follows the line of the Berkshire Downs to the source of the River Kennet in Wiltshire.

Especially in the 18th and 19th centuries, the Icknield Way was used as a drove road, to move sheep from their grazing lands in the Chilterns to markets in East Anglia, particularly Newmarket.

Ickworth

House and 730 ha/1803 acre estate in Suffolk, England, 1 km/0.5 mi southwest of Bury St Edmunds. Ickworth was built by Frederick Augustus Hervey (1730–1803), 4th Earl of Bristol and bishop of Derry, around 1794, and was given to the National Trust by the Treasury in 1956.

Its unusual design comprises an elliptical rotunda with two curved corridors leading to flanking wings. The rotunda was designed to contain the living accommodation, while the wings were designed to house the bishop's collections of furniture, silver, pictures, and sculpture. The collections are now on display in the house, which is open to the public.

ILEA, Inner London Education Authority

Former educational body that administered education in London. It was abolished in 1990 and replaced by smaller borough-based education authorities.

Originally called the School Board for London in 1870, it became part of London County Council (LCC) in 1902. It remained when the LCC became the Greater London Council (GLC) in 1965, and survived the latter's abolition in 1986.

Ilford

Suburb of Greater London, in the borough of ◊Redbridge, 11 km/7 mi northeast of the city centre. Ilford has factories producing photographic materials and scientific instruments.

The hospital of St Mary and St Thomas was originally founded in the 12th century as a hospital for the care of leprosy victims.

Ilfracombe

Resort on the north coast of Devon, southwest England, 17 km/11 mi northwest of Barnstaple; population (1991) 10,400. Features include St Nicholas Chapel, dating from the 14th-century.

Ilfracombe is set amidst impressive cliff scenery, with hills inland. Facilities include a pier, museum, and public gardens; and it is an occasional point of departure for ◊Lundy Island by passenger ferry.

History

From the 14th to 16th centuries Ilfracombe was an important trading port. It supplied six ships and 96 men for the siege of Calais (1347), and was besieged twice during the Civil War. In 1792 a large treasure ship, belonging to the Franco-Spanish fleet taken by Admiral Rodney, was wrecked in Rapparee Cove, just east of Ilfracombe. Gold and silver pieces have since been washed ashore, and a mass grave of black French prisoners-of-war or slaves drowned in the incident has been discovered in the sands. In 1797 four French ships sank all the vessels in the harbour. Ilfracombe developed as a resort in the early 19th century and grew rapidly after the arrival of the railway in 1874.

Ilkeston

Town in southeast Derbyshire, England, 15 km/9 mi northeast of Derby; population (1994 est) 34,300. Part of a former coalmining region, Ilkeston manufactures plastics, clothing, and furnishings, and has pipemaking and iron founding industries.

The town is situated on high ground above the Erewash Valley.

Ilkley, Roman Olicana

Spa town in West Yorkshire, northern England, on the River Wharfe, 16 km/10 mi north of Bradford; population (1996 est) 13,900. The largest town in Wharfedale, it is mainly residential, acting as a dormitory town for Leeds and Bradford. It is a popular centre for touring the Yorkshire Dales. **Ilkley Moor** lies to the south of the town.

Originally the site of an Iron Age settlement, it was later the Roman station of **Olicana**. An Elizabethan manor house, built on the site of the Roman fort, has been restored and now houses the Manor House Museum. All Saints' Church includes three Anglo-Saxon crosses in the churchyard. White Wells, on Ilkley Moor, is the site of a spring and small bath-house. Other features nearby are Bolton Abbey (founded 1151), 8 km/5 mi to the northwest of the town; and the Cow and Calf Rocks to the south. The ballad 'On Ilkla Moor baht'at' was reputedly composed by a church choir from Halifax during the course of picnic beneath the rocks.

Imagism

Movement in Anglo-American poetry that flourished from 1912–14 and affected much US and British poetry and critical thinking thereafter. A central figure in Britain was Richard ⇨Aldington. Poets subsequently influenced by this movement include T S Eliot, William Carlos Williams, Wallace Stevens, and Marianne Moore. Imagism established modernism in English-language verse.

immigration

Major subject of political debate in the UK in the 20th century. Following World War II Britain welcomed immigrants from the Commonwealth to help rebuild the economy with cheap labour; see ⇨*Empire Windrush*. However the size of the immigrant population became a matter for concern in the 1960s, leading to Commonwealth Immigration Acts, passed 1962 and 1968, subsequently replaced by a single system of control under the Immigration Act of 1971. The British Nationality Act 1981 further restricted immigration by ruling that only a British citizen has the right to live in the United Kingdom.

There are five different categories of citizenship, with varying rights. Under the British Nationality Act 1981, amended by the British Nationality (Falkland Islands) Act 1983 and the Hong Kong Act 1985, only a person designated as a **British citizen** has a right of abode in the UK; basically, anyone born in the UK to a parent who is a British citizen, or to a parent who is lawfully settled in the UK. Four other categories of citizenship are defined: **British dependent territories citizenship**, **British overseas citizenship**, **British subject**, and **Commonwealth citizen**. Rights of abode differ widely for each.

See also ⇨population, ⇨Afro=Caribbean, and ⇨Muslim community for a feature detailing Muslim immigration over the past 300 years.

Immingham

Town in North East Lincolnshire, northeast England, on the south side of the Humber estuary, 10 km/6 mi northwest of Grimsby; population (1981) 11,500. It is a bulk cargo handling port, with petrochemical works and oil refineries. Exports include chemicals, iron and steel, vehicles, and petroleum products. The ports of Immingham and Grimsby are managed jointly from ⇨Grimsby, and together deal with 46 million tonnes of freight a year.

Immingham Dock was opened by the Great Central Railway Company in 1912.

Imperial College of Science, Technology, and Medicine, formerly Imperial College of Science and Technology

Institution established in South Kensington, London, in 1907, for advanced scientific training and research, applied especially to industry. Part of the University of London, it comprises three separate colleges, the City and Guilds College (engineering faculty), the Royal College of Science (pure science), and the Royal School of Mines (mining). St Mary's Hospital Medical School was added in 1988, resulting in the change of name.

imperial system

Traditional system of units developed in the UK, based largely on the foot, pound, and second (f.p.s.) system.

In 1991 it was announced that the acre, pint, troy ounce, mile, yard, foot, and inch would remain in use indefinitely for beer, cider, and milk measures, and in road-traffic signs and land registration. Other units, including the fathom and therm, were phased out by 1994.

Imperial War Museum

British military museum, founded in 1917. It includes records of all operations fought by British forces since 1914. Its present building (formerly the Royal Bethlehem, or Bedlam, Hospital) in Lambeth Road, London, was opened in 1936; it was rebuilt and enlarged in 1989.

Importance of Being Earnest, The

Romantic stage comedy by Oscar ⇨Wilde, first performed in 1895. The courtships of two couples are comically complicated by confusions of identity and by the overpowering Lady Bracknell.

Impressionism

Movement in painting which originated in France in the 1860s and had enormous influence on British avant-garde painting in the late 19th century and early 20th century. The Impressionists aimed to depict real life, to paint straight from nature, and to capture the changing effects of light. Notable forerunners of the genre, much admired by the French artists, were the English landscape painters John Constable and J M W Turner.

Many of the British artists influenced were in the circle of Walter Sickert, a charismatic and inspirational figure who spent much of his career in France. His friend and contemporary Philip Wilson Steer is generally regarded as the most outstanding British exponent of Impressionism. James Whistler, although associated with the movement, never became a true Impressionist, painting from memory and mixing his colours on the palette rather than applying pure colour direct.

Ince, Paul Emerson Carlyle (1967–)

English footballer. An energetic, hard-tackling midfield player, he made his full international debut in September 1992 and the following June became the first black footballer to captain England. By the end of the 1998 World Cup finals he had won 43 England caps scoring 2 goals. He has played for West Ham United 1986–88, Manchester United 1989–95, Inter Milan 1994–97, before joining Liverpool at the start of the 1997–98 season.

inch

Imperial unit of linear measure, a twelfth of a foot, equal to 2.54 centimetres.

It was defined in statute by Edward II of England as the length of three barley grains laid end to end.

income support

◊Social security benefit payable to people who are unemployed or who work for less than 24 hours per week and whose financial resources fall below a certain level. It replaced supplementary benefit in 1988. Originally payable to anyone over 18 not in full-time employment and without adequate resources, as of October 1996 it was restricted to group such as pensioners or long-term disabled who were not required to be available for work. Payments were reduced if savings exceeded a set amount.

The number of people living on income support virtually doubled between 1979 (4.4 million) and 1992 (8.7 million).

income tax

Direct tax levied on personal income. In 1997 there were three rates of income tax: 20%, 23%, and 40%. Individuals are permitted to earn a certain amount of income tax free – this is known as their tax allowance; employees' tax is deducted under the ◊PAYE system. The rates of UK tax and allowances are set out yearly in the annual Finance Act, which implements the recommendations agreed to by the House of Commons in the budget presented by the chancellor of the Exchequer.

Self-assessment system

A major change in the UK system of taxation was introduced on 6 April 1996. The self-assessment system, in force since the tax year 1996–97, does not affect the amount of tax payable, but requires the taxpayer to deliver a completed tax return and optionally also calculate the amount of income tax due. The impact of self-assessment is largely limited to those who are self-employed, those with investment income liable to a higher income-tax rate, and those receiving income from the exploitation of land – about 8 million people. For the most part, employees whose tax is deducted under the PAYE system are not affected by the new system.

History

Income tax was introduced by the Tory prime minister William Pitt in 1799 and levied until 1801 to finance the wars with revolutionary France; it was re-imposed from 1803 to 1816 for the same purpose, and was so unpopular that all records of it were destroyed when it was abolished. The Conservative prime minister Robert Peel reintroduced the tax in 1842 and it has been levied ever since, forming an important part of government finance. At its lowest, 1874–76, it was 0.83%; at its highest, 1941–46, the standard rate was 50%.

independent dance

Another term for ◊new dance.

Independent Labour Party, ILP

British socialist party, founded in Bradford in 1893 by the British politician Keir ◊Hardie. In 1900 it joined with trades unions and Fabians in founding the Labour Representation Committee, the nucleus of the ◊Labour Party. Many members left the ILP to join the Communist Party in 1921, and in 1932 all connections with the Labour Party were severed. After World War II the ILP dwindled, eventually becoming extinct. James Maxton (1885–1946) was its chair 1926–46.

independent school

School run privately without direct assistance from the state.

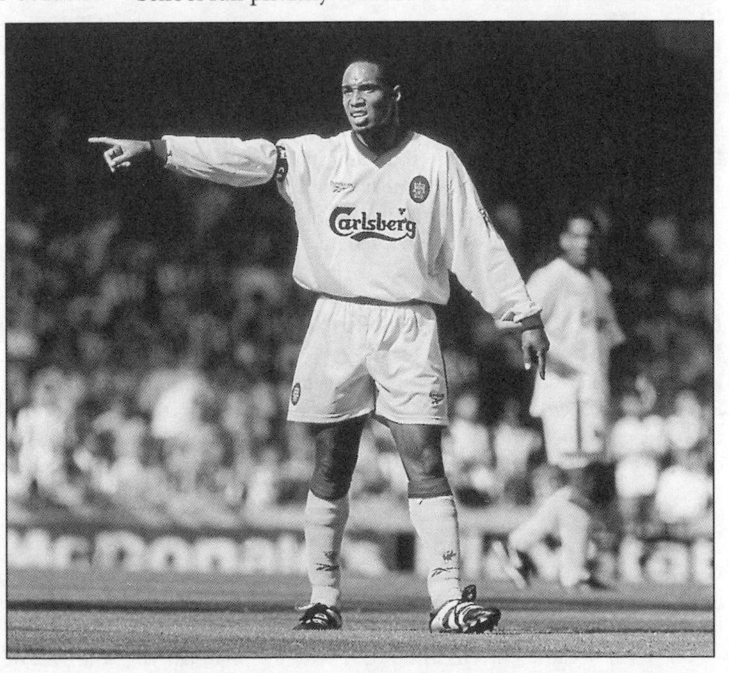

INCE, PAUL *The Liverpool and England midfielder Paul Ince made history in 1992, when he became the first black footballer to captain England. He has a tenacious style of play and can deliver ferocious long-distance strikes on goal. He gained invaluable experience of continental European football during his three-year spell with the Italian club Inter Milan. Marc Aspland/ Rex*

Just over 7% of children (1998) attend private fee-paying schools. There are some 2,420 independent schools in Britain, with about 600,000 pupils. A group of old-established and prestigious independent schools are known as ◊public schools.

The independent sector includes most boarding education in the UK. Although most independent secondary schools operate a highly selective admissions policy for entrants at the age of 11 or 13, some specialize in the teaching of slow learners or difficult children and a few follow particular philosophies of progressive education.

Independent Television Commission, ITC, formerly the Independent Broadcasting Authority

Public body responsible for licensing and regulating commercial television services in the UK, including ITV, Channel 4, and Channel 5, as well as Teletext and a number of cable and satellite services. It is not responsible for licensing S4C, the fourth Welsh channel. Its duties include implementing a code of practice, ensuring adequate quality of services, reporting on complaints, and ensuring competition. It is funded by payments from its licensees; it was paid £315 million in 1995. Members of the Commission are appointed by the government.

Independent, The

Daily quality newspaper established in 1986 to compete with *The Times*, *The Daily Telegraph* and *The Guardian*. Owned by the Mirror Group Consortium, the paper aims to be politically independent. Its circulation in 1998 was over 250,000. A sister paper, *The Independent on Sunday*, was established in 1990 and had a circulation of over 270,000 in 1998.

India Acts

Legislation passed in 1858, 1919, and 1935 which formed the basis of British rule in India until independence in 1947. The 1858 Act abolished the administrative functions of the British ◊East India Company, replacing them with direct rule from London. The 1919 Act increased Indian participation at local and provincial levels but did not meet nationalist demands for complete internal self-government (Montagu-Chelmsford reforms). The 1935 Act outlined a federal structure but was never implemented.

Indian Mutiny, also known as the Sepoy Rebellion or Mutiny

Revolt of Indian soldiers (Sepoys) against the British in India from 1857 to 1858. The uprising was confined to the north, from Bengal to the Punjab, and central India. It led to the end of rule by the British ◊East India Company and its replacement by direct British Crown administration.

indie, short for independent

In music, a record label that is neither owned nor distributed by one of the large conglomerates ('majors') that dominate the industry.

The term became current in the UK with the small labels created to disseminate punk rock in the 1970s. In the 1980s they provided a home for the hardcore bands, for uncategorizable bands with cult followings, like the Fall, and for the occasional runaway success like the ◊Smiths. The British music papers publish separate charts of independent record sales.

Indirect Rule

System of colonial government widely employed by the British for the administration of colonies. Indirect rule sought to encourage and govern through local institutions and traditional authorities with a view to promoting self-government in the long term.

industrial music

Avant-garde music that uses electronic distortion, metal percussion, and industrial tools to achieve deafening, discordant effects, often combined with imagery intended to shock or disgust. Leading industrial bands have included Throbbing Gristle (formed in 1976 in the UK), Einstürzende Neubauten (formed in 1980 in Germany), and Non (formed early 1980s in the USA).

A brief fashion for metal-derived, studio-based 'cut-up' industrial music appeared in the early 1990s, in imitation of highly successful US acts like Nine Inch Nails, but nothing of significance emerged in the UK.

Industrial Revolution

Sudden acceleration of technical and economic development that began in Britain in the second half of the 18th century. The traditional agrarian economy was replaced by one dominated by machinery and manufacturing, made possible through technical advances such as the steam engine. This transferred the balance of political power from the landowner to the industrial capitalist and created an urban working class. From 1830 to the early 20th century, the Industrial Revolution spread throughout Europe and the USA and to Japan and the various colonial empires. See chronology opposite and feature on page 464.

The new working conditions led to political changes as wealth moved away from the land and towards the new manufacturing classes and there were massive social changes brought about by internal migration, a rising population, and the growth of urban areas.

Textile industry

The textile industry saw most of the early benefits of these innovations. The flying shuttle was invented in 1738, rendering the old process of carrying the weft through the threads of the warp obsolete and enabling the weaver to double output. This in turn led spinners to seek mechanical aids to meet the increased demand for yarn. These innovations were swiftly followed by others, notably James Hargreaves's 'spinning jenny' about 1764, Richard Arkwright's water-frame spinning roller in 1768, and Samuel Crompton's 'spinning mule', a combination of Hargreaves's jenny and Arkwright's water-frame, in 1779. Edmund Cartwright's power loom was not perfected for another 25

CHRONOLOGY OF THE INDUSTRIAL REVOLUTION IN BRITAIN

1701 The seed drill was invented by Jethro Tull. This was a critical point of the agricultural revolution which freed labour from the fields and lowered crop prices.

1709 Abraham Darby introduced coke smelting to his ironworks at Coalbrookdale in Shropshire.

1712 The first workable steam-powered engine was developed by Thomas Newcomen.

1740 Crucible steelmaking was discovered by Benjamin Huntsman, a clockmaker of Doncaster.

1759 The first Canal Act was passed by the British Parliament; this led to the construction of a national network of inland waterways for transport and industrial supplies. By 1830 there were 6,500 km/4,000 mi of canals in Britain.

c. **1764** The spinning jenny, which greatly accelerated cotton spinning, was invented by James Hargreaves in Blackburn.

1764 Pierre Trosanquet, a French engineer, developed a new method of road building. Similar techniques were used by Thomas Telford in Britain to build modern roads from 1803.

1769 James Watt patented a more reliable and efficient version of the Newcomen engine.

1779 The spinning mule, which made the production of fine yarns by machine possible, was developed in Bolton by Samuel Crompton.

1785 The power loom marked the start of the mechanised textile industry.

1797 The first true industrial lathe was invented, virtually simultaneously, by Henry Maudslay in England and David Wilkinson in the USA.

1802 The first electric battery capable of mass production was designed by William Cruickshank in England.

1811–16 Textile workers known as Luddites staged widespread protests against low pay and unemployment in Nottinghamshire, which involved destroying new machines.

c. **1812** The population of Manchester passed 100,000.

c. **1813** Industrial employment overtook agricultural employment in England for the first time.

1825 The first regular railway services started between Stockton and Darlington in northeast England.

1826 The Journeymen Steam Engine Fitters, the first substantial industrial trade union, was established in Manchester.

1829 With his steam locomotive *Rocket*, English engineer George Stephenson won a contest to design locomotives for the new Manchester–Liverpool railway.

1831–52 British industrial production doubled.

1832 The Reform Act concerning elections to the British Parliament gave representation to the industrial cities.

1833 The first effective Factory Act was passed in Britain regulating child labour in cotton mills.

1842 Cotton-industry workers in England staged a widespread strike.

1846 Repeal of the Corn Law in Britain reduced agricultural prices, thereby helping industry.

1851 Britain celebrated its industrial achievements in the Great Exhibition.

1852–80 British industrial production doubled again.

1858 The 'great stink' of London dramatized the increasing pollution in the cities.

years but by that time his Doncaster factory was equipped with a steam engine and a year or two later hundreds of his looms were selling to Manchester firms. Gradually the power loom began to be used in the woollen industry as well as the cotton trade for which it had been invented.

industry

The prominent trends in industrial activity in Britain from the 1970s onwards have been the growth of the offshore oil and gas industries, the rapid growth of electronic and microelectronic technologies, and a continuous rise in the share of total employment of service industries. At the same time there has been a decline in traditional industries such as ◊steelmaking, ◊shipbuilding, and ◊coal mining. Recessions 1974–75 and 1980–81, due in part to fluctuating energy costs, have been offset by increased productivity, but the increased output was achieved with fewer workers, and unemployment has been a persistent feature of the period.

Electronics and automated controls are now applied extensively throughout industry, particularly in steel mills, oil refineries, coal mines, and chemical plants. The UK is the sixth largest user of industrial robots in the world. Another area of technological strength is biotechnology, using fermentation techniques for food, beverage, and antibiotic production. The main areas of research and development expenditure are electronics, chemicals and pharmaceuticals, aerospace, mechanical engineering, and motor vehicles.

Conservative government policy during the 1980s was to

DARK SATANIC MILLS: THE INDUSTRIAL REVOLUTION

THE BRITISH economy changed dramatically in the late 18th and early 19th centuries. Technological innovation, agricultural development, communications improvements, growing trade, and the increased consumer demand and labour supply afforded by a rising population took Britain to the forefront of economic progress. These changes had a profound impact on the lives and the mental outlook of contemporaries.

Technological development
Though the rate of industrialization in Britain in the late 18th century was less impressive than used to be believed, and was restricted to only a few sectors (notably cotton textiles and metallurgy), a sense of economic change and the possibilities of progress was powerfully obvious to many contemporary observers. A popular metaphor was that of Prometheus Unbound, of extraordinary opportunities offered by technological innovation.

John Kay's flying shuttle of 1733, which was in general use in Yorkshire by the 1780s, increased the productivity of hand-loom weavers. James Hargreaves' spinning jenny (*c.* 1764), Richard Arkwright's 'spinning frame' (1768), and Samuel Crompton's mule (1779) revolutionized textile spinning. Arkwright and his partners built a number of cotton mills in Lancashire and the Midlands with all the characteristic features of factory system, including the precise division of labour and the co-operation of workers in different manufacturing processes. Cotton production grew by nearly 13% in the 1780s.

In 1769 James Watt patented a more energy-efficient use of steam engines. Steam pumps removed water from deep coal mines, and steam-powered winding engines were introduced in the early 1790s. Coal production increased rapidly, allowing a similar increase in the production of iron and lead. Canals and waggon-ways built to move coal prompted a wider revolution in transportation: for example, the 4th Duke of Portland built a new harbour at Troon on the west coast of Scotland in 1808, linked to his coal pits at Kilmarnock by a waggon-way which during 1839 carried over 130,000 tons of coal.

The coalfields attracted new, heavy industry, particularly in South Wales, Strathclyde, Northeast England, West Yorkshire, South Lancashire, the Vale of Trent, and the West Midlands. The smelting of iron and steel using coke, rather than charcoal, freed a major industry from dependence on wood supplies, while technological development spurred by Britain's wars and the demands of an Empire revolutionized the secondary metallurgical industries, especially gun founding. The percentage of the male labour force employed in industry rose from 19 in 1700 to 30 in 1800.

The social dimension
The strains of industrialization in the early 19th century caused much social and political tension. Improvements in working conditions brought about by technological changes were very gradual, with the result that general living standards only began to rise noticeably after mid-century. The social – and indeed biological – pressure placed on the bulk of the population by the emergence of industrial work methods and economics is indicated by a marked decline in the height of army recruits in the second quarter of the century. Working conditions were often unpleasant and hazardous with, for example, numerous fatalities in mining accidents. The Factory Acts regulating conditions of employment in the textile industry still left work there both long and arduous. The 1833 Act established a factory inspectorate and prevented the employment of under-9s, but 9–13 year olds could still work 8-hour days, and 13–17 year olds 12 hours. The 1844 Act cut that of under-13s to 6 and a half hours, and of 18-year olds and all women to 12; those of 1847 and 1850 reduced the hours of women and under-18s to 10 hours. Despite such legislation, there were still about 5,000 half-timers under 13 in the Bradford worsted industry in 1907. If the bulk of the working population faced difficult circumstances, the situation was even worse for those more marginal to the new economy. 'Hell is a city much like London – A populous and a smoky city;' wrote the poet Shelley in *Peter Bell the Third* (1819). Fast-expanding towns became crowded and polluted, a breeding ground for disease. In 1852, 8,032 of the 9,453 houses in Newcastle lacked toilets.

Britain the world leader
The Industrial Revolution gave Britain a distinctive economy. It became the world leader in industrial production and foreign trade. The annual averages of coal and lignite production, in million metric tons, for 1820–24 were 18 for Britain, compared with 2 for France, Germany, Belgium, and Russia combined. The comparable figures for 1855–59 were 68 and 32, and for 1880–84 159 and 108. The annual production of pig-iron in million metric tons in 1820 was 0.4 for Britain and the same for the rest of Europe, in 1850 2.3 and 0.9, and in 1880 7.9 and 5.4. Raw cotton consumption in thousand metric tons in 1850 was 267 for Britain and 162 for the rest of Europe. Britain was the workshop of the world.

BY JEREMY BLACK

encourage economic recovery by improving performance in the face of the open market, through the ◊privatization (selling shares to the public) of public sector industry. British Telecom was sold in 1985, British Gas in 1986, British Airways in early 1987, the water boards in 1989, electricity boards in 1992, and British Rail in 1996, but the Post Office remains in public ownership. As a member of the European Union (EU), Britain has received grants from the European Regional Development Fund, which was established in 1975 to assist in the development of new or declining industrial regions.

In the mid-1980s manufacturing, construction, and the

INDUSTRY *Welding a large-bore pipe in an engineering factory. As the cradle of the Industrial Revolution, Britain became known as the 'workshop of the world'. Though manufacturing industry is still a major employment sector, in the late 20th century the country's economy has come to rely increasingly on service industries, such as retailing and financial services. John Cole/Impact*

service industries accounted for 88% of gross domestic product, and employed 26%, 5%, and 65% of the labour force respectively. The highest growth in manufacturing since then has been in the chemical, electrical, and instrument engineering sectors. In 1988 the number of people employed in the manufacturing industry dropped below 5 million for the first time since the 19th century.

Mineral products

The British Steel Corporation accounts for 82–85% of Britain's steel output by volume, and is the world's fourth largest steel company. The sector is strong in the manufacture of special steels, alloys, and finished products for the engineering industries. Manipulation of materials by smelting, casting, rolling, extruding, and drawing is also carried out.

Chemicals

Accounting for about 10% of manufacturing net output, this industry produces a complete range of products including fertilizers, plastics, pharmaceuticals, soap, toiletries, and explosives.

Mechanical engineering

Machine tools, industrial engines, mechanical handling equipment, construction equipment, and industrial plant are all significant products in this area. Britain is the Western world's largest producer of agricultural tractors.

Motor vehicles

Recent years have seen a large increase in the volume of imports in this sector, notably from Europe and Japan, but more foreign makes are being assembled in the UK. British manufacturers still provide a major export. In 1995 1.5 million cars were made in the UK, a record production for 20 years.

Aerospace

In order to compete with the USA in this area, Britain resorted to European and multinational cooperative ventures, including the Airbus passenger airliner and the Ariane rocket for the launching of satellites, but it pulled out of both Airbus and Ariane in 1987. The space industry's major strength at present is the manufacture of satellites. Aircraft (civil and military), helicopters, aero-engines, and guided weapons are major products, supported by a comprehensive range of aircraft and airfield equipment and systems.

Construction

Building, repair, alteration and maintenance of buildings, highways, bridges, tunnels, drainage and sewage systems, docks, harbours, and offshore structures are included, together with ancillary services such as wiring, heating, ventilation, and air conditioning.

Top 25 Companies in the UK in 1997

This table is ranked by market capitalization. Market capitalization is the market value of a company's issued. Share capital, that is the quoted price of its shares multiplied by the number of shares issued. (Information as of 22 January 1998.)

Rank	Company	Market capitalization (£ millions)	Rank	Company	Market capitalization (£ millions)
1	HSBC Holdings	56,986.6	14	Unilever	14,782.8
2	British Petroleum	53,596.1	15	Abbey National	13,475.8
3	Glaxo Wellcome	49,734.7	16	Prudential Corporation	13,362.6
4	Shell Transport and Trading	45,093.8	17	Grand Metropolitan	12,489.5
5	Lloyds TSB Group	44,980.0	18	Reuters Holdings	12,439.6
6	SmithKline Beecham	33,256.4	19	Cable & Wireless	11,981.2
7	British Telecommunications	26,214.7	20	BG	11,960.0
8	Barclays	25,352.8	21	Guinness	11,075.4
9	Zeneca	19,175.7	22	General Electric Company	10,900.8
10	Halifax	18,323.0	23	Rio Tinto	10,617.0
11	Marks and Spencer	18,064.5	24	Tesco	10,282.0
12	BAT Industries	16,868.5	25	Vodaphone Group	10,214.7
13	National Westminster Bank	16,044.6			

Source: *FT500, FT Surveys, Financial Times*

Service industries

The fastest growing sectors during the 1970s (measured by employment) were financial and business services, professional and scientific services (including health and education), and leisure. In the 1980s finance continued to grow strongly, and franchising, particularly in labour-intensive areas such as hotel, catering, and cleaning businesses, became a widespread new form of organization.

inheritance tax

A tax charged on the value of an individual's estate on his or her death, including gifts made within the previous seven years. It replaced capital transfer tax in 1986 (which in turn replaced estate duty in 1974).

INLA

Abbreviation for ◊Irish National Liberation Army.

Innes-Ker

Family name of the dukes of Roxburghe; seated at Floors Castle, Roxburghshire, Scotland.

Inns of Court

Four private legal societies in London: Lincoln's Inn, Gray's Inn, Inner Temple, and Middle Temple. All barristers (advocates in the English legal system) must belong to one of the Inns of Court. The main function of each Inn is the education, government, and protection of its members. Each is under the administration of a body of Benchers (judges and senior barristers).

Institute of Management, or IM

Central institution of professional management in the UK, established on government initiative in 1947.

Originally the British Institute of Management, in 1958 it absorbed the Institute of Industrial Administration and in 1978 received the Institution of Works Managers as an affiliate, later incorporating it and adopting the title Institute of Management. It has over 11,000 corporate and 60,000 individual members and, as well as representing managers, provides conference, training, education, and consultancy services.

International Development Department, or IDD

Official body (until 1997 the **Overseas Development Administration**) that deals with development assistance to overseas countries, including financial aid on concessionary terms and technical assistance, usually in the form of sending specialists to other countries and giving training in the UK.

International Petroleum Exchange

Commodity market in the City of London that trades in petroleum. It was established in 1980.

internment

Detention of suspected criminals without trial. Foreign citizens are often interned during times of war or civil unrest.

Internment was introduced for the detention of people suspected of terrorist acts in Northern Ireland by the UK government in 1971. It has now been discontinued.

Inveraray

Former county town and royal burgh in Argyll and Bute unitary authority, Scotland, situated on Loch Fyne, 37 km/23 mi northwest of Greenock; population (1991) 500. A popular tourist centre, the town was originally laid out on a grand scale in 1743 by Archibald, 3rd Duke of Argyll; it was sited close to **Inveraray Castle**, his ancestral seat.

The castle, initially constructed in the 15th century as the stronghold of the 1st Earl of Argyll, head of the clan Campbell, was also redesigned in 1745 by the 3rd duke to provide a stately home.

Inverclyde

Unitary authority in western Scotland, created in 1996 from Inverclyde district in Strathclyde region

Area 161 sq km/62 sq mi

Towns ◊Greenock (administrative headquarters), Port Glasgow, Gourock

Physical coastal lowland on the Firth of Clyde estuary, rising sharply to an inland plateau of 305 m/1,000 ft

Features Inverkip Marina

Industries electronics

Population (1995) 88,700

History key part in the industrial history of Scotland as a port and a heavy engineering centre.

Economy

It is predominantly a de-industrializing urban area with more affluent villages on the southern side of the area and low-quality agricultural land away from the coastal plain. Regeneration has been led by high technology.

Environment

There are four Sites of Special Scientific Interest and one regional park.

Administrative history

Prior to 1975, the area was part of Renfrewshire.

Invergordon Mutiny

Incident in the British Atlantic Fleet, Cromarty Firth, Scotland, on 15 September 1931. Ratings refused to prepare the ships for sea following the government's cuts in their pay; the cuts were consequently modified.

Inverness

Main town in, and the administrative centre of, ◊Highland unitary authority, Scotland, at the head of the Moray Firth, lying in a sheltered site at the mouth of the River Ness; population (1991) 41,200. It is a tourist centre with tanning, oil-related engineering, distilling, and electronics industries. Culloden Moor, scene of the massacre of clansmen loyal to Charles Edward Stuart by the English Army in April 1746, is situated to the east of Inverness.

Iona

Island in the Inner Hebrides; area 850 hectares/2,100 acres. A centre of early Christianity, it is the site of a monastery founded 563 by St ◊Columba. It later became a burial ground for Irish, Scottish, and Norwegian kings. It has a 13th-century abbey.

Ipswich, Saxon Gyppeswyk

River port and administrative headquarters of ◊Suffolk, eastern England, on the Orwell estuary, 111 km/69 mi northeast of London; population (1996 est) 113,000. An important wool port in the 16th century, it now provides financial and distribution services, and is the location of British Telecom's laboratories. Other industries include engineering, and the manufacture of computer software, machinery, beer, flour, fibre optics, videotape and multimedia products, building materials, plastics, and electrical goods.

Shipping services encompass port support, freight forwarding, and other distribution. Engineering products include grass cutting machinery for golf courses, water control equipment for large-scale irrigation schemes, roller mills, grain driers, air compressors, refrigerating plant, and central heating equipment. Automotive components, audio speakers, plywood, wall boards, garden furniture, yeast, and fertilizers are also manufactured. Part of the University of East Anglia is sited here.

History

Originally the site of a small Roman settlement, **Gyppeswyk** prospered as a port and agricultural centre throughout the Saxon period. The Danes were defeated at sea off the mouth of the Orwell in 885 by King Alfred, but in 991 and 1010 they invaded the town and set fire to it. In 1200 King John granted Ipswich its first charter. During the reign of Edward III weavers and wool workers from the Netherlands settled in the area and the Suffolk woollen industry grew rapidly. In 1518 Henry VIII granted a charter confirming the corporation's jurisdiction over the Orwell estuary as far as what is now the port of Harwich.

Features

Much of the centre of Ipswich has been rebuilt and many modern buildings have been constructed around the medieval core of the town. The centre is Cornhill, formerly the site of the Saxon market. In the Butter Market is the Ancient House (1567), or Sparrowe's House, which includes a fine example of pargeting (ornamental carving of the plasterwork on its facade). To the north of the centre is Christchurch Mansion (1548–50), which now houses a museum and gallery including paintings by the Suffolk artists John Constable and Thomas Gainsborough. Wolsey's Gateway (1528) is the only remaining fragment of Cardinal Wolsey's plan to found a college in Ipswich. Ipswich Museum includes geological and archaeological exhibits. The Great White Horse Inn features in the *Pickwick Papers* of Charles Dickens. The library was built in 1924, and is an important repository for Suffolk records. **Ipswich School** (now a private school) was established in 1477 or earlier in the precincts of the Blackfriars monastery; it moved to its present site in 1851.

Churches

The town has many medieval churches. St Margaret's dates from the early 13th century; the Perpendicular St Peter's was renovated and extended in 1878 under Gilbert Scott; and the church of St Nicholas has a 14th-century nave and aisles. Other churches include St Mary-le-Tower, where King John's charter was received in 1200 by the bailiffs and burgesses; the 15th-century St Mary-at-the-Quay; and St Lawrence, a lofty Perpendicular church, with an embattled tower and five medieval bells.

Famous people

Ipswich was the birthplace of Cardinal Wolsey in about 1475, and the home of the painter Thomas Gainsborough.

IRA, or Irish Republican Army

Militant Irish nationalist organization formed in 1919, the paramilitary wing of ⯑Sinn Féin. Its aim is to create a united Irish socialist republic including Ulster. To this end, the IRA has habitually carried out bombings and shootings. Despite its close association with Sinn Féin, it is not certain that the politicians have direct control of the military, the IRA usually speaking as a separate, independent organization. The chief common factor shared by Sinn Féin and the IRA is the aim of a united Ireland.

In 1969 the IRA split into two wings, one 'official' and the other 'provisional'. The official wing sought reunification by political means, while the **Provisional IRA**, or Provos, carried on with terrorist activities, their objective being the expulsion of the British from Northern Ireland. It is this wing, of younger, strongly sectarian Ulster Catholics, who are now generally regarded and spoken of as the IRA.

The IRA was founded in 1919 by Michael ⯑Collins. The IRA strategy was to make British rule ineffective by the use of armed force, the belief being that political activity alone would not achieve this end. During the War of Irish Independence 1919–21, employing guerrilla tactics, it forced the British government to negotiate a political settlement which involved the creation of the Irish Free State in the south. This settlement proved unacceptable to some IRA members and the organization split into two groups. The larger, which supported the settlement, and the rest, styled 'the Irregulars', began a campaign of violence against the new independent government in the south. A civil war ensued 1922–23 which, after heavy fighting, ended with the defeat of the Irregulars. The IRA did not disband or surrender its arms but remained a clandestine organization, turning its efforts towards achieving the unification of Ireland. It was declared illegal in 1936, but came to the fore again in 1939 with a bombing campaign in Britain. Its activities intensified from 1968 onwards.

The left-wing Irish Republican Socialist Party, with its paramilitary wing, the Irish National Liberation Army, split from the IRA in 1974.

The IRA has carried out bombings and shootings in Northern Ireland as well as bombings in mainland Britain and in British military bases in continental Europe. In 1979 it murdered Louis ⯑Mountbatten, and its bomb attacks in Britain included an attempt to kill members of the UK cabinet during the 1984 Conservative Party conference in Brighton.

Ireland

One of the British Isles, lying to the west of Great Britain, from which it is separated by the Irish Sea. It comprises the provinces of Ulster, Leinster, Munster, and Connacht, and is divided into the Republic of Ireland (which occupies the south, centre, and northwest of the island) and ⯑Northern Ireland (which occupies the northeastern corner and forms part of the United Kingdom). See the chronology of Ireland's history (page 470), and features on Ireland under the Stuarts (page 469), and the later struggle for home rule (page 470).

Ireland, Northern

See ⯑Northern Ireland.

Ireton, Henry (1611–1651)

English general. During the Civil War he joined the parliamentary forces and fought at ⯑Edgehill in 1642, Gainsborough in 1643, and ⯑Naseby in 1645. After the Battle of Naseby, Ireton, who was opposed to both the extreme republicans and ⯑Levellers, strove for a compromise with Charles I, but then played a leading role in his trial and execution. He married his leader Cromwell's daughter in

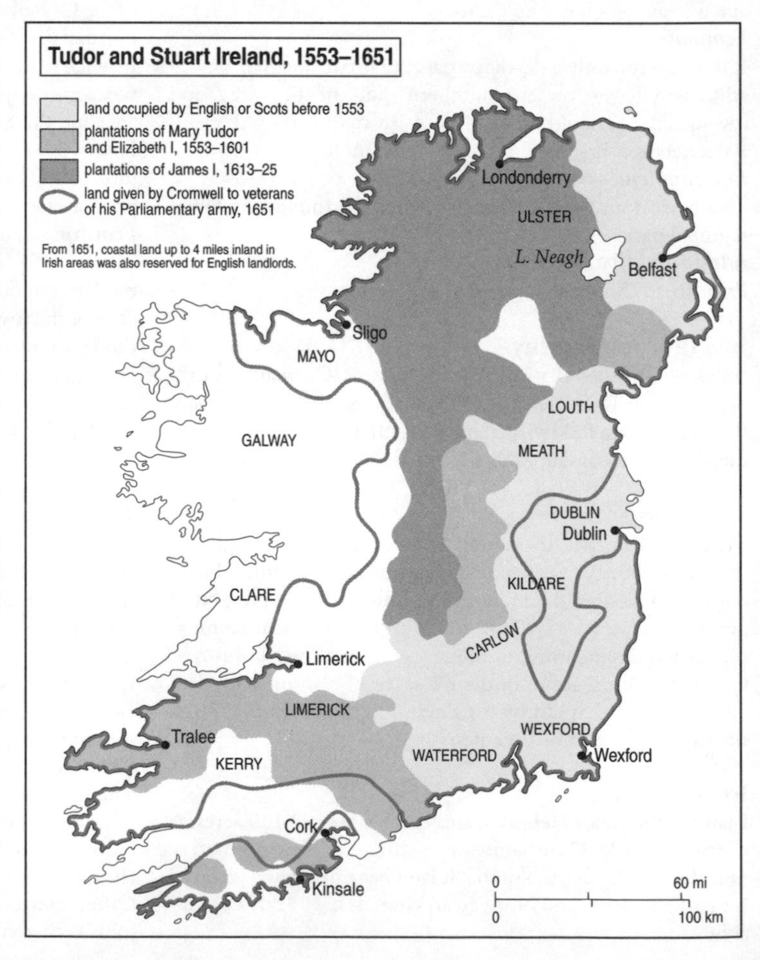

THE ROOTS OF SECTARIANISM: IRELAND UNDER THE STUARTS

From the accession of James I in 1603 to the death of Anne in 1714, Ireland witnessed a significant expansion of the authority of the Dublin administration in both political and religious life, at a time of conflict and dramatic economic growth.

The new English

Sixteenth-century Ireland had been a fragmented polity, dominated by individual native and Anglo-Irish lords. The defeat in the Nine Years War (1594–1603) of a coalition of native lords under Hugh O'Neill, Earl of Tyrone, ensured that royal authority and the common law were finally extended throughout the whole country. The aim in Dublin was an English style 'commonwealth', promoted by unplanned settlement from England and Scotland in areas such as East Ulster, and more regulated plantation, notably in Ulster after the flight of O'Neill and other lords in 1607. The emerging New English settler group, mainly Protestant in religion, challenged the traditional political elite, the Old English Catholic community, just as their identity was being reinforced by the European Counter-Reformation.

Despite increasing economic influence through a trade boom, the Old English were losing political power. They responded with appeals to Charles I as king of Ireland. In the late 1620s a political compromise, the Graces, was devised but not implemented.

Formal plantation and informal New English settlement, along with the growth in Old English landowning power, resulted in the replacement of the 16th-century lords by a new overmighty group of mixed New and Old English lords by the 1630s. The arrival of Thomas Wentworth, Earl of Strafford, as Lord Deputy, intent on re-establishing royal power, upset the precarious political balance. All groups in Ireland combined with allies in the English parliament to impeach Strafford, who was impeached in 1640 and executed. However, the Irish parliament failed to agree on a new polity, and some Irish Catholics, many now well integrated into the new order, feared that they would suffer under an increasingly vociferous Protestant parliament in England. This, combined with a downturn in economic fortunes, drove a number of the most prominent of the Irish Catholics into a 'loyal rebellion' in October 1641 to protect the king's interests against parliament.

The Cromwellian intervention

The Catholic camp operated under the umbrella of the Confederation of Kilkenny. In practice there were political divisions within this group, notably between Old English and native Irish Catholics. As the war continued it became more radical and the issue of religion more divisive. The papacy became involved, providing both funds for the war and a nuncio to ensure its own rights were protected.

The war quickly became inextricably linked with the civil war in England. By 1649 the Confederation had been dissolved and both religious groups formed a united royalist front, forcing the Cromwellian intervention. Ten years of Cromwellian government saw a transfer of land and power from royalist losers, both Protestant and Catholic, to parliamentary winners, as well as punitive taxation. The abolition of the Irish parliament also undermined the existing political framework. This, together with the economic effects of war in the 1640s, effectively resolved the problem of overmighty lords. It introduced other problems, however, notably the emergence of dissent in the form of Quaker, Presbyterian, Baptist, and Independent congregations in a society in which Protestantism had hitherto been the exclusive preserve of the Established Church.

The Anglo-Irish

From the 1660s the political and social life of Ireland was rebuilt, in favourable economic conditions generated by diversification and increased specialization of the economy. Protestant settlers monopolized parliament and were the main beneficiaries of the Acts of Settlement (1663) and Explanation (1665).

The result was a growing identification of the settlers with Ireland and the emergence of an Anglo-Irish identity, manifested in opposition to the London administration in the parliament of 1692, and in the early 18th-century ideology of 'colonial nationalism'. Irish Protestants were prepared to support James II as king of Ireland after his deposition from the English throne in 1688 despite the Catholicization of corporations and the army after 1685. It was James's attempt to undermine the land settlement in the Jacobite parliament of 1689 which finally drove his Protestant supporters into the William of Orange's camp and made inevitable a reconquest of Ireland.

After 1692 the Ascendancy, fearful of another judgement of God (as they interpreted the events of 1688–91), attempted reform by establishing religious societies and enacting a number of bills against Catholicism, culminating in a comprehensive act in 1704 to reduce Catholic landownership. But other problems loomed: prolonged economic recession after 1700 was attributed by many to the English parliament's prohibition of Irish wool exports. Such grievances, ironically, led the Anglo-Irish to adopt in the 18th century the ideas and tactics of the Old English whom they had ousted in the early 17th century.

BY RAYMOND GILLESPIE

1646. Lord Deputy in Ireland from 1650, he died after the capture of Limerick.

Irish Free State

Former name (1922–37) of Southern Ireland, now the Republic of Ireland.

Irish National Liberation Army, or INLA

Guerrilla organization committed to the end of British rule in Northern Ireland and the incorporation of Ulster into the Irish Republic. The INLA was a 1974 offshoot of the Irish Republican Army (IRA). Among the INLA's activities was the killing of British politician Airey Neave in 1979. The

Ireland: Chronology

432 or 456 St Patrick's mission to Ireland.

563 St Columba founds the monastery at Iona.

585 St Columban sails to France.

795 First Viking raids on Ireland.

840 Vikings found Dublin.

1002 Brian Boru acknowledged High King of Ireland.

1014 Brian Boru killed as he defeats Norsemen at Battle of Clontarf.

1169 Norman invasion of Ireland begins.

1172 Henry II lands at Waterford.

1175 Treaty of Windsor.

1315 Edward Bruce invades Ireland.

1318 Edward Bruce killed at Battle of Dundalk.

1394 First visit of Richard II to Ireland.

1399 Second visit of Richard II to Ireland.

1491 Poyning's law makes Irish legislature dependent on England.

1541 Irish parliament confirms Henry VIII as king of Ireland.

1569 First Desmond rebellion against Protestant 'plantations' or settlements.

1579 Second Desmond rebellion.

1586 Plantation of Munster by English and Scottish settlers.

1594 Rebellion of Hugh O'Neill, Earl of Tyrone.

1598 Battle of the Yellow Ford, supported by Spanish troops, O'Neill annihilates an English force.

1601 Battle of Kinsale; O'Neill defeated by Lord Mountjoy.

1603 Treaty of Mellifont; a general amnesty follows.

1607 Flight of the Earls; the earls of Tyrone and Tyrconnel flee to Spain.

1609 Plantation of Ulster.

1633 Sir Thomas Wentworth becomes Lord Deputy of Ireland.

1641 Ulster rising begins; Ulster Protestants are massacred.

1642 Confederation of Kilkenny formed; an independent Irish parliament.

1646 Owen Roe O'Neill defeats a Scottish army led by Robert Monro at the Battle of Benburb.

1649 Oliver Cromwell captures Drogheda and Wexford.

1652 Land confiscation begins.

1681 Irish Jesuit and Primate of Ireland Oliver Plunkett executed in London.

1689 Unsuccessful siege of Londonderry by forces of James II.

1690 William III wins the Battle of the Boyne.

1691 Treaty of Limerick, followed by land confiscation.

1695 Penal laws introduced against Catholics.

1720 Act declaring British parliament's right to legislate for Ireland passed.

1779 Volunteers parade in Dublin; trade restrictions repealed.

1782 Convention of Volunteers at Dungannon; Irish parliamentary independence conceded.

1791 Society of United Irishmen formed.

1792 Catholic Relief Acts ease penal laws against Catholics.

1795 Orange Order founded in Co Armagh.

1798 United Irishmen's rising fails; a prominent member, Wolfe Tone, commits suicide.

1800 Act of Union establishes United Kingdom of Great Britain and Ireland; effective 1801. End of Grattan's parliament.

1823 Catholic Association founded by Daniel O'Connell to campaign for Catholic political rights.

1828 O'Connell elected for County Clare; forces granting of rights for Catholics to sit in Parliament.

1829 Catholic Emancipation Act.

1838 Tithe Act (abolishing payment) removed a major source of discontent.

1840 Franchise in Ireland reformed. 'Young Ireland' formed.

1846–51 Potato famine resulted in widespread death and emigration. Population reduced by 20%.

1850 Irish Franchise Act extended voters from 61,000 to 165,000.

1858 Fenian Brotherhood formed.

1867 Fenian insurrection failed.

1869 Church of Ireland disestablished.

1870 Land Act provided greater security for tenants but failed to halt agrarian disorders. Protestant Isaac Butt formed Home Government Association (Home Rule League).

1874 Home Rule League won 59 Parliamentary seats and adopted a policy of obstruction.

1880 Charles Stuart Parnell became leader of Home Rulers, dominated by Catholic groups. 'Boycotts' against landlords unwilling to agree to fair rents.

1881 Land Act greeted with hostility. Parnell imprisoned. 'No Rent' movement began.

1882 'Kilmainham Treaty' between government and Parnell agreed conciliation. Chief Secretary Cavendish and Under Secretary Burke murdered in Phoenix Park, Dublin.

1885 Franchise Reform gave Home Rulers 85 seats in new parliament and balance between Liberals and Tories. Home Rule Bill rejected.

1886 Home Rule Bill rejected again.

1890 Parnell cited in divorce case, which split Home Rule movement.

1893 Second Home Rule Bill defeated in House of Lords; Gaelic League founded.

1900 Irish Nationalists reunited under Redmond. 82 MPs elected.

1902 Sinn Féin founded by Arthur Griffith.

1906 Bill for devolution of power to Ireland rejected by Nationalists.

1910 Sir Edward Carson led Unionist opposition to Home Rule.

1912 Home Rule Bill for whole of Ireland introduced. (Protestant) Ulster Volunteers formed to resist.

1913 Home Rule Bill defeated in House of Lords but overridden. (Catholic) Irish Volunteers founded in the South.

1914 Nationalists persuaded to exclude Ulster from Bill for six years but Carson rejected it. Curragh 'mutiny' cast doubt on reliability of British troops against Protestants. Extensive gun-running by both sides. World War I deferred implementation.

1916 Easter Rising by members of Irish Republican Brotherhood. Suppressed by troops and leaders executed.

1919 Irish Republican Army (IRA) formed.

1921 Partition of Ireland; creation of Irish Free State.

INLA refused to participate in the August 1994 cease-fire declared by Sinn Féin, the political wing of the Irish Republican Army, but in April 1995 announced that it was renouncing the use of violence.

The group's leader, Gino Gallagher, was shot and killed in Belfast on January 1996, allegedly by feuding INLA members.

Irish News

Daily morning newspaper covering all Ireland, published in Belfast. Established in 1891, it had a circulation of over 48,000 in 1998. A politically independent newspaper, it sells mainly to the nationalist community.

Irish Republican Army

See ⇨IRA.

Irish Sea

Arm of the North Atlantic Ocean separating England and Wales from Ireland; area 103,600 sq km/39,990 sq mi. Its greatest width, between Morecambe Bay, Lancashire, and Dundalk Bay, Louth, is 240 km/150 mi. It joins the Atlantic to the south by St George's Channel and to the north by the North Channel.

Ironbridge Gorge

Site in the Telford and Wrekin unitary authority, England, on the River Severn, south of Telford; it is the site of the Iron Bridge (1777–79) designed by Abraham Darby III (1750–89). The bridge was the world's first iron bridge, and is one of the first and most striking products of the Industrial Revolution in Britain. Designated a British National Monument, it forms the centrepiece of the Ironbridge Gorge World Heritage Site, a series of museums of industrial archaeology in and near the villages of Ironbridge (population (1991) 2,200) and ⇨Coalbrookdale.

Abraham Darby III constructed the Iron Bridge from castings made in his pioneering iron foundry at nearby Coalbrookdale. It was here that Abraham Darby I had first used coke rather than the more expensive charcoal in the iron smelting process, so allowing for increased production. Abraham Darby II (1711–63) later succeeded in making iron suitable for forging as well as casting. The area fell into decline in the 20th century until it was restored as an open-air museum, a major tourist attraction which recreates the heyday of this 'cradle of the Industrial Revolution'. Features include the Coalbrookdale Museum of Iron, Blists Hill Museum, Coalport China Museum, and Jackfield Tile Museum.

Irons, Jeremy (1948–)

English actor. A hint of ambiguity under his surface sheen made him perfect for such film roles as Claus von Bulow in *Reversal of Fortune* (1990; Academy Award) and the twin brothers in *Dead Ringers* (1988). Other films include *The French Lieutenant's Woman* (1981), *The Mission* (1986), and *Damage* (1992).

His aristocratic bearing, immaculate grooming, and precise diction have led to frequent casting as a repressed, upper-class character. He came to prominence in a television adaptation of Evelyn Waugh's *Brideshead Revisited* (1981). His other screen appearances include *Moonlighting* (1982), *Un Amour de Swann/Swann in Love* (1984), and *The House of the Spirits* and *M. Butterfly* (both 1993). Recent films include *Stealing Beauty* (1996), the role of Humbert Humbert in Adrian Lyne's controversial adaptation of *Lolita* (1997), and the mainstream blockbusters *Die Hard: With a Vengeance* (1996) and *The Man in the Iron Mask* (1998).

Ironside, (William) Edmund, 1st Baron Ironside (1880–1959)

Scottish field marshal. He served in the South African War 1899–1902 and World War I. In 1939 during World War II, he replaced Viscount Gort as Chief of the Imperial General Staff because the minister of war, Leslie Hore-Belisha, found him more congenial. In May 1940 he sided with Gort against Churchill in a disagreement over the possibility of the British Expeditionary Force breaking out to the south. Churchill transferred Ironside to the Home Forces, but he handed the post over to Alanbrooke in July 1940 and retired.

Irvine

Administrative headquarters of ⇨North Ayrshire, western Scotland, designated a 'new town' in 1966; population (1991) 33,000. Industries include the manufacture of electronics and pharmaceuticals. It is the birthplace of the novelist John Galt, and the poet James Montgomery.

There are several tourist attractions, including the Magnum

THE CONTINUING QUEST: IRELAND AND THE STRUGGLE FOR HOME RULE

The Irish rebellion of 1798 demonstrated that the Protestant Ascendancy could not keep Ireland stable, and prompted British moves toward union. The Act of Union 1800 abolished the Irish Parliament in return for Irish representation at Westminster. However, Pitt the Younger's attempt to admit Catholics to public office was thwarted by George III; Catholics could not become MPs in the new Parliament until 1829, which created much resentment. The Union ensured that the politics of Ireland were more closely linked with those of Britain than ever before.

A brief survey of Ireland in this period might centre on hardship and discord: the potato famine of 1845–48 and the struggle for Irish political autonomy were both of great importance. Yet Ireland remained within the British Empire, there was no collapse into anarchy or civil war, and the Irish economy developed as part of the growing imperial economy, even while Ireland's Catholic areas became more socially and culturally distinct.

The closing decades of the century brought economic and social change, and reform as in mainland Britain. The (Anglican) Church of Ireland was disestablished 1869, and the position of the Catholic church markedly improved. By 1914 Ireland had gained a large share of economic independence. Legislation from 1860 to 1903 progressively broke the power of the landlords: farmers increasingly owned their holdings. Local government was also transferred to the control of the largely Catholic majority.

Irish nationalism

Nationalism was revived as a political issue by Daniel O'Connell, who campaigned in the 1830s and 1840s for the repeal of the Act of Union. The government responded by attempts at reform and by limiting extra-parliamentary agitation. Nonetheless, the potato famine led to allegations of government neglect as about 800,000 people died from starvation or diseases made more deadly by malnutrition.

The extension of the franchise in 1867 and 1884 greatly increased the number of Catholic voters; most supported Home Rule, which would have given an Irish Parliament control of all policy matters bar defence and foreign policy. The Home Government Association of 1870 was followed by the Home Rule League in 1873. Charles Stuart Parnell became leader of an organized and powerful parliamentary pro-Home Rule party 1879, with 61 MPs by 1880, 86 by 1885, and 85 by 1886.

Home Rule proposals introduced by Gladstone in 1886 and 1893 were defeated at Westminster. Conservatives led the resistance, renaming their party the Conservative and Unionist Party in 1886, but the defeat of the First Home Rule Bill in 1886 was due to the defection of 93 'Liberal Unionists' from Gladstone's government.

Nationalist agitation also had a violent dimension. In 1848 the Young Ireland movement attempted an insurrection. The Fenians, a secret organization founded in 1858, tried to launch a rebellion in Ireland in 1867 and were responsible for terrorist acts in Britain and an attempted invasion of Canada from the United States. Reconstituted as the Irish Republican Brotherhood in 1873, they continued to mount terrorist attacks, and in 1882 another secret society, the Invincibles, murdered Lord Frederick Cavendish, the Chief Secretary for Ireland, in Phoenix Park, Dublin. Some Irishmen served with the Boers during the South African War of 1899–1902.

The Easter Rising

Another Liberal government, dependent on Irish Nationalist support, introduced a Home Rule Bill in 1912. Twice rejected by the Conservative-dominated House of Lords, the Bill was passed in an amended form in 1914 with the proviso that it was not to be implemented until after the war. Protestant Ulster was determined to resist Home Rule. The formation of the Ulster Unionist Council in 1905 and the Ulster Volunteer Force in 1913 revealed an unwillingness of the Ulster Protestants to subordinate their identity to Irish nationalism. In 1914 the country came to the brink of civil war.

Half a million men of Irish descent, both Protestant and Catholic, volunteered to fight for Britain in 1914; fewer than 2,000 rose in the Easter Rising of 1916 in Dublin. The planned nationalist uprising failed to materialize outside Dublin. The British response, however, served to radicalize Irish public opinion. Martial law was declared and a series of trials, executions, and internments provided martyrs for the nationalist cause. In the 1918 general election 73 out of the 105 Irish parliamentary seats were won by Sinn Féin (Nationalists) under Eámon de Valera.

In January 1919 a unilateral Declaration of Independence was issued by a new national assembly (Dail Eireann) and the nationalist Irish Volunteers, soon to rename themselves the Irish Republican Army, staged their first fatal ambush. A brutal civil war ensued (1919–21), followed by the Anglo-Irish Treaty in December 1921, which brought partition and effective independence for the new Irish Free State. Six counties in Ulster opted out as Northern Ireland, which remained part of the United Kingdom.

by Jeremy Black

Leisure Centre, once the largest in Europe, Irvine Beach Park, and the Scottish Maritime Museum.

Irvine, Andrew Robertson (1951–)
Scottish rugby union player who held the world record for the most points scored in senior international rugby with 301 (273 for Scotland, 28 for the British Lions) between 1972 and 1982.

Irving, Henry stage name of John Henry Brodribb (1838–1905)
English actor. He established his reputation from 1871,

IRVING, HENRY *The leading English actor of the Victorian stage, Henry Irving was best known for his Shakespearean roles – he is shown here playing Shylock. He was held in such high esteem that he became the first English actor to be knighted. Linda Proud*

chiefly at the Lyceum Theatre in London, where he became manager in 1878. He staged a series of successful Shakespearean productions, including *Romeo and Juliet* (1882), with himself and Ellen ◊Terry playing the leading roles. He was the first actor to be knighted, in 1895.

Irwell

River in Lancashire, England; length 48 km/30 mi. The Irwell rises in the Rossendale upland, 3 km/2 mi south of Burnley, and flows into the Manchester Ship Canal.

In the 19th century it was described as 'the most hard-worked river in the world', because so many cotton mills used its water. As a result, it was also one of the most polluted, but with the decline of local heavy industry it has become much cleaner.

Isaacs, Alick (1921–1967)

Scottish virologist who, with Swiss colleague Jean Lindemann, in 1957 discovered interferon, a naturally occurring antiviral substance produced by cells infected with viruses. The full implications of this discovery are still being investigated.

Isaacs, Jeremy (1932–)

English television producer, and television and opera administrator. His television career began with ITV in current affairs, and from there he went on to produce the major historical documentary series *The World at War* for Thames TV, for whom he worked for a decade from 1968. He was appointed chief executive of Channel 4, which began broadcasting in 1982. In 1988 he left to be director of the Royal Opera House, Covent Garden where he stayed until 1997, subsequently producing another major documentary series, *Cold War* (1998), for the BBC.

As Channel 4's first chief executive he played a large part in establishing its alternative approach and championed the slot for newly commissioned film drama, *Film on Four*, which was to kick-start the British film industry after a fallow period. He was knighted in 1996.

Isherwood, Christopher (William Bradshaw) (1904–1986)

English novelist. He lived in Germany from 1929–33 just before Hitler's rise to power, a period that inspired *Mr Norris Changes Trains* (1935) and *Goodbye to Berlin* (1939), creating the character of Sally Bowles, the basis of the musical *Cabaret* (1968). Returning to England, he collaborated with W H ◊Auden in three verse plays.

Isherwood was born in Disley, Cheshire, and educated at Cambridge University. After temporary employment as a private secretary and tutor, he went to Berlin. His first novel, *All the Conspirators*, was published in 1928, and was followed by *The Memorial* (1932). His next novel, *Mr Norris Changes Trains*, established his reputation, consolidated by *Goodbye to Berlin*.

In 1938 he went with Auden to China to write a book with him about conditions there, *Journey to a War* (1939).

Isherwood afterwards lived in California, becoming a US citizen in 1946.

Ishiguro, Kazuo (1954–)

Japanese-born British novelist. His novel *An Artist of the Floating World* won the 1986 Whitbread Prize, and *The Remains of the Day*, about an English butler coming to realize the extent of his self-sacrifice and self-deception, won the 1989 Booker Prize and was made into a successful film in 1993. His work is characterized by a sensitive style and subtle structure.

Ishiguro moved with his family to England in 1960 and has worked briefly as a social worker. He attended the creative writing course established by Malcolm ◊Bradbury and Angus ◊Wilson at the University of East Anglia 1979–80. His first novel, *A Pale View of Hills* (1982), takes place mainly in his native Nagasaki, dealing obliquely with the aftermath of the atom bomb. A recent work is *The Unconsoled* (1995).

Isis
Local name for the River ◊Thames around Oxford.

Islandmagee
Peninsula on the coast of Antrim, Northern Ireland, near Larne; area 11 km/7 mi by 3 km/2 mi. There are large basalt cliffs on the east side, a section of which is known as the Gobbins.

There is a dolmen (Neolithic stone chamber) known as the Druid's Chair, at which a number of ornaments and funeral urns have been found.

In 1642 the inhabitants of Islandmagee were killed by forces from Carrickfergus, some reputedly by being thrown off the cliffs. Slaughterford Bridge commemorates this event.

Islay
Southernmost island of the Inner ◊Hebrides, on the west coast of Scotland, in Argyll and Bute, separated from Jura by the Sound of Islay; area 610 sq km/235 sq mi; population (1991) 3,500. The principal towns are Bowmore, Port Charlotte, and Port Ellen. It is renowned for its malt whisky and its wildlife, which includes eagles and rare wintering geese.

The highest summit is Beinn Bheigeir (491 m/1,611 ft). Loch Finlaggan, near Port Askaig in the north, was once the site of the principal seat of the 'Lord of the Isles' during the 14th and 15th centuries. The Kidalton Cross, 11 km/7 mi northeast of Port Ellen, is one of the best-preserved Celtic crosses in Scotland. There are seven whisky distilleries on the island.

Car ferry services connect Islay (Port Askaig) to Oban on the mainland via Scalascaig (Colonsay), and Port Askaig and Port Ellen to Kennacraig on the mainland.

Isle of Man
See ◊Man, Isle of.

Isle of Wight
See ◊Wight, Isle of.

Isles, Lord of the
Title adopted by successive heads of the MacDonald clan to assert their dominance over the Scottish highlands and the Western Isles, and independence from the king of Scots. James IV acquired their rights in 1493 and today the title is held by the Prince of Wales as heir to the monarch in Scotland.

Islington
Inner borough of north Greater London. It includes the suburbs of Finsbury, Barnsbury, and Holloway.

Features
Sadler's Wells music hall, built in 1638 when Clerkenwell springs were exploited and Islington Spa became famous; present Sadler's Wells theatre (1927–31), where opera and ballet companies were established under direction of Lilian ◊Baylis; 16th-century St John's Gate at Clerkenwell; 17th-century houses at Newington Green; 18th- and 19th-century squares and terraces in Canonbury, Highbury, and Barnsbury; Wesley's Chapel (1777, restored 1978), with museum of Methodism and John Wesley's house; Regents Canal, with tunnel 886 m/2,910 ft long; Tower Theatre (1952) in early 16th-century Canonbury Tower; Kings Head, pioneer of public-house theatres in the late 1960s; Almeida Theatre; Packington estate; Business Design Centre; Chapel Market; Pentonville and Holloway prisons; Camden Passage (antiques centre)

Famous people
Duncan Grant, Vanessa Bell, George Weedon Grossmith, Basil Spence, and Yehudi Menuhin all lived here; Tony Blair

Population (1991) 164,700.

Issigonis, Alec (Alexander Arnold Constantine) (1906–1988)
Turkish-born British engineer who designed the Morris Minor (1948) and the Mini-Minor (1959) cars, comfortable yet cheaper to run than their predecessors. He is credited with adding the word 'mini' to the English language.

Overseeing the separate approaches of styling, interior packaging, body engineering, and chassis layout, Issigonis conceived the overall vehicle; specialists in his team then designed and engineered the subsystems of the car. His designs gave much greater space for the occupants together with greatly increased dynamic handling stability. He was knighted in 1969.

ITC
Abbreviation for ◊**Independent Television Commission**.

ITV, or Independent Television
Independent television in the UK, paid for by advertising, dating from 1955. In 1998 there were 16 ITV licensees:

ISSIGONIS, ALEC *The Mini, one of the most successful small cars in the history of motoring, was the brainchild of the engineer Alec Issigonis. He anticipated the needs of the city driver by designing a practical runabout vehicle that was manoeuvrable in traffic and easy to park. The Mini's clean lines and urban chic made it an instant hit in the 1960s, and it has remained popular ever since. Corel*

Anglia, Border, Carlton, Central, Channel, GMTV, Grampian, Granada, HTV, London Weekend, Meridian, Scottish, Tyne Tees, Ulster, West Country, and Yorkshire. Their 10-year licences were granted from January 1993. Independent television companies are regulated by the ◊Independent Television Commission (ITC), and are required to provide quality, independent productions, with provision for viewers with disabilities.

Independent television broadcasting in the UK began on 22 September 1955. It was set up by the 1954 Television Act, which created a regulatory body called the Independent Television Authority (ITA), subsequently called the Independent Broadcasting Authority (IBA), and then the Independent Television Commission (ITC). Franchises were awarded on a regional basis, the first franchise being the London area, and with other regions added progressively until the whole country was covered in 1965. At first there were few changes to the franchises, but in 1993 the franchise system was changed to require companies to bid competitively for the franchise in each area (subject to each bid meeting the ITC's standards for programme quality and a satisfactory business plan). Thames TV, the franchise owner for weekdays in the London area, lost its franchise to Carlton Communications; although Granada TV was outbid by another consortium, it retained its franchise.

See also ◊television and ◊comedy.

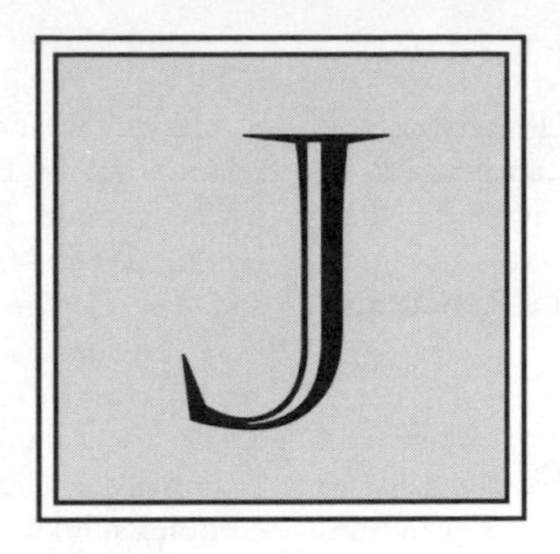

Jackson, Barry Vincent (1879–1961)

English theatre director. He built the Birmingham Repertory Theatre in 1913 and ran it until his death. He also founded the Malvern Festival, providing the annual productions 1929–37. From 1945 to 1948 he was director of the theatre at Stratford-upon-Avon, Warwickshire. He was knighted in 1925.

Jackson, Glenda (1936–)

English actress and politician, Labour member of Parliament from 1992 and parliamentary under-secretary for transport from 1997. Her many stage appearances for the Royal Shakespeare Company include *Marat/Sade* (1966), Hedda in *Hedda Gabler* (1975), and Cleopatra in *Antony and Cleopatra* (1978). Among her films are the Oscar-winning *Women in Love* (1969), *Sunday Bloody Sunday* (1971), and *A Touch of Class* (1973). On television she played Queen Elizabeth I in *Elizabeth R* (1971).

Jackson, John Hughlings (1835–1911)

English neurologist and neurophysiologist. As a result of his studies of epilepsy, Jackson demonstrated that specific areas of the cerebral cortex (outer mantle of the brain) control the functioning of particular organs and limbs.

He also demonstrated that Helmholtz's ophthalmoscope is a crucial diagnostic tool for disorders of the nervous system.

Jack the Ripper

Popular name for the unidentified mutilator and murderer of at least five women prostitutes in the Whitechapel area of London in 1888.

The murders understandably provoked public outrage; the police were heavily criticized, which later led to a reassessment of police procedures. Jack the Ripper's identity has never been discovered, although several suspects have been proposed, including members of the royal household.

Jacobean

Style in the arts, particularly in architecture and furniture, during the reign of James I (1603–25) in England. Following the general lines of Elizabethan design, the Jacobean period was one of transition, using classical features with greater complexity and with more profuse ornamentation, and adopting many motifs from Italian Renaissance design.

An extreme example is the 'Tower of the Five Orders' (1613–18) at the Bodleian Library, Oxford, where the Classical Orders decorate a building with mullioned windows, battlements, and pinnacles.

A sudden change to full-blown Italian Renaissance architecture occurred early in the 17th century with the arrival of the Classical architect Inigo Jones, designer of the Queen's House, Greenwich (1617–35), and the Banqueting House, Whitehall (1619–22). Other notable Jacobean buildings include ◊Hatfield House, Hertfordshire (1607–12), and Blicking Hall, Norfolk (completed 1628), both by Robert Lyminge.

The most important example of ecclesiastical building is St John's Church, Leeds (1634), which is entirely Gothic in structure and general design, but contains magnificent Jacobean (strictly 'Carolean') interior woodwork fittings.

Jacobi, Derek (George) (1938–)

English actor. His powerful and sensitive talent has ensured a succession of leading roles in Shakespearean and other mainly serious drama on stage, television, and film. In the theatre he has several times played the title role in *Hamlet*, notably in 1979 at the Old Vic in London. Television appearances include the title role in *I, Claudius* (1976).

Other stage work includes *The Tempest* and *Peer Gynt* (1982), *Cyrano de Bergerac* (1983), *Much Ado About Nothing* (1985), *Richard II* (1988), *Richard III* (1989), *Becket* (1991), *Macbeth* (1993–94), and the role of Claudius in Kenneth Branagh's adaption of *Hamlet* (1996). Films include *Day of the Jackal* (1973), *Little Dorrit* (1987), *Henry V* (1989), and *Dead Again* (1991). He recently starred as Francis Bacon in the British biopic *Love Is the Devil* (1998).

He has starred on British television as the medieval sleuth in *Cadfael* since 1994.

Jacobite

Supporter of the royal house of Stuart after the deposition of James II in 1688. They include the Scottish Highlanders, who rose unsuccessfully under ◊Claverhouse in 1689; and those who rose in Scotland and northern England in 1715 under the leadership of ◊James Edward Stuart, the Old Pretender, and followed his son ◊Charles Edward Stuart in an invasion of England from 1745 to 1746 that reached Derby. After their final defeat at ◊Culloden, Jacobitism disappeared as a political force. The two risings are known as the **Jacobite Rebellions**.

Jacobson, Dan (1929–)

South African born British novelist, short-story writer, and critic. After being a teacher in London and a journalist in South Africa, he settled in Britain in 1958. His earlier fiction, beginning with *The Trap* (1955), and including *The Evidence of Love* (1960) and the short-story collection *Beggar My Neighbour* (1964), have South African themes. He has subsequently explored alternative narrative techniques and biblical and historical themes in *The Rape of Tamar* (1970), *The God-Fearer* (1992), and other novels.

Jacobson was born in Johannesburg, the son of Jewish immigrants from Lithuania, and educated at Witwatersrand University. He was appointed a lecturer at University College, London in 1976, reader in English in 1980, professor in 1988, and professor emeritus in 1994. *The Story of Stories* (1982) and *Adult Pleasures* (1988) are works of criticism. *The Electric Elephant* (1994) is a travel book. *Time and Time Again* (1985) is an autobiography.

Jaffrey, Saeed (1929–)

Indian actor. He has become a mainstay of British screen productions exploring both contemporary Asian-British culture and the period of British rule in India. A long-serving character actor, he featured as Billy Fish in *The Man Who Would Be King* (1975) and as a slick crime boss in Stephen Frears's slice of 1980s Britain *My Beautiful Laundrette* (1986). His other films include *Bollywood* (1994), *The Journey* (1997), and *Guru in Seven* (1998).

He also appeared in the television miniseries *The Jewel in the Crown* and *The Far Pavillions* (both 1984). In the 1990s, he divided his time between Indian, North American, and British projects.

Jagger, Mick (Michael Philip) (1943–)

English singer and songwriter, lead singer of the rock band the ◊Rolling Stones.

Jaguar

British car manufacturer that has enjoyed a long association with motor racing; owned by Ford from 1989. One of the most successful companies in the 1950s, Jaguar won the Le Mans 24-hour race five times 1951–58. They enjoyed a comeback at Le Mans in the late 1980s winning in 1988 and 1990.

The legendary XK120 was built in 1949. In the 1960s Jaguar were unable to compete with more powerful Ferrari sports cars and they did not make a comeback until the 1980s. In 1989 the company was bought by Ford for £1.6 billion.

James, Henry (1843–1916)

US novelist, who lived in Europe from 1875 and became a naturalized British subject in 1915. His novels deal with the social, moral, and aesthetic issues arising from the complex relationship of European to American culture. His major novels include *The Portrait of a Lady* (1881), *The Bostonians* (1886), *What Maisie Knew* (1887), *The Ambassadors* (1903), and *The Golden Bowl* (1904). He also wrote more than a hundred shorter works of fiction, notably the novella *The Aspern Papers* (1888) and the supernatural/psychological riddle *The Turn of the Screw* (1898).

Initially a master of psychological realism, noted for the complex subtlety of his prose style, James became increasingly experimental, writing some of the essential works of early Modernism. Other major novels include *Roderick Hudson* (1876), *The American* (1877), *Washington Square* (1881), *The Tragic Muse* (1890), *The Spoils of Poynton* (1897), *The Awkward Age* (1899), and *The Wings of the Dove* (1902). He also wrote travel sketches, including *The American Scene* (1906), which records his impressions on returning to the USA after 20 years' absence, and literary criticism, including *Notes on Novelists* (1914).

James, M(ontague) R(hodes) (1862–1936)

English writer, theologian, linguist, and medievalist. He is best known for his frightening ghost tales, including *Ghost Stories of an Antiquary* (1904) and other supernatural tales. His collected stories were published in 1931.

James, P(hyllis) D(orothy), Baroness James of Holland Park (1920–)

English detective novelist. She created the characters Superintendent Adam Dalgliesh and private investigator Cordelia Gray. She was a tax official, hospital administrator, and civil servant in the Home Office, involved with police matters, before turning to writing. Her books include *Death of an Expert Witness* (1977), *The Skull Beneath the Skin* (1982), *A Taste for Death* (1986), *Original Sin* (1994), and *Certain Justice* (1997). She became a baroness in 1991.

James

Two kings of Britain:

James I (1566–1625)

King of England from 1603 and Scotland (as **James VI**) from 1567. The son of Mary Queen of Scots and her second husband, Lord Darnley, he succeeded to the Scottish throne on the enforced abdication of his mother and assumed power in 1583. He established a strong centralized authority, and in 1589 married Anne of Denmark (1574–1619).

As successor to Elizabeth I in England, he alienated the Puritans by his High Church views and Parliament by his assertion of ◊divine right, and was generally unpopular because of his favourites, such as George Villiers, 1st Duke of ◊Buckingham, and his schemes for an alliance with Spain. He was succeeded by his son Charles I.

As king of Scotland, he curbed the power of the nobility, although his attempts to limit the authority of the Kirk (Church of Scotland) were less successful.

Upon his accession to the English throne on the death of Elizabeth I, James acted mainly upon the advice of Robert

JAMES I *The son of Mary, Queen of Scots, James I of England was already King of Scotland when he came to the throne in England in 1603. Private collection*

Cecil, Earl of Salisbury, but on the latter's death all restraint vanished.

His religious policy consisted of asserting the supreme authority of the crown and suppressing both Puritans and Catholics who objected. The preparation of the Authorized Version of the Bible in English, published in 1611, was ordered by James.

He thwarted Guy Fawkes's plot to blow up Parliament during its opening in 1605. The ◊gunpowder plot, with its anti-Catholic reaction, gave James a temporary popularity which soon dissipated. His foreign policy, aimed primarily at achieving closer relations with Spain, was also disliked.

James II (1633–1701)

King of England and Scotland (as **James VII**) from 1685. The second son of Charles I, he succeeded his brother, Charles II. In 1660 James married Anne Hyde (1637–1671, mother of Mary II and Anne) and in 1673 ◊Mary of Modena (mother of James Edward Stuart). He became a Catholic in 1671, which led first to attempts to exclude him from the succession, then to the rebellions of ◊Monmouth and Argyll, and finally to the Whig and Tory leaders' invitation to William of Orange to take the throne in 1688. James fled to France, then led an uprising in Ireland in 1689, but after defeat at the Battle of the Boyne (1690) remained in exile in France.

At the Restoration in 1660 he was appointed lord high admiral and warden of the Cinque Ports, but after the passing of the ◊Test Act in 1673 (which excluded Catholics from public office) he was forced to give up his offices. On his accession to the throne he promised to defend the Church of England, and his reign began peacefully enough. However, the unnecessarily savage repression of the Monmouth rising in 1685 by Judge Jeffreys' ◊Bloody Assizes alienated many supporters, and the birth of his son in 1688 further destroyed English hopes of a Protestant succession, prompting the invitation to William of Orange to claim the throne in the ◊Glorious Revolution.

James

Seven kings of Scotland:

James I (1394–1437)

King of Scotland 1406–37, who assumed power in 1424. He was a cultured and strong monarch whose improvements in the administration of justice brought him popularity among the common people. He was assassinated by a group of conspirators led by the Earl of Atholl, and was succeeded by his son James II.

James II (1430–1460)

King of Scotland from 1437, who assumed power in 1449. The only surviving son of James I, he was supported by most of the nobles and parliament. He sympathized with the Lancastrians during the Wars of the ◊Roses, and attacked English possessions in southern Scotland. He was killed while besieging Roxburgh Castle.

Almost continual civil war raged during the period of his minority; the prize of the victors was the custody of the king. In 1449 he married Mary, daughter of the Duke of Gueldres. He was succeeded by his son James III.

James III (1451–1488)

King of Scotland from 1460, who assumed power 1469. His reign was marked by rebellions by the nobles, including his brother Alexander, Duke of Albany. He was murdered during a rebellion supported by his son, who then ascended the throne as James IV.

Eldest son of James II, he became king at the age of nine. In 1469 he married Margaret, daughter of King Christian I of Denmark.

James IV (1473–1513)

King of Scotland from 1488. He came to the throne after his followers murdered his father, James III, at Sauchieburn. His reign was internally peaceful, but he allied himself with France against England, invaded in 1513, and was defeated and killed at the Battle of ◊Flodden. James IV was a patron of poets and architects as well as a military leader.

In 1503 he married Margaret Tudor (1489–1541, daughter of Henry VII), which eventually led to his descendants succeeding to the English crown. He was succeeded by his son James V.

James V (1512–1542)

King of Scotland from 1513, who assumed power in 1528. During the long period of his minority, he was caught in a struggle between pro-French and pro-English factions. When he assumed power, he allied himself with France and upheld Catholicism against the Protestants. Following an attack on Scottish territory by Henry VIII's forces, he was defeated near the border at Solway Moss in 1542.

Son of James IV and Margaret Tudor, he succeeded his father at the age of one year. His first wife, Madeline, daughter of King Francis I of France, died in 1537; the following year he married Mary of Guise. Their daughter, Mary Queen of Scots, succeeded him.

James VI

Of Scotland. See ◊James I of England.

James VII

Of Scotland. See ◊James II of England.

James Francis Edward Stuart (1688–1766)

British prince, known as the **Old Pretender** (for the ◊Jacobites, he was James III). Son of James II, he was born at St James's Palace and after the revolution of 1688 was taken to France. He landed in Scotland in 1715 to head a Jacobite rebellion but withdrew through lack of support. In his later years he settled in Rome.

Jameson, (Margaret) Storm (1897–1986)

English novelist. Among her finest books are *The Lovely Ship* (1927), *The Voyage Home* (1930), and *A Richer Dust* (1931), which form a trilogy telling of a shipbuilding family like her own; others are *The Black Laurel* (1948), *The Hidden River* (1955), *Last Score* (1961), and *The White Crow* (1968). *Full Circle* (1928) is a one-act play and *No Time Like the Present* (1933) is an autobiography.

Jameson, Leander Starr (1853–1917)

Scottish colonial administrator. In South Africa, early in 1896, he led the **Jameson Raid** from Mafeking into the Transvaal to support the non-Boer colonists there, in an attempt to overthrow the government (for which he served some months in prison). Returning to South Africa, he succeeded Cecil ◊Rhodes as leader of the Progressive Party of Cape Colony, where he was prime minister 1904–08.

Jamiroquai

English pop group formed in 1992. Influenced by funk groups, including the Isley Brothers and Earth Wind and Fire, their album *Emergency On Planet Earth* (1993) was an instant UK chart success. Subsequent albums include *Jay's Selection* (1996) and *Travelling Without Moving* (1996).

The group's members are Jason Kay (1969–) (vocals), Simon Katz (1971–) (guitar), Stuart Zender (1974–) (bass), Toby Smith (1970–) (keyboards), Wallis Buchannan (1965–) (didgeridoo), and Derrick McKenzie (1962–) (drums).

Jane Eyre

Novel (1847) by Charlotte ◊Brontë. The orphan Jane becomes governess to the ward of Mr Rochester. Employer and governess fight a mutual fascination until Jane agrees to marriage. The revelation that Mr Rochester already has a wife, the mad Bertha, who is imprisoned in his attic, causes Jane's flight. She returns to marry Rochester after Bertha has killed herself by setting the house on fire. In this ever popular book, romantic themes derive distinction from Brontë's powerful intellect and imagination.

Jarman, Derek (1942–1994)

English avant-garde film director. Jarman made several low-budget, highly innovative features. His homosexuality was a dominant refrain in his work and he was a committed campaigner for gay rights. His films include *Sebastiane* (1975), with dialogue spoken in Latin; *Caravaggio* (1986); *Edward II* (1991), a free adaptation of Christopher Marlowe's play; and his biography of the philosopher *Wittgenstein* (1993).

Jarman's films often deal with historical subjects using deliberate elements of anachronism and contemporary comment, to provocative effect. His work provoked strong reactions, ranging from admiration for his formal daring, to rejection for what was seen as wilful obscurity. **Derek Jarman's Garden** lies near the old lighthouse at Dungeness in Kent, England.

Jarrow (Saxon 'marsh' or 'fen')

Town in Tyne and Wear, northeast England, on the south bank of the River Tyne, 10 km/6 mi east of Newcastle and connected with the north bank by the Tyne Tunnel (1967); population (1991) 29,300. Industries include the production of chemicals, oil, iron and steel, processed foods, industrial pipework, and paper. In 1933 the closure of Palmer's shipyard in Jarrow prompted the ◊Jarrow Crusade of 1936, a landmark event of the Depression.

The Venerable ◊Bede lived in a monastery here from about 682 until his death in 735.

Features

The chancel of St Paul's Church incorporates part of the original 7th-century monastic foundation, as well as a Saxon window with Saxon stained glass. Bede's World illustrates the history of the monastery and the life of Bede.

Early history

The marsh for which Jarrow is named is the **Jarrow Slake** (a corruption of Jarrow's Lake), an estuary of the Tyne to the east of the town. Bede wrote his *Historia Ecclesiastica Gentis Anglorum/Ecclesiastical History of the English People* (731) while living in the monastery.

Industrial history

In the 19th century coalmining began in the area, the shipbuilding industry was established by the Palmer brothers, and iron works were founded alongside the shipyards. The world's first oil tanker was produced here and some 900 ships were launched from Jarrow prior to 1933. However, demand for ships and steel declined after World War I and many of the workforce became unemployed.

Jarrow Crusade

March in 1936 from Jarrow to London, protesting at the high level of unemployment following the closure of Palmer's shipyard in the town.

The march was led by Labour MP Ellen Wilkinson, and it proved a landmark event of the 1930s Depression. In 1986, on the fiftieth anniversary of the event, a similar march was held to protest at the high levels of unemployment in the 1980s.

Jason, David stage name of David White (1949–)

English actor specializing in comic TV roles with enduring appeal, but who is equally adept at straight acting. Best known as the cockney wideboy Del Boy Trotter in the long-running BBC sitcom *Only Fools And Horses* (from 1981, Christmas special 1993), he also took a lead role in *Open All Hours* (from 1976) and played Pop Larkin in *The Darling Buds of May* (1991). His portrayal of a quirky, widowed detective in several series of *A Touch of Frost* in the 1990s underlined his versatility.

Jeans, James Hopwood (1877–1946)

English mathematician and scientist. In physics he worked on the kinetic theory of gases, and on forms of energy radiation; in astronomy, his work focused on giant and dwarf stars, the nature of spiral nebulae, and the origin of the cosmos. He did much to popularize astronomy. He was knighted in 1928.

Jedburgh

Small town in the Scottish Borders unitary authority, Scotland, on **Jed Water**, 77 km/48 mi south of Edinburgh; population (1991) 4,100. It has the remains of a 12th-century abbey. Jedburgh is a woollen manufacturing centre.

The town's medieval castle was destroyed in 1409, and a prison built on its site in 1823. The fortified town house where Mary Queen of Scots stayed in 1566 is now a museum. The abbey was originally a church attached to an Augustinian priory founded by David I. The Spread Eagle is reputed to be the oldest hotel in Scotland and the fourth oldest in the British Isles.

Jedburgh has associations with Charles Edward Stuart, and with the poet Robert Burns. The town is more popularly known locally as either Jethart or Jeddart. 'Jeddart Justice' means to hang a person first, and try them afterwards.

Jefferies, (John) Richard (1848–1887)

English naturalist and writer. His books on the countryside include *Gamekeeper at Home* (1878), *The Life of the Fields* (1884), and his best-known collection of essays, *The Open Air* (1885). *Bevis: The Story of a Boy* (1882) is a nostalgic novel of the countryside. *Story of My Heart* (1883) is an autobiographical study.

In depicting the countryside and wildlife surviving in the face of modern civilization, there have been few English novelists to equal Jefferies. His work underwent a critical revaluation in the later 20th century and is often compared with that of Thomas ◊Hardy.

Jeffrey, Francis, Lord Jeffrey (1773–1850)

Scottish lawyer and literary critic. He was a founder of the *Edinburgh Review* in 1802 and editor from 1803–29. In 1830 he was made Lord Advocate, and in 1834 a Scottish law lord. Among his critical works are *Samuel Richardson* (1852) and *Jonathan Swift* (1853). He was hostile to the Romantic poets, and wrote of Wordsworth's *Excursion*: 'This will never do.'

Jeffreys, Alec John (1950–)

British geneticist who discovered the DNA probes necessary for accurate ◊genetic fingerprinting so that a murderer or rapist could be identified by, for example, traces of blood, tissue, or semen.

Jeffreys of Wem, George, 1st Baron Jeffreys of Wem (1644–1689)

Welsh judge, popularly known as 'the hanging judge'. He became Chief Justice of the King's Bench in 1683, and presided over many political trials, notably those of Philip Sidney, Titus Oates, and Richard Baxter, becoming notorious for his brutality.

Jeffreys was born in Denbighshire. In 1685 he became Lord Chancellor and, after ◊Monmouth's rebellion, conducted the 'bloody assizes' during which 320 rebels were executed and hundreds more flogged, imprisoned, or transported. He was captured when attempting to flee the country after the revolution of 1688, and died in the Tower of London. He was knighted in 1677 and was made a baron in 1685.

Jeffries, Lionel (1926–)

English actor, writer, and film director. Much-loved for his comic performances in films such as *Blue Murder at St Trinian's* (1957) and *Chitty Chitty Bang Bang* (1968), he also played the occasional horror role before directing a series of popular children's films, including *The Railway Children* (1972), which he also scripted, and *The Water Babies* (1978).

He continued to act throughout the 1980s and 1990s, appearing, for example, in *A Chorus of Disapproval* (1988), although much of his recent work has been on television.

Jekyll, Gertrude (1843–1932)

English landscape gardener and writer. She created over 300 gardens, many in collaboration with the architect Edwin ◊Lutyens. In her books, she advocated colour design in garden planning and natural gardens of the cottage type, with plentiful herbaceous borders.

Originally a painter and embroiderer, she took up landscape design at the age of 48 when her eyesight deteriorated. Her home at Munstead Wood, Surrey, was designed for her by Lutyens.

Jellicoe, Geoffrey Alan (1900–1996)

English architect, landscape architect, and historian. His contribution to 20th-century thinking on landscapes and gardens has been mainly through his writings, notably *The Landscape of Man* (1975). However, he also made an impact as a designer, working in a contemplative and poetic vein and frequently incorporating water and sculptures. Representative of his work are the Kennedy Memorial (1965) at Runnymede, Berkshire, where a granite path winds uphill to a memorial stone by an American Scarlet oak; and the Sutton Place gardens, Sussex (1980–84).

Jellicoe's designs show the influence of modern artists, such as Paul Klee and Ben Nicholson, while his information centre and restaurant at Cheddar Gorge, Somerset, built in 1934, reflects the work of German architect Erich Mendelsohn. He was knighted in 1979.

Jenkins, Neil Roger (1971–)

Welsh rugby union player. A brilliant goal kicker who usually plays at stand-off though has sometimes been selected at full-back, he made his international debut in 1991, and by the end of the 1998 Five Nations championship had scored 594 points in 57 games, 290 more than any other Welshman has achieved. One of the stars of the triumphant British Lions tour of South Africa in 1997, he scored 41 of the Lions' 59 points in the three-test series.

He has scored over 1,800 points in the Welsh league for Pontypridd, 1990–98, and led the club to the SWALEC Cup in 1996 and the Welsh league in 1997.

Jenkins, Roy Harris, Baron Jenkins of Hillhead (1920–)

British politician. He became a Labour minister in 1964, was home secretary 1965–67 and 1974–76, and chancellor of the Exchequer 1967–70. He was president of the European Commission 1977–81. In 1981 he became one of the founders of the Social Democratic Party and was elected as an SDP MP in 1982, but lost his seat in 1987. In the same year, he was elected chancellor of Oxford University and made a life peer. In 1997 he was appointed head of a commission, set up by the Labour government, to recommend, in 1998, a new voting system for United Kingdom Westminster elections.

JENNER, EDWARD *English physician Edward Jenner, who discovered the technique of inoculation to produce immunity against smallpox and other diseases. Smallpox, which was once a major cause of death throughout the world, has since been irradicated. Corbis*

Jenkins was a leading member of the pro-European supporters in the referendum campaign of 1975. He unsuccessfully contested the Labour leadership in 1976.

Jenkins's Ear, War of

War in 1739 between Britain and Spain, arising from Britain's illicit trade in Spanish America; it merged into the War of the Austrian Succession 1740–48. The name derives from the claim of Robert Jenkins, a merchant captain, that his ear had been cut off by Spanish coastguards near Jamaica. The incident was seized on by opponents of Robert ◊Walpole who wanted to embarrass his government's antiwar policy and force war with Spain.

Jenner, Edward (1749–1823)

English physician who pioneered vaccination. In Jenner's day, smallpox was a major killer. His discovery in 1796 that inoculation with cowpox gives immunity to smallpox was a great medical breakthrough.

Jenner observed that people who worked with cattle and contracted cowpox from them never subsequently caught smallpox. In 1798 he published his findings that a child inoculated with cowpox, then two months later with smallpox, did not get smallpox. He coined the word 'vaccination' from the Latin word for cowpox, *vaccinia*.

Jennings, Pat (Patrick) (1945–)

Irish footballer. In his 21-year career he was an outstanding goalkeeper. He won a British record 119 international caps for Northern Ireland 1964–86 (now surpassed by Peter ◊Shilton), and played League football for Watford, Tottenham Hotspur, and Arsenal.

Jerome, Jerome K(lapka) (1859–1927)

English journalist and writer. His works include the novel *Three Men in a Boat* (1889), a humorous account of a trip on the Thames from Kingston to Oxford; the humorous essays 'Idle Thoughts of an Idle Fellow' (1889); and the play *The Passing of the Third Floor Back* (story 1908, dramatized version 1910).

Three Men in a Boat was followed by *Three Men on the Bummel* (1900), a less entertaining account of a tour in Germany.

Jersey

Largest of the ◊Channel Islands; capital St Helier; area 117 sq km/45 sq mi; population (1991) 58,900. It is governed by a lieutenant governor representing the English crown and an assembly. Jersey cattle were originally bred here. Jersey gave its name to a woollen garment

The island was occupied from 1940 until 1945 by German forces. Jersey zoo (founded in 1959 by Gerald Durrell) is engaged in breeding some of the world's endangered species.

Jersey
Breed of small short-horned dairy cows originating in Jersey, Channel Islands, probably descended from French cattle. They are usually a shade of fawn or cream in colour, are adaptable to a wide range of conditions, and are found worldwide. Their milk is very rich in butterfat but they are not desirable producers of beef.

Jervaulx Abbey
Ruined Cistercian monastery in North Yorkshire, England, on the banks of the River Ure, 8 km/5 mi southeast of Leyburn. The abbey was founded in 1156. The remains of the cruciform church, the cloistral courts, chapter-house, refectory, and nine-windowed dormitory, belong to the Transitional Norman or Early English period.

The last abbot was hanged in 1537 because he was implicated in the Pilgrimage of Grace (1536–37), a rebellion against Henry VIII.

Jervis, John, 1st Earl of St Vincent (1735–1823)
English admiral who secured the blockage of Toulon, France, in 1795 during the Revolutionary Wars, and the defeat of the Spanish fleet off Cape St Vincent in 1797, in which Admiral ◊Nelson played a key part. Jervis was a rigid disciplinarian.

JET, Joint European Torus
Research facility at Culham, near Abingdon, Oxfordshire, that conducts experiments on nuclear fusion. It is the focus of the European effort to produce a safe and environmentally sound fusion-power reactor. On 9 November 1991 the JET tokamak, operating with a mixture of deuterium and iritium, produced a 1.7 megawatt pulse of power in an experiment that lasted two seconds. In 1997 isotopes of deuterium and tritium were fused to produce a record 21 megajoule of nuclear fusion power. JET has tested the first large-scale plant of the type needed to process and supply tritium in a future fusion power station.

Jewish community
The Jewish community in Britain numbers about 285,000 (1998); it is the largest in western Europe after that in France. The main groups are in Greater London (183,000), Manchester and Salford (28,000), Leeds (10,000), and Brighton and Hove (6,000). About 70% are affiliated to synagogues.

Jews first settled in Britain at the time of the Norman

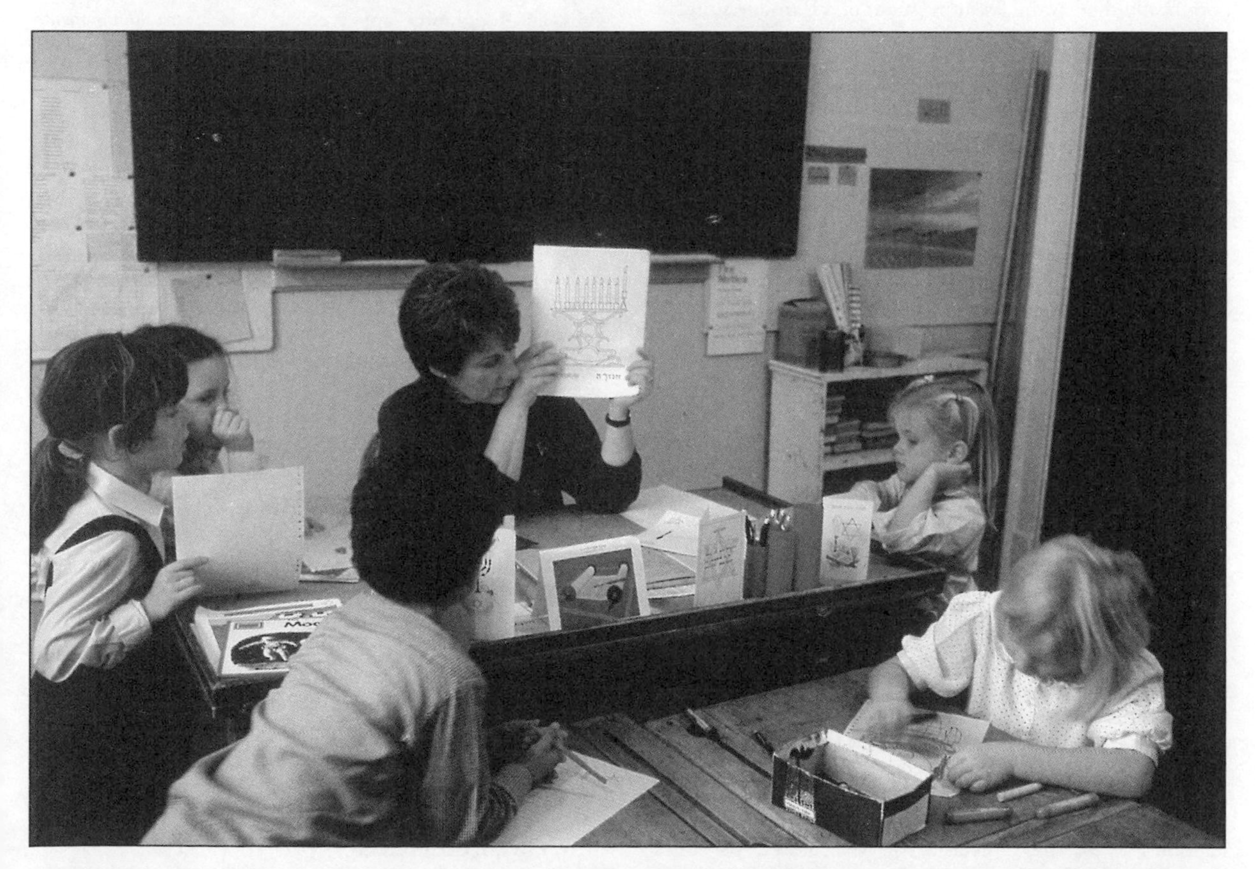

JEWISH COMMUNITY *A Jewish elementary school. Certain areas of Britain are strongly identified with the Jewish community, for example the Golders Green and Mansion House districts of North London (with sizeable numbers of orthodox Hassidic Jews). As tailoring was a traditional Jewish profession, communities also developed in centres of the garment industry such as Manchester and Leeds. Jewish leaders are concerned that numbers may dwindle as more Jews marry and raise children outside the faith. Liba Taylor/Collections*

Conquest and remained until 1290, when they were banished by a royal decree. The present-day community was founded by Jews of Spanish and Portuguese origin, known as the Sephardim, who arrived in Britain in 1656; these now account for some 3% of the community. Later, more settlers came from Germany and eastern Europe. These are known as the Ashkenazim.

Most Ashkenazi Jews (63%) acknowledge the authority of the Chief Rabbi (from 1991 Dr Jonathan Sacks), while the more strictly observant (7%) have their own spiritual leaders, as do the Separdhim. There are about 360 Jewish congregations in Britain, and the officially recognized representative body for all groups is the Board of Deputies of British Jews, founded in 1760.

Reform Judaism, a branch of Judaism, has some 40 affiliated synagogues in the UK, collectively known as the Reform Synagogues of Great Britain. Their chief executive is Tony Bayfield, and in 1998 Mark Weiner was appointed Rabbi at the West London Synagogue.

jig

Dance popular in the British Isles during the 16th century, which is thought to have developed into the **gigue**, later commonly used as the last movement of a Baroque suite.

jingoism

Blinkered, war-mongering patriotism. The term originated in 1878, when the British prime minister Disraeli developed a pro-Turkish policy, which nearly involved the UK in war with Russia. His supporters' war song included the line 'We don't want to fight, but by jingo if we do ...'.

Jiricna, Eva (1939–)

Czech architect who has worked in the UK since 1968. Her fashion shops, bars, and cafés for the Joseph chain are built in a highly refined Modernist style.

jobseekers allowance

Social security benefit included by the Conservative government in the Jobseekers Act, 1995. The allowance became effective from October 1996. It replaced unemployment benefit and ◊income support, combining them into one payment for the unemployed. The Labour government inherited the jobseekers allowance after winning the May 1997 general election.

Jockey Club

Governing body of English ◊horse racing until 1993, when the British Horseracing Board was formed. The Jockey Club still oversees licensing and regulation. It was founded about 1750 at the Star and Garter, Pall Mall, London.

Jodrell Bank

Site in Cheshire, England, of the Nuffield Radio Astronomy Laboratories of the University of Manchester. Its largest instrument is the 76 m/250 ft radio dish (the Lovell Telescope), completed in 1957 and modified in 1970. A 38 × 25 m/125 × 82 ft elliptical radio dish was introduced in 1964, capable of working at shorter wave lengths.

These radio telescopes are used in conjunction with six smaller dishes up to 230 km/143 mi apart in an array called MERLIN (**m**ulti-**e**lement **r**adio-**l**inked **i**nterferometer **n**etwork) to produce detailed maps of radio sources.

John, Augustus Edwin (1878–1961)

Welsh painter. He is known for his vivacious portraits, including *The Smiling Woman* (1910; Tate Gallery, London), portraying his second wife, Dorelia McNeill. His sitters included such literary figures as Thomas Hardy, Dylan Thomas, W B Yeats, T E Lawrence, and James Joyce.

From 1910 to 1919 John led a nomadic existence in Ireland, Dorset, and Wales, producing many poetic small oil paintings of figures in landscape. His cartoon for a mural decoration, *Galway* (1916; Tate Gallery), shows an inclination for large-scale work which was never fully realized. During World War I he was an official artist to the Canadian Corps.

John's portraits are outstanding in their combined certainty of drawing and temperamental handling of paint. His sense of colour and a modified Post-Impressionism appear in their most assured in his landscapes of the south of France and his flower pieces. He produced beautiful drawings of the figure at every stage of his career, and also some etchings.

His autobiography appeared in two parts: *Chiaroscuro* (1952) and *Finishing Touches* (1964). He received the Order of Merit in 1942. His sister was the artist Gwen ◊John.

John, Barry (1945–)

Welsh rugby union player. One in a line of great Welsh fly-halves, he played a leading role in the British Lions' first ever series win in New Zealand 1971. He was first capped for Wales against Australia 1966, and gained a total of 25 caps, nearly all in combination with his Cardiff team mate Gareth ◊Edwards. In 1968 he toured South Africa with the British Lions, playing in one test. Three years later he scored a record 188 points on the Lions' unbeaten tour of Australia and New Zealand. He retired in 1972.

John, Elton stage name of Reginald Kenneth Dwight (1947–)

English pop singer, pianist, and composer whose long and flamboyant career reached unparalleled heights in 1997 when he rewrote his 'Candle in the Wind' hit for the funeral of Diana, Princess of Wales, a personal friend. In the 1970s he had seven consecutive hit albums. *Goodbye Yellow Brick Road* (1973) includes the hit 'Bennie and the Jets'; among his many other highly successful songs are 'Rocket Man', 'Crocodile Rock', and 'Daniel' (all 1972), 'Candle in the Wind' (1973), 'Pinball Wizard' (1975), 'Blue Eyes' (1982), 'Nikita' (1985), and 'Sacrifice' (1989), the last from his album *Sleeping with the Past*.

John, Gwen(dolen Mary) (1876–1939)

Welsh painter. She lived in France for most of her life. Many of her paintings depict young women or nuns (she converted to Catholicism in 1913), but she also painted calm, muted interiors.

Her style was characterized by a sensitive use of colour and of tone.

John (I) Lackland (1167–1216)

King of England from 1199 and acting king from 1189 during his brother Richard the Lion-Heart's absence on the Third Crusade.

He lost Normandy and almost all the other English possessions in France to Philip II of France by 1205. His repressive policies and excessive taxation brought him into conflict with his barons, and he was forced to seal the ◊Magna Carta in 1215. Later repudiation of it led to the first Barons' War 1215–17, during which he died. He was succeedeed by his son Henry III.

John's subsequent bad reputation was only partially deserved. It resulted from his intrigues against his brother Richard I, his complicity in the death of his nephew Arthur, Duke of Brittany (1187–1203), a rival for the English throne, and the effectiveness of his ruthless taxation policy, as well as his provoking Pope Innocent III to excommunicate England 1208–13. John's attempt to limit the papacy's right of interference in episcopal elections, which traditionally were the preserve of English kings, was resented by monastic sources, and these provided much of the evidence upon which his reign was later judged.

John Bull

Imaginary figure who is a personification of England. He is represented in cartoons and caricatures as a prosperous farmer of the 18th century.

The name was popularized by Dr John ◊Arbuthnot's political satire *History of John Bull* (1712), advocating the Tory policy of peace with France.

John Lewis Partnership

Organization that owns 22 department stores and 111 Waitrose supermarkets in the UK, employing more than 41,100 people (1995) on a profit-sharing basis. It was set up as a trust in 1929.

The first John Lewis store was opened in 1864 by John Lewis (1836–1928), a Somerset draper and haberdasher, joined in 1904 by his son John Spedan Lewis (1885–1963). They devised a profit-sharing scheme that was the precursor of the present partnership.

John of Gaunt (1340–1399)

English noble and politician, fourth (and third surviving) son of Edward III, Duke of Lancaster from 1362. He distinguished himself during the Hundred Years' War. During Edward's last years, and the years before Richard II attained the age of majority, he acted as head of government, and Parliament protested against his corrupt rule.

In 1359 he married Blanche, daughter of Henry, Duke of Lancaster (died 1361), whose title passed to John of Gaunt in 1362; their son became Henry IV of England. Blanche died in 1369 and three years later he married Constance, daughter of Pedro III of Castile. Their daughter Philippa (1359–1415) married King John I of Portugal (1357–1433). John of Gaunt assumed the title of King of Castile in 1372, but his efforts to establish his claim against his rival, Henry of Trastamare, proved unsuccessful; in 1387 he renounced all claims in favour of his daughter Catherine, who married Henry III of Castile (1379–1406) in 1393.

Constance died in 1394, and John of Gaunt married his mistress of long standing, Katharine Swynford (*c.* 1350–1403), with whom he already had four children; they were legitimized in 1397 by charter of Richard II, and founded the house of Beaufort, from whom Henry VII was descended.

John of Salisbury (*c.* 1115–1180)

English philosopher and historian. His *Policraticus* portrayed the church as the guarantee of liberty against the unjust claims of secular authority.

He studied in France 1130–1153, in Paris with Abelard, and at Chartres. He became secretary to Thomas à Becket and supported him against Henry II; he fled to France after Becket's murder, and became bishop of Chartres in 1176.

John o' Groats

Village in the northeast of Highland unitary authority, Scotland, about 3 km/2 mi west of Duncansby Head, Britain's northernmost point. It is the furthest point from Land's End on the British mainland.

It is named after the Dutchman John de Groot, who built a house there in the 16th century. There are ferry connections to Burwick on South Ronaldsay.

Johns, W(illiam) E(arl) known as 'Captain' Johns (1893–1968)

English author. From 1932 he wrote popular novels about World War I flying ace 'Biggles', now sometimes criticized for chauvinism, racism, and sexism. Johns was a flying officer in the RAF (there is no rank of captain) until his retirement in 1930.

Johnson, Amy (1903–1941)

English aviator. She made a solo flight from England to Australia in 1930, in 9 ½ days, and in 1932 made the fastest ever solo flight from England to Cape Town, South Africa. Her plane disappeared over the English Channel in World War II while she was serving with the Air Transport Auxiliary.

Johnson, Celia (1908–1982)

English stage and film actress. Much of her film work tended towards screen adaptations of stage productions, and she appeared in the Noël Coward pieces *In Which We Serve* (1942), *This Happy Breed* (1944), and *Brief Encounter* (1945). She also appeared in *The Prime of Miss Jean Brodie* (1969), her last film.

Johnson, Martin Osborne (1970–)

English rugby union second row forward who captained the British Lions on their victorious tour of South Africa in 1997. At 6ft 6in and 18 stone he has been a bulwark of the England scrum since making his international debut in 1993, and was a

JOHNSON, CELIA *English actress Celia Johnson playing Joan of Arc at the New Theatre, London. Johnson is perhaps best remembered for her role in David Lean's film* Brief Encounter. *Corbis*

key member of the England team which won four successive Triple Crowns in the Five Nations championship between 1995 and 1998, including the Grand Slam in 1995.

Johnson, Robert Sherlaw (1932–)

English composer and pianist. He studied at Durham University, the Royal Academy of Music, and in Paris. He has taught at Leeds and York Universities and, from 1970, Oxford.

Works include the opera *The Lambton Worm* (produced Oxford, 1978); *Carmen Vernalia* for soprano and chamber orchestra (1972); *Where the Wild things Are* for soprano and tape (1974); *Festival Mass of the Resurrection* for chorus and orchestra (1974); and *Veritas veritatis* for six voices (1980); piano concerto (1983).

Johnson, Samuel Dr Johnson (1709–1784)

English lexicographer, author, and critic. He was also a brilliant conversationalist and the dominant figure in 18th-century London literary society. His *Dictionary* (1755), provided in its method the pedigree for subsequent lexicography and remained authoritative for over a century. In 1764 he founded, at the suggestion of the painter Joshua Reynolds, a club, known from 1779 as the Literary Club, whose members at various times included the political philosopher Edmund Burke, the dramatist Oliver Goldsmith, the actor David Garrick, and James ◊Boswell, Johnson's biographer.

Johnson's first meeting with Boswell was in 1763. A visit with Boswell to Scotland and the Hebrides in 1773 was recorded in *A Journey to the Western Isles of Scotland* (1775). Other works include a satire imitating Juvenal, *The Vanity of Human Wishes* (1749), the philosophical romance *Rasselas* (1759), an edition of Shakespeare (1765), and the classic *Lives of the English Poets* (1779–81).

Johnson's prose style is balanced, judicious, and sometimes ponderous, and as a critic he displayed great creative insight. His edition of Shakespeare is the forerunner of modern scholarly editions and his 'Preface to Shakespeare' remains a classic critical essay of permanent value. His well-known wit and humanity are documented in Boswell's classic *The Life of Samuel Johnson LL.D* (1791).

Johnston, Brian Alexander (1912–1994)

English broadcaster, writer, and entertainer. Considered the 'voice of cricket' for nearly half a century, Johnston began commentating for the BBC in 1946, and was a commentator on Radio 3's *Test Match Special* from 1970. His genuine love of cricket and cheerful, friendly manner made him a popular broadcaster.

From 1972 to 1987 he hosted the radio series *Down Your Way*.

Jones, Allen (1937–)

English painter, sculptor, and printmaker. He was a leading figure in the ◊Pop art movement of the 1960s. His colourful paintings are executed in the style of commercial advertising, and unabashedly celebrate the female form, for example, *Perfect Match* (1966–67; Wallraf-Richartz Museum, Cologne). One of the most committed exponents of Pop art, he has continued to work in this vein into the 1990s.

His witty, abbreviated imagery of women clad in bustiers, garter-belts, stocking tops, and stiletto-heeled shoes is intended as a comment on male fantasies and sexual fetishes.

Oats A grain, which in England is generally given to horses, but in Scotland supports the people.

SAMUEL JOHNSON English lexicographer, author, and critic.
Dictionary of the English Language (1755)

Jones, Daniel (Jenkyn) (1912–1993)

Welsh composer. He began composing at a very early age and later produced a large quantity of music, including 12 symphonies, eight string quartets, and five string trios.

Jones, Inigo (1573–1652)

English Classical architect. He introduced the ◊Palladian style to England. He was employed by James I to design scenery for Ben Jonson's masques and was appointed Surveyor of the King's Works from 1615 to 1642. He designed the Queen's House, Greenwich (1616–35), and his English Renaissance masterpiece, the Banqueting House, Whitehall (1619–22).

His work was to provide the inspiration for the Palladian Revival a century later.

Jones travelled a great deal, notably in Italy. Through his designs for masques and plays presented at Court, he introduced Italian perspective scenery into England, developing his own system of movable backcloths, and the proscenium arch.

Jones, Thomas Gwynn (1871–1949)

Welsh poet. He won the National Eisteddfod chair at Bangor in 1902 with 'Ymadawiad Arthur' ('The Passing of Arthur'), a poem which, for its application of a modern creative mind to traditional strict metre, heralded a new era in Welsh literature, and won again in 1909 with 'Gwlad y Bryniau' ('The Land of the Hills'); from then his place in Welsh literature was assured.

Jones, Tom stage name of Thomas Jones Woodward (1940–)

Welsh pop singer with a big voice whose hits in an enduring career include the UK chart-topping 'It's Not Unusual' (1964), 'Green Green Grass Of Home' (1966), and 'Delilah' (1968).

Jonestown

Commune of the **People's Temple Sect**, northwestern of Georgetown, Guyana, established in 1974 by the American Jim Jones (1933–1978), who originally founded the sect among San Francisco's black community. After a visiting US congressman was shot dead, Jones enforced mass suicide on his followers by instructing them to drink cyanide; 914 died, including over 240 children.

Jonson, Ben(jamin) (1572–1637)

English dramatist, poet, and critic. *Every Man in his Humour* (1598) established the English 'comedy of humours', in which each character embodies a 'humour', or vice, such as greed, lust, or avarice. This was followed by *Cynthia's Revels* (1600) and *The Poetaster* (1601). His first extant tragedy is *Sejanus* (1603), with Burbage and Shakespeare as members of the original cast. His great comedies are *Volpone, or The Fox* (1606), *The Alchemist* (1610), and *Bartholomew Fair* (1614).

He wrote extensively for court entertainment in the form of masques produced with scenic designer Inigo Jones.

Jonson had a unique comic vision and a remarkable technical mastery of form. His work has had a profound influence on English drama and literature for example, on the Restoration dramatists and on novelists such as Henry ◊Fielding and Tobias ◊Smollett. As an outspoken and biting critic of folly, particularly those aspects associated with a materialistic society, Jonson's work continues to be influential and popular.

He was born in Westminster, London, and entered the theatre as an actor and dramatist in 1597. In 1598 he narrowly escaped the gallows for killing a fellow player in a duel; his goods were confiscated and he was imprisoned. In prison he became a Catholic, but 12 years later reverted to Protestantism. His first comedy, *Every Man in his Humour*, was performed by the Lord Chamberlain's Servants at the Globe Theatre, London. The play was successful, and Jonson was at once enrolled on the list of the leading dramatists. His next plays were *Every Man out of his Humour* (1599), *Cynthia's Revels*, *The Poetaster*, and *Sejanus*. These were followed by *Volpone*, *Epicoene, or The Silent Woman* (1609), *The Alchemist*, and *Bartholomew Fair*. These are regarded as Jonson's greatest plays, in which he most brilliantly and profoundly exposes the nature of folly, and subtly but pervasively offers a standard of moral sanity by which to judge all excess. They were followed by *The Devil is an Ass* (1616) and, after a long absence from the stage, *The Staple of News* (1626), *The New Inn* (1629), *The Magnetic Lady* (1632), and *The Sad Shepherd* (1635).

Jonson collaborated with Marston and Chapman in *Eastward Ho!* (1605) and shared their imprisonment when official exception was taken to the satirization of James I's Scottish policy. He also wrote numerous poems ('Drink to me only with thine eyes'), and some works in prose. In 1619 he received the laureateship and a small pension from the king, but he died in poverty. He was buried in Westminster Abbey.

JONSON, BEN *A portrait of the English writer and critic Ben Jonson. He was born in London, and was a bricklayer and a soldier before becoming involved in theatre as an actor and a playwright. His eventful life also included killing a man in a duel, narrowly escaping hanging, and being imprisoned for writing seditious material. Corbis*

Joseph, Keith Sinjohn, Baron Joseph (1918–1994)

British Conservative politician. A barrister, he entered Parliament in 1956. He held ministerial posts 1962–64, 1970–74, 1979–81, and was secretary of state for education and science 1981–86. He was made a life peer in 1987.

He served in the governments of Harold Macmillan, Alec Douglas-Home, and Edward Heath during the 1960s and 1970s, but it was not until Margaret Thatcher came to office in 1979 that he found a prime minister truly receptive to his views and willing to translate them into policies. With her, he founded the right-wing Centre for Policy Studies, which sought to discover and apply the secrets of the successful market economies of West Germany and Japan.

Joseph was educated at Harrow public school and Magdalen College, Oxford, and was elected a fellow of All Souls. After war service, he studied to become a barrister, then immersed himself in Conservative politics, first at local level and then in Parliament, entering the House of Commons in 1956. After holding various junior offices he was minister of Housing and Local Government from 1962 to 1964. In 1970 he became secretary of state for Social Services, a post he held until the Conservatives' defeat in 1974.

He enjoyed more success as a theoretician than as a practical minister; his political legacy is not so much what he did as what others did at his inspiration. He was the principal author of the Conservative Party's 'New Right' ideology which became the seedbed of Thatcherism.

Josephs, Wilfred (1927–1997)

English composer. As well as film and television music, he wrote nine symphonies, concertos, and chamber music. His works include the *Jewish Requiem* (1969) and the opera *Rebecca* (1983).

Josephson, Brian David (1940–)

Welsh physicist, a leading authority on superconductivity. In 1973 he shared a Nobel prize for his theoretical predictions of the properties of a supercurrent through a tunnel barrier (the **Josephson effect**), which led to the development of the **Josephson junction**.

Joule, James Prescott (1818–1889)

English physicist. His work on the relations between electrical, mechanical, and chemical effects led to the discovery of the first law of thermodynamics.

He determined the mechanical equivalent of heat (**Joule's equivalent**) in 1843, and the SI unit of energy, the joule, is named after him. He also discovered **Joule's law**, which defines the relation between heat and electricity; and with Irish physicist Lord Kelvin in 1852 the **Joule–Kelvin** (or **Joule–Thomson**) effect.

judge

Person invested with power to hear and determine legal disputes.

In the UK, judges are chosen from barristers of long standing, but solicitors can be appointed circuit judges. Judges of the High Court, the crown courts, and the county courts are appointed at the advice of the Lord Chancellor, and those of the Court of Appeal and the House of Lords at the advice of the prime minister, although all judges are appointed by the crown. The independence of the higher judiciary is ensured by the principle that they hold their office during good behaviour and not at the pleasure of the crown. They can be removed from office only by a resolution of both houses of Parliament.

judicial review

In English law, action in the High Court to review the decisions of lower courts, tribunals, and administrative bodies. Various court orders can be made: **certiorari** (which quashes the decision); **mandamus** (which commands a duty to be performed); **prohibition** (which commands that an action should not be performed because it is unauthorized); a **declaration** (which sets out the legal rights or obligations); or an **injunction**.

Julian of Norwich (*c.* 1342–after 1413)

English mystic. She lived as a recluse, and recorded her visions in *The Revelation of Divine Love* (1403), which shows the influence of neo-Platonism.

jungle

Dance music that combines techno with African and Caribbean elements, also called ◊drum 'n' bass after the predominant instruments. Jungle originated in the UK in 1992 and quickly split into subgenres. Exponents include L T J Bukem and Dillinja.

Jungle Book, The

Collection of short stories for children by Rudyard ◊Kipling, published in two volumes in 1894 and 1895. Set in India, the stories feature a boy, Mowgli, reared by wolves and the animals he encounters in the jungle. The stories inspired the formation by Baden Powell of the Wolf Cub division of the Boy Scout movement.

Jura

Island of the Inner ◊Hebrides, Argyll and Bute; area 380 sq km/147 sq mi; population (1991) 196. It is separated from the Scottish mainland by the **Sound of Jura**. The whirlpool Corryvreckan (Gaelic 'Brecan's cauldron') is off the north coast. It has a range of mountains known as the 'Paps of Jura', the highest of which is Beinn an Oir at 784 m/2,572 ft.

Jura is the only major Scottish island without a direct link to the mainland.

jury

Body of lay people (usually 12) sworn to decide the facts of a case and reach a verdict in a court of law. Juries, used mainly in English-speaking countries, are implemented primarily in criminal cases, but also sometimes in civil cases; for example, inquests and libel trials.

The British jury derived from Germanic custom. It was introduced into England by the Normans. Originally it was a body of neighbours who gave their opinion on the basis of being familiar with the protagonists and background of a case.

Eventually it developed into an impartial panel, giving a verdict based solely on evidence heard in court. The jury's duty is to decide the facts of a case: the judge directs them on matters of law. The basic principles of the British system have been adopted in the USA, most Commonwealth countries, and some European countries (for example, France).

In England, jurors are selected at random from the electoral roll. Certain people are ineligible for jury service (such as lawyers and clerics), and others can be excused (such as members of Parliament and doctors). If the jury cannot reach a unanimous verdict it can give a majority verdict (at least 10 of the 12). In Scotland the jury numbers 15, and may return a verdict of 'not proven'.

justice of the peace, or JP

In England, an unpaid ◊magistrate.

Just So Stories

Collection of stories for small children by Rudyard ◊Kipling, published in 1902. Many of the stories offer amusing explanations of how certain animals acquired their characteristic appearance, such as 'How the Leopard got his Spots' and 'How the Camel got his Hump'. They originated in stories that the author told his children.

Just William

Children's book published in 1922, the first of a series by English author Richmal ◊Crompton, featuring the character ◊William. A radio adaptation read by Martin Jarvis in the 1980s gave the books a new lease of life.

Jute

Member of a Germanic people who originated in Jutland but later settled in Frankish territory. They occupied Kent, southeast England, in about 450, according to tradition under Hengist and Horsa, and conquered the Isle of Wight and the opposite coast of Hampshire in the early 6th century.

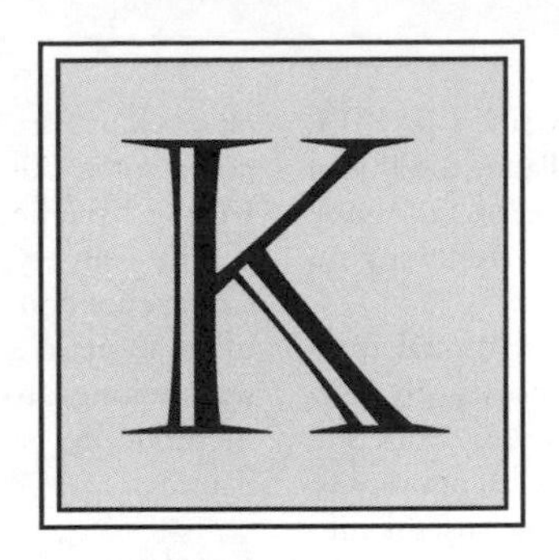

Kapoor, Anish (1954–)

Indian-born British abstract sculptor. His early work was usually in light materials and was often brightly coloured, but from the late 1980s he began using much heavier materials such as stone in big, bold pieces. He won the Turner Prize in 1991.

He settled in London in 1973.

Katz, Bernard (1911–)

German-born British biophysicist. He shared the 1970 Nobel Prize for Physiology or Medicine for work on the biochemistry of the transmission and control of signals in the nervous system, vital in the search for remedies for nervous and mental disorders. He was knighted in 1969.

Kauffmann, (Maria Anna Catherina) Angelica (1741–1807)

Swiss Neo-Classical painter. She worked extensively in England, with the keen support of Joshua ◊Reynolds, and became a founder-member of the Royal Academy in 1768. She was in great demand as a portraitist, but also painted mythological scenes for large country houses.

Kauffman lived in Italy for three years as a child, painting precociously. On a second visit (1763–66) she painted the portrait of the art historian Johann Winckelmann and was no doubt strongly influenced by his Neo-Classicism. After visiting Milan, Rome, Bologna, and Venice, she arrived in London in 1766, one of her first sitters being the actor David Garrick.

Her work became widely known through the engravings of Francesco Bartolozzi (1727–1815) and others, and was extensively adapted in the Adam style of interior decoration in wall and ceiling panels, on painted furniture, and in porcelain.

Kavanagh, Dan

Pseudonym of the English writer Julian ◊Barnes, under which he has written detective novels.

Kay, John (1704–*c.* 1780)

English inventor who developed the flying shuttle, a machine to speed up the work of hand-loom weaving. He patented his invention in 1733.

KBE

Abbreviation for **Knight (Commander of the Order) of the British Empire**.

Kean, Edmund (1787–1833)

English tragic actor. He was noted for his portrayal of villainy in the Shakespearean roles of Shylock, Richard III, and Iago. He died on stage, playing Othello opposite his son as Iago.

Keats, John (1795–1821)

English Romantic poet. He produced work of the highest quality and promise before dying at the age of 25. *Poems* (1817), *Endymion* (1818), the great odes (particularly 'Ode to a

KEATS, JOHN *English romantic poet John Keats, who wrote most of his best-known poems during a concentrated spell in 1818. At this time he fell in love with Fanny Brawne, with whom he remained infatuated until his death. Today his letters, which are witty, warm, and insightful, are almost as highly regarded as his poetry. Corbis*

Nightingale' and 'Ode on a Grecian Urn' written in 1819, published in 1820), and the narratives 'Isabella; or the Pot of Basil' (1818), 'Lamia' (1819), and 'The Eve of St Agnes' (1820), show his lyrical richness and talent for drawing on both classical mythology and medieval lore.

Born in London, Keats studied at Guy's Hospital from 1815–17, but then abandoned medicine for poetry. In 1819 he fell in love with Fanny Brawne (1802–1865). Suffering from tuberculosis, he sailed to Italy in 1820 in an attempt to regain his health, but died in Rome. Valuable insight into Keats's poetic development is provided by his *Letters*, published in 1848.

Keats's poetry often deals with the relationship between love and death, beauty and decay. While 'The Eve of St Agnes', with its sensuous, pictorial language and romantic narrative, had immense influence on later 19th-century poetry, it is the odes which are Keats's most distinctive achievement, reflecting his feelings about human mortality. 'Ode to a Nightingale' is a symbol of beauty's power to surmount death, a theme which reappears in 'Ode on a Grecian Urn', where the figures on the vase are seen to epitomize an enduring truth, while 'Ode to Autumn' asserts the fulfilment of complete fruition and ripeness.

Keble, John (1792–1866)

Anglican priest and religious poet. His sermon on the decline of religious faith in Britain, preached in 1833, heralded the start of the ◊Oxford Movement, a Catholic revival in the Church of England. He wrote four of the *Tracts for the Times* (theological treatises in support of the movement), and was professor of poetry at Oxford 1831–41. His book of poems, *The Christian Year* (1827), was very popular in the 19th century. Keble College, Oxford, was founded in 1870 in his memory.

Keegan, (Joseph) Kevin (1951–)

English footballer and football manager. He played for Scunthorpe United 1968–71, Liverpool 1971–77, SV Hamburg (Germany) 1977–80, Southampton 1980–82, and Newcastle United 1982–84, winning 63 full England caps, scoring 21 goals, and captaining his country. He was Footballer of the Year and PFA Player of the Year 1976, European Footballer of the Year 1978 and 1979, and PFA Player of the Year 1982. He became manager of Newcastle United 1992.

Keeler, Christine (1942–)

Englishwoman who became notorious in 1963 after revelations of affairs with both a Soviet attaché and the war minister John ◊Profumo, who resigned after admitting lying to the House of Commons about their relationship.

Her patron, the osteopath Stephen Ward, convicted of living on immoral earnings, committed suicide and Keeler was subsequently imprisoned for related offences.

Keeper of the Great Seal

In the Middle Ages, an officer who had charge of the great seal of England (the official seal authenticating state documents).

During the Middle Ages the great seal was entrusted to the chancellor. Later, a special Lord Keeper was appointed to take charge of it, but since 1761 the posts of Lord Chancellor and Keeper have been combined.

The delivery of the great seal into the hands of the Lord Chancellor confers the chancellorship upon him. On a demise of the monarch, when a new great seal must be made, the old seal belongs to the Lord Chancellor, though it is first theoretically broken or 'damasked' by a light blow with a hammer.

Keighley

Industrial town in West Yorkshire, northern England, 14 km/9 mi northwest of Bradford, on the River Aire; population (1996) 39,600. ◊Haworth, home of the Brontë family of writers, is now part of Keighley. Industries include the manufacture of woollens and worsteds, textile machinery, and machine tools; service sector activities are increasing in importance.

The Keighley and Worth Valley Railway, reopened by a local preservation society in 1968, runs 8 km/5 mi from Keighley to Haworth and Oxenhope.

Keller, Hans (1919–1985)

Austrian-born British journalist and critic. In 1959 he joined the British Broadcasting Corporation (BBC) in London. He had much influence on broadcasting policy, and in his programmes of functional analysis he sought to elucidate structure and ideas by musical example, rather than verbal explanation.

After studying in Vienna he fled to England in 1938; he played the violin and viola in various ensembles before joining the BBC. An apparent mastery of his adopted language led to a prolific career as a journalist; natives were sometimes bemused by a certain subjectivity and love of paradox. He wrote the libretto for Benjamin Frankel's opera *Marching Song* (BBC 1983), and *The Great Haydn Quartets* (1986).

Kells, Book of

8th-century illuminated manuscript of the Gospels produced at the monastery of Kells in County Meath, Ireland. It is now in Trinity College library, Dublin.

Kelly, Gerald Festus (1879–1972)

English painter. He specialized in portraits, his sitters including George VI, Elizabeth II, and the writer Somerset Maugham. He also painted numerous studies of Burmese girls and dancers. He was knighted in 1945.

Kelman, James (1946–)

Scottish novelist and short-story writer. His works are angry, compassionate, and ironic, and make effective use of the trenchant speech patterns of his native Glasgow. These include the novels *The Busconductor Hines* (1984), *A Disaffection* (1989), and *How Late It Was, How Late* (1994; Booker Prize); *The Good times* (1998) comprises 21 'narratives' in which men try to come to terms with their redundancy in life.

kelpie ('tangle' or 'shelly coat')

In Scottish folklore, a water spirit in the form of a shaggy horse (sometimes a man) who appears as a warning to those destined to be drowned. He sometimes entices travellers to ride on his back, then plunges into a river so that the rider is drowned.

Kemble, (John) Philip (1757–1823)

English actor and theatre manager. He excelled in tragedy, including the Shakespearean roles of Hamlet and Coriolanus. As manager of Drury Lane 1788–1803 and Covent Garden 1803–17 in London, he introduced many innovations in theatrical management, costume, and scenery.

He was the son of the strolling player Roger Kemble (1721–1802), whose children included the actors Charles Kemble and Mrs ◊Siddons.

Kempe, Margerie born Brunham (*c.* 1373–*c.* 1439)

English Christian mystic. She converted to religious life after a period of mental derangement, and travelled widely as a pilgrim. Her *Boke of Margery Kempe* (about 1420) describes her life and experiences, both religious and worldly. It has been called the first autobiography in English.

Kendal

Town in Cumbria, northwest England, on the River Kent, 35 km/22 mi north of Lancaster; population (1991) 24,900. Light industrial activities include the production of footwear, specialist paper, carpets, snuff, and confectionery. Insurance services are also important. The town is a tourist centre for visitors to the ◊Lake District.

Kendal was an important woollen textile centre from the 14th century. **Kendal mint cake**, made from sugar and peppermint oil, comes from here. The town was the birthplace of Catherine Parr, the sixth wife of Henry VIII.

Features include the remains of a Norman castle and Abbot Hall Art Gallery and Museum of Lakeland Life and Industry. The restored Sizergh Castle lies to the south of the town. **Kendal green**, mentioned in William Shakespeare's *Henry IV*, was a woollen cloth worn by English archers.

Kendrew, John Cowdery (1917–1997)

English biochemist who determined the structure of the muscle protein myoglobin. For this work Kendrew shared the 1962 Nobel Prize for Chemistry with his colleague Max Perutz. He was knighted in 1974.

Kenilworth

Town in Warwickshire, central England, 8 km/5 mi north of Warwick; population (1991) 21,000. Industries include motor and agricultural engineering. The Norman castle, celebrated in Walter Scott's novel *Kenilworth*, became a royal residence. Edward II relinquished his crown here in 1327. The castle was enlarged by John of Gaunt and later by the Earl of Leicester – who entertained Elizabeth I here in 1575 – but was dismantled after the English Civil War.

There are some remains of an Augustinian priory dating from about 1122. The ruins of the castle were given to the British nation by the first Lord Kenilworth in 1937.

Kennedy, Margaret (1896–1967)

English novelist. She became known for *The Constant Nymph* (1924), which was later dramatized and filmed. Among her other novels are *Red Sky at Morning* (1927), *Troy Chimneys* (1953; Tait Black Memorial Prize), *A Night in Cold Harbour* (1961), and *Not in the Calendar* (1964).

Kennet and Avon Canal

Waterway in southwest UK linking the Thames at Reading with the Avon at Bath, a distance of 145 km/90 mi. Designed by Scottish engineer John ◊Rennie, the canal was built in 1810, closed in the 1950s, and reopened in 1990.

Kenneth

Two kings of Scotland:

Kenneth I called MacAlpin (died 860)

King of Scotland from about 844. Traditionally, he is regarded as the founder of the Scottish kingdom (Alba) by virtue of his final defeat of the Picts about 844. He invaded Northumbria six times, and drove the Angles and the Britons over the River Tweed.

Kenneth II (died 995)

King of Scotland from 971, son of Malcolm I. He invaded Northumbria several times, and his chiefs were in constant conflict with Sigurd the Norwegian over the area of Scotland north of the River Spey. He is believed to have been murdered by his subjects.

KENNET AND AVON CANAL *A narrowboat on the Kennet and Avon Canal. This waterway passes through some of the most tranquil countryside of southern Britain, such as the chalk downlands of Wiltshire, and was reopened for navigation in 1990. Many of the canals of Britain, once arteries of the Industrial Revolution, are now used for leisure activities, especially during the summer months. Corel*

Kennington, Eric Henri (1888–1960)

English artist and sculptor. He was official war artist 1916–19 and 1940–43, and is best known for his perceptive portraits of soldiers. His memorial to T E Lawrence is in Wareham, Dorset.

Kensington and Chelsea

Inner borough of central Greater London

Features Holland House (about 1606) and Holland Park; Camden House (about 1612); Kensington Palace, Jacobean house redesigned by Christopher Wren for William and Mary (1689); Kensington Gardens, with statue of Peter Pan; Leighton House (1866); Imperial College of Science and Technology (1907); Kensington and Chelsea Town Hall (1976) designed by Basil ◊Spence; museums – Victoria and Albert, Natural History, Science, and Geology; Royal College of Music; Royal College of Art; annual Notting Hill Carnival, held each August, is the largest street carnival in Europe

Population (1991) 138,400

Famous people William Wilberforce lived here.

Kensington Palace

Palace in London, part of the royal household. Formerly Nottingham House, the home of Heneage Finch (1621–82), 1st Earl of Nottingham, it was purchased in 1689 by William III. The latter had it remodelled by Christopher ◊Wren, whose work survives mainly in the south front and northeast wing. Under George I there was further reconstruction by William Benson (1682–1754) and William Kent (northeast and southeast wings). George II was the last sovereign to use the palace.

Diana, Princess of Wales, lived at Kensington Palace and had her offices here following her separation from Prince Charles.

Kent

County of southeast England, known as the 'garden of England' (since April 1998 Medway Towns has been a separate unitary authority)

Area 3,730 sq km/1,440 sq mi

Towns and cities ◊Maidstone (administrative headquarters), Ashford, Canterbury, Deal, Dover (ferry terminus), Gravesend, Hythe, New Ash Green (a new town), Sevenoaks, Royal Tunbridge Wells; resorts: Folkestone, Margate, Ramsgate

Physical the North Downs; White Cliffs of Dover; rivers: Thames, Darent, Medway (traditionally, a 'man of Kent' comes from east of the Medway and a 'Kentish man' from west Kent), Stour; marshes (especially Romney Marsh); the Isles of Grain, Thanet and Sheppey (on which is the resort of Sheerness, formerly a royal dockyard); the Weald (an agricultural area); Dungeness (peninsula and headland)

Features Leeds Castle (converted to a palace by Henry VIII); Ightham Mote; Hever Castle (where Henry VIII courted Anne Boleyn); Chartwell (Churchill's country home), Knole, Sissinghurst Castle and gardens; the Brogdale Experimental Horticulture Station at Faversham has the world's finest collection of apple and other fruit trees; the former RAF Manston became Kent International Airport in 1989; Dungeness nuclear power station

Agriculture cereals, hops, apples, soft fruit, vegetables; in Kent are found about half the orchards, half the hops, and one fifth of the soft fruit grown in England and Wales; livestock production

Industries cement (Gravesend), paper, oil refining, shipbuilding, tourism. The East Kent coalfield ceased production in 1989.

Population (1994) 1,551,300

History St Thomas à ◊Becket was murdered in Canterbury Cathedral, and his shrine became a place of pilgrimage until the Reformation.

Famous people Christopher Marlowe, Edward Heath

Topography

Kent is bounded by Thurrock and Medway Towns to the north; by London and Surrey to the west, and by East Sussex to the south. It is a county of great geographical contrast, and the arrival point in England for thousands of foreign visitors. A long-distance footpath follows the crest of the North Downs and some of the ◊Pilgrims' Way, and near Ashford a loop goes off to take in Canterbury and the surrounding orchard country. The gentle northward chalk slopes of the North Downs provide the excellent conditions for Kent's fruit farming, especially around Faversham and Sittingbourne. The rocks of the Tertiary period found in this area are also found in the isles at Grain, Sheppey, and Thanet. To the south of the North Downs is the ◊Weald, which extends into Surrey and Sussex and has a complement of small towns such as Cranbrook and Hawkhurst with half-timbered yeomen's houses set in rolling, wooded countryside. Parts of northwest Kent have now been absorbed into outskirts of London, or lie within the commuter belt.

Historical events

Kent's proximity to the continent and to London has meant that many historically important events have taken place in the county. It was on the coast of Kent that Caesar landed in 55 BC; to which ◊Hengist and Horsa brought their Saxon mercenaries; and to which St Augustine led his followers. The archbishop of Canterbury traces his descent as Primate of all England from St Augustine. Canterbury is of great antiquity and evidence has been found here for continuity of settlement from Roman to Jute and Frankish times. The influences of these groups reflected in Kent's language, custom, and settlement pattern, which contrast with those of the more predominantly Saxon Surrey and Sussex. Parts of Kent are open countryside, which could easily be invaded, and the former Royal Military Canal was cut across Romney Marsh as a defence against Napoleon.

Kent, Edward George Nicholas Paul Patrick, 2nd Duke of Kent (1935–)

British prince, grandson of George V. His father, Prince George (1902–1942), was created Duke of Kent just before his marriage in 1934 to Princess Marina of Greece and Denmark (1906–1968). Edward succeeded to the title when his father was killed in an air crash on active service with the RAF.

In 1961 he married Katharine Worsley (1933–) and his heir is George (1962–), Earl of St Andrews.

Kent, William (1685–1748)

English architect, landscape gardener, and interior designer. Working closely with Richard ◊Burlington, he was foremost in introducing the ◊Palladian style to Britain from Italy, excelling in richly carved, sumptuous interiors and furnishings, as at ◊Holkham Hall, Norfolk, begun in 1734.

Immensely versatile, he also worked in a Neo-Gothic style, and was a pioneer of Romantic landscape gardening, for example, the grounds of Stowe House, Buckinghamshire, and Rousham Park, Oxfordshire (1738–40). Horace Walpole called him 'the father of modern gardening'.

Kent, kingdom of

Anglo-Saxon kingdom in southeast England, founded by the Jutes when they arrived in Britain as foederati under Hengest and Horsa in the 5th century AD. Kent was the first English kingdom to convert to Christianity in 597 under its king, Ethelbert, although when he died in 616 much of the kingdom reverted to paganism. Kent was divided from 686–90 and then came under the control of Mercia around 762 before being absorbed by Wessex in 825.

Kenwood House

Mansion on the east side of ◊Hampstead Heath, London. It was enlarged by the Earl of Mansfield after he received the estate in 1765. Robert ◊Adam designed two façades and the superb library, with lesser rooms, around 1766.

The house contains the art collection of the 1st Earl of Iveagh, including works by Rembrandt, Vermeer, Hals, Gainsborough, Reynolds, Turner, and Stubbs. English Heritage now manage the house and art collection, which were bequeathed to the nation in 1927.

Kenwright, Bill (1945–)

English theatre producer. He has produced over 500 plays and musicals, including *Joseph and his Amazing Technicolour Dreamcoat* (1979) and *Shirley Valentine* (1989).

Kerr, Deborah (Jane) (1921–)

Scottish actress. She often played genteel, ladylike roles. Her performance in such British films as *Major Barbara* (1940), *The Life and Death of Colonel Blimp* (1943), and *Black Narcissus* (1946) led to starring parts in Hollywood: *Quo Vadis* (1951), *From Here to Eternity* (1953), *The King and I* (1956), and *An Affair to Remember* (1957). She was presented with an Academy Award for lifetime achievement in 1993.

Keswick

Market town and tourist centre in Cumbria, England, 35 km/22 mi southwest of Carlisle; population (1991) 4,600. The town is in the centre of the ◊Lake District and offers accommodation for walkers and holidaymakers. Another industry is the manufacture of pencils.

Derwent Water is adjacent to the town and a number of high hills are within easy reach. Skiddaw (930 m/3,052 ft), immediately north of Keswick, gives fine views.

Kettering

Market town in Northamptonshire, England, 20 km/12 mi northeast of Northampton; population (1991) 73,800. Its principal industries are the manufacture of footwear and clothing, and engineering.

Wicksteed Park, covering 1 sq km/0.4 sq mi, lies to the south of the town. It was purchased by Charles Wicksteed at the end of the 19th century, to be used as a public park.

Kew Gardens

Popular name for the Royal Botanic Gardens, Kew, Surrey, England. They were founded in 1759 by Augusta of Saxe-Coburg (1719–1772), the mother of King George III, as a small garden and were passed to the nation by Queen Victoria in 1840. By then they had expanded to almost their present size of 149 hectares/368 acres and since 1841 have been open daily to the public. They contain a collection of over 25,000 living plant species and many fine buildings. The gardens are also a centre for botanical research.

The herbarium is the biggest in the world, with over 5 million dried plant specimens. Kew also has a vast botanical library, the Jodrell Laboratory, and three museums. The buildings include the majestic Palm House (1848), the Temperate House (1862), both designed by Decimus Burton, and the Chinese Pagoda, some 50 m/165 ft tall, designed by William Chambers in 1761. More recently, two additions have been made to the glasshouses: the Alpine House (1981) and the Princess of Wales Conservatory, a futuristic building for plants from ten different climatic zones, built in 1987. Much of the collection of trees at Kew was destroyed by a gale in 1987.

Since 1964 there have been additional grounds at Wakehurst Place, Ardingly, West Sussex. The seeds of 5,000 species are preserved there in the seed physiology department, 2% of those known to exist in the world. Kew received £21 million from the Millennium Commission in December 1995 to construct a new seed bank.

Keynes, John Maynard, 1st Baron Keynes (1883–1946)

English economist. His *General Theory of Employment, Interest, and Money* (1936) proposed the prevention of financial crises and unemployment by adjusting demand through government control of credit and currency. He is responsible for that part of economics which studies whole economies, now known as macroeconomics.

Keynes led the British delegation at the Bretton Woods Conference in 1944, which set up the International Monetary Fund.

His theories were widely accepted in the aftermath of World War II, and he was one of the most influential economists of the 20th century. His ideas are today often contrasted with monetarism, the theory that economic policy should be based on control of the money supply. He was made a baron in 1942.

KEW GARDENS *The large glass Palm House of Kew Gardens in London, England, covers 24,000 sq ft and houses a collection of palm trees and waterlilies. Kew Gardens has an area of 300 acres and contains plants from all over the world. Liz Stares/Collections*

Keynsham

Town in the unitary authority of Bath and North East Somerset, England, lying midway between Bristol and Bath on the River Avon; population (1991) 15,200. Local industries include the manufacture of chocolate and paper. A Roman villa has been excavated here, and there are also ruins of a 12th-century abbey.

key stage

National curriculum term for the stages of a pupil's progress through school. There are four key stages, each ending with a national standard attainment test (SAT). The key stages are the years 5–7, 7–11, 11–14, and 14–17. GCSE is the test for pupils at the end of Key Stage 4.

khaki

Dust-coloured uniform of British and Indian troops in India from about 1850, adopted as camouflage during the South African War (1899–1902), and later standard for military uniforms worldwide.

Kidd, 'Captain' William (*c.* 1645–1701)

Scottish pirate. He spent his youth privateering for the British against the French off the North American coast, and in 1695 was given a royal commission to suppress piracy in the Indian Ocean. Instead, he joined a group of pirates in Madagascar. In 1699, on his way to Boston, Massachusetts, he was arrested, taken to England, and hanged.

His execution marked the end of some 200 years of semi-official condoning of piracy by the British government.

Kidderminster

Market town in Worcester, England, on the River Stour, 22 km/14 mi north of Worcester; population (1991) 54,600. Its carpet industry dates from about 1735, and associated activities include the manufacture of woollen and worsted yarns, and dyeing. Other industries include steel forging, pleasure boat building, and the manufacture of plastic and ceramic products, sugar, and chemicals. Small high-tech businesses are proliferating.

History

From the early 13th century the town was important for cloth weaving. Its charter of incorporation, granted by Charles I in 1636, describes it is 'an ancient borough of great commerce for the making and manufacture of cloth'.

Features

The Perpendicular church of St Mary and All Saints dates mainly from about 1450. The Staffordshire and Worcestershire Canal passes through the town, and it is also the southern terminus of the Severn Valley Railway. Kidderminster is known for the manufacture of Wilton, Axminster, Brussels, and tufted carpets.

Famous people
Rowland Hill, originator of the penny post, was born here in 1795, and the Nonconformist cleric Richard Baxter (1615–91) was a lecturer (minister) in the town from 1639 to 1662.

Killiecrankie, Battle of

During the first ◊Jacobite uprising, defeat on 7 May 1689 of General Mackay (for William of Orange) by John Graham of ◊Claverhouse, a supporter of James II, at Killiecrankie, Scotland. Despite the victory, Claverhouse was killed and the revolt soon petered out; the remaining forces were routed on 21 August.

Kilmainham Treaty

In Irish history, an informal secret agreement in April 1882 that secured the release of the nationalist Charles ◊Parnell from Kilmainham jail, Dublin, where he had been imprisoned for six months for supporting Irish tenant farmers who had joined the Land League's campaign for agricultural reform.

The British government realized that Parnell could quell violence more easily out of prison than in it. In return for his release, he agreed to accept the Land Act of 1861. The Kilmainham Treaty marked a change in British policy in Ireland from confrontation to cooperation, with the government attempting to conciliate landowners and their tenants, who were refusing to pay rent. This strategy was subsequently threatened by the ◊Phoenix Park Murders.

Kilmarnock

Administrative headquarters of ◊East Ayrshire, Scotland, on the River Irvine, 32 km/20 mi southwest of Glasgow; population (1991) 44,300. Industries include biotechnology and whisky. Robert Burns's first book of poems was printed here in 1786, and became known as the 'Kilmarnock edition'.

Kilmartin

Village in Argyll and Bute unitary authority, Scotland, situated near the southern end of Loch Awe, straddling the natural route to Oban, 11 km/7 mi north of Lochgilphead. Some of Scotland's most important prehistoric sites are found in the vicinity, including chambered cairns, sculptured slabs and crosses, and Bronze Age cairns.

The capital of the ancient Dalriada kingdom, established around AD 500, was situated at nearby Dunadd Fort.

Kinder Scout

Mountain in Derbyshire, central England; height 636 m/2,087 ft. It is the highest point in the ◊Peak District. The summit is an extensive peat-covered plateau.

'King and Country' debate

Controversial debate in Britain in February 1933 in which the Oxford Union, the university's debating society, passed the motion 'this House will in no circumstances fight for its King and its Country'. The debate sent shockwaves throughout the country as many saw it as signalling that Britain's young elite had lost their sense of patriotism, although it probably more accurately reflected a commitment to disarmament after the horrors of World War I.

King Lear
Tragedy by William ◊Shakespeare, first performed in 1605–06. Lear, king of Britain, favours his grasping daughters Goneril and Regan with shares of his kingdom but refuses his third, honest daughter Cordelia a share because she will not falsely flatter him. Rejected by Goneril and Regan, the old and unbalanced Lear is reunited with Cordelia but dies of grief when she is murdered.

King/Queen's Champion

In English history, ceremonial office held by virtue of possessing the lordship of Scrivelsby, Lincolnshire. Sir John Dymoke established his right to champion the monarch on coronation day in 1377 and it is still held by his descendant.

A document of 1332–33 described the champion as 'an armed knight on horseback to prove by his body, if necessary, against whomsoever, the King who is crowned that day is the true and right heir of the kingdom'. This office was last performed on the coronation of King George IV in 1821, at a banquet in Westminster Hall. The gold cup from which the king drank at the banquet was the champion's fee.

King's Counsel

In England, a ◊barrister of senior rank; the term is used when a king is on the throne and ◊Queen's Counsel when the monarch is a queen.

King's Langley

Village in Hertfordshire, England, 6 km/4 mi northwest of Watford; population (1991) 4,600. King's Langley is the site of a former royal palace, the residence of English sovereigns from Henry III to Richard II (early 13th–late 14th centuries).

Kingsley, Ben stage name of Krishna Banji (1943–)

English film actor. An accomplished character actor, he won an Academy Award for his performance in the title role of *Gandhi* (1982), and appeared in *Betrayal* (1982), *Testimony* (1987), *Pascali's Island* (1988), *Bugsy* (1991), *Schindler's List* (1993), and *Death and the Maiden* (1994).

Largely confined to minor support roles in recent years, he has appeared in *Species* (1995), *The Assignment* (1997), and Michael Winner's black comedy *Parting Shots* (1998).

> *I love British cinema like a doctor loves his dying patient.*
>
> BEN KINGSLEY English actor. Remark at Dinard, 29 September 1990

Kingsley, Charles (1819–1875)

English author. A rector, he was known as the 'Chartist clergyman' because of such social novels as *Yeast* (1848) and *Alton Locke* (1850). His historical novels include *Westward Ho!* (1855) and *Hereward the Wake* (1866). He also wrote, for children, *The* ◊*Water Babies* (1863).

He was deeply interested in social questions, and threw

himself wholeheartedly into the schemes of social relief which were supported under the name of Christian Socialism, writing many tracts and articles as 'Parson Lot'.

King's Lynn formerly Bishop's Lynn

Port and market town in Norfolk, eastern England, at the mouth of the River Great Ouse, 56 km/35 mi northeast of Peterborough; population (1996) 40,200. Industries include food-processing, fishing, engineering, light manufacturing (valves, catering refrigerators), and the production of chemicals. It was a thriving port in medieval times, named **Bishop's Lynn** until it became royal property during the reign of Henry VIII.

Features

St George's Guildhall, dating from the early 15th century, has been restored as a theatre, annual festival centre, and art gallery; it is believed to be the oldest surviving guildhall in England. Other features include Trinity Guildhall, dating from 1421; the Saturday Market Place and the Tuesday Market Place; the Old Gaol House (1784), now housing a museum; and Thoresby College (1500), originally a monastic house. Merchant buildings include Hampton Court, originally a 14th-century warehouse; the Hanseatic Warehouse (1428); Greenland Fishery House (1605); Clifton House (12th–18th centuries), with fine 14th-century tiled floors and a five-storey brick watch-tower, constructed in about 1600; and Custom House, built in 1683.

Churches

The church of St Margaret, originally founded in about 1100, was rebuilt in the 13th century; it has two towers at the western end and two of the largest brasses in England. The octagonal Red Mount Chapel (1485) originally served as a stopping place for pilgrims on their way to Walsingham. St Nicholas's Chapel was originally founded in 1146, but dates mainly from the 15th century.

King's proctor

In England, the official representing the crown in certain court cases; the term is used when a king is on the throne, and Queen's Proctor when the monarch is a queen.

Kingston upon Hull, or Hull

City, port, and unitary authority (created in 1996 from part of the former county of Humberside) situated where the River Hull flows into the north side of the Humber estuary, northeast England; unitary authority area 71 sq km/27 sq mi; population (1996) 265,000. It is linked with the south bank of the estuary by the ⇨Humber Bridge, the world's longest single-span suspension bridge. Industries include fish processing, flour milling, sawmilling, marine engineering, food processing, and the manufacture of electrical goods, vegetable oils, paint, pharmaceuticals, chemicals, caravans, aircraft, and paper. There are 11 km/7 mi of modern docks located on the Humber estuary. The largest timber port in the UK, it also handles grain, oilseeds, wool, and the export/import of manufactured goods.

Features include the 13th-century Holy Trinity Church; the Town Docks Museum; the Ferens Art Gallery (1927), the University of Hull (1954), and the University of Humberside (1992), formerly Humberside Polytechnic. The humanitarian reformer William Wilberforce was born here.

There are ferries to Rotterdam and Zeebrugge. Following the building of the Queen Elizabeth Dock in 1971, the port's roll-on/roll-off freight traffic expanded rapidly in the 1980s.

Features

Holy Trinity church, one of the largest parish churches in England, has an Early English chancel which is said to be one of the oldest brick buildings in England still in use for its original purpose. The rest is of stone (mainly late Perpendicular). St Mary's church dates from the early 14th century. Wilberforce House, an Elizabethan manor and the birthplace of William Wilberforce, now houses a museum and memorial to Wilberforce. The dockland area has been restored.

History

The site of the present city was held at the end of the 12th century by Cistercian monks. Their settlement, then known as Wyke, was acquired by Edward I in 1293, and its name was changed to Kingston upon Hull. In 1299 its first charter made the town a free borough, and it grew into a flourishing seaport. New quays were built, internal communications improved, a ferry to the southern shore of the Humber established, and in 1322 the town was enclosed and fortified. In 1440 a charter of Henry VI incorporated the town. During the reign of Henry VIII new fortifications to protect the harbour were built. They were largely devised by the king himself and instructions in his handwriting are still extant. During the Civil War the first forcible resistance to Charles I was the closing of the gates of Hull against him in 1642, and the town sustained two Royalist sieges. It continued to maintain its position as a port and thriving commercial centre, and between 1774 and 1829 three docks were built to make a ring of water around the old town. The largest dock in Hull, the King George, was opened by George V in 1914. The town was made a city in 1897. During World War II the central area of Hull was severely damaged in bombing raids, and much reconstruction has taken place.

Charters

The city has a collection of royal charters and letters patent dating from Edward I (1299) to George V (1914). Of 37 granted to the town by various sovereigns, 32 are still preserved in the Guildhall. The charter of 1661 became the charter under which the town was governed until the Municipal Corporations Act of 1835.

Museums and galleries

The city is home to several museums and galleries, including the Maritime Museum, housed in the old Town Docks offices; Wilberforce House, the former home of William Wilberforce; Streetlife, the Hull Museum of Transport, which includes among its exhibits rare trams such as the Ryde Pier and Kitson; and the Ferens Art Gallery, which houses an eclectic collection dating from the 16th-century Dutch masters to the present day. The old Grammar School has also been converted into a museum and houses collections dedicated to Victorian Britain and the history of Hull and its people.

Famous people
Kingston upon Hull was the birthplace of the aviator Amy Johnson and of the poet Stevie Smith. From 1955 until his death in 1985, the poet Philip Larkin was librarian at the University of Hull.

Kingston upon Thames

Outer borough of southwest Greater London; administrative headquarters of ◊Surrey, although not in the county
Features seven Saxon kings, from Edward the Elder in 900 to Ethelred the Unready in 979, were crowned at Kingston; their coronation stone is preserved here, set with seven silver pennies; oldest of the three Royal Boroughs of England, with ancient right to elect own High Steward and Recorder; Kingston Grammar School, founded by Elizabeth I in 1561
Industries mainly public sector administration and services; finance and business services, and retailing; small manufacturing sector (8% of workforce): chemicals, engineering, plastics, printing
Population (1997 est) 144,600
History
Athelstan, king of the Mercians and West Saxons, was crowned king here in 925. In medieval times Kingston was an important Thames crossing place and market centre. The present bridge was opened in 1828, but a bridge existed here in the 13th century, providing the furthest downstream access across the river above London Bridge until 1750. The earliest surviving town charter is dated 1200, and it was granted a fair by Henry III and market charters by James I and Charles II.

Kingsway

Thoroughfare in central London, connecting Holborn with the Strand. Opened in 1905, it was named after King Edward VII. The street runs from High Holborn, opposite Southampton Row, to Aldwych.

A tunnel, formerly for tramways, ran below Kingsway, connecting Theobalds Road with the Thames Embankment. Part of is now the Strand underpass (opened 1964), which runs from the northern end of Waterloo Bridge and emerges about halfway up Kingsway.

If Margaret Thatcher wins on Thursday, I warn you not to be ordinary, I warn you not to be young, I warn you not to fall ill, and I warn you not to grow old.

NEIL KINNOCK British Labour politician.
Speech at Bridgend 7 June 1983

Kinks, The

British pop-rock group led by the Davies brothers Ray (1944–) and David (1947–), whose songs include 'You Really Got Me' (1964), 'Tired of Waiting For You' (1965), and 'Waterloo Sunset' (1967).

Kinnock, Neil Gordon (1942–)

British Labour politician, party leader 1983–92. Born and educated in Wales, he was elected to represent a Welsh constituency in Parliament in 1970 (Islwyn from 1983). He was further left than prime ministers Wilson and Callaghan, but as party leader (in succession to Michael Foot) adopted a moderate position, initiating a major policy review 1988–89. He resigned as party leader after Labour's defeat in the 1992 general election. In 1994 he left parliament to become a European commissioner and was given the transport portfolio.

Kinross-shire

Former county of east-central Scotland, merged in 1975 in Tayside Region. Kinross was the county town.

There's a whisper down the field where the year has shot her yield, / And the ricks stand grey to the sun, / Singing: 'Over then, come over, for the bee has quit the clover, / And your English summer's done.'

RUDYARD KIPLING English writer.
'The Long Trail'

Kintyre, or Cantire

Longest peninsula in Scotland, in Argyll and Bute unitary authority, lying between the Firth of Clyde and the Atlantic. Joined to the Argyll mainland by the isthmus of Tarbert, it extends southwest for a distance of 70 km/43 mi, with an average width of 10 km/6 mi. Agriculture, fishing, tourism, forestry, and stone quarrying are the main occupations in the area, and its largest centre is Campbeltown. The southernmost headland of the peninsula is the **Mull of Kintyre**.

Kipling, (Joseph) Rudyard (1865–1936)

English writer, born in India. *Plain Tales from the Hills* (1888), about Anglo-Indian society, contains the earliest of his masterly short stories. His books for children, including *The Jungle Book* (1894–95), *Just So Stories* (1902), *Puck of Pook's Hill* (1906), and the picaresque novel *Kim* (1901), reveal his imaginative identification with the exotic. Poems such as 'If–', 'Danny Deever', and 'Gunga Din', express an empathy with common experience, which contributed to his great popularity, together with a vivid sense of 'Englishness' (sometimes denigrated as a kind of jingoist imperialism).

Born in Bombay, Kipling was educated at the United Services College at Westward Ho!, Devon, England, which provided the background for *Stalky and Co* (1899). He worked as a journalist in India from 1882 to 1889 and lived largely in the USA from 1892 to 1999, where he produced the two *Jungle Books* and *Captains Courageous* (1897). Settling in Sussex, southeast England, he published *Kim*, usually regarded as his greatest work of fiction; the *Just So Stories*; *Puck of Pook's Hill*; and *Rewards and Fairies* (1910).

Kipling's work is increasingly valued for its complex characterization and subtle moral viewpoints. He was awarded the Nobel Prize for Literature in 1907.

Kipping, Frederic Stanley (1863–1949)
English chemist who pioneered the study of the organic compounds of silicon; he invented the term 'silicone', which is now applied to the entire class of oxygen-containing polymers.

Kirbye, George (*c.* 1565–1634)
English composer. He first appeared as the most copious contributor, except John Farmer, to Thomas East's psalter *The Whole Book of Psalmes* (1592). In 1598 he married Anne Saxye, and he seems to have lived at that time at Rushbrooke near Bury St Edmunds, Suffolk, as domestic musician at the residence of Sir Robert Jermyn. In 1597 he dedicated his book of 24 madrigals to Jermyn's daughters. In 1601 he contributed a madrigal to *The Triumphes of Oriana.*

Works include motets, a hymn, madrigals, and pavan for viols.

Kirkby-in-Ashfield
Town in Nottinghamshire, England, 19 km/12 mi northeast of Nottingham; population (1991) 18,400. It was formerly the centre of an extensive coal-mining area.

Kirkcaldy
Seaport on the north side of the Firth of Forth, Fife, Scotland, 24 km/15 mi north of Edinburgh across the Forth; population (1991) 47,200. Industries include the manufacture of linoleum, paper, and whisky. It is the birthplace of the economist Adam Smith (1723) and where he retired to write his treatise *The Wealth of Nations*. It is also the birthplace of the architect Robert Adam.

The town has been called 'Lang Toun'; its main street is about 6 km/4 mi long. Every April it hosts the Links Market, reputed to be the longest street fair in Europe.

Kirkintilloch
Industrial and commuter town, and administrative headquarters of ◊East Dunbartonshire unitary authority, Scotland, situated on the Forth and Clyde Canal, 11 km/7 mi northeast of Glasgow; population (1991) 31,300. It has iron and steel foundries and a ferro-concrete works, and also manufactures hosiery and waterproof materials.

Kirkoswald
Village in South Ayrshire unitary authority, Scotland, 6 km/4 mi southwest of Maybole; population (1991) 300. The poet Robert Burns studied here briefly and two of his fictional characters, Tam o'Shanter and Souter Johnnie, are supposed to be modelled on people he met: Douglas Graham of Shanter Farm and John Davidson the shoemaker (souter). Their graves are in Kirkoswald churchyard. Souter Johnnie's cottage now belongs to the National Trust of Scotland and is open to the public.

Kirkwall
Administrative headquarters and port of the ◊Orkney Islands, Scotland, on the north coast of the largest island, Mainland; population (1991) 6,700. The main industry is distilling. The Norse cathedral of St Magnus dates from 1137. The Bishop's Palace is also 12th-century, and the Earl's Palace was completed in 1606.

Every Christmas and New Year's Day, a unique football match, known as the Ba', is played. The match can involve 200 players and last for seven hours.

Kitaj, R(onald) B(rooks) (1932–)
US painter and graphic artist, active in Britain. His work is mainly figurative, and employs a wide range of allusions to art, history, and literature. *The Autumn of Central Paris (After Walter Benjamin)* (1972–74) is a typical work. His distinctive use of colour and economy of line was in part inspired by studies of the Impressionist painter Degas, and has similarities with oriental art.

Much of Kitaj's work is outside the predominant avant-garde trend and inspired by diverse historical styles. Some compositions are in triptych form.

Kit-Cat Club
Club founded in London in 1703 to encourage literature and art, and named after Christopher Cat (or Katt), at whose tavern it met. Ultimately it became a Whig society to promote the Hanoverian succession. Among its original 39 members were the Duke of Marlborough, Robert Walpole, Joseph Addison, Richard Steele, and William Congreve. The membership later increased to 48.

> *I don't mind your being killed, but I object to your being taken prisoner.*
>
> Horatio Herbert Kitchener, Earl Kitchener of Khartoum
> Irish soldier and administrator.
> To the Prince of Wales (later Edward VIII) when he asked to go to the Front in World War I, quoted in Viscount Esher's *Journal* 18 December 1914

Kitchener, Horatio (Herbert), 1st Earl Kitchener of Khartoum (1850–1916)
Irish soldier and administrator. He defeated the Sudanese at the Battle of Omdurman in 1898 and reoccupied Khartoum. In South Africa, he was commander in chief 1900–02 during the Boer War, and he commanded the forces in India 1902–09. Appointed war minister on the outbreak of World War I, he was successful in his campaign calling for voluntary recruitment.

Kitchener was born in County Kerry, Ireland. He was commissioned in 1871, and transferred to the Egyptian army in 1882. Promoted to commander in chief in 1892, he forced a French expedition to withdraw from the Sudan in the Fashoda Incident. During the South African War he acted first as Lord Roberts's Chief of Staff and then as commander in chief. He conducted war by a scorched-earth policy and created the earliest concentration camps for civilians. Subsequently he commanded the forces in India and acted as British agent in Egypt, and in 1914 received an earldom. As British secretary of state for war from 1914, he modernized the British forces. He was one of the first to realize that the war would not be 'over by Christmas' and planned for a three-year war, for which he began raising new armies. He bears some responsibility for the failure of the Gallipoli campaign, having initially refused any troops for the venture, and from then on his influence declined. He drowned when his ship struck a German mine on the way to Russia.

kitchen-sink movement

Loose-knit group of British painters, active in the late 1940s and early 1950s. They depicted drab, everyday scenes with an aggressive technique and often brilliant, 'crude' colour. The name was coined in 1954 by the art critic David Sylvester.

The best known were John ◊Bratby, Derrick Greaves (1927–), Edward Middleditch (1923–1987), and Jack Smith (1928–). These painters had something in common with the 'Angry Young Men' writers of the same time, and playwrights such as John Osborne are sometimes described as 'kitchen sink dramatists'.

Knaresborough

Market town in North Yorkshire, northern England, on the River Nidd, 6 km/4 mi northeast of Harrogate; population (1991) 13,600. It has a diverse range of service sector and light industries, including the manufacture of circuit boards, plastic products (double glazing), stainless steel goods, hi-fi speakers, and flags and bunting.There is an outstanding railway viaduct, and the remains of a castle first established around 1070.

Most of the castle ruins date from the 14th century, and there is a well-preserved dungeon. To the south of the town is a 'dropping well' where the water has petrifying qualities, immersed items becoming coated with calcium carbonate. Nearby is the cave where the prophet Mother Shipton is said to have lived. St Robert's Cave, or Eugene Aram's Cave, is where the convicted murderer Eugene Aram is said to have hidden the corpse of Daniel Clark, a local shoemaker, in 1745. The chapel of Our Lady in the Crag lies near St Robert's Cave.

Knebworth

Town in Hertfordshire, England, 14 km/9 mi east of Luton; population (1991) 4,200. Knebworth has been used as a location for many rock music festivals. At **Knebworth House**, home of the Lytton family since 1492, Edward Bulwer-Lytton wrote many of his novels.

Kneller, Godfrey born Gottfried Kniller (1646–1723)

German-born portrait painter who lived in England from 1674. A successful and prolific painter of nearly 6,000 portraits, he dominated English portraiture of the late 17th and early 18th centuries. He was court painter to Charles II, James II, William III, and George I.

Among his paintings are the series *Hampton Court Beauties* (Hampton Court, Surrey), a sequel to Peter Lely's *Windsor Beauties*; and 48 portraits of the members of the Whig Kit Cat Club (1702–17; National Portrait Gallery, London). His studio, which was attended by most of the outstanding English artists of the 18th century, was the immediate forerunner of the first real drawing school in London. He was knighted in 1692 and made a baronet in 1715.

Knight, Laura born Johnson (1877–1970)

English painter. Her reputation was based on her detailed, narrative scenes of Romany, fairground, and circus life, and the ballet. During World War II she was an official war artist.

Born in Long Eaton, Derbyshire, she studied at Nottingham School of Art, and then at South Kensington School of Art. She first exhibited at the Royal Academy in 1903, and in 1936 she became the first woman since Angelica Kauffmann and Mary Moser to become a full member of the Academy.

Her autobiography, *Oil Paint and Grease Paint*, was published in 1936. Other publications were *A Proper Circus Omie* (1962) and *The Magic of a Line* (1965). She was made DBE in 1929.

knighthood, orders of

Fraternity carrying with it the rank of knight, admission to which is granted as a mark of royal favour or as a reward for public services. During the Middle Ages in Europe such fraternities fell into two classes: religious and secular. The first class, including the **Templars** and the Knights of **St John**, consisted of knights who had taken religious vows and devoted themselves to military service against the Saracens (Arabs) or other non-Christians. The secular orders probably arose from bands of knights engaged in the service of a prince or great noble.

These knights wore the badge of their patrons or the emblems of their patron saints. A **knight bachelor** belongs to the lowest stage of knighthood, not being a member of any specially named order. See ◊honours list for a table of the orders of chivalry.

The Order of the ◊Garter, founded in 1348, is the oldest now in existence; other British orders include the Thistle, founded in 1687, the Bath (see ◊Bath, Order of the), founded in 1725, the St Patrick (1788), the St Michael and St George (1818), the Star of India (1861), the Indian Empire (1878), the Royal Victorian Order (1896), and the Order of the British Empire (OBE), founded in 1917, and the Order of Merit (see ◊Merit, Order of) (OM), founded in 1902.

Most of the ancient European orders, such as the Order of the Golden Fleece, have disappeared as a result of political changes.

In addition to the orders listed above, the Military Knights of Windsor consist of retired officers with outstanding service records; they are attached to the Order of the Garter. The **Most Illustrious Order of St Patrick**, the national order of Ireland, was founded in 1783 by George III. It was formed on the model of the Garter, and named after the Irish patron saint. The motto is 'Quis separabit' ('Who shall separate'). The insignia are the star of the cross of St Patrick on a field argent, charged with three imperial crowns within a circle azure, with motto above. There have been no elections to the order since 1924.

The **Royal Victorian Order** was founded in 1896 by Queen Victoria. It is awarded 'for personal services to the queen and her successors'. The motto is 'Victoria'. The order uses the Chapel Royal of the Savoy, London. The **Most Eminent Order of the Indian Empire** was established in 1878 under the grandmastership of the viceroy of India, to commemorate Queen Victoria's assumption of the title Empress of India. It was awarded for services to the Indian Empire. The collar is composed of elephants, peacocks, and Indian roses. The motto is '*Imperatricis auspiciis*' ('Under the auspices of the empress'). No appointments have been made since 1947.

The **Imperial Order of the Crown of India** was founded in 1878 by Queen Victoria and limited to women of the royal house and high-ranking women in India, either British or Indian; it carried no rank or title. There have been no elections since the Queen and Princess Margaret were appointed in 1947. The **Most Exalted Order of the Star of India**, instituted in 1861, comprised knights grand commanders, knights commanders, and companions. The collar of the star consists of links of lotus flowers, red and white roses, and palm branches. The motto is 'Heaven's Light our Guide'. No appointments have been made since 1947. A ◊Companion of Honour receives no title or precedence. **Knights Bachelor** do not constitute a royal order, but comprise the surviving representation of the ancient state order of knighthood.

The Register of Knights Bachelor, instituted by James I in the 17th century, lapsed, and a voluntary association, known as the Imperial Society of Knights Bachelor by royal command, was formed in 1908 with the primary objects of continuing the various registers dating from 1257, and obtaining the uniform registration of every created knight. A badge to be worn by Knights Bachelor was adopted in 1926.

Knights of the Round Table

In British legend, the knights of King Arthur; see ◊Round Table.

Knole

House in Kent, England, situated 1.5 km/1 mi from Sevenoaks. One of the largest private houses in England, it was begun by Thomas Bourchier (*c.* 1404–1486), archbishop of Canterbury, in 1456, but greatly extended around 1603 by Thomas Sackville, to whom it was granted by Queen Elizabeth I. It was given in 1946 by the 4th Lord Sackville to the National Trust.

The state rooms contain a large number of historic pictures, rare furniture (including the Knole settee), rugs, and tapestries.

Knox, John (*c.* 1505–1572)

Scottish Protestant reformer, founder of the Church of Scotland. He spent several years in exile for his beliefs, including a period in Geneva where he met John Calvin. He returned to Scotland in 1559 to promote Presbyterianism. His books include *First Blast of the Trumpet Against the Monstrous Regiment of Women* (1558).

Originally a Roman Catholic priest, Knox is thought to have been converted by the reformer George Wishart. When Wishart was burned for heresy, Knox went into hiding, but later preached the reformed doctrines.

Captured by French troops in Scotland in 1547, he was imprisoned in France, sentenced to the galleys, and released only by the intercession of the British government in 1549. In England he assisted in compiling the Prayer Book, as a royal chaplain from 1551. On the accession of Mary I in 1553 he fled the country and in 1557 was, in his absence, condemned to be burned. In 1559 he returned to Scotland. He was tried for treason but acquitted in 1563. He wrote a *History of the Reformation in Scotland* (1586).

Knox, Ronald Arbuthnott (1888–1957)

English Roman Catholic scholar whose translation of the Bible (1945–49) was officially approved by the Roman Catholic Church.

KNOX, JOHN *The 16th-century Scottish Protestant reformer and founder of Presbyterianism, John Knox. Originally a Roman Catholic, Knox spent some years in exile after the accession of Mary Queen of Scots and met Calvin in Geneva. Knox was an outspoken and zealous preacher, and his influence on the Scottish Reformation was seminal. Corbis*

A fellow of Trinity College, Oxford 1910–17, he became Anglican chaplain to the University of Oxford on his ordination in 1912, but resigned in 1917 on his conversion, and was Catholic chaplain 1926–39. He wrote six detective stories.

Knussen, (Stuart) Oliver (1952–)

English composer and conductor. An eclectic and prolific composer, his works include the operas *Where the Wild Things Are* (1983), based on the children's story by Maurice Sendak, and *Higglety Pigglety Pop!* (1990). He was made a CBE in 1994.

Knutsford

Town in Cheshire, northwest England, 25 km/16 mi southwest of Manchester; population (1991) 13,400. Its engineering manufactures are particularly associated with the nuclear industry and power stations; diverse light industrial products include scientific instruments. The town is also a centre for financial, information technology, and business services. The novelist Elizabeth Gaskell, who lived in Knutsford for 22 years and is buried here, chose it as the setting for her novel *Cranford*.

Nearby to the north is Tatton Park, which includes Tatton Hall, built at the end of the 18th century.

Kollmann, August Friedrich Christoph (1756–1829)

German organist, theorist, and composer. He held a post at Lüne, near Lüneburg, but in 1782 went to London, where he was appointed sacristan and cantor of the German Chapel, St James's. He wrote many theoretical works, and also composed a piano concerto and chamber music.

Korda, Alexander (Laszlo) (1893–1956)

Hungarian-born British film producer and director. He was a dominant figure in the British film industry during the 1930s and 1940s. His films as director include *Marius* (1931), in France, and *The Private Life of Henry VIII* (1933), in England. He was the producer of *The Scarlet Pimpernel* (1935), *The Thief of Bagdad* (1940), *The Third Man* (1949), and *Richard III* (1956), among many others.

Korda formed London Film Productions in 1932, later linking his company with Metro-Goldwyn-Mayer to form MGM-British Productions. He did much to make British films the equal of the Hollywood product.

Krebs, Hans Adolf (1900–1981)

German-born British biochemist. He discovered the citric acid cycle, also known as the **Krebs cycle**, the final pathway by which food molecules are converted into energy in living tissues. For this work he shared the 1953 Nobel Prize for Physiology or Medicine.

Krebs first became interested in the process by which the body degrades amino acids. He discovered that nitrogen atoms are the first to be removed (deamination) and are then excreted as urea in the urine. He then investigated the processes involved in the production of urea from the removed nitrogen atoms, and by 1932 he had worked out the basic steps in the urea cycle. He was knighted in 1958.

Kubrick, Stanley (1928–)

US film director, producer, and screenwriter, based in England for much of his filmmaking career. His work is eclectic in subject matter and ambitious in scale and technique. It includes *Paths of Glory* (1957), *Dr Strangelove* (1964), *2001: A Space Odyssey* (1968), *A Clockwork Orange* (1971), and *Full Metal Jacket* (1987).

A former photographer in the USA, Kubrick has been critically acclaimed and much admired among his filmmaking peers; he is responsible for *Killer's Kiss* (1955), *The Killing* (1956), *Lolita* (1962), and *The Shining* (1980). His latest work is *Eyes Wide Shut*, starring Tom Cruise and Nicole Kidman, which began shooting in late 1996.

Kureishi, Hanif (1954–)

English dramatist, filmmaker, and novelist. Much of his work explores the interaction of Asian and Anglo communities living in Britain. His early plays *Outskirts* (1981) and *Birds of Passage* (1983) were followed by the screenplays for the films *My Beautiful Laundrette* (1985) and *Sammy and Rosie Get Laid* (1987), both directed by Stephen ◊Frears. He wrote and directed the film *London Kills Me* (1991).

Kureishi's novel *The Buddha of Suburbia* (1990) was adapted to the screen in a popular television miniseries in 1993. He also wrote *The Black Album* (1995), and adapted his novel *My Son the Fanatic* into a movie screenplay in 1998.

Kyle of Lochalsh

Coastal village in west Highland unitary authority, Scotland, 100 km/63 mi west of Inverness; population (1991) 900. It is a railway terminus. The Skye Road Bridge stands 2 km/1 mi to the north of the village.

Built using private sector money, the bridge was opened in 1995, and has resulted in the closure of the Calmac ferry service, which was based at the village's ferry port.

Laban, Rudolf von (1879–1958)

Hungarian dancer, choreographer, and dance and movement theoretician. A seminal influence on dance theatre in Europe, he emigrated to England shortly after having created the dances for the 1936 Berlin Olympic Games, to concentrate on developing his theories on educational dance and movement analysis. In 1946 he established with Lisa Ullmann what was later to become the Laban Centre for Movement and Research, based in southeast London. His theories continue to have great influence, as does the system of Labanotation that he developed, first published in the 1920s, which formalized annotation of dance and movement.

Labour Party

Political party based on socialist principles, originally formed to represent workers. It was founded in 1900 and first held office in 1924. The first majority Labour government 1945–51 introduced nationalization and the National Health Service, and expanded ◊social security. Labour was again in power 1964–70, 1974–79 and from 1997. The party leader (Tony ◊Blair from 1994) is elected by an electoral college, with a weighted representation of the Parliamentary Labour Party (30%), constituency parties (30%), and trade unions (40%).

In 1900 a conference representing the trade unions, the Independent Labour Party (ILP), and the ◊Fabian Society, founded the Labour Party, known until 1906, when 29 seats were gained, as the Labour Representation Committee. All but a pacifist minority of the Labour Party supported World War I, and in 1918 a socialist programme was first adopted, with local branches of the party set up to which individual members were admitted. By 1922 the Labour Party was recognized as the official opposition, and in 1924 formed a minority government (with Liberal support) for a few months under the party's first secretary Ramsay MacDonald.

A second minority government in 1929 followed a conservative policy, and in 1931 MacDonald and other leaders, faced with a financial crisis, left the party to support the national government. The ILP seceded in 1932.

From 1936 to 1939 there was internal dissension on foreign policy; the leadership's support of nonintervention in Spain was strongly criticized and Stafford Cripps, Aneurin Bevan, and others were expelled for advocating an alliance of all left-wing parties against the government of Neville Chamberlain. The Labour Party supported Winston Churchill's wartime coalition, but then withdrew and took office for the first time as a majority government under Clement Attlee, party leader from 1935, after the 1945 elections. The welfare state was developed by nationalization of essential services and industries, a system of national insurance was established in 1946, and the National Health Service was founded in 1948. Defeated in 1951, Labour was split by disagreements on further nationalization, and unilateral or multilateral disarmament, but achieved unity under Hugh Gaitskell's leadership 1955–63.

Under Harold Wilson the party returned to power 1964–70 and, with a very slender majority, 1974–79. James Callaghan, who had succeeded Wilson in 1976, was forced to a general election in 1979 and lost. Michael Foot was elected to the leadership in 1980; Neil Kinnock succeeded him in 1983 after Labour had lost another general election. The party adopted a policy of unilateral nuclear disarmament in 1986 and expelled the left-wing faction Militant Tendency, but rifts remained. Labour lost the 1987 general election, a major reason being its non-nuclear policy. In spite of the Conservative government's declining popularity, Labour was defeated in the 1992 general election, following which Neil Kinnock stepped down as party leader; John Smith succeeded him July in 1992 but died suddenly in May 1994. Tony Blair was elected to succeed him in July 1994, in the first fully democratic elections to the post, and launched a campaign to revise the party's constitution by scrapping Clause 4, concerning common ownership of the means of production, and ending trade union direct sponsorship of MPs; a new charter was approved in April 1995.

We are not here just to manage capitalism but to change society and to define its finer values.

TONY BENN British Labour politician.
Speech, Labour Party Conference 1975

Under the title **New Labour**, Blair sought to move the party nearer to the 'middle ground' of politics to secure the 'middle England' vote. By 1996 Labour Party membership was 365,000 and rising and it led the Conservatives in the opinion polls by more than 20 points. The Labour Party returned to power after a landslide victory in the May 1997 general election. Membership peaked in January 1998, at 405,000, and began to gradually decline for the first time since Blair became leader, amid concerns among traditionalist members that control over the party had become too centralized.

The Labour Party's anthem is 'The Red Flag', written by the Irish socialist Jim Connell (1850–1929) during the London strike in 1889.

Labour Representation Committee

Forerunner (1900–06) of the Labour Party. The committee was founded in February 1900 after a resolution drafted by Ramsay ◊MacDonald, moved by the Amalgamated Society of Railway Workers (now the National Union of Railwaymen), and was carried at the 1899 Trades Union Congress (TUC). The resolution called for a special congress of the TUC parliamentary committee to campaign for more Labour members of Parliament. Ramsay MacDonald became its secretary.

Following his efforts, 29 Labour members of Parliament were elected in the 1906 general election, and the Labour Representation Committee was renamed the Labour Party.

lacemaking

Following the development of lace in the late 15th and early 16th centuries, attempts were made from 1589 to produce a machine-made product. In 1809 this was achieved by John Heathcoat (1783–1861) using a bobbin net machine, the principles of which continue today in the manufacture of plain net. The earliest machine for making true lace (bobbin or pillow lace), reproducing the movements of the workers' fingers, was invented by John Leavers in 1813. It had a wooden frame with mostly wooden moving parts, but worked on the same principle as the modern machines in Nottingham, the centre of machine-made lace.

Lacock

Village in Wiltshire, England, mostly owned by the National Trust, including **Lacock Abbey**, Manor Farm, and Bewley Common, about 130 ha/321 acres in all. Lacock Abbey was a nunnery for Augustinian canonesses, and the 13th-century cloisters, sacristy, chapter-house, and nuns' parlour remain. After the Reformation, around 1540, William Sharrington built a Tudor mansion around these monastic ruins, the chief features of which are the octagonal tower overlooking the River Avon and the large courtyard with half-timbered gables and clock-house.

It was at Lacock that William Henry Fox ◊Talbot pioneered his photographic process, and a museum of his work is now open at the Abbey.

Lady

Formal title of the daughter of an earl, marquess, or duke, and of any woman whose husband's rank is above that of baronet or knight; the title 'Lady' is prefixed to her first name. The wife of a baronet or a knight is also called 'Lady', but uses the title by courtesy only, and has it prefixed to her surname.

Lady Chatterley's Lover

Novel by D H ◊Lawrence, printed privately in Florence in 1928 and in an expurgated form in England in 1932; in its original form it was not published until 1959 in the United States and 1960 in Britain after the obscenity laws had been successfully challenged. The novel explores the love affair between Constance Chatterley and her husband's gamekeeper, Oliver Mellors, and was suppressed owing to its detailed descriptions of the sexual act and its uncompromising language.

In 1960 Penguin Books were prosecuted under the Obscene Publications Act of 1959, but after a celebrated trial, in which authors such as E M Forster defended the book's publication, Penguin Books were found not guilty of publishing an obscene book, so breaking the ban on the book's publication in Britain.

Laing, R(onald) D(avid) (1927–1989)

Scottish psychoanalyst. He was the originator of the social theory of mental illness; for example, that schizophrenia is promoted by family pressure for its members to conform to standards alien to themselves. His books include *The Divided Self* (1960) and *The Politics of the Family* (1971).

Influenced by existentialist philosophy, Laing inspired the antipsychiatry movement. He observed interactions between people in an attempt to understand and describe their experience and thinking. In *The Divided Self* he criticized the psychiatrist's role as one that, with its objective scientific outlook, depersonalized the patient. By investigating the personal interactions within the families of diagnosed schizophrenics, he found that the seemingly bizarre behaviour normally regarded as indicating the illness began to make sense.

Lake District

Region in Cumbria, northwest England. It contains the principal English lakes, separated by wild uplands rising to many peaks, including ◊Scafell Pike (978 m/3,210 ft), the highest peak in England. The area was made a national park in 1951, covering 2,292 sq km/882 sq mi, and is a popular tourist destination.

The Lake District has associations with the writers William Wordsworth, Samuel Taylor Coleridge, Robert Southey, Thomas De Quincey, John Ruskin, and Beatrix Potter. The principal lakes are ◊Windermere, the largest lake in England; ◊Ullswater; ◊Derwent Water; ◊Coniston Water; Bassenthwaite; and Thirlmere. Peaks include Helvellyn (950 m/3,118 ft) and Great Gable (899 m/2,949 ft). The main tourist centres are Windermere, ◊Keswick, ◊Ambleside, and ◊Grasmere. The overall population is 41,600, and growing slowly.

Thirlmere, Hawes Water, and some other smaller lakes are managed as reservoirs for some of England's major conurbations, including Manchester.

The Lake District has a radial system of valleys, deepened by glaciers. Windermere, in the southeast, is connected with Rydal Water and Grasmere. The westerly Scafell range extends south to the Old Man of Coniston overlooking Coniston Water, and north to Wastwater. Ullswater lies in the northeast of the district, on the east side of Helvellyn peak, with Hawes Water and Thirlmere nearby. The River Derwent flows north through Borrowdale forming Derwentwater and Bassenthwaite. West of Borrowdale lie Buttermere, Crummock Water, and, beyond, Ennerdale Water. Woodland includes broadleaf species, partly naturally occurring; and the plantations (mainly coniferous) of the Forestry Commission. Much of the scenery is relatively wild and very attractive.

Conservation

There are 100 Sites of Special Scientific Interest, and 82 regionally important geological or geomorphological sites, making the area of enormous conservation interest. There are also nearly 2,000 listed buildings. Much of the land in the area is owned by the National Trust, and the National Park owns 8,600 ha/3,481 acres of the land under their jurisdiction.

Economy

Agriculture (particularly sheep farming), foresty, and fishing employ about 10% of the working population, with a further 5% employed in energy, water, and mining. Manufacturing industries employ about 10%, and the construction industry another 8%, but almost 38% of the population is supported by retailing, tourism, and catering, with another 30% in general service industries.

History

Before 1974 the Lake District formed part of Cumberland, Westmorland, and the Furness district of Lancashire.

Laker, Jim (James Charles) (1922–1986)

English cricketer who in the 4th Test against Australia at Manchester in 1956 returned figures of 9–37 and 10–53 to become the first bowler to take 19 wickets in a Test or first-class match, and to take 10 wickets in Test match innings, records which have never been equalled. A tall, right-arm off-spinner with a classical action, he took 193 wickets in 46 Tests, 1948–59, at an average of 21.24.

A vital member of the formidable Surrey team which won a record seven consecutive County Championships between 1952 and 1958, he later became a respected TV commentator on the game.

Lallans

Variant of 'lowlands' and a name for Lowland Scots, whether conceived as a language in its own right or as a northern dialect of English. Because of its rustic associations, Lallans has been known since the 18th century as 'the Doric', in contrast with the 'Attic' usage of Edinburgh ('the Athens of the North'). See ◊Scots language.

Lamb, Charles (1775–1834)

English essayist and critic. He collaborated with his sister **Mary Lamb** (1764–1847) on *Tales from Shakespeare* (1807), and his *Specimens of English Dramatic Poets Contemporary with Shakespeare, with Notes* (1808) revealed him as a penetrating critic and helped to revive interest in Elizabethan plays. As 'Elia' he contributed essays to the *London Magazine* from 1820 (collected 1823 and 1833).

Lamb's essays are still widely read and admired; they include 'A Dissertation on Roast Pig', 'Mrs Battle's Opinions on Whist', 'Dream Children', and 'The Supernatural Man'.

As a friend of Coleridge, some of his poems were included in the second edition of *Poems on Various Subjects* (1797). He was a clerk with the East India Company at India House 1792–1825, when he retired to Enfield. His sister Mary stabbed their mother to death in a fit of insanity in 1796, and Charles cared for her between her periodic returns to an asylum.

Lamb, Henry (1885–1960)

English painter. He is best known for his portraits, in particular *Lytton Strachey* (1914; Tate Gallery, London), and for paintings of war in Palestine and Salonika made from 1919 to 1920.

Associated with the ◊Bloomsbury Group and the Camden Town painters, he painted in a number of genres. His portraiture is especially notable for its family groups, such as *The Anrep Family* (1921). In World War II he was an official war artist and his work is well represented in the Imperial War Museum.

Lambeth

Inner borough of south central Greater London. It includes the districts of Waterloo, Kennington, Clapham, Stockwell, and Brixton

Features Lambeth Palace, chief residence of the archbishop of Canterbury since 1200, with brick Tudor gatehouse (1495); Tradescant museum of gardening history; the ◊South Bank, including Royal Festival Hall, Hayward Gallery, National Theatre, the Art Deco Oxo Wharf Tower (1928), now converted into mixed-use development; the Oval (headquarters of Surrey County Cricket Club from 1846) at Kennington, where the first England–Australia test match was played 1880; Old Vic theatre (1816–18); Brixton Prison; Anti-Slavery Archive in Brixton; Channel Tunnel rail terminal at Waterloo; London Aquarium opened 1997 in part of converted County Hall

Population (1991) 244,800

Lambeth Palace

London residence of the archbishops of Canterbury, situated by Lambeth Bridge in the London borough of Lambeth. Building was begun by Archbishop Hubert ◊Walter at the end of the 12th century, although Stephen ◊Langton was the first archbishop to live here. The chapel dates from around 1230 with stalls erected byArchbishop Laud in 1634, and beneath it is a crypt built around 1200.

Lollards Tower was built as a water tower in 1434–35, but was so called in the belief that Lollards (followers of the English religious reformer John Wycliffe in the 14th century) were imprisoned there. The guard chamber has a 14th-century roof and contains portraits of all archbishops since

1503. The entrance is by Morton's Tower, a red brick gatehouse built around 1490. The Great Hall was rebuilt in the medieval style by Archbishop Juxon in 1663 and now houses the library, whichs was founded by Archbishop Bancroft in 1610. The residential part dates from 1829 to 1838.

Lammermuir Hills

Range of hills dividing East Lothian and Scottish Borders, Scotland, running northeast from Gala Water to St Abb's Head on the North Sea. The highest summits are Meikle Says Law (535 m/1,755 ft) and Lammer Law (527 m/1,730 ft).

Lamont, Norman Stewart Hughson (1942–)

British Conservative politician, chief secretary of the Treasury 1989–90, chancellor of the Exchequer 1990–93. In September 1992, despite earlier assurances to the contrary, he was forced to suspend Britain's membership of the European Community (now the European Union) Exchange Rate Mechanism (ERM). He was replaced as chancellor by Kenneth Clarke in May 1993, after which he became a fierce right-wing critic of the Major administration. He lost his House of Commons seat in the May 1997 general election.

Lampeter (Welsh Llanbedr Pont Steffan)

Market town in Ceredigion (Cardiganshire), central Wales, on the River Teifi; population (1991) 2,000. The name **Pont Steffan** is derived from an ancient stone bridge over the river. St David's University College, founded at Lampeter in 1822, is part of the University of Wales.

Lanark

Town in South Lanarkshire, Scotland, on the Clyde; population (1991) 8,900. **New Lanark** to the south, near the Falls of Clyde, was founded as a cotton-spinning centre and was developed as a 'model community' by Robert Owen and Richard Arkwright at the end of the 18th century, with the aim of providing decent conditions for workers and their families. Although there are a few light industries, the town is principally important for agricultural economies.

There is a golfcourse and a racecourse. Lanark was one of the four original royal burghs of Scotland created by David I. William Wallace once lived here, and later returned to burn the town and kill the English sheriff.

David Dale was originally in partnership with Richard Arkwright at New Lanark, but was replaced by Robert Owen after arguments with Arkwright.

Lancashire

County of northwest England (since April 1998 Blackpool and Blackburn have been separate unitary authorities)

Area 3,040 sq km/1,173 sq mi

Towns and cities Preston (administrative headquarters), which forms part of Central Lancashire New Town from

LANCASHIRE COTTON MILL *Male factory workers spinning yarn in a Lancashire cotton mill in the 1890s. Along with the metal industries, textile manufacturing had been central to the industrial revolution a consequence of which had been a steep increase in population during the 19th century. Private collection*

1970 (together with Fulwood, Bamber Bridge, Leyland, and Chorley); Lancaster, Accrington, Burnley; ports Fleetwood and Heysham; seaside resorts Morecambe and Southport
Features the River Ribble; the Pennines; the Forest of Bowland (moors and farming valleys); Pendle Hill
Industries formerly a world centre of cotton manufacture, now replaced with high-technology aerospace, nuclear fuels, and electronics industries. There is dairy farming and market gardening
Population (1994) 1,424,000
Famous people Kathleen Ferrier, Gracie Fields, George Formby, Rex Harrison.

Lancaster

British heavy bomber of World War II made by the Avro company. It was first flown in June 1941 and developed into the RAF's best heavy bomber of the war. Lancaster bombers were responsible for the sinking of the *Tirpitz* and the 'dambuster' raids in 1944.

A heavy four-engine bomber, it was capable of carrying up to 6,350 kg/14,000 lbs of bombs at a speed of 462 kph/287 mph for 2,575 km/1,600 mi. Highly adaptable, it could carry the 5,500 kg/12,000 lb Tallboy bomb and took the bouncing bomb used in the 'dambuster' raids on the Ruhr dams.

Lancaster

City in Lancashire, northwest England, on the River Lune; population (1991) 44,500. Until 1974 it was the county town of Lancashire (now Preston). Industries include the manufacture of paper, furniture, plastics, chemicals, textiles, and wall and floor coverings (linoleum). The service sector is the largest employer, and there is an important livestock market. Education facilities include the University of Lancaster (1964) and St Martin's College. The city's castle was originally established in the 11th century on the site of a Roman fort.

Features

The Norman keep was built in about 1170 and restored in the late 16th century. The castle was enlarged by John of Gaunt, Duke of Lancaster from 1362, and father of Henry IV. It was a parliamentary stronghold during the Civil War. Now much altered it is used as a court and prison. Some of the early structure survives, including the keep and the 13th-century Hadrian's Tower. The priory church of St Mary was founded as a Benedictine priory in 1094. It has a Saxon doorway, but dates mainly from the 15th century. Many of the city's buildings are Georgian, reflecting the period of prosperity in the 18th century when Lancaster was an important port for trade with the West Indies. Other features include St George's Quay, and Custom House (1764) which now houses a museum. The old town hall, now a museum, dates from 1781 to 1783. The Catholic cathedral (1859) has a spire 73 m/239 ft high. The Anglo-Italian Baroque-style Ashton Memorial (1906–09) in Williamson Park was built by Lord Ashton, whose family were linoleum manufacturers. The University of Lancaster contains the Ruskin Library (1996), housing a collection of works by the 19th-century art and social critic John Ruskin. The River Lune Millennium Park is being created by the City Council.

Environs

The nuclear industry at nearby Heysham provides significant employment in the area.

Lancaster, Osbert (1908–1986)

English cartoonist and writer. In 1939 he began producing daily 'pocket cartoons' for the *Daily Express*, in which he satirized current social mores through such characters as Maudie Littlehampton. He was originally a book illustrator and muralist.

In the 1930s and 1940s Lancaster produced several tongue-in-cheek guides to architectural fashion, such as *Homes, Sweet Homes* (1939) and *Drayneflete Revisited* (1949), from which a number of descriptive terms, such as Pont Street Dutch and Stockbroker Tudor, have entered the language. He was knighted in 1975.

Lancaster, House of

English royal house, a branch of the Plantagenets.

It originated in 1267 when Edmund (died 1296), the younger son of Henry III, was granted the earldom of Lancaster. Converted to a duchy for Henry of Grosmont (died 1361), it passed to John of Gaunt in 1362 by his marriage to Blanche, Henry's daughter. John's son, Henry IV, established the royal dynasty of Lancaster in 1399, and he was followed by two more Lancastrian kings, Henry V and Henry VI.

See genealogy on page 510.

Lancelot of the Lake

In British legend, one of King Arthur's knights, the lover of Queen Guinevere. Originally a folk hero, he first appeared in the Arthurian cycle of tales in the 12th century.

Lanchester, Frederick William (1868–1946)

English engineer who began producing motorcars in 1896. His work on stability was fundamental to aviation and he formulated the first comprehensive theory of lift and drag. From early on, Lanchester manufactured his cars with interchangeable parts.

Land Acts, Irish

Series of 19th-century laws designed to improve the lot of the Irish peasantry. The first act in 1870 awarded tenants compensation for improvements they had made to land, but offered no protection against increased rents or eviction. The second act in 1881 introduced the 'three fs' – fair rents, fixity of tenure, and freedom of sale. The third act in 1885, part of Gladstone's abortive plans for Home Rule, provided £5 million for tenants to buy out their landlords. This scheme was further strengthened by the Wyndham Act of 1903 which offered inducements to landlords to sell. Before the end of the Union with Britain, some 11 million acres were purchased with government assistance.

Land League

Irish peasant-rights organization, formed in 1879 by Michael ◊Davitt and Charles ◊Parnell to fight against tenant evictions.

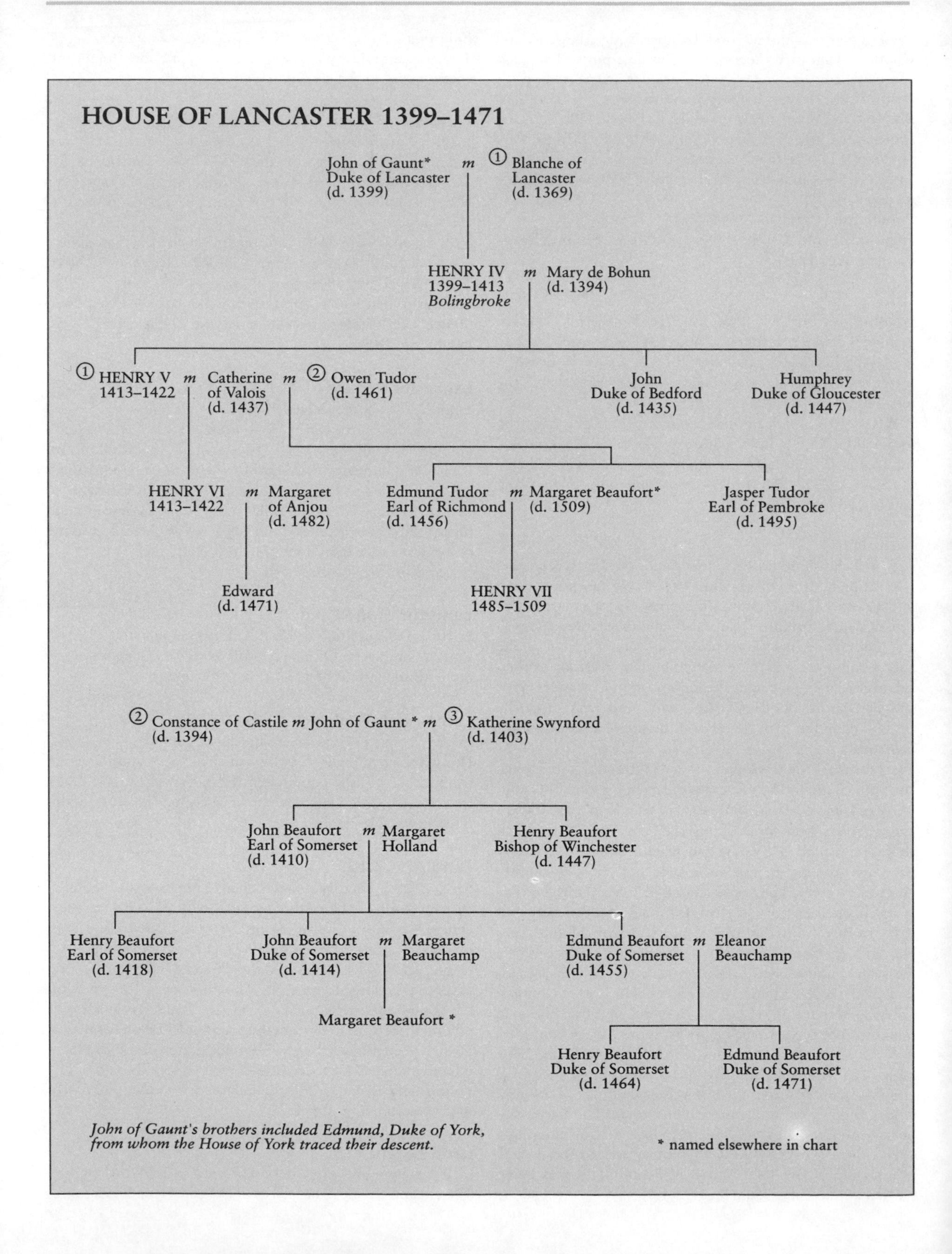
HOUSE OF LANCASTER 1399–1471
John of Gaunt* Duke of Lancaster (d. 1399) m ① Blanche of Lancaster (d. 1369)
HENRY IV 1399–1413 Bolingbroke m Mary de Bohun (d. 1394)
① HENRY V 1413–1422 m Catherine of Valois (d. 1437) m ② Owen Tudor (d. 1461)
John Duke of Bedford (d. 1435)
Humphrey Duke of Gloucester (d. 1447)
HENRY VI 1413–1422 m Margaret of Anjou (d. 1482)
Edmund Tudor Earl of Richmond (d. 1456) m Margaret Beaufort* (d. 1509)
Jasper Tudor Earl of Pembroke (d. 1495)
Edward (d. 1471)
HENRY VII 1485–1509
② Constance of Castile (d. 1394) m John of Gaunt * m ③ Katherine Swynford (d. 1403)
John Beaufort Earl of Somerset (d. 1410) m Margaret Holland
Henry Beaufort Bishop of Winchester (d. 1447)
Henry Beaufort Earl of Somerset (d. 1418)
John Beaufort Duke of Somerset (d. 1414) m Margaret Beauchamp
Edmund Beaufort Duke of Somerset (d. 1455) m Eleanor Beauchamp
Margaret Beaufort *
Henry Beaufort Duke of Somerset (d. 1464)
Edmund Beaufort Duke of Somerset (d. 1471)
John of Gaunt's brothers included Edmund, Duke of York, from whom the House of York traced their descent.
* named elsewhere in chart

Through its skilful use of the boycott against anyone who took a farm from which another had been evicted, it forced Gladstone's government to introduce a law in 1881 restricting rents and granting tenants security of tenure.

Landor, Walter Savage (1775–1864)

English poet and essayist. He lived much of his life abroad, dying in Florence, where he had fled to avoid a libel suit in 1858. His works include the epic poem *Gebir* (1798), the tragedy *Count Julian* (1812), and *Imaginary Conversations of Literary Men and Statesmen* (1824–29). Landor has a high place among prose writers for his restrained and finished style; his shorter poems have the same classic simplicity.

Land Registry, HM

Official body set up 1925 to register legal rights to land in England and Wales. There has been a gradual introduction, since 1925, of compulsory registration of land in different areas of the country. This requires the purchaser of land to register details of his or her title and all other rights (such as mortgages and easements) relating to the land. Once registered, the title to the land is guaranteed by the Land Registry, subject to those interests that cannot be registered; this makes the buying and selling of land easier and cheaper. The records are open to public inspection (since December 1990).

landscape painting

British landscape painting was much influenced by the Dutch, and attained its great development in the 18th and early 19th centuries. Wilson, Crome, the Norwich School, Gainsborough, Constable, and Turner appear in succession and their work in oils is paralleled by that of watercolour landscapists – Paul Sandby, John Cozens, Cotman, Girtin, Bonington, and a host of others.

At the end of the 19th century and beginning of the 20th century, Impressionism and Post-Impressionism influenced British landscape painting, notably in the work of Philip Wilson Steer and several of the members of the Camden Town Group. In the period between the two world wars, Paul Nash and Graham Sutherland were among the artists who maintained the English romantic landscape tradition whilst responding to modern currents, infusing their work with a sense of Surrealist strangeness. Victor Pasmore and John Piper were among the other leading modern exponents of landscape. In the 1950s there was a fashion for gritty realism in landscape, paralleling the work of the 'kitchen sink' school, but a more lyrical approach has prevailed in, for example, the work of Roger de Grey.

Landseer, Edwin Henry (1802–1873)

English painter, sculptor, and engraver of animal studies. Much of his work reflects the Victorian taste for sentimental and moralistic pictures, for example *Dignity and Impudence* (1839; Tate Gallery, London). His sculptures include the lions at the base of Nelson's Column in Trafalgar Square, London (1857–67).

His works show close knowledge of animal forms and he established a vogue for Highland animal and sporting scenes, much encouraged by Queen Victoria's patronage. Among his best-known works are *The Old Shepherd's Chief Mourner* (1837); *Monarch of the Glen* (1851), painted for the House of Lords; and *The Stag at Bay* (1846). He was knighted in 1850.

Land's End

Promontory of southwest Cornwall, 15 km/9 mi southwest of Penzance, the westernmost point of England.

A group of dangerous rocks, the Longships, extend 0.6 km/1 mi out beyond Land's End; and are marked by a lighthouse (1793).

Land's End is a turf slope ending in a granite cliff about 18 m/59 ft high. A natural tunnel pierces the headland, and there are caves which are accessible at low tide. The Longships include the Carn Bras, Meinek, Tal-y-maen, Kettle's Bottom, and Armed Knight rocks.

The area has been under private ownership since 1987.

Lang, Andrew (1844–1912)

Scottish historian and folklore scholar. His writings include historical works; anthropological studies, such as *Myth, Ritual and Religion* (1887) and *The Making of Religion* (1898), which involved him in controversy with the anthropologist James G ◊Frazer; novels; and the series of children's books which he inspired and edited, beginning with *The Blue Fairy Book* (1889).

His earliest published work was a volume of graceful verse, *The Ballads and Lyrics of Old France* (1872), which was followed by other similar volumes. Lang was also a classical scholar of high standing, apparent in *Homer and the Epic* (1893) and *Homer and his Age* (1906), and in his translations (with others) of the *Odyssey* (1879) and the *Iliad* (1883).

Langdale Pikes

Three fells (hills) at the head of Great Langdale in Cumbria, England: Harrison Stickle (732 m/2,400 ft), Pavey Ark (697 m/2,288 ft), and Pike o'Stickle (710 m/2,330 ft).

Langland, William (*c.* 1332–*c.* 1400)

English poet. His alliterative *The Vision of William Concerning Piers the Plowman* (see *Piers Plowman*) was written in three (or possibly four) versions between about 1367 and 1386. The poem forms a series of allegorical visions, in which Piers develops from the typical poor peasant to a symbol of Jesus, and condemns the social and moral evils of 14th-century England. It is a masterpiece in combining the depiction of a spiritual pilgrimage with scenes of contemporary social life for a satirical purpose.

Born in the West Midlands, Langland was educated at the Benedictine monastery in Malvern, became a clerk in minor orders, and went to London where he lived with his wife and daughters in Cornhill. He made a precarious living as a scrivener, by singing requiems for the dead, and sometimes by begging. His experience of poverty and hardship is revealed in the vivid sincerity of the descriptions he gives in his work. He became progressively critical of the Church, whose corruptions he wanted to reform, although his faith remained orthodox.

Langley, John Newport (1852–1925)
English physiologist who investigated the structure and function of the autonomic nervous system, the involuntary part of the nervous system, that controls the striated and cardiac muscles and the organs of the gastrointestinal, cardiovascular, excretory, and endocrine systems. He went on to divide up the autonomic nervous system into the **sympathetic** and **parasympathetic** branches, with specific functions being apportioned to each.

Langton, Stephen (*c.* 1150–1228)
English priest who was mainly responsible for drafting the charter of rights, the ◊Magna Carta.

He studied in Paris, where he became chancellor of the university, and in 1206 was created a cardinal. When in 1207 Pope Innocent III secured Langton's election as archbishop of Canterbury, King John refused to recognize him, and he was not allowed to enter England until 1213. He supported the barons in their struggle against John and worked for revisions to both church and state policies.

Langtry, Lillie stage name of Emilie Charlotte le Breton (1853–1929)
English actress. She was the mistress of the future Edward VII. She was known as the 'Jersey Lily' from her birthplace in the Channel Islands and considered to be one of the most beautiful women of her time.

She was the daughter of a rector, and married Edward Langtry (died 1897) in 1874. She first appeared professionally in London in 1881, and had her greatest success as Rosalind in Shakespeare's *As You Like It*. In 1899 she married Sir Hugo de Bathe.

Lanhydrock House
House in Cornwall, England, 3 km/2 mi southeast of Bodmin. The original 17th-century house was largely destroyed by fire in 1881, but the north wing and detached granite gatehouse survived, and the house was rebuilt within four years. Gilbert ◊Scott laid out the formal gardens in 1857. The 7th Viscount Clifden gave the house and 220 ha/543 acres to the National Trust in 1953.

Lankester, Edwin Ray (1847–1929)
English zoologist who made clear morphological distinctions between the different orders of invertebrates. He distinguished between the haemocoel (blood-containing cavity) in Mollusca and Arthropoda and the coelom (fluid-filled cavity) in worms and vertebrates for the first time, showing that whilst functionally similar they have different origins.

Lansbury, George (1859–1940)
British Labour politician, leader in the Commons 1931–35. He was a member of Parliament for Bow 1910–12 – when he resigned to force a by-election on the issue of votes for women, which he lost – and again 1922–40. In 1921, while mayor of the London borough of Poplar, he went to prison with most of the council rather than modify their policy of more generous unemployment relief.

Lansbury founded the *Daily Herald* in 1912, and edited it until 1922, carrying it on as a weekly through World War I.

Lansdowne, Henry Charles Keith Petty-Fitzmaurice, 5th Marquis of Lansdowne (1845–1927)
British Liberal Unionist politician, governor-general of Canada 1883–88, viceroy of India 1888–93, war minister 1895–1900, and foreign secretary 1900–06. While at the Foreign Office he abandoned Britain's isolationist policy by forming an alliance with Japan and an entente cordiale with

LANGTRY, LILLIE *English actress Lillie Langtry in her stage debut, as Kate Hardcastle in Oliver Goldsmith's* She Stoops to Conquer, *performed at the Haymarket Theatre, London, in 1881. Langtry was eventually to become the mistress of the English king Edward VII.* *Corbis*

France. His letter of 1917 suggesting an offer of peace to Germany created a controversy.

La Plante, Lynda born Lynda Titchmarsh, stage name Lynda Marchal (1946–)

British television writer, producer, novelist, and occasional actress. She earned a reputation on the back of writing hard-hitting dramatic miniseries such as *Widows* (1983) and *Prime Suspect* (1990), which feature tough female protagonists. In addition to sequels to both these television productions, she wrote the miniseries *She's Out* (1995), *Bella Mafia* (1997), and *Killer Net* (1998), also writing the novels for the latter two.

She has written the screenplays for a number of television movies, and has acted under the stage name of Lynda Marchal, appearing in Peter Greenaway's *The Draughtsman's Contract* (1982).

Largs

Town and resort in North Ayrshire unitary authority, Scotland, situated on the Firth of Clyde, 19 km/12 mi southwest of Greenock; population (1991) 10,900. A busy tourist centre, its services include sailing facilities and car ferries to the island of Great Cumbrae.

In 1263 a sea battle between Scotland and Norway was fought off the coast of Largs.

Larkin, Philip Arthur (1922–1985)

English poet. His perfectionist, pessimistic verse appeared in *The Less Deceived* (1955), and in the later volumes *The Whitsun Weddings* (1964), and *High Windows* (1974) which confirmed him as one of the most powerful and influential of 20th-century English poets. After his death, his letters and other writings, which he had instructed should be destroyed, revealed an intolerance and misanthropy not found in his published material. From 1955 until his death he was librarian at the University of Hull.

He edited *The Oxford Book of 20th-Century English Verse* (1973). *Collected Poems* was published in 1988.

Larne

Seaport and industrial town of County Antrim, Northern Ireland, on **Lough Larne**, 30 km/19 mi north of Belfast; population (1991) 17,500. It is the terminus of sea routes to Stranraer, Liverpool, Dublin, and other places, and has a turbine generator works and an electronics industry.

The Curran is a raised gravel beach running south from Larne, on which many Neolithic flint implements have been found. The Norse used Lough Larne in the 10th and 11th centuries as a port. Edward Bruce (brother of Robert) landed at Larne with his army in 1315; his campaign was supported by the Bissett family whose castle (Olderfleet, dating from the 13th century) and lands were confiscated by the British crown as a result. The ruins of Olderfleet Castle can still be seen on the Curran.

Lasdun, Denys Louis (1914–)

English Modernist architect. Many of his designs emphasize the horizontal layering of a building, creating the effect of geological strata extending into the surrounding city or landscape. This effect can be seen in his designs for the University of East Anglia, Norwich (1962–68); and the National Theatre (1967–76) on London's South Bank.

From 1938 he was a member of Berthold ◊Lubetkin's Tecton Group until its dissolution in 1948. His first significant work, Hallfield Housing Estate, Paddington, London (1951–59), shows Tecton influence. He was was knighted in 1976 and awarded the Gold Medal of the RIBA in 1977.

Laski, Harold Joseph (1893–1950)

English political theorist. Professor of political science at the London School of Economics from 1926, he taught a modified Marxism and published *A Grammar of Politics* (1925) and *The American Presidency* (1940). He was chair of the Labour Party 1945–46.

Laski, Marghanita (1915–1988)

English writer and broadcaster. Her first novel was *Love on the Supertax* (1944), which was followed by, among others, *Tory Heaven* (1948), *Little Boy Lost* (1949), *The Victorian Chaise-Longue* (1953), and a play, *The Offshore Island* (1959). A prominent agnostic controversialist, she published *Ecstasy: A Study of Some Secular and Religious Experiences* (1961) and *The Secular Responsibility* (1969). Her critical works include *Jane Austen and her World* (1969). She was the daughter of Harold ◊Laski.

Latimer, Hugh (*c.* 1485–1555)

English Christian church reformer and bishop. After his conversion to Protestantism in 1524 he was imprisoned several times but was protected by Cardinal Wolsey and Henry VIII. After the accession of the Catholic Mary I, he was burned for heresy.

> *Be of good comfort, Master Ridley, and play the man; we shall this day light such a candle, by God's grace, in England as I trust shall never be put out.*
>
> HUGH LATIMER English church reformer and bishop. Attributed remark, to Nicholas Ridley as they were about to be burned at the stake

Laud, William (1573–1645)

English priest; archbishop of Canterbury from 1633. Laud's High Church policy, support for Charles I's unparliamentary rule, censorship of the press, and persecution of the Puritans all aroused bitter opposition, while his strict enforcement of the statutes against enclosures and of laws regulating wages and prices alienated the propertied classes. His attempt to impose the use of the Prayer Book on the Scots precipitated the English ◊Civil War. Impeached by Parliament in 1640, he was imprisoned in the Tower of London, summarily condemned to death, and beheaded.

Lauder, Harry stage name of Hugh MacLennan Lauder (1870–1950)
Scottish music-hall comedian and singer. He began his career as an 'Irish' comedian. He was knighted in 1919.

Lauderdale, John Maitland, 1st Duke of Lauderdale (1616–1682)
Scottish politician. Formerly a zealous Covenanter, he joined the Royalists 1647, and as high commissioner for Scotland 1667–79 persecuted the Covenanters. He was created Duke of Lauderdale in 1672, and was a member of the ◊Cabal ministry 1667–73.

Laugharne, Welsh **Talacharn**
Village at the mouth of the River Taf, Carmarthenshire, Wales. The Boathouse, the home of the poet Dylan ◊Thomas, is here, as is his grave, at the 14th-century church of St Martin. The village features in his work 'Under Milk Wood'.

Laugharne Castle, now in ruins, was built around 1300 on the site of an earlier castle built in the 12th-century. There is also the remains of a 15th-century church.

Laughton, Charles (1899–1962)
English actor who became a US citizen in 1950. Initially a classical stage actor, he joined the Old Vic in 1933. His films include such roles as the king in *The Private Life of Henry VIII* (1933; Academy Award), Captain Bligh in *Mutiny on the Bounty* (1935), and Quasimodo in *The Hunchback of Notre Dame* (1939). In 1955 he directed *Night of the Hunter* and in 1962 appeared in *Advise and Consent*.

Laura Ashley
Fashion and home-furnishing company, founded in 1953 by Welsh designer Laura Ashley (1925–85) with her husband Bernard (1926–). She established and gave her name to a Neo-Victorian country style in clothes, fabrics, and furnishings. The first Laura Ashley shop opened in London in 1968. The business expanded into a successful international chain, and by 1990 there were nearly 500 shops worldwide. The company has suffered some financial difficulties in the 1990s.

Laurel, Stan stage name of Arthur Stanley Jefferson (1890–1965)
English-born US film comedian, who with Oliver Hardy (1892–1957) created one of the most successful comedy teams in film history (Laurel was slim, Hardy rotund). Their partnership began in 1927, survived the transition from silent films to sound, and resulted in more than 200 short and feature-length films. Among these are *Pack Up Your Troubles* (1932), *Our Relations* (1936), and *A Chump at Oxford* (1940). *The Music Box* (1932) won an Academy Award as Best Short Film. Laurel received a special Academy Award in 1960.

Laurel, a British-born former music-hall comedian, produced several of their feature films, notably *Way Out West* (1937). He was born in Ulverston.

Lavenham
Village in Suffolk, England, 16 km/10 mi south of Bury St Edmunds; population (1991) 1,600. It is much visited by tourists. In the 16th century Lavenham had a thriving woollen industry, and the surviving medieval buildings reflect the prosperity of that period. The village has streets of timbered houses, a late 15th-century guildhall, and a church which is a fine example of the late Perpendicular style.

Lavery, John (1856–1941)
Irish portrait-painter of Edwardian society. He studied in Glasgow, London, and Paris and was influenced by the Impressionists and Whistler.

Born in Belfast, he studied in Glasgow, London, and Paris, and was associated with the Glasgow School. He was knighted in 1918.

law, the
See ◊legal system,◊English law and ◊Scottish law.

Law, Andrew Bonar (1858–1923)
British Conservative politician. He was elected leader of the opposition in 1911, became colonial secretary in Asquith's coalition government 1915–16, chancellor of the Exchequer 1916–19, and Lord Privy Seal 1919–21 in Lloyd George's coalition. He formed a Conservative Cabinet in 1922, but resigned on health grounds.

Law was born in New Brunswick, Canada. He made a fortune in Scotland as a banker and iron-merchant before entering Parliament in 1900.

Law Commission
Either of two statutory bodies established in 1965 (one for England and Wales and one for Scotland) which consider proposals for law reform and publish their findings. They also keep British law under constant review, systematically developing and reforming it by, for example, the repeal of obsolete and unnecessary enactments.

law courts
Bodies that adjudicate in legal disputes.

In England and Wales the court system was reorganized under the Courts Act (1971). The higher courts are: the **House of Lords** (the highest court for the whole of Britain), which deals with both civil and criminal appeals; the **Court of Appeal**, which is divided between criminal and civil appeal courts; the **High Court of Justice** dealing with important civil cases; **crown courts**, which handle criminal cases; and **county courts**, which deal with civil matters. **Magistrates' courts** deal with minor criminal cases and are served by ◊justices of the peace or stipendiary (paid) magistrates; and **juvenile courts** are presided over by specially qualified justices. There are also special courts, such as the Restrictive Practices Court and the Employment Appeal Tribunal.

The courts are organized in six circuits. The towns of each circuit are first-tier (High Court and circuit judges dealing with both criminal and civil cases), second-tier (High Court and circuit judges dealing with criminal cases only), or third-tier (circuit judges dealing with criminal cases only). Cases are allotted according to gravity among High Court and circuit judges and recorders (part-time judges with the same jurisdiction as circuit judges). In 1971 solicitors were allowed for the first time to appear in and conduct cases at the level of the crown courts, and solicitors as well as barristers of ten years' standing became eligible for appointment as recorders, who after five years become eligible as circuit judges. In the UK in 1989 there were 5,500 barristers and 47,000 solicitors. In Scotland, the supreme civil court is the **Court of Session**, with appeal to the House of Lords; the highest criminal court is the **High Court of Justiciary**, with no appeal to the House of Lords. See also ◊legal system for a table of courts and glossary of the legal system.

law lords

In England, the ten Lords of Appeal in Ordinary who, together with the Lord Chancellor and other peers, make up the House of Lords in its judicial capacity. The House of Lords is the final court of appeal in both criminal and civil cases. Law lords rank as life peers.

> *Curse the blasted jelly-boned swines, the slimy belly-wriggling invertebrates, the miserable sodding rotters, the flaming sods, the snivelling, dribbling, dithering, palsied pulseless lot that make up England today. ... Why, why, why was I born an Englishman?*
>
> D H LAWRENCE English writer.
> Letter to Edward Garnett, 3 July 1912

Lawrence, D(avid) H(erbert) (1885–1930)

English writer. His work expresses his belief in emotion and the sexual impulse as creative and true to human nature, but his ideal of the complete, passionate life is seen to be threatened by the encroachment of the modern and technological world. His writing first received attention after the publication of the semi-autobiographical *The White Peaco.ck* (1911) and *Sons and Lovers* (1913). Other novels include *The Rainbow* (1915), *Women in Love* (1921), and ◊*Lady Chatterley's Lover*, printed privately in 1928.

Lawrence tried to forge a new kind of novel, with a structure and content so intense that it would reflect emotion and passion more genuinely than ever before. This often led to conflict with official and unofficial prudery, and his interest in sex as a life force and bond was often censured. *The Rainbow* was suppressed for obscenity, and *Lady Chatterley's Lover* could only be published in an expurgated form in the UK in 1932. Not until 1960, when the obscenity law was successfully challenged, was it published in the original text.

The son of a Nottinghamshire miner, Lawrence studied at University College, Nottingham. He became a clerk and later a teacher. On going to London in 1908, he wrote under the pseudonym of Lawrence H Davidson. His first novel, *The White Peacock*, was published on the recommendation of Ford Madox ◊Ford. In 1914 he married Frieda von Richthofen, ex-wife of his university professor. She was the model for Ursula Brangwen in *The Rainbow* and its sequel, *Women in Love*. Lawrence's travels resulted in a series of fine travel essays, including *Sea and Sardinia* (1921) and *Mornings in Mexico* (1927). His sympathy with the traditions of the Aztec civilization encouraged him in an attempt to found an ideal community in Mexico, and in his Mexican novel *The Plumed Serpent* (1926) he expounds a mystical and yet physically satisfying religion. Lawrence suffered from tuberculosis, from which he eventually died near Nice, France.

Lawrence, Gertrude Alexandra Dagma born Klasen (1898–1952)

English actress. She was much in demand for revues, both in London and in New York, where she co-starred with Beatrice Lillie (1894–1989). She was also successful in straight plays, appearing with Noël Coward in *Private Lives* (1930) and *Tonight at 8.30* (1936). Her last success was as Anna in the musical *The King and I* (1951).

Lawrence, T(homas) E(dward) known as Lawrence of Arabia (1888–1935)

British soldier, scholar, writer, and translator. Appointed to

LAWRENCE, D H *English writer D H Lawrence, photographed in the early 20th century. Controversy surrounded him for much of his creative life; the frankly sexual novel* Lady Chatterley's Lover *was banned in England until 1960;* The Rainbow *(1915) was also accused of obscenity. As well as his novels, Lawrence wrote short stories, travel books, and poetry. Corbis*

the military intelligence department in Cairo, Egypt, during World War I, he took part in negotiations for an Arab revolt against the Ottoman Turks, and in 1916 attached himself to the emir Faisal. He became a guerrilla leader of genius, combining raids on Turkish communications with the organization of a joint Arab revolt, described in his book *The Seven Pillars of Wisdom* (1926). At the end of the war he was awarded the DSO for his services, and became adviser to the Foreign Office on Arab affairs. Disappointed by the Paris Peace Conference's failure to establish Arab independence, he joined the Royal Air Force in 1922 as an aircraftman under the name Ross, transferring to the tank corps under the name T E Shaw in 1923 when his identity became known. In 1935 he was killed in a motorcycle accident.

Lawrence, Thomas (1769–1830)

English painter. He was the leading portraitist of his day, becoming painter to George III in 1792 and president of the Royal Academy from 1820 to 1830. One of his finest portraits is *Queen Charlotte* (1789; National Gallery, London).

An infant prodigy, he was already successful and celebrated for his likenesses at Bath before he was twelve. After the Napoleonic wars he was commissioned by the Prince Regent to paint the allied sovereigns and dignitaries, travelling to Aix-la-Chapelle, Vienna, and Rome; the portraits are now in the Waterloo Room, Windsor, and include some of his most brilliant works, for example the *Pope Pius VII*.

He belongs to the Romantic period in the restless glitter of his style, which interested both Géricault and Delacroix, although it descends in some paintings into a superficial showiness. His collection of old master drawings, especially rich in Michelangelos and Raphaels, realized £20,000 in the sale after his death; part of it is now in the Ashmolean Museum. He was knighted in 1815.

Law Society

Professional governing body of solicitors in England and Wales. It also functions as a trade union for its 51,000 members. The society, incorporated in 1831, regulates training, discipline, and standards of professional conduct.

Lawson, Nigel, Baron Lawson of Blaby (1932–)

British Conservative politician. A former financial journalist, he was financial secretary to the Treasury 1979–81, secretary of state for energy 1981–83, and chancellor of the Exchequer 1983–89. He resigned after criticism by government adviser Alan Walters over his policy of British membership of the ◊European Monetary System.

Layamon

English poet. His name means 'law man' or 'judge', and according to his own account he was a priest of Areley (now Areley Kings), Worcestershire. He was the author of the *Brut*, a chronicle of about 16,000 alliterative lines on the history of Britain from the arrival of Brutus, the legendary Roman senator and general, to ◊Cadwalader, which gives the earliest version of the Arthurian legend in English.

The first important poem written in Middle English, the *Brut* is written mainly in alliterative lines but occasionally uses rhyme and assonance; it therefore shows English verse in transition. Two composite manuscript copies survive (housed in the British Museum).

Lea, or Lee

River that rises north of Luton, England, and joins the River Thames at Poplar; length 74 km/46 mi. It is the source of one-sixth of London's water supply.

The Lea flows southeast passing Luton, east past Hertford and Ware, and then south between Hertfordshire and Essex, before emptying into the Thames. The river valley is used for intensive horticultural cultivation under glass, especially of tomatoes.

The river is navigable for 45 km/28 mi. It was used from Roman times as a waterway, and canalized at a later date.

LEA

Abbreviation for **local education authority**, the body of local government responsible for the state schools and further education establishments in a district.

Leach, Bernard Howell (1887–1979)

English potter. His simple designs of stoneware and *raku* ware, inspired by a period of study in Japan from 1909 to 1920, pioneered a revival of studio pottery in Britain. In 1920 he established the Leach Pottery, a communally-run workshop at St Ives, Cornwall, with the Japanese potter Shoji Hamada (1894–1978).

Having worked with trailed slip designs on *raku* ware in Japan, he also revived the 17th-century technique of moulding plates with slip decorations.

Leach, Edmund Ronald (1910–1989)

English anthropologist. Leach's *Political Systems of Highland Burma* (1954), based on fieldwork among the Kachin of Burma, overturned the orthodox notion that the structure of society was stable or in equilibrium by demonstrating that this was an ideal model which people alter in their pursuit of power. Equilibrium could be assumed only for purposes of analysis. He was professor of anthropology at Cambridge University 1972–78.

Leamington, officially Royal Leamington Spa

Town and former health resort in Warwickshire, England, adjoining Warwick, on the River Leam, southeast of Birmingham; population (1991) 42,300. Public administration and services, distribution, tourism, and leisure industries provide the main employment. Manufacturing is more significant than the national average and includes engineering and automotive industries, producing brakes, steering, transmission, and other components. The Royal Pump Room offers spa treatment.

With mineral springs (saline, chalybeate) first recorded in 1586, Leamington developed as a spa in the late 18th century, and it became a royal spa after Queen Victoria visited the town in 1838. Leamington has extensive parks, gardens, and spacious avenues with Regency-style terraces.

The University of Warwick is located nearby.

Lean, David (1908–1991)

English film director. His films, painstakingly crafted, include early work codirected with the playwright Noël Coward, such as *Brief Encounter* (1946). Among his later films are such accomplished epics as *The Bridge on the River Kwai* (1957; Academy Award), *Lawrence of Arabia* (1962; Academy Award), and *Dr Zhivago* (1965).

The unfavourable reaction to *Ryan's Daughter* (1970) caused him to withdraw from filmmaking for over a decade, but *A Passage to India* (1984) represented a return to form. He was knighted in 1984.

Lear, Edward (1812–1888)

English artist and humorist. His *Book of Nonsense* (1846) popularized the limerick (a five-line humorous verse). His *Nonsense Songs, Botany and Alphabets* (1871), includes two of his best-known poems, 'The Owl and the Pussycat' and 'The Jumblies'.

He first attracted attention by his paintings of birds, and later turned to landscapes. He travelled to Italy, Greece, Egypt, and India, publishing books on his travels with his own illustrations, and spent most of his later life in Italy.

Born in Holloway, London, of Danish descent, Lear was the 20th of 21 children and was brought up by an elder sister. His father was declared bankrupt when he was four, he had only five years of schooling, and he was both epileptic and asthmatic. He gave drawing lessons to Queen Victoria in 1846.

They dined on mince, and slices of quince, / Which they ate with a runcible spoon; / And hand in hand, on the edge of the sand, / They danced by the light of the moon.

EDWARD LEAR English artist and humorist.
Nonsense Songs, 'The Owl and the Pussy-Cat'

Leatherhead

Town in Surrey, England, southwest of London, on the River Mole at the foot of the North Downs; population (1991) 9,700. Industries include engineering, high technology, industrial research (paper, electronics, food), and the manufacture of electrical equipment. It is the headquarters of a number of international corporations, including Esso. The Thorndike Theatre (1968) and the Royal School for the Blind (1799) are located here.

The town has an early 13th-century church.

Leavis, F(rank) R(aymond) (1895–1978)

English literary critic. With his wife Q(ueenie) D(orothy) Leavis (1906–1981), he cofounded and edited the influential literary review *Scrutiny* (1932–53). He championed the work of D H Lawrence and James Joyce and in 1962 attacked C P Snow's theory of 'the two cultures' (the natural alienation of the arts and sciences in intellectual life). His critical works, introducing a new seriousness to the study of literature, include *New Bearings in English Poetry* (1932), which placed T S ◊Eliot centrally in the modern poetic tradition, *The Great Tradition* (1948), and *The Common Pursuit* (1952).

Le Carré, John pen name of David John Moore Cornwell (1931–)

English writer of thrillers. His low-key realistic accounts of complex espionage include *The Spy Who Came in from the Cold* (1963), *Tinker Tailor Soldier Spy* (1974), *Smiley's People* (1980), *The Russia House* (1989), *The Night Manager* (1993), *Our Game* (1995), and *The Tailor of Panama* (1996). He was a member of the Foreign Service 1960–64.

Led Zeppelin

UK rock group 1969–80, founders of the heavy metal genre. Their overblown style, with long solos, was based on rhythm and blues; songs like 'Stairway to Heaven' have become classics.

Jimmy Page (1944–), a former member of the Yardbirds, had been an important 1960s session guitarist; the drumming of John Bonham (1948–1980) is said to have been sampled more often than any other. The vocalist was Robert Plant (1948–).

Lee, Christopher (Frank Carandini) (1922–)

English film actor. His gaunt figure was memorable in the title role of *Dracula* (1958) and several of its sequels. He has not lost his sinister image in subsequent Hollywood productions. His numerous other films include *Hamlet* (1948), *The Mummy* (1959), *Julius Caesar* (1970), and *The Man with the Golden Gun* (1974).

Lee, Jennie (Janet), Baroness Lee of Asheridge (1904–1988)

British socialist politician. She became a member of Parliament for the Independent Labour Party at the age of 24, and in 1934 married Aneurin ◊Bevan. On the left wing of the Labour Party, she was on its National Executive Committee 1958–70 and was minister of education 1967–70, during which time she was responsible for founding the Open University in 1969. She was made a baroness in 1970.

Lee, Laurie (1914–1997)

English writer. His autobiographical *Cider with Rosie* (1959) is a classic evocation of childhood: subsequent volumes are *As I Walked Out One Summer Morning* (1969), and *A Moment of War* (1991), in which he describes the horrors of the Spanish Civil War in 1936. His travel writing includes *A Rose for Winter* (1955). *Selected Poems* was published in 1983.

Leeds

Industrial city and metropolitan borough in West Yorkshire, England, 40 km/25 mi southwest of York, on the River Aire; population (1991) 424,200 (city), 680,700 (district). Industries include engineering, printing, chemicals, glass, woollens, clothing, plastics, paper, metal goods, and leather goods. Notable buildings include the Town Hall (1858) designed by Cuthbert Brodrick, the University of Leeds (1904), the Leeds City Art Gallery (1888), Temple Newsam House (early 16th century, altered in about 1630), and the Cistercian Abbey of Kirkstall (1147). It is a centre of communications where road, rail, and canals (to Liverpool and Goole) meet.

Opera North is based here. The Leeds Music Festival and the Leeds International Pianoforte Competition are held here every three years. The City of Leeds Open Brass Band Championships take place each May. The Royal Armouries Museum opened in 1996, housing a national collection of arms and armour formerly in the White Tower at the Tower of London. There is a famous cricket ground at Headingly.

Industries

Leeds is an important regional centre, with about three quarters of its working population employed in insurance, banking, national and local government, and the distributive trades. Important employers are the clothing industry (for which Leeds is a large centre); engineering (which ranges from metal casting to the manufacture of scientific instruments); and the textile manufacturing industry. Leeds is also an important centre for the printing trade and furnituremaking (Thomas ◊Chippendale began his business here); among its other industries are the manufacture of chemicals, soap, leather, coaches, ferro-concrete, medicines, hairdressing apparatus, cardboard boxes, mineral waters, carpets, jams and sauces, hats, brushes, clocks and watches, buttons, and electrical appliances and accessories.

City layout and landmarks

Among the chief shopping streets are Briggate, Bond Street, Boar Lane, and Commercial Street. Another, Kirkgate, leads to the markets and to the parish church of St Peter (rebuilt 1841). The church is said to be the fourth to be built on this site since the Domesday Book recorded that Leeds possessed 'a priest, a church, and a mill'. In the church is a pre-Conquest cross, the oldest monument in Leeds. Crossing Briggate is a wide street, the Headrow, and nearby is the Merrion shopping centre. Most of the shopping area is restricted to pedestrian traffic, and much through traffic is diverted along the inner ring road.

Above the Headrow is St John's Church, which was built and endowed in 1634 by John Harrison; it is a fine example of 17th-century Gothic architecture, and contains a famous English Renaissance screen. Other churches include St Anne's Roman Catholic cathedral near Park Row, and Holy Trinity church (1727). On the south side of the Headrow is the site of the Red Hall, a mansion where Charles I is said to have stayed in 1646 as a prisoner of the Scots. In the centre of City Square stands Brock's equestrian figure (1899) of the Black Prince, whose father, Edward III, did much to establish the wool industry. The City Museum, in Park Row, contains an Egyptian mummy of 1070 BC, pottery, Yorkshire tokens, Roman artefacts, and zoological specimens. Leeds Industrial Museum in Armley Mill (once the largest textile mill in the world) is now a museum of the textile, clothing, and engineering industries. There is also a folk museum at Abbey House, Kirkstall.

The town hall was opened by Queen Victoria in 1858; it has a tower 69 m/226 ft high. At the rear of the town hall is the civic hall, which was opened by King George V in August 1933. The main frontage has a portico with six columns, and the twin towers are 52 m/170 ft high, each surmounted by a large gilt owl, which is part of the arms of the local government. Opposite the town hall are the municipal buildings, occupied by the central reference and lending libraries, and the specialist libraries for science, commerce, technology, art, music, as well as the Leeds City Art Gallery (founded 1888), with the adjoining Henry Moore Institute (1993), the largest gallery in Europe devoted solely to sculpture.

Educational facilities

The city has two universities, the University of Leeds, and Leeds Metropolitan University. The Carnegie Physical Training College in Beckett Park was the first of its kind in the country. There is a girls' high school (1876) and a grammar school (1552; enlarged in 1663).

Parks and woodland

The two principal parks are at Roundhay (255 ha/637 acres) and Temple Newsam (378 ha/945 acres). Roundhay Park has natural woodlands, two lakes, and an open-air swimming pool, and was formerly a royal hunting ground. Temple Newsam House and grounds were acquired in 1922 from the 1st Earl of Halifax. Middleton Park (128 ha/320 acres) lies to the south of the city near an industrial district.

Transport

Leeds, with its inner ring road to the north of the city centre, and an urban motorway system south of the river, has good access to the national motorway system: the M1 for London and the Midlands, and the M62 for Liverpool and Hull. Leeds and Bradford airport is nearby at Yeadon.

History

The early history of Leeds is obscure; its original name was Loidis, and at the coming of the Normans it was an agricultural village of 400 ha/1,000 acres cultivated by 35 farmers. In the 12th century, the monks of Kirkstall Abbey traded in wool, and in the 14th century Flemish immigrants introduced the art of weaving and cloth manufacture. The first royal charter, which formed the town and parish into a municipal borough, was granted by Charles I in 1626.

Leeds owes its modern development to its industries. The city benefited from its communication with Liverpool (via the Leeds and Liverpool Canal, completed in 1816), and with the Humber (via the Aire and Calder Navigation system). The proximity of the great coal-and iron-fields, developed during the Industrial Revolution, was an important factor in establishing the city's prosperity. Engineering developed during the 19th century, in particular railway engineering, on account of the city's central position in the national railway system. Leeds was made a county borough in 1889 and a city in 1893.

leek

A national symbol of Wales, appearing on pound coins and worn on St David's Day (1 March). The reason for its choice as an emblem is uncertain. It was reputedly adopted in the 7th century, when the Welsh, under Cadwalader, wore leeks in their caps to distinguish their forces from the Saxon invaders. Folklore also tells of a Welsh victory in some battle in a garden of leeks, a legend referred to by Shakespeare in *Henry V*. The growing of giant leeks for autumn shows in northeast England has been a popular pastime since the 1880s.

Leek

Town in north Staffordshire, England, 15 km/9.3 mi northeast of Stoke-on-Trent; population (1991) 19,300. Sewing thread, silk dye, silks, and ribbons are manufactured here.

Rudyard Lake is 5 km/3 mi to the north, and 10 km/6 mi north are the spectacular rocks known as the Roaches and Hen Cloud. These are outcrops of gritstone (coarse sandstone) used for practice climbs.

legal system

See below for a glossary of the UK legal system. See also ◊English law and ◊Scottish law.

Lehmann, Rosamond Nina (1901–1990)

English novelist. Her books include *Dusty Answer* (1927), *The Weather in the Streets* (1936), *The Echoing Grove* (1953), and, following a long silence, *A Sea-Grape Tree* (1976), a sequel to *The Ballad and the Source* (1944). Once neglected as too romantic, her novels regained popularity in the 1980s because of their sensitive portrayal of female emotions. She was the sister of the poet and essayist John Lehmann.

A Glossary of the Legal System in Britain: Courts, Professionals, and Important Bodies

In England and Wales the court system was reorganized under the Courts Act 1971.
(– = not applicable.)

Term	Definition	Other
Admiralty Court	English court that tries and gives judgement in maritime causes	the court is now incorporated within the Queen's Bench Division of the High Court and deals with such matters as salvage and damages arising from collisions between ships
Attorney General	principal law officer of the crown and head of the English Bar	the post is one of great political importance
Barrister	a lawyer qualified by study at the Inns of Court to plead for a client in court	barristers also undertake the writing of opinions on the prospects of a case before trial; they act for clients through the intermediary of solicitors
Central Criminal Court	crown court in the City of London, able to try all treasons and serious offences committed in the City or Greater London	–
Chambers	in the UK, rented offices used by a group of barristers	chambers in London are usually within the precincts of one of the four law courts
Chancery	a division of the High Court that deals with such matters as the administration of the estates of deceased persons, the execution of trusts, the enforcement of sales of land, and foreclosure of mortgages	–
Circuit	the geographic district that constitutes a particular area of jurisdiction	in England and Wales the six different centres to which High Court and circuit judges travel to try civil and criminal cases are: Midland and Oxford, Northeastern, Northern, Southeastern, Wales and Chester, and Western
Circuit judge	full-time judicial officer; sits as court judge in civil cases and presiding judge in the crown court	circuit judges must have been barristers for ten years or recorders for three years
Commissioner for oaths	a person appointed by the Lord Chancellor with power to administer oaths or take affidavits	all practising solicitors have these powers but must not use them in proceedings in which they are acting for any of the parties or in which they have an interest
Common law	that part of the English law not embodied in legislation. Consists of rules of law based on common custom and usage and on judicial decisions	English common law became the basis of law in the USA and many other English-speaking countries
Coroner	official who investigates the deaths of persons who have died suddenly by acts of violence or under suspicious circumstances, by holding an inquest or ordering a postmortem examination (autopsy)	–

continued on page 520

A Glossary of the Legal System in Britain: Courts, Professionals, and Important Bodies

continued from page 519

Term	Definition	Other
County court	English court of law; exists to try civil cases; presided over by one or more circuit judges	there are 250 county courts which deal with civil matters. Cases are heard before District Judges, who hear uncontested and smaller value claims; higher value claims being dealt with by Circuit Judges
Court of Appeal	law court comprising a Civil Division and a Criminal Division, set up under the Criminal Appeals Act 1968	sits in London at the Royal Courts of Justice. The Criminal Division deals with appeals from the Crown Court, and is presided over by the Lord Chief Justice. It has the power to revise sentences or quash a conviction on the grounds that in all the circumstances of the case the verdict is unsafe or unsatisfactory, or that the judgement of the original trial judge was wrong in law, or that there was a material irregularity during the course of the trial. The 25 Lord Justices of Appeal are assisted by High Court judges when required
Court of Arches	ecclesiastical court of the archbishop of Canterbury; the presiding judge is the dean of the Arches	–
Court of Protection	in English law, a department of the High Court that deals with the estates of people who are incapable, by reason of mental disorder, of managing their own property and affairs	–
Court of Session	supreme civil court in Scotland, established in 1532	the court sits in Edinburgh
Criminal Injuries Compensation Board	board established 1964 to administer financial compensation by the state for victims of crimes of violence	–
Crown court	in England and Wales, any of several courts that hear serious criminal cases referred from magistrates' courts after committal proceedings	these courts sit in over ninety permanent centres throughout England and Wales, each centre being designated as first, second or third tier, reflecting the seriousness of the offences tried. Trial of cases is by a jury. They are directed on matters of law by a judge, who may be any one of the eighty-four High Court Judges, 478 Circuit Judges, 787 Recorders and 454 Assistant Recorders (the latter two being part-time appointments), which handle criminal cases
Crown Prosecution Service	body established by the Prosecution of Offences Act 1985, responsible for prosecuting all criminal offences in England and Wales; headed by the Director of Public Prosecutions (DPP)	–
Director of Public Prosecutions	the head of the Crown Prosecution Service (established 1985), responsible for the conduct of all criminal prosecutions in England and Wales	–
Ecclesiastical law	in England, the Church of England has special ecclesiastical courts to administer church law	–
Employment appeal tribunal	statutory bodies that adjudicate in disputes between employers and employees or trade unions and deal with complaints concerning unfair dismissal, sex or race discrimination, and equal pay	–
European Court of Human Rights	court that hears cases referred from the European Commission of Human Rights, if the Commission has failed to negotiate a friendly settlement in a case where individuals' rights have been violated by a member state, as defined in the 1950 European Convention on Human Rights; the court sits in Strasbourg and comprises one judge for every state that is a party to the 1950 convention	Britain has never incorporated the Human Rights Convention into its laws, which means that a statute that directly contradicts the convention will always prevail over a Strasbourg decision in a British court; in practice, however, the UK has always passed the necessary legislation to make its laws comply with the court's decisions

Term	Definition	Other
European Court of Justice	the court of the European Union (EU); it sits in Luxembourg with judges from the member states	–
Faculty of Professional Advocates	organization for Scottish advocates	incorporated 1532
High Court of Justice	deals with important civil cases	sits at the Royal Courts of Justice and at County courts around the country; land, patent issues, industrial disputes, property and inheritance matters are dealt with by its Cancery Division. The Queen's Bench Division deals with common law business such as tort and contractual issues. There is also a Family Division. Appeal is to the Court of Appeal (Civil Division), which also hears appeals from the County courts and from tribunals
High Court of Justiciary	in Scotland, court that tries the most serious criminal cases and also sits as the Court of Criminal Appeal (with no appeal to the Lords)	–
House of Lords	highest court for the whole of Britain, deals with both civil and criminal appeals	–
Inns of Court	four private legal societies in London, England: Lincoln's Inn, Gray's Inn, Inner Temple, and Middle Temple; all barristers (advocates in the English legal system) must belong to one of the Inns of Court	the main function of each Inn is the education, government, and protection of its members; each is under the administration of a body of Benchers (judges and senior barristers)
Judge	person invested with power to hear and determine legal disputes	in the UK, judges are chosen from barristers of long standing, but solicitors can be appointed circuit judges; the independence of the higher judiciary is ensured by the principle that they hold their office during good behaviour and not at the pleasure of the crown; they can be removed from office only by a resolution of both houses of Parliament
Jury	body of 12 (15 in Scotland) lay people sworn to decide the facts of a case and reach a verdict in a court of law	in England, jurors are selected at random from the electoral roll; certain people are ineligible for jury service (such as lawyers and clerics), and others can be excused (such as members of Parliament and doctors) if the jury cannot reach a unanimous verdict it can give a majority verdict (at least 10 of the 12); in Scotland a verdict of 'not proven' can be given
Justice of the peace	an unpaid magistrate	–
Juvenile court	special court for young people under the age of 17	presided over by specially qualified justices; members of the public are not admitted and the name of the juvenile may not be disclosed in any report of the proceedings. A juvenile under the age of 10 may not be found guilty of an offence
Land Registry, HM	official body set up 1925 to register legal rights to land in England and Wales	the records are open to public inspection (since December 1990)
Law Commission	either of two statutory bodies established 1965 (one for England and Wales and one for Scotland) which consider proposals for law reform and publish their findings	they also keep British law under constant review, systematically developing and reforming it by, for example, the repeal of obsolete and unnecessary enactments
Law lords	in England, the ten Lords of Appeal who, together with the Lord Chancellor and other peers, make up the House of Lords in its judicial capacity	the House of Lords is the final court of appeal in both criminal and civil cases; law lords rank as life peers
Law Society	professional governing body of solicitors in England and Wales	it also functions as a trade union for its members; the society, incorporated in 1831, regulates training, discipline, and standards of professional conduct

continued on page 522

A Glossary of the Legal System in Britain: Courts, Professionals, and Important Bodies

continued from page 521

Term	Definition	Other
Lord Advocate	chief law officer of the crown in Scotland who has ultimate responsibility for criminal prosecutions in Scotland	–
Lord Chancellor	head of the judiciary	a political appointment, the Lord Chancellor is also a member of the cabinet and holds the office of Keeper of the Great Seal
Lord Chief Justice of England	head of the Queen's Bench	most senior judge in England and Wales; ranks second only to the Lord Chancellor
Lord Justice of Appeal	in England and Wales, one of 14 lords justices who form, together with the Lord Chancellor, the Lord Chief Justice of England, the Master of the Rolls, and the president of the Family Division as ex officio members, the penultimate court of appeal (the Court of Appeal) for England and Wales.	–
Lord Lieutenant	the sovereign's representative in a county, who recommends magistrates for appointment	it is an unpaid position and the retirement age is 75
Magistrate	a person who presides in a magistrates' court: either a justice of the peace or astipendiary magistrates	–
Magistrates' court	in England and Wales, a local law court that mainly deals with minor criminal cases; lowest tier of criminal court	a magistrates' court consists of between two and seven lay justices of the peace (who are advised on the law by a clerk to the justices), or a single paid lawyer called a stipendiary magistrate. The 450 courts are funded jointly by local and central government and deal with about 98% of all criminal cases
Master of the Rolls	English judge who is the president of the civil division of the Court of Appeal, besides being responsible for Chancery records and for the admission of solicitors	–
Notary public	legal practitioner who attests or certifies deeds and other documents. British diplomatic and consular officials may exercise notarial functions outside the UK	–
Old Bailey	popular term for the Central Criminal Court	–
Police Complaints Authority	an independent group of people set up under the Police and Criminal Evidence Act 1984 to supervise the investigation of complaints against the police by members of the public	–
Probate	formal proof of a will	–
Procurator fiscal	officer of a Scottish sheriff's court who (combining the role of public prosecutor and coroner) inquires into suspicious deaths and carries out the preliminary questioning of witnesses to crime	–
Queen's Counsel (QC)	in England, a barrister of senior rank	the title QC is awarded by the Queen on the recommendation of the Lord Chancellor; a QC wears a silk gown, and takes precedence over a junior member of the Bar. When the monarch is a king, the title is King's Council
Recorder	in the English legal system, a part-time judge who usually sits in the crown courts in less serious cases but may also sit in the county courts or the High Court	–
Restrictive practices court	court presiding over cases concerning restrictive practices – any agreement between people in a particular trade or business that restricts free trade in a market. A restrictive trade practice can be legal if found to be in the public interest by the Restrictive practices court	–

Term	Definition	Other
Royal assent	formal consent given by a British sovereign to the passage of a bill through Parliament	last instance of a royal refusal was the rejection of the Scottish Militia Bill of 1702 by Queen Anne
Royal prerogative	powers, immunities, and privileges recognized in common law as belonging to the crown	most prerogative acts in the UK are now performed by the government on behalf of the crown
Serious Fraud Office	set up in 1987 to investigate and prosecute serious or complex criminal fraud cases	–
Sheriff	in England and Wales, the crown's chief executive officer in a county for ceremonial purposes; in Scotland, the equivalent of the English county-court judge, but also dealing with criminal cases	–
Silk	in UK law, a Queen's Counsel, a senior barrister entitled to wear a silk gown in court	–
Slander	spoken defamatory statement	if written, or broadcast on radio or television, it constitutes libel
Solicitor	member of one of the two branches of the English legal profession who provides all-round legal services (making wills, winding up estates, conveyancing, divorce, and litigation)	a solicitor cannot appear at High Court level, but must brief a barrister on behalf of his or her client; solicitors may become circuit judges and recorders
Solicitor General	a law officer of the Crown, deputy to the Attorney General, a political appointee with ministerial rank	–
Stipendiary magistrate	paid, qualified lawyers, working mainly in London and major cities	–
The Bar	the profession of barristers collectively; to be called to the Bar is to become a barrister	–
Treasury counsel	in the UK, a group of barristers who receive briefs from the DPP to appear for the prosecution in criminal trials at the Central Criminal Court	–
Treasury solicitor	the official representing the crown in matrimonial, probate, and admiralty cases	Queen's Proctor is an obsolete term for treasury solicitor
Tribunal	in English law for a body appointed by the government to arbitrate in disputes, or investigate certain matters	tribunals usually consist of a lawyer as chair, sitting with two lay assessors
Writers to the Signet	society of Scottish solicitors	–

Leicester

Industrial city and unitary authority in central England, on the River Soar; unitary authority area 73 sq km/28 sq mi; population (1996) 295,700, urban area (1991) 417,900 . It was part of the county of Leicestershire to 1997. Industries include engineering, food processing, electronics, chemicals, and the manufacture of hosiery, footwear, knitwear, plastics, scientific and medical instruments, electrical products, and construction and woodworking machinery. In 1990 Leicester was designated Britain's first Environment City by the Wildlife Trust (a national environmental charity).

Leicester was founded in AD 50 as the Roman **Ratae Coritanorum**. It developed as a centre of the hosiery trade after the stocking frame was introduced in the late 17th century.

Features

There is a 14th-century Guildhall, St Martin's Cathedral, and two universitites; the University of Leicester was established in 1957, and De Montfort University, formerly Leicester Polytechnic, was established in 1992. Bradgate House, the home of Lady Jane Grey, is located in Bradgate Park, 10 km/6 mi northwest of Leicester. There is an Eco House in the city; an environment-friendly show home, which demonstrates ways in which people can reduce the ecological impact of their homes.

Architectural features

The earliest portions of the half-timbered guildhall were erected towards the end of the 14th century by the Corpus Christi Guild, an important religious fraternity which had its chapel in St Martin's church. The building remained the official headquarters of Leicester until 1876. The Clock Tower dates from 1868. De Montfort Hall is a venue for meetings and large concerts. In Victoria Park is the war memorial designed by the English architect Edwin Lutyens. The Jewry Wall is a large section of Roman masonry. The site to the west of the Jewry Wall was excavated in 1936–38, and

LEICESTER *Although it is now forms part of a museum of industry and technology and is no longer in regular use, the richly ornamented Abbey pumping station in Leicester bears witness to the industrial past that saw the city boom during the 19th century. Leicester became known particularly for manufacturing hosiery and footwear. McQuillan & Brown/Collections*

extensive foundations were revealed. It is believed that there were public baths with a colonnade, and perhaps a basilica on the site of an earlier forum. Other excavations have revealed the plan of part of Leicester Abbey, founded in 1143 for canons of the order of St Augustine, at Abbey Park. In the Newarke area is the Trinity Hospital almshouse. The main part of the hospital chapel is the original building of 1331, and portions of the old arcades remain embedded in the present modern structure. The Newarke gateway (14th century) was the main entry to an ecclesiastical enclosure which contained the Church of the Annunciation and its collegiate buildings, now destroyed, together with the associated almshouses and Newarke Hospital. Bradgate House, dating from the 15th century, was built by Lady Jane's father, Sir Thomas Grey. Bradgate Park contains part of Charnwood Forest, and was a hunting ground in the 12th century.

Castle

It is thought that the earliest castle at Leicester was erected by the first of the four Beaumont overlords who ruled Leicester throughout the 12th century. The castle was later enlarged and improved but the building fell into decay after 1399, when Henry IV, Duke of Lancaster and Earl of Leicester, ascended to the throne. Little now remains of the medieval structure; the ruined Turret Gateway dates from 1423 and there are remains of the 12th-century Great Hall.

Cathedral, churches, and temples

St Martin's Cathedral, dating from Norman times, was substantially modified in the 19th century and received cathedral status in 1926. It has a fine medieval wooden roof and north porch. The partly Norman church of St Mary de Castro has a 12th-century chancel and a large Early English tower and nave. St Nicholas's church has a Saxon nave and Norman tower, partly built of Roman material. The Jain Centre in Leicester contains one of the few Jain temples in Western Europe.

Museums and galleries

The Leicestershire Museum and Art Gallery includes a large collection of German Expressionist paintings, and an Egyptian Gallery. The Jewry Wall and Archaeology Museum illustrates the history of the city to the Middle Ages. Exhibits include sections of mosaic pavement, wall paintings, and milestones from the Fosse Way. Newarke Houses Museum, situated in an early 17th-century house, traces the industrial and social history of Leicestershire from the 16th century to the present day. Other museums include a costume museum housed in Wygston House, and the Museum of Technology.

History

In the Roman period Leicester was a wealthy town, located on the Fosse Way between Lincoln and Cirencester, with large public buildings and rich mosaic or tessellated pavements. After the Roman withdrawal the town was called 'Legerceastre' by the Saxons, and it was the seat of the East Mercian bishopric until 874. The bishopric was transferred to Dorchester when the Danes held Leicester, Derby, and other towns in the Midlands. At the time of the Domesday survey of 1086 the town had 322 houses and six churches, and a population of about 2,000. In the 12th century the castle was built, and Henry II besieged and partly destroyed the town. In the 13th century the castle was the base of Simon de ◊Montfort, 1st Earl of Leicester. In 1201 a meeting of barons took place, which was a forerunner to the meeting in 1215 at Runnymede, when King John signed the Magna Carta. Three parliaments were held in Leicester in the 15th century. During the Civil War Leicester supported the Parliamentarians. It was captured by the Royalist Prince Rupert but it was retaken by Oliver Cromwell after the Battle of ◊Naseby.

Famous people
Leicester was the birthplace of the novelist C P Snow and the dramatist Joe Orton.

Leicester, Robert Dudley, Earl of Leicester (*c.* 1532–1588)

English courtier. Son of the Duke of Northumberland, he was created Earl of Leicester in 1564. He led the disastrous military expedition 1585–87 sent to help the Netherlands against Spain. Despite this failure, he retained the favour of Queen Elizabeth I, who gave him command of the army prepared to resist the threat of Spanish invasion in 1588.

His father was executed in 1553 for supporting Lady Jane Grey's claim to the throne, and Leicester was himself briefly imprisoned in the Tower of London. His good looks attracted Queen Elizabeth, who made him Master of the Horse in 1558 and a privy councillor in 1559. He was a supporter of the Protestant cause.

Elizabeth might have married him if he had not been already married to Amy Robsart. When his wife died in 1560 after a fall downstairs, Leicester was suspected of murdering her. In 1578 he secretly married the widow of the Earl of Essex.

Leicester City

Unitary authority in north central England since April 1997; see ◊Leicester.

Leicestershire

County of central England (since April 1997 Leicester City and Rutland have been separate unitary authorities)
Area 2,084 sq km/804 sq mi
Towns and cities Loughborough, Melton Mowbray, Market Harborough (administrative headquarters at Glenfield, Leicester)
Physical rivers Soar and Wreake; Charnwood Forest (in the northwest); Vale of Belvoir (under which are large coal deposits)
Features Belvoir Castle, seat of the dukes of Rutland since the time of Henry VIII, rebuilt by James Wyatt in 1816; Donington Park motor-racing circuit, Castle Donington; Leicestershire has traditionally had several fox-hunts, including the Quorn hunt
Industries engineering (Loughborough); hosiery (at Earl Shilton, Hinckley, and Loughborough); footwear; bell founding; coal (Asfordby); quarrying of limestone (Barrow-on-Soar, Breedon-on-the-Hill), ironstone (in the northwest), and granite (Enderby, Stoney, and Mountsorrel, known for its paving stones)
Agriculture good pasture with horses, cattle, and sheep (especially the New Leicester breed, first bred by Robert Bakewell in the 18th century at Dishley); dairy products (including Stilton cheese at Melton Mowbray); cereals
Population (1995) 592,700
Famous people Titus Oates, Thomas Babington Macaulay, C P Snow
History Richard III was defeated by Henry VII at the Battle of Bosworth in 1485.

Topography
Leicestershire is bounded on the north by Nottinghamshire; on the east by Lincolnshire and Rutland; on the southeast by Northamptonshire; on the southwest by Warwickshire; and on the northwest by Derbyshire; it contains Leicester City. The broad valley of the River Soar is one of the county's chief physical features, running from south to north, and separating the Charnwood Forest area from the uplands of the east. The Wreake valley, which runs from east to west, cuts through these eastern uplands. The highest point in the county is Bardon Hill (278 m/912 ft), in the Charnwood Forest.

Historic remains
There is only slight evidence of prehistoric settlement in the county. In the 9th century the district was in the hands of the Danish invaders, and there are many place-names of Scandinavian origin.

Industrial past
Leicestershire was famous for its wool as early as 1343, and with the introduction of the hand knitting frame in the 17th century the county soon established itself as the main area for hosiery manufacture in the country.

Leigh

Town in Greater Manchester, England, 9 km/6 mi southeast of Wigan; population (1991) 24,500. It has engineering industries, chiefly electrical. Leigh was traditionally a coal and cotton town.

Leigh, Mike (1943–)

English dramatist and filmmaker. He directs his own plays, which evolve through improvisation before they are scripted. His films, sharp social satires, include *Life Is Sweet* (1991) and *Secrets and Lies* (1995).

His work for television includes *Nuts in May* (1976) and *Abigail's Party* (1977); other feature films are *High Hopes* (1989), *Naked* (1993), a bleak depiction of a Homeric journey through modern London, and *Career Girls* (1997).

Leigh, Vivien stage name of Vivien Mary Hartley (1913–1967)

Indian-born English actress. She won Academy Awards for her performances as Scarlett O'Hara in *Gone With the Wind* (1939) and as Blanche du Bois in *A Streetcar Named Desire* (1951). She was married to Laurence ◊Olivier 1940–60, and starred with him in the play *Antony and Cleopatra* (1951).

Leigh appeared on the stage in London and New York. Her other films include *Lady Hamilton* (1941), *Anna Karenina* (1948), and *Ship of Fools* (1965).

Leighton, Frederic Stretton, 1st Baron Leighton of Stretton (1830–1896)

English painter and sculptor. One of the most highly respected artists of his day, he specialized in recreations of Classical Greek subjects, such as his *Captive Andromache* (1888; Manchester City Art Gallery) and *The Garden of the Hesperides* (1892; Lady Lever Art Gallery, Liverpool). The style of his works is Neo-Classical, the mood dreamily Romantic. He became president of the Royal Academy in 1878. His house in Holland Park, London, is now a museum.

Comprehensively trained in Florence, Frankfurt, Brussels, and Paris (under the Nazarene Eduard von Steinle), he became the main representative of Classicism in its late-Victorian form, painting subject pictures inspired by ancient Greece and the Parthenon frieze. Many landscapes also resulted from his extensive travels, and his visits to the Middle East suggested the *décor* of the Arab Hall at his London house. His decorative art in fresco and mosaic may be studied in the Victoria and Albert Museum, and his bronzes *The Sluggard* and *Athlete Struggling with a Python* (1877) at the Tate Gallery, London. His varied talents, learning, and personal charm contributed to make him a great success as president of the Royal Academy.

Knighted in 1878 and made a baron in 1896, he is the only English painter to have been made a lord.

Leighton, Kenneth (1929–1988)

English composer. He was lecturer at Edinburgh University 1956–68, and at Oxford University 1968–70. From 1970 he was professor at Edinburgh University. His output includes three piano concertos and the Fantasy-Octet, 'Homage to Percy Grainger' (1982).

He studied at Queen's College, Oxford and with Petrassi in Rome. He won several prizes for composition.

Other works include the opera *Columba* (1980); concerto for strings; two symphonies (1964, 1974); three piano concertos (1951–69), violin concerto, cello concerto; string quartet, two violin sonatas; three piano sonatas; Fantasy-Octet; choral works.

Leighton Buzzard

Market town in Bedfordshire, England, 64 km/40 mi northwest of London. The principal industries are sand quarrying and tilemaking; there is also clothing manufacture and light engineering. Leighton Buzzard has a market cross and a fine Early English cruciform church (built in the shape of a cross).

leisure

See feature on the British at play.

England is the paradise of individuality, eccentricity, heresy, anomalies, hobbies, and humours.

GEORGE SANTAYANA Spanish-born US philosopher and critic.
Soliloquies in England (1922)

Leith

Port in City of Edinburgh unitary authority, Scotland, south of the Firth of Forth, which was incorporated into Edinburgh in 1920. Leith was granted to Edinburgh as its port by Robert the Bruce in 1329. By the 15th century, Leith dominated the maritime commerce of the Lothian area, and several times served as a military strongpoint. The port is now a zone for service sector development.

Leith Hill

Highest point in southeast England (height 294 m/965 ft), 9 km/5.6 mi southeast of Dorking, Surrey. From the tower on the top of the hill (20 m/66 ft high and built in 1766) the English Channel may be seen.

Lely, Peter adopted name of Pieter van der Faes (1618–1680)

Dutch painter. He was active in England from 1641, painting fashionable portraits in the style of van Dyck. His subjects included Charles I, Cromwell, and Charles II. He painted a series of admirals, *Flagmen* (National Maritime Museum, London), and one of *The Windsor Beauties* (Hampton Court, Richmond), fashionable women of Charles II's court.

Lely painted Charles I during his captivity at Hampton Court, and worked throughout the Commonwealth era, though reverting to a plainer manner as in his portrait of Oliver Cromwell. However, he is mainly associated with the Restoration period when his output was huge, his replicas alone employing a full-time army of assistants. His popular portraits of the ladies of Charles II's court were turned out to such a standardized pattern as to be often indistinguishable, but his male portraits show a more individual character.

He was knighted in 1679.

Leng (born Holgate; now Elliott), Virginia Helen Antoinette (1955–)

British three-day eventer (rider in horse trials), born in Malta. She has won world, European, and most major British championships.

She was a member of the British team at two world championships (1982 and 1986) and was the individual champion in 1986 on Priceless. She won the European individual title twice (1985 and 1989), the Badminton horse trials in the same years, and Burghley Horse Trials in 1983, 1984, and 1986.

Lennon, John Winston (1940–1980)

Rock singer, songwriter, and guitarist; a founder member of the ◊Beatles. He lived in the USA from 1971. Both before the band's break-up in 1970 and in his solo career, he collaborated intermittently with his wife **Yoko Ono** (1933–). 'Give Peace a Chance', a hit in 1969, became an anthem of the peace movement. His solo work alternated between the confessional and the political, as on the album *Imagine* (1971). He was shot dead by a fan.

Idealism was evident in Lennon's life outside the Beatles, with publicity stunts like the 1969 'bed-in for peace' (he and Ono stayed in bed in an Amsterdam hotel for a week, receiving the press). His first solo album, *John Lennon/Plastic Ono Band* (1970), contained deeply personal songs like 'Mother' and 'Working Class Hero'; subsequent work, though uneven, included big hits like 'Whatever Gets You Through the Night' (1974).

THE BRITISH AT PLAY

'IN ORDER to form a just estimation of the character of any particular people, it is absolutely necessary to investigate the Sports and Pastimes most generally prevalent among them.'

So wrote Joseph Strutt in 1801 in his introduction to *The Sports and Pastimes of the People of England*. While Strutt then went on to give an authoritative account of the various ways in which the British have amused themselves at play from Roman times onwards, neither he nor any subsequent researcher has truly succeeded in describing the British at play.

With competitions covering everything from soccer to worm-charming, games from conkers to gut-barging, and clubs ranging from the noble values of the Queen's English Society to the somewhat more esoteric interests of the International Correspondence of Corkscrew Addicts, the breadth of our leisure activities makes the task formidable. Even the question of what is Britain's favourite pastime is impossible to answer. In recent years, chess, bridge, darts, and fishing have all claimed around three million adherents, though such a figure begs the question of how committed a participant one needs to be in order to be included. In chess, for example, distinct surveys have shown that about eight million homes have chess sets, about three million people say they play occasionally, up to 50,000 are members of chess clubs, but only a little over 10,000 participate frequently in organized events. Bridge, darts, and fishing would produce comparable figures to these, but they are all probably beaten by the armies of crossword solvers whom no-one has ever succeeded in quantifying.

We do know, however, that the British rate game-playing highly. In a recent survey, 'playing traditional family board games' was ranked fourth among responses to the question: 'What is your favourite Christmas Day pastime?' Only 'eating without guilt', 'drinking', and 'opening presents' were viewed more positively. 'Making love' was in fifth place, and 'watching television' ended as low as tenth. There were similar responses to the question: 'What is essential to a traditional British Christmas?' A Christmas tree and Father Christmas took the first two places, but 'traditional family board games' came ahead of both a 'fat turkey' and 'Christmas stockings'.

Walking tops the chart

The most thorough recent account of what Britons do in their spare time is to be found in the 'General Household Survey' for 1996 (published in 1998 by the Office for National Statistics). This revealed high rates of participation in sporting activities with 64% of adults having taken part in some sport or physical activity in the four week period prior to the survey and 81% having done so at some time in the previous 12 months. Those figures dropped to 46% and 66%, however, if the single most popular activity, walking (which specifically was defined as taking a leisure walk of two miles or more), was excluded from consideration.

A long way behind walking (which 45% of adults claimed to have done in the month before the survey), indoor swimming was the next most popular activity (at 13%), followed by keep fit or yoga classes (12%), pool, snooker, or billiards (11%) and cycling (11%). Over the same four-week period, 71% of men and 58% of women took part in some physical activity, with more women participating in keep fit classes, but more men in every other area.

For men, the most common leisure activities involving some element of physical exertion were: 1. Walking; 2. Snooker (or other cue game); 3. Indoor swimming; 4. Cycling; 5. Golf; 6–7. Tenpin bowling and soccer; 8. Outdoor Swimming; 9. Weight training; 10. Running or jogging. For women the top ten were: 1. Walking; 2. Indoor swimming; 3. Keep fit or yoga; 4. Cycling; 5. Outdoor swimming; 6. Tenpin bowling; 7. Snooker (or other cue game); 8–10. Weight training, badminton and tennis.

Over a whole year, the average adult went cycling 11.6 times, went to a keep fit or yoga class 10.8 times, went for 8.2 swims, played 6.6 games of snooker, lifted weights 5.3 times jogged or ran 3.5 times and took to the soccer pitch 3.3 times.

The 'General Household Survey' also investigated the participation rates over a range of non-physical leisure activities. The most popular activity was watching television, which 99% of respondents had done in the four weeks prior to their interview. Almost as many (96%) had visited or entertained friends or relations, while 88% had listened to the radio, 78% had listened to records or tapes, and 65% had read books. Those were the only categories included in the survey which topped 50%, though gardening, at 48%, only narrowly failed to be among those things that more than half the country do in an average month.

However, while participation in most forms of physical activity declines with age, gardening is something we tend to do more of as we get older. Only 15% of 16–19-year-olds did any gardening, but the figure steadily rises with age reaching its peak at 61% for the 60–69 age group. Only after 70 do the exertions of gardening begin to take their toll, when the figure drops back to the national average of 48%.

Bee-keeping to knot-tying

Yet all the above figures do no more than scratch the surface of the Great British public at leisure, for they neglect the many minor sports and activities which individually may appear negligible, yet taken together add up to a mountain of unclassified leisure. Looking, for example, at the clubs and societies in Hampshire – a county that includes only about 2% of the population – we find clubs for battle reenactments, beekeepers and bellringers, groups to cater for anyone interested in rabbits, railways or rambling, cigarette cards or computing. The official web site for the county lists 21 dance groups, including seven troops of Morris Dancers. There are three groups specializing in arts and crafts, including a branch of the International Guild of Knot Tyers. Stamp collectors may choose between two clubs, while anyone wanting to join a knitting circle has three from which to select. And then, of course, there are even more groups who have not bothered to get themselves onto the local council's list. The British are without doubt a playful nation, and especially skilled at the game of frustrating leisure researchers.

BY BILL HARTSTON

LENNON, JOHN *English singer, songwriter, and guitarist John Lennon was one of the most charismatic figures in the history of popular music. Apart from his musical activities, he was famous for his outspoken views on world events, particularly for his hatred of warfare. He also made headlines because of his involvement in drugs and mystical religion. Corbis*

Leno, Dan stage name of George Galvin (1860–1904)

English comedian. A former acrobat, he became the idol of the music halls, and was considered the greatest of pantomime 'dames'.

Leppard, Raymond John (1927–)

English conductor and musicologist. His imaginative reconstructions of Monteverdi and Cavalli operas did much to generate popular interest in early opera and to stimulate academic investigation of the performance implications of early music manuscript scores.

leprechaun (Old Irish 'small body')

In Irish folklore, a fairy in the shape of an old man, sometimes conceived as a cobbler, with a hidden store of gold. If caught by a human he can be forced to reveal his treasure, but he is usually clever enough to trick his captor into looking away, enabling him to vanish.

Lerwick

Port in Shetland, Scotland; population (1991) 7,300. It is the administrative headquarters of the Shetland Islands. The main occupations include fishing and oil supply services. Hand-knitted shawls are a speciality.

The annual fire festival of Up-Helly-Aa, is held in Lerwick at the end of January. A replica of a Viking longship is burned after a torch-light procession through the town. The festival dates from Victorian times and is based on Viking traditions.

Lerwick, the most northerly town in the UK, is on a natural harbour on the east coast of Mainland, Shetland, sheltered by the island of Bressay.

Lessing, Doris May born Tayler (1919–)

English novelist and short-story writer, brought up in Rhodesia. Concerned with social and political themes, particularly the place of women in society, her work includes *The Grass is Singing* (1950), the five-novel series *Children of Violence* (1952–69), *The Golden Notebook* (1962), *The Good Terrorist* (1985), *The Fifth Child* (1988), *London Observed* (1992), and *Love Again. Under My Skin* (1994) and *Walking in the Shade* (1997) are volumes of autobiography.

She has also written an 'inner space fiction' series *Canopus in Argus: Archives* (1979–83), and under the pen name 'Jane Somers', *The Diary of a Good Neighbour* (1981).

Letchworth

Town in Hertfordshire, southeast England, 56 km/35 mi north of London; population (1997 est) 33,700. It was founded in 1903 as the first English ◊garden city (built in a rural area, designed to combine the advantages of the town and the country). The town is an administrative centre for local government. Industries include printing and the manufacture of clothing, furniture, scientific instruments, light metal goods, chemicals and gases, and rubber.

History

Letchworth was developed as an industrial and residential town by the Letchworth urban district council and First Garden City Limited, on an estate of 1,983 ha/4,900 acres. In 1963, under a special parliamentary act of 1962, Letchworth Garden City Corporation took over the Letchworth estate with the statutory obligation of managing, developing, and extending the undertaking as a public service. A permanent rural belt surrounds the town.

letter

Written or printed message, chiefly a personal communication, which are often valuable as reflections of social conditions and of literary and political life. Outstanding examples in Britain include in the 16th century the letters of Edmund Spenser and Philip Sidney; in the 17th century those of John Donne, John Milton, and Oliver Cromwell; in the 18th century those of Alexander Pope, Horace Walpole, Jonathan Swift, William Cowper, and Thomas Gray; in the 19th century those of George Byron, Charles Lamb, John Keats, Edward Fitzgerald, and R L Stevenson; and in the 20th century those of T E Lawrence, G B Shaw, Ellen Terry, and Katherine Mansfield.

Levellers

Democratic party in the English Civil War. The Levellers found wide support among Cromwell's New Model Army and the yeoman farmers, artisans, and small traders, and proved a powerful political force 1647–49. Their programme included the establishment of a republic, government by a parliament of one house elected by male suffrage, religious toleration, and sweeping social reforms.

Cromwell's refusal to implement this programme led to mutinies by Levellers in the army, which, when suppressed by Cromwell in 1649, ended the movement. They were led by John ◊Lilburne.

True Levellers (also known as ◊Diggers) were denounced by the Levellers because of their more radical methods.

Leven

Town in Fife, Scotland, at the mouth of the **River Leven**, where it meets the Firth of Forth; population (1991) 8,300. It has timber-related, papermaking, and engineering industries. Facilities include a sandy beach and golf-links.

Leven, Alexander Leslie, 1st Earl of Leven (*c.* 1580–1661)

Scottish general in the English Civil War. He led the Covenanters' army which invaded England in 1640, commanded the Scottish army sent to aid the English Puritans in 1643–46, and shared in the Parliamentarians' victory over the Royalists in the Battle of Marston Moor.

Leven, Loch

Lake in Perth and Kinross, Scotland; area 16 sq km/6 sq mi. The River Leven flows from Loch Leven. It has six islands; Mary Queen of Scots was imprisoned on Castle Island until she escaped in 1568. The whole loch has been a National Nature Reserve since 1964. The loch is known for its trout fisheries.

St Serf's, the largest island in the loch, contains the ruins of an old priory.

Leverson, Ada born Beddington (1862–1933)

English novelist. Following the publication of articles and sketches, she branched out into fiction. Her six novels, of which the first was *The Twelfth Hour* (1907) and the last *The Bird of Paradise* (1914), are amusing, well-characterized studies of marriage; three of them feature the Ottleys, later issued together as *The Little Ottleys* (1962). She was a close friend of Oscar Wilde, who called her 'The Sphinx'.

Levi, Peter (1931–)

English poet, prose writer, critic, and classical scholar. In 1977 he resigned from the priesthood and from the Society of Jesus, of which he had been a member since 1948. His first volume of verse was *The Gravel Ponds* (1960). His poetry has striking images, and draws on classical and archaeological themes, Christianity, and nature. *Collected Poems 1955–1975* was published in 1976. He has written critical biographies of Tennyson (1993), Lear (1995), Milton (1996), and Horace (1997).

Levin, Bernard (1928–)

English journalist and commentator especially interested in moral issues, with a strong liking for opera. He wrote for several newspapers and magazines, among them *The Times*, the *Observer*, and the *Spectator*. His views were also often heard on radio and television.

Lewes

Market town and administrative headquarters of ◊East Sussex, southeast England, on the River Ouse, 80 km/50 mi south of London; population (1991) 15,400. Industries include light engineering, brewing, printing, and the manufacture of pharmaceuticals. It is a centre for legal services, being the headquarters of the Sussex police and site of **Lewes Prison**. Simon de Montfort defeated Henry III at the ◊Battle of Lewes (1264). The Glyndebourne Festival is held nearby, and a new opera house was opened in 1994.

Features include remains of a Norman castle, and a house which belonged to Anne of Cleves, the fourth wife of Henry VIII. The town is known for its 5th November celebrations.

There are remains of a Cluniac priory, founded in 1078. Barbican House, dating from the 16th century, houses a museum of the Sussex Archaeological Society. An obelisk on Cliffe Hill commemorates the 17 Protestants who were burned at the stake here in 1556, during the reign of Mary I.

The University of Sussex lies nearby.

Once, when a British Prime Minister sneezed, men half a world away would blow their noses. Now when a British Prime Minister sneezes nobody else will even say 'Bless You'.

BERNARD LEVIN English journalist.
The Times 1976

Lewes, Battle of

Battle in 1264 caused by the baronial opposition to Henry III, led by Simon de Montfort, Earl of Leicester (1208–65). The king was defeated and captured at the battle.

The barons objected to Henry's patronage of French nobles in the English court, his weak foreign policy, and his support for the papacy against the Holy Roman Empire. In 1258 they forced him to issue the Provisions of Oxford, and when he later refused to implement them, they revolted. They defeated and captured the king at Lewes in Sussex. Their revolt was broken by de Montfort's death and defeat at Evesham in 1265.

Lewis, or Lewis-with-Harris

Largest and most northerly island in the Outer ◊Hebrides, Western Isles; area 2,220 sq km/857 sq mi; population (1991) 21,700. Its main town is Stornoway. It is separated from northwest Scotland by the Minch. The island is 80 km/50 mi long from north to south, and its greatest breadth is 45 km/28 mi. There are many lochs and peat moors. The Callanish standing stones on the west coast are thought to be up to 5,000 years old, second only to Stonehenge in archaeological significance in the UK.

Harris and Lewis are often assumed to be two separate islands, but they are linked by a narrow neck of land.

The coast is indented on the east and west coasts. The most northerly point is the **Butt of Lewis**. Much of the south and southwest of the island is rugged and mountainous, while northern and central Lewis are dominated by an undulating peat bog.

The chief occupations are crofting and fishing. Oats and potatoes are grown, and sheep and cattle are raised. There are many archaeological remains; the standing stones at Callanish, a circle of 47 stones 24 km/15 mi west of Stornaway, are thought to date from between 3,000 and 1,500 BC. Lews Castle (1856–63) was presented to the town by Lord Leverhulme, and now houses a technical college.

Daily flights link the island with Inverness and Glasgow. A car ferry service connects Stornaway to Ullapool on the mainland.

Lewis, C Day

Irish poet; see Cecil ◊Day-Lewis.

Lewis, C(live) S(taples) (1898–1963)

English academic and writer, born in Belfast. He became a committed Christian in 1931 and wrote the Chronicles of Narnia, a series of seven novels of Christian allegory for children set in the magic land of Narnia, beginning with *The Lion, the Witch, and the Wardrobe* (1950).

His other works include the medieval study *The Allegory of Love* (1936) and the space fiction *Out of the Silent Planet* (1938). He wrote essays in popular theology such as *The Screwtape Letters* (1942) and *Mere Christianity* (1952), and the autobiographical *Surprised by Joy* (1955).

Lewis was a fellow of Magdalen College, Oxford, from 1924–54 and professor of Medieval and Renaissance English at Cambridge from 1954–63.

Lewis, Lennox Claudius (1966–)

English boxer who won the WBC world heavyweight title 1992, becoming the first British boxer to do so this century. He was awarded the title when the reigning champion, Riddick Bowe, refused to fight him. After defending the title successfully for nearly 2 years, he lost to Oliver McCall in September 1994. However, he regained the title in February 1997.

Lewis, Thomas (1881–1945)

Welsh cardiologist and clinical scientist who discovered that histamine, an amine compound, is released as an initial event in the inflammatory response. He was knighted in 1921.

Lewis, (Percy) Wyndham (1882–1957)

English writer and artist. He pioneered ◊Vorticism, which, with its feeling of movement, sought to reflect the age of industry. He had a hard and aggressive style in both his writing and his painting. His literary works include the novel *The Apes of God* (1930); the essay collection *Time and Western Man* (1927); and an autobiography, *Blasting and Bombardiering* (1937). In addition to paintings of a semi-abstract kind, he made a number of portraits; among his sitters were the poets Edith Sitwell, Ezra Pound, and T S Eliot.

Through Vorticism, a variant of Cubist and Futurist ideas, Lewis opposed the 'everyday visual real' and favoured machinelike forms. He edited *Blast* from 1914 to 1915, a literary and artistic magazine which proclaimed the principles of the movement. Both in his paintings and in his numerous written works – including the novels *Tarr* (1918) and *The Childermass* (1928) – he was an intellectual independent, and one of his later literary products, *The Demon of Progress in the Arts* (1954), was an attack on formalized extremism. His painting *The Surrender of Barcelona* (1936; Tate Gallery, London) applies mechanistic treatment to an imagined scene of the past.

Lewisham

Inner borough of southeast Greater London. It includes the suburbs of ◊Blackheath, Sydenham, Catford, and ◊Deptford

Features Deptford shipbuilding yard (1512–1869); Armoury Mill produced steel for armour in the 16th century, musket barrels in the Napoleonic Wars, and gold and silver thread for Victorian uniforms

Population (1991) 215,300

Famous people birthplace of James Elroy Fletcher; home of Samuel Smiles, Arthur Sullivan, W G Grace, Ernest Dowson, Ernest Shackleton.

Leyland

Industrial town in Lancashire, northwest England, 11 km/7 mi south of Preston; population (1991) 33,000. It is the administrative centre for South Ribble borough council. Industries include the manufacture of motor vehicles, rubber components, and diverse light industrial products. The headquarters of Leyland Trucks is here.

Liberal Democrats

In politics, common name for the ◊Social and Liberal Democrats.

Liberal Party

British political party, the successor to the ◊Whig Party, with an ideology of liberalism. In the 19th century it represented the interests of commerce and industry. Its outstanding leaders were Palmerston, Gladstone, and Lloyd George. From 1914 it declined, and the rise of the Labour Party pushed the Liberals into the middle ground. The Liberals joined forces with the Social Democratic Party (SDP) as the Alliance for the 1983 and 1987 elections. In 1988 a majority of the SDP voted to merge with the Liberals to form the ◊Social and Liberal Democrats.

The term 'Liberal', used officially from about 1840 and unofficially from about 1815, marked a shift of support for the party from aristocrats to include also progressive industrialists, backed by supporters of the utilitarian reformer Jeremy ◊Bentham, Nonconformists (especially in Welsh and Scottish constituencies), and the middle classes. During the Liberals' first period of power, from 1830 to 1841, they promoted parliamentary and municipal government reform and the abolition of slavery, but their *laissez-faire* theories led to the harsh Poor Law of 1834. Except for two short periods, the Liberals were in power from 1846 to 1866, but the only major change was the general adoption of free trade. Liberal pressure forced Peel to repeal the Corn Laws of 1846, thereby splitting the Tory party.

Extended franchise (1867) and Gladstone's emergence as leader began a new phase, dominated by the Manchester school with a programme of 'peace, retrenchment, and reform'. Gladstone's 1868–74 government introduced many important reforms, including elementary education and vote by ballot. The party's left, mainly composed of working-class Radicals and led by Charles ⇨Bradlaugh (a lawyer's clerk) and Joseph ⇨Chamberlain (a wealthy manufacturer), repudiated *laissez faire* and inclined towards republicanism, but in 1886 the Liberals were split over the policy of Home Rule for Ireland, and many became Liberal Unionists or joined the Conservatives.

Except for the period 1892 to 1895, the Liberals remained out of power until 1906, when, reinforced by Labour and Irish support, they returned with a huge majority. Old-age pensions, National Insurance, limitation of the powers of the Lords, and the Irish Home Rule Bill followed. Lloyd George's alliance with the Conservatives from 1916 to 1922 divided the Liberal Party between him and his predecessor Asquith, and although reunited in 1923 the Liberals continued to lose votes. They briefly joined the National Government (1931–32). After World War II they were reduced to a handful of members of Parliament.

A revival began under the leadership (1956–67) of Jo Grimond and continued under Jeremy Thorpe, who resigned after a period of controversy within the party in 1976. After a caretaker return by Grimond, David Steel became the first party leader in British politics to be elected by party members who were not MPs. Between 1977 and 1978 Steel entered into an agreement to support Labour in any vote of confidence in return for consultation on measures undertaken. He resigned in 1988 and was replaced by Paddy Ashdown.

Liberty, Arthur Lasenby (1843–1917)

English shopkeeper and founder of a shop of the same name in London in 1875. Originally importing Oriental goods, it gradually started selling British Arts and Crafts and Art Nouveau furniture, tableware, and fabrics. Art Nouveau is still sometimes called *stile Liberty* in Italy.

A draper's son, Liberty trained at Farmer & Rogers' Cloak and Shawl Emporium. He was knighted in 1913.

libraries

In 1998 there were some 5,000 public libraries in Britain, nearly 700 libraries in higher and further education, and over 3,000 specialized libraries in other organizations, as well as three national libraries. Altogether they employ around 42,500 people. In England about 60% of adults are members of their local library, half of these borrowing books at least once a month. See chronology of some key dates, on page 532.

Lending or circulating libraries became widespread in the 19th century. The first documented free public library in the UK was established in Manchester in 1852, after the 1850 Public Library Act. See also ⇨British Library.

licensing laws

Legislation governing the sale of alcoholic drinks. In Britain, sales can only be made by pubs, restaurants, shops, and clubs which hold licences obtained from licensing justices. The hours during which alcoholic drinks can be sold are restricted: licensed premises can sell alcohol between 11am and 11pm Monday to Saturday, and 12 noon to 3pm and 7pm to 10.30pm on Sundays. These hours may be extended for special occasions, by application to the licensing justices.

From the late 19th century, temperance and nonconformist movements lobbied for tighter restrictions on the consumption of alcohol. In Wales Sunday closing was enforced from 1881, and in 1913 Scotland was permitted to hold local referenda on licensing issues. Restrictions on pub hours in England was initially introduced as a temporary war measure in World War I, not as a morality act, but to improve efficiency on the home front, but the regulations were retained after the war.

Lichfield

Cathedral city in Staffordshire, central England, in the Trent Valley, 25 km/16 mi northeast of Birmingham; population (1996 est) 31,800. It offers financial and banking services, and has a mixed industrial base. Substantial military barracks are located on the edge of the city. The cathedral (13th–14th century) has three spires. The writer Samuel Johnson was born in Lichfield in 1709.

The Early English and Decorated-style cathedral contains the *Lichfield Gospels* (a manuscript dating from the 8th century) and *The Sleeping Children* (1817) of Francis Chantrey. The birthplace of Samuel Johnson is now a museum. On the edge of Stowe Pool is the church and well of St Chad, who settled here in 669 and became the first bishop of Lichfield. There is a statue to Capt Edward Smith of the *Titanic* in the city park.

Famous people

The antiquarian Elias Ashmole was born here in 1617. The writer Joseph Addison and the actor David Garrick lived in Lichfield.

Lichfield, Patrick Anson, 5th Earl of Lichfield (1939–)

English photographer. Since 1981 he has been known for his travel and publicity shots as well as his royal portraits.

life expectancy

Average lifespan that can be presumed of a person at birth. It depends on nutrition, disease control, environmental contaminants, war, stress, and living standards in general. In the UK, average life expectancy currently stands at 74 for males and about 80 for females.

LIBRARIES: SOME KEY DATES

1608 The first municipal public library in England is established in Norwich. It contains mainly religious works.

1653 English merchant Humphrey Chetham establishes the Chetham Library in Manchester, England. It is the first library to be fully open to the public and soon carries books in a broad range of subjects.

1682 The Advocates Library in Edinburgh is founded by the Scottish jurist George MacKenzie. It opens in 1698, and later forms the nucleus of the National Library of Scotland.

1684 Trinity College Library at Cambridge University, designed by the English architect Christopher Wren, is completed.

1689 The Advocates Library in Edinburgh, opens. It was founded in 1682.

1697 The English scholar and bibliographer Edward Bernard publishes *Catalogi Librorum Manuscriptorum Angliae et Hiberniae/ Catalogue of English and Scottish Books and Manuscripts*, a library catalogue of English and Scottish manuscripts.

1726 The Scottish poet Allan Ramsay opens the first commercial lending library in Britain, in Edinburgh.

1729 The Doctor William's Library is founded in London in memory of the nonconformist minister Daniel Williams, for students of religion and philosophy.

1749 The Radcliffe Camera in Oxford, a library designed by the English architect James Gibbs, is completed. It is one of the finest examples of English Baroque architecture.

1753 The extensive library of Sir Robert Bruce Cotton is transferred to the British Museum Library.

1768 Britain's first privately owned library open to the public is set up, in Liverpool, with members paying an annual subscription to borrow books. Libraries in Sheffield, Hull, Bristol, and Birmingham soon follow.

1823 The English educationalist and doctor George Birkbeck founds the Mechanics' Institute in Britain to provide libraries, reading rooms, and other educational facilities for workers.

5 May 1841 The London Library opens as a private subscription circulating library in England.

1842 The English bibliophile Charles Edward Mudie's popular circulating library is founded in London.

1850 The English politician William Ewart sponsors an act of Parliament in Britain to establish the first public libraries.

1851 The rates are increased for the funding of public library facilities in England and Wales.

1852 The Manchester Free Library opens, the first free public library in Britain.

1859 The Warrington Mechanics' Institution start the first mobile library in Britain.

1862 The first children's library in Britain opens at the Campfield Reference Library in Manchester.

24 October 1946 King George VI opens the New Bodleian Library in Oxford.

1973 The British Library is created.

1984 Public lending right (PLR) comes into operation in Britain, where authors are paid a fee based on the number of loans of their books by libraries.

1997–99 The reading rooms of the new British Library building at St Pancras, London, open in stages.

LIFFE, London International Financial Futures and Options Exchange

One of the exchanges in London where futures contracts are traded. It opened in September 1982. By 1998 it was the largest futures and options exchange in Europe.

It provides a worldwide exchange for futures dealers and investors, and began options trading in 1985. It was a forerunner of the ◊Big Bang in bringing US-style 'open-house' dealing (as opposed to telephone dealing) to the UK. In 1996 it merged with the London Commodity Exchange and in 1997 joined with the Chicago Board of Trade.

Lighthill, (Michael) James (1924–)

British mathematician who specialized in the application of mathematics to high-speed aerodynamics and jet propulsion. He also studied the theory of jet noise and his work influenced the design of silencers in jet exhausts. He was knighted in 1971.

Lilburne, John (*c.* 1614–1657)

English republican agitator. He was imprisoned 1638–40 for circulating Puritan pamphlets, fought in the Parliamentary army in the Civil War, and by his advocacy of a democratic republic won the leadership of the ◊Levellers, the democratic party in the English Civil War.

In 1640 Oliver Cromwell made a speech in favour of Lilburne to get him released, and in 1641, Lilburne received an indemnity of £3,000. He rose to the rank of lieutenant colonel in the army, but resigned in 1645 because of the number of Presbyterians. In 1647 he was put in the Tower of London for accusations against Cromwell. He was banished in 1652 and arrested again on his return in 1653. He was acquitted, but still imprisoned until 1655 for 'the peace of the nation'.

Limehouse

District in east London; part of ◊Tower Hamlets. It takes its name from the kilns which preceded shipping as the main industry. In the 1890s it was the home of Chinese sailors working from the West India Docks. Bomb damage during World War II led to a decline in population, especially after closure of the docks. The Limehouse docks now form part of the Docklands urban development area. The Limehouse Link motorway and tunnel, linking Tower Hill and Canary Wharf, opened in 1993.

limerick

Five-line humorous verse, often nonsensical and with a strict rhyme scheme, which first appeared in England in about 1820 and was popularized by Edward ◊Lear. An example is: 'There was a young lady of Riga, Who rode with a smile on a tiger; They returned from the ride With the lady inside, And the smile on the face of the tiger.'

Linacre, Thomas (*c.* 1460–1524)

English humanist, physician to Henry VIII, from whom he obtained a charter in 1518 to found the Royal College of Physicians, of which he was the first president.

Lincoln

Industrial and cathedral city, administrative headquarters of ◊Lincolnshire, England, situated on the River Witham, 210 km/130 mi north of London; population (1991) 80,300. Products include bricks, excavators, cranes, gas turbines, radios, vehicle components, cattle feed, matting, pharmaceuticals, power units for oil platforms, and cosmetics. Other industries include heavy engineering, iron foundries, seed milling, and food processing.

During the Roman period, Lincoln was the flourishing colony of **Lindum**, and in the Middle Ages it was a centre for the wool trade. Paulinus built a church here in the 7th century, and the 11th–15th-century cathedral has the earliest Gothic work in Britain. The 12th-century High Bridge is the oldest in Britain still to have buildings on it.

A Roman colony

The first settlement on the site of Lincoln was the ancient British settlement of Lindos (meaning marsh or pool); the Romans latinized the name as **Lindum**. The settlement was at the junction of ◊Ermine Street and ◊Fosse Way, and the Roman presence dates from AD 48. The first permanent fortress of the IXth Legion, whose defences have been located by excavations, was established on the hill top. The title of colonia was conferred in about AD 96. The Roman colony was in the territory of the Coritani, whose capital was at Leicester. The walls of the colony were extended down the hill slope almost to the river in the first half of the 3rd century; coin evidence shows that Roman occupation extended into the 5th century. Newport Arch, which was the north gate to the Roman colony, is the only Roman archway in the British Isles which still spans a main road used by modern traffic.

Under the Normans

Lincoln never attained any great size, although at the Norman Conquest it was one of the six largest towns in the kingdom, with a considerable trade in wool. Under the Danish settlement Lincoln was one of the five boroughs of the ◊Danelaw. William the Conqueror decided to build a castle there, and Lincoln was chosen as the seat of a bishopric. At that time the city was divided into separate jurisdictions of which only one, the manor of Hungate, or Beaumont Fee, survived into modern times. Other communities, civil and ecclesiastical, developed, including the Jewish community, a reminder of whose presence is the Jew's House. Later came the religious houses: Monks Abbey, a cell of the Benedictine abbey of St Mary of York; St Catherine's priory of the order of St Gilbert of Sempringham; and the friars' houses, the only remaining example being the beautiful Grey Friars (founded in 1090), which was later used as the grammar school and is now the museum.

Lincoln Cathedral

The cathedral is built on the highest part of the city. Around 1073 the see of the bishops of Lindsey was moved from Dorchester to Lincoln by Remigius, an appointee of William I. Restoration was needed following a fire in 1141 and a devastating earthquake in 1185, after which the cathedral was greatly rebuilt in the ◊Early English style, although some Norman features remain. Its chapter-house, begun around 1220, is the earliest Gothic example of polygonal pattern. The Angel Choir (1256), one of the most celebrated achievements of English Gothic architecture, is named after the 30 angels decorating the triforium arches.

LINCOLN CATHEDRAL *The second-largest cathedral in England (after York). Destroyed by an earthquake in 1185, it was rebuilt (beginning in 1192) by Bishop Hugh, who made it a masterpiece of Gothic architecture. The remarkable west front, framed by twin towers, is thought to symbolize the gates of heaven. Linda Proud*

The library above the cloister was designed by Christopher Wren. One of the four original copies of Magna Carta is held in the cathedral.

From the Middle Ages to the 19th century

Lincoln received its first royal charter in 1154. In 1301 Edward I granted the city a new charter, and after this there gradually developed a select body of common councilmen, who from the 16th century onwards met in the present guildhall over the Stonebow gatehouse. Many years elapsed before this gatehouse was completed, and the south face with figures depicting the Annunciation was not built before about 1520; the royal arms above the arch probably commemorated the visit of James I in 1617.

The prosperity of medieval Lincoln was based on the wool trade. The raw wool was brought to Lincoln mainly along the waterways (the Fossdyke connecting the Witham with the Trent, and the Cardyke connecting the Nene and the Witham), and was there made up for export to Flanders and the Hanseatic towns. Cloth was being made in Lincoln by 1157, at which date there was a guild of weavers. From 1369 Boston became the centre of the wool trade, and Lincoln declined in importance until improved fen drainage in the 19th century made Lincoln an important agricultural centre. The first railway line to reach Lincoln was opened in 1846, and industry soon developed. Initially, agricultural machinery was manufactured, and later, heavy engineering products.

Lincoln Castle

The castle was built by William the Conqueror in 1068 to supplement the defences of the city, whose Roman walls and gates had for the most part survived. The upper town was annexed to the new castle as a kind of outer bailey, which gave rise to the modern name 'Bailgate'. The castle had two gateways, the east gate opening upon Castle Hill, inside the city, and the west leading to open country. The east gate is still in use though the round Norman arch has been covered by a 14th-century pointed arch with flanking turrets. Lincoln Castle departs from the usual Norman plan in having two mounds instead of one; both stand on the south side of the castle yard, their bases being only about 60 m apart. The Stonebow, the southern gateway to Lincoln, stands on the site of the southern gate of the lower Roman enclosure. On the roof is the mote bell (1371), still rung to summon council meetings. The castle houses one of the four surviving copies of Magna Carta.

The Jewish quarter

The most interesting buildings on Steep Hill are the Jews' houses. In the Strait is the one actually known as the Jew's House; the facade has been mutilated, but it does preserve its beautifully moulded doorway with interlacing pattern. Next door to it is the Jew's Court, rescued from destruction under slum clearance legislation and restored by the Lincolnshire Architectural and Archaeological Society. These houses and that popularly known as Aaron's House date from the 12th century, when Lincoln was at the height of its prosperity as a centre of the wool trade.

Other landmarks

The Usher Art Gallery contains important permanent collections, including the Usher and Tennyson collections and a collection of works by Peter ◊de Wint, the water-colourist. The High Bridge spans the Witham, and its central portion dates from the 12th century. On the west of the bridge are half-timbered houses built in about 1540, and on the eastern side once stood the wayside chapel of St Thomas of Canterbury, built in the 13th century, and demolished in 1763. The Grey Friars is approached from the Stonebow by way of Saltergate, but all that now remains is the chapel built in about 1230. Adjoining the museum is the central public library, built in 1913. The three most interesting medieval parish churches, St Benedict, St Mary-le-Wigford, and St Peter-at-Gowts, are all south of the river. In front of St Benedict's is the city war memorial. St Mary-le-Wigford and St Peter-at-Gowts both possess notable Saxon towers. Lincoln also boasts a bronze statue of Alfred, Lord Tennyson (1905). In 1995 construction began on a new university for Lincolnshire.

Lincolnshire

County of eastern England

Area 5,890 sq km/2,274 sq mi

Towns and cities ◊Lincoln (administrative headquarters), Skegness, Boston, Stamford

Physical hills of Lincoln Edge and the Wolds; marshy coastline; the Fens in the southeast; rivers Trent, Welland, Witham

Features Belton House, a Restoration mansion; Gibraltar Point National Nature Reserve

Agriculture cattle, sheep, horses; cereals (mainly barley); flower bulbs (largest bulb-growing industry in the UK, around Spalding); vegetables

Population (1994) 605,600

Famous people Isaac Newton, John Wesley, Alfred Tennyson, Margaret Thatcher

Topography

Lincolnshire is bounded on the east by the North Sea and the Wash; to the north by Northeast Lincolnshire and North Lincolnshire; to the west by Nottinghamshire, Leicestershire, and Rutland; and to the south by Peterborough, Cambridgeshire and Norfolk. The coastline, though mostly marshy, has long stretches of sand. The county generally is flat, a considerable part being marshes. Lincoln Edge (also known as the Heights, or the Cliff) runs from Grantham to Lincoln, and on to the River Humber; the Wolds run from Spilsby to Barton-upon-Humber.

Lindisfarne

Site of a monastery off the coast of Northumberland, England; see ◊Holy Island.

Lindisfarne Gospels, or St Cuthbert's Evangelistarium

Celtic manuscript conceived as a memorial volume to St Cuthbert, who died in 687, held in the British Museum, London. It was produced at the Anglo-Irish monastery of Lindisfarne on ◊Holy Island, Northumberland. Its decorative interlaced ornament is similar in style to that of the Book of Kells, now in Trinity College, Dublin.

Under Ethelwold, bishop of Lindisfarne, the manuscript was enriched early in the 8th century by an elaborate painting of an evangelist to each of the four Gospels and by illuminated capital letters at the commencement of each book.

Lineker, Gary (1960–)

English footballer. He scored over 250 goals in 550 games for Leicester, Everton, Barcelona, and Tottenham. With 48 goals in 80 internationals he failed by one goal to equal Bobby Charlton's record of 49 goals for England. Lineker was elected Footballer of the Year in 1986 and 1992, and was leading scorer at the 1986 World Cup finals. In 1993 he moved to Japan to play for Nagoya Grampus Eight but retired a year later.

Linlithgow

Town in West Lothian, Scotland, 28 km/17 mi west of Edinburgh; population (1991) 11,900. **Linlithgow Palace**, now in ruins, was once a royal residence, and Mary Queen of Scots was born there.

The palace, with 13th-century origins, dates in its present form from the 15th to 17th centuries. It is a quadrangular building, with a tower at each corner. It overlooks **Loch Linlithgow**, which is 1.6 km/1 mi in length.

Linnhe, Loch

Sea-inlet on the west coast of Scotland, 56 km/35 mi long and 2–8 km/1–5 mi wide, forming part of the border between Highland, and Argyll and Bute unitary authorities. Fort William stands at the head of the loch, at the junction with Loch Eil and the beginning of the ◊Caledonian Canal system.

Its waters are divided by the Corran Narrows, with Loch Leven entering the lower half. The island of Lismore lies within the mouth of Loch Linnhe as it joins the Firth of Lorn.

linoleum (Latin *lini oleum* 'linseed oil')

Floor covering made from linseed oil, tall oil, rosin, cork, woodflour, chalk, clay, and pigments, pressed into sheets with a jute backing. Linoleum tiles have a backing made of polyester and glass.

Linoleum was invented in England in 1860 by Frederick Walton. In the early 20th century he invented a straight-line inlay machine which was able to produce patterned linoleum. Today, the manufacture of linoleum still follows the basic principles of Walton's process although production is much faster. Synthetic floor coverings are now popular and the use of linoleum has declined.

lion

The most important heraldic animal, associated with valour and strength. The **lion rampant** (standing on hind legs) in the arms of Scotland derives from the earls of Northumberland and Huntingdon, from whom some Scottish monarchs were descended. Two of the three **lions passant gardant** (walking, full-faced) in the shield of England derive from William the Conqueror, and Henry II added the third. The lion and the unicorn have been supporters of the royal arms since 1603.

Lion, the Witch and the Wardrobe, The

Novel (1950) by C S ◊Lewis, the first of the Chronicles of ◊Narnia.

Lisburn

Town in County Antrim, Northern Ireland, on the River Lagan, 14 km/9 mi from Belfast; population (1991) 27,400. The main industries are engineering and the production of soft drinks, yarn and thread, and packaging; it is a busy shopping centre. Many inhabitants commute to Belfast. Lisburn was founded in the 17th century and planted with English settlers and French Huguenot refugees.

The development of the linen industry, which came to be important in the town, owed much to the Huguenot settlers. The Church of Ireland cathedral was built in 1623.

There is a monument to Bishop Jeremy Taylor (died 1667) in the cathedral; Lisburn is the seat of the bishop of Connor. Lisburn Museum in the Assembly Rooms has exhibitions on the linen industry, and 2 km/1 mi from Lisburn in Lambeg village is a linen research institute.

Lismore

Island off the west coast of Argyll and Bute unitary authority, Scotland, situated at the mouth of Loch Linnhe, 8 km/5 mi northwest of Oban on the mainland; population (1991) 100. It covers an area 15 km/9 mi long and about 2 km/1 mi wide.

Achadun Castle, now in ruins, was once the seat of the bishops of Argyll.

Lister, Joseph, 1st Baron Lister (1827–1912)

English surgeon. He was the founder of antiseptic surgery, influenced by Louis Pasteur's work on bacteria. He introduced dressings soaked in carbolic acid and strict rules of hygiene to combat wound sepsis in hospitals.

The number of surgical operations greatly increased following the introduction of anaesthetics, but death rates were more than 40%. Under Lister's regime they fell dramatically.

Lister was born in Upton, Essex, and studied at University College, London. He was professor of surgery at Glasgow 1860–69, at Edinburgh 1869–77, and at King's College, London 1877–92. In 1891 he became chair of the newly formed British Institute of Preventive Medicine (later the Lister Institute).

Sepsis was at this time thought to be a kind of combustion caused by exposing moist body tissues to oxygen. Learning of Pasteur's discovery of microorganisms, however, Lister began to use carbolic acid as a disinfectant. In 1867 he announced that his wards in the Glasgow Royal Infirmary had remained clear of sepsis for nine months. Later he adopted the method developed by Robert Koch in Germany of using steam to sterilize surgical instruments and dressings.He became a baronet in 1883, and baron in 1897.

Littlehampton

Seaside resort in West Sussex, southeast England, at the mouth of the River Arun, 16 km/10 mi southeast of Chichester; population (1996 est) 25,100. Industries include light engineering, food production, electronics, commercial horticulture, and the manufacture of Formula 1 racing car bodies. It is the headquarters of Body Shop, an international cosmetics firm with an explicit ethical trading and environmental policy founded by Anita Roddick in 1976.

Little John

In English legend, a companion of ◊Robin Hood.

Little Moreton Hall

Outstanding black-and-white Tudor house near Congleton, Cheshire, England. It was built in stages throughout the 16th century, the oldest part dating from about 1520. The somewhat random structure is surrounded by a moat, while inside the hall and gallery are decorated with carving and plasterwork. The Hall was presented to the National Trust in 1938.

Littlewood, Joan Maud (1914–)

English theatre director. She established the Theatre Workshop in 1945 and was responsible for many vigorous productions at the Theatre Royal, Stratford, London, 1953–75, such as *A Taste of Honey* (1959), Brendan Behan's *The Hostage* (1959–60), and *Oh, What a Lovely War* (1963).

Lively, Penelope Margaret (1933–)

British writer, born in Cairo. She has written many novels for children (*A Stitch in Time* (1976) won the Whitbread Literary Award) and, from 1977, for adults (*Moon Tiger* (1987) won the Booker Prize). Her fiction is characterized by an absorption in the influence of the past on the present.

Liverpool

City, seaport, and metropolitan borough in Merseyside, northwest England; population (1991) 481,800. Liverpool is the UK's chief Atlantic port with miles of specialized, mechanized quays on the River Mersey, and 2,100 ha/5,187 acres of dockland. The port handles 27.8 million tonnes/28.25 million tons of cargo annually. Imports include crude oil, grain, ores, edible oils, timber, and containers. There are ferries to Ireland and the Isle of Man. Traditional industries, such as ship-repairing, have declined. Present-day industries include flour-milling, sugar refining, electrical engineering, food processing, and tanning; products include chemicals, soap, margarine, and motor vehicles. There are industrial estates at Aintree, Kirkby, and Speke. A rail tunnel, and Queensway Tunnel (1934) link Liverpool and Birkenhead; Kingsway Tunnel (1971), also known as the Mersey Tunnel, links Liverpool and Wallasey.

Features

Landmarks include the Bluecoat Chambers (1717); the Town Hall (1754); St George's Hall (1838–54), a good example of classical architecture; the Brown Library and Museum (1860); the Picton Library (1879); the Anglican Cathedral, designed by George Gilbert Scott (begun 1904, completed 1980); the Roman Catholic Metropolitan Cathedral of Christ the King, designed by Frederick ◊Gibberd, consecrated in 1967; and the Tate Gallery in the North in the former Albert Dock (now restored as a shopping and leisure area), opened in 1987. The Walker Art Gallery (1877) and the Liverpool Philharmonic Orchestra, (founded in 1840, the Royal LPO since 1957), are here. The Grand National steeplechase takes place at ◊Aintree. Outstanding buildings include the 16th-century Speke Hall, the Victoria Building of the University of Liverpool, the Dock Offices, the Port of Liverpool building (1907), Royal Liver Building (1911), and the Cunard Building (1916) on Pier Head. In the Canning Conservation Area, 600 Georgian and Victorian houses are being restored.

The Central Libraries (a conglomerate of several libraries) constitute one of the best public libraries in the country; the Picton Library (1879) for the humanities is a 19th-century building. There are two universities: the University of Liverpool (opened in 1903) and John Moores University. Britain's first International Garden Festival was held here in 1984. The ◊Beatles were born here. The Liverpool Institute for the Performing Arts, set up by former Beatle Paul McCartney and opened in 1995, occupies the old Liverpool Institute for Boys, where Paul McCartney and George Harrison went to school. If offers a bachelor's degree in the performing arts.

History

Liverpool grew in importance during the 18th century as a centre of the slave trade, and until the early 20th century through the export of the textiles from Lancashire and Yorkshire.

Middle Ages

Liverpool became a county borough in 1207, and from its beginnings as a port it was associated with the transport of soldiers and military supplies to Ireland, and with general trade. The original port was probably a sheltered creek, the 'Pool', long since filled in, and the original town was small, clustered around the church of St Nicholas (still surviving through many rebuildings and restorations) and a former castle. Although by 1445 Liverpool's trade was injuring the prosperity of ◊Chester as a port, it remained small, and even the church was within the parish of Walton until 1699.

17th–19th centuries

Liverpool developed under Charles II (1630–85) with the developing trade with America and the West Indies, and became the chief centre of the slave trade. Its growth was observed by various travellers, including Gibson in 1695 who related 'the vast growth of this town in recent years' to the trade with Ireland and the West Indies, and also to the development of the manufacturing industry. Even so, in 1668 it was a town of only seven streets though a map by Chadwick in 1725 shows some 37. In 1715 the 'Old Dock' was opened, on the site of the Custom House. This dock was condemned as unsafe in 1811 and was filled up in 1826.

During the 18th century Liverpool grew rapidly. Daniel Defoe, in 1725, found it at least equal to Bristol in 'the trade to Virginia and the English Island Colonies in America', and notes that there was considerable trade with Norwegian and Baltic ports as well as with Hamburg and the ports of the Low Countries. The port of Liverpool had long since eclipsed Chester in importance, and the area surrounding was also growing in importance, with industrial areas to the north (including the Cheshire salt deposits), the textile areas of the Pennines and their fringes, and the metallurgical areas of the Midlands.

The position of Liverpool was strengthened by the building of canals to the River Mersey, including the Sankey Canal from St Helens (1757), the Bridgewater from Manchester to Runcorn (1773), the Trent and Mersey (1777), and the Leeds and Liverpool (which reached Wigan in 1774 but Liverpool only in 1816). The Mersey was navigable to Warrington by 1700, but the Mersey and Irwell navigation system to Manchester was not completed until 1720. Road transport was less satisfactory; the first stage-coach reached Liverpool from London only in 1765 although turnpikes were added later. Like other British cities that were growing rapidly in the 18th century and afterwards, Liverpool presented an aspect of prosperity and elegance in its main streets but poorer housing was abundant in less obvious areas, though in time these areas swamped many of the elegant residential quarters. Meanwhile the dock area was expanding, at first from 1715 to 1797 when several docks south of the Pier Head were built. The Pier Head is the great river focus of Liverpool, for here the Mersey narrows to a mere 915 m/3,000 ft. To Pier Head came the ferries, the tramway, and later bus services, as well as a station on the Mersey railway, giving convenient transport to all parts of the city. Docks were built north of Pier Head from 1821, eventually extending for 11 km/7 mi. In 1893 the overhead railway was built, providing transport for the vast number of people working on ships and in the many warehouses and factories of the dock belt; it was closed in 1956.

By the time of the 1801 census, Liverpool, with 78,000 inhabitants, was larger than Bristol with 64,000. The city grew throughout the 19th century continued and by 1901 its population was 704,134.

The 20th century

A major problem in Liverpool between World War I and II was its housing, for the population had increased to 856,072 in 1931. During the inter-war years, the Queen's Drive was completed as an outer circular road, and beside it a number of large local authority housing estates were built. From 1931 to 1951 the population declined to 780,835, with a further decline to 745,750 by 1961. Slum clearance in the city centre reduced the population there. When a survey was made of housing in the 1950s it was estimated that two fifths of the city's dwellings were below acceptable standards. People began to move to places beyond the perimeter of the city, such as Kirkby and Huyton-with-Roby; this process had in fact begun in central wards as early as the 1840s when houses were cleared for new roads, factories, and public buildings.

Industries

Much of Liverpool's industry was concerned with imported raw materials: timber, flour and grain, chemicals, rubber, leather, foodstuffs, and animal feed. The Leeds and Liverpool Canal, no longer used commercially, was an important route for the raw materials. Railways were also built to carry raw materials from the docks to factory areas scattered through Liverpool. Modern industries, especially in engineering, chemicals, and rubber, are located on outlying estates at Kirkby and Speke, with the addition of the motor industry at Halewood, east of Speke.

Landmarks and layout

Liverpool lacks the medieval grandeur of Bristol, but despite constant rebuilding much survives from the 18th century, though it is difficult to visualize the elegant town that existed on the sandstone hill now crowned by the city's two cathedrals. Some streets that were originally residential, for example Renshaw Street, became commercial, but Rodney Street, built from 1782, has some elegant houses including one of 1796, and is rather more ornate than its neighbours; the Victorian prime minister W E Gladstone was born here. Various churches were built in the 18th century, but many have been demolished. One building of special interest is the former Bluecoat School of 1716–17, a brick building known as Bluecoat Chambers, and used as a cultural centre.

The municipal centre of Liverpool is adjacent to its shopping centre, and between these two and Pier Head lies the office quarter. This area contains the 18th-century town hall and many other major buildings including the Exchange, built in 1863–67. Best known of all the office buildings, perhaps, are those on the waterfront beside the Pier Head: the Royal Liver Building of 1910 topped by the liver bird (a legendary creature regarded by some as romantically expressing the spirit of Liverpool); the Cunard building (1913); and the Mersey Docks and Harbour Board building of 1907, with a copper dome.

The historic waterfront is now a major tourist attraction; the Albert Dock includes the Merseyside Maritime Museum, and the Beatles story, as well as the Tate Gallery in the North.

The cathedrals

From the river, the skyline of Liverpool is dominated by its cathedrals. The Anglican cathedral is Gothic in inspiration. The Roman Catholic metropolitan cathedral consists of a circular nave formed by 16 reinforced concrete columns and buttresses supporting a conical roof with a lantern tower 21 m/69 ft high over the central high altar. Beneath the cathedral there is the crypt of the earlier building, designed by Sir Edwin ◊Lutyens as a vast Romanesque structure. After World War II his plans had to be abandoned as economically unviable.

Liverpool, Robert Banks Jenkinson, 2nd Earl Liverpool (1770–1828)

British Tory politician. He entered Parliament in 1790 and was foreign secretary 1801–03, home secretary 1804–06 and 1807–09, war minister 1809–12, and prime minister 1812–27. His government conducted the Napoleonic Wars to a successful conclusion, but its ruthless suppression of freedom of speech and of the press aroused such opposition that during 1815–20 revolution frequently seemed imminent.

livery companies

Guilds (organizations of traders and artisans) of the City of London. Their role is now social rather than industrial. Many administer charities, especially educational ones. Each livery company is governed by an annually elected court, typically composed as follows: The Master (elected from the Wardens); Upper Warden; Middle Warden; Lower Warden (elected from the Court assistant); between 10 and 20 Court Assistants (elected from the Livery); a Clerk (to keep the records); a Beadle (to keep order).

After years of dispute, an order of precedence for livery companies was settled in 1515, starting with Mercers at number 1 and so on down to number 48. Merchant Taylors and Skinners, however, continued to alternate between numbers 6 and 7 in alternate years, following a compromise reached some 30 years earlier. Numbers 1 to 12 inclusive are known as the Great Twelve. Through choice, the companies of Parish Clerks and Watermen and Lightermen remain City Guilds without grant of livery.

Livery companies in order of precedence Mercers (general merchants); Grocers; Drapers; Fishmongers; Goldsmiths; Merchant Taylors (tailors); Skinners (fur trade); Haberdashers; Salters; Ironmongers; Vintners; Clothworkers; Dyers; Brewers; Leathersellers; Pewterers; Barbers (also surgeons and dentists); Cutlers; Bakers; Waxchandlers; Tallowchandlers; Armourers and Brasiers (armour-makers and workers in brass); Girdlers (girdles and belts as clothing); Butchers; Saddlers; Carpenters; Cordwainers (workers in fine leather); Painter Stainers; Curriers (dressers of tanned leather); Masons; Plumbers; Innholders; Founders; Poulters; Cooks; Coopers (barrel makers); Tylers and Bricklayers; Bowyers (longbow makers); Fletchers (arrow makers); Blacksmiths; Joiners; Weavers; Woolmen (winders and packers of wool); Scriveners (writers of court letters and legal documents); Fruiterers; Plaisterers (plasterers); Stationers and Newspaper Makers; Broderers (embroiderers); Upholders (upholsterers); Musicians; Turners; Basketmakers; Glaziers; Horners; Farriers (shoers of horses/veterinary surgeons); Paviors (paving, highways); Loriners (stirrups and other harness for horses); Apothecaries (medicine); Shipwrights; Spectaclemakers; Clockmakers; Glovers; Feltmakers (hats); Framework Knitters; Needlemakers; Gardeners; Tinplate Workers; Wheelwrights; Distillers; Pattenmakers (makers of wooden clog-style footwear); Glass Sellers; Coachmakers and Coach Harness Makers; Gunmakers; Gold and Silver Wyre Drawers (gold and silver braid for uniforms); Makers of Playing Cards; Fan Makers; Carmen; Master Mariners; Solicitors; Farmers; Air Pilots and Air Navigators; Tobacco Pipe Makers and Tobacco Blenders; Furniture Makers; Scientific Instrument Makers; Chartered Surveyors; Chartered Accountants; Chartered Secretaries and Administrators; Builders Merchants; Launderers; Marketors; Actuaries; Insurers; Arbitrators; Engineers; Fuellers; Lightmongers; Environmental Cleaners; Chartered Architects; Constructors; Information Technologists.

Livingston

Administrative headquarters of ◊West Lothian, Scotland, 47 km/29 mi from Glasgow, ◊new town established in 1962; population (1991) 41,600. Industries include electronics, engineering, paper, steel, scientific instruments, and industrial research.

Livingstone, David (1813–1873)

Scottish missionary explorer. In 1841 he went to Africa, reaching Lake Ngami in 1849. He followed the Zambezi to its mouth, saw the Victoria Falls in 1855, and went to East and Central Africa 1858–64, reaching Lakes Shirwa and Nyasa. From 1866, he tried to find the source of the River Nile, and reached Ujiji in Tanganyika in November 1871. British explorer Henry Stanley joined Livingstone in Ujiji.

Livingstone not only mapped a great deal of the African continent but also helped to end the Arab slave trade.

He died in Old Chitambo (now in Zambia) and was buried in Westminster Abbey, London.

Part of the problem is that many MPs never see the London that exists beyond the wine bars and brothels of Westminster.

KEN LIVINGSTONE British left-wing Labour politician. Quoted in *Observer* 22 February 1987

Livingstone, Ken(neth) (1945–)

British left-wing Labour politician. He was leader of the Greater London Council (GLC) 1981–86 and a member of Parliament from 1987. He stood as a candidate for the Labour

LIVINGSTONE, DAVID *Scottish missionary and explorer David Livingstone hoped to abolish the slave trade in Africa by spreading Christianity, and during his travels he discovered the Zambesi River (1851) and Victoria Falls (1855). He became a national hero in Britain and played a major role in shaping European attitudes towards Africa. Corbis*

Party leadership elections 1992 and has declared himmself to be a candidate for the mayorship of London, although he lacks backing from the Labour Party's leadership.

As leader of the GLC until its abolition in 1986, he displayed outside GLC headquarters current unemployment figures so that they were clearly visible to MPs in the Palace of Westminster across the River Thames.

Lizard Point

Southernmost point of mainland England in Cornwall. The coast is broken into small bays, overlooked by two cliff lighthouses.

Lizard Point is notable for Cornish heath and other plants similar to those found in southwest Europe.

The headland is formed largely of greenish serpentine rock. Goonhilly Downs nearby is the site of a satellite communications centre. The village of **Lizard** lies 17 km/11 mi south of Helston. Kynance Cove lies to the northwest of Lizard Point. The Lion's Den is a chasm formed in 1847 by the collapse of a cave. Lizard Point is situated at latitude 49° 57' 30' N and longitude 5° 12' W.

Llanberis

Village in Gwynedd, northwest Wales, situated 5 km/3 mi east of Caernarfon. It is the point of departure for the ascent of Mount ⇨Snowdon (1,085 m/3,560 ft), either on foot or using the mountain railway which starts here.

There are two lakes in the vicinity, and Llanberis is also a resort for fishermen. The pass of Llanberis travels between the crags of the Glyders and the lower slopes of Snowdon to link the village with Capel Curig. The road reaches a height of 357 m/222 ft at Pen-y-Pas, 1km/0.6 mi from the top on the Capel Curig side, where the Pen-y-Gwryd Hotel has many climbing associations. Close to the pass and the lake of Llyn Padarn sits the solitary tower of the ruined Dolbadarn Castle, probably built in the 13th-century by Llewelyn the Great. Much quarrying was formerly carried on and the landscape is characterised by disused quarries.

Llandaff, Welsh Llandaf

Town in south Wales, 5 km/3 mi northwest of Cardiff, of which it forms part. The 12th-century cathedral, heavily restored, contains Jacob Epstein's sculpture *Christ in Majesty*, crowning a 20th-century arch of reinforced concrete.

Construction of the cathedral began around 1120 on the site of a small church built in 560. A substantial part of the design was in the Norman style, but building continued throughout the medieval period. Although carefully restored between 1844 and 1869, after having been almost in ruins since the 17th century, it was damaged by bombing in 1941. After the World War II restoration began anew, and its completion was celebrated on 6 August 1960 at a service of thanksgiving in the presence of HM the Queen. The Welsh Regiment Memorial Chapel, a gift of the regiment, was added on the north side of the cathedral in 1956.

Llandrindod Wells

Administrative centre of ⇨Powys, east Wales; population (1991) 4,400. Situated on the River Ithon, it is a popular health resort possessing medicinal springs.

Llandudno

Seaside resort in Gwynedd, north Wales, situated on Conwy Bay. Lying on the Creuddyn Peninsula, it has two sandy beaches and is a touring centre. Great Orme's Head is a spectacular limestone headland encircled by a marine 'drive'.

Llanelli, formerly Llanelly

Industrial port in Carmarthenshire, south Wales, situated on Burry Inlet 16 km/10 mi northwest of Swansea; population (1991) 45,000. Industries include copper smelting, and the manufacture of tin plate, chemicals, bricks, and lenses.

Bryncaerau Castle is now a museum housing an art gallery, a pottery collection and a display showing the history of the tinplate industry. The port was closed for trading purposes in 1951.

Llanfair P G

Village in Anglesey, northwest Wales, 24 km/15 mi east of Holyhead; full name **Llanfairpwllgwyngyllgogerychwyrndrobwllllantysiliogogogoch** (St Mary's church in the hollow of the white hazel near the rapid whirlpool of St Tysillio's church, by the red cave), the longest place name in the UK.

Llangefni

Town and administrative headquarters of the Isle of ⇨Anglesey, northwest Wales, situated in the centre of the island; population (1991) 4,600.

Llangollen

Town in Denbighshire, northeast Wales, on the River Dee, 15 km/9 mi southwest of Wrexham; population (1991) 3,300. It is a summer resort. The annual international musical ⇨eisteddfod (festival) is held here. The Vale of Llangollen includes places of historic interest, such as the ruins of Valle Crucis Abbey. Other local features include the Llangollen Canal and the scenic Llangollen Railway.

Llantwit Major, Welsh Llanilltyd Fawr

Small town in the Vale of Glamorgan, south Wales, 11 km/7 mi southeast of Bridgend; population (1991) 12,500. It is built on the site of a 6th-century monastery founded by St Illtyd (fl. 520).

Llewelyn

Two princes of Wales:

Llewelyn I (1173–1240)

Prince of Wales from 1194. He extended his rule to all Wales not in Norman hands, driving the English from northern Wales in 1212, and taking Shrewsbury in 1215. During the early part of Henry III's reign, he was several times attacked by English armies. He was married to Joanna, the illegitimate daughter of King John.

Llewelyn II ap Gruffydd (*c.* 1225–1282)

Prince of Wales from 1246, grandson of Llewelyn I. In 1277 Edward I of England compelled Llewelyn to acknowledge him as overlord and to surrender southern Wales. His death while leading a national uprising ended Welsh independence.

Lleyn Peninsula, Welsh Llŷn

Westward-extending peninsula in north Wales, between Cardigan Bay and Caernarfon Bay. Its coastline is designated as a National Heritage Coastline and an Area of Outstanding Natural Beauty. It includes the resort of ◊Pwllheli. ◊Bardsey Island, at its tip, is the traditional burial place of 20,000 saints.

It is a low plateau with a number of mountains, of which Yr Eifl (564 m/1,850 ft) is the highest. The area is rural with a predominantly Welsh-speaking population. Other resorts along the coast include Criccieth, Abersoch, Aberdaron, and Nefyn. Activities include surfing, sailing, and sea angling.

Lloyd, Marie stage name of Matilda Alice Victoria Wood (1870–1922)

English music-hall artist. Her Cockney songs embodied the music-hall traditions of 1890s comedy.

Lloyd, Selwyn

See ◊Selwyn Lloyd, British Conservative politician.

The last champion of Welsh liberty ... Brave, active and strenuous ... perhaps, better able to conceive than to carry out an elaborate policy.

T F TOUT
Dictionary of National Biography, on Llewelyn ap Gruffydd

Lloyd George, David, 1st Earl Lloyd-George of Dwyfor (1863–1945)

British Liberal politician, prime minister of Britain from 1916 to 1922. A pioneer of social reform and the welfare state, as chancellor of the Exchequer (1908–15) he introduced old-age pensions in 1908 and health and unemployment insurance in 1911. High unemployment, intervention in the Russian Civil War, and use of the military police force, the ◊Black and Tans, in Ireland eroded his support as prime minister, and the creation of the Irish Free State in 1921 and his pro-Greek policy against the Turks caused the collapse of his coalition government.

Lloyd George was born in Manchester, became a solicitor, and was member of Parliament for Caernarvon Boroughs from 1890. During the Boer War, he was prominent as a pro-Boer. His 1909 budget (with graduated direct taxes and taxing land values) provoked the Lords to reject it, and resulted in the Act of 1911 limiting their powers. He held ministerial posts during World War I until 1916 when there was an open breach between him and Prime Minister ◊Asquith, and he became prime minister of a coalition government. Securing a unified Allied command, he enabled the Allies to withstand the last German offensive and achieve victory. After World War I he had a major role in the Versailles peace treaty. In the 1918 elections, he achieved a huge majority over Labour and Asquith's followers. He had become largely distrusted within his own party by 1922, and never regained power. He was made an earl in 1945.

Lloyd's of London

International insurance market and centre of shipping intelligence, based in London. Lloyd's was established in 1688 and named after Edward Lloyd, whose coffee-house was a meeting place for those interested in shipping. Lloyd's accounts for half of all international insurance premiums underwritten in the London market. Lloyd's moved into a new building in the City of London, designed by the architect Richard Rogers, in 1986.

Members of Lloyd's (known as 'names') are organized into syndicates, and pledge personal fortunes in return for premiums. There is no limit to a name's liability, but risks are spread among the members of a syndicate, so that no individual takes too great a personal risk. However, during the late 1980s and early 1990s, Lloyd's suffered a series of losses (Piper Alpha, Hurricane Hugo, the *Exxon Valdez* oil spill, European storms in 1990), and many names faced large bills to meet the insurance cover. 1988 saw the first loss (£510 million) since 1967. Some names took Lloyd's to court, but a financial settlement was reached in 1996.

Famous risks undertaken by the company include the *Titanic*, the *Lutine* (whose bell, salvaged in 1859, is at the Lloyd's headquarters), and space satellites.

Lloyd Webber, Andrew (1948–)

English composer of hugely popular musicals. His early musicals, with lyrics by Tim Rice, include *Joseph and the Amazing Technicolor Dreamcoat* (1968), *Jesus Christ Superstar* (1971), and *Evita* (1978), based on the life of the Argentine leader Eva Perón. He also wrote *Cats* (1981), based on T S Eliot's *Old Possum's Book of Practical Cats*, *Starlight Express* (1984), *The Phantom of the Opera* (1986), and *Aspects of Love* (1989).

What is our task? To make Britain a fit country for heroes to live in.

DAVID LLOYD GEORGE British Liberal prime minister.
Speech at Wolverhampton 24 November 1918

Loach, Ken(neth) (1936–)

English film and television director. Loach became known for his trenchantly realistic treatment of social issues with television dramas such as *Cathy Come Home* (1966), concerning the plight of homeless people.

His first film was *Poor Cow* (1967); its successor, *Kes* (1971), dealing with working-class life in the north of England, was more favourably received. During the 1970s he was mainly active in television but returned to the cinema in the early 1990s, directing *Hidden Agenda* (1990), about the Northern

Ireland troubles; the comedy *Riff Raff* (1991); and *Raining Stones* (1993). His *Tierra y Libertad/Land and Freedom* (1995), a period piece set in the Spanish Civil War, was followed by the Spanish-funded *Carla's Song* (1996). Loach has recently filmed *My Name is Joe* (1998).

local government

See ◊England, ◊Scotland, ◊Wales, and ◊Northern Ireland for details of the local government divisions.

With the latest reorganization of local government culminating in 1998, the emphasis is on single-tier unitary bodies, each providing a full range of local services. Wales has 22 Unitary Councils and Scotland 29, alongside the 3 existing Island Authority Areas; Northern Ireland has a single-tier system of 26 district councils. The latest pattern for England came into effect on 1 April 1998 with the creation of 47 unitary authorities, replacing former borough or city-councils which were previously part of two-tier structures. There were also, in 1998, 34 county councils in England, 36 metropolitan borough councils, and 33 London borough councils.

Under the Local Government Act (1972) the upper range of local government for England and Wales was established on a two-tier basis, with 46 counties in England and eight in Wales. London and six other English cities were created metropolitan areas (their metropolitan county councils were abolished in 1986, and their already limited functions redistributed to **metropolitan district councils**), and the counties had ◊**county councils**. The counties were subdivided into districts (of which there are 300, each with a ◊**district council**, replacing the former county borough, borough, and urban and rural district councils) and then, in rural areas, into parishes and, in Wales, into 'communities' across the country, each again with its own council (see ◊parish council) dealing with local matters. A major process of restructuring was started in 1993 to be effective from 1997. The Labour government, from 1997, had plans to introduce directly elected mayors for the major cities.

Under the Local Government Act (1974) a Commission for Local Administration for England and Wales was set up, creating an **ombudsman** for complaints about local government.

Only 15% of the money spent by local government is raised by local taxes (1995). ◊Council tax is a local tax based on property values but taking account of the number of inhabitants of a property. This superseded the **community charge** or ◊**poll tax** in 1993, which had earlier replaced a system of local property taxes known as ◊rates. In the mid-1980s the Thatcher administration sought to remove many services from the aegis of local authorities and offer them for tender to private companies; thus in many areas school-meals provision was privatized, as were maintenance of council vehicles, street cleaning, and upkeep of parks and sports facilities. In 1987 a code of practice was issued to restrict the ability of local authorities to promote 'partisan' activities. In the May 1998 local elections, turnout fell to an average of only 27%.

Lochgilphead

Administrative centre of ◊Argyll and Bute unitary authority, Scotland, on Loch Fyne, 38 km/24 mi southwest of Inveraray; population (1991) 2,400. It provides market and service functions for the surrounding area.

Loch Ness

Scottish lake; see ◊Ness, Loch.

Locke, John (1632–1704)

English philosopher. His *Essay concerning Human Understanding* (1690) maintained that experience is the only source of knowledge (empiricism), and that 'we can have knowledge no farther than we have ideas' prompted by such experience. *Two Treatises on Government* (1690) helped to form contemporary ideas of liberal democracy.

For Locke, the physical universe was a mechanical system of material bodies, composed of corpuscules, or 'invisible particles'. He believed that at birth the mind was a blank, and that all ideas came from sense impressions.

His *Two Treatises on Government* supplied the classical statement of Whig theory and enjoyed great influence in America and France. It supposed that governments derive their authority from popular consent (regarded as a 'contract'), so that a government may be rightly overthrown if it infringes such fundamental rights of the people as religious freedom.

Locke, or Lock, Matthew (*c.* 1622–1677)

English composer. He is remembered for the music he wrote for masques such as Shirley's *Cupid and Death* (1653), and his incidental and vocal music for plays, notably *Psyche* (1675). He was a vigorous and acrimonious defender of 'modern' music.

Lockerbie

Town and former burgh in Dumfries and Galloway unitary authority, Scotland, 19 km/12 mi northeast of Dumfries; population (1991) 4,000. It hosts the largest lamb fair in Scotland, held annually in August. On 21 December 1988 the bombing over Lockerbie of Pan-Am Flight 103 to New York killed 270 people, including 11 on the ground.

Lockwood, Margaret (Mary) (1916–1990)

English actress. Between 1937 and 1949 she acted exclusively in the cinema, appearing in Alfred Hitchcock's *The Lady Vanishes* (1938) and in *The Wicked Lady* (1945). After 1955 she made only one film, *The Slipper and the Rose* (1976), although she periodically appeared on stage and on television until her retirement in 1980.

Lockyer, (Joseph) Norman (1836–1920)

English scientist. He studied the spectra of solar prominences and sunspots. Through his pioneering work in spectroscopy, he discovered the existence of helium. He was made a KCB in 1897.

Lodge, David John (1935–)

English novelist, short-story writer, dramatist, and critic. Much of his fiction concerns the role of Catholicism in mid-20th-century England, exploring the situation both through broad comedy and parody, as in *The British Museum is Falling Down* (1967), and realistically, as in *How Far Can You Go?* (1980). *Nice Work* (1988) was short-listed for the Booker Prize.

Lollard

Follower of the English religious reformer John ◊Wycliffe in the 14th century. The Lollards condemned the doctrine of the transubstantiation of the bread and wine of the Eucharist, advocated the diversion of ecclesiastical property to charitable uses, and denounced war and capital punishment. They were active from about 1377; after the passing of the statute *De heretico comburendo* ('The Necessity of Burning Heretics') in 1401 many Lollards were burned, and in 1414 they raised an unsuccessful revolt in London, known as Oldcastle's Rebellion.

The name is derived from the Dutch *lollaert* (mumbler), applied to earlier European groups accused of combining pious pretensions with heretical belief. Lollardy lingered on in London and East Anglia, and in the 16th century became absorbed into the Protestant movement.

Lomond, Loch

Largest freshwater Scottish lake, 37 km/21 mi long, area 70 sq km/27 sq mi. It is overlooked by the mountain **Ben Lomond** (973 m/3,192 ft) and is linked to the Clyde estuary.

London

Capital of England and the United Kingdom, located on the River Thames.

Since 1965 its metropolitan area has been known as ◊Greater London, consisting of the City of London and 32 boroughs; total area 1,580 sq km/610 sq mi; combined population (1995) for 31 boroughs, excluding the cities of London and Westminster, 7,001,900. The **City of London**, known as the 'square mile', is the financial and commercial centre of the UK; area 2.7 sq km/1 sq mi. London is the only major European capital without a strategic authority covering the whole area. Popular tourist attractions include the **Tower of London**, St Paul's Cathedral, Buckingham Palace, and Westminster Abbey. The ◊Millennium Dome at Greenwich is the centrepiece of Britain's millennium celebrations.

History

Roman **Londinium** was established soon after the Roman invasion in AD 43; in the 2nd century London became a walled city; by the 11th century it was the main city of England and gradually extended beyond the walls to link with the originally separate Westminster. Throughout the 19th century London had the largest city-based population in the world. London's history is essentially that of two cities: Westminster, the UK's political and administrative centre, seat of the government and royal court; and the City of London, the capital's economic centre, with a separately evolved administration in the corporation of the City of London. London became the administrative capital of the British Empire and the economic nerve centre of Britain's great trading empire.

Features

The **Tower of London** was built by William the Conqueror on a Roman site, and now houses the crown jewels and the royal armouries; it is a World Heritage Site. Other features include the 15th-century Guildhall; the Monument, a column designed by Christopher Wren, which marks the site in Pudding Lane where the Fire of London began in 1666; Mansion House, the residence of the lord mayor; the Barbican arts and conference centre; the Houses of ◊Parliament and Big Ben; the Old Bailey (Central Criminal Court); and the Inns of Court. Covent Garden, once a vegetable market, is now a tourist, shopping, and entertainment area.

Architecture

London contains buildings in all styles of English architecture dating back to the 11th century.

Norman: the White Tower, Tower of London; St Bartholomew's, Smithfield; the Temple Church.

Gothic: Westminster Abbey; Westminster Hall; Lambeth Palace; Southwark Cathedral.

Tudor: St James's Palace; Staple Inn.

17th century: Banqueting Hall, Whitehall (Inigo Jones); St Paul's; Kensington Palace; many City churches (Sir Christopher Wren).

18th century: Somerset House (Chambers); St Martin-in-the-Fields; Buckingham Palace.

19th century: British Museum (Neo-Classical); Houses of Parliament; Law Courts (Neo-Gothic); Westminster Cathedral (Byzantine style).

20th century: Lloyd's of London (High Tech); Millennium Dome.

LOCH LOMOND *Situated in the Strathclyde region of western Scotland, Loch Lomond is set in dramatic mountainous scenery. The lake has always had a romantic image, promoted by a traditional Scottish lament in which the singer wistfully recalls happy times spent on its banks. Corel*

Government
Since 1986, when the Greater London Council was abolished, there has been no central authority for Greater London. Responsibility is divided between central government and 32 London boroughs, which are unitary and deal with matters such as building regulations, environmental health, education, leisure services, local roads, museums, and refuse collection.

The Corporation of the City of London is the local authority for the City of London, and dates back to the 12th century. It is governed by the Court of the Common Council, comprising the lord mayor, 24 aldermen, and 130 common councilmen. The lord mayor and two sheriffs are nominated annually by the councillors and elected by the aldermen in November (although in the late 1990s it was proposed that London's mayor should be elected by the people of London). After being sworn in at the Guildhall, he or she is presented the next day to the lord chief justice at the Royal Courts of Justice in Westminster, an event marked by the ceremonial procession of the Lord Mayor's Show. There are over 100 city guilds (◊livery companies) covering an array of occupations, including, in order of civic precedence, mercers, grocers, drapers, fishmongers, goldsmiths, merchant taylors, skinners, haberdashers, salters, ironmongers, vintners (wine merchants), and clothworkers. The original purpose of the guilds was to administer apprenticeships and oversee production. Although many of the professions are now in decline, there are still more than 23,000 liverymen entitled to vote at Common Hall, the ruling body of the Corporation of the City of London. The Corporation has the same functions as the boroughs and also runs the **City of London Police** and the health authority for the Port of London. It is also responsible for health controls on animal imports throughout Greater London, including Heathrow airport, runs the Central Criminal Court and the large markets, and owns and manages public open spaces throughout Greater London.

Commerce and industry
From Saxon times the **Port of London** dominated the Thames from Tower Bridge to Tilbury. Its activity is now centred outside the metropolitan area, and downstream Tilbury has been extended to cope with container traffic. The prime economic importance of modern London is as a financial centre. There are various industries, mainly on the outskirts. There are also recording, broadcasting, television, and film studios; publishing companies; and the works and offices of the national press. Tourism is important.

Some of the docks in the East End of London, once the busiest in the world, were sold to the Docklands Development Corporation, which has built offices, houses, factories, and a railway. The world's largest office development project is at ◊Canary Wharf. The City Thameslink station, the first mainline railway station to be built in London for nearly a century, opened in 1991.

Education and entertainment
London has many museums, including the British Museum, the Victoria and Albert Museum, the Natural History Museum, and the Science Museum. Galleries include the National Gallery, National Portrait Gallery, Tate Gallery, Hayward Gallery, Wallace Collection, and Courtauld Institute. The former Bankside power station, opposite St Paul's Cathedral, is being converted into the Tate Gallery of Modern Art. London University is the largest in Britain. The Inns of Court have been the training school for lawyers since the 13th century. London has been the centre of English drama since its first theatre was built by James Burbage in 1576. A re-creation of the ◊Globe Theatre opened in Southwark in 1996.

LONDON *Two classic images of London: 'bobbies' on patrol stand in front of 'Big Ben' at the Houses of Parliament. The nickname for the police derives from their founder, Sir Robert Peel; the popular name for the clocktower only refers, strictly speaking, to the bell inside it, but has come to be applied to the whole structure. Corel*

Boroughs
The inner London boroughs of Greater London are Camden, Hackney, Hammersmith and Fulham, Haringey, Islington, Kensington and Chelsea, Lambeth, Lewisham, Newham, Southwark, Tower Hamlets, Wandsworth, and the City of Westminster. The outer London boroughs of Greater London are Barking and Dagenham, Barnet, Bexley, Brent, Bromley, Croydon, Ealing, Enfield, Greenwich, Harrow, Havering, Hillingdon, Hounslow, Kingston upon Thames, Merton, Redbridge, Richmond upon Thames, Sutton, and Waltham Forest.

Location and climate

London lies about 60 km/37 mi from the mouth of the Thames estuary on the North Sea, the principal entry into England from mainland Europe since prehistoric times. Situated in the **London Basin**, a downfold in the chalk formations lining the course of the River Thames, the city occupies both sides of the river, the larger part being on the left or north bank. It is underlain by a mixture of sands, clays, gravels and alluvium. The original settlement occupied an island of river gravel surrounding the two small rises of Cornhill and Ludgate Hill on the northern bank of the Thames, an area defended by marshland and by tributaries of the Thames, the Lea to the east and the Fleet to the west. The Romans, who wished to bridge the Thames, originally chose this fordable site as one which was accessible from the sea and had a solid soil that would support wooden bridge foundations. Another tract of gravel on the south bank became Southwark. The ◊Thames barrier (1982), the largest movable flood barrier in the world, was constructed to protect London from the threat of high tides.

The average annual rainfall in central London is 594 mm/23 in, while daily sunshine averages about 4.4 hours. January temperatures average 5°C/41°F, and July temperatures 18°C/65°F. The high incidence of smog resulting from domestic fires and industrial furnaces was greatly reduced by the Clean Air Act of 1956, but the incidence of photochemical smogs arising from the reaction of strong sunlight on vehicle exhaust fumes has increased.

Population

London is an immensely cosmopolitan city. Almost half the UK's ethnic minority population resides in the Greater London area, representing about 30% of the capital's total population. The East End has been a first base for incoming communities since the late 17th century, when Spitalfields became the sanctuary for thousands of French Protestant Huguenots fleeing religious persecution. As people disperse to other districts, the dominant cultural group changes. London's long-established Jewish community, the majority of whom arrived in the East End at the end of the 19th century to escape the pogroms (massacres) in Russia, is now mainly concentrated in the northern suburbs of Golders Green and Stamford Hill. Brick Lane in Spitalfields is the focal point of the city's Bangladeshi population, and there is also a large Bangladeshi, Indian, and Pakistani population centred on Woolwich. The area around Gerrard Street in Soho is known as London's Chinatown. Immigration from the West Indies after World War II made Brixton the centre of London's Caribbean culture. The City of London's resident population is only around 5,000, but about 300,000 people commute to the area for work.

The inner London population has been gradually declining since World War II. In 1938 the population numbered 6.25 million. Between 1961 and 1971 over half a million people (7%) left; between 1971 and 1981 three-quarters of a million (10%) left; by 1981 Greater London had nearly 2 million fewer people than in 1938. This postwar decline was partly the result of government policies. For example, Patrick Abercrombie's **Greater London Plan** of the 1940s proposed building ten new towns beyond London's Green Belt (among them Stevenage, Hemel Hempstead, Harlow, and Basildon), with the aim of moving people out of London to reduce traffic congestion and tackle problems such as declining housing stock. These new towns were intended to serve both as commuter towns, with people opting to move out of central London and travel to work on a daily basis, and as industrial centres themselves, with new companies being established in the new towns and existing businesses opting to shift their base from the capital to beyond the Green Belt.

From the late 1950s there was a steady decline of rented accommodation in the city and an increase in the number of owner-occupied houses and flats. The 'gentrification' of such areas as Highbury and Notting Hill by the middle class resulted in the renovation of declining properties, but also meant fewer people were now occupying each property, resulting in a lower population density. The gentrification also pushed up property prices, forcing more people to leave the capital. By the late 1980s and early 1990s, 350,000 Londoners were leaving the capital every year, with only 250,000 provincials and immigrants moving into the city.

Inner city landscape

The **City of London**, the oldest part of the capital, lies on the north bank of the Thames between Tower Bridge to the east and London Bridge (last rebuilt in 1964) to the west, the only bridge on the Thames until the late 18th century. It is the financial and business heart of the capital, and contains the law courts of the Old Bailey (Central Criminal Court) and Royal Courts of Justice. The 11th-century ◊Tower of London stands just outside the southeast corner of the City, beyond the former city walls; St Paul's Cathedral (1675–1710) is in the centre; and the Barbican residential and arts complex (1982) lies to the north.

Just outside Temple Bar, the former western gateway of the City of London leading to the Strand, are the Inns of Court, the hub of the legal profession, including the four private legal societies: Lincoln's Inn, Gray's Inn, Inner Temple, and Middle Temple. Following the curve of the river, the Strand runs southwest towards the administrative and government centres of the City of ◊Westminster and Whitehall. It terminates in Trafalgar Square, site of Nelson's Column and the National Gallery. The Houses of ◊Parliament (1840–60), containing the bell-tower of Big Ben (1858), line the riverfront. ◊Westminster Abbey (1050–1745), the coronation and burial place of many of Britain's monarchs, lies nearby. Westminster is also the London seat of the royal court, whose principal residences are Buckingham Palace and St James's Palace. Further to the west are the wealthy residential districts of Knightsbridge and Belgravia.

To the west of the City, London's West End contains most of the capital's hotel, shopping, restaurant, and theatre venues. It is bounded to the north by Regent's Park, to the west by Hyde Park, and to the south by St James's Park. The area incorporates Soho and Covent Garden, notable for their nightlife and restaurants, and Marylebone, Piccadilly, and Mayfair. Further west, the Royal Borough of ◊Kensington and Chelsea extends from Notting Hill in the north to the riverfront of ◊Chelsea. Many of the capital's museums are

LONDON: *Looking east over Regent's Park, which lies to the north of Oxford Street, one of the city's key east–west thoroughfares. Laid out in the early nineteenth century by John Nash for the Prince Regent (later George IV), the park is over 450 acres in size. To the right, the golden dome of the Regent's Park Mosque (completed 1977) is visible. Simon Hazelgrove/ Collections*

concentrated in South Kensington. Northwest of the City, Bloomsbury's cultural centres include the British Museum and parts of London University.

The East End of London includes the boroughs of ◊Hackney to the north and ◊Tower Hamlets to the south, including the ◊Docklands districts of Wapping, Limehouse, and the Isle of Dogs, once the centre of London's port facilities. The area presents a sharp contrast between its traditional small business concerns and low-cost housing, and the multi-million office landscape and exclusive residential facilities of the redeveloped Docklands region.

At the southern end of London Bridge lies ◊Southwark, the oldest borough in London apart from the City, and site of the reconstructed ◊Globe Theatre. ◊Lambeth, to the west, contains the South Bank cultural complex and Lambeth Palace, chief residence of the archbishop of Canterbury since 1200.

Economy

Finance, business, and commerce are London's principal economic activities. It is the world's leading international financial centre, with more than 565 foreign banks. Banking and insurance are concentrated in the City of London, and parts of Finsbury and Holborn. The City is home to the ◊Bank of England (1694), banker to the clearing banks and the UK government. The City of London is the European centre for gold distribution and holds the gold and dollar reserves of the sterling countries, although the bulk of its formerly extensive gold reserves shifted to other countries during world wars I and II.

The Royal Exchange (1567), London's international stock exchange, is also based in the City. It is the world's largest centre for trading foreign equities, accounting for 60% of global turnover in 1996. In the 1960s London was the world's largest single borrowing source. In 1979 the abolition of foreign exchange controls enabled UK savings institutions to invest money overseas, meaning the London Stock Exchange's member firms were exposed for the first time to competition from overseas brokers, culminating in the 'Big Bang' of October 1986. At the same time the name was changed from the London Stock Exchange to the International Stock Exchange and face-to-face dealing on the trading floor was replaced by computerized electronic trading. Many firms were bought by banks, which invested capital. These were boom times, until October 1987, when the stock market crashed and the recession set in. By 1990 losses ran into hundreds of millions of pounds and thousands of redundancies. Nevertheless, London's daily turnover remained higher than that of New York and Tokyo.

Other London-based exchanges include the London Metal Exchange, which, with the Commodity Exchange of New York, is the world's most important market for copper, nickel, and zinc; the Baltic Exchange, which deals with shipping and air freight, and which was the target of an IRA terrorist attack in 1992; and the London Futures and Options Exchange (until 1987 the London Commodity Exchange), which deals in non-metal commodities such as petroleum, coffee, and wool.

London is the location of the world's largest insurance market, with a net premium income of £14 billion in 1996. 28% of world marine insurance and 38% of aviation insurance are traded in London. Lloyd's of London, established in the 1680s by Edward Lloyd, accounts for half of all international insurance premiums underwritten in the London market. Although London was formerly the UK's foremost commercial centre, deriving its prosperity from the vast national and international trade conducted through the **Port of London**, it now handles only 10% of the country's imports and exports. The port, nevertheless, remains the country's largest and is the eighth largest in Europe, comprising 84 independently-run wharves and terminals, overseen by the Port of London Authority. The Authority has jurisdiction from Teddington, 108 km/67 mi inland, to the sea, but, with the growth of container traffic, the bulk of distribution has shifted to container depots downstream, such as those at Chobham Farm and Tilbury. All the docks between Tower Bridge and Barking Creek were shut down, beginning with the East India Dock in 1967 and ending with the Royal Docks in 1981, and many have been the target of commercial and residential redevelopment, including St Katharine's Dock, Tobacco Dock, and Canary Wharf.

Commercial, manufacturing, and professional bodies have congregated in specific areas of inner London over the centuries, although increasing property prices and considerations of access have forced many to relocate to the suburbs and elsewhere. In the postwar years industries that had relied on imperial preference failed to compete against the USA, the postwar economies of France and Germany, and an increase in imports from China and the Pacific Rim. They also found that Britain's failure to join the EEC until 1971 restricted their continental trade. Many of London's traditional employers either collapsed or moved out of the capital, not only to nearby towns such as Basingstoke and Luton, but, in the case of some insurance and banking companies, as far afield as Brighton and Bath, to escape traffic congestion and high office costs. The dispersal of both companies and population from inner to outer London and beyond had a profound effect on the economy. The drain of skilled labour left inner London with a high concentration of unskilled workers and an escalating unemployment problem.

London's wholesale and retail centres include Leadenhall Market, dealing with meat and poultry, and some grocery; Smithfield, the largest meat market in the world; and Hatton Garden, centre of the diamond trade. In 1973 London's fruit and vegetable market moved to Nine Elms in Wandsworth from its original site in Covent Garden, the square subsequently becoming a shopping and restaurant complex notable for its street entertainment. Billingsgate, London's principal fish market, moved from its 900-year-old City site to new premises in the former West India Dock in 1982.

Printing and publishing form a major part of London's economy. Until the mid-1980s Fleet Street was the centre of Britain's newspaper industry, but most of its printing concerns have relocated to other premises in the London region, some to the newly developed Docklands area. Other media-related businesses include television and radio broadcasting, film production, and music-recording. The British Broadcasting Corporation (BBC) has a television centre at Wood Lane, a World Service centre at Bush House, and a radio-broadcasting centre at Portland Place. Channel 4, Channel 5, and the Independent Television (ITV) Network Centre are all based in London, as are the television broadcasting companies Carlton UK, GMTV Ltd, and London Weekend Television. 24 radio stations are based in London, nine of which have national coverage, the remainder catering to local listeners.

Although manufacturing has declined, various light industries remain in the London boroughs, including the production of electronic goods, computer software, pharmaceuticals, and beer.

As one of the world's principal historic and cultural centres, tourism is a major industry. Hotel, restaurant, and shopping facilities are chiefly concentrated in the West End. Some of London's most opulent hotels are located in this area, including Claridges Hotel (1855), the Savoy Hotel (1889), the Ritz Hotel (1906), and the Hilton (1963). The main retail areas are Covent Garden; Oxford Street, Bond Street, and Regent Street; and Knightsbridge, Kensington High Street, and King's Road, Chelsea. Soho is the city's most cosmopolitan restaurant area. Dockland developments have also incorporated hotel and conference centres, shops, and other tourist venues.

Medical services, consulting physicians, surgeons, and private clinics are mainly sited in and around Harley Street in Marylebone.

Transport and communications

London Transport is a holding corporation with two wholly-owned subsidiaries, London Underground Ltd (LUL) and Victoria Coach Station (VCS). It is responsible for an operating area measuring 1,631 sq km/630 sq mi. A third subsidiary, London Buses Ltd (LBL), effectively ceased to trade in 1994 when ten component companies were sold to the private sector. However, buses remain firmly managed and restricted, so the effect of deregulation has not been as great as in other British cities. Between 1994 and 1997 the number of kilometres travelled by buses rose, but the number

LONDON *Canary Wharf in the Docklands redevelopment region of east London. Once commercial shipping became containerized from the 1960s onwards, new port facilities were built downriver at Tilbury and the old London docks around Wapping, Limehouse, and the Isle of Dogs became derelict. In the 1980s, the Conservative administrations of Margaret Thatcher promoted the area as a showcase financial and residential district. Robert Hallmann/Collections*

of passengers fell. In Central London 8% of commuters use buses, compared with 29% using the 'tube'. Since 1986 the volume of daily commuters has declined, but the system is still overcrowded.

The London Underground (or 'tube') was the world's first underground railway, and is now the world's longest, with 12 lines and over 391 km/243 mi of routes serving the city and its suburbs. Work on the largest single addition to the underground in 25 years, the Jubilee Line Extension, began in December 1993. The extension involves almost ten miles of new line from Green Park to Stratford and 11 new stations, providing a direct link from the International Rail Terminal at Waterloo to Docklands and the Millennium Festival site in Greenwich (see ◊Millennium Dome). The Docklands Light Railway (DLR) was opened by London Transport in 1987 and transferred to the London Docklands Development Corporation in 1992.

Transport proposals include an extension of the Docklands Light Railway south under the Thames to connect with the surface railway network at Greenwich, and the Croydon Tramlink, a proposed 29 km/18 mi link between East and West Croydon, Wimbledon, Beckenham, and New Addington.

London is the hub of the UK rail network; seven main lines converge on the capital, and their principal termini are within easy reach of any part of the inner London area. The City Thameslink station (1991) was the first mainline railway station to be built in London for nearly a century. Eurostar, a high-speed train service through the Channel Tunnel, has linked London (Waterloo) to Paris and Brussels since 1994.

River boats travel from Charing Cross, Tower Bridge, and Westminster to Greenwich. Barges also transport sewage and garbage along the river. The Millennium Project includes significant investment in new river boat services to run in the year 2000 (see ◊Millennium Dome). The Thames is navigable by small boats to Lechlade, Gloucestershire; and the Regent and Grand Union canals connect London to the Midlands. Inland river and canal traffic is now mainly confined to leisure craft. Road access across the Thames is provided by 21 bridges and six tunnels in the Greater London area. London is served by three international airports: Heathrow to the west, Gatwick to the south, and Stansted to the north. The London City airport, built on the former Royal Docks and opened late in 1987, has national and European connections.

Museums and galleries

London is one of the world's principal cultural centres, and its long-established collections cover all branches of knowledge and the arts. The oldest museums are the British Museum (1759), the largest in the UK; the Natural History Museum (1856); the Science Museum (1853); the Victoria and Albert Museum (1852), housing one of the world's largest collections of the decorative arts; and the waxworks of Madame Tussaud (1802). London's history is celebrated at the **Museum of London** (1976), and the development of film at the Museum of the Moving Image. Military museums include the Imperial War Museum (1917), for operations from 1914, and the ◊National Army Museum (1960), covering the period 1485–1914. The *Cutty Sark*, a tea clipper launched in 1869, and the World War II battleship *HMS Belfast* are moored in the Thames and are open to the public. The National Maritime Museum in Greenwich incorporates the Old Royal Observatory, the point from which ◊Greenwich Mean Time was originally established. The National Gallery (1824) houses pre-20th-century art and the most comprehensive collection of Italian Gothic and Renaissance works outside Italy, and the National Portrait Gallery (1856) is devoted to distinguished British figures. Art from the 17th century to the modern era is displayed at the Tate Gallery (1897), while the Courtauld Institute (1931) is notable for its Impressionist and Post-Impressionist collections. The Wallace Collection (1897) contains one of the world's finest displays of 18th-century French art. Contemporary works are shown by the Hayward Gallery on the South Bank, and at the annual summer exhibition of the Royal Academy of Arts. The Millennium Project includes the provision of funds for a permanent collection of contemporary art to be displayed at the proposed Tate Gallery of Modern Art from the turn of the century.

The reference division of the new British Library (1997), St Pancras, houses 12 million volumes; another department, the National Sound Archive (1947), is located in South Kensington.

The people of London with one voice would say to Hitler: ... You do your worst – and we will do our best.

WINSTON CHURCHILL British Conservative prime minister.
Speech at County Hall, London 14 July 1942

Music and the performing arts

London was the UK's foremost musical centre by the early 16th century, and has been considered a leading international venue since the 18th century. Major foreign composers such as Handel, Bach, and Haydn lived and worked in the city, and Italian opera found an enthusiastic audience. Today the city houses the UK's two leading colleges of music, the Royal College of Music and Royal Academy of Music. London has five professional symphony orchestras: the London Philharmonic, the London Symphony, the Philharmonia, the Royal Philharmonic, and the BBC Symphony. London's main opera and ballet houses are the Coliseum, home of the English National Opera company and where the English National Ballet Performs, and the Royal Opera House (Covent Garden). English National Ballet also performs at the Royal Albert Hall. Classical and contemporary dance is performed at Sadler's Wells. London's numerous concert halls include the Royal Festival Hall in the South Bank complex; the Barbican arts centre; the Wigmore Hall recital rooms; and the Royal Albert Hall, from 1895 home to the Henry Wood promenade concerts. Open-air concerts take place in the grounds of Kenwood House and Holland Park.

As a centre of English drama since the 16th century, London has many theatres, particularly in and around

Piccadilly, Shaftesbury Avenue, and Leicester Square. Historic West End theatres include the Haymarket (1821), Criterion (1874), Drury Lane (1663), and Her Majesty's (1897). Others include the Old Vic (1818), in south London; the Garrick Theatre (1889), in Charing Cross; and the west London playhouses of the Lyric (1870), in Hammersmith, and the Royal Court (1898), in Sloane Square. Modern theatres include the National Theatre (1963) in the South Bank complex, containing three separate houses, and the Barbican. In-the-round stages are found at the New Vic and the 17th-century-style Globe Theatre (1996). London is also the headquarters of the British Film Institute (BFI), established in 1931, and the National Film Theatre (1951), centre of London's annual film festival in November.

This is a London particular. ... A fog, miss.

CHARLES DICKENS English novelist.
Bleak House ch 3

Educational institutions

University College was founded in 1826 and King's College in 1828. The University of London was established in 1836 to set examinations and grant degrees to students from both these colleges. The University of London now incorporates 26 colleges and 19 affiliated centres, including the Imperial College of Science, Technology, and Medicine (1907), the London School of Economics (LSE), and the School of Oriental and African Studies (SOAS). Other universities in the Greater London area include the City University (1966), the University of Greenwich (1992), the University of North London (1992), the South Bank University (1992), Thames Valley University (1992), the University of East London (1992), and the London Guildhall University (1993).

Specialist institutions include the London teaching hospitals; the Royal Academy schools of painting, sculpture, architecture, and music; the Royal colleges of music and art; the Architectural Association School of Architecture; the Slade School of Fine Art (1871) at University College; the City and Guilds of London Art School; and the Royal Academy of Dramatic Art (RADA). The teaching of law is mainly conducted through the Inns of Court. Although not a statutory authority under the Education Acts, the corporation of the City of London has been engaged in education for more than a century. It maintains two City of London public schools for girls and boys: the City of London Freemen's School, founded for the orphans of freemen; and the Guildhall School of Music and Drama.

Parks, sports, and events

London has numerous lakes and parks, many of which were former royal preserves. The main central parks are Regent's Park, site of London Zoo and an open-air theatre; Hyde Park, containing the Serpentine Lake; Holland Park; and St James's Park. Open areas on the edge of the city include Hampstead Heath; Richmond Park, the largest urban park in Britain; and ◊Kew Gardens (or the Royal Botanic Gardens). Wimbledon is the home of the All England Lawn Tennis and Croquet Club and site of the international Lawn Tennis championship; the Lord's and Oval cricket grounds host the Test matches; Twickenham is the home of English rugby union; and various sporting and cultural events are held at the international arenas of Wembley Stadium and Crystal Palace. Official ceremonies include the Trooping of the Colour, marking the queen's official birthday in June, and the Lord Mayor's Show, a procession of over 140 floats led by the golden Lord Mayor's Coach in November. Other annual events are the Notting Hill Carnival, a Caribbean-style street festival held in August; the Boat Race, on the Thames between Putney and Mortlake, held since 1829 between the universities of Oxford and Cambridge; the London Marathon, established in 1981; and the New Year's Eve celebrations in Trafalgar Square, televised throughout the country.

London has hosted a number of major festivals and sporting events: the Great Exhibition (1851); the Festival of Britain (1951); the Olympic Games (1948); the football World Cup Final (1966); the Rugby Union World Cup Final (1991). The Millennium Festival and Experience will be sited at Greenwich in the year 2000.

When a man is tired of London, he is tired of life; for there is in London all that life can afford.

SAMUEL JOHNSON English lexicographer, author, and critic.
Boswell's *Life of Johnson* vol III

London Contemporary Dance Theatre, LCDT

British modern dance company formed by entrepreneur Robin Howard in 1967. Its aim was to introduce modern dance based on the principles of Martha Graham to Britain. Its first artistic director was Robert Cohan, an American from Graham's company. He left in 1989, but returned to the company as artistic adviser 1992–94. The company was disbanded in 1994. Several important choreographers and dancers have emerged from the company and its school, most notably Richard ◊Alston and Siobhan ◊Davies.

Howard established the London School of Contemporary Dance in 1966, the only European institution authorized to teach the Graham method. The school continues its work at the Place, near Euston Station, London, and is now one of the UK's national dance agencies and a focus for education, creativity, and performance.

Another American, Dan Wagoner, took over artistic direction of LCDT from Cohan in 1989; he was succeeded by Nancy Duncan, from Pentacle in New York. Cohan returned to the company during a troubled period when the company lacked an artistic director.

Other choreographers to have emerged from LCDT include Anthony van Laast, Micha Bergese, Jonathan Lunn, and Paul Douglas; outstanding dancers include Lauren Potter, Gill Clarke, David Hughes, and Darshan Singh Bhuller.

London County Council, LCC

Former administrative authority for London created in 1888

by the Local Government Act; it incorporated parts of Kent, Surrey, and Middlesex in the metropolis. It was replaced by the Greater London Council 1964–86.

Relations between the LCC and the government of the day were frequently discordant, in part because more often than not the two were in the hands of opposing parties.

Londonderry, also known as **Derry** (Irish 'oakwood'); until the 10th century known as **Derry-Calgaich**, 'the oak wood of Calgaich' (a fierce warrior)

Historic city and port on the River Foyle, 35 km/22 mi from Lough Foyle, county town of County ◊Londonderry, Northern Ireland; population (1991) 95,400. Industries include the manufacture of textiles, chemicals, food processing, shirt manufacturing, and acetylene from naphtha.

Features

The Protestant Cathedral of St Columba dating from 1633; the Gothic revival Roman Catholic Cathedral of St Eugene (completed in 1833); the Guildhall (rebuilt in 1912), containing stained glass windows presented by livery companies of the City of London; the city walls, on which are modern iron statues by Anthony Gormley; four gates into the city still survive.

History

Londonderry dates from the foundation of a monastery there by St Columba in AD 546. The city was subject to a number of sieges by the Danes between the 9th and 11th centuries, and by the Anglo-Normans in the 12th century; however, these were unsuccessful until James I of England captured the city in 1608. The king granted the borough and surrounding land to the citizens of London. The Irish Society was formed to build and administer the city and a large colony of English Protestants was established. The city, then governed by Major Henry Baker and the Reverend George Walker, was unsuccessfully besieged in 1689 by the armies of James II, who had fled England when William of Orange was declared joint sovereign with James' daughter Mary. James' army was led by Richard Talbot, Earl of Tyrconnell, in a conflict known as the **Siege of Derry**, when 13 Derry apprentices and citizens loyal to William of Orange locked the city gates against the Jacobite army. The siege lasted 15 weeks, during which many of the inhabitants died of starvation and disease because of the blockade.

Topography

The old city walls that still surround Londonderry extend for over 1 km/0.5 mi and include seven gates and several bastions. The waterside, the part of the city on the right bank of the Foyle, is connected to the old city by the Craigavon Bridge (opened in 1933), which carries a roadway 360 m/1,180 ft long. The original eight bells in the tower of the Cathedral of St Columba were recast in 1929 and another five were added. Among the parks are Brooke Park in which is situated the municipal library, St Columba's Park, and Meenan Park.

From Derry to Londonderry

Derry was pillaged by the Danes on several occasions. In 1164 Abbot O'Brolchain, the first bishop of Derry, built the Teampall Mor or 'great church', and in 1311 the town was granted to Richard de Burgo, Earl of Ulster. An uneventful period of several centuries followed until the rebellion in 1566 of Shane O'Neill, Earl of Tyrone. O'Neill suffered a crushing defeat at the hands of Edward Randolph, commander of the English forces, and was killed. However, Randolph's successor, Edward St Low, abandoned Derry in 1568, after an accidental explosion in which the town and fort, including the Teampall Mor, were blown up.

The town of Derry was fortified and garrisoned by the English, and made a city in 1608. In 1609, during the ◊Plantation of Ireland, James I granted Derry, Coleraine, and a large tract of land between to the City of London. The land was distributed among the London ◊livery companies, but in order to avoid jealousy among the companies, the City of London Corporation retained the boroughs of Londonderry and Coleraine. The Irish Society was formed in 1613 to administer the boroughs; its members were appointed from within the City of London Corporation. The Society was incorporated by royal charter in 1613 and was trustee for the Corporation. Its court consisted of a governor, a deputy governor, and 24 assistants, in addition to the Recorder of London. It was on account of the connection with the City of London Corporation that the name of the city was changed from Derry to Londonderry.

The port was a major naval base during World War II, but has declined in importance since.

Londonderry, also known as **Derry**

County of Northern Ireland

Area 2,070 sq km/799 sq mi

Towns and cities ◊Londonderry (county town), Coleraine, Portstewart, Limavady

Physical hilly moorland, coniferous forest; Sperrin Mountains; rivers Foyle, Bann, Roe, and Faughan; borders Lough Neagh

Industries stone and lime quarrying, food processing, textiles and synthetic fibres, shirt manufacturing, light engineering, chemicals

Agriculture farming is hindered by the very heavy rainfall; flax, cattle, sheep grazing on moorland, salmon and eel fisheries on the Bann

Population (1981) 187,000

Famous people Joyce Cary, Seamus Heaney, William Massey, former prime minister of New Zealand

Topography

Londonderry is bounded on the north by the Atlantic, and is dominated by the Sperrin Mountains which run in an arc from southwest to northeast, dividing the lowlands fringing the River Bann from those of the Foyle. Mount Sawell (670 m/2,198 ft) in the Sperrin Mountains is the county's highest peak. The Roe and the Faughan are the main westward flowing streams, while the Bann forms the eastern border for most of its length.

London, Greater

Metropolitan area of ◊London, England, comprising the City of London, which forms a self-governing enclave, and 32 surrounding boroughs; area 1,580 sq km/610 sq mi; population (1991) 6,679,700. The population of Inner London is 2,504,500 and that of Outer London 4,175,200. Certain powers were exercised over this whole area by the Greater London Council (GLC) 1974–86.

London Metal Exchange

Commodity market for trade in metals, incorporated in 1881. With the Commodity Exchange of New York, it is the world's most important for copper, nickel, and zinc. It also trades in futures, and organizes the storage of metals. In 1993 $1 million million was traded on the London Metal Exchange.

London, Museum of

Museum of London's history. It was formed by the amalgamation of the former Guildhall (Roman and medieval) and London (Tudor and later) Museums, housed from 1976 in a building at the junction of London Wall and Aldersgate, near the Barbican.

London Underground

First underground rail line in the world, opened in 1863. At first it was essentially a roofed-in trench. The London Underground is still the world's longest subway, with over 250 mi/400 km of routes.

London University

University that originated in 1826 with the founding of University College to provide higher education free from religious tests. In 1836 a charter set up an examining body with power to grant degrees. London University opened all its degrees to women in 1878, the first British university to do so.

Its complex substructure of smaller colleges had by 1991 been rationalized to 24 colleges, medical schools, and major institutes, plus 19 affiliated centres.

London Working Men's Association or LWMA

Campaigning organization for political reform, founded in June 1836 in the UK by William Lovett and others, who in 1837 drew up the first version of the People's Charter (see ◊Chartism). It was founded in the belief that popular education, achieved through discussion and access to a cheap and honest press, was a means of obtaining political reform. By 1837 the LWMA had 100 members.

Long, Richard (1945–)

English Conceptual artist. In the vanguard of 1960s artists wishing to break away from studio-created art, he has worked both outdoors and on the spot in galleries. He uses natural materials such as stone, slate, wood, and mud to represent the ritualized traces of early peoples, notably in *River Avon Driftwood* (1977; Museum of Contemporary Art, Ghent). Only photographic records remain of much of his work. He won the Turner Prize in 1991.

His celebrated stone circles and rivers of sticks were created during walks in remote areas of Ireland, the Himalayas, Africa, and Iceland.

longbow

Longer than the standard bow, made of yew, introduced in the 12th century. They were favoured by English archers in preference to the cross bow, as the longer bow allowed arrows of greater weight to be fired further and more accurately. They were highly effective in the Hundred Years' War, to the extent that the French took to removing the first two fingers of prisoners so that they would never again be able to draw a bow.

Long Eaton

Town in Derbyshire, England, midway between Derby and Nottingham in the Trent valley. Its main industry is the manufacture of fabrics, such as lace, braid, upholstery, elastic web, and corsetry. Other industries include the manufacture of metal tubing, stainless-steel sinks, spring seating, piano actions, and pencils.

Longford, Frank (Francis Aungier) Pakenham, 7th Earl of Longford (1905–)

British Labour politician. He was brought up a Protestant but is now a leading Catholic. He is an advocate of penal reform.

He worked in the Conservative Party Economic Research Department 1930–32, yet became a member of the Labour Party and held ministerial posts 1948–51 and 1964–68. He succeeded as earl in 1961.

Longleat

Elizabethan house situated in Wiltshire between Warminster and Frome; the seat of the Marquess of Bath. Begun in 1568 by John Thynne (died 1580), it was revolutionary in its classic symmetry and simplicity, and allocation of most of the wall to window space. Only the exterior survives intact: the interior decoration is now mainly 19th century. Stables were added by Jeffrey Wyatville (1807–11), and the park was laid out by Capability Brown. The estate contains a safari park, the first of its kind in England.

Long, Loch

Sea-loch on the west coast of Scotland, in Argyll and Bute unitary authority. It is a branch of the Firth of Clyde, extending about 28 km/18 mi north from Holy Loch to Arrochar, with an average width of 1 km/0.6 mi. Exceptionally deep, it is used by ocean-going tankers discharging oil at Finnart for transfer by pipeline to Grangemouth on the Firth of Forth.

Long Parliament

English Parliament 1640–53 and 1659–60, which continued through the Civil War. After the Royalists withdrew in 1642 and the Presbyterian right was excluded in 1648, the remaining ◊Rump ruled England until expelled by Oliver Cromwell in 1653. Reassembled in 1659–60, the Long Parliament initiated the negotiations for the restoration of the monarchy.

Longton

Town that makes up part of ◊Stoke-on-Trent, Staffordshire, England; population (1991) 12,500. It is a large producer of pottery, the manufacture of bone china being concentrated here.

The Gladstone Pottery in Longton is a Victorian pottery with traditional bottle kilns. It has been preserved in full working order, and serves as an educational museum.

Lonsdale, Frederick, adopted name of Frederick Leonard (1881–1954)

British dramatist. He wrote many comedies and collaborated on several musical comedies, of which *The Maid of the Mountains* (1917) was the most successful.

Lonsdale, Hugh Cecil Lowther, 5th Earl of Lonsdale (1857–1944)

English sporting enthusiast. **Lonsdale Belts** in boxing, first presented in 1909, are named after him. Any fighter who wins three British title fights in one weight division retains a Lonsdale Belt. A former president of the National Sporting Club, he presented his first belt to the club in 1909, and it was won by Freddie Welsh (lightweight) later that year.

Look Back in Anger

Play by John ◊Osborne, first performed in 1956 at the Royal Court Theatre, and published in 1957. Set in a one-room flat in a Midlands town, its central characters are the working-class university graduate Jimmy Porter and his wife Alison. As a reaction against the English establishment and the social mores of the time, the play was a landmark which launched a new wave in British theatre and established Osborne as the leader of the ◊Angry Young Men. The play was made into a successful film in 1959 starring Richard Burton.

Look Back in Anger was the first of John Osborne's works to be seen in London.

Lord (Old English *hlaford* 'bread keeper')

Prefix used informally as a less formal alternative to the full title of a marquess, earl, or viscount, for example 'Lord Salisbury' instead of 'the Marquess of Salisbury'. Barons are normally referred to as lords, the term baron being used for foreign holders of that rank. 'Lord' is also used as a ◊courtesy title before the forename and surname of younger sons of dukes and marquesses.

It is prefixed to many official titles, for example, Lord High Steward, Lord Chamberlain, and Lord High Chancellor. Where a board has taken the place of an office of state, the members of that board are known as 'lords commissioners', or more commonly, lords of the particular office, for example 'lords of the Admiralty'.

Bishops, whether members of the House of Lords or not, are addressed as 'My Lord Bishop' or 'The Lord Bishop of ...'. All judges of the high court are addressed throughout the UK as 'My Lord' when acting in their official capacity. Mayors of certain large towns may use the prefix 'Lord'.

Historically the term was equivalent to the Latin *dominus* ('master'), and referred to rulers, heads of households, and owners of land. In medieval times 'lord' was the common term for a feudal superior, hence 'lord of the manor', and the king was often referred to as 'the lord king'.

Lord Advocate

Chief law officer of the crown in Scotland who has ultimate responsibility for criminal prosecutions in Scotland. The Lord Advocate does not usually act in inferior courts, where prosecution is carried out by procurators-fiscal acting under the Lord Advocate's instructions.

Lord Chancellor

State official; see ◊Chancellor, Lord.

Lord Lieutenant

The sovereign's representative in a county, who recommends magistrates for appointment. It is an unpaid position and the retirement age is 75.

The Lord Lieutenant of a county is nominated by the sovereign by patent under the great seal. He or she stands as the permanent local representative of the Crown, and as such takes precedence in the county. This title was first created in the reign of Henry VIII, and entailed many responsibilities. The Lord Lieutenant had to maintain the efficiency of the militia of the county, and had the right of appointing his own officers. These rights were withdrawn in 1871 and revested in the Crown.

The chief duties imposed on the Lord Lieutenant at present consist in the recommendation for the appointment of magistrates for the county bench, the appointment of deputy lieutenants, and the raising of the militia, if need be, in times of riot or invasion. He or she is head of the Commission of the Peace for the county. The prefix 'Lord' is colloquial only.

Lord of the Rings, The

Trilogy by J R R ◊Tolkien, published 1954–55. Set in the mythological world of 'Middle Earth', peopled with strange magical creatures, hobbits, and dwarves, it became an international bestseller and achieved cult status in the 1960s. Its success contributed to the growth in popularity of fantasy fiction.

Lord's

Cricket ground in St John's Wood, London. One of England's test-match grounds and the headquarters of one of cricket's governing bodies, the Marylebone Cricket Club (MCC), since 1788 when the MCC was formed following the folding of the White Conduit Club.

The ground is named after Yorkshireman **Thomas Lord** (1757–1832) who developed the first site at Dorset Square in 1787. He moved the ground to a field at North Bank, Regent's Park, in 1811, and in 1814 developed the ground at its present site at St John's Wood. Lord's is also the home of the Middlesex Cricket Club.

On 28 September 1998, the MCC voted in favour of admitting women for the first time in its 211-year history.

Lords, House of

The upper chamber of Parliament. See feature on next page on how the House of Lords operates.

Lorimer, Robert Stodart (1864–1929)

Scottish architect. The most prolific architect representative

HOW THE HOUSE OF LORDS OPERATES

THE HOUSE of Lords is the upper chamber of Parliament. In 1998 there were 1,134 members, including the two archbishops and 24 bishops, 631 hereditary peers, and 477 life peers, of whom 26 are 'law lords'. In total there were 86 women peers. The Labour government elected in May 1997 introduced legislation in 1999 to end the right of hereditary peers to sit and vote in the chamber. This will be the first stage in its democratization. The legislative powers of the Lords will not be changed.

Its members are unelected and in early 1999 comprise the **temporal peers**: all hereditary peers of England created to 1707, all hereditary peers of Great Britain created 1707–1800, and all hereditary peers of the UK from 1801 onwards; all hereditary Scottish peers (under the Peerage Act 1963); all peeresses in their own right (under the same act); all life peers (both the law lords and those created under the Life Peerages Act 1958); and the **spiritual peers**: the two archbishops and 24 of the bishops (London, Durham, and Winchester by right, and the rest by seniority). Since the Parliament Act 1911 the powers of the Lords have been restricted in that they may delay a bill passed by the Commons but not reject it. The Lords are presided over by the Lord Chancellor.

Membership

By the Appellate Jurisdiction Act 1876 (as amended) the Crown is enabled to create life peers to serve as lords of appeal in ordinary (11 at present). By the Life Peerages Act 1958 the Crown may confer life peerages on both men and women. The Peerage Act 1963 enabled hereditary peers to disclaim their peerages for life and a number of peerages have since been disclaimed.

The Life Peerages Act enabled those who objected to the hereditary principle to accept membership of the House of Lords. In particular it enabled many Labour supporters to accept peerages. The Act also facilitated the membership of many individuals prominent in walks of life outside politics. Thus, although the House of Lords has traditionally been regarded as a bastion of Conservatism, the Conservative Party has not had an absolute majority in the Upper House for some time.

In practice a large proportion of the 1,300 potential members, especially among the hereditary peers, do not attend the House regularly, the average attendance being 380. Members of the House of Lords do not receive a salary, but have been entitled to daily expenses since 1957.

Officers

The principal officers of the House of Lords are:

(1) The Speaker, the Lord Chancellor. The Speaker of the House of Lords does not have the wide powers of his or her counterpart in the Lower House; questions of order are determined by the House, and in debate the House and not the Speaker is addressed. The Lord Chancellor, as one of the principal members of the government takes a leading part in the deliberations of the House.

(2) The chairman of Committees, who holds office during the lifetime of a session. He or she takes the chair when the House goes into committee, and superintends all committees and matters appertaining to private bills. In the absence of the Lord Chancellor he or she acts as Speaker.

(3) The clerk of the Parliaments, appointed by letters patent, who keeps the journals of the House, makes minutes of the proceedings, acts as registrar of the House sitting in its judicial capacity, has charge of all records and documents, and signifies the royal assent to bills that have passed both houses.

(4) Gentleman Usher of the Black Rod, who is appointed by letters patent. He or she assists at the introduction of peers, summons the attendance of the Commons when necessary, and executes warrants of commitment.

(5) The Yeoman Usher of the Black Rod, who is Black Rod's deputy.

Functions and powers

The functions of the House of Lords as summarized by the report of the Bryce Conference of 1917–18 are: (1) the examination and revision of bills from the House of Commons, especially those which have been subject to limited debate; (2) the initiation of non-controversial bills; (3) the full and free discussion of large and important questions, especially, but not exclusively, those which the lower House cannot find time to debate; and (4) the delaying of legislation in order to allow public opinion to be heard.

To these must be added the judicial role of the House of Lords as the final court of appeal. This latter function, however, is carried out by lords of appeal or **law lords** (the Lord Chancellor and any former Lord Chancellors, the 11 lords of appeal in ordinary, and any former lords of appeal). Appeals in both civil and criminal cases are heard by at least three lords of appeal.

History

The House of Lords was originally the more important of the two Houses of Parliament. In the latter half of the 19th century and the early part of the 20th there were increasing clashes between Lords and Commons, culminating in the rejection by the upper House of Lloyd George's People's Budget in 1909. This resulted in a fierce constitutional struggle and in the passing of the Parliament Act 1911. The preamble of the latter stated that it was the government's intention to reform the composition of the House of Lords, but this was never done.

The Act of 1911 did drastically curb the powers of the upper House, however, by laying down that any bill rejected or amended by the Lords, but which was passed by the Commons in three successive sessions over not less than two calendar years, should receive the royal assent, and by limiting the Lords' power to delay money bills to one month.

In 1947, the Labour government introduced a Parliament Bill which became the Parliament Act 1949. This effectively reduced the Lords' veto from two years to nine months. Further attempts at reform during the 1950s and 1960s were unsuccessful.

of the Scottish Arts and Crafts movement, Lorimer drew particularly from Scottish vernacular buildings of the 16th and 17th centuries to create a series of mansions and houses, practically planned, with picturesque, turreted exteriors. Examples of his work include Ardkinglas House, Argyll (1906); and Ruwallan House, Ayrshire (1902). He was knighted in 1911.

Lossiemouth

Fishing port and resort in Moray, Scotland, at the mouth of the River Lossie on the Moray Firth; population (1991) 7,200. The first Labour prime minister James Ramsay MacDonald was born at Lossiemouth in 1866 and is buried here.

There is an RAF base nearby. The Moray Firth at Lossiemouth is home to one of only two resident populations of bottle-nosed dolphins in Britain.

Lothian

Former region of Scotland (1975–96), which was replaced by East Lothian, Midlothian, West Lothian, and City of Edinburgh unitary authorities.

The new unitary authorities were formerly the four districts of Lothian region (1975–96), which were previously counties in their own right.

lottery

See ◊National Lottery.

Loughborough

Industrial town in Leicestershire, central England, 18 km/11 mi northwest of Leicester, on the River Soar; population (1995 est) 55,300. Industries include engineering, bell-founding, children's book publishing, brickmaking, and the manufacture of heavy duty electrical goods and power generators, knitwear, hosiery, pharmaceuticals, and medical supplies.

Loughborough University of Technology was established in 1966 (formerly the College of Technology, and incorporating the college of education). A grammar school was founded here in 1495. Great Paul, the bell of St Paul's Cathedral, London, was cast in Loughborough.

Louis, Prince of Battenberg (1854–1921)

German-born British admiral who took British nationality in 1917 and translated his name to Mountbatten. He married Princess Victoria, granddaughter of Queen Victoria, and was the father of Louis, 1st Earl Mountbatten of Burma.

He was First Sea Lord 1912–14, but was forced to resign because of anti-German sentiment. In 1917 he was created marquess of Milford Haven, and made admiral of the fleet in 1921.

Lovelace, Richard (1618–1657)

English poet. Imprisoned in 1642 for petitioning for the restoration of royal rule, he wrote 'To Althea, from Prison', and during a second term in jail in 1648 arranged the publication of his collection *Lucasta* (1649). His poetry is varied in style and content, some in the 'metaphysical' style of conceits, some more courtly and graceful.

Lovell, (Alfred Charles) Bernard (1913–)

English radio astronomer, director 1951–81 of ◊Jodrell Bank Experimental Station (now Nuffield Radio Astronomy Laboratories).

During World War II Lovell worked on developing a radar system to improve the aim of bombers in night raids. After the war he showed that radar could be a useful tool in astronomy, and lobbied for the setting-up of a radio-astronomy station. Jodrell Bank was built near Manchester 1951–57. Several large radio telescopes were constructed, including a 76-m/250-ft instrument. Although its high cost was criticized, its public success after tracking the Soviet satellite *Sputnik I* in 1957 assured its future. He was knighted in 1961.

Lovelock, James (1919–)

British scientist who began the study of CFCs in the atmosphere in the 1960s, and who later elaborated the 'Gaia hypothesis' – the concept of the Earth as a single organism, or ecosystem. The Gaia hypothesis, named after an ancient Greek earth goddess, views the planet as a self-regulating system in which all the individual elements coexist in a symbiotic relationship. In developing this theory (first published in 1968), Lovelock realized that the damage effected by humans on many of the Earth's ecosystems was posing a threat to the viability of the planet itself.

Lovelock invented the electron capture detector in the 1950s, a device for measuring minute traces of atmospheric gases. He developed the Gaia hypothesis while researching the possibility of life on Mars for NASA's space programme; it was not named 'Gaia' until some years later, at the suggestion of the writer William Golding.

Low, David Alexander Cecil (1891–1963)

New Zealand-born British political cartoonist, creator (in newspapers such as the London *Evening Standard*) of the characters Colonel Blimp, the TUC Carthorse, and others.

Low's work is remarkably free from the conventional devices of the professional cartoonist, and in drawings of celebrities in various walks of life, which appeared in the *New Statesman*, he showed a gift for genially humorous portraiture. He was knighted in 1962.

Lowe, John (1947–)

English darts player. He has won most of the major titles including the world championships in 1979 and 1987. In 1986 he achieved the first televised nine-dart finish at the MFI Championship at Reading.

Lower, Richard (1631–1691)

English physician and physiologist who performed the first direct transfusion of blood in 1666 and was the first to link the process of respiration with the blood.

Lowestoft (Old Norse Hloover's Toft 'dwelling belonging to Hloover')

Resort town and port in Suffolk, England, 62 km/38 mi

northeast of Ipswich, the most easterly town in Britain; population (1996 est) 66,300. Offshore oil and gas fields provide significant employment related to production and exploration, including oil platform construction and supply services. Historically a fishing port, the industry is still active but has declined dramatically. Fish- and food-processing (especially freezing), tourism, and the manufacture of radar, electrical equipment, and televisions are also important. **Lowestoft Ness** is the most easterly point in England.

The older part of Lowestoft is built on the cliff overlooking the sea, the later development after the opening of the railway in 1847 being further south.

The composer Benjamin Britten was born here in 1913.

History

The name Lowestoft appears in the Domesday Book of 1086 as **Lothu Wistoft**, derived from **Hloover's Toft**, Hloover being an Old Norse name. In 1916 during World War I the town was attacked by German warships, and it was damaged during World War II. Its role as a large naval base and the headquarters of the minesweeping service is marked by the Royal Naval Patrol Service Memorial in Belle Vue Park. Kirkley was incorporated in Lowestoft in 1854 and Oulton Broad in 1921. Lowestoft china was made here from 1757 to 1802.

Harbour

The harbour was formed by linking Lake Lothing, now known as the Inner Harbour, with the sea in 1831. The construction of Trawler Basin in 1846, Waveney Basin in 1883, and Hamilton Dock in 1906 greatly extended the quay space. Mutford Lock at the western end of the Inner Harbour is linked to Oulton Broad, a boating centre. Large coast protection schemes have been carried out to the north and south of the harbour.

Lowry, L(aurence) S(tephen) (1887–1976)

English painter. His works depict life in the industrial towns of the north of England. In the 1920s he developed a naive style characterized by matchstick figures, often in animated groups, and gaunt simplified factories and terraced houses, painted in an almost monochrome palette. *The Pond* (1950; Tate Gallery, London) is an example.

He also painted remote seascapes, lonely hill landscapes and some striking portraits, for example *A Manchester Man* (1936).

Born in Manchester, he spent the rest of his life in nearby Salford, earning his living as a rent collector. Although he was a legend in his lifetime, he remained an elusive, retiring figure, rarely venturing beyond his native towns. Building of a Lowry Centre in Salford began in the late 1990s.

Loyalist

Member of approximately 30% of the US population who remained loyal to Britain in the ⇨American Revolution. Many Loyalists went to eastern Ontario, Canada, after 1783. Known as Tories, most were crown officials, Anglican clergy, and economically advantaged, although they were represented in every segment of colonial society.

The term also refers to people in Northern Ireland who wish to remain part of the United Kingdom rather than unifying with the Republic of Ireland.

Lubetkin, Berthold Romanovich (1901–1990)

Russian-born architect. He settled in the UK in 1930 and formed, with six young architects, a group called **Tecton**. His pioneering designs include Highpoint I (1933–35), a block of flats in Highgate, London; and the curved lines of the Penguin Pool (1933) at London Zoo, which employ reinforced concrete to sculptural effect.

During the 1930s Tecton was responsible for many buildings erected in England in the International Style then flourishing elsewhere in Europe, including the Gorilla House (1937) at the London Zoo and a health centre for the London borough of Finsbury in 1938. The group was also a training ground for the avant-garde architects of the next generation, such as Denys Lasdun.

During World War II Lubetkin became a farmer in Gloucestershire where, at the request of the London Zoo, he provided a temporary home for a number of rare birds and animals.

Lucan, Richard John Bingham, 7th Earl of Lucan (1934–)

English aristocrat and professional gambler. On 7 November 1974 his wife was attacked and their children's nanny murdered. No trace of Lucan has since been found, and there has been no solution to the murder. He succeeded as earl in 1964.

Lucas, Keith (1879–1916)

English neurophysiologist who investigated the transmission of nerve impulses. He demonstrated that the contraction of muscle fibres follows the 'all or none' law: a certain amount of stimulus is needed in order to induce a nerve impulse and subsequent muscle contraction. Any stimulus below that threshold has no effect regardless of its duration.

Lucas showed that when two successive stimuli are given, the response to the second stimulus cannot be evoked if the first nerve impulse is still in progress. He also demonstrated that following a contraction there is a period of diminished excitability during which the muscle cannot be induced to contract again. This is due to the chemical transmission of impulses over synaptic clefts (the junction between two individual neurons).

Luce Bay

Sea-inlet in Dumfries and Galloway unitary authority, Scotland, penetrating 32 km/20 mi inland and widening to about 30 km/19 mi at its mouth with the Irish Sea. The village of Glenluce lies at the head of the bay.

Luddite

One of a group of people involved in machine-wrecking riots in northern England 1811–16. The organizer of the Luddites was referred to as **General Ludd**, but may not have existed. Many Luddites were hanged or transported to penal colonies, such as Australia.

The movement, which began in Nottinghamshire and spread to Lancashire, Cheshire, Derbyshire, Leicestershire, and Yorkshire, was primarily a revolt against the unemployment caused by the introduction of machines in the Industrial Revolution.

Ludlow

Market town in Shropshire, England, on the rivers Teme and Corve, near the Welsh border, 42 km/26 mi south of Shrewsbury; population (1991) 9,000. Industries include precision engineering, cabinet making, and the manufacture of agricultural machinery. Tourism is important, particularly retailing to the town's visitors.

Features

Ludlow Castle, on a hill overlooking the rivers Teme and Corve, was built as a stronghold of the Welsh Marches in about 1086 and has a large Norman keep. John Milton's masque *Comus* was first presented in the castle in 1634, and an arts festival is held here each year. The large 15th-century St Laurence's Church, with its 41-m/135-ft tower, reflects the town's prosperity as a centre of the wool trade in the Middle Ages. The poet A E Housman is buried in the churchyard. The town has many half-timbered buildings, notably the Jacobean Feathers Hotel. Its grammar school, founded in 1282, is now a sixth form college. The ◊Clee Hills lie east and northeast of the town.

Lulworth, West and East

Two villages in Dorset, southwest England. **West Lulworth** is 12 km/7 mi east of Wareham. Nearby are **Lulworth Cove**, a bay about 450 m/1,500 ft across almost enclosed by hills, and the natural rock arch known as Durdle Door. **East Lulworth** includes the ruins of Lulworth Castle (destroyed by fire in 1929). There is an army tank firing range in the vicinity.

The Roman Catholic chapel in East Lulworth, built in 1786, was the first to be built by royal permission after the Reformation (apart from those attached to foreign embassies).

Lumley, Joanna (1946–)

Indian-born English screen actress, model, and writer. A poised, elegant screen presence, she rose to fame as Purdey on *The New Avengers* (1976–77) and as one half of the detective team in *Sapphire and Steel* (1979–82). She appeared for a short stint in the British soap opera *Coronation Street* in 1973. In the 1990s, her career revived with her role as the objectionable, carefree alcoholic Patsy Stone in the British sitcom ◊*Absolutely Fabulous*, in which she starred with Jennifer ◊Saunders.

Lumley presented the adventurous television series *Girl Friday* (1994), in which she attempts to develop survival techniques while abandoned on an island; and *Joanna Lumley in the Kingdom of the Thunder Dragon* (1997). She has written books to accompany both series, and has also published her autobiography *Stare Back and Smile*. Her film credits include *Shirley Valentine* (1989), the television movie *Cold Comfort Farm* (1995), and the British black comedy *Parting Shots* (1998).

Lundy Island

Rocky, granite island at the entrance to the Bristol Channel; 19 km/12 mi northwest of Hartland Point, Devon, southwest England; area 9.6 sq km/3.7 sq mi; population (1975) 40. Formerly used by pirates and privateers as a lair, it is now the site of a bird sanctuary and the first British Marine Nature Reserve (1986). It has Bronze and Iron Age field systems, which can be traced by their boundaries which stand up above the surface.

The land is used mainly as pasture for sheep and goats, and the island has large breeding colonies of sea birds, including puffins and peregrines, and a thriving population of grey seals. At the northern and southern extremities are lighthouses, and there are the remains of the 13th-century Marisco Castle. The island was bought by the Landmark Trust in 1969. The population increases significantly during the summer tourist season. Visitors are mostly based in local, restored buildings, including the old lighthouse. Contact with the Devon mainland is mainly by ferry to Bideford or Ilfracombe.

Lupino

English family of actors and acrobats. They included **George Lupino** (1853–1932), his sons **Barry Lupino** (1882–1962) and **Stanley Lupino** (1893–1922), and the latter's daughter Ida Lupino. **Henry George Lupino** (1892–1959) was known as **Lupino Lane**. He was a great success in 1937 in the musical *Me and My Girl*, in which he created 'The Lambeth Walk'.

Lutine

British bullion ship that sank in the North Sea in 1799. Its bell, salvaged in 1859, is at the headquarters in Lloyd's of London, the insurance organization. It is sounded once when a ship is missing and twice for good news.

Luton

Industrial town and unitary authority in south-central England, 48 km/30 mi north of London; unitary authority area 43 sq km/17 sq mi; population (1997) 181,400. It was part of the county of Bedfordshire to 1997. **Luton airport** is a secondary airport for London. Local industry has traditionally been associated with the manufacture of hats, but cars and trucks, chemicals, engineering components, and electrical goods are also produced.

Features

The large church of St Mary (13th–15th centuries) is a cruciform building largely in the Decorated and Perpendicular styles. It has a 13th-century font, a unique canopied baptistry of the Decorated period, and a 14th-century tower. The **Luton Hoo** mansion (1767) is located to the south of the town. The mansion was originally designed and built by Robert ◊Adam. Its park was laid out by 'Capability' Brown. Luton Hoo houses the Wernher art collection, including china, glass, jewellery, tapestries, and paintings.

History

Luton was known as **Lygetune** by the Saxons, and in the Domesday Book of 1086 it was called **Loitoine**. The straw and fashion hat industry was responsible for Luton's prosperity in the 19th century. The town was incorporated as a municipal borough in 1876, and became a county borough in

1964, with extended boundaries. In 1974 it became a district of the county of Bedfordshire.

Lutyens, (Agnes) Elizabeth (1906–1983)

English composer. Her works, using the twelve-tone system, are expressive and tightly organized, and include chamber music, stage, and orchestral works. Her choral and vocal works include a setting of the Austrian philosopher Ludwig Wittgenstein's *Tractatus* and a cantata *The Tears of Night*. She also composed much film and incidental music.

Lutyens, Edwin Landseer (1869–1944)

English architect. His designs ranged from the picturesque, such as ◊Castle Drogo (1910–30), Devon, to Renaissance-style country houses, and ultimately evolved into a Classical style as seen in the Cenotaph, London (1919). His complex use of space, interest in tradition, and distorted Classical language have proved of great interest to a number of Post-Modern architects, especially Robert Venturi.

His first commission was a country cottage, Munstead Wood (1896), for Gertrude ◊Jekyll, who greatly influenced his earlier work. His later designs displayed a more formal Georgian or Queen Anne style, a particularly dignified example being Heathcote, Ilkley (1906). Lutyens was knighted in 1918, and was President of the Royal Academy from 1938 to 1944.

Lydford

Village in Devon, England, 18 km/11 mi east of Launceston; population (1991) 1,700. It was a walled town before the Norman Conquest, and Jeffreys of Wem (the 17th-century 'hanging judge') held his assizes at the castle. For many years it was the capital of Devonshire stannary (see ◊stannaries), because of its important position on the edge of the great tin-mining district of Dartmoor.

Lyell, Charles (1797–1875)

Scottish geologist. In his *Principles of Geology* (1830–33), he opposed the French anatomist Georges Cuvier's theory that the features of the Earth were formed by a series of catastrophes, and expounded the Scottish geologist James ◊Hutton's view, known as uniformitarianism, that past events were brought about by the same processes that occur today – a view that influenced Charles ◊Darwin's theory of evolution.

Lyell suggested that the Earth was as much as 240 million years old (in contrast to the 6,000 years of prevalent contemporary theory), and provided the first detailed description of the Tertiary period, dividing it into the Eocene, Miocene, and older and younger Pliocene periods. He was knighted in 1848.

Lyle, Sandy (Alexander Walter Barr) (1958–)

Scottish golfer who came to prominence in 1978 when he won the Rookie of the Year award. He won the British Open in 1985 and added the Masters and World Match-Play titles in 1988. He was Europe's leading money winner in 1979, 1980, and 1985 and has played in five Ryder Cups.

Lyme Park

House in Disley, Cheshire, England. It is partly Elizabethan with 18th- and 19th-century additions by Giacomo Leoni (*c.* 1686–1746) and Lewis Wyatt (1814–17). The house stands in 530 ha/1309 acres of park and moorland, and was given to the National Trust in 1947. The largest house in Cheshire, it has four centuries of period interiors.

Its collections include tapestries, carvings by Grinling Gibbons, and a collection of clocks. The house is set in gardens with an orangery by Wyatt, a lake, and a Dutch garden.

Lyme Park is managed by the National Trust, but is partly financed by Stockport Metropolitan Borough Council.

Lyme Regis

Seaport and resort in Dorset, southern England; population (1993 est) 3,600. Tourism and fishing are the main industries, but employment in information technology is increasingly important. The town was formerly a major port, and the rebel Duke of Monmouth, claimant to the English crown, landed here in 1685. The Cobb (a massive stone pier) features in Jane Austen's *Persuasion* (1818) and John Fowles's *The French Lieutenant's Woman* (1969).

The Lias (Lower Jurassic) rocks nearby are rich in fossils and have yielded remains of ichthyosaur and plesiosaur dinosaurs. The first ichthyosaur was found by Mary Anning in 1819; and in 1995 the fossilized end of an ichthyosaur's body and tail was recovered, containing petrified traces of soft tissues, including the outline of the tail fin.

History

The Cobb was first mentioned in the mid-13th century, when it formed an artificial harbour. Edward I gave Lyme Regis its charter in 1284 and it was incorporated by Elizabeth I. The port's most prosperous historical period was between 1500 and 1700 when trade flourished with the Mediterranean, West Indies, and Americas; even as late as 1780 it was larger than the port of Liverpool. During the English Civil War Lyme Regis withstood a Royalist siege, and 23 rebels were later hung and quartered on the beach.

The philanthropist Thomas Coram, founder of the Foundling Hospital in London, was born here in 1668.

Lymington

Port and yachting centre in Hampshire, southern England, on the River Lymington, 19 km/12 mi southwest of Southampton; population (1998 est) 14,300. It has light engineering and marine-related industries, including a marina, yacht repair yards, sailmaking, and chandlery businesses. There is a ferry link to Yarmouth on the Isle of Wight.

Lyndhurst

Village in Hampshire, England, at the centre of the New Forest, 13 km/8 mi southwest of Southampton; population (1991) 2,900. The Queen's House, now an office of the Forestry Commission, is where the Verderer's Court (an ancient body that looks after the well-being of open forest land) is held.

Lynn, Vera Margaret Lewis (1917–)

English singer. Known during World War II as the 'Forces' Sweetheart', she became famous with such songs as 'We'll Meet Again', 'White Cliffs of Dover', and in 1952 'Auf Wiederseh'n, Sweetheart'. She was made a DBE in 1975.

Lynton and Lynmouth

Twin resort towns on the north coast of Devon, southwest England, on the Bristol Channel, 19 km/12 mi east of Ilfracombe; population (est 1995) 1,700. The fishing village of Lynmouth, on the shore, is linked by a steep road and cliff railway (1890) to Lynton, 152 m/500 ft above at the top of a cliff.

In August 1952, 22.5 cm/9 in of rainfall within 24 hours on Exmoor caused disastrous flooding at Lynmouth, leaving 31 people dead and the harbour and over 100 buildings severely damaged. The harbour and much of the town were later rebuilt.

Silver used to be mined nearby at Combe Martin, west of Lynton.

Lyon, Mary Frances (1925–)

English mouse geneticist who is best known for her theory, now known as the **Lyon hypothesis**, that one of the X chromosomes (female sex chromosomes) is inactivated during early embryonic development of a female mammal. She also helped establish the mouse as a valid experimental model for investigating the genetic basis of inherited diseases.

Lytes Cary

Medieval manor house in Somerset, England, 10 km/6 mi north of Yeovil. Additional buildings were added to the house in almost every century from the 14th. Walter Jenner designed the Elizabethan-style garden, and left the house, contents and 145 ha/358 acres to the National Trust in 1949. The house includes a 14th-century chapel, a 15th-century hall, and a 16th-century 'great chamber'.

Lytes Cary was the home of the Lyte family for five centuries until it was sold in the 18th century. Henry Lyte, horticulturist and antiquary, wrote his *Niewe Herball* here and dedicated it to Elizabeth I. His botanic garden has not survived.

Lytham St Annes

Town and resort in Lancashire, northwest England, on the Ribble estuary, 10 km/6 mi southeast of Blackpool; population (1991) 41,400. The town has government offices and a financial services industry, as well as being a centre for the aerospace industry, with assembly and testing of planes. Tourism is important. Lytham St Annes has a championship golf course.

Lyttleton, Raymond Arthur (1911–1995)

English astronomer and theoretical physicist who focused on stellar evolution and composition, as well as the nature of the Solar System.

In 1939 Lyttleton and astronomer Frederick Hoyle demonstrated the presence of interstellar hydrogen on a large scale, at a time when most astronomers believed space to be devoid of interstellar gas. In the early 1940s they applied the new advances in nuclear physics to the problem of energy generation in stars.

In 1953 Lyttleton published a monograph on the stability of rotating liquid masses, and later postulated that the Earth's liquid core was produced by a phase change resulting from the combined effects of intense pressure and temperature. He also stressed the hydrodynamic significance of the liquid core in the processes of precession and nutation.

In 1959 with cosmologist Hermann ◊Bondi he proposed the electrostatic theory of the expanding universe.

Mabinogion, The (Welsh *mabinogi* 'instruction for young poets')

Collection of medieval Welsh myths and folk tales put together in the mid-19th century and drawn from two manuscripts: *The White Book of Rhydderch* (1300–25) and *The Red Book of Hergest* (1375–1425).

The Mabinogion proper consists of four tales, three of which concern a hero named Pryderi. Other stories in the medieval source manuscripts touch on the legendary court of King ◊Arthur.

McAdam, John Loudon (1756–1836)

Scottish engineer, inventor of the **macadam** road surface. It originally consisted of broken granite bound together with slag or gravel, raised for drainage. Today, it is bound with tar or asphalt.

McAdam introduced a method of road building that raised the road above the surrounding terrain, compounding a surface of small stones bound with gravel on a firm base of large stones. A camber, making the road slightly convex in section, ensured that rainwater rapidly drained off the road and did not penetrate the foundation. By the end of the 19th century, most of the main roads in Europe were built in this way.

McAdam was also responsible for reforms in road administration, and advised many turnpike trusts. He ensured that public roads became the responsibility of the government, financed out of taxes for the benefit of everyone.

Macaulay, (Emilie) Rose (1881–1958)

English novelist. The serious vein of her early novels changed to light satire in *Potterism* (1920) and *Keeping up Appearances* (1928). Her later books include *The World My Wilderness* (1950) and *The Towers of Trebizond* (1956; Tait Black Memorial Prize). Her work reflects the contemporary scene with wit and a shrewd understanding. She was made a DBE in 1958.

Macaulay, Thomas Babington, 1st Baron Macaulay (1800–1859)

British historian, essayist, poet, and politician, secretary of war 1839–41. His monumental *History of England from the Accession of James II* was intended to go up to 1830, but only five volumes, up to 1702, were published (1849–61). He was the first to popularize history by force of narrative, vivid characterization, and graphic detail, the fruits of considerable research.

Called to the bar in 1826, he became famous through his essays in the Whig journal *Edinburgh Review* (1825–44), in which he commented on literary and political topics. His most popular work was *Lays of Ancient Rome* (1842), with their thumping rhythms. His *History*, which took as its starting point the principle that the 1688 Revolution was the least violent and most beneficial of all revolutions, has a Whig bias. He entered Parliament as a liberal Whig in 1830. In India from 1834–38, he redrafted the Indian penal code. He sat again in Parliament from 1839 to 1847 and from 1852 to 1856, and in 1857 accepted a peerage.

We know no spectacle so ridiculous as the British public in one of its periodical fits of morality.

Thomas Macaulay English historian, essayist, poet, and politician.
Literary Essays, Moore's 'Life of Lord Byron'

Macbeth (*c.* 1005–1057)

King of Scotland from 1040. The son of Findlaech, hereditary ruler of Moray and Ross, he was commander of the forces of Duncan I, King of Scotland, whom he killed in battle in 1040. His reign was prosperous until Duncan's son Malcolm III led an invasion and killed him at Lumphanan in Aberdeenshire.

He was probably the grandson of Kenneth II and married Gruoch, the granddaughter of Kenneth III.

Macbeth

Tragedy by William ◊Shakespeare, first performed in 1605–06. Acting on a prophecy by three witches that he will be king of Scotland, Macbeth, egged on by Lady Macbeth, murders King Duncan and becomes king but is eventually killed by Macduff. The play was based on the 16th-century historian ◊Holinshed's *Chronicles*.

McBride, Willie John (William James) (1940–)
Irish Rugby Union player. Born in County Antrim, Northern Ireland, he was capped 63 times by Ireland, and won a record 17 British Lions caps. He played on five Lions tours, 1962, 1966, 1968, 1971, and in 1974 as captain when they returned from South Africa undefeated.

MacCaig, Norman (1910–1996)
Scottish poet. He began as a poet in revolt against the influence of W H ◊Auden in *Far Cry* (1943); in *The Inward Eye* (1946) there was a change to a poetic, metaphysic standpoint. He compensated for what seemed to be a lack of deep feeling with wit, wordplay, and lavish imagery. His many works included *Riding Lights* (1957), *Measures* (1965), *A Man in My Position* (1969), *The White Bird* (1973), *The Equal Skies* (1980), and *Voice-Over* (1988).

He was born in Edinburgh and educated there at the Royal High School and university. After teaching in schools, he became a lecturer at Stirling University.

McCarthy, John (1957–)
English journalist who in 1986 was taken prisoner in Lebanon by the militant group Islamic Jihad. His then girlfriend, Jill Morrell, and other friends campaigned for his release, though this did not take place until 1991. With Jill Morrell he wrote *Some Other Rainbow* (1992) recording in counterpoint the experience of captivity and the prolonged efforts made for his release.

McCartney, (James) Paul (1942–)
Rock singer, songwriter, and bass guitarist. He was a member of the ◊Beatles, and leader of the pop group Wings 1971–81, in which his US-born wife Linda (1942–1998) also performed. His subsequent albums include *Off the Ground* (1993) and *Flaming Pie* (1997). Solo hits have included collaborations with Michael Jackson and Elvis Costello. Together with composer Carl Davis, McCartney wrote the *Liverpool Oratorio* (1991), his first work of classical music. Another classical composition, *Standing Stones*, achieved considerable success in the USA in the same year. He was knighted in 1997.

I still don't know what Sergeant Pepper was about. We always thought of ourselves as just happy little song writers. ... Unfortunately it gets more important than that after you've been to America, and got knighted.

Paul McCartney English pop musician.
Quoted in Palmer, *All You Need is Love*

Macclesfield
Industrial town in Cheshire, northwest England, on the River Bollin on the edge of the Pennines, 28 km/17 mi south of Manchester; population (1991 est) 69,700. Formerly the centre of the English silk industry, it has light engineering industries, including the production of textile machinery, and its chief products are paper, chemicals and pharmaceuticals, and plastics. Several multinational companies have offices here.

There are two working silk museums, one producing silk for sale.

McColgan, Elizabeth (1964–)
Scottish long-distance runner who became the 1992 world 10,000 metres champion. She won consecutive gold medals at the Commonwealth Games in 1986 and 1990 at the same distance.

McCowen, Alec (Alexander Duncan) (1925–)
English actor. His Shakespearean roles include Richard II and the Fool in *King Lear*, he is also known for his dramatic one-man shows.

McCoy, Tony (1974–)
Northern Irish National Hunt jockey who in March 1998 broke Peter Scudamore's all-time record of riding 221 winners in a British season. Born in County Antrim, the son of a horse breeder, he came to Britain in August 1994 and in his first season was the leading conditional jockey with a record 74 winners. He was champion jockey in 1995–96 with 175 winners and in 1996–97 with 197.

McCullin, Don(ald) (1935–)
English war photographer. He started out as a freelance photojournalist for the Sunday newspapers. His coverage of hostilities in the Congo in 1967, Vietnam in 1968, Biafra in 1968 and 1970, and Cambodia in 1970 are notable for their pessimistic vision. He has published several books of his work, among them *Destruction Business*.

MacDiarmid, Hugh pen name of Christopher Murray Grieve (1892–1978)
Scottish poet. A nationalist and Marxist, he was one of the founders in 1928 of the National Party of Scotland. His works include *A Drunk Man looks at the Thistle* (1926) and the collections *First Hymn to Lenin* (1931) and *Second Hymn to Lenin* (1935), in which poetry is made relevant to politics. He developed a form of modern poetic Scots, based on an amalgam of Middle and Modern Scots, and was the leader of the Scottish literary renaissance of the 1920s and 1930s. *Complete Poems 1920–1976* was published in 1978 and *Selected Poems* in 1992.

Macdonald, Flora (1722–1790)
Scottish heroine. She rescued Prince Charles Edward Stuart, the Young Pretender, after his defeat at Culloden in 1746. Disguising him as her maid, she escorted him from her home on South Uist in the Hebrides, to France. She was arrested and imprisoned in the Tower of London, but released in 1747.

Macdonald, George (1824–1905)
Scottish novelist and children's writer. *David Elginbrod* (1863) and *Robert Falconer* (1868) are characteristic novels but his children's stories, including *At the Back of the North Wind*

(1871) and *The Princess and the Goblin* (1872), are now better known. He was much influenced by the German Romantics, and mystical imagination pervades all his books, most notably *Lilith* (1895). His work inspired later writers including G K ◊Chesterton, C S ◊Lewis, and J R R ◊Tolkien.

MacDonald, (James) Ramsay (1866–1937)
British politician, first Labour prime minister January–October 1924 and 1929–31. Failing to deal with worsening economic conditions, he left the party to form a coalition government in 1931, which was increasingly dominated by Conservatives, until he was replaced by Stanley Baldwin in 1935.

MacDonald joined the ◊Independent Labour Party in 1894, and became first secretary of the new Labour Party in 1900. In Parliament he led the party 1906–14 and 1922–31 and was prime minister of the first two Labour governments.

MacDonald was born in Scotland, the son of a labourer. He was elected to Parliament in 1906, and led the party until 1914, when his opposition to World War I lost him the leadership. This he recovered in 1922, and in January 1924 he formed a government dependent on the support of the Liberal Party. When this was withdrawn in October the same year, he was forced to resign. He returned to office in 1929, again as leader of a minority government, which collapsed in 1931 as a result of the economic crisis. MacDonald left the Labour Party to form a national government with backing from both Liberal and Conservative parties. He resigned the premiership in 1935.

McDowell, Malcolm adopted name of Malcolm Taylor (1943–)
English actor. He played the rebellious hero in Lindsay ◊Anderson's film *If …* (1968) and confirmed his acting abilities in Stanley Kubrick's *A Clockwork Orange* (1971). Other films include *O Lucky Man* (1973), *Caligula* (1979), *Blue Thunder* (1983), *The Player* (1992), *Star Trek: Generations* (1994), and *World of Moss* (1998).

He has worked widely in television, featuring in the British miniseries *Our Friends in the North* (1996) and *Fantasy Island* (1998). Other films include *Jezebel's Kiss* (1990), *Chain of Desire* (1992), *Mr Magoo* (1997), and *Beings* (1998).

McEwan, Ian Russell (1948–)
English novelist and short-story writer. His works often have sinister or macabre undertones and contain elements of violence and bizarre sexuality, as in the short stories in *First Love, Last Rites* (1975). His novels include *The Comfort of Strangers* (1981), *The Child in Time* (1987), *Black Dogs* (1992; short-listed for the Booker Prize), *Enduring Love* (1997), and *Amsterdam* (1998; winner of the Booker Prize). *The Daydreamer* (1994) is a novel for children. He has also published *Short Stories* (1995).

McGeechan, Ian Robert (1946–)
Scottish rugby union player and coach. At fly-half or centre he won 32 Scotland caps and eight for the British Lions 1972–79. Appointed Scotland's head coach in 1988 he masterminded the team's Five Nations Grand Slam in 1990. He coached the British Lions in Australia in 1989, New Zealand in 1993, and most notably in South Africa in 1997 when he guided the team to a memorable series victory.

McGough, Roger (1937–)
English poet, dramatist, songwriter, and performer, one of the group known as the 'Liverpool Poets'. He came to prominence in the late 1960s as a singer in the pop group Scaffold, and he wrote many of their songs (including their hit 'Lily the Pink'). His poems were strongly influenced by the pop culture of the 1960s, and he later became noted for his poetry readings. His poetry collections include *Gig* (1973) and *Waving at Trains* (1982). He has also written several plays, often with music, and a range of children's books.

McGrath, John Peter (1935–)
Scottish dramatist and director. He founded the socialist 7:84 Theatre Companies in England in 1971 and Scotland in 1973, and is the author of such plays as *Events Guarding the Bofors Gun* (1966); *The Cheviot, the Stag, and the Black, Black Oil* (1973), a musical account of the economic exploitation of the Scottish highlands; and *The Garden of England* (1985).

McGrath has published two books arguing the case for popular and radical theatre: *A Good Night Out* (1981) and *The Bone Won't Break* (1990).

McGregor, Ewan (1971–)
Scottish screen actor, one of the leading talents of his generation on both sides of the Atlantic. He played a cynical Scottish yuppie in *Shallow Grave* (1994), the first of several collaborations with director Danny Boyle, writer John Hodge, and producer Andrew Macdonald, including ◊*Trainspotting* (1996), in which he played a heroin addict, and the comedy *A Life Less Ordinary* (1997), in which he played an incompetent kidnapper. He also featured in Todd Haynes's glam-rock film *Velvet Goldmine* (1998).

McGregor has effortlessly switched from comic to dramatic roles, featuring in both mainstream and low-budget independent productions in the UK and the USA. His other credits include *The Pillow Book* (1995), the Jane Austen adaptation *Emma* (1996), *Brassed Off* (1996), and the US thriller *Nightwatch* (1998).

He first demonstrated his versatility in two television miniseries, Dennis Potter's 1950s nostalgia piece *Lipstick on Your Collar* and the BBC costume drama *Scarlet and Black*. A guest star appearance in the US hospital drama *ER* in 1994 confirmed his celebrity status. With a diversity of roles and the alternating of period and contemporary pieces, he has avoided the pitfalls of being stereotyped.

MacGregor, Joanna (1959–)
English pianist and composer. She has written music for theatre, radio, and television. In 1993 she gave the premiere of Birtwistle's *Antiphonies*, under Boulez, and has performed other modern repertory by Berio, Xenakis, Ligeti, and Takemitsu.

McGuire, Edward (1948–)

Scottish composer. He studied at the Royal Academy of Music 1966–70 and in Stockholm. He played flute with the folk group The Whistlebinkies from 1973. His music has been performed at the Edinburgh Festival and London Promenade concerts. Recent works include *A Glasgow Symphony* and a trombone concerto (1991).

Machynlleth

Town in Powys, central Wales, situated on the River Dovey, 17 km/10 mi south of Dolgellau; population (1991) 2,000. Agriculture and forestry were formerly the main local economic activities, but tourism has also become an important industry. The Centre for Alternative Technology, an educational charity, attracts large numbers of visitors, and there is also a craft centre and a nature reserve.

Owen Glendower summoned a parliament here in 1402.

Macintosh, Charles (1766–1843)

Scottish manufacturing chemist who invented a waterproof fabric, lined with rubber, that was used for raincoats – hence **mackintosh**. Other waterproofing processes have now largely superseded this method.

In 1797 Macintosh set up the first alum works in Scotland, and in 1799 invented a process for making bleaching powder. While investigating uses for the waste products of the new Glasgow gasworks in 1818, he noticed coal-tar naphtha dissolved India rubber. He experimented by sandwiching wool fabric with this substance to make a waterproof material, and invented the mackintosh. The material was hard in winter and sticky in summer, and awaited the discovery of vulcanization of rubber by Charles Goodyear in 1839 for success.

Mackay of Clashfern, James Peter Hymers Mackay, Baron Mackay of Clashfern (1927–)

British Conservative politician and lawyer. He became Lord Chancellor in 1987 and in 1989 announced a reform package to end legal restrictive practices.

He became a QC in 1965 and in 1979 was unexpectedly made Lord Advocate for Scotland and a life peer. His reform package included ending the barristers' monopoly of advocacy in the higher courts; promoting the combination of the work of barristers and solicitors in 'mixed' practices; and allowing building societies and banks to do property conveyancing, formerly limited to solicitors. The plans met with fierce opposition.

McKellen, Ian Murray (1939–)

English actor. Acclaimed as the leading Shakespearean player of his generation, his stage roles include Richard II (1968), Macbeth (1977), Max in Martin Sherman's *Bent* (1979), Platonov in Chekhov's *Wild Honey* (1986), Iago in *Othello* (1989), and Richard III (1990); recently he has appeared in *Uncle Vanya* (1992) and *Enemy of the People* (1998). His films include *Priest of Love* (1982), *Plenty* (1985), *Scandal* (1990), *The Ballad of Little Jo* (1991), and *Last Action Hero* (1993). He was knighted in 1991.

Mackendrick, Alexander (1912–1993)

US-born Scottish film director and teacher. He was responsible for some of ◊Ealing Studios' finest films, including *Whisky Galore!* (1949) and *The Man in the White Suit* (1951). He went on to Hollywood to direct *Sweet Smell of Success* (1957), an acerbic portrayal of a powerful New York gossip columnist.

Mackendrick's *The Ladykillers* (1955), which proved to be Ealing's last major film, possesses a macabre eccentricity that places it in the front rank of British comedy.

Mackenzie, Alexander (Campbell) (1847–1935)

Scottish composer. He composed prolifically in all genres, perhaps his most notable works being the operas *Colomba* (1883), *The Cricket on the Hearth* (1914), and *The Eve of St John* (1924), and the oratorio *The Rose of Sharon* (1884). He published his autobiography, *A Musician's Narrative*, in 1927.

Mackenzie, Compton adopted name of Edward Montague Compton (1883–1972)

Scottish writer. He published his first novel, *The Passionate Elopement*, in 1911. Subsequent novels included *Carnival* (1912), a melodrama of stage life, the semi-autobiographical *Sinister Street* (1913–14), the sequence *The Four Winds of Love* (1937–45), and the comedy *Whisky Galore!* (1947; filmed in 1949).

During World War I he served in the secret service; his *Greek Memories* (1932) was withdrawn after his trial under the Official Secrets Act. He published his autobiography, *My Life and Times*, in ten volumes from 1963–71.

Mackenzie, James (1848–1924)

Scottish physician and cardiologist who was a pioneer of modern cardiac medicine. He was the first to identify a large number of irregularities in the heart's beat and establish which were caused by serious disease and which were of no consequence. He was knighted in 1915.

McKenzie, Julia (1941–)

English actress and singer. She has starred in plays and musicals on stage and television, including many productions of the musicals of Stephen Sondheim. Her stage performances include *The Norman Conquests* (1978), *Guys and Dolls* (1982), *Into the Woods* (1990), and *Sweeney Todd* (1993); television performances include *Blott on the Landscape* (1985) and *Hotel du Lac* (1986). Her film roles include *Shirley Valentine* (1989).

McKern, (Reginald) Leo (1920–)

Australian character actor. Active in the UK, he is probably best known for his portrayal of the barrister Rumpole in the television series *Rumpole of the Bailey*. His films include *Moll Flanders* (1965), *A Man for All Seasons* (1966), and *Ryan's Daughter* (1970).

Other films include *Omen II* (1978) and *The French Lieutenant's Woman* (1981). On stage he has acted in *Uncle Vanya* and *Crime and Punishment* (both 1978), *The Housekeeper* (1982), and *Boswell for the Defence* (1989). He also acted in the television series *Reilly, Ace of Spies* (1983) and *A Foreign Field* (1994).

MACKINTOSH, CHARLES RENNIE *The Scottish architect and designer Charles Rennie Mackintosh was a leading exponent of the international style known as Art Nouveau. He believed that all elements within a building, including furniture and even cutlery, should be integrated into the overall design. This principle is embodied in the Willow Tea Rooms in Glasgow's main thoroughfare, Sauchiehall Street. George Wright/ Collections*

Mackintosh, Charles Rennie (1868–1928)

Scottish architect, designer, and painter, whose highly original work represents a dramatic break with the late Victorian style. He worked initially in the ◊Art Nouveau idiom but later developed a unique style, both rational and expressive.

Influenced by the ◊Arts and Crafts movement, he designed furniture and fittings, cutlery, and lighting to go with his interiors. Mackintosh was initially influential, particularly on Austrian architects such as Joseph Maria Olbrich and Josef Hoffman. However, he was not successful in his lifetime, and has only recently come to be regarded as a pioneer of modern design.

Mackintosh was born and educated in Glasgow, and also travelled in Italy. In 1896 he won the competition for the Glasgow School of Art (completed 1909). Other major works include the Cranston tea rooms, Glasgow (1897–1909); and Hill House, Helensburgh (1902–03). After 1913 he devoted himself to painting and eventually abandoned architecture and design altogether.

Mackintosh, Elizabeth (1896–1952)

Scottish novelist, dramatist, and biographer. As **Gordon Daviot** she wrote the plays *Richard of Bordeaux* (1933), which John Gielgud directed and starred in; *Queen of Scots* (1934), with Laurence Olivier; and the biography *Claverhouse* (1937). Her detective novels, written as **Josephine Tey**, include *The Franchise Affair* (1948), *Brat Farrar* (1949), and *The Daughter of Time* (1951).

She was born in Inverness. Refusing to go to university, she took a course in physical training, which she taught in schools in England before returning home to look after her father after her mother's death. *The Daughter of Time* re-examines the case of the little princes in the Tower of London.

McLaren

British racing-car manufacturer, which made its debut in Formula One in 1970. The team won the Constructors' championship seven times between 1974 and 1991, and the Driver's title nine times within the same years. From 1988 to 1991 it dominated the sport, winning both titles for four consecutive years. Notable drivers for McLaren have included Ayrton Senna, Alain Prost, and James ◊Hunt. Mika Hakkinen won the Driver's title in 1998 in a McLaren, securing the constructors' title for the company as well.

Maclean, Alistair (1922–1987)

Scottish adventure novelist. His first novel, *HMS Ulysses* (1955), was based on wartime experience. It was followed by *The Guns of Navarone* (1957) and several other best-selling adventure novels. Many of his books were made into films.

His work is meticulously accurate in detail as well as being full of suspense. Among his other novels are *Fear is the Key* (1961), *Ice Station Zebra* (1963), and *Where Eagles Dare* (1967).

Maclean served in the Royal Navy from 1941–46, by his own account 'from the Arctic to the Far East with many places in between'. He became a writer after winning a short-story competition in the *Glasgow Herald* in 1954.

Maclean, Donald Duart (1913–1983)

English spy who worked for the USSR while in the UK civil service. He defected to the USSR in 1951 together with Guy ◊Burgess.

Maclean, brought up in a strict Presbyterian family, was educated at Cambridge, where he was recruited by the Soviet KGB. He worked for the UK Foreign Office in Washington in 1944 and then Cairo in 1948 before returning to London, becoming head of the American Department at the Foreign Office in 1950.

MacLellan, Robert (1907–)

Scottish playwright. His plays are well constructed with a strong historical sense and good characterization, but because they are written in Scots have had only a limited readership. They include *Jeddart Justice* (1934); *The Changeling* (1935); *Toom Byres* (1936); *Jamie the Saxt* (1937); *The Flouers o Edinburgh* (1947); *Rab Mossgiel* (1959), about Robert Burns; *Young Auchinleck* (1962), about James Boswell; and *The Hypocrite* (1970).

Macleod, John James Rickard (1876–1935)

Scottish physiologist who shared the Nobel Prize for Physiology or Medicine with Frederick Banting in 1923 for their part in the discovery of insulin, the hormone in the pancreas that reduces blood glucose (sugar) levels. Since its discovery, insulin has been used extensively as the main treatment for diabetes.

Macmillan, (Maurice) Harold, 1st Earl of Stockton (1894–1986)

British Conservative politician, prime minister 1957–63; foreign secretary 1955 and chancellor of the Exchequer 1955–57. In 1963 he attempted to negotiate British entry into the European Economic Community (EEC), but was blocked by the French president Charles de Gaulle. Much of his career as prime minister was spent defending the retention of a UK nuclear weapon, and he was responsible for the purchase of US Polaris missiles in 1962.

Macmillan was MP for Stockton 1924–29 and 1931–45, and for Bromley 1945–64. As minister of housing 1951–54 he achieved the construction of 300,000 new houses a year. He became prime minister on the resignation of Anthony Eden after the ◊Suez Crisis, and led the Conservative Party to victory in the 1959 elections on the slogan 'You've never had it so good' (the phrase was borrowed from a US election campaign). Internationally, his realization of the 'wind of change' in Africa advanced the independence of former colonies. Macmillan's nickname **Supermac** was coined by the cartoonist Vicky.

Macmillan, a member of a family of publishers, was educated at Eton public school and Oxford, and served with distinction in World War I. He entered Parliament as a Unionist in 1924. During the interwar years, he was one of the severest critics of his party leaders' foreign appeasement policy, and in 1936 he voted against the National Government's decision to abandon the sanctions towards Italy that its aggressive Ethiopian policy had prompted. Macmillan was also interested in social reform, his views being generally in advance of his party at the time. He set out his ideas on combating poverty in *The Middle Way* (1938).

He was parliamentary undersecretary at the Ministry of Supply from 1940 to 1942, when he became parliamentary undersecretary for the colonies. Later that same year he was made minister resident at Allied headquarters in northwest Africa, a position he held until 1945, when he became a conspicuous member of the Conservative opposition. When the Conservatives returned to power in 1951, he was appointed minister of housing and local government. He was minister of defence 1954–55, and then became foreign secretary. He held this post only until December 1955, when he was appointed chancellor of the Exchequer in succession to R A Butler. His 1956 budget, although intended to rectify the unstable economic situation at that time, was popularly remembered for the introduction of Premium Savings Bonds.

When Eden resigned the premiership in January 1957, Macmillan was appointed his successor in preference to the more senior Butler. However, his party's division over the Suez issue combined with inflationary pressures to cause domestic discontent. Between taking office and the general election of 1959, Macmillan made a highly successful Commonwealth tour and also visited Moscow and Washington, DC, becoming an influential figure in world politics.

Meanwhile, in the UK, tax reductions and industrial expansion pushed inflation into the background; Macmillan fought the 1959 election on the theme of belief in an affluent society, and actually increased the Conservative majority. However, his government suffered a subsequent series of setbacks: in 1961 the 'wages pause', an early attempt to control pay rises, caused bitterness but failed to halt inflation; Britain's failure to enter the EEC left the government in a virtual policy vacuum; and the ◊Profumo scandal of June 1963 almost brought the government down. In October 1963 Macmillan was forced to resign through ill health and was succeeded by Alec ◊Douglas-Home. He remained in the Commons until the general election of October 1964, when he announced his retirement from politics. He became chancellor of Oxford University in 1960.

MacMillan, James (1959–)

Scottish composer. In works such as *The Confessions of Isobel Gowdie*, premiered at the London Promenade concerts in 1990, he has forsaken modern orthodoxies for a more popular approach.

MacMillan, Kenneth (1929–1992)

Scottish choreographer. After studying at the Sadler's Wells Ballet School, he was director of the Royal Ballet 1970–77 and then principal choreographer 1977–92. He was also director of Berlin's German Opera ballet company 1966–69. A daring stylist, he often took risks with his choreography, expanding the ballet's vocabulary with his frequent use of historical sources, religious music, and occasional use of dialogue. His works include *Romeo and Juliet* (1965, filmed 1966) for Margot Fonteyn and Rudolf Nureyev. He was knighted in 1983.

MacMillan, Kirkpatrick (1813–1878)

Scottish blacksmith who invented the bicycle in 1839. His invention consisted of a 'hobby-horse' that was fitted with treadles and propelled by pedalling.

McNaught, William (1813–1881)

Scottish mechanical engineer who invented the compound steam engine in 1845. This type of engine extracts the maximum energy from the hot steam by effectively using it twice – once in a high-pressure cylinder (or cylinders) and then, when exhausted from this, in a second, low-pressure cylinder.

MacNeice, (Frederick) Louis (1907–1963)

Northern Irish poet, born in Belfast. He made his debut with *Blind Fireworks* (1929) and developed a polished ease of expression, reflecting his classical training, as in the autobiographical and topical *Autumn Journal* (1939). He is noted for his low-key, socially committed but politically uncommitted verse; and his ability to reflect the spirit of his times in his own emotional experience earned him an appreciative public.

Later works include the play *The Dark Tower* (1947), written for radio (he was employed by the BBC features department from 1941–61); a verse translation of Goethe's

Faust (1949); and the collections *Springboard* (1944) and *Solstices* (1961). *Collected Poems* (1966) was revised in 1979 and *Selected Plays* appeared in 1993.

Maconchy, Elizabeth (1907–1994)

English composer of Irish descent. Several of her works were performed abroad and she had particular success in Belgium and eastern Europe. She composed a great deal of chamber music, including a remarkable series of thirteen string quartets, and three one-act operas, *The Sofa* (1957), *The Departure* (1961), and *The Three Strangers* (1967).

She was born at Broxbourne, Hertfordshire. She studied composition under Vaughan Williams and Charles Wood, and piano under Arthur Alexander at the Royal College of Music in London. Later she went to Prague on a Blumenthal scholarship, where she studied under Karel Jirák in Prague. She married William LeFanu, who translated poems by the Greek poet Anacreon for her. She was awarded the Daily Telegraph medal for chamber music in 1933, and a medal for distinguished service to chamber music from the Worshipful Company of Musicians in 1970. Her *And Death Shall Have No Dominion*, for chorus and brass, was performed at the Three Choirs Festival in 1969. The composer Nicola LeFanu is her daughter.

Macpherson, James (1736–1796)

Scottish writer. He published *Fragments of Ancient Poetry Collected in the Highlands of Scotland* in 1760, followed by the epics *Fingal* in 1761 and *Temora* in 1763, which he claimed as the work of the 3rd-century bard Ossian. After his death they were shown largely, but not entirely, to be forgeries.

When publicly challenged by Samuel ◊Johnson, Macpherson failed to produce his originals, and a committee established in 1797 decided in 1805 that he had combined fragmentary materials with oral tradition. Nevertheless, the works of 'Ossian' influenced the development of the Romantic movement in Britain and in Europe.

McRae, Colin (1968–)

Scottish rally driver who in 1995, driving a Subaru Impreza, became the first ever British driver to win the world rally championship. At 27 years old he was also the youngest ever champion. In 1994 he had become the first British driver since Roger Clark in 1976 to win the RAC Rally, a race he won again in 1995 and 1997. In 1998 he announced that he would drive for Ford from the following year.

MacWhirter, John (1839–1911)

Scottish landscape painter. His works include *June in the Austrian Tyrol*, *Spindrift* (Tate Gallery, London), and various watercolours of Highland landscapes.

McWhirter, Norris Dewar (1925–)

British editor and compiler; with his twin brother, **Ross McWhirter** (1925–1975), he was founding editor of the *Guinness Book of Records* in 1955.

Maesteg

Town in the county borough of Bridgend, south Wales, 13 km/8 mi southeast of Neath; population (1991) 20,600. Industrial activity includes paper milling, engineering, and the manufacture of ceramics.

Mafeking, Siege of

Boer siege, during the South African War, of the British-held town (now **Mafikeng**) 12 October 1899–17 May 1900. The British commander Col Robert Baden-Powell held the Boers off and kept morale high until a relief column arrived and relieved the town. The raising of the siege was a great boost to morale in Britain.

The British garrison, about 750 soldiers under Col Robert Baden-Powell, 1,700 townspeople, and about 7,000 Africans, was besieged by a 10,000-strong Boer force under General Piet Cronje. The siege was not pressed very hard, the town was never completely invested, and the only serious attack the Boers attempted failed. The announcement of the town's relief led to wild scenes of celebration in London and across Britain, far out of proportion to the actual strategic value of the operation, and even led to the coining of a new verb – 'to maffick', meaning to celebrate intemperately.

MAFF

Abbreviation for the **Ministry of ◊Agriculture, Fisheries, and Food.**

magazines

Current top-selling weekly magazines in Britain are *What's on TV*, *Radio Times*, and *TV Times*, each with a circulation figure of over 1 million. *Reader's Digest* is the best-selling monthly magazine, with a circulation of 1.5 million. See tables on pages 567–568 for general and women's magazines attracting over 500,000 readers, and a chronology on page 566.

History

The first magazine in Britain was a penny weekly, the *Athenian Gazette*, better known later as the *Athenian Mercury* (1690–97). This was produced by a London publisher, John Dunton, to resolve 'all the most Nice and Curious Questions'. It was soon followed by the *Gentleman's Journal* (1692–94), started by the French-born Peter Anthony Motteux, with a monthly blend of news, prose, and poetry.

The earliest illustrations were wood engravings; the half-tone process was invented in 1882 and photogravure was used commercially from 1895. Printing and paper-manufacturing techniques progressed during the 19th century, making larger print runs possible. Advertising began to appear in magazines around 1800; it was a significant factor by 1850 and crucial to most magazines' finances by 1880. Specialist magazines for different interests and hobbies, and comic books, appeared in the 20th century.

The 1930s saw the introduction of colour printing. The development of cheap offset litho printing made possible the flourishing of the **underground press** in the 1960s, although it was limited by unorthodox distribution methods such as street sales. Prosecutions and economic recession largely killed the underground press; the main survivors in Britain are

MAGAZINES: SOME KEY DATES

1690 The *Athenian Gazette* is Britain's first magazine, aiming to resolve 'Nice and Curious Questions'.

1701 A Baldwin publishes *Memoirs for the Curious* in London, England, the first illustrated magazine.

3 March 1770 *Trysorfa Gwybodaeth neu Eurgrawn Cymraeg*, the first Welsh language magazine to enjoy ongoing publication, is published.

April 1771 The *Ladies Magazine* features the first colour fashion plate, 'Spring Dress', in London, England.

July 1828 The *Spectator*, a weekly magazine covering politics and the arts, is launched in London, with Robert S Rintoul as editor.

1832 The *Penny Magazine* is launched by Charles Knight in London. The first mass-circulation magazine, it quickly reaches sales in excess of 100,000.

1841 Henry Mayhew launches the weekly comic magazine *Punch*, in London, with Mark Lemon as editor and John Leech as chief illustrator.

May 1842 The *Illustrated London News* is launched by Herbert Ingram, in London.

September 1843 *The Economist* magazine is launched, with James Wilson as editor, in London.

1852 Publisher Samuel Orchart Beeton launches the first mass-market women's magazine, the *Englishwoman's Domestic Magazine*. Its popularity is partly due to the contributions of his wife, Isabella Beeton, on domestic management.

1855 Samuel Orchart Beeton launches the *Boy's Own Magazine*. The first children's magazine to be concerned with entertainment rather than education, its main subjects are adventure stories and sports, and it is very successful.

1893 The *Phonogram* is the first record magazine in Britain.

1904 The *Optical Lantern and Cinematograph Journal*, the first cinema magazine in Britain, is launched.

1916 A British edition of the US magazine *Vogue* is published.

1922 A British edition of the US magazine *Good Housekeeping* is published.

1923 The *Radio Times*, a listeners' guide to radio programmes, is launched.

1926 The magazine *Melody Maker* is founded: it plays an important role in promoting the spread of jazz in the country.

1929 *The Listener*, a magazine reprinting talks from BBC radio programmes, is launched.

1938 Edward Hulton founds the illustrated news magazine *Picture Post*.

14 November 1952 The popular music magazine *New Musical Express* publishes Britain's first pop singles chart.

1978 The music magazine *Smash Hits* is launched; it will become the most successful magazine for the teenage market in the UK.

1979 The scurrilous magazine *Viz* begins publication.

September 1996 The magazine *Punch*, originally published 1841–1992, is resurrected.

the satirical *Private Eye* (1961), and the London listings guide *Time Out* (1968).

Women's magazines

From the *Ladies' Mercury* (1693) until the first feminist publications of the late 1960s, the content of mass-circulation women's magazines in Britain was largely confined to the domestic sphere – housekeeping, recipes, beauty and fashion, advice columns, patterns – and gossip. In the late 18th century, women's magazines reflected society's temporary acceptance of women as intellectually equal to men, discussing public affairs and subjects of general interest, but by 1825 the trend had reversed. Around 1900 publications for working women began to appear, lurid weekly novelettes known as 'penny dreadfuls'. The first colour magazine for women in Britain, *Woman*, appeared in 1937. By the 1990s women's magazines were an extremely strong part of the whole magazine market, with several weeklies reaching between 1.5 and 3 million readers, and over a dozen monthlies reaching between 1 and 2 million readers.

magistrate

In English law, a person who presides in a magistrates' court: either a justice of the peace (with no legal qualifications, and unpaid) or a stipendiary magistrate. Stipendiary magistrates are paid, qualified lawyers working mainly in London and major cities.

magistrates' court

In England and Wales, a local law court that mainly deals with minor criminal cases. A magistrates' court consists of between two and seven lay justices of the peace (who are advised on the law by a clerk to the justices), or a single stipendiary magistrate.

It deals with some civil matters, too, such as licensing certain domestic and matrimonial proceedings, and may include a juvenile court.

In committal proceedings, a magistrates' court decides whether more serious criminal cases should be referred to the crown court. See ◊legal system.

Magna Carta (Latin 'great charter')

In English history, the charter granted by King John in 1215, traditionally seen as guaranteeing human rights against the excessive use of royal power. As a reply to the king's demands for excessive feudal dues and attacks on the privileges of the church, Archbishop Langton proposed to the barons the

General Magazines With a Readership of Over 500,000

Figures are from an unweighted sample of 38,349 adults aged 15 and over. An unweighted sample is 'raw' data which has not been 'weighted' to represent the full population (that is, taking into account age, social grades, etc.). For this survey, the estimated population was 46.15 million and did not include Northern Ireland. Adult coverage is the percentage of the total population aged 15 and over in Great Britain, but not Northern Ireland.

July 1996–June 1997

Periodical	Adult readers	Adult coverage (%)
Weekly		
Radio Times	4,270,000	9.3
What's on TV	4,048,000	8.8
TV Times	3,665,000	7.9
TV Quick	2,385,000	5.2
Auto Trader	2,012,000	4.4
Exchange & Mart	1,122,000	2.4
The Big Issue	1,061,000	2.3
TV & Satellite Week	816,000	1.8
NME (New Musical Express)	675,000	1.5
Motorcycle News	652,000	1.4
Shoot	638,000	1.4
TES (Times Educational Supplement)	637,000	1.4
Time Out	616,000	1.3
Weekly News	598,000	1.3
Match	597,000	1.3
Angling Times	554,000	1.2
Any general weekly	19,398,000	42.0
Fortnightly		
Smash Hits	819,000	1.8
Private Eye	661,000	1.4
Monthly		
SkyTVguide	5,895,000	12.8
Reader's Digest	5,169,000	11.2
Cable Guide	2,162,000	4.7
BBC Gardener's World	1,850,000	4.0
National Geographic	1,787,000	3.9
BBC Top Gear	1,706,000	3.7
FHM (For Him Magazine)	1,580,000	3.4
Saga Magazine	1,516,000	3.3
What Car?	1,437,000	3.1

July 1996–June 1997

Periodical	Adult readers	Adult coverage (%)
Monthly		
Loaded	1,364,000	3.0
Max Power	1,359,000	2.9
Sky	1,211,000	2.6
Classic Cars	961,000	2.1
Practical Gardening	927,000	2.0
Golf Monthly	811,000	1.8
GQ	798,000	1.7
Q	796,000	1.7
Performance Bikes	731,000	1.6
Top of the Pops Magazine	706,000	1.5
Performance Car	694,000	1.5
What Hi-Fi?	665,000	1.4
High Life	653,000	1.4
BBC Wildlife	649,000	1.4
FourFourTwo	618,000	1.3
TV Hits	604,000	1.3
Car	582,000	1.3
Empire	576,000	1.2
Golf World	568,000	1.2
Superbike	532,000	1.2
Goal	522,000	1.1
Garden Answers	517,000	1.1
Any general monthly	23,315,000	50.5
Bi-monthly		
Viz	2,102,000	4.6
Quarterly		
AA Magazine	4,247,000	9.2
The Ford Magazine	1,045,000	2.3
Upbeat	616,000	1.3

Source: National Readership Survey – Top Line

Women's Magazines With a Readership of Over 500,000

Figures are from an unweighted sample of 38,349 adults aged 15 and over. An unweighted sample is 'raw' data which has not been 'weighted' to represent the full population (that is, taking into account age, social grades, etc.). For this survey, the estimated population was 46.15 million and did not include Northern Ireland. Adult coverage is the percentage of the total population aged 15 and over in Great Britain, but not Northern Ireland.

July 1996–June 1997

Periodical	Women readers	Women coverage (%)
	Weekly	
Take a Break	3,792,000	16.0
Woman's Own	3,092,000	13.0
Bella	2,641,000	11.1
Woman	2,388,000	10.1
Woman's Weekly	1,930,000	8.1
Best	1,891,000	8.0
Hello!	1,877,000	7.9
Chat	1,608,000	6.8
My Weekly	1,306,000	5.5
The People's Friend	1,086,000	4.6
Woman's Realm	1,007,000	4.2
Eva	792,000	3.3
That's Life	733,000	3.1
Any women's weekly	9,942,000	41.9
	Fortnightly	
More!	1,049,000	4.4
Inside Soap	513,000	2.2
	Monthly	
Sainsbury's Magazine	2,127,000	9.0
A Taste of Safeway	1,848,000	7.8
Good Houskeeping	1,811,000	7.6
Cosmopolitan	1,690,000	7.1
Prima	1,533,000	6.5
The Somerfield Magazine	1,475,000	6.2
Marie Claire	1,468,000	6.2
Vogue	1,375,000	5.8
Ideal Home	1,338,000	5.6
BBC Good Food	1,144,000	4.8
Homes & Gardens	1,140,000	4.8
Homes & Ideas	1,117,000	4.7

July 1996–June 1997

Periodical	Women readers	Women coverage (%)
	Monthly	
Woman & Home	1,082,000	4.6
Just Seventeen	1,060,000	4.5
Family Circle	1,039,000	4.4
Sugar	1,024,000	4.3
Elle	935,000	3.9
She	935,000	3.9
Essentials	906,000	3.8
House & Garden	863,000	3.6
House Beautiful	823,000	3.5
Clothes Show Magazine	762,000	3.2
Company	709,000	3.0
Mother & Baby	682,000	2.9
'19'	634,000	2.7
New Woman	627,000	2.6
It's Bliss	611,000	2.6
Country Living	594,000	2.5
Candis	576,000	2.4
Looks	553,000	2.3
Top Santé Health & Beauty	537,000	2.3
Needlecraft	507,000	2.1
Any women's monthly	12,331,000	52.0
	Bi-Monthly	
Weight Watchers	1,092,000	4.6
Hair	939,000	4.0
R Conley Diet/Fitness Magazine	569,000	2.4
	Quarterly	
The M&S Magazine	3,332,000	14.0
Good Idea!	772,000	3.3

Source: National Readership Survey – Top Line

drawing-up of a binding document in 1213. John was forced to accept this at Runnymede (now in Surrey) on 15 June 1215.

Magna Carta begins by reaffirming the rights of the church. Certain clauses guard against infringements of feudal custom: for example, the king was prevented from making excessive demands for money from his barons without their consent. Others are designed to check extortions by officials or maladministration of justice: for example, no freeman to be arrested, imprisoned, or punished except by the judgement of his peers or the law of the land. The privileges of London and the cities were also guaranteed.

As feudalism declined, Magna Carta lost its significance, and under the Tudors was almost forgotten. During the 17th century it was rediscovered and reinterpreted by the Parliamentary party as a democratic document. Four original copies exist, one each in Salisbury and Lincoln cathedrals and two in the British Library.

Magnox

Early type of nuclear reactor used in the UK, for example in Calder Hall, the world's first commercial nuclear power station. This type of reactor uses uranium fuel encased in tubes of magnesium alloy called Magnox. Carbon dioxide gas is used as a coolant to extract heat from the reactor core.

In 1998 there were six nuclear power stations run by Magnox Electric plc, which had decommissioned three.

Maguire Seven

Seven Irish victims of a miscarriage of justice. In 1976 Annie Maguire, five members of her family, and a family friend were imprisoned in London for possessing explosives. All seven of the convictions were overturned in June 1991.

Maiden Castle

Prehistoric hillfort with later additional earthworks 3 km/1.8 mi southwest of Dorchester in Dorset, England. The site was occupied from 4000 BC, although the first identifiable settlement is late Neolithic (New Stone Age, about 2000 BC). The fort was stormed by the Romans in AD 43. The site was systematically excavated 1934–37 by the English archaeologist Mortimer Wheeler.

History of occupation

The first identifiable settlement existed in the late Neolithic period, with earthen banks and ditches built on top of a long series of remains demonstrating occupation from 4000 BC. After its desertion, a great Neolithic earthwork, over 150 m/490 ft long, was constructed across the ridge. There is evidence of further occupation by late Neolithic cultures and ◊Beaker people of the early Bronze Age, but it was not until about 350 BC, in the early Iron Age, that the hillfort was extensively developed. Initially an enclosure was built at the east end to encompass a small settlement. During the Iron Age the settlement area extended west, and the east and west entrances to the hillfort were given additional protection in the form of projecting earthworks. The most impressive phase of the site was in the 2nd century BC, with circular houses in rows and extensive areas given over to grain silos, suggesting a large population. By the time of the Roman occupation, the eastern entrance had one of the largest and richest cemeteries in southern England, including those who had met a violent death. The ramparts were about 18 m/60 ft high.

Maidenhead

Town in southern England, on the River Thames, 40 km/25 mi west of London; it became part of ◊Windsor and Maidenhead unitary authority in April 1998; population (1991) 59,600. Industries include electronics, printing, and the production of computer software, pharmaceuticals, board, and paper. It is a major centre for the telecommunications industry. The leisure industry is more limited than in nearby Windsor, but the river is a focus for some tourism.

Two bridges cross the River Thames at Maidenhead, a seven-arched road bridge completed in 1777, and a railway bridge (1838), designed by Isambard Kingdom Brunel. The town is bounded on the west by **Maidenhead Thicket**, once part of Windsor Forest and now preserved by the National Trust.

maid of honour

The closest attendant on a queen. They are chosen generally from the daughters and granddaughters of peers, but in the absence of another title bear that of Honourable.

The appointment dates from the Plantagenet kings and included a mistress of the robes (almost invariably a duchess) and ladies-in-waiting (officially styled 'ladies and women of the bedchamber').

Maidstone

Town and administrative headquarters of ◊Kent, southeast England, on the River Medway; population (1991) 90,900. Industries include the manufacture of agricultural machinery, and paper and card for packaging.

Features

There are a number of medieval buildings, among them the parish church of All Saints', the late 14th-century Archbishop's Palace (a former residence of the archbishops of Canterbury), and the College of Priests (1395–98) built of Kentish ragstone from quarries to the west of the town. The Elizabethan Chillington Manor is an art gallery and museum. A range of 18th-century buildings include Sir John Banks' Almshouses (1700), a Unitarian church, and the Town Hall (1762–63). The Palace stables and tithe barn house the Tyrwhitt-Drake Carriage Museum, containing a collection of 17th–19th-century carriages.

History

Wat Tyler, leader of the Peasants' Revolt (1381), came from Maidstone. The town appointed its first mayor in 1549. When the town supported Sir Thomas Wyatt's Protestant uprising in 1554, its Charter of Incorporation was withdrawn, and was not granted again until 15 years later, when the town was made into a borough by Elizabeth I. The town supported the royalist cause during the Civil War. The essayist William Hazlitt was born here in 1778.

Mainland

Largest of the ◊Orkney Islands, situated about 30 km/19 mi off the north coast of Scotland, population (1991) 15,100. Extending over an area of 380 sq km/146 sq mi, it is divided from the southern islands of Hoy, Flotta, and South Ronaldsay by ◊Scapa Flow. Agriculture, trout-fishing, and sea-fishing are the principal occupations. The main harbour towns are ◊Kirkwall, the island capital, and Stromness.

The terrain is hilly, with extensive lowland tracts and lochs, and the climate windy but relatively frost-free (unlike the western Highlands, Mainland benefits from the warm North Atlantic Drift ocean current, which keeps frost to a minimum).

Evidence of prehistoric settlement includes the Neolithic (Stone Age) village of ◊Skara Brae on the Bay of Skaill, 13 km/8 mi from Stromness, and the megalithic monuments of the Ring of Brodgar, Stenness Standing Stones, and Maes Howe burial chamber. This last contains a wealth of later Viking runic inscriptions.

Occasionally the island is referred to as Pomona, arising from the misreading of a Latin text by the 16th-century Scottish humanist George Buchanan.

Major, John (1943–)

British Conservative politician, prime minister 1990–97.

He was foreign secretary in 1989 and chancellor of the Exchequer 1989–90. As chancellor he led Britain into the European Exchange Rate Mechanism (ERM) in October 1990. The following month he became prime minister on winning the Conservative Party leadership election in a contest with Michael Heseltine and Douglas Hurd, after the resignation of Margaret Thatcher.

His initial positive approach to European Community matters was hindered from 1991 by divisions within the Conservative Party. Despite continuing public dissatisfaction with the poll tax, the National Health Service, and the recession, Major was returned to power in the April 1992 general election. Although victorious, he subsequently faced mounting public dissatisfaction over a range of issues, including the sudden withdrawal of the pound from the ERM, a drastic pit-closure programme, and past sales of arms to Iraq. In addition, Major had to deal with 'Eurosceptics' within his own party who fiercely opposed any moves which they saw as ceding national sovereignty to Brussels. His subsequent handling of a series of domestic crises called into question his ability to govern the country effectively, but he won backing for his launch of a joint UK-Irish peace initiative on Northern Ireland in 1993, which led to a general cease-fire in 1994. His success in Northern Ireland did much to improve his standing, but delays in progressing peace talks resulted in criticism of his cautious approach. On the domestic front, local and European election defeats and continuing divisions within the Conservative Party led to his dramatic and unexpected resignation of the party leadership in June 1995 in a desperate bid for party unity. He was narrowly re-elected to the post the following month.

Criticized for weak leadership of his divided party, he resigned as leader of the Conservative Party after a crushing defeat in the 1997 general election. He has remained a back-bench MP.

Malcolm

Four Celtic kings of Scotland:

Malcolm I (943–954)

King of Scotland, who succeeded his father Donald II.

Malcolm II (*c.* 954–1034)

King of Scotland from 1005. The son of Kenneth II, he was succeeded by his grandson ◊Duncan I.

Malcolm III, called Canmore (*c.* 1031–1093)

King of Scotland from 1058, the son of Duncan I. He fled to England in 1040 when the throne was usurped by ◊Macbeth, but recovered southern Scotland and killed Macbeth in battle in 1057. In 1070 he married Margaret (*c.* 1045–1093), sister of Edgar Atheling of England; their daughter Matilda (d. 1118)

MAJOR, JOHN *British prime minister John Major, who succeeded Margaret Thatcher in 1990, was re-elected in 1992, and resigned as leader of the Conservative Party after Labour swept to power in the 1997 general election. Features of his premiership include Britain's participation in the Gulf War, a greater commitment to the European Union, replacement of the poll tax with the council tax, worsening unemployment and recession, and the highly criticized management policy of the National Health Service and the coal industry. United Nations*

married Henry I of England. Malcolm was killed at Alnwick while invading Northumberland, England.

Malcolm IV the Maiden (1141–1165)

King of Scotland from 1153. The son of Henry, eldest son of ◊David I, he was succeeded by his brother William the Lion.

Maldon

English market town in Essex, at the mouth of the River Chelmer. It was the scene of a battle commemorated in a 325-line fragment of an Anglo-Saxon poem *The Battle of Maldon*, describing the defeat and death of Ealdorman Byrhtnoth by the Vikings in 991.

Malham

Village in North Yorkshire, England, 10 km/6 mi east of Settle on the River Aire. The Craven Fault, a displacement of limestone, forms two amphitheatres of rock, Malham Cove and Gordale Scar, 2 km/1 mi from the village. The cliffs of **Malham Cove** are nearly 100 m/328 ft high; the River Aire rises at their foot. **Malham Tarn**, north of the cove, is an upland lake.

Malinowski, Bronislaw Kasper (1884–1942)

Polish-born British anthropologist. Malinowski was one of the principal founders of the theory of functionalism in the social sciences. During expeditions to the Trobriand Islands, Papua New Guinea, in 1914–16 and 1917–18 his detailed studies of the islanders led him to see customs and practices in terms of their function in creating and maintaining social order.

His fieldwork involved a revolutionary system of 'participant observation' whereby the researcher became completely involved in the life of the people he studied. He was reader in social anthropology 1924–27 and professor from 1927 at the University of London, and was visiting professor at Yale, USA, from 1938.

Mallaig

Fishing port on the west coast of Highland unitary authority, Scotland, 50 km/31 mi northwest of Fort William; population (1991) 900. Winter herring and prawns are the major catches. The town, lying at the end of the 'Road to the Isles', is the terminus of the West Highland railway.

A car ferry crosses the Sound of Sleat from here to Armadale on the Isle of Skye. Loch Morar, Scotland's deepest loch, lies southeast of Mallaig.

The local heritage centre houses exhibitions focusing on the history and culture of the West Highlands of Scotland.

Mall, The

Road in London extending from the Victoria Memorial in front of Buckingham Palace to Admiralty Arch. The Mall in its present form was designed by Aston Webb 1903–04. It is London's main processional route, being the first stage of the monarch's journey to the Houses of Parliament, Westminster Abbey, or Horse Guards Parade.

The Mall was first laid out as a fashionable avenue in the 1660s.

Malmesbury

Ancient hill-top market town in Wiltshire, southwest England, on the River Avon, 30 km/19 mi northwest of Bath; population (1991) 4,700. Tourism is a key source of income; there is also a vacuum-cleaner factory. The 12th-century church was built on the site of a Saxon abbey church, founded in the 7th century; it was the burial place of Athelstan, grandson of Alfred the Great and king of the Mercians and West Saxons in the 10th century.

The church's elaborate 12th-century south porch includes some of the finest Romanesque sculpture in Britain, depicting scenes from the Bible. The interior has stained glass by William Morris and Edward Burne-Jones. The town's market cross dates from around 1490.

Malmesbury's charter of 924 granted by Edward the Elder is one of the oldest in England. St Aldhelm was abbot from 673, and the historian William of Malmesbury (1095–1143) was a monk of the abbey. The philosopher Thomas Hobbes was born at nearby Westport. Nancy Hanks, mother of Abraham Lincoln, was born in Malmesbury.

Malory, Thomas (*c.* 1410–1471)

English author. He is known for the prose romance ◊*Le Morte D'Arthur* written in about 1470, printed in 1485. It is the fullest version of the legends of King ◊Arthur, the knights of the Round Table and the quest for the ◊Holy Grail, and it is a notable contribution to English prose.

Malory's identity is uncertain. He is thought to have been the Warwickshire landowner of that name who was member of Parliament for Warwick in 1445 and was subsequently charged with rape, theft, and attempted murder. If that is so, he must have compiled *Le Morte D'Arthur* during his 20 years in and out of prison. He became a knight of the shire in 1445.

Malvern

English spa town in Worcester, on the east side of the **Malvern Hills**, which extend for about 16 km/10 mi and have their high point in Worcester Beacon 425 m/1,395 ft; population (1991) 31,500. The **Malvern Festival** 1929–39, associated with the playwright G B Shaw and the composer Edward Elgar, was revived in 1977. Elgar lived and was buried here.

Malvern College (1863) and the Royal Radar Establishment are here.

Manchester

Metropolitan district of Greater Manchester, and city in northwest England, on the River Irwell, 50 km/31 mi east of Liverpool; population (1991) 402,900. A financial and manufacturing centre, its industries include banking and insurance; the production of cotton and man-made textiles, petrochemicals, rubber, paper, machine tools, and processed foods; and heavy, light, and electrical engineering, also printing. It is linked to the River Mersey and the Irish Sea by the **Manchester Ship Canal**, opened in 1894. Only one dock is now open.

Features

Manchester is the home of the Hallé Orchestra, the Royal

Northern College of Music, Chetham's School of Music, and Bridgewater Hall; Manchester Grammar School (1515), and four universities (the University of Manchester, UMIST, Manchester Metropolitan University, and the University of Salford); Manchester United Football Club and Manchester Arena (the largest indoor arena in Europe); the Royal Exchange (built in 1869, now a theatre); the Town Hall (1877) designed by Alfred ◊Waterhouse, and the Free Trade Hall (1856); Liverpool Road station (the world's oldest surviving passenger station); the Whitworth Art Gallery, the Cotton Exchange (now a leisure centre), the Central Library designed by Frank Lloyd Wright (1934, the world's largest municipal library), and the John Rylands Library (1900). The Castlefield Urban Heritage Park includes the Granada television studios, including the set of the soap opera *Coronation Street*, open to visitors, and also the Museum of Science and Industry.

History

Originally a Roman camp (**Mancunium** or **Mamucium**), Manchester is mentioned in the Domesday Book, and by the 13th century was already a centre for the wool trade. Its damp climate and many waterways made it ideal for the production of cotton, introduced in the 16th century, and from the mid-18th century onwards the Manchester area was a world centre of manufacture, using cotton imported from North America and India. Unrest after the Napoleonic Wars led to the ◊Peterloo Massacre in 1819 when troops charged a political meeting at St Peter's Fields. In the 19th century Manchester was the centre for a school of political economists, including John Bright and Richard Cobden, who campaigned for the repeal of the Corn Laws in the first half of the century. Manchester was also the original home of the *Guardian* newspaper (founded as the *Manchester Guardian* in 1821).

After 1945 there was a sharp decline in the cotton industry, and many disused mills have been refurbished to provide alternative industrial uses. The pop music scene flourished in the 1960s and 1980s. Metrolink, a light rail system, was opened in 1992. The Commonwealth Games are to be held in Manchester in 2002. New sports facilities include the National Cycling Centre.

Rivers, roads, and the early growth of the city

The Roman settlement was on an area of dry sandstone, at the southern end of Deansgate, a main thoroughfare of the city thought to be on the line of a Roman road. The Saxon town developed on a similar patch of dry ground at the northern end of Deansgate, where the cathedral now stands. Nearby there is an easy crossing place on the River Irwell to Salford, which has never been absorbed into Manchester. The city stands in the centre of a basin flanked on the north by the

MANCHESTER *In an attempt to solve the problem of inner-city traffic congestion, Manchester inaugurated the Metrolink in 1992. This integrated urban transit system reintroduced the tram as a viable means of public transport. Here, a tram arrives in St Peter's Square in the heart of the city.* *Liz Stares/Collections*

Rossendale upland, and on the east by the Pennines; lowlands lie to the south and west. The basin contains numerous rivers: the Irwell, Mersey, Irk, Medlock, and Tib flow through the modern city, though the last two of these are now mainly underground. Rivers contributed to the city's industrial growth, supplying water for the textile industry, but were not part of the commercial network, as many of the valleys are narrow. The ports at Chester and Liverpool, were accessed by road and canal; the roads were sited above the river valleys and crossed them with fords and bridges at suitable places.

Canals

The Mersey–Irwell Canal was established under an Act of Parliament of 1720 to give better communications between Liverpool and Manchester. Previously, goods had been brought to Warrington by water and then by road. In 1763 the Bridgewater Canal was opened from Worsley to Manchester, carrying coal from the Duke's collieries to the city at half the previous cost. The extension westwards of the Bridgewater Canal in 1766 to Runcorn gave a further reduction in transport costs, and also a passenger service twice daily. In the last years of the 18th century, canals were built to Bolton, Rochdale, Todmorden (connecting at Sowerby Bridge with the Calder Canal), Huddersfield, and Oldham. The Manchester Ship Canal connects the city with the Mersey estuary, and it has been a significant port, despite its location 55 km/34 mi from the sea. Though the canals through central Manchester are now hidden by massive buildings or even partially filled in, maps of the early 19th century show that they dominated much of the central area and were surrounded by numerous factories, warehouses, timber yards, and other industrial areas.

Development of the railways

Manchester attracted railways as readily as canals. In 1830 the Liverpool and Manchester line was built to a terminus in Liverpool Road which is still in use. In 1838 a line was opened to Bolton, and in 1839 the Manchester and Leeds railway was built from a station in Oldham Road, completed in 1841. The London link was made in 1842 by the Manchester and Birmingham railway through Stockport and Crewe, and in 1845 the Sheffield and Lincolnshire railway was opened. Many companies were involved and one result of this free enterprise was that, as early as 1842, Manchester had four terminal stations, one each for Liverpool, Bolton, Leeds, and London. However, in 1844 Exchange Station (now closed) was built, and connected in 1845 by a long platform to its larger neighbour, Victoria Station. Central station (now also closed) was begun in 1867 and London Road, now known as Piccadilly station, developed from the Store Street station of 1842. Manchester's canal and railway links contributed to its rapid growth.

19th-century development

In 1801 Manchester's population, with Salford, was 84,000, more than Liverpool (78,000) or Birmingham (74,000), and by 1851 its population was 303,382. Its growth, however, was not in isolation from the area that eventually (in 1951) was defined as the conurbation, which had 322,000 inhabitants in 1801, and 1,063,000 in 1851. Significantly, more than one tenth of Manchester's population in 1851 (30,304) had been born in Ireland: its was a time of immigration on a large scale.

In the middle of the 19th century, central Manchester was very congested. The old nucleus around its parish church, which became a cathedral when the diocese was formed in 1847, had several streets with Tudor buildings, almost all of which were destroyed by bombing in 1940. The cathedral itself dates from the 15th century. Little remains of 18th-century Manchester, though there is the church of St Ann, and also St John Street with two fairly complete Georgian terraces. Many more town houses of the same period were demolished. Behind the main streets of the early Victorian town, and over shops or other premises, there was a warren of residential premises, but as the various public buildings, factories, railway extensions, warehouses, and new roads were added, so houses were bought up and demolished, and replaced by others more distant from the centre. Quarters that had previously been solely residential became more congested as a result, and this process continued, though with improving standards of housing, into the early 20th century.

Meanwhile the more affluent citizens looked for homes further away from the working-class areas. They settled in suburbs such as Withington, Fallowfield, and Didsbury to the south (the least industrial side of Manchester), and in places as much as 16 km/19 mi from the city centre, particularly places beside the railway line to Altrincham (opened in 1849). The city of Manchester became part of a conurbation of which the population by 1901 was 2,150,000. Notable 19th-century buildings are the town hall by Alfred Waterhouse (completed in 1877), with a spire 87 m/285 ft high; the earlier Free Trade Hall (a building in Renaissance style); and the solid block of the Young Men's Christian Association (built in 1909); not far away is the massive Midland Hotel of 1898.

20th-century development

Reconstruction and rebuilding in Manchester began in earnest after World War I. That much of its housing was obsolete was well known, though the endless streets of sub-standard homes did not finally disappear until the 1960s. The first signs of improvement in the standard of amenities available to lower socio-economic groups came in the building of housing estates on the fringes of built-up areas. In 1931, 23 sq km/9 sq mi of Cheshire were incorporated into the city, and the building of Wythenshawe began. Considerable areas were allocated to industry. In 1931 the population was 766,311, but it had declined to 661,791 by 1961. The decrease of almost a quarter of a million meant that the old congestion was alleviated, despite the social disadvantages of the new tower blocks of the 1950s and the flats of the 1960s that replaced the former narrow streets with their small houses. Manchester's water supply is piped from Thirlmere and Haweswater in the Lake District. Manchester International airport is the largest municipally-owned airport in the country.

In the central area are a number of massive buildings, including the Cooperative building, with towers of 25 and 14 storeys beside a one-storey conference hall. There is also the Piccadilly Plaza with shops, offices, and a hotel, and several other high-rise offices. The city centre was devastated in June

1996 when an IRA bomb exploded in the Arndale Shopping Centre. An international competition was held to select a designer for a new city centre, which is to be rebuilt at a cost of about £1 billion. The winning design, announced in November 1996, includes a Millennium centre, a Millennium quarter around the cathedral, a winter garden, and shops and flats.

Pollution

An Irish study 1993–95 found Manchester to be the European city worst affected by acid rain, with building stones being dissolved faster than elsewhere (other cities in the study included Athens, Copenhagen, Amsterdam, Padua, and Donegal). During the study period Manchester's rainfall was amongst the lowest recorded, but the rain falling was the most acid.

Manchester, Greater

Metropolitan county of northwest England, created 1974; in 1986, most of the functions of the former county council were transferred to metropolitan district councils

Area 1,290 sq km/498 sq mi

Towns and cities Manchester, Bolton, Oldham, Rochdale, Salford, Stockport, and Wigan

Features Manchester Ship Canal links it with the River Mersey and the sea; Old Trafford cricket ground at Stretford, and the football ground of Manchester United; a second terminal opened at Manchester Airport 1993

Industries engineering, textiles, textile machinery, chemicals, plastics, electrical goods, electronic equipment, paper, printing, rubber, and asbestos

Population (1991) 2,499,400

Famous people John Dalton, James Joule, Emmeline Pankhurst, Gracie Fields, Anthony Burgess.

Manchester Ship Canal

Waterway which links the city of Manchester with the River Mersey and the sea; length 57 km/35.5 mi, width 14–24 m/45–80 ft, depth 9 m/28.3 ft. It has five locks. The canal was opened in 1894, linking Manchester to Eastham in Merseyside.

The canal transformed Lancashire's economy by making Manchester accessible to ocean-going craft. In particular, it led to the development of the cotton industry as raw cotton was transported east along the canal to Manchester and the finished textile products were shipped west to the Merseyside ports. Although the area has suffered industrial decline, the canal is still in effect the 'port of Manchester', handling approximately 16 million tons per year.

Mandelson, Peter (Benjamin) (1953–)

British Labour politician, minister without portfolio 1997–98, appointed secretary of state for Trade and Industry in 1998; he resigned his post at the end of that year after a loan from the paymaster-general was disclosed. He entered the House of Commons in 1992, representing Hartlepool. Before that he had been an influential backroom figure within the Labour Party as Director of Campaigns and Communications 1985–90. His organizational talents were demonstrated in Labour's victory campaign in the 1997 general election. As minister without portfolio he worked closely on the Millennium Dome project at Greenwich.

Manic Street Preachers

Welsh rock band, whose songs combine emotional intensity with intelligent lyrics, often touching on political and philosophical issues. The original members are singer and guitarist James Dean Bradfield (1969–), guitarist and lyricist Richey James (1968–), bassist Nicky Wire (1969–), and drummer Sean Moore (1968–). Their 1996 album *Everything Must Go* was received with great critical acclaim, winning the band two 1997 Brit awards. Its success was marred, however, by the fact that it was recorded without Richey James, who disappeared in February 1996.

Albums include *Generation Terrorists* (1992), *Gold Against the Soul* (1993), and *The Holy Bible* (1994).

Man, Isle of Gaelic Ellan Vannin

Island in the Irish Sea, a dependency of the British crown, but not part of the UK

Area 570 sq km/220 sq mi

Capital Douglas

Towns and cities Ramsey, Peel, Castletown

Features Snaefell 620 m/2,035 ft; annual TT (Tourist Trophy) motorcycle races; gambling casinos, tax haven; tailless Manx cat

Industries light engineering products; agriculture, fishing, tourism, banking, and insurance are important

Currency the island produces its own coins and notes in UK currency denominations

Population (1991) 69,800

Language English (Manx, nearer to Scottish than Irish Gaelic, has been almost extinct since the 1970s)

Government crown-appointed lieutenant-governor, a legislative council, and the representative House of Keys, which together make up the Court of Tynwald, passing laws subject to the royal assent. Laws passed at Westminster only affect the island if specifically so provided

History Norwegian until 1266, when the island was ceded to Scotland; it came under UK administration in 1765.

Manners

Family name of the dukes of Rutland; seated at Belvoir Castle, Lincolnshire, England.

Manning, Olivia Mary (1908–1980)

English novelist. Among her books are the semi-autobiographical series set during World War II. These include *The Great Fortune* (1960), *The Spoilt City* (1962), and *Friends and Heroes* (1965), forming the 'Balkan trilogy', and a later 'Levant trilogy'.

manor

Basic economic unit in ◊feudalism in Europe, established in England under the Norman conquest. It consisted of the lord's house and cultivated land, land rented by free tenants, land held by villagers, common land, woodland, and waste land.

Here and there traces of the system survive in England – the common land may have become an area for public recreation – but the documents sometimes sold at auction and entitling the owner to be called 'lord of the manor' seldom have any rights attached to them.

Manpower Services Commission

Former name of the ◊Training Agency, UK organization for retraining the unemployed.

Mansell, Nigel (1954–)

English motor-racing driver. He started his Formula One career with Lotus in 1980. Runner-up in the world championship on two occasions, he became world champion in 1992 and in the same year announced his retirement from Formula One racing, having won a British record of 30 Grand Prix races. He won the PPG Indycar series in the USA in 1993 before returning to Formula One racing in 1994.

Mansfield

Industrial town in Nottinghamshire, England, on the River Maun, 22 km/14 mi north of Nottingham; population (1991) 71,900. It is a retail centre for the area. The most important industries are brewing and light engineering, especially the production of car components, while minor industries include quarrying, moulding sand and sand lime bricks, and the manufacture of coal tar products.

Formerly a coal-mining area, Mansfield now has no active collieries. Shoemaking and textile production have also declined.

Sherwood Forest lies to the east.

Mansion House

Official residence of the Lord Mayor of London, opposite the Bank of England. It was built 1739–53 by George Dance the Elder on the site of the old Stocks Market.

Manson, Patrick (1844–1922)

Scottish physician who showed that insects are responsible for the spread of diseases like elephantiasis and malaria.

In 1876 Manson began studying filariasis infection in humans. Having gained a clear idea of the life history of the invading parasite, he correctly conjectured that the disease was transmitted by an insect, a common brown mosquito. He went on to study other parasitic infections; for instance, the fluke parasite, ringworms, and guinea worm. He developed the thesis that malaria was also spread by a mosquito in 1894; the work that proved this was carried out by Manson and British physician Ronald ◊Ross. He was made a KCMG in 1903.

manufacturing industry, or secondary industry

Industry that involves the processing of raw materials or the assembly of components. Examples are aluminium smelting, car assembly, and computer assembly. In the UK many traditional manufacturing industries, built up in the Industrial Revolution, are now declining in importance; for example, shipbuilding.

Manufacturing accounted for about 21% of gross domestic product (GDP) in 1996 and for 18% of employment. More than four-fifths of visible exports consisted of manufactured or semi-manufactured goods. Almost all manufacturing is carried out by private sector businesses. Overseas companies are responsible for one-third of the manufacturing investment in Britain, nearly one-fifth of manufacturing employment, a quarter of net output and two-fifths of exports.

The recession in the early 1990s led to a serious decline in manufacturing output, but it began to rise again in 1993 and by 1996 was well above the 1990 level. Employment in manufacturing in 1996 was 4.1 million. Total capital investment was £5,388 million.

The construction industry contributes around 5% of GDP and provides employment for some 800,000 people. Following a period of marked decline as recession affected the industry in the early 1990s, output has picked up slightly since 1993 while remaining some way below pre-recession levels. Total domestic fixed capital investment was £1,165 million in 1996, 42% higher than the figure for the previous year.

Manx Gaelic

◊Gaelic language of the Isle of Man.

Mappa Mundi

14th-century symbolic map of the world. It is circular and shows Asia at the top, with Europe and Africa below and Jerusalem at the centre (reflecting Christian religious rather than geographical belief). It was drawn by David de Bello, a canon at Hereford Cathedral, England, who left the map to the cathedral, where it was used as an altarpiece.

maps

See chronology on page 576 for some key dates in British mapping.

Mar, John Erskine, 11th Earl of (1672–1732)

Scottish noble and leader of the Jacobite rising of 1715. He raised an army of episcopalian and Catholic highlanders in support of James Edward Stuart, the Old Pretender, after being dismissed from office by George I. He was forced to retreat after an indecisive battle at Sherriffmuir and went into exile in France. He was known as 'Bobbing John' because of his changes of political allegiance.

Marble Arch

Triumphal arch in London in the style of the Arch of Constantine. It was designed by John ◊Nash and John Flaxman (1755–1826) in 1828 to commemorate Nelson's and Wellington's victories, and was originally intended as a ceremonial entry to ◊Buckingham Palace. In 1851, after the completion of Buckingham Palace, it was moved by Edward Blore to the northeast corner of Hyde Park at the end of Oxford Street.

Marcher Lords

Semi-independent nobles on the Welsh–English border, granted special privileges in return for protecting the border area. In William the Conqueror's reign, strong lords were

MAPPING: SOME KEY DATES

1314 The *Mappa Mundi/Map of the World* of Hereford Cathedral, England, is compiled. This is a famous symbolic map of the world showing Jerusalem at its centre, in accordance with the Bible.

1350 The 'Gough Map', an early map of England, is drawn by an unknown cartographer.

c. **1550** The first street map of London appears, engraved by Anthonius van den Wyngaerde.

1563 The Flemish cartographer Gerardus Mercator completes a map of the British Isles.

1579 The English cartographer Christopher Saxton publishes his *County Atlas of England and Wales*, the first detailed regional atlas.

1593 Royal Surveyor John Norden publishes *Speculum Britanniae/The Mirror of Britain*, a survey of England featuring panoramic maps of London and Westminster, among others.

1607 The English cartographer John Norden publishes *The Surveyors Dialogue*, a manual of surveying.

1610 The British historian and cartographer John Speed publishes a collection of 54 maps, the *Theatre of the Empire of Great Britain*.

1675 English map-maker John Ogilby produces *Britannia*, the first road map of Britain, showing rivers, bridges and towns.

1686 The English scientist Edmond Halley publishes a map of the world showing the directions of prevailing winds in different regions – the first meteorological chart.

1703 The Scottish surveyor and cartographer John Adair publishes *Description of the Sea Coasts and Islands of Scotland*.

1791 The Trigonometrical Survey (later named the Ordnance Survey) is established to produce maps of Great Britain.

1830 The first accurate maps produced by the Trigonometrical Survey appear; they are drawn to a scale of 1 inch to the mile (1:63,000).

1858 The Ordnance Survey adopts the scale of 1:2,500 for the mapping of Great Britain and Ireland.

1869 The English meteorologist Alexander Buchan produces the first weather maps to show the average monthly and annual air pressure for the world. They provide information about the atmosphere's circulation.

1989 The Ordnance Survey begins using a computerized system for creating and updating their maps.

placed in Chester, Shrewsbury, and Hereford to protect England from Celtic or Saxon incursions. They began to usurp power in their own right, making wars of their own, particularly in the valleys of South Wales, and claiming rights of conquest. After Edward I subjugated Wales, the Marcher Lords no longer played a vital role in the protection of the realm and Edward sought to restrict their independence. They increasingly lost influence during the 12th and 13th centuries but remained important in moments of crisis for the Crown, such as the Marshall Rebellion or the Wars of the Roses. By the end of the 15th century most of the lordships had come into the possession of the crown and the last independent lordship, Brecon, was taken by the crown in 1521. They were formally united with England in 1536.

Marches
Boundary areas of England with Wales, and England with Scotland. For several centuries from the time of William the Conqueror, these troubled frontier regions were held by lords of the Marches, those on the Welsh frontier called ◊Marcher Lords, sometimes called *marchiones*, and those on the Scottish border known as earls of March. The first Marcher Lord was Roger de Mortimer (about 1286–1330); the first earl of March, Patrick Dunbar (died in 1285).

Marconi Scandal
Scandal in 1912 in which chancellor Lloyd George and two other government ministers were found by a French newspaper to have dealt in shares of the US Marconi company shortly before it was announced that the Post Office had accepted the British Marconi company's bid to construct an imperial wireless chain.

A parliamentary select committee, biased towards the Liberal government's interests, found that the other four wireless systems were technically inadequate and therefore the decision to adopt Marconi's tender was not the result of ministerial corruption. The scandal did irreparable harm to Lloyd George's reputation.

Maree, Loch
Large lake in Wester Ross, Highland unitary authority, Scotland, extending over a length of 22 km/14 mi and widening to 3 km/2 mi. Its outflow is the River Ewe, which joins the sea-inlet of Loch Ewe. Studded with islands, and bordered by soaring mountain peaks, including Slioch (980 m/3,215 ft), it is considered to be one of Scotland's most beautiful lochs.

Margaret (1283–1290)
Queen of Scotland from 1285. Known as the **the Maid of Norway**, she was the daughter of Eric II, King of Norway, and Princess Margaret of Scotland. When only two years old she became queen of Scotland on the death of her grandfather, Alexander III, but died in the Orkneys on the voyage from Norway to her kingdom.

Her great-uncle Edward I of England arranged her marriage to his son Edward, later Edward II. Edward declared himself overlord of Scotland by virtue of the marriage treaty, and 20 years of civil war and foreign intervention followed.

Margaret, Rose (1930–)

Princess of the UK, younger daughter of George VI and sister of Elizabeth II. In 1960 she married Anthony Armstrong-Jones, later created Lord Snowdon, but they were divorced in 1978. Their children are **David, Viscount Linley** (1961–) and **Lady Sarah Chatto** (1964–).

Margaret of Anjou (1430–1482)

Queen of England from 1445, wife of ◊Henry VI of England. After the outbreak of the Wars of the ◊Roses 1455, she acted as the leader of the Lancastrians, but was defeated and captured at the battle of Tewkesbury 1471 by Edward IV.

Her one object had been to secure the succession of her son, Edward (born 1453), who was killed at Tewkesbury. After five years' imprisonment Margaret was allowed in 1476 to return to her native France, where she died in poverty.

Margaret, St (*c.* 1045–1093)

Queen of Scotland, the granddaughter of King Edmund Ironside of England. She went to Scotland after the Norman Conquest, and soon after married Malcolm III. The marriage of her daughter Matilda to Henry I united the Norman and English royal houses.

Through her influence, the Lowlands, until then purely Celtic, became largely anglicized. She was canonized in 1251 in recognition of her benefactions to the church.

Margate

Town and resort on the north coast of Kent, southeast England, on the Isle of ◊Thanet; population (1991) 38,500. A range of industries includes the manufacture of pharmaceuticals, generators, car components, sign machinery, and inks. It was one of the original ◊Cinque Ports, and developed in the late 18th century as one of the earliest coastal resorts in England.

Benjamin Beale, a Quaker from Margate, invented the bathing machine in the mid-18th century. There is a medieval church with a large collection of brasses. Other features include Dreamland, a large amusement park close to the pier.

Margolyes, Miriam (1941–)

English character actress, who has brought to life a string of comic and eccentric characters on film and British television. Her roles include that of the Spanish Infanta in the first series of the television show *Blackadder*, the matriarch Mrs Mingott in Martin Scorsese's adaptation of *The Age of Innocence* (1993), and the nurse in *William Shakespeare's Romeo + Juliet* (1996).

Her television work has included the miniseries *The History Man* (1981) and *Oliver Twist* (1985), and she featured in the filmic romance *Dreaming of Joseph Lees* (1998).

Market Harborough

Market town in south Leicestershire, England, 25 km/15 mi southeast of Leicester, in the rich grasslands of the River Welland; population (1991) 16,000. The town has light industry and manufactures corsetry, food products, rubber goods, and brushes. Its Gothic parish church has a fine spire, and stands next to the grammar school which was founded in 1614.

Markham, Beryl (1903–1986)

British aviator who made the first solo flight from east to west across the Atlantic in 1936.

Markievicz, Constance Georgina, Countess Markievicz born Gore-Booth (1868–1927)

Irish nationalist who married the Polish count Markievicz in 1900. Her death sentence for taking part in the Easter Rising of 1916 was commuted, and she was released from prison in 1917. She was elected to the Westminster Parliament as a Sinn Féin candidate in 1918 (technically the first British woman member of Parliament), but did not take her seat.

Markova, Alicia adopted name of Lilian Alicia Marks (1910–)

English ballet dancer. She danced with Diaghilev's company 1925–29, was the first resident ballerina of the Vic-Wells Ballet 1933–35, partnered Anton ◊Dolin in their own Markova–Dolin Ballet Company 1935–38, and danced with the Ballets Russes de Monte Carlo 1938–41, American Ballet Theater 1941–46, and the London Festival Ballet 1950–52. A dancer of delicacy and lightness, she is associated with the great classical ballets such as *Giselle*. She was made a DBE in 1963.

Marks & Spencer

Chain store. The company was founded in 1884 by **Michael Marks** (1863–1907). In 1894 he was joined by **Thomas Spencer** (1852–1905), cashier at one of his suppliers. The founder's son Simon Marks, from 1961 1st Baron Marks of Broughton, became chairman in 1916 and with his brother-in-law, Israel (later Lord) Sieff (1899–1972), developed the company from a 'Penny Bazaar' to a national and international chain store.

Michael Marks, a Russian Jewish refugee, first set up a stall in Leeds market place selling homewares under the slogan 'Don't ask the price, it's a penny'. By 1900 he and his partner were operating 24 stalls and 12 shops, mainly in the Midlands and north of England. The business was converted into a private company, Marks & Spencer Ltd, in 1903. The company went public in 1926 and the 'St Michael' trademark was registered in 1928. By 1939 the company owned 239 stores. The company's first stores outside the UK were opened in the 1970s. In 1998 there were 289 stores in the UK, 90 in Europe, 33 in the Far East, and 260 in North America.

Marlborough

Market town in Wiltshire, southwest England, on the River Kennet, 41 km/25 mi northeast of Salisbury; population (1991) 6,800. Local employment largely depends on the service sector, tourism, and Marlborough College (1843), a co-educational private school in the centre of the town.

Nearby are the ancient sites of Avebury, West Kennet, and Silbury Hill.

Marlborough has a broad High Street, with a Perpendicular church at each end, and lined with colonnaded Georgian shops. Former pupils of Marlborough College include William Morris, Siegfried Sassoon, John Betjeman, and William Golding.

Marlborough, John Churchill, 1st Duke of Marlborough (1650–1722)

English soldier, created a duke in 1702 by Queen Anne. He was granted the Blenheim mansion in Oxfordshire in recognition of his services, which included defeating the French army outside Vienna in the Battle of Blenheim in 1704, during the War of the Spanish Succession.

In 1688 he deserted his patron, James II, for William of Orange, but in 1692 fell into disfavour for Jacobite intrigue.

He had married Sarah Jennings (1660–1744), confidante of the future Queen Anne, who created him a duke on her accession. He achieved further victories in Belgium at the battles of Ramillies (1706) and Oudenaarde (1708), and in France at Malplaquet in 1709. However, the return of the Tories to power and his wife's quarrel with the queen led to his dismissal in 1711, and his flight to Holland to avoid charges of corruption. He returned in 1714.

Marlborough House

Mansion in Pall Mall, London, opposite St James's Palace. It was designed by Christopher ◊Wren for the 1st Duke of Marlborough in 1709–10 as his London home.

The house became crown property in 1817 and was used as a residence by Edward VII while Prince of Wales, Queen Alexandra, and Queen Mary. In 1959 the Queen gave the house as a Commonwealth centre for government conferences.

Marley, Bob (Robert Nesta) (1945–1981)

Jamaican reggae singer and songwriter. A Rastafarian, his songs, many of which were topical and political, popularized reggae worldwide in the 1970s. They include 'Get Up, Stand Up' (1973) and 'No Woman No Cry' (1974); his albums include *Natty Dread* (1975) and *Exodus* (1977).

Marlow, or Great Marlow

Town in Buckinghamshire, England, on the River Thames, 8 km/5 mi northwest of Maidenhead; population (1991) 16,400. The river is crossed here by an iron suspension bridge. There are extensive beech woods nearby.

Marlowe, Christopher (1564–1593)

English poet and dramatist. His work includes the blank-verse plays *Tamburlaine the Great* in two parts (1587–88), *The Jew of Malta* (about 1591), *Edward II* (about 1592), and *Dr Faustus* (about 1594); the poem 'Hero and Leander' (1598); and a translation of parts of Ovid's *Amores*. Marlowe transformed the new medium of English blank verse into a powerful, melodic form of expression.

He was born in Canterbury and educated at Cambridge University, where he is thought to have become a government agent. His life was turbulent, with a brief imprisonment in connection with a man's death in a brawl (of which he was cleared), and a charge of atheism (following statements by the dramatist Thomas Kyd under torture). He was murdered in a Deptford tavern, allegedly in a dispute over the bill, but it may have been a political killing.

Marlowe's work, considered as a whole, is remarkable for its varied, and even conflicting moods. Even within individual plays there are striking and often confusing contrasts: in *The Jew of Malta* Machiavellian heroism stands side by side with farcical melodrama, while in *Dr Faustus* comic slapstick is followed by the thrilling poetry of the hero's final speeches. There has been much critical controversy about Marlowe's true intentions and real merits as a dramatist, but modern audiences continue to be intrigued and provoked by his major plays, and there can be no doubt of his formative influence on his Elizabethan contemporaries, including Shakespeare.

marquess, or marquis

Title and rank of a nobleman who in the British peerage ranks below a duke and above an earl. The wife of a marquess is a marchioness.

The first English marquess was created in 1385, but the lords of the Scottish and Welsh ◊Marches were known as *marchiones* before this date.

The premier English marquess is the Marquess of Winchester (title created in 1551).

Married Women's Property Acts

Two acts passed in Britain, in 1870 and 1882, granting women basic rights in the division of property between husband and wife. Until 1870 common law decreed that a wife's property, including money and shares, passed to her husband. The first act allowed women to retain their earnings and the second act allowed women to retain the property they owned at the time of their marriage.

Marryat, Frederick (Captain) (1792–1848)

English naval officer and writer. He was the originator of the British sea story. His adventure stories, taken from personal experience, are full of life, humour, and stirring narrative; they include *Peter Simple* (1834) and *Mr Midshipman Easy* (1836). He also wrote children's books, including *The Children of the New Forest* (1847).

marshal

Title given in some countries to a high officer of state. Originally it meant one who tends horses, in particular one who shoes them.

The ◊Earl Marshal in England organizes state ceremonies; the office is hereditarily held by the duke of Norfolk. The corresponding officer in Scotland was the Earl Marischal.

Marston, John (1576–1634)

English satirist and dramatist. His early plays, the revenge tragedies *Antonio and Mellida* and *Antonio's Revenge* (1599), were followed by a number of satirical comedies distinguished by their harsh and often sombre qualities. The first of these was *What You Will* (1601); *The Malcontent* (1604) and *The Dutch Courtesan* (1605) were among the most notable.

Marston also collaborated with dramatists George Chapman and Ben ◊Jonson in *Eastward Hoe* (1605), which satirized the Scottish followers of James I, and for which the authors were imprisoned. His own satires include *The Metamorphosis of Pygmalion's Image* (1598) and *The Scourge of Villanie* (1598).

He was probably born in Coventry. Educated at Brasenose College, Oxford, he studied law at the Middle Temple. As early as 1601 he was satirized under the name of Demetrius in Jonson's *The Poetaster*. However, in 1604, Marston dedicated *The Malcontent* to Jonson, with expressions of affection and esteem, and a year later he was collaborating with Jonson. The two repeatedly quarrelled and became friends again.

Marston Moor, Battle of

Battle fought in the English Civil War on 2 July 1644 on Marston Moor, 11 km/7 mi west of York. The Royalists were conclusively defeated by the Parliamentarians and Scots.

The Royalist forces were commanded by Prince Rupert and the Duke of Newcastle; their opponents by Oliver Cromwell and Lord Leven. Lord Fairfax, on the right of the Parliamentarians, was routed, but Cromwell's cavalry charges were decisive.

Martello tower

Circular tower for coastal defence. Formerly much used in Europe, many were built along the English coast, especially in Sussex and Kent, in 1804, as a defence against the threatened French invasion. The name is derived from a tower on Cape Mortella, Corsica, which was captured by the British with great difficulty in 1794, and was taken as a model. They are round towers of solid masonry, sometimes moated, with a flat roof for mounted guns.

Martin, (John) Leslie (1908–)

English architect. He was co-editor (with Naum Gabo and Ben ◊Nicholson) of the review *Circle*, which helped to introduce the Modern Movement to England. With Peter Moro (1911–) and Robert Matthew (1905–75), he designed the Royal Festival Hall, London (1951). In 1991 he received a RIBA award for his series of buildings for the Gulbenkian Foundation, Lisbon (completed in 1984), which span a period of 30 years.

Martin was Professor of Architecture at Cambridge University from 1956 to 1972, during which period the department's Centre for Land Use and Built Form Studies exercised considerable influence over the development of architectural theory.

His books include *The Framework of Planning* (1967). He was knighted in 1957.

Martin, Archer John Porter (1910–)

English biochemist who received the 1952 Nobel Prize for Chemistry for work with Richard ◊Synge on paper chromatography in 1944.

Martin, James (1893–1981)

Northern Irish aeronautical engineer who designed and manufactured ejection seats. At the time of his death about 35,000 ejection seats were in service with the air forces and navies of 50 countries. Knighted 1965.

Martin, Kenneth (1905–1984)

English painter and sculptor. Strongly influenced by Constructivism, he turned to geometric abstraction in the late 1940s. From 1951 he began making mobiles, initially under the influence of Alexander Calder; his 'screw mobiles', elements arranged around a single rod, create an illusion of changing form as the work revolves. He often collaborated with his wife, the sculptor Mary Martin (1907–1969).

Public commissions include *Construction in Aluminium* (1967), located outside the engineering laboratory, Cambridge University.

Martineau, Harriet (1802–1876)

English journalist, economist, and novelist. She wrote popular works on economics; several novels, including *Deerbrook* (1839); children's stories, including *Feats on the Fiord* (1844); and articles in favour of the abolition of slavery. Her *Illustrations of Political Economy* (1832–34) consist of theoretical tracts roughly disguised as stories which reveal her passion for social reform. *Poor Laws and Paupers Illustrated* followed in 1833–34. Other works include *Society in America* (1837).

> *But at my back I always hear / Time's wingèd chariot hurrying near. / And yonder all before us lie / Deserts of vast eternity.*
>
> Andrew Marvell English poet and satirist.
> 'To His Coy Mistress'

Marvell, Andrew (1621–1678)

English metaphysical poet and satirist. In 'To His Coy Mistress' (1650–52) and 'An Horatian Ode upon Cromwell's Return from Ireland' (1650) he produced, respectively, the most searching seduction and political poems in the language. He was committed to the Parliamentary cause, and was Member of Parliament for Hull from 1659. He devoted his last years mainly to verse satire and prose works attacking repressive aspects of the state and government.

His reputation in his own day was as a champion of liberty and toleration, and as a polemicist. Today his reputation rests mainly on a small number of skilful and graceful but perplexing and intriguing poems, which were published posthumously as *Miscellaneous Poems* (1681). His prose works include *An Account of the Growth of Popery and Arbitrary Government* (1677), a scathing review of Charles II's reign.

Mary Queen of Scots (1542–1587)

Queen of Scotland 1542–67. Also known as **Mary Stuart**, she was the daughter of James V. Mary's connection with the English royal line from Henry VII made her a threat to Elizabeth I's hold on the English throne, especially as she

MARVELL, ANDREW *English metaphysical poet and satirist Andrew Marvell. He was unofficial poet laureate to Oliver Cromwell and took the post of Latin secretary to the Council of State on Milton's retirement. His 'Upon the Death of his Late Highness the Lord Protector' (1658) mourns the death of Cromwell. After the Restoration, Marvell continued to publish anonymously tracts that were anti-royalist or which attacked courtly corruption. Corbis*

represented a champion of the Catholic cause. She was married three times. After her forced abdication she was imprisoned but escaped in 1568 to England. Elizabeth I held her prisoner, while the Roman Catholics, who regarded Mary as rightful queen of England, formed many conspiracies to place her on the throne, and for complicity in one of these she was executed.

Mary's mother was the French Mary of Guise. Born in Linlithgow (now in Lothian region, Scotland), Mary was sent to France, where she married the dauphin, later Francis II. After his death she returned to Scotland in 1561, which, during her absence, had become Protestant. She married her cousin, the Earl of ◊Darnley, in 1565, but they soon quarrelled, and Darnley took part in the murder of Mary's secretary, ◊Rizzio. In 1567 Darnley was assassinated as the result of a conspiracy formed by the Earl of ◊Bothwell, possibly with Mary's connivance, and shortly after Bothwell married her. A rebellion followed; defeated at Carberry Hill, Mary abdicated and was imprisoned. She escaped in 1568, raised an army, and after its defeat at Langside fled to England, only to be imprisoned again. A plot against Elizabeth I devised by Anthony Babington led to her trial and execution at Fotheringay Castle in 1587.

Mary, Queen (1867–1953)

Consort of George V of Great Britain and Ireland. She was the only daughter of the Duke and Duchess of Teck, the latter a grand-daughter of George III. In 1891 she was engaged to marry Prince Albert Victor (born 1864), Duke of Clarence and eldest son of the Prince of Wales (later Edward VII), but he died in 1892, and in 1893 she married his brother George, Duke of York, who succeeded to the throne in 1910.

During World War I she was active in voluntary work for the war effort, and in 1917 visited military hospitals in France.

Mary

Two queens of England:

Mary I called Bloody Mary (1516–1558)

Queen of England from 1553. She was the eldest daughter of Henry VIII by Catherine of Aragón. When Edward VI died, Mary secured the crown without difficulty in spite of the conspiracy to substitute Lady Jane Grey. In 1554 Mary married Philip II of Spain, and as a devout Roman Catholic obtained the restoration of papal supremacy and sanctioned the persecution of Protestants. She was succeeded by her half-sister Elizabeth I.

Mary II (1662–1694)

Queen of England, Scotland, and Ireland from 1688. She was the Protestant elder daughter of the Catholic ◊James II, and in 1677 was married to her cousin ◊William of Orange. After the 1688 revolution she accepted the crown jointly with William.

During William's absences from England she took charge of the government, and showed courage and resource when invasion seemed possible in 1690 and 1692.

Mary of Guise, or Mary of Lorraine (1515–1560)

French-born second wife of James V of Scotland from 1538, and 1554–59 regent of Scotland for her daughter ◊Mary Queen of Scots. A Catholic, she moved from reconciliation with Scottish Protestants to repression, and died during a Protestant rebellion in Edinburgh.

Daughter of Claude, Duke of Guise, she was first married in 1534 to the Duke of Lorraine, who died in 1537. After James V died in 1542 she played a leading role in Scottish politics, seeking a close union with France, but she was unpopular, and was deposed as regent 1559.

Mary of Modena (1658–1718)

Queen consort of England and Scotland. Born Marie Beatrice d'Este, she was the daughter of the Duke of Modena, Italy, and second wife of James, Duke of York, later James II, whom she married in 1673. The birth of their son James Francis Edward Stuart was the signal for the revolution of 1688 that overthrew James II. Mary fled to France.

Mary Rose

English warship, built for Henry VIII of England, which sank off Southsea, Hampshire, on 19 July 1545, with the loss of most of the 700 on board. The wreck was located in 1971, and raised for preservation in dry dock in Portsmouth harbour (where it had originally been built) in 1982. Preserved in the accumulated silt were over 19,000 objects, including leather and silk items, a unique record of Tudor warfare and daily life. The cause of the disaster is not certain, but the lower gun ports were open after firing, and that, combined with overcrowding, may have caused the sinking.

Masefield, John (1878–1967)

English poet and novelist. His early years in the merchant navy inspired *Salt Water Ballads* (1902) and two further volumes of poetry, and several adventure novels; he also wrote children's books, such as *The Midnight Folk* (1927) and *The Box of Delights* (1935), and plays. *The Everlasting Mercy* (1911), characterized by its forcefully colloquial language, and *Reynard the Fox* (1919) are long verse narratives. He was poet laureate from 1930.

> *Dirty British coaster with a salt-caked smoke stack, / Butting through the Channel in the mad March days, / With a cargo of Tyne coal, / Road-rail, pig-lead, / Firewood, iron-ware, and cheap tin trays.*
>
> JOHN MASEFIELD English poet and novelist. 'Cargoes'

Maskelyne, Nevil (1732–1811)

English astronomer. He made observations to investigate the reliability of the lunar distance method for determining longitude at sea. In 1774 he estimated the mass of the Earth by noting the deflection of a plumb line near Mount Schiehallion in Perthshire, Scotland.

Maskelyne was appointed Astronomer Royal in 1765 and held that office until his death. He began publication in 1766 of the *Nautical Almanac*. This contained astronomical tables and navigational aids, and was probably his most enduring contribution to astronomy.

Mason, James (Neville) (1909–1984)

English film actor. He portrayed romantic villains in British films of the 1940s. After *Odd Man Out* (1947) he worked in the USA, often playing intelligent but troubled, vulnerable men, notably in *A Star Is Born* (1954). In 1960 he returned to Europe, where he made *Lolita* (1962).

Other films include *The Wicked Lady* (1946), *Five Fingers* (1952), *North by Northwest* (1959), *Georgy Girl* (1966), and *Cross of Iron* (1977). His final role was in *The Shooting Party* (1984).

masque

Spectacular court entertainment with a fantastic or mythological theme in which music, dance, and extravagant costumes and scenic design figured larger than plot. Originating in Italy, where members of the court actively participated in the performances, the masque reached its height of popularity at the English court between 1600 and 1640, with the collaboration of Ben Jonson as writer and Inigo Jones as stage designer. John Milton also wrote masque verses. Composers included Thomas Campion, John Coperario, Henry Lawes, William Byrd, and Henry Purcell.

The masque had great influence on the development of ballet and opera, and the elaborate frame in which it was performed developed into the proscenium arch.

Massey, Anna (1937–)

English character actress of the stage and screen. Massey broke into the film industry in the 1960s, featuring, in one of her best-known film roles, as the serial killer's inquisitive neighbour in director Michael Powell's controversial psychological study of insanity *Peeping Tom* (1960). Essentially a dramatic player, she also appeared in the equally disturbing *Bunny Lake is Missing* (1965) and *Frenzy* (1972). She has worked widely in television, including *Mansfield Park* (1983), *A Tale of Two Cities*, and *A Respectable Trade* (1998).

Massive Attack

English group formed in Bristol in 1987, pioneers of 'trip-hop' music which combines dub and jazz with electronic sampling. They had UK chart success with *Blue Lines* (1991) and with *Mezzanine* (1998).

Its members are 3-D, Robert Del Naja (1965–) vocals and programming, Daddy-G, Grant Marshall (1959–) vocals and programming, and Mushroom, Andrew Vowles (1967–) on keyboards and programming.

Master of the King's/Queen's Music(k)

Honorary appointment to the British royal household, the holder composing appropriate music for state occasions. The first was Nicholas Lanier, appointed by Charles I in 1626; later appointments have included Edward Elgar and Arthur Bliss. The present holder, Malcolm ◊Williamson, was appointed in 1975.

Master of the Rolls

English judge who is the president of the civil division of the Court of Appeal, besides being responsible for ◊Chancery records and for the admission of solicitors.

Matilda, the Empress Maud (1102–1167)

Claimant to the throne of England. On the death of her father, Henry I, in 1135, the barons elected her cousin Stephen to be king. Matilda invaded England in 1139, and was crowned by her supporters in 1141. Civil war ensued until Stephen was finally recognized as king in 1153, with Henry II (Matilda's son) as his successor.

Matilda was recognized during the reign of Henry I as his heir. She married first the Holy Roman emperor Henry V and, after his death, Geoffrey Plantagenet, Count of Anjou (1113–1151).

Matlock

Spa town and administrative headquarters of ◊Derbyshire, central England, on the River Derwent, 19 km/12 mi northwest of Derby; population (1996 est) 9,400. It manufactures textiles and high-tech products, and is a centre of tourism on the edge of the Peak District National Park.

Matlock is set in picturesque scenery among gritstone and limestone hills, and the Derwent Gorge extends to the south. The village of **Matlock Bath**, about a mile to the south, has caverns, petrifying wells, thermal water, and illuminations; it is dominated by the High Tor (205 m/673 ft) and the Heights of Abraham.

Nearby to the south is Bonsall, noted for its well-dressing ceremony and its ancient lead mines. Cromford to the south has imposing Black Rocks and in 1771 Richard Arkwright founded his water-powered cotton-spinning factory here.

Matthews, Colin (1946–)

English composer. He studied at Nottingham University and taught at Sussex University 1972–77. He worked with Deryck Cooke on the performing version of Mahler's tenth symphony and edited and issued several early works by Britten, whose assistant he was 1974–76. His output includes several *Sonatas* for orchestra; *Night's Mask* (1984), for soprano and chamber orchestra; and *through the glass* (1994), for ensemble.

He is the brother of the English composer David Matthews.

Matthews, Stanley (1915–)

English footballer who played for Stoke City, Blackpool, and England. He played nearly 700 Football League games, and won 54 international caps. He was the first Footballer of the Year in 1948 (again in 1963), the first European Footballer of the Year in 1956, and the first footballer to be knighted for services to the game in 1965.

An outstanding right-winger, he had the nickname 'the Wizard of the Dribble' because of his ball control. At the age of 38 he won an FA Cup Winners' medal when Blackpool beat Bolton Wanderers 4–3, Matthews laying on three goals in the last 20 minutes. He continued to play first-division football after the age of 50.

Matura, Mustapha (1939–)

Trinidad-born British dramatist. Cofounder of the Black Theatre Cooperative in 1978, his plays deal with problems of ethnic diversity and integration. These include *As Time Goes By* (1971), *Play Mas* (1974), and *Meetings* (1981). Other works include *Playboy of the West Indies* (1984) and *Trinidad Sisters* (1988), adaptations of plays by Synge and Chekhov respectively, and *The Coup* (1991).

Mauchline

Town in East Ayrshire unitary authority, Scotland, situated on the River Ayr, 12 km/7 mi southeast of Kilmarnock; population (1991) 3,900. Agricultural implements and granite curling stones are manufactured here.

The town and surrounding area are rich in connections with the poet Robert ◊Burns. Poosie Nancy's Inn, featured in his writings, still stands in Mauchline, and the poet lived nearby at Mossgiel Farm. A museum and a tower are dedicated to his memory.

Maudling, Reginald (1917–1979)

British Conservative politician, chancellor of the Exchequer 1962–64, contender for the party leadership in 1965, and home secretary 1970–72.

He resigned his office as home secretary when referred to during the bankruptcy proceedings of the architect John Poulson, since (as home secretary) he would have been in charge of the Metropolitan Police investigating the case. In July 1977 Maudling, together with two other MPs, was censured for conduct inconsistent with the standards of the House of Commons in a report of a select committee in relation to the Poulson affair, but the House subsequently overwhelmingly defeated a motion to suspend him. Maudling was the Conservative spokesman on foreign affairs from 1975 to 1976.

Maugham, (William) Somerset (1874–1965)

English writer. His work includes the novels *Of Human Bondage* (1915), *The Moon and Sixpence* (1919), and *Cakes and Ale* (1930); the short-story collections *Ashenden* (1928) and *Rain and Other Stories* (1933); and the plays *Lady Frederick* (1907) and *Our Betters* (1917). There were new editions of *Collected Stories* in 1900 and *Selected Plays* in 1991. A penetrating observer of human behaviour, his writing is essentially anti-romantic and there is a vein of cynicism running through his work.

Maw, Nicholas (1935–)

English composer. His music is largely traditional in character. He studied with Lennox Berkeley at the Royal Academy of Music 1955–58 and with Nadia Boulanger in Paris 1958–59. He has taught at Cambridge University 1966–70 and at Yale, and currently teaches in New York. Important works include *Scenes and Arias* (1962) and *Odyssey*, a massive orchestral work composed 1973–89.

Maxwell, (Ian) Robert born Jan Ludvik Hoch (1923–1991)

Czech-born British publishing and newspaper proprietor and politician, who became a British citizen in 1946. He founded Pergamon Press and owned several UK national newspapers. At the time of his death, in suspicious circumstances, the Maxwell domain carried debts of about $3.9 billion and it was revealed that he had been involved in faudulent practices for much of his career.

After serving in World War II, he came to Britain in 1940, and adopted the name Maxwell in 1945. He formed Pergamon Press in 1951. From 1964 to 1970 he was Labour member of Parliament for Buckingham. In 1980 he took over the British Printing Corporation on the point of financial collapse and turned it into the successful British Printing and Communications Corporation, which, in 1985, became the **Maxwell Communications Corporation**. In the UK the national newspapers owned by the **Maxwell Foundation** between 1984 and 1991 were the tabloids *Daily Mirror*, *Sunday Mirror*, and *People*; in 1990 the weekly *European* was launched.

In late 1991 Maxwell, last seen on his yacht off the Canary Islands, was found dead at sea. His sons Kevin and Ian were named as his successors. In 1991 the Serious Fraud Office started an investigation into pension-fund losses following reports of transfers of over £400 million from the Maxwell pension funds to the private Maxwell firms. Kevin and Ian

Maxwell were arrested, but in 1996 were cleared of all charges.

Maxwell, James Clerk (1831–1879)

Scottish physicist. His main achievement was in the understanding of electromagnetic waves: **Maxwell's equations** bring together electricity, magnetism, and light in one set of relations. He studied gases, optics, and the sensation of colour, and his theoretical work in magnetism prepared the way for wireless telegraphy and telephony.

In developing the kinetic theory of gases, Maxwell gave the final proof that heat resides in the motion of molecules.

Studying colour vision, Maxwell explained how all colours could be built up from mixtures of the primary colours red, green, and blue. Maxwell confirmed English physicist Thomas ◊Young's theory that the eye has three kinds of receptors sensitive to the primary colours, and showed that colour blindness is due to defects in the receptors. In 1861 he produced the first colour photograph to use a three-colour process.

Maxwell was born in Edinburgh and educated there and at Cambridge. He was professor of natural philosophy at Aberdeen 1856–60, and of natural philosophy and astronomy at London 1860–65. From 1871 he was professor of experimental physics at Cambridge, where he set up the Cavendish Laboratory in 1874.

Maxwell studied Saturn's rings 1856–59 and established that they must be composed of many small bodies in orbit.

Having explained all known effects of electromagnetism, Maxwell went on to infer that light consists of electromagnetic waves. He also established that light has a radiation pressure, and suggested that a whole family of electromagnetic radiations must exist, of which light was only one. (This was confirmed in 1888 with the discovery of radio waves.)

Maxwell's mathematical basis for the kinetic theory of gases dates from 1860, when he used a statistical treatment to arrive at a formula to express the distribution of velocity in gas molecules, and related it to temperature. In 1865 Maxwell and his wife carried out experiments to measure the viscosity of gases over a wide range of pressures and temperatures, and their findings led to new equations. Maxwell's kinetic theory still did not fully explain heat conduction, and it was modified by Austrian physicist Ludwig Boltzmann in 1868, resulting in the **Maxwell–Boltzmann distribution law**. Both men thereafter contributed to successive refinements of the kinetic theory and it proved fully applicable to all properties of gases.

Mayall, Rik (1958–)

Comic English screen actor and writer. He rose to fame in the early 1980s in a string of cult television programmes, including *Kevin Turvey Investigates* (1981), in which he gave a series of monologues as a Midlands simpleton; *The Comic Strip Presents* (1982), in which he teamed up with fellow rising British comic talents, most notably Adrian Edmondson (1957–), with whom he has collaborated throughout his career; and the student sitcom *The Young Ones* (1982). He demonstrated an alternative screen persona in the late-1980s in the form of the corrupt Conservative politician Alan B'Stard in *The New Statesman* (1988–93).

As Rick in *The Young Ones*, he created a loud, brash screen persona, indulging in both fast verbal delivery and physical slapstick, that has endured through much of his subsequent work, notably as one half of 'The Dangerous Brothers', a regular comic sketch performed with Edmondson on *Saturday Live* and *Friday Night Live* during the latter half of the 1980s; as Richard Rich of *Filthy, Rich and Catflap* (1987); and as Richie Richard in *Bottom* (1991–). His film credits include *Drop Dead Fred* (1991) and *Bring Me the Head of Mavis Davis* (1998). He also featured in the television miniseries *In the Red* (1998).

May Day

First day of May. Traditionally the first day of summer, in parts of England it is still celebrated as a pre-Christian magical rite; for example, the dance around the maypole (an ancient fertility symbol).

Mayfair

District of Westminster, London, vaguely defined as lying between Piccadilly and Oxford Street, and including Park Lane; formerly a fashionable residential district, but increasingly taken up by offices, hotels, and nightclubs.

Mayfair is bounded to the west by Hyde Park and to the south and east by St James's Park, two of London's largest green areas. Mayfair derives its name from a fair held here in May from Charles II's time until 1809; part of the site is now occupied by Shepherd Market, built in about 1735.

Mayflower

Ship in which the Pilgrims sailed in 1620 from Plymouth, England, to found Plymouth plantation and Plymouth colony in present-day Massachusetts.

The *Mayflower* was one of two ships scheduled for departure in 1620. The second ship, the *Speedwell*, was deemed unseaworthy, so 102 people were crowded into the 27-m/90-foot *Mayflower*, which was bound for Virginia. Tension between Pilgrim and non-Pilgrim passengers threatened to erupt into a mutiny. Blown off course, the ship reached Cape Cod, Massachusetts, in December. The **Mayflower Compact** was drafted to establish self-rule for the Plymouth colony and to protect the rights of all the settlers.

Mayhew, Patrick (Barnabas Burke) (1929–)

British Conservative politician and lawyer, Northern Ireland secretary 1992–97. He was appointed Solicitor General in 1983 and four years later Attorney General, becoming the government's chief legal adviser. His appointment as Northern Ireland secretary came at a propitious time and within two years he had witnessed the voluntary cessation of violence by both Republicans and Loyalists, but allegations of unnecessary delays in the peace process led to the resumption of IRA violence in February 1996.

Maynard Smith, John (1920–)

English geneticist and evolutionary biologist. He applied game theory to animal behaviour and developed the concept of the evolutionary stable strategy as a mathematical technique for studying the evolution of behaviour.

Maynard Smith was born in London and educated at Eton and Cambridge. He graduated as an aeronautical engineer in 1941 and received a degree in zoology from University College, London in 1951. He taught at University College, London 1951–65, and was appointed professor of biology at the University of Sussex in 1965.

His works include *Mathematical Ideas in Biology* (1968), *Models in Ecology* (1974), *Evolution of Sex* (1978) and *Evolution and the Theory of Games* (1983). His popular book *The Theory of Evolution* (1958), was widely influential.

mayor

Title of head of urban administration. In England, Wales, and Northern Ireland, the mayor is the principal officer of a district council that has been granted district-borough status under royal charter. In 1996 the Labour Party floated proposals for directly elected mayors in Britain, which it confirmed when it came into power in 1997. A referendum on establishing an elected mayor of London is scheduled for 1998.

Parish councils that adopt the style of town councils have a chair known as the town mayor. In Scotland the equivalent officer is known as a provost. In certain cases the chair of a city council may have the right to be called Lord Mayor.

maypole

Tall pole with long ribbon streamers attached to the top. It is used for traditional ◊May Day dances to celebrate the arrival of spring.

The maypole probably represents the sacred tree which formed the centrepiece of pagan spring festivals. In modern survivals of the ceremony two circles of dancers, all holding streamers, move in opposite directions, weaving the streamers into a pattern.

MBE

Abbreviation for **Member (of the Order) of the British Empire**, an honour first awarded in 1917.

Meade, Richard John Hannay (1938–)

English equestrian in three-day events who 1972 won gold medals at the Olympic Games for both the individual and team competitions four years after winning a team gold at the 1968 Games. He also helped the British team win the 1970 and 1982 world titles

Meccano

Toy metal construction sets launched in 1901 by the British inventor Frank Hornby (1863–1936) (also the creator of Hornby train sets and Dinky toys), which continued in production until 1979.

Meccano products are now collectors' items.

Medawar, Peter Brian (1915–1987)

Brazilian-born British immunologist who, with Macfarlane Burnet, discovered that the body's resistance to grafted tissue is undeveloped in the newborn child, and studied the way it is acquired. They shared a Nobel prize in 1960.

Medawar's work has been vital in understanding the phenomenon of tissue rejection following transplantation. Knighted 1965.

medicine

See ◊health care and ◊NHS.

Medway

River of southeast England; length about 96 km/60 mi. It rises in Sussex and flows through Kent and **Medway Towns** unitary authority, becoming an estuary at Rochester, before entering the Thames at Sheerness. In local tradition it divides the 'Men of Kent', who live to the east, from the 'Kentish Men', who live to the west. It is polluted by industrial waste.

Medway Towns

Unitary authority in southeast England, created in 1998 by combining the former city council of Rochester upon Medway with Gillingham borough council, both formerly in Kent

Area 194 sq km/75 sq mi

Towns and cities Rochester, Chatham, Gillingham, Strood (administrative headquarters)

Features River Medway flows through Rochester; River Thames forms northern border of authority; reclaimed estuarine mudflats form the Isle of Grain; Charles Dickens Centre (Rochester) is housed in a 16th-century mansion; Royal Naval Dockyard (Chatham); Royal Engineers Museum (Gillingham); Upnor Castle (16th century) at Upper Upnor

Industries oil refineries on Isle of Grain, heavy industry, engineering, maritime industries, Thamesport (privately-owned deep-water container port), avionics, financial services, information technology

Population (1995) 240,000

Mee, Margaret Ursula (1909–1988)

English botanical artist. In the 1950s she went to Brazil, where she accurately and comprehensively painted many plant species of the Amazon basin.

She is thought to have painted more species than any other botanical artist.

Melbourne, (Henry) William Lamb, 2nd Viscount Melbourne (1779–1848)

British Whig politician. Home secretary 1830–34, he was briefly prime minister in 1834 and again 1835–41. Accused in 1836 of seducing Caroline Norton, he lost the favour of William IV.

Melbourne was married 1805–25 to Lady Caroline Ponsonby (1785–1828), the novelist Lady Caroline Lamb. He was an adviser to the young Queen Victoria.

Melford Hall

House in Suffolk, England, 5 km/3 mi north of Sudbury. It was built in the second half of the 16th century, and incorporates the remains of the manor house of the abbots of

St Edmunds. It was given by the Treasury with some contents to the National Trust in 1960. A turreted brick Tudor mansion, it has changed little since it was built in 1578; the interior includes an original panelled banqueting hall.

Later additions include an 18th-century drawing-room, a regency library and a Victorian bedroom. The house has collections of English furniture and Chinese porcelain.

Mellanby, Edward (1884–1955)

English pharmacologist who discovered that rickets (disease characterized by the softening of the bones) is the result of a vitamin deficiency.

In 1918 Mellanby produced puppies with rickets by feeding them a diet which was deficient in a compound found in animal fats. While it had been commonly held until 1900 that rickets was a chronic infectious disease, others had proposed before Mellanby that it was caused by poor living conditions (lack of fresh air, sunlight, and exercise).

Mellanby demonstrated conclusively by his experiments that rickets was the result of a vitamin deficiency and could be cured with cod-liver oil. In 1919, Kurt Huldschinsky in Berlin, demonstrated that rickets could also be cured by artificial sunlight.

Melrose (Celtic **mao ros** 'bare moor')

Town in Scottish Borders, Scotland, 59 km/37 mi southeast of Edinburgh; population (1991) 2,300. Melrose is on the River Tweed at the foot of the Eildon Hills, a range of volcanic origin with three peaks, the highest of which is 450 m/1,476 ft. The heart of Robert I the Bruce is buried here. The ruins of **Melrose Abbey** (1136) are commemorated in verse by Sir Walter Scott.

The Cistercian abbey was founded by David I. It was partly destroyed by Edward II (1322) and Richard II (1385), and it was wrecked during Lord Hereford's expedition in 1545. It has elaborately carved stonework and fine traceried windows. It contains the tombs of Alexander II and the wizard Michael Scot (1175–1234), who is said to have caused the Eildon Hills to break into three.

Old Melrose, 4 km/2.5 mi to the east, is the site of a Columban monastery, established in about 640 by St Aidan. Triumontium, the site of a Roman camp, is 2 km/1 mi to the east at Newstead. About 5 km/3 mi west of Melrose is Abbotsford, home of Walter Scott.

Melton Mowbray

Market town in Leicestershire, central England, on the River Eye, 24 km/15 mi northeast of Leicester; population (1995 est) 24,800. A fox-hunting centre, it has a large cattle market, and is known for pork pies and Stilton cheese. There is pet-food processing and the production of packed sandwiches and other snacks. Ashfordby Colliery nearby closed in the 1990s, with pithead gear being removed in 1998.

Menai Bridge, Welsh **Porth Aethwy**

Small town on the Isle of Anglesey, northwest Wales, on the ◊Menai Strait; population (1991) 3,200. It is a suburb of Bangor, to which it is linked by the suspension bridge across the strait. Its English name is derived from the bridge, which was completed in 1825 to a design by Thomas Telford. The town is a centre for angling and fishing. An annual fair, held in October, dates from 1691.

The bridge was the world's first example of a large iron suspension bridge.

Menai Strait, Welsh **Afon Menai**

Channel of the Irish Sea dividing ◊Anglesey from the Welsh mainland; about 22 km/14 mi long and up to 3 km/2 mi wide. It is crossed by two bridges. Thomas Telford's suspension bridge (521 m1,710 ft long) was opened in 1826 but was reconstructed to the original design in 1940, and freed from tolls. Robert Stephenson's tubular rail bridge (420 m/1,378 ft long) was opened in 1850, and is known as the Britannia Bridge.

Men Behaving Badly

Television sitcom (1992–). It focuses on two flat-sharing thirty-somethings, their friendship, 'laddishness', and love of beer, television, toys, and women. The series, directed by Martin Dennis, originally featured Martin Clunes (Gary) and

MEN BEHAVING BADLY *This popular television sitcom, written by Simon Nye, took a wry look at the 'lad culture' of 1990s Britain. It showed the dissolute lifestyle of two London flatmates, and the vain attempts by their girlfriends to get them to act more responsibly. Pictured from left to right are the show's stars Neil Morrissey, Leslie Ash, Caroline Quentin, and Martin Clunes. Brendan O' Sullivan/Rex*

comedian Harry Enfield (Dermot). From the second season Clunes's flatmate was played by Neil Morrissey (Tony). Actresses Caroline Quentin (Dorothy) and Leslie Ash (Deborah) co-star as Gary's long-suffering girlfriend and the neighbour who becomes the object of Tony's affection respectively. A US version of the show premiered in 1996.

Mencap

Charity, founded in 1946, providing a range of services for people with learning disabilities.

Mendip Hills, or Mendips

Range of limestone hills in southern England, stretching nearly 40 km/25 mi southeast–northwest from Wells in Somerset towards the Bristol Channel. There are many cliffs, scars, and caverns, notably ◊Cheddar Gorge. The highest peak is Blackdown (326 m/1,068 ft).

The range includes Burrington Coombe, and Wookey Hole caves. The hills are mainly composed of carboniferous limestone, with old red sandstone.

Mensa International

Organization founded in the UK in 1945 with membership limited to those passing an 'intelligence' test. It has been criticized by many who believe that intelligence is not satisfactorily measured by IQ (intelligence quotient) tests alone. In recent years, Mensa has started to fund special schools and activities for high-IQ children in the UK.

Menuhin, Yehudi, Baron Menuhin (1916–)

US-born British violinist and conductor. His solo repertoire extends from Vivaldi to George Enescu. He recorded the Elgar *Violin Concerto* in 1932 with the composer conducting, and commissioned the *Sonata* for violin solo in 1944 from an ailing Bartók. He has appeared in concert with sitar virtuoso Ravi Shankar, and with jazz violinist Stephane Grappelli. In March 1997 he was awarded Germany's highest honour, the Great Order of Merit. He first played in Berlin in 1928, and was the first Jewish artist to play with the Berlin Philharmonic after World War II.

He made his debut with an orchestra at the age of 11 in New York. A child prodigy, he achieved great depth of interpretation, and was often accompanied on the piano by his sister **Hephzibah** (1921–1981). In 1959 he moved to London, becoming a British subject in 1985. He founded the **Yehudi Menuhin School of Music**, at Stoke d'Abernon, Surrey, in 1963.

Merbecke, or Marbeck, John (*c.* 1505–*c.* 1585)

English composer and writer. He compiled *The Booke of Common Praier Noted* (1550), the first musical setting of an Anglican prayer book. He was lay clerk and organist at St George's Chapel, Windsor from 1531. In 1543 he was arrested and in 1544 tried and condemned for heresy as a Calvinist, but he was pardoned and allowed to retain his office.

Mercer, David (1928–1980)

English dramatist. He first became known for his television plays, including *A Suitable Case for Treatment* (1962), filmed as *Morgan, A Suitable Case for Treatment* (1966); stage plays include *After Haggerty* (1970).

merchant banking

Type of ◊banking that specializes in corporate finance and financial and advisory services for business, particularly when companies merge, are taken over, or undergo major restructuring. Originally developed in the UK in the 19th century, merchant banks now offer many of the services provided by the commercial banks.

The oldest merchant bank in London is ◊Baring Brothers.

Merchant of Venice, The

Comedy by William ◊Shakespeare, first performed in 1596–97. Antonio, a rich merchant, borrows money from Shylock, a Jewish moneylender, promising a pound of flesh if the sum is not repaid; when Shylock presses his claim, the heroine, Portia, disguised as a lawyer, saves Antonio's life.

Merchants Adventurers

English trading company founded in 1407, which controlled the export of cloth to continental Europe. It comprised guilds and traders in many northern European ports. In direct opposition to the Hanseatic League, it came to control 75% of English overseas trade by 1550. In 1689 it lost its charter for furthering the traders' own interests at the expense of the English economy. The company was finally dissolved in 1806.

Mercia

Anglo-Saxon kingdom that emerged in the 6th century. By the late 8th century it dominated all England south of the Humber, but from about 825 came under the power of ◊Wessex. Mercia eventually came to denote an area bounded by the Welsh border, the River Humber, East Anglia, and the River Thames.

Meredith, George (1828–1909)

English novelist and poet. His realistic psychological novel *The Ordeal of Richard Feverel* (1859) engendered both scandal and critical praise. His best-known novel, *The Egoist* (1879), is superbly plotted and dissects the hero's self-centredness with merciless glee. The sonnet sequence *Modern Love* (1862) reflects the failure of his own marriage to the daughter of Thomas Love ◊Peacock. Other novels include *Evan Harrington* (1861), *Diana of the Crossways* (1885), and *The Amazing Marriage* (1895). His verse also includes *Poems and Lyrics of the Joy of Earth* (1883).

Although Meredith's writings have never been generally popular, his genius was immediately recognized by discerning critics. His style is characterized by great fastidiousness in the choice of words, phrases, and condensation of thought; few other writers have attempted to charge sentences, and even words, so heavily with meaning.

Merit, Order of

British order (see ◊knighthood, order of), instituted in 1902 and limited in number to 24 men and women of eminence. It confers no precedence or knighthood.

The ribbon is blue and red. There are both military or civil classes, the badge of the former having crossed swords and the latter oak leaves. Members place the letters OM after their names, following the first class of the Order of the Bath and preceding the letters designating membership of the inferior classes of the Bath and all classes of the remaining orders of knighthood. An Indian Order of Merit was instituted in 1837 for Indian officers and other ranks.

Mersey

River in northwest England; length 112 km/70 mi. Formed by the confluence of the Goyt and Tame rivers at Stockport, it flows west through the south of Manchester, is joined by the Irwell at Flixton and by the Weaver at Runcorn, and enters the Irish Sea at Liverpool Bay. It drains large areas of the Lancashire and Cheshire plains. The Mersey is linked to the Manchester Ship Canal. Although plans were announced in 1990 to build a 1,800-m/5,907-ft barrage across the Mersey estuary to generate electricity from tides, these were abandoned in 1992 for financial reasons.

The river lies entirely below 45 m/150 ft. It is artificially modified (as part of the Manchester Ship Canal) as far as Warrington, where it becomes tidal. The Mersey is polluted by industrial waste, sewage, and chemicals.

The Mersey became an artery of communications from the 18th century. Boats for passengers and goods used the river, with its major tributary the Irwell, between Liverpool and Manchester from 1720; the Bridgewater Canal acquired this traffic in the late 18th century. The Mersey had passenger services until the development of the railway in the middle of the 19th century. In the estuary (which has an area of over 78 sq km/30 sq mi), steam ferries provided transport for commuters from the residential areas of Cheshire to Liverpool from 1815. In 1934 the first road tunnel under the Mersey was opened. Until the 1920s the river formed the boundary between Lancashire and Cheshire.

Mersey beat

Pop music of the mid-1960s that originated in the northwest of England. It was also known as the Liverpool sound or ◊beat music in the UK. It was almost exclusively performed by all-male groups, the most popular being the Beatles.

Merseyside

Metropolitan county of northwest England, created in 1974; in 1986, most of the functions of the former county council were transferred to metropolitan borough councils (The Wirral, Sefton, Liverpool, Knowsley, St Helens)

Area 650 sq km/251 sq mi

Towns and cities Liverpool, Bootle, Birkenhead, St Helens, Wallasey, Southport

Physical River Mersey

Features Merseyside Innovation Centre (MIC), linked with Liverpool and John Moores Universities; Prescot Museum of clock- and watch-making; Speke Hall (Tudor), and Croxteth Hall and Country Park (a working country estate open to the public)

Industries brewing, chemicals, electrical goods, glassmaking, metal-working, pharmaceutical products, tanning, vehicles

Famous people George Stubbs, William Ewart Gladstone, the Beatles

History

St Helens has a long industrial past: glassmaking here dates back more than 200 years, and coal has been mined since the 16th century; in 1757 the Sankey Canal was constructed to carry coal to Liverpool, Warrington, and also Northwich for the then growing salt industry. The chemical and copper industries left large areas of derelict land in St Helens, which have now cleared. Knowsley originally grew up around Knowsley Hall, the home of the Stanley family (Earls of Derby) since 1835.

Merthyr Tydfil

Unitary authority in south Wales, created in 1996 from part of the former county of Mid Glamorgan

Area 111 sq km/43 sq mi

Towns ◊Merthyr Tydfil (administrative headquarters)

Features area includes part of ◊Brecon Beacons National Park

Industries light engineering, and the manufacture of electrical goods.

Population (1996) 60,000

The authority is based mainly around the upper valley of the River ◊Taff. It was formerly a centre of the Welsh coal and steel industries. The area has the largest land-reclamation scheme in Europe.

Merthyr Tydfil

Industrial town and administrative centre of ◊Merthyr Tydfil unitary authority in south Wales, situated 39 km/24 mi northwest of Cardiff on the River ◊Taff; population (1991) 39,500. Its industries include light engineering and the manufacture of electrical goods. It was formerly a centre of the Welsh coal and steel industries. It had the world's first steam railway in 1804 and the largest ironworks in the world in the mid-19th century.

The town is named after a 5th-century Welsh christian princess, **Tudful the Martyr**, who was killed here. The ruins of 13th-century Morlais Castle, which was probably never finished, sit on a hill overlooking the town. The area was the subject of a land dispute between the Earl of Hereford and the Earl of Gloucester, who built the castle, and caused conflict between the two. The dispute reached the court of Edward I.

Merton

Outer borough of southwest Greater London comprising the suburbs of ◊Wimbledon, Mitcham, and Morden

Features the Augustinian priory, founded in 1114, where Thomas à Becket and Walter de Merton, founder of Merton College, Oxford, were educated (it was demolished at the dissolution and the stones used by Henry VIII to build Nonsuch Palace); Merton Place, where Admiral Nelson lived; Merton Park, laid out in the mid-19th century, claimed

as the forerunner of garden suburbs; Wimbledon Common, includes Caesar's Camp – an Iron Age fort; All England Lawn Tennis Club (founded 1877)
Population (1991) 168,500
History Merton was created as a borough on 1 April 1965, comprising the former municipal boroughs of Mitcham and Wimbledon and the urban districts of Merton and Morden.
From Roman times to 20th century
The first traces of settlement in the area are Roman; it is possible there was a staging post along the Roman Stane Street in what is now Merton High Street. In Saxon times it is thought that Cynewulf, King of Wessex, was murdered here in 786 and that in 871 King Ethelred was mortally wounded by the Danish armies in the battle of Merton. Merton remained a small village until 1117 when Merton Priory, a house of Augustinian Canons, was built. This was patronized by most English kings; major international conferences and royal councils were often held here and a major constitutional document, the **Statute of Merton**, which stated causes of baronial opposition to the king, was promulgated in 1236. The monastery was dissolved in 1536 and few ruins remain. In the late 19th century William Morris established a factory on the River Wandle to produce his designs for household and ecclesiastical furnishings; this was closed in 1936. Shortly afterwards Liberty & Co, the Regent Street cloth and fashion manufacturers, established a factory nearby.

Mitcham was also settled in Saxon times but until the 18th century it was mainly an agricultural community, although its fair dates probably from the 16th century, after which time it became the residence of wealthy Londoners. From the 17th century the River Wandle supplied water power for flour mills, bleachers, and calico printers.

Settlement in Morden dates from early times; there is a Romano-British burial mound at Morden Park. Morden manor was given by King Edgar to Westminster Abbey in 968 and remained the Abbey's property until 1553. From the 18th century Morden was a popular residential area for wealthy London bankers and merchants, and with the extension of the underground railway to Morden in 1926 it became a commuter area. The manor house, demolished in 1946, had many distinguished owners, including Queen Henrietta Maria and the Duke of Somerset, who entertained Queen Victoria here on numerous occasions.

Wimbledon is best known for its annual international lawn tennis championships, run by the All England Lawn Tennis Club, which had its origins in the local All England Croquet Club founded in 1868. Buildings of historic interest include the Old Rectory (1500), Eagle House (1613), and the mid-17th-century Rose and Crown public house. The Wimbledon Literary and Scientific Society was founded in 1891. Famous residents include Thomas Cecil, Captain Marryat, and William Wilberforce. Although now mostly a residential area, the main industries are light engineering, and the manufacture of chemicals and food.
Recreation
Extensive recreational areas are provided by Wimbledon, Mitcham, and Cannon Hill commons. Wimbledon Common has a windmill (1817) where Baden-Powell wrote *Scouting for Boys* (1908). Cannizaro Park has a fine collection of azaleas, rhododendrons, and rare plants. The four golf courses in the area include the Royal Wimbledon course adjacent to the Common. Wimbledon stadium is used for football, speedway, stockcar racing, and greyhound racing.

Meteorological Office, or Met Office

Organization based at Bracknell, producing weather reports for the media and conducting specialist work for industry, agriculture, and transport. It was established in London in 1855. Kew is the main meteorological observatory in the British Isles, but other observatories are at Eskdalemuir in the southern uplands of Scotland, Lerwick in the Shetlands, and Valentia in southwest Ireland.

The first weather map in England, showing the trade winds and monsoons, was made in 1688, and the first telegraphic weather report appeared in 1848. The first daily telegraphic weather map was prepared at the Great Exhibition in 1851. The first regular daily collections of weather observations by telegraph and the first British daily weather reports were made in 1860, and the first daily printed maps appeared 1868.

Methodism

Evangelical Protestant Christian movement that was founded by John ◊Wesley in 1739 within the Church of England, but became a separate body in 1795. The Methodist Episcopal Church was founded in the USA in 1784. There are over 50 million Methodists worldwide.

The itinerant, open-air preaching of John and Charles Wesley and George Whitefield drew immense crowds and led to a revival of faith among members of the English working and agricultural classes who were alienated from the formalism and conservatism of the Church of England. Methodist doctrines are contained in Wesley's sermons and 'Notes on the New Testament'. A series of doctrinal divisions in the early 19th century were reconciled by a conference in London in 1932 that brought Wesleyan methodists, primitive methodists, and United methodists into the Methodist Church. The church government is presbyterian in Britain and episcopal in the USA.

metropolitan county

In England, a group of six counties established under the Local Government Act of 1972 in the largest urban areas outside London: Tyne and Wear, South Yorkshire, Merseyside, West Midlands, Greater Manchester, and West Yorkshire. Their elected assemblies (county councils) were abolished in 1986 when most of their responsibilities reverted to metropolitan borough councils.

MI5

Abbreviation for **Military Intelligence, section five**, the counter-intelligence agency of the British intelligence services. Its role is to prevent or investigate espionage, subversion, and sabotage.

MI6

Abbreviation for **Military Intelligence, section six**, the

MI6 *With the end of the Cold War in the 1990s, the British intelligence services adopted a policy of greater openness, revealing the names of their operational heads for the first time. MI6 also moved into these high-profile new offices at Vauxhall Bridge in London. None the less, many feel that the culture of official secrecy still holds sway in Britain, which has no Freedom of Information Act. Simon Shepheard/Impact*

secret intelligence agency of the British intelligence services which operates largely under Foreign Office control.

Middle English

The period of the ◊English language from about 1050 to 1550.

Middlesbrough

Industrial town, port, and unitary authority, on the estuary of the River Tees, northeast England; unitary authority area 54 sq km/21 sq mi; population (1996) 146,000. The town was the administrative headquarters of the county of Cleveland to 1996. The unitary authority was created in 1996 from part of the former county of Cleveland. It is the commercial and cultural centre of the Teesside industrial area, which also includes Stockton-on-Tees, Redcar, Billingham, Thornaby, and Eston. Formerly a centre of heavy industry, it diversified its products in the 1960s; there are constructional, electronics, engineering, and shipbuilding industries, and iron, steel, and chemicals are produced.

Features

The Transporter Bridge (1911) transports cars and passengers across the Tees to Hartlepool in a cable car. Newport Bridge (1934) was the first vertical lift bridge in England. The University of Teesside, formerly Teesside Polytechnic, was established in 1992. The Captain Cook Birthplace Museum commemorates the life of the naval explorer James Cook, who was born in Middlesbrough in 1728. The National Trust-owned Ormesby Hall, an 18th-century house, is located nearby.

History

Middlesbrough developed rapidly in the 19th century after it was decided in 1828 to extend the Stockton and Darlington railway by 6 km/4 mi to reach deeper anchorage on the river. A wet dock was built and trade began in 1830. The original town, between the railway and river, proved too small and the main commercial centre was extended to the south of the docks, in a strictly rectangular layout.

Middleton, Thomas (1580–1627)

English dramatist. He produced numerous romantic plays, tragedies, and realistic comedies, both alone and in collaboration, including *A Fair Quarrel* (1617), *The Changeling* (1622), and *The Spanish Gypsy* (1623) with William Rowley; *The Roaring Girl* (1611) with Thomas ◊Dekker; and (alone) *Women Beware Women* (1621). He also composed many pageants and masques.

Other plays include *A Trick to Catch the Old One* (about 1604–07), *Your Five Gallants* (1604–07), *The Familie of Love* (1608), *A Mad World, My Masters* (1609), *A Chaste Maid in*

Cheapside (about 1611), *No Wit, No Help Like a Woman's* (about 1613), *More Dissemblers Besides Women* (about 1615), and *The Witch* (about 1615).

Middleton's work is wide-ranging and varied in quality. His work shows a particular sympathy with and insight into female psychology.

He was born in London and educated at Queen's College, Oxford. He started his writing career in 1597 with a poem, 'The Wisdom of Solomon Paraphrased'. Soon he became a professional writer for the theatre, collaborating with Thomas Dekker, John Webster, William Rowley, and others. He also wrote verse satires and satirical prose pamphlets such as *The Black Book* (1604). Middleton was employed writing masques and entertainments for civic occasions in London, finally being appointed city chronologer in 1620. In 1624, his satirical anti-Spanish comedy *A Game at Chess*, which represented prominent politicians as chess pieces, played for nine days to packed crowds before being banned by the Privy Council.

Mid Glamorgan, Welsh Morgannwg Ganol

Former county of south Wales, 1974–1996, now divided between ◊Rhondda Cynon Taff, ◊Merthyr Tydfil, ◊Bridgend, and Vale of Glamorgan unitary authorities.

Midlands

Area of central England corresponding roughly to the Anglo-Saxon kingdom of ◊Mercia. The **East Midlands** comprises Derbyshire, Leicestershire, Northamptonshire, and Nottinghamshire. The **West Midlands** covers the metropolitan district of ◊West Midlands created from parts of Staffordshire, Warwickshire, and Worcestershire, and split into the metropolitan boroughs of Dudley, Sandwell, Coventry, Birmingham, Walsall, Solihull, and Wolverhampton; and (often included) the **South Midlands** comprising Bedfordshire, Buckinghamshire, and Oxfordshire.

Midlothian

Unitary authority in southeast Scotland, south of the Firth of Forth, which was previously a district within Lothian region (1975–96) and a county until 1974

Area 363 sq km/140 sq mi

Towns ◊Dalkeith (administrative headquarters), Penicuik, Bonnyrigg

Physical inland area rising toward the Moorfoot Hills in the south; River Esk

Features Crichton Castle, Roslin Castle, Rosslyn Chapel, Newtongrange Mining Museum

Industries glass and crystal, coal mining (declining), light manufacturing, food-processing

Agriculture productive agriculturally to the north (arable and dairy), less productive and intensive toward the hills in the south

Population (1995) 79,900

History historically important mining area, with Scottish Mining Museum at Newtongrange.

Economy

The area is diversifying as it adjusts to the demise of the coal industry. Development is on a small to medium scale.

Environment

There are 14 Sites of Special Scientific Interest, two Ramsars (wetland sites), one regional park, and three country parks.

Architecture

Crichton Castle, now in ruins, is on the Tyne, 19 km/12 mi east of Edinburgh. The 14th-century tower house, mentioned by Walter Scott in his story *Marmion* (1808), was rebuilt in 1585 in Italianate style by Francis Stuart, 5th Earl of Bothwell. The 15th-century chapel at Roslin, built by William Sinclair, has intricate stone carvings and sculptures, including the allegorical 'Dance of Death', and the Late Gothic 'Prentice Pilar'.

Industrial heritage

The Scottish Mining Museum at Lady Victoria Colliery near Newtongrange, was a working mine from 1890 until its closure in 1981. It contains the 'Grant-Richie' winding engine which could lift coal from almost 500 m/1,640 ft below the surface.

Administrative history

The county of Midlothian was more extensive than the present unitary authority and included land now belonging to each of its four neighbouring authorities, East Lothian, West Lothian, Scottish Borders and the City of Edinburgh.

Midsummer Night's Dream, A

Comedy by William ◊Shakespeare, first performed in 1595–96. Hermia, Lysander, Demetrius, and Helena in their various romantic endeavours are subjected to the playful manipulations of the fairies Puck and Oberon in a wood near Athens. Titania, queen of the fairies, is similarly bewitched and falls in love with Bottom, a stupid weaver, whose head has been replaced with that of an ass.

Mikado, The, or *The Town of Titipu*

Operetta by Sullivan (libretto by W S Gilbert), first produced in London at the Savoy Theatre on 14 March 1885. Nanki-Poo loves Yum-Yum, against the Mikado's wishes. However, she must marry Ko-Ko, the Lord High Executioner. The lovers marry and escape decapitation.

Mildenhall

Market town in Suffolk, England, 19 km/12 mi from Bury St Edmunds, situated on the River Lark. Mildenhall airfield was used by the Royal Air Force (RAF) until 1945, and is now operated by the RAF for use by the US air force.

Mildenhall airfield is also the headquarters of the European Tanker Task Force. In 1934 it was the starting point of the Britain to Australia air race.

Mildenhall treasure

Hoard of 4th-century Romano-British silverware discovered in 1942 at Mildenhall in Suffolk, England. The hoard consisted of 34 pieces of silver kitchenware, ornamented with hunting scenes and embossed figures. Some pieces contain Christian motifs. The hoard was probably buried by a wealthy family as protection against the Saxon raids. It is now housed in the British Museum.

Mile End

Area of the East End of London, in the district of Stepney, now part of the London borough of ◊Tower Hamlets. **Mile End Green** (now Stepney Green) was the scene of Richard II's meeting with the rebel peasants in 1381, and in later centuries was the exercise ground of the London 'trained bands', or militia.

A millennium project is planned to revitalize **Mile End Park**, providing a 'green bridge' (with trees on top) to span the busy road which presently bisects the park; wind generators, an art pavilion and an amphitheatre.

Miles, Bernard James, Baron Miles (1907–1991)

English actor and producer. He appeared on stage as Briggs in *Thunder Rock* (1940) and Iago in *Othello* (1942), and his films include *Great Expectations* (1947). He founded a trust that in 1959 built the City of London's first new theatre for 300 years, the Mermaid, which presents a mixed classical and modern repertoire. He was knighted in 1969 and was made a baron in 1979.

Milford Haven, Welsh Aberdaugleddau

Seaport in Pembrokeshire, southwest Wales, on the estuary of the east and west Cleddau rivers 13 km/8 mi southwest of Haverfordwest; population (1991) 13,200. It has oil refineries, and a terminal for giant tankers linked by pipeline with Llandarcy, near Swansea. There is a fishing industry.

The town was originally founded by a colony of Quaker whalers from Nantucket in Massachusetts, USA, as a whaling centre. Later it became a naval dockyard (afterwards moved to Pembroke Dock) and was used as a naval base in both world wars. The natural harbour, one of the finest in the world, runs inland for some 35 km/22 mi and varies in breadth from 1.5–3.5 km/1–2.2 mi with a depth of 29–37 m/95–121 ft. It can accommodate ships of 275,000 tonnes. Development of Milford Haven as a major oil port began in 1957, and it has become the largest oil-importing port in the UK. The Milford Haven Conservancy Board has been set up to control navigation in the harbour.

Militant Tendency

In British politics, left-wing faction originally within the Labour Party, aligned with the publication *Militant*. It became active in the 1970s, with radical socialist policies based on Trotskyism, and gained some success in local government, for example in the inner-city area of Liverpool. In the mid-1980s the Labour Party considered it to be a separate organization within the party and banned it.

Mill, John Stuart (1806–1873)

English philosopher and economist who wrote *On Liberty* (1859), the classic philosophical defence of liberalism, and *Utilitarianism* (1863), a version of the 'greatest happiness for the greatest number' principle in ethics.

On Liberty moved away from the Utilitarian notion that individual liberty was necessary for economic and governmental efficiency and advanced the classic defence of individual freedom as a value in itself and the mark of a mature society. In *Utilitarianism*, he states that actions are right if they bring about happiness and wrong if they bring about the reverse of happiness. His progressive views inspired *On the Subjection of Women* (1869).

Mill was born in London, the son of the Scottish philosopher **James Mill**, from whom he received a rigorously intellectual education. He sat in Parliament as a Radical 1865–68 and introduced a motion for women's suffrage.

Continental people have sex life; the English have hot-water bottles.

GEORGE MIKES Hungarian-born US humorist and writer.
How to be an Alien (1946)

Millais, John Everett (1829–1896)

English painter, a founder member of the ◊**Pre-Raphaelite Brotherhood** in 1848. Among his best known works are *Ophelia* (1852; National Gallery, London) and *Autumn Leaves* (1856; City Art Galleries, Manchester). By the late 1860s he had left the Brotherhood, developing a more fluid and conventional style which appealed strongly to Victorian tastes.

Precocious in talent, he was a student at the Royal Academy Schools at the age of 11. Early acquaintanceship with Holman ◊Hunt and Dante Gabriel ◊Rossetti led to the founding of the Pre-Raphaelite Brotherhood and, inspired by its doctrine of 'truth to nature', he produced some of his best works during the 1950s, among them the painting of Miss Siddell as Ophelia and *Christ in the House of His Parents* (1850; Tate Gallery, London); the latter caused an outcry on its first showing, since its realistic detail was considered unfitting to a sacred subject.

His marriage to Euphemia Gray in 1855 after the annulment of her marriage to John Ruskin estranged him from that early mentor and the *milieu* of Pre-Raphaelite idealism. His illustrations for the Moxon Tennyson (1857) and Trollope's *Orley Farm* (1863) show the change from Pre-Raphaelite principle to mid-Victorian Academicism. Though appealing to popular sentiment, his original style and quality disappeared from his later subject pictures and portraits, which include *The Boyhood of Raleigh* (1870; Tate Gallery, London) and the hugely successful *Bubbles* (1885), used as an advertisement by the Pears soap company. He became a baronet in 1885, and president of the Royal Academy in 1896.

Millar, Gertie (1879–1952)

English actress, one of the most popular leading ladies of musical comedy in the Edwardian era. She was leading lady at the second Gaiety Theatre 1901–08 and 1909–10. She starred at the Adelphi in *The Quaker Girl* in 1910, at Daly's Theatre in *Gypsy Love* in 1914, and also in variety at the Coliseum and the Palace Theatre. She retired from the stage in 1918.

Millennium Commission

Organization set up in 1993 that receives money from the

◊National Lottery, and gives it to projects and awards to mark the millennium and beyond. Money goes towards capital projects, to smaller community projects, and to the **Millennium Experience Festival**, of which the **New Millennium Experience** at ◊Greenwich is the centrepiece. The Commission is chaired by Chris Smith, secretary of state for culture, media, and sport. The Commission is partly funding the British Museum Great Court Project, by which the museum's Great Court will be renovated and roofed to create a new public space in the capital, and the creation of the Tate Gallery of Modern Art, a national gallery that will display the ◊Tate Gallery's modern collection on a permanent basis.

Capital projects funded by the Commission include: rebuilding of ◊Cardiff Arms Park stadium; further development of ◊Portsmouth docks as a maritime museum; development work in ◊Sheffield city centre; the Eden project in ◊Cornwall; and reopening the Forth and Clyde Canal and the Union Canal, to link Glasgow and Edinburgh.

Millennium Dome

Giant structure serving as the centrepiece of Great Britain's Millennium Festival and Experience celebrating the year 2000. Located on a 732,483 sq m/181-acre festival site in Greenwich, southeast London, the Dome is on the Greenwich Prime Meridian (0° longitude). The Dome is 320 m/1,050 ft in diameter, 50 m/164 ft in height, and covers an area of 80,425 sq m/19.86 acres. It has been designed by the Richard Rogers Partnership (architects of another London landmark, the Lloyd's Building), and is twice as big as the world's former largest dome, the Georgia Dome in Atlanta, USA. It is scheduled to open on 31 December 1999.

Inside the Dome several exhibition areas will be arranged around a central performance arena with a seating capacity of 12,500. Situated next to the Dome will be a 6,000-seat amphitheatre. The Dome will be divided into zones, with exhibitions combining education and leisure. Dominating the 'Body Zone' will be a 50-metre-high human figure holding a baby. As well as a sound and light show the 13 zones will include a 'Spirit Level' recognizing the importance of Christianity and other faiths, and 'Licensed to Skill', where visitors will see how they meet the career challenges of the future. The 'Learning Curve' will explore the classroom of the future. 'Serious Play' will be an interactive game-style multimedia experience, and 'Living Island' will take visitors on a seaside trip which allows them to explore the effect on the environment of everyday choices; while in the 'Dreamscape' zone 'visitors float along a river of dreams through environments intended to surprise, excite and entertain, setting minds free in a way that only dreams can achieve'. The Millennium Commission, set up in 1993 and benefiting from ◊national lottery funds, is responsible for financing the Millennium Festival and Experience as well as several other projects in the UK.

The site

The 732,483 sq m/181-acre Greenwich Peninsula site is on waste land, a former gasworks, in a bend of the River Thames. Work began on cleaning up the site in July 1996 and construction started on 23 June 1997. Access to the site will include a new Underground station (the largest in Europe) at North Greenwich on the Jubilee Line, river boats from the site to central London and Greenwich and park and ride (and 'sail and ride') facilities.

Millennium Festival and Experience

The Greenwich festival site is the focal point of the nation's millennium celebrations. The Millennium Experience Visitor's Centre in the Royal Naval College at Greenwich offers a preview of the forthcoming events and buildings, and includes a millennium countdown clock and a model of the Dome.

The Dome

With a circumference of 1.005 km/0.6 mi, the Dome will have a floor area of 80,425 sq m/19.86 acres, equivalent to 13 Albert Halls or two Wembley Stadiums. It will hold 37,000 people. The organizers expect 12 million visitors, and facilities are planned for up to 70,000 people per day. The dome canopy will be made of panels of teflon-coated PTFE, supported by 12 steel masts, each 100 m/328 ft long. Installation of the exhibition and attractions was planned to begin in October 1998.

Ferris Wheel

At the end of 1999 the Ferris Wheel, a 151 m/495 ft-diameter vertical wheel located beside the River Thames near Waterloo Station and County Hall and opposite the Houses of Parliament, is scheduled to begin operation.

River transport

In March 1998 it was announced that new river boat services would run during the year 2000 from Waterloo, site of the Millennium Wheel, to Blackfriars, and from there to a new pier at the Millennium Dome. Each boat will have the capacity to carry 500 passengers. There will also be a shuttle service running at ten-minute intervals between the *Cutty Sark* pier at Greenwich and the Dome, with each boat equipped for 60 passengers. A 'Hopper Service' in central London will link up to ten piers at key attractions and transport interchanges.

Management of the project

The Dome was conceived in 1992 under the Conservative government of John Major, and received the support of the new Labour administration from May 1997, with Minister without Portfolio Peter ◊Mandelson in charge of the project. The Millennium Dome and Experience are run by the New Millennium Experience Company, which is wholly owned by the government, under Chief Executive Jennie Page. The project is part-funded by the Millennium Commission, through lottery funds.

Controversy

In December 1997 Stephen Bayley, the consultant creative director, resigned from the project after disagreements over Exhibition contents and management. Critics have attacked the accessibility of the site, the fact that the Dome began construction before the contents were decided, lack of an early announcement of the proposed contents, and their quality. Some feared a 'dumbing down' of the Exhibition following a fact-finding visit by Peter Mandelson to Disney

World in Florida in January 1998; others attacked such views as elitist. Also in January the Bishop of Oxford, Richard Harries, said that the millennium commemorated the birth of Christ and urged that Christian celebration should be significantly present in the Exhibition. Peter Mandelson wrote that the impact of Christianity would be 'central' to the Millennium Experience, sparking further controversy among non-Christian faiths in the UK.

Miller, Jonathan (1934–)
English theatre and opera producer. He co-authored and performed in the satirical revue *Beyond the Fringe* (1961), with Alan Bennett, Peter Cook, and Dudley Moore. He produced many plays during the 1960s, before turning to opera in the 1970s, including work for English National Opera from 1974. He wrote and presented the medical series *The Body in Question* (1978) for BBC television, and produced a BBC Shakespeare series 1979–81.

It is not an event that has very much to do with Christianity. It is to do with time.

TERENCE CONRAN English designer; creative consultant to the Millennium Dome, Greenwich. Comment on the Millennium; *Daily Telegraph*, 12 January 1998. Peter Mandelson later wrote that the impact of Christianity would be 'central' to the Millennium Experience

---

Miller, William (1801–1880)
Welsh crystallographer, developer of the **Miller indices**, a coordinate system of mapping the shapes and surfaces of crystals.

Milligan, Spike stage name of Terence Alan Milligan (1918–)
Indian-born English writer and radio and screen comedian. He rose to fame as a member of radio's comic team on *The Goon Show* (1949–60), in collaboration with Peter Sellers, Harry Secombe, and Michael Bentine, helping overhaul the rules of comedy both as writer and performer. He featured in a variety of television and film productions, including *The Goon Movie* (1953), the television series Q (1969–80), and *The Life of Brian* (1979). He has published several books including children's poetry, novels, and several volumes of autobiography.

He was born into a military family and himself served in the British army during World War II.

Mills, John (Lewis Ernest Watts) (1908–)
English actor. A very versatile performer, he appeared in films such as *In Which We Serve* (1942), *The Rocking Horse Winner* (1949), *The Wrong Box* (1966), and *Oh! What a Lovely War* (1969). He received an Academy Award for *Ryan's Daughter* (1970).

He is the father of actresses Hayley Mills and Juliet Mills.

Milne, A(lan) A(lexander) (1882–1956)
English writer. He is best known as the author of ◊ *Winnie-the-Pooh* (1926) and *The House at Pooh Corner* (1928), based on the teddy bear and other toys of his son Christopher Robin, with illustrations by E H Shepard. He also wrote children's verse, including *When We Were Very Young* (1924) and *Now We Are Six* (1927). He was an accomplished dramatist whose plays included *Wurzel-Flummery* (1917), *Mr Pim Passes By* (1920), *The Dover Road* (1922), and *Toad of Toad Hall* (1929), an adaptation of Kenneth ◊Grahame's *The Wind in the Willows*.

Milton, John (1608–1674)
English poet and prose writer. His epic ◊ *Paradise Lost* (1667) is one of the landmarks of English literature. Early poems, including *Comus* (a masque performed 1634) and *Lycidas* (an elegy, 1638), showed Milton's superlative lyric gift. He also wrote many pamphlets and prose works, including *Areopagitica* (1644), which opposed press censorship, and he was Latin secretary to Oliver ◊Cromwell and the Council of State from 1649 until the restoration of Charles II.

MILTON, JOHN *A portrait of the English poet John Milton by Jonathan Richardson. Milton's poetic career was interrupted by the exigencies of the English civil war, during which he wrote a number of pamphlets concerned with religious, civil, and domestic liberties. A passionate supporter of republicanism, Milton devoted his life to poetry following the Restoration. Corbis*

Born in Cheapside, London, and educated at St Paul's School and Christ's College, Cambridge, Milton was a scholarly poet, ambitious to match the classical epics, and with strong theological views. Of polemical temperament, he published prose works on republicanism and church government. His middle years were devoted to the Puritan cause and writing pamphlets, including *The Doctrine and Discipline of Divorce* (1643), which may have been based on his own experience of marital unhappiness. During his time as secretary to Cromwell and the Council of State his assistants, as his sight failed, included Andrew ◊Marvell. *Paradise Lost* and the less successful sequel *Paradise Regained* (1671) were written when he was blind and in some political danger (after the restoration of Charles II), as was the dramatic poem *Samson Agonistes* (1671).

Milton's early poems have a baroque exuberance, while his later works are more sober, the blank verse more measured in its mixture of classical and English diction. His stated intention in writing *Paradise Lost* was to 'assert eternal Providence/And justify the ways of God to men'.

Milton Keynes

Industrial ◊new town and administrative headquarters of ◊Milton Keynes unitary authority in south-central England, 80 km/50 mi northeast of London and 100 km/62 mi southwest from Birmingham; population (1995) 192,900. It was part of the county of Buckinghamshire until 1997. It was developed as a new town in 1967 around the old village of the same name, following a grid design. It is the headquarters of the Open University (founded in 1969). Industries include electronics, the manufacture of machine tools, machinery, and pharmaceuticals, and also insurance and financial services.

The M1 motorway and the mainline railway from London to Crewe and Glasgow pass through Milton Keynes.

Milton Keynes was one of the second generation of new towns designed to handle London's overspill population. It includes the towns of Bletchley (population (1991) 40,600), Newport Pagnell (population (1991) 12,100), Stony Stratford (population with Wolverton (1991) 54,500), Wolverton, and Winslow (population (1991) 22,300).

Milton Keynes

Unitary authority in central England, formerly part of Buckinghamshire

Area 311 sq km/120 sq mi

Towns and cities Milton Keynes (administrative headquarters), Newport Pagnell, Olney, Bletchley, Stony Stratford, Woburn Sands, Wolverton

Features Grand Union Canal; River Great Ouse; River Tove; Open University (established in Milton Keynes 1971); Milton Keynes National Bowl (venue for outdoor events); National Badminton Centre (Milton Keynes); Bletchley Park, government centre of code-breaking during World War II; Ouse Valley Park with wetland habitats; Peace Pagoda (Milton Keynes), first to be built in northern hemisphere and surrounded by a thousand cherry and cedar trees planted in memory of all war victims; Milton Keynes' famous concrete cows, constructed in 1978 by a community artist and local school children

Industries financial services, telecommunications, soft drinks, high technology industries, motor vehicle parts and manufacture (Aston Martin-Lagonda, Mercedes-Benz, Volkswagen-Audi), education (Open University and De Montfort University campuses), vellum and parchment

Population (Milton Keynes town, 1995) 192,900

Minch, or Minsh

Arm of the Atlantic Ocean separating the northwest mainland of Scotland from the Outer Hebrides. The channel runs for more than 90 km/56 mi, northeast to southwest, and extends to a width of 30–75 km/19–47 mi. It incorporates the **Little Minch**, a passage separating the island of Skye, in the Inner Hebrides group, from the middle islands of the Outer Hebrides: South Harris, North Uist, and Benbecula.

Mind officially the National Association for Mental Health

A charity, founded in the UK in 1946, that promotes the health and welfare of people who are mentally ill.

Minehead

Seaside resort in Somerset, England, 4 km/2.5 mi northwest of Dunster; population (1991) 6,200. It is situated within the Exmoor National Park, of which it is the main tourist centre. Minehead harbour is used for boating and sailing.

The West Somerset steam railway runs along the coast from Minehead to the village of Blue Anchor.

miners' strike

British strike against pit closures that lasted almost a year from April 1984. The prime minister Margaret Thatcher was determined to make a stand against the miners and in April 1995 members of the National Union of Miners (NUM) returned to work.

The NUM, led by its Marxist president, Arthur ◊Scargill called the strike in April 1994 without a ballot, in protest against pit closures and as part of a campaign for a better basic wage. Support was strong in south Wales, Scotland, Yorkshire, and Kent but pits in Nottinghamshire and Leicestershire continued to operate. Some NUM members left the union and founded the Union of Democratic Mineworkers.

Minghella, Anthony (1954–)

English director, screenwriter, and playwright. In 1992 he won international acclaim for writing and directing *Truly Madly Deeply*, a low-budget television film noteworthy for its understated visual style and the strength of the actors' performances. Its success led to work in the USA, where he filmed *Mr Wonderful* (1993). This was followed by the adaptation of *The English Patient* (1996), another film celebrated for its high-calibre performances and which earned him Academy Awards for screenplay and direction.

He began his career working as a script editor on the British soap opera *Eastenders* during the 1980s, during which time he also wrote such plays as *Made in Bangkok* (1987).

Mini

Originally called the **Mini-Minor**, best-selling car designed by Alec ◊Issigonis in 1959. It was made by the British Motor Corporation.

minimum wage

Minimum level of pay for workers, usually set by government. In the UK, minimum pay for many groups of workers has been fixed by wages councils. Minimum wages are set to prevent low-paid workers from being exploited by employers who would otherwise pay them even lower wages. However, minimum wages are argued by some economists to cause unemployment because if wages were allowed to fall below the minimum wage level, some employers would be prepared to take on more factors.

The UK government in June 1998 announced the level of the national minimum wage at £3.60 an hour for those aged 21 and over. Persons aged 18 to 21 would be covered by a minimum of just £3 an hour which would increase to £3.20 in June 2000. All 16- and 17-year-olds would be exempt from the law and so would all those participating in officially-approved apprenticeship schemes.

Minster in Sheppey

Town and resort on the Isle of Sheppey, Kent, England; population (1991) 6,200. The town has one of England's oldest existing places of worship, the Church of St Mary and St Sexburga. St Mary and St Sexburga are effectively two churches, the latter being originally associated with a nunnery founded about AD 664.

mint

Place where coins are made under government authority; in the UK the **Royal Mint**. The Royal Mint also manufactures coinages, official medals, and seals for Commonwealth countries.

For centuries in the Tower of London, the Royal Mint was housed in a building on Tower Hill from 1810 until the new Royal Mint was opened at Llantrisant, near Cardiff, in 1968.

Minton, Thomas (1765–1836)

English potter. After an apprenticeship as an engraver for transfer printing at Caughley and working for the potter Josiah Spode, he established himself at Stoke-on-Trent as an engraver of designs in 1789. The Chinese-style blue and white 'willow pattern' was reputedly originated by Minton. In 1796 he founded a pottery, producing a cream-base blue-decorated earthenware and (from 1798) high-quality porcelain and bone china, decorated with flowers and fruit. Chinaware became the chief production under his son Herbert Minton (1792–1858).

Mirfield

Town in West Yorkshire, England, on the River Calder, 7 km/4 mi northeast of Huddersfield; population (1991) 15,100. Principal industries are chemicals, the manufacture of woollen textiles, and dyeing. The Community of the Resurrection, an Anglican theological college founded in Oxford, moved to Mirfield in 1898.

The poet and hymn writer James Montgomery worked at Mirfield as a boy, and the Brontë sisters attended school here. St Peter's College, Roe Head, is a junior seminary for the Verona Fathers, a missionary order founded in 1872.

Mirren, Helen (1945–)

English actress. She has played both modern and classical stage roles. Her Shakespearean roles include Lady Macbeth, Isabella in *Measure for Measure*, and Cleopatra in *Antony and Cleopatra* (1964, 1983, and 1998). Her films include *The Long Good Friday* (1981), *Cal* (1984), *Where Angels Fear to Tread* (1991), *The Madness of King George* (1994), and *Some Mother's Son* (1996). She is widely known for her role as Jane Tennison in the television series and films *Prime Suspect* (1990–97).

Mirror, the, formerly *Daily Mirror*

British tabloid newspaper established in 1903. Politically, it is an independent national newspaper, broadly supporting the Labour party. Owned by the Mirror Group, it had a circulation of over 2 million in 1998. Its sister paper, the *Sunday Mirror* was established in 1963 and had a circulation of over 2,200,000 in 1998.

Founded by Lord ◊Northcliffe, as a journal for 'gentlewomen', it was a failure after three months until he transformed it into the world's first daily illustrated paper. In the 1930s the newspaper changed again, by imitating the *New York Mirror* (1924–63) and becoming a tabloid. The *Daily Mirror* adopted characteristically big, bold headlines and vivid treatment of news and pictures which brought about a further rapid increase in sales to give it the largest daily circulation in Britain until challenged by *The Sun* in the 1970s.

mission

Office of a government representative accredited to another government. Britain's missions include high commissions headed by British high commissioners in Commonwealth countries and embassies headed by ambassadors in other countries. Reciprocally Commonwealth governments are represented in London by high commissioners and other governments by ambassadors.

missionary societies

Religious societies established to organize and finance Christian evangelization in the former British Empire. The Anglican Society for Promoting Christian Knowledge (SPCK) was founded in 1698, followed by the Society for the Propagation of the Gospel (SPG) in 1701. As the Empire grew, so did the number of societies. The London Missionary Society (LMS) was founded in 1795, followed by the Church Missionary Society (CMS) in 1799, and the British and Foreign Bible Society (BFBS) in 1804. The Anglo-Catholic

Universities Mission to Central Africa (UMCA) was founded in 1859 in response to the challenge sent out by David Livingstone. In 1965 it joined with the SPG to become the United Society for the Propagation of the Gospel (USPG). Outside the Church of England, the Methodist Missionary Society dates from 1786 and the Baptist Missionary Society from 1792.

Mitchell, Adrian (1932–)

English writer. His witty and political work includes the verse collections *Poems* (1964), *The Apeman Cometh* (1975), *For Beauty Douglas: Collected Poems 1953–1979* (1982), and *Greatest Hits* (1991); several novels; and a number of plays, including *Tiger* (1971) and *Man Friday* (1972) (filmed 1975).

Mitchell first came to notice with *Poems* (1955), a collection of politically committed, left-wing lyrics which recall the work of Bertolt Brecht and W H Auden in the 1930s. Among his novels is *The Bodyguard* (1970), a funny yet chilling science-fiction story set in Britain in the 1980s. He has also written television scripts.

Mitchell, Juliet (1940–)

New Zealand-born British psychoanalyst and writer. Her article in *New Left Review* (1966) entitled 'Women: The Longest Revolution' was one of the first attempts to combine socialism and feminism, using Marxist theory to explain the reasons behind women's oppression. She published *Women's Estate* in 1971 and *Psychoanalysis and Feminism* in 1974.

Other books (with Ann Oakley) include *The Rights and Wrongs of Women* (1976) and (ed.) *What is Feminism?* (1986).

Mitchell, Peter Dennis (1920–1992)

English chemist. He received a Nobel prize in 1978 for work on the conservation of energy by plants during respiration and photosynthesis. He showed that the transfer of energy during life processes is not random but directed.

Mitchell, R(eginald) J(oseph) (1895–1937)

English aircraft designer whose Spitfire fighter was a major factor in winning the Battle of Britain during World War II. He developed world-beating sea-planes for the Schneider Trophy races (1922–23) and won speed records with several of the S-model planes in the 1920s. The single-engined Spitfire prototype was produced in 1936. More than 19,000 Spitfires were eventually built. The manoeuvrability and adaptability of the Spitfire accounted for its success.

Mitchison, Naomi Mary Margaret born Haldane (1897–)

Scottish writer. She wrote more than 70 books, including *The Conquered* (1923), *The Corn King and the Spring Queen* (1931), and *The Blood of the Martyrs* (1939), novels evoking ancient Greece and Rome. A socialist activist, she also campaigned for birth control.

The settings of other novels range from prehistoric Scotland and the Holy Roman Empire to Africa (she was made a tribal adviser in Botswana 1963), and even distant galaxies as in *Memoirs of a Spacewoman* (1962). She has also written short stories, plays, poetry, and five volumes of autobiography, culminating in *As It Was* (1988).

She was born in Edinburgh, the sister of the geneticist J B S Haldane, and brought up in Oxford. In 1916 she married G R Mitchison, a barrister who was made a life peer in 1964, and from 1937 lived in western Scotland, where she was active in local politics. For her historical novels, although she had little formal classical knowledge, she made great use of histories and translations to produce a clear, direct, unsentimental narrative; she also wrote a biography of the Byzantine princess *Anna Comnena* (1928). Mitchison went on publishing novels into her nineties.

Mitford sisters

The six daughters of British aristocrat 2nd Lord Redesdale, including: **Nancy** (1904–1973), author of the semi-autobiographical *The Pursuit of Love* (1945) and *Love in a Cold Climate* (1949), and editor and part author of the satirical essays collected in *Noblesse Oblige* (1956) elucidating 'U' (upper-class) and 'non-U' behaviour; **Diana** (1910–), who married Oswald ◊Mosley; **Unity** (1914–1948), who became an admirer of Hitler; and **Jessica** (1917–), author of the autobiographical *Hons and Rebels* (1960) and *The American Way of Death* (1963).

mixed-ability teaching

Practice of teaching children of all abilities in a single class.

Mixed-ability teaching is normal practice in British primary schools but most secondary schools begin to divide children according to ability, either in single-subject sets or, more rarely, streams across all subjects, as they approach public examinations at 16.

Mo, Timothy (1950–)

British novelist. His works are mainly set in Hong Kong (where he was born) and the East Indies, though *Sour Sweet* (1982) describes a Triad-threatened Chinese family of restaurateurs in London, and is full of realistic detail and brisk humour.

An Insular Possession (1986) is a comprehensive historical novel about the Opium Wars; *The Redundancy of Courage* (1991) deals with guerrillas in East Timor; and *Brownout on Breadfruit Boulevard* (1995), which he published himself, is a political comedy with a scatological sideline.

mod

Traditional Scottish annual arts festival, similar to the Welsh ◊eisteddfod. Mods are held in the autumn and prizes are awarded for Gaelic compositions, both literary and musical, recitation, singing, and playing.

mod

British youth subculture that originated in London and Brighton in the early 1960s; it was revived in the late 1970s. Mods were smart, fashion-conscious, speedy, and upwardly mobile; they favoured scooters and soul music.

Mods and rockers (motorcycle gangs) have traditionally fought pitched battles at certain English seaside resorts on summer bank holidays.

Model Parliament

English parliament set up in 1295 by Edward I; it was the first to include representatives from outside the clergy and aristocracy, and was established because Edward needed the support of the whole country against his opponents: Wales, France, and Scotland. His sole aim was to raise money for military purposes, and the parliament did not pass any legislation.

The parliament comprised archbishops, bishops, abbots, earls, and barons (all summoned by special writ, and later forming the basis of the House of Lords); also present were the lower clergy (heads of chapters, archdeacons, two clerics from each diocese, and one from each cathedral) and representatives of the shires, cities, and boroughs (two knights from every shire, two representatives from each city, and two burghers from each borough).

modern dance

Dance idiom pioneered in the USA in the early 20th century that evolved in opposition to traditional ballet by those seeking a freer and more immediate means of dance expression. In the UK, the London Contemporary Dance Theatre and school was set up in 1966–67 and flourished under the artistic direction of Robert Cohan, pupil of Martha Graham, the foremost US exponent of modern dance. The school is the only European institute authorized to teach the Graham technique. In 1966 the Ballet Rambert became a modern-dance company. See also ◊contemporary dance.

Recent and often experimental work is known as ◊new dance or independent dance, or described as avant-garde dance.

Moffat, Alfred (1866–1950)

Scottish composer and editor. He studied in Berlin, where he worked for a time. He settled in London in the 1890s and edited a large collection of early string music, including many English and French works, also several volumes of Scottish, Welsh, and Irish folksongs.

Mold, Welsh Yr Wyddgrung

Market town and administrative centre of ◊Flintshire, northeast Wales, on the River Alyn; population (1991) 8,750. It has light industries. There are two theatres.

It was the birthplace of Daniel Rowlands, one of the most noted of Welsh novelists. Richard Wilson, the 18th-century landscape painter, is buried at the 15th-century church of St Mary.

Molyneaux, Jim (James Henry) (1920–)

Northern Ireland Unionist politician, leader of the Official Ulster Unionist Party (the largest Northern Ireland party) 1979–95. A member of the House of Commons from 1970, he temporarily relinquished his seat 1983–85 in protest at the Anglo-Irish Agreement. He resigned as party leader in 1995 and retired from parliament in 1997. Although a fervent supporter of the union between Britain and Northern Ireland, he was regarded as one of the more moderate Loyalists. Knighted in 1996, given a life peerage in 1997.

monarchy

See feature on the British monarchy on page 601, also tables listing members of the Royal Family on pages 598 and 599. See also ◊Elizabeth II, ◊constitution and House of ◊Windsor, for genealogy.

The Succession to the Throne

British succession rules were determined following the end of the Commonwealth in the 17th century by the Bill of Rights of 1689. This was amended by the Act of Settlement in 1701 which laid down that only Protestant descendants of Princess Sophia – the Electress of Hanover, granddaughter of James I – can succeed. Sons of the Sovereign and their descendants have precedence over daughters, in succeeding to the Throne. Daughters take precedence over the Sovereign's brothers. When a daughter succeeds, she becomes Queen Regnant and has the same powers as a King. In 1998, however, it was announced that Queen Elizabeth II supports plans to remove gender bias from the succession.

Order of succession	Relationship
The Prince of Wales	Eldest son of Her Majesty The Queen
Prince William of Wales	Eldest son of The Prince of Wales
Prince Henry of Wales	Second son of The Prince of Wales
The Duke of York	Second son of Her Majesty The Queen
Princess Beatrice of York	Eldest daughter of The Duke of York
Princess Eugenie of York	Second daughter of The Duke of York
The Prince Edward	Third son of Her Majesty The Queen
The Princess Royal	Only daughter, second child of Her Majesty The Queen
Peter Phillips	Only son, eldest child, of The Princess Royal
Zara Phillips	Only daughter of The Princess Royal

Monck or Monk, George, 1st Duke of Albemarle (1608–1670)

English soldier. During the English Civil War he fought for King Charles I, but after being captured changed sides and took command of the Parliamentary forces in Ireland. Under Oliver ◊Cromwell he became commander in chief in Scotland, and in 1660 he led his army into England and brought about the restoration of Charles II.

Monmouth, Welsh Trefynwy

Market town in Monmouthshire, southeast Wales, 25 km/16 mi north of Chepstow at the confluence of the Rivers ◊Wye and Monnow; population (1991) 75,000. It is a tourist and fishing centre, and has some light industry. Henry V was born in Monmouth Castle in 1388.

A picturesque bridge, unique in its two-storeyed fortified gatehouse, crosses the Monnow. There are still some remains of the 12th-century castle, one of a number built by William FitzOsbern after the Norman Conquest. The castle keep fell down in 1647 and was replaced, in 1673, by Great Castle House, which became the headquarters of the Royal

Members of The Royal Family

Senior members of the Royal Family are all related to the three middle sons of King George V: King George VI (1895–1952); Henry, Duke of Gloucester (1900–1974); George, Duke of Kent (1902–1942); the eldest son, the Duke of Windsor (1894–1972), who abdicated from the throne as King Edward VIII in 1936 died childless.
(– = not applicable.)

Name and titles	Married	Date of birth	Official residence(s)	Issue
		Family of George VI		
The Sovereign: Her Majesty Queen Elizabeth II, of The United Kingdom of Great Britain and Northern Ireland and of her other Realms and Territories, Queen, Head of the Commonwealth, Defender of the Faith	His Royal Highness The Duke of Edinburgh, 20 November 1947	21 April 1926	Buckingham Palace, Windsor Castle, Palace of Holyrood House	Prince Charles, Princess Anne, Prince Andrew, Prince Edward
Husband Of The Queen: His Royal Highness, The Prince Philip, Duke of Edinburgh, KG, KT, OM, GBE, AC, QSO, PC, Ranger of Windsor Great Park	Her Majesty The Queen, 20 November 1947	10 June 1921		
Mother of The Queen: Her Majesty Queen Elizabeth The Queen Mother, Lady of The Garter, Lady of The Thistle, CI, GCVO, GBE, Dame Grand Cross of the Order of St John, Royal Victorian Chain, Lord Warden and Admiral of the Cinque Ports, Constable of Dover Castle	Prince Albert, Duke of York (later King George VI; died 1952), 26 April 1923	4 August 1900	Clarence House; Royal Lodge, Windsor; Castle of Mey	Queen Elizabeth II, Princess Margaret
		Children of The Queen		
His Royal Highness The Prince of Wales (Prince Charles), KG, KT, GCB and Great Master of the Order of the Bath, AK, QSO, PC, ADP (P)	Lady Diana Spencer (later Diana, Princess of Wales; died 1997), 29 July 1981, marriage dissolved 1996	14 November 1948	St James' Palace, Highgrove, Tetbury	His Royal Highness Prince William of Wales (born 21 June 1982), His Royal Highness Prince Henry of Wales (born 15 September 1984)
Her Royal Highness The Princess Royal (Princess Anne), KG, GCVO	Captain Mark Phillips, 14 November 1973, marriage dissolved 1992; Captain Timothy Laurence, 12 December 1992	15 August 1950	Gatcombe Park, Minchinhampton	Peter Phillips (born 15 November 1977), Zara Phillips (born 15 May 1981)
His Royal Highness The Duke of York (Prince Andrew), CVO, ADC(P)	Sarah Ferguson (now Sarah, Duchess of York), 23 July 1986, marriage dissolved 1996	19 February 1960	Buckingham Palace; Sunninghill Park, Ascot	Princess Beatrice (born 8 August 1988), Princess Eugenie (born 23 March 1990)
His Royal Highness The Prince Edward, CVO	Engaged to Sophie Rhys-Jones, January 1999; to be married June 1999	10 March 1964	Buckingham Palace	none

Name and titles	Married	Date of birth	Official residence(s)	Issue
		Sister of The Queen		
Her Royal Highness The Princess Margaret, Countess of Snowdon, CI, GCVO, Royal Victorian Chain, Dame Grand Cross of the Order of St John of Jerusalem	Antony Armstrong-Jones (later Earl of Snowdon), 6 May 1960, marriage dissolved 1978	21 August 1930	Kensington Palace	David, Viscount Linley (born 3 November 1961), Lady Sarah Chatto[1] (born 1 May 1964)
		Family of Henry, Duke of Gloucester		
		Aunt of The Queen		
Her Royal Highness Princess Alice, Duchess of Gloucester, GCB, CI, GCVO, GBE	Prince Henry, Duke of Gloucester (died 1974), 6 November 1935	25 December 1901	Kensington Palace	Prince William (1941–72), Richard, Duke of Gloucester
		Cousin of The Queen		
His Royal Highness The Duke of Gloucester (Prince Richard), KG, GCV, Grand Prior of the Order of St John of Jerusalem	Birgitte Eva van Deurs (now HRH The Duchess of Gloucester), 8 July 1972	26 August 1944	Kensington Palace	Alexander, Earl Of Ulster (born 24 October 1974), Lady Davina Windsor (born 19 November 1977), Lady Rose Windsor (born 1 March 1980)
		Family of George, Duke of Kent		
His Royal Highness The Duke of Kent (Prince Edward), KG, GCMG, GCVO, ADC (P)	Katherine Worsley (now HRH The Duchess of Kent), 8 June 1961	9 October 1935	Wren House, London	George, Earl of St Andrews[2] (born 26 June 1962), Lady Helen Taylor[3] (born 28 April 1964), Lord Nicholas Windsor (born 25 July 1970)
Her Royal Highness Princess Alexandra, The Honourable Lady Ogilvy, GCVO	The Right Honourable Sir Angus Ogilvy, 24 April 1963	25 December 1936	Thatched House Lodge, Richmond Park, Surrey	James Ogilvy[4] (born 29 February 1964), Marina Mowatt[5] (born 31 July 1966)
His Royal Highness Prince Michael of Kent, KCVO	Baroness Marie-Christine von Reibnitz (now HRH Princess Michael of Kent), 30 June 1978	4 July 1942	Kensington Palace; Nether Lypiatt Manor, Stroud	Lord Frederick Windsor (born 6 April 1979), Lady Gabriella Windsor (born 23 April 1981)

[1] Has one son: Daniel Chatto (born 28 July 1996). [2] Has three children: Lady Marina Windsor (born 30 September 1982), Edward, Baron Downpatrick (born 2 December 1988), Lady Amelia Windsor (born 24 August 1995). [3] Has two children: Columbus Taylor (born 6 August 1994), Cassius Taylor (born 26 December 1996). [4] Has two children: Flora Ogilvy (born 15 December 1994), Alexander Ogilvy (born 12 November 1996). [5] Has two children: Zenouska Mowatt (born 26 May 1990), Christian Mowatt (born 4 June 1993).

Monmouthshire Engineer Militia (now the Royal Monmouthshire Regiment) in 1875.

Monmouth, James Scott, 1st Duke of Monmouth (1649–1685)

Claimant to the English crown, the illegitimate son of Charles II and Lucy Walter. After James II's accession in 1685, Monmouth landed in England at Lyme Regis, Dorset, claimed the crown, and raised a rebellion, which was crushed at ◊Sedgemoor in Somerset. He was executed with 320 of his accomplices.

When ◊James II converted to Catholicism, the Whig opposition attempted unsuccessfully to secure Monmouth the succession to the crown by the Exclusion Bill, and having

MONARCHY *Hundreds of thousands of bunches of flowers left by mourners outside Kensington Palace, London after the death of Diana, Princess of Wales in August 1997. David Halford*

become implicated in a Whig conspiracy, the ◊Rye House Plot in 1683, he fled to Holland.

Monmouthshire, Welsh Trefynwy

Unitary authority in southeast Wales. A former county, between 1974 and 1996 it became (except for a small area on the border with Mid Glamorgan) the county of Gwent

Area 851 sq km/328 sq mi

Towns ◊Cwmbran (administrative headquarters), ◊Chepstow

Physical rivers ◊Wye and ◊Usk; mountainous in north

Features ◊Chepstow and Raglan castles, Tintern Abbey, salmon and trout fishing; peak of Pen-y-Fal or Sugar Loaf (596 m/1,955 ft)

Agriculture lowlands have rich mixed farming, with arable crops, including wheat, being important

Population (1996) 80,400

Topography

The coast of Monmouthshire is exposed to high spring tides which rush up the Severn in a 'bore' from the Bristol Channel, rising at Chepstow sometimes to 18 m/60 ft. The southern part, east and west of the Usk, comprises the Caldecot and Wentloog levels, which are protected from the sea by sea walls. North of the Caldecot level, between the Usk and the Wye, the surface is undulating. The north of the county is more mountainous. About 7 km/4.3 mi from ◊Abergavenny is the peaked mountain called Pen-y-Fal or Sugar Loaf (596 m/1,955 ft), over 8.1 sq km/3.1 sq mi of which have been presented to the National Trust. Between Abergavenny and Usk is the wooded hill-fort of Coed-y-Bonedd, one of several Monmouthshire camps. Skirrid Fawr (486 m/1,595 ft), known locally as the Holy Mountain, has views of the Black Mountains, the Usk valley, and the Sugar Loaf.

Historical features

During the Roman occupation the only Roman town in Wales was built at Caerwent. There are also ruins of feudal strongholds at ◊Chepstow, Caldicot, Raglan, and elsewhere, and the remains of Tintern Abbey and the Cistercian abbey of Llanthony are here.

Political history

Medieval Monmouthshire was undoubtedly Welsh. The Act of Union of 1536 created the original county out of 'divers Lordships Marchers within the said Country or Dominion of Wales'. Later, in the Tudor period, it was brought under the jurisdiction of the courts of Westminster in certain matters, while separate courts were provided for the rest of Wales. It

IS THE BRITISH MONARCHY OUT OF TOUCH?

IN THE immediate aftermath of the death of Diana, Princess of Wales, commentators declared that Britain had become a more compassionate and demonstrative society. Did the country any longer want what was seen as an unfeeling and remote monarchy?

On 17 October 1997, *The Times* newspaper reported that: 'The Queen has accepted that the Royal Family must change its image after the death of Diana, Princess of Wales. A source close to the Queen spoke yesterday of the need to demonstrate 'softer, gentler touches' in the wake of what he described as the first royal tragedy to occur in the mass media culture.'

An acrimonious debate

Six weeks earlier, in the immediate aftermath of Diana's fatal accident, far more significant changes had seemed to be afoot. The 'People's Princess' had not been universally popular, but her many fans had found her emotional, informal style a welcome change from the more remote image presented by other members of the Windsor clan. Her death was then followed by an often acrimonious public debate over how the royal family might survive with credibility into the 21st century. There were even suggestions that Prince Charles was so 'out of touch' with the British people that the crown should 'skip a generation' on the death of the present Queen and pass instead to Prince William, Charles's elder son by Diana.

For a short while, amid the tears and flowers, almost anything seemed possible. Since Britain has a highly flexible, unwritten constitution, a major revision of the royal family's role – or indeed its abolition – would not have been impossible.

However, the British monarchy has deep roots, and it has proved to be a tough old plant, ready and able to adapt itself to changes in its social and political environment. Kings and queens have been ruling in Britain since the first millennium AD and for centuries they were seen as superhuman: as late as 1712 Queen Anne was still practising the 'royal touch', a laying-on of hands that was believed to cure diseased skin. By that time, the monarchy had lost much of its real power to Parliament, and it has continued since then to make a slow constitutional retreat, its role becoming ever more symbolic.

A leaner monarchy

But while most monarchies elsewhere were swept away entirely, the British royal family managed to attune itself to democracy. The current queen has reigned since 1952 and is generally thought to have done a difficult job well. Although she lacks the charisma of a Diana, she is perceived to be conscientious and hard-working, and has attracted less criticism over the years than other members of her family such as Princess Michael of Kent, Princess Margaret, and the Duchess of York. A reduction in the number of such 'lesser royals' would, in the eyes of many, make for a leaner, fitter, and more acceptable monarchy.

But even a pared down royal family will now almost certainly be expected to display those 'softer, gentler touches' that were the trademark of Diana. There are 60 million people in Britain and they do not speak with a single voice, but the most vocal part of the nation seems to want a less formal, more 'hands-on' kind of monarchy than exists at present. This may not mean that the Windsors will have to travel around on bicycles, in the modest style of certain royal families in mainland Europe. The British public still expects some pomp and ceremony – an expectation that was lavishly met by the highly dignified funeral of Princess Diana. But it also now expects more informal touches too – such as the inclusion of a song performed by pop star Elton John at the same funeral.

Reforming the Constitution

The new Labour Government is keen to end inequalities in Britain, and it is no friend to privilege. With the House of Lords facing change, the monarchy's future could appear to be in jeopardy too. Yet Prime Minister Tony Blair is not a republican and his relationship with Buckingham Palace is reported to be good. There is also no consensus on who might replace the queen as head of state, if the monarchy were to be abolished.

Just as the Labour Party put itself back in tune with the British electorate, so now – as the prevailing public mood readjusts after the sometimes hysterical outbursts straight after Diana's tragic death – the monarchy could conceivably get in touch with more of its subjects by presenting itself in a less traditional fashion. Some would say that, in Britain, a 'modernized monarchy' is a contradiction in terms. However, all institutions have to make concessions to changing circumstances. In its way, the monarchy in Britain has been doing this for 1500 years – so the Queen and her family know where their responsibilities lie.

BY HAYDN MIDDLETON

has been included in Wales since 1964 when the description Wales and Monmouthshire was dropped.

Monopolies and Mergers Commission, or MMC

Government body re-established in 1973 under the Fair Trading Act and, since 1980, embracing the Competition Act. Its role is to investigate and report when there is a risk of creating a monopoly by a company merger or takeover, or when a newspaper or newspaper assets are transferred. It also investigates companies, nationalized industries, or local authorities that are suspected of operating in a noncompetitive way.

Monster Raving Loony Party

An irreverent, anti-establishment political party, founded by Screamin' Lord Sutch (David Sutch, 1940–), a pop singer in the group, The Raving Savages. Dressed in a top hat and leopardskin suit, Sutch has been a permanent fixture at by-election counts since 1963. He has stood in a record of more than 50 contests, repeatedly losing his deposit, but attracting media attention. The party's motto has been, 'Vote for insanity, you know it makes sense'. Despite the lack of a policy programme, on occasions the 'Loonies' have won seats in local elections. Its activities have prompted consideration of reform of the eligibility rules for parliamentary elections to prevent non-serious fringe parties from standing. At the 1997 general election, Loony Party candidates won 8,000 votes.

Montacute House

Elizabethan house in Somerset, England, 6 km/4 mi west of Yeovil. It was begun in 1588 by Thomas Phelips, and completed about 1601 by his son, Edward Phelips, Speaker of the House of Commons and master of the rolls under James I. The property was presented to the National Trust through the Society for the Protection of Ancient Buildings in 1931. It contains a collection of period furniture, pictures and tapestries.

Features

Montacute House has an H-shaped ground plan and includes contemporary plasterwork, chimney pieces, and other Renaissance features (curvilinear and finialled gables, an open balustraded parapet, and fluted angle columns). The interior has fine 17th- and 18th-century furniture and Elizabethan and Jacobean paintings from the National Portrait Gallery in the Long Gallery and adjoining rooms.

Montagu, Lady Mary Wortley born Pierrepont (1689–1762)

English society hostess. She was well known in literary circles, associating with writers such as English poet Alexander Pope, with whom she later quarrelled. Her witty and erudite letters were renowned. She introduced the practice of inoculation against smallpox into Britain.

Montagu-Douglas-Scott

Family name of the dukes of Buccleuch; seated at Bowhill, Selkirk, Scotland; Boughton House, Northamptonshire, England; and Drumlanrig, Dumfriesshire, Scotland; descended from the Duke of ◊Monmouth.

Montfort, Simon de Montfort, 1st Earl of Leicester (*c.* 1208–1265)

English politician and soldier. From 1258 he led the baronial opposition to Henry III's misrule during the second ◊Barons' War, and in 1264 defeated and captured the king at Lewes, Sussex. In 1265, as head of government, he summoned the first parliament in which the towns were represented; he was killed at the Battle of Evesham during the last of the Barons' Wars.

Initially one of Henry III's favourites, he married the king's sister Eleanor in 1238. He later disagreed with the king's administrative policies, and in 1258 Montfort and his baronial supporters forced Henry to accept the **Provisions of Oxford**, by which the king's powers were in effect transferred to a committee of barons. These provisions were anulled by the **Dictum of Kenilworth** in 1266, after the final defeat of Montfort's followers, and their lands and titles were confiscated.

Born in Normandy, the son of **Simon de Montfort** (*c.* 1160–1218) who led a crusade against the Albigenses, he arrived in England in 1230, and was granted the earldom of Leicester.

Montgomerie, Colin Stuart (1963–)

Scottish golfer who has won the Harry Vardon Trophy as the top-ranked player in the European Order of Merit a record five times in succession, 1993–97. Success in the Major tournaments eluded him, though he was runner-up in the US Open in 1994 and 1997, and the US PGA in 1995 . He has been a member of the Europe Ryder Cup side since 1991 and played a key role in the team's victories in 1995 and 1997.

Montgomery, Bernard Law, 1st Viscount Montgomery of Alamein (1887–1976)

English field marshal. In World War II he commanded the 8th Army in North Africa in the Second Battle of El ◊Alamein in 1942. As commander of British troops in Northern Europe from 1944, he received the German surrender in 1945.

At the start of World War II Montgomery commanded part of the British Expeditionary Force in France 1939–40 and took part in the evacuation from Dunkirk. In August 1942 he took command of the 8th Army, then barring the German advance on Cairo. The victory of El ◊Alamein in October turned the tide in North Africa; it was followed by the expulsion of Field Marshal Rommel from Egypt and rapid Allied advance into Tunisia. In February 1943 Montgomery's forces came under US general Eisenhower's command, and they took part in the conquest of Tunisia and Sicily and the invasion of Italy. Montgomery was promoted to field marshal in 1944. In 1948 he became permanent military chair of the Commanders-in-Chief Committee for Western European defence, and 1951–58 was deputy Supreme Commander Europe. He was created 1st Viscount Montgomery of Alamein in 1946.

Montgomery commanded the Allied armies during the opening phase of the invasion of France in June 1944, and from August the British and imperial troops that liberated the Netherlands, overran northern Germany, and entered Denmark. At his 21st Army Group headquarters on Lüneburg Heath, he received the German surrender on 4 May 1945. He was in command of the British occupation force in Germany until February 1946, when he was appointed chief of the Imperial General Staff. KCB 1942.

Montgomeryshire

Former county of north Wales, included in Powys between 1974 and 1996; now part of ◊Powys unitary authority.

Montrose

Seaport, holiday resort, and former royal burgh in Angus unitary authority, Scotland, 63 km/39 mi southwest of Aberdeen; population (1991) 11,400. The local economy is dependent on fruit- and vegetable-canning, the manufacture of pharmaceuticals and linen textiles, and timber-related occupations. The town is also the venue of a major livestock market.

Montrose stands at the mouth of the River South Esk where it forms the **Montrose Basin**, a tidal pool covering about 3 sq km/1 sq mi. Montrose now incorporates the village of Ferryden on the right bank of the South Esk, which has developed into a large industrial estate servicing North Sea oil production.

Montrose, James Graham, 1st Marquess and 5th Earl of Montrose (1612–1650)

Scottish soldier, son of the 4th Earl of Montrose. He supported the Covenanters against Charles I, but after 1640 changed sides. As lieutenant general in 1644, he rallied the loyalist Highland clans to Charles, defeating the Covenanters' forces at Tipeprmuir and Aberdeen, but his subsequent attempt to raise the Royalist standard in the Lowlands ended in failure at Philiphaugh in 1645, and he escaped to Holland. Returning in 1650 to raise a revolt, he survived shipwreck only to have his weakened forces defeated, and (having been betrayed to the Covenanters) was hanged in Edinburgh.

In defeat, unbeatable; in victory, unbearable.

WINSTON CHURCHILL British Conservative prime minister.
Attributed remark, referring to Field Marshal Montgomery

Monty Python's Flying Circus

English satirical TV comedy series 1969–74, written and performed by John ◊Cleese, Terry Jones, Michael Palin, Eric Idle, Graham Chapman, and the US animator Terry Gilliam. The series became a cult and the group made several films: *Monty Python and the Holy Grail* (1975), *The Life of Brian* (1979), and *The Meaning of Life* (1983).

Moody Blues

Innovative English rock band formed in 1964. Their singles include 'Knights in White Satin' (1967) and their album hits include *Days Of Future Passed* (1967), *On The Threshold Of A Dream* (1969), and *A Question Of Balance* (1970).

The group's members are Justin Hayward (1946–), vocals and guitar; John Lodge (1945–); Graeme Edge (1941–), drums; Mike Pinder (1941–), keyboards and vocals; and Ray Thomas (1941–), flute and vocals.

Moorcock, Michael John (1939–)

English writer. Associated with the 1960s new wave in science fiction, he was editor of the magazine *New Worlds* (1964–69). He wrote the Jerry Cornelius novels, collected as *The Cornelius Chronicles* (1977), and *Gloriana* (1978). Among later novels are *The Revenge of the Rose* (1989) and *Blood* (1994).

Moore, Bobby (Robert Frederick) (1941–1993)

English footballer who led the England team to victory against West Germany in the 1966 World Cup final. A superb defender, he played 108 games for England 1962–70 (until 1978, a world-record number of international appearances) and was captain 90 times. His Football League career, spent at West Ham 1968–74 and Fulham 1974–77, spanned 19 years and 668 matches.

Moore, Dudley (Stuart John) (1935–)

English actor, comedian, and musician. He was teamed 1959–73 with the comedian Peter ◊Cook. Moore became a Hollywood star after appearing in *'10'* (1979). His other films, mostly comedies, include *Bedazzled* (1968), *Arthur* (1981), *Santa Claus* (1985), and *Blame It on the Bellboy* (1992).

He is also an accomplished musician and has given classical piano concerts.

Moore, G(eorge) E(dward) (1873–1958)

English philosopher who generally defended common-sense views of the world and what is said about it in ordinary language. In ethics, he held that any attempt to identify goodness with another concept, such as happiness, was a fallacy – the 'naturalistic fallacy'.

Educated at Cambridge, he was professor of philosophy at the university 1925–39, and edited the journal *Mind*, to which he contributed between 1921 and 1947. His books include *Principia Ethica* (1903), in which he attempted to analyse the moral question 'What is good?', and *Some Main Problems of Philosophy* (1953).

His emphasis on the value of 'the pleasures of human intercourse and the enjoyment of beautiful objects' was immensely influential, in particular on the ◊Bloomsbury Group.

Moore, Henry (Spencer) (1898–1986)

English sculptor. His subjects include the reclining nude, mother-and-child groups, the warrior, and interlocking abstract forms. Many of his post-1945 works are in bronze or marble, such as *Reclining Figure* (1957–58), outside the UNESCO building in Paris, and are often designed to be placed in landscape settings.

Moore claimed to have learned much from archaic South and Central American sculpture, and this is reflected in his work of the 1920s which laid stress on truth to material and the original block, as in *Reclining Figure* (1929; Leeds City Art Gallery). By the early 1930s most of his main themes had emerged, and the Surrealists' preoccupation with organic forms in abstract works proved a strong influence, particularly that of Alberto Giacometti. Moore's hollowed biomorphic wooden shapes strung with wires, such as *The Bride* (1940; Museum of Modern Art, New York), show affinities with sculpture by Hans Arp and Barbara ◊Hepworth. Semi-abstract work suggesting organic structures recurs after World War II, for example in the interwoven bonelike forms of the *Hill Arches* and the bronze *Sheep Pieces* (1970s), set in fields by his studio in Perry Green, Hertfordshire.

Born in Castleford, Yorkshire, Moore studied at Leeds and

the Royal College of Art (1921–24). As an official war artist during World War II, he made a series of drawings of people in London's air-raid shelters. Many of his works are now exhibited in the gardens and fields overlooking his home in Hertfordshire, looked after by the Henry Moore Foundation (set up by the artist, his wife, and daughter in 1977).

Moore, Patrick Alfred Caldwell (1923–)

English broadcaster, writer, and popularizer of astronomy. He began presenting the BBC television series *The Sky at Night* in 1968.

Moore was born in Pinner, Middlesex, now Greater London. He was educated privately. Moore served with the Royal Air Force during World War II, and for seven years after the war he assisted at a training school for pilots. He was director of the Armagh Planetarium, Northern Ireland 1965–68, and became vice president of the British Astronomical Association in 1970.

Moore, Roger (George) (1927–)

English actor. He starred in the television series *The Saint* (1962–70), and assumed the film role of the spy James Bond in 1973 in *Live and Let Die*. His last appearance as Bond was in *A View to a Kill* (1985).

Moorhouse, Adrian (1964–)

English swimmer who won the 100 metres breaststroke at the 1988 Seoul Olympics.

Moor Park

House on the River Wey in Surrey, England, 3 km/2 mi from Farnham. It was the residence of William Temple, a diplomat, and here Jonathan Swift first met 'Stella' (Hester Johnson), and wrote *The Tale of a Tub* and *The Battle of the Books*.

Morar, Loch

Lake on the west coast of Highland unitary authority, Scotland, extending 19 km/12 mi in length, with an outflow across a narrow bridge of land to the Sound of Sleat, 5 km/3 mi south of Mallaig. It is the deepest loch in the British Isles, reaching a maximum depth of 310 m/1,017 ft.

Moray

Another spelling of **Murray**, regent of Scotland 1567–70.

Moray

Unitary authority in northeast Scotland, created in 1996 from the Moray district of Grampian region

Area 2,224 sq km/859 sq mi

Towns ◊Elgin (administrative headquarters), Forres, Buckie, Lossiemouth

Physical the land gradually slopes from the Grampian Mountains in the south (Cairn Gorm 1,245 m/4,085 ft) towards the Moray Firth; extensive coastal lowlands fringe an area of sand-dune formation; part of this land was reclaimed from the sea and is now covered by the Culbin forest. The River Spey reaches the North Sea near Buckie

Features Elgin cathedral; Brodie and Duffus castles; Gordonstoun school

Industries whisky distilling, food processing

Agriculture some fishing (Buckie, Lossiemouth); trout and salmon fishing in rivers; cereals in lowland plain

Population (1995) 87,200

History numerous royal residences and setting for Shakespeare's *Macbeth*.

Economy

The area has a rural economy, with strength in modern management of traditional produce, food and whisky.

Architecture

Brodie Castle, 5 km/3 mi west of Forres, was built in about 1567 for the Brodie family; it was extended in the early 17th and 19th centuries. Duffus Castle, 8 km/5 mi northwest of Elgin, is a good example of a Norman motte and bailey castle, with a water-filled moat.

Environment

There are 33 Sites of Special Scientific Interest, one National Nature Reserve, three Ramsars (wetland sites), two Special Protection Areas, and one National Scenic Area.

Administrative history

Prior to 1975, the area was divided between the three counties of Nairnshire, Morayshire, and Banffshire.

Moray Firth

North Sea inlet in Scotland, between Burghead (Moray) and Tarbat Ness (Highland), 38 km/24 mi wide at its entrance, and 48 km/30 mi from there to the Caledonian Canal. The city of Inverness is situated at the head of the Firth. The Spey, Findhorn, and Nairn are the chief rivers which flow into the Moray Firth.

More, (St) Thomas (1478–1535)

English politician and author. From 1509 he was favoured by ◊Henry VIII and employed on foreign embassies. He was a member of the privy council from 1518 and Lord Chancellor from 1529 but resigned over Henry's break with the pope. For refusing to accept the king as head of the church, he was executed. The title of his political book *Utopia* (1516) has come to mean any supposedly perfect society.

Son of a London judge, More studied Greek, Latin, French, theology, and music at Oxford, and law at Lincoln's Inn, London, and was influenced by the humanists John Colet and Erasmus, who became a friend. In Parliament from 1504, he was made Speaker of the House of Commons in 1523. He was knighted in 1521, and on the fall of Cardinal Wolsey became Lord Chancellor, but resigned in 1532 because he could not agree with the king on his ecclesiastical policy and marriage with Anne Boleyn. In 1534 he refused to take the oath of supremacy to Henry VIII as head of the church, and after a year's imprisonment in the Tower of London he was executed.

Among Thomas More's writings are the Latin *Utopia* (1516), sketching an ideal commonwealth; the English *Dialogue* (1528), a theological argument against the Reformation leader Tyndale; and a *History of Richard III*. He was also a patron of artists, including Holbein. More was canonized in 1935.

More, Kenneth Gilbert (1914–1982)

English actor. A wholesome film star of the 1950s, he was cast as leading man in adventure films and light comedies such as *Genevieve* (1953), *Doctor in the House* (1954), and *Northwest Frontier* (1959). He played war hero Douglas Bader in *Reach for the Sky* (1956).

Morecambe

Town and seaside resort in Lancashire, northwest England, on Morecambe Bay, joined with the port of Heysham, which has a ferry service to the Isle of Man; joint population (1991) 46,700. Tourism is important; other industries include shrimp fishing, engineering, and the manufacture of clothing.

The town developed from the end of the 18th century as people started visiting the villages of Poulton-le-Sands, Torrisholme, and Bare. During the 19th century the arrival of the railway enabled people from the nearby Lancashire mill towns to reach the coast easily. The name Morecambe was adopted in 1889. The town has increasingly drawn more day-visitors than those staying for a holiday; there are illuminations in the autumn, and the ecology and birdlife of **Morecambe Bay** are an attraction. There are dangerous quicksands in the bay and tides advance very quickly.

Morecambe, Eric stage name of John Eric Bartholomew (1926–1984)

English comic actor and writer, who named himself after his northwest home-town of Morecambe. An endearing screen presence, tall of stature, balding, and sporting large spectacles, he was the funnyman to Ernie ◊Wise's straightman. Their television shows included the 1950s *Running Wild*, the 1960s *Two of a Kind* and the long-running *Morecambe & Wise Show* (1961–82), which offered a mixture of stand-up routines, song-and-dance numbers, and comedy sketches. The 'humiliation' of guest stars, notably André Previn and Glenda Jackson, and song-and-dance routines with Angela Rippon and a team of newsreaders and presenters in full evening dress, provided some of television comedy's most memorable moments. Together with Wise he featured in the films *The Intelligence Men* (1965), *That Riviera Touch* (1966), *The Magnificent Two* (1967), and *Night Train to Murder* (1983), the latter of which they co-wrote.

Morecambe Bay

Inlet of the Irish Sea, between the Furness Peninsula (Cumbria) and Lancashire, England, with shallow sands. There are oil wells, and natural gas 50 km/30 mi offshore.

MORECAMBE, ERIC *As half of one of the most celebrated double-acts in British comedy, Eric Morecambe was famous for debunking the pretensions of his pompous 'straight man' Ernie Wise (left). Morecambe crafted his comedy with great attention to detail, but overwork brought on a heart attack that caused his untimely death in 1984. Rex*

Morgan, Conwy Lloyd (1852–1936)

English psychologist. Of immense influence in the field of comparative psychology, he carried out observational studies of animals in natural settings. In 1894 he was the first to describe **trial-and-error learning** in animals.

Morgan, Henry (*c.* 1635–1688)

Welsh buccaneer in the Caribbean. He made war against Spain, capturing and sacking Panama in 1671. In 1675 he was knighted and appointed lieutenant governor of Jamaica.

Morison, Robert (1620–1683)

Scottish botanist who was the first professor of botany at Oxford University in 1669 and was physician and botanist to England's King Charles II.

Morland, George (1763–1804)

English painter. Strongly influenced by Dutch and Flemish painters of everyday life, he specialized in picturesque rural subjects painted in a fluent easy style, a good example being *Inside of a Stable* (1791; National Gallery, London). His works were widely reproduced in engravings.

Morley

Town in West Yorkshire, England, south of Leeds; population (1991) 46,100. In the 19th century it developed as a large manufacturing town, producing machinery and woollen goods.

Morley, Malcolm (1931–)

English painter; active in New York from 1964. He coined the term **Superrealism** (equivalent to Photorealism) for his work in the 1960s, which was characterized by intense, photographic realism and attention to minute detail. His subjects include landscapes and animals from life combined with mythological motifs; he also paints abstracts. In 1984 he was awarded the first Turner Prize. By this time he had turned away from Superrealism, and was painting in a much looser style.

Morley, Robert (1908–1992)

English actor and dramatist. He was active both in Britain and the USA. His film work consisted mainly of character roles, in such movies as *Marie Antoinette* (1938), *The African Queen* (1952), and *Oscar Wilde* (1960).

Morley, Thomas (*c.* 1557–*c.* 1602)

English composer. He wrote consort music, madrigals, and airs including the lute song 'It was a lover and his lass' for Shakespeare's play *As You Like It* (1599). He published an influential keyboard tutor *A Plaine and Easie Introduction to Practicall Musicke* in 1597. He was also organist at St Paul's Cathedral, London.

Morpeth

Town and administrative headquarters of the county of ◊Northumberland, England, 22 km/14 mi north of Newcastle; population (1991) 13,700. Morpeth has a small iron foundry and a thriving cattle-market. There are remains of a medieval castle, and the town has an ancient chantry and clock tower. Newminster Abbey dates from the 12th century and the parish church of St Mary from the 14th century.

The town hall was designed by John Vanbrugh in 1714. The Chantry Bagpipe Museum includes pipes from Northumberland, the Borders, Ireland, Greece, and Italy.

Morris, Desmond John (1928–)

English zoologist, a writer and broadcaster on animal and human behaviour. His book *The Naked Ape* (1967) was a best seller.

Morris studied at Birmingham and at Oxford, working on animal behaviour under Nikolaas ◊Tinbergen. He became head of the Granada Television and Film Unit at the Zoological Society in London in 1956. Three years later he was appointed Curator of Mammals at London Zoo and from 1967 to 1968 served as director of the Institute of Contemporary Arts in London.

In his book *The Human Zoo* (1969), Morris scrutinizes the society that the naked ape has created for itself. He compares civilized humans with their captive animal counterparts and shows how confined animals seem to demonstrate the same neurotic behaviour patterns as human beings often do in crowded cities. He believes the urban environment of the cities to be the human zoo.

Morris, Jan (1926–)

English travel writer and journalist. Her books display a zestful, witty, and knowledgeable style and offer deftly handled historical perspectives. They include *Coast to Coast* (1956), *Venice* (1960), *Oxford* (1965), *Farewell the Trumpets* (1978), and *Among the Cities* (1985). *Fisher's Face* (1995) is a biography of Admiral of the Fleet Lord Fisher. Born James Morris, her adoption of female gender is described in *Conundrum* (1974), and *Pleasures of a Tangled Life* (1989) is a further autobiographical study.

As a young journalist with the British Everest expedition in 1953 James Morris was the first to send news that the mountain had been conquered.

Morris, William (1834–1896)

English artist, designer, socialist, and writer. A founder of the ◊Arts and Crafts movement, he condemned 19th-century mechanization and sought a revival of traditional crafts. He linked this to a renewal of society based on Socialist principles.

Morris was born in London and educated at Oxford University, where he formed a lasting friendship with the Pre-Raphaelite artist Edward ◊Burne-Jones and was influenced by the art critic John Ruskin and the painter and poet Dante Gabriel ◊Rossetti. He abandoned his first profession, architecture, to study painting, but had a considerable influence on such architects as William Lethaby and Philip Webb. In 1861 he cofounded Morris, Marshall, Faulkner and Company ('the Firm') which designed and produced stained glass, furniture, fabric, carpets, and decorative wallpapers; many of the designs, inspired by medieval, classical, and oriental sources, are still produced today.

Morris's first book of verse was *The Defence of Guenevere* (1858). He published several verse romances, notably *The Life and Death of Jason* (1867) and *The Earthly Paradise* (1868–70). A visit to Iceland in 1871 inspired the epic poem *Sigurd the Volsung* (1876) and general interest in the sagas. His Kelmscott Press, set up in 1890 to print beautifully designed books, influenced printing and book design.

A leading Socialist, his prose romances *A Dream of John Ball* (1888) and utopian *News from Nowhere* (1891) reflected his socialist ideology. He joined the Social Democratic Federation in 1883, but left in 1884 because he found it too moderate, and set up the Socialist League. To this period belong the critical and sociological studies *Signs of Change* (1888) and *Hopes and Fears for Art* (1892). He also lectured on socialism.

Morris dance

Old English folk dance. It derived its name from the Moorish *Moresca* (old English 'morys', 'Moorish'), introduced into England about the 15th century, and may have originated in pre-Christian ritual dances. It partook of a pageant in character and was danced in various kinds of fancy dress, with jingles tied to the dancers' legs. In early times it was usually performed by six men, one of whom wore girl's clothing while another portrayed a horse. In some districts elements of the Sword Dance were introduced into it. The music, a great variety of tunes, was played by a pipe and tabor, or more rarely by a bagpipe or violin. Morris dancing is still popular.

Morrison, Herbert Stanley, Baron Morrison of Lambeth (1888–1965)

British Labour politician. He was a founder member and later secretary of the London Labour Party 1915–45, and a member of the London County Council 1922–45. He entered Parliament in 1923, and organized the Labour Party's general election victory in 1945. He was twice defeated in the contest for leadership of the party, once by Clement Attlee in 1932, and then by Hugh Gaitskell in 1955. A skilful organizer, he lacked the ability to unite the party.

He was minister of transport 1929–31, home secretary

MORRIS DANCING *Morris men from Bampton in Oxfordshire. The precise origins of this ritual folk dance are unclear, but it is believed to derive from a pagan custom. In rural England, the tradition was revived in the 19th century after centuries of neglect. Morris men can often to be seen at country fairs and pubs. Brian Shuel/Collections*

1940–45, Lord President of the Council and leader of the House of Commons 1945–51, and foreign secretary March–Oct 1951.

Morrison, Van (George Ivan) (1945–)

Northern Irish singer and songwriter. His jazz-inflected Celtic soul style was already in evidence on *Astral Weeks* (1968) and has been highly influential. Among other albums are *Tupelo Honey* (1971), *Veedon Fleece* (1974), and *Avalon Sunset* (1989). He continued to release albums throughout the 1990s, with a consistently retrospective tone, the finest being the double CD *Hymns to the Silence* (1991).

Morrison began in the beat-music era by forming the group Them 1964–66, which had two hits, 'Here Comes the Night' and 'Gloria'; the latter became a standard.

Morrissey stage name of Steven Patrick Morrissey (1959–)

English rock singer and lyricist. He was a founder member of the ◊Smiths 1982–87 and subsequently a solo artist. His lyrics reflect on everyday miseries or glumly celebrate the England of his childhood. Solo albums include *Viva Hate* (1987) and *Your Arsenal* (1992). A marked dwindling of interest in the Morrissey world-view in the 1990s saw a rapid diminution in output and returns.

The Smiths' split ended his most successful songwriting partnership with guitarist Johnny Marr, and his solo work has been musically less distinctive, though with his epigrammatic wit still intermittently evident.

Morte D'Arthur, Le

Series of episodes from the legendary life of King Arthur by Thomas ◊Malory, completed in 1470, regarded as the first great prose work in English literature. Only the last of the eight books composing the series is titled *Le Morte D'Arthur.*

Mortensen, Stan(ley) Harding (1921–1991)

English footballer who scored 23 goals in 25 internationals for England, 1947–53, including four on his debut against Portugal. He spent most of his playing career at Blackpool, scoring 197 goals in 317 league appearances.

Mortimer, John Clifford (1923–)

English barrister and writer. His works include the plays *The Dock Brief* (1958) and *A Voyage Round My Father* (1970), and numerous stories about the fictional barrister who first appeared in the volume *Rumpole of the Bailey* (1978) and then in several television series. Subsequent satirical fiction has tended to be developed alongside television, and includes

MORTIMER, JOHN *English writer and lawyer John Mortimer produces popular novels and plays evoking an English middle class in moral decline. His television credits include* I Claudius *(1976),* Brideshead Revisited *(1981), and* Rumpole of the Bailey. *His autobiography,* Clinging to the Wreckage, *appeared in 1982. Penguin Books Limited*

Paradise Postponed (1985) and *Summer's Lease* (1988). *Dunster* (1992) is a mystery story featuring a libel case.

Clinging to the Wreckage (1982) and *Murderers and Other Friends* (1994) are autobiography. Knighted 1998.

> *Matrimony and murder both carry a mandatory life sentence.*
>
> John Mortimer English novelist, TV dramatist, and barrister.
> *Rumpole for the Defence*, 'Rumpole and the Boat People'

Mortimer, Roger de, 8th Baron of Wigmore and 1st Earl of March (*c.* 1287–1330)

English politician and adventurer. He opposed Edward II and with Edward's queen, Isabella, led a rebellion against him in 1326, bringing about his abdication. From 1327 Mortimer ruled England as the queen's lover, until Edward III had him executed.

A rebel, he was imprisoned by Edward II for two years before making his escape from the Tower of London to France. There he joined with the English queen, Isabella, who was conducting negotiations at the French court, and returned with her to England in 1326. Edward fled when they landed with their followers, and Mortimer secured Edward's deposition by Parliament. In 1328 he was created Earl of March. He was popularly supposed responsible for Edward II's murder, and when the young Edward III had him seized while with the Queen at Nottingham Castle, he was hanged, drawn, and quartered at Tyburn, London.

Moshinsky, Elijah (1946–)

Australian-born British opera and theatre producer. He became Associate Producer at the Royal Opera House, London in 1979. He has also produced operas for the English National Opera and Australian Opera. Theatre productions include *Shadowlands* (1989) and plays for the Royal Shakespeare Company and the Royal National Theatre.

Mosley, Oswald (Ernald) (1896–1980)

British politician, founder of the British Union of Fascists (BUF) 1932. He was a member of Parliament 1918–31, then led the BUF until his internment 1940–43 during World War II. In 1946 Mosley was denounced when it became known that Italy had funded his prewar efforts to establish fascism in Britain, but in 1948 he resumed fascist propaganda with his Union Movement, the revived BUF.

His first marriage was to a daughter of the Conservative politician Lord Curzon, his second to Diana Freeman-Mitford, one of the ◊Mitford sisters.

Moss, Stirling (1929–)

English racing-car driver. Despite being one of the best-known names in British motor racing, Moss never won the world championship. He was runner-up on four occasions, losing to Juan Manuel Fangio in 1955, 1956, and 1957, and to fellow Briton Mike Hawthorn (1929–1959) in 1958.

Motherwell

Industrial town and administrative headquarters of ◊North Lanarkshire, Scotland, southeast of Glasgow; population (1991) 60,500. The two burghs of Motherwell and Wishaw were amalgamated in 1920, but the towns retain distinct identities. Formerly a coalmining, iron, and engineering town, industries now include light manufacturing and there is a Eurofreight terminal.

The skyline was formerly dominated by the Ravenscraig iron and steel works which closed in 1992.

The town is named after an old healing well dedicated to the Blessed Virgin.

Motion, Andrew (1952–)

English poet, biographer, and novelist. His volumes of poetry include *The Price of Everything* (1994), and he published the authorized biography of the poet Philip Larkin in 1993.

motoring law

Legislation affecting the use of vehicles on public roads. It covers the licensing of vehicles and drivers, and the criminal offences that can be committed by the owners and drivers of vehicles.

In Britain, all vehicles are subject to road tax and (when over a certain age) to an annual safety check (MOT test). Anyone driving on a public road must have a valid driving licence for that kind of vehicle. There is a wide range of offences: from parking in the wrong place to causing death by dangerous driving. Offences are punishable by fixed penalties: fines; endorsement of the offender's driving licence; disqualification from driving for a period; or imprisonment, depending on the seriousness of the offence. Courts must disqualify drivers convicted of driving while affected by alcohol. Licence endorsements carry penalty points (the number depending on the seriousness of the offence) which are totted up. Once a driver acquires more than 12 points, the court must disqualify him or her from driving.

motor racing

Competitive racing of motor vehicles. It has forms as diverse as hill-climbing, stock-car racing, rallying, sports-car racing, and Formula One Grand Prix racing. A number of Formula One teams are based in Britain, with Oxfordshire a particular centre.

Purpose-built circuits in the UK include: Brands Hatch, Brooklands (to 1939), Donington, and Silverstone.

Rally-driving events in the UK include: the Lombard–RAC Rally (formerly the RAC International Rally of Great Britain), first held in 1927.

The UK government announced in November 1997 that is was exempting Formula One motor racing from its proposed ban on tobacco sponsorship in sport, on the grounds that a ban would put thousands of jobs at risk in the UK where most of the Formula One teams are based. This provoked a storm of protest not just from anti-smoking campaigners but also from the representatives of other sports equally dependent on tobacco sponsorship, such as professional snooker, who were not receiving preferential treatment. The government was put under further pressure in December 1997 when European health ministers agreed on a new directive banning tobacco advertising.

motorway

Road for fast motor traffic, with two or more lanes in each direction, and with special access points (junctions) fed by slip roads. The first motorway in the UK, the Preston by-pass (now part of the M6) was opened in 1958, and the first section of the M1 was opened 1959. In 1992 there were 3,100 km/1,865 mi of motorway in the UK. Their upkeep cost £312 million in 1991, with about 160 km/100 mi needing repair each year. See table on next page for principal motorways in the UK.

Mott, Nevill Francis (1905–1996)

English physicist who researched the electronic properties of metals, semiconductors, and noncrystalline materials. He shared the Nobel Prize for Physics 1977. Knighted 1962.

Mottisfont Abbey

Abbey in Hampshire, England, 15 km/9 mi west of Winchester. The 660 ha/1630 acre estate, which includes most of **Mottisfont village**, the abbey itself, and 162 ha/400 acres of woodland, was given to the National Trust in 1957. The abbey has early 13th-century origins and was an Augustinian priory until the Dissolution of the Monasteries in the 1530s, when it was acquired by Lord Chancellor Sandys and converted into a Tudor mansion. Other major changes were made in the early 18th century.

The house contains 'Gothic' trompe l'oeil paintings by Rex Whistler in the Whistler Room.

A tributary of the River Test which flows through the garden, which together with walled gardens and a collection of old-fashioned types of roses, creates a superb setting.

Mountain Ash, Welsh Aberpennar

Town in the county borough of Rhondda Cynon Taff, south Wales, 6 km/4 mi southeast of Aberdare; population with Abercynon (1991) 21,300. It is in a highly industrialized area, with the industrial villages of Abercwmboi and Aberaman nearby.

Mountbatten, Louis Francis Albert Victor Nicholas, 1st Earl Mountbatten of Burma (1900–1979)

English admiral and administrator, a great-grandson of Queen Victoria. In World War II he became chief of combined operations in 1942 and commander in chief in southeast Asia in 1943. As last viceroy and governor general of India

MOTORWAYS *A paramedic surveying a congested section of the M6 motorway near Birmingham. As traffic levels have steadily increased on Britain's motorways, more provisions have been made for dealing with accidents. Units able to respond rapidly to emergencies include motorcycle paramedics and helicopter ambulances. Steve Connors/ Impact*

Principal Motorways in the UK

Motorway	Destinations	Length
M1	London–Leeds	304 km/189 mi
M11	London–Cambridge	98 km/61 mi
M18	Rotherham–Goole	56 km/35 mi
M180	Doncaster–Grimsby	82 km/51 mi
M2	Gravesend–Faversham	53 km/33 mi
M20	London–Folkestone	117 km/73 mi
M23	London–Crawley	45 km/28 mi
M25	London Orbital	188 km/117 mi
M27	Lyndhurst–Portsmouth	55 km/34 mi
M3	London–Southampton	129 km/80 mi
M4	London–Llanelli	325 km/202 mi
M40	London–Birmingham	193 km/120 mi
M42	Bromsgrove–Ashby-de-la-Zouch	79 km/49 mi
M5	Birmingham–Exeter	266 km/165 mi
M53	Wallasey–Chester	39 km/24 mi
M54	Wolverhampton–Telford	37 km/23 mi
M55	Preston–Blackpool	29 km/18 mi
M56	Manchester–Chester	39 km/24 mi
M6	Rugby–Killington	261 km/162 mi
M6, A74(M)	Killington–Glasgow	251 km/156 mi
M61	Manchester–Preston	50 km/31 mi
M62	Liverpool–Kingston Upon Hull	206 km/128 mi
M63	Salford–Stockport	32 km/20 mi
M65	Bamber Bridge–Colne	45 km/28 mi
M66	Ramsbottom–Stockport	35 km/22 mi
M8	Edinburgh–Greenock	109 km/68 mi
M9	Edinburgh–Dunblane	64 km/40 mi
M90	Rosyth–Perth	48 km/30 mi
A1(M)	London–Newcastle	230 km/143 mi
	Ireland	
M1	Belfast–Dungannon	66 km/41 mi
M2	Belfast–Ballymena	42 km/26 mi

1947–48, he oversaw that country's transition to independence. He was killed by an Irish Republican Army (IRA) bomb aboard his yacht at Mullaghmore, County Sligo, in the Republic of Ireland.

As chief of combined operations he was criticized for the heavy loss of Allied lives in the disastrous Dieppe raid. In southeast Asia he concentrated on the reconquest of Burma, although the campaign was actually conducted by General Slim. Mountbatten accepted the surrender of 750,000 Japanese troops in his area of command at a formal parade in Singapore in September 1945. He was chief of UK Defence Staff 1959–65. KCVO 1922.

Mourne Mountains, or Mountains of Mourne

Mountain range in the south of County Down, Northern Ireland, extending from above Newcastle to Carlingford Lough. The highest summit is Slieve Donard; height 852 m/2795 ft. The mountains are of granite.

Mousetrap, The

Murder mystery play by Agatha ◊Christie, which has run continuously in London since it was first performed at the Ambassador's Theatre in 1952, making it the world's longest-running play. Since 1974 the play has been performed at St Martin's Theatre.

Mow Cop

Hill at the southern end of the Pennines on the Cheshire–Staffordshire border, central England; height 300 m/984 ft. It was the site of an open-air religious gathering on 31 May 1807 that is considered to be the start of Primitive Methodism. It remained a popular location for revivalist meetings.

Features include a folly (1754) in the form of a ruin. Mow Cop is the property of the National Trust.

Mowlam, Marjorie ('Mo') (1949–)

British Labour politician, appointed secretary of state for Northern Ireland in 1997. Her willingness to take risks to promote the peace process, including a January 1998 visit to convicted loyalist terrorists in the Maze prison, helped bring about the 1998 Good Friday Agreement, paving the way for the election of a power-sharing Northern Ireland Assembly.

After studying in Britain and the USA, she embarked on an academic career, at Newcastle University and Northern College, Barnsley, before entering the House of Commons, representing Redcar, at the 1987 general election. She joined Labour's shadow cabinet, covering Northern Ireland 1988–89, Trade and Industry 1989–92, the Citizen's Charter and Women's Affairs 1992–93, National Heritage 1993–94, and Northern Ireland again 1994–97.

As secretary of state for Northern Ireland, she made an immediate impact on politics in the province, initiating a non-ministerial dialogue with Sinn Féin, and taking positive steps towards avoiding the clashes between Catholics and Protestants during the annual 'marching season'.

Moya, Jacko (John Hidalgo) (1920–1994)

US-born British architect. His Modernist work, in partnership with others, includes housing developments, for example, Churchill Gardens, Pimlico, London (1956–92); and Oxbridge college buildings, such as Brasenose College, Oxford (1961). His Skylon (1951), an elegant, lightweight pointed structure suspended on balancing wires above the Thames, was the most visible landmark of the Festival of Britain in London. The Churchill Gardens buildings were technically inventive with district heating from Battersea power station across the river.

Moya's practice developed its clearly Modern direction before less popular Modernist styles such as English Brutalism or system building took hold, and so includes all the eclectic and playful elements of English Modernism. He was awarded the CBE in 1966 and the practice won the RIBA Gold Medal in 1974.

Much Wenlock

Town in Shropshire, England, on the River Severn, 19 km/12 mi southeast of Shrewsbury; population (1991) 3,100. Wenlock is an agricultural centre, and manufactures bricks and tiles. It dates from the Middle Ages. To the southwest of the town is the limestone ridge of **Wenlock Edge** (240 m–290 m/800–950 ft).

The town includes the ruins of Wenlock Priory, originally founded as a convent in the 7th century and later a priory for Cluniac monks. There is also a 16th-century half-timbered guildhall and the church of Holy Trinity, parts of which are Norman. Coal and iron were mined in the area until recently.

Muggeridge, (Thomas) Malcolm (1903–1990)

English journalist and author. He worked for the *Guardian*, the *Calcutta Statesman*, the London *Evening Standard*, and the *Daily Telegraph* before becoming editor of *Punch* 1953–57.

Muir, Edwin (1887–1959)

Scottish poet. He drew mystical inspiration from his Orkney childhood. *First Poems* (1925) was published after an extended period of travel and residence in Europe, which also resulted in translations from German of Franz Kafka and Lion Feuchtwanger, in collaboration with his wife, the novelist Willa Anderson (1890–1970). Dreams, myths, and menaces coexist in his poetry and his *Autobiography* (1954) explores similar themes.

Muir's poetry represents the trend in 20th-century verse to return to a contemplation of the primitive facts of human life on Earth: time, love, and death. His early work is metaphysical, full of symbolism and imagery portraying life as a road of memories from a primeval past, but his later writing is essentially religious.

Muir, Jean Elizabeth (1928–1996)

English fashion designer. She worked as a designer for Jaeger 1956–61 and set up her own fashion house in 1961. In 1991 she launched a knitwear collection. Her clothes are characterized by soft, classic, tailored shapes in leathers and soft fabrics, especially jersey, and by plain, sombre colours, especially navy blue.

Muir began her career as a sales assistant and sketcher at Liberty's. After her fashion house, Jane and Jane, was bought by the textile company Courtaulds in 1966 she formed the **Jean Muir Company**, with her husband Harry Lenckert.

Muldowney, Dominic (1952–)

English composer. He studied with Jonathan Harvey at Southampton and with Birtwistle in London. In 1975 he was appointed assistant music director to Harrison Birtwistle at the Royal National Theatre, London, succeeding as director in 1981. His output includes music for many National Theatre productions; a realisation of *The ◊Beggar's Opera* (1982), and concertos for percussion, oboe, and trumpet (1991, 1991, 1993).

Mull

Second largest island of the Inner ◊Hebrides, Argyll and Bute, Scotland; area 950 sq km/367 sq mi; population (1991) 2,700. It is mountainous, and is separated from the mainland by the **Sound of Mull** and the Firth of Lorne; it lies 11 km/7 mi west of Oban. The main town is Tobermory, from which there are ferry connections to Oban; Craignure is also connected by ferry to Oban. The economy is based on fishing, forestry, tourism, and stock rearing.

The west coast of Mull is indented with sea lochs, of which the main ones are Loch-na-Keal and Loch Scridain. The highest peak is Ben More (966 m/3,171 ft). On the south coast of the island, the Carsaig Arches are a series of columnar black basalt caves and arches, said to have been used as a

MULL *A Celtic cross on the island of Mull in the Inner Hebrides, Scotland. This mountainous granite island, with limited space for grazing and agriculture, nevertheless offered a good defensive position. It was the site of several early settlements, including the ancient castles of Aros and Duart. Corel*

hiding-place by nuns during the Reformation. The island of Mull has the most extensive set of ferry connections among the Scottish islands.

mummers' play, or St George play

Folk drama enacted in dumb show by a masked cast, performed on Christmas Day to celebrate the death of the old year and its rebirth as the new year. The plot usually consists of a duel between St George and an infidel knight, in which one of them is killed but later revived by a doctor. Mummers' plays are still performed in some parts of Britain, often by Morris dance teams.

Munich Agreement

Pact signed on 29 September 1938 by the leaders of the UK (Neville ◊Chamberlain), France (Edouard Daladier), Germany (Hitler), and Italy (Mussolini), under which Czechoslovakia was compelled to surrender its Sudeten-German districts (the **Sudeten**) to Germany. Chamberlain claimed it would guarantee 'peace in our time', but it did not prevent Hitler from seizing the rest of Czechoslovakia in March 1939.

Most districts were not given the option of a plebiscite under the agreement. After World War II the Sudeten was returned to Czechoslovakia, and over 2 million German-speaking people were expelled from the country.

Munnings, Alfred James (1878–1959)

English painter. He excelled in racing and hunting scenes, and painted realistic everyday scenes featuring horses, such as horsefairs or horses grazing. *Epsom Downs* is a notable example. As president of the Royal Academy (1944–51) he was outspoken in his dislike of 'modern art'.

Munrow, David (1942–1976)

English early music specialist and wind-instrument player. He founded the Early Music Consort in 1967 and taught at Leicester University and the Royal Academy of Music, London. He gave frequent performances of medieval and Renaissance music and was a frequent broadcaster. He published *Instruments of the Middle Ages and Renaissance* in 1976.

Murchison, Roderick Impey (1792–1871)

Scottish geologist responsible for naming the Silurian period, the subject of his book *The Silurian System* (1839). Expeditions to Russia 1840–45 led him to define another worldwide system, the Permian, named after the strata of the Perm region.

Murchison was born in Ross-shire. He entered the army at 15 and fought in the Peninsular War. Often accompanied by geologists Adam ◊Sedgwick or Charles ◊Lyell, Murchison made field explorations in Scotland, France, and the Alps. In 1855 he became director-general of the UK Geological Survey. An ardent imperialist, for many years he was also president of the Royal Geographical Society, encouraging African exploration and annexation.

Murchison believed in a universal order of the deposition of strata, indicated by fossils rather than solely by lithological features. Fossils showed a clear progression in complexity. The Silurian system contained, in his view, remains of the earliest life forms. He based it on studies of slate rocks in South Wales. With Sedgwick's cooperation, Murchison also established the Devonian system in southwest England. Knighted 1846, baronet 1866.

Murdoch, (Jean) Iris (1919–)

English novelist, born in Dublin. Her novels combine philosophical speculation with often outrageous situations and tangled human relationships. They include *The Sandcastle* (1957), *The Bell* (1958), *The Sea, The Sea* (1978; winner of the Booker Prize), *Nuns and Soldiers* (1980), *The Message to the Planet* (1989), *The Green Knight* (1993), and *Jackson's Dilemma* (1995).

During World War II she worked at the Treasury, then at refugee camps in Europe. From 1948–63 she was a fellow and tutor in philosophy at St Anne's College, Oxford. Her first work was a philosophical study, *Sartre, Romantic Rationalist* (1953). Her first novel was *Under The Net* (1954), which, with *The Flight from the Enchanter* (1956), made her reputation as a writer of high seriousness of purpose and great wit. She has published other works of philosophy, including *Metaphysics as a Guide to Morals* (1992) and *Existentialists and Mystics* (1997) which is a collection of essays on philosophy and literature. DBE 1987.

Murdock, William (1754–1839)

Scottish inventor and technician. Employed by James ◊Watt and Matthew Boulton to build steam engines, he was the first to develop gas lighting on a commercial scale, holding the gas in gasometers, from the 1790s.

Murray

Family name of dukes of Atholl; seated at Blair Castle, Perthshire, Scotland.

Murray, James Augustus Henry (1837–1915)

Scottish philologist. He was the first editor of the *Oxford English Dictionary* (originally the *New English Dictionary*) from 1878 until his death; the first volume was published in 1884.

He edited more than half the dictionary single-handed, working in a shed (nicknamed the Scriptorium) in his back garden. Knighted 1908.

Murray, or Moray, James Stuart, 1st Earl of Murray (1531–1570)

Regent of Scotland from 1567, an illegitimate son of James V by Lady Margaret Erskine, daughter of the 4th Earl of Mar. He became chief adviser to his half-sister ◊Mary Queen of Scots on her return to Scotland in 1561, but lost her favour when he opposed her marriage in 1565 to Henry, Lord Darnley. He was one of the leaders of the Scottish Reformation, and after the deposition of Mary he became regent. He was assassinated by one of her supporters.

Murrayfield

Scottish rugby football ground and home of the national team.

It staged its first international in 1925 when Scotland beat England 14–11. The capacity is approximately 70,000.

Musgrave, Thea (1928–)

Scottish composer. Her music, in a conservative modern idiom, include concertos, chamber music, and operas, including *Mary, Queen of Scots* (1977), and *Harriet, the Woman Called Moses* (1985). Recent works include the bass clarinet concerto *Autumn Sonata* (1995), and the orchestral piece *Phoenix Rising* (1998).

music

See ◊classical music, ◊chamber music, ◊folk music, ◊pop music, ◊musical, ◊orchestras, ◊ballet, ◊opera, also individual

Music Festivals

(N/A = not available.)

Festival		Date
Aldeburgh Festival of Music and the Arts		June
Arundel Festival		August–September
Bath International Music Festival		May
Buxton Festival		July
Cheltenham International Festival of Music		July
Dartington International Summer School		July–August
Garsington Opera		June–July
Glyndebourne Festival Opera		May–August
Harrogate International Festival		July–August
Henley Festival of Music and the Arts		July
Leicester International Music Festival		June
London	BBC Henry Wood Promenade Concerts	July–September
London	Greenwich and Docklands International Festival	July[1]
London	London Festival of Chamber Music	September–October
London	London Handel Festival	March–May
London	St Ceciliatide International Festival of Music	November
Malvern Elgar Festival		May–June
Manchester	Hallé Proms Festival	June–July
Manchester	Royal Northern College of Music, Manchester International Cello Festival	April–May (biennially)
Norfolk and Norwich Festival		October
Oxford Festival of Contemporary Music		March–April, October–November
Salisbury Festival		May–June
Stratford upon Avon	The English Music Festival	October
Three Choirs Festival[2]		August
Warwick and Leamington Festival		July
York Early Music Festival		July
Ayton	Summer Music at Ayton Castle	July
Edinburgh International Festival		August–September
Glasgow International Early Music Festival		August (biennally)
Highland Festival		May–June
Orkney Islands	St Magnus Festival	June
Scottish Proms		May–June
Aberystwyth Musicfest		July
Beaumaris Festival		May–June
Cardiff Summer Festival		July–August
Carmarthen Festival/Gwyl Caerfyrddin		June–July
Llangollen International Musical Eisteddfod		July
Presteigne Festival of Music and the Arts		August
St David's Cathedral Festival		May
Swansea Festival		October
Wrexham Arts Festival		N/A
Belfast	Festival of Early Music	October (biennially)
Belfast	Sonorities	May
Belfast	Belfast Festival at Queen's	November
Castleward Opera Festival		June
Derry	Two Cathedrals Festival	October
Portstewart	Flowerfield Arts Festival	October[1]

[1] This date is provisional. [2] Gloucester 1998, Worcester 1999, Hereford 2000.

entries. See previous page for a list of music festivals in the UK, and when they take place.

musical

20th-century form of dramatic musical performance, combining elements of song, dance, and the spoken word, often characterized by lavish staging and large casts. It developed from the operettas and musical comedies of the 19th century.

Operetta

The operetta is a light-hearted entertainment with extensive musical content: W S ◊Gilbert and A S ◊Sullivan composed operettas.

Musical comedy and revue

The musical comedy is an anglicization of the French *opéra bouffe*, of which the first was *A Gaiety Girl* (1893), mounted by George Edwardes (1852–1915) at the Gaiety Theatre, London. Noël Coward's revues and musicals included *On With the Dance* (1925) and *Bitter Sweet* (1929), while Ivor Novello wrote *Glamorous Night* (1925), *The Dancing Years* (1939), and *Gay's the Word* (1951).

Musical

Sandy Wilson's *The Boy Friend* (1953) revitalised the British musical and was followed by hits such as Lionel Bart's *Oliver!* (1960). Musicals began to branch into religious and political themes with *Oh, What a Lovely War* (1963), produced by Joan Littlewood and Charles Chiltern, and the Andrew Lloyd Webber musicals *Jesus Christ Superstar* (1971) and *Evita* (1978). Another category of musical, substituting a theme for conventional plotting, is exemplified by Lloyd Webber's *Cats* (1981), using verses by T S Eliot. In the 1980s 19th-century melodrama was popular, for example the long-running *Les Misérables* (first London performance 1985) and *The Phantom of the Opera* (1986). In the 1990s Willy Russell's *Blood Brothers* and Lloyd Webber's *Starlight Express* were popular, as was *Buddy*, on the life on Buddy Holly, and the film-derived *Grease* and *Saturday Night Fever.* See ◊theatre for table showing the musical's dominance of London's West End in the 1990s.

music hall

Light theatrical entertainment, in which singers, dancers, comedians, and acrobats perform in 'turns'. The music hall's heyday was at the beginning of the 20th century, with such artistes as Marie Lloyd, Harry Lauder, and George Formby. The US equivalent is vaudeville.

Many performers had a song with which they were associated, such as Albert Chevalier (1861–1923) ('My Old Dutch'), or a character 'trademark', such as Vesta Tilley's immaculate masculine outfit as Burlington Bertie. Later stars of music hall included Sir George Robey, Gracie Fields, the Crazy Gang, Ted Ray, and the US comedian Danny Kaye.

MUSLIM COMMUNITY *Muslims leaving a mosque in Dalston, northeast London. The Muslim community increased greatly from the 1950s onwards, as immigration from the Indian subcontinent was encouraged, to supplement Britain's workforce. Bangladeshis in the East End of London have replaced earlier generations of immigrants who lived there, such as Jews from eastern Europe. Giles Askham/Impact*

MUSLIMS IN BRITAIN

THERE HAS been a Muslim presence in Britain for at least 300 years. The East India Company recruited seamen from Yemen, Gujarat, Sind, Assam and Bengal, known by the British as 'lascars', and a number of these created small settlements in port towns and cities in Britain, particularly London. Also there were a number of Muslim businesses in the nineteenth century, of which one of the best-known was the fashionable Mahomed's Baths, founded in Brighton by Sake Deen Mohammed (1750–1851).

By 1842 three thousand lascars were visiting Britain every year. Following the opening of the Suez Canal in 1869, seamen originally from Yemen settled in small communities in Cardiff, Liverpool, London, South Shields, and Tyneside and set up zawiyahs (small mosques or prayer rooms). These were the settings for the rites of nikah (marriage), aqikah (birth), khitan (circumcision), and janazah (funeral), and for the celebration of Eid.

Groups of Muslim intellectuals emerged in Britain in the late nineteenth century. In the period 1893 to 1908 a weekly journal, *The Crescent*, was distributed from a base in Liverpool. Its founder was William Henry Quilliam (known within the Muslim community as Shaykh Abdullah Quilliam), who by profession was a lawyer. He had become a Muslim in 1887, following time spent in Algeria and Morocco, and as author of the influential The Faith of Islam was famous throughout the Islamic world. The Liverpool Muslim community set up the Islamic Institute and the Liverpool Mosque in Broughton Terrace, the Medina Home to care for children and orphans, the Muslim College, and a Debating and Literary Society with weekly meetings.

The first purpose-built mosque

In 1889 Britain's first custom-built mosque was established, at Woking in Surrey. The funds for this were largely provided by Shah Jehan, the ruler of Bhopal, India. It was the base for the journal the *Islamic Review* in 1921, and people associated with it included Khwaja Kamal-ud-Din, a barrister originally from Lahore who was seen by the British press as the spiritual leader of all Muslims in Britain; Lord Headley, who had worked in India as a civil engineer and had converted to Islam in 1896; Syed Ameer Ali, an Indian jurist and well-known Islamic scholar, and to the present day the only Muslim privy councillor ever; and Abdullah Yusuf Ali and Marmaduke Pickthall, known for their influential translations of the Koran.

In 1910 a group of prominent British Muslims, including Lord Headley and Syed Ameer Ali, met at a central London hotel and formally established a fund, the London Mosque Fund, to finance the building of a mosque in the capital. In 1941 the East London Mosque Trust purchased three buildings in Commercial Road, Stepney, and converted them into London's first mosque. In the 1980s the East London Mosque moved to its present site in Whitechapel Road.

In the meantime, major purpose-built mosques had been built in Birmingham, Glasgow, and Manchester. The site for the Regents Park mosque in London was donated by the British government in 1944, in recognition of a similar donation by the Egyptian government to the Anglican community in Cairo. The building itself was completed in 1977. The first large mosque in Bradford was established in Howard Street in 1959.

Labour shortages

The migration of Muslims to Britain on a large scale began in the 1950s, mainly involving men in the first instance. In Bradford in 1961, for example, all but 81 of the 3,376 Pakistanis in the city were men. Migration was encouraged because there were major labour shortages in Britain, particularly in the steel and textiles industries of Yorkshire and Lancashire, and particularly for night shifts. The workers who came were needed by the economy, were actually or in effect invited by employers, and as Commonwealth citizens had full rights of entry and residence, and full civic rights. They came principally from the Mirpur district of Azad Kashmir in the country which at that time was known as West Pakistan (now Pakistan), or from the North West Frontier region of Pakistan, or from the Sylhet area of north eastern Bangladesh, known then as East Pakistan. Migrant workers came also from India.

About a sixth of the Indian-background people who came to Britain in the 1950s and 1960s were Muslims, a high proportion of these being from the western state of Gujarat. About 15 per cent of the 150,000 Asians who came from East African countries in the late 1960s and early 1970s were Muslims, with their family roots in Pakistan or Gujarat. It was also in the 1970s that substantial communities from Turkey and Middle Eastern and North African countries began to be established. Latterly, substantial Somali, Iranian, Arab, and Bosnian communities have been established in many cities, and there are considerable numbers of students from Malaysia. There are currently at least ten thousand converts to Islam within Britain, about half of whom are of African-Caribbean origin. Overall, the Muslim population of Britain is estimated to be somewhere between 1.5 and 1.7 million.

BY FUAD NAHDI

History

Music hall originated in the 17th century, when tavern-keepers acquired the organs that the Puritans had banished from churches. On certain nights organ music was played, and this resulted in a weekly entertainment known as the 'free and easy'. Certain theatres in London and the provinces then began to specialize in variety entertainment. With the advent of radio and television, music hall declined, but in the 1960s and 1970s there was a revival in working men's clubs and in pubs.

music theatre

Staged performance of vocal music that deliberately challenges, in style and subject matter, traditional operatic pretensions. Drawing on English music-hall and European cabaret traditions, it flourished during the Depression of the 1920s and 1930s in Europe and the USA. In the 1960s and 1970s in Britain the composers Alexander ◊Goehr, Harrison ◊Birtwistle, and Peter Maxwell ◊Davies wrote several important music theatre pieces, and Birtwistle and Maxwell Davies formed the Pierrot Players (later called The Fires of London) to extend the music theatre repertory. Music theatre has more recently emerged as the favoured idiom for short-term community music projects produced by outreach departments of civic arts centres and opera houses.

Muslim community

Second largest religious community in the UK, with between 750,000 and 2 million followers in Britain (1998). Recent estimates, based on the 1991 census, suggest the population is between 1 million and 1.5 million, while estimates within the Muslim community itself suggest the figure is between 1.5 and 2 million. Most Muslims originate from Pakistan and Bangladesh, while others come from India, Cyprus, the Arab states, Malaysia, and parts of Africa. There are increasing numbers of British-born Muslims, mainly the children of immigrant parents.

There are over 600 mosques and many prayer centres in Britain. The first mosque was established in Woking, Surrey, in 1889. The Central Mosque in Regent's Park, London, has the largest congregation in Britain; during festivals it can number over 30,000. The Islamic Cultural Centre attached to the Central Mosque is one of the most important Muslim institutions in the West. Other important mosques and cultural centres are in Liverpool, Manchester, Leicester, Birmingham, Bradford, Cardiff, Edinburgh, and Glasgow.

Both the Sunni and the Shi'a traditions are represented in Britain, and members of some of the major Sufi traditions have also developed branches. See previous page for a feature on Muslims in Britain.

Musselburgh

Town and former burgh in East Lothian unitary authority, Scotland, situated at the mouth of the River Esk on the Firth of Forth, 8 km/5 mi east of Edinburgh; population (1991) 20,600. It is a prosperous market gardening centre, and also has diverse industries, including the manufacture of nets, twine, wire, and paper. Recreational facilities include a number of fine golf links.

Mutiny Act

An act of Parliament, passed in 1689 and re-enacted annually since then (since 1882 as part of the Army Acts), for the establishment and payment of a standing army. The act is intended to prevent an army from existing in peacetime without Parliament's consent.

Myers, F(rederic) W(illiam) H(enry) (1843–1901)

English psychic researcher, classical scholar, and poet. He coined the word 'telepathy' and was a founder in 1882 and one of the first presidents, in 1900, of the Society for Psychical Research. His main works include *Essays Classical and Modern* (1883), *Phantasms of the Living* (1886), *Science and a Future Life* (1893), and the posthumous *Human Personality and its Survival of Bodily Death* (1903). His best-known poem is 'St Paul' (1867).

NAAFI acronym for Navy, Army, and Air Force Institutes

Non-profit-making association providing canteens for HM British Forces in the UK and abroad.

nabob

18th- and 19th-century nickname for those who made their fortune in India, a corruption of the Mogul royal title *nawab*. The name became widespread when many 'nabobs' returned to England and frustrated attempts to limit the privileges of the East India Company.

Naipaul, V(idiadhar) S(urajprasad) (1932–)

Trinidadian novelist and travel writer living in Britain. His novels include *A House for Mr Biswas* (1961), *The Mimic Men* (1967), *In a Free State* (1971; for which he won the Booker Prize), *A Bend in the River* (1979), *Finding the Centre* (1984), and *A Way in the World* (1994). Knighted 1990.

His brother **Srinivasa ('Shiva') Naipaul** (1945–1985) was also a novelist (*Fireflies*, 1970) and journalist.

Nantwich

Town in Cheshire, England, 7 km/4 mi from Crewe; population of Crewe and Nantwich (1991) 99,500. Industries include the manufacture of footwear and clothing. A market town in the heart of a fertile region, Nantwich was formerly a centre of the salt industry. The 14th-century parish church, much restored, dominates the town centre.

After a disastrous fire in 1583 the town was rebuilt with money provided by a national subscription sponsored by Queen Elizabeth I. Some houses, and the Crown Hotel, date from the period immediately after the fire. Churche's Mansion, a Tudor manor house built in 1577, is located on the edge of the town.

Salt deposits here are said to have been known by the Romans, and the town's brine springs were noted in the Domesday Book of 1087. Nantwich's salt industry was at its most productive in medieval and Tudor times but declined from the 17th century onwards.

NAIPAUL, V S *West Indian-born British writer V S Naipaul, a prolific novelist as well as travel writer and author of works of political journalism. His novels deal with recurrent themes concerning the melancholy side of human nature and the experience of alienation. Corbis*

Napier, John, 8th Laird of Merchiston (1550–1617)

Scottish mathematician who invented logarithms in 1614 and **'Napier's bones'**, an early mechanical calculating device for multiplication and division.

It was Napier who first used and then popularized the decimal point to separate the whole number part from the fractional part of a number.

Napier was born in Merchiston Castle, near Edinburgh, and studied at St Andrews. He never occupied any professional post.

English mathematician Henry ◊Briggs went to Edinburgh

in 1616 and later to discuss the logarithmic tables with Napier. Together they worked out improvements, such as the idea of using the base ten.

Napier, Robert Cornelis, 1st Baron Napier of Magdala (1810–1890)

British field marshal, born in Ceylon. Knighted for his services in relieving Lucknow during the ◊Indian Mutiny, he took part in capturing Peking (Beijing) in 1860 during the war against China. He was commander in chief in India 1870–76 and governor of Gibraltar 1876–82. KCB 1859.

I'm the kind of writer that people think other people are reading.

V S Naipaul Trinidadian-born English writer. *Radio Times* 1979

Napoleonic Wars

Series of European wars (1803–15) conducted by Napoleon I of France against an alliance of Britain, the German states, Spain, Portugal, and Russia, following the ◊Revolutionary Wars, and aiming for French conquest of Europe. At one time nearly all of Europe was under Napoleon's domination. He was finally defeated at the ◊Battle of Waterloo in 1815.

During the Napoleonic Wars, the annual cost of the British army was between 60% and 90% of total government income. About half of Napoleon's army was made up of foreign mercenaries, mainly Swiss and German.

Narnia, Chronicles of

Series of seven books for children by C S ◊Lewis. The first in the series, *The Lion, the Witch and the Wardrobe*, was published in 1950; in it children enter through a wardrobe into an imaginary country, Narnia. There the Christian story is re-enacted in a mythical context, the lion Aslan representing Christ. Further journeys into Narnia feature in the sequels *Prince Caspian* (1951), *The Voyage of the Dawn Treader* (1952), *The Silver Chair* (1953), *The Horse and his Boy* (1954), *The Magician's Nephew* (1955), and *The Last Battle* (1956).

Naseby, Battle of

Decisive battle of the English Civil War on 14 June 1645, when the Royalists, led by Prince Rupert, were defeated by the Parliamentarians ('Roundheads') under Oliver Cromwell and General Fairfax. It is named after the nearby village of Naseby, 32 km/20 mi south of Leicester.

Both armies drew up in similar formation, infantry in the centre, cavalry on the flanks, and reserves behind. The Royalists opened the battle by dashing downhill, across the intervening valley, and up the facing hill to where the Roundheads were massed. Prince Rupert's cavalry broke the Parliamentary right wing and then recklessly pursued them toward the village of Naseby. On the other wing, however, Cromwell's cavalry routed the force opposing them and then turned inward to take the Royalist infantry in the flank. King Charles I ordered his last reserves to charge, but the Earl of Carnwath, seeing this to be a futile move, turned his horse away and led his troops off the field; the Parliamentarians took heart from this, rallied, and completed the victory. Prince Rupert, returning from his chase, found the battle over and could do nothing but follow the king to Leicester. About 1,000 loyalists were killed and 5,000 taken prisoner, together with all their artillery.

Nash, John (1752–1835)

English architect. His large country-house practice, established about 1796 with the landscape gardener Humphry ◊Repton, used a wide variety of styles, and by 1798 he was enjoying the patronage of the Prince of Wales (afterwards George IV). Later he laid out Regent's Park, London, and its approaches, as well as Trafalgar Square and St James's Park. Between 1811 and 1821 he planned Regent Street (later

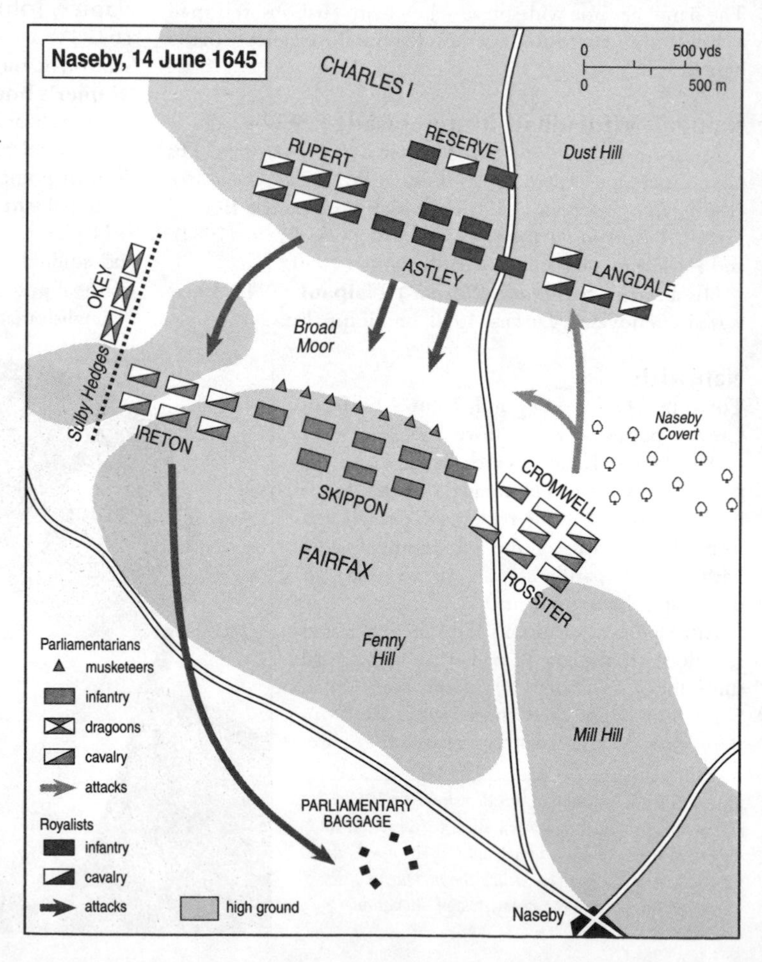

rebuilt), repaired and enlarged ◊Buckingham Palace (for which he designed Marble Arch), and rebuilt the Royal Pavilion, Brighton, in flamboyant oriental style.

For himself he built East Cowes Castle (1798) which greatly influenced the early Gothic Revival.

Nash, John Northcote (1893–1977)

English illustrator, artist, and engraver. He is best known for his watercolour landscapes, his studies of plants, and his illustrations for classic works of literature, such as Edmund Spenser's *Shepheardes Calender* (1930). He was the brother of the artist Paul ◊Nash.

Largely self-taught as an artist, he joined the London Group in 1913. During World War I he served in France, and was commissioned to paint war pictures for the Imperial War Museum.

Nash, Paul (1889–1946)

English painter. He was an official war artist in world wars I and II. In the 1930s he was one of a group of artists promoting avant-garde style, and was deeply influenced by Surrealism. Two works which illustrate the visionary quality of his paintings are *Totes Meer/Dead Sea* (1940–41; Tate Gallery), London; and *Solstice of the Sunflower* (1945; National Gallery of Canada, Ottawa). 'Structural purpose' was an aim which led him into many forms of design, for textiles, ceramics, the stage and the book, but the Surrealist trend of the 1930s and the exhibition of 1936 brought out an imaginative and poetic feeling already apparent in his oils and watercolours.

NASH, PAUL *English artist. A leading figure in English avant-garde art in the 1930s and 1940s, Nash used French Surrealism to revitalize the British landscape tradition. Corbis*

Nash was born in London. In his pictures of World War I, such as *The Menin Road* (Imperial War Museum), he created strange patterns out of the scorched landscape of the Western Front. During World War II he was appointed official war artist to the Air Ministry.

Nash, 'Beau' (Richard) (1674–1762)

Welsh dandy. As master of ceremonies at Bath from 1705, he made the town a fashionable spa resort, and introduced a polished code of manners into polite society.

Nashe, Thomas (1567–1601)

English poet, satirist, and anti-Puritan pamphleteer. He was drawn into the Martin Marprelate controversy (a pamphleteering attack on the clergy of the Church of England by Puritans), and wrote at least three attacks on the Martinists. Among his later works are the satirical *Pierce Pennilesse, his Supplication to the Divell* (1592) and the religious *Christes Teares over Jerusalem* (1593); *The Unfortunate Traveller* (1594) is a picaresque narrative mingling literary parody and mock-historical fantasy.

Nasmyth, James (1808–1890)

Scottish engineer and machine-tool manufacturer whose many inventions included the steam hammer (1839) for making large steel forgings.

Nasmyth was born in Edinburgh and left school at the age of 12. As assistant to English toolmaker Henry Maudslay, he devised a flexible shaft of coiled spring steel for drilling holes in awkward places. After the death of Maudslay in 1831, Nasmyth set up his own workshop, first in Edinburgh, then in Manchester, manufacturing machine tools, locomotives, and other machinery. His steam hammer was first used to make the propeller shaft for Isambard Kingdom Brunel's steamship *Great Britain*.

Nasmyth devised many other tools, including a vertical cylinder-boring machine which speeded up the production of steam engines, and all manner of lateral, transverse, and rotating cutting machines.

Nassau agreement

Treaty signed on 18 December 1962 whereby the USA provided Britain with Polaris missiles, marking a strengthening in Anglo-American relations.

National AIDS Trust

Charity that campaigns for the prevention of AIDS, care for sufferers, and an end to discrimination of people with HIV and AIDS. Diana, Princess of Wales, was its patron from 1991 until her death in 1997, and in 1998 the National AIDS Trust was awarded £1 million from the Diana Memorial Fund.

national anthem

'God Save the King/Queen'. The melody resembles a composition by John Bull and similar words are found from the 16th century. In its present form it was arranged by Dr

'God Save The Queen'

God save our gracious Queen, Long live our noble Queen
God save the Queen!
Send her victorious, Happy and Glorious
Long to reign over us
God save the Queen!

O Lord our God arise, Scatter her enemies
And make them fall
Confound their politics, Frustrate their knavish tricks
On Thee our hopes we fix
Oh, save us all!

Thy choicest gifts in store, On her be pleased to pour
Long may she reign
May she defend our laws, And ever give us cause To sing with heart and voice
God save the Queen!

Not in this land alone, But be God's mercies known
From shore to shore!
Lord make the nations see, That men should brothers be
And form one family
The wide world over.

From every latent foe, From the assassins blow
God save the Queen!
O'er her thine arm extend, For Britain's sake defend
Our mother, prince, and friend
God save the Queen!

The English National Anthem: 'Land of Hope and Glory'

Although this anthem can identify with the whole of the UK by references to the empire 'wider and still wider, shall thy bounds be set', it is also the unofficial national anthem of England, and is used for the English teams at the Commonwealth Games, although the English national football and rugby teams use 'God Save the Queen'.

Words by A C Benson, music by Sir Edward Elgar from 'Pomp & Circumstance March No. 1'.

Dear Land of Hope, thy hope is crowned.
God make thee mightier yet!
On Sov'ran brows, beloved, renowned, Once more thy crown is set.
Thine equal laws, by Freedom gained, Have ruled thee well and long
By Freedom gained, by Truth maintained, Thine Empire shall be strong.

Land of Hope and Glory, Mother of the Free
How shall we extol thee, who are born of thee?
Wider still and wider shall thy bounds be set
God, who made thee mighty, make thee mightier yet
God, who made thee mighty, make thee mightier yet.

Thy fame is ancient as the days, As Ocean large and wide
A pride that dares, and heeds not praise, A stern and silent pride
Not that false joy that dreams content With what our sires have won
The blood a hero sire hath spent, Still nerves a hero son.

Thomas Arne, under the title 'Song for Two Voices'. This version was first performed at Drury Lane Theatre in London on 28 September 1745, following the news of the defeat of the army of King George II by the 'Young Pretender' to the British Throne, Prince Charles Edward Stuart, at the battle of Prestonpans. The song immediately became popular as an anti-Jacobite Party song during the 1745 Jacobite Rebellion.

The words above are those sung in 1745, substituting 'Queen' for 'King' where appropriate. On official occasions, only the first verse is usually sung.

The words of 'Land of Hope and Glory', an unofficial national anthem of England, are also given above right. See ◊Scotland and ◊Wales for their national anthems.

National Army Museum

Official museum, established in 1960 in Chelsea, London, for the British, Indian, and colonial forces 1485–1914. The Imperial War Museum deals with the period from 1914.

national assistance

Term used 1948–66 for a weekly allowance paid by the state to ensure a minimum income.

National Association for Mental Health

Official title of the UK mental health charity, ◊**Mind**.

National Audit Office, or NAO

Independent UK public-spending watchdog, established in 1983 as the successor to the Exchequer and Audit Department. The NAO audits the annual spending of central government departments, ◊Executive Agencies, and ◊quangos. It produces around 50 'Value for Money' (VFM) reports each year, which recommend ways of improving economy, efficiency, and effectiveness in the delivery of government programmes.

National Computing Centre, or NCC

Centre set up in 1966 to offer advice and technical assistance to businesses on every aspect of information technology. The NCC is also the world's largest provider of escrow services for source code, a service necessary for businesses using custom-built software from a single supplier. It is based in Manchester.

National Curriculum

Course of study in ten subjects common to all primary and secondary state schools in the UK. The national curriculum is divided into three core subjects – English, maths, and science – and seven foundation subjects: geography, history, technology, a foreign language (for secondary school pupils), art, music, and physical education. There are four stages, on completion of which the pupil's work is assessed. The stages are for ages 5–7, 7–11, 11–14, and 14–16.

The scheme was set up through the Education Reform Act of 1988. The National Curriculum and testing system was reviewed in 1993 following teachers' complaints of overload and a boycott of tests scheduled for June 1993. The review, conducted by Ron Dearing, head of the Schools Curriculum and Assessment Authority, reduced National Curriculum requirements by about 50%. A revised testing regime was fully implemented with teacher cooperation in 1994. See feature on page 622.

National Dock Labour Scheme
A scheme that guaranteed continued employment and pay for dockworkers, even if there was no work to be done; some 9,000 dockworkers were registered under the scheme, which operated from 1947 until its abolition by the Thatcher government in 1989.

National Front
Extreme right-wing political party founded in 1967. In 1991 the party claimed 3,000 members. Some of its members had links with the National Socialist Movement of the 1960s. It attracted attention during the 1970s through the violence associated with its demonstrations in areas with large black and Asian populations and, in response, the left-wing Anti Nazi League was formed to mount counter protests.

The NF was formed from a merger of the League of Empire Loyalists and the British National Party. In 1982 the NF's leading figure, John Tyndall, left to form a new BNP. This has since eclipsed the NF, winning a local council seat in East London in 1992. Standing on a platform of repatriation of coloured immigrants and national autonomy, the NF won 3% of the vote in national elections in the 1970s, but has since attracted minimal support.

National Galleries of Scotland, the
Three Scottish galleries administered by one director under a single board of trustees. They are the ◊National Gallery of Scotland, the ◊Scottish National Portrait Gallery, and the ◊Scottish National Gallery of Modern Art.

National Gallery
London art gallery housing the British national collection of pictures by artists no longer living, founded in 1824. Its collection covers all major pre-20th-century periods and schools, but it is unique in its collection of Italian Gothic and Renaissance works, which is more comprehensive than any other collection outside Italy.

The present building in Trafalgar Square was designed by William Wilkins and opened in 1838. There have been several extensions, including the Sainsbury Wing, designed by US architect Robert Venturi, which opened in July 1991.

National Gallery of Scotland
Edinburgh art gallery housing the Scottish national collection of old master paintings, opened in 1859. It consists of European and English works from the period 1400–1900, together with a representative collection of Scottish paintings. An important loan of pictures from the Duke of Sutherland includes works by Raphael, Titian, and Rembrandt. The Department of Prints and Drawings contains the Vaughan Bequest, a notable group of Turner watercolours.

National Health Service
See ◊NHS.

National Heritage Memorial Fund
Government fund established in Britain in 1980 to save the countryside, historic houses, and works of art, as a memorial to those who died on military service during World War II.

national insurance
State social-security scheme that provides child allowances, maternity benefits, and payments to the unemployed, sick, and retired, and also covers medical treatment. It is paid for by weekly or monthly contributions from employees and employers.

National Insurance Act
Legislation of 1911, introduced by the Liberal chancellor Lloyd George, which first provided insurance for workers against ill health and unemployment.

Part I of the act introduced compulsory health insurance for all manual workers aged between 16 and 70 and nonmanual workers with incomes below £250 a year who did not claim exemption. Part II of the act provided insurance against unemployment for 2 million workers but excluded domestic servants, agricultural workers, and nonmanual workers exempt from Part I. The schemes were contributory, with employer, employee, and the state making regular contributions. The act provided for medical assistance and maternity benefits, and supplemented recently introduced welfare provisions for disabilities and pensions.

National Liberal Foundation
Central organization of the British ◊Liberal Party, established in 1877 in Birmingham. Its first president was Joseph Chamberlain.

National Lottery
Lottery launched by the British government in November 1994 to raise money for the arts, sports, charities, national heritage, and the Millennium Fund, set up to celebrate the year 2000. Its operators, the Camelot Consortium (led by Cadbury Schweppes plc), predicted total sales of £32 billion over an initial seven-year licence period. Of the weekly takings, 50% is used as prize money, 28% goes to the above causes, 12% is taken in taxes, and the remaining 10% is split between Camelot and an estimated 10,000 retail outlets that sell tickets. An estimated 80% of the adult population play the national lottery, each spending a weekly average of £2.50. From 1997 lottery draws were held twice a week, on Wednesdays and Saturdays.

Lottery tickets cost £1 each; the player chooses six numbers between 1 and 49, which must match at least three of the winning numbers drawn each week to be eligible for a prize. The chances of winning the jackpot (often in excess of £10 million) are around 14 million to one. Instant win tickets are also available, with a jackpot of £50,000.

In February 1997 the National Lottery handed out £137 million to 23 museums and galleries ranging from the Tate Gallery in London to a new National Museum of Football in Preston. The lottery had previously been criticized for favouring high art and the capital at the expense of popular

THE NATIONAL CURRICULUM

THE INTRODUCTION of a National Curriculum in the UK has been a ten-year rollercoaster ride that has not stopped yet. Its introduction was allegedly the result of a chance remark by prime minister Margaret Thatcher, to the effect that it should be possible to spell out what children should know in the basic subjects. But by the time it emerged as part of Secretary of State Kenneth Baker's Education Reform Act in 1988, it offered detailed syllabuses in ten subjects for children from the ages of 5 to 16.

Teachers complained from the beginning that a sensible idea had turned into an uncontrollable monster. Civil servants admitted at the time that the full curriculum actually accounted for 120 percent of the school timetable. Schools agonized over how to fit this quart into a pint pot, and teaching unions complained bitterly of work overload and consequent stress. There were also furious debates about what should be included in the new syllabuses.

There were two particular difficulties that have still not been resolved a decade after the Reform Act. The first concerns the priority that needs to be given to reading, writing, and basic maths in primary schools; the second concerns the number and range of subjects secondary pupils can sensibly cope with up to GCSE level.

A broad and compulsory curriculum

The original National Curriculum was uncompromising. There were to be ten subjects taught: English, maths, science, technology, history, geography, art, music, and PE in all schools; plus a modern language at secondary level. In Wales all children would also study Welsh. And space had to be found for the only other subject that had previously been compulsory: religious education.

In primary schools teachers did not necessarily object to a broad curriculum. Most of them had already been trying to provide that, often in the form of projects that covered aspects of history, geography, and social studies. They accepted that the new dispensation brought method and rigour to the teaching system. Children would no longer find themselves repeating work on the Victorians, or the Wild West, or the Vikings more or less at random as they changed classes or schools.

But primary teachers did complain that the sheer volume of factual knowledge required for teaching the new syllabuses in the humanities, science, and technology was crippling. Most were generalists who were now expected to handle a mountain of specialized knowledge across a wide range of subjects.

At secondary level, difficulties arose at the point where traditionally pupils had chosen some subjects to take at GCSE and had dropped others. Schools struggled to create timetables that would allow pupils to take all the National Curriculum subjects up to the age of 16. Extra classes after school and 'half' GCSE courses were some of the solutions canvassed, as schools struggled to balance depth of study with the new broad curriculum. Where pupils had previously had some choice of subject between the ages of 14 and 16, now there would be none. Specialist teachers of non-compulsory subjects – such as drama, home economics, sociology, and classics – lamented the demise of their subjects in British schools.

A slimmer curriculum with greater choice

Rescue came in the shape of Ron Dearing, a former chairman of the Post Office and an arch-conciliator, who was commissioned to review the whole new curricular edifice. His conclusions, published in 1995, were warmly welcomed by the over-stressed teachers and accepted by the government. He recommended that the primary curriculum should be slimmed down, and that some element of choice

culture and other regions of the country. The Labour government announced that some of the proceeds from the mid-week lottery would be used to fund health-service and education projects. The lottery is regulated by the Office of the National Lottery (◊Oflot).

National Museum of Wales, Welsh Amgueddfa Genedlaethol Cymru

Museum in Cardiff, with outlying museums, namely the Museum of Welsh Life at St Fagans, the Welsh Slate Museum at Llanberis, and the Industrial and Maritime Museum at Cardiff's Bay development.

National Museums of Northern Ireland

Organization that in 1998 brought together the three main museums in Northern Ireland: the Ulster Museum in Belfast, the Ulster Folk and Transport Museum in County Down, and the Ulster–American Folk Park in County Tyrone.

National Museums of Scotland

Collective body made up of the Royal Museum of Scotland, the Scottish United Services Museum, the Scottish Agricultural Museum (all in Edinburgh), the Museum of Flight near North Berwick, and the Museum of Costume near Dumfries. A purpose-built new Museum of Scotland opened next to the Royal Museum in 1998.

national park

Land set aside and conserved for public enjoyment. National parks include not only the most scenic places, but also places distinguished for their historic, prehistoric, or scientific interest, or for their superior recreational assets. They range from areas the size of small countries to pockets of just a few hectares.

In England and Wales under the National Park Act (1949) ten national parks were established including the Peak District, the Lake District, and Snowdonia. National parks are protected from large-scale development, but from time to time pressure to develop land for agriculture, quarrying, or

should be restored for secondary school pupils at the age of 14.

Ironically, his report immediately met with complaints from specialist teachers' groups for subjects such as history and geography, art and music; they had watched their subjects moving from optional to compulsory and back to optional again in the upper years of the secondary schools.

Ron Dearing also recommended that the National Curriculum should not be tampered with again until the year 2000, in order to give schools a period of stability. But he and the schools reckoned without the new Labour government that swept to power with a huge majority in 1997. Tony Blair's dedication to 'education, education, education' has brought more changes for the primary schools.

By the beginning of 1998, schools were being instructed to spend an hour a day on literacy teaching and an hour a day on maths, in order to reach the attainment targets set for the year 2002. Details of how the 'literacy hour' should be spent were published for introduction in the autumn of 1998. These were commitments which made even the newly slimmed down National Curriculum for 5- to 11-year-olds impossible to fit into the school timetable, and for other subjects the regulations were relaxed.

Before the new government was a year old, teachers' organizations and members of the wider public were campaigning again, this time to make sure that subjects like history and music were not squeezed out of primary schools completely. The orchestral conductor Simon Rattle caused such alarm by his pronouncements on what he saw as the threat to Britain's musical heritage that he was immediately appointed as a creative education adviser to the government. Ten years after the Education Reform Act was supposed to have set the school curriculum in stone for a generation, the argument continues as fiercely as ever.

BY MAUREEN O'CONNOR

tourism, or to improve amenities for the local community means that conflicts of interest arise between land users.

Other protected areas include Areas of Outstanding Natural Beauty (see ◊conservation) and ◊Sites of Special Scientific Interest (SSSIs). See table on next page for a list of national parks.

National Physical Laboratory, or NPL

Research establishment, set up in 1900 at Teddington, England, under the control of the Department of Industry; the chair of the visiting committee is the president of the Royal Society. In 1944 it began work on a project to construct a digital computer, called the ACE (Automatic Computing Engine), one of the first ever built. It was completed in 1950, embodying many of the ideas of English mathematician Alan ◊Turing. It was privatized in 1995.

National Portrait Gallery

London art gallery containing portraits of distinguished British men and women. It was founded in 1856 and moved to its present building in St Martin's Place, Trafalgar Square, in 1896.

Overall the collection has over 8,000 original paintings, drawings, and sculptures, and photographs of noted figures from Tudor times onwards, together with an archive and reference library.

National Research Development Council

Former name (to 1981) for the ◊British Technology Group.

National Rivers Authority, or NRA

Government agency launched in 1989. It had responsibility for managing water resources, investigating and regulating pollution, and taking over flood controls and land drainage from the former ten regional water authorities of England and Wales. In April 1996 the NRA was replaced by the ◊Environment Agency, having begun to establish a reputation for being supportive to wildlife projects and tough on polluters.

National Savings

Any of several government savings schemes in the UK, including the National Savings Bank (NSB), which operates through the Post Office; National Savings Certificates; and British Savings Bonds.

national schools

Schools founded from 1811 by the National Society for the Education of the Poor as an Anglican alternative to the nonconformist schools or dissenting academies. The schools used older pupils, known as 'monitors' to supervise the younger children.

national service

◊Conscription into the armed services in peacetime.

National Society for the Prevention of Cruelty to Children, or NSPCC

Charity, founded in 1884, formed with the aim of preventing the ill-treatment of children. It currently has around 50,000 voluntary workers.

National Sound Archive

Department of the British Library, in South Kensington, London. It holds nearly 1 million sound recordings, ranging from birdsong to grand opera. It was founded in 1947 as the British Institute of Recorded Sound.

National Theatre, Royal

National theatre company established in 1963, and the complex, opened in 1976, that houses it on London's South Bank. From 1988 it has been formally called the Royal National Theatre of Great Britain. Trevor ◊Nunn became the artistic director in 1997.

National Trust

British trust founded in 1895 for the preservation of land and buildings of historic interest or beauty, incorporated by an act

National Parks in England and Wales

The Countryside Commission is responsible for designating areas in England as National Parks, and advises Government on policy towards them. There are seven National Parks which, together with The Broads, are managed by a special Authority and cover 7.6 percent (9,934 sq km/3,836 sq mi) of England. They contain some of the country's finest scenery and offer exceptional opportunities for outdoor recreation.

Name	Region	Established (year)	Area		Natural features	Activities
			sq km	sq mi		
England						
The Broads[1]	between Norwich and Great Yarmouth, Norfolk	1989	303	117	fens, waterways, marshes, woodlands	walking, sailing, fishing, birdwatching
Dartmoor	Devon	1951	954	368	boggy plateaux, rocky land, river valleys; prehistoric remains	walking, fishing, riding
Exmoor	Somerset and Devon	1954	693	268	moorlands, cliffs; prehistoric remains	walking, riding, cycling, fishing
Lake District	Cumbria	1951	2,292	885	lakes, mountains, moorlands, fells	walking, climbing, sailing
The New Forest[2]	Hampshire	1990	376	117	forest, woodlands, heathlands	walking, riding, cycling
Northumberland	Northumberland	1956	1,049	405	grass moorlands, deep burn valleys, hills, mountains; Roman antiquities	walking, rock-climbing, canoeing, riding
North York Moors	North Yorkshire, Redcar, Cleveland	1952	1,436	554	open heather moorlands; unique wildlife	walking, riding
Peak District	Derbyshire, Staffordshire, South Yorkshire, Cheshire, West Yorkshire, Greater Manchester	1951	1,438	555	dales, hills, peat moorlands	walking, rock-climbing
Yorkshire Dales	North Yorkshire, Cumbria	1954	1,769	683	limestone cliffs, gorges, and pavements; valleys, waterfalls, caves	walking, caving
Wales						
Breacon Beacons	Powys, Carmarthenshire, Rhondda, Cynon, Taff, Merthyr Tydfil, Blaneau, Gwent, Monmouthshire	1957	1,351	522	mountains, valleys	walking, riding
Pembrokeshire Coast	Pembrokeshire	1952 and 1995	584	225	cliffs, moorlands; includes Skomer Islands	walking, birdwatching, marine life watching
Snowdonia	Gwynedd, Conwy	1951	2,142	827	deep valleys, rugged mountains	hill walking, rock-climbing, riding

[1] The Broads are considered to have equivalent status to National Parks due to Statutory designation. [2] The New Forest does not enjoy Statutory designation, despite planning protection that recognizes its high landscape qualities. Therefore the area does not have equivalent administration or funding to a National Park. 1990 is the date of the establishment of the New Forest Committee.

of Parliament in 1907. It is the largest private landowner in Britain. The National Trust for Scotland was established in 1931.

The total income of the National Trust in 1995–96 was £151 million, of which £77 million was voluntary income (donations, legacies, covenants, Gift Aid, and charity shop income), making it the top-earning charity in the UK.

Under the terms of the 1907 Act, the Trust holds property 'inalienably', meaning that it cannot sell or develop property given to it except by an act of Parliament. In 1934 the Trust set up its Country House Scheme, and in 1947 a gardens fund. In 1997 the Trust in England, Wales, and Northern Ireland opened 300 of its properties to the public and it owned 909 km/565 mi of coastline.

In April 1997 the National Trust's ruling council voted unanimously to ban stag-hunting on its land after a scientific report it had commissioned concluded that the chase caused extreme suffering and exhaustion to the deer. The council has asked the government to set up an expert committee to reappraise the suffering caused by other kinds of hunting in the light of its findings. There are at least 2,500 red deer in the West Country, mostly on Exmoor and in the Quantock Hills, and their numbers have to be controlled otherwise they would destroy their habitat. The National Trust would preserve the red deer herd in good condition by culling and deer management.

National Union of Journalists, or NUJ

British trade union of journalists, the largest association of its kind in the world, with over 25,000 members (1998) in England, Scotland, Wales, and Northern Ireland. Its members include staff of the press media, freelance correspondents and editors, radio and television journalists, press photographers, and editorial designers. It is affiliated to the ◊Trades Union Congress (TUC), the General Federation of Trade Unions (GFTU), and the International Federation of Journalists, and is part of the international labour movement.

The NUJ provides services in the areas of legal advice and support; publications; training and training advice; insurance advice; representation in chapel, branch, industrial sector, national, and international forums.

National Westminster Tower

Building designed by Richard Seifert, located in the City of London. It is 183 m/600 ft high and has 49 storeys. Seen from above it resembles the National Westminster Bank's logo. It was completed in 1979 at a cost of £72 million, and was London's tallest building until 1991.

Natural Environment Research Council, or NERC

UK organization established by royal charter in 1965 to undertake and support research in the earth sciences, to give advice both on exploiting natural resources and on protecting the environment, and to support education and training of scientists in these fields of study.

Research areas include geothermal energy, industrial pollution, waste disposal, satellite surveying, acid rain, biotechnology, atmospheric circulation, and climate. Research is carried out principally within the UK but also in Antarctica and in many developing countries. It comprises 13 research bodies.

nature reserve

Area set aside to protect a habitat and the wildlife that lives within it, with only restricted admission for the public. Under the National Parks Act (1949), the (now defunct) Nature Conservancy Council (NCC) was given the power to designate such areas in Britain; this is now under the control of the Joint Nature Conservation Committee (JNCC). There are both officially designated nature reserves – managed by ◊English Nature, the ◊Countryside Council for Wales, and ◊Scottish Natural Heritage – and those run by a variety of voluntary conservation organizations. In 1997 there were 343 National Nature Reserves (covering more than 490,000 acres); 3 Marine Nature Reserves; over 500 Local Nature Reserves; and nearly 6,2000 ◊Sites of Special Scientific Interest (SSSIs).

Navigation Acts

Series of acts of Parliament passed from 1381 to protect English shipping from foreign competition and to ensure monopoly trading between Britain and its colonies. The last was repealed in 1849 (coastal trade exempt until 1853). The Navigation Acts helped to establish England as a major sea power, although they led to higher prices. They ruined the Dutch merchant fleet in the 17th century, and were one of the causes of the ◊American Revolution.

1650 'Commonwealth Ordinance' forbade foreign ships to trade in English colonies.

1651 Forbade the importation of goods except in English vessels or in vessels of the country of origin of the goods. This act led to the Anglo-Dutch War of 1652–54.

1660 All colonial produce was required to be exported in English vessels.

1663 Colonies were prohibited from receiving goods in foreign (rather than English) vessels.

Naze, the

Headland on the coast of Essex, southeast England, 8 km/5 mi south of the port of Harwich.

Neagh, Lough

Lake in Northern Ireland, 25 km/15 mi west of Belfast; area 396 sq km/153 sq mi. It is the largest lake in the British Isles and Ireland, being 27 km/17 mi long, 16 km/10 mi wide, with an average depth of 12 m/39 ft. The shores are mostly flat and marshy; there are a few islands of which Ram's Island is the largest, on which is an early round tower. The lake is famous for trout and eel fishing, and breeding waterbirds.

Lough Neagh is fed by the rivers Blackwater, Ballinderry, and Upper Bann, and is drained north to the Atlantic through the Lower Bann.

Neagle, Anna born (Florence) Marjorie Robertson (1904–1986)

English actress. She was made a star by her husband Herbert Wilcox (1890–1977), a producer and director. Her films include *Nell Gwyn* (1934), *Victoria the Great* (1937), and *Odette* (1950). She was made a DBE in 1969.

Neath, Welsh Castell-nedd

Town in Neath Port Talbot unitary authority, south Wales, 11 km/7 mi northeast of Swansea near the mouth of the River Neath; population (1991) 46,000. The Roman fort of Nidum was discovered nearby in 1949; there are also remains of a 13th-century Norman castle and Neath Abbey, founded in 1130.

The auxiliary fort of Nidum was established here during the Roman conquest of south Wales in 70–80; two gateways have been preserved. Neath castle was sacked by Llewelyn the Great in 1231, and again in 1321; it was rebuilt in the 14th century. Briton Ferry, at the mouth of the River Neath and part of the town since 1922, was formerly the port for Neath.

Neath Port Talbot

Unitary authority in south Wales, created in 1996 from part of the former county of West Glamorgan
Area 442 sq km/171 sq mi
Towns ◊Port Talbot (administrative headquarters)
Physical the terrain is dominated by the alternation of river valleys and high moorland interfluves
Features Roman fort of Nidum is near ◊Neath
Industries coal mining, chemicals, various metalworks, variety of light industry
Population (1996) 139,400

The county is mainly industrial with coal mining predominating, including anthracite in the upper valleys and metallurgical industries at coastal sites.

Neave, Airey Middleton Sheffield (1916–1979)

British intelligence officer and Conservative member of Parliament 1953–79, a close adviser to former prime minister Margaret Thatcher. During World War II he escaped from Colditz, a German high-security prison camp. As shadow undersecretary of state for Northern Ireland from 1975, he became a target for extremist groups and was assassinated by an Irish terrorist bomb.

Needham, Joseph (1900–1995)

English biochemist and sinologist, historian of Chinese science. He studied at Cambridge, where he spent his academic career, and worked first on problems in embryology. The arrival of some Chinese biochemists in 1936 prompted him to learn their language, and in 1942–46 he travelled through China as head of the British Scientific Mission. He was head of the Division of Natural Sciences at the United Nations 1946–48, after which he returned to Cambridge.

Needham became increasingly interested in the history of science, particularly of Chinese science, and he progressively reduced his biochemical investigations. In *Chemical Embryology* (1931), he concluded that embryonic development is controlled chemically; the discovery of morphogenetic hormones and later of the genetic material DNA confirmed this view.

Needles, the

Group of rocks in the sea, rising to 30 m/100 ft, off the western extremity of the Isle of Wight, southern England.

The origin of the rocks is attributable to the erosion of the steep cliffs which form the western point of the Isle of Wight. The largest of the rocks, which was 36 m/118 ft high, was undermined and fell during a storm in 1764. The rocks are white, but black at their bases, and streaked throughout with black strata of flints. There is a lighthouse rising to 218 m/715 ft above the sea on the outermost rock.

Neeson, Liam (1952–)

Irish film and stage actor. He turned to acting at a relatively late age, appearing on the stage in Belfast and Dublin. He was discovered in the early 1980s by British director John Boorman, who cast him as Sir Gawain in *Excalibur* (1981). He then appeared in the US fantasy film *Krull* (1983), the first of a series of secondary film roles he played throughout the 1980s. In the 1990s he established himself as a leading man. He won acclaim for his performances in Sam Raimi's *Darkman* (1990) and Woody Allen's *Husbands and Wives* (1992), and was nominated for an Academy Award for his role as Oskar Schindler in Steven Spielberg's *Schindler's List* (1993). He has since featured in *Nell* (1994), *Rob Roy* (1995), and *Michael Collins* (1996).

His other films include *The Bounty* (1984), *The Mission* (1986), *Suspect* (1987), *A Prayer for the Dying* (1987), *The Dead Pool* (1988), *Under Suspicion* (1992), *Ethan Frome* (1993), *Before and After* (1996), and *Les Misérables* (1997). He is married to English actress Natasha Richardson.

neighbourhood watch

Local crime-prevention scheme. Under the supervision of police, groups of residents agree to increase watchfulness in order to prevent crimes such as burglary and vandalism in their area.

The first such group in the UK was started in Cheshire in 1982 following a US model. By 1990 there were an estimated 74,000 groups.

Neill, A(lexander) S(utherland) (1883–1973)

Scottish educationist. In 1924, partially in reaction to his own repressive upbringing, he founded a school, Summerhill, where liberal and progressive ideas such as self-government by pupils and the voluntary attendance of lessons achieved remarkable results, especially with problem children.

Nelson, Horatio, 1st Viscount Nelson (1758–1805)

English admiral. He joined the navy in 1770. During the Revolutionary Wars against France he lost the sight in his right eye in 1794 and lost his right arm in 1797. He became a rear admiral and a national hero after the victory off Cape St Vincent, Portugal. In 1798 he tracked the French fleet to Aboukir Bay where he almost entirely destroyed it. In 1801 he won a decisive victory over Denmark at the Battle of ◊Copenhagen, and in 1805, after two years of blockading Toulon, he defeated the Franco-Spanish fleet at the Battle of ◊Trafalgar, near Gibraltar.

Nelson was almost continuously on active service in the Mediterranean 1793–1800; he lingered at Naples for a year, during which he helped to crush a democratic uprising, and fell completely under the influence of Lady ◊Hamilton. In 1800 he returned to England and soon after separated from his wife, Frances Nisbet (1761–1831). He was promoted to vice admiral in 1801, and sent to the Baltic to operate against the Danes, nominally as second in command; in fact, it was Nelson who was responsible for the victory of Copenhagen and for negotiating peace with Denmark. On his return to England he was created a viscount. In 1803 he received the Mediterranean command and for nearly two years blockaded Toulon. When in 1805 his opponent, the French admiral Pierre de Villeneuve (1763–1806), eluded him, Nelson pursued him to the West Indies and back, and on 21 October defeated the combined French and Spanish fleets off Cape Trafalgar, capturing 20 of the enemy ships; Nelson himself was mortally wounded. He is buried in St Paul's Cathedral, London.

I have only one eye, I have a right to be blind sometimes: ...
I really do not see the signal!

HORATIO NELSON British admiral.
At the Battle of Copenhagen 1801

---

nemo me impune lacessit

(Latin 'no one injures me with impunity') the motto of Scotland.

Nene

River rising in the west of Northamptonshire, England, and flowing past Northampton and Peterborough into the Wash (bay of the North Sea between Norfolk and Lincolnshire); length 145 km/90 mi. The Nene is connected with all the central waterways of England by canal.

Neo-Classicism

Movement in art, architecture, and design in Europe and North America, from about 1750 to 1850, characterized by a revival of Classical Greek and Roman styles. In Britain leading figures of Neo-Classicism were the architects Robert Adam, John Soane, Charles Cockerell, James Gibbs, and William Playfair; the painters Angelica Kauffman and Frederic Leighton; the sculptors John Flaxman, Thomas Banks and John Gibson; and the designers Josiah Wedgwood, George Hepplewhite, and Thomas Sheraton.

Neo-Classicism was inspired both by the excavation of the Roman towns of Pompeii and Herculaneum and by the cultural studies of the German art historian Johann J Winckelmann. Neo-Classical artists sought to capture the 'noble simplicity and calm grandeur' of Classical art by conscious emulation of Classical styles and subject matter. They took themes from Homer and Plutarch and were influenced by John Flaxman's austere linear illustrations for the *Iliad* and *Odyssey*.

Nesbit, E(dith) (1858–1924)

English author of children's books. She wrote *The Story of the Treasure Seekers* (1899) and *The Railway Children* (1906). Her stories often have a humorous magical element, as in *Five Children and It* (1902) and *The Phoenix and the Carpet* (1904). *The Treasure Seekers* is the first of several books about the realistically squabbling Bastable children; it was followed by *The Would-be Goods* (1901) and *The New Treasure Seekers* (1904). Nesbit was a Fabian socialist and supported her family by writing. Her stories struck a new note with their naturalistic portrayal of children.

Ness, Loch

Lake in the Highland unitary authority, Scotland, extending northeast to southwest. Forming part of the Caledonian Canal, it is 36 km/22.5 mi long, 2 km/1 mi wide (on average), 229 m/754 ft deep, and is the greatest expanse of fresh water in Europe. There have been unconfirmed reports of a **Loch Ness monster** since the 15th century.

Loch Ness, Loch Lochy and Loch Oich are connected by the ◊Caledonian Canal, and together provide the only navigable channel between the east and west coasts of Scotland.

Nether Stowey

Village in Somerset, England, 14 km/9 mi from Bridgwater, in the Quantock Hills. Coleridge lived here 1796–98, and wrote many of his best-known poems during that period; Wordsworth moved here in 1797. Together, at Nether Stowey, the two poets conceived the *Lyrical Ballads*.

Nevinson, Christopher Richard Wynne (1889–1946)

English painter and graphic artist. He made striking use of a Futurist style in paintings of the Western Front during World War I. His later paintings and etchings, which often employ elaborate allegory, are in a more traditional style.

His war pictures rank with those of Paul Nash, though some met with official disapproval. Nevinson's work is represented in the British Museum; Imperial War Museum; Tate Gallery; Birmingham, and other city art galleries; and also at Harvard University, Massachusetts.

new-age music

Instrumental or ambient music, often semi-acoustic or electronic; less insistent than rock and less difficult than jazz. Clean production, undemanding compositions, and a soft, gentle sound characterize new age.

Widespread from the 1980s, new-age music originated in the mid-1970s with English composer Brian Eno (1948–) who released such albums as *Music for Airports* (1979). Some folk, jazz, and avant-garde rock musicians have all found an outlet in new age.

Newark

Market town in Nottinghamshire, central England, on the River Trent, 25 km/16 mi west of Lincoln; population (1996 est) 24,775. Agriculture is important in the area and there is a cattle market. Industries include engineering, the manufacture of ball and roller bearings, plasterboard and gypsum, and the processing of sugar-beet. There are also some financial services based here. Features include the ruins of a 12th-century castle in which King John died in 1216.

The British Horological Institute is based here. The church of St Mary Magdalene has an Early English tower with a Decorated spire, and a mainly Perpendicular interior.

Newbury

Market town and administrative headquarters of ◊West Berkshire unitary authority in southern England, on the River Kennet, 27 km/17 mi southwest of Reading; population (1991) 33,300. It was part of the county of Berkshire until April 1998. Industries include papermaking, electronics, engineering, and the manufacture of chemicals and plastics; wheat and barley crops are also important to the economy. Newbury has a racecourse and training stables.

Newbury was one of the first industrial textile towns; weaving helped establish the town as a manufacturing centre.

The town was an important centre of the cloth trade in the 16th century. During the Civil War it was the scene of the two indecisive Battles of Newbury (1643 and 1644). Nearby, to the southwest of the town, there is a memorial to Lucius Carey, 2nd Viscount Falkland, who was killed at the battle of 1643. The Jacobean Cloth Hall (1627) houses a museum of local history. Nearby is the hamlet of Speen, built on the site of the Roman settlement Spinae.

Newby, (George) Eric (1919–)

English travel writer and sailor. His books include *A Short Walk in the Hindu Kush* (1958), *The Big Red Train Ride* (1978), *Slowly Down the Ganges* (1966), and *A Traveller's Life* (1985).

Newcastle

Seaside resort in County Down, Northern Ireland; population (1991) 6,300. Situated beneath the slopes of Slieve Donard (in the Mourne Mountains), Newcastle faces the sandy beaches of Dundrum Bay. The town is a centre for golf: the Royal County Down Club is located here.

Tollymore forest park, 3 km/2 mi to the north, includes a natural-history museum and Tollymore Mountain Centre; also nearby is Castlewellan forest park with fine arboreta. At Carncavill, 5 km/3 mi north of Newcastle, is a circular graveyard called Ráth Murbhuilg which contains the ruins of an ancient monastery founded by Bishop Domhaughard, including a church and some remains of a round tower.

Newcastle, Thomas Pelham-Holles, 1st Duke of Newcastle (1693–1768)

British Whig politician, prime minster 1754–56 and 1757–62. He served as secretary of state for 30 years from 1724, then succeeded his younger brother, Henry ◊Pelham, as prime minister in 1754. In 1756 he resigned as a result of setbacks in the Seven Years' War, but returned to office in 1757 with ◊Pitt the Elder (1st Earl of Chatham) taking responsibility for the conduct of the war.

Newcastle-under-Lyme

Market and industrial town in Staffordshire, west-central England, on the River Lyme, 3 km/2 mi west of Stoke-on-Trent; population (1996) 60,000. Manufacturing is important and products include electronics, ceramics, bricks and tiles, clothing, paper, and machinery. Silverdale Colliery was scheduled to close in 1998.

Features

Keele University (established 1962) is nearby to the west. St Giles's Church dates from the 13th century, but was largely rebuilt between 1873 and 1876. A castle was built at Newcastle-under-Lyme 1142–46, of which only the excavated boundaries now remain.

Newcastle upon Tyne

City and metropolitan borough in Tyne and Wear in northeast England on the River Tyne opposite Gateshead, 17 km/10 mi from the North Sea; population city (1991) 189,150, metropolitan district (1994) 274,000. It is the administrative centre of Tyne and Wear and regional centre of northeast England, as well as a centre for retail, commerce, communications, and the arts. Industries include engineering (including offshore technology), food processing, brewing, and the manufacture of electronics. Only 1% of the workforce is now in heavy industry, 80% are in the public or service sectors. The University of Newcastle was founded in 1963, and the University of Northumbria in 1992.

Features

Parts are preserved of a castle built by Henry II 1172–77 on the site of an older castle (1080). Other landmarks include the cathedral, formerly the parish church, which is chiefly 14th-century; a 12th-century church, and the Guildhall (1658); the Metro underground; the Laing Art Gallery; the Newcastle Discovery Museum; the Hancock Museum; fine 19th-century classical buildings. The quayside area with its historic buildings has been restored, and is now a fashionable waterside area known for its nightlife, with clubs and pubs here, as well as in Bigg Market. Newcastle is connected with the neighbouring town of Gateshead by eight bridges and a tunnel.

History

Newcastle stands on the site of a Roman settlement, **Pons Aelius**. Newcastle first began to trade in coal in the 13th century, and was an important centre for coal and shipbuilding until the 1980s. In 1826 ironworks were established by George ◊Stephenson, and the first engine used on the Stockton and Darlington railway was made in Newcastle.

From early times to the 18th century

A Roman bridge encouraged the foundation of the small town called Pons Aelius, several of whose relics are in the Museum of Antiquities. On the foundations of this bridge the Normans built another, with a castle (in 1080) rising above the bridge on the steep river bank. The town grew along the riverside and northwards across the plateau (35 m/115 ft) above the river. There are traces of the medieval street pattern and building plots on the steep slope down to the Tyne, but few buildings remain from this period. From the 13th until the 18th century, Newcastle was walled and traces of the western wall and isolated towers remain. Newcastle provided a military base for English troops during intermittent wars with Scotland and was occupied by the Scots in 1640 and 1644–47. In times of peace Newcastle became a regional trading centre but its chief importance lay as a supplier of coal to London and other North Sea towns. The Newcastle merchants or Hostmen maintained a monopoly of the trade from 1220 until the 18th century.

19th-century development

During the early 19th century the section of the town on the plateau was drastically rebuilt. The walls were partially replaced by wide streets and ravines were filled in to allow new roads to be built including Grainger Street, Clayton, and the curvilinear Grey Street (1834–9) with its impressive Regency architecture. This work was carried out by Richard Grainger (1798–1861), the architect John Dobson, and John Clayton, the town clerk. Grey's monument, at the junction of the main streets commemorates the Reform Act of 1832. At the opposite end of Grainger Street, Dobson's Central Station (1850) complements Robert Stephenson's high-level bridge (1849) which carries the railway and road 34 m/111 ft above the river, and was the largest bridge in the world at the time of its construction. Later in the century a swing bridge (1876), the Redheugh road bridge (1871), the King Edward railway bridge (1906), and the Tyne (road) Bridge (1928) were built within 1 km/0.6 mi of each other.

> *Geordies tell you that the skyline has changed in these parts. The pit-heads have gone. The cranes of the shipyards have disappeared into the history books. The yards that once built a quarter of the world's ships – including the world's first oil tanker at Jarrow – are now almost silent apart from some modest resurgence of ship repair work on the Tyne. The Newcastle that made a living by getting its hands dirty has been allowed to die.*
>
> TONY PARSONS English journalist.
> *Daily Mirror*, 1997

The 20th century

The northern part of the city has been rebuilt since the 1960s and Eldon Square shopping centre was opened in 1976. A motorway circles the east and northeast of the town and there is an underground rapid transit system, the Tyneside Metro. North of the shopping centre lies the administrative and educational precinct with the civic centre (1963) situated between Newcastle University, and the Royal Grammar School (founded 1525). The Town Moor and associated parks, occupying an area of 375 ha/937 acres, separate the commercial town from its northern suburbs in Gosforth. The 19th-century housing has been replaced in Scotswood and Elswick to the west by high-rise flats. In Byker, to the east, a striking continuous block, the 'Byker Wall', provides low-rise accommodation. Millennium Bridge – a steel footbridge which will open like the visor on a motorcycle helmet – is to be built, and will link the quayside with the new international arts complex planned in the old Baltic Flour Mills at Gateshead. There is also to be a new genetics institute, the International Centre for Life (designed by Terry Farrell), due to open in March 2000 as a Millennium Commission Landmark Project.

Churches

St Nicholas Cathedral was formerly the parish church of Newcastle. Tradition has it that the church of St Nicholas was founded by Osmund, bishop of Salisbury, in 1091, but it is believed that a church was standing on the site long before then. The Norman church was destroyed by fire in 1216 and was replaced by a building in the Early English style. The church as it is today is mainly the work of 14th-century builders, with the exception of the Perpendicular tower and steeple, built about 1430. St Mary's Roman Catholic cathedral was built in 1844 from the design of Pugin, and its tall, graceful spire was added in 1872. Other churches include All Saints' church, planned by David Stephenson, and completed in 1796 on the site of an earlier church which had been demolished; St Andrew's church, dating from the middle of the 12th century; the church of St John the Baptist, dating mainly from the 14th and 15th centuries; and St Ann's church, built in 1768 with stones from part of the town wall.

The castle

Although nothing of the Norman castle survives, remains of the Norman wall are still to be seen. Today the expression 'the Castle' denotes only the keep or tower. Of the south wall more extensive remains are extant, including the Postern Gate. The keep was built by Henry II between 1172 and 1177. The original appearance of the building has been entirely altered by the erection of battlements in 1810. The Black Gate is a later addition built by Henry III about 1249. The great hall of the castle has a modern roof, but the chapel is a fine example of late Norman architecture.

The guildhall and its surroundings

The guildhall on the 'Sandhill' is the ancient centre of municipal government of the town. There is evidence of the existence of a guildhall as early as the 13th century. The old guildhall was rebuilt and enlarged in the middle of the 17th century by Robert Trollop, and most of the interior of the present building dates from 1658. In the hall on the upper floor the freemen of the city still hold their annual Michaelmas guild meeting, and the commissions of assize are opened here by the circuit judges, though all cases are normally tried at the County Moot Hall (1810); since 1952 the guildhall has served as an overflow court. Nearby are interesting Elizabethan houses. The commercial exchange is now in Neville Hall. The many public buildings include the Mansion House, Jesmond, and the new city hall and baths (1928).

Nearby is the site of the Barras Bridge, traditionally the site of the long-drawn-out single combat (1388) between Harry Hotspur and the Earl of Douglas before the Battle of Otterburn. Barras Bridge is now the site of Newcastle's civic centre. The Hancock Museum of Natural History in Barras Bridge contains the collections of the Natural History Society of Northumberland, Durham and Newcastle, and also a large series of original work by the wood engraver Thomas Bewick (1753–1828), who was born near Newcastle.

Engineering project

Newcastle University opened a centre for the computer-aided design of complex marine engineering projects in 1990. The Engineering Design Centre for Marine and Other Made-to-order Products is funded jointly by industry and the Social and Economic Research Council, and will be concerned with the computer-aided design of one-off projects such as oil rigs, floating production plants, floating hotels, and also land-based power-generating plants.

Newcomen, Thomas (1663–1729)

English inventor of an early steam engine. His 'fire engine' of 1712 was used for pumping water from mines until James ◊Watt invented one with a separate condenser.

new dance, or independent dance

Modern dance style that overlaps with ◊contemporary dance, but is more usually applied to 'newer' dance artists whose styles stem from release or contact improvisation based work (freer, more organic movement) and more independent styles or fusions. Examples of new or independent dancers are Laurie Booth and other artists influenced by the Brazilian martial arts movement style capoeira.

New English Art Club

Society founded in 1886 to secure better representation for younger painters than was available through the Royal Academy. Its members, most of whom were influenced by Impressionism, included John Singer ◊Sargent, Augustus ◊John, Paul ◊Nash, William Rothenstein, and Walter ◊Sickert.

New Forest

Ancient forest in southwest Hampshire, southern England, and the largest stretch of semi-natural vegetation in lowland Britain. Lying between the River Avon on the west and Southampton Water on the east, its legal boundary encloses 38,000 ha/93,898 acres (1995). Of this area 8,400 ha/20,756 acres is enclosed plantation, and 20,000 ha/49,420 acres is common land, including ancient woodland, heath, grassland, and bog. The remainder is privately owned land and villages. More than six million tourists visit annually.

At least 46 rare plants are found in the New Forest, as well as more than half of Britain's species of butterflies, moths, and beetles.

Features

The principal trees in the forest are oak and beech, with large patches of holly as undergrowth. The area provides a habitat for many breeds of birds, as well as badgers, foxes, and deer. New Forest ponies, a small breed said to have descended from small Spanish horses, graze in the forest. Much of the grazing is unfenced and managed as common land. Natley and Denny is a nature reserve.

The principal town in the New Forest is ◊Lyndhurst. Villages include Brockenhurst, Minstead, and ◊Beaulieu. Other features include the Knightwood Oak, with a circumference of about 7 m/22 ft, and the Rufus Stone, marking the place where William (II) Rufus is thought to have been killed in 1100.

History

A hunting ground in Saxon times, the New Forest was reserved as Crown property in 1079 and William the Conqueror extended its area. His sons William (II) Rufus and Richard were both killed here while hunting. The forest became important as a source of timber for the building of ships in the 17th–19th centuries. In the 20th century the Forestry Commission took over the administration of most of the forest.

Management

The boundary of the New Forest is fenced and gridded, to prevent livestock from crossing, and is known as the New Forest Perambulation, to which the New Forest Acts apply. Within the boundary the Verderers (officers responsible for order in the forest) protect the Rights of Common and the traditional character of the forest. Various other bodies are involved in the forest's management, though none has a remit covering the whole of the New Forest Heritage Area. They include the Forestry Commission, the Ministry of Agriculture, local authorities at county, district and borough level, the Countryside Commission and English Nature. Since 1990 their work in relation to the New Forest has been coordinated by the New Forest Committee.

Newgate

Prison in London, which stood on the site of the Old Bailey central criminal court. Originally a gatehouse (hence the name), it was established in the 12th century, rebuilt after the Great Fire of 1666, and again in 1780. Public executions were held outside it 1783–1868. It was demolished in 1903.

One of the cells is preserved in the Museum of London.

Newham

Inner borough of east Greater London, north of the River Thames. It includes the districts of East and West Ham and the northern part of Woolwich

Features site of former Royal Docks: Victoria (1855), Albert (1880), and King George V (1921); post-war tower blocks (collapse of Ronan Point in 1968 led to official enquiry); Stratford has been chosen as an International Passenger Station for the Channel Tunnel Rail Link

Population (1991) 200,200

Famous people Dick Turpin, Gerard Manley Hopkins

History

From 1671 onwards the borough was associated with the Quakers – from 1704 there was a meeting house in Plaistow, which the Gurneys, Frys, and Barclays attended; it was closed in 1924.

Newhaven

Port in East Sussex, southeast England, at the mouth of the River Ouse, with container facilities and cross-Channel services to Dieppe, France; population (est 1996) 10,700.

Industries include the manufacture of fountain-pens and some light engineering.

Newhaven has a 12th-century Norman church. **Newhaven Fort** was constructed as a defence against Napoleon, and now contains a museum.

New Ireland Forum

Meeting between politicians of the Irish Republic and Northern Ireland in May 1983. It offered three potential solutions to the Northern Irish problem, but all were rejected by the UK the following year.

The Forum was the idea of John Hume (1923–), leader of the Northern Irish Social Democratic Labour Party, and brought together representatives of the three major political parties of the republic, including Fianna Fáil and Fine Gael. The Forum suggested three possibilities for a solution to the Northern Irish problem: unification under a nonsectarian constitution, a federation of North and South, or joint rule from London and Dublin. It recognized that any solution would have to be agreed by a majority in the North, which seemed unlikely. All three options were rejected by the UK government after talks between the former British and Irish leaders, Margaret Thatcher and Garret FitzGerald, in November 1984 (known as the Anglo-Irish summit), although the talks led to improved communication between the two governments.

Newlands, John Alexander Reina (1837–1898)

English chemist who worked as an industrial chemist; he prepared in 1863 the first periodic table of the elements arranged in order of relative atomic masses, and pointed out in 1865 the 'law of octaves' whereby every eighth element has similar properties. He was ridiculed at the time, but five years later Russian chemist Dmitri Mendeleyev published a more developed form of the table, also based on atomic masses, which forms the basis of the one used today (arranged by atomic number).

Newlyn

Working seaport near Penzance, Cornwall, southwest England; population (est 1995) 4,200. Trawler and deep-sea fishing from here is significant, despite the impact of fishing quotas. There is a fish market and also fish-processing and packaging. Tourism is less important than in the adjacent town of Penzance. The town gave its name to the **Newlyn School** of artists 1880–90, who included Stanhope Forbes (1857–1947).

The Ordnance Survey relates heights in the UK to mean sea-level here.

Newman, John Henry (1801–1890)

English Roman Catholic theologian. While still an Anglican, he wrote a series of *Tracts for the Times*, which gave their name to the Tractarian Movement (subsequently called the ◊Oxford Movement) for the revival of Catholicism. He became a Catholic in 1845 and was made a cardinal in 1879. In 1864 his autobiography, *Apologia pro vita sua*, was published.

Newmarket

Town in Suffolk, eastern England, 21 km/13 mi northeast of Cambridge; population (est 1996) 17,100. A centre for horse racing since the reign of James I, it is the headquarters of the Jockey Club and the National Stud and site of the National Horseracing Museum (1983). There are two racecourses, the July course and the Rowley Mile Racecourse, both owned by the Jockey Club, and lying to the southwest. The most important races held at Newmarket are the 1,000 and 2,000 Guineas, the Cambridgeshire, and the Cesarewitch. Approximately a fifth of the town's working population is employed in the racing industry, including veterinary services. Other industries include the manufacture of electronic equipment and agricultural machinery, photographic processing, and light engineering.

New Model Army

Force created in 1645 by Oliver ◊Cromwell to support the cause of Parliament during the English ◊Civil War. It was characterized by organization and discipline. Thomas Fairfax was its first commander.

NEWMARKET *The Suffolk town of Newmarket is the centre of horse racing in Britain. The headquarters of the Jockey Club were established here in 1752, in a building known as the 'Coffee Room'. The Jockey Club was formerly the governing body of flat racing in the country, but ceded control to a new body, the British Horseracing Board, in the 1990s. Bill Weils/Collections*

Newport

Unitary authority in south Wales, created in 1996 from part of the former county of Gwent
Area 190 sq km/73 sq mi
Towns ◊Newport (administrative headquarters)
Physical rivers ◊Usk Ebbw, Afon Llwyd
Features Legionary Museum and Roman amphitheatre at ◊Caerleon
Industries steel and aluminium production, engineering, chemicals, fertilizers, electronics
Population (1996) 133,300

Newport

River port, administrative headquarters of the ◊Isle of Wight unitary authority, southern England, on the River Medina; population (1991) 25,000. Newport is the retail centre for the island and Parkhurst Prison and Camp Hill Prison, in the nearby residential district of Parkhurst, are important sources of employment. Products include electronic current boards and computer parts. Charles I was imprisoned 1647–1648 in nearby Carisbrooke Castle.

Newport formerly imported goods but now has a marina, without major port facilities.

St Thomas's church was built in 1854 on the site of a church originally built during the reign of Henry II; it contains a monument commissioned by Queen Victoria in memory of the Princess Elizabeth, daughter of Charles I, who died in captivity at Carisbrooke Castle in 1650.

Newport, Welsh Casnewydd

Seaport and administrative centre of ◊Newport unitary authority, southeast Wales, situated on the River ◊Usk 30 km/19 mi northwest of Bristol; population (1994 est) 111,000. There is a steelworks at nearby Llanwern, and a high-tech complex at Cleppa Park. Other industries include engineering, and the manufacture of chemicals, fertilizers, aluminium, and electronics.

The Newport Transporter Bridge was built 1906.

It was formerly a walled town defended by a castle, the ruins of which still stand. St Woolos' church, the cathedral of the diocese of Monmouth, dates from Saxon times. The poet W H Davies was born here in 1871.

Newport Pagnell

Market town in Buckinghamshire, southern England, 22 km/14 mi northeast of Buckingham; population (1991) 13,900. Newport Pagnell forms part of the new-town conurbation of ◊Milton Keynes. The main occupation is agriculture, and there are also light industries.

Newport Pagnell is situated on the Great Ouse, at the point where it is joined by the Ousel. It has a 14th-century church.

Newport Riots

Violent demonstrations by the ◊Chartists in 1839 in Newport, Wales, in support of the Peoples' Charter. They were suppressed with the loss of 20 lives.

Newquay

Holiday resort on the Atlantic coast of Cornwall, England, about 18 km/11 mi north of Truro; population (1991) 15,200. It is a centre for surfing.

New Romney

Town in the ◊Romney Marsh area of Kent, southeast England, formed by the amalgamation of Romney with Littlestone on Sea and Greatstone on Sea; population (1991) 8,200. Romney was one of the original ◊Cinque Ports, but its harbour was destroyed by a storm in the 13th century which diverted the course of the River Rother; the town is now more than 2 km/1 mi from the sea.

The medieval wealth of the town is reflected by the Norman church of St Nicholas.

Newry

Town in counties Armagh and Down, Northern Ireland; population (1991) 19,400. It is situated at the head of Carlingford Lough, 53 km/33 mi southwest of Belfast. It manufactures products for veterinary care and also textiles and electrical goods, and has food and drink processing. An important seaport since medieval times, Newry was connected with Lough Neagh by canals in the 18th century.

The first inland canal constructed in Ireland and the UK was at Newry. The canals are now used for angling.

Nothing remains of the Cistercian abbey founded here in 1153 by Maurice MacLoughlin, King of Ireland, and the castle built by de Courcy in 1177. In the 16th century the confiscated lands of Newry were granted to Nicholas Bagenal and the Protestant St Patrick's church includes a tower he built in 1578.

Patrick Brontë, or Prunty (1777–1861), father of the English novelists Anne, Charlotte and Emily Brontë, was born in Ballynaskeagh 24 km/15 mi from Newry.

News Letter

Daily morning newspaper with a unionist slant covering Northern Ireland. Published in Belfast and a sister paper of the *Mirror*, it was established in 1737. It had a circulation of over 34,000 in 1998.

News of the World

Popular Sunday newspaper established in 1843. Owned by News International, it has the highest circulation of any UK newspaper (over 4,400,000 in 1998). It is noted for its reporting of crime, scandals, and sport.

Newson, Lloyd (1954–)

Australian choreographer and dancer, an exponent of avant-garde dance in Britain. He aims to make 'dance about something', and many of his pieces explore psychological and social issues, sexual politics, and gender stereotypes. Strongly influenced by the theatricality of the German avant-garde choreographer Pina Bausch, his choreographic process includes improvisation, frequently devising pieces with the collaboration of dancers and designers. He is the cofounder and director of the DV8 Physical Theatre (1986).

His work for DV8 includes *Dead Dreams of Monochrome Men* (1989), *If Only* . (1990), *Strange Fish* (1992), *MSM* (1993), *Enter Achilles* (1995), and *Bound to Please* (1997). He has collaborated with filmmakers to make award-winning films of several of his pieces for the company.

newspapers

Nearly 60% of the British public over the age of 15 reads a daily paper, over 65% read a Sunday paper, and about 90% read a regional or local paper. The oldest national newspaper currently printed in the UK is the ◊*Observer* (1791); the highest circulation UK newspaper is the Sunday ◊*News of the World* (nearly 5 million copies weekly). See also entries for other individual newspapers.

History

The first English newspaper appeared in 1622, the *Weekly News*, edited by Nicholas Bourne and Thomas Archer. By 1645 there were 14 news weeklies on sale in London, but the first daily was the subsidized progovernment *Daily Courant* (1702). Arrests, seizure of papers, and prosecution for libel or breach of privilege were employed by the government against opposition publications, and taxes and restrictions were imposed 1700–1820 in direct relation to the growth of radical opinion. The last of these taxes, stamp duty, was abolished in 1855.

Improved printing (steam printing in 1814, the rotary press in 1857), newsprint (paper made from woodpulp, used in the UK from the 1880s), and a higher literacy rate led to the growth of newspapers throughout the 19th century. A breakthrough in printing technology was the Linotype machine that cast whole lines of type, introduced in Britain in 1896; and better train services made national breakfast-time circulation possible. There were nine evening papers in the London area at the end of the 19th century, and by 1920, 50% of British adults read a daily paper; by 1947, just before the introduction of television, the average adult read 1.2 daily papers and 2.3 Sunday papers; in 1998 about 60% of adults read a daily paper.

Newspapers in the first half of the 20th century reinforced the traditional model of British society, being aimed at upper,

NEWSPAPERS: SOME KEY DATES

1500 English printer Wynkyn de Worde establishes the first press in Fleet Street, London. The street will become synonymous with printing and newspapers.

1590 The first regular newspaper, the *Mercurius Gallobelgicus*, is printed in London, carrying reports of news from continental Europe.

23 November 1646 The first advertisement in an English newspaper appears in Samuel Pecke's *Perfect Diurniall*. It is for books and Pecke charges 6d per advert.

1701 Francis Burgess founds the *Norwich Post*, the first newspaper in England published outside London.

2 March 1702 E Mallet launches the *Daily Courant*, the first successful daily newspaper published in England.

1730–1807 The *Daily Advertiser* is launched in London. With its dependence on advertisements, this may be regarded as the first modern newspaper.

1751 John Hill, writing as 'The Inspector', begins the first regular newspaper column, in the *London Advertiser and Literary Gazette*.

25 January 1762 Anna Maria Smart is the first British woman to edit a newspaper when she becomes the editor and publisher of the *Reading Mercury* in Britain.

1778 The *Whitehall Evening Post* in London is the first newspaper to carry regular sports reports.

26 March 1780 The *British Gazette and Sunday Monitor* is the first Sunday newspaper in the country.

1 January 1814 The first Welsh language newspaper, *Seren Gomer*, is launched.

1842 The first photograph to be printed in a newspaper appears in the London paper *The Times*.

1875 *The Times* starts publishing the first generally available daily weather forecasts.

25 October 1881 *The Evening Illustrated Newspaper*, the first illustrated newspaper in Britain, is launched.

1900 Cyril Arthur Pearson publishes the *Express* in Britain; one of the paper's innovations is to have news on the front page.

1904 The British newspaper the *Daily Illustrated Mirror* is the first in the world to employ photographers on its staff and to publish photographs of news events.

1915 The first British comic strip appears in the *Daily Mail*, Charles Folkard's 'Adventures of Teddy Tail'.

1920 The Press Association leases telegraph wires for news distribution in Britain.

1967 The *London Daily Express* is transmitted electronically, via telephone lines and satellite, to Puerto Rico. It is the first newspaper to be printed simultaneously in another part of the world.

1969 The Australian businessman Rupert Murdoch buys the *Sun*, which is relaunched as a tabloid.

1977 *Gay News* (launched 1972) is prosecuted for blasphemy in a private case brought by Mary Whitehouse.

1981 Rupert Murdoch's News International buys *The Times*.

August 1989 The Associated Newspapers group – *Evening Standard*, *Daily Mail* and *Mail on Sunday* – are the first to print newspapers in nonsmudge ink in Britain.

13 December 1990 The *Northern Echo* in Darlington, England is the first British newspaper to appear on CD-ROM.

middle, or working-class readers. During World War II and until 1958, newsprint rationing prevented market forces from killing off the weaker papers. Polarization into 'quality' and 'tabloid' newspapers followed. Sales of national newspapers that have closed, such as the *News Chronicle*, were more than 1 million; they were popular with the public but not with advertisers. Papers with a smaller circulation, such as *The Times* and the *Independent*, survive because their readership is comparatively well off, so advertising space can be sold at higher rates. The *Guardian* is owned by a nonprofit trust. Colour supplements have proliferated since their introduction by some Sunday papers in the 1960s. The sales of the mass-circulation papers are boosted by lotteries and photographs of naked women; their news content is small. Some claim not to be newspapers in the traditional sense; their editorial policy is to entertain rather than inform.

Press regulation

British newspapers cover a political spectrum from the moderate left to the far right. Investigative reporting is restricted by stringent laws of libel and contempt of court and by the Official Secrets Act. The Press Council was established in 1953 to foster 'integrity and a sense of responsibility to the public', but had no power to enforce its recommendations. In December 1989 all major national newspapers agreed on a new code of conduct to prevent possible new legislation by instituting a right of reply, a readers' representative, and prompt correction of mistakes, resulting in the ◊Press Complaints Commission a voluntary regulatory body, from 1991.

Journalism is to England what bullfighting is to Spain: a daring national sport that offers youngsters with the guts for it a chance to pull themselves up out of pedestrian destinies.

IRMA KURTZ US-born journalist.
Dear London (1997)

New Statesman

Weekly periodical, founded in 1913 by Sidney ◊Webb and George Bernard ◊Shaw. In 1931 it absorbed *The Nation* and *Athenaeum*, and in 1934 the *Weekend Review*. Today the *New Statesman* is an influential political and literary review, and is one of the biggest selling left-wing periodicals in Britain.

Newstead

Village in Nottinghamshire, England, 14 km/9 mi north of Nottingham, situated in Sherwood Forest; population (1991) 1,900. A colliery lies within the village. **Newstead Abbey**, founded by Henry II in the 12th century, was granted by Henry VIII to the Byron family, who held it until 1818 when the 6th Lord Byron (the poet) sold it. The house and gardens have since been restored.

Newton, Isaac (1642–1727)

English physicist and mathematician who laid the foundations of physics as a modern discipline. During 1665–66, he discovered the binomial theorem, differential and integral calculus, and that white light is composed of many colours. He developed the three standard laws of motion and the universal law of gravitation, set out in *Philosophiae naturalis principia mathematica* (1687), usually referred to as the *Principia*.

Newton's greatest achievement was to demonstrate that scientific principles are of universal application. He clearly defined the nature of mass, weight, force, inertia, and acceleration.

In 1679 Newton calculated the Moon's motion on the basis of his theory of gravity and also found that his theory explained the laws of planetary motion that had been derived by German astronomer Johannes Kepler on the basis of observations of the planets.

Newton was born at Woolsthorpe Manor, Lincolnshire, and studied at Cambridge, where he became professor at the age of 26. He resisted James II's attacks on the liberties of the universities, and sat in the parliaments of 1689 and 1701–02 as a Whig. Appointed warden of the Royal Mint in 1696, and master in 1699, he carried through a reform of the coinage. Most of the last 30 years of his life were taken up by studies of theology and chronology, and experiments in alchemy.

Newton began to investigate the phenomenon of gravitation in 1665, inspired, legend has it, by seeing an apple fall from a tree. But he was also active in algebra and number theory, classical and analytical geometry, computation, approximation, and even probability. He was knighted in 1705.

Newton Abbot

Town in Devon, England, on the estuary of the River Teign, 25 km/15 mi southwest of Exeter; population (1991) 21,000. Pipeclay and fine china clay (kaolin) are obtained in the area.

William (III) of Orange was proclaimed King of England here in 1688, at the market cross. Bradley Manor, west of the town, is a fine example of 15th-century architecture.

Newton Aycliffe

Town in Durham, northeast England, on the River Skerne, 8 km/5 mi north of Darlington; population (1995) 28,500. It was designated a ◊new town in 1947. Products include washing machines, lawn mowers, microelectronics, and vehicle axles.

Newton Aycliffe was developed on the site of the former Aycliffe Royal Ordnance factory in order to provide work and housing for some of the population of the declining coalfield in southwest Durham. The Aycliffe and Peterlee Development Corporation, responsible for the planning of the new town from 1947, was wound up in 1988.

Newton-John, Olivia (1948–)

English-born Australian pop singer. She was born in Cambridge, England, and emigrated to Australia at the age of 5 with her family. She achieved success with the single 'If Not For You' (1971) and a number of singles and albums followed which were hits in the UK and USA. She starred alongside

John Travolta in the film *Grease* (1978) and 'You're The One That I Want', a song from the film, was an international hit.

new town

Centrally planned urban area. Based on schemes initiated by Patrick ◊Abercrombie, new towns such as Milton Keynes and Stevenage were built after World War II to accommodate the overspill from cities and large towns, at a time when the population was rapidly expanding and inner-city centres had either decayed or been destroyed. In 1976 the policy, which had been criticized for disrupting family groupings and local communities, destroying small shops and specialist industries, and furthering the decay of city centres, was abandoned.

New towns are characterized by a regular street pattern and the presence of a number of self-contained neighbourhood units, consisting of houses, shops, and other local services.

Newtown, Welsh Drenewydd

Manufacturing and market town in Powys, central Wales, 20 km/12 mi southwest of Welshpool, situated on the River Severn; population (1991) 10,500. It was the first town to be expanded by the Mid-Wales Development Corporation; it now has a growing range of light industry, including textiles.

Newtown was the birthplace of the socialist Robert Owen (whose ideas stimulated the cooperative movement in the 19th century).

Newtownards

Town in County Down, Northern Ireland, near the head of Strangford Lough; population (1991) 21,000. Synthetic fibre, linen yarn, carpets, and jeans are manufactured here. The town is a shopping centre for a rich farming district and there is food processing. Newtownards was planned in the 17th century, centred on a large square.

The ruins of a Dominican friary founded in 1244 by Walter de Burgh can be seen here, but most of the present town originated during the plantation period.

Scrabo Hill, (165 m/540 ft) 2 km/1 mi from Newtownards, is a red sandstone and basalt hill. On its summit is Scrabo Tower, erected as a memorial to the marquis of Londonderry in 1857.

Newtownards has a small airfield.

Newtown St Boswells

Administrative headquarters of ◊Scottish Borders unitary authority, southeast Scotland; population (1981) 1,100.

Next Steps agency

◊Executive Agency allocated responsibility for work previously done by a government department, such as the Benefits Agency, Contributions Agency, Employment Service, the Passport Agency, the Child Support Agency, the Prison Service, the Defence Research Agency, and the Meteorological Office. Their chief executives are appointed by ministers. The first were created in the late 1980s following the publication of an Efficiency Unit Report 'Improving Management in Government: The Next Steps' in 1988. By September 1997 there were 136 Next Steps agencies employing 360,000 (76%) of civil servants.

NHS, or National Health Service

One of the biggest public health organizations in the world, set up in 1948 to provide free health care for everybody in Britain. The hopes of its founders, that it would so improve public health that its cost could be easily contained, have proved in vain. Better and more expensive treatments have sent costs soaring, though it has succeeded in its basic aims. The Labour government elected in 1997 announced that it would cut waiting lists, reduce the running costs of the service, and by 1999 would end the internal market introduced by the previous government.

> *I do not know what I may appear to the world, but to myself I seem to have been only a boy playing on the sea-shore, and diverting myself in now and then finding a smoother pebble or a prettier shell than ordinary, whilst the great ocean of truth lay all undiscovered before me.*
>
> Isaac Newton English physicist and mathematician. Quoted in L T More's *Isaac Newton*

History and structure

When the NHS began there were a number of counties without even one consulting physician, surgeon, or obstetrician, and many other specialities were also lacking. Now all parts of the country have good medical facilities. In spite of the existence of the NHS, some people prefer to pay into private health schemes, such as BUPA, to avoid long waiting lists for treatment.

The National Health Service Act (1946) was largely the work of Aneurin ◊Bevan, Labour minister of health. It instituted a health service from July 1948 that sought to provide free medical, dental, and optical treatment. Successive governments, both Labour and Conservative, introduced charges for some services. The NHS offers free hospital care, but limited fees are made for ordinary doctors' prescriptions, eye tests and spectacles, and dental treatment, except for children and people on very low incomes.

A White Paper introduced by the Conservative government in 1989 proposed legislation for decentralizing the control of hospitals and changes in general practice giving greater responsibilities to doctors to manage their general practice. Following the NHS and Community Care Act (1990), health authorities and some general practitioners (over 50% by April 1997) were in receipt of funding to purchase health care for their patients from health care providers. Hospitals became self-governing NHS Trusts, financing their work from income from contracts to provide services to the health authorities and GPs.

In 1998 the NHS was administered by 100 health authorities in England, five in Wales, 15 health boards in

Scotland and four health and social services boards in Northern Ireland. The devolution of central government power to the ◊Northern Ireland Assembly, ◊Welsh Assembly and ◊Scottish Parliament will have an impact on the organization of health care in these areas.

Vital statistics

The NHS employs about 1 million people, including part-timers. In 1996–97 it spent £34,900 million. It offers free health care to the population at a cost of 5.8% of the GDP (gross domestic product), compared with an average cost among developed countries of 7.6% of GDP. However, the number of available hospital beds in public hospitals decreased by 25% between 1971 and 1987, while the number of private hospital beds increased by 157%. On average, 317,000 beds are occupied in NHS hospitals. The number of frontline NHS staff (nurses and midwives) on hospital wards fell by 13%, to 349,800, between 1985 and 1995, while the number of managerial and administrative staff increased from 110,900 to 161,000 in England and from 14,315 to 19,778 in Scotland.

Nichols, Peter Richard (1927–)

English dramatist. His first stage play, *A Day in the Death of Joe Egg* (1967), explored the life of a couple with a paraplegic child, while *The National Health* (1969) dramatized life in the face of death from cancer. *Privates on Parade* (1977), about the British army in Malaya, was followed by the middle-class comedy *Passion Play* (1981) and *Poppy* (1982), a musical satire on the Opium Wars in China in the 19th century.

Nicholson, Ben(jamin Lauder) (1894–1982)

English abstract artist. After early experiments influenced by Cubism and the Dutch De Stijl group, Nicholson developed an elegant style of geometrical reliefs, notably a series of white reliefs (1933–38). He won the first Guggenheim Award in 1957.

Son of artist William ◊Nicholson, he studied briefly at the Slade School of Art, London, and travelled in Europe and in California from 1912 to 1918. He married the sculptor Barbara ◊Hepworth in 1934 and was a leading member of the ◊St Ives School.

Nicholson, William Newzam Prior (1872–1949)

English artist. He studied art in Paris, and under the name 'The Beggarstaff Brothers', he developed the art of poster design in partnership with his brother-in-law, James Pryde, their simplified cut-paper designs being noted for their striking simplicity.

Another early graphic achievement was his woodcuts series in colour, which included *Queen Victoria* and *London Types*. He subsequently painted in oils, producing portraits, *Miss Jekyll* (Tate Gallery) being a notable example; landscapes; and glowing still lifes with a fine technical quality, such as *Mushrooms* (Tate Gallery). He was the father of the artist Ben Nicholson. He was knighted in 1936.

Nightingale, Florence (1820–1910)

English nurse, the founder of nursing as a profession. She took a team of nurses to Scutari (now Üsküdar, Turkey) in 1854 and reduced the ◊Crimean War hospital death rate from 42% to 2%. In 1856 she founded the Nightingale School and Home for Nurses in London.

Born in Florence, Italy, she trained in Germany and France. Florence Nightingale was involved with philanthropic and social work in England from an early age, and in 1844 she visited many hospitals and reformatories in Europe. In 1851 she trained as a nurse at an institution of the Protestant Deaconesses at Kaiserswerth, on the River Rhine, Germany, and on her return to England devoted herself to the Governesses' Sanatorium in connection with the London Institute.

At the beginning of the Crimean War, appalled by the sufferings of the wounded, Florence Nightingale volunteered her services and sailed in 1854 with a party of 38 nurses, including Sisters of Mercy from England and Ireland. Her self-sacrificing services to the wounded made her name famous throughout Europe. She wrote several pamphlets on nursing and hospitals, and established a fund in 1857 for the purpose of training nurses at the St Thomas's and King's College hospitals, London. She was the author of the classic *Notes on Nursing* (1860), the first textbook for nurses. In 1907 she was awarded the Order of Merit.

The Verney–Nightingale papers afford interesting details of her relations with Benjamin Jowett, an Oxford University professor who wished to marry her; the politician and philanthropist Richard Monckton Milnes (1809–1885), a great admirer; and her friends Sidney Herbert, the politician who was responsible for sending her to the Crimean front, and the poet Arthur Hugh Clough.

> *It may seem a strange principle to enunciate as the very first requirement in a Hospital that it should do the sick no harm.*
>
> FLORENCE NIGHTINGALE English founder of nursing. Notes on Hospitals

Nineteen Eighty-Four

Futuristic novel by George ◊Orwell, published in 1949, which tells of an individual's battle against, and eventual surrender to, a totalitarian state where Big Brother rules. It is a dystopia (the opposite of a utopia) and many of the words and concepts in it have passed into common usage (for example, newspeak, doublethink, thought police).

Nineteen Propositions

Demands presented by the English Parliament to Charles I in 1642. They were designed to limit the powers of the crown, and their rejection represented the beginning of the Civil War.

1922 Committee

Body made up of all the Conservative Party's backbench MPs, who hold neither portfolios in the government or shadow cabinet. It originated in a meeting in October 1922 at the

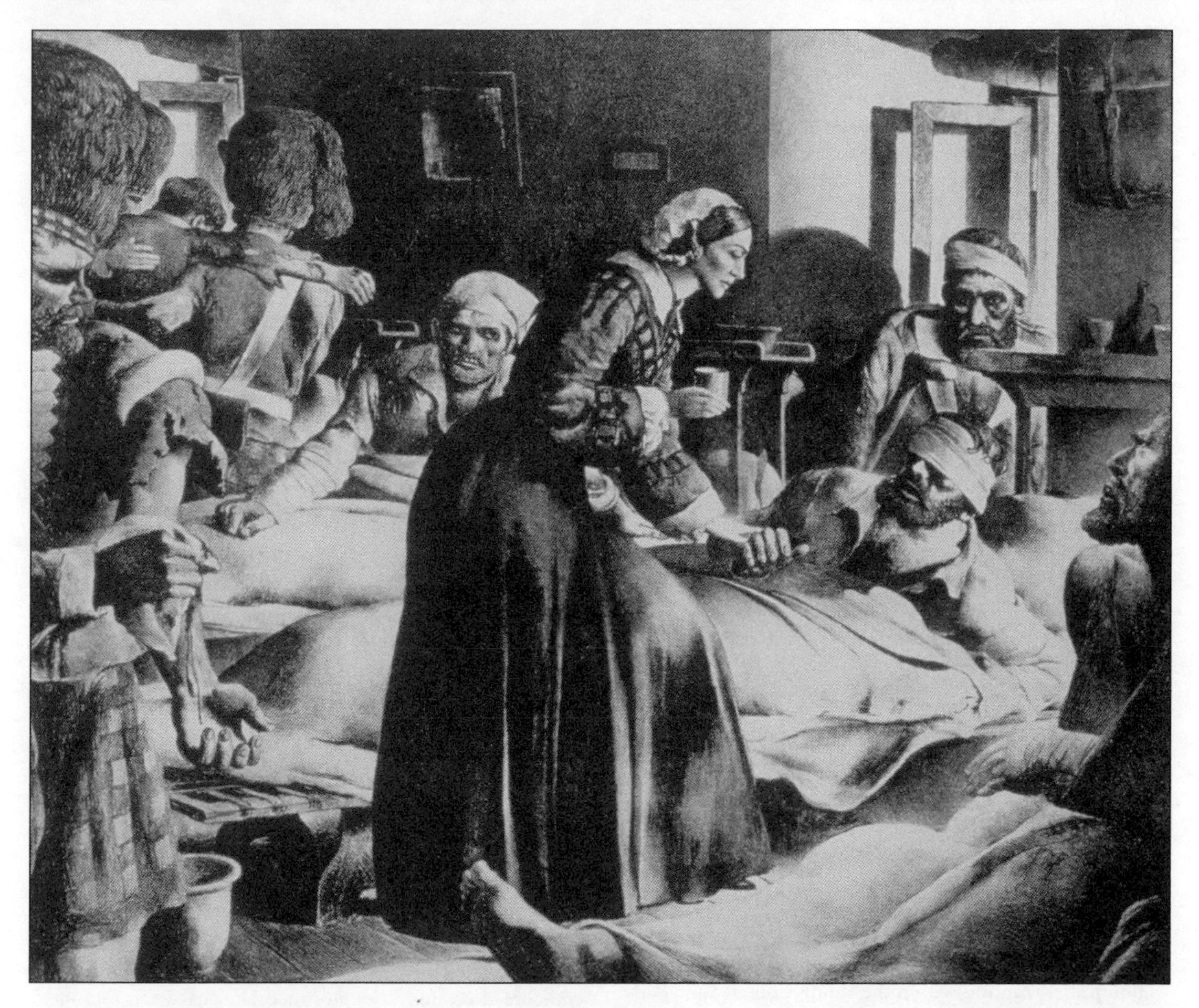

NIGHTINGALE, FLORENCE *A 19th-century lithograph of the English nurse, hospital reformer, and philanthropist, Florence Nightingale, known as 'the Lady of the Lamp'. She organized the barracks hospital at Scutari during the Crimean War, greatly reducing the mortality rate of wounded soldiers by improvements in nursing discipline and sanitation. Corbis*

party's Carlton Club in London, when the party's MPs voted against the policy of the Conservative leader, Austen ◊Chamberlain to remain in the coalition government led by the Liberal, ◊Lloyd George. In the 1990s the Committee comprised an elected chairman and an executive which meets weekly when the House of Commons is sitting. The Committee exerts considerable influence in relaying backbencher concerns to the party's leadership and in the process of removing unpopular leaders.

Ninian, St (*c.* 360–432)

First Christian missionary to Scotland. He appears to have been the son of a Cumbrian chief, but was educated in Rome. He was made a bishop by the pope in 394 and sent to convert Britain. According to Bede, he converted the Picts of southern Scotland, and founded the monastery at Whithorn in about 397.

Nith

River of southern Scotland, rising in East Ayrshire unitary authority, about 13 km/8 mi south of Cumnock, and flowing southeast for about 112 km/70 mi through the valley of Nithsdale in Dumfries and Galloway unitary authority, before entering the Solway Firth 13 km/8 mi south of Dumfries.

Niven, (James) David (Graham) (1910–1983)

Scottish-born US film actor. A suave and sophisticated leading man, he made films in Hollywood and Britain from the 1930s, often featuring in witty comedies and war films. His films include *Wuthering Heights* (1939), *Around the World in 80 Days* (1956), *Separate Tables* (1958) (Academy Award), *The Guns of Navarone* (1961), and *The Pink Panther* (1964).

nobility

Ranks of society who originally enjoyed certain hereditary

privileges. Their wealth was mainly derived from land. In many societies until the 20th century, they provided the elite personnel of government and the military. In the UK members of the ◊peerage sit in the House of Lords.

The English nobility of the Norman Conquest and the Middle Ages was essentially feudal and military, and based on the foundations of landed property. Like that of the feudal nobility of the Normans and Germans, its origins lie in the personal relationship between lord and vassal, and in the system of commendation by which the lord, in return for the allegiance and personal services (generally military) of his vassal, awarded him land and guaranteed a reciprocal protection.

The modern nobility of England resembles the old feudal nobility in no other respect than in the fact that it may possess landed estates; for the rest it consists of a heterogeneous body of peers, some with patents entitling them to sit in the House of Lords and some without, and baronets and knights, the great majority of whom possess titles of recent creation, awarded for political or other public services. Only a few of the existing English peerages go back before the time of William Pitt the Younger (twice prime minister between 1783 and 1806), who himself advised the creation of more than 100.

Noble, Adrian (1950–)

English theatre director. He has been director of the Royal Shakespeare Company since 1991, and is best known for his productions of Shakespeare and other classics, including the plays of Anton Chekhov and Henrik Ibsen.

Nolan Committee

Standing committee set up in October 1994 by prime minister John Major to examine and report on standards in British public life. Its appointment, under Patrick Nolan (1928–), a lord justice of appeal, followed media allegations of political corruption within the ruling Conservative Party. The results of its first round of investigations found no evidence of 'systematic corruption within British public life', but made several recommendations intended to avert future possible conflicts of interest. In his second report in May 1996 he said that there was no 'fundamental malaise' in the quangos he had been asked to examine.

Having completed its first round of investigations into the finances of ministers, members of Parliament, civil servants, and council members, the Committee moved on to examine standards in local government and quangos (quasi-autonomous nongovernmental organizations).

Nore, the

Sandbank at the mouth of the River Thames. It was the site of the first lightship in 1732.

Formerly marked by lightships, the sandbank is now marked by many buoys. In World War II seven towers were erected near the Nore as part of the Thames defences, and the lightship stationed at the eastern end of the sandbank, northeast of Sheerness, was removed. The towers were demolished between 1956 and 1958. The Nore mutiny took place in the vicinity in 1797.

Norfolk

County of eastern England

Area 5,360 sq km/2,069 sq mi

Towns and cities ◊Norwich (administrative headquarters), King's Lynn, Great Yarmouth (ports); Cromer, Hunstanton (resorts)

Physical low-lying with the Fens in the west and the ◊Norfolk Broads in the east; rivers Bure, Ouse, Waveney, Yare

Features the Broads (a series of lakes famous for fishing and water fowl, and for boating); Halvergate Marshes wildlife area; traditional reed thatching; Grime's Graves (Neolithic flint mines); shrine of Our Lady of Walsingham, a medieval and present-day centre of pilgrimage; Blickling Hall (Jacobean, built 1619–24, situated 14 km/7 mi south of Cromer); residence of Elizabeth II at Sandringham (built 1869–71)

Industries agricultural implements; boots and shoes; brewing and malting; offshore natural gas; tanning; there are flour mills and mustard works

Agriculture cereals (wheat and barley); fruit and vegetables (beans, sugar beets, swedes, turnips); turkeys, geese, cattle; fishing centred on Great Yarmouth

Population (1994) 768,500

Famous people Fanny Burney, Thomas Paine, Horatio Nelson, John Crome ('Old Crome'), John Sell Cotman, Rider Haggard

History The earliest record of the term 'North Folk' is dated 1040, but the county's division from Suffolk is almost certainly earlier. Norfolk suffered many incursions from the Danes.

Topography

Norfolk is bounded to the north and northeast by the North Sea; to the northwest by Lincolnshire and the Wash; to the west by Cambridgeshire; and to the south by Suffolk. The coastline is mainly flat and low, and has suffered from widespread erosion, though much land has been reclaimed from the Wash around King's Lynn. There are long stretches of sand, and few inlets; the coast is dangerous owing to numerous sandbanks. Inland the surface is mostly level, and includes in the west a part of the Fens known as the Bedford Level. The many windmills which once stood in this area are now largely derelict; however, several have been restored under a scheme sponsored by Norfolk county council. The soil is varied with chalk, sand, and loam being prevalent in different districts.

Resources 'Gingerbread stone', the local building stone, is quarried near Snettisham, and limestone at Marham. Clay is dug for bricks and tiles at Hunstanton and Snettisham; flints are worked for facing walls.

Historic buildings

Norfolk has many fine churches, among them the beautiful Norman cathedral at Norwich, originally part of a Benedictine monastery. The village churches in the marshland areas are notable for both their grandness of scale and length of nave. The most notable examples are at Emneth, Walsoken, and West Walton (all near Wisbech); at Terrington St Clement and Tilney All Saints (near King's Lynn); at Cley, and at Walpole St Peter, which is also remarkable for its battlement-like parapets and gargoyles. At Castle Rising there is a fine Norman church and the ruins of a Norman castle. Other feudal and monastic ruins are the well-preserved castle at Norwich; Castle Acre; Bacton Abbey; and the ruins of the Augustinian priory at Walsingham.

Norfolk, Miles Francis Stapleton Fitzalan-Howard, 17th Duke of Norfolk (1915–)

Earl marshal of England, and premier duke and earl; seated at Arundel Castle, Sussex, England. As earl marshal, he is responsible for the organization of ceremonial on major state occasions. He became a baron in 1971, and duke in 1975.

Norfolk Broads

Area of interlinked shallow freshwater lakes in East Anglia, eastern England, between Norwich, Sea Palling, and Lowestoft. The area has about 200 km/125 mi of navigable waterways, and the region is a popular tourist destination for boating and fishing.

The lakes formed some 600 years ago when medieval peat diggings were flooded as a result of a rise in the water level. They are connected by 'dykes' to the six rivers which intersect the region: the Bure, Yare, Waveney, Thurne, Ant, and Chet. The Upper Bure is where motorcruising developed and many of the smaller broads open out from here. It is an important wetland region supporting a rich variety of wildlife, including swallowtail butterflies and many breeds of birds. Reeds which grow around the margins of the lakes are used for thatching; Thurne has the most extensive reedbeds. Much of the water has been affected by excessively high levels of phosphates and nitrates draining off from agricultural land, and sewage pollution.

Principal lakes

Hickling Broad (about 3 km/2 mi long) is the largest of the Norfolk Broads. Others include South Walsham, Wroxham, Barton, Salhouse, Blackhorse, Malthouse, Surlingham, Rockland, Horsey (the nearest to the coast in the northeast),
Ormesby, Rollesby, Filby, and Somerton. Oulton is the largest of the Suffolk Broads. Breydon Water and Oulton Broad are segments of estuaries that have been converted into tidal lakes.

Nature reserves

There are nature reserves at Hickling, Horsey, and Strumpshaw Fen, with huge wildfowl populations, including ducks, waders, and geese, and at Upton fen where wild flora are important.

Norman

Any of the descendants of the Norsemen (to whose chief, Rollo, Normandy was granted by Charles III of France in 911) who adopted French language and culture. During the 11th and 12th centuries they conquered England in 1066 (under William the Conqueror), Scotland in 1072, parts of Wales and Ireland, southern Italy, Sicily, and Malta, and took a prominent part in the Crusades.

They introduced feudalism, Latin as the language of government, and Norman French as the language of literature. Church architecture and organization were also influenced by the Normans, although they ceased to exist as a distinct people after the 13th century. See feature on next page on their impact on Britain, and pages 642–644 for genealogies.

Norman architecture

Style of architecture used in England in the 11th and 12th centuries, also known as Romanesque. Norman buildings are massive, with round arches (although trefoil arches are sometimes used for small openings). Buttresses are of slight projection, and vaults are barrel-roofed. Examples include the Keep of the Tower of London and parts of the cathedrals of Chichester, Gloucester, and Ely.

The so-called 'Jews' Houses' at Lincoln, built of stone, are among the few remaining examples of domestic architecture.

Norman Conquest

Invasion and settlement of England by the ◊Normans, following the victory of ◊William the Conqueror at the Battle of ◊Hastings in 1066.

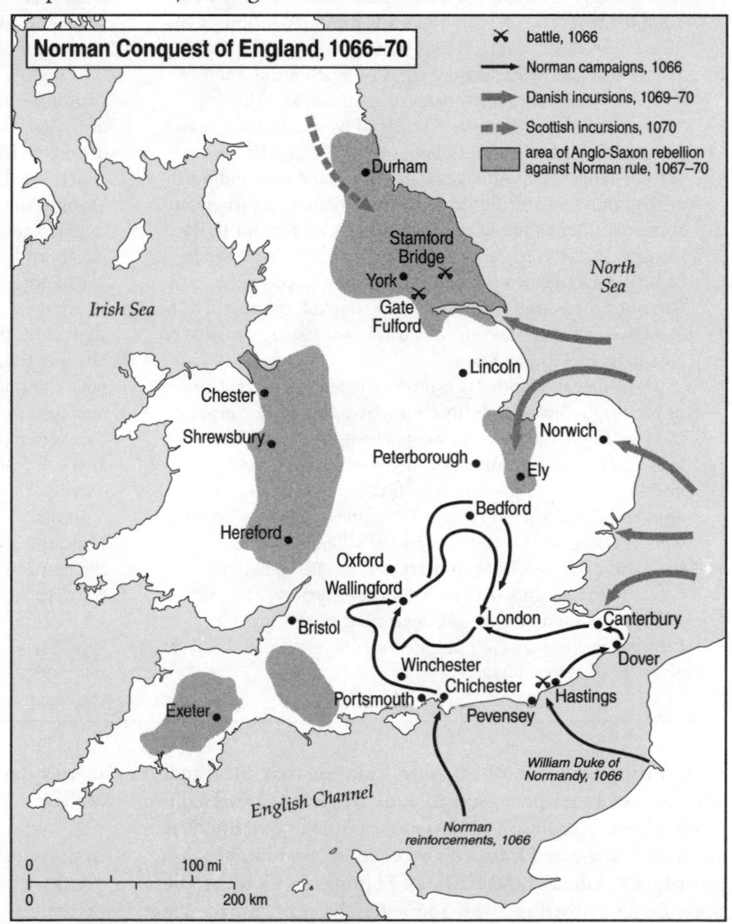

THE NEW ORDER: THE IMPACT OF THE NORMANS

Of all dates, 1066 is probably the best remembered in English history. But exactly what impact the Norman Conquest really had has always been controversial. Did it represent a clear break in the history of Anglo-Saxon England, or were the Normans quickly assimilated, simply hastening developments already underway, and even learning from them?

In a more nationalistic age than ours, many English historians felt instinctively that the virtues and institutions long thought to be characteristically English ought somehow to be traceable to a purely English past – a past that predated the arrival of the 'French' Normans. Detailed research into the survival of pre-Conquest institutions such as shire- and hundred-based local government, the common law, an efficient royal administration, and a national taxation system (Danegeld), led to the argument that the Norman Conquest did little to change an already highly sophisticated society. A less nationalistic view, however, reveals the Norman Conquest as a manifestation of wider changes in Western Europe as a whole, in social and cultural terms, in military terms, and in religious terms.

Society and culture

Changes already taking place in Anglo-Saxon society by 1066 made it less 'English' than was previously thought. As recently as 1042, England had been ruled by a Danish king. The Danes had brought new types of landholding (and therefore social status) to parts of England, and the Anglo-Saxon term 'thane' had been replaced by the Scandinavian 'housecarl' for the warrior class, perhaps also reflecting a social change. Scandinavian influence in the east and north of the country contributed to the lukewarm support which some chroniclers noted in those regions for Harold II, the former Earl of Wessex. A surviving legal case from the reign of William I features a landowner dispossessed in the Conquest who argues that his land should be returned as he is a Dane, and was therefore neutral in the struggle between Normans and Anglo-Saxons.

The Norman Conquest brought the wholesale replacement of the Anglo-Saxon nobility, but it also brought changes in the way English society was conceived. Above all, the ancient Germanic concept of the free peasant owing personal military service to his king was finally brought to an end: after the Conquest, the Anglo-Scandinavian free peasants were reduced to the status of feudal villeins, bound to the land and excluded from military service. Elsewhere in western Europe this new conception of society, central to what we call feudalism, had developed since the 10th century; in England, the older conceptions were only swept away by the Normans.

Military change

The events of 1066 can be seen as part of a wider colonization of the borderlands of Europe by a military elite from Western Europe. The Battle of Hastings was one of the key points of conflict between two of the three distinct military systems of 11th-century Europe. In Scandinavia and Anglo-Scandinavian England the heavy infantryman had dominated the battlefield, armed with the two-handed axe. On the Celtic fringe, mobile light infantrymen, expert with bows, were characteristic. And in feudal Western Europe the warrior par excellence was the heavy horseman, the knight. The knight's charge, with his lance held firm (couched) so as to focus the whole weight of man and charging horse at its point, was the classic tactical device of medieval warfare. Its use at Hastings can be seen in the Bayeux Tapestry. The *Anglo-Saxon Chronicle* confirms the novelty in post-Conquest England of both knights and castles, the two defining features of feudal warfare.

Religious change

Some of the most obvious changes in post-Conquest England were in the church. Most notably, church lands exempt from taxation or military service to the Anglo-Saxon kings were brought within the feudal system of knight-service. Under Lanfranc, appointed archbishop of Canterbury in 1070, the English church itself was thoroughly reorganized. He enforced unity and discipline within the church and the monasteries under the authority of Canterbury, established regular councils and synods, and introduced a whole system of canonical law and separate courts for the church. Above all, the bishops and abbots brought in to replace Anglo-Saxon prelates re-integrated England into the cultural and intellectual mainstream of Northern France.

The ideological importance of these changes cannot be stressed enough. The late Anglo-Saxon church, despite significant reform, had become moribund in a way that was obvious to many of its members; the Norman church in post-Conquest England was perceived even by those nostalgic for the old ways as a positive, dynamic influence. Changes in the church impressed contemporaries as much as the spread of castles or the organization of the Domesday survey.

In many respects, then, it is possible to view the Norman Conquest as a reintegration of the kingdom of England into the cultural, intellectual, military, and religious world of Western Europe, itself on the verge of great changes in the 12th century.

by Simon Hall

William, Duke of Normandy, claimed that the English throne had been promised to him by his maternal cousin Edward the Confessor (died January 1066), but the Witan (Parliament) elected Edward's brother-in-law Harold as king. Harold was killed at the Battle of Hastings in October 1066, and Edgar Atheling was immediately proclaimed king; he was never crowned, renouncing his claim in favour of William. There were several rebellions against William's rule, especially from the north, which he ruthlessly suppressed.

Under Norman rule the English gradually lost their landed possessions and were excluded from administrative posts. In

NORMAN CONQUEST *The south door of the church of St Mary, Iffley, Oxfordshire, England, showing the typical rounded arch and concentric mouldings of Norman architecture. Linda Proud*

1085 William instigated the compilation of the ◊Domesday Book, a recorded survey of land and property in the English shires.

Norman French

Form of French used by the Normans in Normandy from the 10th century, and by the Norman ruling class in England after the Conquest in 1066. It remained the language of the English court until the 15th century, the official language of the law courts until the 17th century, and is still used in the Channel Islands.

Norrington, Roger Arthur Carver (1934–)

English conductor. An early music enthusiast, he has promoted the use of period instruments in his many recordings. He is noted for his interpretations of the Mozart and Beethoven symphonies.

Norrish, Ronald George Wreyford (1897–1978)

English physical chemist who studied fast chemical reactions, particularly those initiated by light. He shared the 1967 Nobel Prize for Chemistry with his co-worker George ◊Porter. Norrish was largely responsible for the advance of reaction kinetics to a distinct discipline within physical chemistry.

Norsemen

Early inhabitants of Norway. The term Norsemen is also applied to Scandinavian ◊Vikings who during the 8th–11th centuries raided and settled in Britain, Ireland, France, Russia, Iceland, and Greenland.

North, Frederick, 2nd Earl of Guilford, known as Lord North (1732–1792)

English Tory politician. He entered Parliament in 1754, became chancellor of the Exchequer in 1767, and was prime minister in a government of Tories and 'king's friends' from 1770. His hard line against the American colonies was supported by George III, but in 1782 he was forced to resign by the failure of his policy. In 1783 he returned to office in a coalition with Charles ◊Fox. After its defeat, he retired from politics.

Northallerton

Market town and administrative headquarters of ◊North Yorkshire, England, between York and Darlington; population (est 1996) 18,000. Employment is largely in the service sector but manufacturing industries include flour-milling, trailer-manufacture and light engineering;

All Saints' church dates from the 12th century and has a Perpendicular bell tower. There are remains of a Norman castle, and the ruins of a Carthusian priory are nearby.

Northampton

Market town and administrative headquarters of ◊Northamptonshire, central England, on the River Nene, 108 km/67 mi northwest of London; population (1996 est) 192,400. The major employers are public administration, financial services and the distribution trade. The manufacture of boots and shoes was historically important, but engineering has taken over as the key industry; other industries include food processing, brewing, and the manufacture of shoe machinery, cosmetics, leather goods, and car accessories.

Northampton was designated a ◊new town in 1968 and is still growing rapidly. The Development Corporation was wound up in the 1980s. The town's Riverside Park is to house a National Fairground Museum.

History

Northampton was held by the Danes at the beginning of the 10th century, and was burned by them in 1010. After the Norman Conquest Simon de Senlis, 1st Earl of Northampton, built a castle here (now destroyed) which became a favourite resort of the Norman and Angevin kings. The town became important for shoe and bootmaking during the Civil War, when it provided boots for Parliamentary troops. Many of Northampton's buildings were destroyed in a fire of 1675. The town expanded greatly in the 19th century with the development of road and rail links and with the growth of the shoe and boot industry.

Features

St Peter's church is a fine example of late Norman work, and the church of St Sepulchre, dating from the 12th century, is one of four surviving round churches in England. All Saints church was rebuilt following the fire of 1675 and has an Ionic

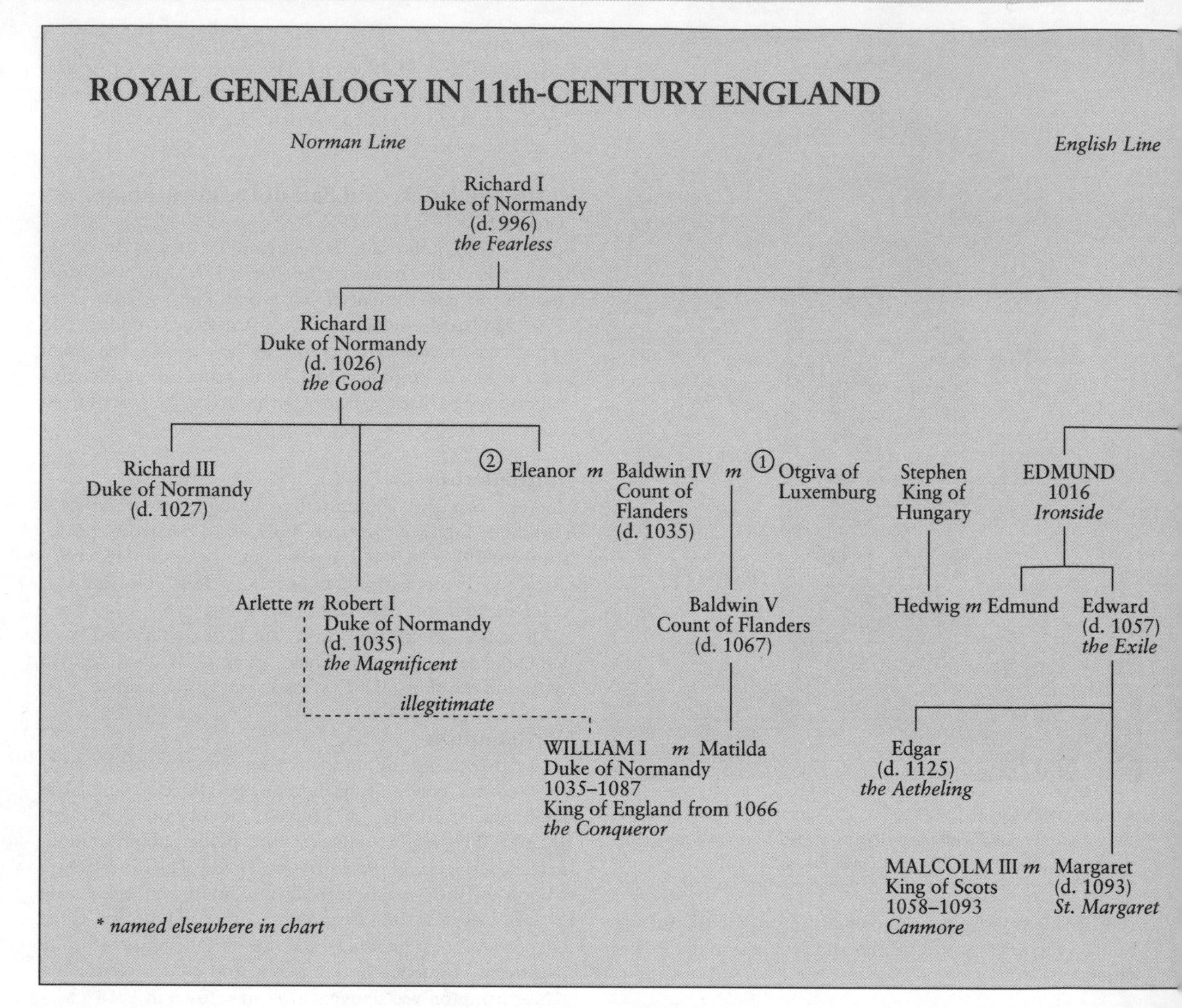

portico with a statue of Charles II wearing Roman costume. The Central Museum and Art Gallery traces the town's industrial history and includes a large collection of shoes. Other features include the County Hall (1682), the Victorian Gothic Guildhall (1864), and the Roman Catholic Cathedral, designed by Augustus Pugin.

Northamptonshire

County of central England

Area 2,370 sq km/915 sq mi

Towns and cities ◊Northampton (administrative headquarters), Kettering, Corby, Daventry, Wellingborough

Physical rivers Avon, Cherwell, Leam, Nene, Ouse, and Welland

Features Althorp Park, Spencer family home and burial place of Diana, Princess of Wales; Canons Ashby, Tudor house, home of the Drydens for 400 years; churches with broached spires (an octagonal spire on a square tower)

Industries engineering, food processing, printing, shoemaking; Northampton is the centre of the leather trade in England

Agriculture cereals (wheat and barley), sugar beet, sheep rearing; cattle rearing, especially in the Nene and Welland valleys, where there is rich pasture

Population (1994) 594,800

Famous people Richard III, Robert Browne, John Dryden; the family of George Washington, first president of the USA, originated at Sulgrave Manor

History The Battle of Naseby, the decisive battle of the English Civil War in 1645, in which Oliver Cromwell defeated the Royalists, was fought at Naseby 32 km/20 mi south of Leicester.

Topography

Northamptonshire is bounded on the north by Rutland and Leicestershire; on the east by Peterborough, Cambridgeshire, Bedfordshire, and Milton Keynes; on the south by Buckinghamshire and Oxfordshire; and on the west by Warwickshire. The surface of the county is mainly level, with occasional low hills and woodland. The Grand Union Canal crosses the county. The climate is mild.

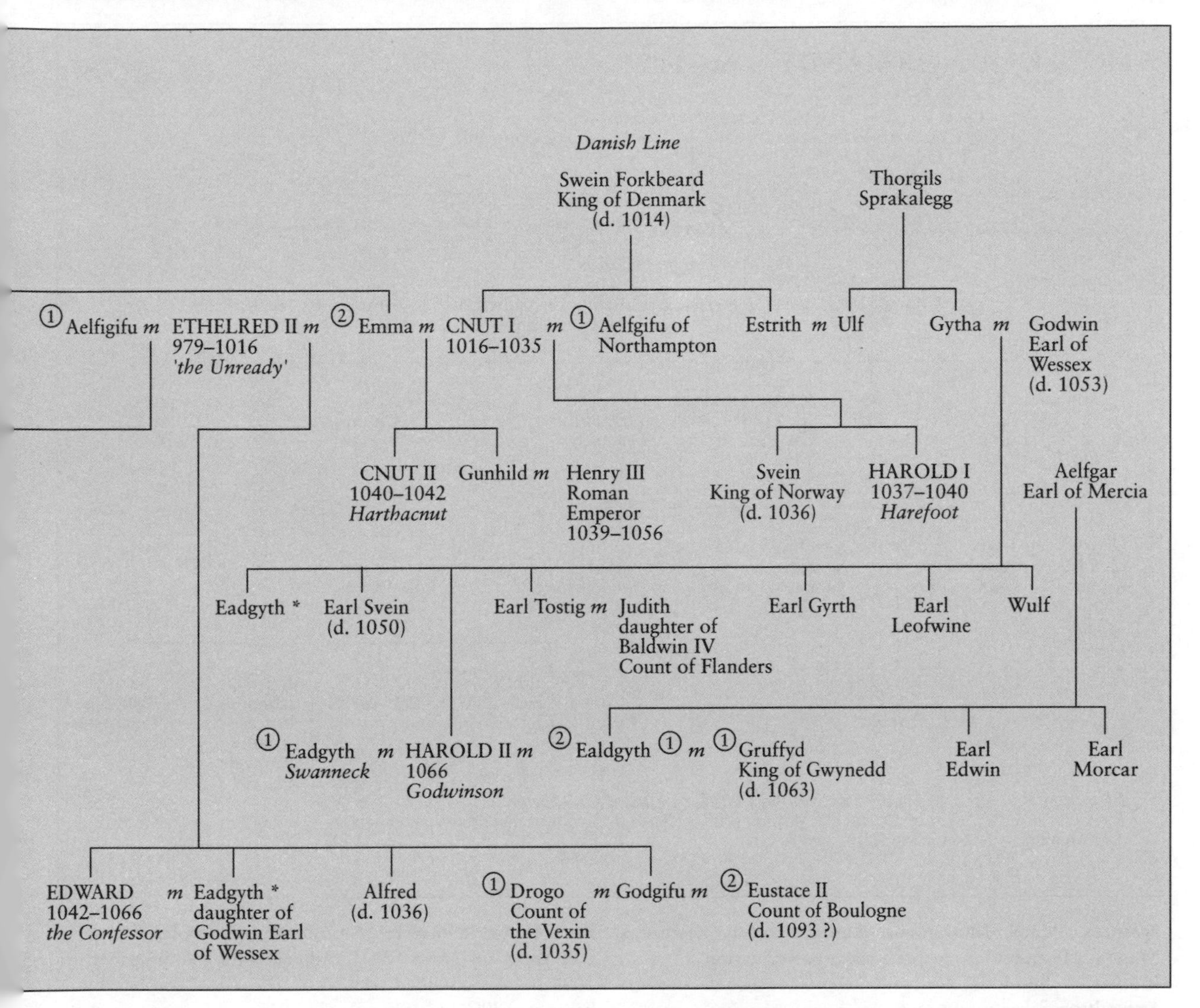

Resources
Ironstone is quarried in large quantities, especially near Kettering and Wellingborough. Weldon stone (a type of building stone), limestone and clay are also quarried. Iron ore was quarried at Corby from 1933, but the town's steel works closed in 1979.

Early history
At Draughton there is evidence of occupation in the early Iron Age. Prehistoric and Roman remains have been found, and Watling Street and Ermine Street both cross the county. Northamptonshire was part of the Anglo-Saxon kingdom of Mercia, and in the 11th century was part of the earldom of ◊Tostig. In 1215 the barons besieged Northampton Castle, held by King John, and in 1264 the castle was taken from Simon de Montfort, leader of the baronial opposition to the king, by Henry III. Henry VI was defeated at Northampton during the Wars of the Roses.

Historic buildings
Northamptonshire has few monastic remains, but there are Norman churches. There are market crosses at Brigstock, Helpston, Higham Ferrers, and Irthlingborough, and at Hardingstone and Geddington are two of the crosses built by Edward I in memory of his wife, Queen Eleanor. The ruins of Fotheringhay Castle, where Mary Queen of Scots was executed, are also in the county. Mansions include Althorp Park, Burghley House, Rushton Hall, Rockingham Castle, Castle Ashby, Dingley Hall, Deene Park, and the ruined Kirby Hall.

North Ayrshire
Unitary authority in western Scotland, created in 1996 from Cunninghame district in Strathclyde region
Area 889 sq km/343 sq mi
Towns ◊Irvine (administrative headquarters), Kilwinning, Saltcoats, Largs, Kilbirnie
Physical low-lying coastal plain on the mainland, rising inland to a plateau of over 305 m/1,000 ft; the islands of the Firth of Clyde are Arran, Holy Isle, Cumbraes; the rivers Irvine and Garnock reach the sea at Irvine; Goat Fell (874 m/2,867 ft)

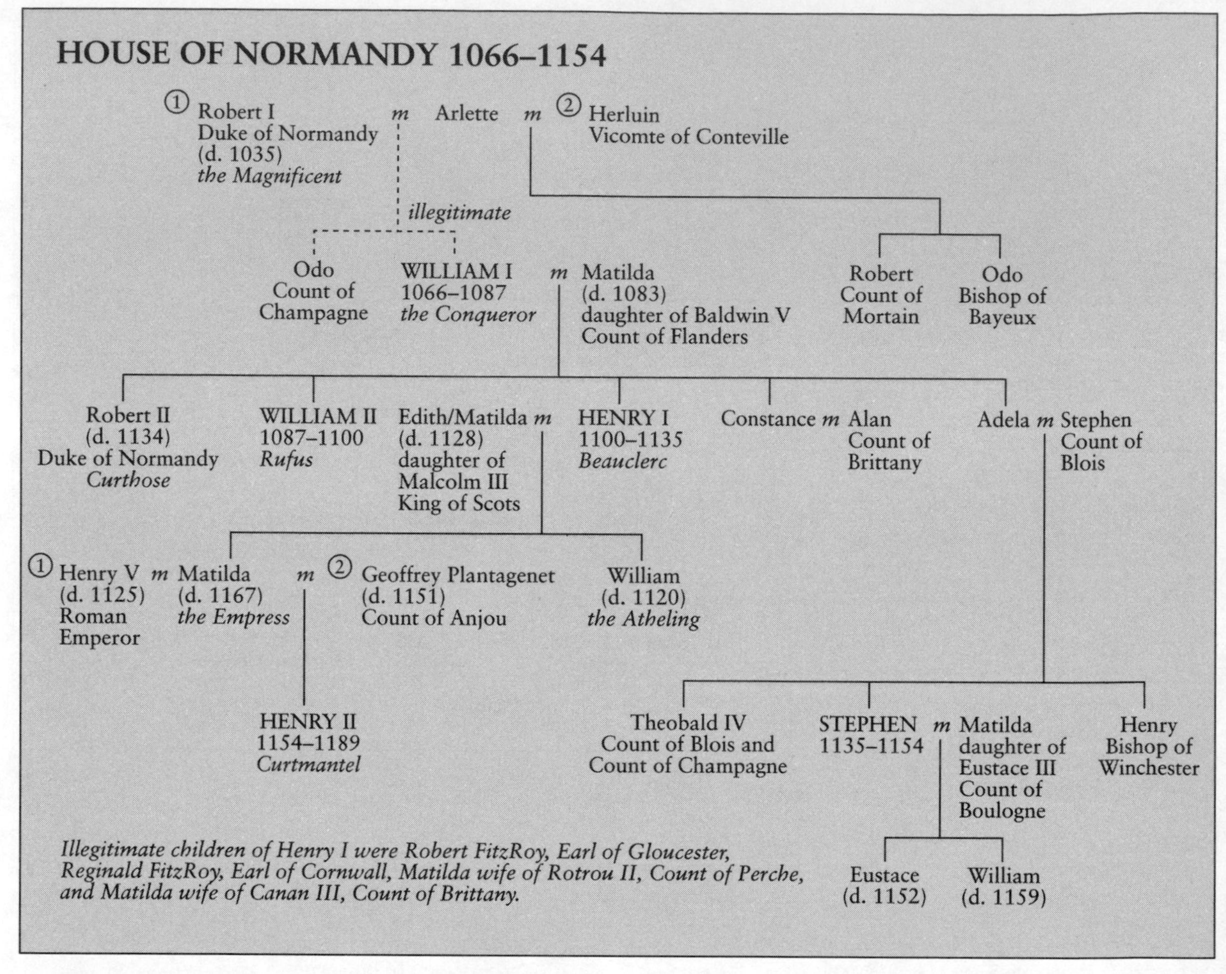

Features Pencil Monument, Largs; Scottish Maritime Museum, Irvine; Hunterston nuclear power station
Industries chemicals, electronics, computer manufacturing
Agriculture dairying, potatoes
Population (1995) 139,500
History Eglinton Tournament (19th century); Battle of Largs (1263), when the Scots captured the Hebrides from the Norwegians.

Economy

The towns of the Garnock Valley have suffered from de-industrialization, despite diversification of the economy. Irvine New Town is the focus for electronics and chemical industries. The area is within the Glasgow commuter zone.

Environment

There are 27 Sites of Special Scientific Interest, one National Nature Reserve, one National Scenic Area, one regional park, and two country parks.

Administrative history

Prior to 1975, the mainland was part of the county of Ayrshire, and Arran was part of the county of Bute.

Northcliffe, Alfred Charles William Harmsworth, 1st Viscount Northcliffe (1865–1922)

British newspaper proprietor, born in Dublin. Founding the *Daily Mail* in 1896, he revolutionized popular journalism, and with the *Daily Mirror* (1903) originated the picture paper. In 1908 he also obtained control of *The Times*. He became a baron in 1905, and a viscount in 1917.

His brother **Harold Sidney Harmsworth, 1st Viscount Rothermere** (1868–1940), was associated with him in many of his newspapers. He became a baron in 1914, and a viscount in 1919.

North Downs

Line of chalk hills in southeast England, extending from Salisbury Plain across Hampshire, Surrey, and Kent. They face the ◊South Downs across the Weald of Kent and Sussex and are much used for sheep pasture.

The downs run from Andover (on the edge of Salisbury Plain) in the west to the cliffs of South Foreland in the east. The North Downs Way is a long-distance footpath (length 227 km/141 mi) which runs along the crest of the North Downs, coinciding in places with the Pilgrims' Way (an ancient track running from Winchester to Canterbury). The Surrey Hills and the Kent Downs are both designated areas of outstanding natural beauty, and at Wye and Crundale Downs there is a national nature reserve. The rivers Stour, Medway, Darent, Mole, and Wey cut through the chalk creating natural routes and important centres, as at Guildford, Reigate, Maidstone, Ashford, and Canterbury.

North East Lincolnshire

Unitary authority in eastern England created in 1996 from part of the former county of Humberside
Area 192 sq km/74 sq mi
Towns and cities ◊Grimsby (administrative headquarters), Immingham, Cleethorpes, Humberston, New Waltham, Waltham, Healing, Laceby
Features Humber Estuary forms east border of authority; River Freshney; Immingham Museum; National Fishing Heritage Centre (Grimsby)
Industries fishing and associated industries, docks and shipping services at Immingham and Grimsby), chemical manufacture, heavy engineering, marine engineering, oil refining, tourism (Cleethorpes)
Population (1996 est) 164,000.

Northern Ireland

Constituent part of the United Kingdom
Area 13,460 sq km/5,196 sq mi
Capital Belfast
Towns and cities Londonderry, Enniskillen, Omagh, Newry, Armagh, Coleraine
Features Mourne Mountains, Belfast Lough and Lough Neagh; Giant's Causeway; comprises the six counties (Antrim, Armagh, Down, Fermanagh, Londonderry, and Tyrone) that form part of Ireland's northernmost province of Ulster
Exports engineering, shipbuilding, textile machinery, aircraft components; linen and synthetic textiles; processed foods, especially dairy and poultry products; rubber products, chemicals
Currency pound sterling
Population (1993 est) 1,632,000
Language English; 5.3% Irish-speaking
Religion Protestant 51%, Roman Catholic 38%
Famous people Viscount Montgomery, Lord Alanbrooke
Government direct rule from the UK since 1972. Northern Ireland is entitled to send 18 members to the Westminster Parliament. Local government: 26 district councils. The province costs the UK government £3 billion annually. Under the terms of the 1998 Good Friday Agreement, Northern Ireland now has a 108-member assembly, elected by proportional representation, exercising devolved executive and legislative authority in areas including health, social security, education and agriculture. There are provisions to ensure that all sections of the community participate in the government and that minority rights are protected.

History

The creation of Northern Ireland dates from 1921 when the Irish Free State (subsequently the Republic of Ireland) was established separately from the mainly Protestant counties of north and northeastern Ireland (six out of the nine counties of the province of Ulster), which were given limited self-government as Northern Ireland, but continued to send members to the House of Commons in Westminster.

Northern Irish governments to 1963

The Northern Ireland Parliament (known as Stormont, from the location where it met from 1932 onwards) met for the first time in 1921, the first prime minister being James ◊Craig, later Viscount Craigavon, who headed a Unionist government until his death in 1940. Northern Ireland continued to be ruled by Unionist governments until direct rule was imposed from Westminster in 1972.

Craig was a fervent champion of continued union with the United Kingdom and during the early years of the Irish Free State, when civil strife spread over the border into Northern

Northern Ireland: Counties

County	County town	Area		Population (1991)
		sq km	sq mi	
Antrim	Belfast	2,830	1,092	44,500
Armagh	Armagh	1,250	482	51,800
Down	Downpatrick	2,470	953	58,000
Fermanagh	Enniskillen	1,680	648	54,000
Londonderry	Londonderry	2,070	799	95,400
Tyrone	Omagh	3,136	1,211	158,500

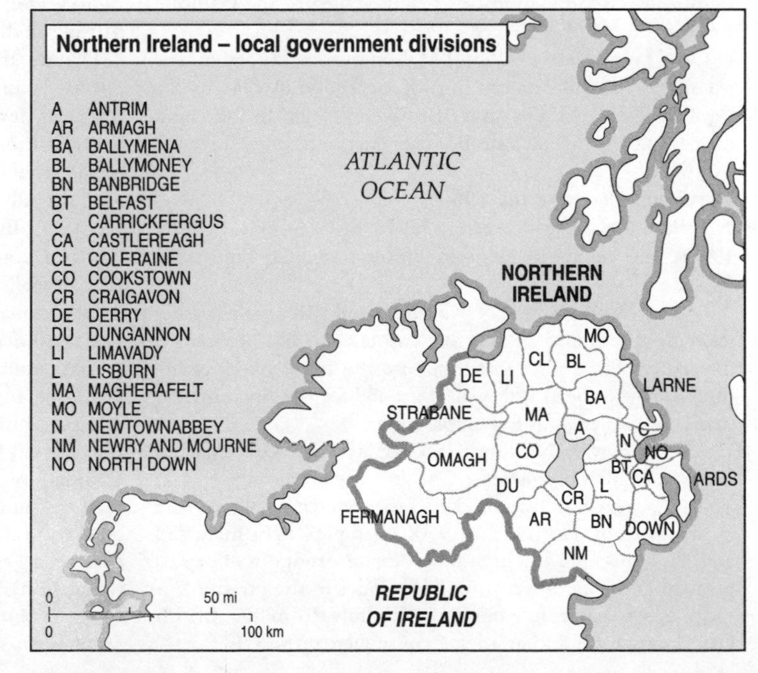

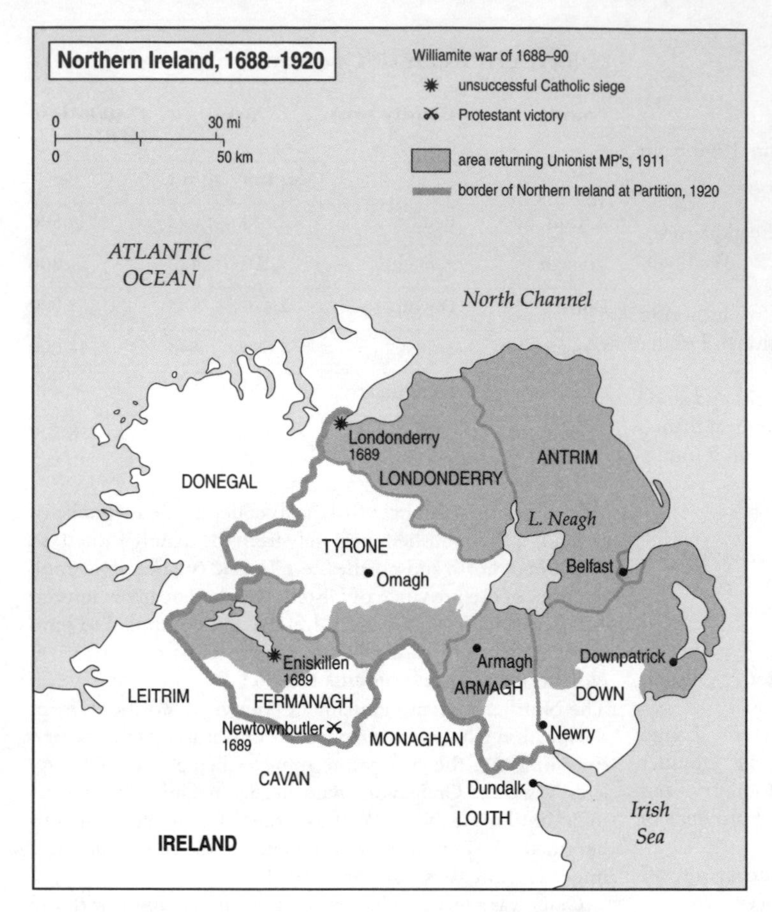

Ireland, his forceful character had a steadying influence on Northern Ireland politics. Under Unionist governments, significant discrimination was practised against the Catholic minority.

On Craig's death in 1940, J M Andrews succeeded him as premier, and Andrews was in turn succeeded in 1943 by Sir Basil Brooke, later Viscount ◊Brookeborough. Brooke held office until 1963, when he was succeeded by Terence ◊O'Neill.

Developments up to the 1960s

Northern Ireland was severely hit by the depression of the 1930s, and unemployment in Ulster remained high until 1939.

During World War II Northern Ireland had a considerable strategic importance, filling the gap created by the South's neutrality. The country's agriculture and industries contributed much to the British war effort and for the first time for many years there was full employment.

After the war, Northern Ireland, like the UK, enacted legislation in the spheres of health, social insurance, and housing, which transformed it into a welfare state on the British pattern. During the 1950s unemployment increased and has continued at a high level despite strenuous efforts to persuade new industries to build factories in the province.

In 1949 the Irish Republic withdrew from the British Commonwealth and as a legal consequence the UK Parliament passed the 1949 Northern Ireland Act, which declared that Northern Ireland remained part of the United Kingdom and would not cease to be such without the consent of the Parliament of Northern Ireland. This confirmation of the breach with the Republic was followed by six years of ◊Irish Republican Army (IRA) activity on the border (1956–62).

Many attempts were made to improve relations between the North and South, particularly by Terence O'Neill, who in 1965 met the prime minister of the Republic, Sean Lemass, in Belfast, the first meeting of two Irish premiers since the establishment of Stormont. But all such developments lapsed with the spread of civil disorder in the North from 1968 (the 'Troubles'), and the inevitable identification of the South with the Catholic minority in Ulster.

The beginning of the Troubles

The summer of 1968 saw the first disturbances resulting from a civil rights campaign against anti-Catholic discrimination in voting, housing, and employment, and the counter-demonstrations of Protestant extremists led by Ian Paisley. The justice of the civil rights campaign was tacitly admitted and reforms promised. O'Neill, although reelected on a reform platform, lost the confidence of the Unionist Party and was replaced in April 1969 by James Chichester-Clark. After further rioting British troops were called in to maintain law and order – and to protect Catholics – in August 1969. The most prominent civil rights leader, Bernadette Devlin, was later imprisoned for her part in the disturbances.

Despite the disbandment of the (largely) Protestant B Special volunteer constabulary, and the announcement of a five-year development and reform programme, rioting and street fighting took place intermittently in 1970. As a reaction to the troubles, two new political parties were formed that year: the Alliance Party, which aimed to unite Protestants and Roman Catholics on a platform of moderate policies, and the ◊Social Democratic and Labour Party (SDLP), whose moderate nationalist policy aimed at the reunification of Ireland by constitutional means.

The crisis deepens

As the country drifted from civil disturbance to the edge of civil war in 1971, there were an increasing number of sectarian murders and evidence of struggles between the Official and Provisional wings of the IRA for control of the Catholic areas of Belfast (the IRA had split in 1969 at the same time as ◊Sinn Féin). Violence became a part of everyday life in that city and, with the UK and Northern Irish governments disagreeing on security measures, a political crisis led to the resignation of Chichester-Clark, who was succeeded by Brian Faulkner. Internment of suspects without trial, chiefly at the Long Kesh camp, was introduced, to the outrage of the

Catholic community, and open warfare on the Belfast streets followed.

A significant political development in 1971 (and a pointer to the hardening of some Unionist attitudes) was the establishment by Ian Paisley of the Democratic Unionist Party (DUP) as a more hardline rival to the ruling dominant Ulster Unionist Party.

The following year, 1972, was the worst so far experienced in the violence. It began with the demonstration in Londonderry that produced 'Bloody Sunday', in which 14 demonstrators were killed by British soldiers. By the end of the year 467 people had been murdered. In March Stormont was suspended; in future Ulster was to be governed direct from Westminster through the secretary of state for Ireland. Brian Faulkner and his whole cabinet resigned and the Unionist Party and many other Protestants reacted bitterly to what they saw as British betrayal.

While the British government attempted to conciliate Catholic opinion, following a policy of phasing out internment and holding the army in check, the IRA's activities increased and an opposition emerged in the shape of the Protestant paramilitary Ulster Defence Association. Now both communities possessed an armed, potentially aggressive force and a wave of sectarian, reprisal killings followed.

The power-sharing experiment

In 1973 there were attempts to find a political solution in a new, democratically elected, authority. A poll on the issue of staying in the UK or joining the Republic gave a massive majority for the former, while elections to the new Irish assembly fragmented the Unionist Party and gave the SDLP a powerful voice. Talks continued on the formation of a 'power-sharing' Northern Ireland Executive Council with representatives from all parties and a Council of Ireland consisting of representatives from both North and South Ireland. Agreement on the latter between the British government, Northern Ireland, and the Republic was eventually reached after talks at Sunningdale in 1973.

The new Executive, a coalition of Protestants and Catholics led by Brian Faulkner, took office in 1974, but was repudiated days later by the Unionist Party. It was finally brought down six months later, after a massive strike by Protestant workers against it and the Sunningdale agreement had paralyzed Northern Ireland. Direct rule from Westminster was reimposed.

While attempts to find a new political solution continued, so did the campaign of violence, which spread increasingly to mainland Britain and to the Republic, where, in 1976, the British ambassador was murdered. Other instances of republican violence included the 1979 murder of Lord Mountbatten and the 1984 bombing of the Conservative Party conference at the Grand Hotel in Brighton. In the early 1980s republican hunger strikes in prison raised political tension, and led the republican movement to embark on a more sustained and successful political campaign, to complement its paramilitary activities. Fears in London and Dublin that Sinn Féin might overtake the more moderate Social Democratic and Labour Party (SDLP) as the party representatives of most Northern Irish nationalists, led to a major intergovernmental initiative in the form of the 1985 Anglo-Irish Agreement.

The Anglo-Irish Agreement

Under the Anglo-Irish Agreement of 1985, the Republic of Ireland was given a consultative role (via an Anglo-Irish conference) in the government of Northern Ireland, but agreed that there should be no change in its status except by majority consent. The agreement was approved by Parliament, but all 12 Ulster members gave up their seats, so that by-elections could be fought as a form of 'referendum' on the views of the province itself. A similar boycotting of the Northern Ireland Assembly led to its dissolution in 1986 by the UK government.

Job discrimination was outlawed under the Fair Employment Act of 1975, but in 1987 Catholics in Northern Ireland were two and a half times more likely to be unemployed than their Protestant counterparts – a differential that had not improved since 1971. In 1993, unemployment was running at 14.2%, and 75% of the unemployed were Catholic. Residential integration was still sparse: in 1993 650,000 people lived in areas that were 90% Catholic or Protestant.

Towards the Downing Street Declaration

Against the backdrop of continuing loyalist and republican paramilitary violence, the question of Northern Ireland's political future was debated in talks held in Belfast in April–September 1991 – the first direct negotiations between the political parties for 16 years. Follow-up talks between the British government and the main Northern Ireland parties in September–November 1992 made little progress.

In September 1993 it emerged that the Catholic nationalist Social Democratic Labour Party (SDLP) and Sinn Féin (political wing of the outlawed IRA) had held talks aimed at achieving a political settlement. This revelation prompted the British government to engage in bilateral talks with the main Northern Ireland parties, and in December 1993 London and Dublin issued a joint peace proposal, the ◊Downing Street Declaration, for consideration by all parties.

The first IRA cease-fire

In August 1994 the Provisional IRA announced a unilateral cease-fire, apparently in an attempt to reach a non-violent solution. A framework document, intended to form a basis for peace negotiations, was issued jointly by the London and Dublin governments in February 1995. Its proposal for an Ulster–Ireland legislative body with limited powers was countered by the Irish government rescinding its constitutional claim to Ulster and the UK government giving its support to a separate Northern Ireland assembly.

In May 1995 Sinn Féin engaged in the first public talks with British government officials since 1973. However, the deadlock over the issues of decommissioning of IRA weapons continued, and Sinn Féin continued to refuse the original British government–Unionist demand that all-party talks could not proceed until the IRA had begun decommissioning their arms. A UK–Unionist proposal for elections of a body to provide the representation in all-party talks was rejected by the SDLP and Sinn Féin.

Amid the deadlock, the IRA broke the cease-fire with a renewed campaign of violence in London; a bomb exploded in an office building in Docklands in February 1996, killing two people and injuring 100. Nine days later, a bomb exploded on a bus in the West End, killing one person and injuring eight. Efforts to find a solution intensified, and by the end of February a firm date for the start of all-party talks had been announced, and a compromise agreed under which Northern Ireland political parties could hold preliminary meetings to discuss the elections, with Sinn Féin being permitted to participate if the IRA reinstated its cease-fire. In June 1996 an IRA bomb exploded in Manchester's Arndale Centre, and in October 1996 two IRA car bombs exploded at the British army's headquarters in Lisburn, Co Antrim, Northern Ireland, killing one British soldier (the first to die since the IRA cease-fire was announced in August 1994) and injuring 30 people.

The second IRA cease-fire

In a changed political climate after Labour victory in the UK general election of May 1997, the IRA announced a renewal of its August 1994 cease-fire with effect from noon 20 July 1997. The move was cautiously welcome, and British contact with Sinn Féin, which had been severed in June after murders in Lurgan, was resumed the following day.

During the second half of December 1997 violence in Northern Ireland appeared to be spreading, with potentially damaging effects on the Ulster peace process. Londonderry experienced its worst violence since the restoration of the IRA cease-fire in July, when riots broke out as nationalists protested at a Protestant Apprentice Boys parade through the city centre mid-December 1997. In late December Billy Wright, Northern Ireland's most notorious loyalist terrorist, was assassinated by republicans inside the Maze prison, near Belfast. The Irish National Liberation Army claimed responsibility for Wright's killing. Wright's organization, the Loyalist Volunteer Force, in turn claimed responsibility for two retaliatory attacks in which two men were killed and eight injured.

Multi-party talks

Despite fears that the growing violence would derail the multi-party talks, scheduled to resume at Stormont Castle, Belfast, on 12 January 1998, the political process was saved following a visit to convicted loyalist terrorists in Maze prison by Mo Mowlam, secretary of state for Northern Ireland. At the end of their meeting with Mowlam, the prisoners announced that they had dropped their opposition to the talks process and were willing to give negotiations another chance. Mowlam's dramatic action and its equally dramatic result meant that the Stormont multi-party talks could resume with much of the tension of recent weeks drained from the air.

One day after their resumption, the Northern Ireland

NORTHERN IRELAND *One of Northern Ireland's principal museums is the Ulster Folk and Transport Museum at Holywood in County Down. This incorporates displays and demonstrations of how people in the province once lived and worked, such as this traditional method of gathering hay bales from the field. Bob Brien/Image Ireland/Collections*

Trooping the Colour, a parade of troops in ceremonial dress which takes place every year on Horse Guards Parade in central London on the Queen's official birthday in early June.
Roger Scruton/Collections

Judges at an annual breakfast parade. The higher echelons of the judiciary in Britain wear a variety of flamboyant ceremonial clothes, which traditionalists regard as part of the law's necessary pomp and majesty. Modernizers argue that the outmoded dress detracts from the function of legal proceedings.
Peter Arkell/Impact

The London Marathon, the nation's foremost mass-participation sporting event. The course includes the rejuvenated Docklands area of the city. Alongside celebrated distance runners, participants include disabled athletes and thousands of fun-runners raising money for charity.
Ray Roberts/Impact

A Welsh rugby match. Rugby Union is played and followed with intense passion in Wales, especially in the south, where it first became popular among Welsh miners and factory workers. Rugby League traditionally draws support from the English northern industrial heartlands of Lancashire, Yorkshire, and Tyneside.
Robert Eames/Impact

The Handsworth Carnival is held in an inner-city area of Birmingham long associated with the Afro-Caribbean community. *Richard Whitehead/Collections*

A very British spectacle: racegoers at the four-day horseracing meeting in June known as Royal Ascot. Attended by royalty, it is a mixture of sporting event and social gathering. The dress code is a key element, with some men wearing morning suits and women traditionally wearing flamboyant hats.
Ben Edwards/Impact

Shopping has developed into a major national pastime, reflecting the increase in people's leisure time and disposable income. In some cities this has led to a spate of urban renewal, as in Leeds. Above, in the Victorian Quarter, a glass canopy installed in 1990 covers an entire street. Despite the welcome regeneration, some critics denounce the rise of a US-style 'mall culture'. *Joe Cornish.*

The pub is a feature unique to the British social scene. Though trends in decor and atmosphere come and go, at its best the pub remains a focal point for the local community.
Lionel Derimais/Impact.

Unexpected tranquillity in the inner city. Angling continues to grow as a leisure activity, ranging from fishing on free pitches on canals, lakes, and streams, to costly fly-fishing on the country's premier trout and salmon rivers. As early as 1653, Izaak Walton praised the quiet relaxation angling brings, in his book ***The Compleat Angler***. *Simon Shepheard/Impact*

Parks and other green areas, such as Hampstead Heath in London, shown here, provide vital breathing space for city-dwellers.
Simon Shepheard/Impact

Homeless people, especially the young and old, are a familiar sight in Britain's cities. Mental illness and drug or drink addiction often compound other personal problems such as family breakdown or unemployment.
John Cole/Impact

An 'eco-village', created by young environmentalists opposed to the profit motive behind property speculation. Constructed on former brewery land in south London in the mid-1990s, the village demonstrated that a simpler, more resourceful lifestyle was possible even in the capital city.
Andy Johnstone/Impact

Working on a Millennium tapestry at Maldon in Essex, in anticipation of the year 2000. *Julian Calder/ Impact.*

School children represent the citizens of tomorrow. With society becoming more fragmented, and means of communication less personal, there are calls for children's formal schooling and vocational education to be supplemented by lessons in good citizenship and pro-social behaviour. *Peter Arkell/ Impact*

political talks surmounted a significant hurdle when all parties involved – including Sinn Féin – agreed on a document jointly proposed by the British and Irish governments as a basis for negotiation. The document provided a suggested outline of a scheme with institutions to link not only Belfast, Dublin and London but Glasgow and Cardiff as well. However, Sinn Féin made it clear that accepting it as a basis for negotiation did not imply approval of its contents.

The British and Irish governments and local political parties early March 1998 sought to shelter the peace process from the shock generated by a double killing in a small pub in Poyntzpass. Loyalist extremists, in their efforts to damage the process, killed two men – a Catholic and a Protestant – who were close personal friends. Unionist and nationalist leaders combined in unusual singleness of purpose in expressing their condemnation. The two killings were carried out by the Loyalist Volunteer Force, the group founded by the assassinated loyalist Billy Wright.

Sinn Féin was barred in February 1998 from the multi-party talks for a two-week period. The expulsion came after two recent killings allegedly carried out by the IRA. However, penalizing Sinn Féin had little effect in preventing two further IRA bombings later that same month.

Northern Ireland Political Talks Document

Sinn Féin returned to the Stormont talks on 23 March 1998, and the negotiations continued. Although the Stormont talks missed their midnight deadline of 9 April, negotiators decided to plough on through the night in a search for a full agreement. Prime minister Tony Blair had flown to Belfast two days earlier for last-ditch talks after UUP leader David Trimble had rejected the framework document. On 10 April, the multi-party talks were concluded, and the Northern Ireland Political Talks Document was released. The people of Northern Ireland were to give their verdict on the proposed settlement in a referendum 22 May; a parallel referendum was scheduled to be held in the Republic of Ireland.

The comprehensive agreement reached on Good Friday was heralded as a historic breakthrough, which could bring about a new era of peaceful coexistence and constructive co-operation. Among the principal elements of the agreement were the devolution of a wide range of executive and legislative powers to a Northern Ireland Assembly, in which executive posts would be shared on a proportional basis; the establishment of a North/South Ministerial Council, accountable to the Assembly and the Irish Parliament; and a British-Irish Council to bring together the two governments and representatives of devolved administrations in Northern Ireland, Scotland, and Wales. There would also be a new British Irish Agreement to replace the Anglo-Irish Agreement signed in 1985.

The agreement also included a range of measures to enhance the proper protection of basic human rights, to reduce the profile of security measures and emergency legislation, and to consider an appropriate policing service. It established a clear process for the decommissioning of illegal weapons and the means to achieve the decommissioning of all paramilitary arms within two years of the referendum, and committed both Governments to put in place mechanisms to provide for an accelerated programme for the release of prisoners.

On 10 May Sinn Féin decided to support the 'Yes' vote in the referendum. A special party's conference chose to change Sinn Féin's constitution in order to enable party members take seats in the new Belfast assembly envisaged in the Good Friday agreement.

Ian Paisley's Democratic Unionist Party and the Orange Order strongly opposed the deal. David Trimble, leader of the Ulster Unionist Party, overcame bitter internal criticism and decided to accept the agreement. The Ulster Unionist Council voted on 18 April to endorse the settlement, suggesting a comfortable majority in favour of the settlement should be assured in the May referendum. The IRA, on the other hand, remained opposed to the decommissioning of weapons.

Referendum result

On 22 May 1998 the Good Friday agreement was overwhelmingly endorsed by 71.12% of voters (676,966 votes) in Northern Ireland and 94.39% (1,442,583 votes) in the Republic of Ireland. 28.88% of the electorate (274,879 voters) in Northern Ireland and 5.61% (85,748 voters) in the Republic voted 'No' to the agreement. Total turnout in Northern Ireland reached 80.98%, that is, 951,845 out of 1,175,403 people eligible to vote. The vote met with support and relief expressed by Tony Blair (who campained for the 'Yes' vote in the course of his visits to the province in May), Mo Mowlam, US president Bill Clinton, David Trimble, John Hume and other political leaders. Gerry Adams expressed cautious optimism, and came closer than he had ever before to suggesting that IRA arms might be decommissioned.

Assembly elections

In the June 1998 elections to the 108-seat Belfast assembly, SDLP gained 22%, OUP 21.3%, DUP 18.1%, and Sinn Féin 17.6%. The central and most powerful figures in the new institution were the Ulster Unionist leader, David Trimble, and John Hume, leader of the SDLP. Trimble and SDLP deputy leader Seamus Mallon were elected first minister and deputy first minister on 1 July by the first meeting of the new assembly.

This took place against a backdrop of rising tension surrounding Orange Order's parades at Dumcree, Co Armagh, where the traditional route had been banned by the Parades Commission. During the first half of July, the Orange Order staged a stand-off at Dumcree parish church in Portadown; talks between the Order's leaders and British prime minister Tony Blair failed to bring a peaceful solution to the crisis, and by 10 July the total number of incidents of disorder and violence rose to almost 1,700. The Orange celebrations finally took place on 12 July, in a sombre and subdued mood, following the killing of three young brothers in a Loyalist arson attack the night before. The controversial march through the lower Ormeau area of south Belfast passed peacefully, and at Dumcree itself the number of protesters was greatly reduced.

In the following months, despite the tragic ◊Omagh

bombing in August, believed to be the work of an extreme IRA splinter group 'Real IRA', the peace process in Northern Ireland continued. In September Sinn Féin appointed Martin McGuinness its main negotiator with the international committee overseeing the decommissioning of arms; a historic meeting between David Trimble and Gerry Adams took place; and the first group of terrorist prisoners, consisting of three republicans and three royalists, was released from the Maze prison.

A timetable for the IRA and other paramilitary groups to begin surrendering their arms was being worked on during late September and early October 1998 to break the deadlock in the peace process but, despite the intervention of Tony Blair, there was no sign of progress. The prime minister met the main party leaders, including the Sinn Féin representative Gerry Adams, at Labour's 1998 conference in Blackpool to try to force the pace of the peace settlement amid fears that it was becoming bogged down over the IRA's failure to begin decommissioning its weapons. In October 1998, the Nobel Peace Prize was awarded jointly to David Trimble and John Hume for their part in the peace process.

Northern Ireland Assembly

Power-sharing assembly based in Belfast and created by the 1998 Good Friday Agreement between leaders of the contending Unionist and Irish Nationalist communities in Northern Ireland. It was first elected in June 1998. The Assembly comprises 108 members, elected by proportional representation, and exercises devolved executive and legislative authority in areas including health, social security, education and agriculture.

The assembly has effectively taken over much of the work of the Northern Ireland Office, although the post of Secretary of State for Northern Ireland remains. Special provisions ensure that all sections of the community participate in the Assembly's operations. In addition, the Assembly, which has elected David ◊Trimble, leader of the Ulster Unionist Party, as its 'First Minister', has been charged with establishing, with the Irish government, a joint North–South ministerial council to cooperate and take decisions on matters of mutual interest.

Northern Ireland Office, or NIO

Government department established in 1972. It is responsible for direct government of Northern Ireland, including administration of security, law and order, and economic, industrial, and social policies. Its secretary of state from 1997 is Marjorie Mowlam. Under the terms of the 1998 Good Friday Agreement, there is now power-sharing with an executive drawn from the Northern Ireland Assembly.

Northern rebellion, or Rebellion of the Earls

In English history, rising in 1569–70 led by the earls of Northumberland and Westmorland in support of the Catholic Mary Queen of Scots. They demanded that Mary be declared Elizabeth's successor and the restoration of Catholicism. The bishop of Durham was seized and the mass was restored, but promised Spanish support did not arrive and the rising was suppressed. The earls were forced to flee to Scotland and 400 rebels were executed.

North Lanarkshire

Unitary authority in central Scotland, created in 1996 from three districts of Strathclyde region
Area 475 sq km/183 sq mi
Towns Airdrie, Coatbridge, Cumbernauld, Motherwell (administrative headquarters)
Physical low-lying, heavily urbanized area; River Clyde
Industries paper, pharmaceuticals, engineering, electronics, light manufacturing, food and drink processing
Agriculture dairying (around urban environment)
Population (1995) 326,700
History former industrial region of central Scotland.

Economy

It is an area of contrasting economic fortunes. To the north in Cumbernauld New Town, prestige industrial estates attract high technology investment, while to the south, the impacts of de-industrialization are felt, despite concerted efforts to regenerate the area. It is overwhelmingly an urban economy.

Environment

There are eight Sites of Special Scientific Interest and three country parks.

Administrative history

The districts of Motherwell, Monklands, and Cumbernauld and Kilsyth were merged into North Lanarkshire in 1996. Prior to 1975 the area was part of the counties of Lanarkshire, Renfrewshire, and Stirlingshire.

North Lincolnshire

Unitary authority in eastern England created in 1996 from part of the former county of Humberside
Area 850 sq km/328 sq mi
Towns and cities ◊Scunthorpe (administrative headquarters), Brigg, Barton-upon-Humber, Barrow upon Humber, Epworth
Features Humber Estuary forms north border; River Trent; Isle of Axholme; Stainforth and Keadby Canal; River Torne; Humber Bridge southern landfall at Barton upon Humber; Julian's Bower (near Alkborough) – medieval maze cut in turf; wetland nature reserves at Barton Waterside and Blackroft Sands; Sandtoft Transport Centre with 60 trolley buses running on own circuit; Old Rectory (Epworth) where John Wesley, founder of Methodism, was born
Industries steelworks and manufacture of steel products, computer equipment and electronics, food processing (Golden Wonder)
Population (1996) 153,000

North Sea

Sea to the east of Britain and bounded by the coasts of Belgium, The Netherlands, Germany, Denmark, and Norway; part of the Atlantic Ocean. The Dogger Bank extends east to west with shallows of as little as 11 m/36 ft, forming a traditionally well-stocked fishing ground. In the northeast the North Sea joins the Norwegian Sea, and in the south it meets the Strait of Dover. It has 300 oil platforms, 10,000 km/

6,200 mi of gas pipeline (gas was discovered in 1965), and fisheries (especially mackerel and herring). Overfishing is a growing problem.

Pollution

In 1987 Britain dumped more than 4,700 tonnes of sewage sludge into the North Sea; Britain agreed in 1994 to stop the dumping of sludge by 1998 (5% of sewage released is untreated). Britain is also responsible for the highest input of radioactive isotopes, atmospheric nitrogen, and hydrocarbons. In 1991 the North Sea received more than 2 million tonnes of liquid chemical waste. The effects of pollution are most noted along the east coast of the North Sea. The North Sea is heavily polluted with oil and toxic metals (such as cadmium) and chemicals (such as tributyl tin and polychlorinated biphenyl), and many fish are deformed or diseased. Fertilizer runoff has been known to cause algal blooms that starve fish of oxygen.

Rising sea level

A gradual lowering of the British coastline since the Ice Age has meant a gradual rise in the sea level, producing floods in 1881, 1928, 1953, and 1978. It is believed that the melting of the polar ice cap as a result of the greenhouse effect will increase this rise in sea level.

North Sea oil

There has been a large growth in production of oil which is likely to continue to the end of the 1990s. UK reserves stand at 2 billion tonnes, which is as much as has been produced since the early 1970s. Oil reserves are forecast to last until 2020.

North Shields

Industrial town and fishing port in ◊Tyne and Wear, northeast England, 7 mi/11 km east of Newcastle upon Tyne; it is part of the Tyneside urban area, on the north bank of the River Tyne; population (1991) 37,500. Industries include engineering, ship maintenance, printing and publishing, and seafood processing. North Shields was the 'birthplace' of the steam trawler.

The wet docks at North Shields were built in the late 19th century. These have been replaced by oil-storage facilities and by roll-on roll-off berths for ferries to Denmark and Norway. There are ship-repair yards and a fish quay.

North Somerset

Unitary authority in southwest England created in 1996 from part of the former county of Avon

Area 372 sq km/144 sq mi

Towns and cities ◊Weston-Super-Mare (administrative headquarters), Clevedon, Portishead, Yatton, Congresbury

Features Severn Estuary forms northwest border of authority; River Yea, River Avon forms northeast border; west end of the Mendips including Bleadon Hill (134 m/440 ft); Clevedon Court – 14th/15th century manor house owned by Elton family; Weston Woods and Worlebury Hill iron age sites (Weston-Super-Mare); International Helicopter Museum (Weston-Super-Mare)

Industries automotive components, rubber and plastics manufacture

Population (1996) 177,000

North Uist

Island of the Outer ◊Hebrides, Western Isles, Scotland. Lochmaddy is the main port and town. There is a Royal Society for the Protection of Birds reserve at Balranald.

North Uist is connected to Benbecula to the south by the island of Grimsay and two stone causeways. The crofting population is found on the north and west coasts. The interior consists of peat bogs and many lochs. Eaval (347 m/1,138 ft), on the southeast coast, rises abruptly from the generally lowland landscape.

There are many important Iron Age sites, especially on the Machair lands of the north and west coasts. In the southwest, at Carinish, there are the ruins of a 13th-century monastery and college, Trinity Temple (1203). Balranald is home to the corncrake, one of Europe's most endangered species.

North Uist is served by car ferries to Berneray (from Otternish), Uig on Skye (from Lochmaddy), and Leverburgh on Harris.

Northumberland

County of northern England

Area 5,030 sq km/1,942 sq mi

Towns and cities ◊Morpeth (administrative headquarters), Berwick-upon-Tweed, Hexham

Physical Cheviot Hills; rivers Aln, Coquet, Rede, Till, Tweed, upper Tyne; Northumberland National Park in the west

Features ◊Holy Island (Lindisfarne); the ◊Farne island group 8 km/5 mi east of Bamburgh, which is home to large seal and bird colonies; part of Hadrian's Wall (a World Heritage site), including Housesteads Fort; Alnwick and Bamburgh castles; Thomas ◊Bewick museum; Hexham Abbey; the walls of Berwick-upon-Tweed; large moorland areas used for military manoeuvres; Longstone Lighthouse from which Grace Darling rowed to rescue the crew of the *Forfarshire*; wild white cattle of Chillingham; Kielder Water (1982), the largest artificial lake in northern Europe

Industry manufacturing of computer monitors (Cramlington); coal was formerly mined at several locations

Agriculture sheep, cattle; fishing

Population (1994) 307,700

Famous people Thomas Bewick, Grace Darling, Jack and Bobby Charlton.

Topography

The greater part of the county, comprising the districts of Berwick, Alnwick, and Tynedale, is rural. The Cheviot Hills, along the Anglo-Scottish border, rise to 810 m/2,657 ft; further east there are uplands rising to a height of 250–450 m/820–1,476 ft above sea-level. They are composed of coarse sandstones which dip towards a low coastal plateau, meeting the North Sea in low cliffs and shallow bays backed by sand dunes. There are extensive forests in the west of Northumberland, and much of the upland is used by the army. South of the River Coquet, coal is found underneath the coastal plateau in the districts of Wansbeck, Blyth, and Castle Morpeth.

Northumberland, John Dudley, Duke of Northumberland (*c.* 1502–1553)

English politician. He was chief minister from 1551 until Edward VI's death in 1553. He tried to place his daughter-in-law Lady Jane Grey on the throne, and was executed on Mary I's accession.

Son of the privy councillor Edmund Dudley (beheaded 1510), he overthrew Edward Seymour, Duke of Somerset, as protector to the young Edward VI and, having married one of his sons to Lady Jane Grey (fifth in line to the throne), persuaded the king to sign a document excluding his half-sisters from the succession, thereby hoping to retain his authority after Edward's death. He was knighted in 1523.

Another of his sons, Robert, Earl of Leicester, became one of Elizabeth I's favourites.

Northumbria

Anglo-Saxon kingdom that covered northeast England and southeast Scotland. Comprising the 6th-century kingdoms of Bernicia (Forth–Tees) and Deira (Tees–Humber), united in the 7th century, it accepted the supremacy of Wessex in 827 and was conquered by the Danes in the late 9th century. It was not until the reign of William the Conqueror that Northumbria became an integral part of England.

Influenced by Irish missionaries, it was a cultural and religious centre until the 8th century with priests such as Bede, Cuthbert, and Wilfrid.

North Yorkshire

County of northeast England, created in 1974 from most of the North Riding and parts of the East and West Ridings of Yorkshire (since April 1996 York has been a separate unitary authority)

Area 8,037 sq km/3,102 sq mi

Towns and cities ◊Northallerton (administrative headquarters); resorts: Harrogate, Scarborough, Whitby

Physical England's largest county; rivers Derwent, Esk, Ouse; includes part of the Pennines; the Vale of York (a vast plain); the Cleveland Hills; North Yorkshire Moors, which form a national park (within which is Fylingdales radar station to give early warning – 4 minutes – of nuclear attack)

Features Rievaulx Abbey; Yorkshire Dales National Park (including Swaledale, Wensleydale, and Bolton Abbey in Wharfedale); Fountains Abbey near Ripon, with Studley Royal Gardens (a World Heritage site); Castle Howard, designed by Vanbrugh, has Britain's largest collection of 18th–20th-century costume; largest accessible cavern in Britain, the Battlefield Chamber, Ingleton

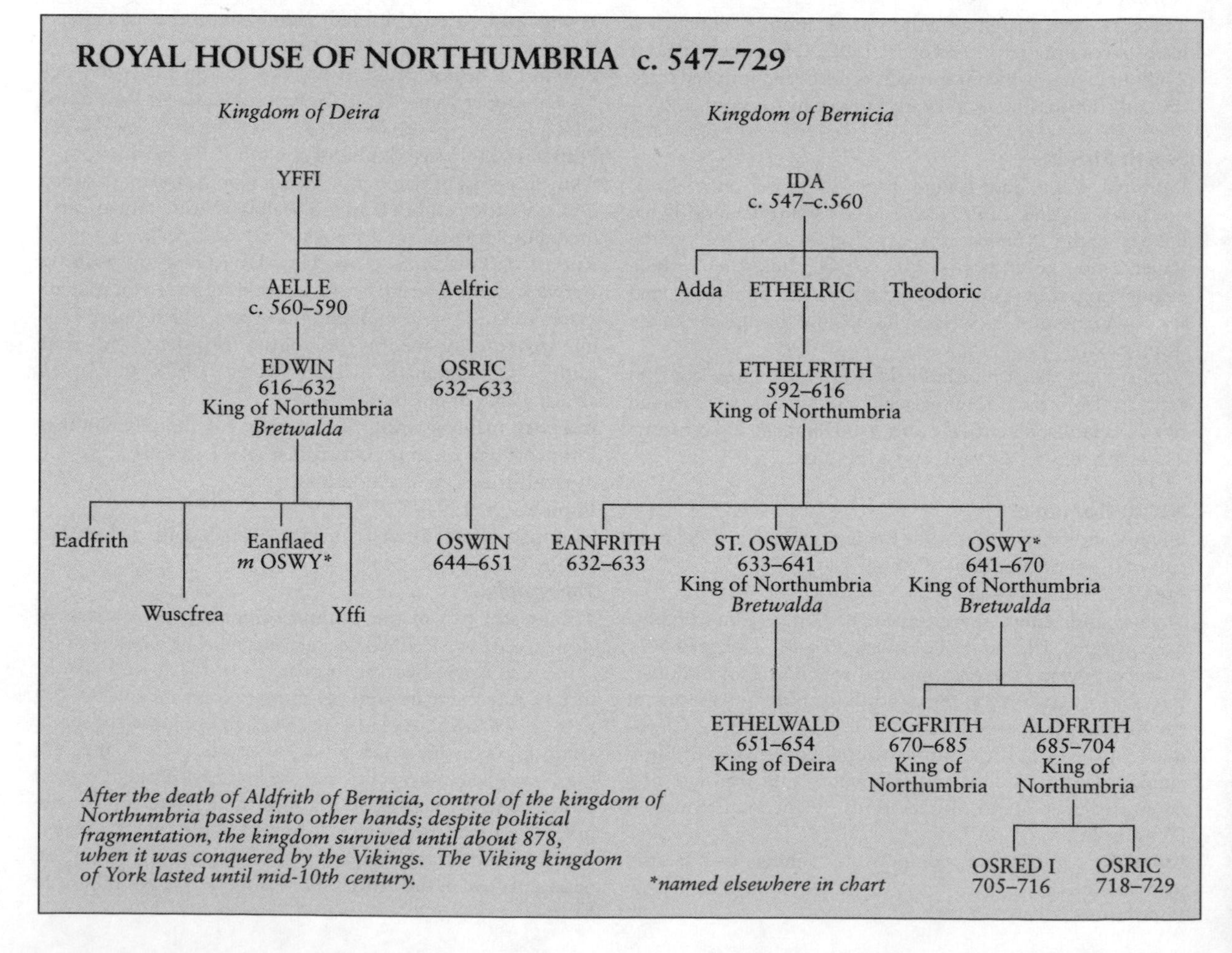

Agriculture cereals, dairy products (Vale of York, Pickering); wool and meat from sheep (North York Moors)
Industries coal, footwear, clothing, vehicles, plastics, foodstuffs, high technology industries, light industry
Population (1995) 556,200
Famous people Alcuin, Guy Fawkes, W H Auden

Topography

North Yorkshire is divided into eight districts. The Pennines are in the west part of the county. There are several beautiful dales, which together constitute the Yorkshire Dales National Park, the principal ones being Swaledale, Wensleydale, Nidderdale, Airedale, and Ribblesdale. The relief of the east part of the county is varied. To the northeast are the Cleveland Hills and the valley of the River Esk, which flows to the North Sea; south of Esk lies Fylingdales Moor, the Hambleton Hills, and the North Yorkshire Moors. From these moors, several valleys, such as Bilsdale and Farndale, run down to the Vale of Pickering, through which runs the River Derwent, which flows southwest from near the coast to join the Ouse between Selby and Goole. The county extends south of the Vale of Pickering to the Yorkshire Wolds (an area of moorland). The coast from Runswick Bay in the north to Filey Bay in the south is varied; the stretch between Whitby and Scarborough, with its high cliffs, is especially attractive.

Tourism

With its pleasant coastline, National Parks, and rural landscapes, North Yorkshire is an important centre for tourism. In addition to the coastal resorts at Scarborough and Whitby, several smaller places attract tourists. Visitors come to the numerous small market towns and villages within the two National Parks, and to nearby towns, particularly Richmond, Ripon, Harrogate, and Pickering.

History

Yorkshire as a whole formed part of the Brigantian kingdom with the Parisii on the Wolds and in Holderness. It was conquered by the Romans in the 1st century AD, and by the Danes in the 9th century, and came under the rule of Harold of England in 1066 after the Battle of Stamford Bridge. Large areas were devastated by the Normans. Since then the county has been the scene of many battles. During the Wars of the Roses one of the bloodiest battles ever to have been fought in Britain took place at Towton Field. During the Civil War the county was divided, and the principal battle was fought at Marston Moor, where the Royalists were defeated.

Historic monuments

Important monuments in the county include the great Iron Age camp at Stanwix, and the Roman town at Aldborough. Among many castles the best known are Richmond, Bolton, Skipton, Knaresborough, and Scarborough. Middleham Castle was a residence of Warwick 'The King Maker'. Of the ecclesiastical remains the most important are the Cistercian abbeys of Fountains, Rievaulx, and Jervaulx; the Augustinian priories of Bolton and Kirkham; and the Premonstratensian House at Easby. There were Benedictine foundations at Selby and Whitby.

Norton, Mary (1903–)

English writer of books of children. *The Magic Bedknob* (1943) and *Bonfires and Broomsticks* (1947) were later adapted for film and reissued as *Bedknobs and Broomsticks* in 1970. She established her reputation and won the Carnegie Medal with ◊ *The Borrowers* (1952), the first of a series of five books which describe a family of tiny people who live beneath the floorboards of a large house.

Norwich

Cathedral city and administrative headquarters of ◊Norfolk, eastern England, on the River Wensum, 160 km/100 mi northeast of London; population (1991) 172,600. Industries include financial services and insurance, tourism, television and radio broadcasting, engineering, printing, high-technology industries, and the manufacture of shoes, mustard, clothing, chemicals, and confectionery. It is the largest medieval walled city in England.

Features

Norwich has a Norman castle, the 11th-century Norwich Cathedral, a 15th-century Guildhall, over 30 medieval churches, Tudor houses, and a Georgian Assembly House. Its City Hall dates from 1938. The University of East Anglia (established in 1963) includes the Sainsbury Centre for Visual Arts (1978), designed by Norman Foster, and the Sainsbury Laboratory for Molecular Research (1987) – in association with the John Innes Institute – designed by Denys Lasdun. New Technopolis, a business and education centre planned for a site near the cathedral, will be a Millennium Commission Landmark Project.

History

First fortified by the Saxons in the 9th century, Norwich was settled in medieval times by Flemish weavers and it became the centre of the worsted trade in the 14th century. As northern manufacturing towns expanded during the Industrial Revolution, Norwich lost some of its importance. During World War II Norwich was heavily damaged.

Administration

Norwich is administered by a lord mayor and 48 councillors, and returns two members to Parliament.

Architectural features

The city has an irregular street plan dating from Saxon times, and some cobbled streets are preserved. Fragments of the ancient walls, which were 6 km/4 mi in circuit, remain. The Guildhall, a flint-and-stone building, dates from 1407–1413. It contains a display of civic regalia including a sword presented to the city by Admiral Horatio Nelson. The 15th-century St Andrew's Hall and Blackfriars' Hall were originally the nave and chancel of the church of the Dominicans. The fine Georgian Assembly House was restored in 1950 as an arts centre. Other features include Tombland, the marketplace of the original Anglo-Saxon settlement of Norwich; the 15th-century Maid's Head Hotel; the Stranger's Hall, a 14th-century merchant's house, now a folk museum; Suckling House, a 16th-century banqueting hall; Erpingham Gate (1420); Ethelbert Gate, commemorating a riot between monks and citizens (1272); the Bridewell, built in 1370, now a museum of local industries; Pull's Ferry, an ancient water gate; and the 13th-century Bishop's Bridge, one of the oldest bridges in England. The City Hall, opened in

1938, has a clock tower which is 56 m/184 ft high. Theatres include the Maddermarket, home of the Norwich Players, and the Theatre Royal.

Norwich Cathedral

The largely Norman cathedral was begun in 1096 as part of a Benedictine house by Herbert de Losinga, first bishop of Norwich. Norwich is unusual among cathedrals in retaining its Norman chancel, transepts, crossing and tower, in addition to its nave. It has a 15th-century octagonal spire (96 m/315 ft high), the second highest in England after that of Salisbury Cathedral. The Cathedral's cloisters, dating from 1297, are the only two-storey monastic cloisters surviving in England.

University of East Anglia

The Sainsbury Centre for Visual Arts houses a collection of paintings given to the University of East Anglia in 1973 by Robert and Lisa Sainsbury. It includes modern European paintings as well as a collection of ethnographic art. The building was designed to display openly its steel structure, one of the first examples of its kind.

Castle and castle museum

The 12th-century castle keep stands on a mound which existed before 1100. The originally Norman structure, built soon after the Norman Conquest to dominate East Anglia, was destroyed in the Earl of Norfolk's rebellion against William I, and the present building, an almost cubic block, dates from about 1120. It was captured by Flemish forces in 1174 and by French troops in the reign of King John (I). It was given to the county of Norfolk by George III and was used as a jail until 1887. Refaced in 1834–39, the keep was opened in 1894 as the Norwich Castle Museum. It contains a large collection of ceramic teapots and the art gallery contains a collection of paintings by the ◊Norwich School (John Sell Cotman and John Crome).

Churches

Norwich's medieval churches are mostly built of flint in late Decorated or Perpendicular style. The largest is St Peter (Mancroft), built in 1430–1455. Its tower is 31 m/102 ft, and it has a peal of 13 bells. Its east window contains 15th-century glass, and the church contains the tomb of the writer and physician Thomas Browne, whose statue stands on the Haymarket nearby. St Andrew's church, rebuilt in 1506, contains a memorial tablet to Abraham Lincoln, 16th president of the USA. The 15th-century church of St Peter (Hungate) is now an ecclesiastical museum. The church of St Julian is associated with the mystic Julian of Norwich; the church was rebuilt following World War II bomb damage.

Parks

The chief parks are Eaton Park and Earlham Park. Other parks and open spaces include Mousehold Heath, Chapelfield Garden (the central public garden of Norwich), and Waterloo Park.

Industries

Anglia Television, BBC TV East, Radio Broadland, and Radio Norfolk are all based in Norwich. The nearby Norwich Research Park at Colney is a major centre for biotechnology.

Norwich School

English regional school of landscape painters, inspired by the 17th-century Dutch realist tradition of landscape painting, notably the work of Ruisdael. Founded in 1803, the school was made up of both professional and amateur artists and flourished until the 1830s. Its leading members were John Sell ◊Cotman and John ◊Crome.

They constituted a local school of landscape unique in the history of British art. The many minor but interesting artists of the school included Crome's son John Berney Crome, George Vincent, James Stark, Joseph and Alfred Stannard, John Thirtle, Thomas Lound, Henry Ninham, and Samuel David Colkett.

Nostell Priory

Outstanding Palladian house in West Yorkshire, England, 8 km/5 mi east of Wakefield. It was built in 1733 by James Paine for Rowland Winn, 4th Baronet, on the site of a 12th-century priory. Later in the century the 5th Baronet commissioned Adam to add four large wings to the house. Of these only the northeast was built, as the work was curtailed when the 5th Baronet died. Nostell was given to the National Trust in 1955 by the 4th Lord St Oswald.

The state rooms, decorated by Robert Adam, Joseph Rose (1745–99), and Zucchi (1726–95), contain notable pictures and ◊Chippendale furniture that was made especially for the house. It is thought that Chippendale began his career at Nostell.

Nottingham

Industrial city and unitary authority in central England, on the River Trent, 200 km/124 mi northwest of London; unitary authority area 74 sq km/29 sq mi; population (1994 est) 285,000. It was the administrative headquarters of the county of Nottinghamshire to April 1998. Industries include tourism, engineering, and the manufacture of bicycles, textiles, knitwear, pharmaceuticals, tobacco, lace, hosiery, and electronics. The English Civil War began here in 1642, and the city expanded rapidly in the late 18th century as a centre of the lace industry.

Features

Among the city's cultural attractions are the Nottingham Playhouse (1963), the Theatre Royal (1866), the Royal Concert Hall (1982), and the Castle Museum. There are two universities, the University of Nottingham (1881) and the Nottingham Trent University (1992), formerly the Trent Polytechnic. The Goose Fair, dating from the Middle Ages, is held here every October. The National Water Sports Centre is located to the east of the city, near the village of Holme Pierrepont. A Tudor mansion, Holme Pierrepont Hall, is also situated in the village. Nottingham has a racecourse, and test matches are played on the Trent Bridge cricket ground. The Harvey Haddon sports stadium opened in 1964.

Nottingham Castle

The heavily restored 13th-century gatehouse is all that remains of the original castle. Built on Castle Rock 40 m/130 ft above the city soon after the Norman Conquest, the castle became a royal palace and fortress, but it was dismantled after the Civil War in 1651. A mansion was built on the site during 1674–78, but was burned during riots in 1831. It was restored and opened as a museum in 1878 as England's first provincial museum and art gallery. The collections include examples of Nottingham alabaster carving, a local industry of the 14th and 15th centuries.

Architectural features and museums

The 'Trip to Jerusalem' Inn, below the castle, is said to be the oldest inn in England. The church of St Mary dates from the 15th century; St Peter's church is partly 12th and partly 15th century; and the church of St Nicholas was built in 1678. The Roman Catholic cathedral of St Barnabas was designed by Augustus Pugin. Other features include the old Lace Market with 19th-century warehouses, the Lace Hall museum, the Costume Museum, and the restored Green's Mill, where the mathematician George Green was once a miller. Wollaton Park (300 ha/741 acres) includes Wollaton Hall, an Elizabethan mansion, now a natural history museum. The former home of the writer D H Lawrence is located nearby at Eastwood. Newstead Abbey, to the north of the city, was once the home of the poet George Byron. The remains of ◊Sherwood Forest, formerly a royal forest and the legendary home of Robin Hood, also lie to the north of the city.

Early history

From the 6th century Nottingham was a Saxon settlement known as 'Snotingham'. It was occupied by the Danes in 868, and William the Conqueror occupied the town in 1086. Richard III had his headquarters at Nottingham Castle before the Battle of Bosworth. Charles I raised his standard here in 1642, and in 1643 the town and castle were taken by the Parliamentarians.

Industrial history

In 1589 the Reverend William Lee invented the first stocking-frame in Nottingham. Richard Arkwright introduced his first spinning-frames here in the late 18th century and James Hargreaves set up his spinning jenny in a small Nottingham cotton mill after being driven from his family home in Blackburn in the late 1760s. From the late 18th century the city's population grew rapidly with the expansion of the lace and hosiery industries. ◊Luddite riots, caused by the introduction of machinery, took place in 1811–12 and 1816–17. In 1863 Jesse Boot, the pharmacist, took over his father's shop selling medicinal herbs, and began the manufacture of drugs in 1892.

Famous people

Nottingham was the birthplace of William Booth, founder of the Salvation Army, and of the writer Alan Sillitoe. The city is associated with the legendary outlaw ◊Robin Hood.

Nottingham City

Unitary authority in north central England since April 1998; see ◊Nottingham.

Nottinghamshire

County of central England, which has contained the unitary authority Nottingham City since April 1998

Area 2,160 sq km/834 sq mi

Towns and cities West Bridgford (administrative headquarters), Mansfield, Newark, Worksop

Physical rivers: Erewash, Idle, Soar, Trent

Features the remaining areas of Sherwood Forest (home of ◊Robin Hood) are included in the ◊Dukeries, an area of estates; originally 32 km/20 mi long and 12 km/7 mi wide, the forest was formerly a royal hunting ground; Cresswell Crags (remains of prehistoric humans); D H Lawrence commemorative walk from Eastwood (where he lived) to Old Brinsley Colliery

Agriculture cereals (barley, wheat), market gardening (potatoes), sugar beet; cattle, sheep; there are many orchards

Industries cigarettes, coal mining, engineering, footwear, furniture, gravel, gypsum, ironstone, light engineering, limestone, oil, pharmaceuticals, sandstone, textiles

Population (1994) 1,031,900

Famous people William Booth, D H Lawrence, Alan Sillitoe

History During World War II Nottinghamshire produced the only oil out of U-boat reach, and drilling was revived in the 1980s.

Topography

Nottinghamshire is bounded on the west by Derbyshire, Rotherham, and Doncaster; on the north by North Lincolnshire; on the east by Lincolnshire; and on the south by Leicestershire. The county forms part of the extensive lowland to the east of the southern Pennines, the greater part being between 30 and 120 m (98 and 427 ft) above sea-level. Only in the west, around Mansfield, is there hilly country, which reaches a height of 180 m (591 ft).

Early history

In Saxon times Nottinghamshire was part of the kingdom of ◊Mercia, and after the Danish invasions it formed part of the ◊Danelaw. At the time of the Dissolution of the Monasteries there were 16 religious houses in Nottinghamshire, but the only important remains are those of Newstead Abbey. There are some fine churches, including Southwell Minster, of Norman construction.

Notting Hill Carnival

Largest street festival in Europe, held in the Notting Hill area of London each August. Traditionally a celebration of the end of slavery in the West Indies, the Carnival began among the West Indian community in London in the early 1960s and today involves 70–100 bands in masquerade. Over one million people attend each year.

Notting Hill Riots

Racial fighting in the Notting Hill area of London in August and September 1958 involving up to 2,000 youths. The riots were the culmination of constant attacks by whites against blacks common in the area in the late 1950s. Along with a similar riot in Nottingham in 1958, the riots brought racial issues to prominence and were cited as arguments for restricting further immigration. They influenced the development of the Commonwealth Immigrants Act (1962) which restricted immigration of non-whites.

novel

Extended fictional prose narrative, usually between 30,000

NOTTING HILL CARNIVAL *The principal annual festival of Britain's Afro-Caribbean community is the carnival that takes place in Notting Hill, a district of west London once heavily settled by immigrants from the West Indies. This huge event involves detailed planning, and the many music and dance troupes work for months to perfect their elaborate costumes and routines. Javed A Jafferji/Impact*

and 100,000 words, that deals imaginatively with human experience through the psychological development of the central characters and of their relationship with a broader world. From the 18th century, the novel has gone with the English language into all parts of the world. As the main form of narrative fiction in the 20th century, the novel is frequently classified according to genres and subgenres such as the ◊historical novel, detective fiction, fantasy, and ◊science fiction.

Origins

The modern novel took its name and inspiration from the Italian *novella*, the short tale of varied character which became popular in the late 13th century. A major period of the novel's development came during the late Italian Renaissance. The works of the Italian writers such as Boccaccio were translated into English and inspired the Elizabethan novelists, including Philip Sidney, Thomas Nash, and Thomas Lodge. With the growth of literacy and cheaper book production, the novel developed rapidly. Although the novels of Daniel ◊Defoe show many signs of the highest art and organization, they remain in some respects works of journalism rather than fiction, relating sequences of events with little development of the characters.

18th century

Most critics acknowledge the true birth of the English novel with the publication of Samuel ◊Richardson's *Pamela* (1740), and by the close of the 18th century most of the possibilities inherent in the novel had been mapped out by authors such as Tobias ◊Smollett, Laurence ◊Sterne, and Oliver Goldsmith. The first of the modern romantic school was Horace ◊Walpole, and one of the greatest exponents in the modern romantic form, which came to be called the 'Gothic novel', was Mrs ◊Radcliffe, whose *Mysteries of Udolpho* (1794) had a profound influence on the taste of generations of readers.

19th century

In the early 19th century Walter ◊Scott developed the historical novel, and Jane ◊Austen wrote perceptive 'novels of manners'. English fiction had an immediate impact throughout Europe and beyond. Given such impetus, the Victorian novel in England rapidly became institutionalized. Celebrated British novelists of the Victorian age include Charles ◊Dickens, William ◊Thackeray, the ◊Brontës, George ◊Eliot, Anthony ◊Trollope, and Robert Louis ◊Stevenson.

20th century

The 20th century novel is distinguished by variety and experiment. After 1920 it is no longer possible simply to analyse the novel in terms of plot and characters. The principal influence was French, and the high level of art to which the French novel had aspired in the second half of the 19th century. Radically new methods of handling time, space, consciousness, relationship, story, and even words themselves, were tried. There was a reaction to ultra-realism which resulted in Virginia ◊Woolf's *The Voyage Out* (1915). The stream of consciousness technique enabled Woolf to make an intimate exploration of her characters' thought and motivation, exemplified particularly in *Mrs Dalloway* (1925) and *The Waves* (1931). However, tradition continued – E M ◊Forster, in method, was a mid-19th-century novelist, displaying an orderly unfolding of story and character. Two other important figures in the 20th-century English novel are D H ◊Lawrence and Aldous ◊Huxley.

During the 1950s a group of novelists who chose working-class settings for their books attracted attention, and were loosely referred to as the ◊Angry Young Men. They included Kingsley ◊Amis, John ◊Braine, Alan ◊Sillitoe, and David Storey.

The novel continues to flourish as a form. The distinction between 'literary' and 'popular' novels has become increasingly blurred, with detective novels such as the Sherlock Holmes stories by Arthur Conan ◊Doyle now regarded as classics and 'serious' novelists like Graham ◊Greene employing the techniques traditionally associated with genres such as the thriller and science fiction. Recent writers of note include Anthony Powell, John Fowles, Kingsley and Martin Amis, Anthony Burgess, Iris Murdoch, Doris Lessing, Salman Rushdie, and Vikram Seth.

Novello, Ivor stage name of Ivor Novello Davies (1893–1951)

Welsh composer and actor-manager. He wrote popular songs, such as 'Keep the Home Fires Burning', in World War I, and musicals in which he often appeared as the romantic lead, including *Glamorous Night* (1925), *The Dancing Years* (1939), and *Gay's the Word* (1951).

Novello, Vincent (1781–1861)

English composer, organist, editor, and publisher, father of the soprano Clara Novello. He founded the music publishing firm of Novello & Company in London in 1811. He edited valuable collections of music including Masses by Haydn and Mozart, and composed church music and cantatas.

Nuffield, William Richard Morris, 1st Viscount Nuffield (1877–1963)

English manufacturer and philanthropist. Starting with a small cycle-repairing business, in 1910 he designed a car that could be produced cheaply, and built up **Morris Motors Ltd** at Cowley, Oxford.

He endowed **Nuffield College**, Oxford, in 1937 and the **Nuffield Foundation** for medical, social, and scientific research in 1943. Baronet 1929, Baron 1934, Viscount 1938.

Nuneaton

Industrial town in Warwickshire, central England, on the River Anker, 15 km/9 mi northeast of Coventry; population (1991) 65,900. Industries include engineering, electronics, and the manufacture of tiles and textiles.

The church of St Nicholas is Early English and Perpendicular, and has a square embattled tower and pinnacles. The church of St Mary the Virgin (1877) was built on the site of the ruins of a Benedictine nunnery founded in 1150, from which the town derives its name. Arbury Hall, to the southwest of the town, is a fine example of Gothic Revival architecture. Nuneaton's former grammar school, dating from the 16th century, was largely rebuilt following serious damage during World War II and is now used as parish offices. The novelist George Eliot was born nearby at Astley in 1819.

Nunn, Trevor Robert (1940–)

English stage director. He succeeded Richard Eyre as artistic director of the National Theatre, London, in 1997. Previously, he was artistic director of the Royal Shakespeare Company 1968–86. He received a Tony award (with John Caird (1948–)) for his production of *Nicholas Nickleby* (1982) and for the musical *Les Misérables* (1985). He directed Andrew Lloyd Webber's musical *Cats* (1981), followed by *Starlight Express* (1984), *Chess* (1986), and *Aspects of Love* (1989).

Other plays directed by Nunn include *The Fair Maid of the West* (1986–87), *Othello* (1989), *Timon of Athens* (1991), *Measure for Measure* (1991–92), and *Heartbreak House* (1992). For television he directed *The Comedy of Errors* (1990).

Nurse, Paul Maxime (1949–)

English microbiologist who has contributed to knowledge of the molecular mechanisms of cell growth. He worked on the genetic and enzymatic control of the cell cycle in yeast, a microorganism that he used as a model system for mammalian cells.

Nurse showed that genes for protein kinases (a family of enzymes that chemically bond a phosphate molecule to other

NUFFIELD, WILLIAM RICHARD MORRIS *English car manufacturer and philanthropist Lord Nuffield. He began his career manufacturing bicycles in 1895 with just £5 of capital. Philip Sauvain Picture Collection*

NURSERY RHYMES – ROBUST AND IRREVERENT SURVIVORS

Nursery rhymes are one of the glories of children's literature, as sparky, irreverent and irrepressible today as they have always been in the past. But paradoxically few were composed with children specifically in mind. Because babies particularly like the sound of the human voice, mothers and other adults involved with looking after infants have always talked and sung to them, sometimes in order to soothe, at other times to entertain. The songs and rhymes used on these occasions have varied from family to family. Today they might include television jingles, football chants, and pop songs, but chosen, as in the past, because they are the first things that come to mind rather than because they are thought particularly suitable for young children.

Curly locks, curly locks,
Wilt thou be mine?
Thou shalt not wash dishes,
Nor yet feed the swine
But sit on a cushion
And sew a fine seam
And dine upon strawberries,
Sugar and cream.

Historically, such scraps came from different sources. To quote Peter and Iona Opie, the world's leading authorities on this topic, nursery rhymes originated from 'unrelated snatches of worldly songs, adult jests, lampoons, proverbial maxims, charms, and country ballads.' Infants usually forget most early songs and chants over the years, but sometimes particular family favourites will stick in the memory. The sole reason why today's nursery rhymes dating from the remote past managed to survive in a pre-print culture was because enough parents remembered them from their own childhood and then passed them on to the next generation. To quote Andrew Lang, a former collector of nursery rhymes, they are like 'smooth stones from the brook of time, worn round by constant friction of tongues long silent.'

Jack Spratt could eat not fat
His wife could eat no lean
And so between them both
you see
They licked the platter clean

The move into print

When nursery rhymes eventually made their way into print they were not always of the best quality. The earliest anthology *Tom Thumb's Pretty Song Book*, published in 1744, contained two versions still too indelicate to publish for children today. The first really comprehensive nursery rhyme anthology had to wait till 1842, when it was assembled by a folklorist named James Halliwell. But he had not reckoned on the enthusiasm with which child readers would greet his collection, even though it was not addressed to them in the first instance. In the succeeding editions he quickly brought out in order to satisfy demand, he was forced to alter some of the more racy rhymes originally included. Extra violent rhymes and a couple with anti-Semitic themes were also dropped or cut. Subsequent anthologists generally chose from Halliwell's collection in its final edition, also dropping other rhymes that had come to seem too violent or otherwise objectionable over time.

Eventually every anthology was concentrating on the same old popular favourites, from 'Jack and Jill' to 'Mary had a little lamb'. But in the 1960s a new generation of tough-minded illustrators like Raymond Briggs brought back some of those older rhymes once thought too outspoken for modern children into the anthologies coming out at the time. In the public mind, however, a fixed cannon of nursery rhyme favourites had by now become well established. Since no-one was collecting any new ones from whatever modern parents were choosing to sing to infants from the top of their heads, further developments in the genre stopped altogether. That is why today's selections of nursery rhymes derive from a past culture mostly involving rural agriculture. But this unchanging traditionalism has some advantages: glimpses of a past village life make for attractive accompanying pictures, and almost all Britain's best illustrators have designed their own collection over the years. Nursery rhymes also provide details of remote social history interesting in their own right for small children who might otherwise get to know very little about the past.

Not everyone has always approved of nursery rhymes. Some critics have objected to their violence, occasionally

cellular proteins) were crucial in controlled cell growth. His work is significant for cancer research as it contributes to the understanding of why cancer cells might undergo uncontrolled cell growth and how this might be prevented by new, highly specific drugs.

nursery rhyme

Short traditional poem or song for children. Usually limited to a couplet or quatrain with strongly marked rhythm and rhymes, nursery rhymes have often been handed down by oral tradition.

Some of the oldest nursery rhymes are connected with a traditional tune and were sung as accompaniment to ancient ring games, such as 'Here we go round the mulberry bush', which was part of the May Day festivities. See feature on the origins of nursery rhymes, above.

nursing

Organized nursing training originated in 1836 in Germany, and was developed in Britain by the work of Florence ◊Nightingale, who, during the Crimean War, established standards of scientific, humanitarian care in military hospitals.

attempting to substitute their own reformed rhymes instead. In one such version, for example, the rhyme 'Three blind mice' was re-written as 'Three kind mice'. These rodents now get on very well with the farmer's wife, with no danger to their tails at all. But these cleaned up versions have never taken off: infants seem to prefer traditional nursery rhymes, along with their odd moments of violence. They also like their bouncy rhythms, particularly when these are accompanied by real bouncing on a parent's lap. It does not matter if they don't understand all the accompanying words at the same time. As the poet Dylan Thomas once wrote, 'The first poems I knew were nursery rhymes, and before I could read them for myself I had come to love just the words of them... 'Ride a cock-horse to Banbury Cross' was haunting to me who did not know then what a cock horse was or cared a damn where Banbury Cross might be.'

Still thriving in the electronic age

Nursery rhymes continue to be part of a British culture that almost everyone recognizes. When politicians compare each other to Little Jack Horner or Miss Muffet they still trust that most people will understand what they mean. Modern parents may not know as many rhymes by heart as they once did, but nursery rhyme anthologies are much in use in today's nurseries and infant schools, offering an ideal introduction to early reading skills while also providing good fun at the same time. Having survived attacks from Puritans in the past, who did not approve of teaching nonsense to infants in place of hard common sense, nursery rhymes still seem strong enough to continue to thrive in a world of video and computers.

Their long-term appeal is not based on any far-fetched theory, like the idea that nursery rhymes once offered coded glimpses from British history (the notion that 'Ring-a-ring o' roses' marks a folk memory of dying from the Great Plague has long been discredited). Nursery rhymes survive because children have always liked them, whether the rhyme concerned makes sense or not (no-one for example has ever worked out what exactly 'Pop goes the weasel' is really about).

For nursery rhymes have been chosen by as well as for children: a marked contrast to other children's literature written by adults especially for children, whether young readers themselves always like it or not.

BY NICHOLAS TUCKER

Nurses give day-to-day care and carry out routine medical and surgical duties under the supervision of doctors.

In the UK there are four National Boards (England, Scotland, Wales, and Northern Ireland) for Nursing, Midwifery, and Health Visiting, and the Royal College of Nursing (1916) is the professional body.

Nutter, Tommy (1943–1992)

English tailor. His trend-setting suits became famous in the 1960s and 1970s. Although employing conventional tecniques, he made a distinct break with many traditions of tailoring when he produced suits with wide lapels and flared trousers and experimented with fabrics, for example cutting pinstripes on the horizontal and mixing gamekeeper tweeds in three-piece suits.

In 1969 he opened his own tailoring shop in Savile Row, London, where he attracted many celebrity clients such as the Beatles, Mick and Bianca Jagger, Elton John, and the fashion designer Hardy Amies. Among his designs are the suits worn by the Beatles on the cover of their *Abbey Road* album.

NVQ, national vocational qualification

Certificate of attainment of a standardized level of skill and competence. A national council for NVQs was set up 1986 in an effort by the government in cooperation with employers to rationalize the many unrelated vocational qualifications then on offer. The Scottish equivalent is the Scottish Vocational Qualification (SVQ).

In 1991 NVQs were established in colleges of further education, with companies arranging them for employees; points are awarded for previous experience. Qualifications gained are roughly equivalent to the GCSE, A level, and degree system of academic qualifications.

Nyman, Michael (1944–)

English composer. His highly stylized music is characterized by processes of gradual modification by repetition of complex musical formulae (known as minimalism). His compositions include scores for English filmmaker Peter Greenaway and New Zealand filmmaker Jane Campion (*The Piano* 1993); a chamber opera, *The Man Who Mistook His Wife for a Hat* (1989); and three string quartets.

Nyren, John (1764–1837)

English writer on cricket, the son of Richard Nyren, cricketer and captain of the famous Hambledon Club, Hampshire. A moderate cricketer himself, his fame rests on his account of the Hambledon players, *The Cricketers of My Time*, which is regarded as a classic of English sporting literature. The work was first published in 1833 as part of *The Young Cricketer's Tutor*, edited by Charles Cowden Clarke and first published in 1833.

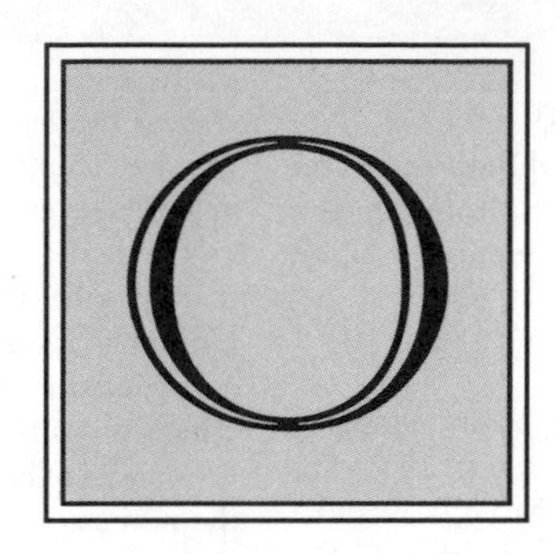

oak

Unofficial emblem of England, appearing as a 'national' plant on pound coins. Its folklore is confined to three areas: weather rhymes, such as 'Oak before ash, We'll have a splash'; legends concerning individual trees, for instance the **Major Oak** of Sherwood Forest where Robin Hood reputedly hid; and the wearing of an oakleaf or oakapple on **Oak Apple Day** (29 May) to commemorate the restoration of the monarchy in 1660 – Charles II had hidden in an oak at Boscobel after his defeat at the Battle of Worcester (1651).

Oakham

Town in Rutland, England, in the Vale of Catmose, 26 km/16 mi east of Leicester; population (1991) 8,300. Shoes and knitted garments are manufactured here. Oakham Castle dates from the 12th century and has a Norman hall. There is an independent school founded in 1584.

Oaks

Horse race, one of the English classics, run at Epsom racecourse in June, now run two days before the ◊Derby, for three-year-old fillies only. The race is named after the Epsom home of the 12th Earl of Derby.

Oasis

English pop group. Although often derivative of 1960s rock and roll groups such as the Beatles and T-Rex, their confident reworking of the genre has won them much praise. Members are brothers Liam (1972–) (vocals) and Noel Gallagher (1967–) (guitar and vocals), guitarist Paul Arthurs (1965–), bassist Paul McGuigan (1971–), and drummer Alan White (1972–).

Albums include *Definitely Maybe* (1994) and *(What's the Story) Morning Glory?* (1995).

oast house

Traditional building containing kilns for drying hops. The hops were placed on horse-hair covered floors, which were heated from below, and the oast house was constructed to allow a constant draught of warm air to pass through and out at the top. Circular oast houses with conical roofs are seen in hop-growing districts, for example Kent, England.

OAST HOUSE *With their conical roofs surmounted by wooden cowls, oast houses (kilns in which hops for beer-making were dried) are a familiar sight in the southeastern county of Kent. As local breweries declined and drinking habits changed in the 1960s, with foreign hop varieties being imported to make lager, many oast houses became redundant and were converted into highly distinctive living space. Corel*

Oates, Laurence Edward Grace (1880–1912)
English Antarctic explorer who accompanied Robert Falcon ◊Scott on his second expedition to the South Pole. On the return journey, suffering from frostbite, he went out alone into the blizzard to die rather than delay the others.

Oates, Titus (1648–1705)
English conspirator. A priest, he entered the Jesuit colleges at Valladolid, Spain, and St Omer, France, as a spy in 1677–78, and on his return to England announced he had discovered a 'Popish Plot' to murder Charles II and re-establish Catholicism. Although this story was almost entirely false, many innocent Roman Catholics were executed during 1678–80 on Oates's evidence.

In 1685 Oates was flogged, pilloried, and imprisoned for perjury. He was pardoned and granted a pension after the revolution of 1688.

I am just going outside and may be some time.

Laurence Oates English Antarctic explorer. Last words, quoted in R F Scott's *Diary* 16–17 March 1912

Oban
Seaport and resort in Argyll and Bute, western Scotland; population (1991) 8,200. It is an important service, tourist, and communications centre to the Hebridean islands. The main industries are whisky distilling and tweed manufacture; fishing is also carried on.

The island of Kerrera shelters Oban's harbour from the Atlantic gales. The unfinished folly McCaig's Tower is a conspicuous landmark, which overlooks the harbour.

Car and passenger ferries sail to the islands of Islay, Colonsay, Gigha, Coll, Tiree, Mull, Lismore, Barra, and South Uist and to Kennacraig, Argyll, and Bute on the mainland.

OBE
Abbreviation for **Officer of the Order of the British Empire**, a British honour.

Oberon, Merle stage name of Estelle Merle O'Brien Thompson (1911–1979)
Indian-born British actress. She starred in several films by Alexander ◊Korda (to whom she was briefly married 1939–45), including *The Scarlet Pimpernel* (1935). She played Catherine to Laurence Olivier's Heathcliff in *Wuthering Heights* (1939), and after 1940 worked in the USA.

Observer, The
Oldest surviving English Sunday newspaper, founded in 1791. Its long record of newsgathering and liberal comment includes coverage of the execution of Marie Antoinette, Nelson's victory at Trafalgar, the exposure of the framing of Alfred Dreyfus, and condemnation of Britain's Suez campaign. It is a sibling of the daily *Guardian* newspaper and is owned by the Guardian Media Group, which bought *The Observer* from Lonrho, the international media conglomerate, in 1993. Its circulation in 1998 was over 450,000.

The paper retains a largely independent journalistic staff, sharing only its foreign correspondents with the *The Guardian*. Uniquely among British newspapers, the editorial independence of the two titles is safeguarded by a nonprofit trust which owns the Guardian Media Group; the trust appoints the editors of both titles but has no role in the daily running of the newspapers.

The paper was founded by a young Irishman, W S Bourne, in 1791; by 1799 it had established a circulation in London and the provinces. Early in the 19th century the paper was acquired by W L Clement, a pioneer in the field of pictorial journalism and the first man to establish a newspaper syndicate. In 1870 it was bought by Julius Beer, who, with his son, achieved for the paper much of the status and quality for which it remains known. In 1905 *The Observer* was bought by Lord ◊Northcliffe, who appointed J L Garvin as editor. The first Lord Astor acquired *The Observer* in 1911 and in 1945 his son David Astor vested the ownership of the paper in a trust.

Occam or Ockham, William of (*c.* 1300–1349)
English philosopher and scholastic logician who revived the fundamentals of nominalism (the theory that denies that universals really exist). The principle of reducing assumptions to the absolute minimum is known as **Occam's razor**. As a Franciscan monk he defended evangelical poverty against Pope John XXII, becoming known as the Invincible Doctor. He was imprisoned in Avignon, France, on charges of heresy in 1328 but escaped to Munich, Germany, where he died.

Ochil Hills
Mountain range in Scotland, extending from the Firth of Tay, in Fife unitary authority, about 40 km/25 mi southwest to Bridge of Allan, in Stirling unitary authority. The highest summit is Ben Cleuch, rising to 721 m/2,365 ft. Coal, iron, copper, and lead were extensively mined in the past, but most of the land has now been turned over to rich sheep and cattle pasture.

Ockham, William
English philosopher; see ◊Occam.

O'Connell, Daniel (1775–1847)
Irish politician, called 'the Liberator'. Although ineligible, as a Roman Catholic, to take his seat (there had been a ban on Catholics holding public office since the 'Popish Plot' allegedly discovered by Titus ◊Oates in 1678), he was elected member of Parliament for County Clare in 1828 and was instrumental in forcing the UK government to grant Catholic emancipation. In Parliament he cooperated with the Whigs in the hope of obtaining concessions until 1841, when he launched his campaign for repeal of the 1801 union with Great Britain.

In 1823 O'Connell founded the Catholic Association to press Roman Catholic claims. His reserved and vacillating leadership and conservative outlook on social questions alienated his most active supporters, who broke away and formed the nationalist Young Ireland movement.

O'Connor, Feargus Edward (1794–1855)

Irish parliamentarian, a follower of Daniel ◊O'Connell. He sat in Parliament 1832–35, and as editor of the *Northern Star* became an influential figure of the radical working-class Chartist movement (see ◊Chartism).

Ode for St Cecilia's Day

Setting by Handel of Dryden's poem, produced in London, Theatre in Lincoln's Inn Fields, on 22 November 1739.

Odington, Walter de (or Walter of Evesham) (fl. 1298–1316)

English monk, musician, and astronomer. He entered the Benedictine monastery at Evesham and wrote a treatise *Summa de speculatione musicae*.

OED

Abbreviation for ◊*Oxford English Dictionary*.

Offa (died *c.* 796)

King of Mercia, England, from 757. He conquered Essex, Kent, Sussex, and Surrey; defeated the Welsh and the West Saxons; and established Mercian supremacy over all England south of the River Humber.

Offa's Dyke

Defensive earthwork dyke along the English–Welsh border, of which there are remains from the mouth of the River Dee to that of the River ◊Severn. It was built about AD 785 by King ◊Offa of Mercia, England, and represents the boundary secured by his wars with Wales.

The dyke covered a distance of 240 km/149 mi, of which 130 km/81 mi are still standing. It consists of a large rampart and ditch, the latter usually on the Welsh side, and was laid out to take advantage of natural physical features.

Offer

Acronym for **Office of Electricity Regulation**, a regulatory body in the UK that supervises the privatized electricity companies.

It was established under the Competition and Service (Utilities) Act 1992, as a means of controlling the monopolistic powers of the privatized utilities.

Offiah, Martin Nwokocha (1966–)

English rugby league player who on 1 March 1998 scored his 442nd try to become the fifth highest try scorer in the history of the game. A winger of exceptional pace, he began his career in rugby union with Rosslyn Park and was capped by England B. In 1986 he changed codes, winning Division One titles twice and the Premiership Trophy three times with Widnes. In 1991 he joined Wigan for a world record fee of £400,000, instantly repaying his fee with victories for Wigan in the Challenge Cup Final and the Premiership Trophy in 1992. He was transferred from Wigan to London Broncos in July 1996.

Office of Fair Trading

UK government department established in 1973 to keep commercial activities under review. It covers the areas of consumer affairs and credit, monopolies and mergers, and anticompetitive and restrictive trade practices.

Official Secrets Act

UK act of Parliament 1989, prohibiting the disclosure of confidential material from government sources by employees; it remains an absolute offence for a member or former member of the security and intelligence services (or those working closely with them) to disclose information about their work. There is no public-interest defence, and disclosure of information already in the public domain is still a crime. Journalists who repeat disclosures may also be prosecuted.

> *[Taking] drugs is like getting up and having a cup of tea in the morning.*
>
> NOEL GALLAGHER Singer with the pop group Oasis. BBC Radio One, February 1997

Ofgas

Acronym for **Office of Gas Security**, a regulatory body in the UK that supervises the privatized ◊gas industry.

It was established under the Competition and Service (Utilities) Act 1992, as a means of controlling the monopolistic powers of the privatized utilities.

Oflot

The Office of the National Lottery. It was established in 1993 by the then Secretary of State for National Heritage, Peter Brooke. Its first task was to issue a licence to the ◊National Lottery operator and thereafter to monitor its performance. In May 1994 a licence was issued to the Camelot Group, a consortium which included Cadbury-Schweppes, Racal Electronics, the bank note printers, De La Rue, ICL, and an experienced US lottery group, G-Tech.

On 22 October 1993 Peter Davies, a deputy chairman of Abbey National plc, was appointed as its director-general. The high-profile entrepreneur Richard ◊Branson, who had earlier offered to operate a non-profitmaking lottery, won a libel case in February 1998 against a director of Camelot who, he said, had tried to bribe him to drop his lottery bid, and on the following day the Oflot director-general, who had been under considerable pressure to do so, resigned.

Oftel

Acronym for **Office of Telecommunications**, a regulatory body in the UK that supervises the privatized telephone industry.

It was established under the Competition and Service (Utilities) Act 1992, as a means of controlling the monopolistic powers of the privatized utilities.

Ofwat

Acronym for **Office of Water Services**, a regulatory body in the UK that supervises the privatized water companies.

It was established under the Competition and Service (Utilities) Act 1992, as a means of controlling the monopolistic powers of the privatized utilities.

Ogden, C(harles) K(ay) (1889–1957)

English writer and scholar. With I A ◊Richards he developed the simplified form of English known as ◊Basic English, built on a vocabulary of just 850 words. Together they wrote *Foundations of Aesthetics* (1921) and *The Meaning of Meaning* (1923).

Ogdon, John Andrew Howard (1937–1989)

English pianist and composer. A contemporary of Alexander Goehr and Peter Maxwell Davies at Manchester University, he won early recognition at the Moscow Tchaikovsky Piano Competition in 1962 and went on to become an ebullient champion of neglected virtuoso repertoire by Alkan, Bartók, Busoni, and Sorabji.

For a number of years unable to perform as a result of depression, he recovered to make a successful return to the concert hall shortly before his death.

Ogham

Early Celtic alphabet, comprising in its basic form 20 letters made up of straight lines at a right angle or an oblique angle to a base line. It has been found in Cornwall, Wales, and Scotland, and dates from the 4th century AD.

Ogilby, John (1600–1676)

English map-maker. He produced the first road map in Britain, *Britannia* (1675), which showed major roads in strip form. These maps were freshly surveyed, and included accurate details of bridges, rivers, and towns. Ogilby concentrated on roads radiating out from London. His atlas was also an innovation in using the statute mile, introduced in 1593 but not in widespread use at that time. His maps remained the standard for almost one hundred years.

old-age pension

Regular payment made by the state or a private institution to persons who have reached a specified age and are eligible for such assistance. In 1908 the British Parliament passed the Old Age Pensions Act that provided a weekly pension of five shillings to people over 70 years of age (7s 6d for a married couple) with an income of less than ten shillings a week. Old-age pensions are a form of ◊social security.

Old Bailey

Popular name for the Central Criminal Court in London, situated in a street of that name in the City of London, off Ludgate Hill.

'Old Contemptibles'

Name adopted by British soldiers who survived the retreat from Mons in 1914 and other early battles of World War I.

The name came from Kaiser Wilhelm's angry outburst at his forces in Belgium being held up by 'Sir John French's contemptible little army'. The troops seized on this with delight and named their post-war veterans' association 'The Old Contemptibles'.

Old English

General name for the range of dialects spoken by Germanic settlers in England between the 5th and 12th centuries AD, also known as Anglo-Saxon. The literature of the period includes *Beowulf*, an epic in West Saxon dialect.

Old English written records may be divided into three or four dialectal groups: the southern English dialects and the Anglian dialects, divided into Northumbrian (being dialects of the Angles north of the Humber) and Mercian (the dialects of the Angles of the Midlands). There were probably also East Anglian dialects, but nothing is known of their early form. Of the southern dialects the most important by far is that of Wessex, or West Saxon, which became dominant for literary purposes during the early 10th century and maintained its supremacy until the close of the Old English period. See also ◊Old English literature.

Old English literature

Poetry and prose in the various dialects of Old English written between AD 449 and 1066. Poetry (alliterative, without rhyme) was composed and delivered orally; much has therefore been lost. What remains owes its survival to monastic scribes who favoured verse with a Christian motivation or flavour. Prose in Old English was a later achievement, essentially beginning in the reign of Alfred the Great.

The greatest surviving epic poem is ◊*Beowulf* (*c.* 700), which recounts the hero's battles with mythical foes such as the man-eating Grendel and his mother. *Widsith/The Wanderer, Finnsburgh* (about a tragic battle), and *Waldhere* (fragments of a lost epic), all written in the mid-7th century, also belong to the the earlier centuries and express the bleakness and melancholy of life. *The Battle of Maldon*, written soon after the event in 991, extols heroic values of courage in defeat.

One of the earliest attributed short poems consists of six lines by ◊Caedmon the herder, reputedly inspired to sing about the Creation by a vision. 'The Dream of the Rood' (about 698) shows the cult of the Cross, as does ◊Cynewulf's 'Elene'. Elegies, including 'The Seafarer', written before 940, express the sense of loneliness in exile and an inflexible Fate.

Prose in Old English dates from Alfred the Great's translations of St Gregory, Boethius, and Bede's *History of the English Peoples* (first published in Latin in 731, translated between 871 and 899). Historical writing began with the ◊*Anglo-Saxon Chronicle*, at first brief notes of yearly events but later a dignified and even poetic narrative. Dating from the 10th and 11th centuries are sermons by ◊Aelfric, a Dorset monk who also translated the Old Testament, and those by the prelate Wulfstan (died 1023). Some spells and riddles have also survived.

Oldfield, Bruce (1950–)

English fashion designer. He set up his own business in 1975.

His evening wear has been popular with the British royal family, film stars, and socialites.

Oldfield, Mike (1953–)

English pop music composer. His album *Tubular Bells* (1973) sold 16 million copies. *Tubular Bells II* and *III* were released in 1992 and 1997.

Oldham

Industrial town in Greater Manchester, England, 10 km/6 mi northeast of Manchester, on the lower slopes of the Pennine upland; population (1991) 102,300. Industries include the manufacture of plastics, electrical goods, and electronic equipment. It was traditionally a cotton-spinning town.

In 1900 Winston Churchill was elected Conservative member of Parliament for Oldham, his first constituency. Oldham was the birthplace in 1902 of the composer William Walton.

Oldman, Garry (1958–)

English character actor of the stage and screen. He broke into the British film scene in the 1980s, working with such leading directors as Mike Leigh, Alex Cox, and Stephen Frears. In the 1990s Oldman gravitated towards US productions, including playing Lee Harvey Oswald in *JFK* (1991) and a corrupt police officer in *Romeo is Bleeding* (1994). Oldman won international acclaim for his debut as writer-director with the raw, London-set study of domestic violence *Nil By Mouth* (1997).

He worked with Cox and Frears on their two biopics of punk musician Sid Vicious and playwright Joe Orton, *Sid and Nancy* (1986) and *Prick Up Your Ears* (1987) respectively. His performance in *Romeo is Bleeding* included a convincing American-accented voiceover narrated by his untrustworthy protagonist, and is one of several examples in his work of a willingness to experiment in his performances. Some of his recent roles have tended towards caricature, notably in *True Romance* (1993) and *Lost in Space* (1998).

OLDFIELD, BRUCE *English fashion designer Bruce Oldfield , who worked for Yves Saint-Laurent before showing his first collection in 1975. He has received international acclaim for both his custom-made clothes and his ready-to-wear designs. The Hamling Company*

Old Moore's Almanac

Annual publication in the UK containing prophecies of the events of the following year. It was first published in 1700 under the title *Vox Stellarum/Voices of the Stars*, by Francis Moore (1657–*c.* 1715).

Old Pretender

Nickname of ◊James Edward Stuart, the son of James II of England.

Old Sarum

Iron Age fortified hill settlement north of Salisbury, Wiltshire. Used as a fortress in Roman, Saxon, and Norman times, the settlement gained importance on the completion of a cathedral under St Osmund in 1092. A new cathedral was built in the valley in 1220 (using stones from the original), and Old Sarum was eventually abandoned.

Old Trafford

Two sporting centres in Manchester, England. **Old Trafford football ground** is the home of Manchester United FC and was opened in 1910. The record attendance was 76,692 at an FA Semifinal match in March 1939; the capacity was later reduced to 55,800. It was used for the 1966 World Cup competition and the 1996 European Championships and has also hosted one FA Cup Final and two FA Cup Final replays. A rugby union international was staged at the stadium for the first time in November 1997 when England played New Zealand. **Old Trafford cricket ground** was opened in 1857 and has staged Test matches regularly since 1884. The ground capacity is approximately 21,000.

Old Vic

Theatre in south London, former home of the National Theatre (1963–76). It was founded in 1818 as the Coburg. Taken over by Emma Cons in 1880 (as the Royal Victoria Hall), it became a popular centre for opera and drama, and was affectionately dubbed the Old Vic.

In 1898 Lilian ◊Baylis, niece of Emma Cons, assumed the management, and in 1914 began a celebrated series of Shakespeare productions. Badly damaged in air raids in 1940, the Old Vic reopened 1950–81. In 1963 it became the home of the National Theatre until the latter moved to its South Bank building in 1976. In 1983 the Old Vic was bought by Ed Mirvish, a Canadian entrepreneur, and was refurbished in 1985.

O level, General Certificate of Education, or Ordinary level

Formerly an examination taken by British school children at the age of 16. It was superseded by the ◊GCSE in 1988.

Oliphant, Margaret born Wilson (1828–1897)

Scottish writer. The author of 98 novels, 25 nonfictional works, 50 short stories, and 300 articles, she was one of the first women writers to live entirely by writing, which she did while bringing up her children and other dependants unaided, following her husband's death. Her major novels are the series *The Chronicles of Carlingford* (1863–66) (including *The Perpetual Curate*, 1864, and *Miss Marjoribanks*, 1866) and *Effie Ogilvie* (1886).

Oliver, Isaac (*c.* 1560–1617)

English painter of miniatures. A Huguenot refugee, he studied under Nicholas ◊Hilliard. He introduced light and shade into miniatures, his style closer to that of the Continental Baroque portraitists. A popular court artist to James I, he was Hilliard's main rival from about 1600. His sitters included the poet John Donne. Examples of his work may be seen at the Victoria and Albert Museum, London. His son **Peter Oliver** (1594–1648) was also 'limner' (painter of miniatures) to the Stuart Court, working in his father's style.

Olivier, Laurence (Kerr), Baron Olivier (1907–1989)

English actor and director. For many years associated with the Old Vic Theatre, he was director of the National Theatre company 1962–73 (see ◊National Theatre, Royal). His stage roles include Henry V, Hamlet, Richard III, and Archie Rice in John Osborne's *The Entertainer* (1957; filmed 1960). He directed and starred in filmed versions of Shakespeare's plays; for example, *Henry V* (1944) and *Hamlet* (1948) (Academy Award). He was knighted in 1947 and created a baron in 1970.

Olivier appeared in many films, including *Wuthering Heights* (1939), *Rebecca* (1940), *Sleuth* (1972), *Marathon Man* (1976), and *The Boys from Brazil* (1978).

The Olivier Theatre (part of the National Theatre on the South Bank, London) is named after him. He was married to the actress Vivien Leigh 1940–60, and to the actress Joan Plowright from 1961 until his death.

> *What is acting but lying and what is good acting but convincing lying?*
>
> LAURENCE OLIVIER English actor and director. *Autobiography*

Omagh

County town of County ◊Tyrone, Northern Ireland, in the foothills of the Sperrin Mountains, on the River Strule, 48 km/30 mi south of Londonderry; population (1991) 17,300. Industries include dairy produce, food processing, footwear, shirt manufacturing, and engineering. Omagh was planned in the early 17th century; its chief buildings are the Catholic church, with its irregular twin spires, the courthouse, built in Classical style, and the County Hall. It is now a tourist centre, and there is salmon fishing.

Omagh became the scene of a terrorist attack when a republican car bomb exploded on 15 August 1998 in a busy shopping area, killing 29 people and injuring scores of others. The breakaway republican group, the Real IRA, claimed responsibility for the bombing. This tragic incident appeared to have a bonding and strengthening effect which spurred the Northern Ireland process forward. Over 50,000 people gathered in Omagh for the remembrance ceremony, and in September the Real IRA announced a permanent ceasefire.

Omega Workshops

Group of early 20th-century English artists (1913–20), led by Roger ◊Fry, who brought them together to design and make interiors, furnishings, and craft objects. The workshops included members of the ◊Bloomsbury Group, such as Vanessa Bell, Duncan Grant, Wyndham Lewis, and Henri Gaudier-Brzeska.

The articles they made were often primitive – both in design and execution – and brightly coloured. Some members moved to Charleston, a house in the South Downs which they decorated and fitted out with their creations.

O'Neill, Terence, Baron O'Neill of the Maine (1914–1990)

Northern Irish Unionist politician. In the Ulster government he was minister of finance 1956–63, then prime minister 1963–69. He resigned when opposed by his party on measures to extend rights to Roman Catholics, including a universal franchise.

Open College

A network launched in 1987 by the Manpower Services Commission (now the Training Agency) to enable people to gain and update technical and vocational skills by means of distance teaching, such as correspondence, radio, and television.

open-field system

System of agriculture in lowland areas of England during the Middle Ages. A village would normally have three large fields throughout which each farmer's land was distributed in scattered strips, while another area was set aside for common grazing. By the early 19th century, ◊enclosure meant that most farmland had been consolidated into individual holdings.

Farming activity in each village or manor was coordinated by the landowner's steward. Two fields would be cultivated (usually with corn) each year, the third being left fallow to recover its fertility. The small scattered strips, theoretically intended to share good and bad land fairly, made efficient farming difficult, and common grazing made it easy for disease to spread quickly among livestock. A form of the open-field system survives at Laxton in Nottinghamshire.

Open University

Institution established in the UK in 1969 to enable mature students without qualifications to study to degree level without regular attendance. Open University teaching is based on a mixture of correspondence courses, TV and radio lectures and demonstrations, personal tuition organized on a regional basis, and summer schools.

Announced by Harold Wilson in 1963 as a 'university of the air', it was largely created by Jennie ⇨Lee, minister for the arts, from 1965.

opera

Dramatic musical work in which singing takes the place of speech. In opera the music accompanying the action has paramount importance, although dancing and spectacular staging may also play their parts. The form seems to have originated in late 16th-century Florence.

In Elizabethan times, English drama frequently had singing and dancing, although these were not essential to the plot. An early masterpiece in English, albeit in the French style, was Purcell's *Dido and Aeneas*. Italian opera became very popular among the upper classes in London at the start of the 18th century, with Handel its most prominent exponent. The ⇨*Beggar's Opera*, a ballad opera (a play interspersed with popular tunes that did not disturb the flow of the plot), had a huge success in 1728. The influence of this form continued to be felt long after, with ballads being included in various types of drama and even opera. The form was revived in the 20th century by ⇨Vaughan Williams, ⇨Holst, ⇨Tippett, and ⇨Bush.

Italian opera maintained its position and cachet throughout most of the 19th century. Opera in German began to gain ground after the first London performance of Wagner's Ring cycle in 1882. Very little opera (in the sense of drama entirely set to music) in English had been composed in the later 18th and 19th centuries, although the ballad opera did develop in complexity, with the introduction of finales, and arias borrowed from foreign opera; plots were also often borrowed from foreign sources. Several attempts were made by various companies in the mid-19th century to commission and perform full-length operas in English; however, a lack of patronage from the upper classes meant that these ventures did not last long.

In 1875 opera companies were founded by both Carl Rosa and Richard D'Oyly Carte, who produced many operas by Gilbert and ⇨Sullivan. These operas had English elements (ballads and ⇨glees for example), as well as elements of French operetta (which had been performed in London from the 1860s) and influences from Mendelssohn and Schubert.

English opera at the start of the 20th century was influenced by Wagner, and Ethyl Smyth's *The Wreckers* (1906) is a notable work. The changes in social conditions after World War I were partly responsible for the advent of chamber and one-act operas, as well as works written specifically for amateurs. ⇨Sadler's Wells opened in 1931, presenting opera in English; the company moved to the Coliseum in 1968, and became the ⇨English National Opera in 1974. The company has supported new work by British composers, and important English opera composers in the latter half of the 20th century include ⇨Britten, ⇨Goehr, Maxwell ⇨Davies, ⇨Tippett, and ⇨Birtwistle.

Among the first operas produced in Scotland were those brought by the Carl Rosa company after 1877. ⇨Scottish Opera was founded in 1962, and ⇨Welsh National Opera in 1946.

See page 668 for lists of opera companies, and most popular operas.

OPERA *Open-air opera in the picturesque setting of Garsington Manor, near Oxford. A relatively recent addition to the venues in Britain for live opera, the small village of Garsington plays host to an increasingly popular annual festival. Caroline Penn/Impact*

Opera Factory

Opera company founded in 1981 under the umbrella of the English National Opera; in 1991 it became resident at the Queen Elizabeth Hall, South Bank, London. It had an iconoclastic approach to classic operas and performed several new works. Its director was David Freeman (1952–). The company's last performances took place in May 1998.

Some Major Opera Companies in the UK

Company	Director
British Youth Opera	Timothy Dean
Central Festival Opera Ltd	Tom Hawkes
City of Birmingham Touring Opera	Graham Vick
Dorset Opera	Patrick Shelley
English Festival Opera	Simon Gray
English National Opera	Dennis Marks
English Touring Opera	Andrew Greenwood
European Chamber Opera	Stefan Paul Sanchez
First Act Opera International	Elaine Holden
Garsington Opera Ltd	Leonard Ingrams
Glyndebourne Festival Opera	Andrew Davis
Glyndebourne Touring Opera	Louis Langrée
London Chamber Opera	David Wordsworth
London Community Opera	Peter Bridges
Midsummer Opera	David Roblou
Millenium Opera	James Kelleher
Music Theatre London	Tony Britten
Music Theatre Wales	Michael Rafferty
National Youth Music Theatre	Jeremy James Taylor
New Chamber Opera	Gary Cooper
New Sussex Opera	David Angus
Northern Opera Ltd	Richard Bloodworth
Opera Box Ltd	Fraser Goulding
Opera da Camera	Derek Barnes
Opera Europa	John Gibbons
Opera Factory	David Freeman
Opera North	Richard Mantle
Opera Northern Ireland	Stephen Barlow
Opera Restor'd	Peter Holman
Pimlico Opera	Wasfi Kani
Pocket Opera	Michael Armitage
Royal Opera	
Scottish Early Music Consort	Warwick Edwards
Scottish Opera	Richard Armstrong
South Yorkshire Opera Ltd	Nita White
Surrey Opera	Jonathan Butcher
Travelling Opera	Peter Knapp
Welsh National Opera	Carlo Rizzi

Top 5 Most Popular Operas Performed in the UK 1996–97

April 1996–March 1997

Rank	Opera	Tickets sold
1	*La Bohème*	105,436
2	*La Traviata*	92,608
3	*The Marriage of Figaro*	72,294
4	*Rigoletto*	61,287
5	*Madam Butterfly*	46,987

Source: Arts Councils of England, Scotland, Wales, and Northern Ireland

Opera North
British opera company based in Leeds. It tours mainly in the north of England.

Opera Northern Ireland
Opera company based at the Grand Opera House in Belfast. It regularly tours the province.

Opium Wars
Two wars, the First Opium War 1839–42 and the Second Opium War 1856–60, waged by Britain against China to enforce the opening of Chinese ports to trade in opium. Opium from British India paid for Britain's imports from China, such as porcelain, silk, and, above all, tea.

The **First Opium War** resulted in the cession of Hong Kong to Britain and the opening of five treaty ports. Other European states were also subsequently given concessions. The **Second Opium War** followed with Britain and France in alliance against China, when there was further Chinese resistance to the opium trade. China was forced to give the European states greater trading privileges, at the expense of its people.

Opposition
Party in opposition to the government, usually the second largest party in the House of Commons. The leader of this party has the official title of leader of Her Majesty's Opposition and is assisted by the 'shadow cabinet', which consists of colleagues appointed by the leader to be spokesmen for the party in various policy areas. Since 1989 the leader of the Opposition has received a government salary, starting at

£98,000 (from 1997). William Hague has been leader of the Opposition since 1997.

The Opposition is allocated 29 'supply days' each parliamentary session or year. These are days on which the estimates (of public expenditure) or supply are discussed, but which are in practice used by the Opposition to debate any subject it chooses. Cooperation and negotiation between the government and the Opposition take place through the 'usual channels' or 'behind the Speaker's chair', the terms used to describe discussions between the party ◊whips.

In presenting itself as an alternative government the Opposition does not normally expect to defeat the government in the House of Commons, although it sometimes seeks to do so in a 'snap' vote, but so to damage the government's credibility that the electorate will be persuaded to elect the opposition party to power at the next general election. The Opposition also seeks and sometimes succeeds in securing the modification of government policy and may resort to obstructive tactics in Parliament to demonstrate the strength of its feeling.

opus anglicanum (Latin 'English work')

Ecclesiastical embroidery made in England about 900–1500. It typically depicts birds and animals on highly coloured silks, using gold thread. It was popular throughout medieval Europe, being much in demand at the papal court.

Orangeman

In Northern Ireland, a member of the Ulster Protestant **Orange Society** established in 1795 in opposition to the United Irishmen and the Roman Catholic secret societies. It was a revival of the Orange Institution (founded in 1688), formed in support of William (III) of Orange, whose victory over the Catholic James II at the Battle of the Boyne in 1690 is commemorated annually by Protestants in parades on 12 July.

Orange Prize

British literary prize of £30,000. The controversial award, established in January 1996, is open to women only of any nationality. In its first year, it was won by British author Helen Dunmore for *A Spell of Winter*. The 1997 winner was the Canadian Anne Michaels, author of *Fugitive Pieces*.

oratorio

Dramatic, non-scenic musical setting of religious texts, scored for orchestra, chorus, and solo voices. Its origins lie in the *Laude spirituali*, musical settings of religious subjects performed by St Philip Neri's Oratory in Rome in the 16th century. Although dramatic works of a sacred nature existed in England at the begining of the 17th century, the first major exponent of the form was Handel, who used the styles and forms both of Italian opera and English sacred choral music. His best known work, unusually one with no dramatic narrative, is his *Messiah*, which has remained popular ever since. Not many oratorios were composed in Britain in the 18th century after Handel's death. During the 19th century, music festivals, particularly those in Leeds and Birmingham, promoted the composition of oratorios and performances of such works by major European composers. Mendelssohn's *Elijah* received its first performance in Birmingham in 1846. Oratorios continued to be written in the 20th century. Important examples include Elgar's trilogy *The Dream of Gerontius* (1900), *The Apostles* (1903), and *The Kingdom* (1906); *Belshazzar's Feast* (1931), by William Walton; and *Child of our Time* (1941), by Michael Tippett.

orchestras

See table on page 670 for some of the leading symphony and chamber orchestras in the UK, and their directors.

order in council

An order issued by the sovereign with the advice of the ◊Privy Council; in practice it is issued only on the advice of the cabinet. Acts of Parliament often provide for the issue of orders in council to regulate the detailed administration of their provisions.

Order of Merit, OM

British order of chivalry founded in 1902 by Edward VII and limited in number to 24 at any one time within the British Isles, plus additional honorary OMs for overseas peoples. It ranks below a knighthood. There are two types of OM, military and civil.

Ordnance Survey, OS

Official body responsible for the mapping of Britain. It was established in 1791 as the **Trigonometrical Survey** to continue work initiated in 1784 by Scottish military surveyor General William Roy (1726–1790). Its first accurate maps appeared in 1830, drawn to a scale of 1 in to the mile (1:63,000). In 1858 the OS settled on a scale of 1:2,500 for the mapping of Great Britain and Ireland (higher for urban areas, lower for uncultivated areas).

Subsequent revisions and editions include the 1:50,000 Landranger series of 1971–86. In 1989, the OS began using a computerized system for the creation and continuous revision of maps. Customers can now have maps drafted to their own specifications, choosing from over 50 features (such as houses, roads, and vegetation). Since 1988 the OS has had a target imposed by the government to recover all its costs from sales.

Orford, 1st Earl of

Title of the British politician Robert ◊Walpole.

Organ, (Harold) Bryan (1935–)

English portraitist. He works in a solidly traditional style although his portraits often have a modern air in their informality of pose. His subjects have included Harold Macmillan, Michael Tippett, Elton John, and the Prince and Princess of Wales. Examples of his work may be found at the National Portrait Gallery, London.

Orkney Causeway, or Churchill Barriers

Construction in northern Scotland, put up in World War II, completed in 1943, joining four of the Orkney Islands. It was built to protect the British fleet from intrusion through the eastern entrances to Scapa Flow.

Selected Symphony and Chamber Orchestras in the UK

Orchestra	Director
The Academy of Ancient Music	Christopher Hogwood
Academy of London	Richard Stamp
Academy of St Martin in the Fields	Neville Marriner
Academy of the London Mozarteum	Robert Hamwee
Ambache Chamber Orchestra	Diana Ambache
BBC Concert Orchestra	Barry Wordsworth
BBC National Orchestra of Wales	Mark Wigglesworth
BBC Philharmonic	Yan Pascal Tortelier
BBC Scottish Symphony Orchestra	Osmo Vänskä
BBC Symphony Orchestra	Andrew Davis
Bournemouth Sinfonietta	Alexander Polianichko
Bournemouth Symphony Orchestra	Yakov Kreizberg
The Brandenburg Consort	Roy Goodman
The Brandenburg Orchestra	Robert Porter
The Britten Sinfonia	Nicholas Cleobury
CBSO (City of Birmingham Symphony Orchestra)	Sakari Oramo
Charivari Agréable Simfonie	Kah-Ming Ng
City of London Sinfonia	Richard Hickox
City of Oxford Orchestra	Marios Papadopoulos
Corydon Orchestra	Matthew Best
East of England Orchestra	Nicholas Kok
English Baroque Orchestra	Leon Lovett
English Camerata	Elizabeth Altman
English Classical Players	Jonathan Brett
English National Opera Orchestra	Paul Daniel
English Northern Philharmonia	Richard Mantle
English Sinfonia	Bramwell Tovey
English String Orchestra	William Boughton
English Symphony Orchestra	William Boughton
European Women's Orchestra	Odaline de la Martinez
Fiori Musicali	Penelope Rapson
Gabrieli Consort and Players	Paul McCreesh
Glyndebourne Touring Opera Orchestra	Ivor Bolton
Guildford Philharmonic Orchestra	En Shao
The Hallé Orchestra	Kent Nagano
The Hanover Band	Caroline Brown
The King's Consort	Robert King
London Chamber Orchestra	Christopher Warren-Green
London Handel Orchestra	Denys Darlow
London Jupiter Orchestra	Gregory Rose
London Mozart Players	Matthias Bamert
London Philharmonic Orchestra	Bernard Haitink
London Pro Arte Orchestra	Murray Stewart
London Sinfonietta	Markus Stenz
London Symphony Orchestra	Colin Davis
Manchester Camerata	Sachio Fujioka
Mozart Orchestra	Gordon Heard
New London Orchestra	Ronald Corp
New Queen's Hall Orchestra	John Boyden
Northern Sinfonia	Jean-Bernard Pommier
Orchestra da Camera	Kenneth Page
Orchestra of St John's Smith Square	John Lubbock
Orchestra of the Age of Enlightenment	Marshall Marcus
Orchestre Révolutionnaire et Romantique	John Eliot Gardiner
Oxford Orchestra da Camera	Patricia Bavaud
Philharmonia Orchestra	Christoph von Dohnányi
Philomusica of London	David Littaur
The Royal Liverpool Philharmonic Orchestra	Petr Altrichter
Royal Opera House Orchestra	
Royal Philharmonic Concert Orchestra	Thomas Siracusa
Royal Scottish National Orchestra	Alexander Lazarev
The Scottish Chamber Orchestra	Joseph Swensen
Sinfonia 21	Dennis Stevenson
Taverner Players	Andrew Parrott
Ulster Orchestra	Michael Henson
Welsh Chamber Orchestra	Anthony Hose
Welsh National Opera Orchestra	Carlo Rizzi
Welsh Philharmonic Orchestra	G J Harries

The Orkney Causeway links the islands of mainland Orkney with Lamb Holm, Glims Holm, and Burray.

Orkney Islands

Island group and unitary authority off the northeast coast of Scotland

Area 1,014 sq km/391 sq mi

Towns ◊Kirkwall (administrative headquarters), Stromness, both on Mainland (Pomona)

Physical group of 90 islands and inlets. The surface of the islands is irregular and indented by many arms of the sea. Next to Mainland, the most important of the islands are North and South Ronaldsay, Hoy, Rousay, Stronsay, Flotta, Shapinsay, Eday, Sanday, and Westray. The highest peak is Ward Hill in Hoy, which has an elevation of 479 m/1,572 ft. The Old Man of Hoy is an isolated stack of red sandstone 137 m/450 ft high, off Hoy's northwest coast

Features Skara Brae Neolithic village, and Maes Howe burial chamber; Scapa Flow; oil terminal on Flotta

Industries offshore oil, woollen weaving, wind-powered electricity generation, distilling, boat-building, fish curing

Agriculture fishing, beef cattle, dairy products

ORKNEY ISLANDS *The Ring of Brogar is one of several ancient monuments on Mainland, in the Orkney Islands. It comprises a great circle of 60 prehistoric standing stones, some 27 of which remain upright. Nearby is another circle known as the stones of Stenness and the gigantic burial mound of Maes Howe. Corel*

Population (1995) 19,900

Famous people Edwin Muir, John Rae

History population of Scandinavian descent; Harald I (Fairhair) of Norway conquered the islands in 876; pledged to James III of Scotland in 1468 for the dowry of Margaret of Denmark; Scapa Flow, between Mainland and Hoy, was a naval base in both world wars, the German fleet scuttled itself here on 21 June 1919.

Scotland is a foreign country, from their point of view.

JO GRIMOND British Liberal politician. On the people in his constituency of Orkney and Shetland, who voted 'no' in the devolution referendum of 1979

Demography

The population, long falling, has in recent years risen as the islands' remoteness from the rest of the world attracts new settlers.

Energy

Burgar Hill has the world's most productive wind-powered generator; a 300 kW wind turbine with blades 60 m/197 ft in diameter, capable of producing 20% of the islands' energy needs.

Archaeology

Many brochs, chambered cairns, and burial mounds remain as evidence of prehistoric and Norse settlements. The Neolithic dwellings of Skara Brae are important examples.

Early history

The Orkneys, under the name 'Orcades', are mentioned by ancient geographical writers, including Pliny and Ptolemy. In 876 Harold I (Harald Haarfager) conquered the Orkneys and the Hebrides. During most of the 10th century the Orkney Islands were ruled by independent Scandinavian jarls (earls), but in 1098 became subject to the Norwegian crown and remained Scandinavian until 1468, when they were given to James III as security for his wife's dowry. In 1590, on the marriage of James VI with the Danish Princess Anne, Denmark formally resigned all pretensions to the sovereignty of the Orkneys. However, during their long connection with Norway and Denmark, all traces of the primitive Celtic population disappeared, and the present inhabitants are of Scandinavian stock.

Later history

In the mid-19th century there was a big influx of farmers from Aberdeenshire and other parts of northeast Scotland, and two world wars also brought many others to reside permanently in Orkney. Scapa Flow, between Mainland and Hoy, was a naval base in both world wars, and the German fleet scuttled itself here on 21 June 1919.

Climate

The climate of the Orkney Islands is mild, owing to the Gulf Stream. At the season of the longest day, there is almost no darkness for about six weeks, and during the summer solstice photographs can be taken at midnight.

Economy
The area has a buoyant mixed economy. While the predominant industry is agriculture and other 'community' industries, such as fishing, crafts, and knitwear, are important, the economic vitality of the islands is largely attributable to the development of the oil industry in the 1980s.
Environment
There are 34 Sites of Special Scientific Interest, five Special Protection Areas, and one National Scenic Area.

> *NO we don't speak Gaelic and never have done, YES we have electricity, NO our eyebrows don't meet in the middle and our toes aren't webbed.*
>
> Duncan MacLean Writer and adoptive Orcadian. On popular misconceptions of Orkney and Shetland; the *Independent on Sunday*, September 1998

Orkneys, South
Islands in the British Antarctic Territory.

Orme's Head
Limestone promontories near Llandudno, in Conwy county borough, north Wales. **Great Orme's Head**, lying to the west of Llandudno, rises to 207 m/680 ft above the Irish Sea. A cable tramway runs to the summit. The lighthouse has been converted to a hotel and there is a country park with nature trails. Bronze-Age copper mines are open to visitors. **Little Orme's Head**, 141 m/463 ft, lies to the east of Llandudno.

Ormskirk
Town in Lancashire, England, 20 km/12 mi from Liverpool. Situated in a rich agricultural area, it is principally a market town and residential centre. Industries include brass foundries and confectionery. Ormskirk has a street market thought to date from the 13th century. The parish church, with both tower and spire, has tombs of the Earls of Derby.

Orton, Joe (John Kingsley) (1933–1967)
English dramatist. In his black comedies, surreal and violent action takes place in genteel and unlikely settings. Plays include *Entertaining Mr Sloane* (1964), *Loot* (1966), and *What the Butler Saw* (1968). His diaries deal frankly with his personal life. He was murdered by his lover Kenneth Halliwell.

Orwell
River in Suffolk, England. It rises, as the River Gipping, a few kilometres north of Stowmarket, through which it passes. It flows through Needham Market to Ipswich, where it becomes tidal and takes the name Orwell. Below Ipswich it joins the River Stour and forms the estuary on which the port of Harwich is situated. The river is navigable to Ipswich.

Orwell, George pen name of Eric Arthur Blair (1903–1950)
English writer. His books include the satirical fable ◊*Animal Farm* (1945) (an attack on the Soviet Union and its leader Stalin), which included such slogans as 'All animals are equal, but some are more equal than others', and the prophetic ◊*Nineteen Eighty-Four* (1949) (targeting Cold War politics), which portrays the catastrophic excesses of state control over the individual. He also wrote numerous essays. Orwell was distrustful of all political parties and ideologies and a deep sense of social conscience and antipathy towards political dictatorship characterize his work.
Life
Orwell was born in India, and served in Burma with the Indian Imperial Police from 1922–27, an experience reflected in the novel *Burmese Days* (1934). In horrified retreat from imperialism, he moved towards socialism and even anarchism. A period of poverty, during which he was successively tutor, teacher, dishwasher, tramp, and bookshop assistant, is described in *Down and Out in Paris and London* (1933), and also provided him with material for *The Road to Wigan Pier* (1937) and *Keep the Aspidistra Flying* (1936). In 1936 he fought on the Republican side in the Spanish Civil War and was wounded; these experience are related in *Homage to Catalonia* (1938). During World War II, Orwell worked for the BBC, writing and monitoring propaganda.

> *A family with the wrong members in control – that, perhaps, is as near as one can come to describing England in a phrase.*
>
> George Orwell English author. *The Lion and the Unicorn* (1941)

Osborne, John James (1929–1994)
English dramatist. He became one of the first ◊Angry Young Men (anti-establishment writers of the 1950s) of British theatre with his debut play, *Look Back in Anger* (1956), which caught the mood of a generation disillusioned by the gulf between their expectations and the drab reality of a postwar Britain in decline. Other plays include *The Entertainer* (1957), *Luther* (1960), *Inadmissible Evidence* (1964), and *A Patriot for Me* (1965).

Osborne's plays are first and foremost character studies, although they also reflect broader social issues. Other works include *Hotel in Amsterdam* (1968), *West of Suez* (1971), *Watch It Come Down* (1976), and *Too Young to Fight, Too Old to Forget* (1985). With *Déjà-Vu* (1992) he returned unsuccessfully to Jimmy Porter, the hero of the epoch-making *Look Back in Anger*.

Osborne also formed a film company with the director Tony ◊Richardson and made highly acclaimed versions of *Look Back in Anger*, starring Richard Burton, and *The Entertainer*, starring Laurence Olivier. His adaptations for cinema include *Tom Jones* (1963), which brought him an Oscar for best screenplay, *Hedda Gabler* (1972), and *The Picture of Dorian Gray* (1973).

Osborne, Nigel (1948–)
English composer. He studied at Oxford with Egon Wellesz

and Kenneth ◊Leighton and in Poland with Witold Rodziński. He lectured at Nottingham University from 1978. He is best known for his vivid and iconoclastic stage works, which include the operas *The Electrification of the Soviet Union* (1986) and *Sarajevo* (1994).

Other works include: *Byzantine Epigrams* for chorus (1969); *Seven Words*, cantata (1971); *Charivari* for orchestra (1973); *Chansonnier* for chamber ensemble (1975); *I am Goya* for baritone and instruments (1977); *Concert Piece* for cello and orchestra (1977); *In Camera* for 13 instruments (1979); *Gnostic Passion* for 36 voices (1980); Flute concerto (1980); *The Cage* for tenor and ensemble (1981); *Sinfonia* for orchestra (1982); *Alba* for mezzo, instruments, and tape (1984); *Zansa* for ensemble (1985); *Pornography* for mezzo and ensemble (1985); *Esquisse I and II* for strings (1987–88); violin concerto (1990); *The Sun of Venice* for orchestra (1991); and the opera *Terrible Mouth* (1992).

Osborne House

House on the Isle of Wight, England, 1.6 km/1 mi southeast of Cowes. It was the preferred residence of Queen Victoria, for whom it was built in 1845. The house was designed by Prince Albert and Thomas Cubitt. Queen Victoria died there in 1901, and the estate passed to the Prince of Wales who, on his coronation as Edward VII in 1902, made a gift of the building and grounds to the nation, to be used as a convalescent home for officers of the Army and Navy. The state apartments are now open to the public.

Osterley Park

House and 16 ha/40 acre estate in western Greater London, 5 km/3 mi northwest of Richmond; one of the last great houses with its estate intact in the London area. The house is Elizabethan, but was extensively remodelled into an 18th-century villa with Neo-Classical interiors by Robert ◊Adam around 1760–80.

The interior includes the Etruscan Room and the sumptuous Tapestry Room, the latter hung with 18th-century Gobelins tapestries after designs by François Boucher (1769). Osterley Park was given to the National Trust in 1949 by the 9th Earl of Derby.

Oswald, St (*c.* 605–642)

King of Northumbria from 634, after killing the Welsh king Cadwallon. He became a Christian convert during exile on the Scottish island of Iona. With the help of St ◊Aidan he furthered the spread of Christianity in northern England. Feast day 9 August.

Oswaldtwistle

Town in Lancashire, England, to the east of Blackburn. Traditionally a cotton town, it now has chemical and engineering works. James Hargreaves invented the 'spinning jenny' (a machine which allowed several threads to be spun simultaneously) here in 1764.

Robert Peel, Conservative politician and founder of the modern police force, was born here in 1788.

Oswestry

Market town in north Shropshire, England, 32 km/20 mi northwest of Shrewsbury, 8 km/5 mi from the Welsh border; population (1991) 15,600. Industries include the manufacture of agricultural machinery, plastics, and insulated equipment, tanning, printing, livestock marketing, and some tourism. The town is named after St Oswald, King of Northumbria, who was killed here in 642 at the Battle of Maserfelth.

It was the site of much border warfare between the Welsh and English in the Middle Ages, and the town was twice burned to the ground. Old Oswestry, nearby to the north, is the site of an Iron Age earthwork. Oswestry was the birthplace of the poet Wilfred Owen, and the town was the original seat of the family of Fitz-Alan, from whom descended the Earls of Arundel.

Othello

Tragedy by William ◊Shakespeare, first performed in 1604–05. Othello, a Moorish commander in the Venetian army, is persuaded by Iago that his wife Desdemona is having an affair with his friend Cassio. Othello murders Desdemona; on discovering her innocence, he kills himself.

Otley

Town in West Yorkshire, England, 15 km/9 mi northwest of Leeds, on the River Wharfe; population (1991) 22,200. Otley has an agricultural trade and manufactures leather goods and machinery. Nearby are woollen and worsted mills.

Near to the town is Farnley Hall, where the painter William Turner produced many of his works; it contains a fine private collection of his paintings. Otley has a 17th-century grammar school. The seat of the Fairfax family is at Denton Park nearby.

O'Toole, Peter (Seamus) (1932–)

Irish-born British actor. He made his name in the title role of *Lawrence of Arabia* (1962), and then starred in such films as *Becket* (1964) and *The Lion in Winter* (1968), moving effortlessly from comic to dramatic roles – from the philanderer of *What's New Pussycat?* (1965) to his King Henry II of *The Lion in Winter*. Subsequent appearances include *The Ruling Class* (1972), *The Stuntman* (1980), and *High Spirits* (1988).

His career was severely hampered by his alcoholism in the 1970s, and although he has given fine performances since going teetotal, notably in *The Stunt Man*, he has tended towards caricature in recent years.

Otterburn

Village in Northumberland, England, on the River Rede, 51 km/32 mi northwest of Newcastle. Nearby is the site of the Battle of Otterburn, fought in 1388 between the English and the Scots, in which the English army under Henry 'Hotspur' Percy was defeated by the Earl of Douglas and his troops.

Otterburn, Battle of, or Chevy Chase

Battle on 15 August 1388 in which an inferior Scottish army heavily defeated an English army under Henry 'Hotspur'

Percy, who was himself taken prisoner. The Scottish commander, the 3rd Earl of Douglas, was killed in the battle.

Ottery St Mary

Town in Devon, England, 19 km/12 mi east of Exeter, on the River Otter; population (1991) 8,100. The church of St Mary dates from 1061 and has a Norman font. The poet Samuel Coleridge was born in Ottery St Mary. The Vale of Otter is noted for its scenery and trout fishing.

Examples of Elizabethan architecture are found in the area at Cadhay and Knightstone. Escot Grange was the 'Fairoaks' of *Pendennis* by William Thackeray. An annual carnival, said to have originated in 1688, is held on 5 November.

In the 14th century Bishop Grandison (1292–1369) rebuilt much of the church's 13th-century structure, transforming it into a collegiate church; it held this status until the Reformation. The building bears striking similarities to Exeter Cathedral, on which Grandison also worked.

Oughtred, William (1575–1660)

English mathematician, credited as the inventor of the slide rule in 1622. His major work *Clavis mathematicae/The Key to Mathematics* (1631) was a survey of the entire body of mathematical knowledge of his day. It introduced the '×' symbol for multiplication, as well as the abbreviations 'sin' for sine and 'cos' for cosine.

Oulton Broad

Resort in Suffolk, England, incorporated in Lowestoft; population (1991) 6,200. It attracts visitors for yachting, motor-boat racing, and fishing. The lake (broad) of the same name connects with the sea via locks at Lowestoft, and with the ◊Norfolk Broads via Oulton Dyke.

Ouse

River in southeast England; length 48 km/30 mi; it rises between Horsham and Cuckfield in the Weald of West Sussex and flows southwards through the South Downs to enter the English Channel at Newhaven. Uckfield and Lewes are the principal towns on its banks. The River Uck is its only main tributary.

The Sussex Ouse derives its name from the town of Lewes, the river being known in early charters as *aqua de Lewes*, later misunderstood as 'de l'Ouse'.

Ouse (Celtic 'water')

River in northern England; length 87 km/54 mi. It is formed by the junction of the rivers Ure and Swale near Boroughbridge in North Yorkshire and flows in a southeasterly direction through York City and the East Riding of Yorkshire to unite with the Trent 13 km/8 mi east of Goole. The two rivers then form the ◊Humber.

The chief tributaries are the Nidd, Wharfe, Aire, and Don from the northwest, and the Derwent from the northeast. Navigation on the Ouse is connected via the Aire and Calder to Leeds and Dewsbury.

Ouse, Great (Celtic 'water')

River which rises near Brackley in Northamptonshire, central England, and flows eastwards through Buckinghamshire, Bedfordshire, Cambridgeshire, and Norfolk, before entering the Wash north of King's Lynn; length 250 km/160 mi. A large sluice across the Great Ouse, near King's Lynn, was built as part of extensive flood-control works in 1959.

The chief tributaries of the Great Ouse are the Ivel, Cam, Lark, Little Ouse, Wissey, and Nar, all of which come from the south or east. The Bedfordshire Ouse was diverted in the 17th century from its devious course through Ely via two new channels called the New and Old Bedford rivers, 32 km/20 mi long, running in a direct line from Earith near St Ives to Denver Sluice near Downham Market.

outlawry

In medieval England, a declaration that a criminal was outside the protection of the law, with his or her lands and goods forfeited to the crown, and all civil rights being set aside. It was a lucrative royal 'privilege'; ◊Magna Carta restricted its use, and under Edward III it was further modified. Some outlaws, such as ◊Robin Hood, became popular heroes.

Oval, the

Cricket ground in Kennington, London, the home of Surrey County Cricket Club. In 1880 it was the venue for the first Test match to be held in England (between England and Australia).

overseas civil service

Civil services of Britain's remaining colonial and dependent territories which are, for the most part, recruited locally. Overseas staff are recruited only for posts for which suitable local candidates cannot be found. They are mostly appointed on fixed-term contracts, but a number, including most of the senior officials still serving, are members of HM Overseas Civil Service.

Overseas Development Administration, ODA

See ◊**International Development Department (IDD)**.

Ovett, Steve(n) Michael James (1955–)

English middle-distance runner who won the 800 metres gold and the 1500 metres bronze at the 1980 Olympics. He was also European 1500 metres champion in 1978 and Commonwealth 5,000 metres champion in 1986.

Owen, David Anthony Llewellyn (1938–)

British politician, Labour foreign secretary 1977–79. In 1981 he was one of the founders of the ◊Social Democratic Party (SDP), and became its leader in 1983. Opposed to the decision of the majority of the party to merge with the Liberals in 1987, Owen stood down, but emerged in 1988 as leader of a rump SDP, which was eventually disbanded in 1990.

In 1992 he replaced Lord Carrington as European Community (now European Union) mediator in the peace talks on Bosnia-Herzegovina. He resigned from the post in 1995, and retired from active politics. He received a life peerage in 1992.

Owen, Michael (1979–)

English footballer. A striker of exceptional pace, he made his full England debut in February 1998 at the age of 18 years 59 days, then three months later became England's youngest ever goalscorer. He scored two goals at the 1998 World Cup finals, including what was widely regarded as the goal of the tournament against Argentina. Owen made his first team debut for Liverpool in May 1997, and in his first full season (1997–98) finished as the Premier League's equal top scorer with 18 goals.

Owen, Robert (1771–1858)

British socialist, born in Wales. In 1800 he became manager of a mill at New Lanark in Scotland, where, by improving working and housing conditions and providing schools, he created a model community. His ideas stimulated the cooperative movement (the pooling of resources for joint economic benefit).

From 1817 Owen proposed that 'villages of cooperation', self-supporting communities run on socialist lines, should be founded; these, he believed, would ultimately replace private ownership. His later attempt to run such a community in the USA (called New Harmony) failed.

He organized the Grand National Consolidated Trades Union in 1833, in order that the unions might take over industry and run it cooperatively, but this scheme collapsed in 1834. In *A New View of Society* (1813), he claimed that personal character is wholly determined by environment. He had earlier abolished child employment, established sickness and old-age insurance, and opened educational and recreational facilities at his cotton mills in the north of England.

OWEN, WILFRED *English poet Wilfred Owen (left). Admired for the bleak realism of his World War I poetry, Owen's work exemplifies his horror at the brutalities of warfare. He fought on the Somme, won the Military Cross, and was killed in action in 1918, one week before the Armistice. Corbis*

Owen, Wilfred Edward Salter (1893–1918)

English poet. His verse, owing much to the encouragement of Siegfried ◊Sassoon, is among the most moving of World War I poetry; it shatters the illusion of the glory of war, revealing its hollowness and cruel destruction of beauty. Only four poems were published during his lifetime; he was killed in action a week before the Armistice. After Owen's death Sassoon collected and edited his *Poems* (1920). Among the best known are 'Dulce et Decorum Est' and 'Anthem for Doomed Youth', published in 1921. Benjamin ◊Britten used several of the poems in his *War Requiem* (1962).

In technique Owen's work is distinguished by the extensive use of assonance in place of rhyme, anticipating the later school of W H ◊Auden and Stephen ◊Spender.

'Owl and the Pussycat'

Nonsense poem by Edward ◊Lear, published in *Nonsense Songs, Stories, Botany and Alphabets* (1871). It describes how an owl and a pussycat set off in their 'beautiful pea-green boat', sail 'for a year and a day', and are married in the 'land where the Bong-tree grows'.

Oxbridge

Generic term for Oxford and Cambridge universities, the two oldest universities in the UK. They are still distinctive because of their academic and social prestige, their ancient collegiate structure, their separate entrance procedures, and their high proportion of students from private schools compared to all other higher education.

Oxburgh Hall

House in Norfolk, England, 13 km/8 mi east of Downham Market. It was built about 1482, but was damaged in the English Civil War, and repairs continued for the next hundred years. It was substantially rebuilt and restored in the 18th and 19th centuries, although its outward appearance is much the same as in Tudor times. The 24 m/79 ft gate tower is virtually unaltered. Oxburgh was given to the National Trust in 1952 by Lady Bedingfeld.

It has been the home of the Bedingfeld family for nearly 500 years.

Oxfam

Charity, established in Oxford in 1942, aiming to put an end to poverty worldwide. It provides assistance for development and relief by working in partnership with local groups, helping poor people to help themselves. Oxfam campaigns internationally, gives poor people channels to voice their concerns, funds long-term projects such as education and training, and provides emergency aid. The organization operates in over 70 countries. Oxfam UK is a member of Oxfam International.

Oxford

University city and administrative centre of ◊Oxfordshire in south central England, at the confluence of the rivers Thames (called the Isis around Oxford) and Cherwell, 84 km/52 mi northwest of London; population (1994 est) 121,000. ◊Oxford University has 36 colleges, the oldest being University College (1249). Industries include motor vehicles at Cowley, steel products, electrical goods, publishing (Oxford University Press, Blackwells), and English language schools. Tourism is important.

Features

These include Christ Church cathedral (12th century); the Divinity School and Duke Humphrey's Library (1488); the Sheldonian Theatre, designed by Christopher ◊Wren 1663–69; the Ashmolean museum (1845); and the 17th-century Bodleian Library. Other museums include the University Museum (1855–60), designed by Benjamin Woodward, the Pitt-Rivers Museum, and the Museum of Modern Art. Features of the colleges include the 14th-century Mob Quad and library at Merton College; the Canterbury Quad (1636) and gardens laid out by 'Capability' Brown at St John's College; and Holman Hunt's *The Light of the World* in Keble College. The Bate Collection of Historical Instruments is housed at the Faculty of Music. The Botanic Gardens (laid out in 1621) are the oldest in Britain. On 1 May (May morning) madrigals are sung at the top of Magdalen College tower. St Giles fair takes place every September.

History

The town was first occupied in Saxon times as a fording point, and is first mentioned in written records in the Anglo-Saxon Chronicle of 912. The University of Oxford, the oldest in England, is first mentioned in the 12th century, when its growth was encouraged by the influx of English students expelled from Paris in 1167. The fame of the university grew steadily, until by the 14th century it was the equal of any in Europe. As the university grew, there was increasing antagonism between it and the town. Most of the university's buildings were built during the 15th, 16th, and 17th centuries. Oxford's earliest colleges were University College (1249), Balliol (1263), and Merton (1264).

During the Civil War, the university supported the Royalist cause while the city declared for Parliament. Oxford became the headquarters of the king and court in 1642, but yielded to the Parliamentary commander in chief, Gen Fairfax, in 1646.

OXFORD *The Sheldonian Theatre, Oxford, one of Christopher Wren's earliest buildings, designed while he was professor of astronomy and mathematics at Oxford. Built 1662–63, a few years before Wren was introduced to the Baroque architecture of Paris, it is based on ancient Roman models. Its innovative trussed roof, however, beneath which there had to be a self-supporting ceiling covering a wide span, was designed using his own mathematical researches. Linda Proud*

By the beginning of the 20th century, the city had experienced rapid expansion and industrialization, and printing and publishing industries had become firmly established. In the 1920s the English industrial magnate William Morris (1877–1963), later Lord Nuffield, began a motor-car industry at Cowley, just outside the city, which became the headquarters of the Austin-Rover group.

Early importance

Though the town is now famous chiefly for Oxford University, it was also of some importance prior to the founding of the university. It was situated between Mercia and Wessex, on one of the best of the fords across the Thames. Oxford's importance in early times is shown by the first mention of the city in recorded history, the Anglo-Saxon Chronicle of 912, where it is recorded that in that year Edward, son of Ethelred, took possession 'of London and Oxford and all the lands obedient to those cities'. The town probably made a stubborn resistance to the Norman invaders, and the Domesday Book shows the reprisals which followed. To prevent further revolt the Norman governor, Robert D'Oilly, built huge works to keep the town in submission. The remains of these are to be seen in the castle tower and parts of the churches of St Michael, St Peter in the East, and St Cross. The city again figures prominently in the troubles of Stephen's reign, and in 1142 the Empress Matilda (or Maud) was besieged here, escaping over the river on the ice. But, with unimportant exceptions, the fortress was not again seriously attacked till the 17th century, after which it ceased to rank as a place of strength and rapidly fell into decay, though D'Oilly's tower has successfully weathered the storms of 800 years, and even now is practically intact. In 1258 the Provisions of Oxford were drawn up here for the guidance of Henry III, and the Montfort rebellion was partly due to these. In the Civil War of Charles I's reign, Oxford figures as the chief royalist centre, enthusiastic in its support of the king.

20th century expansion

Before 1914 Oxford was regarded solely as a university city and market town, printing being then its only considerable industry. Between the two wars the Oxford motor industry expanded rapidly, and the city's population rose from 67,000 in 1921 to 94,000 in 1938. By 1945 Oxford itself contained a population of 100,000. In 1962 Donnington Bridge, linking east and south Oxford, was opened to motor traffic. The university franchise, whereby Oxford University returned two members to Parliament, was discontinued in 1948.

City layout and landmarks

The old town of Oxford is built almost entirely in the angle formed by the Cherwell and the Thames, here called the Isis. The four main roads of the town meet at the place known as Carfax (derived from Latin *quadrifurcus*, 'four-forked'). Carfax Tower, said to have been built in the reign of Edward III, may have been built at a much earlier date. It was renovated in 1896, and the curious 'Quarter Boys', relic of the past, restored to use. North from Carfax runs Cornmarket Street, continued further north as Magdalen Street. Where Cornmarket Street runs into Magdalen Street it is crossed by a single thoroughfare with several names, which are (east to west) George Street, Broad Street, Holywell Street, and Longwall Street. It sweeps round in a large curve, and roughly marks the boundaries of the ancient city in that direction. Some fragments of the old wall still remain, notably as part of the wall of Merton Gardens. West from Carfax runs Queen Street, continued as New Road. In Cornmarket Street is St Michael's church, the tower of which dates to the late 11th-century. Not far from it is the church of St Mary Magdalene, an interesting building of various dates. Nearby is the Martyrs' Memorial, a monument commemorating the martyrdom of bishops Ridley, Latimer, and Cranmer (1556), designed by Sir Gilbert Scott. South runs St Aldate's as far as Folly Bridge. Until near the end of the 18th century, an ancient water-tower, known as Friar Bacon's Study, rose over the old bridge.

Eastwards from Carfax runs the High Street, off which is the university church of St Mary the Virgin, built between the 13th and 15th centuries, except for the Baroque porch, erected by the Laud's chaplain, Dr Morgan Owen, in 1637. It was to St Mary's that the remains of Amy Robsart, wife of Robert Dudley, Earl of Leicester, were brought from Cumnor in 1560 – Dudley was suspected of murdering her; and from St Mary's pulpit the Anglican priest and religious poet John Keble preached his sermon on national apostasy in 1833.

High Street passes over Magdalen Bridge, which commands fine views north and south, the former toward the wooded heights of Headington Hill, with St Clement's church (1828) in the middle distance, the latter toward Magdalen College School playing fields and a section of the botanic gardens. In High Street are the examination schools, used in the world wars as a military hospital, designed by Sir Thomas Graham Jackson, who also designed Oxford's 'Bridge of Sighs' (1913–14), connecting the two sections of Hertford College.

Opposite to Hertford is the **Bodleian Library** (1488), most of which was designed by Holt of York. Near it is the Clarendon Building which was for many years the home of the Oxford University Press. Designed by John Vanbrugh, both of its main elevations are stately; that on the south contains a figure of Lord Clarendon, from the proceeds of whose book, the *History of the Rebellion*, the building was erected. The New Bodleian, designed by Giles Gilbert Scott, was opened in 1947.

Christ Church cathedral, the smallest, but one of the most beautiful of English cathedrals, is a good example of English church architecture. The pier arches are early 12th-century work, as are the transepts and choir aisles. Originally the church of St Frideswide's Priory, it was incorporated by the English cleric and politician Thomas Wolsey into his collegiate foundation in the 16th century, and later designated the cathedral of Oxford by Henry VIII. Tom Tower contains the famous bell from which the tower gets its name; the upper part of the tower (1681–82) was designed by Christopher Wren.

Oxford has expanded to take in many suburbs: Osney to the west, Grandpont to the south, St Clement's, Cowley, Headington, and Iffley to the east, and St Giles's, Sum-

Oxford University Colleges

date[1]	college	note
full colleges		
1249	University	
1263–8	Balliol	
1264	Merton	
c. 1278	St Edmund Hall	
1314	Exeter	
1326	Oriel	the last men-only college to go mixed, in 1984
1340	The Queen's	
1379	New	
1427	Lincoln	
1438	All Souls	has no students – for fellows only
1458	Magdalen	
1509	Brasenose	
1517	Corpus Christi	the smallest college in terms of number of students
1546	Christ Church	
1554–5	Trinity	
1555	St John's	
1571	Jesus	
1612	Wadham	
1624	Pembroke	
1714	Worcester	
1740	Hertford	
1870	Keble	
1878	Lady Margaret Hall	
1879	Somerville	women only up until Oct 1994
1886	St Hugh's	
1893	St Anne's	
1893	St Hilda's	women only
1929	St Peter's	
1953	St Anthony's	graduate college
1958	Nuffield	graduate college
1962	Linacre	graduate college
1963	St Catherine's	the largest college in terms of numbers of students
1965	St Cross	graduate college; date of establishment given as no charter yet granted
1979	Green	graduate college; date of establishment given as no charter yet granted
1981	Wolfson	graduate college
1984	Templeton	graduate college for management studies
1990	Kellogg College	graduate college for part-time students
permanent private halls		
Not affiliated to the University as full colleges, but students study for the same degrees.		
1221	Blackfriars	mainly for members of the Dominican Order
1786	Manchester	moving towards full college status
1810	Regent's Park	
1886	Mansfield	moving towards full college status
1896	Campion Hall	mainly for members of the Society of Jesus
1897	St Benet's Hall	mainly for members of the Benedictine community
1910	Greyfriars	mainly for members of the Franciscan Order

[1]date of college's foundation or of recognition as a full college; for permanent private halls the date of foundation is given.

mertown, and Wolvercote, which form a popular residential district, to the north.

Schools

There are several well-known schools in Oxford. Magdalen College School was founded in 1480 by William of Waynflete for instruction in grammar; the college choristers, not originally members of the school, have since 1849 been boarded in the master's house at the expense of the college. St Edward's School, founded in 1863, was originally in New Inn Hall Street, being moved to Summertown in 1873. Others schools include Headington School, Milham Ford School, and Oxford High School for Girls.

Oxford and Asquith, Earl of

Title of British Liberal politician Herbert Henry ◊Asquith.

Oxford English Dictionary, The, OED

Multi-volume English ◊dictionary, which provides a detailed historical record of each word, with usage and senses illustrated by quotations. It is subject to continuous revision (and now computerization). Originally called the *New English Dictionary on Historical Principles*, it was first conceived by the Philological Society in 1858. The first part appeared in 1884 under the editorship of James ◊Murray and the final volume appeared in 1928.

Oxford Movement, also known as Tractarian Movement or Catholic Revival

Movement that attempted to revive Catholic religion in the Church of England. Cardinal Newman dated the movement from ◊Keble's sermon in Oxford in 1833. The Oxford Movement by the turn of the century had transformed the Anglican communion, and survives today as Anglo-Catholicism.

Oxfordshire

County of south central England

Area 2,610 sq km/1,007 sq mi

Towns and cities ◊Oxford (administrative headquarters), Abingdon, Banbury, Goring, Henley-on-Thames, Wallingford, Witney, Woodstock, Wantage, Chipping Norton, Thame

Physical River Thames and tributaries (the Cherwell, Evenlode, Ock, Thame, and Windrush); Cotswold Hills (in the north) and Chiltern Hills (in the southeast)

Features Vale of the White Horse (with a chalk hill figure 114 m/374 ft, below the hill camp known as Uffington Castle); Oxford University; Blenheim Palace (a World Heritage site), Woodstock (started in 1705 by Vanbrugh with help from Nicholas Hawksmoor, completed in 1722), with landscaped grounds by Capability ◊Brown; early 14th-century Broughton Castle; Rousham Park (1635), remodelled by William ◊Kent (1738–40), with landscaped garden; Ditchley Park, designed by James Gibbs in 1720; Europe's major fusion project JET (Joint European Torus) at the UK Atomic Energy Authority's fusion laboratories at Culham; the Manor House, Kelmscott (country house of William Morris, leader of the Arts and Crafts movement); Henley Regatta

Agriculture cereals, sheep, dairy farming

Industries agricultural implements (at Banbury); aluminium (at Banbury); bricks; cars (Cowley); cement; iron ore (in the north); high technology industries; medical electronic equipment; paper; publishing; nuclear research (Harwell); biotechnology

Population (1994) 590,200

Famous people William Davenant, Flora Thompson, Winston Churchill, William Morris

History Oxford was the chief stronghold of the Royalists during the Civil War (1642–46), and was the scene of many battles.

Topography

Oxfordshire is bounded to the south by Swindon, West Berkshire, Reading, and Wokingham, to the east by Buckinghamshire, to the northeast by Northamptonshire, to the northwest by Warwickshire, and to the west by Gloucestershire. The county was considerably increased in size by transfers from Berkshire (as it then was) at the time of local government reorganization in April 1974.

Historic remains

There are several prehistoric remains in Oxfordshire, including the Rollright stones, and the Devil's Quoits. There are also several Roman villas, such as North Leigh. Few old monastic buildings or castles remain, the most important being the abbey church at Dorchester-on-Thames, and the castles at Shirburn and Broughton, near Banbury. There are remains of famous houses at Greys Court, Minster Lovell, and Rycote. Churches of note include those in Oxford itself, and those at Adderbury, Iffley, and Minster Lovell.

Oxford Street

A main road in central London; one of London's principal shopping thoroughfares, containing department stores as Selfridges and John Lewis. It forms the boundary between the City of Westminster and the former borough of St Marylebone. It is crossed halfway along its length by Regent Street. Oxford Street follows the site of a Roman road that ran from London to Silchester.

The Pantheon, a fashionable entertainment centre, stood near the eastern end of the street from 1772 until 1867. The eastern extension, known as New Oxford Street, was added in 1847.

The street has been known at different times as 'the way from Uxbridge', 'the road to Oxford', and 'Tyburn road' (as it led to the gallows at ◊Tyburn). It was eventually named after Edward Harley, 2nd Earl of Oxford, who married the daughter of the Duke of Newcastle, who owned land in St Marylebone.

Oxford University

Oldest British university, established during the 12th century, the earliest existing college being founded in 1249. After suffering from land confiscation during the Reformation, it was reorganized by Elizabeth I in 1571. In 1996–97 there were 15,641 undergraduates in residence. All colleges, with the exception of St Hilda's (women only), are now coeducational. See table opposite.

Besides the colleges, notable academic buildings are the Bodleian Library (including the New Bodleian, opened in 1946, with a capacity of 5 million books), the Divinity School, the Radcliffe Camera, and the Sheldonian Theatre.

Packwood House

Mid-16th-century timber-framed house with 17th-century additions in Warwickshire, England, 8 km/5 mi southeast of Solihull. Packwood was given to the National Trust in 1941 and contains collections of tapestries, needlework, and furniture.

The yew topiary in the garden was designed by John Fetherston in the 17th century to represent the Sermon on the Mount.

Paddington Bear

Bear who features in a series of children's stories by English writer Michael Bond (1926–), beginning with *A Bear called Paddington* (1958). The bear is found abandoned on Paddington Station in London by the Brown family, who adopt him; he likes marmalade sandwiches and customarily wears a hat, duffel coat, and Wellington boots.

Page, Frederick Handley (1885–1962)

English aeronautical engineer, see ◊Handley Page.

Paget, James (1814–1899)

English surgeon, one of the founders of pathology. He described two conditions now named after him: Paget's disease of the nipple and Paget's disease of the bone. Baronet 1871.

Paget was born in Great Yarmouth, Norfolk, and studied at St Bartholomew's Hospital in London. He was one of the original 300 fellows of the Royal College of Surgeons of England in 1843, and was professor there 1847–52. Having tended the Princess of Wales in 1878, he was appointed surgeon extraordinary to Queen Victoria.

Paige, Elaine born Elaine Bickerstaff (1948–)

English actress and singer. She made her West End début in *Hair* (1969), followed by the roles of Eva Perón in *Evita* (1978), Grizabella in *Cats* (1981), and Edith Piaf in *Piaf* (1993). She was the Variety Club Showbusiness Personality of the Year 1978, and was awarded the OBE in 1995.

Paine, Thomas (1737–1809)

English left-wing political writer. He was active in the American and French revolutions. His pamphlet *Common Sense* (1776) ignited passions in the American Revolution; others include *The Rights of Man* (1791) and *The Age of Reason* (1793). He advocated republicanism, deism, the abolition of slavery, and the emancipation of women.

Paine, born in Thetford, Norfolk, was a friend of US

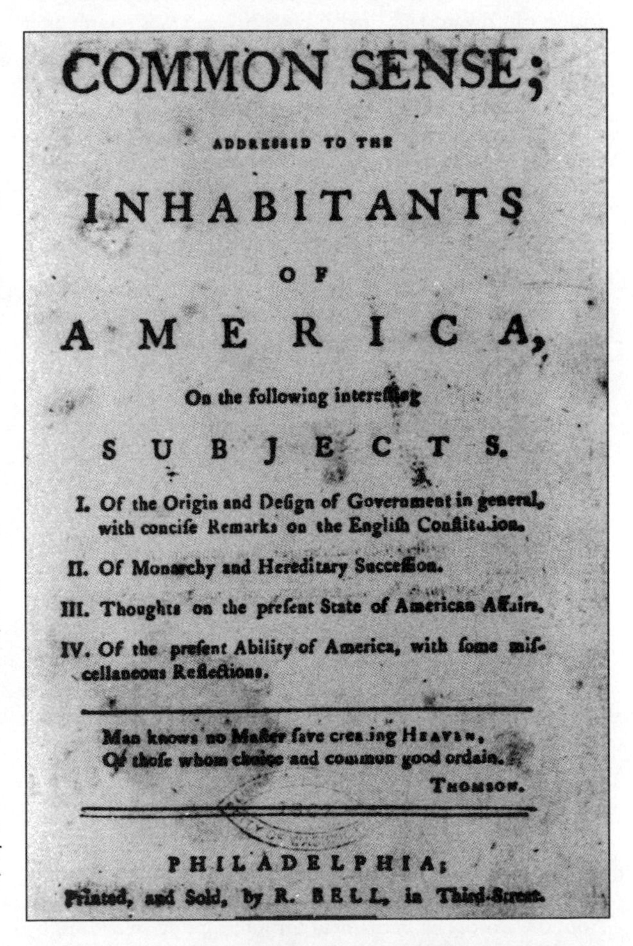

COMMON SENSE;

ADDRESSED TO THE

INHABITANTS

OF

AMERICA,

On the following interesting

SUBJECTS.

I. Of the Origin and Deſign of Government in general, with conciſe Remarks on the Engliſh Conſtitution.

II. Of Monarchy and Hereditary Succeſſion.

III. Thoughts on the preſent State of American Affairs.

IV. Of the preſent Ability of America, with ſome miſcellaneous Reflections.

Man knows no Maſter ſave creating HEAVEN,
Or thoſe whom choice and common good ordain.
THOMSON.

PHILADELPHIA;
Printed, and Sold, by R. BELL, in Third-Street.

PAINE, THOMAS *The title page of Thomas Paine's pamphlet* Common Sense. *Written in America in 1776, it advocated independence and resistance to Britain and encouraged the American Revolution. Corbis*

scientist and politician Benjamin Franklin and went to America in 1774, where he published several republican pamphlets and fought for the colonists in the revolution. In 1787 he returned to Britain. *The Rights of Man* is an answer to the conservative theorist Burke's *Reflections on the Revolution in France*. In 1792, Paine was indicted for treason and escaped to France, to represent Calais in the National Convention. Narrowly escaping the guillotine, he regained his seat after the fall of Robespierre. Paine returned to the USA in 1802 and died in New York.

Paisley (Roman Vanduara)

Administrative headquarters of ◊Renfrewshire, Scotland, part of the Clydeside urban area, on the banks of the White Cart Water, 11 km/7 mi southwest of Glasgow; population (1991) 75,500. It is the largest town in Scotland. Industries include textiles and pharmaceuticals. It was an important centre for the manufacture of textiles, especially the woollen Paisley shawl, with a pattern based on the shape of a palm shoot.

The Paisley Museum and Art Gallery includes a collection of shawls. The 12th-century abbey was destroyed on the orders of Edward I of England in 1307, but was rebuilt after the Battle of Bannockburn in 1314.

A 15th-century decorated nave is almost all that remains of the old abbey, which has since served as a parish church. It was founded in 1163 by Walter Fitzalan as a Cluniac monastery, but was damaged during the Reformation. Paisley has a 16th-century grammar school and a university.

In the early 18th century the town was already noted for its manufacture of shawls, silk gauze, muslin, and linen. Near the town is Glasgow airport (Abbotsinch).

Paisley, Ian (Richard Kyle) (1926–)

Northern Ireland politician, cleric, and leader of the Democratic Unionist Party (DUP) from 1971. An imposing and deeply influential member of the Protestant community, he is staunchly committed to the union with the UK and opposed to the Good Friday Agreement. His political career has been one of high drama, marked by protests, resignations, fierce oratory, and a pugnacious and forthright manner.

Paisley was influential in the actions of the Ulster Workers' Council and their general strike which destroyed the Sunningdale Power Sharing Initiative in 1974. Paisley's powerful speeches and image of strength won him great support within the Protestant community and he scored overwhelming victories in both the 1979 and 1984 European elections, polling around one-third of the first-preference votes each time.

Throughout the 1980s, Paisley stuck rigidly to his 'no surrender' policies, resigning his seat in 1985 in protest at the Anglo-Irish Agreement. He re-entered Parliament early the following year. His Presbyterian beliefs are inextricably bound up with his political aims, and in 1988 he was ejected from the European Parliament for interrupting an address by Pope John Paul II. Paisley has been deeply sceptical of the various initiatives to solve the problems of Northern Ireland, particularly those involving any 'sellout', in his view, to the Dublin government or Sinn Féin and the Irish Republican Army (IRA).

He has opposed the 1998 Good Friday Agreement on power-sharing in Northern Ireland and in the May 1998 referendum his North Antrim constituency was the only one of Northern Ireland's 18 seats in which there was a majority against the accord. He now leads the opposition to the agreement with the new Northern Ireland Assembly.

Paley, William (1743–1805)

English Christian theologian and philosopher. He put forward the argument for design theory, which reasons that the complexity of the universe necessitates a superhuman creator and that the existence of this being (God) can be deduced from a 'design' seen in all living creatures. His views were widely held until challenged by Charles ◊Darwin.

His major treatises include *The Principles of Moral and Political Philosophy* (1785), *A View of the Evidences of Christianity* (1794), and *Natural Theology* (1802).

Palladian

Style of revivalist architecture influenced by the work of the Italian Renaissance architect Andrea Palladio. Inigo Jones introduced Palladianism to England with his Queen's House, Greenwich (1616–35), but the true Palladian revival began in the early 18th century when Richard Boyle ◊Burlington and Colen ◊Campbell 'rediscovered' the Palladio–Jones link. Campbell's Mereworth Castle, Kent (1722–25), is an example of the style.

Pall Mall

Main road in London, running from the southern end of St James's Street to the southern end of Haymarket. It is a centre of social clubs, including the Athenaeum, the Reform, the Travellers, and the Royal Automobile Club. The street derives its name from the French game of *paille maille* (from which croquet is believed to have developed), played here at least as early as 1635, when Pall Mall was part of St James's Park. The game was discontinued during the rule of Oliver Cromwell, and there was a considerable increase of building in the area.

The original name of Pall Mall was 'The Mall'. Pall Mall was the first London street lit by gas, in 1807.

Former inhabitants of Pall Mall include the actress (and mistress of Charles II) Nell Gwyn, the 1st Duke of Marlborough, the historian Edward Gibbon, and the painter Thomas Gainsborough.

Palmer, Samuel (1805–1881)

English landscape painter and etcher. He was largely self-taught as an artist, though given some instruction by John Linnell, whose daughter he married. His early works, small pastoral scenes mostly painted in watercolour and sepia, have an intense, visionary quality, greatly influenced by a meeting with the aged William Blake, and the latter's engravings for Thornton's *Virgil*. From 1826 to 1835 he lived in Shoreham, Kent, with a group of artists who followed Blake, styling themselves 'the Ancients'.

His works from this period, now highly regarded, have had a distinct influence on the imaginative treatment of landscape in modern English art, and fine examples may be found in the Tate Gallery and the Victoria and Albert Museum, London, and the Ashmolean Museum, Oxford.

Palmerston, Henry John Temple, 3rd Viscount Palmerston (1784–1865)

British politician. He was prime minister 1855–58 (when he rectified Aberdeen's mismanagement of the Crimean War, suppressed the ◊Indian Mutiny, and carried through the Second Opium War) and 1859–65 (when he almost involved Britain in the American Civil War on the side of the South). Initially a Tory, in Parliament from 1807, he was secretary-at-war 1809–28. He broke with the Tories in 1830 and sat in the Whig cabinets of 1830–34, 1835–41, and 1846–51 as foreign secretary.

Palmerston succeeded to an Irish peerage in 1802. He served under five Tory prime ministers before joining the Whigs. His foreign policy was marked by distrust of France and Russia, against whose designs he backed the independence of Belgium and Turkey. He became home secretary in the coalition government of 1852, and prime minister on its fall, and was responsible for the warship *Alabama* going to the Confederate side in the American Civil War. He was popular with the people and made good use of the press, but his high-handed attitude annoyed Queen Victoria and other ministers.

Palumbo, Peter Garth (1935–)

English property developer. As chair of the Arts Council from 1989 to 1994, he advocated a close partnership between public and private funding of the arts, and a greater role for the regions.

His planned skyscraper by the German architect Ludwig Mies van der Rohe beside the Mansion House, London, was condemned by Prince Charles as 'a giant glass stump'.

pamphlet

Small unbound booklet or leaflet, used to spread information and opinion. In 16th century the pamphlet became the principal means of stimulating public debate on a wide range of political, religious, and cultural issues. It remained an effective method of widespread communication until the advent of mass media.

As in continental Europe, the first pamphlets in Britain concerned religious and constitutional matters; among these was the Scots Presbyterian John Knox's *First Blast of the Trumpet Against the Monstrous Regiment of Women* (1558). Political pamphlets and news-sheets made their first appearance in England in the 17th century, multiplying rapidly during the Civil War, when leading Puritans such as John Milton used them to expound their views. In the early 18th century, a period that the lexicographer Samuel Johnson dubbed 'the age of pamphlets', writers such as Joseph ◊Addison, Richard ◊Steele, and Jonathan ◊Swift produced numerous pamphlets. The form continued throughout the 19th century in Britain, until the rise of national newspapers signalled the demise of the political pamphlet.

Pankhurst, Emmeline born Goulden (1858–1928)

English ◊suffragette. Founder of the Women's Social and Political Union (WSPU) in 1903, she launched the militant suffragette campaign in 1905. In 1926 she joined the Conservative Party and was a prospective Parliamentary candidate.

In 1879 she married **Richard Marsden Pankhurst** (died 1898), a lawyer, and they served together on the committee that promoted the Married Women's Property Act. From 1906, as a militant, she was frequently arrested and in 1913 was sentenced to three years' penal servitude in connection with the blowing up of Lloyd George's house at Walton.

She was supported by her daughters **Christabel Pankhurst** (1880–1958), political leader of the movement, and **Sylvia Pankhurst** (1882–1960). The latter was imprisoned nine times under the 'Cat and Mouse Act', and was a pacifist in World War I.

> *We women suffragists have a great mission – the greatest mission the world has ever known. It is to free half the human race, and through that freedom save the rest.*
>
> EMMELINE PANKHURST English women's rights campaigner.
> Speech, published in *Votes for Women* 25 October 1912

pantomime

In the British theatre, a traditional Christmas entertainment. It has its origins in the harlequin spectacle of the 18th century and burlesque of the 19th century, which gave rise to the tradition of the principal boy being played by an actress and the dame by an actor. The harlequin's role diminished altogether as themes developed on folk tales such as 'The Sleeping Beauty' and 'Cinderella', and with the introduction of additional material such as popular songs, topical comedy, and audience participation. Popular television stars regularly feature in modern pantomime

After World War II, pantomimes on ice became popular. The term 'pantomime' was also applied to Roman dumbshows performed by a masked actor, to 18th-century ballets with mythical themes, and, in 19th-century France, to the wordless Pierrot plays from which modern mime developed.

Panufnik, Andrzej (1914–1991)

Polish-born composer and conductor. His music is based on the dramatic interplay of symbolic motifs. His works include *Mistica* (1977), *Votiva* (1981), no. 9, and *Sinfonia di Speranza* (1986).

Paolozzi, Eduardo Luigi (1924–)

Scottish sculptor and graphic artist. He was an important figure in the Pop-art movement in London in the 1950s and

1960s. During the 1940s he produced collages using images taken from popular magazines. From the 1950s he worked primarily as a sculptor, typically using bronze casts of machinery to create sinister, robotlike figures, such as *Cyclops* (1957; Tate Gallery, London). From the 1960s his work became more abstract and lighter in mood.

The mural decorations for Tottenham Court Road tube station, London (installed 1983–85), and a huge bronze *The Wealth of Nations* (1993; Royal Bank of Scotland, Edinburgh) are among his many public commissions. He was knighted in 1989.

Paradise Lost

Epic poem in 12 books, by John ⇨Milton, first published in 1667. The poem describes the Fall of Man and the battle between God and Satan, as enacted through the story of Adam and Eve in the Garden of Eden. A sequel, *Paradise Regained*, was published in 1671 and relates the temptation of Christ in the wilderness.

> *There's no other country in the world where you have pantomime with men dressed as women and women dressed as men and everyone thinks this is perfectly suitable entertainment for children.*
>
> Angela Carter English writer. Interviewed in *New Writing* (1992)

Parcelforce

Department of the Post Office that handles the collection and delivery of parcels. It handles over 140 million items a year.

pargeting

Fine, relief-patterned plasterwork used for the external decoration of timber-framed buildings. Originating in the Elizabethan period, it is commonly found on 16th- and 17th-century buildings in East Anglia. The design was modelled on wet plaster and then colour-washed.

Paris, Matthew (*c.* 1200–1259)

English chronicler. He entered St Albans Abbey in 1217, and wrote a valuable history of England up to 1259.

parish

A subdivision of a county often coinciding with an original territorial subdivision in Christian church administration, served by a parish church. The origins of the parish lie in early medieval Italian cities, and by the 12th century, most of Christian Europe was divided into parishes. The parish has frequently been the centre of community life, especially in rural areas.

parish council

Lowest, neighbourhood, unit of local government in England and Wales, based on church parishes. They developed as units for local government with the introduction of the Poor Law in the 17th century. In Wales and Scotland they are commonly called **community councils**. In England approximately 8,200 out of the 10,000 parishes have elected councils. There are 730 community councils in Wales and about 1,000 in Scotland, which, unlike their English and Welsh counterparts, do not have statutory powers.

Parish councils provide and maintain monuments, playing fields, footpaths, and churchyards, administer local charities, may impose a limited local rate, are elected every four years, and function in parishes of 200 or more electors. Parish councils were established by the Local Government Act 1894, but most of their legal powers were abolished by the 1972 Local Government Act.

Park, Merle Florence (1937–)

Rhodesian-born English ballerina. She joined the Sadler's Wells Ballet in 1954, and by 1959 was a principal soloist with the Royal Ballet. She combined elegance with sympathetic appeal in such roles as Cinderella. She became director of the Royal Ballet School in 1986 and was created a DBE in the same year.

Park, Mungo (1771–1806)

Scottish explorer who traced the course of the Niger River 1795–97. He disappeared and probably drowned during a second African expedition 1805–06. He published *Travels in the Interior of Africa* (1799).

Park spent 18 months in the Niger Basin while tracing the river. Even though he did not achieve his goal of reaching Timbuktu, he proved that it was feasible to travel through the interior of Africa.

Park, Nick (1958–)

English animator, specializing in stop-motion animation using clay figures. His creation of the much-loved characters ⇨Wallace and Gromit earned him international fame. He met with early success with his first two shorts, *A Grand Day Out* (1989) – the first to star Wallace and his faithful canine side-kick Gromit – and *Creature Comforts* (1990), for which he won an Academy Award. The next two Wallace and Gromit instalments, *The Wrong Trousers* (1993) and *A Close Shave* (1995), both earned him further Academy Awards.

Park lights and photographs his films as if they were real action features and he mixes genres (slapstick, soap opera, *film noir*, science fiction) to immense comic effect. Every film is packed with a wealth of often humorous detail especially in the props and decor.

Parker, Alan (1944–)

English film writer and director. After starting his career in the advertising industry, Parker broke into feature films with the children's gangster musical *Bugsy Malone* (1976). In an eclectic career which has seen him flit from musicals to political thrillers, dramas to comedies, and work on both sides of the Atlantic, Parker has turned out a series of popular successes. These include *Midnight Express* (1978) and the screen adaptations *Birdy* (1984), *Angel Heart* (1987), *The Commitments* (1991), a Dublin-set tale of aspiring musicians based on

PARK, NICK *As a founder of the company Aardman Animations, Nick Park won acclaim, including three Oscars, for his claymation films featuring the characters Wallace and Gromit. In* The Wrong Trousers *(1993), Wallace's invention of a pair of automated trousers for walking his dog Gromit goes disastrously wrong. Ronald Grant*

Roddy Doyle's novel, and *Evita* (1996), based on Andrew Lloyd-Webber's stage musical.

He is currently chairman of the British Film Institute (1998).

Parkinson, Cecil (Edward) (1931–)
British Conservative politician, chairman of the Conservative Party (1981–83 and 1997–). He was a minister for trade and industry, but resigned in October 1984 following disclosure of an affair with his secretary. In 1987 he rejoined the cabinet as secretary of state for energy, and in 1989 became transport secretary. He left the cabinet when John Major became prime minister in 1990 and later announced his intention to retire from active politics and enter business. He received a life peerage in 1992.

In 1997 at the request of the new Conservative Party leader, William Hague, he returned to politics as a senior statesman.

Parkinson, Cyril Northcote (1909–1993)
English writer and historian, celebrated for his study of public and business administration, *Parkinson's Law* (1958), which included the dictum: 'Work expands to fill the time available for its completion.'

Parkinson, James (1755–1824)
British neurologist who in 1817 gave the first description of paralysis agitans, or Parkinson's disease.

Parkinson, Norman adopted name of Ronald William Smith (1913–1990)
English fashion and portrait photographer. He caught the essential glamour of each decade from the 1930s to the 1980s. Long associated with the magazines *Vogue* and *Queen*, he was best known for his colour work, and from the late 1960s took many official portraits of the royal family.

Parkinson's law
Formula invented by the English political analyst Cecil Northcote Parkinson (1909–1993), which states that 'work expands so as to fill the time available for its completion'.

Parliament (French 'speaking')
The supreme legislature, meeting in the Palace of Westminster, comprising the House of ◊Commons and the House of

Parliamentary Glossary

Term	Description
Abstention	refusal by an MP to vote for or against a motion
Act of Parliament	bill passed by the Houses of Parliament (Commons and Lords) and signed by the Queen
Address	formal message to the Crown, presented to the Monarch by a Commons whip when the House of Commons wishes to make a point to the Monarch; the message is answered by the Monarch and returned to the Commons by a whip or to the Lords by the Lord Chamberlain
Adjournment of the House	request by an MP in the House of Commons to terminate the days proceedings
Admonition	reprimand to an MP who has done something wrong, made by the Speaker of the House of Commons
Amendment	alteration proposed in a motion or a bill; amendments can be voted on in order to change what is written in a bill
Back Bencher	MP who does not hold office in the Government, or any senior position on the leading opposition party
Ballot	paper on which an MP registers their vote in matters requiring the use of ballots to decide issues in Parliament
Bar of the House	marked by a leather strip, the Bar of the House is the line at the entrance to the House of Commons which non-MPs must not cross
Bill	draft of an Act of Parliament, presented to either the House of Commons or the House of Lords to vote on. If successful, the bill is forwarded for Royal Assent; if granted, it becomes an Act
Black Rod	officer of the Royal Household who looks after the doorkeepers and messengers of the House of Lords; Black Rod also issues the orders for entry into the Stranger's Gallery
Budget	annual financial statement of the Chancellor of the Exchequer
By-election	election to fill a vacancy in a constituency that arises during the course of a Parliament, usually as a result of the death or resignation of an MP
Catching the Speaker's Eye	any MP who wishes to speak in the Houses of Commons must stand and wait for the Speaker to see them and give them permission to speak
Clause	subdivision of an Act or Bill
Count	if there are less that 40 MPs present in the House of Commons, the Speaker can close the House
Crossing the floor	changing allegiance from one political party to another is signified by 'crossing the floor' of the House and taking a seat with an opposing party
Dissolution	bringing to an end the Parliament of the Houses of Commons and Lords by the Monarch; it is followed by a general election
Father of the House	longest serving MP in the House of Commons, currently Sir Edward Heath
Front Benches	benches where members of the Government and senior opposition members sit in the House of Commons; nearest to the centre of the Table of the Commons
Galleries	areas in the House of Commons set aside for the public and press to attend sittings
General election	election of a new government by all eligible voters in the country following the dissolution of Parliament
Government bill	bill introduced by a Government Minister
Hansard	House of Commons' written reports
Houses of Parliament	Palace housing the House of Commons and the House of Lords
Independent Member	elected MP who is not a member of any recognized political party. MPs can also leave or be expelled by a political party during a Parliament and sit as independents
Maiden speech	first speech in the House of Commons by a new member; traditionally, a new MP standing will be given preference over others by the Speaker
Majority government	government formed by the party with the majority of seats in the House of Commons

Term	Description
Minority government	government formed by a party that does not hold a majority of seats; it must maintain the confidence of the House in order to remain in government
Oath of allegiance	oath of loyalty to the Sovereign that must be made by an MP before they can take their seat in the House of Commons
Order Paper	daily timetable of events in the House of Commons and the House of Lords
Pairs	if an MP does not wish to vote in the Chamber, they have to come to an arrangement with an opposition MP who will not vote either. The overall vote is then reduced by one on each side
Parliamentary procedure	rules by which the House of Commons and the House of Lords conduct their business
Passage of a bill	process by which a bill obtains Parliamentary approval and becomes law. Once Parliamentary approval has been granted, the bill is forwarded to the Monarch for Royal assent
Point of order	technical or procedural breach of order can be brought to the attention of the Speaker by an MP at any time during a debate or as House business is being conducted; the Speaker decides on the validity of the matter raised and his/her decision is final
Portfolio	responsibilities of a Cabinet minister
Question Time	time when government ministers have to answer questions put by members of the House of Commons and the House of Lords. Prime Ministers' questions are on Wednesdays; other days are rotated among other government departments
Recess	period between the end of one Parliament and the start of another
Royal Assent	approval by the Monarch of a bill passed by the House of Commons and the House of Lords, making it an Act of Parliament
Teller	appointed by the Speaker to count the number of ayes and noes in a vote
Ten-Minute Rule	MPs are given ten minutes in which to make their comments or statements. The Speaker keeps time and ends the session at the end of the ten minutes
Whip	member who makes sure that fellow party members vote according to party wishes; they are paid a higher salary than normal back-bench MPs

◊Lords. The origins of Parliament are in the 13th century, but its powers were not established until the late 17th century. The powers of the Lords were curtailed in 1911, and the duration of parliaments was fixed at five years, but any parliament may extend its own life, as happened during both world wars. See Parliamentary glossary table above, and chronology of Parliamentary reform on page 688. See also ◊constitution.

History

Parliament originated under the Norman kings as the Great Council of royal tenants-in-chief, to which in the 13th century representatives of the shires were sometimes summoned. The Parliament summoned by Simon de Montfort in 1265 (as head of government in the Barons' War) set a precedent by including representatives of the boroughs as well as the shires. Under Edward III the burgesses and knights of the shires began to meet separately from the barons, thus forming the House of Commons.

By the 15th century Parliament had acquired the right to legislate, vote, and appropriate supplies, examine public accounts, and impeach royal ministers. The powers of Parliament were much diminished under the Yorkists and Tudors but under Elizabeth I a new spirit of independence appeared. The revolutions of 1640 and 1688 established parliamentary control over the executive and judiciary, and finally abolished all royal claim to tax or legislate without parliamentary consent. During these struggles the two great parties (Whig and Tory) emerged, and after 1688 it became customary for the sovereign to choose ministers from the party dominant in the Commons. The English Parliament was united with the Scottish in 1707, and with the Irish 1801–1922. The ◊franchise was extended to the middle classes in 1832, to the urban working classes in 1867, to agricultural labourers in 1884, and to women in 1918 and 1928. The duration of parliaments was fixed at three years in 1694, at seven in 1716, and at five in 1911. Payment of MPs was introduced in 1911. A **public bill** that has been passed is an ◊act of Parliament.

Parliament Act 1911

Statute severely curtailing the power of the House of Lords and asserting the primacy of the House of Commons. The law, introduced after the Lords rejected Lloyd George's radical People's Budget of 1909, prohibited the Lords from interfering with financial legislation and abolished their power to reject other types of legislation passed by the Commons, restricting them to delaying it for up to two years. The law also reduced the maximum life of a parliament from seven years to five.

CHRONOLOGY OF PARLIAMENTARY REFORM

1822 Lord John Russell proposed a redistribution of seats. Whig Party espoused cause of reform.

1830 Duke of Wellington resigned as prime minister, bringing in Whig ministry under Lord Grey, committed to reform. (Electorate 516,000 = 2% of population.)

1832 Reform Act involved redistribution of parliamentary seats from 'rotten boroughs' to urban constituencies. Franchise extended to householders paying £10 per year rent in towns and 40-shilling freeholders in counties. (Electorate 813,000 = 3% of population.)

1867 Reform Act involved further redistribution of seats and extension of franchise to all ratepayers in boroughs. (Electorate 2,500,000 = 8% of population.)

1872 Ballot Act introduced secret ballots for elections.

1883 Corrupt and Illegal Practices Act set limits to election expenses.

1884 Reform Act again involved redistribution of seats and equalization of franchise for boroughs and counties, to include all householders and ratepayers. (Electorate 5,600,000 = 16% of population.)

1885 Further redistribution of parliamentary seats.

1918 Representation of the People Act gave the vote to all men over 21 and all women ratepayers (or wives of ratepayers) over 30.

1928 Representation of the People (Equal Franchise) Act gave the vote to all women over 21.

1948 Plural voting abolished. Permanent Boundary Commission established.

1971 Voting age reduced to 18.

1979 Constituencies established for direct election to European Parliament in Strasbourg.

1983 Number of parliamentary seats raised from 635 to 650.

1985 Representation of the People Act gave the vote to British citizens living abroad for a period of five years after they have left Britain.

1989 Representation of the People Act extended the period during which British citizens abroad may vote to 20 years after leaving Britain. Live televising of House of Commons proceedings approved.

1992 Number of parliamentary seats raised from 650 to 651.

1994 Number of UK seats in European parliament raised from 81 to 87.

1998 Jenkins report on proportional representation.

parliamentary agents

People who act on behalf of those promoting or petitioning against private bills in Parliament. The parliamentary agents perform the useful function of examining bills on behalf of those affected who have neither the skill nor the time to do it themselves. Many organizations, such as the major industrial associations and associations of employees, employ parliamentary agents to watch their interests.

parliamentary paper

An official document, such as a White Paper or a report of a select committee, which is prepared for the information of members of Parliament.

parliamentary reform acts

UK acts of Parliament 1918, 1928, and 1971. The 19th century witnessed the gradual reform of the voting system in Britain and suffrage was extended in the 20th century. In 1918 the Representation of the People Act gave the vote in the UK to men over 21 years and to women over 30. In 1928 a further act gave women the vote from the age of 21. In 1971 the voting age for men and women was lowered to the age of 18. See above for a chronology of parliamentary reform; see also ◊Reform Acts, with a feature on 19th-century reform.

parliamentary sovereignty, or parliamentary supremacy

Doctrine defined by A V Dicey (1835–1922), in his book *Law of the Constitution* (1885), as the doctrine that Parliament has 'the right to make or unmake any law whatever . . . and . . . no person or body is recognised by the Law of England as having the right to override or set aside the legislation of Parliament'.

Parliament in this context consists of the sovereign, the House of Lords, and the House of Commons. Any act of Parliament properly passed by both Houses of Parliament (or by the House of Commons under the terms of the Parliament Acts 1911 and 1949), and which receives ◊royal assent, is legally binding on all people and property which comes within the jurisdiction of the UK.

The UK's closer integration within the European Union has meant that, during recent decades, there has been some cession of parliamentary sovereignty, as EU regulations, policed by the European Court of Justice, take precedence over national laws. Further sovereignty has been ceded since 1997 by the new Labour government, which has given the Bank of England full control over the setting of interest rates and has devolved certain powers to new assemblies in Scotland, Wales, and Northern Ireland.

Parliament, Houses of

Building where the legislative assembly meets. The present Houses of Parliament in London, designed in Gothic Revival style by the architects Charles ◊Barry and A W N ◊Pugin, were built 1840–60, the previous building having burned down in 1834. It incorporates portions of the medieval Palace of Westminster.

The House of Commons debating chamber was destroyed by incendiary bombs in 1941: the rebuilt chamber (opened in 1950) is the work of architect Giles Gilbert ◊Scott and preserves its former character.

House of Lords
The thrones for the sovereign and consort, designed by Pugin, stand at its southern end, and in front of them is the Lord Chancellor's ◊woolsack. In front of the chancellor's woolsack are two other woolsacks on which the judges sit at the opening of Parliament. At the other end of the chamber is the bar, at which the members of the Commons attend to hear the speech from the throne at the opening of Parliament and to hear the royal assent to acts of Parliament. See ◊Lords, House of, for how the House operates.
House of Commons
The Speaker's chair is at the northern end. The benches on his or her right are occupied by the members of the party in power, those on the left by the party in opposition, the front benches being occupied by cabinet ministers and Opposition leaders respectively. In front of the Speaker's chair is the clerk's table, upon which the Mace (symbol of the Speaker's authority from the sovereign) is placed when the House sits as a house, but below which the Mace is put when the House goes into committee. Above are the public galleries. When the House is sitting a light shows at night from the clock tower. See ◊Commons, House of, for how the House operates.

Parnell, Charles Stewart (1846–1891)
Irish nationalist politician. He supported a policy of obstruction and violence to attain ◊Home Rule, and became the president of the Nationalist Party in 1877. In 1879 he approved the ◊Land League, and his attitude led to his imprisonment in 1881. His career was ruined in 1890 when he was cited as co-respondent in a divorce case.

Parnell, born in County Wicklow, was elected member of Parliament for Meath in 1875. He welcomed Gladstone's Home Rule Bill, and continued his agitation after its defeat in 1886. In 1887 his reputation suffered from an unfounded accusation by *The Times* of complicity in the murder of Lord Frederick ◊Cavendish, chief secretary to the Lord Lieutenant of Ireland. Three years later came the adultery scandal, and for fear of losing the support of Gladstone, Parnell's party deposed him. He died suddenly of rheumatic fever at the age of 45.

No man has a right to fix the boundary of the march of a nation; no man has a right to say to his country – thus far shalt thou go and no further.

Charles Stewart Parnell Irish politician.
Speech in Cork 1885

Parr, Catherine (1512–1548)
Sixth wife of Henry VIII of England. She had already lost two husbands when in 1543 she married Henry. She survived him, and in 1547 married the Lord High Admiral Thomas Seymour of Sudeley (1508–1549).

Parry, (Charles) Hubert (Hastings) (1848–1918)
English composer. His works include songs, motets, and the setting of Milton's 'Blest Pair of Sirens' and Blake's 'Jerusalem'.

Parsons, Charles Algernon (1854–1931)
English engineer who invented the Parsons steam turbine in 1884, a landmark in marine engineering and later universally used in electricity generation to drive an alternator. He was created a KCB in 1911.

Parsons developed more efficient screw propellers for ships and suitable gearing to widen the turbine's usefulness, both on land and sea. He also designed searchlights and optical instruments, and developed methods for the production of optical glass.

Pasmore, (Edwin John) Victor (1908–1998)
English painter. In the 1930s he was a founder-member of the ◊Euston Road School, which favoured a subdued representational style. He painted landscapes and, from 1947, three-dimenstional abstract reliefs and constructions, reviving the early ideas of the Constructivists.

Even at its most severe, his work contained a romantic element which attracted a wider appreciation during the late 1950s and early 1960s than most similar art. He was awarded the CBE in 1959.

Passchendaele, Battle of
In World War I, successful but costly British operation to capture the Passchendaele ridge in western Flanders, part of the third battle of ◊Ypres October–November 1917; British casualties numbered nearly 400,000. The name is often erroneously applied to the whole of the Battle of Ypres, but Passchendaele was in fact just part of that battle.

The ridge, some 60 m/200 ft high, had been captured and fortified by the Germans in October 1914. It was a vital strategic gain as it gave them command of the Allied lines. Hence, its capture was an important target of the British strategy during the third battle of Ypres, despite the strong resistance offered by the German defenders. It was re-taken by the Germans in March 1918 and recovered again by the Belgians in October 1918.

Paston Letters
Correspondence of a Norfolk family, together with state papers and other documents, covering the period 1422–1509. They form an invaluable source of information on 15th-century life and manners, and on conditions during the Wars of the Roses, as well as giving vivid portraits of some members of the Paston family.

Pater, Walter Horatio (1839–1894)
English scholar, essayist, and art critic. He published *Studies in the History of the Renaissance* (1873), which expressed the idea of 'art for art's sake' that influenced the ◊Aesthetic Movement.

Paton, Joseph Noel (1821–1901)
Scottish painter. Taking his subjects largely from legend and history, he painted in a detailed style that was close to the

approach of the ⟩Pre-Raphaelite Brotherhood (⟩Millais was a lifelong friend). One of his most popular works was *The Fairy Raid* (1867; Glasgow City Art Gallery).

patronage

Power to give a favoured appointment to an office or position in politics, business, or the church; or sponsorship of the arts. Patronage was for centuries bestowed mainly by individuals (in Europe often royal or noble) or by the church. In the 20th century, patrons have tended to be political parties, the state, and – in the arts – private industry and foundations.

In Britain, where it was nicknamed 'Old Corruption', patronage existed in the 16th century, but was most common from the Restoration of 1660 to the 19th century, when it was used to manage elections and ensure party support. Patronage was used not only for the preferment of friends, but also as a means of social justice, often favouring, for example, the families of those in adversity. Political patronage has largely been replaced by a system of meritocracy (in which selection is by open competition rather than by personal recommendation).

Ecclesiastical patronage was the right of selecting a person to a living or benefice, termed an advowson.

Salaried patronage was the nomination to a salaried post: at court, in government, the Church of England, the civil service, the armed services, or to the East India Company. The Northcote-Trevelyan report of 1854 on the civil service advised the replacement of patronage in the civil service by open competitive examination, although its recommendations were carried out only later in the century. Commissions in the British army were bought and sold openly until the practice was abolished in 1871. Church livings were bought and sold as late as 1874.

Patronage survives today in the political honours system (awards granted to party supporters) and the appointment of university professors, leaders of national corporations, and government bodies or ⟩quangos, which is often by invitation rather than by formal application. Selection on grounds other than solely the basis of ability lives on today with the practice of positive discrimination.

Patten, Brian (1946–)

English poet. In the 1960s, with Roger ⟩McGough and Adrian ⟩Henri, he became known as one of the 'Liverpool Poets' who, strongly influenced by the pop culture of the period, promoted poetry as a performance art. A collection of their work appeared in *The Mersey Sound* (1967).

Patten, Chris(topher Francis) (1944–)

British Conservative politician, governor of Hong Kong 1992–97. He was Conservative Party chairman 1990–92, orchestrating the party's campaign for the 1992 general election, in which he lost his parliamentary seat. He accepted the governorship of Hong Kong for the crucial five years prior to its transfer to China in 1997. He is currently helping to oversee the reform of the Royal Ulster Constabulary.

As environment secretary 1989–90, he was responsible for administering the ⟩poll tax. As governor of Hong Kong, Patten's proposals for greater democracy – which resulted in the first fully democratic elections to legislative bodies in 1994 – were welcomed by Hong Kong's Legislative Council but strongly opposed by the Chinese government. His prodemocracy, anti-Chinese stance won the backing of many Hong Kong residents, but was criticized by members of its business community.

Patterson, Harry (1929–)

English novelist. He has written many thrillers under his own name, including *Dillinger* (1983), as well as under the pseudonym Jack Higgins, including *The Eagle Has Landed* (1975).

Pay-As-You-Earn, PAYE

System of tax collection in the UK in which income tax is deducted on a regular basis by the employer from wages before they are paid.

PAYE tax deductions are calculated so that when added up they will approximately equal the total amount of tax likely to be due in that year. Income tax is transferred to the Inland Revenue, reliefs due being notified to the employer by a code number for each employee. PAYE was introduced in Britain in 1944 to spread the tax burden over the year for the increasing number of wage earners becoming liable.

Paycocke's

Early 16th-century merchant's house in Essex, England, 13 km/8 mi west of Colchester. It is half-timbered, and remarkable for the richness of the panelling and wood-carving inside. Lord Noel-Buxton gave Paycocke's to the National Trust in 1924, and it is now furnished with 16th- and 17th-century furniture from the Grigsby Collection.

It is thought that John Paycocke (after whom the house was named) was, in addition to being a butcher, also a clothier. There was a flourishing cloth industry in the area at the time, and the Buxton family, who later owned the house, were also clothiers.

PAYE

Abbreviation for ⟩**Pay-As-You-Earn**.

paymaster-general

Head of the Paymaster-General's Office, the British government department (established in 1835) that acts as paying agent for most other departments.

The current paymaster-general, Geoffrey Robinson (1997–), played a key role in devising a 'windfall tax' on privatized utilities and a tax-free saving scheme for private investors.

Peacock, Thomas Love (1785–1866)

English satirical novelist and poet. His unique whimsical novels are full of paradox, prejudice, curious learning, and witty dialogue, interspersed with occasional poems, and he satirizes contemporary ideas, outlooks, and attitudes in a prevailing comic tone. They include *Headlong Hall* (1816), *Melincourt* (1817), and *Nightmare Abbey* (1818), which has very little plot, consisting almost entirely of conversation expressing points of view on contemporary controversies and society.

He published two romances, *Maid Marian* (1822) and *Misfortunes of Elphin* (1829), but returned to the form of *Headlong Hall* with his last and best novels, *Crotchet Castle* (1831) and *Gryll Grange* (1860).

Peak District

Elevated plateau of the south ◊Pennines in northwest Derbyshire, central England; area 1,438 sq km/555 sq mi. It is a tourist region and part of it forms a national park. The highest point is Kinder Scout (636 m/2,087 ft), part of High Peak. In the surrounding area the main cities are Manchester, Sheffield, and Derby, and the town of Bakewell is located within the Peak District.

The Peak District National Park, established in 1951, was Britain's first national park. Britain's first long-distance footpath, the Pennine Way (opened in 1965), traverses much of the region, from north to south. In addition to tourism, which includes rock climbing, exploring caverns, and grouse hunting, industries include sheep farming and mineral extraction. Limestone is quarried, particularly in the vicinity of Buxton, and the area also produces potters clay and Blue John (a type of fluorspar).

The Peak District covers the plateau north of Buxton. The rocks are formed of millstone grit and shale grit, underlain by limestone. The northern area, with underlying gritstone, is sometimes known as **Dark Peak**, while the southern part, predominantly limestone, is known as **White Peak**. High Peak is the highest elevation in the south Pennines; other peaks include Axe Edge (566 m/1,857 ft) and Mam Tor (518 m/1,699 ft), and approximately half of the **Derbyshire Dales** lie within the Peak District. The rivers Derwent, Dove, and Wye rise in the area. The village of Chapel-en-le-Frith is known as 'the capital of the Peak'. The Peak Cavern nearby goes 450 m/1,476 ft into the limestone. Rock-climbing edges are found at Laddow in the Woodhead valley, Stanage near Sheffield, Windgather, Castle Naze, Black Rocks, and Cratcliffe Tor.

Peake, Mervyn Laurence (1911–1968)

English writer and illustrator. His novels include the grotesque fantasy trilogy *Titus Groan* (1946), *Gormenghast* (1950), and *Titus Alone* (1959), together creating an allegory of the decline of modern civilization. He illustrated most of his own work and produced drawings for an edition of *Treasure Island* (1949), and other works. Among his collections of verse are *The Glassblowers* (1950) and the posthumous *A Book of Nonsense* (1972). He also wrote a play, *The Wit to Woo* (1957).

Pearsall, Robert (Lucas) (1795–1856)

English composer. He studied law and became a barrister in 1821, but had already composed. In 1825 he settled at Mainz, devoting himself entirely to music. Another year in England, 1829–30, was his last, except for visits.

Pearse, Patrick (Henry) (1879–1916)

Irish nationalist poet. He was prominent in the Gaelic revival, and a leader of the ◊Easter Rising in 1916. Proclaimed president of the provisional government, he was court-martialled and shot after its suppression.

Pearse was born in Dublin, and became a member of the Gaelic League. He founded St Enda's College in 1908, a school for boys; its teachings were based on Irish traditions and culture. In 1914 he became a member of the supreme council of the Irish Republican Brotherhood.

Pearson, Karl (1857–1936)

English statistician who followed Francis ◊Galton in introducing statistics and probability into genetics and who developed the concept of eugenics (improving the human race by selective breeding). He introduced the term standard deviation into statistics.

Peasants' Revolt

The rising of the English peasantry in June 1381, the result of economic, social, and political disillusionment. It was sparked off by the imposition of a new poll tax, three times the rates of those imposed in 1377 and 1379. Led by Wat ◊Tyler and John ◊Ball, rebels from southeast England marched on London and demanded reforms. The authorities put down the revolt by deceit and force.

Following the plague of the Black Death, a shortage of agricultural workers led to higher wages. The Statute of Labourers (1351), attempted to return wages to pre-plague levels. When the third poll tax was enforced in 1381, riots broke out all over England, especially in Essex and Kent. Wat Tyler and John Ball emerged as leaders and the rebels went on to London, where they continued plundering, burning John of Gaunt's palace at the Savoy, and taking the prisons at Newgate and Fleet. The young king Richard II attempted to appease the mob, who demanded an end to serfdom and feudalism. The rebels then took the Tower of London and murdered Archbishop Sudbury and Robert Hales. Again the king attempted to make peace at Smithfield, but Tyler was stabbed to death by William Walworth, the Lord Mayor of London. The king made concessions to the rebels, and they dispersed, but the concessions were revoked immediately.

Peebles

Wool town and former royal burgh in Scottish Borders unitary authority, Scotland, situated at the confluence of the rivers Eddleston and Tweed, 37 km/23 mi south of Edinburgh; population (1991) 7,100. Favoured by Scottish royalty, Peebles probably received its charter in 1367 from Alexander III, and later became the capital of the former county of Peeblesshire.

The massive ruined keep of the 14th-century Neidpath Castle lies about 2 km/1 mi to the west.

Peel

Fishing port in the Isle of Man, 19 km/12 mi northwest of Douglas. Peel Castle was the seat of the rulers of the Norse kingdom of Mann and the Isles in the 11th century.

Within the castle walls are the ruins of an 11th-century church and round tower, a Viking palace, and a 13th-century cathedral. A causeway links the town with St Patrick's Isle, where the castle stands.

Peel, John (1947–)

English disc jockey and broadcaster who has presented pop shows for BBC radio since the advent of its pop channel, Radio 1, in 1967. An enthusiast for new music, he has never settled into complacency and predictability, becoming something of a folk hero with a strong following for his weekend shows. In the 1990s he presented a BBC television documentary series about the traumas of moving house.

Peel, Robert (1788–1850)

British Conservative politician. As home secretary 1822–27 and 1828–30, he founded the modern police force and in 1829 introduced Roman Catholic emancipation. He was prime minister 1834–35 and 1841–46, when his repeal of the ◊Corn Laws caused him and his followers to break with the party.

Peel, born in Lancashire, entered Parliament as a Tory in 1809. After the passing of the Reform Bill of 1832, which he had resisted, he reformed the Tories under the name of the Conservative Party, on a basis of accepting necessary changes and seeking middle-class support. He fell from prime ministerial office because his repeal of the Corn Laws in 1846 was opposed by the majority of his party. He and his followers then formed a third party standing between the Liberals and Conservatives; the majority of the Peelites, including Gladstone, subsequently joined the Liberals.

PEEL, JOHN *Known for his laconic, wry style, the Liverpool-born disc jockey John Peel became a cult favourite in the 1970s and 1980s with listeners to Radio 1. Over the years, his late-night show premiered many new bands. From 1998, he hosted a talk show on Radio 4 on the foibles of family life,* Home Truths. *Rex Features*

peerage

The high ◊nobility; in the UK, holders, in descending order, of the titles of duke, marquess, earl, viscount, and baron. Most hereditary peerages pass on death to the nearest male relative, but some of these titles may be held by a woman in default of a male heir; no title can be passed on to the untitled husband of a woman peer. In the late 19th century the peerage was augmented by the Lords of Appeal in Ordinary (the nonhereditary life peers) and, from 1958, by a number of specially created life peers of either sex (usually long-standing members of the House of Commons). Since 1963 peers have been able to disclaim their titles, usually to enable them to take a seat in the Commons (where peers are disqualified from membership).

Unelected Irish peers and peeresses in their own right are members of the peerage but not 'Lords of Parliament'.

Medieval hereditary peerages were created by a writ of summons to Parliament, provided persons so summoned actually took their seats there. Today all peerages are created by letters patent, which specify the line of descent of the dignity, and the heir specified in the patent succeeds even if the grantee dies before taking his or her seat. Peeresses in their own right who marry commoners retain their titles, but peeresses by marriage lose their titles by remarriage.

Pelham, Henry (1696–1754)

English Whig politician. He held a succession of offices in Robert Walpole's cabinet 1721–42, and was prime minister 1743–54. His influence in the House of Commons was based on systematic corruption rather than ability. He concluded the War of the Austrian Succession and was an able financier.

Having held a number of posts in the Treasury, Pelham was appointed secretary for war in 1724, and in 1743 First Lord of the Treasury and chancellor of the Exchequer, despite the opposition of Walpole's successor John Carteret (1690–1763). Pelham's period in office was one of general pacification. Opposition (including that of King George II) was overcome, an alliance was forged with the Dutch in 1744, and then peace concluded with the French in the treaty of Aix-la-Chapelle in 1748. This having been established, Pelham devoted himself wholeheartedly to the reduction of national expenditure and the reorganization of the finances.

Pembroke, Welsh Penfro ('land's end')

Seaport and engineering centre in Pembrokeshire, southwest Wales; population (1991) 8,650. Henry VII was born in Pembroke Castle in 1457. Pembroke Dock was created in 1814 in conjunction with the Royal Navy dockyard, and there is now some light industry in the refurbished dock areas. Tourism is a growing industry. A car ferry operates between here and Rosslare in the Republic of Ireland.

Originally founded in 1090 by the Norman Lord Grimley

The Peerage

Duke
The title originated in England in 1337, when Edward III created his son Edward, Duke of Cornwall
Coronet: eight strawberry leaves
Title: His Grace, The Duke of
Wife's title: Her Grace, The Duchess of
Eldest son's title: takes his father's second title (Marquess, Earl, or Viscount) as a courtesy title
Younger sons' title: 'Lord' before forename and family name
Daughters' title: 'Lady' before forename and family name.

Marquess

The first English marquess was created in 1385, but the lords of the Scottish and Welsh Marches were known as marchiones before this date.
Coronet: four strawberry leaves alternating with four silver balls
Title: The Most Honourable, The Marquess of
Wife's title: The Most Honourable, The Marchioness of
Eldest son's title: takes his father's second title (Earl or Viscount) as a courtesy title
Younger sons' title: 'Lord' before forename and family name
Daughters' title: 'Lady' before forename and family name

Earl

Earldoms first became hereditary during the Norman period, and the title of earl was the highest hereditary dignity until 1337.
Coronet: eight silver balls on stalks alternating with eight gold strawberry leaves
Title: The Right Honourable, The Earl of
Wife's title: The Right Honourable, The Countess of
Eldest son's title: takes his father's second title as a courtesy title
Younger sons' title: 'The Honourable' before forename and family name
Daughters' title: 'Lady' before forename and family name

Viscount

The title was first granted in England in 1440 to John, Lord Beaumont. Originally the title was given to the deputy sheriff, who acted on behalf of an earl within his estate.
Coronet: sixteen silver balls
Title: The Right Honourable, The Viscount of
Wife's title: The Right Honourable, The Viscountess of
Eldest son's title: takes his father's second title as a courtesy title
Younger sons' title: 'The Honourable' before forename and family name
Daughters' title: 'The Honourable' before forename and family name

Baron

Historically, a baron is any member of the higher nobility, a direct vassal (feudal servant) of the king, not bearing other titles such as duke or count. Life peers, created under the Act of 1958, are always of this rank.
Coronet: six silver balls
Title: The Right Honourable, The Lord
Wife's title: The Right Honourable, The Lady
Eldest son's title: 'The Honourable' before forename and family name
Younger sons' title: 'The Honourable' before forename and family name
Daughters' title: 'The Honourable' before forename and family name.
For Royal Dukes, His Royal Highness and Her Royal Highness are used instead of His or Her Grace. In Scotland, Marquis is used for peers created before the Union with England. In Scotland, 'The Master of' followed by the Viscount's title can be used. The title Baron does not exist in Scotland.

---

de Montgomery, the castle was completely rebuilt around 1207 by William Marshall, the greatest English knight of the Middle Ages, and remains largely unaltered today. There is a bridge crossing the River Cleddau, an arm of Milford Haven.

Pembrokeshire, Welsh Sir Benfro

Unitary authority in southwest Wales; a former county, from 1974 to 1996 it was part of the county of Dyfed
Area 1,588 sq km/613 sq mi
Towns ◊Haverfordwest (administrative headquarters), ◊Milford Haven
Physical bounded on the south by the Bristol Channel; valleys and hills inland; rivers East and West Cleddau
Features Pembrokeshire Coast National Park
Industries oil refinery at ◊Milford Haven, agriculture, fishing, woollen milling.
Population (1996) 117,700
The coast
Pembrokeshire is bounded on the south by the Bristol Channel and on the west and north by ◊St George's Channel, into which protrudes St David's Head. The chief bays are Milford Haven and St Bride's, the coast of which is part of the national park; smaller bays include Fishguard and Newport. All have good anchorage. A number of islands lie off the coast, including ◊Skokholm, ◊Skomer, ◊Caldey, Ramsey, and ◊Grassholm, as well as many rocky islets, including the group known as the Bishops and Clerks, which has a lighthouse. The south coast is wild and precipitous, fronted by high cliffs.
Inland
Pembrokeshire is undulating, consisting of green hills alternating with fertile valleys. The main relief is the ◊Preseli Hills in the northeast; the most important rivers are the East and West Cleddau, which unite and form a navigable portion of Milford Haven. There are many prehistoric monuments in the district.

Penda (*c.* 577–654)

King of Mercia, an Anglo-Saxon kingdom in England, from about 632. He raised Mercia to a powerful kingdom, and defeated and killed two Northumbrian kings, Edwin in 632 and ◊Oswald in 642. He was killed in battle by Oswy, King of Northumbria.

Penguin Books

Publishing house founded in 1935 by Allen Lane (1902–1970) and his two brothers, John and Richard, to produce paperback reprints of fiction. Within two years over 100

Penguin titles had been published at sixpence a volume (equivalent to 2.5p in decimal currency). In 1937 Penguin started a complementary imprint, Pelican Books, for sociological and scientific subjects. Subsequent Penguin imprints included Penguin Classics; Puffins, for children; Penguin Modern Classics; the Penguin Shakespeare; and the Pelican History of Art. Early Penguins, with their characteristic orange-banded covers, have become collectors' items. Allen Lane was knighted in 1952.

Peninsular War

War of 1808–14 caused by the French emperor Napoleon's invasion of Portugal and Spain. British expeditionary forces under Sir Arthur Wellesley (Duke of ◊Wellington), combined with Spanish and Portuguese resistance, succeeded in defeating the French at Vimeiro in 1808, Talavera in 1809, Salamanca in 1812, and Vittoria in 1813. The results were inconclusive, and the war was ended by Napoleon's forced abdication in 1814.

Penistone

Town in South Yorkshire, England, on the River Don, 21 km/13 mi northwest of Sheffield; population (1991) 19,000. Agriculture and the manufacture of steel goods are the main industries.

Penn, William (1644–1718)

English member of the Society of Friends (Quakers), born in London. He joined the Society in 1667, and in 1681 obtained a grant of land in America (in settlement of a debt owed by the king to his father) on which he established the colony of Pennsylvania as a refuge for persecuted Quakers.

Penn made religious tolerance a cornerstone of his administration of the colony. He maintained good relations with neighbouring colonies and with the Native Americans in the area, but his utopian ideals were not successful for the most part. In 1697 he presented a plan, never acted upon, for a union among the colonies. In 1701 he established, with his Charter of Privileges, a bicameral legislature as the government for Pennsylvania.

Penney, William George (1909–1991)

English scientist who worked at Los Alamos, New Mexico, 1944–45, developing the US atomic bomb. He also headed the team that constructed Britain's first atomic bomb and directed its testing programme at the Monte Bello Islands off Western Australia in 1952. He subsequently directed the UK hydrogen bomb project, tested on Christmas Island in 1957, and developed the advanced gas-cooled nuclear reactor used in some UK power stations. KBE 1952, Baron 1967.

Pennines, the

Range of hills in northern England, known as the 'the backbone of England'; length (from the Scottish border to the Peaks in Derbyshire) 400 km/250 mi. The highest peak in the Pennines (which are sometimes referred to mountains rather than hills) is Cross Fell (893 m/2,930 ft). It is the watershed for the main rivers of northeast England. The rocks are carboniferous limestone and millstone grit, the land high moorland and fell.

The **Pennine Way**, Britain's first long-distance footpath (opened in 1965), extends along the length of the range.

The rivers Eden, Kibble, and Mersey rise in the Pennines and flow westwards towards the Atlantic, while the Tyne, Tees, Swale, Aire, Don, and Trent, which also rise in the region, flow eastwards to the North Sea. Principal summits of the Pennines include Whernside (736 m/2,415 ft), Ingleborough (723 m/2,372 ft), Pen-y-ghent (693 m/2,274 ft), and Kinder Scout (636 m/2,087 ft). Underground caverns and watercourses have developed as a result of water action. Among these caverns and chasms are Gaping Hill (over 107 m/350 ft deep) and Rowten Pot (111 m/365 ft deep).

penny

Basic coin of English currency from about the 6th century, apparently named after Penda, King of Mercia. The penny was the only coin in general circulation until the 13th century and was defined in terms of a pound (libra) of silver, the equivalent of 240 pennies. One side showed the king's head, the other displayed the mark of the mint.

penny post

First prepaid postal service, introduced 1840. Until then, postage was paid by the recipient according to the distance travelled. Rowland Hill of Shrewsbury suggested a new service which would be paid for by the sender of the letter or package according to its weight. The **Penny Black** stamp was introduced May 1840, and bore the sovereign's portrait in the manner of coins.

Penrhyn Castle

Huge neo-Norman castle near Bangor, Gwynedd, North Wales, designed 1820–40 by Thomas Hopper (1776–1856). Penrhyn was given to the National Trust in 1951 by the Treasury, with the 17,000 ha/41,989 acre Ysbyty Estate. The castle contains 'Norman' furniture, panelling, and plasterwork designed by Hopper, and one of the best private collections of paintings in Wales.

There are also collections of dolls, stuffed birds, and animals; an exhibition of locomotives in the grounds; and a Victorian walled garden.

The keep is said to have been inspired by Castle Hedingham in Essex.

Penrith

Town in Cumbria, England, 28 km/17 mi southeast of Carlisle, on a hilly site above the River Eamont; population (1991) 12,800. Penrith manufactures agricultural machinery. The M6 motorway runs immediately to the west of the town and Penrith railway station is on the main London–Glasgow line.

There are ruins of a 15th-century castle, and an 18th-century church.

Penrose, Roger (1931–)

English mathematician who formulated some of the fundamental theorems that describe black holes, including the singularity theorems, developed jointly with English physicist Stephen ◊Hawking, which state that once the gravitational collapse of a star has proceeded to a certain degree, singularities (which form the centre of black holes) are inevitable. Penrose has also proposed a new model of the universe.

Penshurst

Village in Kent, England, northwest of Tunbridge Wells; population (1991) 1,400. **Penshurst Place**, a 14th-century manor house, was the birthplace of the Elizabethan poet Philip Sidney.

The house has a Barons' Hall, Elizabethan Long Gallery, and many portraits. The village church has an ancient lych-gate.

Pentland Firth

Channel separating the Orkney Islands from the northern mainland of Scotland. It is 20 km/12 mi long and 8–13 km/5–8 mi wide. Ferries cross the Firth, but strong tidal currents and whirlpools render navigation dangerous.

The **Pentland Skerries**, 8 km/5 mi northeast of Duncansby Head, include two islets, one of which has a lighthouse.

Pentland Hills

Mountainous ridge in southeast Scotland running from Carnwath in South Lanarkshire unitary authority, 30 km/19 mi northeast to the city of Edinburgh. Its average height is above 300 m/985 ft, and its breadth is 6–10 km/4–6 mi. Scald Law, rising to 579 m/1,900 ft, and Carnethy Hill, at 576 m/1,890 ft, are the highest points.

A large dry ski-slope has been established at Hillend at the northern end of the ridge. Significant archaeological remains are located on the slopes of Castlelaw, height 486 m/1,594 ft.

Penzance

Seaport and resort in Cornwall, southwest England, on Mount's Bay 38 km/24 mi southwest of Truro; population (1991) 19,700. The most westerly town in England, it has a ferry link with the Scilly Isles. It is the centre of a market-gardening and agricultural area, and early fruit, flowers, and vegetables are produced. It now incorporates the seaport of ◊Newlyn. It is known as the 'Cornish Riviera'.

Features

Penzance has a mild climate in which palm trees flourish, and subtropical plants are grown in Morrab Gardens. There is a museum of the Royal Geological Society of Cornwall, and Penlee Park includes an art gallery and museum containing a natural history collection and paintings by members of the Newlyn School. In front of the domed market house (1836) is a marble statue of Humphry Davy, inventor of the miner's safety lamp, who came from Penzance. The town overlooks St Michael's Mount in the bay.

Churches include St Mary's (1832); St Paul's (1843), built in 13th-century style; the Roman Catholic church (1847); and St John's (1881), built in the Early English style.

History

In 1332 Edward III granted Penzance a weekly market and a fair of seven days. In 1512 Henry VIII gave Penzance a charter granting it ship dues on condition that the town maintained the quays in repair. Another grant of a market was received in 1592 from Elizabeth I. Penzance was burned by the Spanish in 1595 and was incorporated by James I in 1614. Formerly important in the tin trade, it developed with the growth of tourism from the early 19th century, and further expansion followed the arrival of the railway in the 1850s.

The occasional pirate raids that Penzance experienced during the 17th century, due to its location on a sheltered bay on England's southwest point, made it the location for Gilbert and Sullivan's operetta *The Pirates of Penzance*.

People's Budget

The Liberal government's budget of 1909 to finance social reforms and naval rearmament. The chancellor of the Exchequer David Lloyd George proposed graded and increased income tax and a 'supertax' on high incomes. The budget aroused great debate and precipitated a constitutional crisis.

The People's Budget was passed in the House of Commons but rejected by the House of Lords. The prime minister Herbert Henry Asquith denounced the House of Lords for a breach of the constitution over the finance bill and obtained the dissolution of Parliament. The Liberals were returned to power in the general election of 1910. In 1911 the Parliament Act greatly reduced the power of the House of Lords.

People's Charter

The key document of ◊Chartism, a movement for reform of the British political system in the 1830s. It was used to mobilize working-class support following the restricted extension of the franchise specified by the 1832 Reform Act. It was drawn up in February 1837.

People, The

Popular Sunday newspaper established in 1881. Owned by Mirror Group, it had a circulation of over 1,900,000 in 1998. It is noted for its sports coverage and popular features.

Peploe, Samuel John (1871–1935)

Scottish painter. He is best known for his still lifes (often flowers in vases) and landscapes, his strong colours and creamy brushwork being derived from Cézanne and also the Fauves. An early example is *Boats at Royan* (1910; National Gallery of Scotland, Edinburgh).

Pepusch, Johann Christoph (1667–1752)

German composer. He settled in England about 1700 and contributed to John Gay's ballad operas *The Beggar's Opera* and *Polly*.

Pepys, Samuel (1633–1703)

English naval administrator and diarist. His *Diary* (1660–69) is a unique record of the daily life of the period, the historical events of the Restoration, the manners and scandals of the court, naval administration, and Pepys's own interests, weaknesses, and intimate feelings. Written in shorthand, it was not deciphered until 1825.

PEPYS, SAMUEL *Portrait of the English diarist Samuel Pepys in 1666 by John Hayls, National Portrait Gallery, London. The private diaries of Pepys, who was an energetic public servant, express a relish for life and its full range of experiences. His account of the last great plague epidemic in 1665 and of the Fire of London in 1666 are particularly valuable as social history. Topham Picture Source*

Pepys entered the Navy Office in 1660 and was secretary to the Admiralty from 1672–79. He was imprisoned in 1679 in the Tower of London on suspicion of being connected with the Popish Plot (see Titus ◊Oates). He was reinstated as secretary to the Admiralty in 1684, but was finally deprived of his post after the 1688 Revolution. He published *Memoires of the Navy* in 1690. Pepys abandoned writing his diary because he believed, mistakenly, that his eyesight was about to fail – in fact, it continued to serve him for 30 or more years of active life.

The original manuscript of the *Diary*, preserved in Cambridge together with other papers, is in six volumes, containing more than 3,000 pages. It is closely written in cipher (a form of shorthand), which Pepys probably used in case his journal should fall into unfriendly hands during his life or be rashly published after his death. Highlights include his accounts of the Great Plague of London in 1665, the Fire of London in 1666, and the sailing up the Thames of the Dutch fleet in 1667.

Perceval, Spencer (1762–1812)

British Tory politician. He became chancellor of the Exchequer in 1807 and prime minister in 1809. He was shot in the lobby of the House of Commons in 1812 by a merchant who blamed government measures for his bankruptcy.

Percival, or Perceval

In British legend, one of King Arthur's knights, particularly associated with the quest for the ◊Holy Grail. Based on the Welsh hero Peredur, he first appeared in Chrétien de Troyes's *Perceval, ou le conte du Graal* about 1190.

Brought up in a Welsh forest by his widowed mother, a chance meeting with some knights prompts his departure for Arthur's court. Later he is knighted, falls in love with Blanchefleur, and encounters the wounded Fisher King. His failure to ask about the lance and Holy Grail which he sees during dinner with the Fisher King lead to destruction and suffering.

His story, incomplete in Chrétien de Troyes's work, inspired various elaborations by later writers. In Manessier's continuation of Chrétien's poem, in Wolfram von Eschenbach's *Parzival* (which inspired Wagner's opera), and in the Didot *Perceval* he achieves the Grail quest, while in another prose romance, *Perlesvaus*, he delivers the Grail Castle from a hostile king.

Percy

Family name of dukes of Northumberland; seated at Alnwick Castle, Northumberland, England.

Percy, Henry 'Hotspur' (1364–1403)

English soldier, son of the 1st Earl of Northumberland. In repelling a border raid, he defeated the Scots at Homildon Hill, Durham, in 1402. He was killed at the Battle of Shrewsbury while in revolt against Henry IV.

Percy, Thomas (1729–1811)

English scholar; bishop of Dromore, Ireland, from 1782. He was given a manuscript collection of songs, ballads, and romances, which became the basis of the *Reliques of Ancient English Poetry* (1765). The Percy collection renewed interest in ballads and was influential in the Romantic revival and inspired Walter ◊Scott's *Minstrelsy of the Scottish Border*.

Pergau Dam

Hydroelectric dam on the Pergau River in Malaysia, near the Thai border. Building work began in 1991 with money from the UK foreign aid budget. Concurrently, the Malaysian government bought around £1 billion worth of arms from the UK. The suggested linkage of arms deals to aid become the subject of a UK government enquiry from March 1994. In November 1994 a High Court ruled as illegal British foreign secretary Douglas ◊Hurd's allocation of £234 million towards the funding of the dam, on the grounds that it was not of economic or humanitarian benefit to the Malaysian people.

The dam is the largest aid project ever financed by the UK.

Perkin, William Henry (1838–1907)

English chemist. In 1856 he discovered mauve, the dye that originated the aniline-dye industry and the British synthetic-dyestuffs industry generally. Knighted 1906.

Perpendicular

Period of English Gothic architecture lasting from the end of the 14th century to the mid-16th century. It is characterized by window tracery consisting chiefly of vertical members, two or four arc arches, lavishly decorated vaults, and the use of traceried panels. Examples include the choir, transepts, and cloister of Gloucester Cathedral (about 1331–1412); and King's College Chapel, Cambridge, built in three phases: 1446–61, 1477–85, and 1508–15.

> *But Lord! to see the absurd nature of Englishmen, that cannot forbear laughing and jeering at everything that looks strange.*
>
> Samuel Pepys English diarist.
> *Diary* 27 November 1662

Perry, Fred (Frederick John) (1909–1995)

English lawn-tennis player, the last Briton to win the men's singles at Wimbledon, in 1936. He also won the world table-tennis title in 1929. Perry later became a television commentator and a sports-goods manufacturer.

Perth

Town and administrative headquarters of ◊Perth and Kinross, central Scotland, on the River Tay, 70 km/43 mi northwest of Edinburgh; population (1991) 41,500. It is known as the 'fair city'. Industries include dyeing, textiles, whisky distilling, and light engineering. It is an important agricultural centre, noted for the sale of pedigree livestock, particularly young beef cattle. It was the capital of Scotland from the 12th century until 1452. James I of Scotland was assassinated here in 1437.

Reputed to have been founded by Agricola in AD 70, Perth is believed to have been occupied by the Romans for 320 years. The town was known as 'St John's Toun' until the Reformation. The oldest building in Perth is the cruciform church of St John, which was founded in 1126.

Perth was the scene of the murder of the Duke of Cornwall by his brother, Edward III of England, in 1335, and of the battle between the clans Quhele and Chattan described in Walter Scott's novel *The Fair Maid of Perth* (1828). John Knox preached a sermon on idolatry at St John's church in 1559, thus initiating the Scottish Reformation.

The Tay is spanned by two fine bridges, and along its banks are two public parks known as the North and South Inches.

Perth and Kinross

Unitary authority in central Scotland, created in 1996 from the district bearing the same name in Tayside region

Area 5,388 sq km/2,080 sq mi

Towns Blairgowrie, Crieff, Kinross, ◊Perth (administrative headquarters), Pitlochry, Aberfeldy

Physical the geological fault which gives the distinctive character to lowland and highland Scotland passes through the area from southwest to northeast. The population is largely centred in the lowlands, along wide fertile valleys such as Strathearn, and the Carse of Gowrie. To the north and west are the Grampians intersected by narrow glens with lochs in their valley floors. Among the highest elevations in the Grampian Mountains are Ben Lawers (1,214 m/3,984 ft) and Schiehallion (1,083 m/3,554 ft); in the south are the lower Ochil and Sidlaw Hills

Features Highland Games at Pitlochry; Dunkeld Cathedral; Scone Palace; Glenshee Ski Development

Industries woollen manufacture, whisky distilling and blending

Agriculture highly productive and varied agricultural area with soft fruit (Carse of Gowrie), arable crops (to the south), livestock, salmon fisheries (to the north)

Population (1995) 132,800

History Macbeth defeated in Dunsinane in 1054; victory of Scots (under Viscount Dundee) over English at Killiecrankie in 1689; Mary Queen of Scots' escape from Loch Leven castle in 1568.

Economy

To the north, there is afforestation and 14 hydroelectric power installations. The attractions of the natural scenery of mountains and lochs has made tourism an important part of northern Perth and Kinross' economy. In the south, agriculture plays a more central role in the local economy.

Architecture

Dunkeld Cathedral was founded in 1107, and the church of St John, Perth, in 1126. The area is particularly rich in fine mansions, such as Kinross House (17th century), designed by William Bruce; and Scone Palace (1803–08); there are also many good examples of castles, such as Grandtully (1560) and Blair (1269).

Environment

There are 111 Sites of Special Scientific Interest, six National Nature Reserves, three Ramsars (wetland sites), one Special Protection Area, and five National Scenic Areas.

Archaeology

There are many remains of prehistoric stone circles and standing stones, and several Roman sites of great interest, notably Ardoch Roman Camp, near Braco.

Administrative history

Prior to 1975, the area was divided between the counties of Perthshire and Kinross-shire.

pesticide

Any chemical used in farming, gardening, or indoors to combat pests. Pesticides are of three main types: **insecticides** (to kill insects), **fungicides** (to kill fungal diseases), and **herbicides** (to kill plants, mainly those considered weeds).

Many pesticides remain in the soil, since they are not biodegradable, and are then passed on to foods. In the UK, more than half of all potatoes sampled in 1995 contained residues of a storage pesticide; seven different pesticides were found in carrots, with concentrations up to 25 times the permitted level; and 40% of bread contained pesticide residues. There are around 4,000 cases of acute pesticide poisoning a year in the UK.

The Pesticide Safety Directorate, an executive agency of the Ministry of Agriculture, Fisheries and Food (MAFF) is responsible for the evaluation and approval of pesticides in Great Britain and provides policy advice.

Peterborough

Unitary authority in eastern England, created in 1998 from part of Cambridgeshire

Area 334 sq km/129 sq mi

Towns and cities ◊Peterborough (administrative headquarters), Wittering, Old Fletton, Thorney, Glinton, Northborough, Peakirk

Features River Nene; western margins of the Fens; St Peter's Cathedral (Peterborough), 12th century, containing Catherine of Aragon's tomb; Wildfowl and Wetlands Centre at Peakirk

Industries aluminium founding and manufacture, electronics, domestic appliances, plastics and rubber manufacture, precision engineering, telecommunications equipment, food manufacture and processing

Population (1995) 159,300

Peterborough

City in eastern England, on the River Nene, 64 km/40 mi northeast of Northampton, and from April 1998 administrative headquarters of ◊Peterborough unitary authority; population (1994 est) 139,000. Situated on the edge of the ◊Fens in the centre of an agricultural area, it is one of the fastest growing cities in Europe. Industries include sugar-beet refining, foodstuffs, aluminium founding and manufacturing, agricultural machinery, engineering, brick-making, diesel engines, and refrigerators. It has an advanced electronics industry. It is noted for its 12th-century cathedral. Nearby Flag Fen disclosed in 1985 a well-preserved Bronze Age settlement of 660 BC. The 17th-century Thorpe Hall is a cultural and leisure centre.

The plans for Hampton Township (formerly known as Peterborough Southern Township), the largest town in Europe built by the private sector, threatened the world's largest colony of great crested newts in old clay pits. Work has begun on the town, and the first people moved in in 1997.

The cathedral

The cathedral, begun in 1117, was formerly the church of a Benedictine monastery. Architectural styles range from the Norman to the Perpendicular period, and prior to the Reformation it was considered one of the most magnificent in Britain. The first monastery was founded in 655, but was totally destroyed by the Danes in 870. In 972 a new monastery, founded by Aethelwold, Bishop of Winchester, was endowed by Edgar the Peaceful, and, fortified by Abbot Kenulph, acquired the name of Burgh. The Peterborough Chronicle, or later Anglo-Saxon Chronicle, was composed by monks here. Somewhat parochial in outlook, it nevertheless gives a vivid account of the troubles of Stephen's reign. The second church was destroyed by fire in 1117, and in the following year the building of a third church began. The three-arched west front was completed in the reign of John, and many additions and alterations to the building were made almost up to the time of the surrender of the monastery in 1539, when the church was selected as one of the six cathedrals to be refounded from monastic churches in 1541 by Henry VIII, on the advice of Cranmer. The remains of Catherine of Aragon, wife of Henry VIII, lie in the cathedral, and those of Mary Queen of Scots lay buried here for a quarter of a century, before being moved to Westminster Abbey by her son, James I, in 1612. In 1643 the cathedral was ransacked by Oliver Cromwell and his soldiers, who destroyed most of the monuments and stained glass.

Growth of the city

Before the Dissolution there had been a small borough dating back to the Norman era, the town growing up round the monastery. Both town and monastery were sacked by Hereward the Wake and the Danes in 1071, and the abbey tenants took part in the Peasants' Revolt during the reign of Edward II. The city itself was created by letters patent of Henry VIII on 4 September 1541. Growth in the 19th century was the result of improved drainage of the fens, and the arrival of the railway; growth in the 20th century was largely due to the brickworks at Fletton. Peterborough has always been the marketing centre for an important agricultural area.

Local government

Formerly the powers of local government in Peterborough were divided between the dean and chapter (whose steward presided over a court held in and for the city); a rival parochial authority, which held certain town estates known as the *feoffees*; and governors of the town lands and stock. In 1874 the city became a municipal corporation. The justices for the Soke of Peterborough have by long-standing commissions (especially preserved by the Justices of the Peace Act, 1949) full powers of judges of assize, though in practice do not exercise their rights in the most serious category of cases.

The modern city

Peterborough is a busy railway town being a junction for the northeastern and midland regions, situated on the London–Edinburgh line. It has large railway workshops. It is an industrial centre and an important wholesale and retail centre with the indoor Queensgate shopping centre. Nene Park, a 200 ha/500 acre country park, offers outdoor leisure facilities; the Nene Valley Steam Railway runs through it. The East of England agricultural show is held in July. Peterborough was designated a New Town (planned to absorb overspill population) in 1967.

Peterhead

Port in Aberdeenshire, Scotland, 54 km/33 mi northeast of Aberdeen; population (1991) 18,700. The port is Europe's busiest fishing port. The harbour is used by service industries for North Sea oil, a daily fish market and a marina. It is the most easterly town in Scotland, built of locally quarried Peterhead pink granite. Peterhead was formerly a whaling port. James Edward Stuart, the Old Pretender, landed here in 1715.

There is a submarine cable between Peterhead and Egersund in southern Norway. The town also has a high security prison. The island headland of Keith Inch is linked by a bridge to the town proper. White fishing has developed since 1945.

The main industries now are those related to the oil industry in the North Sea; spare parts, food and domestic equipment, precision tools, and all appliances required by the offshore industry are manufactured and, in some cases, stored at Peterhead.

Peterlee

Town in County Durham, northeast England, between Sunderland and Hartlepool, designated a ◊new town in 1948; population (1991) 31,100. Industries include the manufacture of transport equipment, textiles, engineering, and mining; there is also some agricultural activity, particularly dairy farming, in the area. The town was named after Peter Lee (1864–1935), a miner's leader and the first Labour chair of the county council.

Peterlee was established in 1948 to replace some of the 19th-century housing in the mining villages of the district, to provide alternative industrial employment, and to act as a service centre.

Peterloo massacre

The events in St Peter's Fields in Manchester, England, on 16 August 1819, when an open-air meeting in support of parliamentary reform was charged by yeomanry and hussars. Eleven people were killed and 500 wounded. The name was given in analogy with the Battle of Waterloo.

Peter Pan, or *The Boy Who Wouldn't Grow Up*

Play for children by James ◊Barrie, first performed in 1904. Peter Pan, an orphan with magical powers, arrives in the night nursery of the Darling children, Wendy, John, and Michael. He teaches them to fly and introduces them to the Never Never Land inhabited by fantastic characters, including the fairy Tinkerbell, the Lost Boys, and the pirate Captain Hook. The play was followed by a story, *Peter Pan in Kensington Gardens* (1906), and a book of the play (1911).

Peter Rabbit, full title *The Tale of Peter Rabbit*

First of the children's stories written and illustrated by English author Beatrix ◊Potter, published in 1900.

Peters, Ellis pen name of Edith Pargeter (1913–1995)

English novelist and translator. Early novels of contemporary issues included *She Goes to War* (1942). Subsequently she alternated thrillers with historical novels until 1978, when, as Ellis Peters, she published the first Brother Cadfael novel, *A Morbid Taste for Bones*, set in Shropshire and the Welsh borders. There followed 19 further medieval detective stories about him, in which the crime is only one element of tales of rich characterization with underlying philosophical and theological truths.

Petrie, (William Matthew) Flinders (1853–1942)

English archaeologist who excavated sites in Egypt (the pyramids at Gîza, the temple at Tanis, the Greek city of Naucratis in the Nile delta, Tell el Amarna, Naqada, Abydos, and Memphis) and Palestine from 1880.

Petrie's work was exacting and systematic, and he developed dating sequences of pottery styles that correlated with dynastic and predynastic events.

petrol

Mixture of hydrocarbons derived from petroleum, mainly used as a fuel for internal-combustion engines. It is colourless and highly volatile. **Leaded petrol** contains antiknock (a mixture of tetraethyl lead and dibromoethane), which improves the combustion of petrol and the performance of a car engine. The lead from the exhaust fumes enters the atmosphere, mostly as simple lead compounds. There is strong evidence that it can act as a nerve poison on young children and cause mental impairment. This has prompted a gradual switch to the use of **unleaded petrol** in the UK.

The changeover from leaded petrol gained momentum from 1989 owing to a change in the tax on petrol, making it cheaper to buy unleaded fuel. Unleaded petrol contains a different mixture of hydrocarbons, and has a lower octane rating than leaded petrol. Leaded petrol cannot be used in cars fitted with a catalytic converter.

Petworth

Town in West Sussex, England; population (1991) 3,700. It has many old timber-framed buildings, including several around the market square.

Petworth House

Late 17th-century mansion in West Sussex, England, 21 km/13 mi northeast of Chichester. It was rebuilt 1688–96 by the 6th Duke of Somerset. The west front of the house is 98 m/321 ft long. In 1947 the 3rd Lord Leconfield gave the house and 300 ha/740 acres of park to the National Trust.

Much of the furniture and contents of the house was lent to the Trust by the Treasury, including many paintings by J M W Turner who was a friend of the 3rd Lord Egremont and often stayed at Petworth. There are also paintings here by Van Dyck, Claude, and Poussin, a large collection of antique and 18th-century sculpture, and a room carved by Grinling ◊Gibbons.

Pevensey

English village in East Sussex, 8 km/5 mi northeast of Eastbourne, the site of the Norman king William the Conqueror's landing in 1066. The walls remain of the Roman fortress of Anderida, later a Norman castle, which was prepared against German invasion in World War II.

Pevsner, Nikolaus Bernhard Leon (1902–1983)
Anglo-German art historian. Born in Leipzig, he fled from the Nazis to England. He became an authority on architecture, especially English. His *Outline of European Architecture* was published in 1942, followed by numerous other editions. In his series *The Buildings of England* (46 volumes; 1951–74), he built up a first-hand report on every notable building in the country.

Philby, Kim (Harold Adrian Russell) (1912–1988)
British intelligence officer from 1940 and Soviet agent from 1933. He was liaison officer in Washington 1949–51, when he was confirmed to be a double agent and asked to resign. Named in 1963 as having warned Guy Burgess and Donald Maclean (also double agents) that their activities were known, he fled to the USSR and became a Soviet citizen and general in the KGB. A fourth member of the ring was Anthony Blunt.

Philip, Duke of Edinburgh (1921–)
Prince of the UK, husband of Elizabeth II, a grandson of George I of Greece and a great-great-grandson of Queen Victoria. He was born in Corfu, Greece, but brought up in England.

He was educated at Gordonstoun and Dartmouth Naval College. During World War II he served in the Mediterranean, taking part in the battle of Matapan, and in the Pacific. A naturalized British subject, taking the surname Mountbatten in March 1947, he married Princess Elizabeth in Westminster Abbey on 20 November 1947, having the previous day received the title Duke of Edinburgh. In 1956 he founded the Duke of Edinburgh's Award Scheme to encourage creative achievement among young people. He was created a prince of the UK in 1957, and awarded the Order of Merit in 1968.

Philips, Peter (1561–1628)
English organist and composer. He was famous as an organist throughout the Netherlands, and was probably the best-known English composer in northern Europe. His collections of madrigals and motets are Roman in style, with Italianate word-painting and polyphony; they were reprinted many times in Antwerp.

His works include masses, 106 motets published in

PHILBY, KIM *British double agent Kim Philby facing the press. Philby became a communist at Cambridge, like Burgess, Maclean, and Blunt. He worked for British Intelligence during and after World War II, and then at the British embassy in Washington, where he liaised with the CIA. During this time he was supplying secret intelligence information to the Russians. He was uncovered as a double agent in 1951 and asked to resign. He disappeared to the USSR in 1963. Corbis*

Paradisus sacris cantionibus (Antwerp, 1628), hymns, *Sacrae cantiones*; madrigals; fantasies, pavans, and galliards for various instruments; organ and virginal pieces.

Phillips, Caryl (1958–)

West Indian-born novelist and playwright who moved to England in 1959. His work, which explores the conflicts of race and heritage and the themes of loss and persecution, includes the plays *Strange Fruit* (1981), *Where There is Darkness* (1982), and *The Shelter* (1984), and the novels *The Final Passage* (1985), *A State of Independence* (1986), *Higher Ground* (1989), *Cambridge* (1991), and *The Nature of Blood* (1997).

He has also written screenplays and radio plays, including *Crossing the River* (1985), and he is chief editor of the Faber and Faber Caribbean Writers' series.

Phillips, Peter (1953–)

English choral director. With the Tallis Scholars, he has won renown for recordings of such works as Gesualdo's *Tenebrae Responsories*, *Missa Pastores* by Clemens non Papa, Byrd's *Great Service* and three Masses, the English anthems of Tallis, and the Masses of Josquin Desprez and Palestrina.

Phiz pseudonym of Hablot Knight Browne (1815–1882)

English artist who illustrated the greater part of the *Pickwick Papers* and other works by Charles Dickens.

Phoenix Park Murders

The murder of several prominent members of the British government in Phoenix Park, Dublin, on 6 May 1882. The murders threatened the cooperation between the Liberal government and the Irish nationalist members at Westminster which had been secured by the ◊Kilmainham Treaty.

The murders began with the stabbing of Thomas Burke, the permanent under-secretary for Ireland, and Lord Frederick Cavendish, chief secretary to the viceroy. A murderous campaign was continued by the Irish National Invincibles until some members turned 'Queen's evidence'.

Burke and Cavendish were hacked to death by nine assassins wielding surgical knives. One informer, James Carey, a Dublin Corporation councillor, was murdered aboard a ship taking him to South Africa by Patrick O'Donnell who, like five of the Phoenix Park murderers, was tried by the British and hanged. The English press suggested Parnell was implicated but he was awarded damages after bringing a successful libel action against *The Times* which was shown to have cited forged letters. Gladstone's government responded to the killings in Ireland with the Prevention of Crimes Act which suspended trial by jury and gave the police exceptional powers for three years. In the long run an important consequence was the strengthened resolve of Spencer Compton Cavendish, Marquess of Hartington, future Duke of Devonshire and elder brother of the ill-fated Lord Frederick, who was later to lead the Liberal Unionists.

phoney war

The period in World War II between September 1939, when the Germans had occupied Poland, and April 1940, when the invasions of Denmark and Norway took place. During this time there were few signs of hostilities in Western Europe; indeed, Hitler made some attempts to arrange a peace settlement with Britain and France.

photography

Britain has produced a number of pioneers in the development and application of photography, the most significant advances occurring in the first half of the 19th century.

Development

As early as 1790 Thomas Wedgewood made **photograms** on leather sensitized with silver nitrate, and in 1807 William Wollaston (1868–1828) developed the *camera lucida* for copying drawings, using light reflected through a prism to create an image. These inventions proved inspirational to William ◊Fox Talbot, one of the foremost pioneers of photography. By 1841 he had patented the **calotype** process, the first multi-copy method of photography using a negative/positive process, and in 1851 he used a one-thousandth per second exposure to demonstrate high speed photography. The first three-colour photograph was produced in 1861 by Scottish physicist James Clerk Maxwell (1831–1879), and the first twin-lens reflex camera made in London in 1880. One of the greatest landmarks of the 20th century was the demonstration of the principles of holography (three-dimensional photography) by physicist Dennis ◊Gabor in 1947.

Application

The first book illustrated with photographs was Fox Talbot's *The Pencil of Nature* (1844–46). Notable pioneers of photographic portraiture were David Hill (1802–1870) and Robert Adamson (1821–1848) who worked together in Edinburgh between 1843 and 1848, producing some 2,500 calotypes. In 1855 photographer Roger Fenton (1819–1861) comprehensively documented the Crimean War from a specially constructed caravan with a portable darkroom. Early innovators in photographic technique included Henry Robinson (1830–1901), who from 1851 produced images which closely imitated Victorian painting by combining several negatives in one print; and Julia Cameron (1815–1879), who used long lenses for her dramatic portraits of the Victorian intelligentsia. Differential focusing was used by English landscape photographer Peter Emerson (1856–1936) to produce naturalistic images in which only part of the picture was sharply focused. *Picture Post*, introduced in 1938, was the first UK magazine devoted to photo-journalism. Notable photographers of the 20th century include the war photographer Don McCullin; fashion photographers David Bailey and Norman Parkinson; and Anthony Snowdon, who is especially known for his portraits.

Photographic processes found early application in the field of astronomy. Warren de la Rue invented the first heliographic photograph, and took the first photograph of a solar eclipse in 1860, and William Huggins (1824–1910) pioneered the use of photography in stellar spectography. The cataloguing of stars through photography was led by Scottish astronomer David Gill in 1882. In archaeology Kenneth St Joseph (1912–1994) pioneered the use of aerial photography, discovering thousands of previously unknown sites.

Collections

In 1851 the Great Exhibition in London contained one of the first public displays of photography. The Photographers Gallery was established in London in 1971, and in 1983 the National Museum of Photography, Film, and Television opened in Bradford.

Piccadilly

A main road in London, running between Piccadilly Circus and the southeast corner of Hyde Park. In Piccadilly are St James's Church, designed by Christopher Wren; Burlington House, home of the Royal Academy of Arts; and the Ritz Hotel. In Piccadilly Circus, at the eastern end of Piccadilly, is a fountain with a statue, popularly known as Eros, erected in memory of the 7th Earl of Shaftesbury.

Piccadilly was extensively developed and made fashionable in the late 17th century, when the life of the court centred on nearby St James's Palace.

Pict

Roman term for a member of the peoples of northern Scotland, possibly meaning 'painted' (tattooed). Of pre-Celtic origin, and speaking a Celtic language which died out in about the 10th century, the Picts are thought to have inhabited much of England before the arrival of the Celtic Britons. They were united with the Celtic Scots under the rule of Kenneth MacAlpin in 844. Their greatest monument is a series of carved stones, whose symbols remain undeciphered.

pidgin English

Originally a trade jargon developed between the British and the Chinese in the 19th century, but now commonly and loosely used to mean any kind of 'broken' or 'native' version of the English language.

Pidgin is believed to have been a Chinese pronunciation of the English word *business*. There have been many forms of pidgin English, often with common elements because of the wide range of contacts made by commercial shipping. The original pidgin English of the Chinese ports combined words of English with a rough-and-ready Chinese grammatical structure. Melanesian pidgin English (also known as Tok Pisin) combines English and the syntax of local Melanesian languages. For example, the English pronoun 'we' becomes both *yumi* (you and me) and *mifela* (me and fellow, excluding you).

pier

Structure built out into the sea from the coastline for use as a landing place or promenade.

The first British pier was built at Ryde, Isle of Wight, in 1814. Eugenius Birch (1818–1883) designed the West Pier, Brighton, in 1866 (339 m/1,115 ft); Margate Pier 1856; and the North Pier, Blackpool, 1863.

Piers Plowman, full title *The Vision of William Concerning Piers the Plowman*

Medieval English alliterative poem, written in about 1367–86 by William ◊Langland. It tells of a wanderer who falls asleep in the Malvern Hills and dreams of the means to Christian salvation. Piers Plowman represents Christ and other characters include the personified seven deadly sins. As an allegory it has flashes of poetic quality rather than a consistent and coherent poetic effect. The longest of several versions is over 7,200 lines.

The work is structured in two parts, divided into books or *passus*. In Part I, the poet dreams of events in contemporary secular society in which personified abstractions such as Lady Holy Church, Lady Meed, Conscience, Reason, and the Seven Deadly Sins take part, alongside the idealized figure of Piers the ploughman himself. Part II shows the dreamer searching for Do-well, Do-bet, and Do-best, the good, better, and best ways of life, on the basis of his earlier experience.

Piggott, Lester Keith (1935–)

English jockey. He adopted a unique high riding style and is renowned as a brilliant tactician. A champion jockey 11 times between 1960 and 1982, he rode a record nine ◊Derby winners. Piggott retired from riding in 1985 and took up training. In 1987 he was imprisoned for tax evasion. He returned to racing in 1990 and has ridden 4,460 winners, including a record 30 classics to the start of the 1994 season. He retired as a jockey for the second time in September 1995.

Pike, Magnus Alfred (1908–1992)

British food scientist and broadcaster. He enjoyed an extraordinary period of celebrity following his retirement in 1973, co-presenting *Don't Ask Me*, which became the most popular science series on British television.

Pike was author of the standard work *The Manual of Nutrition* (1945). He ran Genochil Research Station, Scotland, 1955–73, after which he became Secretary of the British Association for the Advancement of Science.

Pike had a mission to explain, which he achieved brilliantly. Much in demand as a lecturer, his arms flailed as he sought the clearest answers to the questions his audience asked.

He referred to his period of fame as a television scientist as his 'sixth life'. His 'fifth life' was spent working for Distillers Company in Scotland and bringing up his family; the fourth was marked by the publication of *The Manual of Nutrition*. His 'third life' was passed in Canada, working as a farm labourer in the summer, and studying at McGill University in the winter; his second was his education at St Paul's School, London; while the first encompassed his early childhood in west London. His 'seventh life' began when *Don't Just Sit There* – a further highly successful television series – ended, and he retired again, in 1980.

Pilcher, Percy Sinclair (1867–1899)

English aviator who was the first Briton to make a successful flight in a heavier-than-air craft, called the *Bat*, in 1895. Like Otto Lilienthal, Pilcher made flights only downhill from gliders, using craft resembling the modern hang glider. Pilcher's next successful aircraft was the *Hawk*, launched in 1896 at Eynsford, Kent, by a tow line. He was killed in 1899 flying the *Hawk* near Rugby in the Midlands.

Pilgrimage of Grace

Rebellion against Henry VIII of England 1536–37, originating in Yorkshire and Lincolnshire. The uprising was directed against the policies of the monarch (such as the dissolution of the monasteries and the effects of the enclosure of common land).

At the height of the rebellion, the rebels controlled York and included the archbishop there among their number. A truce was arranged in December 1536 and the rebels dispersed, but their demands were not met, and a further revolt broke out in 1537, which was severely suppressed, with the execution of over 200 of the rebels, including the leader, Robert Aske.

Pilgrim's Progress

Allegory by John Bunyan, published in 1678–84, that describes the journey through life to the Celestial City of a man called Christian. On his way through the Slough of Despond, the House Beautiful, Vanity Fair, Doubting Castle, and other landmarks, he meets a number of allegorical figures.

In *The Pilgrim's Progress* the worlds of biblical and English rural culture are successfully fused; the simple plot has taken on the quality of a myth, and the symbols have become a continuing part of the language. For a long time the book was read by ordinary people as a devotional manual and was often, with the Authorized Version of the Bible, the only book in the household; in the literary world its quality was recognized only by a few. Opinion began to change with Southey's preface to his 1830 edition of *The Pilgrim's Progress*, and references to it permeate 19th-century fiction; its influence, for example, lies behind works as diverse as Charlotte Brontë's *Jane Eyre*, Louisa Alcott's *Little Women*, and Mark Twain's *Huckleberry Finn*.

Pilgrims' Way

Track running from Winchester to Canterbury, England, which was the route taken by medieval pilgrims visiting the shrine of Thomas à Becket. It was some 195 km/120 mi long, and can still be traced for most of its length.

Piltdown man, or *Eoanthropus dawsoni*

Fossil skull and jaw fragments 'discovered' by Charles Dawson at Piltdown, East Sussex, England, between 1908 and 1912, and believed to be the earliest European human remains until proved a hoax in 1953. The jaw was that of an orang-utan with the teeth filed flat, and the skull bones were human but from an ancient deposit; both had been stained to match the Piltdown gravel deposits.

Pinero, Arthur Wing (1855–1934)

English dramatist. A leading exponent of the 'well-made' play, he enjoyed great contemporary success with his farces, beginning with *The Magistrate* (1885). More substantial social drama followed with *The Second Mrs Tanqueray* (1893), and comedies including *Trelawny of the 'Wells'* (1898). He was knighted in 1909.

PILGRIM'S WAY *Medieval pilgrims on their way to the shrine of St Thomas à Becket at Canterbury. Pilgrimage, immortalized by Geoffrey Chaucer, was a remarkably common activity throughout medieval Europe, at all social levels. Canterbury was the most important English pilgrimage site, attracting pilgrims from elsewhere in Europe too. Philip Sauvain Picture Collection*

Pink Floyd

British psychedelic rock group, formed in 1965. The original members were Syd Barrett (1946–), Roger Waters (1944–), Richard Wright (1945–), and Nick Mason (1945–). Their albums include *The Dark Side of the Moon* (1973) and *The Wall* (1979), with its spin-off film starring Bob Geldof.

They were the most successful group to emerge from London's hippie scene in the late 1960s.

Pinkie, Battle of

Battle of 10 September 1547 near Musselburgh, Lothian, Scotland, in which the Scots were defeated by the English under the Duke of Somerset.

Pinnock, Trevor (1946–)

English harpsichordist and conductor. He founded the English Concert in 1973, giving performances of early music.

In 1980 he began conducting. Recordings include Purcell's *King Arthur* and the complete Mozart symphonies.

Pinter, Harold (1930–)

English dramatist, originally an actor. He specializes in the tragicomedy of the breakdown of communication, broadly in the tradition of the Theatre of the Absurd – for example, *The Birthday Party* (1958) and *The Caretaker* (1960). Later plays include *The Homecoming* (1965), *Old Times* (1971), *Betrayal* (1978), and *Moonlight* (1993).

piobaireachd

Scots Gaelic term meaning *piping*. Its anglicized form *pibroch* denotes a specific category of music for the Scottish Highland pipes.

Pipe, Martin Charles (1945–)

English racehorse trainer. He was the leading National Hunt trainer for a record 12 successive years, 1986–98. In 1988–89 he became the first person to saddle 200 winners in a season, and in 1990–91, when he had a record 230 winners, he became the first National Hunt trainer to earn over a million pounds in prize money in a season.

Piper, John Egerton Christmas (1903–1992)

English painter, printmaker, and designer. A leading figure of the Neo-Romantic movement (1935–55), which revived the spirit of 19th-century Romanticism in a more modern idiom, he became known in the 1940s for his dramatic views of landscape and architecture, usually in watercolour or aquatint.

A leading abstract painter in the 1930s, by the 1940s he had returned to figurative art, becoming well known for his pictures of air-raid destruction in World War II, particularly those of the House of Commons and of the city of Bath. Among his designs are those for stained glass at Coventry Cathedral, Llandaff Cathedral, and the Catholic Cathedral, Liverpool; and theatre sets for Benjamin Britten's opera *Death in Venice*.

pipe rolls

Records of the Exchequer 1130–1832, which record the sheriff's annual accounts for each county. They form the longest series of public records in England. The term was also used by important ecclesiastics, such as the bishop of Winchester, for estate records.

Pippard, (Alfred) Brian (1920–)

English physicist who applied microwaves to the study of superconductivity. The research he initiated has transformed understanding of the dynamical laws governing the motion of electrons in metals. Knighted in 1975.

pirate radio

Illegal radio broadcasting set up to promote an alternative to the state-owned monopoly. The early pirate radio stations broadcast from offshore ships, outside territorial waters; the first was Radio Atlanta (later Radio Caroline), set up in 1964.

Pirates of Penzance, The or *The Slave of Duty*

Operetta by Sullivan (libretto by W S Gilbert), produced Paignton, Bijou Theatre, 30 December 1879; pirated performance, New York, Fifth Avenue Theatre, 31 December 1879; first London performance, Opéra-Comique, 3 April 1880. Frederic, mistakenly apprenticed to some pirates, intends to turn in the outlaws when he comes of age. However, he discovers he was born on 29 February in a leap year, and is consequently not yet 21; he must remain an apprentice.

Pitcairn Islands

British colony in Polynesia, 5,300 km/3,300 mi northeast of New Zealand; area 27 sq km/10 sq mi; population (1994) 56. The islands were visited by British sailor Philip Carteret in 1767. They were settled in 1790 by nine mutineers from the British ship the *Bounty* together with some Tahitians; their occupation remained unknown until 1808.

Pitman, Isaac (1813–1897)

English teacher and inventor of Pitman's shorthand. He studied Samuel Taylor's scheme for shorthand writing, and in 1837 published his own system, *Stenographic Soundhand*, fast, accurate, and adapted for use in many languages. Knighted in 1894.

Pitt, William, the Elder, 1st Earl of Chatham (1708–1778)

British Whig politician, 'the Great Commoner'. As paymaster of the forces 1746–55, he broke with tradition by refusing to enrich himself; he was dismissed for attacking the Duke of Newcastle, the prime minister. He served effectively as prime minister in coalition governments 1756–61 (successfully conducting the Seven Years' War) and 1766–68.

Entering Parliament in 1735, Pitt led the Patriot faction opposed to the Whig prime minister Robert Walpole and attacked Walpole's successor, Carteret, for his conduct of the War of the Austrian Succession. Recalled by popular demand to form a government on the outbreak of the Seven Years' War in 1756, he was forced to form a coalition with Newcastle in 1757. A 'year of victories' ensued in 1759, and the French were expelled from India and Canada. In 1761 Pitt wished to escalate the war by a declaration of war on Spain, George III disagreed, and Pitt resigned, but was again recalled to form an all-party government in 1766. He championed the Americans against the king, though rejecting independence, and collapsed during his last speech in the House of Lords – opposing the withdrawal of British troops – and died a month later.

Pitt, William, the Younger (1759–1806)

British Tory prime minister 1783–1801 and 1804–06. He raised the importance of the House of Commons, clamped down on corruption, carried out fiscal reforms, and effected the union with Ireland. He attempted to keep Britain at peace but underestimated the importance of the French Revolution and became embroiled in wars with France from 1793; he died on hearing of Napoleon's victory at Austerlitz.

Son of William Pitt the Elder, he entered Cambridge University at age 14 and Parliament at age 22. He was the Whig Shelburne's chancellor of the Exchequer 1782–83, and with the support of the Tories and king's friends became Britain's youngest prime minister in 1783. He reorganized the country's finances and negotiated reciprocal tariff reduction with France. In 1793, however, the new French republic declared war and England fared badly. Pitt's policy in Ireland led to the 1798 revolt, and he tried to solve the Irish question by the Act of Union of 1800, but George III rejected the Catholic emancipation Pitt had promised as a condition, and Pitt resigned in 1801.

On his return to office in 1804, he organized an alliance with Austria, Russia, and Sweden against Napoleon, which was shattered at Austerlitz. In declining health, he died on hearing the news, saying: 'Oh, my country! How I leave my country!' He was buried in Westminster Abbey.

Necessity is the plea for every infringement of human freedom. It is the argument of tyrants; it is the creed of slaves.

William Pitt the Younger British Tory prime minister.
Speech, House of Commons 18 November 1783

---

pixie, or pixy
In the folklore of Devon and Cornwall, England, a kind of fairy. Pixies were believed to kidnap children and to lead travellers astray.

plague
See ◊Black Death.

Plaid Cymru (Welsh 'Party of Wales')
Welsh nationalist political party established in 1925, dedicated to an independent Wales. In 1966 the first Plaid Cymru member of Parliament was elected. Four Plaid Cymru MPs were returned in the 1997 general election. The Labour Party's 1997 devolution proposals for Wales were criticized by Plaid Cymru as being too cautious. Nevertheless, the party supported the 'Yes' vote in the subsequent referendum.

Plaid Cymru is the Welsh political movement dedicated to separation from and independence of the United Kingdom in order to safeguard the culture, language, and economic life of Wales. Founded in 1925, Plaid Cymru has contested parliamentary elections in Wales since 1929, but did not gain representation in Westminster until 1966, when it won the Carmarthen by-election. This seat was lost in 1970, but in the two general elections of February and October 1974 Plaid Cymru won two and three seats respectively.

Plaidy, Jean pen name of Eleanor Hibbert (*c.* 1910–1993)
English historical novelist. A prolific writer, she produced popular historical novels under three different pseudonyms: Jean Plaidy, Victoria Holt, and Philippa Carr.

Hibbert never revealed her date of birth nor her maiden name. Her first novel, *Beyond the Blue Mountains*, was not published until 1947. The 90 novels she wrote under the name Jean Plaidy were fictionalized English history and were often particularly concerned with episodes involving queens and princesses. Some 30 more Victoria Holt novels were published, all of them set in the second half of the 19th century. Under the name Philippa Carr she wrote a series of novels set in various historical periods from Tudor times to World War II.

Planets, The
Suite by Holst for orchestra with organ and (in final section) female chorus. 1. *Mars, the Bringer of War*; 2. *Venus, the Bringer of Peace*; 3. *Mercury, the Winged Messenger*; 4. *Jupiter, the Bringer of Jollity*; 5. *Saturn, the Bringer of Old Age*; 6. *Uranus, the Magician*; 7. *Neptune, the Mystic*. First (private) performance, London, Queen's Hall, 29 September 1918; first public performance, London, 15 November 1920. The idea of writing music on the planets was not new: Buxtehude wrote a harpsichord suite on them; but Holst dealt with them from the astrological aspect.

Plantagenet
English royal house, reigning 1154–1399, whose name comes from the nickname of Geoffrey, Count of Anjou (1113–1151), father of Henry II, who often wore in his hat a sprig of broom, *planta genista*. In the 1450s, Richard, Duke of York, took 'Plantagenet' as a surname to emphasize his superior claim to the throne over that of Henry VI. See genealogy on page 706.

Plantation of Ireland
Colonization and conquest of Ireland by English and Scottish settlers from 1556 to 1660. There were several rebellions against the plantation by the Irish and the Anglo-Irish aristocracy. The final stages of the conquest took place under ◊Cromwell.

Plater, Alan Frederick (1935–)
English dramatist. He is best known as a writer for television (18 episodes of *Z Cars* and 30 episodes of *Softly Softly*). His TV and radio scripts and plays reflect his northern working-class origins, left-wing political beliefs, and love of jazz.

Playfair, William Henry (1789–1857)
Scottish Neo-Classical architect. He was responsible for much of the design of Edinburgh New Town in the early 19th century. His buildings there, mostly in Neo-Greek style, included the Calton Hill Memorial, the Advocates' Library, the Royal Institution (1822; altered 1831; now the Royal Scottish Academy), the College of Surgeons, and the National Gallery of Scotland (1850).

Pleasence, Donald (1919–1995)
English character actor. He specialized in sinister or mysterious roles; for example, the devious, aggressive tramp in Harold Pinter's *The Caretaker* (1960), which he also played in

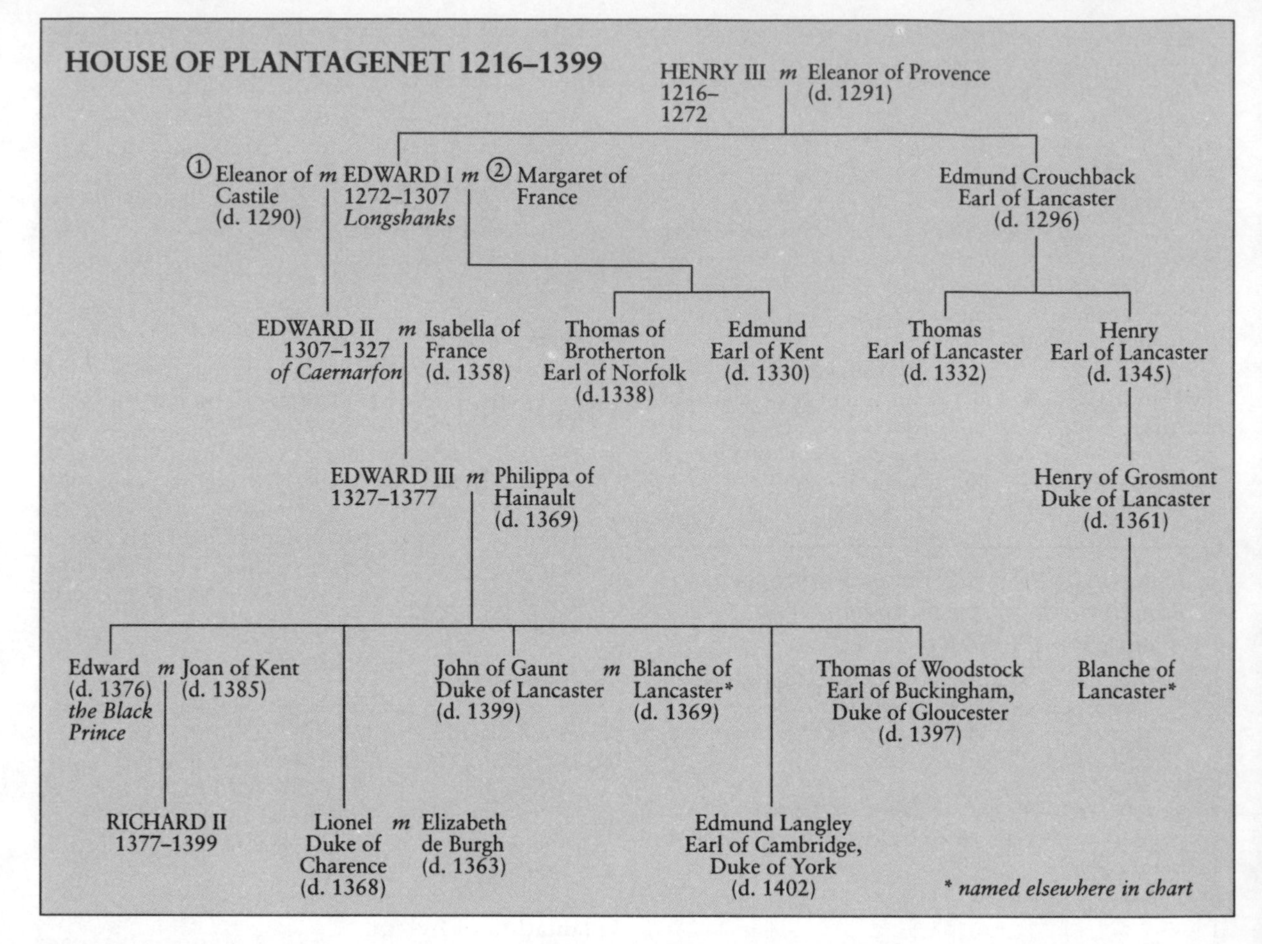

the film version of 1963. His other films include *Dr Crippen* (1962), *Will Penny* (1968), and *The Eagle Has Landed* (1976), in which he played the Nazi Himmler.

Pleasence made his first film appearance in 1954 and, after graduating to featured roles, only occasionally returned to the stage, though he had success as a Nazi war criminal in *The Man in the Glass Booth* (1968), and in 1990 reprised the tramp's role in a revival of *The Caretaker*. In more sympathetic guise, he played the investigating psychiatrist in the influential horror film *Halloween* (1978). Other films include Roman Polanski's *Cul de Sac* (1966), *Soldier Blue* (1970), *The Last Tycoon* (1976), and he played James Bond's adversary Blofeld in *You Only Live Twice* (1967). He was one of the most prolific of British film and television actors.

Plimsoll, Samuel (1824–1898)

English social reformer, born in Bristol. He sat in Parliament as a Radical from 1868 until 1880, and through his efforts the Merchant Shipping Act was passed in 1876, providing for Board of Trade inspection of ships, and the compulsory painting of a **Plimsoll line** (a circular disc with a horizontal line drawn through its centre) to indicate safe loading limits.

Plowright, Joan (1929–)

English stage and screen actress. One of the leading classical actresses of the British stage, she has also enjoyed a lengthy film career, making her screen debut in *Moby Dick* (1956). She worked in both US and British productions, mixing comic and dramatic roles, including an adaptation of John Osborne's play *The Entertainer* (1960), *Drowning By Numbers* (1987), and *Enchanted April* (1991). She also featured in the live action *101 Dalmations* (1996) and the television series *Encore! Encore!*. She was married to English actor Laurence ◊Olivier.

Plymouth

City, seaport, and unitary authority in southwest England, at the mouth of the River Plym; unitary authority area 79 sq km/31 sq mi; population (1994 est) 257,000. Until April 1998 it was part of the county of Devon. It has a dockyard, barracks, and a naval base at Devonport. There are marine and machine tools industries, and clothing, radio equipment, and processed foods are produced. The city rises north of the Hoe headland where tradition has it that the explorer Francis Drake played bowls as the Spanish Armada approached in 1588. The *Mayflower* Pilgrims sailed from here to North America in 1620.

The city centre was reconstructed after heavy bombing in World War II. Plymouth has ferry links with France and Spain. Plymouth University, formerly South West Polytechnic, was established in 1992.

PLYMOUTH *The Hoe, the level headland overlooking Plymouth Sound, is reputed to be the place where the naval hero Sir Francis Drake played bowls while waiting for the onslaught of the Spanish Armada on Britain in 1588. The lighthouse (Smeaton's Tower) was moved here from Eddystone Rocks, and is merely a decorative feature. Corel*

The three separate towns of Devonport, East Stonehouse, and Plymouth were amalgamated in 1914 under the inclusive name of Plymouth. There are three harbours, Sutton Pool, Catwater (Cattewater), and the Hamoaze, which unite in **Plymouth Sound**, a spacious bay which has a breakwater over 1 km/0.6 mi in length across the entrance.

Features

Dominating the city are the ramparts of the 17th-century citadel, built to guard the harbour soon after the long sieges when Plymouth successfully withstood Royalist attacks during the Civil War. The Eddystone Rocks lighthouse is 22 km/14 mi to the south. The Hoe, an esplanade overlooking Plymouth Sound, has many monuments including a statue of Sir Francis Drake, and Smeaton's Tower, originally erected in 1759 on the Eddystone Rocks and replaced in 1882. Plymouth Dome illustrates the history of the city. There is an aquarium of the Marine Biological Association, which has its headquarters in Plymouth. The Devonport dockyard is used for the refitting of commissioned and the stripping of decommissioned nuclear submarines.

History

The naval explorer James Cook led his first (1768–71) and third (1776–79) Pacific voyages from Plymouth. The first meeting in England of the fundamentalist Christian Protestant sect, the ◊Plymouth Brethren, was held here in 1831.

Famous people

The navigator John Hawkins and the painter John Northcote were born in Plymouth in 1532 and 1746 respectively. Robert Falcon Scott (Scott of the Antarctic) was born in Devonport in 1868.

Plymouth Brethren

Fundamentalist Christian Protestant sect characterized by extreme simplicity of belief, founded in Dublin about 1827 by the Reverend John Nelson Darby (1800–1882). The Plymouth Brethren have no ordained priesthood, affirming the ministry of all believers, and maintain no church buildings. They hold prayer meetings and Bible study in members' houses.

An assembly of Brethren was held in Plymouth in 1831 to celebrate the sect's arrival in England, but by 1848 the movement had split into 'Open' and 'Closed' Brethren. The latter refuse communion with those not of their persuasion. A further subset of the Closed Brethren is the 'Exclusive' Brethren, who have strict rules regarding dress and conduct.

In the UK, the Plymouth Brethren are mainly found in the fishing villages of northeast Scotland. Worldwide membership is about 1.5 million (1993), including members in the Caribbean, India, and Myanmar.

Plymouth Sound, or the Sound

Arm of the English Channel between Devon and Cornwall, covering an area of 2,226 ha/5,500 acres. It provides good anchorage. Its inlets include the Catwater (or ' Cattewater'), Sutton Pool, Mill Bay, Stonehouse Pool, the Hamoaze (a naval harbour at the estuary of the River Tamar), and Cawsand Bay. A long breakwater was completed 4 km/2.5 mi south of the Hoe in 1845, to provide shelter from southwesterly gales.

Plympton

Market town in Devon, England, 7 km/4 mi northeast of Plymouth; population (1991) 26,900. Plympton, a 'stannary' (tin-mining) town (see ◊stannaries), comprises the parishes of Plympton St Mary and Plympton St Maurice. It has an ancient guildhall, and there are ruins of an old castle.

Plympton St Maurice was the headquarters of Prince Maurice (a Royalist appointed in 1643 to the command of the Cornish army), and the birthplace of the painter Joshua Reynolds. Reynolds was educated at the grammar school, which was founded in 1658.

Plynlimon, Welsh Pumlumon

Mountain in Ceredigion, central Wales, with three summits; the highest is 752 m/2,468 ft. The rivers ◊Wye, ◊Severn, Lynfant, Rheidol, and Ystwyth rise on its slopes.

It is chiefly formed of clay-slate with veins of lead. Its heights form a commanding viewpoint.

Poel, William (1852–1934)

English actor and producer. He formed the Elizabethan Stage Society in 1895, whose productions influenced the work of other actors and producers. He favoured a bare stage, fine verse speaking, and a swift, unbroken progress through the play. One of his most successful productions was a revival of the medieval morality play *Everyman* in 1901.

Dame Edith ◊Evans made an appearance, as an amateur, as Cressida in his production of Shakespeare's *Troilus and Cressida*, and he trained a number of actors noted for their good diction.

poet laureate

Poet of the British royal household, so called because of the laurel wreath awarded to eminent poets in the Graeco-Roman world. Early UK poets with unofficial status were John Skelton, Samuel Daniel, Ben ◊Jonson, and William Davenant. John ◊Dryden was the first to receive the title by letters-patent in 1668 and from then on the post became a regular institution. Ted ◊Hughes was poet laureate 1984–98.

There is a stipend of £70 a year, plus £27 in lieu of the traditional butt of sack (cask of wine). See table below.

point-to-point

A form of horse racing over fences, organized by local hunts in Britain. It is open only to amateurs riding horses that have been regularly used in hunts. The point-to-point season lasts January to May.

Poitevin

In English history, relating to the reigns of King John and King Henry III. The term is derived from the region of France south of the Loire (Poitou), which was controlled by the English for most of this period.

Poets Laureate

Appointed	Poet Laureate
1668	John Dryden (1631–1700)
1689	Thomas Shadwell (c 1642–1692)
1692	Nahum Tate (1652–1715)
1715	Nicholas Rowe (1674–1718)
1718	Laurence Eusden (1688–1730)
1730	Colley Cibber (1671–1757)
1757	William Whitehead (1715–1785)
1785	Thomas Warton (1728–1790)
1790	Henry James Pye (1745–1813)
1813	Robert Southey (1774–1843)
1843	William Wordsworth (1770–1850)
1850	Alfred, Lord Tennyson (1809–1892)
1896	Alfred Austin (1835–1913)
1913	Robert Bridges (1844–1930)
1930	John Masefield (1878–1967)
1968	Cecil Day-Lewis (1904–1972)
1972	Sir John Betjeman (1906–1984)
1984	Ted Hughes (1930–1998)

Polesden Lacey

Villa near Dorking, Surrey, England. Originally an elegant 1820s villa, the house was extensively remodelled after 1906, and bequeathed to the National Trust in 1942, with 365 ha/902 acres, by the Hon Mrs Ronald Greville (a well-known Edwardian hostess). The house contains her collection of paintings, furniture, porcelain, and silver. The gardens include a walled rose garden and tree-lined walks.

King George VI and Queen Elizabeth (now the Queen Mother) spent part of their honeymoon here in 1923.

Richard Brinsley ◊Sheridan bought the original Caroline house in 1797, and his son sold the property in 1818 to Joseph Bonsor, who built the present house.

police

Civil law-and-order force. It is responsible to the Home Office, with 56 autonomous police forces, generally organized on a county basis; mutual aid is given in circumstances such as mass picketing in the 1984–85 miners' strike, but there is no national police force or police riot unit. The predecessors of these forces were the ineffective medieval watch and London's Bow Street runners, introduced in 1749 by Henry ◊Fielding which formed a model for the London police force established by Robert ◊Peel's government in 1829 (hence 'peelers' or 'bobbies'); the system was introduced throughout the country from 1856.

Landmarks include: **Criminal Investigation Department** detective branch of the London Metropolitan Police (New Scotland Yard) (established in 1878), recruited from the uniformed branch (such departments now exist in all UK forces); women police (1919); motorcycle patrols (1921); two-way radio cars (1927); personal radio on the beat (1965); and **Special Patrol Groups** (SPG) (1970), squads of experienced officers concentrating on a specific problem. Unlike most other police forces, the British are armed only on special occasions, but arms issues grow more frequent. In 1997 the London Metropolitan Police Force had about 27,000 officers, one for every 255 citizens.

Police expenditure increased by 55% in real terms in the period 1979–90. The police had an annual budget of £6.5 billion and a staff of 127,000 in 1995.

In 1991, the force claimed to clear up 26% of all recorded crimes, although this is estimated to be only 7% of the total committed.

The 3 million criminal records held by the British police on microfiche were entered on a national computer system called Phoenix in 1994.

Police Complaints Authority

An independent group of a dozen people set up under the Police and Criminal Evidence Act 1984 to supervise the investigation of complaints against the police by members of the public.

When the investigation of a complaint is completed the authority must make a public declaration of its decision. It can order disciplinary action to be taken against police officers. The total number of complaints in 1989 was 11,155, of which 1.7% resulted in disciplinary charges. Alternatively, a complainant may take a case to court. The number of successful civil actions against the police rises every year. In England and Wales in 1992 there were 35,000 recorded complaints against the police, but not all of these were forwarded to the authority.

Pollen, Arabella (1961–)

English fashion designer. She achieved instant success in 1981 when she sold one of her first coat designs to the Princess of Wales. She has become familiar for her classic styles – tailored, sophisticated shapes in bright-coloured wool and cotton. In 1991 she launched Pollen B, a line of clothing directed at a younger market, which is simpler in design and cheaper than her main collection.

poll tax

Tax levied on every individual, without reference to income or property. Being simple to administer, it was among the earliest sorts of tax (introduced in England in 1379), but because of its indiscriminate nature (it is a regressive tax, in that it falls proportionately more on poorer people) it has often proved unpopular. The **community charge**, a type of poll tax, was introduced in Scotland by the British government in April 1989, and in England and Wales in 1990, replacing the property-based local taxation (the ◊rates). Its unpopularity contributed to the downfall of the then prime minister Margaret Thatcher. It was replaced from 1993 to 1994 by a ◊council tax, based both on property values and on the size of households.

The poll tax of 1379 contributed to the ◊Peasants' Revolt of 1381 and was abolished in England in 1698.

The British government's decision to abolish the community charge followed widespread opposition and regional demonstrations, notably the central London anti-poll-tax rally in March 1990, which culminated in police–civilian violence and high-street looting. The combined cost of its collection and abolition was estimated at £4 billion.

pollution

The greatest single cause of **air pollution** in the UK is the car, which is responsible for 85% of the carbon monoxide and 45% of the oxides of nitrogen present in the atmosphere. In 1987 carbon monoxide emission from road transport was measured at 5.26 million tonnes. According to a UK government report in 1998, air pollution causes up to 24,000 deaths in Britain per year. **Water pollution** is controlled by the Environment Agency (since 1996).

In 1989 the regional water authorities of England and Wales were privatized to form ten water and sewerage companies. Following concern that some of these companies were failing to meet EU drinking-water standards on nitrate and pesticide levels, the companies were served with enforcement notices by the government Drinking Water Inspectorate. The existence of 1,300 toxic waste tips in the UK in 1990 posed a considerable threat for increased water pollution.

polytechnic

Formerly an institution for higher education offering courses mainly at degree level and concentrating on full-time vocational courses, although many polytechnics provided a wide range of part-time courses at advanced levels.

In April 1989 the polytechnics in England and Wales became independent corporations. In 1992 all polytechnics and some colleges of higher education became universities, and from 1993 all universities began to compete for funding on an equal basis.

From 1992 public funds became the responsibility of the new Universities and Colleges Funding Council. Academic validation of courses was transferred from the Council for National Academic Awards to the individual institutions. The new UK university sector consisted of 104 institutions.

Pomp and Circumstance

Five military marches by Elgar, originally intended as a set of 6. 1–4 were composed 1901–07, 5 in 1930. The first contains, as a trio, the tune afterwards used in the *Coronation Ode* to the words 'Land of hope and glory'.

Pontefract

Industrial town in West Yorkshire, northern England, 34 km/21 mi southwest of York, near the junction of the rivers Aire and Calder; population (1991) 28,400. Industries include coalmining, iron founding, engineering, tanning, brewing, corn milling, market gardening, and the manufacture of furniture and confectionery. The town gives its name to liquorice Pontefract or Pomfret cakes. Features include the remains of the Norman castle (built in 1069) where Richard II was murdered in 1399.

History

The first borough charter was granted at the end of the 12th century. The castle was a Royalist stronghold during the English Civil War, sustaining three sieges in the mid-17th century before the Royalists surrendered. It was destroyed in 1649.

Pontypool, Welsh Pontypwl

Industrial town and administrative centre of ◊Torfaen unitary authority, southeast Wales, situated on the Afon Llwyd 15 km/9 mi north of Newport; population (1991) 35,600. Products include iron and steel goods, tinplate, glass, synthetic textiles, and scientific instruments. The first tinplate to be made in Britain was produced here in 1703

The town is made up of a series of semi-independent industrial villages including Varteg, Garndiffaith, Abersychan, Pontymoel, Griffithstown, New Inn, and Sebastopol. It is bordered on the south by the new town of ◊Cwmbran.

Pontypridd (Welsh 'old bridge')

Industrial town in Rhondda Cynon Taff, south Wales, situated at the junction of the rivers ◊Taff and ◊Rhondda; population (1990 est) 33,600. Industries include chain and cable works, iron and brass founding, chemicals, and light industry on the Treforest trading estate 3 km/1.9 mi from the centre.

The town is industrial in character, but possesses the spacious Ynysangharad Park. The 'Old Bridge' (from which the town takes its name) was erected in 1755, and has a single span of 43 m/140 ft; it is no longer in use.

Poole

Industrial town, port, and since 1997, a unitary authority in southern England, 8 km/5 mi west of Bournemouth; area 64 sq km/25 sq mi; population (1996) 138,100. It was part of the county of Dorset until 1997. Poole Harbour is a centre for yachting. In addition to tourism, the town's industries include engineering, boatbuilding, and the manufacture of caravans, sail cloth, packaging materials, tiles, and pottery from local clay.

Features Furzey Island, within the harbour, is part of Wytch Farm, Britain's largest onshore oil development; the River Stour which forms the northern border of the authority; Poole Harbour; Holes Bay; Pergins Island; Maritime Museum (Poole); Compton Acres themed gardens (including water, rock, heather, Japanese, Roman, Italian); Canford Heath, tumuli field; Sandbanks spit guarding entrance to harbour; ferry from Poole to Brownsea Island and the Channel Islands.

The first Scout camp was held in 1907 on Brownsea Island in the harbour; the island is now owned by the National Trust. Brownsea Island has a large bird sanctuary, and Furzey Island is a haven for the red squirrel.

poor law

English system for poor relief, established by the Poor Relief Act of 1601. Each parish was responsible for its own poor, paid for by a parish tax. The care of the poor was transferred to the Ministry of Health in 1918, but the poor law remained in force until 1930.

Poor law was reformed in the 19th century. After the Royal Commission on the Poor Law of 1834, 'outdoor' relief for able-bodied paupers was abolished and replaced by workhouses run by unions of parishes. Conditions in such workhouses were designed to act as a deterrent for all but the genuinely destitute, but the Andover workhouse scandal of 1847 removed some of the greatest corruptions and evils of the system.

Pop art

Movement in modern art that took its imagery from the glossy world of advertising and from popular culture such as comic strips, films, and television; it developed in the 1950s and flourished in the 1960s, notably in Britain and the USA. The term was coined by the British critic Lawrence Alloway (1926–1990) in about 1955, to refer to works of art that drew upon popular culture. Richard Hamilton, one of the leading British pioneers and exponents of Pop art, defined it in 1957 as 'popular, transient, expendable, low-cost, mass-produced, young, witty, sexy, gimmicky, glamorous, and Big Business'. In its eclecticism and sense of irony and playfulness, Pop art helped to prepare the way for the Post-Modernism that has been a feature of Western culture since the 1970s.

Pop art was an expression of a time of relative affluence that followed a period of austerity after World War II. It was often comical in mood, sometimes deliberately debunking the values of the art world.

Leading British figures included Peter Blake, David Hockney, Allen Jones, and Eduardo Paolozzi. For some of these artists, such as Hockney, Pop art represented a brief stage in their career, but others have solidly committed themselves to the style.

Pop design

Design movement of the 1960s which was characterized by its use of bright colours, expressive forms, synthetic materials, and throwaway objects.

Pop design centred on fashion – exemplified by the work of Mary ◊Quant and John Stephen who opened a number of boutiques in Carnaby Street – and graphics, as in the work of the psychedelic poster artists Michael English (1942–) and Nigel Weymouth. In essence, Pop design set out to challenge and subvert establishment design values.

Pope, Alexander (1688–1744)

English poet and satirist. He established his poetic reputation with the precocious *Pastorals* (1709) and *An Essay on Criticism* (1711), which were followed by a parody of the heroic epic, *The Rape of the Lock* (1712–14), *The Temple of Fame* (1715), and 'Eloisa to Abelard' (1717). The highly Neo-Classical translations of Homer's *Iliad* and *Odyssey* (1715–26) were very successful but his edition of Shakespeare (1725) attracted scholarly ridicule, which led Pope to write a satire on scholarly dullness, *The Dunciad* (1728). His finest mature works are his *Imitations of the Satires of Horace* (1733–38) and his personal letters.

Pope had a biting wit, expressed in the heroic couplet, of which he was a master. His couplets have an epigrammatic quality ('True wit is nature to advantage dressed/What oft was thought, but ne'er so well expressed'), and many of his observations have passed into the language as proverbs, for example 'A little learning is a dang'rous thing'. His philosophical verse, including *An Essay on Man* (1733–34) and *Moral Essays* (1731–35), was influenced by the political philosopher Henry ◊Bolingbroke. As a Catholic, he was subject to discrimination, and he was embittered by a deformity of the spine caused by childhood illness. Among his friends were the writers Jonathan ◊Swift, John ◊Arbuthnot, and John ◊Gay, and with them he was a member of the Scriblerus Club.

pop festival

Outdoor concert usually spanning a weekend and featuring a number of bands; pop, rock, heavy-metal, and world-music festivals have become regular events in many countries since the 1960s. British pop festivals include Glastonbury (established in 1970) and Reading (1971).

pop music

A key British industry at the end of the 20th century. See feature on a brief history of British pop music (pp. 712–713) and the chronology of some pop highlights (p. 711).

Popper, Karl Raimund (1902–1994)

British philosopher of science, who was born in Austria and became a naturalized British subject in 1945. His theory of falsificationism states that although scientific generalizations cannot be conclusively verified, they can be conclusively

Pop music: some key dates

1952 *Hit Parade* is the first television pop music show on British television.

14 November 1952 The popular music magazine *New Musical Express* publishes Britain's first pop singles chart.

1956 Rock 'n' roll music dominates dance floors in Britain.

1957 The US rock singer Elvis Presley's single 'All Shook Up' becomes his first number one in Britain.

3 March 1957 *The Eurovision Song Contest*, which started in 1956, is shown for the first time on British television.

1960–69 The Beatles' song 'She Loves You' is the best-selling single of the 1960s in Britain. The Beatles are responsible for five out of the top six singles in Britain in the 1960s.

1961 The British rock group the Rolling Stones is formed.

1961 The Shadows become the first British rock group to top the UK album charts, with *The Shadows*.

1963 Rhythm and blues music becomes popular in Britain, with key acts including Chuck Berry and Bo Diddley.

1964 *Top of the Pops*, to date the longest-running rock and pop music programme on British television, starts broadcasting. It has a significant influence on sales.

29 March 1964 Radio Caroline, the first offshore 'pirate' radio station broadcasting to Britain, begins transmissions from a ship in the North Sea. Modelled on Radio Luxembourg with its nonstop diet of pop music, it is Britain's first pop music station.

1966 Soul is fashionable in Britain, with the music of James Brown, Wilson Pickett, Otis Redding, and Stevie Wonder very popular.

30 September 1967 The BBC launches a national pop music station, Radio 1. The first programme is *The Breakfast Show*, presented by Tony Blackburn, and the first record played is 'Flowers in the Rain' by the Move.

1969 The British rock group the Beatles make their last ever public appearance on the roof of the Apple Records building in London, England. It is recorded as part of their film *Let It Be*.

1971 Glam rock emerges. A reaction against progressive rock, it is characterized by elaborate costumes, makeup, and stage posturing, as exemplified by British bands such as T Rex and the Sweet.

1971 The first Glastonbury music festival takes place.

1972 Groups such as the Bay City Rollers, the Jackson Five, the Osmonds, and David Cassidy mark the era of 'Teenybop', with the bands appealing particularly to teenage girls.

1972 The first rock concert at Wembley Stadium in London, England, takes place. Artists appearing include Bill Haley and Chuck Berry and a film of the event, *The London Rock and Roll Show*, is released.

20 December 1975 The British pop group Queen promotes its song 'Bohemian Rhapsody', from the album *A Night at the Opera*, with the first pop video. The video, produced by Bruce Gowers on a £4,500 budget, debuts on the television programme *Top of the Pops*.

1977 Punk music comes to prominence in the UK, with the emergence of bands such as the Sex Pistols, the Clash, the Buzzcocks, the Damned, and the Stranglers.

1978 The music magazine *Smash Hits* is launched; it will become the most successful magazine for the teenage market in the UK.

1982 *The Tube*, Britain's most influential television music programme of the 1980s, starts on BBC2, with presenters Paula Yates and Jools Holland.

13 July 1985 Live Aid, organized by Band Aid to raise funds for famine-relief in Africa, is a day-long concert held simultaneously at Wembley Stadium in London and JFK Stadium in Philadelphia, USA. Over $70 million is raised worldwide.

20 September 1997 The English pop star Elton John releases the single 'Candle in the Wind 1997' as a tribute to Diana, Princess of Wales. It goes immediately to number one and becomes the best-selling single of all time.

falsified by a counterinstance; therefore, science is not certain knowledge but a series of 'conjectures and refutations', approaching, though never reaching, a definitive truth. For Popper, psychoanalysis and Marxism are falsifiable and therefore unscientific.

Popper is one of the most widely read philosophers of the 20th century. His book *The Open Society and its Enemies* (1945) became a modern classic. In it he investigated the long history of attempts to formulate a theory of the state. Animated by a dislike of the views of Freud and Marx, Popper believed he could show that their hypotheses about hidden social and psychological processes were falsifiable.

His major work on the philosophy of science is *The Logic of Scientific Discovery* (1935). Other works include *The Poverty of Historicism* (1957) (about the philosophy of social science), *Conjectures and Refutations* (1963), and *Objective Knowledge* (1972). Popper was professor of logic and scientific method at the London School of Economics (LSE) 1949–69. Knighted 1965.

population

The UK's population in 1997 was 59 million. See related tables and map, pages 714–717.

FROM ROCK 'N' ROLL TO BRITPOP: A BRIEF HISTORY OF BRITISH POP MUSIC

Rock 'n' roll first came to Britain as an imported luxury that alleviated post-war austerity. According to Keith Richards of the Rolling Stones, 'There was nothing for kids after the war. Nothing in the shops. No sweets. The only music was 'I'm a Pink Toothbrush'. Then you heard Chuck Berry, Eddie Cochran, and Elvis and boom! That was it. Everything changed.'

Attempts made in the mid- to late-1950s to copy American records were successful in the home market but not in the USA. Tommy Steele and Cliff Richard did not possess the same raw conviction as the US originals and in truth were a continuation of 'light entertainment' by other means. Besides, only imported US goods had real hipster cachet, whether in rock 'n' roll, jazz, rhythm and blues (R&B), or blues.

However, as economic prosperity and music-industrial efficiency burgeoned in the USA in the late-1950s, causing the tougher rock acts to be displaced in public taste by sweeter, more romantic fare (for example, doo-wop), British pop assumed the role of torch-bearer for more fundamental values. In the northwest of the early to mid-1960s, the so-called Merseybeat scene – musically predicated on punchy, guitar-driven, R&B-pop songs played for the benefit of dancers in clubs – gave rise to such groups as Gerry and the Pacemakers and, crucially, the Beatles. The latter began as copyists of authentic US styles but through the early part of the 1960s began to write more of their own material and, by 1965, Lennon and McCartney stood as the most accomplished and sophisticated pop composers yet seen.

During this period, in the southeast (chiefly in London and its suburbs), hipster devotion to black American blues and R&B reached fever pitch. Leaders in the field were the Rolling Stones and 'Mod' stylists the Who, pursued by such hardcore bluesologists as the Yardbirds, Pretty Things and John Mayall's Bluesbreakers, plus the Animals from the northeast and Them (featuring Van Morrison) from Belfast. The British 'blues boom' coincided with the economic prosperity of mid-1960s 'swinging London'. Instrumental virtuosity became a major issue for the first time in pop, giving rise to the competitive marketing of such guitar heroes as Eric Clapton, Jeff Beck, and Jimmy Page, all of whom played in the Yardbirds at some point or other. This was 'rock' music.

In the black metropolitan centres, meanwhile, imported Jamaican bluebeat and ska was beginning to be heard more and more, and appreciated by sharp working-class whites in the same way that imported American blues records were appreciated half a decade earlier.

Psychedelia

The increased availability of drugs, both hard and soft but particularly hallucinogenic, had immense impact in the mid-1960s. The Beatles, as ever, were market leaders, recording the first truly psychedelic British album in 1967 (*Sgt Pepper's Lonely Hearts Club Band*) and seeming to embrace the hippy ideal with alacrity. Also, Messrs Page, Clapton, and Beck suddenly found themselves upstaged on their own patch by a wild, black American guitar virtuoso with true psychedelic style, Jimi Hendrix, who had acquired a British manager and chosen the ostensibly 'cooler' London scene as a base for operations. In an increasingly competitive climate, Clapton formed supergroup Cream, Page formed Led Zeppelin, and Beck the Jeff Beck Group, and for a while rock music became instrumentally otiose, diminishing somewhat the impact of the poppier, bouncier efforts of Steve Marriott's Small Faces.

As hippy values spread throughout the late-1960s, so rock music adopted a more pastoral attitude. English folk-rock emerged with such groups as Traffic and Fairport Convention, and experimental electronics were heard in psychedelic clubs to complement extravagant light shows. The technically limited but imaginatively gifted (and resoundingly middle-class) Pink Floyd were leaders in the field and helped pave the way for what came to be known as 'progressive rock' in the 1970s.

Marauding punks

Prog rock's greatest failing lay in its reluctance to edit itself. Instrumental virtuosity became, for some groups, the essence of what rock might become, and so musicians' excesses compromised even the best efforts of Prog's leading exponents, Yes and Genesis. Prog was also often mystical, technically overblown, unequivocally English, largely middle-class in personnel, and therefore was a sitting target for those with a radical agenda. Prog died a terrible death in the UK in 1976–77 at the hands of marauding punks.

The ground had been prepared for punk in the early 1970s by the anarcho-androgyny that was Glam Rock. The London suburbanite David Bowie had used pop during this period as a tool with which to explore his art of confounding expectations, and had written some classic pop songs to boot. He was profoundly influenced by the Pop art world of Andy Warhol and the Velvet Underground in New York, as were Glam rivals Roxy Music. But Glam also restored pop purism to the agenda, and groups like Slade, T Rex, Gary Glitter, Sweet, and Mott the Hoople counterbalanced any perceived artiness with a decidedly camp-proletarian stance.

The punks, however, adopted a minimalist policy with regard to musical aesthetics. The Sex Pistols, Clash, Damned, Buzzcocks, and so on could barely play their instruments and so refocussed the pop agenda on to socio-political issues and the output of raw energy. They also aligned themselves explicitly with the growing force of Jamaican reggae, led by Bob Marley and the Wailers and taken up by British acts such as Aswad and Steel Pulse.

As punk's initial energy dissipated in the face of fierce commercial exploitation, the Anglo-Caribbean connection grew in symbolic importance, resulting in the brief but powerful 'Two Tone' explosion. In 1979–81, the Specials, Selecter, Madness, and the Beat all made multiracialism a cornerstone of their aesthetic and borrowed heavily on traditional hip working-class tastes for Jamaican ska and US R&B, creating in the process an apposite soundtrack for the social disturbances of the period.

Danceability

The immense global success of disco in the 1970s had reinvigorated club culture, which had largely been engulfed in the 1960s by the tidal success of rock music. Disco, however, had no social geography as such, and it was this equity of the dance floor that gave rise to the New Romantic scene of the early 1980s. New Romanticism somehow fused the sartorial principles of Glam with the musical values of disco. Spandau Ballet, Culture Club, Duran Duran, the Human League, and ABC defined mid-1980s UK pop with a theatricalized, high camp, low-brow brand of semi-ironic performance pop, in which musical value was subordinated to the visual impact of the group and the danceability of the beat. Their success set in train the mechanism by which club culture would come to dominate the popular music agenda.

In the meantime, the huge success of Bob Geldof's Live Aid event in 1985 completed the globalization of pop music. From 1985 it was possible to observe that there was not a nation on Earth which did not sustain a healthy trade in CDs by Dire Straits, Michael Jackson, and Madonna.

1990s fragmentation

The local response in the UK was to go underground again, once more with imported American dance records, and create what came to be known as the 'rave' scene. Groups, singers, and all visual epiphenomena were deemed crass and exploitative, and the home-made, technically limited 12-inch dance record became the hub of a new DIY aesthetic. The DJ replaced the old-fashioned pop star as bearer of the creative torch. Clubs or open fields, as opposed to concert halls and stadia, became the venues of choice. Melody largely went out of pop music.

Meanwhile, the multicultural fusions set in train by the punks, the advent of homegrown reggae and soul, and the Two Toners resulted in the absolute fragmentation of taste. In the early 1990s, longstanding rock groups like U2 made albums with dance beats, while certain structural elements long associated with rock (like distorted electric guitars) would turn up, in edited, manipulated form, in the middle of dance records. Drum 'n' bass (initially known as 'jungle') became the first truly British formal invention in pop – and it was a hybrid.

The rise of such explicitly retrospective Britpop rock groups as Blur, Oasis, and Suede during the middle of the decade was testament partly to the lack of focus in the UK pop scene in the face of such fragmentation, and partly to the acceptability of conservative taste some forty years on from the advent of Elvis Presley. Similarly, a vast nostalgia market has grown over the past decade.

BY NICK COLEMAN

The Manchester band Oasis has been one of British pop's most consistent success stories in the 1990s. However, press coverage has focused as much on the off-stage escapades and private lives of the group's front-men, the brothers Liam and Noel Gallagher, as on their music.
Simon Walker/Rex

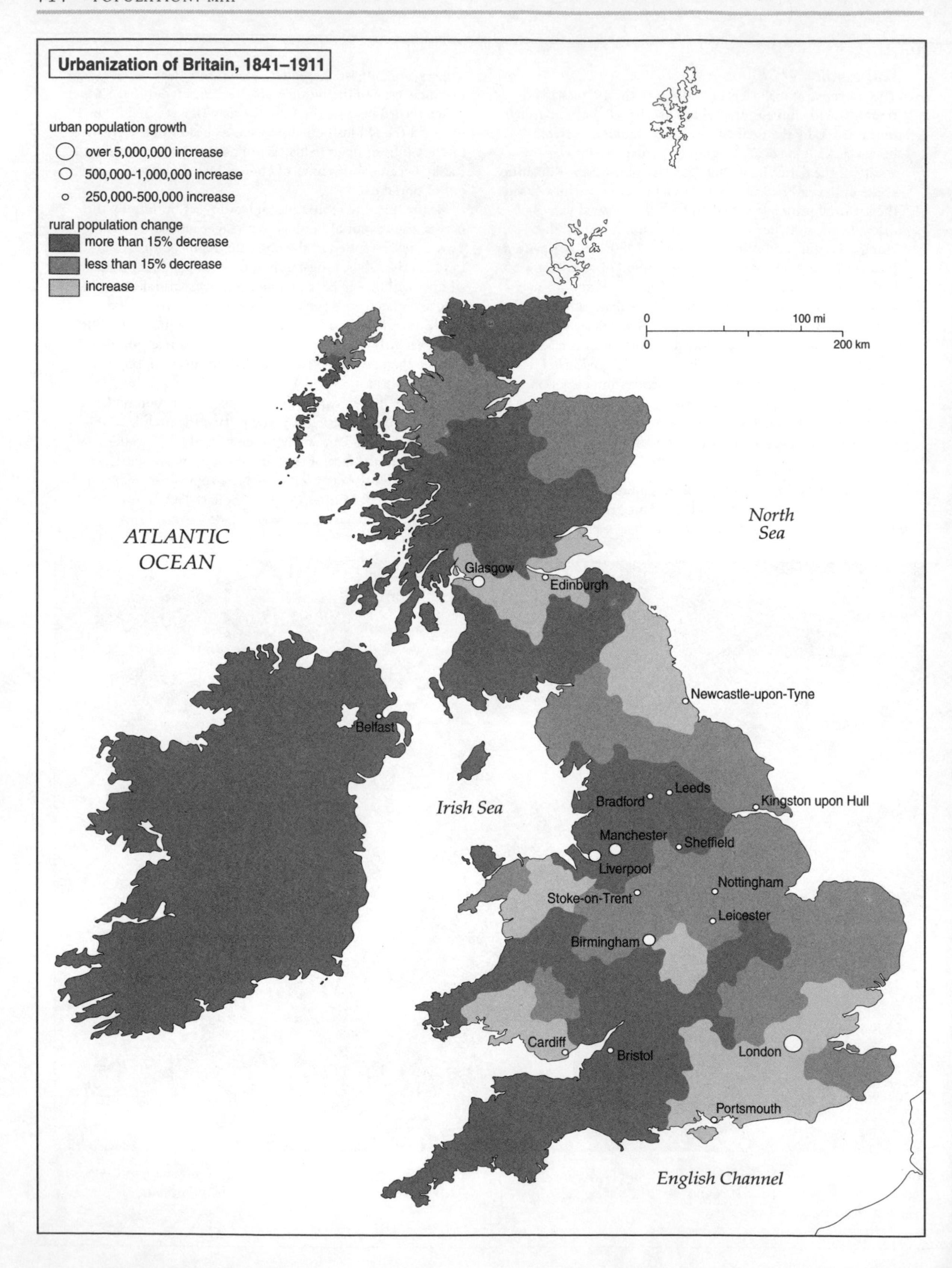
Urbanization of Britain, 1841–1911
urban population growth
over 5,000,000 increase
500,000-1,000,000 increase
250,000-500,000 increase
rural population change
more than 15% decrease
less than 15% decrease
increase
0
100 mi
0
200 km
ATLANTIC OCEAN
North Sea
Irish Sea
English Channel
Glasgow
Edinburgh
Belfast
Newcastle-upon-Tyne
Leeds
Bradford
Kingston upon Hull
Manchester
Sheffield
Liverpool
Nottingham
Stoke-on-Trent
Leicester
Birmingham
Cardiff
Bristol
London
Portsmouth

Porlock

Village in Somerset, England, on the edge of Exmoor; population (1991) 1,300. It is noted for the steep gradient (25%/1 in 4) of Porlock Hill. The village has a Perpendicular church and some thatched houses. Porlock Bay is an opening of the Bristol Channel, 7.2 km/4.5 mi wide, with Porlock Weir, the old harbour, at the western end.

porphyria

Group of rare genetic disorders caused by an enzyme defect. Porphyria affects the digestive tract, causing abdominal distress; the nervous system, causing psychotic disorder, epilepsy, and weakness; the circulatory system, causing high blood pressure; and the skin, causing extreme sensitivity to light. It is known as the 'royal disease' because sufferers are believed to have included Mary Queen of Scots, James I, and George III.

Porritt, Jonathon (1950–)

British environmental campaigner, director of ◊Friends of the Earth 1984–90. He has stood in both British and European elections as a Green (formerly Ecology) Party candidate.

Portadown

Part of the new town of ◊Craigavon in County Armagh, Northern Ireland; population (1991) 21,400. It is situated on the River Bann, 40 km/25 mi southwest of Belfast, and was joined with Lurgan to form Craigavon in 1965. Manufactures include domestic appliances, plastics, and clothing; and there

Population Summary of the UK

Source: *Annual Abstract of Statistics, 1998*, Office for National Statistics, © Crown copyright 1998

Year	Male	Female	Total
Enumerated Population: Census Figures			
1851	11,404,000	10,855,000	22,259,000
1901	19,745,000	18,492,000	38,237,000
1911	21,725,000	20,357,000	42,082,000
1921	22,994,000	21,033,000	44,027,000
1931	23,978,000	22,060,000	46,038,000
1951	26,107,000	24,118,000	50,225,000
1961	27,228,000	25,481,000	52,709,000
Resident Population: Mid-Year Estimates			
1964	27,800,000	26,191,000	53,991,000
1965	27,982,000	26,368,000	54,350,000
1966	28,132,000	26,511,000	54,643,000
1967	28,286,000	26,673,000	54,214,000
1968	28,429,000	26,784,000	55,214,000
1969	28,553,000	26,908,000	55,461,000
1970	28,641,000	26,992,000	55,632,000
1971	28,761,000	27,167,000	55,928,000
1972	28,837,000	27,259,000	56,709,000
1973	28,891,000	27,332,000	56,223,000
1974	28,887,000	27,349,000	56,236,000
1975	28,865,000	27,361,000	56,226,000
1976	28,856,000	27,360,000	56,216,000
1977	28,845,000	27,345,000	56,190,000
1978	28,849,000	27,330,000	56,178,000

Year	Male	Female	Total
1979	28,867,000	27,373,000	56,240,000
1980	28,919,000	27,411,000	56,330,000
1981	28,943,000	27,409,000	56,352,000
1982	28,927,000	27,391,000	56,318,000
1983	28,948,000	27,429,000	56,377,000
1984	28,995,000	27,511,000	56,506,000
1985	29,074,000	27,611,000	56,685,000
1986	29,153,000	27,698,000	56,852,000
1987	29,220,000	27,789,000	57,009,000
1988	29,282,000	27,876,000	57,158,000
1989	29,368,000	27,989,000	57,358,000
1990	29,443,000	28,118,000	57,561,000
1991	29,562,000	28,246,000	57,808,000
192	29,645,000	28,362,000	58,006,000
1993	29,718,000	28,474,000	58,191,000
1994	29,803,000	28,592,000	58,395,000
1995	29,878,000	28,727,000	58,606,000
1996	29,946,000	28,856,000	58,801,000
Resident Population: Projections (Mid-Year)[1]			
2001	30,241,000	29,377,000	59,618,000
2006	30,477,000	29,809,000	60,287,000
2011	30,723,000	30,206,000	60,929,000
2021	31,328,000	30,916,000	62,244,000

[1] These projections are 1996-based.

Age Distribution of the UK

Source: *Annual Abstract of Statistics, 1998*, Office for National Statistics, © Crown copyright 1998

	1996		
Age	**Male**	**Female**	**Total**
Under 1	369,000	350,000	719,000
1–4	1,560,000	1,484,000	3,044,000
5–9	2,002,000	1,903,000	3,905,000
10–14	1,895,000	1,795,000	3,690,000
15–19	1,810,000	1,713,000	3,522,000
20–29	4,289,000	4,091,000	8,380,000
30–44	6,538,000	6,397,000	12,935,000
45–59	5,270,000	5,312,000	10,582,000
60–64	1,355,000	1,418,000	2,772,000
65–74	2,310,000	2,748,000	5,058,000
75–84	1,185,000	1,940,000	3,125,000
85 and over	273,000	794,000	1,067,000
School ages (5–15)	4,276,000	4,059,000	8,335,000
Under 18	6,957,000	6,604,000	13,561,000
Pensionable age	3,768,000	6,900,000	10,668,000
All ages	28,856,000	29,946,000	58,801,000

Migration into and out of the UK

Source: *Annual Abstract of Statistics, 1998*, Office for National Statistics, © Crown copyright 1998

Year	Inflow	Outflow	Balance
1985	232,000	174,000	59,000
1986	250,000	213,000	37,000
1987	212,000	210,000	2,000
1988	216,000	237,000	–21,000
1989	250,000	205,000	44,000
1990	267,000	231,000	36,000
1991	267,000	239,000	28,000
1992	216,000	227,000	–11,000
1993	213,000	216,000	–2,000
1994	253,000	191,000	62,000
1995	245,000	192,000	54,000

Population by Ethnic Group in Great Britain

(Average over the period Spring 1993 to Spring 1996.)
Source: *Annual Abstract of Statistics, 1998*, Office for National Statistics, © Crown copyright 1998

Ethnic group		Number
Black	Caribbean	503,000
	African	273,000
	other (non-mixed)	85,000
	mixed	131,000
Indian		872,000
Pakistani		547,000
Bangladeshi		181,000
Chinese		137,000
Other	Asian (non-mixed)	169,000
	other (non-mixed)	131,000
	mixed	190,000
All ethnic minority groups		3,220,000
White		52,747,000
All ethnic groups[1]		55,981,000

[1] Figure includes ethnic groups not stated.

are service industries, food processing, and newspaper printing and publishing.

Portadown developed first as a result of the construction of the Lough Neagh canal in the 1730s and later as a result of the linen industry and as a railway junction in the 19th century.

Porteous riots

Riots in Edinburgh, Scotland on 14 April 1736, after Lieutenant John Porteous, captain of the Edinburgh militia, ordered his men to open fire on a crowd rioting in protest at the execution of smugglers. Six members of the crowd were killed and Porteous was sentenced to death but was later reprieved. The prison in which Porteous was being held was stormed on 8 September by an angry mob which dragged him out and lynched him. The city was fined £2,000 and the Lord Provost was dismissed. As a result of the affair Walpole lost the crucial support of the Duke of Argyll, who led Scottish peers in the House of Lords.

Porter, Andrew (1928–)

English music critic and scholar. He studied at Oxford University and worked for various newspapers and journals from 1949 (edited *Musical Times* 1960–67). He is noted for his research on Verdi and has prepared for performance much material for *Don Carlos* which Verdi discarded at the first production in 1867; he worked on several translations of Verdi's libretti. His translation of Wagner's *Ring* was heard at

United Kingdom: Breakdown of Population from 1801 (Millions)

year	United Kingdom	England and Wales	Scotland	Northern Ireland
1801	–	8.893	1.608	–
1811	13.368	10.165	1.806	–
1821	15.472	12.000	2.092	–
1831	17.835	13.897	2.364	–
1841	20.183	15.914	2.620	1.649
1851	22.259	17.928	2.889	1.443
1861	24.525	20.066	3.062	1.569
1871	27.431	22.712	3.360	1.359
1881	31.015	25.974	3.736	1.305
1891	34.264	29.003	4.026	1.236
1901	38.237	32.528	4.472	1.237
1911	42.082	36.070	4.761	1.251
1921	44.027	37.887	4.882	1.258
1931	46.038	39.952	4.843	1.243
1951	50.225	43.578	5.096	1.371
1961	52.709	46.105	5.179	1.425
1971	55.515	48.750	5.229	1.536
1981	55.848	49.155	5.131	1.533
1991	56.487	49.890	4.999	1.578

estimated population of England only in earlier years

year	population (millions)
1570	4.160
1600	4.811
1630	5.600
1670	5.773
1700	6.045
1750	6.517

the Coliseum, London, in 1973, and his version of the *Parsifal* libretto was given there in 1986. Critic for the *Observer* from 1992; five volumes of criticism were published 1974–91.

Porter, Eric (1928–1995)

English actor. His numerous classical roles include title roles in *Uncle Vanya, Volpone*, and *King Lear*; on television he played Soames Forsyte in *The Forsyte Saga*.

Porter, George (1920–)

English chemist. From 1947 he and Ronald ◊Norrish developed a technique by which flashes of high energy are used to bring about extremely fast chemical reactions. They shared a Nobel prize in 1967. Knighted 1972.

Porter, Rodney Robert (1917–1985)

English biochemist. In 1962 he proposed a structure for human immunoglobulin (antibody) in which the molecule was seen as consisting of four chains. He was awarded the 1972 Nobel Prize for Physiology or Medicine.

Port Glasgow

Town in Inverclyde unitary authority, Scotland, situated on the southern shore of the Firth of Clyde, 30 km/18 mi northwest of Glasgow; population (1991) 19,700. Founded in 1668, it has developed a worldwide reputation for shipbuilding and ship repairs, and has one of the largest dry docks in Europe. Other industries include light engineering and the manufacture of clothing, textiles, outdoor equipment, and temporary structures such as tents.

Portillo, Michael (Denzil Xavier) (1953–)

British Conservative politician, employment secretary 1994–95, and defence secretary 1995–97. Representative of the right wing of the party in John Major's government, his progress up the ministerial ladder was swift. He lost his House of Commons seat of Enfield Southgate in the 1997 general election.

Portland, William Henry Cavendish Bentinck, 3rd Duke of Portland (1738–1809)

English Whig politician. He was prime minister in 1783 and 1807–09, each time as titular leader of a government dominated by stronger characters. He served as home secretary in William Pitt's Tory administration 1794–1801.

Portland, Isle of

Limestone peninsula on the coast of Dorset, southern England, joined to the mainland by the bank of shingle, ◊Chesil Bank; length 7 km/4 mi. The naval base, founded in 1845, closed in 1995. Portland stone, used for St Paul's Cathedral, London, is still quarried here. Portland Harbour is Europe's largest artificial harbour. Portland Castle was built by Henry VIII in 1539–40.

The principal villages on the peninsula are Easton and Fortuneswell. Portland Harbour is enclosed by Portland Breakwater, built from Portland stone by convicts in 1849–72. At the southernmost tip of the peninsula, known as **Portland Bill**, is a lighthouse (1906). With a height of 35 m/115 ft, the lighthouse was designed to send out a 30-km/18-mi beam of light. It is now a bird-watching station.

The novelist Thomas Hardy referred to the Isle of Portland as the 'Isle of Slingers'.

Portland Vase

Glass vessel of *c.* 25 BC, a fine example of Roman glass-blowing. Made of cobalt-blue glass decorated with figures in relief in white opaque glass, the vase imitates the appearance and craftsmanship of cameo-cut vessels of semiprecious stone. It is 24.8 cm/9.8 in high and 18.4 cm/7.2 in in diameter. Discovered in a sarcophagus near Rome in the 17th century, the vase is now housed in the British Museum, London.

Following its discovery, the vase was placed in the Barberini Palace in Rome, and subsequently purchased by British antiquary William Hamilton in 1770. He sold it to the Duchess of Portland and in 1810 it was lent to the British Museum, where it was destroyed by a vandal in 1845. It was skillfully repaired, and, after having been on loan for 136 years, it was sold to the British Museum in 1946.

The English pottery manufacturer Josiah Wedgwood made a copy of the vase in a blue-black jasper stoneware in 1790. It is thought that 50 copies were made in his lifetime, some of which may be seen at the Victoria and Albert Museum, London, and the Wedgwood Museum, Barleton, Staffordshire.

Portmeirion

Holiday resort in Gwynedd, north Wales, built by the architect Clough ◊Williams-Ellis in Italianate fantasy style on a private headland overlooking Tremadoc Bay; it was the setting of the 1967 cult television series *The Prisoner*.

portraiture

The secular spirit of art after the Reformation helped to to give portraiture special importance in Britain from the 16th century onwards, as exemplified by the work of Hans Holbein the Younger while painter to Henry VIII. Holbein also introduced the art of miniature painting to England. In the 17th century Anthony van Dyck produced numerous portraits of royalty and aristocrats, such as *Charles I on Horseback* (about 1638; National Gallery, London).

This long tradition found its greatest expression in the 18th century with William Hogarth, Thomas Gainsborough, Joshua Reynolds, George Romney, Allan Ramsay, Henry Raeburn, Thomas Lawrence, and others. A special growth was the intimate 'conversation piece'.

The decline of portraiture began in the 19th century. The invention of photography was obviously a contributory factor, and artists were becoming preoccupied with ideas and styles that paid a decreasing attention to likeness of the sitter. However, the tradition was maintained into the 20th century by artists such as John Singer Sargent, who brilliantly depicted affluent late-Victorian and Edwardian society, Augustus John, and Wiliam Orpen. Their kind of traditional society portraiture had become something of an anachronism by the second half of the 20th century, although it still had distinguished practitioners such as Gerald Kelly. Other artists produced portraits in a more modern and subjective vein, for example Graham Sutherland, Lucian Freud, Francis Bacon, and later David Hockney. Artists who have broken further away from the conventional idea of portraiture include Marc Quinn, whose *Self* (1991; Saatchi Collection, London) is a cast of his head made from his own frozen blood (it is displayed in a refrigerated cabinet).

Portree

Town on the island of ◊Skye, in Highland unitary authority, Scotland, situated on the east coast opposite the island of Raasay; population (1991) 2,100. It specializes in the manufacture of woollens, and has an expanding tourist industry. Portree was the administrative centre of the former Skye and Lochalsh District.

Portsea Island

Island off the coast of Hampshire, England. It lies between Portsmouth Harbour and Langstone Harbour, two inlets of the English Channel. The southwestern part of the island is occupied by a naval station.

Portsmouth

City, naval port, and unitary authority in southern England, 118 km/73 mi southwest of London, on the peninsula of Portsea Island, opposite the Isle of Wight; unitary authority area 42 sq km/16 sq mi; population (1996) 189,300. It was part of the county of Hampshire to 1997. The naval dockyard was closed in 1981, although some naval facilities remain. It is a continental ferry port. There are high-technology and manufacturing industries, including aircraft engineering, electronics, shipbuilding, and ship maintenance.

The world's first dry dock was constructed here in 1495. The Tudor warship *Mary Rose* and Admiral Horatio Nelson's flagship, HMS *Victory*, are exhibited here. The cathedral, dating from the 12th century, was enlarged with a new west front and consecrated in 1991. Portsmouth is the UK headquarters of IBM (UK) Ltd, Pall Europe Ltd, and Zurich Insurance Group. It has won a Millennium Award for a harbour development that will create a maritime leisure complex. Portsmouth University, formerly Portsmouth Polytechnic, was established in 1992. The novelist Charles Dickens was born in the Portsmouth suburb of Landport in 1812.

Portsmouth was made a city in 1926, and it includes Landport, Portsea, Southsea, Cosham, Paulsgrove and Farlington. The harbour has a narrow entrance, but expands into a basin 6 km/4 mi by 3 km/2 mi. On the opposite side of the harbour is Gosport. Portsmouth has ferry links with the Isle of Wight, France, and the Channel Islands.

Features

The Historic Ships complex includes the HMS *Warrior* (1860), Britain's first armoured battleship, and the Royal Naval Museum, which illustrates naval history from the 16th century. Near the museum is Double Ropehouse, which was the longest building in the world when it was completed in 1776. The building where Charles Dickens was born now houses a museum. Porchester Castle nearby is the site of a Roman fort founded in the 3rd century. The Australian Settlers Memorial is a chain-link sculpture commemorating the departure of the first convict ships to Australia in 1787.

Millennium Project

Work began in the late 1990s on an £86 million project to develop the harbour and create an extensive maritime leisure complex; the development work will continue well into the next century. The renaissance of the harbour was chosen by the Millennium Commission as one of 12 Landmark Projects. Among the features will be 6 km/4 mi of new public promenades on both sides of the harbour; Gunwharf Quay, a former Ministry of Defence training establishment, which will be transformed into a festival waterfront area with cafés, bars, restaurants, hotels, and houses; and the Millennium Tower (approximately 165 m/541 ft high), which will be located at Gunwharf Quay, close to the harbour entrance, and will have an observation gallery.

History

Portsmouth was already a port in the days of King Alfred, but in 1194 Richard I recognized its strategic importance and created a settlement on Portsea Island. By the beginning of the 13th century Portsmouth had become an important naval station, the docks enclosed by a strong wall, accommodating the royal galleys. In 1545 the English fleet assembled at Portsmouth prior to the naval engagement with the French off Spithead. In 1662 the marriage of Charles II with Catherine of Braganza took place here. George Villiers, the 1st Duke of Buckingham, was assassinated in Portsmouth in 1628, and Admiral John Byng was executed here in 1757. In September 1805 Admiral Horatio Nelson and his fleet departed from Portsmouth for Trafalgar.

During World War II Portsmouth was a principal embarkation point in the ◊D-day operation. It was an important military target, and, of 70,000 buildings, 65,000 suffered some damage in air raids. 6,650 were totally destroyed.

Famous people

Portsmouth was the birthplace of the writers Captain Frederick Marryat, George Meredith, and Walter Besant, the engineer Isambard Kingdom Brunel, and the philanthropist Jonas Hanway.

Port Sunlight

Housing estate built as a model village in 1888 by W H Lever (1851–1925) for workers at the Lever Brothers (now Unilever) soap factory on the Wirral Peninsula at Birkenhead, near Liverpool, northwest England. It is now part of ◊Bebington, Merseyside. A model example of a village created by philanthropic industrialists, it has nearly 900 houses, set in gardens with extensive open spaces. It was designed for a population of 3,000 and includes an art gallery, church, library, and social hall.

Port Talbot

Industrial port and administrative centre of ◊Neath Port Talbot unitary authority, south Wales, situated 11 km/7 mi east of Swansea where the River Afan enters the Bristol Channel; population (1991) 37,600. Industries include tinplate, chemicals, and steel-strip milling. The port accommodates bulk carriers of iron ore.

There are beaches at Aberavon and Margam. Margam Park is wooded, and contains the remains of a Cistercian abbey and the ruins of the chapter house and other 12th-century buildings. The nave of the abbey church now forms the parish church.

postal service

System for delivering mail. In Britain regular permanent systems were not created until the emergence of the modern nation state. Henry VIII in 1516 appointed Sir Brian Tuke as Master of the Posts, to maintain a regular service on the main roads from London. Postmasters (usually innkeepers) passed the mail to the next post, and supplied horses for the royal couriers. In 1635 a royal proclamation established the first public service. Private services were discouraged to avoid losing revenue for the state service and assisting treasonable activities, the latter point being stressed by the act establishing the Post Office, passed under Oliver ◊Cromwell in 1657. Mail coaches first ran in 1784, and in 1840 Rowland Hill's prepaid penny postage stamp, for any distance within the UK, led to a massive increase in use. Services were extended to registered post in 1841; post boxes in 1855; savings bank in 1861; postcards in 1870; postal orders in 1881; parcel post in 1883; air mail in 1911; telephone in 1912; data processing by computer in 1967; and giro in 1968. In 1969 the original General Post Office ceased to be a government department, and in 1981 it split into two, the Post Office and the telecommunications corporation ◊British Telecom (privatized in 1984). The Post Office lost its monopoly in 1987. International cooperation is through the Universal Postal Union (1875) at Bern, Switzerland.

In the 1830s, a letter from England to India took from five to eight months to arrive; by the 1850s, this was reduced to 30–45 days; by 1870, a telegram could be sent in under five hours.

postcard

Card with space for a written message that can be sent through the mail without an envelope. The postcard's inventor was Emmanual Hermann, of Vienna, who in 1869 proposed a 'postal telegram', sent at a lower fee than a normal letter with an envelope. The first picture postcard was produced in 1894.

The postcard, typically 14 x 9 cm/5½ x 3½ ins, rapidly gained popularity after the introduction of the picture postcard. From 1902 the address could be written on the back, leaving the whole of the front for the illustration. Subjects included topographical views, reproductions of paintings, photographs of film stars, and sentimental drawings; common in Britain was the seaside comic postcard, typically illustrated by Donald McGill (1875–1962). Postcards were also a popular means of communication during World War I.

poster art

Ancestors of the modern poster were handbills with woodcut illustrations. One of the first English posters by a distinguished artist, Frederick Walker's design announcing *The Woman in White* (1871), was engraved on wood. The 1890s were the classic age of the poster, exponents being the Art Nouveau illustrator Aubrey Beardsley, and the 'Beggarstaff Brothers' (William Nicholson and James Pryde), whose strikingly simple designs evolved from cut-paper shapes, subsequently lithographed. In the early 20th century Frank Brangwyn, Duncan Grant, Graham Sutherland, and Paul Nash, and patrons such as London Transport and Shell-Mex, contributed to the development of poster design. The advent of Psychedelic art, especially in the work of Michael English (1942–), popularized poster art in the 1960s.

Post Office, PO

Government department or authority with responsibility for postal services; see ◊postal service. The Post Office in the UK also has responsibility for paying out social security and collecting revenue for state insurance schemes. Post Office activities were divided in 1981 and in 1984 telecommunications activities were privatized, forming a new company, British Telecom. Plans to privatize the Royal Mail, including customer services and parcel deliveries, were revived in 1996 by the Conservatives before they lost the general election.

Poston, Elizabeth (1905–1987)

English composer. She was a student at the Royal College of Music in London and studied piano with Harold Samuel. In 1925 she published seven songs and in 1927 a prize-work, a violin and piano sonata, was broadcast. From 1940 to 1945 she was director of music in the foreign service of the British Broadcasting Corporation (BBC).

potato famine

Famine in Ireland 1845–48 caused by the failure of the potato crop, the staple of the Irish diet. Nearly a million people died from malnutrition-related diseases such as a cholera, dysentery, and typhus and at least the same number again emigrated, mainly to America. The former Irish population of 8 million had thus fallen by at least 2 million. The famine devastated Ireland for many years after. The British government was slow to provide relief and provoked Irish hostility in consequence.

Potter, (Helen) Beatrix (1866–1943)

English writer and illustrator of children's books. Her first book was *The Tale of Peter Rabbit* (1900), followed by *The Tailor of Gloucester* (1902), based on her observation of family pets and wildlife. Other books in the series include *The Tale of Mrs Tiggy-Winkle* (1904), *The Tale of Jeremy Fisher* (1906), and a sequel to Peter Rabbit, *The Tale of the Flopsy Bunnies* (1909). Her tales are told with a childlike wonder, devoid of sentimentality, and accompanied by delicate illustrations.

Potter was also an accomplished mycologist. She was the first person to report the symbiotic relationship between lichen and fungi, and to catalogue the fungi of the British Isles. She was excluded from professional scientific societies because of her sex.

She had a quiet and restrained childhood in London, relieved by holidays in Scotland, Wales, and the Lake District, during which she studied and painted the countryside and its animals and plants. From 1905 she lived in the Lake District, where she bred hill-sheep and was an active conservationist. Her diaries, written in a secret code, were translated and published in 1966. She left her extensive estate to the National Trust, and her Lake District home at Sawrey is now a museum.

Potter, Dennis Christopher George (1935–1994)

English dramatist and journalist. His most important work was written for television, extending the boundaries of the art form. Serials include *Pennies from Heaven* (1978) (feature film 1981), and *The Singing Detective* (1986); *Brimstone and Treacle* (1976) (transmitted 1987, feature film 1982), was a play.

Potter's television dramas exhibit a serious concern for social issues, and are characterized by a marked avoidance of euphemism or delicacy. Highly inventive in form, they explore the medium's technical possibilities, employing devices such as overlap, fantasy sequences, and flashback. His posthumous plays were *Cold Lazarus* and *Karaoke* (both 1995). Potter often incorporated popular music into his works, for example in *Pennies from Heaven*, in which the action is interrupted by songs lip-mimed by the characters.

Potteries, the

Home of the china and earthenware industries, in central England. Wedgwood and Minton are factory names associated with the Potteries.

The Potteries lie in the upper Trent basin of north Staffordshire, covering the area around Stoke-on-Trent, and include the formerly separate towns of Burslem, Hanley, Longton, Fenton, and Tunstall.

pound

British standard monetary unit, issued as a gold

POTTER, BEATRIX *The author of a series of children's classic stories about animals, Beatrix Potter was also an accomplished watercolourist, who illustrated all her own works, and a gifted natural scientist. Her books continue to have a wide appeal, and have been adapted for both stage and screen. Seen here, from the film version of her tales, is the frog, Jeremy Fisher. Ronald Grant*

sovereign before 1914, as a note 1914–83, and as a circular yellow metal-alloy coin from 1983.

The edge inscriptions on the pound coin are: 1983 *Decus et tutamen* 'An ornament and a safeguard'; 1984 (Scottish) *Nemo me impune lacessit* 'No one injures me with impunity'; 1985 (Welsh) *Pleidiol wyf i'm gwlad* 'True am I to my country', from the national anthem. A new £2 coin, the UK's first bi-coloured coin, was introduced in 1998.

The **green pound** is the European Union exchange rate for conversion of EU farm prices to sterling.

> *Money speaks sense in a language all nations understand.*
>
> Aphra Behn English novelist and playwright.
> *The Rover* pt II, III.i

Powell, (John) Enoch (1912–1998)

British Conservative politician. He was minister of health 1960–63, and contested the party leadership in 1965. In 1968 he made a speech against immigration that led to his dismissal from the shadow cabinet. He resigned from the party in 1974, and was Official Unionist Party member for South Down, Northern Ireland, 1974–87.

He was an MP for Wolverhampton from 1950 and subsequently a member of the cabinet. He refused to serve under Sir Alec Douglas-Home, but subsequently, in Opposition, became one of the Conservative Party's principal spokesmen. In 1965 he stood as a candidate at the election of a new Conservative leader, but came third to Edward Heath and Reginald Maudling. His radical views on the social services and prices and incomes policy often conflicted with those of the Conservatism of the day and from 1968 his attitude towards immigrants and his repatriation proposals made him a controversial figure. He was dismissed from the shadow cabinet by Edward Heath, following his controversial speech on immigration, and was not offered a post in the Conservative administration of 1970–74. He was an opponent of British membership of the European Economic Community. Declining to stand in the February 1974 election, he attacked the Heath government and resigned.

> *All political lives, unless they are cut off in midstream at a happy juncture, end in failure, because that is the nature of politics and of human affairs.*
>
> Enoch Powell British Conservative politician.
> *Joseph Chamberlain*, epilogue

Powell, Anthony Dymoke (1905–)

English novelist and critic. He wrote the series of 12 volumes *A Dance to the Music of Time* (1951–75) that begins shortly after World War I and chronicles a period of 50 years in the lives of Nicholas Jenkins and his circle of upper- and middle-class friends and acquaintances. It is written in an elegant style which sets off the blend of the comic, the melancholic, and the tragic in the situations he describes.

Powell, Cecil Frank (1903–1969)

English physicist who investigated the charged subatomic particles in cosmic radiation by using photographic emulsions carried in weather balloons. This led to his discovery of the pion (??? meson) in 1947, a particle whose existence had been predicted by Japanese physicist Hideki Yukawa in 1935. Powell was awarded a Nobel prize in 1950.

Powell, Michael (Latham) (1905–1990)

English film director and producer. In collaboration with the Hungarian-born screenwriter Emeric Pressburger, he produced a succession of ambitious and richly imaginative films, including *I Know Where I'm Going!* (1945), *A Matter of Life and Death* (1946), and *The Red Shoes* (1948).

Their work has gained a burgeoning reputation with subsequent generations of filmmakers and critics for its striking employment of both Technicolor and black-and-white cinematography, its vivid Expressionism, and its imaginative fusion of cinema with the other art forms (music, painting, ballet, opera, even poetry in *A Matter of Life and Death*). Among their other films are *The Life and Death of Colonel Blimp* (1943), *A Canterbury Tale* (1944), *Black Narcissus* (1947), and *The Tales of Hoffman* (1951).

Powis Castle

Medieval castle in Welshpool, Powys, Wales, owned by the National Trust. The late 13th-century walls and bastions remain, but the castle was adapted in Elizabethan times and again in the latter half of the 17th century. It became the home of Robert Clive, created Earl of Powis, and contains many of his relics. The house contains the Clive Museum; the garden has late 17th-century terraces.

The 4th Earl remodelled the interior, and made further modifications to the castle before giving it to the National Trust in 1952.

Powys

Unitary authority in central Wales, created in 1996 from the former county of Powys

Area 5,179 sq km/1,999 sq mi

Towns ◊Llandrindod Wells (administrative headquarters), Brecon, Builth Wells, ◊Newtown, Welshpool

Physical mountainous to the north, Black Mountains, rivers ◊Wye and ◊Severn, which both rise on the eastern slopes of Plynlimon

Features the ◊Brecon Beacons National Park, Lake Vyrnwy (an artificial reservoir supplying Liverpool and Birmingham), alternative-technology centre near ◊Machynlleth

Industries agriculture, tourism

Agriculture arable and dairy farming, sheep-rearing

Population (1996) 123,600

Agriculture and commerce

Agriculture is the main occupation of the area. Much arable and dairy farming is undertaken on the lower valley lands, especially on the fertile alluvial soils of the Usk and Wye region. The central district belongs almost entirely to the basin of the Severn, where a pure breed of Welsh ponies is reared and where Welsh flannel manufacture was extensively carried out. The River Teme has good trout fishing. Afforestation has been undertaken extensively in the north; forestry and quarrying are undertaken in the south; and limestone is worked in the central areas.

Other features

Knighton and Rhayader are important market towns. Some 5 km/3 mi west of Brecon is Y Gaer, the Roman Bannium, an excavated walled fort. The 14th-century fortified manor house of Tretower Court and the adjacent Norman tower 5 km/3 mi from Crickhowell are ancient monuments. In the Vale of Ewyas are the ruins of Llanthony Abbey, which was founded early in the 12th century. The writer and MP George Herbert lived in the region, as did the philanthropist and manufacturer Robert ◊Owen.

Topography

Other main rivers include Dovey, ◊Taff, Tawe, Teme, and ◊Usk. Near Rhayader are the Elan Valley and Claerwen reservoirs. The highest peaks of the area are Pen y Fan (885 m/2,904 ft) in the Brecon Beacons, Waun Fach (811 m/2,660 ft) in the ◊Black Mountains, and Carmarthen Van (802 m/2,630 ft) in the ◊Black Mountain range. The north is almost wholly mountainous, a large portion consisting of bleak elevated moorland, but towards the English border there are several open, fertile, and well-wooded valleys. Over one-half of the central district is 300 m/1,000 ft or more above sea-level, the highest point being at 660 m/2,165 ft in Radnor Forest. In the south the main geological formation is that of the Old Red Sandstone (Devonian System). On the southern boundary this is overlain by Carboniferous limestone. In more central areas older Silurian rocks are exposed. There is evidence that the area was heavily glaciated.

Powys, House of

Ancient kingdom in Wales, bordering England in the east. It was frequently threatened from the east, and lands in the present English counties of Herefordshire, Worcestershire, and Shropshire were lost following the incursion of the Mercians in the period leading up to the construction in the late 8th century of Offa's Dyke between the two countries. The rulers of Powys often fought those of neighbouring Gwynedd. The last ruler of Powys as an intact kingdom was Madog ap Maredudd. His successors ruled over a Powys divided into north and south. The name was restored for the present county of Powys, formed in 1974 from the counties of Breconshire, Mongomeryshire, and Radnorshire. See genealogy on page 723.

Poynter, Edward John (1836–1919)

English painter. First engaged in decorative design, he later produced decorous nudes, mosaic panels for Westminster Palace (1870), and scenes from ancient Greece and Rome, as in *Visit to Aesculapius* (1880; Tate Gallery, London).

He was the first head of the Slade School of Fine Art, London, from 1871 to 1875; director of the National Gallery, London, from 1894 to 1905; and president of the Royal Academy in succession to John Everett Millais from 1896 to 1918. He was knighted in 1896.

Poynting, John Henry (1852–1914)

English physicist, mathematician, and inventor. He devised an equation by which the rate of flow of electromagnetic energy (now called the **Poynting vector**) can be determined.

In 1891 he made an accurate measurement of Isaac ◊Newton's gravitational constant.

Pratchett, Terry (Terence David John) (1948–)

English writer of bestselling science fantasy fiction whose books have achieved cult status. He is the creator of the imaginary 'Discworld', a flat, circular planet which is carried through space by a giant turtle and four elephants. *The Colour of Magic* (1983) was the first of the Discworld series which also includes *Wyrd Sisters* (1988), *Guards! Guards!* (1983), *Jingo* (1997), and *The Last Continent* (1998). Several of his works have been successfully serialized for radio and adapted for the stage.

His first novel *The Carpet People* (1971, rewritten 1992) was a children's bestseller. *Truckers* (1989) was the first of the 'Gnomes' trilogy for children and adults, which also includes *Diggers* (1990) and *Wings* (1990).

precedence

Order or rank in which people should be placed on ceremonial occasions, depending partly upon letters patent and partly upon ancient custom. Questions of precedence are the responsibility of the Earl Marshal in England and Wales, and the ◊Court of the Lord Lyon in Scotland. Precedence cannot be derived from a female, except in the case of a peeress in her own right.

The official table of precedence is found in such reference books as *Burke's Peerage*. The sovereign is at the head, followed by the Prince of Wales and other male members of the royal family. Then come ambassadors, the Archbishop of Canterbury, the Lord Chancellor, the Archbishop of York, the prime minister (dating only from 1905, however), the Lord President of the Council, the Speaker of the House of Commons, and so on to include holders of offices of state, members of the peerage, secretaries of state, various officers of the royal household, Knights of the Garter, privy councillors, holders of various judicial offices, and members of various orders of chivalry.

Premium Savings Bond

British government bond introduced in 1956 whose purchaser is eligible for a prize-winning lottery. The prize money is funded from interest payable on the bond.

Pre-Raphaelite Brotherhood, PRB

Group of British painters (1848–53); Dante Gabriel ◊Rossetti, John Everett ◊Millais, and Holman Hunt – at this time young students at the Royal Academy – were the leading figures among the seven founders. They aimed to paint serious subjects, to study nature closely, and to return to the sincerity of spirit of painters before the time of Raphael Sanzio

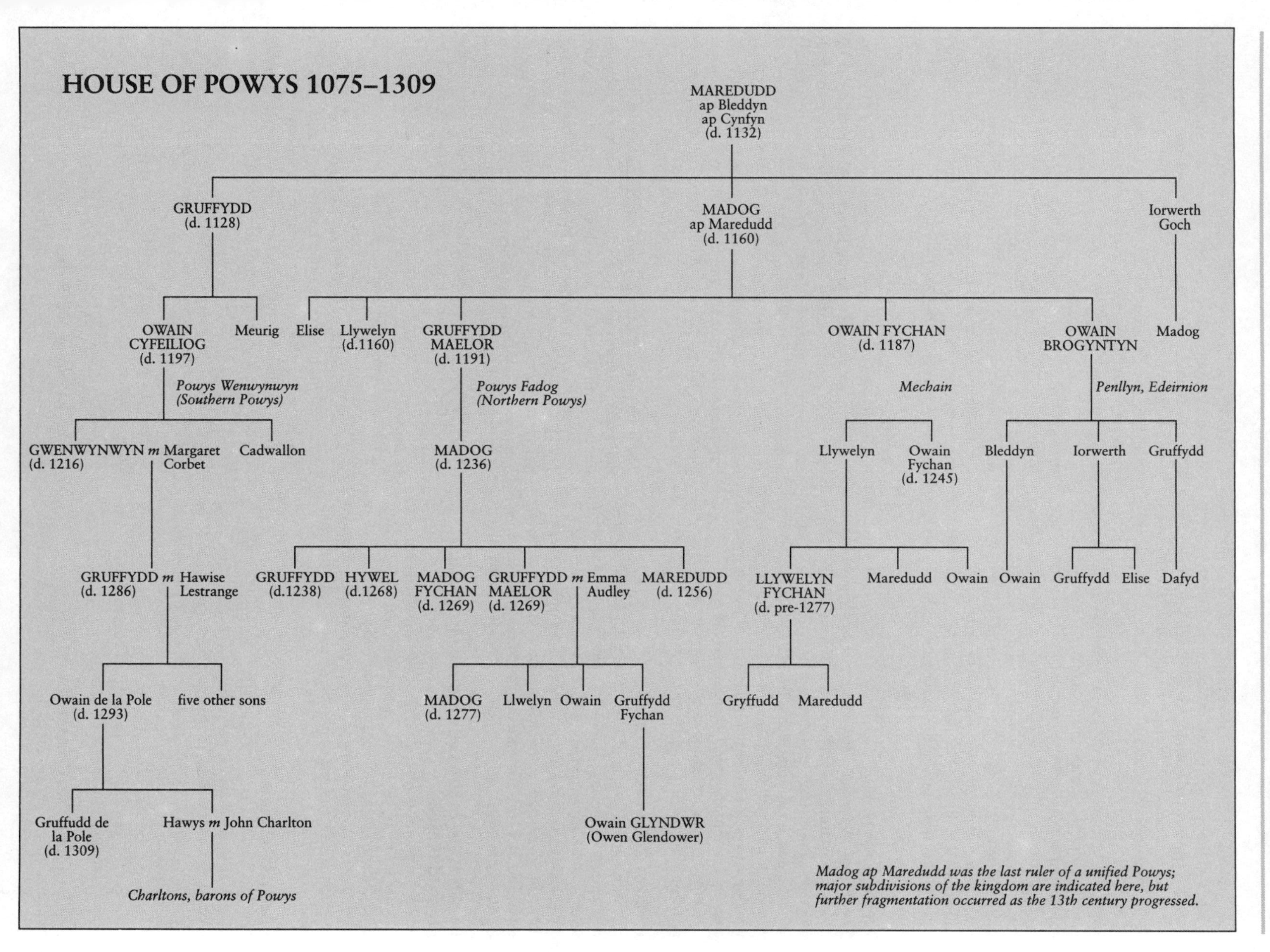
HOUSE OF POWYS 1075–1309
MAREDUDD ap Bleddyn ap Cynfyn (d. 1132)
GRUFFYDD (d. 1128)
MADOG ap Maredudd (d. 1160)
Iorwerth Goch
OWAIN CYFEILIOG (d. 1197)
Meurig
Elise
Llywelyn (d.1160)
GRUFFYDD MAELOR (d. 1191)
OWAIN FYCHAN (d. 1187)
OWAIN BROGYNTYN
Madog
Powys Wenwynwyn (Southern Powys)
Powys Fadog (Northern Powys)
Mechain
Penllyn, Edeirnion
GWENWYNWYN m Margaret Corbet (d. 1216)
Cadwallon
MADOG (d. 1236)
Llywelyn
Owain Fychan (d. 1245)
Bleddyn
Iorwerth
Gruffydd
GRUFFYDD m Hawise Lestrange (d. 1286)
GRUFFYDD (d.1238)
HYWEL (d.1268)
MADOG FYCHAN (d. 1269)
GRUFFYDD MAELOR m Emma Audley (d. 1269)
MAREDUDD (d. 1256)
LLYWELYN FYCHAN (d. pre-1277)
Maredudd
Owain
Owain
Gruffydd
Elise
Dafyd
Owain de la Pole (d. 1293)
five other sons
MADOG (d. 1277)
Llwelyn
Owain
Gruffydd Fychan
Gryffudd
Maredudd
Gruffudd de la Pole (d. 1309)
Hawys m John Charlton
Owain GLYNDWR (Owen Glendower)
Charltons, barons of Powys
Madog ap Maredudd was the last ruler of a unified Powys; major subdivisions of the kingdom are indicated here, but further fragmentation occurred as the 13th century progressed.

(1483–1520). Their subjects were mainly biblical and literary, painted with obsessive naturalism and attention to detail. The group was short-lived but added a new realism to the art of the 1850s, and influenced many painters including W H Deverell, W L Windus, John Brett, W S Burton, and Robert Martineau.

In his later work only Hunt remained true to Pre-Raphaelite ideals, but the name stuck to Rossetti, the least committed of the original group, and was applied to his later dreamily romantic pictures although these had moved away from the movement's founding ideas. A 'second wave' of Pre-Raphaelitism in the late 19th century, stimulated by Ruskin and Rossetti, was associated with the revival of handicrafts and the art of design. William Morris and Edward Burne-Jones were among the many artists influenced at this time.

Presbyterianism

System of Christian Protestant church government, expounded during the Reformation by John Calvin, which gives its name to the established Church of Scotland, and is also practised in England, Wales, Ireland, Switzerland, North America, and elsewhere. There is no compulsory form of worship and each congregation is governed by presbyters or elders (clerical or lay), who are of equal rank.

Congregations are grouped in presbyteries, synods, and general assemblies.

Prescott, John Leslie (1938–)

British Labour Party politician, deputy leader from 1994, deputy prime minister from 1997. He unsuccessfully contested for the party leadership in 1988 and 1992. After the 1997 Labour victory, he was given a key appointment in Tony Blair's new government, combining the role of deputy prime minister with responsibility for transport, the environment, and the regions.

Preseli Hills, or Prescelly Mountains, Welsh Mynydd Preseli

Range of hills in Pembrokeshire, southwest Wales, rising to 536 m/1,759 ft (at Foel Cwmcerwyn) and crossed by a primitive trackway. A site of Neolithic settlement, the eastern section of these hills is thought to have provided the bluestone of ◊Stonehenge; this is the only known place in Britain where bluestone is found.

Press Association, PA

National news agency of the UK, founded in 1868. It provides comprehensive around-the-clock news and sports services for newspapers, magazines, broadcasters, and the electronic media. It also works with a wide range of commercial organizations, local and central government, and the public relations industry. It employs about 1,000 people (1998). PA New Media is a major UK content provider for online, Internet, and digital formats.

Press Complaints Commission

Non-statutory body set up in 1991 by the newspaper and periodical industry following a report on privacy and the press by an independent committee. It deals with complaints about the content and conduct of newspapers and magazines and operates a code of conduct agreed by editors. The commission's members are drawn from the public and the press.

In 1995 the government rejected proposals for legislation giving the right to privacy, favouring self-regulation of the industry instead.

press gang

Method used to recruit soldiers and sailors into the British armed forces in the 18th and early 19th centuries. In effect it was a form of kidnapping carried out by the services or their agents, often with the aid of armed men. This was similar to the practice of 'shanghaiing' sailors for duty in the merchant marine, especially in the Far East.

Preston

Industrial town and administrative headquarters of ◊Lancashire, northwest England, on the River Ribble, 34 km/21 mi south of Lancaster, at the highest navigable point of the Irish Sea estuary; population (1991) 126,100. Industries include textiles, chemicals, electrical goods, aircraft, plastics, and engineering; it is also an agricultural market centre. Oliver Cromwell defeated the Royalists at Preston in 1648. It is the birthplace of Richard Arkwright, inventor of cotton-spinning machinery, and was a centre of the cotton industry in the 18th century.

Location

The main part of the town is on high ground above the river floodplain, which is used partly for parks and sports grounds. On the north side of the town there is the extensive former Town Moor. Part of the river floodplain is used for industries and also for the Preston Docks, whose freight trade with Ireland is significant. A fine communications centre, Preston suffered for many years from acute traffic congestion on its roads, especially during summer when thousands of motorists passed through it to Blackpool, but the M6 motorway to the east of the town with its spur to Blackpool alleviated its problems.

Features

There are numerous churches, and Preston's skyline is dominated by the fine slender spire of St Walburge's, over 92 m/302 ft high and designed by Joseph Hansom (perhaps more famous for his cabs). The town centre has been rebuilt and includes a shopping precinct. Preston has spread beyond its previous boundaries into adjacent urban districts, notably Fulwood and Walton (south of the Ribble).

History

Preston grew up near the site of a Roman fort. It was originally a market town, and is mentioned in the Domesday Book; in 1179 it was given the first of its various royal charters by Henry II. Apart from the right to hold regular markets, a fair was established by a charter of 1179, which now takes place every 20 years. From its original, but long since obsolete, relation with the rights of traders and burgesses it became known as the Preston Guild. A Royalist town, Preston was the site of one of Cromwell's victories in 1648; the town was equally unfortunate in its Jacobite sympathies later, when the 'Old Pretender', James Edward Stuart, was proclaimed king in its market square.

There are few visual traces of Preston's early history, as even the mansions of its nobility were swamped by early industrialization. Cotton was for many decades the mainstay of the industrial life of Preston; the first cotton spinning mill was established in 1777, and by 1835 there were 40 factories spinning cotton. There was also wool and linen weaving. In 1939 rayon manufacture began; Preston is home to the largest rayon factory in Europe. It is known in Lancashire as 'Proud Preston' and its central position partly accounts for its choice as the administrative centre for Lancashire. Although much of the 19th-century housing has been cleared, the town centre and the former dock areas have been redeveloped recently.

Preston, Peter John (1938–)

British newspaper editor and executive. In 1975 he became editor of the moderate left-wing daily *Guardian* and from 1988 he was also its company chair.

Preston, Battle of

Battle of 17–19 August 1648 at Preston, Lancashire, in which the English defeated the Scots. The Scots invaded England under the Duke of ◊Hamilton, but were cut off from Scotland by ◊Cromwell and fled in a series of running fights. Hamilton was captured and executed.

Prestwick

Town in South Ayrshire, southwest Scotland, on the Firth of Clyde, adjacent to Ayr; population (1991) 13,700. Industries include aerospace engineering. Glasgow Prestwick International Airport resumed passenger services in the 1990s, having previously been the main transatlantic gateway to North America in the 1970s. The inaugural Open Golf Championship was held at the Old Course in Prestwick in 1860. Today, Prestwick has three golf courses and a long sandy beach.

pretender

Claimant to a throne. In British history, the term is widely used to describe the Old Pretender (◊James Edward Stuart) and his son, the Young Pretender (◊Charles Edward Stuart).

Pride and Prejudice

Novel by Jane ◊Austen, published in 1813. Mr and Mrs Bennet, whose property is due to pass to a male cousin, William Collins, are anxious to secure good marriage settlements for their five daughters. Central to the story is the romance between the witty Elizabeth Bennet and the proud Mr Darcy.

Priestley, J(ohn) B(oynton) (1894–1984)

English novelist and dramatist. His first success was a novel about travelling theatre, *The Good Companions* (1929). He followed it with a realist novel about London life, *Angel Pavement* (1930). His career as a dramatist began with *Dangerous Corner* (1932), one of several plays in which time is a preoccupation. His best-known plays are the enigmatic *An Inspector Calls* (1945) and *The Linden Tree* (1948), a study of postwar social issues.

Priestley had a gift for family comedy; for example, the play *When We Are Married* (1938). He was also known for his wartime broadcasts and literary criticism, such as *Literature and Western Man* (1960).

Priestley, Joseph (1733–1804)

English chemist and Unitarian minister. He identified oxygen in 1774 and several other gases. Dissolving carbon dioxide under pressure in water, he began a European craze for soda water.

Gases

Swedish chemist Karl Scheele independently prepared oxygen in 1772, but his tardiness in publication resulted in Priestley being credited with the discovery.

Priestley discovered nitric oxide (nitrogen monoxide, NO) in 1772 and reduced it to nitrous oxide (dinitrogen monoxide, N_2O). In the same year he became the first person to isolate gaseous ammonia by collecting it over mercury (previously ammonia was known only in aqueous solution). In 1774 he found a method for producing sulphur dioxide (SO_2).

priest's hole

Hiding place, in private homes, for Catholic priests in the 16th–17th centuries when there were penal laws against them in Britain. Many still exist, for example at Speke Hall, near Liverpool.

Primal Scream

British rock/dance group formed in 1984. Their early albums *Sonic Flower Groove* (1987) and *Primal Scream* (1989) won them an audience among fans of both indie and acid house music. The rock-dance crossover album *Screamadelica* (1991) reached the UK Top 10. They achieved success with 'The Scream Team Meets The Barmy Army Uptown', the title track of the film *Trainspotting* (1996), and the hit album *Vanishing Point* (1997).

Its members are Bobby Gillespie (1964–) (vocals), Martin Duffy (keyboards), Andrew Innes (guitar), Throb (Robert Young) (guitar), and Mani (Gary Mounfield 1962–) (bass).

prime minister, or premier

Head of the parliamentary government, usually the leader of the largest party. The first prime minister in Britain is usually considered to have been Robert ◊Walpole, but the office was not officially recognized until 1905. In the late 20th century, the office became increasingly presidential, with the prime minister being supported by a large private office and No 10 Policy Unit. Tony ◊Blair became Britain's prime minister in 1997.

The prime minister is appointed by the sovereign, but in asking someone to form a government the sovereign is constitutionally bound to invite the leader of the party with a majority of seats in the House of Commons (see ◊Commons, House of), a situation which is normally determined by a

Prime Ministers of Great Britain and the United Kingdom

Term	Name	Party
1721–42	Robert Walpole[1]	Whig
1742–43	Spencer Compton, Earl of Wilmington	Whig
1743–54	Henry Pelham	Whig
1754–56	Thomas Pelham-Holles, 1st Duke of Newcastle	Whig
1756–57	William Cavendish, 4th Duke of Devonshire	Whig
1757–62	Thomas Pelham-Holles, 1st Duke of Newcastle	Whig
1762–63	John Stuart, 3rd Earl of Bute	Tory
1763–65	George Grenville	Whig
1765–66	Charles Watson Wentworth, 2nd Marquess of Rockingham	Whig
1766–68	William Pitt, 1st Earl of Chatham	Tory
1768–70	Augustus Henry Fitzroy, 3rd Duke of Grafton	Whig
1770–82	Frederick North, Lord North[2]	Tory
1782	Charles Watson Wentworth, 2nd Marquess of Rockingham	Whig
1782–83	William Petty-Fitzmaurice, 2nd Earl of Shelburne[3]	Whig
1783	William Henry Cavendish-Bentinck, 3rd Duke of Portland	Whig
1783–1801	William Pitt, The Younger	Tory
1801–04	Henry Addington	Tory
1804–06	William Pitt, The Younger	Tory
1806–07	William Wyndham Grenville, 1st Baron Grenville	Whig
1807–09	William Henry Cavendish-Bentinck, 3rd Duke of Portland	Whig
1809–12	Spencer Perceval	Tory
1812–27	Robert Banks Jenkinson, 2nd Earl of Liverpool	Tory
1827	George Canning	Tory
1827–28	Frederick John Robinson, 1st Viscount Goderich	Tory
1828–30	Arthur Wellesley, 1st Duke of Wellington	Tory
1830–34	Charles Grey, 2nd Earl Grey	Whig
1834	William Lamb, 2nd Viscount Melbourne	Whig
1834	Arthur Wellesley, 1st Duke of Wellington	Tory
1834–35	Sir Robert Peel, 2nd Baronet	Tory
1835–41	William Lamb, 2nd Viscount Melbourne	Whig
1841–46	Sir Robert Peel, 2nd Baronet	Conservative
1846–52	John Russell, Lord Russell	Whig-Liberal
1852	Edward Geoffrey Stanley, 14th Earl of Derby	Conservative
1852–55	George Hamilton-Gordon, 4th Earl of Aberdeen	Peelite
1855–58	Henry John Temple, 3rd Viscount Palmerston	Liberal
1858–59	Edward Geoffrey Stanley, 14th Earl of Derby	Conservative
1859–65	Henry John Temple, 3rd Viscount Palmerston	Liberal
1865–66	John Russell, 1st Earl Russell	Liberal
1866–68	Edward Geoffrey Stanley, 14th Earl of Derby	Conservative
1868	Benjamin Disraeli	Conservative
1868–74	William Ewart Gladstone	Liberal
1874–80	Benjamin Disraeli[4]	Conservative
1880–85	William Ewart Gladstone	Liberal
1885–86	Robert Cecil, 3rd Marquess of Salisbury	Conservative
1886	William Ewart Gladstone	Liberal
1886–92	Robert Cecil, 3rd Marquess of Salisbury	Conservative
1892–94	William Ewart Gladstone	Liberal
1894–95	Archibald Philip Primrose, 5th Earl of Rosebery	Liberal
1895–1902	Robert Cecil, 3rd Marquess of Salisbury	Conservative
1902–05	Arthur James Balfour	Conservative
1905–08	Sir Henry Campbell-Bannerman	Liberal
1908–16	H H Asquith	Liberal
1916–22	David Lloyd George	Liberal
1922–23	Bonar Law	Conservative
1923–24	Stanley Baldwin	Conservative
1924	Ramsay Macdonald	Labour

Term	Name	Party
1924–29	Stanley Baldwin	Conservative
1929–35	Ramsay Macdonald	Labour
1935–37	Stanley Baldwin	Conservative
1937–40	Neville Chamberlain	Conservative
1940–45	Winston Churchill	Conservative
1945–51	Clement Atlee	Labour
1951–55	Winston Churchill[5]	Conservative
1955–57	Sir Anthony Eden	Conservative
1957–63	Harold Macmillan	Conservative
1963–64	Sir Alec Douglas-Home	Conservative
1964–70	Harold Wilson	Labour
1970–74	Edward Heath	Conservative
1974–76	Harold Wilson	Labour
1976–79	James Callaghan	Labour
1979–90	Margaret Thatcher	Conservative
1990–97	John Major	Conservative
1997–	Tony Blair	Labour

[1] From 1725, Sir Robert Walpole. [2] From 1790, 2nd Earl of Guilford. [3] From 1784, 1st Marquess of Lansdowne. [4] From 1876, Earl of Beaconsfield. [5] From 1953, Sir Winston Churchill.

general election. If no party has a majority then the sovereign normally invites the leader of the party with the largest number of seats to form a government, and, failing this, may consult various party leaders and elder statesmen. If the prime minister dies or resigns between elections the sovereign waits until the party concerned has elected a new leader. All governmental appointments are made by the sovereign on the advice of the prime minister.

Sir Robert ◊Walpole is widely regarded as the first prime minister, but Walpole's career set a precedent for the post rather than establishing it firmly as part of the machinery of government. The first prime minister in the modern sense was probably William Pitt the Younger (see ◊Pitt, William, the Younger), who clearly established the role of the prime minister as the dominant figure in the cabinet.

The post of prime minister is largely the product of constitutional convention, although the office was recognized in formal precedence in 1905 and has been mentioned in various acts of Parliament since 1918. The prime minister normally holds the post of First Lord of the Treasury, and, in the past, sometimes held a major departmental portfolio. The last prime minister to do so was Sir Winston Churchill, who held the post of minister of Defence between 1951 and 1952, although Harold Wilson was minister for the Civil Service between 1968 and 1970.

Princes in the Tower

Popular name for King ◊Edward V and his younger brother Richard, Duke of York (1472–1483). They are said to have been murdered in the Tower of London by order of their uncle, the Duke of Gloucester, so that he could succeed to the throne as ◊Richard III.

Princess Mary's Royal Air Force Nursing Service

Air force support service which offers commissions to Registered General Nurses.

Princess Royal

Title borne only by the eldest daughter of the British sovereign, granted by royal declaration. It was first borne by Mary, eldest daughter of Charles I, probably in imitation of the French court, where the eldest daughter of the king was styled 'Madame Royale'. The title is currently held by Princess Anne.

Princes Street

Main street in central Edinburgh, Scotland, which has many shops and restaurants. It was named after the young sons of George III. The gardens along its south side are a memorial to Sir Walter Scott.

Princetown

Village in the centre of ◊Dartmoor, Devon, southwest England, part of Dartmoor Forest; population of Dartmoor Forest (1996 est) 1,300. Industries include tourism and farming. It is the site of Dartmoor high-security prison (opened in 1809).

Princetown lies at one of the highest points on Dartmoor (400 m/1,300 ft). Dartmoor prison was built (by French and American prisoners) during the Napoleonic Wars for French prisoners of war. It has been used as a high-security prison since the 19th century. St Michael's church was built by convicts in 1813.

printmaking

The **woodcut** is the oldest form of print found in Britain, followed by **line engraving** from the 15th century. In the 17th century Hogarth used **etching** as well as line-engraving; and Rowlandson and Gillray etched in outline, their prints being completed by hand-colouring. In 1637 the Bohemian engraver Wenceslaus Hollar (1607–1677) introduced landscape engraving to England, recording views of London before the Great Fire of 1666. Crome, Girtin, Cotman, and Turner give later landscape examples.

The **mezzotint** medium was introduced to England by Prince Rupert, nephew of Charles I. Many of the earliest practitioners were English, and by the end of the 17th century it was generally known as *la manière anglaise*. Pioneers of the process included John Smith (born 1652), who engraved over 100 portraits by Godfrey Kneller. Notable landscape mezzotints of the 19th century are those of Turner's *Liber Studiorum*.

In the 18th century Thomas Bewick was one of the first exponents of **wood engraving**, an allied but finer technique to the earlier woodcut, the cuts being made across the end-grain of a block. The Dalziel family continued the tradition in the 19th century, producing illustrations for classic works of literature and for magazines. **Aquatint** also became common in the 18th century, Thomas Gainsborough being one of the first to experiment with the process. It had a vogue in the early 19th century, as in the topographical prints published by Rudolph Ackermann, and was used for colour as well as black-and-white. After long disuse aquatint had some revival in the 20th century with such artists as John Piper.

The invention of **colour lithography** in 1796 encouraged the 19th-century development of poster art. The 'Beggarstaff Brothers', William Nicholson and James Pryde, created paper cut-out designs, later lithographed, which were noted for their striking simplicity. There was a great revival of etching in the late 19th and early 20th century, led by Whistler and Sickert, and new techniques have been invented or popularized in the 20th century, notably linocut and screenprinting. The most significant figure in modern British printmaking has been Stanley ◊Hayter who set up Atelier 17, an experimental printmaking workshop, in Paris. Many distinguished artists learned printmaking techniques here and were encouraged to use printmaking as a means of original expression rather than simply a method of creating multiple copies.

Prior, Matthew (1664–1721)

British poet and diplomat. He was associated under the Whigs with the negotiation of the treaty of Ryswick (1697) ending the war with France and under the Tories with that of Utrecht (1714) ('Matt's Peace') ending the War of the Spanish Succession, but on the Whigs' return to power he was imprisoned by the government leader Walpole from 1715–17. His gift as a writer was for light occasional verses, epigrams, and tales, in a graceful yet colloquial manner.

prisons

The average number of people in prison in the UK in 1995 was 58,375; 12,669 on remand (awaiting trial or sentence), 45,052 sentenced, and 654 other. Of these, 56,189 were male and 2,186 female. In the late 1990s there were 134 prison establishments in England and Wales, 22 in Scotland, and 5 in Northern Ireland.

PRISONS: SOME KEY DATES

Late 18th century Criminal prisons begin to replace places of detention for those awaiting trial or confined for political reasons. Previously criminals were commonly sentenced to death, mutilation, or transportation rather than imprisonment.

1778 The British reformer John Howard's Prison Act establishes the principle of separate confinement combined with work in an attempt at reform.

1791 The English philosopher and social reformer Jeremy Bentham designs a 'panopticon' prison, allowing for efficient supervision of inmates.

1813 Elizabeth Fry, the English campaigner for improvement in prison conditions, begins to visit Newgate Prison, London, and is appalled at the squalor she finds there.

4 July 1823 The British home secretary Robert Peel allows the employment of transported convicts in the colonies instead of confining them to prison ships

10 July 1823 The British Parliament passes the home secretary Robert Peel's Gaols Act, which improves conditions in prisons.

1842 Pentonville prison is built, the first to put into practice the Prison Act of 1778.

1857 Penal servitude is introduced after the colonies refuse to accept transported convicts.

1903 The Poor Prisoners' Defence Act creates the first legal-aid scheme in Britain.

1948 Penal servitude and hard labour are abolished by the Criminal Justice Act 1948.

1967 The Criminal Justice Act 1967 allows courts to suspend prison sentences of two years or less. Persistent offenders may receive an extended sentence for the protection of the public. After serving one-third of their sentence (a minimum of 12 months), selected prisoners may be released on parole.

1971 People suspected of terrorism in Northern Ireland can be sentenced without trial.

1972 The Criminal Justice Act 1972 requires the courts to consider information about an offender before sentencing them to prison for the first time, and introduces the concept of community service to replace prison for nonviolent offenders, and of day-training centres for the social education of those who are unable to integrate into society.

18 January 1978 The European Court of Human Rights clears the British government of torture but finds it guilty of inhuman and degrading treatment of prisoners in Northern Ireland.

13 March 1997 The prison ship *Weare* arrives off Portland, Dorset, as part of an attempt to address the problem of prison overcrowding in Britain.

20 November 1997 British Home Secretary Jack Straw announces plans to increase the electronic tagging of convicts to help reduce the prison population. The plan would enable criminals serving short sentences to be released up to two months ahead of schedule, fitted with electronic bracelets to record their movements.

Experiments have been made in the UK in 'open prisons' without bars, which have included releasing prisoners in the final stages of their sentence to work in ordinary jobs outside the prison, and the provision of aftercare on release.

Attempts to deal with the increasing number of young offenders include, from 1982, accommodation in community homes in the case of minor offences, with (in more serious cases) 'short, sharp shock' treatment in detention centres (although the latter was subsequently found to have little effect on reconviction rates).

In 1990 there was widespread rioting in several prisons in the UK, notably the 25-day siege at Strangeways Prison in Manchester; this was the longest ever prison siege in the UK, during which several prisoners died.

Pritchard, John (1921–1989)

English conductor. He studied in Italy and went to Glyndebourne in 1947; gave three Mozart operas there in 1951; and was music director 1969–77. He conducted the first performances of Benjamin Britten's *Gloriana* and Michael Tippett's *Midsummer Marriage* at Covent Garden, and *King Priam* with the company at Coventry in 1962. He made his US debut in 1953 with the Pittsburgh Symphony Orchestra; New York Metropolitan Opera 1971. He was music director of the London Philharmonic Orchestra 1962–66; BBC Symphony Orchestra from 1981; and principal conductor of the Cologne Opera from 1978.

Pritchett, V(ictor) S(awdon) (1900–1997)

English short-story writer, novelist, and critic. His style was often witty and satirical. Many of his short stories were set in London and southeast England, among them *The Spanish Virgin* (1930), *Blind Love* (1969), and *The Camberwell Beauty* (1974). His critical works included *The Living Novel* (1946) and biographies of the Russian writers Turgenev (1977) and Chekhov (1988).

The Complete Stories was published in 1990 and *The Complete Essays* in 1991. Knighted 1975.

privacy

The right of the individual to be free from secret surveillance (by scientific devices or other means) and from the disclosure to unauthorized persons of personal data, as accumulated in computer data banks.

Under the Data Protection Act 1984 a register is kept of all businesses and organizations that store and process personal information, and they are subject to a code of practice set out in the act.

A bill to curb invasions of privacy by the media failed to reach the statute book in 1989. It would have enabled legal

PRISON *Women prisoners with their babies in the exercise yard at Wormwood Scrubs prison on the western outskirts of London, England, in the late 1890s. Women who received custodial sentences were allowed to see their infants for only a short period each day. Private collection*

action against publication, or attempted publication, of private information without consent. A new campaign to stabilize privacy law began after the death of Diana, Princess of Wales, in 1997.

private finance initiative, PFI

An idea floated by the Labour Party when in opposition before 1997, and particularly by the deputy leader, John ◊Prescott, who argued that the country's infrastructure could be improved by combining public expenditure with private finance. Since assuming office in May 1997 the Labour government has kept the initiative alive by gaining the support of major companies for its investment plans and inviting prominent industrialists to work in or with the administration.

In PFI deals, the public sector decides what service is required and the private sector is challenged to bid for the design, building, financing, and operation of the service. The government aims to have agreed £14 billion of PFI deals by the end of 1998–99. A recent example of PFI has been a £150 million deal to build and operate a new national insurance records system for the Department of Social Security.

privatization

Policy or process of selling or transferring state-owned or public assets and services (notably nationalized industries) to private investors. Privatization of services involves the government contracting private firms to supply services previously supplied by public authorities. The policy of privatization has been pursued by the post-1979 Conservative and Labour administrations.

Supporters of privatization argue that the public benefits from theoretically greater efficiency from firms already in the competitive market, and the release of resources for more appropriate use by government. Those against privatization believe that it transfers a country's assets from all the people to a controlling minority, that public utilities such as gas and water become private monopolies, and that a profit-making state-owned company raises revenue for the government.

Industries in the UK privatized since 1979:
British Telecom
British Gas Corporation
British National Oil Corporation
British Airways
British Airports Authority
British Aerospace
British Shipbuilders
British Steel
British Transport Docks Board
British Water Board
National Freight Company
Enterprise Oil
Jaguar
National Freight Company
Rover Group
Water Supply
Electricity and gas companies
British Rail

Privy Council

Council composed originally of the chief royal officials of the Norman kings in Britain; under the Tudors and early Stuarts it became the chief governing body. It was replaced from 1688 by the cabinet, originally a committee of the council, and the council itself now retains only formal powers in issuing royal proclamations and orders in council. In 1998 there were over 200 Privy Counsellors. Cabinet ministers are automatically members, and it is presided over by the Lord President of the Council.

Composition

The modern Privy Council consists of some three hundred people who hold or have held high legal or political offices (including all members of the cabinet who are appointed privy councillors on assuming ministerial office of cabinet rank), together with the archbishops of Canterbury and York, the Speaker of the House of Commons, a number of Commonwealth statesmen, and British ambassadors. Appointment is made by letters patent, and is normally for life.

Functions

The full Privy Council now meets only to sign the proclamation of a new sovereign and when a sovereign announces his or her intention to marry. The latter last occurred in 1839, when Queen Victoria announced her forthcoming marriage to Prince Albert of Saxe-Coburg-Gotha.

The Lord President of the Council is responsible for presenting the business to the Queen, who by convention gives her approval. The Lord President is also the member of the cabinet in charge of the Privy Council Office and, since 1964, he has also been the leader of the House of Commons and therefore in charge of the government's business in the lower House. Because he or she has minimal departmental responsibilities the Lord President also presides over one or more important cabinet committees.

privy purse

Personal expenditure of the British sovereign, which derives from his/her own resources (as distinct from the ◊civil list, which now finances only expenses incurred in pursuance of official functions and duties). The office that deals with this expenditure is also known as the Privy Purse.

Privy Seal, Lord

Until 1884, the UK officer of state in charge of the ◊great seal to prevent its misuse. The honorary title is now held by a senior cabinet minister who has special non-departmental duties.

Until the reign of Henry VIII the office was usually held by a churchman. He was appointed originally to keep the privy seal of the king, so that no independent grants might be made without the knowledge of the king's council. His duties were abolished in 1884, but the office still exists and is generally held by a member of the cabinet, who is entrusted with special duties. The current (1998) Lord Privy Seal is also the leader of the House of Lords, the Labour peer Lord Richard.

proclamation

Constitutional mode of declaring the will of the chief

executive of a state. All British proclamations are made by the monarch as an ◊order in council and must pass under the ◊great seal. For the most part proclamations can be binding on the subject only in so far as they are based on the law of the land.

Proclamations are principally used for declarations of war, peace, or state of emergency, for proroguing, dissolving, and summoning Parliament, and on ceremonial occasions such as the accession of the monarch.

procurator fiscal

Officer of a Scottish sheriff's court who (combining the role of public prosecutor and coroner) inquires into suspicious deaths and carries out the preliminary questioning of witnesses to crime.

Prodigy

English pop group formed in 1990. Following early success with 'Charley' and the album *The Prodigy Experience* (1992), they have achieved worldwide success as their style has become more aggressive, combining heavy metal and dance. The single 'Firestarter' (1996) reached number one in the UK chart and was followed by the hit album *The Fat of the Land* (1997).

The group's members are Liam Howlett (1971–) (keyboards), Keith Flint (1969–) (vocals and dancing), Maxim Reality (Keith Palmer, 1967–) (vocals and dancing), and Leeroy Thornhill (1969–) (dancing).

Profumo, John Dennis (1915–)

British Conservative politician, secretary of state for war from 1960 to June 1963. He resigned following disclosure of his involvement with Christine Keeler, mistress also of a Soviet naval attaché, and admitted he had deceived the House of Commons about the affair. The scandal caused great damage to the Macmillan government, contributing to its downfall. In 1982 Profumo became administrator of the social and educational settlement Toynbee Hall in London.

Proms, the

Popular name for the Henry Wood Promenade Concerts held annually between July and September in the Royal Albert Hall, London. The Proms were launched by the English conductor Henry ◊Wood at Queen's Hall, London, in 1895; they have been held at the Albert Hall since 1941. The concerts have been sponsored and broadcast by the BBC since 1927. A proportion of the audience stands during performances.

The eight-week concert season features mainly classical music, with regular premieres of new works. Henry Wood conducted the Proms 1895–1944; he was succeeded by Malcolm ◊Sargent 1944–67. The **Last Night of the Proms** is a traditionally patriotic occasion, with Elgar's *Land of Hope and Glory*, Henry Wood's *Fantasia on British Sea Songs*, Thomas Arne's *Rule, Britannia!*, and Hubert Parry's *Jerusalem* stirringly performed by the BBC Symphony Orchestra, under the baton of chief conductor Andrew Davis (1944–) since 1989. The audience, particularly those standing – the 'Prommers' – wave flags, bob up and down, and participate enthusiastically.

proportional representation, PR

Electoral system in which distribution of party seats corresponds to their proportion of the total votes cast, and minority votes are not wasted (as opposed to a simple majority, or 'first past the post', system). Forms include:

Party list (PLS) or additional member system (AMS). As recommended by the Hansard Society in 1976 for introduction in the UK, three-quarters of the members would be elected in single-member constituencies on the traditional majority-vote system, and the remaining seats be allocated according to the overall number of votes cast for each party. Proportional representation is to be used for the new Scottish Parliament and Welsh Assembly, to be elected in 1999, and for the next European Parliament elections in Britain.

Single transferable vote (STV), in which candidates are numbered in order of preference by the voter, and any votes surplus to the minimum required for a candidate to win are transferred to second preferences, as are second-preference votes from the successive candidates at the bottom of the poll until the required number of elected candidates is achieved. This is in use for European Parliament elections in Northern Ireland.

In Britain the growth in the vote for third parties, especially the Liberals, in the 1960s and 1970s, revived interest in a pressure for some form of proportional representation. Before assuming office in May 1997, the Labour Party established a commission to review and advise on possible future changes to the electoral system. The commission was chaired by the Liberal Democrat peer, Lord Jenkins.

prorogation

The termination of a session of Parliament and the setting of the date for a new session. All business, including bills before Parliament, is terminated by prorogation and must, if desired, be reintroduced in the following session. The only exceptions to this are impeachment proceedings by the House of Commons (now obsolete) and appeals before the House of Lords. The period between sessions is known as a 'recess'.

prosecution

In law, the party instituting legal proceedings. In the UK, the prosecution of a criminal case is begun by bringing the accused (defendant) before a magistrate, either by warrant or summons, or by arrest without warrant. Most criminal prosecutions are conducted by the ◊Crown Prosecution Service, although other government departments may also prosecute some cases; for example, the Department of Inland Revenue. An individual may bring a private prosecution, usually for assault.

Prosecution Service, Crown

Body established by the Prosecution of Offences Act 1985, responsible for prosecuting all criminal offences in England and Wales. It is headed by the Director of Public Prosecutions (DPP), and brings England and Wales in line with Scotland (see ◊procurator fiscal) in having a prosecution service independent of the police.

In most cases the decision to prosecute is made on the basis of evidence presented by the police to local crown prosecutors in each of 43 police authority areas. Before the 1985 act, the DPP took action (under the guidance of the attorney general) only in cases of special difficulty or importance.

Prout, William (1785–1850)

British physician and chemist. In 1815 Prout published his hypothesis that the relative atomic mass of every atom is an exact and integral multiple of the mass of the hydrogen atom. The discovery of isotopes (atoms of the same element that have different masses) in the 20th century bore out his idea.

In 1827, Prout became the first scientist to classify the components of food into the three major divisions of carbohydrates, fats, and proteins.

Provisional IRA

Radical faction of the ◊IRA.

provisional order

Form of delegated legislation exercised in Britain by ministers under existing statutory powers, but which must be confirmed by the passing of a Provisional Order Confirmation Bill. They apply particularly to powers granted to individual local authorities which would otherwise have to be granted by means of private bills promoted by the local authority concerned.

provost (Latin *praepositus* 'prefect, the chief of a body or community')

Chief magistrate of a Scottish burgh, approximate equivalent of an English mayor.

The provosts of Aberdeen, Dundee, Edinburgh, Glasgow, and Perth are entitled **Lord Provost**. In the Scottish Episcopal Church the title 'provost' is the equivalent of 'dean'. In some English dioceses it is used in the place of dean for the head of the cathedral chapter. These cathedrals are also parish churches, and the provost is the incumbent. The title is also used for the heads of certain colleges in the universities of Oxford, Cambridge, and London, and there is a provost of Eton College.

Pryce, Jonathan (1947–)

Welsh character actor of the stage and screen. He rose to international renown following his roles as a journalist in *The Ploughman's Lunch* (1983) and as a Kafkaesque clerk in *Brazil* (1985). A prolific performer in the 1990s, Pryce has brought intelligent poise to minor roles in films such as *The Age of Innocence* (1993), and lent a comic touch in his role as a corrupt media mogul in the James Bond film *Tomorrow Never Dies* (1997). Other feature roles include the period pieces *Carrington* (1995) and *Regeneration* (1997), and his role as the Argentine dictator Juan Perón in the musical film *Evita* (1996).

Pryde, James (1866–1941)

Scottish painter. With William ◊Nicholson, he produced the **Beggarstaff Brothers** posters from 1894 to 1896.

As a painter, he created pictures of Romantic gloom in which, to echoes of William Hogarth or Giambattista Piranesi, he added an urban fantasy of his own. *The Slum* is among the most striking of his variations on the architectural theme.

Public Health Acts

Legislation enacted by Parliament in 1848, 1872, and 1875 to deal with squalor and disease and to establish a code of sanitary law. The first act, in 1848, established a central board of health with three members who were responsible to Parliament to impose local boards of health in districts where the death rate was above the national average and to make provision for other local boards of health to be established by petition. The 1872 act made it obligatory for every local authority to appoint a medical officer of health. The 1875 act consolidated previous acts and provided a comprehensive code for public health.

public house, or pub

Building licensed for consumption of liquor. In Britain a pub is either 'free' (when the licensee has free choice of suppliers) or, more often, 'tied' to a brewery company owning the house. There are some 77,100 pubs in Britain (1998), many of which also serve food. Legal opening hours are 11.00–23.00 Monday to Saturday and 12.00–22.30 on Sunday. See feature on page 734.

public inquiry

In English law, a legal investigation where witnesses are called and evidence is produced in a similar fashion to a court of law. Inquiries may be held as part of legal procedure, or into a matter of public concern.

Inquiries that are part of certain legal procedures, such as where planning permission is disputed, or where an inquiry is required by an act of Parliament, are headed by an inspector appointed by the secretary of state concerned, who then makes a decision based on the inspector's report (although this report is not binding). The longest and most expensive inquiry ever held was the Sizewell B nuclear-plant inquiry, which lasted for two and a quarter years (approved 1987). Inquiries into a matter of public concern are usually headed by a senior judge. Examples include the **Scarman inquiry** following inner-city riots in 1981, an inquiry into the King's Cross Underground fire in 1987, and an inquiry into child abuse in Cleveland in 1988.

public lending right, PLR

Method of paying a royalty to authors when books are borrowed from libraries, similar to a royalty on performance of a play or piece of music. Payment to the copyright holder for such borrowings was introduced in Australia in 1974 and in the UK in 1984.

Public Order Act

UK act of Parliament 1986 that abolished the common-law offences of riot, rout, unlawful assembly, and affray and created a new expanded range of statutory offences: riot, violent disorder, affray, threatening behaviour, and disorderly conduct. These are all arrestable offences that may be committed in both private and public places. Prosecution for riot requires the consent of the Director of Public Prosecutions.

Public Order Acts were also passed in 1936 and 1963. The first act was passed at a time when various paramilitary organizations, in imitation of the Fascists and Nazis, adopted black, brown, green, or other distinctive shirts, marched in procession, and held political meetings which not infrequently led to disturbances of the peace.

The Public Order Act 1936 prohibited both paramilitary organizations and the wearing of uniforms in connection with political objectives. It also gave powers to the police for the preservation of public order on the occasion of processions. No conditions, however, restricting the display of flags, banners, or emblems were imposed by the act, except such as were reasonably necessary to prevent risk of a breach of the peace. The act also prohibited the carrying of offensive weapons without lawful authority at public meetings and offensive conduct conducive to breaches of the peace. The Public Order Act of 1963 increased the penalties for offences under the 1936 Act.

public school

In England and Wales, a prestigious fee-paying independent school. In Scotland a 'public' school is a state-maintained school, and independent schools are generally known as 'private' schools.

Some English public schools (for example Eton, Harrow, Rugby, Winchester) are ancient foundations, usually originally intended for poor male scholars; others developed in the 18th–19th centuries. Among those for girls are Roedean and Benenden. Many public schools are coeducational in the sixth form, and some boys' schools now admit girls at 13. Some discipline (less than formerly) is in the hands of senior boys and girls (prefects).

Originally, UK public schools stressed a classical education, character training, and sports, but the curriculum is now closer allied to state education, although with generally a wider range of subjects offered and a lower pupil-to-teacher ratio.

puddings

The British repertoire of puddings is unrivalled. It includes steamed puddings, fruit pies, tarts, trifles, flans and flummeries, rice pudding, treacle tart, bread and butter pudding with real custard, and apple pie with clotted cream (or in Yorkshire, a slice of cheese).

Most British puddings trace their origin back to one of two ancient confections; the 'pye' or pudding filled with dried fruit and nuts plus shredded meat (hence the term 'mincemeat'), or a soft, jellied milk pudding, made from wheat or barley, called 'frumenty'. As available ingredients increased, so did the fashion for encasing the pudding in a thick pastry crust or 'coffyn'.

Pies grew increasingly spectacular, but by the end of the 17th century tastes became more rustic and regionalized. Batter and steamed puddings and plate pies were all popular, and local fairs or 'junkets' gave their name to a popular dish that could be made on the spot with milk warm from the cow. This fondness for sweet creamy things still manifests itself in desserts such as gooseberry fool, Trinity or burnt cream, Eton Mess, and the Scottish cranachan made with oatmeal, whisky, and raspberries, as well as the brown bread ice cream that was an Edwardian favourite.

In the late 20th century traditional 'nursery' puddings enjoyed something of a revival (Queen of puddings, spotted dick, Sussex pond pudding, and sticky toffee pudding) but the greatest, Christmas pudding, has never fallen out of favour since it first decorated tables in the 18th century.

It is not that the Englishman can't feel – it is that he is afraid to feel. He has been taught at his public school that feeling is bad form.

E M FORSTER English novelist.
Abinger Harvest, 'Notes on English Character'

Pudsey

Town in West Yorkshire, England, west of Leeds; population (1991) 22,400. It has an important woollen and worsted trade, and there are dyeing and fulling mills. Iron and brass foundries are located here and machinery is made. Fulneck, a Moravian settlement since 1745, lies within the town.

In the early 6th century Pudsey and the neighbourhood are thought to have been the centre of the kingdom of Elmete, which retained its independence for more than 200 years after other kingdoms had been subdued by the Saxons. The name Pudsey occurs in the Domesday Book.

The cricketer Len Hutton was born in Pudsey.

Pugin, Augustus Welby Northmore (1812–1852)

English architect and designer. He collaborated with Charles ◊Barry in the detailed design of the New Palace of Westminster (Houses of Parliament). He did much to instigate the ◊Gothic Revival in England, largely through his book *Contrasts* (1836). Pugin believed in a close connection between Christianity and Gothic architecture, and attacked what he held to be the 'pagan' method of Classical architecture. He became a Roman Catholic, and designed many Roman Catholic churches, including the cathedral of St George at Southwark (severely damaged during World War II).

Punch (Italian *Pulcinella*)

Male character in the traditional puppet play *Punch and Judy*, a humpbacked, hooknosed figure who fights with his wife, Judy.

Punch generally overcomes or outwits all opponents. The play is performed by means of glove puppets, manipulated by a single operator concealed in a portable canvas stage frame, who uses a squeaky voice for Punch. Punch originated in Italy, and was probably introduced to England at the time of the Restoration.

THE PUB – A NATIONAL INSTITUTION

THE WORD 'pub' is instantly and universally recognized, a term of verbal shorthand. On the 'must-do' list of every visitor to Britain, alongside a ride on a red London bus or in a black taxi, will be a visit to a pub. Other countries have bars, cafés, and kellers, but only Britain has its public houses, over 70,000 of them in towns, cities, villages, and hamlets, with names that express the deep roots the institution has in the country's history, community, and culture. Many attempts have been made to export 'the English pub', often with risible results, but it flourishes only on its native soil.

Photo: Corel

Ale-houses and taverns
The public house is a comparatively modern term, dating from Victorian times, when large and imposing new licensed premises were built by rich brewers with government backing to offer a relatively sober alternative to sordid gin shops. Until the development of the public house, people drank in ale houses, inns, and taverns, an overlapping and interconnected system of drinking places as old as the island race. Brewing for centuries was a domestic activity, usually carried out by women who made ale for home consumption as naturally as they made bread. The Roman invaders built their *tabernae* where wine was drunk, but such establishments were not open to the natives, though they duly noted the name and later adopted it for their own use. The Danes, Vikings, and Saxons who followed the Romans brought with them a passion for ale drinking that became deeply embedded in the way of life of the emerging nation. Gradually the ale wives or brewsters who made the best beer would offer it to others in their local communities: when a fresh brew was ready,a pole with a garland of evergreens on the end would emerge from a window. These rudimentary drinking places were forced to grow, with additional rooms added to accommodate willing customers. The ale house was born.

With the spread of Christianity, brewing came under the control of the church. Monasteries had their own large breweries and the monks built adjoining inns to provide accommodation for pilgrims and travellers. Innkeepers gave their houses names, often taken from the coats of arms of the local nobility. As towns and cities grew, inns were built to refresh the urban masses, and often took as their inn signs the names of the guilds and associations formed by city craftsmen, such as the Bakers Arms, Lamb and Flag (merchant tailors), Three Compasses (carpenters), and the Elephant and Castle (master cutlers). It also became the custom to name inns after the monarch of the day, which is why Britain still has a profusion of Queen's and King's Head pubs bearing the visage of the chosen monarch.

The types of drinking establishments were strictly codified in medieval England: an ale house could sell only beer, while a tavern had to serve food as well as drink, and an inn offered accommodation as well, an important consideration as a network of roads developed and coaches took people on long journeys that required regular stops for refreshment and sleep.

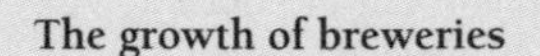

The growth of breweries
During the Tudor period, commercial or 'common' brewers appeared who supplied ale to casual callers and to innkeepers. But most innkeepers made their own ale in tiny brewhouses, a habit that did not start to decline until the 18th century when the spread of vast cities created a

The British satirical magazine *Punch* was founded in 1841, ceased publication in 1992, and was resurrected in 1996.

punk
Movement of disaffected youth of the late 1970s, manifesting itself in fashions and music designed to shock or intimidate.

demand for beer that innkeepers could not meet. Commercial brewing became big business and the owners bought pubs to create a captive market for their products. In spite of government efforts to stop the spread of brewery-owned pubs in the 19th century, by the turn of that century the 'tied house' system was deeply entrenched, with the biggest and wealthiest brewers building large estates of houses.

For most of the 20th century the pub scene remained largely unaltered, divided between tied houses owned by brewers and 'free houses' run by independent small businessmen. The system worked well as long as there were several hundred breweries offering choice and diversity in their houses. Choice declined rapidly from the 1970s onward as a series of mergers and takeovers created half a dozen giant national companies, each owning thousands of pubs and restricting them to a handful of beers. Efforts by successive governments in the 1980s and 1990s to break the stranglehold of the national brewers had only limited success. Rather than improve choice as a result of government diktat, the brewers sold off most of their tied estates, creating new quasi-independent pub groups. In some, the choice of beer has improved; in others, the same old national brands dominate.

Restricted choice goes hand in hand with the tunnel vision of both brewers and pub owners who think that young people are the only customers worthy of note. The late 1990s has seen a rash of 'circuit pubs' and 'theme pubs' that allow teenagers and those in their early twenties to roam the streets in search of strong alcohol and high-decibel entertainment. Deafening music, strobe lights, and bouncers on the door make a mockery of the notion of a public house open to all. But as the century draws to an end there are signs that even younger people are tiring of the excesses of circuit drinking; the public house, that most enduring of institutions seems set to survive into the 21st century, once again providing good beer, simple food, and the opportunity for people to throw off the stresses of modern life. In the pub, heaven knows, even the English talk to one another.

Scotland and Ireland

The pub is mainly confined to England and Wales. It exists in the Scottish Borders and the great cities of Aberdeen and Edinburgh in Scotland, but elsewhere serious drinking is done in hotels and spartan bars. The Irish, too, both North and South, tend to talk of bars rather than pubs: they are named after their owners rather than kings, queens, and half-forgotten battles, and the rural and small-town versions often sell groceries as well as beer. The great cities of Belfast, Cork, and Dublin have large, ornate drinking places, full of polished wood, alcoves, snugs, vast mirrors, cut glass, sudden outbreaks of live music, and that special kind of Irish conversation, an intertwining of humour, politics, and pathos that is known as 'the craic'.

BY ROGER PROTZ

Punk rock began in the UK and stressed aggressive performance within a three-chord, three-minute format, as exemplified by the Sex Pistols. The punk aesthetic continued to be revived periodically with the nostalgia boom of the 1990s, supported by the growth of a neo-punk movement in the USA and by groups such as the Clash being accorded the status of rock 'n' roll 'classics'.

Purbeck, Isle of

Peninsula in southeast Dorset, southern England, between Poole Harbour and the English Channel, terminating at St Aldhelm's Head (or St Alban's Head). Purbeck marble and china clay are obtained from the area, which includes the villages of Corfe Castle and Swanage.

The northern ridge of the chalk Purbeck Hills traverses the peninsula from east to west. Purbeck was once a deer forest, but the land is now mainly heath and downs.

Purcell, Daniel (*c.* 1663–1717)

English organist and composer. He finished the opera *The Indian Queen*, which his brother Henry ◊Purcell had left unfinished at his death. After a busy career writing music for plays, he became organist of St Andrew's Church, Holborn, London, in 1713.

Purcell, Henry (*c.* 1659–1695)

English Baroque composer. His music balances high formality with melodic expression of controlled intensity, for example, the opera *Dido and Aeneas* (1689) and music for Dryden's *King Arthur* (1691) and for *The Fairy Queen* (1692). He wrote more than 500 works, ranging from secular operas and incidental music for plays to cantatas and church music.

Born at Westminster, he became a chorister at the Chapel Royal, and subsequently was a pupil of Dr John Blow. In 1677 he was appointed composer to the Chapel Royal, and in 1679 organist at Westminster Abbey. As composer to the king, Purcell set odes or anthems to music.

Pusey, Edward Bouverie (1800–1882)

English Church of England priest and theologian. In 1835 he joined J H ◊Newman in the ◊Oxford Movement, and contributed to the series *Tracts for the Times*. After Newman's conversion to Roman Catholicism in 1845, Pusey became leader of the High Church Party, or Puseyites, striving until his death to keep them from conversion.

His work is continued through Pusey House at Oxford, founded in his memory, which contains his library.

Educated at Christ Church, Oxford, he was elected a fellow of Oriel College, Oxford, in 1823. Ordained in 1828, he became professor of Hebrew at Oxford University.

Puttnam, David (Terence) (1941–)

English film producer. He played a major role in reviving the British film industry internationally in the 1980s, and has been involved in an eclectic range of films with a variety of filmmakers. They include *Midnight Express* (1978), *Chariots of Fire* (1981) (Academy Award for best film), *The Killing Fields* (1984), and *Memphis Belle* (1990). He was head of Columbia Pictures 1986–87.

In the 1990s he produced *Meeting Venus* (1991), *Le Confessional* (1995), and *The World of Moss* (1998). He was made a life peer in 1997.

Pwllheli

Market town and resort in Gwynedd unitary authority, northwest Wales, situated on the south coast of the ▷Lleyn Peninsula and on Cardigan Bay, 30 km/19 mi southwest of Caernarfon. The Welsh National Party, Plaid Cymru, was founded here in 1925. Nearby is a very large holiday camp.

Pym, Barbara Mary Crampton (1913–1980)

English novelist. Her closely observed novels of village life include *Some Tame Gazelle* (1950), *The Sweet Dove Died* (1978), and *A Few Green Leaves* (1980).

Pym, John (1584–1643)

English Parliamentarian, largely responsible for the Petition of Right in 1628. As leader of the Puritan opposition in the ▷Long Parliament from 1640, he moved the impeachment of Charles I's advisers the Earl of Strafford and William Laud, drew up the ▷Grand Remonstrance, and was the chief of five members of Parliament Charles I wanted arrested in 1642. The five hid themselves and then emerged triumphant when the king left London.

Quaker

Popular name, originally derogatory, for a member of the Society of ⇨Friends.

quango, acronym for quasi-autonomous nongovernmental organization

Any administrative body that is nominally independent but relies on government funding; for example, the British Council (1935) and the Equal Opportunities Commission (1975).

In 1996 in the UK, there were more than 6,000 quangos, spending £45 billion annually (equivalent to one-third of central government spending). The growth of quangos in the UK represented one aspect of the Conservative government's (1979–97) policy of reducing the size of the central government machine.

Quangos have been criticized for a lack of popular accountability, and face few of the statutory obligations that apply to local authorities.

Quant, Mary (1934–)

English fashion designer. She popularized the miniskirt in the UK and was one of the first designers to make clothes specifically for the teenage and early twenties market, producing bold, simple outfits which were in tune with the 'swinging London' of the 1960s. Her designs were sharp, angular, and streetwise, and she combined spots, stripes, and checks in an original way. Her boutique in Chelsea's King's Road, opened in 1955, was named Bazaar. In the 1970s she extended into cosmetics and textile design.

Born in London, Quant studied at Goldsmith's College of Art. An exhibition, **Mary Quant's London**, was held at the Museum of London in 1973–74. In 1990 she won the British Fashion Council's Hall of Fame award. Her cosmetics company became part of the Max Factor empire.

QUANT, MARY *The international reputation that British fashion designers now enjoy is partly due to pioneers such as Mary Quant, who helped promote abroad the fresh, uncomplicated styles adopted by fashionable young people in London in the 1960s. These included the boyish, short-haired look for women, and the mini skirt. Rex*

Quantock Hills, or the Quantocks

Range of hills in northwest Somerset, England, extending 13 km/8 mi between Taunton and the Bristol Channel. They form a series of irregular ridges, chiefly of greywacke (dark sandstone or grit) and limestone. The highest point is Willsneck (387 m/1,270 ft).

quarantine (from French *quarantaine* '40 days')

Any period for which people, animals, plants, or vessels may be detained in isolation to prevent the spread of contagious disease. In the UK, imported animals are quarantined to prevent the spread of ◊rabies.

In September 1998 Britain announced that its quarantine regulations would be changing to allow animals from the European Union and rabies-free islands, such as Australia and New Zealand, into the country without a period of quarantine. This would apply only to microchipped animals with vaccination certificates.

quarter session

Former local criminal court in England, replaced in 1972 by crown courts (see also ◊law courts).

Quayle, (John) Anthony (1913–1989)

English actor and director. From 1948–56 he directed at the Shakespeare Memorial Theatre, and appeared as Falstaff in *Henry IV*, Petruchio in *The Taming of the Shrew*, and played the title role in *Othello*. He played nonclassical parts in *Galileo*, *Sleuth*, and *Old World*. He founded the Compass Company in 1984. His numerous film appearances include *Lawrence of Arabia* (1962). He was knighted in 1985.

Queen

British glam-rock group 1971–91 credited with making the first successful pop video, for their hit 'Bohemian Rhapsody' (1975). The operatic flamboyance of lead singer Freddie Mercury (1946–1991) was the cornerstone of their popularity. Among their other hits are 'We Will Rock You' (1977) and the rockabilly pastiche 'Crazy Little Thing Called Love' (1980).

Mercury was accorded saintly status following his death from AIDS-related illness. His career as a solo artist was negligible, but his contribution within the group as a technically gifted singer and musician, and a self-aware icon of British high camp, established him as a mainstream cultural figure whose wide appeal was only truly apparent after his death.

Queen, the

See ◊Elizabeth II and ◊monarchy.

Queen Alexandra's Royal Army Nursing Corps, QARANC

Army support service whose members serve in Ministry of Defence hospital units in the UK and in military hospitals both in the UK and abroad. Service in the Corps was opened to men in 1992. The Corps was founded in 1902 as Queen Alexandra's Imperial Military Nursing Service and gained its current title in 1949. The Corps has trained nurses and trains and employs health care assistants.

Queen Alexandra's Royal Naval Nursing Service, QARNNS

Naval support service which gained its title in 1902, nursing sisters having first been appointed to naval hospitals in 1884. Men were integrated into the Service in 1982; female medical assistants were introduced in 1987. QARNNS ratings, both male and female, enlist on the 'Open Engagement' to complete 22 years of active service with the option to leave at 18 months notice at the completion of a minimum of 2½ years productive service.

Queen Anne style

Decorative art style in England (1700–20), characterized by plain, simple lines, mainly in silver and furniture.

Queenborough

Town in Kent, England, on the western side of the Isle of Sheppey; population 7,200. It has a deep water port, a ferrous sulphate (iron (II) sulphate or copperas) factory, and engineering and pharmaceutical factories. Founded in the 14th century against French raids, the town has a castle, built 1361–77.

Queenborough was named after Queen Philippa of Hainault, wife of Edward III.

Queen's Award

British award for industrial excellence established in 1965 as the Queen's Award to Industry, and replaced from 1976 by two separate awards, for export achievement and for technological achievement.

Made to organizations, not individuals, the Queen's Award entitles the holder to display a special emblem for five years. Awards are made annually in April.

Queensberry, John Sholto Douglas, 8th Marquess of Queensberry (1844–1900)

British patron of boxing. In 1867 he gave his name to a new set of boxing rules. Devised by the pioneering British sports administrator John Chambers (1841–1883), the **Queensberry Rules** form the basis of today's boxing rules.

He was the father of Lord Alfred ◊Douglas and it was his misspelled insult to Oscar Wilde that set in motion the events leading to the playwright's imprisonment. He became Marquess in 1858.

Queensbury

Town in West Yorkshire, England, southwest of Bradford; population (1991) 15,700. Worsted (a fabric made from wool) is manufactured here and stone is quarried.

Queen's Counsel

(QC) in England, a barrister appointed to senior rank by the Lord Chancellor. When the monarch is a king the term is **King's Counsel (KC)**. A QC wears a silk gown, and takes precedence over a junior member of the Bar.

Quiller-Couch, Arthur (Thomas) (1863–1944)

English scholar and writer, who wrote under the pseudonym **Q**. He edited several anthologies, including the original edition of *The Oxford Book of English Verse* (1900), and wrote a number of critical studies, such as *On the Art of Writing* (1916) and *On the Art of Reading* (1920). He was professor of English literature at Cambridge University from 1912 until his death. Knighted 1910.

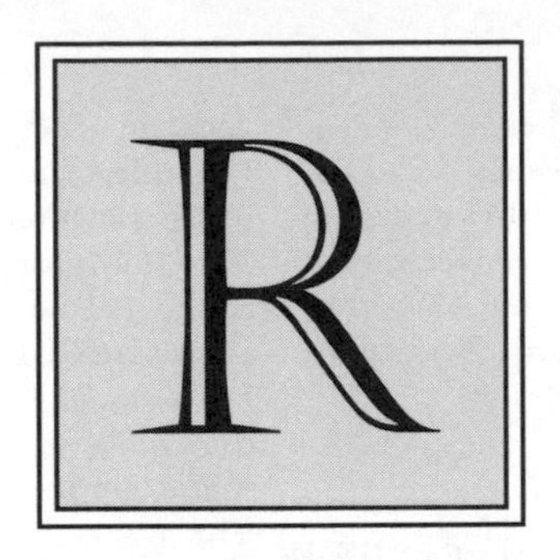

rabies, or **hydrophobia** (Greek 'fear of water')
Viral disease of the central nervous system that can afflict all warm-blooded creatures. It is caused by a lyssavirus, and is almost invariably fatal once symptoms have developed. Its transmission to humans is generally by a bite from an infected animal. Rabies continues to kill hundreds of thousands of people every year; almost all these deaths occur in Asia, Africa, and South America.

In Britain, no human rabies has been transmitted since 1902. Britain and Ireland are the only countries in the European Union to ◊quarantine all incoming pets (for a six-month period), following the decisions of Sweden and Norway to replace their four-month quarantine period with a vaccination scheme in 1994.

According to the European Commission, the number of cases of rabies in animals in EU member states was reduced by 70% between 1990 and 1994. In 1996 the Commission also began examining ways of controlling rabies in bats, which were identified as possible carriers in the early 1990s.

In September 1998 Britain announced that its quarantine regulations would be changing to allow animals from the European Union and rabies-free islands, such as Australia and New Zealand, into the country without a period of quarantine. This would apply only to microchipped animals with vaccination certificates.

RAC
Abbreviation for the British **Royal Automobile Club**, founded in 1897 as the **Automobile Club of Great Britain and Northern Ireland**. It became the RAC in 1907. Its aim is 'to advance the automobile movement in the UK'.

race-relations acts
Acts of Parliament of 1965, 1968, and 1976 to combat discrimination. The Race Relations Act 1976 prohibits discrimination on the grounds of colour, race, nationality, or ethnic origin. Indirect as well as direct discrimination is prohibited in the provision of goods, services, facilities, employment, accommodation, and advertisements. The ◊Commission for Racial Equality was set up under the act to investigate complaints of discrimination.

rackets, or **racquets**
Indoor game played on an enclosed court. Although first played in the Middle Ages, rackets developed in the 18th century and was played against the walls of London buildings. It is considered the forerunner of many racket and ball games, particularly squash.

The game is played on a court usually 18.3 m/60 ft long by 9.1 m/30 ft wide, by two or four persons each with a racket about 75 cm/2.5 ft long, weighing 255 g/9 oz. The ball is 25 mm/1 in in diameter and weighs 28 g/1 oz. Play begins from a service box – one is marked at each side of mid-court – and the ball must hit the end wall above a 2.75 m/9 ft line high. After service it may be played anywhere above a line 68.5 cm/27 in high on the end wall, the general rules of tennis applying thereafter.

Rackham, Arthur (1867–1939)
English illustrator. Influenced by ◊Art Nouveau, he developed an ornate and delicate style. He illustrated a wide range of books, but is best remembered for his illustrations for children's classics, including *Peter Pan* (1906) and *Andersen's Fairy Tales* (1932).

Radcliffe
Town in Greater Manchester, England, on the River Irwell close to Bury; population (1991) 32,500. It developed as a cotton-weaving centre, but engineering is now the main industry. Residential development has been limited by fears of subsidence from former mining activity.

Radcliffe, Ann born Ward (1764–1823)
English novelist. An exponent of the Gothic novel or 'romance of terror', she wrote, for example, *The Mysteries of Udolpho* (1794). She excelled in depicting scenes of mystery and terror, and was one of the first novelists to include vivid descriptions of landscape and weather.

Her other novels include *A Sicilian Romance* (1790), *The Romance of the Forest* 1791, and *The Italian* (1797). Her work was very popular in her day.

Radical
Supporter of parliamentary reform before the Reform Bill of 1832. As a group the Radicals later became the progressive

wing of the Liberal Party. During the 1860s (led by Cobden, Bright, and J S Mill) they campaigned for extension of the franchise, free trade, and *laissez-faire*, but after 1870, under the leadership of Joseph Chamberlain and Charles Dilke, they adopted a republican and semi-socialist programme. With the growth of socialism in the later 19th century, Radicalism ceased to exist as an organized movement.

radio

Radio channels, both national and local, are run by the ◊BBC and by a mix of independent commercial companies who play on-air advertising. The five BBC national radio stations are Radio 1 (pop), Radio 2 (mainstream music), Radio 3 (predominantly classical music and some talk), Radio 4 (mostly speech: news and current affairs, features, drama), and Radio 5 Live (sport and news). In addition the BBC runs a range of local radio stations and the World Service, which in 1998 broadcasted in 47 languages, including English.

In the independent sector the national stations are Virgin (music), Talk Radio, and Classic FM (music), while the local commercial stations include Capital, in London. Commercial radio stations are licensed by the Radio Authority, created in 1991 to take on radio responsibilities from the Independent Broadcasting Authority.

History

Guglielmo Marconi successfully transmitted radio signals across the English Channel in 1898, and in 1901 established communication with St John's, Newfoundland, from Poldhu in Cornwall. The BBC began radio broadcasts in 1927, and started the World Service in English in 1932. It consolidated its UK output into the Home Service in 1939. A year later, to cater especially for those involved in the war, a new BBC radio entertainment channel was started, called the Forces Programme; it was renamed the Light Programme after World War II. The Third Programme for music and some speech began broadcasting in 1946.

These three became Radios 2, 3, and 4 (Home Service) in 1967, when the BBC also launched its pop channel, Radio 1, to compete with pirate radio stations broadcasting from offshore ships, outside territorial waters; the first of these was Radio Atlanta (later Radio Caroline), set up in 1964. The commercial station Radio Luxembourg was another competitor, broadcast from Luxembourg using UK disc jockeys.

Commercial radio proper began in the UK in 1972, under the terms of the Sound Broadcasting Act.

Radiohead

English rock group formed in Oxford in 1987. Following the success of 'Creep' (1992) in the USA, they gained a large following for their music which combines angst and epic balladry. Albums include *The Bends* (1995) and the critically acclaimed *OK Computer* (1997) which reached number one in the UK chart; hit singles in the UK include 'Karma Police'.

Members are Thom Yorke (1968–) (vocals, keyboards, and guitar), Jonny Greenwood (1971–) (guitar and keyboards), Colin Greenwood (1969–) (bass), Ed O'Brien (1968–) (guitar), and Phil Selway (1967–).

radon

Colourless, odourless, gaseous, radioactive, nonmetallic element, symbol Rn, atomic number 86, relative atomic mass 222. It is grouped with the inert gases and was formerly considered nonreactive, but is now known to form some compounds with fluorine. Of the 20 known isotopes, only three occur in nature; the longest half-life is 3.82 days (Rn-222).

Radiation levels

The average radon radiation level found in a study of 40 British limestone caves was 2,900 Bequerels per cubic metre. This compares with the National Radiological Protection Board (NRPB)'s set level of 200 Bequerels per cubic metre, at which removal of radon from homes is recommended. The highest levels were found in the Giant's Hole in Derbyshire, with values of around 155,000 Bequerels per cubic metre during the summer, which is the highest level ever recorded from a natural limestone cave. Levels up to 2.8 million Bequerels per cubic metre were recorded in abandoned mines in southwest England – 14,000 times the NRPB action level for homes.

It is estimated that there are about 100,000 homes in Britain

RAFFLES, STAMFORD *Statue in Singapore of the British colonial administrator Stamford Raffles, who founded Singapore in 1819 and thereby secured British control of Malaya. He wrote a* History of Java *(1817) and was a keen natural history collector; he founded the Zoological Society of London in 1826 and was its first president. Corbis*

where radon is believed to give off hazardous levels of radioactivity. The NRPB estimated in 1998 that between 1,800 and 2,500 people die per year in Britain due to radon exposure.

Raeburn, Henry (1756–1823)

Scottish painter. One of the leading portrait painters of the 18th century, his technique of painting with broad brushstrokes directly on the canvas, without preparatory drawing, gave his works an air of freshness and spontaneity. *The Reverend Robert Walker Skating* (about 1784; National Gallery of Scotland, Edinburgh) is typical.

Raeburn was active mainly in Edinburgh, his subjects being the notable figures of literature and law, and the chieftains of the Highland clans. He excelled in male rather than female portraits, his style being well adapted to convey their rugged dignity. He was knighted in 1822 and appointed painter to George IV in 1823.

Raffles, (Thomas) Stamford (1781–1826)

British colonial administrator, born in Jamaica. He served in the British ⇨East India Company, took part in the capture of Java from the Dutch in 1811, and while governor of Sumatra 1818–23 was responsible for the acquisition and founding of Singapore in 1819. Knighted 1817.

ragged schools

Schools founded by John Pounds (1766–1839) dedicated to the education of poor and delinquent children in industrial areas.

Raglan, FitzRoy James Henry Somerset, 1st Baron Raglan (788–1855)

English general. He took part in the Peninsular War under Wellington, and lost his right arm at Waterloo. He commanded the British forces in the Crimean War from 1854. The **raglan sleeve**, cut right up to the neckline with no shoulder seam, is named after him.

Raikes, Robert (1735–1811)

English printer who started the first Sunday school (for religious purposes) in Gloucester in 1780 and who stimulated the growth of weekday voluntary 'ragged schools' for poor children.

Railtrack

Company responsible for the commercial operation of the railway network (track and stations) in Britain. In May 1996, as part of privatization, the 20 British Rail service companies that had previously provided Railtrack's infrastructure support functions were sold into the private sector.

Railtrack does not operate train services, but is responsible for timetabling and signalling, and owns the freehold of stations. Following privatization, passenger services were divided into 25 train-operating units to be franchised to private sector operators, enabling the private sector to eventually run completely new services. The three subsidiary companies that were responsible for British Rail's passenger rolling stock were privatized in February 1996.

railways

Following the work of British steam pioneers such as Scottish engineer James ⇨Watt, English engineer George ⇨Stephenson built the first public steam railway, from Stockton to Darlington, England, in 1825. This heralded extensive railway building in Britain, continental Europe, and North America, providing a fast and economical means of transport and communication. After World War II, steam engines were replaced by electric and diesel engines. At the same time, the growth of road building, air services, and car ownership destroyed the supremacy of the railways.

Growth years

Four years after building the first steam railway, Stephenson opened the first steam passenger line, inaugurating it with his locomotive *Rocket*, which achieved speeds of 50 kph/30 mph. The railway construction that followed resulted in 250

RAILWAYS Over London by Rail *(1872), an engraving by the French artist Gustave Doré. Though most of his works are book illustrations, in the 1870s Doré engraved a series depicting the grim realities of slum life in London. His images were so powerful they were used in British government reports on the conditions of the poor. Corbis*

separate companies in Britain, which resolved into four systems in 1921 and became the nationalized British Railways in 1948, known as British Rail from 1965.

Gauge

Railway tracks were at first made of wood but later of iron or steel, with ties wedging them apart and keeping them parallel. The distance between the wheels is known as the gauge. Since much of the early development of the railway took place in Tyneside, England, the gauge of local coal wagons, 1.24 m/4 ft 8.5 in, was adopted in 1824 for the Stockton–Darlington railway, and most other early railways followed suit. The main exception was the Great Western Railway (GWR) of Isambard Kingdom ◊Brunel, opened in 1841, with a gauge of 2.13 m/7 ft. The narrow gauge won legal backing in the UK in 1846, but parts of GWR carried on with Brunel's broad gauge until 1892. British engineers building railways overseas tended to use the narrow gauge, and it became the standard in the USA from 1885. Other countries, such as Ireland and Finland, favoured the broad gauge.

Decline of railways

With the increasing use of private cars and government-encouraged road haulage after World War II, and the demise of steam, rising costs on the railways meant higher fares, fewer passengers, and declining freight traffic. In the UK many rural rail services closed down on the recommendations of the Beeching Report of 1963, reducing the size of the network by more than 20% between 1965 and 1970, from a peak of 24,102 km/14,977 mi. In the 1970s, national railway companies began investing in faster intercity services: in the UK, the diesel high-speed train (HST) was introduced.

The process of rail privatization in Britain, begun in 1992, was formally completed in April 1997 when the British Rail chairman signed papers handing over ScotRail to National Express. National Express, with five of the 25 franchises, extending from London to the Highlands, became the biggest single buyer of BR.

Railtrack is now responsible for the track and infrastructure. There are three rolling stock companies which lease locomotives and passenger coaches; 25 train operating companies; four freight service providers; seven infrastructure maintenance companies and six track renewal companies.

Raj, the

The period of British rule in India before independence in 1947.

Raleigh, or Ralegh, Walter (*c.* 1552–1618)

English adventurer, writer, and courtier to Queen Elizabeth I.

He organized expeditions to colonize North America 1584–87, all unsuccessful, and made exploratory voyages to South America in 1595 and 1616. His aggressive actions against Spanish interests, including attacks on Spanish ports, brought him into conflict with the pacific James I. He was imprisoned for treason 1603–16 and executed on his return from an unsuccessful final expedition to South America. He is traditionally credited with introducing the potato to Europe and popularizing the use of tobacco.

Born in Devon, Raleigh became a confidant of Queen Elizabeth I and was knighted in 1584. After initiating several unsuccessful attempts 1584–87 to establish a colony in North America, he led a gold-seeking expedition to the Orinoco River in South America in 1595 (described in his *Discoverie of Guiana* 1596). He distinguished himself in expeditions against Spain in Cádiz in 1596 and the Azores in 1597.

After James I's accession to the English throne in 1603, Raleigh was condemned to death on a charge of conspiracy, but was reprieved and imprisoned in the Tower of London, where he wrote his unfinished *History of the World*. Released in 1616 to lead a second expedition to the Orinoco, which failed disastrously, he was beheaded on his return under the charges of his former sentence.

Rambert, Marie adopted name of Cyvia Myriam Rambam (1888–1982)

Polish-born British ballet dancer and teacher. One of the major innovative and influential figures in modern ballet, she worked with Vaslav Nijinsky on *The Rite of Spring* for the Diaghilev ballet in Paris 1912–13, opened the Rambert School in London in 1920, and in 1926 founded the Ballet Rambert which she directed. It became a modern-dance company from 1966 and was renamed the Rambert Dance Company in 1987. Rambert became a British citizen in 1918. She was created a DBE in 1962.

Rambert Dance Company

British modern-dance company, founded as the Ballet Rambert by Marie ◊Rambert in 1926. In 1966 she handed the direction over to her protégé Norman Morrice, who began the process of transforming the company into one more focused on new creations and modern work. Richard ◊Alston was appointed artistic director in 1986 and changed the company name to Rambert Dance Company in 1987. The company was relaunched on an expanded scale in 1994 under the direction of Christopher ◊Bruce, working from a more 'classical' contemporary base.

During the tenure of Norman Morrice, seminal work was created for the company by the US choreographer Glen Tetley, among others. From 1974, artistic direction was successively in the hands of Christopher Bruce, John Chesworth, Robert North, and Richard Alston, who left in 1992.

Ramblers' Association

Society founded in Britain in 1935 to conserve the countryside and ensure that footpaths remain open.

Rampling, Charlotte (1946–)

English film actress. She has appeared in, among others, *Georgy Girl* (1966), *The Damned* (1969), *The Night Porter/Il Portiere di Notti* (1974), *Farewell My Lovely* (1975), and *D.O.A.* (1988).

Ramsay, Allan (1713–1784)

Scottish painter. Having studied in Edinburgh and then in Italy, he settled in London, becoming one of the most successful portrait painters of his day. Unlike his younger contemporary and rival, Joshua Reynolds, he sought for grace rather than grandeur in European models, acquiring in his earlier work a Baroque elegance from his studies in Naples and Rome, later delighting in the Rococo delicacy of the French.

He is particularly noted for the charm and elegance of his female portraiture, especially in the period 1754–66, as in his masterpiece *The Artist's Wife* (1755; National Gallery of Scotland, Edinburgh), a portrait of Margaret Lindsay, his second wife. He was devoted to drawing, and the value of this study can be seen in his full-length portraits, for example of Lady Mary Coke (Marquess of Bute collection). He became artist to George III in 1760 and played an active role in London's literary and intellectual life, becoming a member of Dr Johnson's circle.

Ramsay, William (1852–1916)

Scottish chemist who, with Lord ◊Rayleigh, discovered argon in 1894. In 1895 Ramsay produced helium and in 1898, in cooperation with Morris ◊Travers, identified neon, krypton, and xenon. In 1903, with Frederick ◊Soddy, he noted the transmutation of radium into helium, which led to the discovery of the density and relative atomic mass of radium. He was awarded a Nobel prize in 1904. He was made a KCB in 1902.

Ramsbottom

Town in Greater Manchester, England, on the River Irwell north of Bury; population (1991) 13,300. It is situated on the southern side of the Rossendale upland. Industries include textiles and the manufacture of paper.

Ramsey, Alf(red) Ernest (1920–)

English football player and manager. England's most successful manager ever, he won the World Cup in 1966. Of the 123 matches in which he was in charge of the national side between 1963 and 1974, England had 78 victories and only 13 defeats. Shrewd, pragmatic and single-minded, he was not afraid to go against traditional football wisdom, most notably in 1966 when he decided to play without wingers; a step which was greeted with widespread scepticism, but subsequently was hailed as a masterstroke when England won the World Cup. He led England to the quarter-finals of the 1970 World Cup, but was sacked four years later after the team failed to qualify for the 1974 finals.

Ramsey Island

Island in St George's Channel, 2 km/1.2 mi off the coast of Pembrokeshire, southwest Wales. Farming used to take place here, but the island is now owned by the Royal Society for the Protection of Birds. There is much wildlife, particularly seabirds and seals, and the island has a breeding colony of lapwings.

Ramsgate

Seaside resort and cross-Channel port in the Isle of Thanet, northeast Kent, southeast England; population (1991) 37,100. It is a centre for yachting and fishing. Features include St Augustine's Roman Catholic church (1850), designed by Augustus Pugin. Ramsgate became popular as a resort following George IV's visit in 1827. There are ferry links with France and Belgium.

St Augustine, sent by the Pope to convert England to Christianity, is said to have landed here in 597.

Features

Augustus Pugin built his home, the Grange, here in the 1840s, and he is buried in St Augustine's church. The Clock House Maritime Museum illustrates the maritime history of Ramsgate from Roman times. A replica of the Viking ship *Hugin* commemorates the landing in about 449 of Hengist and Horsa, the first Anglo-Saxon settlers in Britain, at nearby Ebbsfleet. A commemorative voyage of the ship took place in 1949. A Celtic cross marks the spot where St Augustine is said to have met King Ethelbert when he landed in 597.

The harbour was completed in 1763. The hoverport was opened in 1969 for passenger and vehicle transfer to Calais, France. The cross-Channel ferry terminal opened in 1981.

Ranjitsinhji, K S, Maharajah Jamsaheb of Nawanagar (1872–1933)

Indian prince and cricketer, popularly known as 'Ranji', who played for Sussex and England. A top batsman renowned for his elegant and innovative strokeplay between 1896 and 1920 he scored 24,692 runs at an average of 56.37. In 15 Tests for England, 1896–1902, he scored 985 runs at an average of 44.95. He hit over 3,000 runs in successive English seasons 1899–1900. After 1904 he only played occasionally, especially after 1907 when he became the Maharajah of Nawangar.

Rank, J(oseph) Arthur, 1st Baron Rank (1888–1972)

English film magnate. Having entered films in 1933 to promote the Methodist cause, by the mid-1940s he controlled, through the Rank Organization, half the British studios and more than 1,000 cinemas. The Rank Organization still owns the Odeon chain of cinemas, although film is now a minor part of its activities. He was created a baron in 1957.

Rankine, William John Macquorn (1820–1872)

Scottish engineer and physicist who was one of the founders of the science of thermodynamics, especially in reference to the theory of steam engines.

Rannoch, Loch

Lake in Perth and Kinross unitary authority, Scotland, lying 204 m/669 ft above sea level, and extending over an area 15 km/9 mi long and about 2 km/1 mi wide. The River Tummel, a tributary of the River Tay, flows through the loch from west to east.

Ransome, Arthur (Michell) (1884–1967)

English writer of adventure stories for children. His children's novels feature sailing and include ◊*Swallows and Amazons* (1930) and *Peter Duck* (1932). A journalist, he was correspondent in Russia for the *Daily News* during World War I and the Revolution.

He was also a student of folklore, and the stories he collected while working in Russia were published in 1916 as *Old Peter's Russian Tales*.

rates

A local government tax levied on industrial and commercial property (business rates) and, until the introduction of the community charge (see ◊poll tax) 1989–90, also on residential property to pay for local amenities such as roads, footpaths, refuse collection and disposal, and community and welfare activities. The water companies also use a rating system to charge most householders for water supply.

The Conservative government replaced the rate with a **community charge** or poll tax on each individual (introduced in Scotland in 1989 and England in 1990). This in turn was superseded by a **council tax** in 1993, based on property values but taking into account the number of occupiers.

In January 1990 the UK government revised all valuations of business property in England and Wales as part of its new Uniform Business Rate. All commercial property users were to pay 34.8% of the valuation. Rates were revalued proportionately higher in the south than the north.

Rathbone, (Philip St John) Basil (1892–1967)

South African-born British character actor. He specialized in playing villains, and also played Sherlock ◊Holmes (the fictional detective created by Arthur Conan Doyle) in a series of films. He worked mainly in Hollywood, in such films as *The Adventures of Robin Hood* (1938) and *The Hound of the Baskervilles* (1939).

Rathlin Island

Island in Northern Ireland, 10 km/6 mi off the north coast of County Antrim, opposite Ballycastle. Its main industries are fishing and tourism.

The Kebble national nature reserve is a breeding ground for such seabirds as razorbills and puffins. There is also a scuba-diving centre here.

Rathlin Island has had a long history of conflict: it was raided by Vikings in 790 and later by the Campbells of Scotland; later still, English forces slaughtered the inhabitants in 1597. In 1617 Rathlin Island was subject to a legal dispute over ownership between Scotland and Ireland which finally settled it as Irish.

The island was the refuge of Robert ◊Bruce, King of Scotland, in 1306. Legend has it that this is where the exiled king learned his lesson in perseverance from watching a spider weave its web in a basalt cave now known as Bruce's Cave.

rationing

Restricted allowance of provisions or other supplies in time of war or shortage. Food rationing was introduced in Britain during World War I. During World War II food rationing, organized by the government, began in Britain in 1940. Each person was issued with a ration book of coupons. Bacon, butter, and sugar were restricted, followed by other goods, including sweets, petrol, clothing, soap, and furniture. All food rationing finally ended in Britain in 1954. During the Suez Crisis of 1956, petrol rationing was reintroduced in Britain.

Rattigan, Terence Mervyn (1911–1977)

English dramatist. His play *Ross* (1960) was based on the character of T E Lawrence (Lawrence of Arabia). Rattigan's work ranges from the comedy *French Without Tears* (1936) to the psychological intensity of *The Winslow Boy* (1946). Other plays include *The Browning Version* (1948) and *Separate Tables* (1954). Knighted 1971.

Rattle, Simon (1955–)

English conductor, principal conductor of the City of Birmingham Symphony Orchestra (CBSO) 1979–98. He built the CBSO into a world class orchestra, with a core repertoire of early 20th-century music; he also commissioned new works. A popular and dynamic conductor, he achieves a characteristically clear and precise sound.

RATTLE, SIMON *English conductor Simon Rattle. He worked closely with the City of Birmingham Symphony Orchestra 1978–98 and is renowned for his eclectic programmes, which favour music of the 20th century. In recent years his repertory has widened and he has performed 19th-century classics in his distinctive energetic style. EMI*

He was assistant conductor with the Bournemouth Symphony Orchestra 1974–76 and with the BBC Scottish Symphony Orchestra 1977–79. He was the driving force behind the funding and building of a new concert hall for the CBSO, Symphony Hall, completed in 1991. Knighted 1998.

Ravenscraig

Former major iron and steel works in Scotland, near ◊Motherwell and Wishaw in North Lanarkshire unitary authority. Built between 1951 and 1957, it became one of the largest integrated iron and steel works in Europe, employing over 5,000 workers. It was the only hot strip mill in Scotland. It was closed in 1992, bringing an end to steelmaking in Scotland.

The idea behind the works was that, with the establishment of a car plant at Linwood in 1963, the area would become a major industrial development and achieve self-sustaining growth. This failed, partly because related component industries were not attracted to the area. The Linwood car plant closed in 1981, further reducing local demand for steel. International competition and the British Steel Corporation's reluctance to modernize the Ravenscraig plant led to the eventual closure of the works. The original installation began on a greenfield site, and included the hot strip mill, in production in 1962, and a slabbing mill. Coal and iron ore were imported by rail. The cold reduction mill at Gartcosh near Coatbridge was associated with the complex.

Ray, John (1627–1705)

English naturalist who devised a classification system accounting for some 18,000 plant species. It was the first system to divide flowering plants into monocotyledons and dicotyledons, with additional divisions made on the basis of leaf and flower characters and fruit types.

In *Methodus plantarum nova* (1682), Ray first set out his system. He also established the species as the fundamental unit of classification.

Ray believed that fossils are the petrified remains of dead animals and plants. This concept, which appeared in his theological writings, did not gain general acceptance until the late 18th century.

Rayleigh, John William Strutt, 3rd Baron Rayleigh (1842–1919)

English physicist who wrote the standard treatise *The Theory of Sound* (1877–78), experimented in optics and microscopy, and, with William ◊Ramsay, discovered argon. He was awarded a Nobel prize in 1904. Baron 1873.

Rayleigh was born in Essex and studied at Cambridge. He set up a laboratory at his home and was professor of experimental physics at Cambridge 1879–84, making the Cavendish Laboratory an important research centre.

In 1871, Rayleigh explained that the blue colour of the sky arises from the scattering of light by dust particles in the air, and was able to relate the degree of scattering to the wavelength of the light. He also made the first accurate definition of the resolving power of diffraction gratings, which led to improvements in the spectroscope. He completed in 1884 the standardization of the three basic electrical units: the ohm, ampere, and volt. His insistence on accuracy prompted the designing of more precise electrical instruments.

Read, Herbert (Edward) (1893–1968)

English critic and poet. His reputation as an art critic was established in the 1930s and 1940s, when he was a keen supporter of such artists as Henry ◊Moore, Barbara ◊Hepworth, and Ben ◊Nicholson. His many books and essays, which helped to make modern art accessible to a wider public, include *The Meaning of Art* (1931) and the influential *Education through Art* (1943). Knighted 1953.

Reading

Industrial town and unitary authority in southern England, on the River Thames where it meets the Kennet, 61 km/38 mi west of London; unitary authority area 37 sq km/14 sq mi; population (1994 est) 131,000. It was the administrative headquarters of the county of Berkshire until April 1998. Industries include the manufacture of biscuits, brewing, boats, engineering, printing, and electronics. It is an agricultural and horticultural centre with seed-testing grounds, and is a major bulb producer.

Reading was extensively rebuilt after World War II. Reading University was established in 1892 as a college affiliated to the University of Oxford. It gained independent university status in 1926.

Features

There are remains of a 12th-century Benedictine abbey where Henry I is buried. The Museum of Reading includes Roman and Saxon relics, and a full-size Victorian reproduction of the Bayeaux Tapestry. The Museum of English Rural Life is also located here.

History

It was a Danish encampment in 871. By the time of the Domesday survey of 1086, 'Radynges' as it was then known, had 30 religious houses. The Benedictine abbey was founded here in 1121, consecrated in 1164, and solemnized by Thomas à Becket in the presence of Henry II. In the 16th century the town was important in the cloth industry.

Famous people

The writer Oscar Wilde spent two years in Reading jail (1895–97). Reading was the birthplace of William Laud, archbishop of Canterbury from 1633.

Real IRA

An extremist Irish Republican terrorist group which split away from the ◊IRA in 1997. Based in the Republican stronghold of Dundalk, County Louth, in the Irish Republic, close to the border with Northern Ireland, its political mouthpiece has been the 32 County Sovereignty Committee. On 15 August 1998 it was responsible for the deadliest terrorist atrocity in Northern Ireland's history, when 28 innocent bystanders were killed by a car bomb detonated in the shopping centre of Omagh, County Tyrone. Following condemnation of the attack by ◊Sinn Féin and revulsion within Dundalk, the Real IRA apologized for the deaths and claimed that the warnings given had not been misleading, as the media and police claimed. Soon afterwards, it announced a suspension to its military operations.

Reardon, Ray (1932–)

Welsh snooker player. One of the leading players of the 1970s, he was six times world champion 1970–78.

Rebecca Riots

Disturbances in southwest Wales 1842–44. They were primarily a protest against toll charges on public roads, but were also a symptom of general unrest following the ◊Poor Law Amendment Act of 1834, which made obtaining poor relief much harder. The rioters, many disguised as women, destroyed the tollhouses and gates. Each leader was known as 'Rebecca' and followers were 'her daughters'. They took their name from the biblical prophecy that the seed of Rebekah would 'possess the gate of those which hate them' (Genesis 24,60).

received pronunciation, RP

A term used to describe national and international English accents which are associated with ◊Standard English. Spoken by royalty and representatives of the church, the government, and the law courts, RP is the language of official authority.

Record Office, Public

Government office containing the English and Welsh national records since the Norman Conquest, brought together from courts of law and government departments, including the Domesday Book, the Gunpowder Plot papers, and the log of HMS *Victory* at Trafalgar. It was established in 1838 in Chancery Lane, London; records dating from the 18th century onwards have been housed at Kew, London, since 1976.

The Scottish Records Office is situated in Edinburgh and the Public Record Office of Northern Ireland is in Belfast. Scotland's national archives were established in the 13th century, with the appointment of a Clerk of the Rolls. There are also Public Record Offices for each county.

Reculver

Village on the north coast of Kent, England, and the site of the Roman fort of Regulbium; population (1991) 8,400. A 7th-century church was enlarged in the 12th century with two towers and a west front, which are all that remain. They act as a guide to shipping approaching the Thames estuary. In the 19th century much of the church's fabric was removed to St Mary's at Hillborough.

recusant

In England, those who refused to attend Anglican church services, especially applied to Catholics. The Acts of Uniformity of 1552 and 1559 imposed fines on those who refused to attend, and it was not until the reign of Elizabeth I that the idea of a large and permanent Catholic minority gradually began to be accepted. Even then, an act of 1587 provided for the seizure of up to two-thirds of a recusant's property, although this was only enforced in times of crisis. The fines later became a means of raising revenue rather than a matter of religious policy. Recusants were often associated with the houses of gentry in certain parts of the country, such as the West Midlands which had a strong Catholic community.

Redbridge

Outer borough of northeast Greater London. It includes the suburbs of Ilford, Wanstead, and Woodford, and parts of Chigwell and Dagenham

Features takes its name from old Red Bridge over the River Roding; Leper Hospital, founded in about 1140, with 14th-century chapel and 18th-century almshouses; Friends Burial Ground, Wanstead; part of Epping Forest; Hainault Forest

Population (1991) 226,200

Industries light industry and manufacture of defence equipment

Famous people

William Penn, Richard Brinsley Sheridan, and Thomas Hood lived in Wanstead. Winston Churchill was member of Parliament for Woodford for 40 years.

Redcar and Cleveland

Unitary authority in northeast England created in 1996 from part of the former county of Cleveland

Area 240 sq km/93 sq mi

Towns and cities Redcar (administrative headquarters), Skelton, Guisborough, Marske-by-the-Sea, Saltburn-by-the-Sea, Brotton, Loftus

Features North Sea coast; River Tees forms northwest border; Boulby Cliffs are highest cliffs on England's east coast (203 m/666 ft); 12th-century Priory at Guisborough; Cleveland Way long-distance path reaches coast at Saltburn; RNLI Zetland Lifeboat Museum (Redcar); Ironstone Mining Museum (Saltburn-by-the-Sea)

Industries manufacture of steel products (British Steel), engineering, fertilizers and potash products, textiles

Population (1996) 144,000

Redditch

Industrial town in Worcestershire, 19 km/12 mi south of Birmingham; population (1991) 72,700. It was designated a ◊new town in 1964 to take overspill population from Birmingham. Industries include engineering, electronics, and the production of electrical equipment, car and aircraft components, motorcycles, and fishing tackle.

Red Dwarf

Comic science-fiction television programme (1988–). It concerns the plight of Dave Lister (Craig Charles), a 23rd-century reveller who, seeking to return home to Earth after a drinking binge, finds work on the space ship *Red Dwarf*. The series follows the fortunes of the space ship's eclectic crew on their adventurous journey through space.

Disciplined for breaking quarantine regulations, Lister is placed in stasis for the trip back to Earth, only to be revived some 3 million years later accompanied by the ship's senile computer Holly, a humanoid descendant of his pet cat (Danny John-Jules), and a hologram of his former supervisor Arnold Rimmer (Chris Barrie).

Redgrave, Lynn (1943–)

English-born stage and screen actress, a US citizen from 1998. She first rose to prominence in *Georgy Girl* (1966). She starred as Gillian Helfgott in the acclaimed Australian film *Shine* (1996) and has featured in the new British television series *Rude Awakening* (1998). She has worked extensively on US television, featuring prominently in US Weight Watchers advertising campaigns. She is the daughter of Michael Redgrave and sister of Vanessa Redgrave.

Redgrave, Michael (Scudamore) (1908–1985)

English actor. His stage roles included Hamlet and Lear (Shakespeare), Uncle Vanya (Chekhov), and the schoolmaster in Terence Rattigan's *The Browning Version* (filmed 1951). On screen he appeared in *The Lady Vanishes* (1938), *The Importance of Being Earnest* (1952), and *Goodbye Mr Chips* (1969). He was knighted in 1959.

He was the father of the actresses Vanessa and Lynn Redgrave.

> *To be an Englishman is to belong to the most exclusive club there is.*
>
> OGDEN NASH US poet. *England Expects* (1950)

Redgrave, Steven Geoffrey (1962–)

English oarsman. He was a gold medallist at four successive Olympics, winning the coxed fours in 1984 and the coxless pairs in 1988 and 1992. He also won four gold medals at the World Championships 1986–93, gold at the World Indoor Championships in 1991, and was a member of the winning four-man bobsleigh team at the national bobsleigh championships in 1989.

He won the coxless pairs for the UK with Matthew Pinsent at the world championships in 1991, 1993–95, and the gold medal at the Atlanta Olympics in 1996, becoming only the fourth person to win gold medals at four consecutive Olympics. Together with Matthew Pinsent, he was a member of the British coxless fours team which won a gold medal at the final of the inaugural World Cup Regatta in 1997. Rowing in UK's coxless four he won the World Championships in Cologne, Germany, in 1998.

Redgrave, Vanessa (1937–)

English actress. She has played Shakespeare's Lady Macbeth and Cleopatra on the stage, Ellida in Ibsen's *Lady From the Sea* (1976 and 1979), and Olga in Chekhov's *Three Sisters* (1990). She won an Academy Award for best supporting actress for the title role in the film *Julia* (1976); other films include *Wetherby* (1985), *Howards End* (1992), *Mother's Boys* (1994), *The House of the Spirits* (1993), and *A Month by the Lake* (1995). She is active in left-wing politics.

Other stage plays include *Heartbreak House* (1992) and *Vita and Virginia* (1994), and television films include *They* (1993) and *Down Came a Blackbird* (1995).

Redhead, Brian (1929–1994)

English journalist and broadcaster, best known as co-host of Radio 4's *Today* programme 1975–94, where he won over listeners with his jaunty, confident manner and often idiosyncratic interviewing style. Redhead worked for the *Manchester Guardian* from 1954, becoming northern editor in 1964, and he was appointed editor of the *Manchester Evening News* in 1969. He left newspaper journalism to join the *Today* team in 1975. His highly idiosyncratic and unpredictable broadcasts gained a large and devoted following.

Redhill

Town in Surrey, England, at the foot of the North Downs. With Reigate, Redhill forms a residential suburb of London. Gatwick airport is nearby, 5 km/3 mi to the south. The town developed into a commercial centre with the advent of the railway.

Redmond, John Edward (1856–1918)

Irish nationalist politician, leader of the Irish Parliamentary Party (IPP) 1900–18. He rallied his party after Charles Stewart ◊Parnell's imprisonment in 1881, and came close to achieving Home Rule for all Ireland in 1914. However, the pressure of World War I, Unionist intransigence, and the fallout of the 1916 ◊Easter Rising destroyed both his career and his party.

Red Rum

Racehorse whose exploits in the ◊Grand National at ◊Aintree won him national fame. The only horse to win the race three times, with victories in 1973, 1974, and 1977, he also finished second in 1975 and 1976. He died in 1995 at the age of 30, and is buried at Aintree near to the winning post.

Redruth

Town in Cornwall, southwest England, part of the combined town of ◊Camborne-Redruth.

Redwood, John (1951–)

British Conservative politician. He was Welsh Secretary 1993–95, when he resigned to contest the Conservative leadership following John Major's decision to challenge his critics within the party by forcing a leadership election. Positioned on the far-right wing of the party, Redwood contested the leadership again, unsuccessfully, in 1997.

Although he was defeated, Redwood fought a creditable campaign, increasing his public profile and establishing himself as a serious potential leader from the right of the party. His seemingly unemotional character, which earned him the nickname 'Vulcan', was to some extent dispelled by his performance during the campaign, and even his fiercest critics have had to acknowledge his intellectual ability.

Reed, (Robert) Oliver (1938–)

English actor. He appeared in the films *Women in Love* (1969), *The Devils* (1971), and *Castaway* (1987). He is the nephew of the director Carol ◊Reed.

Reed, Carol (1906–1976)

English film producer and director. He was an influential figure in the British film industry of the 1940s. His films include *Odd Man Out* (1946), *The Fallen Idol* (1948), *The Third Man* (1949), *Our Man in Havana* (1959), and the Academy Award-winning musical *Oliver!* (1968).

Reed reached the pinnacle of his career in conjunction with producer Alexander ◊Korda. *Odd Man Out* was a brooding drama set in Belfast, with Expressionist imagery and an outstanding performance from James Mason as a wounded IRA man. Next came two features scripted by the novelist and former film critic Graham Greene. *The Fallen Idol*, about a small boy trying to protect the family butler from a murder charge, earned Reed an Academy Award nomination, as did *The Third Man*, a stylish thriller about penicillin racketeering in Vienna just after World War II, which became an instant classic.

reel

A Scottish, Irish, and Scandinavian dance, either of Celtic or Scandinavian origin. It is performed with the dancers standing face to face and the music is in quick 2–4 or 4–4, occasionally 6–8, time and divided into regular eight-bar phrases. A musical characteristic of many reels is a drop into the triad of the subdominant unprepared by modulation.

Rees, Merlyn (1920–)

British Labour politician. From 1972 to 1974 he was Opposition spokesman on Northern Ireland affairs and in March 1974 became secretary of state for Northern Ireland, a post he retained until he was appointed home secretary in September 1976.

He was educated at Harrow Weald Grammar School, Goldsmiths' College, University of London, and the London School of Economics and Political Science. After war service he went to university and became a lecturer in economics. In 1963 he succeeded Hugh Gaitskell as Labour MP for Leeds South. Between 1965 and 1970 he was successively parliamentary under-secretary, Ministry of Defence, and parliamentary under-secretary at the Home Office.

Rees-Mogg, Lord William (1928–)

English journalist, editor of *The Times* 1967–81, chair of the Arts Council 1982–89, and from 1988 chair of the ◊Broadcasting Standards Council. In 1993 he challenged the government over ratification of the Maastricht Treaty, notably the government's right to transfer foreign policy decisions to European Community (now European Union) institutions. His challenge was rejected by the High Court.

reeve

In Anglo-Saxon England, an official charged with the administration of a shire or burgh, fulfilling functions similar to those of the later sheriff. After the Norman Conquest, the term tended to be restricted to the person elected by the villeins (feudal tenants) to oversee the work of the manor and to communicate with the manorial lord.

Reeve, William (1757–1815)

English composer. He studied with Richardson, the organist at St James's Church, Westminster, and was organist at Totnes, Devon, 1781–83. After various engagements at London theatres, he joined the Covent Garden chorus, and there was asked to complete the ballet-pantomime *Oscar and Malvina* (after Ossian) left unfinished by Shield in 1791 on account of differences with the management. He then became composer at Covent Garden and in 1802 part-owner of Sadler's Wells Theatre. In one of his more popular pieces, *The Caravan* (1803), a child was rescued from a tank of water by a well-trained dog; the music of his theatre pieces failed to gain as much attention.

Referendum Party

Single-issue political party formed by the billionaire Anglo-French financier James ◊Goldsmith, whose aim was to force the government into holding a plebiscite on the issue of whether Britain should be part of a federal Europe or a bloc of independent trading nations. Its founding was announced in November 1994 and it was formally launched in October 1996.

The party attracted several high-profile defectors from the right-wing of the Conservative Party, including Alan Walters, an economics adviser during the 1980s to Prime Minister Thatcher, and, briefly, the MP George Gardiner. However, despite extensive media advertising, funded by Goldsmith, who invested 20 million of his personal fortune, the party's support in national opinion polls failed to rise above 1%. In the May 1997 general election, only 30 of its 545 candidates saved their deposits and, in capturing 810,000 votes, the party is believed to have been a decisive factor in the loss of 20 Conservative Party seats. Goldsmith died in July 1997.

Reform Acts

Acts of Parliament in 1832, 1867, and 1884 that extended voting rights and redistributed parliamentary seats; also known as ◊Representation of the People Acts.

The 1832 act abolished the pocket, or ◊rotten borough, which had formed unrepresentative constituencies, redistributed seats on a more equitable basis in the counties, and formed some new boroughs. The franchise was extended to male householders in property worth £10 a year or more in the boroughs and to owners of freehold property worth £2 a year, £10 copyholders, or £50 leaseholders in the counties. The 1867 act redistributed seats from corrupt and small boroughs to the counties and large urban areas. It also extended the franchise in boroughs to adult male heads of households, and in counties to males who owned, or held on long leases, land worth £5 a year, or who occupied land worth £12 on which they paid poor rates. The 1884 act extended the franchise to male agricultural labourers. See feature on page 750, and ◊parliamentary reform for a chronology of key dates.

Reform Acts: Growth of the Electorate in 19th-Century Britain

Year	UK voters	Approximate percentage of population enfranchised
1831	515,920	2%
1833	809,374	3%
1866	1,367,845	5%
1869	2,445,847	8%
1883	3,155,143	9%
1886	5,674,964	16%

Reformation

Religious and political movement in 16th-century Europe to reform the Roman Catholic Church, which led to the establishment of Protestant churches. Anticipated from the 12th century by the Waldenses, Lollards, and Hussites, it was set off by German priest Martin Luther in 1517, and became effective when the absolute monarchies gave it support by challenging the political power of the papacy and confiscating church wealth. See feature on page 751.

> *The Reformation was the greatest revolution in English history. It meant that England was suddenly separated from the Europe of western Christendom, of which it had formed an important part for more than a millennium. This was the first element in the establishment of an independent nation-state which was to be isolated from Europe until 1973.*
>
> EDWIN JONES English historian.
> *The English Nation: the Great Myth* (1998)

Reformation Parliament

English parliament of November 1529–April 1536 which passed Thomas Cromwell's antipapal legislation. It acknowledged the sovereign as head of the Church in place of the pope, and empowered Henry VIII to abolish payments to Rome of the first year's income of all newly installed bishops, as had hitherto been the practice. It sanctioned the installation of Thomas Cranmer as primate of the English church, and enabled Henry to divorce Catherine of Aragón in 1533 and have Anne Boleyn executed in 1536, so that he at last had a male heir (Edward) in 1537 by Jane Seymour. The dissolution of the monasteries followed 1636–40. The Parliament lasted an unprecedented seven years and altogether enacted 137 statues, 32 of which were of vital importance.

Regency

The years 1811–20 during which ◊George IV (then Prince of Wales) acted as regent for his father ◊George III.

Regency style

Style of architecture and interior furnishings popular in England during the late 18th and early 19th centuries. It is

THE AGE OF REFORM: POLITICS AND SOCIAL CHANGE IN 19TH-CENTURY BRITAIN

Reform was the leading political issue of 19th-century Britain – reform of the protectionist system, reform of the franchise, and reform of society. It was an issue which politicized British society, and increased middle-class social awareness, to a level not seen since the 1640s.

The repeal of the protectionist Corn Laws (which had controlled movements of grain in order to keep domestic prices high) by Sir Robert Peel in 1846 split the governing Tories, but reflected the extent to which the interests of an increasingly urbanized and literate society set the political agenda.

The Reform Acts

Successive extensions of the franchise (right to vote) created a mass electorate, though it was still all-male until the following century. The First Reform Act of 1832, described by its authors as final, fixed a more uniform right to vote that brought the franchise to the middle class, and reorganized the distribution of seats in order to reward growing towns, such as Birmingham, Bradford, and Manchester, and counties, at the expense of 'rotten' boroughs, seats with a small population that were open to corruption. The electorate increased greatly, to about one-fifth of all English adult males.

The Second Reform Act 1867 nearly doubled the existing electorate and, by offering household suffrage, gave the right to vote to about 60% of adult males in boroughs. The Third Reform Act of 1884 extended this franchise to the counties.

Changes in the franchise led naturally to further changes: to Liberal election victories in 1868 and 1886, and to changes in the nature of the political system itself. A growing democratization of society led to a far greater emphasis in government on the conditions and attitudes of the people.

Society and environment

A society influenced by both religious evangelism and the teachings of Charles Darwin (whose *Origin of the Species* appeared in 1859) was increasingly aware of the importance of environment, and thus living standards. At the same time, a belief in progress and perfectibility was widespread. It was taken up by both politicians and commentators, such as novelists. Charles Dickens was a supporter of reform in fields such as capital punishment, prisons, housing, and prostitution. His novel *Bleak House* (1852–53) was an indictment of the coldness of law and church; *Little Dorrit* (1855–57) was an attack on snobbery, imprisonment for debt, business fraud, and bureaucracy. The novels of Wilkie Collins (1824–89) dealt with divorce, vivisection, and the impact of heredity and environment. Moral campaigns, against slavery, alcohol, and cruelty to animals, aroused widespread support, fuelling a major expansion in the voluntary societies that characterized Victorian Britain. Though compromise and the search for short-term advantage played a major role in political reform, idealism was also genuine and important.

Reform was in part a desire to control the new, more dangerous, society and environment of Victorian Britain. Peel's Metropolitan Police Act 1829 created a uniformed and paid force for London. The County and Borough Police Act 1856 made the formation of paid forces obligatory. The Poor Law Amendment Act 1834 sought to control the poor, introducing a national system of workhouses. Cholera and typhoid led to the public health movement of the 1840s. The Health of Towns Act 1848 created a Great Board of Health and an administrative structure to improve sanitation, especially water supply.

An interventionist state

The pace of reform accelerated after the Liberal victory of 1868. The first government of William Gladstone pushed through the disestablishment of the Irish Church in 1869, the introduction of open competition in the Civil Service in 1870, and the secret ballot in 1872. The 1870 Education Act set a minimum level of educational provision, introducing school district authorities where existing parish provision was inadequate. In 1872 the powers of turnpike trusts were ended and road maintenance was placed totally under public control.

The Tories, or Conservatives, came to power under Benjamin Disraeli in 1874 and maintained the pace of reform. Legislation on factories in 1874, and Public Health, Artisans' Dwellings, and Pure Food and Drugs Acts in 1875, systematized and extended the regulation of important aspects of public health and social welfare. Building on the Factory Acts of 1833, 1844, 1847, and 1850, those of 1874 and 1878 limited work hours for women and children in industry. The Prison Act 1877 established central government control of prisons.

A collectivist state was developing, and in some respects it looked toward the later Welfare State. State intervention in education helped to reduce illiteracy. Greater social intervention by the new, more formal and responsive, mechanisms of local government established under the Local Government Act 1888 (which created directly elected county councils and county boroughs) encouraged, by the end of the century, a general expectation of state intervention in the life of the people, in health, education, and housing.

BY JEREMY BLACK

characterized by restrained simplicity and the imitation of ancient classical elements, often Greek.

Architects of this period include Decimus Burton (1800–1881), Henry Holland (1746–1806), and John ◊Nash.

regent

Person who carries out the duties of a sovereign during the sovereign's minority, incapacity, or lengthy absence from the country. In England since the time of Henry VIII, Parliament

SOVEREIGNS AND PURITANS: THE BRITISH REFORMATION

The conventional history of the British Reformation, written by the victorious Protestants, is a tale of how a decaying, corrupt, and unpopular medieval Church was bowled over by an irresistible movement of reform and renewal. Recent research has destroyed this picture completely. Historians are now certain that in 1520 the Church in Britain was a thriving, dynamic, and well-loved institution. Parish churches were the foci of intense local devotion, ecclesiastical courts were respected and much in demand, and there were more applicants for the priesthood than there were jobs. To be sure, there were also problems: too many religious houses, clashes with the growing numbers of common lawyers, and the persistence of small groups of people in southern England, collectively called Lollards, who privately rejected aspects of the official religion. None of these, however, represented a serious weakness.

Royal involvement

The real issue after 1520 was not that the old Church was going wrong, but that an increasing number of people started to think that it had never been right. It depended upon the doctrine that Christians could best get to heaven by performing ritual works: by joining in ceremonies, by beautifying churches, and by revering saints as personal divine patrons. Over the centuries this behaviour had become ever more elaborate, intense, and expensive. The argument of Protestantism, as first preached by Martin Luther in Germany in 1517, was that it was all a confidence trick, for the Bible suggested that none of it was necessary. Indeed, to Protestants it was actually evil, for it diverted attention from direct concern with God and Scripture.

Nonetheless, popular Protestantism was so weak in Britain before 1550 that it would have made little impact had not the English Crown embraced the new ideas. All over Europe in this period monarchs were increasing their control over the Church within their realms. This could be accomplished perfectly well by allying with it against Protestantism, and such a line was taken by Henry VIII of England during the 1520s. In 1529, however, he quarrelled with the Pope over the latter's refusal to grant him a divorce, and resolved to take over the Church in England himself. His avowed aim was to reform it within a Catholic tradition, but he came increasingly to rely upon Protestant advisers and the latter took control when Henry died, on behalf of his young son Edward VI.

Counter-Reformation

Under Henry the monasteries were dissolved and the cult of the saints destroyed, while Edward's regime removed the old ornaments and rituals altogether. Both encountered fierce resistance, Henry provoking the huge northern rising known as the Pilgrimage of Grace and Edward's ministers facing the Western Rebellion in 1549. The first was defeated by trickery and the second in pitched battles. By early 1550 a majority of the English, especially in the southeast, had probably ceased to believe in the old Church, but only a minority had acquired any active commitment to the new faith. In Scotland, the association of Protestantism with England, the old enemy, had kept the traditional religion in power even though a growing number of Scots were turning against it.

There was therefore a real potential for the Reformation to be reversed, and so it was when Edward died in 1553 and was succeeded by his Catholic sister Mary. She restored her Church, with more streamlining and central control than before, and persecuted Protestants with a savagery unique in British religious history, burning about 300. It seems likely that had she lived for a further 20 years then Britain would be Catholic to this day, but she died after only 5 years and left her Protestant sister, Elizabeth, to take over.

The Elizabethan compromise

The English Catholics were demoralized by the lack of any alternative heir and comforted by promises of good treatment. The Scottish Protestants now chose their moment to rebel and Elizabeth sent an English army to help them into power. Another English expeditionary force in 1573 secured their position, and the young king of the Scots, James VI, was brought up in the Protestant tradition and inherited England when Elizabeth died in 1603.

It was the sheer length of Elizabeth's reign which allowed the Reformation to triumph in Britain, so that by the 1580s the majority of its people had been so thoroughly re-educated in the new faith that they genuinely identified with it. It never, however, achieved the unity of the old one. The Church of England reflected Elizabeth's wish for compromise, yoking Protestant doctrine to a Catholic structure of bishops, cathedrals, and festivals. Many Protestants remained deeply unhappy with it. The Church of Scotland, formed in revolution, made a more radical departure, to a presbyterian structure and a complete abolition of the old festivals and vestments. The defeat of Catholicism in Britain made certain a future struggle between the different strands of Protestantism.

BY RONALD HUTTON

has always appointed a regent or council of regency when necessary.

Regencies were established during the minorities of Henry III, Edward III, Richard II, Henry VI, Edward V, and Edward VI, and during the insanity of Henry VI. The most recent period of prolonged regency occurred during the reign of George III, whose mental illness in 1788 and after 1810 led to the nomination of the Prince of Wales as regent.

Legislation was passed to deal with particular contingencies during the reigns of William IV, Victoria, and George V, but comprehensive provision for the incapacity, illness, or absence of the sovereign was not passed until 1937. The Regency Acts 1937–53 now provide for the delegation of royal function to counsellors of state, who may be the wife or husband of the sovereign, the four people next in succession to the throne, and, since 1953, Queen Elizabeth the Queen Mother. Counsellors of state may not, however, dissolve Parliament nor grant peerages. The same legislation also provides for the establishment of a regency where the sovereign is under 18 years of age and in the event of the mental or physical incapacity of the sovereign.

Regent's Park

Park in London, covering 188 ha/464 acres. It contains London Zoo. Regent's Canal runs through the park, which was laid out by John Nash for the Prince Regent, later George IV. Grand terraced residences, which overlook the park, were designed by Nash and by Decimus Burton (1800–81).

The park was developed on the site of Marylebone Gardens and pasture land. It formed part of a scheme, begun in 1812, to connect the Prince's residence (Carlton House) in the Mall, via Regent Street, with another residence (never built) in the new park. The park was opened to the public in 1838.

Bedford College (now part of Royal Holloway College) was located here 1909–85. There is an open-air theatre in the Inner Circle of the park.

Regent Street

Shopping street in London, running from Pall Mall to Langham Place, crossing Piccadilly Circus and Oxford Street. It was designed by John Nash between 1813 and 1820 for the Prince Regent, later George IV, to connect the Prince's residence (Carlton House) in the Mall with another residence (never built) in Regent's Park. Since then it has been completely rebuilt.

The curved area north of Piccadilly Circus, known as the Quadrant, was redesigned in 1925–26 by Reginald Blomfield (1856–1942).

The Café Royal in Regent Street was the haunt of many literary and artistic figures in the late 19th century and early 20th century; among them were Augustus John, Aubrey Beardsley, and Max Beerbohm. The Liberty shop, with its mock Tudor facade, was designed in 1924 by E T and E S Hall. On the Great Marlborough Street side of the building (north) is a public clock on which St George and the Dragon appear each hour.

reggae

Predominant form of West Indian popular music of the 1970s and 1980s, characterized by a heavily accented offbeat and a thick bass line. The lyrics often refer to Rastafarianism. The UK was the most important market for reggae outside the Caribbean.

Musicians include Bob Marley, Lee 'Scratch' Perry (1940– , performer and producer), and the group Black Uhuru (1974–). Reggae is also played in the UK, South Africa, and elsewhere.

There are several reggae styles. The practice of issuing singles with, on the B-side, a **dub** version, or stripped-down instrumental remix, was designed for use in clubs, where disc jockeys who added a spoken vocal part became known as **toasters**; they in turn released records. A fast reggae-rap style called **ragga** emerged in the early 1990s. Like rap texts, reggae lyrics tend to be political-historical (Burning Spear, Gregory Isaacs), sexually explicit (Shabba Ranks), or describe ghetto violence (Cobra).

During the late 1970s, a number of accomplished UK reggae acts grew to rival the popularity of their Jamaican counterparts, chief among them being Steel Pulse and Aswad (who later had UK pop hits in the late 1980s and early 1990s). The softer, more melodious 'crossover' efforts of UB40 continued to realize commercial success through the 1980s and into the 1990s. The tough, rap-influenced dancehall/ragga styles of this period ensured that reggae has not diminished in popularity at the grassroots level, and is in a position to cross-fertilize with other forms (demonstrated by the success of the Bristolian 'trip-hop' group Massive Attack and the fine 1998 drum 'n' bass/roots-reggae album by the 1970s singer Junior Delgado, *Fearless*). Also of note is a growing retrospective market for 1970s roots material, as exemplified by the UK reissue of the label Blood & Fire.

regicides

The forty-nine signatories on the instrument of execution for Charles I of England in 1649, together with the two executioners (who were anonymous). After the Restoration in 1660, twenty-nine of these men were put on trial and ten were sentenced to death.

Regional Crime Squad

Local police force that deals with serious crime; see ⇨Scotland Yard, New.

Reigate

Town in Surrey, southeast England, at the foot of the North Downs; population (1991, with Redhill) 46,300. Situated 30 km/19 mi south of London, it is primarily a commuter town.

An 18th-century gatehouse marks the site of a castle built here in the 12th century. Man-made tunnels associated with the castle were used as air-raid shelters and for storage during World War II. The Town Hall dates from 1728, and the church of St Mary Magdalene includes a late 12th-century nave. Reigate Priory to the west of the town was founded in the 13th century. An 18th-century windmill (no longer used as such) stands on Reigate Heath.

Reith, John Charles Walsham, 1st Baron (1889–1971)

Scottish broadcasting pioneer, the first general manager 1922–27 and director general 1927–38 of the British Broadcasting Corporation (BBC). He was enormously influential in the early development of the BBC and established its high-minded principles of public service broadcasting. He held several ministerial posts in government during World War II, including minister of information in 1940, transport in 1940, and minister of works 1940–42.

Remembrance Sunday, Armistice Day until 1945

National day of remembrance for those killed in both world

wars and later conflicts, on the second Sunday of November. Remembrance Sunday is observed by a two-minute silence at the time of the signature of the armistice with Germany that ended World War I: 11:00 am, 11 November 1918 (although since 1956 the day of commemoration has been the Sunday). There are ceremonies at the Cenotaph in Whitehall, London, and elsewhere. 'Flanders poppies', symbolic of the blood shed, are sold in aid of war invalids and their dependants.

Renaissance architecture

Style of architecture which began in 15th-century Italy, based on the revival of Classical, especially Roman, architecture developed by Brunelleschi. Renaissance architecture in England is exemplified by the Queen's House at Greenwich, London, built by Inigo Jones in 1637.

Renault, Mary pen name of (Eileen) Mary Challans (1905–1983)

English historical novelist. She specialized in stories about ancient Greece, with two novels on the mythical hero Theseus – *The King Must Die* (1958) and *The Bull from the Sea* (1962) – and two on Alexander the Great: *Fire from Heaven* (1970) and *The Persian Boy* (1972).

Rendell, Ruth Barbara (1930–)

English novelist and short-story writer. She is the author of a popular detective series featuring Chief Inspector Wexford, of which *Road Rage* (1997) was the 16th. Her psychological crime novels explore the minds of people who commit murder, often through obsession or social inadequacy, as in *A Demon in my View* (1976), *Heartstones* (1987), *The Keys to the Street* (1996), and *A Sight for Sore Eyes* (1998). Many of her works have been adapted for television.

Lake of Darkness (1980) won the Arts Council National Book Award (Genre Fiction) for that year. She also writes under the pseudonym Barbara Vine. She was created a baroness in 1997.

Renfrew

Town on the Clyde, in Renfrewshire, Scotland, 8 km/5 mi northwest of Glasgow; population (1991) 20,300. It was formerly the county town of Renfrewshire, and was once an important Clyde port. Near the town is Glasgow airport (Abbotsinch).

Renfrewshire

Unitary authority in west central Scotland, bordering the Firth of Clyde, which was formed from the northern and western parts of Renfrew district in Strathclyde region (1975–96), which in turn was formed from the former county of Renfrewshire (until 1974)

Area 260 sq km/100 sq mi

Towns ◊Paisley (administrative headquarters), Renfrew, Johnstone, Erskine

Physical mainly low lying, but hilly in the west, rising to Hill of Stake (525 m/1,723 ft); rivers Clyde, Gryfe, White Cart, Black Cart

Features sculptural stones at Inchinnan, near Erskine; Glasgow International Airport

Industries engineering, computers, electronics, chemicals

Agriculture sheep on grassy uplands; dairy farming on lowlands

Population (1995) 178,300

History once part of the ancient kingdom of Strathclyde; name given to Stuart heirs since Robert III made his son Baron of Renfrew.

Economy

While dominated by large industrial and de-industrializing towns, the area also covers an affluent belt of small towns and villages that are within the Glasgow commuter belt.

Environment

There are seven Sites of Special Scientific Interest, one regional park, and three country parks.

Administrative history

The county of Renfrewshire covered a more extensive area than the unitary authority of the same name, as it also included the lands now of Inverclyde and East Renfrewshire, which are unitary authorities in their own right.

Rennie, John (1761–1821)

Scottish engineer who built three bridges over the River Thames in London, later demolished: Waterloo Bridge 1811–17, Southwark Bridge 1814–19, and London Bridge 1824–34; he also built bridges, canals, dams (Rudyard dam, Staffordshire, 1800), and harbours.

reply, right of

Right of a member of the public to respond to a media statement. A statutory right of reply, enforceable by a Press Commission, as exists in many Western European countries, failed to reach the statute book in the UK in 1989. There is no legal provision in the UK that any correction should receive the same prominence as the original statement and legal aid is not available in defamation cases, so that only the wealthy are able to sue. However, the major newspapers signed a Code of Practice in 1989 that promised some public protection.

Representation of the People Acts

Series of UK acts of Parliament from 1867 that extended voting rights, creating universal suffrage in 1928. The 1867 and 1884 acts are known as the second and third ◊Reform Acts.

The 1918 act gave the vote to men over the age of 21 and women over the age of 30, and the 1928 act extended the vote to women over the age of 21. Certain people had the right to more than one vote; this was abolished by the 1948 act. The 1969 act reduced the minimum age of voting to 18.

Repton

Village in Derbyshire, England, on the River Trent, 12 km/7 mi southwest of Derby; population (1991) 3,500. The kings of Mercia (the Anglo-Saxon kingdom that emerged in the 6th century) had a palace at Repton and three kings were buried at the monastery. The parish church contains a Saxon crypt.

Repton, Humphry (1752–1818)

English garden designer. He worked for some years in partnership with English architect John ◊Nash. Repton preferred more formal landscaping than his predecessor Capability ◊Brown, and was responsible for the landscaping of some 200 gardens and parks. He coined the term 'landscape gardening'.

He laid out Russell Square and Bloomsbury Square in London around 1800, and published many books on landscape.

research

The primary activity in science, a combination of theory and experimentation directed towards finding scientific explanations of phenomena. It is commonly classified into two types: **pure research**, involving theories with little apparent relevance to human concerns; and **applied research**, concerned with finding solutions to problems of social or commercial importance – for instance in medicine and engineering. The two types are linked in that theories developed from pure research may eventually be found to be of great value to society.

Financing research

Scientific research is most often funded by government and industry, and so a nation's wealth and priorities are likely to have a strong influence on the kind of work undertaken. In the UK in 1995 £14.3 billion or 2.05% of gross domestic product (GDP) was spent on research of which £12.2 billion was spent on civil research and development. Of the total funding for research, 48% was provided by industry and 33% by the government. A further 14% came from abroad. Between 1990 and 1995 defence spending on research and development declined from 0.5 to 0.3% of GDP. The 1997–98 budgets for Biotechnology and Biological Sciences Research Council (BBSRC) was £183 million; Natural Environment Research Council (NERC) £167 million; Economic and Social Research Council (ESRC) £65 million; Council for the Central Laboratory of Research Councils (CCLRC) £110 million.

Restoration

In English history, the period when the monarchy, in the person of Charles II, was re-established after the English Civil War and the fall of the Protectorate in 1660.

Restoration comedy

Style of English theatre, dating from the Restoration (1660). It witnessed the first appearance of women on the English stage, most notably in the 'breeches part', specially created in order to costume the actress in male attire, thus revealing her figure to its best advantage. The genre placed much emphasis on wit and sexual intrigues. Examples include Wycherley's *The Country Wife* (1675), Congreve's *The Way of the World* (1700), and Farquhar's *The Beaux' Stratagem* (1707).

Retford

Market town in Nottinghamshire, England, on the River Idle, 32 km/20 mi northwest of Newark; population (1991) 20,000. Industries include engineering and the manufacture of paper, dyes, rubber, and iron castings. The town also has a large agricultural trade.

Retford became a borough (unit of local government) in the Middle Ages, and was noted for its markets and fairs. The grammar school was founded in 1551.

Revolutionary Wars

Series of wars from 1791 to 1802 between France and the combined armies of England, Austria, Prussia, and others, during the period of the French Revolution and Napoleon's campaign to conquer Europe.

Revolution, the Glorious

Events surrounding the removal of James II from the throne and his replacement in 1689 by his daughter Mary and William of Orange as joint sovereigns (◊Mary II and ◊William III), bound by the ◊Bill of Rights. See feature.

James had become increasingly unpopular on account of his unconstitutional behaviour and Catholicism. Various elements in England, including seven prominent politicians, plotted to invite the Protestant William to invade. Arriving at Torbay on 5 November 1688, William rapidly gained support and James was allowed to flee to France after the army deserted him. Support for James in Scotland and Ireland was forcibly suppressed 1689–90. William and Mary accepted in 1689 a new constitutional settlement, the Bill of Rights, which assured the ascendancy of parliamentary power over sovereign rule. The Act of ◊Settlement of 1701 ensured future Protestant succession to the throne, and William was succeeded by Anne, second daughter of James II.

Reynolds, Joshua (1723–1792)

English painter. One of the greatest portraitists of the 18th century, he displayed a facility for striking and characterful compositions in the 'Grand Manner', a style based on Classical and Renaissance art. He often borrowed Classical poses, for example *Mrs Siddons as the Tragic Muse* (1784; San Marino, California). His elegant portraits are mostly of wealthy patrons, though he also painted such figures as the writers Laurence Sterne and Dr Johnson, and the actor David Garrick. Active in London from 1752, he became the first president of the Royal Academy in 1768 and founded the Royal Academy schools.

Reynolds was particularly influenced by Classical antiquity and the High Renaissance masters, Michelangelo, Raphael, Titian, and Leonardo da Vinci. In his *Discourses on Art*, based on lectures given at the Royal Academy from 1769 to 1791, he argued that art should be of the Grand Manner, presenting the ideal rather than the mundane and realistic. Some of his finest portraits, however, combine Classical form with a keen awareness of individuality, as in his *Lord Heathfield* (1787; National Gallery, London) and *Admiral Keppel* (1753–54; National Maritime Museum, London). Certain works – such as his *Self-Portrait* (about 1773; Royal Academy, London) – appear closer to Rembrandt than to Renaissance artists. He was knighted in 1769.

Rhodes, Cecil John (1853–1902)

South African politician, born in the UK, prime minister of Cape Colony 1890–96. Aiming at the formation of a South African federation and the creation of a block of British territory from the Cape to Cairo, he was responsible for the

THE EMERGENCE OF A GREAT POWER: ENGLAND AFTER 1688

William III's seizure of power in England was opposed in both Scotland and Ireland, where supporters of James II (known as 'Jacobites' from *Jacobus*, Latin for James) fought a bitter war before finally being defeated in 1690. The Jacobites were to stage major risings in 1715 and 1745, but they were both defeated. The Glorious Revolution therefore led to English domination of the British Isles, albeit a domination supported by and identified with important sections of the Irish and Scottish population: Irish Anglicans and Scottish Presbyterians.

This process led to the Union of 1707 of England and Scotland: the Scottish Parliament was abolished and Scotland was thereafter represented in the Westminster Parliament. The Scottish Privy Council was also abolished 1708. Protestantism, war with France, and the benefits of empire helped to create a British consciousness alongside the still strong senses of English, Scottish, Irish, and Welsh identity. Parliamentary union with Ireland followed in 1800–01.

Wars with France

William III led England into war with Louis XIV of France, the War of the League of Augsburg (or Nine Years' War) of 1689–97, fought to stop France overrunning the Low Countries. Conflict resumed with the War of the Spanish Succession (1701–14) in which John Churchill, 1st Duke of Marlborough, heavily defeated the French in a number of battles, particularly Blenheim in 1704. The Royal Navy also emerged during this period as the leading European navy.

Naval strength was crucial in seeing off the French threat during the War of the Austrian Succession (Britain's involvement lasted 1743–48) and the Seven Years' War 1756–63. The latter war ended with the Thirteen Colonies on the eastern seaboard of North America, and the British possessions in India, secure; with Canada, Florida, and many Caribbean islands acquired; and with Britain as the leading maritime power in the world, thus fulfilling what James Thomson had seen as the national destiny in his song *Rule Britannia* (1740): 'Rule, Britannia, rule the waves; Britons never will be slaves.'

This was the achievement of the ministry of William Pitt the Elder and the Duke of Newcastle (1757–62), and of a number of able military leaders, including Wolfe, Clive, Hawke, and Boscawen. Robert Clive's victory at Plassey in 1757, over the vastly more numerous forces of the Indian Prince, Suraja Dowla, laid the basis for the virtual control of Bengal, Bihar, and Orissa by the East India Company (French forces in India were finally defeated in 1760–61, and Britain emerged as the leading European power in the subcontinent). A French attempt to invade Britain on behalf of the Jacobites was crushed by British naval victories at Lagos and Quiberon Bay in 1759. That year, British troops also defeated the French at Minden in Germany, while James Wolfe's troops scaled the Heights of Abraham near Québec to capture France's most important possession in Canada. The bell ringers at York Minster were paid four times between 21 August and 22 October that year for celebrating triumphs.

In 1762 British forces campaigned round the globe. They helped the Portuguese resist a Spanish invasion, fought the French in Germany, and captured Martinique from France and Havana and Manila from Spain, an extraordinary testimony to the global reach of British power, particularly naval power, and the strength of the British state.

The growth of empire

British control of the eastern seaboard of North America north of Florida had been expanded and consolidated with the gain of New York from the Dutch in 1664, the French recognition of Nova Scotia, Newfoundland, and Hudson Bay as British in 1713, and the foundation of colonies including Maryland in 1634, Pennsylvania in 1681, Carolina in 1663, and Georgia in 1732. Possibly 200,000 people emigrated from the British Isles to North America during the 17th century, far outnumbering the French settlers in Canada and Louisiana, and the settlements founded included Charleston in 1672, Philadelphia in 1682, Baltimore in 1729, and Savannah in 1733.

The English also made a major impact in their West Indian islands and developed there a sugar economy based on slave labour brought from West Africa, where British settlements included Accra (settled in 1672). The East India Company, chartered in 1600, was the basis of British commercial activity, and later political power, in the Indian Ocean. Bombay was gained in 1661, followed by Calcutta in 1698. Trade outside Europe became increasingly important to the British economy, and played a major role in the growth of such ports as Bristol, Glasgow, Liverpool, and Whitehaven. The mercantile marine grew from 280,000 tonnes in 1695 to 609,000 in 1760.

By 1763 Britain was the leading maritime state in the world, unified at home and secure in the possession of a large trade-based empire. With France and Spain both vanquished, Britain's position as the world's leading power seemed beyond serious challenge.

BY JEREMY BLACK

annexation of Bechuanaland (now Botswana) in 1885. He formed the British South Africa Company in 1889, which occupied Mashonaland and Matabeleland, thus forming **Rhodesia** (now Zambia and Zimbabwe).

Rhodes went to Natal in 1870. As head of De Beers Consolidated Mines and Goldfields of South Africa Ltd, he amassed a large fortune. He entered the Cape legislature in 1881, and became prime minister in 1890, but the discovery of his complicity in the ◊Jameson Raid forced him to resign in 1896. Advocating Anglo-Afrikaner cooperation, he was less alive to the rights of black Africans, despite the final 1898 wording of his dictum: 'Equal rights for every civilized man south of the Zambezi.'

The **Rhodes scholarships** were founded at Oxford University, UK, under his will, for students from the Commonwealth, the USA, and Germany.

Rhodes, Wilfred (1877–1973)

English cricketer. A slow left-arm spin bowler, he took more first-class wickets than anyone else in the game – 4,187 wickets 1898–1930 – and also scored 39,802 first-class runs.

Playing for Yorkshire, Rhodes made a record 763 appearances in the county championship. He took 100 wickets in a season 23 times and completed the 'double' of 1,000 runs and 100 wickets in a season 16 times (both records). He played his 58th and final game for England, against the West Indies in 1930, when he was 52 years old, the oldest ever Test cricketer.

Rhodes, Zandra Lindsey (1940–)

English fashion designer. She is known for the extravagant fantasy and luxury of her dress creations. She founded her own fashion house in 1968.

After studying at the Royal College of Art, Rhodes began designing and printing highly individual textiles. Her fabrics – chiffon, silk, and tulle – are frequently handprinted with squiggles, zigzags, and other patterns. Her evening dresses are often characterized by their uneven handkerchief hems. She designs wedding and evening dresses embroidered in India, and saris for the top end of the Indian fashion market.

Since 1976 she has licensed her name in the UK and abroad, expanding into textile design, furnishing fabrics, and cosmetics. In 1984 she won an Emmy award for her costumes for the televised production of *Romeo and Juliet on Ice*. She won the British Fashion Council's Hall of Fame Award in 1995.

Rhondda

Industrial town in Rhondda Cynon Taff, south Wales, situated 26 km/16 mi northwest of Cardiff; population (1991) 59,900. Light industries have replaced coal mining, formerly the main source of employment in the area. The closure of the Maerdy mine (opened 1875) in 1990 ended mining in the valley; Rhondda's coal powered 90% of the Royal Navy's ships in World War I. The Rhondda Heritage Park recreates a 1920s-style mining village for visitors.

Rhondda Cynon Taff

Unitary authority in south Wales, created in 1996 from part of the former county of Mid Glamorgan
Area 440 sq km/170 sq mi
Towns Clydach Vale (administrative headquarters)
Physical rivers Rhondda Fawr and Rhondda Fach
Industries light industries
Population (1996) 232,600

It consists of a series of linear settlements following the two rivers, Rhondda Fawr and Rhondda Fach. A variety of new light industries have been attracted here, and there are two major industrial estates, one at Treforest near Pontypridd and the other at Hirwaun near ◊Aberdare. To the south is the lowland plateau, or Bro Morgannwg, a rich agricultural area of mixed farming and large villages which is traversed by the M4 motorway. This was formerly an important coal mining area. The Royal Mint is at Llantrisant.

Rhyl

Seaside holiday resort in Denbighshire, north Wales, situated 50 km/31 mi northwest of Chester near the mouth of the River Clwyd; population (1991) 24,900. Products include furniture manufacture; tourism is important.

The world's first scheduled hovercraft service began in 1962 between here and Wallasey near Birkenhead, England.

RIBA

Abbreviation for **Royal Institute of British Architects**, institute whose object is 'the advancement of Architecture and the promotion of the acquirement of the knowledge of the Arts and Sciences connected therewith'. The RIBA Gold Medal is the world's most prestigious award for architecture.

The institute received its charter in 1837; it is the custodian of the British Architectural Library and the Drawings Collection – the largest body of architectural designs in the world, with a quarter of a million drawings from the Renaissance to the present day.

Ribble

River in northern England, formed by the confluence of the Gayle and Cam; length 120 km/75 mi. From its source in the Pennine hills, North Yorkshire, it flows south and southwest past Preston, Lancashire, to join the Irish Sea.

The Ribble Estuary National Nature Reserve is the largest in England. It is a wintering ground for migrating waterfowl. It has salt marshes and sandflats.

The river is contaminated with radioactive waste from the British Nuclear Fuels plant at Springfield. Monitoring takes place every two months.

Ricardo, Harry Ralph (1885–1974)

English engineer who played a leading role in the development of the internal-combustion engine. During World War I and World War II, his work enabled British forces to fight with the advantage of technically superior engines. His work on combustion and detonation led to the octane-rating system for classifying fuels for petrol engines. Knighted 1948.

Rice, Tim (Timothy Miles Bindon) (1944–)

English lyricist. He has collaborated extensively with composer Andrew Lloyd ◊Webber, writing the lyrics for three of Webber's early musicals – *Joseph and the Amazing Technicolour Dreamcoat* (1968), *Jesus Christ Superstar* (1970), and *Evita* (1976). His work with other composers includes the lyrics for *Chess* (1984) and the film *The Lion King* (1994), with music by Elton John. He was knighted in 1994.

Richard, Cliff stage name of Harry Roger Webb (1940–)

English pop singer. Initially influenced by Elvis Presley, he soon became a Christian family entertainer. One of his best-selling early records was 'Livin' Doll' (1959); it was followed by a string of other successful singles. His original backing group was the Shadows (1958–68 and later reformed). During the 1960s he starred in a number of musical films including *The Young Ones* (1962) and *Summer Holiday* (1963). Fulfilling a personal ambition, he produced the musical *Heathcliff* (1997) in which he played the title role.

Other best-selling singles include 'Congratulations' (1968),

'Power to all our Friends' (1973), 'We Don't Talk Anymore' (1979), 'Daddy's Home' (1981), and 'Mistletoe and Wine' (1988).

Richard

Three kings of England:

Richard (I) the Lion-Heart (French *Coeur-de-Lion*) (1157–1199)

King of England from 1189. He spent all but six months of his reign abroad. He was the third son of Henry II, against whom he twice rebelled. In the third Crusade 1191–92 he won victories at Cyprus, Acre, and Arsuf (against Saladin), but failed to recover Jerusalem. While returning overland he was captured by the Duke of Austria, who handed him over to the emperor Henry VI, and he was held prisoner until a large ransom was raised. He then returned briefly to England, where his brother John had been ruling in his stead. His later years were spent in warfare in France, where he was killed.

Himself a poet, he became a hero of legends after his death. He was succeeded by his brother John I.

Richard II, or Richard of Bordeaux (1367–1400)

King of England from 1377, effectively from 1389, son of Edward the Black Prince. He reigned in conflict with Parliament; they executed some of his associates in 1388, and he executed some of the opposing barons in 1397, whereupon he made himself absolute. Two years later, forced to abdicate in favour of ◊Henry IV, he was jailed and probably assassinated.

In 1381 Richard was faced with the ◊Peasants' Revolt, a result of the imposition of the Poll Tax in 1380. The leader of the Revolt, Wat Tyler, was stabbed and killed at Smithfield by the Lord Mayor of London, fearing for the safety of the king. Richard's apparent courage in facing the mobs gathered at Mile End and Smithfield also contributed to the failure of the uprising.

Richard was born in Bordeaux. He succeeded his grandfather Edward III when only ten, the government being in the hands of a council of regency. His fondness for favourites resulted in conflicts with Parliament, and in 1388 the baronial party, headed by the Duke of Gloucester, had many of his friends executed. Richard recovered control in 1389, and ruled moderately until 1397, when he had Gloucester murdered and his other leading opponents executed or banished, and assumed absolute power. In 1399 his cousin Henry Bolingbroke, Duke of Hereford (later Henry IV), returned from exile to lead a revolt; Richard II was deposed by Parliament and imprisoned in Pontefract Castle, where he died mysteriously.

RICHARD (I) THE LION-HEART *The Great Seal of King Richard I who spent most of his reign away from England. He was a notable soldier who fought in the third Crusade 1191–92, defeating the Muslim leader Saladin and capturing Acre. Philip Sauvain Picture Collection*

Richard III (1452–1485)

King of England from 1483. The son of Richard, Duke of York, he was created Duke of Gloucester by his brother Edward IV, and distinguished himself in the Wars of the ◊Roses. On Edward's death in 1483 he became protector to his nephew Edward V, and soon secured the crown for himself on the plea that Edward IV's sons were illegitimate. He proved a capable ruler, but the suspicion that he had murdered Edward V and his brother undermined his popularity. In 1485 Henry, Earl of Richmond (later ◊Henry VII), raised a rebellion, and Richard III was defeated and killed at ◊Bosworth.

Scholars now tend to minimize the evidence for his crimes as Tudor propaganda.

Richards, Gordon (1904–1986)

English jockey and trainer who was champion on the flat a record 26 times between 1925 and 1953.

He started riding in 1920 and rode 4,870 winners from 21,834 mounts before retiring in 1954 and taking up training. He rode the winners of all the classic races but only once won the Epsom ◊Derby (on Pinza, 1953). In 1947 he rode a record 269 winners in a season and in 1933 at Nottingham/ Chepstow he rode 11 consecutive winners. Knighted 1953.

Richards, I(vor) A(rmstrong) (1893–1979)

English literary critic. He collaborated with C K ◊Ogden on two books and wrote *Principles of Literary Criticism* (1924). With Ogden, he founded the simplified form of English known as ◊Basic English. In 1939 he went to Harvard University, USA, where he taught detailed attention to the text and had a strong influence on contemporary US literary criticism.

Richardson, Dorothy (Miller) (1873–1957)

English novelist. Her sequence of 12 autobiographical novels was published together as *Pilgrimage* in 1938. It began with *Pointed Roofs* (1915), in which she was one of the first English novelists to use the 'stream of consciousness' technique.

Her contemporary, the English novelist and critic Virginia ◊Woolf, recognized and shared this technique as part of the current effort to express women's perceptions in spite of the resistance of man-made language, and she credited Richardson with having invented 'the sentence of the feminine gender'.

Richardson, Ian William (1934–)

English actor. He joined the Shakespeare Memorial Theatre (later the Royal Shakespeare Company) in 1960. At the RSC his many performances included Richard II (1973), when he alternated the roles of Richard and Bolingbroke with Richard Pasco. He has also acted in films and television plays, including *Porterhouse Blue* (1987) and *House of Cards* (for which he won the BAFTA Best Actor Award in 1991).

Born in Edinburgh, Richardson trained at the College of Dramatic Art, Glasgow, before joining the Birmingham Repertory Company in 1958.

Richardson, Miranda (1958–)

English stage, film, and television actress. Her credits span both comic and serious parts, from Elizabeth I in the black-comedy television series *Blackadder* (1986–87) to the murderess Ruth Ellis in her first film *Dance with a Stranger* (1985) and the unbalanced wife of the poet T S Eliot in *Tom and Viv* (1994).

Richardson made her West End stage debut in 1980. Plays include *A Lie of the Mind* (1987), *Etta Jenks* (1990), *The Changeling* and *Mountain Language* (both 1988), and *The Designated Mourner* (1996). Other films include *Empire of the Sun* (1987), *Enchanted April* (1991), *The Crying Game* (1992), *Damage* (◊BAFTA award for best supporting actress) and *Century* (both 1993), *Kansas City* and *Swann* (both 1995), and *Evening Star* (1996).

Richardson, Owen Willans (1879–1959)

British physicist. He studied the emission of electricity from hot bodies, giving the name thermionics to the subject. At Cambridge University, he worked under J J ◊Thomson in the Cavendish Laboratory. He was awarded a Nobel prize in 1928. Knighted 1939.

Richardson, Ralph (David) (1902–1983)

English actor. He played many stage parts, including Falstaff (Shakespeare), Peer Gynt (Ibsen), and Cyrano de Bergerac (Rostand). He shared the management of the Old Vic Theatre with Laurence ◊Olivier 1944–50. In later years he revealed himself as an accomplished deadpan comic.

Later stage successes include David Storey's *Home* (1970) and Harold Pinter's *No Man's Land* (1976). His films include *Things to Come* (1936), *Richard III* (1956), *Our Man in Havana* (1959), *The Wrong Box* (1966), *The Bed-Sitting Room* (1969), and *O Lucky Man!* (1973). He was knighted in 1947.

Richardson, Samuel (1689–1761)

English novelist. He was one of the founders of the modern novel. *Pamela* (1740–41), written in the form of a series of letters and containing much dramatic conversation, was sensationally popular all across Europe, and was followed by *Clarissa* (1747–48) and *Sir Charles Grandison* (1753–54).

He set up his own printing business in London in 1719, becoming printer to the House of Commons.

Richardson, Tony (Cecil Antonio) (1928–1991)

English director and producer. With George Devine he established the English Stage Company in 1955 at the Royal Court Theatre, London, with such productions as John Osborne's *Look Back in Anger* (1956). He was a leading figure in the English realist cinema of the late 1950s and early 1960s, with such films as *Look Back in Anger* (1958), his feature debut, *Saturday Night and Sunday Morning* (1960), *A Taste of Honey* (1961), and *Tom Jones* (1963) (Academy Award).

He also made *The Loneliness of the Long Distance Runner* (1962), *Joseph Andrews* (1977), and *Blue Sky* (shot 1991, released 1994, in the USA).

He was married to Vanessa ◊Redgrave and was the father of the actresses Natasha (born 1963) and Joely Richardson (born 1965).

Other films are *The Border* (1982) and *The Hotel New Hampshire* (1984), which he adapted for the screen from John Irving's novel.

Richborough

Former port in Kent, southeast England, 3 km/2 mi from Sandwich. Now marooned in salt marshes, it was used as a military site in World Wars I and II.

Richborough was the site of the Roman port **Reputiae**, the principal Roman port on the east coast of England in the 2nd and 3rd centuries; to the north of Sandwich on the River Stour are the remains of **Richborough Castle**, a Roman fort built in the 3rd century to defend the port.

A transport depot was established here in 1916, and Richborough served as an embarkation port for the invasion of Normandy in World War II. The nearby power station was completed in 1963.

Richmond

Market town in North Yorkshire, northern England, on the River Swale, 17 km/11 mi southwest of Darlington; population (1991) 7,800. It is the centre of the surrounding farming district and is also the main tourist centre of the Yorkshire Dales National Park. Features include a restored Georgian theatre (1788).

It has the remains – only the keep – of a Norman castle, built in 1071 on a promontory overlooking the River Swale. To the southeast of Richmond are the ruins of Easby Abbey (1152). Also nearby is Catterick Camp, a large military camp.

Richmond-upon-Thames

Outer borough of southwest Greater London, the only London borough with land on both sides of the River Thames, including the districts of Kew, Teddington, ◊Twickenham, and Hampton

Features Royal Botanic gardens, Kew; Richmond Park, 1,000 hectares/2,470 acres with 11 gates, the largest urban park in Britain, enclosed by Charles I for hunting, with ancient oaks, deer, and White Lodge, home of the Royal Ballet School; Maids of Honour Row, Richmond (1724), terrace of four houses for maids of honour attending the Princess of Wales; early 18th-century houses around Richmond green; gatehouse of former Richmond Palace; Richmond Theatre (1899); Garrick's Villa, Hampton, acquired by David Garrick in 1754 and altered by Robert Adam; Old Court House, Hampton, last home of Christopher Wren; Faraday House, Hampton, home of Michael Faraday; Hampton Court Palace, begun by Thomas Wolsey in 1514; Bushy Park (acquired by Wolsey in 1514) containing Bushy House, built in 1665 and remodelled *c.*1720, which now houses the National Physical Laboratory; highest tidal point of River Thames at Teddington; Ham House, Petersham (1610), with 17th-century garden; Twickenham Rugby football ground, headquarters of the Rugby Football Union; Barnes Common; 18th- and 19th-century Barnes terrace, facing River Thames; Kneller Hall, Twickenham, is the home of the Royal Military School of Music

Industries brewing, printing, electrical engineering

Population (1991) 160,700

Famous people

Virginia and Leonard Woolf set up the Hogarth Press here. Thomas Traherne and R D Blackmore lived in Teddington; Henry Fielding in Barnes.

Places of historical interest

Richmond is a royal borough and Edward I built a palace here in the 13th century. It was rebuilt and enlarged by Henry VII, who held a tournament in Richmond in 1492. An archway, Wardrobe Court, and the Gatehouse are the only remains of the palace of Sheen, in which Edward III and Elizabeth I both died. Near these remains, forming one side of Richmond Green, is Maids of Honour Row, built to house the ladies of the court during George I's reign. Richmond Hill, on which Joshua Reynolds once lived, commands a famous view of the meadows, uplands, woods, and of the islands of the winding Thames, on whose bank the town stands. Reynolds and Joseph Turner are among the many artists to have painted this view. Richmond Park was enclosed as a hunting and pleasure ground by Charles I, and still shelters herds of wild deer. Edmund Kean, who leased Richmond Theatre (first established in 1719), is buried in the parish churchyard, as is the author of 'The Seasons', James Thomson. Ham House, built in 1610 by Sir Thomas Vavasour, stands on the banks of the Thames in the nearby village of Petersham. The house was greatly extended in the 18th century by the Countess of Dysart and her husband, the Duke of Lauderdale. It is now open to the public, under the Victoria and Albert Museum, and has fine furniture and works by the Dutch painter Peter Lely. The church of St Mary the Virgin at Mortlake, which was founded in 1348, rebuilt in 1543, and often enlarged, contains memorials to Sir Philip Francis, the bitter opponent of Warren Hastings, and Sir John Temple, besides many tombs of celebrities, notably of John Dee, the 16th-century philosopher and astrologer. Mortlake was famous for its tapestry works in the 17th century and Charles I was a patron of the factory. Mortlake is the finishing point of the annual boat race between Oxford and Cambridge Universities.

Twickenham

Twickenham is mentioned in the second oldest Middlesex charter (704), when the land was granted to the Bishop of London. It became fashionable in the 17th century and maintained and strengthened its attractions in the 18th. Among its residents have been the philosopher and writer Sir Francis Bacon, the dramatist John Gay, the novelist Henry Fielding, the society hostess Lady Mary Wortley Montagu, the actress Kitty Clive, Charles Dickens, J M W Turner, Charles Tennyson (poet and elder brother of Alfred Tennyson), and Walter de la Mare. York House, built in the late-17th century and now municipal offices, was once owned by James, Duke of York; Queen Anne lived there as a child. Kneller Hall, built between 1709 and 1711 and since altered, was the house of the painter Godfrey Kneller, and is now the headquarters of the Royal Military School of Music. Marble Hill, an example of the English Palladian style, standing in beautiful grounds on the banks of the Thames, was restored in 1966. The house was built by the Duchess of Suffolk, the mistress of George II, and was at one time occupied by Mrs Fitzherbert, George IV's morganatic wife.

Twickenham is chiefly noted for its associations with the poet Alexander Pope and the politician Horace Walpole. Pope's Villa, where he lived from 1719 until his death in 1744, and where many celebrities of his day met, was pulled down in 1807. All that now remains of the once-famous Grotto is a passage under the road, now used to connect the two halves of a school that has been built on the site. Walpole settled in a cottage close by in 1747, and in 1750 began to reconstruct it in a Gothic style, progressively enlarging it with the help of several architects, until the fantastic mixture of mansion and castle was completed in 1776. Strawberry Hill, as the castle was named, had a considerable influence on architectural taste in the 19th century. It is now St Mary's Training College, a Roman Catholic teacher-training establishment. The oldest surviving building in Twickenham is the 15th-century tower of the parish church, which was retained when the church was rebuilt in 1714–15. Pope is buried in the church.

Hampton

In the early 13th century the manor of Hampton passed to the order of St John of Jerusalem, from whom Cardinal Wolsey obtained a 99-year lease in 1514 in order to build his palace. In the 18th-century Hampton became a fashionable residential area. The actor David Garrick lived there from 1754 until his death in 1779. His house near the river, now called Garrick Villa, was enlarged by Robert Adam. Facing Hampton Court Green, which is just by ◊Hampton Court Palace, are some very good examples of domestic architecture, including the Old Court House, where the architect Christopher Wren lived from 1706 until he died in 1723, and Faraday House, where the scientist Michael Faraday lived between 1858 and 1867. The parish church at Hampton-on-Thames, built in 1830 on the site of an older church, contains monuments of notable people, including residents of Hampton Court Palace. The bridge over the Thames at Hampton Court was designed in 1933 by Sir Edwin Lutyens.

Teddington

Teddington belonged to the abbey of Westminster until the

Dissolution. It is the highest tidal point on the Thames, and its lock (built in 1811) is the largest (198 m/650 ft by 7.6 m/25 ft) on the river. Teddington is the point where the discharge is gauged, and is the limit of the jurisdiction of the Port of London Authority. The National Physical Laboratory is at Teddington.

Bushy Park (445 ha/1,112 acres), which lies between Teddington and Hampton Court, was laid out in its present form by William III.

Riding, from the old Norse 'thrithjungs'

One of the three former administrative divisions of the county of Yorkshire until 1974: West Riding, North Riding, and East Riding; in 1974 they were reorganized into the counties of North Yorkshire and Humberside, and the metropolitan counties of West Yorkshire and South Yorkshire. In 1996 Humberside was abolished and the new unitary authority of the East Riding of Yorkshire was created. At the same time the City and County of York was created from the southern part of North Yorkshire, around York.

Ridley, Nicholas (*c.* 1500–1555)

English Protestant bishop. He became chaplain to Henry VIII in 1541, and bishop of London in 1550. He took an active part in the Reformation and supported Lady Jane Grey's claim to the throne. After Mary's accession he was arrested and burned as a heretic.

Ridolfi Plot

Conspiracy of 1571 led by the Italian banker Roberto Ridolfi with Spanish and papal backing to replace Elizabeth I with Mary Queen of Scots. Spanish troops in the Netherlands were to invade England and lead a Catholic uprising against Elizabeth. The plot was discovered before it became a serious threat. Ridolfi was overseas at the time but another conspirator, Thomas Howard, Duke of Norfolk, was executed the following year. Mary was placed in stricter confinement as a result of the plot.

Rie, Lucie born Gomperz. (1902–1995)

Austrian-born potter. She worked in England from the 1930s. Her pottery, exhibited all over the world, is simple and pure in form, showing a debt to English potter Bernard ◊Leach.

Rievaulx Abbey, or **Rivaulx Abbey**

Ruined Cistercian foundation situated near Helmsley, North Yorkshire, England. It dates from 1131, and has a magnificent chancel date from around 1230 and extensive remains among the monastic buildings.

The word means 'valley of the Rye' from a small river that flows by the ruins. There is also a village of Rievaulx.

Rifkind, Malcolm Leslie (1946–)

British lawyer and Conservative politician, foreign secretary 1995–97. As defence secretary 1992–95, his incisive intellect enabled him to manage the 'peace dividend', with its inevitable rundown of parts of the armed forces, more successfully than some of his predecessors. He lost his parliamentary seat of Edinburgh Pentlands in the 1997 general election.

Rigg, Diana (1938–)

English actress. Her stage roles include Bianca in *The Taming of the Shrew* (1961), Cordelia in *King Lear* (1964), Héloïse in *Abelard and Héloïse* (1970), and the title roles in *Medea* (1993–94) and *Mother Courage* (1995); she also appeared in *Who's Afraid of Virginia Woolf?* (1996).

In 1990 she won the ◊BAFTA award for best actress for her role in the BBC production *Mother Love*. Television credits include *Bleak House* (1985), *Genghis Cohen* (1993), and *Moll Flanders* (1996). DBE 1998.

right of way

The right to pass over land belonging to another. Other rights of way are licences (where personal permission is given) and easements.

In English law public rights of way are acquired by long use, by specific grant, or by statute. They are shown in definitive

Diana Rigg *The actress Diana Rigg began her career in classical Shakespearean drama, but came into the wider public eye in the 1960s, playing the role of the debonair and athletic secret agent Emma Peel in the comedy thriller television series* The Avengers. *Returning to the stage, she won great praise for her interpretation of a wide variety of parts, and was made a Dame of the British Empire (DBE) in 1998. Greg Williams/Rex*

maps (which are conclusive evidence of the existence of the rights of way) maintained by the relevant local authority. A court ruling in 1991 established that right of navigation is equivalent to right of way.

Riley, Bridget Louise (1931–)

English painter. A pioneer of Op art, she developed her characteristic style in the early 1960s, arranging hard-edged black lines in regular patterns to create disturbing effects of scintillating light and movement. *Fission* (1963; Museum of Modern Art, New York) is an example.

In the late 1960s she introduced colour and experimented with silk-screen prints on Perspex, though she continued to create works in her familiar black-and-white style. Her work has also included stage design, notably for the ballet *Colour Moves* (1983).

Riley trained at Goldsmiths' School of Art and the Royal College.

Riley, or Ryley, John (1646–1691)

English portrait painter. Charles II, James II, and Samuel Pepys were among his sitters and, with Godfrey Kneller, he became court painter to William and Mary.

He occasionally painted minor domestic members of the royal household, and his portrait of Charles II was candid enough to have evoked – it is said – the royal comment: 'Odd's fish, I'm an ugly fellow.' His works may be seen in the National Portrait Gallery, London, in the Royal Collection, and in Oxford.

Rimington, Stella (1935–)

British public servant and director-general of the counter-intelligence security service (MI5) 1992–96. She was the first head of MI5 to be named publicly, and in July 1993 published a booklet containing hitherto undisclosed details on the service, including its history, organization, and constitutional role. She was the first woman to hold the top post.

riot

Riots formerly suppressed under the Riot Act are now governed by the Public Order Act 1986. Methods of riot control include plastic bullets, stun bags (soft canvas pouches filled with buckshot which spread out in flight), water cannon, and CS gas (tear gas).

Riots in Britain include the Spitalfields weavers' riot in 1736, the Gordon riots in 1780, the Newport riots in 1839, and riots over the Reform Bill in Hyde Park, London, in 1866; in the 1980s inner-city riots occurred in Toxteth, Liverpool; St Paul's, Bristol; Broadwater Farm, Tottenham, and Brixton, London; and in 1990 rioting took place in London and several other cities after demonstrations against the ◊poll tax. Race-related riots erupted in Brixton again in December 1995, arising from a demonstration after a black man died in police custody.

Riot Act

Act of Parliament passed in 1714 to suppress the ◊Jacobite disorders. If three or more persons assembled unlawfully to the disturbance of the public peace, a magistrate could read a proclamation ordering them to disperse ('reading the Riot Act'), after which they might be dispersed by force. It was superseded by the Public Order Act 1986, which was instituted in response to several inner-city riots in the early 1980s, and greatly extends police powers to control marches and demonstrations by rerouting them, restricting their size and duration, or by making arrests. Under the act a person is guilty of riot if in a crowd of 12 or more, threatening violence; the maximum sentence is ten years' imprisonment.

Ripon

City and market centre in North Yorkshire, northern England, on the River Ure; population (1991) 14,200. Agricultural produce is traded here. Features include a cathedral (1154–1520), and nearby are the 12th-century ruins of ◊Fountains Abbey, among the finest monastic ruins in Europe.

Features

Each evening at nine o'clock a horn is blown in the market square, an ancient custom which is said to date from before the 11th century. There is a 28 m/90 ft obelisk (1780) in the market square, and the town hall (1801) was designed by James Wyatt. Other features include the Norman chapel of St Mary Magdalen. St Wilfrid's Feast is celebrated annually in August with a large procession through the streets.

Ripon cathedral

The cathedral, built on the site of a Saxon church, includes a crypt built by St Wilfrid in 672, and fine 15th-century misericords (ledges projecting from the underside of the hinged seat of choir stalls, for support during standing). General restoration was carried out by George Gilbert Scott in the 19th century.

History

Ripon grew up around the abbey which was founded in the 7th century. The first abbot was St Wilfrid. The town became known for its markets and fairs, which belonged to the Archbishop of York and the ecclesiastical commissioners until 1800. In 1640 Charles I made the treaty of Ripon with the Scots here, ending the second Bishop's War.

Ritz Hotel

Hotel in Piccadilly, London, opened in 1906 to the specifications of Swiss hotelier César Ritz (1850–1918) and named after him. The hotel is renowned for its rich and opulent interior; the word 'ritzy' derives from it, meaning 'showily smart'.

Rivers, William Halse Rivers (1864–1922)

English anthropologist and psychologist. His systematic study of kinship relations and his emphasis on fieldwork helped to establish anthropology as a more scientific discipline. As a psychologist he argued that perception was culturally conditioned, and he applied the theories of Sigmund Freud in his treatment of World War I shell-shock victims.

Rivers is a central character in Pat Barker's 'Regeneration' trilogy, which includes a fictionalized account of his encounter with the poet Siegfried ◊Sassoon at Craiglockhart War Hospital outside Edinburgh.

Rix, Brian Norman Roger (1924–)

English actor and manager. He first became known for his series of farces at London's Whitehall Theatre, notably *Dry Rot* (1954–58). He made several films for cinema and television, including *A Roof Over My Head* (1977), and promotes charities for the mentally disabled. He was knighted in 1986.

Rizzio, David (*c.* 1533–1566)

Italian adventurer and musician. He arrived at the court of Mary Queen of Scots in 1561 in the train of the ambassador of the Duke of Savoy. Mary appointed him her French secretary in 1564, and he soon acquired great influence and to some degree directed her policy. This angered her husband ◊Darnley, and, on suspicion of being the Queen's lover, he was seized in her presence and murdered by Darnley and his friends.

RNIB

See ◊Royal National Institute for the Blind.

RNID

See ◊Royal National Institute for the Deaf.

RNLI

See ◊Royal National Lifeboat Institution.

Robert II (*c.* 1054–1134)

Eldest son of ◊William the Conqueror, succeeding him as Duke of Normandy (but not on the English throne) in 1087. His brother ◊William II ascended the English throne, and they warred until 1096, after which Robert took part in the First Crusade. When his other brother ◊Henry I claimed the English throne in 1100, Robert contested the claim and invaded England unsuccessfully in 1101. Henry invaded Normandy in 1106, and captured Robert, who remained a prisoner in England until his death.

Robert

Three kings of Scotland:

Robert (I) the Bruce (1274–1329)

King of Scotland from 1306, and grandson of Robert de ◊Bruce. He shared in the national uprising led by William ◊Wallace and, after Wallace's execution in 1305, rose once more against Edward I of England and was crowned at Scone in 1306. He defeated Edward II at ◊Bannockburn in 1314. In 1328 the Treaty of Northampton recognized Scotland's independence and Robert as king.

Robert II (1316–1390)

King of Scotland from 1371. He was the son of Walter (1293–1326), steward of Scotland, and Marjory, daughter of Robert the Bruce. He acted as regent during the exile and captivity of his uncle David II, whom he eventually succeeded. He was the first king of the house of Stuart.

Robert III (*c.* 1340–1406)

King of Scotland from 1390, son of Robert II. He was unable to control the nobles, and the government fell largely into the hands of his brother, Robert, Duke of Albany (*c.* 1340–1420).

Roberts, Richard John (1943–)

British molecular biologist who shared the 1993 Nobel Prize for Physiology or Medicine with Phillip Sharp for the discovery of split genes (genes interrupted by nonsense segments of DNA).

They glory in their warhorses and equipment. For us the name of the Lord must be our hope of victory in battle.

Robert (I) the Bruce King of Scotland. Addressing his troops before the Battle of Bannockburn 1314

Robertson, George Islay MacNeill (1946–)

British Labour politician, secretary of state for Defence (1997–). He entered the House of Commons, representing Hamilton, in 1978. After serving as parliamentary private secretary (PPS) to the secretary of state for Social Services in the last months of the Callaghan government, 1979, when Labour went into opposition, he became shadow spokesman on Scotland 1979–80, on Defence 1980–81, on Foreign and Commonwealth Affairs 1981–93, and on European and Community Affairs 1985–93. He was shadow Scottish Secretary 1993–97.

Robey, George stage name of George Edward Wade (1869–1954)

English music-hall comedian. He came to fame in 1891 with his comic interpretation of the song 'The Simple Dimple'. He took part in many revues and films and had some success as a serious actor, notably as Falstaff in Shakespeare's *Henry IV* in 1935. He was knighted in 1954.

In his early days he was extremely acrobatic, especially in his parody of Lottie Collins in 'Ta-Ra-Ra-Boom-De-Ay!'.

Robin Hood

In English legend, an outlaw and champion of the poor against the rich, said to have lived in Sherwood Forest, Nottinghamshire, during the reign of Richard I (1189–99). He feuded with the sheriff of Nottingham, accompanied by Maid Marian and a band of followers traditionally known as his 'merry men', including Little John (so called because of his huge stature), Friar Tuck (a jovial cleric), and Alan a Dale. He appears in many popular ballads from the 13th century, but his first datable appearance is in William Langland's *Piers Plowman* in the late 14th century.

To judge from the references to him and his legendary associates in ballads and other popular literature, and in records of ritualistic summer games, his name became well known both in England and Scotland in the 15th century.

Traditionally he is a nobleman who remained loyal to

Richard during his exile and opposed the oppression of King John. There may be some historical basis for the legend. He has been identified both as an earl of Huntingdon born in about 1160 and as the defendant in a court case in 1354 awaiting trial on a charge of the theft of foliage and venison from a forest in Northamptonshire, but many of the customs and practices associated with his name suggest that he is a character of May Day celebrations. He is claimed to have been buried at Kirklees Hall, Yorkshire.

Robin Hood's Bay

Village on a wide bay on the coast of North Yorkshire, England, between Scarborough and Whitby. It is an example of a large wave-cut platform. The village is surrounded by moorland.

Robinson, Robert (1886–1975)

English chemist, Nobel prizewinner in 1947 for his research in organic chemistry on the structure of many natural products, including flower pigments and alkaloids. He formulated the electronic theory now used in organic chemistry.

Robinson's studies of the sex hormones, bile acids, and sterols were fundamental to the methods now used to investigate steroid compounds. His discovery that certain synthetic steroids could produce the same biological effects as the natural oestrogenic sex hormones paved the way for the contraceptive pill. Knighted 1939.

Robinson, W(illiam) Heath (1872–1944)

English cartoonist and illustrator. He made humorous drawings of bizarre machinery for performing simple tasks, such as raising one's hat. A clumsily designed apparatus is often described as a 'Heath Robinson' contraption.

Robinson Crusoe, full title *The Life and Strange and Surprising Adventures of Robinson Crusoe*

Novel by Daniel ◊Defoe, published in 1719. It tells the story of a man shipwrecked alone on a desert island. His attempts to ensure his physical and mental survival are thoroughly documented before he meets another castaway, 'Man Friday', who he treats as his pupil and servant. Defoe freely embroiders the real-life ordeal of Alexander ◊Selkirk which inspired the book. *Robinson Crusoe* is generally regarded as the first major English novel.

Rob Roy nickname of Robert MacGregor (1671–1734)

Scottish Highland ◊Jacobite outlaw. After losing his estates, he lived by cattle theft and extortion. Captured, he was sentenced to transportation but pardoned in 1727. He is a central character in Walter Scott's historical novel *Rob Roy* 1817. A film of *Rob Roy* was made in 1995, starring Liam Neeson.

Robson, Bobby (Robert William) (1933–)

English footballer and manager who coached England from 1982 to 1990 before enjoying considerable success in Europe at PSV Eindhoven, Porto, and Barcelona. As a player he scored 133 goals in 584 league appearances for West Bromwich Albion and Fulham, 1951–67, and 4 goals in 20 full internationals for England, 1957–62.

Robson, Flora (McKenzie) (1902–1984)

English actress. A stalwart of both stage and screen, she excelled as Queen Elizabeth I in the film *Fire Over England* (1937) and as Mrs Alving in *Ghosts* (1958), a film adaptation of the play by the Norwegian dramatist Henrik Ibsen.

Rochdale

Industrial town in Greater Manchester, northwest England, on the River Roch, 16 km/10 mi northeast of Manchester; population (1994 est) 138,000. It was formerly an important cotton-spinning town; industries now include textiles and the manufacture of machinery and asbestos. The Rochdale Pioneers founded the first Co-operative Society in England here in 1844.

ROBINSON CRUSOE *A woodcut for the title page of* Robinson Crusoe *(1719), by the English writer Daniel Defoe. The novel is a fictionalized account of the adventures of the Scottish sailor Alexander Selkirk, who was marooned in the South Pacific. Corbis*

Situated at the southern end of the Rossendale upland, with the Pennines to the east, Rochdale is an ancient market town which was traditionally associated with the wool trade. Its prosperity as a cotton-spinning town in the Victorian period is expressed in its large Gothic-style town hall (completed in 1871). Other features include the Rochdale Pioneers Museum, housed in the building in Toad Lane where the first Co-operative Society shop was established. The extensively restored church of St Chad dates from the 12th century. The singer Gracie Fields was born here in 1898, and there is a Gracie Fields collection within the Rochdale Museum.

Roche, Jerome (1942–1994)

English musicologist. Early Italian music was at the centre of his research and he published books on Palestrina (1971), the Italian madigral (1972), and Lassus (1982).

Rochester

City in southeastern England, on the Medway estuary, in Medway Towns unitary authority; population (1991) 24,000. Rochester upon Medway district joined with Gillingham to form the Medway Towns unitary authority in April 1998. Rochester was a Roman town, **Durobrivae**. It has a 12th-century Norman castle keep (the largest in England), a 12th–15th-century cathedral (containing a memorial to Charles Dickens), and many timbered buildings. Industries include aeronautical, electrical, and mechanical engineering; cement; paper; and paint and varnish. The Charles Dickens Centre (1982) commemorates the town's links with the novelist Charles Dickens, whose home was at Gad's Hill.

Traces of the walls of Roman **Durobrivae** exist, standing where Watling Street crosses the tidal Medway. In 604 the second bishopric in the kingdom was established here by St Augustine and a church endowed by King Ethelbert. A Norman cathedral, Benedictine priory, and later a castle were built, all of which have important remains. The west doorway of the cathedral, with its highly decorative carving, is unique in England. Extension to the fabric was made possible by rich offerings to the shrine of William of Perth, a pious baker who was murdered close to Rochester in 1201 during a pilgrimage. He was buried in the cathedral; miracles took place at his tomb and he was canonized in 1256. Of the castle, the impressive keep remains, 39 m/128 ft high, dominating its surroundings. There is a 17th-century guildhall.

Associations with Dickens

Charles Dickens spent some of his childhood at Chatham, and the last years of his life at Gad's Hill Place, on the Rochester–Gravesend road, where he died in 1870. Although Gad's Hill is also the scene of the adventures of Falstaff and Prince Hal in Shakespeare's Henry IV, it is Dickens who is best remembered for his associations with the area. Chertsey Gate, one of three leading from the cathedral to the High Street is known as 'Jaspers Gate', under which name it appeared in the unfinished *Mystery of Edwin Drood.* Other parts of the city appear in *Pickwick Papers*, *Great Expectations*, and *The Uncommercial Traveller.*

Rockall

British islet in the Atlantic, 24 m/80 ft across and 22 m/65 ft high, part of the Hatton-Rockall bank, and 370 km/230 mi west of North Uist in the Hebrides. The bank is part of a fragment of Greenland that broke away 60 million years ago. It is in a potentially rich oil/gas area. A party of British marines landed in 1955 formally to annex Rockall, but Denmark, Iceland, and Ireland challenge Britain's claims for mineral, oil, and fishing rights. The **Rockall Trough** between Rockall and Ireland, 250 km/155 mi wide and up to 3,000 m/10,000 ft deep, forms an ideal marine laboratory.

A 1995 study by the Natural History Museum of 17 seabed sites (including the Great Barrier Reef and the San Diego Trough) revealed that the Rockall Trough had more species than any other site, and greater biodiversity than a coral reef. In 4 cubic metres/5 cubic yards of sediment there were 325 species of worm.

Rockingham

Village in Northamptonshire, England, 5 km/3 mi northwest of Corby. It was formerly the centre of a royal forest. **Rockingham Castle**, built by William (I) the Conqueror on the site of earlier earthworks, dominates the Welland valley. The village has many 17th-century and 18th-century houses.

Rockingham, Charles Watson Wentworth, 2nd Marquess of Rockingham (1730–1782)

British Whig politician, prime minister 1765–66 and 1782 (when he died in office); he supported the American claim to independence.

Roddick, Anita Lucia born Perilli (1942–)

English entrepreneur, founder of the ◊Body Shop. She campaigns on green issues and is an advocate of 'caring capitalism'.

Roe, (Edwin) Alliott Verdon (1877–1958)

English aircraft designer, the first Briton to construct and fly an aeroplane, in 1908. He designed the Avro series of aircraft from 1912.

Roeg, Nicolas (Jack) (1928–)

English film director and writer. He was initially a cinematographer working on such films as *The Masque of the Red Death* (1964), François Truffaut's *Fahrenheit 451* (1966), and *Far From the Madding Crowd* (1967). His striking visual style as a director is often combined with fractured, disturbing plots, as in *Performance* (1970), *Don't Look Now* (1973), *The Man Who Fell to Earth* (1976), and *The Witches* (1989). His other films include *Walkabout* (1970), *Bad Timing* (1980), *Castaway* (1986), and *Track 29* (1988).

Rogers, Richard George (1933–)

English High Tech architect. His works include the Pompidou Centre in Paris (1977), with Renzo Piano; the Lloyd's of London building in London (1986); and the Reuters building at Blackwall Yard, London (1992), which won him a RIBA award. The Richard Rogers Partnership designed the ◊Millennium Dome, situated on the Millennium Festival site in Greenwich, and in October 1998, the Partnership's design concept was chosen for the National Assembly for Wales building at Cardiff Bay. Rogers was knighted in 1991 and was subsequently made a life peer under the title Lord Rogers of Riverside.

Roget, Peter Mark (1779–1869)

English physician and scholar, one of the founders of the University of London, and author of a *Thesaurus of English Words and Phrases* (1852), a text constantly revised and still in print, offering a range of words classified according to underlying concepts and meanings, as an aid to more effective expression and communication.

Rolling Stones, the

British band formed in 1962, once notorious as the 'bad boys' of rock. Original members were Mick Jagger (1943–), Keith Richards (1943–), Brian Jones (1942–1969), Bill Wyman (1936–), Charlie Watts (1941–), and the pianist Ian Stewart (1938–1985). A rock-and-roll institution, the Rolling Stones were still performing and recording in the 1990s.

The Stones' earthy sound was based on rhythm and blues. Classic early hits include 'Satisfaction' (1965) and 'Jumpin' Jack Flash' (1968). The albums from *Beggars Banquet* (1968) to *Exile on Main Street* (1972) have been rated among their best work; others include *Some Girls* (1978), *Steel Wheels* (1989), and *Stripped* (1996), which plays as a normal CD in an audio player and as an interactive video when played in a CD-ROM drive.

The Rolling Stones toured 33 cities in the USA in 1997 to promote their 36th album, *Bridges to Babylon*.

Rolls, Charles Stewart (1877–1910)

British engineer who joined with Henry ◊Royce in 1905 to design and produce cars. In 1906 a light model 20, driven by Rolls, won the Tourist Trophy and also broke the Monte Carlo-to-London record.

Rolls trained as a mechanical engineer at Cambridge, where he developed a passion for engines of all kinds. After working at the railway works in Crewe, he set up a business in 1902 as a motor dealer. Rolls was the first to fly nonstop across the English Channel and back in 1910. Before the business could flourish, he died in a flying accident.

Rolls, Master of the

British judge; see ◊Master of the Rolls.

Rolls-Royce

Industrial company manufacturing cars and aeroplane engines, founded in 1906 by Henry ◊Royce and Charles Rolls. The Silver Ghost car model was designed in 1906, and produced until 1925, when the Phantom was introduced. In 1914 Royce designed the Eagle aircraft engine, used extensively in World War I. Royce also designed the Merlin engine, used in Spitfires and Hurricanes in World War II. Jet engines followed, and became an important part of the company.

From 1994, BMW of Germany were to build a percentage of the engines for Rolls-Royce and Bentley cars, as well as providing engineering consultation.

Roman architecture

Building erected during the Roman occupation (AD 43–around 410). Features were similar to Roman architecture in other provinces of the Empire, being less ambitious and elaborate than those of the city of Rome.

Most examples are to be found in the larger Roman towns: Camulodunum (Colchester), Verulamium (St Albans), Aquae Sulis (Bath), Calleva Atrebatum (Silchester), Viroconium (Wroxeter), and Isca Silurum (Caerwent). Other important towns such as Londinium (London), Eboracum (York), Ratae (Leicester), Lindum (Lincoln), Glevum (Gloucester), and Corinium (Cirencester) have yielded comparatively few remains; usually because later building has smothered or destroyed the Roman work, or because they have not yet been thoroughly excavated.

Public buildings were generally grouped round the forum or market-place, as at St Albans. Notable remains include the amphitheatre at Caerwent; the theatre at St Albans; secular basilicas at Cirencester, Silchester, Wroxeter, and Caerwent; the largest basilica north of the Alps, found under Gracechurch Street, London; and public baths, especially at Bath, but also at Leicester, Silchester, and Wroxeter. No temples remain above ground but the foundations of a large construction have been found at Colchester, and there are numerous temples to the oriental deity Mithras, such as that in Walbrook, London. A fragment of a small basilican church at Silchester, dating from about 410, is the only surviving Christian church of the period.

Domestic town-houses are best studied at St Albans; the streets form a chess-board pattern and contain centrally heated houses, baths, and mosaic floors. Larger dwellings include palaces, such as Fishbourne near Chichester, villas, and farmhouses, some of them having over 50 rooms. They are chiefly situated south and east of a line from York to Exeter, the best examples being at Bignor, Sussex; Brading, Isle of Wight; Chedworth, Gloucestershire; Folkestone, Kent; and Northleigh and Woodchester in Oxfordshire.

Roman Britain

Period in British history from the two expeditions by Julius Caesar in 55 and 54 BC to the early 5th century AD. Roman relations with Britain began with Caesar's expeditions, but the actual conquest was not begun until AD 43. During the reign of the emperor Domitian, the governer of the province, Agricola, campaigned in Scotland. After several unsuccessful attempts to conquer Scotland, the northern frontier was fixed between the Solway and the Tyne at ◊Hadrian's Wall.

The process of Romanization was enhanced by the establishment of Roman colonies and other major urban centres. Most notable was the city of Colchester (Camulodunum), which was the location of the temple dedicated to the Divine Claudius, and the focus of the revolt of Boudicca. Other settlements included London, York, Chester, St Albans, Lincoln, and Gloucester, as well as the spa at Bath,

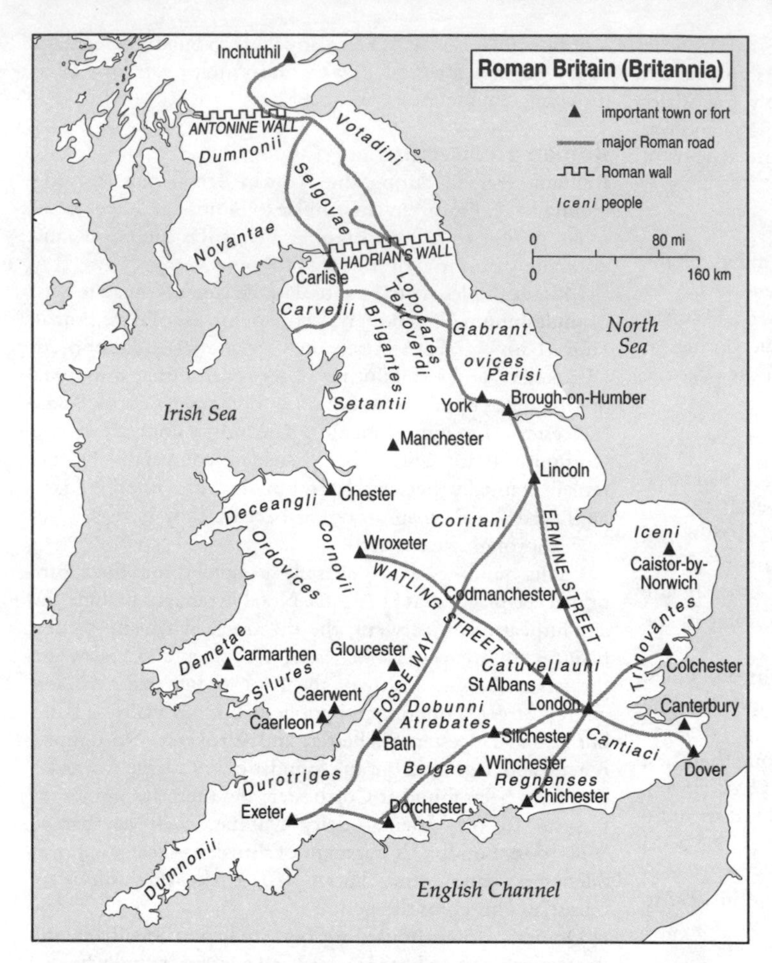

dedicated to the worship of Sulis Minerva, a combination of local and Roman deities. England was rapidly Romanized, but north of York few remains of Roman civilization have been found.

The province was garrisoned by three Roman legions based at Caerleon in South Wales, Chester, and York. These troops were supplemented by auxiliaries placed on the frontier regions such as Wales and northern Britain, especially along Hadrian's Wall. The development of the province was aided by the creation of a network of roads. These still form the basis of some of the main routes of the country, such as ◊Watling Street from London to Wroxeter (near Shrewsbury), the Fosse Way which runs southwest through places such as Cirencester, and Ermine Street from London to Lincoln and York.

During the 4th century Britain was raided by the Saxons, Picts, and Scots. The Roman armies were withdrawn in 407, and the emperor Honorius wrote a famous letter telling the province to look to its own defence, but there were partial reoccupations from 417 to about 427 and about 450.

Roman Catholicism

Religion professed by about 10% of the British population. Roman Catholicism is one of the main divisions of the Christian religion, separate from the Eastern Orthodox Church from 1054, and headed by the pope, currently John Paul II, based in Rome. The head of the Roman Catholic Church in Britain is Cardinal Basil Hume.

Organization

In Great Britain the Roman Catholic Church is organized into seven provinces and 30 dioceses (22 in England and Wales, 8 in Scotland), each of which is headed by a bishop responsible to the pope. Within the dioceses there are 3,319 parishes and about 4,800 priests. Northern Ireland has six dioceses.

History

The Protestant churches separated from the Catholic with the Reformation in the 16th century. In England, for more than two centuries after the Reformation, scattered Catholics were served by missionary priests, whose activities were subject to penal laws. Toleration was officially extended to Catholics by the Catholic Emancipation Act 1829, and a Roman Catholic episcopate was restored in England and Wales in 1850, and in Scotland in 1878.

Irish immigration (chiefly as a result of the potato famine in the mid-19th century) played a major role in determining the subsequent development and character of English Roman Catholicism. Today, its demonstrative worship and apostolic fervour contrast forcibly with the sober and unobtrusive English Catholicism of penal times.

Roman roads

Network of well built roads constructed across Britain by the Romans, to facilitate rapid troop movements and communications, as well as trade. The best known are Ermine Street, Watling Street, and Fosse Way. Many Roman roads were constructed afresh; others, such as the Icknield Way, were based on ancient routes. The roads were usually as straight as possible to aid speed of travel, and were built from large kerb stones between smaller stones covered with river gravel, often accompanied by drainage ditches. Many of the roads continued in use throughout the Middle Ages.

Romanticism

Late-18th- and early-19th-century cultural movement which emphasized the imagination and emotions of the individual, in a reaction against the restraint of 18th-century Classicism and Neo-Classicism. Major themes included a love of atmospheric landscapes; nostalgia for the past, particularly Gothic forms (leading to ◊Gothic Revival architecture); cult of the hero figure; romantic passion; mysticism; and a fascination with death. The poets Thomas Gray, William Cowper, and William Bowles, and the landscape painters Paul Sandby and Thomas Girtin, are regarded as forerunners of the movement in Britain. Romanticism also gained inspiration

THE EDGE OF THE WORLD: BRITAIN AND THE COMING OF ROME

THE EXPEDITIONS of Julius Caesar and the conquest under Claudius brought most of Britain (but not Ireland) within the political, cultural, and economic system of the Mediterranean-based empire of Rome. But the Roman conquest of Britain was a long process, and cultural domination, at first no more than superficial, was established only slowly.

Britain before the conquest

The *Cassiterides* or 'Tin Islands' known to Greek writers are generally identified with southwest Britain. During his conquest of Gaul, Julius Caesar crossed to Britain in 55 and 54 BC. This was more for the propaganda effect at Rome of invading the mysterious island in the Ocean than with any serious intent to conquer the island. For the next hundred years the peoples of the southeast of Britain were increasingly influenced by the Romans, and native kings such as Cunobelin (Shakespeare's Cymbeline) maintained diplomatic relations with them. In AD 43 the new emperor Claudius rewarded the army which had placed him on the throne by taking up the work of his ancestor Caesar and invading Britain with a view to conquest.

Conquest, resistance, and domination

The initial invasion of AD 43 under its commander Aulus Plautius soon overran the southeast of Britain, taking Camulodunum (Colchester) the centre for the most powerful tribe. Its leader, Caractacus, escaped to the Silures of south Wales, where he stirred up resistance until his defeat and capture in AD 51, when he was sent to Rome. Resistance continued in Wales, particularly inspired by the Druids, the priests and law-givers of the Celtic peoples. The Romans depict them as practising barbarous rites such as human sacrifice, but this may be more of an attempt to blacken the image of leaders of resistance than the truth.

The next serious resistance to Rome came from the Iceni of East Anglia. When their king Prasutagus died in 60 or 61, their territory was forcibly annexed to the province of Britannia and Prasutagus' widow Boudicca (Boadicea) and her daughters abused. The Iceni and their southern neighbours the Trinovantes of Essex rose in revolt and sacked the now Roman-style towns at Colchester, London, and Verulamium (St Albans) before being slaughtered in battle by Roman troops under the governor Suetonius Paullinus. This was the last concerted effort to shake off Roman rule, though it was not until the 70s that the Romans completed the conquest of what are now England and Wales.

Scotland and the walls

In the early 80s Roman power was advanced into Scotland under the governor Gnaeus Julius Agricola, the best-known governor of Britain as the biography by his son-in-law the historian Tacitus has survived. Agricola defeated the Caledonian tribes under their leader Calgacus at the battle of Mons Graupius in northeastern Scotland, but over the next 40 years the Romans gradually gave up their conquests in Scotland. In 122 the emperor Hadrian visited Britain and commanded the construction of a wall from sea to sea. Hadrian's Wall ran from Newcastle to west of Carlisle. With a gate (milecastle) every mile as well as watch-towers and forts, it was designed to control movement across the frontier, supervise the tribes to the north, and stand as a great monument to the might of Hadrian and Rome. At Hadrian's death in 138, his successor Antoninus Pius abandoned the newly completed Wall and advanced to a new line from the Forth to the Clyde, the Antonine Wall. But with the death of its originator in 161 the Antonine Wall was abandoned, and thereafter Hadrian's Wall marked the northern boundary of Rome in Britain.

The development of Britannia

The initial conquest was long drawn out and occasionally bloody, and the Romans never succeeded in subduing all the island. Thus there was always a substantial military garrison in Britain and resistance by unconquered tribes. But the great majority of the people of Britain soon settled down to Roman rule and adapted to the style of their conquerors. Under Roman influence towns appear in Britain, including colonies for military veterans such as Colchester, Gloucester, and Lincoln, the great port of London and other towns which have remained important to the present such as Canterbury and York. Roman fashions can also be seen in the introduction of temples, altars, and sculpture for the worship of native gods, new burial practices, the construction of Roman-style country residences (villas), and the importation of luxuries such as spices or glass from elsewhere in the empire. This 'Romanization' of Britain principally affected the aristocracy, who used Roman manners to please their overlords and to impress the rest of the populace. But the great majority of the people continued to live on the land and eke out a living as peasants, relatively little touched by the forms of Roman civilization.

BY SIMON ESMONDE CLEARY

from the medieval poetry and short life of Thomas Chatterton, Thomas Percy's manuscript collection of ballads and romances, and James Macpherson's poetry, attributed to the 3rd-century Gaelic bard Ossian.

In **literature**, leading figures of full-blown Romanticism were William Wordsworth, Samuel Taylor Coleridge, Percy Bysshe Shelley, John Keats, and Walter Scott. Byron became a symbol of British Romanticism and political liberalism throughout 19th-century Europe. The movement also led to the rise of English melodrama, marked by Thomas Holcroft's *A Tale of Mystery* (1802).

In **art**, J M W Turner was an outstanding landscape painter of the Romantic tradition, while the poet, artist, and visionary William Blake represented a mystical and fantastic trend. Other leading Romantic artists of the period were John Martin and Thomas Lawrence. The movement was also influenced by John Constable, his paintings, such as *The Haywain*, epitomizing a Wordsworthian return to nature and the study of natural phenomena.

The Romantic tradition of British art continued into the 20th century with the work of James Pryde, and John Piper's dramatic views of landscape and architecture. Piper was part of a movement called **Neo-Romanticism** (around 1935–55), in which British artists revived the spirit of 19th-century Romanticism in a more modern idiom, particularly in landscapes. Other leading figures of the movement were Graham Sutherland and Keith Vaughan.

Romeo and Juliet

Romantic tragedy by William ◊Shakespeare, first performed in 1594–95. The play is concerned with the doomed love of teenagers Romeo and Juliet, victims of the bitter enmity between their respective families in Verona.

Romney, George (1734–1802)

English painter. Active in London from 1762, he became, with Thomas Gainsborough and Joshua Reynolds, one of the most successful portrait painters of the late 18th century. His best work is to be found in the straightforward realism of *The Beaumont Family* (National Gallery, London) or the simple charm of *The Parson's Daughter* (Tate Gallery, London).

A visit to Italy (1773–75) filled him with the ambition to paint Classical and imaginative compositions, and from 1782 to 1785 he drew and painted Lady Hamilton, mistress of Lord Nelson, whom he admired obsessively, in many preliminary studies for mythological or allegorical themes he was ill-fitted to carry out. He retired to his home county of Lancashire in 1789.

Romney Marsh

Stretch of drained marshland on the Kent coast, southeast England, between ◊Hythe and Rye, used for sheep pasture. From Hythe in the north it extends to the ◊Dungeness promontory in the south, and includes Denge Marsh and Walland Marsh. Reclamation of the land began in Roman times. The principal settlement in the area is ◊New Romney.

The Romney, Hythe, and Dymchurch narrow-gauge railway, one of the world's smallest public railways, was opened in 1927. The Rhee Wall, between Appledore and New Romney, is thought to be Roman in origin.

Romney Marsh was formerly a bay extending from Hythe in Kent and to Fairlight in Sussex, England. Shingle spits grew outwards from the headlands to form a bar behind which sedimentation took place. There is an area of shingle, Dungeness Foreland, in which old shorelines can be found, and an area of former marshland which had been almost completely reclaimed by the 17th century to give rich pasture for Romney Marsh sheep.

Romsey

Market town in Hampshire, southern England, 13 km/8 mi northwest of Southampton, on the River Test; population (1991) 16,600. Industries include brewing, carpet manufacture, computer consultancy, and farming. The Norman church of Romsey Abbey (founded by Edward the Elder in 907) survives, as does King John's Hunting Box of about 1206 (now a museum, King John's House).

Nearby Broadlands was the seat of Earl Mountbatten and Lord Palmerston.

rose

A symbol of England, where it is occasionally worn on St George's Day (23 April), and of love. The rose has been associated with England since the Wars of the Roses of the 15th century, when the Yorkists bore the white rose and the Lancastrians the red. The badges were united by the marriage of Henry VII to Elizabeth of York to form the **Tudor rose**, which remains an English royal emblem. The **red rose** was also adopted in 1986 as a symbol of the Labour Party. Roses are placed on the shrine of St Alban at St Albans on the Sunday nearest his feast day, 22 June, and roses are often used in children's naming ceremonies in Unitarian chapels.

Rosebery, Archibald Philip Primrose, 5th Earl of Rosebery (1847–1929)

British Liberal politician. He was foreign secretary in 1886 and 1892–94, when he succeeded Gladstone as prime minister, but his government survived less than a year. After 1896 his imperialist views gradually placed him further from the mainstream of the Liberal Party.

Rosenberg, Isaac (1890–1918)

English poet. His poems of World War I reflect the horror of life on the front line, as in 'Louse Hunting', and fleeting philosophical moments, as in 'Break of Day in the Trenches'.

Like that of his contemporary Wilfred ◊Owen, Rosenberg's war poetry now ranks with the finest of World War I, although it was largely unpublished during his lifetime. After serving for 20 months at the front, he was killed on the Somme. His *Collected Works* appeared in 1937.

Roses, Wars of the

Civil wars in England from 1455 to 1485 between the houses of ◊Lancaster (badge, red rose) and ◊York (badge, white rose), both of whom claimed the throne through descent from the sons of Edward III. As a result of ◊Henry VI's lapse into insanity in 1453, Richard, Duke of York, was installed as protector of the realm. Upon his recovery, Henry forced York to take up arms in self-defence. The name Wars of the Roses was given in the 19th century by novelist Walter Scott.

Rose Theatre

Former London theatre near Southwark Bridge where many of Shakespeare's plays were performed. The excavation and preservation of the remains of the theatre, discovered in 1989, caused controversy between government bodies and archaeologists.

The theatre was built in 1587 by the impresario Philip Henslowe (*c.* 1550–1616), who managed it until 1603; the theatre was the site of the first performances of Shakespeare's plays *Henry VI* and *Titus Andronicus*.

Ross, Ronald (1857–1932)

British physician and bacteriologist, born in India. From 1881 to 1899 he served in the Indian Medical Service, and during 1895–98 identified mosquitoes of the genus *Anopheles* as being responsible for the spread of malaria. He was awarded a Nobel prize in 1902. KCB 1911.

Ross studied at St Bartholomew's Hospital in London. On retiring from the Indian Medical Service in 1899, he returned to Britain, eventually becoming professor of tropical medicine at Liverpool. During World War I he was consultant on malaria to the War Office, and when the Ross Institute of Tropical Diseases was opened in 1926, he became its first director.

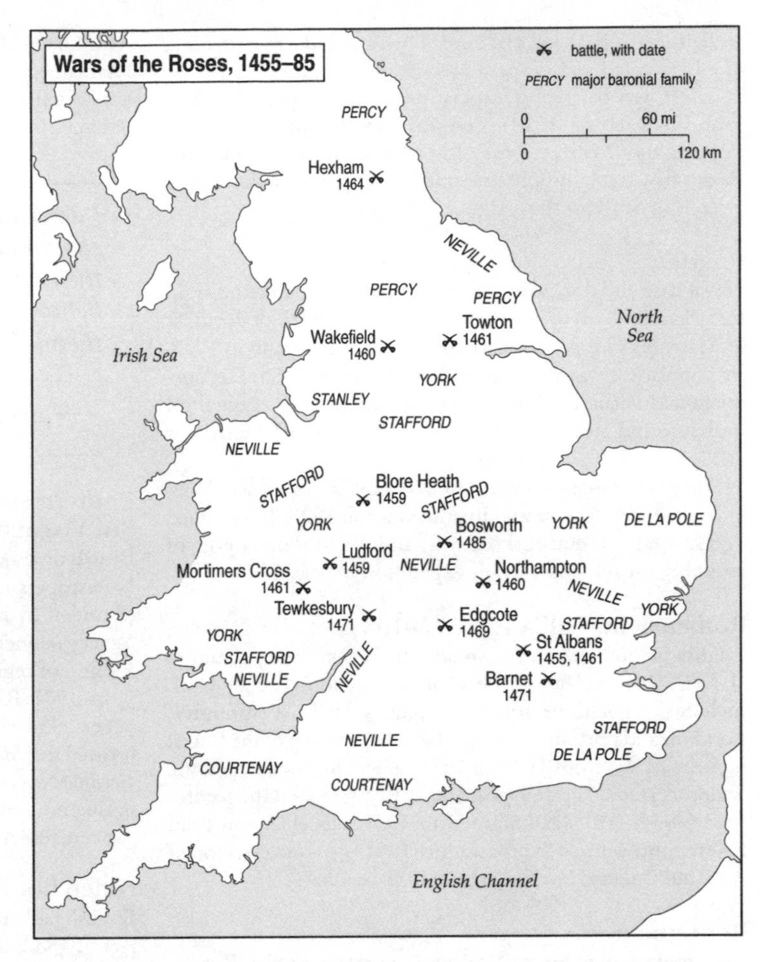

Rossendale

Upland area that gave its name in 1974 to a borough in southeast Lancashire, England; population (1991) 64,000. It takes its name from the ancient forest of Rossendale. The upland area includes significant areas of moorland where hill farming takes place. Although the area developed in the 18th and 19th centuries with the cotton and textile industries, textiles and footwear now coexist with new industries such as light engineering.

Rossetti, Christina Georgina (1830–1894)

English poet and a devout High Anglican (see ◊Oxford movement). Her best-known work is *Goblin Market and Other Poems* (1862); among others are *The Prince's Progress* (1866), *Annus Domini* (1874), and *A Pageant* (1881). Her verse expresses unfulfilled spiritual yearning and frustrated love. She was a skilful technician and made use of irregular rhyme and line length. She was the sister of Dante Gabriel ◊Rossetti.

Her first recorded poem was completed at the age of 12. In 1847 a volume of her verses was privately printed, and in 1850, using the pseudonym Ellen Alleyne, she contributed to the famous but short-lived Pre-Raphaelite periodical *The Germ*. The sadness that pervades her writing may be due to an unhappy love affair in her youth, and to the ill health she constantly suffered.

Rossetti, Dante Gabriel (1828–1882)

English painter and poet. Although a founding member of the **◊Pre-Raphaelite Brotherhood** in 1848, he produced only two deliberately Pre-Raphaelite pictures: *The Girlhood of Mary Virgin* (1849) and *Ecce Ancilla Domini* (1850), both in the Tate Gallery, London. He went on to develop a broader romantic style and a personal subject matter related to his poetry, but the term Pre-Raphaelite continued to be applied to his painting.

Rossetti was a friend of the critic John ◊Ruskin and William Morris, with whom he initiated a second phase of Pre-Raphaelitism associated with the Arts and Crafts movement.

Between 1850 and 1860 he produced many of his best pictures, mainly in watercolour; his subjects were mainly from Dante or the *Morte D'Arthur* and his chief model was the painter Elizabeth Siddal (1834–1862), who became his wife in 1860. His later works concentrated on single studies of allegorical females such as the *Beata Beatrix* (1864), *Proserpine* (Tate Gallery, London), *Astarte Syriaca* (Manchester City Art Gallery), and *The Day Dream* (Victoria and Albert Museum), his most important model being William Morris's wife, Jane, who became his lover.

Rossetti's early verse includes 'The Blessed Damozel' (1850). His *Poems* (1870) were disinterred from the grave of Elizabeth Siddal, but were attacked as being of 'the fleshly school of poetry'. After this he became addicted to the use of chloral; he attempted suicide in 1872 and suffered from partial paralysis from 1881. His sister was the poet Christina ◊Rossetti.

Ross-on-Wye

Market town in Hereford and Worcester, England, on the River Wye, 19 km/12 mi southeast of Hereford; population (1991) 9,200. Factories for agricultural implements and for seed processing are located here. The town has a fine example of a Decorated and Perpendicular church.

The town has many associations with the philanthropist John Kyrle (1637–1724), described by the poet Alexander Pope as the 'Man of Ross'. John Kyrle was responsible for Ross's first water-supply system and for the restoration of the church of St Mary the Virgin.

Rosyth

Naval base and dockyard used for nuclear submarine refits, in Fife, Scotland, on the northern shore of the Firth of Forth, at St Margaret's Hope. Construction of the base began in 1903. Its population was affected by defence cuts in 1994. Decommissioned *Polaris* nuclear submarines will be stored here until underground storage facilities are complete, scheduled for 2012.

Rosyth became important in World War I as a repair base; it was reduced to care and maintenance in 1925. It reopened in 1939 on the outbreak of war, and was the main port of assembly for the Norwegian expedition of May 1940.

Rothenstein, William (1872–1945)

English painter and writer on art. His best-known painting is *A Doll's House* (1899; Tate Gallery, London). Other work includes decorations for St Stephen's Hall, Westminster, London, and portrait drawings. He was principal of the Royal College of Art from 1920 to 1935, where he encouraged the sculptors Jacob ◊Epstein and Henry ◊Moore, and the painter Paul ◊Nash. He was knighted in 1931. His elder son John Knewstub Maurice Rothenstein (1901–) was director of the Tate Gallery, London, from 1938 to 1964.

Rotherham

Industrial town in South Yorkshire, northern England, at the confluence of the rivers Don and Rother, 10 km/6 mi northeast of Sheffield; population (1994) 154,000. Industries include engineering, pottery, glass, iron and steel, brassware, machinery, and coal.

Features

The Perpendicular church of All Saints was built on the site of an earlier Saxon church; it contains 15th-century stalls and benches, and a fine pulpit (1603). The Chapel of Our Lady, built in about 1483 on the old Rotherham Bridge, is one of only four surviving bridge chapels in England. The chapel was later used as the town prison, but in 1924 it was restored and re-dedicated. Clifton House (1783) in Clifton Park houses a museum which includes displays of Roman relics and local Rockingham Pottery. Other features nearby include Conisbrough Castle and Roche Abbey.

History

There was a Roman post near the present town. In the Domesday Book of 1086 Rotherham is mentioned as having a church and a mill. The town developed during the Industrial Revolution after an ironworks was established in 1746.

Rotherhithe Tunnel

Road tunnel extending 1,481 m/4,860 ft under the River Thames east of Wapping, London, connecting Rotherhithe with Shadwell. It was built 1904–08 to a design by Maurice Fitzmaurice (1861–1924). The top of the tunnel is 14.6 m/48 ft below the Trinity high-water mark to allow for the passage of large ships.

I don't think the British public are sanctimonious. They love to read humbug, their appetite for it is limitless, but I don't believe they are actually humbugs themselves.

Lord Rothermere British newspaper proprietor. Interviewed a month before his death in the *Daily Telegraph*, August 1998

Rothermere, Vere Harold Esmond Harmsworth, 3rd Viscount Rothermere (1925–1998)

British newspaper proprietor. He became chair of Associated Newspapers in 1971, controlling the right-wing *Daily Mail* (founded by his great-uncle Lord ◊Northcliffe) and *Mail on Sunday* (launched in 1982), the London *Evening Standard*, and a string of regional newspapers. Viscount 1978.

In 1971 Rothermere took control of the family newspapers. He closed the *Daily Sketch* and successfully transformed the *Mail* into a tabloid. In 1977 he closed the London *Evening News* with heavy loss of jobs, but obtained a half-share of the more successful *Evening Standard*, and gained control of the remainder in 1985.

rotten borough

English parliamentary constituency, before the Great Reform Act of 1832, that returned members to Parliament in spite of having small numbers of electors. Such a borough could easily be manipulated by those with sufficient money or influence.

Rottingdean

Coastal village near Brighton, East Sussex, England; population (1991) 8,300. Rudyard Kipling, the writer, lived here for a time, as did the painter Edward Burne-Jones. Rottingdean has a museum displaying toys and Kipling memorabilia.

Roundhead

Member of the Parliamentary party during the English Civil War 1640–60, opposing the royalist Cavaliers. The term referred to the short hair then worn only by men of the lower classes.

Round Table

In British legend, the table of the knights of King ◊Arthur's court. According to tradition, they quarrelled for precedence and a round table was designed so that all could sit equally. It had one vacant place, the 'Siege Perilous', or 'dangerous seat', awaiting the arrival of the Grail hero Galahad.

The Great Hall in Winchester, Hampshire, contains a Round Table which was presented to Henry VIII; it was known to have existed in Henry III's reign; it has seats for the king and 24 knights. It is probably the relic of a joust, as the

Round Table gave its name, from the 12th century, to a form of tournament where knights may have played the part of Arthurian characters.

Routledge, Patricia (1929–)

English actress. She plays mainly comedy roles, including that of Hyacinth Bucket in *Keeping Up Appearances* (from 1990) on television. Other television roles include Alan Bennett's *Talking Heads* (1988 and 1998) and *Hetty Wainthropp Investigates* (1996). She also sang and appeared in *Cowardy Custard* (1972), a stage celebration of Noel Coward's revues and plays. Her performance in *Candide* (1988) at the Old Vic won her the Laurence Olivier Award.

Born in Birkenhead, she trained at the Bristol Old Vic Theatre School, and acted in repertory for a number of years.

Rowe, Nicholas (1674–1718)

English dramatist and poet. His dramas include *The Fair Penitent* (1703) and *The Tragedy of Jane Shore* (1714), in which English actress Mrs Siddons played. He edited Shakespeare, and was poet laureate from 1715.

Rowland, Tiny (Roland W) adopted name of Roland Fuhrhop (1917–1998)

British entrepreneur, co-chief executive and managing director of Lonrho 1961–1994, and owner of the *Observer* Sunday newspaper from 1981 to 1993.

Born in India, he emigrated to Rhodesia in 1947. In 1961 he merged his business interests with the London and Rhodesian Mining and Land Company, now known as Lonrho. After acquiring the *Observer*, he made an unsuccessful bid for the Harrods department store in London. In November 1994, following a long-running power struggle with his joint-chief executive, Roland provoked the Lonrho board into dismissing him as managing director.

Rowlandson, Thomas (1757–1827)

English painter and illustrator. One of the greatest caricaturists of 18th-century England, his fame rests on his humorous, often bawdy, depictions of the vanities and vices of Georgian social life. He illustrated many books, including *Tour of Dr Syntax in Search of the Picturesque* (1809), which was followed by two sequels between 1812 and 1821.

Born in London, Rowlandson studied at the Royal Academy schools and in Paris and in 1777 settled in London as a portrait painter. Impoverished by gambling, he turned to caricature around 1780. Other works include *The Dance of Death* (1815–16) and illustrations for works by the writers Tobias Smollett, Oliver Goldsmith, and Laurence Sterne.

Rowntree, B(enjamin) Seebohm (1871–1954)

English entrepreneur and philanthropist. He used much of the money he acquired as chair (1925–41) of the family firm of confectioners, H I Rowntree, to fund investigations into social conditions. His writings include *Poverty, A Study of Town Life* (1900), a landmark in empirical sociology. The three **Rowntree Trusts**, which were founded by his father **Joseph Rowntree** (1836–1925) in 1904, fund research into housing, social care, and social policy, support projects relating to social justice, and give grants to pressure groups working in these areas.

Rowse, A(lfred) L(eslie) (1903–1997)

English historian. He published a biography of Shakespeare in 1963, and in *Shakespeare's Sonnets: The Problems Solved* (1973) controversially identified the 'Dark Lady' of Shakespeare's sonnets as Emilia Lanier, half-Italian daughter of a court musician, with whom the Bard is alleged to have had an affair in 1593–95.

His other works include the scholarly *Tudor Cornwall: Portrait of a Society* (1941, 1969) and *Shakespeare the Man* (1973). He was also a minor poet of Celtic themes and traditional forms of verse: he published *A Life: Collected Poems* in 1981.

Roxburgh, William (1751–1815)

Scottish botanist who enlarged the Royal Botanic Gardens in Calcutta, India. Until he took over the care of these gardens they had served a simply commercial purpose; the East India Company had established them in order to acclimatize plants that they wished to introduce to the Indian subcontinent. Roxburgh brought specimens from all over India and developed a large herbarium.

Royal Academy of Arts, RA

British society founded by George III in London in 1768 to encourage painting, sculpture, and architecture; its first president was Joshua ⇨Reynolds. It is now housed in Old Burlington House, Piccadilly. There is an annual summer exhibition for contemporary artists, and tuition is provided at the Royal Academy schools.

Royal Academy of Dramatic Art, RADA

British college founded by Herbert Beerbohm Tree in 1904 to train young actors. Since 1905 its headquarters have been in Gower Street, London. A royal charter was granted in 1920.

Royal Academy of Music, RAM

Conservatoire of international standing in London, founded in 1822 by John Fane, Lord Burghesh, later 11th Earl of Westmorland. It was granted a royal charter in 1830. Based in Marylebone Road, it provides full-time training leading to performing and academic qualifications. The current principal is Curtis Price.

Royal Aeronautical Society

Oldest British aviation body, formed in 1866. Its members discussed and explored the possibilities of flight long before its successful achievement.

Royal Agricultural Society of England

Premier association in England for the agricultural industry. Founded in 1839, the society is based at the National Agricultural Centre, Stoneleigh, Warwickshire, where it holds a four-day agricultural show every July.

Royal Air Force, RAF

See ◊armed forces.

Royal Albert Hall

Large oval hall situated south of Kensington Gardens, London, opposite the ◊Albert Memorial. It was built 1867–71 from the surplus of funds collected for the Albert Memorial. The architect was Francis Fowke (1823–1865). It is usually referred to as the Albert Hall. It holds 6,800 people and is used for concerts, meetings, boxing-matches and other events. It has one of the largest organs in the world.

royal assent

Formal consent given by a British sovereign to the passage of a bill through Parliament, after which it becomes an ◊act of Parliament. The last instance of a royal refusal was the rejection of the Scottish Militia Bill of 1702 by Queen Anne.

When a bill has passed through both Houses of Parliament in the same session it does not become the law of the land until the sovereign has signified his or her consent, by letters patent under the ◊great seal signed with the sovereign's own hand. This is known as the royal assent. The Parliament Act 1949 provides that where a bill has passed the Commons twice in two successive sessions, such a bill may be presented direct to the sovereign for his or her assent even if the Lords refuse to agree to its passage.

The granting of the royal assent may be given by the sovereign in person, but this has not occurred since 1854. Under the Royal Assent by Commission Act 1541 the royal assent could be pronounced by lords commissioners, usually the Lord Chancellor and three or four peers who were also privy councillors. This act has been superseded by the Royal Assent Act 1967, by which the royal assent may be given by the sovereign in person, by the lords commissioners, or, what is now the normal practice, announced by the Lord Chancellor and the Speaker of the House of Commons in the Houses of Parliament. Prior to this the proceedings of the Commons were interrupted several times each session by a summons, conveyed by Black Rod, to attend at the bar of the House of Lords to hear the royal assent. This ceremony now occurs at the end of a parliamentary session.

The assent is given in Norman-French. After the title of the bill is read by the clerk of the Crown, the clerk of the Parliaments says *Le Roy (or La Reyne) le veult*. An expression of thanks for the 'benevolence' of *ses bon sujets* is coupled to the assent to a money bill, and there is yet another formula for assenting to a private bill. Should the sovereign refuse his or her assent to a bill the form of the announcement is *Le Roy (or, La Reyne) s'avisera* (the king, or queen, will consider it). But as the sovereign can now act only on the advice of his or her ministers (the cabinet) this contingency never arises.

In former times the refusal of the royal assent was a common enough occurrence. Queen Elizabeth I once refused to assent to 48 bills out of a total of 91 presented to her at the end of a session.

Royal Auxiliary Air Force, RAUXAF

Air force support service which was formed in 1924 and merged with the Royal Air Force Volunteer Reserve in 1997. It supports the RAF in air and ground defence of airfields, air movements, maritime air operations, and medical evacuations by air.

Royal Ballet

Leading British ballet company and school, based at the Royal Opera House, Covent Garden, London. Until 1956 it was known as the Sadler's Wells Ballet. It was founded in 1931 by Ninette ◊de Valois, who established her school and company at the Sadler's Wells Theatre. It moved to Covent Garden in 1946. Frederick ◊Ashton became principal choreographer in 1935, providing the company with its uniquely English ballet style. Leading dancers included Margot Fonteyn, Rudolf Nureyev, Alicia Markova, and Antoinette Sibley. Anthony ◊Dowell became artistic director of the company in 1986.

The company's roots can be traced to the invitation by Lilian ◊Baylis to Ninette de Valois to establish her school and company at the rebuilt

ROYAL ALBERT HALL *The Royal Albert Hall in Kensington, London, was built as a memorial to Queen Victoria's royal consort Prince Albert, who died prematurely in 1861. It is most famous as the venue (since 1941) of the annual Sir Henry Wood promenade concerts, or 'Proms', a two-month season of classical concerts that attracts a devoted following. Corel*

Sadler's Wells Theatre in 1931. The Vic-Wells Ballet, as it was then known, developed its popularity largely through the performances of Alicia ◊Markova and through de Valois' shrewd artistic policies and organizational prowess. In 1946, the company changed its name to Sadler's Wells Ballet and shifted base from the Wells Theatre to the Royal Opera House, Covent Garden. The same year saw the founding of a second, touring troupe, the Sadler's Wells Opera Ballet (later Theatre Ballet). The touring company again changed its name in 1976 to Sadler's Wells Royal Ballet, and in 1990 it became the Birmingham Royal Ballet. In 1963 de Valois resigned in favour of Frederick Ashton as director. He was responsible for creating such ballets as *Marguerite and Armand* for Margot ◊Fonteyn, whose partnership with Rudolf Nureyev ushered in the Royal Ballet's golden age. Kenneth ◊MacMillan took over from Ashton in 1970 and strengthened both companies' modern-ballet styles with works from US choreographers such as Jerome Robbins and Glen Tetley.

Norman Morrice was artistic director 1977–86, when Anthony Dowell took over and declared a policy of rejuvenating the classics, as in his *Swan Lake* (1987). Dowell persuaded Frederick Ashton to agree to the 1988 revival of his *Ondine* (created for Margot Fonteyn), and in the 1994/95 seasons the company remounted full evening programmes devoted to Ashton's repertoire in tribute. Among new works, the Royal Ballet commissioned Kenneth MacMillan's *The Prince of the Pagodas* (1989), David Bintley's *Cyrano* (1991) and *Tombeux* (1993), and Twyla Tharp's *Mr Worldly Wise* (1995). The Royal Ballet also acquired its first William Forsythe ballet, *In the Middle, Somewhat Elevated*, in 1992, later joined by three other Forsythe ballets, which showed several of the Royal Ballet dancers excelling in the extended technique required in these works.

In 1997–98, due to the redevelopment of the Royal Opera House, the company performed at a range of London venues.

Royal British Legion

Full name of the ◊British Legion, a nonpolitical body promoting the welfare of war veterans and their dependants.

Royal College of Music, RCM

Conservatoire of international standing in London, founded in 1882 in Kensington. It provides full-time training leading to performing and academic qualifications. The current principal is Dr Janet Ritterman.

Royal College of Organists

College founded in London in 1864, and currently located in Kensington. Towards the end of the 19th century, it was influential in standardization of organ design. It is an important examining body, and also organizes lectures.

The college was originally set up to provide a central organization for the organ profession; to provide an examinations system for the church; to provide opportunities for meetings and lectures; and to promote composition of church music.

royal commission

A group of people appointed by the government (nominally by the sovereign) to investigate a matter of public concern and make recommendations on any actions to be taken in connection with it, including changes in the law. In cases where agreement on recommendations cannot be reached, a minority report can be submitted by dissenters.

Royal commissions are usually chaired by someone eminent in public life, often someone favourable to the government's position. No royal commissions were set up during the Thatcher administration (1979–90) but the practice was revived by her successor, John Major (1990–97), who appointed, in 1991, a royal commission on criminal justice, chaired by Lord Runciman, which reported in 1993.

In 1997, the Labour government of Tony Blair appointed a royal commission to examine the system of long-term care for the elderly in Scotland and an independent commission, chaired by Lord Jenkins, to recommend a new 'broadly proportional' system of voting for Westminster elections.

Royal Court Theatre

Theatre in Sloane Square, London. As the home of the ◊English Stage Company from 1956, it is associated with productions of new work.

The Royal Court had its first success with Arthur Pinero's *Trelawny of the 'Wells'* in 1898. It thrived under the managing partnership of John Vedrenne (1867–1930) and Harley ◊Granville-Barker 1904–07, with productions of plays by Shakespeare, George Bernard Shaw, John Galsworthy, and others, and under George Devine 1956–64.

Royal Family

See ◊monarchy.

Royal Flying Corps, RFC

Forerunner of the ◊Royal Air Force, created in 1912 from the Air Battalion, Royal Engineers, as the air arm of the British army.

Royal Greenwich Observatory

The national astronomical observatory of the UK, founded in 1675 at Greenwich, southeast London, to provide navigational information for sailors. After World War II it was moved to Herstmonceux Castle, Sussex; in 1990 it was transferred to Cambridge. It also operates telescopes on La Palma in the Canary Islands, including the 4.2-m/165-in William Herschel Telescope, commissioned in 1987.

In 1998 the Particle Physics and Astronomy Research Council decided to return some of the Royal Observatory's work back to the original Greenwich site from Cambridge (other technical work will go to a new UK Astronomy Technology Centre in Edinburgh).

The observatory was founded by King Charles II. The eminence of its work resulted in Greenwich Time and the Greenwich Meridian being adopted as international standards of reference in 1884.

Royal Horticultural Society, RHS

British society established in 1804 for the improvement of horticulture. The annual Chelsea Flower Show, held in the grounds of the Royal Hospital, London, is also a social event, and another flower show is held at Vincent Square, London. There are gardens, orchards, and trial grounds at Wisley, Surrey, and the Lindley Library has one of the world's finest horticultural collections.

royal household

Personal staff of a sovereign. In Britain the chief officers are the Lord Chamberlain, the Lord Steward, and the Master of the Horse. The other principal members of the royal family also maintain their own households. The ◊civil list provides for the maintenance of the royal household.

History

The royal household probably had its origin in the *comitatus* described by the Roman historian Tacitus. This consisted of *comites* or companions who were the personal attendants of the Teutonic chieftain. In England before the Norman Conquest the *comites* had been replaced by thanes, while in Normandy a similar arrangement had been established, and each duke had his seneschal, his chamberlain, and his constable. After the Conquest this ducal household was reproduced in the royal household of England.

Royal Institution of Great Britain

Organization for the promotion, diffusion, and extension of science and knowledge, founded in London in 1799 by the Anglo-American physicist Count Rumford (1753–1814). In 1998 it appointed Susan Greenfield (1951–) as its first woman director.

English chemists Michael ◊Faraday and Humphry ◊Davy were among its directors.

Royal Mail

Department of the UK Post Office that handles the collection and delivery of letters. The Royal Mail delivers to 26 million addresses in Britain, handling over 2 million letters a day. Collections are made from over 120,000 sites.

Royal Marines

British military force trained for amphibious warfare.

Royal Military Academy

British officer training college popularly known as ◊Sandhurst.

Royal Musical Association

A society formed to promote the investigation of all aspects of music. It was founded in London in 1874 as the Musical Association and became 'Royal' in 1944. The Association published the *Proceedings of the RMA* (until 1956–57), and now publishes the *Journal of the RMA* (from 1987), the *RMA Research Chronicle* (from 1961), *RMA Monographs* (from 1985), and initiated *Musica Britannica* in 1951. It holds two conferences each year, one being for research students.

The society awards the Dent medal annually in association with the International Musicological Society to a musicologist of international repute.

Royal National Institute for the Blind, RNIB

Charity, founded in 1868, providing specialized services for blind and partially-sighted people.

Royal National Institute for the Deaf, RNID

Charity, founded in 1911, providing specialized services for deaf people.

Royal National Lifeboat Institution, RNLI

Charity, founded in 1824, operating a 24-hour lifeboat rescue service around the coasts of Britain and Ireland. In 1998 it had 2,000 fundraising branches and 100,000 members.

Royal Naval Air Service, RNAS

Air arm of the British Royal Navy during World War I, formed in July 1914 from naval officers and elements of the ◊Royal Flying Corps. The RNAS performed patrol duties over the North Sea, pioneered the use of aircraft carriers, and was also responsible for the air defence of Britain until 1916. It pioneered strategic bombing, attacking German airship bases as early as 1914.

Royal Naval Reserve

See ◊armed forces.

Royal Navy

The navy of Britain. For the navy today, see ◊armed forces.

Founding of the Navy

Alfred the Great established a navy in the 9th century, and by the 13th century there was already an official styled 'keeper of the king's ships'. This office grew to become the Navy Board in 1546, the body responsible for administering the fleet of Henry VIII, some 80 ships, with the *Great Harry* as his flagship. The Navy Board administered the navy until 1832, when the Board of Admiralty was instituted. The government head of the Admiralty was the First Lord of the Admiralty, while the senior serving officer in command of the navy was the First Sea Lord (now known as Chief of Naval Staff and First Sea Lord). The Admiralty was abolished in 1964 and replaced by the naval department of the Ministry of Defence.

> *The Royal Navy of England has ever been its greatest defence and ornament; it is its ancient and natural strength, the floating bulwark of the island.*
>
> William Blackstone English jurist. *Commentaries on the Laws of England*

A national force

It was only in the reign of Elizabeth I (1558–1603) that the navy grew from Henry's private fleet to become a national defensive force. It gained the title Royal Navy in the reign of Charles II (1660–85). During the 18th century the Royal Navy successfully vied for maritime supremacy with the French navy, leading Britain to victory in four separate wars between 1688 and 1763. It played a key role in Britain's stand against Napoleon and was never again challenged by the French after Trafalgar in 1805. Meanwhile the navy had been the means by which the British Empire extended round the world from the 17th century. The Royal Navy continued to be the world's most powerful navy well into the 20th century. In World War I its main task was to protect shipping from submarine attack. After World War II the Royal Navy was second in size only to the US Navy and continued to be a world leader, especially in submarine warfare. By the 1980s, however, as a result of defence cuts, the Royal Navy had declined to third in world size, after the USA and USSR. Despite this smaller presence, the Royal Navy has been responsible for Britain's nuclear deterrence from 1969 and in 1995 had a fleet of four nuclear submarines. As a fighting force in recent times the Royal Navy played a vital national role in the Falklands War in 1982 and also formed part of an international force in the Korean War 1950–53, Gulf War 1990–91, and Balkans War 1992–95.

Royal Opera

Opera company based at the Royal Opera House in Covent Garden, London. The opera was granted its royal charter in 1968. Lottery funds have been granted for major building work at the Opera House, but continuing financial difficulties have cast doubt over the future of both the company and theatre. Bernard Haitink resigned as musical director in September 1998, after it was proposed the company close for a year.

Royal Opera House

Britain's leading opera house, sited at Covent Garden, London.

The original theatre opened in 1732, was destroyed by fire in 1808 and reopened in 1809. It was again destroyed by fire in 1856, and the third and present building dates from 1858. It has been the home of the Royal Opera and the Royal Ballet since 1946.

Royal Pavilion, or Brighton Pavilion

Palace in Brighton, England, built in 1784 and bought in the early 19th century for the Prince Regent (the future George IV) who had it extensively rebuilt in a mix of classical and Indian styles. Queen Victoria was the last monarch to use it and it is now municipal property.

royal prerogative

Powers, immunities, and privileges recognized in common law as belonging to the crown. Most prerogative acts in the UK are now performed by the government on behalf of the crown. The royal prerogative belongs to the Queen as a person as well as to the institution called the crown, and the award of some honours and dignities remain her personal choice. As by prerogative 'the king can do no wrong', the monarch is immune from prosecution.

The royal prerogative is traceable to the days before Parliament existed. Examples include the conduct of foreign relations, making war and peace, the dissolution of Parliament, assent to bills, and the choice of ministers.

ROYAL PAVILION, BRIGHTON *The Royal Pavilion, rebuilt between 1815 and 1821 for the pleasure-loving Prince of Wales (later George IV). The Prince's favourite architect, John Nash, employed an exotic hybrid style that has been dubbed 'Hindoo-Gothic'. Philip Sauvain Picture Collection*

Royal Scottish Academy of Music and Drama

Institution in Scotland training musicians, actors, and other professionals in music and drama. Based in state-of-the-art premises in Glasgow, it is the only conservatoire in Scotland. Its principal is Dr Philip Ledger.

Royal Scottish National Orchestra

Orchestra based in Glasgow and regularly touring to other locations in Scotland, England, and beyond. Its principal conductor is Alexander Lazarev.

Royal Shakespeare Company, RSC

British professional theatre company that performs Shakespearean and other plays. It was founded in 1961 from the company at the Shakespeare Memorial Theatre (1932, now the Royal Shakespeare Theatre) in Stratford-upon-Avon, Warwickshire, England, and produces plays in Stratford and the Barbican Centre in London.

The RSC initially presented mainly Shakespeare at Stratford; these productions were usually transferred to the Aldwych Theatre, London, where the company also performed modern plays and non-Shakespearean classics. In 1982 it moved into a permanent London headquarters at the Barbican. A second large theatre in Stratford, the Swan, opened in 1986 with an auditorium similar to theatres of Shakespeare's day.

The first director of the RSC was Peter Hall. In 1968 Trevor Nunn replaced him, and in 1986 Nunn was succeeded by Terry Hands. Adrian Noble has been director since 1990.

Royal Society

Oldest and premier scientific society in Britain, originating in 1645 and chartered in 1662; Robert Boyle, Christopher ◊Wren, and Isaac ◊Newton were prominent early members. Its Scottish equivalent is the **Royal Society of Edinburgh** (1783).

Royal Society for the Protection of Birds, RSPB

UK charity, founded in 1889, aiming to conserve and protect wild birds, both in the UK and overseas. It has a network of reserves in all types of habitat (73,000 ha/180,000 acres), and is the largest voluntary wildlife-conservation body in Europe, with a membership of 827,000 (1990).

Royal Society of Chemistry

Society formed in the UK in 1980, merging the Chemical Society (founded in 1841) and the Royal Institute of Chemistry (founded in 1877). The society's object, as stated in its royal charter, is the general advancement of chemical science and its applications, serving to that end as a learned society, a professional body, and a representative body. It is recognized in the UK and internationally as an authoritative voice of chemistry and chemists.

Royce, (Frederick) Henry (1863–1933)

British engineer who so impressed Charles ◊Rolls with the car he built in 1904 that ◊Rolls-Royce Ltd was formed in 1906 to produce automobiles and aeroengines. Baronet 1930.

Royston

Town in Hertfordshire, England, 21 km/13 mi southwest of Cambridge; population (1991) 13,600. It is situated on the pre-Roman ◊Icknield Way. Royston has a 13th-century church.

The **Royston Cave**, a Roman burial place and oratory, was discovered in 1742. It is dug out of the chalk, is 8 m/26 ft high and 5 m/16 ft in diameter, and contains rough figures and coloured reliefs of saints, kings, and queens. Most figures were made at the time of the Crusades (12th and 13th centuries).

Therfield Heath, to the southwest of the town, is a rolling heathland of 168 ha/415 acres open to the public, where golf and other games are played. Hunting and coursing take place here.

RSI

Abbreviation for ◊repetitive strain injury, a condition affecting workers, such as typists, who repeatedly perform certain movements with their hands and wrists.

RSPCA, Royal Society for the Prevention of Cruelty to Animals

British organization formed in 1824 to safeguard the welfare of animals; it promotes legislation, has an inspectorate to secure enforcement of existing laws, and runs clinics. In 1997 it had 43,000 members, 1,200 paid staff, an income of £43.4 million, and annual expenditure of £40.8 million.

Rt Hon

Abbreviation for **Right Honourable**, title of members of the Privy Council (including all present and former UK Cabinet members).

Rubbra, Edmund (1901–1986)

English composer. He studied under the composer Gustav Holst and specialized in contrapuntal writing, as exemplified in his study *Counterpoint* (1960). His compositions include 11 symphonies, chamber music, and songs. In 1948 he became a Roman Catholic, and his later music shows the influence of Catholic mysticism.

rugby

Contact sport that is traditionally believed to have originated at Rugby School, England, in 1823 when a boy, William Webb Ellis, picked up the ball and ran with it while playing football (now soccer). Rugby is played with an oval ball. It is now played in two forms: ◊**Rugby League** and ◊**Rugby Union**.

Rugby

Market town and railway junction in Warwickshire, central England, on the River Avon, 19 km/12 southeast of Coventry; population (1991) 60,500. Industries include engineering and the manufacture of cement, and the town has a cattle market. **Rugby School** (1567), a private school for boys, established its reputation under headmaster Thomas Arnold; it was described in Thomas Hughes' semi-autobiographical classic *Tom Brown's Schooldays*. ◊Rugby football originated at the school in 1823. The poet Rupert Brooke was born here in 1887.

A village until the early 19th century, Rugby expanded with the advent of the London–Birmingham railway in 1838.

Rugby League

Professional form of rugby football founded in England in 1895 as the Northern Union when a dispute about pay caused northern clubs to break away from the Rugby Football Union. The game is similar to ◊Rugby Union, but the number of players was reduced from 15 to 13 in 1906, and other rule changes have made the game more open and fast-moving.

Major events include the Challenge Cup final, first held in 1897 and since 1929 staged at Wembley Stadium, and the Premiership Trophy, introduced at the end of the 1974–75 season, which is a knockout competition involving the top eight clubs in the first division. In March 1996 the game was played during the summer season for the first time, when the Super League began in the UK comprised of 12 teams, including Paris. In 1997 a world club championship between teams from the British and Australian Super League (which includes teams from New Zealand) was inaugurated.

Rugby Union

Form of rugby in which there are 15 players on each side. Points are scored by 'tries', scored by 'touching down' the ball beyond the goal line or by kicking goals from penalties. The

Rugby Football Union was formed in 1871 and has its headquarters in England (Twickenham, Middlesex). Formerly an amateur game, the game's status was revoked in August 1995 by the International Rugby Football Board, which lifted restrictions on players moving between Rugby Union and Rugby League.

The first World Cup, the William Webb Ellis trophy, held in Australia and New Zealand in 1987, was won by New Zealand. Other major events include the International Championship (Five Nations), instituted in 1884, now a tournament between England, France, Ireland, Scotland, and Wales (to be expanded in 2000 to include Italy); the Tetley Bitter Cup, the SWALEC Cup, and the Tennents Cup, the club knockout tournaments of the English, Welsh, and Scottish rugby unions. Each of the home countries also stage league championships. Rugby Union (along with cricket) was introduced to the Commonwealth Games for the first time at Kuala Lumpur, Malaysia, in September 1998.

Rugeley

Town on the edge of Cannock Chase in Staffordshire, England, 14 km/9 mi southeast of Stafford, on the River Trent; population (1991) 40,000. Electronic equipment is manufactured here, and the town also has iron foundries and tanneries. Lea Hall colliery, sunk in the early 1960s, was closed in 1990 along with the adjacent power station. The grammar school was founded in the 17th century.

Lea Hall colliery was a large pit producing over a million tons of coal per annum. Much of this was consumed directly in the adjacent power station. A large industrial estate now lies on the site of the former colliery.

'Rule, Britannia'

A patriotic song by Thomas Arne, now almost a second British national anthem, originally part of the masque *Alfred*, produced on 1 August 1740, at Cliefden (now Cliveden) House near Maidenhead, the residence of Frederick, Prince of Wales.

Rule Britannia

Words by James Thomson.

When Britain first, at heaven's command
Arose from out the azure main
This was the charter the charter of the land
And guardian Angels sung this strain:

Rule, Britannia, rule the waves
Britons never will be slaves.

The nations, not so blest as thee
Must, in their turns, to tyrants fall
While thou shalt flourish great and free
The dread and envy of them all.

Still more majestic shalt thou rise
More dreadful, from each foreign stroke
As the loud blast that tears the skies
Serves but to root thy native oak.

Thee haughty tyrants ne'er shall tame
All their attempts to bend thee down
Will but arouse thy generous flame
But work their woe, and thy renown.

To thee belongs the rural reign
Thy cities shall with commerce shine
All thine shall be the subject main
And every shore it circles thine.

The Muses, still with freedom found
Shall to thy happy coast repair
Blest isle! with matchless beauty crowned
And manly hearts to guard the fair.

Rum, or Rhum

Island of the Inner ◊Hebrides, Highland unitary authority, Scotland, area 110 sq km/42 sq mi, a nature reserve since 1957. Askival is 810 m/2,658 ft high.

The island is owned by Scottish National Heritage, known as the Nature Conservatory Council when it was purchased in 1957. It is served by passenger ferries from the port of Kinloch to Muck, Canna, Eigg, and Mallaig on the mainland.

Rumford, Benjamin Thompson, Count von Rumford (1753–1814)

American-born British physicist and inventor. In 1798, impressed by the seemingly inexhaustible amounts of heat generated in the boring of a cannon, he published his theory that heat is a mode of vibratory motion, not a substance.

Rumford spied for the British in the American Revolution, and was forced to flee from America to England in 1776. He travelled in Europe, and was knighted and created a count of the Holy Roman Empire for services to the Elector of Bavaria in 1784.

Rumford devised the domestic range – the 'fire in a box' – and fireplaces incorporating all the features now considered essential in open fires and chimneys, such as the smoke shelf and damper.

Rump, the

English parliament formed between December 1648 and November 1653 after Pride's purge of the ◊Long Parliament to ensure a majority in favour of trying Charles I. It was dismissed in 1653 by Cromwell, who replaced it with the ◊Barebones Parliament.

Reinstated after the Protectorate ended in 1659 and the full membership of the Long Parliament was restored in 1660, the Rump dissolved itself shortly afterwards and was replaced by the Convention Parliament, which brought about the restoration of the monarchy.

Runcie, Robert Alexander Kennedy, Baron Runcie (1921–)

English cleric, archbishop of Canterbury 1980–91, the first to be appointed on the suggestion of the Church Crown Appointments Commission (formed in 1977) rather than by political consultation. He favoured ecclesiastical remarriage for the divorced and the eventual introduction of the ordination of women. Baron 1991.

Runcorn

Industrial town in Cheshire, northwest England, on the River Mersey and the Manchester Ship Canal, 24 km/15 mi from

Liverpool; population (1991) 63,000. Designated a ◊new town in 1964, it has received Merseyside overspill. Industries include brewing, the production of chemicals, and high-technology industries.

Runnymede

Meadow on the south bank of the River Thames near Egham in Surrey, England, where on 15 June 1215 King John put his seal to the ◊Magna Carta.

Runrig

Scottish folk/rock group formed in 1973. Their music, mainly sung in Gaelic, has won an international following and reflects Gaelic cultural, musical, and historical traditions. Their albums include *Recovery* (1981), *The Big Wheel* (1991), and *The Gaelic Collection* (1998). Their single ' An Unbal As Airde' was the first Gaelic single to reach the UK Top 20.

The Canadian vocalist Bruce Guthro joined the group in 1998 following the departure of Donnie Monro who left the group in 1997 to become a politician.

Rupert, Prince, or Rupert of the Rhine (1619–1682)

English Royalist general and admiral, born in Prague, son of the Elector Palatine Frederick V and James I's daughter Elizabeth. Defeated by Cromwell at ◊Marston Moor and ◊Naseby in the Civil War, he commanded a privateering fleet 1649–52, until routed by Admiral Robert Blake, and, returning after the Restoration, was a distinguished admiral in the Dutch Wars. He founded the Hudson's Bay Company.

Rusedski, Greg(ory) (1973–)

Canadian-born British tennis player. A left-hander renowned for his world record-breaking fast serves, in September 1997 he became the first Briton to reach a final of a Grand Slam men's singles tournament since Fred ◊Perry in 1936 when he was runner-up to Patrick Rafter in the US Open. A month later Rusedski advanced to fourth place in the ATP world rankings, the highest position by a British male since the ranking system was introduced in 1973. In November 1998 he defeated Pete Sampras, the world's number one tennis player, at the Paris Indoor Open.

Rushdie, (Ahmed) Salman (1947–)

British writer. He was born in Bombay, India, of a Muslim family, and later lived in Pakistan before moving to the UK. *Midnight's Children* (1981), deals with India from the date of independence and won the Booker Prize. His novel *The Satanic Verses* (1988) (the title refers to verses deleted from the Koran) offended many Muslims with alleged blasphemy. In 1989 the Ayatollah Khomeini of Iran placed a religious *fatwa* on Rushdie, calling for him and his publishers to be killed, and the furore caused by the publication of the book led to the withdrawal of British diplomats from Iran. In India and elsewhere, people were killed in demonstrations against the book and Rushdie was forced to go into hiding. In September 1998 the Iranian government pledged formally to dissociate itself from the *fatwa* placed on Rushdie by the late Ayatollah Khomeini. The *fatwa*, however, continued to stand. The agreement which had been under secret negotiation between the two governments since early 1998, ended nearly ten years of diplomatic chill between Britain and Iran. Both sides agreed on the normalization of diplomatic relations and the imminent exchange of ambassadors.

Rushdie's publications produced while he was in hiding include *Haroun and the Sea of Stories* (1990) (for children), *Imaginary Homelands* (1991) (essays and criticism), *East and West* (1994) (short stories), and a further novel, *The Moor's Last Sigh* (1995).

Ruskin, John (1819–1900)

English art and social critic. Much of his finest art criticism appeared in two widely influential works, *Modern Painters* (1843–60) and *The Seven Lamps of Architecture* (1849). He was a keen advocate of painters considered unorthodox at the time, such as J M W ◊Turner and members of the ◊Pre-Raphaelite Brotherhood. His later writings were concerned with social and economic problems.

Ruskin was one of the major figures of 19th-century British intellectual life. Like his contemporaries Thomas

RUSKIN, JOHN *English art critic John Ruskin, photographed in old age. He was an enormously prolific writer and was far and away the most influential British writer on art in the 19th century. He was also a talented watercolour painter, but he devoted much of his later life to social reform rather than art. His personal life was wretched, marked by disappointment in love and later by mental illness. Corbis*

◊Carlyle and Matthew ◊Arnold, he was an outspoken critic of Victorian society, and, like them, called for a renewal of British moral, intellectual, and artistic life. His early works were concerned with architecture and painting: his support both for the Pre-Raphaelite Brotherhood and the ◊Gothic Revival had a profound effect on Victorian art, architecture, and crafts.

From these aesthetic concerns he increasingly drew social and moral views, and from the 1860s he devoted himself to political and economic problems, condemning *laissez-faire* economics, and extolling both the dignity of labour and the moral and aesthetic value of 'craftsmanship'. His beliefs took a practical turn, and he played a leading role in providing education and decent housing for working people.

Russell, Bertrand Arthur William, 3rd Earl Russell (1872–1970)

English philosopher and mathematician. He contributed to the development of modern mathematical logic and wrote about social issues. His works include *Principia Mathematica* (with A N ◊Whitehead, 1910–13), in which he attempted to show that mathematics could be reduced to a branch of logic; *The Problems of Philosophy* (1912); and *A History of Western Philosophy* (1946). He was an outspoken liberal pacifist.

Russell, Dora Winifred born Black (1894–1986)

English feminist who married Bertrand Russell in 1921. The 'openness' of their marriage (she subsequently had children by another man) was a matter of controversy. She was a founding member of the National Council for Civil Liberties in 1934.

Russell, Frederick Stratten (1897–1984)

English marine biologist who studied the life histories and distribution of plankton. He also discovered a means of distinguishing between different species of fish shortly after they have hatched, when they are almost identical in appearance. Knighted 1965.

The British are distinguished among the nations of modern Europe, on the one hand by the excellence of their philosophers, and on the other hand by their contempt for philosophy. In both respects they show their wisdom.

Bertrand Russell English philosopher and mathematician. *Unpopular Essays* (1950)

Russell, 'Jack' Robert Charles (1963–)

English cricketer. The finest wicketkeeper in England of his generation, he made his Test debut in 1988, and at the end of the 1998 English season had achieved 165 dismissals in 54 Tests. He would have won more caps than this if his batting had been more highly regarded by the England selectors, however he has still managed two Test centuries. At Johannesburg in 1995–96 against South Africa he set a new Test record of 11 dismissals in a match. He made his first-class debut for Gloucestershire in 1981 and was appointed county captain in 1995.

Russell, John, 1st Earl Russell known until 1861 as **Lord John Russell** (1792–1878)

British Liberal politician, son of the 6th Duke of Bedford. He entered the House of Commons in 1813 and supported Catholic emancipation and the Reform Bill. He held cabinet posts 1830–41, became prime minister 1846–52, and was again a cabinet minister until becoming prime minister again 1865–66. He retired after the defeat of his Reform Bill in 1866.

As foreign secretary in Aberdeen's coalition in 1852 and in Palmerston's second government 1859–65, Russell assisted Italy's struggle for unity, although his indecisive policies on Poland, Denmark, and the American Civil War provoked much criticism. He had a strained relationship with Palmerston.

Russell, Ken (Henry Kenneth Alfred) (1927–)

English film director. His work, typified by stylistic extravagance, includes *Women in Love* (1969), *The Music Lovers* (1971), *Tommy* (1975), *Lisztomania* (1975), and *Gothic* (1986). His work is often criticized for self-indulgence, containing gratuitous sex and violence, but is also highly regarded for its vitality and imagination.

Russell has made television biographies of the lives of the composers Edward Elgar, Frederick Delius, and Richard Strauss. In the 1990s he worked widely in television, directing *Lady Chatterley* (1992) and *Dogboys* (1998), among others.

Russell, William, Lord (1639–1683)

British Whig politician. Son of the 1st Duke of Bedford, he was among the founders of the Whig Party, and actively supported attempts in Parliament to exclude the Roman Catholic James II from succeeding to the throne. In 1683 he was accused, on dubious evidence, of complicity in the ◊Rye House Plot to murder Charles II, and was executed. He used the courtesy title Lord Russell from 1678.

Russell, Willy (William Martin) (1947–)

English playwright. His best-known plays are *Educating Rita* (1979) and *Shirley Valentine* (1986), both of which were made into successful films. He also wrote the musicals *John, Paul, George, Ringo, and Bert* (1974) and *Blood Brothers* (1983).

He worked as a ladies' hairdresser until 1969, which he said taught him invaluable lessons about how women perceive and talk about their lives.

Russell Beale, Simon (1961–)

Scottish-born actor. He joined the Royal Shakespeare Company in 1986, where his roles have included Konstantin in Anton Chekhov's *The Seagull* (1990) and the title role in *Richard III* (1992). His roles at the Royal National Theatre have included Iago in *Othello* (1997). He won the Royal Television Society Award and the BAFTA Best Actor Award for his acting of Widmerpool in *Dance to the Music of Time* (1996).

Born in Edinburgh, Russell Beale trained at the Guildhall School of Music and Drama. He first came to notice for his performance in *Women Beware Women* (1986) at the Royal Court Theatre. He is an Associate of the Royal Shakespeare Company.

Rutherford, Ernest, 1st Baron Rutherford of Nelson (1871–1937)

New Zealand-born British physicist. He was a pioneer of modern atomic science. His main research was in the field of radioactivity, and he discovered alpha, beta, and gamma rays. He was the first to recognize the nuclear nature of the atom in 1911. He was awarded a Nobel prize in 1908. Knighted 1914, Baron 1931.

Rutherford produced the first artificial transformation, changing one element to another (1919), bombarding nitrogen with alpha particles and getting hydrogen and oxygen. After further research he announced that the nucleus of any atom must be composed of hydrogen nuclei; at Rutherford's suggestion, the name 'proton' was given to the hydrogen nucleus in 1920. He speculated that uncharged particles (neutrons) must also exist in the nucleus.

In 1934, using heavy water, Rutherford and his co-workers bombarded deuterium with deuterons and produced tritium. This may be considered the first nuclear fusion reaction.

Rutherford, Margaret (1892–1972)

English film and theatre actress. She specialized in formidable yet jovially eccentric roles. She played Agatha Christie's Miss Marple in four films in the early 1960s and won an Academy Award for her role in *The VIPs* (1963). She was made a DBE in 1967.

Rutland

Unitary authority in central England, formerly the smallest English county, which was part of ◊Leicestershire 1974–1997
Area 394 sq km/152 sq mi
Towns and cities ◊Oakham (administrative headquarters), Uppingham
Physical rivers Chater, Eye, Gwash, and Welland
Features Rutland Water, a large reservoir in the valley of the Gwash at Empingham, with outdoor leisure facilities (sailing, cycling, bird watching); historic villages and churches including Braunston-in-Rutland, Preston, Wing, and Exton.
Industries clothing, engineering, and plastics; limestone and ironstone are quarried
Agriculture cereals (barley, wheat), sugar beet, potatoes; sheep and cattle are reared, and Stilton cheese is produced
Population (1997) 34,600

Topography

Rutland is bounded to the north and east by Lincolnshire; to the north and west by Leicestershire; and on the southeast by Northamptonshire. The surface is broken by low hills forming valleys, of which the chief is the Vale of Catmose. Between Oakham and Uppingham the county was at one time covered by Lyfield or Leafield Forest, part of which formed the hunting land of Beaumont Chase.

Rutter, John (1945–)

English composer and choral director. He has written carols, anthems, and other choral music (mostly sacred) for use by non-professional choirs. He edited and recorded the original version of Fauré's Requiem in 1984 and composed his own Requiem the following year.

He studied at Cambridge and founded the Cambridge Singers in 1981; they made their US debut in 1990.

Ryde

English resort on the northeast coast of the Isle of Wight, on the Solent opposite Portsmouth, with which there is ferry and hovercraft connection; population (1991) 20,500.

Ryder, Susan (1923–)

British philanthropist and founder of the **Sue Ryder Foundation**, a charity which helps the sick and disabled of all ages. In 1959 she married Leonard ◊Cheshire. She became a life peeress in 1978.

Ryder Cup

Golf tournament for professional men's teams from the USA and Europe. It is played every two years, and the match is made up of a series of singles, foursomes, and fourballs played over three days.

Named after entrepreneur Samuel Ryder, who donated the trophy in 1927, the tournament is played alternately in the USA and Europe. The match was between the USA and Great Britain 1927–71; USA v. Great Britain and Ireland 1973–77, and USA v. Europe from 1979.

Rye

Town in East Sussex, southeast England; population (1991) 3,700. It was formerly a flourishing port (and one of the ◊Cinque Ports), but silt washed down by the River Rother has left it 3 km/2 mi inland. Rye has a pottery, but there are no major industries.

Features

Rye has picturesque cobbled streets and medieval, Tudor, and Georgian buildings. Ypres Tower, built as a fort in about 1250, now houses a museum of local history. The Mermaid Inn, in the cobbled Mermaid Street, dates from the early 15th century. St Mary's church, of Norman to Perpendicular origins, includes a clock which is said to have the oldest functioning pendulum in England (dating from about 1560). The 18th-century Lamb House was once the home of the US novelist Henry James, and it was later the residence of the writer E F Benson (mayor of Rye 1934–37). Peacock's School was established in 1636. To the south are the remains of Camber Castle, built by Henry VIII.

History

In medieval times Rye was a major port, handling iron and timber and the cross-Channel trade. It suffered many naval attacks and was burned by the French in 1377. It became a full member of the Cinque Ports confederation in 1350, but its importance declined as the Rother began to silt up in the 16th century.

Famous people

The dramatist John Fletcher was born here in 1579.

Rye House Plot

Conspiracy of 1683 by English Whig extremists against Charles II for his Roman Catholic leanings. They intended to murder Charles and his brother James, Duke of York, at Rye House, Hoddesdon, Hertfordshire, but the plot was betrayed. The Duke of ◊Monmouth was involved, and alleged conspirators, including Lord William ◊Russell and Algernon Sidney (1622–1683), were executed for complicity.

Rylance, Mark (1960–)

English actor and director. In 1995 he became the first artistic director of the reconstructed ◊Globe Theatre, London. He has played leading roles in classical and modern plays with the Royal Shakespeare Company (RSC). His films include *Prospero's Books* (1991) and *Angels and Insects* (1995). In 1991 he formed his own theatre company, Phoebus Cart.

He received the 1994 Olivier Award for best actor for his role as Benedick in *Much Ado About Nothing*. Critics were equally thrilled by his more modern roles, in such productions as Gogol's *Gamblers* (1992) and Sam Shepard's *True West* (1994). Rylance has also appeared in several television films, including *The Grass Arena* (1993), *Institute Bejamenta* (1994), and *Loving* (1995).

Ryle, Gilbert (1900–1976)

British philosopher. His *The Concept of Mind* (1949) set out to show that the distinction between an inner and an outer world in philosophy and psychology cannot be sustained. He ridiculed the mind–body dualism of the French philosopher René Descartes as the doctrine of 'the Ghost in the Machine'.

Ryle, Martin (1918–1984)

English radio astronomer. At the Mullard Radio Astronomy Observatory, Cambridge, he developed the technique of sky-mapping using 'aperture synthesis', combining smaller dish aerials to give the characteristics of one large one. His work on the distribution of radio sources in the universe brought confirmation of the Big Bang theory. He was knighted in 1966, and won, with his co-worker Antony ◊Hewish, the Nobel Prize for Physics in 1974.

Rysbrack, Jan Michiel (1694–1770)

Dutch-born sculptor, settled in England from 1720. Working in a style of restrained Baroque, he established an extensive practice in monumental sculpture, his work being found in many English churches. Some of his portraits and tombs are in Westminster Abbey, London, including the monument to the scientist Isaac Newton (1731). He also created the equestrian statue of William III in Queen Square, Bristol (1735).

S4C, Sianel Pedwar Cymru (Channel Four Wales)
Welsh television station with a duty to transmit programmes in Welsh, especially in the evening. At other times it shows Channel 4 programmes. Based in Cardiff, it began broadcasting in 1982 and is financed by a government grant and income from advertising. S4C is regulated by the Welsh Fourth Channel Authority, whose members are appointed by government.

Saatchi & Saatchi plc
British advertising, communications, and consulting company. Founded by the brothers Charles (1943–) and Maurice Saatchi (1946–) in 1970, by the mid-1980s it had become the world's largest advertising company. In 1995 the Saatchi & Saatchi group changed its name to Cordiant plc, after the departure of the founding brothers to form the New Saatchi Agency.

Saatchi & Saatchi is particularly associated with the Conservative Party under Margaret Thatcher; it produced the party's successful election campaign in 1979 (and also helped her in 1983). One advertisement showed a long line of unemployed workers and said, in a simple pun: 'Labour isn't working'.

Saatchi Collection
Large UK collection of contemporary art, including much British art. It was formed by the businessman Charles Saatchi (1943–) and opened to the public in 1985 in a converted warehouse in north London. Saatchi's huge wealth enabled him to become a major British patron of contemporary art. He has been praised for supporting artists, but also criticized for helping to create an art market based on superficial trends and the investment value of works rather than on serious aesthetic merit.

The controversial Sensation exhibition of avant-garde British art at the Royal Academy, London, in 1997 was drawn from works in the Saatchi Collection.

Sacks, Jonathan Henry (1948–)
English rabbi, Chief Rabbi of the United Hebrew Congregations of the British Commonwealth of Nations since 1991. He was a lecturer at Jews College, London, from 1973 until 1982, when he was appointed the first Sir Immanuel (later Lord) Jakobovits Professor of Modern Jewish Thought. His books include *Crisis and Covenant* (1992), *One People? Tradition, Modernity, and Jewish Unity* (1993), and *The Politics of Hope* (1997).

Sackville-West, Vita (Victoria Mary) (1892–1962)
English writer. Her novels include *The Edwardians* (1930) and *All Passion Spent* (1931); she also wrote the long pastoral poem

SACKVILLE-WEST, VITA *English novelist and poet Vita Sackville-West. One of the most colourful and flamboyant figures of English literary life in the 1920s and 1930s, she was the model for the central character in the novel Orlando (1928) by her close friend Virginia Woolf. Corbis*

The Land (1926). The fine gardens around her home at Sissinghurst, Kent, were created by her and her husband Harold Nicolson.

Virginia ◊Woolf was a close friend and based the novel *Orlando* (1928) on her.

Sadler's Wells

Theatre in Islington, north London, built in the 17th century. Originally a music hall, it was developed by Lilian Baylis as a northern annexe to the ◊Old Vic in 1931. For many years it housed the Sadler's Wells Opera Company (relocated to the London Coliseum in 1969 and known as the English National Opera Company from 1974) and the Sadler's Wells Ballet, which later became the ◊Royal Ballet.

Sadler's Wells Royal Ballet

Former name of the ◊Birmingham Royal Ballet.

Saffron Walden

Town in Essex, England, 26 km/16 mi southeast of Cambridge, and 74 km/46 mi northeast of London; population (1991) 13,400. Its church, the largest in Essex, dates from the 15th century and has a spire that was added in 1832. Nearby are the remains of a Norman keep. The town takes its name from the saffron crocus, which was once cultivated here.

The Sun Inn was the headquarters of Oliver Cromwell and Thomas Fairfax in 1647. The grammar school, endowed in 1525, was re-established by Edward VI. A museum, built in 1834, houses local and other antiquities.

The Guild of Our Lady of Pity, which founded and managed an almshouse for 13 residents, was granted a royal charter in 1400. In 1513 Henry VII replaced this by a charter, giving wider powers, to the Guild of the Holy Trinity. This charter was renewed by Edward VI in 1549, by James II in 1685, and by William and Mary in 1694.

About 2 km/1 mi from Saffron Walden is Audley End, a 16th-century house with 40 ha/98 acres of parkland and gardens. It was enlarged in the reign of James I, and takes its name from Thomas Audley, Speaker of the Commons from 1529 to 1532, and later lord chancellor, to whom in 1538 Henry VIII granted the manor of Walden. The property is now in the care of English Heritage.

Sainsbury's

Britain's largest supermarket chain, with 398 stores in the UK (1998) and 82,345 employees by 1997. It was founded in 1869 by John James Sainsbury (1844–1928), a grocer who from one dairy shop in Drury Lane, London, expanded to owning 14 food stores in London by 1891.

The corporation has provided financial backing for major projects in the arts, including Norman ◊Foster's High-Tech design for the Sainsbury Centre for Visual Arts (1978) and the Sainsbury Laboratory for molecular research (1987) (both in Norwich, Norfolk), and the Sainsbury Wing of the National Gallery, London (1991).

In January 1995 the company purchased the hardware firm, Texas Homecare Ltd, from the Ladbroke Group.

St Albans

City in Hertfordshire, England, on the River Ver, 40 km/25 mi northwest of London; population (1991) 80,400. The chief industries are electrical engineering, hosiery, clothing, information and legal services, musical instruments, and orchid culture. Printing is very important: one of the early presses set up in the late 15th century by the 'Scolemaster Printer', and his *The Book of St Albans* contains the earliest example of colour printing in England. There are the ruins of the Roman city of ◊Verulamium on Watling Street. A Benedictine abbey was founded in 793 in honour of St Alban, and it became a cathedral in 1878. Other features include the Clock Tower (1411) in the High Street; the Royal National Rose Society headquarters and gardens; Rothamsted Park agricultural research centre; the Organ Museum of mechanical musical instruments; and the Verulamium Museum, with its collection of Roman remains.

St Albans is the successor to the important Romano-British town of **Verulamium**. The martyrdom of St Alban traditionally took place there in 303; recent scholarship puts the date at about 254 or 209. St Alban was a Roman convert and the first Christian martyr in England. Offa, King of Mercia, is said to have rediscovered the coffin containing his bones. The Benedictine abbey founded by Offa in honour of the saint in about 793 and the medieval town, arose on the opposite side of the valley from Verulamium, that being the spot to which, according to tradition, St Alban was led for execution. Matthew Paris (died 1259), the historian monk of St Albans, mentions the benefactions of Abbot Wulsin or Ulsinus, who founded (950) the three parish churches, St Peter's, St Michael's, and St Stephen's, the abbey school, from which the present St Albans school claims direct succession, and the market. St Michael's church, which stands on part of the site of the forum of Verulamium contains a monument to Francis Bacon, Baron Verulam and Viscount St Albans (died 1626). Nearby are the impressive remains of the Roman theatre.

The cathedral

The abbey church, the present cathedral, has one of the longest naves in Europe. The tower is built of thin Roman bricks taken from the ruined buildings of Verulamium. The Saxon church was rebuilt at the end of the 11th century by Paul of Caen, the first Norman abbot, whose Norman work is among the earliest in the country. In contrast to the massive unadorned forms of the Norman arches is the presbytery, with its delicate late Gothic reredos, and Abbot Ramryge's (died 1520) chantry chapel. Further contrasts are afforded by the nave arcades of various periods, and owing to its great length the nave gains from this piecemeal rebuilding. The series of wall paintings on the west and south sides of the Norman piers in the north arcade of the nave belong in part to the time of Walter of Colchester, sacrist, 1213–48, and Matthew Paris. In the abbey is the tomb of Humphrey, Duke of Gloucester (died 1447), and an inscription to Sir John Mandeville.

The abbey gatehouse of stone and flint was built about 1360, supposedly from the designs of Henry Yevele, the king's master mason. Since 1871 it has formed part of the buildings of St Albans school, for the previous 300 years housed in the lady chapel of the abbey. The school was refounded in 1545 by Richard Boreman. Among its pupils were Alexander Neckam, foster brother of Richard the Lion-Heart, and possibly Nicholas Breakspear (the only English pope, as Adrian IV, 1154), and John Mandeville. The abbey and St Michael's and St Peter's churches alterations by Edmund Beckett, afterwards Lord Grimthorpe. In 1877 the abbey church was raised to cathedral status on the formation of the new diocese, though it is still widely known as the abbey.

The modern city

The market established in Saxon times is still held in the market place near the abbey. In spite of modern shop fronts and some rebuilding, some old houses still survive near the clock tower, which has dominated the scene for more than 500 years.

St Andrews

Town in Fife, Scotland, 19 km/12 mi southeast of Dundee; population (1991) 11,100. Its university (1411) is the oldest in Scotland. It is considered to be the 'home of golf', with a famous Old Course. The Royal and Ancient Club (1754) is the ruling body of golf. There is a cathedral, founded in 1160 and consecrated in 1318.

There are six golf courses, four of which, the Old, New, Eden, and Jubilee, are owned by the Links Trust; the Old Course dates from the 16th century. The Royal and Ancient Golf Club was so named in 1834, 80 years after its inception as the Society of St Andrews Golfers.

The town is named after St Andrew, the patron saint of Scotland. There are ruins of a castle (originally built in 1200). A fragment of wall and some archways are the only remnants of a wealthy Augustinian priory which Bishop Robert founded here in 1144.

The cathedral suffered iconoclastic damage provoked by a sermon by John Knox in the town's parish church Holy Trinity in 1559. In the 9th century, St Andrews was a bishopric.

St Austell

Market town in Cornwall, southwest England, 22 km/14 mi northeast of Truro; population (1991, with Fowey, with which it is administered) 21,600. It is the centre of the china-clay industry, which supplies the Staffordshire potteries.

The Eden Project, due to open in 2000, will create two 'biomes' (miniature ecosystems) – tropical rainforest and Mediterranea – in a giant greenhouse in a disused china-clay pit near St Austell; it is a Millennium Commission Landmark Project.

St Austell was formerly the centre of a tin- and copper-mining district. The Early English church has a fine Perpendicular tower. Part of the Parliamentary army had quarters here during the Civil War, shortly before the capture of Charles I in 1644. Originally called Trenance, the town takes its present name from St Austel, a hermit. Debris and slag heaps created by the china-clay industry are much in evidence in the surrounding landscape.

St David's, Welsh Tyddewi

Small town in Pembrokeshire, southwest Wales, situated on the River Alun just 2 km/1.2 mi from the sea. Its cathedral, founded by ◊St David, the patron saint of Wales, was rebuilt between 1180 and 1522. Formerly the resort of pilgrims, the town is now a summer tourist centre.

St David settled here in the 6th century. His relics are preserved in the sandstone cathedral, which contains the stone screen of Bishop Gower (died 1347), the carved stalls of Bishop Tully (died 1481), and the fan-vaulting of Bishop Vaughan (died 1522). There are also splendid ruins of Bishop Gower's 14th-century palace.

St George's Channel

Stretch of water between southwest Wales and southeast Ireland, linking the ◊Irish Sea with the Atlantic Ocean. It is 160 km/100 mi long and 80–150 km/50–90 mi wide.

ST DAVID'S *Situated in Pembrokeshire, west Wales, St David's is remarkable for being the smallest cathedral city in the British Isles. The cathedral itself is a huge building constructed mainly of sandstone, but with a highly ornate flat timber ceiling dating from the late 15th century. John D. Beldom/Collections*

St Helena

British island in the south Atlantic, 1,900 km/1,200 mi west of Africa, area 122 sq km/47 sq mi; population (1997) 5,644. Ascension and Tristan da Cunha are dependencies. St Helena became a British possession in 1673, and a colony in 1834.

St Helens

Town in Merseyside, northwest England, 19 km/12 mi northeast of Liverpool, and connected to the River Mersey by canal; population (1991) 104,700. Formerly a coalmining town, St Helens is now a major centre for the manufacture of sheet glass. Other industries include the manufacture of tiles, engineering, and pharmaceuticals.

The history of glass manufacture in St Helens, dating back to the late 18th century, is illustrated in the Pilkington Glass Museum. Coalmining began in the 16th century, and in 1757 the Sankey Canal was constructed to carry coal from St Helens to Liverpool, Warrington, and to Northwich for the growing salt industry.

St Helier

Resort and capital of Jersey, Channel Islands; population (1991) 28,100. The 'States of Jersey', the island legislature, sits here in the *salle des états*.

St Ives

Fishing port and resort in Cornwall; population (1991) 10,100. Its artists' colony, founded by Walter Sickert and James Whistler, later included Naum Gabo, Barbara ◊Hepworth (a museum and sculpture gardens commemorate her), and Ben Nicholson. A branch of the Tate Gallery opened here in 1993, displaying works of art from the Tate's collection by artists connected with St Ives.

St Ives

Market town in Cambridgeshire, eastern England, on the River Ouse, 18 km/11 mi east of Huntingdon; population (1991) 14,700. There is a 15th-century church and a 15th-century bridge, in the centre of which is a restored two-storey chapel.

A priory was founded here in the 12th century. Historically, St Ives owed its importance to the annual St Ives Fair, first held in 1110.

St Ives School

Ill-defined group of English artists, working in a wide range of styles, who lived in the fishing port of St Ives, Cornwall, after the outbreak of World War II. The group included Ben ◊Nicholson and Barbara ◊Hepworth.

St James's Palace

Palace in London. It was commissioned by Henry VIII in 1530 on the site of a hospital for leprous women founded at about the time of the Norman Conquest. Of Henry's palace only the imposing gateway survives, since much was destroyed by fire in 1809. It became the official residence of the sovereign from 1698, after Whitehall Palace was destroyed by fire, until 1837 when Queen Victoria chose Buckingham Palace.

The British Court is still officially styled 'the Court of St James'; the palace is now used for apartments for court officials. **St James's Park** (enlarged by Charles II) formed the palace grounds.

Charles I spent his last night here. Adjacent is the Queen's Chapel (1623–27) by Inigo Jones.

St John's Wood

Residential suburb of northwest London. It is the site of Lord's cricket ground, headquarters of the Marylebone Cricket Club (MCC).

St Kilda

Archipelago of four islands, sea stacks, and skerries, the most westerly of the Outer ◊Hebrides, Western Isles, 200 km/124 mi west of the Scottish mainland. They were populated from prehistory until 1930, and now form a National Nature Reserve belonging to the National Trust of Scotland. They have the world's largest colony of gannets, the oldest and largest colony of fulmars in the British Isles, and a large population of puffins. St Kilda is a World Heritage Site.

On Hirta, the largest island, there is a radar base for tracking guided missiles from the rocket range on South Uist. The cliffs at Conachair, 425 m/1,394 ft high, are the tallest in Britain. The islands are populated by about 1,400 Soay sheep.

In 1957, the Marquis of Bute bequeathed St Kilda to the National Trust of Scotland who leased them to the then Nature Conservatory Council as a National Nature Reserve. St Kilda is also a Biosphere Reserve (1976), a National Scenic Area (1981), a Site of Special Scientific Interest (1984) and a European Community Special Protection Area (1992).

St Leger

Horse race held at Doncaster, England, every September. It is a flat race over 2.8 km/3,060 yd, and is the last classic of the season. First held in 1776, it is the oldest of the English classic races.

St Leonards

Seaside town near ◊Hastings, England.

St Mary's

Largest of the Isles of ◊Scilly, off the coast of Cornwall, southwest England, 48 km/30 mi from Land's End; population (1991) 1,500. Tourism and the cultivation and export of flowers are important. The island's largest town, Hugh Town, is the capital of the Scilly Isles. A helicopter service runs between the aerodrome on St Mary's and Penzance, Cornwall.

St Michael and St George

British orders of ◊knighthood.

St Michael's Mount

Small island in Mount's Bay, Cornwall, southwest England; population (1981) 26. It is linked to Marazion on the mainland by a causeway which is submerged at high tide

St Michael's Mount, owned by the National Trust, is

formed of granite and slate rock. There is a castle on the summit (76 m/250 ft) which includes a 14th-century chapel. It is thought that a church was built here in the 5th century, and it was the site of a Celtic monastery in the 8th century. In the 11th century the island was given by Edward the Confessor to the Benedictine abbey of Mont St Michel off the coast of northwest France. It remained a priory of this abbey until the reign of Henry V.

St Paul's Cathedral

Cathedral church of the City of London, the largest Protestant church in England, and a national mausoleum second only to Westminster Abbey. An earlier Norman building, which had replaced the original 7th-century Saxon church, was burned down in the Great Fire of 1666. The present cathedral, a magnificent combination of Gothic plan and Classic detail, was designed by Christopher ◊Wren and built from 1675 to 1711. His assistants included Nicholas Hawksmoor, Grinling Gibbons, Caius Gabriel Cibber, and Jean Tijou, the Huguenot iron worker.

The lantern of the dome is ingeniously supported on a brick cone, concealed between the inner dome and the outer, and curves almost hemispherically. Its ceiling is decorated with scenes from the life of St Paul by James ◊Thornhill. Wren's chapter-house was destroyed in the German raids of 1940–41, which also damaged the choir and high altar.

The **Old St Paul's**, completed in 1287, had the tallest spire and was probably the largest church in Christendom.

St Peter Port

Only town of Guernsey, Channel Islands; population (1991) 16,650.

Saki pen name of H(ector) H(ugh) Munro (1870–1916)

Burmese-born British writer. He produced ingeniously witty and bizarre short stories, often with surprise endings. He also wrote two novels, *The Unbearable Bassington* (1912) and *When William Came* (1913).

He served with the Military Police in Burma, and was foreign correspondent of the *Morning Post* 1902–08. He was killed in action on the western front in World War I.

Salford

Industrial city in Greater Manchester, northwest England, on the west bank of the River Irwell and the Manchester Ship Canal; population (1991) 80,600. Industries include engineering and the manufacture of electrical goods and textiles.

Features include the Roman Catholic Cathedral of St John (1844–48) and Salford University (1966), founded in 1896 as the Royal Technical Institute. The artist L S Lowry lived in Salford for much of his life; a new arts centre, the Lowry Centre, is being developed as a Millennium Commission Landmark Project

Features

The city Art Gallery and Museum contains a large collection of paintings by L S Lowry. Building of the Lowry Centre began in the late 1990s. It has a waterfront location at the site of Salford Quays, and is the first purpose-built centre in the UK to integrate the visual and performing arts, with two theatres to seat 1,650 and 400, and a gallery to house the Lowry collection. A National Industrial Centre for Visual Reality is to be sited adjacent to the Lowry Centre.

Part of the docks area has been redeveloped to provide leisure facilities and housing. The Lancashire Mining Museum is housed in a building designed (1825–29) by Charles Barry. The Neo-Classical St Philip's Church (1825) was designed by Robert Smirke. Among the Georgian houses in the Crescent is the former home of the scientist James Prescott Joule. Ordsall Hall (1350), close to the docks, has a 15th-century interior.

History

Traditionally regarded as separate from Manchester, Salford became a county borough in 1888, and in 1926 it became a city to celebrate the seventh centenary of its original charter. With the growth of the cotton, textile, and engineering industries in the 19th century, the city's population expanded rapidly and social problems resulted from overcrowding and the building of much poor quality housing. Salford reached its population peak of 234,000 in 1921. Many of the 19th-century houses were demolished after World War II, and the population declined dramatically in the second half of the 20th century.

Famous people

Salford was the birthplace of the scientist James Prescott Joule, the conductor John Barbirolli, and the novelist Walter Greenwood. A 17th-century draper and astronomer, William Crabtree, is said to have sighted Venus for the first time here in 1639.

Salisbury

City and market town in Wiltshire, south England, on the edge of Salisbury Plain 135 km/84 mi southwest of London; population (1991) 39,300. Salisbury is an agricultural centre, and industries include brewing and engineering. The nearby Wilton Royal Carpet factory closed in 1995. The cathedral of St Mary, built 1220–66, is an example of Early English architecture; its decorated spire 123 m/404 ft is the highest in England; its clock (1386) is one of the oldest still working. The cathedral library contains one of only four copies of the *Magna Carta*.

Another name for the modern city of Salisbury is **New Sarum**, Sarum being an abbreviated form of the medieval Latin corruption ('Sarisburiensis') of the ancient Roman name Sorbiodonum. **Old Sarum**, site of an Iron Age fort, cathedral, and town on a 90-m/300-ft hill to the north, was abandoned in 1220. Old Sarum was the most famous of the 'rotten boroughs' prior to the 1832 Reform Act.

Location

The city lies amid level meadowlands, at the confluence of the Avon with three small rivers, the Nadder, Bourne, and Wylye, and surrounded by hills.

Salisbury Cathedral

With the exception of its crowning tower and spire, it is a building of uniform ◊Early English design, built to one plan between 1220 and 1258 (unlike any other English cathedral except Exeter). The cathedral was dedicated to the Virgin Mary on completion. Its 123-m/404-ft spire is the tallest in England.

The **cathedral close** is surrounded on three sides by a great wall, built partly of stone from the cathedral church of Old Sarum; the River Avon completes the boundary. The close is entered by the four old gates: the High Street, St Ann's Gate, Harnham Gate, and the private gate to the bishop's palace. It contains several colleges and some beautiful houses, including the college of matrons, provided by Bishop Seth Ward in 1682 for the widows of priests of the diocese.

Features

Salisbury was moved from Old Sarum at the beginning of the 13th century, and built on a settled plan 3 km/1.8 mi below the old citadel by Bishop Poore. The planning is indicated by the many straight and wide streets running north to south and east to west, forming 'chequers' or 'squares', with a fine open marketplace in the centre. Audley House, once owned by Mervin, Lord Audley, is a beautiful building, now used as the church house. 'The Hall of John Halle' was built in 1407 by the wool merchant John Halle. Poultry Cross is believed to have been erected in the early 16th century by a nobleman as an act of penance. It is in the form of an open hexagon with six arches and six piers, heavily buttressed. The Old George Hotel, built 15th–16th-century, was perhaps a lodging for pilgrims to the cathedral. The guildhall is on the site of the 14th-century guildhall and city jail. One of the finest examples of timber framing in Salisbury is the house of John A 'Port, built in 1425 by a merchant of that name, who was six times mayor of the city.

The Shoemakers' Guildhall, built in 1638, was added to the timber-framed house left to the Shoemakers' Company by one Philip Crewe, a schoolmaster. This house still overhangs the highway as it did centuries ago. The council house, Bourne Hill, off the London Road, is the historically interesting former college of St Edmund. In the grounds is the only remaining portion of the city rampart. In St Ann Street is the Salisbury, Southern Wiltshire, and Blackmore Museum, containing a large and representative collection of local exhibits. The finely timbered Joiners' Hall, also in St Ann Street, is one of the old halls of the ancient trade guilds of the city. It is Elizabethan, and was purchased by the National Trust in 1898. The Salisbury diocesan training college is on the site of the old deanery in the Close. Salisbury is the 'Melchester' of Thomas Hardy novels and the 'Barchester' of Anthony Trollope's.

Churches

Apart from the cathedral, the three oldest churches of the city are St Martin's, St Thomas's of Canterbury, and St Edmund's. The tower, chancel, and font of St Martin's are Early English, the nave and aisles are 15th century. The present 15th-century Perpendicular church of St Thomas replaced a 13th-century church. From early times it was a chapel of ease to the cathedral. About the end of the 15th century the great west window and finely carved Tudor roof were added to the nave, and later the remarkable fresco of the Last Judgement over the chancel was executed. St Edmund's, which adjoins the Council House, is dedicated to St Edmund of Abingdon, Archbishop of Canterbury. It is part of a large collegiate church which was built in 1407 to replace one built in the 13th century.

Salisbury, Robert Cecil, 1st Earl of Salisbury

Title conferred on Robert ◊Cecil, secretary of state to Elizabeth I of England.

Salisbury, Robert Arthur Talbot Gascoyne-Cecil, 3rd Marquess of Salisbury (1830–1903)

British Conservative politician. He entered the Commons in 1853 and succeeded to his title in 1868. As foreign secretary 1878–80, he took part in the Congress of Berlin, and as prime minister 1885–86, 1886–92, and 1895–1902 gave his main attention to foreign policy, remaining also as foreign secretary for most of this time.

English policy is to float lazily downstream, occasionally putting out a diplomatic boat-hook to avoid collisions.

Robert, 3rd Marquess of Salisbury British Conservative politician.
Attributed remark during his period as foreign secretary

Salisbury, Robert Arthur James Gascoyne-Cecil, 5th Marquess of Salisbury (1893–1972)

British Conservative politician. He was Dominions secretary 1940–42 and 1943–45, colonial secretary 1942, Lord Privy Seal 1942–43 and 1951–52, and Lord President of the Council 1952–57. Baron 1941, Marquess 1947.

Salisbury Plain

Undulating plateau between Salisbury and Devizes in Wiltshire, southwest England; area 775 sq km/300 sq mi. It rises to 235 m/770 ft in Westbury Down. Since the mid-19th century it has been a military training area. ◊Stonehenge stands on Salisbury Plain.

Features

A tract of open chalk downs, Salisbury Plain is rich in prehistoric burial mounds and earthworks, particularly of the Bronze and Early Iron Ages. There are extensive remains of Celtic field systems and of Roman settlements.

Military training

Salisbury Plain has been used as an army training area since the time of the Napoleonic Wars. A permanent camp was started at Tidworth in 1902. During World War I and World War II many training camps were established in the area, and soldiers were prepared for active service here. The airfields at Upavon and Netheravon have been in use since 1912 and are amongst the oldest in Britain. The main army establishments are the Royal Armoured Corps camp at Tidworth, the Royal Artillery camp at Larkhill, the School of Infantry at Warminster, and the Research Centre at Ponton Down, Britain's centre for chemical and biological warfare.

Salmond, Alex (Alexander Elliott Anderson) (1954–)

Scottish politician, leader of the Scottish National Party (SNP) from 1990. The SNP won six of Scotland's 72 seats and over one-fifth of the Scottish vote in the 1997 general election. The SNP supported the new Labour government's proposals for Scottish devolution, viewing it as a stepping-stone towards independence, and are expected to poll strongly in 1999 elections to Scotland's new parliament.

Salmond joined the SNP and in 1987 was elected to the House of Commons, representing Banff and Buchan. He became SNP leader in 1990 and, through his ability to project a moderate image, did much to improve his party's credibility, even though its proposals to make Scotland an independent member of the European Union (EU) went far beyond the limits of what the majority of Scottish electors would support.

salmonella

Any of a very varied group of bacteria, genus *Salmonella*, that colonize the intestines of humans and some animals. Some strains cause typhoid and paratyphoid fevers, while others cause salmonella ◊food poisoning, which is characterized by stomach pains, vomiting, diarrhoea, and headache. It can be fatal in elderly people, but others usually recover in a few days without antibiotics. Most cases are caused by contaminated animal products, especially poultry meat.

In 1989 the British government was forced to take action after it was claimed that nearly all English eggs were infected with salmonella. Many chickens were slaughtered and consumers were advised to hardboil eggs. In 1998, 1 in 700 British eggs contained *Salmonella*. This shows very little improvement on the situation at the beginning of the 1990s when 1 in 650 eggs was contaminated.

The number of notified cases of *Salmonella* poisoning reached almost 40,000 in Britain during 1997.

Saltaire

Model town in West Yorkshire, England, on the River Aire near Shipley. Saltaire was founded in 1853 by the manufacturer Titus Salt (1803–1876), who owned large worsted works. One of Salt's mills now houses a large collection of works by Bradford-born artist David Hockney.

Saltcoats

Residential and holiday town in North Ayrshire unitary authority, Scotland, situated on the Firth of Clyde, 48 km/30 mi southwest of Glasgow; population (1991) 11,900. It merges with the seaport of Ardrossan to the northwest. The town was a major salt producer from the end of the 17th to the beginning of the 19th century.

Saltram

House owned by the National Trust in Devon, England, 5 km/3 mi east of Plymouth. Classical façades were added to the original Tudor house around 1750, and Robert ◊Adam designed the saloon and dining-room in 1768. The house is set in a landscaped park and has gardens with an orangery and summer-house. The large picture collection includes 14 portraits by Joshua Reynolds, a frequent visitor. The Parker family lived here from 1712 until 1962.

Salvation Army

Christian evangelical, social-service, and social-reform organization, originating in 1865 in London, with the work of William ◊Booth. Originally called the Christian Revival Association, it was renamed the East London Christian Mission in 1870 and from 1878 has been known as the Salvation Army, now a worldwide organization. It has military titles for its officials, is renowned for its brass bands, and its weekly journal is the *War Cry*.

Sandbach

Town in Cheshire, England, 8 km/5 mi northeast of Crewe; population (1991) 15,200. It has a chemicals industry. There are two 7th-century Saxon crosses in the market place, and a grammar school founded in 1594.

Sandby, Paul (1725–1809)

English painter and etcher. He is often called 'the father of English watercolour'. He specialized in Classical landscapes, using watercolour and gouache, and helped to introduce the technique of aquatint to England.

Working as a topographical surveyor for the Army, he travelled widely in Britain, painting Scottish scenes following the survey of the Scottish Highlands after the 1745 rebellion, and being one of the first to depict Welsh scenery. Subsequently he often stayed in Windsor with his brother, **Thomas Sandby** (1721–1798), who was appointed Deputy Ranger of Windsor Forest, and some of his best work (Royal Collection) is of Windsor Castle and its environs. He was a founder-member of the Royal Academy in 1768. The romantic features in his paintings, such as ruined castles and stormy skies, paved the way for the full-bodied Romanticism of ◊Girtin and ◊Turner.

Sandhurst

Town in Bracknell Forest unitary authority, southern England, 14 km/9 mi north of Aldershot; population (1981) 13,500. Nearby are the Royal Military Academy (the British military officer training college), founded in 1799, the National Army Museum, and also the military camp of Aldershot.

Sandringham House

Private residence of the British sovereign in Norfolk, England, 13 km/8 mi northeast of King's Lynn. In 1862 King Edward VII, then Prince of Wales, bought an estate here, and in 1867–70 built a house which is still a private country residence of the royal family.

Sandwich

Resort and market town in Kent, southeast England, 18 km/11 mi east of Canterbury; population (1981) 4,200. It has many medieval buildings and was one of the original ◊Cinque Ports. Industries include pharmaceutical research and manufacture, and also market gardening. Features include the

Guildhall (1578) which now houses a museum, and two town gates, the Barbican and Fisher Gate.

Silting up of the River Stour left the harbour useless by the 16th century. From the 16th century Sandwich prospered as a centre of the cloth industry established by refugee Huguenot cloth workers. It is a golfing centre, with the Royal St George's Golf Club nearby. To the north of the town is the Gazen Salts Nature Reserve, and also nearby to the north are the remains of Richborough Castle, a 3rd-century Roman fort.

Sandwich, John Montagu, 4th Earl of Sandwich (1718–1792)

British politician. He was an inept First Lord of the Admiralty 1771–82 during the American Revolution, and his corrupt practices were blamed for the British navy's inadequacies.

The Sandwich Islands (Hawaii) were named after him, as are sandwiches, which he invented so that he could eat without leaving the gaming table.

Sanger, Frederick (1918–)

English biochemist. He was the first person to win a Nobel Prize for Chemistry twice: the first in 1958 for determining the structure of insulin, and the second in 1980 for work on the chemical structure of genes.

Sanger's second Nobel prize was shared with two US scientists, Paul Berg and Walter Gilbert, for establishing methods of determining the sequence of nucleotides strung together along strands of RNA and DNA. He also worked out the structures of various enzymes and other proteins.

Sargent, (Harold) Malcolm (Watts) (1895–1967)

English conductor. He was professor at the Royal College of Music from 1923, chief conductor of the BBC Symphony Orchestra 1950–57, and continued as conductor in chief of the annual Henry Wood promenade concerts at the Royal Albert Hall.

Sargent, John Singer (1856–1925)

US portrait painter. Born in Florence, Italy, of American parents, he studied there and in Paris, and settled in England in 1885. He quickly became a fashionable and prolific painter, though not in the sense that he flattered: he brilliantly depicted affluent late Victorian and Edwardian society, British and American.

Dominant influences on his style were Frans Hals, Velázquez, and Monet, all artists whose free handling of paint gives a lively spontaneity to their works. His paintings of the Wertheimer family (Tate Gallery, London) constitute a remarkable family record, and for 25 years he portrayed a long series of celebrities, including Chamberlain, and Ellen Terry.

In various ways he reacted against the demands of portraiture: in the much criticized murals for the Boston Library (1890); in his war pictures, for example *Gassed* (1920; Imperial War Museum, London); and in the watercolours in which after 1910 he found his main pleasure, his views of Venice in this medium being notable works. The superficiality of which he is often accused could be said to reflect that of the society he depicted, and he remains an outstanding recorder of his age.

Sark

One of the ◊Channel Islands, 10 km/6 mi east of Guernsey; area 5 sq km/2 sq mi; population (1991) 575.

There is no town or village. It is divided into Great and Little Sark, linked by an isthmus, and is of great natural beauty. The Seigneurie of Sark was established by Elizabeth I, the ruler being known as Seigneur/Dame, and has its own parliament, the Chief Pleas.

There is no income tax, divorce and cars are forbidden, and immigration is controlled.

SAS

Abbreviation for Special Air Service, see ◊armed forces.

Sassoon, Siegfried Loraine (1886–1967)

English poet. His anti-war poems which appeared in *The Old Huntsman* (1917), *Counter-Attack* (1918), and later volumes, were begun in the trenches during World War I and express the disillusionment of his generation. His later poetry tended towards the reflective and the spiritual. His three fictionalized autobiographical studies (including *Memoirs of a Fox-Hunting Man*, 1928, *Memoirs of an Infantry Officer*, 1930, and *Sherston's Progress*, 1936) were published together as *The Complete Memoirs of George Sherston* (1937).

Educated at Cambridge, Sassoon enlisted in the army in 1915, serving in France and Palestine. Decorated and then wounded in France, he published a manifesto severely criticizing the authorities, 'A Soldier's Declaration' (1917). He was diagnosed as suffering from shell-shock and returned to duty.

He wrote volumes of genuine autobiography, *The Old Century and Seven More Years* (1938), *The Weald of Youth* (1942), and *Siegfried's Journey* (1945). He also wrote a biography of the novelist George Meredith (1948) and *Collected Poems 1908–1956* (second edition) was published in 1961.

Sassoon, Vidal (1928–)

English hairdresser. He was patronized by pop stars and models from the early 1950s and stopped cutting in 1974.

He created many new hairstyles, including the 'shape' (1959), a layered cut tailored to the bone structure – a radical change from the beehive hairstyles of the 1950s; the Nancy Kwan, a graduated bob longer at the front than at the back (1963); and the feather cut (1964).

Sassoon moved his corporate headquarters from London to New York in 1968 then to California in 1974, when he retired. His second wife continued working for the organization.

satellite television

See ◊television.

satire

Literary or dramatic work that ridicules human pretensions or exposes social evils. Satire is related to parody in its intention to mock, but satire tends to be more subtle and to mock an attitude or a belief, whereas parody tends to mock a particular work (such as a poem) by imitating its style, often with purely comic intent. The intention is to mock a person or a system out of its follies.

In Britain, Alexander Pope and Jonathan Swift are among the best-known satirists. *Gulliver's Travels* is an extended satire on the weaknesses of humanity. Swift also satirized the English exploitation of the Irish in the pamphlet *A Modest Proposal*, which advocated selling Irish babies as a luxury food for English lords. More recent exponents of satire are Hilaire ◊Belloc, G K ◊Chesterton, Evelyn ◊Waugh, Angus ◊Wilson, and Kingsley ◊Amis.

During the 1960s the form flourished on the television and radio, and in the theatre, following the revue *Beyond the Fringe* (1959–64), with Alan ◊Bennett, Peter ◊Cook, Dudley Moore, and Jonathan Miller. In 1960 'The Establishment', Britain's first satirical nightclub, opened and the satirical magazine *Private Eye* was first published in 1962. See also ◊comedy and ◊Spitting Image.

Saul

Village in County Down, Northern Ireland, 3 km/2 mi northeast of Downpatrick. St Patrick is reputed to have landed at Saul in 432. Sliabh Padraig Hill (126 m/415 ft) west of Saul is a pilgrimage site; there is an altar and on the summit a granite statue of the saint.

Some 4 km/2 mi from Saul are the ruins of Raholp church said to have been founded by St Tassach, and 2 km/1 mi south of Saul are the ruins of a church, well, and bathhouses, known as St Patrick's Wells, another site of pilgrimage.

Above the village of Saul is a modern Protestant church dedicated to St Patrick.

Saunders, Cicely Mary Strode (1918–)

English philanthropist, founder of the hospice movement, which aims to provide a caring and comfortable environment in which people with terminal illnesses can die. She was the medical director of St Christopher's Hospice in Sydenham, south London 1967–85, and later became its chair. She wrote *Care of the Dying* (1960). DBE 1980.

Saunders, Jennifer (1958–)

British comedienne, actress, and writer. She rose to fame in partnership with Dawn ◊French with whom she appeared on the British stand-up comedy circuit, the television series *The Comic Strip Presents* (1982), and subsequently their own long-running television show. She won international acclaim for her writing and performances in the widely popular sitcom ◊*Absolutely Fabulous*, in which she starred with Joanna ◊Lumley.

Savernake Forest

Large area of woodland in Wiltshire, England, lying about 5 km/3 mi southeast of Marlborough. Covering 1,620 ha/4,000 acres, it is wooded primarily with beech trees, and abounds in deer and game.

Savery, Thomas (*c.* 1650–1715)

British engineer who invented the steam-driven water pump in 1696. It was the world's first working steam engine, though the boiler was heated by an open fire.

The pump used a boiler to raise steam, which was condensed (in a separate condenser) by an external spray of cold water. The partial vacuum created sucked water up a pipe; steam pressure was then used to force the water away, after which the cycle was repeated. Savery patented his invention in 1698, but it appears that poor-quality work and materials made his engines impractical.

Save the Children

Organization established in 1919 to promote the rights of children to care, good health, material welfare, and moral, spiritual, and educational development. It operates in more than 50 Third World countries and the UK; projects include the provision of health care, education, community development, and emergency relief. In 1997 Save the Children had an income of £78.4 million. Its headquarters are in London.

The charity was founded by Eglantyne Jebb (1876–1928), a nurse who had been working in Turkey. She drafted a charter on children's rights, which formed the basis of the Convention on the Rights of the Child adopted by the United Nations in 1989.

Savile, Jimmy (1926–)

British radio disc-jockey and cigar-toting TV presenter who from 1964 was one of the regular presenters the BBC's *Top of the Pops* before moving on to his own show, *Jim'll Fix It* (1975–94). This broke new ground in bringing members of the public to the screen to fulfil their ambitions with Jim's help. Jimmy Savile has taken special interest in fund-raising for, and helping in, hospitals. Knighted 1990.

Savile Row

Street in London, situated north of Piccadilly. It is a centre of the tailoring trade and synonymous with fine-quality work. It was built in about 1735 by the 3rd Earl of Burlington, and named after his wife, Dorothy Savile, who died in 1717. For many years it was the favoured business location for leading members of the medical profession.

The playwright Richard Sheridan died in Savile Row in 1816.

Savoy Hotel

Hotel in the Strand, London, opened in 1889. It is next to the Savoy Theatre and is noted for its rich, famous, and idiosyncratic guests. The first manager was César Ritz (subsequent founder of the ◊Ritz Hotel), and its Grill Room is one of the leading traditional restaurants in London.

Savoy Theatre

Theatre in London, opened in 1881. Its first production was Gilbert and Sullivan's *Patience*, under the management of F R D'Oyly Carte. The theatre was for long the home of the D'Oyly Carte Opera Company, and saw the production of all the Gilbert and Sullivan operettas.

Saxon

Member of a Germanic tribe once inhabiting the Danish peninsula and northern Germany. The Saxons migrated from their homelands in the early Middle Ages, under pressure from the Franks, and spread into various parts of Europe, including Britain (see ◊Anglo-Saxon). They also undertook piracy in the North Sea and the English Channel.

According to the English historian Bede, the Saxons arrived in Britain in 449, and the archaeological evidence and sparse literary sources suggest the years around 450 as marking the end of their piratical raids, and the establishment of their first settlements in southern England.

Bede states that the tribes who came to Britain at the invitation of the British chieftain Vortigern, to help defend his

THE SAXON SHORE: THE END OF ROMAN BRITAIN

In the 3rd century AD the European provinces of the Roman Empire suffered greatly from barbarian invasion and political turmoil. Though Britain was relatively immune, these events set in motion the longer-term dissolution of the Western Roman Empire.

The sea wolves

The 3rd century AD was a time of peace on the northern frontier of Roman Britain. Treaties and the garrisons of Hadrian's Wall held the northern tribes in check, but at the same time Gaul and Germany were afflicted by invasions, and the fringes of the storm reached Britain. From across the North Sea came Saxon raiders, threatening the villas and settlements of the southeastern coasts. To fend them off a series of strong, new forts, the forts of the Saxon Shore, were built in the late 3rd century around the coasts of East Anglia and the southeast, from Brancaster in Norfolk via the Straits of Dover to Portchester in Hampshire. They show the high walls and towers of late Roman defences and were associated with both land and sea forces to intercept and repel invaders.

By the 4th century the northern frontier was again giving concern, with the Picts and powerful new peoples such as the Scots menacing Hadrian's Wall, which was refurbished to meet the threat. Occasionally the defensive system based on the Wall failed, most notably in the great 'Barbarian Conspiracy' of 367. In this year the Picts, Scots, and Saxons combined to attack Britain from all sides and the army in Britain temporarily collapsed, having to be restored by the general Theodosius (father of the emperor of the same name).

Britain in the 4th century

A 4th-century writer refers to Britain as 'a very wealthy island' and its importance to the politics and economy of the late Roman west are clear. The island spawned a succession of claimants to the imperial throne, starting success- fully with Constantine I, the first Christian emperor, proclaimed at York in 306. Less successful were Magnentius (350–53) and Magnus Maximus (383–88), both of whom may have removed troops to the continent, and whose suppression brought reprisals upon Britain.

Nonetheless, excavations on the towns and villas of Britain have shown that the first half of the 4th century was their heyday and the time of greatest prosperity and stability for Roman Britain. The villas in particular were at their most numerous and elaborate, with palatial residences such as Bignor (Sussex) or Woodchester (Gloucestershire). Both villas and town-houses were embellished with mosaics whose designs drew on themes from Greco-Roman mythology or the newly fashionable Christianity. The well-to-do proprietors of these villas enjoyed a Roman lifestyle comparable with their peers in Gaul, Spain, or Italy. Finds of silver plate such as that from Corbridge (Northumberland) and Mildenhall (Suffolk) or of jewellery from Hoxne and Thetford (both Suffolk) attest to the wealth and the artistic and religious tastes of British aristocrats.

Decline and fall

By the late 4th century the archaeological evidence shows that the glory days of Roman Britain were passing. Villas were becoming dilapidated or were abandoned, damaged mosaics went unpatched, and the streets and services of the towns fell into decay. The critical moment came early in the 5th century. In 406 the army in Britain proclaimed another claimant to the imperial purple, Constantine III. He took part of the army with him to Gaul, where he was defeated and killed in 411. At the time Gaul was in turmoil through barbarian invasions, and the central Roman authorities were unable to re-establish control or re-garrison Britain.

Though the Romans never formally abandoned Britain (the famous 410 letter of the emperor Honorius urging the British to look to their own defences may actually refer to Bruttium in southern Italy), it slipped from their grasp in the early 5th century and was never recovered. Despite the level of success of Roman civilization among the British upper classes, the removal of military protection and the imperial system dealt this way of life a body-blow which it could not withstand, and the decay and dilapidation of the late 4th century hastened the final collapse of Roman-style living in the early 5th century.

The Dark Ages

There is an almost total lack of contemporary historical sources for the mid- and late 5th centuries. Yet it is in this time that the Anglo-Saxons became established in Britain. One story has it that some were brought over by a post-Roman ruler in Kent, Vortigern, to protect his kingdom against other raiders. Because of Vortigern's treachery they turned against him and took the kingdom for themselves. This has also been seen as the time of the 'historical' King Arthur, a post-Roman war-leader rallying the Britons against the Anglo-Saxon invaders, the last standard-bearer of Rome in Britain.

by Simon Esmonde Cleary

country against Pictish and Irish invaders, were from three powerful Germanic peoples, the Saxons, Angles, and Jutes.

Saxon cemeteries that have been located show a wide settlement in eastern England, stretching roughly from the Tees to the Thames, penetrating deeply into the Midlands and the upper Thames, and in the south from Kent to north Hampshire and east Wiltshire. Settlers heading inland from the coast sailed up the rivers Thames, Trent, and Ouse; they also travelled along some Roman roads, particularly in Leicestershire, Warwickshire, and Yorkshire. By the end of the 6th century much of England was in Anglo-Saxon hands. Kent, East Anglia, Wessex, Bernicia, Deira, and finally Mercia had all developed into separate kingdoms.

The name Saxon is said to be derived from their national weapon, the *seax*, a short thrusting sword, in the same way that the Franks, the spearmen, took their name from the Old English *franca*, a javelin.

Sayers, Dorothy L(eigh) (1893–1957)

English writer of detective fiction, playwright, and translator. Her books, which feature the detective Lord Peter Wimsey and the heroine Harriet Vane, include classics of the detective fiction genre such as *Strong Poison* (1930), *Murder Must Advertise* (1933), *The Nine Tailors* (1934), and *Gaudy Night* (1935).

Scafell Pike

Highest mountain in England, in the ◊Lake District, Cumbria, northwest England; height 978 m/3,210 ft. It is separated from Scafell (964 m/3,164 ft) by a ridge called Mickledore.

The summit of Scafell Pike was presented to the National Trust by the third Lord Leconfield, as a war memorial, in 1919.

Scales, Prunella (1932–)

English actress, best-known for her role as Sybil Fawlty in the much-repeated television comedy series *Fawlty Towers* (1975, 1978). Her stage performances include her one-woman show *An Evening with Queen Victoria* (1980) and her role as the Queen in Alan Bennett's *A Question of Attribution* (1988) – the first time the Queen had been portrayed on stage.

Born in Surrey, she trained at the Old Vic Theatre School and the Herbert Berghof Studio, New York. In the 1960s she was teamed with Richard Briers in the television comedy *Marriage Lines*. She was awarded the CBE in 1992.

Scapa Flow

Large protected sea area in the Orkney Islands, Scotland, between Mainland, Flotta, South Ronaldsay, and Hoy, until 1957 a base of the Royal Navy. It was the main base of the Grand Fleet during World War I and in 1919 was the scene of the scuttling of 74 surrendered German warships (62 of which have since been salvaged). It was reactivated as a base in World War II. It is now an attraction for scuba divers.

A German U-boat penetrated the anchorage on 14 October 1939, and sank the battleship *Royal Oak* with the loss of 810 men.

Scarborough

Spa and holiday resort on the North Sea coast of North Yorkshire, northern England, 56 km/35 mi northeast of York; population (1991) 38,900. It is a touring centre for the Yorkshire Moors, and is also centre for fishing. A ruined 12th-century Norman castle overlooks the town.

The playwright Alan Ayckbourn has a long association with Scarborough as artistic director of the Stephen Joseph Theatre, and many of his plays have been premiered in the theatre in the round.

Features

The Norman castle was built on a rocky headland (87 m/285 ft high) which separates Scarborough's north and south bays. Bronze Age and Iron Age relics have been recovered from the site and in the castle yard are the remains of a Roman signal station. Remains of the Norman castle include the 12th-century keep and the 13th-century barbican. Other features include St Mary's church dating from about 1180; a house where King Richard III is said to have stayed; and Wood End, formerly a home of the Sitwell family, which now houses a museum.

History

During the Civil War the castle surrendered to Parliamentary forces after a siege in 1645. George Fox, the founder of the Society of Friends, was imprisoned in the castle from 1665 to 1666. Scarborough developed as a resort after the discovery of mineral spring water in 1620.

Famous people

Scarborough was the birthplace of the poet Edith Sitwell. The novelist Anne Brontë is buried in the churchyard of St Mary's church.

Scarfe, Gerald (1936–)

English cartoonist and animator. He became known in the 1960s as a cartoonist for the satirical magazine *Private Eye*. The cruellest British cartoonist since James ◊Gillray, his subjects are treated with extreme and highly inventive distortion. His collection of cartoons *Gerald Scarfe People* was published in 1966. He also animated parts of the film *Pink Floyd: The Wall* (1982), and later experimented with instant photography. His work has also included sculpture, and stage and film design, notably the animation of Disney's *Hercules* (1997).

Scargill, Arthur (1938–)

British trade-union leader. Elected president of the National Union of Miners (NUM) in 1981, he embarked on a collision course with the Conservative government of Margaret Thatcher. The damaging strike of 1984–85 split the miners' movement. In 1995, criticizing what he saw as the Labour Party's lurch to the right, he announced that he would establish a rival, the independent Socialist Labour Party. This proved to be largely ineffectual, and made little impact in consequent elections. By 1997 membership of the NUM had falled to 10,000.

Scarlet Pimpernel, The

Historical adventure novel by Baroness Orczy published in the UK in 1905. Set in Paris during the Reign of Terror

(1793–94), it describes the exploits of a group of Britons, called the League of the Scarlet Pimpernel, and their leader, Sir Percy Blakeney, who saved aristocrats from the Revolution.

Scarman, Leslie George, Baron Scarman (1911–)

English judge and legal reformer. A successful barrister, he was a High Court judge 1961–73 and an appeal-court judge 1973–77, prior to becoming a law lord. He was the first chairman of the Law Commission for the reform of English law, 1965–73.

He gradually shifted from a traditional position to a more reformist one, calling for liberalization of divorce laws in 1965 and campaigning for a bill of rights in 1974. As chair of the inquiry into the Brixton riots in 1981, he proposed positive discrimination in favour of black people. He campaigned for the release of the ◊Birmingham Six and the ◊Guildford Four. Knighted 1961, Baron 1977.

Schlesinger, John (Richard) (1926–)

English film and television director. His eclectic career embraces British social conscience films of the 1960s, comedies, thrillers, and nostalgic period pieces. Early films include *Billy Liar* (1963) and *Darling* (1965). His first US film, *Midnight Cowboy* (1969) (Academy Award), was a big commercial success and was followed by *Sunday, Bloody Sunday* (1971), *Marathon Man* (1978), *Yanks* (1979), *Pacific Heights* (1990), and *Eye for an Eye* (1996).

Schumacher, Fritz (Ernst Friedrich) (1911–1977)

German economist who made his career in the UK. He believed that the increasing size of institutions, coupled with unchecked economic growth, creates a range of social and environmental problems. He argued his case in books such as *Small is Beautiful* (1973), and established the Intermediate Technology Development Group.

Schumacher studied at Oxford and held academic posts there and in the USA at Columbia in the 1930s and 1940s. After World War II he was economic adviser to the British Control Commission in Germany 1946–50 and to the UK National Coal Board 1950–70.

science fiction, or speculative fiction (also known as SF or sci-fi)

Genre of fiction and film with an imaginary scientific, technological, or futuristic basis. It is sometimes held to have its roots in the works of Mary ◊Shelley, notably *Frankenstein* (1818), but the form as it is now known did not emerge until the late 19th century.

H G ◊Wells was one of the early practitioners in Britain, and following World War II John Wyndham and Arthur C Clarke became prominent. A consensus of 'pure storytelling' and traditional values was disrupted by writers associated with the British magazine *New Worlds*, including Brian ◊Aldiss, Michael ◊Moorcock, and J G ◊Ballard, who used the form for serious literary purposes and for political and sexual radicalism. Douglas Adams' *Hitch-Hiker's Guide to the Galaxy* began as a radio serial in 1978. and became a best-seller in 1979. In the 1980s the 'cyberpunk' school spread from the USA.

Science Museum

British museum of science and technology in South Kensington, London. Founded in 1853 as the National Museum of Science and Industry, it houses exhibits from all areas of science.

Scilly, Isles of, or Scilly Isles/Islands, or Scillies

Group of 140 islands and islets lying 40 km/25 mi southwest of Land's End, England; administered by the Duchy of Cornwall; area 16 sq km/6.3 sq mi; population (1991) 2,050. The five inhabited islands are **St Mary's**, the largest, on which is ◊Hugh Town, capital of the Scillies; **Tresco**, the second largest, with subtropical gardens; **St Martin's**, noted for its beautiful shells; **St Agnes**; and **Bryher**.

Products include vegetables and early spring flowers, and tourism is important. The islands have remains of Bronze Age settlements. The numerous wreck sites off the islands include many of Cloudesley Shovell's fleet (1707). The islands are an important birdwatching centre with breeding sea birds in the summer and rare migrants in the spring and autumn.

Ownership

The islands are the property of the Crown (with the exception of Hugh Town, St Mary's, the property in which was sold freehold to the occupiers in 1949) and are administered by the Duchy of Cornwall. However, the island of Tresco, the most beautiful, is leased to R A Dorrien-Smith, together with the uninhabited islands of the group.

Agriculture

Farms are small, but well equipped. The average holding is approximately 8 ha/20 acres, with the land divided into small squares surrounded by tall hedges of *Pittosporum*, a New Zealand plant with a thick evergreen foliage. These hedges protect the crops from the Atlantic gales. Much land has been drowned by the encroaching sea and by slow subsidence.

Climate

Frost and snow are a rare occurrence. The climate is an important factor in the islands' main industry, the growing of spring flowers for market.

Transport

There is an air service between Penzance airport on the mainland and St Mary's, and a boat service between St Mary's and Penzance.

Early history

The islands are crowded with prehistoric burial chambers, menhirs (upright stone monuments), middens, and hut villages. The stone-chambered barrows evidently represent a provincial extension of the great megalithic culture of Brittany, as might be inferred from the geographical setting of the islands. It is thought possible that they may have been the special home of the dead, known in Celtic mythology. The English antiquary William Camden (1551–1623) identified the Scilly Isles with the fabled islands called the Cassiterides, to which came the Phoenician traders, but there is no proof. Tin was worked in Cornwall in the early Iron Age and in Roman

SCOFIELD, PAUL *English actor Paul Scofield. Acclaimed for his performances both on stage and on film, Scofield is pictured here in the eponymous role of the 1970 Royal Court Theatre production of* Uncle Vanya. *Corbis*

times, but there is no trace of tin workings in the Scilly Isles. Some, at least, of the villages belong to the Bronze Age, and to this time also may be attributed the ancient walls of an early field system, examples of which are occasionally to be seen below present sea level.

Scofield, (David) Paul (1922–)

English actor. His wide-ranging roles include the drunken priest in Graham Greene's *The Power and the Glory* (1956), Lear in *King Lear* (1962), Salieri in Peter Shaffer's *Amadeus* (1979), Othello (1980), and Shotov in *Heartbreak House* (1992). He appeared as Sir Thomas More in both stage and film versions of Robert Bolt's *A Man for All Seasons* (stage 1960–61, film 1966).

Other films include *When the Whales Come* (1989), *Hamlet* (1990), *Utz* (1993), and *Quiz Show* (1994). He played the part of Karenin in the television film *Anna Karenina* (1985).

Scone

Site of the ancient **Scone Palace** (destroyed in 1559), near the village of New Scone, Perth and Kinross, where many of the Scottish kings were crowned on the Stone of Destiny. The coronation stone was removed to Westminster Abbey, London, by Edward I in 1297, but was returned to Scotland in 1996 and is on display at Edinburgh Castle.

Scotch snap

The technical name for rhythmic figures inverting the order of dotted notes, the short note coming first instead of last. Its name in England, which is also **Scots catch**, is no doubt due to the fact that the Scotch snap is a feature in the Scottish strathspey (folk dance). It was popular in Italy in the 17th and 18th centuries and was called by German writers the 'Lombardy rhythm'.

Scotland, Roman Caledonia

The northernmost part of Britain, formerly an independent country, now part of the UK
Area 78,470 sq km/30,297 sq mi
Capital Edinburgh
Towns Glasgow, Dundee, Aberdeen
Features the Highlands in the north (with the ◊Grampian Mountains); central Lowlands, including valleys of the Clyde and Forth, with most of the country's population and industries; Southern Uplands (including the ◊Lammermuir Hills); and islands of the Orkneys, Shetlands, and Western Isles; the world's greatest concentration of nuclear weapons are at the UK and US bases on the Clyde, near Glasgow; 8,000-year-old pinewood forests once covered 1,500,000 ha/3,706,500 acres, now reduced to 12,500 ha/30,900 acres; there were at least 104,876 ha/259,150 acres of native woodlands remaining in the Highlands in 1994, covering only 2% of the total area. The 1995 Millennium Commission award will fund the creation of the Millennium Forest, and double Scotland's forests
Industry electronics, marine and aircraft engines, oil, natural gas, chemicals, textiles, clothing, printing, paper, food processing, tourism, whisky, coal, computer industries (Scotland's 'Silicon Glen' produces over 35% of Europe's personal computers)
Currency pound sterling
Population (1993 est) 5,120,000
Languages English; Scots, a lowland dialect (derived from Northumbrian Anglo-Saxon); Gaelic spoken by 1.3%, mainly in the Highlands
Religions Presbyterian (Church of Scotland), Roman Catholic
Famous people Robert Bruce, Walter Scott, Robert Burns, Robert Louis Stevenson, Adam Smith
Government Scotland sends 72 members to the UK Parliament at Westminster. The Local Government (Scotland) Bill of 1994 abolished the two-tier system of local government. Since 1996 there have been 32 unitary authorities; see map (page 797) and list (page 796). See also table of historic counties (page 802). There is a differing legal system to England (see ◊Scottish law).

Scots voted overwhelmingly in favour of a Scottish parliament and the beginning of devolution in a referendum held in September 1997. Scotland's last legislature vanished with the Union of 1707. The ◊Scottish Parliament was backed by 75% of the 2.4 million people who voted in the two-question referendum and 63% agreed that it should have tax-varying powers. There was a 61.4% turnout.

Elections to the 129-member assembly were planned for spring 1999, with the Parliament coming into being on a site in Edinburgh to be decided by the turn of the millennium. It will have charge over most of Scotland's domestic affairs,

Scotland: Local Government

The Local Government (Scotland) Bill of 1994 abolished the two-tier system of local government that had been established for the nine Scottish regions in 1975. Since April 1996 there have been 29 mainland unitary authorities; the 3 island areas (the Orkney Islands, Shetland Islands, and Western Isles) retained their existing single-tier administrative divisions.

Local authority	Administrative headquarters	Area		Population (1996)
		sq km	sq mi	
Aberdeen City	Aberdeen	184	71	219,100
Aberdeenshire	Aberdeen	6,289	2,428	226,500
Angus	Forfar	2,184	843	111,300
Argyll and Bute	Lochgilphead	4,001	1,545	89,300
Clackmannanshire	Alloa	161	62	47,700
Dumfries and Galloway	Dumfries	6,394	2,468	147,800
Dundee City	Dundee	65	25	155,000
East Ayrshire	Kilmarnock	1,271	491	124,000
East Dunbartonshire	Kirkintilloch	202	78	110,000
East Lothian	Haddington	681	263	85,500
East Renfrewshire	Giffnock	172	66	86,800
Edinburgh, City of	Edinburgh	261	101	477,550
Falkirk	Falkirk	294	114	142,500
Fife	Glenrothes	1,340	517	351,200
Glasgow City	Glasgow	177	68	618,400
Highland	Inverness	25,304	9,767	207,500
Inverclyde	Greenock	157	60	90,000
Midlothian	Dalkeith	355	137	79,900
Moray	Elgin	2,217	856	85,000
North Ayrshire	Irvine	878	339	139,200
North Lanarkshire	Motherwell	466	180	326,750
Orkney Islands	Kirkwall	970	375	19,600
Perth and Kinross	Perth	5,328	2,058	131,800
Renfrewshire	Paisley	261	101	176,970[1]
Scottish Borders	Newtown St Boswells	4,712	1,819	105,300
Shetland Islands	Lerwick	1,400	541	22,500
South Ayrshire	Ayr	1,202	464	114,000
South Lanarkshire	Hamilton	1,776	686	307,100
Stirling	Stirling	2,195	848	82,000
West Dunbartonshire	Dumbarton	155	60	97,800
Western Isles	Stornoway	2,900	1,120	27,800
West Lothian	Livingston	475	183	147,900

[1] 1993.

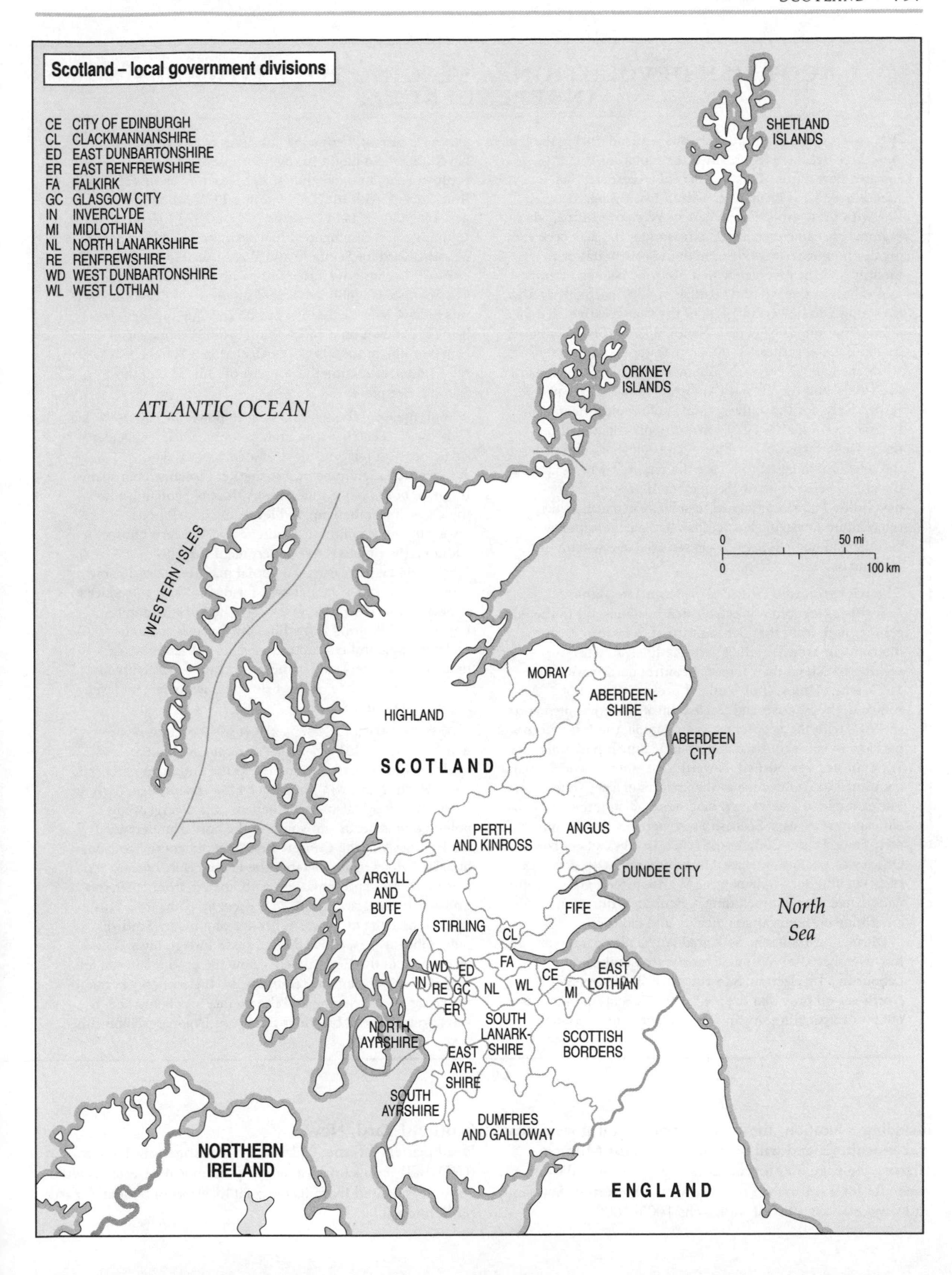
Scotland – local government divisions
CE CITY OF EDINBURGH
CL CLACKMANNANSHIRE
ED EAST DUNBARTONSHIRE
ER EAST RENFREWSHIRE
FA FALKIRK
GC GLASGOW CITY
IN INVERCLYDE
MI MIDLOTHIAN
NL NORTH LANARKSHIRE
RE RENFREWSHIRE
WD WEST DUNBARTONSHIRE
WL WEST LOTHIAN
SHETLAND ISLANDS
ORKNEY ISLANDS
ATLANTIC OCEAN
WESTERN ISLES
0 50 mi
0 100 km
MORAY
ABERDEENSHIRE
HIGHLAND
ABERDEEN CITY
SCOTLAND
PERTH AND KINROSS
ANGUS
DUNDEE CITY
ARGYLL AND BUTE
FIFE
North Sea
STIRLING
CL
WD
ED
FA
CE
EAST LOTHIAN
IN
RE
GC
NL
WL
MI
ER
NORTH AYRSHIRE
SOUTH LANARKSHIRE
SCOTTISH BORDERS
EAST AYRSHIRE
SOUTH AYRSHIRE
DUMFRIES AND GALLOWAY
NORTHERN IRELAND
ENGLAND

SCOTTISH DEVOLUTION: A STAGING POST TOWARDS INDEPENDENCE?

PRESSURE EMANATING from within Scotland during the last three decades has provided the motor for the drive towards devolution. This was part of a broader modernization of Britain's constitutional arrangements, in line with those typical elsewhere in Western Europe, where regional parliaments exist. The reason for this has been the greater homogeneity and strength of Scottish national identity and the divergence that occurred between trends and values in English and Scottish politics, particularly after the coming to power, in 1979, of the Conservative Thatcher administration. The Scottish National Party (SNP), founded in 1934, has spearheaded the drive towards independence, while the Labour Party, the dominant force in Scotland since the 1960s, and the Liberal Democrats have campaigned, respectively, for the halfway houses of devolution and federalism. In March 1979 a majority of Scots voted narrowly in favour of establishing a Scottish assembly, but the referendum failed to secure the required 40% support of the eligible electorate. By September 1997 support for devolution had strengthened to such an extent that the referendum to establish a Scottish parliament with law-making and tax-varying powers received overwhelming backing of 74%.

The background to the 1997 devolution plans

A Scottish kingdom was established by Kenneth I in the 9th century and, from the 13th century, it came into intermittent armed conflict with the English, who were seeking to extend their imperial control northwards. In 1603, when James VI of Scotland became James I of England, the Scottish and English thrones were united and in 1707, with the negotiated Act of Union, the Edinburgh parliament was abolished and a single British parliament, at Westminster, established. Nevertheless, after union, Scotland continued to retain some of the features of a separate state. For example, it had its own bank notes, distinctive legal and education systems, a Scottish Presbyterian Church, and its own Trade Union Congress (STUC). In 1885 a Scottish Office was established, based in Edinburgh, with devolved responsibility for implementing Westminster legislation in a wide range of areas, including agriculture, education, environment, home affairs, health, and industry.

During the 1960s the SNP gradually built up support and in November 1967 Winnie Ewing won Hamilton from Labour in a by-election. Subsequently, the discovery of North Sea oil provided the SNP with 'It's Scotland's Oil' as a potent campaigning slogan and enabled it to argue that, although currently enjoying subsidies from English tax-payers, Scotland might in the future become more prosperous as an independent state. As well as this challenge from the left, with the SNP winning 11 of Scotland's 71 parliamentary seats in October 1974, a 1973 Royal Commission recommended that separate assemblies should be established for Scotland and Wales. In response, the 1974–79 Labour government drew up plans for devolution. The Scottish assembly envisaged by the 1978 devolution act was to have some legislative but no revenue-raising powers, being dependent on a 'block grant' from Westminster. However, the proposals were defeated in a March 1979 referendum, attracting the support of only 33% of the Scottish electorate.

With the Conservatives coming to power in May 1979, led by Margaret Thatcher – an arch unionist 'Little Englander' – Anglo-Scottish relations deteriorated rapidly. The Thatcherite programme of free-market capitalism ran against the grain of the more collectivist values of Scotland, where trade union membership and levels of council house ownership were amongst the highest in Western Europe. In addition, the Conservative government came to treat Scotland in an increasingly colonial manner, most notably using it as an experimental base for the poll tax, introduced to Scotland in 1989, one year before its introduction to England and Wales. Meanwhile, the Scottish economy underwent painful restructuring, as its old 'smokestack' industries were replaced by newer technologies centred in 'Silicon Glen', in the Central Belt: the unemployment level exceeded 11% in 1988.

Between 1979 and 1997, support for the Conservatives – which had exceeded 50% in 1955 – collapsed in Scotland, while Labour became entrenched as the dominant party. The SNP, which from 1983 campaigned for 'independence within a federal Europe', also strengthened. This divergence in polling trends north and south of the border undermined the legitimacy of the Conservative government in Scotland, but also helped bring together the Labour, Liberal, and SNP parties, whose representatives participated, from 1989, in a Constitutional Convention. This drew up plans for a future Scottish parliament. It was reflective of growing Scottish self-confidence, as, assisted by massive foreign inward investment in the Central Belt – now the production site for 30% of Europe's personal computers – the economy began to revive, and broadcasting and the literary arts flourished. It was also influenced by wider European Union developments,

including education, the health service, local government, and agriculture, and will be headed by a First Minister.

History see page 800 for a chronology of Scotland's history, page 803 for a feature on the medieval kingdom of Scotland, and page 801 for a list of monarchs 1005–1603.

Scotland Yard, New

Headquarters of the ◊Criminal Investigation Department (CID) of Britain's London Metropolitan Police, established in 1878. It is named from its original location in Scotland Yard, off Whitehall.

with 'subsidiarity', or the devolving of decision-making from the centre to the lowest level possible, being promoted as a particularly effective form of government.

The 1997 Scottish parliament proposals and referendum result

In the May 1997 general election, Labour won a stunning victory both across Britain and in Scotland. In contrast, running on a strongly unionist platform, the Conservatives, led by Prime Minister John Major, failed, for the first time ever, to secure the election of any Scottish members of Parliament and attracted only 18% of the Scottish vote. The SNP, with 22% of the vote and advocating separation by the year 2007 (the 300th anniversary of the Union) polled strongly and won six of Scotland's 72 seats. The 'New' Labour government, with Scots occupying its four most senior positions, including the Edinburgh-born Tony Blair as prime minister, was the most Scottish in British history and it made an early priority in pushing through legislation on devolution.

The Scottish act provided for the creation of a 129-member (MSP) Scottish Parliament, based in Edinburgh. Seventy-three MSPs would be elected from the existing 72 Westminster constituencies, with an extra seat being created by dividing the Orkney and Shetland constituency into two, while 56 would be elected, by proportional representation, from party lists in the eight Scottish European parliamentary constituencies. The parliament's law-making powers would cover all areas except defence, foreign affairs, the constitution, social security, company regulation, economic management, and taxation; and its ministers would be able to sit with British ministers at negotiating meetings in Brussels whenever Scottish interests were affected. In addition, if approved by the electorate, it would have the authority to vary the basic rate of income tax in Scotland by up to 3p to supplement a block grant equivalent to the current Scottish Office budget of £14 billion.

The proposals were surprisingly bold and were sufficient to ensure that the campaign for a 'Yes, Yes' vote on the two referendum questions, on a Scottish parliament and tax-varying powers, were supported by the SNP. The referendum was held auspiciously on 11 September 1997, which was the 700th anniversary of William 'Braveheart' Wallace's victory over English troops at Stirling Bridge. Scotland's voters responded by giving resounding backing to each question, with 74.3% and 63.5% support, respectively. With turnout at 60%, about 45% of the total electorate voted 'Yes' to the devolved parliament. All 32 of the local authority areas in Scotland supported home rule, including the traditional pockets of resistance, in the Borders and Dumfries and Galloway (adjoining England), Aberdeen, Tayside, Orkney, and Shetlands, which had voted 'No' in 1979. The result was a personal triumph for Scottish Secretary Donald Dewar, who announced later that he intended to step down from Westminster to contest the elections for the Scottish parliament in 1999, with the aim of becoming Scotland's first minister (prime minister).

Scottish devolution is likely to have wider, but unpredictable, consequences for the British polity. Donald Dewar described the results of 11 September 1997 as a vote to strengthen the union between England and Scotland, since it would remove a source of resentment and tension. In contrast, Alex Salmond, leader of the SNP, which is expected to win at least one-third of the vote in the May 1999 elections, saw it as a vote to 'weaken the union' and as the first step in what he hoped was an unstoppable march towards independence. Indeed, opinion polls held during March 1998 suggested that up to two-thirds of Scots believed that independence would be achieved within two decades. From a different perspective, the Conservatives also believe that devolution has the risk of leading to the eventual break-up of the United Kingdom.

The Impact on Westminster

In the shorter term, the new Scottish parliament seems set to promote coalition politics, since, with proportional representation, no single party is likely to achieve an overall majority in 1999. There is also scope for fiscal disputes between the Edinburgh and Westminster parliaments if the 3p 'Tartan tax' proves inadequate for Scottish spending needs. Additionally, Scotland's current overrepresentation, on a demographic basis, in the Westminster parliament will be ended at the election after next, with a reduction in its quota of members of Parliament by between 12 and 14. This will weaken Labour's position in Westminster. Indeed, if, as the Conservatives have demanded, Scottish members of Parliament are also debarred, after the year 2000, from voting on issues which affect only English interests (the 'West Midlothian question'), there exists the future prospect that a Westminster parliament might return a government with a voting majority for British issues, but not for purely English matters. However, with the development of national assemblies in Wales and Northern Ireland, and the prospect of regional assemblies in England, the logical outcome of Scottish devolution may eventually be not the break-up of the United Kingdom, but the creation of a federal state.

BY IAN DERBYSHIRE

Scots language

The form of the English language as traditionally spoken and written in Scotland, regarded by some scholars as a distinct language. Scots derives from the Northumbrian dialect of Anglo-Saxon or Old English, and has been a literary language since the 14th century.

It is also known as **Inglis** (now archaic, and a variant of 'English'), ◊**Lallans** ('Lowlands'), **Lowland Scots** (in contrast with the Gaelic of the Highlands and Islands), and '**the Doric**' (as a rustic language in contrast with the 'Attic' or 'Athenian' language of Edinburgh's literati, especially in the 18th century). It is also often referred to as Broad

Scotland: Chronology

3,000 BC Neolithic settlements include Beaker people and Skara Brae on Orkney.

1st millennium BC The Picts reached Scotland from mainland Europe.

1st century AD Picts prevented Romans from penetrating far into Scotland.

122–128 Hadrian's Wall built to keep northern tribes out of England.

500 The Scots, a Gaelic-speaking tribe from Ireland, settled in the Kingdom of Dalriada (Argyll).

563 St Colomba founded the monastery on Iona and began to convert the Picts to Christianity.

9th century Norsemen conquered Orkney, Shetland, Western Isles, and much of Highlands.

c. **843** Kenneth McAlpin unified the Scots and Picts to become first king of Scotland.

1040 King Duncan murdered by Macbeth.

1263 Scots defeated Norwegian invaders at Battle of Largs.

1295 First treaty between Scotland and France (the Auld Alliance).

1296 Edward I of England invaded and declared himself King of Scotland.

1297 William Wallace and Andrew Moray defeated English at Battle of Stirling Bridge.

1314 Robert the Bruce defeated the English at Battle of Bannockburn.

1328 Scottish independence recognized by England.

1371 Robert II became first king of the House of Stuart.

1513 Battle of Flodden: Scots defeated by the English and James IV killed.

1542 Mary Queen of Scots succeeded to throne when less than a week old.

1540s John Knox introduced Calvinism to Scotland.

1557 The First Covenant established the Protestant faith in Scotland.

1567 Queen Mary abdicated, later fleeing to England, where she was beheaded in 1587.

1603 Union of crowns: James VI of Scotland became James I of England.

1638 Scots rebelled after National Covenant condemned Charles I's changes to church ritual.

1643 Solemn League and Covenant allied the Scots with Parliament in the English Civil War.

1650 Cromwell invaded and defeated the Scots at Dunbar.

1679 Presbyterian Covenanters defeated by Episcopalians at Battle of Bothwell Brig.

1689 Jacobite victory at Killiecrankie, but rebellion against William III collapsed soon after.

1692 Campbells massacred the Macdonalds at Glencoe.

1698 Unsuccessful Scottish colony founded at Darien in Central America.

1707 Act of Union united the Scottish and English Parliaments.

1715 'The Fifteen': Jacobite rebellion in support of James Edward Stuart.

1745 'The Forty-Five': Charles Edward Stuart led Jacobite rebels as far south as Derby.

1746 Jacobites defeated at Battle of Culloden by English forces under Duke of Cumberland.

1747 Act of Prescription banned Highland costume until repeal in 1782.

c. **1780–1860** Highland clearances: crofters evicted to make way for sheep.

1822 George IV made state visit to Scotland.

1843 The Disruption: 400 ministers left the Church of Scotland to form the Free Church of Scotland.

1885 Scottish Office created.

1886 Crofters Act provided security of tenure for crofters.

1926 Scottish Secretary upgraded to Secretary of State.

1928 National Party of Scotland formed (became Scottish National Party in 1932).

1939 Headquarters of Scottish Office moved from London to Edinburgh.

1945 First Scottish Nationalist MP elected.

1970s Aberdeen became centre of North Sea oil development.

1979 Referendum failed to approve devolution of power to a Scottish Assembly.

1990 'Constitutional Convention' of Labour and Liberal Parties demanded a Scottish Parliament.

1994 Scottish Grand Committee of MPs given additional powers.

1996 Local government reform: unitary authorities replaced regional and district councils.

1997 Referendum supported plans for a Scottish Parliament and its tax-varying powers.

Scots in contrast to the anglicized language of the middle classes.

Scots has been spoken in southeast Scotland since the 7th century. During the Middle Ages it spread to the far north, blending with the Norn dialects of Orkney and Shetland (once distinct varieties of Norse). Scots has a wide range of poetry, ballads, and prose records, including two national epic poems: John Barbour's *Brus* and Blind Harry's *Wallace*. With the transfer of the court to England upon the Union of the Crowns in 1603 and the dissemination of the King James Bible, Scots ceased to be a national and court language, but has retained its vitality among the general population and in various literary and linguistic revivals.

Words originating in Scots that are now widely used in English include *bonnie* (= good-looking), *glamour, raid*, and *wee* (= small). In Scotland a wide range of traditional Scots usage intermixes with standard English.

Scottish Monarchs 1005–1603

This table covers the period from the unification of Scotland to the union of the crowns of Scotland and England.

Reign	Name
	Celtic Kings
1005–34	Malcolm II
1034–40	Duncan I
1040–57	Macbeth
1057–93	Malcolm III Canmore
1093–94	Donald III Donalbane
1094	Duncan II
1094–97	Donald III (restored)
1097–1107	Edgar
1107–24	Alexander I
1124–53	David I
1153–65	Malcolm IV
1165–1214	William the Lion
1214–49	Alexander II
1249–86	Alexander III
1286–90	Margaret of Norway
	English Domination
1292–96	John Baliol
1296–1306	annexed to England
	House of Bruce
1306–29	Robert I the Bruce
1329–71	David II
	House of Stuart
1371–90	Robert II
1390–1406	Robert III
1406–37	James I
1437–60	James II
1460–88	James III
1488–1513	James IV
1513–42	James V
1542–67	Mary
1567–1625	James VI
1603	union of crowns

Scotland The Brave

Hark where the night is falling
Hark hear the pipes a calling
Loudly and proudly calling down thru the glen
There where the hills are sleeping
Now feel the blood a leaping
High as the spirits of the old highland men

Towering in gallant fame
Scotland my mountain hame
High may your proud standards gloriously wave
Land of my high endeavour
Land of the shining river
Land of my heart forever, Scotland the Brave

High in the misty mountains
Out by the purple highlands
Brave are the hearts that beat beneath Scottish skies
Wild are the winds to meet you
Staunch are the friends that greet you
Kind as the love that shines from fair maidens eyes

The Scottish National Anthem: 'Flower of Scotland'

Although modern, this anthem commemorates the Battle of Bannockburn in 1314 when the Scottish Army under Robert (I) the Bruce King of Scots defeated Edward II, King of England.

O Flower of Scotland, When will we see Your like again
That fought and died for, Your wee bit Hill and Glen
And stood against him, Proud Edward's Army
And sent him homeward, Tae think again.

The Hills are bare now, and Autumn leaves lie thick and still
O'er land that is lost now, Which those so dearly held
That stood against him, Proud Edward's Army
And sent him homeward, Tae think again.

Those days are past now, And in the past they must remain
But we can still rise now, And be the nation again
That stood against him, Proud Edward's Army
And sent him homeward, Tae think again.

Flower of Scotland, When will we see Your like again
That fought and died for, Your wee bit Hill and Glen
And stood against him, Proud Edward's Army
And sent him homeward, Tae think again.

Scotsman, The

Daily morning newspaper covering Scotland, published in Edinburgh. Established in 1817, it had a circulation of over 80,000 in 1998. *The Scotsman* was the first newspaper to achieve distribution throughout Scotland. The Sunday sister paper, *Scotland on Sunday*, was established in 1988 and had a circulation of over 120,000 in 1998.

Scott, (George) Gilbert (1811–1878)

English architect. As the leading practical architect of the mid-19th-century ◊Gothic Revival in England, Scott was responsible for the building or restoration of many public buildings and monuments, including the Albert Memorial (1863–72), the Foreign Office in Whitehall (1862–73), and the St Pancras Station Hotel (1868–74), all in London.

Scotland: Historic Counties

Aberdeen	Lanark
Angus (fomerly Forfar)	Midlothian
Argyll	Moray
Ayr	Nairn
Banff	Orkney
Berwick	Peebles
Bute	Perth
Caithness	Renfrew
Clackmannan	Rose and Cromarty
Dumfries	Roxburgh
Dunbarton	Selkirk
East Lothian	Stirling
Fife	Sutherland
Inverness	West Lothian
Kincardine	Wigtown
Kinross	Zetland
Kirkcudbright	

Scott established himself as a restoration architect; his work began in earnest with Ely Cathedral in 1847, and was followed by many other restorations, some 40 cathedrals and 'minsters' in all.

Scott, Giles Gilbert (1880–1960)
English architect. He was the grandson of Gilbert ⇨Scott. He designed Liverpool Anglican Cathedral (begun 1903; completed 1978), Cambridge University Library (1931–34), and Waterloo Bridge, London (1939–45). He also designed and supervised the rebuilding of the House of Commons chamber at the Palace of Westminster in a modern Gothic style after World War II.

His design for Battersea Power Station (1932–34) set the pattern for British power stations and his red telephone boxes in London became a part of British tradition.

Scotland, land of the omnipotent No.

ALAN BOLD Scottish poet.
A Memory of Death (1969)

Scott, Paul Mark (1920–1978)
English novelist. He was the author of *The Raj Quartet* consisting of *The Jewel in the Crown* (1966), *The Day of the Scorpion* (1968), *The Towers of Silence* (1972), and *A Division of the Spoils* (1975), dealing with the British Raj in India. Other novels include *Staying On* (1977), set in post-independence India, for which he won the Booker Prize.

Scott, Peter Markham (1909–1989)
English naturalist, artist, and explorer, founder of the Wildfowl Trust at Slimbridge, Gloucestershire, England, in 1946, and a founder of the World Wildlife Fund (now World Wide Fund for Nature). Knighted 1973.

He was the son of Antarctic explorer Robert Falcon Scott; he studied at Cambridge, in Germany, and at the Royal Academy School, London. In 1936 he represented Britain in the Olympic Games, gaining a bronze medal for the single-handed sailing event. During World War II he served with the Royal Navy. In 1949 he led his first expedition, which was to explore the uncharted Perry River area in the Canadian Arctic. Scott also led ornithological expeditions to Iceland, Australasia, the Galápagos Islands, the Seychelles, and the Antarctic. He was the first president of the World Wildlife Fund 1961–67.

At no period of its history has Scotland ever stood as high in the scale of nations.

HUME BROWN
on David's reign in *History of Scotland* 1899. vol i

Scott, Ridley (1939–)
English film director and producer. His work includes some of the most visually spectacular and influential films of the 1980s and 1990s, such as *Alien* (1979) and *Blade Runner*

THE LONG RIVALRY: THE MEDIEVAL KINGDOM OF SCOTLAND

The only royal rivals of the medieval English kings in the British Isles lay in the north. The kings of the Scots claimed to be the heirs to a line of over 100 royal forebears, rulers of a people unconquered by invaders. From 1300, relations between the two realms of Britain were dictated by rival claims to land and power in the north of the island, claims which fuelled long-running war.

Clients and rivals

After the emergence of both kingdoms in the 9th century, Anglo-Scottish relations rested on a balance: between an English desire to bring Scotland into its political orbit, and Scottish territorial ambitions in northern England. These ambitions had by the 11th century encouraged Scotland's expansion from its heartlands north of the Forth. The annexation of Strathclyde and of English-settled Lothian marked out Scotland as an aggressive power with designs on Cumbria and Northumberland. After 1058, Scotland, unlike the other Celtic kingdoms, was ruled by a single dynasty; though challenged by rival claimants, the Canmores moved from being kings of an unruly federation to masters of their kingdom.

The Normans recognized this situation and there was no Norman conquest of Scotland. Instead the Norman kings sought to increase their influence with the Canmores. David I (1124–1153), as brother-in-law and vassal of Henry I of England, was part of the Anglo-Norman world. The politics and culture of 12th-century Scotland were transformed by the arrival of the personnel and practices of Norman nobility, church, government, and trade. If change was not entirely peaceful, in Scotland it did not sweep away native power.

The Canmores used the new techniques of war and administration to increase royal authority. Although influenced heavily by their powerful neighbour, neither David I nor his successors became vassal rulers; from 1124 to 1286, designs on northern England were still pursued and English claims to be lords of Scotland still resisted.

The long war

In the last decades of the 13th century, the end of the Canmore dynasty and Edward I of England's search for real influence in Scotland combined to sweep away the balance between English claims and Scottish independence. From 1296 until 1560 war was the normal state of relations between the two kingdoms.

English aims varied between the destruction of the Scottish kingdom and its reduction to a vassal-state. The greatest efforts to achieve these goals came in the half-century up to 1346, but claims to overlordship were never abandoned. English kings continued to press these claims and from 1544 union based on war was revived in the 'Rough Wooing' of Scotland by Henry VIII.

The demands of a war for survival shaped late medieval Scotland. The language of resistance to Edward I and his heirs stressed the existence of Scotland as a community whose rights were under threat. The usurpation of Robert the Bruce in 1306 harnessed effective royal leadership to this sense of grievance. Bruce's military success against English forces was exploited to create a bond between his kingship and the aristocratic community. This bond was cemented by the rise of families, like the Stewarts and Douglases, who had been closest to Bruce's cause. In the century after his death in 1329, when the Scots lacked a similar royal leader, these noble families combined private aggrandizement with a patriotic cause, the maintenance of the kingdom. Scotland's place in diplomacy was defined by a role as the hereditary enemy of England and as the ally of England's enemy, France. By the mid-14th century, British conflict and European conflict had become intertwined.

Kingdom and community

History and geography combined to make medieval Scotland seem little more than a collection of provinces by comparison with England. Areas like Argyll, Moray, and Galloway retained significance and identity into the 15th century. While the Canmores had added Caithness and the Hebrides to their realm, the highland areas of the kingdom remained under only limited control. Sustained war and, from 1329, weak kingship strengthened the power of regional lords.

In the west and north this meant a resurgence of Gaelic power built around the Lordship of the Isles, which stretched from Ulster to Inverness. The threat from the Isles fostered a growing cultural divide between lowland and highland Scotland after 1400.

Traditions of kingship did not sit comfortably in a realm which by 1400 was dominated by great lords. The subsequent century witnessed a series of aggressive rulers of the Stewart dynasty asserting the rights of the Crown to the full. Two of the five kings between 1406 and 1542 died at their subjects' hands, and all faced opposition. However, they ultimately restored royal primacy. By 1500 Scotland seemed secure as a small but stable kingdom with connections in diplomacy, trade, and culture which stretched beyond the British Isles.

by Michael Brown

(1982). Criticized for sacrificing storyline and character development in favour of ornate sets, Scott replied with *Thelma and Louise* (1991), a carefully wrought story of female bonding and adventure.

Having started as a set designer, Scott graduated to directing episodes of the television series *Z Cars* before leaving the BBC in 1967. He completed his first film, *The Duellists*, in 1977. Among his other films are *Legend* (1985), *Someone to Watch Over Me* (1987), *Black Rain* (1989), *1492 – The Conquest of Paradise* (1992), *White Squall* (1996), and *G.I. Jane* (1997).

Scott, Robert Falcon, known as Scott of the Antarctic (1868–1912)

English explorer who commanded two Antarctic expeditions, 1901–04 and 1910–12. On 18 January 1912 he reached the South Pole, shortly after the Norwegian Roald

Amundsen, but on the return journey he and his companions died in a blizzard only a few miles from their base camp. His journal was recovered and published in 1913.

Born in Devonport, he entered the navy in 1882. With Scott on the final expedition were Edward Wilson (1872–1912), Laurence ◊Oates, H R Bowers, and E Evans. The Scott Polar Research Institute in Cambridge was founded in 1920 out of funds donated by the public following Scott's death, as a memorial to him and his companions.

Scott, Samuel (1702–1772)

English painter. He painted topographical views, particularly of the River Thames, and depicted ships and sea fights in the Dutch style (14 are in the National Maritime Museum, Greenwich, London).

From about 1735 he turned to views of London and the Thames. Many of his subjects were later painted by the Venetian artist Canaletto, who came to London in 1746. Although Scott admired Canaletto, his style is distinct.

Scott, Terry stage name of Owen John Scott (1927–1994)

English comic actor. He achieved popularity on television partnering June Whitfield in *Happy Ever After* and *Terry and June* (1974–88), in which he epitomized suburban man, by turns timorous and truculent. His wide-ranging career also encompassed theatre, films, and radio.

Scott, Walter (1771–1832)

Scottish novelist and poet. His first works were translations of German ballads and collections of Scottish ballads, which he followed with narrative poems of his own, such as *The Lay of the Last Minstrel* (1805), *Marmion* (1808), and *The Lady of the Lake* (1810). He gained a European reputation for his historical novels such as *Waverley* (1814), *Rob Roy* (1817), *The ◊Heart of Midlothian* (1818), and *Ivanhoe* (1819), all published anonymously.

SCOTT, WALTER *Scottish novelist and poet Sir Walter Scott, whose early romantic ballads made him the most popular author of his day after Byron.* Waverley *(1814) was the first in a long series of historical novels which Scott wrote anonymously until 1827. He was created a baronet in 1820. Corbis*

Scott exerted a strong influence on the imaginative life of his country. He stimulated an interest in Scottish history and materially affected the literary movement of his time: his unconventional manner of writing and his total freedom from the academic point of view were largely instrumental in arousing the French Romantic movement. Scott was also the creator of the historical novel, combining naturalness and realism with the historical and romantic element of adventure and the marvels of superstition.

Scott was crippled for life following an early attack of poliomyelitis. Educated at Edinburgh University, he became a lawyer, and in 1799 was appointed a sheriff-depute of Selkirkshire. His *Minstrelsy of the Scottish Border* appeared in 1802–03, and from then he combined writing with his legal profession. He supplied half the capital for starting the publishing house of Ballantyne & Co, and purchased and rebuilt the house of Abbotsford on the Tweed. In 1820 he was elected president of the Royal Society of Scotland. His last years were marked by frantic writing to pay off his debts after the bankruptcy of the printing and publishing business, and continuous overwork ended in a nervous breakdown.

Scott, William Bell (1811–1890)

Scottish painter, illustrator, and poet. He painted historical themes, his major works being scenes of Northumberland history, and he was closely associated with the ◊Pre-Raphaelite Brotherhood, though he regarded himself as a 'realist'.

Scottish Ballet

Ballet company founded in 1956 as the Western Theatre Ballet, based in Glasgow. It tours Scotland and northern England.

Scottish Borders

Unitary authority in southeast Scotland, created in 1996 to replace the former Borders region

Area 4,733 sq km/1,827 sq mi

Towns Galashiels, Hawick, Jedburgh, Kelso, Newtown St Boswells (administrative headquarters), Peebles, Selkirk

Physical much of the west part of the area is upland (Lammermuir, Moorfoot and Pentland Hills); Broad Law (840 m/2,756 ft), near Tweedsmuir, is the highest point. The principal river, the Tweed, traverses the region from west to east; its tributaries include the River Teviot. The largest loch is St Mary's, and the only substantial area of low-lying agricultural land is the Merse in the southeast, near the English border. The coastline is generally precipitous

Features Walter Scott's home at Abbotsford; Field Marshal

Haig and Walter Scott buried at Dryburgh Abbey; Melrose Abbey (12th century)
Famous people Mungo Park, James Hogg (Scottish poet 'the Ettrick Shepherd'), Walter Scott
Industries electronics, timber, knitwear, tweed
Agriculture sheep and cattle; cereals and root crops; fishing
Population (1995) 106,200

Archaeology
The area has been occupied since early hunter-gatherers moved into Scotland; early monuments include many hill-forts, of which Eildon Hill North, near Melrose, is the most impressive.

Architecture
There are medieval abbeys at Melrose, Jedburgh, Dryburgh, and Kelso. A series of stone-built castles, including Hermitage in Liddesdale (*c.* 13th century), testify to the insecurity of the border area well into the 16th century. Later buildings include Abbotsford, created by Walter Scott (1822), and Floors Castle, built by William Adam (1721–25) and altered by Playfair in the 1840s.

Border unrest
The Raid of the Redeswire (1575), an English defeat at the hands of Jedburgh's provost and townspeople, was the last major engagement of this kind. At Philiphaugh on Yarrow Water, the Covenanter General Leslie defeated the Marquis of Montrose in 1645.

Economy
Lacking coal, the border area was largely bypassed in the industrialization which took place during the 19th century. The tweed industry, however, contributed to the expansion of the mill towns. The area is essentially rural; limited afforestation is now taking place.

Environment
There are 88 Sites of Special Scientific Interest, three National Nature Reserves, three Ramsars (wetland sites), three Special Protection Areas, and two National Scenic Areas.

Scottish Gaelic language

See ◊Gaelic language.

Scottish Gaelic literature

The earliest examples of Scottish Gaelic prose belong to the period 1000–1150, but the most significant early original composition is the history of the MacDonalds in the Red and Black Books at Clanranald. The first printed book in Scottish Gaelic was a translation of Knox's Prayer Book (1567). Prose Gaelic is at its best in the folk tales, proverbs, and essays by writers such as Norman MacLeod in the 19th and Donald Lamont in the 20th century.

Scottish Gaelic poetry falls into two main categories. The older, syllabic verse was composed by professional bards. The chief sources of our knowledge of this are the Book of the Dean of Lismore (16th century), which is also the main early source for the Ossianic ballads; the panegyrics in the Books of Clanranald; and the Fernaig manuscript. Modern Scottish Gaelic stressed poetry began in the 17th century but reached its zenith during the Jacobite period with Alexander MacDonald, Duncan Macintyre, Rob Donn, and Dugald Buchanan. Only William Livingstone (1808–1870) kept alive the old nationalistic spirit in the 19th century. During and after World War II a new school emerged, including Somhairle MacGilleathain, George Campbell-Hay, and Ruaraidh MacThómais.

In Scotland there is no shadow even of representation. There is neither a representation of property for the counties, nor of population for the towns.

Charles James Fox English Whig politician. Quoted in Cobbett's *Parliamentary History of England*

Scottish law

The legal system of Scotland. Owing to its separate development, Scotland has a system differing from the rest of the UK, being based on civil law. Its continued separate existence was guaranteed by the Act of Union with England in 1707.

In the latter part of the 20th century England adopted some features already existing in Scottish law, for example, majority jury verdicts and the replacement of police prosecution by a system of public prosecution (see ◊procurator fiscal). There is no separate system of ◊equity. The supreme civil court is the House of Lords, below which comes the ◊Court of Session, and then the sheriff court (in some respects similar to the English county court, but with criminal as well as civil jurisdiction). More serious criminal cases are heard by the High Court of Justiciary which also sits as a Court of Criminal Appeal (with no appeal to the Lords). Juries have 15 members, and a verdict of 'not proven' can be given. There is no coroner, inquiries into deaths being undertaken by the procurator fiscal.

Scottish National Gallery of Modern Art

Edinburgh gallery housing the Scottish national collection from 1900 to the present day, founded in 1960. It comprises the most concentrated collection of international modern art in Britain outside London, together with a representative display of modern Scottish art. The collection is especially rich in sculpture, with works by Bourdelle, Moore, Arp, and Giacometti. The permanent collection is constantly supplemented by temporary exhibitions.

Scottish National Party, SNP

Nationalist party, advocating the separation of Scotland from the UK as an independent state within the European Union. It was formed by the amalgamation of several early nationalist parties in 1934 and at first advocated only autonomy within the UK. It is second only to the Labour Party in Scotland, having forced the Conservatives into third place.

The party gained its first parliamentary victory in 1945 but did not make serious headway in parliament until the 1970s when it became an influential bloc at Westminster, and its support was crucial to James Callaghan's Labour government. At the 1983 general election, SNP support in Scotland fell back to 12%. However, after subsequently adopting the stance of 'independence within a federal Europe', its support climbed steadily, reaching 22% of the Scottish vote in May 1997, when it won six of Scotland's 72 seats. Led since 1990 by Alex Salmond, the SNP advocates separation by 2007, the 300th anniversary of the Act of Union with England, and is expected to poll strongly in the 1999 elections to the new devolved Scottish parliament.

Scottish National Portrait Gallery

Edinburgh art gallery, founded in 1882. It aims to illustrate Scottish history with portraits of Scots distinguished in any activity, and paintings which illustrate the history of Scottish dress and other historical developments such as topographical changes. The sequence of portraits starts in the 16th century with Mary Queen of Scots, and continues without serious breaks to the present day (though living people are excepted).

> *Fully 83% said they feel no dislike of the English.*
>
> David MacCrone Projessor at Edinburgh University. On the findings of an opinion poll in Scotland; the *Sunday Times*, June 1998

Scottish Natural Heritage

Scottish nature conservation body formed in 1991 after the break-up of the national Nature Conservancy Council. It is government-funded.

Scottish Office

Government department established in 1707 in England, and in 1938 in Scotland. The ◊Scottish Parliament is scheduled to take over its role. In 1998 the Scottish office employed nearly 5,000 people. Its secretary of state from 1997 was Donald Dewar.

After elections in 1999 to the Scottish Parliament, Scotland will have its own elected executive, headed by a first minister, with considerable powers.

Scottish Opera

Scottish opera company founded in 1962 and based in Glasgow. Richard Armstrong became its music director in 1993. It tours in Scotland and northern England.

Scottish Parliament

129-member devolved body, approved overwhelmingly in a September 1997 Scottish referendum, when it was agreed the parliament would be based in Edinburgh, and that elections would take place in May 1999, with the first meeting of the Scottish Parliament scheduled for 2000. The parliament has law-making powers in all areas, except those of defence, foreign affairs, the constitution, social security, company regulation, economic management, and taxation. It also has the authority to vary the basic rate of income tax in Scotland by up to 3p to supplement a block grant equivalent to the current Scottish Office budget of £14 billion.

A first minister (prime minister) will be drawn from the majority grouping within the parliament, and relevant ministers will sit with their UK government counterparts at negotiating meetings in Brussels whenever Scottish interests are affected. The parliament will be elected by a mixture of first-past-the-post for 73 members (from existing Westminster constituencies, with an extra seat created through dividing the Orkney and Shetland constituency into two), and proportional representation for 56 members from party lists in the eight Scottish European Parliament constituencies.

Scott Report

Report in 1996 resulting from an inquiry into alleged British government complicity in secretly allowing sales of arms or arms-related equipment to Iraq in the period leading up to the invasion of Kuwait in August 1990. Headed by Lord Justice Richard Scott (1934–), the board of inquiry heard evidence from a succession of senior officials and politicians.

The report was published in February 1996. Its length and style obscured its conclusions, but it was clear that there had been considerable duplicity on the part of highly placed government officials, and a general tendency to hide from Parliament and the public any information that might show the government in a bad light.

Scott Thomas, Kristin (1960–)

English screen actress. She spent much of her early career working on film and television productions in France, and rose to international prominence in the 1990s, an aloof presence of refined good looks in such successes as *Four Weddings and a Funeral* (1994), *Angels and Insects* (1995), *Mission: Impossible* (1996), and *The English Patient* (1996). She also featured in *The Horse Whisperer* (1998).

Scouts

Worldwide youth organization that emphasizes character, citizenship, and outdoor life. It was founded (as the Boy Scouts) in England in 1908 by Robert ◊Baden-Powell. His book *Scouting for Boys* (1908) led to the incorporation in the UK of the Boy Scout Association by royal charter in 1912. There are some 25 million members of the World Organization of the Scout Movement (1998).

There are four branches: Beaver Scouts (aged 6–8), Cub Scouts (aged 8–10½), Scouts (10½–15½), and Venture Scouts (15½–20). Girls were admitted to the Venture Scouts in 1976 and to the other branches in 1991 (see also ◊Girl Guides). In 1966 the rules of the Boy Scout Association (now the Scout Association) were revised to embody a more adult and 20th-century image, and the dress was updated; for example, the traditional shorts were exchanged for long trousers. There are over 607,000 members of the Scout Association in the UK (1998).

scrapie

Fatal disease of sheep and goats that attacks the central nervous system, causing deterioration of the brain cells, and leading to the characteristic staggering gait and other behavioural abnormalities, before death. It is related to ◊bovine spongiform encephalopathy, and ◊Creutzfeldt–Jakob disease in humans. It is a transmissible spongiform encephalopathy.

UK farmers have a statutory duty to report all cases of scrapie but it was reported that very few actually comply with it. In 1996, only 453 cases were confirmed in England and Wales, whereas the real incidence was probably much higher.

Scruton, Roger Vernon (1944–)

British philosopher and right-wing social critic, professor of aesthetics at Birkbeck College, London, from 1985. Advocating the political theories of Edmund ◊Burke in such books as *The Meaning of Conservatism* (1980), he influenced the free-market movements in eastern Europe.

He makes frequent appearances as a guest on BBC radio discussion programmes.

Scudamore, Peter Michael (1958–)

British National Hunt jockey. He was champion jockey in 1982 (shared with John ◊Francome) and from 1986 to 1992. In 1988–89 he rode a record 221 winners, a total surpassed in 1997–98 by Tony ◊McCoy. In April 1993 he announced his retirement from the sport, with a world record 1,677 winners.

sculpture

Historically sculpture has been mainly religious or monumental in purpose, the large Celtic stone crosses of the early Christian period (from AD 597) being among the earliest sculptures in Britain. During the medieval period sculpture was epitomized by niche figures carved in stone for churches and by delicate ivory carvings. Following the Reformation, sculpture became increasingly secularized along with the other visual arts. In the late 17th and early 18th centuries Baroque design favoured relief rather than free-standing sculptures, Grinling Gibbons producing carved wooden panels (mainly birds, flowers, and fruit) for St Paul's Cathedral and many large country houses. The Neo-Classical sculptors of the 18th century concentrated on smooth perfection of form and surface. Leading Neo-Classicists were Thomas Banks, John Flaxman, and John Gibson.

In the late 19th century the English 'New Sculpture' movement (1890–1915) was characterized by naturalistic modelling and the influence of Symbolism. One of its leading figures was George Frampton, sculptor of *Peter Pan* in Kensington Gardens, London.

In the 20th century various techniques for 'constructing' sculptures were developed, for example metal welding and assemblage. Sculptors such as Henry Moore, Barbara Hepworth, and Jacob Epstein used traditional materials and techniques to create forms inspired by 'primitive' art and nature. Followers of the non-representational school included Reg Butler and Anthony Caro. Traditional sculpture continued, as represented by Frank Dobson (1888–1963), whose work powerfully expresses the Modernist idiom.

Other sculptors have broken with the past entirely, rejecting both carving and modelling. Today the term sculpture applies to the mobiles of Lynn Chadwick and Kenneth Martin, assemblages of various materials, 'environment sculpture' and earthworks, and 'installations'. Contemporary sculptors who work in a variety of unconventional techniques include Damien ◊Hirst and Rachel Whiteread. Another development has been the sculpture garden or park, for example the Grizedale Forest sculpture project in the Lake District.

Scunthorpe

Industrial town and administrative headquarters of ◊North Lincolnshire, England, 39 km/24 mi west of Grimsby; population (1991) 74,700. It has one of Europe's largest iron and steel works, which has been greatly expanded with assistance from the European Union. Other industries include engineering, electronics, food processing, clothing, and furniture.

The first ironworks were opened here in 1864 and steelmaking began in 1890.

SDLP

Abbreviation for ◊**Social Democratic Labour Party**, a Northern Ireland political party.

SDP

Abbreviation for ◊**Social Democratic Party**, a former British political party.

Seaford

Resort in East Sussex, England, 13 km/8 mi west of Eastbourne on the South ◊Downs; population (1991) 19,800. The Seven Sisters chalk cliffs are nearby.

Seaford was once the outlet for the lower River Ouse and an important port, but in 1570 a great storm shifted the course of the lower Ouse westwards, resulting in the development of a new port, Newhaven.

Seaforth, Loch

Sea-inlet on the island of ◊Lewis, in the Outer Hebrides, Western Isles unitary authority, Scotland, penetrating inland from the southeast for a distance of about 25 km/16 mi.

Seaham

Seaport in Durham, northeast England, 8 km/5 mi south of Sunderland; population (1991) 21,800. It has had an engineering industry since the 19th century, and the town also has shipping services. The poet George Byron married Anne Isabella Milbanke at **Seaham Hall** nearby.

Seaham was formerly a coalmining town; the Vane Tempest Colliery (the last coal mine in the Durham coalfield) closed in 1992. A regeneration project is intended to re-develop this site and that of the former Seaham Colliery.

Seaman, David Andrew (1963–)

English footballer whose brilliant goalkeeping performances in the 1996 European Championships won him recognition as a world-class player. He made his England debut in 1988 and by August 1998 had gained 44 caps. An Arsenal player from 1990, he helped the club to win six major trophies including two league championships. He had previously played for Leeds United, Peterborough United, Birmingham City, and Queen's Park Rangers.

Searle, Ronald William Fordham (1920–)

English cartoonist and illustrator. He created the schoolgirls of St Trinian's characters in 1941 and has made numerous cartoons of cats. His drawings as a Japanese prisoner of war during World War II established him as a serious artist. His sketches of places and people include *Paris Sketch Book* (1950) and *Rake's Progress* (1955).

seaside

Favourite destination for many Britons, especially for day-trips. The seaside became especially popular with the advent of direct travel by rail. See chronology below for some seaside highlights.

Seathwaite

Hamlet at the head of Borrowdale, in the English ◊Lake District, Cumbria, 13 km/8 mi southwest of Keswick. With an average of 3,300 mm/130 ins per year, Seathwaite has the highest annual rainfall in England.

Seathwaite marks the beginning of the ascent by foot to Sty Head Pass, from where many of the peaks in the region may be climbed.

secretary of state

A title held by a number of ministers; for example, the secretary of state for foreign and commonwealth affairs.

Each secretary of state is a member of the cabinet and is assisted by at least one minister of state, one or more parliamentary under-secretaries, and by a permanent under-secretary and official staff.

Historically secretaries of state were the constitutional channel of communication between the crown and its subjects. The office resulted from the expansion of the royal household as the king's business grew. A king's secretary existed in the reign of Henry III. Under Henry VIII the office was considerably enhanced and its holder designated principal secretary.

The title 'secretary of state' appears to have developed in the 18th century. In 1801 there was one for home affairs, one for foreign matters, and a third for war and colonial work; in modern times the number of secretaries of state has been considerably increased.

Scotland

Scottish affairs were originally the responsibility of the home secretary and various other departments, but a Scottish Office and secretary for Scotland were created in 1885, and the latter became a secretary of state in 1926. The secretary of state for Scotland is responsible for agriculture, education, health and social services, and home affairs in Scotland.

Wales

A minister of Welsh Affairs was created in 1951, but the post was usually combined with another portfolio. In 1964, however, a Welsh Office was established and a secretary of state for Wales appointed. Until the Welsh Assembly sits, the latter is responsible for housing, town and country planning, local government, roads, and primary and secondary education in Wales.

Secret Diary of Adrian Mole Aged 13¾, The

Bestselling novel by English author Sue ◊Townsend, published in 1982, in which the fictional teenager Adrian Mole reveals his innermost thoughts and feelings about the problems of his existence, from spots to his parents' marriage. It was the highest selling paperback in the UK in the 1980s (over

THE SEASIDE IN BRITAIN: SOME KEY DATES

1620 The discovery of a mineral spring leads Scarborough to develop as a spa resort.

1750s 'Beale's bathing machines', wagons pulled by horses into the sea at Margate, allow bathers of either sex to enter the water discreetly, from under the cover of a large hood. Similar wagons are still in use over a century later.

1870s Having hitherto bathed in the sea naked, men are expected to wear drawers or long bathing costumes.

18 September 1879 The first illuminations at the seaside resort of Blackpool, Lancashire, are switched on.

1889 Southend pier is opened. Extended in 1929, it becomes the longest pier in the world.

1894 The first holiday camp on a permanent site is opened near Douglas, Isle of Man, by Joseph Cunningham. The campers are all male and no alcohol is allowed.

1903 The first mixed-bathing in Britain is introduced, at Bexhill-on-Sea, Sussex.

c. **1903** Postcards become very popular in Britain as more people go to the seaside for holidays. Donald McGill begins producing a series of saucy seaside postcards.

1929 The resort of Bognor adds 'Regis' to its name after George V convalesces nearby at Aldwick.

1935 Skegness becomes the site of the first Butlin's holiday camp.

1963 Tony Hancock's film *The Punch and Judy Man* shows traditional seaside entertainments in decline.

30 March 1964 Fights between rival Mods and Rockers break out in Clacton, Essex, and other seaside resorts during the Easter weekend.

9 August 1979 Brighton, East Sussex, is the first British seaside resort to provide an area designated for nudists.

1988 Following concern for the conditions of bathing beaches, the subject of a directive from the European Economic Community on water quality, beaches in the UK that are free of industrial pollution, litter, and sewage, and with water of the highest quality, have the right to fly a blue flag.

3 million copies sold). The book was adapted for the stage in 1985 and has had several sequels including *The Growing Pains of Adrian Mole* (1984).

Secret Garden, The

Novel for children by Frances Hodgson ⇨Burnett first published in the USA in 1911. Mary, a spoilt, sickly orphan, is sent from India to England to live at the house of her uncle, a crippled recluse. Her cultivation of the secret garden from a forgotten wilderness helps to transform her health and outlook and leads her to effect a similar change in her cousin Colin, who believed himself to be an invalid.

Securities and Investment Board

Body with the overall responsibility for policing financial dealings in the City of London. Introduced in 1987 following the deregulation process of the so-called ⇨Big Bang, it acts as an umbrella organization to such self-regulating bodies as the Stock Exchange.

sedan chair

Enclosed chair for one passenger carried on poles by two or more bearers. Introduced into England by Sanders Duns-combe in 1634, by the 18th century it was the equivalent of a one-person taxi. The name derives from southern Italy rather than from the French town of Sedan.

Sedgefield

Town in County Durham, northeast England, 13 km/8 mi northwest of Stockton; population (1991) 88,400. There is a racecourse nearby. Sedgefield lies in a former mining district, and local limestone quarries used to supply the steel industry.

Tony Blair, UK Prime Minister from 1997, became MP for the Sedgefield parliamentary constituency in 1983.

Sedgemoor, Battle of

In English history, a battle on 6 July 1685 in which ⇨Monmouth' s rebellion was crushed by the forces of James II, on a tract of marshy land 5 km/3 mi southeast of Bridgwater, Somerset.

Sedgwick, Adam (1785–1873)

English geologist who contributed greatly to understanding the stratigraphy of the British Isles, using fossils as an index of relative time. Together with Scottish geologist Roderick ⇨Murchison, he identified the Devonian system in southwest England.

Segal, Walter (1907–1985)

Swiss-born British architect. He pioneered community architecture in the UK. From the 1960s he developed proposals for end-users to design and build their own housing, using simple construction methods and standardized low-tech building components, such as timber framing and pre-cut cladding boards. Houses built by the Lewisham Self-Build Housing Association, London (1977–80), are examples of his system in practice.

Selborne

Village in Hampshire, southern England, 8 km/5 mi southeast of Alton; population (1995 est) 1,300. Gilbert White, author of *The Natural History of Selborne* (1789), was born here. The Selborne Society (founded in 1885) promotes the study of wildlife. Brewing is carried out here, and there is also some cultivation of hops.

The Wakes, the house where Gilbert White lived, contains a museum. West of the village, between Selborne and Newton Valence, is Selborne Hill (property of the National Trust) where Gilbert White made many of his observations.

Selby

Market town on the River Ouse, in York unitary authority, northern England, 22 km/14 mi south of York; population (1991) 15,000. Industries include sugar-beet refining, ship-building, paper, and chemicals. It was formerly a coalmining town; the nearby Selby coalfield (discovered in 1967) – once the largest new coalfield in Europe, producing 12 million tonnes of coal a year – was closed in 1992. Features include a 12th-century abbey church.

The church of St Mary was the abbey church of a Benedictine abbey founded in 1069; it was restored in 1906.

select committee

Any of several long-standing committees of the House of Commons, such as the Environment Committee and the Treasury and Civil Service Committee. These were intended to restore parliamentary control of the executive, improve the quality of legislation, and scrutinize public spending and the work of government departments. Select committees represent the major parliamentary reform of the 20th century, and a possible means – through their all-party membership – of avoiding the automatic repeal of one government's measures by its successor.

Select committees, normally consisting of not more than 15 members in proportion to the parties in the House, are appointed to consider particular matters and, more rarely, to take the committee stage of a bill. Apart from those select committees which are concerned primarily with the internal affairs of the House of Commons (for example, the select committees on privileges, procedure, standing orders, and the House of Commons (services)), select committees are used to investigate various matters or policies. In some cases a select committee is established to deal with a particular matter, and once it has reported back to the House it ceases to exist. In other cases, however, select committees have a more or less continuous existence.

Select committees operate less formally than standing committees, are less partisan in atmosphere, sometimes have the assistance of ad hoc advisers, may receive oral and written evidence, and may demand the production of certain documents and records. Departmental ministers attend to answer questions, and if information is withheld on a matter of wide concern, a debate of the whole House may be called. In short, select committees are one of Parliament's principal means of scrutinizing the activities and policies of the government.

Selkirk, Alexander (1676–1721)

Scottish sailor marooned 1704–09 in the Juan Fernández Islands in the south Pacific. His story inspired Daniel Defoe to write *Robinson Crusoe.*

Sellafield

Site of a nuclear power station on the coast of Cumbria, northwest England. It was known as **Windscale** until 1971, when the management of the site was transferred from the UK Atomic Energy Authority to British Nuclear Fuels Ltd. It reprocesses more than 1,000 tonnes of spent fuel from nuclear reactors annually. The plant is the world's greatest discharger of radioactive waste: between 1968 and 1979, 180 kg/400 lb of plutonium was discharged into the Irish Sea.

In 1996, British Nuclear Fuels was fined £25,000 after admitting 'serious and significant' failures in safety that left a Sellafield plant worker contaminated with radioactivity.

In 1998, the Norwegian environment minister called for a ban on the release of technetium-99 into the sea. It is being released from Sellafield and causing raised concentrations along the coast of Norway.

The thermal oxide reprocessing (THORP) unit at Sellafield has been given the Health and Safety Executive's nuclear inspectorate's 'consent to operate' and already has advance orders worth £12 billion, two-thirds of which are from overseas.

Sellers, Peter stage name of Richard Henry Sellers (1925–1980)

English comedian and film actor. He was particularly skilled at mimicry. He made his name in the madcap British radio programme *The Goon Show* (1949–60). His films include *The Ladykillers* (1955), *I'm All Right Jack* (1960), *Dr Strangelove* (1964), five *Pink Panther* films (1964–78) (as the bumbling Inspector Clouseau), and *Being There* (1979).

Selsey, or Selsea ('seal island')

Fishing village in West Sussex, England, 11 km/7 mi south of Chichester; population (1991) 8,400. The Selsey peninsula has yachting and beaches, and there is a wildlife sanctuary at Pagham Harbour. The headland of **Selsey Bill** projects to the south of the village.

Selsey has been severely affected by coastal erosion. It was a Saxon bishopric before 1075, but the cathedral is now beneath the sea.

Selwyn Lloyd, (John) Selwyn Brooke Lloyd, Baron Selwyn Lloyd (1904–1978)

British Conservative politician. He was foreign secretary 1955–60 and chancellor of the Exchequer 1960–62.

He was responsible for the creation of the National Economic Development Council, but the unpopularity of his policy of wage restraint in an attempt to defeat inflation forced his resignation. He was Speaker of the House of Commons 1971–76.

Sepoy Rebellion

Alternative name for the ◊Indian Mutiny, a revolt of Indian soldiers against the British in India 1857–58.

Serjeant at Arms

Officer appointed to the House of Commons by the sovereign to attend on the Speaker while Parliament is sitting. The Serjeant at Arms precedes the Speaker with the mace on the Speaker's entering or leaving the House, and bears the mace on formal occasions at the bar of the House. Until 1971 there was a Serjeant at Arms in the House of Lords but those duties are now carried out by Black Rod.

The Serjeant at Arms was originally an officer of the Crown and who possessed broad executive functions and later attended the sovereign upon certain ceremonial occasions. A Serjeant at Arms was first assigned to the House of Commons in the 15th century. Under the direction of the Speaker, the Serjeant at Arms is responsible for seeing to the removal of people (including members on occasions) who are directed to withdraw but decline to do so; for the admission of strangers to the House; and for the custody of people the House commits for contempt. The police and the messengers on duty in the House are under the Serjeant at Arms's direction.

The Serjeant at Arms is responsible for serving orders of the House on those whom they concern, and is 'housekeeper' of the House, and as such has charge of committee and other rooms. While the House is sitting a chair at the bar is occupied by the Serjeant at Arms or one of the three deputies.

Serota, Nicholas Andrew (1946–)

British art-gallery director. He has been director successively of the Museum of Modern Art, Oxford (1973–76), the Whitechapel Art Gallery (1976–87), and the Tate Gallery, London (from 1988). At the Tate he became controversial for instituting annual re-hangs of the collection, which sometimes relegated established favourite works to storage.

SERPS

Acronym for **State Earnings-Related Pension Schemes**, the UK state pension scheme.

Pension schemes operated by private companies may now be run in conjunction with SERPS; if they are 'contracted in', part of an employee's National Insurance contributions go towards the pension, which is linked to final salary.

Session, Court of

One of the civil courts in Scotland; see ◊Court of Session.

Settlement, Act of

A law passed in 1701 during the reign of King William III, designed to ensure a Protestant succession to the throne by excluding the Roman Catholic descendants of James II in favour of the Protestant House of Hanover. Elizabeth II still reigns under this act.

Sevenoaks

Town in Kent, southeast England, 32 km/20 mi southeast of London, population (1991) 24,000. Industries include chemical manufacture, financial services, and insurance. Nearby are the houses of Knole (1456) and Chevening (17th century).

Most of the oak trees from which the town derives its name were blown down in the gales which struck southern England in October 1987.

Sevenoaks prospered in the 15th century with the building of the Archbishop of Canterbury's palace at Knole, southeast of the town. The mansion became the property of the crown in 1532, and in 1566 Elizabeth I presented it to her cousin, Thomas Sackville, later Earl of Dorset. In 1946 the fourth Lord Sackville presented it to the National Trust. Knole is set in a park of about 405 ha/1,000 acres.

The predominantly Perpendicular church of St Nicholas includes Saxon stonework and a 13th-century nave. Sevenoaks School was established in the 15th-century. The Vine is one of England's oldest cricket grounds.

Severn, Welsh Hafren

River in Britain, which rises on the slopes of Plynlimon, in Ceredigion, west Wales, and flows east and then south, finally forming a long estuary leading into the Bristol Channel; length 336 km/208 mi. The Severn is navigable for 290 km/180 mi, up to Welshpool (Trallwng) on the Welsh border. The principal towns on its course are Shrewsbury, Worcester, and Gloucester. England and South Wales are linked by two road bridges and a railway tunnel crossing the Severn (see ◊Severn Bridge. A remarkable feature of the river is a tidal wave known as the 'Severn Bore' that flows for some miles upstream and can reach a height of 2 m/6 ft.

The Severn rail tunnel was built 1873–85. The first of the road bridges to be built opened in 1966, and carries the M4 motorway linking London and South Wales. A second road bridge was opened in 1996 and carries the M48 motorway. Scottish researchers estimate that in 1998, the Severn Estuary was contaminated with the radioactive isotope of carbon, carbon-14. The isotope, which is at five times the normal background level, was discharged from a medical isotope production plant in Cardiff.

Course

From its source, the Severn passes east through Powys and enters Shropshire near the Brythen Hills. Southeast of Shrewsbury, the river passes through ◊Ironbridge Gorge, 'cradle of the Industrial Revolution' and now a tourist attraction. Thereafter, it runs through Worcestershire and Gloucestershire, widening considerably after it passes Newnham. The Severn is navigable by larger ships (of around 8,000 tonnes) as far as Sharpness, and by smaller vessels (up to 700 tonnes) to Gloucester, while barges of 350 tonnes capacity can negotiate its upper reaches as far as Stourport. The Severn is connected with the rivers Trent and Mersey via the Staffordshire and Worcestershire Canal, and with the canal network around Birmingham via the Worcester and Birmingham Canal, which joins the Severn at Worcester. Between Gloucester and Sharpness, the treacherous nature of the riverbed necessitated the construction, in 1827, of the 26km-/16 mi-long, lock-free Sharpness and Gloucester Ship Canal. Tributaries of the Severn include the Teme, Stour, ◊Wye, Vyrnwy, Tern, and ◊Avon; in total, the river basin covers an area of 11,420 sq km/4,409 sq mi.

Crossings

Between 1873 and 1885, a rail tunnel was dug underneath the Severn near Chepstow, running for a distance of 7.2 km/4.4 mi, from New Passage to Portskewett; this crossing greatly facilitated travel between Bristol and the Welsh capital Cardiff. A road suspension bridge (see ◊Severn Bridge) was opened nearby, from Aust to Beachley, in 1966; this crossing carries the main M4 motorway linking London and South Wales and is subject to payment of a toll by users. Because of the increase in traffic volume, construction of a new road bridge was started in 1992 and completed five years later.

Hydroelectric power

In 1933, a committee recommended the construction of a hydroelectric power station on a river barrage at English Stones reef, which would utilize the tidal flow of the Severn. This plan, which was interrupted by World War II, was revived in 1945, when engineers confirmed the practicability of the scheme and projected an output of some 2,190,000,000 kWh. However, no tidal power plant has yet been built.

Severn Bridge

Bridge linking England with south Wales across the Severn estuary, constructed 1961–66 at a cost of £8 million. A second bridge was built 1992–96, crossing from Severn Beach to New Passage. The construction of the second bridge followed a 63% increase in traffic across the original bridge from 1982 to 1992.

The central span of the original Severn bridge is 988 m/3,241 ft long, and it has two side spans, each of 305 m/1,000 ft. The vertical clearance for shipping is 34 m/112 ft above high-water level near the towers, and

SEVERN BRIDGE *The Severn Bridge is a suspension bridge that carries the M4 motorway over the River Severn, linking the West Country of England and South Wales. A toll is payable for all vehicles using the bridge. A second road crossing spanning the Severn to the southwest of the original bridge, was opened in 1996 to relieve congestion on this busy route. Corel*

about 37 m/121 ft in the centre. The bridge has two carriageways, each 7.3 m/24 ft wide, as well as a cycle track, and a footpath. The second bridge spans a distance of 5 km/3 mi.

Seward, Albert Charles (1863–1941)

English palaeobotanist whose work on Palaeozoic and Mesozoic plants established the new field of palaeobotany. His *Fossil Plants as Tests of Climate* (1892) was one of the earliest works of biogeochemistry and along with *Jurassic Flora* (1900–03) was widely acclaimed. Knighted 1936.

Sewell, Anna (1820–1878)

English writer. Her only published work, the novel ◊*Black Beauty* (1877), tells the life story of a horse. It was a bestseller and became a children's classic. Her aim in writing the book was 'to induce kindness, sympathy, and understanding treatment of horses'.

Sex Pistols, the

Punk-rock group (1975–78) that became notorious under the guidance of their manager Malcolm McLaren (1946–). Their first singles, 'Anarchy in the UK' (1976) and 'God Save the Queen' (1977), unbridled attacks on contemporary Britain, made the Pistols into figures the media loved to hate.

Seymour

Family names of the dukes of Somerset (seated at Maiden Bradley, Wiltshire, England), and marquesses of Hertford (seated at Ragley Hall, Warwickshire, England); they first came to prominence through the marriage of Jane Seymour to Henry VIII.

Seymour, Jane (*c.* 1509–1537)

English noble, third wife of Henry VIII, whom she married in 1536. She died soon after the birth of her son Edward VI.

Daughter of John Seymour and sister of Edward, Duke of Somerset, she was a lady-in-waiting to Henry VIII's first two wives, Catherine of Aragón and Anne Boleyn. She married Henry a few days after Anne's execution.

Shackleton, Ernest Henry (1874–1922)

Irish Antarctic explorer. In 1907–09, he commanded an expedition that reached 88° 23′ S latitude, located the magnetic South Pole, and climbed Mount Erebus. Knighted 1909.

He was a member of Scott's Antarctic expedition 1901–04, and also commanded the expedition 1914–16 to cross the Antarctic, when he had to abandon his ship, the *Endurance*, crushed in the ice of the Weddell Sea. He died on board the *Quest* on his fourth expedition 1921–22 to the Antarctic.

shadow cabinet

The chief members of the British parliamentary opposition, each of whom is responsible for commenting on the policies and performance of a government ministry.

Shaffer, Peter Levin (1926–)

English dramatist. His psychological dramas include *Five Finger Exercise* (1958), the historical epic *The Royal Hunt of the Sun* (1964), *Equus* (1973), *Amadeus* (1979), about the envy provoked by the composer Mozart, and *Gift of the Gorgon* (1993).

Shaftesbury, or Shaston

Market town and agricultural centre in Dorset, southwest England, 30 km/19 mi southwest of Salisbury; population (1991) 6,200. Industries include tourism. King Alfred is said to have founded an abbey on the site in 880 (consecrated in 888); King Canute died at Shaftesbury in 1035.

Features

Excavations have revealed the foundations of the abbey and the plan of the abbey church. The earliest part of St Peter's church dates from the 14th century (and an even older building is underneath); other parts date largely from the 15th century. Gold Hill Wall is part of the old town wall, built in Saxon times and later buttressed.

History

It is said that King Alfred's second daughter Ethelgiva was the first abbess of the Benedictine abbey. In 979 the remains of Edward the Martyr (who died in 978 and was initially buried

SHAKESPEARE, WILLIAM *English dramatist and poet William Shakespeare. This portrait appeared on the title page of the edition of his works published in 1623. Philip Sauvain Picture Collection*

at Wareham) were re-interred at the abbey, and a shrine was built in 1001. This became an important place of pilgrimage, and the town became known for a time as St Edwardstowe. The abbey was demolished soon after its dissolution in 1539. Shaftesbury is mentioned as a borough in the Domesday Book of 1086, being then more important than Exeter or Dorchester. The town received its first charter in 1252, and two others followed (in 1604 and 1664).

Shaftesbury, Anthony Ashley Cooper, 1st Earl of Shaftesbury (1621–1683)

English politician, a supporter of the Restoration of the monarchy. He became Lord Chancellor in 1672, but went into opposition in 1673 and began to organize the ◊Whig Party. He headed the Whigs' demand for the exclusion of the future James II from the succession, secured the passing of the Habeas Corpus Act of 1679, then, when accused of treason in 1681, fled to Holland.

Shaftesbury, Anthony Ashley Cooper, 7th Earl of Shaftesbury (1801–1885)

British Tory politician. He strongly supported the Ten Hours Act of 1847 and other factory legislation, including the 1842 act forbidding the employment of women and children underground in mines. He was also associated with the movement to provide free education for the poor.

Shakespeare, William (1564–1616)

English dramatist and poet. He is considered the greatest English dramatist. His plays, written in blank verse with some prose, can be broadly divided into lyric plays, including *Romeo and Juliet* and *A Midsummer Night's Dream*; comedies,

Shakespeare's Plays

Title	Performed/written (approximate)
Early Plays	
Henry VI Part I	1589–92
Henry VI Part II	1590–91
Henry VI Part III	1590–92
The Comedy of Errors	1591–93
The Taming of the Shrew	1593–94
Titus Andronicus	1593–94
The Two Gentlemen of Verona	1590–95
Love's Labour's Lost	1593–95
Romeo and Juliet	1594–95
Histories	
Richard III	1592–93
Richard II	1595–97
King John	1595–97
Henry IV Part I	1596–97
Henry IV Part II	1596–97
Henry V	1599
Roman Plays	
Julius Caesar	1599
Antony and Cleopatra	1606–07
Coriolanus	1608

Title	Performed/written (approximate)
The 'Great' or 'Middle' Comedies	
A Midsummer Night's Dream	1594–95
The Merchant of Venice	1596–98
Much Ado About Nothing	1598
As You Like It	1599–1600
The Merry Wives of Windsor	1597
Twelfth Night	1600–02
The Great Tragedies	
Hamlet	1601–02
Othello	1604
King Lear	1605–06
Macbeth	1606
Timon of Athens	1607–08
The 'Dark' Comedies	
Troilus and Cressida	1601–02
All's Well That Ends Well	1602–03
Measure for Measure	1604
Late Plays	
Pericles	1606–08
Cymbeline	1609–10
The Winter's Tale	1611
The Tempest	1611
Henry VIII	1613

including *The Comedy of Errors*, *As You Like It*, *Much Ado About Nothing*, and *Measure For Measure*; historical plays, such as *Henry VI* (in three parts), *Richard III*, and *Henry IV* (in two parts), which often showed cynical political wisdom; and tragedies, including ◊*Hamlet*, *Othello*, ◊*King Lear*, and *Macbeth*. He also wrote numerous sonnets.

Born in Stratford-on-Avon, the son of a wool dealer, he was educated at the grammar school, and in 1582 married Anne ◊Hathaway. They had a daughter, Susanna, in 1583, and in 1585 twins, Hamnet (died 1596) and Judith. By 1592 Shakespeare was established in London as an actor and a dramatist, and from 1594 he was an important member of the Lord Chamberlain's Company of actors. In 1598 the Company tore down their regular playhouse, the Theatre, and used the timber to build the ◊Globe Theatre in Southwark. Shakespeare became a 'sharer' in the venture, which entitled him to a percentage of the profits. In 1603 the Company became the King's Men. By this time Shakespeare was the leading playwright of the company and one of its business directors; he also continued to act. He retired to Stratford about 1610, where he died on 23 April 1616. He was buried in the chancel of Holy Trinity, Stratford.

The extraordinary thing about English literature is that actually our greatest writer is the intellectual equivalent of bubble-gum, but can make twelve-year old girls cry, can foment revolution in Africa, can be translated into Japanese and leave not a dry eye in the house.

ANGELA CARTER English writer.
On Shakespeare, interviewed in *New Writing* (1992)

Early plays

In the plays written around 1589–94, Shakespeare may be regarded as a young writer learning the techniques of his art and experimenting with different forms. These include the three parts of *Henry VI*; the comedies *The Comedy of Errors*, *The Taming of the Shrew*, and *The Two Gentlemen of Verona*; the Senecan revenge tragedy *Titus Andronicus*; and *Richard III*. About 1593 he came under the patronage of the Earl of Southampton, to whom he dedicated his long poems *Venus and Adonis* (1593) and *The Rape of Lucrece* (1594); he also wrote for him the comedy *Love's Labour's Lost*, satirizing the explorer Walter Raleigh's circle, and seems to have dedicated to him his sonnets written around 1593–96, in which the mysterious 'Dark Lady' appears.

Lyric plays

The lyric plays *Romeo and Juliet*, *A Midsummer Night's Dream*, and *Richard II* (which explores the relationship between the private man and the public life of the state) 1594–97 were followed by *King John* (again exploring the ironies and problems of politics) and *The Merchant of Venice* 1596–97. The Falstaff plays of 1597–1600 – *Henry IV* (parts I and II, juxtaposing the comic world of the tavern and the dilemmas and responsibilities attending kingship and political ambition), *Henry V* (a portrait of King Hal as the ideal soldier-king), and *The Merry Wives of Windsor* (said to have been written at the request of Elizabeth I, to show Falstaff in love) – brought his fame to its height. He wrote *Julius Caesar* in 1599 (anticipating the great tragedies in its concentration on a central theme and plot: the conspiracy to assassinate Caesar, and the confrontation between political rivals, in which the more ruthless win). The period ended with the lyrically witty *Much Ado About Nothing*, *As You Like It*, and ◊*Twelfth Night*, about 1598–1601.

Follow your spirit; and, upon this charge / Cry 'God for Harry! England and Saint George!'

WILLIAM SHAKESPEARE English dramatist and poet.
Henry V III. i 33

Tragedies and late plays

With *Hamlet* begins the period of the great tragedies, 1601–08: *Othello*, *King Lear*, *Macbeth*, *Timon of Athens*, ◊*Antony and Cleopatra*, and *Coriolanus* (the hero of which comes into disastrous conflict with the Roman people through his overriding sense of personal honour). This 'darker' period is also reflected in the comedies *Troilus and Cressida* (a sardonic exploration of the concept of chivalric honour in relation to sexual conduct and the war between Greece and Troy), *All's Well That Ends Well*, and *Measure for Measure* around 1601–04. It is thought that Shakespeare was only part author of *Pericles*, which is grouped with the other plays of around 1608–11 – *Cymbeline* (set in ancient Britain, when Augustus Caesar ruled in Rome and Christ was born in Palestine), *The Winter's Tale* (a refashioning of a romance by an envious rival, Robert Greene), and *The Tempest* – as the mature romance or 'reconciliation' plays of the end of his career. It is thought that *The Tempest* may have been based on the real-life story of William Strachey, who was shipwrecked off Bermuda in 1609. During 1613 it is thought that Shakespeare collaborated with John ◊Fletcher on *Henry VIII* (in which the theme of reconciliation and regeneration after

Top 5 Shakespeare Plays by Tickets Sold

Source: Arts Council of England

April 1996–March 1997

Rank	Production	Tickets sold[1]
1	*Macbeth*	166,232
2	*As You Like It*	154,651
3	*A Midsummer Night's Dream*	96,906
4	*Romeo and Juliet*	74,276
5	*Troilus and Cressida*	35,470

[1] This data covers all theatre activity within the subsidized sector in England and does not include the rest of the UK, the West End, or the commercial sector.

strife is played out in historical terms, so that the young child who represents hope for the future is none other than Elizabeth I) and *The Two Noble Kinsmen*.

For the first 200 years after his death, Shakespeare's plays were frequently performed in cut or revised form (Nahum Tate's *King Lear* was given a happy ending), and it was not until the 19th century, with the critical assessment of Samuel ◊Coleridge and William ◊Hazlitt, that the original texts were restored.

Appreciation of Shakespeare's plays in the 20th century became analytical, examining in detail such aspects as language, structure, contemporary theatrical conditions, and the social and intellectual context of his work. His plays were collected and edited by John Hemige and Henry Condell, two of Shakespeare's former colleagues from the King's company, into the *First Folio* (1623). Later editions were published in 1632, 1664, and 1685 as the *Second*, *Third*, and *Fourth Folios*, respectively.

shamrock

Unofficial emblem of the Irish and their descendants overseas, traditionally worn on St Patrick's Day (17 March), when many people try to gather their own wild plant. Its association with St Patrick stems from his preaching about the Holy Trinity. The shamrock has been commercially adopted to promote a number of Irish products.

Sharp, Cecil (James) (1859–1924)

English collector and compiler of folk songs and dances. He visited the USA 1916–18 to collect songs in the Appalachian mountains, where many English songs were still preserved in their early form by descendants of 17th-century emigrants. His work ensured that the English folk-music revival became established throughout the English-speaking world.

He led a movement to record a threatened folk-song tradition for posterity, publishing *English Folk Song* (1907; two volumes).

Sharp, Granville (1735–1813)

English philanthropist. He was prominent in the anti-slavery movement and in 1772 secured a legal decision 'that as soon as any slave sets foot on English territory he becomes free'.

Sharpe, Tom (Thomas Ridley) (1928–)

English satirical novelist. Sharpe uses satire and farcical plots to explore the eccentricities and social manners of the English middle classes, in works such as *Porterhouse Blue* (1973), *Blott on the Landscape* (1975), *Wilt* (1976), and *Vintage Stuff* (1982). Many of his works have been successfully adapted for television.

Sharpey-Schafer, Edward Albert born Schäfer (1850–1935)

English physiologist, one of the founders of endocrinology. He made important discoveries relating to the hormone adrenaline, and to the pituitary and other endocrine, or ductless, glands. Knighted 1913.

Shaw, (William) Napier (1854–1945)

English meteorologist who introduced the millibar as the meteorological unit of atmospheric pressure (in 1909, but not used internationally until 1929). He also invented the tephigram, a thermodynamic diagram widely used in meteorology, in about 1915. Knighted 1915.

Shaw, George Bernard (1856–1950)

Irish dramatist. He was also a critic and novelist, and an early member of the socialist ◊Fabian Society. His plays combine comedy with political, philosophical, and polemic aspects, aiming to make an impact on his audience's social conscience as well as their emotions. They include *Arms and the Man* (1894), *Devil's Disciple* (1897), *Man and Superman* (1903), *Pygmalion* (1913), and *St Joan* (1923).

Shaw was born in Dublin, and went to London in 1876, where he became a brilliant debater and supporter of the Fabians, and worked as a music and drama critic. He wrote five unsuccessful novels before his first play, *Widowers' Houses*, was privately produced in 1892. Attacking slum landlords, it allied him with the realistic, political, and polemical movement in the theatre, pointing to people's responsibility to improve themselves and their social environment. His first public production was *Arms and the Man*, a cynical view of war.

The volume *Plays: Pleasant and Unpleasant* (1898) also included *The Philanderer, Mrs Warren's Profession*, dealing with prostitution and banned until 1902, and *Arms and the Man*. *Three Plays for Puritans* (1901) contained *The Devil's Disciple*, *Caesar and Cleopatra* (a companion piece to Shakespeare's *Antony and Cleopatra*), and *Captain Brassbound's Conversion*, written for the actress Ellen ◊Terry. *Man and Superman* expounds his ideas of evolution by following the character of Don Juan into hell for a debate with the devil.

The 'anti-romantic' comedy *Pygmalion*, first performed in 1913, was written for the actress Mrs Patrick ◊Campbell (and after Shaw's death converted to a musical as *My Fair Lady*). Later plays included *Heartbreak House* (1920), *Back to Methuselah* (1922), and the historical *St Joan*.

Altogether Shaw wrote more than 50 plays and became a byword for wit. He was awarded the Nobel prize in 1925.

How can what an Englishman believes be heresy? It is a contradiction in terms.

GEORGE BERNARD SHAW Irish dramatist.
St Joan IV

Shaw, (Richard) Norman (1831–1912)

English architect, born in Edinburgh. He was the leader of the trend away from Gothic and Tudor styles back to Georgian designs. In partnership with W E Nesfield (1835–1888), he began working in the ◊Arts and Crafts tradition, designing simple country houses using local materials, in a style known as Old English. The two then went on to develop the Queen Anne style, inspired by 17th-century Dutch domestic architecture of which Shaw's design for Swan House, Chelsea,

London (1876) is a fine example. Shaw's later style was Imperial Baroque, as in the Piccadilly Hotel (1905).

Shearer, Alan (1970–)

English footballer. In 1996 he was transferred to Newcastle United from Blackburn Rovers for what was then a world record fee of £15 million. A strongly-built centre-forward, he made his England debut in 1992 and by the end of the 1998 World Cup had scored 20 goals in 43 appearances.

Although he scored a hat trick on his league debut for Southampton at the age of 17 it was not until he joined Blackburn Rovers in July 1992 that he established his reputation as a prolific goal scorer. He scored over 30 league goals in three consecutive seasons, a feat not performed since before World War II. His 34 goals in the 1994/95 season helped Blackburn secure the Premier League. He scored on his full England debut in 1992, but did not score regularly at international level until the 1996 European Championships, when he finished as the tournament's top scorer with five goals. In 1998 he was named among the first players to be inducted into the FA Premier League's Hall of Fame.

Shearer, Moira stage name of Moira Shearer King (1926–)

Scottish actress and ballerina. Primarily a dancer, Shearer starred in the Michael Powell and Emeric Pressburger British screen classic *The Red Shoes* (1947), which served to establish her international reputation as both ballerina and actress. She worked again with Powell and Pressburger in their opera-dance adaptation *The Tales of Hoffmann* (1951) and with Powell on his solo horror project *Peeping Tom* (1960).

Throughout the 1940s and early 1950s she danced in a series of classic and new ballet productions, and was a member of the Sadler's Wells troupe from the age of 16. She has worked in theatre and television and has lectured on the history of ballet.

Sheerness

Seaport and resort on the Isle of ◊Sheppey, Kent, southeast England, 21 km/13 mi northwest of Whitstable; population (1991) 11,300. Situated at the confluence of the rivers Thames and Medway, it was originally a fortress in the 1660s, and was briefly held by the Dutch admiral de Ruyter in 1667. It was a 19th century 'dockyard town', and was a naval dockyard until 1960. Sheerness has a freight ferry service to Vlissingen, the Netherlands, and the port is one of the fastest expanding ports in the UK. There is some tourism.

The dockyard is now an industrial estate. The boatstore (1859) in the dockyard is a very early example of a multi-storey iron-framed building.

Sheffield

Industrial city and metropolitan borough on the River Don, South Yorkshire, England; population of metropolitan district (1991) 501,200. From the 12th century, iron smelting was the chief industry, and by the 14th century, Sheffield cutlery, silverware, and plate were being made. During the Industrial Revolution the iron and steel industries developed rapidly. It now produces alloys and special steels, cutlery of all kinds, permanent magnets, drills, and precision tools. Other industries include electroplating, type-founding, and the manufacture of optical glass. It is an important conference centre. On 15 April 1989, a major disaster occurred when 95 football fans died at Hillsborough football ground as a result of overcrowding. 200 people were injured.

Features

The parish church of St Peter and St Paul (14th–15th centuries) is the cathedral of Sheffield bishopric established in 1914. Mary Queen of Scots was imprisoned in Sheffield 1570–84, part of the time in the Norman castle, which was captured by the Parliamentarians in 1644 and subsequently destroyed. There are two art galleries (Graves Art Gallery and Mappin Art Gallery); the Ruskin museum, opened in 1877 and revived in 1985; and the Cutlers' Hall. There are also three theatres (the Crucible (1971); the Lyric, designed by W R Sprague in 1897; and the restored Lyceum, reopened in 1990) and two universities (the University of Sheffield and Sheffield Hallam University). The Sheffield Supertram, Britain's most modern light rail system, opened in 1995. The city is a touring centre for the Peak District. The Meadowhall shopping centre in the old steel works area is one of the largest shopping centres in the UK. In 1997 Sheffield was chosen as the site for the new National Sports Institute. A Millennium Gallery and Museum are to be built as part of a project to revitalize the city centre.

Location

Situated on coal measures with workable seams, including the famous Silkstone seam within the city boundary, Sheffield is bisected by the Don and its tributaries, the Loxley, Rivelin, Porter, and Sheaf, flowing from the millstone grit to the west. Sheffield is flanked to the west and south by moorlands, including the Peak District National Park, and the southern Pennines.

Places of interest

A few old grinding mills still stand beside the streams; one, Shepherd Wheel in Whiteley Woods, has been completely restored. On the River Sheaf the Abbeydale Industrial Hamlet is a restored industrial complex with its millponds, water-wheels, and numerous workshops for a wide variety of old craft industries; Kelham Island Industrial Museum on the River Don has a working steam engine. The remains of Beauchief Abbey are within the city boundary. Public buildings include the town hall, opened in 1897 and extended in 1923, with sites now being developed for a civic centre; the Cutlers' Hall, erected in 1832 on the site of previous buildings; the city hall, opened in 1932, with six halls including the magnificent oval hall seating 2,500; the Castle Market Building completed in 1959; and the Central Library and Graves Art Gallery, opened in 1934. In addition to an extensive green belt, over 1,375 ha/3,437 acres of the city are publicly owned parks and open space. Over 240 ha/600 acres of the Peak District National Park are within the city boundary. The city museum in Weston Park has unique collections of cutlery and old Sheffield plate and an important collection of British antiquities particularly rich in Bronze Age specimens. The 'Grice' collection of Chinese ivories is displayed in the Graves Art Gallery. The Botanical Gardens have glass houses (1836) designed by Joseph Paxton, which are to be restored with money from the Heritage Lottery Fund.

The Fitzwilliam muniments (title deeds) from Wentworth Woodhouse, the Arundel Castle muniments, and the Crewe muniments are all in the Sheffield Archives.

The cathedrals

The parish church of St Peter and St Paul, a 12th-century foundation, became the cathedral in 1914 when the diocese of Sheffield was created from part of that of York. Enlargement of the cathedral, begun in 1937, was partially completed in 1942 and further building began in 1963. There is also a Roman Catholic cathedral, the church of St Marie (1847) which was made a cathedral for the new diocese of Hallam in 1980.

The Cutlers' Company

'The Master, Wardens, Searchers, Assistants and Commonalty of the Company of Cutlers in Hallamshire in the County of York' was incorporated in 1624. The Company owns the trademark 'Sheffield', and elects a Master Cutler annually. This office is regarded in the city as second only to that of Lord Mayor. The Cutlers' Feast, Forfeit Feast, and installation of the Master are important events in the calendar of the Cutlers' Company.

History

Thomas de Furnival granted Sheffield a charter in 1297. Under the Talbot Earls of Shrewsbury, it was closely connected with one of the foremost noble families until 1616. The Talbot Earls often resided in the town, and in the early 16th century built the Manor Lodge and the Shrewsbury chapel in the parish church. In 1616 the manor passed to the Howard family; the present Duke of Norfolk retains considerable interests in the city as ground landlord. Mary Queen of Scots was held in custody in the manor and castle, 1569–83, by the sixth Earl of Shrewsbury.

In 1843 Sheffield was incorporated as a borough, and made a city 50 years later. It was first represented in Parliament in 1832.

Industrial history

Iron was worked in the vicinity in the 12th century, and Sheffield was famed for its knives by the time of Chaucer. Cutlery long remained the industry of the 'little mester', but the 18th century saw many industrial changes. The invention by Thomas Boulsover in 1742 of the method of coating copper with silver to form 'old Sheffield plate', established an industry which flourished until it was superseded by electroplating in the 1850s. In 1740 Benjamin Huntsman invented the process for making crucible steel and later established his works at Attercliffe. At the same time coke began to be widely used for smelting; even more important was Henry Bessemer's converter of 1856. At the same time there arose a demand for steel for railways, armaments, and constructional purposes.

Present-day industry

Little steel for general purposes is produced today. Sheffield's unique position depends on its production of alloy and special steels made to withstand high pressures or temperatures, to be acid-resistant, or possess other unusual qualities. Most were invented in Sheffield laboratories and works (including stainless steel). Much emphasis is placed on the importance of research in the industry. Sheffield has a high reputation for craftsmanship, apparent also in its heavy engineering industry. Melting shops, heavy forges, rolling mills, plate and wire mills make up the industrial conurbation of Sheffield. Its cutlery industry includes knives, razors, scissors, surgical instruments, agricultural and other machine knives, joiners', carvers', mechanics', and garden tools, and coal-cutting and boring tools. The production of silver and electroplated goods, with silver and gold refining, forms another group of industries. There are important subsidiary industries including typefounding, snuff, confectionery, food, refractory materials, and cardboard-box making, and media-related industries in the new Cultural Industries Quarter.

Shelburne, William Petty, 2nd Earl of Shelburne (1737–1805)

British Whig politician. He was an opponent of George III's American policy, and, as prime minister in 1783, he concluded peace with the United States of America.

Shelley, Mary Wollstonecraft born Godwin (1797–1851)

English writer. She is best known as the author of the Gothic horror story ⇨*Frankenstein* (1818), which is considered to be the origin of modern science fiction, and her other novels include *The Last Man* (1826) and *Valperga* (1823). In 1814 she eloped to Switzerland with the poet Percy Bysshe Shelley, whom she married in 1816 on the death of his first wife Harriet. She was the daughter of Mary Wollstonecraft and William Godwin.

Shelley, Percy Bysshe (1792–1822)

English lyric poet and critic. With his skill in poetic form and metre, his intellectual capacity and searching mind, his rebellious but constructive nature, and his notorious moral nonconformity, he is a commanding figure of the Romantic movement. He fought all his life against religion and for political freedom. This is reflected in his early poems such as *Queen Mab* (1813). He later wrote tragedies including *The Cenci* (1818), lyric dramas such as *Prometheus Unbound* (1820), and lyrical poems such as 'Ode to the West Wind'. He drowned while sailing in Italy.

Born near Horsham, Sussex, he was educated at Eton and Oxford, where his collaboration in a pamphlet *The Necessity of Atheism* (1811) caused his expulsion. While living in London he fell in love with 16-year-old Harriet Westbrook, whom he married in 1811. He visited Ireland and Wales, writing pamphlets defending vegetarianism and political freedom, and in 1813 published privately *Queen Mab*, a poem with political freedom as its theme. Meanwhile he had become estranged from his wife and in 1814 left England with Mary Wollstonecraft Godwin, whom he married after Harriet drowned herself in 1816. By 1818 Shelley was living in Italy where he produced *The Cenci*; the satire on Wordsworth, *Peter Bell the Third* (1819); and *Prometheus Unbound*. Other works of the period are 'Ode to the West Wind' (1819); 'The Cloud' and

SHELLEY, PERCY BYSSHE *English Romantic poet Percy Bysshe Shelley, whose creativity was fuelled by his radical thinking and eccentric behaviour. Shelley attempted to establish radical communes in Devon and Wales, then eloped with 16-year-old Harriet Westbrook. His second marriage to Mary Wollstonecraft Godwin was marked by tragedy – two of his children died in infancy and Mary suffered a nervous breakdown. Corbis*

'The Skylark' (both 1820); the lyric drama *Hellas* (1822); and the prose *Defence of Poetry* (1821). In July 1822 Shelley was drowned while sailing near Viareggio, and his ashes were buried in Rome.

Shelter, officially the National Campaign for Homeless People

UK charity, founded in 1966, providing homes or temporary accommodation for people who have nowhere to live.

Shepard, E(rnest) H(oward) (1879–1976)

English illustrator and cartoonist. He worked for *Punch*, but is best remembered for his illustrations for children's classics, including A A Milne's *Winnie-the-Pooh* (1926) and Kenneth Grahame's *The Wind in the Willows* (1908).

Shephard, Gillian Patricia (1940–)

British Conservative politician, education and employment secretary 1995–97. She became education secretary in 1994 at a time when relations between government and the profession were particularly fraught.

After a career in education as an extra-mural lecturer and an education officer and schools' inspector, Shephard entered politics in her mid-forties, winning the South-West Norfolk seat in 1987. She made steady progress through ministerial ranks, entering the cabinet as secretary of state for employment in 1992, and then moved rapidly through agriculture to education. Her open conciliatory approach did much initially to alleviate the situation, although teachers' patience rapidly dissipated in the face of on-going cuts in education budgets. In the cabinet reshuffle that followed Prime Minister John Major's successful re-election bid for the party leadership in July 1995, she was also given responsiblity for employment.

Shepperton

Village in Surrey, southeast England, on the north bank of the River Thames; population (1991) 5,900. Shepperton has extensive film studios. Parts of the church date from the 13th century.

Sheppey

Island off the north coast of Kent, southeast England; area 80 sq km/31 sq mi; population (est) 27,000. Situated at the mouth of the River Medway, it is linked with the mainland by Kingsferry Bridge (road and rail, completed in 1960) over the River Swale. The resort and port of ◊Sheerness is here. There is a nature reserve in the southern part of the island.

Arable farming is important in the north of the island; in the south of the island the reclaimed marshes are used for grassland farming, particularly sheep grazing. Agricultural produce includes cereals and vegetables. Other industries include tourism, and – in west Sheppey – ceramics, pharmaceuticals, and steelmaking.

Sheraton, Thomas (1751–1806)

English designer of elegant inlaid Neo-Classical furniture. He was influenced by his predecessors ◊Hepplewhite and ◊Chippendale. He published the *Cabinet-maker's and Upholsterer's Drawing Book* in 1791.

Sherborne

Town in Dorset, southwest England, 10 km/6 mi east of Yeovil; population (1991) 7,200. It is a tourist centre. Features include Sherborne Castle, built by the 16th-century adventurer Walter Raleigh, and the ruins of a Norman castle. The abbey church of St Mary the Virgin, founded in the 8th century, contains traces of Anglo-Saxon work.

Early in the 12th century the Anglo-Saxon church building was replaced by a Norman church, and much of this structure is still standing. In the 15th century the Norman choir was demolished and replaced by a Perpendicular Gothic choir with fan vaulting. The nave was also rebuilt in this period.

A silk-weaving mill was built at Sherborne in 1740 by Huguenot refugees (French Protestants). Sherborne School, a private school for boys, was founded here in 1550.

Sheridan, Richard Brinsley (1751–1816)

Irish dramatist and politician. His social comedies include *The Rivals* (1775), celebrated for the character of Mrs Malaprop, and *The School for Scandal* (1777). He also wrote a burlesque, *The Critic* (1779). In 1776 he became lessee of the Drury Lane Theatre. He became a member of Parliament in 1780.

sheriff (Old English *scīr* 'shire', *gerēfa* 'reeve')

In England and Wales, the crown's chief executive officer in a county for ceremonial purposes; in Scotland, the equivalent of the English county-court judge, but also dealing with criminal cases; and in the USA the popularly elected head law-enforcement officer of a county, combining judicial authority with administrative duties.

In England, the office (elective until Edward II) dates from before the Norman Conquest. The sheriff, who is appointed annually by royal patent, and is chosen from the leading landowners, acts as returning officer for parliamentary elections, and attends the judges on circuit. The duties of keeping prisoners in safe custody, preparing panels of jurors for assizes, and executing writs, are supervised by the under-sheriff. The City of London has two sheriffs elected by members of the ◊livery companies.

> *Mr Speaker, I said the honourable member was a liar it is true and I am sorry for it. The honourable member may place the punctuation where he pleases.*
>
> RICHARD BRINSLEY SHERIDAN Irish dramatist and politician.
> Attributed remark, when asked to apologize for calling a fellow Member of Parliament a liar

Sherriff, R(obert) C(edric) (1896–1975)

English dramatist. He is remembered for the antiheroic war play *Journey's End* (1928). Later plays include *Badger's Green* (1930) and *Home at Seven* (1950).

Sherrington, Charles Scott (1857–1952)

English neurophysiologist who studied the structure and function of the nervous system. *The Integrative Action of the Nervous System* (1906) formulated the principles of reflex action. He was awarded the Nobel Prize for Physiology or Medicine in 1932. GBE 1922.

He showed that when one set of antagonistic muscles is activated, the opposing set is inhibited. This theory of reciprocal innervation is known as **Sherrington's law**. He also identified the regions of the brain that govern movement and sensation in particular parts of the body.

Sherwood Forest

Hilly stretch of parkland in west Nottinghamshire, central England; area about 520 sq km/200 sq mi. Formerly an ancient royal forest extending from Nottingham to Worksop, it is associated with the legendary outlaw ◊Robin Hood. According to the Forestry Commission, Sherwood Forest is over 1,000 years old.

It was once a vast royal forest of oak, birch, and bracken, covering all of west Nottinghamshire. The great 'Shire Wood' stretched 32 km/20 mi from Nottingham north to Worksop, and was up to 13 km/8 mi wide. Kings and queens of England used it as a hunting ground from medieval times. It was cleared in the 18th century, although parts of it remain from Nottingham to Mansfield and to Worksop.

Shetland Islands (Old Norse Hjaltland 'high land' or 'Hjalte's land')

Islands and unitary authority off the north coast of Scotland, 80 km/50 mi northeast of the Orkney Islands, an important centre of the North Sea oil industry, and the most northerly part of the UK

Area 1,452 sq km/560 sq mi

Towns ◊Lerwick (administrative headquarters), on Mainland, largest of 12 inhabited islands

Physical the 100 islands are mostly bleak, hilly, and clad in moorland. The climate is moist, cool, and windy; in summer there is almost perpetual daylight, whilst winter days are very short. On clear winter nights, the aurora borealis ('northern lights') can frequently be seen in the sky

Industries processed fish, handknits from Fair Isle and Unst, herring fishing, salmon farming, cattle and sheep farming; large oil and gas fields west of Shetland; Europe's largest oil port is Sullom Voe, Mainland; production at Foinaven oilfield, the first to be developed in Atlantic waters; tourism

Population (1995) 23,100

History dialect derived from Norse, the islands having been a Norse dependency from the 9th century until 1472 when they were annexed by Scotland.

Economy

A buoyant mixed economy which had prospered with the development of the North Sea oil industry. Traditional sectors still play an important part in the economy.

Archaeology

Shetland is rich in archaeological sites, the best known of which are Jarlshof, Mousa, and Clickhimin Broch. Clickhimin Broch forms an island at the end of a causeway near Lerwick and was inhabited from *c.* 6 BC to AD 5. At Mousa, the Picts successfully sought refuge from Roman slave hunters. The settlement site at Jarlshof dates from the Bronze Age.

Environment

In 1993 the *Braer* ran aground on Shetland spilling 85,000 tonnes of oil. By February 1994, 50,000 birds, mostly guillemots and other fish-eating species, were washed up around the Islands. They appeared to have starved to death. There are 78 Sites of Special Scientific Interest, three National Nature Reserves, nine Special Protection Areas, and one National Scenic Area.

Shiel, Loch

Narrow lake in southwest Highland unitary authority, Scotland, extending 27 km/17 mi in length, and widening to less than 1 km/0.6 mi. It marked the boundary between the former counties of Inverness and Argyll.

A monument stands at Glenfinnan, at the head of the loch, marking the place where Prince Charles Edward Stuart raised his standard on 19 August 1745 in his bid for the throne.

shilling

English coin worth 12 pennies (there were 20 shillings to one pound), first minted under Henry VII. Although the demonination of a shilling was abolished with the advent of decimalization in 1971, the coins remained in circulation as five-pence pieces.

Shilton, Peter (1949–)

English international footballer, an outstanding goalkeeper, who has set records for the highest number of Football League appearances (1,005) and England caps (125). First capped by England in 1970, he retired from international football after the 1990 World Cup finals. He was manager of Plymouth Argyle 1992–95.

shinty, Gaelic *camanachd*

Stick-and-ball game resembling hurling, popular in the Scottish Highlands. It is played between teams of 12 players each, on a field 132–183 m/144–200 yd long and 64–91 m/70–99 yd wide. A curved stick (*caman*) is used to propel a leather-covered cork and worsted ball into the opposing team's goal (*hail*). The premier tournament, the Camanachd Cup, was instituted in 1896.

Shipley

Town in West Yorkshire, England, northwest of Bradford, on the River Aire; population (1991) 28,700. It has woollen and engineering industries.

ship money

Tax for support of the navy, levied on the coastal districts of England in the Middle Ages. Ship money was declared illegal by Parliament in 1641.

Charles I's attempts to levy it on the whole country in 1634–36, without parliamentary consent and in time of peace, aroused strong opposition from the member of Parliament John Hampden and others, who refused to pay.

ships

Building ships has historically been a major concern for Britain, surrounded as it is by sea. See chronology opposite for some key dates in the history of British ships. The earliest ships were rafts or dug-out canoes, and date from prehistoric times.

Development of sailing ships

The invention of the stern rudder during the 12th century, together with the developments made in sailing during the Crusades, enabled the use of sails to almost completely supersede that of oars. Following the invention of the compass, the development of sailing ships advanced quickly during the 14th century. In the 15th century Henry VIII built the *Great Harry*, the first double-decked English warship.

In the 16th century ships were short and high-sterned, and despite Pett's three-decker in the 17th century, English ships

ships *A supertanker under construction at the Swan Hunter shipyard at Wallsend on the River Tyne in northeast England. Ships built in this yard included the liner* Mauretania *in 1906 and the aircraft carrier HMS* Ark Royal *in 1981. The closure of Swan Hunter in the late 1990s signalled the final demise of shipbuilding on the Tyne, once one of the most productive such areas in the world. Brian Shuel/Collections*

SHIPS AND SHIPBUILDING: SOME KEY DATES

1647 The Royal Navy adopts a flag code for communication between ships.

1715 The first dock is built at Liverpool, a city that will become one of the world's most important ports in the coming industrial revolution.

1726 The English coffee house owner Edward Lloyd first issues the twice-weekly *Lloyd's List*, a list of shipping news for the merchants and ship owners who frequent his establishment.

1802 Scottish engineer William Symington launches the world's first paddlewheel steamer, the *Charlotte Dundas*, which acts as a tug on the Forth and Clyde Canal. The 17-m/56-ft long steam-driven vessel runs at 13 kph/8 mph and uses a piston rod connected directly to the crankshaft.

1812 Scottish engineer Henry Bell's steamship *Comet* plies the Clyde River. The first commercially successful steamship in Europe, it heralds the era of steam navigation in Europe.

1821 The world's first iron-hulled steamship, the *Aaron Manby*, steams from Birmingham, England, to Paris, France, where it enters service on the Seine.

23 April 1838 The *Great Western* and *Sirius*, both built by the English engineer Isambard Kingdom Brunel, are the first steamships to cross the Atlantic entirely under steam, arriving in New York only hours apart. The *Sirius*, which arrives first, uses a condenser to recover fresh water from the boiler, and the *Great Western* is a wooden paddle steamer driven by two engines.

19 July 1843 Isambard Kingdom Brunel's ship *Great Britain* is launched. It is the world's largest ship (98 m/322 ft long; weighing 3,332 tonnes/3,270 tons), with six masts and a screw propeller, and becomes the first propeller-driven iron ship to cross the Atlantic.

1860 British engineer John Russel builds the *Warrior*, the world's first iron-hulled battleship.

1869 The British clipper ship *Cutty Sark* is launched. It is one of the largest sailing ships at 65 m/212 ft long.

1877 The Royal Navy's first torpedo boat, the *Lightning*, is completed by British engineer John Isaac Thornycroft.

1886 The British submarine *Nautilus* is launched. The first electric-powered submarine, it uses two electric 50 horsepower motors powered by a 100 cell storage battery to achieve a speed of 6 knots. The need for frequent battery recharges limits its range to 130 km/80 mi.

1893 The first British destroyers begin to be built.

1899 The first icebreaker, the *Ermak*, is built in Britain for the Russian government. It has 38 mm/1.5 in steel plating on its hull, and serves as the prototype for all other icebreakers.

14–15 April 1912 The British luxury liner *Titanic*, carrying 2,224 people on its maiden transatlantic voyage, hits an iceberg 640 km/400 mi off the coast of Newfoundland and sinks causing the deaths of between 1,503 and 1,517 people (estimates vary). The accident leads to the first international convention for safety at sea, held in London the following year, which draws up safety standards.

September 1918 The Royal Navy launches the first aircraft carrier, the *Argus*. A converted merchant ship, it has a flight deck measuring 170.7 m/560 ft and a hangar that can house 20 aeroplanes.

1919 The British ship *Hermes* is launched. It is the first purpose-built aircraft carrier.

1939 English archaeologists discover the remains of a 7th-century Anglo-Saxon ship burial at Sutton Hoo, Suffolk. The ship is 27 m/88.6 ft long and was crewed by 28–40 oarsmen.

1948 Radar is installed at Liverpool Docks to supervise shipping approaches in fog.

18 March 1967 The Liberian-registered tanker *Torrey Canyon* strikes a submerged reef off the coast of Cornwall, England, and spills 860,000 barrels of crude oil into the sea. It is the biggest oil spill to date.

20 September 1967 The Queen launches the Cunard liner *Queen Elizabeth II*.

15 March 1977 The British government nationalizes the shipbuilding industry.

11 October 1982 The *Mary Rose*, King Henry VIII's flagship which was sunk by the French on 19 July 1545, is raised from the bottom of Portsmouth harbour.

11 December 1997 The British royal yacht, the *Britannia*, is formally retired at a decommissioning ceremony in Portsmouth, England.

did not bear comparison with the Spanish and Dutch until the early 19th century. In the 1840s iron began replacing wood in shipbuilding, pioneered by British engineer Isambard Kingdom ◊Brunel's *Great Britain* in 1845. Throughout the 19th century, improvements were made in warships, including the evolution of the elliptical stern. However, increased rivalry between US and British owners for possession of the Chinese and Indian tea trade led to improvements also being made to the merchant vessel.

The first clipper, the *Ann McKim*, was built in Baltimore in 1832, and Britain soon adopted this type of fast-sailing ship.

Steamships

Early steamers depended partly on sails for auxiliary power. In 1802 the paddle-wheel steamer *Charlotte Dundas*, constructed by William Symington, was launched on the Forth and Clyde Canal, Scotland. However, the effort was halted amid fears that the wash produced by the paddle would damage the canal banks. In 1812 the *Comet*, built in Scotland in 1804 by Bell,

Napier, and Robertson, was launched. This ship, which had a paddle on each side, was a commercial success, and two others were built for service from Glasgow. From this time the steamship-building industry rapidly developed on the banks of the Clyde.

The first steamship to cross the Atlantic was the Dutch vessel *Curaçao*, a wooden paddler built at Dover in 1826, which left Rotterdam in April 1827, and took one month to cross. The next transatlantic steamer, the *Royal William*, crossed from Quebec to London in 17 days in 1833. Britain's entry into the transatlantic efforts began with ◊Brunel's *Great Western* paddle-steamer, which achieved recognition when it completed the journey from Bristol to New York in 15 days – three days faster than a clipper.

The first great iron steamship, *Rainbow*, was launched in 1838. In the following year, Pettit Smith designed the *Archimedes*, the first steamer to use a screw propeller, followed quickly by Brunel's *Great Britain*, which crossed from Liverpool to New York in 14.5 days in 1845.

In 1862 the Cunard Company obtained permission to fit mail steamers with propellers, which suffered less from the rolling of the ship, and the paddle-wheel was relegated to comparatively smooth water. The opening of the Suez Canal in 1869, together with the simultaneous introduction of the compound engine, raised steamships to superiority over sailing ships. In 1902 the turbine engine was employed on passenger steamers on the Clyde, and in 1905 was applied to the transatlantic service. This was followed by the introduction of the internal combustion engine.

Tankers

Following World War II, when reconstruction and industrial development created a great demand for oil, the tanker was developed to carry supplies to the areas of consumption. The shipyards of the world were flooded with orders for tankers; due to economic demands, the size of the tankers became increasingly large. The Suez Canal crisis of 1956, with its disruption of the free flow of the world's oil supplies, focused attention on the possibility of working giant tankers over the Cape route. The prolonged closure of the Suez Canal after 1967 and the great increase in oil consumption led to the development of the very large tanker, or 'supertanker'.

More recently ◊hovercraft and hydrofoil boats have been developed for specialized purposes, particularly as short-distance ferries – for example, the catamarans introduced in 1991 by Hoverspeed cross the English Channel from Dover to Calais in 35 minutes, cruising at a speed of 35 knots (84.5 kph/52.5 mph). Sailing ships in automated form for cargo purposes, and maglev ships, were in development in the early 1990s.

shire

Administrative area formed in Britain for the purpose of raising taxes in Anglo-Saxon times. By AD 1000 most of southern England had been divided into shires with fortified strongholds at their centres. The Midland counties of England are still known as **the Shires**; for example Derbyshire, Nottinghamshire, and Staffordshire.

shopping

Napoleon famously described the British as 'a nation of shopkeepers' and at the end of the 20th century shopping is acknowledged as a prime leisure pastime. The debate as to whether out-of-town shopping centres are killing town centres continues. See chronology opposite for some highlights of shops and shopping.

Shoreham-by-Sea

Seaport and resort in West Sussex, England, between Worthing and Brighton; population (1991) 20,000. The small cargo ships that use the port, at the mouth of the River Adur, can go out only at high tide. Fishing has become more important in the 1990s.

In the 16th–17th centuries, Shoreham was the most important English Channel port. Trade now is mainly with Baltic and Mediterranean ports.

Short, Clare (1946–)

British Labour politician, secretary of state for International Development (1997–). Formerly a career civil servant in the Home Office 1970–75, she became the director of community organizations concerned with race and urban deprivation in Birmingham 1976–77 and youth aid 1979–83. She was then elected MP for her home constituency, Birmingham Ladywood, in 1983. In the House of Commons she was Opposition spokesperson on Employment 1985–88, Social Security 1989–91, Environmental Protection 1992–93, Women 1993–95, Transport 1995–96, and shadow minister for Overseas Development 1996–97.

She was born in Ladywood, Birmingham, and educated at Keele and Leeds Universities. She faced criticism in 1997 for her handling of the crisis in Montserrat following a volcanic eruption.

Short Parliament

The English Parliament that was summoned by Charles I on 13 April 1640 to raise funds for his war against the Scots. It was succeeded later in the year by the ◊Long Parliament.

When it became clear that the parliament opposed the war and would not grant him any money, he dissolved it on 5 May and arrested some of its leaders.

Shotton

Urban area in Flintshire, northeast Wales; population with Hawarden (1991) 23,300. Light industry predominates now, although there was formerly a major foundry here. Steel production has ceased but plate and strip-milled steel products are still manufactured.

Shrapnel, Henry (1761–1842)

British army officer who invented shells containing bullets, to increase the spread of casualties, first used in 1804; hence the word **shrapnel** to describe shell fragments.

Shrapnel was born in Bradford-on-Avon, Wiltshire. He received a commission in the Royal Artillery in 1779, and in the following year he went to Newfoundland, returning to England in 1783. He served in the Duke of York's unsuccessful campaign against France in 1793, being wounded in the

SHOPS AND SHOPPING IN BRITAIN: SOME KEY DATES

1848 English stationery company W H Smith and Sons agrees a deal with the London and North Western Railway Company to set up bookstalls at all their stations. This will be the foundation of the profitable W H Smith stationery and bookshop chain.

1849 English tea wholesaler Henry Charles Harrod buys a grocery store in London, which will grow to become one of the world's most famous department stores.

1863 William Whiteley opens the Universal Provider, in London, under the slogan 'Everything from a pin to an elephant'. This is essentially the first department store in Britain.

1874 Jesse Boot expands his mother's shop in Britain, aiming to produce cheap high-quality products, in particular drugs. This will grow into the Boots pharmaceutical chain.

1876 Scottish grocer Thomas Lipton opens his first shop, in Glasgow, the first step towards the creation of a grocery store chain that will make him a millionaire at the age of 29.

28 September 1894 Michael Marks and Tom Spencer open their first Penny Bazaar, a stall selling a wide range of domestic products, in Manchester. Building on a network of stalls, they open their first Marks & Spencer shop in 1922: this will grow to become Britain's most successful chain of department stores.

1897 The second-hand clothes shop Moss Bros starts a formal-clothing hire service in Britain.

1907 British tobacconist Alfred Dunhill opens his world-famous tobacco shop in London.

1909 The first Woolworth's store in Britain is opened in Liverpool.

15 March 1909 The US businessman H G Selfridge opens the first modern department store in Britain, Selfridge's in London, using the slogan, 'All your shopping under one roof'.

1931 Jack Cohen opens the first Tesco shop, in London. Later the title of his authorised biography sums up his approach: *Pile It High and Sell It Cheap*.

12 January 1948 The London Co-operative Society opens the first supermarket in Britain, at Manor Park in London.

31 July 1950 J Sainsbury's, the British supermarket chain, opens its first self-service shop in Croydon, south London.

1972 At Caerphilly in Wales, Carrefour becomes the first hypermarket to open in Britain.

1976 Brent Cross shopping centre opens, the first regional shopping centre in Europe.

1990 Westminster Cable launches Metrochannel. It is the first television shopping channel in Britain, covering central London.

1 October 1993 The satellite station BSkyB launches QVC, the first national home shopping channel in Britain.

1995 Sunday shopping laws are modified in England and Wales, permitting shops to open for a maximum of six hours.

siege of Dunkirk. In 1804, he was appointed inspector of artillery at the Royal Arsenal in Woolwich, London. He retired with the rank of lieutenant general. Shrapnel had spent several thousand pounds of his own money in perfecting his inventions. The Treasury eventually granted him a pension of £1,200 a year for life.

Shrapnel's shell was fused and filled with musket balls, plus a small charge of black powder to explode the container after a predetermined period of time. The first shells were round; later they were of an elongated form with added velocity. Shrapnel's shells continued to be used until World War I.

Shrewsbury

Market town on the River Severn, Shropshire, England, 244 km/152 mi northwest of London; population (1991) 64,200. It is the administrative headquarters of Shropshire. There are service industries and light manufacturing, and tourism is important. To the east at Wroxeter is the site of the Roman city of **Viroconium**.

Features

Landmarks include Clive House Museum, the 18th-century residence of Robert Clive (of India) and the church of St Mary with its 14th-century Jesse window. The castle dates from 1070.

History

In the 5th century, as **Pengwern**, Shrewsbury was capital of the kingdom of Powys, which later became part of Mercia. In the Battle of Shrewsbury in 1403, Henry IV defeated the rebels led by Henry 'Hotspur' ◊Percy. The city declined an invitation in 1539, at the dissolution of the monasteries, to become a cathedral city.

Layout and landmarks

The town centre is on a peninsula of rising ground within a horseshoe bend of the Severn; suburbs beyond the river are reached by two principal bridges which from their position on the main east–west highway are known respectively as the English Bridge and the Welsh Bridge. Shrewsbury retains much of its medieval character, particularly in the centre of the town, with its black and white timber-frame buildings, which sometimes lean out and almost touch, and its unusual street names.

At the narrowest point of the peninsula stands the **castle**, founded about 1070 by Roger de Montgomery; it served as a royal fortress until the time of Charles II, but was rebuilt by Telford.

Roger de Montgomery also founded a **Benedictine monastery** at Shrewsbury in 1083, but at the dissolution the monastic buildings were demolished, together with the east end of the abbey church of SS Peter and Paul, the west end being spared as a parish church.

The **church of St Mary**, part Norman and part Early English, possesses some remarkable glass, including a 14th-century Jesse window of English glass, and stained glass from Trier (Trèves), Germany.

The town was formerly walled, though now only a portion of the original wall can be seen. Substantial remains of a unique 13th-century town house, probably the 'Bennetteshalle' known to have belonged to the abbots of Haughmond, were investigated in 1957, prior to demolition. The ruins of **Haughmond Abbey**, founded in 1135 by William Fitz-Alan for Augustinian canons, lie 5 km/3 mi northeast of the town.

During the time of Elizabeth I many of the timber-framed mansions which survive today were built, for example Ireland's Mansion (1575) and Owen's Mansion (1592). Rowley's House (1595), another 16th-century timber-framed building, houses the museum of Roman antiquities from the city of Viroconium at Wroxeter near Shrewsbury.

By the river is Shrewsbury School, originally situated in the town (the 17th-century school buildings are now the borough library and museum). Charles Darwin was a pupil here. There is also a high school for girls, founded in 1872.

Industries

Industries include precision engineering, malting, the manufacture of diesel engines, locomotives, machine tools, electrical equipment, and agricultural implements. The main heavy industries are located in the northern suburbs along garden-city lines. The cattle market, one of the busiest in England, was moved to a new and larger site in the northern suburbs.

From early times to the 17th century

Shrewsbury was occupied by a British community, who called it Pengwern; later the Saxons renamed the site Scrobbesbyrig (alternatively Salopesberia, from which the name Salop derives). Offa made Shrewsbury part of his kingdom of Mercia at the end of the 8th century; in the Saxon and Norman periods it was frequently raided by the Welsh. Early in the 13th century Llewelyn the Great twice captured Shrewsbury; Edward I made it his seat of government (1277–83), and here Dafydd, last Welsh royal prince, was tried and executed (1283). At the Battle of Shrewsbury (1403), which took place just outside the modern town, Henry 'Hotspur' Percy was defeated and killed. Charles I set up his headquarters here in 1642, but the town fell to the Parliamentarians in 1645.

Shrewsbury, Earl of

Title in the peerage of England, held by the family of Talbot since 1442. It is the premier earldom of England.

Shropshire

County of western England, which has contained the unitary authority Telford and Wrekin since April 1998. Sometimes abbreviated to **Salop**, Shropshire was officially known by this name from 1974 until local protest reversed the decision in 1980.

Area 3,490 sq km/1,347 sq mi

Towns ◊Shrewsbury (administrative headquarters), Ludlow, Oswestry, Telford

Physical Shropshire is bisected, on the Welsh border, northwest–southeast by the River Severn; River Teme; Ellesmere (47 ha/116 acres), the largest of several lakes; the Clee Hills rise to about 610 m/1,800 ft (Brown Clee) in the southwest

Features Ironbridge Gorge open-air museum of industrial archaeology, with the Iron Bridge (1779), the world's first cast-iron bridge; Market Drayton is famous for its gingerbread, and Wem for its sweet peas

Agriculture cereals (barley, oats, wheat), sugar beet, mangolds (a root vegetable used for cattle feed), vegetables (turnips, swedes), sheep and cattle; dairy farming; forestry

Industries brick-making; engineering; limestone; manufacturing: machine tools and agricultural implements (Shrewsbury, Market Drayton, Prees, Whitchurch, Ellesmere), carpets and radio receivers (Bridgnorth), clocks (Whitchurch); Shropshire is the principal iron-producing county of England

Population (1995) 419,900

Famous people Charles Darwin, A E Housman, Wilfred Owen, Gordon Richards

History Shropshire became a county in the 10th century, as part of the kingdom of Mercia in its defence against the Danes. During the Middle Ages, it was part of the Welsh Marches and saw much conflict between the lords of the Marches and the Welsh.

Topography

English county on the Welsh border, bounded on the north by Cheshire; on the south by Herefordshire and Worcestershire; on the east by Staffordshire; and on the west by Powys. The name Salop derives from Salopesberia (a variant of the Saxon name Scrobbesbyrig for the town Shrewsbury). The market towns of Shrewsbury, Oswestry, Ludlow, Bridgnorth, Ellesmere, Whitchurch, Wellington, and Bishop's Castle serve as centres for the agricultural districts.

In the south and west the county is hilly, the chief features other than the Clee Hills being the Stiperstones (527 m/1,729 ft), the Long Mynd plateau (517 m/1,696 ft), the Caradoc range, and Wenlock Edge. Geologically the county displays a greater variety of rocks than any other county in England; this diversity gives rise to great variety of landscape and scenery.

History

On the evidence of its numerous hill-top forts, Shropshire had a considerable population in the Early Iron Age. It was settled by the Romans, who established at Wroxeter the third largest city of Roman Britain, and was subsequently added to the Saxon kingdom of Mercia by Offa in the 8th century. There are several sections of ◊Offa's Dyke, marking the boundary between Mercia and Wales, in the west of the county. Near Shrewsbury was fought the battle between Henry IV and the Percys (1403) at which Henry 'Hotspur' ◊Percy was killed; the place is now marked by the church and village of Battlefield.

Chuches and manor houses

The county contains many beautiful ruins, such as Haughmond, Buildwas, and Lilleshall abbeys and Much Wenlock

Priory. There is a large number of castles, of which only fragments generally remain; Ludlow is the finest. Stokesay House is perhaps the best example in the country of a fortified manor house of the 13th century. There are many other manor houses of the 16th to 18th centuries, and many examples of the traditional timber-framed architecture characteristic of the area. Shropshire's churches display a range of architectural styles: Heath Chapel, Edstaston, and Holgate are Norman; Acton Burnell is a perfect example of Early English; and the church at Tong is in the Perpendicular style.

Shugborough

House in Staffordshire, England, 9 km/6 mi southeast of Stafford. It has been the home of the Anson family, later to become Earls of Lichfield, from 1624 until the present day. The present late 17th-century house, with 18th-century alterations, contains plasterwork by Vassali and Joseph Rose (1745–99). Shugborough was acquired by the National Trust.

Sibley, Antoinette (1939–)

English dancer. She joined the Royal Ballet in 1956 and became principal soloist in 1960. Her roles included Odette/Odile in *Swan Lake*, Giselle, and the title role in Kenneth MacMillan's *Manon* (1974). A dancer of exceptional musicality and grace, she excelled in Frederick ◊Ashton's *The Dream* (1964). She formed an ideal partnership with Anthony ◊Dowell. She continues to work as a ballet coach and mentor.

Sickert, Walter Richard (1860–1942)

English artist. His works, broadly Impressionist in style, capture subtleties of tone and light, often with a melancholic atmosphere, their most familiar subjects being the rather shabby cityscapes and domestic and music-hall interiors of late Victorian and Edwardian London. *Ennui* (about 1913; Tate Gallery, London) is a typical interior painting.

Sickert learned his craft from James Whistler in London and then from Degas in Paris. Though often described as an Impressionist, he was only so to the same limited extent as Degas, constructing pictures from swift notes made on the spot, and never painting in the open air.

He worked in Dieppe from 1885 to 1905, with occasional visits to Venice, and produced music-hall paintings and views of Venice and Dieppe in dark, rich tones. In his 'Camden Town' period (1905–14), he explored the back rooms and dingy streets of North London. His zest for urban life and his personality drew together a group of younger artists who formed the nucleus of the ◊Camden Town Group, which played a leading role in bringing Post-Impressionism into English art.

His later work became broader in treatment and lighter in tone, a late innovation being the 'Echoes', in which he freely adapted the work of Victorian illustrators.

Siddons, Sarah born Kemble (1755–1831)

English actress. Her majestic presence made her suited to tragic and heroic roles such as Lady Macbeth, Zara in Congreve's *The Mourning Bride*, and Constance in *King John*.

She toured the provinces with her father Roger Kemble (1721–1802), until she appeared in London to immediate acclaim in Otway's *Venice Preserv'd* (1774). This led to her appearing with David ◊Garrick at Drury Lane. She retired in 1812.

Sidlaw Hills

Range of hills spanning Perth and Kinross, Angus, and Aberdeenshire unitary authorities, Scotland. They extend in a northeasterly direction from Kinnoul Hill near Perth to the North Sea coast, between Red Head and Stonehaven. The highest points are Craigow Hill, rising to 455 m/1,493 ft, and King's Seat, which reaches 377 m/1,237 ft.

Sidney, Philip (1554–1586)

English poet and soldier. In about 1580 he began an unfinished prose romance, known as *Arcadia*, published in a shortened version in 1590, and more fully in 1593. At the same time he wrote an essay on the state of English poetry, published in 1595 both as 'The Defence of Poesie' and 'An Apologie for Poetrie', one of the earliest examples of English literary criticism to be published and the best at least until Dryden. In about 1581 he composed to a lost love the first major sonnet sequence in English, published as *Astrophel and Stella* (1591).

Silbury Hill

Artificial mound of the Neolithic (New Stone Age) period, around 2800 BC, situated just south of ◊Avebury in Wiltshire, England. Steep and rounded, it towers 40 m/130 ft high with a surrounding ditch approximately 6 m/20 ft deep, made when quarrying for the structure. It is the largest ancient artificial mound in Europe.

Local legend suggested that the hill contained a lifesize statue of King Sil and his horse, but no significant finds have ever been made.

Silchester

Archaeological site, a major town in Roman Britain. It is 10 km/6 mi north of Basingstoke, Hampshire.

Silicon Glen

Area in central Scotland, around Glenrothes ◊new town, where there are many electronics firms. By 1986 Glenrothes had over 21% of its workforce employed in electrical engineering, especially high-tech firms. Many of the firms here are owned by US and other foreign companies.

silk

In UK law, a ◊Queen's Counsel, a senior barrister entitled to wear a silk gown in court.

Silkin, Jon (1930–)

English poet. His works include *The Re-ordering of the Stones* (1961) and *Nature With Man* (1965). His mature style is marked by slow, rhythmic movements alternating with sharp, dramatic statements, as in the collections *The Principle of Water* (1974) and *The Lens-Breakers* (1992). He founded the literary magazine *Stand* in 1952.

Sillitoe, Alan (1928–)
English novelist. He wrote *Saturday Night and Sunday Morning* (1958) about a working-class man in Nottingham, Sillitoe's home town. *The Loneliness of the Long Distance Runner* is the title story of a collection of short stories published in 1959.

Sillitoe published several collections of verse, including *Sun Before Departure: Poems 1974 to 1982* (1984), but is most widely acclaimed for his novels and stories about working-class life. His later novels deal with characters from other sections of society, but always view the plight of individuals trapped in a stifling social environment.

Among his novels are *A Start in Life* (1970) and *Raw Material* (1972) (fictionalized memoirs), *The Flame of Life* (1974), and *Last Loves* (1990). *Life Without Armour* (1995) is an early autobiography.

Silures
Celtic tribe of southeast Wales which joined with the Ordovices tribe in resisting the Romans. They were eventually subjugated about AD 75 and were recognized as a Roman Empire civitas (provincial town or community with full privileges of citizenship), with their capital at Venta Silurum (Caerwent).

Silverstone
Britain's oldest motor-racing circuit, opened on 2 October 1948. It is situated near Towcester, Northamptonshire, and was built on a disused airfield after World War II. It staged the first officially-titled British Grand Prix in 1948 and on 13 May 1950 hosted the inaugural Grand Prix of the Formula 1 World Drivers' Championship. In 1987 it became the permanent home of the British Grand Prix. Celebrations took place on the weekend of 3 October 1998 to mark the racetrack's 50th anniversary.

Sim, Alastair (George Bell) (1900–1976)
Scottish comedy actor. Possessed of a marvellously expressive face, he was ideally cast in eccentric roles, as in the title role in *Scrooge* (1951). His other films include *Inspector Hornleigh* (1939), *Green for Danger* (1945), and *The Belles of St Trinians* (1954).

Simmons, Jean (1929–)
English actress. Of dark, elegant looks, she played Ophelia in Laurence Olivier's film of *Hamlet* (1948), and later in Hollywood starred in such films as *Black Narcissus* (1947), *Guys and Dolls* (1955), and *Spartacus* (1960).

Simnel, Lambert (*c.* 1475–*c.* 1535)
English impostor, a carpenter's son who under the influence of an Oxford priest claimed to be Prince Edward, one of the ◊Princes in the Tower. ◊Henry VII discovered the plot and released the real Edward for one day to show him to the public. Simnel had a keen following and was crowned as Edward VI in Dublin 1487. He came with forces to England to fight the royal army, and attacked it near Stoke-on-Trent on 16 June 1487. He was defeated and captured, but was contemptuously pardoned. He is then said to have worked in the king's kitchen.

SIM, ALASTAIR *Scottish stage and screen actor Alastair Sim. An adept and witty character actor who entered the profession relatively late at the age of 30, he made his stage debut in* Othello *with Paul Robeson and Peggy Ashcroft. He is seen here in a 1960 TV play. Corbis*

Simon, John (1816–1904)
English surgeon and public health reformer who cleaned up the City of London in the 19th century. The eight annual reports that Simon presented to the Corporation of London are the most famous health reports ever written. They embody an incredible record of success, and years later legislation was based on them, culminating in the great Public Health Act of 1875.

Simple Minds
Scottish rock band formed in 1977 and fronted by Jim Kerr (1959–), whose songs include 'Don't You (Forget About Me)'. Their album hits include *Sparkle In The Rain* (1984) and *Street Fighting Years* (1989).

Simpson, (Cedric) Keith (1907–1985)
British forensic scientist, head of department at Guy's Hospital, London 1962–72. His evidence sent John Haig (an acid-bath murderer) and Neville Heath to the gallows. In 1965 he identified the first 'battered baby' murder in England.

Simpson, James Young (1811–1870)
Scottish physician, the first to use ether as an anaesthetic in childbirth in 1847, and the discoverer, later the same year, of

the anaesthetic properties of chloroform, which he tested by experiments on himself. Baronet 1866.

Simpson was born near Linlithgow and studied at Edinburgh, where he became professor of midwifery in 1840. From 1847 he was requested to attend Queen Victoria during her stays in Scotland. By this time he had a thriving private practice and was making pioneering advances in gynaecology; he was eventually appointed physician to Queen Victoria.

Simpson's *Account of a New Anaesthetic Agent* (1847) aroused opposition from Calvinists, who regarded labour pains as God-given. It was Queen Victoria's endorsement of Simpson's use of chloroform during the birth of her seventh child in 1853 that made his techniques universally adopted.

Simpson, N(orman) F(rederick) (1919–)

English dramatist. His plays *A Resounding Tinkle* (1957), *The Hole* (1958), and *One Way Pendulum* (1959) show the logical development of an abnormal situation, and belong to the Theatre of the Absurd. He also wrote a novel, *Harry Bleachbaker* (1976).

Simpson, Robert (Wilfred Levick) (1921–)

English composer and music critic. He studied privately with ◊Howells and was active in the BBC. He wrote on music, especially that of Bruckner, Nielsen, and Sibelius. His music displays tonal stability and an emphasis on organic unity, influenced by Beethoven and Bruckner. His output includes 11 symphonies (1951-90) and 15 string quartets (1952-91). Other works include *Nielsen Variations* (1986); concertos for violin (1959), piano (1967), flute (1989), and cello; *Variations and Fugue on a theme of Bach* for strings (1991); a fantasia for strings; and piano music.

Simpson, Thomas (1710–1761)

English mathematician and writer who devised **Simpson's rule**, which simplifies the calculation of areas under graphic curves. He also worked out a formula that can be used to find the volume of any solid bounded by a ruled surface and two parallel planes.

Simpson, Tommy (1937–1967)

English cyclist. He won the 1965 world professional road race championship.

He turned professional in 1960, winning his first classic race, the Tour of Flanders, a year later. In 1962 he became the first British rider to wear the leader's yellow jersey in the Tour de France. He reinforced his reputation as a top road-racer with wins in the Bordeaux–Paris event in 1963 and the Milan–San Remo classic in 1964. His best year was 1965, when he won both the world professional road race and the Tour of Lombardy. He died tragically after collapsing on Mount Ventoux in the Tour de France, his death precipitated by the use of stimulants.

Sinclair, Clive Marles (1940–)

British electronics engineer. He produced the first widely available pocket calculator, pocket and wristwatch televisions, a series of home computers, and the innovative but commercially disastrous C5 personal transport (a low cyclelike three-wheeled vehicle powered by a washing-machine motor). Knighted 1983.

Sinclair, May (1870–1946)

English writer. Her realistic novels include *The Divine Fire* (1904) and *The Creators* (1910), both about the artist in society. *Mary Olivier: A Life* (1919), which is autobiographical, and *Life and Death of Harriett Frean* (1922) follow the lives of single women, using a stream of consciousness technique.

Sinden, Donald Alfred (1923–)

English actor. A performer of great versatility and resonant voice, his roles ranged from Shakespearean tragedies to light comedies, such as *There's a Girl in My Soup* (1966), *Present Laughter* (1981), and the television series *Two's Company*.

Singleton

Village in the South ◊Downs in West Sussex, England. It is the site of the Weald and Downland Open Air Museum, which has historical exhibits including reconstructed farmhouses, a smithy, and barns.

Sinn Féin (Gaelic 'we ourselves')

Irish political party founded in 1905, whose aim is the creation of a united republican Ireland. The driving political force behind Irish nationalism between 1916 and 1921, Sinn Féin returned to prominence with the outbreak of violence ('the Troubles') in ◊Northern Ireland in the late 1960s, when it split into 'Provisional' and 'Official' wings at the same time as the ◊Irish Republican Army (IRA), with which it is closely associated. From the late 1970s 'Provisional' Sinn Féin assumed a more active political role, putting up candidates to stand in local and national elections. Sinn Féin won two seats in the 1997 UK general election and one seat in the 1997 Irish general election. Gerry ◊Adams became party president in 1978. Sinn Féin participated in the multi-party negotiations (known as the Stormont Talks) and became a signatory of the agreement reached on Good Friday, 10 April 1998. It secured 18 of the 108 seats in the new Northern Ireland Assembly, elected in June 1998. In September a historic meeting between Gerry Adams and the Ulster Unionist leader, David Trimble, took place at Stormont; Sinn Féin also agreed to appoint a contact with the international body overseeing the decommissioning of arms – the party's chief negotiator, Martin McGuinness.

Sinn Féin was founded by Arthur Griffith (1872–1922). Eamon ◊de Valera became its president in 1917. Sinn Féin MPs won a majority of the Irish seats in the 1918 UK general election, set up a secessionist Dáil (Irish parliament) in Dublin, and declared Irish independence in January 1919. The party split over the 1921 Anglo-Irish Treaty which created the Irish Free State and partitioned Ireland. The refusal of a section of Sinn Féin, led by de Valera, to accept the terms of the treaty, led to armed conflict between his followers and the forces of the new Free State. In the aftermath of the Irish Civil War, Sinn Féin pursued a policy of abstention from the Dáil. The party rapidly declined in importance after Eamon de Valera resigned the presidency of Sinn Féin to form his new Fianna Fáil party in 1926.

Talks in 1993 between Provisional Sinn Féin and the moderate nationalist ◊Social Democratic and Labour Party (SDLP) were followed by the ◊Downing Street Declaration and the IRA cease-fire of August 1994. In May 1995 Sinn Féin engaged in the first talks with British government officials since 1973, but the 'peace process' remained deadlocked over Sinn Féin's refusal to accept the demands that all-party talks could not proceed until the IRA had begun decommissioning their arms.

Sinn Féin won two seats in the May 1997 UK general election, though neither of their elected MPs, Gerry Adams and Martin MacGuinness, was permitted to take up his seat in the Westminster parliament because of their refusal to swear the traditional oath of allegiance to the British crown. A second IRA cease-fire was declared in July 1997 to prepare the way for all-party talks. Although the IRA maintained that its cease-fire was intact, the killings of loyalists resulted in Sinn Féin's temporary exclusion from the all-party talks in early 1998. In February, however, the party returned to the negotiations and became a signatory of the Good Friday Agreement.

On 10 May 1998 Sinn Féin decided to opt for involvement in a new Northern Ireland government and to campaign for a 'Yes' vote in the May referenda.

Sissinghurst

Village in Kent, southeast England, south of Maidstone, near Cranbrook. The Elizabethan mansion **Sissinghurst Castle**, nearby to the northeast of the village, was the home from 1930 of the writer Vita Sackville-West. Together with her husband Harold Nicolson, she restored the mansion and created extensive gardens in the grounds. The gardens attract many visitors, and have been in the care of the National Trust since 1966.

Site of Special Scientific Interest, SSSI

Land that has been identified as having animals, plants, or geological features that need to be protected and conserved. From 1991 these sites were designated and administered by English Nature, Scottish Natural Heritage, and the Countryside Council for Wales.

Numbers fluctuate, but in 1998 Britain had almost 5,000 SSSIs, two-thirds of which were privately owned. Although SSSIs enjoy some legal protection, this does not in practice always prevent damage or destruction; during 1992, for example, 40% of SSSIs were damaged by development, farming, public access, and neglect. A report by English Nature estimated that a quarter of the total area of SSSIs, over 1 million acres, had been damaged by acid rain. Around 1% of SSSIs are irreparably damaged each year. In 1995–96 7% of Welsh SSSIs and 4.2% of English SSSIs experienced damage.

Sittingbourne

Town in Kent, England, between Gillingham and Canterbury; population (1991) 56,300. It is in a fruit-growing area; local industries include fruit packing and preserving, and the manufacture of paper, cement, bricks, and clothing. There is also a large agricultural research station here.

Sitwell, (Francis) Osbert (Sacheverell) (1892–1969)

English poet and author. He was the elder brother of Edith and Sacheverell Sitwell. He published volumes of verse, including *Selected Poems* (1943); art criticism; and novels including *Miracle on Sinai* (1933). His greatest literary achievement is a series of autobiographical memoirs (1944–62).

Sitwell, Edith (Louisa) (1887–1964)

English poet, biographer, and critic. Her verse has an imaginative and rhythmic intensity. Her series of poems *Façade* (1922) was performed as recitations to the specially written music of William ◊Walton (1923).

Her *Collected Poems* appeared in 1930 (new edition 1993). Her prose works include *Aspects of Modern Poetry* (1934) and *The Queens and the Hive* (1962).

Sitwell edited the poetry journal *Wheels* (1916–21), a showcase for young poets fighting an artistic revolt against pastoral Georgian verse. The visual imagery and verbal music of her verse influenced T S Eliot and W B Yeats. She was the sister of Osbert and Sacheverell Sitwell. DBE 1954.

The British Bourgeoisie / Is not born, / And does not die, / But, if it is ill, / It has a frightened look in its eyes.

Osbert Sitwell English writer and poet.
'At the House of Mrs Kinfoot'

Six Acts

Acts of Parliament passed in 1819 by Lord Liverpool's Tory administration to curtail political radicalism in the aftermath of the ◊Peterloo massacre and during a period of agitation for reform when ◊habeas corpus was suspended and the powers of magistrates extended.

The acts curtailed the rights of the accused by stipulating trial within a year; increased the penalties for seditious libel; imposed a newspaper stamp duty on all pamphlets and circulars containing news; specified strict limitations on public meetings; banned training with guns and other arms; and empowered magistrates to search and seize arms.

Six Articles

Act introduced by Henry VIII in England in 1539 to settle disputes over dogma in the English church.

The articles affirmed belief in transubstantiation, communion in one kind only, auricular confession, monastic vows, celibacy of the clergy, and private masses; those who rejected transubstantiation were to be burned at the stake. The act was repealed in 1547, replaced by 42 articles in 1551, and by an act of Thirty-Nine Articles in 1571.

Six Counties

The six counties that form Northern Ireland: Antrim, Armagh, Down, Fermanagh, Londonderry, and Tyrone.

Sizergh Castle
Castle in Cumbria, England, 5 km/3 mi southwest of Kendal. The 14th-century pele tower (square fortified tower typical of the Border counties) was built for defence against Border raids, but the castle is largely Tudor, containing panelling, old English furniture, and Stuart and Jacobite relics. The castle was given to the National Trust with 632 ha/1,562 acres by the Hornyold-Strickland family in 1950.

Sizewell
Nuclear power station in Suffolk, eastern England, 3 km/2 mi east of Leiston. Sizewell A, a ◊Magnox nuclear power station, came into operation in 1966. Sizewell B, Britain's first pressurized-water nuclear reactor (PWR) and among the most advanced nuclear power stations in the world, reached full load in June 1995. Plans to build Sizewell C were abandoned by the British government in December 1995.

Sizewell B has an electrical output of 1,188 MW. It cost £2,030 million to construct (in 1987).

The Primary Protection System (PPS) of Sizewell B nuclear plant involves extensive integration of modern digital control equipment. Criticism of this software and controversy regarding its potential negative effect on the overall safety of the system led to a long public enquiry. However, this did not stop operation of the plant. There is now an information centre open to the public.

ska, or bluebeat
Jamaican pop music, a precursor of ◊reggae, mingling the local calypso, *mento*, with rhythm and blues. Ska emerged in the early 1960s (a slower style, **rock steady**, evolved 1966–68) and enjoyed a revival in the UK in the late 1970s. Prince Buster (1938–) was an influential ska singer. A fascination with the beginnings of Jamaican music continued well into the 1990s.

In the late 1980s the term **skacid** was coined for a speeded-up ska with rap and electronic effects.

Skara Brae
Preserved Neolithic village built of stone slabs on ◊Mainland in the Orkney Islands, Scotland.

Skegness
Holiday resort on the North Sea coast of Lincolnshire, eastern England; population (1998) 16,400. It was the site of the first ◊Butlin holiday camp in 1936. An annual carnival is held here in the summer.

SKARA BRAE *The ancient Pictish settlement at Skara Brae on Mainland in the Orkney Islands dates from the Stone Age. It was preserved after a storm buried it in sand; once uncovered, in around 1850, the one-room houses of the village were found to contain a wealth of stone artefacts and furniture, such as cupboards and tables. Robert Hallmann/Collections*

Skelmersdale
Town in Lancashire, northern England, 12 km/8 mi west of Wigan; population (1991) 42,100. Industries include engineering and the manufacture of textiles, rubber, and glass; it also has many light industries, including electronics. Formerly a coalmining village, Skelmersdale was designated a ◊new town in 1961 and received overspill population from Liverpool.

It lies at the foot of Ashurst Beacon, which has Beacon Country Park.

Skelton, John (*c.* 1460–1529)
English poet. He was tutor to the future Henry VIII, under whom he became poet laureate in effect, if not in name. His satirical poetry includes political attacks on Cardinal Wolsey, such as *Collyn Cloute* (1522). He also wrote *Magnyfycence* (1516), the first secular morality play in English.

Skiddaw
Mountain in the ◊Lake District, Cumbria, northwest England, north of Keswick, on the shore of Derwent Water; height 930 m/3,053 ft. It is the fourth-highest peak in the Lake District, although only slightly lower than Scafell Pike (987 m/3,210 ft, the highest point in England).

skiffle
British popular music style, introduced by singer and banjo player Lonnie Donegan (1931–) in the mid-1950s, using improvised percussion instruments such as tea chests and washboards. Donegan popularized US folk songs like 'Rock Island Line' (1953; a UK hit in 1955 and US hit in 1956) and

'Cumberland Gap' (1957). Skiffle gave way to beat music in the early 1960s.

Skipton

Industrial town in North Yorkshire, northern England, 32 km/20 mi northwest of Bradford; population (1991) 13,600. Industries include engineering and textiles. There is an 11th-century castle.

Skokholm

Small island, 5 km/3 mi off the west coast of Pembrokeshire, southwest Wales. The first migratory-bird-marking station in Great Britain was established here in 1927. Skokholm is leased by the West Wales Field Society; in 1946 it was established as Skokholm Bird Observatory, and it is now leased to and managed by the Wildlife Trust for West Wales.

Skomer

Small island in Pembrokeshire, southwest Wales, off the southern arm of St Bride's Bay. It contains many hut-circles (circles of earth or stones representing the sites of prehistoric huts). The surrounding waters are a marine nature reserve. There are colonies of grey seals and several species of birds, including puffins.

Sky

See ◊television.

Skye

Largest island of the Inner ◊Hebrides, Highland region, off the west coast of Scotland; area 1,740 sq km/672 sq mi; population (1991) 8,900. It is separated from the mainland to the southeast by the Sound of Sleat and by the islands of Raasay and Scalpay to the northeast. The chief port and town is Portree. The economy is based on crofting, craft industries, tourism, and livestock. The **Skye Bridge**, a privately financed toll bridge to Kyleakin on the island from the Kyle of Lochalsh, was completed in 1995. The island has a Gaelic college.

Bonnie Prince Charlie (◊Charles Edward Stuart) took refuge here after the Battle of ◊Culloden.

Much of the island is underlain by Tertiary volcanic rocks, and the scenery of the central part is very mountainous; Sgurr Alasdair (993 m/3,257 ft) in the Cuillin Hills is the highest point. The coastline is deeply indented by numerous sea lochs, and most of the settlements are coastal. Large areas of the northern and central western parts of the island have now been planted as forest. The island is 75 km/47 mi long and 25 km/16 mi wide.

Numerous car ferries serve the island: Armadale is connected to Mallaig on the mainland; Uig to Tarbert (Harris); Uig to Lochmaddy (North Uist); and Sconser to Raasay.

Dunvegan Castle (13th–14th centuries) in the west of the island, is home to the chiefs of the Scottish clan Macleod.

Slade, Felix (1790–1868)

English art collector. He bequeathed his collections of engravings, glass, and pottery to the British Museum, and endowed Slade professorships in fine art at Oxford, Cambridge, and University College, London. The Slade School of Fine Arts, which opened in 1871, is a branch of University College.

slave trade

The transport of slaves from one country to work in another. British slaves were taken to Rome during the Roman occupation of Britain, and slaves from Ireland were imported to work in Bristol before the 11th century. The transportation of slaves from Africa to work in plantations in the New World began in the early 16th century. This stimulated a lucrative trade in slaves and the need for slaves to work the British plantations in the Americas led to the development of the Atlantic triangle trade. By the late 17th century, when sugar plantations in the West Indies had become profitable, much of the slave trade was being organized by the British.

From the late 17th century gradual opposition to the slave trade began in Britain. The Mansfield judgement of 1772 stated that a slave held on a ship on the Thames after escaping had become free on setting foot in Britain. The Society for the Abolition of the Slave Trade was founded in 1787 with William ◊Wilberforce as a leading member. After persistent campaigning by abolitionists, an Act of Parliament in 1807 made it illegal for British ships to carry slaves or for the British colonies to import them. Finally the Abolition Act of 1833 provided for slaves in British colonies to be freed and for their owners to be compensated.

SLD

Abbreviation for ◊**Social and Liberal Democrats**, British political party.

Sleat, Sound of

Narrow strait dividing the island of Skye in the Inner Hebrides, Highland unitary authority, from mainland Scotland, extending 32 km/20 mi in length and varying in width from less than 1 km/0.6 mi to 12 km/8 mi.

Sleep, Wayne (1948–)

English dancer. He was a principal dancer with the Royal Ballet 1973–83. He formed his own company, Dash, in 1980. Noted for his technical virtuosity, speed, and the relish with which he embraced a range of character roles, he adapted his TV *Hot Shoe Show* for the stage in 1983, fusing classical, modern, jazz, tap, and disco, and appeared in the original productions of the West End hit musicals *Cats* (1981) and *Song and Dance* (1983), and in the revival of *Carousel* (1986).

The solo *A Tribute to Diana* (1998) recalls the occasion when he danced with Princess Diana on the stage of the Royal Opera House at a gala event in 1985.

Sloane, Hans (1660–1753)

British physician, born in County Down, Ireland. He settled in London, and in 1721 founded the Chelsea Physic Garden. He was president of the Royal College of Physicians 1719–35, and in 1727 succeeded the physicist Isaac ◊Newton as president of the Royal Society. His library, which he bequeathed to the nation, formed the nucleus of the British Museum. Baronet 1716.

Slough

Industrial town and unitary authority in southern England, near Windsor, 32 km/20 west of London; unitary authority area 28 sq km/11 sq mi; population (1994) 105,000. It was part of the county of Berkshire to April 1998. Industries include pharmaceuticals, electronics, engineering, aviation support services, and the manufacture of chocolate, paint, and power tools. A trading estate was developed here in the 1920s, the first of its kind to be established in England.

Features

The home of astronomer William Herschel is now a museum. The history of the town is recorded in Slough Museum.

History

A small market town until the beginning of the 20th century, Slough developed into a large residential and industrial area following the conversion of a government mechanical transport depot into a trading estate of 280 ha/692 acres, containing some 290 factories. It was granted a borough charter in 1938.

Smeaton, John (1724–1792)

England's first civil engineer. He rebuilt the Eddystone lighthouse in the English Channel 1756–59, having rediscovered high-quality cement, unknown since Roman times.

Smeaton adopted the term 'civil engineer' in contradistinction to the fast-growing number of engineers graduating from military colleges. He was also a consultant in the field of structural engineering, and from 1757 onwards he was responsible for projects including bridges, power stations operated by water or wind, steam engines, and river and harbour facilities.

Smethwick

Town in the West Midlands, England, 5 km/3 mi northwest of Birmingham, of which it is now effectively a suburb; population (1991) 11,300. Its principal industries are engineering, brewing, and the manufacture of weighing machines, metals, screws, nuts and bolts, and optical, technical, and domestic glass. There are also foundries.

Smethwick was the site of the factory where some of the leading engineers of the ◊Industrial Revolution – Matthew Boulton, James Watt, and William Murdock – developed their innovations in steam power and gas lighting.

Smith, Adam (1723–1790)

Scottish economist. He is often regarded as the founder of political economy. His *The Wealth of Nations* (1776) defined national wealth in terms of consumable goods and the labour that produces them, rather than in terms of bullion, as prevailing economic theories assumed. The ultimate cause of economic growth is explained by the division of labour – dividing a production process into several repetitive operations, each carried out by different workers, is more efficient. Smith advocated the free working of individual enterprise, and the necessity of 'free trade'.

In *Theory of Moral Sentiments* (1759), Smith argued that the correct way to discern the morally right is to ask what a hypothetical impartial spectator would regard as fitting or proper. The Adam Smith Institute, an organization which studies economic trends, is named after him.

SMITH, ADAM *Scottish economist Adam Smith, the founder of political economy as a separate discipline. In* The Wealth of Nations *(1776) he argued that individual self-interest is the prime motive of human action, but that this leads naturally – through the creation of prosperity and a healthy economy – to the good of society as a whole. Linda Proud*

Smith, Christopher Robert ('Chris') (1951–)

British Labour politician, secretary of state for Culture, Media, and the Arts 1997– . He entered the House of Commons in 1983, representing Islington South and Finsbury. He was shadow Treasury minister 1987–92, shadow secretary of state for the Environment 1992–94, for National Heritage 1994–95, for Social Security 1995–96, and for Health 1996–97.

Smith, Francis Graham (1923–)

English radio astronomer who with his colleague Martin ◊Ryle mapped the radio sources in the sky in the 1950s. Smith discovered the strongly polarized nature of radiation from pulsars in 1968, and estimated the strength of the magnetic field in interstellar space. He was Astronomer Royal 1982–90. Knighted 1986.

Smith, John (1580–1631)

English colonist. After an adventurous early life he took part in the colonization of Virginia, acting as president of the North American colony 1608–09. He explored New England in 1614, which he named, and published pamphlets on America and an autobiography. His trade with the Indians may have kept the colonists alive in the early years.

During an expedition among the American Indians he was captured, and his life is said to have been saved by the intervention of the chief's daughter Pocahontas.

Smith, John (1938–1994)

British Labour politician, party leader 1992–94. He was trade and industry secretary 1978–79 and from 1979 held various shadow cabinet posts, culminating in that of shadow chancellor 1987–92. When Neil Kinnock resigned the leadership after losing the 1992 general election, Smith was readily elected as his successor. During his two years as leader, building on Kinnock's efforts, he drew together the two wings of the Labour Party to make it a highly electable proposition. He won the trust and support of colleagues of all shades of opinion, and built a formidable front-bench team. His sudden death from a heart attack shocked British politicians of all parties.

Smith, John Maynard

British biologist, see ◊Maynard Smith.

Smith, Maggie (Margaret Natalie Cross) (1934–)

English actress. She has a commanding presence, and delivers throwaway lines in a fluting voice. Her films include *The Prime of Miss Jean Brodie* (1969) (Academy Award), *California Suite* (1978), *A Private Function* (1984), *A Room with a View* and *The Lonely Passion of Judith Hearne* (both 1987), *Sister Act* (1992), *Richard III* (1995), and *Washington Square* (1997). She was created a DBE in 1990.

Smith, Matthew Arnold Bracy (1879–1959)

English artist. Influenced by the Fauves, he is known for his exuberant treatment of nudes, luscious fruits and flowers, and his landscapes of Cornwall and southern France. His works display a sumptuousness of colour which have no modern British rival. He was knighted in 1954.

Smith studied at the Slade School and in Paris, working for a short time in Matisse's school in 1911. His mature style developed in the 1920s.

Smith, Michael (1932–)

British molecular biologist who received the Nobel Prize for Chemistry in 1993 for his technique **site-specific mutagenesis**, a technique that replaced the way scientists established the function of a particular protein or gene, by using single strands of viral DNA to mutate the genetic code at precise locations.

Smith, Paul (1946–)

English clothes designer. His clothes are stylistically simple and practical. He opened his first shop in his native Nottingham in 1970, selling designer menswear alongside his own designs, and showed his first collection in Paris in 1976. He launched a toiletry range in 1986, a children's wear collection in 1991, and women's wear in 1994.

In 1997 Smith was wholesaling in 34 countries and there were Paul Smith shops worldwide, including 201 in Japan. He won the British Designer for Industry Award in 1991.

Smith, Richard (1931–)

English abstract artist. His use of advertising imagery in the 1960s linked him briefy to ◊Pop art. He spent long periods in the USA, turning to abstract work and developing the use of shaped canvases. From the 1970s he sometimes worked on a very large scale, turning his paintings into architectural decorations.

Smith was born at Letchworth and educated at Luton and St Albans schools of art before going to the Royal College of Art. His painting alludes to the scale and colour of commercial imagery but does not quote from or parody it.

Smith, Stevie (Florence Margaret) (1902–1971)

English poet and novelist. She made her debut with *Novel on Yellow Paper* (1936). She wrote nine volumes of eccentrically direct verse illustrated with her equally eccentric line drawings, including *Not Waving but Drowning* (1957), and two more novels.

Smith was born in Hull, educated in London, and worked for many years in a publishing house. She published her first collection of poems, *A Good Time Was Had by All*, in 1937; *Collected Poems* was published in 1975.

Smith, William (1769–1839)

English geologist. He produced the first geological maps of England and Wales, thus setting the pattern for geological cartography. While working as a canal engineer, Smith observed that different beds of rock could be identified by their fossils, and so established the basis of stratigraphical geology. From 1816–24 he determined the succession of English strata across the whole country, from the Carboniferous up to the Cretaceous.

Smithfield

Site of a meat market from 1868 and poultry and provision market from 1889, in the City of London. The market now handles fruit and fish in addition to meat and poultry. Formerly an open space used as a tournament ground and cattle market, it was the scene of the murder of Wat Tyler, leader of the Peasants' Revolt in 1381, and the execution of many Protestant martyrs in the 16th century under Mary I.

The annual Bartholomew Fair, a major London market, was held here from 1614 to 1855.

Smiths, the

English four-piece rock group (1982–87) from Manchester. Their songs, with lyrics by singer ◊Morrissey and tunes by guitarist Johnny Marr (1964–), drew on diverse sources such as rockabilly and Mersey beat, with confessional humour and images of urban desolation. They had an intensely dedicated following in Britain and were one of the most popular ◊indie bands.

Albums include *Hatful of Hollow* (1984), *Meat is Murder* (1985), *The Queen is Dead* (1986), and *Strangeways, Here We Come* (1987).

Smithson, Alison Margaret born Gill (1928–1993) and Peter Denham (1923–)

English architects, teachers, and theorists. They are known for their development in the 1950s and 1960s of the style known as Brutalism, for example, Hunstanton School, Norfolk (1954). Notable among their other designs are the Economist Building, London (1964), Robin Hood Gardens, London (1968–72), and the Garden Building at St Hilda's College, Oxford (1970).

Their style reflected the influence of Le Corbusier and Mies van der Rohe in its symmetry and clarity of form. Their *House of the Future* at the 1956 Ideal Home Exhibition, London, drew on futuristic car design and innovative mechanical services.

Smithson, James Louis Macie (1765–1829)

British chemist and mineralogist whose bequest of $100,000 led to the establishment of the Smithsonian Institution.

Smith, W H

Chain of newsagent, book, and record shops developed from a newspaper and stationery business set up 1820. In 1986 W H Smith bought the Our Price chain of record shops and in 1988 acquired 74 of the Virgin record outlets, plus in 1991 a half share in the Virgin megastores, giving the company more than 25% of the UK music market. W H Smith supplied about a third of all newspapers and magazines in the UK in 1996, and had 33,625 employees.

Two newsvendor's sons, Henry Edward Smith and William Henry Smith (died 1865), ran the first shop in the Strand, London, 1820–28, after which William Henry Smith continued alone. In 1846 he was joined by his son William Henry Smith (1825–1891), and they opened the first railway bookstall at Euston Station, London, in 1848.

smoking

In the UK in 1988 33% of men and 30% of women were smokers (a decrease on the 1972 figures of 52% and 41%). UK figures in 1991 showed that smoking kills around 113,000 people per year from related diseases, more than the entire number of deaths from road accidents, drug misuse, AIDS, and alcohol put together. The National Health Service spends up to £500 million a year caring for people with severe illnesses directly related to smoking. Evidence from a study of smoking in British male doctors 1951–94 showed that the death rate in middle age was three times as high as in those who have never smoked. Approximately 50% of smokers die as a result of smoking related diseases.

Passive smoking

UK studies in 1991 showed that passive smoking is a cause of lung cancer. Children whose parents smoke suffer an increased risk of asthma and respiratory infections. A UK study into the smoking habits of parents whose children have died of cancer concluded that the fathers were more likely to have been heavy smokers. As the mothers' smoking habits seemed to have little influence, the researchers concluded in 1996 that the cancers arose, not as a result of passive smoking by the children but because of mutations within the fathers' sperm.

Smollett, Tobias George (1721–1771)

Scottish novelist. He wrote the picaresque novels *Roderick Random* (1748), *Peregrine Pickle* (1751), *Ferdinand Count Fathom* (1753), *Sir Launcelot Greaves* (1760–62), and *Humphrey Clinker* (1771). His novels are full of gusto and vivid characterization.

Smythson, Robert (*c.* 1535–1614)

English architect. He built Elizabethan country houses, including Longleat (1568–75), Wollaton Hall (1580–88), and Hardwick Hall (1590–97). Their castlelike silhouettes, symmetry, and large gridded windows are a uniquely romantic English version of Classicism.

Snaefell

Highest mountain in the Isle of ⇨Man, 620 m/2,035 ft.

snooker

Indoor game derived from billiards (via pool). It is played with 22 balls: 15 red, one each of yellow, green, brown, blue, pink, and black, and one white cueball. A tapered pole (cue) is used to move the balls across the table. The world amateur championship was first held in 1963. The International Olympic Committee recognized snooker as an Olympic sport in 1998; snooker will make its Olympic debut at the Athens games in 2004.

The game was invented by British army officers serving with the Devonshire Regiment in Jubbulpore, India, in 1875 and derived from the game of black pool. It did not gain popularity until the 1920s when Joe ⇨Davis introduced new techniques. Since then it has become one of the biggest television sports in the UK. A season-long series of ranking tournaments culminates in the World Professional Championship at the Crucible Theatre, Sheffield, England, every April.

Snow, C(harles) P(ercy), Baron Snow (1905–1980)

English novelist and physicist. He held government scientific posts in World War II and from 1964–66. His sequence of novels *Strangers and Brothers* (1940–70) portrayed English life from 1920 onwards. *The Two Cultures and the Scientific Revolution* (Cambridge Rede lectures, 1959) discussed the absence of communication between literary and scientific intellectuals in the West, and added the phrase 'the two cultures' to the language. Knighted 1957; baron 1964.

Snowdon, Welsh Eryri

Highest mountain in Wales, 1,085 m/3,560 ft above sea level. Situated 16 km/10 mi southeast of the Menai Strait, it consists of a cluster of five peaks. At the foot of Snowdon are the Llanberis, Aberglaslyn, and Rhyd-ddu passes. A rack railway ascends to the summit from ⇨Llanberis. ⇨Snowdonia, the surrounding mountain range, was made a national park in 1951. It covers 2,188 sq km/845 sq mi of mountain, lakes, and forest land.

The five main peaks are Y Wyddfa (1,085 m/3,560 ft), Carnedd Ungain (1,065 m/3,494 ft), Crib Goch (921 m/3,022 ft), Y Lliwedd (898 m/2,946 ft), and Llechog (884 m/2,900 ft). Shaped roughly like an octopus, the massif extends six tentacles or arms around 12 lakes. It is extremely popular for both family walkers and mountaineers. There is a restaurant at the summit of Y Wyddfa.

Snowdon, Anthony Charles Robert Armstrong-Jones, 1st Earl of Snowdon (1930–)

English photographer. He is especially known for his portraits. He was consultant to the Council of Industrial Design and editorial adviser to *Design Magazine* from 1961 to 1987; artistic adviser to Sunday Times Publications from 1962 to 1990; and photographer for the *Telegraph Magazine* from 1990. He has also made several films for television. In 1960 he married Princess Margaret; they were divorced in 1978. He was created earl in 1961.

Snowdonia

Mountainous region of north Wales, comprising three massifs above 1,000 m/3,280 ft divided by the passes of Llanberis and Nant Ffrancon: ⇨Snowdon, the Glyders, and the Carnedds (including Carnedd Dafydd and Carnedd Llewelyn). Snowdonia was designated a National Park in 1951. The park area of 2,188 sq km/845 sq mi dominates Gwynedd and extends eastwards into Conwy county borough.

Snowshill Manor

Tudor Cotswold manor house in Gloucestershire, England, 10 km/6 mi southeast of Evesham. The house has an early 18th-century façade, but is primarily of interest because it belonged to Charles Paget Wade, an inveterate collector of anything and everything that appealed to him, including clocks, toys, bicycles, orientalia, musical instruments, craft tools, and bygones. Wade left Snowshill and its contents to the National Trust in 1951.

Soane, John (1753–1837)

English architect. His refined Neo-Classical designs anticipated contemporary taste. Soane was a master of the established conventions of Classical architecture, he also developed a highly individual style based on an elegantly mannered interpretation of Neo-Classicism. He designed his own house in Lincoln's Inn Fields, London (1812–13), now **Sir John Soane's Museum**, which he bequeathed to the nation in 1835, together with his collection of antiques, architectural elements and casts, papers, and drawings. Little remains of his extensive work at the Bank of England, London (rebuilt 1930–40).

soap

Mixture of the sodium salts of various fatty acids. Soap was manufactured in Britain from the 14th century, but better-quality soap was imported from Castile or Venice. The Soapmakers' Company, London, was incorporated in 1638. Soap was taxed in England from the time of Cromwell in the 17th century to 1853.

soap operas

On-going TV dramas, a mainstay of British TV schedules, drawing large audiences. At the end of the 1990s the home-grown stalwarts were *Coronation Street* (began 1961), *Emmerdale* (began 1972 as *Emmerdale Farm*), *Brookside* (began 1982), and *EastEnders* (began 1985). *Brookside* was the first soap to be made entirely on location, and has dabbled the most in new ways of presentation: in 1987 a deliberately short-lived soap 'bubble' story, *Damon and Debbie*, 'floated off' from the main story, and extended programmes have covered dramatic storylines.

Not all long-running soaps survive indefinitely: the *Crossroads* Motel closed its doors 23 years after the series began in 1964. Shorter-lived successes have included *Emergency Ward Ten* (from 1957), while *Eldorado* (began 1992), set in Spain, lasted just a year.

Take the High Road (began 1981), later renamed *High Road*, is a Scottish soap; *Pobol y Cwm* is Welsh.

Soar

River in Leicestershire, central England; length 65 km/40 mi. It rises just within the Warwickshire borders and flows through Leicester and Loughborough to Ratcliff, where it joins the River ⇨Trent, 14 km/9 mi southwest of Nottingham and 17 km/11 mi southeast of Derby. It is navigable as far as Leicester.

Sobers, Garry (Garfield St Auburn) (1936–)

West Indian Test cricketer, arguably the world's finest ever all rounder. He held the world individual record for the highest Test innings with 365 not out, until beaten by Brian Lara 1994. He played county cricket for Nottinghamshire and, in a match against Glamorgan at Swansea 1968, he became the first to score six sixes in an over in first-class cricket. He played for the West Indies on 93 occasions, and was captain 39 times. He was knighted for services to cricket 1975. Sobers started playing first-class cricket in 1952.

Social and Liberal Democrats

Official name for the British political party formed in 1988 from the former Liberal Party and most of the Social Democratic Party. The common name for the party is the **Liberal Democrats**. Its leader (from July 1988) is Paddy ⇨Ashdown.

social contract

The idea that government authority derives originally from an agreement between ruler and ruled in which the former agrees to provide order in return for obedience from the latter. It has been used to support both absolutism (Thomas ⇨Hobbes) and democracy (John ⇨Locke, Jean-Jacques Rousseau).

The term was revived in the UK in 1974 when a head-on clash between the Conservative government and the trade unions resulted in a general election which enabled a Labour government to take power. It now denotes an unofficial agreement (hence also called 'social compact') between a government and organized labour that, in return for control of prices, rents, and so on, the unions would refrain from economically disruptive wage demands.

SOAP OPERAS *Some of the cast of the long-running soap opera* Coronation Street. *This programme, produced by Granada Television in Manchester, along with its rivals, such as the BBC's* Eastenders, *attracts huge audiences. The British viewing public's fascination with soaps is fuelled by extensive coverage in the tabloid press of the stars' private lives. Julian Makey/Rex*

Social Democratic and Labour Party, SDLP

Northern Ireland left-of-centre political party, formed in 1970. It aims ultimately at Irish unification, but has distanced itself from violent tactics, adopting a constitutional, conciliatory role. Its leader, John ◊Hume, played a key role in the negotiations which ended in the 1998 Good Friday Agreement on power-sharing. It secured 24 of the 108 seats in the new Northern Ireland Assembly, elected in June 1998; the party's deputy leader, Seamus Mallon, was voted deputy first minister (to Ulster Unionist David Trimble) by the first meeting of the Assembly.

The SDLP, led by John Hume, was responsible for setting up the ◊New Ireland Forum in 1983, and for initiating talks with the leader of Sinn Féin (the political wing of the IRA), Gerry Adams, in 1993, which prompted a joint UK-Irish peace initiative and set in motion a Northern Ireland cease-fire 1994–96. The party won three seats in the 1997 general election. In October 1998 John Hume was, jointly with David Trimble, awarded the Nobel Peace Prize for his part in the Northern Ireland Peace Process.

Social Democratic Federation, SDF

A socialist society founded as the Democratic Federation in 1881 and renamed in 1884. It was led by H M Hyndman (1842–1921), a former conservative journalist and stockbroker who claimed Karl Marx as his inspiration without obtaining recognition from his mentor. In 1911 it became the British Socialist Party.

Social Democratic Party, SDP

British centrist political party 1981–90, formed by members of Parliament who resigned from the Labour Party. The 1983 and 1987 general elections were fought in alliance with the Liberal Party as the **Liberal/SDP Alliance**. A merger of the two parties was voted for by the SDP in 1987, and the new party became the ◊Social and Liberal Democrats, leaving a rump SDP that folded in 1990.

The SDP founders, known as the 'Gang of Four', were Roy ◊Jenkins (its first leader), David ◊Owen (leader from 1983), Shirley ◊Williams, and William Rodgers. The Alliance had limited electoral success (1983, six seats, 11.6% of the vote; 1987, five seats, 9.8% of the vote). David Owen resigned the leadership during the negotiations concerning the merger and was replaced by Robert Maclennan, but continued to lead a separate SDP with two other MPs.

social security

State provision of financial aid to alleviate poverty. In Britain the term was first used officially in 1944, and following the

◊Beveridge Report (1942) a series of acts was passed from 1945 to widen the scope of social security. Basic entitlements of those paying National Insurance contributions in Britain include an old-age pension, unemployment benefit (known as jobseeker's allowance from October 1996), widow's pension, incapacity benefit, and payment during a period of sickness in one's working life (Statutory Sick Pay). Other benefits, which are non-contributory, include family credit, ◊income support, child benefit, and attendance allowance for those looking after sick or disabled people.

Entitlements under National Insurance, such as unemployment benefit, are paid at flat rates regardless of need; other benefits, such as income support, are 'means-tested', that is, claimants' income must be below a certain level. Payments are made by the Benefit Agency and the Contributions Agency, which were formed in 1991 and are accountable to the Department of Social Security (DSS).

In 1997, 42% of the social security budget was spent on the elderly, 24% on the sick and disabled, and 9% on the unemployed. It was announced in the March 1998 budget that family credit and the disabled working allowance would be replaced from October 1999 by a working families tax credit and disabled persons tax credit, to be administered by the Inland Revenue.

The income-support scheme, known originally as national assistance, was called supplementary benefit 1966–88. Family credit was known as family income supplement, and child benefit was known until 1977 as family allowance. In 1987–88 further changes in the social-security system included the abolition of death and maternity grants, to be replaced by means-tested payments from a new Social Fund; and the replacement of maternity allowances by statutory maternity pay, paid by employers, not the DSS.

Social Security, Department of, DSS

Government department established in 1988, after being part of the Department of Health and Social Security. It is responsible for administration of social-service policies, including pensions, unemployment, income support, and disability benefits. In 1998 it employed 89,000 staff, including 69,000 in the Benefits Agency. The secretary of state for social security from 1998 is Alistair Darling.

Since 1991 much of its administrative work had been undertaken by agencies, notably the Benefit Agency, Contributions Agency, and Child Support Agency (established in 1993).

Soddy, Frederick (1877–1956)

English physical chemist who pioneered research into atomic disintegration and coined the term isotope. He was awarded a Nobel prize in 1921 for investigating the origin and nature of isotopes.

The displacement law, introduced by Soddy in 1913, explains the changes in atomic mass and atomic number for all the radioactive intermediates in the decay processes.

Soho

District of central London, in the City of Westminster, which houses the offices of publishing, film, and recording companies; restaurants; nightclubs; and a decreasing number of sex shops. There is a flourishing Chinese community in the area around Gerrard Street.

Soil Association

Pioneer British ecological organization founded in 1946, which campaigns against pesticides and promotes organic farming.

Solemn League and Covenant

Alliance between the Scots and English Parliamentarians on 25 September 1643; both sides agreed to abolish episcopacy and introduce Presbyterianism. In return for £30,000, the Scots provided another army against Charles I, and their cavalry was instrumental in the royalist defeat at Marston Moor in 1644.

Our English countryside is one of the most heavily man-made habitats in Europe. To make it into a green museum would be to belie its whole history.

Nicholas Ridley British Conservative politician.
Speech, November 1988

Solent, the

Channel between the coast of Hampshire, southern England, and the Isle of ◊Wight. It is a yachting centre.

The Solent is 27 km/17 mi long and 1.6–8 km/1–5 mi wide. ◊Spithead is within the Solent, at the eastern end, between Portsmouth and the Isle of Wight (Rye area).

solicitor

A member of one of the two branches of the English legal profession, the other being a ◊barrister.

A solicitor is a lawyer who provides all-round legal services (making wills, winding up estates, conveyancing, divorce, and litigation). A solicitor cannot appear at High Court level, but must brief a barrister on behalf of his or her client. Solicitors may become circuit judges and recorders.

The Courts and Legal Services Act 1990 leaves to a committee of lawyers and lay people, chaired by Lord Griffiths, the work of deciding the extent to which solicitors and employed barristers should be allowed into the higher courts.

Solicitor General

A law officer of the crown, deputy to the ◊Attorney General, a political appointee with ministerial rank.

Solihull

Industrial and residential town in the county of West Midlands, England, 11 km/7 mi southeast of Birmingham; population (1991) 192,200. The area includes Birmingham Airport and the National Exhibition Centre.

Solti, Georg (1912–1997)

Hungarian-born British conductor. He was music director at the Royal Opera House, Covent Garden, London, 1961–71, and director of the Chicago Symphony Orchestra (1969–91). He was also principal conductor of the London Philharmonic Orchestra 1979–83. KBE 1971.

Solway Firth

Inlet of the Irish Sea, formed by the estuaries of the rivers Eden and Esk, at the western end of the border between England and Scotland, separating Cumbria in England from Dumfries and Galloway in Scotland. Solway Firth is in part the estuary of the River Esk, and in part an inlet of the Irish Sea.

At its mouth the firth is over 40 km/25 mi wide; at its narrowest point it is 3 km/2 mi wide. The tides ebb and flow with great rapidity, creating a bore (high wave moving up a narrow estuary, caused by the tide) of some 16 kph/10 mph. There are salmon fisheries.

Solway Moss, Battle of

Crushing defeat on 24 November 1542 of the Scots by an invading English force under the Duke of Norfolk. Some 500 Scottish prisoners were captured including two earls and five barons, and the shame is said to have led to James V's death three weeks later. The Treaty of Greenwich, by which the infant Mary Queen of Scots would marry Edward, Prince of Wales, was signed in the aftermath of the battle.

Somerset

County of southwest England

Area 3,460 sq km/1,336 sq mi

Towns ◊Taunton (administrative headquarters); Bridgwater, Frome, Glastonbury, Wells, Yeovil; Burnham-on-Sea, Minehead (coastal resorts)

Physical rivers Avon, Axe, Brue, Exe, Parret (the principal river), and Yeo; marshy coastline on the Bristol Channel; Mendip Hills; Quantock Hills; Exmoor; Blackdown Hills

Features Cheddar Gorge and Wookey Hole, a series of limestone caves where Stone Age flint implements and bones of extinct animals have been found; Glastonbury Tor

Agriculture apples; dairy farming; cereals (wheat, barley, oats), vegetables (turnips, mangolds (a root vegetable used as animal feed)); cider; cattle and sheep rearing; willows (withies) for wicker-work

Industries agricultural implements; Bath-bricks (manufactured at Bridgwater from the sand of the Parret); chemicals; dairy products (including Cheddar cheese); engineering; food processing; helicopters; leather; mineral working (iron, lead, zinc); stone quarrying (slate); textiles; tourism

Population (1994) 477,900

Famous people John Pym, Henry Fielding, Ernest Bevin

History at the Battle of Sedgemoor in 1685, James II defeated the Duke of Monmouth, a claimant to the English crown who had been proclaimed king at Taunton that year.

Topography

Somerset is bounded on the southwest by Devon; on the southeast by Dorset; on the east by Wiltshire; on the northeast by Bath and North East Somerset, and North Somerset; and on the northwest by the Bristol Channel. There are low cliffs along the northern coast, which has long sandy beaches and mud tracts at low tide, particularly in the northwest. Bridgwater Bay is the chief inlet; the only important harbour is at the mouth of the River Parret.

The Quantock Hills, the highest point of which is Willsneck (387 m/1,270 ft), extend from Taunton northwest towards the sea. In the south of the county is the second largest area of fen country in England, the **Somerset Levels**, which includes the area known as Sedgemoor; peat was formerly cut here.

The wild forest of ◊Exmoor lies partly in the extreme west of the county and partly in Devon. ◊Dunkery Beacon (518 m/1,700 ft), the highest point in the county, is on the edge of Exmoor.

Fauna

There is a breed of hardy ponies peculiar to the Exmoor district; red deer are also found there. There is good river fishing, including salmon fishing, particularly in the west of the county.

From the Romans to the English Civil War

There are many notable Roman remains in Somerset, including a large mosaic pavement near Langport, and many later Saxon stone carvings in the church at Milborne Port. Somerset was originally part of the kingdom of Wessex, and figured largely in King Alfred's struggle against the Danes. Somerset contains several abbeys, and castles, notably at Glastonbury and Dunster, and an important cathedral at Wells. A battle was fought at Allermoor in 1645 during the Civil War.

Somerset

Family name of the dukes of Beaufort, seated at Badminton in Gloucestershire, England; they are descended in an illegitimate line from King Edward III.

Somerset, Edward Seymour, 1st Duke of Somerset (*c.* 1506–1552)

English politician. Created Earl of Hertford after Henry VIII's marriage to his sister Jane, he became Duke of Somerset and protector (regent) for Edward VI in 1547. His attempt to check ◊enclosure (the transfer of land from common to private ownership) offended landowners and his moderation in religion upset the Protestants, and he was beheaded on a fake treason charge in 1552. Knighted 1523, viscount 1536, earl 1537.

Somerset House

Government office in the Strand, London, built in 1775. It is used by the Inland Revenue, the Principal Probate Registry, where wills are kept, and by the University of London. Somerset House is also the home of the Courtauld Institute Collection of paintings. The river façade was designed by the Scottish architect William Chambers (1726-1796).

The General Register Office (births, marriages, and deaths), formerly at Somerset House, was merged with the Government Social Survey Department as the Office of Population Censuses and Surveys in 1970, and transferred to St Catherine's House, also in the Strand.

Somervell, Arthur (1863–1937)
English composer and educationist. His songs, especially settings of lyrics from Tennyson's 'Maud', Housman's 'A Shropshire Lad', and Browning's 'James Lee's Wife', are his best-known works. He also composed two Masses, choral works, including a setting of Wordsworth's 'Intimations of Immortality', and a symphony, and edited *Songs of the Four Nations* and other folk songs.

Somerville, Mary born Fairfax (1780–1872)
Scottish scientific writer who produced several widely used textbooks, despite having just one year of formal education. Somerville College, Oxford, is named after her.

Somes, Michael George (1917–1994)
British ballet dancer, teacher, *répétiteur*, and guardian of the Royal Ballet's Frederick Ashton repertoire. Somes was praised by critics for his elegant deportment, superb elevation, and exceptional musicality. He was also an important long-time partner of Margot Fonteyn.

Somme, Battle of the
Allied offensive in World War I during July–November 1916 on the River Somme in northern France, during which severe losses were suffered by both sides. It was planned by the Marshal of France, Joseph Joffre, and UK commander in chief Douglas Haig; the Allies lost over 600,000 soldiers and advanced 13 km/8 mi. It was the first battle in which tanks were used. The German offensive around St Quentin during March–April 1918 is sometimes called the Second Battle of the Somme.

Sons and Lovers
Novel (1913) by D H ◊Lawrence. The central character is Paul Morel, the artistic son of a stormy marriage between a coal miner and his sensitive and ambitious wife. He grows up attempting to maintain a strong connection with his mother while failing in his sexual relationships, firstly with the virginal Miriam Leivers and then with the married feminist Clara Dawes. The largely autobiographical material is illuminated and shaped by Lawrence's confidently original imagination.

Soper, Donald Oliver, Baron Soper (1903–)
British Methodist minister, superintendent of the West London Mission, Kingsway Hall, 1936–78.

A pacifist, he had a ready wit in debate and made many television appearances. His books include *All His Grace* (1957) and *Aflame with Faith*. He was a regular speaker at Hyde Park Corner. In 1965 he became a life peer.

Sopwith, Thomas Octave Murdoch (1888–1989)
English designer of the Sopwith Camel biplane, used in World War I, and joint developer of the Hawker Hurricane fighter plane used in World War II. Knighted 1953.

From a Northumbrian engineering family, Sopwith gained a pilot's licence in 1910 and soon after set a British aerial duration record for a flight of 3 hours 12 minutes. In 1912 he founded the Sopwith Aviation Company, which in 1920 he wound up and reopened as the Hawker Company, named after the chief test pilot Harry Hawker. The Hawker Company was responsible for the Hawker Hart bomber, the Hurricane, and eventually the vertical takeoff ◊Harrier jump jet.

Sorby, Henry Clifton (1826–1908)
English geologist whose discovery in 1863 of the crystalline nature of steel led to the study of metallography. Thin-slicing of hard minerals enabled him to study the constituent minerals microscopically in transmitted light. He later employed the same techniques in the study of iron and steel under stress.

South, James (1785–1867)
English astronomer. He published two catalogues of double stars in 1824 and 1826, the former with John ◊Herschel. For this catalogue, they were awarded the Gold Medal of the Astronomical Society in 1826. Knighted 1830.

South African Wars
Two wars between the Boers (settlers of Dutch origin) and the British; essentially fought for the gold and diamonds of the Transvaal.

The **War of 1881** was triggered by the attempt of the Boers of the Transvaal to reassert the independence surrendered in 1877 in return for British aid against African peoples. The British were defeated at Majuba, and the Transvaal again became independent.

The **War of 1899–1902**, also known as the **Boer War**, was preceded by the armed Jameson Raid into the Boer Transvaal; a failed attempt, inspired by the Cape Colony prime minister Cecil Rhodes, to precipitate a revolt against Paul Kruger, the Transvaal president. The *uitlanders* (non-Boer immigrants) were still not given the vote by the Boers, negotiations failed, and the Boers invaded British territory, besieging Ladysmith, Mafeking (now Mafikeng), and Kimberley. The war ended with the Peace of Vereeniging following the Boer defeat.

British commander ◊Kitchener countered Boer guerrilla warfare by putting the noncombatants who supported them into concentration camps, where about 26,000 women and children died of sickness.

Southampton
Industrial city, seaport, and unitary authority in southern England, at the head of **Southampton Water**, 20 km/12 mi southwest of Winchester; unitary authority area 52 sq km/20 sq mi; population (1997 est) 207,100. It was part of the county of Hampshire to 1997. Industries include marine engineering, chemicals, plastics, flour-milling, tobacco, the manufacture of cables and electrical goods, and financial services. It is a major passenger and container port. There is an oil refinery nearby at Fawley.

The *Mayflower* originally set sail from here en route to North America in 1620 (bad weather forced it to stop at Plymouth), as did the *Titanic* on its fateful maiden voyage in 1912. Southampton University was established in 1952. There is a ferry link to the Isle of Wight. The port is a base for many liners, including P&O's *Oriana*. The *QE II* was also

SOUTHAMPTON *A sailing ship moored at the south coast port of Southampton. The quayside she is lying alongside, in the Old Docks area, was once the Cunard Line's Ocean Terminal, serving liners such as the* Queen Elizabeth *and* Queen Mary. *Though the transatlantic passenger trade is long gone, Southampton continues to thrive as one of Britain's main ports for containerized freight. Robert Hallmann/ Collections*

formerly based here. Approximately 250,000 people pass through the city docks every year on cruise business.

Features

Southampton City Art Gallery includes a fine collection of 20th-century British art. Some parts of the medieval town wall survive including four of the town-wall towers, and Bargate, the elaborate old north gateway to the city. The partly Norman St Michael's Church has an 18th-century spire which is 50 m/164 ft high. The 14th-century Wool House, originally a warehouse for wool, now houses a maritime museum. The Tudor House Museum is situated in a half-timbered 15th-century building and illustrates the social history of Southampton. The hospital of God's House was originally founded in 1185 for pilgrims going either to the shrine of St Swithin at Winchester, or to Canterbury. God's House Tower dates from the 15th century and now houses a museum of archaeology. The Norman House and Canute's Palace are among the oldest examples of Norman domestic architecture in Britain. A memorial column marks the place of embarkation of the Pilgrim Fathers on the *Mayflower*. The headquarters of the mapping agency, the Ordnance Survey, is located here.

History

A walled town was established on the peninsula between the Test and the Itchen after the Norman Conquest. A charter of incorporation was granted to the town by Henry I, and it was created a county by Henry VI. Trade with Mediterranean ports was the basis of the town's economy by the 15th century. In the early 19th century Southampton developed as a spa and, following the building of the docks in the 1840s, the city replaced Falmouth as a mail-packet station. Southampton was frequently bombed during World War II, and it was the main port of embarkation for troops in the ◊D-day operation of 1944.

Docks

The building of the modern system of docks began in 1838. The Old Docks, covering some 80 ha/198 acres, contain three large tidal basins, known as the Ocean, Empress, and Outer Docks. The New Docks, facing the River Test, were completed in 1934. At the western end of the New Docks is the King George V graving (dry) dock, built primarily for the *Queen Mary*. The Princess Alexandra Dock has been redeveloped as a marina and shopping centre.

Southampton Water

Inlet of the English Channel, stretching from the ◊Solent and Spithead into Hampshire, southern England. It is about 18 km/11 mi long and its greatest breadth is 3.2 km/2 mi.

Southampton Water forms a natural harbour, with the Isle of Wight a natural breakwater, giving the area a double high tide. The rivers Itchen and Test flow into Southampton Water.

South Ayrshire

Unitary authority in southwest Scotland, created in 1996 from Kyle and Carrick district (1975–96), Strathclyde region

Area 1,245 sq km/480 sq mi

Towns ◊Ayr (administrative headquarters), Prestwick, Girvan, Troon, Maybole

Physical coastal plain which rises to higher ground inland (500 m/1,640 ft); rivers Ayr, Stinchar, Water of Girvan; Brown Carrick Hill (287 m/942 ft); Ailsa Craig; many beaches interspersed with cliffs and caves

Features Glasgow Prestwick Airport; Culzean Castle; Crossraguel Abbey; Royal Troon and Turnberry championship golf courses; Ayr racecourse

Industries aerospace, high technology, tourism

Agriculture fishing (Ayr), dairying, beef cattle, potatoes

Population (1995) 114,600

History birthplace of Robert Burns.

Economy

It is an affluent area with a diverse and prosperous agricultural sector, particularly to the south. The north is dominated by the buoyant economy of Ayr, which combines service sector, tourist, technology, and traditional (fishing) enterprise.

Environment
There are 31 Sites of Special Scientific Interest, one Special Protection Area, and one country park.
Administrative history
Prior to 1975, the area was part of the county of Ayrshire.
Architecture
Culzean Castle, 19 km/12 mi south of Ayr, was built by Robert Adam in the late 18th century for the 10th Earl of Cassillis. The ruins of Crossraguel Abbey (1244), a Cluniac monastery, lie near Maybole.

South Bank

Area of London south of the River Thames, between Waterloo Bridge and Hungerford Bridge. It was the site of the Festival of Britain in 1951, and is now a cultural centre. Buildings include the Royal Festival Hall (1951, Robert Matthew and Leslie Martin), the Queen Elizabeth Hall and the Purcell Room (1967), the National Theatre (1976, Denys Lasdun), the Hayward Gallery (1967), the National Film Theatre (1970), and the Museum of the Moving Image (1988), all connected by a series of walkways. It was announced in 1991 that the Queen Elizabeth Hall was to be demolished to create a new South Bank Arts Centre. The South Bank Centre is to be refurbished by the architect Richard Rogers.

Southcott, Joanna (1750–1814)

English religious fanatic whose prophecies attracted thousands of followers in the early 19th century. She began prophesying in 1792 in her native Devon, but only gained a widespread reputation after moving to London in 1802. In 1814 she announced she was to give birth to a 'Prince of Peace' but died shortly after.

South Downs

Line of chalk hills in southeast England, running from near Petersfield, Hampshire, across Sussex to the south coast at Beachy Head near Eastbourne. They face the ◊North Downs across the Weald and are used as sheep pasture.

The South Downs long-distance footpath traverses the area. In the west of the range Butser Hill, the highest point, rises to 271 m/887 ft and Duncton Down to 255 m/836 ft; in the east Ditchling Beacon rises to 248 m/813 ft. The rivers Cuckmere, Ouse, Adur, and Arun cut transversely through the chalk, and there are towns at the crossing points such as Lewes and Arundle.

Southend

Resort and unitary authority in eastern England, on the Thames estuary, 60 km/37 mi east of London, the nearest seaside resort to London; area 42 sq km/16 sq mi; population (1994 est) 171,000. It was part of the county of Essex to April 1998. Features include a pier, 2 km/1.25 mi long, said to be the longest in the world. Industries include tourism, financial services, light engineering, and boatbuilding.

Southend-on-Sea developed as a resort (at the 'south end' of the village of Prittlewell) at the beginning of the 19th century. The Southend unitary authority now includes the neighbouring villages of Westcliff, Leigh, Thorpe Bay, Shoeburyness, Southchurch, Eastwood, Cambridge Town, and Prittlewell. It attracts nearly 3 million visitors a year.
Features
There are 11 km/7 mi of seafront, as well as an aquarium, amusement facilities, and many public parks and gardens, including the Cliff Gardens. Southend is well known for its floral features, including carpet bedding displays and a Floral Trail Tour. Nearly one-third of all land in the area is actively managed for nature conservation, including Belfairs Wood Nature Reserve and Leigh National Nature Reserve on Two Tree Island.
Architecture
Southchurch Hall, a 13th-century building, on the site of an earlier Saxon building, was the residence of Sir Richard de Southchurch, Sheriff of Essex in 1265. The Cluniac priory of St Mary's at Prittlewell was founded about 1110 as a cell of the priory at Lewes, East Sussex. The church of St Mary the Virgin, Prittlewell, dates from the 7th century; the present Norman nave was erected in the 11th century, the processional aisle in the 12th century, and the chancel tower in the 15th century; the 15th-century Jesus Chapel has a fine stained-glass window attributed to the German artist Albrecht Dürer, and was formerly in the church of St Ouen, Rouen.
History
There were successive occupations in the area by Celts, Romans, Saxons, and Danes. The Saxons settled in the area from 500 to 650, and in 894 King Alfred defeated the Danes at Benfleet, driving them across the site of modern Southend to Shoeburyness, where they formed a settlement. The name 'Southende' was first used in a legal document during the reign of Henry VIII. The rise of the town as a health resort dates from about 1794, when it became a fashionable place for sea-bathing. After the arrival of the railway in the 19th century, Southend developed rapidly as a seaside resort, popular with holidaymakers from London.

Southern Uplands

One of the three geographical divisions of Scotland, being most of the hilly Scottish borderland to the south of a geological fault line that stretches from Dunbar, East Lothian, on the North Sea to Girvan, South Ayrshire, on the Firth of Clyde. The Southern Uplands, largely formed by rocks of the Silurian and Ordovician age, are intersected by the broad valleys of the Nith and Tweed rivers.

Southey, Robert (1774–1843)

English poet and author. He is sometimes regarded as one of the 'Lake poets', more because of his friendship with Samuel Taylor ◊Coleridge and William ◊Wordsworth and residence in Keswick, in the English Lake District, than for any Romantic influence in his work. In 1813 he became poet laureate, but he is better known for his *Life of Nelson* (1813) and for his letters.

He was an early admirer of the French Revolution, whose aims he supported in the epic poem *Joan of Arc* (1796). He joined with Coleridge in planning the utopian 'Pantisocracy', a scheme for a radical community in the USA, which came to nothing, and married Edith Fricker (1795). He later abandoned his revolutionary views, and from 1808 contributed regularly to the Tory *Quarterly Review*. He wrote long epic poems reflecting the contemporary fashion for exotic melodrama, and short poems including 'The Battle of Blenheim' and 'The Inchcape Rock'.

South Georgia

Island in the South Atlantic, a British crown colony administered, with the South Sandwich Islands, from the Falkland Islands; area 3,757 sq km/1,450 sq mi. There has been no permanent population since the whaling station was abandoned in 1966. The British Antarctic Survey has a station on nearby Bird Island.

In 1993, the UK provoked an outcry from Argentina when it announced it was extending the territorial waters around South Georgia and the South Sandwich Islands from 19 to 322 km/12 to 200 mi to protect fish stocks from foreign fleets.

South Glamorgan, Welsh De Morgannwg

Former county of south Wales, 1974–1996, now divided between ◊Cardiff and ◊Vale of Glamorgan unitary authorities.

South Gloucestershire

Unitary authority in southwest England created in 1996 from part of the former county of Avon
Area 497 sq km/192 sq mi
Towns and cities Thornbury (administrative headquarters), Patchway, Yate, Chipping Sodbury
Features River Severn borders northwest; Vale of Berkeley; Severn Road Bridge; Marshfield has one of Britain's longest village streets with 17th-century almshouses; 13th-century church of St Peter (Dyrham); late 17th-century Dyrham Park Mansion
Industries agriculture and associated industries
Population (1996) 220,000.

South Lanarkshire

Unitary authority in south central Scotland, created in 1996 from three districts of Strathclyde region
Area 1,772 sq km/684 sq mi
Towns ◊Hamilton (administrative headquarters), Lanark, Rutherglen, East Kilbride, Carluke, Cambuslang
Physical area of stark contrast: predominantly rural to the south and urban to the north. The River Clyde flows through the area. Tinto (707 m/2,320 ft) is a key landmark to the south
Features Craignethan Castle; Carstairs State Hospital, New Lanark
Industries textiles, electronics, engineering
Agriculture fruit cultivation in the valleys of the Clyde; less intensive grazing and stock rearing in the upland south; dairying around the urban core in the north
Population (1995) 307,400
History New Lanark village is a World Heritage Site, significant for the attempt to improve living conditions for workers and their families.

Economy

The northern part contains de-industrializing towns, towns within the Glasgow economic system, and the new town of East Kilbride. To the south, a more rural economy prevails, focused aroung the market town of Lanark. The area is one of economic contrast.

Environment

There are 38 Sites of Special Scientific Interest, two National Nature Reserves, and three country parks.

Administrative history

The districts of Clydesdale, East Kilbride, and Hamilton were merged into South Lanarkshire in 1996. Prior to 1975, this area was part of the county of Lanarkshire.

Southport

Resort town on the Irish Sea coast in Merseyside, northwest England, 25 km/16 mi north of Liverpool; population (1981) 98,000. Tourism is important and other industries include engineering and the manufacture of clothing and food. Southport pier (1859) was the first pier to be built for pleasure rather than as a landing stage.

The town is built mainly on old sand dunes, and the peat mosslands away from the coastal belt are used for market gardening. A large area has been reclaimed for gardens, a marine lake, swimming pools, and other recreational facilities.

Southport was laid out in a rectangular pattern of tree-lined streets. It acquired its first hotel for visitors in the 18th century, but the town did not expand greatly until the railway to Liverpool was built in 1848, and the line to Wigan and Manchester in 1855. At 1,100 m/1,200 yd, the pier is the second longest in England.

South Ronaldsay

Southernmost of the ◊Orkney Islands, Scotland, situated 9 km/6 mi northeast of Duncansby Head on the Scottish mainland; population (1991) 900. Its surface is flat and well cultivated, covering an area of 46 sq km/18 sq mi. St Margaret's Hope, the main harbour and settlement, lies in the north of the island.

South Ronaldsay is connected to Burray and Mainland, the largest of the Orkney Islands, by the ◊Orkney Causeway (or Churchill Barrier), constructed during World War II to close off the eastern arm of ◊Scapa Flow.

South Sandwich Islands

Actively volcanic uninhabited British Dependent Territory; area 337 sq km/130 sq mi. Along with ◊South Georgia, 750 km/470 mi to the northwest, it is administered from the Falkland Islands. They were claimed by Captain Cook in 1775 and named after his patron John Montagu, the 4th Earl of Sandwich.

South Sea Bubble

Financial crisis in Britain in 1720. The South Sea Company, founded in 1711, which had a monopoly of trade with South America, offered in 1719 to take over more than half the national debt in return for further concessions. Its 100 shares rapidly rose to 1,000, and an orgy of speculation followed. When the 'bubble' burst, thousands were ruined.

The discovery that cabinet ministers had been guilty of corruption led to a political crisis. Robert Walpole became prime minister, protected the royal family and members of the government from scandal, and restored financial confidence.

South Shields

Manufacturing port in Tyne and Wear, northeast England, on the south side of the Tyne estuary opposite North Shields and east of Gateshead; population (1991) 82,400. Shipbuilding has declined and industries now include electrical goods, cables, chemicals, and paint.

It was the site of a Roman fort **Arbeia**, and the Roman Museum displays relics excavated from the site. South Shields was founded by the Convent of Durham in the 13th century. A river port in medieval times, South Shields was a centre of the salt and glass industries in the 17th and 18th centuries, and developed as a resort and coal port in the 19th century.

Famous people

Children's adventure story writer, Elinor Brent-Dyer, author of the *Chalet School* stories, was born here in 1894. It was also the birthplace of William Wouldhave, inventor of the modern lifeboat.

South Uist

Second largest island in the Outer ◊Hebrides, Western Isles, Scotland, separated from North Uist by the island of Benbecula. The main town and port with connections to the mainland is Lochboisdale. Most of the population live in crofting townships on the west coast. There are hundreds of lochs in the central area of the island; the east coast is mountainous and dissected by sea lochs.

The island is connected by car ferries from Lochboisdale to Castlebay (Barra), Eriskay, and Mallaig and Oban on the mainland.

Southwark

Inner borough of south Greater London. It includes the districts of Camberwell, ◊Dulwich, and Walworth. It is the oldest borough in London (after the City of London) and was the first to send representatives to Parliament.

Features large Roman baths complex, about AD 120, and fine wall paintings have been excavated; Southwark Cathedral (1220), earliest Gothic church in London, with nave built in the 1890s (formerly a parish church, it became a cathedral in 1905); inns and alehouses, including the Tabard Inn, where Chaucer's pilgrims met, and the George Inn (1677), the last galleried inn in London; formerly seven prisons, including the Clink and the Marshalsea; site of Globe Theatre (built on Bankside in 1599 by Burbage, Shakespeare, and others, burned down in 1613, rebuilt in 1995); the International Shakespeare Globe Centre is planned to open in 1999; Imperial War Museum; Dulwich Picture Gallery; Horniman Museum; Elephant and Castle public house, Walworth; Labour Party headquarters in Walworth Road; former Bankside power station to be transformed into the Tate Gallery of Modern Art (Swiss architects Herzog and de Meuron) with the help of a Millennium Award

Famous people John Harvard (1607–1638), founder of Harvard College, Massachusetts, USA – he is commemorated in Harvard Chapel, Southwark Cathedral; Joseph Chamberlain

Population (1991) 218,500.

Southwell

Small town in Nottinghamshire, England, 24 km/15 mi northeast of Nottingham; population (1991) 6,600. The main industries are lacemaking, milling, and agriculture. The town is dominated by Southwell Minster (begun about 1110), which was designated a cathedral in 1884.

It is claimed that a church was first established here in 630 by Paulinus, the second bishop of York. The present church shows architectural styles from Norman (the nave) to Perpendicular Gothic, with 13th-century foliage carving in the chapter house, and a 14th-century screen.

In the town's Old Market Place is the Saracen's Head Hotel, an old coaching inn. From here, on 5 May 1647, Charles I went under escort to nearby Kelham and surrendered to the Scottish army. Bishop's Manor is the official residence of the bishop and there is an ancient grammar school.

South Yorkshire

Metropolitan county of northeast England, created in 1974; in 1986, most of the functions of the former county council were transferred to the metropolitan borough councils

Area 1,560 sq km/602 sq mi

Towns Barnsley, Doncaster, Rotherham, Sheffield (all administrative centres for the districts of the same name)

Physical River Don; part of Peak District National Park; the county contains a rich diversity of rural landscapes formed between the barren Pennine moors in the southwest and the very low, flat carr-lands (a mixture of marsh and copses) in the east

Features a 1995 Millennium Commission award will enable the Earth Centre for Environmental Research to be built near Doncaster

Agriculture sheep; dairy and arable farming

Industries metal-work, coal, engineering, iron, and steel

Population (1995) 1,298,000

Famous people Ian Botham, Arthur Scargill

Population and industry

The overall rate of increase in population in the South Yorkshire area in recent years has been below the national average due to outward migration. Over 90% of the population resides in the urban areas, which are concentrated along the valley of the River Don, which runs from southwest to northeast, and along the valleys of the Don's main tributaries, the Dearne and the Rother. There is a high level of unemployment; most employed persons are engaged in coal-mining, steel manufacturing and processing, and in the glass, brass, wire, and various engineering industries. Sheffield is especially noted for its high-quality alloy steels, machine tools, heavy engineering, and cutlery.

sovereign

British gold coin, introduced by Henry VII, which became the standard monetary unit in 1817. Minting ceased for currency purposes in the UK in 1914, but the sovereign continued to be used as 'unofficial' currency in the Middle East. It was minted for the last time in 1987 and has now been replaced by the **Britannia**.

The value is notionally £1, but the actual value is that of the weight of the gold at current rates. Sovereigns are bought by investors suspicious of falling values of paper currencies.

Spa Fields riots

Riots in London on 2 December 1816 provoked by demands for parliamentary reform. Discontent was widespread at the time due to an economic depression at the end of the Napoleonic Wars. The orator Henry Hunt was due to address a mass meeting calling for universal suffrage and reform of parliament in Spa Fields, London, but radical agitators led the crowd on the City of London. They were confronted by the lord mayor at the head of a force of police and the ensuing riot was eventually broken up by troops.

Spaghetti Junction

Nickname for a complex system of motorway flyovers and interchanges at Gravelly Hill, north Birmingham, in West Midlands, central England. It was opened in May 1972.

Spalding

Market town in the Lincolnshire fens, eastern England, on both banks of the River Welland, 23 km/14 mi southwest of Boston; population (1991) 18,700. It is an agricultural and horticultural centre, with bulb farms. Flower-growing fields occupy an area of over 4,000 ha/10,000 acres. Industries include the manufacture of agricultural implements and tractors. A flower festival is held annually here in May.

The church of St Mary and St Nicholas dates from the 13th century. The 15th-century Ayscoughfee Hall houses a museum of agriculture illustrating the history of the fens. Spalding Gentleman's Society, founded in 1710, is the oldest antiquarian society in England.

Spanish Armada

Fleet sent by Philip II of Spain against England in 1588. Consisting of 130 ships, it sailed from Lisbon, Portugal, and carried on a running fight up the Channel with the English fleet of 197 small ships under Howard of Effingham and Francis ◊Drake. The Armada anchored off Calais, France, but fire ships forced it to put to sea, and a general action followed off Gravelines. What remained of the Armada escaped around the north of Scotland and west of Ireland, suffering many losses by storm and shipwreck on the way. Only about half the original fleet returned to Spain.

Philip II had resolved to mount an invasion of England in response to the English army supporting the Netherlands in their revolt against Spain. A fleet assembled at Cádiz, Spain, for this purpose was largely destroyed by Sir Francis Drake's raid in April 1587. The Spanish assembled another fleet, the Great Armada, late in the year, which the Admiral Santa Cruz refused to risk in the winter gales of the Bay of Biscay. By spring 1588 Santa Cruz had died and command was given to the Duke of Medina Sidonia, who set sail on 12 July with 130 ships carrying 20,000 soldiers.

The English fleet, consisting of 34 Queen's ships and 163 mainly small privateers, had been ready since February. Sidonia's orders were to sail up the English Channel to the Netherlands and there embark more troops from the Spanish army operating in the Low Countries; the English fleet's objective was to break up the Armada before it reached the Netherlands.

Spark, Muriel (Sarah) born Camberg (1918–)

Scottish-born novelist. After writing poetry and critical and biographical works, she was encouraged to embark upon fiction after winning the *Observer* short-story competition in 1951 and her conversion to Catholicism in 1954. Many of her characters are misfits, such as feature in *The Comforters* (1957) (her first novel), *The Prime of Miss Jean Brodie* (1961), and *A Far Cry from Kensington* (1988). Blacker satire is in *Memento Mori* (1959), *Symposium* (1990), and *Realities and Dreams* (1996). *Collected Poems* appeared in 1967 and *The Collected Stories* was published in 1994.

Her early novels, such as *The Comforters* and *The Girls of Slender Means* (1963), are dark and witty fantasies; later novels, such as *Memento Mori*, *The Mandelbaum Gate* (1965), and *The Driver's Seat* (1970), deal with deeper themes. *Curriculum Vitae* (1992) is an autobiography to 1957. She has lived in Italy since 1967. In 1997 she won the British Literature Prize. DBE 1993.

Spark, Muriel *Scottish novelist Muriel Spark, photographed in 1960. Her* The Prime of Miss Jean Brodie *(1961), about an Edinburgh schoolteacher and the influence she has on her pupils, was made into an Academy Award-winning film starring Maggie Smith in 1969. Spark has written short stories, poetry, and plays as well as novels. Corbis*

Speaker
Presiding officer charged with the preservation of order in the House of Commons. The equivalent of the Speaker in the House of Lords is the Lord Chancellor; in the House of Commons the Speaker is elected for each parliament, usually on an agreed basis among the parties, but often holds the office for many years. The original appointment dates from 1377. In 1992 Betty ◊Boothroyd became the first female Speaker of the House of Commons.

Speakers never vote except when the votes are equal. Their powers are substantial, especially in rulings as to procedure. The Speaker acts independently of all party considerations; this impartiality is of nearly two centuries' standing. Other functions include maintaining order, signing warrants of committal for contempt, reprimanding members, and signing warrants for by-election writs. The Speaker ranks as the 'third commoner'; on retirement he or she is usually created a peer, and is given an annuity.

Spear, Ruskin (1911–1990)
English artist. His portraits include Laurence Olivier (as Macbeth), Francis Bacon, and satirical representations of Margaret Thatcher.

Special Branch
Section of the British police originally established in 1883 to deal with Irish Fenian activists. All 42 police forces in Britain now have their own Special Branches. They act as the executive arm of MI5 (British intelligence) in its duty of preventing or investigating espionage, subversion, and sabotage; carry out duties at air and sea ports in respect of naturalization and immigration; and provide armed bodyguards for public figures.

Special Operations Executive, SOE
British intelligence organization established in June 1940 to gather intelligence and carry out sabotage missions inside German-occupied Europe during World War II.

Speke, John Hanning (1827–1864)
British explorer. He joined British traveller Richard ◊Burton on an African expedition in which they reached Lake Tanganyika in 1858; Speke became the first European to see Lake Victoria.

His claim that it was the source of the Nile was disputed by Burton, even after Speke and James Grant made a second confirming expedition 1860–63. Speke accidentally shot himself, in England, the day before he was due to debate the matter publicly with Burton.

Speke Hall
House in Merseyside, England, 10 km/6 mi southeast of Liverpool. The manor of Speke was mentioned in the Domesday Book and was therefore in existence in 1066. The present 16th-century house is notable for its Tudor half-timbering and plasterwork. Speke Hall was given to the National Trust in 1944.

Spence, Basil Urwin (1907–1976)
Scottish architect. For nearly 20 years his work comprised houses, factories, theatres, and the Scottish Pavilion at the Empire Exhibition in 1938. In 1951 he won the competition for Coventry Cathedral, and in 1952 began the Nuclear Physics Building at Glasgow University. He was professor of architecture at the Royal Academy, London, from 1961 to 1968. He was knighted in 1960 and awarded the Order of Merit in 1962.

Spencer, Charles (1966–)
9th Earl Spencer, British aristocrat, brother of Diana, Princess of Wales. At Diana's funeral in 1997 he delivered an address that criticized the press for their insatiable appetite for information on Diana, and made a plea for the Spencer family to be allowed to take a part in the upbringing of her two sons, Prince William and Prince Harry. Applause audible from crowds outside Westminster Abbey spread to those inside the Abbey.

In 1998 Earl Spencer opened a museum commemorating Diana at the family home, Althorp Park in Northamptonshire, where the Princess is buried on a small island in a lake.

Spencer, Stanley (1891–1959)
English painter. He was born and lived in Cookham-on-Thames, Berkshire, and recreated the Christian story in a Cookham setting. Typically his dreamlike compositions combine a dry, meticulously detailed, and often humorous depiction of everyday life with an elaborate religious symbolism, as in *The Resurrection, Cookham* (1924–26; Tate Gallery, London).

He studied at the Slade School from 1910 to 1914, and served in World War I. The influence of his military service is evident in his great mural paintings for the Memorial Chapel, All Soul's, at Burghclere, Hampshire, which depict crowded and active scenes of military life and the Resurrection, a recurrent theme in his work. Other major works include *Christ Carrying the Cross* (1920; Tate Gallery, London), and intimate scenes such as *Self-portrait with Patricia Preece* (1936; Fitzwilliam Museum, Cambridge) and *The Dustman, or The Lovers* (1934; Laing Art Gallery, Newcastle-upon-Tyne). He was knighted in 1959.

Spencer-Churchill
Family name of the dukes of Marlborough, whose seat is Blenheim Palace in Oxfordshire, England.

Spender, Stephen (Harold) (1909–1995)
English poet and critic. His early poetry has a left-wing political content. With Cyril Connolly he founded the magazine *Horizon* (of which he was co-editor 1939–41), and Spender was co-editor of *Encounter* 1953–66. His *Journals 1939–83* and *Collected Poems 1928–1985* were published in 1985.

In the late 1920s and 1930s he was closely associated with the writers W H Auden, Christopher Isherwood, Louis MacNeice, and Cecil Day-Lewis, sharing their concern with socialism. Later his work became more personal and introspective, and increasingly his public literary activities were as an editor and critic. Knighted 1983.

Spenser, Edmund (*c.* 1552–1599)

English poet. His major work is the moral allegory *The Faerie Queene*, of which six books survive (three published in 1590 and three in 1596). Other works include *The Shepheardes Calender* (1579), an excursion into pastoral verse which echoes the language of Chaucer, the sonnet sequence *Amoretti*, and the magnificent wedding hymn 'Epithalamion' (1595) celebrating his own courtship and marriage. He is with Shakespeare the greatest poet of the Elzabethan age, and is a link between the poetry of the Middle Ages and that of Milton and beyond to the Romantics.

Other important works include 'Prothalamion' (1596), a wedding song commissioned for the double marriage of the daughters of the Earl of Worcester. He has been called the 'poet's poet' because of his rich imagery and command of versification.

Spey

Second longest river in Scotland. It flows through Highland and Moray, rising 14 km/8 mi southeast of Fort Augustus, for 172 km/107 mi to the Moray Firth between Lossiemouth and Buckie. It has salmon fisheries at its mouth.

The upper river augments the Lochaber hydroelectric scheme. Whisky is distilled in the Spey valley.

Spice Girls

British vocal pop group. Their songs combine dance and funk rhythms with lyrics extolling the virtues of what the group call 'girl power'. Group members are Melanie Janine Brown (or 'Scary Spice', 1975–), Victoria Adams (or 'Posh Spice', 1975–), Emma Lee Bunton (or 'Baby Spice', 1976–), and Melanie Jayne Chisholm (or 'Sporty Spice', 1974–). A fifth member, Geraldine Estelle Halliwell (or 'Ginger Spice', 1972–), left the group in May 1998; she went on to campaign for breast cancer awareness and was appointed a United Nations goodwill ambassador.

spinning jenny

Machine invented in Britain by James Hargreaves about 1764 which allowed several threads to be spun simultaneously. At first the machine, patented in 1770, could operate 16 spindles at the same time, and, less than 15 years later, 80 spindles could be used. The machine was named after his wife.

Spitalfields

District in the Greater London borough of ⟡Tower Hamlets. It was once the home of Huguenot silk weavers.

Spitfire

See ⟡Supermarine.

Spithead

Partly sheltered anchorage in the English Channel between the mainland of England and the Isle of ⟡Wight. It is part of the ⟡Solent.

In 1545 a battle was fought here between the English and French fleets in which the French were defeated. Spithead has been the scene of many Royal Navy reviews.

Spitting Image

Television series. First broadcast in 1983, it used grotesque rubbery-faced puppets in satirical sketches about people in the public eye – including politicians, members of the royal family, sports personalities, and entertainers. The puppets are the creation of the caricaturists Peter Fluck (1941–) and Roger Law (1941–).

Fluck and Law (who work under the name 'Luck and Flaw') met as students at Cambridge School of Art in the 1950s and began collaborating in 1975.

Spode, Josiah (1754–1827)

English potter. Around 1800, he developed bone porcelain (made from bone ash, china stone, and china clay), which was produced at all English factories in the 19th century. He became potter to King George III in 1806.

His father, Josiah Spode the elder (1733–1797), founded the Spode factory at Stoke-on-Trent in 1770. He succeeded to the firm in 1797, and added porcelain and, in 1805, stone-china to its production. The Spode works were taken over by W T Copeland in 1833.

Spooner, William Archibald (1844–1930)

English academic after whom the phenomenon of spoonerism is named. He was an Anglican cleric and warden of New College, Oxford, from 1903–24, with a tendency to transpose the initial sounds of words, as in 'Let us drink to the queer old Dean' (dear old Queen). Most spoonerisms are apocryphal.

Spooner was elected a fellow of New College in 1867, and lectured on ancient history, philosophy, and divinity. 'You have tasted two whole worms, hissed all my mystery lectures, and been caught fighting a liar in the quad. You must leave Oxford by the next town drain' is often cited as an example of a spoonerism, though he probably never said it.

sport

See feature on page 846 on Britain's contribution to modern sport.

Spurn Head

Promontory at the southeast extremity of the East Riding of Yorkshire, northeast England, on the estuary of the River ⟡Humber. There are two lighthouses on the promontory. The area is much used by migrating sea birds in spring and autumn.

Spycatcher

Controversial memoirs (published in 1987) of former UK intelligence officer Peter ⟡Wright. The Law Lords unanimously rejected the UK government's attempt to prevent allegations of MI5 misconduct being reported in the British media. Unsuccessful worldwide litigation to suppress *Spycatcher* cost the UK taxpayer over £1 million and gave rise to the phrase 'economical with the truth' (Robert Armstrong).

MODERN SPORT – A SPECIAL CONTRIBUTION

It is a difficult task to trace the precise origins and genealogy of most sports. Rudimentary versions of games such as football, hockey, or bowls were played all over the world from ancient times. However, it is safe to say that an extraordinary number of what may be called 'modern' sports were pioneered or first organized by the British in the 18th and 19th centuries. Remarkable in range and extent, this is one of Britain's most important contributions to the modern world. From association football (or soccer), the most popular and widely diffused sport in the world, to golf – a game first organized in 1754 and today one of the world's fastest-growing sports with over 20 million players in the USA alone – to boxing, thoroughbred horse racing, and to sports with a more limited appeal, such as darts, curling, lawn bowls, billiards, and snooker, the British contribution has been immense. Many of the major racket sports were developed in Britain, from tennis to badminton, to squash and table tennis, the latter surely one of the most popular sports in the world by virtue of the many millions who play it in China alone.

Team games

Team games too were pioneered in Britain; many of them developed in private schools. As well as association football, rugby union, rugby league, hockey, water polo, and of course cricket, were British-made. Polo, an ancient sport of Indian or Persian origin, was revived and modernized by the British army officers and planters in the Indian subcontinent, and the game's governing body, the Hurlingham Association, was founded in London in the 1870s. Oddly, netball, a staple of girls' school sport in Britain and in parts of the Commonwealth, was imported to Britain from the USA in the 1890s as a version of basketball suitable for women. However, the game as it is played now is based on the laws drawn up in 1899 by the British physical education organization, the Ling Association.

Competitions, clubs, and rules

The British were also at the forefront in the development of many other sports, whether by organizing competitions, forming clubs, or establishing rule-making bodies. For example, the first national track and field championships in modern times were held in England in 1866, and the first national track and field organization, the Amateur Athletic Association, was founded in 1880. The British pioneered competitive cross-country running, staging the first national championships in 1876. The first national swimming association, the Metropolitan Swimming Clubs Association (later renamed the Amateur Swimming Association), was founded in England in 1869. Rowing as a modern sport is often dated from the establishment of Doggett's Coat and Badge in 1715, a race for scullers on the Thames, still held today in a modified form. The first known regatta took place on the Thames in 1775, the first Oxford and Cambridge University boat race took place in 1829, and ten years later the Henley Regatta was inaugurated.

Equally, Britain was at the forefront in developing yacht racing in the 19th century, and the sport's most famous trophy, the America's Cup, was donated by the British Royal Yacht Squadron in 1851. Canoeing as a sport was pioneered by John MacGregor, who founded the Canoe Club (later renamed the Royal Canoe Club), in Surrey in 1866. Archery was revived as a sport with the formation of the Toxophilite Society of London in 1781, and the first national archery championships were held at York in 1844. Croquet, a game thought to have been imported to Britain from France via Ireland, was organized at Wimbledon in 1868 with the formation of the All England Croquet Club. The foundation of mountaineering as a sport in the mid-19th century is deemed to have begun with the Englishman Alfred Wills's ascent of the Wetterhorn in the Alps in 1854, while the first known bobsleigh races were staged by the British in the Swiss Alps in the 1880s. And hard though it may be to believe, the British even had a vital role in the development of competitive alpine skiing: in the 1920s the English travel agent Arnold Lunn devised the slalom event and then campaigned successfully to get slalom and downhill racing recognized by the International Ski Federation. And there are other sports, such as cycling, motor car, motor cycle, powerboat, and aeroplane racing, in which the British shared a pioneering role with other countries, notably France and the USA.

Sports as a product of modern society

That many of today's sports appeared first in Britain is in simple terms a product of the country being the first modern – that is predominantly urban and industrial – society. Sports evolve like everything else, in response to changing social and economic conditions. Association football would not have emerged as the first mass spectator-sport in Britain in the late 19th century had it not met the leisure needs of a rapidly expanding population increasingly concentrated in the new industrial urban areas. In turn, games like lawn tennis, badminton, and croquet suited the new suburban middle classes, being far more genteel and in the most part

stadium rock

Epic style of rock music developed in the 1980s. As live audiences grew, performers had to adapt their delivery and material to the size of the auditorium. Stadium rock is a music of broad gesture, windswept and brooding. The Irish band U2 and Scottish band Simple Minds (formed in 1977) are formative stadium-rock bands.

Staffa

Uninhabited island in the Inner Hebrides, west of Mull. It has a rugged coastline and many caves, including ◊Fingal's Cave.

Stafford

County town of ◊Staffordshire, England, population (1991) 113,400. Stafford lies on the River Sow, in the green belt

more gentle forms of physical recreation. The nation's factories and workshops could easily supply the equipment needed to play these games. Improved transport and communications, most importantly the development of the railways, greatly facilitated the modernization and diffusion of sport, in part by enabling and encouraging the establishment of regional and national competition whether in leagues or knockout cups.

British sports around the world

That British sports then became so widely diffused throughout the world was in part a consequence of Britain's political and economic hegemony in the 19th century. Sports like cricket and rugby were established in the colonies, especially the English-speaking ones. Businessmen, bankers, engineers, teachers, soldiers, and sailors exported football to Europe and South America. In this sense sport was one of the ways in which Britain exerted its cultural influence – though the local population may have appreciated the opportunity to beat the incomers at their own games. Traditional Gaelic sports were revived by the newly-formed Gaelic Athletic Association in the 1880s in part to resist what some Irish nationalists considered to be the pernicious colonial influence of British sports. While the rescued sports did thrive in Ireland, so did rugby and football.

Sporting pioneers

Such political and socio-economic explanations of Britain's sporting influence are valid but should not eclipse the individual efforts of Britain's many sporting pioneers, figures like John Chambers, who drafted the Marquess of Queensbury's rules for boxing in 1865, and organized championships in sports as diverse as athletics, billiards, cycling, and billiards. Or Charles Alcock, who devised the FA Cup in 1871, the first ever national knockout cup in any sport, and in 1880 organized the first cricket Test match to be played in England. Without the energy, missionary zeal, and enthusiasm of such people, the country's contribution to modern sporting life would have been considerably less. Moreover, the British had a peculiar genius for eventing games that can adapt to changing times and conditions. It is remarkable that a game like football, with its modern origins in the country's elite private schools, should have become by the end of the 19th century the devoted sport of the country's industrial masses, and by the end of the 20th century is played or followed by billions of people worldwide, its popularity still growing – reportedly, it has taken over from table tennis as China's most popular sport.

BY BEN RAMOS

between Wolverhampton and Stoke-on-Trent; it is a rail centre, and is served by the M6 motorway. Its chief industries include electrical engineering, shoemaking, salt, adhesives, grinding wheels, concrete reinforcement, and other engineering products. Staffordshire University is located here.

The town dates from the 10th century. The writer Izaak ◊Walton was born in Stafford.

History

Stafford is mentioned in the Anglo-Saxon Chronicle of AD 913 as Betheney. A royal mint existed on the site in about 940. In the Domesday Book the town appears as Stadford. Stafford's first town charter was granted by King John in 1206. In 1643, during the English Civil War, Parliamentary forces destroyed the town walls and Stafford Castle after their victory at Hopton Heath. A later castle built on the same site has also been demolished. The High House is said to have been built in 1555. Chetwynd House, now the head post office, has associations with the Irish dramatist Richard ◊Sheridan, who was member of Parliament for the town 1780–1806.

Stafford-Clark, Max (1941–)

English theatre director. He founded the Out of Joint Theatre Company in 1993. He worked at the Traverse Theatre until he founded the Joint Stock Theatre Group in 1974 with David Hare and William Gaskill. He was artistic director of the English Stage Company at the Royal Court Theatre 1979–93. His productions include *Cloud 9* (1980) and *Tom and Viv* (1984).

Staffordshire

County of west central England (since April 1997 Stoke-on-Trent has been a separate unitary authority)

Area 2,623 sq km/1,012 sq mi

Towns ◊Stafford (administrative headquarters), Newcastle-under-Lyme, Lichfield, Tamworth, Leek, Uttoxeter

Physical largely flat, with hilly regions in the north (part of the Peak district) and southwest; River Trent and its tributaries (the Churnet, Dove, Penk, Sow, and Tame); Cannock Chase (a large open area in the middle of the county)

Features castles at Chartley, Tamworth, and Tutbury; Lichfield Cathedral; Keele University (1962); Shugborough Hall (17th century), seat of the earls of Lichfield; Staffordshire bull terriers

Industries breweries (Burton-upon-Trent); china and earthenware in the ◊Potteries and the upper Trent basin (including Wedgwood); tractors and agricultural equipment (Uttoxeter); electrical engineering; electronics

Agriculture dairy farming

Population (1995) 802,100

Famous people Arnold Bennett, Peter de Wint, David Garrick, John Jervis, Samuel Johnson, Robert Peel, Isaak Walton, Josiah Wedgwood, Clarice Cliff

History In Anglo-Saxon times, Staffordshire formed part of the kingdom of Mercia; the Mercian kings had their residence at Tamworth; Stoke-on-Trent, heart of the Potteries manufacturing district, used to be part of Staffordshire but is now a separate unitary authority.

Topography

Staffordshire is bounded on the northeast by Derbyshire; on the southeast by Warwickshire; on the south by the West Midlands and Worcestershire; on the west by Shropshire; and on the northwest by Cheshire. It contains Stoke-on-Trent. The Staffordshire and Worcestershire canal crosses the county.

STAFFORDSHIRE *The county of Staffordshire has long been famous as the centre of the British pottery industry, concentrated in the 'five towns' of Tunstall, Hanley, Burslem, Stoke-upon-Trent, and Longton (which merged into Stoke-on-Trent in 1910). Here, gilders are seen putting the final touches to some of the porcelain tableware produced at the Minton factory. McQuillan & Brown/Collections*

Historical remains

There is evidence of pre-Roman and Roman occupation of the county, and Wall (**Letocetum**) was a Roman station on Watling Street near Lichfield.

Staines

Residential town in Surrey, southeast England, at the junction of the rivers Thames and Colne, 29 km/18 mi west of London; population (1991) 53,000. A bridge across the River Thames existed here in the 13th century and a more recent bridge was completed in 1962. Heathrow Airport is nearby.

stakeholder economy

An idea floated by Will Hutton, former economics editor of *The Guardian* newspaper, and subsequently editor of *The Observer*, which put forward the prospect of greater worker involvement in companies on something of the German model. In his best-selling book *The State We're In* (1996), Hutton ranged far wider than industrial democracy and called for a major review of Britain's constitution.

Tony ◊Blair, in a speech he made when Leader of the Opposition, took up the theme in a political context, arguing that people should feel they had a stake in the country and its future.

Stalker affair

Inquiry begun in 1984 by John Stalker, deputy chief constable in Manchester, England, into the killing of six unarmed men in 1982 by Royal Ulster Constabulary special units in Northern Ireland. The inquiry was halted and Stalker suspended from duty in 1986. Although he was later reinstated, the inquiry did not reopen, and no reason for his suspension was given.

Stalybridge

Town in the metropolitan county of Greater Manchester, England, 12 km/7 mi northeast of Stockport; population (1991) 21,500. Its indus tries include electrical engineering, metallurgy, and the manufacture of paper, rubber, and plastics. Stalybridge was originally a cotton town (a cotton mill was built here in 1776).

Stamford

Market town on the River Welland in Lincolnshire, east-central England, 20 km/12 mi northwest of Peterborough; population (1991) 4,800. Agriculture, engineering, plastics, and the timber and stone trades are important.

Founded by the Danes in the 7th century, Stamford became an important town in the wool trade in the Middle Ages. Its many old buildings include 17th–19th-century houses and public buildings, and medieval churches.

Stamford became a royal borough in 972. Part of the earthworks of a Norman castle may still be seen. Seventeen parish churches were built here in the Middle Ages, of which six survive.

Burghley House, south of the town, was begun in 1575 by Elizabeth I's adviser William Cecil ◊Burghley. During the Middle Ages a number of monasteries were founded; the Benedictine priory of St Leonard retains a Norman arcade and a fine west front. Browne's Hospital, dating from the time of Edward IV (late 15th century), is noteworthy for its glass and screen in the chapel.

The *Lincoln, Rutland, and Stamford Mercury* is one of the oldest newspapers in the country, and is said to have been established in 1695.

Stamford Bridge, Battle of

Battle on 25 September 1066 at Stamford Bridge, a crossing of the Derwent 14 km/9 mi northeast of York, England, at which ◊Harold II defeated and killed Harald Hardraada, King of Norway, and ◊Tostig, the English king's exiled brother. Harold then marched south to face the Normans at the Battle of ◊Hastings.

Stamp Act

Act of Parliament in 1765 that sought to raise enough money from the American colonies to cover the cost of their defence. The act taxed (by requiring an official stamp) all publications and legal documents published in British colonies.

Refusal to use the required tax stamps and a blockade of British merchant shipping in the colonies forced repeal of the act the following year. It helped to precipitate the ◊American Revolution.

The act provoked vandalism and looting in America, and

the **Stamp Act Congress** in October 1765 (the first intercolonial congress) declared the act unconstitutional, with the slogan 'No taxation without representation', because the colonies were not represented in the British Parliament.

Standard English

Form of English that in its grammar, syntax, vocabulary, and spelling system does not identify the speaker or writer with a particular geographical area or social grouping. In Britain, the accent associated with Standard English is ◊received pronunciation. All forms of slang, dialect, and grammatical deviation are non-Standard.

standing committee

Committee of the House of Commons that examines parliamentary bills (proposed acts of Parliament) for detailed correction and amendment. The committee comprises members of Parliament from the main political parties, with a majority usually held by the government. Several standing committees may be in existence at any time, each usually created for a particular bill.

Under standing orders, standing committees consist of between 16 and 50 members, but the tendency in recent years has been for them to be of 20 members or less on most bills, with larger committees for more important or controversial bills. Despite the term 'standing', each committee, which is designated by a letter of the alphabet, is reconstituted for each bill. There are usually between eight and ten standing committees set up each session, one or two of which deal exclusively with the committee stage of bills relating to Scotland and another of which deals only with private members' bills. In effect each committee is a miniature of the House of Commons, following basically the same procedures and operating on the adversary principle, with government and opposition MPs sitting opposite one another and speakers being called from each side.

Each committee is presided over by a chair drawn from a panel of MPs nominated by the Speaker. Standing committee chairs operate in the same way as the Speaker and vote only in the case of a tie. Meetings are usually, but not exclusively, held in the mornings, when the House is not sitting and, unlike select committees, standing committees may not receive evidence in the form of written briefs nor hear witnesses.

standing orders

The printed rules for regulating the proceedings of both Houses of Parliament, which, unless repealed, remain in force from parliament to parliament. They may be supplemented from time to time by sessional or temporary orders and resolutions.

Stanford, Charles Villiers (1852–1924)

Irish composer and teacher. He was a leading figure in the 19th-century renaissance of British music. His many works include operas such as *Shamus O'Brien* (1896), seven symphonies, chamber music, and church music. Among his pupils were Vaughan Williams, Gustav Holst, and Frank Bridge.

He received a doctorate from Oxford in 1883 and in 1888 from Cambridge, where he had succeeded Macfarren as professor of music in 1887. He was also conductor of the Bach Choir in London and professor of composition at the Royal College of Music, where he conducted the orchestral and opera classes.

Stanhope, Hester Lucy (1776–1839)

English traveller who left England in 1810 to tour the east Mediterranean with Bedouins and eventually settled there. She adopted local dress and became involved in Middle Eastern politics.

Stanley, Henry Morton adopted name of John Rowlands (1841–1904)

Welsh-born explorer and journalist, who emigrated to the USA when he was 18. In 1871 he was sent by the editor of the *New York Herald* James Gordon Bennett (1795–1872) to find the ailing David ◊Livingstone, which he did on 10 November. He and Livingstone explored Lake Tanganyika. In three further expeditions to Africa he traced the course of the Congo-Zaïre River to the sea (1874–77), established the Congo Free State (Democratic Republic of Congo) (1879–84), and charted much of the interior (1887–89). From Africa he returned to the UK and was a member of Parliament 1895–1900. GCB 1899.

stannaries

Tin mines in Devon and Cornwall, England, which belonged to the Duchy of Cornwall. The workers had the right to have their cases heard in their own stannaries court and the administration of the area was largely delegated to the court under a special privilege granted by Edward I in 1305. In recent times, attempts have been made to impede legislation from Westminster on the grounds that the ancient rights of the stannaries have been ignored. They have been unsuccessful.

Stansfield, Lisa (1965–)

English pop singer. Her soulful vocals with slick productions have won her several of the UK record industry's Brit Awards. She had a UK number-one hit with 'All Around the World' (1989). Her albums *Affection* (1989) and *Real Love* (1992) also enjoyed chart success in the UK and the USA. By the mid-1990s Stansfield's star had diminished somewhat in the face of more contemporary sounding dance fusions.

Stansted

London's third international airport, in Essex, southeast England.

As a civilian airport from 1957, offering a limited international service, it featured in three government inquiries before the 1985 decision to make it London's third airport. The passenger terminal, designed by Norman Foster and opened in March 1991, is the centrepiece of a £400 million development, which has taken the airport's annual capacity to 5.5 million passengers (in 1998).

The original runway was built by US forces during World War II and became operational in 1944.

Star Chamber

A civil and criminal court, named after the star-shaped ceiling decoration of the room in the Palace of Westminster, London, where its first meetings were held. Created in 1487 by Henry VII, the Star Chamber comprised some 20 or 30 judges. It was abolished in 1641 by the ◊Long Parliament.

The Star Chamber became notorious under Charles I for judgements favourable to the king and to Archbishop Laud (for example, the branding on both cheeks of William Prynne in 1637 for seditious libel). Under the Thatcher government 1979–90 the term was revived for private ministerial meetings at which disputes between the Treasury and high-spending departments were resolved.

Stark, Freya Madeline (1893–1993)

English traveller, mountaineer, and writer. Often travelling alone in dangerous territories, she described her explorations in the Middle East in many books, including *The Valley of the Assassins* (1934), *The Southern Gates of Arabia* (1936), and *A Winter in Arabia* (1940).

In her 70s and 80s she travelled to Afghanistan, Nepal, and again to Iraq for a journey on a raft down the River Euphrates. The first volume of her autobiography, *The Traveller's Prelude*, which she began soon after World War II, was published in 1950, followed by *Beyond Euphrates* (1951), *The Coast of Incense* (1953), and *Dust in the Lion's Paw* (1961). Her last book, *Rivers in Time*, appeared in 1982.

Starling, Ernest Henry (1866–1927)

English physiologist who, with William ◊Bayliss, discovered secretin and in 1905 coined the word 'hormone'. He formulated **Starling's law**, which states that the force of the heart's contraction is a function of the length of the muscle fibres. He is considered one of the founders of endocrinology.

Starling and Bayliss researched the nervous mechanisms that control the activities of the organs of the chest and abdomen, and together they discovered the peristaltic wave in the intestine. In 1902 they found the hormone secretin. It was the first time that a specific chemical substance had been seen to act as a stimulus for an organ at a distance from its site of origin.

Stationery Office

Organization established in 1786 to supply books and stationery to British government departments, and to superintend the printing of government reports and other papers, and books and pamphlets on subjects ranging from national works of art to industrial and agricultural processes. Formerly His/Her Majesty's Stationery Office, HMSO.

Statute of Westminster

In the history of the British Empire, legislation enacted in 1931 which gave the dominions of the British Empire complete autonomy in their conduct of external affairs. It made them self-governing states whose only allegiance was to the British crown.

St Clement Danes

Parish and church of London. The body of the church was built on the site of an older church in 1680–82, from designs by Christopher ◊Wren; the spire was added in 1719. It is now the central church of the Royal Air Force.

The church is traditionally associated with the rhyme 'Oranges and lemons, Say the bells of St Clemens'. St Clement was the patron saint of sailors; the affix 'Danes' may refer to a local settlement of Danes.

Steadman, Alison (1946–)

English character actress. She has worked on a variety of comic and dramatic British television and film roles. An accomplished stage performer, she came to the attention of a wider audience in Dennis Potter's *The Singing Detective* (1986) and as the suburban matriarch in her husband Mike ◊Leigh's *Life is Sweet* (1991). Other films include the period drama *Pride and Prejudice* (1995) and the comedies *Clockwise* (1986) and *Shirley Valentine* (1989).

Steadman, Ralph (1936–)

English caricaturist, designer, and writer. He has worked for several newspapers and magazines and has also illustrated numerous books, including his own writings, such as *I, Leonardo* (1983). His cartoons are noted for their anarchic homour and sharp satire.

steel

Historically a major UK ◊industry; see chronology opposite.

Steel, David Martin Scott (1938–)

British politician, leader of the Liberal Party 1976–88. He entered into a compact with the Labour government 1977–78, and into an alliance with the Social Democratic Party (SDP) in 1983. Having supported the Liberal-SDP merger (forming the ◊Social and Liberal Democrats), he resigned the leadership in 1988, becoming the party's foreign affairs spokesman. At the 1994 party conference, he announced that he would not seek re-election to the next parliament. He is the president of Liberal International. He entered the House of Lords in 1997.

Steele, Richard (1672–1729)

Irish essayist, playwright, and politician. He founded the journal *The Tatler* (1709–11), in which Joseph ◊Addison collaborated. They continued their joint work in the *Spectator*, also founded by Steele (1711–12), and the *Guardian* (1713). He also wrote plays, such as *The Conscious Lovers* (1722).

Born in Dublin, he entered the Life Guards, and then settled in London. In 1713 he was elected to Parliament. Knighted 1715.

Steer, Philip Wilson (1860–1942)

English artist. The son of Philip Steer, a portrait painter, he studied art in Paris and was influenced by the French Impressionists and Neo-Impressionism of the 1880s. He became a leader (with Walter ◊Sickert) of the English Impressionist movement and a founder-member of the ◊New English Art Club. In beauty of colour and effective simplicity of design his paintings of Walberswick (Tate Gallery,

Steel Production: Some Key Dates

1740 English clockmaker Benjamin Huntsman rediscovers the principle of producing steel in a crucible. Huntsman's Sheffield steel is far superior to any other being made.

1856 English inventor Henry Bessemer obtains a patent for the Bessemer converter which converts cast iron into steel by injecting air into molten iron to remove carbon and increase the temperature of the molten mass. It allows iron to be poured and thus shaped and brings down prices.

1856 German-born British engineer William Siemens invents a regenerative smelting furnace which preheats the air supplied to a furnace resulting in high-temperature flames. Patented in 1858, it permits the production of ductile steel for boiler plating.

1861 Steel mills in England begin to process steel in continuous rods.

1864 French engineers Pierre and Emile Martin, and British engineer William Siemens, simultaneously develop the open-hearth process for making steel using a regenerative gas-fired furnace. By using hot waste gases to heat the furnace, high quality steel is produced in bulk, and scrap steel can be melted and reused.

1870 The world production of steel is 560,000 tons, half of which is produced by Great Britain.

1878 German-born British inventor Charles William Siemens invents the electric arc furnace, the first to use electricity to make steel.

1878 British metallurgists Sidney Thomas and Percy Gilchrist perfect the 'basic' process for steel production by lining the Bessemer furnace with dolomite, which removes phosphorous oxides that otherwise result in the production of brittle steel.

1883 British metallurgist Robert Abbott Hadfield patents manganese steel, the first special alloy of steel, and one that is exceptionally hard.

1913 The first stainless steel is cast in Britain, by Harry Brearley in Sheffield.

1934 The British Iron and Steel Federation is founded to set prices and plan the future development of industry.

1953 The steel industry (nationalized by the Labour government in 1951) is denationalized by the Conservative government.

1966 The British steel industry is renationalized, and the Industrial Reorganization Corporation is founded to aid mergers.

30 November 1979 British Steel announces the loss of 50,000 jobs in Britain.

29 July 1980 British Steel announces record losses of £545 million in Britain.

London), Suffolk, and Cowes, Isle of Wight, executed between 1886 and 1892, were a major contribution to the early exhibitions of the Club.

Later he returned to English tradition, leaning towards Constable and Turner, as in his *Chepstow Castle* (Tate Gallery, London). He revived the art of direct watercolour painting, and also painted portraits and figure studies in the style of Gainsborough's 'fancy pictures', but is mainly of note as an English Impressionist in landscape.

Stein, Jock (John) (1922–1985)

Scottish football player and manager. The most successful manager in the history of Scottish football, between 1965 and 1977 he guided Glasgow Celtic to ten league championships, eight Scottish Cups, and six League Cups. His crowning achievement came in 1967 when Celtic defeated Inter Milan in Lisbon to become the first British team to win the European Cup.

Stenness

Prehistoric site on Mainland, in the Orkney Islands, Scotland, 17 km/11 mi northwest of Kirkwall. Its ancient monuments include the Ring of Brodgar, the largest stone circle in Scotland, which comprises 27 stones and has a diameter of 104 m/3,431 ft, and the Stenness Standing Stones, comprising 12 slabs, the tallest of which stands at 1.8 m/6 ft.

Maes Howe, a chambered tomb with dry stone walling, and associated with the Boyne megalithic culture of Ireland, lies 4 km/2.5 mi to the east.

Stephen (*c.* 1097–1154)

King of England from 1135. A grandson of William the Conqueror, he was elected king in 1135, although he had previously recognized Henry I's daughter ◊Matilda as heiress to the throne. Matilda landed in England in 1139, and civil war disrupted the country until 1153, when Stephen acknowledged Matilda's son, Henry II, as his own heir.

Stephens, Robert Graham (1931–1995)

English actor. He performed with the National Theatre Company at the Old Vic during the 1960s, where his most famous role was as Atahualpa in *The Royal Hunt of the Sun* (1964). Once tipped as Laurence Olivier's heir, he faded from the limelight until the 1990s, when he was acclaimed for his Falstaff in *Henry IV* parts I and 2 (for which he won the Laurence Olivier Best Actor Award in 1992), and his King Lear with the Royal Shakespeare Company in 1993.

Born in Bristol, Stephens trained at Bradford Civic Theatre School. He joined the English Stage Company in the 1950s. He frequently played opposite Maggie Smith (to whom he was married for eight years). He was knighted in 1995.

Stephenson, George (1781–1848)

English engineer. He built the first successful steam locomotive. He also invented a safety lamp independently of Humphrey ◊Davy in 1815. He was appointed engineer of the Stockton and Darlington Railway, the world's first public railway, in 1821, and of the Liverpool and Manchester Railway in 1826. In 1829 he won a prize with his locomotive *Rocket*.

Experimenting with various gradients, Stephenson found that a slope of 1 in 200, common enough on roads, reduced the haulage power of a locomotive by 50% (on a completely even surface, a tractive force of less than 5 kg/11 lb would move a tonne). Friction was virtually independent of speed. It followed that railway gradients should always be as low as possible, and cuttings, tunnels, and embankments were therefore necessary. He also advocated the use of malleable iron rails instead of cast iron. The gauge for the Stockton and Darlington Railway was set by Stephenson at 1.4 m/4 ft 8 in, which became the standard gauge for railways in most of the world.

Stephenson was born near Newcastle-upon-Tyne and received no formal education. He worked at a coal mine, servicing the steam pumping engine, and it was there he built his first locomotive in 1814. After the Liverpool and Manchester Railway opened in 1830, he worked as a consultant engineer to several newly emerging railway companies, all in the north of England or the Midlands.

In his first locomotive, Stephenson introduced a system by which exhaust steam was redirected into the chimney through a blast pipe, bringing in air with it and increasing the draught through the fire. This development made the locomotive truly practical.

With his son Robert, he established locomotive works in Newcastle. The Stockton and Darlington Railway was opened in 1825 by Stephenson's engine *Locomotion*, travelling at a top speed of 24 kph/15 mph.

Stephenson was engaged to design the railway from Manchester to Liverpool, but there was an open competition for the most efficient locomotive. Three other engines were entered, but on the day of the trials the *Rocket* was the only locomotive ready on time. It weighed 4.2 tonnes, half the weight of *Locomotion*.

Stephenson, Robert (1803–1859)

English civil engineer. He constructed railway bridges such as the high-level bridge at Newcastle-upon-Tyne, England, and the Menai and Conway tubular bridges in Wales. He was the son of George ◊Stephenson. The successful *Rocket* steam locomotive was built under his direction in 1829, as were subsequent improvements to it.

Stephenson was born near Newcastle-upon-Tyne, and began his working life assisting his father in the survey of the Stockton and Darlington Railway in 1821. He managed the locomotive factory his father had established in Newcastle, with a three-year break in South America, superintending some gold and silver mines in Colombia. In 1833 he became engineer for a projected railway from Birmingham to London. The line was completed in 1838, and from then on he was engaged on railway work for the rest of his life.

In 1844 construction began, under Stephenson's supervision, of a railway line from Chester to Holyhead. His bridge for the Menai Straits, in which the railway tracks were completely enclosed in parallel iron tubes, was so successful that he adopted the same design for other bridges. One such, the Victoria Bridge over the St Lawrence at Montréal, Canada, built 1854–59, was for many years the longest bridge in the world.

Stepney

District of London, now part of the borough of ◊Tower Hamlets, north of the Thames, and east of the City of London.

Steptoe, Patrick Christopher (1913–1988)

English obstetrician who pioneered in vitro fertilization. Steptoe, together with biologist Robert ◊Edwards, was the first to succeed in implanting in the womb an egg fertilized outside the body. The first 'test-tube baby' was born in 1978.

Steptoe developed laparoscopy for exploring the interior of the abdomen without a major operation.

Steptoe and Son

Television sitcom (1962–74) by Ray Galton and Alan Simpson. The show documents the endless bickering and run-ins of father and son rag-and-bonemen Steptoe (Wilfrid Brambell), a dirty, uncouth old man, and his middle-aged son

STEPTOE, PATRICK *English obstetrician Patrick Steptoe and biologist Robert Edwards, pioneers of in vitro fertilization. They are pictured here at a press conference, shortly after the birth of the first baby by this technique in 1978. Corbis*

Harold (Harry H Corbett), a man deluded by his sense of superiority and culture. Brambell and Corbett starred in two feature-length spin-offs, *Steptoe and Son* (1972) and *Steptoe and Son Ride Again.*

Sterne, Laurence (1713–1768)

Irish writer. He took orders in 1737 and became vicar of Sutton-in-the-Forest, Yorkshire, the following year. He created the comic anti-hero Tristram Shandy in *The Life and Opinions of Tristram Shandy, Gent* (1759–67), an eccentrically whimsical and bawdy novel in which associations of ideas on the principles of John Locke, and other devices, foreshadow in part some of the techniques associated with the 20th-century novel such as stream-of-consciousness. His other works include *A Sentimental Journey through France and Italy* (1768).

Stevenage

Town in Hertfordshire, southeast England, 45 km/28 mi north of London; population (1991) 75,000. Industries include the manufacture of electrical components, pharmaceuticals, and management services. The town dates from medieval times. In 1946 Stevenage was the first place in England to be designated a ◊new town (to accommodate population overspill).

The church of St Nicholas is mainly Early English. Stevenage has an annual fair dating back to 1280. The Six Hills are round barrows possibly of Roman origin.

Stevens, Cat born Steven Georgiou, now Yusef Islam (1947–)

English singer songwriter. His songs include 'Father And Son' (1970), 'Moon Shadow' (1971), and 'Peace Train' (1971). He became dedicated to the Islamic cause in 1977.

Stevens, David Robert Stevens, Baron Stevens of Ludgate (1936–)

British financier and newspaper publisher, chair of United News & Media (formerly United Newspapers), a provincial newspaper and magazine group based in the north of England, from 1981 and of Express Newspapers from 1985 (the right-wing *Daily Express* and *Sunday Express*, the tabloid *Daily Star*, and a few provincial papers).

Stevenson, Juliet (Anne Virginia) (1956–)

English stage and film actress. She was a member of the Royal Shakespeare Company 1978–86, and her later stage work includes *Yerma* (1987), *Hedda Gabler* (1988), *Death and the Maiden* (1991–92), and *The Duchess of Malfi* (1995). Film roles include *Truly, Madly, Deeply* (1991), *The Trial* (1993), *The Secret Rapture* (1994), and *Emma* (1996).

Stevenson, Robert (1772–1850)

Scottish engineer who built many lighthouses, including the Bell Rock lighthouse 1807–11.

Stevenson, Robert Louis Balfour (1850–1894)

Scottish novelist and poet. He wrote the adventure stories ◊*Treasure Island* (1883), *Kidnapped* (1886) and *The Master of Ballantrae* (1889), notable for their characterization as well as their action. He was a master also of shorter fiction such as *The Strange Case of Dr Jekyll and Mr Hyde* (1886), and of stories of the supernatural such as *Thrawn Janet* (1881).

In depth of character and power, his unfinished novel *Weir of Hermiston* might have exceeded all his other works. *A Child's Garden of Verses* (1885) is a collection of nostalgic poetry reflecting childhood.

Stevenson was born in Edinburgh. He studied at the university there and qualified as a lawyer, but never practised. Early works include *An Island Voyage* (1878) and *Travels with a Donkey* (1879). In 1879 he met the American Fanny Osbourne in France and they married in 1880.

Stevenston

Industrial and residential town in North Ayrshire unitary authority, Scotland, situated on the Firth of Clyde, 45 km/28 mi southwest of Glasgow; population (1991) 10,200. Local industries are mainly chemical-related. An explosives factory located at nearby Ardeer Mains to the southeast of the town was established by the Swedish chemist and inventor Alfred Nobel.

Owned by Imperial Chemical Industries (ICI), the factory is also known as Nobel's Explosive Co. Ltd.

Stewart, Alec James (1963–)

English cricketer. A stylish right-handed batsman who plays county cricket for Surrey, he made his Test debut in 1990 and by the start of the 1998 English season had scored 5,153 runs in 75 Tests at an average of 41.22. These figures would probably have been higher if he had not on several occasions been burdened with the additional responsibility of keeping wicket. Nevertheless, he is a fine wicketkeeper (in 1989 playing for Surrey he equalled the world record with 11 catches in a match), and his ability to perform this twin role has made him a particularly important member of England's one-day international team. He was appointed England captain in succession to Mike Atherton in May 1998. MBE 1998.

Stewart, Jackie (John Young) (1939–)

Scottish motor-racing driver. Until surpassed by Alain Prost (France) in 1987, Stewart held the record for the most Formula One Grand Prix wins (27). He entered a Formula 1 team in partnership with his son Paul for the 1997 and 1998 championships.

Stewart, Rod (David) (1945–)

English rock singer and songwriter who was lead singer of the Faces 1965–75. He achieved success as a solo artist following the album *Every Picture Tells A Story* (1971), which reached number one in the UK, and his songs include 'You Wear It Well' (1972), 'Sailing' (1975), and 'Maggie May' (1971).

Stewartby

Town in Bedfordshire, southern England, 8 km/5 mi south of Bedford. There are large brickworks here, using the clay of the blue Oxford clay belt. A model village was built for the employees of the brickworks in 1927.

Stilton

High-fat cheese (30–50% fat) with an internal blue mould; it is made from ripened whole milk and contains 33–35% water. It has a mellow flavour and is cured for four to six months. Stilton cheese is still made in and around Melton Mowbray in Leicestershire, England, where it originated, but takes its name from a village in Cambridgeshire, 10 km/6 mi southwest of Peterborough; the cheeses were taken there in coaching days for transport to London.

The name 'Stilton Cheese' was registered as a trademark in 1966 and can only be used for Stilton cheeses produced in Leicestershire, Derbyshire, or Nottinghamshire.

Sting stage name of Gordon Sumner (1951–)

English pop singer, songwriter, bass player, and actor. As a member of the trio the Police 1977–83, he had UK number-one hits with 'Message in a Bottle' (1979), 'Walking on the Moon' (1979), and 'Every Breath You Take' (1983). 'Don't Stand So Close to Me' was the best-selling single in the UK in 1980. In his solo career he has often drawn on jazz, as on the albums *The Dream of Blue Turtles* (1985), *Nothing Like the Sun* (1987), and *Soul Cages* (1991).

Emerging during the punk era, the Police were one of the first white pop groups to use a reggae-based sound. In his solo work, Sting has continued to blend music styles from all over the world into a Western rock format. His films include *Quadrophenia* (1979), *Brimstone and Treacle* (1982), and *Dune* (1984).

Stirling

Unitary authority in central Scotland, created in 1996 from Stirling district, Central region

Area 2,196 sq km/848 sq mi

Towns Dunblane, ◊Stirling (administrative headquarters), Aberfoyle

Physical mountainous to the north, including the forested Trossachs, and the open moorland north and west of Breadalbane, within the flood plain of the River Forth to the south around Sterling. The area contains many famous Scottish lochs (Tay, Katrine, Lomond) and Scotland's only lake (Lake of Menteith). Peaks include Ben More (1,174 m/3,852 ft) and Ben Venue (727 m/2,385 ft)

Features Bannockburn Heritage Centre; Stirling Castle (most visited paid attraction in Scotland outside Edinburgh)

Industries tourism, light engineering

Agriculture forestry and stock rearing in the uplands, while in the lowlands some of the richest agricultural lands in Scotland may be found, including the Carse of Gowrie

Population (1995) 82,300

History William Wallace won Battle of Stirling Bridge in 1297; English defeated at Bannockburn by Robert the Bruce in 1314; Battle at Sheriffmuir in 1715 between Jacobites and Hanoverians.

Economy

Large-scale afforestation has occurred in Breadalbane and the Trossachs, and the attraction of the natural scenery of loch, mountain, and river, has led to the development of a considerable tourist industry concentrated on Aberfoyle and Callander. The Stirling area benefits from the presence of the university and from tourism.

Architecture

There are many fine examples of early religious establishments, including Dunblane Cathedral (13th century with a 12th-century tower), Cambuskenneth Abbey (12th century), and the Church of the Holy Rude in Stirling town (15th century). **Stirling Castle**, whose main buildings date from the 15th and 16th centuries, and Doune Castle, dating from the 14th century, are good examples of castle-building of that period.

Environment

There are 68 Sites of Special Scientific Interest, four National Nature Reserves, one Special Protection Area, three National Scenic Areas, one regional park, and one country park.

Administrative history

Prior to 1975, the area was part of the counties of Perthshire and Stirlingshire.

Stirling

Administrative headquarters of Stirling unitary authority, Scotland, on the River Forth, 43 km/27 mi northeast of Glasgow; population (1991) 30,500. Industries include the manufacture of agricultural machinery, textiles, chemicals, and carpets. The Stirling skyline is noted for its castle, which guarded a key crossing of the river, and the (William) Wallace Monument, erected in 1870 to commemorate the Scots' victory of the English at nearby **Stirling Bridge** in 1297. Edward I of England (in raising a Scottish siege of the town) went into battle at Bannockburn in 1314 and was defeated by Robert (I) the Bruce, in the Scots' greatest victory over the English.

The castle predates the 12th century and was long a Scottish royal residence.

The Augustinian abbey at Cambuskenneth was founded by David I in the 12th century (*c.* 1140); in 1326 Robert the Bruce held his parliament in the abbey, and James III and his queen, Margaret, are buried there. At St Ninians there is the site of the 'Borestone Rotunda' on which it is claimed Robert the Bruce's standard was set up after the Battle of Bannockburn. A university was established at Stirling in 1967.

Stirling, James Frazer (1926–1992)

Scottish architect. He was possibly the most influential of his generation. While in partnership with James Gowan (1924–), he designed an influential housing estate at Ham Common, Richmond (1958), and the Leicester University Engineering Building (1959–63) in a Constructivist vein. He later adopted a more eclectic approach, exemplified in his considered masterpiece, the Staatsgalerie, Stuttgart, Germany (1977–83), which blended Constructivism, Modernism, and several strands of Classicism. He also designed the Clore Gallery (1980–86) extension to the Tate Gallery, London. He was knighted in 1983.

Stirling, Robert (1790–1878)

Scottish inventor of the first practicable hot-air engine in 1816. The Stirling engine has a high thermal efficiency and a large number of inherent advantages, such as flexibility in the choice of fuel, that could make it as important as the internal-combustion engine.

Stirling Bridge, Battle of

Scottish rebel William Wallace's victory over English forces led by John de Warenne on 11 September 1297. Although the Scottish king John Balliol had surrendered Scotland to Edward I the previous year, the English conquest had to be recommenced after this defeat.

stock exchange

London's stock exchange is one of the three largest in the world and was founded in 1801.

Stockport

Town in Greater Manchester, northwest England, 10 km/6 mi southeast of Manchester; population (1991) 130,800. The rivers Tame and Goyt join here to form the Mersey. Formerly important in the textile industry, Stockport now manufactures electrical machinery, paper, plastics, hats, and some cotton textiles; other industries include electronics, chemicals, and engineering.

Features

A large railway viaduct across the Mersey, built in 1841 (0.5 km/0.3 mi across the town centre, with 27 arches), dominates the town. The riverside area, once lined with mills, and surrounded by poor-quality housing, has been redeveloped. The church of St Mary, dating originally from the 12th century, was rebuilt in the early 19th century but retains a 14th-century chancel. The nave and tower were rebuilt in 1813 after a partial collapse which was blamed on an extended bell-ringing session to celebrate Nelson's Trafalgar Victory (1805). Nearby to the south is Bramall Hall, a well-preserved black-and-white mansion dating mainly from the 16th century.

History

The old town was built on a sandstone ridge overlooking the Mersey. It was granted a charter in 1220 and thrived as a market town, becoming a centre of cotton textiles and hat manufacture in the 19th century. Although the production of hats has now declined, one manufacturer remains.

Stockton-on-Tees

Unitary authority in northeast England created in 1996 from part of the former county of Cleveland

Area 200 sq km/77 sq mi

Towns and cities ◊Stockton-on-Tees (administrative headquarters), Billingham, Yarm, Longnewton

Features River Tees forms east border; Tees Barrage; Yarm viaduct; Preston Hall Museum and Park (Stockton); Castlegate Quay (Stockton) includes full-scale replica of *HMS Endeavour*

Industries chemicals, polythene film, light and heavy engineering, insulation products, plastics, electronics

Population (1996) 176,600.

Stockton-on-Tees

Town, port, and administrative headquarters of ◊Stockton-on-Tees metropolitan borough, on the River Tees, 5 km/3 mi west of Middlesbrough, northeast England; population (1991) 82,400. There are ship-repairing, steel, and chemical industries. It was the starting point for the Stockton–Darlington railway, the world's first passenger railway, which opened in 1825.

The town has the oldest railway-station building in the world, and there are many Georgian buildings.

The town is believed to have received its charter of incorporation as a borough between the years 1201 and 1208, and its first market charter was granted in 1310. The town hall dates from 1735. Stockton-on-Tees was the birthplace of the cabinet maker Thomas Sheraton, and of John Walker, inventor of the first friction match.

Stoke-on-Trent

City and unitary authority in central England, on the River Trent, 23 km/14 mi north of Stafford; unitary authority area 93 sq km/36 sq mi; population (1996) 254,200. It was part of the county of Staffordshire to 1997. It is the heart of the ◊Potteries, a major ceramic centre, and the largest clayware producer in the world. Other industries include the manufacture of steel, chemicals, engineering machinery, paper, rubber, and tyres. Michelin has its headquarters in the town.

Stoke was formed in 1910 from Burslem, Hanley, Longton, Stoke-upon-Trent, Fenton, and Tunstall. The ceramics factories of ◊Minton, ◊Wedgwood, Spode, and Royal Doulton are all based here.

The Gladstone Pottery Museum is a working pottery museum. The novelist Arnold Bennett was born near Hanley in 1867. Many of his novels are set in the region.

Stoke Poges

Village in Buckinghamshire, southern England, 3 km/2 mi north of Slough; population (1991) 4,900. Stoke Poges inspired Thomas ◊Gray to write his 'Elegy in a Country Churchyard'; the poet is buried in St Giles church.

Stoker, Bram (Abraham) (1847–1912)

Irish novelist, actor, theatre manager, and author. A civil servant from 1866–78, he subsequently became business manager to the theatre producer Henry Irving at the Lyceum Theatre in London from 1878 to 1905. His novel *Dracula* (1897) crystallized most aspects of the traditional vampire legend and became the source for all subsequent fiction and films on the subject.

Stoker wrote a number of other stories and novels of fantasy and horror, such as *The Lady of the Shroud* (1909).

Stone

Market town in Staffordshire, central England, on the River Trent, 11 km/7 mi north of Stafford. Industries include brewing and the manufacture of ceramics, glass, and footwear.

There was formerly a priory and a grammar school established in 1558.

Stone, Nicholas (1586–1647)

English sculptor and painter. He was appointed master mason for building the new banqueting house of Whitehall, London

(1619), and in 1626 master mason of Windsor Castle. His tombs include those of the poets Edmund Spenser (Westminster Abbey) and John Donne (St Paul's).

His son **Henry Stone** (died 1653) was also a sculptor and painter. His second son **Nicholas Stone** (died 1647), also a sculptor, worked under the Baroque sculptor and architect Bernini in Rome.

Stonehaven, or Stanehive

Port, seaside resort, and former burgh, in Aberdeenshire unitary authority, Scotland, situated on Stonehaven Bay, 24 km/15 mi south of Aberdeen; population (1991) 9,400. A market centre for the surrounding area, it possesses a secure harbour servicing a small fishing industry.

The cliff-top ruins of Dunnottar Castle, once the home of the Earls Mareschal of Scotland, lie 2 km/1 mi to the south.

Stonehenge (Old English 'hanging stones')

Megalithic monument on Salisbury Plain, 3 km/1.9 mi west of Amesbury in Wiltshire, England. The site developed over various periods from a simple henge (earthwork circle and ditch), dating from about 3000 BC, to a complex stone structure, from about 2100 BC, which included a circle of 30 upright stones, their tops linked by lintel stones to form a continuous circle about 30 m/100 ft across. It has been suggested that Stonehenge was constructed as an observatory.

Within the sandstone or sarsen circle (**peristyle**) was a horseshoe arrangement of five sarsen **trilithons** (two uprights plus a lintel, set as five separate entities), and the so-called 'Altar Stone' – an upright pillar – on the axis of the horseshoe at the open, northeast end, which faces in the direction of the rising sun. A further horseshoe and circle within the sarsen peristyle were constructed from bluestone relocated from previous outer circles.

Local sandstone, or sarsen, was used for the uprights, which measure 5.5 by 2 m/18 by 7 ft and weigh some 26 tonnes each. The bluestone was transported from the Prescelly Mountains, Pembrokeshire, Wales.

Stonehenge is one of the best-known archaeological sites in the world. Its conservation poses problems and the decision to close the circle to the public has caused controversy, in particular with regard to the Midsummer solstice ceremony held there. It is apparent that whatever the original intention of the builders, it has been given ritual significance in later years and is regarded as a 'sacred site'. Stonehenge, Avebury and associated sites were named a World Heritage site in 1986.

Stopes, Marie Charlotte Carmichael (1880–1958)

Scottish birth-control campaigner. With her second husband H V Roe (1878–1949), an aircraft manufacturer, she founded

STONEHENGE *The stone circle of Stonehenge in southern England. The earliest erections at Stonehenge date from about 3000 BC. The Stonehenge complex, which includes a long avenue and other nearby circles, is thought to have been used to predict various astronomical events and to have been important in worship of the sky and the sun. The building of the main part, about 2000 BC, would have required complex organization, and coincided with the beginnings of chiefdoms in Britain. Corbis*

Britain's first birth-control clinic in London in 1921. In her best-selling manual *Married Love* (1918) she urged women to enjoy sexual intercourse within their marriage, a revolutionary view for the time. She also wrote plays and verse.

She was a palaeontologist (a student of extinct forms of life) and taught at the University of Manchester from 1905 to 1911, the first woman to be appointed to its science staff.

Stoppard, Tom adopted name of Thomas Straussler (1937–)

Czechoslovak-born British dramatist. His works use wit and wordplay to explore logical and philosophical ideas. His play *Rosencrantz and Guildenstern are Dead* (1967) was followed by comedies including *The Real Inspector Hound* (1968), *Jumpers* (1972), *Travesties* (1974), *Dirty Linen* (1976), *The Real Thing* (1982), *Hapgood* (1988), *Arcadia* (1993), and *Indian Ink* (1995). He has also written for radio, television, and the cinema.

I wish I could bring Stonehenge to Nyasaland to show there was a time when Britain had a savage culture.

HASTINGS BANDA Malawi politician and physician.
Observer 10 March 1963

Storey, David Malcolm (1933–)

English dramatist and novelist. His plays include *In Celebration* (1969), *Home* (1970), *Early Days* (1980), *The March on Russia* (1989), and *Stages* (1992). Novels include *This Sporting Life* (1960).

Stormont

Village 8 km/5 mi east of Belfast, Northern Ireland. It is the site of the new Northern Ireland Assembly, elected as a result of the Good Friday Agreement in 1998. It was the seat of the government of Northern Ireland 1921–72.

The official residence of the prime minister of Northern Ireland was at Stormont, and parliament met in Parliament House, a large white Neo-Classical building, completed in 1932. Following increasing civil unrest from 1968, the UK government suspended the constitution and parliament of Northern Ireland in 1972, and imposed direct rule from London. By the Northern Ireland Act 1972 the UK Parliament was to approve all legislation for Northern Ireland, and the Northern Ireland department was placed under the direction of the Secretary of State for Northern Ireland, with an office at Stormont Castle.

Stornoway

Air and sea port on the island of Lewis in the Outer ◊Hebrides, Scotland; population (1991) 6,000. It is the main administrative and shopping centre for the Western Isles unitary authority. The economy is based on fishing, tourism, and tweeds. Stornoway was founded by James VI of Scotland (James I of England).

Stornoway airport links Lewis with Glasgow, Inverness, and with the smaller islands of Benbecula and Barra. Car ferries sail from here to Ullapool on the Scottish mainland. Lews Castle (mid-19th century), presented to the town by Lord Leverhulme, is now a technical college.

Stothard, Thomas (1755–1834)

English painter and illustrator. His painting of *The Canterbury Pilgrims* was particularly popular. Among the many books he illustrated were editions of Daniel Defoe's *Robinson Crusoe*, Alain-René Le Sage's *Gil Blas*, and John Bunyan's *The Pilgrim's Progress*. His graceful drawings had some influence on John Flaxman and William Blake.

Stour

River in southwest England, a tributary of the ◊Avon; length 88 km/55 mi. It rises near Stourhead in Wiltshire, flows through Dorset and joins the Avon at Christchurch, just before it flows into the English Channel.

Stourbridge

Market town in West Midlands, central England, on the River Stour, 19 km/12 mi southwest of Birmingham; population (1991) 54,700. Stourbridge was incorporated in Dudley in 1974. It is part of the ◊Black Country. Although industrial activity has declined, allowing more space for housing, warehousing, and parks, some industries remain; these include the manufacture of glass (especially crystal), bricks, fire clay, iron products, and galvanized and enamelled hollowware (such as pots, jugs, and kettles). There is some tourism, including canal-boating.

The Stourbridge Canal was formerly used for the transportation of coal.

The glass manufacturing industry was established in Stourbridge by Hungarian immigrants in about 1557. The Edward VI Grammar School (founded in 1552) was attended by the lexicographer Dr Samuel Johnson from 1725 to 1726.

Stourhead

House in Wiltshire, England, 13 km/8 mi south of Frome. Henry Hoare, the banker, commissioned Colen ◊Campbell to build the house in 1722, and the landscaped gardens were laid out 1741–50. The house and its contents, and the estate of 1,000 ha/2,470 acres, including the gardens and the villages of Stourton and Kilmington, were given to the National Trust by Lord Hoare in 1946.

The house contains works of art and furniture by Thomas Chippendale the Younger.

Strabane

Market town in County Tyrone, Northern Ireland; population (1991) 10,800. It is situated on the River Mourne, 32 km/20 mi north of Omagh. Clothing is manufactured, and there is a food-processing industry. The town was developed by the Abercorn family in the 18th century as a linen-manufacturing centre.

The novelist Flann O'Brien was born here. Strabane was also the birthplace of John Dunlap (1747–1812), the printer who printed the American Declaration of Independence and founded one of the first daily newspapers in the USA, the *Pennsylvania Packet*. James Wilson, grandfather of the US president Woodrow Wilson, worked in the printing trade in Strabane and his home is open to the public. The hymn writer Frances Alexander, author of 'There is a green hill far away', was also born in Strabane.

Sion Mills village 5 km/3 mi south of Strabane is a planned settlement of half-timbered housing established in the 1840s to promote the textile industry.

Strachey, (Giles) Lytton (1880–1932)

English critic and biographer. He was a member of the ◊Bloomsbury Group of writers and artists. His *Landmarks in French Literature* was written in 1912. The mocking and witty treatment of Cardinal Manning, Florence Nightingale, Thomas Arnold, and General Gordon in *Eminent Victorians* (1918) won him recognition. His biography of *Queen Victoria* (1921) was more affectionate.

Strafford, Thomas Wentworth, 1st Earl of Strafford (1593–1641)

English politician. He was originally an opponent of Charles I, but from 1628 he was on the Royalist side. He ruled despotically as Lord Deputy of Ireland 1632–39, when he returned to England as Charles's chief adviser and received an earldom. He was impeached in 1640 by Parliament, abandoned by Charles as a scapegoat, and beheaded. Knighted 1611.

Strand, the

Street in central London, between ◊Charing Cross and ◊Fleet Street. It was originally a track along the strand, or margin, of the River Thames, connecting the cities of London and Westminster.

The road does not appear to have been paved before the time of Richard II (1367–1400). From early times, but especially in the Tudor and Stuart periods, it was lined with mansions. There are two churches in the Strand: St Clement Danes and St Mary-le-Strand, the former by Christopher Wren 1680–82 and James Gibbs 1719, and the latter wholly by Gibbs 1714–17. There are also banks, theatres, and hotels, including the Savoy 1889. Somerset House 1776–86 by William Chambers, at the foot of Waterloo Bridge, houses the Courtauld art collection. The ◊Adelphi 18th-century housing development is off the Strand.

Strangford Lough

Island-dotted inlet in the east of County Down, Northern Ireland. The entrance to the lough lies between Strangford and Portaferry in the south, and it is bounded from the sea on the east by the Ards Peninsula, 32 km/20 mi long by 8 km/5 mi.

Violent tides enter the lough through the narrow inlet. Strangford Lough is an important habitat for wildlife, especially for overwintering Arctic birds. Queen's University, Belfast, has a marine biological research station and sea-water aquarium at Portaferry on the south of Ards Peninsula. There are many monastic and castle ruins along the shores of Strangford Lough. On Mahee Island, reached by a causeway, are the ruins of Nendrum monastery founded in the 5th century. The Nendrum Bell is now in Belfast Museum.

Stranraer

Port in Dumfries and Galloway, Scotland, on Loch Ryan; population (1991) 11,300. There is a ferry service to Belfast in Northern Ireland, and a summer service to the Isle of Man.

The Northwest Castle, now a hotel, was once the home of Sir John Ross, the Arctic explorer.

Stratfield Saye House

House in Hampshire, England, 11 km/7 mi south of Reading. The central portion of the present house was built about 1630. It is the seat of the Duke of Wellington. Wellington chose Stratfield Saye when Parliament voted him a country estate, and after 1817 he filled the house with his acquisitions from Paris, Spain, and contemporary London. The house contains a collection of French and English furniture and Roman mosaic pavements from Silchester.

Stratford-upon-Avon

Market town on the River Avon, in Warwickshire, England, 35 km/22 mi southeast of Birmingham; population (1991) 22,200. It is the birthplace of William ◊Shakespeare and has the Royal Shakespeare Theatre (1932), the Swan Theatre, and The Other Place. Stratford receives over 2 million tourists a year. Industries include canning, aluminium ware, and boat building.

The Royal Shakespeare Theatre replaced an earlier building (1877–79) that burned down in 1926. Shakespeare's birthplace contains relics of his life and times. His grave is in the parish church; his wife Anne ◊Hathaway's cottage is nearby.

Shakespeare landmarks

Shakespeare's reputed birthplace is in Henley Street, purchased for the nation in 1847 for £3,000, (it is administered by the Shakespeare Birthplace Trust, which also runs the adjoining library and study centre, opened in 1964, and several other Shakespeare-related buildings); Anne Hathaway's cottage, 1.5 km/1 mi from the centre of the town; the graves of the poet and his wife in the chancel of Holy Trinity; 'The Cage', which was for 36 years the home of Judith, Shakespeare's younger daughter, wife of Thomas Quiney, vintner; Hall's Croft, old-timbered residence of Susanna, the poet's elder daughter, who married Dr John Hall, his executor, which now houses the offices of the British Council and a Festival Club; Wilmcote, the house of Shakespeare's mother Mary Arden, a fine timbered farmhouse of the Tudor period, 5 km/3 mi outside the town; Nash's House, restored in 17th-century style, with the adjoining vacant site of Shakespeare's house, New Place, and its Elizabethan garden; and King Edward VI Grammar School, endowed in 1482 by Rev Thomas Jolyffe, MA, of Stratford, and re-endowed by Edward VI.

Royal Shakespeare Theatre and surroundings

The original theatre built by public subscription as the

Shakespeare Memorial Theatre, a redbrick building which opened in 1879 for annual summer seasons of Shakespeare's plays, was destroyed by fire in 1926. The present building, which changed its name in 1961 to the Royal Shakespeare Theatre, was designed by Elizabeth Scott and opened in 1932. The buildings adjoining the theatre were not seriously damaged by the fire. They include the library, which, mainly donated by C E Flower (1830–1892) and his wife, contains some 10,000 volumes of Shakespeare editions and dramatic literature, and a number of pictures, including the 'Droeshout' portrait. There is also the art gallery and museum, containing pictures and exhibits illustrating the history of the theatre and Shakespeare productions. Mason Croft, once the home of Marie Corelli, is now the Institute of Shakespeare Studies, run by the University of Birmingham.

Other features

The Chapel of the Guild of the Holy Cross dates from the 13th century. Holy Trinity church occupies the site of a Saxon monastery, and also dates from the 13th century. The town hall, first erected in 1633, was rebuilt in 1767; it has complete records of the sequence of bailiffs, mayors, and town clerks from 1553 (including Shakespeare's father, John Shakespeare), and of high stewards from 1610. The town trades in cattle and agricultural produce. Charlecote Park and its 16th-century house lies 6 km/3.7 mi east of the town; the park was acquired by the National Trust in 1945.The river is crossed by a fine bridge, erected during the reign of Henry VII by Sir Hugh Clopton, Lord Mayor of London.

Strathclyde

Former region of Scotland (1975–96), which consisted of 19 districts and was replaced in 1996 by the 12 unitary authorities of Argyll and Bute, Renfrewshire, East Ayrshire, East Dunbartonshire, East Renfrewshire, Glasgow City, Inverclyde, North Ayrshire, North Lanarkshire, South Ayrshire, South Lanarkshire, and West Dunbartonshire.

The districts of Argyll and Bute, Dumbarton, Inverclyde, Renfrew, Cunninghame, Kyle and Carrick, Cumnock and Doon Valley, Kilmarnock and Loudoun, East Kilbride, Eastwood, Hamilton, Motherwell, Clydesdale, City of Glasgow, Monklands, Clydebank, Bearsden and Milngavie, Cumbernauld and Kilsyth, and Strathkelvin made up Strathclyde region. The region was formed from the counties of Argyllshire, Bute, Ayrshire, Lanarkshire, Renfrewshire, Dunbartonshire, Stirlingshire, and Glasgow City.

strathspey

A Scottish folk dance in quick common time, similar to the reel, but with dotted rhythms. The name derives from the strath (valley) of Spey and is first heard of in 1780, though dances of the kind are much older.

Straw, Jack (1946–)

British Labour lawyer and politician, home secretary 1997– . After graduating in law he qualified as a barrister 1972. He became a member of Labour's front bench team in 1980, and then shadow education secretary 1987–92, shadow environment secretary 1992–94 and shadow home secretary 1994–97.

Street

Town in Somerset, England, 3 km/2 mi southwest of Glastonbury; population (1991) 9,200. Shoes, leather, and sheepskin goods are made here. A private school, Millfield School, is situated near Street.

Stretford

Town in Greater ◊Manchester, northwest England, southwest of Manchester; population (1991) 42,400. It includes the Old Trafford cricket ground. There are engineering, chemical, and textile industries.

strikes

Stoppage of work by employees, often as members of a trade union, to obtain or resist change in wages, hours, or conditions. Strikes may be 'official' (union-authorized) or 'wildcat' (undertaken spontaneously). In a 'sympathetic' strike, action is in support of other workers on strike elsewhere, possibly in a different industry.

Under the ◊Thatcher government, various measures to curb trade-union power to strike were introduced, for example, the act of 1984 that provided for loss of immunity from legal action if a secret ballot of members is not held before a strike. However, profit-sharing and co-ownership have been increasingly adopted. A general strike was last held in the UK in 1926; the last serious major strike was the ◊miners' strike 1984–85.

In the UK, 1.3 million working days were lost in 1996 through industrial disputes, in contrast to the 1970s, when the average loss was 12.9 million days, peaking at 29.5 million during the 'Winter of Discontent' in 1979. The UK's labour relations record during the 1990s has been one of the best among developed OECD countries.

Stroud

Town in Gloucestershire, southwest England, in the Cotswolds 13 km/8 mi southeast of Gloucester, on the River Frome; population (1981) 38,230. For many centuries broadcloth and scarlet-dyed cloth have been made in the area, and are still produced for military uniforms. There are also engineering works, woollen mills, sawmills, and factories making plastics and fibre board.

Strutt, John William

English physicist; see ◊Rayleigh.

Stuart, or Stewart

Royal family who inherited the Scottish throne in 1371 and the English throne in 1603, holding it until 1714, when Queen Anne died without heirs; the house of Stuart was replaced by the house of ◊Hanover. See pages 860 and 861 for a genealogy.

Stubbs, George (1724–1806)

English artist. He is renowned for his paintings of horses, such as *Mares and Foals* (about 1763; Tate Gallery, London). After the publication of his book of engravings *The Anatomy of the Horse* (1766), he was widely commissioned as an animal painter. The dramatic *Lion Attacking a Horse* (1770; Yale

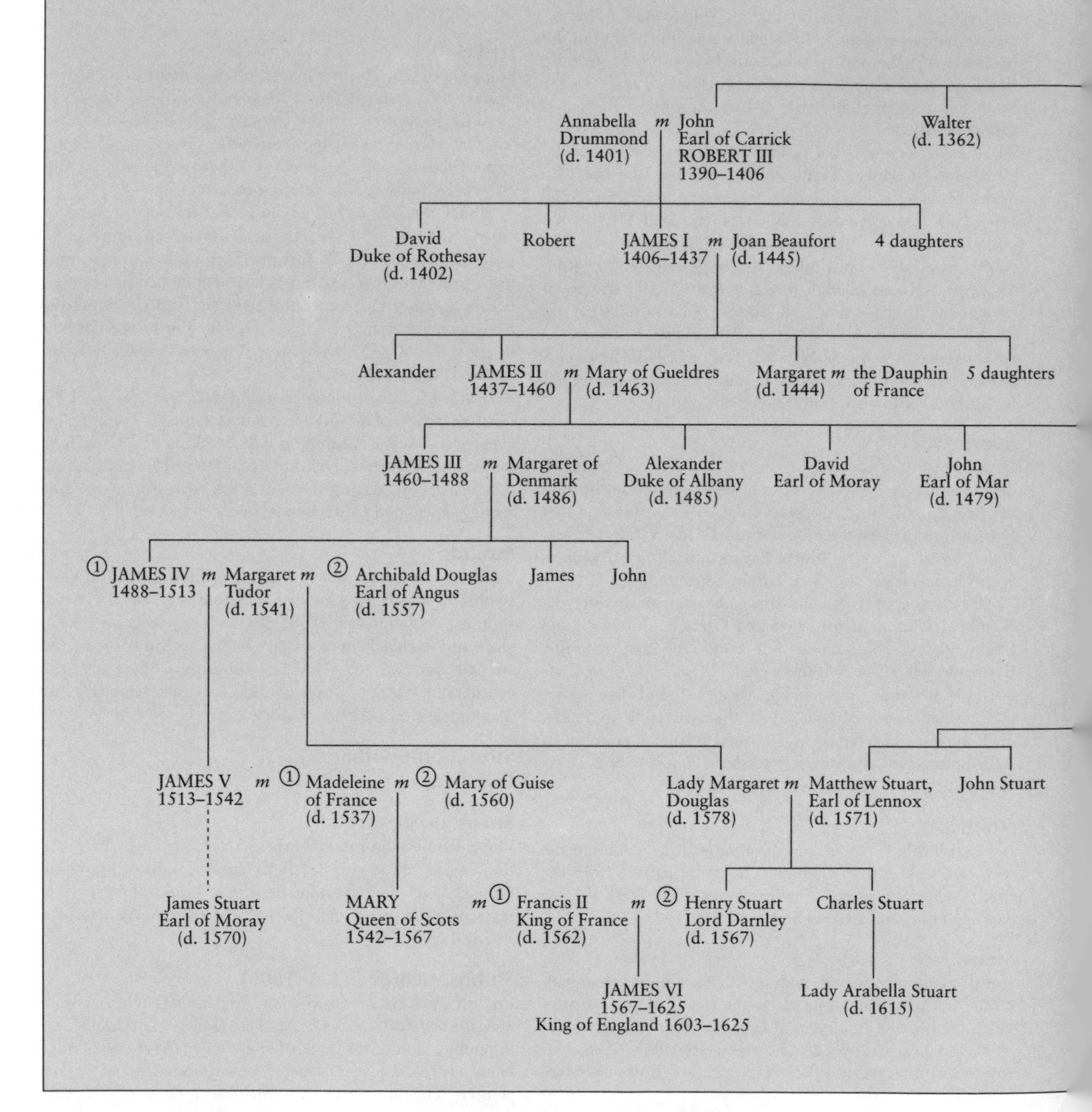
HOUSE OF STEWART 1309–1625
Annabella Drummond (d. 1401) m John Earl of Carrick ROBERT III 1390–1406
Walter (d. 1362)
David Duke of Rothesay (d. 1402)
Robert
JAMES I 1406–1437 m Joan Beaufort (d. 1445)
4 daughters
Alexander
JAMES II 1437–1460 m Mary of Gueldres (d. 1463)
Margaret (d. 1444) m the Dauphin of France
5 daughters
JAMES III 1460–1488 m Margaret of Denmark (d. 1486)
Alexander Duke of Albany (d. 1485)
David Earl of Moray
John Earl of Mar (d. 1479)
① JAMES IV 1488–1513 m Margaret Tudor (d. 1541) m ② Archibald Douglas Earl of Angus (d. 1557)
James
John
JAMES V 1513–1542 m ① Madeleine of France (d. 1537) m ② Mary of Guise (d. 1560)
Lady Margaret Douglas (d. 1578) m Matthew Stuart, Earl of Lennox (d. 1571)
John Stuart
James Stuart Earl of Moray (d. 1570)
MARY Queen of Scots 1542–1567 m ① Francis II King of France (d. 1562) m ② Henry Stuart Lord Darnley (d. 1567)
Charles Stuart
JAMES VI 1567–1625 King of England 1603–1625
Lady Arabella Stuart (d. 1615)

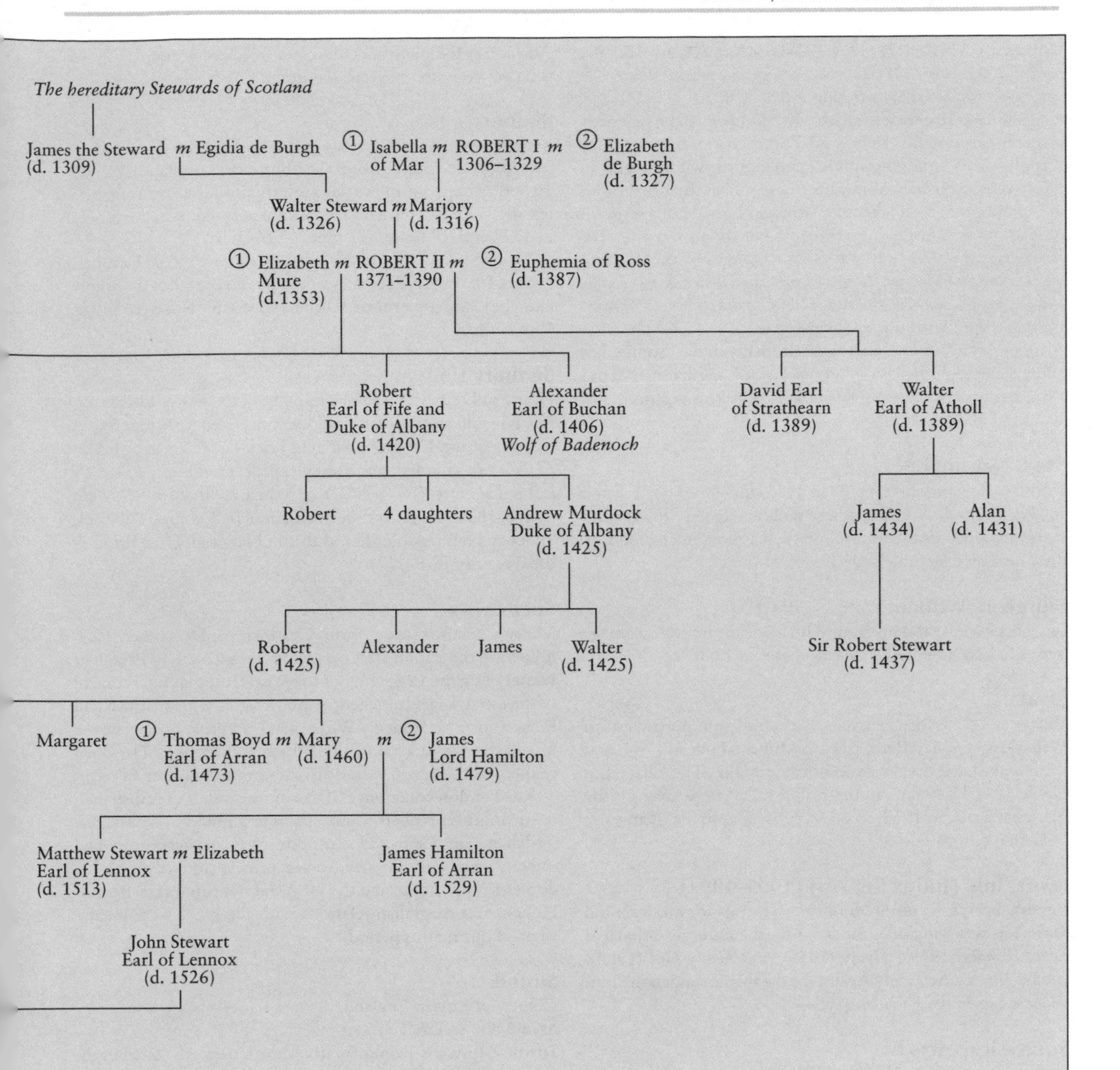

The House of Stewart changed the spelling of their name to Stuart during the reign of James V, in recognition of the difficulty their French allies found in pronouncing the letter W.

University Art Gallery, New Haven, Connecticut) and the peaceful *Reapers* (1786; Tate Gallery, London) show the variety of mood in his painting.

Stubbs was largely self-taught. As a young man he practised portrait painting in York and elsewhere in the north of England while studying human and animal anatomy, and in 1754 went to Rome, continuing these studies. Before settling in London in 1759 he rented a farm and carried out a series of dissections of horses, the results of which appeared in *The Anatomy of the Horse*. He was often employed by the sporting aristocracy to paint racehorses, *Gimcrack with a Groom, Jockey and Stable-lad on Newmarket Heath*, painted for Viscount Bolingbroke, being a notable example.

Once seen as only an expert animal painter, Stubbs has come to be regarded as one of the major English artists of the 18th century in power of design and composition and all-round ability.

Stud, National

British establishment founded in 1915, and since 1964 located at ◊Newmarket, Suffolk, where stallions are kept for visiting mares in order to breed racehorses. It is now maintained by the Horserace Betting Levy Board.

Sturgeon, William (1783–1850)

English physicist and inventor who made the first electromagnets. He also invented a galvanometer in 1836.

Styal

Village in Cheshire, England, 2 km/1 mi northwest of Wilmslow. Quarry Bank Cotton Mill was built in 1784, and the remainder of Styal village shortly after this. The village and 100 ha/247 acre estate in the Bollin valley were given to the National Trust in 1939, to preserve as an example of an early industrial community.

Styne, Jule (Julius Kerwin) (1905–1994)

English-born US composer of songs, mainly for musicals and films. His work includes the score for the musicals *Gentlemen Prefer Blondes* (1949), *Gypsy* (1959), and *Funny Girl* (1964), and he won an Academy Award for the theme song to the film *Three Coins in the Fountain* (1954).

Succession, Acts of

Legislation of Henry VIII to establish the line of succession to the throne. The first act was passed in 1534, giving Anne Boleyn's children precedence over Princess Mary, Henry VIII's child by Catherine of Aragón. The king's subsequent marriages required further legislation, and in 1544 he was given the power to bequeath the throne by will, which he did, naming his children in the order of Edward, Mary, and finally Elizabeth. The Act of Settlement of 1701 established a Protestant succession.

Suckling, John (1609–1641)

English Cavalier poet and dramatist. An ardent Royalist, he played an active part in the Civil War, fleeing to France where he may have committed suicide. His chief lyrics appeared in *Fragmenta Aurea* and include his best-known one, 'Why so pale and wan, fond lover?' Knighted 1630.

Sudbury

Market town in Suffolk, eastern England, on the River Stour, 26 km/16 mi south of Bury St Edmunds; population (1991) 10,900. The main industries are flour-milling, malting, and textiles. The painter Thomas ◊Gainsborough was born here in 1727 and his house is a tourist attraction.

Woollen manufacture was introduced here by the Flemings in the 14th century. The town has three Perpendicular Gothic churches, and a grammar school was established here in the 15th century.

Sudbury Hall

House in Derbyshire, England, 7 km/4 mi east of Uttoxeter. It was begun around 1613 but not completed until much later in the century. It is built of diaper brick (a design using bricks of different colours), and contains plaster ceilings painted by Louis Laguerre (1663–1721), a staircase carved by Edward Pierce (1630–1695), and an overmantel by Grinling Gibbons. Sudbury Hall was transferred to the National Trust through the Treasury in 1967.

Suez Crisis

Military confrontation from October to December 1956 following the nationalization of the Suez Canal by President Nasser of Egypt. In an attempt to reassert international control of the canal, Israel launched an attack, after which British and French troops landed. Widespread international censure forced the withdrawal of the British and French. The crisis resulted in the resignation of British prime minister Eden.

At a London conference of maritime powers the Australian prime minister Robert Menzies was appointed to negotiate a settlement in Cairo. His mission was unsuccessful. The military intervention met Soviet protest and considerable domestic opposition, and the USA did not support it. British, French, and Australian relations with the USA were greatly strained during this period.

Suffolk

County of eastern England

Area 3,800 sq km/1,467 sq mi

Towns ◊Ipswich (administrative headquarters), Aldeburgh, Beccles, Bury St Edmunds, Felixstowe, Lowestoft, Sudbury, Southwold

Physical undulating lowlands in the south and west; flat coastline; rivers Waveney (the boundary with Norfolk), Alde, Deben, Orwell, Stour (the boundary with Essex), Little Ouse; part of the Norfolk Broads

Features Minsmere marshland bird reserve, near Aldeburgh; the Sandlings (heathlands and birds); bloodstock rearing and horse racing at Newmarket; ◊Sutton Hoo (7th-century ship burial); Sizewell B, Britain's first pressurized-water nuclear reactor plant; Aldeburgh Festival, held every June at Snape Maltings

Industries agricultural machinery; chemicals; coconut matting; electronics; fertilizers; food processing; motor vehicle

SUFFOLK *The magnificent 15th century Church of the Holy Trinity in Long Melford, Suffolk, is built in the Perpendicular style of architecture (the final stage of development of the English Gothic). Such imposing parish churches are typical of the county; other fine examples can be seen at Blythburgh and Southwold. Liz Stares/Collections*

components; North Sea oil and gas exploration; printing; telecommunications research; silk; timber; brewing

Agriculture cereals (barley, oats, wheat), sugar beet; cattle, sheep, and pig rearing; fishing (for which Lowestoft is the main centre)

Population (1994) 649,500

Famous people Thomas Gainsborough, George Crabbe, John Constable, Elizabeth Garrett Anderson, Benjamin Britten

History during the 14th century Suffolk became one of the richest counties in England, based on its wool and cloth production, the latter developing with the influx of Flemish weavers. During the Civil War it was a stronghold of Parliament.

Topography

Suffolk is bounded by Norfolk to the north; by Cambridgeshire to the west; by Essex to the south; and by the North Sea to the east. The coastline, which is generally low and regular, has been encroached upon by the sea in places, notably at Dunwich. Lowestoft, Southwold, Aldeburgh, and Felixstowe are seaside resorts. In the extreme northwest, near Mildenhall, is a small area of fenland, and southeast of Mildenhall, at Rede, is the highest point (128 m/420 ft) in the county. Around Brandon is an area known as the Breckland, which was an ancient heath, but is now largely covered in forest or reclaimed for agriculture. Ipswich, Felixstowe, and Lowestoft are ports. The River Orwell is navigable by large vessels as far as Ipswich dock; there is yachting on some rivers. Smaller towns include Bungay, Hadleigh, Halesworth, Haverhill, Saxmundham, Leiston, and Woodbridge.

Early history

Relics of prehistoric man have been found near Brandon. Suffolk derives its name from settlement by the South Folk in the latter part of the 5th century AD. The county suffered much from the later incursions of the Danes. Walton was the scene of the landing of the Earl of Leicester in 1173 when he marched against Henry II.

Historic buildings

Because Suffolk was settled at an early date and subsequently became prosperous, it is rich in buildings of architectural and historic interest. There are monastic remains at Bury St Edmunds (Benedictine); Leiston (Premonstratensian); Kersey, Butley, and Ixworth (Augustinian); Sibton (Cistercian); and Clare (Austin Friary). There are castles at Framlingham and Orford; a Roman fort, known as Burgh Castle, near Great Yarmouth; and fortified manor houses at Mettingham and Wingfield. The many large churches are frequently ornamented with patterns in flint work, and over 40 of them have round towers, many of which date from the 12th century. The village of Lavenham is probably unrivalled in Britain in its wealth of medieval buildings. Suffolk also has historic examples of domestic architecture, the earliest being Moyses' Hall, Bury St Edmunds (dating from the 12th century), and Little Wenham Hall (dating from the13th century). Tudor houses include Hengrave Hall, Hengrave, and Melford Hall and Kentwell Hall, Long Melford. Ickworth Hall (5 km/3 mi from Bury St Edmunds) is an 18th-century mansion in the Classical style.

Suffolk

Breed of medium-wool, dark-faced, hornless sheep developed in Suffolk, England, in the first half of the 19th century by mating Norfolk horned ewes with Southdown rams. They are excellent producers of mutton but are not desirable for wool production.

Suffolk Punch

Smallest breed of draught horse, originating in Suffolk, England. Suffolks are unusually compact and rotund with thick short necks, legs, and backs, and are docile but powerful. Their coat is always chestnut-coloured.

suffragette, or suffragist

Woman fighting for the right to vote. Women's suffrage bills were repeatedly introduced and defeated in Parliament between 1886 and 1911, and a militant campaign was launched in 1906 by Emmeline ◊Pankhurst and her daughters. In 1918 women were granted limited franchise; in 1928 it was extended to all women over 21.

Suffragettes (the term was coined by a *Daily Mail* reporter) chained themselves to railings, heckled political meetings, refused to pay taxes, and in 1913 bombed the home of Lloyd George, then chancellor of the Exchequer. One woman, Emily ◊Davison, threw herself under the king's horse at the Derby horse race in 1913 and was killed. Many suffragettes were imprisoned and were force-fed when they went on hunger strike; under the notorious 'Cat and Mouse Act' of 1913 they could be repeatedly released to regain their health and then rearrested. The struggle was called off on the outbreak of World War I.

Sugar, Alan Michael (1947–)

English entrepreneur who founded the electronics company ◊Amstrad in 1968. In 1996 Sugar became non-executive chairman of the consumer electronics group Betacom and non-executive director of the computer company Viglen. He became executive chairman of Amstrad in 1997. In 1991 he became chair of Tottenham Hotspur Football Club.

Sulgrave Manor

House in Northamptonshire, England, 11 km/7 mi northeast of Banbury. It was built by Lawrence Washington in 1560 on the site of a dissolved priory. The present house, altered and restored, was bought by the British public in 1914 to commemorate the Treaty of Ghent.

John Washington, a descendant of the first owner, emigrated to Virginia in 1656, and his great-grandson, George Washington, became the first president of the USA. The house was later endowed in perpetuity by the Society of the Colonial Dames of America. It is open to the public, and contains portraits of Washington and some of his possessions.

Sullivan, Arthur Seymour (1842–1900)

English composer. He wrote operettas in collaboration with William ◊Gilbert, including *HMS Pinafore* (1878), *The Pirates of Penzance* (1879), and *The Mikado* (1885). Their partnership broke down in 1896. Sullivan also composed serious instrumental, choral, and operatic works – for example, the opera *Ivanhoe* (1890) – which he valued more highly than the operettas.

Other Gilbert and Sullivan operettas include *Patience* (which ridiculed the Aesthetic Movement) (1881), *The Yeomen of the Guard* (1888), and *The Gondoliers* (1889).

Sullivan, Jim (1903–1977)

Welsh-born rugby player. A great goal-kicker, he kicked a record 2,867 points in a 25-year Rugby League career covering 928 matches.

He played rugby union for Cardiff before joining Wigan Rugby League Club in 1921. He kicked 193 goals in 1933–34 (a record at the time) and against Flimby and Fothergill in 1925 he kicked 22 goals, still a record.

Sullom Voe

Long, deep sea-inlet on Mainland, in the Shetland Islands, Scotland, penetrating into the northern part of the island, 35 km/22 mi north of Lerwick. It is 12 km/7 mi in length. A vast complex for the storage and transhipment of North Sea oil has been constructed on its shores. This is fed by submarine pipelines from northern offshore fields, and has the capacity to take supertankers. This oil terminal, built between 1975 and 1982, is the largest of its kind in Europe.

The inlet reaches its head at Mavis Grind, a narrow neck of land connecting the northernmost part of Mainland to the remainder of the island. During World War II Sullom Voe was used as a base for the Norwegian Air Force and RAF seaplanes.

'Sumer is icumen in', *Summer has come*

An English song in parts, dating from around 1270 and known as the Reading Rota (round). It is a canon for four voices and there are two additional bass voices adding a pes or ground-bass, also in canon. In the manuscript the tune is also provided with Latin words, beginning *Perspice, Christicola*, but the accompanying voices (or pes) merely have 'Sing cuccu nu' in both versions, though the music they sing is actually part of an Easter antiphon.

summer time

Practice introduced in the UK in 1916 whereby legal time from spring to autumn is an hour in advance of Greenwich Mean Time.

Continental Europe 'puts the clock back' a month earlier than the UK in autumn. British summer time was permanently in force February 1940–October 1945 and February 1968–October 1971. Double summer time (2 hours in advance) was in force during the summers of 1941–45 and 1947.

Sunbury-on-Thames

Market town in Surrey, southeast England, on the River Thames, 22 km/14 mi southeast of London; population (1991) 27,400. It is primarily residential, and is a centre for boating. Kempton Park racecourse is nearby.

Sunday Telegraph, The

British Sunday newspaper, founded in 1961 under the same ownership as the ◊*Daily Telegraph*, but with a largely different editorial staff. Its circulation in 1998 was over 800,000.

Sunday Times, The

British Sunday newspaper, founded in 1822. The paper is noted for the quality of its literary, dramatic, and musical criticism, as well as for its articles on world affairs, politics, art, economics and finance, and women's issues. Daily Internet editions of both *The Sunday Times* and *The Times* were launched in 1996. Owned by News International, it had a circulation of over 1,300,000 in 1998.

The paper was at one time owned by Mrs Julius Beer, whose husband owned the *Observer*. It passed to Herman Schmidt, who in 1897 had started the *Sunday Special*, which amalgamated with *The Sunday Times* in 1904. It was bought in 1915 by Viscount Camrose and Viscount Kemsley and, coming into the sole control of the latter in 1937, entered a period of rapid development. This continued after Lord Thomson of Fleet bought the paper in 1959; it became the first newspaper in Britain to be printed in separate sections and, in 1962, to include a separate colour magazine.

Sunday trading

Buying and selling on Sunday; this was banned in the UK by the Shops Act 1950, but the ban may have been in breach of Article 30 of the Treaty of Rome as amounting to an unlawful restraint on the free movement of goods. Following the defeat of a bill to enable widespread Sunday trading in April 1986, compromise legislation was introduced in 1994 in Britain which allowed shops to open but restricted larger stores (over 280 sq m/3,014 sq ft) to a maximum of six hours. Shops in Scotland, where Sunday trading is fully deregulated, retained the right to open at any time.

Sunderland

City and port in Tyne and Wear, northeast England, at the mouth of the River Wear; population (1991) 183,200. A former coalmining and shipbuilding centre, Sunderland now has electronics, engineering, and brewing industries, and manufactures glass, pottery, chemicals, paper, furniture, and cars. It also has some tourism.

Sunderland was granted city status by Royal Charter in 1992. Features include the Sunderland Empire Theatre (1907), and the University of Sunderland (established in 1992), formerly Sunderland Polytechnic.

History

The town of Sunderland developed around the villages of Monkwearmouth, Bishopwearmouth, and Sunderland. Churches were first built at Monkwearmouth on the north bank of the Wear in 674 and at Sunderland on the south bank later in the 7th century. Sunderland developed as a port during the Middle Ages, with a charter dating from 1154. During the Civil War Sunderland was held by the Parliamentarians. Records of shipbuilding in Sunderland go back to 1346. The first shipyard was established in 1775 and the wet dock was built in 1840. During the 19th century several shipyards were built on the river frontage, and Sunderland became the world's largest shipbuilding town in the 19th century. The shipbuilding industry was hit by the depression of the 1930s, went further into decline after World War II, and ceased completely in the 1990s. Coal was mined in Sunderland from the 14th century onwards. It was hit by the depression of the 1930s, although less severely than shipbuilding was. Mining gradually declined since, ceasing altogether by 1990.

Famous people

Joseph Swan, inventor of the incandescent-filament electric lamp, was born here in 1828.

Sunningdale Agreement

Pact of December 1973 between the UK and Irish governments, together with the Northern Ireland executive, drawn up in Sunningdale, England.

The agreement included provisions for a power-sharing executive in Northern Ireland. However, the executive lasted only five weeks before the UK government was defeated in a general election, and a general strike in May 1974 brought down the Northern Ireland government.

Sun, The

UK daily tabloid newspaper established in 1964. Owned by News International, it has the highest circulation of any UK daily paper (over 3,800,000 in 1998). It is noted for popular features on celebrities and other public figures and many photographs.

Supermarine

British aircraft company famous for the Supermarine **Spitfire** fighter aircraft of World War II.

This single engine, eight-gun monoplane was designed by R J ◊Mitchell in 1936 and went into service with the RAF in August in 1938. It was the only British combat aircraft to remain in production throughout the war years, over 20,000 being built, and 19 squadrons were equipped with it in the Battle of Britain in 1940. It was progressively improved, adopting cannon instead of machine guns, and was modified into an attack bomber, photo-reconnaissance aircraft, and, as the **Seafire**, a naval carrier fighter. The Mark IX of 1944 flew at 655 kph/408 mph, carried cannon and .5 in machine guns, and had a range of 700 km/435 mi.

supplementary benefit

Former name (1966–88) for ◊**income support**; weekly ◊social security payments by the state to those with low incomes.

The payments were called national assistance 1948–66 in Britain and consisted of a weekly payment made by the government to individuals whose income was considered to be lower than a legally determined minimum and who did not qualify for contributory pensions such as unemployment benefit or earnings-related pensions. Until 1983 it included housing subsidies. The theory of such a system, to catch those falling through the benefits 'act', formed part of the ◊Beveridge Report.

Supremacy, Acts of

Two UK acts of Parliament 1534 and 1559, which established Henry VIII and Elizabeth I respectively as head of the English church in place of the pope.

Surrey

County of southern England

Area 1,660 sq km/641 sq mi

Towns ◊Kingston upon Thames (administrative headquarters), Farnham, Guildford, Leatherhead, Reigate, Woking, Epsom, Dorking

Physical rivers Mole, Thames, and Wey; Box Hill (183 m/600 ft), Gibbet Hill (277 m/909 ft), and Leith Hill (299 m/981 ft, 5 km/3 mi south of Dorking, the highest hill in southeast England); North Downs

Features Kew Palace and Royal Botanic Gardens, Kew; Yehudi Menuhin School (one of four specialist music schools in England)

Agriculture vegetables; sheep rearing; dairy farming; horticulture

Industries service industries; sand and gravel quarrying; fuller's earth extraction (near Reigate)

Population (1994) 1,041,200

Famous people John Galsworthy, Aldous Huxley, Laurence Olivier, Eric Clapton

History King John signed the Magna Carta at Runnymede in 1215.

Topography

Surrey is bounded on the north by Greater London, Windsor and Maidenhead, and Bracknell Forest; on the east by Kent; on the south by East and West Sussex; and on the west by Hampshire. Historically, the northern boundary was the Thames, but Surrey has no other natural boundaries and no natural centre; its principal settlements were Guildford to the west, Croydon to the east, and the Thames settlements at Kingston-upon-Thames and Southwark. Boundary changes in 1888 placed parts of what was then Surrey (Battersea, Camberwell) within what is now Greater London; further changes in 1974 placed Gatwick in West Sussex.

Geologically, Surrey forms the northern counterpart of Sussex, and the main strata repeat those of Sussex in the reverse direction. They are, from south to north: ◊Weald clay; lower greensand (a type of sandstone); narrow belts of gault (a type of clay) and upper greensand; chalk forming the North Downs and passing through the centre of the county along the line Reigate–Dorking–Guildford–Farnham; and London clay. The county's landmarks include Newlands Corner (164 m/538 ft), near Guildford, and the Devil's Punch Bowl, near Hindhead, beneath Gibbet Hill and Leith Hill. There are large areas of heath and common land, especially in the west.

Surrey is densely populated, particularly in the northeast and along the main commuter road and rail links to London. The rural areas are mainly south of the Downs, and most of the county is now protected from further urban encroachment; undeveloped areas are either National Trust land, or have been designated as 'open space', common land, areas of outstanding natural beauty, or metropolitan green belt. In total about 14,500 ha/35,800 acres are open to the public, including the North Downs footpath, that runs east from Farnham.

Historic remains and buildings

Archaeologically, Surrey is of national importance for finds of flints near Farnham, dating to the Palaeolithic period, and other finds from the Thames gravels and elsewhere, dating to the Mesolithic period. There are pre-Roman earthworks at Hascombe and Holmbury Hills, and remains from the Roman period include many villas, such as those at Ashtead, Farnham, Rapsley, and Titsey. A royal castle was established at Guildford after the Norman conquest, and there were others at Abinger, Bletchingley, Farnham, and Reigate. Of the many royal and ecclesiastical palaces built in Surrey, Farnham Castle, now a college, is one of the few surviving examples still in use; Henry VIII's palace at Nonsuch Park (begun 1538) was demolished in 1687. Major religious sites include Waverley Abbey, near Farnham, (the first Cistercian foundation in this country), and successful excavations have been carried out at the Dominican friary site at Guildford.

In the Tudor period, many London professional and business men had a country home in Surrey; Sutton Place, Great Tangley Manor, and Loseley Park, all near Guildford, are examples. Other great houses of later date are Clandon Park (1731), Hatchlands (1759), Nonsuch Park (1802–06), and Polesden Lacey, a Regency villa near Dorking. There are also many excellent examples of humbler dwellings, ranging from typical 17th-century tile-hung and timber-framed Surrey cottages, to dignified Georgian brick houses, examples of which can be seen in Farnham. Surrey became increasingly residential with the coming of the railway, and many houses by well-known architects were built, such as Goddards, near Dorking, designed by Edwin ◊Lutyens.

surrogacy

Practice whereby a woman is sought, and usually paid, to bear a child for an infertile couple or a single parent.

In the UK, the Warnock Report 1984 on embryo research condemned surrogacy. Under the Surrogacy Arrangements Act 1985 it became illegal for third parties to negotiate or facilitate any surrogacy for payment. The act did not affect noncommercial surrogacy agencies nor did it regulate negotiations directly made between the mother and the commissioning parents. Under the Human Fertilization and Embryo Bill 1989 a statutory licensing authority was established to regulate research and treatment in human infertility and embryology. The act enabled any established surrogacy services to be brought within the control of the authority.

Surtees, John (1934–)

English motor racing driver and motorcyclist, the only person to win world titles on two and four wheels. After winning four 500 cc and three 350 cc world motorcycling titles 1956–60, he turned to motor racing, and driving for Ferrari, won the Formula 1 World Drivers' Championship in 1964. He later produced his own racing cars.

Surtees, R(obert) S(mith) (1805–1864)

English novelist. He created Jorrocks, a sporting grocer, and in 1838 published *Jorrocks's Jaunts and Jollities*. He excels in the satirical observation of characters and situations from rural society life, such as he demonstrated also in *Hillingdon Hall* (1845), and *Mr Sponge's Sporting Tour* (1853).

Sussex

Former county of England, on the south coast, now divided into ◊East Sussex and ◊West Sussex.

According to tradition, the Saxon Ella landed here in 477, defeated the inhabitants, and founded the kingdom of the South Saxons, which was absorbed by Wessex in 825.

Sutcliff, Rosemary (1920–1992)

English historical novelist. She wrote for both adults and children, and her books include *The Eagle of the Ninth* (1954), *Tristan and Iseult* (1971), and *The Road to Camlann* (1981). Her settings range from the Bronze Age to the 18th century, but her favourite period was the Roman occupation of Britain.

Sutcliffe, Herbert (1894–1978)

English cricketer. A prolific right-handed opening batsman from Yorkshire whose Test career average of 60.73 is the highest achieved by an Englishman batting in 10 or more innings. One of only seven players to have scored over 50,000 first class runs, he established famous opening partnerships with Percy Holmes for Yorkshire and with Jack Hobbs for England.

Sutherland, Graham Vivian (1903–1980)

English painter, graphic artist, and designer. He was active mainly in France from the 1940s. A leading figure of the Neo-Romantic movement (1935–55), which revived the spirit of 19th-century Romanticism in a more modern idiom, he executed portraits, landscapes, and religious subjects, often using a semi-abstract style.

Sutherland first studied engraving and etching, his early prints showing some affinity with the work of Samuel ◊Palmer. He began to paint from 1930, and during that decade acquired a Surrealist appreciation of the strangeness and metaphorical suggestion of natural form. This developed into the characteristic thorns, sinister tree shapes, and distillations of his Neo-Romantic landscapes of the 1940s. An official war artist from 1941, his sense of strangeness found vivid expression in paintings of bomb devastation. In the late 1940s he turned increasingly to portraiture.

Varied aspects of his work are shown in his *Crucifixion* (1946; the church of St Matthew, Northampton); his *Origins of the Land* (1951; Tate Gallery, London), for the Festival of Britain; his characterful portrait of the writer *Somerset Maugham* (1949; Tate Gallery, London); and his *Christ in Glory* tapestry (1962; Coventry Cathedral). His portrait of Winston Churchill (1954) was disliked by its subject and eventually burned on the instructions of Lady Churchill (studies survive). He also created designs for posters, stage costumes, and theatre sets. He was awarded the OM in 1960.

Sutton

Outer borough of south Greater London, created in 1965 and comprising the former municipal boroughs of Beddington and Wallington, Sutton and Cheam, and the urban district of Carshalton.

Features site of Nonsuch Palace, built by Henry VIII, demolished in the 17th century; parish church of St Nicholas, rebuilt in 1862; All Saints Church (1865); one of the first nursery schools in England, founded in 1909; the central library, opened in 1975; a large shopping mall, St Nicholas Centre, built in 1991

Industries engineering, building, electronics, and the manufacture of plastics, vinyls, perfumes, chemicals, audio-visual equipment, cricket bats

Population (1991) 168,900

History Sutton was probably a Saxon settlement in 6th and 7th centuries. It expanded in the mid-19th century, after construction of a railway line, and became an early commuter town. It has remained a residential area.

Places of historical interest

Settlement in the area dates from the Stone Age; a camp of this period has been excavated at Queen Mary's Hospital, Carshalton, and Roman remains have been found in many parts of the borough. Beddington consisted of two manors in Domesday, one of the manor houses still survives, its great hall dating from the 15th century; it is now Carew Manor Special School. One owner of the house was Sir Francis Carew, the famous horticulturalist. Elizabeth I came twice to visit his gardens, where he grew plants brought back by Sir Walter Raleigh from the New World. The 13th-century church contains many memorials to the Carew family. Cheam was given by King Athelstan to Christchurch monastery at Canterbury. In 1018 Archbishop Lanfranc appropriated half the manor and at the Reformation both parts passed into secular hands. Between Cheam and Ewell was the site of Nonsuch Palace, built by Henry VIII to rival the palaces of Francis I of France. Elizabeth I used it often, but subsequent sovereigns did not, and it was demolished in the 1680s. The site was excavated in 1959–60. Cheam School, attended by Prince Charles, seems to have originated in a school moved from London at the time of the 1665 plague, but the present buildings are modern. Sutton was held by Chertsey Abbey from the 7th century until 1537. Wallington too had medieval origins. These were all small agriculturally based communities until the mid-19th century when the advent of railways led to their rapid development as residential suburbs of London.

Sutton Coldfield

Residential part of the West Midlands conurbation around ◊Birmingham, central England; population (1991) 103,900.

Sutton Coldfield was incorporated in the city of Birmingham in 1974. Sutton Park, to the west of the town, is a large open space (approximately 1,000 ha/2,400 acres) including woodland, lakes, heathland, and wetland. The park is a remnant of an extensive forest that formerly covered much of the Midlands region. The ancient Roman Rykmild Street runs through it.

Sutton Park was given to the townspeople in the 16th century by King Henry VIII. It formerly belonged to Richard Neville, Earl of Warwick, who died in 1471 and whose land went to the crown. In 1528 Bishop Vessey, whose home town was Sutton, obtained from Henry VIII a charter of incorporation which entrusted the government of the town to a warden and 24 local inhabitants, known together as 'The Warden and Society of the Royal Town of Sutton Coldfield'.

Sutton Hoo

Archaeological site in Suffolk, England, where in 1939 a Saxon ship burial was excavated. It may be the funeral monument of Raedwald, King of the East Angles, who died about 624 or 625. The jewellery, armour, and weapons discovered were placed in the British Museum, London.

Sutton-in-Ashfield

Town in Nottinghamshire, central England, 22 km/14 mi northwest of Nottingham; population (1990 est) 40,200. Industries include the manufacture of hosiery, plastics, and light engineering products.

The church of St Mary Magdalene was built in the 12th century and restored in the 19th century.

Sutton-Pringle, John William (1912–1982)

British zoologist who established much of our knowledge of the anatomical mechanisms involved in insect flight.

Swaledale

River valley extending from Keld to Richmond, in the Yorkshire ◊Dales national park, North Yorkshire, England; length 32 km/20 mi. It is the narrowest of the northwest dales. A former lead-mining area, Swaledale is now chiefly agricultural, though tourism is also a major industry. It gives its name to a breed of horned sheep. Buttertubs Pass (526 m/1, 726 ft) connects Swaledale and Wensleydale.

Arkengarthdale, a branch dale, starts from the village of Reeth and leads to Tan Hill Inn, England's highest inn (527 m/1,728 ft). Below Reeth are the ruined nunneries of Marrick and Ellerton.

Swallows and Amazons

The first of a series of novels for children by English author Arthur ◊Ransome, published in the UK from 1930–47. The novels describe the adventures of children on holiday, set in the English Lake District and East Anglia, and always involve boats.

Swallows and Amazons introduces the two families featuring in most of the series, the Walkers and the Blacketts, and their sailing dinghies, *Swallow* and *Amazon* respectively. Later books in the series include *Peter Duck* (1932), *Pigeon Post* (1936), and *We Didn't Mean to Go to Sea* (1937).

Swan, Joseph Wilson (1828–1914)

English inventor of the incandescent-filament electric lamp and of bromide paper for use in developing photographs. Knighted 1904.

Other inventions

Swan took out more than 70 patents. He made a miner's electric safety lamp which was the ancestor of the modern miner's lamp. In the course of this invention he devised a new lead cell (battery) which would not spill acid. He also attempted to make an early type of fuel cell.

The filament lamp

Swan was born in Sunderland and went to work in a chemical firm. Interested in electric lighting from about 1845, he began making filaments by cutting strips of paper and baking them at high temperatures to produce a carbon fibre. In making the first lamps, he connected the ends of a filament to wire (itself a difficult task), placed the filament in a glass bottle, and attempted to evacuate the air and seal the bottle with a cork. Usually the filament burned away very quickly in the remaining air, blackening the glass at the same time. Only after the invention of the vacuum pump in 1865 was Swan able to produce a fairly durable incandescent lamp. For this he made a new type of filament from cotton thread partly dissolved by sulphuric acid. He patented the process in 1880 and began manufacturing lamps. In 1882 US inventor Thomas Edison initiated litigation for patent infringement against Swan, but this was dismissed and the joint company Edison and Swan United Electric Light Company came into being in 1883.

Photography

A wet process for producing photographic prints, using a gelatine film impregnated with carbon or other pigment granules and photosensitized using potassium dichromate, was patented by Swan in 1864. This was known as the carbon or autotype process.

Swanage

Town and resort on the ◊Isle of Purbeck, Dorset, southern England; population (1991) 10,500. Purbeck stone is quarried nearby.

Swann, Donald (Ibrahim) (1923–1994)

British composer, pianist, and entertainer. With his lyricist partner Michael Flanders, he created a series of witty revues 1956–67 with 'Drop of a Hat' in the title. When the partnership ended in 1967, Swann tried his hand at more serious works – opera, a *Te Deum*, more songs – though none became quite so popular.

Swansea

Unitary authority in south Wales, created in 1996 from part of the former county of West Glamorgan

Area 377 sq km/156 sq mi

Towns ◊Swansea (administrative headquarters)

Physical River Tawe

Features ◊Gower Peninsula (an area of outstanding natural beauty)

Industries tinplate manufacture, chemicals, oil refineries

Population (1996) 232,000.

The western boundary of the authority is determined by the River Loughor and its estuary. The main river is the Tawe. The Gower Peninsula remains mainly rural and its coastal scenery makes it a tourist area, but the suburbs of Swansea have spread west into Gower. The whole complex of urban-industrial development in the area is sometimes referred to as Swansea Bay City. The area has natural resources in limestone, silica, brick-earth, shales, and sand. Its metallurgical importance was founded on copper ore, and copper works multiplied from the early 18th century. The scientific process of refining the ore was initiated in the region.

Swansea, Welsh Abertawe

Port and administrative centre of ◊Swansea unitary authority, south Wales, at the mouth of the River Tawe 70 km/43 mi west of Cardiff; population (1994 est) 172,000. It is the second-largest city in Wales. It has oil refineries, chemicals, metallurgical industries, and tin plate manufacturing, and has produced stained glass since 1936. It is the vehicle-licensing centre of the UK.

Swansea received its first charter in 1210 and a new charter in 1655; it was made a city in 1970. The University College of Swansea, a constituent college of the University of Wales, was established here in 1920. The scientific process of refining copper ore was initiated in the Swansea region.

Development

Swansea grew up around the Norman castle of **Swinesaye**, which no longer exists, but the ruins of a castle built next to it do still stand. The latter was built by Henry Gower, Bishop of St David's, between 1328 and 1347. The town suffered greatly from air raids in 1941 and much of the town centre has been rebuilt. The industrial and maritime activities of Swansea are carried on to the east of the High Street, the works and wharves being in the valleys beyond and down at the mouth of the Tawe. The residential parts of Swansea, with their wide streets and parkland, have spread along the bay and over the hills behind. The residential and holiday area of The Mumbles is 8 km/5 mi to the southwest.

Features

The old guildhall or town hall, built in 1847 near the docks, is in the Italian style. The civic building, with its lofty central tower, in Victoria Park, embraces the new guildhall, law courts, and Brangwyn Hall. Other notable buildings are the Royal Institution of South Wales, with a museum and a library; the public library, which includes the corporation art gallery; the Glynn Vivian Art Gallery; and the Exchange Buildings or Chamber of Commerce. Some educational institutions have been combined into a West Glamorgan Institute of Higher Education. The poet Dylan Thomas was born here in 1914.

Industry and commerce

Long recognized as the chief metal port of Great Britain, Swansea is now also a large oil port, while remaining the leading centre of the tin-plate trade. The largest docks are the Queen's, opened in 1920 (0.61 sq km/0.24 sq mi), and the King's (0.29 sq km/0.11 sq mi), the former being used for the oil trade. There is also a municipal dry dock for vessels up to 2,000 tons, and a number of privately-owned dry docks. Swansea's metallurgical importance was founded on copper ore, and copper works multiplied from the early 18th century. The oil-refining industry yields a wide range of products.

Swift, Graham (1949–)

English novelist. His first two novels, *The Sweet-Shop Owner* (1980) and *Shuttlecock* (1981), earned him a reputation as one of the most promising English novelists of his generation. He won wide critical acclaim with his third novel, *Waterland* (1983). Its theme – the struggle to understand and come to terms with the past – is central to his other novels, such as *Last Orders* (1996), which won the Booker Prize for Fiction.

Swift, Jonathan (1667–1745)

Irish satirist and Anglican cleric. He wrote ◊*Gulliver's Travels* (1726), an allegory describing travel to lands inhabited by giants, miniature people, and intelligent horses. His other works include *The Tale of a Tub* (1704), attacking corruption in religion and learning and the satirical pamphlet *A Modest Proposal* (1729), which suggested that children of the poor should be eaten. His lucid prose style is simple and controlled and he imparted his views with fierce indignation and wit.

Swift, born in Dublin, became secretary to the diplomat William Temple (1628–1699) at Moor Park, Surrey, where his friendship with the child 'Stella' (Esther Johnson 1681–1728) began in 1689. Returning to Ireland, he was ordained in the Church of England in 1694, and in 1699 was made a prebendary of St Patrick's, Dublin. He made contributions to the Tory paper *The Examiner*, of which he was editor from 1710–11. He obtained the deanery of St Patrick in 1713. His *Journal to Stella* is a series of intimate letters (1710–13), in which he described his life in London. From about 1738 his mind began to fail.

Swinburne, Algernon Charles (1837–1909)

English poet. He attracted attention with the choruses of his Greek-style tragedy *Atalanta in Calydon* (1865), but he and ◊Rossetti were attacked in 1871 as leaders of 'the fleshly school of poetry', and the revolutionary politics of *Songs before Sunrise* (1871) alienated others. His verse is notable for its emotion and opulent language.

Swindon

Town and administrative headquarters of ◊Swindon unitary authority in southwest England, 124 km/77 mi west of London; population (1996) 170,000; it was part of the county of Wiltshire until 1997. The site of a major railway engineering works 1841–1986 on the Great Western Railway, the town has diversified since 1950 into such industries as heavy engineering, electronics, electrical manufacture, cars, and also insurance.

There is a railway museum, and the ◊White Horse of Uffington, an ancient hill figure on the chalk downs, is nearby.

Swindon Rail Works specializes in repair work for steam-railway preservation societies.

Swindon

Unitary authority in southwest England, created in 1997 from the former district council of Thamesdown

Area 223 sq km/86 sq mi

Towns and cities ◊Swindon (administrative headquarters); villages of Stanton, Fitzwarren, Highworth

Features River Thames forms northern border of authority; Barbury Castle, Iron Age hillfort on Marlborough Downs; Great Western Railway Museum and National Monuments Records Centre (Swindon)

Industries insurance, motor vehicle manufacturing, publishing, energy services, high technology industries, information technology
Population (1995) 173,800

Swing Riots

Uprising of farm workers in southern and eastern England 1830–31. Farm labourers protested at the introduction of new threshing machines, which jeopardized their livelihood. They fired ricks, smashed the machines, and sent threatening letters to farmers. They invented a Captain Swing as their leader, and he became a figure of fear to the landed gentry. The riots were suppressed by the government, with 19 executions and almost 500 transportations.

Swithun, or Swithin, St (*c.* 800–*c.* 862)

English priest, chancellor of King Ethelwolf and bishop of Winchester from 852. According to legend, the weather on his feast day (15 July) determines the weather for the next 40 days.

Sydenham, Thomas (1624–1689)

English physician, the first person to describe measles and to recommend the use of quinine for relieving symptoms of malaria. His original reputation as the 'English Hippocrates' rested upon his belief that careful observation is more useful than speculation. His *Observationes medicae* was published in 1676.

Sylvester, James Joseph (1814–1897)

English mathematician who was one of the discoverers of the theory of algebraic invariants. He coined the term 'matrix' in 1850 to describe a rectangular array of numbers out of which determinants can be formed.

Symington, William (1763–1831)

Scottish engineer who built the first successful steamboat. He invented the steam road locomotive in 1787 and a steamboat engine in 1788. His steamboat *Charlotte Dundas* was completed in 1802.

Symons, Julian (Gustave) (1912–1994)

English novelist, poet, and critic. In 1937 he founded, and edited until 1939, the magazine *Twentieth Century Verse. Confusions about X* (1939) was his own first book of poetry, of which over the years he published four more. At first a conscientious objector during World War II, he subsequently served in the 57th Tank regiment. *The Immaterial Murder Case* (1945) was the first of his many crime novels. He was instrumental in the founding of the Crime Writers' Association (1953) and was president of the Detection Club 1976–85.

Symons was born in London, younger brother of A J A Symons (1900–1941), biographer of Frederick Rolfe and bibliographer. After leaving school at 14, he went out to work as a clerk while reading widely. He succeeded George Orwell in 1947 as literary columnist on the *Manchester Evening News*.

Synge, Richard Laurence Millington (1914–1994)

British biochemist who improved paper chromatography (a means of separating mixtures) to the point where individual amino acids could be identified. He developed the technique, known as partition chromatography, with his colleague Archer ⇨Martin in 1944. They shared the 1952 Nobel Prize for Chemistry.

Martin and Synge worked together at Cambridge and at the Wool Industries Research Association in Leeds, Yorkshire. Their chromatographic method became an immediate success, widely adopted. It was soon demonstrated that not only the type but the concentration of each amino acid can be determined.

table entertainment

18th-century English entertainment, only partly musical in character, given by a single performer sitting at a table and telling stories and jokes, giving displays of mimicry, singing songs, and so on. The first table entertainments on record are those of George Alexander Steevens at Dublin in 1752. Dibdin began a series in London in 1789 and continued for 20 years, introducing most of his songs in this way.

Taff, Welsh Taf

River in south Wales rising in the Brecon Beacons and flowing south to enter the Bristol Channel at Cardiff; length 64 km/40 mi; catchment area 526 sq km/203 sq mi. The towns of Merthyr Tydfil, Pontypridd, Aberdare, and the city of Cardiff all lie on the banks of the Taff or its tributaries. The Rhondda joins the Taff at Pontypridd.

Take That

British pop group formed in 1991. Its members were Gary Barlow (1971–) (vocals and keyboards), Robbie Williams (1974–) (vocals), Mark Owen (1974–) (vocals), Jason Orange (1970–) (vocals), and Howard Donald (1970–) (vocals). Following the 1992 hit singles 'It Only Takes A Minute ' and 'A Million Love Songs', they rose to become one of the most successful of all 'boy bands' in the UK, with a string of number one UK hits. Williams left in 1995 and the group disbanded in 1996.

Following the announcement of the break-up of the group in February 1996 helplines run by Childline and the Samaritans were set up to offer support to distressed fans.

Talbot, William Henry Fox (1800–1877)

English pioneer of photography. He invented the paper-based calotype process in 1841, the first negative/positive method. Talbot made photograms several years before Louis Daguerre's invention was announced.

In 1851 he made instantaneous photographs by electric light and in 1852 photo engravings. *The Pencil of Nature* (1844–46) by Talbot was the first book illustrated with photographs to be published.

He was elected Liberal member of Parliament for Chippenham in 1833. During a trip to Italy he tried to capture the images obtained in a camera obscura and by 1835 had succeeded in fixing outlines of objects laid on sensitized paper. Images of his home, Lacock Abbey, Wiltshire, followed.

Talbot was also a mathematician and classical scholar, and was one of the first to decipher the cuneiform inscriptions of Nineveh, Assyria.

A museum of his work was opened at Lacock Abbey, Wiltshire, in 1975.

Tallis, Thomas (*c.* 1505–1585)

English composer. He was a master of counterpoint. His works include *Tallis's Canon* ('Glory to thee my God this night') (1567) and the antiphonal *Spem in alium non habui* (about 1573) for 40 voices. He published a collection of 34 motets, *Cantiones sacrae*, (1575), of which 16 are by Tallis and 18 by Byrd. He was one of the earliest composers to write for the Anglican liturgy (1547–53) but some of his most ornate music, including the Mass *Puer natus est nobis*, dates from the brief Catholic reign of Mary Tudor (1553–58). A tune written for Archbishop Parker's Psalter of 1567 was used by Vaughan Williams in his celebrated *Fantasia on a Theme of Thomas Tallis*.

Tamar

River rising in north Cornwall, southwest England; length 97 km/60 mi. For most of its length it forms the Devon–Cornwall border; it forms the Hamoaze estuary at Devonport and flows into Plymouth Sound.

Taming of the Shrew, The

Comedy by William ◊Shakespeare, first performed in 1593–94. Bianca, who has many suitors, must not marry until her elder sister Katherina (the shrew) has done so. Petruchio agrees to woo Katherina so that his friend Hortensio may marry Bianca. Petruchio succeeds in 'taming' Katherina but Bianca marries another.

Tamworth

Town in Staffordshire, central England, at the junction of the rivers Tame and Anker, 24 km/15 mi northeast of Birmingham; population (1991) 67,500. Industries include agricultural engineering and the manufacture of paper, clothing, bricks, tiles, and aluminium products.

TALBOT, WILLIAM HENRY FOX *Pioneering English photographer William Henry Fox Talbot (far right) at work. He was a gentleman scientist with the financial means to pursue his intellectual interests and he was more concerned with solving technical problems than in the artistic potential of photography. Corbis*

Features

The castle has a Norman keep and a Jacobean great hall, and it includes a museum of local history. The tower of the 14th-century church of St Editha contains an unusual double spiral staircase. The town hall was built in 1701 by Thomas Guy (*c.*1644–1724), founder of Guy's Hospital and also member of Parliament for Tamworth 1695–1707, who was educated at Tamworth. In front of the town hall is a statue of the Conservative politician and prime minister Robert Peel, who represented Tamworth from 1830 until his death in 1850.

History

Once the capital of the Anglo-Saxon kingdom of Mercia, Tamworth was the site of a palace and mint of Offa, King of Mercia, in the 8th century. It was one of the places where King Athelstan held his councils in the early 10th century, and Ethelfleda, daughter of King Alfred, fortified the town. Robert Peel's election address in 1834, the Tamworth Manifesto, was adopted as the blueprint for Tory party philosophy.

Tandy, Jessica (1909–1994)

English film and theatre actress. One of the greatest classical theatre actresses of her day, she played all the major Shakespearean heroines, including Ophelia alongside John Gielgud's Hamlet in 1934. She won an Academy Award for the film *Driving Miss Daisy* (1989). She was created a DBE in 1990.

Tansley, Arthur George (1871–1955)

English botanist, a pioneer in the science of plant ecology. He coordinated a large project to map the vegetation of the British Isles; the results were published in *Types of British Vegetation* (1911). He was also instrumental in the formation of organizations devoted to the study of ecology and the protection of wildlife. Knighted 1950.

tartan

Woollen cloth woven in specific chequered patterns individual to Scottish clans, with stripes of different widths and colours crisscrossing on a coloured background; it is used in making skirts, kilts, trousers, and other articles of clothing.

Developed in the 17th century, tartan was banned after the 1745 ⇨Jacobite rebellion, and not legalized again until 1782.

Tate, Jeffrey Philip (1943–)

English conductor. He was appointed chief conductor and artistic director of the Rotterdam Philharmonic Orchestra in 1991. He assisted at Covent Garden, London 1970–77 and under Boulez at Bayreuth, Germany in 1976 before making a remarkable operatic debut at the New York Metropolitan Opera in 1980 with Berg's expressionist masterpiece *Lulu*.

Principal conductor of the English Chamber Orchestra in 1985, principal conductor of the Royal Opera House, Covent Garden, London, 1986–91, and principal guest conductor since 1991, he has specialized in Mozart symphonies and piano concertos, the latter with his wife Mitsuko Uchida as soloist.

Tate, Phyllis Margaret Duncan (1911–1987)

English composer. Her works include *Concerto for Saxophone and Strings* (1944), the opera *The Lodger* (1960), based on the story of Jack the Ripper, and *Serenade to Christmas* for soprano, chorus, and orchestra (1972). Her works were generally small in scale, and carefully crafted.

She studied composition with Harry Farjeon at the Royal Academy of Music in London 1928–32. Several of her works were performed when she was still a student, and in 1933 her cello concerto was her first work heard at a public concert.

Tate & Lyle

British sugar-manufacturing company which grew from the grocery business set up in Liverpool 1839 by Henry Tate (1819–1899). In 1869 Tate turned to sugar refining and in 1876 moved his company to London and opened a new refinery there. In 1921 Tate merged with the sugar refinery business founded in London in 1881 by Abram Lyle (1820–1891), a former shipowner and refiner in Greenock, Scotland. In 1882 Abram Lyle launched his best-known product, Lyle's Golden Syrup.

In 1897 Henry Tate, as a wealthy art collector, gave his collection of modern paintings to the nation and founded the Tate Gallery in London to house them.

Tate Gallery

Art gallery in London, housing British art from the late 16th century and international art from 1810. Endowed by the sugar merchant Henry Tate (1819–1899), it was opened in 1897. A Liverpool branch of the Tate Gallery opened in 1988, and the St Ives extension in 1993. Increased display space will be provided by the new Tate Gallery of Modern Art at Bankside, London; scheduled to open in 2000. Lars Nittve was appointed as its first director in 1998; in 1998 Stephen Deuchar was appointed director of the Tate Gallery of British Art, at the main Millbank site.

The Tate Gallery has unique collections of the work of J M W Turner and William Blake, also one of the best collections of Pre-Raphaelite painting. The Clore Gallery extension for Turner's paintings was opened in 1987.

Tattersall's

British auctioneers of racehorses based at Knightsbridge Green, southwest London, since 1864. The firm is named after Richard Tattersall (1724–1795), who founded Tattersall's at Hyde Park Corner in 1766.

Tatton Park

House in Cheshire, England, 5 km/3 mi north of Knutsford. Originally built in the 17th century, Tatton Park was rebuilt from 1780 to 1813 by Samuel (1737–1807)and Lewis William Wyatt (1777–1853). The house, furniture, silver, and paintings, as well as a 22 ha/54 acre garden, were bequeathed to the National Trust by the 4th Lord Egerton of Tatton, and subsequently the 800 ha/1,976 acre estate came to the Trust through the Treasury, in 1960. Humphry Repton designed the park and garden.

Taunton

Market town and administrative headquarters of ◊Somerset, southwest England, 50 km/31 mi northeast of Exeter, on the River Tone; population (1991) 56,400. Products include cider, leather, optical instruments, computer software, aeronautical instruments, and concrete; other industries include light engineering, and there is a weekly cattle market. Taunton is the main market centre for west Somerset and east Devon. The remains of Taunton Castle include the Elizabethan hall in which Judge ◊Jeffreys held his Bloody Assizes in 1685 after the Duke of Monmouth's rebellion.

Location

Taunton is situated in the heart of the fertile valley of Taunton Deane, and is sheltered on the north and south by the Quantock and Blackdown hills.

Features

The large Perpendicular 15th-century church of St Mary Magdalene has double aisles and an elaborately sculptured tower which is 49 m/163 ft high. Taunton Castle is a Norman and Edwardian building built on the site of a Saxon fort; it now houses the county museum. Other features include a 12th–13th-century leper hospital, Priory Barn which formed part of a 12th-century Augustinian priory, and Gray's Almshouses (1635). The Admiralty Hydrographic Establishment is located at Taunton. The town formerly had army barracks, but these have now been converted to flats. There is a Marines base nearby at Norton-Fitzwarren.

History

Taunton existed as a West Saxon stronghold in the early 8th century, and had a market before the Norman Conquest, receiving its first charter in the reign of Stephen. During the Civil War Taunton was held by the Parliamentarians and its castle held out against a Royalist siege. In 1685 the Duke of Monmouth was proclaimed king here before his defeat at the Battle of Sedgemoor, and inhabitants of Taunton were among the rebels executed following the assizes of Judge Jeffreys.

Tavener, John Kenneth (1944–)

English composer. He has written austere vocal works including the dramatic cantata *The Whale* (1968) and the opera *Thérèse* (1979). *The Protecting Veil*, composed in 1987 for cello and strings alone, became a best-selling classical recording. Recent works include *Vlepondas* for soprano, bass and cello, and *Feast of Feasts* for chorus, both 1996.

Tavistock

Market town in Devon, southwest England, on the west of Dartmoor, 24 km/15 mi north of Plymouth, on the River Tavy; population (1991) 10,100.

Features

The architecture of the town is predominantly Victorian,

although there are remains of a Benedictine Abbey founded in the 10th century, and the church of St Eustachius dates from the 15th century. An annual 'Goose Fair' is held under royal charter, granted by Henry I in 1105.

History

Tavistock became a stannary town (see ◊stannaries) in 1305, and it was a centre of the cloth industry from about 1500 until the end of the 18th century. The town prospered in the 19th century after the discovery of copper deposits here, but most of the copper mines had closed by the beginning of the 20th century.

Famous people

The explorer Francis Drake was born nearby.

taxation

Raising of money from individuals and organizations by the state in order to pay for the goods and services it provides. Taxation can be **direct** (a deduction from income) or **indirect** (added to the purchase price of goods or services, that is, a tax on consumption). The standard form of indirect taxation in Europe is **value-added tax (VAT)**. **◊Income tax** is the most common form of direct taxation.

The proportions of direct and indirect taxation in the total tax revenue vary widely from country to country. By varying the effect of a tax on the richer and poorer members of society, a government can attempt to redistribute wealth from the richer to the poorer, both by taxing the rich more severely and by returning some of the collected wealth in the form of **benefits**. A **progressive** tax is one that falls proportionally more on the rich; most income taxes, for example, have higher rates for those with higher incomes. A **regressive** tax, on the other hand, affects the poor proportionally more than the rich.

In Britain, taxation is below average by comparison with other members of the Organization for Economic Cooperation and Development (OECD). Income tax is collected by the Inland Revenue, as are the other direct taxes, namely **corporation tax** on company profits; **capital gains tax**, introduced to prevent the use of capital as untaxed income in 1961; and **inheritance tax** (which replaced capital transfer tax). Levels of taxation on land and inherited wealth in Britain were in 1994 among the lowest in the world. The UK has a high proportion of direct taxation compared, for example, with the USA which has a higher proportion of indirect taxation.

VAT is based on the French TVA (*taxe sur la valeur ajoutée*), and was introduced in the UK in 1973. It is paid on the value added to any goods or services at each particular stage of the process of production or distribution and, although collected from traders at each stage, it is in effect a tax on consumer expenditure. In the UK, a ◊council tax, based on property values, is the form of taxation that pays for local government spending. It replaced the unpopular **poll tax** or community charge of 1989–93, levied on each person of voting age. In Britain taxes are also levied on tobacco, wine, beer, and petrol, in the form of **excise duties**.

The UK tax system has been criticized in many respects; alternatives include an **expenditure tax**, which would be imposed only on income spent, and the **tax-credit system** under which all are guaranteed an income bolstered as necessary by social-security benefits, taxation beginning only above that level, hence eliminating the 'poverty trap', by which the unemployed receiving state benefits may have a net loss in income if they take employment at a low wage.

Tay

Longest river in Scotland; length 193 km/120 mi, it flows northeast through **Loch Tay**, then east and southeast past Perth to the **Firth of Tay**, crossed at Dundee by the **Tay Bridge**, before joining the North Sea. The Tay has salmon fisheries; its main tributaries are the Tummel, Isla, and Earn, Braan, and Almond.

The drainage basin of the Tay and its tributaries forms one of the most fully integrated hydroelectric developments in the north of Scotland.

The first Tay Bridge, opened in 1878, on the then longest span over water in the world, was blown into the river in 1879, along with a train which was passing over it. The bridge was rebuilt 1883–88, and a road bridge, from Newport-on-Tay to Dundee, was completed in 1966.

Taylor, A(lan) J(ohn) P(ercivale) (1906–1990)

English historian and television lecturer. His books include *The Struggle for Mastery in Europe 1848–1918* (1954), *The Origins of the Second World War* (1961), and *English History 1914–1945* (1965).

Taylor lectured at Manchester University 1930–38 and was a fellow of Magdalen College, Oxford, 1938–76. As international history lecturer at Oxford University 1953–63, he established himself as an authority on modern British and European history and did much to popularize the subject, giving the first televised history lectures.

Taylor, Ann (1947–)

British Labour politician, President of the Council and Leader of the House of Commons 1997–98, chief whip 1998– . She was a whip, 1977–79, in the government of James Callaghan, and, in opposition, spokesperson on Education 1979–81, on Housing 1981–83, on the Home Office 1987–88, on the Environment 1988–92, shadow secretary of state for Education 1992–94, spokesperson on the Citizen's Charter 1994–96, and shadow Leader of the House 1996–97. She is the first woman to hold the post of government chief whip.

Taylor, C(ecil) P(hilip) (1929–1981)

Scottish dramatist. His stage plays include *Bread and Butter* (1966), *And a Nightingale Sang...* (1979), and *Good* (1981), a study of intellectual complicity in Nazi Germany. His work was first produced by the Traverse Theatre in Edinburgh; he also wrote extensively for television and radio.

Taylor, Elizabeth (Rosemond) (1932–)

English-born US actress. She graduated from juvenile leads to dramatic roles, becoming one of the most glamorous stars of the 1950s and 1960s. Her films include *National Velvet* (1944),

Cat on a Hot Tin Roof (1958), *BUtterfield 8* (1960) (Academy Award), *Cleopatra* (1963), and *Who's Afraid of Virginia Woolf?* (1966) (Academy Award).

Her husbands have included Michael Wilding (1912–1979) and Richard Burton (twice).

Tayside

Former region of Scotland (1975–96); replaced by Angus, Dundee City, and Perth and Kinross unitary authorities.

The new unitary authorities were formerly the three districts of Tayside region (1975–96). Tayside region was formed from the counties of Perthshire, Kinross-shire, Angusshire, and the city of Dundee.

> *Until 1914 a sensible, law-abiding Englishman could pass through life and hardly notice the existence of the state, beyond the post office and the policeman.*
>
> A J P Taylor English historian.
> *England 1914–1945* (1965)

teacher training

Training of teachers either by means of the four-year Bachelor of Education (BEd) degree, which integrates professional training and the study of academic subjects, or by means of the Postgraduate Certificate of Education (PGCE), which offers one year of professional training to follow a degree course in a specialist subject. The majority of BEd students train to teach in primary schools; two-thirds of PGCE students train to teach specialist subjects in secondary schools. In 1995, 20,400 trainee teachers successfully completed a postgraduate course and 11,700 a course for non-graduates.

The numbers of teacher training places fell sharply in line with school pupil numbers in the 1970s. By the late 1980s there were considerable difficulties in filling all training places, especially in such subjects as science, maths, and technology. By 1993, however, demand for training places had increased and the teacher shortage had largely disappeared as a result of rising graduate unemployment.

Tebbit, Norman Beresford, Baron Tebbit (1931–)

British Conservative politician. He was minister for employment 1981–83, minister for trade and industry 1983–85, chancellor of the Duchy of Lancaster 1985–87, and chairman of the party 1985–87. As his relations with Margaret Thatcher cooled, he returned to the back benches in 1987. Created a life peer in 1992, he went on to carve out a new career in business.

Tedder, Arthur William, 1st Baron Tedder (1890–1967)

Marshal of the Royal Air Force in World War II. He was air officer commanding RAF Middle East 1941–43, where his method of pattern bombing became known as 'Tedder's carpet'. As deputy supreme commander under US general Eisenhower 1943–45, he was largely responsible for the initial success of the 1944 Normandy landings. KCB 1942.

Teddington

Part of Twickenham, in the Greater London borough of ◊Richmond-upon-Thames; site of the National Physical Laboratory, established 1900.

Tees

River flowing from the Pennines in Cumbria, northwest England, to the North Sea via Tees Bay, Middlesborough unitary authority, in northeast England; length 130 km/80 mi. Its port, Teesport, handles in excess of 42 million tonnes per annum, with port trade mainly chemical-related.

Although much of the river is polluted with industrial waste, sewage, and chemicals, the Tees Barrage (opened in 1985, cost of construction £50 million) enables a 16-km/10-mi stretch of the river to provide clean, non-tidal water. This is used for white-water sports, including canoeing.

The Tees rises in the north Pennines at Tees Head, on the easterly reaches of Cross Fell, Cumbria, and flows southeast and then northeast through Stockton-on-Tees and Middlesbrough, entering the Tees Mouth estuary to join the North Sea. It is navigable to Middlesbrough. Its main tributaries are the Lune, Balder, and Greta. The river valley, known as Teesdale, includes Mickle Fell (790 m/2,326 ft), the highest point in County Durham, and the waterfall of High Force.

The Tees has a unique transporter bridge (a bridge consisting of a movable platform suspended from cables), opened in 1911, which has 49 m/160 ft clearance above the water. Its central section transports cars and people across the Tees towards Hartlepool. It is the sole working example in England.

Teesside

Industrial area at the mouth of the River Tees, northeast England; population (1994 est) 323,000. It includes the towns of ◊Stockton-on-Tees, ◊Middlesbrough, ◊Billingham, and Thornaby. There are high-technology industries, as well as petrochemicals, electronics, steelmaking, and plastics. The area includes an oil-fuel terminal and the main North Sea natural gas terminal.

Enron Power Station, a gas-fired plant opened in the area in 1993, is the largest combined heat and power plant in the world. The University of Teesside (formerly Teesside Polytechnic) was established in 1992.

The traditional industries of shipbuilding and heavy engineering have declined, and Teesside now rivals Rotterdam as Europe's largest petrochemicals complex.

Teifi, or Teivy

River in Wales, rising at 455 m/1,493 ft in Llyn Teifi in Ceredigion (Cardiganshire); length 118 km/73 mi; catchment area 1,007 sq km/389 sq mi. It flows southwest through Lampeter and Llanybydder and then west to enter Cardigan Bay in a wide estuary. At Cenarth, the river is confined by a rocky outcrop leading to picturesque rapids and falls.

Teignmouth

Port and resort in south Devon, southwest England, 20 km/13 mi from Exeter, at the mouth of the River Teign; population (1991) 13,400. The port handles imports of animal feed and fertilizers, and exports of Poole Clay. There is some commercial salmon-fishing in the Teign. Leisure industries here include a yachting centre.

Teignmouth extends onto the tongue of land between the Teign and the sea, and it has a sea-wall 3 km/2 mi long. It developed as a resort at the end of the 18th century.

telecommunciations

The UK was one of the first countries in the world to break up telecommunications and postal services within its state-owned monopoly and allow competition by issuing licences to new Public Telecommunications Operators (PTOs) of fixed networks and mobile networks.

Two events in 1981 heralded the beginning of deregulation and increased competition in the UK telecommunications industry: the government sold shares in Cable, and postal and telecommunications services, which had both been run by the Post Office, were separated and British Telecommunications plc (BT) was formed.

Privatization of BT took place in stages, beginning in 1984 when the government sold 51% of its shares in BT to the public. In the same year, BT lost its monopoly on telecommunications provision and services in the UK when Mercury Communications was granted an operator's licence. The introduction of Vodafone and Cellnet cellular radio networks in 1985 provided the BT and Mercury duopoly with some competition, encouraging the development of new markets. Cable television operators were also granted licences to provide telecommunications services, but only as agents for BT and Mercury.

The BT/Mercury duopoly on fixed services continued until 1991 when the government decided to accept applications for licences from new operators. Vodafone and Cellnet were issued with licences to provide fixed services, and cable television networks were allowed to offer services in their own right.

Restrictions on the use of leased lines for the provision of international services were lifted in 1991. Further competition was encouraged with the creation of International Simple Resale (ISR). This system allows operators of international leased lines to interconnect with public networks between designated countries and re-sell their services to both residential and business customers.

In 1996 the Department of Trade and Industry removed the BT/Mercury duopoly on the provision of international telecommunications services and opened the telecommunications industry to full competition.

telecommuting

Working from home using a telephone, fax, and modem to

TELEVISION *Cable television, delivered via underground cables, began in earnest in Britain in the 1980s, and can now potentially be received by some 80 percent of homes. Consumers pay by subscription, and can access between 30 and 65 television channels (including satellite broadcasts) as well as a wide range of telecommunications services, such as home shopping, e-mail, and Internet access. Piers Cavendish/Impact*

TELEVISION *The comedy drama series* All Creatures Great and Small, *based on the novels by James Herriot about a veterinary practice in Yorkshire in the 1930s, was hugely popular on British television in the 1980s, and was sold worldwide. Its success gave rise to other dramas with a strong regional flavour. Rex*

keep in touch with the office of the employing company. In the mid-1990s, it was estimated that 2.3% (600,000) of the British workforce were telecommuters.

Most telecommuters are self-employed, or sales people spending much of their time on the road. However, the number of part-time telecommuters, for example working one day per week at home, is growing.

Telecom Tower, formerly Post Office Tower

Building in London, 189 m/620 ft high. Completed in 1966, it is a microwave relay tower capable of handling up to 150,000 simultaneous telephone conversations and over 40 television channels.

telephone tapping, or telephone bugging

Listening in on a telephone conversation, without the knowledge of the participants; in the UK this is a criminal offence if done without a warrant or the consent of the person concerned.

In Britain, the Interception of Communications Act 1985 allows a tribunal to investigate a complaint from any person who believes they have been subject to an interception. There were 893 warrants for telephone tapping issued in England and Wales in 1993 and 112 in Scotland.

television

See also ◊BBC, ◊ITV, ◊Channel 4, ◊Channel 5, and ◊Independent Television Commission (ITC). See table for average daily viewing 1969-96.

Since television began in Britain in 1936 it has had a huge impact on the nation, providing a shared experience of programmes that has created a talking-point and a common cultural understanding. Significant television 'moments' are remembered long after the event, whether favourite comedy sketches, a tough interview, a shocking documentary, or a sporting win. Live coverage of ceremonies, particularly the 1953 coronation and the funerals of key figures – Churchill; Kennedy; Diana, Princess of Wales, the latter reaching a record worldwide audience – have united the country. A few programmes have prompted action or change: the 1966 Wednesday Play *Cathy Come Home* broke new ground showing something of what it is like to be homeless, and helped Shelter on its way to becoming a major charity and campaigning group. Television has also raised millions of pounds for charities, either via single appeals, or an evening of special programmes to benefit a range of themed charities. Successful examples of the latter are the BBC's annual *Children in Need* appeal, and *Comic Relief*.

Programmes

Soap operas, films, comedies, and sport dominate the ratings. Most costly to produce are drama and comedy, which has encouraged braodcasters to repeat popular programmes alongside new material. As the satellite and digital age of television gets underway, the vast bank of quality programmes produced when only three channels existed is reaching a new audience in addition to those who can remember them first time round. While classics such as *Z Cars* (produced from 1962) and its successor *Softly Softly*, may be beyond recall, satellite schedules in late 1998 included *The Persuaders* (from 1971), *All Creatures Great and Small* (first shown in 1977; it prompted a wave of nostalgia series and alerted producers to the value of regional scenery), *Lillie* (1978), about Lillie

Average Daily Television Usage per Household in the UK

(– = not applicable. In hours.)

Year	Total	ITV	BBC1	BBC2	Channel 4
1969	4.5	2.4	2.1	–	–
1972	4.8	2.7	1.9	0.3	–
1976	5.1	2.7	2.1	0.4	–
1980	5.1	2.5	2.0	0.6	–
1982	4.9	2.4	1.9	0.6	–
1986	5.3	2.4	1.9	0.6	0.5
1990	5.1	2.3	1.9	0.5	0.5
1993	5.8	2.3	1.9	0.6	0.7
1994	5.8	2.3	1.9	0.7	0.7
1995	5.9	2.2	1.9	0.7	0.7
1996	5.8	2.0	1.9	0.7	0.7

Source: Taylor Nelson AGB/BARB

Langtry, the genial *Minder* (from 1979), the nurses soap *Angels* (from 1979), and the Jersey-based *Bergerac* (from 1981). Also with potential for repetition are the lavish costume dramas, such as *Elizabeth R* (1972) with Glenda Jackson, the long-running and much-exported *Upstairs Downstairs* (from 1973), *Edward and Mrs Simpson* (1978), and *Brideshead Revisited*, plus the BBC's many successful adaptations of novels, such as *Middlemarch*.

Among other home-grown drama series that have made their mark are *The Sweeney* (from 1975), *Secret Army* (1977), *Rumpole of the Bailey* (from 1978) *When the Boat Comes In* and *Bouquet of Barbed Wire* (both 1979), *Casualty* (from 1986), the series of *Poirot* dramas (from 1989), *Darling Buds of May* (1991), and *London's Burning* (from 1994). See also ◊comedy, for some of the most successful sitcoms and sketch shows.

> *The culture that brought us the warmth, skill and benevolent didacticism of David Attenborough is being subsumed by a new, democratised, 'interactive' fashion where TV executives can shrug their shoulders and say 'I don't know what they want. Why don't we give them all a camera and they can film what they want?'*
>
> RORY BREMNER British comedian. Writing in the *New Statesman*, September 1998, describing a 'karaoke' culture where participation is valued over ability and popularity over excellence

History

In 1873 it was realized that, since the electrical properties of the nonmetallic chemical element selenium vary according to the amount of light to which it is exposed, light could be converted into electrical impulses, making it possible to transmit such impulses over a distance and then reconvert them into light. The chief difficulty was seen to be the 'splitting of the picture' so that the infinite variety of light and shade values might be transmitted and reproduced. In 1908 it was found that cathode-ray tubes would best effect transmission and reception. Mechanical devices were used at the first practical demonstration of television, given by the Scottish engineer J L Baird in London on 27 January 1926, and cathode-ray tubes were used experimentally in the UK from 1934.

The world's first public television service was started from the BBC station at Alexandra Palace in North London, on 2 November 1936.

Colour television

Baird gave a demonstration of colour TV in London 1928, but it was not until December 1953 that the first successful system was adopted for broadcasting, in the USA. Colour television did not arrive in the UK until the start of BBC2, in 1964.

Satellite television

This is transmission of broadcast signals through communications satellites. Mainly positioned in geostationary orbit, satellites have been used since the 1960s to relay television pictures around the world. Higher-power satellites have more recently been developed to broadcast signals to cable systems or directly to people's homes, requiring a satellite dish.

Direct broadcasting by satellite began in the UK in February 1989 with the introduction of Rupert Murdoch's Sky Television service; its rival British Satellite Broadcasting (BSB) was launched in April 1990, and they merged in November of the same year, becoming British Sky Broadcasting (BSkyB). BSkyB dwarfs the schedules of both ITV and BBC. Broadcasting Hollywood films and top sporting events has fuelled subscriptions.

Digital television

This is a system of transmitting television programmes in digital codes. Until the late 1980s it was considered impossible to convert a TV signal into digital code because of the sheer amount of information needed to represent a visual image. However, data compression techniques were developed to reduce the number of bits that needed to be transmitted each second. As a result, digital technology was developed that offers sharper pictures on wider screens, with image quality comparable to a cinema. A common world standard for digital TV, the MPEG–2, was agreed in April 1993 at a meeting of engineers representing manufacturers and broadcasters from 18 countries.

Digital television offers the possibility of far more channels being available than hitherto. Digital television is available by satellite, cable, or terrestrial means. The 1996 Broadcasting Act provided for the licensing by the ITC of at least 18 national digital terrestrial TV channels, transmitted on six frequency channels or 'multiplexes', and 12 digital radio stations. The licences for running the multiplexes are also granted by the ITC.

The existing public service broadcasting channels – BBC1, BBC2, ITV, Channel 4 (S4C in Wales), and Channel 5 – are all available digitally at no extra charge beyond the cost of the receiving equipment. This is either a box fixed to an existing TV to decode the signal, or a new television set with the decoder built in. These existing services are described as 'free-to-air' services, and there will be room for more free services.

At the end of 1998 the two main operators in the UK digital market were Sky Digital, promising up to 200 digital channels available by satellite, and paid for either by subscription or pay-per-view, and ONdigital, a terrestrial digital operator, owned by two ITV companies, Carlton and Granada, operated largely by subscription, though some pay-per-view services may be included. This was offering some 30 channels.

Available via Sky Digital and ONdigital are the BBC's own digital-only services, initially BBC Choice and BBC News 24, while an ITV channel for youth and sports programming is available via ONdigital, and may be contracted to Sky Digital as well.

Take-up of digital television will be assessed by the government in order to decide when the former type of analogue transmissions could cease, though this is unlikely to be for ten years after digital's launch.

Telford

Town, administrative headquarters of ◊ Telford and Wrekin unitary authority, in west-central England, 52 km/32 mi northwest of Birmingham; population (1991) 100,000. Founded as Dawley New Town in 1963, it was extended and renamed Telford in 1968. ◊Ironbridge Gorge is nearby.

Telford and Wrekin

Unitary authority in west England, created in 1998 from part of Shropshire
Area 291 sq km/112 sq mi
Towns and cities ◊Telford (administrative headquarters), Newport
Features the **Wrekin**, isolated hill (407 m/1,334 ft); Ironbridge Gorge (World Heritage Site) includes world's first iron bridge, built across River Severn in 1779 by Abraham Darby, and Ironbridge Gorge Museum Trust (seven industrial history museums including Museum of the River, Museum of Iron, Blists Hill Open Air Museum, Coalport China Museum)
Industries iron founding, agriculture, dairy farming, food processing, confectionery, audio and tape manufacture, electronic tools and equipment, vehicle parts, plastics, clothing manufacture, information technology
Population (1995) 144,600.

Telford, Thomas (1757–1834)

Scottish civil engineer. He opened up northern Scotland by building roads and waterways. He constructed many aqueducts and canals, including the Caledonian Canal (1802–23), and erected the Menai road suspension bridge between Wales and Anglesey 1819–26, a type of structure scarcely tried previously in the UK. In Scotland he constructed over 1,600 km/1,000 mi of road and 1,200 bridges, churches, and harbours.

In 1786, Telford was appointed official surveyor to the county of Shropshire. There he built three bridges over the River Severn, among other structures. He also rebuilt many Roman roads to meet the need for faster travel.

As engineer to the Ellesmere Canal Company from 1793, Telford was responsible for the building of aqueducts over the Ceirog and Dee valleys in Wales, using a new method of construction consisting of troughs made from cast-iron plates and fixed in masonry.

Tempest, The

Romantic drama by William ◊Shakespeare, first performed in 1611–12, in London. Prospero, usurped as Duke of Milan by his brother Antonio, lives on a remote island with his daughter Miranda and Caliban, a deformed creature. Prospero uses magic to shipwreck Antonio and his party on the island and, with the help of the spirit Ariel, regains his dukedom.

Temple Bar

Former western gateway of the City of London, between Fleet Street and the Strand (site marked by a stone griffin); the heads of traitors were formerly displayed above it on spikes. It was rebuilt by Christopher Wren in 1672, and moved to Theobald's Park, Hertfordshire, in 1878.

tenant farming

System whereby farmers rent their holdings from a landowner in return for the use of agricultural land.

In 19th-century Britain, most farmland was organized into landed estates containing tenanted farms. A marked change began after World War I when, owing to the agricultural depression, many landowners sold off all or part of their estates, often to the sitting tenant farmers. Although in 1950 50% of the country's farms were still rented, the current figure is less than 25%.

Tenby, Welsh Dinbych-y-pysgod

Coastal resort in Pembrokeshire, southwest Wales, 15 km/9 mi east of Pembroke; population (1991) 5,600. It is situated on a narrow promontory jutting out into Carmarthen Bay. By the late 15th century Tenby was a prosperous small port. Part of the castle and most of the 13th-century town walls still exist.

Tenniel, John (1820–1914)

English illustrator and cartoonist. He is known for his cartoons for *Punch* magazine and for his illustrations for Lewis Carroll's *Alice's Adventures in Wonderland* (1865) and *Through the Looking-Glass* (1872). He was knighted in 1893.

tennis, or lawn tennis

Racket-and-ball game invented towards the end of the 19th century, derived from real tennis. See chronology on page 880 for some key dates in tennis, and also ◊sport for feature on Britain's contribution to modern sport.

Although played on different surfaces (grass, wood, shale, clay, concrete), it is also called 'lawn tennis'. The aim of the two or four players is to strike the ball into the prescribed area of the court, with oval-headed rackets (strung with gut or nylon), in such a way that it cannot be returned. Until the mid-1970s, tennis rackets were made from wood or moulded from aluminium. In 1976, the Prince racket, made from sandwiched layers of aluminium and glass fibre, doubled the racket area to 839 sq cm/130 sq in. Today, rackets are made from graphite and glass fibre.

Major events include the annual All England Tennis Club championships (originating in 1877), an open event for players of both sexes at ◊Wimbledon, one of the four **Grand Slam** events; the others are the US Open, the French Championships, and the Australian Championships.

Tennis was introduced by Major Walter Clopton Wingfield at a Christmas party at Nantclwyn, Wales, in 1873. His game was then called 'Sphairistike'. The game is won by those first winning four points (called 15, 30, 40, game), unless both sides reach 40 (deuce), when two consecutive points are needed to win. A set is won by winning six games with a margin of two over opponents, though a tie-break system operates, that is at six games to each side (or in some cases eight) except in the final set. A match lasts a maximum of five sets for men, three for women.

Tennis in Britain: Some Key Dates

1529–30 A real (or royal) tennis court, the oldest still in existence in England, is built at Hampton Court Palace near London. Real tennis courts were usually a covered courtyard.

1873 The British major Walter Clopton Wingfield invents the game of 'Sphairistiké', a direct precursor of lawn tennis, largely based on real tennis, squash, and badminton. The game becomes known as lawn tennis or tennis-on-the-lawn, and his rules for the game, as revised by the Marylebone Cricket Club, form the basis of the code drafted in 1877 by the All England Croquet and Lawn Tennis Club for the first Wimbledon tournament.

5–19 July 1884 At the Wimbledon tennis championships in London, the British player Maud Watson wins the first ever women's singles event and James and William Renshaw, also from Britain, win the first ever men's doubles.

13 July 1886 The British tennis player William Renshaw wins the men's singles at the Wimbledon championships for the sixth successive year, a feat that has never been equalled.

6 July 1887 The British tennis player Lottie Dod, aged 15 years and 8 months, wins the women's singles at the Wimbledon championships.

1888 The Lawn Tennis Association is established in Britain. It is the governing body for the game in England, Scotland, and Wales, and also serves as the international ruling body until the formation of the International Lawn Tennis Federation in 1913.

1895 Peter Latham, the English world champion at rackets since 1887, wins the real tennis world championship, a title which he holds until 1905.

23 June–4 July 1913 Women's doubles and mixed doubles events are held for the first time at the Wimbledon lawn tennis championships.

4 July 1914 The English tennis player Dorothea Lambert Chambers wins her fourth women's singles title in five years at the Wimbledon lawn tennis championships.

1922 The All England Lawn Tennis and Croquet Club moves from Worple Road, Wimbledon, London, to new premises in nearby Church Road. The newly built Centre Court has 9,989 seats and standing room for 3,600 spectators.

1934 British tennis player Fred Perry wins the men's singles titles at Wimbledon, the US, and the Australian championhips.

21 June 1937 The Wimbledon tennis championships are televised for the first time in the UK.

8 July 1961 In the first all-British women's singles final since 1914 at Wimbledon, Angela Mortimer defeats Christine Truman in three sets. Mortimer is also the first British winner of a singles title at the championships since 1937.

5 October 1967 The British Lawn Tennis Association abolishes the distinction between amateurs and professionals, paving the way for open competition.

2–27 April 1968 A month after the International Lawn Tennis Federation accepts open competition between amateurs and professionals, the world's first officially sanctioned open tennis tournament, the Hard Court Championships of Great Britain, is held in Bournemouth, Dorset. The English player Virginia Wade wins the women's singles.

4 July 1969 Ann Jones of Great Britain defeats Billie Jean King of the USA in three sets in the final of the women's singles at Wimbledon; she is the first British winner of the title since Angela Mortimer in 1961.

1 July 1977 The English tennis player Virginia Wade wins the women's singles title at the Centenary Wimbledon Tennis Championships.

12 December 1982 Virginia Wade becomes the first woman to be elected to the All England Lawn Tennis Club.

25 June–8 July 1984 Total prize money at the Wimbledon tennis championships exceeds £1 million for the first time.

7 July 1984 Georgina Clark becomes the first woman to umpire a final on the centre court at Wimbledon.

20 June–3 July 1988 For the first time at the Wimbledon tennis championships, no player uses a wooden racquet.

21 June–4 July 1993 Prize money at Wimbledon reaches the £5 million mark for the first time.

1 July 1996 The English tennis player Tim Henman becomes the first Briton to reach the quarter finals of the men's singles at Wimbledon since Roger Taylor in 1973.

7 September 1997 Patrick Rafter of Australia defeats Britain's Greg Rusedski in the final of the men's singles tournament at the US Open tennis championships. Rusedski is the first Briton to reach a Grand Slam final since 1936.

Tennyson, Alfred, 1st Baron Tennyson (1809–1892)

English poet. He was poet laureate from 1850 to 1892. His verse has a majestic, musical quality, and few poets have surpassed his precision and delicacy of language. His works include 'The Lady of Shalott' (1833), 'The Lotus Eaters' (1833), 'Ulysses' (1842), 'Break, Break, Break' (1842), and 'The Charge of the Light Brigade' (1854); the longer narratives *Locksley Hall* (1832) and *Maud* (1855); the elegy *In Memoriam* (1850); and a long series of poems on the Arthurian legends, *The Idylls of the King* (1859–89).

Tennyson's poetry is characterized by a wide range of interests; an intense sympathy with the deepest feelings and aspirations of humanity; an exquisite sense of beauty; and a marvellous power of vivid and minute description, often

TENNYSON, ALFRED *A portrait of the English poet by the Swedish photographer Oscar Gustav Rejlander. Tennyson became poet laureate in 1850 and is admired for the lyrical quality of his work. His preference for narrative and epic form is demonstrated in such works as 'The Lotus Eaters' and 'Morte D'Arthur'. Corbis*

achieved by a single phrase, and heightened by the perfect matching of sense and sound.

At Cambridge, Tennyson won the chancellor's medal for English verse (1829), and the following year he produced a volume of *Poems Chiefly Lyrical*, containing some verse of great promise. In 1930 he toured Europe with Arthur Hallam, and the impressions he gained inspired many of his works. *The Princess* (1847), a serio-comic epic containing some of his finest lyrical poems, was his first popular success, running through five editions in six years. He was made a peer in 1884.

Terrence Higgins Trust

Charity established in 1983 that provides services for people living with HIV and AIDS. It has a network of volunteers and runs a helpline.

Territorial Army

See ◊armed forces.

Terry, (Alice) Ellen (1847–1928)

English actress. She was leading lady to Henry ◊Irving from 1878. She excelled in Shakespearean roles, such as Ophelia in *Hamlet*. She was a correspondent of longstanding with the dramatist George Bernard Shaw. She was awarded the GCBE in 1925.

Terry, (John) Quinlan (1937–)

English Post-Modernist architect. He works in a Neo-Classical idiom. His projects include country houses, for example Merks Hall, Great Dunmow, Essex (1982), and the larger-scale riverside project at Richmond, London (commissioned 1984).

Terry-Thomas stage name of Thomas Terry Hoar Stevens (1911–1990)

English film comedy actor. He portrayed upper-class English fools and cads in such films as *I'm All Right Jack* (1959), *It's a Mad, Mad, Mad, Mad World* (1963), and *How to Murder Your Wife* (1965).

Terylene

Trade name for a synthetic polyester fibre produced by the chemicals company ICI. It is made by polymerizing ethylene glycol and terephthalic acid. Cloth made from Terylene keeps its shape after washing and is hard-wearing.

Terylene was the first wholly synthetic fibre invented in Britain. It was created by the chemist J R Whinfield of Accrington in 1941. In 1942 the rights were sold to ICI (Du Pont in the USA) and bulk production began in 1955. Since 1970 it has been the most widely produced synthetic fibre, often under the generic name polyester. In 1989 8.4 million tonnes were produced, constituting over 50% of world synthetic fibre output.

Tesco

British supermarket chain founded by Jack Cohen (1898–1979) in 1931 in London. The name was a combination of Cohen's name and that of his supplier, T E S Stockwell. In 1998 the chain had 600 stores and 160,000 staff.

TESSA, acronym for tax-exempt special savings account

Scheme, introduced in 1991, to encourage longer-term savings by making interest tax-free on deposits of up to £9,000 over five years.

Test Act

Act of Parliament passed in England in 1673, more than 100 years after similar legislation in Scotland, requiring holders of public office to renounce the doctrine of transubstantiation and take the sacrament in an Anglican church, thus excluding Catholics, Nonconformists, and non-Christians from office. Its clauses were repealed in 1828–29. Scottish tests were abolished in 1889. In Ireland the Test Act was introduced in 1704 and English legislation on oaths of allegiance and religious declarations were made valid there in 1782. All these provisions were abolished in 1871.

The University Test Act of 1871 abolished the theological test required for the MA degree and for Oxford University and College offices.

Test match

Sporting contest between two nations, the most familiar being those played between the nine nations that play Test cricket

(England, Australia, West Indies, India, New Zealand, Pakistan, South Africa, Sri Lanka, and Zimbabwe). Test matches can also be found in Rugby League and Rugby Union. A cricket Test match lasts a maximum of five days and a Test series usually consists of four to six matches. The first cricket Test match was between Australia and England in Melbourne, Australia, 1877.

Tewkesbury

Market town in Gloucestershire, southwest England, between Cheltenham and Worcester; population (1991) 67,700. It is situated on the River Avon close to the point where it joins the Severn, 16 km/10 mi northeast of Gloucester. It is an agricultural centre. Its abbey church, begun in 1092, was part of a Benedictine abbey erected here on an Anglo-Saxon foundation.

Tewkesbury was settled in Roman times and in 1087 was a borough and market. The 'Bloody Meadow' on the southern side of the town was the site of the Battle of Tewkesbury in the Wars of the Roses.

Monuments in the abbey church include the Beauchamp Chantry (1422) and the tomb of Hugh Le Despenser, Earl of Winchester (died 1349). Prince Edward, son of Henry VI, is reputed to be buried under the tower. A grammar school was founded in Tewkesbury in the 16th century. In Tudor times the town produced mustard. Mrs Craik's novel *John Halifax, Gentleman* (1856) is set in Tewkesbury.

Tey, Josephine

See Elizabeth ◊Mackintosh.

Thackeray, William Makepeace (1811–1863)

English novelist and essayist. He was a regular contributor to *Fraser's Magazine* and *Punch*. His first novel was ◊ *Vanity Fair* (1847–48), significant for the breadth of its canvas as well as for the depth of the characterization. This was followed by *Pendennis* (1848), *Henry Esmond* (1852) (and its sequel *The Virginians*, 1857–59), and *The Newcomes* (1853–55), in which Thackeray's tendency to sentimentality is most marked.

Other works include *The Book of Snobs* (1848) and the fairy tale *The Rose and the Ring* (1855).

Thames

River in south England, flowing through London; length 338 km/210 mi. The longest river in England, it rises in the Cotswold Hills above Cirencester and is tidal as far as Teddington. Below London there is protection from flooding by means of the ◊Thames barrier. The headstreams unite at Lechlade.

Tributaries from the north are the Windrush, Evenlode, Cherwell, Thame, Colne, Lea, and Roding; and from the south, the Kennet, Loddon, Wey, Mole, Darent, and Medway. Around Oxford the river is sometimes poetically called the **Isis**. The construction of a 11-km/7-mi flood alleviation channel between Maidenhead and Eton was approved in 1994.

Source, course, and estuary

The Thames rises near Cirencester in the Cotswold Hills and follows a course of 330 km/205 mi to the ◊Nore, where it flows into the North Sea. At Gravesend, the head of the estuary, it has a width of 1 km/0.6 mi, gradually increasing to 16 km/10 mi at the Nore. Lying some 5 km/3 mi southwest of the Nore is the mouth of the Medway estuary, at the head of which lie Chatham with important naval dockyards, Gillingham, and Rochester. Gravesend on the south bank of the river, some 40 km/25 mi from the Nore, developed at a point where vessels used to await the turn of the tide. Tidal waters reach Teddington, 100 km/62 mi from its mouth, where the first lock from the sea (except for the tidal lock at Richmond) is located. There are in all 47 locks, St John's Lock, Lechlade, being nearest the source.

The London Thames

The normal rise and fall of the tide is from 4.5 m/15 ft to 7 m/23 ft at London Bridge and from 4 m/13 ft to 6 m/20 ft at Tilbury. Until Tower Bridge was built, London Bridge was the lowest in the course; the reach between these two bridges is known as the 'Pool of London'. Tilbury, Fort and Docks, important as the main London container terminal, lies opposite Gravesend on the northern bank. At Woolwich, some 30 km/19 mi above Tilbury, is the arsenal; Greenwich, a little farther upriver, has the Royal Naval College. Between Tilbury and London Bridge (some 40 km/ 25 mi upstream) stretches the London dock

THACKERAY, WILLIAM MAKEPEACE *British novelist, William Makepeace Thackeray, photographed in 1862. His great contemporary Anthony Trollope wrote of him: 'Among all our novelists his style is the purest, as to my ear it is also the most harmonious. The reader, without labour, knows what he means, and knows all that he means.' Corbis*

System (see also ◊Docklands. The Thames has been frozen over at various times, the earliest recorded occasion being 1150.

The embankments of the Thames in London were the work of Joseph Bazalgette (1819–1891), chief engineer of the Metropolitan Board of Works. The Albert Embankment on the south side was completed in 1869, the Victoria Embankment from Westminster to Blackfriars in 1870, and the Chelsea Embankment from the Royal Hospital to Battersea Bridge in 1874. In January 1949 work was started on a new embankment, designed by J Rawlinson, chief engineer of the former London County Council, on the south side from County Hall to Waterloo Bridge. These embankments were raised after 1974. There are walkways (formerly towpaths) from Teddington to Cricklade.

The Port of London Authority is responsible for the control and conservation of the river below Teddington. Above Teddington the Environment Agency is the responsible authority; there is some barge traffic on this stretch of the river. The Thames is of great importance to the water supply of London, partly because the many springs in the chalk usually maintain a steady flow in summer. Salmon returned to the Thames in 1974.

London bridges

The river is spanned by 20 road and 9 rail bridges between Hampton Court and the Tower of London. These include Tower Bridge (which has a drawbridge mechanism to enable large vessels to pass) and a suspension bridge at Hammersmith. The Queen Elizabeth II Bridge, opened in 1991, joins the counties of Essex and Kent. The Millennium Bridge, a footbridge linking St Paul's Cathedral to the new Tate Gallery on the south bank of the Thames, is to be built by May 2000; its designers are sculptor Anthony Caro and architect Norman Foster.

THAMES *Swans on the River Thames. Swans throughout Britain came to be regarded as royal property in around 1100, but some birds on the Thames were granted to two city livery companies, the Vintners and the Dyers. They still catch and mark their quota of swans in an ancient annual ceremony that takes place on the river between Sunbury and Abingdon and is known as 'swan-upping'. Corel*

London tunnels

The chief tunnels under the Thames are the Thames Tunnel, completed by Marc Isambard Brunel in 1843, now used by the East London Line of the London Underground; the Blackwall Tunnel (1897) from East India Dock Road to East Greenwich, the Rotherhithe Tunnel (1918) from Shadwell to Rotherhithe, and the Dartford tunnel completed in 1963.

Upstream

There are regular boats from Kingston to Folly Bridge, Oxford, during the summer. There is some beautiful scenery along this part of the river, for example at Cliveden, Cookham, Sonning, and Pangbourne. There are fine bridges at Richmond, Hampton Court, Chertsey, Maidenhead, and Shillingford. Henley, Wallingford, Dorchester, Abingdon, Eton, and Windsor are attractive. Along the 80 km/50 mi from its source beneath a tree in 'Trewsbury Mead' to Oxford, the Thames glides through meadows, its course interrupted only by the small towns of Lechlade and Cricklade and the pretty stone-built hamlets of Kelmscott and Ashton Keynes. In these upper reaches there are two medieval bridges, New Bridge and Radcot Bridge. Motor launches can reach Lechlade; beyond that point it is possible to canoe up to Cricklade, but the final 16 km/10 mi to the source of the Thames is best done on foot. One particularly attractive section is the steep-sided valley through the chalk hills between Goring and Reading, known as the Goring Gap.

Thames barrier

Movable barrier built across the River Thames at Woolwich, London, as part of the city's flood defences. Completed in 1982, the barrier comprises curved flood gates which are rotated 90° into position from beneath the water to form a barrier when exceptionally high tides are expected. It is 520 m/1,706 ft long, with steel gates 20 m/66 ft high.

Thames Tunnel

Tunnel extending 365 m/1,200 ft under the River Thames, London, linking Rotherhithe with Wapping; the first underwater tunnel in the world. It was designed by Marc Isambard Brunel and was completed in 1843. Originally intended as a road tunnel, it remained a pedestrian tunnel, for lack of funds, until the 1860s, when it was converted into a railway tunnel for the East London Railway. Today it carries underground trains.

Thanet, Isle of

Northeast corner of Kent, southeast England, bounded by the North Sea at the Thames estuary, and the rivers Stour and

Wantsum. It was an island until the 16th century, and includes the coastal resorts of ◊Broadstairs, ◊Margate, and ◊Ramsgate. Traditionally a cereal-growing area, it has now become a major area for the cultivation of vegetables. In addition to agriculture, industries include toymaking, signmaking, and plastics.

The main vegetable crops are cauliflowers and potatoes. There is a co-operative of local farmers. Much investment in the Isle of Thanet has been encouraged through attaining 'Assisted Area' status in 1993.

Ebbsfleet, near Ramsgate, is said to have been the landing place of the Saxons in AD 449, and St Augustine is said to have landed in the same area in 597. Manston, originally a US Air Force base, is now a civil airport.

Thatcher, Margaret Hilda, Baroness Thatcher born Roberts (1925–)

British Conservative politician, prime minister 1979–90. She was education minister 1970–74 and Conservative Party leader 1975–90. In 1982 she sent British troops to recapture the Falkland Islands from Argentina. She confronted trade-union power during the miners' strike 1984–85, sold off majority stakes in many public utilities to the private sector, and reduced the influence of local government through such measures as the abolition of metropolitan councils, the control of expenditure through 'rate-capping', and the introduction of the community charge, or ◊poll tax, in 1989. In 1990, splits in the cabinet over the issues of Europe and consensus government forced her resignation. An astute Parliamentary tactician, she tolerated little disagreement, either from the opposition or from within her own party.

Thatcher was the most influential peacetime Conservative prime minister of the 20th century. She claimed to have 'rolled back the frontiers of the state' by reducing income-tax rates, selling off council houses, and allowing for greater individual choice in areas such as education. However, such initiatives often resulted paradoxically in greater central government control. She left the Opposition Labour Party in disarray, and forced it to a fundamental review of its policies. Her vindictiveness against the left was revealed in her crusade against local councils, which she pursued at the cost of a concern for social equity. She was created a life peer in 1992. Her first speech in the House of Lords was an attack on the government's policies.

Margaret Thatcher was an unexpected victor in the 1975 leadership election when she defeated Edward Heath. As prime minister she sharply reduced public spending to bring down inflation, but at the cost of generating a recession: manufacturing output fell by a fifth, and unemployment rose to over 3 million. Her popularity revived after her sending a naval force to recapture the Falkland Islands in 1982. Her second term of office was marked by the miners' strike 1984–85, which ended in defeat for the miners and indicated a shifted balance of power away from the unions. In October 1984 she narrowly avoided an IRA bomb that exploded during the Conservative Party conference. Her election victory in 1987 made her the first prime minister in 160 years to be elected for a third term, but she became increasingly isolated by her autocratic, aloof stance, which allowed little time for cabinet debate. In 1986 defence minister Michael Heseltine resigned after supporting a European-led plan for the rescue of the Westland helicopter company. In 1989 Nigel Lawson resigned as chancellor when she publicly supported her financial adviser Alan Walters against him. The introduction of the poll tax from 1989 was widely unpopular. Finally, Geoffrey Howe resigned as deputy prime minister in November 1990 over her public denial of an earlier cabinet consensus over the single European currency.

Thatcherism

Political outlook comprising a belief in the efficacy of market forces, the need for strong central government, and a conviction that self-help is preferable to reliance on the state, combined with a strong element of nationalism. The ideology is associated with the former UK premier Margaret Thatcher, but stems from an individualist view found in Britain's 19th-century Liberal and 20th-century Conservative parties, and is no longer confined to Britain. Since leaving public office, Baroness Thatcher has established her own 'Foundation'.

Elements of Thatcherism, particularly the emphasis on controlling public expenditure and promoting opportunities for personal achievement, have been incorporated into the

THATCHER, MARGARET *Conservative politician and former prime minister, whose brand of Conservatism and European policy eventually provoked a crisis in her party and the government. The 1990 leadership challenge led to her resignation as prime minister, an office she had held since 1979, and her replacement as leader of the Conservative Party, a post she had held for nearly 16 years. United Nations*

THEATRE *English actor and director Laurence Olivier, unparalleled in British theatre in the 20th century, pictured here in the title role of a 1948 production of* Hamlet. *During a career that spanned nearly 60 years, Olivier played both Shakespearean and modern roles and was director of the Old Vic, London, the Chichester Festival Theatre, and the National Theatre, London, which he helped found. Corbis*

policy approach of the 'New Labour' government of Tony Blair, from 1997. However, it has sought to include a greater emphasis on social justice and assistance for the socially excluded, in what has been termed the 'third way'.

thatching

Method of roofing using reeds or straw, fixed to the roof timbers with hazel pegs and metal hooks. Heather and gorse may also be used. Thatch was the main roofing material in rural areas until the 18th–19th centuries, particularly in England and Wales, and remained the common finish for buildings constructed with ◊cob (sun-baked clay and straw).

Reed thatch, such as that found in Norfolk, has a sharply angled appearance with a heavy ridge. **Wheat straw** appears softer and more rounded. In Kent, Essex, and parts of Sussex it is traditionally laid with the heads and butt-ends randomly, then raked to give a flowing surface and ridged with criss-cross stitching. Alternatively it is arranged with the butt-end downwards to give a neatly cropped appearance, a method known as combed wheat reed, or Dorset or Devon reed after its areas of origin. In exposed regions, such as the Isle of Man and the Atlantic coast of Scotland, thatched roofs are held down by a lattice of ropes.

theatre

One of the earliest known forms of drama in Europe was the Christian **liturgical drama**. The earliest English example was written by Ethelwold, bishop of Winchester, in about 970. The staging of liturgical plays, which were sung, was governed by the physical restrictions of the church or cathedral in which they were performed. Visual symbols, such as the Christmas crib or everyday objects, were endowed with or used for their spiritual significance. More complicated liturgical narratives involved several different locations within the building at different positions down the nave. In such cases the spectators may have been placed in the side aisles.

Secularization of drama

Religious cycle-plays performed in English may have developed from liturgical drama, but their informal conventions, such as the scurrying of 'devils' around the acting area and into the audience, were probably influenced by popular performance techniques. Priests were forbidden to appear on a public stage after 1210, which led to a secularization of drama. Simple plays or farces were probably performed by itinerant secular actors on rudimentary booth stages.

Miracle play cycles, morality plays, and saints' plays conformed in general to the conventions of liturgical drama, but were performed in one of two ways: either in 'station-to-station' form, in which moveable pageant wagons, which were richly decorated and had sophisticated machinery, were used for performances at different locations in the town; or on stationary 'place-and-scaffold' structures, one for every scene, set up in churches and market squares.

> *State socialism is totally alien to the British character.*
>
> MARGARET THATCHER British Conservative prime minister.
> *The Times* 1983

Religious plays continued to be staged regularly in England until the end of the 16th century, while professional itinerant actors performed on stages erected against the hall-screens of Tudor halls and on curtained booth stages wherever they could find an audience.

Commedia dell'arte

This popular form of knockabout improvised comedy, which

emerged from Italy in the 16th century, quickly won widespread popularity. Performed by trained troupes of actors and involving stock characters and situations, it influenced the later genres of **harlequinade** (popular in the 18th and 19th centuries) and pantomime, a traditional Christmas entertainment in the 20th century.

Elizabethan theatre

The Elizabethan age witnessed a great advance in the development of drama in London, and saw the advent of the open-air ◊Elizabethan playhouse. William ◊Shakespeare was attached as actor/writer to the Lord Chamberlain's Men, a theatre company formed in 1594 and renamed the King's Men in 1603. Rather than being characterized by almost bare stages in soberly timbered playhouses, Elizabethan theatre was probably sumptuously decorated, with coloured architecture, and stages occupied by the same impressive scenic emblems used in contemporary court entertainments and religious and civic pageantry. A list of properties (dated 1598) survives in the papers of Philip Henslowe (died 1616), owner of the Fortune, Rose, and Hope theatres.

New ideas from Italy

During the 17th century Italian innovations such as perspective scenery, the use of elaborate machinery to create spectacular effects, and the proscenium-arch stage, were introduced in England. The architect Inigo Jones, who had trained in Italy, was employed by James I to design scenery for Court masques and plays in collaboration with Ben Johnson. Jones developed a system of flats moving in grooves in and above the stage, the backcloth being formed of two shutters which could open to reveal another elaborate scene behind.

At this time Jonson established the English 'comedy of humours', notably in *Volpone* (1606) and *St Bartholomew's Fair* (1614), which was to have a profound influence on Restoration drama.

Theatre banned

At the outbreak of the Civil War in 1642, Parliament banned all plays and theatre ceased for almost 20 years. On the reopening of the English theatres at the Restoration (1660), the tradition of Elizabethan open-air theatre was superseded by ◊Restoration comedy and other European-style drama performed in indoor playhouses. Women were finally admitted to the stage.

Developments in staging

Perspective scenery and proscenium stages were used, though at first a traditional apron stage protruded in front of the proscenium arch. The apron stage diminished in size gradually, although it did not disappear entirely until the middle of the 19th century. Towards the end of the 18th century there was a movement towards greater historical realism in costume and scenery.

19th-century melodrama

The influence of ◊Romanticism was responsible for the rise of English melodrama in the 19th century, with its emphasis on the imagination and emotions. Spectacle was also the keynote, and elaborate machinery was invented to reproduce such sensational effects as train crashes, horse races, and ships in storm-tossed seas. There were many technical advances: elevator platforms, sliding stages, and revolving platforms were developed.

Sentimental problem drama (as in the work of James Knowles) enjoyed great popularity in the middle of the century. The movement towards greater historical accuracy continued, and the pageantry of historical spectacles attracted large audiences.

Box sets and new lighting

The box set arrangement of painted flats joined together to form three walls, with realistic doors, windows, fireplaces, and other items, was introduced by Thomas Robertson (1829–1871) in his domestic melodramas of the 1860s.

During the second half of the 19th century, first limelight and then electric lighting were introduced. As a result, the darkened auditorium and the illuminated and realistically decorated stage became entirely separate entities. Naturalism in scenery, costume, and acting was the logical culmination of the lengthy movement in the 19th century towards a more convincing illusion of reality.

The 20th century

British theatre in the 20th century has been characterized by experiment and innovation, as much in staging methods as in artistic and intellectual terms. The early reaction against naturalism is linked with Gordon ◊Craig, who rejected illusion and advocated a theatre of romantic 'mood', in which dance and mime would be prominent. European influences included the work of French director Jacques Copeau during and after World War I, who placed emphasis on the art of acting. His productions used only lighting and a few key props to establish the setting, and his style heavily influenced that of Peter ◊Brook.

Repertory

Repertory theatres, running a different play every few weeks, proliferated throughout Britain until World War II, the ◊Old Vic in London being an example. Although the repertory

Top Ten Longest-Running West End Theatre Productions at February 1998

Rank	Production	Category	Years	Months
1	*The Mousetrap*	whodunnit	45	3
2	*Cats*	musical	16	9
3	*Starlight Express*	musical	13	11
4	*Les Misérables*	musical	12	4
5	*The Phantom of the Opera*	musical	11	4
6	*Blood Brothers*	musical	9	6
7	*The Woman in Black*	thriller	9	0
8	*Miss Saigon*	musical	8	5
9	*Buddy*	musical	8	4
10	*Grease*	musical	4	6

Source: Society of London Theatre

Some Important Regional Theatres

Birmingham Repertory Theatre Centenary Square, Broad Street, Birmingham; artistic director: Bill Alexander

Theatre Royal King Street, Bristol; artistic director: Andy Hay

Royal Lyceum Theatre Grindlay Street, Edinburgh; artistic director: Kenny Ireland

Citizen's Theatre Gorbals, Glasgow; artistic director: Giles Havergal

West Yorkshire Playhouse Playhouse Square, Quarry Hill, Leeds; artistic director: Jude Kelly

Haymarket Theatre Belgrave Gate, Leicester; artistic director: Paul Kerryson

Royal Exchange Theatre Upper Campfield Market, Liverpool Road, Manchester; artistic directors: Braham Murray, Greg Hersov

Nottingham Playhouse Wellington Circus, Nottingham; artistic director: Martin Duncan

Theatre Royal Royal Parade, Plymouth, Devon

Stephen Joseph Theatre Westborough, Scarborough; artistic director: Alan Ayckbourn

movement declined from the 1950s with the spread of cinema and television, a number of regional community theatres did subsequently develop.

1950s and 1960s

In 1953 Sandy Wilson's *The Boyfriend* marked a revival of the British ◊musical, a form subsequently taken up by Andrew ◊Lloyd Webber and Tim Rice, who produced a series of successful musicals from the late 1960s. The 1950s also saw the advent of the realistic dramas of the working classes, typified by *Look Back in Anger* written by John ◊Osborne, performed in 1956 by the ◊English Stage Company at the Royal Court Theatre. He, Arnold ◊Wesker, and Alan ◊Sillitoe, were dubbed 'Angry Young Men'. At much the same time, Harold ◊Pinter's long writing career was beginning.

In 1968 Edward Bond's *Early Morning* was the last play to be banned by the Lord Chamberlain, whose powers of censorship under the Theatres Act ended that year. From then laws relating to obscenity, blasphemy, and libel acted as a form of censorship.

1970s to the late 1990s

In counterpoint to the founding of the Royal Shakespeare Company and the opening of the ◊National Theatre, the 1970s saw the growth of **alternative theatre** functioning outside the commercial mainstream, usually in an anti-establishment or experimental style and in unconventional venues (converted warehouses and pubs, for example). The movement is also known as **fringe theatre**, a term originating in the 1960s from performances on the 'fringe' of the Edinburgh Festival. One facet of alternative theatre in the 1970s was **women's theatre**, performed by women and about women's lives.

Many of the playwrights who dominated the mainstream theatre in the 1970s and 1980s continued to write and be performed in the 1990s, among them Michael ◊Frayn, Tom ◊Stoppard, Alan ◊Ayckbourn, Peter ◊Shaffer, and Willy ◊Russell. Plays by John Godber (1956–), artistic director Hull Truck theatre company were especially popular. Musicals, however, tended to dominate London's West End, as the table below shows.

Staging in the late 20th century

Numerous theatres have been built which dispense with the proscenium arch and combine features associated with medieval and Elizabethan stages together with the facilities offered by modern technology. Alternative types of performing space include open stage, thrust stage, theatre in the round, and studio theatre. Theatres are often associated with a university or are part of a larger cultural centre. Staging conventions in commercial theatre which were once regarded as experimental are now regularly employed in a suitably adapted form, though traditional naturalistic settings are still much in evidence. See table opposite for the longest-running West End productions at February 1998; see table above for some important regional theatres.

Théâtre de Complicité

English touring company, founded in 1983. It originally specialized in small-scale theatre using mime techniques, but has expanded into larger-scale productions of classic texts and pieces devised specifically for the company, while still remaining characteristically innovatory and dynamic. Notable productions have included Dürrenmatt's *The Visit* (1988–89); a devised show *The Street of Crocodiles* (1992–94), based on the writings of Bruno Schulz, *The Three Lives of Lucie Cabrol* (1994–96), adapted from a short story by John Berger, and a new translation of Eugène Ionesco's *The Chairs* (1997–98).

Theatre Museum

Museum housing memorabilia from the worlds of the theatre, opera, ballet, dance, circus, puppetry, pop, and rock and roll. It opened in Covent Garden, London, in 1987.

theme park

Amusement park devised around a central theme or themes. The first theme park, Disneyland, opened in 1955 in Anaheim, California, USA, and features Walt Disney's cartoon characters; other Disney parks exist in Florida, Japan, and France.

Disneyland covers 30 hectares/74 acres. Walt Disney World (approximately 11,000 hectares/27,000 acres) opened in 1971 near Orlando, Florida; it was later enhanced by the creation of an adjacent Experimental Prototype Community of Tomorrow (EPCOT) centre (1982), featuring displays of advanced technology and re-creations of historical landmarks, and the Animal Kingdom (1998), one of the world's largest live-animal theme parks. Other ventures continuing the Disney theme include the Tokyo Disneyland (1983) and Euro Disney, near Paris (1992), which covers an area one-fifth the size of Paris. Features to be found in most theme parks include animatronics, robots which look like animals and people, all of which are programmed to perform lifelike movements and gestures to the accompaniment of a soundtrack (a technique developed by Walt Disney in the 1960s and first used at the World's Fair).

There are some 15 theme parks in the UK, attracting more than 15 million visitors a year. The three largest, all multi-themed, are Alton Towers in Staffordshire (1979), which attracted 2.7 million visitors in 1996–97, and Thorpe Park (1980) and Chessington World of Adventure (1987), both in Surrey.

Thetford

Market town in Norfolk, eastern England, between Cambridge and Norwich, at the junction of the rivers Little Ouse and Thet; population (1991) 19,800. There is light industry and printing. It was the capital of the Anglo-Saxon kingdom of East Anglia and the birthplace in 1737 of the radical political writer Thomas Paine.

Features

The town is situated on the edge of **Thetford Forest Park**. Castle Hill was the site of Iron Age earthworks. Relics excavated from the site of the Saxon town are displayed at the Ancient House Museum. The ruins of a Cluniac priory (founded in about 1103) stand on the banks of the Little Ouse, and there are remains of the Benedictine nunnery of St George, and of the monastery of the Canons of the Holy Sepulchre.

This Life

British television drama (1996–97) that followed the lives of five young professionals sharing a house. With its infidelities, office romances, major career changes, recreational drug use, and treatment of homosexuality, the series documented the varying fortunes of a predominantly privileged, legally-trained, twenty-something group of characters in both their work and private lives. The cast included Jack Davenport, Amita Dhiri, Andrew Lincoln, Daniela Nardini, Jason Hughes, and Ramon Tikaram.

thistle

Emblem of Scotland, appearing on pound coins. The history of the emblem and the identity of the species of thistle are confused. It is said to date from the 8th century, after Stirling Castle was saved from a Danish night assault when one of the attackers cried out as he trod on the plant, though it is not recorded as a royal emblem until the 15th century. The name Scottish or Scotch thistle has been given to *Onopordum acanthium*, also known as the cotton thistle. The association of this thistle with Scotland dates particularly from George IV's visit to the country in 1822, when a wealth of Scottish pageantry was generated.

Thistle, Order of the

Scottish order of ◊knighthood.

Thomas, (Philip) Edward (1878–1917)

English poet and prose writer. He met the US poet Robert Frost and began writing poetry under his influence. His essays and his poems (including 'Adlestrop') were quiet, stern, melancholy evocations of rural life. *Poems* was published in October 1917 after his death in World War I, followed by *Last Poems* in 1918.

Thomas, Dylan Marlais (1914–1953)

Welsh poet. His poems, characterized by complex imagery and a strong musicality, include the celebration of his 30th birthday 'Poem in October' and the evocation of his youth 'Fern Hill' (1946). His 'play for voices' *Under Milk Wood* (1954) describes with humour and compassion a day in the life of the residents of a small Welsh fishing village, Llareggub. The short stories of *Portrait of the Artist as a Young Dog* (1940) are autobiographical.

He was born in Swansea, the son of the English teacher at the local grammar school where he was educated. He worked as a reporter on the *South Wales Evening Post*, then became a journalist in London and published his first volume *Eighteen Poems* in 1934. He returned periodically to Wales, to the village of ◊Laugharne, from 1938, with his wife Caitlin (born Macnamara, 1913–1994), moving into the Boat House in 1949. Here he wrote most of *Under Milk Wood*, several major poems, and some short stories. He collapsed and died during a lecture tour of the USA.

The land of my fathers. My fathers can have it.

DYLAN THOMAS Welsh poet.
On Wales; quoted in *Dylan Thomas*, by John Ackerman

Thomas, R(onald) S(tuart) (1913–)

Welsh poet. His verse contrasts traditional Welsh values with encroaching 'English' sterility. His poems, including *The Stones of the Field* (1946), *Song at the Year's Turning* (1955), and *Laboratories of the Spirit* (1975), excel at the portrayal of the wild beauty of the Welsh landscape and the religious spirit that the harshness of life there engenders. His *Collected Poems* appeared in 1993.

Thomas, Sidney Gilchrist (1850–1885)

English metallurgist and inventor who, with his cousin Percy ◊Gilchrist, developed a process for removing phosphorus impurities from the iron melted during steel manufacture.

Thomas the Tank Engine

Best-known character in the 'Railway series' of books for young children by Rev W V Awdry (1911–1997). The series features a number of train characters who converse through their funnels and are supervised by the Fat Controller. The first of the 26 volumes in the series was *The Three Railway Engines* (1945), and others include *Gordon, the Big Engine* (1953), *Edward the Blue Engine* (1954), and *Tramway Engines* (1972).

A television series, followed by videos and a range of Thomas products, have contributed to the continuing popularity of the books.

The train characters in the *Thomas the Tank Engine* series form the basis of Andrew Lloyd Webber and Richard Stilgoe's musical *Starlight Express* (1984).

Thompson, Daley Francis Morgan (1958–)
English decathlete who broke the world record four times since winning the Commonwealth Games decathlon title in 1978. He won two more Commonwealth titles (1982, 1986), two Olympic gold medals (1980, 1984), three European medals (silver 1978; gold 1982, 1986), and a world title (1983). He retired in 1992.

Thompson, Emma (1959–)
English actress. She has worked in cinema, theatre, and television, ranging from song-and-dance to Shakespeare, often playing variations on the independent woman. She won an Academy Award for her performance in *Howards End* (1992) and another for her film adaptation (1995) of Jane Austen's novel *Sense and Sensibility*, in which she also played the role of Elinor.

In 1989 Thompson married the actor and director Kenneth ◊Branagh, and appeared in his films, including the role of Katharine in *Henry V* (1989), a dual role in *Dead Again* (1991), and as Beatrice in *Much Ado About Nothing* (1993); the couple separated in 1995. Away from Branagh, she has appeared in the film version of *The Remains of the Day* (1993), Alan Rickman's British film *The Winter Guest* (1997), and the US comedy *Primary Colors* (1998), in a role loosely based on Hilary Clinton.

EMMA THOMPSON *The English actress Emma Thompson, seen here in the film of* Howard's End *(1992) plays strong-willed characters on screen, and is admired for speaking her mind in real life. Named without her consent as a 'role-model' for young women in Britain in a government-sponsored initiative in 1998, she joked that she would behave outrageously to lose the dubious honour. Rex*

Thompson, Flora Jane (1876–1947)
English novelist. Her trilogy *Lark Rise to Candleford* (1945) describes Victorian rural life.

Thompson, Richard (1949–)
English virtuoso guitarist, songwriter, and singer. His work spans rock, folk, and avant-garde. He was a member of pioneering folk-rock group Fairport Convention 1966–71, contributing to albums like *What We Did on Our Holidays* (1968). With his wife Linda Thompson he made several albums, among them *Shoot Out the Lights* (1982). Later solo work includes *Rumor and Sigh* (1991). He continued to release critically acclaimed work in various musical contexts throughout the 1990s, including an ingenious renaissance/rock album with wind-player and early musicologist Philip Pickett in 1998, *The Bones of All Men*.

Thomson, George Paget (1892–1975)
English physicist whose work on interference phenomena in the scattering of electrons by crystals helped to confirm the wavelike nature of particles. He shared a Nobel prize in 1937. He was the son of J J ◊Thomson. Knighted 1943.

Thomson, J(oseph) J(ohn) (1856–1940)
English physicist. He discovered the electron in 1897. His work inaugurated the electrical theory of the atom, and his elucidation of positive rays and their application to an analysis of neon led to the discovery of isotopes. He was awarded a Nobel prize in 1906. His son was George Paget ◊Thomson. Knighted 1908.

Using magnetic and electric fields to deflect positive rays, Thomson found in 1912 that ions of neon gas are deflected by different amounts, indicating that they consist of a mixture of ions with different charge-to-mass ratios. English chemist Frederick ◊Soddy had earlier proposed the existence of isotopes and Thomson proved this idea correct when he identified, also in 1912, the isotope neon-22. This work was continued by his student Francis ◊Aston.

Thomson, James (1700–1748)
Scottish poet. His descriptive blank verse poem *The Seasons* (1726–30) was a forerunner of the Romantic movement. He also wrote the words of 'Rule, Britannia'.

Thorndike, (Agnes) Sybil (1882–1976)
English actress. George Bernard Shaw wrote *St Joan* for her. The Thorndike Theatre (1969), Leatherhead, Surrey, England, is named after her. She was created a DBE in 1931.

Thornhill, James (1676–1734)
English painter. Styling himself on Italian Baroque artists, he painted a number of large, decorative commissions. They included designs for the interior of the dome of St Paul's Cathedral, London, and the great hall at Blenheim Palace, Oxfordshire.

Thornhill studied under Thomas Highmore (died 1720), whom he succeeded in 1720 as serjeant-painter to Queen Anne, working on St Paul's and the princesses' apartments at Hampton Court. He set up a drawing school in Covent Garden, London, where William Hogarth was one of his pupils. Thornhill's son, also James, became serjeant-painter to George II.

THORP, Thermal Oxide Reprocessing Plant

Nuclear plant built at ◊Sellafield for reprocessing spent fuel from countries around the world, with plutonium as the end product. The plant began operating in 1994, despite a court action by Greenpeace.

Thorpe, (John) Jeremy (1929–)

British Liberal politician, leader of the Liberal Party 1967–76.

From a family of MPs, Thorpe first trained as a barrister, then became a Liberal MP in 1959 and party leader in 1967. A flamboyant campaigner, party fortunes advanced under his leadership, but he was forced to step down in 1976 following allegations that he had had a homosexual affair with Norman Scott, and that he had conspired in an attempted murder of his lover. He was acquitted of all charges in 1979, but lost his parliamentary seat at the general election.

Thorpe, Graham Paul (1969–)

English cricketer. A reliable and consistent left-handed batsman who began his Test career in 1993 with a century against Australia. At the beginning of the 1998 English season he had scored 3,303 runs in 49 Tests at an average of 42.34. He has played county cricket for Surrey since 1988.

Threadneedle Street

Street in the City of ◊London, England, running eastwards from the ◊Bank of England. The name of the street probably indicates that the property once belonged to the Needlemakers' Company. The dramatist Richard Sheridan gave the Bank of England the nickname 'the Old Lady of Threadneedle Street'.

At the east end where Threadneedle Street joins Old Broad Street is the Stock Exchange Building.

three-day week

The policy adopted by Prime Minister Edward ◊Heath in January 1974 to combat an economic crisis and coal miners' strike.

A shortage of electrical power led to the allocation of energy to industry for only three days each week. A general election was called in February 1974, which the government lost.

Thrust SCC

Jet-propelled car in which British driver Richard Noble attempted to break the sound barrier in 1996. *Thrust SCC* has two Rolls-Royce Spey engines (the same kind used in RAF Phantom jets) that provide 110,000 horsepower; it weighs 6,350 kg/13,970 lb, and is 16.5 m/54 ft in length. It was driven by RAF fighter pilot Andy Green to break the sound barrier in September 1997, at a record speed of 1,149.272 kph/714.144 mph. *Thrust 2* was an earlier version in which Noble set a world land speed record in the Black Rock desert of Nevada, USA, on 4 October 1983. The record speed was 1,019.4 kph/633.468 mph. See on page 892 for feature on the land speed record.

Thurrock

Unitary authority in eastern England, created in 1998 from part of Essex
Area 163 sq km/63 sq mi
Towns and cities Grays (administrative headquarters), Purfleet, Tilbury, Chadwell, St Mary, Stanford-le-Hope, Corringham, South Ockendon
Features located on north bank of River Thames; Holehaven Creek forms eastern border of authority; Tilbury Marshes; Mucking Marshes; Dartford Tunnel and Queen Elizabeth II bridge have northern approach through Thurrock; 17th-century Tilbury Fort, with three moats; Alexandra Lake; Lakeside shopping centre
Industries oil refineries, power station at west Tilbury Marshes, sand and gravel extraction, cement works, soap, margarine, timber products
Population (1995) 131,600

Thurso

Port in the Highland unitary authority, Scotland, 140 km/87 mi northeast of Inverness; population (1991) 8,500. It is the principal town of Scotland's north coast. The experimental nuclear reactor site of Dounreay, 14 km/8 mi to the west, was decommissioned in 1994 and replaced by a nuclear waste reprocessing plant. Ferries operate between Scrabster, on **Thurso Bay**, and Stromness in the Orkney Islands.

Dounreay was the site of the Atomic Energy Authority's first experimental fast-breeder reactor and a nuclear processing plant. Just offshore is an ocean swell-powered renewable energy generating station (OSPREY), the first commercial operation of its type in the world, which began producing electricity in 1995.

Thurso was the centre of Norse power on the mainland in the 11th century until it integrated with the rest of Scotland after the Battle of Largs in 1263. Its former industry of quarrying and exporting Caithness flagstones was in decline at the end of the 19th century, but has now been revived; in 1998 there were 10 working quarries.

Thynne

Family name of the marquesses of Bath, seated at Longleat in Wiltshire, England.

Tilbury

Port in Thurrock unitary authority, eastern England, on the north bank of the River Thames 42 km/26 mi downstream from London Bridge, opposite Gravesend; population (1991) 11,700. Greatly extended in 1976, it became London's largest container port. It includes **Tilbury fort**, originally built by Henry VIII, now in the care of English Heritage.

Tilbury fort
Built in 1539, the fort was rebuilt by Charles II in 1670–83 as a defence against the Dutch and French. The troops raised in anticipation of a Spanish invasion were reviewed here by Elizabeth I in 1588.
Docks
The docks were opened in 1886; they originally belonged to the London and East India Dock Company but came under the control of the Port of London Authority in 1909. From 1917 to 1929 the Port of London Authority extended the main dock 442 m/1,450 ft, enabling London to compete for the large ocean-liner traffic.

Till Death Us Do Part

British comedy series, originally broadcast by the BBC in 1966. The series follows the foul-mouthed, bigoted, West Ham Football Club-loving Alf Garnett (Warren Mitchell) as he does battle with the world, constantly in conflict with officialdom, his family, and the young. His long-suffering wife Else is played by Dandy Nichols, their daughter by Una Stubbs, and her boyfriend by Anthony Booth.

The series was the model for the equally popular US show *All in the Family* (1971–79). Other spin-offs include the films *Till Death Us Do Part* (1969) and *The Alf Garnett Saga* (1972), and the sequel series, also starring Warren Mitchell, *In Sickness and in Health* (1985–92).

Times, The

The UK's oldest surviving daily national newspaper, founded in 1785. Along with *The ◊Sunday Times*, it was bought in 1981 by News International from Lord Thomson, and by 1998 its circulation had grown to over 700,000. The paper also publishes *The Times Educational Supplement*, founded in 1910 as a monthly insert in *The Times* and published as a separate weekly in 1916; and the *Higher Education Supplement*, published separately in 1972. Covering education and teaching, their advertisements act as national notice boards for educational appointments. *The Times Literary Supplement*, founded in 1902, began to be published by Times Newspapers Limited in 1967; it is one of the leading literary weeklies in the UK.

In 1996 *The Times* and *The Sunday Times* became the first UK newspapers to publish comprehensive editions on the Internet and become leading online content providers.

The paper was founded as the *Daily Universal Register* by the publisher John Walter. Walter intended to establish himself as a book publisher by promoting a more economic method of typesetting, using units of words or groups of letters as well as single letters. The 'logographic' invention was a failure, but the news-sheet printed as an advertisement was a success, and on 1 January 1788 it was retitled *The Times*.

In 1803 the management, and in 1812 the ownership, passed to his second son, John Walter, under whom the paper maintained its independence and secured a leading position. In 1817 Thomas Barnes was appointed editor. He became the outstanding journalist of the century, and, as the champion of middle-class opinion, won for *The Times* the nickname of 'The Thunderer'. The third John Walter succeeded his father as proprietor in 1847. His editor, John Delane, claimed for the press a responsibility in national affairs that was demonstrated by the newspaper's successful agitation for the proper equipment and care of troops in the Crimea.

The competition of cheaper journals after the repeal of the Stamp Act of 1855 was severe, but John Walter refused to endanger the independence or inclusiveness of the paper. During the editorship of G E Buckle, *The Times* suffered a serious setback to its reputation when it mistakenly indicted Irish politician Charles ◊Parnell on the basis of a letter which turned out to be forged. In 1908 the paper was publicly sold; though the Walter interest was retained, the paper came under the control of Lord ◊Northcliffe. On Northcliffe's death in 1922 control was acquired by J J Astor (later Lord Astor), in association with the fourth John Walter. In 1966, in an attempt to increase circulation, *The Times* modernized its layout and news replaced classified advertisements on the front page. But these efforts failed to overcome the paper's financial difficulties and in 1967 it was taken over by Lord Thomson of Fleet who brought it under the control of Times Newspapers Limited, part of the Thomson organization.

Tinbergen, Niko(laas) (1907–1988)

Dutch-born British zoologist. He specialized in the study of instinctive behaviour in animals. One of the founders of ethology, the scientific study of animal behaviour in natural surroundings, he shared a Nobel prize in 1973 with Konrad Lorenz (with whom he worked on several projects) and Karl von Frisch.

Tinbergen investigated other aspects of animal behaviour, such as learning, and also studied human behaviour, particularly aggression, which he believed to be an inherited instinct that developed when humans changed from being predominantly herbivorous to being hunting carnivores.

Tintagel

Village resort on the coast of north Cornwall, southwest England. There are castle ruins, and legend has it that King ◊Arthur was born and held court here.

Formerly known as Trevena, Tintagel has been associated with King Arthur since medieval times. The castle ruins stand on Tintagel Head, a promontory 91 m/299 ft high on the Atlantic coast. It was a Norman stronghold from the mid-12th century, and the keep dates from the 13th century. Excavations have revealed evidence of a Celtic monastery on the site. It is thought that this may have existed from AD 350 to 850. The Old Post Office building dates from the 14th century.

Tintern Abbey

Ruined abbey in Monmouthshire, Wales, beautifully situated on the Wye River, 7 km/4 mi north of Chepstow. The ruins date from 1131, when Walter de Clare founded a Cistercian house which became one of the wealthiest foundations in England. The building was mainly erected between 1269 and 1287 by Roger Bigod, Earl of Norfolk, but work continued until 1320.

The chief remains are the ruins of the magnificent

Thrust: Breaking the Land Speed Record

The attempt to break the sound barrier in a car, and in doing so establish a new land speed record, began in 1991. The idea was sparked off in the mind of Richard Noble, the UK driver who had established a new record of 960.9 kph/600.6 mph, when Craig Breedlove – the US rival whose record Noble had just broken – announced that he intended to break the sound barrier. Noble recalled later: 'From that moment, I knew we had to mount a challenge. I could not let Breedlove beat me to what is the last great challenge to man.'

The history behind land speed record attempts
The history of the land speed record began on 18 December 1898, when Gaston Chasseloup-Laubat of France, driving an electric vehicle at Acheres, achieved 62.792 kph/39.245 mph. Since 15 September 1924, it has been held either by a Briton or an American – increasing 32 times from its value then of 234 kph/146 mph.

How the speed is measured
The measurement process has become increasingly precise: it now uses laser interferometry for timing and distance. Today, a valid attempt must be made twice over a measured mile. The two runs, one in each direction, must be completed within one hour; the final speed is the average of the two runs. For a jet-fuelled car such as Noble's, or Craig Breedlove's *Spirit of America*, that 'turnaround' time represented a considerable challenge, even though covering the distance itself takes only a few seconds.

Work begins on *Thrust*
In June 1994 work started on *Thrust SSC* ('SuperSonic Car'). By the time Noble had succeeded in his mission, it had cost £5 million. In many ways it was a revolutionary design, but the black *Thrust SSC* could hardly be called pretty. The Rolls-Royce jet engines, with their long tubular intakes and afterburners mounted either side of the needle-shaped body, came from a Phantom jet fighter. The steering was done by the rear wheels – a bit like a supermarket shopping trolley or forklift truck – the feasibility of which was first tested on a Mini. The car was driven by Andy
Green, normally a Tornado jet pilot with the UK Royal Air Force.

The team heads for Nevada
After testing during June 1997 in the Jordanian desert, the *Thrust SSC* team left for Black Rocks, Nevada, in September. They were short of cash – a call for £200,000 was made as the team left – but determined to break the record. Also heading there was Craig Breedlove, with the *Spirit of America II*. He too intended to break the record and go supersonic. The thin air of Black Rock's high-altitude setting, and its flat, dry desert provides the ideal location for speed attempts, even though the teams had to drive more than 160 km/100 mi every day from their lodgings to the site.

Craig Breedlove's many attempts and successes at breaking the record
Breedlove has a long history of setting the land speed record: he broke the 640 kph/400 mph, 800 kph/500 mph, and 960 kph/600 mph barriers. In October 1996 his car was hurtling across the Black Rock desert at 1,080 kph/675 mph, within seconds of setting a new record, when it crashed. Breedlove survived. The car didn't.

Craig Breedlove's 1997 version was powered by a single 48,000 horsepower fighter jet engine. In early testing he managed 549 kph/343 mph. But there was intense speculation among observers and engineers about whether Breedlove's car was stable enough. He admitted that if he was not confident enough to ride in it, he would try to pilot the car by a remote control link at up

Thrust SSC *The world land speed record was captured for Britain in October 1997 by the jet-powered car* Thrust SSC, *driven by Andy Green. So great was the speed of the car as it broke the sound barrier (Mach 1) during its record-breaking run that it pushed a shock wave ahead of it across the Nevada desert. Charles Ommanney/Rex*

cruciform church, the chapter-house, and refectory. The great west window is one of the finest examples of curvilinear tracery. The site was purchased by the crown in 1901.

Tippett, Michael Kemp (1905–1998)

English composer. With Britten, he became the foremost English composer of his generation. His works include the operas *The Midsummer Marriage* (1952), *The Knot Garden* (1970), and *New Year* (1989); four symphonies; *Songs for Ariel* (1962); and choral music including *The Mask of Time* (1982).

Tippett was very deliberate and highly self-critical, so that his works appeared in slow succession, but always showed closely concentrated craftsmanship and great originality. Amidst many contemporaries whose music could be described as static, one gains above all from Tippett's music a sense of movement.

Tiree

Island of the Inner Hebrides, in Argyll and Bute unitary authority, Scotland, 21 km/13 mi west of Mull and 2 km/1 mi

to 1,120 kph/700 mph – an idea that Noble insisted was dangerous.

Testing, checking, and repairing
Because the tiniest fault could be deadly at high speeds, the teams spent long hours checking and repairing any problems that turned up in low-speed testing. Such is the sophistication of modern cars that some of the 'repairs' involved computer code – controlling the suspension and engines – rather than anything physical. But after nearly a month, the *Thrust SSC*, driven by Green, was ready to make a serious attempt.

***Thrust* goes supersonic**
The attempt to break the record succeeded on 25 September when the car broke Noble's 1993 record of 1,013 kph/633 mph by the remarkable margin of 130 kph/81 mph, as Green drove the car at 1,120/700 mph on the first run and 1,165 kph/728 mph on the second for a 1,142 kph/714 mph average. The Queen sent her congratulations from Buckingham Palace. But the team had greater aims. The car had only been using 70 % of its power: they were convinced it could go supersonic.

The media were interested in what the experience was like. Green replied: 'The world looks the same at that speed. The mountains are still in the distance, the ground just moves past you a little faster.'

The training runs went on. Then on Monday 13 October the car broke the speed of sound on each run – but a parachute failure meant the car rolled more than a mile past its intended stopping place. It took 61 minutes to complete the second run – rendering it invalid as a record by 60 seconds, according to the international rules. The speeds were 1,222.669 kph/764.168 mph – or 1.007 % above the speed of sound – and 1,216.245 kph/760.153 mph.

But on Wednesday 15 October, during the first run at 9.07 a.m. local time, the car hit 1,214.932 kph/759.333 mph. The return speed of 1,225.774 kph/766.109 mph, completed in the time limit, set the new record at 1,220.354 kph/762.721 mph.

Congratulations for the team
Among the first to congratulate the team was the UK prime minister Tony Blair, who sent a message calling it 'a triumph in which the nation can share and take pride. This success is an excellent example of Britain at its best'.

Noble flew back to the UK, and welcomed the team when they returned with the car on 30 October. 'I think we were all actually quite pleased that it went so smoothly,' he said. And did he have any more plans – for 800 mph and upwards, perhaps? He refused to be drawn. 'We have got something planned but there's a lot of research to do first,' he replied.

BY CHARLES ARTHUR

southwest of Coll; population (1991) 800. An elevated area rises to the west, but the majority of its terrain is flat and low-lying, three-quarters of Tiree's 77 sq km/48 sq mi being less than 20 m/66 ft above sea level. The main settlement is Scarinish on the east coast.

Sand dunes and fertile machair (shoreline grasslands) cover a third of the island, and its dry, sunny climate encourages the farming of rich fodder crops and cattle stock, as well as a thriving tourist industry.

Island connections include an air service to Glasgow from Reef airfield, and ferry links to the islands of Coll, Mull, and mainland Oban.

Titanic

British passenger liner, supposedly unsinkable, that struck an iceberg and sank off the Grand Banks of Newfoundland on its first voyage 14–15 April 1912; estimates of the number of lives lost, largely due to the inadequate provision of lifeboats, vary between 1,503 and 1,517. In 1985 it was located by robot submarine 4 km/2.5 mi down in an ocean canyon, preserved by the cold environment. In 1987 salvage operations began.

In August 1996 salvage divers eased a 15-tonne section of the liner's steel hull away from the sea floor and raised it more than 2 mi/3.2 km from the seabed using flotation balloons. The high-tech expedition appeared to be on the verge of success when the balloons lost pressure and the liner returned to the ocean floor. By 1996, the cost of the project to raise the wreck stood at £3.3 million.

The results of the first ultrasonic scan of the front of the *Titanic*, much of which is buried in mud, showed that a series of six short slits was the only damage inflicted on the ship by the iceberg, and not, as has always been thought, a gaping 91-m/300-ft gash. The total area of openings was found to be only about 1.1 or 1.2 sq m/12 or 13 sq ft. The unexpected discovery, which emerged from an expedition to the seabed by a team of scientists and engineers in August 1996, will force a re-writing of the countless histories of the disaster. Although small, the gaps would have been roughly 6 m/20 ft below the water line. The high pressure would have forced the ocean through the holes fast enough to flood the ship with about 39,000 tonnes of water before it finally went down.

tithe

Formerly, payment exacted from the inhabitants of a parish for the maintenance of the church and its incumbent; some religious groups continue the practice by giving 10% of members' incomes to charity.

It was originally the grant of a tenth of all agricultural produce made to priests in Hebrew society. In the Middle Ages the tithe was adopted as a tax in kind paid to the local parish church, usually for the support of the incumbent, and stored in a special tithe barn; as such, it survived into contemporary times in Europe and Britain. In Protestant countries, these payments were often appropriated by lay landlords.

In Britain in the 19th century a rent charge was substituted. By the Tithe Commutation Act of 1836, tithes were abolished and replaced by 'redemption annuities' payable to the crown, government stock being issued to tithe-owners.

Toby Jug

Mug or jug shaped like an old man wearing a tri-cornered hat. Originally made in Staffordshire, England, it is reputedly named after **Toby Philpot**, a character in an 18th-century ballad.

TITANIC *British passenger steamer, the* Titanic *under construction. The* Titanic *sank on its first voyage with the tragic loss of over 1,500 lives. The ship was 265 m/882 ft long, weighed 45,000 tons, and was designed to carry 2,500 passengers and 860 crew. Efforts have been made to salvage the wreck from the seabed. Corbis*

Todd, Alexander Robertus, Baron Todd (1907–)

Scottish organic chemist who won a Nobel prize in 1957 for his work on the role of nucleic acids in genetics. He also synthesized vitamins B_1, B_{12}, and E. Knighted 1954, created baron 1962.

Todd was born in Glasgow and studied there and in Germany at Frankfurt. He was professor at Manchester 1938–44 and Cambridge 1944–71. He began his work on the synthesis of organic molecules in 1934 with vitamin B_1. In the late 1940s and early 1950s he worked on nucleotides; he synthesized adenosine triphosphate (ATP) and adenosine diphosphate (ADP), the key substances in generating energy in the body. He developed new methods for the synthesis of all the major nucleotides and their related coenzymes, and established in detail the chemical structures of the nucleic acids, such as DNA (deoxyribonucleic acid), the hereditary material of cell nuclei. During the course of this work, which provided the essential basis for further developments in the fields of genetics and of protein synthesis in living cells, Todd also devised an approach to the synthesis of the nucleic acids themselves.

Todd, Ron(ald) (1927–)

British trade-union leader. He rose from shop steward to general secretary of Britain's largest trade union, the Transport and General Workers' Union, a post he held 1985–92. Although a Labour Party supporter, he criticized its attitude toward nuclear disarmament.

Tolkien, J(ohn) R(onald) R(euel) (1892–1973)

English writer and scholar. To express his theological and philosophical beliefs, and as a vehicle for his linguistic scholarship, he created a complete mythological world of 'Middle Earth', on which he drew for his children's fantasy *The Hobbit* (1937), and the trilogy ◊*The Lord of the Rings* (1954–55), nominated in a UK bookselling chain's survey in 1997 as the 'greatest book of the 20th century'. His work developed a cult following in the 1960s and had many imitators. At Oxford University he was professor of Anglo-Saxon from 1925–45 and Merton professor of English from 1945–59.

Tolpuddle Martyrs

Six farm labourers of Tolpuddle, a village in Dorset, south-west England, who were transported to Australia in 1834 after being sentenced for 'administering unlawful oaths' – as a 'union', they had threatened to withdraw their labour unless their pay was guaranteed, and had been prepared to put this in writing. They were pardoned two years later, after nationwide agitation. They returned to England and all but one migrated to Canada.

Tom Brown's Schooldays

Novel by Thomas ◊Hughes, published in 1857. Through the experiences of Tom Brown and his friends East and Arthur, and the school bully Flashman, Hughes recalls his time at Rugby School under Thomas ◊Arnold, and presents a boarding school ethos combining Christian principles, patriotism, physical courage, and school loyalty. The book established a new tradition of school stories for boys.

Tom Jones, full title *The History of Tom Jones, a Foundling*

Novel (1749) by Henry ◊Fielding. The story tells of a foundling, Tom Jones, led astray by the impetuousness of his own nature. He has many adventures, which take him through scenes of uproarious 18th-century life, until he is finally redeemed by his own good heart and the love of the beautiful Sophia Western. A large, self-indulgent work, full of broad, high-spirited effects, it is one of the early great landmarks of the novel form.

Tonbridge

Town on the River ◊Medway in Kent, southeast England, between Tunbridge Wells and Sevenoaks; population (1991) 99,100. The town is a market centre and industries include printing, tanning, distilling, and the manufacture of bricks. The ruins of the castle, which has Norman origins, include a large 14th-century gatehouse.

The Medway is navigable up to here for pleasure craft. Tonbridge School was founded in 1553 by Andrew Judd, and George Austen, father of the novelist Jane Austen, was a teacher there.

Tone, (Theobald) Wolfe (1763–1798)

Irish nationalist, prominent in the revolutionary society of the United Irishmen. In 1798 he accompanied the French invasion of Ireland, was captured and condemned to death, but slit his own throat in prison.

Torbay

Urban area and unitary authority in southwest England created in April 1998 from part of the county of Devon
Towns and cities Paignton, ◊Torquay (administrative headquarters), Brixham
Features Tor Bay; English Channel coast; 23 beaches including Goodrington Sands; Oldway Mansion (Paignton) modelled partly on Versailles; 12th-century Torre Abbey (Torquay); replica of Drake's *Golden Hind* (Brixham); Abbey Mansion (17th/18th century); Paignton Zoo
Industries tourism, fishing, electronics, radio equipment, iron founding, horticultural products
Population (1994 est) 128,000.

Torfaen

Unitary authority in south Wales, created in 1996 from part of the former county of Gwent
Area 98 sq km/38 sq mi
Towns ◊Pontypool (administrative headquarters), ◊Cwmbran (the first new town in Wales)
Physical Coity Mountain in the north, River Afon Llwyd
Industries advanced electronics, automotive, engineering
Population (1996) 90,700.

Torness

Site of an advanced gas-cooled nuclear reactor 7 km/4.5 mi southwest of Dunbar, East Lothian, Scotland. It started to generate power in 1987 and is the largest technological project ever carried out in Scotland. It is open to the public.

> *My Lord, if we have violated any law it was not done intentionally. We have injured no man's reputation, character, person or property. We were meeting together to preserve ourselves, our wives, and our children from utter degradation and starvation.*
>
> George Loveless One of the Tolpuddle Martyrs. At their trial March 1833

Torquay

Resort in southern England, 41 km/25 mi south of Exeter; from April 1998, administrative headquarters of ◊Torbay unitary authority; population (1991) 59,600. It is a sailing centre and has an annual regatta in August. Tourism is very important. Torquay lies in the area known as the English Riviera on account of its mild climate and exotic plants, including palm trees.

The Domesday survey identifies part of the site of Torquay with the Norman period, recording that William I gave the manor of Cockintone (now Cockington) to a follower, Hostiarius. But by far the earliest link with the past is Kent's Cavern, in the Ilsham valley. A large and fine collection of the remains of extinct animals and Old Stone Age implements forms part of the exhibits at the Museum of the Torquay Natural History Society. In 1196 the Premonstratensians (a Roman Catholic monastic order) founded Torre Abbey, the ruins of which, together with the restored Monastic Barn and the Mansion House (dating in some parts from about the 15th century), are a conspicuous feature today on the seafront. The development of Torquay as a modern seaside resort dates back to the end of the 18th century when 'Tor Kay' or 'Tor Key' was no more than a cluster of fishermen's huts on the shore, with the village of Tor (or Torre) a short way inland. To deal with the threat of invasion by Napoleon, ships of the fleet constantly used Torbay as an anchorage, and houses were built on the shores of the bay for the accommodation of officers' families. Terracotta clay and marble are found near the town.

Torvill and Dean, Jayne Torvill (1957–) and Christopher Dean (1959–)

English ice-dance champions. They won the world title four

times 1981–84 and were the 1984 Olympic champions. They turned professional shortly thereafter, but returned to international competition in 1994 and immediately won the European Championship. They retired again from competitive ice dance after a bronze medal in the same year at the Olympic Games in Lillehammer, Norway.

Tory Party

The forerunner of the British ⟡Conservative Party about 1680–1830. It was the party of the squire and parson, as opposed to the Whigs (supported by the trading classes and Nonconformists). The name is still applied colloquially to the Conservative Party.

The original Tories were Irish guerrillas who attacked the English, and the name was applied (at first insultingly) to royalists who opposed the Exclusion Bill (see under Duke of ⟡Monmouth). Although largely supporting the 1688 revolution, the Tories were suspected of ⟡Jacobite sympathies, and were kept from power 1714–60, but then held office almost continuously until 1830.

Tostig

Anglo-Saxon ruler, the son of Earl Godwin and brother of ⟡Harold II. He was made Earl of Northumbria in 1055 by his brother-in-law, ⟡Edward the Confessor, but was outlawed and exiled because of his severity. He joined Harold Hardrada of Norway in the invasion in 1066 of northern England, but they were both defeated and killed the same year by Harold II at the Battle of ⟡Stamford Bridge.

Tottenham

District of the Greater London borough of ⟡Haringey.

tournament

In medieval England, martial competition between knights. Until the accession of the Stuarts to the English throne, chivalric contests were a feature of court life. Jousting and hand-to-hand combat took place, and a lord might dedicate himself to one of the ladies present. In the early part of his reign, Henry VIII participated in tournaments personally, much to the consternation of his counsellors.

Tovey, Donald (Francis) (1875–1940)

English music scholar, pianist, and composer. His music is classical in form and style; as a pianist he was for some time in the front rank with his interpretations of Bach, Beethoven, and Brahms. He was Reid professor of music at Edinburgh University from 1914, and conducted the Reid orchestral concerts there. He wrote several books, including six volumes of *Essays in Musical Analysis*, which were notes for performances by the Reid Orchestra.

Tower Bridge

Bridge over the River ⟡Thames in London, between the Tower of London and Bermondsey. Designed by Horace Jones and John Wolfe Barry, it was built in 1886–94. The central span between two towers consists of two drawbridges which can be raised to allow vessels to pass to and from the Pool of London.

Tower Bridge is the most easterly of the London Thames bridges. It has two high Gothic Revival towers 70 m/200 ft apart, and is connected with each bank by single-span suspension bridges.

Tower Hamlets

Inner borough of east Greater London. It includes the districts of Limehouse, Spitalfields, Bethnal Green, ⟡Wapping, Poplar, Stepney, and the Isle of Dogs. Large parts of the borough's dockland areas have been redeveloped for business and residential use.

Features Tower of London; the Isle of Dogs, bounded on three sides by the Thames; ⟡Docklands redevelopment area (including ⟡Canary Wharf); site of ⟡Billingsgate fish market; Limehouse, the main centre of 18th- and 19th-century shipbuilding, which in the 1890s became a focal point for

TOWER BRIDGE *Tower Bridge across the Thames stands just downstream of the Tower of London. Its Gothic towers are façades hiding the steel framework and opening mechanism. A distinctive landmark, it is sometimes misidentified; popular rumour maintains that, when US entrepreneurs purchased the old London Bridge in the 1960s, it was in the mistaken belief that they were buying Tower Bridge. Simon Hazelgrove/ Collections*

Chinese sailors working from West India Docks; Spitalfields, which derives its name from the priory and hospital of St Mary's Spital (1197), where silk weaving developed following the influx of Huguenot refugees to the area after 1685 (the industry collapsed in the mid-19th century); Spitalfields Market (formerly a fruit and vegetable market) is being developed by Norman Foster for LIFFE (London International Financial Futures Exchange); Bethnal Green Museum of Childhood (1872); Victoria Park (1840s)
Industries chemicals, matches, paints, glasswork, paper, foodstuffs, engineering, clothing; Canary Wharf is the focus for national newspapers: 12 papers are published and 8 printed in Tower Hamlets
Population (1991) 161,100
History Richard II met the Essex rebels at Mile End Green (now Stepney Green) during the Peasants' Revolt in 1381. In the 17th century, the name Tower Hamlets referred to the East London military district of 21 hamlets from which the Lieutenant of the Tower of London had the right to muster militia.

Historical landmarks

Settlement in the area dates from the time of the Romans. **Stepney** was a London suburb as early as the composition of the Domesday Book, when it had a population of about 800. The Royal Mint and the Tower of London both lay just outside the City of London and within the borough. Another early foundation was the Royal Hospital of St Katherine by the Tower, which, founded by Queen Matilda in 1148, has always had queens as its patrons. It was founded for the sick and elderly, and in the 1820s, when the site was used for St Katherine's Dock, it was moved to Regent's Park. In the 1950s it moved back to Stepney and is now located in Butcher Row, partly housed in an 18th-century merchant's house. The chapel still has medieval stalls and carvings. St Dunstan's church dates from the Middle Ages, and the manor house at Bromley from the 15th century. Ratcliff, a Stepney hamlet, has long been a dock area and it was from here in the 16th century that the explorers Frobisher and Willoughby sailed to Russia while searching for the northwest passage. Later this section of riverside became notorious for its rowdy public houses.

Wapping, an adjacent hamlet, was the site of execution docks, where people such as Captain Kidd were executed for crimes on the high seas. The Thames tunnel, built between 1824 and 1843, links Wapping and Rotherhithe. Blackwall docks were built in 1612–14, followed by the West India Docks in 1799–1802, the East India Docks in 1803–06, and Milwall Docks in 1868. The area of the West India and Millwall docks is a peninsula known as the **Isle of Dogs**. Ships were built here, one of the most famous being the *Great Eastern*, which was launched in 1858. The construction of Limehouse Cut in 1770 linking the River Lea and the Thames, and the Regent's Canal between 1812 and 1820, helped further the progress of industrialization.

Limehouse, an area adjacent to the docks, received the name from the lime kilns which were in use from the Middle Ages until the 19th century. Bow had a porcelain factory in the 18th century producing 'Bow China'. **Bethnal Green** was mostly farmland in the 18th century until, it became largely residential. Bells have been cast at Whitechapel Bell Foundry for over 400 years, and these hang in many famous churches including Westminster Abbey. The Liberty Bell, which was rung to mark the acceptance by the US Congress of the Declaration of Independence, was cast in Whitechapel in 1752.

Tower of London

Fortress on the bank of the River Thames to the east of the City of London. The keep, or White Tower, was built in about 1078 by Bishop Gundulf on the site of British and Roman fortifications. It is surrounded by two strong walls and a moat (now dry), and was for centuries a royal residence and the principal state prison.

Thomas More, Anne Boleyn, Catherine Howard, Lady Jane Grey, earls Essex and Strafford, Bishop Laud, and the Duke of Monmouth were among those imprisoned and executed at the Tower. Today it is a barracks, an armoury, and a museum. In 1994 the crown jewels, traditionally kept in a bunker in the keep, were moved to a specially designed showcase, the Jewel House, situated above ground level. In 1996 the collection of arms and armour formerly kept in the White Tower was moved to the new Royal Armouries Museum in Leeds.

Townsend, Sue (Susan) (1946–)

English humorous novelist and playwright. She is the author of the best-selling *The Secret Diary of Adrian Mole, aged 13¾* (1982) (adapted for the stage in 1985) and later sequels. Other novels include *Rebuilding Coventry* (1985), *The Queen and I* (1992), about a dethroned royal family in a republican Britain (also adapted for the stage, 1994), and the haunting tale *Ghost Children* (1997).

Townshend, Charles, 2nd Viscount Townshend (known as 'Turnip' Townshend) (1674–1738)

English politician and agriculturalist. He was secretary of state under George I from 1714 to 1717, when he was dismissed for opposing the king's foreign policy; and from 1721 to 1730, after which he retired to his farm and did valuable work in developing crop rotation and cultivating winter feeds for cattle (hence his nickname).

Townshend, Charles (1725–1767)

British politician, chancellor of the Exchequer 1766–67. The **Townshend Acts**, designed to assert Britain's traditional authority over its colonies, resulted in widespread resistance. Among other things they levied taxes on imports (such as tea, glass, and paper) into the North American colonies. Opposition in the colonies to taxation without representation (see ◊Stamp Act) precipitated the American Revolution.

Townshend, Pete(r Dennis Blandford) (1945–)

UK rock musician. He was a founder member of the ◊Who. His solo albums include *Empty Glass* (1980).

Townswomen's Guilds, National Union of

An urban version of the ◊Women's Institute. It was founded in 1929.

Towy, Welsh Tywi

River in Wales, rising in the Tywi hills between Ceredigion (Cardiganshire) and Powys; length 111 km/69 mi. It flows south, passing Llandovery and Carmarthen, and enters Carmarthen Bay at Llanstephan. Sailing, game fishing, and commercial cockle-fishing take place in the estuary.

Toynbee, Arnold (1852–1883)

English economic historian who coined the term 'industrial revolution' in his 'Lectures on the Industrial Revolution', published in 1884.

Toynbee Hall, an education settlement in the east end of London, was named after him.

Trade and Industry, Department of, DTI

Government department established in 1970, bringing together the Board of Trade, founded in 1786, and the Ministry of Technology, formed in 1964; it took over the responsibilities of the Department of Energy in 1992. Including agencies, such as the Patent Office, the departmeent employs more than 8,000 staff. The current secretary of state (from 1998) is Peter Mandelson, who has dispensed with the title president of the Board of Trade.

The department is responsible for administration of policies on international trade, industry, competition, industrial research and assistance to exporters.

Trade Descriptions Acts 1968 and 1972

Acts of Parliament which make it a legal offence for businesses to give false or misleading descriptions of goods or services for sale to consumers. For example, a glue described as being suitable for wood must be capable of gluing wood. Businesses which offend against the acts can be prosecuted and fined.

Tradescant, John (1570–*c.* 1638)

English gardener and botanist who travelled widely in Europe and is thought to have introduced the cos lettuce to England from the Greek island of that name. He was appointed gardener to Charles I and was succeeded by his son, **John Tradescant the Younger** (1608–1662). The younger Tradescant undertook three plant-collecting trips to Virginia in North America.

The Tradescants introduced many new plants to Britain, including the acacia, lilac, and occidental plane. Tradescant senior is generally considered the earliest collector of plants and other natural-history objects.

The Largest Trade Unions in the UK

Source: Labour Force Survey

Rank	1990		1995			
	Union	**Membership**	**Union**	**Membership**	**Male (%)**	**Female (%)**
1	Transport and General Workers Union	1,224,000	UNISON – The Public Service Union	1,355,000	28	72
2	General Municipal Boilermakers' Union	865,000	Transport and General Workers Union	897,000	81	19
3	National and Local Government Officers Association	744,000	General Municipal Boilermakers' Union	740,000	64	36
4	Amalgamated Engineering Union	702,000	Amalgamated Engineering and Electrical Union	726,000	94	6
5	Manufacturing Science and Finance Union	653,000	Manufacturing Science and Finance Union	446,000	69	31
6	National Union of Public Employees	579,000	Royal College of Nursing of the UK	300,000	8	92
7	Electrical Electronic Telecommunication and Plumbing Union	367,000	Union of Shop Distributive and Allied Workers	283,000	42	58
8	Union of Shop Distributive and Allied Workers	362,000	Communication Workers Union	275,000	81	19
9	Royal College of Nursing of the UK	289,000	National Union of Teachers	248,000	25	75
10	National Union of Teachers	218,000	National Association of School Masters and Union of Women Teachers	234,000	47	53

Trades Union Congress, TUC

Voluntary organization of trade unions, founded in the UK in 1868, in which delegates of affiliated unions meet annually to consider matters affecting their members. In 1997 there were 67 affiliated unions, with an aggregate membership of 6 million.

30% of the employees in the UK belong to trade unions (25% in the private sector, and 60% in the public sector). In September 1993 John Monks became the TUC's general secretary.

trade unions

Organizations of workers that exist to promote and defend the interests of its members. Trade unions are particularly concerned with pay, working conditions, job security, and redundancy. Four types of trade union are often distinguished: general unions, craft unions, industrial unions, and white-collar unions.

Trade-union members in a place of work elect a shop steward to represent them and their concerns to the management. Trade unions also employ full-time trade-union officers who tend to cover a geographical area. Top trade-union officials must be elected by a secret ballot of members.

Unions negotiate with employers over any differences they may have. Both parties may invite an outside body such as the ◊Advisory, Conciliation and Arbitration Service (ACAS) to conciliate or arbitrate in an industrial dispute. Alternatively, trade-union members may take industrial action.

History

Under the Trade Union Act of 1871 unions became full legal

TRADE UNIONS: CHRONOLOGY

1799 The Combination Act outlawed organizations of workers combining for the purpose of improving conditions or raising wages. The act was slightly modified in 1800.

1811 Luddite machine-breaking campaign against hosiers began; it was ended by arrests and military action in 1812.

1818 Weavers and spinners formed the General Union of Trades in Lancashire.

1824 The Combination Act repealed most of the restrictive legislation but an upsurge of violent activity led to a further act 1825. Trade unions could only bargain peacefully over working hours and conditions.

1830 The General Union of Trades became the National Association for the Protection of Labour; it collapsed in 1832.

1834 Formation of the Grand National Consolidated Trade Union, which lasted only a few months. Six agricultural labourers from Tolpuddle, Dorset, were convicted of swearing illegal oaths and transported to Australia.

1842 The 'Plug Plot' (removing plugs from boilers) took on the appearance of a general strike in support of a People's Charter.

1851 The foundation of the Amalgamated Society of Engineers marked the beginning of the 'New Model Unionism' of skilled workers.

1866 The 'Sheffield outrages' (attacks on nonunion labour) led to a royal commission. The Hornby v. Close case cast doubt on the legal status of unions.

1867 Amendments to the Master and Servant Act gave more scope for trade unions, and the royal commission recommended they be given formal legal status.

1868 The first Trades Union Congress (TUC) was held in Manchester.

1871 The Trade Union Act gave unions legal recognition.

1888 Beginnings of 'new unionism' and the organization of unskilled workers.

1901 Taff Vale case re-established union liability for damage done by strikes; this was reversed by the Trade Disputes Act 1906.

1909 Osborne judgements ruled against unions using funds for political purposes; this was reversed by the Trade Union Act 1913.

1918–20 Widespread industrial unrest on return to a peacetime economy.

1926 A general strike was called by the TUC in support of the miners.

1930–34 Union membership fell as a result of economic recession. The Transport and General Workers replaced the Miners Federation as the largest single union.

1965 The Trade Disputes Act gave unions further immunities.

1969 The TUC successfully stopped the Labour government white paper *In Place of Strife*.

1971 The Conservative government passed the Industrial Relations Act, limiting union powers.

1973–74 'Winter of Discontent'. Strikes brought about electoral defeat for the Conservative government. Labour introduced the 'social contract'.

1980 The Conservatives introduced the Employment Act, severely restricting the powers of unions to picket or enforce closed shop; this was extended in 1982.

1984 The miners' strike led to widespread confrontation and divisions within the miners' union.

1984–90 The Conservative government continued to limit the powers of trade unions through various legislative acts, notably the Trade Union Act of 1984 and a further extension of the Employment Act of 1988.

1998 The Labour government decided that employers had to recognize a union if at least 40% of the entire workforce voted in favour of union representation.

organizations. The TUC was for many years representative mainly of unions of skilled workers, but in the 1890s the organization of unskilled labour spread rapidly.

In 1926, the TUC called a general strike in support of the miners; this collapsed and after nine days, leaving the miners' union to continue the strike alone for a further six months. Under the Trade Disputes and Trade Union Act of 1927 general strikes or strikes called in sympathy with other workers were made illegal.

The period after World War II was marked by increased unionism among white-collar workers. From the 1960s onwards there were confrontations between the government and the trade unions, and unofficial, or wildcat, strikes set public opinion against the trade-union movement. Acts of Parliament in 1975 and 1976 increased the involvement of the government in industrial relations. ACAS was set up in 1975 to arbitrate in industrial disputes. In 1979 trade union membership in the UK peaked at 13.5 million, representing 54% of the workforce.

The Thatcher government, in the Employment Acts of 1980 and 1982, restricted the closed shop, picketing, secondary action, immunity of trade unions in respect of unlawful activity by their officials, and the definition of a trade dispute, which must be between workers and employers, not between workers. The Trade Union Act 1984 made it compulsory to have secret ballots for elections and before strikes. Picketing was limited to the establishment at which strikes were taking place. The Employment Act 1988 contains further provisions regulating union affairs.

A report drawn up by the Trades Union Congress (TUC) in February 1997 stated that union membership had dropped by more than 1.7 million since 1989 and stood at 7.3 million in 1995. The report blamed the drop on the decline in the manufacturing industry, more part-time and temporary jobs, high unemployment and a hostile political climate during the 1980s.

In May 1998 the Labour government announced that an employer would be required to recognize a union if a minimum of 40% of the total workforce vote in favour of union representation.

See chronology of unions in the UK (page 899), and list of the largest trade unions in the UK (page 898).

Trafalgar, Battle of

During the ◊Napoleonic Wars, victory of the British fleet, commanded by Admiral Horatio Nelson, over a combined French and Spanish fleet on 21 October 1805; Nelson was mortally wounded during the action. The victory laid the foundation for British naval supremacy throughout the 19th century. It is named after Cape Trafalgar, a low headland in southwest Spain, near the western entrance to the Straits of Gibraltar.

The British fleet consisted of 27 ships mounting 2,138 guns; the Franco-Spanish fleet consisted of 33 ships with 2,640 guns under Admiral Pierre de Villeneuve. The French were sailing in a loose line formation and Nelson divided his force into two parts which he intended to drive through the French line at different points. The manoeuvre was successful, Nelson's flagship *Victory* passing the stern of the French flagship *Bucentaure* and discharging its broadside at a range of 11 m/12 yd, causing 400 casualties, and other British ships used similar tactics of close-quarter gunnery. The battle commenced at about 12 noon, and at 1.30 p.m. Nelson was mortally wounded by a musket-shot. By 3 p.m. the battle was over, and the surviving French and Spanish ships were concentrating on escape. Of their number, 15 had been sunk, and of the 18 which escaped 2 were wrecked on 24 October and 4 taken by a British squadron on 3 November. The British lost no ships and sustained casualties of 449 killed and 1,242 wounded; French and Spanish casualties amounted to about 14,000.

Trafalgar Square

London square commemorating the victory of the British fleet, led by Admiral Nelson, over a combined French and Spanish force at the Battle of ◊Trafalgar. Its centrepiece is

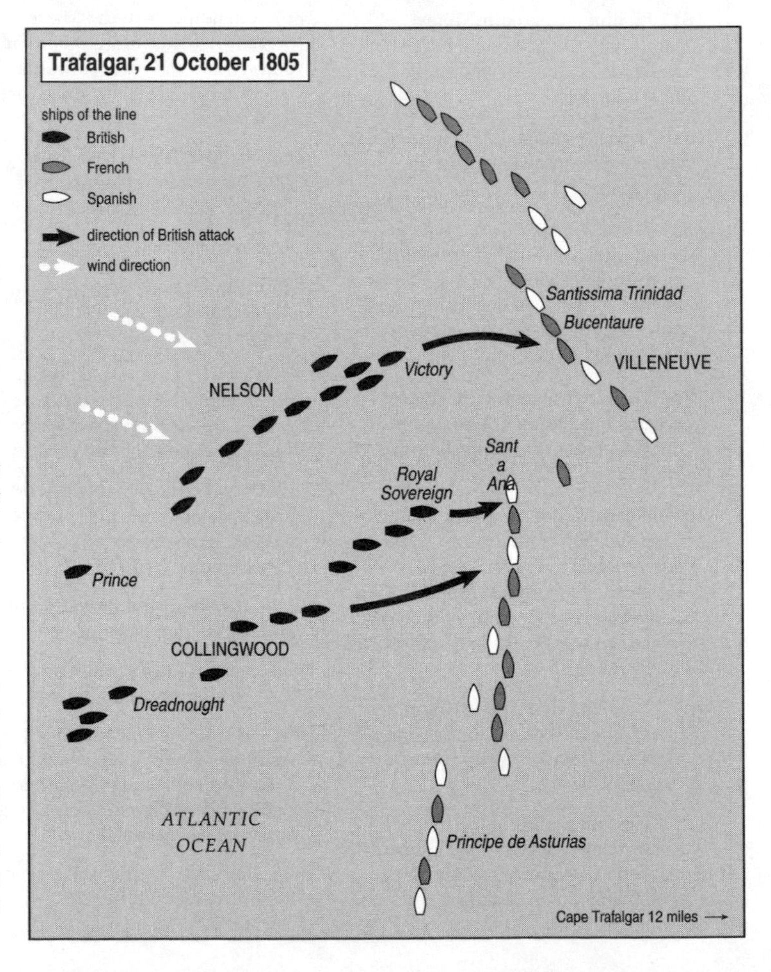

Nelson's Column bearing a statue by Edward Baily (1788–1867); four lions by Edwin Landseer recline at the base. The square and its fountains have become the London focus for New Year's Eve and other national celebrations.

Trafalgar Square is London's only metric square, laid out as one hectare.

Traherne, Thomas (*c.* 1637–1674)

English Christian mystic, religious poet, and essayist. His lyric poetry was not published until 1903, and his prose *Centuries of Meditations* until 1908.

Training Agency

Government-sponsored organization responsible for retraining of unemployed workers. Founded as the **Manpower Services Commission** in 1974, the organization has operated such schemes as the Training Opportunities Scheme (TOPS) (1974), the Youth Opportunities Programme (YOP) (1978), the Youth Training Scheme (YTS) (1983), and the Technical and Vocational Initiative (TVEI) (1983).

In the early 1990s the government set up Training and Enterprise Councils (TECs) to channel state funds for employment-related training. There are 79 TECs in England and Wales and 22 similar Local Enterprise Councils (LECs) in Scotland.

Trainspotting

Landmark film in recent British cinema history, released in 1995. Cementing the collaborative partnership of director Danny Boyle, screenwriter John Hodge, producer Andrew Macdonald, and actor Ewan ◊McGregor (who had all previously worked together on *Shallow Grave* in 1994), the film centres on a group of young working-class heroin addicts in Edinburgh. Experimental in its visual style, editing, and use of voice-over, the film fuses both comedy, drama, and realism. It is adapted from the novel of the same title by Irvine ◊Welsh. Other actors include Ewen Bremner, Robert ◊Carlyle, and Kelly Macdonald.

tramway

Transport system for use in cities, where wheeled vehicles run along parallel rails. Trams are powered either by electric conductor rails below ground or by conductor arms connected to overhead wires. Greater manoeuvrability is achieved with the ◊trolley bus, similarly powered by conductor arms overhead but without tracks.

Trams originated in collieries in the 18th century, and the earliest passenger system was in use in New York in 1832. Tramways were widespread in Europe and the USA from the late 19th to the mid-20th century after which they were phased out, especially in the UK and the USA, under pressure from the motor-transport lobby. In the 1990s both trams and trolley buses were being revived in some areas and are still found in many cities on the continent; in the Netherlands several neighbouring towns share an extensive tram network. Trams and trolley buses have the advantage of being nonpolluting to the local environment, though they require electricity generation, which is polluting at source.

Trams returned to the UK in 1992 after an absence of 40 years, when the Metrolink scheme in Manchester, connecting two commuter railways by 3 km/2 mi of track through the centre of the city, was completed. Another tramway was constructed in Sheffield, and around 40 other areas are considering plans.

Transport and General Workers' Union, TGWU

UK trade union founded in 1921 by the amalgamation of a number of dockers' and road-transport workers' unions, previously associated in the Transport Workers' Federation. With more than 900,000 members, it ranks behind the public employers' union, UNISON, as the second largest trade union in Britain. The current leader is Bill Morris (1938–).

transportation

Punishment of sending convicted persons to overseas territories to serve their sentences. It was introduced in England towards the end of the 17th century and although it was abolished in 1857 after many thousands had been transported, mostly to Australia, sentences of penal servitude continued to be partly carried out in Western Australia up until 1867. Transportation was used for punishment of criminals by France until 1938.

The first British convict ship to reach Austrlia arrived at Sydney Cove, New South Wales, in January 1788 with 736 convicts surviving the journey. The last convict ship to arrive in Australia was the *Hougoumont* which brought 279 prisoners to Fremantle, Western Australia, in 1868. In all, about 137,000 male and 25,000 female convicts were transported to Australia.

Most convicts went into private service under the assignment system. Misbehaviour was punished by flogging, working in government chain gangs, usually on road building, or by confinement in a special penal settlement such as was set up at Newcastle, later moved to Moreton Bay, Norfolk Island, and Port Arthur. Many convicts managed to escape to the bush, some becoming bushrangers.

Criticism of the convict system on various grounds, including its leniency and inefficiency in deterring crime in England, led to an inquiry by a select committee of the House of Commons in 1837 after which the British government decided to abolish assignment and stop transportation to New South Wales.

In the 1850s transportation to all the colonies (South Australia was never a convict settlement) ceased except in Western Australia which became the last Australian colony to receive convicts.

Transport, Department of, DOT

UK government department established in 1975, which merged with the Department of the Environment in 1997 to form the ◊Department of the Environment, Transport, and the Regions.

Travers, Ben(jamin) (1886–1980)

English dramatist. He wrote (for actors Tom Walls, Ralph Lynn, and Robertson Hare) the 'Aldwych farces' of the 1920s, so named from the London theatre in which they were played. They include *A Cuckoo in the Nest* (1925) and *Rookery Nook* (1926).

Travers, Morris William (1872–1961)

English chemist who, with Scottish chemist William ◊Ramsay, between 1894 and 1908 first identified what were called the inert or noble gases: krypton, xenon, and radon.

treadmill

Wheel turned by foot power (often by a domesticated animal) and used, for instance, to raise water from a well or grind grain.

The human treadmill was used as a form of labour discipline in British prisons during the 19th century. In 1818, William Cubitt (1785–1861) introduced a large cylinder to be operated by convicts treading on steps on its periphery. Such treadmills went out of use early in the 20th century.

Treasure Island

Adventure story for children by R L ◊Stevenson, published in 1883. Jim Hawkins, the story's narrator, sets sail with Squire Trelawney in the *Hispaniola*, armed with a map showing the location of buried treasure. Attempts by the ship's crew of pirates, including Long John Silver, to seize the map are foiled after much fighting and the squire finds the treasure.

Treasury

Government department established in 1612 to collect and manage the public revenue and coordinate national economic policy. Technically, the prime minister is the first lord of the Treasury, but the chancellor of the Exchequer is the acting financial head.

Tredegar

Town in Blaenau Gwent county borough, south Wales, on the River Sirhowy, 42 km/26 mi north of Cardiff; population (1991) 15,400. Its chief industries were formerly coal mining and light engineering, and tourism related to the town's industrial heritage is now an important source of income. A visitor centre is located at Parc Bryn Bach. Tredegar has a cast-iron clock and tower, 22 m/ 72 ft high, which was completed in 1859.

The Welsh Hang-Gliding Centre is located here. Tredegar is the birthplace of the politician Aneurin Bevan.

The title of Baron Tredegar has been borne by the family of Morgan since 1859, the family seat being **Tredegar Park**, near Newport.

Tree, Herbert Draper Beerbohm (1853–1917)

English actor and theatre manager. Noted for his lavish Shakespeare productions, he was founder of the ◊Royal Academy of Dramatic Art (RADA). He was the half-brother of Max ◊Beerbohm. He was knighted in 1909.

Tremain, Rose (1943–)

English novelist, short-story writer, and playwright. The historical novel *Restoration* (1989), perhaps her best-known work, was shortlisted for the Booker Prize, and filmed in 1995. Short-story collections include *The Colonel's Daughter* (1982), *The Garden of the Villa Mollini* (1986), and *Evangelista's Fan* (1994). Other novels include *Sacred Country* (1992) and *The Way I Found Her* (1997).

Trent

Third longest river of England; length 275 km/170 mi. Rising in the south Pennines (at Norton in the Moors) by the Staffordshire–Cheshire border, it flows south and then northeast through Derbyshire, along the county boundary of Leicestershire, and through Nottinghamshire and Lincolnshire, joining the Ouse east of Goole to form the Humber estuary, and entering the North Sea below Spurn Head. Its drainage basin covers more than 10,000 sq km/4,000 sq mi. Main tributaries are the Churnet, Dove, and Derwent.

It is navigable by barge for nearly 160 km/100 mi.

The principal towns and cities along its course are Burton upon Trent, Stoke-on-Trent, Nottingham, and Newark. It is connected with other rivers and with the Birmingham and Lancashire districts by the Trent and Mersey Canal and the Grand Union Canal. The Trent valley includes extensive gravel workings and many electric power stations.

Trent Bridge

Test-cricket ground in Nottingham, home of the Nottinghamshire county side. One of the oldest cricket grounds in Britain, it was opened in 1838.

The ground covers approximately 2.5 hectares/6.2 acres and the present-day capacity is around 30,000. It has staged Test cricket since 1899. A crowd of 101,886 watched the England–Australia Test match in 1948.

Tresco

Second largest of the Isles of ◊Scilly, off the coast of Cornwall, southwest England; population (1991) 158. The island lies 1.6 km/1 mi northwest of the largest island in the group, St Mary's. Features include Tresco Abbey, which has subtropical gardens and the ruins of a Benedictine priory.

Trevithick, Richard (1771–1833)

English engineer, constructor of a steam road locomotive in 1801, the first to carry passengers, and probably the first steam engine to run on rails in 1804. He also built steamboats, river dredgers, and threshing machines.

Trevithick was born in Illogan, Cornwall. As a boy he was fascinated by mining machinery and the large stationary steam engines that worked the pumps. He made a working model of a steam road locomotive in 1797 and went on to build various full-sized engines.

Trevithick's road locomotive *Puffing Devil* made its debut on Christmas Eve 1801, but burned out while he and his friends were celebrating their success at a nearby inn. He then made a larger version which he drove from Cornwall to London the following year, at a top speed of 19 kph/12 mph.

By 1804 he had produced his first railway locomotive, able to haul 10 tonnes and 70 people for 15 km/9.5 mi on rails used by horse-drawn trains at a mine in Wales. He set up in London in 1808 giving novelty rides on the engine *Catch-me-who-can*. Then in 1816 he left England for Peru. When he returned, after making and losing a fortune, he found that steam transport had become a thriving concern. Trevithick had been overtaken, and he died a poor man.

T-Rex

Influential English glam rock band, formed in 1968 and fronted by lead singer and songwriter Marc Bolan (1947–1977). Their songs include 'Ride a White Swan' and their UK number one hits 'Hot Love' and 'Get It On'. Bolan was killed in a motor accident in London.

Trimble, David (1944–)

Northern Ireland politician, leader of the ◊Ulster Unionist party (UUP) from 1995 and Northern Ireland's first minister from 1998. Representing the Upper Bann constituency in the House of Commons from 1990, he won the leadership of the UUP in August 1995, when James ◊Molyneaux decided to retire at the age of 75.

Trimble, originally seen as a hard-liner and not likely to move easily into Molyneaux's seat, proved to be more flexible and tolerant than had been predicted. Following his election as UUP leader, he sought to give an impetus to the Northern Ireland peace process, meeting UK prime minister John Major, Irish taoiseach John Bruton, and US president Bill Clinton. Still emphasizing the need for the Irish Republican Army (IRA) to decommission its weaponry, he nevertheless suggested a route to all-party talks through elections, although this proposal was opposed by republican spokesmen.

He accepted the 1998 Good Friday Agreement on power-sharing, which was rejected by the more extreme Democratic Unionist Party, led by Ian Paisley, and the United Kingdom Unionist Party, led by Robert McCartney. He was chosen as Northern Ireland's first minister, after the newly elected Northern Ireland Assembly met in June 1998, and seemed determined to make the peace agreement work. In the first meeting between Unionist and Republican leaders for several generations he met the president of Sinn Féin, Gerry Adams, at Stormont in September 1998. In October 1998 he was, jointly with John Hume of the Social Democratic Labour Party (SDLP), awarded the Nobel Peace Prize for his part in the Northern Ireland peace process.

Tring

Market town in Hertfordshire, southeast England, in the Chiltern Hills, between Hemel Hempstead and Aylesbury; population (1991) 12,000. Trade in agricultural produce is important and there is a flour mill and a light engineering works. Features include Tring Park and the Zoological Museum, which is part of the British Museum's natural-history section. Tring reservoirs are a national nature reserve.

Trinity College of Music

A school of music in London incorporated in 1875. Famous students include Sir John Barbirolli. Gavin Henderson has been principal since 1993. Together with his predecessor he has helped prevent the college being merged with another institution, and managed to keep it on its current site through the purchase of the lease.

trip-hop

Pop music combining electronic sampling with rap and jazz stylings for a languid, spacy effect. It originated in Bristol, England, in the 1990s. Exponents include Tricky, Massive Attack, and Portishead, whose debut album *Dummy* (1994) introduced the genre to a wide audience.

Tristan da Cunha

Group of islands in the south Atlantic, part of the British dependency of ◊St Helena, comprising four islands: Tristan, Gough, Inaccessible, and Nightingale; population (1996) 292; area 110 sq km/42 sq mi. Tristan consists of a single volcano 2,060 m/6,761 ft; it is an important meteorological and radio station. Gough Island Wildlife Reserve is a World Heritage Site. They were annexed by Britain in 1816.

We are not saying that, simply because someone has a past, they can't have a future. We always acknowledge that people have to change.

DAVID TRIMBLE Northern Ireland politician, leader of the Ulster Unionists.
Accepting his election as first minister of the Northern Ireland Assembly, *Daily Telegraph*, July 1998

Tristram Shandy, full title *The Life and Opinions of Tristram Shandy, Gent.*

Novel by Laurence ◊Sterne, published 1759–67. The work, a forerunner of the 20th-century stream-of-consciousness novel, has no coherent plot and uses typographical devices to emphasize the author's disdain for the structured novels of his contemporaries.

trolley bus

Bus driven by electric power collected from overhead wires. It has greater manoeuvrability than a tram (see ◊tramway).

Its obstructiveness in present-day traffic conditions led to its withdrawal in the UK.

Trollope, Anthony (1815–1882)

English novelist. He delineated provincial English middle-class society in a series of novels set in or around the imaginary cathedral city of Barchester. *The Warden* (1855) began the series, which includes *Barchester Towers* (1857), *Doctor Thorne* (1858), and *The Last Chronicle of Barset* (1867). His political novels include *Can You Forgive Her?* (1864), *Phineas Finn* (1867–69), and *The Prime Minister* (1875–76).

Trollope became a post office clerk in 1834, introduced the pillar box in 1853, and achieved the position of surveyor before retiring in 1867.

Trollope, Joanna (1943–)

English novelist. Her books, which explore the fortunes and

TROLLOPE, ANTHONY *English novelist Anthony Trollope, who produced a remarkable quantity of fine novels, biographies, and travel books while pursuing a successful career as a civil servant in the Post Office. Trollope introduced the pillar box for letters to Britain and stood unsuccessfully for Parliament in 1868. Corbis*

misfortunes of the upper-middle classes, include *The Choir* (1988) (televised in 1995), *The Rector's Wife* (1991) (televised in 1994), *The Men and the Girls* (1992), *The Best of Friends* (1995), and *Next of Kin* (1996). *Britannia's Daughters* (1983) is a study of women in the British Empire. Under the name Caroline Harvey she has written romantic period sagas.

Troon

Harbour town and holiday resort in South Ayrshire unitary authority, Scotland, situated on the Firth of Clyde, opposite the island of Arran; population (1991) 15,200. Originally a small fishing hamlet, the settlement expanded into a port and shipbuilding centre with the construction of its harbour in 1808. Tourism is now a major industry. Visitor attractions include golf courses and other sports facilities. Royal Troon, founded in 1878, is a championship golf course.

Trossachs ('bristled terrain')

Woodland glen between lochs Katrine and Achray in Stirling unitary authority, Scotland, 3 km/2 mi long. Overlooking it are Ben Venue (727 m/2,386 ft) and Ben A'an (369 m/1,211 ft), a popular climbing venue, which rests against Meall Gainmheich (564 m/1,851 ft). Featured in the novels of Walter Scott, it has become a favoured tourist spot.

Trowbridge

Market town and administrative headquarters of ◊Wiltshire, southwest England, 12 km/7 mi southeast of Bath; population (1991) 28,800. It produces bacon, ham, and dairy produce, and other industries include brewing, printing, and light engineering.

Trowbridge was important in the cloth industry, particularly the woollen trade, from medieval times. There were still five mills in the town until the 1950s, but these had all closed by 1982. The town has many fine stone houses of the 18th and early 19th centuries. The poet George Crabbe was rector at the restored 15th-century church of St James. Trowbridge was the birthplace of Isaac Pitman, inventor of Pitman's shorthand.

Trueman, Fred(erick Sewards) (1931–)

English cricketer. A right-arm fast bowler of great hostility, he played for Yorkshire 1949–68, and in 67 Tests for England 1952–65. Through much of his Test career he formed a fine opening bowling partnership with Brian Statham of Lancashire. In 1964 at the Oval, London, he gained special fame by becoming the first bowler to take 300 wickets in Test cricket, and his final total was 307 at an average of 21.57. After a few one-day appearances for Derbyshire in 1972, he retired from competitive cricket. Altogether he took 2,304 wickets in first-class matches.

Truro

Market town in ◊Cornwall, England, and administrative headquarters of the county, on the River Truro, a branch of the Fal, 14 km/9 mi north of Falmouth; population (1991) 19,000. It is a business centre.

Truro was the traditional meeting place of the Stannary (local parliament; see ◊Cornwall), and was formerly a centre and port for the now defunct tin-mining industry. The cathedral, designed by J L Pearson (1817–1897) dates from 1880–1910, and the museum and art gallery has works by John Opie. Present industries include pottery, biscuit manufacturing, and seaweed fertilizer.

Places of historical interest

Truro is the Treuru of the Domesday Book. The old borough comprised the parish of St Mary, on land at the junction of the Allen and Kenwyn rivers, but even in Tudor times the township had grown beyond these narrow limits. John Leland (in about 1535) mentions 'Kenwyn Streate' and 'Clementes Streate', suburbs of Truro. They were not formally incorporated until 1835. The Allen is still a noticeable feature with its three bridges. Kenwyn River runs underground through the centre of the city, but there is an attractive walk to the Victoria Gardens along the river's upper reaches. Lemon Street (*c.* 1795), named after an 18th-century merchant, is a splendidly planned street mentioned under the name of 'Orange Street' in Hugh Walpole's novels. In Prince's Street, named after the Regent, is the house of Mr Lemon, with its massive mahogany woodwork. Henry Martyn, the missionary philologist, was born here, and is commemorated in the cathedral by the baptistry. Nearby is the site of the old Coinage Hall, where for 500 years until 1837 royal officials came to examine the smelted tin and where the Stannary held its often stormy gatherings. Welsey also preached there. The County Museum and Art Gallery contains many paintings by John Opie (1761–1807) and by modern Cornish artists. Near the museum is the site of the Dominican Friary, of which the church was dedicated in 1259. The cattle market, the most important in the county, was built in 1840 on the site of Truro Castle. Notable schools are the high school for girls founded in 1880 by Bishop Benson; the Cathedral School for boys founded in 1549 or earlier, as the Truro grammar school; and, on a hill above the cathedral and city, the Truro School, founded in 1879.

The cathedral

The whole city is dominated by the cathedral whose central tower is 76 m/250 ft high. The ancient diocese was re-established in 1876, and the cathedral was the first erected in Britain after the rebuilding of St Paul's in the reign of Charles II. The foundation stone was laid on 20 May 1880, by the Duke of Cornwall (later Edward VII). In 1903 the nave was added and the central tower in 1904. In 1910 the western towers, named after Edward VII and Queen Alexandra, were dedicated.

Tudor and Elizabethan architecture

English architecture during the reign of the Tudor dynasty, from 1485 to 1603. The first stage of transition from Gothic to Renaissance is referred to as **Tudor**, the period 1558–1603 is commonly known as **Elizabethan**. The Renaissance movement in Italy began to influence English architecture early in the 16th century, but at first was confined to small ornamental details imported from Italy (for example the terracotta busts of Roman emperors at Hampton Court, about 1520) or carried out by imported Italian craftsmen (for example Torrigiano's tomb for Henry VII in Westminster Abbey, 1512). Italian ornamental features soon came to be copied by English craftsmen, and books of engravings of the 'Orders of Architecture' and other Roman architectural details were compiled, mainly in Germany and the Netherlands, and were studied in England.

The period saw a great boom and revolution in the building of houses and of grammar schools and colleges. The castlelike silhouettes, symmetry, and large gridded windows of Longleat (1568–75), Wollaton Hall (1580–88), and Hardwick Hall (1590–97), built by Robert Smythson, display a uniquely romantic English version of Classicism.

Tudor dynasty

English dynasty 1485–1603, founded by Henry VII, who became king by overthrowing Richard III (the last of the York dynasty) at the Battle of Bosworth. Henry VII reigned from 1485 to 1509, and was succeeded by Henry VIII (reigned 1509–47); Edward VI (reigned 1547–53); Mary (reigned 1553–58); and Elizabeth I (reigned 1558–1603). Elizabeth died childless and the throne of England passed to her cousin James VI of Scotland, who thus became James I of England and the first of the Stuart line. See page 906 for a genealogy.

The dynasty was descended from the Welsh adventurer Owen Tudor (*c.* 1400–1461), who fought on the Lancastrian side in the ⇨Wars of the Roses. Owen Tudor later became the second husband of Catherine of Valois (widow of Henry V of England). Their son Edmund, Earl of Richmond, married Margaret Beaufort (1443–1509), the great-granddaughter of ⇨John of Gaunt, who was the fourth son of Edward III. Henry VII, the founder of the Tudor dynasty, was the son of Edmund, Earl of Richmond, and Margaret Beaufort.

The dynasty's symbol, the Tudor rose, combines the red and white roses of the Lancastrian and Yorkist houses, and symbolizes the union of the two factions which was cemented by Henry VII in January 1486 when he married Elizabeth of York, the eldest daughter of Edward IV.

Tull, Jethro (1674–1741)

English agriculturist who about 1701 developed a drill that enabled seeds to be sown mechanically and spaced so that cultivation between rows was possible in the growth period. His chief work, *Horse-Hoeing Husbandry*, was published in 1733.

Tull also developed a plough with blades set in such a way that grass and roots were pulled up and left on the surface to dry. Basically the design of a plough is much the same today.

Tull was born in Berkshire, studied at Oxford and qualified as a barrister, but took up farming about 1700.

The seed drill was a revolutionary piece of equipment, designed to incorporate three previously separate actions into one: drilling, sowing, and covering the seeds. The drill consisted of a box capable of delivering the seed in a regulated amount, a hopper mounted above it for holding the seed, and a plough and harrow for cutting the drill (groove in the soil) and turning over the soil to cover the sown seeds.

Tunbridge Wells, Royal

Spa and commuter town in Kent, southeast England, between London and Hastings; population (1991) 60,300. It has a light industrial estate. The town developed after the discovery of iron-rich springs here in 1606. The **Pantiles** or shopping parade (paved with tiles in the reign of Queen Anne), was a fashionable resort; visited by Queen Victoria, the town has been named 'Royal' since 1909.

Following the discovery of the chalybeate (containing iron salts) springs in the area visitors at first stayed at Tonbridge or Southborough to the north, but in the 1630s large houses were built near the springs and shaded walks were laid out. **Tunbridge ware**, wooden boxes whose mosaic lids are decorated with rural scenes and ornamental borders, was produced here from the 17th century. A fine collection of Tunbridge ware, which is no longer made, is housed in the museum and art gallery. There was an Iron Age hill-fort at High Rocks nearby. The common is over 100 ha/247 acres.

Tunnicliffe, C(harles) F(rederick) (1901–1979)

English painter of birds. He worked in Anglesey. His many books include *Bird Portraiture* (1945) and *Shorelands Summer Diary* (1952). He also illustrated Henry Williamson's *Tarka the Otter* (1927) and *Salar the Salmon* (1935) with wood engravings.

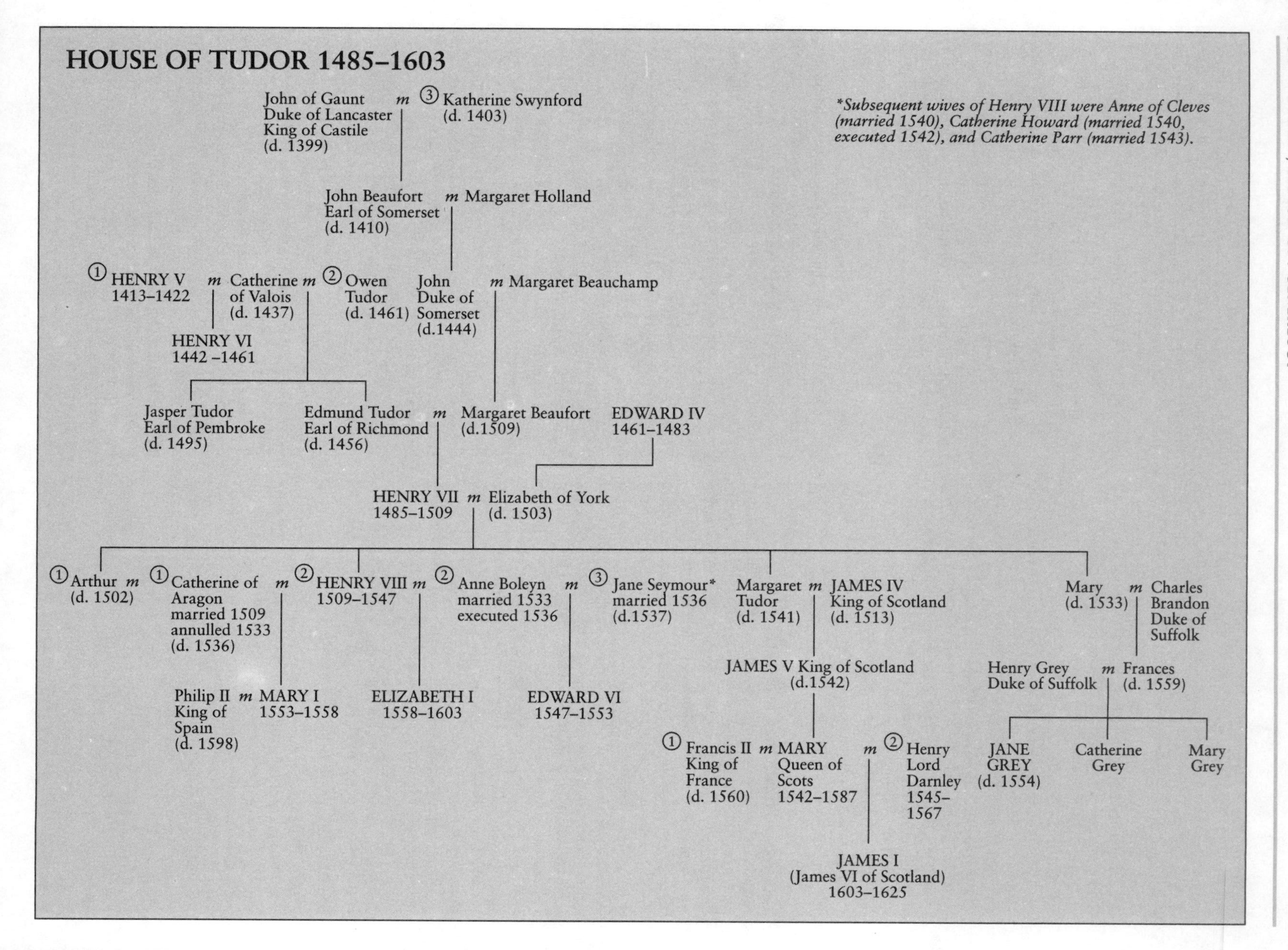
HOUSE OF TUDOR 1485–1603
John of Gaunt Duke of Lancaster King of Castile (d. 1399)
m
③ Katherine Swynford (d. 1403)
*Subsequent wives of Henry VIII were Anne of Cleves (married 1540), Catherine Howard (married 1540, executed 1542), and Catherine Parr (married 1543).
John Beaufort Earl of Somerset (d. 1410)
m Margaret Holland
① HENRY V 1413–1422
m Catherine of Valois (d. 1437)
m ② Owen Tudor (d. 1461)
John Duke of Somerset (d.1444)
m Margaret Beauchamp
HENRY VI 1442 –1461
Jasper Tudor Earl of Pembroke (d. 1495)
Edmund Tudor Earl of Richmond (d. 1456)
m Margaret Beaufort (d.1509)
EDWARD IV 1461–1483
HENRY VII 1485–1509
m Elizabeth of York (d. 1503)
① Arthur m (d. 1502)
① Catherine of Aragon married 1509 annulled 1533 (d. 1536)
m ② HENRY VIII 1509–1547
m ② Anne Boleyn married 1533 executed 1536
m ③ Jane Seymour* married 1536 (d.1537)
Margaret Tudor (d. 1541)
m JAMES IV King of Scotland (d. 1513)
Mary (d. 1533)
m Charles Brandon Duke of Suffolk
Philip II King of Spain (d. 1598)
m MARY I 1553–1558
ELIZABETH I 1558–1603
EDWARD VI 1547–1553
JAMES V King of Scotland (d.1542)
Henry Grey Duke of Suffolk
m Frances (d. 1559)
① Francis II King of France (d. 1560)
m MARY Queen of Scots 1542–1587
m ② Henry Lord Darnley 1545–1567
JANE GREY (d. 1554)
Catherine Grey
Mary Grey
JAMES I (James VI of Scotland) 1603–1625

Tunstall

Part of ◊Stoke-on-Trent, in Staffordshire, central England, 6 km/4 mi from Newcastle-under-Lyme. It is a centre for tile and earthenware manufacture and is one of the towns around Stoke-on-Trent known collectively as the ◊Potteries.

Turing, Alan Mathison (1912–1954)

English mathematician and logician. In 1936 he described a 'universal computing machine' that could theoretically be programmed to solve any problem capable of solution by a specially designed machine. This concept, now called the **Turing machine**, foreshadowed the digital computer.

Turing is believed to have been the first to suggest (in 1950) the possibility of machine learning and artificial intelligence. His test for distinguishing between real (human) and simulated (computer) thought is known as the **Turing test**: with a person in one room and the machine in another, an interrogator in a third room asks questions of both to try to identify them. When the interrogator cannot distinguish between them by questioning, the machine will have reached a state of humanlike intelligence.

Turks and Caicos Islands

British crown colony in the West Indies, the southeastern archipelago of the Bahamas; area 430 sq km/166 sq mi; population (1990 est) 12,400, 90% of African descent. British settlers from Bermuda established a salt panning industry in 1678. Secured by Britain in 1766 against French and Spanish claims, the islands were a Jamaican dependency from 1873 to 1962, and became a separate colony in 1962.

Turnage, Mark-Anthony (1960–)

English composer. He studied at the Royal College of Music with Oliver ◊Knussen 1974–78, and with Henze and Schuller at Tanglewood. His music admits a wide range of influences, including popular elements. His opera *Greek*, performed at Munich and Edinburgh in 1988, was a major success, and his other works include a saxophone concerto (1993), and *Three Screaming Popes* (1989), for orchestra.

He was composer-in-association with the City of Birmingham Symphony Orchestra 1989–93; and was featured composer at the 1986 Bath Festival and 1987 Glasgow Musica Viva.

Turnbull, William (1922–)

Scottish painter and sculptor. He became internationally known in his early career for his primitive, totemlike figures. From 1962, he explored Minimalist form, employing identical, pre-fabricated units to produce austere, vertical, and repetitive structures grouped on a mathematically devised ground plan, as in *5 x 1* (1966; Tate Gallery, London). His later work has generally been more intimate in feeling.

Turnbull was a founder-member of the Independent Group at the Institute of Contemporary Arts (ICA), London, in 1952.

Turner, Eva (1892–1990)

English operatic soprano. She was prima donna of the Carl Rosa Opera Company 1916–24. Her incomparable top range and generous tone survive in a magnificent *Turandot* recorded in 1928 under Thomas Beecham.

Turner, Joseph Mallord William (1775–1851)

English painter. He was one of the most original artists of his day. He travelled widely in Europe, and his landscapes became increasingly Romantic, with the subject often transformed in scale and flooded with brilliant, hazy light. Many later works anticipate Impressionism, for example *Rain, Steam and Speed* (1844; National Gallery, London).

A precocious talent, Turner entered the Royal Academy schools in 1789. In 1792 he made the first of several European tours from which numerous watercolour sketches survive. His early oil paintings show Dutch influence (such as that of van de Velde), but by the 1800s he had begun to paint landscapes in the 'Grand Manner', reflecting the Italianate influences of Claude Lorrain and Richard ◊Wilson.

Many of his most dramatic works are set in Europe or at sea, for example, *Shipwreck* (1805), *Snowstorm: Hannibal Crossing the Alps* (1812), and *Destruction of Sodom* (1805), all at the Tate Gallery, London; and *The Slave Ship* (1839; Museum of Fine Arts, Boston, Massachusetts). Turner was also devoted to literary themes and mythologies, such as *Ulysses Deriding Polyphemus* (1829; Tate Gallery, London).

His use of colour was enhanced by trips to Italy (1919, 1828, 1835, and 1840), and his brushwork became increasingly free, allowing him to capture both the subtlest effects of light and atmosphere and also the most violent forces of nature. Although encouraged by the portraitist Thomas Lawrence and others early in his career, he failed to achieve recognition, and it was not until he was championed by the critic John ◊Ruskin in *Modern Painters* (1843) that his originality was fully appreciated.

In his old age he lived as a recluse in Chelsea, London, under an assumed name. He died there, leaving to the nation more than 300 paintings, nearly 20,000 watercolours, and over 19,000 drawings. In 1987 the Clore Gallery extension to the Tate Gallery, London, was opened to display his bequest.

Turner Prize

Annual prize established in 1984 to encourage discussion about new developments in contemporary British art. £20,000 is awarded to a British artist under the age of 50 for an outstanding exhibition or other presentation of his or her work in the preceding 12 months; the winner is usually announced in November or early December. The Turner Prize has often attracted criticism for not celebrating what is traditionally considered to be art.

The prize was established by the Patrons of New Art, and is named after the British artist J M W ◊Turner. Artists are shortlisted by a jury and their work is exhibited at the Tate Gallery, London. Originally sponsored by an individual, it is now sponsored by Channel 4, which televises the award.

See table of winners on page 908.

turnpike road

Road with a gate or barrier preventing access until a toll had been paid, common from the mid-16th–19th centuries. In

Turner Prize

Year	Winner
1984	Malcolm Morley
1985	Howard Hodgkin
1986	Gilbert and George
1987	Richard Deacon
1988	Tony Cragg
1989	Richard Long
1990	no award
1991	Anish Kapoor
1992	Grenville Davey
1993	Rachel Whiteread
1994	Antony Gormley
1995	Damien Hirst
1996	Douglas Gordon
1997	Gillian Wearing
1998	Chris Ofili

1991, a plan for the first turnpike road to be built in the UK since the 18th century was announced: the privately funded Birmingham northern relief road, 50 km/31 mi long.

Turpin, Dick (Richard) (1705–1739)

English highwayman. The son of an innkeeper, he turned to highway robbery, cattle-thieving, and smuggling, and was hanged at York, England.

His legendary ride from London to York on his mare Black Bess is probably based on one of about 305 km/190 mi from Gad's Hill to York completed in 15 hours in 1676 by highwayman John Nevison (1639–1684).

Tussaud, Madame born Anne Marie Grosholtz (1761–1850)

French wax-modeller. In 1802 she established an exhibition of wax models of celebrities in London. It was destroyed by fire in 1925, but reopened in 1928. The exhibition was transferred to Baker Street in 1883 and to its present site in Marylebone Road in 1884, where it remains one of London's top fee-paying attractions.

Born in Strasbourg, she went to Paris as a young girl in 1766 to live with her wax-modeller uncle, Philippe Curtius, whom she soon surpassed in working with wax. During the French Revolution they were forced to take death masks of many victims and leaders (some still exist in the Chamber of Horrors).

Tutin, Dorothy (1931–)

English actress. Her roles include most of Shakespeare's leading heroines (among them Portia, Viola, and Juliet) for the Royal Shakespeare Company, and Lady Macbeth for the National Theatre Company. She has also acted in the first productions of plays by John Osborne and Harold Pinter.

In the 1990s she appeared in *A Little Night Music* (1989) and *Party Time* (1991).

tweed

Cloth made of woollen yarn, usually of several shades, but in its original form without a regular pattern and woven on a hand loom in the more remote parts of Ireland, Wales, and Scotland. **Harris tweed** is made on the island of Harris in the Outer Hebrides; it is highly durable and largely weatherproof.

Tweed

River rising in the Tweedsmuir Hills, 10 km/6 mi north of Moffat, southwest Scottish Borders, Scotland, and entering the North Sea at Berwick-upon-Tweed, Northumberland; length 156 km/97 mi. It flows in a northeasterly direction, and from Coldstream until near Berwick-upon-Tweed it forms the border between England and Scotland.

It is the fourth longest river in Scotland and is one of the best salmon rivers.

Twelfth Night

Comedy by William ◊Shakespeare, first performed in 1601–02. The plot builds on misunderstandings and mistaken identities, leading to the successful romantic unions of Viola and her twin brother Sebastian with Duke Orsino and Olivia respectively, and the downfall of Olivia's steward Malvolio.

Twickenham

District in the Greater London borough of ◊Richmond-upon-Thames. Twickenham Rugby football ground, headquarters of the Rugby Football Union, is here. Buildings include Marble Hill House (1723), a Palladian villa (home of the duchess of Suffolk, mistress of George II), and Horace Walpole's home Strawberry Hill (1748–77), an early example of the Gothic Revival style of architecture. The Royal Military School of Music is at Kneller Hall. Alexander Pope is buried in the church.

Twickenham

Stadium in southwest London, the ground at which England play home Rugby-Union internationals. It first staged an international match in 1910. The Rugby Football Union has its headquarters at Twickenham, and the Harlequins club used to play some of its home matches there. The ground was extensively rebuilt in the 1990s it now holds 75,000.

Twort, Frederick William (1877–1950)

English bacteriologist, the original discoverer in 1915 of bacteriophages (often called phages), the relatively large viruses that attack and destroy bacteria. He also researched into Johne's disease, a chronic intestinal infection of cattle.

Tyburn

Stream in London, near which (at the junction of the present Oxford Street and Edgware Road) Tyburn gallows stood from the 12th century until 1783. The Tyburn now flows underground.

A tributary of the River Thames, the Tyburn was formed originally by the confluence of two streams from the Hampstead heights. It entered the flood plain of the Thames near the western end of St James's Park, then divided into three mouths, two of them forming the island of Thorney on which Westminster Abbey was built.

Tyburn gallows

The first recorded execution using the Tyburn gallows took place in 1196, the last in 1783, after which the place of execution was moved to Newgate Prison. A permanent gallows stood at the junction of Oxford Street and Edgware Road from 1571 to 1759. Among those executed here were Perkin Warbeck and Jack Sheppard and, in the 16th and 17th centuries, many English Catholics.

Tyler, Wat (died 1381)

English leader of the ◊Peasants' Revolt of 1381. He was probably born in Kent or Essex, and may have served in the French wars. After taking Canterbury, he led the peasant army to Blackheath, outside London, and went on to invade the city. King Richard II met the rebels at Mile End and promised to redress their grievances, which included the imposition of a poll tax. At a further conference at Smithfield, London, Tyler was murdered.

Tylor, Edward Burnett (1832–1917)

English anthropologist. Often called 'the father of anthropology', he was the leading evolutionary anthropologist of the 19th century. His definition of culture in his book *Primitive Culture* (1871) was the first anthropological definition of the term; most modern definitions have derived from it.

His *Anthropology* (1881) was the first textbook on the subject, and in 1884 he became the first person to hold an academic position in anthropology when he became a lecturer at Oxford.

Tynan, Kenneth Peacock (1927–1980)

English theatre critic and author, a leading cultural figure of the radical 1960s. A strong opponent of censorship, he devised the nude revue *Oh Calcutta!* (1969), first staged in New York, USA. His publications include *A View of the English Stage 1944–63* (1975).

Tyndale, William (*c.* 1492–1536)

English translator of the Bible. The printing of his New Testament (the basis of the Authorized Version) was begun in Cologne, Germany, in 1525 and, after he had been forced to flee, completed in Worms. Tyndale introduced some of the most familiar phrases to the English language, such as 'filthy lucre', and 'God forbid'. He was strangled and burned as a heretic at Vilvorde in Belgium.

Tyne

River of northeast England formed by the union of the North Tyne (rising in the Cheviot Hills) and South Tyne (rising near Cross Fell in Cumbria) near Hexham, Northumberland, and reaching the North Sea at Tynemouth; length 72 km/45 mi. Kielder Water (1980) in the North Tyne Valley is Europe's largest artificial lake, 12 km/7.5 mi long and 0.8 km/0.5 mi wide, and supplies the industries of Tyneside, Wearside, and Teesside. As well as functioning as a reservoir, it is a major resource for recreational use.

The principal tributary of the Tyne is the River Derwent, and the chief towns and cities along its course are Newcastle upon Tyne, Gateshead, Jarrow, and South Shields. Much of the Tyne basin lies within the Northumberland National Park. Along the lower reaches the Tyneside conurbation developed in the 19th century around shipyards, iron works, and chemical industries.

Tyne and Wear

Metropolitan county of northeast England, created 1974; in 1986, most of the functions of the former county council were transferred to the metropolitan borough councils

Area 540 sq km/208 sq mi

Towns and cities Newcastle upon Tyne, Gateshead, Sunderland (administrative centres for the districts of the same name), South Shields (administrative centre of South Tyneside district), North Shields (administrative centre of North Tyneside district)

Physical rivers: Tyne and Wear

Features part of ◊Hadrian's Wall; Newcastle and Gateshead, linked with each other and with the coast on both sides by the Tyne and Wear Metro (a light railway using existing suburban lines, extending 54 km/34 mi); Tyneside International Film Festival

Industries Once a centre of heavy industry, Tyne and Wear's industry is now being redeveloped and diversified, with car manufacturing on Wearside, electronics, offshore technology (floating production vessels), automobile components, pharmaceuticals, and computers

Population (1991) 1,095,200

Famous people Thomas Bewick, Robert Stephenson, Harry Patterson ('Jack Higgins')

The Tyne and the Wear

Tyne and Wear county was formed in 1974 through the reorganization of the counties of Durham and Northumberland as they were then, uniting the interests of neighbouring industrial towns along the estuaries of the rivers Tyne and Wear. These rivers enter the North Sea within 11 km/7 mi of each other. The Tyne is tidal for 30 km/19 mi, the Wear for 13 km/8 mi; both have relatively narrow, steep-sided valleys with river banks rising to 30–50 m/98–160 ft. The Tyne cuts across a plateau formed largely of sandstone; both rivers cut gorges through a magnesian limestone plateau at their mouths. Both rivers have general merchandise quays. The Tyne has fishing berths, a wet dock, and roll-on/roll-off berths for ferries to ports between Bergen and Esbjerg.

History

Several of the towns of Tyne and Wear originated as Anglo-Saxon settlements from the 7th century. These include the fortified monastery at Tynemouth, the monastery at Jarrow, Gateshead at the southern end of the Tyne crossing, North and South Shields by the sheltered waters upstream of the Tyne River mouth, and Monkwearmouth and Sunderland, respectively north and south of the Wear gorge. The Normans built a castle in 1080 at the easiest crossing point of the Tyne (◊Newcastle upon Tyne), 16 km/10 mi inland, and later built a bridge at the same place on Roman foundations. This site remained the crossing point of the Tyne nearest to sea-level until the construction of the Tyne Tunnel in 1967.

The coal industry

Coal shipments began in the 13th century, as the Tyne and Wear were the only rivers in the area of the North Sea and the Baltic where coal outcrops were within reach of sheltered water. London was the largest market but supplies also went to Antwerp, the Netherlands, and eventually to Scandinavia and Russia. The merchants of Newcastle did their utmost to control the whole coal trade but the occupation of their town by Royalist and Scottish forces during the Civil War of 1642–49 allowed Sunderland a share in the trade. During the 18th century long wagonways were built to enable coal from mines up to 35 km/22 mi inland to be brought to the staithes (wooden coal wharves) along the estuaries. The local invention of the iron-screw collier (a coal transport ship driven by an iron-screw propeller) in 1852 reduced the cost of transport of coal to London and overseas markets by sea. On land, the development of the railway enabled other inland coalfields in other parts of the country to compete in markets once monopolized by supplies from the Tyne and Wear region.

19th-century industrial developments

Riverside sites were attractive to 19th-century industry because of its dependence on large inputs of coal and bulky raw materials, which has to be transported by water. The short waterfront of the Wear was soon lined with shipyards. On the Tyne, the narrowing and deepening of the channel allowed shipyards room to develop inland on either side of the estuary between Felling and Jarrow, a distance of 3–11 km/2–7 mi. Further upstream there was a large chemical industry, with heavy engineering and armaments above Newcastle upon Tyne. The population of the Tyne and Wear area rose from 178,000 in 1821 to 1,170,000 in 1921. Housing took the form of dense terraces built as closely as possible to mines, factories, and shipyards. Building and chemical pollution destroyed much of the natural vegetation of the river banks. Although the Tyneside chemical industry was in decline at the turn of the century, the production of coal, ships, and engineering components rose until the end of the World War I.

The 20th century

Growth of the local economy, which was almost entirely based on coal and raw materials, could not be sustained in the 20th century. Unemployment was widespread during the interwar period. Population growth has been negligible since 1921. Government aid began in 1935, which led to the establishment of a number of industrial trading estates in some areas. Newcastle upon Tyne has become the major office centre of the northern region of England and one of the chief shopping centres in the county.

Much of the population has been rehoused at lower densities since 1945, with the result that the Tyne and Wear area is almost entirely urban. In addition to peripheral housing estates there has been major redevelopment of the older suburbs of Newcastle upon Tyne and Sunderland. New towns were established at Washington (originally a group of mining and industrial villages) and at Killingworth, 9 km/6 mi northeast of Newcastle upon Tyne. Communications within the county were improved by the construction of the Tyne Tunnel (in 1967), motorway systems, and the Tyneside Metro (an integration of Newcastle upon Tyne's suburban rail network through underground lines beneath the city).

Tynemouth

Port and resort in ◊Tyne and Wear, England; population (1991) 17,100. There are remains of a Norman castle and Benedictine priory.

A monastery was first established here in the 7th century and in the 11th century it was refounded as a Benedictine priory and fortified. Tynemouth is a chiefly residential area with cliffs overlooking the mouth of the River Tyne. The residential area extends northwards through the resort of Whitley Bay.

Tyneside

Industrial conurbation in Tyne and Wear, northeast England, on the River Tyne. North Tyneside and South Tyneside are metropolitan boroughs of Tyne and Wear. The area extends from ◊South Shields to ◊Newcastle upon Tyne and is characterized by heavy industry such as shipbuilding and repairing, and fish canneries.

Tyrone

County of Northern Ireland

Area 3,160 sq km/1,220 sq mi

Towns and cities Omagh (county town), Dungannon, Strabane, Cookstown

Features rivers: Derg, Blackwater, Foyle; Lough Neagh; Sperrin Mountains

Industries mainly agricultural: barley, flax, potatoes, turnips, cattle, sheep, brick making, linen, hosiery, shirts

Population (1991) 158,500.

Tyrrell

British motor-racing team founded by Ken Tyrrell in 1970. He formed a partnership with Jackie ◊Stewart and the celebrated driver won all three of his world titles in Tyrrell-run teams. The team won the Formula One World Constructors' title in 1971.

Tywi, or Towy

River in Carmarthenshire, southwest Wales; length 108 km/68 mi. It rises in the Cambrian Mountains of central Wales and flows southwest through ◊Carmarthen before entering ◊Carmarthen Bay.

U2

Irish rock group formed in 1977 by singer Bono Vox (born Paul Hewson, 1960–), guitarist Dave 'The Edge' Evans (1961–), bassist Adam Clayton (1960–), and drummer Larry Mullen (1961–). The band's albums include *The Unforgettable Fire* (1984), *The Joshua Tree* (1987), and *Achtung Baby* (1992).

Uckfield

Town in East Sussex, southeast England, 13 km/8 mi northeast of Lewes; population (1991) 11,500. To the south is the Bentley Wildfowl Trust and to the northwest is Sheffield Park, with fine gardens and the Bluebell Line railway.

UDA

Abbreviation for ◊Ulster Defence Association.

Uddin, Pola Manzila, Baroness Udin (1959–)

Bangladeshi-born English Labour working peer, one of three Muslim members of the House of Lords. She was elected to Tower Hamlets Borough Council in 1990, the first Bangladeshi-born woman to sit on a local authority in the UK, and became deputy leader of the council. She left Tower Hamlets to become a social services manager for the London Borough of Newham. She was created Baroness in 1998.

Uist

Two small islands, part of Western Isles unitary authority, in the Outer ◊Hebrides, Scotland: North Uist and South Uist.

Ullswater

Second largest lake in the Cumbrian ◊Lake District, northwest England, on the east side of ◊Helvellyn ridge; length 13 km/8 mi, width 1 km/0.6 mi. The former lead-mining and quarrying villages of Patterdale and Glenridding to the south of the lake now consist mainly of hotels and guesthouses for tourists.

Ulster

A former kingdom and province in the north of Ireland, annexed by England in 1461, from Jacobean times a centre of English, and later Scottish, settlement on land confiscated from its owners; divided in 1921 into Northern Ireland (counties Antrim, Armagh, Down, Fermanagh, Londonderry, and Tyrone) and the Republic of Ireland (counties Cavan, Donegal, and Monaghan).

Ulster Defence Association, UDA

Northern Ireland Protestant paramilitary organization responsible for a number of sectarian killings. Fanatically loyalist, it established a paramilitary wing (the Ulster Freedom Fighters) to combat the ◊Irish Republican Army (IRA) on its own terms and by its own methods. No political party has acknowledged any links with the UDA. In 1994, following a cessation of military activities by the IRA, the UDA, along with other Protestant paramilitary organizations, declared a cease-fire.

Ulster Unionist Party, UUP, also known as the Official Unionist Party (OUP)

The largest political party in ◊Northern Ireland. Right-of-centre in orientation, it advocates equality for Northern Ireland within the UK and opposes union with the Republic of Ireland. The party has the broadest support of any Ulster party, and has consistently won a large proportion of parliamentary and local seats. Its central organization, dating from 1905, is formally called the Ulster Unionist Council. Its leader from 1995 is David ◊Trimble. It secured 28 of the 108 seats in the new Northern Ireland Assembly, elected in June 1998, and Trimble was elected Northern Ireland's first minister at the Assembly's first meeting on 1 July.

Policies

The party advocates equal local-government rights for the people of Ulster compared with the rest of the UK. The need for tough law-and-order measures is also a strong party theme, with many of its leaders in favour of reintroducing capital punishment. The party has been generally hostile to the terms of the UK's membership of the European Union (EU), and believes that it has a negative impact on Ulster. Within Westminster the Ulster Unionist members of Parliament have generally voted with the Conservative Party.

Influence in the UK Parliament

In the 1974–79 UK Parliament, the Unionist MPs held an important bargaining position, and the Conservatives could no longer rely on their support – in 1979 two Unionists supported the Labour government in a vote of confidence.

The Ulster Unionist Party totally rejected the Anglo-Irish Agreement in 1985, and joined forces with the Democratic Unionist Party (DUP) to campaign against it. All its MPs resigned their seats in order to demonstrate the degree of Unionist hostility to the agreement.

In February 1995 the Ulster Unionists rejected the British and Irish governments' published proposals on the future of Northern Ireland and threatened to withdraw their support of the government. Under Trimble's leadership, from 1995, the UUP became more accommodating in the peace negotiations and accepted the 1998 Good Friday Agreement on power-sharing.

Ulverston

Market town on the ◊Furness peninsula, in the South Lakeland district of Cumbria, England; population (1991) 11,500. The town has a wide range of industries, including electrical engineering, and products include oils, chemicals, plastics, and medical supplies.

Ulverston has a church reputed to contain, perhaps in the tower of 1540, some of the stones from Furness Abbey. John Rennie built a ship canal (1793–96) here, long since disused. Ulverston was the birthplace of John Barrow (1764–1848), founder of the Royal Geographical Society, and the comedian Stan Laurel (of Laurel and Hardy).

Underwood, Rory (1963–)

English Rugby Union player. A wing-threequarter, he is England's most capped player and highest try scorer with 49 tries in 85 internationals, 1984–1996. Underwood helped England to win Grand Slams in 1991, 1992, and 1995.

unemployment

Since September 1988, unemployment in Britain has been measured as the total or percentage of the working population unemployed and claiming benefit. This only includes people aged 18 or over, since the under-18s are assumed to be in full-time education or training, which is not always the case. In 1997 there were 1,651,400 unemployed, 5.9% of the workforce. Of these, 1,342,200 were in England, 82,400 in Wales, 162,000 in Scotland, and 64,800 in Northern Ireland.

History

For at least 150 years before 1939, the supply of labour in the UK always exceeded demand except in wartime, and economic crises accompanied by mass unemployment were recurrent from 1785. The percentage of unemployed in trade unions averaged 6% during 1883–1913 and 14.2% (of those covered by the old Unemployment Insurance Acts) 1921–38. World War II and the rebuilding and expansion that followed meant shortage of labour rather than unemployment in the Western world, and in Britain in the 1950s the unemployment rate fell to 1.5%. Fluctuation in employment returned in the 1960s, and in the recession of the mid-1970s to 1980s was a worldwide problem. In Britain deflationary economic measures tended to exacerbate the trend, and in the mid-1980s the rate had risen to 14% (although the basis on which it is calculated has in recent years been changed several times and many commentators argue that the real rate is higher).

As the British economy experienced significant economic growth between 1986 and 1989, the rate of unemployment fell to a low of 5.6% in April 1990 (using the post-1988 definition) but rose again during the subsequent recession, reaching a peak of 10.5% in April 1993. As the economy recovered, it fell once again, to 9.5% in April 1994, and to 8.7% in 1995.

unicorn

Heraldic animal represented as a horse with a twisted horn, a deer's hooves, a goat's beard, and a lion's tail. When James VI of Scotland became James I of England in 1606, one of the two supporting unicorns on the Scottish arms replaced the Welsh dragon on the English shield, the other supporter being the lion. The legendary animosity between the lion and the unicorn relates to former rivalry between England and Scotland.

Uniformity, Acts of

Two acts of Parliament in England. The first in 1559 imposed the Prayer Book on the whole English kingdom; the second in 1662 required the Prayer Book to be used in all churches, and some 2,000 ministers who refused to comply were ejected.

Unilever

Multinational food, drink, and detergent company formed in 1930 in a merger between British and Dutch companies. The merger took in Lever Brothers, founded in 1885 by William Hesketh Lever (1851–1935) and James Darcy Lever, who built ◊Port Sunlight. By 1996 Unilever employed 304,000 people worldwide, with 21,422 in the UK. The 1995 turnover was £29,666,000,000, and pretax profits were £2,383,000,000. Unilever's headquarters are in Rotterdam, the Netherlands.

Union, Acts of

Acts of Parliament that accomplished the joining of England with Wales (1536), England and Wales with Scotland (1707), and Great Britain with Ireland (1800). See display text opposite for detail.

Union Jack

Popular name for the British national flag, properly called the **Union flag**. Strictly speaking, the term Union Jack should be used only when the flag is flown on the jackstaff of a warship. The flag unites the crosses of St George, St Andrew, and St Patrick, representing England, Scotland, and Ireland. The union flag was introduced after the union of England and Scotland in 1707, and at first bore the crosses of St George and St Andrew. At the union with Ireland in 1801, St Patrick's cross – a red diagonal cross on a white ground – was added, forming what has ever since been the UK national flag.

Union Movement

British political group. Founded as the **New Party** by Oswald ◊Mosley and a number of Labour members of Parliament in

Acts of Union

Act of Union of 1536

The Act of Union passed in 1536, during the reign of King Henry VIII, the second English monarch descended from the Welsh House of Tudor, formally united England and Wales. By its terms, the Welsh Marches, estates held for centuries by semi-independent Marcher lords, became several new counties or were added to older counties. Counties and boroughs in Wales were granted representation in the English Parliament.

Act of Union of 1707

The Act of Union passed in 1707 by the parliaments of England and Scotland created the Kingdom of Great Britain. Although Scotland retained its judicial system and its Presbyterian church, its parliament was joined with that of England. The crowns of the two countries had been united in 1603 when James Stuart (James VI of Scotland) succeeded Elizabeth I as James I of England, but the kingdoms otherwise remained separate.

Act of Union of 1800

The Act of Union, which was passed in 1800 and went into effect on 1 January 1801, joined the Kingdom of Great Britain and all of Ireland into the United Kingdom of Great Britain and Ireland. The act was revoked when the Irish Free State was constituted in 1922.

1931, it developed into the **British Union of Fascists** in 1932. In 1940 the organization was declared illegal and its leaders interned, but it was revived as the Union Movement in 1948, characterized by racist doctrines including anti-Semitism.

An attempt by the 'blackshirts' to march through the East End of London in 1936 led to prohibition of the wearing of such political uniforms.

UNISON

Britain's largest trade union with 1,368,796 members (1998): 966,370 female and 402,426 male. It was formed on 1 July 1993 by the merging of the National Union of Public Employees (NUPE), the Confederation of Health Service Employees, and the National Local Government Officers Association (NALGO). Its general secretary is Rodney Bickerstaffe.

unitary authority

Administrative unit of Great Britain. Since 1996 the two-tier structure of local government has ceased to exist in Scotland and Wales, and in some parts of England, and has been replaced by unitary authorities, responsible for all local government services.

Following the review of local government structure by the Local Government Commission set up by the Local Government Act 1992, the counties of Avon, Cleveland, and Humberside, their districts, and the district of York City were abolished, and 13 unitary authorities were created in their place. These came into existence in April 1996. In 1997 13 further unitary authorities were established, and 19 in 1998, making a total of 46 unitary authorities in England, in addition to the existing London and Metropolitan boroughs, which already had unitary powers. The Isle of Wight became a unitary authority in 1995. In some counties the two-tier structure has been retained. The act also abolished the counties and their districts in Wales, creating 22 unitary authorities in their place from 1996, and abolished the regional councils and their districts in Scotland, creating 29 new unitary authorities from 1996, making a total of 32.

United Irishmen

Society formed in 1791 by Wolfe ◊Tone to campaign for parliamentary reform in Ireland. It later became a secret revolutionary group.

Inspired by the republican ideals of the French Revolution, the United Irishmen was initially a debating society, calling for reforms such as the right of Catholics to vote in Irish elections, but after an attempt to suppress it in 1793, the organization became secret, looking to France for military aid. An attempted insurrection in 1798 was quickly defeated and the leaders captured.

United Kingdom, UK

Official name for country comprising ◊England, ◊Scotland, ◊Wales, and Northern ◊Ireland, which is sometimes colloquially referred to as Britain or Great Britain. See Acts of ◊Union for when the constituent parts were joined. For history, see constituent parts, also the chronology from 1707 in Appendices. For topographical features of the UK, see individual entries.

> *Here is a country that fought and won a noble war, dismantled a mighty empire in a generally benign and enlightened way, created a far-seeing welfare state – in short, did nearly everything right – and then spent the rest of the century looking on itself as a chronic failure. The fact is that this is still the best place in the world for most things.*
>
> BILL BRYSON US writer.
> *Notes From a Small Island* (1995)

United Kingdom Atomic Energy Authority, UKAEA

National authority, established in 1954 to be responsible for research and development of all nonmilitary aspects of nuclear energy. The authority also provided private industry with contract research and development, and specialized technical and advanced engineering services. The research function was split off into a new company, **AEA Technology**, which was put up for sale in September 1996 as part of the government's privatization programme. UKAEA now manages its nuclear installations and is responsible for decommissioning and maximizing the return on property.

The main areas of research are: thermal reactors, fast reactors, fusion, decommissioning of plants and radioactive waste management, nuclear fuels, and environmental and energy technology. The principal establishments are at the Atomic Energy Research Establishment, Harwell, Oxfordshire; the Culham Laboratory, Oxfordshire; Dounreay, Scotland; Risley, Cheshire; and Winfrith, Dorset.

unleaded petrol

Petrol manufactured without the addition of antiknock. It has a slightly lower octane rating than leaded petrol, but has the advantage of not polluting the atmosphere with lead compounds. Many cars can be converted to run on unleaded petrol by altering the timing of the engine, and most new cars are designed to do so. Cars fitted with a catalytic converter must use unleaded fuel.

Aromatic hydrocarbons and alkenes are added to unleaded petrol instead of lead compounds to increase the octane rating. After combustion the hydrocarbons produce volatile organic compounds. These have been linked to cancer, and are involved in the formation of phytochemical smog. A low-lead fuel is less toxic than unleaded petrol for use in cars that are not fitted with a catalytic converter.

The use of unleaded petrol is increasing in the UK (encouraged by a lower rate of tax than that levied on leaded petrol). In 1987 only 5% of petrol sold in the UK was unleaded; by 1992 this had risen to 45%. Lead emissions in the UK fell from 7,500 tonnes in 1980 to 1,000 tonnes in 1996.

Unst

Northernmost of the Shetland Islands, Scotland, and most northerly of the British Isles, 64 km/40 mi northeast of Lerwick; population (1991) 1,100. It covers an area of 120 sq km/46 sq mi, including the islands of Uyea and Muckle Flugga, and is separated from the island of Yell by Bluemull Sound. The main occupations are fishing and the production of knitwear. Former talc and chromate mining activities have now ceased. Norwick, Haroldswick, and Baltasound (site of an RAF base) are the largest settlements.

An operational automatic lighthouse stands on Muckle Flugga, just off the northern headland of Hermaness; the promontory is now a nature reserve. On the southwest coast lies the 16th-century stronghold of Muness Castle.

Unwin, Raymond (1863–1940)

English architect and leading town planner of his time. He put the ⇨garden city ideals of Ebenezer ⇨Howard into practice, overseeing Letchworth, Hertfordshire (begun 1903), Hampstead Garden Suburb, outside London (begun 1907), and Wythenshawe, outside Manchester (begun 1927). He was president of the Royal Institute of British Architects (RIBA) from 1931 to 1933, and was awarded the Royal Gold Medal in 1937. He was knighted in 1932.

Uppark

Late 17th-century house in West Sussex, England, 8 km/5 mi south of Petersfield. Uppark was given to the National Trust in 1954 and retains much of the original decorations and furnishings, including flock wallpapers and damask curtains. However, a high proportion of this was destroyed by fire in August 1989. The house was reopened in 1995 following a complete restoration.

It was the home of the Fetherstonhaugh family from 1747, and its many famous visitors included Emma Hart (later Lady Hamilton and Nelson's mistress), Charles Greville, the Prince Regent, and H G Wells, whose mother was housekeeper there for several years.

The restoration of the house was revolutionary in that it attempted to restore the house to its exact state the day before the fire. Modern reproductions and replacements of features such as wallpaper were 'aged' by the incorporation of original fragments.

Usk, Welsh Wysg

River in south Wales, rising in the Black Mountain on the boundary between Carmarthenshire and Powys; length 137 km/85 mi; catchment area 1,358 sq km/524 sq mi. It flows south through Powys and Monmouthshire, passing through the towns of Abergevenny, Usk, and Caerlon, and enters the Bristol Channel at Newport.

The Usk valley, of which the upper half is in the Brecon Beacons National Park, has fine scenery and good fishing.

Ustinov, Peter (Alexander) (1921–)

English stage and film actor, writer, and director, of Russian descent. He has an impressive screen presence, either as comic chat show raconteur or dramatic actor. He won Academy Awards as best supporting actor for *Spartacus* (1960) and *Topkapi* (1964). He has written, produced, directed, and acted in several films, including *Romanoff and Juliet* (1961), *Billy Budd* (1962), and *Lady L* (1965).

Other film appearances include *Death on the Nile* (1978), in which he first played the Belgian detective Hercule Poirot, and *Evil under the Sun* (1981). In the 1980s he revived the role of Hercule Poirot in such British television productions as *Murder in Three Acts* (1986) and *Appointment with Death* (1988). He continued to act throughout the 1990s, appearing in the films *Lorenzo's Oil* (1992) and *Stiff Upper Lips* (1996). He was knighted in 1990.

Uttoxeter

Town in eastern Staffordshire, England, 19 km/12 mi northeast of Stafford; population (1991) 11,000. Products include biscuits, dairy produce, and agricultural implements. There is a racecourse at Uttoxeter.

V1, V2 (German *Vergeltungswaffe* 'revenge weapons')

German flying bombs of World War II, launched against Britain in 1944 and 1945. The V1, also called the **doodlebug** and **buzz bomb**, was an uncrewed monoplane carrying a bomb, powered by a simple kind of jet engine called a pulse jet. The V2, a rocket bomb with a preset guidance system, was the first long-range ballistic missile. It was 14 m/47 ft long, carried a 1-tonne warhead, and hit its target at a speed of 5,000 kph/3,000 mph.

Vale of Glamorgan

Unitary authority in south Wales, created in 1996 from parts of the former counties of Mid Glamorgan and South Glamorgan

Area 337 sq km/130 sq mi
Towns ◊Barry (administrative headquarters), Penarth
Physical lowland area
Agriculture sheep farming, varied agriculture
Population (1996) 119,500

Cardiff Airport is situated near the coast at Roose, west of Barry.

Valera, Éamon de

Irish politician; see ◊de Valera.

Vanbrugh, John (1664–1726)

English Baroque architect, dramatist, and soldier. Although entirely untrained as an architect, he designed the huge mansions of Castle Howard (1699–1726), Blenheim (1705–16; completed by Nicholas Hawksmoor 1722–25), Seaton Delaval (1720–29), and many others, as well as much of Greenwich Hospital (1718 onwards). He also wrote the comic dramas *The Relapse* (1696) and *The Provok'd Wife* (1697).

He was imprisoned in Paris 1688–93 as a political hostage during the war between France and the Grand Alliance (including Britain). In 1704 Vanbrugh built his own theatre, the Queen's Theatre or Italian Opera House in the Haymarket, London (now destroyed). From this point playwriting displaced architecture as his principal activity. He was knighted in 1714.

Vancouver, George (1757–1798)

English navigator who made extensive exploration of the west coast of North America. The city of Vancouver was named after him. He accompanied James ◊Cook on two voyages, and served in the West Indies. He also surveyed parts of Australia, New Zealand, Tahiti, and Hawaii.

Vane, Henry (1613–1662)

English politician. In 1640 he was elected a member of the ◊Long Parliament, and was knighted in the same year. He was prominent in the impeachment of Archbishop Laud and in 1643–53 was in effect the civilian head of the Parliamentary government. At the Restoration of the monarchy he was executed.

Vane, John Robert (1927–)

English pharmacologist who discovered the wide role of prostaglandins in the human body, produced in response to illness and stress. He shared the 1982 Nobel Prize for Physiology or Medicine with Sune Bergström and Bengt Samuelsson of Sweden.

Vanity Fair

Novel by William Makepeace ◊Thackeray, published in the UK in 1847–48. It deals with the contrasting fortunes of the tough orphan Becky Sharp and the soft-hearted, privileged Amelia Sedley, who first meet at Miss Pinkerton's Academy for young ladies.

Vanwall

British motor-racing team and manufacturer; the first winners of the Formula One Constructors' Championship in 1958. The company was started by Tony Vandervell and it launched its first car in 1954. It was designed around a Ferrari chassis with a Norton engine. Stirling ◊Moss drove for Vanwall and won the 1956 International Trophy.

VANBRUGH, JOHN *Castle Howard, North Yorkshire, England. It was designed by John Vanbrugh and Nicholas Hawksmoor for the Earl of Carlisle in 1699. Corbis*

Vardon, Harry (Henry William) (1870–1937)

British golfer, born in Jersey. He won the British Open a record six times 1896–1914. Vardon was the first UK golfer to win the US Open in 1900.

Varley, John (1778–1842)

English painter. One of the leading early watercolour artists, he is best known for his picturesque views of North Wales. He was a friend of the poet and artist William ◊Blake.

In his youth he was a protégé of the art collector Dr Thomas Monro (1759–1833), and he later became known as an art teacher in London, David ◊Cox, John Linnell, and Samuel ◊Palmer being among his many students. Views of North Wales, painted in the 'sublime manner', are among his most important works, but his large output tended towards a mechanical facility. It was for him that Blake drew his famous 'visionary heads'.

His brother **Cornelius Varley** (1781–1873) was a watercolour painter of landscape, marine, and architectural subjects. His younger brother **William Fleetwood** (1785–1856), his son **Albert Fleetwood**, and two grandsons were also watercolourists.

Vaughan, Henry (1622–1695)

Welsh poet. He published several volumes of metaphysical religious verse and prose devotions. His best-known work, *Silex Scintillans: Sacred Poems and Private Ejaculations* (1650), contains the exquisite short poem 'The Retreat'. His mystical outlook on nature influenced later poets, including William Wordsworth.

Vaughan Williams, Ralph (1872–1958)

English composer. His style was tonal and often evocative of the English countryside through the use of folk themes. Among his works are the orchestral *Fantasia on a Theme by Thomas Tallis* (1910); the opera *Sir John in Love* (1929), featuring the Elizabethan song 'Greensleeves'; and nine symphonies (1909–57).

The English pastoral tradition was revived in his 3rd symphony (1921), and the complementary, visionary source of his inspiration was renewed in such sacred works as the Mass in G minor, *Sancta Civitas*, and *Benedicite*. His two best-known symphonies, nos. 4 and 5, were composed between 1934 and 1943; the angularity and fierce accents of the earlier work lead to the repose and serenity of its companion. The last four symphonies continue the composer's spiritual quest, already begun in *The Pilgrim's Progress*. Although Vaughan Williams' compositions are usually classified broadly as pastoral, making use of folk melodies, or at least the lyrical and often model aspects of such melodies, he was conscious of contemporary musical developments and often involved a greater degree of dissonance in his later works.

VE Day, Victory in Europe

Anniversary of the surrender of Germany at the end of ◊World War II, 8 May 1945. The day is celebrated as a commemoration of the victory of the Allied powers in the European theatre. The war continued in the Pacific theatre until Japan's surrender on 15 August which is marked by VJ Day.

Venables, Terry (Terence Frederick) (1943–)

English footballer and coach. He was the England football manager 1994–96.

Although Venables had a solid playing career with Chelsea, Tottenham, Queens Park Rangers, and Crystal Palace, and won two full England caps, it is as a coach that his reputation lies. He won promotion to the first division for Crystal Palace (1978–79) and then Queens Park Rangers (1982–83), before taking Barcelona (1984–87) to the Spanish League title in 1984–85. After winning the FA Cup with Tottenham Hotspur in 1991 he became the club's chief executive, but was sacked two years later over alleged financial misdealing. These allegations plagued him throughout his time as England manager and led to his decision in January 1996 to relinquish his post after the European Championships later that year. He became the owner of Portsmouth Football Club in 1997. In the same year, he failed to steer Australia to the 1998 World Cup finals, losing a two-leg playoff to Iran on the goals away rule. In early 1998 Venables stood down as chairman of Portsmouth Football Club and severed all his connections with the club. Shortly afterwards, he was also disqualified in the High Court from acting as a company director for seven years after agreeing not to contest allegations of serious misconduct brought by the Department of Trade and Industry arising from his management of Tottenham Hotspur Football Club and three other companies. In June 1998 he was re-appointed coach of Crystal Palace, a club he had managed 1976–80.

While his tenure as England coach ended with defeat by Germany in the semi-final, he was generally applauded for improving the style and effectiveness of the team.

Venn, John (1834–1923)

English logician whose diagram, known as the Venn diagram, is much used in the teaching of elementary mathematics.

Verulamium

Romano-British town near St Albans, Hertfordshire, occupied until about AD 450. Verulamium superseded a nearby Belgic settlement and was first occupied by the Romans in 44–43 BC. The earliest English martyr, St Alban, was martyred here, perhaps during the reign of Septimus Severus. A fragmentary inscription from the site of the forum records the name of the Roman governor ◊Agricola. The site became deserted in the late 5th or 6th century.

Verulamium was sacked by the Iceni under ◊Boudicca in AD 61, but the timber shops were rebuilt and a basilica erected in AD 79. The town plan of the late 1st century was almost rectangular. The town wall, built of masonry with solid projecting bastions and elaborate gateways, was not erected until the 3rd century. Building activity continued until the end of the 5th century. Only the southeastern gate foundations and adjoining wall, a mosaic pavement with its hypocaust or heating system, and the remains of a large house and the theatre with adjoining shops, are visible today.

Verve, the

English rock group formed in 1990. Their first hit single was 'On Your Own' (1995) but, following a temporary split, they secured their reputation in 1997 with the singles 'Bitter Sweet Symphony' and 'Drugs Don't Work' (which entered the UK chart at number one), and with the award-winning album *Urban Hymns* (1997).

The group's members are Richard Ashcroft (1971–) (vocals and guitar), Simon Jones (1972–) (bass), Simon Tong (guitar and keyboards), and Peter Salisbury (1971–) (drums). Nick McCabe (1971–) (guitar), left the band for a second time during their 1998 tour.

Vickers

British engineering company, prominent in the manufacture of munitions. In addition to naval and land artillery, the company gave its name to the 'Vickers gun', a modified form of the Maxim machine gun, adopted by the British army in 1912, as well as to a series of aircraft in both world wars.

Vicky pen name of Victor Weisz (1913–1966)

Hungarian cartoonist who settled in England from 1935. He worked for a number of British papers but is best known for his contributions to the *New Statesman* from 1954 and the *Evening Standard* from 1958. His satirical cartoons attacked power and privilege, and his serious drawings exposed the plight of the poor and oppressed.

Victoria (1819–1901)

Queen of the UK from 1837, when she succeeded her uncle William IV, and Empress of India from 1877. In 1840 she married Prince ◊Albert of Saxe-Coburg and Gotha. Her relations with her prime ministers ranged from the affectionate (Melbourne and Disraeli) to the stormy (Peel, Palmerston, and Gladstone). Her golden jubilee in 1887 and diamond jubilee in 1897 marked a waning of republican sentiment, which had developed with her withdrawal from public life on Albert's death in 1861.

The only child of Edward, Duke of Kent, fourth son of George III, she was born on 24 May 1819 at Kensington Palace, London. She and Albert had four sons and five daughters. After Albert's death she lived mainly in retirement. Nevertheless, she kept control of affairs, refusing the Prince of Wales (Edward VII) any active role. From 1848 she regularly visited the Scottish Highlands, where she had a house at Balmoral built to Prince Albert's designs. She died at ◊Osborne House, her home in the Isle of Wight, on 22 January 1901, and was buried at Windsor. See also ◊Victorian period.

Victoria and Albert Museum, V & A

Museum of decorative arts in South Kensington, London, founded in 1852. It houses prints, paintings, and temporary exhibitions, as well as one of the largest collections of decorative arts in the world.

Originally called the Museum of Ornamental Art, it had developed from the Museum of Manufacturers at Marlborough House, which had been founded in the aftermath of the Great Exhibition of 1851. In 1857 it became part of the South Kensington Museum, and was renamed the Victoria and Albert Museum in 1899. The museum was inspired by Prince ◊Albert and Henry Cole (1808–1882), English industrial designer and writer on decorative arts. He selected the museum's first acquisitions and became its first director. In 1990 the Nehru Indian Gallery was opened, displaying a selection of the museum's Indian collection, which derives from the East India Company's Museum, acquired in 1858.

Victoria Cross

British decoration for conspicuous bravery in wartime, instituted by Queen Victoria in 1856.

It is bronze, with a 4 cm/1.5 in diameter, and has a crimson ribbon. Victoria Crosses are struck from the metal of guns captured from the Russians at Sevastopol during the Crimean War.

Victorian period

Mid- and late 19th century in England, covering the reign of Queen Victoria from 1837 to 1901. This period was one of significant industrial and urban development in Britain, and also saw a massive expansion of the ◊British Empire. In domestic politics the period is particularly notable for the rivalry between the Conservative prime minister Benjamin ◊Disraeli and his Liberal successor William Ewart ◊Gladstone.

Queen Victoria

Victoria became queen on 20 June 1837, and enjoyed the longest reign of any British monarch. In domestic affairs and politics she relied initially on the shrewd advice of her Whig prime minister Lord ◊Melbourne, but later clashed with his Tory successor Robert ◊Peel, the founder of the modern police force. She was also strongly influenced by the views of her husband, Prince Albert of Saxe-Coburg-Gotha, whom she married in 1840. The high point of her reign came in 1851 with the opening of the ◊Great Exhibition in Hyde Park, London, which was organized by Albert. The exhibition was designed in order to display 'the Industries of all Nations', but in fact came to symbolize the technological and industrial achievements of Victorian England.

Colonial expansion

During Queen Victoria's reign the British Empire was extended significantly, and often by means of military force, in Asia, Africa, and the Middle East. Hong Kong, for example, became part of the Empire as a result of the first ◊Opium Wars of 1839 to 1842, and Kowloon was later added to the colony after a second Opium War of 1856 to 1858. Other additions to the Empire made in the same period include New Zealand (1840), Northern Somalia (1884), Burma (1886), and Egypt, which became a British protectorate after the opening of the Suez Canal in 1869. The centre of the Empire, however, was India, which was controlled by the ◊East India Company until 1858. Control of India eventually passed to the British crown after the ◊Indian Mutiny of 1857, and, in 1877, Benjamin Disraeli's government conferred the title of Empress of India upon Queen Victoria.

Domestic politics

In domestic politics the Victorian period saw the development of a number of extra-parliamentary pressure groups, such as the ◊Anti-Corn Law League of 1838, and the Chartist movement (see ◊Chartism), which flourished in the period from 1838 to 1848. The latter movement supported a democratic ◊People's Charter, which demanded universal male suffrage, equal electoral districts, and other reform measures, and also organized violent demonstrations in Wales in 1839 (see ◊Newport Riots).

Further riots occurred in Wales between 1842 and 1844 (see ◊Rebecca Riots), which resulted in part from general unrest concerning the unpopular Poor Law Amendment Act of 1834. However, a number of more positive and liberalizing acts were also passed within Parliament during the same period. These include the Abolition Act of 1833, which provided for slaves in British colonies to be freed; the ◊Representation of the People Acts of 1832, 1867, and 1884, which extended voting rights and redistributed parliamentary seats; and the 1846 repeal of the Corn Laws, which was effected by the Tory prime minister Robert Peel and came about partly as a result of the Irish potato famine of 1846 to 1851. The Liberal prime minister William Gladstone also introduced elementary education in 1870 and, between 1880 to 1894, agitated (unsuccessfully) for Irish Home Rule.

Victorian style

Style of architecture, furnituremaking, and decorative art of the reign of Queen Victoria, from 1837 to 1901. The era was influenced by significant industrial and urban development, and the massive expansion of the ◊British Empire.

Victorian style was often very ornate, markedly so in architecture, where there was more than one 'revival' of earlier styles, beginning with a lengthy competition between the **Classic** and **Gothic** schools. ◊Gothic Revival drew on the original Gothic architecture of medieval times. The Gothic boom had begun in 1818, when Parliament voted a million pounds for building 214 new Anglican churches. No less than 174 of them were constructed in a Gothic or near-Gothic style, and for nearly a century, most churches in England were Gothic in design. Despite the popularity of extravagant decoration, Renaissance or Classic styles were also favoured for public buildings, examples being St George's Hall, Liverpool (1815), and Birmingham Town Hall (1832–50).

Many people, such as John ◊Ruskin, believed in designing objects and architecture primarily for their function, and not for mere appearance. Increasing mass production by machines threatened the existence of craft skills, and encouraged the development of the ◊Arts and Crafts movement, with its nostalgia for the medieval way of life. In the last quarter of the century there were revivals of **Jacobean** and finally of **Queen Anne** architecture.

Victory
British battleship, the flagship of Admiral Nelson at Trafalgar. Weighing 2,198 tonnes/2,164 tons, it was launched in 1765; it is now in dry dock in Portsmouth harbour, England.

Video Standards Council, VSC
Council established in 1989 as a standards body for the UK video industry. It is responsible for ensuring compliance with the law and proper trading standards. It is concerned with all aspects of the video industry, from good conduct by video retail and rental outlets, to videotape content. It also liaises with the ◊British Board of Film Classification.

Viking, or Norseman
Inhabitant of Scandinavia in the period 800–1100. The Vikings traded with, and raided, much of Europe, and often settled there. In their narrow, shallow-draught, highly manoeuvrable longships, the Vikings penetrated far inland along rivers. They plundered for gold and land, and were equally energetic as colonists – with colonies stretching from North America to central Russia – and as traders, with main trading posts at Birka (near Stockholm) and Hedeby (near Schleswig). The Vikings had a sophisticated literary culture, with sagas and runic inscriptions, and an organized system of government with an assembly ('thing'). Their kings and chieftains were buried with their ships, together with their possessions.

In France the Vikings were given Normandy. Under Sweyn I they conquered England (where they were known as 'Danes') in 1013, and his son Canute was king of England as well as Denmark and Norway. As ◊'Normans' they achieved a second conquest of England in 1066.

In Ireland the Vikings founded the cities of Dublin (841), Cork, and Limerick. They were halted, however, by their defeat at the battle of Clontarf in 1014.

See feature on page 920 on the Vikings in Britain.

Viking art
In Britain Viking art did not replace contemporary ◊Celtic art and Anglo-Saxon art of the 8th to 11th century, and made no marked influence until the latter part of the 10th century. It is noted for its woodcarving and finely wrought ornaments in gold and silver, and for an intricate interlacing decorative style similar to Celtic art. A dragonlike creature, known as the 'Great Beast', is a recurring motif; an early 11th-century rune-inscribed sculpture of a Great Beast and serpent (now in the Guildhall (City of London) Museum) was found on a tomb in St Paul's Cathedral churchyard in 1852 .

The three styles of Viking art are all represented in Britain: **Jellinge**, based on heavy animal designs, as found on a 2-m/6.5-ft-high standing cross in Gosforth, Cumberland; **Ringerike**, characterized by elaborate foliage ornament and interlacing, as seen in the Winchester school of illuminated manuscripts; and **Urnes**, notable in English Christian carving.

villeinage
System of serfdom that prevailed in Europe in the Middle Ages.

A villein was a peasant who gave dues and services to his lord in exchange for land. In France until the 13th century, 'villeins' could refer to rural or urban non-nobles, but after this, it came to mean exclusively rural non-noble freemen. In Norman England, it referred to free peasants of relatively high status. At the time of the Domesday Book, the villeins were the most numerous element in the English population, providing the labour force for the manors.

Their social position declined until, by the early 14th century, their personal and juridical status was close to that of serfs. After the mid-14th century, as the effects of the Black Death led to a severe labour shortage, their status improved. By the 15th century villeinage had been supplanted by a system of free tenure and labour in England.

Virgin
Company founded and owned by Richard ◊Branson. Branson started Virgin in 1969 as a mail-order business and the first Virgin record store opened in 1971. The company developed quickly, diversifying from retailing records to the airline business, then to radio, operating rail franchises, and offering financial services.

Branson started the Virgin record label in 1973. In 1984 he moved into the airline business, founding **Virgin Atlantic Airways**, which was followed by **Virgin Express**, which operates flights to Europe. The **Virgin Music Group** was sold to Thorn EMI in 1992. **Virgin FM**, the UK's second independent national radio station, opened in 1993, but **Virgin Radio** was sold to Capital Radio in 1997. In 1995 Virgin bought the MGM UK chain of 116 cinemas. **Virgin Rail Group Ltd** was formed in 1996, and operates the west coast rail franchise and cross-country services radiating from Birmingham. The company diversified into financial services in 1995, with the launch of **Virgin Direct**. In 1997 Branson announced that Virgin was expanding into banking, setting up a **Virgin One** bank account in partnership with the Royal Bank of Scotland. **Virgin Vie** stores sell cosmetics and toiletries, and the **Virgin Clothing Company** was scheduled for launch in 1998.

Viroconium, or Uriconium
Roman-British town, the remains of which have been excavated at Wroxeter, Shropshire, England. It was the fourth largest town in Roman Britain, and was founded in about AD 48 as a legionary camp fortress during Roman campaigns against the Welsh.

Viroconium became a town in about 80, when the Cornovii were forced to leave their own hill city on the Wrekin. It became the tribal capital of the Cornovii. A forum and basilica were built by 130, and baths and other public buildings followed. Much of the town was destroyed by fire in about 300, but the site was occupied until the 4th century.

viscount (medieval Latin *vicecomes* 'in place of a count/earl')
In the UK ◊peerage, the fourth degree of nobility, between earl and baron.

The title was first granted in England in 1440 to John, Lord Beaumont. Originally the title was given to the deputy sheriff, who acted on behalf of an earl within his estate.

THE SCOURGE OF THE NORTH: THE VIKINGS IN BRITAIN

The Viking Age in the British Isles began in the late 8th century with a series of raids by Scandinavian pirates on coastal monasteries such as Lindisfarne (sacked 793) and Iona (sacked 795). These hit-and-run raids were virtually impossible to prevent: by the time an army had gathered to counterattack, the Vikings had taken their plunder and set sail for home.

In the 840s Viking activity intensified. The Vikings came in larger numbers and founded permanent bases, such as Dublin in 841, from which they could campaign all year round. They were now interested as much in settlement as in plunder. The first areas to be settled were Scotland's northern and western isles, but the largest settlements took place in eastern and northern England after the Danes overran the Anglo-Saxon kingdoms of East Anglia, Northumbria, and Mercia in 865–74. The Vikings were greatly aided in this period by the disunity of the native kingdoms in Britain and Ireland, which failed absolutely to bury their differences and unite against the common enemy.

As the 9th century drew to a close, Viking activity declined. This was partly because many Vikings had now settled down as farmers and partly because of stiffening native resistance, such as that of Wessex under the leadership of Alfred the Great. Once the Vikings had settled down they lost their main advantage over the natives: their mobility. Between 912 and 954 Wessex conquered the Danelaw, as the Viking-settled area of eastern England was known, and the Viking kingdom of York. In Ireland the Vikings of Dublin struggled to maintain their independence and often paid tribute to Irish kings.

The late 10th century saw a resumption of large-scale Viking raiding, directed mostly at England. At first the raiders were content to extract Danegeld (protection money) but as English defences crumbled, the Danish king Sweyn I Forkbeard conquered the country in 1014. A resurgence of English resistance was put down by his son Canute in 1016 and England remained under Danish rule until 1042. The last major Viking invasion of the British Isles was Norwegian King Harald Hardrada's attempt to seize the English throne in 1066: he was defeated and killed by Harold I Godwinson at Stamford Bridge just days before William the Conqueror launched his own successful invasion.

The cultural impact

Most of our historical sources for Viking Age Britain were written by monks. Monasteries were the main cultural centres of early medieval Britain and Ireland: they were also wealthy and unprotected and this made them a favourite target of Viking raids. Not surprisingly therefore, monastic chroniclers dwelt mainly on the violence and destruction wrought by the Vikings. Some modern historians have argued that these chroniclers were prejudiced against the Vikings because of their paganism and greatly exaggerated the violence of their raids. However, contemporary accounts of Viking raids from Francia, the Byzantine Empire, and the Islamic lands, and Viking poetry, all agree that Viking raiders were extremely violent and destructive. Much of the damage caused by Viking raids was temporary, but their attacks on monasteries were devastating for cultural life: works of art and literature were destroyed, and the communities of learned monks were dispersed. In England, monasticism made a strong recovery in the 10th century, but the brilliant monastic civilization of early Christian Ireland, which had produced masterpieces like the *Book of Kells*, never recovered from the Viking raids.

Perhaps the most important effect of the Viking invasions was that they broke up the existing power structures of the British Isles. Viking raids on western Scotland encouraged the Scots to expand inland, conquering the Picts, thus creating the kingdom of Scotland. By destroying their rivals the Vikings also greatly aided the creation of a unified English kingdom by the kings of Wessex in the 10th century.

The abiding influence

The Vikings were not only warriors and pirates, however, but also merchants, farmers and settlers, and skilled craftsmen. Viking traders stimulated the growth of trading centres like York and the foundation of new towns like Dublin. Viking art styles influenced and enriched Celtic and Anglo-Saxon art. The English language was also greatly enriched by Danish loan words, including 'sky', 'egg', and 'sister'. After the initial violence of conquest, the Viking settlers farmed peacefully alongside their Celtic or Anglo-Saxon neighbours and, through conversion to Christianity and intermarriage, were quickly assimilated.

The Viking settlements have left few physical remains, but their locations and density can be inferred from the distribution of Scandinavian placenames. For example, Danish placenames (typically ending in '-by' or '-thorpe') are common in much of eastern England, while Norwegian placename elements (such as 'fell') are common in northwest England and the Hebrides. In Orkney and Shetland almost all placenames are of Scandinavian origin, pointing to a particularly dense Viking settlement.

BY JOHN HAYWOOD

visitor

Officer or superior whose duty it is to visit an English corporation, civil or ecclesiastical, in order to see that its rules and regulations are being observed, and that there is no serious default.

The visitation of civil corporations is the work of the crown, which acts through the medium of the Court of Queen's Bench. The bishop is the visitor of his or her diocese. On account of the number of parishes, however, the visitation is usually left to the archdeacons.

Viz

Adult comic, founded and edited by Chris Donald in 1979. Often described as Britain's rudest comic, it includes such controversial characters as Sid the Sexist, the Fat Slags, and the Topless Skateboard Nuns. By 1996 it was selling 916,000 copies to a mainly male readership.

Voice, The

Weekly newspaper established in 1982 for black Britons; in 1997 it had a circulation of just over 39,000.

Vorticism

Short-lived British literary and artistic movement (1912–15), influenced by Cubism and Futurism and led by Wyndham ◊Lewis. The aim was to build up 'a visual language as abstract as music' and also to make use of machine forms, which constituted as real a world to the artist as the forms of nature. Its manifesto appeared in the publication *Blast* in June 1914, of which only one other issue came out, in 1915. Lewis believed that painting should reflect the complexity and rapid change of the modern world; he painted in a harsh, angular, semi-abstract style. A number of distinguished artists had some association with the movement, including Henri Gaudier Brzeska, William Roberts, Edward Wadsworth, and David Bomberg. World War I halted Vorticist activity, but a number of Lewis's associates were later prominent in the London Group. The last Vorticist exhibition was held in 1915.

voting

Expression of opinion by ballot. All British subjects over 18, except peers, the insane, and felons, are entitled to vote in UK local government and parliamentary elections. A register of voters is prepared annually, and since 1872 voting has been by secret ballot.

Under the Corrupt and Illegal Practices Act 1883, any candidate attempting to influence voters by gifts, loans or promises, or by intimidation, is liable to a fine or imprisonment. The voting system is by a simple majority in single-member constituencies. Critics point out that under this system many electors have no say, since votes for a defeated candidate are wasted, and governments may take office with a minority of the total vote. When there are two main parties, divided along class lines, the one in power often undoes the legislation of its predecessor. Supporters of the system argue the danger of increasing party fragmentation, and they believe continual coalition governments would be ineffective. In the 1997 election, turnout was 71% of registered voters.

Systems of proportional representation have been introduced, since 1997, for elections to the new assemblies in Scotland, Wales, and Northern Ireland and for future elections to the European Parliament. In December 1997, the Labour government of Tony Blair, established an independent commission, chaired by Lord Jenkins, to propose a 'more proportional' electoral system for the United Kingdom Westminster parliament.

Voysey, Charles Francis Annesley (1857–1941)

English architect and designer. From 1888 to about 1914 he had an international reputation as a designer of houses of extreme simplicity, in contrast to mid-Victorian pretentiousness. His country houses are characteristically asymmetrical with massive buttresses, long sloping roofs, and roughcast walls, for example The Cottage, Bishop's Itchington, Warwickshire (1888–89). He also designed textiles and wallpaper in the ◊Arts and Crafts tradition, his work showing the influence of William Morris and Arthur Mackmurdo. He designed his houses in minute detail, including the furniture, fireplaces, door handles, and other features.

VSC

Abbreviation for the ◊Video Standards Council.

Vyne, the

House in Hampshire, England, 6 km/4 mi north of Basingstoke. It was built by the Sandys family 1500–20, and a classic portico (large porch with a pediment) was added around 1654 (the earliest added to a country house in England). The house has a 16th-century oak gallery and chapel with Renaissance glass, a Palladian staircase, and some 18th-century Rococo rooms. The Vyne was acquired by the National Trust, together with 445 ha/1,099 acres, in 1956.

Waddesdon Manor

Late Victorian Renaissance-style house in Buckinghamshire, England, 8 km/5 mi northwest of Aylesbury. It was built for Baron Ferdinand de Rothschild, and was bequeathed to the National Trust in 1957, with a collection of pictures, furniture, and china. The grounds contain an 18th-century aviary.

Wade, (Sarah) Virginia (1945–)

English tennis player who won the Wimbledon singles title in the Silver Jubilee year of 1977 after 15 years of striving. She also won the US Open in 1968 and the 1972 Australian Open. She holds a record number of appearances for the Wightman and Federation Cup teams and her total of eight Grand Slam titles is a post-war British record equalled only by Ann Jones.

Wadsworth, Edward Alexander (1889–1949)

English artist. Associated with the Vorticists, he first produced brightly coloured linear abstracts and made a remarkable series of semi-abstract woodcuts from 1913 to 1914. By the 1920s he had developed a crisp, realistic style in which inanimate objects (often connected with sailing) have a Surrealistic quality, as in his well-known *North Sea* (1928; private collection).

Wain, John (Barrington) (1925–1994)

English poet and novelist. His first novel, *Hurry on Down* (1953), expresses the radical political views of the ◊Angry Young Men of the 1950s. He published several volumes of witty and ironic verse, collected in *Poems 1949–79* (1981), and was professor of poetry at Oxford University from 1973 to 1980.

wait

Double-reed wind instrument of the oboe type, similar to the shawm, used in England by the Christmas waits and, in the 13th century, by the keepers of the City of London gates and other town gates for the purpose of sending signals such as 'All's well'.

Waite, Terry (Terence Hardy) (1939–)

British religious adviser to the archbishop of Canterbury (then Dr Robert ◊Runcie) 1980–87.

As the archbishop's special envoy, Waite disappeared on 20 January 1987 while engaged in secret negotiations to free European hostages in Beirut, Lebanon. He was taken hostage by an Islamic group and released on 18 November 1991.

His kidnapping followed six conversations he held with the US agent Col Oliver North, who appeared to be hoping to ransom US hostages through Waite.

Wakefield

Industrial city in West Yorkshire, northern England, on the River Calder, south of Leeds; population (1991) 73,600. Industries include chemicals, machine tools, wool textiles, coal mining, and the manufacture of clothing, wire-rope, and sheet metal. Lancastrian forces defeated and killed Richard of York here in 1460, during the Wars of the ◊Roses. The National Coal Mining Museum is here.

Features

All Saints' cathedral, founded originally in the 13th century, dates largely from the 15th century; it is chiefly Perpendicular with a crocketed spire (75 m/246 ft). On the bridge over the Calder stands the chapel of St Mary, one of only four surviving bridge chapels in England; it dates originally from the 14th century and was rebuilt in 1847 in a rich Decorated style. Queen Elizabeth Grammar School, said to be the descendant of a 13th-century school, was founded here by a royal charter of Elizabeth I in 1591. Wakefield includes the suburb of Sandal Magna.

History

A medieval town of some importance, Wakefield became a prominent centre for the cloth trade in the 16th century. It became a municipal borough in 1848, and a city in 1888, when a diocese was created and the parish church of All Saints became a cathedral.

Famous people

Wakefield was the birthplace of the writer George Gissing and of the physician Dr John Radcliffe (1652–1714).

Walden, (Alastair) Brian (1932–)

British journalist and, from 1977, television presenter. He was a Labour member of Parliament 1964–77.

Walden was a university lecturer before entering Parliament. Disillusioned with party politics, he cut short his parliamentary career in 1977 and became presenter of the current-affairs TV programme *Weekend World*, with a direct and uninhibited style of interviewing public figures.

He also contributes to the *Sunday Times* and *Evening Standard* newspapers.

Wales, Welsh Cymru

Principality of; constituent part of the UK, in the west between the British Channel and the Irish Sea
Area 20,780 sq km/8,021 sq mi
Capital Cardiff
Towns and cities Swansea, Wrexham, Newport, Carmarthen
Features Snowdonia Mountains (Snowdon 1,085 m/3,560 ft, the highest point in England and Wales) in the northwest and in the southeast the Black Mountains, Brecon Beacons, and Black Forest ranges; rivers Severn, Wye, Usk, and Dee
Industries traditional industries have declined, but varied modern and high-technology ventures are being developed. There are oil refineries and open-cast coal mining. The last deep coal mine in north Wales closed in 1996. Wales has the largest concentration of Japanese-owned plants in the UK. It also has the highest density of sheep in the world and a dairy industry; tourism is important
Currency pound sterling
Population (1993 est) 2,906,000
Language English, 19% Welsh-speaking
Religion Nonconformist Protestant denominations; Roman Catholic minority
Government returns 40 members to the UK Parliament; in April 1996, the 8 counties were replaced by 22 county and county borough unitary authorities (see table on page 927).

See below for chronology of key dates, page 928 for list of sovereigns and princes, and page 926 for a feature on Welsh devolution.

Wales, Church in

The Welsh Anglican Church, independent from the ◊Church of England.

The Welsh church became strongly Protestant in the 16th century, but in the 17th and 18th centuries declined from being led by a succession of English-appointed bishops. Disestablished by an act of Parliament in 1920, with its endowments appropriated, the Church in Wales today comprises six dioceses (with bishops elected by an electoral college of clergy and lay people) with an archbishop elected from among the six bishops.

The six dioceses are: St David's, Llandaff, Bangor, St Asaph, Monmouth, and Swansea and Brecon (a diocese which, with Monmouth, was formed after 1920). Until the Welsh Church Acts of 1914 and 1919, Wales was included in the province of

WALES: CHRONOLOGY

For ancient history, see also Ancient Britain.

c. 400 BC Wales occupied by Celts from central Europe.

AD 50–60 Wales became part of the Roman Empire.

c. 200 Christianity adopted.

c. 450–600 Wales became the chief Celtic stronghold in the west since the Saxons invaded and settled in southern Britain. The Celtic tribes united against England.

8th century Frontier pushed back to Offa's Dyke.

9th–11th centuries Vikings raided the coasts. At this time Wales was divided into small states organized on a clan basis, although princes such as Rhodri (844–878), Howel the Good (*c.* 904–949), and Griffith ap Llewelyn (1039–1063) temporarily united the country.

11th–12th centuries Continual pressure on Wales from the Normans across the English border was resisted, notably by Llewelyn I and II.

1277 Edward I of England accepted as overlord by the Welsh.

1284 Edward I completed the conquest of Wales that had been begun by the Normans.

1294 Revolt against English rule put down by Edward I.

1350–1500 Welsh nationalist uprisings against the English; the most notable was that led by Owen Glendower.

1485 Henry Tudor, a Welshman, became Henry VII of England.

1536–43 Acts of Union united England and Wales after conquest under Henry VIII. Wales sent representatives to the English Parliament; English law was established in Wales; English became the official language.

18th century Evangelical revival made Nonconformism a powerful factor in Welsh life. A strong coal and iron industry developed in the south.

19th century The miners and ironworkers were militant supporters of Chartism, and Wales became a stronghold of trade unionism and socialism.

1893 University of Wales founded.

1920s–30s Wales suffered from industrial depression; unemployment reached 21% 1937, and a considerable exodus of population took place.

post-1945 Growing nationalist movement and a revival of the language, earlier suppressed or discouraged.

1966 Plaid Cymru, the Welsh National Party, returned its first member to Westminster.

1979 Referendum rejected a proposal for limited home rule.

1988 Bombing campaign against estate agents selling Welsh properties to English buyers.

1997 Referendum endorsed devolution proposals by a narrow margin of 50.3%.

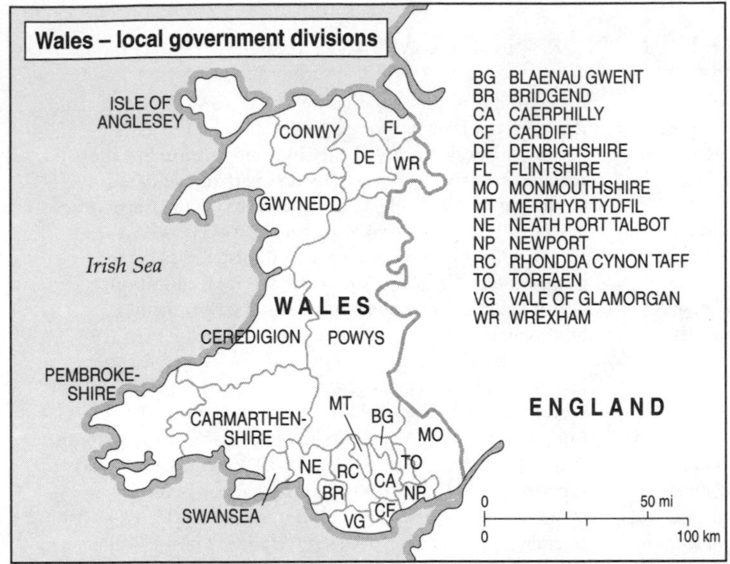

Canterbury; the Welsh archbishopric was formed on disestablishment.

Wales, Prince of

Title conferred on the eldest son of the UK's sovereign. Prince ⇨Charles was invested as 21st prince of Wales at Caernarfon in 1969 by his mother, Elizabeth II.

The conferment is sometimes accompanied or followed by a ceremony of investiture at Caernarfon Castle, north Wales. Edward (afterwards King Edward II), son and heir apparent, was summoned to and sat in Parliament as Prince of Wales; his presentation at Caernarfon is legendary. The earliest documented grantee was Edward II's grandson, Edward the Black Prince, with limitation 'to him and his heirs the kings of England'. Consequently, when a Prince of Wales succeeds to the throne, his title merges in the crown and requires a new creation for its separate existence. See table on page 928.

Wall, Max stage name of Maxwell George Lorimer (1908–1990)

English music-hall comedian. Towards the end of his career he appeared in starring roles as a serious actor, in John Osborne's *The Entertainer* (1974), in Harold Pinter's *The Caretaker* (1977), and in Samuel Beckett's *Waiting for Godot* (1980). In his solo comedy performances his trademark was an eccentric walk.

Wallace, (Richard Horatio) Edgar (1875–1932)

English writer of thrillers. His prolific output includes *The Four Just Men* (1905) and *The Mind of Mr J G Reeder* (1925); stories such as those in *Sanders of the River* (1911), set in Africa, and sequels; and melodramas such as *The Ringer* (1926), from his own novel *The Gaunt Stranger* (1925).

Wallace was born in London, left school at 12, and did unskilled work before joining the army. He served in South Africa from 1896–99, after which he became a journalist. He wrote or dictated over 175 novels and volumes of stories in the space of 20 years, finding his true medium in thrillers, which he himself described as 'pirate stories in modern dress'.

Wallace, Alfred Russel (1823–1913)

Welsh naturalist who collected animal and plant specimens in South America and South-East Asia, and independently arrived at a theory of evolution by natural selection similar to that proposed by Charles ⇨Darwin.

Wallace and Darwin

In 1858, Wallace wrote an essay outlining his ideas on evolution and sent it to Darwin, who had not yet published his. Together they presented a paper to the Linnaean Society that year. Wallace's section, entitled 'On the

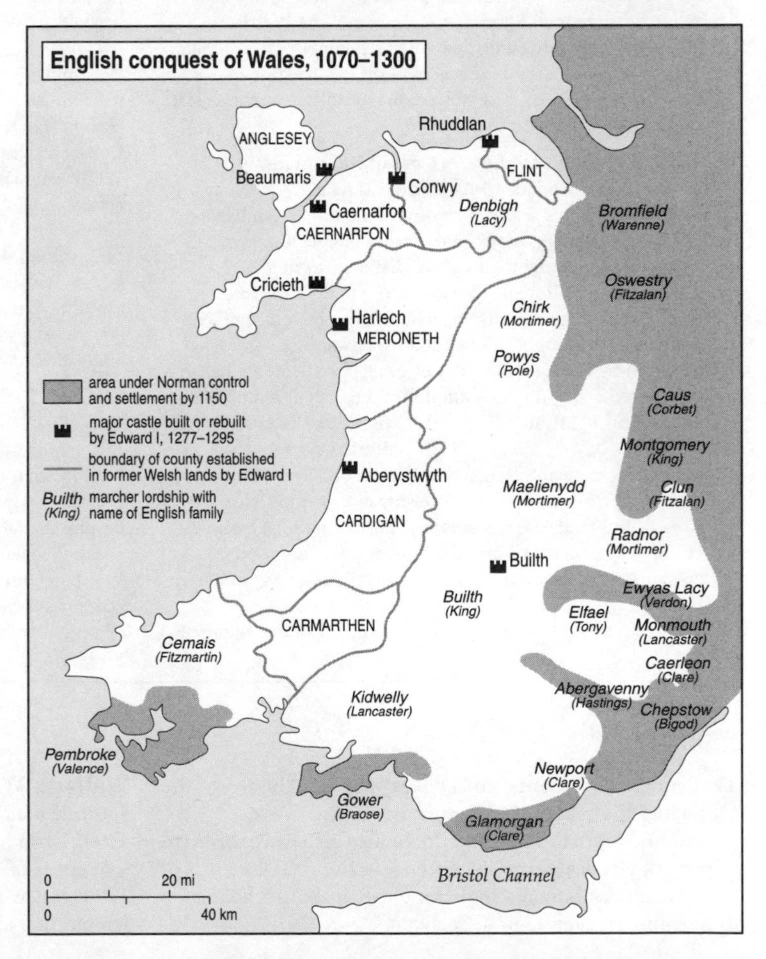

WELSH DEVOLUTION: A HESITANT 'YES'

With its Celtic language, still spoken by one-fifth of the population, and its early history as an outpost largely free from Roman and Anglo-Saxon occupation, Wales has a distinctive culture and history. It has its own flag, centred on the Welsh dragon, a prince, national sports teams, and thriving arts. However, Welsh national identity lacks the cohesiveness of Scots. The reason for this has been that many centuries of immigration from England, to the northeast and south, has, in effect, created three Waleses: 'British' Wales, the heavily anglicized east and northeast, where most of the people are either English-born or work in the neighbouring English cities of Bristol and Manchester; Welsh Wales, the former mining valleys of the south, where the people feel Welsh but do not speak it and where there is a distinctive tradition of radical non-conformism; and Welsh-speaking Wales, the highland regions of the interior and northwest, which held out longest against English conquest and settlement during the medieval period and where, centred on Gwynedd, a Welsh principality was established in 1244 by David ap Llewelyn.

The lack of a homogenous identity has long hampered Plaid Cymru, the Welsh Nationalist Party, a centre-left party which was set up in Gwynedd in 1925 to campaign for self-government and greater promotion of the Welsh language. These divisions remained prominent in September 1997, when a referendum was held on the question of establishing a Welsh assembly, nearly resulting in the defeat of the devolution plans.

The background to the 1997 devolution plans

Between the 11th and 13th centuries, England's Norman and Plantagenet kings set up earldoms along the Welsh border, but Welsh soldiers, based in the mountainous interior, successfully resisted the English challenge to their independence, allowing Welsh culture to flourish and a principality to be established. The English conquest of Wales was finally accomplished in 1282 by Edward I and was followed by the establishment of English settlements in the conquered areas, the introduction of English common law, and the titling, from 1301, of the King's eldest son as 'Prince of Wales'. During the early 15th century, Owen Glendower led an armed revolt against the English overlords, but from 1485, when Henry Tudor, a Welshman, became Henry VII, King of England, the ties between the two nations became closer. The process of the administrative assimilation culminated in the signing, by Henry VIII, of an Act of Union in 1536.

During the 19th century, with the revival of the National Eisteddfod of Wales, a gathering of poets and musicians, and the novels of Daniel Owen, a Welsh cultural renaissance began. This was promoted later by Plaid Cymru, but the nationalist party did not win its first parliamentary seat until the triumph of its leader, Gwynfor Evans, in the Carmarthen by-election of 1966. Two years earlier, a Welsh Office was set up, which, headed by a cabinet minister, was given responsibility for health and social services, education, the Welsh language, arts and culture, local government, housing, agriculture, roads, and tourism.

From the 1960s, support for Plaid Cymru and for the Labour and Liberal parties, which proposed devolving powers to a Welsh assembly, strengthened. Only the Conservative Party, which has long been a minority party in Wales, has opposed devolution. In 1978, with Liberal Party support, James Callaghan's minority Labour government secured the passage of legislation to create an elected Welsh assembly to take over the executive powers of the Welsh Office. However, in the referendum held in March 1979, only 20% voted 'Yes' for devolution, with turnout of 59%. Divisions within Labour's ranks over the devolution issue contributed to the failure of this referendum, but so did public apathy, the desire for self-government being clearly weaker in Wales than in Scotland.

During the subsequent 18 years of Conservative rule in Westminster, Wales continued to return large Labour majorities and between 1980 and 1992 the party had Welsh leaders: Michael Foot, followed by Neil Kinnock. The Conservatives reluctantly agreed to the introduction of a Welsh language TV channel, S4C, in 1982, but their other actions, including their crushing of the miners' strike in 1984–85 and the unprecedented appointment, in 1987, of an Englishman, Peter Walker, as Welsh Secretary, did little to attract Welsh support. Consequently, in the 1992 general election, Conservative support in Wales fell to 29%, compared with Labour's 50% share, while Plaid Cymru, with 9% of the vote, won a record four of Wales' 38 Westminster seats.

The 1997 Welsh assembly proposals

At the May 1997 general election, Conservative support fell even further, to 19% of the Welsh vote, and for the first time ever the party failed to win any Welsh seats. This was despite the fact that, although traditional industries such as coal and steel had been decimated, recent years had seen a Welsh economic revival, founded on foreign inward economic investment in the automobile, electronics, and computer industries.

Tendency of Varieties to Depart Indefinitely from the Original Type', described the survival of the fittest.

Although both thought that the human race had evolved to its present physical form by natural selection, Wallace was of the opinion that humans' higher mental capabilities had arisen from some 'metabiological' agency.

Wallace, William (1272–1305)

Scottish nationalist who led a revolt against English rule in 1297, won a victory at Stirling, and assumed the title 'governor of Scotland'. Edward I defeated him at Falkirk in 1298, and Wallace was captured and executed. He was styled Knight in a charter of 1298.

The 'New' Labour government swiftly secured passage of devolution bills for Scotland and Wales, but the proposals for Wales fell far short of those offered to Scotland. Instead of a parliament with law-making and tax-varying powers, Wales was offered a 60-seat assembly designed chiefly to take over the functions of the Welsh Office, implementing Westminster laws, spending its £7 billion budget, and making quasi-nongovernmental organizations, which had proliferated during the Conservative years, more accountable. The assembly, which will be based in Cardiff and will be elected in 1999 (one-third by proportional representation), will not have primary law-making powers even in respect to the Welsh language.

A disappointing turnout

The proposals were attacked by Plaid Cymru and the Liberal Democrats as too cautious, but nevertheless secured their broad support. This left the 'No' campaign backed by only the Conservative Party and six dissident Labour Members of Parliament. Campaigning was low-key and was disrupted by the death of Princess Diana. The strong vote for devolution in the Scottish referendum, held a week earlier, may have had a crucial impact on the Welsh 'Yes' campaign. Nevertheless, when the referendum was held, on 18 September 1997, turnout was disappointingly low, at just 51.3% of the electorate. The outcome remained undecided until the final declaration, in Carmarthenshire, which, by giving strong support to the 'Yes' campaign, resulted in an overall 50.3% support for a devolved assembly. Nevertheless, in 11 of the nation's 22 unitary authorities, concentrated in the east and far southwest, there was a majority against devolution. Essentially, the 'Yes' vote was brought about through an alliance of the Welsh-speaking interior and northwest and the Labour strongholds in the southern valleys.

The narrowness of the 'Yes' vote in September 1997 persuaded the then Welsh Secretary Ron Davies to pursue an 'inclusive strategy' for the assembly, which will start functioning in 2000. An all-party commission is to be established to devise the assembly's rules, while powerful regional committees will also be set up to placate North Wales fears that the assembly will be dominated by the populous south. The weakness and ambiguity of the September 1997 result also suggests that while, over time, the Welsh assembly is likely to form an accepted and useful addition to the Welsh government system, it is unlikely to be form a 'staging post' towards eventual independence.

BY IAN DERBYSHIRE

Wales: Local Government

In April 1996, the 8 counties of Wales – Clwyd, Dyfed, Gwent, Gwynned, Mid Glamorgan, Powys, South Glamorgan, and West Glamorgan – were replaced with 22 counties and county borough unitary authorities.

Local authority	Administrative headquarters	Area		Population (1996)
		sq km	sq mi	
Blaenau Gwent	Ebbw Vale	109	42	73,000
Bridgend	Bridgend	40	15	128,300
Caerphilly	Ystrad Mynach	270	104	172,000
Cardiff	Cardiff	139	54	306,500
Carmarthenshire	Carmarthen	2,390	923	68,900
Ceredigion	Aberaeron	1,793	692	68,900
Conwy	Conwy	1,107	427	113,000
Denbighshire	Ruthin	844	326	91,000
Flintshire	Mold	437	167	144,000
Gwynedd	Caernafon	2,546	983	116,000
Isle of Anglesey	Llangefni	720	278	71,100
Merthyr Tydfil	Merthyr Tydfil	111	43	60,000
Monmouthshire	Cwmbran	851	328	80,400
Neath Port Talbot	Port Talbot	442	171	139,400
Newport	Newport	190	73	133,300
Pembrokeshire	Haverfordwest	1,588	613	117,700
Powys	Llandrindod Wells	5,179	1,999	123,600
Rhondda Cynon Taff	Clydach Vale	440	170	232,600
Swansea	Swansea	377	156	232,000
Torfaen	Pontypool	98	38	90,700
Vale of Glamorgan	Barry	337	130	119,500
Wrexham	Wrexham	500	193	123,500

Wallace, William (1860–1940)

Scottish music author and composer. He was educated at Edinburgh and Glasgow Universities and in Vienna as an eye specialist. He began to practise in 1888, but gave up his profession for music except during World War I. In 1889 he entered the Royal Academy of Music in London for a brief course in composition, and later he became successively secretary and trustee of the Philharmonic Society. His books include *The Threshold of Music* (1908), *The Musical Faculty* (1914), *Richard Wagner as He Lived* (1925), and *Liszt, Wagner and the Princess* (1927).

Wallace and Gromit

Animated clay characters created by English animator Nick ◊Park. Wallace, a northern working-class inventor, and his canine sidekick Gromit starred in *A Grand Day Out* (1989), in which they build a space rocket to the Moon in search of

Wales: Historic Counties

Anglesey
Brecknockshire
Caernarvonshire
Cardiganshire
Carmarthenshire
Denbighshire
Flintshire
Glamorgan
Merioneth
Monmouthshire
Montgomeryshire
Pembrokeshire
Radnorshire

Wales, Princes of (since 1301; date given is when title was conferred)

1301	Edward (II)
1343	Edward (the Black Prince)
1376	Richard (II)
1399	Henry of Monmouth (V)
1454	Edward of Westminster
1471	Edward of Westminster (V)
1483	Edward
1489	Arthur Tudor
1504	Henry Tudor (VIII)
1610	Henry Stuart
1616	Charles Stuart (I)
c. 1638	Charles (II)
1688	James Francis Edward (Old Pretender)
1714	George Augustus (II)
1729	Frederick Lewis
1751	George William Frederick (III)
1762	George Augustus Frederick (IV)
1841	Albert Edward (Edward VII)
1901	George (V)
1910	Edward (VIII)
1958	Charles Philip Arthur George

Wales: Sovereigns and Princes 844–1282

844–78	Rhodri the Great
878–916	Anarawd
915–50	Hywel Dda (Hywel the Good)
950–79	Iago ab Idwal
979–85	Hywel ab Ieuaf (Hywel the Bad)
985–86	Cadwallon
986–99	Maredudd ab Owain ap Hywel Dda
999–1008	Cynan ap Hywel ab Ieuaf
1018–23	Llywelyn ap Seisyll
1023–39	Iago ab Idwal ap Meurig
1039–63	Gruffydd ap Llywelyn ap Seisyll
1063–75	Bleddyn ap Cynfyn
1075–81	Trahaern ap Caradog
1081–1137	Gruffydd ap Cynan ab Iago
1137–70	Owain Gwynedd
1170–94	Dafydd ab Owain Gwynedd
1194–1240	Llywelyn Fawr (Llywelyn the Great)
1240–46	Dafydd ap Llywellyn
1246–82	Llywellyn ap Gruffydd ap Llywellyn

cheese; *The Wrong Trousers* (1993), in which they capture a criminal mastermind; and *A Close Shave* (1995), in which they save a flock of sheep from an evil robot dog. *The Wrong Trousers* and *A Close Shave* won Academy Awards.

Wallace Collection

Collection of paintings and art objects on display in Hertford House, Manchester Square, London. The works were collected by Richard Wallace (1818–1890), and donated to the nation in 1897. It is one of the finest collections of 18th-century French art.

Much of the collection comes from the royal châteaux, and includes sculpture, furniture, and small *objets d'art*, as well as paintings by Watteau, Boucher, Fragonard, and others. There are also many fine paintings of various national schools, including *Lady with a Fan* by Velázquez and *The Laughing Cavalier* by Frans Hals, and collections of European and Oriental armour.

Wallasey

Residential town in the metropolitan county of ◊Merseyside, northwest England, on the northeast extremity of the Wirral peninsula, at the mouth of the River Mersey; population (1991) 15,000. Since the 1820s there have been ferries from here to Liverpool across the Mersey, with railway services through the Mersey tunnel from 1885, and road tunnels from 1934.

Wallasey derives its name from an old village within which several districts developed, including Egremont, Seacombe, Liscard, and New Brighton. Mainly residential, these centres grew and joined together as suburbs for Liverpool and Birkenhead.

It's cool to be Welsh these days – well, almost.

PATRICK HANNAN Welsh broadcaster. *Daily Telegraph*, September 1998

Wallington

House and estate in Northumberland, England, 18 km/11 mi west of Morpeth. The house contains collections of porcelain, paintings and furniture. There is a conservatory in the walled garden. The 5,250 ha/12,967 acre estate was given to the National Trust by Charles Trevelyan in 1942. The estate includes 16 farms and most of the village of Cambo besides the late 17th-century house which was largely redesigned around 1740.

Wallis, Alfred (1855–1942)

English naive painter. Having spent much of his life as a sailor, he started painting when he was 70 and living in St Ives in Cornwall, southwest England. Often using household or ship paints and scraps of cardboard, he painted ships and harbours with a childlike simplicity of form and composition. *Voyage to Labrador* (about 1935; Tate Gallery, London) is typical.

In the late 1920s he attracted the attention of the painters Ben ◊Nicholson and Christopher Wood, both of whom were directly influenced by his work.

Wallis, Barnes Neville (1887–1979)

British aeronautical engineer who designed the airship R-100, and during World War II perfected the 'bouncing bombs' used by the Royal Air Force Dambusters Squadron to destroy the German Möhne and Eder dams in 1943. He also assisted in the development of the Concorde supersonic airliner and developed the swing wing aircraft. Knighted 1968.

Wallsend

Town in Tyne and Wear, northeast England, on the River Tyne at the east end of Hadrian's Wall; population (1991) 44,500. Industries include engineering, floating oil-production platforms for the North Sea, ship repairs, electronics, and the manufacture of transport equipment. The Swan Hunter shipyards were closed in 1994 following the launch of the last ship to be built in the northeast.

Wallsend was the site of the Roman fort of **Segedunum**; relics excavated from the site are displayed in a heritage centre. The 19th-century engineer George Stephenson, and his son Robert who was also an engineer, lived here.

Walmer

Resort in Kent, southeast England, south of Deal; population (1991) 2,300. Its castle, built for Henry VIII in about 1539, has been the official residence of the Lord Warden of the ◊Cinque Ports since the 18th century. The Duke of Wellington died here in 1852. Walmer is a reputed landing place of Julius Caesar in 55 BC.

Walney Island

Island off the coast of Cumbria, northwest England; population (1991) 11,200. It is connected by a bridge to the industrial seaport of ◊Barrow-in-Furness, and except for the suburb of Vickerstown it is mainly an agricultural area, with some tourism.

Walney Island has at its southern tip the largest colony of gulls in Europe and is an important nesting site for the eider duck.

Walpole, Horace, 4th Earl of Orford (1717–1797)

English novelist, letter writer and politician, the son of Robert Walpole. He was a Whig member of Parliament 1741–67.

He converted his house at Strawberry Hill, Twickenham (then a separate town southwest of London), into a Gothic castle; his *The Castle of Otranto* (1764) established the genre of the Gothic, or 'romance of terror', novel. More than 4,000 of his letters have been published.

Walpole, Robert, 1st Earl of Orford (1676–1745)

British Whig politician, the first 'prime minister'. As First Lord of the Treasury and chancellor of the Exchequer (1715–17 and 1721–42) he encouraged trade and tried to avoid foreign disputes (until forced into the War of Jenkins' Ear with Spain in 1739).

Opponents thought his foreign policies worked to the advantage of France. He held favour with George I and George II, struggling against ◊Jacobite intrigues, and received an earldom when he eventually retired in 1742.

Walsall

Industrial town in West Midlands, central England, 13 km/8 mi northwest of Birmingham; population (1991) 172,600. It has a leather industry and also produces castings. Until the 1930s coal was mined here. Walsall's art gallery contains the Garman–Ryan collection, over 350 paintings including works by Jacob Epstein. The writer Jerome K Jerome was born here in 1859.

The Garman–Ryan collection was bequeathed to the art gallery in 1974 – with the aim of providing a 'bright light' in the Black Country – by Kathleen Garman, Jacob Epstein's second wife, who was born in the town. Other features include a canal museum and a leather museum. There are also plans to build a £21 million New Art Gallery by the canal, as part of the 'Town Wharf' development.

Walsingham

Village in Norfolk, England, 8 km/5 mi north of Fakenham; population (1991) 1,300. There are ruins of an Augustinian priory founded in 1153, which was a centre of pilgrimage until the time of the Reformation. Pilgrimages to Walsingham were revived in 1921; they centre on the Slipper Chapel (Roman Catholic) 2 km/1 mi from the village, and on an Anglican shrine in the village.

According to tradition, the Virgin Mary appeared before the lady of the manor in 1061, and a shrine was built to 'Our Lady of Walsingham', later incorporated in the church of the Augustinian priory. The shrine, priory, and a Franciscan friary, dating from the late 13th century, were destroyed at the time of the Reformation.

> *I have never felt truly at ease or at home anywhere but in Wales. I fell in love with the land as I believe people are expected to fall in love with other people.*
>
> Alice Thomas Ellis British writer. *A Welsh Childhood* (1990)

Walsingham, Francis (*c.* 1530–1590)

English politician who, as secretary of state from 1573, both advocated a strong anti-Spanish policy and ran the efficient government spy system that made it work. Knighted 1577.

Walter, Hubert (died 1205)

Archbishop of Canterbury 1193–1205. As justiciar (chief political and legal officer) 1193–98, he ruled England during Richard I's absence and introduced the offices of coroner and justice of the peace.

Walters, Julie (1950–)

English stage and screen actress. She has worked extensively on British film and television, displaying adept skill in both comic and dramatic roles. She established her reputation in her role of a a down-trodden housewife seeking to expand her intellectual horizons in *Educating Rita* (1983). Comic performances such as that of the brothel madam Christine Painter in *Personal Services* (1987) were subsequently alternated with dramatic roles in television miniseries such as *GBH* (1991) and *Jake's Progress* (1995). She also featured in the television series *Dinner Ladies* (1998).

Waltham Forest

Outer borough of north Greater London. It includes the suburbs of Chingford, Leyton, and Walthamstow

Features takes its name from former name for Epping Forest, referring to forest around Waltham Abbey; Lea Valley Regional Park (1967), including Walthamstow Marshes; Water House, Walthamstow, home of William Morris, now the William Morris Gallery

Population (1991) 212,000

Famous people Martin Frobisher. Cardinal Wiseman lived in Leyton.

Walton, Izaak (1593–1683)

English writer. He is known for his classic fishing compendium *The Compleat Angler, or the Contemplative Man's Recreation* (1653). He also wrote lives of the poets John Donne (1658) and George Herbert (1670) and the theologian Richard Hooker (1665).

The Compleat Angler is an autobiographical and philosophical study in the form of a dialogue between an angler, a fowler, and a hunter, with verses, anecdotes, and extracts from folklore.

Walton, William Turner (1902–1983)

English composer. Among his works are *Façade* (1923), a series of instrumental pieces designed to be played in conjunction with the recitation of surrealist poems by Edith Sitwell; the oratorio *Belshazzar's Feast* (1931); and *Variations on a Theme by Hindemith* (1963).

Wandsworth

Inner borough of southwest central Greater London

Features made famous for hats in the 18th century by influx of Huguenot refugees who were skilled hatters (Roman cardinals ordered their hats from here); mills on River Wandle; Wandsworth Prison (1857); brewing industry (important since the 16th century); Battersea Park and Putney Heath are both in the borough; Battersea Power Station (1937, designed by Giles Gilbert Scott)

Industries light engineering, brewing, paint, candles, computers

Population (1991) 252,400.

Wapping

District of the Greater London borough of ◊Tower Hamlets. The redevelopment of the London ◊Docklands began here 1969 with work on St Katherine Dock. From the mid-1980s it has been a centre of the newspaper industry.

The Times newspaper moved its offices here and built an 80 million printing plant in February 1986; it became the headquarters of Rupert Murdoch's News International group. The plant gained the nickname 'Fortress Wapping' after disputes with the print unions over the introduction of new technology led to the sacking of over 5,000 print workers and a bitter year-long strike led to picketing and often violent clashes with police.

Warbeck, Perkin (*c.* 1474–1499)

Flemish pretender to the English throne. Claiming to be Richard, brother of Edward V, he led a rising against Henry VII 1497, and was hanged after attempting to escape from the Tower of London.

Warchus, Matthew (1967–)

English theatre director. His productions include *Who's Afraid of Virginia Woolf?* (1992), *The Life of Stuff* (1993), *Henry V* and *Volpone* (both 1995, Evening Standard Best Director Award), *Art* (1996, Evening Standard Best Comedy Award, 1998 Tony Best Play Award), and *Hamlet* (1997). He has directed plays for the National Youth Theatre, the Bristol Old Vic Theatre, the Donmar Warehouse, the Royal Shakespeare Company, the Royal National Theatre; and operas for the

WAPPING *In the 1980s, Wapping in the east London area of Docklands became the scene of mass protests, after the Australian newspaper magnate Rupert Murdoch moved production of the* Times *and other titles to a new plant and dispensed with traditional print-union labour. This was one of the key anti-trade union moves that characterized the Thatcher era. Peter Arkell/Impact*

English National Opera, Opera North, and the Welsh National Opera.

He is an associate director for the West Yorkshire Playhouse. He won the 1993 Shakespeare's Globe Most Promising Newcomer Award for his production of *Much Ado About Nothing* (Queen's Theatre).

Ward, Leslie (1851–1922)

English caricaturist. He became famous as 'Spy', the caricaturist for *Vanity Fair* from 1873 to 1909. Among his most characteristic drawings were those of lawyers. His *Forty Years of Spy* was published in 1915. He was knighted in 1918.

Wardens of the Marches

Officials responsible for the security of the Anglo-Scottish border from the 14th century. They were appointed separately in England and Scotland for the East, West, and Middle Marches. Usually local noblemen, their duty was not only to defend their respective borders but, more usually, to maintain peace and settle disputes. The offices lapsed with James VI's accession to the English throne in 1603.

wardrobe

Financial department of the British royal household, originally a secure place for royal robes and other valuable items. As the Exchequer became a formal department of state, monarchs needed to maintain a privy treasury under their personal supervision and the wardrobe was secure enough to hold money. By the time of Henry III's reign, the wardrobe was so important that the barons demanded all income should be officially accounted for in the Exchequer. Under Edward I, it became a war treasury and was used to pay the armies on major expeditions. However, from the time of Edward IV, and more especially the Tudors, it was largely replaced by the Chamber as a form of 'current account'.

Ware

Town in the county of Hertfordshire, England, on the River Lea, 3 km/2 mi northeast of Hertford; population (1991) 16,500. Industries include pharmaceuticals, malting, engineering, the manufacture of plastics and stationery, and glovemaking.

The **Great Bed of Ware**, a piece of medieval furniture formerly at the Saracen's Head public house, is now in the Victoria and Albert Museum, London.

Warlock, Peter pen name of Philip Arnold Heseltine (1894–1930)

English composer. His style was influenced by the music of the Elizabethan age and by that of Delius. His works include the orchestral suite *Capriol* (1926) based on 16th-century dances, and the song cycle *The Curlew* (1920–22). His works of musical theory and criticism were published under his real name.

Warminster

Market town in Wiltshire, southwest England, at the southwestern extremity of Salisbury Plain, midway between Bath and Salisbury; population (1991) 15,400. There is an army training centre and silk, gloves, and agricultural machinery are produced.

Warminster prospered in the 18th century as a wool town and corn market. A grammar school was founded here in 1707, at which Thomas ◊Arnold, later headmaster of Rugby School, was a pupil. The town has an early 14th-century church. Cley Hill, an Iron Age hillfort 244 m/800 ft high, is about 5 km/3 mi west of the town, and the Elizabethan mansion Longleat House is 8 km/5 mi to the southwest.

The theological college of St Boniface is in Warminster.

Warner, Deborah (1959–)

English theatre director. She founded the Kick Theatre company in 1980. Discarding period costume and furnished sets, she adopted an uncluttered approach to the classics, including productions of many Shakespeare plays and Sophocles' *Electra* (1989).

She has directed *King Lear* (1985 and 1989), *Coriolanus* (1986 and 1993), *The Swan* (1987), *Titus Andronicus* (1988, Olivier Award for best director), *King John* and *The Good Person of Szechuan* (both 1989), *Hedda Gabler* (1991), and *Woyzeck* (1993).

War Office

Former British government department controlling military affairs. The Board of Ordnance, which existed in the 14th century, was absorbed into the War Department after the Crimean War and the whole named the War Office. In 1964 its core became a subordinate branch of the newly established **Ministry of ◊Defence**.

Warrack, Guy (Douglas Hamilton) (1900–1986)

Scottish composer and conductor. He studied at Oxford and with Boult and Vaughan Williams at the Royal College of Music, and taught there 1925–35. He made his debut as conductor in London, in 1925, and conducted the British Broadcasting Corporation (BBC) Scottish Orchestra 1936–45 and the Sadler's Wells Ballet 1948–51. He wrote music for various documentary films, including the official film of the 1953 coronation.

Warren, Frank (1952–)

British boxing promoter who helped bring world-title fights to commercial television. Among boxers he has represented is Naseem ◊Hamed. He set up the London Arena in the Docklands which became a major venue for sporting and other events. In 1989 he was seriously wounded in a shotgun attack. He acquired Bedford Rugby club in 1996.

Warrenpoint

Seaside resort in County Down, Northern Ireland, on the northern shore of Carlingford Lough; population (1991) 4,800. It succeeded Newry as the main port in this area, and has facilities for container shipments to England. Warrenpoint is also a centre for yachting and sea angling.

Narrow Water Castle 2 km/1 mi northwest was built by the Duke of Ormonde in 1663 on the site of a castle constructed here by John Savicky in 1560; it is now an art gallery.

Warrington

Unitary authority in northwest England, created in 1998 from part of Cheshire

Area 176 sq km/68 sq mi

Towns and cities ◊Warrington (administrative headquarters), Lymm, Great Sankey

Features River Mersey; Manchester Ship Canal; Warrington Museum and Art Gallery includes over 1,000 paintings; Risley Moss bog and woodland with nature trails and visitors' centre

Industries chemicals, food and soft drinks processing, brewing, printing, manufacturing of clothing, leather, metal goods, timber products

Population (town, 1995) 188,000

Warrington

Industrial town and from April 1998 administrative headquarters of ◊Warrington unitary authority in northwest England, on the River Mersey, 25 km/16 mi from both Liverpool and Manchester; population (1994 est) 151,000. It was part of the county of Cheshire to April 1998. Industries include the manufacture of metal goods and chemicals, brewing, iron founding, tanning, engineering, and high technology industries. A trading centre since Roman times, it was designated a ◊new town in 1968.

In 1993 bombs planted here by the Irish Republican Army (IRA) killed two boys (one a three-year-old, believed to be the youngest victim of IRA violence in Britain) and wounded more than 50 other people.

The industrial tradition of Warrington dates back to the medieval period, when it was important for the production of textiles and tools. Industrial expansion took place after the Mersey was made navigable in the 18th century and the Manchester Ship Canal opened in 1894. Features include a town hall (1750), designed by the Scottish architect James Gibbs.

Warwick

Market town, administrative headquarters of ◊Warwickshire, central England, 33 km/21 mi southeast of Birmingham, on the River Avon; population (1991) 22,300. Industries include agriculture and tourism. Founded in 914, it has many fine medieval buildings, including a 14th-century castle.

The University of Warwick was founded in 1965. It has a student population (1998) of 15,600.

Features

The castle stands on a site fortified in Saxon times. The main castle gateway and towers are fine examples of 14th-century military architecture. The church of St Mary was largely burned down in a fire which destroyed most of the centre of Warwick in 1694, but its fine Perpendicular Beauchamp Chapel (1443–64) survived. The Hospital of Lord Leycester was founded by Robert Dudley, Earl of Leicester, in 1571; the hospital's half-timbered buildings date from the late 15th century. Warwick Grammar School claims its descent from a school possibly dating from the 11th century.

Warwick, Richard Neville, 1st or 16th Earl of Warwick (1428–1471)

English politician, called **the Kingmaker**. During the Wars of the ◊Roses he fought at first on the Yorkist side against the Lancastrians, and was largely responsible for placing Edward IV on the throne. Having quarrelled with him, he restored Henry VI 1470, but was defeated and killed by Edward at Barnet, Hertfordshire. Earl 1449.

Warwick Castle

Castle in England, on the River Avon, 32 km/20 mi southeast of Birmingham. The first defences were erected here in Saxon times, and a wooden castle with a ditch built around 1065–67 by the Earl of Warwick. The fortifications were strengthened in 1068 by William (I) the Conqueror, and construction of the present stone castle began in 1345. The interior was completely rebuilt in the 17th century, and the Avon-side grounds landscaped in the 18th century by Capability Brown.

Considered one of the finest medieval castles in England, Warwick contains state rooms, a fine collection of armour, silver vault, dungeon, and ghost tower.

Warwickshire

County of central England

Area 1,980 sq km/764 sq mi

Towns and cities ◊Warwick (administrative headquarters), Nuneaton, Royal Leamington Spa, Rugby, Stratford-upon-Avon (the birthplace of Shakespeare)

Physical rivers Avon, Stour, and Tame; remains of the 'Forest of Arden' (portrayed by Shakespeare in *As You Like It*)

Features Kenilworth and Warwick castles; Edgehill, site of the Battle of Edgehill in 1642, during the English Civil War; annual Royal Agricultural Show held at Stoneleigh

WARWICKSHIRE *Stoneleigh Park in Warwickshire, six miles south of the city of Coventry, is the permanent site of the Royal Agricultural Society's annual show. This gathering features the showing of prize livestock, exhibitions of farming machinery, and a showjumping competition. Corel*

Agriculture cereals (oats and wheat); dairy farming; fruit; market gardening
Industries cement; engineering; ironstone, and lime are worked in the east and south; motor industry; textiles; tourism
Population (1994) 496,300
Famous people William Shakespeare, George Eliot, Rupert Brooke

Topography

Warwickshire is bounded on the north by Staffordshire, and Derbyshire; on the east by Leicestershire and Northamptonshire; on the south by Gloucestershire and Oxfordshire; and on the west by Worcestershire and the West Midlands. The surface is not very flat, though the highest point, Ebrington Hill, is only 260 m/853 ft.

Ecclesiastical buildings

The Beauchamp Chapel of St Mary's church, Warwick, is noteworthy, and there are the remains of a Cistercian monastery at Coombe Abbey, and of other religious houses at Kenilworth, Maxstoke, Merevale, Stoneleigh, and Wroxall.

Wasdale

Valley in Cumbria, northwest England, southwest of Keswick, in the ⟡Lake District. The valley includes **Wastwater Lake**, the deepest English lake, 5 km/3 mi long with high screes lining its southeastern side.

The upper part of the valley has a few farms and the hamlet of **Wasdale Head**, a centre for climbing ⟡Scafell Pike. Tracks from Wasdale Head also lead towards Great Gable (899 m/2,949 ft) and other Lake District mountains.

Wash, the

Bay of the North Sea between Norfolk and Lincolnshire, eastern England; 24 km/15 mi long, 40 km/25 mi wide. The rivers Nene, Ouse, Welland, and Witham drain into the Wash. In 1992, 10,120 ha/25,000 acres of the mudflats, marshes, and sand banks on its shores were designated a national nature reserve.

Much of the land adjacent to the Wash has been reclaimed. King John is said to have lost his baggage and treasure while crossing it in 1216.

Washington

Town in Tyne and Wear, northeast England, 8 km/5 mi southeast of Newcastle upon Tyne; population (1991) 58,000. The chief industry is the manufacture of cars. Washington was designated a new town in 1963 in what was then an industrial and mining area,

Washington was developed to rehouse people from the locality, Gateshead, and Sunderland, to attract industry to the area, which is close to the motorway and rail-freight networks of northeast England, and to provide out-of-town shopping and entertainment facilities for the southern part of Tyne and Wear.

Washington Old Hall is a largely 17th-century house, near the centre of the town. It has medieval origins and in the 14th century it was the home of the ancestors of George Washington, the first president of the USA. There is a Wildfowl and Wetland Trust nature park to the east of the town.

waste disposal

The average Briton throws away about ten times his or her own body weight in household refuse each year. Collectively the country generates about 50 million tonnes of waste per annum. Methods of waste disposal vary, although the use of landfill sites has been the preferred option for many years; up to 90% of domestic rubbish is disposed of in this fashion. In principle, over 50% of household waste could be recycled, although less then 5% is currently recovered.

The industrial waste dumped every year by the UK in the North Sea includes 550,000 tonnes of fly ash from coal-fired power stations. The British government agreed in 1989 to stop North Sea dumping from 1993, but dumping in the heavily polluted Irish Sea continues. Industrial pollution is suspected of causing ecological problems, including an epidemic that killed hundreds of seals in 1989. The Irish Sea currently receives 80 tonnes of uranium a year from phosphate rock processing, and 300 million gallons of sewage every day, 80% of it untreated or merely screened.

Britain imported 41,000 tonnes of hazardous waste for disposal in 1989, according to official estimates (which exclude chlorinated solvents and nonferrous metals). Greenpeace estimates that in 1991 Britain imported 50,000 tonnes from Europe alone. Most of these imported wastes are put into landfill sites without treatment. Between 1946 and 1982 Britain dumped into the North Atlantic an estimated 35,000 tonnes of chemical weapons, nearly 1 million tonnes of obsolete munitions, and 75,000 tonnes of nuclear waste. Of all the known radioactive waste dumped at sea by 13 Western nations, Britain is responsible for 76%.

Waste Land, The

Poem by T S ⟡Eliot, first published in 1922. A long, complex, and innovative poem, it expressed the prevalent mood of disillusionment after World War I and is a key work of Modernism in literature.

Water Babies, The

Fantasy by English author Charles ⟡Kingsley, published in England in 1863. Tom, an orphan child who works as a chimney sweep, inadvertently frightens a girl, Ellie, and runs away. He drowns and is immortalized as an amphibious 'water baby'. After redeeming his moral character by the instruction of Mrs Bedonebyasyoudid and Mrs Doasyouwouldbedoneby, Tom is reunited with Ellie, who strikes her head on the rocks after a fall at the seashore. She dies a few days later, joining Tom as a water baby.

watercolour painting

Although watercolours are internationally popular, it is perhaps still in Britain – its traditional home – that the medium has the strongest appeal. The art of painting with pigments mixed with water, as practised today, began in England in the 18th century with the work of Paul Sandby, and was developed by Thomas Girtin, John Sell Cotman, and J M W Turner. The technique, which was was known in China as early as the 3rd century, requires great skill since its transparency rules out overpainting. Artists excelling in watercolour include J R Cozens, Peter de Wint, John Constable, David Cox, John Singer Sargent, and Philip Wilson Steer. Paul Nash and John Piper were among the greatest 20th-century exponents, and in his celebrated World War II drawings of Londoners sheltering in the Underground, Henry Moore used a novel combination of ink, watercolour, and wax. More recently, David Hockney and R B Kitaj have made memorable use of the medium.

The Royal Society of Painters in Water Colours was founded in 1804.

Waterhouse, Alfred (1830–1905)

English architect. He was a leading exponent of Victorian Neo-Gothic, typically using multicoloured tiles and bricks. His works include the Natural History Museum, London (1868).

Waterhouse, Keith Spencer (1929–)

English journalist, novelist, and dramatist. His second novel, *Billy Liar* (1959), an account of a whimsical day in the life of a fantasy-prone undertaker's clerk, became a successful play and film. His play *Jeffrey Bernard Is Unwell* (1989) was based on the dissolute life of a *Spectator* columnist. Waterhouse was a journalist on the *Daily Mirror* from 1970 to 1986, when he moved to the *Daily Mail*.

Born in Leeds, Waterhouse's Yorkshire working-class background and early job experience helped produce *Billy Liar*, which he adapted for the stage in collaboration with Willis Hall (1929–). They went on to write a long line of plays, musical revues, and films together; for example, the screenplays *Whistle Down the Wind* (1961) and *A Kind of Loving* (1962) (adapted from a novel by Stan Barstow).

Waterloo, Battle of

Final battle of the Napoleonic Wars on 18 June 1815 in which a coalition force of British, Prussian, and Dutch troops under the Duke of Wellington defeated Napoleon near the village of Waterloo, 13 km/8 mi south of Brussels, Belgium. Napoleon found Wellington's army isolated from his allies and began a direct offensive to smash them, but the British held on until joined by the Prussians under Marshal Gebhard von Blücher. Four days later Napoleon abdicated for the second and final time.

Napoleon's 120,000-strong army was amassed on the French–Belgian frontier on 12 June; Wellington had about 90,000 troops at Brussels, of whom 30,000 were British, and was expecting Napoleon to march on Brussels to attack him. However, on their way to attack Wellington, the French fought the Prussians at Ligny, and also fought a combined Dutch–Belgian army at Quatre Bras, all of which delayed Napoleon and enabled Wellington to concentrate his forces at Waterloo, in anticipation of the arrival of Marshal Blücher with the Prussian army. Napoleon despatched the Marquis de Grouchy with 33,000 troops to block the road upon which the Prussians were expected to arrive and took the rest of his army to face the Allies.

The forces actually facing each other on the field were 67,000 Allies and 74,000 French, the latter being stronger in artillery and cavalry. The French opened the battle at 11.30 a.m. on 18 June, and a fierce struggle developed for Hougoumont Farm. On the left, a long bombardment by French artillery, followed by an infantry assault, forced the Dutch and Belgians to give way, but the situation was saved by a charge of British cavalry under General Thomas Picton. In the centre, the action revolved around the farmhouse of La Haye Sainte, where the British stubbornly beat off the French until about 6 p.m., when the French managed to seize the farmhouse, although they were evicted from it shortly afterwards. The French cavalry, meanwhile, was expending its energy against the British infantry squares: they failed to break the formations but inflicted heavy casualties. The first elements of Blücher's Prussians arrived in the afternoon, but Grouchy managed to push them back. Napoleon then made his last attempt, ordering the Guard, under Marshal Michel Ney, to advance against the British Guards division. These stood firm until the French were very close, then at Wellington's orders fired a devastating volley, followed by a bayonet charge. The French attack was thrown into confusion, and at this moment Blücher's main force thrust Grouchy aside and came onto the field. British cavalry charged forward, the French broke, and were pursued off the field by the Prussians.

Waterloo Bridge

Bridge spanning the River Thames, between Blackfriars Bridge and Charing Cross, in central London. It was designed by Giles Gilbert ◊Scott, and opened in 1945.

A previous bridge on this site was built 1811–17 by John ◊Rennie (who also built the former London Bridge), and was demolished in 1934.

Waterloo Cup

The principal coursing event (chasing of hares by greyhounds) in England, known as the 'courser's Derby'. Staged at Altcar, near Formby, Merseyside, each year, it is named after the nearby Waterloo Hotel whose proprietor originated the race in 1936.

It is also the name of the trophy given to the winner of the **Waterloo Handicap**, a Crown Green bowls competition held at the Waterloo Hotel, Blackpool, every year.

Water Music

A set of instrumental pieces by Handel, first performed in London, in 1715, on a boat following the royal barge on the Thames. The music is said to have reconciled George I to Handel after the latter's desertion from the court of Hanover, but the story is doubtful.

Waterston, John James (1811–1883)

Scottish physicist who first formulated the essential features of the kinetic theory of gases 1843–45. He also estimated the temperature of the Sun in 1857.

water supply

Since 1989 ten privatized water companies have statutory responsibility for water supply, sewerage, and sewerage treatment in England and Wales, under the supervision of the industry's regulatory body, Ofwat. In Scotland the responsibility for all water and sewerage services rests with three public water authorities, while in Northern Ireland the Department of the Environment holds this brief. About 75% of Britain's water supplies are obtained from mountain lakes, reservoirs, and rivers; the rest comes from underground sources. 1995–97 was the driest two-year period in over 200 years and, as a result, there was a severe depletion in Britain's water supplies. The Environment Agency, which is responsible for monitoring and protecting water resources, has since introduced statutory efficiency measures which the water companies are now obliged to follow.

Water consumption

The water supply companies in England and Wales provide almost 4.6 million household with water; over 75% of commercial and industrial customers pay for water and sewerage services on the basis of their metered consumption. 1% of total water provided by these companies is used for drinking; 2% for cooking; 3% for gardening; and 49% in bathrooms. Following concern that some of the water companies were were failing to meet EU drinking-water standards on nitrate and pesticide levels, the companies were served with enforcement notices by the government Drinking Water Inspectorate.

Watford

Industrial town in Hertfordshire, southeast England, on the River Colne, 24 km/15 mi northwest of London; population (1991) 110,500. It is a commuter town for London. Industries include printing and publishing, engineering, electronics, and brewing.

St Mary's church, dating from the 13th century, includes the 16th-century Essex chapel. Other features include almshouses dating from 1590; Monmouth House (17th century); Free School (1704); and Frogmore House (1715).

Watling Street

Roman road running from London to Wroxeter (*Viroconium*) near Shrewsbury, in central England. Its name derives from *Waetlingacaester*, the Anglo-Saxon name for St Albans, through which it passed.

Watson, David Meredith Seares (1886–1973)

English embryologist and palaeobiologist who provided the first evidence that mammals evolved from reptiles. From the fossilized remains of primitive reptiles and mammals collected on trips to South Africa and Australia 1911–14, he pieced together the evolutionary line linking reptiles to early mammals.

Watson-Watt, Robert Alexander (1892–1973)

Scottish physicist who developed a forerunner of radar. He proposed in 1935 a method of radiolocation of aircraft – a key factor in the Allied victory over German aircraft in World War II. Knighted 1942.

Watt, James (1736–1819)

Scottish engineer who developed the steam engine in the 1760s, making Thomas ◊Newcomen's engine vastly more efficient by cooling the used steam in a condenser separate from the main cylinder. He eventually made a double-acting machine that supplied power with both directions of the piston and developed rotary motion. He also invented devices associated with the steam engine, artistic instruments and a copying process, and devised the horsepower as a description of an engine's rate of working. The modern unit of power, the watt, is named after him.

At Glasgow University, Watt was asked to repair a small working model of Newcomen's steam engine, which was temperamental and difficult to operate without air entering the cylinder and destroying the vacuum. It was also extremely costly to run in terms of the coal required to keep a sufficient head of steam in a practical engine. In Newcomen's engine, the steam in the cylinder was condensed by a jet of water, creating a vacuum. The vacuum, in turn, was filled during the power stroke by the atmosphere pressing the piston to the bottom of the cylinder. On each stroke the cylinder was heated by the steam and cooled by the injected water, thus absorbing a tremendous amount of heat. Watt investigated the properties of steam and made measurements of boilers and pistons. He had the idea of a separate condenser (separate from the piston) that would allow the cylinder to be kept hot, and the condenser fairly cold by lagging, thus improving the thermal efficiency.

Working with manufacturer Matthew Boulton in 1782, Watt improved his machine by making it double-acting. Using a mechanical linkage known as 'parallel motion' and an extra set of valves, the engine was made to drive on both the forward and backward strokes of the piston, and a 'sun-and-planet' gear (also devised by Watt) allowed rotatory motion to be produced. This new and highly adaptable engine was quickly adopted by cotton and woollen mills.

During the period 1775–90, Watt invented an automatic centrifugal governor, which cut off the steam when the engine began to work too quickly and turned it on again when it had slowed sufficiently. He also devised a steam engine indicator that showed steam pressure and the degree of vacuum within the cylinder. Because of the secretarial duties connected with his business, Watt invented a way of copying letters and drawings with a chemical process that was displaced only with the advent of the typewriter and photocopier.

Watt devised a rational method to rate the capability of his engines by considering the rate at which horses worked. After many experiments, he concluded that a 'horsepower' was 33,000 lb (15,000 kg) raised through 1 ft (0.3 m) each minute. The English-speaking world used horsepower to describe the capability of an engine until recent years.

Watt was born in Greenock (now in Strathclyde) and trained as an instrument-maker. Between 1767 and 1774, he made his living as a canal surveyor. In 1775 Boulton and Watt went into partnership and manufactured Watt's engines at the Soho Foundry, near Birmingham. Watt's original engine of 1765 is now in the Science Museum, London.

Watts, George Frederick (1817–1904)

English painter and sculptor. Influenced by the Venetian

masters, he painted biblical and Classical subjects, but his fame was based largely on his moralizing allegories, such as *Hope* (1886; Tate Gallery, London). He was also a portrait painter, his works including *Gladstone* and *Tennyson* (National Portrait Gallery, London). As a sculptor he executed *Physical Energy* (1904) for Cecil Rhodes's memorial in Cape Town, South Africa; a replica is in Kensington Gardens, London. He was a forerunner of Symbolism.

In 1842 he won £300 in the competition for murals for Westminster with his cartoon of *Caractacus*. He went to Italy and met Lord and Lady Holland, with whom he stayed in Florence, and who became his patrons. The Renaissance pattern of patron and household genius was later repeated during his 30-year stay at Little Holland House, Kensington, with Thoby Prinsep and his wife. Insulated from the world, Watts worked on allegories, symbolic frescoes, and portraits of those he admired.

His studies of eminent Victorians combine idealism and reality, while his portrayal of the actress Ellen Terry, his first wife, is sensitive and perceptive.

He is best known for the cloudily philosophic works of the 1880s such as *Love and Death* (Tate Gallery, London), while his *Mammon* shows the Victorian desire to teach and uplift. The Watts Gallery at Compton, Surrey, founded by his second wife, contains a permanent collection of his work.

Waugh, Evelyn (Arthur St John) (1903–1966)

English novelist. His humorous social satires include *Decline and Fall* (1928), *Vile Bodies* (1930), *Scoop* (1938), and *The Loved One* (1948). He developed a serious concern with religious issues in ◊*Brideshead Revisited* (1945) (successfully dramatized for television in the 1980s). *The Ordeal of Gilbert Pinfold* (1957) is largely autobiographical.

Waugh was born in London and studied at Oxford University. He was an art student and a schoolteacher for a time, but soon began to travel and devote himself to writing. In 1927 he published a life of the Pre-Raphaelite Dante Gabriel Rossetti, and in 1928 the first of his satirical novels, *Decline and Fall*; others are *Black Mischief* (1932), *A Handful of Dust* (1934), and *Put Out More Flags* (1942). These novels are witty and at the same time biting attacks on contemporary society.

After World War II his writing took a more intentionally serious turn, and he produced the trilogy *Men at Arms* (1952), *Officers and Gentlemen* (1955), and *Unconditional Surrender* (1961), in which he attempted to analyse the war as a struggle between good and evil.

Wavell, Archibald Percival, 1st Earl Wavell (1883–1950)

British field marshal in World War II. As commander in chief in the Middle East, he successfully defended Egypt against Italy in July 1939 and successfully conducted the North African war against Italy 1940–41. He was transferred as commander in chief in India in July 1941, and became Allied Supreme Commander after Japan entered the war. He was unable to prevent Japanese advances in Malaya and Burma and Churchill became disillusioned with him. He was made viceroy of India 1943–47. KCB 1939.

Waveney

River in England that forms part of the boundary between Norfolk and Suffolk; length 80 km/50 mi. The Waveney rises near the Little Ouse and flows past the towns of Diss, Bungay, and Beccles. It is navigable as far as Geldeston. It joins the Yare 6 km/4 mi southwest of Great Yarmouth.

Waverley, John Anderson, 1st Viscount Waverley (1882–1958)

British administrator. He organized civil defence for World War II, becoming home secretary and minister for home security in 1939. **Anderson shelters**, home outdoor air-raid shelters, were named after him. He was chancellor of the Exchequer 1943–45. KCB 1919.

Any one who has been to an English public school will always feel comparatively at home in prison.

EVELYN WAUGH English novelist.
Decline and Fall pt 3, ch 4

Ways and Means, Chairman of

The Chairman of Ways and Means, or deputy Speaker, takes the chair in the House of Commons when it goes into committee, maintains order in committee, and acts as deputy Speaker of the House in the absence of the Speaker. Chairmen of Ways and Means are elected by the House and, like the Speaker, hold office until a dissolution. When acting in committee, they can apply the closure.

They also have important duties in conjunction with the chair of committees in the upper House in regard to private bills. In their absence one of the two deputy chairmen acts for them, and shares with the chairman duties in the House when the Speaker is absent.

Weald, the, or **the Kent Weald** (Old English 'forest')

Area between the North and South Downs, England, a raised tract of forest 64 km/40 mi wide. It forms part of Kent, Sussex, Surrey, and Hampshire. Once thickly wooded, it is now an agricultural area producing fruit, hops, and vegetables. Crowborough and Wadhurst are the largest villages in the area. In the Middle Ages its timber and iron ore made it the industrial heart of England.

The village of Penshurst, 8 km/5 mi northwest of Tunbridge Wells, is a tourist centre. Features include Hever Castle and Penshurst Place. Other villages in the Weald include Forrest Row, Cranbrook, Mayfield, Hawkhurst, and Tenterden.

Iron ore was mined here in Saxon times and wood provided charcoal and oak for shipbuilding. In medieval times the Weald was a major provider of armaments. Ashdown Forest, originally a Norman hunting forest, is a tourist destination.

The oldest rocks in the area have been exposed by denudation at the centre and are surrounded by horseshoe-shaped outcrops of progressively younger rocks giving the Wealden Series, Weald Clay, and the complex Hastings Beds formation (Tunbridge Wells Sands, Wadhurst Clay, Ashdown Sand, with subordinate beds).

Wear

River in northeast England; length 107 km/67 mi. From its source near Wearhead in the Pennines in County Durham, it flows eastwards along a narrow valley, Weardale, to Bishop Auckland and then northeast past Durham and Chester-le-Street, to meet the North Sea at Sunderland.

Weardale is moorland in its upper reaches at Stanhope and Wolsingham. At Sunderland the Wear cuts a gorge 30 m/98 ft deep through the local magnesian limestone plateau to reach the North Sea. The city of Durham is built along the Wear, and its castle and cathedral (a World Heritage site) stand 30 m/100 ft above the river on an incised meander.

Wearing, Gillian (1963–)

English artist. Her basic media are photography and video, which she uses in a documentary fashion to explore how people think and behave. The subjects can be people stopped in the street and asked to write a personal message, as in the series of photographs *For signs that say what you want them to say and not signs that say what someone else wants you to say* (1992–93); or respondents to newspaper advertisements, as in *Confess All On Video. Don't Worry You Will Be In Disguise. Intrigued? Call Gillian* (1994). She won the Turner Prize in 1997.

Born in Birmingham, Wearing graduated from Goldsmiths' College, London, in 1990. She has had solo exhibitions in London and New York, and has shown in group shows in London, Milan, Le Havre, New York, Manchester, Glasgow, Berlin, Naples, Geneva, Hamburg, and Minneapolis.

weather

The climate of Britain is notoriously variable and changeable from day to day. Weather is generally cool to mild with frequent cloud and rain, but occasional settled spells of weather occur at all seasons. Visitors are often surprised by the long summer days, which are a consequence of the northerly latitude; in the north of Scotland in midsummer the day is 18 hours long and twilight lasts all night. Conversely, winter days are short.

While the south is usually a little warmer than the north and the west wetter than the east, the continual changes of weather mean that, on occasions, these differences may be reversed. Extremes of weather are rare but they do occur. For example, in December 1981 and January 1982, parts of southern and central England experienced for a few days lower temperatures than central Europe and Moscow. During the long spells of hot, sunny weather in the summers of 1975 and 1976 parts of Britain were drier and warmer than many places in the western Mediterranean.

The greatest extremes of weather and climate occur in the mountains of Scotland, Wales, and northern England. Here at altitudes exceeding 600 m/2,000 ft conditions are wet and cloudy for much of the year with annual rainfall exceeding 1,500 mm/60 in and in places reaching as much as 5,000 mm/200 in. These are among the wettest places in Europe. Winter conditions may be severe with very strong winds, driving rain, or snow blizzards.

In spite of occasional heavy snowfalls on the Scottish mountains, conditions are not reliable for skiing and there has been only a limited development of winter sports resorts. Because of the severe conditions which can arise very suddenly on mountains, walkers and climbers who go unprepared face the risk of exposure or even frostbite. Conditions may be vastly different from those suggested by the weather at lower levels.

Settlement level

Virtually all permanent settlement in Britain lies below 300 m/1,000 ft, and at these levels weather conditions are usually much more congenial. As a general rule the western side of Britain is cloudier, wetter, and milder in winter, than the east, with cooler summers. The eastern side of Britain is drier, with a tendency for summer rain to be heavier than that of winter. Much of central England has very similar weather to that of the east and south of the country. Southwestern England shares the greater summer warmth of southern England but experiences rather milder and wetter winters than the east of the country.

The average number of hours of sunshine is greatest in the south and southeast of England. Western Scotland, Wales, and Northern Ireland have rather less sunshine than most of England. Generally, daily sunshine hours range from between one and two in midwinter to between five and seven in midsummer. Winter sunshine is much reduced because of frequent fogs and low cloud. This is a consequence of winds from the Atlantic and seas surrounding Britain, which bring high humidity. For the same reason the mountain areas are particularly cloudy and wet.

Snow may occur anywhere in Britain in winter or even spring but, except on the hills, it rarely lies for more than a few days. In some winters there may be very little snow, but every 15 or 20 years it may lie for some weeks during a prolonged cold spell.

Northern Ireland

Northern Ireland shares with the rest of the British Isles a mild, changeable climate with very rare extremes of heat or cold. Ireland is even more influenced by the warm waters of the North Atlantic than England and, consequently, its climate is a little wetter the year round, milder in winter and cooler and cloudier in summer. This mild, rainy climate is particularly favourable to the growth of grass and moss and for this reason Ireland has been called the Emerald Isle.

In the wetter west of the country rain is frequent but on many days it is very light and in the form of drizzle. The sunniest parts of the country are the east and south coasts, with sunshine hours averaging from two a day in winter to six in midsummer. Over most of Ireland spring is the driest time of the year and May is the sunniest month. Except in the extreme east around Dublin, autumn and winter are the wettest seasons. Occasional severe weather in winter takes two forms: storms and gales which particularly affect the west; and rare

BRITISH WEATHER: SOME KEY DATES AND EXTREME CONDITIONS

1703 A great storm sweeps across Britain, devastating the countryside, killing thousands of people, and destroying the Eddystone Lighthouse at Plymouth.

1869 English meteorologist Alexander Buchan produces the first weather maps showing the average monthly and annual air pressure for the world. They provide information about the atmosphere's circulation.

1875 *The Times* newspaper starts publishing the first generally available daily weather forecasts.

1922 The British meteorologist Lewis Fry Richardson publishes *Weather Prediction by Numerical Process*, in which he applies the first mathematical techniques to weather forecasting.

26 March 1923 The BBC begins broadcasting daily weather forecasts in Britain.

1947 Severe winter weather badly disrupts the sporting programme in Britain. All racing fixtures between 22 January and 15 March are called off, and the English Football League season is not concluded until 14 June.

29 July 1949 The first weather forecast is broadcast on British television: it consists of a voice-over only.

December 1952 Smog hits London: weather conditions and industrial and domestic pollution combine to produce a haze of toxic pollutants, which limit visibility to a few feet. It lasts for three weeks, and over 4,000 people, mostly elderly, die from respiratory problems caused by poor air quality. The disaster leads to antipollution legislation.

August 1952 22.5 cm/9 in of rainfall within 24 hours on Exmoor causes disastrous flooding at Lynmouth, leaving 34 people dead and the harbour and over 100 buildings severely damaged.

11 January 1954 George Cowling of the Meteorological Office becomes the first weather forecaster to appear on British television.

May 1961 The Atlas computer, the world's largest (with one megabyte of memory), is installed at Harwell, Oxfordshire; as well as undertaking atomic research, it aids weather forecasting.

15 January 1962 British weather reports start giving temperatures in centigrade as well as Fahrenheit.

1973–82 The Thames flood barrier in London, England, is constructed.

16 October 1987 A great storm, which weather forecasters fail to predict, sweeps across southeast England, killing 17 people and felling 15 million trees. Reckoned to be the worst storm in Britain for 300 years, it does £1.7 billion of damage.

24–26 December 1997 A fierce storm with winds up to 130 kph/80 mph hits southern England, killing 13 people and leaving thousands of homes without electricity.

3–4 January 1998 Violent storms sweep through Britain and Ireland, bringing winds up to 160 kph/100 mph and claiming two lives.

10–11 April 1998 The eastern and central regions of England experience the worst flooding in 50 years, resulting in five deaths and estimated damage of up to £500 million.

spells with frost and snow when cold easterly or northerly winds bring severe weather to the whole British Isles.

Webb, (Martha) Beatrice born Potter (1858–1943) and Sidney James, 1st Baron Passfield (1859–1947)

English social reformers, writers, and founders of the London School of Economics (LSE) in 1895. They were early members of the socialist ◊Fabian Society, and were married in 1892. They argued for social insurance in their minority report (1909) of the Poor Law Commission, and wrote many influential books, including *The History of Trade Unionism* (1894), *English Local Government* (1906–29), and *Soviet Communism* (1935).

Sidney Webb was a member of the Labour Party executive from 1915 to 1925, entered Parliament in 1922, and held several government posts.

Webb, Mary (Gladys) born Meredith (1881–1927)

English novelist. She wrote of country life and characters, as in *Precious Bane* (1924), a rustic novel of primitive passions, with a heroine who suffers, as she herself did, from a harelip; it was parodied by Stella ◊Gibbons in *Cold Comfort Farm* (1932).

She was born in Leighton, Shropshire, the scene of all her novels.

Webb, Philip Speakman (1831–1915)

English architect and designer. He was a leading figure (along with Richard Norman ◊Shaw and Charles ◊Voysey) of the Arts and Crafts movement, which was instrumental in the revival of English domestic architecture in the late 19th century. He mostly designed private houses, notably the Red House, Bexleyheath, Kent (1859), for William ◊Morris.

Webber, Andrew Lloyd

English composer of musicals; see ◊Lloyd Webber.

Webster, John (*c.* 1580–*c.* 1625)

English dramatist. His reputation rests on two tragedies, *The White Devil* (1612) and *The Duchess of Malfi* (*c.*1613). Though both show the preoccupation with melodramatic violence and horror typical of the Jacobean revenge tragedy, they are also remarkable for their poetry and psychological insight. He collaborated with a number of other dramatists, notably with Thomas ◊Dekker on the comedy *Westward Ho* (*c.*1606).

Born in London, he was the son of a tailor and was

apprenticed to the same trade, becoming a freeman of the Merchant Taylors' Company in 1603. But he was also active in the theatre by 1602, working on collaborations and perhaps also acting. His first independent work was *The White Devil*, printed (and probably first performed) in 1612.

Little is known of his life, and the details and dates of his various collaborations are still unclear. Among those usually credited to him (apart from the two major tragedies) are the following:

Comedies: *Northward Ho* (*c.*1605) and *Westward Ho* (both with Dekker), *Any Thing for a Quiet Life* (*c.*1621) (with Thomas Middleton), and *A Cure for a Cuckold* (*c.*1624) (with William Rowley).

Tragedies: *The Famous History of Sir Thomas Wyatt* (*c.*1606) (with Dekker), and *Appius and Virginia* (*c.*1608) (probably with John Heywood).

Tragicomedy: *The Devil's Law Case* (*c.*1610).

Wedgwood, Josiah (1730–1795)

English pottery manufacturer. He set up business in Staffordshire in the early 1760s to produce his agateware as well as unglazed blue or green stoneware (jasper) decorated with white neo-Classical designs, using pigments of his own invention.

Wedgwood was born in Burslem, Staffordshire, and worked in the family pottery. Eventually he set up in business on his own at the Ivy House Factory in Burslem, and there he perfected cream-colonial earthenware, which became known as queen's ware because of the interest and patronage of Queen Charlotte in 1765. In 1768 he expanded the company into the Brick House Bell Works Factory. He then built the Etruria Factory, using his engineering skills in the design of machinery and the high-temperature beehive-shaped kilns, which were more than 4 m/12 ft wide.

Wednesbury

Town in the county of West Midlands, England, 12 km/7 mi northwest of Birmingham; population (1991) 24,300. Industries include engineering and the manufacture of railway rolling stock, boiler plates, axles, springs, bridges, and girders. Lighter industries include the manufacture of electrical goods, motor-vehicle components, metal windows, and household accessories. In Anglo-Saxon times Wednesbury was a fortified stronghold, and it is mentioned in the Domesday Book.

The church, part of which dates from the 12th century, is one of the oldest in the industrial ◊Black Country.

Weekly Journal, The

Weekly newspaper for black professionals living in Britain, covering UK and international news, as well as business news, sport, and other general subject matter. It was established in 1992 and in 1998 had a circulation of 25,000.

Weelkes, Thomas (*c.* 1576–1623)

English composer. He wrote ten Anglican services and around 40 anthems, including 'When David heard'. He was also one of the most significant madrigalists of his time, and his madrigals, often for four, five, and six voices, demonstrate his intricate style, fine counterpoint, and brilliant imagery.

Weight, Carel (1908–1997)

English figurative painter. His most characteristic works are street scenes that superficially seem ordinary but have an underlying feeling of tension or menace. His other subjects included landscapes and portraits.

He taught at the Royal College of Art, London, from 1947 to 1973, from 1967 as professor of painting.

Weir, Judith (1954–)

Scottish composer. She studied with John Tavener and worked with computer music at the Massachusetts Institute of Technology in 1973. Later she studied with Robin Holloway at Cambridge. Her compositions include *A Night at The Chinese Opera* (1987); *The Art of Touching the Keyboard* (1983), for piano; and *The Bagpiper's String Trio* (1985).

Weldon, Fay (1931–)

English novelist and dramatist. Her work deals with feminist themes, often in an ironic or comic manner. Novels include *The Fat Woman's Joke* (1967), *Female Friends* (1975), *Remember Me* (1976), *Puffball* (1980), *The Life and Loves of a She-Devil* (1984) (made into a film in 1990), *The Hearts and Lives of Men* (1987), *Splitting* (1995), *Worst Fears* (1996), and *Big Women* (1998) (also a television series).

Short stories are in *Wicken Women* (1995) and *A Hard Time to be a Father* (1998). She has also written plays for the stage, radio, and television.

Weldon, George (1906–1963)

English conductor. He studied at the Royal College of Music with Malcolm Sargent, and conducted various provincial orchestras, in 1943 becoming conductor of the City of Birmingham Symphony Orchestra (CBSO), a post he held until 1951; he was later assistant conductor of the Hallé Orchestra under Barbirolli.

Welfare to Work

Programme introduced by the ◊Labour Party to reduce unemployment, particularly among young people, by getting them off welfare into work. In January 1998, the chancellor of the Exchequer, Gordon ◊Brown, announced a 'national crusade to end unemployment', targeting at first the under-25s, and then older people.

The expenditure of some £3.5 billion was partly met by proceeds from the 'windfall tax' on privatized utilities. The philosophy of making people less dependent on the state, and more self-reliant, has been criticized by left-wing Labour supporters.

Wellesley

Family name of the dukes of ◊Wellington, seated at Stratfield Saye in Berkshire, England.

Wellesley, Richard Colley, Marquess Wellesley (1760–1842)

British administrator; brother of the 1st Duke of Wellington. He was governor general of India 1798–1805, and by his victories over the Marathas of western India greatly extended the territory under British rule. He was foreign secretary 1809–12, and lord lieutenant of Ireland 1821–28 and 1833–34.

Wellesz, Egon Joseph (1885–1974)

Austrian-born British composer and musicologist. He taught at Vienna University 1913–38, specializing in the history of Byzantine, Renaissance, and modern music. He moved to England in 1938 and lectured at Oxford from 1943. His compositions include operas such as *Alkestis* (1924); symphonies, notably the Fifth (1957); ballet music; and a series of string quartets.

Wellingborough

Market town in Northamptonshire, England, on the River Nene, 16 km/10 mi northeast of Northampton; population (1991) 65,600. Industries include agriculture and the manufacture of footwear. Iron ore is mined nearby.

Wellington, Arthur Wellesley, 1st Duke of Wellington (1769–1852)

British soldier and Tory politician. As commander in the ◊Peninsular War, he expelled the French from Spain in 1814. He defeated Napoleon Bonaparte at Quatre-Bras and Waterloo in 1815, and was a member of the Congress of Vienna. As prime minister 1828–30, he was forced to concede Roman Catholic emancipation.

Wellington was born in Ireland, the son of an Irish peer, and sat for a time in the Irish parliament. He was knighted for his army service in India and became a national hero with his victories of 1808–14 in the Peninsular War and as general of the allies against Napoleon. At the Congress of Vienna he opposed the dismemberment of France and supported restoration of the Bourbons. As prime minister he modified the Corn Laws but became unpopular for his opposition to parliamentary reform and his lack of opposition to Catholic emancipation. He was foreign secretary 1834–35 and a member of the cabinet 1841–46. He held the office of commander in chief of the forces at various times from 1827 and for life from 1842. His home was Apsley House in London.

Wells

Cathedral city and market town in Somerset, southwest England, at the foot of the Mendip Hills; population (1991) 9,900. Although tourism is the economic mainstay, there is some other industry, including printing and electronics and the production of paper, cheese, textiles, and animal foodstuffs. The cathedral, built near the site of a Saxon church in the 12th and 13th centuries, has a west front with 386 carved figures. Wells was made the seat of a bishopric about 909 (Bath and Wells from 1244) and has a 13th-century bishop's palace.

Ine, King of Wessex, is said to have founded the first church in Wells in 704. The bishop's palace, the residence of the Bishop of Bath and Wells, is moated and surrounded by a defensive wall. It includes the natural wells from which the town derives its name. Other features include the 15th-century deanery and Vicar's Close, a well-preserved medieval street. See also ◊Wells Cathedral.

Wells, H(erbert) G(eorge) (1866–1946)

English writer. He was a pioneer of ◊science fiction with such novels as *The Time Machine* (1895) and *The War of the Worlds* (1898), which describes a Martian invasion of Earth and brought him nationwide recognition. His later novels had an anti-establishment, anti-conventional humour remarkable in its day, for example *Kipps* (1905) and *Tono-Bungay* (1909).

Wells was a prophet of world organization. His theme was the need for humans to impose their mastery upon their own creations and to establish benevolent systems and structures by which to rule themselves, and in pursuing this concept he became a leading advocate of social planning. A number of prophecies described in fictional works such as *The First Men in the Moon* (1901) and *The Shape of Things to Come* (1933), as well as in *The Outline of History* (1920) and other popular nonfiction works, have been fulfilled; among them, the significance of aviation, tank warfare, World War II, and the atomic bomb. He also wrote many short stories.

His social novels explored with humour and sympathy the condition of ordinary lower middle- and working-class people. They include *Love and Mr Lewisham* (1900), *Ann Veronica* (1909), a feminist novel, *The History of Mr Polly* (1910), and *Marriage* (1912).

> *In England we have come to rely upon a comfortable time lag of fifty years or a century intervening between the perception that something ought to be done and a serious attempt to do it.*
>
> H G WELLS English writer. 'The Work, Wealth and Happiness of Mankind' (1932)

Wells Cathedral

Cathedral of the diocese of Bath and ◊Wells, England. It was begun in the late 12th century, and the central parts of the building are in the transitional style of that period. Jocelin, bishop from 1206 to 1242, built the rest of the nave, the west front, and the north porch, all of which are superb examples of Early English architecture.

The west front, once painted, has a gallery of medieval statuary unrivalled in England;. The cathedral also contains excellent 14th-century stained glass, misericord seats of around 1340, and a clock of around 1390.

Welsh, Irvine (1959–)

Scottish novelist, best known as the author of ◊*Trainspotting* (1993); his works are characterized by an uncompromising treatment of controversial subjects. His other works include *The Acid House* (1994), *Marabou Stork Nightmares* (1995), the trio of novellas *Ecstasy* (1996), and *Filth* (1998).

Welsh assembly

60-seat devolved body, based in Cardiff, taking over the functions of the ⇨Welsh Office, spending its £7 billion budget. The National Assembly for Wales, which was narrowly approved in a September 1997 referendum, will implement Westminster laws and will not have primary law-making powers, even in respect to the Welsh language. However, it will oversee quangos, which proliferated during the Conservative years, making them more accountable. The assembly is due to be elected in 1999, with a third of its seats being selected by proportional representation. In October 1998, the design concept put forward by the Richard Rogers Partnership was chosen for the National Assembly for Wales building, to be located at Cardiff Bay.

Welsh language, in Welsh, Cymraeg

Member of the Celtic branch of the Indo-European language family, spoken chiefly in the rural north and west of Wales. Spoken by 18.7% of the Welsh population, it is the strongest of the surviving ⇨Celtic languages.

Welsh has been in decline in the face of English expansion since the accession of the Welsh Henry Tudor (as Henry VII) to the throne of England in 1485. Nowadays, few Welsh people speak only Welsh; they are either bilingual or speak only English.

During the 20th century the decline of Welsh has been slowed: from about 900,000 speakers at the turn of the century, the number had shrunk to half a million in 1995. However, due to vigorous campaigning and efforts to promote the language, made by the S4C (Sianel Pedwar Cymru) television network, and the Welsh Language Society, and to some extent elsewhere in literature and the media, the numbers speaking Welsh has stabilized. According to a survey, in 1995 21% of the Welsh population spoke the national tongue; of that number, it was the mother tongue of 55%. Use of the language among young people increased as a result of its inclusion in the national curriculum; in 1993–94, 78.4% of Welsh pupils learnt it as either first or second language. See table of Welsh words borrowed into English, on page 943.

Welsh literature

The prose and poetry of Wales, written predominantly in Welsh but also, more recently, in English. Characteristic of Welsh poetry is the bardic system. In the 18th century the ⇨eisteddfod (literary festival) movement brought a revival of classical forms.

Ancient literature

The chief remains of early Welsh literature are contained in the Four Ancient Books of Wales – the *Black Book of*

WELSH LANGUAGE *Welsh is spoken by around 500,000 inhabitants of the principality, mainly in the north and west. To promote Welsh as a vigorous living language, it was made a compulsory element of the National Curriculum for Wales, and bilingual education is encouraged in schools. Bruce Stephens/Impact*

The Welsh National Anthem: 'Wlad Fy Nhadau/Land Of My Fathers'

The words are given in Welsh and English.

Wlad Fy Nhadau

Mae hen wlad fy nhadau yn annwyl i mi
Gwlad beirdd a chantorion, enwogion o fri
Ei gwrol ryfelwyr, gwladgarwyr tra mad
Tros ryddid collasant eu gwaed.
Gwlad, gwlad, pleidiol wyf i'm gwlad
Tra mor yn fur i'r bur hoffbau
O bydded i'r heniaith barhau.
Hen Gymru fynyddig, paradwys y bardd
Pob dyffryn, pob clogwyn i'm golwg sydd hardd
Trwy deimlad gwladgarol, mor swynol yw si
Ei nentydd, afonydd, i mi.
Os treisiodd y gelyn fy ngwlad tan ei droed
Mae hen iaith y Cymry mor fyw ag erioed
Ni luddiwyd yr awen gan erchyll law brad
Na thelyn berseiniol fy ngwlad.

Land of My Fathers

The land of my fathers is dear unto me
Old land where the minstrels are honoured and free
Its warring defenders so gallant and brave
For freedom their life's blood they gave.
Home, home, true am I to home
While seas secure the land so pure
O may the old language endure.
Old land of the mountains, the Eden of bards
Each gorge and each valley a loveliness guards
Through love of my country, charmed voices will be
Its streams, and its rivers, to me.
Though foemen have trampled my land 'neath their feet
The language of Cambria still knows no retreat
The muse is not vanquished by traitor's fell hand.

Welsh Words Borrowed into English

cromlech	17th century	('arched stone') a megalithic chamber tomb or dolmen; standing stone(s)
englyn	17th century	a four-line stanza of prescribed form written in *cynghanedd* metre
flummery	17th century	(unknown origin) a pudding made with coagulated wheatflour or oatmeal; mere flattery or nonsense
gorsedd	18th century	('throne') a meeting of bards and druids, preliminary to an *eisteddfod*
cynghanedd	19th century	a complex form of alliterative metre
cwm	19th century	a valley; a deep rounded hollow with a steep side formed by a glacier; a cirque
eisteddfod	19th century	('session') a festival of poetry, singing, and music; a congress of Welsh bards and minstrels
hwyl	19th century	emotional fervour, characteristic of poetry recitation
corgi	20th century	('dwarf-dog') either of two breeds of short-legged dogs, originally from Wales

Carmarthen, the *Book of Taliesin*, the *Book of Aneirin*, and the *Red Book of Hergest* – anthologies of prose and verse of the 6th–14th centuries. The bardic system ensured the continuance of traditional conventions; most celebrated of the 12th-century bards was Cynddelw Brydydd Mawr (active 1155–1200).

Literature after the English conquest

The English conquest of 1282 involved the fall of the princes who supported these bards, but after a period of decline a new school arose in South Wales with a new freedom in form and sentiment, the most celebrated poet in the 14th-century being Dafydd ap Gwilym, and in the next century the classical metrist Dafydd ap Edmwnd (active 1450–1459). With the Reformation, biblical translations were undertaken, and Morgan Llwyd (1619–1659) and Ellis Wynne (1671–1734) wrote religious prose. Popular metres resembling those of England developed – for example, the poems of Huw Morys (1622–1709).

Classical revival

Goronwy Owen revived the classical poetic forms in the 18th century, and the eisteddfod movement began: popular measures were used by the hymn writer William Williams Pantycelyn (1717–1791).

Second revival

The 19th century saw few notable figures, but the foundation of a Welsh university and the work there of John Morris Jones (1864–1929) produced a 20th-century revival, including T Gwynn ◊Jones, W J Gruffydd (1881–1954), and R Williams Parry (1884–1956). Later writers included the poet J Kitchener Davies (1902–1952), the dramatist and poet Saunders Lewis (1893–1985), and the novelist and short-story writer Kate Roberts (1891–1985). Among writers of the period after World War II are the poets Waldo Williams (1904–1971), Euros Bowen (1904–), and Bobi Jones (1929–), and the novelists Islwyn Ffowc Elis (1924–) and Jane Edwards (1938–).

Welsh writers in English

Those who have expressed the Welsh spirit in English include the poets Edward ◊Thomas, Vernon Watkins (1906–67), Dylan ◊Thomas, R S ◊Thomas, and Dannie Abse (1923–), and the novelist Emyr Humphreys (1919–).

Welsh National Opera, Opera Cenedlaethol Cymru

Welsh opera company founded in 1946 and based in Cardiff. It tours regularly in Wales and England.

Welsh Office

Government department, responsible until late 1999 for

administration in Wales of policies on agriculture, education, health and social services, local government, planning, sport, and tourism. In 1999 its functions pass to the Welsh Assembly. Established in 1951, in 1998 it employed 2,000 staff. Its secretary of state 1997–98 was Ron Davies, from 1998 Alun Michael. From 1975 it sponsored the Welsh Development Agency.

Welwyn Garden City

Industrial town in Hertfordshire, southeast England, 32 km/20 mi north of London; population (1991) 41,400. Industries include electrical engineering and the manufacture of chemicals, plastics, clothing, food, and pharmaceuticals. It was founded as a ◊garden city in 1919–20 by Ebenezer Howard, and designated a ◊new town in 1948.

Welwyn Garden City was the second of the garden cities established by Ebenezer Howard (after Letchworth). The town was planned for a population of 40,000–50,000 as a satellite town to provide for the decentralization of population and industry from London; the original population on the estate was 400. In 1948 a development corporation was appointed to take over the town and to complete it, and the estate was transferred to the New Town Commission in 1966.

Wembley

Residential district of the outer borough of ◊Brent, Greater London, site of ◊Wembley Stadium. The stadium was chosen in 1997 as England's new National Sports Stadium, designed by Norman Foster. It will be completely rebuilt, except for the famous 'twin towers', after the Football Association (FA) Cup Final in May 1999.

Brent council, the planning authority for the Wembley area, has set up a special advisory group 'Sustadium' to help ensure that the building of the new National Stadium in Wembley does not have a detrimental effect on the local environment.

Wembley Stadium

Sports ground in north London, completed in 1923 for the British Empire Exhibition 1924–25. It has been the scene of the annual Football Association (FA) Cup final since 1923. The 1948 Olympic Games and many concerts, including the Live Aid concert of 1985, were held here. Adjacent to the main stadium, which holds 79,000 people all seated, are the Wembley indoor arena (which holds about 10,000, depending on the event) and conference centre.

The largest recorded crowd at Wembley is 126,047 for its first FA Cup final; the capacity has since been reduced by additional seating. England play most of their home soccer matches at Wembley. Other sports events over the years have included show jumping, American football, Rugby League, Rugby Union, hockey, Gaelic football, hurling, and baseball.

Wensleydale

Upper valley of the River Ure in North Yorkshire, England, within the Pennine highlands. It lies largely in the Yorkshire ◊Dales national park, beginning southeast of Middleham and extending to near the source of the river northwest of Hawes, one of the area's largest towns. The dale gives its name to a type of cheese and a breed of sheep with long wool.

The village of **Wensley** has a 15th-century bridge across the Ure and a 13th-century church. Bolton Castle nearby is a 14th-century fortified mansion, where Mary Queen of Scots was imprisoned in 1568.

Wesker, Arnold (1932–)

English dramatist. His socialist beliefs were reflected in the successful trilogy *Chicken Soup with Barley*, *Roots*, and *I'm Talking About Jerusalem* (1958–60). He established a catchphrase with *Chips with Everything* (1962). His autobiography, *As Much as I Dare* was published in 1994.

In 1961 Wesker tried unsuccessfully to establish a working-class theatre with trade-union backing at the Round House in London. Later plays include *The Merchant* (1978) and *Lady Othello* (1987). He wrote the screenplay for *Maudie* (1995).

Wesley, John (1703–1791)

English founder of ◊Methodism. When the pulpits of the Church of England were closed to him and his followers, he took the gospel to the people. For 50 years he rode about the country on horseback, preaching daily, largely in the open air. His sermons became the doctrinal standard of the Wesleyan Methodist Church.

Wesley went to Oxford University together with his brother Charles, where their circle was nicknamed Metho-

WESLEY, JOHN *John Wesley was founder of the evangelical Christian Methodist movement. The movement was named after its strict adherence to methodical devotion and study. Wesley travelled throughout Britain, preaching in the open air. By the time he died, Methodist societies, independent of the established Church, had been set up in Britain and the USA. Corbis*

dists because of their religious observances. He was ordained in the Church of England in 1728 and in 1735 he went to Georgia, USA, as a missionary. On his return he experienced 'conversion' in 1738, and from being rigidly High Church developed into an ardent Evangelical.

Wesker, unusually for a British playwright, had a very overt, idealist-socialist 'message'.

ARTHUR MARWICK.
On Arnold Wesker, in *British Society since 1945* (1982)

Wesley, Mary pseudonym of Mary Aline Siepmann (born Farmer) (1912–)
English novelist. Her novels are characterized by the ironic and detached treatment of her middle-class characters. She wrote children's books before turning to adult fiction (at the age of 70) with *Jumping the Queue* (1983). Her other works include *The Camomile Lawn* (1984) (televised in 1991) set in World War II, *A Sensible Life* (1990), *An Imaginative Experience* (1994), and *Part of the Furniture* (1997).

Mary Wesley was born near Windsor and educated at the London School of Economics. During World War II she worked in the War Office.

Wessex
The kingdom of the West Saxons in Britain, said to have been founded by Cerdic about AD 500, covering present-day Hampshire, Dorset, Wiltshire, Berkshire, Somerset, and Devon. In 829 Egbert established West Saxon supremacy over all England. See genealogy below.

Thomas ◊Hardy used the term Wessex in his novels for the southwest counties of England; drawing on England's west country, the heartland was Dorset but its outlying boundary

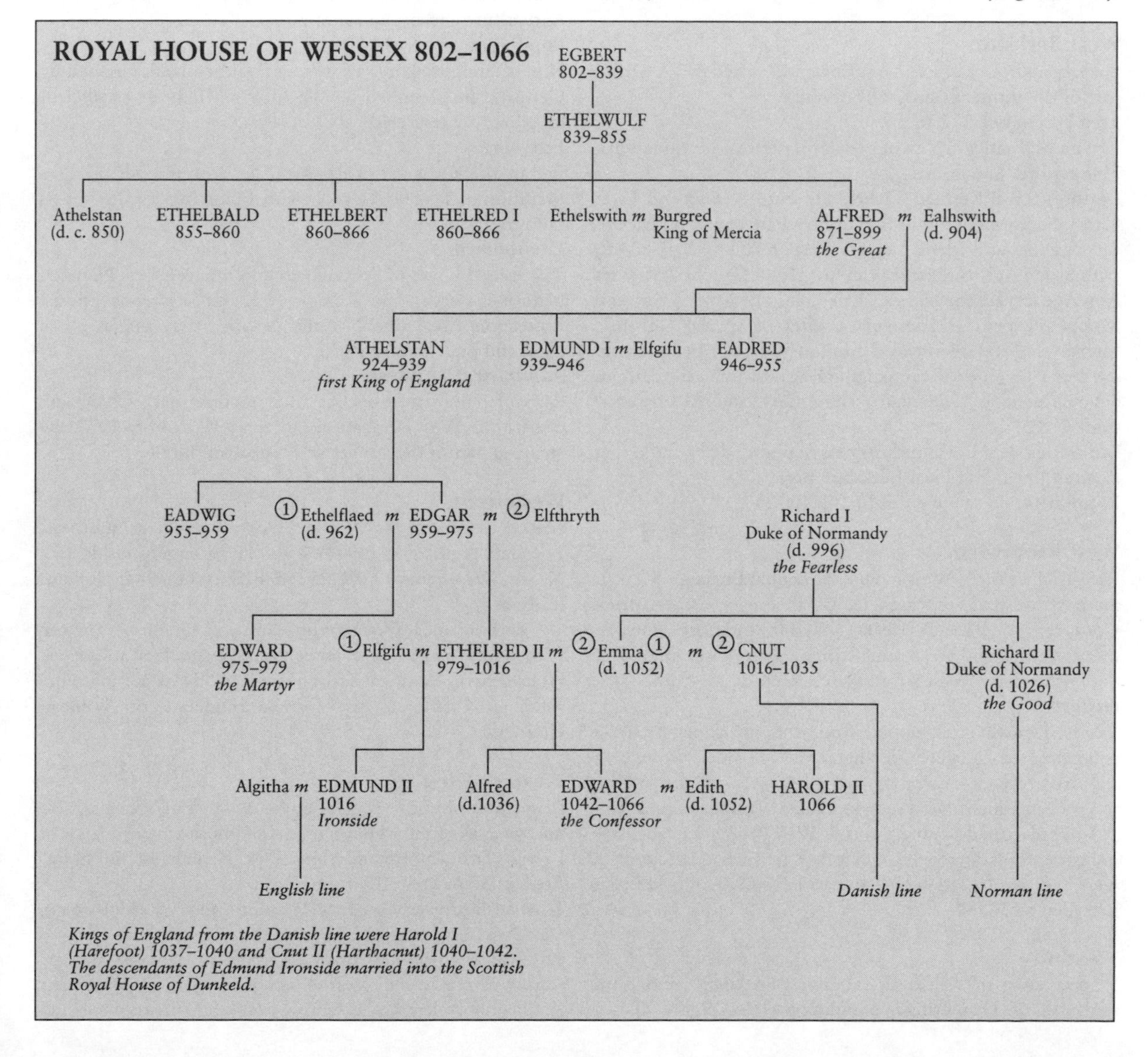

markers were Plymouth, Bath, Oxford, and Southampton. He gave fictional names to such real places as Dorchester (Casterbridge), Salisbury (Melchester) and Bournemouth (Sandbourne) but mixed these with a sprinkling of real names such as Stonehenge, the River Frome, and Nettlecombe Tout.

West, Rebecca pen name of Cicily Isabel Fairfield (1892–1983)

English journalist and novelist, an active feminist from 1911. Her novels, of which the semi-autobiographical *The Fountain Overflows* (1956) and *The Birds Fall Down* (1966) are regarded as the best, demonstrate a social and political awareness.

The Meaning of Treason (1947) was reissued as *The New Meaning of Treason* in 1964, which included material on the spies Guy ◊Burgess and Donald ◊Maclean.

Rebecca West had a close relationship with H G Wells; their son, Anthony West, was born in 1914. DBE 1959.

West Berkshire

Unitary authority in southeast England, created in 1998 from part of the former county of Berkshire
Area 705 sq km/272 sq mi
Towns and cities ◊Newbury (administrative headquarters), Hungerford, Lambourn
Features River Kennet; River Cambourn; Kennet and Avon Canal; Snelsmore Common Country Park covers 59 ha/146 acres including wetland habitats; Inkpen Hill (291 m/854 ft) with Stone Age tomb and Walbury Hill (297 m/974 ft) with Iron Age fort are the highest chalk hills in England; Thatcham Moors reedbeds are designated Sites of Special Scientific Interest (SSSI); Greenham Common Women's Peace Camp has been the site of campaigning against nuclear weapons development at Greenham, Burghfield, and Aldermaston since 1981
Industries race horse industry, agriculture, dairy cattle, pig farming (including local Berkshire pig)
Population (Newbury, 1995) 142,600.

West Bromwich

Industrial town in West Midlands, central England, 9 km/6 mi northwest of Birmingham, on the edge of the ◊Black Country; population (1991) 144,700. Industries include metalworking and the manufacture of springs and tubes. It is the home of the West Bromwich Albion soccer team.

History

West Bromwich developed from the amalgamation of a collection of hamlets on the Tame as small ironworks appeared; the discovery of coal in the vicinity led to the town's subsequent rapid development. With the completion in 1769 of a canal passing through West Bromwich, ancillary industries soon developed, and forges, furnaces, and foundries were erected. In 1819 the population was 9,000; by 1854 it had risen to 36,500.

Westbury

Market town in Wiltshire, southwest England, 8 km/5 mi southeast of Trowbridge; population (1991) 9,500. It is a railway junction; industries include leather working, food processing, and the manufacture of cloth, gloves, cement, and electric clocks, and there is a large engineering contracting firm. The town has a Perpendicular Gothic church.

East of the town is the **White Horse of Westbury**, cut into the chalk of Westbury Hill, dating in its present form from the 18th century.

West Dunbartonshire

Unitary authority in west central Scotland, created in 1996 from parts of two districts of Strathclyde region
Area 177 sq km/68 sq mi
Towns ◊Dumbarton (administrative headquarters), Clydebank, Alexandria
Physical Leven valley and coastal land of Firth of Clyde rise toward the upland plateau of the Kilpatrick Hills
Features Dumbarton Castle
Industries whisky distilling, light manufacturing
Agriculture sheep; not significant
Population (1995) 96,300
History industrial area of west central Scotland, targeted by Germans and bombed in World War II; heart of ancient kingdom of Strathclyde

Economy

within the Glasgow economy. The area is undergoing a transition as it seeks to redevelop following the loss of its industrial base.

Environment

There are 14 Sites of Special Scientific Interest, one National Nature Reserve, one Ramsar (wetland site), one Special Protection Area, one National Scenic Area, one regional park, and one country Park.

Administrative history

Parts of Dumbarton district were merged with Clydebank district into West Dunbartonshire in 1996. Prior to 1975, the area was part of the county of Dunbartonshire.

Westerham

Market town in the North ◊Downs of Kent, southeast England; population (1991) 3,700. It is largely residential. Nearby **Westerham Hill** (252 m/827 ft) is the highest point in Kent.

General James Wolfe, who captured Québec from the French in 1759, was born at the vicarage and lived at Québec House, now a National Trust property; 2.5 km/1.5 mi to the south is Chartwell, the former residence of Winston Churchill.

Western Isles

Island administrative unitary authority area in Scotland, also known as the Outer Hebrides, including the major islands of Lewis, Harris, North and South Uist, Benbecula, and Barra
Area 3,057 sq km/1,180 sq mi
Towns ◊Stornoway on Lewis (administrative headquarters), Castlebay, Lochboisdale, Lochmaddy, Tarbert
Physical open to the Atlantic Ocean on the west and the stormy Minch to the east, the islands are now almost treeless and mainly covered by extensive peat bogs. Areas of hills and

mountains are found on all the islands. The only fertile land is the sandy Machair on the west coast. The islands are almost entirely composed of the oldest rock in Britain, the Lewisian gneiss. Lewis is divided from the mainland by the Minch channel. The islands south of Lewis are divided from the Inner Hebrides by the Little Minch and the Sea of the Hebrides; uninhabited islands include St Kilda, Rockall
Features Callanish monolithic Stone Age circles on Lewis
Industries Harris tweed, tourism
Agriculture sheep, cattle, fishing
Population (1995) 29,000.

Harris and Lewis are often assumed to be two islands, but they are linked by a narrow neck of land.

History

A long history of settlement has left Stone, Bronze, and Iron Age remains, including those at Callanish. From the 8th to 13th centuries the area remained subject to the Scandinavians; sites with remains are rare but language, customs, and place names are strongly related to this period. Associations with strong clans such as Macdonald, MacNeil, and MacLeod, the escape of Bonnie Prince Charlie (Prince Charles Edward Stuart), the formation of large estates and the 'clearances' are all integral parts of the history of this area.

Economy

The main occupations of farming, weaving, and fishing are related to the crofting form of land holding and settlement. The larger settlements are all ports on the indented east side of all the main islands. Apart from the Harris tweed mills, there is little industry. Tourism is increasingly important. There are good air and sea connections from the larger islands.

Environment

There are 53 Sites of Special Scientific Interest, four National Nature Reserves, two Ramsars (wetland sites), seven Special Protection Areas, two Biosphere Reserves, one World Heritage Site, and three National Scenic Areas.

Everything that is most beautiful in Britain has always been in private hands.

MALCOLM RIFKIND British Conservative politician. Saying of the Week, the *Observer*, January 1988

Western Mail, The

Daily morning newspaper covering Wales, published in Cardiff. Established in 1869, it had a circulation of over 60,000 in 1998. The Sunday sister paper, *Wales on Sunday*, was established in 1989 and had a circulation over 57,000 in 1998.

West Glamorgan, Welsh Gorllewin Morgannwg

Former county of southwest Wales, 1974–1996, now divided into ◊Neath Port Talbot, and ◊Swansea unitary authorities.

Westland affair

The events surrounding the takeover of the British Westland helicopter company 1985–86. There was much political acrimony in the cabinet and allegations of malpractice. The affair led to the resignation of two cabinet ministers: Michael Heseltine, minister of defence, and the secretary for trade and industry, Leon Brittan.

West Lothian

Unitary authority in central Scotland, south of the Firth of Forth, which was previously a district within Lothian region (1975–96) and a county until 1974
Area 428 sq km/165 sq mi
Towns Bathgate, Linlithgow, ◊Livingston (administrative headquarters)
Physical low-lying, undulating area through which the River Almond flows; Cairnpapple Hill
Features Linlithgow Palace; prehistoric ritual site at Cairnpapple Hill, near Torpichen
Industries electronics, engineering, coal mining, food processing
Agriculture productive area of arable farming
Population (1995) 149,500
History royal connections with Linlithgow.

Economy

The area has a buoyant economy with the expansion of the development of the electronics industry.

Environment

There are 17 Sites of Special Scientific Interest, one National Nature Reserve, one regional park, and three country parks.

Administrative history

The unitary authority of West Lothian is more extensive than the county of the same name, as it includes parts of the county of Midlothian.

West Midlands

Metropolitan county of central England, created in 1974; in 1986, most of the functions of the former county council were transferred to the metropolitan borough councils
Area 900 sq km/347 sq mi
Towns and cities Birmingham, Coventry, Dudley, Solihull, Walsall, Wolverhampton (all administrative centres for districts of the same name), Oldbury (administrative centre for Sandwell)
Industries aircraft components; chemicals; coal mining; engineering; electrical equipment; glass; machine tools; motor vehicles, including Land Rover at Solihull; motor components
Population (1995) 2,637,300
Famous people Edward Burne-Jones, Neville Chamberlain, Philip Larkin.

Development of the West Midlands

Although the West Midlands area was sparsely inhabited for centuries, it is now almost entirely one urban conurbation. Towards the end of the Middle Ages, Coventry became an important centre of the cloth trade. Metalworking began at Birmingham in the 16th century, but the town remained very small until the Industrial Revolution, when the presence of coal and iron ore transformed it into an industrial boom town. The Birmingham area and the nearby ◊Black Country became highly industrialized, notoriously grimy, and densely populated area. An enormous range of metal goods was

WEST LOTHIAN *The great cantilever Forth Railway Bridge crosses the river at Queensferry and was built in 1890. So much steel was used in its construction that the phrase 'painting the Forth Bridge' has come to denote a never-ending task. On film, the bridge was the scene of a daring escape from a train by Richard Hannay, hero of Alfred Hitchcock's 1935 thriller* The Thirty-Nine Steps. *Corel*

manufactured. Redevelopment in the 20th century included a massive programme of high-rise building and new shopping centres, and population pressure was relieved by the development of new towns such as Telford.

Westminster, City of

Inner borough of central Greater London, on the north bank of the River Thames between Kensington and the City of London. It encompasses Bayswater, Belgravia, Mayfair, Paddington, Pimlico, Soho, St John's Wood, and Westminster

Population (1991) 174,800

Features:

Bayswater a residential and hotel area north of Kensington Gardens; Tyburn, near Marble Arch, site of public executions until 1783.

Belgravia bounded to the north by Knightsbridge, has squares laid out 1825–30 by Thomas Cubitt; Grosvenor estate.

Mayfair between Oxford Street and Piccadilly, includes Park Lane and Grosvenor Square (with the US embassy).

Paddington includes Little Venice on the Grand Union Canal.

Pimlico has the Tate Gallery (Turner collection, British, and modern art); developed by Thomas Cubitt in 1830s.

Soho has many restaurants and a Chinese community around Gerrard Street. It was formerly known for strip clubs and sex shops.

St John's Wood has Lord's cricket ground and the studios at 3 Abbey Road where the Beatles recorded their music; famous residents included Edwin Landseer, Thomas Henry Huxley, George Frampton.

Westminster encompasses Buckingham Palace (royal residence), Green Park, St James's Park and St James's Palace (16th century), Marlborough House, Westminster Abbey, Westminster Hall (1097–1401), the only surviving part of the Palace of Westminster built by William II, the Houses of Parliament with Big Ben, Whitehall (government offices), Downing Street (homes of the prime minister at number 10 and the chancellor of the Exchequer at number 11), Hyde Park with the Albert Memorial (1876) opposite the Royal Albert Hall (1871), Trafalgar Square with the National Gallery, the National Portrait Gallery, and the church of St Martin in the Fields (designed by James Gibb 1722–24). The Palace of Westminster, Westminster Abbey, and St Margaret's Church are a World Heritage site.

Westminster Abbey

Gothic church in central London, officially the Collegiate Church of St Peter. It was built 1050–1745 and consecrated under Edward the Confessor in 1065. Since William I nearly all English monarchs have been crowned in the abbey, and several are buried here, including Edward the Confessor, Henry III, Edward I, Henry VII, Elizabeth I, Mary Queen of Scots, Charles II, William III, Anne, and George II. Some 30 scientists, among them Isaac Newton and James Prescott, are also interred or commemorated here. Poets' Corner was established with the burial of Edmund Spenser in 1599. In the centre of the nave is the tomb of an 'Unknown Warrior' of World War I.

Fragments of Edward the Confessor's immense Romanesque church are embodied in the present building which was begun in 1245 by Henry III. Structurally, it is a French church, but much of the detail is English. The chapter-house was built from 1245 to 1250 and is one of the largest in England. From the reign of Edward I until 1547 Parliament generally met here. It was completely restored by Gilbert Scott in 1865. The king's treasure chamber was once the crypt under the chapter-house. The west towers are by Nicholas ◊Hawksmoor, completed after his death in 1745.

Until recently the Coronation Chair included the Stone of ◊Scone on which Scottish kings were crowned, and which was brought here by Edward I in 1296. On the back of the tomb of Philippa of Hainault is the Westminster Retable, a 13th-century oak altarpiece with what is considered to be probably the finest early medieval painting in Europe.

Westminster School, a public school with ancient and modern buildings nearby, was once the abbey school. The Norman undercroft of the dormitory is now the abbey museum.

Westminster Bridge

Bridge spanning the River Thames in central London, overlooking the House of Commons. Designed by Thomas Page between 1854 and 1862, it is a steel bridge 247 m/810 ft long. At its western end is a large statue of Boudicca, Queen of the Iceni, (1902) by Thomas Thorneycroft.

The original Westminster Bridge was built between 1739 and 1750 by the Swiss architect Charles Labelye. Before that, the only bridge across the Thames in London was ◊London Bridge.

The original bridge inspired the sonnet by William Wordsworth 'Upon Westminster Bridge' (1802).

Westminster Cathedral

Roman Catholic Metropolitan church in London. The site, part of what was once known as Tothill Fields, was acquired by Cardinal Manning. His successor, Cardinal Vaughan, supervised the building of the cathedral, from 1895 to 1903. The architect, John Francis Bentley, designed a remarkable building in Early Byzantine style. The Stations of the Cross on the piers were carved by Eric Gill.

Weston-super-Mare

Seaside resort and administrative headquarters of ◊North Somerset, southwest England, 32 km/20 mi from Bristol, on the Bristol Channel; population (1991) 68,800. Industries include plastics and engineering.

Weston-super-Mare was a small fishing hamlet until it expanded rapidly as a resort in the late 19th century; it had become one of the most popular resorts in the southwest of England by Edwardian times. Amenities include sandy beaches, the Grand Pier (completed in 1904), public parks and gardens, and sports facilities.

Westrup, Jack (Allan) (1904–1975)

English musicologist, critic, composer, and conductor. He was educated at Dulwich College and Balliol College, Oxford, where as an undergraduate he edited Monteverdi's *Orfeo* and *Incoronazione di Poppea* for performance by the Oxford University Opera Club. He taught classics at Dulwich College 1928–34, and was an assistant music critic on the *Daily Telegraph* 1934–40. From 1941 to 1944 he was lecturer in music at King's College, Newcastle-upon-Tyne, 1944–46 professor of music at Birmingham University and 1947–71 professor at Oxford. He conducted *Idomeneo* and *Les Troyens*, the first performance of E Wellesz's *Incognita* and the first UK performance of *Hans Heiling* and *L'Enfant et les sortilèges*. He was chairman of the editorial board of the *New Oxford History of Music* and editor of the sixth volume thereof; he was also

WESTMINSTER ABBEY *Situated near the Houses of Parliament in London, Westminster Abbey is the burial place of many eminent Britons, including monarchs, scientists, and artists. In September 1997, the funeral service for Diana, Princess of Wales, was held here. Corel*

editor of *Music and Letters* from 1959. Other literary work includes a book on Purcell and the fourth and fifth editions of the *Everyman Dictionary of Music* (1962 and 1971).

West Sussex

County of southern England, created in 1974, formerly part of Sussex
Area 2,020 sq km/780 sq mi
Towns and cities ◊Chichester (administrative headquarters), Crawley, Horsham, Haywards Heath, Shoreham (port); Bognor Regis, Littlehampton, Worthing (resorts)
Physical the ◊Weald; South Downs; rivers Adur, Arun, and West Rother
Features Arundel and Bramber castles; Chichester cathedral; Goodwood House and racecourse; Petworth House (17th century); Wakehurst Place, where the Royal Botanic Gardens, Kew, have additional grounds; Uppark House (1685–90); the Weald and Downland Open Air Museum at Singleton; Fishbourne villa (important Roman site near Chichester); Selsey (reputed landing place of the South Saxons in 447); Gatwick Airport
Agriculture cereals (wheat and barley); fruit; market gardening (mainly on the coastal plain); dairy produce; forestry
Industries electronics; light engineering
Population (1996) 737,300
Famous people Percy Bysshe Shelley, William Collins, Richard Cobden

Topography

West Sussex is bounded on the north by Surrey; on the east by East Sussex and Brighton and Hove; on the west by Hampshire; and on the south by the English Channel. Part of the Weald lies in West Sussex, and there are large tracts of lower greensand (a type of sandstone) country. The county contains part of the Downs, which are more wooded than in East Sussex, with beeches predominating in the Goodwood-Charlton area. Parts of the county are marshy, and there is a wide and fertile coastal plain stretching westwards from Worthing. Along the coast there are beaches, as at Littlehampton and Bognor Regis, and shallow inlets, such as those at Pagham Harbour and Chichester Harbour, with its intricate channels. There is a port at Shoreham.

Westward Ho!

Resort on the north coast of Devon, southwest England, 3 km/2 mi northwest of Bideford; population (1991) 1,400. Westward Ho! was named after a novel by Charles ◊Kingsley published in 1855.

The writer Rudyard ◊Kipling was educated at the United Services College (now a terrace of houses), which provided the background to his book of schoolboy stories *Stalky and Co* (1899). Pebble Ridge, jutting out into the Taw-Torridge estuary, is 3 km/2 mi long.

Westwood, Vivienne (1941–)

English fashion designer of international renown. She first attracted attention in the mid-1970s as co-owner of a shop with the rock-music entrepreneur Malcolm McLaren (1946–), which became a focus for the punk movement in London. Early in the 1980s her 'Pirate' and 'New Romantics' looks gained her international recognition.

Westwood's dramatic clothes continue to have a wide influence on the public and other designers. She has designed clothes and accessories for mail-order companies and young people's high-street fashion stores.

Her partnership with McLaren ended in 1983. In 1990 she opened a shop in Mayfair, London.

West Yorkshire

Metropolitan county of northeast England, created in 1974; in 1986, most of the functions of the former county council were transferred to the metropolitan borough councils
Area 2,040 sq km/787 sq mi
Towns and cities Bradford, Leeds, and Wakefield (administrative centres for districts of the same name); Halifax (administrative centre of Calderdale district); and Huddersfield (administrative centre of Kirklees district)
Physical Ilkley Moor, Haworth Moor; high Pennine moorlands in the west, Vale of York to the east; rivers: Aire, Calder, Colne, Wharfe
Features Haworth Parsonage; part of the Peak District National Park; British Library, Boston Spa (scientific, technical, and business documents)
Industries woollen textiles, financial services; coal mining is in decline
Population (1995) 2,105,700
Famous people the Brontës, J B Priestley, Henry Moore, David Hockney

Industrial past

Leeds, Bradford, Halifax, Huddersfield, Dewsbury, and Wakefield were formerly all built-up manufacturing centres. The coal that was extensively mined in the vicinity of these towns in the 19th century provided a foundation for West Yorkshire's prosperity. The area already had a long-established domestic clothing industry. The application of steam power to carding, combing, spinning, and weaving led to a rapid transformation of the wool textiles industry, and to a certain degree of specialization in several centres. The local coal-pits met the textile manufacturers' coal needs, and the huge supplies of soft water required in the manufacturing process could be obtained from moorland reservoirs. The coal measures were also exploited for ironstone (a type of iron ore) which gave rise to the production of crude and pure forms of iron. These, in turn, contributed to the development of textile machinery and other engineering products.

Inevitably, the coal seams were exhausted; iron smelting, which reached its zenith about 1875, had disappeared by 1930. Fortunately, the mechanical and electrical engineering trades continued to expand and are found in all the major centres. The wool textile industry transformed itself into an industry dealing in all types of textile, but its importance has declined and many old mills have been demolished or been converted for other purposes.

The landscape

West Yorkshire's landscape was mainly industrial, with much of the of the county (203,914 ha/503,658 acres) remaining semi-rural in character. In the west, there are unspoilt heather-clad moorlands, such as Ilkley Moor and Haworth Moor, intertwined with valleys along which sprawl textile villages; and in the east, arable and pastoral land is interspersed with former coal-mining villages.

wet

A derogatory term used to describe a moderate or left-wing supporter of the Conservative Party, especially those who opposed the monetary or other hardline policies of its former leader Margaret Thatcher.

Wetherby

Town in West Yorkshire, England, on the River Wharfe, 17 km/11 mi northeast of Leeds; population (1991) 23,300. It has mineral-water, light engineering, nylon-weaving, food-canning, electronic instrument, and prepacked-food industries, a cattle market, and a trade in agricultural produce. There is a racecourse nearby.

wetland

Naturally flooding area that is managed for agriculture or wildlife. Wetlands include areas of marsh, fen, bog, flood plain, and shallow coastal areas. Wetlands are extremely fertile areas, and provide warm, sheltered waters for fisheries, lush vegetation for grazing livestock, and an abundance of wildlife. The Royal Society for the Protection of Birds (RSPB) manages 2,800 hectares/7,000 acres of wetland, using sluice gates and flood-control devices to produce sanctuaries for wading birds and wild flowers. Some of these wetland sites are of international importance, and have been designated for protection under the EU Birds Directive known as the 'Ramsar Convention'. There are currently over 100 Ramsar sites in Britain.

Weymouth

Seaport and resort in Dorset, on the south coast of England, at the mouth of the River Wey; population (1991) 45,900. It is linked by ferry to France and the Channel Islands. Industries include the quarrying of Portland stone, sailmaking, brewing, fishing, electronics, and engineering. Weymouth, dating from the 10th century, was the first place in England to suffer from the Black Death in 1348. It was popularized as a bathing resort by George III.

Weymouth stands on both banks of the Wey, incorporating the area formerly known as Melcombe Regis. George III stayed at the Gloucester Hotel during his summer visits in Weymouth. To the south of Weymouth Bay is the limestone peninsula the Isle of ◊Portland.

Wharfedale

Valley in West and North Yorkshire, England, in the Yorkshire ◊Dales national park, extending from Wetherby to the source of the River Wharfe on Cam Fell. Lower Wharfedale is a rich agricultural district.

The area includes Harewood, where there is a ruined medieval castle, and ◊Ilkley, the largest town in the dale. Upper Wharfedale, above the ruins of Bolton Abbey, a priory founded in 1151, includes the village of Grassington. The village of Hubberholme lies at the northern end of the dale at the entrance to Langstrothdale.

Wheatley, Dennis Yates (1897–1977)

English thriller and adventure novelist. His works include a series dealing with black magic and occultism, but he also wrote crime novels in which the reader was invited to play the detective, as in *Murder off Miami* (1936), with real clues such as ticket stubs.

Wheatstone, Charles (1802–1875)

English physicist and inventor. With William Cooke, he patented a railway telegraph in 1837, and, developing an idea of Samuel Christie (1784–1865), devised the **Wheatstone bridge**, an electrical network for measuring resistance. He also invented the concertina.

In 1834 Wheatstone made the first determination of the velocity of electricity along a wire. He also improved on early versions of the dynamo so that current was generated continuously. Knighted 1868.

Whernside

Mountain in North Yorkshire, England; height 736 m/2,415 ft. One of the highest peaks of the ◊Pennines, it stands in the moorlands at the junction of Yorkshire with Cumbria and Lancashire.

Whewell, William (1794–1866)

British physicist and philosopher who coined the term 'scientist' along with such words as 'Eocene' and 'Miocene', 'electrode', 'cathode', and 'anode'. He produced two works of great scholarship, *The History of the Inductive Sciences* (1837) and *The Philosophy of the Inductive Sciences* (1840).

Most of his career was connected with Cambridge University, where he became the Master of Trinity College.

Whig Party

Predecessor of the Liberal Party. The name was first used of rebel Covenanters and then of those who wished to exclude James II from the English succession (as a Roman Catholic). They were in power continuously 1714–60 and pressed for industrial and commercial development, a vigorous foreign policy, and religious toleration. During the French Revolution, the Whigs demanded parliamentary reform in Britain, and from the passing of the Reform Bill 1832 became known as Liberals.

whip (the whipper-in of hounds at a foxhunt)

The member of Parliament who ensures the presence of colleagues in the party when there is to be a vote in Parliament at the end of a debate. The written appeal sent by the whips to MPs is also called a whip; this letter is underlined once, twice, or three times to indicate its importance. A **three-line whip** is the most urgent, and every MP is expected to attend and vote with their party. An MP who fails to attend may be temporarily suspended from the party, a penalty known as 'having the whip withdrawn'.

The government chief whip and the three junior whips are

salaried officials; some opposition whips also receive a salary. Conservative whips are chosen by the leader of the party; Labour whips are chosen by the prime minister when the party is in office, otherwise by election. The chief whip from 1998 is Ann Taylor, the first woman to hold the post.

Whips are officials of British parliamentary parties through whom party discipline in matters of attendance and voting is exercised. They are also channels of information between leaders and party members, and through them 'pairing' arrangements to assist MPs unable to attend any particular sitting are made.

Whipsnade

Wild animal park in Bedfordshire, England, 5 km/3 mi south of Dunstable, on the edge of Dunstable Downs. Wild animals and birds are exhibited in spacious open-air enclosures intended to provide conditions resembling their natural state. The 240-ha/600-acre park, opened in 1931, is the property of the Zoological Society of London and runs conservation and breeding programmes for endangered species.

whisky, or whiskey (Gaelic *uisge beatha*, water of life)

Distilled spirit made from cereals: Scotch whisky from malted barley, Irish whiskey usually from barley, and North American whiskey and bourbon from maize and rye. Scotch is usually blended; pure malt whisky is more expensive. Whisky is generally aged in wooden casks for 4–12 years.

The spelling 'whisky' usually refers to Scotch or Canadian drink and 'whiskey' to Irish or American. The earliest written record of whisky comes from Scotland in 1494 but the art of distillation is thought to have been known before this time.

Types of whisky:

Scotch whisky is made primarily from barley, malted, then heated over a peat fire. The flavoured malt is combined with water to make a mash, fermented to beer, then distilled twice to make whisky at 70% alcohol; this is reduced with water to 43% of volume.

Irish whiskey is made as Scotch, except that the malt is not exposed to the peat fire and thus does not have a smoky quality, and it is distilled three times. Irish whiskey is usually blended.

Canadian whisky was introduced early in the 19th century and is a blend of flavoured and neutral whiskies made from mashes of maize, rye, wheat, and barley malt. It is usually aged for six years.

American whiskey was introduced in the 18th century and is made from barley malt with maize and rye, made into a beer, then distilled to 80% alcohol and reduced to 50–52% with water, and is aged in unused, charred white-oak barrels. Bourbon is characterized by the flavour of maize.

Japanese whisky is made by the Scotch process and blended.

Straight whisky is unmixed or mixed with whisky from the same distillery or period; **blended whisky** is a mixture of neutral products with straight whiskies or may contain small quantities of sherry, fruit juice, and other flavours.

Grain whisky is made from unmalted grain mixed with malt.

Chemistry of whisky

There are 600–800 different flavour compounds in whisky, mainly fatty acids, esters, alcohols, and aldehydes.

Whistler, James Abbott McNeill (1834–1903)

US painter and etcher. Active in London from 1859, he was a leading figure in the ◊Aesthetic Movement. Influenced by Japanese prints, he painted riverscapes and portraits that show subtle composition and colour harmonies, for example *Arrangement in Grey and Black: Portrait of the Painter's Mother* (1871; Musée d'Orsay, Paris).

He settled in Chelsea, London, and painted views of the Thames including *Old Battersea Bridge* (about 1872–75; Tate Gallery, London). In 1877 the art critic John ◊Ruskin published an article on his *Nocturne in Black and Gold: The Falling Rocket* (Detroit Institute of Arts) which led to a trial in which Whistler sued Ruskin for libel, claiming £1,000; he was awarded symbolic damages of a farthing (a quarter of an old penny). Whistler described the trial in his book *The Gentle Art of Making Enemies* (1890).

Whistler, Rex (Reginald John) (1905–1944)

English artist, illustrator, and stage designer. He painted fanciful murals, for example *In Pursuit of Rare Meats* (1926–27) in the restaurant of the Tate Gallery, London. His illustrations include editions of *Gulliver's Travels* and Hans Andersen's *Fairy Tales*.

His stage work includes sets for *The Tempest* (Stratford, 1934) and *The Rake's Progress* (Sadler's Wells, 1935). His brother **Laurence Whistler** (1912–) was a glass engraver and poet.

Whitbread Literary Award

Annual prize of £23,000 open to writers in the UK and Ireland. Nominations are in four categories: novel, first novel, autobiography/biography, and poetry, each receiving £2,000. The overall winner receives a further £21,000. The award, which is administered by the Booksellers Association, was founded in 1971 by Whitbread, the UK brewing, food, and leisure company. The Whitbread Children's Book of the Year is a separate award worth £10,000.

The first overall winner in 1984 was the poet Douglas Dunn for his *Elegies*. In 1992 Jeff Torrington won the overall prize for his novel *Swing Hammer, Swing*. In 1993 a woman won the overall prize for the first time: Joan Brady for her novel *Theory of War*. Ted Hughes won the 1997 overall prize for *Tales from Ovid*, and the 1997 Whitbread Children's Book of the Year was *Aquila* by Andrew Norriss. See table of winners on page 953.

Whitby

Port and resort in North Yorkshire, northern England, on the North Sea coast, at the mouth of the River Esk, 32 km/20 mi northwest of Scarborough; population (1991) 13,800. Industries include tourism, boat building, fishing (particularly herring), and plastics. There are remains of a 13th-century abbey. Captain James Cook served his apprenticeship in Whitby and he sailed from here on his voyage to the Pacific Ocean in 1768. Bram Stoker's *Dracula* (1897) was set here.

Whitbread Literary Award Book of the Year

Winners are announced in November each year, and the overall winner (The Book of the Year) is awarded the £21,000 prize the following January.

Year	Winner	Awarded for
1987	Christopher Nolan	*Under the Eye of the Clock*
1988	Paul Sayer	*The Comforts of Madness*
1989	Richard Holmes	*Coleridge: Early Visions*
1990	Nicholas Mosley	*Hopeful Monsters*
1991	John Richardson	*A Life of Picasso*
1992	Jeff Torrington	*Swing Hammer Swing!*
1993	Joan Brady	*Theory of War*
1994	William Trevor	*Felicia's Journey*
1995	Kate Atkinson	*Behind the Scenes at the Museum*
1996	Seamus Heaney	*The Spirit Level*
1997	Ted Hughes	*Tales from Ovid*

Whitby was an important whaling centre and shipbuilding town in the 18th and 19th centuries. Mineral resources include jet, and Whitby also has potash reserves which run under the sea.

In 664 the Synod of Whitby, which affected the course of Christianity in England, was held here. The abbey was built on the site of a Saxon foundation established in 657 by St Hilda and destroyed by the Danes in 867. A Benedictine abbey was established in 1078, and the present ruins, reached from the town by 199 steps, date from 1220. Caedmon, the earliest-known English Christian poet, worked in the abbey in the 7th century. Near the abbey ruins stands the partly Norman parish church of St Mary. Captain Cook's ship *Resolution* was built in Whitby, and the Captain Cook Memorial Museum commemorates the life of the explorer. Other features include the Pannet Park Museum and Art Gallery and the Whitby Lifeboat Museum. The novelist Storm Jameson was born in Whitby in 1897.

Whitchurch

Market town in Shropshire, England, 30 km/19 mi north of Shrewsbury; population (1991) 9,000. Industries include structural engineering and the manufacture of milk products. There is a long tradition of the making and maintenance of clocks, including railway clocks and large tower clocks.

White, Gilbert (1720–1793)

English naturalist and cleric. He was the author of *The Natural History and Antiquities of Selborne* (1789), which records the flora and fauna of an area of Hampshire.

White's book is based on a diary of his observations and on letters to two naturalist friends over a period of about 20 years. Elegantly written, *The Natural History* contains descriptions of rural life and acute observations of a wide variety of natural-history subjects, such as the migration of swallows, the recognition of three distinct species of British leaf warblers, and the identification of the harvest mouse and the noctule bat as British species.

Whitehall

Street in Westminster, central London, between Trafalgar Square and the Houses of Parliament; it includes many of Britain's principal government offices and the Cenotaph war memorial.

The street derives its name from **Whitehall Palace** which was largely destroyed by fire in 1698. Of the palace only the Palladian Banqueting House (1622) survives, designed by Inigo Jones for James I. Whitehall is also the site of the headquarters (1753) of ◊Horse Guards, the Household Cavalry. Among the many government offices in Whitehall are the Admiralty, Home Office, and Ministry of Defence.

Whitehall Palace

A mansion was built here in the early 13th century by the justiciary, Hubert de Burgh. It was the residence of the archbishops of York from about 1250 until it was taken from Cardinal Wolsey by Henry VIII, who enlarged it and renamed it Whitehall; it remained the chief royal residence in London for about 150 years. The fine Banqueting House includes a ceiling painted by Rubens. From a window in the hall Charles I stepped onto the scaffold for his execution in the street below.

> *You must not miss Whitehall. At one end you will find a statue of one of our kings who was beheaded; at the other a monument to the man who did it. This is just an example of our attempts to be fair to everybody.*
>
> EDWARD APPLETON British physicist. Referring to Charles I and Oliver Cromwell; speech, Stockholm, January 1948

Whitehaven

Town and port in Cumbria, northwest England, on the Irish Sea coast, southwest of Carlisle; population (1991) 26,400. Industries include chemicals, printing, textiles, and food processing. Britain's first nuclear power station was sited in 1956 at Calder Hall to the southeast. Sellafield nuclear power station (formerly known as Windscale) is also nearby.

The Renaissance of Whitehaven millennium project will include an event centre, a history centre, and a mast 40 m/130 ft high which will transmit a panoramic view to a circular building at its base.

Whitehead, Alfred North (1861–1947)

English philosopher and mathematician. In his 'theory of organism', he attempted a synthesis of metaphysics and science. His works include *Principia Mathematica* (1910–13) (with Bertrand Russell), *The Concept of Nature* (1920), and *Adventures of Ideas* (1933).

Whitehead was professor of applied mathematics at London University 1914–24 and professor of philosophy at

WHITEHEAD, ALFRED NORTH *English mathematician and philosopher Alfred North Whitehead whose* Principia Mathematica *(written with Bertrand Russell) was an attempt to set out the foundations of mathematics on a logical basis. Whitehead later developed a philosophy of physical science and investigated the historical role of metaphysical ideas in civilization. Corbis*

Harvard University, USA, 1924–37. His research in mathematics involved a highly original attempt – incorporating the principles of logic – to create an extension of ordinary algebra to universal algebra (*A Treatise of Universal Algebra* (1898)), and a meticulous re-examination of the relativity theory of Albert Einstein.

Whitehead, Robert (1823–1905)

English engineer who invented the self-propelled torpedo in 1866. He devised methods of accurately firing torpedoes either above or below water from the fastest ships, no matter what the speed or bearing of the target.

Whitehead developed the torpedo for the Austrian Empire. Typically it was 4 m/13 ft long, could carry a 9-kg/20-lb dynamite warhead, and by 1889 had a speed of 29 knots. It was powered by compressed air and had a balancing mechanism and, later, gyroscopic controls. In 1876 he developed a servomotor, which controlled the steering gear and gave the torpedo a truer path through the water.

White Horse

Any of 17 ◊hill figures in England, found particularly in the southern chalk downlands. The Uffington White Horse below Uffington Castle, a hillfort on the Berkshire Downs, is 110 m/360 ft long and probably a tribal totem of the late Bronze Age.

The **Westbury Horse** on Bratton Hill, Wiltshire, was made in 1778 on the site of an older horse, said to commemorate Alfred the Great's victory over the Danes at Ethandun in AD 878.

Uffington White Horse

The Uffington Horse has inspired many imitations, many of which date from the 18th and early 19th centuries. It has been known historically since at least AD 1084, when it was noted as a landmark in a charter of the Abbey of Abingdon, and by the 14th century it had given its name to the Vale of the White Horse. Theories regarding its origins have suggested that it was cut by Alfred the Great to celebrate his victory over the Danes at Ashdown in AD 871; that it was a memorial of the conversion of the Saxons to Christianity; and that it was made for some unknown purpose by the Druids or the Romans.

There is a stylistic similarity between the Uffington Horse and the horse represented on the gold and silver coins current in southeast England at the end of the early Iron Age. Similar horses appear on two artefacts of the same period, the Aylesford and Marlborough buckets. The nearby hillfort of Uffington Castle is also from the early Iron Age. According to recent excavation, the site has been used extensively since the Bronze Age, although the White Horse may not be contemporaneous with this, but a later modification to the landscape. Current opinion is that the Uffington Horse was a totem or cult object of the Belgae, a people who occupied much of southeast England between 50 BC and AD 50.

Whitehouse, Mary (1910–)

British media activist. A founder of the National Viewers' and Listeners' Association, she has campaigned to censor radio and television for their treatment of sex and violence.

Whitelaw, William Stephen Ian, 1st Viscount Whitelaw (1918–)

British Conservative politician. As secretary of state for Northern Ireland he introduced the concept of power sharing. He was chief Conservative whip 1964–70, and leader of the House of Commons 1970–72. He became secretary of state for employment 1973–74, but failed to conciliate the trade unions. He was chair of the Conservative Party in 1974 and home secretary 1979–83, when he was made a peer.

He was educated at Winchester and Trinity College, Cambridge. He is a farmer and landowner and was elected Conservative MP for Penrith and Border in 1955. He became a government whip in 1959 and was parliamentary secretary, Ministry of Labour 1962–64. From 1964 to 1970 he was Opposition chief whip, becoming Lord President of the Council and leader of the House of Commons in 1970. In 1972 he became secretary of state for Northern Ireland, following the imposition of direct rule.

He made strenuous efforts to secure a solution to the problems of Northern Ireland: the 'no-go' areas of Belfast and Londonderry were cleared and a constitutional settlement appeared to have been reached between the Unionist Party and the SDLP at the Sunningdale Conference of 1973, but the agreement was to break down later.

Prior to the miners' strike of 1974 he was appointed secretary of state for Employment, but was unable to avert the strike. In 1975 he unsuccessfully contested the Conservative leadership.

White Paper
An official document that expresses government policy on an issue. It is usually preparatory to the introduction of a parliamentary bill (a proposed act of Parliament). Its name derives from its having fewer pages than a government blue book, and therefore needing no blue paper cover. A White Paper does not incorporate final cabinet decisions and comes to the House of Commons as a basis for discussion.

Whiteread, Rachel (1963–)
English sculptor. Her work consists mainly of casts of objects or the spaces around them or contained within them. She came to public attention with her cast of a whole house in 1993, which was controversially demolished soon afterwards. She won the Turner Prize in 1993, the first woman to win this award.

Whithorn
Town and former royal burgh in Dumfries and Galloway unitary authority, Scotland, 18 km/11 mi south of Wigtown; population (1991) 1,000. Whithorn and Isle of Whithorn, a small port on Wigtown Bay lying 7 km/4 mi to the southeast, are associated with St ◊Ninian, Scotland's earliest Christian missionary and bishop, who landed nearby around 397.

Candida Casa, his monastery and burial place, became a place of pilgrimage for many hundreds of years. **Whithorn Priory**, now in ruins, was built in the 12th century, and St Ninian's Chapel, founded in the 13th century, still stands at Isle of Whithorn. St Ninian's Cave lies on Port Castle Bay 4 km/2.5 mi to the southwest.

Whitstable
Resort in Kent, southeast England, at the mouth of the River Swale, noted for its oysters; population (1991) 28,500. It is a yachting centre. In the Middle Ages it was a stopping place for pilgrims travelling to Canterbury, 11 km/7 mi to the southeast.

Whitten-Brown, Arthur (1886–1948)
British aviator. After serving in World War I, he took part in the first nonstop flight across the Atlantic as navigator to Captain John ◊Alcock in 1919. KBE 1919.

Whittington, Dick (Richard) (*c.* 1358–1423)
English cloth merchant who was mayor of London 1397–98, 1406–07, and 1419–20. According to legend, he came to London as a poor boy with his cat when he heard that the streets were paved with gold and silver. His cat first appears in a play from 1605.

Whittle, Frank (1907–1996)
British engineer. He patented the basic design for the turbojet engine in 1930. In the Royal Air Force he worked on jet propulsion 1937–46. In May 1941 the Gloster E 28/39 aircraft first flew with the Whittle jet engine. Both the German (first operational jet planes) and the US jet aircraft were built using his principles. Knighted 1948.

Whittle was born in Coventry and joined the RAF as an apprentice, later training as a fighter pilot. He had the idea for a jet engine in 1928 but could not persuade the Air Ministry of its potential until 1935, when he formed the Power Jets Company. He retired from the RAF with the rank of air commodore in 1948 and took up a university appointment in the USA.

Whitworth, Joseph (1803–1887)
English engineer who established new standards of accuracy in the production of machine tools and precision measuring instruments. He devised standard gauges and screw threads, and introduced new methods of making gun barrels. Baronet 1869.

Who, the
English rock group, formed in 1964, with a hard, aggressive sound, high harmonies, and a propensity for destroying their instruments on stage. Their albums include *Tommy* (1969), *Who's Next* (1971), and *Quadrophenia* (1973).

Originally a mod band, the Who comprised Pete ◊Townshend (1945–), guitar and songwriter; Roger Daltrey (1944–), vocals; John Entwistle (1944–), bass; and Keith Moon (1947–1978), drums. The group was reconstituted for various performances in the 1990s, to a mixed reception.

WI
Abbreviation for ◊Women's Institute.

Wick
Fishing port and industrial town in the Highland unitary authority, northeast Scotland, at the mouth of the River Wick; population about 8,000. Industries include shipping, distilleries, glassware, knitwear, and North Sea oil. Air services to the Orkney and Shetland islands operate from here. An opera house at 15th-century Ackergill Tower opened in 1994.

Wick was once the busiest herring port in Europe. Pultenytown is the name given to the part of the town designed by Telford in the 1800s as a model village.

Widnes
Industrial town in Cheshire, England; population (1991) 56,000. It is linked with ◊Runcorn on the other side of the River Mersey by road and rail bridges. Widnes is the centre of the British chemical industry, and produces metals.

Wigan
Industrial town in Greater Manchester, northwest England, between Liverpool and Manchester, on the River Douglas; population (1991) 84,700. Industries include food processing, engineering, the manufacture of paper, fibreglass, and carpet tiles, tourism and leisure, and retail. The traditional coal and cotton industries have declined.

Wigan Pier was made famous by the writer George Orwell in *The Road to Wigan Pier* (1937). The pier has been redeveloped to include a heritage centre. This includes an exhibition, research centre, geological centre, history shop, souvenir bookshop, and meeting room. It was extended in

1996 with the addition of an art gallery, partly funded by the National Lottery.

Features
Wigan Pier, the area of the Leeds–Liverpool Canal basin, including Tencherfield Mill, the world's largest working mill steam-engine; Town Hall (1867); Market Hall (1877); Royal Albert Edward Infirmary (1873); Wigan Alps recreation area with ski slopes and water sports created from industrial dereliction including colliery spoil heaps; large complex at Robin Park for sports, leisure, and retail

Industries
Major companies in the borough of Wigan include Heinz (one of the largest food companies in Europe), Shearings, and Girobank.

History
Wigan was the site of Roman and Saxon settlements; it was the Roman garrison Coccium. The town was granted borough status by charter of Henry III in 1246. It became an important trading centre in medieval times, on the road north through Lancashire between Warrington and Preston. Coal-mining began in the area in the 15th century and Wigan prospered in the 19th century during the Industrial Revolution from the development of the cotton and engineering industries. Coal was distributed from here via the Liverpool–Leeds Canal to the Lancashire cotton mills. The Wigan School of Mines was founded in 1857. Thomas Linacre, one of the finest scholars of the 16th century and the first president of the Royal College of Physicians, was rector of Wigan 1519–24.

Wight, Isle of

Island and unitary authority of southern England

Area area 380 sq km/147 sq mi

Towns ◊Newport (the administrative headquarters); Ryde, Sandown, Shanklin, and Ventnor (all resorts)

Physical chalk cliffs and downs, and deep ravines, known locally as 'chines'; the highest point is St Boniface Down (240 m/787 ft); the Needles, a group of pointed chalk rocks up to 30 m/100 ft high in the sea to the west; the Solent, the sea channel between Hampshire and the island

Features Benedictine monastery at Quarr Abbey; Parkhurst Prison, just outside Newport; Cowes, venue of Regatta Week and headquarters of the Royal Yacht Squadron; Osborne House, built for Queen Victoria in 1845

Industries aircraft components; electronics; marine engineering; plastics; boatbuilding; sawmills; tourism

Agriculture fruit and vegetables grown in south of island

Population population (1996) 130,000

Famous people Robert Hooke and Thomas Arnold were born on the Isle of Wight, and Alfred Tennyson had a home at Farringford, near Freshwater.

History The Isle of Wight was called **Vectis** ('separate division') by the Romans, who conquered it in AD 43; there are Roman villas at Newport and Brading. Charles I was imprisoned (1647–48) in Carisbrooke Castle, now ruined.

Wightman Cup

Annual tennis competition between international women's teams from the USA and the UK. The trophy, first contested in 1923, was donated by Hazel Hotchkiss Wightman (1886–1974), a former US tennis player who won singles, doubles, and mixed-doubles titles in the US Championships 1909–1911. Because of US domination of the contest it was abandoned in 1990.

Wightwick Manor

19th-century half-timbered house in the West Midlands, England, 5 km/3 mi west of Wolverhampton. It contains fabrics and wallpaper designed by William Morris, Pre-Raphaelite paintings, de Morgan ware, and Kempe glass. Geoffrey Mander gave the house and 7 ha/17 acres to the National Trust in 1937.

Wigley, Dafydd (1943–)

Welsh politician, president of Plaid Cymru, the Welsh nationalist party, 1981–84 and from 1991. He aims to see Wales as a self-governing nation within the European Community. He has been Plaid Cymru member of Parliament for Caernarfon since February 1974, and sponsored the Disabled Persons Act 1981.

Wilberforce, William (1759–1833)

English reformer. He was instrumental in abolishing slavery in the British Empire. He entered Parliament in 1780; in 1807 his bill banning the trade in slaves from the West Indies was passed, and in 1833, largely through his efforts, slavery was

WILBERFORCE, WILLIAM *A leading member of the Evangelical Movement, which sought to promote Christian values in late 18th–early 19th century English society, William Wilberforce fought from 1788 to abolish British involvement in the slave trade. Having achieved this in 1807, he began campaigning for the abolition of the slave trade abroad and the total abolition of slavery. Slavery in the British Empire ended in 1833, the year of his death. Corbis*

eradicated throughout the empire. He died shortly before the Slavery Abolition Act was passed.

Wilberforce was a member of a humanitarian group called the Clapham Sect, which exercised considerable influence on public policy, being closely identified with Sunday schools, and the British and Foreign Bible Society, as well as the issue of slavery.

Wilbye, John (1574–1638)

English composer. He was not only one of the first English composers to write madrigals, but also one of the finest. Among his most characteristic works are the popular madrigals 'Draw on Sweet Night' and 'Sweet honey sucking bees', both 1609.

Other works include: two sacred vocal pieces contributed to Leighton's *Teares or Lamentacions*; two books of 64 madrigals (1598, 1609), madrigal 'The Lady Oriana' contributed to *The Triumphes of Oriana*; five sacred works; three fantasies for viols (incomplete), lute lessons (lost).

Wilde, Oscar (Fingal O'Flahertie Wills) (1854–1900)

Irish writer. With his flamboyant style and quotable conversation, he dazzled London society and, on his lecture tour in 1882, the USA. He published his only novel, *The Picture of Dorian Gray*, in 1891, followed by a series of sharp comedies, including *A Woman of No Importance* (1893) and *The Importance of Being Earnest* (1895). In 1895 he was imprisoned for two years for homosexual offences; he died in exile.

Wilde studied at Dublin and Oxford, where he became known as a supporter of the Aesthetic movement ('art for art's sake'). He published *Poems* (1881), and also wrote fairy tales and other stories, criticism, and a long, anarchic political essay, 'The Soul of Man Under Socialism' (1891). His elegant social comedies include *Lady Windermere's Fan* (1892) and *An Ideal Husband* (1895). The drama *Salome* (1893), based on the biblical character, was written in French; considered scandalous by the British censor, it was first performed in Paris in 1896 with the actress Sarah Bernhardt in the title role.

Among his lovers was Lord Alfred ◊Douglas, whose father provoked Wilde into a lawsuit that led to his social and financial ruin and imprisonment. The long poem *Ballad of Reading Gaol* (1898) and a letter published as *De Profundis* (1905) were written in jail to explain his side of the relationship. After his release from prison in 1897, he lived in France. He is buried in the Père Lachaise cemetery, Paris.

Wilkes, John (1727–1797)

British Radical politician, imprisoned for his political views; member of Parliament 1757–64 and from 1774. He championed parliamentary reform, religious tolerance, and US independence.

Wilkes, born in Clerkenwell, London, entered Parliament as a Whig in 1757. His attacks on the Tory prime minister Bute in his paper *The North Briton* led to his being outlawed in 1764; he fled to France, and on his return in 1768 was imprisoned. He was four times elected MP for Middlesex, but the Commons refused to admit him and finally declared his opponent elected. This secured him strong working- and middle-class support, and in 1774 he was allowed to take his seat in Parliament.

Wilkes, Maurice Vincent (1913–)

English mathematician who led the team at Cambridge University that built the EDSAC (electronic delay storage automatic calculator) in 1949, one of the earliest of the British electronic computers.

Wilkie, David (1785–1841)

Scottish painter. Active in London from 1805, he became famous for his depictions of everyday life, such as *The Blind Fiddler* (1806; Tate Gallery, London) and *The Letter of Introduction* (1813; National Gallery of Scotland, Edinburgh), executed in the 17th-century Dutch tradition.

Born in Cults, Fife, he was the son of a parish minister. He studied at the Trustees' Academy, Edinburgh, and the Royal Academy schools, but engravings after the Dutch painters David Teniers and Adriaen van Ostade suggested the popular subjects in which he was to excel. *The Village Politicians* (1805; private collection) won instant success and was followed by such other works as *The Penny Wedding* (Royal Collection). In 1823 he was appointed king's limner in Scotland.

After 1825, when he visited Italy and Spain, his style changed under the influence of Velázquez and Murillo. He was made painter-in-ordinary to William IV in 1830. He died at sea during his return from travels in Turkey and Palestine.

They charge me with fanaticism. If to be feelingly alive to the sufferings of my fellow-creatures is to be a fanatic, I am one of the most incurable fanatics ever permitted to be at large.

William Wilberforce English reformer.
Speech, 1816

Wilkins, Maurice Hugh Frederick (1916–)

New Zealand-born British molecular biologist. In 1962 he shared the Nobel Prize for Physiology or Medicine with Francis ◊Crick and James Watson for his work on the molecular structure of nucleic acids, particularly DNA, using X-ray diffraction.

Wilkins began his career as a physicist working on luminescence and phosphorescence, radar, and the separation of uranium isotopes, and worked in the USA during World War II on the development of the atomic bomb. After the war he turned his attention from nuclear physics to molecular biology, and studied the genetic effects of ultrasonic waves, nucleic acids, and viruses by using ultraviolet light.

Wilkins, William (1778–1839)

English architect. He pioneered the Greek Revival in England with his design for Downing College, Cambridge (1807–20). His other works include Haileybury College (1806–09); and in London, the main block of University

College (1827–28), the National Gallery (1834–38), and St George's Hospital (1828–29). All these buildings are Classical in style, but in his extensions of Corpus, King's, and Trinity colleges at Cambridge he adopted the Gothic style.

Wilkins was born in Norwich, the son of an architect. After graduating from Cambridge, he travelled in Greece and Italy from 1801 to 1805. He started practice in about 1806.

Wilkinson, Geoffrey (1921–1996)

English inorganic chemist who shared a Nobel prize in 1973 for his pioneering work on the organometallic compounds of the transition metals. Knighted 1976.

Willenhall

Town in the metropolitan county of West Midlands, England, between Walsall and Wolverhampton; population (1991) 26,200. The town has a long history of lockmaking, which is still the principal industry. Coal was dug here in the 16th century.

William

The badly behaved schoolboy hero of a series of children's books by English author Richmal ◊Crompton, published from 1922–70. William rebels against conventional English family life and, with his fellow 'Outlaws', Henry, Douglas, and Ginger, has many mishaps from which there is no honourable escape. Violet Elizabeth Bott, a 'soppy' girl, is an unwelcome addition to the Outlaws.

William full name William Arthur Philip Louis (1982–)

Prince of the UK, first child of the Prince and Princess of Wales.

William

Four kings of England:

William (I) the Conqueror (*c.* 1027–1087)

King of England from 1066. He was the illegitimate son of Duke Robert the Devil and succeeded his father as Duke of Normandy in 1035. Claiming that his relative King Edward the Confessor had bequeathed him the English throne, William invaded the country in 1066, defeating ◊Harold II at Hastings, Sussex, and was crowned king of England.

William's coronation took place in Westminster Abbey on Christmas Day 1066. He completed the establishment of feudalism in England, compiling detailed records of land and property in the Domesday Book, and kept the barons firmly under control. He died in Rouen after a fall from his horse and is buried in Caen, France. He was succeeded by his son William II.

William (II) Rufus, 'the Red' (*c.* 1056–1100)

King of England from 1087, the third son of William the Conqueror. He spent most of his reign attempting to capture Normandy from his brother ◊Robert II, Duke of Normandy. His extortion of money led his barons to revolt and caused confrontation with Bishop Anselm. He was killed while hunting in the New Forest, Hampshire, and was succeeded by his brother Henry I.

> *By the splendour of God I have taken possession of my realm; the earth of England is in my two hands.*
>
> William the Conqueror King of England from 1066. Said when he fell as he landed in England. Attributed

William (III) of Orange (1650–1702)

King of Great Britain and Ireland from 1688, the son of William II of Orange and Mary, daughter of Charles I. He was offered the English crown by the parliamentary opposition to James II. He invaded England in 1688 and in 1689 became joint sovereign with his wife, ◊Mary II. He spent much of his reign campaigning, first in Ireland, where he defeated James II at the Battle of the Boyne in 1690, and later against the French in Flanders. He was succeeded by Mary's sister, Anne.

Born in the Netherlands, William was made *stadtholder* (chief magistrate) in 1672 to resist the French invasion. He forced Louis XIV to make peace in 1678 and then concentrated on building up a European alliance against France. In

WILLIAM (I) THE CONQUEROR *The Great Seal of William I, the Norman king who mounted the last successful conquest of England. He subdued the country and imposed a new system of government dominated by an aristocratic Norman elite. Philip Sauvain Picture Collection*

1677 he married his cousin Mary, daughter of the future James II. When invited by both Whig and Tory leaders to take the crown from James, he landed with a large force at Torbay, Devon. James fled to France, and his Scottish and Irish supporters were defeated at the battles of Dunkeld in 1689 and the Boyne in 1690.

William IV (1765–1837)

King of Great Britain and Ireland from 1830, when he succeeded his brother George IV. Third son of George III, he was created Duke of Clarence in 1789, and married Adelaide of Saxe-Meiningen (1792–1849) in 1818. During the Reform Bill crisis he secured its passage by agreeing to create new peers to overcome the hostile majority in the House of Lords. He was succeeded by his niece Victoria.

William the Lion (1143–1214)

King of Scotland from 1165. He was captured by Henry II while invading England in 1174, and forced to do homage, but Richard I abandoned the English claim to suzerainty for a money payment in 1189. In 1209 William was forced by King John to renounce his claim to Northumberland.

> *Almost all the chief towns of modern Scotland trace their erection or the grant of privileges to his reign.*
>
> A J G MACKAY
> *Dictionary of National Biography* referring to William the Lion

William of Malmesbury (*c.* 1080–*c.* 1143)

English historian and monk. He compiled the *Gesta regum/ Deeds of the Kings* (*c.*1120–40) and *Historia novella*, which together formed a history of England to 1142.

William of Wykeham (*c.* 1323–1404)

English politician and clergyman. Appointed bishop of Winchester in 1367, he was twice Lord Chancellor (1367–72 and 1389–91), and founded Winchester College (public school) in 1378 and New College, Oxford, in 1379.

Williams, (George) Emlyn (1905–1987)

Welsh actor and dramatist. His plays, in which he appeared, include *Night Must Fall* (1935) and *The Corn Is Green* (1938). He was also acclaimed for his solo performance as the author Charles Dickens. Williams gave early encouragement to the actor Richard Burton.

Williams, J(ohn) P(eter) R(hys) (1949–)

Welsh Rugby Union player. A strong-running full-back, he won 55 caps for Wales and a further eight for the British Lions. He played in three Grand Slam winning teams and twice toured with winning British Lions teams. He played for Bridgend and London Welsh.

Williams, Kenneth (1926–1988)

English comedian and actor who was a mainstay of the ◊*Carry On* films, made from 1958. His mobile face, haughty air, and mannered speech combined to create a unique, mocking persona that was also much in demand for television talk-shows, where he would recount long, quirky anecdotes, and quizzes, such as the long-running radio show *Just a Minute*.

Born in London, he worked as a cartographer before moving into acting, initially on stage, and then on radio comedy show *Round the Horne*. While the *Carry On* films brought a steady income over two decades, he also worked in cabaret. His diaries were published after his death.

Williams

British racing-car manufacturing company started by Frank Williams in 1969 when he modified a Brabham BT26A. The first Williams Grand Prix car was designed by Patrick Head in 1978 and since then the team has been one of the most successful in Grand Prix racing, winning the Formula One Constructors' title a record-equalling nine times 1980–97.

Williams, John Christopher (1942–)

Australian guitarist. He has been resident in London since 1952. After studying with the Spanish virtuoso guitarist Andrés Segovia (1893-1987), he made his formal debut in 1958. His extensive repertoire includes contemporary music and jazz; he recorded the Rodrigo *Concerto de Aranjuez* (1939) three times. He was a founder member of the pop group Sky 1979–84.

Williams, Shirley Vivien Teresa Brittain, Baroness Williams of Crosby (1930–)

British Liberal Democrat Party politician. She was Labour minister for prices and consumer protection 1974–76, and education and science 1976–79. She became a founder member of the SDP (Social Democrat Party) in 1981 and its president in 1982, but lost her parliamentary seat in 1983. In 1988 she joined the newly-merged Social and Liberal Democratic Party (SLDP). She is the daughter of the socialist writer Vera ◊Brittain. She was made a life peer in 1993.

She was educated at St Paul's Girls' School, Somerville College, Oxford, and Columbia University, New York. She was general secretary of the Fabian Society 1960–64, and was elected Labour MP for Hitchin in 1964, and was MP for Hertford and Stevenage from 1974. Between 1966 and 1970 she was successively parliamentary secretary, Ministry of Labour, minister of state, Department of Education and Science, and minister of state at the Home Office. From 1970 to 1974 Mrs Williams was an Opposition spokesperson on social services, home affairs, and prices and consumer protection.

In March 1974 she entered the cabinet as secretary of state for Prices and Consumer Protection. In addition to this post she was appointed paymaster-general and chair of several important cabinet committees by James Callaghan, following his appointment as prime minister in 1976. Later in 1976 Mrs Williams became secretary of state for Education and Science, still retaining the office of paymaster-general.

Williams-Ellis, (Bertram) Clough (1883–1978)
English architect. He designed the fantasy resort of Portmeirion, North Wales. He was knighted in 1972.

Williamson, Alexander William (1824–1904)
English organic chemist who made significant discoveries concerning alcohols and ethers, catalysis, and reversible reactions. He was the first to explain the action of a catalyst in terms of the formation of an intermediate compound.

Williamson, Henry (1895–1977)
English writer. His stories of animal life include *Tarka the Otter* (1927). He wrote the fictional 15-volume sequence *A Chronicle of Ancient Sunlight* (1951–69), and described his own experiences in three autobiographies: *The Children of Shallowford* (1939), *The Story of a Norfolk Farm* (1941), and *A Clear Water Stream* (1958).

Williamson was born in London. After serving in World War I, he worked briefly as a journalist, but preferred country life, moving first to north Devon, then to Norfolk. He published the tetralogy *The Flax of Dreams* (1921–28), but is best known for his animal stories, which include *The Peregrine's Saga* (1923), *The Old Stag* (1926), *Salar the Salmon* (1935), and *Tales of Moorland and Estuary* (1953). Other works include *The Patriot's Progress* (1930).

Williamson, Malcolm (Benjamin Graham Christopher) (1931–)
Australian composer, pianist, and organist. Williamson studied with Eugene Goossens at the Sydney Conservatory and with Elisabeth ◊Lutyens in London, where he settled in 1953, and became an organist. His works include operas such as *Our Man in Havana* (1963), two symphonies, and chamber music. He was appointed ◊Master of the Queen's Musick in 1975.

His music draws on a wide range of influences, moving from an awareness of the avant garde to a more popular style, and includes several operas, a ballet *The Display*, concertos, church music, and dramatic works for children.

Other works include: the operas *English Eccentrics* (1964), *The Violins of St Jacques* (1966), *Lucky Peter's Journey* (1969); concerto for organ and orchestra, four piano concertos (1957–94), violin concerto (1965), seven symphonies (1957–84); *Santiago de Espada*, overture for orchestra; *Mass of Christ the King*, for soloists, chorus, and orchestra (1975–78); *Mass of St Etheldreda* (1990), *A Year of Birds* for soprano and orchestra (1995); chamber music; and piano and organ works.

Williamson, William Crawford (1816–1895)
English botanist, surgeon, zoologist, and palaeontologist who was regarded as one of the founders of modern palaeobotany. His research included work on deep-sea deposits, protozoans (single-celled animals), and cryptogams (plants that grow from spores, such as algae, ferns, or mosses). He showed that not all plant fossils containing secondary wood were necessarily spermatophytes (seed plants), but that some were spore-bearing.

William the Marshall, 1st Earl of Pembroke (*c.* 1146–1219)
English knight, regent of England from 1216. After supporting the dying Henry II against Richard (later Richard I), he went on a crusade to Palestine, was pardoned by Richard, and was granted an earldom in 1189. On King John's death he was appointed guardian of the future Henry III, and defeated the French under Louis VIII to enable Henry to gain the throne.

Willis, Norman David (1933–)
English trade-union leader. A trade-union official since leaving school, he was the general secretary of the Trades Union Congress (TUC) 1984–93.

He presided over the TUC at a time of falling union membership, hostile legislation from the Conservative government, and a major review of the role and policies of the Labour Party.

Willis, Thomas (1621–1673)
English physician and a founding member of the Royal Society who contributed much to our knowledge of the nervous system and cardiovascular system. He carried out a detailed study of the circulation of the brain, including the cerebral arterial circle, which he discovered under the base of the brain, that bears his name.

Willis wrote extensively about many diseases, including the mental disorders hypochondria, hysteria, and melancholia. He rediscovered the sweetness of urine excreted from patients with diabetes mellitus (which had originally been identified by physicians in India around 400 BC).

Wilmington
Village in East Sussex, southeast England, 8 km/5 mi northwest of Eastbourne. A ruined Benedictine monastery is now an agricultural museum. Nearby on the South ◊Downs is a ◊hill figure cut into the chalk of Windover Hill, the **Long Man of Wilmington**.

Wilmslow
Town in the district of Macclesfield, Cheshire, England, on the southern residential fringe of Greater Manchester; population (1991) 48,100.

Wilson, Richard (1936–)
Scottish actor who became famous in the 1990s for his portrayal of the grumpy pensioner Victor Meldrew in the BBC sitcom *One Foot in the Grave*. Prior to that he had a long theatrical career and also appeared in the off-beat comedy drama *Tutti Frutti*.

Wilson, Angus (Frank Johnstone) (1913–1991)
English novelist, short-story writer, and biographer. His acidly humorous books include *Anglo-Saxon Attitudes* (1956) and *The Old Men at the Zoo* (1961). In his detailed portrayal of English society, he extracted high comedy from its social and moral grotesqueries.

Wilson was deputy superintendent of the British Museum Reading Room from 1949–55, then worked as a full-time

WILSON, ANGUS *English writer Angus Wilson working in the British Museum reading room, London in 1952. Wilson joined the staff of the British Museum library in 1937, and in 1955 gave up his post as deputy superintendent of the reading room to devote himself to writing. He produced novels, criticism, short stories, and biography. Corbis*

writer. He was professor of English literature at the University of East Anglia from 1966–78.

His first published works were the short-story collections *The Wrong Set* (1949) and *Such Darling Dodos* (1950). His other major novels include *Late Call* (1964), *No Laughing Matter* (1967), and *Setting the World on Fire* (1980). Knighted 1980.

Wilson, Charles Thomson Rees (1869–1959)

Scottish physicist who in 1911 invented the Wilson cloud chamber, an apparatus for studying subatomic particles. He shared a Nobel prize in 1927.

Wilson, Colin Henry (1931–)

English author. He wrote *The Outsider* (1956) and thrillers, including *Necessary Doubt* (1964). Later works, such as *Mysteries* (1978), are about the occult.

Wilson, (James) Harold, Baron Wilson of Rievaulx (1916–1995)

British Labour politician, party leader from 1963, prime minister 1964–70 and 1974–76. His premiership was dominated by the issue of UK admission to membership of the European Community (now the European Union), the social contract (unofficial agreement with the trade unions), and economic difficulties.

Wilson, born in Huddersfield, West Yorkshire, studied at Jesus College, Oxford, where he gained a first-class degree in philosophy, politics, and economics. During World War II he worked as a civil servant, and in 1945 stood for Parliament and won the marginal seat of Ormskirk. Assigned by Prime Minister Clement Attlee to a junior post in the Ministry of Works, he progressed to become president of the Board of Trade 1947–51 (when he resigned because of social-service cuts). In 1963 he succeeded Hugh Gaitskell as Labour leader and became prime minister the following year, increasing his majority in 1966. He formed a minority government in February 1974 and achieved a majority of three in October 1974. He resigned in 1976 and was succeeded by James Callaghan. He was knighted in 1976 and made a peer in 1983.

A week is a long time in politics.

HAROLD WILSON British Labour prime minister. Attributed remark

---

Wilson, Richard (1714–1782)

Welsh painter. His landscapes, infused with an Italianate atmosphere, are painted in a Classical manner. His work influenced the development of English landscape painting, and Turner in particular.

Until 1750 he practised portraiture with some success, painting the Prince of Wales (George III) and his brother, the Duke of York (National Portrait Gallery, London), as well as Flora Macdonald (National Gallery of Scotland).

He also painted some landscapes before going to Italy in 1750, where he was encouraged to devote himself to this genre. He worked in Rome and Naples, producing a type of 'classical landscape' derived in part from Claude Lorrain, but also from Aelbert Cuyp, whose golden light Wilson greatly admired; his convention for painting foliage seems to have been based on Jacob Ruisdael. His originality, however, lay in a structural simplicity of design, breadth of treatment, and luminous atmosphere directly studied in nature.

It is possible that this departure from the artificialities then in vogue accounts for his lack of success when he returned to England in 1756. His work was uneven in quality and his attempts to introducing mythology, as in *The Destruction of the Children of Niobe* (1760; Yale Center for British Art), were often unsuccessful. Yet he created masterpieces, among them *The River Dee* (Barber Institute, Birmingham), *Cader Idris* (National Gallery, London), and *Snowdon from Llyn Nantlle* (versions in Walker Art Gallery, Liverpool, and Castle Museum, Nottingham).

He retired shortly before his death to live near Llanberis. His achievement was only fully appreciated by the following generation.

Wilton

Market town in Wiltshire, southwest England, 5 km/3 mi west of Salisbury; population (1991) 3,600. It manufactured carpets from the 16th century until 1995, when the Wilton Royal Carpet Factory closed. **Wilton House**, the seat of the earls of Pembroke, was built from designs by Hans Holbein and Inigo Jones.

Wilton was the seat of a bishopric until 1075, and was the capital of Wessex and the county town of Wiltshire in medieval times. The name of the county of Wiltshire is derived from 'Wiltonshire'.

Wilton House is associated with Shakespeare and with the Elizabethan courtier and poet Sir Philip Sidney. It is thought that the first performance of Shakespeare's play *As You Like It* took place at Wilton House in 1603 in front of James I. Sidney wrote part of his prose romance *Arcadia* (1590) in Wilton House. Scenes from the book are illustrated in the dado round the Single Cube Room.

Wilton

Type of cut-pile carpet originally made in Wilton, Wiltshire. It resembled a Brussels carpet, with a backing of linen and wool face, but the loop was cut open into an elastic velvet pile. Wilton manufactured carpets from the 16th century and was a major centre from the 18th century. The Wilton Royal Carpet Factory closed in 1995.

Wiltshire

County of southwest England (since April 1997 Swindon has been a separate unitary authority)

Area 3,255 sq km/1,256 sq mi

Towns and cities ◊Trowbridge (administrative headquarters), Salisbury, Wilton, Devizes, Chippenham, Warminster

Physical Marlborough Downs; Savernake Forest; rivers Kennet, Wylye, Avons (Salisbury and Bristol); Salisbury Plain (32 km/20 mi by 25 km/16 mi, lying at about 120 m/394 ft above sea-level), a military training area used since Napoleonic times

Features Longleat House (Marquess of Bath); Wilton House (Earl of Pembroke); Stourhead, with 18th-century gardens; Neolithic Stonehenge, Avebury, Silbury Hill, West Kennet Long Barrow, finest example of a long barrow in Wiltshire, dating from the 3rd millennium BC; Stonehenge, Avebury, and associated sites are a World Heritage site; Salisbury Cathedral, which has the tallest spire in Britain (123 m/404 ft)

Industries brewing (Devizes); computing; electronics; engineering (Chippenham); pharmaceuticals; plastics; quarrying (Portland stone); rubber (Bradford-upon-Avon, Melksham); tobacco (Devizes)

Agriculture cereals (wheat); cattle; dairy-farming (condensed milk, cheese); pig and sheep farming

Population (1997 est) 424,600

Famous people Christopher Wren, William Talbot, Isaac Pitman

Topography

Wiltshire is bounded on the north by Gloucestershire, and Swindon; on the east by West Berkshire and Hampshire; on the south by Dorset; and on the west by Somerset, Bath and North Somerset, and South Gloucestershire.

Wimbledon

District of the Greater London borough of ◊Merton. The headquarters of the All-England Lawn Tennis and Croquet Club are here, and the Wimbledon Championships are played in June.

On Wimbledon Common there is an Iron Age fort, Caesar's Camp, and a windmill where Robert ◊Baden-Powell wrote *Scouting for Boys*. Among its buildings are the Old Rectory (about 1500), Eagle House (1613), and the mid-17th century Rose and Crown public house. Famous residents have included Capt Frederick Marryat and William Wilberforce.

Wimbledon

English lawn-tennis centre used for international championship matches, situated in south London. There are currently 18 courts.

The first centre was at Worple Road when it was the home of the All England Croquet Club. Tennis was first played there in 1875, and in 1877 the club was renamed the All England Lawn Tennis and Croquet Club. The first all England championship was held in the same year. The club and championship moved to their present site in Church Road in 1922. The Wimbledon championship is one of the sport's four **Grand Slam** events; the others are the US Open, first held in 1881 as the US Championships, becoming the US Open in 1968; the French Championships, and the Australian Championships.

Wimborne Minster

Market town in Dorset, southwest England, 10 km/6 mi north of Poole, on the River Stour. Agriculture is the principal economic activity. The minster, or collegiate church, dating from Norman times, has a 14th-century clock.

About 6 km/4 mi to the west of the town is Badbury Rings, an Iron Age fortification which was once a Roman encampment.

Near Wimborne Minster is Canford Magna. Canford School, a private school for boys founded in1923, is housed in a 19th-century Gothic Revival mansion.

Winchelsea

Town in East Sussex, southeast England, about 3 km/2 mi from Rye; population (1991) 2,300. The town was formerly one of the ◊Cinque Ports. During the 16th century the inlet to the sea became silted up, and Winchelsea is now more than 1 km/0.6 mi from the sea.

New Winchelsea was laid out in about 1290 by Edward I to replace Old Winchelsea, which was submerged by the sea in 1287. The plans were never the completed because harbour silted up, and the church of St Thomas was also never finished, although the 14th-century chancel can still be seen.

Winchester

Cathedral city and administrative headquarters of ◊Hampshire, England, on the River Itchen, 19 km/12 mi northeast of Southampton; population (1991) 36,100. Tourism is important, and there is also light industry. Originally a Roman town, Winchester was capital of the Anglo-Saxon kingdom of Wessex, and later of England. Winchester Cathedral (1079–93) is the longest medieval church in Europe and was remodelled from Norman-Romanesque to Perpendicular Gothic under the patronage of William of Wykeham (founder of Winchester College in 1382), who is buried there, as are Saxon kings, St ◊Swithun, and the writers Izaac Walton and Jane Austen.

Winchester was a tribal centre of the Britons under the name **Caer Gwent**. On St Catherine's Hill can be seen the rampart and ditch made for defence by an Iron Age settlement in the 3rd century BC. Winchester was later one of the largest Roman settlements in Britain. It became capital of Wessex in 519 and under Alfred the Great and Canute was the seat of government. In 827 Egbert was crowned first king of all England here. Under William the Conqueror, Winchester was declared dual capital of England with London. A medieval 'reconstruction' of Arthur's Round Table is preserved in the 13th-century hall (all that survives) of the castle.

Roman Winchester

During the Roman occupation of Britain, Winchester, called **Venta Belgarum**, was a route-centre and the commercial and administrative capital of a district. Many Roman finds from the city are in the city museum, and remains of Roman buildings were discovered during excavations from 1953 to 1963. The forum was found north of the cathedral in 1961 and 1963.

The cathedral

The Saxon kings of Wessex are said to have been crowned in the old cathedral, which has now been fully excavated. Among kings of England crowned or recrowned at Winchester were William the Conqueror, and Richard I after his return from captivity. Here also Queen Mary was married to Philip of Spain. Not far from the cathedral lie the 12th-century ruins of the episcopal castle of Wolvesey, and adjoining them is the present official residence of the bishop, a building of the late-17th century. During the Saxon period the Winchester illuminators became famous. The most notable work produced was the Benedictional of St Aethelwold (created probably 975–80), formerly at Chatsworth and since 1957 in the British Museum. Another outstanding book is the 12th-century Winchester Bible, still in the cathedral library.

Places of historical interest

North of the city was Hyde Abbey, in which King Alfred was buried. Of Winchester Castle, the only part remaining above ground is the hall, the finest 13th-century hall in England, in which is the famous King Arthur's Round Table, made in the Middle Ages. The Westgate, one of the two remaining gates of the city, is now a museum, in which there is the finest civic collection of old weights and measures in England; the other gate is the Kingsgate, surmounted by St Swithun's church. St Cross Hospital was founded in 1136 by Bishop Henry de Blois; Cardinal Beaufort endowed it in 1446 for the Brethren of Noble Poverty. The church of the Hospital is a fine example of transitional Norman work. Winchester College was founded by William of Wykeham in 1394, and St Swithun's School for girls in 1884. The most interesting parish church in Winchester is St John's, which contains medieval woodwork (screens and pulpit). The old city mill, which for hundreds of years has spanned the Itchen above the City Bridge, has been preserved by the National Trust.

Windermere

Largest lake in England, in the ◊Lake District, Cumbria, northwest England; length 17 km/10.5 mi; width 1.6 km/1 mi. Windermere is the principal centre of tourism in the Lake District. The town of the same name extends towards Bowness on the eastern shore of the lake.

Wholly in Cumbria since 1974, Windermere was formerly in Westmorland, with its southeastern shore and western shores in Lancashire. The shores are well-wooded, and the lake drains southwards into Morecambe Bay via the River Leven. The town of Windermere (population (1991) 7,700) developed around the railway station which was built in 1847; combined with Bowness, it is a tourist resort. There is a car ferry service from Bowness across the lake to Sawrey.

windfall tax

One-off levy, introduced in 1997 by the UK Labour government, on the excess profits earned by 33 UK utilities privatized by public flotation since 1983, and regulated by statute. The tax was designed to raise, in two equal instalments (December 1997 and December 1998) £5.2 billion, to be used to fund the Welfare to Work programme, helping the young and long-term unemployed back into work.

The justification provided for the tax was that investors in the privatized utilities had secured excess profits, as shares had been underpriced when originally issued and subsequent regulation of the companies had been lax. The utilities affected by the levy included the regional water and electricity companies, the power-generators, British Gas (and its successors), British Telecommunications, Railtrack, and the British Airports Authority. It was not imposed on enterprises privatized through management buy-outs or third-party sales, such as the National Freight Company and rolling stock leasing companies (although investors made substantial profits in such cases), or on privatized bodies such as British Steel and British Airways, which operate in competitive markets. The Conservatives have criticized the tax for being retrospective and affecting the current shareholders 'unlucky enough to be holding the parcel when the music stops', rather than the early investors who had secured the windfall profits.

Wind in the Willows, The

Fantasy for children by Scottish author Kenneth ◊Grahame (1908). The story relates the adventures of a group of humanlike animals – Rat, Mole, Badger, and Toad. It was dramatized by A A ◊Milne as *Toad of Toad Hall* (1929) and by Alan Bennett (1990).

Windmill Theatre

Theatre in London, opened in 1932 for the presentation of nonstop variety. During World War II the Windmill Theatre adopted the motto 'We Never Close', and became famous as the only theatre to remain open during the whole of the

London Blitz. In 1964, however, the theatre was closed and later reopened as a cinema. It has now reverted to stage performances.

Windrush

BBC television series; see ♢*Empire Windrush*.

Windsor

Town in southern England, on the River Thames, 35 km/22 mi west of London; population (1991, with Eton) 30,600. Formerly in Berkshire, it joined with Maidenhead to become ♢Windsor and Maidenhead unitary authority in April 1998. Industries include tourism, computer services, and financial services. It is the site of ♢Windsor Castle, a royal residence, and a 17th-century guildhall designed by Christopher Wren. Nearby is the prestigious private school Eton College (founded in 1440).

The administrative headquarters of Windsor and Maidenhead unitary authority are in Maidenhead. The state apartments of Windsor Castle were badly damaged by fire in 1992. Legoland Windsor opened in 1996 on the site of the former Windsor Safari Park.

Features

The church of St John the Baptist (rebuilt in 1822) includes fine examples of woodcarvings by the Dutch woodcarver Grinling Gibbons, and a Jubilee statue of Queen Victoria. The parish church of Clewer St Andrew is a fine example of Norman architecture.

Windsor and Maidenhead

Unitary authority in southeast England, created in 1998 from part of the former county of Berkshire

Area 198 sq km/76 sq mi

Towns and cities Windsor, ♢Maidenhead (administrative headquarters)

Features River Thames; Windsor Castle, royal residence originally built by William the Conqueror; Windsor Great Park, remnant of royal hunting ground; Eton College,

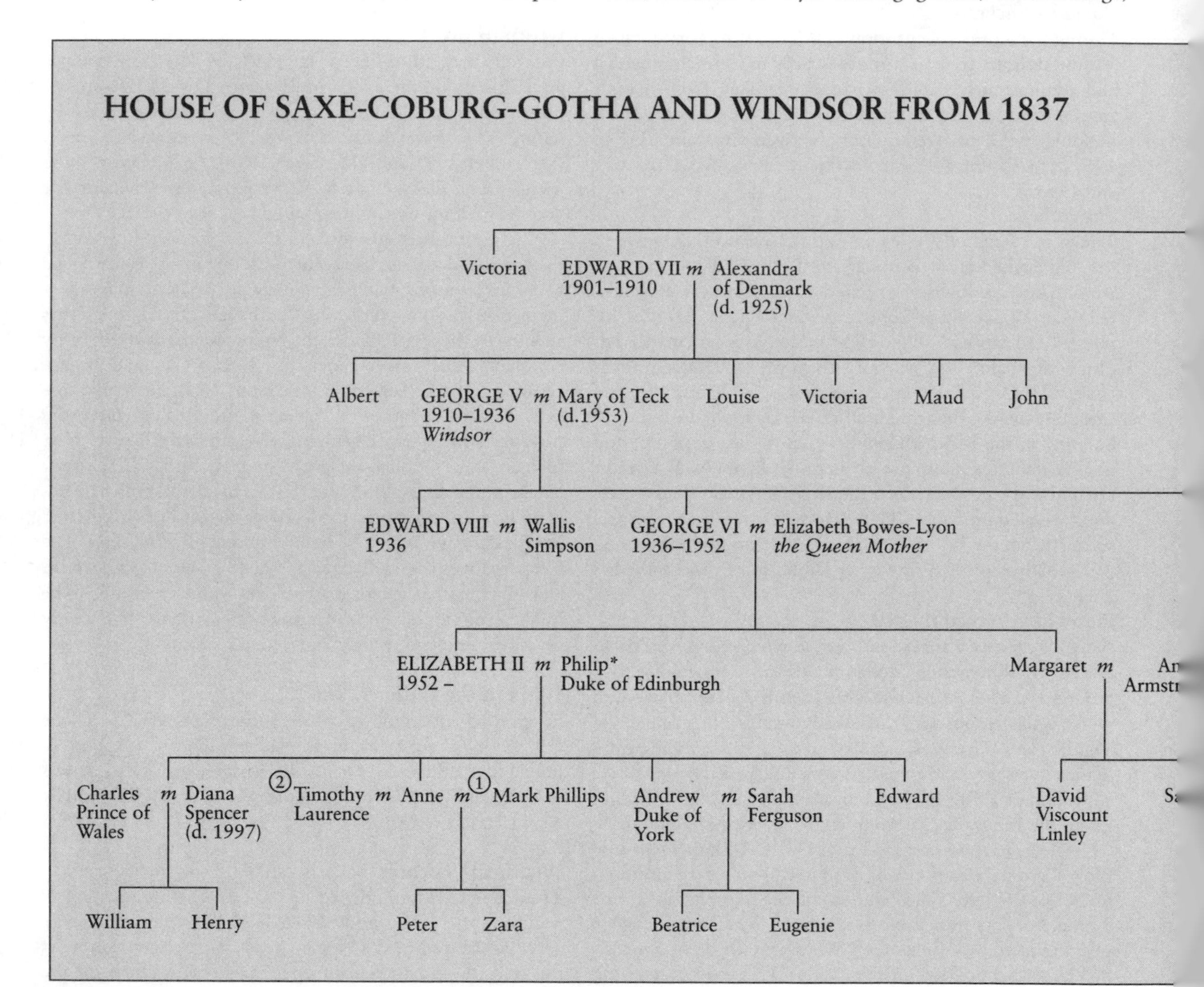

founded by Henry VI in 1440; Household Cavalry Museum (Windsor); Stanley Spencer Gallery (Cookham on Thames); Ascot Racecourse
Industries tourism and service industries, electrical systems and components, chemicals, motor vehicle components, telecommunications, publishing, scientific equipment
Population (1995) 140,200.

Windsor Castle

British royal residence in Windsor, Windsor and Maidenhead unitary authority, founded by William the Conqueror on the site of an earlier fortress. It includes the Perpendicular Gothic St George's Chapel and the Albert Memorial Chapel, beneath which George III, George IV, and William IV are buried. In the Home Park adjoining the castle is the Royal Mausoleum, Frogmore, where Queen Victoria and Prince Albert are buried.

Beyond the Round Tower or Keep are the state apartments and the sovereign's private apartments. **Windsor Great Park** lies to the south. In 1990 the royal residence Frogmore House, near Windsor Castle, as well as the Royal Mausoleum, were opened to the public.

On 20 November 1992 the castle was heavily damaged by a fire in its 14th-century St George's Hall. In April 1993 the Queen decided to open Buckingham Palace to the public to raise money for the necessary repair work. St George's Hall was reopened in 1998.

Windsor, House of

Official name of the British royal family since 1917, adopted in place of Saxe-Coburg-Gotha. Since 1960 those descendants of Elizabeth II not entitled to the prefix HRH (His/Her Royal Highness) have all borne the surname of Mountbatten-Windsor. See genealogy below.

Winnie-the-Pooh

Collection of children's stories by English author A A ◊Milne, published in 1926, illustrated by E H Shepard. The stories

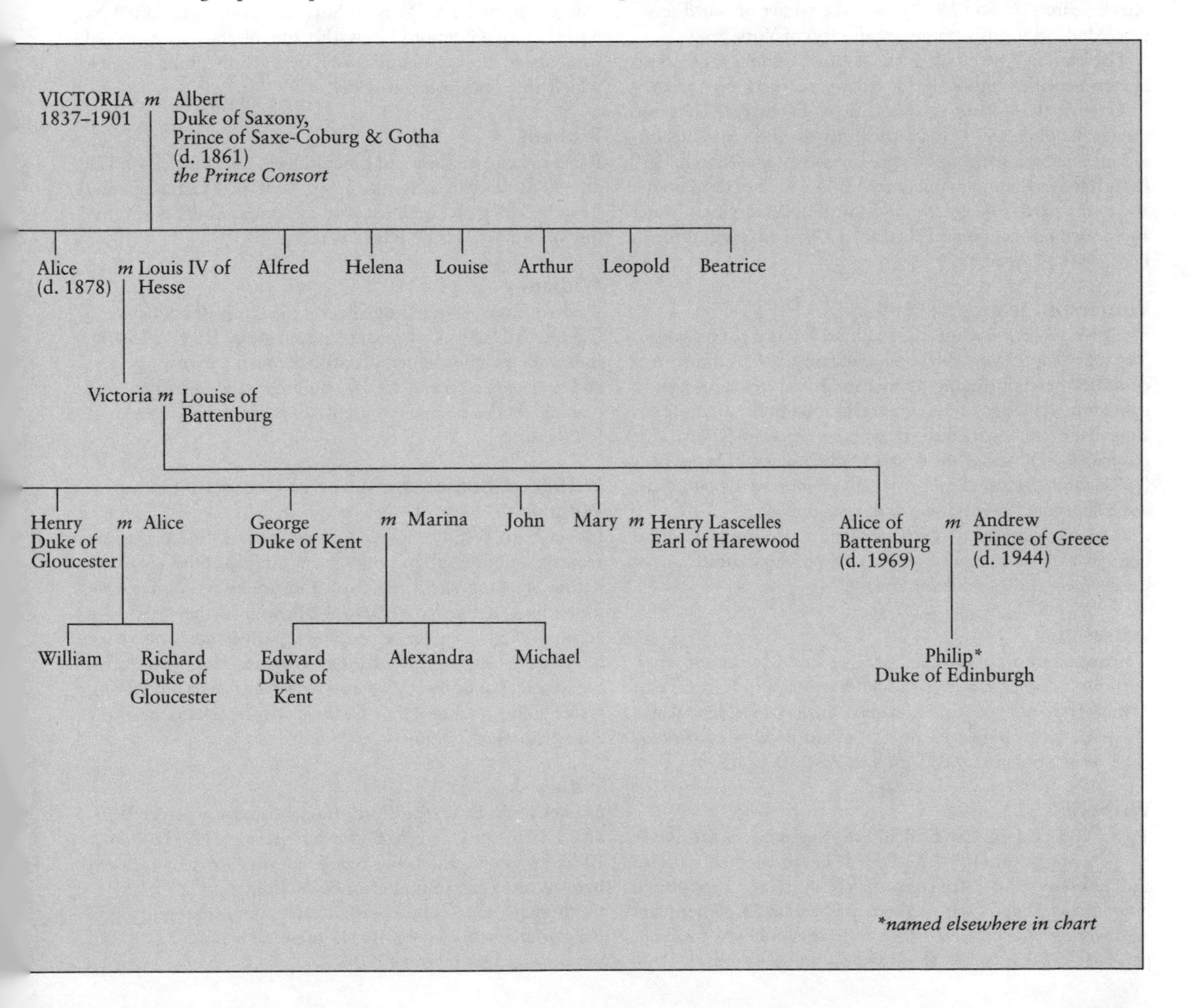

feature the author's son Christopher Robin, his teddy bear Winnie-the-Pooh, and a group of toy animals, Piglet, Eeyore, Rabbit, Owl, Kanga and Roo, and Tigger. Further stories appeared in *The House at Pooh Corner* (1928).

Winslet, Kate (1975–)

English screen actress. She made her film debut in the New Zealand period piece *Heavenly Creatures* (1994) based on the real-life stories of two school girls whose obsessive friendship drives them to commit murder. This was followed by her performance in the adaptation of Jane Austen's *Sense and Sensibility* (1995) and a star role in the blockbuster *Titanic* (1997). Her other films include *Jude* (1996) and *Hamlet* (1997), in which she played Ophelia.

winter of discontent

The winter of 1978–79 in Britain, marked by a series of strikes that contributed to the defeat of the Labour government in the general election of spring 1979. The phrase is from Shakespeare's *Richard III*: 'Now is the winter of our discontent/Made glorious summer by this sun of York.'

The strikes included Ford Motor Company workers September–November 1978, bakery workers November–December 1978, lorry drivers January–February 1979, train drivers January 1979, local-authority workers and health-service ancillaries and ambulance crews January–March 1979 (which led to the much publicized failure to bury dead bodies and to the partial breakdown of some hospital services), water and sewerage workers February 1979, and civil servants February and April 1979.

Winterson, Jeanette (1959–)

English novelist. Her autobiographical first novel *Oranges Are Not the Only Fruit* (1985, televised in 1990) humorously describes her upbringing as an Evangelical Pentecostalist in Lancashire, and her subsequent realization of her homosexuality. Later novels include *Boating for Beginners* (1986), *The Passion* (1987), *Sexing the Cherry* (1989), *Written On the Body* (1992), and *Art and Lies* (1994). *Art Objects: Essays on Ecstasy and Effrontery* (1995) is a work of non-fiction.

After working for two years driving an ice-cream van and one year in a mental hospital, Winterson studied at St Catherine's College, Oxford.

Wirral, the

Narrow peninsula between the Dee and Mersey estuaries, northwest England; population (1991) 316,300. It forms part of the Merseyside conurbation and is mainly a residential area but with some industrial development, notably at Birkenhead, Port Sunlight, and Ellesmere Port.

Wisbech

Town and port in Cambridgeshire, England, on the River Nene; population (1991) 17,900. It lies in the centre of an agricultural and fruit-growing district; agricultural implements, beer, and baskets are produced. There are engineering works, and other industries include canning, preserving, can-making, shipbuilding, and printing.

There are many Georgian houses on the North Brink and South Brink, near the Nene quay, some of which have Dutch characteristics.

Wise, Ernie stage name of Ernest Wiseman (1925–)

English comic actor and writer. He played the straightman to Eric ◊Morecambe's out-and-out comedian in their partnership, his screen persona always aspiring to writing and performance celebrity. Their television shows included the 1950s *Running Wild*, the 1960s *Two of a Kind*, and the long-running *Morecambe & Wise*, which featured a mixture of stand-up routines, song-and-dance numbers, 'humiliation' of guest stars, and comedy sketches. Together with Morecambe he starred in the films *The Intelligence Men* (1965), *That Riviera Touch* (1966), *The Magnificent Two* (1967), and *Night Train to Murder* (1983), the last of which they co-wrote.

Wisley

Village on the River Wey in Surrey, England, 12 km/8 mi northeast of Guildford. It is the site of the experimental gardens and laboratories of the ◊Royal Horticultural Society, which were established in 1904.

Witham

River in Leicestershire and Lincolnshire, England; length 129 km/80 mi. It rises in Rutland and flows past Grantham and Lincoln, and then southeast past Tattershall and Boston into the Wash north of the River Welland.

Witham

Town in Essex, eastern England, on the River Brain, between Chelmsford and Colchester; population (1991) 26,100. Industries include the manufacture of metal windows, gloves, and fruit juice; there is also milling, seed growing, and malting. There are ancient earthworks around the church of St Nicholas.

Withers, Googie stage name of Georgette Lizette Withers (1917–)

Indian-born British stage and screen actress. She began her career as a chorus girl in London's West End at the age of 12, before breaking into the British film industry in a series of short films directed by Michael ◊Powell in the 1930s. An accomplished character actress, she is perhaps best known for her role as a bitter hostess aspiring to run her own night club in the classic London-set *film noir Night and the City* (1950). Other films include the *Dead of Night* (1945) and the Australian *Shine* (1996).

Witney

Market town in Oxfordshire, England, on the River Windrush, 16 km/10 mi from Oxford; population (1991) 18,400. Blankets, gloves, and other woollen goods are manufactured here. Witney has a number of old buildings.

There is a 13th-century cruciform church (restored 1867), the grammar school (1663), the Blue Coat School (1723), and the Blanket Hall (about 1720).

The small roofed open-air shelter known as the Butter Cross in the market place, near to the Town Hall, was erected in 1683, replacing the old Butter Cross which formerly stood on this site.

Wittgenstein, Ludwig Josef Johann (1889–1951)

Austrian-born philosopher who taught at Cambridge University from 1929. *Tractatus Logico-Philosophicus* (1922) postulated the 'picture theory' of language: that words represent things according to social agreement. He subsequently rejected this idea, and developed the idea that usage was more important than convention: words are used according to different rules in a variety of human activities – different 'language games' are played with them.

Wittgenstein was born in Vienna and studied in the UK at Cambridge, becoming professor in 1939. His *Philosophical Investigations* (1953) and *On Certainty* (1969) were published posthumously.

Woburn

Small town in Bedfordshire, England, southwest of Bedford; population (1991) 1,500. Nearby is ◊**Woburn Abbey**, the home of the Duke of Bedford. The grounds, landscaped by Humphrey Repton (1752–1818), include a safari park.

Straw-plaiting was formerly an important occupation in Woburn.

Woburn Abbey

House in Bedfordshire, England, 12 km/7 mi southeast of Milton Keynes. The present building contains an altered 17th-century wing but is otherwise of the 18th century, its main west range (1747–61) by Henry Flitcroft, who also built the stables, and its south range (1787–90) built by William Chambers or Henry Holland. Woburn attracts a large number of visitors, not only to the house, but also to the safari park in the grounds, and other entertainments.

The house contains many treasures, including 24 paintings by Canaletto, and works by Poussin, Claude, Reynolds, and Gainsborough. Woburn has been the seat of the earls and dukes of Bedford since 1547.

Wodehouse, P(elham) G(renville) (1881–1975)

English novelist. He became a US citizen in 1955. His humorous novels and stories portray the accident-prone world of such characters as the socialite Bertie Wooster and his invaluable and impeccable manservant Jeeves, and Lord Emsworth of Blandings Castle with his prize pig, the Empress of Blandings.

From 1906, Wodehouse also collaborated on the lyrics of Broadway musicals by Jerome Kern, Gershwin, and others. Staying in France in 1941, during World War II, he was interned by the Germans; he made some humorous broadcasts from Berlin, which were taken amiss in Britain at the time, but he was exonerated later and was knighted in 1975. His work is admired for its style, erudition, and geniality, and includes *Indiscretions of Archie* (1921), *The Clicking of Cuthbert* (1922), *The Inimitable Jeeves* (1932), and *Uncle Fred in the Springtime* (1939).

Wogan, Terry born Michael Terence Wogan (1938–)

Irish presenter and radio disc jockey who after a long stint as the breakfast-show presenter on BBC's Radio 2 in the 1970s, became British TV's leading chat show host in the 1980s. Starting with one programme per week in 1984, he moved to thrice-weekly shows in 1985. A long-standing presenter of *Come Dancing* and the *Eurovision Song Contest*, he found a new niche in the 1990s bringing *Auntie's Bloomers* (programme out-takes) to the screen.

> *It is never difficult to distinguish between a Scotsman with a grievance and a ray of sunshine.*
>
> P G WODEHOUSE English novelist. Quoted in *Wodehouse at Work to the End*, by Richard Usborne

Woking

Town in Surrey, southeast England, 37 km/23 mi southwest of London; population (1991) 82,300. It is largely residential and owes its growth to railway development after 1838 when a station opened 3 km/2 mi from Old Woking.

There is a large mosque (1889) here, and many commons and parks. In Old Woking the church of St Peter has Norman origins.

Wokingham

Unitary authority in southeast England, created in 1998 from part of the former county of Berkshire

Area 179 sq km/69 sq mi

Towns and cities ◊Wokingham (administrative headquarters), Twyford

Features River Thames forms northern border of authority; Royal Electrical and Mechanical Engineering Corps Museum (Arborfield); Swallowfield Park, house built for 2nd Earl of Clarendon in 1690; National Dairy Museum; Henley Regatta course; large areas of mixed woodland including remnants of old Royal Chase of Windsor Forest and tree-lined avenues; Finchampstead Ridges

Industries light engineering, electronics and information technology, telecommunications, computer components and software, plastics

Population (1995) 142,000.

Wokingham, formerly Oakingham or Ockingham

Town, administrative centre of ◊Wokingham unitary authority, in southern England, between Reading and Bracknell; population (1991) 31,900. The chief forest town of Windsor Forest, it has been a market centre for over 700 years.

All Saints' church has a carved Perpendicular Gothic font, and there are almshouses in the town, some of which date from 1451.

The poets John ◊Gay, Pope, Swift, and Arbuthnot are said to have composed the ballad of 'Molly Mog' at the local Rose Inn.

wold (Old English *wald* 'forest')
Open, hilly country. The term refers specifically to certain areas in England, notably the Yorkshire and Lincolnshire Wolds and the ◊Cotswold Hills.

Wolfe, James (1727–1759)
English soldier. He served in Canada and commanded a victorious expedition against the French general Montcalm in Quebec on the Plains of Abraham, during which both commanders were killed. The British victory established their supremacy over Canada.

Wolfe fought at the battles of Dettingen, Falkirk, and ◊Culloden. With the outbreak of the Seven Years' War (the French and Indian War in North America), he was posted to Canada and played a conspicuous part in the siege of the French stronghold of Louisburg in 1758. He was promoted to major general in 1759.

Wolfenden Report
The findings, published 1957, of a British royal commission on homosexuality and prostitution. The report recommended legalizing homosexual acts between consenting adults of 21 and over, in private. This became law in 1967.

Wolfit, Donald (1902–1968)
English actor and manager. He formed his own theatre company in 1937, and excelled in the Shakespearean roles of Shylock and Lear, and Volpone (in Ben Jonson's play). He was knighted in 1957.

Wolfson, Isaac (1897–1991)
British store magnate and philanthropist, chair of Great Universal Stores from 1946. He established the **Wolfson Foundation** (1955) to promote health, education, and youth activities, founded **Wolfson College**, Cambridge, in 1965, and (with the Ford Foundation) endowed **Wolfson College**, Oxford, in 1966. Baronet 1962.

Wollaston, William Hyde (1766–1828)
English chemist and physicist who discovered in 1804 how to make malleable platinum. He went on to discover the new elements palladium in 1804 and rhodium in 1805. He also contributed to optics through the invention of a number of ingenious and still useful measuring instruments.

Wollstonecraft, Mary (1759–1797)
British feminist. She was a member of a group of radical intellectuals called the English Jacobins. Her book *A Vindication of the Rights of Women* (1792) demanded equal educational opportunities for women. She married William ◊Godwin in 1797 and died giving birth to a daughter, Mary (later Mary ◊Shelley).

WOLLSTONECRAFT, MARY *English author and early feminist Mary Wollstonecraft. Her best-known work is* A Vindication of the Rights of Woman, *written in 1792. She was also the mother of Mary Shelley. Corbis*

Wolsey, Thomas (*c.* 1475–1530)
English cleric and politician. In Henry VIII's service from 1509, he became archbishop of York in 1514, cardinal and lord chancellor in 1515, and began the dissolution of the monasteries.

His reluctance to further Henry's divorce from Catherine of Aragón led to his downfall in 1529. He was charged with high treason in 1530 but died before being tried.

I do not wish them [women] to have power over men; but over themselves.

MARY WOLLSTONECRAFT English feminist and writer.
Vindication of the Rights of Woman ch 4

Wolverhampton
Industrial town in West Midlands, central England, 20 km/12 mi northwest of Birmingham; population (1994) 256,100. Industries include metalworking, engineering, and the manufacture of chemicals, tyres, aircraft, bicycles, locks and keys, and commercial vehicles. Europe's first power station fuelled by waste tyres opened here in 1993.

The University of Wolverhampton (formerly Wolverhampton Polytechnic) was established in 1992.

Features

St Peter's church was founded in 994 and some of its present structure dates from the 13th century. Wightwick Manor nearby to the west was begun in 1887; it includes embroideries, carpets, and wallpapers designed by William Morris. Moseley Old Hall to the north is an Elizabethan timber-framed house in which Charles II stayed in 1651 when escaping from the Battle of Worcester.

History

Wolverhampton was a wool town in the Middle Ages and, situated at the heart of the industrial ◊Black Country, it was a centre of the iron industry from the 18th century.

Women's Institute, WI

National organization with branches in many towns and villages for the 'development of community welfare and the practice of rural crafts', found in Britain and Commonwealth countries.

The first such institute was founded in 1897 at Stoney Creek, Ontario, Canada, under the presidency of Adelaide Hoodless; the National Federation of Women's Institutes in the UK was founded in 1915. The **National Union of Townswomen's Guilds**, founded in 1929, is the urban equivalent. The WI is not associated with any religious faith or political party.

Women's Land Army

Organization founded in 1916 for the recruitment of women to work on farms during World War I. At its peak in September 1918 it had 16,000 members. It re-formed June in 1939, before the outbreak of World War II. Many 'Land Girls' joined up to help the war effort and, by August 1943, 87,000 were employed in farm work.

women's movement

Campaign for the rights of women, including social, political, and economic equality with men. Early European campaigners of the 17th–19th centuries fought for women's right to own property, to have access to higher education, and to vote (see ◊suffragette). Once women's suffrage was achieved in the 20th century, the emphasis of the movement shifted to the goals of equal social and economic opportunities for women, including employment. A continuing area of concern in industrialized countries is the contradiction between the now generally accepted principle of equality and the inequalities that remain between the sexes in state policies and in everyday life.

History

Pioneer 19th-century feminists, considered radical for their belief in the equality of the sexes, included Mary ◊Wollstonecraft and Emmeline ◊Pankhurst in the UK. The women's movement was also supported in principle by the English philosopher John Stuart Mill, in his essay *On the Subjugation of Women* (1869), although he also believed that the political advocacy of the women's cause was not possible in the climate of opinion prevailing at that time.

In 1993 women made up 49.5% of the UK workforce, yet only 5% of judges, 9% of MPs, and 5% and 7% of professors at Oxford and Cambridge universities respectively. The average female worker earns nearly 40% less than the average male earner, and women managers (less than 3% of all managers) earn 16% less than their male counterparts. In 1995, British companies had on average 3.7% women board members. The economic value of women's unpaid work has been estimated at £2 trillion annually. In 1994 girls outperformed boys at every level of education. In 1995, 90% of part-time workers in the UK were women.

UK legislation

In Britain, the denial of a woman's right to own property was eventually overcome by the Married Women's Property Act of 1882. Legislation for giving the vote to women was passed several times by the House of Commons from 1886 until 1911, but was always vetoed by the House of Lords. The organized protests of women in the suffragette movement were abruptly terminated by the beginning of World War I in 1914, but opinion later turned in their favour owing to the work women did during the war. In 1918 a bill granting limited franchise was passed, and ten years later full equality in this respect was attained. In the UK since 1975 discrimination against women in employment, education, housing, and provision of goods, facilities, and services to the public has been illegal under the Sex Discrimination and Equal Pay Acts.

See chronology of key dates on page 970.

Wood, Henry Joseph (1869–1944)

English conductor. From 1895 until his death, he conducted the London Promenade Concerts, now named after him. He promoted a national interest in music and encouraged many young composers. As a composer he is remembered for the *Fantasia on British Sea Songs* (1905), which ends each Promenade season.

Wood, John, the Elder (*c.* 1705–1754)

English architect. He was known as 'Wood of Bath' because of his many works in that city. His plan to restore the Roman character of Bath in strict Palladian style was only partially realized. His designs include Queen Square (1729–36) and the Circus (1754), a circular space with streets radiating out from it, which was not yet built by the time he died.

His son **John Wood, the Younger** (1728–1782) carried on his work, and himself designed the Royal Crescent (1767–75), the New Assembly Rooms (1769–71), and the Hot Baths (1776–78).

Wood, Victoria (1953–)

English writer, comedienne, and singer who rose to prominence in the 1980s as one of British TV's leading comics. First appearing in the talent show *New Faces*, she went on to a number of her own shows, including *Wood and Walters*, in partnership with Julie Walters, and *Victoria Wood on TV*. In 1998 she starred in her sitcom *Dinner Ladies*. In the 1990s she continued to tour an extremely successful live, essentially solo show.

WOMEN'S MOVEMENT IN BRITAIN: SOME KEY DATES

1775 King George III orders women and young children out of coal and salt mines.

1792 The English writer and feminist Mary Wollstonecraft publishes her *Vindication of the Rights of Woman*.

11 June 1847 Millicent Garrett Fawcett (–1929), English suffragette leader for over 50 years, is born in Aldeburgh, Suffolk.

1857 The Matrimonial Causes Act sets up divorce courts, allowing divorcees to remarry without recourse to a private act of Parliament, and outlines terms for divorce: men must prove adultery and women adultery and cruelty or desertion.

14 July 1858 Emmeline Pankhurst (–1928), militant English suffragette, is born in Manchester.

9 August 1870 The Married Women's Property Act is passed recognizing a woman's right to keep any money she earns and some of her own possessions.

1871 The English educationalist Anne Clough provides a house of residence for the first women students at the University of Cambridge, which becomes Newnham College in 1875.

1873 Legislation extends women's rights to claim custody of their children in divorce proceedings.

1875 The London Medical School for Women is founded (women having previously been excluded from studying medicine).

1882 The Married Women's Property Act gives married women the right of separate ownership of property of all kinds.

23 October 1906 Women suffragettes demonstrate in the outer lobby of the House of Commons. Ten of the demonstrators are charged the following day, and sent to prison.

1909 The suffragette Marion Wallace Dunlop becomes the first hunger striker in Britain: she is released after 91 hours.

4 June 1913 The suffragette Emily Davidson is killed when she runs under the king's horse at the Derby.

28 November 1919 Lady Nancy Astor is elected in a by-election and becomes the first woman member of Parliament to take her seat.

2 July 1928 Women's suffrage rights are extended to become equal with those of men.

30 May 1929 In a general election, the first held under universal adult suffrage, the Labour Party wins 287 seats, Conservatives 260, Liberals, 59, others, 9.

1930 Gertrude Denman, who introduced the Inter-uterine device (IUD) for birth control and published the best-selling *The Sex Factor in Marriage* earlier this year, becomes chair of the National Birth Control Council.

23 May 1937 The Matrimonial Causes Act, introduced by the author, lawyer, and politician A P Herbert, gives women equality with men in divorce proceedings in England and Wales.

1939 Dorothy Garrod becomes the first woman to receive a professorship at Cambridge University. She serves as professor of archaeology until 1952.

6 November 1946 A royal commission favours equal pay for women.

6 December 1947 Cambridge University votes to admit women to membership and degree courses.

27 October 1967 Laws governing abortion are relaxed.

23 April 1969 The government concedes universal adult suffrage in local elections in Northern Ireland, in response to Catholic civil-rights activists' demands.

28 February 1972 English women's football clubs are officially recognized by the English Football Association (FA) under the assurance that no matches are to be allowed between mixed teams or between men's teams and women's teams. The FA had banned women from playing at the grounds of clubs under its jurisdiction in 1921.

1973 The women's publishing house Virago is founded.

October 1974 Five male colleges at Oxford University – Brasenose, Jesus, Wadham, Hertford, and St Catherine's – admit women for the first time.

29 December 1975 The Sex Discrimination Act establishes the Equal Opportunities Commission.

1979 The House of Commons has 19 women out of 635 members and the House of Lords has 51 women out of 1,107 members.

4 May 1979 Conservative leader Margaret Thatcher becomes Britain's first woman prime minister.

3 January 1980 A report shows that half of married British women go out to work, the largest proportion anywhere in the European Community.

March 1984 Brenda Dean is the first woman to lead a major British union, when she is elected leader of print union SOGAT '82.

1985 The General Synod of the Church of England approves by a large majority the ordination of women as deacons.

1990 Britain introduces separate taxation for married women.

27 April 1992 The Labour politician Betty Boothroyd becomes the first woman Speaker of the House of Commons.

5 November 1993 Legislation to allow the Church of England to ordain women priests gains the royal assent.

27 February 1998 The Home Office announces that Queen Elizabeth II supports plans to remove the gender bias from British succession rules which currently states that succession goes to the first-born son.

woodland

Area in which trees grow more or less thickly; generally smaller than a forest. Woodland covers about 2.4 million hectares/6 million acres in the UK: about 8% of England, 15% of Scotland, 12% of Wales, and 6% of Northern Ireland. This is over 10% of the total land area – well below the 25% average in the rest of Europe. An estimated 33% of ancient woodland has been destroyed in Britain since 1945. The Forestry Commission aims to double the area of woodlands in England by the middle of the next century.

wool

The natural hair covering of the sheep, and also of the llama, angora goat, and some other mammals. The domestic sheep *Ovis aries* provides the great bulk of the fibres used in textile production. Lanolin is a by-product.

Types of wool

In Britain there are some 40 breeds of sheep, and the wool is classified as lustre (including Lincoln, Leicester, South Devon, Cotswold, Dartmoor), demi-lustre (Cheviot, Exmoor Horn, Romney Marsh), down (Dorset, Oxford, Suffolk, Hampshire, Southdown), and mountain (Blackface, Swaledale, Welsh White, Welsh Black).

Lustre wools are used for making worsted dress fabrics, linings, and braids. Demi-lustre wools are rather finer in quality, and are used for suitings, overcoats, and costumes, and worsted serge fabrics. Finest of English-grown wools are the down; they are used for hosiery yarns, and some for woollen cloths. Mountain wools are coarse and poor in quality, often comprising wool and hair mixed; they are useful for making carpets, homespun tweeds, and low-quality woollen suits and socks.

Woolf, (Adeline) Virginia born Stephen (1882–1941)

English novelist and critic. In novels such as *Mrs Dalloway* (1925), *To the Lighthouse* (1927), and *The Waves* (1931), she used a 'stream of consciousness' technique to render inner experience. In *A Room of One's Own* (1929) (nonfiction), *Orlando* (1928), and *The Years* (1937), she examines the importance of economic independence for women and other feminist principles.

Her first novel, *The Voyage Out* (1915), explored the tensions experienced by women who want marriage and a career. *Night and Day* was published in 1919, but her first really characteristic work was *Jacob's Room* (1922). After the death of her father, Leslie Stephen, she and her siblings moved to Bloomsbury, forming the nucleus of the ◊Bloomsbury Group. She produced a succession of novels, short stories, and critical essays, included in *The Common Reader* (1925 and 1932). She was plagued by bouts of depression and committed suicide in 1941.

In 1912 Woolf married the writer **Leonard Woolf** (1880–1969), with whom she founded the Hogarth Press in 1917.

Woolner, Thomas (1825–1892)

English sculptor and poet. He was an original member of the ◊Pre-Raphaelite Brotherhood, and wrote poems for the *Germ*, a short-lived Pre-Raphaelite literary journal. His statues and portrait busts include those of the writers Tennyson, Thomas Carlyle, and John Stuart Mill.

Woolner was born at Hadleigh, Suffolk, and studied under William Behnes and at the Royal Academy.

woolsack

The seat of the Lord Chancellor in the House of Lords. The woolsack is a large square bag of wool, with a backrest but no arms, covered with red cloth. It is traditionally held to have been placed in the House during the reign of Edward III as a mark of the importance of the wool trade.

Woolwich

District in east London, cut through by the River Thames, the northern part being in the borough of ◊Newham and the southern part in the borough of ◊Greenwich. The Thames barrier (a flood barrier, constructed in 1982) is here.

The Woolwich Royal Arsenal, an ordnance depot from 1518 and centre for the manufacture and testing of arms, is still partly in use. The Royal Military Academy and the Royal Artillery Institution Museum are located here. The Town Hall (1905) is the administrative centre for the borough of Greenwich.

Woolwich in the Middle Ages was a fishing village but it expanded in the 15th century when it became the site of a royal dockyard and the Royal Arsenal (developed from the Royal Laboratory, Carriage Department, and a Powder House, probably established about the same time as the dockyard). The main government foundry was moved here from Moorfields in 1716–17. The Royal Military Academy, established originally inside the Arsenal in 1741, was the first military school in Britain; it was amalgamated with the Royal Military College at Sandhurst in 1946. The population of Woolwich increased greatly after many factories were established here as a result of the Crimean War and World War I.

Woosnam, Ian (1958–)

Welsh golfer who, in 1987, became the first UK player to win the World Match-Play Championship. He has since won many tournaments, including the World Cup 1987, World Match-Play 1990, and US Masters 1991. Woosnam was Europe's leading moneywinner in 1987 (as a result of winning the $1 million Sun City Open in South Africa) and again in 1990. He was ranked Number One in the world for 50 weeks in 1991–92.

Wootton, Barbara Frances, Baroness Wootton of Abinger (1897–1988)

English educationist and economist. She taught at London University, and worked in the fields of politics, media, social welfare, and penal reform. Her books include *Freedom under Planning* (1945), *Testament for Social Science*, and *Social Science and Social Pathology* (1959). She was given a life peerage in 1958.

Worcester

Cathedral city in west central England on the River Severn, and administrative headquarters of the county of ◊Worcestershire, 35 km/22 mi southwest of Birmingham; population (1991) 82,700. Industries include the manufacture of shoes, Worcestershire sauce, and Royal Worcester porcelain. The cathedral dates from the 13th and 14th centuries. Much of the city centre was redeveloped in the 1960s. The birthplace of the composer Elgar at nearby Broadheath is a museum. At the **Battle of Worcester** in 1651 Oliver Cromwell defeated Charles II.

History

Worcester was important as early as the 7th century owing to its situation on a ford in the Severn. The city motto, 'Faithful in war and peace', commemorates the royalist support given by Worcester during the civil wars. In 1651 Charles II lodged in the city, and from the cathedral tower watched his forces being routed by Cromwell's troops. Many royalist soldiers were imprisoned in the cathedral after the battle. Worcester has been an episcopal see since 680, but its early history is obscure. In 964 St Oswald founded a new church there for Benedictine monks, and Bishop Wulfstan began rebuilding on a large scale in 1084. King John is buried between the shrines of Oswald and Wulfstan. From medieval times Worcester was the centre of a prosperous glove trade. The firms of Dent's and Fownes', founded in the 18th century, carry on this tradition. The Royal Worcester Porcelain Factory founded in 1751 by 'John Wall, doctor of Physic, and William Davis, Apothecary'; Wall was also connected with Worcester Royal Infirmary, which opened in a house in Silver Street in 1745. Berrow's *Worcester Journal* traces its history to 1690, and is therefore one of the oldest newspapers in England.

The cathedral

The Cathedral of Christ and St Mary the Virgin includes a Norman crypt, an impressive geometrical west window, and a Perpendicular cloister with a well-preserved lavatorium and some carved bosses on the vaulted roof. The circular Norman chapter house and the original refectory, now used by the King's School, remain. The external length of the cathedral is 126 m/413 ft and the central tower (completed 1364) is 60 m/197 ft high. The exterior was extensively restored between 1857 and 1874. The building of the Early English choir and Lady chapel began in 1224, and was effected by bishops De Blois and Cantelupe, whose effigies are in the chapel. The last important addition to the cathedral was Prince Arthur's Chantry, with a magnificent Perpendicular screen, erected by Henry VII in memory of his eldest son. The Three Choirs Festival is held here once every three years.

Churches

St Helen's is the oldest church in Worcester, dating back to 680, but rebuilt in the 13th and 15th centuries. St Andrew's

WORCESTER CATHEDRAL *One of the most beautifully situated of English cathedrals, seen from across the River Severn. The oldest part of the building, the crypt, was begun in 1084, but predominantly the cathedral dates from the 13th and 14th centuries, harmoniously blending a variety of styles. Corbis*

and St Albans are other medieval ecclesiastical structures, but these three churches are not now used as places of worship.

The Commandery

The Commandery, formerly called the Hospital of St Wulfstan, was founded by Wulfstan (1085) for a master, priests, and brethren, under the rule of St Augustine; the present structure is 15th century. At the Battle of Worcester in 1651, the Commandery was the headquarters of the royal forces under the Duke of Hamilton, and the royal standard was raised on the hill known as Fort Royal, which at that time was part of the grounds.

Other features

Medieval buildings still remain in New Street and Friar Street, the most important being that built in about 1480 by the Grey Friars. In 'King Charles's House' Charles II is said to have hidden after his defeat at Worcester. From 'Queen Elizabeth's House', Queen Elizabeth I, according to tradition, addressed the people when she visited Worcester in 1574. Worcester is rich in Georgian buildings. The Guildhall (1721–23) is the work of Thomas White, a native of Worcester. The Royal Grammar School dates back to the 13th century, when it was supported by the merchants of the Trinity Guild; Elizabeth I granted it a charter in 1561. The Worcester Cathedral King's School was established and endowed out of the monastic funds by Henry VIII in 1541, and reorganized in 1884. More modern buildings include the Shire Hall, the Worcester Royal Infirmary, the Victoria Institute, and Crown Gate, a shopping precinct (1992).

Worcester Porcelain Factory

English porcelain factory, since 1862 the Royal Worcester Porcelain Factory. The factory was founded in 1751 and produced a hard-wearing type of softpaste porcelain, mainly as tableware and decorative china and also white Parian ware figures. It employed advanced transfer printing techniques on a variety of shapes often based on Chinese porcelain.

Worcestershire

Two-tier county of west central England. Herefordshire and Worcestershire existed as counties until 1974, when they were amalgamated to form the county of Hereford and Worcester; in 1998 this county was divided back into Worcestershire and Herefordshire, which regained their pre-1974 boundaries.

Area approximately 1,640 sq km/1,020 sq mi

Towns and cities ◊Worcester (administrative headquarters), Bewdley, Bromsgrove, Evesham, Kidderminster, Pershore, Stourport, Tenbury Wells

Physical Malvern Hills in the southwest (highest point Worcester Beacon 425 m/1,394 ft); rivers: Severn with tributaries Stour, Teme, and Avon (running through the fertile Vale of Evesham)

Features Droitwich, once a Victorian spa, reopened its baths in 1985 (the town lies over a subterranean brine reservoir); Three Choirs Festival at Great Malvern

Agriculture cereals (oats, wheat), fruit (apples, pears), hops, vegetables; cider; much of the county is under cultivation, a large part being devoted to permanent pasture, notably for Hereford cattle

Industries carpets (Kidderminster), chemicals, engineering, food processing, needles and fishing tackle (Redditch), porcelain (Worcester), salt

Population (1994) 699,900

Famous people Richard Baxter, Samuel Butler (author of *Hudibras*), Edward Elgar, A E Housman, William Langland (author of the *Vision of Piers Plowman*), Francis Brett Young

Topography

Worcestershire is bounded to the north by West Midlands, Staffordshire, and Shropshire; to the west by Herefordshire; to the southwest by Gloucestershire; and to the east by Warwickshire. The surface of Worcestershire varies, the south and southwest being hilly, while through the centre run the river valleys, with the Lickey Hills and the Clent Hills in the north. The North Cotswold Hills and Bredon Hill lie along the southeast border of the county. Worcestershire is well wooded and contains the two ancient forests of Wyre and Malvern Chase. Canals connect the Severn with the Midland canal system.

Ecclesiastical history

The greater part of the county was at one time in the hands of the church, and there were no less than 13 great monastic foundations. Of these there are ruins at Pershore and Evesham, both dating from the 8th century; Worcester Cathedral, and the priory church at Malvern, also of the same date; and ruins at Bordesley and Astley dating from the 13th century.

Architecture

The county is rich in domestic architecture of the Tudor and Georgian periods, and possesses a number of notable country houses.

Wordsworth, Dorothy (1771–1855)

English writer. She was the only sister of William ◊Wordsworth and lived with him (and later his wife) as a companion and support from 1795 until his death. Her journals describe their life in Alfoxden, Somerset (of which only a small section remains), and at Grasmere in the Lake District, and their travels, which provided inspiration and material for his poetry.

Wordsworth, William (1770–1850)

English Romantic poet. In 1797 he moved with his sister Dorothy ◊Wordsworth to Somerset, where he lived near Samuel Taylor ◊Coleridge and collaborated with him on *Lyrical Ballads* (1798) (which included 'Tintern Abbey', a meditation on his response to nature). His most notable individual poems were published in *Poems* (1807) (including 'Intimations of Immortality'). At intervals between then and 1839 he revised *The Prelude* (posthumously published in 1850), the first part of his uncompleted philosophical, creative, and spiritual autobiography in verse. He was appointed poet laureate in 1843.

Wordsworth's first published works appeared in 1793, *The Evening Walk* and *Descriptive Sketches of a Pedestrian Tour in the*

Alps. With his sister Dorothy he settled in Racedown, Dorset, then in Alfoxden in Somerset, near Nether Stowey where Coleridge was living. With the profits he made from the publication of *Lyrical Ballads* he went with Dorothy and Coleridge to Germany where he wrote some of his best short poems, including 'Strange fits...' and 'A slumber did my spirit seal'. In 1799 he and Dorothy moved to Dove Cottage in Grasmere, in the Lake District, and in 1802 he married his cousin Mary Hutchinson (1770–1859). In 1813 the Wordsworths moved to Rydal Mount. His later years were marred by his sister's ill health and the death of his daughter Dora in 1847.

A leader of the Romantic movement, Wordsworth is best known as the poet who reawakened his readers to the beauty of nature, describing the emotions and perceptive insights which natural beauty arouses in the sensitive observer. He advocated a poetry of simple feeling and the use of the language of ordinary speech, demonstrated in the unadorned simplicity of lyrics such as 'To the cuckoo' and 'I wandered lonely as a cloud'. At a deeper level, he saw himself as a philosophical poet and his nature mysticism had a strong, though diffuse, effect on his successors.

We saw a raven very high above us. It called out, and the dome of the sky seemed to echo the sound.

DOROTHY WORDSWORTH English writer.
Journals 27 July 1800

Workington

Seaport and market town at the mouth of the River Derwent, in Cumbria, northwest England, 48 km/30 mi southwest of Carlisle; population (1991) 26,000. Its industries include steel, metallurgy, engineering, and the manufacture of carpets.

The port centres on the Prince of Wales dock.

Worksop

Market and industrial town in Nottinghamshire, central England, on the River Ryton; population (1991) 37,100. Industries include coalmining, light engineering, and the manufacture of chemicals and food products. Mary Queen of Scots was imprisoned at Worksop Manor, which was burned in 1761.

The church, which formerly belonged to an Augustinian priory, includes a Norman nave and the 13th-century Lady Chapel. The priory gatehouse dates from the early 14th century. The ◊Dukeries, an area of estates with large stately homes, lies to the south.

World Heritage sites

There are 17 UK World Heritage sites, a term determined in 1972 by UNESCO. Their formal titles are, in order of designation:

1986 The Giant's Causeway and Causeway coast
1986 Durham Castle and Cathedral
1986 Ironbridge Gorge
1986 Studley Royal Park, including the ruins of Fountains Abbey
1986 Stonehenge, Avebury, and associated sites
1986 The castles and town walls of King Edward in Gwynedd
1986 St Kilda
1987 Blenheim Palace
1987 City of Bath
1987 Hadrian's Wall
1987 Palace of Westminster, Abbey of Westminster, and St Margaret's church
1988 Henderson Island (in the South Pacific)
1988 The Tower of London
1988 Canterbury Cathedral, St Augustine's abbey, and St Martin's church
1995 Old and New Towns of Edinburgh
1995 Gough Island Wildlife Reserve (in the Atlantic)
1997 Maritime Greenwich

World War I, 1914–1918

War between the Central Powers (Germany, Austria-Hungary, and allies) on one side, and the Triple Entente (Britain and the British Empire, France, and Russia) and their allies on the other. An estimated 10 million lives were lost and twice that number were wounded. It was fought on the eastern and western fronts, in the Middle East, in Africa, and at sea. Russia withdrew in 1917 because of the Russian Revolution; in the same year the USA entered the war on the side of Britain and France. The peace treaty of Versailles in 1919 was the formal end to the war.

The war was set in motion by the assassination in Sarajevo of the heir to the Austrian throne, Archduke Franz Ferdinand, by a Serbian nationalist in June 1914. Tension had already been mounting over many years between the major European powers who were divided, by a series of alliances, into two rival camps: one led by Germany and Austria-Hungary, and the other containing France, Britain, and Russia. Germany and Britain had both recently modernized their navies, and imperialist rivalries had led to a series of international crises: Russia against Austria over Bosnia 1908–09, and Germany against France and Britain over Agadir in 1911. When Austria declared war on Serbia on 28 July 1914, Russia mobilized along the German and Austrian frontier. Germany then declared war on Russia and France, taking a short cut in the west by invading neutral Belgium; on 4 August Britain declared war on Germany. The war against Germany was concentrated on the Western Front; the German advance was initially halted by the ◊British Expeditionary Force under Sir John French at Mons and, following an allied counterattack at the Marne, the Germans were driven back to the Aisne River. The opposing lines then settled into trench warfare with neither side advancing more than a few miles over the next three years. Poison gas was first employed by the Germans at the second Battle of Ypres in 1915, and the British introduced tanks at the Battle of the Somme in 1916.

THE EMBATTLED ISLAND: BRITAIN IN THE WORLD WARS

War is often cited as a catalyst for change, and Britain's experience during the World Wars seems to prove the maxim. If World War I saw the birth of modern British society, World War II, to continue the analogy, saw its maturation.

'The War to End all Wars'

The events of July 1914 caught most of Britain by surprise. Despite Sir Edward Grey's apocalyptic remark 'the lamps are going out all over Europe; we shall not see them lit again in our lifetime', the majority of British people adhered to the popular belief that the European war would be over by Christmas. This belief goes some way to explain why the military encounter which consumed the next four years was so difficult for Britain; it proved to be a war of stalemate which established military thinking was powerless to break.

Reactions to the new reality of war were slow; neither British military nor political leaders were equipped for a major challenge to their accepted ideas. The prime minister, Asquith, was at first unwilling to treat the war as 'total', and then unable to implement the necessary control measures. The creation of Lloyd George's coalition in 1916 saw the first real political incursion into civilian life, ending the 'business as usual' attitude which had hampered the war effort until then.

The length of the conflict meant that resources were paramount, especially as Britain had traditionally been an importer of raw materials. Great efforts were made from 1916 to co-ordinate the country's requirements with industry's capabilities, and the rapid technical development which accompanied the war was effectively harnessed. The success of British agriculture is best shown in the delay of rationing until 1918, despite the threat of starvation caused by the German U-boat campaign of 1917.

Britain's most valuable resource in a war of attrition was its population. Kitchener's volunteer army had raised half a million by September 1914, but it was necessary to introduce conscription in 1916 for all males aged between 18 and 41. The labour market was filled by the allocation of women to the agricultural and industrial sectors, and their achievements gave weight to the call for emancipation, finally met in 1918.

World War I is remembered for its horrific casualties. It is estimated that of those who served 40% were either killed or suffered serious injuries. Both the reality and the image of these casualties haunted British society for decades afterwards.

The interwar years

'What is our task? To make Britain a fit country for heroes to live in.' Lloyd George's slogan of 1918 reflected an admirable sentiment, but it proved unobtainable in the postwar world. By 1917, the war was costing Britain £7 million per day, the money coming largely from American loans. By 1918, the country was economically exhausted, and the impact of the war upon the international economy meant that Britain's usual revenue from exports was severely curtailed. The worldwide interwar depression further diminished Britain's economic standing, leaving the country facing the threat of Hitler in 1939 with limited resources, but at least with the experience of total war gleaned from the earlier conflict.

The Finest Hour

During the 1930s, despite the policy of appeasement, Britain had been preparing for war; this is clearly demonstrated by the issue of gas masks as early as 1937. In May 1940, a coalition government was formed, with a War Cabinet of five. Led by Winston Churchill, this administration proved to be the most competent since the turn of the century. Conscription was introduced as soon as war broke out. In 1940 the Emergency Powers Act was enacted, effectively giving the government unlimited powers.

Although military casualties in World War II were about one-third of those suffered in World War I, the home population also faced direct attack. Fear of invasion and the horrors of the Blitz greatly increased civilian hardship caused by strict rationing, but tight government control of information ensured that no social breakdown occurred. Churchill's carefully contrived morale-boosting broadcasts also helped to maintain a spirit of national unity which transcended social divisions. As in World War I, effective management of resources was essential, and in Ernest Bevin Britain had an ideal minister of labour, directing workers nationally. Despite significant wage increases, inflation was prevented by strict controls.

The financial consequence of a lengthy war was nevertheless a bankrupt Britain, and the war had highlighted huge social problems. Beveridge, working from the premise that 'warfare necessitates welfare', produced a report in 1942 which formed the blueprint for the Welfare State. Central to this plan was the creation of a system of universal secondary education, achieved by the 1944 Education Act, but many other welfare provisions were also floated. Thus on VE Day the British people really believed that they were entering a period of prosperity.

BY PETER MARTLAND

On the Eastern Front the major Allied offensive was the Gallipoli campaign in 1915 which attempted to break through the Dardanelles and open up a route to assist Russia in its fight against the Turks. The failure of the campaign, and the great loss of mainly Australian and New Zealand troops, led to Winston Churchill's resignation as First Lord of the Admiralty. The Turks were also under attack in Mesopotamia, with Baghdad finally falling in 1917, and in Palestine where General ◊Allenby, assisted by the Arab Revolt, won a series of victories that resulted in the Turkish armistice in October 1918.

The war at sea involved, almost exclusively, the British and German navies, but the major sea battle at Jutland in 1916 was indecisive. The main impact at sea was by German U-boats (submarines) which, from January 1917, attempted to destroy Britain's merchant fleet and succeeded in bringing the country close to starvation. They were countered by the introduction, by British prime minister Lloyd George, of the convoy system, in which groups of vessels were protected by warships. As a result of the submarine threat the USA entered the war in April 1917.

Fifty years were spent in the process of making Europe explosive. Five days were enough to detonate it.

Basil Liddell Hart British military strategist. *The Real War, 1914–1918*

In the spring of 1918 Germany launched a major offensive on the Western Front, which was halted at the second Battle of the Marne in August 1918, while in Italy the Austro-Hungarian army was defeated at Vittorio-Veneto. German capitulation began with naval mutinies at Kiel in October 1918, followed by uprisings in the major cities. Kaiser Wilhelm II abdicated, and on 11 November the armistice was signed. The peace conference at Versailles began in January 1919, and the treaty was signed by Germany in June 1919.

The terms of peace were negotiated separately with each of the Central Powers in the course of the next few years:

Treaty of Versailles between the Allies and Germany, signed on 29 June 1919, and ratified in Paris on 19 January 1920;

Treaty of St Germain between the Allies and Austria, signed on 10 September 1919, and ratified in Paris on 16 July 1920;

Treaty of Trianon between the Allies and Hungary, signed on 4 June 1920;

Treaty of Sèvres between the Allies and Turkey, signed on 10 August 1920, not ratified and superseded by the Treaty of Lausanne;

Treaty of Lausanne between the Allies and Turkey, signed on 24 July 1923, and ratified in the same year.

World War II, 1939–45

War between Germany, Italy, and Japan (the Axis powers) on one side, and Britain, the Commonwealth, France, the USA, the USSR, and China (the Allied powers) on the other. The main theatres of war were Europe, the USSR, North Africa, and the Pacific and Atlantic seaboards. An estimated 55 million lives were lost, including 20 million citizens of the USSR and 6 million Jews killed in the holocaust. Germany surrendered in May 1945, but Japan fought on until the USA dropped atomic bombs on Hiroshima and Nagasaki in August.

The war's origins lay in Germany's reluctance to accept the frontiers laid down at the peace of Versailles in 1920, and in the highly aggressive foreign policy of Adolf Hitler (German Chancellor from 1933). Britain and France declared war on Germany on 3 September 1939, two days after German forces had invaded Poland. In the following months (the 'phoney' war) little fighting took place, until April 1940 when the Germans invaded Denmark and Norway. The failure of the Allied resistance led to the replacement of British prime minister Neville Chamberlain by Winston Churchill. By the end of May, Germany had invaded Holland, Belgium, and France, and 337,131 Allied troops had to be evacuated from the beaches of Dunkirk to England. Following the aerial bombardment of British cities, known as the ◊Blitz, German air attacks on British air bases were successfully resisted by the RAF in the Battle of ◊Britain, and the planned invasion of Britain was abandoned.

The Germans then moved east, invading Yugoslavia and Greece in April 1941, and launching an attack on the Russian front in June; by the end of the year they had come within 40 km/25 mi of Moscow and had begun to besiege Leningrad (now St Petersburg). After their initial success in the USSR, the Germans were gradually repulsed; Leningrad lost about a third of its population while resisting the German siege for nearly two years. The Germans were finally expelled from the USSR in August 1944.

The USA entered the war in December 1941 following the Japanese bombing of the US naval base at Pearl Harbour, Hawaii. The Japanese then took control of southeast Asia and Burma, capturing some 90,000 British and Commonwealth prisoners. They were only checked in June 1942 with a series of US naval victories culminating in the defeat of the Japanese

world war ii *During World War II parachute troops often proved vitally important. These parachutists, landing in the Netherlands in September 1944, were some of the 20,000 airborne troops who were landed as part of the Allied invasion of Europe. Library of Congress*

BREAKING WITH THE PAST: BRITAIN FROM ATTLEE TO THATCHER

Britain emerged victorious from World War II, with its Empire intact. 'Now Win the Peace', said the election posters. The new Labour government promised planned economic growth, Keynesian remedies for unemployment, modernization of industry by nationalization, and welfare 'From the Cradle to the Grave'. It was little short of a social revolution, but high hopes were soon tempered by reality.

The end of Empire

Internationally, the 'Big Three' were at best the 'Two-and-a-half'. The USA and USSR had contributed most to victory. When their rivalry turned into Cold War, Britain could not hope to compete in the arms race for long. At home, the staple British export industries (coal, steel, textiles, and ship-building) were in long-term decline. Markets lost during the war would never be fully recovered, and economic problems seemed endemic. These issues were linked: how could a nation with chronic balance of payments difficulties afford to remain a global power?

Despite austerity policies, by 1949 Britain had been forced to devalue the pound and reduce its overseas commitments by withdrawing from India and Palestine. Departure from these trouble-spots did not mean wholesale retreat. The government hoped to transform the British Empire into a freely co-operating Commonwealth of Nations with real political and economic significance. The aim was to satisfy colonial nationalism, while preserving a network of military bases and a trading bloc making international payments in sterling.

The weakness of this strategy was revealed by the Suez Crisis. When Britain attempted to exercise neo-imperial dominance in the Middle East by force, it failed and unleashed a wave of anti-British feeling. Harold Macmillan accelerated decolonization and accepted that the Commonwealth was going to be a very loose association. By 1964 most of the Empire had become independent. The 'special relationship' with the USA suffered as a result: Britain minus the colonies was simply not so valuable an ally. Fearing isolation, Britain turned to the European Community, only to find its application for membership vetoed by France. 'Great Britain has lost an Empire and has not yet found a role', observed Dean Acheson in 1962.

'East of Suez'

Britain meanwhile shared in the remarkable post-war economic recovery of the western world. 'Most of our people have never had it so good', said Macmillan in 1957. Both Conservatives and Labour were broadly committed to maintaining the mixed economy, the welfare state, and full employment. While living standards rose, governments shrank from tackling the underlying problems of an uncompetitive economy with high wage demands and low investment. The Treasury merely operated short-term 'stop-go' policies as each spurt of growth ended in balance of payments deficits. These necessitated a second devaluation in 1967 and drastic cuts in overseas defence spending. All significant commitments 'East of Suez' were to be abandoned by 1971. Thus Britain broke through the status barrier: it was a world power no longer. Late-1960s society may have been affluent and permissive, but the nation seemed in decline – the word itself was becoming a cliché.

Edward Heath swung foreign policy decisively toward Europe. Britain entered the EC in 1973 but found it difficult to adjust to its institutions and policies. EC membership did not bring the dramatic material benefits expected. Nor did the discovery of North Sea oil. Rising unemployment, record levels of inflation, an energy crisis, widespread industrial disputes, and violence in Northern Ireland all deepened the mood of demoralization.

The Thatcher years

The post-war consensus crumbled as politicians in both parties tried to find new policies. This plunged Labour into a decade of internal strife and permanent opposition from 1979. The Conservatives, led by Margaret Thatcher, adopted a radical 'monetarist' programme intended to revitalize the economy through rapid deflation, deregulation, privatization, and the reduction of trade union power. But this economic shock treatment coincided with a global recession. British unemployment topped 3 million, amid signs of a growing divide between the depressed north and relatively prosperous south. Productivity improved and enterprise was encouraged in an economy increasingly based on services, but the 'economic miracle' of the mid-1980s proved short-lived, and unemployment remained high.

Thatcher sought to re-assert British influence in international affairs, but the prestige derived from the Falklands War and a revival of the 'special relationship' was not sustainable. When the end of the Cold War prompted further European integration British doubts about the EC resurfaced in the politics of the 1990s.

Britain has been transformed since 1945. The British Empire, built up over four centuries, came to an end in the 1960s. Traditional industries, chief sources of national wealth since the Industrial Revolution, withered away and all but died in the 1980s. The nation faced these historic changes with some reluctance, but the era of empire and industry is now over. A new era has begun.

by Jason Tomes

fleet at Leyte Gulf in October 1944. The major turning point for the Allies occurred in North Africa, where German successes under Rommel were reversed when the British Eighth Army under ◊Montgomery won the decisive Battle of El ◊Alamein in October–November 1942; by May 1943 the German army in Africa had surrendered. This left the Allies free to invade Sicily and, after the fall of the Italian dictator Mussolini in July 1943, mainland Italy. Rome fell in June 1944, and the Germans in Italy finally surrendered after the fall of Trieste in May 1945. The Allies launched the successful

D-Day invasion of Normandy on 6 June 1945 under the command of Eisenhower; Paris was liberated by August and, in spite of the setback at Arnhem, the Allies pressed forward across the pre-war German frontier to link up in April 1945 with the Soviet army on the Elbe. The Germans surrendered at Rheims on 7 May. The Japanese continued to fight, despite the loss of Burma and the Philippines in 1945, and only surrendered after US atonm bombs were dropped on the cities of Hiroshima and Nagasaki.

The British people have taken for themselves this motto – 'Business carried on as usual during alterations on the map of Europe'.

WINSTON CHURCHILL British Conservative prime minister.
Speech at the Guildhall 9 November 1914

Worthing

Seaside resort in West Sussex, southeast England, 23 km/14 mi west of Brighton, at the foot of the South Downs; population (1991) 94,000. Industries include financial and business services, electronics, engineering, the manufacture of plastics and furniture, horticulture, retail, tourism, and leisure. There are traces of prehistoric and Roman occupation in the vicinity. The headquarters of the English Bowling Association is at Worthing.

Worthing developed from a small fishing hamlet into a popular resort in the late 18th century. Regency terraces and crescents were built, including Park Crescent. Features include the Connaught Theatre, and a museum which contains Roman relics discovered in the area. Worthing includes the former separate villages of Broadwater, Durrington, and West Tarring.

Wren, Christopher (1632–1723)

English architect. His ingenious use of a refined and sober Baroque style can be seen in his best-known work, St Paul's Cathedral, London (1675–1711), and in the many churches he built in London including St Mary-le-Bow, Cheapside (1670–77), and St Bride's, Fleet Street (1671–78). His other works include the Sheldonian Theatre, Oxford (1664–69), Greenwich Hospital, London (begun 1694), and Marlborough House, London (1709–10; now much altered).

After studying science and mathematics at Oxford, he became Professor of Astronomy at Gresham College, London, in 1657 and Savilian Professor of Astronomy, Oxford, in 1661.

He turned to architecture in about 1662, when he designed the chapel of Pembroke College, Cambridge. After the Great Fire of London in 1666, he prepared a plan for rebuilding the city on Classical lines, incorporating piazzas and broad avenues, but it was not adopted. Instead, he was commissioned to rebuild St Paul's and 51 City churches. He showed great skill both in fitting his buildings into the irregular sites of the destroyed churches, and in varying the designs, giving them a series of towers which characterized the London skyline until World War II.

In 1669 Wren became surveyor-general of the King's Works, his commissions including building and renovations at Hampton Court, Kensington, St James's, Westminster, Whitehall, Winchester, Windsor Castle, and Chelsea Hospital (1682–85).

Wrexham

Unitary authority in northeast Wales, created in 1996 from part of the former county of Clywd

Area 500 sq km/193 sq mi

Towns ◊Wrexham (administrative headquarters), Holt, Ruabon

Physical western side is mountainous, including Ruabon Mountain; River Dee

Features Clywedog Valley, with notable countryside and industrial archaeology

Industries food manufacture, plastics, pharmaceuticals, high-technology industries

Population (1996) 123,500.

Wrexham, Welsh Wrecsam

Administrative centre of ◊Wrexham unitary authority, northeast Wales, situated on the Clywedog River 19 km/12 mi southwest of Chester; population (1991) 40,600. Industries include coal, electronics, pharmaceuticals, chemicals, cables, and metal goods. It is the seat of the Roman Catholic bishopric of Menevia (Wales). Elihu Yale, founder of Yale University, USA, died in Wrexham and is buried in the 15th-century church of St Giles.

St Giles, which was rebuilt about 1470, has a 41-m/136-ft pinnacled tower. Much of the town's industry is situated on the large industrial estate at Marchwiel to the east, but Wrexham is also a market town and the centre of an agricultural district.

Wright, Almroth Edward (1861–1947)

English bacteriologist who developed a vaccine against typhoid fever. He established a new discipline within medicine, that of therapeutic immunization by vaccination, which was aimed at treating microbial diseases rather than preventing them. Knighted 1906.

Wright, Billy (William Ambrose) (1924–1994)

English footballer. A versatile player, equally strong in midfield or central defence, he won 105 caps for England 1946–59 including a record 90 as captain. He made 490 appearances for Wolverhampton Wanderers 1946–59, and led the club to the FA Cup in 1949 and the league championship in 1954, 1958, and 1959.

Wright, Joseph (1734–1797)

English painter. He was known as **Wright of Derby**, from his birthplace. He painted portraits, landscapes, and groups performing scientific experiments. His work is often dramatically lit – by fire, candlelight, or even volcanic explosion.

Several of his subjects are highly original, for example *The Experiment on a Bird in the Air Pump* (1768; National Gallery,

London). His portraits include the reclining figure of *Sir Brooke Boothby* (1781; Tate Gallery, London).

Wright, Thomas (1711–1786)

English astronomer and teacher. He was the first to propose that the Milky Way is a layer of stars, including the Sun, in his *An Original Theory or New Hypothesis of the Universe* (1750).

Wright was born near Durham and apprenticed to a clockmaker. He taught mathematics and lectured on popular scientific subjects.

In his book, Wright described the Milky Way as a flattened disc, in which the Sun does not occupy a central position. Furthermore, he stated that nebulae lie outside the Milky Way. These views were more than 150 years ahead of their time. However, he believed that the centre of the system was occupied by a divine presence.

Wright's other work included thoughts on the particulate nature of the rings of Saturn, and reflections on such diverse fields as architecture and reincarnation.

Wright, Peter (1916–1995)

English intelligence agent. His book *Spycatcher* (1987), written after his retirement, caused an international stir when the British government tried unsuccessfully to block its publication anywhere in the world because of its damaging revelations about the secret service.

Wright joined MI5 in 1955 and was a consultant to the director-general 1973–76, when he retired. In *Spycatcher* he claimed, among other things, that Roger Hollis, head of MI5 (1955–65), had been a Soviet double agent; this was later denied by the KGB.

wrought iron

Fairly pure iron containing some beads of slag, widely used for construction work before the days of cheap steel. It is strong, tough, and easy to machine. It is made in a puddling furnace, invented by Henry Colt in England in 1784. Pig iron is remelted and heated strongly in air with iron ore, burning out the carbon in the metal, leaving relatively pure iron and a slag containing impurities. The resulting pasty metal is then hammered to remove as much of the remaining slag as possible. It is still used in fences and gratings.

Wuthering Heights

Novel (1847) by Emily ◊Brontë. The orphan Heathcliff is loved by Catherine, the daughter of his adopted father, Mr Earnshaw of Wuthering Heights. Ill-treated after Earnshaw's death, Heathcliff's extremes of love and hate are played out in the relationship between himself, the Earnshaws, and the Lintons of Thrushcross Grange and their stories. There is an ultimate reconciliation of conflicts when the daughter of the dead Catherine marries the son of Heathcliff and Isabella Linton. The novel's high reputation is based on its outstanding originality and power. It was Emily Brontë's only novel.

Wyatt, Thomas (*c.* 1503–1542)

English poet. He was employed on diplomatic missions by Henry VIII, and in 1536 was imprisoned for a time in the Tower of London, suspected of having been the lover of Henry's second wife, Anne Boleyn. In 1541 Wyatt was again imprisoned on charges of treason. With the Earl of Surrey, he introduced the sonnet to England. Knighted 1537.

Wycherley, William (1640–*c.* 1716)

English Restoration dramatist. His first comedy, *Love in a Wood*, won him court favour in 1671, and later bawdy works include *The Country Wife* (1675) and *The Plain Dealer* (1676).

Wycliffe, John (*c.* 1320–1384)

English religious reformer. Allying himself with the party of John of Gaunt, which was opposed to ecclesiastical influence at court, he attacked abuses in the church, maintaining that the Bible rather than the church was the supreme authority. He criticized such fundamental doctrines as priestly absolution, confession, and indulgences, and set disciples to work on the first translation of the Bible into English. He wrote many popular tracts in English (rather than Latin). His followers were known as Lollards.

Wycombe, West

Village in Buckinghamshire, now forming part of the borough of High Wycombe. Most of the village, which contains many 17th- and 18th-century buildings, belongs to the National Trust. The latter also owns West Wycombe Park, 3 km/2 mi west of High Wycombe.

On the hill is a curious church, built in 1763, surmounted by a golden ball capable of holding 12 people, which has associations with the English courtier Francis Dashwood (1708–1781), as do the caves in the hillside.

Wye, Welsh Gwy

River in Wales and England; length 208 km/130 mi. It rises on ◊Plynlimon in northeast Ceredigion, flows southeast and east through Powys and Hereford and Worcester, and follows the Gwent–Gloucestershire border before joining the River ◊Severn 4 km/2.5 mi south of Chepstow. It has salmon fisheries and is noted for its scenery.

Other rivers of the same name in the UK are found in Buckinghamshire (15 km/9 mi) and Derbyshire (32 km/20 mi).

Wyndham, John pen name of John Wyndham Parkes Lucas Beynon Harris (1903–1969)

English science-fiction writer. He wrote *The Day of the Triffids* (1951), describing the invasion of Earth by a strange plant mutation; *The Chrysalids* (1955); and *The Midwich Cuckoos* (1957). A recurrent theme in his work is people's response to disaster, whether caused by nature, aliens, or human error.

Yarmouth

Small seaport on the northwest coast of the ◊Isle of Wight, England, 16 km/10 mi west of Newport at the mouth of the River Yar; population (1991) 820. Yarmouth is a yachting centre; there is a car-ferry service from here across the Solent to Lymington.

Yell

Second largest of the Shetland Islands, Scotland, 3 km/2 mi north of Mainland; population (1991) 1,100. It extends over an area of 208 sq km/80 sq mi, including the island of Hascosay. Peat moorland, cut locally for fuel, covers most of the interior. Crofting (a form of subsistence farming) is confined to the more fertile coastal plains. Trout and sea fishing also form a valuable part of the island's economy. Its main settlement is the harbour town of Burravoe.

yeoman

In England, a small landowner who farmed his own fields – a system that formed a bridge between the break-up of feudalism and the agricultural revolution of the 18th–19th centuries.

Yeomen of the Guard

English military corps, popularly known as **Beefeaters**, the sovereign's bodyguard since the corps was founded by Henry VII in 1485. Its duties are now purely ceremonial.

There are Yeomen warders at the Tower of London, and the uniform and weapons are much as they were in Tudor times. The nickname 'Beefeaters' is supposed to have originated in 1669 when the Grand Duke of Tuscany ascribed their fine appearance to beef.

Yeovil

Market town in Somerset, southwest England, on the River Yeo; population (1991) 27,200. Gloves and leather goods are produced, the headquarters of Westland Aircraft is here, and other industries include engineering, electronics, the manufacture of hovercraft, and food processing.

The church of St John the Baptist is a 14th-century example of the Perpendicular Gothic style.

Yes

English progressive rock band formed in 1968. Members are Jon Anderson (1944–) (vocals), Steve Howe (1947–) (guitar), Chris Squire (1948–) (bass), Alan White (1949–) (drums), and Rick Wakeman (1949–) (keyboards). Their albums include *The Yes Album* (1971), *Close To The Edge* (1972), and *Going For The One* (1977).

YMCA, Young Men's Christian Association

International organization founded in 1844 by George Williams (1821–1905) in London. It aims at self-improvement – spiritual, intellectual, and physical. YMCAs provide dormitories and rooms for both transients and residents; educational, sports, and civic programmes; and recreation facilities for members and for military troops in wartime.

From 1971 women were accepted as members.

York

Cathedral and industrial city and administrative headquarters of ◊York unitary authority in northern England, on the River Ouse; population (1991) 127,700. It was the administrative headquarters of the county of North Yorkshire until 1996. Industries include tourism and the manufacture of scientific instruments, sugar, chocolate, and glass. Founded in AD 71 as the Roman provincial capital **Eboracum**, York retains many of its medieval streets and buildings and much of its 14th-century city wall; the Gothic York Minster, England's largest medieval cathedral, includes fine 15th-century stained glass. The city is visited by some 3 million tourists a year.

Features

The south transept of the York Minster has been restored following severe damage caused by a fire in 1984. Four gates or 'bars' of the city wall survive, as well as the medieval streets including the Shambles. The Jorvik Viking Centre (opened in 1984) contains wooden remains of Viking houses. Other features include the Theatre Royal, site of a theatre since 1765; the Castle Museum; the National Railway Museum; and York University (1963).

History

Recent excavations of the Roman city have revealed the fortress, baths, and temples to Serapis and Mithras. The Roman missionary Paulinus became the first archbishop of

YORK MINSTER *The historic city of York is dominated by York Minster, seen here from the River Ouse. The vast cathedral is particularly noted for its stained glass. When fire, caused by a lightning strike, swept the south transept of the building in 1984, the famous Rose Window there was severely damaged, but has since been restored. Roger Scruton/Collections*

York in 633. In 867 it became the Viking settlement of **Jorvik**. During the Middle Ages it was important in the wool trade. An active Quaker element in the 18th and 19th centuries included the Rowntree family, which founded a chocolate factory. In the 19th century it developed as a railway centre. Britain's last train-building factory closed in 1995.

York Minster

It is thought that a wooden chapel was erected on the site of the present Minster in 627 for the baptism of King Edwin of Northumbria. A Norman structure was begun in about 1080, but the oldest surviving part of the present building dates from about 1220, and the central tower was completed in about 1480. Among English churches York Minster is preeminent in the amount, range, and quality of its surviving glass from around 1150 to the present century. The chief glory of the whole collection is the Great East Window (1405–08), the work of John Thornton of Coventry; it is 24 m/80 ft by 10 m/32 ft, and each of the 117 main panels measure almost 1 m/3 ft square. Its various panels represent scenes from the Old Testament and the Apocalypse. It is thought to be the largest medieval stained-glass window in the world.

The Minster Library contains a varied and ancient collection of manuscripts, archives, and 30,000 printed books. The south transept was severely damaged by fire in 1984, but has been restored.

The octagonal Chapter House, dating from 1260 to 1300, has no central supporting column. The choir screen, dating from the late 15th century, depicts kings of England from William I to Henry VI.

Churches

All Saints' Church (North Street) has 14th- and 15th-century glass and a graceful spire; All Saints' (in Pavement) is the only church in York to have a lantern tower. The last to be built before the Reformation, St Michael-le-Belfry (1535), has in its register an entry recording the baptism in 1570 of Guy Fawkes, the conspirator in the Gunpowder Plot. St Olave's Church was established in the 11th century and contains 15th-century stained glass.

Schools

St Peter's School is one of the oldest private schools in England, and has claims to link it with the school of St Peter founded in 627. There are two Society of Friends' (Quaker) schools; the Mount School for girls (1785) and Bootham School (1823), formerly a boys' school but now co-educational.

Architectural features

The medieval Guildhall, built in 1448, was destroyed by

bombing in 1942, but was restored to its former state in 1960. Three other guildhalls remain: the Merchant Adventurers Hall, built by York's most powerful guild which in the 15th–17th centuries controlled the export of cloth from the north of England; the Merchant Tailors' Hall which has a 17th–18th-century exterior and a 14th-century roof; and the 15th-century St Anthony's Hall.

The city walls, built on earlier foundations, extend for 4.4 km/2.7 mi, and date mainly from the 14th century, although the gates include Norman work. The four main gateways or 'bars' are Walmgate Bar, Bootham Bar, Monk Bar, and Mickelgate Bar. Walmgate retains its barbican, whilst Bootham and Monk each has its portcullis. Micklegate was the chief of the four gates and on it was impaled the head of Richard of York in 1460.

The basement of the Yorkshire Museum incorporates the chapter house and fireplace of the Benedictine St Mary's Abbey (founded about 1080). In the gardens of the museum are more remains of the Abbey, including the ruins of the church (1259) and gatehouse. Clifford's Tower (1245–1262) is all that remains of York Castle. It was built to replace the wooden tower built by William the Conqueror which was destroyed in 1190 when, during anti-Jewish riots in the city, 150 members of the Jewish population were put there and took their own lives by setting fire to the tower rather than fall into the hands of the mob. The network of narrow medieval streets in the centre of York includes Stonegate, and the Shambles, the street of the butchers. The Shambles includes the house of Margaret Clitherow who was martyred in 1586 after being accused of providing a refuge for Jesuit priests; the house has been restored by Catholics of York as a shrine.

Museums and galleries

The Yorkshire Museum contains fine archaeological, natural history, and geological collections. There is a richly stocked Roman gallery as well as Anglo-Saxon and Viking relics. The City Art Gallery contains a large collection of European paintings, including the Lycett Green collection of old masters, which provides a continuous series of examples of the development of European art. The Castle Museum, occupying two former prison buildings built in the 18th century, is a folk museum which includes reconstructed 19th-century streets. The Jorvik Viking Centre, opened after excavations at Coppergate (1976–81), depicts life in York in the time of the Vikings and displays the archaeological remains discovered during the excavations. The National Railway Museum contains a large collection of locomotives, dating from 1829, as well as royal carriages and a replica of a section of the Channel Tunnel.

Roman period to the Middle Ages

The Roman **Eboracum** was an important administrative centre, and the base for the northern campaigns of Hadrian. The emperor Septimus Severus died in the city, and following the death here of the emperor Constantine Chlorus in 306, the troops proclaimed his son Constantine the Great emperor of the Western Roman Empire. The Romans withdrew in 407. Under the Saxons York was known as **Eoforwic** and it became a Christian stronghold. The Roman missionary Paulinus baptized King Edwin of Northumbria here in 627. In the 8th century York was renowned as a seat of learning; Alcuin, the headmaster of its school of St Peter, was called by Charlemagne (Roman emperor from 800) to found a school at Aquisgranum (now Aachen, Germany), and a system of education for the Holy Roman Empire. The Danes captured the city in 867, and it became the Viking trading centre of **Jorvik**. At the Battle of Stamford Bridge (1066), 14 km/9mi northeast of York, Harold II defeated the army of King Harold of Norway.

At the time of the Norman Conquest the population was estimated to be 8,000, second in size only to that of London. An important commercial city in medieval times, it became a centre of the wool trade, and the small ships of its merchant adventurers sailed from the wharves of York to those of the Hanseatic towns (confederation of north European trading centres from the 12th to the 17th centuries). As the size of ships increased the city's European trade declined, and York lost its commercial importance, whilst retaining its ecclesiastical and much of its political importance. Parliaments were held here, and Edward I, Edward II, and Edward III made York their base for wars against the Scots. In the 15th century Richard, Duke of York (1411–60), founded the dynasty of ◊York which ruled England from 1461 to 1485.

16th–19th centuries

At the height of the ◊Pilgrimage of Grace, the rebellion against Henry VIII in 1536–37, the city was controlled by rebels. Following their suppression, Robert Aske, leader of the rebellion, was executed in the city in 1537. In the same year Henry VIII established in York the headquarters of the Council of the North, to oversee the introduction of Protestantism in the north. The city was a Royalist stronghold during the Civil War; in 1644 it was besieged by Parliamentary forces and surrendered after the Battle of Marston Moor. In the 18th century York became a fashionable resort, and in the 19th century its prosperity was again established when it became a railway centre.

Famous people

York was the birthplace of the conspirator Guy Fawkes, the poet W H Auden, the painter William Etty, and the sculptor John Flaxman. Dick Turpin, the highwayman, was hanged here in 1739.

York

Unitary authority in northeast England created in 1996 from part of the county of North Yorkshire

Area 271 sq km/105 sq mi

Towns ◊York (administrative headquarters)

Features River Ouse; River Fosse; York Minster –largest medieval cathedral in England, with 15th-century stained glass; York Castle and Museum; National Railway Museum; city walls built by Henry III in 13th century with 4 gates and 39 towers; Jorvik Viking Centre; the Shambles medieval streets

Industries agriculture and agricultural services, mechanical engineering, circuit boards, tourism, scientific instruments, confectionery, glass

Population (1996) 174,800.

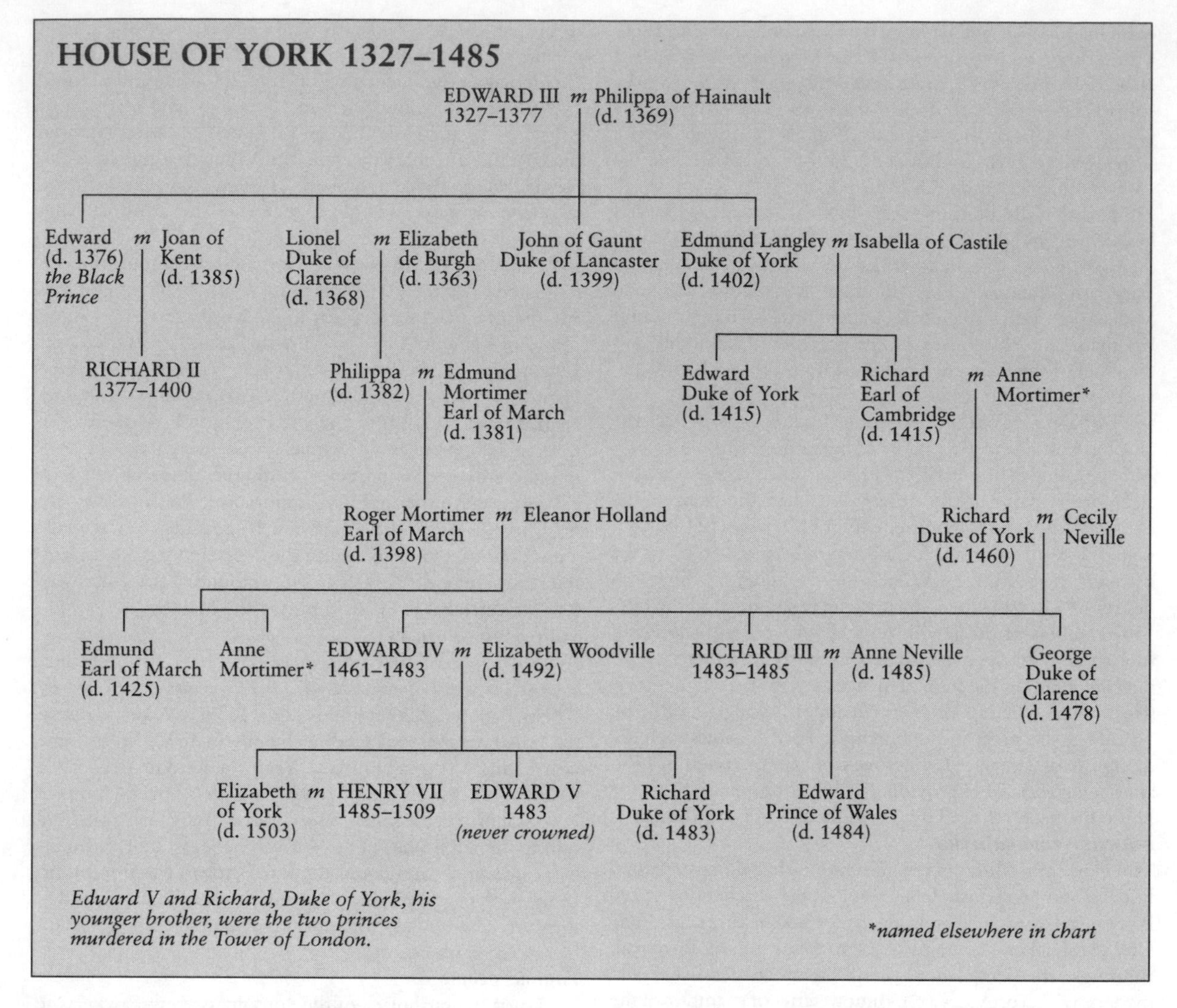

York, House of

English dynasty founded by Richard, Duke of York (1411–60). He claimed the throne through his descent from Lionel, Duke of Clarence (1338–1368), third son of Edward III, whereas the reigning monarch, Henry VI of the rival house of Lancaster, was descended from the fourth son, John of Gaunt. The argument was fought out in the Wars of the ◊Roses. York was killed at the Battle of Wakefield in 1460, but the following year his son became King Edward IV. Edward was succeeded by his son Edward V and then by his brother Richard III, with whose death at Bosworth the line ended. The Lancastrian victor in that battle was crowned Henry VII, and consolidated his claim by marrying Edward IV's eldest daughter, Elizabeth, thus founding the House of Tudor.

See genealogy above.

York, Duchess of

Title borne by the wife of the Duke of York. Sarah Ferguson (1959–) became Duchess of York when she married Prince ◊Andrew in 1986. They have two daughters, Princess Beatrice (1988–) and Princess Eugenie (1990–). The Yorks divorced in 1996. Sarah, Duchess of York has written children's books and appeared as a TV chat-show host in the US.

York, Duke of

Title often borne by younger sons of British sovereigns, for example George V, George VI, and Prince ◊Andrew from 1986.

York, Frederick Augustus, Duke of York (1763–1827)

Second son of George III. He was an unsuccessful commander in the Netherlands 1793–99 and British commander in chief 1798–1809.

The nursery rhyme about the 'grand old duke of York' who marched his troops up the hill and down again commemorates him, as does the Duke of York's column in Waterloo Place, London.

York, archbishop of

Metropolitan (archbishop with authority over bishops) of the northern province of the Anglican Church in England, hence primate of England.

The first archbishop of York was Egbert (732–66). The first Norman archbishop was Thomas of Bayeux (1070–1100). Pope Innocent VI (1352–62) decided that the archbishop of Canterbury should have precedence over the archbishop of York, with the title 'Primate of All England' as distinct from 'Primate of England' for York.

Recent noted archbishops of York have included Cosmo Gordon Lang (1908–28), William Temple (1929–42), and Arthur Michael Ramsey (1956–61), all of whom went on to become archbishop of Canterbury. The current archbishop of York is David M Hope (appointed in 1995).

Yorkshire

Former county in northeast England on the North Sea divided administratively into North, East, and West Ridings (thirds), but reorganized to form a number of new counties in 1974: the major part of **Cleveland** and **Humberside**, **North Yorkshire**, **South Yorkshire**, and **West Yorkshire**. Small outlying areas also went to Durham, Cumbria, Lancashire, and Greater Manchester. In 1996 Cleveland and Humberside were abolished, and a number of unitary authorities were created to replace them.

Young, Arthur (1741–1820)

English writer and publicizer of the new farm practices associated with the ◊agricultural revolution. When the Board of Agriculture was established in 1792, Young was appointed secretary, and was the guiding force behind the production of a county-by-county survey of British agriculture.

His early works, such as *Farmer's Tour through the East of England* and *A Six Months' Tour through the North of England*, contained extensive comment and observations gathered during the course of a series of journeys around the country. He published the *Farmers' Calendar* (1771), and in 1784 began the *Annals of Agriculture*, which ran for 45 volumes, and contained contributions from many eminent farmers of the day.

Young, David Ivor, Baron Young of Graffham (1932–)

British Conservative politician, chair of the Manpower Services Commission (MSC) 1982–84, secretary for employment from 1985, trade and industry secretary 1987–89, when he retired from politics for a new career in business. He was subsequently criticized by a House of Commons select committee over aspects of the privatization of the Rover car company. Baron 1984.

Young, J(ohn) Z(achary) (1907–1997)

English zoologist who discovered and studied the giant nerve fibres in squids, contributing greatly to knowledge of nerve structure and function. He also did research on the central nervous system of octopuses, demonstrating that memory stores are located in the brain.

Young was born in Bristol and studied at Oxford and the zoological station in Naples, Italy. He set up a unit at Oxford to study nerve regeneration in mammals. In 1945 he became the first nonmedical scientist in Britain to hold a professorship in anatomy, at London.

Young discovered that certain nerve fibres of squids are about 100 times the diameter of mammalian neurons and are covered with a relatively thin myelin sheath (unlike mammalian nerve fibres, which have thick sheaths). These properties make them easy to experiment on and to obtain intracellular nerve material.

Turning his attention to the central nervous system, Young showed that octopuses can learn to discriminate between different orientations of the same object. When presented with horizontal and vertical rectangles, for example, the octopuses attacked one but avoided the other. He also demonstrated that octopuses can learn to recognize objects by touch. In addition, Young proposed a model to explain the processes involved in memory.

Young published the textbooks *The Life of Vertebrates* (1950) and *The Life of Mammals* (1957).

Young, Thomas (1773–1829)

British physicist, physician, and Egyptologist who revived the wave theory of light and identified the phenomenon of interference in 1801. He also established many important concepts in mechanics.

In 1793, Young recognized that focusing of the eye (accommodation) is achieved by a change of shape in the lens of the eye, the lens being composed of muscle fibres. He also showed that astigmatism is due to irregular curvature of the cornea. In 1801, he became the first to recognize that colour sensation is due to the presence in the retina of structures that respond to the three colours red, green, and violet.

Young was born in Milverton, Somerset. A child prodigy, he had learned most European and many ancient languages by the age of 20. He studied medicine in London and at Edinburgh and Göttingen, Germany. He was professor of natural philosophy at the Royal Institution 1801–03 and worked as a physician at St George's Hospital, London, from 1811.

Young assumed that light waves are propagated in a similar way to sound waves, and proposed that different colours consist of different frequencies. He obtained experimental proof for the principle of interference by passing light through extremely narrow openings and observing the interference patterns produced.

In mechanics, Young was the first to use the terms 'energy' for the product of the mass of a body with the square of its velocity and 'labour expended' for the product of the force exerted on a body 'with the distance through which it moved'. He also stated that these two products are proportional to each other. He introduced an absolute measurement in elasticity, now known as **Young's modulus**.

From 1815 onwards, Young published papers on Egyptology; his account of the Rosetta stone played a crucial role in the stone's eventual decipherment.

Young Farmers' Clubs

Organization that seeks to promote among young people a

practical interest in agriculture and the countryside. It is open to anyone between the ages of 10 and 26.

England, Wales, Scotland, and Northern Ireland all have YFC Federations under the general guidance of a National Federation, and there are hundreds of active local branches. Originally the YFC had a strong farming bias, but more recently the emphasis has broadened to include country crafts, conservation, and a general concern with rural life.

Young Pretender

Nickname of ◊Charles Edward Stuart, claimant to the Scottish and English thrones.

Youth Hostels Association, YHA

Registered charity founded in Britain in 1930 to promote knowledge and care of the countryside by providing cheap overnight accommodation for young people on active holidays (such as walking or cycling). Types of accommodation range from castles to log cabins.

YHA membership is open to individuals of 14 or over (or 5 if accompanied by an adult). There are 260 hostels in England and Wales. In addition to basic accommodation, YHA provides sporting activities including climbing, windsurfing, hang-gliding, and horse riding.

Ypres, Battles of, Flemish Ieper

In World War I, three major battles 1914–17 between German and Allied forces near Ypres, a Belgian town in western Flanders, 40 km/25 mi south of Ostend. Neither side made much progress in any of the battles, despite heavy casualties, but the third battle in particular (also known as Passchendaele) July–November 1917 stands out as an enormous waste of life for little return. The Menin Gate (1927) is a memorial to British soldiers lost in these battles.

October–November 1914 A British offensive aimed at securing the Channel ports of Dunkirk and Ostend clashed with a German offensive aimed at taking those ports. The subsequent fighting was extremely heavy and ended with the Germans gaining the Messines Ridge and other commanding ground but with the British and French holding a salient around Ypres extending into the German line. German losses were estimated at 150,000 troops, British and French at about the same number.

April–May 1915 Battle opened with a German chlorine gas attack; this made a huge gap in the Allied lines but the Germans were unprepared for this success and were unable to exploit it before the Allies rushed in reserves. More gas attacks followed, and the British were driven to shorten their line, so making the Ypres salient a smaller incursion into the German line.

July–November 1917 An Allied offensive, including British, Canadian, and Australian troops, was launched under British commander in chief Field Marshal Douglas Haig, in an attempt to capture ports on the Belgian coast held by Germans. The long and bitter battle, fought in appalling conditions of driving rain and waterlogged ground, achieved an advance of only 8 km/5 mi of territory that was of no strategic significance, but the Allies alone lost more than 300,000 casualties.

YWCA, Young Women's Christian Association

Organization for the welfare of women and girls, founded in London in 1855. Its facilities and activities are similar to those of the YMCA.

Zircon

Codename for a British signals-intelligence satellite originally intended to be launched in 1988. The revelation of the existence of the Zircon project (which had been concealed by the government), and the government's subsequent efforts to suppress a programme about it on BBC television, caused much controversy in 1987. Its intended function was to intercept radio and other signals from the USSR, Europe, and the Middle East and transmit them to the Government Communications Headquarters (GCHQ) in Cheltenham, England.

Zoffany, Johann (or John) (1733–1810)

German portrait painter who worked in London from about 1761. Under the patronage of George III he painted many portraits of the royal family and the English aristocracy, and became a founder-member of the Royal Academy in 1768.

Initially a painter of theatrical scenes, he soon became successful as a painter of portraits and crowded conversation pieces, such as *The Academicians of the Royal Academy* (1772; Windsor Castle) and *The Tribuna of the Uffizi* (1780; Windsor Castle), showing the old master paintings and antiques which were used for study at the Royal Academy, and groups of connoisseurs and students.

Appendices

Some key international organizations of which the UK is a member

Bank for International Settlements
CAB International (formerly C'wealth Agricultural Bureaux)
Commonwealth, the British
Council of Europe
European Bank for Reconstruction and Development
European Free Trade Association
European Organization for Nuclear Research (CERN)
European Space Agency
European Union
Food and Agriculture Organization of the United Nations
Inmarsat (formerly International Mobile Satellite Organization)
International Atomic Energy Agency
International Civic Aviation Organization
International Confederation of Free Trade Unions
International Criminal Police Organization (Interpol)
International Energy Agency
International Fund for Agricultural Development
International Fund for Ireland
International Labour Organization
International Maritime Organization
International Monetary Fund
International Red Cross and Red Crescent Movement
International Telecommunications Satellite Organization
International Telecommunication Union
North Atlantic Treaty Organization
Organization for Economic Co-operation and Development
Organization for Security and Co-operation in Europe
South Pacific Commission
United Nations
United Nations Educational Scientific and Cultural Organization
United Nations Industrial Development Organization
Universal Postal Union
Western European Union
World Bank
World Council of Churches
World Health Organization
World Intellectual Property Organization
World Meteorological Organization
World Trade Organization

Leading Sports Clubs

COUNTY CRICKET CLUBS

Essex
Winners of 13 major trophies (all since 1979) including six County Championship titles. Founded: 1876. Headquarters: Chelmsford. Famous players include Trevor Bailey, Keith Fletcher, John Lever, and Graham Gooch.

Kent
Winners of nine limited overs trophies and seven county championships (once as joint champions). Founded: 1858 (reorganized 1870). Headquarters: St Lawrence Ground, Canterbury. Famous players include Frank Woolley, Leslie Ames, Godfrey Evans, Colin Cowdrey, and Alan Knott.

Lancashire
Eight times winners of the County Championship (once as joint champions) and a record 15 limited overs titles. Founded: 1864 Headquarters: Old Trafford, Manchester. Famous players include: Ernest Tyldesley, Brian Statham, Clive Lloyd, and Michael Atherton.

Leicestershire
Founded 1879 they waited until 1972 for their first trophy when they won the inaugural Benson & Hedges Cup final. Subsequently they have won two County Championship titles and four limited overs titles. Headquarters: Grace Road, Leicester. Famous players include Graham McKenzie, Ray Illingworth, and David Gower.

Middlesex
Winners of 12 County Championships (twice as joint champions) and seven limited overs titles. Founded: 1864. Headquarters: Lord's. Famous players include Patsy Hendren, Denis Compton, Bill Edrich, and Mike Gatting.

Nottinghamshire
Four times winners of the County Championship. Founded: 1841 (reorganized 1866) Headquarters: Trent Bridge, Nottingham. Famous players include Harold Larwood, Bill Voce, Gary Sobers, Clive Rice, and Derek Randall.

Surrey
The inaugural winners of the County Championship 1890 they have won the title 16 times in all (including one shared title). They dominated county cricket in the 1950s winning seven successive County titles, 1952–58. Founded: 1845. Headquarters: The Oval. Famous players include Jack Hobbs, Alec Bedser, Jim Laker, Ken Barrington, and Alec Stewart.

Warwickshire
Winners of 13 major titles, including five County Championships. In 1994 they became the first side to win three major trophies in one season. Founded 1882 (reorganized 1884). Headquarters: Edgbaston, Birmingham. Famous players include Bob Wyatt, Dennis Amiss, Bob Willis, Brian Lara, and Allan Donald.

Yorkshire
Winners of a record 30 County Championship titles (including one shared title), 1893–1968. Founded 1863 (reorganized 1891) Headquarters: Headingley, Leeds. Famous players include: Wilfred Rhodes, Herbert Sutcliffe, Len Hutton, Fred Trueman, and Geoff Boycott.

FOOTBALL CLUBS

Aberdeen
Nicknamed 'The Dons', they have won the Scottish league title four times and the Scottish Cup seven times. Founded: 1903. Ground: Pittodrie (current capacity 21,634). Famous players include Joe Harper, Gordon Strachan, Willie Miller, and Alex McLeish.

Arsenal
North London team, nicknamed 'The Gunners', who have won 22 major trophies including the league championship 11 times and the FA Cup seven times. Achieved the cup and league 'double' in 1970–71 and 1997–98. Founded: 1886 (1891–1914 known as Woolwich Arsenal). Ground: Highbury (current capacity 38,500) Famous players include Alex James, George Eastham, Liam Brady, and Dennis Bergkamp.

Aston Villa
Birmingham club nicknamed 'The Villans'. Seven times winners of the league championship and FA Cup, and the 1982 European Cup winners. Ground: Villa Park (current capacity 39,372). Famous players include George Ramsey, 'Pongo' Waring, Charlie Aitken, and David Platt.

Blackburn Rovers
Lancashire club nicknamed 'The Rovers'. Three times league champions and six times FA Cup winners. Founded 1875. Ground: Ewood Park (current capacity 31,300) Famous players include Jimmy Brown, Bob Crompton, Simon Garner, and Alan Shearer.

Chelsea
West London club, nicknamed 'The Blues'. League champions, 1954-55, FA Cup winners in 1970 and 1997, European Cup Winners' Cup winners 1971 and 1998. Founded: 1905. Ground: Stamford Bridge (current capacity 34,750). Famous players include Roy Bentley, Charlie Cooke, Peter Osgood, Ruud Gullit, and Gianfranco Zola.

Everton
Liverpool club, nicknamed 'The Toffees'. Nine times league champions and five times FA Cup winners. Founded: 1878 (as St Domingo FC) Ground: Goodison Park (current capacity 40,200) Famous players include Dixie Dean, Alan Ball, Howard Kendall, and Neville Southall.

Glasgow Celtic
Nicknamed 'The Bhoys', they have won the Scottish league championship 36 times, the Scottish Cup a record 30 times, and the Scottish league cup nine times. In 1967 under manager Jock Stein they became the first British club to win the European Cup. Founded: 1888. Ground: Celtic Park (current capacity 60,294) Famous players include Jimmy McGrory, Jimmy Johnstone, Billy McNeill, and Kenny Dalglish.

Glasgow Rangers
Nicknamed 'The Gers' they have won the Scottish league championship a record 46 times, the Scottish Cup 27 times, and the Scottish league cup a record 20 times. Founded: 1873. Ground: Ibrox Park (current capacity 50,500). Famous players include George Young, Jim Baxter, John Greig, and Ally McCoist.

Heart of Midlothian
Edinburgh club nicknamed 'Hearts', they have won the Scottish league title four times and the Scottish Cup six times. Founded: 1874. Ground: Tynecastle Park (current capacity 18,300). Famous players include Bobby Walker, Gary Mackay, and John Robertson.

Leeds United
Yorkshire club, nicknamed 'United', they won the league championship 1969, 1974 and 1992. Founded: 1919 (following the disbandment of Leeds City (formed 1904) Ground: Elland Road (current capacity: 40,000) Famous players include John Charles, Bobby Collins, Jack Charlton, and Billy Bremner.

Liverpool
Nicknamed 'The Reds' they have won a record 18 English league titles. European Cup winners 1977, 1978, 1981, and 1984, they have also won the FA and league cups five times each, and the UEFA Cup twice. Founded: 1892. Ground: Anfield (current capacity 45,362). Famous players include Billy Liddell, Roger Hunt, Kevin Keegan, Kenny Dalglish and Ian Rush.

Manchester United
Nicknamed 'The Red Devils', they have won the English league championship 11 times and the FA Cup a record nine times. The first English side to win the European Cup 1968. Founded: 1880 as Newton Heath (present name from 1902) Ground: Old Trafford (current capacity 56,387) Famous players include Johnny Carey, Bobby Charlton, Denis Law, George Best, and Eric Cantona.

Newcastle United
Nicknamed 'The Magpies', they have been league champions five times and FA Cup winners six times. Founded: 1881 (as Stanley, 1882–92 as Newcastle East End) Ground: St James's Park (current capacity 36,834) Famous players include Hughie Gallacher, Jackie Milburn, Kevin Keegan, and Alan Shearer.

Nottingham Forest
Nicknamed 'Reds', they won the European Cup in 1979 and 1980. Founded: 1865. Ground: The City Ground (current capacity 30,602). Famous players include Ian Storey Moore, Kenny Burns, Trevor Francis, and Stuart Pearce.

Sheffield Wednesday
Yorkshire club nicknamed 'The Owls', they have won the league championship four times and the FA Cup three times. Founded: 1867. Ground: Hillsborough (current capacity 39,859) Famous players include Andy Wilson, Ron Springett, Chris Waddle, and Benito Carbone.

Tottenham Hotspur
North London side nicknamed 'Spurs' 1960–61 became the first team since 1897 to achieve the league and cup double. Eight times winners of the FA Cup. Founded: 1882 Ground: White Hart Lane (current capacity 36,200) Famous players include Danny Blanchflower, Jimmy Greaves, Glen Hoddle and Jürgen Klinsmann.

West Ham United
East London club nicknamed 'The Hammers'. Winners of the FA Cup 1964, 1975, and 1980, and the European Cup Winners' Cup 1965. Ground: Upton Park (current capacity 26,012) Famous West Ham players include Vic Watson, Bobby Moore, Geoff Hurst, and Martin Peters.

RUGBY LEAGUE CLUBS

Bradford Bulls
Three times league champions (including the Super League in 1997) and four times Challenge Cup winners. First season: 1895–96 (renamed Bradford Northern 1907–08) and Bradford Bulls 1995–96.) Ground: Odsal Stadium. Famous players include Keith Mumby, Jack McLean, Ernest Ward, and Robbie Paul.

Leeds Rhinos
10 times Challenge Cup winners and three times league champions. First season: 1895–96 (renamed Leeds Rhinos 1997) Ground: Headingley Famous players include Lewis Jones, Eric Harris, John Atkinson, and Garry Schofield.

St Helens
Seven times Challenge Cup winners and eight times league champions including the inaugural Super League in 1996. First season: 1895–96 Ground: Knowsley Road. Famous players include Kel Coslett, Tom Van Vollenhoven, Cliff Watson, and Alex Murphy.

Salford Reds
Six times league champions, they have only won the Challenge Cup once (1938). First season: 1896–97 (renamed Salford Reds 1995–96). Ground: The Willows. Famous players include Gus Risman, David Watkins, and Maurice Richards.

Wigan Warriors
Lancashire side who have won the Challenge Cup a record 16 times and the league championship a record 17 times. First season: 1895–96 (renamed Wigan Warriors 1997). Ground: Central Park. Famous players include: Jim Sullivan, Billy Boston, Ellery Hanley, Shaun Edwards, and Jason Robinson.

RUGBY UNION CLUBS

Bath
English knockout cup winners a record 10 times, and English league champions a record six times. In 1998 they became the first British side to win the European Cup. Founded: 1865. Ground: Recreation Ground. Famous players include: John Hall, Stuart Barnes, Jeremy Guscott, and Jon Callard.

Cardiff
Welsh league champions in 1995, and seven times winners of the SWALEC Cup. Founded: 1876. Ground: Cardiff Arms Park. Famous players include: Bleddyn Williams, Cliff Morgan, Gareth Edwards, and Barry John.

Harlequins
Founded: 1866. Winners of the English knockout cup in 1988 and 1991. Ground: The Stoop Memorial Ground, Twickenham. Famous players include Wavell Wakefield, Bob Hiller, Peter Winterbottom, and Will Carling.

Leicester
Five times winners of the English knockout cup and twice English league champions. Founded: 1880. Ground: Welford Road. Famous players include: Dusty Hare, Rory Underwood, Dean Richards, Joel Stransky, and Martin Johnson.

Llanelli
Welsh club who have won the SWALEC Cup a record ten times. Founded: 1872 Ground: Stradey Park. Famous players include: Ivor Jones, Phil Bennett, Jonathan Davies, and Ieun Evans.

Newcastle
English league champions, 1997/98. English knockout cup winners, 1976 and 1977. Founded: 1877 (as Newcastle Gosforth; reformed 1995) Ground: Gateshead International Stadium. Famous players include: Roger Uttley, Rob Andrew, Gary Armstrong, and Va'aiga Tuigamala

Saracens
1998 English knockout cup winners. Founded: 1876. Ground: Vicarage Road, Watford. Famous players include: Philippe Sella, Michael Lynagh, and François Pienaar.

Swansea
Welsh league champions in 1992 and 1994 and SWALEC Cup winners 1978 and 1995.

Founded 1873. Ground: St Helen's Ground. Famous players include: Dewi Bebb, Mervyn Davies, and Robert Jones.

Wasps
English league champions in 1990 and 1997. Founded: 1867 Ground: Loftus Road, Shepherds Bush. Famous players include: Maurice Colclough, Rob Andrew, and Lawrence Dallaglio.

Contemporary writers, film actors and directors, and sports men and women

WRITERS

Ahlberg, Allan (1938–) English writer of numerous successful books for children, many illustrated by his wife Janet (died 1994), including *Each Peach Pear Plum* (1978) and *The Jolly Postman.*

Aiken, Joan (Delano) (1924) English novelist and writer of critically acclaimed historical and mystery books for children including *The Wolves of Willoughby Chase* (1962) and more recently *The Jewel Seed* (1997).

Atkinson, Kate (Katherine) (1951–) English novelist who established her reputation and won the Whitbread Book of the Year prize with her first novel *Behind the Scenes at the Museum* (1995).

Berry, James (1924–) leading contemporary poet, novelist, and writer of books for children, born in Jamaica and settled in England in 1948, who has published acclaimed collections poetry as well as anthologies of West Indian–British poetry.

Bond, Michael (1926–) English author of books for children, best known as the creator of the character 'Paddington Bear'.

Boyd, William (Andrew Murray) (1952–) British novelist and short-story writer, born in Ghana, who has won wide critical success since *A Good Man in Africa* (1981) won the Whitbread Award for best first novel.

Bradford, Barbara Taylor (1933–) English novelist (now living in the USA), author of numerous works of bestselling romantic fiction following her first novel *A Woman of Substance* (1979).

Briggs, Raymond (Redvers) (1934–) English writer and illustrator of children's books including *Father Christmas* (1973) and *The Snowman* (1979), both of which use his hallmark comic-strip format and have been made into successful animated films.

Burgess, Melvin (1954–) English author whose books for children and teenagers have received wide critical acclaim, including *Junk* (1997) which focuses on heroin addiction and won the Carnegie Medal.

Cross, Gillian (Clare) (1945–) award-winning English writer of children's books including *Wolf* (1990) (Carnegie Medal) and *The Great Elephant Chase* (1992) (Whitbread Children's Novel Award).

Cunliffe, John (1933–) English writer and illustrator of books for children, the creator of the characters 'Postman Pat' (from 1981) and 'Rosie and Jim' (from 1991).

Cooper, Jilly (1937–) English author and journalist, perhaps best known for her bestselling popular romantic fiction including *The Man Who Made Husbands Jealous* (1993).

Dexter, Colin (1930–) English author of bestselling detective fiction and creator of Inspector Morse, who first appeared in the book *Last Bus to Woodstock* (1975) and later became the central character in a popular television series.

Dunnett, Dorothy (1923–) Scottish author best known for her historical adventures 'The Lymond Chronicles', featuring Francis Crawford of Lymond.

Emecheta, (Florence Onye) Buchi (1944–) British novelist, born in Nigeria and settled in Britain in 1962, who has achieved critical acclaim for her works championing the rights of women.

Fenton, James (Martin) (1949–) English poet and journalist who has achieved wide recognition for his mainly political and satirical poetry, winning the Whitbread Award for poetry with *Out of Danger* (1993).

Fielding, Helen English writer who achieved great popular success with the bestselling comic novel *Bridget Jones's Diary* (1996).

Follett, Ken (1949–) award-winning English writer of historical epic sagas and suspense thrillers such as *Eye of the Needle* (1978), an international bestseller.

Fine, Anne (1947–) English writer of books for children and teenagers who won the Carnegie Medal with *Goggle Eyes* (1989) and with *Flour Babies* (1992), and whose *Madame Doubtfire* (1988) was filmed as *Mrs Doubtfire* (1994).

Hegley, John (1953–) contemporary English comic poet who has achieved popular and critical success as a performer of his work as well as for collections of his poems such as *Glad to Wear Glasses* (1990).

Hornby, Nick (1957–) English author whose book *Fever Pitch* (1992), about football, became a major bestseller (filmed in 1997) and was followed by his highly acclaimed first novel *High Fidelity* (1995).

Howatch, Susan (1940–) English writer of bestselling fiction focusing on the Church of England in the 20th century, including *Absolute Truths* (1995).

Johnson, Linton Kwesi (1952–) poet born in Jamaica and came to Britain in 1963, whose dub poetry, characterized by an aggressive urban style, has a wide following.

Keating, H R F (Henry Reymond Fitzwalter) (1926–) English writer of bestselling classic detective fiction, known especially for his Inspector Ghote series set in India.

King-Smith, Dick (Ronald Gordon) (1922–) English author of over 90 books for children, many of which have been inspired by his experiences as a farmer, including *The Sheep-Pig* (1984) which was filmed as *Babe* (1995).

Morpurgo, Michael English writer of over 50 books for children and young teenagers including *Why the Whales Came* (1985) which was made into a successful film.

Pearce, (Ann) Philippa (1920–) English writer of critically acclaimed books for children including the classic *Tom's Midnight Garden* (1958) which won the Carnegie Medal.

Pilcher, Rosamunde (1924–) English novelist and short-story writer, who won wide recognition with her bestselling romantic novel *The Shell Seekers* (1987).

Pullman, Philip (1946–) English writer of fiction for children and teenagers including *Northern Lights* which won the Carnegie Medal.

Raine, Craig (Anthony) (1944–) leading contemporary British poet who has achieved critical success with his work which treats familiar objects in unusual ways, as in *A Martian Sends a Postcard Home* (1979).

Rankin, Ian (1960–) Scottish writer of bestselling crime thrillers featuring the detective Inspector Rebus, including the award-winning *Black and Blue* (1997).

Raven, Simon (Arthur Noël) (1927–) English novelist and playwright, perhaps best known for the ten-volume series of novels *Alms for Oblivion* (1964–1976) depicting post-war life from 1945 to 1973.

Rosen, Michael (1946) English writer of poems and books for children, performer, and broadcaster, whose works include the popular *We're Going on a Bear Hunt* (1989) (illustrated by Helen Oxenbury) and *You Wait 'Til I'm Older Than You* (1996).

Ross, Tony (1938) English writer and illustrator of books for children including the bestselling classic *I Want My Potty* (1986).

Self, Will English author who established his reputation with his debut novel, the satirical *The Quantity Theory of Insanity* (1991).

Tennant, Emma (Christina) (1937–) English novelist who has achieved critical success for her works using fantasy and stream of consciousness to explore extreme psychological states as well as for her more conventional works.

Waddell, Martin (1941–) British writer of books for young children, including the bestselling picture book *Can't You Sleep Little Bear* (1988) (illustrated by Barbara Firth).

Williams, Hugo (1942–) leading contemporary English poet who has achieved critical acclaim for his vivacious and lucid poetry as in *Self-Portrait with a Slide* (1990).

FILM ACTORS AND DIRECTORS

Agutter, Jenny (1952–) English film actress, who rose to fame as a teenager in *Walkabout* and *The Railway Children*.

Apted, Michael (1941–) English film and television director, whose works have included *Coal Miner's Daughter* and *Gorillas in the Mist*.

Baxendale, Helen (1970–) English screen actress who gained stardom in the British miniseries *An Unsuitable Job For a Woman* and on the US sitcom *Friends*.

Bean, Sean (1959–) English stage and film actor who, since 1993, has starred as Richard Sharpe in a series of ITV costume dramas.

Boyle, Danny (1956–) English film director and producer, and a key member of the British team behind *Shallow Grave* and *Trainspotting*.

Byrne, Gabriel (1950–) Irish film actor who has featured in a number of British and US films, including *Defence of the Realm* and *Miller's Crossing*.

Carroll, Madeleine (1906–1987) British born screen actress, whose aloof blonde in *The 39 Steps* became the female archetype for future Hitchcock thrillers.

Cavalcanti, Alberto (de Almeida) (1897–1982) Brazilian-born film director, screenwriter, and producer, who, during the course of a nomadic career, made a significant contribution to the British cinema of the 1940s with films like *Went the Day Well?*.

Cox, Alex (1954–) English film director, screenwriter, and television presenter who, with *Repo Man* and *Sid and Nancy*, has carved a niche as a cult filmmaker.

Cox, Brian (1946–) British character actor, whose distinctive voice has been widely used for documentary and advertising voice-overs. His on-screen film credits include *Manhunter* and *Desperate Measures*.

Crichton, Charles (1910–) English director whose career has spanned several decades of British filmmaking, ranging from a string of 1950s Ealing comedies to the 1980s' *A Fish Called Wanda*.

Cusack, Sinéad (1948–) Irish actress and daughter of Cyril Cusack. She has starred opposite her husband Jeremy Irons in *Waterland* and *Stealing Beauty*.

Dalton, Timothy (1946–) Welsh stage and screen actor, whose international reputation was established when he assumed the Bond mantle in *The Living Daylights*.

Dunbar, Adrian (1958–) Irish actor who co-wrote and starred in *Hear My Song*, before featuring in the television miniseries *Melissa* and the latest instalment of George Lucas' *Star Wars* cycle.

Eccleston, Christopher (1964–) versatile English actor, who won acclaim for his performances in the films *Let Him Have It* and *Shallow Grave* and the television series *Our Friends in the North*.

Figgis, Mike (Michael) (1949–) Kenyan-born English film director and music composer who won critical acclaim for his stylish adaptation of *Leaving Las Vegas*.

Fitzgerald, Tara (born Tara Callaby) (1967–) leading English actress who rose to fame in *The Camomile Lawn* before starring in the films *Sirens* and *Brassed Off*.

Fox, Edward (1937–) English screen actor, who gave a chilling performance as the assassin in *The Day of the Jackal*. He is brother of fellow film actor James Fox.

Fox, Kerry (1966–) New Zealand-born actress who rose to stardom following her performance as Janet Frame in *An Angel at My Table* and has since featured in such British films as *Shallow Grave* and *Welcome to Sarajevo*.

Gough, Michael (1917–) versatile Malayan-born British stage and screen actor, whose career has embraced prominent stage and television productions, Hammer horror films, and the recent big screen *Batman* productions.

Grant, Richard E (1957–) Swaziland-born British actor and writer, who made his feature film debut with a manic performance in *Withnail and I*.

Hamer, Robert (1911–1963) English filmmaker who worked his way up the studio ranks from clapper-boy to director and co-screenwriter of the 1940s' classic *Kind Hearts and Coronets*.

Hart, Ian (1964–) English actor who, before starring in *Land and Freedom*, played John Lennon in two films, *The Hours and Times* and *Backbeat*.

Horrocks, Jane (1964–) versatile comic English actress who has played a bulimic chocoholic in Mike Leigh's *Life is Sweet*, the dizzy Bubbles in *Absolutely Fabulous*, and the title role in *Little Voice*.

Howitt, Peter (1958–) English actor, writer, and director who rose to fame on British television as Joey Boswell in *Bread*, then in 1998 wrote and directed the film *Sliding Doors*.

Kensit, Patsy (1968–) English actress and singer, who rose to fame as a child performer in the 1970s.

Lloyd, Emily (1970–) English actress who burst on the scene as the extrovert heroine of *Wish You Were Here*, going on to perform in such US films as *A River Runs Through It*.

Lyne, Adrian (1941–) English film director, who graduated from the British advertising scene of the 1970s to direct such Hollywood films as *Fatal Attraction* and the controversial *Lolita*.

McGann, Paul (1960–) English film and television actor whose credits include *Withnail and I* and *Dr Who*.

Meadows, Shane (1973–) promising English film director, who followed the popular shorts *Smalltime* and *Where's the Money Ronnie?* with the feature *twentyfourseven*.

Molina, Alfred (1953–) English stage and screen character actor who won acclaim for his performance as Joe Orton's lover, Kenneth Halliwell, in *Prick Up Your Ears*.

Newell, Mike (1942–) English film and television director whose credits include the acclaimed drama *Dance With a Stranger* and the popular comedy *Four Weddings and a Funeral*.

Ormond, Julia (1965–) English screen actress who graduated from British television to star in such Hollywood hits as *Legends of the Fall* and *First Knight*.

Paterson, Bill (1945–) Scottish character actor, whose illustrious television credits include *Auf Wiedersehen, Pet*, *The Singing Detective*, and the miniseries *The Crow Road*.

Postlethwaite, Peter (1945–) English stage and screen actor who, since the success of *Distant Voices, Still Lives*, has enjoyed a prolific film career in both Britain and the USA.

Potter, Sally (1949–) English film director, writer, and editor, whose works include the avant-garde feminist film *Thriller* and an adaptation of *Orlando*.

Radford, Michael (1946–) Indian-born British film director, who followed *1984* and *White Mischief* with the acclaimed Italian-language film *Il Postino/The Postman*.

Rea, Stephen (1949–) Irish stage and film actor, who has enjoyed a long-running collaborative relationship with writer-director Neil Jordan, most notably in *The Crying Game*.

Rickman, Alan (1946–) English stage and screen actor, whose RSC and Broadway successes led to a series of prominent film roles in the USA and Britain.

Roth, Tim (1961–) English film and television actor who has performed in a number of innovative, low-budget British and American productions with such filmmakers as Stephen Frears, Peter Greenaway, Robert Altman, and Quentin Tarantino.

Scacchi, Greta (1960–) Italian-born and Australian and British-educated screen actress whose credits include *White Mischief* and *The Player*.

Scott, Tony (1944–) English film director who, like his brother Ridley, graduated from the British advertising scene, directing such US commercial successes as *Top Gun* and *Crimson Tide*.

Staunton, Imelda (1956–) English stage and screen actress who has featured on television in *The Singing Detective* and on film in *Peter's Friends*.

Thewlis, David (1963–) English stage and screen actor who won international acclaim for his acerbic performance in Mike Leigh's film *Naked*.

Whalley, Joanne (1964–) English stage and screen actress who followed appearances in the television miniseries *Edge of Darkness* and *The Singing Detective* with leading roles in the films *Scandal* and *Kill Me Again*.

Wilkinson, Tom (1948–) long-serving English character actor whose reputation was enhanced in the late 1990s by his performances in the Dickens adaptation *Martin Chuzzlewit* and the hit comedy film *The Full Monty*.

SPORTS MEN AND WOMEN

Adams, Tony (1966–) England footballer who captained Arsenal to the league championship in 1989, 1991 and 1998. He has won 55 England caps since his debut in 1987.

Ainslie, Ben (1977–) English sailor who won the men's singlehanded gold medal at the 1998 ISAF World Championships, and a silver in the Laser class at the 1996 Olympic Games.

Barnes, John (1963–) Jamaican-born English footballer who has won 79 England caps since his debut in 1983.

Brown, Karen (1963–) English hockey player who since her international debut 1982 has won 152 caps for England and 140 for Great Britain.

Calzaghe, Joe (1972–) Welsh boxer who won the WBO world super middleweight title in October 1997.

Campbell, Sol (1974–) Tottenham and England footballer who has won 20 caps since making his full international debut 1995.

Cork, Dominic (1971–) Derbyshire and England cricketer. A right-arm fast bowler, he took a hat-trick on his England Test debut 1995.

Coulthard, David (1971–) Scottish motor racing driver who has driven for the McLaren Formula 1 team since 1996. He made his Formula 1 debut with Williams 1994.

Dawson, Matt (1971–) English rugby union player who 1997 scored two tries in British Lions 2–1 series win over South Africa. He made his England debut 1995.

Evans, Ieun (1964–) Welsh rugby union player. He scored a Welsh record 33 tries in 72 internationals 1987–98.

Fogarty, Carl (1965–) English motor cyclist who won the World Superbike Championship in 1994, 1995 and 1998.

Gibbs, Scott (1971–) Welsh rugby player who was the British Lions' Man of the Series against South Africa 1997. He has been capped by Wales at both rugby union and rugby league.

Giggs, Ryan (1973–) Welsh footballer. who has won four league championships with Manchester United 1993–97. Capped 21 times by Wales since making his debut as a 17 year old in 1991.

Hide, Herbie (1972–) English boxer. The WBO world heavyweight champion 1994–95, and since June 1997.

Higgins, John (1975–) Scottish snooker player who won the 1998 Embassy World Championship.

Howey, Kate (1973–) English judo black belt who won the women's 66kg event at the 1997 World Judo Championships.

Howley, Robert (1970–) Welsh rugby union player. The Welsh Player of the year in 1996 and 1997.

Hussain, Nasser (1968–) Essex and England cricketer who in 1998 scored his 2,000th run in Test cricket.

Hughes, Mark (1984–) Welsh footballer who has won a record four FA Cup winners' medals for Manchester United and Chelsea, 1990–1997. He has won 66 international caps since 1984.

Irvine, Eddie (1965–) Northern Irish motor racing driver who has driven for the Ferrari Formula 1 team since 1996. He made his Formula 1 debut for Jordan in 1993.

Jackson, Colin (1967–) Welsh athlete who won the 1993 World 110-metre hurdles title in a world record time of 12.91 sec.

Jones, Robert (1965–) Welsh rugby union player who has won 54 caps for Wales and three for the British Lions since making his full international debut 1986.

Leonard, Justin (1968–) English rugby union player. England's most capped prop forward with 59 full international appearances since making his debut in 1990. He has also won three British Lions caps.

Lessing, Simon (1971–) South African-born British triathlete who was world triathlon champion in 1992, 1995, 1996, and 1998.

Lewis, Denise (1972–) English athlete. The 1998 European heptathlon champion, she won a silver medal at the 1997 World Championships.

McCoist, Ally (1972–) Scottish footballer who in 1992 became the first player to score 200 goals in the Scottish Premier Division. He has scored 19 goals in 59 Scotland internationals since 1986.

Nicol, Peter (1973–) Scottish squash player who 1998 became the first Briton to top the men's world squash rankings, and also the first Briton since 1973 to win the men's British Open.

Nicholas, Alison (1962–) English golfer who in 1996 became only the second Briton to win a women's major when she won the US Women's Open.

O'Sullivan, Ronnie (1975–) English snooker player who has won 12 titles since turning professional in 1992 including the UK Championship in 1993 and 1997.

Ramprakash, Mark (1969–) Middlesex and England cricketer. A right-handed batsman he has scored 1,195 runs in 29 Tests since making his Test debut in 1991.

Robinson, Jason (1974–) Wigan and Great Britain rugby league player.

Rose, Justin (1981–) English golfer who as a 17 year-old amateur finished equal fourth in the 1998 British Open, a year after becoming the youngest player to compete in the Walker Cup.

Sixsmith, Jane (1967–) English hockey player who since 1987 has scored 38 goals in 139 appearances for England, and 46 in 123 appearances for Great Britain.

Thomas, Iwan (1974–) Welsh runner. The 1998 European 400 metres champion and silver medalist in the 4 × 400 metre relay at the 1996 Olympic Games and the 1997 World Championships.

Townsend, Gregor (1975–) Northampton, Scotland and British Lions rugby union player. He made his Scotland debut 1993 and 1997 was a member of the triumphant British Lions tour of South Africa.

Westwood, Lee (1973–) English golfer. Winner of eight tournaments worldwide since turning professional in 1993.

Whitaker, John (1955–) English showjumper who won the Volvo World Cup 1990 and 1991. His brother Michael (1960–) has won the King George V Gold Cup four times 1982–94.

Wright, Ian (1963–) English footballer who in 1997 broke Cliff Bastin's Arsenal club scoring record of 178 goals. He has scored 9 goals in 31 England internationals.

TV personalities past and present

Abbott, Russ (stage name of Russ Roberts) (1948–) English comedian and comic actor who emerged in the 1980s as one of Britain's most popular TV entertainers.

Alexander, Jean (1926–) English actress who played Hilda Ogden in the ITV soap opera *Coronation Street* (1964–87).

Allen, Dave (1936–) (stage name of David Tynan O'Mahony) Irish comedian whose sharply observed humour has been popular on British TV since the late 1960s.

Anderson, Clive (1953–) English chat show host and presenter who has also chaired the Channel 4 improvisation game show *Whose Line is it Anyway?* since 1988.

Andrews, Eamonn (1922–1987) Irish presenter, chat show host, and sports commentator who rose to prominence in British TV in the 1950s as the host of panel game *What's My Line?*.

Aspel, Michael (stage name of Michael Terence) (1933–) laidback English presenter and chat show host who has presented *This Is Your Life* since its revival in 1994.

Baker, Richard (1925–) English newsreader and classical music presenter who, in 1954, became one of BBC TV's first 'in-vision' newsreaders, a position he held until 1982.

Bakewell, Joan (born Joan Dawson) (1933–) distinguished English broadcaster who presents the BBC TV's moral issue series *Heart of the Matter*.

Barrymore, Michael (1952–) energetic English comedian and entertainer who hosts the ITV game show *Strike It Lucky*.

Baxter, Stanley (1926–) inventive Scottish TV comedian renowned for his elaborate parodies of the film world.

Beadle, Jeremy (1948–) English TV entertainer who has presented humorous excerpts from viewers' home videos on ITV's peak-time show *You've Been Framed*.

Bellamy, David (1933–) popular English TV naturalist and environmental campaigner.

Berry, Nick (1963–) English actor who starred as PC Nick Rowan in the popular ITV drama series *Heartbeat*.

Bewes, Rodney (1938–) English actor who co-starred with James Bolam in the BBC sitcom *The Likely Lads*.

Black, Cilla (stage name of Priscilla White) (1943–) English presenter, entertainer, and former pop star who hosts two of ITV's most popular programmes, *Blind Date* and *Surprise, Surprise*.

Braden, Bernard (1916–1993) Canadian actor and presenter who pioneered consumer programming on British television in the late 1960s with his show *Braden's Week* and *The Braden Beat*.

Brambell, Wilfrid (1912–1985) Irish-born actor who is famous for his role as the coarse, manipulative father Albert Steptoe in the BBC sitcom *Steptoe and Son*.

Bremner, Rory (1961–) inventive Scottish-born TV impressionist who specializes in topical and political satire.

Burnet, Alastair (adopted name of James William Alexander) (1928–) distinguished Scottish current affairs presenter and journalist who anchored ITN's *News at Ten* for many years.

Carpenter, Harry (1925–) esteemed English sports commentator who commentated on boxing and other sports on BBC TV for over 40 years.

Carrott, Jasper (stage name of Robert Davies) (1945–) English comedian who has been popular on British TV since the 1970s.

Carson, Violet (1898–1983) English actress who played the formidable Ena Sharples for over 20 years in the ITV soap opera *Coronation Street*.

Chalmers, Judith (1935–) English presenter who hosted the ITV holiday programme *Wish You Were Here* for over 20 years.

Clarkson, Jeremy (1960–) English motoring journalist, star presenter of BBC's car programme *Top Gear* and budding chat show host.

Cole, George (1925–) enduring English actor best known for his portrayal of the spiv entrepreneur Arthur Daley in the ITV comedy drama *Minder*.

Coleman, David (1926–) veteran English sports presenter and commentator who also hosted the popular BBC quiz show *A Question of Sport* for over 20 years.

Coogan, Steve (1958–) English comic actor and writer whose 1997 BBC comedy *It's Alan Partridge* has confirmed his reputation as one of British TV's brightest new talents.

Cook, Roger (1943–) New Zealand-born investigative reporter famous for his face-to-face confrontations with fraudsters and other criminals on his long-running ITV series *The Cook Report*.

Cooper, Tommy (1922–1984) Welsh comedian whose deliberately bad jokes and hilariously unsuccessful magic tricks performed in his trademark fez made him one of British TV's most adored personalities.

Cotton, Billy (1899–1969) English bandleader and entertainer who was a permanent fixture of BBC TV's variety revues in the 1950s and 1960s.

Cradock, Fanny (1909–1994) pioneering English TV cook who is less remembered for her recipes than for her comically strident manner and brusque on-screen treatment of her embattled husband Johnny.

Daniels, Paul (1938–) English magician and entertainer who won the Golden Rose of Montreaux award in 1985 for *The Paul Daniels Magic Show*.

Davidson, Jim (1953–) English comedian and entertainer who hosts the BBC game shows *Big Break* and *Jim Davidson's Generation Game*.

Dawson, Les (1934–1993) English comedian whose brand of dry, deadpan wit brought him high ratings on British TV in the 1980s.

Day, Robin (1923–) eminent English broadcast journalist who pioneered the probing political interview on British TV in the 1950s.

Deayton, Angus (1956–) English actor, writer, and presenter who has hosted the humorous topical quiz show *Have I Got News For You* on BBC TV since 1990.

Dennis, Les (1954–) English comedian and impressionist who has hosted the ITV game show *Family Fortunes* since 1987.

Dodd, Ken (1927–) English comic entertainer and singer, who appeared on TV from the 1950s to the 1990s, often with diminutive characters called Diddymen.

Doonican, Val (1929–) wholesome Irish singer and entertainer who enjoyed peak-time success on British TV in the 1960s and early 1970s.

Edmonds, Noel (1948–) English entertainer and former radio disc jockey who hosts the highly popular BBC TV show *Noel's House Party*.

Emery, Dick (1917–1983) English comic actor whose *Dick Emery Show* was a mainstay of BBC TV's comedy output in the 1960s and 1970s, making him allegedly TV's highest paid star of the time.

Ford, Anna (1943–) English broadcaster who has been one of British TV's leading newsreaders since the late 1970s.

Fry, Stephen (1957–) English actor, comedian, and writer who came to the fore in the 1980s on British TV alongside comedy partner Hugh Laurie.

Gascoigne, Bamber (1935–) author and broadcaster who chaired the student quiz show *University Challenge* (1962–87).

Gordon, Noele (1923–1985) English actress who starred as motel proprietress Meg Richardson in the ITV soap opera *Crossroads* (1964–81).

Grayson, Larry (1923–1995) camp English comedian and entertainer who enjoyed peak time success as a host of BBC's *Generation Game* (1978–82).

Greene, Hughie (1920–1997) Canadian-born presenter and quiz show host who compered the ITV talent show *Opportunity Knocks* for 21 years from 1956.

Harding, Gilbert (1907–1990) English broadcaster who, as an outspoken panellist on the TV quiz *What's My Line?*, became perhaps the leading personality on British TV in the 1950s.

Harris, Rolf (1930–) Australian entertainer and presenter who has enjoyed a long and successful career on British TV.

Harty, Russell (1934–1988) English presenter whose relaxed and deadpan style made him one of Britain's leading chat show hosts of the 1970s and 1980s.

Humphries, Barry (1934–) Australian comedian who has enjoyed great success on stage and TV in the guise of Australian 'housewife megastar' Dame Edna Everage.

Inman, John (1935–) English comic actor who is best known for his portrayal of the camp menswear assistant Mr Humphries in the BBC sitcom *Are You Being Served?*

James, Clive (1939–) Australian presenter, chat show host, and author whose British TV programmes (taking a humorous look at TV around the world) have been much imitated.

Kendal, Felicity (1946–) English actress who in the mid-1970s played one of the lead characters in the much-repeated BBC television comedy *The Good Life* but also plays straight roles for television and in the theatre.

Kennedy, Ludovic (1919–) British current affairs journalist, presenter, and author whose distinguished career on British TV began in the 1950s.

Lawley, Sue (1946–) English current affairs presenter and host of the BBC radio series *Desert Island Discs*.

Lipman, Maureen (1946–) English actress specialising in comedy, who has appeared in television plays by her husband, Jack Rosenthal; she also writes sharply observed commentaries on life for magazines and in her own books.

Lowe, Arthur (1915–1982) English actor best known for his portrayal of the bumptious Captain Mainwaring in the classic BBC sitcom *Dad's Army*.

Lynam, Des (1942–) suave, Irish-born BBC sports presenter with a droll wit and impeccable delivery.

Lyndhurst, Nicholas (1961–) English comic actor, a star of the BBC sitcoms *Only Fools and Horses* and *Goodnight Sweetheart*.

MacDonald, Trevor (1939–) Trinidadian-born newsreader, the main presenter of ITV's *News at Ten*.

McGoohan, Patrick (1928–) US-born British actor who created and starred in the cult British TV drama *The Prisoner*.

McNee, Patrick (1922–) English actor who starred as the suave gentleman agent in the ITV action drama *The Avengers* (1961–69) and in *The New Avengers* (1976–77).

Magnusson, Magnus (1929–) Icelandic broadcaster who chaired the compelling BBC quiz show *Mastermind* (1972–97).

Merton, Paul (1957–) Comic writer and performer whose droll demeanour and speedy wit is displayed to effect on the television quiz *Have I Got News For You* and the radio quiz *Just a Minute*.

Michelmore, Cliff Arthur (1919–) English current affairs journalist, presenter, and producer who enjoyed a long and distinguished career on BBC TV.

Mitchell, Warren (1926–) English actor whose bigoted cockney Alf Garnett in the long-running sitcom *Till Death Us Do Part* became a national institution.

Monkhouse, Bob (1928–) English comedian, actor, writer, and entertainer whose long and varied career on British TV began in 1954 and has included being host of the long-running quizzes *The Golden Shot* and *Celebrity Squares*.

Morris, Johnny (1916–) Welsh-born broadcaster who made the animals talk on the long running BBC children's programme *Animal Magic*.

Muir, Frank (1920–1998) polished English broadcaster and leading comedy writer on radio and TV, often working in partnership with Denis Norden, who is best remembered on TV as a panellist on the BBC quiz show *Call My Bluff*.

Norden, Denis (1922–) English broadcaster and leading comedy writer, who had a long writing partnership Frank Muir; best known latterly on TV for his humorous compilations of TV out-takes on ITV's *It'll Be Alright on the Night*.

Norman, Barry (1933–) English broadcaster, writer, and journalist who presented BBC TV's *Film* movie review series from the early 1970s until 1998, when he moved to Sky.

O'Connor, Des (1932–) English singer and entertainer who established himself as a leading celebrity chat show host with his series *Des O'Connor Tonight*, which began in the 1980s on BBC and later transferred to ITV in the 1990s.

Owen, Bill (stage name of William John Owen Rowbotham) (1914–) veteran English actor who plays the part of the jovial scruff Compo in the whimsical BBC sitcom *Last of the Summer Wine*.

Palin, Michael (1943–) English comic actor and presenter who rose to prominence in TV and film as a member of *Monty Python's Flying Circus*, and who in recent years has enjoyed high ratings for his globe-trotting TV travelogues.

Parkinson, Michael (1935–) English journalist and chat show host whose long-running BBC chat show *Parkinson* was revived in 1998 after a gap of 15 years.

Paxman, Jeremy (1950–) English current affairs presenter and writer who presents BBC's *Newsnight* and has chaired the quiz show *University Challenge* since its revival in 1994.

Rantzen, Esther (1940–) English broadcaster who presented and edited the long-running BBC consumer programme *That's Life* (1973–84).

Reeves, Vic (stage name of Jim Moir) (1959–) English comedian and writer who hosts the award-winning alternative celebrity quiz show *Shooting Stars* with regular comedy partner Bob Mortimer.

Rhys, Jones Griff (1953–) Welsh-born comedian and comic actor who has enjoyed a long and successful TV comedy partnership with Mel Smith.

Rippon, Angela (1944–) English broadcaster who in the 1970s became BBC TV's first female newsreader and is also remembered for her high-kicking dance routine on *Morecambe & Wise*.

Roache, William (1932–) English actor who, in the part Ken Barlow, is the only surviving original cast member of the first episode of the ITV soap opera *Coronation Street*.

Ross, Jonathan (1960–) English broadcaster and producer who rose to prominence in the late 1980s as the host of the Channel 4 chat show *The Last Resort*.

Rossiter, Leonard (1926–1984) English actor who enjoyed great success in the 1970s in the title role of the BBC comedy *The Fall and Rise of Reginald Perrin*, and as the seedy landlord Rigsby in the ITV sitcom *Rising Damp*.

Savage, Lily Persona created by Paul O'Grady, English entertainer from Liverpool, who won mainstream recognition in the 1990s with *The Lily Savage Show* on BBC, and has presented the BBC's celebrity quiz *Blankety Blank*.

Secombe, Harry (1921–) Welsh-born singer, entertainer, presenter, and comedian who rose to fame on the 1950s radio show *The Goon Show*.

Singleton, Valerie (1937–) English presenter who came to the fore in the 1960s as a presenter of the BBC children's programme *Blue Peter* and subsequently presented *The Money Programme*, also for the BBC.

Sykes, Eric (1923–) English comedian, comic actor, and writer whose BBC sitcom *Sykes*, co-starring Hattie Jacques, ran for 16 years between 1961 and 1979.

Tarrant, Chris English TV presenter and star radio DJ with a comic slant, who presented *Tiswas* and *OTT*, and in 1998 fronted *Man O Man*, a game show where girls pick chaps.

Thaw, John (1942–) English actor who is best known for his police detective roles in the ITV dramas *The Sweeney* and *Inspector Morse*.

Vorderman, Carol (1960–) English television presenter who works on a wide variety of programmes, who came to prominence as the mathematically speedy co-presenter of the Channel Four game of mental calculations, *Countdown*.

Walden, Brian (1932–) English current affairs broadcaster and former Labour MP who became one of British TV's toughest political interviewers.

Warner, Jack (stage name of Horace John Waters) (1895–1981) English actor who played the part of the reliable neighbourhood bobby George Dixon in the BBC drama *Dixon of Dock Green* for 21 years from 1955.

Wax, Ruby (1953–) sassy US comedian, TV editor, and presenter who specializes in 'at home' TV interviews of celebrities.

Wheldon, Huw (1916–1986) eminent Welsh broadcaster who made a long and lasting contribution to the BBC as a presenter, editor, producer, and senior executive.

Whicker, Alan (1925–) globe-trotting English broadcaster who, in 1993, became the first person to be named in the Royal Television Society's Hall of Fame for making an outstanding creative contribution to British TV.

Whitehouse, Paul (1958–) English comedian and writer who stars in the cult BBC TV comedy sketch show *The Fast Show* and in *Harry Enfield and Chums*.

Worth, Harry (stage name of Harry Illingsworth) (1920–1989) English comedian and comic actor who was a mainstay on British TV in the 1960s and 1970s.

Yarwood, Mike (1941–) English impressionist who enjoyed high ratings on British TV in the 1970s.

Useful Web sites

Some selected sites relating to main encyclopedia entries, grouped by title in three main categories: Arts, Science and Technology, and Society.

ARTS

Architecture

Big Ben
http://www.virtual-london.co.uk/attractions/bigben.html

Buckingham Palace
http://www.royal.gov.uk/palaces/bp.htm

Pugin, Augustus
http://www.hubcom.com/pugin/

Shakespeare's Globe
http://www.rdg.ac.uk/globe/Globe.html

Sir John Soane's Museum
http://www.demon.co.uk/heritage/soanes/

St James's Palace
http://www.royal.gov.uk/palaces/stjamess.htm

Virtual Tour of the Tower of London
http://www.itw.com/~dravyk/toltour/

Wren, Sir Christopher
http://www-groups.dcs.st-and.ac.uk/history/Mathematicians/Wren.html

Arts and Crafts

Arts and Crafts Society
http://www.arts-crafts.com/

Bayeux Tapestry
http://blah.bsuvc.bsu.edu/bt

Welcome to the Story of Spode
http://www.spode.co.uk/

Cinema

Alien
http://www.godamongdirectors.com/scripts/alien.shtml

BAFTA Awards
http://www.bafta.org/

Carry Online
http://www.carryonline.com/

Charlie Chaplin Filmography
http://www.cs.monash.edu.au/~pringle/silent/chaplin/filmography.html

Completely Unauthorized Hugh Grant Page
http://www.wkgroup.com/~blake/hugh/

Connery, Sean
http://www.mcs.net/~klast/www/connery.html

Cook, Peter
http://www.scream.demon.co.uk/pcook.html

Daniel Day-Lewis
http://www.danielday.org/

Darla's Peter Sellers Tribute Page
http://members.aol.com/damsel16/sellers.html

Dr Who
http://www.dwguide.demon.co.uk/listjava.htm

Harrison, Rex
http://www.reelclassics.com/Actors/Rex/rex.htm

Hitchcock Page
http://www.primenet.com/~mwc/

Hope Enterprises
http://bobhope.com/

James Bond, Agent 007
http://www.mcs.net/~klast/www/bond.html

Julie Andrews Resource Page
http://www.geocities.com/Hollywood/7308/intro.htm

Kerr, Deborah
http://www.reelclassics.com/Actresses/Kerr/kerr.htm

Kubrick Multimedia Film Guide
http://www.lehigh.edu/~pjl2/kubrick.html

Leigh, Vivien
http://www.dycks.com/vivienleigh/

Monty Python and the Holy Grail
http://www.intriguing.com/mp/scripts/mp-holy.txt

Monty Python's Flying Circus in Australia
http://www.dcscomp.com.au/sdp/mainpage.htm

Moore, Roger
http://www.mcs.net/~klast/www/moore.html

Neeson, Liam
http://www.celebsite.com/people/liamneeson/content/bio.html

O'Toole, Peter
http://www.reelclassics.com/Actors/O'Toole/otoole.htm

Taylor, Elizabeth
http://www.reelclassics.com/Actresses/Liz-Taylor/liz.htm

Thompson, Emma
http://ziff.shore.net/~courses/mulder/emma/index.html

Tony Hancock Home Page
http://www.achilles.net/~howardm/tony.html

Welcome to the Ultimate Cary Grant Pages
http://www.ifb.co.uk/~pingu/cg/c-grant.htm

Wendy's Audrey Hepburn Page
http://www.geocities.com/Hollywood/Boulevard/4452/audrey.html

Classical Music

Andrew Lloyd Webber Online Magazine
http://www.serve.com/dougmac/

Bagpipes of the World
http://www.rootsworld.com/rw/feature/gaida.html

Bantock Society
http://www.edu.coventry.ac.uk/music/bantock/index.htm

Britten, Benjamin
http://www.geocities.com/Vienna/Strasse/1523/britten.htm

Ceolas Celtic Music Archive
http://celtic.stanford.edu/ceolas.html

D'Oyly Carte Family
http://math.idbsu.edu/gas/html/carte.html

Elgar Society and Elgar Foundation
http://www.elgar.org/

Folk Music Home Page
http://www.jg.org/folk/

George Frideric Handel Home Page
http://www.intr.net/bleissa/handel/home.html

Gustav Holst Site
http://wso.williams.edu/~ktaylor/gholst

Howells, Herbert
http://www.gprep.pvt.k12.md.us/~gldaum/howells/howells1.html

Malcolm Arnold Society
http://www.edu.coventry.ac.uk/music/arnold/arnold.htm

Nyman, Michael
http://www.december.org/nyman/index.htm

Purcell, Henry
http://portico.bl.uk/exhibitions/purcell/overview.html

Ralph Vaughan Williams Web Page
http://www.cs.qub.ac.uk/~J. Collis/RVW.html

Royal Opera House
http://195.26.96.12/house/welcome.html

Walton, William
http://www.geocities.com/Vienna/5827/walton.htm

William Alwyn Society
http://www.edu.coventry.ac.uk/music/alwyn/index.htm

Painting

Bacon, Francis (artist)
http://www.oir.ucf.edu/wm/paint/auth/bacon/

Beardsley, Aubrey
http://www.stg.brown.edu/projects/hypertext/landow/victorian/decadence/ab/beardsleyov.html

Blake, William
http://www.oir.ucf.edu/wm/paint/auth/blake/

Brown, Ford Madox
http://www.oir.ucf.edu/wm/paint/auth/brown/

Burne-Jones, Sir Edward Coley
http://sunsite.unc.edu/wm/paint/auth/burne-jones/

Constable, John
http://www.oir.ucf.edu/wm/paint/auth/constable/

Dyck, Sir Anthony van
http://www.oir.ucf.edu/wm/paint/auth/dyck/

Freud, Lucian
http://www.oir.ucf.edu/wm/paint/auth/freud/

Gainsborough, Thomas
http://www.oir.ucf.edu/wm/paint/auth/gainsborough/

Hockney, David
http://www.oir.ucf.edu/wm/paint/auth/hockney/

Kauffmann, Angelica
http://www.knight.org/advent/cathen/08609b.htm

Kitaj, R B
http://www.oir.ucf.edu/wm/paint/auth/kitaj/

National Portrait Gallery
http://www.npg.org.uk/index.htm

New Atlantis, The
http://wiretap.spies.com/ftp.items/Library/Classic/atlantis.txt

Pre-Raphaelite Critic
http://www.engl.duq.edu/servus/PR-Critic/

Royal Academy of Arts
http://www.royalacademy.org.uk/

Ruskin on Turner
http://www4.torget.se/artbin/art/oruskincontents.html

Sargent, John Singer
http://www.oir.ucf.edu/wm/paint/auth/sargent/

Selected Hogarth Prints
http://www.english.upenn.edu/~jlynch/hogarth.html

Tate Gallery
http://www.tate.org.uk/menu.htm

Turner, Joseph Mallord William
http://www.oir.ucf.edu/wm/paint/auth/turner/

Victoria and Albert Museum
http://www.vam.ac.uk/

Victorian Web
http://www.stg.brown.edu/projects/hypertext/landow/victorian/victov.html

Whistler, James Abbott McNeill
http://www.oir.ucf.edu/wm/paint/auth/whistler/

William Blake Archive
http://jefferson.village.virginia.edu/blake/

Wright, Joseph
http://www.oir.ucf.edu/wm/paint/auth/wright/

Photography

Beaton, Cecil
http://www.harrowschool.org.uk/harrow/beaton.htm

Fox Talbot Museum
http://www.r-cube.co.uk/fox-talbot/

Pop Music

Bagism
http://www.bagism.com/

Behind Blue Eyes—A Life of Pete Townshend
http://www.thewho.net/Chris/Who20.html

Bhangra Network
http://www.bhangra.co.uk/index.htm

Blurspace
http://www.parlophone.co.uk/blur/

BM's Bob Marley Pages
http://www.jswd.net/marley/

Cemetery Gates
http://moz.pair.com/

Cliff Richard Home Page
http://www.dds.nl/~cliff/

Cure, The
http://weber.u.washington.edu/~pianoman/index.html

David Bowie: Teenage Wildlife
http://www.etete.com/Bowie/

Electric Magic
http://www.led-zeppelin.com/

Elvis Costello Home Page
http://east.isx.com/~schnitzi/ec/index.html

Gilbert and Sullivan Home Page
http://math.idbsu.edu/gas/GaS.html

Hypertext Who
http://www.thewho.net/hyper/

Illustrated Elton John Discography
http://ej.kylz.com/

Internet Beatles Album
http://www.primenet.com/~dhaber/bmain.html

Manic Street Preachers Home Page
http://www.tmtm.com/manics/

Official Oasis Home Page
http://www.oasisinet.com/

Pink Floyd—Set the Controls
http://www.mtnlake.com/~robp/floyd1.html

Punk Page
http://www.webtrax.com/punk/

Queen Home Page
http://queen-fip.com/

Real Jamaica Ska
http://www.slip.net/~skajam/

Reggae Update
http://www.earthchannel.com/reggaesupersite/

Rolling Stones: Get Yer Ya-Ya's Out
http://homepage.seas.upenn.edu/~demarco/stones/breakfast.html

Shrine to the Sex Pistols
http://pcstraining.uts.ohio-state.edu/consult/decarlo.7/pistols.htm

Slowhand's Realm
http://www.geocities.com/SunsetStrip/Towers/8488/index.html

Tuff Gong
http://www.bobmarley-foundation.com/main.html

Van Morrison Home Page
http://www.harbour.sfu.ca/~hayward/van/

Theatre

Hamlet
http://the-tech.mit.edu/Shakespeare/Tragedy/hamlet/hamlet.html

Howerd, Frankie
http://www.carryonline.com/carry/howerd.html

King Lear
http://the-tech.mit.edu/Shakespeare/Tragedy/kinglear/kinglear.html

Major Barbara by Bernard Shaw
http://www.best.com/~hansen/DrPseudocryptonym/Shaw-MajorBarbara.html

Misalliance
http://www.ul.cs.cmu.edu/gutenberg/etext97/msali10.txt

Official Sir Anthony Hopkins Page
http://www.nasser.net/osahp-html/osahp.html

Olivier, Laurence
http://www.reelclassics.com/Actors/Oliver/olivier.htm

Oroonoko
http://english.hss.cmu.edu/fiction/oroonoko/

Oscariana
http://www.jonno.com/oscariana/1.html

Peter and Wendy by J M Barrie
http://www.hoboes.com/html/FireBlade/Peter/chapter1.html

Peter Pan
http://www.inform.umd.edu/EdRes/ReadingRoom/Fiction/Barrie/PeterPan/

Poems of Oscar Wilde
http://www.cc.columbia.edu/acis/bartleby/wilde/

Pygmalion
http://www.cc.columbia.edu/acis/bartleby/shaw/

Redgrave, Vanessa
http://www.geocities.com/Hollywood/9766/redgrave.html

Rosencrantz and Guildenstern Are Dead
http://www.susqu.edu/ac-depts/arts-sci/english/lharris/class/stoppard/rose.htm

Royal Academy of Dramatic Art
http://rada.drama.ac.uk/

Royal Court Theatre
http://www.royal-court.org.uk/

Royal Shakespeare Company
http://www.stratford.co.uk/rsc/

Shakespeare's Globe
http://www.rdg.ac.uk/globe/Globe.html

Sir Derek Jacobi Home Page
http://www.dabbler.com/jacobi/home.html

The City Heiress
http://etext.lib.virginia.edu/etcbin/browse-mixed-new?id=BehCity&tag=public&images=images/modeng&data=/texts/english/modeng/parsed

Trevor Nunn Profile
http://www.achievement.org/autodoc/page/nun0pro-1

British History

1956—The Suez Crisis and the Peacekeeping Debut
http://www.screen.com/mnet/eng/med/class/teamedia/peace/Part1/P1-11.htm

Abdication Crisis
http://web.bham.ac.uk/maddendp/abdicatn.htm

Anglo-Saxon Chronicle
http://sunsite.berkeley.edu/OMACL/Anglo/

Arthur of Britain
http://www.angelfire.com/ak/auden/arthur.html

Ashmolean Museum
http://www.ashmol.ox.ac.uk/

Battle of Naseby 1645
http://web.ukonline.co.uk/glenn.foard/index.html

Bolingbroke, Henry St John
http://socserv2.socsci.mcmaster.ca/~econ/ugcm/3ll3/bolingbroke/index.html

Camelot Project
http://www.lib.rochester.edu:80/camelot/CPHOME.stm

Castle of Otranto, The
http://www.ul.cs.cmu.edu/gutenberg/etext96/cotrt10.txt

Chamberlain, Sir Joseph Austen
http://www.nobel.se/laureates/peace-1925-1-bio.html

Collins, Michael
http://www.thebigfella.com/texts/history.html

Commemoration of the Great Famine
http://www.toad.net/~sticker/nosurrender/PotatCom.html

Conquest of Ireland
http://www.fordham.edu/halsall/source/geraldwales1.html

Considerations on the Propriety of Imposing Taxes in the British Colonies
http://odur.let.rug.nl/~usa/D/1751-1775/stampact/consid.htm

Corn Laws by T R Malthus
http://www.yale.edu/lawweb/avalon/econ/corframe.htm

Country Joe McDonald's Florence Nightingale Tribute
http://www.dnai.com/~borneo/nightingale/

Duke of Wellington's Correspondence
http://www.wtj.com/pl/pages/welling2.htm

Earl of Shaftesbury, Anthony Ashley Cooper
http://www.utm.edu/research/iep/s/shaftes.htm

Edmund Burke: Speech on Conciliation with America
http://odur.let.rug.nl/~usa/D/1751-1775/libertydebate/burk.htm

English Civil War
http://history.idbsu.edu/westciv/english

Extracts from the Declaration of Rights (February 1689)
http://history.hanover.edu/early/decright.htm

Freemasonry on the Internet
http://www.chrysalis.org/masonry/

Glorious Revolution of 1688
http://www.lawsch.uga.edu/~glorious/

Gunpowder Plot Pages
http://www.bcpl.lib.md.us/~cbladey/guy/html/main.html

Hadrian's Wall
http://www.northumbria-tourist-board.org.uk/hadrian/

Hampton Court Palace
http://www.the-eye.com/hcintro.htm

HMS Victory
http://home.att.net/~ronfraser/

Industrial Revolution: A Trip to the Past
http://members.aol.com/mhirotsu/kevin/trip2.html

International Churchill Societies Online
http://www.winstonchurchill.org/

Kells, Book of
http://www.exotique.com/fringe/art/symbolic/BookKell/kells.htm

King George III—Proclamation of Rebellion, 1775
http://douglass.speech.nwu.edu/proc-a52.htm

Landings of Caesar in Britain, 55 and 54 BC
http://www.athenapub.com/caesar1.htm

Laws of William the Conqueror
http://www.fordham.edu/halsall/source/will1-lawsb.html

'Lectures on The Industrial Revolution'
http://socserv2.socsci.mcmaster.ca/~econ/ugcm/3ll3/toynbee/indrev

Letter from a Farmer Regarding the Townshend Act
http://odur.let.rug.nl/~usa/D/1751-1775/townshend/dickII.htm

Letters and Dispatches of Lord Horatio Nelson
http://www.wtj.com/pl/pages/nelson2.htm

Life of the Industrial Worker in 19th-Century England
http://ab.edu/~delcol-l/worker.html

Lollards
http://www.knight.org/advent/cathen/09333a.htm

Magna Carta
http://www.yale.edu/lawweb/avalon/magframe.htm

Mary Rose
http://www.compulink.co.uk/~mary-rose/

Memoirs of General Savary, the Duke of Rovigo
http://www.wtj.com/pl/pages/savary.htm

Munich Pact
http://www.yale.edu/lawweb/avalon/imt/munich1.htm

Murder of Thomas Becket, 1170
http://www.ibiscom.com/becket.htm#TOP

Mutiny on the HMS Bounty
http://wavefront.wavefront.com/~pjlareau/bounty1.html

Neville Chamberlain WAVS
http://earthstation1.simplenet.com/Chamberlain.html

Nightingale Letters
http://www.kumc.edu/service/clendening/florence/florence.html

Oates's Plot
http://www.knight.org/advent/cathen/11173c.htm

Our Modern Commonwealth
http://www.rhouse.co.uk/rhouse/rcs/modcom/

Paris, Matthew
http://www.knight.org/advent/cathen/11499a.htm

Past Features—Britain
http://www.buckinghamgate.com/events/features/past-features.html

Peel, Sir Robert
http://madhatter.chch.ox.ac.uk/chch/people/peel.html

Philosophy of the Manufacturers, 1835
http://www.fordham.edu/halsall/mod/1835ure.html

Plea for Atheism
http://www.infidels.org/library/historical/charles-bradlaugh/plea-for-atheism.html

'Reflections on the Revolution In France'
http://english-www.hss.cmu.edu/18th/burke.txt

Regency Fashion Page
http://locutus.ucr.edu/~cathy/reg3.html

Resolutions of the Stamp Act Congress
http://odur.let.rug.nl/~usa/D/1751-1775/stampact/sa.htm

RMS Titanic, Inc
http://www.titanic-online.com/

Robert Owen: 'A New View of Society'
http://socserv2.socsci.mcmaster.ca/~econ/ugcm/3ll3/owen/index.html

Roman Military Sites in Britain
http://www.morgue.demon.co.uk/index.htm

Secrets of the Norman Invasion
http://www.cablenet.net/pages/book/index.htm

Selected Poetry of Matthew Prior (1664-1721)
http://library.utoronto.ca/www/utel/rp/authors/prior.html

Social Contract
http://www.utm.edu/research/iep/s/soc-cont.htm

South Sea Bubble
http://is.dal.ca/~dmcneil/sketch.html

Speech Delivered by King William of England to Parliament
http://odur.let.rug.nl/~usa/D/1701-1725/england/french.htm

Speeches of Winston Churchill Sounds Page
http://earthstation1.simplenet.com/churchil.html

St Edward the Confessor
http://www.knight.org/advent/cathen/05322a.htm

Thomas Paine National Historical Association
http://www.mediapro.net/cdadesign/paine/

Thomas Paine: American Crisis, 1780-1783
http://odur.let.rug.nl/~usa/D/1776-1800/paine/AC/crisisxx.htm

Timeline of Arthurian Britain
http://www.britannia.com/history/timearth.html

Tolpuddle
http://www.dorset-cc.gov.uk/tolpudd.htm

True Interest of America
http://odur.let.rug.nl/~usa/D/1776-1800/libertydebate/inglis.htm

Views of the Famine
http://vassun.vassar.edu/~sttaylor/FAMINE/

'Wages Theory of the Anti-Corn Law League, The'
http://leftside.uwc.ac.za/Archive/1881-ls/ls07.htm

Walter Bagehot: 'A New Standard of Value'
http://socserv2.socsci.mcmaster.ca/~econ/ugcm/3ll3/jevons/bagehot.htm

Welcome to the John Hampden Society
http://www.westberks.demon.co.uk/jhs/

William Pitt: Speech on the Stamp Act
http://odur.let.rug.nl/~usa/D/1751-1775/stampact/sapitt.htm

Exploration

Bonington.com
http://www.bonington.com/index2.htm

Cook's First Voyage 1768-1771
http://pacific.vita.org/pacific/cook/cook1.htm

Dampier, William
http://pacific.vita.org/pacific/dampier/dampier.htm

Endeavour
http://www.greenwichuk.com/endeavour/

Fiennes, Sir Ranulph
http://www.speakers.co.uk/6071.htm

Livingstone—Man of Africa
http://www.rmplc.co.uk/eduweb/sites/blantyre/living/livmenu.html

Missionary Travels and Researches in South Africa by David Livingstone
http://src.doc.ic.ac.uk/media/literary/collections/project-gutenberg/gutenberg/etext97/mtrav10.txt

William Baffin and Robert Bylot—1615, 1616
http://www.schoolnet.ca/collections/arctic/explore/baffin.htm

The Monarchy

Althorp
http://www.althorp-house.co.uk/welcome.html

British Monarchy
http://www.royal.gov.uk/

Duke of York
http://www.royal.gov.uk/family/york.htm

Funeral of Diana, Princess of Wales
http://earthstation1.simplenet.com/Princess-Diana.html

Her Majesty Queen Elizabeth the Queen Mother
http://www.royal.gov.uk/family/mother.htm

Her Majesty the Queen
http://www.royal.gov.uk/family/hmqueen.htm

Prince Edward
http://www.royal.gov.uk/family/edward.htm

Prince of Wales
http://www.royal.gov.uk/family/wales.htm

Prince Philip, Duke of Edinburgh
http://www.royal.gov.uk/family/philip.htm

Prince's Trust
http://www.princes-trust.org.uk/n3-index.htm

Princess Royal
http://www.royal.gov.uk/family/royal.htm

St James's Palace
http://www.royal.gov.uk/palaces/stjamess.htm

Windsor Castle
http://www.hotelnet.co.uk/windsor/home.htm

War

Battle of Trafalgar
http://www.compulink.co.uk/~flagship/battle.htm

D-Day
http://www.pbs.org/wgbh/pages/amex/dday/index.html

Imperial War Museum
http://www.iwm.org.uk/

'Napoleon and England'
http://www.napoleon.org/us/us-cd/bib/articles/textes/SN400/us-SN400-napoleon-anglet.html

Radio Broadcast of the D-Day Landing at Normandy
http://www.otr.com/hicks.html

Royal British Legion
http://www.britishlegion.org.uk/

Use of Poison Gas on the Western Front
http://www.lib.byu.edu/~rdh/wwi/1915/chlorgas.html

Language

Brief History of the English Language
http://www.m-w.com/about/look.htm

Etymological Dictionary of the Gaelic Language
http://www.smo.uhi.ac.uk/gaidhlig/faclair/macbain

Gaelic and Gaelic Culture
http://sunsite.unc.edu/gaelic/gaelic.html

Labyrinth Library: Middle English Bookcase
http://www.georgetown.edu/labyrinth/library/me/me.html

Modern English to Old English Vocabulary
http://www.mun.ca/Ansaxdat/vocab/wordlist.html

Welsh Course
http://www.cs.brown.edu/fun/welsh/home.html

Word Page
http://users.aol.com/jomnet/words.html

World Wide Words
http://www.quinion.demon.co.uk/words/index.htm

Literature

A S Byatt's Possession
http://www.sjsu.edu/depts/jwss.old/possession/

Alice's Adventures in Wonderland by Lewis Carroll
http://www.cstone.net/library/alice/aliceinwonderland.html

American Chesterton Society
http://www.chesterton.org/

Arbuthnot, John
http://www-history.mcs.st-and.ac.uk/history/Mathematicians/Arbuthnot.html

Auden, W H
http://www.lit.kobe-u.ac.jp/~hishika/auden.htm

'Ballad of Reading Gaol, The'
http://www.bibliomania.com/Fiction/wilde/ReadingGaol/index.html

Ballard, J G
http://www.geocities.com/Area51/Corridor/4085/ballard.html

Barnes, Julian
http://alexia.lis.uiuc.edu/~roberts/barnes/home.htm

Beggar's Opera
http://darkwing.uoregon.edu/~rbear/beggar.html

Bentham, Jeremy
http://socserv2.socsci.mcmaster.ca/~econ/ugcm/3ll3/bentham/index.html

'Beowulf'
http://etext.lib.virginia.edu/cgibin/browse-mixed?id=AnoBeow&tag=public&images=images/modeng&data=/lv1/Archive/eng-parsed

'Best' of Edward Gibbon's Decline and Fall of the Roman Empire
http://alumni.caltech.edu/~zimm/gibbon.html

Betjeman, John
http://ourworld.compuserve.com/homepages/StevePhillips/homepage.htm

Black Beauty by Anna Sewell
http://tom.cs.cmu.edu/cgi-bin/book/lookup?num=271

Blue Fairy Book, The
http://etext.lib.virginia.edu/etcbin/browse-mixed-new?id=LanBlue&images=images/modeng&data=/texts/english/modeng/parsed&tag=public

Booker Prize Winners and Shortlisted Title Page
http://www.suntech.com/brad/booker.htm

Bride of Lammermoor, The
http://www.ul.cs.cmu.edu/gutenberg/etext96/brlam10.txt

Brontë Sisters
http://www2.sbbs.se/hp/cfalk/bronteng.htm

'Caedmon's Hymn': Northumbrian version
http://www.georgetown.edu/labyrinth/library/oe/texts/a32.1.html

Can You Forgive Her?
http://etext.lib.virginia.edu/etcbin/browse-mixed-new?id=TroForg&tag=public&images=images/modeng&data=/texts/english/modeng/parsed

Canterbury Tales
http://etext.lib.virginia.edu/cgibin/toccer?id=Cha2Can&tag=public&images=images/modeng&data =/lv1/Archive/mideng-parsed&part=0

Captain Frederick Marryat—A Biography
http://www.cronab.demon.co.uk/mary.htm

Case Book of Sherlock Holmes, The by Arthur Conan Doyle
http://wiretap.spies.com/ftp.items/Library/Classic/casebook.dyl

'Charge of the Light Brigade'
http://etext.lib.virginia.edu/britpo/tennyson/TenChar.html

Chimes, The
http://etext.lib.virginia.edu/cgibin/browse-mixed?id=DicChim&tag=public&images=images/modeng&data=/lv1/Archive/eng-parsed

Christie, Agatha
http://members.aol.com/mg4273/chris1.htm

Christmas Carol, A
http://etext.lib.virginia.edu/cgibin/browse-mixed?id=DicChri&tag=public&images=images/modeng&data=/lv1/Archive/eng-parsed

Coleridge Companion: An Introduction to the Major Poems and the Biographia Literaria
http://www.uottawa.ca/~phoenix/ccomp.htm

Collected Poems of Rupert Brooke
http://src.doc.ic.ac.uk/media/literary/collections/project–gutenberg/gutenberg/etext95/rupbr10.txt

Compleat Angler, or the Contemplative Man's Recreation, The
http://www.ul.cs.cmu.edu/gutenberg/etext96/tcang10.txt

Complete Collection of Poems by Robert Louis Stevenson
http://www.rit.edu/~exb1874/mine/stevenson/stevenson–ind.html

Complete Collection of Poems by Rudyard Kipling
http://www.rit.edu/%7Eexb1874/mine/kipling/kipling–ind.html

Complete Poetical Works of Percy Bysshe Shelley
http://www.cc.columbia.edu/acis/bartleby/shelley/

Complete Poetical Works of William Wordsworth
http://www.cc.columbia.edu/acis/bartleby/wordsworth/index.html

Complete Shorter Fiction of Oscar Wilde
http://www.bibliomania.com/Fiction/wilde/stories/index.html

Conan Doyles' The Memoirs of Sherlock Holmes: electronic edition
http://www.hti.umich.edu/bin/pd-idx?type=header&id=DoyleMemoi

Confessions of an English Opium-Eater by Thomas de Quincey
http://www.lycaeum.org/~sputnik/Ludlow/Texts/Opium/

Cricket on the Hearth, The
http://wiretap.spies.com/ftp.items/Library/Classic/cricket.txt

Cyfarwydd—Storyteller
http://snowcrash.cymru.net/~nwi/cfarwydd.htm

Daniel Defoe: 'Giving Alms No Charity'
http://socserv2.socsci.mcmaster.ca/~econ/ugcm/3ll3/defoe/index.html

de la Mare, Walter
http://www.columbia.edu/acis/bartleby/mbp/48.html

Diary of a Nobody by George Grossmith and Weedon Grossmith
http://src.doc.ic.ac.uk/media/literary/collections/project–gutenberg/gutenberg/etext97/dnbdy10.txt

Dickens House Museum
http://www.rmplc.co.uk/orgs/dickens/dickenshouse/

Dickens, Charles
http://www.stg.brown.edu/projects/hypertext/landow/victorian/dickens/dickbioov.html

Dombey and Son
http://www.bibliomania.com/Fiction/dickens/Dombey/index.html

Don Juan
http://english.hss.cmu.edu/poetry/don-juan.txt

Dr Jekyll and Mr Hyde
http://www.bibliomania.com/Fiction/stevensn/drjekyll/index.html

Dr Johnson and Fanny Burney
http://etext.lib.virginia.edu/etcbin/browse-mixed-new?id=BurJohn&images=images/modeng&data=/lv1/Archive/eng-parsed&tag=public

Drabble, Margaret
http://tile.net/drabble/

Dream Days
http://etext.lib.virginia.edu/cgibin/browse-mixed?id=GraDrea&tag=public&images=images/modeng&data=/lv1/Archive/eng-parsed

'Dream of the Rood'
http://www.georgetown.edu/labyrinth/library/oe/texts/a2.5.html#n4

Elizabeth Barrett Browning: An Overview
http://www.stg.brown.edu/projects/hypertext/landow/victorian/ebb/browning2ov.html

Elizabeth Gaskell—The Life of Charlotte Brontë
http://lang.nagoya-u.ac.jp/~matsuoka/EG-Charlotte-1.html

English Literature Main Page
http://humanitas.ucsb.edu/shuttle/english.html

Fairies and Fusiliers
http://www.cc.columbia.edu/acis/bartleby/graves/

Far from the Madding Crowd
http://www.bibliomania.com/Fiction/hardy/crowd/index.html

Fleming, Ian
http://www.mcs.net/~klast/www/fleming.html

Forster's A Room with a View
http://www.hti.umich.edu/bin/pd-idx?type=header&id=ForstRoomV

Forster's Howard's End
http://www.hti.umich.edu/bin/pd-idx?type=header&id=ForstHowar

Frankenstein
http://etext.lib.virginia.edu/etcbin/browse-mixed-new?id=SheFran&tag=public&images=images/modeng&data=/texts/english/modeng/parsed

Gaskell Web
http://lang.nagoya-u.ac.jp/~matsuoka/Gaskell.html

'George Eliot' by Virginia Woolf
http://www.cs.cmu.edu/People/mmbt/women/VW-Eliot.html

George Gissing, New Grub Street
http://lang.nagoya-u.ac.jp/~matsuoka/GG-NGS.html

George Gissing, The Private Papers of Henry Ryecroft
http://lang.nagoya-u.ac.jp/~matsuoka/GG-PPHR.html

Gissing, George
http://ernie.lang.nagoya-u.ac.jp/~matsuoka/Gissing.html

Godwin, William
http://www.english.upenn.edu/~jlynch/Frank/Godwin/bio.html

Golden Age, The
http://etext.lib.virginia.edu/cgibin/browse-mixed?id=GraGold&tag=public&images=images/modeng&data=/lv1/Archive/eng-parsed

Golden Key: The George MacDonald WWW Page
http://dspace.dial.pipex.com/town/plaza/ev90481/md-index.htm

Gormenghast (Castle) Page
http://www.gate.net/~zacharyp/gormenghast/

Graham Swift: An Overview
http://www.stg.brown.edu/projects/hypertext/landow/post/uk/gswift/gsov.html

Great Expectations
http://www.bibliomania.com/Fiction/dickens/greatexp/index.html

Guide to Samuel Johnson
http://www.english.upenn.edu/~jlynch/Johnson/Guide/

Gulliver's Travels
http://english-server.hss.cmu.edu/fiction/gulliver.txt

Hamlet
http://the-tech.mit.edu/Shakespeare/Tragedy/hamlet/hamlet.html

Herbert, George
http://www.luminarium.org/sevenlit/herbert/index.html

Heretics
http://ccel.wheaton.edu/c/chesterton/heretics/heretics.html

His Last Bow by Arthur Conan Doyle
http://wiretap.spies.com/ftp.items/Library/Classic/lastbow.dyl

History of Tom Jones, a Foundling by Henry Fielding
http://dev.library.utoronto.ca/utel/fiction/fieldingh-tj/tj-titlepage.html

Hopkins, Gerald Manley
http://www.knight.org/advent/cathen/16045b.htm

Hound of the Baskervilles, The
http://www.bibliomania.com/Fiction/Doyle/Hound/index.html

Hunting of the Snark—An Agony in Eight Fits, The
http://www.math.hr/~urbiha/LewisCarroll/eng-parsed.html

Hypertextualised Tolkien FAQ
http://www.daimi.aau.dk/~bouvin/tolkienfaq.html

Idylls of the King
http://www.ul.cs.cmu.edu/gutenberg/etext96/idyll10.txt

Invisible Man, The
http://etext.lib.virginia.edu/etcbin/browse-mixed-new?id=WelInvi&tag=public&images=images/modeng&data=/texts/english/modeng/parsed

Ivanhoe
http://etext.lib.virginia.edu/etcbin/browse-mixed-new?id=ScoIvan&tag=public&images=images/modeng&data=/texts/english/modeng/parsed

Jane Austen Information Page
http://uts.cc.utexas.edu/~churchh/janeinfo.html

Jane Austen: Emma
http://www.w3.org/hypertext/DataSources/bySubject/Literature/Gutenberg/etext9 4/emma10.txt

Jane Austen: Pride and Prejudice
http://www.bibliomania.com/Fiction/Austen/Pride/index.html

John Arbuthnot: 'An Argument for Divine Providence'
http://panoramix.univ-paris1.fr/CHPE/Textes/Arbuthnot/Arbuthnot.html

John Clare Page
http://human.ntu.ac.uk/foh/ems/clare.html

Jonathan Swift Essays
http://socserv2.socsci.mcmaster.ca/~econ/ugcm/3ll3/swift/index.html

Jude the Obscure
http://wiretap.spies.com/ftp.items/Library/Classic/jude.th

Jungle Book
http://wiretap.spies.com/ftp.items/Library/Classic/jungle.rk

Keats, John
http://www.cc.columbia.edu/acis/bartleby/keats/

Kidnapped
http://www.ul.cs.cmu.edu/gutenberg/etext96/kdnpd10.txt

King Lear
http://the-tech.mit.edu/Shakespeare/Tragedy/kinglear/kinglear.html

King Solomon's Mines
http://wiretap.spies.com/ftp.items/Library/Classic/solomon.hrh

Lady Chatterley's Lover
http://www.bibliomania.com/Fiction/dhl/chat/index.html

Lady Susan
http://www.pemberley.com/janeinfo/ladysusn.html

Lancelot and Elaine
http://etext.lib.virginia.edu/etcbin/browse-mixed-new?id=TenLanc&tag=public&images=images/modeng&data=/texts/english/modeng/parsed

Last Man, The
http://etext.lib.virginia.edu/etcbin/browse-mixed-new?id=SheLast&tag=public&images=images/modeng&data=/texts/english/modeng/parsed

Lawrence, D H
http://home.clara.net/rananim/lawrence/

Letters of Jane Austen—Brabourne Edition
http://www.pemberley.com/janeinfo/brablets.html

Lewis Carroll Home Page
http://www.lewiscarroll.org/carroll.html

Lewis, C S
http://cslewis. DrZeus.net/

Life and Opinions of Tristram Shandy, Gent, The
http://www.gifu-u.ac.jp/~masaru/TS/contents.html#start

Life of Nelson
http://www.ul.cs.cmu.edu/gutenberg/etext97/hnlsn10.txt

Life of Scott by J G Lockhart
http://eng.hss.cmu.edu/fiction/life-of-scott.txt

Little Princess, A
http://wiretap.spies.com/ftp.items/Library/Classic/crewe.txt

Lord Jim
http://www.bibliomania.com/Fiction/conrad/LordJim/index.html

Lorna Doone: A Romance of Exmoor by R D Blackmore
http://src.doc.ic.ac.uk/media/literary/collections/project-gutenberg/gutenberg/etext97/lorna10.txt

Love and Friendship
http://www.pemberley.com/janeinfo/lovfrend.html

Mansfield Park
http://wiretap.spies.com/ftp.items/Library/Classic/mansfield.ja

Martin Amis Web
http://www.albion.edu/fac/engl/diedrick/amispge.htm

Martin Chuzzlewit
http://www.bibliomania.com/Fiction/dickens/Chuzzlewit/index.html

Marvell, Andrew
http://www.luminarium.org/sevenlit/marvell/index.html

Mary Shelley Resource Page
http://www.desert=fairy.com/maryshel.htm

Master of Ballantrae, The
http://www.ul.cs.cmu.edu/gutenberg/etext97/blntr10.txt

Mayor of Casterbridge, The
http://www.bibliomania.com/Fiction/hardy/mayor/index.html

Meredith, George
http://www.stg.brown.edu/projects/hypertext/landow/victorian/meredith/biograph.html

Meredith's The Ordeal of Richard Feverel
http://www.ul.cs.cmu.edu/books/MeredFever/ordeal.txt

Mill on the Floss, The
http://www.bibliomania.com/Fiction/eliot/mill/index.html

Milton, John
http://www.luminarium.org/sevenlit/milton/index.html

'Modest Proposal, A'
http://english-server.hss.cmu.edu/18th/swift-modest.txt

Moon and Sixpence by W Somerset Maugham
http://tom.cs.cmu.edu/cgi-bin/book/lookup?num=222

Moonstone, The
http://www.bibliomania.com/Fiction/collins/Moonstone/index.html

Mother Goose Pages
http://pubweb.acns.nwu.edu/~pfa/dreamhouse/nursery/rhymes.html

New Arabian Nights, The
http://www.ul.cs.cmu.edu/gutenberg/etext97/narab10.txt

Nicholas Nickleby
http://www.bibliomania.com/Fiction/dickens/Nickleby/index.html

Northanger Abbey
http://wiretap.spies.com/ftp.items/Library/Classic/nabby.ja

Nostromo
http://www.bibliomania.com/Fiction/conrad/Nostromo/index.html

Of Human Bondage
http://www.bibliomania.com/Fiction/Maugham/Human/index.html

Orthodoxy
http://ccel.wheaton.edu/c/chesterton/orthodoxy/orthodoxy.html

Oscariana
http://www.jonno.com/oscariana/1.html

P G Wodehouse Fan Club
http://www.serv.net/~camel/wodehouse/

Page at Pooh Corner
http://chaos.trxinc.com/jmilne/Pooh/

Pair of Blue Eyes, A
http://www.ul.cs.cmu.edu/gutenberg/etext95/pblue10.txt

Pater, Walter
http://www.crl.com/~subir/pater/

Pearse, Patrick
http://wwwvms.utexas.edu/~jdana/pearsehist.html

Persuasion
http://wiretap.spies.com/ftp.items/Library/Classic/persuasion.ja

Peter Rabbit Web Site
http://www.peterrabbit.co.uk/

Phineas Finn
http://etext.lib.virginia.edu/etcbin/
browse-mixed-new?id=TroFinn&tag=public&images=images/modeng&data=/texts/english/modeng/parsed

Pickwick Papers, The
http://www.bibliomania.com/Fiction/dickens/Pickwick/index.html

Pilgrim's Progress
http://ccel.wheaton.edu/b/bunyan/pilgrims-progress/title.html

Poems of D H Lawrence
http://www.cc.columbia.edu/acis/bartleby/lawrence/

Poems of Gerard Manley Hopkins
http://www.cc.columbia.edu/acis/bartleby/hopkins/

Poems of Oscar Wilde
http://www.cc.columbia.edu/acis/bartleby/wilde/

Poems of Siegfried Sassoon
http://www.cc.columbia.edu/acis/bartleby/sassoon/

'Politics of T S Eliot, The'
http://www.frc.org/townhall/hall-of-fame/kirk/kirk182.html

Prince Otto
http://www.bibliomania.com/Fiction/stevensn/Otto

Princess and Curdie, The
http://sunsite.unc.edu/pub/docs/books/gutenberg/etext96/prcur10.txt

Princess, The
http://www.ul.cs.cmu.edu/gutenberg/etext97/prncs09.txt

Prisoner of Zenda by Anthony Hope
http://www.teachersoft.com/Library/lit/hope/contents.htm

Return of the Native
http://wiretap.spies.com/ftp.items/Library/Classic/native.th

Robin Hood Project
http://www.lib.rochester.edu:80/camelot/rh/rhhome.stm

Robinson Crusoe
http://www.bibliomania.com/Fiction/defoe/robin/index.html

Rose and the Ring, The
http://www.ul.cs.cmu.edu/gutenberg/etext97/rsrng10.txt

Rudyard Kipling: 'The White Man's Burden' and Its Critics
http://www.rochester.ican.net/~fjzwick/kipling/

Rushdie, Salman
http://www.crl.com/~subir/rushdie.html

Ruskin on Turner
http://www4.torget.se/artbin/art/oruskincontents.html

Ruskin, John
http://www.stg.brown.edu/projects/hypertext/landow/victorian/ruskin/ruskinov.html

Sassoon, Siegfried
http://www.geocities.com/CapitolHill/8103/index.html

'Seafarer, The'
http://www.georgetown.edu/labyrinth/library/oe/texts/a3.9.html

Seamus Heaney Page
http://sunsite.unc.edu/dykki/poetry/heaney/heaney-cov.html

Secret Agent, The
http://www.bibliomania.com/Fiction/conrad/agent/index.html

Secret Garden, The
http://wiretap.spies.com/ftp.items/Library/Classic/garden.txt

Secret Sharer, The
http://wiretap.spies.com/ftp.items/Library/Classic/sharer.txt

Selected Poetry and Prose of John Dryden
http://library.utoronto.ca/utel/rp/authors/dryden.html
This utoronto *site has associated sites for over 40 authors featured in this encyclopedia.*

Sentimental Journey through France and Italy, A
http://src.doc.ic.ac.uk/media/literary/collections/project-gutenberg/gutenberg/etext97/senjr09.txt

Shavian Ideal: George Bernard Shaw's Man and Superman
http://www.fas.harvard.edu/~art/super1.html

She
http://wiretap.spies.com/ftp.items/Library/Classic/she.hrh

Sherlockian HolmePage
http://watserv1.uwaterloo.ca/~credmond/sh.html

Shropshire Lad, A
http://www.cc.columbia.edu/acis/bartleby/housman/

Silas Marner
http://www.inform.umd.edu/EdRes/ReadingRoom/Fiction/Eliot/SilasMarner/

Silva by John Evelyn
http://www.british-trees.com/p10.htm

Sir Walter Scott: Heart of Mid-Lothian
http://www.ul.cs.cmu.edu/books/ScottLothi/heart-lothian.txt

Sir Walter Scott: Waverley
http://english-www.hss.cmu.edu/fiction/waverley.txt

Sons and Lovers by D H Lawrence
http://www.bibliomania.com/Fiction/dhl/Sons/index.html

Stanley Kubrick's A Clockwork Orange
http://jake.chem.unsw.edu.au/~michaels/Orange/

Study in Scarlet, A
http://etext.lib.virginia.edu/cgibin/
browse-mixed?id=DoyScar&tag=public&images=images/modeng&data=/lv1/Archive/eng-parsed

Swinburne, Algernon Charles
http://www.stg.brown.edu/projects/hypertext/landow/victorian/decadence/swinburne/acsov.html

Sylvie and Bruno
http://www.bibliomania.com/Fiction/Caroll/Sylvie

Tale of Two Cities
http://www.bibliomania.com/Fiction/dickens/TaleOf2Cities/index.html

Tales From Shakespeare
http://eldred.ne.mediaone.net/cml/tfs.html

Tenant of Wildfell Hall, The
http://www.bibliomania.com/Fiction/Bronte/Tenant

Tennyson, Alfred Lord
http://www.stg.brown.edu/projects/hypertext/landow/victorian/tennyson/tennyov.html

Thirty-Nine Steps
http://www.cc.columbia.edu/acis/bartleby/buchan/

Thomas Carlyle: An Overview
http://www.stg.brown.edu/projects/hypertext/landow/victo rian/carlyle/carlyleov.html

Thomas Hardy Resource Library
http://pages.ripco.com/~mws//hardy.html

Thomas, Dylan
http://pcug.org.au/~wwhatman/dylan-thomas.html

Three Men in a Boat by Jerome K Jerome
http://src.doc.ic.ac.uk/media/literary/collections/project-gutenberg/gutenberg/etext95/3boat10.txt

Through the Looking Glass by Lewis Carroll
http://www.cstone.net/library/glass/alice-lg.html

Time Machine, The
http://www.inform.umd.edu/EdRes/ReadingRoom/Fiction/Wells/TimeMachine/

Treasure Island
http://www.bibliomania.com/Fiction/stevensn/island/index.html

Treatise on Parents and Children, A
http://www.ul.cs.cmu.edu/gutenberg/etext97/topac10.txt

Tribute to William Golding
http://www.geocities.com/Athens/Forum/6249/index.html

Trollope's Lady Anna: electronic edition
http://www.hti.umich.edu/bin/pd-idx?type=header&id=TrollLadyA

TSEbase: The Online Concordance to T S Eliot's Collected Poems
http://www.missouri.edu/~enggf/tsebase.html

Vanity Fair
http://www.ul.cs.cmu.edu/gutenberg/etext96/vfair10.txt

Vicar of Wakefield, The
http://etext.lib.virginia.edu/cgibin/browse-mixed?id=GolVica&tag=public&images=images/modeng&data=/lv1/Archive/eng-parsed

Virginia Woolf and the Bloomsbury Group
http://www.lm.com/~kaydee/Bloomsbury.html

Virginia Woolf Chronology
http://www.aianet.or.jp/~orlando/VWW/vwlife.html

Vision of Piers Plowman
http://etext.lib.virginia.edu/cgibin/browse-mixed?id=LanPier&tag=public&images=images/mideng&data=/lv1/Archive/mideng-parsed

Voyage Out, The
http://wiretap.spies.com/ftp.items/Library/Classic/voyage.vw

W H Auden's Poetry
http://www.sat.dundee.ac.uk/~arb/speleo/auden.html

War of the Worlds, The
http://www.fourmilab.ch/etexts/www/warworlds/warw.html

Washington Square
http://www.newpaltz.edu/~hathaway/washsq.html

Water Babies, The
http://src.doc.ic.ac.uk/media/literary/collections/project-gutenberg/gutenberg/etext97/wtrbs10.txt

Watsons, The
http://www.pemberley.com/janeinfo/watsons1.html

Weldon, Fay
http://tile.net/weldon/index.html

Welsh Literature: Introduction
http://www.britannia.com/wales/lit/intro.html

Wessex poems and Other Verses
http://www.cc.columbia.edu/acis/bartleby/hardy/

'What Won't Go Away: Waterland and Traditional Psychotherapy'
http://www.student.gu.se/~jawi0004/grahams.html

Wilkie Collins Appreciation Page
http://www.ozemail.com.au/~drgrigg/wilkie.html

William Blake Archive
http://jefferson.village.virginia.edu/blake/

Wind in the Willows, The
http://etext.lib.virginia.edu/etcbin/browse-mixed-new?id=GraWind&images=images/modeng&data=/lv1/Archive/eng-parsed&tag=public

Woman in White, The
http://www.bibliomania.com/Fiction/collins/WomanInWhite/index.html

Woodlanders, The
http://www.ul.cs.cmu.edu/gutenberg/etext96/woodl10.txt

Wuthering Heights
http://www.bibliomania.com/Fiction/Bronte/Wuthering/index.html

SCIENCE AND TECHNOLOGY

Astronomy

Adams, John Couch
http://www-history.mcs.st-and.ac.uk/history/Mathematicians/Adams.html

Airy, George Biddell
http://www-history.mcs.st-and.ac.uk/%7Ehistory/Mathematicians/Airy.html

Arthur C Clarke Foundation
http://www.cequel.co.uk/acclarke/

Eddington, Arthur Stanley
http://www-groups.dcs.st-and.ac.uk/history/Mathematicians/Eddington.html

Flamsteed, John
http://www-history.mcs.st-and.ac.uk/history/Mathematicians/Flamsteed.html

Halley, Edmond
http://es.rice.edu/ES/humsoc/Galileo/Catalog/Files/halley.html

Herschel, Caroline
http://www.scottlan.edu/lriddle/women/herschel.htm

Little Green Men, White Dwarfs, or Pulsars?
http://www.bigear.org/vol1no1/burnell.htm

Maskelyne, Nevil
http://www-groups.dcs.st-and.ac.uk/history/Mathematicians/Maskelyne.html

Nuffield Radio Astronomy Observatories
http://www.jb.man.ac.uk/

Royal Greenwich Observatory
http://www.ast.cam.ac.uk/RGO/

Biology

Crick, Francis Harry Compton
http://kroeber.anthro.mankato.msus.edu/bio/francis-crick.htm

Darwin Buffet
http://eve.chem.wesleyan.edu/Chem350/Buffet/default.html

Darwin, Charles
http://www.literature.org/Works/Charles-Darwin

Darwin, Charles
userwww.sfsu.edu/~rsauzier/Darwin.html

Dawkins, Richard
http://www.spacelab.net/~catalj/

Hopkins, Sir Frederick Gowland
http://web.calstatela.edu/faculty/nthomas/hopkins.htm

Chemistry

Davy Discovers Sodium and Potassium
http://dbhs.wvusd.k12.ca.us/Chem-History/Davy-Na&K-1808.html

Electrical Decomposition by Michael Faraday
http://dbhs.wvusd.k12.ca.us/Chem-History/Faraday-electrochem.html

Joseph Priestley on Making Carbonated Water (1772)
http://dbhs.wvusd.k12.ca.us/Chem-History/Priestley-1772/Priestley-1772-Start.html

Molecular Expressions: The Pesticide Collection
http://micro.magnet.fsu.edu/pesticides/index.html

Royal Society of Chemistry
http://www.rsc.org/

Computing

Alan Turing Home Page
http://www.turing.org.uk/turing/

Babbage, Charles
http://ei.cs.vt.edu/~history/Babbage.html

Earth Science and Environment

Charles Elton: 'Early Forms of Landholding'
http://socserv2.socsci.mcmaster.ca/~econ/ugcm/3ll3/misc/elton.html

Corn Laws by T R Malthus
http://www.yale.edu/lawweb/avalon/econ/corframe.htm

Countryside Commission
http://www.countryside.gov.uk/

English Heritage
http://www.english-heritage.org.uk/dminterface/dmindex.asp

English Nature—Facts and Figures
http://www.english-nature.org.uk/facts.htm

Friends of the Earth Home Page
http://www.foe.co.uk/

Lord Boyd Orr of Brechin
http://www.nobel.se/laureates/peace-1949-bio.html

Royal Agricultural Society of England
http://www.rase.org.uk/

Royal Horticultural Society
http://www.rhs.org.uk/

Schumacher Society
http://www.oneworld.org/schumachersoc/

General Science

Fisheries
http://www.fao.org/WAICENT/FAOINFO/FISHERY/FISHERY. HTM

From Smithson to Smithsonian—Birth of an Institution
http://www.sil.si.edu/exhibits/smithson/intro.html

History of the Royal Society
http://www-history.mcs.st-and.ac.uk/~history/Societies/RShistory.html

Royal Institution
http://www.ri.ac.uk/

Science Museum—Online Features
http://www.nmsi.ac.uk/on-line/

Barrow, Isaac
http://www-groups.dcs.st-and.ac.uk/history/Mathematicians/Barrow.html

Bayes, Thomas
http://www-groups.dcs.st-and.ac.uk/history/Mathematicians/Bayes.html

Boole, George
http://www-history.mcs.st-and.ac.uk/history/Mathematicians/Boole.html

Gosset, William
http://www-history.mcs.st-and.ac.uk/history/Mathematicians/Gosset.html

Green, George
http://www-groups.dcs.st-and.ac.uk/history/Mathematicians/Green.html

Hardy, Godfrey Harold
http://www-groups.dcs.st-and.ac.uk/history/Mathematicians/Hardy.html

Oughtred, William
http://www-history.mcs.st-and.ac.uk/history/Mathematicians/Oughtred.html

Pearson, Karl
http://www-groups.dcs.st-and.ac.uk/history/Mathematicians/Pearson.html

Simpson, Thomas
http://www-groups.dcs.st-and.ac.uk/history/Mathematicians/Simpson.html

Sylvester, James Joseph
http://www-history.mcs.st-and.ac.uk/history/Mathematicians/Sylvester.html

Venn, John
http://www-groups.dcs.st-and.ac.uk/history/Mathematicians/Venn.html

Medicine

Black Death
http://history.idbsu.edu/westciv/plague/

Childhood Infections—Rabies
http://kidshealth.org/parent/common/rabies.html

Creutzfeldt-Jakob Disease & Bovine Spongiform Encephalopathy
http://www.open.gov.uk/doh/cjd/cjd1.htm

Ecstasy.org
http://www.ecstasy.org/

Gulf War Syndrome
http://www.cais.com/cfs-news/gulfwar.htm#TALK

Repetitive Strain Injury
http://engr-www.unl.edu/ee/eeshop/rsi.html

Tobacco Alert
http://www.who.ch/programmes/psa/toh/Alert/apr96/index.html

Physics

Aston Isotopes and Atomic Weights

Blackett, Patrick Maynard Stuart
http://www.nobel.se/laureates/physics-1948-1-bio.html

Hawking, Stephen
http://www.damtp.cam.ac.uk/DAMTP/user/hawking/home.html

Heat is a Form of Motion: An Experiment in Boring Cannon
http://dbhs.wvusd.k12.ca.us/Chem-History/Rumford-1798.html

Heaviside, Oliver
http://www-history.mcs.st-and.ac.uk/history/Mathematicians/Heaviside.html

Jeans, Sir James Hopwood
http://www-groups.dcs.st-and.ac.uk/history/Mathematicians/Jeans.html

Maxwell, James Clerk
http://www-history.mcs.st-and.ac.uk/history/Mathematicians/Maxwell.html

Newton's birthplace: Woolsthorpe Manor, Lincolnshire
http://wwwcn.cern.ch/~mcnab/n/W/index.html

Rutherford on the Discovery of Alpha and Beta Radiation
http://dbhs.wvusd.k12.ca.us/Chem-History/Rutherford-Alpha&Beta.html

Supersonic Spies
http://www.pbs.org/wgbh/nova/supersonic/

Thomson on the Number of Corpuscles in an Atom
http://dbhs.wvusd.k12.ca.us/Chem-History/Thomson-1906/Thomson-1906.html

Visit to James Clerk Maxwell's House
http://www-history.mcs.st-and.ac.uk/~history/HistTopics/Maxwell-House.html

Whitehead, Alfred North
http://plato.stanford.edu/entries/whitehead/

Technology

Alexander Graham Bell's Path to the Telephone
http://jefferson.village.virginia.edu/albell/homepage.html

Henry Bessemer FRS, An Autobiography
http://www.bibliomania.com/NonFiction/Bessemer/Autobiography/

Independent Television Commission
http://www.itc.org.uk/

JET World Wide Web Page
http://www.jet.uk/

Penney, William George
http://www-groups.dcs.st-and.ac.uk/history/Mathematicians/Penney.html

Thames Barrier
http://www.environment-agency.gov.uk/info/barrier.html

Young, Arthur M
http://www.arthuryoung.com/

Transport

Build a Real Working Hovercraft
http://www.flash.net/~spartech/ReekoScience/ExpHoverCraft.htm

European Railway Server
http://mercurio.iet.unipi.it/home.html

National Railway Museum, York
http://www.nmsi.ac.uk/nrm/page2.html

Railtrack—The Heart of the Railway
http://www.railtrack.co.uk/home.html

Welcome to BAA
http://www.baa.co.uk/

Society and Social Sciences Anthropology Asatru—Norse Paganism
http://www.religioustolerance.org/asatru.htm

Malinowski, Bronislaw
http://kroeber.anthro.mankato.msus.edu/bio/Malinowski.htm

Piltdown Man
http://www.tiac.net/users/cri/piltdown.html

Tylor, Edward
http://kroeber.anthro.mankato.msus.edu/bio/tylor.htm

SOCIETY

Business and Economics

Adam Smith: Excerpt from The Wealth of Nations: Regarding the Cost of Empire
http://odur.let.rug.nl/~usa/D/1776-1800/adamsmith/wealth02.htm

Bank of England—Banknote Printing
http://www.bankofengland.co.uk/print.htm#top

CA Net
http://www.dss.gov.uk/ca/index.htm

Economic Consequences of the Peace, The
http://socserv2.socsci.mcmaster.ca/~econ/ugcm/3ll3/keynes/peace

Office of Fair Trading
http://www.oft.gov.uk/

Oftel
http://www.oftel.gov.uk/

OFWAT—Office of Water Services
http://www.open.gov.uk/ofwat/index.htm

Secrets of Making Money
http://www.pbs.org/wgbh/nova/moolah/

'Wealth of Nations, The'
http://english-www.hss.cmu.edu/18th/wealth-of-nations.txt

Education
Amy and Jon's Oxford University Tour

Harrow School Ezine
http://www.harrowschool.org.uk/

Independent Schools Information Service
http://www.isis.org.uk/

Nothing Matters
http://www.serve.com/Nowhere/

Open University
http://www.open.ac.uk/

University of Oxford Museums
http://www.ox.ac.uk/museums.html

Varsity Online
http://www.varsity.cam.ac.uk/

Media

75 years of the BBC
http://www.bbc.co.uk/info/75years.htm

BBC Online
http://www.bbc.co.uk

Channel Four
http://www.channel4.com/

Daily Telegraph, The
http://www.telegraph.co.uk

Guardian, The
http://www.guardian.co.uk

Independent, The
http://www.independent.co.uk

Independent Television Commission
http://www.itc.org.uk/

Times, The
http://www.the-times.co.uk

Welcome to ITV Online
http://www.itv.co.uk

Religion

Archbishop of Canterbury
http://www.church-of-england.org/main/lambeth/abchome.htm

Autobiography of George Fox
http://ccel.wheaton.edu/fox/autobiography/autobiography.html

Bible Gateway
http://www.gospelcom.net/bible

Church of England
http://www.church-of-england.org/

Cuthbert, St
http://www.knight.org/advent/cathen/04578a.htm

Mission of St Augustine of Canterbury to the British
http://users.aol.com/butrousch/augustine/index.htm

Newman, John Henry
http://www.knight.org/advent/cathen/10794a.htm

On Pusey
http://www.stg.brown.edu/projects/hypertext/landow/victorian/religion/pusey.html

Oxford Movement
http://www.knight.org/advent/cathen/11370a.htm

Paley, William
http://www.utm.edu/research/iep/p/paley.htm

Religious Society of Friends
http://www.quaker.org/

Salvation Army
http://www.salvationarmy.org/aboutus.htm

Selected Poetry of John Henry Newman (Cardinal; 1801-1890)
http://library.utoronto.ca/www/utel/rp/authors/newman.html

Selected Poetry of John Wesley (1703-1791)
http://library.utoronto.ca/www/utel/rp/authors/wesleyj.html

Worldwide Study Bible
http://ccel.wheaton.edu/wwsb/index.html

General

10 Downing Street
http://www.number-10.gov.uk/index.html

About the National Trust
http://www.nationaltrust.org.uk/aboutnt.htm

ActionAid Home Page
http://www.oneworld.org/actionaid/

Amnesty International Online
http://www.amnesty.org/

Aphra Behn Page
http://ourworld.compuserve.com/homepages/r-nestvold/

Bacon, Roger
http://www-groups.dcs.st-and.ac.uk/history/Mathematicians/Bacon.html

BAFTA Awards
http://www.bafta.org/

Bentham Archive of British Law
http://www.ndirect.co.uk/~law/bentham.htm

Bentham, Jeremy
http://socserv2.socsci.mcmaster.ca/~econ/ugcm/3ll3/bentham/index.html

British Library
http://www.bl.uk/

British Museum
http://www.british-museum.ac.uk/

Campaign for Nuclear Disarmament
http://www.mcb.net/cnd/welcome.htm

Charter 88
http://www.charter88.org.uk/home.html

Citizen's Charter Unit
http://www.open.gov.uk/charter/ccuhome.htm

Claim of Englishwomen to the Suffrage Constitutionally Considered (1867)
http://www.indiana.edu/~letrs/vwwp/taylor/suffrage.html

Crown Prosecution Service—Working in the Interests of Justice
http://www.cps.gov.uk/

Cryptozoo Archives: Lake Monsters
http://www.ncf.carleton.ca/~bz050/HomePage.lm.html

Debate Between Thomas Hobbes and John Locke: A Creative Essay
http://www.yucc.yorku.ca/~rickg/academics/hobesvlo.html

Essay Concerning Civil Government
http://odur.let.rug.nl/~usa/D/1651-1700/locke/ECCG/governxx.htm

Essay Concerning Human Understanding
http://www.ilt.columbia.edu/academic/digitexts/locke/understanding/title.html

Fawcett Library special Collections: Josephine Butler Society Library
http://www.lgu.ac.uk/fawcett/main.htm

FCO Online
http://www.fco.gov.uk/news/

Freemasonry on the Internet
http://www.chrysalis.org/masonry/

Friends of the Earth Home Page
http://www.foe.co.uk/

Godwin, William
http://www.english.upenn.edu/~jlynch/Frank/Godwin/bio.html

Hallowe'en on the Net
http://www.holidays.net/halloween/

Hands Up—The Online Rollercoaster Magazine
http://www.rollercoaster.co.uk/

Hansard—House of Commons Debates
http://www.parliament.the-stationery-office.co.uk/pa/cm/cmhansrd.htm

Heath Under Attack
http://www-leland.stanford.edu/~cjacoby/heath.html

History of the Scottish Kilt
http://www.mhc.edu/users/jet/kilthist.htm

HM Land Registry
http://www.open.gov.uk/landreg/home.htm

Holy Grail
http://www.knight.org/advent/cathen/06719a.htm

HSE—Health and Safety Executive
http://www.open.gov.uk/hse/hsehome.htm

Hume Archives
http://www.utm.edu/research/hume/hume.html

Law Commission—Working for Better Law
http://www.gtnet.gov.uk/lawcomm/misc/about.htm#consolidation

'Lectures on The Industrial Revolution'
http://socserv2.socsci.mcmaster.ca/~econ/ugcm/3ll3/toynbee/indrev

Letter Concerning Toleration
http://odur.let.rug.nl/~usa/D/1651-1700/locke/ECT/toleraxx.htm

Liberal Democrats
http://www.libdems.org.uk

Ministry of Agriculture, Food, and Fisheries
http://www.maff.gov.uk/maffhome.htm

NIO Online
http://www.nio.gov.uk/index.htm

Notting Hill Carnival
http://www.nottinghillcarnival.net.uk

Old Postcard Exhibition
http://www.algonet.se/~stenborg/postcard.html

Origins of Halloween
http://www.geocities.com/Athens/Forum/5452/hallorig.html

Our Modern Commonwealth
http://www.rhouse.co.uk/rhouse/rcs/modcom/

Plaid Cymru, the Party of Wales
http://www.plaidcymru.org/

Plan of Union
http://odur.let.rug.nl/~usa/D/1651-1700/union/penn.htm

Right of Way
http://www.ramblers.org.uk/rightsofway.html

Robin Hood Project
http://www.lib.rochester.edu:80/camelot/rh/rhhome.stm

Save the Children Fund
http://www.oneworld.org/scf/

Schumacher Society
http://www.oneworld.org/schumachersoc/

Social Contract
http://www.utm.edu/research/iep/s/soc-cont.htm

Some Fruits of Solitude
http://etext.lib.virginia.edu/cgibin/browse-mixed?id=PenSoli&tag=public&images=images/modeng&data=/lv1/Archive/eng-parsed

Symbolism of Freemasonry
http://www.umdl.umich.edu/cgi-bin/moa/sgml/moa-idx?notisid=AHK6822

The City Heiress
http://etext.lib.virginia.edu/etcbin/browse-mixed-new?id=BehCity&tag=public&images=images/modeng&data=/texts/english/modeng/parsed

Trades Union Congress
http://www.tuc.org.uk/

Ulster Unionist Party
http://www.uup.org/

Vindication of the Rights of Woman, A
http://www.cc.columbia.edu/acis/bartleby/wollstonecraft/

Votes for Women: Suffrage Pictures, 1850-1920
http://lcweb2.loc.gov/ammem/vfwhtml/vfwhome.html

Voyage Out, The
http://wiretap.spies.com/ftp.items/Library/Classic/voyage.vw

Walter Bagehot: 'A New Standard of Value'
http://socserv2.socsci.mcmaster.ca/~econ/ugcm/3ll3/jevons/bagehot.htm

Welcome to CNT
http://www.cnt.org.uk/

Welcome to ITV Online
http://www.itv.co.uk

Welcome to IYHF
http://www.iyhf.org/iyhf/ehome.html

Welcome to Oxfam UK and Ireland
http://www.oxfam.org/

Westwood, Vivienne
http://si.ims.net/pgeek/viv/vivwest.html

Whitehead, Alfred North
http://plato.stanford.edu/entries/whitehead/

Who was Fawcett?
http://www.lgu.ac.uk/phil/fawbiog.htm#MILLICENT

Women on the March
http://www.onf.ca/FMT/E/58/58053.html

Women Win the Vote
http://www.inform.umd.edu/EdRes/Topic/WomensStudies/ReadingRoom/History/Vote.html

Women's National Commission
http://www.thewnc.org.uk/

Women's Web
http://www.womweb.com/

Work of the Audit Commission
http://www.audit-commission.gov.uk/

Sport

Aintree Racecourse
http://www.aintree.co.uk/

Badminton Home Page
http://mid1.external.hp.com/stanb/badminton.html

Champagne Mumm Admiral's Cup
http://www.admiralscup.com/

CricInfo: The Home of Cricket on the Internet
http://www-uk.cricket.org/

Edwards, Gareth
http://www.sportszineuk.co.uk/rugbynews/hallfeb.htm

Faldo, Nick
http://www.pga97.com/champ97/players/bio01326.html

GolfWeb
http://www.golfweb.com/

Goodwood Experience
http://www.goodwood.co.uk/

History of the Ryder Cup
http://infotu.com/ryder/ryhistor.htm

Introduction to the Game of Rugby
http://blaise.anderson.edu/~adekunle/rugby/index.html

Irvine, Andy
http://www.sportszineuk.co.uk/rugbynews/hallaug.htm

Jockey Club
http://www.jockeyclub.com/

Lawn Bowling
http://www.tcn.net/~jdevons/test1.html

Lord's—The Home of Cricket
http://lords.msn.com/news/headlines/

Major League Soccer
http://www.mlsnet.com/index.html

Manchester 2002 XVII Commonwealth Games
http://www.poptel.org.uk/commonwealth2002/index.html

Mansell, Nigel
http://cool.virtual-pc.com/williams/WGPE/PROFILES/mansell.htm

Mining Co Guide to Horse Racing
http://horseracing.miningco.com/

Molecular Expressions: The Beershots Photogallery
http://micro.magnet.fsu.edu/beershots/index.html

Motor Racing Regulations
http://www.fia.com/homepage/regle-a.htm

Official Site of the Championships—Wimbledon
http://www.wimbledon.org/

Orright Guv'nor?—The Many Faces of Terry Venables
http://www.theage.com.au/daily/971128/sport/sport4.html

Redgrave, Steve
http://gruffle.comlab.ox.ac.uk/archive/other/rowing/redgrave.html

Regatta—The Oxford-Cambridge Boat Race
http://www.boatrace.co.uk/

RugbyInfo
http://www.uidaho.edu/clubs/womens-rugby/RugbyRoot/

Rules, Skills, and Objectives of Rugby League Explained
http://www.senet.com.au/~emjay/rules.htm#

Scottish Highland Games
http://users.deltanet.com/~hilander/games.html

Vardon, Harry
http://tour.golf.com/tour/pgae/britishopen/history/bios/harry-vardon.htm

Chronology of British history 1707–1998

Events involving Britain and Ireland

1707 Union of Scotland and England.

1715 Jacobite Rebellion.
1716 Septennial Act: maximum length of English parliament extended to seven years.

1720 South Sea Bubble.
1721–42 Second ministry of Sir Robert Walpole.

1745 Jacobite Rebellion.

1756–63 Seven Years' War, ending with the Treaty of Paris.

1776 American Declaration of Independence from Britain.

1781 Americans force British army to surrender at Yorktown.

1793 Revolutionary government in France declared war on Britain.
1798 Battle of the Nile: Royal Navy defeated French navy in Egypt.

1801 Union of Britain and Ireland.
1802 Britain made peace with France.

1805 Battle of Trafalgar: Royal Navy defeated French and Spanish fleets.

1815 Battle of Waterloo: Britain and allies defeated French.

1829 Catholic Emancipation.

1832 Great Reform Act.

Other events

1709 Battle of Poltava: Russians inflicted major defeat on Swedish invaders.

1740 War of Austrian Succession: Prussia conquered Silesia.

1772 First Partition of Poland.

1789 Outbreak of French Revolution.

1792–97 War of the First Coalition.
1793, 1795 Second and Third Partitions of Poland.
1798–1801 War of the Second Coalition.
1799 In France, Napoleon overthrew the Directory.

1805–7 War of the Third Coalition.

1813–14 War of the Fourth Coalition, ending with the abdication of Napoleon.
1815 Napoleon's 'Hundred Days' as restored emperor of France; Treaty of Vienna.

1829 Greek kingdom established.
1830 July Revolution in France: Louis Philippe replaced Charles X.

Society, economy, and science

1709 Abraham Darby used coke to smelt iron.

1712 Last execution for witchcraft in England.

1721 Lady Mary Wortley Montague introduced inoculation for smallpox into England.

1733 James Kay patented the 'flying shuttle', for use in weaving.
1738 John Wesley received call to evangelism.

1750 Foundation of the English Jockey Club and of the Hambledon Cricket Club.
1754 Foundation of the Royal and Ancient Golf Club, St Andrew's.

1768–71 James Cook's first voyage of discovery.

1773–79 Construction of the cast-iron bridge at Ironbridge, Shropshire.
1774 Joseph Priestley discovered oxygen.
1776 Adam Smith, *An Inquiry into the Nature and Causes of the Wealth of Nations.*

1787 Marylebone Cricket Club (MCC) founded.
1789 Jeremy Bentham, *Introduction to the Principles of Morals and Legislation.*
1790 Edmund Burke, *Reflections on the Revolution in France.*

1798 Thomas Malthus, *Essay on the Principle of Population.*

1802 John Dalton proposed atomic theory and compiled tables of atomic weights; William Paley, *Natural Theology.*

1811 Luddite attacks on textile machinery in Nottingham and Yorkshire.

1825 Opening of the Stockton and Darlington Railway.
1829 Foundation of the Metropolitan Police force (London).

1833 John Keble begins the Oxford Movement in the Church of England.
1834 Poor Law Amendment Act.

Cultural history

1710 George Berkeley, *A Treatise Concerning the Principles of Human Knowledge.*
1712 Alexander Pope, *The Rape of the Lock.*

1719 Daniel Defoe, *Robinson Crusoe.*

1724 Foundation of Three Choirs Festival (for choirs in Gloucester, Hereford, and Worcester).
1726 Jonathan Swift, *Gulliver's Travels.*
1728 John Gay, *Beggar's Opera.*

1739 David Hume, *Treatise on Human Nature.*

1741 George Frideric Handel, *Messiah.*

1749 Henry Fielding, *The History of Tom Jones, A Foundling.*

1759 Opening of British Museum.

1776 Edward Gibbon, *Decline and Fall of the Roman Empire* (–1788).

1791 James Boswell, *Life of Johnson.*

1813 Jane Austen, *Pride and Prejudice.*

1817 Foundation of *The Scotsman.*

1818 Lord Byron, *Don Juan* (–1823); Mary Shelley, *Frankenstein.*
1821 John Constable, *The Hay Wain.*
1824 Foundation of the National Gallery, London.

Events involving Britain and Ireland	*Other events*
1845–46 Great Famine in Ireland. **1846** Abolition of Corn Laws; Conservative Party split.	
	1848 Revolutions in Europe; republic established in France.
1854–56 Crimean War: Britain and France fight Russia.	
	1861–65 American Civil War. **1861** Kingdom of Italy proclaimed.
1867 Second Reform Act.	
	1870–71 Franco–Prussian War. **1871** German Empire proclaimed; Third Republic established in France.
1884 Third Reform Act. **1885** Redistribution Act creates single-member constituencies. **1886** Gladstone's first Home Rule Bill for Ireland defeated; Liberal Party split.	
	1894 Franco–Russian Alliance formed.
1899–1902 Boer War.	
1902 Anglo–Japanese Alliance formed.	
1904 Anglo–French entente.	
	1905 Attempted Revolution in Russia.
1907 Anglo–Russian entente.	
	1908 Austria-Hungary annexed Bosnia-Herzegovina.
1909 Rejection of David Lloyd George's 'People's Budget' by Lords started constitutional crisis. **1911** Parliament Act reduced power of Lords. **1914** Irish Home Rule Act on statute book, but was suspended. **1914** Start of World War I: British forces involved in campaigns in NE France.	**1914** Assassination of Austrian Archduke Franz-Ferdinand in Sarajevo led to outbreak of World War I.
1915 Dardanelles campaign.	**1915** Italy joined War on Allied side.
1916 Easter Rising in Dublin; Battle of Jutland; Battle of the Somme.	**1916** Battle of Verdun on Western Front; Brusilov Offensive on Eastern Front.
1917 Third Battle of Ypres (Passchendaele).	**1917** 'February Revolution' in Russia (March), followed by the Bolshevik (Communist) 'October Revolution' (November) and civil war; USA enters War.
1918 Counter-offensive against the Central Powers.	**1918** Treaty of Brest-Litovsk between Russia and Germany; end of War with Armistice of 11 November. **1919** Treaty of Versailles, including creation of the League of Nations. **1920** Russian Civil War ended with Bolshevik victory.
1921 Partition of Ireland with separate governments in the north and the Irish Free State.	
	1922 Benito Mussolini appointed prime minister of Italy.
1924 First Labour government, with Ramsay MacDonald as prime minister.	
1926 General Strike.	**1925** Locarno Pact: Rhineland made a demilitarized zone.

Society, economy, and science	Cultural history
	1836 Charles Dickens, *Sketches by Boz* and start of *Pickwick Papers.*
1838 Working Men's Association draws up the People's Charter.	
1840 Introduction of Penny Postage.	**1841** Publication of *Punch.*
1843 Great Disruption in Scottish Church.	
1844 Foundation of the Co-operative Society.	
	1847 W M Thackeray, *Vanity Fair* (–1848).
1851 Great Exhibition held in Hyde Park, London, in Joseph Paxton's Crystal Palace.	
1857 Matrimonial Causes Act established divorce courts in England and Wales.	**1857** Anthony Trollope,*Barchester Towers.*
1859 Charles Darwin, *The Origin of Species*; J S Mill, *On Liberty.*	
1865 Debut of W G Grace, cricketer.	**1865** Lewis Carroll, *Alice's Adventures in Wonderland.*
1867 Karl Marx, *Das Kapital*, Vol. 1 (Vol. 2, 1885; Vol. 3, 1895).	
1871 Bank Holidays introduced in England and Wales.	**1871** George Eliot, *Middlemarch* (–1872).
	1872 Thomas Hardy, *Under The Greenwood Tree.*
1882 Married Women's Property Act.	
	1889 J K Jerome, *Three Men in a Boat.*
	1892 A Conan Doyle, *The Adventures of Sherlock Holmes.*
	1895 Oscar Wilde, *The Importance of Being Earnest*; first series of Promenade Concerts at Queen's Hall, London, conducted by Henry Wood.
	1899 Edward Elgar, *Enigma Variations.*
1901 Guglielmo Marconi transmitted wireless message from Poldhu, Cornwall, to Newfoundland.	
1902 Balfour Education Act provided state secondary education and integrated state and church schools.	**1902** Publication of the *Times Literary Supplement.*
	1903 G E Moore, *Principia Ethica.*
1905 Foundation of the Automobile Association.	
	1906 John Galsworthy, *The Man of Property* (Vol. I of The Forsyte Saga).
1907 Formation of Boy Scouts (Girl Guides formed 1909).	
	1908 Kenneth Grahame, *The Wind in the Willows.*
1911 Ernest Rutherford identified nuclear atom.	**1911** Max Beerbohm, *Zuleika Dobson.*
1914 British government granted emergency powers.	
1916 Marie Stopes, *Married Love.*	
1918 School leaving age increased to 14.	**1918** Lytton Strachey, *Eminent Victorians.*
1919 John Maynard Keynes, *The Economic Consequences of the Peace.*	**1919** Edward Elgar, *Cello Concerto.*
1922 Foundation of the British Broadcasting Company (Corporation from 1927).	**1922** T S Eliot, *The Waste Land*; James Joyce, *Ulysses.*
	1923 William Walton, *Façade.*
1925 UK divorce laws made inoperative in Irish Free State.	
1926 John Logie Baird demonstrated television.	**1926** A A Milne, *Winnie the Pooh.*

Events involving Britain and Ireland	***Other events***
1929 Second Labour government, with Ramsay MacDonald as prime minister.	**1929** Wall Street Crash and start of the Great Depression.
1931 Formation of coalition National Government, with Ramsay MacDonald as prime minister.	
	1933 Adolf Hitler appointed chancellor of Germany. **1934** Stalin started purge of political enemies and others in USSR.
1936 Abdication crisis: Edward VIII abdicates.	**1936–9** Spanish Civil War.
	1937 Japanese invasion of China.
1938 Munich crisis: Prime Minister Neville Chamberlain agreed to Hitler's demands on Czechoslovakia. **1939** Following German invasion of Poland, Britain declared war on Germany.	**1939** Soviet–German Pact; outbreak of World War II.
1940 Churchill appointed prime minister of coalition government; British withdrawal from Dunkirk; Battle of Britain.	**1940** German invasion of Low Countries and France.
	1941 German invasion of USSR; Japan bombed Pearl Harbor and occupied SE Asia.
1942 Battle of El Alamein: British army defeated Germans under Erwin Rommel.	**1942** US Navy defeated Japan in Battle of Midway.
1943 Anglo-American invasion of Italy. **1944** D-Day invasion of France.	**1943** German army surrendered to Russians at Stalingrad.
1945 End of World War II.	**1945** Foundation of United Nations; end of World War II in Europe; atomic bombs halted war in Asia. **1946–8** Communist governments established in E European countries.
1947 Britain granted independence to India, Pakistan, and Burma. **1949** Formation of NATO with Britain as member; southern Ireland became fully independent. **1951** Festival of Britain.	
	1955 Warsaw Pact signed.
1956 Suez crisis.	
	1957 Creation of the European Economic Community.
1962 'Night of Long Knives': Prime Minister Macmillan dismissed 7 of 21 cabinet ministers.	**1962** Cuban missile crisis.
1963 British application to join European Common Market vetoed by France; Profumo Scandal.	**1963** In USA, assassination of President John F Kennedy.
1964 Creation of the Welsh Office. **1965** Rhodesia made Unilateral Declaration of Independence from Britain.	**1964** Growth of US involvement in Vietnam War. **1965** Cultural Revolution in China.
1967 Sterling devalued.	**1967** Six-Day War between Israel and Arab countries.
1968 Enoch Powell's 'rivers of blood' speech advocating repatriation of immigrants. **1969** Outbreak of 'the troubles' in Northern Ireland.	**1968** Student unrest in France.
1973 Britain joined the European Economic Community. **1974** Britain established direct rule of Northern Ireland.	**1973** USA withdrew from Vietnam War.
	1975 In Spain, death of General Franco; succeeded by King Juan Carlos.
1979 'Winter of discontent': widespread strikes by public workers discredited Labour government; Margaret Thatcher elected first woman prime minister.	**1979** Peace Treaty between Egypt and Israel; USSR invaded Afghanistan.

Society, economy, and science

1929 Most Scottish Presbyterian churches united as Church of Scotland.
1930 First British Empire Games held (in Canada).

1932 James Chadwick discovered the neutron.
1933 Controversial 'bodyline' MCC cricket tour of Australia.

1935 First successful experiments with radar.
1936 Billy Butlin opened first holiday camp, near Skegness; BBC started television broadcasting.

1940 Howard Florey developed penicillin for medical use.

1942 William Beveridge, Social Security and Allied Services (the Beveridge Report); William Temple, *Christianity and the Social Order.*

1944 'Butler' Education Act, creating three-school system of secondary education.

1946 London Airport opened at Heathrow.

1949 Maiden flight of the Comet, the first jet airliner.

1953 Francis Crick and James Watson announced double-helix structure of DNA.
1954 Roger Bannister's four-minute mile.

1956 Nuclear power station at Calder Hall opened.

1958 Munich air crash killed eight Manchester United players.
1959 Mini Minor on sale.
1960 Trial ruled that *Lady Chatterley's Lover* by D H Lawrence is not obscene.
1961 First betting shop opened; Michael Ramsey became 100th archbishop of Canterbury.

1963 Beeching Report proposed closure of quarter of railway network.

1966 England won World Cup.
1967 Completion of Cathedral of Christ the King, Liverpool; colour television introduced.

1969 Maiden flights of Concorde supersonic airliner; Open University founded.
1970 Age of majority reduced from 21 to 18.

1973 Introduction of commercial radio.

1975 Equal pay for both sexes compulsory.

1978 First test-tube baby born.

Cultural history

1928 Virginia Woolf, *Orlando.*
1929 Noel Coward, *Bitter Sweet*; Robert Graves, *Goodbye to All That.*
1930 W H Auden, *Poems.*

1932 Aldous Huxley, *Brave New World.*

1936 A J Ayer, *Language, Truth and Logic.*

1938 Graham Greene, *Brighton Rock.*

1943 T S Eliot, *Four Quartets.*

1945 Benjamin Britten, *Peter Grimes.*

1947 First Edinburgh Festival of the Arts.
1949 George Orwell, *Nineteen Eighty-four.*

1954 Kingsley Amis, *Lucky Jim*; William Golding, *Lord of the Flies.*
1955 Samuel Beckett, *Waiting for Godot*; Philip Larkin, *The Less Deceived.*
1956 John Osborne, *Look Back in Anger.*
1957 Richard Hoggart, *The Uses of Literacy.*
1958 John Betjeman, *Collected Poems.*

1961 Debut of The Beatles.

1962 Anthony Burgess, *A Clockwork Orange*; BBC broadcast *That Was The Week That Was.*
1963 John le Carré, *The Spy Who Came in from the Cold.*

1969 *Civilisation*, television series presented by Kenneth Clark; Rupert Murdoch purchased *The Sun.*
1970 Ted Hughes, *Crow.*
1972 Frederick Forsyth, *The Day of the Jackal.*

1978 *Evita*, musical by Tim Rice and Andrew Lloyd Webber.

Events involving Britain and Ireland	*Other events*
	1980 Death of President Tito of Yugoslavia; Ronald Reagan elected president of the USA.
1981 Riots in Brixton (London) and Toxteth (Liverpool).	
1982 Falklands War.	**1982** Martial Law declared in Poland and Solidarity Union suppressed.
1984–5 Miners' strike.	**1984** Prime Minister Indira Gandhi of India assassinated.
1985 Anglo–Irish Agreement.	**1985** Mikhail Gorbachev appointed secretary general of Soviet Communist Party.
	1989 Tienanmen Square massacre in Beijing, China.
	1989–90 Collapse of Communism in E Europe.
1990 Resignation of Mrs Thatcher; succeeded by John Major.	**1990–91** Gulf War.
	1991 Collapse of Soviet Union; formation of the Confederation of Independent States; Maastricht Treaty agreed.
1992 Conservative Party's fourth consecutive victory in general election.	
1994 Paramilitary organizations declared cease-fire in Northern Ireland.	**1994** Non-racial general election held in South Africa.
1996 Northern Ireland ceasefire collapsed.	
1997 Victory of Labour Party in general election; Tony Blair became prime minister.	
1997 Paramilitary ceasefire resumed; multi-party talks on Northern Ireland began.	
1997 Following referendums in Wales and Scotland, the government announced plans for a Welsh Assembly and a Scottish Parliament.	
1998 Home Office announced that Queen Elizabeth II supports plans to remove the gender bias from British succession rules.	**1998** Pakistan exploded five nuclear devices.
1998 Ireland, Britain, and political parties in Northern Ireland reached peace agreement over Northern Ireland involving the devolution of a wide range of powers to a Northern Ireland Assembly. Surrender of arms by the IRA, however, was a stumbling block.	**1998** Australian Constitutional Convention voted to replace the Queen as head of state with a president.

Society, economy, and science

1982 First papal visit to Britain.

1986 GCSE examinations replaced O level and CSE.
1989 Ayatollah Khomeini of Iran issued fatwa sentencing British writer Salman Rushdie to death for blasphemy in his novel *The Satanic Verses*.

1991 Polytechnics permitted to become universities.

1992 Church of England voted to allow ordination of women to the priesthood.
1993 Queen Elizabeth II and Prince of Wales volunteered to pay income tax; Buckingham Palace was opened to the public.
1994 Privatization of British coal mines.
1994 Channel Tunnel opened.
1995 Baring's, Britain's oldest merchant bank, collapsed.
1996 Geneticists at the Roslin Institute in Edinburgh, Scotland, cloned an adult sheep, named Dolly.
1997 Death in a car accident in Paris of Diana, Princess of Wales.

Cultural history

1982 *Gandhi*, film directed by Richard Attenborough.

1984 First payments to authors on library loans under Public Lending Right.
1985 *Triumph of the West*, television series on world history presented by J M Roberts.

1989 John Tavener, *The Protecting Veil* for cello and string orchestra.

1990 Glasgow is 'Cultural Capital of Europe' for 1990.
1991 Closure of the *Listener* magazine (founded 1929).

1993 Rachel Whiteread awarded Turner Prize for *House* (plaster cast of inside of London house).

1995 Irish poet Seamus Heaney won Nobel Prize for Literature.

1997 Elton John's single 'Candle in the Wind' 97, a tribute to Diana, Princess of Wales, became the best-selling single of all time.
1997 *The Full Monty*, by Peter Cattaneo, became the biggest-grossing British film in the UK.

1998 David Trimble and John Hume jointly awarded Nobel peace prize for their part in the Northern Ireland peace process.